THE PEOPLE'S ALMANAC # 3

THE PEOPLE'S ALMANAC #3

by
David Wallechinsky
and
Irving Wallace

The exact contrary of what is generally believed is often the truth.

—*Jean de La Bruyère (1645–1696)*

BANTAM BOOKS
TORONTO • NEW YORK • LONDON • SYDNEY

THE PEOPLE'S ALMANAC® #3
A Bantam Book

First printing/October 1981

Book design by Gene Siegel

Library of Congress Cataloging in Publication Data
Main entry under title:
The People's almanac #3.
Includes index.
1. Handbooks, vade-mecums, etc. I. Wallechinsky, David, 1948- . II. Wallace, Irving, 1916- .
AG106.P466 1981 031'.02 81-43093
ISBN 0-553-01352-1 AACR2

Published in association with William Morrow and Company, Inc.
Published simultaneously in the United States and Canada

Bantam Books are published by Bantam Books, Inc. Its trademark, consisting of the words "Bantam Books" and the portrayal of a rooster, is Registered in United States Patent and Trademark Office and in other countries. Marca Registrada. Bantam Books, Inc., 666 Fifth Avenue, New York, New York, 10103.

Printed in the United States of America
0 9 8 7 6 5 4 3 2 1

Executive Editor: Carol Orsag
Almanac Managing Editor: Vicki Scott
Associate Editors: Kristine H. Johnson, Diane Brown Shepard
Senior Editors: Fern Bryant, Elizebethe Kempthorne
Staff Writers and Researchers: Loreen Leo, Karen Pedersen, Linda Schallan
Staff Researchers: Helen Ginsburg, Anita Taylor, Sue Ann Power, Lee Clayton
Assistant Editor: Judy Knipe
Editorial Aides: Joanne Maloney, Linda Laucella
Photograph Editor: Danny Biederman
Copy Editor: Wayne Lawson
Designer: Gene Siegel

They Wrote the Original Material

When "The Eds." is used, it means the material has been contributed by the editors of the *Almanac.*

A.E. Ann Elwood
A.K. Aaron Kass
A.T. Anita Taylor
A.W. Amy Wallace
B.B. Barbara Bedway
B.F. Bruce Felton
B.O.B. Bruce O. Boston
C.D. Carol Dunlap
C.H.S. Charles H. Salzberg
C.L.C. Clarence L. Crist
C.O. Carol Orsag
C.S. Carl Sifakis
D.B. David Barash
D.B.S. Diane Brown Shepard
D.G.I. Dennis G. Iberman
D.L. Don Lessem
D.R. Dan Riley
D.W. David Wallechinsky
E.F. Ed Fishbein
F.B. Fern Bryant
F.S. Fred Setterberg
G.G. George Gamester
I.F. Ira Feldschneider
I.W. Irving Wallace
J.A. John Ascenzi
J.E. John Eastman
J.H. Jannika Hurwitt
J.H.W. John H. Womeldorf

J.N.	Jim Natal	M.S.S.	Michael S. Smith
J.W.B.	James W. Blair	N.C.S.	Nancy C. Sorel
K.H.J.	Kristine H. Johnson	P.A.R.	Patricia A. Ryan
K.P.	Karen Pedersen	P.H.	Paul Hoffman
L.C.	Loren Coleman	R.J.F.	Rodger J. Fadness
L.Ch.	Linda Chase	R.K.R.	R. Kent Rasmussen
L.K.S.	Laurie K. Strand	R.R.	Robert Reginald
L.L.	Loreen Leo	S.D.	Sally Darnowsky
L.P.	Lillie Parkin	S.M.	Susan Marks
L.S.	Lenny Siegel	V.B.	Vincent Buranelli
L.Sc.	Linda Schallan	V.S.	Vicki Scott
M.B.T.	Marguerite B. Thompson	W.A.D.	William A. DeGregorio
M.J.T.	Michael J. Toohey	W.J.C.	Warwick J. Carter
M.S.	Michael Sheeter	W.K.	Walter Kempthorne
M.S.M.	Michael S. Medved		

CONTENTS

HELLO, PEOPLE

Welcome to *The People's Almanac #3*. For those of you who are new to our books, as well as those of you who have been with us the past few years, a little history: In 1971 we conceived the idea for a new kind of almanac. Our goal was to create a reference book that could be read for pleasure, a volume of facts that would entertain as well as educate. We decided to call our project *The People's Almanac*. We chose this name for several reasons. First of all, other almanacs and reference books tended to tell only the history of military and political leaders and the wealthy. So, in preparing our "U.S.A.—Year by Year," as well as other chapters of *The People's Almanac*, we concentrated on incidents in the history of the rest of the people. And when we talked about famous people, we tried to bring out their human side, to flesh out the two-dimensional images presented in textbooks and other reference works. Our final reason for choosing the title *The People's Almanac* was our hope that subsequent editions would include the participation of our readers.

After four and a half years of work, *The People's Almanac* was finally published in November of 1975. To our delight, people began buying our books faster than the publisher could print them. And thousands of you accepted our invitation to write to us, telling us what you liked and didn't like, sending us new ideas and stories. Encouraged by your response, we set to work on *The People's Almanac #2*. We decided not to just update our first volume, but to create an all-new book. This took a lot of work, but with the help of over 200 writers, readers, staff researchers, and editors we were able to complete *The People's Almanac #2* in 1978. This edition got a warm reception from the reading public, and like its predecessor, it became a #1 best-seller.

Now three more years have passed and you have before you *The People's Almanac #3*. Once again we have produced a book filled with new material rather than repeating or merely updating our previous works. *People's Almanac* aficionados will recognize some familiar and popular sections, such as "Mysterious Happenings" and "Footnote People in U.S. and World History." But the subjects covered in these sections are new. We have also continued our summary of the Nations of the World, presenting under the heading "Who Really Rules?" the political and economic realities that other almanacs choose to ignore. In line with our philosophy of writing about topics that are usually avoided in reference books, we have created a new chapter, "Controversies," which deals with such diverse issues as abortion, the death of Karen Silkwood, and "Who Really Invented the Airplane?" In other chapters we have included articles about sex manuals, the afterlife, *Time* magazine, and Ronald Reagan.

As in *The People's Almanac #2,* we have chosen to close this book with a chapter called "The Voice of the People." This chapter includes contributions from our readers as well as "Solutions—Practical Proposals and Brand-New Approaches to a Multitude of Problems." We hope you will share with us your own solutions and opinions, as well as fresh factual information you have to offer. If we publish your material, we will credit you and pay you, of course. Our address is:

The People's Almanac #3
P.O. Box 49699
Los Angeles, Calif. 90049

Now, before you cross the threshold into the world of *The People's Almanac,* we would like you to take along something we picked up from the philosopher Friedrich Nietzsche: "The surest way to corrupt a young man is to teach him to esteem more highly those who think alike than those who think differently." And that goes for a young woman, too.

Until next time—

David Wallechinsky
Irving Wallace

1

CONTROVERSIES

WERE THEY MURDERED?

WARREN G. HARDING

Victim: Born on Nov. 2, 1865, in what is now Blooming Grove, O., Harding at 19 joined two partners in buying the failing Marion, O., *Star*. Behind Harding, managing the day-to-day operations of the newspaper and unceasingly boosting the career of her big, lovable "Wurr'n," was his wife, Florence Kling DeWolfe Harding, a strong-willed, blunt, domineering matron five years older than him. They married in 1891. Harding's charm and affability won him many friends, and he soon became active in civic affairs and the local Republican party. Through machine connections he was elected state senator in 1899, lieutenant governor in 1903, and U.S. senator in 1914. A lazy legislator, Harding had one of the poorest attendance records in the Senate and introduced not a single significant bill during his six-year term. He was a gifted orator, but his speeches were filled with what Sen. William McAdoo called "pompous phrases moving over the landscape in search of an idea." His biggest asset was that he looked like a statesman. In 1920 Harding emerged as a compromise candidate for president at the deadlocked Republican Party convention in Chicago. In a smoke-filled room at the Blackstone Hotel, party bosses chose Harding, who went on to smother the Democratic nominee James M. Cox in the general election. Harding's presidency was an utter failure. His "friends," rewarded with government posts, used their office for personal enrichment in the Teapot Dome and other swindles. Only dimly aware of the enormity of the crisis, Harding set out on a cross-country "Voyage of Understanding" in June, 1923. He died suddenly in San Francisco on Aug. 2, thereby eluding disgrace and possible impeachment.

His Death: Returning south from Alaska during his trip, Harding complained of severe cramps and indigestion, a condition the President's physician, Charles Sawyer, misdiagnosed as food poisoning. The cross-country tour had exhausted him. On doctor's orders, he canceled scheduled speeches and sped on to San Francisco. There, in room 8064 on the eighth floor of the Palace Hotel, he was put to bed. On July 30 his temperature climbed to 102°, his pulse raced 120 beats per minute, pneumonia settled in his right lung. However, next day he rallied and by Aug. 1 he was sitting up, his temperature normal, his pulse below 100. Dr. Sawyer pronounced the crisis over. On Aug. 2 Harding's spirits continued to improve. He talked eagerly of going deep-sea fishing. That evening, alone with Mrs. Harding, he listened contentedly as his wife read him an article from *The Saturday Evening Post,* "A Calm View of a Calm Man," a flattering portrait of the President by Samuel Blythe. "That's good," Harding said. "Go on, read some more." Mrs. Harding finished the piece, then left the room for her own quarters across the hall. Moments later Nurse Ruth Powderly entered the President's room with a glass of water. As she approached him his face suddenly twitched, his jaw dropped, and his head rolled to the right. The nurse called for Mrs. Harding. Mrs. Harding yelled for Dr. Joel Boone. The President was pronounced dead at about 7:30 P.M.

Official Version: Five doctors—Sawyer and Boone, as well as Ray Lyman Wilbur, Charles Minor Cooper, and Hubert Work—signed a statement asserting the apparent cause of death to be "some brain evolvement, probably an apoplexy"; in other words, a sudden stroke. The official version of Harding's death, generally accepted by historians, is that distress over the treachery of his friends and the rigors of a transcontinental tour combined to break down an already overworked cardiovascular system. Harding suffered from high blood pressure, and previous examinations had revealed an enlarged heart. His Voyage of Understanding was a grueling undertaking. He delivered 85 speeches in six weeks. At outdoor events he often spent hours hatless under the broiling summer sun. In Tacoma, Wash., he spoke in the rain. During a speech in Seattle he flubbed his lines and at one point dropped his text to the floor and grabbed the lectern for support. Contributing to his failing health was a growing awareness that his administration was rotten and scandal-ridden. In Kansas City he met for almost an hour with Emma Fall, wife of his corrupt secretary of the interior, Albert Fall, and was said to have left the meeting visibly shaken. To newsman William Allen White he complained, "My God, this is a hell of a job! I can take care of my enemies. . . . But my God-damn friends, they're the ones that keep me walking the floor nights." And on the way to Alaska he asked Secretary of Commerce Herbert Hoover whether a president ought to expose or cover up any scandal discovered in his administration. This stress and strain, plus his known medical history, supported the official version of his death.

Theories and Unanswered Questions: The exact cause of Harding's death was never learned because Mrs. Harding refused to allow an autopsy. She also declined the casting of a death mask. And the body was embalmed immediately, before it ever left the hotel. All this led to rumors that Mrs. Harding had poisoned the President while they were alone together shortly before his death, perhaps with the help or knowledge of Dr. Sawyer. In 1924 eyebrows once again were raised. Dr. Charles Sawyer died suddenly—and his death was strikingly similar to that of President Harding—while Mrs. Harding was visiting the Sawyer home. Had she slipped something into Sawyer's drink, too, perhaps to ensure his silence? Mrs. Harding herself died in November, 1924, before the ugly rumors of her role in the President's death ever reached print. In 1930 Gaston Means, an unscrupulous detective and convicted swindler, published *The Strange Death of President Harding,* in which he claimed he had been hired by Mrs. Harding to serve as her personal investigator. One of his most important tasks was to follow Harding's longtime mistress Nan Britton, who had borne the President's only child, out of wedlock. The widely read book broadly hinted that Mrs. Harding, seeking revenge for this affair and for Harding's many other infidelities during their marriage, had poisoned her husband. Means also suggested that Mrs. Harding had another motive, a more compassionate one: to spare the President the disgrace of the political scandals about to be disclosed. "My love for Warren has turned to hate," she supposedly told Means. "The President deserves to die. He is not fit to live . . . and he knows it." Means claimed that after the President's death Mrs. Harding confided to him, "Warren Harding died in honor. . . . Had he lived 24 hours longer he might have been impeached. . . . I have not betrayed my country or the party. . . . They are saved . . . I have no regrets. I have fulfilled my destiny."

—W.A.D.

BRUCE LEE

Victim: The Little Dragon was born in San Francisco on Nov. 27, 1940, but he was raised in Hong Kong, where he began making movies at the age of six. At 13 his interest in the martial arts began in earnest, and he worked on toughening himself up by pounding his fists on a stool near the table during dinners and conversations at home. In order to retain his American citizenship he returned to the U.S. when he was 18. He enrolled as a philosophy major at the University of Washington, but increasingly his time was taken up with giving lessons in his personal version of kung fu, "jeet kune do," an amalgam of classical kung fu techniques and American boxing. In August, 1964, he married Linda Emery, one of his students, and soon he quit school and set off to seek a film career in Hollywood. During the 1966–1967 television season, he was seen as Kato in *The Green Hornet* TV series. When he wasn't acting out his karate moves in front of the cameras, he was giving private lessons at $150 an hour to some of Hollywood's biggest names, Lee Marvin, Steve McQueen, James Garner, and James Coburn among them. However, Hollywood moneymen refused to grant him the stardom he thought he deserved—especially Warner Bros., which claimed he was too inexperienced for the leading role in its *Kung Fu* TV series. So Lee returned to Hong Kong, determined to become a worldwide superstar. There he teamed up with producer Raymond Chow, who had defected from Run Run Shaw's all-powerful Shaw Bros. production company. Liberal doses of Chinese jingoism injected into the action-packed plots of Lee's man-against-the-mob martial arts pictures helped Lee and Chow become the major force in the Hong Kong film trade. With the stunning success of Lee's films (*Big Boss,* 1972; *The Chinese Connec-*

Bruce Lee.

tion, 1972; and *The Way of the Dragon,* 1973), Warner Bros. came calling and brought along major financing for *Enter the Dragon,* the breakthrough film Lee coveted. He died before its release in 1973.

His Death: On May 10, 1973, Lee suffered a mysterious collapse while dubbing *Enter the Dragon* in Hong Kong. During the crisis he experienced great difficulty in breathing, a series of convulsions, and a swelling of the brain. Lee was treated with the drug Mannitol, and within a few hours he began to show signs of recovery, so emergency surgery was deemed not necessary. A week later Lee, feeling fit as ever, was examined in Los Angeles by Dr. David Reisbord, who did a brain scan, a brain flow study, an EEG, and a complete physical. The doctor concluded that Lee had suffered a grand mal seizure of no known origin, but that overall he was in extraordinarily good health. However, friends were worried by the fact that he was rapidly losing weight. Two months later, on July 20, Lee complained of a headache while working on a script at the Hong Kong apartment of his co-star, Betty Ting-pei. The actress gave Lee the painkiller Equagesic, which had been prescribed for her by her doctor. Lee then went off to nap on her bed—and never woke up again. He was found at 9:30 P.M. by Raymond Chow, who had come to pick him up for a dinner engagement. A doctor was called, but efforts to revive Lee were in vain. He was taken to Queen Elizabeth Hospital, where he was pronounced dead.

Official Version: Reasons for suspicion: Lee was not taken to the hospital closest to his co-star's apartment; Raymond Chow announced to the press that Lee had died at his own home; Lee had acted erratically and had publicly attacked director Lo Wei on the eve of his death; traces of cannabis were found in his system; and, at the time, he was regarded as "the fittest man in the world." Since there was no discernible reason for his death, an official coroner's inquest was convened on Sept. 3, 1973. The findings were as follows: that Dr. Chu, who had been called to the scene, determined that Lee was already dead, so the choice of hospital was immaterial; that Chow had refrained from mentioning Betty Ting-pei's apartment in the death announcement as a face-saving gesture to protect Lee's wife, Linda, since Lee had been romantically linked with his co-star; that Lee's attack on director Lo Wei had been simply the climax of their long-simmering hostility; that the amount of cannabis found in Lee's system was too insignificant to have played any part in his death; and that the fittest man in the world probably died because of a hypersensitivity to some component of the painkiller Equagesic—either meprobamate or aspirin or a combination of the two. The official verdict after the inquest: death by "misadventure."

Theories and Unanswered Questions: Bruce Lee cultists have refused to believe that a man who could do one-finger push-ups and was fanatical about his diet of raw beef and egg shakes could die of such a minor cause. They have, as a result, made a parlor game out of his death, not unlike "Is Paul Dead?," which was played by Beatles fans in the 1960s. Some of Lee's fans are sure that the whole thing was a hoax. A tribe in Malaysia is so convinced he is still alive that they continue to wait patiently for his reemergence. Those closest to Lee, who accept his death as a grim reality, scoff at the sensational stories that attribute his early demise to an overindulgence in sex or drugs—notably cocaine. They are convinced, instead, that the hard-driven actor simply burned himself out.

In Alex Ben Block's book *The Legend of Bruce Lee* (1974), some intriguing theories are put forth. Lee may have been done in by kung fu traditionalists, who were offended because he arrogantly flaunted the secrets of their sect. Another theory points the finger at rival Hong Kong filmmakers who saw him becoming a serious competitor. Block contends that either of these groups would have had access to herbal poisons that could work without detection long after they had been administered. Block also casts a shadow of suspicion on the Ninja, a centuries-old organization of Japanese assassins so skillful at covert killing that people once believed its members were invisible. The motive here, says Block, would have been the traditional Chinese-Japanese rivalry which Lee exploited in his films. It has also been suggested that Bruce Lee was killed when he refused to give a share of his income to the Chinese "Mafia."

Block's most exotic theory, however, involves the dreaded Malaysian art of "the vibrating palm." In this, a practitioner of the art can convert internal energy into resonating vibrations and, through a mere touch, cause a victim's death at a predetermined future time. According to *Black Belt* magazine, these vibrations can be transmitted "through the hand to the victim's body cavity," where "they systematically disrupt blood flow and lung structure." Block adds, parenthetically, that Lee had "strange broken blood vessels in his lungs" at the time of his death.

In *Bruce Lee, King of Kung Fu* (1974), authors Felix Dennis and Don Atyeo point out that, during the last months of his life, Lee had been warned of inauspicious omens connected with the location of his house; the title of his final movie, *The Game of Death;* and the name of his co-star, Betty Ting-pei. Even in death bad luck continued to plague Lee; his coffin was scratched, and its silk lining was stained in the process of being shipped back to Seattle. According to Chinese beliefs, this final mishap reveals that the soul of the Little Dragon is still not at peace.

—D.R.

JAN MASARYK

Victim: He was born in Prague on Sept. 14, 1886, the son of Tomáš Masaryk, founder of Czechoslovakia's Golden Republic and patron saint of Czech nationalism. After Tomáš Masaryk's death in 1937 and the subsequent Nazi takeover of Czechoslovakia, freedom-loving Czechs transferred their affections and yearnings for independence to Jan. He answered their call from England, where he was a member of the Czech democratic government in exile. With the charismatic voice of a Roosevelt or a Churchill, Masaryk inspired his countrymen through underground radio broadcasts to Czechoslovakia. In August, 1945, he returned to a liberated Prague, happy to serve in the new government but wary of the conditions of peace which made Czechoslovakia a protectorate of Russia. Within two years his fears were confirmed; he met Stalin in Moscow in July, 1947, and was told that the Czechs must not accept Marshall Plan assistance. "I went to Moscow as the foreign minister of a sovereign state and I came back a stooge of Stalin," he complained. This incident and the truth it revealed to him about his country's diminished standing in the world helped form the backdrop for one of the most perplexing political deaths in history.

His Death: In September, 1947, two months after his meeting with Stalin, Masaryk and two other democratic leaders received anonymous gift boxes marked "Perfume" which contained crude bombs. An investigation by Minister of Justice Prokop Drtina linked the unsuccessful bomb plot to the Czech Communist party and Alexeja Čepička, son-in-law of party boss and prime minister Klement Gottwald. On Feb. 25, 1948, the Communists assumed total control of Czechoslovakia, and Gottwald ousted Drtina as minister of justice and replaced him with Čepička. The next night Drtina allegedly attempted suicide by jumping from a third-story window. Masaryk, a friend of Drtina, characterized the action as "a servant girl's way to die." Masaryk's comment proved highly significant, because two weeks later—at 6:25 A.M. on Mar. 10—his own body was found sprawled in the courtyard of the Czerin Palace, the apparent result of a suicide jump from a third-story bathroom window.

Official Version: At noon on Mar. 10, Communist Minister of the In-

Jan Masaryk two years before his death.

The window from which Masaryk is alleged to have jumped.

terior Vaclav Nosek appeared before the Czech parliament and reported that Masaryk had committed suicide because of criticism he had received for remaining in the cabinet after the Communist coup. "During the night," Nosek said, "Mr. Masaryk must have read a number of letters and telegrams from his former friends in England and America full of reproaches about their disappointment over his uncompromising attitude during the recent crisis." The Communists said that a verdict of death by suicide was inescapable since the window from which Masaryk fell was inconveniently located behind a couch; therefore, he could not have fallen out of it accidentally.

Theories and Unanswered Questions: The endless array of questions concerning Masaryk's death begins with the bathroom window. There was not only a couch in front of it, but also a radiator. In addition, it was very hard to open and only half the size of an easily accessible window in Masaryk's private bedroom—a key factor when one considers that Masaryk was a 200-lb. six-footer who would have had to squeeze his bulk through the bathroom window. From here the questions go off in a hundred different directions. Why were there smears of excrement on the bathroom windowsill and on Masaryk's body when forensic experts agree that people about to commit suicide don't lose control of their bowels? (Those who are in the final stages of suffocation, however, normally do lose control.) Why were there paint chips under Masaryk's fingernails and scratches on his hands and stomach, indicating a struggle? Why were there signs of violence in his apartment—furniture overturned and vials of medicine trampled all over the bathroom floor? How could Masaryk's large body have landed with enough impact to shatter the heel bones but not telescope the legs up into the torso, as is usually the case when victims of high falls land on their feet? Why did the police physician, Dr. Jaramír Teplý, describe the heels as having been beaten "repeatedly with a very heavy instrument, for example a hammer"? Why would Masaryk, known as an unusually fastidious man with an inordinate fear of physical pain, choose to throw himself out a window clad only in a mismatched pair of pajamas when he had 50 to 60 sleeping pills and a loaded revolver by his bed? And, if he had planned on killing himself, why would he spend his last night working on a future speech instead of a suicide note, take two sleeping pills, and ask his butler to wake him at 8:30 in the morning?

In her book *The Masaryk Case*, Claire Sterling theorizes that Masaryk was planning to escape from Czechoslovakia and denounce the Communists when he was safe in the free world. He had already sent his fiancée, novelist Marcia Davenport, out of the country with the promise that he would join her in London. Sterling says that the Communists—who had Masaryk under constant surveillance—learned of his plan and, in order to avoid being embarrassed by Czechoslovakia's most famous citizen, dispatched two party thugs to his room to talk him out of a window. A struggle ensued which ended in the bathroom, where the thugs subdued him by placing a pillow over his face and then dragged his body to the bathroom window and shoved it out. The inquiry into Masaryk's death was reopened when Czechoslovakia was liberalized under Alexander Dubček in the first half of 1968. By that time 16 Czechs who could have supplied the investigator with valuable information were dead. Ten had been executed, one had died in prison, another had been released from jail only to die from the physical abuse he had suffered there, one had committed suicide, and three were most likely murdered—among them Dr. Teplý, who died at police headquarters after he allegedly injected himself with gasoline. No one knows how many other witnesses were too frightened to tell what they knew about the Masaryk case. The taxi driver who took three security officers to the palace the morning Masaryk's body was discovered and stayed to gather heel bone fragments spent two years in a penitentiary. He was never charged or tried, but was informed he had been "punished as a warning" when he was set free.

The puzzle of Jan Masaryk's death was still officially unsolved when Soviet tanks started rolling through Prague in August, 1968, and it was left to the next regime to concoct an acceptable explanation. The Communists' sensitivity to the Masaryk mystery became apparent when in 1969 they replaced the original finding of death by suicide with the following imaginative scenario: "Masaryk . . . most likely fell accidentally from a windowsill where he had been sitting in a yoga position to combat insomnia."

—D.R.

MARILYN MONROE

Victim: The sex symbol of a generation, Marilyn Monroe began life as Norma Jean Mortenson, daughter of Gladys Baker and Edward Mortenson, on June 1, 1926, in Los Angeles, Calif. At age 16, after a childhood spent in foster homes, Marilyn married Jim Dougherty, who later became a Los Angeles policeman. Having worked as a photographer's model, she broke into the movies, in which she was initially cast as a beautiful but dumb blonde. From bit parts, she rose to stardom in the 1950s in such films as *Gentlemen Prefer Blondes* (1953) and *Some Like It Hot* (1959).

Her Death: On Saturday, Aug. 4, 1962, Marilyn Monroe puttered around her newly purchased Spanish-style home in the exclusive Brentwood area of Los Angeles. She chatted with her friend and press agent Patricia Newcomb—who had been her overnight houseguest—by the swimming pool. Her psychiatrist, Dr. Ralph Greenson, stopped by and spoke privately with her at about five in the afternoon. Miss Newcomb left about 6:00 P.M. and Dr. Greenson left at 6:30. Neighbors also reported having seen Robert Kennedy there late in the day. Marilyn received a number of phone calls—from her lawyer, from Peter Lawford, and from Joe DiMaggio, Jr.—after which she told her housekeeper, Mrs. Eunice Murray, that she was going to retire early. At eight that evening she went to her bedroom. Sometime after that Marilyn apparently tried to call Ralph Roberts, her masseur. His answering service later gave him the message that a "fuzzy-voiced and troubled" woman had tried to contact him.

At 4:25 A.M. the Los Angeles Police Dept. received a call from Dr. Hyman Engelberg, Marilyn's personal physician, who reported that he had pronounced the star dead at 3:40 A.M.

Official Version: The Los Angeles Police report stated that Mrs. Murray awoke about 3:30 A.M. and noticed that a light was still on in Marilyn's bedroom. After knocking on the door and getting no response, Mrs. Murray went to the bedroom window and saw Marilyn lying naked on her bed. Sensing something was wrong, she called Dr. Greenson, the psychiatrist, who told her to call Dr. Engelberg. Greenson entered the bedroom at approximately 3:40 and found Marilyn's body. Dr. Engelberg arrived shortly thereafter and pronounced her dead.

The subsequent coroner's report, issued by Los Angeles Deputy Medical Examiner Dr. Thomas Noguchi, gave the cause of death as "acute barbiturate poisoning, ingestion of overdose." The toxicologist's report, prepared by R. J. Abernathy of the Los Angeles County Coroner's Office, recorded 4.5 mg. percent of barbiturates in the blood and 13 mg. percent in the liver.

Dr. Greenson stated that Marilyn had been despondent recently, particularly on Saturday. Also, Dr. Engelberg noted that he had given her a prescription for 50 Nembutals (a barbiturate) a couple of days earlier. Police found the Nembutal vial among 15 other prescription bottles next to her bed, with only three capsules left in it.

An unofficial suicide investigation was conducted to try to ascertain whether the overdose was accidental or intentional. This investigation revealed that Marilyn had attempted suicide previously as a means of getting attention but that she had always called someone to rescue her. In this case, Dr. Greenson noted on discovering her body that she had the telephone receiver in her hand. The conclusion of the investigators was that she had repeated her past pattern, but had been overcome by the effect of the drugs before she could call anyone to help her.

Theories and Unanswered Questions: Since Marilyn Monroe's death, a number of investigators have asserted that she did not commit suicide but was murdered. They point to inconsistencies and contradictions in the statements made by the various people involved and in the official reports of the police and coroner, which clearly indicate that Marilyn Monroe was a homicide, not a suicide, victim.

The center of the controversy is the Los Angeles County coroner's report. It gives the cause of death as *ingestion* of barbiturates, yet when the coroner examined the stomach and duodenum on that Sunday morning, he found no trace of pills. In fact, the stomach contained nothing but an ounce of brownish liquid. An analysis for refractile crystals, which should have been left as a residue of the barbiturates, came back negative. The coroner noted that the small intestine appeared normal. In other words, the digestive system showed no signs of ingestion of barbiturates. The toxicologist's report showed barbiturates only in the blood and liver. Dr. Sidney Weinberg, a noted forensic pathologist, has stated, "There is no way Marilyn Monroe could have orally taken the drugs she allegedly took without some of them being present in her [digestive] system."

The official ingestion theory falls short on other points. The suicide investigation team stated: "We estimate that she took one gulp [of the alleged 47 Nembutals] within—let's say—a period of seconds." Dr. Engelberg's statement that he had given her a prescription for 50 Nembutal capsules was incorrect. Pharmacy records show that the prescription was for only 25 Nembutals, not the lethal 50. And though no one admitted moving her, Marilyn's body was neatly stretched out with no signs of the convulsions normally associated with such a death.

What all this suggests, as Dr. Weinberg and other pathologists have concluded, is the possibility that Marilyn Monroe died of an *injected* overdose of barbiturates. No syringe was found in her house, and she was never known to have given herself an injection. The only recent injections she had had were 13 of various drugs given to her by Dr. Engelberg over the previous month and a half. The coroner's report stated there were no injection marks on her body. This is quite strange, for the bill Dr. Engelberg filed against her estate shows that he gave her an injection the day before her death. The mark from that injection should have been easily detected.

Another discrepancy is the time of death. The police and coroner reports give it as Sunday at 3:40 A.M., when Engelberg pronounced her dead. However, when Engelberg arrived it was obvious to him that rigor mortis had set in and that Marilyn had been dead for three to six hours. Death most likely came in the late hours of Saturday night.

The motive for suicide, or even a faked suicide, rests on Dr. Greenson's comment that Marilyn seemed despondent on Saturday. But housekeeper Eunice Murray, Peter Lawford, press agent Pat Newcomb, and Joe DiMaggio, Jr., all reported that she seemed happy and positive when they talked to her on Saturday. Despite problems on her current picture, Marilyn was receiving more offers of roles than she could possibly handle. Financially she was well off, and she had just bought her first permanent home and was busy decorating it. The only area in which she was having problems was her love life, and this leads to even further questions about her death.

That Marilyn Monroe was having an affair with Attorney General Robert Kennedy, and most probably had had one with President John Kennedy earlier, is almost undisputed now. For several weeks, possibly a month, before her death, Robert Kennedy had attempted to break off the affair, but Marilyn had persistently tried to reach him at the Justice Dept. A few days before her death Marilyn had told a friend, writer Robert Slatzer, "If he [Robert Kennedy] keeps avoiding me, I might just call a press conference and tell them about it . . . and my future plans." In his biography of Marilyn, Slatzer asserts that Bobby actually visited her on the Saturday before she died, having flown down to Los Angeles from San Francisco, where he was officially supposed to be, and that he spent that night at his brother-in-law Peter Lawford's home in Santa Monica.

The Kennedy connection is a confusing and sensitive area. It is believed that Marilyn's phone had been tapped both by Robert Kennedy through the Justice Dept. and by his enemy, teamster boss Jimmy Hoffa.

(Telephone toll tickets, which might have shed light on the case, have disappeared.) That a cover-up was enacted by the Los Angeles police and coroner is suspected. Sgt. Jack Clemmons, who was the first police officer to arrive at Marilyn's house the night of her death, later stated, "She was murdered by needle injection by someone she knew and probably trusted. I have no doubt of it. This was the cover-up crime of the century—a matter of [Los Angeles Chief of Police] Bill Parker and other officials here protecting a famous political family of the East who had good reason to shut Monroe's mouth." Deputy Coroner Lionel Grandison, who signed Marilyn's death certificate, later stated, "The whole thing was organized to hide the truth. An original autopsy file vanished, a scrawled note that Marilyn Monroe wrote and which did not speak of suicide also vanished, and so did the first [Sgt. Clemmons's] police report. I was told to sign the official report—or I'd find myself in a position I couldn't get out of." It is also interesting to note that two key witnesses were not available for questioning after Marilyn's death. Mrs. Murray moved out of her apartment the next day, leaving no forwarding address. She later reported that she had come into some money and had taken an extended trip to Europe. Pat Newcomb, Marilyn's press agent, had an argument with reporters the Sunday when the body was discovered, and was fired from her job by the firm that employed her. She immediately accepted an invitation to visit the Kennedy compound at Hyannis Port, after which she also took a long European vacation. When she returned she went to work for the Justice Dept. in an office next door to Bobby Kennedy's.

In his book *Who Killed Marilyn?* (1976), Tony Sciacca presents a number of murder theories. One is that Kennedy loyalists in either the Justice Dept. or the CIA—possibly through Mafia connections—killed Marilyn Monroe with a lethal dose of injected barbiturates in order to protect the Kennedy brothers from the threat of scandal. Sciacca strenuously argues that he believes Robert Kennedy would have known nothing about this, that he was not involved in any way. Another theory is that rightist groups within the CIA killed Marilyn to expose the scandal and possibly frame Robert and John Kennedy. After their plot failed, they decided on more drastic measures against the Kennedys, which eventually led to Dallas and Los Angeles.

A number of writers, including Norman Mailer, relate other, sometimes bizarre, theories. One is that Jimmy Hoffa and the teamsters were involved in an effort to discredit or blackmail Robert Kennedy. A second is that Cuban agents murdered Monroe as a reprisal against the Kennedys for the CIA-initiated Mafia contract that was put out on Fidel Castro. Yet another outlandish theory attributes her death to Communist conspirators who sought to ruin the Kennedy brothers by linking them to murder.

—R.J.F.

JACK RUBY

Victim: Jacob Rubenstein was born in Chicago in 1911, the son of im-

Jack Ruby.

migrant Polish Jews. Young Jacob grew up in an explosive family atmosphere in which his carousing father often beat up his mentally unstable wife until the couple separated in 1921. At that time 10-year-old Jacob and his seven siblings were placed in foster homes. He quit school at 16 to hustle a living on the streets of Chicago. Nicknamed Sparky for his feisty temperament, he scalped sports tickets, sold pirated sheet music, and reportedly ran messages for Al Capone. In 1937 he was hired as an organizer for the newly formed Scrap Iron and Junk Handlers' Union for $22.50 a week. Drafted in 1943, he spent the war in the U.S. as an aircraft mechanic. He changed his name to Jack Ruby in 1947 while setting up a small-time business partnership with his brothers—a venture that failed. Later that year he moved to Dallas because, as he often boasted later, the Chicago crime syndicate had assigned him there. For the next 16 years he operated a number of sleazy nightclubs, the last being the Carousel, a walk-up strip joint at 1312½ Commerce Street, which he opened in 1960. His anemic profit margin there relied on such rip-offs as selling $1.60-a-bottle champagne for $17.50. Ruby relished serving as his own bouncer, since he enjoyed pistol-whipping rowdy drunks. In one club brawl, the tip of Ruby's right index finger was bitten off. Although arrested nine times in 16 years on a variety of charges, including assaulting a police officer, he never was convicted of a crime. For the most part, he maintained friendly relations with the Dallas police, who got their drinks free or at a cut rate when they visited Ruby's clubs. On Nov. 24, 1963, he somehow slipped into the basement of the Dallas jail, where TV cameramen were awaiting the appearance of Lee Harvey Oswald, who two days before allegedly had assassinated President John F. Kennedy. In what is still television's most chilling live spectacle, Ruby stepped forward to fire one fatal shot from a snub-nosed .38 caliber revolver into Oswald's left side. Convicted of murder on Mar. 14, 1964, Ruby was sentenced to death, but on Oct. 5, 1966, the Texas Court of Criminal Appeals overturned his conviction, citing judicial error. Before he could be tried a second time, Ruby died suddenly on Jan. 3, 1967.

His Death: While awaiting retrial, Ruby began complaining of a persistent cough and nausea. On Dec. 9, 1966, he was transferred from the Dallas County Jail to Parkland Hospital, where doctors initially diagnosed his trouble as pneumonia. The next day, however, it was learned that Ruby had terminal cancer. A team of doctors under the direction of Dr. Eugene P. Frenkel reportedly considered the disease so far advanced that they ruled out surgery or radiation treatment as useless and instead injected Ruby regularly with 5-fluorouracil to retard the cancer's progress. Late in the evening of Jan. 2, 1967, doctors suspected that blood clots were forming; they administered oxygen, and by the next morning Ruby seemed in high spirits. Then about 9:00 A.M. he suffered a spasm. Despite emergency procedures, he was dead by 10:30 A.M.

Official Version: After performing an autopsy, Dallas County Medical Examiner Dr. Earl Rose ruled the immediate cause of death to be pulmonary embolism. He said a massive blood clot had formed in the leg, passed through the heart, and lodged in the lungs. He also found evidence of cancer in the right lung, which he listed as a contributing cause of death. But much to the surprise of Ruby's doctors, who believed that the disease had originated in the pancreas, Dr. Rose found the pancreas perfectly normal.

Theories and Unanswered Questions: In 1979 the House Select Committee on Assassinations, after a two-and-a-half-year inquiry, asserted that a conspiracy to assassinate President Kennedy likely did exist, probably involving elements of organized crime. Thus arises the theory that some crime figure contracted Oswald to kill the President, hired Ruby to silence Oswald, and then ordered a third party to eliminate Ruby. Supporting this theory are Ruby's long-standing, though loose, ties to various underworld figures. Just three weeks before Kennedy's death, for example, Ruby placed a call to the New Orleans office of the Tropical Court Tourist Park, operated by Nofio Pecora, a lieutenant of New Orleans *capo* Carlos Marcello. The House committee also concluded that one of Ruby's police pals probably helped him slip into the Dallas jail basement through which Oswald was to pass, perhaps unaware of Ruby's murderous intent. Also troubling is Ruby's sudden financial solvency. Chronically hard-pressed for cash, he owed some $40,000 in back taxes, but suddenly, days before Kennedy was shot, he was flashing $7,000 in cash and bragging about having a connection who would bail him out of his tax problems. While in jail Ruby often repeated his story that he had shot Oswald spontaneously and out of compassion for Mrs. Kennedy, most notably in a taped conversation with his brother Earl a couple of weeks before his death. But when representatives of the Warren Commission saw Ruby in Dallas, he begged to be moved to Washington for the interview so that he could tell the *real* story. And in papers smuggled out of his Dallas jail cell, Ruby wrote, "Don't believe the Warren Report. That was only put out to . . . throw the Americans and all the European countries off guard. They have found a means and ways to frame me, by deception, etc., and they have succeeded." He also claimed that he had been injected with live cancer cells by those who were afraid he would talk. Another unsettling aspect of the Ruby case is the fact that Broadway gossip columnist Dorothy Kilgallen paid a celebrated visit to Ruby during his trial. During the next year and a half, Kilgallen continued her investigation of the Kennedy assassination. On Nov. 8, 1965, she was found dead in her apartment, a death officially attributed to a combination of barbiturates and alcohol. No notes of her interview with Ruby ever turned up. Still, for all the unanswered questions, how could Ruby have been killed? His autopsy seemed to rule out poison or external violence, although Ruby had frequently charged that officials were systematically poisoning him. One possibility is that the mob may have leaned on Ruby's doctors to "overlook" his cancer until it had advanced beyond control.

Ruby himself had this to say in a filmed interview shortly before his death: "The world will never know the true facts of what occurred—my motives. . . . Unfortunately, the people that had so much to gain and had such an ulterior motive, and who put me in the position I'm in, will never let the true facts come aboveboard to the world."

—W.A.D.

KAREN SILKWOOD

Victim: Karen Gay Silkwood was a 28-year-old laboratory worker in the Kerr-McGee Corporation's Cimarron facility, a plant near Oklahoma City which manufactures highly radioactive plutonium fuel for nuclear reactors. She had begun work at the plant in the fall of 1972, after her six-year marriage had broken up. Her three children were left in the custody of their father after he remarried.

Silkwood joined the Oil, Chemical and Atomic Workers' Union (OCAW) and was elected to the union's governing committee in the spring of 1974. Throughout that summer she noticed a rapid decline in safety standards at the plant after a production speed-up caused a high worker turnover. As a result, newly hired employees assumed positions for which they had received little training. She started taking notes on what she saw and interviewing workers who had become contaminated or who had reported safety violations. Silkwood herself became contaminated by airborne particles and had to go through the decontamination process. She and two other members of the union's steering committee were invited to Washington to the OCAW national offices, where she told union legislative officials that the plant's procedures were sloppy and unsafe. These officials were the first to inform her that

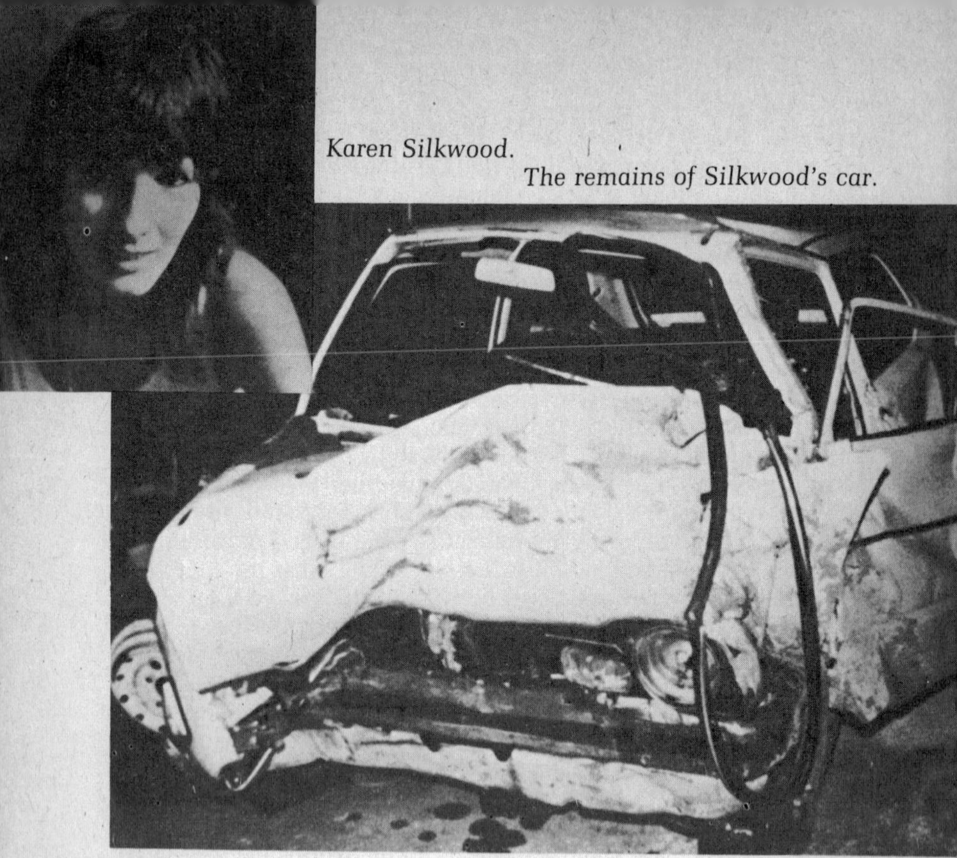

Karen Silkwood.

The remains of Silkwood's car.

plutonium, one of the most toxic substances known, was believed to cause cancer. The officials asked her to work undercover to gather company files as corroborating evidence of mismanagement. She continued to take notes at the lab and relayed her findings to union official Steve Wodka in Washington when she had collected contamination reports and information on defective rods. After she again became contaminated and no source at the plant was discovered, inspectors went to her apartment, where both her bathroom and kitchen were found to be extremely "hot." Since plutonium by law has to be kept under the strictest security, questions arose as to how any had escaped from the nuclear facility.

During the six days before she died Silkwood spoke to investigators from the Atomic Energy Commission and the Oklahoma State Health Dept., attempting to explain how she had gotten contaminated in her own home. Silkwood supporters later claimed that Kerr-McGee had planted the plutonium in her apartment to scare her off her union activities, while Kerr-McGee maintained that Silkwood herself had carried it back to her apartment in order to make the company look bad. When doctors informed her that she was infected with "less than one-half of the maximum permissible body burden" of plutonium, her fears were assuaged somewhat. She returned to work at the lab and went through with her plans on the night of Nov. 13 to meet with a *New York Times* reporter and Steve Wodka and give them the documents she had collected.

Her Death: Shortly after six o'clock that evening, Silkwood left a union meeting at the Hub Café in Crescent to meet with the *Times* reporter and Steve Wodka in Oklahoma City, about 30 mi. away. She was driving her white Honda Civic about 50 mph down Highway 74 when the car went off the left side of the road, ran 240 to 270 ft. along a ditch, and hit the south wall of a concrete culvert. The car traveled approximately 24 ft. into the air, then crashed on the culvert's north wall at about 45 mph. Silkwood died instantly.

Official Version: The Oklahoma State Highway Patrol ruled that Silkwood had fallen asleep at the wheel and drifted off the left side of the road to her death. Although a drifting car tends to pull to the right, a 1974 *Consumer Reports* review of the Honda Civic Hatchback described its tendency during acceleration "to lunge and pull to the left." The patrol also cites an autopsy report showing that methaqualone, a sleep-inducing drug prescribed for Silkwood to combat stress, was present in her blood, stomach, and liver. This explains why Silkwood made no effort to apply the brakes or veer away from the concrete culvert. A dent discovered in the car's rear bumper was said to have been caused by the wrecker that dragged the Honda over the concrete wall. Later, Justice Dept. and FBI investigations agreed that there was no foul play, and two congressional subcommittees subsequently dropped their investigations.

Theories and Unanswered Questions: The union's accident investigator found that the Honda's tire tracks showed that the car had skidded violently off the left side of the highway, then had straightened and driven along the shoulder for nearly 100 yd. He cites this as evidence that Silkwood was prevented from returning to the highway by the presence of another car. Not until she saw the culvert did she frantically try to steer the car back onto the road. The investigator argues that a drifting car would have veered into a field before it reached the culvert, and that the highway's center-line crest would have deflected a drifting car to the right, not the left. The "drifting car" theory is also disputed by eight independent toxicologists interviewed separately by investigating reporters. They agreed that Silkwood had built up such a tolerance to methaqualone that the small amount of the drug found in her body would not have lulled her to sleep. An auto-crash expert hired by OCAW found that the dent in the car's rear bumper resulted from "contact between two metal surfaces." Under magnification, the dent showed scratch marks leading from the rear of the car toward the front, an indication that the car had been struck.

Other curiosities surround her death. A *Rolling Stone* investigation suggests that the Kerr-McGee plant was missing substantial amounts of plutonium from its inventory—enough to bring millions of dollars in a potential nuclear black market. The magazine speculates that Silkwood may have unwittingly stumbled across falsified Kerr-McGee inventory records as she was gathering information for the union. One of the last people to see her alive described in a sworn affidavit the documents Silkwood had with her the night of her death, contained in a brown manila folder and a large notebook. They have never been found.

The mysteries surrounding the Silkwood death remained unsolved when the suit brought by her parents finally reached the courts in March, 1979. The presiding judge allowed only one issue to be decided: Kerr-McGee's negligence in Silkwood's contamination. Other counts, which might have uncovered possible liability for her death, were thrown out. Lawyers for the Silkwood case theorize from the pattern of circumstantial evidence that Silkwood was under surveillance by Kerr-McGee, who knew about her special union assignment. The lawyers were not allowed to present a Kerr-McGee official's testimony that documents with the plant insignia had been found in the car and that—according to the owner of the garage where Silkwood's car was towed—only police, government, and Kerr-McGee officials visited the wreck during the night of the accident.

Though the jury decided on May 18, 1979, to award $10 million in punitive damages to the Silkwood estate (Kerr-McGee has apealed the decision), there is still no resolution to the question of whether she was murdered and, if so, by whom. In November, 1980, the case was reopened when congressional investigator Peter Stockton filed a suit against the FBI and officials of Kerr-McGee, claiming that they had conspired to put an end to any further inquiry into Silkwood's death.

—B.B.

HISTORICAL CONTROVERSIES

WHO REALLY DISCOVERED ANESTHESIA?

THE EXPLOIT

Since the birth of the medical profession, surgery had been a brutally painful affair. For centuries doctors had sought ways to eliminate—or at least lessen—the pain experienced during operations. Induced temporary asphyxiation, freezing of surgical areas, hypnotism, inhalation of narcotic plant fumes, and alcoholic stupefaction had all been tried in an effort to combat pain. However, none of these adequately controlled pain. In 1839 the noted French surgeon Alfred Velpeau summarized current medical opinion when he stated, "The abolishment of pain in surgery is a chimera. It is absurd to go on seeking it today. *Knife* and *pain* are two words in surgery that must forever be associated."

Only a few years later, this bleak assessment was totally disproved. In America in the 1840s, two dentists and two doctors were experimenting with chemical agents that would lead to surgical painkillers. The advent of anesthesia—a word coined by Oliver Wendell Holmes, Sr., and derived from the Greek word meaning lack of feeling—was at hand, as was a controversy that has continued into the 20th century.

THE CONTENDERS AND THEIR STORIES

DR. CRAWFORD LONG (1815–1878)

The son of a well-to-do Southerner, Crawford Long was born in Georgia and attended the University of Pennsylvania, after which he practiced surgery in New York City. Although a brilliant young surgeon, Long was forced to return to Georgia because of family problems and assume a rural practice in the hamlet of Jefferson in 1841.

The 26-year-old doctor, a sociable and adventuresome man, became interested in a current craze—nitrous oxide sniffing. Long and several friends tried to obtain nitrous oxide—also known as laughing gas—and when none was available, Long suggested they try another gas, sulfuric ether, which they did. During these "ether frolics," Long noted that some of his friends severely bruised themselves but felt no pain.

Long recalled this observation on Mar. 30, 1842, when James Venable, a fellow ether-sniffer, came to him to have a growth removed from his neck. Long had Venable sniff ether and then cut out the tumor. Venable felt nothing. In his journal, Long recorded: "James Venable, 1842. Ether and excising tumor, $2.00." Over the next four years Long performed seven more operations while his patients were anesthetized with ether. In 1849 he published his results in the *Southern Medical and Surgical Journal*.

Of all the anesthesia-discovery claimants, Long was the one least involved in the controversy. He remained in private practice in Georgia until his death at the age of 62.

HORACE WELLS (1815–1848)

A tall, handsome New Englander, Horace Wells studied dentistry and opened his first practice in Hartford, Conn., in 1836, at the age of 21. Wells gained a solid reputation as a dentist and prospered, but he was disturbed by the pain he inflicted, especially during extractions.

In December of 1844, Wells attended a traveling show at which nitrous oxide demonstrations were performed. Wells noticed that a man who struck his shins while under the influence of the gas felt nothing. Wells invited the laughing-gas showman, Gardner Colton, to meet him at his office the next day. During this visit Wells asked Colton to administer nitrous oxide to him while another dentist extracted one of Wells's teeth. The extraction was painless. Thereafter, Wells learned how to manufacture and administer this gas, and he used it in a number of extractions. He did not patent the gas because he believed it should "be as free as the air we breathe."

With the assistance of his former dental partner, William Morton, Wells demonstrated his discovery at Massachusetts General Hospital in January, 1845. Wells began his extraction before the gas had taken effect, however, and the patient screamed. The attending medical observers jeered Wells, and he was ridiculed as a charlatan in the Boston press.

In December of 1846, Wells printed the results of his studies in anesthesia, but his ostracism by the Boston medical profession had left him an emotionally crippled man. He continued to experiment—on himself—with a variety of gases, including nitrous oxide, ether, and chloroform. These vapor inhalations strongly affected him emotionally, and he deteriorated mentally. In New York City in 1848, he sniffed chloroform, went berserk, and threw acid on the clothes of a prostitute. Jailed for this offense, Wells committed suicide by slashing an artery in his leg.

DR. CHARLES JACKSON (1805–1880)

An eccentric genius, Massachusetts-born Charles Jackson's career embraced both medicine and geology, and he was not only a renowned medical chemist but also a mineralogist.

A flamboyant yet brilliant scientist, Jackson had observed as early as 1834 that chloroform deadened nerves, and in 1837 he had studied the effects of nitrous oxide. In 1842, according to his account, he rendered himself unconscious for 15 minutes by inhaling ether and so realized the anesthetic properties of that gas. On Sept. 30, 1846, Jackson instructed William Morton to use ether in tooth extractions and thus invented anesthesia.

In the decades that followed, Jackson was bitterly embroiled in the unresolved controversy over who had discovered anesthesia. He continued to work as a chemist and geologist until 1873, when he became violently insane, possibly due to his personal experimentation with various gases, and was admitted to an asylum. There he died seven years later.

WILLIAM MORTON (1819–1868)

The son of a New England farmer, William Morton first worked as a clerk and salesman, but his ambitious nature led him to study, and eventually practice, dentistry. In 1842 he became the partner of Horace Wells, who later introduced him to his experiments with nitrous oxide. During 1844 Morton lived in Boston while he studied with Dr. Charles Jackson, who taught him about the chemical properties of gases.

By 1845 Morton had invented an easily manufactured denture, which he planned to market. However, this denture required the removal of all of the patient's teeth, usually an extremely painful process. This problem encouraged Morton to investigate anesthesia. He studied Wells's work with nitrous oxide and observed Wells's failure at Massachusetts General in 1845. Finally, Morton consulted Charles Jackson about the gases available for experimentation. According to Morton, Jackson suggested he try sulfuric ether, which was known to have a localized painkilling effect.

On Sept. 30, 1846, a patient named Eben Frost came to Morton's office. Terrified at the thought of pain, Frost agreed to try Morton's painkiller invention. The subsequent extraction, which utilized sulfuric ether, was painless. A few weeks later Morton was approached by Boston surgeon Henry Bigelow, who had heard of Morton's discovery and wanted to test it in a surgical theater.

On Oct. 16, 1846, Morton used ether at Massachusetts General. The patient was operated on for a vascular tumor while painlessly unconscious, and Morton was promptly proclaimed the inventor of anesthesia by the Boston medical profession. For the next 20 years Morton invested his time and money acquiring and defending patents. At first he called the ether gas "Morton's letheon" and refused to reveal what it was. After it was found to be simple ether, his patents were impossible to defend, and even the U.S. Army ignored them. In fact, with the growing controversy over who discovered anesthesia, the government annulled his patent in 1862 until the matter could be settled—which it never was. Morton's dreams of wealth from his discovery never materialized; he died destitute in New York City of a stroke.

THE CONTROVERSY

Never before or since has a medical discovery generated such heated debate and bitterness. By 1849 the controversy over who discovered anesthesia had become such a public issue that the U.S. Congress was called on to resolve the matter. However, even Congress became deadlocked over the issue. The controversy centers on the definition of discovery. Is discovery of a medical process simply the mental conceptualization of the process, or does it also require a practical application of the process? And does a medical discoverer have to publicize and expose his invention to the medical profession and the world in order to be awarded credit?

PRO LONG

Long supporters point to one simple fact when they back his claim that he was the discoverer of anesthesia. That fact is that on Mar. 30, 1842—before any other claimant—he performed the first surgical operation utilizing anesthesia—in this case, sulfuric ether.

PRO WELLS

Wells advocates, along with those of Jackson and Morton, hold that a discovery is not a discovery if it is not presented to the world. Not until three years after Morton's demonstration in Boston, and after ether had been accepted into general practice, did Long reveal that he had discovered anesthesia. If Long had not heard about the anesthesia debate in Congress in 1849, Wells supporters contend, he never would have published his claims, and knowledge of his "ether frolic" experiments would have died with him.

Wells partisans say that Wells conducted the first operations using anesthesia which led to the general acceptance and use of anesthesia. Wells's work gave medical exposure to anesthesia even if his January, 1845, demonstration was a failure. In fact, Morton's demonstrations were merely a continuation of Wells's experiments and a vindication of his concepts. Wells discovered and presented anesthesia to the world, while Morton gave the first practical demonstration of Wells's work.

PRO JACKSON

The Jackson partisans assert that Jackson, with ether, discovered anesthesia, and that Morton was merely Jackson's assistant in publicly demonstrating the substance.

PRO MORTON

Morton partisans deny that Morton was carrying on the work of either Wells or Jackson, and claim instead that he did his own independent research. Among the many specialists he interviewed was Jackson, who mentioned that ether had been used as a localized painkiller. Morton took these ideas and suggestions from various sources and synthesized them, thus discovering and publicly demonstrating anesthesia to the world.

Morton supporters have vented their full wrath on Jackson. They assert that he was merely a glory-seeker who tried to take credit for the accomplishments of everyone he came into contact with. They point out that, before the anesthesia controversy, Jackson contended that he had invented the telegraph because he had once proposed the concept during a discussion of electricity with Samuel Morse. In actuality, Jackson was just a chemist who gave Morton technical advice. Morton supporters deny the claim that he was Jackson's assistant by pointing to the fact that Jackson advised against and refused to be associated with Morton's Massachusetts General demonstration because it was, in Jackson's words, "too dangerous." Only after Morton had been acknowledged as anesthesia's discoverer did the other claimants publish their results and their challenges. Morton advocates maintain that Morton conceptualized, implemented, demonstrated, and presented anesthesia to the world.

—R.J.F.

WHO REALLY INVENTED THE AIRPLANE?

THE EXPLOIT

For ages people had been fascinated by the thought of aerial flight. Leonardo da Vinci designed a flying machine in the 15th century, and by the 19th century men were airborne in hot-air balloons, gliders, and huge kites. But they still had not built a craft that could fly independent of the forces of nature; flight still depended on the whimsy of the wind. Steam and gasoline engines, however, made it theoretically possible to construct a heavier-than-air craft that could be lifted off the ground and sustained in flight by its own power source. And so, at the end of the 19th century, enthusiasts around the world joined in the race to invent the first flying machine.

THE CONTENDERS AND THEIR STORIES

CLÉMENT ADER (1841–1925)

Clément Ader was intrigued by aerial navigation even as a boy growing up in the south of France. His interest led him to build and design countless kites, and while he was still young he succeeded in producing a kite capable of carrying a man aloft. Ader worked in the Dept. of Public Works for 15 years but quit his job to tinker with his inventions. He designed the first telephone system in Paris, a public-address device, and a microphone, but he never lost his interest in aeronautics. In the early 1870s he created an ornithopter, an engine to which was attached flapping wings, but it failed to fly. Then Ader went to Algeria to study the flight of vultures and discovered that once airborne they rarely flapped their wings. He promptly scrapped the design of the ornithopter as impractical. In order to fly, he decided, a machine must have fixed wings and an engine capable of lifting it off the ground. Back in France, he built his first airplane, the *Éole* (named for Aeolus, the Greek god of the winds).

The *Éole* had bat-shaped wings and was driven by a steam engine attached to a four-blade propeller. Ader tested his airplane near Gretz-Armainvilliers on Oct. 9, 1890, and claimed that he accomplished a takeoff and a powered flight of approximately 165 ft. There were a few witnesses to his feat but they were not familiar with aeronautics, and consequently none of them reported what he saw. Ader asserted that he had tested the *Éole* a second time at the army base at Satory near Versailles in September of 1891 and flew roughly 330 ft. at an altitude of 8 in. above the ground before crashing. There supposedly was only one witness; he did not make a statement to authorities about what he saw. Ader himself did not publicly report this flight until 1906.

Ader kept working to perfect his airplane, and finally, with the financial backing of the French Army, he built *Avion III*, a flying machine similar in design to the *Éole* but with a longer wingspan and two four-blade propellers. On Oct. 14, 1897, Ader tested his *Avion* at Satory with a military observer team present. Ader claimed that that day he had again flown, but three witnesses disagreed with each other about whether Ader actually took off and flew the *Avion* before it crashed. With the destruction of *Avion III*, Ader abandoned his career as an aerial inventor and test pilot. He spent a good portion of his last years trying to prove his claims, and he published two books on military aviation before he died at Toulouse in 1925.

SAMUEL PIERPONT LANGLEY (1834–1906)

Samuel Langley, born in Roxbury, Mass., had a wealthy father who encouraged him to study and to pursue educational hobbies. Langley's childhood love was astronomy, but he eventually chose civil engineering as his occupation. After several years at jobs as a qualified engineer and architect, he changed directions and went back to his study of astronomy and science. He taught mathematics at the U.S. Naval Academy, became director of the Allegheny Observatory, and taught physics and astronomy at the University of Pittsburgh though he had never earned a college degree. In the late 1880s his studies on the effects of the sun on the weather and wind currents led him to aviation.

Langley was soon experimenting with models, the first of which were powered by rubber bands. When he became the secretary of the Smithsonian Institution, he drew on the expertise and knowledge of the technicians and scientists there. The result was the completion of a series of test planes. On May 6, 1896, with his friend Alexander Graham Bell as an observer, Langley sent his *Aerodrome Number* 5 into the air,

Nine days before the Wright brothers' success, Samuel Langley's attempted flight failed.

launched from a catapult on top of a houseboat in the middle of the Potomac River. This 30-lb. craft with a steam engine flew for 1 min. 20 sec. at an altitude of 70 to 100 ft. for a distance of 3,000 ft. It was the first successful flight of an unmanned heavier-than-air flying machine. Langley's *Aerodrome Number 6* had mechanical problems that day, but it flew 4,200 ft. in November of 1896.

In 1898, at President William McKinley's instigation, the U.S. Army awarded Langley $50,000 to develop a plane that would carry a man aloft. In December, 1903, nine days before the Wrights' test at Kitty Hawk, Langley tried out his new gasoline-powered experimental model. A mishap with the catapult caused the airplane to plunge to the bottom of the Potomac, and Langley gave up his experiments after being criticized by the press for the great expense to the taxpayers.

ALBERTO SANTOS-DUMONT (1873–1932)

Jules Verne's fictional accounts of flying machines inspired young Alberto Santos-Dumont, son of a wealthy Brazilian coffee plantation owner, to fantasies about flight. At age 18, when his father's death made him a millionaire, Santos-Dumont sailed for France, where he became engrossed in internal-combustion engines and automobiles. In 1897 he flew in a balloon for the first time and thereafter became one of the foremost balloonists in France.

In 1905 he built an airplane consisting of three box kites connected to each other by bamboo poles, powered by a steam engine. Strapping his machine to the undercarriage of a balloon, Santos-Dumont went aloft, started the airplane's engine, climbed into the cockpit, and cut the plane loose from the balloon. He plummeted to the ground. However, he persevered and built a new model, which he tested outside Paris on Oct. 23, 1906. With the same kite-shaped wings but a lighter gasoline engine, this airplane successfully took off and flew 722 ft. before landing. Qualified witnesses verified and documented the takeoff and flight. The French government recognized this as the first time a human being had flown in a heavier-than-air machine.

For the next four years Santos-Dumont continued his aeronautical experiments, but in 1910 he contracted disseminating sclerosis and never flew again. He returned to Brazil in 1928, became increasingly depressed over the fact that world powers were using airplanes in warfare, and committed suicide four years later.

THE WRIGHT BROTHERS

Orville and Wilbur Wright, the sons of a midwestern minister, displayed a high mechanical aptitude even in their youth. This, coupled with investigative natures, made Orville (1871–1948) and Wilbur (1867–1912) ideal inventors. By their early twenties they had built a printing press and designed a new bicycle, which they also manufactured. They became interested in flight by reading about the glider experiments of German aerialist Otto Lilienthal.

For three years Orville and Wilbur built and tested gliders on the tree-barren sand dunes of Kitty Hawk, N.C. During the winters at their bicycle plant in Dayton, O., they experimented with new wing shapes and control systems in a wind tunnel that they also invented. By December of 1903, the brothers were back at Kitty Hawk with their first powered airplane, a double-winged, box kite–shaped contraption with an undercarriage attached to a stationary monorail track. On Dec. 17 Orville stretched out in the middle of the lower wing and took off on a 12-sec., 120-ft. flight. That same day, Wilbur flew for 59 sec., covering 852 ft. The tests were observed by five witnesses. The brothers continued to perfect their machine, and in 1906 they were granted a U.S. patent for their invention. However, they did not publicly demonstrate their airplane until 1908, after which they were awarded U.S. Army and French commercial contracts to manufacture them.

(L to R) Orville and Wilbur Wright.

THE CONTROVERSY

Controversy still rages over who really invented the first airplane because it's not just a matter of who devised a craft that got off the ground. It depends on how one defines flight. Which of these inventions, if any, took off from the ground and stayed in the air under its own mechanical power rather than depending on forces such as momentum or wind? In order to be considered true flight, did it have to be sustained and well controlled? Does 10 sec. in the air count as much as 10 min.? If the machine lost power and crashed, does that count as much as a three-point landing? Finally, based on modern-day knowledge, were any of these machines compatible with proven theories of aeronautical design?

PRO ADER

Ader's claims are often attacked because of his lack of qualified witnesses, but the Wright brothers in 1903 had only five witnesses, none of whom was a qualified aeronautical engineer. In fact, one of the Wrights' witnesses, A. W. Drinkwater, stated in an interview in the early 1950s that the Wrights had not achieved powered flight but only a powered glide in 1903. They had launched their plane into a strong headwind, down a sand dune, using their monorail undercarriage system; all the engine did was power the plane as a glider once it was airborne. Compared to this, Ader had the testimony of General Mensier of the French Army General Staff, who at one point in time stated that at Satory in 1897 *Avion III* took off by itself from the ground.

Another argument against Ader is that he did not achieve sustained or controlled flight. Ader's supporters counter that any number of qualifications can be added to the definition of flight and that although Ader's machines lacked sophisticated controls and never flew great distances, they still satisfied the basic requirement of taking off under their own power.

Later investigation showed that Ader's steam engine was a highly efficient mechanism, powerful but amazingly light. Some experts, including certain of Ader's detractors, contend that his engine was far more suitable for flight than the engine used by the Wright brothers.

Ader's proponents maintain that, although his flights were largely uncontrolled and brief, he successfully flew at least six years before the Wright brothers.

PRO LANGLEY

Langley's supporters have had to refute two major arguments concerning his claim. First, that his 1896 airplane was unmanned and therefore only a model, while his man-carrying plane was a failure. But his adherents assert that his machines met all requirements for controlled, lengthy flight. The manned airplane failed, not because of any inherent mechanical difficulties, but simply because of the faulty catapult. Second, some argue that Langley's airplanes did not, and could not, use their own motive power for takeoff. Langley partisans claim that he could have ascended from the ground but was concerned with the damage that might occur on landing. It is also asserted that the engine of Langley's flying machine was efficient enough to power a takeoff.

Even Wilbur Wright once admitted that Langley had a stronger claim than any other contender, saying Langley had provided "the first practical demonstration of the possibility of mechanical flight," and that he and his brother were influenced in their work by Langley's skills. The Langley claim is in agreement with the Wrights' claim that Ader's aircraft never flew, but it points out that Langley's machines had achieved flight some seven years before the Wright brothers and ten years before Santos-Dumont.

PRO SANTOS-DUMONT

A number of aviation historians assert that none of these contenders—not Langley or the Wright brothers—was the first to invent a viable heavier-than-air machine. These authorities argue that the Wrights' supporters are correct in their evaluations of Ader. They also claim that Langley's unmanned, unguided, catapult-launched airplane cannot be seriously considered, and that the Wrights achieved only a powered glide in 1903. They contend that Alberto Santos-Dumont on Oct. 23, 1906, became the first man to fly. They point out that the French government, in spite of its later patent award to the Wright brothers, officially recognized this 1906 event as the first witnessed powered flight. Unlike the case with the other claimants, no aeronautics experts dispute the fact that Santos-Dumont's flight met *all* the necessary definitions and criteria. That would make him the father of the airplane.

PRO WRIGHT BROTHERS

Supporters of Orville and Wilbur Wright deny that Ader flew in 1890, in 1891, or in 1897. They underscore the fact that Ader did not press his claims until 1906, when the Wrights were already acknowledged as the inventors of the airplane. Only after Ader could not officially prove that he flew in 1897, since his witnesses disagreed as to whether *Avion III* actually became airborne or simply made short hops off the ground when it was buffeted by crosswinds, did he assert that he had also flown in 1890 and 1891. He named dates and places but could not produce witnesses.

Pro-Wright authorities also contend that Ader's craft lacked the proper aerial design for controlled and sustained flight. Even if his engine could launch the craft, that did not constitute flying, for a sky-rocket powered by gunpowder could do the same. It was not until the Wrights took off in an aeronautically feasible craft, with its well-designed stabilizers and wings, that man flew for the first time, they assert. And in spite of the fact that there were no public or formal demonstrations, Orville and Wilbur had so well mastered aviation that by the fall of 1905 they could claim flights lasting half an hour covering distances of up to 24 mi.

As further proof there are the patents awarded by a French patent court in 1911 and an American patent court in 1914, which named the brothers as the inventors of the airplane. Charles Dollfus, honorary curator of the Paris Air Museum, who was assigned by the French government to examine Ader's papers after his death, stated categorically: "Ader did not fly for a single instant at Satory in the course of the tests of . . . 1897." And, finally, the Wrights went on to prove their claims by perfecting the airplane and producing it commercially.

—R.J.F.

TOPICAL CONTROVERSIES

ABORTION

DEFINITION

Sensationalism naturally results when the abortion issue is raised. Anti-abortion groups send pickled fetuses to their congressmen and publicly display grisly photographs of tiny-dismembered hands and feet from aborted fetuses. The symbol of the National Abortion Rights Action League is a coat hanger, an abortion tool often used by desperate women in the days before liberalized abortion laws. The issue is a gut-level one, and, sensationalism aside, it typifies what may be the central issue of our time: Which is more fundamental to the future of the human race—an arbitrary respect for life or the choice of quality of life over quantity of life? Technological and scientific advances have further complicated the question; for example, doctors can now identify a defective fetus in the womb. In addition, life can be evaluated by cost-effectiveness statistics; the price of keeping one person alive may take life away from others.

In 1800 abortion was not illegal in the U.S. until "quickening," the fetal movement in the womb in the fourth or fifth month—at that time the only certain proof of pregnancy. By 1860 abortion was against the law in most states for various reasons—medical dangers, dropping birthrate, Victorian prudishness. In 1973 the U.S. Supreme Court liberalized abortion laws based on the woman's right to privacy. In the first trimester (three months), the decision to abort is left to the woman and her doctor. In the second trimester, states may intervene to protect the woman's health. In the third trimester, an abortion can be denied. In 1980 the U.S. Supreme Court upheld the 1976 Hyde Amendment, which restricted Medicaid payments for abortion.

The abortion question is this: Does a pregnant woman have the legal right to decide for herself whether to have an induced abortion? On both sides of the issue are strange bedfellows; Feminists for Life, for example, are pro-ERA and anti-abortion. As you read the informal debate that follows, imagine a room in which two anonymous debaters—one anti-abortion and the other pro-abortion—bring forth witnesses who at various times have had something meaningful to say on the issue.

PROS AND CONS

Issue: Which comes first—the woman's right to free choice or the fetus's right to live?

Pro Abortion: A woman has the right to control her own body; she is not just a walking incubator. Her decision to abort or not to abort is a private one. Government has no right to interfere.

Anti Abortion: In civilized societies, people don't have total control over their own bodies. It is against the law to abuse your body with drugs, for example. Some invasions of privacy are legal and acceptable; consider child-abuse laws and control of communicable disease.

Anti-abortion Witness Juli Loesch, Feminist: "Each woman has the right [to use birth control]. . . . But once a woman has conceived, she can no longer choose whether or not to become a mother. Biologically, she already is a mother. . . . The woman's rights are then limited, as every right is limited, by the existence of another human being who also has rights."

Anti-abortion Witness Jesse Jackson, Black Leader: "You could not protest the existence or treatment of slaves on the plantation because that was private and therefore outside of your right to be concerned."

Pro Abortion: In most Protestant and Jewish denominations, the fetus is considered a potential person, not an actual one. According to Talmudic law, for example, a fetus is not a person until born; before its birth, the mother's welfare is primary. Just because the fetus *will be* a person doesn't mean it *is* one.

The fetus is dependent on the woman's body—the placenta and umbilical cord; without her, it would die. Consider Judith Thomson's analogy, given in the article "A Defense of Abortion": A person wakes up to find that he or she has been hooked to a comatose violinist with a kidney ailment. Without the host's blood, the violinist would die. Is the individual morally obligated to stay hooked up to the violinist for nine months? No, says Thomson. In comparison, the fetus has the right to its mother's body only if she grants it.

Pro-abortion Witness Joseph Fletcher, Episcopalian Priest: "There is no such thing as an unborn baby." The fetus is "gametic material."

Pro-abortion Witness Alan Guttmacher, Planned Parenthood: "My feeling is that the fetus, particularly during its early intrauterine life, is merely a group of specialized cells that do not differ materially from other cells."

Anti Abortion: The zygote (fertilized egg) is a masterpiece of God, already a human individual because of its unique genetic code, which came into being when the egg and sperm united. At 4 to 5 weeks, a baby in the womb has a heartbeat. By 8 weeks, all limbs and organs are formed. By 10 weeks, it makes faces. A premature baby, born only 17 weeks after fertilization, has lived outside the womb. It won't be long before artificial wombs will nurture very tiny fetuses. Some aborted babies have survived abortion only to be strangled by physicians.

Anti-abortion Witness Bernard Nathanson, a Physician Who Changed Sides: "Human life exists within the womb from the very onset of pregnancy."

Pro Abortion: It is not so simple as that. Twinning occurs between the 7th and 14th day following fertilization. Can a unique person be split in two? When do we assign the fetus full value with full rights? Philosophers, religious authorities, and physicians disagree on the criteria—social and mental development and other factors—used to determine personhood. As for the horror stories of babies that survive abortions, such babies are extremely rare because 96% of abortions are performed in the first trimester. Later abortions usually involve saving the life of the mother, or severe deformity of the fetus.

Pro-abortion Witness U.S. Supreme Court Justice Harry A. Blackmun, in His Opinion on the 1973 Abortion Decision: "We need not resolve the difficult question of when life begins. When those trained in the respective disciplines of medicine, philosophy, and theology are unable to arrive at any consensus, the judiciary, at this point in the development of man's knowledge, is not in a position to speculate as to the answer."

Issue: Does legalized abortion lead to a general devaluing of human life?

Anti Abortion: Every person—handicapped, senile, eccentric, or unborn—has the right to his or her own life. By allowing abortion we open the door to infanticide, euthanasia, and other types of murder. If abortion is allowed, we will begin to think like Nazis.

Pro Abortion: The right to choose abortion does not lead to the devaluation of human life. A study of 23 preindustrial cultures proves it. In 11 of those cultures abortion was punished, and in the other 12 it was allowed. Yet in the 11 societies that considered abortion to be a crime, slavery, murder, and torture were rampant. Fifteen of the societies practiced infanticide; of those, 8 punished abortion and 7 did not. Abortion does not equal genocide.

Anti-abortion Witness Adolf Hitler, Genocidal Dictator: Anti-abortionists have often accused the other side of having a Hitlerian philosophy. Hitler was against abortion, not in support of it. As he wrote in *Mein Kampf*, "I'll put an end to the idea that a woman's body belongs to her. . . . Nazi ideals demand that the practice of abortion shall be exterminated with a strong hand." (Hitler sentenced Aryan women who had abortions to hard labor after the first offense, to death after the second.)

Anti Abortion: Though hardly ever stated openly by pro-abortion groups, one of the reasons for liberalized abortion is population control, particularly of poor and minority groups. In some states an abortion costs only about 1/17 as much as the cost of paying welfare for a child for one year. As for worldwide overpopulation, more humane solutions exist—contraception and voluntary sterilization, for example.

Anti-abortion Witness Evelyn Eaton, San Francisco's Catholic Council for Life: "What they're saying is that a dead baby is cheaper than a live one."

Pro Abortion: We are asking only that poor women be allowed equal access to abortion, not that they be forced into abortion. In 1970, about 94% of the women whose deaths were caused by criminal abortions in New York County were black and Puerto Rican. White women, statistically of higher income, went to higher-priced and safer criminal abortionists, obtained "legal" abortions under another label (dilation and curettage), or traveled to a country with more liberal abortion laws. Women who want abortions will get them, even if they have to risk their lives to get them.

Issue: Is legal abortion physically or mentally dangerous?

Anti Abortion: Particularly in the last stages, abortion is more dangerous than childbirth. Women who have aborted a child sometimes have difficulty with future pregnancies. If a woman has two or more induced abortions, she is two to three times more likely to miscarry in the first trimester of later pregnancies. Having an abortion causes terrible mental anguish.

Pro Abortion: According to the Center for Disease Control, one death occurs in every 100,000 early abortions, while nearly 20 deaths occur in every 100,000 live deliveries. The suction-curettage abortion, used in the first 12 weeks of pregnancy, is very safe. Only when the cervix is dilated too much, usually in a late abortion, does the woman run some risk of miscarrying in later pregnancies.

Pro-abortion Witness—Study from the Institute of Medicine of the National Academy of Science: "The feelings of guilt, regret, or loss elicited by a legal abortion in some women are generally temporary and appear to be outweighed by positive life changes and feelings of relief."

Issue: Is abortion really necessary with improved contraceptive measures?

Anti Abortion: Contraceptives are now so effective that a woman who becomes pregnant without wanting to is guilty of carelessness. To allow abortion is to open the door to its use as a contraceptive.

Pro Abortion: Birth-control methods do fail. The condom and diaphragm have failure rates of up to 15%, and while the birth-control pill offers greater success rates, it has dangerous side effects for many women. Women do not take abortion lightly. It is humiliating, expensive, and often painful, as anyone who has had one—legal or illegal—can tell you.

Anti Abortion: A study by Dr. Robin Badgley found that twice as many women were having repeat abortions in 1976 as in 1974, the year after the landmark Supreme Court decision. Almost half were not practicing contraception when they became pregnant the second time.

Pro-abortion Witness Dr. Christopher Tietze, Population Council: "There has been a marked increase in the use of contraceptives by both married and unmarried women since legal abortions became available."

Issue: Are abortion laws enforceable?

Pro Abortion: Before the 1973 Supreme Court decision, a million or more American women a year subjected themselves to criminal abortions, many by back-alley butchers. Some tried to abort themselves by forcing a coat hanger or a knitting needle into the uterus. From 5,000 to 10,000 women a year died from illegal abortions, and many developed terrible complications, such as peritonitis. Despite expense, pain, and risk, those women chose criminal abortion over childbirth. Abortion laws are not enforceable.

Anti Abortion: Our statistics show only 500 to 1,000 deaths a year from criminal abortions prior to 1973. Moreover, our concern is for the million innocent fetuses doomed to die. Cynically speaking, if abortion is again made illegal, criminal abortion will be much safer. The suction-curettage method is safe even in the hands of a person without medical training.

Issue: Should the Catholic Church be allowed to force its moral views on all of society?

Pro Abortion: The Catholic position allows abortion only if the death of the fetus is an "indirect consequence" of surgery, such as the removal of a cancerous uterus. Otherwise, the life of the fetus is considered more important than that of the mother, even if she has 10 other children. And why? Because of the belief, originating with early church fathers, that original sin dooms the unbaptized fetus to eternal punishment. The Catholic Church is trying to put its religious beliefs into law so that they

will be imposed on everyone. The Methodists and others tried to do something very similar with Prohibition.
Anti Abortion: Many issues, like civil rights and welfare reform, have moral overtones. A right-to-life amendment would be more like the 13th Amendment, which abolished slavery, than like the 18th, which outlawed liquor. Catholics are not the only people against abortion. We count in our number Protestants, Jews, and atheists.

Issue: Are there preferable alternatives to abortion?

Anti Abortion: Abortion is a poor solution to a problem that is often rooted in economics. Many women abort because they think they can't afford a child. Society must change so that the single pregnant woman and mother can survive more easily. Day care should be available to the working mother. The woman who does not want to keep her baby can put it up for adoption by a childless couple. Dr. Bernard Nathanson suggests that fetuses may be transplanted to host mothers or artificial wombs in the future. Abortion is just one more factor in the weakening of the family.
Pro Abortion: No woman should be forced to bear a child, especially one that she can't love and care for. Every child has the right to be wanted. Even with an enlightened social policy, a woman with several children, living in dire poverty, has a poor chance of doing a good job of raising yet another child. Studies show that children born to women denied abortions are more likely to have mental problems, get in trouble with police, and fail in school. Giving up a child for adoption is far more traumatic than abortion for the natural mother, and it is a form of slavery to make women act as baby factories for other people. As for the transplanted fetus idea, where will you find 1,500,000 sets of parents to adopt the 1,500,000 fetuses that would be transplanted? A Carter administration study group on alternatives to abortion disbanded with the conclusion that the real alternatives to abortion were "suicide, motherhood, and, some would add, madness."

Consider women who have chronic diseases like cancer, diabetes, and epilepsy. Pregnancy often exacerbates the illness, and the side effects of the treatment or the disease itself can cause birth defects in the child. Consider the anguish of bearing an anencephalic child (one without a brain and therefore doomed to die) or other defective infant. Medical tests can give conclusive evidence of birth defects that doom a child to permanent disability or early death. Why not abort if necessary and try again for a healthy child? Certainly those who become pregnant as the result of rape or incest, often children themselves, are entitled to an abortion.
Anti Abortion: The right of every child to live supersedes his right to be wanted, happy, or perfect, and supersedes his mother's right to physical and mental health.

—A.E.

A NATIONAL INITIATIVE

DEFINITION

The initiative is a process whereby a bill or measure is "initiated" by a citizen and, bypassing the legislature, is then voted on directly by the people in an election. Generally, for an initiative to qualify for the ballot, a certain number of valid signatures must be collected to support it. The initiative becomes law if it is approved by a large enough majority of voters.

In 1977 Senators James Abourezk and Mark Hatfield introduced a constitutional amendment to permit national initiatives. Under their proposal, if a bill received the signatures of 3% of the voters in at least 10 states, it would qualify for the ballot of the next general election. If approved by the voters, the new law could not be changed or repealed by Congress for two years, except by a two thirds vote.

Is the voice of the people heard through initiatives liberal or conservative? As might be expected, that depends on how the pendulum of public opinion swings. Experience in what Sen. James Abourezk called the "state laboratory" would seem to indicate that it is politically neutral. When people begin thinking in a liberal way, they tend to vote on the liberal side, and liberals promote the initiative as a liberal tool. The reverse is true, too. State referendums and initiatives have been influential in gaining civil rights, protecting the environment, reforming civil service, and guarding consumer interests. Measures on these issues have also been voted down. A good example is recent experience with property taxes. California's Proposition 13 to limit property taxes passed by a 64% majority in 1978 and set off "tax revolt fever" in other states. Yet while 10 such propositions made state ballots in 1980, only 3 were voted in.

PROS AND CONS (INCLUDING COMMENTS MADE BY AUTHORITIES IN THE PAST)

Issue: What would the Founding Fathers think of a national initiative?

Pro: The first amendment to the Constitution reads: "Congress shall make no law . . . abridging the . . . right of the people . . . to petition the Government for a redress of grievances." Obviously, the Founding Fathers would applaud a national initiative, particularly in view of radical changes produced by events of the last 200 years which make it more feasible—a once rural society gone urban, shifts of power, a technological revolution that has brought with it sophisticated communications systems. Why shouldn't the voice of the people be heard when opinions can so easily be collected and evaluated by computer? Past amendments have extended voting rights, for example, to blacks and women. The national initiative would carry on that trend to let the voice of the people be heard.

Con: You misinterpret the 1st Amendment, which merely states that the people may *petition* Congress. It does not say that the people may make laws. In a representative democracy like ours, lawmaking powers are given over to elected officials. Pure democracy, where everyone votes on everything, is impossible. No town meeting hall is large enough to accommodate millions of people. Even with electronic gadgets, the process would be far too unwieldy and time-consuming. Our republic is based on a delicate system of checks and balances, including the concept that while the minority must accept the decisions of the majority, the majority must not be allowed to impose injustices on the minority. An initiative process would destroy that system.

Columnist George F. Will: "The people are not supposed to govern; they are not supposed to decide issues. They are supposed to decide who will decide."

Pro: Only a gross conception of the popular will—a blanket yes to a particular set of candidates and party—emerges from a general election. Voters may not agree with all the views of a candidate they elect. The national initiative process would allow them to express their opinions and impose their will on specific issues. Therefore, it would expand what the Founding Fathers intended.

Constitutional Scholar Arthur S. Miller: "The Constitution has never been interpreted in ways to give sole authority to the views of the Founding Fathers, even if those views are ascertainable; usually, they are not."

Con: Establishing a national initiative process would irreparably tear the delicate fabric of our governmental system.

Issue: Can the people fight City Hall? Should they?

Pro: A national initiative amendment would give new hope to an alienated and apathetic electorate. At present most of our political leaders emerge from one tiny segment of society—the community of lawyers, whose profession is a natural one for politics. Political hopefuls must enter the system through the party machine. The initiative process at local levels can change that by arousing citizens to action and developing leaders outside our present system. In working to qualify an initiative and get it passed, grass-roots activists develop skills valuable to our political system and may end up in government, where they can offer a much-needed fresh point of view. Ordinary citizens become better informed, more aware, more involved in civic affairs, more likely to vote. With the ability to propose and write their own laws, they have no excuse for alienated passivity. They can fight City Hall, and if they don't win on an issue, at least they have brought it into the public spotlight and there can be a next time. Politics is taken out of the smoke-filled room and brought into the open air.

Con: The nonvoters in our society, who comprise about 50% of us, are so turned off and feel so powerless that it will take more than an initiative to involve them. A badly educated slum dweller, already beaten down by society, sunk in apathy, won't get out of his chair to vote on an issue, much less work for it. His faith in the system is too shattered for him to do that.

Peter Bachrach, Professor of Political Science, Temple University: "I cannot see why a person who is scuffling for a job and who has not voted in the past 10 years is now going to say, 'Ah, the nuclear power issue is a very important one. I have to rush to the polls and vote.' "

Pro: Through the initiative process, John Q. Public can get Congress cracking on stalled legislation and "hot potato" issues. Legislators have direct feedback on what people want, so they can be more responsive to the people's will. And if Congress fails to act, the people themselves can propose and enact a strong law, uncompromised by special-interest groups.

Consumer Activist Ralph Nader: "It's important that the ultimate check in a representative democracy is not revolution. The ultimate check is direct democracy."

Con: The initiative is a two-edged sword. Legislators threatened by an initiative can pass the buck to the electorate, knowing the issue will be settled at the ballot box and they can remain free of the taint of possible bias on a "hot" issue. They can always say they were overridden by the will of the people, and therefore become less accountable for what they do. Subtle compromise, through which legislators settle questions, is a strength of our system. An initiative decision is by definition yes or no, creating winners and losers. There's no chance for a just compromise with something for everyone. Ralph Nader's suggestion could also backfire. Consider what would happen if the electorate passed an initiative forcing women to be housewives and only housewives, and half the housewives in the U.S. rose up in righteous rebellion.

Ernest Barker in Reflections on Government: "If a majority engages in discussion with a minority, and if that discussion is conducted in a spirit of giving and taking, the result will be that the ideas of the majority are widened to include some of the ideas of the minority which have established their truth in the give and take of debate. . . . Some fusion will have taken place; some accommodation will have been attained."

Issue: Can an initiative decision be bought by big money?

Con: The initiative will bring out the promoters of the "hate and fear" issues such as gay rights and capital punishment and will arouse the self-righteous majority to oppress minorities. The disenfranchised will become even more disenfranchised, and the majority will kick aside minority rights. Vested interests and big money will be able to control the process with money. A spot on the ballot is won with signatures, and signatures can be bought at so much each. Companies specializing in signature collection will get them for anyone willing to pay. Expensive media campaigns can manipulate the minds of voters. In 1980 a proposition to create smoking and nonsmoking sections in public places gained a spot on the California ballot. Early polls showed overwhelming support for the proposal, even among smokers. However, the tobacco companies blanketed the state with a sophisticated \$2.3 million media campaign, and the measure went down in defeat. It would cost 10 times as much to influence a national referendum. Large companies could threaten employees with loss of their jobs if they didn't vote the "right" way.

Peter Bachrach: "What it would come to is a contest between money and power groups."

Pro: It wasn't the people who interned the Japanese during W.W. II, but elected officials. Government can be repressive too. And the people, through state initiatives, have often protected the rights of the minorities. In any case, any law that infringes on minority rights can be overturned in the courts. It's naive to think that elected officials are immune to big money influence. Washington crawls with lobbyists. In fact, the cost of influencing a congressional vote is less than the cost of "buying" a bloc of voter minds. Moreover, money does not necessarily buy the results of a proposition on a state ballot, and it is logical to assume that the same would be true of a national initiative. In 1972, Proposition 20, which protected the California coastline, was passed in spite of the fact that the opposition outspent its proponents by 3 to 1. In California from 1972 to 1976, the side that spent the most money won in only 8 out of 16 initiative battles. When voters spot media manipulation, it can backfire. Any bill establishing a national initiative can have campaign finance safeguards and disclosure requirements built into it. Signature requirements could be set low enough so that volunteer grassroots efforts to qualify a measure for the ballot could be successful.

Issue: Can the public be trusted to enact laws without nightmarish consequences?

Con: Imagine an initiative forcing Congress to balance the budget immediately, which would cause national economic catastrophe. Or imagine what would happen if the speed limit were raised to 90 mph. What if health nuts outlawed the sale of junk food? The people might go on a mammoth lawmaking binge with disastrous results.

Pro: Involved people are politically sophisticated enough not to enact bad or silly laws. With government as close as the end of his voting pencil, the voter becomes more careful. Experience with state initiatives tells us that people tend to be judicious. In the 23 states authorizing initiatives, only 500 laws have been passed in 80 years. Most measures never make it to the ballot because the system is set up to sift out the bizarre and frivolous bills without much backing. Any bad law can be repealed in the courts, and the initiative amendment could give Congress the power to overturn bad decisions by a certain majority. Behind what you say lies an elitist distrust of the people, who, when appealed to correctly, will vote rationally.

Sen. James Abourezk: "The initiative process, unique among our democratic rights, is founded on the belief that the citizens of this country are indeed as competent to enact legislation as we are to elect public officials to represent us."

Con: We aren't saying that the people are stupid, just that it is impossible to make a decision on every complicated issue. It's no more stupid to give congressmen the authority to enact laws for us than it is to pay garage mechanics to fix our cars or physicians to take out our tonsils.

Bills in Congress can run as long as 50 pages. Even congressmen consider some issues so complicated as to be best handled by special committee. We do not live in an Athenian society with slaves to do the work while we think about political decisions full-time. Should the expert knowledge of our elected officials be subject to the will of an uninformed electorate? Why should voters have to deal with a long ballot littered with numerous propositions, most of them oversimplified, many too complicated to understand without great study? Why should they have to work their way through such a labyrinthine mess?

Pro: Not every issue needs to be decided through the initiative process, only those most important and fundamental. The sum of individual votes provides a broad, trustworthy base representing a wise, considered decision.

—A.E.

National Initiative: What If . . . ?

If the result of national public-opinion polls can be used to judge the voting in initiative elections, here are some of the things that would be different if a national-initiative law had taken effect in 1950.

By 1952 party conventions would have been eliminated, and presidential candidates would be chosen instead by a nationwide primary election.

In 1953 the voting age would have been lowered to 18. (The politicians didn't get around to doing this until 1971.)

By 1965 all electric and telephone wires would have been moved underground.

The electoral college would have been discarded by the mid-1960s, and presidential elections would be decided by direct popular vote.

In 1969 it would have become illegal to heckle. In the same year, compulsory national service would have been instituted, giving young men the choice between military and nonmilitary service.

U.S. troops would have been withdrawn completely from Vietnam by the end of 1970. (This would have saved 4,852 American lives, kept another 60,000 Americans from being wounded, and prevented over 400,000 Vietnamese, Cambodian, and Laotian casualties.)

The Equal Rights Amendment would have passed in 1975 (or any year since).

The draft would have been reinstituted in 1980, with women included.

The government would be legally obligated to balance the federal budget.

There would be public funding of congressional campaigns, and no private contributions would be allowed.

Able-bodied welfare mothers with no children under the age of 13 would be required to take whatever full-time work was available. (A majority of all segments of the population approve this proposal, including the poor.)

—D.W.

2

THE ALMANAC SPECIAL COLLECTION

HISTORY AROUND THE CLOCK

by Jeremy Beadle

There are basically only two ways one can present events in history—either chronologically or alphabetically. Well, we have found a third way, and we would like to offer it to you here. We want to present some highlights and small lights in history by the *time* of day or night these events happened. Have you ever wondered when the flood hit Johnstown? When the *Lusitania* was torpedoed? When Erwin Rommel was forced to commit suicide? Or, to put it another way, have you ever wondered what fascinating historic events took place at two o'clock in the morning or at 5:30 in the afternoon? Even if you haven't wondered, maybe you should—because time sets history in a new perspective.

So picture before you a giant clock. Let's set it at an hour after midnight, at one o'clock in the morning. Let's find out what took place in history between 1:00 and 2:00 and so on through the morning to noon, and then from noon through the night. Let's follow history around the clock hour by hour. Each given time is based on the local time where the event happened, although space events are based on the time at the Soviet and U.S. space centers. Here we go to London time as a starter.

1:00 in the Morning

Sept. 2, 1666. The Great Fire of London started inside a baker's shop in Pudding Lane. It lasted five days, and nearly 80% of all the buildings within the London Wall were razed. According to the official report, 13,200 houses, 87 parish churches, over 400 streets, and the enormous old St. Paul's Cathedral—one of the wonders of the medieval world—were in ruins. Out of London's 450 acres, only 75 remained untouched. Officials saved many buildings by blowing up rows of houses in order to make fire breaks.

Even before the blaze was contained, police and mobs of angry citizens searched for the culprits who set the fire. It was unsafe for foreigners or Roman Catholics to walk through the devastated city.

Finally a French watchmaker from Rouen, Robert Hubert, confessed to the crime. Since he was not only a foreigner but also a Roman Catholic, the public's wrath was assuaged. One contemporary account of the disaster states that Hubert was "only accused upon his own confession; yet neither the judges nor any present at the trial did believe him guilty, but that he was a poor distracted wretch, weary of his life, and chose to part with it in this way." The Old Bailey jury, however, found that, "not having the fear of God before his eyes, but moved and led away by the instigation of the devil," Hubert had deliberately started the fire. After he was hanged, it was conclusively proved that he had not even arrived in London until two days after the fire broke out.

2:00 in the Morning

Mar. 31, 1918. America lost an hour when it suddenly became 3:00 A.M. Clocks across the continent were set forward one hour in a government move to "save daylight." In 1966 the U.S. Congress provided that daylight saving time would begin the last Sunday in April and that clocks would return to standard time on the following "last Sunday in October."

2:50 in the Morning

Sept. 8, 1934. Smoke was discovered pouring from a ventilator aboard the passenger liner *Morro Castle* as it steamed back to New York after a pleasure cruise to Havana. In the subsequent panic 137 people died.

It was an ill-fated journey. Earlier Capt. Robert Wilmott died of a heart attack. George Rogers, the liner's radio officer, sat with wet towels around his head as he tapped out SOS messages while the radio room exploded and sulfuric acid burned his feet. Many of the passengers

Morro Castle *ablaze as passengers await rescue boats.*

Chief Radio Operator George Rogers.

were drunk after a party and did not take advantage of the lifeboats. Fortunately, other ships came to the rescue.

The cause of the fire was never fully established. After the disaster, George Rogers briefly made a living recounting his heroism in lecture halls. He subsequently opened a radio repair shop, which burned to the ground, but Rogers collected the insurance money. In 1936 he joined the Bayonne, N.J., Police Force and worked in the radio department. Coveting his superior's job, Rogers tried to murder him with a bomb made from a fish-tank heater. Before he was sent to prison, Rogers was questioned about the *Morro Castle* and suggested the suspiciously imaginative idea that the fire was started by an incendiary fountain pen, rigged with a delayed-action device, which had been left in the writing room. He refused to say anything else, and the disaster of the *Morro Castle* remains a mystery. (In 1942 Rogers was paroled, but in 1954 he was convicted of murdering an elderly couple. Four years later he died in the New Jersey State Penitentiary, remaining stubbornly mute about the *Morro Castle*.)

3:20 in the Morning

Mar. 25, 1944. RAF Sgt. Nicholas Alkemade said, "Jesus Christ, I'm alive!" Lighting a cigarette, he checked his watch for the time. Just three hours earlier he had been in the blazing tail of an RAF Lancaster bomber that had been hit after dropping its load on Berlin. The captain ordered the crew to bail out, but a fire in the fuselage made it impossible for Alkemade to reach his parachute. He had to make an instant decision—a roasting hell or an unconscious fall? He pushed open the plane's door and somersaulted backward into the night.

Alkemade jumped at 18,000 ft. without a parachute. He said he had no sensation of falling, that it was "like being at rest on an airy cloud." The last thing he remembered was looking down at his feet, seeing stars, and thinking, "Must be falling headfirst." Plummeting at about 120 mph, he landed in a fir forest, where the thickly interlaced branches broke his fall and an 18-in. layer of snow cushioned his final landing. Found by a German patrol, he was taken prisoner and given a thorough investigation by understandably disbelieving German interrogators. But his story was proved true. Alkemade suffered burned legs, a twisted right knee, splinters in his thigh, a strained back, a scalp wound, and burns on his face and hands—all sustained *before* his 3½-mi. jump.

4:30 in the Morning

Apr. 30, 1943. The corpse of Major Martin was secretly buried at sea from the British submarine *Seraph*. At that moment Martin, the strangest hero of W.W. II, began his first and last battle. He would become the leading actor in a bizarre plan to convince the Germans that the Allied attack on Europe would take place on Sardinia, not Sicily—the most obvious place.

The plan was to put top-secret documents in the clothes of "a shot-down airman," then throw the corpse into the sea off the Spanish coast, where it would fall into enemy hands. British Intelligence officials, faced with the problem of finding a suitable corpse, selected a soldier who had died from pneumonia, for an autopsy would reveal water in the lungs and seem to prove that the victim had drowned. The soldier's relatives agreed to the mission on the condition that his identity never be revealed. British Intelligence named him Major Martin and supplied him with a complete background. For personal papers, they gave him a bank overdraft of £80, a photograph of his supposed fiancée, a £53 bill for an engagement ring, and torn tickets for a London show. Because the corpse looked "too hopelessly dead," a "double" was photographed for the identity card. Most important of all, Martin had a letter personally signed by Lord Mountbatten which ended with a simple pun designed to trick the Germans into believing the Allied assault would be on Sardinia: "Let me have him [Martin] back, please, as soon as the assault is over. He might bring some *sardines* with him—they are on points here!"

Major Martin was buried at sea in a Mae West life jacket. Later in the day the body was found by Spanish fishermen. A postmortem officially established cause of death as "asphyxiation through immersion in the sea." On May 2, 1943, Major Martin was buried with full military honors. He even got a death notice in the London *Times*. However, his papers were not returned until May 13, when it was established that they had been carefully examined. Days later British Intelligence learned that the Germans had begun sending large reinforcements to Sardinia. When the Allies invaded Sicily, Field Marshal Rommel said that the failure of the German defenses was "a result of a diplomatic courier's body being washed up off Spain."

5:12 in the Morning

Apr. 18, 1906. San Francisco was close to the epicenter of an earthquake that for 55 sec. rocked 50,000 sq. mi. of California at a force of 8.3 on the Richter scale. With commendable composure philosopher William James turned to his wife and said, "This is an earthquake, there is no cause for alarm," then slowly dressed himself. Enrico Caruso reputedly sang a few notes to make certain he hadn't lost his voice; then he wrapped a towel around his throat and ran down Market Street, clutching an autographed photograph of Theodore Roosevelt and vowing never to return to San Francisco—which he never did. For the 400,000 residents of San Francisco, each of the two major shocks spelt death and destruction.

The final toll: 4 sq. mi.—520 blocks with 28,000 buildings—were utterly devastated; more than 450 people were dead, 300,000 homeless. The total damage estimate was $500 million. There were only 38 horse-drawn fire engines to cope with the 52 fires in the city. One man, trapped beyond hope of rescue, begged a policeman to shoot him before the flames could reach him. Unwilling to carry out the man's request, the policeman asked a man in the crowd to do it. With amazing courage and fortitude San Francisco rose from the rubble to reassert itself as one of America's most beautiful cities—near the same San Andreas fault that sooner or later will growl again.

6:15 in the Morning

June 21, 1756. The prisoners in the Black Hole of Calcutta were released.

The previous evening Siraj-ud-daula, a young British-hating nabob of Bengal whose childhood hobby was torturing animals, captured the British Fort William at Calcutta where the East India Company based its powerful export empire. He believed a secret treasure was being held. After the fort surrendered, he demanded to know the hiding place. The temporary British commander, John Holwell, a business executive with the East India Company and not really a soldier, informed Siraj-ud-daula that no such fortune existed. The furious nabob ordered that the British be confined in the Black Hole.

This infamous prison cell in Calcutta was 18 ft. by 14 ft. 10 in., with only two small barred windows. Like sardines, 145 men and a girl were packed into the sweltering cell. The girl, Mary Carey, was the 15-year-old Indian wife of Englishman Peter Carey. Two days before Fort William fell, a ship had taken all the European women and children away to safety, but Mary Carey, who had devotedly nursed the wounded, was not allowed on board because she was not white. All through that dreadful night the men, crushed against each other, slowly died of thirst and suffocation. At one point a sympathetic guard offered water through the cell window, but many men died in the ensuing struggle, and Commander Holwell said, "These supplies are like sprinkling water on fire, only served to feed and raise the flames."

The door was unlocked at 5:55, but because it opened inward, it took a full 20 minutes to release the survivors because corpses were packed so tightly against it. Of the 146 prisoners only 23 survived; Holwell and Mary Carey were among the living. They had been in the Black Hole for 10 hours. Holwell was again taken before the nabob, but even under the threat of being shot from the mouth of a cannon he still denied the existence of any treasure. This time the nabob believed him. Holwell remained a prisoner, and Mary Carey became part of the prince's harem.

British revenge was swift and certain. A year later Siraj-ud-daula's remains were placed on an elephant and exposed to the people. The widowed Mary Carey was released and later married another English officer, by whom she had three children.

7:00 in the Morning

May 9, 1671. Col. Thomas Blood stole the British Crown Jewels from the Tower of London.

Blood had spent several weeks disguised as a parson in order to win the confidence of Talbot Edwards, the 77-year-old keeper of the Crown Jewels. On the morning of the robbery Blood arrived with three companions and introduced one of them, his "nephew," to the keeper's daughter. While the nephew was getting acquainted with the young lady, Blood suggested that Edwards might like to show them all the Crown Jewels. Edwards happily agreed and took everyone into the chamber inside Martin Tower, locking the door behind them. Immediately, a cloak was thrown over his head and a wooden plug was thrust into his mouth. To further gag Edwards, the thieves also "fastened an iron hook to his nose that no sound might pass from him that way." Still the keeper struggled until he was flattened with a wooden mallet and then stabbed in the stomach.

Blood used the same mallet to flatten out St. Edward's Crown so that he could hide it beneath his clerical coat. Another conspirator stuffed the orb down his trousers while the third man filed the scepter in two. Just then, by an extraordinary coincidence, Edwards's son, who had been serving in the military in Flanders for several years, returned to visit his parents. The lookout delayed him, then rushed to warn the other conspirators. The gang left hurriedly with the jewels in their pockets, but in the rush they dropped the scepter. At that moment the elder Edwards managed to remove the gag from his mouth and cried out, "Treason! Murder! The crown is stolen!"

The chase was on. Blood shot one yeoman warder who tried to stop them, and the drawbridge guard was so frightened that he dropped his musket and let the gang pass. Blood was finally caught by a Captain Beckman after a "robustious struggle." The crown fell from beneath Blood's cloak during the fight and for some time lay unnoticed in the gutter. The other thieves were quickly caught, and all of them were held in the Tower. Blood refused to talk, saying that he would speak only to the king himself. Finally the king granted him an audience, in which the Irish-born Blood produced such a torrent of blarney that he received not only a royal pardon but also a pension of £500!

8:52 in the Morning

Feb. 10, 1962. The first spy exchange in the cold war took place when Francis Gary Powers, a U.S. pilot-spy, was swapped for top Soviet agent Rudolf Abel.

In 1956 Powers, a civilian employee of the CIA, began making secret illegal flights over the U.S.S.R. In 1960 his plane was shot down 1,300 mi. inside Russia. He managed to parachute to safety, and although he possessed a poisoned needle to end his life, Powers chose to be taken prisoner.

A fierce international argument resulted, and Soviet Premier Nikita Khrushchev canceled a Paris summit meeting with President Dwight Eisenhower. The Russians made brilliant propaganda by successfully forcing the Americans to publicly admit that they had been spying for many years. Ironically, Powers was captured on May Day, the most important day in the Marxist calendar. The American pilot was put through a public trial in which he pleaded guilty and made an apology. Even though Powers could have been sentenced to death, he was only given 10 years in prison.

After two years of top secret negotiations, Powers was exchanged for Colonel Abel, the former KGB resident director in the U.S., who was serving a 30-year sentence in an Atlanta, Ga., prison for spying. The event took place on the Glienicker Bridge, which links the Western sector of Berlin with the Soviet zone of Germany. Russian authorities announced that Powers had been released "as an act of clemency" that would improve Soviet-American relations; they made no mention of Colonel Abel. Powers received $52,000 in back salary and again took to the air, first as a test pilot, later as a reporter of traffic conditions in Los Angeles from a helicopter. He was killed in a flying accident in 1977. It is reported that Abel still works in the Soviet secret service.

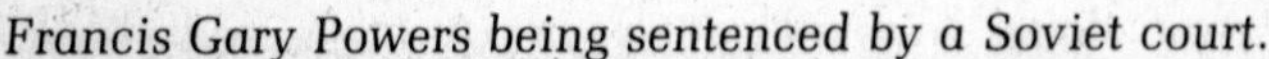
Francis Gary Powers being sentenced by a Soviet court.

9:00 in the Morning

Oct. 23, 4004 B.C. God created the world, according to James Ussher, Archbishop of Armagh and author of *Annals of the Old and New Testaments*, published in 1658. Ussher also claimed that Adam and Eve were created on Friday, Oct. 28. Taught to read by two blind aunts, Ussher had much trouble delivering sermons in later life because he had lost all of his teeth.

9:07 in the Morning

Apr. 12, 1961. Yuri Gagarin left the Soviet launching pad at Baykonur, Western Siberia, inside the 10,416-lb. spaceship Vostok 1 on the world's first successful manned space flight. His words after launch: "I am in good spirits. The machine works perfectly." The spaceship completed a single orbit of the earth in 89.34 minutes and landed in a field near the village of Smelovka in the Saratov region of the U.S.S.R. As he crossed the field, Gagarin met a young woman who had been caring for a calf. She screamed when she saw the strange monster approaching her, and cried out, "Who are you?" The cosmonaut politely doffed his space helmet and said, "A friend, a friend." Gagarin—whose name means "wild duck"—was only 5 ft. 2 in. tall.

10:00 in the Morning

May 19, 1780. The "dark day" of New England. It began like most other mornings, but at 10:00 A.M. a mysterious darkness spread over the land. Although there were no clouds, candles had to be lit inside houses, and outdoor work had to be stopped because people could not see what they were doing. At midday it was impossible to read a book. The darkness continued until the dawn of the following day. The strange phenomenon has never been scientifically explained. However, it is known that there was no eclipse of the sun on that day.

10:03 in the Morning

May 2, 1960. Caryl Chessman entered the gas chamber at San Quentin prison. He had spent 11 years, 10 months, and 1 week on death row—after a record eight stays of execution.

In 1948, the 26-year-old Chessman had been arrested after an 80-mph car chase which ended in a shoot-out that almost took his life when a police bullet grazed his head. He was identified as "the Red Light Bandit" who had terrorized Los Angeles by attacking courting couples, then robbing the men and raping the women. In total Chessman was charged with 18 crimes, including robbery and the kidnapping and sexual assault of two young women (the "kidnapping" consisted of transferring them from their own car to his car for the purpose of rape).

During his trial he frequently complained that his confinement prevented him from collecting evidence that would prove his innocence. He was sentenced to two death penalties for kidnapping plus eight five-year sentences for the robberies. Over the next 11 years Chessman had access to the prison library and a typewriter, and employed what he described as "unparalleled legal black magic" to win eight stays of execution. When the end finally came, a last-minute stay of execution had been agreed upon, but a federal judge's secretary trying to reach San Quentin misdialed the telephone number on her first attempt. Whether those few seconds would have saved Chessman is debatable.

Just before he entered the death chamber, Chessman said, "I specifically state I was not the Red Light Bandit." Sixty witnesses watched the executioner drop the pellets of potassium cyanide into the container beneath the chair. Chessman smiled as he inhaled the hydrocyanic gas. Eight minutes and 15 seconds later, at 10:12 A.M., Chessman was pronounced dead.

The enormous international outrage at the execution was answered by ex-President Harry Truman, who declared that Chessman "ought to have been executed long ago," and that the excitement the case caused "was a lot of hooey stirred up to get your mind off what's happening." In a last written message Chessman said, "Now that the state has had its vengeance, I should like to ask the world to consider what has been gained."

10:22 in the Morning

Jan. 17, 1966. A giant U.S. B-52 bomber with four hydrogen bombs aboard collided with a K-135 air tanker above the Almería coast of eastern Spain. The tanker burst into flames and the B-52 broke up and tumbled to earth. Three of the bombs, each measuring 10 ft. in length and 20 in. in diameter, landed near the village of Palomares.

The U.S. Air Force immediately put operation "Broken Arrow" into action, and over 400 American and Spanish soldiers hunted for the bombs. Within 48 hours the three bombs had been located—one by a local farmer, who kicked the smoldering nuclear bomb. When a Spanish fisherman reported that he had seen "half a man" drop by parachute into the sea, a huge search party—20 ships, 2,200 sailors, and over 130 divers—began to comb the seabed. On Mar. 15 a three-man submarine discovered the bomb at a depth of 2,550 ft. on a narrow 20-ft. ledge. On Apr. 7 American engineers operating under extreme difficulties succeeded in hoisting the bomb to the surface. For the first time in history cameramen were allowed to photograph a nuclear bomb. A major catastrophe had been averted, but many of the villagers in Palomares began to suffer mysterious illnesses. Despite the fact that American authorities had scraped away 1,750 tons of the village's topsoil and buried it in a nuclear cemetery in South Carolina, the Spanish villagers still complain that their land has been contaminated.

11:00 in the Morning

Oct. 25, 1854. The Charge of the Light Brigade at the Battle of Balaklava began. Galloping forward, 675 British horsemen rode into "the valley of death" with 12 Russian guns backed by the complete Russian cavalry awaiting them at the end of the ride. On both sides of the valley the Russian infantry was poised with 22 guns. Eight minutes elapsed before the Light Brigade reached the Russians. Another four minutes were spent in fierce hand-to-hand combat, and it took eight more minutes to return. The suicidal attack so confused the disbelieving Russians that 3,000 of them retreated in complete disorder. Almost 250 men were killed and wounded, and 475 horses lay dead.

The charge resulted from a misunderstood order delivered by a Captain Nolan, who, once he realized the dreadful mistake, tried to stop the advance by galloping ahead and screaming for the men to return. As he did so, Nolan was killed by shrapnel from the first Russian shell. When Lord Cardigan, the officer who led the charge, inspected his troops immediately afterward, he said, "Men, it is a mad-brained trick, but it is no fault of mine." One of the remaining 195 troopers stepped forward and said, "Never mind, my lord, we are ready to go again!" The cavalry cheered in agreement.

12:30 in the Afternoon

Nov. 22, 1963. Riding to the Dallas Trade Mart, U.S. President John Fitzgerald Kennedy was hit in the back of the neck by a rifle bullet which entered slightly to the right of the spine, traveled downward, and exited from the front of his neck, nicking the knot in his necktie. Jackie Kennedy, seated on his left, turned and saw her husband give a "quizzical look" as he raised his left hand to his throat. Texas Governor John Connally, riding in the front seat of the open limousine, started to turn but was hit in the back by another rifle shot, which entered his body just below his right armpit. The bullet exited below his right nipple and continued through his right wrist, which was resting on his lap, finally causing a wound to his left thigh. Another bullet struck Kennedy's head, exiting through the right side of his skull; it made a 5-in. gaping hole and splattered brain tissue all over the car. As Kennedy's body lurched backward, his wife reached out and cradled him in her arms, saying, "Oh, my God, they have shot my husband. I love you, Jack."

Kennedy was rushed to the Parkland Memorial Hospital in Dallas, where his head was covered to prevent anyone from taking photographs. The first doctor who examined the President noted that his skin was a blue-white color. Slow spasmodic breathing was detected, and although Kennedy's eyes were open, the pupils were dilated and did not react to any stimulus. Brain tissue was still oozing out of the massive wound. Despite unflagging efforts by the medical staff, Kennedy died. The official time of his death was 1:00 P.M. The official cause: "Gunshot wound, in the brain."

12:40 in the Afternoon

June 30, 1882. Charles Guiteau, the assassin of President James Garfield, was hanged in Washington, D.C. Approximately 250 people were admitted to watch the execution; some paid up to $300 for the privilege. In his cell Guiteau prepared himself as if he were going on a first date. He carefully brushed his hair and trimmed his bushy beard, then spent some time shining his black shoes to such a high gloss that he whistled with satisfaction.

On the walk to the scaffold his otherwise brave appearance was interrupted by occasional soft sobs. At the foot of the scaffold he told the witnesses that he had shot the President by divine order. His little speech ended with the words "I therefore predict that this nation will go down in blood, and that my murderers from the executive to the hangman will go to hell." After that pronouncement, he recited a poem he had written in the death cell; it was entitled "I Am Going to the Lordy." Guiteau was still talking when the hood was put over his head. His last words were "Glory, glory, glory." The night before his execution Guiteau had written a curious will, which bequeathed his body to the Rev. William Hicks "provided, however, it shall not be used for any mercenary purposes."

12:45 in the Afternoon

Sept. 10, 1897. George Smith, a London taxi driver, after consuming two or three glasses of beer, drove his electric cab up onto the pavement and into the entrance of 165 Bond Street. In court later that day, Smith was fined 20 shillings and earned the honor of becoming the world's first convicted drunk driver.

1:25 in the Afternoon

Oct. 21, 1805. At the Battle of Trafalgar, British Admiral Horatio Nelson was struck by a musket ball. Fired from above, the shot ripped through his epaulet into his left shoulder, passed down through the lungs, split his spine, and finally lodged in the muscles of his back. Nelson fell to his knees with one hand pressing on the deck. Then that arm gave way, and he fell on his side on the very spot where his secretary, John Scott, had been killed earlier. Scott's blood stained Nelson's coat. A fellow officer, Capt. Thomas Hardy, dashed forward and bent over him. Nelson smiled and said, "Hardy, I believe they have done for me at last." "I hope not," said Hardy, but Nelson sensed the end and said, "Yes, my backbone is shot through."

That day, against all advice, Nelson had worn all his military decorations, arranged in the form of a diamond on his breast. (It is not true that he wore a full dress uniform; in fact, the stars and orders were actually embroidered on the coat he wore that day.) The decorations were so brilliant that he was an easy target for enemy snipers. The debilitating shot was fired by a sharpshooter located in the mizzentop of the French flagship *Redoutable*. As the wounded Nelson was carried below, he covered his face and decorations so that his men would not know that their admiral had been shot. When the fatal musket ball was recovered from Nelson's body, a bit of gold lace and part of his epaulet, together with a small piece of Nelson's coat, were found embedded in it. The admiral lingered for three hours, then died. Captain Hardy had the bullet set in a locket and gave it to the surgeon of the *Victory*, Sir William Beatty, the man who had removed it from Nelson's body.

1:25 in the Afternoon

Oct. 14, 1944. Field Marshal Erwin Rommel was found dead on arrival at Ulm Hospital.

That day at noon Gen. Wilhelm Burgdorf and Gen. Ernst Maisel had arrived at the field marshal's home. An hour later Rommel went upstairs to his wife's room and said to her, "In a quarter of an hour I shall be dead." He explained that Hitler had discovered his part in "Operation Valkyrie," a conspiracy of German army leaders to blow up the Führer. The bomb went off 2 yd. from Hitler, wrecked his headquarters, injured 20 men and killed 4 others—but Hitler miraculously escaped. Rommel had been given a choice—immediate death by poison or a public trial. However, Burgdorf had made it perfectly clear that if Rommel chose a court hearing, reprisals would be taken against his family. However, if Rommel elected suicide his family would receive all pensions due and he would get a full military funeral. (Hitler obviously did not want to admit that Germany's most famous general had plotted against him.)

After giving his wife a brief good-bye, Rommel put on his overcoat and walked to the waiting car. On the drive to Ulm, Burgdorf ordered the car to stop and told Maisel and the SS driver to leave for just a moment. When the two men returned, Rommel was dead, probably from a cyanide pill, which would have killed him almost instantly. At his state funeral three days later, the largest wreath came from Hitler.

Footnote: On July 15 Rommel saw the hopelessness of the Normandy situation and demanded that Hitler negotiate an armistice. Forty-eight hours later two planes with British markings attacked Rommel's car and shot it off the road. The one volley hit the car and knocked Rommel out onto the road. The field marshal lived but suffered a fractured skull, a broken cheekbone, an eye injury, and a concussion of the brain. The curious thing is, according to British records, no RAF plane could have been involved. It is possible that Hitler had been planning Rommel's death for some time.

1:40 in the Afternoon

July 14, 1865. The Matterhorn was conquered by the English climber Edward Whymper. The 14,690-ft. Matterhorn, located in the Pennine Alps on the Swiss-Italian border near the town of Zermatt, is neither the highest nor the most difficult mountain to climb, but its four ridges, sharply tapering in a peaked summit, have always beckoned mountaineers.

It was Whymper's seventh attempt, and this time he had competition from an Italian party headed by an ex-friend, the brilliant Italian mountaineer Giovanni Antonio Carrel. Whymper assembled a party of seven men, including himself. Accompanying him was the youthful but experienced English climber Lord Francis Douglas and guides Peter Taugwalder, Sr., and his son, also named Peter. The Rev. Charles Hudson also joined forces with Whymper and brought along 19-year-old novice climber Douglas Hadow. (Hudson insisted that Hadow join the party. Whymper agreed, though later he claimed that he had opposed the inclusion of the youth.) Hudson also brought with him the legendary Alpinist guide Michel Auguste Croz, whom Whymper had originally invited to join his attempt. Croz had at that time refused because he was employed by Hudson.

The party set out at 5:30 A.M. on July 13. By midday they had reached an 11,000-ft. ridge and pitched their tents, waiting for the next day to begin the final 4,000-ft. assault. By 10:00 A.M. on July 14 they had less than 800 ft. to go. After a slow, dangerous climb, the party was within 200 ft. of the summit. With an easy stretch before them, Croz, Hudson, and Whymper ran a neck-and-neck race that ended in a dead heat on the summit. Whymper was delighted that "not a footstep could be

Edward Whymper in 1865.

seen." But the summit of the Matterhorn is a 100-yd.-long ridge. He was on the Swiss end and wanted to be certain that his competition, Carrel's party, had not reached the other end before him. He was delighted to find that it, too, was untrodden. Whymper peered over the edge and could see the Italian party heading toward him. To attract their attention Whymper threw rocks. The bitterly disappointed Italians stopped, turned, and began to descend. Whymper set up a flag, which was seen both in Zermatt and Breuil, where the villagers believed that the Italians had won. The party remained on the summit for "one crowded hour of glorious life." Just before leaving, Whymper broke off the topmost piece of rock from the Matterhorn and put it in his bag. The slow descent began.

Three quarters of an hour later, disaster struck. The inexperienced Hadow slipped and dragged Croz, Hudson, and Douglas down with him. The other three members of the party braced themselves as they watched their companions fall. Then the rope broke and the four falling men plunged 4,000 ft. to their deaths. Paralyzed by shock, Whymper and the two Taugwalders did not budge for half an hour. When they finally began to move, Whymper examined the rope and discovered that they had not been attached by proper heavy climbing rope, but by thin weak rope intended only as a reserve piece of equipment. When they finally reached Zermatt, the hotel owner asked what had happened. Whymper replied, "The Taugwalders and I have returned."

2:05 in the Afternoon

March 31, 1889. The Eiffel Tower was officially opened by its designer, Alexandre Gustave Eiffel, with the unfurling of the tricolor and a 21-gun salute. Eiffel had wanted the ceremony to be a quiet one, attended only by himself and his workers. Instead 400 journalists and various officials and members of Parliament climbed the 1,671 steps to the summit. The procession took 55 minutes to get to the top. The 985-ft. tower was the star attraction of the Paris Universal Exhibition of 1889.

When the plans were first approved, contemporary artists said: "We write to express our indignant protest, in the name of taste, and the threat to the art and history of France, against the erection in the heart of our capital of the useless and monstrous Eiffel Tower, which public malice, so often expressive of common sense and fairness, has already christened the 'Tower of Babel.' Does the City of Paris intend to associate any longer with the baroque and commercial ideas of a machine builder, which can only lead to irreparable ugliness and disgrace? For there is no doubt that the Eiffel Tower, which even America, commercially minded as it is, would refuse to have, is the disgrace of Paris." Among the signatories of this protest were Alexandre Dumas *fils*, Sully Prudhomme, Guy de Maupassant, J. K. Huysmans, and Charles Gounod. The tower took almost 2 years to build and cost precisely 7,799,401 francs and 31 centimes. Still not impressed, Maupassant left home saying, "I have left Paris, and even France, because of the Eiffel Tower."

3:00 in the Afternoon

Apr. 25, 1792. Nicolas Jacques Peletier became the first victim of the guillotine. He had been found guilty of "assaulting a private individual" with several blows of a knife and stealing a wallet containing 800 livres. When sentencing him, the judge offered the following comfort: "The condemned will have nothing to endure but the apprehension of death, which apprehension will be more painful to you than the blow that robs you of life." Peletier wasn't convinced and had to be dragged to the scaffold in a fainting fit. The Place de Grève in Paris was packed with eager spectators, but after the executioner, Charles Henri Sanson, released the blade the crowd gave a groan of disapproval. It had all been too quick. They began chanting, "Give me back my wooden gallows." The inventor, the kindly Dr. Ignace Joseph Guillotin, wasn't too pleased either. From that day on, whenever he was recognized, people would strike the napes of their necks with the palms of their hands. The good doctor even hated having the device named after him, and if anyone ever used the name guillotine in his presence he would always correct the person by calling it "the Maiden." It is also a fact that Dr. Guillotin not only didn't attend the beheading of Peletier but was never present at a single capital execution.

3:15 in the Afternoon

May 25, 1935. After running 41 strides at 4½ strides per sec., the amazing Jesse Owens equaled the 100-yd. record of 9.4 sec. while run-

Jesse Owens in action.

ning for Ohio State in the 35th annual Western Conference meet in Ann Arbor, Mich. Ten minutes later he jumped an incredible 26 ft. 8¼ in., a world record for the broad jump. Twenty minutes later, in the 220-yd. sprint, he not only established a new world record of 20.3 sec. but also simultaneously smashed the 200-meter record. A quarter of an hour later he set a new world record of 22.6 sec. for the 220-yd. low hurdles and at the same time broke the 200-meter record. In 45 minutes of breathless athletic brilliance, Jesse Owens set or matched six world records.

3:53 in the Afternoon

Dec. 4, 1958. The world's longest air flight began when Robert Timm and John Cook took off from McCarran Airfield, Las Vegas, Nev., in a Cessna 172 Hacienda. Without once touching the ground, they landed back at the same airport on Feb. 7 of the following year! Their flight had lasted 64 days, 22 hours, 19 minutes, and 5 seconds. By continual airborne refueling they managed to fly the equivalent of six times around the world.

4:07 in the Afternoon

Sept. 6, 1901. As U.S. President William McKinley passed along a line of well-wishers in the Temple of Music at the Pan-American Exposition in Buffalo, a 28-year-old anarchist named Leon Czolgosz (pronounced chol′ gosh) stepped forward and pumped two bullets into the Chief Executive. One struck the President's breastbone while the other zipped through the left side of his abdomen, perforating both the front and rear walls of the stomach and lodging itself somewhere in the gristle of his back muscles. Czolgosz had fired from such a short range—about 3 ft.—that the gunpowder stained McKinley's vest. Eight men leaped on the tiny Czolgosz and began to beat him. Just before McKinley collapsed he said, "Be easy with him, boys."

The President was rushed by ambulance to an emergency hospital, where surgeons struggled in vain to locate the bullet. The medical team finally settled for suturing the stomach walls and closing the abdominal wound. McKinley died eight days later. When police interrogated Czolgosz and asked for his name, he replied, "Fred Nieman—Fred Nobody—nobody killed the President." When he was brought before the Supreme Court, he pleaded guilty. The judge refused to accept the plea, and an understandably confused Czolgosz was forced to plead not guilty. It made no difference for he was executed anyway. One of the men who had jumped on Czolgosz later said, "We thumped him and slapped his face, and I took a knife out of my pocket and started to cut his throat, but he never flinched. Gamest man I ever saw in my life."

5:30 in the Afternoon

Sept. 7, 1822. King Pedro of Brazil, inspired by his country's newly gained independence from Portugal, took pen to paper in an effort to commemorate the event. By 9:00 P.M. he had produced the words and music of the *Himno da Carta*. Later in the evening, backed by a full chorus, he gave a personal rendition to the court. Delighted with his own work, he decreed that from that day on it would be the official national anthem of Brazil. However, in 1826 Pedro succeeded his father, John VI, as king of Portugal. When he arrived in his new kingdom he had with him the *Himno da Carta* and decreed that it was to become the national anthem of Portugal. This act left the Brazilians without an anthem for nearly a century. The *Himno da Carta* has the unique double distinction of being the only national anthem composed by a reigning monarch, as well as being almost certainly the most quickly composed.

6:57 in the Evening

May 26, 1940. Operation Dynamo, the evacuation of trapped Allied forces from the beach of Dunkerque, began. This W.W. II plan became the greatest evacuation in military history and one of the most complex and hazardous sea maneuvers ever attempted. It was organized by Admiral Bertram Ramsay with a staff of only 16 from his operational headquarters cut deep into the White Cliffs of Dover. Here the most unusual fleet in naval history was assembled. Any boat that could possibly make the Channel crossing was requisitioned for the operation. They included coasters, colliers, paddle steamers, tugs, Thames fire floats, lifeboats, pleasure steamers, barges, fishing vessels, yachts, and cabin cruisers. The boats were manned by the most diverse crew imaginable—doctors, dentists, truck drivers, civil servants, bankers, bakers, and retired businessmen.

Against all odds and with very little chance of survival, the Dunkerque armada sailed for France. Despite ferocious German air attacks and unrelenting bombardment from land for the next nine days, this fleet of 848 craft evacuated 338,226 men. Back and forth in the face of heavy artillery fire, the little boats continually ferried men from the beach to the big ships in deep water. Sixty-five big ships, including nine destroyers, were sunk, most of them by direct German air attack. The little fleet lost 240 vessels. The spirit of Dunkerque inspired Winston Churchill on June 4 to make one of his most dramatic speeches: "We shall not flag nor fail. We shall go on to the end. . . . We shall fight on the seas and oceans, we shall fight with growing confidence and growing strength in the air; we shall defend our island whatever the cost may be. We shall fight on the beaches, we shall fight on the landing grounds, we shall fight in the streets, we shall fight in the hills; we shall never surrender."

7:27 in the Evening

Jan. 17, 1950. One of the Brink's cashiers managed to loosen his bonds and set off the emergency button which announced the greatest bank robbery in U.S. history. After 18 months of detailed organization, which included several dry runs, seven bandits wearing grotesque Halloween masks, gloves, rubbers, and navy pea coats, entered the Brink's headquarters in Boston, Mass. Reaching the vaults, they found five cashiers counting money and checking papers. The gunmen ordered the employees to lie down and then tied them up. The total haul was $2,775,395.12, of which $1,218,211.19 was in actual cash. During the raid the robbers also noticed a big heavy metal box marked "General Electric." Lacking the necessary tools to open it, they left it behind. (The box contained $800,000 in untraceable payroll cash.)

The 11-man gang was headed by chief planner Anthony Pino, who because of his size was affectionately known as the Pig. It seemed like a perfect robbery. Although the FBI and local police suspected the men involved, they had no proof against them. The state statute limit would be up on Jan. 17, 1953; after that none of the bandits could be prosecuted. But on Jan. 6, with only 11 days to go, one of the gang, Specs O'Keefe, sour at being tricked out of $63,000, turned informer. Within days the entire gang was arrested. Eight of them were sentenced to life prison terms. In 1960 Specs was released, having given state's evidence. When reporters asked him to comment, he said, "Nothing to say." After his release, there were at least three known efforts to murder him.

8:00 in the Evening

Mar. 9, 1566. David Rizzio, secretary to Mary, Queen of Scots, was hacked to pieces in the most sensational political murder in British history.

Twenty-three-year-old Mary Queen of Scots was six months pregnant, and the birth of her child would have dashed the hopes of her husband, Henry Lord Darnley, to become the crown matrimonial of Scotland. With ruthless cunning, he planned to force Mary into having a miscarriage by watching her favorite, the Italian secretary, David Rizzio, brutally murdered.

Under the pretense that Rizzio was Mary's lover, an armed party of six Scottish noblemen with swords and daggers went to the palace of Holyrood in Edinburgh and made their way to where the queen was having supper with her half brother, her half sister, and Rizzio. The men rushed into the room and dragged Rizzio, who was clinging to Mary's skirts, to the door. There he was stabbed with 56 dagger thrusts, the first being with Darnley's own weapon, which was left in his heart. But the conspirators had failed to allow for Mary's resilience. She cunningly organized a formal reconciliation with Darnley and later gave birth to a child who afterward became James I of Great Britain. On Feb. 9, 1567, Darnley was murdered, almost certainly with Mary's knowledge.

8:40 in the Evening

Mar. 24, 1944. The greatest mass escape of W.W. II began at Stalag Luft III in what is now Zagań, Poland. A total of 76 Allied airmen dressed as workmen and office workers (and even a German corporal) edged their way along the 320-ft. escape tunnel—the longest built in either of the world wars. As the 76th escapee was about to emerge from the hole, German guards spotted others running into the woods beyond the prison camp. Most of the fugitives were caught within a day, although some got as far south as Munich. The German reprisal for the mass escape was barbaric despite the Geneva Convention's rule respecting the right to escape. Of the 76 escapees, 50 were shot. Later 15 men were returned to Stalag Luft III; 8 were interned inside the notorious Oranienburg concentration camp, where they again tunneled out; and 3 made it back home.

9:15 in the Evening

June 5, 1944. The BBC radio news was interrupted by this report: "Eileen is married to Jo. . . . It is hot in Suez. . . . The compass points north. . . . The dice are on the table." To thousands of listeners, including many Germans, this message was utter nonsense. To the French underground, however, it was the signal that D-Day was imminent. Over 5,000 French resistance workers, each carrying two packages of TNT, went out into the night and blasted important railway targets. In addition, 74 telephone exchanges were destroyed, and roads that German reinforcements would have to travel along were blown up.

10:10 in the Evening

July 1, 1941. The world's first television commercial was broadcast by WNBT in New York City. The screen showed a Bulova watch as an announcer extolled its virtues and ended by reading the time. The 20-second advertisement cost $9.

10:15 in the Evening

Apr. 14, 1865. John Wilkes Booth assassinated Abraham Lincoln as he sat in the presidential box of Ford's Theater watching the light comedy *Our American Cousin.*

10:22 in the Evening

May 21, 1927. Charles Lindbergh landed at Le Bourget airfield in Paris after becoming the first man to make a solo flight across the Atlantic Ocean. The 3,610-mi. flight took 33 hr. 29½ min. By the time Lindbergh reached Paris, he was so tired and confused that he circled the Eiffel Tower in order to get his bearings. When the plane touched down at the airfield, 20,000 French people surged forward. Lindbergh later reported that the enthusiastic reception was the most dangerous part of the flight. Lindbergh was the 79th man to cross the Atlantic by air but the first to do it alone.

11:00 in the Evening

June 27, 1787. After 22 years of painstaking work, Edward Gibbon finished his *Decline and Fall of the Roman Empire.* He conceived the book—the greatest classical work of historical literature in the English language—on Oct. 15, 1764, "at Rome . . . as I sat musing amidst the ruins of the Capitol, while the barefooted friars were singing vespers in a Temple of Jupiter." Gibbon finished the last lines of the last page in a summerhouse in his garden and celebrated by taking a walk among his acacias.

11:53 in the Evening

May 31, 1962. Karl Adolf Eichmann was hanged inside Ramleh Prison, near Tel Aviv, Israel, for the mass murder of 6 million Jews. Of all the Nazi exterminating machines, Eichmann was the most efficient and enthusiastic. After the war he escaped to find political asylum in Argentina. On May 11, 1960, Israeli Secret Service agents kidnapped him, and nine days later he was smuggled out of the country on board an El Al Britannia plane officially described as a "diplomatic charter flight." The Israeli government was informed of the capture by a cable: BEAST IN CHAINS. Ironically, Eichmann's Jewish appearance once caused him to be violently beaten by Nazi sympathizers, and when he first joined the Socialists he was thought to be a Jewish spy. One wonders if, on the gallows, he was still proud of the boast he made in 1944: "I shall leap into my grave laughing, because the feeling I have that the deaths of 5 million people on my conscience will be for me a source of extraordinary satisfaction."

11:55 in the Evening

Nov. 4, 1605. Guy Fawkes attempted to blow up the English Houses of Parliament but was arrested in the cellars directly beneath the Lords' Chamber.

With other conspirators disguised as coal merchants, Fawkes had smuggled 36 barrels of gunpowder into the vaulted cellars and hidden them under bundles of wood, and empty bottles. One of the Catholic conspirators, however, decided to write to Lord Monteagle, a Catholic peer, warning him not to attend the opening of Parliament, which was set for Nov. 5. The anonymous letter read: "Retire to the country, for though there may be no appearance of any stir, yet I say they shall receive a terrible *blow* this Parliament, yet shall they not see who hurt them."

Monteagle immediately informed the authorities. At first a search of Parliament revealed nothing, but Monteagle decided to make one final check. Just before midnight Fawkes was found in the cellar, claiming he was just a servant looking for his master. But Monteagle noticed that the woodpile seemed out of proportion. He also thought Fawkes to be "a very tall and desperate fellow." The explosives were found and Fawkes was arrested. King James I ordered particularly brutal tortures for Guy Fawkes: "The gentler tortours are to be first usid unto him, *et sic per gradus ad ima tenditur* [and by degrees into hell] and so God spede your goode worke." After suffering extreme agony on the rack, Fawkes signed a confession and named the other conspirators. The following January he was hanged and drawn and quartered in front of the Houses of Parliament.

12:13 in the Morning

Sept. 18, 1961. A DC-6B airliner carrying 56-year-old Dag Hammarskjöld, the Swedish secretary-general of the U.N., crashed in a jungle near Ndola in present-day Zambia. On board were a six-man crew plus Hammarskjöld's staff of eight men and one woman. All were killed instantly except for Hammarskjöld and an aide, who were both thrown clear. Although the plane was several hours overdue and a police inspector telephoned the airport to describe a mysterious flash, no search party was organized until 10:00 A.M. The wreckage was sighted at 3:10 P.M. Hammarskjöld had died during the night, but his aide, Sgt. Harold Julien, a security officer, survived for five days, during which time he raved about explosions and sparks in the sky.

A postmortem established that two of the victims were riddled by bullets—officially from a box of ammunition that had exploded on impact. The official verdict was "pilot error." However, due to the acute political crisis at that time in the Congo, rumor of assassination has never died. Harry S Truman, former U.S. president, said, "Dag Hammarskjöld was on the point of getting something done when they killed him. Notice that I said, 'when they killed him.' "

12:17 in the Morning

June 30, 1908. One of the most baffling natural catastrophes in history occurred in the area of Vanavara on the Stony Tunguska River in Siberia. A massive explosion totally devastated an area of 1,500 sq. mi. Scientists have attributed the explosion to a comet or meteorites, though recently a more imaginative guess has suggested the holocaust was caused by antimatter. Two small villages disappeared in the explosion, millions of forest trees were blown down, and thousands of reindeer perished. Perhaps the most surprising feature of this mysterious catastrophe was that, although the shock was felt more than 600 mi. away, Russian scientists did not bother to investigate until 1927.

Opposite: Siberian forest 20 years after the Tunguska explosion.

UNUSUAL FIRSTS

THE FIRST STUDENT PROTEST IN THE U.S.

Henry David Thoreau's grandfather, Asa Dunbar, set the pattern for American student rebellions over 200 years ago. In 1766 he protested against the quality of Harvard College food with the slogan "Behold, our butter stinketh!" After the faculty condemned him for "the sin of insubordination," Dunbar and his followers conducted an eat-out. They breakfasted off campus.

THE FIRST USE OF TEMPORARY INSANITY AS A DEFENSE IN THE U.S.

On Feb. 25, 1859, Congressman Daniel Sickles learned that his wife had been having an affair with Philip Key, son of Francis Scott Key who wrote "The Star-Spangled Banner." Two days later the enraged Sickles confronted Key and shot him twice, killing him. During the trial Attorney James T. Brady defended his client with the plea of "temporary insanity." Sickles was acquitted and later became a distinguished Union general in the Civil War.

THE FIRST AMERICAN ACCIDENT INSURANCE POLICY

Travelers Insurance Co. sold the nation's first accident insurance policy in 1864 to James Bolter of Hartford, Conn. The $1,000 policy covered only the time Bolter spent walking from the post office to his home on Buckingham Street. The premium was 2¢.

THE FIRST USE OF A CABLEGRAM TO CAPTURE A MURDERER

In April, 1885, Hugh Brooks, the son of a prosperous English merchant, registered at the elegant Southern Hotel in St. Louis, Mo. While staying there, he became a good friend of C. Arthur Preller, a wealthy compatriot. A few days after Brooks left St. Louis for New Zealand, police discovered Preller's body stuffed inside a trunk in his hotel room. Suspecting Brooks, Police Chief Larry Harrigan sent a 133-word wire costing $400 to the U.S. consul in Auckland. When Brooks arrived there, officials seized him and returned him to the U.S. in irons. Lawyers at the trial proved that Brooks, despite his family background, had little money, and had killed Preller in order to steal $600 from him. Brooks was hanged at the St. Louis Four Courts Jail in 1888, but before he died, he quipped, "America was certainly not the land of opportunity for me."

THE FIRST GIDEON BIBLE

Members of Gideons International, a laymen's organization formed in 1899, placed its first Bible in a room at the Superior Hotel in Iron Mountain, Mont., on Nov. 10, 1908. Since then, they have been responsible for distributing Bibles to prisons, hospitals, and schools, as well as motels and hotels.

THE FIRST AIRLINE MEALS

Britain's Handley Page Transport became the first airline to serve in-flight meals when it offered lunch boxes on its London-to-Paris flight on Oct. 11, 1919.

THE FIRST AMERICAN NEON ADVERTISEMENT

The first neon-tube advertising sign in the U.S. appeared on the marquee of the Cosmopolitan Theater in New York City in July, 1923. It announced Marion Davies in the leading role of *Little Old New York*. A patent for the neon lighting was granted to French physicist and chemist Georges Claude.

THE FIRST IN-FLIGHT MOVIES

During an Imperial Airways flight to the Continent in April, 1925, the first in-flight movie, First National's production of Sir Arthur Conan Doyle's *The Lost World*, was featured. Regular in-flight movies began on July 19, 1961, with the showing of *By Love Possessed* on a TWA flight between New York and Los Angeles.

THE FIRST FOOD STAMPS

On May 29, 1961, Chloe and Alderson Muncy, along with 13 of their 15 children, went to Welch, W.Va., to receive the nation's first food stamps from Secretary of Agriculture Orville Freeman. Accompanied by reporters and television crews, the Muncys proceeded to a grocery store after receiving $95 worth of stamps. They finished their shopping only after the Hale family, the country's second recipient of food stamps and the first family to pay for the stamps, had been to the checkout counter before them. Sponsored by the Kennedy administration, the food stamp program grew out of the shock that JFK experienced when campaigning in poverty-stricken areas of West Virginia in 1960.

THE FIRST X-RATED MOVIE IN CHINA

As a sign of a more tolerant intellectual climate, the first X-rated movie allowed inside the People's Republic of China was shown throughout the country in 1978. The Japanese-made film depicted the struggles of a young girl sold into prostitution by her parents. The nation's most respected cultural journal defended the movie, explaining that it had "enlightened and educated" its audiences by expanding the narrow view of morality imposed by Mao's wife and other members of the notorious "Gang of Four."

THE FIRST NUNS TO BE A U.S. AIR FORCE CAPTAIN AND A U.S. MAYOR

Mary Hargrafen, also known as Sister Mary Carl, was the first nun to become a captain in the U.S. Air Force. She was attached to the 2nd Air Medical Evacuation Squadron at Rhine-Main Air Base in West Germany in March, 1978. A member of the Sisters of St. Francis in Dubuque, Ia., Sister Mary Carl turned over most of her annual $20,000 salary to her convent. In 1980 Dubuque also had the distinction of electing the first nun as mayor of an American city—Sister Carol Farrell.

THE FIRST ARTIFICIAL BLOOD TRANSFUSION IN THE U.S.

A spokesman for the University of Minnesota Hospital announced on Nov. 20, 1979, that one of its doctors, Dr. Robert Anderson, had been the first in the country to give a patient a transfusion of artificial blood. The patient suffered a severe loss of blood after having undergone surgery for vascular disease. As a Jehovah's Witness, he refused on religious grounds to receive a transfusion of real blood, so the doctor injected a milky blood substitute called Fluosol, which was developed and tested in Japan.

—C.L.C. and L.L.

MY SEARCH FOR EINSTEIN'S BRAIN

by Steven Levy

Albert Einstein lived in Princeton, N.J. A small house, address 112 Mercer Street. He was a familiar figure in the town, usually walking around in a ragged sweater and tennis shoes, thin gray hair awry, thoughts entangled in a complex mathematical labyrinth. Children loved him; he would occasionally help them with their homework.

In 1955 he was working on a theory of gravitation that he would never perfect. He had turned down the presidency of Israel three years earlier and was now involved in drafting a letter with Bertrand Russell imploring the nations of the world to abolish war. He was noted as the greatest thinker in the world. He had changed our conception of time and space. But at 76 his health was failing.

The doctors called it a hardened aorta. It leaked blood. He had known about the fault in his heart for several years. When first hearing that the artery might develop an aneurysm that could burst, he said, "Let it burst." On Apr. 13 it looked as if it might.

His physician, Dr. Guy K. Dean, called in two consultants, and the three doctors concluded that unless surgery was attempted, the outlook was grim. The creator of the theory of relativity refused. On Friday, Apr. 15, Einstein was persuaded to move his sickbed from Mercer Street to the Princeton Hospital.

During the weekend things began to look better. Einstein's son, Hans Albert, flew in from California. His stepdaughter Margot was already in the hospital, being treated for a minor illness. On Sunday it looked as if the aneurysm might heal temporarily. Dr. Dean took a look at his patient at eleven P.M. He was sleeping peacefully.

The nurse assigned to Einstein was named Alberta Roszel. After midnight she noticed some troubled breathing in her patient. She went to get help. The bed was cranked up. Pale and emaciated, Albert Einstein

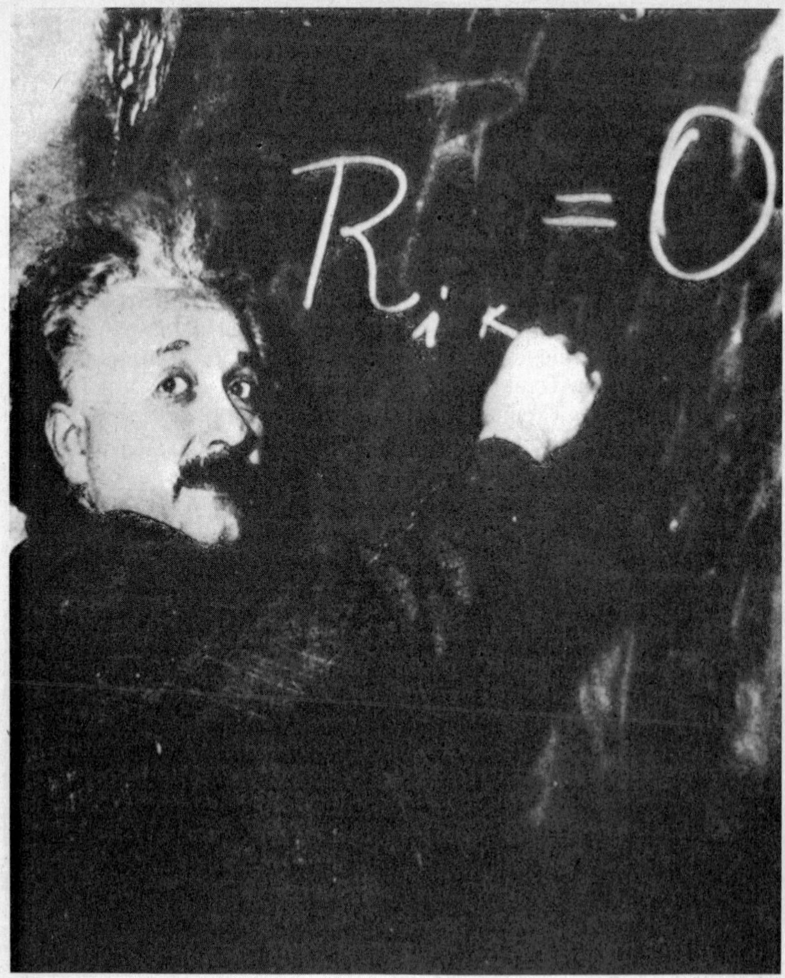

Albert Einstein, 1931.

was muttering something in German, a language Alberta Roszel did not understand. He took two deep breaths and died.

Princeton Hospital in 1955 was not the major facility it would become in later years. A major mobilization was needed to handle publicity on the occasion of the death of such a well-known international figure. Almost seven hours after the death, the hospital announced it and set up a news conference at 11:15. During the hours between the death and the release of details, the Einstein family, their friends, and the hospital officials worked in concert to deny the reporters then flooding to Princeton any scenes to witness, any physical evidence to describe to the millions who craved more than cold facts. Einstein had specifically asked that he not become the subject of a "personality cult."

He did not want 112 Mercer Street to become a museum. He did not want his remains available to admirers making pilgrimages. His family shared his zeal for privacy. By the time the news conference began, an autopsy had been performed. The hospital pathologist, Dr. Thomas S. Harvey, had presided. He worked alone, under the eyes of Dr. Otto Nathan, a friend and colleague of the deceased, who was the designated executor of the Einstein literary estate. For a period of time Dr. Dean was also in the autopsy room. It was Dr. Dean who signed the death certificate. Official cause: rupture of the arteriosclerotic. Birthplace: Ulm, Germany. Citizen of: U.S.A. Occupation: scientist.

If the assembled reporters hoped for any details of the autopsy, they were disappointed; they learned only the cause of Einstein's death. The body was not available for viewing. It was taken to the Mather Funeral Home in Princeton, where it sat for an hour and a half, until it was driven to the Ewing Crematory in Trenton. At four-thirty in the afternoon the body was cremated. Later Dr. Nathan took the ashes and dispersed them in a river, presumably the Delaware.

But part of the remains were spared. Einstein had requested his brain be removed for posthumous study, and his family bid it be done at the autopsy. It was placed in a jar. A *New York Times* reporter on Apr. 20 wrote an article headlined "Key Sought in Einstein Brain." It talked of a study to be performed on the brain and the possible implications. The study, said the story, "may shed light on one of nature's greatest mysteries—the secret of genius." More details were to be released on how the study would be performed. Another press conference was scheduled for the following week.

The Einstein family was upset by the article and told the doctors entrusted with the brain that there was to be no publicity whatsoever concerning the study. The press conference never took place. Einstein's brain had gone into hiding.

"I want you to find Einstein's brain."

Of course I knew who Albert Einstein was. I knew, like most people, about the theory of relativity, but could provide little detail. Something about *e* equaling mc^2, and something about atomic energy, and something about how time and space differed depending on your point of view. I knew it changed the world, and I knew that although it was responsible for nuclear weapons, the theory itself was a step forward, and Einstein was recognized as a humanitarian as well as a genius. I didn't know that his brain was still around.

Neither, really, did my editor. He had done some work on the subject of the brain and had wondered what had happened to this brain of brains, this organic masterpiece of gray matter and cerebral cortex. He had read the last pages of Ronald Clark's *Einstein: The Life and Times*, where the author says of Einstein, "He had insisted his brain be used for research," and then drops the subject. And my editor had heard all sorts of rumors. Einstein's brain was lost. Einstein's brain was examined and found to be normal. Einstein's brain was hidden in a vault, frozen for cloning. And so on.

So the editor had written to Clark, asking him what happened to the brain. The author of Einstein's standard biography wrote back saying, "I'm afraid I don't know the answer, but have a recollection that it *was* preserved somewhere." He suggested contacting Otto Nathan, the executor of the Einstein estate. Nathan replied promptly. His one-paragraph letter confirmed that the brain had been removed before cremation, and stated that the pathologist in charge had been a Dr. Thomas Harvey.

The letter was a year old. Now my editor wanted to know where the brain was. And he wanted me to find it.

"Sure," I said.

I had to wait a long time. Then a voice came over the phone. "Mr. Seligman will be right with you," it said. While someone in the hospital paged him, I read some more of a book explaining relativity. The brain I was looking for had changed our perception of the universe, and since Walter Seligman was a vice-president of the Princeton Medical Center, where the brain had been removed from the highly recognizable head of Albert Einstein, I hoped for a clue.

Finally he reached a phone. "Yes, the operation took place here," he conceded. "But there are no records." He paused. "The only person who would know anything about it would be the pathologist who performed the operation. Dr. Thomas Harvey."

Where would Dr. Harvey be found?

"I'm afraid I don't know. He left here years ago."

"You're looking for Einstein's brain?" said a co-worker. "I have a friend who saw a picture of it."

What?

"She's a medical student in California. Her teacher had slides of it. Here's her number."

I called. The woman, it seemed, had not seen the slide, but had once been invited to by her instructor, a Dr. Moore. Supposedly he had in his possession slides that pictured Einstein's brain. She wasn't sure how he got them. She gave me his number.

Dr. Moore was willing to talk.

"I worked on the study of the brain," he said. "In Chicago. Sets of the section were sent to various experts for analysis. The man I was working for, Dr. Sidney Schulman, specialized in the thalamus, and we got portions of Einstein's thalamus, sectioned and stained for microscopic study."

The thalamus is a part of the brain which transmits impulses to the cerebral cortex.

"As far as the thalamus is concerned," said Dr. Moore, "Einstein's brain cells were like anyone else's at that age. If you showed the slides blind to someone, he would say that they came from any old man. Even so, I took Kodachromes of a couple slides to show to my students."

I wondered if Dr. Moore knew where the brain section came from and whether he knew of parts of the brain that might still be around.

"I'm not sure. I think the stuff we got was from some pathologist from Princeton—"

"A Dr. Thomas Harvey?"

"*That's* the name."

"Have you heard anything from Dr. Harvey? Do you know where he is?"

"No, I haven't heard from him since he took back the samples. And I have never seen anything published. Do *you* know where to reach him?"

No, I didn't know where to reach him. But I had one last idea. Since my man was a doctor, he must be a member of the American Medical Association. Surely they keep track of their members.

There was a tense pause when I asked the man who came to the phone whether he was the same Dr. Harvey who had worked at Princeton Hospital in the mid-1950s. Almost as if he had been considering a denial, he slowly said yes. I told him I was interested in Einstein's brain and I was willing to visit him to talk about it.

Throughout the conversation Dr. Harvey had sounded very uncomfortable, so I hadn't asked him some obvious questions. Like why nothing had been published. Like why the subject was still so touchy. Like whether he still had any of the brain in his possession.

These questions I would ask in Wichita.

What the reporters weren't told in 1955 was that Dr. Harvey was enlisting some brain experts to assist him in studying the most significant chunk of "gross material," as Harvey put it, ever to become available to medical science.

The first step in the process was an exacting measurement and complete photographing of the whole brain. This was done at Princeton Hospital, which had agreed to partially fund the study. From these measurements, there was apparently no difference between Einstein's brain and a "normal" one. Certainly it was no bigger and, at 2.64 lb., it was no heavier. This was no surprise; the real work would take place in microscopic studies of the dissected brain.

So sometime in the early fall of 1955 Dr. Harvey packed up the brain of Albert Einstein, made sure it was well cushioned in its formaldehyde-filled jar, and drove—very, very carefully—from Princeton to Philadelphia, where the brain would be sectioned in a laboratory at the University of Pennsylvania.

From there, the sections of the brain, some in small chunks preserved in celloidin (a gelatinous material), some on microscopic slides, went off to various parts of the country to be studied by specialists. "I usually delivered the pieces myself," said Harvey. "It could have been handled by mail, I guess, but I wanted to meet these men."

The idea was that the specialists would eventually publish papers on the brain parts they studied. Meanwhile, Harvey would perform his own tests, some paralleling the other work and some that no one was duplicating.

"In order to do a study like this," said Dr. Harvey, "you have to have seen enough of the normal brain to have a pretty good idea what would be extraordinary. Unfortunately, not a lot of brains have been studied completely. Less than a dozen. Of course, when it comes to genius . . . not even that many. It really is a mammoth task. There's a tremendous number of cells in the brain. You don't examine every one of them in detail, but you look at an awful lot of sections. Almost all the brain now is in sections. There's a little left as brain tissue, but very little."

How little? I wondered to myself. And where was it? All this history had been fascinating, but I wanted to *view* the damn thing. Of course, you couldn't just bust in on a guy and demand to see a brain. Somehow I had to steer things toward the "gross material" itself. I asked Dr. Harvey if it might be possible to see a slide, perhaps.

"I don't really have any slides here in this office," he said. "So you can't do it here."

Perhaps I could have accepted not seeing the brain if I knew that it didn't exist. But to leave Wichita knowing that there might well be some brain to see? Unthinkable. Dr. Harvey noted my obvious dismay, and almost as a consolation asked me if I had any more questions about the study.

Well, all right. Why had things been taking so long?

"We had no urgency to publish. And the actual examination didn't take this long, of course. Though there is some work still to be done. You see, my career since I did the autopsy has been sort of interrupted. I left Princeton Hospital in 1960 and moved to Freehold. And for the past few years I've been here in Wichita. I don't work on it as much as I used to. But we're getting closer to publication."

Has the study found the brain to be . . . different?

Dr. Harvey thought a bit before answering. "So far it's fallen within normal limits for a man his age. There are some changes that occur within the brain with age. And his brain showed these. No more so than the average man. The anatomical variations," he said, "are within normal limits."

Another uneasy silence followed. Dr. Harvey shifted in his seat. He seemed to have something he wanted to say, but was agonizing over whether to voice it or not.

"Do you have a *photograph* of it here?" I blurted out.

"No, I don't," he said. "I don't have any material here." Then he paused. A shy grin came over his face. "I *do* have a little bit of the gross here," he said, almost apologetically.

"Pardon?"

"Gross material. Unsectioned. But that's all."

Here? *In this office we're sitting in?*

Without another word, Dr. Harvey rose from his seat and walked around the desk, crossing in front of me to get to the corner of the room. He bent down over the clutter on the floor, stopping at the red plastic cooler. He picked it up and put it on a chair next to me.

Einstein's brain in a beer cooler?

No. He turned away from the cooler, going back to the corner. Of the two cardboard boxes stacked there, he picked up the top one and moved it to the side. Then he bent down over the bottom box, which had a logo reading "Costa Cider" on the side. There was no top to the box, and it looked filled with crumpled newspapers. Harvey, still wearing a sheepish grin, thrust his hand into the newspapers and emerged with a large mason jar. Floating inside the jar, in a clear liquid solution, were several pieces of matter. A conch shell–shaped mass of wrinkly material the color of clay after kiln firing. A fist-sized chunk of grayish, lined substance, the apparent consistency of sponge. And in a separate pouch, a mass of pinkish-white strings resembling bloated dental floss. All the material was recognizably brain matter.

Dr. Harvey pointed out that the conch-shaped mass was Einstein's cerebellum, the gray blob a chunk of cerebral cortex, and the stringy stuff a group of aortic vessels.

"It's all in sections, except for this," he said. I had risen up to look into the jar, but now I was sunk in my chair, speechless. My eyes were fixed upon that jar as I tried to comprehend that these pieces of gunk bobbing up and down had caused a revolution in physics and quite possibly changed the course of civilization. *There it was!* Before I could regain my wits, Dr. Harvey had reached back into the box for another jar. This one was larger, and since it was not a mason jar, the top had been fixed in place by yellowed masking tape. Inside it were dozens of rectangular translucent blocks, the size of Goldenberg's Peanut Chews, each with a little sticker reading "Cerebral Cortex" and bearing a number. Encased in every block was a shriveled blob of gray matter.

All along, I had feared that if I ever did get to see Einstein's brain, the experience would be a terrific letdown. My fears were unjustified. For a moment, with the brain before me, I had been granted a rare peek into an organic crystal ball. Swirling in formaldehyde was the power of the smashed atom, the mystery of the universe's black holes, the utter miracle of human achievement.

Whether you see it or merely contemplate it, there is something very awesome in the postmortem remains of Albert Einstein's brain. It is something of ourselves at our best, or something of what we humans can be—using our own awesome powers to work out the relation between ourselves and our surroundings. The fact that 23 years of study indicate that Einstein's brain is physiologically no different from yours or mine seems to bear this out. "God does not play dice with the universe," Albert Einstein liked to say, and he spent the bulk of his life trying to prove it. I think that he would be happy to find that, with no better a roll than most of us, he managed to beat the house!

SOURCE: *New Jersey Monthly*, August 1978.

THE MICHAEL ROCKEFELLER RIDDLE

by John Godwin

Our helicopter danced and leaped crazily, buffeted by blasts of hot, moist air. Below, as far as our eyes could see, the jungle stretched like a crumpled green rug, the solid mass of treetops broken only by mud-brown patches of *loraro* and mangrove swamps. This was the Asmat coastline of southern New Guinea, the region known as "the land of the lapping death." A tangled morass of bog and forest, thick with insects and leeches but unmarred by a single road, airfield, or telephone wire.

Down there lived an estimated 18,000 natives, but no sign of human habitation was visible from above. Most of the villages lay so deeply buried in the jungle that their people rarely saw the sun.

It was mid-November, 1961, and I knew that the greatest search operation in the island's history was running full gear: Dutch and Australian aircraft crisscrossing the sky, canoes and launches nosing along the rivers, thousands of marines, police troopers, and tribesmen beating through the bush. But all this might have been happening in another country. From where we sat, there was nothing but the infinity of vegetation.

Before starting out I had asked Sergeant Gerig, the Dutch patrol officer flying with us, how he rated our chances of finding any lone man in this wilderness.

He shrugged. "About as good as finding half a needle in a thousand haystacks, *mijnheer.*"

The man we were searching for, however, wasn't just "any" lone man. His name was Michael Clark Rockefeller, and he happened to be the son of the governor of New York and heir to one of the largest fortunes on earth.

Michael was a Harvard graduate, but otherwise refused to follow in his father's footsteps. After graduating cum laude and serving a hitch in the army, he went to New Guinea as a member of the Harvard Peabody Museum expedition. As he explained it, "I have the desire to do something romantic and adventurous at a time when frontiers in the real sense of the word are disappearing."

He couldn't have picked a better place to fulfill that particular desire. New Guinea is an island about as large as Texas and New York State combined, perched on the northern tip of Australia. It remains one of the least explored areas in the world; vast patches are as unmapped as the mountains of the moon. The island has never had an accurate census; the population is believed to number approximately 4 million.

Rockefeller's first expedition went to the Baliem Valley in the central highlands, a region of clouds and constant drizzle and perpetually warring Dani tribesmen, so secluded that explorers had tagged it "Shangri-

Michael Rockefeller in New Guinea, 1961, the year of his disappearance.

la." The Harvard men stayed there until September, 1961, filming bloody tribal battles and collecting Dani weaponry and artifacts.

Michael returned home for a brief rest, but New Guinea seemed to draw him like a magnet. Two months later he was back, this time on behalf of the New York Museum of Primitive Art. He headed for the Asmat coast in the South. His object was to purchase some of the decorated *bis* poles which the natives carve in memory of their ancestors. Above all, he wanted samples of the human skulls that serve the Asmat warriors as tokens of prowess in combat as well as hut decorations.

For the Asmats were headhunters (some of them were also cannibals), but their treatment of the trophies varied sharply from that of other head-takers in different parts of the world. The Asmats didn't shrink heads. Instead they stripped heads down to the skull, let them bleach in the sun, then painted them in artistic designs and stuck them on poles to proclaim their machismo.

Michael Rockefeller was 23 when he returned to New Guinea, a rangy, bearded lad whose round spectacles gave him a deceptively indoorish appearance. Actually he was an outstanding athlete in peak physical condition, untroubled by the murderous climate of the region (the humidity, I remember, was such that a cigarette pack I put under my bed at night showed a film of mildew by morning).

Unfortunately the young American knew little about the dangers of the Asmat coast. He took risks that made some of the more experienced locals blanch. And he rarely took warning.

The last persons to caution him were the Dutch Crozier fathers at the mission station of Agats. Michael arrived there in a 30-ft. catamaran made of two native canoes lashed together by planks and powered by a single 18-hp outboard motor. It was a highly maneuverable craft, but quite unsuitable for what he had in mind. The mission fathers shook their heads when they learned that he intended to cruise in it to the village of Atsj, 25 mi. down the coast.

They explained that this journey would take him across the mouth of the Eilanden River where it empties into the Arafura Sea. At this point the coastal tides often rolled out in waves up to 20 ft. high. No place for a fragile makeshift craft, heavily laden with trading goods.

On the morning of Thursday, Nov. 16, Michael started out just the same. His only companions were a Dutch anthropologist named René Wassing and two Asmat helpers. Around noon, just as they were passing across the mouth of the Eilanden, the warning of the missionaries came true. A huge wave suddenly surged over the boat, swamping the outboard motor. Now the vessel was drifting helplessly, the fierce tidal rip sweeping it out into the Arafura Sea. The two natives dived overboard almost immediately and reached land. But the white men hung on, stubbornly trying to tinker the engine back to life.

Twenty-four hours later they were still drifting with a dead motor. Both of them believed that the Asmats had simply left them to their fate—falsely, as it turned out, because the natives had already alerted the Dutch authorities. But the helpless drifting and the beckoning shoreline were too much for Michael's active temperament. He told his companion that he'd try to swim to the coast.

Wassing warned him against the attempt. The mangrove swamps of the coast were only about 3 mi. away, but the water was known to contain both sharks and crocodiles. Michael merely grinned and made his preparations. He stripped down to his shorts, tied his glasses firmly to his ears, and strapped on a jerry can and an empty gas container to make an impromptu float. He was an excellent swimmer, and with these supports the 3 mi. to land seemed easy.

Wassing watched him disappear—the last *confirmed* witness to see the young man alive. For with this swim Michael Rockefeller joined Ambrose Bierce, Colonel Fawcett, and Amelia Earhart on the mystery list of vanished celebrities.

Late that afternoon Wassing was picked up by a Royal Netherlands

Navy flying boat. His first question was about young Rockefeller. The navy pilots shrugged. Nothing had been seen or heard of him.

As soon as the flying boat docked, New Guinea's meager communications network began to hum. The Dutch administrator at Agats raised his superior at Merauke, 240 mi. away, by shortwave radio. Merauke radioed Hollandia [now Djajapura], the colony's capital. The governor informed The Hague, in far-off Holland. From there the message went to the Dutch embassy in Washington. And the ambassador telephoned Gov. Nelson Rockefeller in New York.

The governor immediately chartered a jet for $38,000 to fly him and Michael's twin sister, Mary, to the scene, more than 10,000 mi. from New York. Even before he arrived there, an immense search apparatus leaped into action.

Dutch Gov. P. J. Platteel mobilized every aircraft at his disposal, ordered out marines, police troopers, and every naval patrol craft to scour the area. Australia dispatched helicopters and a squadron of air force transport planes. Most important, some 5,000 local Asmats joined the search voluntarily, fired by the royal reward of 250 sticks of trading tobacco offered for any clue to Michael's whereabouts.

Also on the spot were nearly 100 reporters and cameramen (including me) representing the world's press, television, and radio.

Merauke, a small cluster of huts with normally 3,000 inhabitants, became search headquarters, and temporarily the most overcrowded spot in the Southern Hemisphere. The temperature hovered around 100° in the shade, air conditioning was unknown, ants ate through flashlight batteries, mosquitoes feasted on every exposed inch of skin, and newsmen slept four to a room. The water supply broke down immediately, so everyone went dirty and stank. The only drink available was lukewarm beer.

The main search area lay 240 mi. to the north and encompassed 1,400 sq. mi. of swamp and jungle. Governor Rockefeller exchanged his jet for a lumbering Dakota, slowly circling over the endless greenish-brown curtain under which his son had vanished. He and Mary took turns peering down with field glasses, scanning the treetops . . . hoping.

Those of us using helicopters got a closer view—occasionally a little too close for comfort. Whenever our pilot spotted what could pass for a clearing near a few huts, we went down.

The scene was always the same. Thick, steamy heat that engulfed you like a moist towel. Branch huts built on stilts over reeking, dark brown mud. A wide, cautious circle of people staring at us as we climbed from our machine. The Asmats were totally naked—not so much as a loincloth among them. The men fingered flintstone knives and whipped 12-ft. spears with serrated shark's-teeth tips. Some of the women nursed a baby on one breast and a piglet on the other.

Our helicopter didn't seem to astonish them unduly. Other things did. I created a sensation by lighting my pipe with a match; you could hear them drawing their breaths in wonder. We always broke the ice by passing out the standard currency of the region: sticks of tobacco that could be smoked or chewed or bartered for something else.

Sergeant Gerig spoke a few words of their language and used gestures to explain the purpose of our visit. We were looking for a bearded young man wearing glasses. His hands indicated hair on his face and rings around his eyes. He pointed to his own fair skin—a white man. Had they seen such a man?

The Asmat warriors exchanged a few rapid grunts. Then one of them—usually a headman with a boar's tusk stuck through his nose—replied. Yes, they had heard of such a man, but they hadn't seen him. He was *agai, agai*—farther away—which might mean anything from 1 to 100 mi.

The Asmats were quite friendly, particularly after we'd distributed the tobacco. But you couldn't help noticing the skulls. Some yellow with age, others gleaming white and fresh. Most of them displayed on poles outside the huts, but a few lying around casually, like household utensils. I also noticed that Gerig kept his leather gun holster in a handy position.

Later I asked him about those skulls. "I thought you'd outlawed head-hunting around here?"

"Oh, certainly. Only the nearest police post is 140 mi. away. So we cannot control very well. Also, *mijnheer*," he added, "we have no way of telling which skull belonged to a slain enemy or somebody's grandfather who died of old age. They often keep a relative's skull. Like—how do you say?—for memento."

We whirred from one swampy clearing to another, handing out tobacco, always asking the same questions, always getting the same maddening *agai, agai* for an answer. The white man had been seen . . . found . . . farther inland . . . farther down the coast . . . anywhere except the place we were at.

The other search teams were getting the same elusive reply. We saw the crocodiles basking on the mud banks, the skulls grinning at us from the village poles, the incredible clouds of sparrows rising like locusts from the trees, and felt our hopes fading.

They revived briefly when a patrol craft fished an empty gasoline can from the sea 120 mi. down the coast. But they found no sign of Michael, and it still isn't certain that the can was his.

Gov. Nelson Rockefeller held a press conference in Merauke. He looked as if he hadn't slept for days and seemed totally exhausted. But his quiet courtesy never cracked. He was one of the bravest men I'd ever seen. He thanked the Dutch and Australian governments—and all of us—for our help. Then he patiently answered a barrage of questions. Then he flew back to New York.

After 10 days the Dutch authorities called off the search. They were satisfied, they declared, that Michael had either drowned or been taken by a shark or crocodile. Most of the press corps pulled out. Only a few of us stayed on, held by a lingering doubt about the correctness of the official verdict. It was mostly instinctive—we had no real clues to go by—but we had the distinct feeling that this case wasn't as closed as some people wanted us to believe.

Only after the turmoil of the search had died down did it become apparent that a large number of people shared our opinion. There was, in fact, a sharp split between Dutch officialdom and the local white civilians as to young Rockefeller's fate. Those who lived in the area—resident missionaries, medical men, traders—were convinced that, whatever else may have happened, Michael had *not* perished in the water.

The first person to confirm my private doubts was Dr. Ary Kemper, who specialized in tropical medicine and had lived in the Asmat for 11 years.

"That young man was a powerful swimmer, and with those floats on his back he could not have drowned," said the doctor. "Sharks and crocodiles? Yes, there are plenty. But, you know, in all the years here I have never heard of *one* human being attacked. The natives swim and fish without fear of them. They just don't seem to be man-eaters. Not along this part of the coast. Believe me, I would have learned of any such attack."

"Well, what do you think happened?" I asked.

"I think he reached land. And I think he was killed there," Kemper said grimly. "By the Asmats. Perhaps for his head. Or perhaps he was eaten. One man alone—unarmed—wandering on this coast, now that *is* risky."

"Then why are the government people so adamant about him being lost at sea?"

Kemper grinned wryly. "Because they don't wish the world to know that they are not in control of the entire territory. Officially there is no head-hunting, no cannibalism, no tribal warfare, you understand? No white man is ever murdered. And such an important person—a billionaire's son—this must not have occurred! It would look very bad at the United Nations, you understand?"

I understood even better after talking to a Dutch administration officer. Over half a bottle of *jonge genever* he gave me a view of Michael that had not hitherto been voiced.

"He was a likable boy, very courageous and sincere, but sometimes very foolish. He came to the Asmat and offered six, seven steel axes per skull for his museum. He offered this to natives who hardly know any metal. Six steel axes—why, *gottverdomme*, that is a fortune! They could buy two wives for that price!"

The official went on to describe how—as soon as word of the offer spread—head-hunting flared up along the entire coast. "I don't think Rockefeller realized what he was doing," he went on. "But some tribesmen actually approached me for permission to go raiding—'only one night, two night, no more.' And when I refused, they went just the same. They just couldn't resist that offer."

Although the administrator didn't say so, his implication was that Michael had perished in trouble of his own making. To the Asmat warriors a head was a head; they couldn't have known that the half-naked white man on the shore was the source of those steel hatchets.

The more locals I interviewed, the stronger grew the impression that Michael had indeed been slain rather than drowned. One missionary priest, Father Jan Smit—who knew Rockefeller well—told me he had actually seen a warrior wearing the young man's shorts. Father Smit, who was himself killed by the Asmats in 1965, was the first person who pinpointed the murder scene for me: the coastal village of Otsjanep.

The place had a sinister reputation for general violence as well as cannibalism. A French movie team chose it as the location for their epic New Guinea film *The Sky Above, the Mud Below,* because there they were able to get shots of warriors sleeping with their heads pillowed on human skulls.

Yet during our search operation the Dutch authorities had paid very little attention to Otsjanep—despite the fact that it lay in the area where Michael could have reached shore. Later on they actually barred strangers from the vicinity. Why?

The more I learned about this village the more puzzling the whole matter became. For Michael Rockefeller and his team had done most of their initial research right there! If the Otsjanep tribesmen wished to kill them, they must have missed a dozen earlier opportunities to do so.

Hospitality is a sacred institution among the Asmats. Your worst enemy becomes an honored guest as long as he dwells in your village. Thus the Rockefeller team was sacrosanct just as long as they remained in Otsjanep. As soon as it left, any of them became fair game.

It was Michael's tragic bad luck that he should have reached land just at a point where a fishing party of his former hosts was hunting for sea turtles. They were not a war party, but their long barbed fishing spears were just as deadly for humans.

According to one story, one of the warriors speared the American while he was still in the water. Then the others joined in and dragged their wounded victim ashore to finish him off. They took the head, cooked and ate parts of the body, and buried the remains.

This account, I learned, was based mainly on the boasting of an Otsjanep fight chief named Ajik or Ajim. While the search operation was going on, the men involved kept very quiet about their deed. But as soon as things calmed down, Ajik went around proclaiming how he had killed an "important wizard" of the whites and taken his head, thereby inheriting some of his powers. Simultaneously two other warriors spread the same story, also claiming to be the killers and now possessors of some of Rockefeller's "magic." In evidence one of them, called Fin, allegedly showed Michael's spectacles to his audience.

I could only surmise the reason why the Dutch authorities failed to search Otsjanep. Possibly because the incident of the trigger-happy patrol that had opened fire on a throng of villagers earlier might then have come to light. More probably because the searchers might have had to fight their way in. Either way it would have made a pretty bad impression on the representatives of the international media.

This undoubtedly was what lay behind officialdom's insistence on Rockefeller's death by drowning. They had to cling to that theory in order to avoid having to raid Otsjanep by force. It also accounted for the fact that neither Ajik nor Fin nor any of the other boasters were ever arrested or even interrogated.

The missionaries, who knew their Asmats, took these boasts quite seriously. Father Gerald Hekman of the Evangelical Aid Mission even offered a substantial reward in axes and tobacco to anyone who brought in Michael's skull. There were no takers.

Some rumors, based on second-, third-, or even fourth-hand accounts, had it that Michael was *alive*, that he was being held captive by one of the coastal tribes, who were now even more isolated and unapproachable than they had been during the Dutch regime.

What made these stories so tantalizing was both their elusiveness and their persistence. Plus the fact that similar episodes *have* occurred in New Guinea.

During the W.W. II fighting in the Pacific, the Eilanden River region marked the most southerly point of advance for the Japanese armies. When U.S., Australian, and Dutch troops finally recaptured Merauke in 1945, thousands of Nipponese soldiers fled into the Asmat. The Japanese War Office wrote them off as dead. But an amazing number of them were very much alive. Most of their comrades either perished in the jungle or by Asmat spears. A few survivors, however, were taken in by the villagers and treated kindly for reasons it took them years to understand.

The Asmats believe that odd-looking and unusual people offer protection against their main dread—the *adat*, or forest demons. They like to keep such creatures in their villages as good-luck charms because the *adat* won't approach a settlement that harbors them. To the Asmats some of the Japanese must have looked very odd indeed. They were kept as part prisoners, part guests. They were given wives and whatever food the tribe possessed—but carefully watched and never allowed to leave a certain area. The Asmats often keep their own albinos in similar captivity as mascots against the jungle spirits. As the years passed, the Japanese grew accustomed to tribal life and made no serious efforts to escape. Those who did usually owed their getaway to the confusion of a tribal war. Others died in the villages without the outside world's ever learning of their existence.

There was thus at least a *possibility* of Rockefeller's survival somewhere in the Asmat wilderness. But until one of the rumors came up with some concrete geographical data there was no chance for a follow-through.

Then, in October, 1968, a very tough-looking individual who called himself John Donahue walked into the New York office of *Argosy* magazine, demanding to see the editor. The executive editor was Milt Machlin, a chunky globe-trotting adventurer who had nosed around the remotest corners of the Pacific. To him Donahue confided that he, personally, had seen Michael Rockefeller alive only 10 weeks earlier! What's more, he had talked to him.

The man began his story by admitting that he was a wanted criminal, a professional smuggler and gunrunner. He certainly looked the part. On his most recent operation he and two companions stopped at a small island called Kanaboora, one of the Trobriand group lying off the northeastern tip of New Guinea. There, Donahue claimed, he met a half-crippled white man with a long sandy beard, whom the natives were keeping in their tribal council house.

The bearded man, who was wearing only a native lap-lap, peered at them shortsightedly, then introduced himself: "I am Michael Rockefeller. Can you help me?" According to Donahue he related how he had reached the Asmat shore after diving overboard and stumbled through the mangroves for three days, sleeping in the trees at night. He broke both his legs when a branch snapped under him, and lost his glasses. Eventually he was captured by a party of Trobriand Islanders, a seafaring tribe that often made long coastal journeys. They had brought him back to their home island and kept him there, believing him to be an "important sorcerer."

Donahue couldn't do anything for him at the time. He would have run the risk of drawing attention to his illicit cargo. But perhaps Machlin could.

Most magazine editors would have treated the story as just one more yarn spun by a roving crank. But Milt Machlin was not the average editor. He asked for names and details—and got them. Without quite believing the tale, he assured himself that Donahue had actually been to New Guinea recently and that he really was some sort of outlaw. Where exactly was that island? "About a hundred and fifty degrees east longitude by around eight degrees south," came the prompt answer.

Machlin was no armchair journalist. He knew enough about the region and the background of Rockefeller's disappearance to realize that—while wildly improbable—the story was not *impossible*. Donahue wanted neither a reward nor a fee for his information. Why, then, would he bother to make up such a saga?

As Machlin put it: "There was only one way to check out Donahue's story—go out and see." Whatever the outcome, the investigation would make a splendid article for his magazine. (It did.)

For a start the editor discovered that Donahue had made a mistake about the name of the island. There was no "Kanaboora" at the location given. But there *was* a minute speck called Kanapu in almost precisely that position.

Machlin got there by jet liner, prop plane, and diesel schooner, only to discover that the tiny islet was uninhabited. The searchers found old campfire sites, a couple of abandoned palm shelters, but not a living soul. Some natives had obviously been there, but they had gone. Where to and who with was anybody's guess.

This was the end of what Machlin dubbed the "Donahue saga." It had served merely to add yet another mystery touch to the Rockefeller enigma.

Rumors concerning Michael Rockefeller continued to surface. Most of them were the usual secondhand legends, long on fantasy and short on facts, all the more difficult to verify because the Indonesian government was busily manufacturing tales of its own, aimed at discrediting the former Dutch administration. One of them had it that the American was actually a CIA agent and that his disappearance had been an elaborately staged fraud designed to plant him in West Irian, where he was now fomenting unrest among the natives.

But in December, 1972, I tracked down an eyewitness account that pushed the whole guessing game back to square one. It came from a veteran Australian island trader named Roy Hogan, who was taking a brief vacation in Sydney before returning to his route. His "run," as he called it, extended into the Arafura Sea from Australian Papua and occasionally included the Asmat coast. His boat, the 60-ft. *Rosemary M.*, was a former pearling lugger fitted with an improved cargo hold that enabled him to carry anything from copra to light machinery.

The previous month he had visited the Ewta River region in the Asmat. Hogan and his crew—a Chinese and a Papuan—were doing some fishing at a bivouac called Mirinaup.

"Around five in the afternoon we saw a whole bunch of natives coming toward the bivouac," Hogan told me. "We were sheltered behind some scrub, so they didn't spot us until they were almost on top of us. A big bunch—about 30 of 'em—but evidently peaceful because they had women and small children with them. The moment we stood up they stopped dead; they were pretty surprised, judging by the looks on their faces.

"We made peace signs with our palms open—no weapons—and they stood still; kind of hesitant. I got a long, close look at them. And that's when I saw the white bloke."

Hogan raised his hand to forestall my interjection. "I know what you're going to say—he might have been an albino. But I've seen plenty of Asmat albinos, and I'm telling you this fellow was *white*. First of all, he wore specs—glasses. Then he had straight blond hair, not curly, and a big straggly beard. The Asmats can't grow beards. He was taller than the rest. And he wore a strip of cloth around his waist; the others weren't wearing a stitch between 'em.

"He was staring directly at us, but he gave us no special greeting, no sign of recognition. He just stared like the rest. After a few moments the whole bunch turned away from us, heading back the way they'd come. Well, I was pretty curious and followed them a few steps. That's when some of the bucks turned nasty. I saw them raising those long barbed spears of theirs, shaking them up and down the way they do when they're getting ready to throw.

"That was enough for me. I got back to my mates as fast as I could. We had no guns or anything on us. And that crowd disappeared in the scrub. We never saw them again.

"The funny thing is," Hogan added, "that I never thought of young Rockefeller until we got back to Australian territory, to Port Moresby. I looked up his picture in a newspaper file. And let me tell you—if that geezer wasn't him, it must have been his bloody twin brother!"

When I matched Hogan's account with the mass of similar snippets in circulation, I was struck by two alternative solutions nobody seems to have considered so far.

There may be several *other* white men living a tribal existence in the remoter regions of New Guinea. This would explain the bewildering change of locale in these stories that had Michael cropping up in places hundreds of miles apart.

The second solution is admittedly the most way-out of all. Those who knew Michael Rockefeller have found it impossible to believe in his prolonged captivity. They reason that anyone as intelligent and enterprising as he would have managed to escape or at least send out a message of some kind.

Quite true—providing he *wanted* to escape. But there remains the bare possibility that Michael has deliberately renounced civilization. That he decided to make his way in a land where his family's name and wealth counted for nothing . . . where he would be valued for himself alone. He was, by nature, a passionate outdoorsman, fascinated by the primitive life and constantly drawn toward the wilderness. He could, conceivably, have made friends with the Asmats and become a kind of honorary tribal member. And he must have realized that if the outside world learned of this, they would pressure him into returning to the plastic artificiality he had shaken off.

It is, as stated, a way-out solution. But then, New Guinea is a way-out country. Stranger things have happened there than a billionaire's son's return to nature in the raw.

WHO'S IN CHARGE?—SIX POSSIBLE CONTENDERS

THE BILDERBERG GROUP

The Enterprise: Often called "the most exclusive club of the Western establishment," the Bilderberg Group is a mixed collection of some of the world's most powerful financiers, industrialists, statesmen, and intellectuals, who get together each year for a private conference on world affairs. The meetings provide an informal, off-the-record opportunity for international leaders to mingle, and are notorious for the cloak of secrecy they are held under.

History: A Polish political philosopher who was an avid crusader for a united Europe first conceived of the idea for a private gathering of the world's elite. Worried over a rising tide of anti-American feeling in Europe, Dr. Joseph H. Retinger approached Prince Bernhard of the Netherlands in 1952 with a proposal to chair a series of meetings aimed at reestablishing and redefining American and European relations. Bernhard enthusiastically embraced the plan, and the two drew up a list of representatives from Western Europe and the U.S., their original intention being to invite two people from each country to give both the

The Bilderberg Group as drawn by Feliks Topolski, 1956.

conservative and liberal viewpoints. However, the Americans were just then embroiled in the 1952 presidential campaign and brushed aside the proposal. After two years of contacting various Americans and Europeans, Retinger's dream finally bore fruit. In 1954 a collection of carefully selected business and political leaders from Europe and the U.S. met near Arnhem in the Netherlands at the Hotel de Bilderberg, from which the group derived its name. Shrouded in secrecy, the meeting received little attention despite the phenomenon of so many of the leading citizens of the industrialized world being gathered in one place. One of the concerns of the original meeting was the wave of McCarthyism that was sweeping America at the time. American representatives reassured their European counterparts that the anticommunist fanaticism was merely a short-term trend that would soon die out.

The first meeting was such a success that they decided to meet once a year and establish a steering committee whose primary function would be to choose the roster for the next year's meeting. Participation in the Bilderberg Group is by invitation only, and just because a person is invited one year does not necessarily mean he or she will be invited the next. There are no permanent members except the 25 to 30 people on the steering committee who retain their seats unless they take a government office, at which time they nominate a successor for the vacated post. In the early days, the Bilderberg Group drew 50 to 60 people, but in recent years it has attracted well over 120. Out-of-the-way, exclusive spots, such as the Villa d'Este at Lake Como in Italy and St. Simons Island off the Georgia coast, are favored for the annual meetings. The group usually takes over an entire hotel, which is closely watched by security guards, and the members live, eat, and drink together for three days. Wives and husbands of the group are not invited. Each member pays his own way to the meeting, although impoverished academics are given air fare. Basic operating expenses for a small office in The Hague are covered by contributions from wealthy members or their companies. The group has met every year since 1954 except for 1976, when a Lockheed bribery scandal involving Prince Bernhard caused an embarrassed steering committee to postpone the event. Although committee members anxiously debated at the time whether to abandon the whole idea, they decided against it, and people accepted invitations to the next year's meeting as eagerly as ever.

Exploits: Bilderbergers have shielded their privacy with such zealousness and skill over the years that it's been hard for outsiders to guess at what really goes on at meetings that include such leading world figures as British Prime Minister Margaret Thatcher, West German leader Helmut Schmidt, and former U.S. Secretary of State Henry Kissinger. Papers assigned by the steering committee on such topics as world inflation, the Middle East, and the West's relationship with the third world are presented at each meeting but are never published and are given little importance by members. No votes are taken and no official positions are formulated on any issues. Bilderbergers who are willing to talk often say that making "contacts" is the single greatest benefit of attending a conference. Since the steering committee aims for a 20% turnover of new faces at each gathering, those who attend are able to meet people they might not otherwise have come in contact with. Former Under Secretary of State George W. Ball noted that Bilderberg meetings provide an "opportunity for responsible people in industry, statecraft, or politics to have a frank discussion where they will not be publicly quoted and are able to give their personal views without their remarks being considered official." President Eisenhower, who always sent one of his advisers to the conferences, said, "The Bilderberg meetings enlightened me; I'd get viewpoints from other than official channels."

Both right-wing and left-wing groups have alleged that Bilderberg leaders meet secretly to plan events that later appear to just happen. The John Birch Society has frequently claimed that the group is part of an international conspiracy, with the ultimate goal of founding a totally planned world economy and political system ruled by members of the Bilderberg Group and the Council on Foreign Relations. Birchers say the Bilderberg Group was responsible for the liberation of oil-rich Algeria and other oil-laden countries, and point out that the Algerian revolt in 1954 began a mere six months after the first Bilderberg Group meeting. Apparently members within the group control the sources of energy for the major industries of France and West Germany. The Treaty of Rome, which brought the Common Market into existence, is also said to have been nurtured at Bilderberg meetings, as is the formation of an international corporation to finance industrial development in the Near East. At least one tangible result can be traced to a Bilderberg meeting, and that is the formation of the Trilateral Commission, sometimes referred to as the "child of Bilderberg." For it was at a Bilderberg meeting that American financier David Rockefeller first broached the subject of forming a group of private individuals to work at strengthening an economic partnership involving North America, Europe, and Japan.

Bilderbergers stoutly refute charges of behind-the-scenes wheeling and dealing; they say they are merely leading world citizens who meet to create a better understanding of the issues affecting Western nations and are without any real power or influence. But if they are really without power and if nothing much really goes on at their meetings, then why have they devoted so much energy toward keeping their sessions secret?

Famous Members: Whatever denials Bilderbergers put forth, it's hard to ignore the fact that the group has succeeded in attracting some of the wealthiest and most powerful men and women in the Western world. Before becoming president, France's Valéry Giscard D'Estaing attended meetings, as did former U.S. President Gerald Ford when he was a congressman. President Kennedy's State Dept. was heavily staffed with Bilderberg alumni, including Secretary of State Dean Rusk, Under Secretary of State George Ball, and National Security Adviser McGeorge Bundy. David Rockefeller is virtually guaranteed an invitation each year, as are many other directors from American financial institutions such as First National City Bank and Morgan Guaranty Trust Co. and industrial leaders from Ford Motor Co., Standard Oil, and Du Pont. French financier Baron Edmond de Rothschild and Italian Fiat president Giovanni Agnelli have both made appearances at the annual meetings, and a top official of NATO nearly always attends. Although little is said of the group in the press, some media representatives are invited to the meetings, including James Reston and Thomas Wicker. (All journalists are, of course, sworn to secrecy.)

How Much Power: Many powerful bankers, industrialists, and politicians attend the Bilderberg meetings. However, the shroud of mystery surrounding what they like to call an "informal get-together" has never been lifted. The influence of the Bilderberg conclave on our daily lives remains to be determined. But as John R. Rarick (D-La.) pointed out to his fellow congressmen in 1971, "The limited information available about what transpires at these meetings reveals that they discuss matters of vital importance which affect the lives of all citizens."

BUSINESS ROUNDTABLE

The Enterprise: The Business Roundtable is the most commanding political syndicate of corporate America, counting some 200 of the nation's largest firms as members in an unprecedented effort to present a united business front. As the voice of big business, it has proved successful in influencing U.S. economic and legislative policy, both through the executive branch and the legislature. Its power and position increase in direct relation to setbacks in the areas of labor reform, consumer protection, and environmental issues.

History: Although the Roundtable now represents a broad range of business interests, its seeds of origin were planted in the chaos that prevailed in the construction industry in the late 1960s. Skyrocketing labor costs had thrown many of the building trades into disarray. The last straw was the erection of a General Motors plant in Ohio, where lucrative union overtime attracted workers from all over the Midwest, putting a cramp on other contractors in the region. With that culminating factor, the Construction Users Anti-Inflation Roundtable was formed in August, 1969, bringing some of the largest corporations in America into cooperation with building contractors. As the influence of the Users Roundtable grew, its original membership of some 50 firms more than doubled. Then in the early 1970s a loosely knit, informal group of chief executive officers from some major American firms who were concerned over the declining position of the U.S. in the world market began meeting. Calling themselves the March Group, under the chairmanship of General Electric's Fred Borch, they strove to reach a consolidated strategy in areas ranging from taxation to international trade to environmental concerns. Corporate membership among the Users Roundtable and the March Group overlapped with each other as well as with the Labor Law Study Group, an organization of prominent companies that had united to protect business interests against encroaching labor legislation. Foreseeing the need for a coordinated body representing big-business concerns, and encouraged by then Treasury Secretary John Connally, the three groups moved toward a merger and formed the Business Roundtable in late 1972. When the Roundtable held its first annual meeting in June, 1973, it was well on its way to becoming a political powerhouse for corporate America.

Headquartered in New York, with an office in Washington, D.C., the Roundtable holds regular annual meetings each June. It has a small permanent staff of about 20, and the organization's activities are funded through dues, which member firms pay on a sliding scale based on the volume of their sales and worth of the company. A policy committee of 45 members is the principal governing body; it elects a chairman and three co-chairmen. Other members serve on a series of task forces to study a wide variety of issues, including government regulations, taxation, inflation, energy use, national health, employment, antitrust cases, and corporate responsibility. The task forces prepare position papers, which are reviewed by the policy committee, and if approved, are circulated to other members and to the government. Although the Roundtable presents a united front, there is dissension within the group, with particular tensions between oil company members and some of the other firms, such as General Electric. But, overall, the Roundtable holds a powerful lobbying position, strengthened by the sheer number of large corporations it represents.

Exploits: Again and again in the late 1970s, the Roundtable demonstrated its deftness in guiding public policy—through lobbying Congress, advising the president, and initiating legislation. Its predecessor, the Users Roundtable, was successful in eroding much of the power of the building trades unions in many parts of the country, with a growth in dollar volume and industrial percentage of nonunion construction throughout the 1970s. One of Business Roundtable's undertakings has been a public-relations campaign to tell its side of the story concerning the American economy. The Roundtable has supported efforts through the Joint Council on Economic Education to promote the teaching of economics from the kindergarten level on up. The Roundtable has also attempted to make greater use of the press to foster pro-business sentiment and has sponsored a series of articles in the *Reader's Digest* on the virtues of free enterprise and high worker productivity and the evils of inflation.

The Roundtable commands a flank of skilled lobbyists and has succeeded in undoing the Labor Law Reform bill, rewording one of the federal clean-air acts, and bottling up antitrust bills. In 1978 it attacked a Consumer Protection Agency bill and succeeded in defeating the legislation, thereby virtually emasculating the agency. In addition to backing various tax bills before Congress, such as President Carter's proposal to reduce *corporate* taxes, Roundtable representatives helped design Carter's first tax program, blocked attempts to audit the Federal Reserve, and promoted the deregulation of natural gas prices. Its task forces produce studies on such topics as how much federal regulations cost companies each year, using the studies to back up their viewpoints. In an effort to make it easier for businessmen to accept appointments to federal regulatory agencies such as the Interstate Commerce Commission, the Roundtable completed a study providing recommendations dealing with conflict-of-interest problems that make industrial leaders leery of taking regulatory jobs. Other areas in which the Roundtable pursues an active interest include investment tax credits and the acceleration of industrial plant depreciation schedules. So far, it has shied away from formulating major policy recommendations on divisive issues like trade with Communist bloc countries and national defense spending.

Famous Members: The Business Roundtable brings together representatives from nearly every area of industry and business imaginable. Well-known corporate executives such as William M. Agee of the Bendix Corporation, George P. Shultz of Bechtel, and A. W. Clausen of BankAmerica serve on its policy committee. So does Donald Regan, secretary of the treasury in the Reagan administration. Almost every major oil company belongs, with Standard Oil, Exxon, Texaco, Atlantic Richfield, Gulf Oil, and Shell leading the pack. Heavy industries like U.S. Steel, Bethlehem Steel, the Boeing Co., and the Caterpillar Tractor Corp. are represented. The membership role includes manufacturing conglomerates like Johnson & Johnson, and Procter & Gamble; financial institutions such as Citicorp and J. P. Morgan and Co.; and utilities such as AT&T and Pacific Gas & Electric Co. A large number of food manufacturers belong to the Roundtable, including General Foods, General Mills, Coca-Cola Co., Campbell Soup Co., Kraft, Inc., and Nabisco Co. Department store chains such as Macy's, J. C. Penney, and Sears, Roebuck and Co. are members, as are a miscellany of insurance companies such as Metropolitan Life and Prudential. General Motors and Ford Motor Co. belong, as do Trans World Airlines and Eastern Airlines. Chemical and pharmaceutical companies abound, including Dow Chemical, Allied Chemical Corp., Du Pont, and Eli Lilly & Co.

How Much Power: The Roundtable's activities intrude on almost every aspect of daily life. It seeks to undo regulations regarding safety on the job, clean air standards, and consumer protection—in order to benefit the corporate structure. As Thomas Ferguson and Joel Rogers wrote in *The Nation*, "[The Roundtable] is more powerful than the small-enterprise-dominated National Association of Manufacturers and U.S. Chamber of Commerce, more visible and broadly active than the Business Council, more capable of mounting a far-reaching program of Big Business demands than any of the flourishing single-issue groups."

COUNCIL ON FOREIGN RELATIONS

The Enterprise: The foremost flank of America's foreign policy establishment for more than half a century, the Council on Foreign Relations is a private organization of business executives, scholars, and political leaders that studies global problems and plays a key role in developing U.S. foreign policy. The CFR is one of the most powerful semiofficial groups concerned with America's role in international affairs.

History: Following the Versailles Conference after W.W. I, a group of Americans and Britons decided to organize a continued study of international relations, and in 1919 formed the Institute of International Affairs. Although the British organization forged ahead, the American sector faltered. At the same time, the Council on Foreign Relations, which had started as a New York dinner club that sponsored distinguished foreign speakers, was suffering from inactivity. The two groups' leaders suggested a merger and in August, 1921, they were officially joined under the name Council on Foreign Relations. Aided by funds from a variety of sources, including J. P. Morgan and Co., the Carnegie Endowment, the Rockefeller family, and other Wall Street banking interests, the council had firmly established itself as a foreign policy institution within its first 15 years. Although the group's intent was "to guide American policy" through a diversity of ideas rather than taking a single policy stance, there was general agreement among members that the U.S. should hold a dominant place in world affairs. In 1922 the council began publishing *Foreign Affairs*, which rapidly became the authoritative American review of international relations and foreign policy. The council itself soon gained such a prestigious position that, beginning with Herbert Hoover's administration, council members were repeatedly called upon to fill many top State Dept. spots. There were several major criteria for being selected as a member; one had to be male and American and show a strong predilection for foreign affairs. Members also had to abide by a "confidentiality" code and could have their membership terminated for publicly disclosing anything that was said at a council meeting.

Over the years the council developed a wide range of activities centered in its Pratt House headquarters on East 68th Street in New York. "Study groups" became one of the council's most important vehicles for developing policy recommendations, which were often written up in book form and published by the council. In addition to holding round-table seminars and weekly meetings, the council sponsored luncheons and dinners that featured such speakers as Cuba's Fidel Castro, Britain's Edward Heath, Israel's Moshe Dayan, and West Germany's Willy Brandt. A corporation service program was founded by the council in 1953; it provided seminars for corporate executives to expose them to international policy decisions that affected their businesses. And in an attempt to branch out beyond its East Coast nucleus, the council established a number of affiliated organizations called Committees on Foreign Relations, composed of local leaders in cities throughout the country. By 1980 there were 37 such groups with over 3,500 members.

After controlling American foreign policy development for over four decades, the council's influence started to slip in the late 1960s as the Vietnam War shattered consensus among the elite. By 1968 most of the establishment was against escalation of the war, with the resulting effect that the council had little decision-making power within the Nixon administration. The council's position was further weakened by a proliferation of other international relations organizations such as the Brookings Institution. The CFR came to be viewed by some as a stuffy eastern men's club. "I regard it as a nostalgic convocation of people who are trying to recapture their days of greatness," said economist John Kenneth Galbraith, a 24-year member until he resigned "out of boredom." In 1977 Zbigniew Brzezinski was quoted as saying, "If you were a member of the council 15 years ago . . . you knew damn well that the conversation either was policy or would be policy. Today it is just interesting talk." To fight such growing lethargy and regain its place of power, the council began a massive recruitment drive in the 1970s, opening up its doors to more radical academics and non-Easterners and admitting women for the first time. Membership leaped from 1,200 in 1970 to more than 2,030 in 1980, and the council recently announced new plans to reach an even larger audience, by allowing occasional CFR speakers to be quoted "on the record," by permitting outsiders to attend certain meetings, and by developing council programs for public television.

Exploits: Since its inception, the Council on Foreign Relations has aimed at creating a worldwide cooperative system controlled by multinational corporations and financiers. That charge is backed up by the council's overriding policy of "liberal internationalism" and its influence in establishing global organizations. The idea of forming international economic institutions originated within the council, and it provided much of the input on decisions about the creation of the U.N., the International Monetary Fund, and the World Bank. The council also played a key role in the decision to use the atomic bomb in W.W. II, since a presidential committee established in 1945 to make recommendations on the bomb was heavily dominated by CFR members. The council also wielded a good deal of power during the post-W.W. II era. A special-studies project by the council, which recommended "moderate" peace terms for Germany and Germany's reintegration into the world economy, was adopted almost part and parcel by the Truman administration. A special conference on training for foreign service held by the CFR in 1945 for the State Dept. resulted in the creation of the Foreign Service Institute. So many council members were tapped by the executive branch for policy-making positions that insiders called the council the "real" state department. "Whenever we needed a new man, we just thumbed through the roll of council members and put through a call to New York," said John McCloy, foreign policy adviser to six presidents and former CFR chairman. The council embarked on its most extensive research and publishing project in 1973. More than 300 people were involved in the "1980s project," which was recently completed. The ambitious undertaking outlined what a desirable international environment would consist of in the 1980s and offered conclusions about changes that are needed in national policy to deal with projected food and energy shortages.

Famous Members: A survey of its membership roster for the past 50 years amply demonstrates that the council has been a fertile training and selection ground for the State Dept. Beginning with John Foster Dulles, all of the secretaries of state except one have belonged to the council, including Dean Rusk, Cyrus Vance, Edmund Muskie, Henry Kissinger, and Alexander Haig. Indeed, Kissinger started on his route to global diplomatic stardom through his association with the council. A young, unknown scholar at the time, Kissinger took a job as study director in 1955 for a council panel set up to explore methods short of war for coping with the Soviets in a nuclear age. Besides providing background material and funding for his best-seller, *Nuclear Weapons and Foreign Policy*, the council enabled Kissinger to meet a number of powerful individuals he wouldn't otherwise have met, including David Rockefeller. Rockefeller himself has been a prominent member of the CFR, both as a director and as chairman.

Another government body that has always had strong ties to the council is the CIA. Forty-year CFR director Allen W. Dulles helped establish the CIA and subsequently became its director. Nearly *all* CIA chiefs since then have been former council members, including Richard Helms, William Colby, George Bush, and William Casey. A number of presidential candidates and presidents have belonged to the council, including Richard Nixon, Dwight Eisenhower, Adlai Stevenson, Hubert Humphrey, George McGovern, and John Anderson. Vice-Presidents Nelson Rockefeller and Walter Mondale were also members. Although Ronald Reagan was not a member, he appointed many people to his administration who were. Besides Haig, and Casey, and Donald Regan, Secretary of Commerce Malcolm Baldrige and special trade representative William Brock belonged to the CFR.

Many of the council's members have a personal financial interest in foreign relations, principally because it is their property and investments that are guarded by the State Dept. and the military. There is a heavy predominance of corporate leaders, bankers, and top corporate lawyers from such firms as ITT, IBM, and Standard Oil on the council's roster. In addition, almost all of the major media in the country have connections with the council. Former *New York Times* publisher Arthur Hays Sulzberger was a member; so are journalists James Reston and Bill Moyers, former *Time* magazine editor in chief Hedley Donovan, *Washington Post* publisher Katharine Graham, CBS chairman William S. Paley, and NBC newscaster John Chancellor.

How Much Power: The CFR's audience, one council member contends, is "the most influential in the world." The interests of its members are inextricably woven with the vital interests of the U.S. because their own personal financial ventures overseas often hinge on the direction of American foreign policy. In spite of its relatively low public profile, it is a high-impact organization. In fact, in the 1952, 1956, 1968, and 1972 U.S. presidential elections, both major parties nominated candidates who had been members of the CFR.

INTERNATIONAL MONETARY FUND

The Enterprise: Acting arbitrarily as global overseer of the world's economy, the International Monetary Fund's realm of influence extends over the finances of dozens of industrialized nations and developing countries. In addition to forcing fiscal cooperation between countries, the IMF functions as a short-term lending bank and doles out economic "advice" to its member nations. That advice has often taken the form of harsh preconditions which governments must meet before loans are granted. Three times the IMF refused to grant Italy a loan. There was speculation that the Italian government would fall if the IMF continued its financial squeeze play. Italy apparently capitulated to Fund pressures, and the loan finally went through. Similar situations have occurred in Mexico, Portugal, and Zaire. And in 1980 the IMF approved a $1.6 billion loan to Pakistan. It was the largest single loan ever made by the organization.

History: Founded along with the World Bank in 1944 at a U.N. conference at Bretton Woods, N.H., the IMF's initial job was to stabilize exchange rates and expand the international flow of currency. At its inception, IMF helped trigger an open international economy, as member nations agreed not to alter the exchange value of their currencies without permission from the IMF. Membership in the IMF expanded from 29 countries which signed the original agreement to more than 141 in 1980. Each nation's voting power is determined by its "quota," that is, the amount of its contribution to the Fund in gold and paper money. Historically, the IMF has been dominated by Western nations, with the largest 10 industrialized countries jointly controlling the majority of votes. As the chief Fund contributor, the U.S. controls about 20% of the IMF's vote, giving it veto power over Fund policy. Twenty executive directors, of whom five are appointed by the U.S., Great Britain, France, Germany, and Japan (the nations with the largest quotas), oversee a staff of 1,400 based at IMF headquarters in Washington.

Besides acting as an exchange-rate enforcer, the IMF empowered itself with the authority to make short-term balance-of-payments loans to member nations. Traditionally, the Fund would attach conditions to its loans, requiring that borrowers take IMF-prescribed steps to reduce their payment imbalance. But, never intended as a major lending institution, the IMF simply didn't have assets to sustain such loans, and began to lose its influence in the 1950s, overshadowed by its sister organization, the World Bank. Then, deprived of its original role of managing international exchange rates in 1973 when major industrialized nations abandoned fixed rates and began to allow their currencies to float, the Fund's future looked dim. Eventually the IMF's lending began to pick up again when it rushed in to help countries buffer OPEC price hikes in the mid-1970s, but its power remained in a decline. In fact, so few conditions were attached to IMF loans that a West German finance minister remarked that the IMF had become a "self-service supermarket, where the customers just help themselves to the products on the shelves." But then, as even developed countries reeled under quadrupled OPEC price increases in late 1973, IMF began experiencing a rebirth. As private banks reached the hilt of their lending capacity, IMF stepped in to fill the void. U.S. Treasury and Federal Reserve officials decided the IMF was the agency to act as the world's financial "big brother," and IMF's lending capacity was expanded. In 1976 the Fund conducted the first gold sale in its history, with much of the money going for low-interest loans to poorer nations with international payment difficulties. As a consequence, countries with ongoing deficits have gotten further into debt. IMF's influence rapidly reached such a peak that it gained the title of "the most powerful supranational government in the world."

Exploits: As the IMF's power mounted, so did criticism. The Fund is seen as a repressive tool of the industrialized nations, which use it to manipulate poorer countries' economies. Although a Fund spokesman responds to such charges by saying, "The IMF is a private club and members must accept its rules," third-world members say they really have no choice but to join, since otherwise they face being cut off from World Bank aid as well as credit from banks that balk at giving loans to non-IMF nations. The Fund says it only sets broad economic targets for borrowing countries—such as cutting inflation by a certain amount. But the IMF attaches stringent conditions to its loans, such as devaluing the currency and reducing government spending. Fund-ordered cutbacks in social welfare programs are said to have provoked mass uprisings in cities such as Cairo, where riots occurred when the Egyptian government tried to comply with an IMF demand that it cut back on food subsidies. Many corrupt governments secretly approve of Fund policies, which they know will be unpopular among their poorer population, and are glad to let the IMF take the blame for their dirty work. The IMF also is accused of having double standards in its lending conditions. It tells developing countries to limit armament spending if they want to receive loans, while ignoring similar expenditures in more favored European nations. Human rights activists come down hard on the Fund's policy of making liberal loans to repressive countries such as Argentina and South Africa without even attempting to impose any conditions regarding individual liberties. The IMF is the only international agency in which the U.S. delegation is not bound by any human rights terms.

One of the IMF's most unique achievements was its creation of an international reserve asset in the late 1960s, in the form of "Special Drawing Rights." SDRs served to enlarge member countries' quotas without requiring them to contribute additional subscriptions in gold or currency, thus enabling them to borrow a greater amount. Unlike the World Bank, some of the Fund's major customers have been industrialized countries. The U.S. has been the second-largest user of the Fund's SDRs, and since 1963 has made withdrawals from the Fund 24 times for about $7.5 billion. The IMF came to the aid of economically troubled Great Britain in 1976 and of Italy in 1977. However, both countries paid a heavy price by agreeing to strict IMF terms to cut government spending and slow down inflation.

In order to further expand its role as enforcer of the international economy, the IMF recently initiated a surveillance program, in which it assesses the performance of member countries against an agreed-upon global policy. Under the program, the Fund encourages any nation with a large payment imbalance to submit to an IMF analysis to show how it should deal with that imbalance. The IMF also began acting as an intermediary between OPEC countries and less developed countries whose oil debts skyrocketed in the 1970s. Its attempts to coax Saudi Arabia and other OPEC countries to pitch in and invest their surpluses with the IMF for loans to deficit countries suffered a setback, however, when the IMF and World Bank voted to bar the Palestinian Liberation Organization from their 1980 annual meeting—a move which displeased Saudi Arabia. OPEC countries have also been unenthusiastic about active participation in the IMF unless they are guaranteed some semblance of power in the organization—a condition that the Western-dominated Fund has been reluctant to grant.

Famous Members: Renowned economist Lord John Maynard Keynes had a grand vision of the IMF as a central world bank that would issue legal tender and provide centralized economic direction to the world. Although Keynes's idea was squelched by the U.S. delegation at the original Bretton Woods conference, the Fund today bears a curious resemblance to Keynes's original proposition. When H. Johannes Witteveen, an economics professor and former finance minister of the Netherlands, took over as IMF managing director in September, 1973, the Fund was at its nadir. Although Witteveen, an austere, somewhat withdrawn man, didn't endear himself to IMF staffers as did his predecessor, Pierre Paul Schweitzer, the Dutch economist succeeded where Schweitzer had not—in creating a clear mission for the IMF. An advocate of expanding the Fund's resources and activities, Witteveen was committed to the idea of the IMF's eventually becoming a centralized global bank with control over some of the activities of national central banks. One of Witteveen's ambitious projects was to establish $16 billion in new financing for the IMF, which became known as the "Witteveen facility." Although Witteveen did much to recoup IMF's status in the world, he was also faulted for perpetuating the Fund's conservative economic outlook, viewing the cure for inflation as holding down demand rather than controlling prices. Jacques de Larosière, former director of the treasury in France, became managing director of the IMF on June 17, 1978. His economic policies seem to follow the same conservative path as Witteveen's. He feels that the U.S. should slow economic growth in order to reduce inflation. The IMF's continued conservative path has caused a Brookings Institution economist, Robert Solomon, to remark that the Fund tends "to apply classical, well-accepted policies when something more innovative, imaginative, and less traditional is needed."

How Much Power: Although the IMF supposedly was established to aid the international financial situation, third-world debt skyrocketed from some $64 billion to $376 billion between 1970 and 1979. It is certainly not the world's financial elite who will be repaying the IMF at a rate of 6.875% interest for a five-year loan. It will be the poor of borrowing nations who will be (and have been) forced to suffer through painful austerity programs for the sake of IMF favors.

TRILATERAL COMMISSION

The Enterprise: An elite group of nearly 300 prominent business, political, and intellectual decision makers of Western Europe, North America, and Japan, the Trilateral Commission is a private agency that works to build up political and economic cooperation among the three regions. Its grand design is a new world order.

History: The Trilateral Commission was the brainchild of American banking magnate David Rockefeller, who along with others in the financial world was concerned over the weakening of the Western alliance due to policies of the Nixon administration. The devaluation of the dollar, imposition of surcharges on imports, and the opening of the door to China—all had led to deteriorating U.S. relations with Japan. Trilateral relations had been further jarred by OPEC price hikes. After putting out feelers at a Bilderberg Group meeting in 1972 about forming a private group of trilateral leaders, Rockefeller set about gathering international financiers, political figures, and a sprinkling of academics for membership in the commission. Aided in his recruiting by his intellectual cohort Zbigniew Brzezinski, Rockefeller gathered his political alter egos together for the first official meeting of the executive committee in Tokyo in October, 1973. Brzezinski became the commission's director, and under his and Rockefeller's leadership the group went full steam ahead in its ambitious promotion of an active partnership among trilateral nations. "Liberal internationalism is our creed," stated commission member C. Fred Bergsten.

Three commission headquarters with small full-time staffs were established in New York, Paris, and Tokyo, and each trilateral area was given responsibility for funding its own activities. In 1977 Rockefeller became chairman of the North American section, which was funded

(L to R) President Gerald Ford, David Rockefeller, and future national security adviser Zbigniew Brzezinski at a meeting of the Trilateral Commission Executive Committee, 1974.

through contributions from individuals, foundations, and corporations such as Exxon, General Motors, Bechtel, and Time, Inc., with the Rockefeller name conspicuous on the list of donors. Rotating among the three regions, the full commission meets once a year for several days in sessions that are closed to the public. A 30-member executive committee with representatives from each country manages the commission's activities. An in-house bulletin of the group's activities is published under the name *Trialogue*, and commission task forces issue a stream of policy recommendation reports, called "Triangle Papers," which deal with such topics as international trade, energy, monetary reform, and labor management. As it continued to draw influential members capable of swaying world decision makers, the commission's realm or power in policymaking expanded to such a point that rumors of its conspiratorial nature began to circulate. The Trilateral Commission became a recurrent issue in the 1980 presidential campaign. Independent candidate John Anderson was criticized for his membership, as was Republican candidate George Bush, while Jimmy Carter battled accusations that his three-year membership prior to taking the presidency made him an Eastern establishment pawn.

Exploits: The Trilateral Commission's tentacles have reached so far afield in the political and economic sphere that it has been described by some as a cabal of powerful men out to control the world by creating a supernational community dominated by the multinational corporations. Nowhere has the commission's influence been more evident than within the Carter administration. Carter became one of the group's original members in 1973, after the up-and-coming Georgia governor was brought to the attention of Rockefeller. It's been noted that Carter's ascent to the White House was greatly aided by the powerful network of financial leaders he gained access to through membership in the commission. Even one of Carter's own deputy campaign chiefs acknowledged that fact when he remarked, "David Rockefeller and Zbigniew have both agreed that Carter is the ideal politician to build on." Carter himself treated the commission as a crash course in foreign policy, saying that it "provided me with a splendid learning opportunity." Many of Carter's campaign speeches on foreign policy, often written by Brzezinski, reflected Trilateral thinking, most notably one in 1976 in which he remarked, "The time has come for us to seek a partnership between North America, Western Europe, and Japan." His recurrent election platform on foreign affairs also had a Trilateral ring to it: "We must replace balance-of-power politics with world-order politics." Carter drew heavily on Trilateral members to stock his administration, with no fewer than 25 top officials having ties to the commission. Carter's support from the commission was not without a price, however. Rockefeller and fellow Trilateral member Henry Kissinger were said to have pressured Carter to let the deposed Shah of Iran into the U.S. for medical treatment, an event which triggered the taking of American hostages in Tehran in 1979.

Although the commission's influence peaked with the Carter administration, it was widespread for several years previously. One of its primary aims has been to revitalize international institutions that can "make the world safe for interdependence," according to a Triangle Paper. As part of that program the commission has supported the strengthening of global financial institutions such as the World Bank and the International Monetary Fund, and it advocated the IMF's selling off its gold stock to raise money for loans to developing countries long before it actually did so. The Trilateral Commission also played a key role in reconciling French and American attitudes on energy and monetary matters in 1975. The commission's emphasis on an international economy is not entirely disinterested, since the oil crisis forced many developing countries with doubtful repayment abilities to borrow heavily from many of the financial institutions represented amongst commission members (not the least of which is Rockefeller's Chase Manhattan Bank), which have all together lent nearly $52 billion to developing countries.

The group's most controversial paper has fueled charges that the commission is devoted to the idea of a few elite ruling the world. *The Crisis of Democracy* outlines inherent weaknesses of the democratic system and cites the need for leaders of "expertise, seniority, experience, and special talents" to take over in certain situations and "override the claims of democracy."

Famous Members: One of the Trilateral Commission's greatest successes was its ability to place key thinkers in top policymaking posts in the Carter administration. The list of Carter cabinet members who formerly belonged to the commission include Vice-President Walter

Mondale, Secretary of State Cyrus Vance, Under Secretary of State Warren Christopher, Treasury Secretary W. Michael Blumenthal, Defense Secretary Harold Brown, U.S. representative to the U.N. Andrew Young, and, of course, Carter's national security adviser, Zbigniew Brzezinski. One of President Ronald Reagan's key economic advisers and Defense Dept. head, Caspar Weinberger, was also part of the Trilateral clan. The commission's American membership overlaps heavily with the Council on Foreign Relations. Former Under Secretary of State George Ball, former chairman of the Federal Reserve Board Arthur Burns, and AFL-CIO president Lane Kirkland belong to both organizations. Familiar Bilderberg Group names such as Fiat president Giovanni Agnelli and French financier Baron Edmond de Rothschild pop up on its international roster. The ruling classes of Japan and Western Europe are represented on the council with corporate executives from the Bank of Tokyo, Fuji Bank, Bank of Madrid, and Royal Dutch Petroleum, and multinational corporations such as Boeing, Coca-Cola, Sony, and Toyota all have members on the commission as well. A number of media representatives also belong, including ones from *La Stampa*, *Die Zeit*, the *Chicago Sun-Times*, and the *Minneapolis Star and Tribune*.

How Much Power: Though no tax money goes directly toward its operation and the public has no say concerning its membership or its policies, the Trilateral Commission may be one of the most powerful international organizations in the world. It is out to build an interlocking global economy controlled by a handful of multinational corporations. Trilateralists themselves have called repeatedly for the establishment of a supranational institution that would regulate foreign investments.

WORLD BANK

The Enterprise: The International Bank for Reconstruction and Development, better known as simply the World Bank, is a powerful global financial institution that lends billions of dollars each year for economic development projects in the underdeveloped countries of the world. That in itself is an honorable undertaking. But the World Bank has also funded such projects as India's attempt at reducing its birth rates. The World Bank sank $25 million into the plan before realizing that it knew nothing about the subject. In one year alone, 11% of World Bank's programs ran into similar major problems. The bank has also lavished large sums of money on the repressive governments of Romania and Communist Vietnam. Moreover, the World Bank does not try to hide the fact that its resources have gone toward the uprooting of entire populations and the formation of collective farms. But the funds the bank plays with are tax dollars. In its last year, the Carter administration sought a 44% budget increase in the amount of money to go into such international financial schemes.

History: Originally set up as a tool to help war-torn countries get back on their feet following W.W. II, the World Bank was conceived at a U.N. Monetary and Financial Conference at Bretton Woods, N.H., in

July, 1944, when 44 nations met to plan for international economic cooperation in the postwar years. The international bank officially began operating in June, 1946, with its first loans going for reconstruction projects, mostly in Western Europe. By 1949, however, the emphasis had shifted toward giving loans for economic development to countries throughout the world, with most of the money going for improvements in transportation, electric power, and water supply systems. In recent years the bank has also turned to financing an increasing number of agricultural and rural development projects. Loans are made directly to governments, or to private enterprises with the local government's guarantee, with the capital often provided through the bank's soft loan affiliate, the International Development Association.

World Bank membership has climbed to include over 130 nations in recent years. Before becoming eligible for World Bank aid, countries must first join the bank's sister organization, the International Monetary Fund, which was set up at the same 1944 U.N. conference. World Bank works hand in hand with IMF; the two institutions share headquarters in Washington, publish a quarterly magazine called *Finance and Development*, and hold a joint annual meeting. Although World Bank policy is made by a board of governors, with one governor appointed by each member nation, the board relegates most of its powers to executive directors, who are based at the bank's headquarters and oversee a staff of 4,500 recruited from over 100 countries. Voting power is proportionate to a country's capital subscription, with the U.S. topping the list in terms of influence. In the beginning, the U.S. subscribed nearly 40% of the bank's capital, making it the only country with a large enough contribution to give it veto power over bank policy. However, in recent years the U.S.'s share of the bank's capital has sunk to about 21%, and it stands to lose its veto power if its capital drops below 20%. The Soviet Union has disdained membership in the World Bank, calling it a tool of capitalistic imperialism, but the People's Republic of China joined in 1980, taking over the seat held by Taiwan.

The bank's lending skyrocketed under the leadership of former U.S. Defense Secretary Robert McNamara, who became World Bank president in 1968. Long-term loans to developing countries increased by 400% and money was doled out to nearly 100 countries during McNamara's first five-year term. By 1980 the bank was overseeing more than 1,600 projects in the third world at a cost of over $100 billion, and its capital had grown from $45 billion to $80 billion, causing some U.S. officials to wonder whether the bank would someday have the potential to destabilize U.S. money markets.

World Bank is a "Western rich man's club" wielding enormous political power over indebted countries' economies. The U.S. apparently used its influence in the bank to cut off World Bank aid to Chile during Salvador Allende's three-year socialist regime. The bank has supported questionable projects such as Indira Gandhi's compulsory sterilization program in India. The bank is also probably guilty of financing the shift of millions of peasants in Vietnam, which triggered the flood of refugees known as the Boat People. Third-world members have little say in World Bank policy, even though most of the bank's programs are directed at them. Congressman C. W. Bill Young (R-Fla.) has remarked that "through the international banks . . . we created a high-living group of international money changers accountable to no one."

Exploits: World Bank contends that it has helped improve the quality of life for millions of people in the world's less developed countries. Since the early 1970s the bank has financed over 40 urban projects aimed at improving living conditions for several million people. The bank lent $36 million to the Philippines in 1976 to upgrade slum sites and services in Manila. However, World Bank also played a large part in the establishment of martial law in the Philippines by its strong support of the Marcos regime, thereby protecting its investment as well as that of many major U.S. corporations. Such inconsistencies run through a number of the bank's loan practices in relation to its overall stated goals. Five of the top eight recipients of World Bank loans have been right-wing dictatorships with poor human rights records. A striking, though small, example was a $2.5 million loan the bank made to the Central African Empire (now Republic), one of the world's worst human rights violators, where Amnesty International has protested the merciless beatings and killings of thousands of children.

World Bank's development projects have both directly and indirectly benefited the economic interests of the U.S. and other industrialized Western nations. As one World Bank observer noted, by financing enterprises in third-world countries, the industrialized world is assured of having access to needed raw materials and supplies provided by developing regions. Many of the borrowing countries are also important markets for U.S. goods and services. Thus World Bank money eventually comes full circle, being paid back to the industrial nations. That the U.S. plays a dominant role in deciding what money goes where is documented by the large share of World Bank funds that are channeled into countries in which the U.S. has strategic and diplomatic interests, such as India and certain African and South American countries.

Recently World Bank has gotten into the energy business. After a bank study showed that 70 developing countries probably have about 60 billion barrels of recoverable oil, but have only found about 10 billion barrels, the bank decided to invest small amounts in exploratory drilling. The increasing rise in poorer nations' import-oil debts, as well as continued inflation, has set World Bank officials clamoring that in order to meet rising needs its lending authority must be increased substantially. Loans the bank made during 1980 came in at just under $12 billion, and its tentative schedule calls for the bank's lending commitments to increase to around $20 billion by 1985.

Famous Members: World Bank presidents have always been Americans, with former Defense Secretary Robert McNamara perhaps doing the most to shape bank policy during his 1968–1981 term. (A. W. Clausen, president of BankAmerica, took over the post in June, 1981.) While acting as the bank's head, McNamara, a self-made expert on third-world problems, was praised for showing a "concern for humanity and a sympathy for the poor that most bankers lack." Not everyone looked upon McNamara's term with favor, however. *Barrons* called him an "autocratic ruler," under whose guidance billions of dollars were lavished on projects with little hope of return on the investment. A *Forbes* editorial noted, "Perhaps the cruelest thing that can be said about McNamara is that he may be a brilliant man without much common sense."

How Much Power: Today the World Bank supervises some 1,600 programs throughout the third world, at a cost of $100 billion. Of course, it seeks to protect those investments. There is no better example of the bank's pervasive power than its entanglement in the government machinery in the Philippines. In 1970 the Marcos regime, under threat of losing its credit rating, took the unpopular step of devaluing its peso. Martial law was imposed in 1972 with the active participation of the bank. By 1975 the World Bank was pouring some $208 million a year into the Philippines. The bank's power, needless to say, now permeates every political and economic sector of that nation. And the Philippines is just one small tip of the iceberg.

—L.K.S.

3

U.S.A.—RED, WHITE, AND WHO

WHAT DO YOU KNOW ABOUT THE U.S.?

1. Can you name the one U.S. president who never voted in a presidential election?
2. Where is the bank that honors a man who held it up?
3. What U.S. coin was the first to bear the motto "In God We Trust"?
4. Where in the U.S. are you allowed to look for diamonds—and keep them if you find them?
5. What state in the U.S. has no official motto?
6. Which state was the first in the U.S. to elect a woman governor?
7. In what state can you be fined $300 for picking a wild flower?
8. Which is the nation's largest privately owned university?
9. Did any U.S. president ever serve in the Confederate government?
10. Has there ever been a U.S. president who had no brothers or sisters?
11. Where did the first yellow pages in the telephone book appear?
12. Why does Illinois block off 3 mi. of road to public traffic for an entire month every autumn?
13. Only one restaurant in the U.S. is forced by law to serve bean soup every day. What is that restaurant?
14. A city in what state elected the first woman mayor in U.S. history?
15. What state had its capital changed 15 times?
16. What two states in the U.S. do not have daylight saving time?
17. In 1865 George Mortimer Pullman spent $18,000 to build the first railroad sleeping car, called the *Pioneer*, in Chicago, but it was a failure because no one could use it. It had been built too wide to go through stations and too high to go under bridges. What national event saved Pullman from bankruptcy and made him a millionaire?
18. How many buffalo were there in the old Wild West of the U.S.?
19. How many slaves were there in the U.S. at the time Abraham Lincoln issued his Emancipation Proclamation?
20. Who created the name United States of America?

Answers

1. Gen. Zachary Taylor, the hero of the Seminole and Mexican wars, was eligible to vote in 10 presidential elections—and voted in none

of them. He did not even vote for himself when he became the 12th President.

2. Liberty, Mo., was where Jesse James robbed his first bank. Thirty years later the same bank was turned into the Jesse James Bank Museum, displaying mementos of the bandit's criminal career.
3. On Apr. 22, 1864, the motto first appeared on a bronze 2¢ piece.
4. Crater of Diamonds State Park in Arkansas, producing the only real diamonds in the U.S., invites visitors to hunt for diamonds on its 867 acres. The park advertises: "Bring any find you suspect to be a diamond to the park office for a free weight and certification. And anything you find is yours, no matter the value." On the average, 200 diamonds are found each year.
5. Alaska.
6. In 1924 Mrs. Nellie Tayloe Ross took office as governor of Wyoming. Later, she was appointed director of the U.S. Mint and served in that position for 20 years. As far back as 1869, the Wyoming territorial legislature had granted universal female suffrage, the first government in the world to do so.
7. Colorado. The state treasures its beautiful wild flowers, such as the columbine, the state flower. Authorities feel that the thoughtless destruction of the flowers reduces their chances for reproduction.
8. Brigham Young University in Provo, U.
9. Yes, one did. President John Tyler, who left the White House in 1845, served in the provisional Confederate Congress and was elected by his fellow Virginians to the Confederate House of Representatives in 1861, but he died before taking his seat.
10. No president was ever an only child.
11. Cheyenne, Wyo., in 1883.
12. This small road east of State Route 3 in Union County is closed at Winter's Pond to allow hundreds of turtles and rattlesnakes to migrate west safely to their winter quarters in the Ozark rocks.
13. By law the Congressional cafeteria in Washington, D.C., must have Yankee soup—plain bean soup—on the menu every day.
14. Kansas. In 1887 the town of Argonia elected 27-year-old Susanna Medora Salter the nation's first female mayor.
15. Texas.
16. Hawaii and Alaska.
17. The assassination of Abraham Lincoln saved George Pullman. Eager to offer its best to its fallen native son, Illinois decided to add Pullman's luxurious sleeping car to the funeral train carrying Lincoln's body from Chicago to its final resting place in Springfield. Immediately, railway platforms were modified, bridges across the lines were raised, and the Pullman car was on its way to fame and fortune.
18. There were none. Those were bison. You'd have to go to Africa or Asia to see a buffalo.
19. About 4 million.
20. The man who coined the name United States of America was once indicted for treason in England, came to America in 1774, and was

later jailed in France. His pamphlets, among them *Common Sense*, propagandized for the American Revolutionary War. Called an atheist, he died impoverished and largely forgotten in 1809. His name was Thomas Paine.

—I.W.

PROFILES OF THE PRESIDENTS

For detailed profiles of Presidents George Washington, Abraham Lincoln, Franklin D. Roosevelt, Harry S Truman, John F. Kennedy, Richard M. Nixon, and Gerald R. Ford, see *The People's Almanac #1*, pages 278 to 339.

For detailed profiles of Presidents Thomas Jefferson, Andrew Jackson, Theodore Roosevelt, Warren G. Harding, Dwight D. Eisenhower, Lyndon B. Johnson, and James Earl Carter, see *The People's Almanac #2*, pages 167 to 212.

2nd President
JOHN ADAMS

VITAL STATISTICS

Born: Oct. 30, 1735, at the family farm in Braintree (now Quincy), Mass.

Died: July 4, 1826, at his Braintree home at the age of 90 years, 247 days. It is ironic that this lifelong hypochondriac, who suffered so many premonitions of an early death, should live longer than any other president. While still a young man of 35 he complained that his health was "feeble"; at 37 he described himself as "an infirm man"; and 50 years later he was still complaining, though alert and alive. The year before his death he took great pride in the inauguration of his son, John Quincy Adams, as the sixth president of the U.S., and he also lived to see the 50th anniversary of the Declaration of Independence, which he had helped to draft. On the afternoon of the 4th of July he told his daughter-in-law, "It is a great day; it is a good day," and then sat down in his favorite chair in the upstairs study, not far from the noise of a nearby celebration. About 1:00 in the afternoon, his thoughts turned to an old friend and associate from revolutionary days. "Thomas Jefferson survives," he said. Adams had no way of knowing that Jefferson had died a few hours before in faraway Virginia. At 6:00 P.M. Adams's heart stopped beating.

The house in which Adams died is part of the Adams National Historic Site, administered by the National Park Service. Located at 135 Adams Street, Quincy, Mass., it is open to the public.

BEFORE THE PRESIDENCY

Career: For four generations Adams's ancestors had been obscure

John Adams.

New England farmers, and young John was the first member of his family to receive a college education. At age 19 he graduated from Harvard and got a job teaching school in Worcester, Mass. His family hoped that after a few years of teaching he would go on to study for the ministry; however, not only did he hate his students ("little runtlings, just capable of lisping A, B, C and troubling the master"), but also he could not accept the Calvinist orthodoxy of the Massachusetts clergy. By the time he was 21 Adams was lecturing himself in his diary, with characteristic immodesty: "The pulpit is no place for you, young man! And the sooner you give up all thoughts of it the better for you, though the worse for it." In 1756 he began studying law, and two years later he was admitted to the bar in Boston. Adams soon combined his natural intelligence with a growing reputation for integrity (which was rare for lawyers, even in that age) to build one of the finest law practices in Massachusetts. Among his many prominent clients was John Hancock, the richest man in the province. When one of Hancock's ships was seized by British authorities on smuggling charges, Adams successfully defended the merchant on the grounds that the colonial trade regulations were in themselves improper. This case, along with two widely read essays asserting colonial rights, established Adams as a leader in the growing movement protesting "taxation without representation." He jeopardized this position in 1770, however, when he agreed to defend the hated British soldiers who had fired on a crowd in the riot popularly known as the Boston Massacre. In the trial, Adams proved that the frightened redcoats had acted in self-defense. He won acquittal for his clients, but he was sure that popular resentment over the outcome of the case would mean an end to his political prominence. On the contrary, the people of Boston, admiring Adams's courage and impressed with the extensive publicity the trial had received, elected him to the legislature by a 4-to-1 margin. When the first Continental Congress was called in 1774 to plan united colonial action to deal with the worsening crisis, Adams was one of five men selected to represent Massachusetts.

Personal Life: At the age of 26, lawyer Adams fell in love with the 17-year-old daughter of a village parson. On her mother's side, however, Abigail Smith was a Quincy, and thereby related to one of New England's leading families. Her parents considered Adams—because of his humble origins—unworthy of their daughter, but Abigail was not the type to be easily dissuaded. A brilliant, independent woman, she had thoroughly educated herself in philosophy, literature, and history in an age when a concern for books was considered "unfeminine." In Adams, Abigail not only recognized her intellectual equal but also found the same sort of pride and stubbornness that marked her own personality. It was two years before the objections of her parents melted away, but the couple was finally married on Oct. 25, 1764. Over the next 54 years John and Abigail established one of the most remarkable marriages in history—a marriage that can only be described as a love feast. Though often cold and uncompromising in political life, John Adams was passionate, devoted, and tender as a husband. He was never intimidated by his wife's intelligence—he gloried in it, and he loved talking politics with her. His habit of listening to Abigail's advice became so well known, in fact, that Adams was publicly criticized for it. The furious opposition labeled her Mrs. President. The opposition would have been even more furious had it known that she privately advocated the complete abolition of slavery and favored women's suffrage. The Adamses were always conscious of their role in history and carefully saved all of their letters to each other. Today these letters—numbering in the hundreds—are justly celebrated not only for their remarkable philosophic and political insights, but for the freshness and intensity of the love the couple expressed, even after years of marriage. In one typical exchange, shortly after John had left for Europe on a diplomatic mission, Abigail teased her aging husband with the line: "No man, even if he *is* 60, ought to live more than three months at a time from his family." Adams wrote back immediately: "How dare you hint or lisp a word about '60 years of age.' If I were near I would soon convince you that I am not above 40."

Whenever they traveled, the Adamses were homesick for their modest farm in Braintree. With John away much of the time on political business, Abigail supervised the farm's hired help and took personal charge of educating their four children. In middle age the Adamses suffered notably over these children. Their beautiful daughter, who had inherited Abigail's finely chiseled nose, arched eyebrows, and independent spirit, fell in love with an unsuitable young man, and both parents moved in to squelch the romance. Even worse, their younger son, Charles, unable to live up to the demanding standards set by his parents, became an alcoholic in his 20s and died of cirrhosis at age 30. The pride and joy for both John and Abigail was, of course, their brilliant son John Quincy. When only 10 years old, the boy began accompanying his lonely father on missions to Europe. Shortly after the Adamses celebrated their 52nd anniversary, John Quincy was named U.S. secretary of state. Abigail died in 1818 at age 73 and missed the ultimate satisfaction of seeing her son in the White House.

On the Way to the White House: For years Boston had been the center of revolutionary agitation, and it was only to be expected that a Massachusetts man would play the leading role at the Continental Congress in Philadelphia. It soon became clear that John Adams was that man. He personally pushed through the appointment of George Washington as commander in chief, won approval for the Declaration of Independence drafted by his friend Thomas Jefferson, and served as chairman of the Board of War and Ordnance—in effect as secretary of war. When it became clear that the success of the revolution depended upon European aid and Congress had to send its best men abroad, Adams sailed for Europe. In Paris he quarreled with Benjamin Franklin, the other American representative (a jealous nature was always part of the Adams character), but moving on to Holland, he negotiated a key loan that kept the revolution afloat. Later Adams was one of the three Americans who negotiated the final treaty of peace with Great Britain, and he served as the first American minister to London. Somehow, in the midst of this activity, he found time to draft a new constitution for Massachusetts and to write several lengthy and highly influential essays in support of the American war effort. Small wonder that Adams won the sobriquet of the Atlas of American Independence. Of all the founding fathers, only Washington had done more for the cause. When Washington was unanimously elected president in 1789, Adams was the obvious choice for the vice-presidency. Over a period of eight years Adams established himself as a vigorous, if not always popular, vice-president. He dreamed of the top office for himself and presided over the Senate like an impatient New England schoolmaster. Before debate on any issue could begin, the Vice-President always lectured the senators on their constitutional responsibilities. Before a vote could be taken, he insisted on summarizing the issue, as if talking to children, and frequently instructed the senators on how to vote.

His Person: With his round face, puckered lips, sharp nose, and heavy, curved brows, Adams was never considered personally attractive. Bald at the top, his forehead was high and shiny. Standing 5 ft. 7 in., Adams was always stocky, but after middle age he grew notoriously plump. Once as vice-president he asked the Senate what his formal title should be. Behind his back, several of the senators suggested "His Rotundity." Adams was not the man to take this sort of teasing lightly. Once, when asked to provide a physical description of himself, he wrote back: "I have one head, four limbs, and five senses, like any other man, and *nothing peculiar in any of them*. . . . I have no miniature and have been too much abused by painters ever to sit to anyone again." As president, Adams, like Washington, received visitors in full dress—a suit of black velvet with silk stockings, silver knee and shoe buckles, white waistcoat, powdered hair, and gloves. He considered it beneath his dignity to shake hands with his guests, but bowed to them, as Washington had done. Such supercilious manners never failed to irritate his colleagues. William Maclay of Pennsylvania offered a memorable description of Adams holding court over the Senate. Seated in his chair, the Vice-President would "look on one side, then on the other, then down on the knees of his breeches, then dimple his visage with the most silly kind of half-smile, which I cannot well express in English. The Scotch-Irish have a word that hits it exactly—smudging."

PRESIDENCY

Election: Winter, 1796 . . .

When factionalism fractured American politics in the 1790s, Vice-President Adams identified himself with the Federalist party, and in 1796, after Washington had announced his retirement, Adams was the Federalist candidate for president. Adams's chief competition came from Thomas Jefferson, the Republican candidate, who was billed as the "uniform advocate of equal rights among citizens" while Adams was portrayed as the "champion of rank, titles, and hereditary distinctions." Nevertheless, Adams's long service to the cause of independence and his status as heir apparent to Washington made him the odds-on favorite.

The situation was complicated, however, by divisions in the Federalist party. Alexander Hamilton distrusted the stubborn streak in Adams and wanted a president he could control more easily. He developed a complicated plot centering on Thomas Pinckney, the Federalist candidate for vice-president. According to Hamilton's plan, Federalist electors from Pinckney's native South Carolina would secretly drop Adams's name from their ballots, while still voting for Pinckney. Thus the Federalists' number-two man would receive more votes than Adams, and so be elected president. When New England electors got wind of this conspiracy, they retaliated by dropping Pinckney from their ballots, in order to insure that Adams would come out on top after all. The result of this manipulation was that both Adams and Pinckney lost votes, and the election was almost thrown to Jefferson. The final tally in the electoral college showed Adams with 71 votes, while Jefferson, right behind him with 68, was automatically elected vice-president under the old system. Pinckney, who had lost his chance at the vice-presidency because of Hamilton's treachery, finished third with 59 electoral votes.

Term of Office: Mar. 4, 1797 . . .

Adams was driven to his inauguration in a gilded coach drawn by six white horses. He was sworn in by Chief Justice Oliver Ellsworth in the chamber of the House of Representatives in Philadelphia, then capital of the U.S. The government did not move to Washington until the end of Adams's term, and Adams was the first president to occupy the executive mansion.

During his term, Adams enjoyed Federalist majorities in both houses of Congress and did not veto a single bill. He was the first of eight presidents who never used the veto power.

His 4 Years as President:

PRO

In order to head off the threat of war, Adams built up the armed forces of the U.S. to respectable proportions; he has justly been called the Father of the American Navy. In a series of naval skirmishes with France, only one of the new American ships was lost, while 85 French vessels were sunk or captured. This formidable military establishment (later dismantled by Jefferson) helped protect American independence and ensured peace during Adams's term.

CON

The military buildup under Adams went far beyond what was necessary, and the people—especially poor farmers—paid dearly for it in increased taxes. In both his military and financial programs, Adams was often unable to control his own cabinet, which was unduly influenced by his archenemy, Alexander Hamilton.

PRO

Adams showed remarkable courage and defied his own party in heading off a full-scale war with France. While much of the country clamored hysterically for war, Adams concluded a treaty of peace, and then showed skill and determination in forcing the restless country to accept it. Though this responsible statesmanship probably cost him reelection, Adams understood that keeping the peace was his most valuable contribution to his country. He once suggested that his epitaph should read: "Here lies John Adams, who took upon himself the responsibility of peace with France in the year 1800."

CON

Although Adams is certainly to be commended for stopping short at the brink of war, it was Adams himself who led the country so dangerously close to that disaster. If he had not overreacted to relatively minor French provocations, the war hysteria would never have gotten started. Actually, Adams seems to have been more interested in discrediting his pro-French, Republican opponents than in conducting a sensible and consistent foreign policy.

PRO

Adams has been blamed unfairly for the Alien and Sedition Acts, passed during his administration to curb criticism of the government. He did not initiate these measures, he signed them reluctantly, and he then resisted the Federalist clamor for a more vigorous crackdown on the administration's opponents. Actually, the acts were passed in anticipation of war with France, and in many respects they resembled the necessary limitations on free speech imposed by the government during future wars.

CON

Whatever the extenuating circumstances, Adams formally approved the Alien and Sedition Acts and thereby showed his complete disregard for fundamental civil liberties. Many prominent Americans were fined or imprisoned for their criticism of the government under the Federalist "Reign of Terror." One Republican editor from New York was marched in chains over 200 mi. in order to serve his prison term for "sedition." Even more shocking was the case of Matthew Lyon, a Republican congressman from Vermont, who was arrested and imprisoned for criticizing the President in a private letter. Luckily Adams's defeat and the election of Jefferson in 1800 preserved the basic guarantee of free speech.

PRO

Adams deserves credit for his appointment of John Marshall, the greatest chief justice in the history of the U.S. Supreme Court.

CON

Along with Marshall, Adams also appointed a score of "midnight judges" in the last hours before the inauguration of his successor. This was a transparent attempt to stack the judiciary with entrenched Federalists and to thwart the will of the people as expressed in the recent election.

AFTER THE PRESIDENCY

Although the election of 1800 has often been represented by historians as a sweeping rejection of Adams and his policies, the final outcome was remarkably close. Despite the open hostility of Alexander Hamilton and other members of his own party, Adams ran as head of the Federalist ticket, and if a single bitterly contested state—New York—had voted differently, he would have been reelected. Instead, Thomas Jefferson became president, and Adams retired to his Massachusetts farm, wrote eloquent defenses of his stormy term as president, and watched with satisfaction the career of his son. In 1811, at age 76, Adams had mellowed to the point where he wanted to resume contact with his onetime friend Thomas Jefferson. In Revolutionary days, Jefferson had been particularly close to the whole Adams family, and Abigail had called him "one of the choice ones of the earth," but years of increasingly bitter political competition had left both Adams and Jefferson with bad feelings. Now, three years after Jefferson had left the White House, Adams was ready to break the ice; he wrote a cordial letter just before Christmas. Along with the note, Adams proudly sent off two volumes on political theory written by his son John Quincy, which he described as "two pieces of homespun, lately produced in this quarter by one who was honored in his youth by some of your attention and much of your kindness." Jefferson responded warmly, and so began a remarkable correspondence which the Virginian described as "sweetening to the evening of our lives." Although suffering from a host of physical afflictions, Adams's mind remained sharply focused to the end. At the age of 85 he was elected by his neighbors to the state constitutional convention in Boston, called to revise a document that Adams himself had written some 40 years before. The old man spoke forcefully against universal suffrage and in favor of a property tax. Even after failing vision made it difficult for him to write, Adams continued his distinguished correspondence with Jefferson until shortly before the two men died—on the same day—in 1826.

PSYCHOHISTORY

As an adolescent, Adams felt insecure owing to his small size, his plain features, and his low social standing. In an age when Massachusetts was dominated by a handful of leading families, young Adams, with his obscure rural origins, was definitely an outsider. Painfully unsure of himself, he had to remind the world time and again of his talents and virtues. He might freely admit his own shortcomings in the pages of his diary, but he saw any criticism from others as part of a grand conspiracy against him. Although he had rejected much of traditional Calvinism, Adams remained enough of a Puritan to see devils everywhere; few presidents have equaled him in the scale of his paranoia. In 1765, when Great Britain closed the Massachusetts courts, Adams thought the move was aimed particularly at him. He wrote in his diary: "Thirty years of my life are passed in preparation for business. I have had poverty to struggle with—envy and jealousy and malice of enemies to encounter—no friends, or but few to assist me, so that I have groped in dark obscurity, till of late, and had but just become known, and gained a small degree of reputation, when this execrable project was set on foot for my ruin as well as that of America in general." This tone of self-pity appears again and again in Adams's writings. It reflected his desperate need for love, sympathy, and reassurance—a need which not even the devoted Abigail could satisfy completely.

LITTLE-KNOWN FACTS

While Adams served as minister to Great Britain, Jefferson, who was serving in France at the time, crossed the Channel to spend a brief vacation with his friend. Among other things, the two Americans visited Shakespeare's birthplace in Stratford. While touring the house, these great men showed that they were still provincial tourists after all; they cut chips off a chair alleged to have been Shakespeare's and took them home as souvenirs.

John Adams, the first president to occupy the White House, moved into the unfinished executive mansion a few weeks before Abigail arrived in Washington. In a letter home, he reported on the condition of the building and concluded: "I pray heaven to bestow the best of blessings on this house, and all that shall hereafter inhabit it. May none but honest and wise men ever rule under this roof." More than 100 years later, President Franklin Roosevelt asked that this prayer be inscribed over the fireplace in the State Dining Room.

In a letter to her daughter, Abigail reported that the executive mansion was barely habitable at the time she moved in. Permanent stairways had not been installed, and the bedrooms were uncomfortably drafty. The walls were still so wet that seven cords of wood had to be burned in order to dry them out. Showing her practical nature, Abigail used "the great unfinished audience room" (the East Room) as a place to hang the family's laundry.

In 1787 Adams bought a frame house in Quincy known as Peacefield and later passed it on to his son. Over the years, the house was used by four generations of politicians, diplomats, writers, and historians in this most distinguished American family. As the historian Henry Adams was taking a friend through the family's longtime home, he pointed to an old chair and remarked, "This is the chair in which John Adams was stricken." He paused for a moment, then asked, "Do you know how I know?" When the friend shook his head, Adams turned the chair over and showed him a piece of paper tacked onto the bottom. There, in a fine hand, were the words "Father was seated in this chair when he was stricken July 4, 1826. signed John Quincy Adams."

QUOTES FROM ADAMS

"Facts are stubborn things; and whatever may be our wishes, our inclinations, or the dictates of our passions, they cannot alter the state of facts and evidence."—As defense attorney in the Boston Massacre trial, 1770

"Philadelphia, with all its trade and wealth and regularity, is not Boston. The morals of our people are much better; their manners are more polite and agreeable; they are purer English; our language is better, our taste is better, our persons are handsomer; our spirit is greater, our laws are wiser, our religion is superior, our education is better."—1774

"My country has in its wisdom contrived for me the most insignificant office that ever the invention of man contrived or his imagination conceived."—Vice-President Adams to his wife

"I do not say when I became a politician, for that I never was. In every considerable transaction of my public life, I have invariably acted according to my best judgment, and I can look up to God for the sincerity of my intentions."

"Let the human mind loose. It must be loosed; it will be loose. Superstition and despotism cannot confine it."

"The love of God and his creation—delight, joy, triumph, exultation in my own existence, though but an atom in the Universe—these are my religion."

"Had I been chosen president again, I am certain I could not have lived another year."

QUOTES ABOUT HIM

"He is vain, irritable, and a bad calculator of the force and probable effect of the motives which govern men. This is all the ill which can possibly be said of him. He is as disinterested as the Being who made him."—Thomas Jefferson, letter to James Madison, 1787

"Well known are his disgusting egotism, distempered jealousy, ungovernable indiscretion, and vanity without bounds."—Alexander Hamilton, letter to James Madison, 1787

"I cannot sometimes refrain from considering the honors with which he is invested as badges of my unhappiness."—Abigail Adams

"It has been the political career of this man to begin with hypocrisy, proceed with arrogance, and finish with contempt."—Thomas Paine, *Open Letter to the Citizens of the United States,* Nov. 22, 1802

"Here I say I have amused myself in reading and thinking of my absent friend, sometimes with a mixture of pain, sometimes with pleasure, sometimes anticipating a joyful and happy meeting, whilst my heart would bound and palpitate with the pleasing idea, and with the purest affection I have held you to my bosom till my whole soul has dissolved in tenderness and my pen fallen from my hand."—Abigail Adams

"How often do I reflect with pleasure that I hold in possession a Heart equally warm with my own, and full as susceptible of the tenderest impressions, and who, even now whilst he is reading here, feels all I describe."—Abigail Adams

—M.S.M.

28th President

WOODROW WILSON

VITAL STATISTICS

Born: Dec. 28, 1856, in Staunton, Va., the last of eight American Presidents born in Virginia. His given names were Thomas Woodrow and throughout his youth he was known as Tommy. At the age of 24, however, Wilson officially dropped his first name. His birthplace, the former Presbyterian manse in Staunton, is located at 24 North Coalter Street and is open to the public. Admission: $1.

Died: In Washington, D.C., on Feb. 3, 1924, at the age of 67. The cause of death was listed as apoplexy; Wilson had been in poor health and partially paralyzed since suffering a stroke while President in 1919. He is buried in the Washington Cathedral—the only President buried in Washington, D.C. His last words, addressed to his wife, were "Edith, I'm a broken machine, but I'm ready."

BEFORE THE PRESIDENCY

Career: The son of a strong-willed Presbyterian minister, Wilson grew up in Georgia and the Carolinas and always thought of himself as a loyal son of the South. At 16 he entered North Carolina's Davidson College, but left after a few months because of poor health. A year later Wilson enrolled at the College of New Jersey (now Princeton), where he soon won distinction as an orator and debater. By the time he graduated in 1879 he had decided on a political career. As an initial step toward public office, he attended the University of Virginia School of Law, was admitted to the bar, and practiced law for a year in Atlanta, Ga., but he soon found himself bored with the day-to-day details of legal work. At

Woodrow Wilson.

the age of 26 he returned once more to an academic environment—this time as a graduate student in political science at Johns Hopkins University in Baltimore. In 1885 his Ph.D. thesis, *Congressional Government*, was published to widespread critical acclaim, giving young Wilson a preliminary taste of national attention. It also helped him in his teaching career. After brief service at Bryn Mawr College and Wesleyan University, he was appointed a full professor of jurisprudence and political economy at his beloved Princeton. During the next 10 years Wilson emerged as one of the "stars" of the Princeton faculty. During his academic career he produced a total of nine books, including a biography of George Washington and a five-volume *History of the American People*, along with 35 articles. In 1902 the trustees of Princeton unanimously elected Wilson president of the university. He soon launched a program of educational innovation and reform that received much favorable publicity.

Personal Life: In April, 1883, Wilson attended a church service in Rome, Ga., where he met a girl with a "tip-tilted little nose, sweetly curved mouth, and hair like burnished copper." Ellen Axson, like Wilson, was the child of a Presbyterian minister. Along with her devotion to religion, Ellen maintained a strong interest in the fine arts. An accomplished painter, she spent several months studying at the Art Students League in New York, just before her marriage to Wilson. The date of the wedding was June 24, 1885, and two ministers presided jointly over the ceremony, Wilson's father and Ellen's grandfather—the third clergyman in the family! On the surface the Wilsons maintained a pleasant and proper relationship during their 29 years of marriage, and it was not until 1962, when their remarkable love letters were published, that the passionate, obsessive nature of their union became widely known. In one typical letter Wilson declared: "I would a thousand times rather repay you a tithe of the happiness you have brought me than make my name immortal *without* serving you as the chief mission of my life. Ah, my little wife, do you know that my whole self has passed over into my allegiance for you?" Ellen bore Wilson three daughters, which was fortunate, because Wilson generally preferred the company of "clever" women to that of men. In 1914, while Wilson was president, Ellen died of Bright's disease at the age of 54. Wilson sat beside her body for two days and was so stricken with grief that he came close to a nervous breakdown. His seemingly incurable depression was heightened by the fact that W.W. I had begun in Europe the same week that his wife died, and Dr. Cary Grayson, the White House physician, took personal responsibility for providing Wilson with the emotional support and distraction that the President needed. Six months after Ellen's death, Grayson helped to engineer a meeting between Wilson and the beautiful Washington widow Edith Bolling Galt. As a romance quickly developed between the two, Wilson's top aides began to worry that an early remarriage might imperil the President's chances for reelection. Furthermore, it was feared that a new love interest might revive persistent (but totally unfounded) rumors that Wilson, while president of Princeton, had conducted an illicit affair with a divorcée in Bermuda. Despite these warnings, Wilson married Edith Galt in the small, private ceremony at her Washington home on Dec. 18, 1915, one year and four months after Ellen's death. With seemingly little difficulty, Wilson managed to transfer to the elegant and sophisticated Edith all the devotion he had felt for his first wife.

On the Way to the White House: As early as 1906 there was public speculation that the president of Princeton might make a fine president of the U.S. Wilson's original backers were conservatives who saw him as a safe-and-sound member of the eastern establishment and the man to "save" the Democratic party from left-wing reformers. Wilson's long, bitter, and unsuccessful struggle against Princeton's traditional "eating clubs" helped him win a democratic image and popular appeal to go along with his conservative support. As a stepping-stone to the White House, Wilson accepted the New Jersey gubernatorial nomination when the Democratic bosses offered it to him in 1910. With the backing of one of the most corrupt political machines in America, Wilson was elected governor by a large margin, then promptly turned against his former allies and pushed through legislation for direct primaries, workmen's compensation, and regulation of public utilities. In 1912, after a scant two years in public office, Wilson took his progressive record to the people as a candidate for president. His stiff professorial manner, however, seemed to alienate many voters, and in a key primary Wilson was crushed by a 3-to-1 margin. By the time of the Democratic convention, Wilson was still a candidate but a definite underdog in his fight for the nomination.

His Person: Wilson was a tall, lean man with sparse iron-gray hair and blue eyes often hidden behind glittering, rimless glasses. His most prominent feature was his square, heavy lantern jaw, which, combined with a wide straight mouth and arched eyebrows, gave him what he himself described as a "Scotch Presbyterian face." Wilson had been a plain and ungainly youth, and throughout his life he thought of himself as particularly unattractive. He was fond of joking about his own forbidding appearance and liked to recite a self-derogatory limerick to his friends.

For beauty I am not a star;
There are others more handsome by far.
But my face, I don't mind it,
For I am behind it,
It's the people in front that I jar.

Proud of his strong tenor voice (he had been a member of the Princeton Glee Club in his student days), Wilson often joined his daughters Margaret and Eleanor in a singing trio. In private social gatherings, he also did impersonations and was particularly fond of recounting dialect and black folk stories. Appearing cold and rigid in public, Wilson was always plagued by a painful sense of his own isolation. He once wrote: "The president of the U.S. is not made of steel or whipcord or leather. He is more utterly dependent on his friends, on their sympathy and belief in him, than any man he has ever known or read about. . . . He has many counselors, but few loving friends. The fire of life burns in him only as his heart is kept warm."

PRESIDENCY

Nomination: June 25, 1912 . . .

As the Democratic convention began in Baltimore, the leading candidate for the nomination was James Beauchamp "Champ" Clark, the popular Speaker of the House, who—unlike Wilson—had won an impressive string of primary victories. Clark had captured much of William Jennings Bryan's old agrarian constituency, but though he won a majority of the votes on several early ballots, Wilson combined with other minor candidates to prevent him from winning the necessary two thirds. When Bryan himself deserted Clark, a strong trend developed toward Wilson, and the former Princeton professor was finally nominated on the 46th ballot.

Election: Nov. 5, 1912 . . .

Wilson's election was assured from the very beginning by the bitter split in Republican ranks. After an unsuccessful drive to take the Republican nomination away from President Taft, former President Theodore Roosevelt led progressives out of the convention in order to organize their own party. Under Roosevelt's leadership, the resulting Progressive, or "Bull Moose," party was the most powerful third party in the history of presidential elections.

In the public debate on key issues, Wilson assumed a middle ground between the conservative Taft and the radical platform of the Roosevelt Progressives. Under the influence of the crusading lawyer Louis D. Brandeis (later appointed by Wilson to the Supreme Court), Wilson developed a program known as the New Freedom, which was designed to end large business combinations and to return the U.S. to the old days of wide-open opportunity and free-enterprise capitalism. In taking his program to the public, Wilson loosened up considerably; he said that the highlight of the campaign for him was the moment when someone at the back of the crowd in a small town waved his arms at Wilson's train and shouted, "Hello, Woody!" On another occasion, as Wilson reached the climax of his speech and lashed out against the trusts, an unidentified citizen yelled, "Give it to 'em, Doc! You're all right."

Nevertheless, in the final tally Wilson actually polled *fewer* votes than did William Jennings Bryan in any of his three unsuccessful tries as the Democratic candidate, but because of the Republican split, Wilson's 6,301,254 was enough for victory. Third-party candidate Roosevelt finished second with 4,127,788, while incumbent William Howard Taft polled only 3,485,831. In the electoral college, Wilson won easily with 435 votes to 88 for Roosevelt and only 8 (the states of Utah and Vermont) for Taft.

In this already complicated election, a strong fourth party challenge was offered by the Socialists and their standard-bearer, Eugene V. Debs. Debs won nearly a million votes, or an impressive 6% of the national total.

First Term: Mar. 4, 1913 . . .

On a cold and disagreeable day, Woodrow Wilson was sworn in by Chief Justice Edward Douglass White on the east portico of the Capitol. The Wilsons had insisted that there be no inaugural ball, and they retired to the White House for a quiet family evening before going to bed at "a reasonable hour."

Reelection: Nov. 7, 1916 . . .

Despite an impressive record of domestic legislation in his first term, Wilson faced a tough fight for reelection because the Republicans in 1916 were once more united. Their competent, colorless candidate was Supreme Court Justice Charles Evans Hughes, and while Teddy Roosevelt grumbled about Hughes's lack of character and called him "the bearded lady" behind his back, Teddy agreed to lead his Progressives back into the GOP.

Though there had been speculation that Wilson's remarriage would hurt his chances of reelection, it turned out that the President's handsome new wife was a valuable political asset. Gossip about the White House romance served to humanize Wilson and to lend some warmth to his austere presidential image.

The key issue for the Democrats was the fact that the U.S. remained at peace while the bloodiest war in human history raged on in Europe. The slogan "He Kept Us Out of War" was used throughout the country on Wilson's behalf.

Nevertheless, on election night it appeared that Hughes had won by a narrow margin. It was only after late returns arrived from rural California counties that it became clear that Wilson had carried that state by the razor-thin margin of 4,000 votes and thereby won the election. According to one story, when a reporter called the morning after the election to wake Hughes with news from California, an aide loftily said, "The President can't be disturbed." "Well," replied the reporter, "when he wakes up tell him he's no longer president." The closeness of the vote led Republicans to hope that a recount would reverse the outcome, and Hughes waited two weeks before sending a telegram to Wilson conceding the election. Dryly commenting on the delay, Wilson said of the telegram: "It was a little moth-eaten when it got here, but quite legible."

Second Term: Mar. 5, 1917 . . .

The inauguration was delayed one day because, the scheduled Inauguration Day Mar. 4, fell on a Sunday. Wilson was once again sworn in by Chief Justice Edward D. White.

Just one month after the inauguration, the President who "kept us out of war" sent his war message to Congress and led the U.S. into W.W. I.

During his two terms Wilson vetoed 44 bills. Only 6 of these vetoes were overridden by Congress.

His 8 Years as President:

PRO

Wilson pushed through key reform legislation, including a reduction in the tariff; a stronger antitrust law; the establishment of the Federal Trade Commission to regulate unfair competition in business; and the institution of the Federal Reserve System, providing government, rather than private, control of the U.S. banking system.

CON

Wilson's reforms, though significant, were as much a reflection of the progressive temper of the times as of presidential leadership; on several secondary issues Wilson showed his true colors. He attacked Roosevelt's proposal for a minimum-wage law as "paternalistic" and dismissed the question of woman's suffrage as "not a problem that is dealt with by the national government at all." Under Wilson's administration, a policy of racial segregation was instituted for the first time in federal offices. Wilson's attorney general presided over the celebrated "Big Red Scare" in which socialists and other radicals were ruthlessly persecuted in coast-to-coast raids and 249 "undesirables" were deported to Russia.

PRO

Ignoring demands by hysterical interventionists for immediate American entry in the war, Wilson pursued a policy of neutrality that delayed U.S. participation for nearly three years and saved hundreds of thousands of American lives.

CON

Wilson's talk of neutrality was a sham and a fraud; from the beginning, he and his top advisers showed a clear bias for the Allied cause. As American business interests became steadily more involved with Britain and France, Wilson adopted a policy that made war inevitable. While sincere pacifists such as William Jennings Bryan bitterly protested, the U.S., like the European powers, followed a foreign policy designed to protect the interests of major capitalists, even at the risk of war. Wilson's high-handed intervention in Latin American affairs provided yet another illustration of this policy. In 1914 Wilson ordered military action against Mexico which killed 126 Mexicans, led the U.S. to the brink of another Mexican war, and caused lasting resentment south of the border.

PRO

Once the U.S. decided to enter W.W. I, Wilson proved himself an able war leader. His idealistic definition of war aims, including the famous 14 Points, helped to rally international support for the Allied cause. His aggressive action in organizing the home front to ensure victory demonstrated an efficient and imaginative use of the presidential war powers.

CON

Though effective as propaganda, Wilson's lofty speeches about "making the world safe for democracy" were misleading and deceptive. W.W. I was a struggle between self-interested nation-states competing for economic and political advantage, *not* a crusade for justice or democracy. After all, the most backward and repressive ruler in the world, the czar of Russia, had been a key partner in the coalition described by Wilson as "the forces of decency." At the peace conference after the war, the hollow nature of Wilson's idealism was exposed for everyone to see. One by one, the much-heralded 14 Points were abandoned, and a selfish and vindictive peace was imposed—despite Wilson's earlier assurances to the German people. It was the obvious bankruptcy of Wilson's visionary war aims that led to the universal disillusionment which plagued the world after the war.

PRO

At the peace conference in Paris, Wilson struggled valiantly to defend his ideals. Without his influence, the final settlement would have been even harsher than it was. Most important for the future of the world was the fact that the treaty, at Wilson's insistence, included provisions for a League of Nations, designed to resolve future international conflicts in a peaceful manner. When Wilson returned home, however, he found that Senate Republicans—some of them motivated by partisan political considerations—were ready to block Senate approval of the treaty. Wilson knew he was right and so refused to bargain with his political opponents; instead he boldly took his case directly to the people, in the hope of influencing the Senate decision. In the midst of his exhausting coast-to-coast speaking tour, the President suffered a stroke which left him partially paralyzed, a semi-invalid for the rest of his life. With his health broken, Wilson watched the Senate reject the treaty he had worked so hard to produce. Even more than Lincoln, Wilson was a tragic martyr to his ideals.

CON

From the beginning Wilson's role in the peace conference was marked by an unparalleled series of destructive blunders. His first mistake was his decision to attend the peace conference personally; if he had remained in the U.S. "above the battle," he might have been able to exert a greater influence on the proceedings. Second, even though the Republicans controlled Congress, Wilson stubbornly refused to allow a representative of the opposition to join him in the American delegation to the peace conference; instead, he gave the negotiations a partisan flavor by surrounding himself with Democrats who were also yes-men. Finally, and most importantly, Wilson's refusal to compromise with the Senate on even the smallest detail of his policy ensured defeat of the treaty. Nearly all historians are agreed that if Wilson had permitted some key "reservations" to be attached to the Versailles Treaty, the Senate would have surely given its approval and the U.S. would have entered the League. On the most controversial of these reservations—a restatement of the Constitution insisting that only the elected representatives in Congress, and not the League of Nations, could formally commit the U.S. to war—the senators were certainly right, and Wilson's rejection of compromise seems not only impractical but inexplicable. It was Wilson—not the Republican senators—who demanded final rejection of the League, after the key reservations had been attached. The illogical and uneasy peace that Wilson created in 1919 nurtured the seeds of W.W. II. The enormously destructive influence of his neurotic personality must counterbalance the pity to which the President might otherwise be entitled.

"Our First Lady President"

From the time of his collapse during his speaking tour promoting the League in September, 1919, until the end of his term some 17 months later, Wilson was little more than a shadow president. While the Chief Executive lay helpless and paralyzed in the White House, his wife, his doctor, and his private secretary agreed that the nation must never learn the true extent of his illness. The White House gates were closed, sentries were posted, and Edith Galt Wilson assumed active control of the presidency.

There was widespread talk that Vice-President Thomas Marshall (whose only enduring contribution to American history was his statement "What this country needs is a good 5¢ cigar") should take control of the government. Marshall, however, was too timid for such decisive action, especially with the Wilsons obviously unwilling to give up the reins of power. One of the main purposes of the 25th Amendment (ratified in 1967) was to avoid a repeat of the Wilson-Marshall situation, as well as to provide a clear-cut means for the transfer of power in cases of presidential incapacity.

AFTER THE PRESIDENCY

Despite his broken health and the wreckage of his policies, Wilson entertained the incredible idea that the Democrats might nominate him for a third term. Fortunately, the convention turned elsewhere, choosing James M. Cox of Ohio, who agreed nevertheless to champion the cause of the League of Nations and to make the election a referendum on Wilson's leadership. The result was the greatest landslide in American history up to that time—and an emphatic rejection of Wilsonian idealism. After a brief appearance at the inauguration of his Republican successor, the 64-year-old former President retired in bitterness to a private home on S Street in Washington. There Wilson hoped to write a book that would advance his policies and justify his presidency, but he never got further than the first page—a formal dedication to his wife Edith. On Armistice Day, 1923 (three months before his death), a throng of well-wishers gathered in front of his house. Wilson appeared on the balcony and, overcome with emotion, made a brief speech. "I am not one of those that have the least anxiety about the triumph of the principles I have stood for," he concluded. "I have seen fools resist Providence before and I have seen their destruction, as will come upon these again—utter destruction and contempt. That we shall prevail is as sure as that God reigns." The main headline in *The New York Times* the day Wilson's remarks appeared read—across three columns—HITLER FORCES RALLYING NEAR MUNICH.

PSYCHOHISTORY

As a boy, "Tommy" Wilson felt ugly, weak, and stupid, especially in comparison with his brilliant and much-admired father, the Reverend Joseph Ruggles Wilson. The boy developed serious difficulties in school—he did not master reading until he was 11—and became desperately afraid that he might disgrace his parents. Wilson convinced himself that the only way out of his dilemma was constant work—that pushing himself to the point of exhaustion was the road to success. This idea seemed to incorporate the young man's psychic need for self-punishment—punishment "deserved" since he saw himself as imperfect and unworthy when judged against the high standards set by his idealized parents and his grim Calvinist theology. Another result of this low self-esteem was Wilson's need to dominate his immediate environment completely. No one could disagree with him and still remain his friend, and any direct criticism was out of the question. As president, he dropped one by one all of his most trusted advisers and felt comfortable only in the company of sycophants or admiring women. Anyone who dared challenge Wilson or his ideas was considered hopelessly misguided or utterly base. For him compromise was impossible. Sigmund Freud suggested that Wilson unconsciously identified himself as the second member of the Trinity, Jesus Christ, while his father, Joseph Ruggles Wilson, assumed the role of God the Father. In a speech during the treaty negotiations in 1919, Wilson asked his audience: "Why has

Jesus Christ so far not succeeded in inducing the world to follow His teachings? It is because He taught the ideal without devising any practical means of attaining it. That is why I am proposing a practical scheme to carry out His aims." With such a messianic view of his own role, is it any wonder that Wilson seemed to seek ultimate martyrdom?

LITTLE-KNOWN FACTS

When Wilson was an undergraduate at the College of New Jersey (now Princeton), he wrote out on visiting cards: "Thomas Woodrow Wilson, Senator from Virginia." It was another 25 years, however, before he ran for public office and began to realize his political ambitions.

Wilson's first wife, Ellen, an accomplished artist, prepared crayon portraits of five of the men he most admired for her husband's study. Included were Daniel Webster, the American orator and lawyer; William Gladstone, the British statesman; Edmund Burke, British essayist and statesman; Walter Bagehot, British economist; and, of course, the Reverend Joseph Ruggles Wilson, Woodrow's father.

Washington etiquette was of little importance to Wilson. According to tradition, a president always walked ahead of his companions, even if those companions happened to be ladies. But Wilson refused to enter rooms before his wife, saying "a man who is a gentleman before becoming president should remain one afterwards."

In the White House, Wilson's daily breakfast was a glass of grapefruit juice and two raw eggs; his favorite lunch was chicken salad.

Wilson's second wife, Edith, was a Virginia aristocrat who claimed direct descent from Jamestown planter John Rolfe and the celebrated Indian princess Pocahontas.

In 1915 a typographical error in *The Washington Post* made President Wilson the unhappy subject of lewd laughter. Describing an evening at the theater enhanced by the attendance of the President and his new fiancée, a reporter wrote that instead of watching the performance, "the President spent most of his time entertaining Mrs. Galt." The word *entertaining* came out *entering* in the newspaper's earliest edition. Although this edition was hastily retrieved from newsstands—after a White House aide detected the error and placed a desperate phone call to the managing editor—enough copies had been sold to convulse innumerable readers.

In the same vein was a riddle that made the rounds in Washington about the time of Wilson's second marriage:

> "What did Mrs. Galt do when the President proposed to her?"
> "She fell out of bed."

During the grim period following his stroke, Wilson enjoyed few amusements in the White House. Some of his happiest hours were those he spent watching motion pictures, a form of entertainment he loved. One of his special favorites was D. W. Griffith's *Birth of a Nation*, which described Reconstruction with a pro-Southern bias that Wilson shared.

QUOTES FROM WILSON

"And let me again remind you that it is only by working with an energy which is almost superhuman and which looks to uninterested spectators like insanity that we can accomplish anything worth the achievement."—Undergraduate essay, "The Ideal Statesman"

"Tolerance is an admirable intellectual gift; but it is worth little in politics. Politics is a war of causes; a joust of principles."—Wilson at age 21

"I have a sense of power in dealing with men collectively which I do not always feel in dealing with them singly. . . . One feels no sacrifice of pride necessary in courting the favor of an assembly of men such as he would have to make in seeking to please one man."—Wilson at age 27

"The business of government is to organize the common interest against the special interests."—1912

"Segregation is not humiliating but a benefit, and ought to be so regarded by you gentlemen. The only harm that will come will be if you cause the colored people of the country to think it is a humiliation." —President Wilson to a delegation of black leaders, November, 1913

"We are glad, now that we see the facts with no veil of false pretense about them, to fight thus for the ultimate peace of the world and for the liberation of its peoples, the German peoples included; for the rights of nations great and small and the privilege of men everywhere to choose their way of life and of obedience. The world must be made safe for democracy. . . . It is a fearful thing to lead this great peaceful people into war, into the most terrible and disastrous of all wars, civilization itself seeming to be in the balance. But the right is more precious than peace, and we shall fight for the things which we have always carried nearest our hearts."—Declaration of war against Germany, Apr. 2, 1917

"Better a thousand times to go down fighting than to dip your colors to dishonorable compromise."—Wilson to his wife, 1919

"My constant embarrassment is to restrain the emotions that are inside of me. You may not believe it, but I sometimes feel like the fire from a far from extinct volcano, and if the lava does not seem to spill over it is because you are not high enough to see into the basin and see the caldron boil."—Comment at presidential press conference

"If I said what I thought about those fellows in Congress, it would take a piece of asbestos two inches thick to hold it."—On Senate opponents of the Versailles Treaty, Aug. 12, 1919

"My fellow citizens, I believe in Divine Providence. If I did not I would go crazy."—Sept. 17, 1919, one week before his collapse

"Again and again mothers who lost their sons in France have come to me, and, taking my hand, have not only shed tears upon it, but they have added, 'God bless you, Mr. President!' Why should they pray God to bless me? I advised the Congress to create the situation that led to the death of their sons. I ordered their sons overseas. I consented to their sons' being put in the most difficult part of the battle line, where death was certain. . . . Why should they weep upon my hand and call down the blessings of God upon me? Because they believe that their boys died for something that vastly transcends any of the immediate and palpable objects of the war. They believe, and rightly believe, that their sons saved the liberty of the world."—Speech in Pueblo, Colo., September, 1919

QUOTES ABOUT HIM

"He had to hold the reins and do the driving alone; it was the only kind of leadership he knew."—Arthur S. Link in *Wilson: The Road to the White House*

"He is an utterly selfish and cold-blooded politician always."—Former President Theodore Roosevelt

"He thought that lying was justified in some instances, particularly where it involved the honor of a woman. . . . He thought it was also justified where it related to matters of public policy."—Col. E. M. House, Wilson's close friend and top aide

"That mulish enigma, that mountain of egotism and selfishness who lives in the White House."—Former President William Howard Taft

"Father enjoyed the society of women, especially if they were what he called 'charming and conversable.' . . . Father once said, 'No man has ever been a success without having been surrounded by admiring females.' "—Eleanor Wilson McAdoo

"The largest single factor in the war was the mind of Woodrow Wilson."—Mark Sullivan

"Mr. Wilson bores me with his 14 points; why, God Almighty has only 10."—Georges Clemenceau, premier of France

"It would have been easy to lay the treaty and the covenant before the Senate as a bad lot, but the best he could do; but that would have been to confess weakness, to admit failure, something that Wilson could not do. He was schooled in the counsel of perfection and could give his approval to nothing less than perfection. So he brought home the perfect treaty and the impeccable covenant, and laid them both before his countrymen as the work of God."—William Allen White

"Wilson, after all, stood for human decency. He stood weakly for human decency; but he stood where it is an honor to stand."—Sigmund Freud and William Bullit in *Wilson: A Psychological Study*

—M.S.M.

40th President

RONALD WILSON REAGAN

VITAL STATISTICS

Born: Feb. 6, 1911, in Tampico, Ill., a town of about 1,200. When Reagan's father saw his newborn son, he commented, "For such a little bit of a fat Dutchman, he makes a hell of a lot of noise, doesn't he?" and for the next 25 years Dutch was Reagan's nickname. His brother, Neil, two years older, was called Moon. The family kept on the move to various Illinois cities and towns until Reagan was nine. John Edward Reagan—known as Jack—was a gregarious, sentimental Irish Catholic shoe salesman who, largely because of a drinking problem, had difficulty holding a job. His wife, Nelle Wilson Reagan, a Protestant of Scots-English descent, tolerated her husband's weakness for alcohol with unfailing Christian charity and understanding. She was a spiritual anchor for the family—and sometimes for the community as well—employing her dramatic talents to stage literary and inspirational readings for jails, hospitals, and clubs in most of the small towns where the Reagans lived.

In 1920 they settled in Dixon, Ill., a quiet town about 90 mi. from Chicago. It was the age of Warren Harding and Calvin Coolidge, and Dixon's 10,000 citizens were mostly orthodox Republicans abiding by the traditional midwestern small-town values. Jack Reagan was a Democrat, a liberal committed to the rights of the working man and with no tolerance for bigotry. He once stalked out of a hotel when he learned that the management refused to admit Jews. A good son, Reagan accepted and respected his parents' convictions. "I don't think he ever saw the inside of a pool hall," said Neil years later. When the family had money problems, the boys went to work. It was not an easy childhood, but a happy one, with a warm home life and hours spent outdoors, exploring the woods.

In high school Reagan was athletic, joining the Dixon High football team as a freshman, even though he was small for his age. He excelled in basketball and track and was popular with his schoolmates. A friendly, outgoing style and a desire for recognition won him parts in school plays, and by senior year he was president of the student body. As a summer lifeguard, Reagan saved a total of 77 people from drowning. Years later he commented that not one of them had ever thanked him: "I got to recognize that people hate to be saved; almost every one of them later sought me out and angrily denounced me for dragging them to shore."

By 1928 he had earned almost enough money to attend Eureka College, a small church-affiliated school near Peoria, Ill. Assisted by a sports scholarship and dishwashing jobs at his fraternity house (Tau Kappa Epsilon), Reagan plunged into college life. Classes had hardly begun when the school announced a massive budget cut and subsequently pared down the curriculum. Reagan was in the forefront of student opposition to the measure. He attacked the school's shortsighted economics in impassioned speeches before his fellow students and sympathetic faculty and assumed leadership of a protest committee, which voted to strike. (Witnesses to the incident remarked later that the protest actually centered on college rules against dancing and smoking.) Whatever the cause, the strike was a success and Reagan was its hero. Within a few days the school president resigned in defeat.

Reagan continued to occupy center stage all through college. He was on the football, swimming, and track teams. He joined the drama club and was president of the Boosters Club and the student council. He won an acting award for his role in an antiwar play, Edna St. Vincent Millay's *Aria da Capo*. With a decent but undistinguished academic record, Reagan graduated with a B.A. in sociology and economics in 1932.

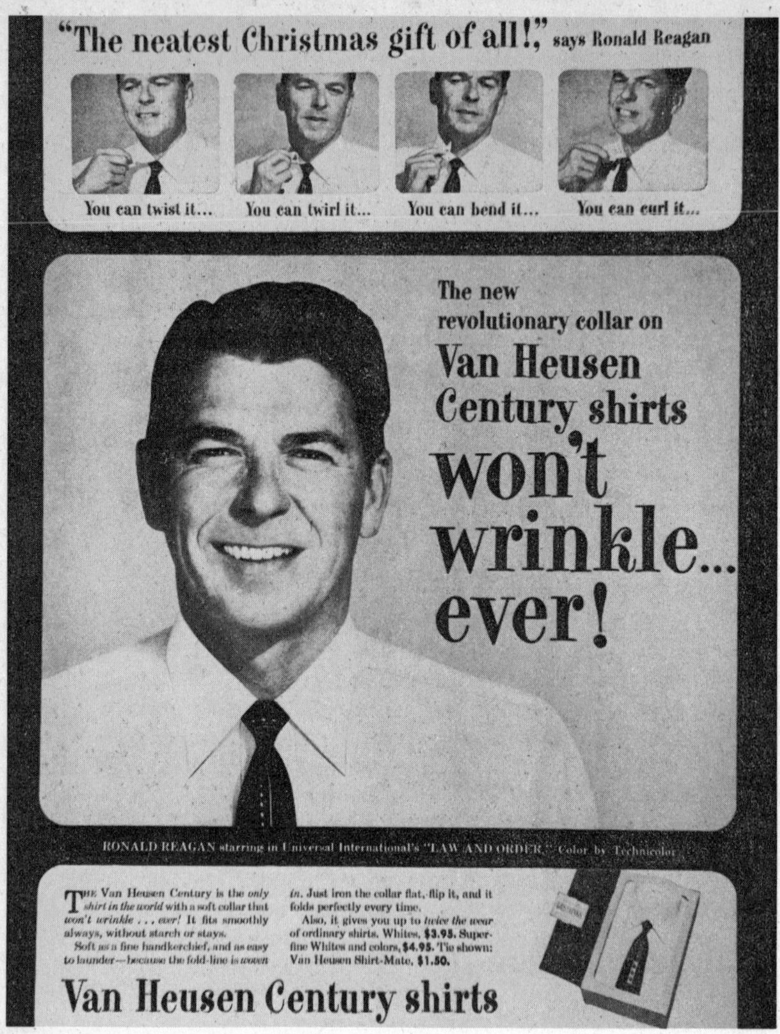

BEFORE THE PRESIDENCY

Career: Armed with his degree and an ambition to act in the movies, Reagan set out to find his first job in the heart of the Great Depression. Without the necessary Hollywood contacts, he decided to aim for a more wide-open entertainment medium—radio. WOC (World of Chiropractic, on the top floor of a chiropractor's office building) in Davenport, Ia., hired him as a sports announcer for $5 a game plus bus fare. He showed style in describing the play-by-play action of the University of Iowa football games, and soon he was promoted to a $100-a-month salary—far more than his father had ever earned selling shoes. When an opening at sister station WHO in Des Moines materialized, Reagan jumped at it, and for four years "Dutch" Reagan was on the air throughout the Midwest. Eventually NBC absorbed WHO, and Reagan's audience and reputation grew to national proportions.

During this time Reagan had not abandoned his Hollywood goal. In 1937 he landed an assignment covering the Chicago Cubs' spring training session on Catalina Island, off the southern California coast. He contacted an agent, Bill Meiklejohn, who, using the line "I have another Robert Taylor sitting in my office," arranged a screen test for Reagan at Warner Bros. Studio. He was hired at $200 a week and started making as many as eight films a year. In his first, *Love Is on the Air,* Reagan played the part of a radio announcer. In the second, *Submarine D-1,* he was cut from the final print. Always the sunny, all-American good guy, he was a safe commercial bet for low-budget films, including *Girls on Probation, Naughty but Nice,* and *Smashing the Money Ring.* Looking back at that time, Reagan called himself "the Errol Flynn of the B's."

In 1940 Reagan reached a turning point in his career and personal life. He married actress Jane Wyman in January and won the role of Notre Dame halfback George Gipp ("the Gipper") in *Knute Rockne—All-American.* At last Reagan's acting earned recognition, and the studio took notice. In 1941 he got another good role in a serious and disturbing work, *King's Row,* which is still considered the finest of Reagan's 53 films. (The director, Sam Wood, got an Oscar nomination.) It seemed as if Reagan's career was finally taking off. But by the time the picture was released in 1942, the U.S. was at war and Reagan had been called up for active duty. Bad eyesight disqualified him for combat, so he was assigned to the Army Air Corps' First Motion Picture Unit. He narrated training films produced at the Hal Roach Studios in Culver City, Calif., for the duration of the war. He also took time out to appear in a few wartime productions, notably Irving Berlin's musical comedy *This Is the Army* in 1943. However, by the time Captain Reagan was discharged in December, 1945, Hollywood—and movie audiences—had changed.

He returned to a film industry beset by labor-management disputes between the unions and the studios. Political turmoil polarized Hollywood into leftist and rightist groups. In the heat of argument, the charge of Communist infiltration of the unions began to be heard. Reagan's own union, the Screen Actors Guild, of which he had become a board member in 1938, was battling the studio bosses for benefits. As a liberal Democrat like his father, opposing communism and adhering to the principles of Franklin D. Roosevelt's New Deal, Reagan projected himself into the controversy. With his career in a holding pattern, he was collecting a star salary of $3,500 a week but being offered no quality roles. Reagan began to develop a consuming interest in film industry politics and joined organizations like the Hollywood Independent Committee for the Arts, Sciences, and Professions; the United World Federalists; and Americans for Democratic Action. He immersed himself in the activities of the Screen Actors Guild. In 1947 he was elected SAG president, a post he held until 1953; he served another term in 1959–1960.

Reagan recalled the mid-1940s as his "hemophilic [*sic*] liberal" days, when he bled for every cause. Discovering that several of these causes were too far left, he resigned his memberships and turned to a new political entity, the House Un-American Activities Committee, in his efforts to preserve Hollywood's freedom. In October, 1947, he testified as a "friendly" witness at the committee's hearings, and he encouraged others to reveal the identities of writers, directors, actors, and union leaders who were supposed agents of an international Communist conspiracy. Said Reagan: "The Communist play for Hollywood was remarkably simple. It was merely to take over the motion picture business, not only for its profits, as the hoodlums had tried—but also for a grand worldwide propaganda base." By 1948 Jane Wyman had filed for divorce, claiming his obsession with politics had undermined their marriage. A year later he was single again, still stalled in his career but involved in the motion picture industry's power centers. In 1949 he was elected chairman of the Motion Picture Industry Council.

With the insight he earlier displayed in choosing radio as the path to success, Reagan again turned to a new medium, television, and by 1950 he had appeared in several TV dramas. The next year he met Nancy Davis, an actress at MGM. Because he was her union president, she asked him to help get her name removed from mailing lists for Communist literature. They were married in 1952. Before long, Reagan had a new family to support. Since 1950 he had made only a few movies each year, hitting a new low in 1951 with *Bedtime for Bonzo,* in which he co-starred with a chimpanzee. Reagan was in debt, and at one point he accepted a two-week Las Vegas nightclub engagement on the same bill with the Continentals, a comedy dance team. His career had lost direction. In 1953, when he retired from the presidency of SAG, someone asked if he intended to enter politics. He answered, "I'd like to keep on making horse operas. I'm a ham—always was, always will be."

But in 1954 Reagan accepted a job which some say was the real beginning of his political career. He became the host of a weekly TV show, *General Electric Theater,* for $125,000 a year. The contract also provided for his services as goodwill ambassador for the General Electric Company, traveling around the U.S. and giving 250,000 minutes' worth of promotional speeches to plant employees. For eight years Reagan was a fixture on national television, and on tour he refined his public-speaking skills.

As defender of the corporate view of free enterprise as the American way, Reagan developed a speech he would repeat throughout his political career. Heartfelt in its view that conservatism equals patriotism, the speech attacked big government as a source of economic, social, and moral decay. Thus Reagan zeroed in on the average man's exasperation with bureaucracy. Eventually his antigovernment opinions inspired him to attack the Tennessee Valley Authority, one of GE's biggest customers. The company gently asked Reagan to drop the subject. He did, but by then his transformation was complete. Reagan had begun as a Democrat, but in 1952 and 1956 he had voted for Eisenhower. In 1960 he gave 200 speeches as a Democrat for Nixon. By 1962 he had officially registered as a Republican.

That same year also found Reagan out of work, since GE's show fell in the ratings and went off the air. His brother, Neil, now a senior vice-president at the McCann Erickson advertising agency and in charge of the Borax soap account, arranged to test viewer reaction to Reagan's presence in a Borax soap commercial. Results showed that women in the audience were highly responsive to Ronald Reagan. *Death Valley Days*, a television weekly sponsored by Borax, had found a new host.

On the Way to the White House: Reagan's rightist politics came into full flower during the 1960s, when issues concerning inflation and recession, the war in Vietnam, student revolt, and racial tension plagued American society. The speech he had honed at GE had by now become a fixture on his Republican after-dinner speaking circuit. In 1962 Reagan managed the unsuccessful primary campaign of Lloyd Wright, an ultraconservative Californian running for a seat in the U.S. Senate. Wright, a John Birch Society–supported candidate who advocated a "preventive war" with the Soviet Union, lost to the moderate Republican incumbent, Thomas Kuchel.

In 1964 Reagan became California chairman of Republican candidate Barry Goldwater's campaign for the presidency. A few days before the election Reagan made a nationally televised 30-minute speech to boost

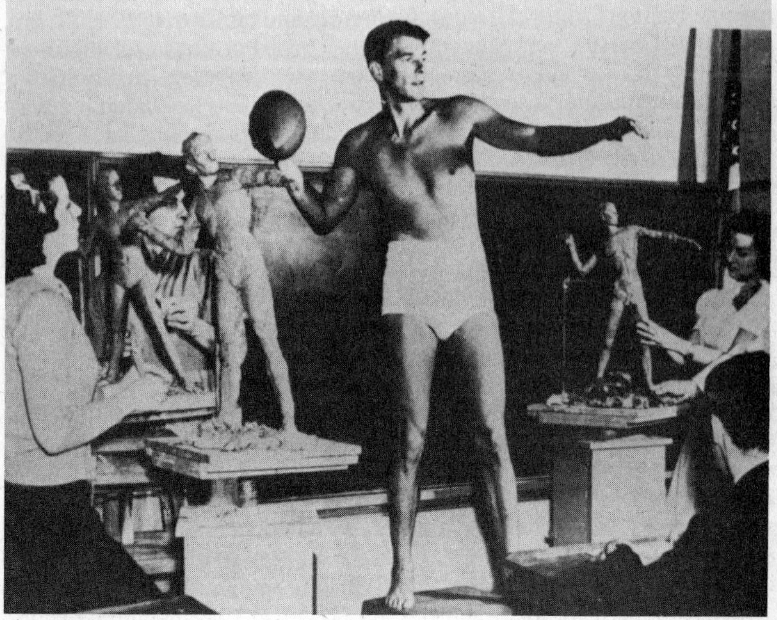

In 1940 the Division of Fine Arts of the University of Southern California selected Ronald Reagan as the possessor of the most nearly perfect male figure.

Goldwater's dim prospects of victory. Entitled "A Time to Choose," it was essentially the GE speech raised to a fine pitch of emotionality. Audiences were electrified and sent in nearly $1 million in campaign contributions. The world also took notice of Ronald Reagan as a political speaker, and so did a group of powerful Republican California businessmen: oil magnate Henry Salvatori, chairman of Union Oil A. C. "Cy" Rubel, and auto dealer Holmes Tuttle. They formed the "Friends of Ronald Reagan" committee and in 1966 encouraged him to run for governor of California.

With money, advice, and support, Reagan's committee of friends sponsored a sophisticated campaign, offering their gubernatorial candidate as an idealistic "citizen-politician" whose views on inflation, welfare, taxes, unemployment, and riots provided the necessary fresh perspective. Incumbent Democratic Gov. Edmund G. "Pat" Brown was accused of aiding the enemy in Vietnam and condoning welfare cheats. Reagan overhauled the GE speech once again, and the taxpaying public loved it. At last there was a candidate voicing their frustration with a system that they believed in but that had turned away from them in favor of blacks, students, and welfare cases. Reagan went on record for free enterprise, law, order, morality, the family, the death penalty, a state hiring freeze, tax cuts, elimination of "waste" and "fraud" in government, the war in Vietnam, and a balanced budget. From his movie and television days he had acquired two invaluable assets, especially in media-oriented California: a public identity and familiarity with TV as a medium of persuasion. Nevertheless, he earned criticism for his cavalier views on certain issues (he called unemployment insurance "a prepaid vacation for a segment of our society which has made it a way of life") and for his tendency to mangle statistics and distort facts. Asked about his qualifications for the office of governor, Reagan replied, "Gee, I don't know. I've never played a governor before."

In Chico, Calif., in 1966, reporters questioned Reagan's stand on discrimination in public housing and his opposition to the federal Civil Rights Act of 1964 and 1965. After giving a confusing answer, Reagan continued, "I'm not sure I know what I'm talking about, I'm so pooped. You're boring in on me, aren't you? You're boring in because you know you've caught me so pooped that I don't know what I'm doing." Said Governor Brown: "What are his excuses? One time he laughs boyishly—no mean trick at our ages—and says he 'goofed.' Another time he admits to being too 'pooped' to think straight, and this was at 3:30 in the afternoon. You can't afford a governor like that. You don't get retakes as governor."

On Nov. 8, 1966, Reagan beat Brown by 845,000 votes. Inaugurated in a midnight ceremony on Jan. 2, 1967, California's 33rd governor turned to his old Hollywood friend George Murphy (then a U.S. senator) and said, "Well, here we are on the late show again." After inaugural festivities arranged by Walt Disney Studios, Reagan set about translating his tax-cutting rhetoric into action. Promising to "squeeze and cut and trim" state expenses, he began with a proposal to reduce the University of California's budget by 25% and introduce tuition to make up the difference—thus obliterating the prestigious university's 100-year tradition of free education for the top 12% of the state's students. Tuition, said the governor, "would help get rid of undesirables." Students and educators saw this plan as retaliation for campus demonstrations. Evidently Reagan agreed with State Superintendent of Public Instruction Max Rafferty, that the University of California offered a "four-year course in sex, drugs, and treason"; moreover, he had tapped a huge reservoir of public resentment against liberalism on campus. With popular support, Reagan arranged the dismissal of UC President Clark Kerr. Before his first month in office was over, Reagan had been hanged in effigy on the Berkeley campus. Reagan relished his war with the universities. When students at San Francisco State College went on strike, demanding the creation of black and ethnic studies departments, Reagan committed 600 police a day to the campus to restore order. When students and locals in Berkeley turned a vacant lot owned by the University of California into a park, Reagan ordered that it be destroyed. Later he lauded the efforts of the police after they fired into a crowd, killing one bystander and wounding 100 other people.

The 25% UC budget cut never materialized; in fact, like other state expenditures, the UC budget actually increased 100% during Reagan's eight-year tenure as governor. By 1975 the state's budget had increased by 122%—the largest hike in any state—and Reagan had signed into law the single biggest tax increase in the history of California: $1 billion, in one jump.

The Reagan administration's first year was riddled with crisis and confrontation. In March, 1967, he proposed shutting down 15 state mental-health facilities and phasing out 3,700 jobs in the Dept. of Mental Hygiene. About 650 California psychiatrists formally protested, pointing out that the agencies slated for closing were the very ones whose treatments were most effective in reducing the number of institutional patients. Reagan called them "head shrinkers" working at the "biggest hotel chain in the state." After Denmark's director of mental health facilities visited a northern California state mental hospital in November, 1967, he told the press of the shocking conditions there, the worst he had seen in a dozen countries. Reagan lost his temper and denied that California had anything but first-rate facilities. He implied that the director was part of a conspiracy to discredit the Reagan administration. A few days later the governor apologized.

In August, 1967, Reagan announced a $200 million Medi-Cal budget cut, saying he didn't condone handouts to the poor, but the California Supreme Court threw it out. Handouts to big business were another matter: In October, 1967, the Associated Farmers, a group of millionaire growers in the central valley, received from the Reagan administration the use of prison labor to harvest strawberries and grapes. Farm workers were outraged; nothing like that had happened since W.W. II.

In November, 1967, Washington columnist Drew Pearson reported that two top Reagan aides had been forced to resign after they were discovered in a homosexual ring with teenage boys. California newspapers had suppressed the story at the request of Reagan's press secretary, Lyn Nofziger, but when out-of-state publications *Time* and *Newsweek* hit the stands, Californians were confronted with the story—and with the governor's denial of it. The credibility gap widened as Reagan hotly called Pearson a liar, then changed his tone and asked that the matter be quietly dropped.

In certain areas of legislation the Reagan administration proved progressive. In 1967 one of the most liberalized abortion bills in the U.S. became law in California. In his eight-year term Reagan increased state spending for higher education by 136%. He added 41 mi. of coastal land to the state park system. He approved the 1971 Welfare Reform Act, which increased benefits to the needy by 43%.

Elected to a second term in 1970 (a year in which he paid no state income taxes) by a margin of 500,000 votes, Reagan continued to represent the prevailing mood of California voters. He used his veto power on fiscal measures 994 times in eight years and addressed the anxious public on issues of taxation and law and order. But since 1968 Reagan and his circle of wealthy backers (his "kitchen cabinet") had been looking to the presidential arena. He made a last-minute bid for the GOP nomination in 1968, but it went to Nixon. When his governorship expired in 1975, Reagan passed up a third term to concentrate on the 1976 presidential race. In spite of his ninth-place rating in a 1975 poll of most-admired Americans, Reagan lost the nomination to Gerald Ford.

For the next four years Reagan cultivated his public image with a newspaper column and television appearances, in which he delivered variations on the basic speech that had been his trademark for over 20 years. At the 1980 Republican convention in Detroit, Mich., Ronald Reagan won the nomination he had sought for 12 years. Henry Kissinger urged him to choose Gerald Ford as a running mate in a sort of "co-presidential" capacity. Reagan consented to Kissinger's idea, and for several days the former secretary of state courted the ex-president. Ford briefly considered the offer, then declined. Reagan then selected George Bush, former director of the CIA, as his vice-presidential choice, despite the fact that in the primary campaign he had denounced Bush as a representative of the "Eastern Liberal Establishment."

Relying on his friendly style and appealing looks, Reagan conducted a campaign that called for the revitalization of America's traditional values, namely, "family, work, neighborhood, freedom, peace," and made use of his characteristic supply of one-liners and questionable data. In fact, all Reagan had to do to get elected was sit back quietly and let Jimmy Carter's record speak for itself. However, the former after-dinner speaker couldn't leave well enough alone, and before long newsmen were catching him in one lie or distortion after another. Speaking to a crowd of evangelists, Reagan announced the discovery of "new evidence" disputing the Darwinian theory of evolution and supporting the fundamental biblical view of creation. When challenged, he was unable to produce this new evidence. While visiting Pittsburgh, he declared that smog had been cleared up in California and that government control of industrial air pollution had gone too far. At that very moment Reagan's hometown of Los Angeles was suffering its worst smog attack in several years.

One of Reagan's most popular crowd pleasers was the following: "Jimmy Carter said we should give back the Panama Canal because nobody would like us if we didn't. . . . Jimmy Carter says we should sign the SALT II treaty because nobody will like us if we don't. . . . Well, I say, isn't it about time we stopped worrying about whether people like us and say, 'We want to be respected again!' " The fact that Jimmy Carter had never said any such thing didn't stop Reagan from using the story over and over, just as he continued to repeat other allegations, even after they had been proved wrong. For example, Reagan incorrectly stated that Alaska has more oil than Saudi Arabia; that trees cause more pollution than industry; that it cost $3 to deliver $1 of welfare (it actually cost 12¢); and that the number of government employees had increased by 131,000 while Carter was president (the true figure was 6,000).

Fortunately for Reagan, Carter's record bothered more people than Reagan's blunders and falsehoods, and on Nov. 4, 1980, Ronald Reagan was elected president of the U.S. in an electoral landslide. With the votes of 43.3 million Americans (a 51% majority) he won in 44 states, compared to Carter's 6 states (plus Washington, D.C.) and 41% (35 million) of the popular vote. Reagan scored 489 electoral votes and Carter only 49. Independent candidate John Anderson (R-Ill.) won 7% (5.6 million) of the popular vote. In the 20th century, only two presidents received a larger electoral majority: Franklin D. Roosevelt in 1936 and Richard Nixon in 1972. However, voter turnout was 54%—the lowest since 1948—and only 27% of the voting-age population actually voted for Reagan.

Personal Life: As the first U.S. president to have been divorced, Reagan nevertheless places a traditional and stable family life at the pinnacle of his moral code and his political program. On Jan. 26, 1940, Reagan and first wife, actress Jane Wyman, were married. Described by Hollywood columnist Louella Parsons as the ideal American couple, they had met in 1937 on the Warner Bros. lot and had co-starred in *Brother Rat* (1938), *Brother Rat and a Baby* (1940), and *An Angel from Texas* (1940). Reagan was not oblivious to the publicity value of his marriage. He consented to *Modern Screen* magazine's publication of his "Letters to Button Nose"—his version of a serviceman's letters home during W.W. II, even though his battle station was in Culver City and he went home to Button Nose every night. Daughter Maureen Reagan was born in 1941, and the Reagans adopted son Michael in 1945.

Wyman's reputation as an actress flourished while Reagan had made only one film, *King's Row,* which received critical acclaim. He was proud of it, though, and often screened it for after-dinner guests. As his film career veered off into politics, Reagan was divorced by Wyman in 1948, the year she won an Oscar for her role in *Johnny Belinda.* Of the divorce, Reagan said, "I suppose there had been warning signs, but small-town boys grow up thinking only other people get divorced."

Wyman blamed his obsessive political activism, claiming, "Finally there was nothing in common between us." She is also reported to have said, "I just couldn't stand to watch that damned *King's Row* one more time." She was granted custody of their children, and Reagan briefly indulged in a bachelor life of nightclubs and parties that ill suited him.

It was his role as the film industry's anti-Communist watchdog that led Reagan to his second wife, Nancy Davis. Ten years younger than Reagan, she was an MGM contract actress who arrived in Hollywood through her parents' contacts. Nancy had grown up in the ultraconservative household of her stepfather, Dr. Loyal Davis, a wealthy Chicago neurosurgeon. She had been a debutante whom acquaintances described as prim and straitlaced. On her own in Hollywood in 1951, she was dismayed to find her name associated with Communist organizations. She appealed to her union president—Ronald Reagan—for help. They soon began dating and were married on Mar. 4, 1952. Daughter Patti was born 7½ months later. In 1957 Reagan and his wife costarred in *Hellcats of the Navy*. It was her last film. The Reagans had a son, Ronald, in 1958. Many observers have said that Nancy Reagan greatly reinforced her husband's conservative views. Acknowledged to be his all-around adviser and the person closest to him, she has also been described by one California Reagan supporter as an "anachronism [who] lives in the 1950s, when it was a man's world and women were there to be perfect wives. She lacks compassion for the issues of the day because they have never been in her sphere of life."

Reagan and his wife remained very close. In 1974 they bought a 688-acre ranch (for $574,000) in California's Santa Ynez Mountains, just north of Santa Barbara. A small ranch house built on the property in 1881 serves as their retreat from the public eye, and they enjoy relaxing there in each other's company. Gardening, chopping wood, and riding horseback serve as Reagan's pastimes. Once he came across a rattlesnake on the property and stamped it to death, only to realize later that he had been wearing sneakers instead of boots. In the evenings Reagan and his wife enjoy watching television, particularly *Little House on the Prairie* and *M*A*S*H*.

The Reagans share unassailable convictions on the sanctity of marriage and traditional family life. Nancy Reagan has been consistently opposed to values at variance with her own; she is against abortion, against ERA, against premarital sex, and against "easy" divorce. Ronald Reagan has stated a belief that big government is responsible for eroding moral stability. In his opinion government interference in private life has caused rising divorce rates and a breakdown in communication between parents and children. If his own divorce was not caused by the government, it was at least caused by politics.

The four Reagan children are aware of the modern communication problems between parents and children. Maureen, the eldest and twice divorced, has campaigned for her father even though she is a feminist and supports the ERA. Michael, a former boat racer, put himself through college when it became clear that tuition money would not be forthcoming from his millionaire father. Michael's parents never attend any of his races. Youngest son, Ron, who left Yale University to join New York's Joffrey School as a ballet dancer. (His parents didn't see him perform until after Reagan became president.) In 1976, when Reagan was voted West Coast Father of the Year, his daughter Patti was not permitted to bring her rock star boyfriend into the family home because they were living together without benefit of marriage.

According to friends and close associates, Reagan in private is very akin to his public self: likable, friendly, conversational, an exceptionally good storyteller, and an optimist. He is a man who sees the world in simple terms, they say. His circle of friends are much like him: wealthy, conservative, and with enormous faith in the work ethic. However, as the oldest (70 a few days after his inauguration) man to assume the presidency, Reagan has continued certain practices observed since his tenure as California governor, namely a nine-to-five workday, punctuated by an afternoon nap. Reagan's friends point out that he is dedicated but not compulsive.

His Person: Ronald Reagan has always been a physically vigorous man, proud of his athletic ability. He has kept his 6-ft. 2-in. frame to a trim 194 lb. Ever since his years as a glamorous face in Hollywood, he has worn contact lenses on his light blue eyes to correct nearsightedness. Reagan has hay fever and takes periodic injections to control symptoms. He quit smoking many years ago, replacing his habit with a more benign fondness for jelly beans. (Reportedly he included 8,000 lb. of jelly beans in his $8 million inauguration day gala.) When he is not dieting, Reagan is fond of such special dishes as spiced hamburger soup, and he loves desserts, especially chocolate brownies. He and Nancy enjoy vodka and orange juice cocktails and an occasional glass of wine.

PSYCHOHISTORY

The question is: How did Ronald Reagan, a young man with working-class parents who were impassioned liberals, whose father had a job thanks to FDR's New Deal, who led a student demonstration and acted in an antiwar play, change into a staunch supporter of the rights of corporations over the rights of the poor, who violently attacked student demonstrators, and who continued to refer to the Vietnam War as "a noble cause" as recently as 1980.

Before W.W. II, Reagan had been an actor who followed orders. In the army he became a captain and learned to give orders. After the war he rose quickly in the ranks of his union and, as its representative, came into increased contact with representatives of the other side. More and more he began to identify with the values of the studio chiefs with whom he was negotiating. During the HUAC investigations, he pleased the motion picture producers by taking up the cause of anticommunism and agreeing to help them clean up Hollywood's image. A few weeks after Reagan's testimony to HUAC, columnist Louella Parsons wrote, "You may be sure Jack Warner, who is fighting communism in Hollywood along with the other producers, is giving Ronnie a break he deserves." By 1954 Reagan had become a spokesman for General Electric, one of the largest and most antiunion corporations in the U.S. Once "Ronnie" crossed over into the world of the wealthy, he kept on the path and never looked back.

In many ways, Ronald Reagan was a dream come true for the leaders of corporate America—a politician who is a *real* actor; a man who started his career by convincing radio audiences that he was actually at a sports event when he was really reading off a ticker-tape machine and inventing the details; a man who made his living following directions and reading from scripts and convincing the American people that the resultant performance was reality. Is it really surprising that Ronald Reagan should graduate from fake broadcasts (which his listeners enjoyed) to fake statistics and fake facts?

One more disturbing aspect of Reagan's psychology is his big-stick paternalism. Although he seems to have been a fairly distant father to his children, he presents the image of a parent who would rather use the rod than spoil the child. As governor of California, Reagan seemed to perceive all students and minorities as his children, and his rod became rifles, tanks, tear gas, and a whole array of experimental crowd-control weapons. As president, Reagan appears to have expanded his conception of his "children" to include the citizens of Third World countries. His support of the authoritarian dictators of many of these nations (South Korea, Philippines, El Salvador, Chile, etc.), coupled with his concern for the interests of U.S. corporations, has led him to ignore considerations of human rights. Having enjoyed the suppression of his unruly "children" as governor, he has shown no hesitation in providing unpopular foreign leaders with the weapons they need to beat down the rebellious masses in their own countries.

In 1953 Reagan was the model in a Van Heusen shirt advertisement ("Won't wrinkle ever!" read the headline), and in reissuing the ad 27 years later the company added a congratulatory message: "The wonderful thing about America is that sooner or later, everyone's dream can come true." President Reagan, whose dreams are in line with corporate interests, would agree. But how does Reagan regard those Americans with differing dreams? Ronald Reagan truly believes in America. Even his critics have not questioned the sincerity of that belief. But certain groups of citizens are wondering if Reagan's America believes in them.

LITTLE-KNOWN FACTS

Ronald Reagan and Ann Sheridan were originally cast for the roles that went to Humphrey Bogart and Ingrid Bergman in *Casablanca*.

In 1940 Reagan was voted by the University of Southern California's Division of Fine Arts as having "the most nearly perfect male figure."

In the 1950s Reagan was $18,000 in debt. He owed the government money, and he had mortgages on both his Pacific Palisades house and his ranch in the Malibu hills. He turned his finances over to his friend, William French Smith, and his problems were finally solved when 20th Century–Fox bought the ranch for $2 million.

The greatest disappointment of Reagan's acting career came in 1970, when he was California governor: No one thought to offer him the starring role in *Patton*.

QUOTES FROM REAGAN

"I discovered that night that an audience has a feel to it and, in the parlance of the theater, that audience and I were together. When I came to actually presenting the motion, there was no need for parliamentary procedures. They came to their feet with a roar—even the faculty members present voted by acclamation. It was heady wine. Hell, with two more lines I could have had them riding through every Middlesex village and farm—without horses yet."—On the 1928 student strike he led at Eureka College

"I'd like to harness their youthful energy with a strap."—Concerning student demonstrations in California, 1966

"The entire graduated income tax structure was created by Karl Marx. It has no justification in getting government revenue."—During the 1966 gubernatorial campaign in California

"We should declare war on North Vietnam. We could pave the whole country and put parking stripes on it, and still be home by Christmas."—1966

"Welfare recipients are a faceless mass waiting for a handout."—1966

"The time has come to stop being our brother's keeper."—Concerning welfare budget cuts in California, 1967

"A tree's a tree. How many do you need to look at?"—Concerning the expansion of California's Redwood National Forest, 1967

"Let me point out that my administration makes no bones about being business-oriented."—As California governor, 1967

"If it's a bloodbath they want, let's get it over with."—Concerning student demonstrations, 1970

"It's just too bad we can't have an epidemic of botulism."—In response to the Hearst family's free food giveaway to the poor as partial ransom for their daughter Patricia, kidnapped by the SLA terrorist group, 1974

"We have a different regard for human life than those monsters do."—On the subject of Communists, 1980

"I'm not smart enough to lie."—Response to an inquiry about his qualifications for the presidency, 1980

QUOTES ABOUT HIM

"No, no, no, no. You've got it all wrong. *Jimmy Stewart* for governor, Ronald Reagan for best friend."—Attributed to Jack Warner when he first learned that Reagan was running for public office, 1966

"Ronald Reagan managed to change his image almost completely between the time he announced for the office of governor and the time he came into the homestretch of the election, a period of some two or three months . . . he came into the election carrying the image of Barry Goldwater. He emerged at the end of the campaign bearing the image of Nelson Rockefeller."—Harry Ashmore, chairman of the Advisory Committee of the California Democratic party, 1967

"For years the American Right had hungered for a national spokesman with political sex appeal. . . . [Reagan] looked sophisticated and urbane, even though his message was corny and parochial."—Joseph Lewis, author of *What Makes Reagan Run*, 1968

"He's simplistic in a positive sense. He sees situations and problems very clearly. The measurements he uses are black and white, even if the problems aren't."—Charles Z. Wick, California investor

"Ron is no genius. He's not a helluva lot smarter than I am, but he has enormously good common sense and he uses it. That's what appeals to the man in the street."—Justin Dart, chairman and chief executive of Dart Industries, Inc., 1980

"I'm dissatisfied with the candidates of the major parties. You have [Carter] . . . and on the other hand you have a man who is difficult to understand because he has his feet in his mouth most of the time." —Stanley Marcus, former chairman of the board of Neiman-Marcus, 1980

"Ronnie knows how to relax. He doesn't take his problems home." —Alfred Bloomingdale, 1980

"External experience seems filtered into his rhetorical shell like Tang to an astronaut—powdered, sanitary, and lifeless."—Robert Scheer, journalist, 1980

"He doesn't make snap decisions, but he doesn't tend to overthink, either."—Nancy Reagan, 1980

"Nancy and Dad have a very close relationship. You'd think they just got married yesterday. It's hard to break that barrier sometimes—not that that's bad. It's great for them because it's their lives."—Michael Reagan, 1980

—K.P. and D.W.

FOOTNOTE PEOPLE IN U.S. HISTORY

HARRY J. ANSLINGER (1892–1975). ***U.S. commissioner of narcotics.***

What J. Edgar Hoover and communism were to the FBI, Harry J. Anslinger and drugs were to the Treasury Dept.'s Bureau of Narcotics. During his 32-year reign as the bureau's first director, his mission was, as he put it, to "get rid of drugs, pushers, and users. Period." His unrelenting attack on marijuana, which he believed to be as dangerous as any hard drug, led to the Marijuana Tax Act of 1937, the first federal attempt to stamp out the weed. He brought his expertise to numerous international conferences on drug control and was described by Sir Leonard Lyle of the International Permanent Central Opium Board as "the greatest living authority on the world narcotic drug traffic."

Born on May 20, 1892, in Altoona, Pa., Anslinger worked his way through two years at Pennsylvania State College by playing background piano at a silent-movie theater. In 1917 he took a job with the War Dept. Transferring to the Treasury Dept., he rose in 1929 to assistant commissioner of prohibition, a post that included drug-law enforcement. When corruption in the narcotics section led to the creation of a separate

Bureau of Narcotics, President Herbert Hoover appointed Anslinger its first commissioner on Aug. 12, 1930.

From the beginning Commissioner Anslinger relentlessly attacked any and all illicit drugs. He singled out marijuana as especially pernicious because of its appeal to youth. In collaboration with Courtney Ryley Cooper, he wrote for the July, 1937, issue of *American Magazine* the classic scare piece "Marijuana, Assassin of Youth." In bold type above the authors' by-line the reader was warned, "A weed that grows wild throughout the country is making dope addicts of thousands of young people." The article presented a train of tragedies: a girl jumps out a window in Chicago, a boy axes his family to death in Florida, a youth shoots an elderly bootblack in Los Angeles—all senseless acts committed while under the influence of marijuana, Anslinger claimed. The authors asserted that marijuana induced temporary insanity that "may take the form of a desire for self-destruction or a persecution complex to be satisfied only by the commission of some heinous crime." Marijuana abuse was so rampant in New Orleans, according to the article, that pot smokers accounted for some 29% of the criminals in that city.

In the magazine article and at congressional hearings, Anslinger pressed for passage of a federal law to stamp out marijuana. He was rewarded with the Marijuana Tax Act, which imposed stiff penalties for possession and effectively ended any further medical use of the plant. Cannabis, as the drug was known among doctors, was eliminated from the *Pharmacopoeia of the United States of America*.

In his single-minded zeal to rid the land of drugs, Commissioner Anslinger had little patience with those who saw drug abuse as a medical problem. It was, he felt, a police problem. While many doctors, lawyers, and judges sought to treat narcotics addicts—like alcoholics—as victims of a disease, Anslinger insisted that users were "immoral, vicious, social lepers" who must be segregated from society. When in 1959 a joint committee of the American Medical Association and the American Bar Association suggested that it might be helpful to treat addicts on an outpatient basis, allowing them to withdraw gradually from the habit, Anslinger bitterly denounced the proposal. If addicts were to be weaned from drugs instead of locked up and forced to kick their habit cold turkey, said Anslinger scornfully, then society might as well set aside "a building where on the first floor there would be a bar for alcoholics, on the second floor licensed prostitution, with the third floor set aside for sexual deviates, and, crowning them all, on the top floor a drug-dispensing station for addicts."

Among the dangers of narcotics, Anslinger concluded, was their potential as a weapon of war. In 1942 he charged that Japan had been encouraging the use of opium in the lands occupied by the Japanese army in order to make their subjects more docile. During W.W. II he marshaled the forces of several U.S. departments to check this "Japanese opium offensive." Two years before the war erupted in Europe, Anslinger began working with opium alkaloid manufacturers in the U.S. to stockpile the massive medical supplies that would be needed to care for Allied casualties.

Also for the war effort, the commissioner suspended his long-standing campaign against marijuana smoking and actually fostered its use—among captured enemy officers. Collaborating with the Office of Strategic Services, he spiked cigarettes with marijuana and had them distributed among selected POWs, who were then interrogated while under the influence.

With Japan's defeat, Anslinger focused his attack on Communist China. Speaking before the U.N. in 1954, he charged that Peking was trying to demoralize the free world by stimulating drug traffic in Southeast Asia.

In 1962 Anslinger reached the then mandatory retirement age of 70 and so was replaced by Henry L. Giordano. Anslinger retired to Hollidaysburg, Pa., near his native Altoona. Although he continued to serve as U.S. representative to the U.N. Commission on Narcotic Drugs, he was powerless to check the growing drug culture of the late 1960s and 1970s. However, Anslinger was quite explicit about why he disapproved of LSD. "Whatever sublime feelings the person on LSD *imagines,*" Anslinger said, "the fact is that he is out of his head. He can't function in any normal way. He couldn't play chess, make a bed, run a cash register."

While the nation began to adopt a more permissive attitude toward marijuana use, the retired commissioner remained until his death in 1975 an unreconstructed opponent of decriminalization. In the August, 1968, issue of *Esquire* magazine, he confided to James Sterba his own personal reason for not smoking pot. "Sometimes," he said, "I get in the mood where I'd like to take care of three certain individuals in this country, because of the damage they've done. . . . If I were in the mood at the time that I smoked a marijuana cigarette, I might do some damage to those fellows."

Fortunately for the three would-be targets—all left unnamed—the commissioner never smoked a joint.

—W.A.D.

JOHN HOWARD GRIFFIN (1920–1980). ***Writer, civil rights activist, musicologist.***

One of the most vivid personal accounts of the experience of being black in America, *Black Like Me,* was written by a white man, John Howard Griffin. In 1959 Griffin went to a New Orleans doctor who administered the drug Oxsoralen, which makes skin turn a dark brown upon exposure to the ultraviolet rays of the sun or a sunlamp. Used in conjunction with a vegetable dye, it allowed Griffin to "pass" for black and find out firsthand the prejudice Negroes had to endure.

"As a Southerner," said Griffin, who was born in Dallas, Tex., in 1920, "I became increasingly tormented by the similarity of our racist attitudes and rationalizations to those I had encountered in Nazi Germany. I began to do studies dealing with the problems and patterns of racism. In 1959, convinced that we were making little progress in resolving the terrible tragedy of racism in America—a tragedy for the white racist as well as for the Negro (and other) victim groups—I had

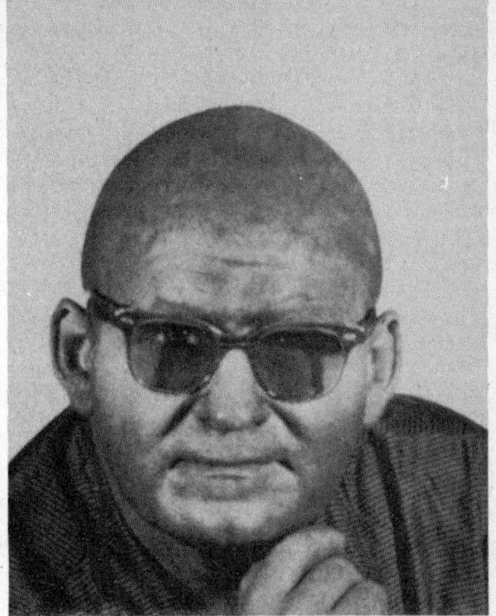

John Howard Griffin before . . . *. . . and after.*

myself medically transformed into a Negro and lived in the states of Louisiana, Mississippi, Alabama, and Georgia.

"I wanted to test whether we really judge men as human or whether we draw up an indictment against a whole group. I kept my name and changed nothing but my pigment."

On assignment from *Sepia* magazine, Griffin hitchhiked, walked, and rode buses through the South for six weeks and discovered to his dismay the extent and intensity of racial hatred that existed.

On one bus ride to Hattiesburg, Miss., he was not allowed to get off at a rest stop with the white passengers. In another incident, this time on a New Orleans city bus, the driver refused to let Griffin out at his requested stop and drove on for eight more blocks before opening the door.

Whenever Griffin managed to hitch rides with whites, they seemed always to turn the conversation toward one general subject—the sexual appetites, preferences, and private parts of blacks. His questioners wanted to know if all the sexual myths about blacks were true and if he had ever had or wanted a white woman. One driver even went so far as to ask Griffin to expose himself because he had never seen a black man completely naked.

Later Griffin was told to "move on" in a public park, was not allowed access to restaurants and rest rooms, had his change thrown on the floor when he tried to purchase a bus ticket, and was given what he called the "hate stare" whenever he came in contact with whites. In general, he learned the daily indignities that blacks had to suffer and it made him sick at heart.

Black Like Me was compiled from Griffin's notes and *Sepia* articles and was well received critically when it was published in 1961. A second edition was published in 1977 with a new epilogue by the author. All together, the book has sold more than 5 million copies, and in 1964 it was made into a movie. The book was not popular with some of Griffin's neighbors; in fact, they hanged him in effigy.

Black Like Me was a remarkable project, but Griffin was a remarkable man. In 1936 he went to France to study at the Lycée Descartes in Tours. He graduated in 1938 and went on to study psychiatry, working as an assistant in an asylum. He worked on experiments using musical therapy to treat the insane, and his research led him to pursue a career in musicology.

At the outbreak of W.W. II, Griffin joined with the Défense Passive, a French organization that helped evacuate Austrian and German Jewish refugees fleeing the Nazis. He was almost caught by the Gestapo but eventually returned safely to America. Once home, he enlisted in the U.S. Army Air Corps and was stationed in the South Pacific. During his tour of duty he studied the ethnology and anthropology of the people of the islands around him. Griffin suffered severe head wounds in a bomber explosion; these later were complicated when the hospital he was in was hit. A a result of these injuries, he began to lose his eyesight in 1946.

Even though partially blind, Griffin resumed his musical studies in France at the Monastery of Solesmes in Sarthe. After earning a *certificat d'études*, he experienced complete loss of vision. He settled on his parents' farm near Fort Worth, Tex. There, at the urging of noted drama critic John Mason Brown, he began to write. His first book, *The Devil Rides Outside*, was a semiautobiographical novel dealing with "the struggle between the spirit and the flesh" of a monastery student. It was banned in some parts of the country and was the subject of an obscenity hearing in the Supreme Court.

Griffin was married in 1953. He later developed spinal malaria and lost the use of his legs for two years. But he continued to write, and his second novel, *Nuni*, was completed in 1956. *Nuni* was again semiautobiographical, the story of an American college professor who crash-lands on a Pacific island inhabited by a primitive tribe. In January of 1957, as he was walking unaided from his workshop to the farmhouse, Griffin suddenly regained his vision after 10 years of blindness. Upon seeing his wife and two children for the first time (he later had two more children) he said, "They are more beautiful than I ever expected. . . . I am astonished, stunned, and thankful."

Shortly afterward Griffin undertook the *Black Like Me* project. Less than a year later he began to suffer bone deterioration and tumors. By 1970 he had undergone 70 operations. But in the interim he worked, lectured, taught, and wrote to correct the racial situation that had so affected him during his weeks as a black man. In 1964 he predicted the "massive and deep bloodshed" that was to come in the black uprisings that soon erupted in cities and towns across the country.

Griffin's failing health slowly forced him to stay closer and closer to home. He kept up his writing, and by the time of his death on Sept. 9,

1980, of diabetes complications he had published several books and numerous shorter works. In one of the last of these he wrote, "I write not because I understand anything and want to expose, but because I understand nothing. . . . I write to seek understanding."

—J.N.

JOE HILL (1879–1915). ***Labor leader and songwriter.***

I dreamed I saw Joe Hill last night,
Alive as you and me.
Says I: "But Joe, you're 10 years dead."
"I never died," said he.

On Nov. 19, 1915, the state of Utah created a legend. It took a penniless migrant worker and turned him into one of the great martyrs of the American labor movement. It achieved this transformation by executing the itinerant songwriter-organizer Joe Hill for a murder he was widely believed not to have committed.

How Joe Hill came to be punished for this crime is one of the more curious stories in American legal history. It began in Sweden, where Joel Emmanuel Haagland was born in 1879. His father was a train conductor whose meager salary supported a wife and nine children. When Joel was eight years old, his father died as the result of a railroad accident and Joel went to work to help support the family, eventually becoming a seaman. After his mother's death in 1902 the family was separated, and Joel and his brother Paul sailed off to a new and better life in America.

An introverted, uneducated man, Haagland apparently had a gift for organizing workers, and he put that talent to use shortly after his arrival in the U.S. He was fired from a job in a Chicago machine shop for attempting to organize his fellow laborers. To escape the blacklist that resulted from the incident, he changed his name to Joseph Hillstrom, which was shortened by his acquaintances to Joe Hill.

For the next few years Hill wandered around the country working at a wide range of jobs. In 1910 he joined the Industrial Workers of the World (the IWW, or Wobblies) a radical organization that had as its goal the destruction of capitalism through a series of general strikes. Hill helped the Wobblies organize workers up and down the West Coast. But his main contribution to the IWW was the songs he wrote for the *Little Red Song Book*, the organization's most effective propaganda tool. Such songs as "Casey Jones—the Union Scab," "Mr. Block," and "The Preacher and the Slave" (which coined the phrase "pie in the sky") inspired workers throughout the country and helped contribute to the growth of Hill's legend.

In 1913 Hill's travels took him to Utah. He was not to leave the state alive because of a murder that occurred in Salt Lake City on Jan. 10, 1914. That particular Saturday night, two armed masked men entered the grocery store of John G. Morrison, who was closing up with his two teenage sons. According to the 13-year-old, the men rushed toward the grocer shouting, "We've got you now." One of the men then shot Morrison, after which his 17-year-old son grabbed a revolver and fired back. Although the younger boy wasn't sure, he thought that one of the assailants had been hit at this point. What he could say with certainty was that his brother's gunfire was returned and that both his father and brother were killed. The men fled without taking anything.

That same night, Joe Hill appeared at the office of a local doctor with a bullet wound. He told the doctor that he had been shot in a quarrel over a woman and that, since he was partly responsible for the incident, he didn't want the authorities brought into it. The physician dressed the wound and sent Hill home. But he had second thoughts about his patient's request for silence, and three days later he told the Salt Lake City police about Hill's visit. The police went to Hill's boardinghouse and arrested him. Four suspects were already in jail when Hill was picked up. However, soon after his arrest they were all released.

The general feeling in Salt Lake City was that the murder of the Morrisons was a crime of revenge. More than once Morrison had been involved in a skirmish with criminals at his store. Additionally, he was a former member of the Salt Lake City police, and a few days before his murder he had stated that he was afraid of being attacked by some of the men he'd arrested. As far as anyone could tell, Hill had never met the grocer. Why, then, did suspicion focus so totally on Hill? Many people who studied the case thought that it was due in part to the anger felt toward the IWW. In Utah the Wobblies had been involved in some very bitter labor disputes, which had triggered intense hostility. Joe Hill's membership in this organization—and the fact that he was from outside the state—didn't enhance his image in the eyes of the local authorities.

The law's attitude toward Hill certainly wasn't rooted in the overwhelming strength of its case. The district attorney in his opening statement at the trial said that his evidence was circumstantial. His major witnesses were Morrison's 13-year-old son and three women who had seen a man resembling Hill near the store at the time of the killings. Not one of these four people, however, had definitely identified Hill as the man seen. Then two of the women significantly altered their testimony from what they had said at the preliminary hearing, somehow becoming far more confident—despite the passage of half a year's time—that the man they had seen was Hill. The state's case had other holes. It was never proved that one of Morrison's assailants had been wounded. Also, the police were unable to find in the store any spent bullets with the capacity to pass through a human body, even though the bullet that had wounded Hill had done just that.

The state's biased case wasn't the only factor working against Hill. What gave his accusers added credibility was Hill's attitude, specifically his consistent refusal to reveal where he was the night of the murders. A number of explanations were possible. Perhaps there really was a quarrel over a woman and Hill was protecting her reputation. (Although he never married, Hill apparently was considered attractive by women, and thus he may have become involved in an explosive situation.) Or perhaps he *was* guilty and decided to become a martyr. Whatever the explanation, he made other mistakes that hurt his case.

During the trial, for example, he stood up one day and attempted to fire the two defense attorneys. Hill thought that they were not aggressive enough in cross-examining the prosecution witnesses and in pointing out the discrepancies between their testimony at the preliminary hearing and their current statements. He contended in court: "I have three prosecuting attorneys here [the district attorney plus his own lawyers] and I intend to get rid of two of them." A compromise was ultimately reached whereby his attorneys remained in the courtroom and questioned witnesses, but Hill conducted some of his own defense. Overall, the jury was not impressed with Hill's behavior.

Despite the unfortunate bickering, Hill might still have been found innocent if the judge hadn't offered a definition of circumstantial evidence that worked against the defense. The judge told the jury that the weakness of individual links in the prosecution's case was not fatal if the general weight of evidence pointed to a guilty verdict. The jury conscientiously followed the judge's instructions, and on June 27, 1914, it found Hill guilty of murder. Two weeks later he was sentenced to death. When the judge gave Joe Hill the option of hanging or facing a firing squad, Hill replied, "I'll take shooting. I'm used to that. I've been shot a few times in the past and I guess I can stand it again."

The appeal process, ultimately unsuccessful, took a year. In that time Hill became a cause célèbre. The IWW, not surprisingly, had been involved in the case since early 1914, picturing their songwriter as an innocent victim of capitalist oppression. As Hill's execution day approached, hundreds of letters and telegrams poured into the governor's office. Since Hill was still a Swedish citizen, the Swedish ambassador became involved. He prevailed upon President Woodrow Wilson to write the governor of Utah, an action that won Hill a temporary reprieve. Before the execution, people as diverse as Helen Keller and American Federation of Labor President Samuel Gompers entered the fray. But Hill's stubborn refusal to reveal how he was wounded doomed him. On Nov. 19, 1915, he was shot by a firing squad.

His legend became a source of inspiration to radical labor movements around the world, and a message he wired to IWW founder "Big Bill" Haywood the night before his execution became a famous slogan. It read: "Don't waste any time in mourning. Organize!"

—E.F.

ROBERT WADLOW (1918–1940). ***Giant.***

Robert Wadlow's brief life is a cautionary tale for any child who daydreams about being a giant. Wadlow is the tallest person in history whose height has been verified. When he died, he was an inch shy of 9 ft. tall, a victim of his own growth.

Wadlow was born in his parents' Alton, Ill., home on Feb. 22, 1918. No one suspected him of being anything but normal. He weighed 8½ lb., and his family had no history of exceptionally tall members. However, his rapid growth began immediately and never abated. At 6 months he weighed 30 lb.; at a year, 44 lb.; at 18 months, 62 lb. His first thorough examination came at age 5, when he stood 5 ft. 4 in. tall and weighed 105 lb. When he entered school at 5½, he was wearing clothes made for 17-year-olds. He reached 6 ft. at age 8, and Wadlow, Sr., was soon wearing *his son's* hand-me-downs. At 10 Wadlow was 6 ft. 5 in., weighed 210 lb., and had to have all his clothes tailor-made. Shoes were a special problem; he occasionally outgrew them before they had been delivered.

It was only when Wadlow was nearing 12 that his rapid growth was diagnosed as excessive pituitary gland secretion. Thereafter the medical school of St. Louis's Washington University kept detailed records of his growth. Wadlow continued to grow about 3 in. every year until he died. He passed 7 ft. before he turned 13, and at 16 was 7 ft. 10½ in.—the tallest person in the U.S. At 19 he became the tallest person ever measured—8 ft. 5½ in. And still he grew. Several weeks before he died, he had reached 8 ft. 11 in.—with a weight of 439 lb., down from his peak of 491 lb.—and his pituitary malfunction might have kept him growing past the age of 30. His early death was probably inevitable since few pituitary giants live past 40. Wadlow was the fastest-growing of them all, so it is not surprising that his death came early. His body simply outgrew its own ability to function properly. The body's organs are not designed to meet the demands of excessive scale. Physical coordination becomes increasingly difficult as size exceeds normal ranges; accidents are frequent, they produce more serious injuries, and the body heals less quickly.

Wadlow's physical problems began early. At two, he was operated on for a congenital double hernia. As he grew older he suffered frequent injuries and serious illnesses. The strain of simply getting along in a normal-sized world was always a problem, and one which accelerated even faster than Wadlow grew. As a 6-ft.-tall 8-year-old he functioned reasonably well in the adult-sized world, but he spent much of his time in school, where he damaged his precarious posture in tiny desks and chairs. By his early teenage years he was outgrowing even the adult world. Everything became too small: furniture, buildings, cars, and anything that he had to use with his hands.

After he had had a series of foot injuries, doctors advised Wadlow to walk a lot to build up his strength; however, walking actually further damaged his arches. Getting around on foot was painful and dangerous. He started attending Shurtleff College in his hometown in hopes of becoming a lawyer, but he dropped out largely because walking between classrooms was too difficult. In the end his foot problems killed him. At 22 he was fitted with an ankle brace. Within a week it had cut into his ankle, causing an infection his overtaxed nervous system failed to detect. By the time the illness was diagnosed, it had advanced too far to halt. He died in Michigan on July 15, 1940.

Wadlow's life was not unrelievably sorrowful. He was intelligent, and he was fortunate in that his parents determined to make his life as normal as possible. He pursued the typical avocations of boyhood: hobbies, sports, Boy Scouts. He was also an avid reader. During his last years he traveled widely throughout the U.S. and mingled with the famous. Despite his inevitable self-consciousness, he impressed every-

Robert Wadlow with his mother, 1939.

one he met with his charm and perceptivity. The unfolding tragedy of his inexorable growth was as obvious to him as to those around him, but he remained cheerful and positive to the end, never giving in to the gloom which typically afflicts pathological giants. His father—the mayor of Alton—became his closest companion and helped him steer his way through the web of publicity which complicated his last years.

The news media weren't aware of Wadlow until he was nine, when the Associated Press discovered his picture in the St. Louis *Globe-Democrat* and circulated his photograph around the country. From that point on, however, Wadlow was a public person, beset by a never-ending stream of journalists, medical researchers, would-be entrepreneurs, and ordinary curiosity-seekers. Each time he celebrated a birthday, newspaper reporters converged on him, and he appeared regularly in newsreels. Theatrical agents pressured him with their lavish offers for his services, but his parents rejected almost every opportunity to cash in on his size. There were two notable exceptions, and both worked out well for him. From the age of 12, Wadlow had had all his shoes specially made by the Peters Shoe Co. of St. Louis. Soon the company was paying Wadlow to wear its shoes and make occasional public appearances. After Wadlow quit college, he traveled more and more for this company, hoping some day to go into the shoe business on his own. Accompanied by his father, he drove more than 300,000 mi. around the U.S. on behalf of Peters Shoes.

In 1937 Wadlow worked briefly for Ringling Brothers Circus in New York and Boston. The conditions of his contract were strict. He made only two 3-minute, center-ring appearances, wearing ordinary street clothes, and he absolutely refused to have anything to do with the sideshow. (He also appeared for churches and charities without recompense.) His only other attempts to profit from his size were selling soft drinks at state fairs during summer vacations and selling autographed pictures to help buy a new pipe organ for the Methodist Church in Alton.

In 1936 a small-town Missouri doctor interested in giantism visited Wadlow to study his condition. The doctor saw him for less than an hour at one of his low points and then published an article in the *Journal of the American Medical Association* which described Wadlow as dull and surly. In order to vindicate his character, Wadlow's family took legal action against the doctor and the journal, but the proceedings dragged on unsatisfactorily until Wadlow's death. The AMA's heavy legal efforts to defend its vituperative member disillusioned Wadlow, who had voluntarily put up with much from doctors all his life. Partly for this reason he wanted his body kept out of the hands of scientists. There was no postmortem examination, and he was buried intact in a custom-built, 10-ft.-long casket in an almost impregnable tomb in his hometown. Over 46,000 people paid their respects at the funeral home.

—R.K.R.

FANNY BULLOCK WORKMAN (1859–1925). ***Traveler and mountain climber.***

A photograph taken in 1912 reveals a great deal about Fanny Bullock Workman. She is dressed with Victorian propriety in a thick skirted costume, sturdy boots, and sun helmet, and she stands—ice ax planted next to her—in the snow on the Silver Throne promontory above the treacherous Siachen Glacier in the trackless wastes of India's Karakoram Mountains near the border of Tibet. In her hand is a newspaper displaying the headline VOTES FOR WOMEN. No other European or American woman ventured into those snowy regions until well after W.W. I. She was ahead of her time, a feminist who believed in athletic liberation but faced "sex antagonism" in her chosen pursuit. For example, the Royal Geographical Society barred women as members—except for a brief period in 1892—until 1913, even though Fanny and others like her were exploring previously uncharted territory.

In 1881 Fanny, a New England blue blood and the daughter of a governor of Massachusetts, married William Hunter Workman, a sober, handsome physician 12 years her elder. The marriage, which appeared to be traditional, was actually much different than the run-of-the-mill upper-class marriage of the time, if only because it was egalitarian.

Three years after their wedding Fanny bore their only child, Rachel, who was cared for by nurses at first and sent to boarding schools in Europe later. In 1888 William, claiming poor health, retired from his practice, and a year later the Workmans were in Europe soaking up culture and climbing the Alps. Then they discovered the bicycle, which

Fanny Bullock Workman in the Himalayas.

by the 1880s had been developed into a safe vehicle. One could travel almost anywhere by bicycle, and the Workmans did. In 1895, carrying her tin teakettle on her handlebars and with heavy Kodak camera equipment in her pack, Fanny set off "awheel" with William on a trip to Algeria, using a steel-cored whip to repel dogs that attacked her skirts and brandishing a gun occasionally to frighten bandits. As with everything, the Workmans shared the writing of their books. Their first two, *Algerian Memories: A Bicycle Tour over the Altas Mountains to the Sahara* and *Sketches Awheel in Modern Iberia,* written with stilted charm, reveal them as adventurous, nature-loving, and snobbish, with a gratuitous sense of Anglo-Saxon superiority. Invited into the living room of an "obese, oily-looking" Spanish woman, they rudely took out their notebooks and started writing when they grew bored.

In 1897 the Workmans sailed to the Far East for a 17,300-mi. bicycle trip through Ceylon, India, Java, Sumatra, and Cochin China (now part of Vietnam). The temperature was fiercely hot, and the terrain rough. They forded rivers, hauled their bicycles through sand, fixed tire punctures—once 40 in one day—and sat up all night on cane couches in railroad stations, "a method of repose which does not serve to relieve fatigue any too well after a hard day's ride."

As a respite from their bicycling, they took a side trip into the Karakoram Mountains, mostly on foot, in the summer of 1898. They fell in love with the "snows." That fall, they tried an expedition into the mountains of Sikkim, but it fell afoul of government delays, late rains, and recalcitrant porters. The Workmans, with their brusque American manners, never learned to deal with Indian servants in the smooth British fashion. They told of a harrowing night on the return journey, trudging in the dark, whipped by a cold wind, down a rain-wet treacherous path which "wound among projecting rocks, was crossed by gigantic tree roots, and was bordered on either side by precipices." Their coolies, carrying supplies, had lagged far behind, and they spent the night sitting up in a primitive cabin. It was during that trip that Fanny fell into a crevasse at Snow Lake and had to be pulled out by ropes, emerging with her hat still on her head. Yet they left with regret, looking back to where, "far within Nepal, Everest, with its giant sister, rose straight and creamy from a lapis lazuli plinth of hill and cloud."

From 1899 to 1912 the Workmans conducted seven expeditions into the Karakoram range and the western Himalayas, about which they wrote five thick mountaineering books. Much of the territory was unmapped. The peaks they scaled were higher than those in Europe, and there were no amenities like alpine huts. Supplies and outfits had to be shipped from Europe. Coolies, porters, guides, assistants, and mapmakers had to be hired. Scientific and photographic projects had to be planned. They split duties. For one expedition, William might take care of ordering and hiring, while Fanny planned scientific and photographic work; for the next, they would switch. They measured altitudes and temperatures, named new peaks, studied glacier movement and structure, recorded the physiological effects of high altitudes, filled in uncharted areas on maps. Sometimes they were wrong. Upon occasion they mistook one peak for another. Nonetheless, their work was immensely valuable to geographers and mountain climbers.

Fanny set a new altitude record for women when, in 1899, she climbed 21,000-ft. Mt. Koser Gunge. On their 1902–1903 expedition to the head of the Chogo Lungma Glacier, she broke her own record by climbing 22,568-ft. Mt. Lungma, and in 1906 on 22,810-ft. Pinnacle Peak in the Nun Kun, she set a record that would last 28 years. The Workmans could claim other records: William set a man's altitude record, and in 1908 they completed the longest ice journey yet made—75 mi.—by traversing the Biafo Glacier and Hispar Pass in the Hunza Nagar region.

In their first mountaineering book Fanny offered advice to women climbers, noting that she was "a slow climber" and "not a light weight." She recommended spending a month in high valleys before braving the thin air at extremely high altitudes. Though she encouraged other women to climb, she was not pleased when Annie Peck, another American climber, claimed she had beaten Fanny's Pinnacle Peak record by conquering Mt. Huascarán in Peru in 1908. In fact, Fanny was so incensed that she financed an expedition to Peru to discredit Peck. Peck's mountain proved to be lower than she had said, and the two women exchanged acerb comments in the pages of *Scientific American*, with Fanny the clear winner.

The Workmans' last expedition, that of the famous "Votes for Women" photograph, took them to the Baltistan and Siachen glaciers in the eastern Karakoram range. In the fall of 1911 they crossed over Bilaphond La, a pass into the Valley of the Siachen. Fanny wrote later: " 'No, I won't come again,' I said as I sat snowed in my tent for two days before returning over the Bilaphond La in September, 1911. But no sooner had I turned my back to the Rose [Siachen] Glacier and reached again the top of the pass on that brilliant September 16th, than my mountain-ego reasserted itself, saying *tant pis* to the obstacles, 'Return you must.' " It was at her instigation that they went back the following year for a triumphant expedition, which she led. Their maps, which they had made with the help of professional mapmakers, were their most accurate yet. During the expedition Chenoz Caesare, an Italian porter, fell to his death in a crevasse right at Fanny's feet. Her reaction, after a period of grief, was typical in its unconscious arrogance: "My own escape from sharing his dire fate was quite miraculous. Those who share the Oriental belief in 'Kismet' might say his passing was fore-ordained, while others, believing in 'survival of the fittest,' might have said that I, having the work to carry on, was, by not taking one step more, and by chance not being roped, saved to accomplish it."

There was little more work to do. W.W. I started, and the Workmans holed up in France. In 1917 Fanny became incurably ill and died eight years later in Cannes. William lived to be 90.

In her will, Fanny left $125,000 to four American women's colleges. Part of this bequest, with some additional money from William, established the Fanny Bullock Workman Traveling Fellowship at Bryn Mawr. Fanny's obituary in the London *Alpine Journal*, written by J. P. Farrar, summed up her character succinctly: "a woman of determination and energy [and] a doughty fighter." One could not, he added, "fail to recognize her warmness of heart, her enthusiasm, her humor, her buoyant delight in doing." Said William in his eulogy: "She was a firm friend and a loyal wife."

—A.E.

U.S. ETHNIC POPULATIONS

Acadians (Cajuns)	820,000
Afghans	2,500
Afro-Americans	25,000,000
Albanians	70,000
Aleuts	1,800
American Indians (173 groups)	
Navaho	160,000
Cherokee	75,000
Sioux	50,000
Chippewa	45,000
Amish	80,000
Arabs	1,000,000
Armenians	400,000
Assyrians	150,000
Australians & New Zealanders	82,000
Austrians	1,000,000
Azerbaijians	200 families
Azoreans	300,000
Bangladeshi	3,500
Basques	75,000
Belgians	130,000*
Belorussians	200,000
Bosnian Muslims	11,000
Bulgarians	70,000
Burmese	70,000
British Canadians	2,000,000
Cape Verdians	300,000
Carpathian Ruthenians	600,000
Central & South Americans	800,000
Chinese	500,000
Copts	85,000
Cossacks	4,000
Croatians	650,000
Cubans	750,000
Czechs	1,000,000
Danes	2,000,000

Group	Number
Dominicans	300,000
Dutch	4,000,000
East Indians	200,000
English	30,000,000
Eskimos	35,000
Estonians	20,000*
Filipinos	450,000
Finns	2,000,000
French	4,000,000
French Canadians	1,500,000
Georgians	1,100
Germans	25,500,000
Germans from Russia	1,000,000
Greeks	1,000,000
Gypsies	500,000
Haitians	300,000
Hawaiians	180,000
Hungarians	2,000,000
Hutterites	6,000
Icelanders	21,000
Indochinese	200,000
Indonesians	10,000
Iranians	75,000
Irish	17,000,000
Italians	8,500,000
Japanese	600,000
Jews	6,000,000
Kalmucks (Mongolian Buddhists)	900
Koreans	275,000
Kurds	750
Latvians	86,000
Lithuanians	1,000,000
Luxembourgers	90,000
Macedonians	50,000
Maltese	70,000
Manx	50,000
Mexicans (Chicanos)	8,000,000
Mormons	1,500,000
North Caucasians	500 families
Norwegians	3,000,000
Pacific Islanders	100,000
Samoans 50,000	
Chamorros 40,000	
Tongans 10,000	
Pakistanis	20,000
Poles	5,500,000
Portuguese	350,000
Puerto Ricans	1,500,000
Romanians	120,000
Russians	1,750,000
Scotch-Irish	8,000,000
Scots	18,500,000
Serbs	250,000
Slovaks	500,000
Slovenes	300,000
South Africans (95% whites)	30,000
Spaniards	1,000,000
Spanish (Mexicanos)	850,000
Swedes	12,000,000
Swiss	220,000
Tatars	5,000
Thais	20,000
Tri-racial Isolates+	200 groups
Lumbees 31,000	
Turkestanis (67% Uzbeks)	150 families
Turks	85,000
Ukrainians	2,000,000
Welsh	150,000
West Indians	315,000

*Represents first- and second-generation group members as counted by the U.S. Bureau of Census. All other figures also include people who are descended from first- and second-generation group members.

+Isolated communities of mixed white, black, and American Indian ancestry, most of whom still live in swamps and inaccessible mountain valleys in the eastern United States. The Lumbees live in Robeson County, N.C. Other groups include the Tennessee Melungeons and the Ramapo Mountain People of New York and New Jersey.

Primary Source: Stephan Thermstrom, editor, *Harvard Encyclopedia of American Ethnic Groups*. Cambridge, Mass: Harvard University Press, 1980.

4

DOLLARS AND SENSE

EXCESSES OF THE RICH

What would you do if you had a million dollars? (After taxes.) This is a question most people have asked themselves at one time or another. But what would you do if you had $20 million, $100 million, half a billion dollars? To dispose of such large sums of money takes a kind of talent—a genius for spending. Neither mere lavishness nor eccentricity can qualify a man or a woman for the ranks of the truly excessive. Before we tell the stories of those who have achieved this distinction, we offer two pieces of advice to the aspiring reader. The first comes from John Jacob Astor I, who said, "A man who has a million dollars is as well off as if he were rich." And Dallas oilman Clint Murchison, Sr., who left his two sons a few hundred million, gave them this advice: "Money is a lot like manure. Pile it all in one place and it stinks like hell. Spread it around, and it does a lot of good."

MRS. ASTOR (1830–1908)

No chronicle of the rich is complete without mention of Mrs. William Backhouse (Caroline) Astor, who married a third-generation Astor, then pompously dropped her forenames and her husband's and was known simply as Mrs. Astor. With social director Ward McAllister as her formidable right hand, she waged war against all other hostesses of the time and won, emerging as the queen bee of society. The most vicious of the battles took place between Caroline and her nephew's wife, Mary Astor, who dared covet the title of *the* Mrs. Astor. Caroline won and so incensed her nephew, William Waldorf Astor, that he and his wife moved to England, stating, "America is not a fit place for a gentleman to live." Before he left, however, William took revenge on his aunt. He tore down the stately mansion he had inherited from his father, John Jacob Astor III, which stood on the northwest corner of Fifth Avenue and Thirty-third Street in New York City, and constructed the 13-story Waldorf Hotel in its place. Since Caroline's mansion was on the southwest corner of Fifth and Thirty-fourth, the heavy traffic the hotel drew disturbed her peace and forced her to move uptown.

Mrs. Astor threw expensive, boring parties with dinners served on a

$75,000 gold service. (After her death, it was discovered that the service was only gold-plated.) Following dinner, Mrs. Astor received her guests from a red silk divan placed on a raised dais, which was simply a modified throne. Mr. Astor rarely attended these parties, escaping instead to his magnificent yacht, the *Nourmahal*.

When Mrs. Astor desired yet another mansion, her husband was mildly irritated by the cost—$1,500,000 for the house, plus $750,000 for the furnishings—but he acquiesced. He died shortly before the structure was completed in 1895, perhaps in an ultimate attempt to avoid his wife's parties.

Mrs. Astor's greatest extravagance was her jewelry collection. She wore emeralds, a diamond necklace worth $60,000 and another worth $80,000, white satin dresses embroidered with pearls and silver, a diamond tiara, and a diamond stomacher that had belonged to Marie Antoinette. Mrs. Astor's impeccable posture was due to the fact that she even wore jewelry down to the waist across her back, which made it painful for her to sit back in her chair.

THE VANDERBILTS

When railroad magnate Cornelius "Commodore" Vanderbilt died in 1877, he left behind $107 million. His son, William H., left $200 million eight years later. At the turn of the century, total Vanderbilt money was estimated at $400 million. So, in 1945, when Gloria Vanderbilt inherited a piddling $4,346,000, the inevitable question was asked: Where did all the money go?

First of all, the Vanderbilts have rightly been called the greatest house-building family in American history. The Vanderbilt wives competed not only with the Astors but also with each other in house building and party throwing. The Commodore's grandson Cornelius II married socialite Alice Claypoole Gwynne; his brother William K. married Southern belle Alva Smith. Cornelius and Alice dropped $10 million into the Breakers, their Newport "summer cottage." The 70-room cottage included a 45-ft.-high hall, a 70-ton front door, and a green marble billiard room. The wrought-iron fence surrounding the Breakers cost $5,000 a year to paint. Inside, guests could choose between salt and fresh water in the bathrooms. The fireplace in the library, with its mantel from Pompeii, cost $75,000.

Alva built Marble House, so named for its white marble driveway and white marble everything. It was modeled after the Temple of the Sun at Baalbek in Lebanon. Here Alva threw a $250,000 costume party that knocked society off its feet. The Vanderbilts gave a distinguished florist, Klunder, carte blanche, and the tab for flowers alone came to $11,000. Although Alice emerged wearing the crown of *the* Mrs. Vanderbilt, William K. and Alva built the most formidable house of all, "Vanderbilt Palace," at 640 Fifth Avenue. It was so lavish as to almost defy description. A team of more than 600 American builders and 250 artisans constructed it in 18 months. The ballroom was a replica of the one at Versailles, and an 8-ft. malachite vase in the house came from the Winter Palace at St. Petersburg. So ultimately expensive was Vanderbilt

Palace that photographs of it were used as models for Tara, Scarlett O'Hara's mansion in *Gone with the Wind*. William K. built himself yet another house on Long Island called Idle Hour. It had 110 rooms plus 45 bathrooms.

Aside from Marble House and Vanderbilt Palace, Alva made another historical purchase. Completely against her daughter's wishes, Alva "bought" her a husband. In one of the most scandalously arranged marriages in history, she literally forced Consuelo Vanderbilt to marry "Sunny," Duke of Marlborough. Consuelo was kept locked in her room the day before the wedding, lest she try to escape and marry the man she really loved (whom her mother had threatened to murder). Consuelo's dowry was $2,500,000 plus funds to restore the Duke of Marlborough's family home.

Beginning with the Commodore, many of the Vanderbilt men had enjoyed yachts. William K.'s yacht had a mechanic to take care of the ice-cream machine. His son, William K. II, built a remarkable yacht in 1931, naming it *Alva* after his mother. It possessed a complete gymnasium and a $60,000 seaplane. The *Alva*'s staterooms were 9 ft. high, and the main living room was 15 ft. high, grandiose dimensions for a mere pleasure boat.

Two tales from John Tebbel's *The Inheritors* may best illustrate what it means to be a Vanderbilt.

> Alice, Cornelius II's wife, was having luncheon one day at the old Ambassador Hotel with her son, Reggie, and his new second wife, Gloria Morgan, when she inquired of the not so freshly minted bridegroom: "Has Gloria received her pearls yet?" He would love to give pearls to Gloria, Reggie answered, but he could not afford the kind he thought worthy of his bride.
>
> "Please bring me a pair of scissors," Alice commanded the maitre d', and when they were produced, she cut off about a third of her own pearls, or roughly $70,000 worth, from the ropes of them that hung around her neck.
>
> "There you are, Gloria," said Alice fondly. "All Vanderbilt women have pearls."

Just as telling is this story about Grace Wilson, who married Cornelius III: "Signing checks one morning which totaled $80,000, Grace casually asked her secretary, 'Do I have this much money?' "

THE ROTHSCHILDS

The name Rothschild connotes riches. These Jewish banking scions rank as one of the wealthiest and most powerful families in history. Overcome with the building mania common to so many of the rich, they competed in producing ostentatious houses, which ranged from the ghastly to the gorgeous as brothers and cousins vied for grandeur.

Baron James built a lavish palace in Paris, where he entertained the likes of Benjamin Disraeli and Heinrich Heine. Heine recalled one visit: "I saw a gold-laced lackey bringing the baronial chamber pot along the corridor. Some speculator from the Bourse, who was passing, reverently

Baron Alfred de Rothschild's English manor—"lavish wealth thrust up your nose."

lifted his hat to the impressive vessel." Baron James later built another palace 25 mi. east of Paris at Ferrières. When William I of Prussia saw it, he said, "Kings could not afford this. It could only belong to a Rothschild."

A certain distinction must belong to Baron Alfred de Rothschild, for the house he built on his father Lionel's 1,400 acres in Halton, England. Visitors to the mansion described it as follows: "Senseless and ill-applied magnificence . . . lavish wealth thrust up your nose! . . . ghastly coarseness." Even Baron Alfred's tea was served in a pretentious manner. A servant would inquire of a guest, "Milk or lemon, sir?" If the guest's reply was milk, he was then asked, "Jersey, Hereford, or Shorthorn, sir?"

ALFRED KRUPP (1812–1887)

Alfred Krupp, the German munitions giant, was the second in a line which the world would come to know as the "merchants of death." Krupp was not an extravagant spender in the usual sense, but like

William Randolph Hearst he had a driving ambition: to immortalize himself by building a great house. Not a mere house, in fact, but a palace, a castle. Krupp himself spent five years designing it, and he built it close to his beloved foundry. What emerged was the Villa Hügel, a perfectly hideous, uncomfortable mansion whose facade sprouted grotesque gargoyles and other weird sculptures.

William Manchester, author of the major book on the Krupps, once attempted to count the rooms in the Villa Hügel, since no reliable estimate existed. Give or take a few secret passages, he counted 300.

Perhaps the one charming aspect of Krupp's creation grew out of his wish to be surrounded by trees. Since the site for the villa stood on a bare hill overlooking a river, Krupp took dramatic measures. As Alan Jenkins wrote in *The Rich Rich:* "Being nearly 60 he could not wait for the saplings to grow. So, many years before tree surgery became a profession, he transplanted a forest of full-grown trees; and such was the force of his will that they budded in their first spring."

JAY GOULD (1836–1892)

The beginning of railway magnate Jay Gould's fortune was reputedly a patented mousetrap. However he began, he went on to connive, cheat, and steal with such ruthless zest that he can truly be labeled the ultimate robber baron. Leaving in his wake countless ruined businessmen, he emerged a multimillionaire. Being primarily interested in money and power, he was a man of relatively few indulgences and left the business of serious spending to his heirs.

However, he did have a few habits which are worthy of mention. He had a weakness for orchids, possessing the largest collection in the world; and for yachts, which culminated in his plush vessel, the *Atalanta*. The *Atalanta*'s staff boasted, among its coterie of French chefs, a Viennese pastry cook whose sole task was to make ladyfingers for Gould, ladyfingers being the only dainty the sickly Gould—on a strict diet—allowed himself. On his railroad car, also named *Atalanta,* he took a private doctor with him at all times. Also accompanying him was a cow—in her own car—whose butterfat content was suited to Gould's ulcerated stomach. But these are trifling matters compared to the one real coup Jay Gould enjoyed with his ill-got gains.

It began when Gould was refused membership in the New York Yacht Club. The blue bloods of this club did not care to have their ranks adulterated by robber baron rapscallions like Gould, no matter *how* rich they were. So Gould started his own organization, the American Yacht Club. However, this was only a portent of things to come.

The "club" that Gould—and many others, such as the Astors, Rockefellers, Morgans, and Vanderbilts—*really* wanted to join was the Academy of Music. It was New York's finest opera house, and the staunchest barricade of elite old money and old snobbery. A box at the academy (and there weren't many) could not be bought at any price. In a great surge of rebellion, Gould joined forces with other snubbed millionaires, and they built the Metropolitan Opera. The box holders at the Met's opening night were said to be worth, collectively, $540 million. In less than two seasons, the academy was ruined and forced to close down.

THE BRADLEY-MARTIN BALL

In February of 1897 Mr. and Mrs. Bradley-Martin of Troy, New York, decided to put themselves on the map. They had moved to Manhattan and had been doggedly social climbing, and now they were ready to go for broke—literally. During a period of serious economic depression, they planned an extravaganza so lavish that it created a major scandal.

The fete was to be a costume party, with each guest representing a historical character, and was to cost in the neighborhood of $200,000. The Bradley-Martins' social secretary composed lyric descriptions of the coming festivities for the newspapers. For example, there were to be "five mirrors on the north side of the ballroom richly but not heavily garlanded in a curtain effect by mauve orchids and the feathery plemusa vine. . . . The profusion of mauve orchids will stream carelessly to the floor, like the untied bonnet strings of a thoughtless child."

While the cream of New York society vied for invitations and began preparing their costumes months in advance, the newspapers and the clergy had a field day. They denounced the Bradley-Martins for spending money frivolously at a time when it might be better used for charitable endeavors. The Bradley-Martins responded to this criticism by pointing out that their ball would "stimulate trade" by giving jobs to out-of-work seamstresses, hairdressers, florists, and other artisans. This rebuttal heightened the controversy, and the upcoming party filled columns of newsprint. One clergyman, deeply affected by the Bradley-Martins' point of view, declared from the pulpit, "The public be damned, let the Bradley-Martins spend their money as they please."

And so they did. The Bradley-Martin ball offered endless culinary delicacies, 6,000 mauve orchids (not to mention the feathery plemusa vine), and 400 carriages to take the guests home. Mrs. Bradley-Martin wore a 20-ft.-long train on her gown, and between $60,000 and $100,000 worth of diamonds (reports varied). However, she was clearly outdone by *the* Mrs. Astor, who sported $200,000 worth of jewels. One London magazine estimated that the ball's feminine revelers used more than 500 lb. of rouge, two and a half flour barrels of powder, and enough powder puffs to make a pile 10 ft. high and 6 ft. wide.

The total cost of the ball was $369,000. Upon discovering this, the New York City tax authority doubled the Bradley-Martins' tax assessment; as a result, the miffed couple left the U.S. permanently for Scotland and England. Oscar Hammerstein I subsequently wrote a farce called *The Bradley-Radley Ball,* and the event is still remembered as one of the most controversial moments in the history of spending.

WILLIAM COLLINS WHITNEY (1841–1904)

William C. Whitney, an American multimillionaire, threw the first gala party after the Bradley-Martin ball to cause a flurry in New York society. He bought a brownstone at 871 Fifth Avenue and proceeded to furnish it in the fashionable manner of the time—by going on a four-year tour of Europe and scouring it for such things as furniture, stained-glass windows, and fireplaces. But he did the average palace-ransacker one better; he imported an entire ballroom from Bordeaux to 871 Fifth Avenue. The room was 63 ft. long and 45 ft. wide and cost $50,000 for the transatlantic shipping. The 500 guests who attended the coming-out party for the ballroom drank 1,200 bottles of vintage champagne. In fact, a fountain gushing the finest champagne became the trademark of Whitney's parties. An excellent host, he retained a domestic staff capable of serving 100 guests at an hour's notice. At one of Whitney's dinners, which cost $20,000, each guest discovered a precious black pearl in one of his or her oysters.

JAMES GORDON BENNETT (1841–1918)

Webster's American Biographies describes James Gordon Bennett as a "publisher, sportsman, and bon vivant." This is a genteel description of the outrageous Bennett, who became rich when he took over his father's newspaper, *The New York Herald,* in 1868. He managed the paper so successfully that he made $1 million a year after taxes (worth at least six times that much in today's currency).

In the annals of the very rich there have been, as we have seen, a number of reckless and extravagant spenders. There have also been a good many wealthy eccentrics. Surprisingly, rarely do the two truly cross. In Bennett is found the best of the breed.

In *The Big Spenders* Lucius Beebe has deliciously described a handful of Bennett's escapades. It would be difficult indeed to improve on Mr. Beebe's selections, so here are some of our favorites in capsule form.

Though a notorious playboy, Bennett became engaged in 1876 to a beautiful socialite, Caroline May, and promised her that he would reform. On New Year's Day, 1877, he attended a party at her family's Manhattan home. Well in his cups, Bennett mistook the fireplace for the toilet, and there relieved himself of some New Year's libations. This faux pas caused such an unspeakable scandal that young Bennett, after fighting a duel with Caroline's brother (both parties intentionally misfired), retired to Paris and environs. Well, not *retired,* exactly—Bennett did nothing in a retiring way.

A wacky, drunk expatriate with money to burn, Bennett became a familiar sight in Paris's best restaurants. Stumbling in pie-eyed, Bennett would walk between the exquisitely laden tables of Maxim's or Voisin, and sometimes pulled hard enough on the surrounding tablecloths to send food, wine, and all crashing to the floor. Then he would command that the costly china, crystal, and food be replaced, send expensive bottles of wine to the tables of the bewildered customers, and order that all cleaning bills be sent to him. After his meal he would offer a wad of bank notes to the restaurant's proprietors, letting them extract what they deemed sufficient.

In 1887 Bennett established the Paris edition of *The New York Herald,* which lost money but gave him power and, one might almost say, prestige. The New York edition, however, was making good money, and with the proceeds Bennett decided to replace his 900-ton yacht

Namouna with a fancier model. The *Lysistrata* was named "for a Greek lady reported to have been very beautiful and very fast." It cost $625,000 to build, the equivalent of over $2 million today. Among many luxuries, it had a full Turkish bath and a 24-hour masseur to ease the publisher's hangovers. Its most customized feature was, according to Lucius Beebe, "a soft padded cell with special seagoing fittings for the ship's cow, an Alderney which . . . supplied the Commodore's table butter and the ingredients for his brandy milk punches at breakfast. An electric fan blew gentle breezes over the cow in tropical climes; the finest of all-wool blankets warmed it in arctic waters." Like Jay Gould's train-traveling bovines, Bennett's cows had to have just the right butter-fat content to suit him.

Though a stingy employer, Bennett could be an ardent tipper. One night he tipped the porter on the Blue Train between Paris and Monte Carlo $14,000. The lucky recipient resigned from his post and opened his own hotel. In a rather different mood, Bennett conducted an interview with a young man who wanted a job on the *Paris Herald*. Throughout their conversation, Bennett appeared to be in physical discomfort, squirming in his seat. Finally he pulled a huge wad of money out of his back trouser pocket and tossed it into the fireplace. Bennett's visitor leapt from his seat, grabbed the thousand-franc notes from the fire, and handed them to the publisher. Throwing them back onto the flames, Bennett snapped, "That's where I wanted them in the first place."

The stories of Bennett's extravagances with the $40 million he spent in his lifetime could go on and on, but there is one in particular that perhaps best illustrates the man.

It begins with Gordon Bennett's passion for a good Southdown mutton chop, for which he searched far and wide. In a small family restaurant in Monte Carlo he found the mutton chop of his dreams. Bennett lunched there daily. But one day he arrived to find his regular terrace table occupied by a large group of drinkers. Bennett had nothing against the consumption of spirits, of course, but he *was* displeased.

He approached the establishment's owner and asked if the restaurant was for sale. He informed the proprietor that he could name his price but that he must sell on the spot. The transaction was completed for $40,000. The drinking party was asked to leave, and Bennett sat down to his mutton chops. After his meal Bennett gave the restaurant to the waiter who had served him—with one provision—that a place be reserved for Bennett each day, and that the mutton chops always be prepared by the same chef. Bennett didn't even know the waiter's name, which, in fact, was Ciro, and three *Ciro's* restaurants were eventually ranked among the world's most famous purveyors of fine European cuisine.

WILLIAM RANDOLPH HEARST (1863–1951)

At the age of 10, little Willie Hearst asked his mother, "When I grow up, Mama, can I live in Windsor Castle?" When told no, he said, "Well then, will you buy me the Louvre?"

Unable to buy or live in either of those institutions, William Randolph Hearst set about producing a facsimile of the two of them combined. San Simeon, his California estate, was the ultimate monument to this attempt.

Hearst inherited $8 million from his father. Putting the money to "good" use, he developed a newspaper-publishing empire founded on a bedrock of yellow journalism. With the immense proceeds from his various ventures, he began his quest for the perfect castle to call home. Listing and detailing all of Hearst's homesteads—most of which he shared with his mistress, actress Marion Davies—would be very time-consuming. It is preferable, then, to limit the descriptions to his major fortresses.

He barely bothered to live in St. Joan, a Long Island château that had belonged to August Belmont. The feature that most intrigued Hearst about the mansion was that it possessed its very own lighthouse.

He preferred St. Donat's, an authentic 11th-century castle on the south coast of Wales. Hearst bought it after seeing a photograph of only one of its rooms, and did not get around to visiting it until three years later, when he stuffed it with antiques and *objets d'art*. He transformed the moat into a croquet lawn. (It was his second house with a moat; the first also had a drawbridge.)

Hearst's mother had once said, "Every time Willie feels bad, he goes out and buys something." He must have felt bad quite often, then, because the accumulation of antiques and *objets d'art* was the ruling passion in Hearst's life, next to Marion Davies. He acquired Charles I's bed, deer antler chandeliers, German armor, mummy cases, prize paintings, and silver—you name it, he bought it. A creative buyer, he even bought a Spanish cloister, sight unseen, for $40,000 and had it dismantled and transported to a warehouse. Unfortunately, it didn't fit into St. Donat's. A Cistercian monastery from Guadalajara wound up being donated to a San Francisco museum because Hearst didn't know what to do with it. In 50 years he spent over $50 million on his art collection alone. If there was not enough room in his houses for some of his 20,000 acquisitions, he stored them in his Bronx warehouses. During his peak buying period of 40 or so years, his purchases represented one quarter of the entire sale of art objects in the world. Hearst also had a pair of plush Rolls-Royces. Each car possessed, proportionately, as many mirrors as Versailles. In the rear, for the passenger, were a duplicate dashboard inlaid in walnut, several built-in thermos bottles, gold vanity cases filled with compacts and combs, a tiny wooden rolltop desk, a miniature table to be pulled out at mealtime, and a portable bar.

But back to the castles. Wyntoon (which Marion disparagingly called Spitoon) was an estate 250 mi. north of San Francisco. Here Hearst built (twice, because once it burned down) a fantasy Bavarian village which could house 60 guests. He gave the chalets names like Bear House, Fairy House, Cinderella House, and Angel House. These he stuffed with cuckoo clocks and other Germanic things, and he strolled about the place in a Tyrolean hat. Marion had a nice little Santa Monica beach house of her own, with 110 rooms plus 55 bathrooms and a 110-ft.-long marble swimming pool.

Then there was San Simeon, which covered over 200,000 acres. Its private zoo housed more than a hundred kinds of animals, including 40 bison. The 6-mi. driveway was lined with signs which read: "Animals have the right-of-way." The Italian gardens were dotted with fountains and statuary. Any time a guest wandering the San Simeon acres wanted a drink, he or she had only to reach for one of the telephones hidden in rocks and trees and place an order. Two acres of cellar underneath the main building housed art objects.

Eventually Hearst fell on troubled times financially and sold nearly two thirds of his art collection. But he had enjoyed his money to the fullest, and had lived true to his motto: "Pleasure is what you can afford to pay for it."

JACKIE AND ARI

When Aristotle Socrates Onassis married Jacqueline Lee Bouvier Kennedy in October, 1968, he took on rather a large expense. Jackie's compulsive spending had caused her first husband to ask a friend, "Isn't there a Shoppers Anonymous?" Jackie complained, "Sometimes the President seems more concerned with my budget than with the budget of the U.S." When the newspapers reported that Jackie had spent $50,000 on clothes alone during her first 15 months in the White House, she retorted, "I couldn't spend that much unless I wore sable underwear." However, this figure was probably accurate. Her spending was uncontrollable, and it drove John Kennedy to distraction.

Aristotle Onassis's Christina *in Monte Carlo harbor.*

If Kennedy was tight by Jackie's standards, at least Ari was no slouch. As an impoverished, uneducated teenager, his first job paid 23¢ an hour. At the time of his marriage to Jackie, the Greek shipping king was worth a minimum of $500 million. He owned a Greek island, Skorpios, as well as houses everywhere and a yacht that may be the most fabulous one in history. This yacht was named *Christina*, after Ari's daughter by his first marriage. Purchased in 1954, the former Canadian frigate was remodeled at a cost variously reported at $2.5 million and $3 million. The *Christina* has baths constructed of Siena marble with gold fixtures, luxurious guest quarters uniquely styled and named after different Greek islands, a lapis lazuli fireplace, two El Greco paintings, 42 phones, teakwood decks, a dry-cleaning plant, a full-sized movie screen, and a seaplane. In the children's playroom, the dolls wore clothes designed by Dior. The yacht's circular bar has its own homey little touches too. The covering for the bar stools is made of whale's testicles, and the footrests on the stools are polished whale teeth. Best of all, there is a mosaic dance floor, a reproduction of a fresco from ancient Crete. Push a button, and the mosaic descends and becomes a swimming pool. In 1971 the *Christina* was estimated to be worth $7 million. Its basic operating costs were $1,140,000 a year. Frank Sinatra, among others, attempted to buy it, but Onassis would not sell. Though Ari was not a big reader, on his desk on the yacht he kept a copy of J. Paul Getty's *How to Be Rich*.

The *Christina* was more or less up to Jackie's standards, and to satisfy these high standards Ari was indulgent with his bride. For a wedding ring he gave her a cabochon ruby "the size of an Easter egg," according to one biographer. Matching earrings were made of heart-shaped rubies surrounded by diamonds. This set cost $1.2 million, not counting a gold bracelet also studded with rubies. A later set of earrings from Ari cost $300,000. For Jackie's 40th birthday, he gave her a 40-carat diamond valued at $1 million. He also gave her a diamond necklace and bracelet costing another million.

Jackie received a set of earrings as a birthday present to commemorate the Apollo 11 mission. Variously reported as a gift from Onassis's jeweler and a gift from Onassis himself, the earrings were unique. In *Jackie Oh!* by Kitty Kelley, they are described for posterity: ". . . a sapphire-studded earth at the ear and a large ruby moon hanging from a chain. The Apollo ship was attached to a thin gold thread which circled the sapphire earth and then dropped to the ruby moon." This trifle cost $150,000. In the first year of their marriage Ari gave Jackie $5 million worth of jewelry. Unfortunately, Jackie could not wear her jewels in the U.S. Since she was an American citizen, bringing them in from Greece would have cost her $1.2 million in duty.

An attentive and adoring husband for the first years of their marriage, Ari made a habit of leaving a little surprise for Jackie on her breakfast tray each morning, even if he was thousands of miles away. Sometimes it was a poem, but more often it was a gold or diamond bracelet. Once she found a string of Japanese cultured pearls wrapped around a roll.

Besides his gifts, Ari happily indulged his wife's spending sprees all over the world. These were no ordinary spending sprees. Free of Jack Kennedy's disapproving glare, Jackie's really heavy binges have been averaged at $300 dollars a minute. Author Fred Sparks has meticulously detailed both Jackie's and Ari's spending in his book *The $20,000,000 Honeymoon: Jackie and Ari's First Year,* which title speaks for itself. Sparks has calculated that this breaks down to $384,615.33 a week. Jackie spent an average of $300,000 a year on clothes, in contrast to the $30,000 a year she spent as First Lady. Neither she nor Ari ever needed to use cash, checks, or credit cards. Their faces sufficed, and Ari received the bills in the mail.

Said Ari, "Jackie can have anything she wants if it makes her happy." Of himself he said, "It's not a question of money. After you reach a certain point, money becomes unimportant. What matters is success. The sensible thing would be for me to stop now. But I can't. I have to keep aiming higher and higher—just for the thrill." And finally, Jackie on Ari: "Ari *never* stops working. He dreams in millions."

THE SHAH'S PARTY

In October of 1971, the late Shah of Iran threw a little bash. The occasion was officially the 2,500th anniversary of the founding of the Persian Empire. The party was also given as "a sign to the rest of the world that Iran is again a nation equal to all the others—and much finer than many." To this end, the shah constructed a well-guarded "tent city" in Persepolis—three enormous "tents" (they were more like mini-buildings) and 59 smaller ones, constructed on a 160-acre area. The 500 guests included Emperor Haile Selassie of Ethiopia, Marshal Tito of Yugoslavia, Princess Grace and Prince Rainier of Monaco, Vice-President Spiro Agnew, nine kings, five queens, sixteen presidents, and two sultans, among others. The shah had commanded "something out of the Arabian nights," and he got it.

The prestigious Jansen of Paris decorated the air-conditioned tents (they had helped Jackie Kennedy redo the White House), which contained Baccarat crystal, Limoges china, Porthault linens, intercoms, Persian carpets, and bidets. These interiors did not live up to the rumors that had preceded them, however; there was no 18th-century French furniture, and only the shah had a marble bathtub.

Despite these inconveniences, the guests managed to enjoy themselves. There were French hairdressers available, armed with 300 wigs and 240 lb. of hairpins. Maxim's of Paris provided 165 chefs and ample refreshments, including 25,000 bottles of wine that were sent to Iran a month in advance to rest. The guests were fed 7,700 lb. of meat, 8,000 lb. of butter and cheese, and 1,000 pints of cream. Among the dishes flown in from Paris by Maxim's were quail eggs and caviar, partridge with foie gras and truffle stuffing, and filet of sole stuffed with caviar. The chefs also boasted that they could whip up and deliver to a tent any dish that anybody wanted; the Sultan Qabus bin Said of Oman ordered and got caviar and kebab.

Some of the guests behaved as regally as they were expected to. Frederick IX of Denmark and Queen Ingrid decided to go "out" for lunch. They walked from their tent to the curb, where a Rolls-Royce was waiting to drive them 500 ft. to the club tent. Nearby, Emperor Haile Selassie, who had arrived with an entourage of 72 rather than an expected 5 guests, gracefully walked his chihuahua Chicheebee, who wore a diamond-studded collar.

In his welcoming speech, the shah said, "Each one of us must try as hard as possible, as much as circumstances allow, to turn the world into one of love, peace, and cooperation for mankind, a world in which every person may enjoy the full amenities of science and civilization." At a time when the per capita income in Iran was $350 a year, the Shah's week-long "Disneyland-in-the-desert," as journalists called the party, cost $100 million.

THE UNITED STATES GOVERNMENT

Based on the $580 billion final budget for 1980, the federal government is spending over one and a half billion dollars a day, or more than 1 million dollars a minute.

—A.W.

MISERABLE MISERS

The Penurious Parliamentarian: JOHN ELWES (1714–1789)

"A name which has become proverbial in the annals of avarice" is how John Elwes was described 150 years ago. The epitaph was not completely fair, however. In self-denial he stood alone, but to others he was often generous to a fault. Elwes's fame as a miser undoubtedly arose from the attention his public life drew to him.

He was born into a respectable English family, received a good education in the classics, and was even something of a socialite during his early life. He was known as one of the best riders in Europe. He inherited his first fortune from his father, a brewer, who died when Elwes was four. Although his mother was left £100,000, she reputedly starved herself to death.

The greatest influence on his life was his miserly uncle, whom Elwes obsequiously imitated to gain favor. The two of them would spend the evening railing against other people's extravagances while they shared a single glass of wine. When Elwes inherited the uncle's entire estate, his net worth was around £500,000, a figure that continued to grow despite Elwes's inept handling of his finances. On assuming his uncle's property, Elwes also assumed his uncle's frugal ways. He wore only ragged clothes, including a wig he found in a gutter. To avoid paying for a coach he would walk in the rain, and then sit in wet clothes to save the cost of a fire to dry them. He so hated to waste anything that he would eat putrefied game before allowing new provisions to be acquired. On one occasion he ate a moorhen that a rat had pulled from a river. In common with many misers, he distrusted physicians, preferring to treat himself in order to save their fees. Elwes's only indulgence was a pack of excellent foxhounds.

Elected to Parliament in 1772 as a compromise candidate, he began the first of three terms. He sat with either party according to his whim, and he never rose to address the House. Fellow members mockingly observed that since Elwes possessed only one suit, they could never accuse him of being a turncoat. After 12 years he retired rather than face the prospect of laying out cash to retain his seat. In the meantime he lost huge sums of money to his colleagues in unrepaid loans, uncollected debts, and dubious investments. He believed that one did not ask a gentleman for money, regardless of the circumstances.

When his parliamentary career was over, he devoted his full energies to being a miser as he moved about among his many properties. At his neglected estates he forbade repairs, joined his tenants in postharvest gleaning, and sat with his servants in the kitchen to save the cost of a fire elsewhere. If a stableboy put out hay for a visitor's horse, Elwes would sneak out and remove it. In his last years he had no fixed abode and frequently shifted his residence between his unrented London properties. The practice nearly cost him his life when he fell desperately ill in one of these houses. No one knew where he was, and only by chance was he rescued.

Elwes had two sons out of wedlock, whom he loved but would not educate. He believed that "putting things into people's heads is the sure way to take money out of their pockets." He did, however, fill their pockets. After having lived on only £50 a year, he left half a million pounds to his sons.

The Perfect Miser: DANIEL DANCER (1716–1794)

Though his countryman Elwes was more famous, Daniel Dancer was a more accomplished and thoroughgoing miser, perhaps because his family set him such a good example. His grandfather and father had been noted misers, and his sister and two brothers were almost equally niggardly. After inheriting the whole of his father's estate in 1736, Dancer had an income of over £3,000 a year, but his sole occupation was hoarding his wealth.

For 30 years Dancer's sister served as his housekeeper, stretching meager Sunday meals with a handful of hard dumplings, which fed them both for the rest of the week. Occasionally Dancer got lucky, such as the time he found a partly decomposed sheep, which his sister transformed into a two-week supply of meat pies. The stench from such cuisine probably eluded Dancer, for he did not bathe, wash his clothes (which he wore until they disintegrated), or allow his house to be cleaned. He let his fields go fallow while he occupied himself with scrounging the countryside for bits of firewood, bones, and cow dung, with which he stuffed his pockets. No expenditure was too slight to be avoided. He obtained an occasional candle by swapping snuff he mooched a pinch at a time. Once a friend sent him a meal, but it congealed in the cold weather. After agonizing over how to reheat the dish without the use of a fire, Dancer placed the food between pewter plates and sat on the top one like a laying hen. He was also alert to the danger of even potential expenditures. A pet dog was his sole indulgence, but he worried about being sued if the dog should get at neighbors' livestock. He eliminated this danger by having the dog's teeth knocked out.

Despite his reputation for meanness, Dancer was credited with great integrity and an aptitude for showing his gratitude. However, his gratitude did not extend to his sister, whom he allowed to die without benefit of medical treatment, which he reasoned would only be a wicked attempt "to counteract the will of Providence." He filled her place in his household with an old servant he paid 18 pence a week (less than £4 a year)—a meager wage but enough for the servant to live more comfortably than Dancer himself.

The classic miser, Dancer lived in constant fear of thieves, who were aware that he hoarded money. Indeed, he was frequently robbed, and he combatted the problem by stashing his money in odd places. After he died, searchers turned up money caches everywhere, even in a dung heap, where they found £2,500.

Honored by a Queen: JOHN CAMDEN NEILD (1780–1852)

In contrast to the many misers who inherited their penny-pinching ways from their forebears, John Camden Neild was the son of a prosperous English goldsmith noted for his philanthropy. Neild received a fine liberal education and was expected to follow his father's beneficent example after he inherited the whole of his £250,000 estate in 1814. However, Neild's sole interest was increasing his fortune, which he doubled before he died. He did everything possible to avoid spending money. His huge house was so poorly furnished that for a time it lacked even a bed. He dressed in rags, refusing to have his clothes brushed for fear of ruining the nap, and he wouldn't wear an overcoat in even the severest weather. He quibbled over every expenditure, however small, and mooched meals and lodging from the tenants of his vast estates in Buckinghamshire. As estate owner he couldn't escape his responsibility for maintaining the church at North Marston, so he had the leaky lead roof resurfaced with calico.

Death rescued Neild from obscurity when it was learned that he had left his entire fortune to Queen Victoria. Victoria increased Neild's meager bequests to his executors and provided for the servants he had forgotten. She also restored the North Marston church properly and had a stained-glass window installed as a memorial to Neild. This distinction earned Neild a place in England's *Dictionary of National Biography,* which courteously described him as simply an "eccentric."

The Witch of Wall Street: HETTY GREEN (1835–1916)

A harsh New England Quaker upbringing taught Hetty Green (née Robinson) the virtues of thrift and self-denial, and her close study of her prosperous family's whaling business and investments taught her the intricacies of finance. Missing from her education, however, were lessons on how to enjoy the vast wealth she was destined to accumulate.

Her father applauded her thrift when she dressed in rags. Although she grew into a voluptuous young woman with an exquisite complexion, she continued her slovenly ways. One potential suitor noted that his ardor quickly cooled when he caught sight of mismatched stockings hanging down around her ankles. As for Hetty, she considered all men fortune hunters.

Hetty came into her own at 30. Her father's death left her a million dollars outright, as well as the income from several million more, the principal of which was to pass on to her children. Soon thereafter she inherited the income from another million dollars, half of an aunt's estate. Hetty was outraged at not receiving the whole thing. She considered the entire estate rightfully hers and spent years trying to break the will. She finally dropped the case when she was accused of forging a document in her aunt's name. Hetty's wrath was increased by a provision in the will calling for the distribution of the principal among relatives on her own death. Visions of greedy relatives awaiting her death made it impossible for Green to relax, for fear of assassination.

In 1867 Hetty married 46-year-old Edward H. Green, a millionaire in his own right. Although Green was wildly extravagant in comparison with his wife, they seemed genuinely happy together. Soon they had two children. Drawing upon her husband's financial expertise, as well as her own sound judgment, Hetty invested in railroads, U.S. gold, bonds, and real estate and quickly doubled her father's fortune. During her peak income years (which were many), she earned enough money in an hour or two to pay all her living expenses for a year. And during the rest of the year she kept on earning money at the same furious rate, 24 hours a day. The surplus she reinvested and hoarded. Her formula for getting rich was simple: "All you have to do is buy cheap and sell dear, act with thrift and shrewdness and be persistent."

Hetty followed her own advice to extremes, particularly the admonition to thrift. As her biographers wrote, "In the spending of money she might have been compared to an athlete who never broke training." A classic miser, she hated to spend a nickel on anything if she could avoid it. When a druggist explained that a bottle of medicine cost 10¢ because the bottle cost 5¢, Green went home to fetch her own bottle. She lived in the simplest hotels, traveled by the cheapest conveyances, ate at the dingiest restaurants, dressed in old clothes, and often washed her own garments in her hotel rooms. After reading the morning paper, she would send her son downtown to resell it.

Green's very wealth ruined her life. Aside from her fear of assassination, she fretted over the possibility of forgers' cleaning out her bank accounts, and she suspected almost everyone with whom she dealt of trying to take advantage of her because she was rich. Therefore, she often feigned poverty, had friends do her shopping, and buttonholed professional people (particularly lawyers) on the street for free advice. When her son was 14, he dislocated his kneecap in a sledding accident. Green first tried to nurse the boy herself, then donned pauper's clothing to present him to a doctor as a charity patient. The leg was eventually amputated—an operation one doctor said could have been avoided if the boy had been treated properly from the start.

Green's eccentricities made her a legend in her own time. She moved frequently from one cheap hotel to another (a practice that helped make it impossible for New York State to prove her a legal resident when her estate was settled), transacting her affairs from the vaults and spare desks of the banks in which she stored her money, papers, and even parts of her dismal wardrobe.

Hetty and her husband separated in 1885 after he committed the unpardonable sin of losing all his money and accumulating debts which she was expected to make good. Although she maintained thereafter that he was absolutely useless and a burden to her, she never lost her affection for him. After his death in 1902 she wore only black—attire which contributed to her nickname, the Witch of Wall Street.

In 1916 Green was the houseguest of a friend whose extravagant spending she relentlessly criticized. Her host ignored her remarks, but the servants were outraged by her rudeness. One day the cook got drunk and told Green off. The verbal blast caused Hetty to have a stroke. She died a few months later. Most of her estimated $100 million estate was split between her children. Her son is reputed to have spent his share on such pleasures as private yachts, teenage girls, and diamond-studded chamber pots. He went through his inheritance at the rate of $3 million a year, making him as great a spender as his mother was a miser.

The Hermits of Harlem: HOMER COLLYER (1881–1947) AND LANGLEY COLLYER (1885–1947)

The discovery, in March, 1947, of Homer Collyer's dead body in the rubble-filled three-story home he had shared with his brother in a once fashionable section of Harlem fascinated New Yorkers. Blind and paralyzed, the former admiralty lawyer had starved to death amidst so much debris that police spent several hours just getting into the house. Neighbors crowded around, hoping for a glimpse of the millions of dollars the legendary Collyer brothers had reputedly stashed away. Official investigators were concerned with another question: Where was Langley Collyer, the former engineer and concert pianist?

The reclusive Collyers had lived in their house since their beloved mother had separated from their father, a wealthy and well-known doctor, in 1909. When the mother died 20 years later, the brothers abandoned their careers completely and grew even more reclusive, allowing all the utilities to be shut off. Homer went blind a few years later and became paralyzed around 1940. He never saw a doctor and was completely dependent on Langley, who thought he could cure Homer's blindness by feeding him 100 oranges a week. Homer never again emerged from the house alive, but Langley was constantly active. He cooked on a kerosene stove, fetched water from a park four blocks away, and roamed the streets at night foraging for food and supplies. Obsessed with a fear of burglars, Langley barricaded the house's doors and windows (how *he* got in and out remains a mystery) and piled up

Langley Collyer unsuccessfully attempting to evade photographers.

mountains of debris inside as barriers and booby traps. Police found the house honeycombed with narrow crawl spaces he must have negotiated like a mole.

While police mounted an interstate search for Langley, sanitation officers slowly cleared away the house's clutter. Working from the basement up, they removed 120 tons of material in the several weeks it took them to reach the second floor, where Homer had died. The news media reveled in the catalog of discoveries: 14 grand pianos, the chassis of a Model-T Ford, old toys, boxes of rotting clothes, thousands of books, bicycles, sewing machines and dressmakers' dummies, a coil of barbed wire, unopened mail, 34 bank books (totaling only $3,007), an arsenal of modern and archaic weapons, the jawbone of a horse, machinery, scrap iron, heaps of coal, two 7-ft. sections of a tree, and endless other items which Langley must have dragged home from back alleys and garbage cans. Dominating the whole mess were tons of newspapers Langley was saving for Homer to read when he regained his sight.

Finally, just 10 ft. from where Homer had been found, officials uncovered the rat-gnawed body of Langley. He had been crushed by one of his own booby traps while crawling through a tunnel to feed Homer. No millions were found, but the Collyers' attorney valued their total property at over $100,000, and scores of relatives appeared to stake their claims.

—R.K.R.

OG MANDINO'S 10 GREATEST HOW-TO-SUCCEED BOOKS

Og Mandino, former executive editor and president of *Success Unlimited* magazine, is the author of *The Greatest Salesman in the World* and *The Greatest Miracle in the World*, two how-to-succeed books that together have sold more than 6 million copies in 17 languages. His other works include *The Gift of Acabar* and *The Christ Commission*.

1. *THINK AND GROW RICH* (1936) by NAPOLEON HILL

Fountainhead of nearly every how-to-succeed book published during the past four decades, Hill's classic, inspired by Andrew Carnegie, who disclosed his secrets of personal achievement to the author, has outlasted several of its publishers, with estimates of total copies printed ranging between 10 and 20 million. "Anybody," Hill wrote, "can wish for riches, and most people do, but only a few know that a definite plan plus a *burning desire* for wealth are the only means of accumulating wealth." Hill's "Thirteen Steps to Riches" provide a working blueprint for anyone willing to pay the price in time and effort. All of today's self-help authors owe Napoleon Hill an incalculable debt. Available in hardcover (Hawthorn Books) and paperback (Fawcett Books).

2. *AS A MAN THINKETH* (1903) by JAMES ALLEN

"Into your hands will be placed the exact results of your own thoughts; you will receive that which you earn; no more, no less. Whatever your present environment may be, you will fall, remain, or rise with your thoughts, your vision, your idea. You will become as small as your controlling desire; as great as your dominant aspiration. . . ." This British professor of languages produced scores of poems, novels, and short stories, but his fame is assured by this single brief essay, which has affected countless lives. "A man is literally *what he thinks*, his character being the complete sum of all his thoughts." Available in numerous editions.

3. *AUTOBIOGRAPHY OF BENJAMIN FRANKLIN* (1868)

Perhaps America's first and greatest success story, Franklin's chronicles of his struggles to overcome serious defects in his personality make fascinating reading for anyone wishing to change his or her life for the better. Franklin was not blind to his own bad habits, traits that he realized were impeding his development and progress. He finally developed a plan to rid himself of them: "I made a little book, in which I allotted a page for each of 13 virtues. I ruled each page with red ink, so as to have seven columns, one for each day of the week, marking each column with a letter for the day. I crossed these columns with 13 red lines, marking the beginning of each line with the first letter of one of the virtues, on which line, and in its proper column, I might mark, by a little black spot, every fault I found upon examination to have been committed respecting that virtue upon that day." Franklin's system still works. Available in countless editions.

4. *HOW TO WIN FRIENDS AND INFLUENCE PEOPLE* (1936) by DALE CARNEGIE

Now past its 10 million-copy milestone with 117 printings, Dale Carnegie's marvelous handbook on dealing with our fellow man is must reading for anyone with ambition to improve his or her life. No one succeeds alone, and our progress up that ladder of achievement is usually measured by our ability to get along with and influence others to do what *we* want them to do. "There is only one way under high heaven to get anybody to do anything. Did you ever stop to think of that? Yes, just one way. And that is by making the other person want to do it. Remember there is no other way." Available in hardcover (Simon & Schuster) and paperback (Pocket Books).

5. *THE POWER OF POSITIVE THINKING* (1952) by NORMAN VINCENT PEALE

Dr. Peale's "positive thinking" message has survived those not so happy "happy days" of our first postwar decade and still sustains countless thousands every day. "The secret," he maintains, "is to fill your mind with thoughts of faith, confidence, and security. This will force out or expel all thoughts of doubt, all lack of confidence." Available in hardcover (Prentice-Hall) and paperback (Fawcett Books).

6. *THE RICHEST MAN IN BABYLON* (1955) by GEORGE CLASON

In 1926 George Clason issued the first of a famous series of pamphlets on thrift and financial success, using parables set in ancient Babylon. These were distributed by banks and insurance companies and finally collected into a book which has no equal in the art of acquiring wealth. Clason's advice, in the parable from which the book title was taken, is a good example of this book's wisdom: "Remember that a part of all you earn is yours to keep. Take whatever portion seems wise but let it be not less than one-tenth and lay it aside. Then, make your treasure work for you. Make it your slave. Make its children and its children's children work for you. Invest your treasure with greatest caution. Counsel with wise men. Let them save you from error. Enjoy life while you are here. Do not overstrain or try to save too much. Let not yourself get niggardly and afraid to spend. Life is good and life is rich with things to enjoy." Available in hardcover and paperback (Hawthorn Books).

7. *YOUR GREATEST POWER* (1953) by J. MARTIN KOHE

"You are the possessor of a great and wonderful power. This power, when properly applied, will bring confidence instead of timidity, calmness instead of confusion, poise instead of restlessness, and peace of mind in place of heartache." What is your greatest power? *The power to choose.* Available in hardcover (Success Unlimited).

8. *PSYCHO-CYBERNETICS* (1960) by MAXWELL MALTZ

Psycho-Cybernetics broke new ground in showing us how our success mechanisms work. Dr. Maltz's experiments in the regrowth of injured tissues disclosed a little-known side effect of plastic surgery: its influence on the human personality and its altering of one's self-image. Change the self-image and the individual is imbued with new capabilities, new talents, and the ability to literally turn failure into success. He went beyond his own patients to study scores of average individuals struggling through life with negative attitudes. Available in hardcover (Prentice-Hall) and paperback (Pocket Books).

9. *THE SUCCESS SYSTEM THAT NEVER FAILS* (1962) by W. CLEMENT STONE

At the age of six he was fighting to survive on the streets of Chicago, peddling newspapers. "Years later," W. Clement Stone wrote, "I used to think of that little boy, almost as if he were not me but some strange friend from long ago. Once, after I had made my fortune and was head of a large insurance empire, I analyzed that boy's actions in the light of what I had learned." Stone's conclusions, that there were three necessary ingredients for success, are the essence of this classic. These three qualities—inspiration to action, know-how, and activity—can be acquired by anyone regardless of his or her current environment, age, color, occupation, or education. "Success," he explains, "is achieved by those who try and keep trying." Available in hardcover (Prentice-Hall) and paperback (Pocket Books).

10. *HOW I RAISED MYSELF FROM FAILURE TO SUCCESS IN SELLING* (1949) by FRANK BETTGER

The ultimate book on salesmanship, whether you're trying to sell an automobile, an insurance policy, your talents, or your charming personality. Bettger's hustle and enthusiasm brought him from the bush leagues to playing third base for the St. Louis Cardinals until one day, while fielding a swinging bunt, something snapped in his arm and his athletic career came to an immediate halt. How he applied his enthusiasm to a new career in selling, until he became the top insurance salesman in the nation, makes this must reading for anyone pursuing the goddess called success. Dale Carnegie called the book's first chapter, "How One Idea Multiplied My Income and Happiness," one of the most inspiring he had ever read on the power of enthusiasm. Available in hardcover (Prentice-Hall) and paperback (Cornerstone).

—Exclusive for *The People's Almanac #3*

6 CURRENT CASH REWARDS THAT YOU MIGHT WIN

1. FOR BALD-EAGLE KILLERS

The Illinois Wildlife Federation offers a standing reward of $500 for information leading to the arrest and conviction of anyone who has killed a bald eagle in that state. As of November, 1980, no one has claimed it. (To claim reward, contact: Illinois Wildlife Federation, 13005 Western Avenue, Blue Island, Ill. 60406.)

2. FOR THE REMAINS OF BIGFOOT

Project Bigfoot in Seattle, Wash., has posted an offer of $1,000 for any verifiable remains, such as the skull, hair, teeth, or bones, of a Bigfoot. The creature, also known as Sasquatch, is described as a 7-ft., 400-lb. giant who inhabits the Pacific Northwest. Local residents have reported sightings of it over the past 160 years. The money has never been collected. (Contact: Project Bigfoot, P.O. Box 444, North Gate Station, Seattle, Wash. 98125.)

3. FOR DELIVERY OF ENEMY WEAPONRY

The People's Republic of China will give as much as $4 million in gold for Taiwanese military craft and weapons. At last report, a person showing up on the mainland with a destroyer in tow will be paid a full $4 million. Other rewards include $2 million for a submarine, $1.4 million for an F-5E jet, and a mere $14,000 for a C-47. Taiwan offers similar rewards. In 1977 a pilot who defected from China received $800,000 in gold for his MIG-19 and military information. (Contact: People's Republic of China Liaison Office, 2300 Connecticut Avenue, Washington, D.C. 20008 or Government Information Office, 3 Chung Hsiao East Road, Section 1, Taipei, Taiwan 100, Republic of China.)

4. FOR INFORMATION LEADING TO THE INDICTMENT OF BANK ROBBERS

Under its "rat on a rat" program, the Washington State Bankers Association pays $1,000 for information leading to the arrest and indictment of a bank robber. Bank employees and law-enforcement officials are ineligible. (Contact: Washington State Bankers Association, 1218 Third Avenue, Suite 505, Seattle, Wash. 98101.)

5. FOR THE CAPTURE OF A UFO

Cutty Sark, the whiskey manufacturer, has offered £1 million to anyone who captures a spaceship or other vehicle that the Science Museum of London can verify as having come from outer space. "We're very serious about this," says the director of the firm, which has taken out several thousand pounds' worth of insurance with Lloyd's of London against paying the reward. BUFORA, the British Unidentified Flying

Object Research Association, rates the chances of someone's collecting as nil. (Contact: Cutty Sark, 3 St. James Street, London SW1, England.)

6. FOR A WORLD CHESS CHAMPION COMPUTER

The Fredkin Charitable Foundation of Boston, Mass., has established a $100,000 reward for the first computer program to defeat the world chess champion. An eminent professor in the computer science field admits that not until 1990 is there even a "50-50 chance" that a computer could become the chess champion of the world.

—B.F. and the Eds.

UNUSUAL COLLECTIONS

BARBED WIRE

Collector: Jesse S. James, Maywood, Calif.

An Illinois farmer named Joseph F. Glidden invented the first practical barbed wire. When it was introduced in 1874 to protect ranchers' crops and animals, it was greeted with rage by many. It inspired bitter feuds when land boundaries were disputed. However, by the time a decade had passed, the concept of the open range had begun to change, and 120 million lb. of barbed wire were being sold each year.

Since 1957 Jesse James has meticulously categorized and arranged his antique barbed wire specimens on six 1½-by-3-ft. panels, each containing 30 pieces which are 18 in. long. Along with the barbed wire, James has a collection of splices made with rare old wires. James has written a book on barbed wire—*Early U.S. Barbed Wire Patents*—which has also become somewhat of a collector's item now that it is out of print.

BEER CANS

Collectors: Peter and Arthur Ressel, St. Louis, Mo.

The Beer Can Collectors of America (BCCA) have a motto: "Don't kick the can." After all, it may be a collector's item.

Peter and Arthur Ressel (father and son) have a miscellaneous collection of over 5,000 different beer cans. The foreign and domestic cans range in size from 7 oz. to 5 liters. The Ressels find their hobby graphically interesting as well as inexpensive.

One of their favorite cans is from 1934. The Krueger Beer Company of Richmond, Va., test-marketed an unnamed prototype which was sent to the breweries to promote the concept of canned beer. The Ressels' 1934 "Brewer Test Can" has never been opened. It took 35 years for canned beer to surpass bottled beer in yearly sales.

BOARD GAMES

Collector: Sid Sackson, New York, N.Y.

Childhood elicits memories of intriguing and challenging games such as *Scrabble, Monopoly,* and *Parcheesi,* among many others. Unfortunately, these games are slowly fading into the background as the fascination with electronic gadgetry brings us video games on home computers.

A traditionalist at heart, Sid Sackson has the largest and most extensive private collection of games in the world. The collection is limited (with very few exceptions) to games that can be played at a bridge table. It totals approximately 50,000 games; nearly half of them are playable, and the remainder are in the form of complete reproductions of equipment and rules. Three whole rooms of Sackson's home are piled from floor to ceiling with his collection. He also has a library of 1,000 game books in 13 languages and over 2,000 magazines.

Sackson has always loved games. He uses his collection as a reference library, inventing and selling his own games to well-known companies such as Milton Bradley and Parker Bros.

BOTTLE CAPS

Collector: Danny Ginsburg, Rancho Palos Verdes, Calif.

The only criterion for Danny Ginsburg's collection is that each bottle cap must have grooved edges—no twist tops allowed.

Ginsburg estimates that his collection numbers around 250,000, but it is growing rapidly at almost 3,000 a month. He has caps from over 35 countries and 800 cities on every continent except Africa and Antarctica.

One of the more unusual caps he has seen includes both a saccharin health warning and a "Kosher for Passover" label written in Hebrew.

DIONNE QUINTUPLET MEMORABILIA

Collectors: Fay and Jimmy Rodolfos, Woburn, Mass.

The birth of quintuplets to Oliva and Elzire Dionne in rural Ontario, Canada, on May 28, 1934, was a human interest story all over the world. The birth was considered something of a miracle, since the quints were the only identical set of quintuplets that had ever survived. Elzire was 25 years old at the time of their birth and had already given birth to six children, the youngest only 11 months old. She had no prenatal care whatsoever until a week before the birth. The first three girls had been delivered by two midwives by the time the doctor arrived to deliver two more girls. A wicker basket was used to hold the babies, who weighed a total of 10 lb., 5½ oz.

Although the quintuplets were always pictured as happy children completely removed from any of life's normal problems, underneath that facade lay a sad story that the public was not aware of. Their exploitation resulted in a rather tragic adulthood for them. Two are already dead. Their mother still lives very close to the place where the quintuplets were born.

Fay and Jimmy Rodolfos have one of the finest collections of Dionne memorabilia in the world. It includes all types of souvenir items—"Famous Five" dolls, postcards, scrapbooks, newspaper and magazine articles, photos, paper dolls, and much more. It all began when they added a set of Dionne dolls to their baby-doll collection. After some

A Dionne Quintuplet lamp from the collection of Fay and Jimmy Rodolfos.

preliminary research, they "were hooked with 'Dionne Quint fever' " and have been collecting ever since.

DREAMS

Collector: Elizabeth Lowe, Middleton, Wis.

Everyone dreams approximately 1,500 dreams a year. Elizabeth Lowe, a librarian and owner of a small mail-order publishing house, is currently assembling "a people's collection of dreams." Lowe has over 2,500 dreams, including her own, which she has been collecting for over 16 years. She eventually hopes to publish an uninterpreted collection, with the dreamers identified only by age and gender. All types of dreams will be included, from the ordinary to the bizarre. Lowe runs ads in newspapers and journals asking people to send her their dreams for her collection. She leaves the interpretation up to the dreamer. Write to Lowe at: Dreams Unlimited, P.O. Box 247, Middletown, Wis. 53562.

One of Lowe's favorite recurring dreams is her own. In it a miniature elephant frolics in her bathtub, making a glorious mess.

MACK TRUCKS

Collector: R. S. "Dick" Kemp, Hillsboro, N.H.

Equipment operator Dick Kemp is the proud owner of over 90 old trucks (mostly Mack) that date back as far as 1916. One 1916 Selden with wooden spokes was once used as a street sprinkler.

Kemp began his collection in 1952 with a 1930 Bulldog Mack which he bought for $50. Only 63 Mack trucks were built in 1947, and he owns 2 of them.

Kemp, a bachelor now 50 years old, has spent his entire life in the house he was born in on the Contoocook River. His father taught him to drive a truck at the age of 14, and he was doing it for a living by the time he was 16.

Visitors come from all over the U.S. and Canada to see Kemp's collection, which is exhibited in a large garage nearby and in a yard next door. He has received countless offers to sell his trucks, but his answer is always the same: "Nothing for sale." He does all his own restoration work ("I just get them so they run and look half decent").

Kemp's Mack Truck Museum is free to all visitors during daylight hours "as long as they don't destroy."

NAILS

Collector: Frank C. Horwath, Joliet, Ill.

At the age of 14, Frank Horwath began collecting nails while sorting them for his father, a carpenter. Today he has over 15,000 varieties—hand-forged, cast, and machine-made—from over 40 countries. All of the nails are documented and mounted on panels of wood in his basement. It is the most complete collection of its kind in existence.

Antique shops, junkyards, swap meets, and flea markets all supply Horwath with antique nails. He is particularly proud of a collection of 48 nails which came from state capitol buildings—each one with a letter from the state's governor. Another rare nail is from the Dome of the Rock, the oldest existing Islamic shrine. Another nail is from the home of William Ellery, one of the signers of the Declaration of Independence. Some of the most valuable nails are the 50 "tie-backs"—nails with inlaid mother-of-pearl or glass in the heads.

TINFOIL BALL

Collectors: Students of Central School, Stirling, N.J.

A huge tinfoil ball is being assembled by all the students at Central School. Mr. Lee Evans, a teacher at the school, is the supervisor of this unusual collection. At the present time the ball weighs 38 lb., has a circumference of over 6 ft., and is growing rapidly. "The students are going wild," says Evans, who challenges anyone to break their record.

USED OIL RAGS

Collector: Ed Haberman, Tama, Ia.

Ed Haberman's interest in grease rags began back in the 1950s, when an ice machine in the family dairy sprang a leak and they bought an oil rag for 8¢ to keep the floor clean. With the replacement of dirty rags with clean ones, Haberman was on his way to having probably the largest known collection of its kind.

No oil rag is ever passed over by Haberman. He's retrieved them from busy streets in many cities. Donations are also gladly accepted. The rags—now totaling well over 13,000—are all washed before being neatly stacked in his garage and basement.

Mrs. Haberman does not share her husband's fascination with the rags. She once "borrowed" one to do some housecleaning. Mr. Haberman discovered the loss and quickly put an end to such behavior. "She hasn't done it since."

Haberman finds great satisfaction in the people who have taken an interest in his unusual collection. One letter is particularly gratifying. It is from some handicapped residents of Northwest Iowa Work Activity Center in Sheldon, Ia.: "One of our jobs is to smooth grease rags for Spencer A & M Laundry. We smooth 20,000 grease rags each week. We would like you to have this grease rag for your collection. If you are in the area you are welcome to visit us at work." The letter is signed by the handicapped workers.

WORLD WAR II RADIO BROADCASTS

Collector: Doug Hodge, Honolulu, Hawaii

Doug Hodge likes to "make history come alive" by listening to the actual radio broadcasts of historical events. His collection of over 20,000 broadcasts has a special emphasis on W.W. II, including documentaries, newscasts, win-the-war campaigns, and war-related commercials.

Just as television made Vietnam a reality in American homes, so radio brought in the sounds of the W.W. II battlefield, allowing listeners to form their own vivid images. One of Hodge's favorite broadcasts dates from May, 1942. The Mauna Loa volcano had erupted on the island of Hawaii, much to the concern of military personnel who were still jittery over the attack on Pearl Harbor. Worried that the spectacular lava flow would serve as a beacon to enemy aircraft, CBS ordered correspondent Webley Edwards to keep this hot news item a secret for almost a month, until the volcanic activity had subsided. The network then allotted Edwards several minutes to give his eyewitness account of the event. He describes it in such graphic detail that listeners can clearly visualize the eruption.

—D.B.S.

5

NATIONS OF THE WORLD

FROM AFGHANISTAN TO ZIMBABWE*

AFGHANISTAN

Location: Landlocked in south central Asia, bordered by Iran, Pakistan, China, and the U.S.S.R. **Size:** 249,999 sq. mi. (647,497 sq. km.). **Population:** 15,000,000.

Who Really Rules: Afghanistan is in the midst of a war between a Soviet occupation army, backing a narrow leftist clique around President Babrak Karmal, and a guerrilla movement made up of diverse political and ethnic factions. The rebels receive some support from Muslim countries, China, and the U.S. The war thus far has been marked by brutality on both sides, and it is unlikely that stability will be reached for many years, even if one side achieves a military victory.

In 1978 a leftist coup, popular in urban areas, overthrew a government which had seized power earlier in the year. The new government met with opposition in many rural areas, not only because it introduced programs to distribute land and liberate women, but because it attempted to extend central government control to areas that were autonomous. Two coups among the Marxist leadership in 1979—one opposed by, and a later one carried out by, the Soviet Union—narrowed the regime's political base. The Soviets launched a full-scale invasion in December, 1979.

ALBANIA

Location: On the western coast of the Balkan Peninsula in southeastern Europe, bordered by Yugoslavia and Greece. **Size:** 11,100 sq. mi. (28,748 sq. km.). **Population:** 2,773,000.

Who Really Rules: Governed by the Albanian Workers' (Communist) party, led by Enver Hoxha, Albania forbids dissent, religious practice, and emigration. In 1978, following Albanian criticism of China's new leadership, China cut off assistance, which had totaled $800 million in 17 years. Since then Albania's state-owned economy has sought new trading links in western and eastern Europe.

*Area figures are latest U.N. statistics. Population figures are estimates.

Albania is energy self-sufficient. It has no income tax and no inflation. The government also makes sure that there are no blue jeans, narrow trousers, or cosmetics. Drugs, premarital sex, and chewing gum are also forbidden.

Albania was a monarchy for a brief time before W.W. II. Now the former king's 6-ft. 9-in. son, Leka, claims the throne. The *Wall Street Journal* reported in 1979 that King Leka was last seen in Zimbabwe, "preparing to direct a guerrilla invasion of Albania from southern Africa."

ALGERIA

Location: In northern Africa, from the Mediterranean coast into the Sahara Desert, between Morocco and Tunisia. **Size:** 919,591 sq. mi. (2,381,741 sq. km.). **Population:** 19,709,000.

Who Really Rules: Algeria is governed by the collective leadership of the socialist FLN (National Liberation Front), the only legal party. In 1979, following the death of longtime president Houari Boumédienne, the Front chose Col. Chadli Benjedid, the army chief, as his successor.

The Algerian economy is controlled by the government, whose officials have a reputation for corruption. The most important enterprise is the state-owned petroleum and natural gas company, Sonatrach.

Periodically, the Berber minority, which comprises one sixth of Algeria's population, has protested the government's suppression of the Berber language and culture. The government's response to the latest uprising, in April, 1980, left 30 dead. Algeria receives arms from the U.S.S.R.; its economy is still closely tied to France, its former colonial master; and it ships fuel to the U.S.

ANDORRA

Location: A ministate in the Pyrenees mountains, between France and Spain. **Size:** 175 sq. mi. (453 sq. km.). **Population:** 37,500 (61% Spanish, 30% Andorran, 6% French).

Who Really Rules: Andorra's elective 24-member General Council is responsible for day-to-day government, but two feudal co-princes are authorized to veto any action. Each year Andorra pays 960 French francs to one co-prince, the French president, and pays the other co-prince, the Spanish Bishop of Seo de Urgel, 460 Spanish pesetas, 6 hams, 12 capons, and 25 slabs of cheese.

In a 1977 referendum, 35% of those voting advocated a change to democracy and self-rule, 31% favored the status quo, and the remainder favored a range of intermediate alternatives.

ANGOLA

Location: On the southwest coast of Africa, between Namibia and Zaire, plus the enclave of Cabinda, on the coast between Zaire and the Congo. **Size:** 481,351 sq. mi. (1,246,700 sq. km.). **Population:** 6,726,000.

Who Really Rules: Most of Angola is governed by the Movement for the Popular Liberation of Angola–Labor party, the Marxist-Leninist liberation movement which gained power after independence was achieved in 1975. Traditionally, the MPLA has been strongest among the Kimbundu tribe and mestizos (of mixed Portuguese and African blood). The U.S.S.R. is a major backer of the MPLA, and Cuban troops still help defend the government.

The southern-based National Union for the Total Independence of Angola (UNITA) has continued to rebel. Centered in the Ovimbundu ethnic group, UNITA guerrillas have hampered rail traffic over the Benguela railway, a lifeline for Zaire and Zambia.

Though the MPLA-Labor government has increased state control over Angola's economy, it has not nationalized Gulf Oil's wells off the shore of Cabinda. Angola could not find experts to take over production, and Gulf concealed operating data, so the government worked out a partnership with its former enemy. Today Angola owns a majority of the operation, but Gulf runs it.

ANGUILLA

Location: An island in the Lesser Antilles, east of the Virgin Islands in the eastern Caribbean. **Size:** 35 sq. mi. (91 sq. km.). **Population:** 7,000.
Who Really Rules: Anguilla is a British dependency, technically part of the associated state of St. Christopher–Nevis–Anguilla, but separate in practice. When St. Kitts–Nevis becomes independent, even that formal link will be removed. Anguilla's seat in the St. Kitts–Nevis Assembly is vacant. The Anguilla United Movement, headed by Prime Minister Ronald Webster, controls Anguilla's own House of Assembly.

ANTIGUA

Location: Three islands in the Leeward group of the eastern Caribbean, north of Guadeloupe. **Size:** 171 sq. mi. (442 sq. km.). **Population:** 76,000.
Who Really Rules: Antigua is presently an associated state of the U.K., but in Nov., 1981 it will become an independent nation. The parliament, essentially a two-party body, is currently in the hands of Prime Minister Vere Bird's conservative Antigua Labor party. Antigua hosts an American communications station which reportedly also serves as an intelligence base covering the eastern Caribbean.

ARGENTINA

Location: In southern South America, east of the Andean crest. **Size:** 1,068,297 sq. mi. (2,766,889 sq. km.). **Population:** 27,709,000.
Who Really Rules: The current military dictatorship, which seized power in 1976, consists of two major factions. The soft-liners, or *blandos*, support the use of unconstitutional means to suppress those attempting to overthrow the military government. The hard-liners, or

duros, support such means to suppress anyone. The Argentine government, even after the defeat of Marxist and Peronist guerrillas in the late 1970s, continues to manhandle the traditionally powerful labor movement, to censor the press, and to intimidate the intelligentsia. In addition to 4,000 acknowledged political prisoners, there are some 15,000 *desaparecidos*, or disappeared persons. Most of these people, suspected critics of the government, were kidnapped by right-wing paramilitary forces linked to the military government. Though a few are eventually released, *desaparecidos* are usually summarily executed or held in clandestine prison camps, where many are tortured.

Despite this record of active repression, it is economic conditions which are actually building opposition to the government. Military-backed economic policies have given Argentina one of the world's highest inflation rates, and they have helped monopoly business interests at the expense of small and medium-sized businesses, as well as at the expense of the working class.

AUSTRALIA

Location: Continent and islands dividing the Pacific and Indian oceans, south of the East Indies. **Size:** 2,967,895 sq. mi. (7,686,848 sq. km.). **Population:** 14,796,000.

Who Really Rules: Australia's parliamentary government is currently controlled by a conservative Liberal-Country party coalition, but the leftist Labor party has a large following, as does the powerful Australian Council of Trade Unions. Australia is a capitalist country with extensive social welfare programs. Much of the industrial economy, including the rapidly expanding mineral sector, is controlled by foreign corporations.

Though the aboriginal population has land rights similar to those held by American Indians, the rights to minerals underneath their lands are controlled by the government. The government has awarded numerous uranium-mining concessions to foreign companies over the objections of the aborigines.

AUSTRIA

Location: Landlocked in the Alps of central Europe. **Size:** 32,374 sq. mi. (83,849 sq. km.). **Population:** 7,476,000.

Who Really Rules: Chancellor Bruno Kreisky's Socialist party holds a majority in the freely elected parliament. Though capitalist and open to foreign investment, Austria has a highly developed social welfare system and a history of labor-management cooperation. As a neutral state situated between the Soviet bloc and the nations of the Common Market, Austria—particularly its capital, Vienna—has prospered with the rise in East-West trade. Though neutral, Austria is a major international supplier of small arms and ground vehicles, including jeeps and tanks. The major arms manufacturer, Puch, is better known in the U.S. for its mopeds, however.

In 1978 Austrians narrowly voted not to begin operating an already constructed nuclear power plant.

AZORES

Location: Three island groups, approximately 800 mi. west of mainland Portugal in the north Atlantic Ocean. **Size:** 902 sq. mi. (2,335 sq. km.). **Population:** 330,000.

Who Really Rules: The Azores are a semiautonomous region of Portugal. Never too happy about mainland neglect of Azores problems, conservative Azorean leaders flirted with the idea of independence in the mid-1970s, when leftists were in power in Portugal.

The U.S. operates the 1,500-man Lajes Air Base on the island of Terceira, as well as two communications stations elsewhere in the Azores. Lajes is an important base for antisubmarine aircraft and a refueling station for transatlantic military transport planes. In 1979 the U.S. and Portugal renewed their base agreement, with the U.S. promising to seek Portuguese approval should it wish to use the base to send war planes to the Middle East. The U.S. supplied Portugal and the Azores with $140 million in aid in exchange for the agreement.

More than 300,000 Azoreans now reside in the U.S.

BAHAMAS

Location: A chain of West Indies islands, northeast of Cuba, southeast of Florida. **Size:** 5,380 sq. mi. (13,935 sq. km.). **Population:** 244,000 (80% black, 10% white, 10% mixed).

Who Really Rules: The traditional white elite still hold top positions in private business and the civil service, but the predominantly black Progressive Liberal party controls the elective House, the key body in the Bahamas' three-party, British-model parliamentary system.

Foreign corporations play a leading role in the economy, which is based upon tourism and gambling, the refining of imported oil, and international finance. More than a mere tax haven, the Bahamas—that is, the capital city of Nassau—have become a major center for international financial activity, where major U.S., Canadian, and European banks conduct unregulated "offshore" lending activity.

BAHRAIN

Location: One major and a number of smaller islands in the Persian Gulf, west of Qatar, about 13 mi. from Saudi Arabia's coast. **Size:** 240 sq. mi. (622 sq. km.). **Population:** 407,000 (80% Arab, 12% Iranian).

Who Really Rules: The ruling emir and his al-Khalifa family allow no political parties, although Bahrain does have a tradition of labor organization. Sunni Muslims, the al-Khalifas have arrested leaders of protest demonstrations staged by pro-Iran members of the majority Shia sect. Bahrain is one of the oldest oil producers in the region, but its production is declining. The government has diversified the economy, however, by building an aluminum smelter and inviting in foreign banks. Bahrain is the Persian Gulf's most important financial center. The U.S. operates its only Persian Gulf base at Bahrain.

BANGLADESH

Location: At the northern tip of the Bay of Bengal (Indian Ocean), between India and Burma. **Size:** 55,598 sq. mi. (143,998 sq. km.). **Population:** 94,170,000 (83% Muslim, 16% Hindu).
Who Really Rules: Lt. Gen. Ziaur Rahman seized power in 1975, and gradually returned the country to civilian rule. He was elected president in 1978, and in 1979 his Bangladesh Nationalist party won the relatively free, contested, parliamentary elections. Rahman was gunned down by troops in June, 1981, and 75-year-old moderate Abdus Sattar became acting president.

Since 1972 most of Bangladesh's finance and industry have been state-owned, but Rahman encouraged the rebirth of the private sector, including selected foreign investment.

BARBADOS

Location: East of St. Vincent in the Lesser Antilles in the Caribbean. **Size:** 166 sq. mi. (580 sq. km.). **Population:** 282,000.
Who Really Rules: Barbados, with a two-party parliamentary democratic system, is currently governed by the middle-class, pro-American Barbados Labor party. Sugar production and tourism are the leading industries, but in the past several years Barbados has welcomed foreign light manufacturing firms. Electronics firms and other export-oriented assembly firms have established factories to take advantage of the island's literate, cheap, English-speaking labor force.

BELAU (PALAU)

Location: Southwest of Yap, in the western Caroline Islands in the western Pacific. **Size:** 192 sq. mi. (500 sq. km.). **Population:** 15,000.
Who Really Rules: On Jan. 1, 1981, Harvath Remelik took office as the first president of the Republic of Belau. The 200 islands of the new nation had been administered for over 30 years as part of the U.S. Trust Territory of the Pacific. Under the new arrangement of "free association," the Belauan economy will continue to be subsidized by the U.S., which will also control matters of defense.

BELGIUM

Location: In western Europe, on the coast of the English Channel (North Sea) between France and the Netherlands. **Size:** 11,781 sq. mi.

(30,513 sq. km.). **Population:** 9,875,000 (55% Flemish, 33% Walloon, 12% mixed or other).

Who Really Rules: Belgium is run by a Brussels-based bureaucracy, tenuously linking two ethnically distinct provinces. In Flanders, the northern province, the Flemish people (Flemings) speak Dutch. In Walloonia, in the south, the Walloons speak French. Brussels, the national capital as well as the headquarters for both NATO (the North Atlantic Treaty Organization) and the European Economic Community (Common Market), is located within Flanders, but most of its residents speak French. Ethnic distrust divides the nation's major political parties, as well as the general population. In 1980 the Belgian parliament approved a plan to turn over 10% of the national budget to two regional governments, one in Flanders, one in Walloonia.

Flemish incomes are generally higher than those in Walloonia, and Flemish business interests tend to dominate the economy. Although integrated into the European Community, the Belgian economy is subordinate to its neighbors, particularly West Germany.

BELIZE

Location: On the Gulf of Honduras (Caribbean Sea) in Central America, between Mexico's Yucatán Peninsula and Guatemala. **Size:** 8,867 sq. mi. (22,965 sq. km.). **Population:** 167,000 (51% black, 22% mestizo, 19% American Indian).

Who Really Rules: Guatemala had claimed Belize since 1859, but more than a century of British rule created a separate Belizean national identity. The fear of a Guatemalan invasion has kept the U.K. and its troops in the country, but a territorial settlement was reached between the three countries early in 1981, paving the way to Belizean independence. Predominantly black, English-speaking Belizeans identify with the formerly British island nations in the Caribbean; in fact, Belize is a member of the Caribbean Common Market.

BENIN

Location: On West Africa's Guinea coast, sandwiched between Nigeria and Togo. **Size:** 43,483 sq. mi. (112,622 sq. km.). **Population:** 3,615,000.

Who Really Rules: Benin, formerly the French colony of Dahomey, is governed by the Marxist-Leninist People's Revolutionary party. Following the November, 1979, election, in which 97.48% of the voters supported the single PRP slate, the seven-year-old military government turned power over to a civilian regime, headed by President Ahmed Kerekou, the lieutenant colonel who formed the PRP after seizing power in 1972. On Sept. 27, 1980, Kerekou converted to Islam while in the presence of Col. Muammar al-Qaddafi of Libya, changing his name from Mathieu to Ahmed.

BERMUDA

Location: An island 570 mi. off the east coast of the U.S. **Size:** 20 sq. mi. (53 sq. km.). **Population:** 64,000 (59% black, 41% white).
Who Really Rules: Though Bermuda is a colony of the U.K., subject to British rule, its economy and government are controlled by an oligarchy of white merchant and professional families. The oligarchy imports several thousand professionals from England to help manage the tourist industry and the financial companies that operate the tax haven. These temporary white residents are eligible to vote and have helped keep the white minority in power. Black Bermudians generally hold menial jobs in the tourist industry.

BHUTAN

Location: In the Himalayas, between eastern India and Tibet (China). **Size:** 18,147 sq. mi. (47,000 sq. km.). **Population:** 1,377,000 (60% Bhutias, 25% Nepalis).
Who Really Rules: King Jigme Singye Wangchuk shares power with a National Assembly consisting of royal appointees, representatives of the Buddhist monasteries, and members elected indirectly. Under a 1949 treaty India has special rights to Bhutan's foreign trade and guides Bhutan's foreign policy. Beginning in 1979, however, Bhutan began to exert an independent voice, disagreeing with India at international forums and establishing diplomatic relations with nearby Bangladesh.

BOLIVIA

Location: Landlocked in central South America. **Size:** 424,163 sq. mi. (1,098,581 sq. km.). **Population:** 5,564,000.
Who Really Rules: On July 17, 1980, the Bolivian government changed hands for the 189th time in 155 years since independence. A three-man military junta, led by Gen. Luis García Meza, voided the June 29 election which had given a moderate-left coalition a plurality. Unlike previous military governments, the García Meza junta began a severe campaign of repression against the regime's opponents, including major political parties, organized labor, the press, and the church. The military government of neighboring Argentina reportedly played a key role in the July, 1980, coup, and both Brazil and Argentina are providing ongoing support for García Meza.

BOTSWANA

Location: Landlocked in southern Africa, surrounded by South Africa, Zimbabwe, and Namibia. **Size:** 231,804 sq. mi. (600,372 sq. km.). **Population:** 821,000.
Who Really Rules: Botswana is a multiparty parliamentary democracy in which only one party, the Botswana Democratic party, has a substan-

Ourou Indians of Lake Titicaca, Bolivia.

tial following. In 1979 the BDP, which is based on Tswana tribal ties, won 29 out of the 32 contested seats in the Legislative Assembly. Sir Seretse Khama, who served as president from the country's independence in 1966 until his death in 1980, had been an important Tswana chief.

Botswana's economy is subordinate to South Africa. More than 40,000 nationals work in South Africa's mines. De Beers, the South African diamond giant, controls Botswana's significant diamond exports, while other foreign companies control other minerals. Cattle, raised by traditional farmers who make up most of the population, are exported to Europe.

BRAZIL

Location: In east central South America. **Size:** 3,286,473 sq. mi. (8,511,965 sq. km.). **Population:** 120,000,000.

Who Really Rules: Brazil's armed forces, in power since a 1964 coup, are presently dominated by a faction favoring "limited liberalization." Under President João Figueiredo, the fifth successive general to hold that office, Brazil has reduced its human rights violations and announced plans to hold open elections in 1982.

Brazil's economy is essentially a joint venture between multinational corporations—from the U.S., Japan, and West Germany—and government-owned enterprises. Under the military, both industry and export-oriented agriculture have expanded rapidly, but the benefits have not sifted down to the vast numbers of urban and rural poor. Critics of military economic policies include Roman Catholic church leaders and organized labor.

BRITISH INDIAN OCEAN TERRITORY (CHAGOS ARCHIPELAGO)

Location: Islands in the middle of the Indian Ocean, south of India. **Size:** 30 sq. mi. (78 sq. km.). **Population:** No permanent inhabitants; a few thousand U.S. military personnel.

Who Really Rules: Britain leases Diego Garcia, the main Chagos island, to the U.S., which uses it as its chief naval logistical base and antisubmarine air station in the Indian Ocean region. Britain severed the islands from Mauritius in 1968, when it granted that west Indian Ocean island independence. Britain paid Mauritius £3 million sterling and moved Diego Garcia's 1,200 to 1,500 inhabitants to Mauritius.

Mauritian leaders, who say that the British promised the islands would be used only for a communications station, are now claiming sovereignty over the territory, and they are backed by the Organization of African Unity.

BRUNEI

Location: Two enclaves on the north coast of the East Indies island of Borneo (Kalimantan). **Size:** 2,226 sq. mi. (5,765 sq. km.). **Population:** 218,000.

Who Really Rules: This oil-rich British protectorate is governed by Sultan Sir Muda Hassanal Bolkiah and his father, former Sultan Sir Omar Ali Saifuddin. The sultan's government is operated largely by British civil servants, and the oil and gas fields are run by Royal Dutch Shell. A battalion of British-controlled Nepalese Gurkhas provides for defense. The sultan still detains, without trial, eight members of the banned *Partai Rakyat Brunei* (People's party), which staged a rebellion in 1962 when the elder sultan refused to let the elected members of the Brunei Legislative Council form a government. British troops suppressed the uprising and arrested 2,500 people.

BULGARIA

Location: On the Black Sea coast of the Balkan Peninsula in southeastern Europe, south of Romania. **Size:** 42,823 sq. mi. (110,912 sq. km.). **Population:** 8,937,000.

Who Really Rules: Bulgaria is a communist state in which all production is socialized, but planning is less centralized than in the Soviet Union. Todor Zhivkov has headed the government and the ruling

Bulgarian Communist party since 1954. The Bulgarian government does not tolerate criticism and places limitations on all organized religions. Bulgaria is a full-fledged member of the Soviet bloc, and its economy has benefited from its links with the Soviet Union. Unlike other Eastern bloc nations, Bulgaria has a history of national friendship with Russia, which drove the Ottoman Turks out of Bulgaria in 1878 after 500 years of control.

BURMA

Location: On the Bay of Bengal (Indian Ocean) in Southeast Asia, between Thailand and the Indian subcontinent. **Size:** 261,217 sq. mi. (676,552 sq. km.). **Population:** 35,656,000 (72% Burman, 7% Karen, 6% Shan, 3% Indian, 2% Kachin, 2% Chin, 1% Chinese).
Who Really Rules: The bureaucracy of the Burma Socialist Program party controls Burma's industrial economy through a number of state-owned enterprises, but most important decisions are made by President U Ne Win, the general who seized power in 1962. Ne Win's government successfully distributed the wealth of the country, but it let the economy stagnate. The black market is not only the source of most imported commodities but also the agency for a huge chunk of Burma's rice crop.

Since Burma achieved its independence in 1949, the central government has been fighting insurgents in several areas of the country. The most significant, in the northeast Shan states, is led by the Burmese Communist party, which seeks a nationwide victory. The Communists use their friendship with China—the chief supplier of armaments—to win allies among the autonomist armies of the Shan, Karen, Mon, and Kachin ethnic groups. These long-simmering insurgencies have hampered Ne Win's limited plans for development by restricting access to the country's valuable mineral and timber resources. Even among the Burmese, the military government is overwhelmingly unpopular.

BURUNDI

Location: Inland in east central Africa, on the shores of Lake Tanganyika, between Tanzania and Zaire. **Size:** 10,747 sq. mi. (27,834 sq. km.). **Population:** 4,578,000 (85% Hutu, 14% Tutsi, 1% Pygmy).
Who Really Rules: The Hamitic Tutsi minority maintains its feudal lordship over the Bantu Hutu subsistence and coffee farmers. In 1972, the Tutsi slaughtered as many as 200,000 Hutu in a Hutu uprising and sent another 200,000 into exile. In 1976 Col. Jean Baptiste Bagaza, a Belgian-trained political scientist, seized power in a bloodless coup. Bagaza attempted to bring the Hutu into his government and abolished some of the worst features of feudalism. In establishing civilian power in his National Unity and Progress party (UPRONA) in 1979, Bagaza recruited a million members and staged public assemblies throughout the country.

CAMEROON

Location: At the bend of Africa, on the Gulf of Guinea between Nigeria and Equatorial Guinea. **Size:** 183,568 sq. mi. (475,442 sq. km.). **Population:** 8,583,000.

Who Really Rules: President Ahmadou Ahidjo rules Cameroon with only disorganized opposition. A Muslim northerner, his major challenge is to balance the various ethnic, religious (including Catholic and Muslim), and regional (particularly British and French) factions. French expatriates hold important positions in government and business, and the southwestern Bamiléké group (one quarter of the population) controls most internal commerce. Most of the economy is in the hands of domestic or foreign private owners, but all is subject to government planning.

France, which placed Ahidjo in power while suppressing a left-wing independence movement, is still the country's major ally and trading partner.

CANADA

Location: The northern tier of North America, from the U.S. border to the Arctic, excluding Alaska. **Size:** 3,851,791 sq. mi. (9,976,139 sq. km.). **Population:** 24,336,000.

Who Really Rules: Canada has traditionally been dominated by an economic elite based in the province of Ontario. In recent years, however, elitists from other provinces have challenged not only the traditional ruling group but also the power of the Canadian central government itself. French-speaking Quebec Province rejected sovereignty in a 1980 advisory referendum, but the forces for autonomy remain strong.

The ruling Liberal party, which generally represents the industrial eastern provinces (including Quebec) in Parliament, carries out policies which favor manufacturing over the resource-oriented industries of Canada's western provinces. Oil-rich Alberta opposes federal suggestions for distributing its wealth. Instead, it is circumventing the federal government by investing its multibillion-dollar Heritage Fund, from oil and gas royalties, in other provinces.

U.S.-based multinational corporations wield a great deal of power in Canada, actually controlling basic industry. Canada's economy is closely linked to that of the U.S. In fact, the two countries are each other's major trading partners.

CANARY ISLANDS

Location: Islands just off the west coast of Africa at the boundary of Morocco and Western Sahara. **Size:** 2,808 sq. mi. (7,273 sq. km.). **Population:** 1,300,000.

Who Really Rules: The islands are governed as part of Spain, but many African nations and a growing number of Canarians consider the islands a colony. In Spain's 1979 election, the Canary Islands independence movement elected one deputy to the Spanish Cortes.

CAPE VERDE

Location: Ten major and five minor islands in the Atlantic Ocean, 300 mi. west of Senegal. **Size:** 1,557 sq. mi. (4,033 sq. km.). **Population:** 332,000.

Who Really Rules: From the attainment of independence from Portugal in 1975 until the November, 1980, coup in Guinea-Bissau, Cape Verde was ruled by the revolutionary left-wing Partido Africano da Independencia da Guinee e Cabo Verde (PAIGC). When the PAIGC was overthrown in Guinea-Bissau, its Cape Verde branch changed its name and reorganized. The party relies on mass mobilization, directed at agricultural production, to build the nation. Since the islands have been experiencing a drought since the late 1960s, the government focuses popular energy on water and soil conservation, but it is also developing its own fishing industry.

More than 300,000 Cape Verdians, mostly men, work in Senegal, the U.S., Europe, and elsewhere. Their remittances are a major source of national income.

CAYMAN ISLANDS

Location: Three major islands in the Caribbean, south of Cuba, west of Jamaica. **Size:** 100 sq. mi. (259 sq. km.). **Population:** 17,000.

Who Really Rules: The Cayman Islands are a British territory. The U.K. takes responsibility for military and international relations. The local government is mixed between elected and appointed officials. With no direct taxes, the Cayman Islands serve as one of the world's leading tax havens for multinational corporations and banks.

CENTRAL AFRICAN REPUBLIC

Location: Landlocked in central Africa, north of the Congo and Zaire. **Size:** 240,534 sq. mi. (622,984 sq. km.). **Population:** 2,565,000.

Who Really Rules: In September, 1979, several hundred French troops overthrew Emperor Jean Bedel Bokassa, a close friend of France whose atrocities had become embarrassing to the French government. The French installed as president David Dacko, who had been deposed by Bokassa in 1966. Though Dacko has promised elections, he has detained a major opposition leader, Ange Patasse, and banned strikes.

CHAD

Location: Landlocked in central Africa, south of Libya. **Size:** 495,753 sq. mi. (1,284,000 sq. km.). **Population:** 4,787,000.

Who Really Rules: Chad alternates between periods of internal warfare and "national unity" government. Political factions are communally based among the 240 tribes from 12 major ethnic groups. Black tribes in the agricultural south ran the country following independence from

France, but the nomadic and seminomadic peoples of the Muslim north have been more successful militarily.

In December, 1980, troops from Libya, which occupies a stretch of Chadian border territory believed to contain uranium, aided the winning faction in Chad's civil war. The following month, Libyan officials announced a merger between the two countries.

CHANNEL ISLANDS

Location: Jersey, Guernsey, and other islands between Britain and France. **Size:** 75 sq. mi. (195 sq. km.). **Population:** 131,000.
Who Really Rules: Though ruled by the British crown and linked economically to Britain, the Channel Islands are not part of the U.K. They are self-governing territories whose lieutenant governors are appointed by the crown. Several British banks have established Channel Islands subsidiaries to take advantage of commercial laws there.

CHILE

Location: Along the Pacific coast of southwestern South America. **Size:** 292,257 sq. mi. (756,945 sq. km.). **Population:** 11,262,000.
Who Really Rules: A four-man military junta, headed by Maj, Gen. Augusto Pinochet Ugarte, has ruled Chile since 1973, when it seized power from an elected leftist government in a bloody CIA-supported coup. Since that time, the Pinochet regime has outlawed most political activity and has repressed leftists at home and abroad. In 1980 the military claimed a 2-to-1 victory in a plebiscite which promised military rule at least until 1989 and authorized it until 1997.

Within Chile, Pinochet is opposed not only by the left but also by the Christian Democrats who supported his coup and even by one of the four members of the original junta.

Since 1973 the government has dismantled Chile's mixed economy and applied the "free market" economics of U.S. economist Milton Friedman. Under the "Chicago Boys," Chilean disciples of Friedman, Chile's economy has grown considerably, but the working class has suffered. Several U.S. banks have made large loans to Chile since the coup, and multinational corporations have upped their investments there. In 1981 the Reagan administration lifted trade sanctions which had been imposed against the Chilean military government by President Carter.

CHINA

Location: In east Asia, south of Siberia (U.S.S.R.) and the Mongolian People's Republic. **Size:** 3,705,390 sq. mi. (9,596,961 sq. km.). **Population:** 1,053,788,000.
Who Really Rules: Nationwide political and economic policies are set by the upper echelons of the Chinese Communist party, as well as by top Communist military officers. At the national level the government tolerates little dissent. Most of China's economy is socialized, although

Camel-drawn cart in Inner Mongolia, China.

unregulated "free markets" exist throughout the country. In many areas local committees make the day-to-day decisions governing factories, agricultural communes, and neighborhoods, but only with the consent of the Communist party.

Within the Communist party, there have been ongoing disputes over the degree of economic centralization, the role of production incentives, and the degree of China's dependence on foreign goods and technology. Several times since the Communists took power in 1949, leading party figures have been discredited. Usually these leaders—such as the "Gang of Four" associated with the 1960s Cultural Revolution—are blamed for a wide range of policy failures, and the rhetoric of party policy shifts sharply. The present dominant faction, led by Deng Xiaoping, advocates "modernization."

China's leadership comes from the Han ethnic group, which makes up 96% of the population. Although divided into regional cultures speaking different dialects of the same written language, the Han are relatively homogeneous. The cultural and political rights of ethnic minorities are protected as long as they do not conflict with the perceived interests of China overall.

COLOMBIA

Location: Northwest corner of South America, straddling the Panamanian isthmus. **Size:** 439,735 sq. mi. (1,138,914 sq. km.). **Population:** 27,600,000.

Who Really Rules: Political power in Colombia is shared by two elite parties, the Liberals and Conservatives, who fought each other for power from 1948 to 1957. In 1978 the Liberal presidential candidate, Julio Cesar Turbay Ayala, won election with 49% of the vote, although only 30% of those eligible voted. In the legislative assembly elections in March, 1980, there was only a 27% voter turnout.

Colombia has been under a state of siege for more than three decades. The government practices torture at 35 military centers throughout the country, the primary victims being peasants, Indians, and trade unionists. When Turbay took office, he followed American advice and imposed additional security measures, ostensibly to crack down on the export of marijuana and cocaine to the U.S. (Colombia exports an estimated $3 billion in drugs each year.) In aiding the Colombian military, the U.S. Drug Enforcement Administration may have planted the seeds of a military government, common in Latin America but unusual in Colombia.

In the March, 1980, elections, a self-proclaimed witch, Regina Betancourt de Liski, was elected to the city councils of both Bogotá and Medellín.

COMOROS

Location: Three islands in the western Indian Ocean between Mozambique and Madagascar—Grande Comore, Anjouan, and Mohéli. **Size:** 693 sq. mi. (1,795 sq. km.). **Population:** 291,000.

Who Really Rules: The government of Ahmad Abdallah was placed in power by a 1978 coup led by French-born mercenary Bob Denard. Several of Denard's mercenaries remain in the Comoros to back up Abdallah's regime. Under the conservative leadership of Abdallah, the Comoros economy is a mixture of free enterprise, price controls, and subsistence agriculture. Mayotte, the predominantly Christian fourth island of the Comoros group, remains a French territory (called Mahore) as a result of a 1975 referendum.

Reportedly, in 1977 a witch doctor warned President Ali Soilah that he would be killed by a man with a dog, so Soilah ordered every dog in the capital city of Moroni slaughtered. A year later, when Denard overthrew Soilah, he was accompanied by an Alsatian mascot. Shortly thereafter, Soilah was killed by Denard's forces.

CONGO

Location: On the west coast of central Africa, between Gabon and Cabinda (Angola). **Size:** 132,046 sq. mi. (342,000 sq. km.). **Population:** 1,608,000 (48% Bakongo, 20% Bateke).

Who Really Rules: The Congo is ruled by the leftist Congo Labor party (PCT), the sole legal party. President Denis Sassou-Nguesso, a leader of the PCT's left wing, eased aside his predecessor, Joachim Yhombi-Opango, in early 1979. Later that year, the government declared an amnesty for all political prisoners except Yhombi-Opango, who remained under house arrest, and the PCT took a number of steps to increase its ethnic and regional base.

In April, 1979, the government came to terms with foreign financial interests by signing a standby agreement pledging domestic austerity with the International Monetary Fund. Though the Congo considers itself the first Marxist-Leninist regime in Africa (since 1963), it permits private commerce. In fact, the economic climate in the Congo is so much freer than in neighboring "capitalist" Zaire that diamond exporters from Zaire prefer to smuggle their gems out through the Congo. Consequently, the Congo is a leading exporter of diamonds although it has no known deposits.

COOK ISLANDS

Location: A Polynesian group of islands in the southwest Pacific, east of Fiji. **Size:** 91 sq. mi. (236 sq. km.). **Population:** 18,000.
Who Really Rules: Since 1965 the Cook Islands have been a self-governing state associated with New Zealand. Technically, Cook Islanders are citizens of New Zealand, and a few thousand islanders live and work there. New Zealand is responsible for the islands' foreign policy and defense, although the Cook Islands government occasionally projects an independent image in its efforts to attract foreign assistance.

From 1965 to 1978, the late Sir Albert Henry governed as premier. In the 1978 parliamentary elections, however, he used government funds to fly in voters from New Zealand. Subsequently, those votes were annulled and Henry was convicted of conspiracy, stripped of his office and knighthood, and fined. Opposition leader Dr. Tom Davis was thus elected premier.

COSTA RICA

Location: In Central America, between Nicaragua and Panama. **Size:** 19,575 sq. mi. (50,700 sq. km.). **Population:** 2,295,000.
Who Really Rules: Costa Rica has a tradition of multiparty democracy, in which transfers of power are usually smooth. It has no standing army—just a poorly armed civil guard. The judiciary, legislature, and presidency are independent. In fact, when the minister of public security authorized the landing of a 35-man U.S. Air Force rescue team near the Nicaraguan border in 1979, he was forced to withdraw permission when the legislature voted to deny it. In 1980 the U.S. Army was forced to dismantle an observation post it had set up near the Nicaraguan border.

All sectors of Costa Rican society supported the Sandinista revolution in neighboring Nicaragua, but the government limited the movement of

Sandinista guerrillas in Costa Rica until Venezuela signed a pact with Costa Rica in effect promising to defend it against retaliatory invasion.

CUBA

Location: An island in the northern Caribbean, about 90 mi. south of Florida. **Size:** 44,218 sq. mi. (114,524 sq. km.). **Population:** 9,985,000.
Who Really Rules: Cuba is run by the Cuban Communist party, headed by charismatic President Fidel Castro, the guerrilla leader who overthrew the Batista dictatorship in 1959. The Communist bureaucracy runs the government and the centralized economy. Opponents are encouraged to emigrate, and the Committees for the Defense of the Revolution, an ever-present militia incorporating most of the adult population, maintain a careful watch for subversion and intervention.

Cuba is a close ally of the U.S.S.R., and it is host to the only Soviet troops in the Western Hemisphere. It receives substantial economic and technical assistance from the Soviet Union.

CYPRUS

Location: An island south of Turkey in the eastern Mediterranean. **Size:** 3,572 sq. mi. (9,251 sq. km.). **Population:** 623,000 (78% Greek, 18% Turkish).
Who Really Rules: Since 1974 the island has been divided into two sectors. Troops from Turkey occupy the northern zone, about 36% of the area. Presently the home of the Turkish Cypriot minority as well as colonists from Turkey, the Turkish sector contains tourist facilities, citrus orchards, and about 70% of the island's overall productive capacity. When the Turks invaded, 180,000 Greek Cypriots fled the northern sector. The government of Cyprus occupies the southern 64% of the island. A majority of the Greek Cypriots reside there. Most of the 45,000 Turkish Cypriots from the southern sector have fled to the north. The southern economy is growing rapidly, but it is incurring a mounting foreign debt.

Representatives of elective governments in both sectors have been negotiating to reunite the country, but segments of both populations support annexation of the zones to Greece and Turkey.

CZECHOSLOVAKIA

Location: Landlocked in eastern Europe, south of Poland, southeast of Germany, and north of Austria and Hungary. **Size:** 49,370 sq. mi. (127,869 sq. km.). **Population:** 15,475,000 (64% Czech, 30% Slovak).
Who Really Rules: Czechoslovakia is ruled by the Czechoslovakian Communist party and the semi-independent Slovakia Communist party. Gustav Husak has been president and party leader since the 1968 Soviet-led invasion removed the reformist regime of Alexander Dubcek. Under Husak, the government has cracked down on all forms of opposition.

Except for the party elite, all workers in the state-owned, centrally planned economy receive essentially the same pay. Production incentives, introduced in 1978, have caught on slowly, but the underground economy and black market thrive.

DENMARK

Location: Jutland Peninsula and adjacent islands north of Germany, south of the Scandinavian Peninsula, in northern Europe. **Size:** 16,629 sq. mi. (43,069 sq. km.). **Population:** 5,157,000.

Who Really Rules: Denmark's welfare state has survived the tax revolt of the early 1970s with only minor changes. Although Denmark is a capitalist country, the government guarantees a wide range of social services and assistance. The labor movement is particularly strong, and the leftist Social Democratic party has for many years been the leading bloc in Denmark's multiparty parliamentary system.

Denmark is an active participant in the North Atlantic Treaty Organization (NATO). However, in 1980, when Denmark failed to increase military spending as required by NATO, U.S. Secretary of Defense Harold Brown threatened to end the U.S. commitment to defend the country.

DJIBOUTI

Location: On the African side of the Bab el Mandeb strait, at the southern end of the Red Sea. **Size:** 8,494 sq. mi. (22,000 sq. km.). **Population:** 333,000 (50% Issa, 40% Afar).

Who Really Rules: Called the French Territory of Afars and Issas until 1977, Djibouti is still essentially a French protectorate, made up of Afars, an Ethiopian ethnic group, and Issas, who are ethnic Somalis. Independence marked the ascendancy of the Issas over the Afars, who were favored during French rule. The president is an Issa; the prime minister is an Afar.

Internal ethnic rivalries are overshadowed by the ongoing hostilities between neighboring Somalia and Ethiopia. Djibouti is officially neutral, but the two groups readily identify with their ethnic brethren. Djibouti also hosts an estimated 35,000 refugees, primarily from the secessionist Ethiopian region of Eritrea.

France and Saudi Arabia both supply millions of dollars to the fledgling nation. France also stations 3,650 air, ground, and naval personnel in Djibouti.

DOMINICA

Location: In the Lesser Antilles (eastern Caribbean), between Guadeloupe and Martinique. **Size:** 290 sq. mi. (751 sq. km.). **Population:** 79,000 (primarily of African descent).

Who Really Rules: In 1980 the conservative, pro-American Freedom party, led by Mary Eugenia Charles, won the country's first parliamentary elections since independence in 1978. Charles is the first woman to become prime minister of a Caribbean nation. Following the election, the Canadian and British governments promised to provide additional training and equipment to the 250-member Dominican police force, reportedly at the request of the U.S. State Dept.

DOMINICAN REPUBLIC

Location: Eastern part of the island of Hispaniola, in the Caribbean Sea between Cuba and Puerto Rico. **Size:** 18,816 sq. mi. (48,734 sq. km.). **Population:** 5,906,000.

Who Really Rules: In 1978 Antonio Guzman defeated military-backed incumbent Joaquín Balaguer in the first honest presidential elections in the Dominican Republic since 1962. Guzman was the candidate for the Revolutionary Dominican party, a social democratic party with labor, peasant, middle-class, and elite constituencies that has moved to the right since being overthrown by the military in 1963.

The American conglomerate Gulf & Western is the Dominican Republic's largest foreign investor, private landowner, and employer. It controls 30% of the nation's sugar crop and most of the tourist industry. In 1980 Guzman negotiated a compromise settlement to a festering dispute with Gulf & Western, in which the company agreed to fund a nonprofit social-services foundation as the country's share of 1975 sugar-trading profits.

ECUADOR

Location: Equatorial Pacific (northwest) coast of South America, between Peru and Colombia, plus the Galapagos Islands, 600 mi. offshore. **Size:** 109,483 sq. mi. (283,561 sq. km.). **Population:** 8,382,000.

Who Really Rules: Until the early 1970s Ecuador was the archetypical "banana republic." The United Fruit Co. dominated the country until the early 1960s, when it pulled out. For the next decade, an oligarchy of landowners and exporters held power, ruling through both military and civilian regimes.

In 1972 the production of oil for export transformed Ecuador economically and politically. The military government that seized power that year joined the Organization of Petroleum Exporting Countries (OPEC) and, under the tutelage of Venezuela, established national control of the country's oil resources.

Since 1979 Ecuador has been governed by an elected, left-of-center coalition government. This is not the first time that reformist parties have controlled the government structure, but it is the first time that the government has had the economic resources—oil revenues—to establish a power base among the middle and lower classes.

EGYPT

Location: Northeastern corner of Africa, fronting both the Mediterranean Sea and the Red Sea. **Size:** 386,660 sq. mi. (1,001,449 sq. km.). **Population:** 41,502,000.

Who Really Rules: Egypt has been ruled since 1970 by President Anwar el-Sadat, who created the National Democratic party in 1978 to bolster his regime. Sadat suppresses opposition from the left, including supporters of the late president, Gamal Nasser, and from the Muslim fundamentalist right. At times immensely popular, Sadat holds on to power through his ability to maintain the expectation of a rising standard of living. His Camp David accords with Israel were popular in Egypt largely because much of the population expected a "peace dividend."

Egypt has a mixed economy, with an open door to foreign investment since 1974. Most Egyptians, however, have not benefited from the rapid growth of international economic activity under the open-door policy.

Since the original Camp David accords in 1978, Arab governments have cut off their official aid programs to Egypt, but the U.S. has become an important source of assistance, as well as a military ally.

EL SALVADOR

Location: On the Pacific coast of Central America, between Guatemala and Honduras. **Size:** 8,124 sq. mi. (21,041 sq. km.). **Population:** 4,991,000.

Who Really Rules: El Salvador is in the midst of a civil war. The U.S.-backed "reformist" military junta, which overthrew another military regime in October, 1979, drifted to the right soon after taking power, so once again power is in the hands of El Salvador's large landowners. Unsafe in their homeland, many members of the Salvadoran elite live in southern Florida, commuting to El Salvador only to complete necessary business transactions. The opposition has coalesced into the Democratic Revolutionary Front, which includes small-business owners, organized labor, peasant organizations, Catholic activists, and armed guerrilla movements.

EQUATORIAL GUINEA

Location: On the west coast of Africa, between Gabon and Cameroon, plus islands in the Gulf of Guinea (Atlantic Ocean). **Size:** 10,831 sq. mi. (28,051 sq. km.). **Population:** 245,000 (there are also 100,000 to 120,000 exiles living in neighboring countries).

Who Really Rules: In August, 1979, Defense Minister Theodore Nguema Mbasogo overthrew and executed his uncle, president-for-life Masie Nguema Biyogo, one of Africa's most brutal despots. The new military government has not yet scheduled any elections or other democratization programs. Officials in Spain, Equatorial Guinea's former colonial master, knew of plans for the coup beforehand, and they have supported the new regime. In addition, troops from Morocco help keep order.

ETHIOPIA

Location: In northeastern Africa, from the Red Sea south to Kenya. **Size:** 471,776 sq. mi. (1,221,900 sq. km.). **Population:** 31,712,000 (there are also 2 million Ethiopian refugees in neighboring Somalia, Sudan, and Djibouti).

Who Really Rules: Lt. Col. Mengistu Haile Mariam heads the all-powerful Provisional Military Administrative Council, or Dergue. Dergue leaders are Amharic, like the late Emperor Haile Selassie, and they have successfully eliminated most of their opponents in central and urban Ethiopia. The Dergue claims to be Marxist, and has in fact carried out massive land-reform programs and established peasant and worker organizations. These mass organizations exercise some local authority, but they also act as arms of the Dergue in implementing repressive government policies.

Since 1977, when Mengistu threw out Ethiopia's American sponsors, the Soviet Union, Cuba, and their allies have propped up the Dergue regime with military hardware and "advisers." However, Ethiopia continues to export a large portion of its coffee to the U.S. and other Western countries.

Breaking Up Is Hard to Do: Liberation Fronts in several regions have challenged the Ethiopian central government. In the Ogaden desert region of the southeast, ethnic Somalis backed by the government of Somalia nearly separated the region before the Soviets and Cubans bolstered the Ethiopian military. Somali forces support annexation by Somalia. The rebels in the mountainous northern province of Tigre, who advocate greater autonomy within Ethiopia, control as much as 85% of their province, while the Oromo Liberation Front in the populous, coffee-growing south is just getting started.

The major regional movements are in Eritrea, that band of Ethiopian territory annexed by Emperor Selassie after W.W. II. Home to 3.5 million people—a half million of whom are refugees in neighboring countries—Eritrea's 45,000 sq. mi. provide Ethiopia with its only seacoast, along the Red Sea. The oldest rebel organization is the Eritrean Liberation Front, which has been fighting for about two decades. The ELF has recently taken a more conciliatory stance toward the Dergue, perhaps accepting regional autonomy, and it has engaged in fighting, on and off, against the newer but larger Eritrean People's Liberation Front. The Marxist-oriented EPLF not only has proven itself effective militarily against the Ethiopian army, but also has established a viable political and economic organization within its territories. In addition, it has provided training for several thousand members of the Tigre People's Liberation Front and the Oromo Liberation Front.

FAEROE ISLANDS

Location: 18 inhabited islands in the North Atlantic, between Iceland and Scotland. **Size:** 540 sq. mi. (1,399 sq. km.). **Population:** 44,000.

Who Really Rules: The Faeroes are a self-governing province of Denmark, with two representatives in the Danish parliament. Primarily a fishing economy, the local government relies on subsidies from the Danish central government for a portion of its budget. The most important issue in the 1980 Faeroe Islands parliamentary elections was whether government-owned ferry service should be extended through the winter.

FALKLAND ISLANDS (ISLAS MALVINAS)

Location: Two major and 200 minor islands in the South Atlantic, northeast of Cape Horn. **Size:** 4,700 sq. mi. (12,173 sq. km.). **Population:** 2,000.

Who Really Rules: The Falkland Islands are a British colony, populated by British colonists who produce wool for export to the U.K. Argentina also claims the islands, calling them the Islas Malvinas, and the Argentinean air force provides the only regular air service.

FIJI

Location: An island group in the Melanesian southwestern Pacific, east of Australia. **Size:** 7,056 sq. mi. (18,274 sq. km.). **Population:** 646,000 (50% Indian; 44% Fijian; 6% European, Chinese, etc.).

Who Really Rules: Fiji's freely elected parliament is chosen according to a formula guaranteeing representation for the various ethnic groups. Indigenous Fijians have the privilege of owning land, but East Indians, the descendants of indentured sugar workers, are only allowed to lease land. Sugar, the islands' major industry, is now under government control, and the government also runs Air Pacific, a regional airline. Much of the economy, however, is privately owned.

FINLAND

Location: In northern Europe, between the Gulf of Bothnia (Baltic Sea) and Karelia (U.S.S.R.). **Size:** 130,119 sq. mi. (337,009 sq. km.). **Population:** 4,786,000.

Who Really Rules: Finland is a multiparty democracy governed by a center-left coalition. The aging president, Urho Kekkonen, is a popular leader, largely because of his ability to maintain Finland's independence while preserving its friendship with the Soviet Union, with which it shares a 1,000-mi. frontier. Finland has a free market economy, but a number of enterprises are state or cooperatively owned, and there is a broad range of social welfare programs.

The reindeer-raising Lapp minority, with 50,000 people in northern Finland, Scandinavia, and the Soviet Kola Peninsula, is losing its culture through exposure to industrial cultures from the south. Finland has created a special Lapp parliament and offers schooling in native languages to slow this trend.

FRANCE

Location: In western Europe, between the Atlantic Ocean and the Mediterranean Sea, including the Mediterranean island of Corsica. **Size:** 211,207 sq. mi. (547,026 sq. km.). **Population:** 53,844,000.
Who Really Rules: Center-right parties held the presidency and National Assembly for 23 years until Socialist Party leader François Mitterrand was elected president in May, 1981 and the left wing won a legislative majority the following month. France operates as a capitalist nation, but the government owns controlling shares of leading corporations in industries such as auto production, banking, and petroleum.

Though a member of NATO, France maintains an independent foreign policy and has its own nuclear weapons program. It is a major supplier of sophisticated arms to much of the third world.

FRENCH GUIANA

Location: On the northern coast of South America, between Surinam and Brazil. **Size:** 35,135 sq. mi. (91,000 sq. km.). **Population:** 65,000.
Who Really Rules: The last colony in South America, French Guiana is technically an overseas department of France, with representation in the French parliament. A penal colony until the late 1940s, French Guiana is the home of France's rocket-launching center.

Most of the work force is employed by the French government. Only Indians and members of the Foreign Legion go into the sparsely populated jungle interior, although France has resettled 100 Laotian tribal families in an inland jungle clearing.

FRENCH POLYNESIA

Location: Islands scattered in the Polynesian southern Pacific, south of Hawaii. **Size:** 1,544 sq. mi. (4,000 sq. km.). **Population:** 150,000 (80% Polynesian).
Who Really Rules: French Polynesia is a territory of France, with representation in the French National Assembly. Since 1980 all political parties, including the Gaullist party of European French residents, have favored either self-government or complete independence. However, the present government of France adamantly rejects this sentiment. Not only do Tahiti and the other islands produce important tourist income, but Mururoa Atoll is the site of all French nuclear weapons tests.

GABON

Location: Between Equatorial Guinea and the Congo on the Atlantic (Gulf of Guinea) coast of Africa. **Size:** 103,346 sq. mi. (267,667 sq. km.). **Population:** 605,000 (excluding recent immigrants).
Who Really Rules: Resource-rich Gabon is ruled by President El Hadj Omar Bongo and his Gabonese Democratic party. Though the country has a minimum wage and a social security system, income levels vary

considerably. Most skilled jobs are held by French nationals—there are about 25,000 in Gabon—and African expatriates. Bongo has amassed a fortune while president. In 1979 he justified the purchase of a $2 million home in Beverly Hills, Calif., by virtue of the fact that his daughters were attending school in Los Angeles.

Gabon is an ally of France, its former master, and takes part in joint military maneuvers. Economic policy is influenced by American and European banks, whose primary concern is that the extraction and export of lumber, manganese, uranium, and petroleum remain undisturbed.

THE GAMBIA

Location: Along the Gambia River on the west coast of Africa, surrounded by Senegal. **Size:** 4,361 sq. mi. (11,295 sq. km.). **Population:** 627,000.

Who Really Rules: The Gambia's multiparty democracy is led by President Sir Alhaji Dawda Kairaba Jawara and his People's Progressive party. Ethnic ties influence politics, so Jawara balances his cabinet appointments among the various tribes. Peanuts are the major export, but tourism also generates significant foreign income as thousands of northern Europeans come to Gambia each year to enjoy its climate and political stability. Since Gambia has no differences with neighboring Senegal, it maintains no armed forces, just an internal police force.

GERMANY, EAST (GERMAN DEMOCRATIC REPUBLIC)

Location: The eastern third of present-day Germany, west of Poland on the Baltic Sea in central Europe. **Size:** 41,768 sq. mi. (108,178 sq. km.). **Population:** 16,756,000.

Who Really Rules: East Germany is a one-party state, ruled by the Social Unity (Communist) party, an elite meritocracy. The government strictly limits emigration and free speech, but it no longer jams Western broadcasts. Many East Germans now watch West German television.

East Germany has a state-owned, centrally planned economy, with a comprehensive social welfare system. The standard of living is the highest in the Communist world.

Since W.W. II East Germany has been occupied by Soviet troops.

GERMANY, WEST (FEDERAL REPUBLIC OF)

Location: The south and western two thirds of present-day Germany, east of France, Belgium, and the Netherlands in central Europe. **Size:** 95,976 sq. mi. (248,577 sq. km.). **Population:** 60,948,000.

Who Really Rules: West Germany is a multiparty parliamentary democracy, governed by a coalition of the labor-oriented Social Democratic party and the liberal Free Democrats. The largest party, the conservative Christian Democratic party leads the opposition.

West Germany has one of the strongest capitalist economies in the world. Though U.S. companies still control important German enterprises, German-based companies are buying into U.S. corporations as well. The German currency, the deutsche mark, anchors the European monetary system. West Germany's major trade partners are its Common Market partners and the U.S., but it also carries on more trade with the Soviet Union than any other Western country. The U.S. still stations 200,000 troops in West Germany, but the Social Democratic government frequently disagrees with U.S. military policy in NATO.

GHANA

Location: On the Gulf of Guinea (Atlantic Ocean), between Togo and the Ivory Coast, in Africa. **Size:** 92,099 sq. mi. (238,537 sq. km.). **Population:** 12,737,000.

Who Really Rules: In September, 1979, the Armed Forces Revolutionary Council, which had been in control for less than four months, turned power over to a freely elected government headed by President Hilla Limann of the People's National party. Limann has done little to curb corruption or bolster the country's sagging economy other than to impose "austerity" measures urged by the International Monetary Fund. Those measures sparked a series of strikes and led to speculation about a right-wing coup or a popular uprising led by former Flight Lt. Jerry Rawlings, the young officer who led the popular military government that preceded Limann.

Volta Aluminum, owned by Kaiser Aluminum and Reynolds Metals, uses 70% of the Akosombo Dam's electrical power to smelt aluminum. The company's 30-year contract for cheap power does not expire until 1997, but it still imports bauxite from Jamaica and ignores Ghana's deposits.

GIBRALTAR

Location: A massive rock at the southern tip of Spain, overlooking the entrance into the Mediterranean Sea from the Atlantic Ocean. **Size:** 2 sq. mi. (6 sq. km.). **Population:** 29,000.

Who Really Rules: Though claimed by Spain, Gibraltar has been a British colony, home to a British naval base, for nearly 270 years. The U.K. is prepared to cede the rock back to Spain should the local population approve, but the Gibraltarians overwhelmingly oppose association with Spain. The Labour party, led by Chief Minister Sir Joshua Hassan, controls the freely elected House of Assembly.

GREECE

Location: The southern section of the Balkan Peninsula, plus surrounding islands—including Crete—in southeastern Europe. **Size:** 50,944 sq. mi. (131,944 sq. km.). **Population:** 9,590,000.

Who Really Rules: Greece's multiparty parliamentary democracy is currently governed by Prime Minister Konstandinos Karamanlis's New Democracy party. In elections scheduled for late 1981, New Democracy is expected to face stiff opposition from the left, especially Andreas Papandreou's Panhellenic Socialist Movement (PASOK).

Greece is scheduled to join the European Common Market in 1981, and European companies are expected to swallow many Greek enterprises. Unlike other recent additions to the Common Market, Greece never held a referendum on the issue. Should PASOK and other leftist parties win a parliamentary majority, they could reverse the decision.

GREENLAND

Location: A large island in the North Atlantic. **Size:** 840,000 sq. mi. (2,175,600 sq. km.). **Population:** 49,000.
Who Really Rules: A province of Denmark, Greenland is an extension of that Scandinavian country's welfare state. Four fifths of its budget comes from Denmark, and continental Danes hold most skilled and professional jobs.

Most of the people of Greenland are of Eskimo descent, but Danish "benevolence" has virtually destroyed the native culture. Greenlanders, predominantly fishing people, live off the sea and the land, so they oppose development of the island's anticipated offshore oil deposits. Not only do they fear pollution, but they have never welcomed foreign investment. These concerns have stimulated a strong native movement for home rule.

GRENADA

Location: One major island and several smaller islands (the Grenadines) at the southern end of the Lesser Antilles, in the eastern Caribbean. **Size:** 133 sq. mi. (344 sq. km.). **Population:** 111,000.
Who Really Rules: Grenada is run by the New JEWEL (Joint Endeavor for Welfare, Education, and Liberation) Movement, headed by Prime Minister Maurice Bishop. Bishop's People's Revolutionary Army seized power from unpopular Prime Minister Eric Gairy in a March, 1979, coup. Since then it has arrested opponents and banned the island's only independent newspaper. The government is socialist, dedicated to improving conditions for the island's poor population, but it has nationalized only one enterprise, a bottling plant, following a labor dispute.

Cuba is supporting the Grenada revolution with guns, technicians, and an airport construction crew, but the New JEWEL Movement has chosen to affiliate with the Socialist International, which includes parties such as the German and Scandinavian Social Democrats as well as the British and Israeli Labour parties.

GUADELOUPE

Location: Several islands in the eastern Caribbean, between Dominica and Antigua. **Size:** 687 sq. mi. (1,779 sq. km.). **Population:** 319,000 (90% black).

Who Really Rules: France governs Guadeloupe as an overseas department, and European French citizens operate the local government and economy. Guadeloupians vote in French elections, but a growing percentage of the native population is urging autonomy or independence. Several thousand young Guadeloupians are employed in France.

GUAM

Location: Southernmost of the Marianas island chain, in the western Pacific, more than 1,400 mi. east of the Philippines. **Size:** 212 sq. mi. (549 sq. km.). **Population:** 110,000.

Who Really Rules: Guam is a self-governing territory of the U.S. and sends a nonvoting representative to the U.S. Congress. The U.S. military, which operates a B-52 base, nuclear submarine base, and other facilities on the island, overshadows all other economic activity. In 1978 local employers attacked the U.S. Labor Dept. for policies that were preventing them from importing construction laborers from the Philippines and South Korea. The U.S. and local governments own two thirds of Guam's land area.

GUATEMALA

Location: Straddling Central America, southeast of Mexico. **Size:** 42,042 sq. mi. (108,889 sq. km.). **Population:** 7,377,000 (41.4% Indian, 58.6% Ladino).

Who Really Rules: Guatemala is governed by the military, the wealthy landowning class, and the growing urban industrial elite. A small number of families own most of the land, producing coffee, cotton, sugar, bananas, and meat for export. The urban working class and the majority of the people who work in agriculture (when they work at all) are impoverished. Conditions are particularly bad for the non-Spanish-speaking Indian population.

Since the late 1960s the U.S. has trained and armed Guatemala's security forces to fight recurring guerrilla movements. In addition to openly sanctioned repression, right-wing death squads with links to the government have killed more than 20,000 people since 1966.

GUINEA

Location: On the west African coast, between Guinea-Bissau and Sierra Leone. **Size:** 94,964 sq. mi. (245,957 sq. km.). **Population:** 5,655,000.

Who Really Rules: Since independence in 1958, Guinea has been governed by President Sékou Touré, leader of its only party, the Democratic party of Guinea. Ostensibly socialist, the country is essentially under Touré's personal rule. Most of the economy is state-run, but following demonstrations by market women in 1977, the government abandoned a two-year experiment in government market control. Touré has released several hundred political prisoners in recent years, but human rights violations continue.

The Soviet Union, which helped develop Guinea's bauxite mines, imports most of the country's bauxite. Guinea does not always toe the Soviet line, and in the mid-1970s Guinea reopened relations with France and its pro-French neighbors.

GUINEA-BISSAU

Location: On the west African coast, between Guinea and Senegal, plus adjacent islands. **Size:** 13,948 sq. mi. (36,125 sq. km.). **Population:** 665,000.

Who Really Rules: Guinea-Bissau is a one-party state, governed by the left-wing PAIGC (Partido Africano da Independencia da Guinee e Cabo Verde) since independence in 1974. During the war for independence, the population in liberated zones was organized into local "political committees." That structure remains today; there are about 1,000 such committees throughout the country.

In November, 1980, a military coup led by Maj. João Bernardo Vieira overthrew the government of revolutionary leader Luis Cabral, who was charged with subordinating the Guinean people to an elite from the Cape Verde Islands, as well as emphasizing industrial development rather than agricultural modernization.

GUYANA

Location: On the northeastern coast of South America, between Venezuela and Surinam. **Size:** 83,000 sq. mi. (214,969 sq. km.). **Population:** 851,000 (53% East Indian, 42% black).

Who Really Rules: President Forbes Burnham and his Peoples National Congress (PNC), placed in power by British authorities and the CIA, have ruled Guyana since independence in 1966. Burnham retains power through violence, electoral fraud, and restrictions such as the outright denial of newsprint to the opposition's formerly daily newspaper. The PNC is predominantly black, while the larger of the two Marxist opposition parties, Cheddi Jagan's Peoples Progressive party, is largely East Indian.

During the mid-1970s Guyana upgraded its relations with Cuba, adopted left-wing rhetoric, and nationalized foreign bauxite and plantation holdings. Although the government now owns 80% of Guyana's economy, the economy is based on exports and financial assistance from the International Monetary Fund and the World Bank. Those international agencies have insisted upon an austerity program in which the government has held down wages and reduced social services and food subsidies.

HAITI

Location: Eastern part of the Caribbean island of Hispaniola, between

Cuba and Puerto Rico. **Size:** 10,714 sq. mi. (27,750 sq. km.). **Population:** 6,018,000 (90% black, 10% mulatto).

Who Really Rules: Haiti is a dictatorship under president-for-life Jean-Claude Duvalier, son of the late dictator François Duvalier. Under Jean-Claude, Haiti's ruling class has divided into two factions. The "Old Guard" landowning class, backed by the paramilitary Tontons Macoute, opposes any liberalization of authoritarian rule or opening to foreign capital. The "Jean-Claudistes," on the other hand, have favored an increased foreign role in the economy including a $41 million loan from the International Monetary Fund. Although the annual income per capita in Haiti is $250, Jean-Claude spent $5 million on his May, 1980, wedding. Anyone convicted of criticizing Jean-Claude in the press is subject to three years' imprisonment.

HONDURAS

Location: In Central America, bordered by Guatemala, El Salvador, and Nicaragua. **Size:** 43,277 sq. mi. (112,088 sq. km.). **Population:** 3,958,000.

Who Really Rules: Honduras is in the early stages of the class conflict that has broken out into civil war in neighboring Central American republics. Though Honduras has been ruled by various military factions since 1972, the U.S., through its military aid program, is promoting the return of civilian rule. In April, 1980, the military organized elections for a constituent assembly from which left-wing and Christian Democratic parties were excluded. Despite predictions that the election would be rigged to favor the oligarchy's right-wing National party, the opposition Liberal party—split between conservative and reformist factions—won a majority. Though Honduras is no longer a "banana republic," Standard Fruit (Castle & Cooke) and United Fruit (United Brands) remain powerful.

HONG KONG

Location: Islands and peninsula on southern coast of China, near the Pearl River estuary. **Size:** 403 sq. mi. (1,045 sq. km.). **Population:** 5,000,000.

Who Really Rules: A crown colony of the United Kingdom, Hong Kong is administered by an appointed governor under the guidance of the ruling party in Great Britain. The Hong Kong economy, traditionally the bastion of British capital and Chinese businessmen who fled China during the revolution, is open to multinational manufacturing and finance ventures from Japan, the U.S., and elsewhere.

China claims sovereignty over the colony, and the largest, least developed section—the New Territories—is scheduled to revert to China when Britain's lease expires in 1997.

HUNGARY

Location: Landlocked in east central Europe, north of Yugoslavia. **Size:** 35,919 sq. mi. (93,030 sq. km.). **Population:** 10,791,000.

Who Really Rules: Since the Soviet Union crushed the 1956 uprising, Hungary's Socialist Workers' party (Communist) government has been led by János Kádár. Despite the presence of 70,000 Soviet troops, Hungary is one of the most liberal of Soviet bloc regimes. The government tolerates social criticism but not political opposition.

All industrial and agricultural production is organized in cooperatives or state-owned firms, but the government allows those enterprises to follow market economics. A large portion of Hungary's economic activity takes place in the "secondary" economy, where service and construction workers moonlight. Even four-story apartment buildings have been built in this unofficial sector.

ICELAND

Location: An island in the North Atlantic between Scandinavia and Greenland. **Size:** 39,768 sq. mi. (103,000 sq. km.). **Population:** 231,000.
Who Really Rules: Iceland's multiparty parliamentary system has a long history. The first parliament, or Althing, met in 930 A.D., but Iceland did not become independent from Denmark until 1944. The labor movement and environmental protection movement are particularly strong. Iceland has no army or navy of its own, but the U.S. operates a strategic naval air station at Keflavik.

INDIA

Location: Large central portion of the Indian subcontinent in southern Asia, plus islands in the eastern Indian Ocean. **Size:** 1,269,340 sq. mi. (3,287,590 sq. km.). **Population:** 683,810,051 (72% Indo-Aryan, 25% Dravidian; 84% Hindu, 11% Muslim, 2% Sikh).
Who Really Rules: India, the world's largest parliamentary democracy, is currently governed by Indira Gandhi and her branch of the Indian National Congress (Congress party). Though deposed by the Janata electoral coalition in 1977, Gandhi's party swept the 1980 national elections, picking up two thirds of the seats in Parliament with 42% of the popular vote. The new government wasted little time in passing a new national security law which allows anyone to be jailed for a year without trial.

Although the caste system has been outlawed, the Hindu elite is still in control of business, the government bureaucracy, and the Congress party. Armed with the help of the Soviet Union, India is the major military power in the Indian Ocean region. As a major trading partner and aid recipient of the capitalist West, however, India's foreign policy is independent.
Breaking Up Is Hard to Do: Nearly surrounded by Burma, Bangladesh, Bhutan, and Tibet (China), the seven Indian states of the northeast are home to 23 million people.

In *Assam*, the most populous state in the region, Bengali immigrants (from Bangladesh as well as from West Bengal) may already outnumber the native Assamese, who fear the influx of outsiders. Though the Communist party that rules *Tripura* has strong followings among the tribal population and the Bengali majority, communal violence broke out there in 1980. Similar conflicts have arisen in *Meghalaya*.

There is also interfaith violence in the three eastern states of *Nagaland, Manipur,* and *Mizoram*, but the Indian central government is more concerned about secessionists. None of the native peoples—Nagas, Meitis, and Mizos—recognized their post–W.W. II absorption into India, and the predominantly Christian Nagas and Mizos have been engaged in sporadic guerrilla warfare ever since. In the late 1970s Meiti rebels took up armed struggle as well. All three movements appear to be left-wing and have received training in China.

Sikkim, an independent kingdom until annexed by India in 1975, is separated from the rest of the region by an arm of the state of West Bengal. There is tension between the Nepalese, the 70% of the population whose forebears arrived in the 18th and 19th centuries, and the indigenous Bhutias and Lepchas. All three ethnic groups resent recent arrivals from the Indian lowlands, and they are suspicious of the Indian central government.

INDONESIA

Location: Most of the East Indies Archipelago, between Australia and mainland Southeast Asia. **Size:** 782,659 sq. mi. (2,027,087 sq. km.) (excluding East Timor). **Population:** 154,000,000.

Who Really Rules: The government and many of the economic enterprises of Indonesia are effectively controlled by active and former top military officials. General Suharto, the president, has balanced the interests of numerous anti-Communist military factions since he seized power in 1965–1966. Whenever the press, student groups, or Muslim activists challenge the authority of the government—usually in protest of high-level corruption—the military cracks down, with arrests and censorship. In the past few years Indonesia has released most of the remaining tens of thousands of leftists held without trial since the late 1960s, but the government watches the former prisoners to ensure that they do not become politically active.

Since the late 1960s Suharto has relied heavily upon U.S. military aid, economic assistance from the U.S. and its allies, and the cooperation of multinational banks and resource corporations, such as Caltex, a joint venture of Standard Oil of California and Texaco. Though foreign capitalist interests support the military because it reversed Indonesia's slide toward communism and economic nationalism, foreign investors don't have much confidence in the managerial abilities of military leaders. For this reason they have insisted that U.S.-trained "technocrats" be given power over the Indonesian economy.

IRAN

Location: In southwestern Asia, between the U.S.S.R. and the Persian Gulf (Indian Ocean). **Size:** 636,293 sq. mi. (1,648,000 sq. km.).

Population: 40,469,000 (50% Persian, 30% Turkic, 10% Kurdish, 3% Arab and other Semitic).

Who Really Rules: The Ayatollah Ruhollah Khomeini, a charismatic Shiite religious leader, is the acknowledged leader of the Iranian revolution that overthrew Shah Mohammed Reza Pahlavi in 1979. His word—at least his interpretation of the Koran—is essentially law, but he does not take part in routine government functions. Political power is split between two Islamic revolutionary factions. In the minority are those with relatively moderate, quasi-socialistic tendencies. On the other side, the Islamic Republican party holds a majority in the Iranian parliament—the Majlis—which was also elected in 1980. The Islamic Republicans are led by nationalist, right-wing fundamentalist clergy.

Leftist political groups that fought to bring down the shah are still active, with bases in factories, universities, and even the peasantry. Many of the workers' councils and peasants' councils established during the revolutionary period are still intact, despite opposition from the Islamic leadership.

Breaking Up Is Hard to Do: Farsi-speaking (ethnic Persian) Iranians make up only half the population. Kurds, who number as many as 14 million—in Iraq, Syria, the U.S.S.R., and Turkey as well as in Iran—are generally Sunni Muslims. Active in the rebellion against the shah, armed Kurdish groups have been fighting the Iranian central government for regional autonomy in their northwestern region.

Turkomans, tribespeople in the northeast, have also been fighting for autonomy. There are about a third of a million Turkomans in Iran, and a million more of this Sunni group in the Soviet Union and Afghanistan. Baluchis in southeastern Iran number 2 million, but there are a million more in neighboring Pakistan and Afghanistan. The Baluchis are also Sunni, and they have rebelled against central control in all three countries where they reside. Other, less populous tribal groups are equally militant.

Some of the ethnic autonomy movements consider autonomy as only part of a second phase of the Iranian revolution, in which Khomeini's theocracy would be replaced. However, links between the various ethnic groups are weak.

IRAQ

Location: In the Tigris and Euphrates valleys, bordered by Iran, Saudi Arabia, and Syria, in the Middle East. **Size:** 167,924 sq. mi. (434,924 sq. km.). **Population:** 14,042,000 (71% Arabs, 18% Kurds; 50% Shia Muslim, 40% Sunni Muslim).

Who Really Rules: Iraq is controlled by the Arab Socialist, or Ba'ath, party of Iraq, which took power in a 1968 coup. President Saddam Hussein's government does not tolerate opposition. In 1979 several Ba'ath leaders were charged with conspiring to overthrow Hussein and executed.

In 1975 the central government brought the Kurdish minority under control, but the predominantly Sunni Ba'ath leadership fears an uprising by the Shia majority, which has been urged to rebel by Iran's Ayatollah Khomeini. In 1980 Hussein executed the leader of Iraq's Shiites. The central government also continues to face opposition from the Kurdish minority, which seeks autonomy.

For many years Iraq received most of its arms from the Soviet Union, but relations have cooled since 1978, when Hussein decimated the Iraq Communist party leadership. Iraq now buys weapons from France and imports technology from Japan. Hussein's hope of using his oil wealth and well-equipped military to lead the Arab region was dealt a serious blow in 1980, when his invading army met stiff resistance from the disorganized Iranian armed forces in Iran's Khuzistan Province.

IRELAND (EIRE)

Location: All but the northeastern corner of the British Isles island of Eire, off the Atlantic coast of Europe. **Size:** 27,136 sq. mi. (70,283 sq. km.). **Population:** 3,349,000.

Who Really Rules: Three parties hold seats in Ireland's democratically elected parliament. Prime Minister Charles Haughey leads the majority Fianna Fáil party. One of the European Common Market's less affluent members, Ireland has encouraged investment by U.S. and Japanese manufacturers wishing to market their products in Europe. By 1980, 70 foreign electronics companies had set up plants in Ireland.

Though public opinion in Ireland supports the return of Ulster (Northern Ireland) to Ireland from the U.K., all major parties oppose the tactics of the revolutionary provisional wing of the Irish Republican Army.

ISLE OF MAN

Location: An island in the Irish Sea, between Great Britain and Ireland. **Size:** 227 sq. mi. (588 sq. km.). **Population:** 65,000.

Who Really Rules: Although a British dependency midway between Liverpool and Belfast, the Isle of Man is not a part of the U.K. Except on foreign affairs and military issues, it is self-governing, and it has a special trading relationship with the Common Market. English is the official language, and less than 300 residents still speak the native Manx. The legislature consists of the Legislative Council, which is appointed and indirectly elected, and the elected House of Key.

ISRAEL

Location: On the southeastern Mediterranean coast, between Egypt and Lebanon. **Size:** 8,019 sq. mi. (20,770 sq. km.) in Israel proper; 2,099 sq. mi. (5,439 sq. km.) in occupied West Bank and Gaza. **Population:** 3,890,000 (85% Jewish) in Israel proper; 750,000 in West Bank and Gaza.

Who Really Rules: Israel is a multiparty parliamentary democracy, currently governed by the right-wing Likud bloc coalition of Prime Minister Menachem Begin. The Labor party (Mapai), which held power from independence in 1948 until 1977, leads a large opposition.

The country has a mixed economy with extensive welfare programs. Histadrut, the labor federation for both Jews and non-Jews (predominantly Arab Muslims), is in fact Israel's largest employer, owning not only cooperatives and agricultural collectives but also corporate enterprises. Well-educated Jews of European descent (Ashkenazim) are generally more affluent than Sephardic (Mediterranean and Middle Eastern) Jews. Non-Jewish Arabs remain at the bottom of the economic and social ladder.

In a constant state of war since before its independence, Israel diverts a huge portion of its national resources to the military. Israel relies heavily on weapons and financial assistance from the U.S. government, as well as on private contributions from American Jewry. Since Israel turned the Sinai oil fields over to Egypt, the U.S. has guaranteed Israel's fuel supply.

West Bank and Gaza: Though Israel also occupies sections of Syria, Egypt, and, indirectly, Lebanon, those areas administered by Jordan and the U.N. from 1948 to 1967 are still considered to be Palestine. The Gaza Strip (south of Tel Aviv on the Mediterranean coast) and the West Bank (the area west of the Jordan River, including Arab—East—Jerusalem) may become a Palestinian (Arab) state or an autonomous region of Israel. Presently, however, the occupied territories are under the arbitrary authority of the Israeli military.

Israelis are divided as to the future of Palestine. While all Israelis reject the official Palestinian program of eliminating the Jewish state, many oppose the establishment of Israeli settlements in the occupied territories. Few Israelis want the West Bank and Gaza to become part of a unitary Israeli state, however, for that would give the vote to hundreds of thousands of Arabs and dilute Jewish power.

ITALY

Location: A peninsula in south central Europe, jutting from the Alps into the Mediterranean Sea, plus the islands of Sardinia and Sicily to the southwest. **Size:** 116,303 sq. mi. (301,225 sq. km.). **Population:** 57,513,000.

Who Really Rules: Italy's multiparty parliamentary democracy is perpetually in crisis. Since W.W. II the Christian Democratic party has led the government, presently in coalition with the Socialists. The independent Communist party is the largest opposition bloc.

Italy's provincial, regional, and local governments have substantial authority. Left-wing, Communist-led coalitions control many of those governments, including those of most of Italy's major cities.

With key U.S. and NATO military bases in Italy, the U.S. has strongly discouraged the Christian Democratic leadership from allowing Communist participation in the government.

IVORY COAST

Location: On the south coast of western Africa, between Liberia and Ghana. **Size:** 124,503 sq. mi. (322,463 sq. km.). **Population:** 8,513,000.
Who Really Rules: Since independence in 1960, the Ivory Coast has been ruled by the firm hand of President Félix Houphouet-Boigny. Not until 1980 did his Democratic party allow candidates not selected by party leadership to run for the National Assembly. In the 1980 legislative elections, only 20 of 147 incumbents were returned to office.

The Ivory Coast has a consistent record of economic growth, based upon export-oriented farm products such as cacao and coffee. Some of the wealth trickles down to the peasantry, but land ownership is becoming more concentrated. Houphouet-Boigny himself has massive holdings. The economy is controlled by French corporations and other foreign investors and by local French and Lebanese. French expatriates hold key positions in Ivory Coast government and industry, and several hundred French troops are stationed there.

JAMAICA

Location: An island in the central Caribbean, south of Cuba, west of Hispaniola. **Size:** 4,244 sq. mi. (10,991 sq. km.). **Population:** 2,313,000 (91% black and Afro-European, 3.4% East Indian and Afro-East Indian, 3.2% white).
Who Really Rules: Prime Minister Edward Seaga's Jamaica Labour party defeated Michael Manley and his ruling People's National party in the October, 1980, parliamentary elections. Under the leadership of Manley, Jamaica had imposed higher taxes and tight controls on the powerful American aluminum companies that mine bauxite on the island. The resulting decline in bauxite exports, rising oil import costs, and other factors hurt the Jamaican economy, so Manley turned to the International Monetary Fund and American banks for assistance. In the late 1970s Manley's government decided that IMF demands for domestic austerity were too strict, and refused to make a new agreement. Meanwhile, the U.S. and Britain, concerned about Manley's friendship with Fidel Castro as well as his economic nationalism, reduced their aid.

The resulting economic downturn was the primary factor in the 57%-to-43% right-wing election victory. Neither of the two major party leaders is black.

JAPAN

Location: Four major and many minor islands off the east coast of Asia, near the Korean Peninsula. **Size:** 143,750 sq. mi. (372,313 sq. km.). **Population:** 118,783,000.
Who Really Rules: The Liberal Democratic party, which holds a solid majority in both houses of the National Diet, has governed Japan since

W.W. II. The pro-business LDP is made up of a number of personality-oriented factions.

Japanese industry is organized into several huge *zaibatsu*, economic groups that descend from the prewar holding companies of "fascist" Japan. Each *zaibatsu* is headed by at least one major bank, which influences member corporations by controlling their financial sources. The presidents of companies in each group meet regularly. The government, through agencies such as the powerful Ministry of International Trade and Industry, cooperates with *zaibutsu* leaders in establishing industrial and government policy. This integrated form of capitalism has been nicknamed "Japan, Inc.," because of the ability of the Japanese government and companies to unite around an apparent single goal.

Japan is the only major capitalist nation with minimal American investment or economic control. The U.S. does exercise considerable influence over Japan, however, through the presence of more than 44,000 air, land, and sea forces.

JORDAN

Location: Landlocked in the Middle East, bordered by Israel, Syria, Iraq, and Saudi Arabia. **Size:** 37,737 sq. mi. (97,740 sq. km.). **Population:** 2,453,000.

Who Really Rules: King Hussein is the ultimate power in Jordan, particularly since 1970, when he liquidated the Jordanian branch of the Palestine Liberation Organization. His major allies are presently Iraq and Saudi Arabia. Hussein has been on the CIA payroll for years. The Jordanian army, loyal to Hussein, has a long friendship with the U.S., which supplies it with advanced weapons. Officially at war with Israel, private Jordanians carry out regular trade with Israel over the Jordan River at the Allenby Bridge.

KAMPUCHEA (CAMBODIA)

Location: On Southeast Asia's Indochina Peninsula, fronting the Gulf of Thailand between Vietnam and Thailand. **Size:** 69,898 sq. mi. (181,035 sq. km.). **Population:** 4,850,000.

Who Really Rules: Since early 1979, when Communist Vietnamese troops drove troops of Democratic Kampuchea (ruled by the Communist Khmer Rouge) from Phnom Penh, the capital city, Kampuchea has been governed by a People's Revolutionary Council headed by Heng Samrin. Heng and his top aides are defectors from the Khmer Rouge regime, but lower-level officials are remnants of the U.S.-backed Gen. Lon Nol government, deposed by the Khmer Rouge in 1975.

Heng Samrin's government is entirely dependent upon Vietnamese military protection, technical assistance from Vietnam and the Soviet bloc, and humanitarian aid from around the world. It is building a state-owned, centrally planned economy. Private commerce, however, has returned to the country, which has been devastated by years of fighting, U.S. bombing, and the harsh rule of the Khmer Rouge.

Khmer Rouge troops, as well as several right-wing guerrilla bands, still resist the Vietnamese occupation. Former neutralist ruler Prince Norodom Sihanouk, overthrown by Lon Nol in 1970, remains on the diplomatic sidelines.

KENYA

Location: On the east coast of equatorial Africa, between Somalia and Tanzania. **Size:** 224,960 sq. mi. (582,646 sq. km.). **Population:** 16,808,000.

Who Really Rules: Kenya's elected government is dominated by leaders of the Kikuyu ethnic group through the Kenya African National Union (KANU) party. Though the KANU leadership selects all National Assembly candidates from those who spend $150 or more to buy "lifetime party memberships," opponents of the Kikuyu leadership have won office. For instance, when in 1979 KANU refused to let Ogiga Odinga, a Luo ethnic group leader and former vice-president, stand for election, his son-in-law and other Luo candidates defeated KANU's national chairman and three other members of the government.

The Kenyan economy is dominated by foreign capital, including British and American-based multinational corporations, and Kenyan citizens of British and American descent. However, the government-backed African commercial class is growing in importance.

KIRIBATI

Location: Micronesian southwest Pacific, midway between Hawaii and Australia, including the former Gilbert Islands, Banaba (Ocean Island), and the Phoenix and Line islands. **Size:** 342 sq. mi. (886 sq. km.). **Population:** 59,000.

Who Really Rules: Kiribati's elective government relies heavily upon assistance from the United Kingdom (its former colonial master), Australia, and New Zealand. It is attempting to take over foreign-owned copra plantations, but it is having difficulty negotiating a price. Islanders from Banaba are due to return there from their exile in Fiji now that the British Phosphate Commission has denuded the island. Banabans are reserved one seat in the Kiribati Assembly. In 1980 the U.S. renounced its claims to 14 islands in Kiribati in exchange for a Kiribati pledge not to allow a third country to use the islands as bases without U.S. permission.

KOREA, NORTH

Location: Northern half of the Korean Peninsula, which juts south from Manchuria (China) into the Pacific Ocean. **Size:** 46,540 sq. mi. (120,538 sq. km.). **Population:** 20,250,000.

Who Really Rules: North Korea is tightly ruled by the Communist Korean Workers' party, headed by Kim Il Sung. More than one tenth of the total population belong to the party, which descends from the anti-

Japanese resistance movement before and during W.W. II. The government and party closely monitor all political activity in the country, restrict travel and access to information, and imprison suspected opponents. Kim Il Sung is glorified by an enormous personality cult in which he is credited for everything that is good in North Korea. Every North Korean (except Kim) wears a badge showing Kim's face; the size of the badge indicates the wearer's status. The ailing Kim is expected to pass his authority on to one of his sons.

An industrial country without unemployment, North Korea is also self-sufficient in most farm goods. The cities are clean, the transportation systems are efficient, and the military is well armed and well trained.

KOREA, SOUTH

Location: Southern half of the Korean Peninsula, plus islands, west of Japan in eastern Asia. **Size:** 38,025 sq. mi. (98,484 sq. km.). **Population:** 40,731,000.

Who Really Rules: President Chun Doo Hwan leads a military regime which tolerates no real opposition and represses union organizing. Following a popular uprising in the southern city of Kwangju, brutally suppressed by troops, Chun's government sentenced opposition leader Kim Dae Jung to life imprisonment. Though Chun's government is unpopular, no South Korean opposition groups identify with the Communist North.

South Korea's manufacturing economy has grown rapidly in the past decade, and so have its debts to foreign banks. Japanese and U.S. corporations operate numerous subsidiaries in South Korea, but the government has supported the emergence of several major Korean-owned industrial groups. The U.S. and Japanese governments may oppose authoritarian rule in Korea, but the export-oriented development strategy which they have encouraged requires low wages and the repressive policies which guarantee them. Chun's regime has been particularly strict about what can be shown on television. Banned have been portrayals of such diverse subjects as extramarital affairs, conflict between the generations, violations of the highway code, and property speculation.

KUWAIT

Location: A small enclave at the northwest end of the Persian Gulf, between Saudi Arabia and Iraq. **Size:** 6,880 sq. mi. (17,818 sq. km.). **Population:** 1,478,000 (including 450,000 native Kuwaitis and 300,000 Palestinians).

Who Really Rules: Kuwait is a Bedouin emirate, ruled by the al-Sabah family. Since 1976, when the emir dissolved the National Assembly, there has been no elective body. The ruling family uses Kuwait's enormous oil revenues to provide essential goods and services to citizens and expatriates free or for nominal cost. Citizens also have the right to own land. There are a number of prosperous merchant families, such as the al-Ghanim family, whose YAAS (Yusuf A. al-Ghanim & Sons) retails cars, airline tickets, television sets, construction equipment, and virtually everything else in Kuwait.

LAOS

Location: Landlocked on Southeast Asia's Indochinese Peninsula, between Vietnam and Thailand. **Size:** 91,429 sq. mi. (236,800 sq. km.). **Population:** 3,500,000.

Who Really Rules: Laos is governed by the Lao People's Revolutionary (Communist) party, led by the Pathet Lao guerrilla movement leadership. The regime's opponents, including former U.S. allies and former Pathet Lao cadre, are sent to reeducation camps, from which they are released once they agree to toe the government line. Armed opposition, particularly among the Hmong (Meo) tribal group that fought for the American CIA, continues in a few areas. Laos has a special relationship with Vietnam, which supports the Lao government with 40,000 troops and technical assistance.

Though the Communists have nationalized industry and imposed central planning, this agricultural subsistence economy is far from socialist. Most peasants still work privately owned land, the free market is tolerated, and private real-estate holdings are legal.

LEBANON

Location: On the eastern Mediterranean coast, between Syria and Israel. **Size:** 4,015 sq. mi. (10,400 sq. km.). **Population:** 3,071,000.

Who Really Rules: For many years Lebanon served as the financial and commercial center of the Middle East, but the prosperity that it brought multinational corporations and the Lebanese merchant class did not spread throughout the society. Ancient religious conflicts, the presence of Palestinian Muslim refugees, and social inequities created the diverse forces that exploded in the 1975–1976 civil war. Although there continues to be fighting, some commerce has returned, but the Lebanese central government and army are having a difficult time establishing authority.

Different zones of the country are governed by right-wing Christian militias; the Lebanese National Movement, a front of leftist Muslims; the Palestine Liberation Organization (PLO); Syrian troops leading an Arab internal peace-keeping force; U.N. troops monitoring areas near the Israeli border; and Maj. Saad Haddad's "Free Lebanon" militia of right-wing Christians and Shiites, which, with Israeli help, controls a 700-sq.-km. area on the Israeli border. In retaliation against Palestinian raids against Israel, Israeli forces frequently bomb or raid Palestinian and leftist zones within Lebanon.

LESOTHO

Location: Surrounded by South Africa, separated from the Indian Ocean by the Bantustan of Transkei. **Size:** 11,720 sq. mi. (30,355 sq. km.). **Population:** 1,380,000.

Who Really Rules: Since independence from Britain in 1966, Lesotho has been governed by Prime Minister Chief Leabua Jonathan and his Basutoland National party. The opposition Basutoland Congress party (BCP), headed by Ntsu Mokhehle, won the 1970 National Assembly elections, but Jonathan charged it with vote fraud and annulled the results. The banned BCP has strong support among lower-level government employees and from a popular church newspaper. In 1979 it launched a guerrilla campaign to depose Jonathan or force new elections.

Surrounded by South Africa, Lesotho must coexist with its powerful white-ruled neighbor. Nevertheless, it openly attacks South Africa's apartheid policy. More than 160,000 Lesotho men work in South Africa. The South African government helped put Jonathan in power.

LIBERIA

Location: On the west African coast between Sierra Leone and the Ivory Coast. **Size:** 43,000 sq. mi. (111,369 sq. km.). **Population:** 1,940,000 (3.5% Americo-Liberian).

Who Really Rules: From 1877 until April, 1980, Liberia was ruled by the True Whig party, run by the descendants of freed American slaves who colonized the area beginning in 1822. Under the corrupt, nepotistic leadership of President William Tolbert, these Americo-Liberians maintained a position of economic, social, and political privilege.

On Apr. 12, 1980, a group of soldiers from Liberia's 5,000-man army, led by 28-year-old Sgt. Samuel Doe, overthrew Tolbert and executed the president and a dozen top officials. Doe heads the People's Redemption Council (PRC), composed of 17 low-level military officers, primarily from indigenous tribes. Though his cabinet includes leaders of the civilian movements that opposed Tolbert, Doe and the PRC set policy.

Under the True Whigs, Liberia maintained close economic links with the U.S., particularly Firestone, which operates the world's largest rubber plantation in Liberia, and U.S. maritime companies, which own most of the 2,500 ships of Liberian registry. Thus far the new regime has not threatened any of those relations. A few months after taking power, the PRC agreed to follow financial policies demanded by the U.S. and the International Monetary Fund as a condition for foreign loans. In November, 1980, Doe ordered all Liberians to forgo at least one month's salary.

LIBYA

Location: On the Mediterranean coast of North Africa, between Tunisia and Egypt. **Size:** 679,359 sq. mi. (1,759,540 sq. km.) (93% desert). **Population:** 3,178,000.

Who Really Rules: Col. Muammar al-Qaddafi and other young military officers who overthrew the Libyan monarchy in 1969 run Libya's central government, oil industry, and foreign policy. Following the principles laid out in Qaddafi's "Green Book," however, the government has encouraged the growth of democratic People's Committees, which have responsibility for local government and small-scale enterprise. Libya is eliminating the private ownership of factories and rental properties.

The bulk of Libya's population has benefited materially from the Qaddafi regime, but those who have lost privileges oppose it vigorously abroad and silently within Libya. The government does not tolerate opposition, and it has even executed opponents in exile.

Though the Soviet bloc supplies most of Libya's military hardware, as well as the personnel to operate it, Libya's economy is oriented to the West. Former colonial ruler Italy, just across the Mediterranean, is its number-one trading partner, and the U.S. gets about one tenth of its oil imports from Libya. Under Qaddafi, Libya has used its wealth to back liberation movements and third-world regimes of varying political complexions, including that of Uganda's Idi Amin. In 1980 Libya announced plans to federate with Syria.

LIECHTENSTEIN

Location: In central Europe, bordered by Switzerland and Austria. **Size:** 61 sq. mi. (157 sq. km.). **Population:** 27,000 (plus 5,000 foreign workers).

Who Really Rules: Liechtenstein is a tiny, wealthy tax haven, which owes much of its prosperity to the fees paid by some 20,000 to 30,000 foreign corporations that maintain letter-box "offices" there. It is a constitutional monarchy, with only male suffrage for most offices.

The principality is tied to Switzerland through a customs union, and it uses the Swiss franc as its currency. Switzerland is also responsible for Liechtenstein's defense and foreign relations. Liechtenstein earns about 8% of its budget from stamp sales.

LUXEMBOURG

Location: In western Europe, bordered by Belgium, France, and West Germany. **Size:** 998 sq. mi. (2,586 sq. km.). **Population:** 360,000.

Who Really Rules: A member of NATO, the Common Market, and the Belgium-Luxembourg Economic Union (BLEU), Luxembourg is dominated by its larger neighbors. One company, ARBED (Aciéries Réunies de Burbach-Eich-Dudelange) Steel, accounts for one half of Luxembourg's exports, one fifth of its gross national product, and one seventh of its work force. During the 1970s Luxembourg's elected government successfully promoted the Grand Duchy as an international financial center.

MACAO

Location: A peninsular enclave of China, plus two small islands on the coast of Kwangtung Province, across the Pearl River estuary from Hong Kong. **Size:** 5 sq. mi. (16 sq. km.). **Population:** 280,000.

Who Really Rules: The Portuguese have ruled Macao since the 16th century, but officially it is a "Chinese territory under the temporary administration of Portugal." The governor, a military officer appointed by the Portuguese government, establishes policy and oversees the small bureaucracy, but neighboring China exercises enormous influence. Members of Macao's partially elected legislative assembly have been stymied in their drive toward parliamentary rule largely by China's open disapproval. China prefers that the colony, which is 99% ethnic Chinese, remain stable and undemocratic.

Macao's booming economy, based on gambling, textiles, and access to China, is dominated by wealthy Portuguese and by Chinese businessmen like Ho Yin, who doubles as Communist China's unofficial representative in Macao.

MADAGASCAR

Location: Large island across Mozambique Channel from southeast Africa. **Size:** 226,656 sq. mi. (587,041 sq. km.). **Population:** 8,872,000.

Who Really Rules: The Socialist military regime of Commander Didier Ratsiraka, which took power in 1975, permits opposition from several parties that supported the 1975 revolution. The government controls finance, a large share of foreign trade, and 30% of industry. However, some 85% of the population is engaged in subsistence agriculture.

Although France remains Madagascar's largest trading partner, the Ratsiraka regime closed France's naval base at Diégo-Suarez and has accused French interests of attempting to destabilize the Madagascar government.

MAHORE

Location: One of the four Comoro Islands, between Mozambique and Madagascar in the western Indian Ocean. **Size:** 145 sq. mi. (375 sq. km.). **Population:** 50,000.

Who Really Rules: In 1976 the predominantly Christian residents of the island, then known as Mayotte, voted to remain in association with France rather than join the other Comoro Islands, which chose independence. Presently it is considered a "special collectivity" by France and sends a deputy to the French National Assembly. In 1984 it will have the option of becoming a full-fledged French department. Neither the Comoros nor the U.N. General Assembly accepts Mahore's secession from the Comoro Islands.

MALAWI

Location: Southeast Africa, along the west coast of Lake Malawi (Nyasa). **Size:** 45,747 sq. mi. (118, 484 sq. km.). **Population:** 6,134,000.
Who Really Rules: Malawi is ruled by Dr. H. Kamuzu Banda, president for life, and his conservative Malawi Congress party. Banda represses active opposition and controls the flow of information in and out of the country. In the 1978 elections, however, more than a third of the sitting members of the National Assembly were defeated by other Congress party candidates.

Foreign companies, chiefly from Britain, run Malawi's tea and tobacco plantations, while South Africans control the tourist industry along Lake Malawi. As many as 200,000 Malawi men work in South Africa.

MALAYSIA

Location: The southern end of the Malay Peninsula and neighboring islands make up the 11 states of peninsular Malaysia, while the East Malaysian states of Sabah and Sarawak follow most of the northern coast of the island of Borneo (Kalimantan). **Size:** 127,316 sq. mi. (329,749 sq. km.). **Population:** 14,513,000 (83% Peninsular, 17% East Malaysia; 50% Malay, 35% ethnic Chinese, 10% East Indian, 5% indigenous tribes and others).
Who Really Rules: Malaysia has the only open parliamentary democracy in Southeast Asia. It is ruled by the interracial National Front, which is dominated by the United Malays National Organization. The government encourages some environmental and consumer activist groups, but it also imprisons some political opponents and strictly controls the labor movement. Though older political leaders are British-trained, U.S.-educated technocrats are gradually taking over the bureaucracy. Since the end of the Indochina War, the U.S. has joined the U.K. and Australia as a major source of military hardware and training.

Though the government, led by Malay Muslims, is dedicated to increasing the Malay role in the economy, ethnic Chinese and investors from the U.S. and England control most of industry, mining, and export-oriented agriculture.

MALDIVES

Location: 1,192 small islands in the Indian Ocean, southwest of India. **Size:** 115 sq. mi. (298 sq. km.). **Population:** 161,000 (on 22 islands).
Who Really Rules: There are no political parties on the Maldives, but the country is ruled by an elected parliament—the Majlis—which selects the republic's president. Since the Maldives are strategically situated in the mid-Indian Ocean, the U.S. and the U.S.S.R. have carefully watched events there ever since 1976, when the British closed their base at Gan, the southernmost island. The island republic has

upgraded its relations with the Soviet Union since then, but it has not accepted a Soviet offer to lease Gan for a reported $1 million a year. Thus far, the Republic of Maldives is committed to demilitarizing the Indian Ocean.

MALI

Location: Landlocked in West Africa, from the Sahara Desert to the upper Niger River basin. **Size:** 478,764 sq. mi. (1,240,000 sq. km.). **Population:** 6,912,000.

Who Really Rules: President Moussa Traoré, head of the single legal party, the Democratic Union of Malian People, has held power since he led a 1968 military coup. Though he returned the country to constitutional government in 1979, the military still reigns supreme, despite its small size (4,500 men). The regime is unpopular among the impoverished population, and there has been active opposition among students, labor, and former members of the Union Soudanaise, the party in power before 1968.

A former French colony, Mali receives assistance from France, the U.S., the Soviet Union, and China, as well as international financial institutions.

MALTA

Location: An island just south of Sicily (Italy), north of Libya, in the Mediterranean Sea. **Size:** 122 sq. mi. (316 sq. km.). **Population:** 338,000.

Who Really Rules: Socialist Prime Minister Dom Mintoff, whose Labor party holds a small majority in the House of Representatives, is leading Malta onto a path of nonalignment. In 1979 Britain closed its bases at Maltese request, and in 1980 Libyan military advisers were expelled from the small island republic. Malta offers its citizens a number of social programs and encourages foreign investment. Mintoff sees the island as an economic bridge between Europe and the Arab world.

MARIANAS, NORTHERN

Location: Six major and several minor islands arcing north from Guam in the Micronesian West Pacific. **Size:** 184 sq. mi. (477 sq. km.). **Population:** 17,000.

Who Really Rules: Since January, 1978, the islands have been an autonomous commonwealth territory of the U.S. The U.S. Defense Dept. retains the right to build a base on the island of Tinian, and federal grants supply about three quarters of the commonwealth budget.

After 30 years of American trusteeship, the Northern Marianas remain undeveloped. Construction workers are imported from Asia, despite widespread underemployment among the native population.

MARSHALL ISLANDS

Location: A double chain of Micronesian atolls in the western Pacific

Ocean, southwest of Hawaii. **Size:** 70 sq. mi. (181 sq. km.). **Population:** 31,000.

Who Really Rules: On Oct. 31, 1980, the Marshall Islands signed a compact of free association with the U.S. The U.S., which had previously ruled the islands as part of the U.N.-mandated Trust Territory of the Pacific, will continue to operate the Kwajalein Missile Range, which cost billions of dollars to build. The Marshalls also include the former nuclear test sites of Bikini and Eniwetok.

MARTINIQUE

Location: An island in the eastern Caribbean, between St. Lucia and Dominica. **Size:** 425 sq. mi. (1,102 sq. km.). **Population:** 315,000 (90% black).

Who Really Rules: An overseas department of France, Martinique is one of the last vestiges of colonialism in the Lesser Antilles. Its citizens vote in French elections, and it is governed by the Paris regime, which subsidizes the island's economy. Thousands of white "Metropolitan" French, who hold skilled and professional jobs in the public and private sector, make up the island's elite, along with several landed Creole families.

Now that neighboring islands have gained independence from Britain, Martinique political parties and labor unions are agitating for independence. France, which originally claimed the island in 1635, intends to hold on, however.

MAURITANIA

Location: West coast of Sahelian Africa, between Senegal and the Western Sahara. **Size:** 397,954 sq. mi. (1,030,700 sq. km.). **Population:** 1,638,000 (30% Moorish, 30% black, 40% mixed).

Who Really Rules: In 1978 a military coup brought down Moktar Ould Daddah, president since the country achieved independence in 1960. Since then, leadership in the ruling Military Committee for National Salvation has shifted several times. The major accomplishment of the military government has been ending Mauritanian participation in the Saharan war by withdrawing its claim to the southern third of Western Sahara.

The Moorish Mauritanians, Arabic-speaking Arabs and Berbers from nomadic backgrounds, have dominated the sedentary black tribes from the southern region and the Haratins ("Emancipated Ones"), a mixed people traditionally servants of the Moors. Black pressures for equality have led the military government to recognize national languages in addition to Arabic and to outlaw slavery in 1980.

MAURITIUS

Location: An island east of Madagascar (and Réunion) in the western

Indian Ocean. **Size:** 790 sq. mi. (2,045 sq. km.). **Population:** 970,000 (67% Indian, 29% Creole).

Who Really Rules: Since independence from Britain in 1968, the elected parliamentary government of Mauritius has been headed by Sir Seewoosagur Ramgoolam. Ramgoolam's Labour party, based on Indian ethnic ties, barely holds on to power through a coalition with the right-wing Social Democratic party. The Mauritian Militant Movement (3M), an interethnic left-wing party with a base among youth and the powerful General Workers' Federation, is the largest party in the National Assembly.

The island's sugar economy is still controlled by a handful of Franco-Mauritian families, part of the republic's 35,000-member white community. Ironically, the leader of the 3M is Paul Bérenger, a young member of that elite who is a veteran of the 1968 uprising in Paris.

MEXICO

Location: Southern portion of North America, between Guatemala and the U.S. **Size:** 761,601 sq. mi. (1,972,547 sq. km.). **Population:** 70,143,000.

Who Really Rules: Though superficially an electoral democracy, every six years the outgoing president of Mexico handpicks his successor from within the ruling Institutional Revolutionary party (PRI). Despite the closed nature of the system, the transition—next scheduled for 1982—often brings dramatic policy shifts. Whatever policies the president pursues, the PRI, which has held power since 1929, has the clout, exercised through leadership, rhetoric, corruption, and force to guarantee implementation.

Mexican presidents build popularity by vilifying wealthy Mexican industrialists, U.S. financial interests, and the U.S. government, but they generally cooperate closely with all three. To encourage investment and obtain credits from the International Monetary Fund and New York private banks, President Lopez Portillo enacted an austerity program that caused hardship for Mexico's lower classes soon after he assumed office in 1976. Mexico's vast oil wealth, controlled by the government, provides the country with new economic options, but it is likely that oil revenues will merely lead to a greater imbalance in the distribution of income.

MICRONESIA

Location: In the western Pacific Ocean, including the central Caroline Island groups of Yap, Truk, Ponape, and Kosrae. **Size:** 271 sq. mi. (702 sq. km.). **Population:** 75,000.

Who Really Rules: The backbone of the former U.S. Trust Territory of the Pacific, the Federated States of Micronesia signed an agreement of free association with the U.S. on Oct. 31, 1980. This agreement bans the establishment of a non-U.S. military base on any of the more than 750 islands. Micronesia receives $3 million a year from Japan for fishing rights.

The second-biggest piece of stone money on the Yap Islands in Micronesia.

MONACO

Location: Enclave on France's Riviera (Mediterranean) coast, near the Italian border. **Size:** .4 sq. mi. (1 sq. km.). **Population:** 28,000 (15% native Monegasque).

Who Really Rules: A principality for most of the last 1,000 years, Monaco is now a constitutional monarchy with an elected National Council. France, however, controls Monaco's foreign policy and reviews the appointment of the minister of state. Should the reigning prince—currently Rainier III—die without leaving a male heir, Monaco would be annexed to France. Fortunately, Rainier's wife, former actress Grace Kelly, has already provided the prince with a son named Albert.

The principality took control of the Monte Carlo Casino and associated real estate in 1967, when it bought out Aristotle Onassis's holding in the *Société des Bains de Mer.*

MONGOLIA

Location: East central Asia, between Siberia (U.S.S.R.) and China. **Size:** 604,247 sq. mi. (1,565,000 sq. km.). **Population:** 1,778,000.
Who Really Rules: Mongolia is a communist state, governed by the Mongolian People's Revolutionary party since declaring independence from China in 1924. President Yumjagiyn Tsedenbal heads both the government and the party, but he actively rejects attempts to build a personality cult around him. The Soviet Union dominates Mongolia, although the two nations have a history of friendship dating back to Lenin's assistance in the fight against Chinese rule. Soviet troops are stationed near the Chinese border, and several thousand Soviet and Eastern European specialists help administer the Mongolian economy and government.

MONTSERRAT

Location: An island in the Lesser Antilles of the eastern Caribbean, between Guadeloupe and Nevis. **Size:** 38 sq. mi. (98 sq. km.). **Population:** 13,000.
Who Really Rules: Montserrat is a British colony with limited self-government. Though a member of the Caribbean Common Market, it has not taken any steps toward national independence.

MOROCCO

Location: Northwest corner of Africa, between Algeria and the Western Sahara (the latter is claimed by Morocco). **Size:** 172,413 sq. mi. (446,550 sq. km.). **Population:** 21,886,000.
Who Really Rules: Morocco is the last monarchy in northern Africa. There is a partially elected National Assembly, but King Hassan II holds real power. Moroccan society is characterized by corruption and an uneven distribution of income. One of the most pro-Western Arab states, Morocco receives arms from the U.S., France, and Egypt. It has intervened militarily in black Africa—Zaire, for instance—to support pro-Western leaders.

When Morocco first claimed control of two thirds of neighboring Western Sahara in 1975, nationalist feeling improved the king's popularity. Today, locked in an unwinnable war of counterinsurgency, many view the venture as too costly. Political fallout from the war could prompt a military coup. Aware of this possibility, Hassan limits the authority of his generals.

MOZAMBIQUE

Location: Southeast African coast, between Tanzania and South Africa. **Size:** 309,494 sq. mi. (801,590 sq. km.). **Population:** 10,750,000.
Who Really Rules: The Mozambique Liberation Front (FRELIMO), the party that spearheaded the armed independence movement against Por-

tuguese colonialism, governs Mozambique and most of its economy. FRELIMO calls itself Marxist-Leninist, but it places a great deal of emphasis on popular participation in the political process, and it has strong popular support. FRELIMO nominates all candidates for People's Assemblies, the local level of the four-tiered representative political structure, but 5% to 10% of the candidates are rejected by public meetings. The regime encourages dissent within FRELIMO, but it restricts public dissent. Political opponents are detained without trial, and in 1979 the government reversed its opposition to the death penalty—unique to Africa—for treason and terrorist murder.

Though the U.S.S.R. has provided military assistance, Mozambique has not permitted the Soviet Union to establish a naval base. Mozambique welcomes foreign investment, and despite its political hostility to South Africa it maintains extensive commercial relations with that country. Most of the port traffic through Maputo, Mozambique's capital, originates in South Africa, and 500,000 Mozambicans work in South Africa.

NAMIBIA

Location: Southwestern Africa, between Angola and South Africa. **Size:** 318,259 sq. mi. (824,292 sq. km.). **Population:** 1,066,000.
Who Really Rules: South Africa administers this territory against the dictates of the U.N. General Assembly. In late 1978 South Africa staged elections giving nominal power to its protégé, the Democratic Turnalle Alliance, but the elections were boycotted by African-led opposition groups. The U.N. and the Organization for African Unity recognize the South West African People's Organization (SWAPO) as representative of Namibia's predominantly black population. SWAPO is engaged in guerrilla warfare against South African troops and their local militia.

Although Namibia is primarily desert, it is rich with minerals such as diamonds and uranium. The diamond industry is controlled by De Beers, the company of South African Harry Oppenheimer, while an international consortium led by Rio Tinto Zinc mines uranium. The largest employer is U.S.-controlled Tsumeb, which produces copper, lead, and zinc.

NAURU

Location: An island in the Micronesian West Pacific, just south of the equator, west of Kiribati (Gilbert Islands). **Size:** 8 sq. mi. (21 sq. km.). **Population:** 8,000 (58% Nauruan).
Who Really Rules: The elected parliament, the indirectly elected president, and the Nauru Phosphate Commission are responsible for the distribution and investment of Nauru's phosphate revenues. Though phosphate exports make Nauru one of the world's richest countries, per capita, the government expects the phosphate deposits to be exhausted by 1993. The government is sinking about half its budget into the unprofitable Air Nauru. Several hundred million dollars, however, are

invested in an Australian-managed trust fund, to revert to government control when the phosphate runs out.

NEPAL

Location: The Himalayan mountain range and environs, in southern Asia between Tibet (China) and India. **Size:** 54,362 sq. mi. (140,797 sq. km.). **Population:** 15,434,000.

Who Really Rules: Nepal is the world's only Hindu monarchy. King Birendra appears to be gradually turning his powers over to the *panchayat* system, a partyless electoral system based upon traditional elites. Demonstrations by students and other urban groups backing Western-style parliamentary democracy forced the king to hold a referendum in May, 1980. Voters, however, rejected partisan politics by a 55% to 45% margin. To win support for the *panchayat* system, King Birendra promised to adopt constitutional reforms protecting freedom of expression. Nearly all of Nepal's external trade goes to or through India, which is able to exert substantial influence on Nepal.

THE NETHERLANDS

Location: North Sea coast of Europe, between Belgium and Germany. **Size:** 15,770 sq. mi. (40,844 sq. km.) (9% inland water). **Population:** 14,233,000.

Who Really Rules: During the 1970s the social democratic Labor party used rising offshore natural gas revenues to finance a comprehensive minimum income program for all retired and working-age citizens. That program, and the Labor party, are backed by the Federation of Dutch Unions (FNV). Rising taxes, however, brought narrow victory to a center-right coalition government in 1977. Headed by the Christian Democrats and backed by the Dutch Employers Federation, the new government has attempted to slow the growth of government spending.

All that remains of the Dutch Empire, which included Indonesia and Surinam, are the Netherlands Antilles. Dutch corporations, however, have kept their own overseas empires. Three of the largest multinational corporations in the world are Dutch-owned—Philips' Gloeilampenfabrieken (electronics), Unilever (food), and Royal Dutch Shell—the latter two being jointly held with British interests.

NETHERLANDS ANTILLES

Location: Caribbean islands, including Aruba, Bonaire, and Curaçao, just north of Venezuela; and Saba, St. Eustatius, and St. Martin's southern half in the Lesser Antilles between St. Kitts and Anguilla. **Size:** 371 sq. mi. (961 sq. km.). **Population:** 247,000.

Who Really Rules: The Netherlands Antilles are in the process of negotiating independence as one or more nations. Aruba, rich from oil revenues, wishes to separate from the other islands. The autonomous local government is run by elected representatives belonging to a number of regional parties. Shell and Exxon petroleum refineries at Curaçao and Aruba are among the largest in the world. Oil accounts for 95% of the islands' exports but less than 8% of total employment.

NEW CALEDONIA

Location: Southwest Pacific, east of Australia. **Size:** 7,358 sq. mi. (19,058 sq. km.). **Population:** 147,000 (43% Kanak, 36% European).
Who Really Rules: New Caledonia is a French territory, administered by the French government with the advice of a locally elected assembly. In July, 1979, New Caledonians, including overseas French citizens, voted against independence, 65% to 35%. Kanak independence leaders, however, claimed that more than 80% of the Melanesian voters supported independence.

Nickel production dominates the economy. As the world's third-largest supplier, tiny New Caledonia is a valuable colony for France. *Société Le Nickel* (SLN), traditionally dominated by Rothschild interests, is the major miner and processor of ore.

NEW ZEALAND

Location: Two major Polynesian islands and numerous smaller ones in the Pacific Ocean, southwest of Australia. **Size:** 103,736 sq. mi. (268,676 sq. km.). **Population:** 3,150,000 (9% Maori and 2% Pacific islanders) plus 60 million sheep and 8 million cattle.
Who Really Rules: "New Zealand," says the *Wall Street Journal*, "is the closest thing there is to a pastoral welfare state." Though an industrial nation, New Zealand has an economy dominated by the raising of livestock and the export of wool, meat, and dairy products. Until 1973, when the United Kingdom joined the European Common Market, New Zealand was "England's farm." Today exports suffer as a result of Common Market import restrictions.

Both major political parties, National and Labour, support the government's social democratic programs, and the society is considered one of the world's most egalitarian. Although New Zealand appears to have overcome social forms of discrimination, ethnic Polynesians (including the native Maoris) remain at the bottom of the economic ladder.

NICARAGUA

Location: Across Central America, between Costa Rica and Honduras. **Size:** 50,193 sq. mi. (130,000 sq. km.). **Population:** 2,683,000.
Who Really Rules: The armed, popular Sandinista Liberation Front took over the reins of power from dictator Anastasio Somoza in July, 1979. Though the leftist Sandinista revolutionaries control the government, they have reserved two seats on their five-man junta for representatives of the business class who opposed Somoza, and the 47-seat Council of State contains representatives from various political parties, unions, and business organizations, as well as the Sandinista.

Major Sandinista programs have included land reform and a massive literacy campaign. The new government has nationalized the holdings of Somoza and his clique, the banks, agricultural export companies, and any lands left out of production. However, it has not altered the export orientation of Nicaraguan agriculture. The ruling junta has announced that no elections will take place before 1985.

NIGER

Location: Landlocked in the Sahelian belt of Africa, north of Nigeria. **Size:** 489,189 sq. mi. (1,267,000 sq. km.). **Population:** 5,744,000.

Who Really Rules: Since 1974 the Niger army, represented by the Supreme Military Council, has ruled the country. Former colonial ruler, France, remains influential, with French troops stationed in the country and French citizens in the civil service. Uranium production, begun in 1971, catapulted Niger onto the list of strategic real-estate countries and provided funds to alleviate some of the widespread poverty of the country. In most mining projects, the official mining agency, Onarem, owns about a third of the equity, and French, U.S., and other foreign interests hold the remainder.

NIGERIA

Location: On the Gulf of Guinea (Atlantic Ocean) in west central Africa, between Benin and Cameroon. **Size:** 356,667 sq. mi. (923,768 sq. km.). **Population:** 80,928,000.

Who Really Rules: On Oct. 1, 1979, the Nigerian military government of Gen. Olusegun Obasanjo achieved its foremost goal, the transfer to civilian rule. In 1978 the military promulgated a new federal constitution, modeled after that of the U.S., providing for independent legislative, executive, and judicial branches at the state and federal levels. The Federal Election Commission approved five political parties in preparation for a series of four elections in the summer of 1979. In those elections Shehu Shagari was elected president, and a coalition of his National party and the People's party won control of both National Assembly houses and 10 of 19 state governorships. Though the National party is considered a conservative party, voting patterns appear to be based upon a mix of political, personal, and ethnic loyalties. Nigeria is an amalgam of more than 250 ethnic groups, including the Hausa-Fulani of the northern region, the Yorubas of the west, and the Ibos of the east (the region which attempted to secede as Biafra).

Most of the federal government's revenue comes from Nigeria's oil exports, and though the federal government plans to share those revenues with the states, the wealth has not trickled down to the population at large. The oil boom has enriched a number of public employees and businessmen, who have a penchant for conspicuous consumption.

NORWAY

Location: Western edge of the Scandinavian Peninsula in northern

Europe, plus islands in the Arctic Ocean. **Size:** 125,181 sq. mi. (324,219 sq. km.). **Population:** 4,115,000.
Who Really Rules: Norway is a constitutional monarchy with a multiparty elected parliament, the Storting. The ruling party is the social democratic Labor party, which has a strong rural and environmentalist base. Most of the economy is privately owned. High taxes support a comprehensive welfare state. With the discovery of oil and gas in the North Sea, the already rich Norwegians were nicknamed Blue-Eyed Arabs, but many Norwegians fear the changes that oil dollars may bring. Norway's petroleum industry is run by the state-owned company Statoil.

Norway is a member of the North Atlantic Treaty Organization (NATO). It operates spy and communications bases and contains "prepositioned" conventional weapons, but it refuses to permit foreign bases operated by its allies.

OMAN

Location: Eastern corner of the Arabian Peninsula, plus a small peninsula at the Strait of Hormuz, south of Iran. **Size:** 82,030 sq. mi. (212, 457 sq. km.). **Population:** 850,000.
Who Really Rules: Although Oman is a traditional absolute monarchy, Sultan Qabus bin Said has undermined traditional economic and social structures through his cooperation with foreign agencies and corporations. British advisers, administrators, military officers, and pilots help run the government, and migrant labor, primarily from India and Pakistan, makes up over a third of the work force and much of the Omani army. Thousands of Omanis work in the neighboring United Arab Emirates and serve as mercenaries in the U.A.E. army. Oman was the only Arab state not to condemn Egypt's Camp David accords with Israel, and it permits U.S. forces to use Omani bases.

PACIFIC ISLANDS (MISCELLANEOUS)

Under Australian Control: Norfolk Island, north of New Zealand, is a self-governing tax haven and home to 1,800 people, primarily descendants of the *Bounty* mutineers and other Pitcairn Island settlers. Most of the islanders oppose an Australian proposal to integrate the island into Australia.
Under British Control: Pitcairn Island is the last remaining British territory in the Pacific (excluding those considered part of Asia). Southeast of Tahiti, 63 people (1980) live on 2 sq. mi. (5 sq. km.). The residents are descendants of *Bounty* mutineers and their Polynesian companions, who returned in 1858 and 1863 after the whole colony had moved to Norfolk Island. In 1981 an informal poll revealed that about half the population favored building an airstrip on Pitcairn.
Under Chilean Control: Easter Island, in the southeastern Pacific, is noted mostly for its massive stone statues of heads. Home to a Polyne-

sian culture that once had its own script, the island now has 1,135 inhabitants on its territory of 50 sq. mi. (130 sq. km.).

Closer to the Chilean mainland is the Juan Fernández group of three islands, one of which was the temporary home of Alexander Selkirk, the original Robinson Crusoe.

Under French Control: The Wallis and Futuna Islands are a small Polynesian group northeast of Fiji. A French territory of 77 sq. mi. (200 sq. km.), its 9,000 people send a deputy to the French National Assembly.

Under Japanese Control: Japan controls the islands of Ogasawara (Bonin) and Kazan Retto (Volcano), two chains south of Japan in the western Pacific. The islands total about 48 sq. mi. (124 sq. km.) and have about 1,400 people. Kazan Retto includes Iwo Jima, conquered by U.S. Marines in W.W. II. Both chains were returned to Japan by the U.S. in 1968.

Under New Zealand Control: Niue (100 sq. mi., or 259 sq. km.; 3,850 population, 1976) is a self-governing territory. East of Tonga, it is actually the westernmost of the Cook Islands. The Tokelau group (4 sq. mi., or 10 sq. km.; 1,575 population, 1976) is administered directly.

Under United States Control: The U.S. holds sovereignty over Howland, Baker, and Jarvis (3 sq. mi., or 8 sq. km.); Johnston and Sand islands (.4 sq. mi., or 1 sq. km.); Kingman Reef; Midway Islands (2 sq. mi., or 5 sq. km.; 468 population, 1980); Palmyra (4 sq. mi., or 10 sq. km.); and Wake (3 sq. mi., or 8 sq. km; 532 population, 1980), all west and south of Hawaii. The U.S. government is considering placing a nuclear waste dump on the islands. Palmyra, which is privately owned, and Wake, which is administered by the air force, have been mentioned as possible sites.

PAKISTAN

Location: South Asia, on the Arabian Sea, west of India, east of Iran and Afghanistan. **Size:** 310,403 sq. mi. (803,943 sq. km.). **Population:** 90,121,000 (60% Punjabi, 25% Sindh, 10% Pushtun, 3% Baluchi).

Who Really Rules: Gen. Mohammad Zia ul-Haq governs Pakistan under martial law. Although his Military Council rules through a civilian bureaucracy, Zia has no sizable popular support. If he were to permit an open election, the "populist" Pakistan People's party (PPP), which he overthrew in 1977, would win easily. (In April, 1979, Zia's government executed PPP Prime Minister Zulfikar Ali Bhutto, having charged him with complicity in murder.)

Ethnic and religious distrust divides the population. Ethnic Sindhis (Bhutto was Sindh) and Baluchi seek greater power from the Punjabi-Pushtun army.

Though Pakistan has historically had close relations with the U.S. and Communist China, Saudi Arabia appears to be its closest ally today. Pakistan provides trained manpower for the Saudi armed forces, and most of the 1.4 million overseas Pakistani workers are employed in Saudi Arabia and other Persian Gulf states.

PANAMA

Location: On the isthmus of Central America, between Colombia and Costa Rica. **Size:** 29,761 sq. mi. (77,082 sq. km.). **Population:** 1,990,000.
Who Really Rules: In 1978 Gen. Omar Torrijos turned over the government to the new president, Aristides Royo, and a team of technocrats, but Torrijos remains the "power behind the throne." During the first eight years of his 10-year rule, Torrijos was considered a populist, providing new rights for the peasantry and urban working class. However, faced with a stagnating economy, he made his peace with the traditional oligarchy in 1976. The government emphasizes private investment and intends to build on Panama's tax-haven history to make the country a "transnational services platform"—an international financial and shipping center.

On Oct. 1, 1979, the U.S. turned the Panama Canal and the surrounding Canal Zone back to Panama. The canal treaties provide for continued U.S. control of canal operations until the year 2000 and for a permanent U.S. right to intervene to defend the canal.

PAPUA NEW GUINEA

Location: Eastern half of East Indies island of New Guinea, plus smaller islands off the main island's east coast, directly north of Queensland, Australia. **Size:** 178,259 sq. mi. (461,691 sq. km.). **Population:** 3,294,000.
Who Really Rules: Papua New Guinea's elected parliament is a mixture of vaguely defined political parties, some of which identify with one or more of the nation's 700 ethnic or tribal groups. Though a foreign consortium operates a huge copper mine on the eastern island of Bougainville, the various coalition governments have preferred to offer incentives to domestic business interests rather than open the country's doors to widespread foreign investment.

Australia, the former colonial administrator of the country, provides military aid and training plus a huge share of the national budget. Though physically part of Southeast Asia, Papua New Guinea's Melanesian and Papuan racial makeup have oriented it towards the Pacific. In 1980 Papua New Guinea sent troops to Vanuatu to put down a secessionist rebellion.

PARAGUAY

Location: South America, landlocked by Bolivia, Brazil, and Argentina. **Size:** 157,047 sq. mi. (406,752 sq. km.). **Population:** 3,395,000.
Who Really Rules: Paraguay is under the personal dictatorial rule of President Alfredo Stroessner, a general who seized power in 1954. Born in 1913, he has made no provision for selecting his successor. Stroessner governs through the military, the police, and the Colorado party, a corrupt network that dominates the country's civilian institutions. The

press is the only major independent force in the country, but writers are subject to imprisonment and their papers to closure for displeasing Stroessner.

Though predominantly a *mestizo* nation, Paraguay is gradually eliminating its native Indian tribes through disease, environmental control, enslavement, and outright murder.

Historically, Argentina has exercised enormous influence over Paraguay, but since the early 1970s Brazil has become more important, particularly with the construction of the Itaipu Dam—the world's largest hydroelectric project—on the Rio Parana border with Brazil. Stroessner has opened large sections of Paraguay's land to soybean farmers from Brazil, to U.S. firms such as Gulf & Western Industries, and to individuals such as the late Nicaraguan dictator Anastasio Somoza. General Stroessner was the winner of The People's Almanac Dictator-of-the-Year Award for 1980.

PERU

Location: West coast of South America, between Ecuador and Chile. **Size:** 496,222 sq. mi. (1,285,216 sq. km.). **Population:** 18,304,000.
Who Really Rules: In 1980 an elected regime headed by President Fernando Belaúnde Terry took the reins of power from the Peruvian military, which had overthrown Belaúnde in 1968. The original military leadership had nationalized key industries and carried out an extensive, expensive land reform program. But in the late 1970s a new military government agreed to economic controls by U.S. banks and the International Monetary Fund as it increased Peru's foreign debt to more than $8 billion.

Those controls further impoverished the Peruvian working class, sparked a series of general strikes, and forced the military to schedule elections for a constitutional convention and eventually a new government.

During military rule Belaúnde and many of his associates lived in exile in the U.S., where they developed links to the American banking community. They can be expected to continue the bank-imposed austerity program, so more labor unrest is likely.

PHILIPPINES

Location: Large island chain in Southeast Asia, across the South China Sea from Indochina. **Size:** 115,830 sq. mi. (300,000 sq. km.). **Population:** 50,718,000.
Who Really Rules: The Philippines has been under the authoritarian rule of President Ferdinand Marcos since he declared martial law in 1972. During martial law, Marcos, his family members, and his associates became notoriously wealthy. For instance, his cousin-in-law Herminio Disini has made millions of dollars on the government's U.S.-financed nuclear reactor project on the Bataan Peninsula.

Under Marcos, the Philippines has adopted an export-oriented economic development strategy based on foreign loans and investment. Economic policy is in the hands of the World Bank and Philippine technocrats friendly to the World Bank. In exchange for permitting the continued operation of strategic bases at Subic Bay (U.S. Navy) and Clark Field (U.S. Air Force), the Philippines receives substantial U.S. economic aid and weapons. Certain areas of the country are controlled by guerrilla forces of the New People's Army, a Communist movement, and the Moro National Liberation Front, representing Muslim autonomists in the south.

POLAND

Location: On the Baltic Sea in eastern Europe, between Germany and the U.S.S.R. **Size:** 120,725 sq. mi. (312, 677 sq. km.). **Population:** 36,094,000.

Who Really Rules: Since W.W. II, Poland has been ruled by the bureaucracy of the United Workers' (Communist) party. Although the government restricts dissent, it has been more open than other Eastern European governments. The party tolerates the influential Roman Catholic Church, but it attempts to keep the Church out of politics. The state owns the industrial and mining sectors of the economy, but more than 70% of Poland's agricultural land is in small, private farms.

The Soviet Union, which maintains an estimated 30,000 troops in Poland, put the Communists in power. Though the Russians and Poles have a long history of mutual distrust, the presence of overwhelming Soviet military and economic power on Poland's eastern border guarantees an ongoing Soviet influence.

Several times since W.W. II. Polish workers have struck for lower food prices. (Instead of adjusting wages, the party raises prices.) Successful strikes in 1970 led the government to borrow huge sums from Western banks and governments to stimulate economic growth. By the end of 1979 Poland owed West German banks and other Western institutions more than $20 billion. Once an answer to growing demands by workers, the loans are now draining the Polish economy. In 1980 the government announced new food price hikes, in part to generate the funds to repay the banks.

Polish workers greeted the price increases with a massive wave of strikes. Unwilling to accept mere economic concessions, the strikers pushed for the formation of unions independent of the Communist leadership and for democratic rights. Though the new independent unions have not openly challenged the Communist system, they have rejected outright the Communist party leadership.

PORTUGAL

Location: West coast of the Iberian Peninsula in southwestern Europe, plus the Madeira and Azores islands in the Atlantic. **Size:** 35,553 sq. mi. (92,082 sq. km.). **Population:** 10,038,000.

Who Really Rules: Political power is divided among the parliament (run by coalitions of the four major parties), the president (who is elected directly by the entire adult population), and the military Revolutionary Council (an outgrowth of the 1974 "Captains' Coup"). The major question in Portuguese politics is whether the nationalization of banks and industries and the land reform following the 1974 revolution will be reversed. Supporting reversal is the International Monetary Fund, which has forced Portugal to accept austerity policies, while the well-organized left-wing labor movement fights to maintain the status quo.

Portugal is a member of NATO, providing the U.S. with important military bases on the Azores Islands, and most political factions hope to win Portuguese admission to the Common Market by 1983.

PUERTO RICO

Location: Major Caribbean island, east of Hispaniola, plus adjacent smaller islands. **Size:** 3,435 sq. mi. (8,897 sq. km.). **Population:** 3,400,000.

Who Really Rules: Puerto Rico is a U.S. territory with limited self-government. It is part of the U.S. customs zone. Puerto Ricans are U.S. citizens, although those who remain on the island do not pay federal taxes and cannot vote in U.S. elections.

In 1980 Gov. Carlos Romero-Barcelo barely won reelection while promising a referendum on possible statehood in the U.S. The pro-Commonwealth party came in a close second, and pro-independence forces trailed. Romero Barcelo argues that annexation will bring additional federal subsidies.

Economically, Puerto Rico is a colony of U.S.-based multinational corporations, particularly the petrochemical and pharmaceutical industries, which take advantage of the island's lax environmental regulations. The U.S. military operates several bases in Puerto Rico, and the U.S. Navy uses the island of Vieques, off the east coast, for target practice.

QATAR

Location: Peninsula jutting from Arabia into the Persian Gulf. **Size:** 4,247 sq. mi. (11,000 sq. km.). **Population:** 181,000 (29% Qatari Arab, 9% other Arab, 15% Iranian, 29% Pakistani).

Who Really Rules: Qatar is a monarchy ruled by an emir from the Al-Thani family, currently Khalifa bin Hamad al-Thani. There are no elections and no political parties. Nearly all state revenue and most of the economy are based upon oil and gas production. The onshore fields are state-owned, but Qatar is still negotiating with Shell on the takeover of offshore production. About 82% of the work force is foreign, including skilled and professional workers from the developed countries. Saudi Arabia, the giant oil producer next door, exerts enormous influence on the emirate.

Modernization has brought 10% of Qatari women into the work force, but they remain socially isolated from men.

RÉUNION

Location: An island east of Madagascar in the Indian Ocean. **Size:** 969 sq. mi. (2,510 sq. km.). **Population:** 521,000.
Who Really Rules: Réunion is an overseas department of France, administered by the French government. Citizens of Réunion vote in French elections. Though left-wing parties favoring home rule are strong, France is unlikely to grant independence, since Réunion hosts one of the last French bases in the Indian Ocean region.

ROMANIA

Location: Eastern Europe, between the U.S.S.R. and the Danube, with 225 km. of Black Sea coastline. **Size:** 91,699 sq. mi. (237,500 sq. km.). **Population:** 22,507,000 (87% ethnic Romanian).
Who Really Rules: Romania, although a member of the Warsaw Pact and Comecon (Soviet bloc military and economic alliance), has earned a reputation for independent diplomatic and international economic policies. Led by President Nicolae Ceauşescu, the Communist party still rules the country with an iron hand.

Despite amnesties for 28,000 prisoners in the late 1970s, political, religious, and labor dissidents face police harassment, job demotion or transfer, and even forced labor or forced psychiatric internment. The government restricts emigration, but it encourages critics to leave the country. Nevertheless, Romania is the only Communist country with a state church, the Romanian Orthodox Church, of which three quarters of the population are members. Although there has been some criticism of the ethnic Romanian majority's treatment of the Hungarian minority (at least 8% of the national population) in Transylvania, Romania provides Hungarian language schools and publishing houses.

In the international arena, Romania is the only Soviet bloc member of the World Bank and International Monetary Fund. Romania refused to take part in the Soviet move into Czechoslovakia in 1968, and since then it has limited its participation in the Warsaw Pact.

RWANDA

Location: Inland in east central Africa, on Lake Kivu, between Zaire and Tanzania. **Size:** 10,169 sq. mi. (26,338 sq. km.). **Population:** 4,912,000 (90% Hutu, 9% Tutsi, 1% Pygmy).
Who Really Rules: Since Rwanda's 1959 antifeudal revolution, the Bantu Hutu peasant class has controlled the political scene, trusting few Hamitic Tutsi, their former overlords. The president, Maj. Gen. Juvenal Habyarimana, seized power in 1973. In 1978 he staged a constitutional referendum and presidential plebiscite, nominally returning the coun-

try to constitutional rule. His National Revolutionary Development Movement (MRND) selected all the candidates for the 1981 National Assembly elections.

SAHARA, WESTERN

Location: West coast of North Africa, between Morocco and Mauritania. **Size:** 102,973 sq. mi. (266,770 sq. km.). **Population:** 150,000.
Who Really Rules: The Polisario (Popular Front for the Liberation of Saguia el Hamra and Rio de Oro) is a left-of-center, Islamic nationalist front that was formed in 1973 to oppose Spanish colonial rule. In 1975, when Morocco and Mauritania carved up the territory, the Polisario evacuated thousands of Saharans to Algeria, which shares a border with the Western Sahara, and stepped up its raids. In 1979 Mauritania signed a peace agreement with the Polisario, agreeing to withdraw, but Morocco merely added the Mauritanian sector to its claim. There are between 50,000 and 80,000 Moroccan troops in the region—most confined to urban areas and garrisons—and an estimated 10,000 or more Polisario fighters. Polisario's call for self-determination is supported by a majority of the members of the Organization of African Unity. Its chief backer is Algeria, which provides funds, Soviet-made weapons, and a base area.

ST. HELENA (AND DEPENDENCIES)

Location: Islands scattered in south Atlantic Ocean. **Size:** St. Helena, 47 sq. mi. (122 sq. km.); Ascension, 34 sq. mi. (88 sq. km.); Tristan da Cunha, 42 sq. mi. (109 sq. km.). **Population:** St. Helena, 6,000; Ascension, 1,200; Tristan da Cunha, 315.
Who Really Rules: St. Helena is a British colony, known primarily for volcanic eruptions and as the site of Napoleon Bonaparte's second exile. With no exports, the islands depend upon British assistance.

ST. KITTS-NEVIS (ST. CHRISTOPHER-NEVIS)

Location: Two islands and the islet of Sombrero between St. Eustatius (Netherlands Antilles) and Montserrat in the Lesser Antilles of the eastern Caribbean. **Size:** 103 sq. mi. (267 sq. km.). **Population:** 59,000.
Who Really Rules: St. Kitts-Nevis is an associated state of the United Kingdom. Its transition to independence has been slowed by secessionist movements. Anguilla seceded in 1967, and Nevis, the smaller of the two islands, is also pressing for self-government. St. Kitts-Nevis has an elected parliament, the unicameral House of Assembly, with full autonomy. Presently the Labour party, based on St. Kitts, controls the Assembly.

ST. LUCIA

Location: Windward Islands of the eastern Caribbean, between St. Vin-

cent and Martinique. **Size:** 238 sq. mi. (616 sq. km.). **Population:** 126,000.
Who Really Rules: In 1979 St. Lucia was granted independence from Great Britian. The St. Lucia Labour Party won parliamentary elections that year, ending 15 years of leadership by the United Workers' Party (UWP). The UWP has formed an alliance with a new Progressive Labour Party and promises to keep Prime Minister Winston Cenac's government in turmoil until the next elections are held in 1984. St. Lucia has a mixed economy open to foreign investment.

ST. PIERRE AND MIQUELON

Location: Eight small islands 15 mi. south of Newfoundland, in the Atlantic. **Size:** 93 sq. mi. (242 sq. km.). **Population:** 6,000.
Who Really Rules: Like other French dependencies in the Western Hemisphere, St. Pierre and Miquelon is governed as a part of metropolitan France. It has an elected local government, and it sends a deputy to the French National Assembly.

ST. VINCENT AND THE GRENADINES

Location: An eastern Caribbean island, between St. Lucia and Grenada, plus the northern Grenadine Islands. **Size:** 150 sq. mi. (388 sq. km.). **Population:** 118,000.
Who Really Rules: St. Vincent is governed by the conservative St. Vincent Labour party, which holds 11 of the 13 seats in the elected legislature. In December, 1979, Barbados sent troops to put down a rebellion allegedly inspired by Grenada's revolutionary government, but it was actually a protest by the Rastafarian sect. Barbados also fired the leader of St. Vincent's socialist opposition from his teaching position at the University of the West Indies.

SAMOA, AMERICAN

Location: Seven easternmost islands of the Samoan island chain, in the southwest Pacific, east of Fiji. **Size:** 76 sq. mi. (197 sq. km.). **Population:** 34,000.
Who Really Rules: American Samoa is a self-governing U.S. territory, headed since January, 1978, by an elective governor. Nearly half the work force is employed by the government, which gets four fifths of its budget from the U.S. federal government. The major private businesses are fish-canning plants owned by Van Camp and Starkist.

Half the residents of American Samoa are immigrants, while as many as 60,000 Samoans, who are American nationals without the right to vote in federal elections, are in Hawaii, California, and the U.S. armed forces.

SAMOA, WESTERN

Location: Savaii, Upolu, and several smaller islands in the Polynesian southwest Pacific, northeast of Fiji. **Size:** 1,097 sq. mi. (2,842 sq. km.). **Population:** 158,000.

Who Really Rules: Western Samoa has an electoral system based upon the traditional social structure. Of 47 members of the Legislative Assembly, 45 are elected by *matais*, the traditional heads of extended families; 2 members without family ties are elected at large.

Western Samoa encourages foreign investment. Potlatch, the American forest-products multinational, operates a timber-cutting concession, a sawmill, and a veneer plant, which threaten the fragile ecology of the rain-forested lands.

SAN MARINO

Location: Landlocked enclave in Italy, southeast of Bologna. **Size:** 24 sq. mi. (61 sq. km.). **Population:** 19,000.

Who Really Rules: A city-state since the 4th century, San Marino is a multiparty parliamentary democracy. Governed by a leftist coalition, it is the only nation in Western Europe with a Communist-led regime. Ethnically Italian, San Marino has close ties, including a customs union, with Italy. Italy subsidizes the San Marinese budget in exchange for an agreement not to market certain commodities in Italy. San Marino, unlike many other ministates, carries out its own foreign policy, with consulates around the world.

SÃO TOMÉ AND PRÍNCIPE

Location: Two major islands in the Gulf of Guinea (Atlantic Ocean), about 125 mi. west of Gabon. **Size:** 372 sq. mi. (964 sq. km.). **Population:** 85,000.

Who Really Rules: Since it declared independence from Portugal in 1975, the Movement for the Liberation of São Tomé and Príncipe (MLSTP) has governed the islands. The Movement, which led the fight against colonialism for 15 years, is the only legal political party, but it does not persecute former opposition groups. The MLSTP nationalized Portuguese cacao plantations when it took over, but Portugal is still the islands' number-one trade partner. Cacao still represents about 90% of exports.

SAUDI ARABIA

Location: All but the southern and eastern portions of the Arabian Peninsula in the Middle East. **Size:** 829,996 sq. mi. (2,149,690 sq. km.). **Population:** 8,725,000.

Who Really Rules: Saudi Arabia is ruled by the Saud royal family, led by the half brothers who are sons of King Ibn Saud, the man who forged the Saudi Arabian nation-state and ruled it until his death in 1953. The royal family maintains its domestic authority through a combination of religious leadership, marriage with other tribes, control of the country's oil wealth, and military power. The government is unwilling to trust military power to citizens who are not members of, or associated with, the royal family, so it contracts for "advisers" from the U.S. and officers from Pakistan. Saudi Arabia's capitalist class, primarily made up of traditional merchant families, owes its vast wealth to the favor of the royal family.

Internationally, Saudi Arabia is considered a friend of the U.S., which provides it with most of its military hardware and training. Although well armed, the untested Saudi military has little regional influence. As the world's largest oil exporter, Saudi Arabia is a leading member of the Organization of Petroleum Exporting Countries (OPEC).

SENEGAL

Location: Horseshoe-shaped on the West African coast, surrounding the Gambia, between Mauritania and Guinea-Bissau. **Size:** 75,750 sq. mi. (196,192 sq. km.). **Population:** 5,886,000.

Who Really Rules: President Léopold Senghor, who had governed Senegal since independence, resigned in 1981 after a 20-year rule. He was replaced by Prime Minister Abdou Diouf—a succession specified by the constitution. Senegal has an active multiparty electoral system, but some leftist parties are outlawed.

Senegal maintains close ties with its former colonial master, France, which stations about 1,700 troops there. When France masterminded the foreign intervention in the Shaba region of Zaire, it brought in a contingent of Senegalese troops. Although Senegal contains large deposits of phosphates and petroleum, its economy is still based upon the export of peanuts. Industry, in general, is foreign-controlled.

SEYCHELLES

Location: About 90 equatorial islands in the western Indian Ocean, about 1,000 mi. east of Kenya and Tanzania. **Size:** 108 sq. mi. (280 sq. km.). **Population:** 68,000.

Who Really Rules: The Seychelles republic is ruled by the Seychelles People's Progressive Front, whose leader, President France Albert René, seized power in 1977. (René was already prime minister.) Under the constitution adopted in June, 1979, no opposition parties are permitted, but one third of all SPPF members of the People's Assembly are former members of the deposed opposition.

The government, which considers itself socialist, has close ties to labor but outlaws strikes. It closed the only political publication in the country in 1979. René's proposal for a mandatory National Youth Service faces widespread opposition.

A U.S.-owned satellite-tracking facility is the islands' largest employer. Though René is an outspoken proponent of Indian Ocean demilitarization, Western diplomats fear he may permit the Soviets to establish a naval base in the Seychelles.

SIERRA LEONE

Location: West African coast, between Guinea and Liberia. **Size:** 27,699 sq. mi. (71,740 sq. km.). **Population:** 3,558,000.
Who Really Rules: In 1978 President Siaka Stevens ordered all opposition parties to join his All People's Congress, making Sierra Leone a one-party state. Economic power lies in the hands of multinational corporations and about 5,000 expatriates, including Lebanese diamond smugglers. (Officially, De Beers has a monopoly on the diamond trade.) Some 1,000 families run the administrative apparatus, doing favors for corporate interests in exchange for graft.

Like many other third-world countries, in 1979 Sierra Leone signed an agreement with the International Monetary Fund to accept economic policies which caused hardship for its population, in this case higher export taxes on agricultural products.

SINGAPORE

Location: An island at the tip of the Malay Peninsula in Southeast Asia. **Size:** 224 sq. mi. (581 sq. km.). **Population:** 2,427,000.
Who Really Rules: Though other parties are allowed to contest elections, Prime Minister Lee Kuan Yew's People's Action party (PAP) runs what is essentially a one-party state. The PAP controls the labor unions and a grass-roots network called Residents Committees. The older leadership of the PAP, which led Singapore to independence while crushing, with British assistance, the Communist opposition, has selected a team of younger technocrats to manage the system when the old guard steps down. The authoritarian government does not tolerate opposition that it considers subversive, and its Corrupt Practices Investigation Bureau wins convictions on cases ranging from a $5 payoff to a policeman to top-level influence peddling.

Although the country was once the site of unskilled-worker assembly factories, the government has forced the upgrading of Singapore's position in the international capitalist division of labor. Today Singapore's workers are better paid and perform more skilled work. Unskilled foreign (Malaysian) workers, when not needed, are merely deported.

SOLOMON ISLANDS

Location: Southeastern part of the Solomon Islands group, including Guadalcanal, in southwestern Pacific, east of New Guinea. **Size:** 10,983 sq. mi. (28,446 sq. km.). **Population:** 236,000 (93% Melanesian, 4% Polynesian).
Who Really Rules: Evangelist lay preacher Peter Kenilorea was elected prime minister after the 1980 parliamentary elections, the first since

independence in 1978. The nascent political parties of the islands are based upon personalities, not policies. Europeans still run the bureaucracy.

Foreign corporations, led by Unilever, control the timber industry, and in 1980 villagers on the island of Kolombangara fought Unilever for control of their lands.

SOMALIA

Location: Eastern horn of Africa, between Ethiopia and Kenya. **Size:** 246,200 sq. mi. (637,657 sq. km.). **Population:** 3,680,000 (plus as many as 1.5 million refugees from Ethiopia).

Who Really Rules: The president, Maj.-Gen. Mohammed Siad Barre, seized power from a divided civilian government in 1969. Now Siad Barre's Somali Revolutionary Socialist party governs. Siad Barre has attempted to carry out a socialist transformation from above but has accomplished little more than a few nationalizations in this primarily agricultural and nomadic society. The government has carried out numerous reforms, including the creation of a Somali script so that it could launch a major literacy campaign.

The internationally recognized borders of Somalia are those of two former colonies, British Somaliland and Italian Somaliland. Somalia, however, claims territories inhabited by Somali people in Djibouti (formerly French Somaliland), northeastern Kenya, and the Ogaden region of Ethiopia. Somali armed forces and a local guerrilla army have been fighting Ethiopian troops for control of the Ogaden.

For several years a close friend of the Soviet Union, Somalia threw out the Soviet military and Soviet advisers in 1977, when the U.S.S.R. befriended Ethiopia's revolutionary government. In 1980 Somalia concluded an agreement with the U.S., offering military bases in exchange for economic aid and military hardware. The U.S., however, recognizes the Ethiopian claim to the Ogaden and insists that Somalia not use these arms in that war.

SOUTH AFRICA

Location: Southern tip of Africa, plus the Walvis Bay enclave on the coast of Namibia. **Size:** 471,443 sq. mi. (1,221,037 sq. km.). **Population:** 29,288,000 (70% black, 18% white, 9% colored, or mixed, and 3% Asian).

Who Really Rules: South African society is based upon apartheid, a system of racial segregation and white social, economic, and political supremacy. Apartheid consists of three types of policies: (1) petty apartheid, social segregation intended to prevent intermarriage; (2) the homelands policy, the eventual concentration of the black majority into semi-independent tribal "Bantustans," or reservations; and (3) tight controls on the movement and activities of blacks within the remaining white areas, which make up 87% of the territory. Blacks are allowed in white areas only to provide cheap labor for affluent whites.

Within the ruling white minority, the Afrikaans people—descendants

The Soweto uprising, South Africa, 1976.

of Dutch and other continental European immigrants—dominate the elected parliamentary government. The Afrikaans-based National party, which runs the government, is split between *verligtes* (liberals) and *verkramptes* (hard-liners). The *verligtes* are willing to compromise away some of their privileges under petty apartheid, while the *verkramptes* oppose any substantial reform. The English-speaking whites, concentrated in the Cape Province, historically favor the liberal position. Leading capitalists, foreign and domestic, as well as Western governments, urge reform, but they are unwilling to take any steps which might endanger white rule.

The government attempts to control any opposition to apartheid by arresting and "banning" (restricting the political rights of) white as well as nonwhite critics. However, opposition within black townships is growing, and the liberation of nearby nations such as Zimbabwe and Mozambique has paved the way for full-scale guerrilla war by African nationalists.

Thus far, South Africa has granted "independence" to three black homelands within its boundaries—Transkei, Bophuthatswana, and Venda. As part of this independence, members of the black ethnic group assigned to each homeland are denied their South African citizenship.

TRANSKEI—A NON-NATION

Location: Three sections of South Africa, between independent Lesotho and the Indian Ocean. **Size:** 17,000 sq. mi. (44,030 sq. km.). **Population:** 2,368,000.

Who Really Rules: Transkei, officially the homeland for nearly 4 million Xhosa-speaking South African blacks, was granted "independence" in October, 1976. Prime Minister Kaiser Mantanzima, chief minister of the homeland before independence, has "governed" the area under a state of emergency since 1960, but the South African government holds real power through its subsidization of the Transkei budget and control of the Xhosa Development Corporation, which administers most of the modern economy in the zone. About 85% of the Xhosa's employed wage workers labor in white South Africa.

BOPHUTHATSWANA—A NON-NATION

Location: Six sections of South Africa, generally near the border of independent Botswana. **Size:** 14,500 sq. mi. (37,555 sq. km.). **Population:** 1,330,000.
Who Really Rules: South Africa awarded Bophuthatswana "independence" in December, 1977, as the homeland of the 2.1 million South African members of the Tswana tribe, which also resides in Botswana. Approximately 1.4 million Tswana live outside of the homeland, and several hundred thousand non-Tswana reside in Bophuthatswana. President Lucas Mangope's Bophuthatswana Democratic party holds most of the seats in the legislative assembly, but it was elected by only a fraction of the eligible voters. Most Tswana, particularly those outside the six zones, boycotted the election. Like Transkei, Bophuthatswana relies on South Africa for its budget and administrative advice.

VENDA—A NON-NATION

Location: Two sections in northeast South Africa, near Mozambique and Zimbabwe. **Size:** 2,510 sq. mi. (6,500 sq. km.). **Population:** 480,000.
Who Really Rules: South Africa granted "independence" to Venda in September, 1979, as the homeland of 600,000 Venda-speaking South African blacks. Venda gets half its food, all its mineral fuel, and five sixths of its budget from South Africa, and two thirds of its male work force is employed in South Africa. President Patrick Mphephu lost in the 1978 elections, but he retained his position by arresting opposition members of the assembly. South Africa has an air force base in Venda, and South African troops guard its border with Zimbabwe.

SPAIN

Location: Most of the Iberian Peninsula, in southwest Europe. **Size:** 194,897 sq. mi. (504,782 sq. km.). **Population:** 38,686,000.
Who Really Rules: Since 1976, following the death of dictator Francisco Franco and the accession of King Juan Carlos I, Adolfo Suárez, head of the center-right Union of the Democratic Center, has served as prime minister. His minority government is supported in parliament by right-wing parties, but left-wing and regional parties also represent nearly half the electorate and control many urban local governments. Though private businessmen and landowners remain powerful, the government controls certain economic sectors such as minerals.

Spain hosts several major U.S. military facilities, but in 1979 it banned the presence of nuclear weapons. Many U.S.-based multinational corporations have built plants in Spain in recent years to take advantage of Spain's impending admission into the European Common Market, scheduled for the mid-1980s.

Breaking Up Is Hard to Do: Autonomy movements are strong in many regions of Spain, but nowhere is sentiment stronger than in the Basque region on the Bay of Biscay. The 2.5 million Basques share a unique culture and language. They occupy four Spanish provinces—Vizcaya, Guipúzcoa, Álava, and Navarra—as well as part of southwestern France. For generations the Basques in Spain enjoyed limited autonomy, and a strong nationalist movement backs a return of those rights. In fact, the ETA (Euzkadi Ta Azkatasuna, meaning Basque Homeland and Liberty) Marxist urban guerrillas lead a movement for total independence for a united Basque nation, Euzkadi. Though many Basque nationalists object to the ETA's violent tactics, a pro-ETA party won 20% of the vote in Vizcaya and Guipúzcoa in the 1979 Spanish national elections. Its three victorious deputies refused to take part in the Cortes (the national legislature).

SPANISH NORTH AFRICA (CEUTA AND MELILLA)

Location: Ceuta is an enclave of Morocco, across the Straits of Gibraltar from Spain, and Melilla is a peninsula and islands further east on the Mediterranean Moroccan coast. **Size:** Ceuta, 7 sq. mi. (19 sq. km.); Melilla, 5 sq. mi. (12.3 sq. km.). **Population:** Ceuta, 70,000; Melilla, 67,500.

Who Really Rules: Both Ceuta and Melilla are considered integral parts of Spain. Both are duty-free ports, however, carrying a substantial portion of the trade and traffic between Spain and Morocco. They are the last pieces of European territory on the African continent.

SRI LANKA

Location: An island in the Indian Ocean, just south of India. **Size:** 25,332 sq. mi. (65,610 sq. km.). **Population:** 15,204,000 (71% Sinhalese, 21% Tamil).

Who Really Rules: Sri Lanka is a multiparty democracy, governed since 1977 by the right-wing United National party. The UNP, working with the World Bank and International Monetary Fund, has opened the Sri Lanka economy to large inflows of foreign goods and investment while reducing social welfare programs. In 1980 the UNP majority declared a state of emergency and expelled former Prime Minister Sirimavo Bandaranaike from parliament, asserting that she had abused her power by postponing elections from 1975 until 1977.

The new 1978 constitution continues to favor the Sinhalese majority over the Tamil minority. Sinhalese remains the national language; Buddhism remains the official religion. About 9% of the population, native-born Tamils descended from Indian plantation workers, are disenfranchised because they are officially Indian citizens.

SUDAN

Location: South of Egypt in northeastern Africa. **Size:** 967,495 sq. mi. (2,505,813 sq. km.), Africa's largest nation. **Population:** 19,573,000 (52% black, 39% Arab, 6% Beja).

Who Really Rules: Gen. Jaafir al-Numeiry, who seized power in 1969, is the president, and his Sudan Socialist Union is the only legal political organization. Numeiry holds power because of his ability to balance the interests of the numerous ethnic and regional groups that make up the Sudan's population, but his grants of regional autonomy have been limited. Coup attempts and repression campaigns are frequent, and they allegedly involve factions backed by various foreign governments, including Libya, Iraq, and the Soviet Union.

Sudan depends heavily upon foreign aid and loans to support its finances. The International Monetary Fund, acting on behalf of Western and Arab financial interests, has imposed cutbacks in government spending. Sudan is cooperating with Egypt to build the massive Jonglei Canal to make additional Nile River water available for irrigation in the arid northern region. Western governments refuse direct participation because of environmental controversies, but their financial aid makes construction possible. Sudan hopes that the canal and other development programs will turn the country into the "breadbasket" of the Middle East.

SURINAME

Location: Northwestern corner of South America, between Guyana and French Guiana. **Size:** 63,037 sq. mi. (163,265 sq. km.). **Population:** 421,000 (37% East Indian, 31% Creole—black and mixed, 15% Javanese, 10% Djuka—descendants of runaway slaves living in interior, 3% American Indian).

Who Really Rules: Leadership of the ruling National Military Council has shifted since its junior officers seized power, ostensibly over pay and work conditions, in February, 1980. Civilian politics are tied to ethnic loyalty, and Creoles are historically dominant. The Netherlands, which granted independence in 1975, is Suriname's major source of foreign aid. Bauxite, mined by subsidiaries of Alcoa and Royal Dutch Shell, is by far the largest sector of the economy. It provides about 40% of government revenues and represents about 85% of all exports. However, the industry employs only 6,000 people.

SWAZILAND

Location: Landlocked in southern Africa, surrounded by South Africa and Mozambique. **Size:** 6,704 sq. mi. (17,363 sq. km.). **Population:** 572,000 (96% black, 3% white, 1% mixed).

Who Really Rules: Since 1973 Swaziland has been under the absolute rule of King Sobhuza II, who has held the throne since 1921. Sobhuza is sick, however, and regardless of who his family chooses as a successor, real power will probably transfer to the surprisingly independent prime minister, Mabandla Dlamini. Dlamini has established an investigation of government corruption, released members of the major leftist opposition party—all parties are outlawed—and improved relations with Mozambique.

Reportedly, whites own 44% of Swaziland's farmland, while the king holds most of the rest in trust for its traditional farmers. The economy is wide open to foreign investors from South Africa, Japan, and elsewhere, and the country is a gambling and tourist center for South Africans.

SWEDEN

Location: Northern Europe, along the eastern half of the Scandinavian Peninsula. **Size:** 173,731 sq. mi. (449,964 sq. km.). **Population:** 8,335,000.

Who Really Rules: While a coalition of three centrist parties holds a one-vote majority over the labor-backed coalition of two left-wing parties, the political programs of the two coalitions are remarkably similar. Both support the continuation of Sweden's welfare state. Both coalitions are divided on the hot issue of phasing out existing nuclear power plants. (No one wants to start new nuclear construction.)

Though governed by a socialist coalition for decades, Sweden's economy is characterized by more private ownership than "capitalist" France and Italy. Unions, however, have direct roles in corporate management, and they are pushing for actual stock ownership. On a recent U.S. tour, King Carl XVI Gustaf avoided crossing labor union picket lines. In late 1978 Sweden signed a 20-year economic pact with neighboring Norway, in which Norway agreed to supply petroleum to Sweden in exchange for timber, technology, and 40% of the Volvo car company.

Although Sweden has an impressive record of respecting human rights, many Swedes criticize the government's practice of assigning each person at birth a "person number," used in the administration of several government programs.

SWITZERLAND

Location: Landlocked in the Alps of central Europe, surrounded by France, Italy, Germany, and Austria. **Size:** 15,941 sq. mi. (41,288 sq. km.). **Population:** 6,300,000.

Who Really Rules: Switzerland is a multiparty parliamentary democracy, but substantial authority is left in the hands of the 23 cantons. In recent years Swiss voters, at the national level, have decided on a multitude of controversial initiative and referendum propositions.

Banking is the leading sector in the Swiss economy. The top three banks—Swiss Bank Corp., Union Bank of Switzerland, and Swiss Credit Bank—and other members of the Swiss Bankers Association control much of the industrial economy. With a history of stability and reliability and a promise of secrecy, the banks have attracted $120 billion in foreign deposits and an equal amount in other holdings. To control the banks, the Social Democratic party has qualified an initiative measure for a national ballot which would remove the shroud of banking secrecy. Switzerland is noted for its neutrality, but it is armed. In fact, it buys sophisticated weapons from the U.S. Voters, however, have rejected the formation of a national police force.

SYRIA

Location: On the eastern Mediterranean coast, between Lebanon and Turkey. **Size:** 71,498 sq. mi. (185,180 sq. km.). **Population:** 9,107,000 (90% Arab; 70% Sunni Muslim, 15% Alawite Muslim, 12% Christian, 3% Druze and others).

Who Really Rules: Despite periodic elections, Syria is essentially a military dictatorship of the Arab Socialist Reconstructionist (Ba'ath) party. The present ruling faction, dominating the military, bureaucracy, and public sector of the economy, is from the Alawite sect. Right-wing Sunni Muslims from the Muslim Brotherhood have spearheaded anti-Alawite forces.

In a permanent state of war with Israel, hostile to Iraq, and with 30,000 troops in Lebanon, Syria expends a huge chunk of its national resources on the military. The Soviet Union is its major arms supplier, and it hopes to get financial aid from Libya, with which it "federated" in 1980.

TAIWAN (REPUBLIC OF CHINA)

Location: An island off the coast of southern China. **Size:** 13,885 sq. mi. (35,962 sq. km.), including the Pescadores. **Population:** 18,342,000, excluding Quemoy and Matsu (84% native Taiwanese, 14% mainlanders, 2% aboriginal).

Who Really Rules: Taiwan, historically a province of China with its own dialect and culture, is ruled by the leaders of the Kuomintang (KMT), or Chinese Nationalists. Since 1949, when the KMT retreated to Taiwan following the Communist victory in the Chinese civil war, it has ruled the island under martial law. Though it has occasionally permitted limited dissent, the KMT maintains power through censorship, imprisonment of opponents, electoral manipulation, and economic harassment.

When the KMT moved to Taiwan, it carried out a land reform program that it had never implemented on the mainland, building a constituency among Taiwanese peasants and eliminating political competition from the local landlord class. However, Taiwan's economic expansion—based on exports such as garments and electronics—actually undermined the KMT's popularity, because it required that rural income be held down and that labor organizing be suppressed.

Although all major powers and most minor ones recognize the Communist government of the People's Republic of China, the KMT still claims to be the government of China. Isolated diplomatically, it retains strong economic links with business interests in Japan and the U.S., and it continues to receive modern arms from the U.S.

TANZANIA

Location: East central coast of Africa, between Kenya and Mozambique, plus the islands of Zanzibar, Pemba, and Mafia just offshore in the Indian Ocean. **Size:** 364,898 sq. mi. (945,087 sq. km.). **Population:** 18,744,000.

Who Really Rules: The Chama Cha Mapinduzi (Revolutionary) party, led by President Julius Nyerere and Aboud Jumbe, is the only political party. In the 1980 elections, almost all constituencies were contested, and a number of incumbents, including former cabinet members, lost their seats.

Tanzania has a socialistic economy, working toward self-reliant food production. Drought, floods, and rising oil prices, coupled with some bureaucratic mismanagement, have created shortages and a blossoming black market. In 1979 the International Monetary Fund attempted to impose a series of "reforms" in exchange for financing, but Tanzania refused. In addition, the British-based Lonrho Corporation asked aid agencies to cut off funds to Tanzania because the government there refused to pay what the company asked when it nationalized Lonrho's tea estates and other holdings in 1978. However, Tanzania and the IMF, as well as the World Bank, settled on a compromise economic program in 1980.

Formerly independent Zanzibar (including Pemba) retains autonomy over its own economy. Profiting from the export of cloves, the island does not face the same economic problems as the mainland. Aboud Jumbe, president of Zanzibar, is vice-president of the United Republic.

THAILAND

Location: In Southeast Asia, between Laos and Burma, and along the isthmus of the Malay Peninsula. **Size:** 198,456 sq. mi. (514,000 sq. km.). **Population:** 50,025,000.

Who Really Rules: Although Thailand presently has an elected two-house legislature, it is actually ruled by a coalition of army officers, wealthy businessmen, and the royal family. Gen. Prem Tinsulanonda is prime minister. Boonchu Rojanasthien, former head of the Bangkok Bank, is deputy premier for economic affairs. King Phumiphon Adunadet's formal powers are limited, but he and his family are still influential.

Since W.W. II Thailand has been governed by regimes—usually headed by army men—sympathetic to the U.S. Although capitalist-oriented, these governments have limited foreign involvement in the economy, choosing to promote their own corrupt state-owned enterprises. In 1980, however, Boonchu announced his "Thailand, Inc."

policy, backed by the World Bank, under which Thailand has swung its economic doors wide open to multinational corporations.

The Thai central government has a long history of administration over the ethnic Thai central plains of the country, but it has never maintained tight control over the remote north, northeast, and southern areas. In those zones, insurgent movements led by the Communist party of Thailand claim control over "liberated areas."

TIMOR, EAST

Location: Eastern half of the East Indies island of Timor, just north of Australia, plus adjacent smaller islands. **Size:** 5,763 sq. mi. (14,925 sq. km.). **Population:** 400,000 to 600,000 (indefinite because of massive war casualties).

Who Really Rules: Indonesia, which invaded the former Portuguese colony in December, 1975, formally annexed East Timor as a province in 1976. However, the annexation has never been recognized by Portugal, the U.N., or the Timorese. Earlier in 1975, leaders of the Revolutionary Front for the Independence of East Timor (FRETILIN) had declared independence, and when forces of their more populous neighbor attacked, they retreated to fight a protracted guerrilla war. From the start, Indonesia has controlled the flow of news from Timor, but refugees report ongoing fighting.

TOGO

Location: On the Gulf of Guinea (Atlantic Ocean) in west Africa, between Ghana and Benin. **Size:** 21,622 sq. mi. (56,000 sq. km.). **Population:** 2,710,000.

Who Really Rules: Togo is ruled by Gen. Gnassingbé Eyadéma, who first seized power in 1963 in independent Africa's first military coup. One-party elections in December, 1979, merely confirmed his position. From a northern ethnic group, Eyadéma has downgraded the role of the traditional Togo elite, made up of southerners from the Mina ethnic group intermarried with descendants of ex-slaves from Brazil. Eyadéma represses the elite, particularly those connected with the previous government, just as the southerners repressed opposition when they were in power.

Togo's major exports are phosphates. France, its former colonial ruler, is its leading trading partner.

TONGA

Location: About 170 islands in the southwestern Pacific, east of Fiji. **Size:** 270 sq. mi. (699 sq. km.). **Population:** 92,500.

Who Really Rules: Tonga is a feudal society, ruled by King Taufa'ahau Tupou IV, his brother Prince Fatafehi Tu'ipelehake (the premier), and 33 hereditary nobles. Only 7 of the 22 members of the Legislative Assembly are elected by the public. Though the king owns all land on the islands, it is allotted to the nobles, who in turn assign 8¼-acre sections to adult male citizens (one parcel each, as available).

TRINIDAD AND TOBAGO

Location: Two main islands, northeast of Venezuela, in the Caribbean. **Size:** 1,981 sq. mi. (5,130 sq. km.). **Population:** 1,182,000 (43% black, 40% East Indian, 14% mixed).

Who Really Rules: Calling itself the Saudi Arabia of the Caribbean, Trinidad indeed is the richest Caribbean state. Not only do the islands have valuable petroleum and gas resources, but Texaco built one of the world's largest refineries there. Since the 1973 oil price jump, Trinidad has used its wealth to build its basic industry and infrastructure in partnership with foreign corporations. The multiparty parliamentary government is controlled by the conservative People's National Movement (PNM), headed by Prime Minister George Chambers. Originally a worker-based national independence movement, the PNM is now the guarantor of the middle class.

TUNISIA

Location: On the Mediterranean coast of North Africa, between Libya and Algeria. **Size:** 63,170 sq. mi. (163,610 sq. km.). **Population:** 6,716,000.

Who Really Rules: Tunisia is governed by President Habib Bourguiba (born in 1903) and his factionalized Destourian Socialist party (PSD). Under Bourguiba, the country's foreign-oriented economic growth policies have brought income inequalities and corruption. To find work, some 200,000 Tunisians have gone to Europe.

Tunisia's labor movement is historically strong; it spearheaded the fight for independence from France. In 1978, when the General Union of Tunisian Workers (UGTT) staged a general strike against government economic policies, the government smashed the union leadership. In 1980, however, the shake-up in the PSD leadership brought a more conciliatory attitude toward the labor movement. Under Prime Minister Mohamed Mzali, the government might even legalize opposition parties, since the political situation is too unstable for the PSD to replace Bourguiba smoothly when he dies. In early 1980, when Libyan-trained Tunisian guerrillas attempted a local insurrection, the U.S. and France speeded military aid to the government.

TURKEY

Location: Asia Minor—the portion of Asia between the Black Sea and the Mediterranean Sea—and the southeastern Europe peninsula of Thrace. **Size:** 301,381 sq. mi. (780,576 sq. km.). **Population:** 47,284,000 (85% Turkish, 12% Kurdish).

Who Really Rules: In September, 1980, the Turkish military seized power, ostensibly to halt political violence from both the Right and Left.

However, the coup also stifled popular opposition to an economic austerity program imposed in conjunction with the International Monetary Fund. Those economic policies continue under the military regime.

Earlier in 1980, the U.S. and Turkey signed a military cooperation agreement in which Turkey allowed the U.S. to reopen several intelligence bases in return for military aid. A member of NATO, Turkey had been in U.S. disfavor because of its conflicts with Greece, another NATO member, and its occupation of northern Cyprus.

TURKS AND CAICOS ISLANDS

Location: Southeasternmost islands in the Bahamas, northeast of Cuba. **Size:** 166 sq. mi. (430 sq. km.). **Population:** 8,000.
Who Really Rules: The Turks and Caicos are British territories dependent upon British funds. Instead of demanding independence, in the early 1970s the elected State Council petitioned unsuccessfully to be joined to Canada. The U.S. operates a navy navigation facility, an oceanographic research center, and a missile test support system from the islands.

TUVALU

Location: South Pacific, midway between Hawaii and Australia. **Size:** 9 sq. mi. (23 sq. km.). **Population:** 7,500.
Who Really Rules: Formerly known as the Ellice Islands, Tuvalu consists of five atolls granted independence by the United Kingdom in 1978 and four disputed atolls ceded by the U.S. in 1980. Governed by a national assembly of only eight members, it still retains close ties to Britain. Its only exports, reports the *Wall Street Journal*, are coconuts, postage stamps, and sea slugs. Shortly after independence, Prime Minister Toalipi Lauti turned over the national treasury of $500,000 to a California real estate investor, who promised a 15% annual yield. In 1980 the government announced that it was recalling the funds to form a joint venture bank with Barclay's, but the investment paid off. Less fortunate, however, were the private Tuvaluans who invested thousands of dollars in worthless Texas real estate, sold by the same investor.

UGANDA

Location: East central Africa, north of Tanzania, west of Kenya. **Size:** 91,134 sq. mi. (236,036 sq. km.). **Population:** 14,119,000.
Who Really Rules: Following the downfall of Idi Amin, the country's brutal military dictator, in April, 1979, Uganda was governed by a factionalized "National Liberation Front," led by men exiled during the Amin regime. Controversial elections in December, 1980, were won by former president Milton Obote's Uganda People's Congress. Uganda's 7,000-man army, led by Brigadier David Oyite Ojok, is a significant force, but the last word on Uganda politics may come from Julius

Nyerere, president of neighboring Tanzania. Tanzanian soldiers spearheaded the drive that ousted Amin, and there are still 10,000 Tanzanian troops in Uganda. Amin's excesses and the war to oust him have left Uganda's economy in shambles and the political situation in chaos; armed bandits—including members of the military—prey upon the population.

UNION OF SOVIET SOCIALIST REPUBLICS

Location: Eastern Europe and northern Asia, from the Baltic Sea to the Bering Sea. **Size:** 8,649,498 sq. mi. (22,402,200 sq. km.). **Population:** 269,302,000 (72% Slavic).

Who Really Rules: The U.S.S.R. consists of 15 union republics, 20 autonomous republics, and numerous smaller political divisions. Each entity is governed by the Communist party, headed by a politburo made up of older male civilians, predominantly of Russian nationality. In theory a federation, U.S.S.R. political authority and economic planning are centralized, with Russians playing an important role even in homelands of other nationalities.

Most of the economy is state-owned, though an underground commerce persists in border republics. The economy, like the government, is run by party bureaucrats, whose material and social privileges increase with performance and promotion. Under the leadership of Leonid Brezhnev, party general secretary and Presidium chairman, the ruling group has delegated decision-making authority to lower-level bureaucrats. Interest groups, based upon industrial affiliation, have emerged, but they remain subordinate to the top party men.

While centralizing the economy and politics, the Russian leadership has protected and promoted the culture and language of the diverse Soviet nationalities. In many regions this had led to a revival of nationalism, but there is no current threat of secession. However, with a much higher birthrate in Muslim central Asia than in the European zones, the country's demographic balance is changing. Ethnic Russians will soon make up less than half of the population, while the Muslim share is 20% and rising.

UNITED ARAB EMIRATES

Location: Along the southern edge of the Persian Gulf, between Qatar and Oman. **Size:** 32,278 sq. mi. (83,600 sq. km.). **Population:** 900,000, 80% of whom are foreign.

Who Really Rules: The U.A.E. is a loose federation of seven princely states, governed by the Supreme Council of the emirs of each state. President Sheikh Zayid, emir of Abu Dhabi, the largest, most populous, and richest state, uses his oil money to promote unification and modernization. He is generally allied with the growing commercial class, which is represented by the appointed, advisory National Council. Sheikh Rashid of Dubai, the second most populous and second-richest emirate, was brought into the Federalist camp in 1979, when he was made prime minister. Great Britain, the former colonial power in the region, still runs the U.A.E. military and advises key ministries, while Saudi Arabia and Kuwait exert direct influence on the Supreme Council.

With perhaps the highest per capita income in the world, the U.A.E. is able to provide basic services for most of its population while wasting huge sums on useless building programs and corruption. Expatriates and immigrants, largely from the Middle East and South Asia, make up most of the work force, but there are no labor unions.

UNITED KINGDOM (OF GREAT BRITAIN AND NORTHERN IRELAND)

Location: An island off the northwestern coast of Europe. Great Britain comprises England, Scotland, and Wales. **Size:** 94,226 sq. mi. (244,046 sq. km.). **Population:** 55,717,000 (85% English, 10% Scottish, 5% Welsh).

Who Really Rules: The United Kingdom, which includes Great Britain and Northern Ireland, has a mixed economy in which the government provides extensive social and health services as well as welfare grants. There is government ownership of major industries that have proven unprofitable, and England remains home to multinational corporations with investments throughout the world, particularly in the former British Empire. In the elective parliamentary system, power has alternated between the Conservatives (Tories), who favor lower taxes and reduced government economic activity, and the Labour party, which is backed by the active Trade Unions Congress.

In 1979 referendums, proponents of greater autonomy in Scotland won a slight majority of those voting, but "lost" because that represented only a third of the electorate. In Wales, supporters of autonomy won about one fifth of the votes. In Northern Ireland, British military and government funds are being used to defuse the ongoing civil war between the minority Catholics, most of whom prefer association with Ireland, and majority Protestants.

UNITED STATES OF AMERICA

Location: Central tier of North America, plus Alaska (northwestern North America and associated Pacific Islands) and Hawaii (mid-Pacific Polynesian islands). **Size:** 3,615,105 sq. mi. (9,363,123 sq. km.). **Population:** 225,195,000.

Who Really Rules: The U.S. government consists of the federal government, divided into three semi-independent branches (executive, legislative, and judicial), 50 state governments with a similar structure, and numerous local agencies, counties, and cities. Each unit has different functions, but the federal executive branch, headed by President Ronald

Reagan, is the center of power, with effective control over the massive federal budget and over the U.S. armed forces.

Although the U.S. has a two-party electoral system with active campaigns, political and economic power is concentrated in a ruling elite of white, predominantly Protestant men. Based in financial centers such as New York City, this elite directly controls most U.S.-based multinational corporations, major media, influential "charitable" foundations, major private universities, and most public utilities. Although much of the elite's wealth is inherited, "membership" is open to capable or newly rich outsiders.

The elite exerts only indirect control over the political system, through campaign contributions, lobbying, and policy-formation study associations, in which it prepares political leaders for higher office. Both the Republican party and the Democratic party draw upon elite members for appointed positions, but rarely is one elected.

The U.S. government regulates and subsidizes the country's capitalist economy and carries out a foreign policy that supports the interests of U.S.-based corporations. The U.S. ruling class has historically been forced to share part of its power in exchange for social stability and economic productivity. Consequently, other groups, such as organized labor, ethnic minorities, small business and professional organizations, and single-issue lobbies, also influence policy.

UPPER VOLTA

Location: Landlocked in Sahelian West Africa, north of the Ivory Coast and Ghana. **Size:** 105,869 sq. mi. (274,200 sq. km.). **Population:** 8,098,000.

Who Really Rules: In November, 1980, the 14-year rule of Gen. Aboubacar Sangoulé Lamizana was ended by a bloodless military coup led by Col. Saye Zerbo. Parliament was dissolved and the three-year-old constitution was suspended.

Traditional tribal structures are still powerful in this subsistence-oriented country. Zerbo has the support of the labor movement and the Catholic Church as well as the leaders and royalty of the Mossi ethnic group, which makes up nearly 40% of the population. Lamizana's party was officially linked to the ruling party in the Ivory Coast, which exercises a great deal of influence over Upper Volta because the Ivory Coast is Upper Volta's major trading partner and employs 500,000 Voltan migrant workers each year.

URUGUAY

Location: Between Brazil and Argentina, on the southeastern coast of South America. **Size:** 68,037 sq. mi. (176,215 sq. km.). **Population:** 2,954,000.

Who Really Rules: Since 1973 real power in Uruguay has been in the hands of the military leaders who make up the National Security Council. Leftist political parties and unions have been banned, and several thousand people have had their political rights suspended until 1991.

The two traditional parties—National, or Blanco, representing the cattle-raising aristocracy, and Colorado, party of the industrial and commercial class—are allowed to operate under military supervision. The military has announced plans for a presidential election in 1981, in which the armed forces will pick a single candidate in conjunction with the Blanco and Colorado parties.

Representatives of the two traditional parties and the leftist Broad Front met in Mexico in late 1980 to form the Democratic Convergency, a united opposition to military rule.

VANUATU

Location: A cluster of islands in the Melanesian southwest Pacific, northeast of Australia. **Size:** 5,700 sq. mi. (14,763 sq. km.). **Population:** 120,000.

Who Really Rules: Vanuatu, formerly the New Hebrides, gained independence on July 30, 1980. Ruled until that date by France and the United Kingdom as a "condominium"—a unique and historically divisive form of joint administration—the population is split into culturally dissimilar English-speaking and French-speaking communities. The large Anglophone community runs the elected government.

Prior to independence, Francophone groups on two islands rebelled, attempting to secede. On the large island of Espiritu Santo rebels were aided by French planters, who feared Anglophone support for Melanesian land rights, and by the U.S.-based Phoenix Foundation, a group with links to the American Libertarian party. French and British forces, brought in to keep peace and neutralize each other, did nothing, but after independence the Vanuatu government used troops from Papua New Guinea, with Australian advisers, to put down the revolt.

VATICAN CITY

Location: Within Rome, Italy. **Size:** .16 sq. mi. (.41 sq. km.). **Population:** 750.

Who Really Rules: The Vatican City is the headquarters of the Roman Catholic Church. Though the pope, elected from and by the College of Cardinals (Catholic leaders worldwide), has full governing powers, he delegates them to a governor. Street access and electrical power are provided by the city of Rome, and the Italian government is responsible for defense, but a detachment of Swiss Guards patrols the Vatican itself.

The Vatican, through its own representatives and church officials around the world, maintains extensive diplomatic contacts. It is a powerful influence anywhere Catholics make up a large portion of the population.

VENEZUELA

Location: Northern coast of South America, between Colombia and Guyana. **Size:** 352,143 sq. mi. (912,050 sq. km.). **Population:** 15,771,000 (excluding as many as 200,000 jungle Indians).
Who Really Rules: Venezuela is one of the most democratic nations in Latin America; two major political parties alternate control of the government. Elections resemble campaigns in the U.S., and the political parties even hire North American media consultants. In the 1970s the spurt in oil revenues greatly increased government control of the economy, but it did little to reduce economic inequality in the population.

Long a preserve of U.S. oil companies, the rise of OPEC in 1973 gave Venezuela sufficient oil revenue to nationalize the industry. Since then Venezuela has used its money and skills to promote economic nationalism and political democracy in Central America (including Nicaragua), the Caribbean, and Ecuador. The government remains friendly to the U.S., but it has awarded a growing share of major public works and industrial development contracts to European and Japanese firms.

VIETNAM

Location: Along the eastern coast of the Indochinese Peninsula in Southeast Asia, south of China. **Size:** 127,242 sq. mi. (329,556 sq. km.). **Population:** 55,172,000.
Who Really Rules: Unified Vietnam is governed by the Vietnam Communist party, essentially the same body that led Vietnamese opposition to French colonialism and U.S. intervention. The Communists have encountered difficulty introducing communism to the southern part of Vietnam, however, even in areas with a long history of revolutionary activity. Many Vietnamese in the south prefer urban squatter shacks to life in "new economic zones"—rural areas that were abandoned during the war against the U.S. Farmers in the Mekong Delta are reluctant to join cooperatives. And the black market in Ho Chi Minh City (Saigon) thrives with goods mailed to family members by Vietnamese refugees in other parts of the world.

Vietnam receives substantial aid, technical advice, and military hardware from the U.S.S.R., but thus far it has not offered to let the Soviets use any former U.S. bases as Pacific naval bases.

VIRGIN ISLANDS, BRITISH

Location: 36 islands in the eastern Caribbean, east of Puerto Rico and south of the U.S. Virgin Islands. **Size:** 59 sq. mi. (153 sq. km.). **Population:** 12,500.
Who Really Rules: The British Virgin Islands is a British colony with limited self-government. Tourism is the major industry.

VIRGIN ISLANDS, U.S.

Location: Three major and several minor islands in the Caribbean, east of Puerto Rico. **Size:** 133 sq. mi. (344 sq. km.). **Population:** 115,000 (12% white, remainder black and Puerto Rican).
Who Really Rules: The U.S. Virgin Islands is a self-governing U.S. territory. The economy is dominated by American hotel companies, the Amerada Hess petroleum corporation (which operates one of the world's largest oil refineries there), and Martin Marietta Alumina. The islands have become a center for drug smuggling from South America to the U.S. The coast is not watched closely, and once goods are on the islands they are within U.S. customs boundaries.

As many as one quarter of the U.S. Virgin Islanders are aliens, immigrants, or temporary workers from other West Indies islands. Disliked by many indigenous residents, these migrants have organized to protect their interests.

YEMEN, NORTH (YEMEN ARAB REPUBLIC)

Location: Southwestern Arabian Peninsula, fronting the Red Sea, in the Middle East. **Size:** 75,290 sq. mi. (195,000 sq. km.). **Population:** 5,371,000.
Who Really Rules: North Yemen (with its capital at San'a) is ruled by a military regime headed by Col. Ali Abdullah Saleh. Its urban economy is capitalist, and thousands of merchants from Aden (South Yemen) have set up business there. Shiite Muslims form the majority of the population. Sections of the country are essentially under tribal rule. Several hundred thousand Yemenis work abroad, primarily in Saudi Arabia. In 1979 they sent home a whopping $1.4 billion in earnings.

Because Yemen is strategically located at the southern entrance to the Red Sea and borders Saudi Arabia, the U.S., U.S.S.R., and Saudi Arabia have all provided financial and/or military assistance to win its friendship. Relations with South Yemen have varied from negotiations aimed at unification to outright border war.

YEMEN, SOUTH (PEOPLE'S DEMOCRATIC REPUBLIC OF)

Location: Southern Arabian Peninsula, fronting the Gulf of Aden (Arabian Sea), in the Middle East. **Size:** 128,559 sq. mi. (332,968 sq. km.). **Population;** 1,866,000.
Who Really Rules: South Yemen (with its capital at Aden) is ruled by the communist Yemeni Socialist party. There have been several leadership changes in the past few years, their long-term result being the replacement of former guerrilla leaders with technocrats. The Aden government seeks unification with North Yemen, under Socialist party leadership, and it has pursued this course through negotiation, border war, and assassination.

South Yemen receives military assistance and advice from the Soviet Union and its allies, and the Soviet fleet in the Indian Ocean regularly refuels at Aden. Reportedly, Russian, East German, and Cuban advisers have had a hand in recent party leadership shake-ups.

YUGOSLAVIA

Location: Adriatic coast of the Balkan Peninsula in southeastern Europe, bordered on the north by Austria and Hungary. **Size:** 98,766 sq. mi. (255,804 sq. km.). **Population:** 22,677,000.
Who Really Rules: Yugoslavia's central government, six republics, and two autonomous provinces are governed by the League of Communists of Yugoslavia (LCY). Although Yugoslavians enjoy substantial economic freedom and contact with Western Europe, the LCY monopolizes the government and harshly limits dissent. Since the death of President Josip Broz (Tito) in 1980, the government and party have been in the hands of a collective leadership representing Yugoslavia's eight major nationalities.

The Yugoslav economy is based upon decentralized, worker-controlled enterprises, with numerous joint ventures with Western capitalists. The relatively free market has encouraged large-scale consumption of consumer goods. Still, the Soviet Union is Yugoslavia's number-one trading partner.

ZAIRE

Location: Equatorial Africa, touching the Atlantic coast at the mouth of the Zaire (Congo) River. **Size:** 905,563 sq. mi. (2,345,409 sq. km.). **Population:** 30,181,000.
Who Really Rules: Since 1965, when the CIA helped Lt. Gen. Mobutu Sese Seko seize power, Zaire has been under Mobutu's personal rule. He maintains control by permitting government officials to siphon off public funds and by suppressing both reformist and revolutionary opposition. Zaire's foreign debt is nearing $5 billion. Consequently, foreign creditors, organized into the "Paris Club," have been able to impose economic policies upon Zaire, requiring cuts in government expenditures and other actions causing hardship for Zairians.
Breaking Up Is Hard to Do: Zaire is the creation of Belgian colonialism. Mobutu has limited control over, and little popularity with, many of the two hundred ethnic groups. Shaba, the southern highlands once known as Katanga, has been the site of recurring rebellions. The predominant Lunda ethnic tribe, also important in Angola and Zambia, does not recognize the Zaire central government. In 1977 and 1978, soldiers of the Congo National Liberation Front (FLNC) occupied much of Shaba, but were driven out by Moroccan and French troops supporting Mobutu. Although FLNC troops have been allied in the past with Belgian economic interests and the Portuguese colonial army, today the Front is considered leftist. Extremely popular in the Shaba region, it hopes to overthrow Mobutu throughout the country.

Shaba is important to Zaire, and Western nations as well, because it is the richest section of the country, with valuable copper and cobalt deposits. Zaire needs its Shaba mining income to pay off its huge foreign debt.

ZAMBIA

Location: Landlocked in southern Africa, east of Angola, south of Zaire. **Size:** 290,585 sq. mi. (752,614 sq. km.). **Population:** 6,113,000.

Who Really Rules: Zambia is governed by President Kenneth Kaunda and his United National Independence party, the single legal party. The only organized opposition has centered in the Bemba tribal group, from Zambia's mining belt.

Zambia's economy is dependent upon the export of copper and cobalt. Although the government owns 51% of the mining operation's shares, foreign corporations are still in control. In addition, foreign banks and governments, working through the International Monetary Fund, exert enormous influence over the Zambian economy in exchange for their loans.

Generally considered pro-Western, Kaunda concluded a major arms purchase agreement with the Soviet Union in early 1980.

ZIMBABWE (FORMERLY RHODESIA)

Location: Landlocked in southeastern Africa, west of Mozambique. **Size:** 150,803 sq. mi. (390,580 sq. km.). **Population:** 7,718,000 (over 70% Shona-speaking blacks, 20%–25% Ndebele-speaking blacks, 4% whites).

Who Really Rules: British mediation in the civil war between the white-run regime of Rhodesia and Zimbabwe nationalist guerrillas led to elections in February, 1980, in which Robert Mugabe's Zimbabwe African National Union and Joshua Nkomo's Zimbabwe African People's Union—members of the guerrilla Patriotic Front—won a huge majority of the black vote. When Mugabe, a Marxist revolutionary, became prime minister, he assumed a conciliatory posture, vowing to protect the rights and investments of the white minority. Mugabe's immediate goal is to bring blacks into positions of political authority.

White Zimbabweans still earn 10 to 20 times as much as blacks, and American, British, and South African corporations still control the economy. Zimbabwe's closest ally is Mozambique, but Britain, the colonial power and mediator, is assisting in the transition, and Zimbabwe has assumed Rhodesia's massive debt to neighboring South Africa.

—L.S.

6

HISTORY LESSONS

THE OTHER SIDE OF HISTORY

The Coming of Pizarro As Seen by the Incas

The Traditional Version: In order to head off a war between Spain and Portugal over discoveries in the New World, Pope Alexander VI divided the territory with an imaginary "line of demarcation" in 1493. The land to the east of the line—which ran north to south several hundred miles west of the Azores and Cape Verdes—belonged to Portugal, while that to the west was given to Spain. Almost 40 years after this papal decree, soldier of fortune Francisco Pizarro set out for Peru to secure the pagan kingdom of the Incas for Charles V of Spain and the Catholic Church.

Accompanied by 168 soldiers, Pizarro disembarked confidently. As the conquistadores, wearing shining armor and mounted on horses, rode inland from the sea toward the Inca city of Cajamarca, they were greeted along the way by awestruck natives. In Cajamarca, Pizarro was to meet with Atahualpa, the tyrannical Inca ruler. However, once inside the city, the Spaniards saw that they were surrounded by thousands of Inca warriors, and they prepared to fight the heathen for the glory of God and Spain. Despite their lesser numbers, Pizarro's men had superior arms and easily routed the primitive Inca army. They took Atahualpa prisoner and later executed him because Pizarro feared the possibility of reprisal. Without their leader, the Incas readily accepted Christianity and Spanish rule.

The Other Side: In many ways Inca civilization was more advanced than that of Western Europe. Inca physicians were performing successful brain surgery while their European counterparts still prescribed leeches. Inca architecture, agriculture, and astronomy had progressed amazingly, too, but perhaps the most remarkable Inca achievement concerned social order. In their society there were no poor people. Widows, orphans, and invalids were cared for by the state, and workers retired at age 50 on pensions of food and clothing. There was little crime because every basic need was met. At the head of this benevolent system was the ruler, or Inca, who demanded in exchange the obedience of his subjects.

When Pizarro landed in Peru in 1532, all he knew of the Incas was that, according to legend, they possessed fabulous wealth. His twin objectives were to loot the empire and to subjugate its people to not only

Christianity but Spanish rule. The conquistadores had arrived at a most opportune time. Both Atahualpa and his half-brother Huáscar had claimed the throne after their father, Huayna Capac, died in 1525 without formally naming his successor. Although Huayna Capac's priest designated Huáscar the ruler, a civil war erupted between the two brothers and lasted until 1532, when Atahualpa's forces captured and imprisoned Huáscar. Huáscar was forced to witness the slaughter of the royal family; hundreds of men, women, and children were killed so Atahualpa could reign without further challenge. Atahualpa's bloody power play disrupted the ordered Inca society, and the natives hailed Pizarro as a son of their white-skinned god Viracocha, who they believed had been sent to avenge Huáscar and his family. The Spaniard did not abuse them. The sound of his cannon added credence to this false identity, since Viracocha controlled the thunder. As the conquistadores plundered their way cross-country, they met with no resistance from the thoroughly intimidated and demoralized Incas.

However, when word of the Spaniards' conduct during their trek to Cajamarca reached Atahualpa, he demanded that the thieves return the goods they had stolen. Instead, they sent him a priest, Brother Vicente, who proceeded to instruct Atahualpa in Western religion. The catechism lesson ended abruptly when Atahualpa hurled a Bible on the ground. At this, the offended Spaniards—who the night before had been whipped into a religious frenzy by Pizarro—attacked and slaughtered the unarmed natives. The Inca warriors stationed outside the city scattered before the onslaught of the Spanish artillery. Atahualpa was taken captive and held for ransom. When he learned that Huáscar was promising the Spanish more gold for his own release, the ruthless Atahualpa secretly ordered his brother's death. During the next nine months, a roomful of gold and silver was delivered to Pizarro to secure Atahualpa's safe return to the throne, but the Spaniard had no intention of releasing his prisoner. Pizarro knew that in order to disrupt and conquer this well-run society, he must kill the Inca leader. After a mock trial at which Atahualpa was found guilty of trumped-up charges, Pizarro offered him a choice: He could elect to be burned alive as a heathen or to be strangled as a Christian. When the Inca ruler chose the latter, he was baptized Juan de Atahualpa in honor of St. John the Baptist. Then he was tied to a stake and garroted. Pizarro and his men gave the Inca a full-scale Catholic funeral.

Eyewitness Account: Huaman Poma, a member of the Inca nobility, lived during the transition to Spanish rule. The following account of the battle at Cajamarca is excerpted from his *Letter to a King*, a description of Inca culture before and after the Spanish conquest.

"Friar Vicente . . . came forward holding a crucifix in his right hand and a breviary in his left and introduced himself as another envoy of the Spanish ruler, who according to his account was a friend of God, and who often worshiped before the cross and believed in the Gospel. Friar Vicente called upon the Inca to renounce all other gods as being a mockery of the truth.

"Atahualpa's reply was that he could not change his belief in the Sun, who was immortal, and in the other Inca divinities. He asked Friar Vicente what authority he had for his own belief, and the friar told him it was all written in the book which he held. The Inca then said: 'Give me the book so that it can speak to me.' The book was handed up to him, and he began to eye it carefully and listen to it page by page. At last he asked: 'Why doesn't the book say anything to me?' Still sitting on his throne, he threw it on the ground with a haughty and petulant gesture.

"Friar Vicente found his voice and called out that the Indians were against the Christian faith. Thereupon Pizarro and Almagro (his lieutenant) began to shout orders to their men, telling them to attack these Indians who rejected God and the Emperor. The Spaniards began to fire their muskets and charged upon the Indians, killing them like ants. At the sound of the explosions and the jingle of bells on the horses' harness, the shock of arms and the whole amazing novelty of their attackers' appearance, the Indians were terror-stricken. The pressure of their numbers caused the walls of the square to crumble and fall. They were desperate to escape from being trampled by the horses, and in their headlong flight a lot of them were crushed to death. So many Indians were killed that it was impracticable to count them. As for the Spaniards, only five of them lost their lives, and these few casualties were not caused by the Indians, who had at no time dared to attack the formidable strangers. The Spaniards' corpses were found clasped together with their Indian victims, and it was assumed that they had been mistakenly trampled to death by their own cavalry."

—M.S.

The American Revolution As Seen by the British

The Traditional Version: "Taxation without representation is tyranny," British colonists protested when Parliament passed the Stamp Act in 1765. Two years earlier, eager settlers and land promoters had been provoked when expansion west of the Allegheny Mountains was blocked by the Proclamation of 1763. Then the Townshend Acts imposed duties on vital colonial imports in 1767. Even with the tax, British tea from India was still cheaper than inferior Dutch tea, but it was the principle involved that prompted the dumping of 342 cases of this disputed commodity into Boston Harbor in 1773. The British Parliament responded with the "Intolerable Acts," which closed the Boston port. When protest and reprisal escalated into armed conflict at Lexington, Concord, and Bunker Hill in 1775, the colonists chose "liberty or death" rather than indefinite "slavery" as a part of the British Empire. According to their Declaration of Independence (1776), they believed that men possessed "certain unalienable rights" and that a government derived its power from the "consent of the governed." These new "Americans" proceeded to secure their rights by force of arms in the modern world's first revolutionary war against a mother country.

The Other Side: "The colonies were acquired with no other view than to be a convenience to us," the London *Chronicle* pointed out in 1764, "and therefore it can never be imagined that we are to consult their interest preferably to our own." In fact, the British considered that their American colonies, having enjoyed an extended period of "salutary neglect" during the 18th century, were practically self-governing. They had only to fulfill their vital function within the mercantile system by providing raw materials and consuming the manufactures of the British Empire. (The laws prohibiting trade between the colonies and foreign countries had never been strictly enforced anyway; therefore, smuggling was a popular avocation.)

There remained the thorny subject of taxation. At considerable expense, Britain had won France's North American territory in the Seven Years' War (1756–1763). Britain now faced a large postwar debt and the responsibility of additional land to protect and govern. Highly burdened by taxes themselves, the British were merely asking the colonies to bear the expense of their own administration and defense. As each proposed revenue bill met with opposition, it was repealed, Parliament being anxious to appease the colonies. But such "lenity" only encouraged additional disobedience, which was skillfully orchestrated by colonial propagandists. The Boston Massacre of 1770, during which redcoats fired on a mob owing to extreme provocation, was played up as if hundreds of colonists had been killed instead of five.

Scarcely noted in the British press at first, the Boston Tea Party was magnified from a simple matter of destruction of property into an intolerable insult to British authority. Chiefly responsible for the incident were Sam Adams, a tough and cunning professional politician, who was said to control two Boston mobs which he exploited for his own personal gain and glory, and the rich and vain businessman John Hancock, later described as "an elegant revolutionary" of the "native governing class of merchants and landowners whose interests were threatened by imperial policies and by the barrier to obtaining western land." These "incendiaries" used all manner of intimidation, even tarring and feathering loyal subjects of the king, to undermine their own current democratic self-rule, although British lawyers determined after careful consideration that the rebels were not guilty of high treason—yet.

According to official accounts of the battles of Lexington and Concord, the British did not fire in self-defense until besieged by rebel mobs who scalped and removed the ears of their victims. These techniques, in addition to such Indian practices as shooting from cover, were considered dishonorable conduct. By 18th-century European standards, opponents were required to mass large formations of troops facing one another on open terrain.

Still maintaining their "magnanimous tolerance" up to the eve of Bunker Hill in 1775, the British offered pardon to all who would lay down their arms—except Adams and Hancock, whose offenses were "of too flagitious a nature to admit of any other consideration than that of condign punishment."

With the Declaration of Independence the colonists "crossed their Rubicon," as historian Edward Gibbon put it. King George III favored armed intervention to put down the "rebellion," while his advisers preferred a naval blockade; wavering between a land or sea strategy, the British never fully implemented either. The opposition Whigs, advocates of trade rather than taxation and with no stomach for the war at all, accused the government of corruption and incompetence. The chief culprits were the rakish Lord Sandwich, who ran a highly idiosyncratic admiralty, and Lord George Germain, the arrogant colonial secretary whose instructions ensured the defeat of Gen. John Burgoyne at Saratoga in 1777. A major blow to British prestige, Saratoga encouraged the French to avenge the humiliation of the Seven Years' War by coming to the aid of the Americans. In fact the French navy—not the colonial farmer—defeated the British navy and cornered Cornwallis at Yorktown in 1781, thus ending the war for all practical purposes. (The outbreak of the French Revolution a few years later was regarded by most Britons as "just desserts.")

Thanks to the political and physical difficulties of conducting such a huge overseas operation, the world's greatest power was defeated by a ragged band of revolutionaries. But the loss of the American colonies, as formalized by the Treaty of Paris in 1783, was taken by the British with characteristic aplomb—rather as if a group of businessmen were closing down an unprofitable branch, it was said.

Eyewitness Accounts: "Well, boys, you've had your Indian caper, haven't you?" Admiral Montague of the Royal Navy remarked to a group of Bostonians after the Boston Tea Party. "But mind, you've got to pay the fiddler yet." British officers in the colonies were at first inclined to express such patriarchal condescension, and had an upper-class contempt for the rough-hewn Americans; letters home revealed their chief concerns to be pay, promotion, and perquisites.

As the war settled in for good and earnest, the British became more bitterly impassioned. "I every day curse Columbus and all the discoverers of this diabolical country," Maj. John Bowater wrote, while a surgeon on board one of His Majesty's ships described the rebel army as "truly nothing but a drunken, canting, lying, praying, hypocritical rabble." A few, however, were moved to admiration of the Americans, particularly for Gen. George Washington and his ragged "banditti," who managed to frustrate the empire's finest. "Come on, Maister Washington," murmured a grizzled old Highland officer in Virginia, "I could na think of gangin' home without a sight of you."

With their defeat at Yorktown, it seemed to the British soldiers like "The World Turned Upside Down"—one of their marching songs in which "ponies rode men" and "grass ate the cows." News of the defeat was received by British prime minister Lord North "as he would have taken a ball in his breast," a colleague reported. "O God! it is all over!" North kept repeating, and it was for him. His government would soon fall. The king, who had threatened to abdicate rather than give the rebels their freedom, steeled himself to receive John Adams, the ambassador from the new nation. Privately, however, he confided, "[I will] never lay my head on my last pillow in peace and quiet so long as I remember the loss of my American colonies."

—C.D.

The Alamo as drawn by a Mexican officer preparing to attack.

The Battle of the Alamo As Seen by the Mexicans

The Traditional Version: Provisions were scanty, ammunition was scarce, and help was nowhere in sight when 185 Texans, barricaded inside an old mission, fought a 4,000-man Mexican army. During the 12 days of siege prior to the final battle, the gallant Americans reinforced the walls, dug trenches, and mounted their 18 cannon while being harassed around the clock by Mexican rifle and artillery fire and scouting parties.

"I feel confident that the determined valor and desperate courage heretofore evinced by my men will not fail them in the last struggle; and although they may be sacrificed to the vengeance of a Gothic enemy, the victory will cost so dear that it will be worse for him than defeat. God and Texas! Victory or death!" So ended the final plea for assistance from the Alamo's commander, Col. William Travis.

After rejecting the Mexican demand for unconditional surrender, Travis assembled his men (including the legendary Jim Bowie and Davy Crockett) and offered them the choice of fighting to certain death or leaving the fort. All chose to stay except one man, who managed to escape through the tightening Mexican encirclement. No other defender would remain alive.

On Mar. 6, 1836, the Mexican army, commanded by Gen. Antonio López de Santa Anna, attacked the fort from three sides. Twice the Texans repulsed them with bullets and cannon, but sheer numbers finally permitted the Mexicans to gain the walls and pour into the fort. The Texans, out of ammunition, used their rifle butts for clubs as they fought hand to hand. Those who survived the assault on the walls retreated slowly, desperately fighting from room to room in the barracks.

Although certain Mexican officers requested clemency for the last surviving Americans, Santa Anna ordered them massacred. Mexican soldiers tossed the Texans' bodies on their bayonets as if they were bales of hay. As a final insult, the Mexicans stripped and burned the corpses.

Although outnumbered 20 to 1, the Alamo defenders indeed made Mexico pay a heavy price. At least 1,500 Mexicans were killed or wounded, and Santa Anna's advance into Texas was delayed for two weeks, which gave Texas enough time to gather the army that defeated Mexico two months later. Thirteen months after the Alamo fell, Texas declared its independence from Mexico's repressive, dictatorial rule, which not only had denied Texas such rights as statehood, trial by jury, public education, and religious freedom but also had proscribed slavery.

The Other Side: Mexico generously opened Texan lands to American settlers who, corrupted by their greed for land and the precious metals it contained, ignored the 1824 Mexican constitution which they had sworn to obey and took advantage of Mexico's internal problems to revolt. The Texans demanded legalization of their despicable practice of slavery, formed unauthorized governing bodies that collected taxes but did not return any of this revenue to the state, continually demanded more and more land, and insisted on rights granted only to sovereign nations.

This bold infringement on the honor and property of Mexico could not be permitted. "The colonists established in Texas," declared a circular distributed by the minister of relations, "have recently given the most unequivocal evidence of the extremity to which perfidy, ingratitude, and the restless spirit that animates them can go, since—forgetting what they owe to the supreme government of the nation which so generously admitted them to its bosom, gave them fertile lands to cultivate, and allowed them all the means to live in comfort and abundance—they have risen against that same government, taking arms against it . . . [while] concealing their criminal purpose of dismembering the territory of the Republic."

General Santa Anna, who had taken control of the government three years earlier, declared that he would "strike in defense of the independence, honor, and rights of my nation." Fired with patriotism, he formed an army and gave this order: "The foreigners who are making war on the Mexican nation in violation of every rule of law are entitled to no consideration whatever, and in consequence no quarter is to be given them."

The enemy took refuge in the Alamo when they saw the Mexican army approaching. After a 12-day siege, four columns of soldiers and reserves quietly positioned themselves on four sides of the fort in the predawn darkness. They were thrust into battle by the ancient Spanish bugle call that signaled "fire and death."

The revolutionaries' barrage of cannon and rifle fire stopped the initial charge and killed valiant officers and soldiers who had won the honor of being among the first to attack. When a second attempt was likewise repulsed, Santa Anna ordered in the reserves. Soon the army surged over the north wall, where wooden planking allowed a foothold, and overran the defenders.

As the Texans retreated to the barracks behind sandbag barriers and trenches, Mexican soldiers followed. Fierce fighting ensued, but the Americans fell quickly, especially when their cannon were turned against them. The wrath of the army abated only after all the foreigners were killed. The number of Mexicans lost in the battle was appalling, but they died for a just and honorable cause.

Eyewitness Report: José Enrique de la Peña, a lieutenant colonel in Santa Anna's army, wrote: "The columns [of soldiers], bravely storming the fort in the midst of a terrible shower of bullets and cannon fire, had reached the base of the walls. . . . Our soldiers, some stimulated by courage and others by fury, burst into the quarters where the enemy had entrenched themselves, from which issued an infernal fire. Behind these came others who, nearing the doors and blind with fury and smoke, fired their shots against friends and enemies alike, and in this way our losses were most grievous. On the other hand, they turned the enemy's own cannon to bring down the doors to the rooms or the rooms themselves; a horrible carnage took place, and some were trampled to death. The tumult was great, the disorder frightful; it seemed as if the furies had descended upon us."

De la Peña's testimony gave the lie to a favorite myth: that Davy Crockett died in the baptistery of the Alamo and was found there, according to a plaque at the site, "with dead Mexicans piled about him, whom he had slain before giving up his life." On the contrary, according to De la Peña (and other soldiers backed his story): "Some seven men had survived the general carnage and . . . they were brought before Santa Anna. Among them . . . was the naturalist Davy Crockett. . . . Santa Anna . . . ordered his execution. . . . Though tortured before they were killed, these unfortunates died without complaining and without humiliating themselves before their torturers."

—P.A.R.

The Spanish-American War As Seen by the Filipinos

The Traditional Version: The standard historical interpretation of the Spanish-American War holds that an outraged American public forced President William McKinley to declare war on Spain on Apr. 21, 1898. U.S. citizens had become inflamed by newspaper reports of the atrocities perpetrated by Spanish troops upon the Cuban people, who were fighting to gain their independence from Spain.

When the war began, this sympathy for a people still under the yoke of Spanish imperialism was extended to the Filipinos, who had also lived under Spanish colonialism for centuries. On May 1, 1898, Adm. George Dewey led a U.S. naval squadron into Manila Bay and destroyed the Spanish fleet stationed there. American troops then arrived in the Philippines, and with the aid of native rebel forces led by Gen. Emilio

Aguinaldo, they defeated Spanish land forces and captured Manila in August, 1898.

With the liberation of the Philippines, a dilemma arose as to its future. President McKinley realized that, left to themselves, these Filipinos who had had no experience in self-rule would probably plunge their country into civil war and anarchy. Also, he believed that some aggressive imperialist power such as Germany or Japan would invade if American forces did not remain to protect the fledgling nation. Therefore, McKinley decided the U.S. had a moral responsibility to stay in the Philippines while introducing modern institutions and preparing and educating the Filipinos for self-government.

Fanatic Filipino patriots, led by General Aguinaldo and others, objected to this policy and waged guerrilla warfare for several years. However, by 1902, with the assistance of the responsible elements in Filipino society and the passive support of the Filipino masses, U.S. troops had put down the minor insurgency, which degenerated into mere bandit raids.

The Other Side: The Filipino view of the Spanish-American War is dramatically different. First of all, to the Filipinos it is known as the

Filipino independence leader General Emilio Aguinaldo.

Filipino War for Independence. In 1896 Filipino insurrectionists—who were members of the Katipunan society headed by Emilio Aguinaldo, the mayor of Cavite—had revolted against Spanish colonialism. This popular widespread rebellion had impelled the Spaniards to call for a truce and to promise reforms in December of 1897. Aguinaldo and other rebel leaders were forced into exile in Hong Kong as part of the truce agreement. By 1898 the Spanish had failed to implement the promised reforms, and the Filipino rebels were preparing to return and continue the struggle for freedom.

At this point Aguinaldo was approached by U.S. diplomatic and military representatives who proposed joint U.S.–Filipino military action against the Spanish in the Philippines. Aguinaldo considered the offer but first asked for guarantees that the U.S. did not plan to annex or colonize any Filipino territory. The American agents reassured him that the U.S. was interested only in defeating Spain and, in the process, helping the Filipinos gain their independence. President McKinley publicly announced that annexation, "by our code of morality, would be criminal aggression." These were, as later events proved, lies.

The U.S. was an expansionist, imperialist power which saw the Philippines as the perfect trade route into Asia. Not only did the islands have a wealth of raw materials to exploit, but they would also provide an untapped consumer base for U.S. manufactured goods. The Philippines were also the perfect target for another American product—racism. The Filipinos were considered "big children" or "little brown brothers." It was the destiny of "enlightened" white Americans to rule them because these "lost" souls were incapable of self-government. McKinley called on God to justify this condescending attitude on which his foreign policy was based. As he explained, "I walked the floor of the White House night after night . . . I went down on my knees and prayed [to] Almighty God for light and guidance. . . . And one night it came to me . . . there was nothing left for us to do but to take them all, and to educate the Filipinos, and to uplift and civilize and Christianize them." This in spite of the fact that the Philippines had been a primarily Catholic country for centuries.

Unaware of McKinley's true goals and sentiments, and armed with false offers of friendship, Aguinaldo returned to the Philippines to lead his people into revolution.

The rebels liberated the southern provinces of the island of Luzon; forced the Spanish into Manila, where they effectively contained them; and declared Filipino independence on June 12, 1898—all before the U.S. troops landed. Late in June the first wave of U.S. soldiers arrived, and by the end of July there were some 10,000 in the Philippines. Their commander, Gen. Wesley Merritt, immediately ordered the Filipino leaders to place themselves under his control. Not wanting to antagonize his new allies, Aguinaldo agreed—a decision he soon regretted. General Merritt entered into secret negotiations with the Spanish that resulted in a sham battle for Manila on Aug. 12, after which the Spanish readily surrendered to the Americans, who entered the city but refused entry to Filipino soldiers.

Tension grew over the next months as it became apparent to the Filipinos that the U.S. was in the Philippines to stay. On Dec. 10 the Treaty of Paris ending the Spanish-American War was signed. In this treaty it was agreed that possession of the Philippines, Cuba, and Guam be transferred from Spain to the U.S. for the price of $20 million. No Filipino representative had been allowed to participate in the negotiations in spite of the fact that the Philippines was, by then, a nation with a congress, a constitution, and local governments. When President McKinley issued the Proclamation of Benevolent Assimilation and ordered the U.S. Army to move out of Manila and occupy the entire country on Dec. 21, the betrayed Filipino rebels opposed this invasion and war erupted anew.

The aristocratic class, which had formerly collaborated with the Spanish, supported the Americans, while the majority of the Filipinos accepted Aguinaldo as their leader. In January of 1899 Aguinaldo formed a democratic nationalist government—the Philippine Republic—dedicated to independence. What followed is very reminiscent of U.S. involvement in Vietnam. By 1901, 126,000 troops had poured into the Philippines. Mass relocation camps were established in order to stop Filipino peasants from supporting the rebel armies. It was estimated that half the population of Luzon (the largest of the islands) starved to death after U.S. troops burned crops to keep them from falling into rebel hands. Torture was used to obtain confessions and information. American soldiers specialized in the "water cure," in which gallons of water were forced down the throats of natives; if the first application didn't have the desired effect, the victim was jumped on to empty his stomach, and the process was started over. The massacre of civilians became commonplace. Brig. Gen. Jacob Smith, commanding forces on the island of Samar, ordered: "I want no prisoners. I wish you to kill and burn: The more you kill and burn the better you will please me."

These brutal tactics succeeded so well that, after 3½ years of savage war, President Theodore Roosevelt announced on Independence Day, July 4, 1902, that the Philippines were "pacified." (In actuality, the rebels continued fighting for many more years.) From the Filipino point of view, their country had been invaded, conquered, and colonized by U.S. imperialists. Some 200,000 Filipinos were killed, while an estimated 400,000 died of war-generated diseases and starvation.

Eyewitness Accounts: A transcript was made of a meeting between Adm. George Dewey and Filipino general José Alejandrino in April of 1898, aboard the cruiser U.S.S. *Olympia* in Hong Kong harbor. Herewith is an excerpt.

Dewey: "The American people, champion of liberty, will undertake this war with the humanitarian purpose of liberating from the Spanish yoke the people which are under it and to give them independence and liberty, as we have already proclaimed before the whole world."

Alejandrino: "We are very thankful for this generous manifestation of the American people, and having come from the mouth of an admiral of her squadron, we give it more value than a written contract and, consequently, we place ourselves at your entire disposal. . . . We are ready to fight on your side for the independence of the Philippines."

Dewey: "America is rich under all concepts; it has territories scarcely populated, aside from the fact that our Constitution does not permit us to expand territorially outside of America. For these reasons, the Filipinos can be sure of their independence and of the fact that they will not be despoiled of any piece of their territory."

The following are excerpts from letters mailed home from U.S. soldiers fighting in the Philippines.

"We bombarded a place called Malabon, and then we went in and killed every native we met, men, women, and children."—Anthony Michea, Third Artillery

"Caloocan was supposed to contain 17,000 inhabitants. The 20th Kansas swept through it, and now Caloocan contains not one living native. Of the buildings, the battered walls of the great church and dismal prison alone remain."—Captain Elliot, Kansas Regiment

"I have seen a shell from our artillery strike a bunch of Filipinos, and then they would go scattering through the air, legs, arms, heads, all disconnected. And such sights actually make our boys laugh and yell, 'That shot was a peach.' "—Charles Weyland, Washington Volunteers, C Company

—R.J.F.

THE HIGH AND THE MIGHTY

Famous and Infamous Rulers in History

QUEEN VICTORIA

Vital Statistics: Victoria's ascension to the British throne in 1837 marked the end of the 123-year Hanoverian (German)/British joint monarchy because of the House of Hanover's law against a woman becoming its ruler. Her sex, though, did not prevent her from becoming one of the most colorful and controversial monarchs of Great Britain, Ireland, and the British Dominions beyond the seas.

Victoria was born in Kensington Palace in London on May 24, 1819, and began her reign in 1837, when she was just over 18 years of age. In 1840 she married her first cousin, Albert, and they had nine children. Albert died in 1861, and Victoria went into a period of seclusion that did not end fully until the 1880s. She died at her favorite home, Osborne House, on the Isle of Wight, on Jan. 22, 1901. She was 81 years old and had been sovereign for nearly 64 years.

Victoria cannot be considered beautiful, but she was attractive in her own way. Called "the little queen," she stood about 5 ft. She had bright blue eyes and long brown hair. However, she had a large, puffy face and a mouth that was amiable only when she smiled. Her appeal lay in her immense intelligence and her iron will, plus her sophistication and wit.

Queen Victoria with Prince Consort Albert, c. 1858.

Personal Life: Queen Victoria was a product of politics. In 1817 Princess Charlotte, granddaughter of George III, died while delivering a stillborn son. Charlotte was the only child of the prince regent, who was to become George IV. Pressure mounted on the remaining sons of George III to produce an heir, and in 1818 his fourth son, the 50-year-old Duke of Kent, reluctantly gave up his mistress of 27 years to marry Victoria of Saxe-Coburg-Saalfeld, a widow 18 years his junior. When the duchess became pregnant, they returned to England from her home in Coburg, Germany, to ensure that the child would be born on British soil.

Victoria had an unhappy childhood. Her father died from pneumonia when she was eight months old, and her mother raised her in Kensington Palace with the help of a governess, Baroness Lehzen, who became Victoria's lifelong friend. However, the comptroller of the household was Sir John Conroy, an ambitious, arrogant Irishman determined to be the power behind the throne when Victoria became queen. Hoping to make the child a weak and dependent person, Conroy devised the "Kensington system." Following this program, Victoria slept in her mother's bedroom, had to have someone hold her hand whenever she descended the stairs, and never held a conversation with anyone unless a third person was present. Victoria also had to endure long journeys with her mother and Conroy, tours of the British Isles calculated to ensure her popularity. These trips tired the child immensely and often made her ill.

In 1830 William IV ascended the throne on the death of his brother. Although William was immensely fond of his young niece, he despised her domineering mother. In 1836 the German princes Albert and Ernest of Saxe-Coburg and Gotha visited England. Victoria's mother hoped to marry her to one of the boys, but the king thought one of the princes of Orange would be far more suitable. He discouraged the stay of Albert and Ernest, but the duchess won out and engineered a three-week visit for the German princes. Victoria's heart did the choosing. While she found the princes of Orange "plain . . . dull . . . and not at all prepossessing," both Albert and Ernest struck her as "extremely merry" and "extremely sensible." Moreover, Albert was also "extremely good-looking." She soon fell madly in love with her "angel" Albert and proposed to him a year after ascending the throne. Theirs was a happy marriage, although Victoria detested being pregnant and later confided to her eldest daughter, "I positively think that those ladies who are always *enceinte* are quite disgusting; it is more like a rabbit or a guinea pig than anything else and really it is not very nice."

Albert had a difficult position as a German prince in Britain. He was a very intelligent and conscientious man, however, and Victoria came to rely more and more on his advice. A philanthropist and good businessman, he was also the architect of Osborne House and planned the enormously successful Great Exhibition of 1851. Albert was raised to the dignity of Prince Consort in 1857, but he remained essentially a reserved and melancholy man who undermined his health through overwork and worry. He was particularly concerned about the morals of Crown Prince Albert, and when he learned of Bertie's affair with an actress he was deeply distressed. His depression was increased by the illness of his son Leopold and the death of his young cousin Pedro V of Portugal. In his despondency he confided to Victoria, "I am sure, if I had a severe illness, I should give up at once." He died of typhoid fever at Windsor Castle on Dec. 14, 1861. He was only 42.

Victoria was shattered. She dressed primarily in black for the rest of her life and always kept a picture of Albert above her pillow. She also maintained his rooms in Windsor Castle as if in anticipation of his return. Each morning she had his clothes laid out for him, and every evening fresh water was placed in his washbasin. Avoiding London, she spent much of her time either at Osborne House or at Balmoral in the Scottish Highlands with her devoted servant and companion, John Brown. Their affection for each other led to a flurry of rumors and accusations. Dr. Michael MacDonald, a Scottish museum curator, contends that they became lovers after Albert's death. He even claims that they were secretly married and that Victoria bore Brown a son, who died a recluse in Paris in the 1950s at the age of 90. Although the story hardly seems likely, it is true that after Victoria's death her papers were stripped of all references to Brown, and that upon ascending the throne Edward VII ordered the destruction of all Brown memorabilia.

The last years of Victoria's reign were bittersweet. Most of her friends, including John Brown, had already died; she had also witnessed the deaths of two of her children, and it looked as if her eldest daughter would reach the grave before her. Still, she gained immense satisfaction as matriarch of her vast brood. At the time of her death, she had 37 great-grandchildren.

Rise to Power: Victoria's heirless uncle, King William IV, died at Windsor Castle on June 20, 1837, and Victoria ascended the throne.

In Power: When the teenage Victoria became queen, she knew little about the ruling of her empire. But in her handsome prime minister, Lord Melbourne, she found the ideal person to instruct her. Victoria thought Melbourne sparkling, merry, and witty, and in a week's time she was calling him "my friend." More than that, Melbourne served as a father figure to Victoria.

Unfortunately, Melbourne was of little help when Victoria faced her first major crisis early in 1839—the "Ladies of the Bedchamber" scandal. The scandal involved Flora Hastings, lady-in-waiting to the Duchess of Kent, who suddenly began showing signs of pregnancy. All eyes turned to John Conroy, who had shared a carriage with her on her return from a family visit. Although doctors certified that Lady Flora was still a virgin, ugly rumors circulated about the immorality of the court. When Victoria drove into Ascot with Lord Melbourne, whose government was falling, the populace taunted the queen with cries of "Mrs. Melbourne!" Lady Flora died in July, and an autopsy revealed that the swelling of her stomach had been caused by a tumor-infested liver.

The tumult died down, and Victoria was soon preoccupied with plans for her wedding to Albert. After their marriage, the royal couple set out on a round of state visits to the other royal families of Europe. They were particularly close to King Louis Philippe of France, who found refuge in Britain in 1848 after a revolution placed Napoleon III in power. In that one fateful year, nearly every government in Europe changed hands.

Another problem was also looming on the horizon. The weakness of Turkey encouraged Czar Nicholas II of Russia to champion the claims that the Russian Orthodox Church had over the Turkish-controlled holy places in Palestine. Britain—and indeed most of Europe—believed that Turkey would be torn apart by Russia, and this led Britain to declare war on Russia on Mar. 24, 1854. Although the Crimean War was in many ways disastrous for Britain, it won new respect for the British soldier. "I feel so much for them, and am so fond of my dear soldiers, and so *proud* of them," Victoria wrote to her uncle. She personally visited the wounded in hospitals and created a medal for outstanding bravery and courage—the Victoria Cross.

Another matter soon claimed Victoria's attention. In 1857 the Sepoy Mutiny broke out after Indian soldiers (Sepoys) were forced to use gun cartridges that were greased with pig or cow fat and that had to be bitten open. Since Hindus consider the cow sacred and Muslims are forbidden to eat pig, it was the final indignation in their struggle against the East India Company, which had ruled India for 99 years. The Sepoys went on a rampage, killing British men, women, and children indiscriminately. Victoria was horrified, but she fought against reprisals once the mutiny had been quashed.

After Albert's death in 1861, Victoria refused to attend the meetings of her Privy Council, instead opting to sit in an adjoining room with the door open. At first she was the subject of worldwide sympathy, but as her mourning dragged on and the rumors of her relationship with John Brown increased, respect for her and for the monarchy declined. It had not been at such a low ebb since the reign of Victoria's "wicked uncle," George IV.

When ill health forced Prime Minister Lord Derby to resign in 1868, he was replaced by Benjamin Disraeli, who proceeded to win the queen over and slowly coax her out of seclusion. "Everyone likes flattery," he told Matthew Arnold, "and when you come to royalty you should lay it on with a trowel." Disraeli called Victoria the "Faery Queen," and she responded by affectionately referring to him as "Dizzy." Two years later, however, her new favorite was replaced by William Gladstone, with whom she clashed over nearly everything. In 1874 the Conservatives—and Disraeli—were returned to power.

Victoria was genuinely fond of Disraeli; she shared his vision of a world empire so vast that no nation would dare tamper with it. It was an age of imperialism, and Victoria gloried in it. In 1876 she added "Empress of All India" to her title. By 1880 Victoria had acquired a huge empire that would build to a peak just before her death. Disraeli's star was again declining, however, and Gladstone and the Liberal party were returned to power in 1880.

Gladstone's anti-imperialist stance enraged her. She became infuriated when he backed out of a war with Afghanistan after the murder of a British diplomat, and they locked horns continually over the Irish question. Gladstone was a firm supporter of Irish home rule while Victoria opposed it.

At least these ministerial crises served to bring Victoria back into the public eye. To the delight of her subjects, she once more took part in the ceremonial aspects of the monarchy. She even began dancing again.

In 1887 Victoria celebrated her Golden Jubilee, marking the 50th year of her reign. It was a grand spectacle. Ten years later festivities were even greater in celebration of her Diamond Jubilee, when she drove in state to St. Paul's Cathedral through streets lined by millions. It was in fact more than a jubilee. It was an extravaganza celebrating the apogee of Pax Britannia.

Victoria's soldiers were back on the battlefield in 1889, this time in the South African Boer War. Although the British emerged victorious, they paid a heavy price. In February, 1900, Victoria visited the Herbert Hospital and gave flowers and candy to her wounded "dear soldiers." She even knitted seven special scarves that were awarded to outstanding veterans of the war. In April she made a long-overdue visit to Ireland to honor the Irish regiments that had fought so bravely. But it was apparent that Victoria was becoming tired.

By January, 1901, her zest for life was gone. On the 13th she made a last entry in her journal, which she had kept faithfully since 1834. She died peacefully at 6:30 P.M. on Jan. 22, 1901, ending, if not the longest, certainly the most triumphant reign in European history.

Little-Known Facts: The tone of sexual repression that characterized the Victorian era was set by Albert, not by the queen. According to the Duke of Wellington, Albert was "extremely straitlaced and a great stickler for morality whereas she was rather the other way."

Victoria was an accomplished artist and produced many paintings and sketches.

The queen was a carrier of hemophilia. Her youngest son, Leopold, succumbed to it at age 31, and her daughters Alice and Beatrice were carriers, who transmitted it to the royal families of Russia and Spain.

There were seven attempts on Victoria's life. In five of the seven cases, the culprits were emotionally disturbed young men who had not even loaded their pistols.

Victoria's immense wealth was a subject of much contention. Particularly during her extended period of mourning, people questioned why they should subsidize her at the rate of £385,000 a year when she had virtually ceased to fulfill the functions expected of a monarch. When she died, she left a personal fortune of nearly £2 million.

Quotes By: Upon hearing that she would one day be queen: "I will be good."

Upon Albert's death: "I never, never shall be able to bear that chilling, dreadful, weary, unnatural life of a widow."

On her Golden Jubilee: "This never-to-be-forgotten day will always leave the most gratifying and heart-stirring memories behind."

And, upon hearing a ribald joke: "We are not amused!"

Quotes About: Lady Lyttelton, royal governess: "A vein of iron runs through her most extraordinary character."

Charlotte Brontë: "A little stout, vivacious lady, very plainly dressed—not much dignity or pretension about her."

Prince Albert: "I . . . regard Victoria as naturally a fine character, but warped in many respects by wrong upbringing."

Benjamin Disraeli: "I love the Queen—perhaps the only person in the world left to me that I do love."

—I.F. and F.B.

JAWAHARLAL NEHRU

Vital Statistics: The man who was to become one of the most powerful and revered leaders in 20th-century Asia sprang from the bluest blood in India. Born in Allahabad on Nov. 14, 1889, Jawaharlal Nehru was the first and only son of Motilal Nehru, one of the most distinguished lawyers and richest men in India. A member of Hindu's highest caste, a Kashmiri Brahman, Nehru exuded an aura of aristocracy.

Slim and tall by Indian standards, with finely sculpted features and an aquiline nose, Nehru was elegantly handsome and somewhat vain about his thinning hair. When dressed in Western clothing in his youth, he more closely resembled a refined young Englishman than an Indian. A man who enjoyed vigorous good health most of his life, Nehru loved active sports such as skiing, swimming, mountain climbing, and horse-back riding, and kept fit by following a daily hatha-yoga regime, which included standing on his head each morning. Although generally a vegetarian, Nehru didn't strictly adhere to his country's religious dietary practices. He would on occasion eat meat, and when he was out of India he would drink wine.

In accordance with Indian custom, Nehru's father arranged his son's marriage to a young woman who also belonged to the Brahman caste, although Nehru himself disparaged the caste system. Nehru was 26 when he married 16-year-old Kamala Kaul in March, 1916. The couple had a son who died when he was two days old and a daughter, Indira, who later followed in her father's footsteps and became India's prime minister in 1966. Nehru's wife was an invalid during much of their marriage and died in 1936. Nehru never remarried.

During the struggle for India's independence from British rule, Nehru was sentenced to prison nine times between 1921 and 1945 and spent a total of nearly nine years behind bars. An almost cultlike adoration sprang up around the nationalist leader, who was affectionately called *Pandit*, ("wise man"). After leading the fight for his country's freedom for two decades, Nehru became prime minister in 1947 and ruled the country nearly single-handedly for almost 17 years until his death on May 27, 1964.

Personal Life: As the only son of a wealthy and influential Indian, Nehru led a pampered childhood in westernized surroundings, growing up on the family's palatial estate, which boasted an indoor swimming pool, riding stables, and magnificent gardens. Because of the 11-year age gap between the first of his two younger sisters and him, he was a lonely child taught by a series of governesses and an English tutor. As was the practice among upper-class Indians, Nehru was sent off to England at the age of 16 for his formal education. While studying at Harrow and Cambridge for the next seven years, Nehru assumed the guise of a fashionable young English gentleman, playing tennis, rowing, and developing a taste for gambling. A rather undistinguished scholar, Nehru was extremely shy; while on the Cambridge debating team, he often paid fines for not speaking during the entire term.

After receiving his law degree he returned to India and married

Jawaharlal Nehru with daughter Indira Gandhi and grandson Sanjay.

Kamala, who in sharp contrast to her husband had little formal education and was quite unsophisticated. Nehru practiced law and moved on the outer edge of politics for the next four years, until he was swept up in the nationalist movement. Plunging into Mahatma Gandhi's civil disobedience campaign, Nehru was horrified by his first real encounter with the true poverty and ignorance of the Indian masses. Traveling through rural India, giving dozens of speeches, Nehru began developing into the politician he would later become. "The peasants took away the shyness from me," he remarked, "and taught me to speak in public." Shedding the last vestiges of his Western upbringing, Nehru abandoned his English style of dress and adopted traditional Indian garb. As a dedicated *Satyagraha* (literally "truth force")—one pledged to disobey the law as a symbol of passive resistance to the British regime—Nehru embarked on the road that was to land him in prison so many times during the next 24 years. Along with some 30,000 other Indians, he first went to jail in 1921 for distributing notices advocating the closing of schools and businesses to protest English rule in India. Caught up in the fervor of nationalism, Nehru looked upon imprisonment as a privilege, saying, "I shall go to jail again most willingly and joyfully. Jail has indeed become a heaven for us, a holy place of pilgrimage." During his periods of imprisonment Nehru wrote several books, including his autobiography, *Toward Freedom*, as well as a series of whimsical letters to his daughter, Indira, about the history of the world, which were later published as a children's book. Because of Nehru's political activity, he was often absent from his family for long stretches of time, although he did accompany his wife periodically to Europe, where she was treated for tuberculosis. Despite their differences, Nehru and his wife enjoyed a close relationship, especially when she too became involved in the civil disobedience movement and went to prison—along with other members of his family, including his father, two sisters, and daughter. Nehru was only in his 40s when Kamala died, but he didn't consider marrying again. His name was rarely linked romantically with anyone. However, he did have several platonic friendships with married women, and he apparently had an affair with Lady Edwina Mountbatten—allegedly with her husband's approval.

As Gandhi's protégé, Nehru rapidly emerged alongside the spiritual leader as one of the primary figures in India's fight for freedom, and at Gandhi's urging he became president of India's Congress in 1935. Although Nehru and Gandhi often disagreed on methods—Nehru wanted to move forward too rapidly and leaned too far away from nonviolence for the Mahatma's liking—the two developed an immutable bond. Impatient at times and quick-tempered, Nehru's impetuosity was actually part of his charm. Impulsive acts such as tearing off a garland of marigolds from around his neck and tossing it to a young girl in a crowd endeared Nehru to the masses, and later in his life he was referred to by some as "our Buddha." Nehru admitted that he was both annoyed and flattered by such devotion, and his family helped him keep a sense of perspective in the matter. They would tease him by saying, "O Jewel of India, what time is it?" or "O Embodiment of Sacrifice, please pass the bread."

Nehru was imprisoned for the last, and longest, time in 1942, after Gandhi drafted the famous "Quit India" resolution at a Congress session in Bombay. Upon Nehru's release from prison in 1945, he played a key role in the intricate planning and negotiations that were necessary before England relinquished its power. When it became clear that it would be impossible to avoid massive civil war without giving in to Muslim factions who wanted a separate state, the pragmatic Nehru resigned himself to the partitioning of India and the resultant creation of Pakistan. "By cutting off the head, we shall get rid of the headache," he told the people. India was then ready to accept its place in the free world, with Nehru at its helm.

Rise to Power: As the first head of state of free India, Nehru assumed the post of prime minister on Aug. 15, 1947, the day that India formally achieved its independence from Great Britain.

In Power: One of Nehru's first tasks as prime minister was to tackle the problem of mass migration and border violence that erupted over the partitioning of India. More than 2 million people were killed in the bloodbath that accompanied the establishment of Pakistan, and Nehru had to deal with the rehabilitation of 5 million Hindu refugees. India's birth as a free nation was further marred by the assassination of Gandhi, who was shot by a Hindu fanatic in 1948. The spiritual leader's death was a personal blow to Nehru, who had come to regard Gandhi as a second father. Choking with emotion, he told the people in a radio broadcast, "The light of our life has gone out."

Nehru wielded supreme power as prime minister, and with the devoted consent of his people he could easily have assumed control as a dictator. Instead, he resolutely held to his belief that India must develop as a free nation through parliamentary methods with the mixed goals of socialism and a capitalistic economy. In addition to the prime ministership, however, he held an array of posts, including foreign minister, president of Congress, chairman of the planning commission, and head of the atomic energy department. Although no great orator, Nehru spoke in public more frequently than nearly any other statesman of his day. A good deal of his time was spent abroad, carrying out missions of diplomacy, and he emerged as the voice of the new Asia after giving an address before the U.N. General Assembly in Paris in 1948. Because of his nonalignment stance, Nehru's relationship with the U.S. was rocky, but he refused to back down from his firm position that India must achieve an independent status and not side with either the U.S.S.R. or the U.S.

Nehru's first and foremost intent was to bring India into the 20th century. Along with encouraging industrialization, he strove for the emancipation of Indian women. With that goal in mind, he advocated birth control programs, made Hindu marriage monogamous, established divorce procedures, and introduced laws that gave daughters an equal share in family estates. Nehru despised the ritualism and mysticism involved in religion and vowed that as long as he was in office India would never become a Hindu state. Under his rule, untouchability was abolished and a bill of rights was established in India's constitution.

Not a physically demonstrative man, Nehru showed his concern indirectly for people he worked with; for instance, he would take care to see that his aides were fed before sitting down to a meal himself. He also disliked lavish displays; upon being presented with a silver- and gold-plated chair at a meeting, he said disgustedly, "What is this? I hate this show—take it away." Perhaps the worst that could be said of him was that he was an inept administrator at times, stubbornly refusing, for instance, to believe reports of corruption about those who served under him.

In later life Nehru became increasingly isolated, the inevitable result of being placed on a pedestal by so many of his peers. He first talked of resigning in 1954, partially to seek reassurance that people didn't feel he was clinging to power. Worried about losing the capacity for being treated as a human being, he confided to a friend that he would like to retire and "wander about as a private person." Twice more, in 1956 and 1957, Nehru offered his resignation but both times gave in at the protest of his colleagues and remained as prime minister. He relied more and more on his daughter, Indira, who became his official hostess and traveling companion as well as his confidante. After ruling a nation of 450 million people for more than 15 years, Nehru was criticized for not training a successor. But the oft-repeated question Who after Nehru? irritated the ruler, who asserted that no great nation is dependent on one man. In January of 1964 the 74-year-old leader suffered a stroke that left him slightly paralyzed on one side. Five months later his aortic artery burst, and he died on May 27. According to his wishes, some of Nehru's ashes were scattered "over the fields where the peasants of India toil, so that they might mingle with the dust and soil . . . and become an indistinguishable part of India."

Little-Known Facts: An animal lover, Nehru kept a private zoo at his residence. His pets included deer, crocodiles, tiger cubs, pigeons, dogs, and squirrels. His special pride was four pet pandas, which he would coax to eat out of his hand. Once after they repeatedly rejected the proffered food, Nehru remarked to a friend with a disgusted grin, "I can't get them to mate either."

During one of his stints in prison, Nehru spun for nearly three hours a day on his own spinning wheel. Then for another two to three hours he did tape weaving. He said he liked such activities because they "soothed the fever of my mind."

Nehru felt more comfortable speaking and writing in English than in any of the Indian languages. He thought in English and wrote all of his books in English. The only Indian language he was reasonably competent at was Urdu, a derivative of Persian and Hindi.

The Indian ruler had a penchant for poetry, and in the latter years of his life took to carrying with him four lines of a poem by Robert Frost:

> The woods are lovely, dark and deep.
> But I have promises to keep,
> And miles to go before I sleep,
> And miles to go before I sleep.

Quotes By: After his first close contact with the peasants of India: "Looking at them and their misery . . . I was filled with shame and sorrow, shame at my own easygoing and comfortable life . . . and sorrow at the degradation and overwhelming poverty of India. A new picture of India seemed to rise before me; naked, starving, crushed, and utterly miserable."

Looking back on one of the lessons he learned in prison: "It is not possible in any vital matter to rely on anyone. One must journey through life alone; to rely on others is to invite heartbreak."

Although affected by the writings of Marx, he wrote: "I am not a Communist chiefly because I resist the communist tendency to treat communism as a holy doctrine; I do not like being told what to think and do. I suppose I am too much of an individualist."

Nehru hated the British system but retained a respect for British culture: "In spite of everything I am a great admirer of the English, and in many things I feel even now that an Englishman can understand me better than the average Indian."

Reflecting on his mixed background: "I have become a queer mixture of the East and West, out of place everywhere, at home nowhere."

Quotes About: A contemporary writer, Krisna Kripalani, drew this portrait of Nehru: "He is at once personal and detached, human and aloof, with the result that now he appears fond, now cold, now proud, now modest. An aristocrat in love with the masses, a nationalist who represents the culture of the foreigner, an intellectual caught up in the maelstrom of an emotional upheaval—the very paradox of his personality has surrounded it with a halo."

Gandhi, in writing a tribute to Nehru: "If he has the dash and rashness of a warrior, he has also the prudence of a statesman. He is undoubtedly an extremist, thinking far ahead of his surroundings. But he is humble enough and practical enough not to force the pace to the breaking point. He is pure as crystal, he is truthful beyond suspicion. He is a knight *sans peur et sans reproche*. The nation is safe in his hands."

In the words of Gandhi's disciple Vinoba Bhave: "After Gandhi's, his is the one name that stands for India—*is* India."

—L.K.S.

FIDEL CASTRO

Vital Statistics: Born Aug. 13, 1926, in Oriente Province, Fidel Castro Ruz grew up on his Spanish-born father's plantation at the rural eastern end of Cuba. A laborer when he first emigrated to Cuba, Ángel Castro had prospered. He married his second wife some time after the birth of Fidel, the fourth of their seven children. Fidel was a 10-lb. baby with dark eyes and curly hair. Throughout his childhood he had an abundance of energy, optimism, and audacity, and he early attained an impressive 6 ft. 2 in. and a substantial girth. His prodigious appetites for food, sports, and talk have remained undiminished through the years. At 32 Castro became the first of his generation to achieve political power in the Western Hemisphere, when in 1959 he overcame tremendous obstacles and overthrew the corrupt dictatorship of Fulgencio Batista. After installing himself as the Jefe Maximo ("maximum leader") of Cuba, Castro retained the beard, rumpled fatigues, and Spartan life-style of his guerrilla days. Fidel's brand of revolution was uniquely his own, and his socialist vision of Cuba has held together largely on the strength of his enormous charisma.

Personal Life: As a boy Castro threatened to burn the house down if his parents didn't send him to school. They relented, and Fidel received a Jesuit education in Havana. According to the school yearbook, he was

Fidel Castro objects to: (a) a speech by President Reagan; (b) news from Angola; or (c) a close call at second base?

"a true athlete, always defending with bravery and pride the flag of his school." In 1944 he was voted Cuba's best all-around school athlete. One of his instructors observed that "the actor in him will not be lacking." Although Castro was later excommunicated by the Catholic Church for political acts against Cuban priests, he was never antireligious—merely indifferent to religion's prominent place in Cuban life.

Fidel excelled not only in sports but also in oratory and in fighting. He simply never gave up, and this persistence became a cornerstone of his brilliance as a revolutionary warrior. In 1945 Castro entered the

University of Havana to study law—a choice made chiefly because of his oratorical talent—and soon immersed himself in radical campus politics. Even as a boy Castro had been an agitator; at 13 he had tried to incite a revolt among his father's cane cutters. As a student he went further; he bought a revolver and in 1947 joined an ill-starred expedition to overthrow Dominican dictator Rafael Trujillo. The following year he went to Colombia and got his first taste of guerrilla fighting in a student uprising. The roughneck image stayed, and rumors circulated that he had killed a priest in Colombia.

Castro earned his doctoral degree in law in 1950 and practiced for a few years, handling cases for political dissidents and the poor. In 1952 he became a candidate for Parliament, but Batista canceled the elections. After that Castro devoted himself to ousting the Batista regime. In his zeal he neglected every aspect of his personal life. Mirta Díaz Balart, who had become Castro's wife in 1948 and had borne him a son—"Fidelito"—in 1949, left for the U.S. Fidel was in prison for anti-Batista activity in 1955 when Mirta—whose family was pro-Batista—divorced him and took Fidelito to Long Island, N.Y. Four years later, father and son were reunited during Fidel's triumphant entry into Havana.

Castro's own father died in 1956. The event seemed to produce no emotion in Castro, who commented only that his father had "played politics for money." During the revolution in 1959, the Castro family plantation was nationalized. This outraged Fidel's mother, who objected loudly and was considered something of a counterrevolutionary for several years. The events of 1959 split the family dramatically. While Fidel's younger sister Juanita went into exile as a vehement anti-Castroite, brothers Raúl and Ramón became his strongest allies. Raúl Castro remains second-in-command of the Cuban government and is clearly slated for leadership should anything happen to Fidel. Castro has warned his ideological enemies against assassinating him because Raúl would succeed him, and "he's more radical than I am."

Castro's mother died in 1965, and since that time the Cuban press has not mentioned any news of his family or personal affairs. There have always been gossip and speculation about attractive women in his life. He had been briefly engaged to a young Cuban woman in Mexico in 1956, but preparations for the overthrow of Batista apparently preempted her. In 1962 Cuban exile newspapers announced his marriage to Isabel Coto. The most enduring speculations have centered on Celia Sánchez, a comrade from the early days. Known until her death in 1980 as Fidel's "constant companion," she held the positions of Secretary of the Central Committee and Secretary of the Council of State and was the most powerful woman in Cuba.

Castro has described himself as "naturally disorderly." He prefers cultivating his image of tireless leader and liberator to bothering with elegant dress and fancy residences. His habit of dropping cigar butts wherever he pleases does not seem to be offensive to colleagues and guests who are invited to the several residences he maintains around Havana. The houses are furnished comfortably but with complete disregard for conventional standards of cleanliness and taste. A fleet of vintage Oldsmobiles and military jeeps is always at Castro's disposal, and he keeps on the move, preferring to come and go without fanfare or public knowledge.

Castro's boundless energy and appetites have become his trademark: 12-hour speeches on public television, impromptu midnight bull sessions with students, gargantuan dinners, the ever-present cigars, marathon domino tournaments, endless baseball games. All vividly attest to his determination to infuse every act with the revolutionary spirit. At an exclusive country-club golf course that had been nationalized, Castro commented: "Now if Kennedy and Eisenhower would like to discuss some problems with us over a game of golf, I'm sure we'll win. We just have to practice a few days, that's all."

Rise to Power: Beginning with the attack on Batista's Moncada Barracks in 1953, Castro alone has created the history—and the mythology—of his movement. That attack, his first attempt to depose Batista, was a fiasco, an almost perfect disaster; about half of the rebels were captured, tortured, and murdered. Castro turned the brutality used in suppressing the attack to his political advantage, and Moncada came to stand as an eloquent symbol of the regime's oppression. On trial, Castro conducted his own four-hour defense, concluding with the now famous words, "Condemn me. It does not matter. History will absolve me."

Fidel drew a 15-year prison sentence but was given amnesty after 22 months. He reorganized his guerrilla followers in Mexico, and they named themselves "the 26th of July Movement" after the Moncada Barracks attack. Since 1959 this date has been celebrated as Cuban independence day. In Mexico, Castro bought a dilapidated American yacht named the *Granma* and planned the next phase of the struggle against Batista. He even announced his planned invasion of Cuba to the public, claiming that psychological warfare was an essential tactic. His force of 82 guerrillas sailed from Mexico on the partially disabled yacht, and on Dec. 2, 1956, they waded ashore on the swampy coast of Castro's native Oriente Province. Government forces were waiting to ambush them, and only 12 of the rebels escaped into the Sierra Maestra mountains and survived. The Batista government announced the rebels' defeat and the death of their leader. Then Castro invited *New York Times* correspondent Herbert Matthews into the rebel camp for an interview, thus astonishing not only the people of Cuba but spectators around the world. The guerrillas gradually built up their strength to 800 men to fight Batista's army of 30,000. After a long period during which survival alone counted as victory, the rebels took the offensive in the spring and summer of 1958. By the end of that year a detachment led by Argentinean radical Ernesto "Che" Guevara had captured the provincial capital of Santa Clara in central Cuba. Incredibly, Batista chose to quit without a confrontation. He packed his bags with cash and fled to the Dominican Republic in the first few hours of the new year, 1959. Like Moses parting the Red Sea, Castro then triumphantly proceeded through Cuba. In the words of U.S. photojournalist Lee Lockwood, an eyewitness, "It was a fabulous time. For a moment, at least, even the most pessimistic suspended their 20th-century cynicism and saw Fidel Castro as the incarnation of a legendary hero surrounded by an aura of magic, a bearded Parsifal who had brought miraculous deliverance to an ailing Cuba."

In Power: Preferring the Havana Hilton to Batista's presidential palace, Castro set up quarters there and proclaimed 1959 as the year of the revolution. He proceeded immediately with the transformation of Cuba. First on the agenda was a public trial of the old regime's "war criminals." Mobilizing the country around a new theme each year, he proclaimed 1960 the year of agriculture and 1961 the year of education. Illiteracy was subsequently reduced from 24% to 4%. Castro envisioned massive changes in Cuban society: the elimination of vice, prostitution, corruption, gambling, and poverty. Initially the regime drew U.S. endorsement for such admirable goals. "I think Fidel Castro has done a magnificent job," said Nelson Rockefeller in August, 1959. But this support withered quickly as Castro forged an alliance with the Soviet Union and placed himself in the forefront of socialist revolution in South America. Castro vehemently denied being a communist and claimed that the purpose of the revolution was Cuba's true independence from any ideological or economic master. Having once served as the U.S.'s sugar factory, Cuba would not now become a Soviet pawn, Castro claimed.

As he developed social, economic, and agricultural reforms, Castro's followers and critics divided sharply into two camps: the Fidelistas and the anti-Castroites, many of whom immediately left Cuba. Anti-Castroites in the U.S. number over 1 million, and they have maintained active opposition to their country's socialist takeover for more than 20 years. At the extremes of protest are terrorist groups like Omega 7, who say they will stop at nothing to get rid of the man they call "the Trujillo of the left." Castro's supporters contend that the CIA is supporting saboteurs, guerrillas, and assassins in Cuba; they point to the Bay of Pigs invasion of April, 1961, as a prime example of U.S. imperialist meddling. Castro's success in repelling this CIA-sponsored invasion force of Cuban exiles made him even more of a hero to his supporters. Seemingly inspired by crisis, Castro capitalized on the victory with rallies and marathon speeches. In televised hearings, he personally interviewed over 1,000 of the captured invasion force. "Now be honest," he said to one prisoner, "surely you must realize that you are the first prisoner in history who has the privilege of arguing in front of the whole population . . . with the head of the government which you came to overthrow." The prisoners were later returned to the U.S. in exchange for several million dollars' worth of supplies.

The U.S. restricted sugar imports in 1960, so Castro sold his sugar to the Soviets. Russian technicians and advisers began to arrive in Cuba, and the presence of Soviet nuclear weapons in Cuba precipitated the missile crisis of October, 1962—the cold war's most horrifying moment. After the Bay of Pigs, Castro announced that he was a Marxist-Leninist and therefore committed to promoting communist rule throughout Latin America, which he called a "continent where revolution is inevitable." That same year marked the beginning of food rationing in Cuba, where it remains an ongoing fact of life. Castro nationalized all business, from sugar factories to shoe-shine parlors, and instituted an extensive secret police force (numbering in the tens of thousands) as well as a large military force. Organized resistance to Castro has a formidable opponent in this government-controlled network, but anti-Castroites continue to plot his overthrow.

Since 1973 the U.S. has officially declined any part in anti-Castro activities, and there has been some attempt at normalizing relations between the two countries. But such efforts have been impeded by Castro's role in African politics. Nearly 45,000 Cuban troops and advisers are in Africa, primarily in Angola and Ethiopia. In spite of Castro's dedication to worldwide socialist revolution, his own soldiers are increasingly going AWOL, and many are involved in black-market sale of military supplies. Some men are evading the draft altogether. After more than 20 years, the new Cuban economy is still unstable, dependent on one crop (sugar), and reliant on strict rationing of all consumer goods. Castro has found ways to keep his country afloat in the face of diplomatic and trade boycotts by almost all Latin American nations, but the price is high.

Dissidents, homosexuals, malcontents, and the mentally disturbed are encouraged to observe a love-it-or-leave-it policy in Cuba. When the social pressures get too great, Castro allows great numbers of troublemakers to leave the country, "like steam from a kettle," commented one exiled leader.

Little-Known Facts: As a left-handed pitcher at Havana University, Castro was given a tryout by the Washington Senators (now Minnesota Twins) baseball team. They turned him down. Like many young Cuban couples, Castro and his first wife spent their 1948 honeymoon in Miami.

In 1956 Castro made another trip to the U.S., that time sneaking in by swimming across the Rio Grande from Mexico to arrange the purchase of the *Granma*. (The ship's name later became the title of Castro's official newspaper.)

In 1960 he attended the U.N. General Assembly in New York. When problems developed about his hotel accommodations, Castro stormed out, took rooms at the Theresa Hotel in Harlem, and captured the attention of the worldwide press for days.

Quotes By: "We represent the first great revolution in a small country, which makes us a privileged generation of Cubans, not only in terms of our own history but in the history of all the peoples of the world." —Speech on Cuban TV, June 5, 1960

"You Americans keep saying that Cuba is 90 mi. from the U.S. I say that the U.S. is 90 mi. from Cuba, and for us that is worse."—To Herbert Matthews, *New York Times* correspondent

"What bothers the U.S. most is that we have made a socialist revolution right under their noses . . . a democratic revolution of the poor, by the poor, and for the poor."—After the Bay of Pigs, April, 1961

"Of course we engage in subversion, the training of guerrillas, propaganda! Why not? This is exactly what you are doing to us."—November, 1963.

"History always favors the intrepid!"—Overheard by U.S. journalist Lee Lockwood as Castro played dominoes

Quotes About: "He ought to be grateful to us. He gave us a kick in the ass and it made him stronger than ever."—President John F. Kennedy, after the Bay of Pigs

"Fidel Castro was more than willing to turn Marxist-Leninist and to make his regime a communist one, but it had to remain *his* revolution and the communism had to be personal, special, revolutionary—and Cuban. There is nothing in the 'socialist world' like Cuban communism. Moscow, echoing Washington, thanks its lucky stars that there is only one Fidel Castro."—Herbert Matthews

—C.D. and K.P.

FOOTNOTE PEOPLE IN WORLD HISTORY

ADRIAN IV (1100?–1159), English pope

A small good-looking man who hid his peasant origins behind a cultivated voice and who satisfied his great personal ambition by rising to the papacy, Adrian IV is recognized as the first, and so far only, Englishman to have been pope. His repeated clashes with the equally ambitious Frederick Barbarossa of Germany, which focused on the domination of Rome, intensified the running debate of the Middle Ages as to whether Church or State should be the supreme power on earth.

Nicholas Breakspear was born around 1100 at Abbot's Langley near St. Albans in Hertfordshire. As a boy he hung around St. Alban's Abbey, hoping to pick up a little learning and eventually enter the monastery. The story goes that his father—who became a monk—disparaged him so much that Nicholas was refused all but the dirtiest work at the abbey and was not considered worth educating. In defiance, he begged his way to France, where he managed to study at the Cathedral School of Paris and in Arles. He chose to enter St. Rufus's, near Valence in Provence, and rose to become abbot.

Taking his new position seriously, Nicholas was such a strict taskmaster that the monks twice complained to Pope Eugenius III about "the most exact . . . regular discipline" imposed by their foreign abbot. Once Nicholas was reprimanded; the second time he was summoned to Rome, but instead of being chastised he was made a papal aide. In 1146 he was made Cardinal-Bishop of Albano, causing one historian to remark on the irony that "he who was refused to be an English monk in England should become an English cardinal in Italy."

After serving in Albano for several years, Nicholas was appointed papal legate to Scandinavia to carry on the work begun there by English missionaries. He returned to Rome most opportunely on Dec. 4, 1154, as Anastasius IV lay dying. The next day the Apostle of the North was unanimously elected pope. Nicholas was invested on Christmas Day, taking the name of Adrian IV, and was immediately forced to face problems caused in part by the weakness of his predecessor.

A republic had been established in Rome, ruled by 56 senators under Arnold of Brescia, a former canon who had been excommunicated by Eugenius III. Arnold's doctrine of separating the Church from civil affairs was especially repugnant to the new pope, who was determined to assert all the rights of his position including that of worldly sovereign. Unable to act against Arnold at once, Adrian waited until an attack on a cardinal in a street brawl demonstrated the apparent failure of the republican government. On the last day of Lent in 1155 Adrian placed the city of Rome, the heart of the Catholic Church, under an interdict which declared it to be unholy. By Easter, Arnold had been ousted from the city, not because the interdict meant inevitable damnation for the Romans, but because it effectively stopped the pilgrim trade during the holiest—and most lucrative—season of the year.

The truce between pope and republicans was an uneasy one. Adrian thought that the new German king, Frederick Barbarossa—who had invaded northern Italy in his attempt to form an empire—might become an ally, a dangerous thought since Frederick considered himself Charlemagne's successor and therefore the lawful possessor of Rome. Frederick agreed to capture Arnold of Brescia in return for being crowned Holy Roman Emperor, and he proceeded to Sutri, where Adrian had gone to escape Roman unrest.

Their meeting on June 7, 1155, was marked by a clash of wills that was to become characteristic. It was the custom for a king to serve as the pope's groom and help him dismount from his horse, thus acknowledging papal superiority; this Frederick refused to do. The standoff lasted two days, until Frederick finally yielded. Satisfied that he had made his point, Adrian secretly crowned Frederick Holy Roman Emperor at St. Peter's on the morning of June 18. When the republicans found out, street fighting erupted, and the pope and the new emperor—who both claimed ownership of Rome—were forced by its citizens to flee the city. Meanwhile, Arnold of Brescia had been captured by Frederick's troops. Frederick had him hanged and cremated, and had his ashes flung into the Tiber.

Adrian had mistakenly assumed that papal recognition of his empire would encourage a grateful Frederick to move against William I, the excommunicated Norman who had inherited the crown of Sicily and was terrorizing southern Italy. But malaria, scanty foraging, and the Italian heat forced Frederick to withdraw to the north. Although Byzantine Emperor Manuel I joined with Adrian against William, their combined armies were defeated at Benevento. The 1156 Treaty of Benevento settled the Norman-papal dispute, conceding to William the kingship of Sicily and parts of southern Italy. In return William acknowledged himself the pope's vassal, vowing to pay tribute and send troops to defend the pope.

Adrian's position as supreme ruler with the right to dispose of domains at will was further reinforced when Henry II of England requested permission to invade Ireland, all Christianized islands being considered the property of the Holy See. Adrian's 1156 bull, *Laudabiliter*, granted this request, urging Henry "to subject [Ireland's] people to the rule of law and to uproot the weeds of vice," and at the same time to collect the annual penny-per-household due to St. Peter. Henry waited until 1171 to conquer Ireland.

Frederick, piqued by what he thought of as the theft of southern Italy from his infant empire, refused to intervene at Adrian's request when an old Swedish acquaintance, the Archbishop of Lund, was held for ransom in Germany. Adrian then sent his chief adviser, Cardinal Roland of Siena, to Frederick's 1157 Diet at Besançon with a letter implying that Frederick owed the pope obedience as a vassal since the pope had given him the empire. An uproar ensued, during which Roland's vehement support of the pope almost cost him his life. The legation was expelled from Germany, and Frederick wrote to Adrian that he owed his power to God alone, not to any mortal representative, and that Adrian's claims amounted to blasphemy.

As Frederick again moved to assert his control over northern Italy, Adrian partially retracted, explaining that the misunderstanding was due to a bad translation of his letter to the Diet, which had been written in Latin. Friendship of a sort was restored until the German's Code of Roncaglia in late 1158 established the emperor as "ruler of the whole world." "If the emperor of the Romans has no rights over Rome," Frederick declared, "he has no rights anywhere." Adrian alerted what allies he had and tried to switch his allegiance from the imperial to the republican faction in Rome; this futile attempt failing, he moved south to Anagni to be closer to William of Sicily. Frederick, however, made common cause with the republicans, agreeing to retain the Senate, and prepared to move against the pope. Adrian was planning to excommunicate Frederick and had put himself at the head of the anti-imperial forces when he died suddenly on Sept. 1, 1159. Frederick won this battle in the Church-versus-State war by setting up an antipope, Victor IV, upon Adrian's death.

Although Adrian is supposed to have said, "I wish I had never left England, or had lived out my life quietly in the cloister of St. Rufus," his dictatorial and ambitious personality makes this unlikely. One cannot help remembering young Nicholas's father, who denied his son the learning he craved and taunted him out of England. It must have been unbearably frustrating for the man Adrian became to rise so far above his father's reach and still be thwarted.

—S.D.

ALICE LIDDELL HARGREAVES (1852–1934), Alice in Wonderland

On July 4, 1862, the Rev. Charles Lutwidge Dodgson, a 30-year-old mathematics lecturer at Christ Church, Oxford, and a colleague named Robinson Duckworth took three little girls on a rowboat trip up the Thames River to Godstow, where they planned to picnic. To entertain the girls on the journey, Dodgson told a fanciful tale about a girl who fell down a rabbit hole into a strange land. The outing was a great success, and the three girls—Alice, Lorina, and Edith Liddell—were held spell-

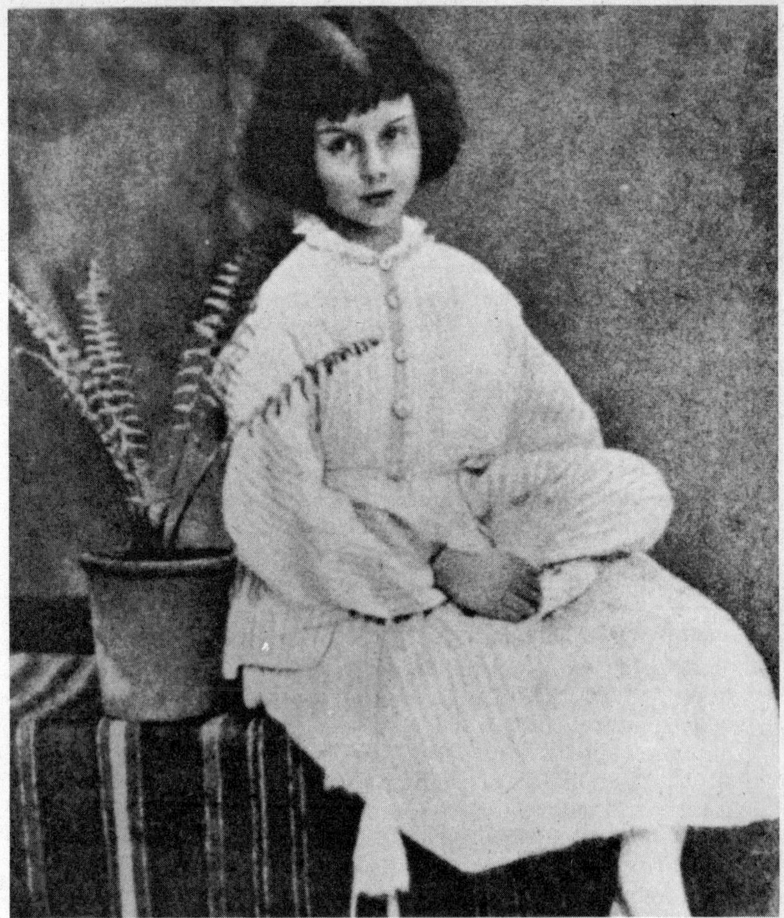

Alice of Wonderland. Photograph by Lewis Carroll, 1862.

bound by Reverend Dodgson's story. Upon returning home, Alice asked Dodgson to write it down, which he did under the pen name Lewis Carroll. Today, *Alice's Adventures in Wonderland* is considered by many to be the greatest children's book ever written.

Alice Liddell, age 10 at the time, was Dodgson's favorite of the three Liddell girls, so he named his heroine after her. She was the daughter of Henry George Liddell, the dean of Christ Church, and his wife, Lorina, who had moved to Oxford in 1855. Alice had large blue eyes and a cherubic oval face. She and her sisters were practically the only children in the vicinity of Christ Church, but Charles Dodgson was always available as their playmate.

Dodgson, an introverted man with a scholarly disposition, was one of England's early photographers. Unlike most of his contemporaries, he preferred children as models. For Dodgson, "children" meant little girls exclusively. "Boys are not in my line: I think they are a mistake: girls are less objectionable," he once wrote. His fondness for prepubescent females was the nearest thing to passion in this Victorian bachelor's existence. As far as we know, Dodgson remained a virgin all his life. While he protested that his fondness for little girls was strictly platonic, he worried more than a few suspicious mothers. In the late 1860s he began photographing some of his little female friends in the nude. Alice was not one of these, though Dodgson photographed her often and occasionally let her come into his darkroom. Alice later told her son, "Much more exciting than being photographed was being allowed to go into the darkroom and watch him develop the large glass plates."

It was perhaps inevitable that Dodgson should appoint himself "uncle" to the Liddell children. He was particularly attracted to Alice because of her trusting nature and her eagerness to accept even the wildest improbabilities. On the day after the picnic, he outlined "Alice's Adventures under Ground" and subsequently presented the little girl with the first version of his masterpiece. It was a 92-page manuscript, hand-lettered by Dodgson and illustrated with his own crude but effective drawings. The author had no thought of publishing the work, but novelist Henry Kingsley, who read the manuscript on a visit to the Liddells, convinced him to reconsider. Dodgson enlarged the story from 18,000 to 35,000 words, and it was promptly accepted by Macmillan. John Tenniel of *Punch* magazine was commissioned to illustrate it.

By the time the book was published, Dodgson's friendship with Alice had begun to cool. Alice's mother, believing that Dodgson's attentions to her daughter were potentially scandalous, had discouraged their relationship. Mrs. Liddell destroyed letters that the eccentric bachelor had written to Alice, and in so doing no doubt destroyed evidence that might have clarified Dodgson's relationship with the girl. Despite Mrs. Liddell's vigilance, the Rev. Dodgson's affection for Alice was doomed to fade when she reached puberty. He wrote, "About nine out of ten of my child-friendships got shipwrecked at the critical point 'where the stream and river meet' and the child-friends, once so affectionate, become uninteresting acquaintances, whom I have no wish to see again." Some theorists have intimated that Dodgson finally broke with the Liddell family after he proposed to Alice and was turned down. There is no evidence of this apart from Liddell family tradition.

Alice grew up, and at age 20 experienced the pains of a frustrated love affair. In 1872 Prince Leopold, fourth in line of succession to the throne, matriculated at Christ Church. Leopold and Alice met, discovered that they shared the same interests in languages and music, and fell in love. Again, Alice's mother stepped in to squelch the affair, since a marriage between Leopold and Alice would have antagonized Queen Victoria. Alice had to accept the fact that Leopold's life was not his own.

The man Alice eventually did marry, on Sept. 15, 1880, was named Reginald Hargreaves. He was very much the country squire, fond of the great outdoors. Alice couldn't have picked a man more basically opposite to the avuncular Charles Dodgson. In 1888, after meeting Hargreaves, Dodgson wrote in his diary, "It is not easy to link in one's mind the new face [Hargreaves] with the olden memory—the stranger with the once-so-intimately known and loved Alice." Alice and her husband settled into his family estate at Cuffnells in Hampshire. There she gave birth to three sons, Alan, Caryl, and Leopold—the namesake of her royal suitor. Dodgson flatly refused to stand as godfather to Leopold.

Alan and Leopold were both killed in W.W. I, and after her husband's death in 1926, Alice's fortunes rapidly declined. In 1928 she timorously approached Sotheby's, noted London auctioneers, with the original 92-page holograph manuscript of *Alice*. The manuscript was acclaimed as a major literary find, and she received a then phenomenal $74,259 for her treasure, which was purchased by an American. The manuscript has since found its way into the British Museum in London.

In 1932, at the age of 80, Alice traveled to the U.S. to attend a Lewis Carroll centenary celebration. She received a doctor of letters degree from Columbia University, and on her return trip to England her Cunard liner displayed a special banner in her honor—a grinning Cheshire cat. Two years later she died quietly at her home in Kent.

—M.S.

EDWARD "NED" KELLY (1854–1880), Australian outlaw

"I'll see you where I'm going, Judge." With the matter-of-factness of a man whose own future is as certain as the sunset, Edward "Ned" Kelly took his leave of Sir Redmond Barry, who had just sentenced him to death for the murder of an Australian policeman. Kelly had no doubt that the hated judge, who had once sentenced Kelly's mother to three years in prison on a trumped-up charge involving another policeman, would have to answer to a higher court. Kelly's prophecy was ironic. Within a fortnight both men were dead: Kelly from the hangman's rope, Sir Redmond of a heart attack.

Little known beyond his native land, Kelly is the most balladed Australian of them all. He combines all the daring, resourcefulness, and drama that Americans find in Jesse James, Billy the Kid, and John Dillinger. Kelly was a crook with style, romance, and a sense of chivalry. Descended from a poor Irish farmer who had been transported to penal servitude in Tasmania for stealing two pigs, Ned grew up on intimate terms with poverty, hardship, and a class system marked by entrenched privilege protected all too often by brutal police.

Ned Kelly was one of eight children of "Red" John Kelly and Ellen Quinn Kelly, who scrabbled out a living in the outback of northeast Victoria, about 150 mi. north of Melbourne. The mostly Irish selectors (small landholders) of the area constantly chafed under the power of the big landowners. Ned's uncles and cousins, the Quinns and the Lloyds, were frequently in and out of jail for rustling cattle, stealing horses, and brawling. By the time he was 21, Ned had become an accomplished bushman. He could break horses, tend cattle, cut timber, and mend fences. He was an expert rider, a crack shot, and a boxer with a mean reputation. He had also served three years for receiving a stolen horse, the result of only one of several brushes with the law.

But Ned had a determination to straighten out his life. For a few years

The controversial Ned Kelly of Australia.

following his release from prison, he rendered a good account of himself as a timber cutter, a prospector, and foreman of a sawmill. However, in 1878 a sequence of events began that would lead him to the gallows.

It started when Ned's younger brother Dan fell under suspicion of horse stealing. One Constable Fitzpatrick, who was dispatched to haul Dan in, ignored the counsel of his superior and enter "Kelly country" alone; he found it prudent, however, to take on some courage at a nearby bar. According to the story, Fitzpatrick made a drunken pass at Ellen Kelly, whereupon he received a coal shovel over the head (from Ellen) and a drubbing (from Dan and two friends) as rewards for his ardor. To counter the embarrassment of returning without his man, Fitzpatrick concocted a story of having been set upon, shot at, and wounded by the notorious Ned, who had not been present at all. Returning with reinforcements, Fitzpatrick found that Dan had "gone bush." Ellen and the two other men were arrested and sentenced to stiff jail terms by Sir Redmond Barry.

Ned and Dan swore vengeance. They were joined in the bush by Joe Byrne and Steve Hart, who had their own grievances against the authorities. Together they took up the life of "bushrangers" (outlaws); Ned was their undisputed leader. An intense police hunt led to a gunfight at Stringybark Creek between the four outlaws and four constables. Three of the lawmen were killed. When the lone survivor returned to tell his tale, the Victoria State Parliament posted a £2,000 reward for the outlaws and passed the Felons Apprehension Act, entitling anyone to shoot the members of the gang on sight.

Two months later (December, 1878) the gang embarked on a series of colorful escapades that increasingly captured the popular imagination. Still dodging the police, Ned and his gang entered Younghusband station (ranch) and locked up its 22 inhabitants. Leaving Byrne as a guard, Ned, Dan, and Steve rode into Euroa and made an unauthorized withdrawal of £2,000 from the bank. The reward jumped to £1,000 per man.

In February of 1879 the gang again crossed the border into New South Wales and pulled their most famous job, the Jerilderie Bank episode. Stealing into town under cover of night, they captured two policemen and took their uniforms. The next day Ned rounded up some 60 townspeople and held them prisoners in the hotel. He then dictated a document he hoped the world would read—the "Jerilderie Letter"—a remarkable blend of autobiography, self-justification, and social criticism. In it Ned railed against the oppression inflicted on the Irish in general and his relatives in particular. He also hinted at "some colonial stratagem which will open the eyes of not only the Victoria police . . . but also the whole British army." Ned's intention was to have the document printed in the local newspaper, but the editor had run away. Instead, he read the 8,300-word manifesto to the captive townspeople and left it behind with a bank teller, who promptly turned it over to the police after the gang had left the bank some £2,000 poorer. The reward jumped to £8,000 for the gang.

The escalating reward soon proved too great a temptation for an old friend of Joe Byrne. The friend was Aaron Sherritt, who informed the police of the gang's whereabouts. Byrne came out of hiding and fatally shot Sherritt. News of the shooting was wired to Melbourne before the gang could cut the telegraph wires. A special police train was dispatched north, and Ned decided the time had come to stand and fight. The result was a battle with every bit of the drama of the gunfight at the OK Corral, and more.

Following the pattern of Euroa and Jerilderie, Ned commandeered a hotel near the Glenrowan railway station and imprisoned several townspeople, most of whom were only too happy to become "prisoners" of Ned Kelly. A weekend of wild partying ensued, during which Ned and his cronies competed in athletic and drinking bouts with the "prisoners."

Kelly's plan was to derail the train over a steep embankment, kill the survivors and, according to one theory, instigate an areawide rebellion that would create an independent republic of Victoria, the "colonial stratagem" promised in the Jerilderie Letter. They planned to outfit themselves and their supporters in suits of armor they had been making for just such a confrontation.

As the train neared Glenrowan, however, the police were warned. The hotel was quickly surrounded and a furious gun battle began. Ned was seriously wounded in the first exchange but fought gamely on. Sometime during the day, Byrne, Hart, and Dan Kelly were also wounded. Desultory firing continued throughout the night. In the early dawn, the police were astonished to see an armor-clad apparition clanging toward them out of the mist, arm extended, firing a gun. The return fire of the police bounced off the armor for a time; then one constable began firing at the figure's unprotected legs. When the mysterious combatant was finally felled, it proved to be Ned himself, dressed in hammered-out plowshares. He had been wounded 28 times.

The police then torched the hotel, but not before the lifeless bodies of Hart, Byrne, and Dan Kelly had been dragged from the flames; they had taken poison, preferring death to surrender.

Whether Ned had tried to escape, repented, and returned to help his mates, or whether he had gone to warn the neighboring selectors that the uprising had been aborted, remains unclear. Whatever his motive for returning on that second morning, his bizarre one-man attack was recognized as an act of great courage.

Kelly was bound over for trial and charged with the murder of one of the three constables killed at Stringybark Creek. He succeeded in enraging the judge by insisting at his sentencing that he would have been acquitted had he been able to conduct his own defense. On Nov. 11, 1880, Ned Kelly mounted the scaffold. True to his mother's final admonition, he "died like a Kelly"; as the hangman adjusted the noose, Ned's last words were "Such is life." His fabled career of bushranging and rebelling against authority, which ended spectacularly in a grand gesture against insuperable odds, has made the epithet "game as Ned Kelly" one of the highest compliments any Australian can bestow.

—B.O.B.

ARTHUR ORTON (1834–1898), English impostor

The story of Arthur Orton is intertwined with that of another man, Sir Roger Charles Doughty Tichborne, member of a wealthy, landed British family. These men had very dissimilar lives; their glaring differences help to make up a remarkable story about one of history's greatest impostures.

Orton, the youngest of 12 children of a Wapping (a district in London) butcher, was born on Mar. 20, 1834. At the age of nine he was terribly frightened by a fire near his home—so much so that he developed nervous twitches later diagnosed as St. Vitus' dance. In 1849 Orton was apprenticed as a seaman because his mother thought the sea air would help his condition. His ship arrived in Valparaíso, Chile, in June of that year. Arthur jumped ship upon arrival and traveled overland to a small town called Melipilla. There he ingratiated himself with two prominent families by telling tales of cruelty and ill treatment aboard his ship. To further get into the good graces of the town's Catholic citizenry, he had himself rebaptized and became a member of the Catholic Church.

Two years later Orton, a little homesick, returned to England. In June, 1851, he reached his hometown and began to work in his father's butcher shop. But Arthur soon decided on other plans for himself, and 18 months later he set out for Australia. He worked for three years as a butcher's assistant in the town of Hobart and, while there, borrowed $35 from a distant relative. By August, 1855, Arthur had disappeared, a fact discovered too late by the relative seeking repayment of the personal loan.

Orton drifted around Australia, employed in various positions including stock driver and butcher in New South Wales. In addition, he became involved in horse stealing. Caught and indicted in 1859, he changed his name to Thomas Castro. Orton later resurfaced in Wagga Wagga, where in 1865, still using the name Castro, he married Mary Ann Bryant, an illiterate servant girl. It was in Wagga Wagga that Roger Tichborne entered the picture.

Tichborne, part of a distinguished English family, was born in his mother's native France. He enjoyed a typical French boyhood until his father removed him from under his mother's smothering influence and sent him to Stonyhurst school in England. After a stint in the army (he purchased a commission), Roger, then 24, decided to leave the country for a variety of reasons; one of them was to forget a complicated love affair with a young cousin. He landed in Valparaíso in 1853, later set out across the Andes, and eventually made his way to Rio de Janeiro in 1854. From there he decided to travel to Mexico by way of the West Indies. On Apr. 20 he took passage aboard the *Bella* bound for Kingston, Jamaica. The ship never arrived. One of its overturned lifeboats was found floating amid wreckage more than 400 mi. off the coast of Brazil.

Roger was presumed lost, and his younger brother eventually became heir to the family fortune. However, Roger's strong-willed mother refused to believe that Roger was dead. Nine years after the ship went down, she advertised for news of him in *The Times*. Undaunted by receiving no replies, she advertised again two years later in an Australian newspaper. This advertisement contained considerable information about Roger and the circumstances surrounding his death.

At the time, Orton was in the process of declaring bankruptcy through a Wagga Wagga solicitor named William Gibbes. During one meeting with Gibbes, Orton let "slip" that he owned some property in England and vaguely mentioned an inheritance, all the while fingering a pipe carved with the initials R.C.T. Gibbes, who had seen Lady Tichborne's advertisement, was hooked. He confronted Orton (who was still using the name Castro), and Orton "admitted" that he was Roger Tichborne. Gibbes immediately wrote to Lady Tichborne and had Orton do the same. Arthur's letter should immediately have cast grave doubt upon his claim. After beginning with "My Dear Mother," Arthur went on to say that he was enclosing a photograph so that she "may see how greatly I have emprove." In closing he wrote, "Hoping my dear Mama to see alive once more. But I am afraid not has I can not get surfience Money to come home with." Incredibly, Lady Tichborne believed the communication to be from her *literate* son and sent money for the trip.

Soon afterward Orton, along with his wife and child, left for England by way of Sydney. There he looked up two former servants of the Tichborne household, who both accepted Orton as Tichborne. Orton hired one of them, a West Indian named Bogle, as his valet. Orton lost no time adopting the style and character of a Tichborne—by spending money lavishly. Before leaving Sydney, he bought the Metropolitan Hotel for £10,000 by writing a check and signing Tichborne's name.

Once in England, Orton learned that Lady Tichborne was in Paris, so he went there to see her. In a darkened hotel room, where Orton claimed to be too sick to leave his bed, the meeting took place. Despite poor lighting and the cataracts that were forming in her eyes, Lady Tichborne identified Orton as her long-lost son.

Orton immediately began litigation to regain his "rightful" title. Orton's bid to become a Tichborne was amazing; the two men looked and acted almost nothing alike. The true Sir Roger was thin, frail, tall, and rather effeminate, with a tattoo on his left arm. He had straight dark hair, was well educated, and spoke French fluently. The fake Sir Roger, on the other hand, was grossly fat, had wavy fair hair, and had virtually no education. Orton failed almost every test in his effort to prove he was Tichborne. For example, the village blacksmith near the Tichborne estate was asked by Orton to verify that he was Roger Tichborne. The blacksmith replied, "If you are, you've changed from a racehorse to a carthorse." Yet, numerous people did believe Orton was Tichborne and supported his claim, and all the while Orton kept gathering details of the life of Roger Tichborne. His following was so large that before the trial, when he was bereft of funds, local citizens supported him by buying Tichborne Bonds. Orton successfully raised £40,000 from investors who were promised repayment after he secured the Tichborne estate.

Unfortunately for Orton, by the time the trial came to court on May 11, 1871, Lady Tichborne had died. In the interim, too, members of the Tichborne family had obtained considerable evidence to show that the "Tichborne claimant" was Arthur Orton. The trial lasted 102 days and cost the Tichborne family £90,000. In the end, Orton lost both the case and his freedom. He was arrested for perjury and, after a second, even longer trial, was sentenced in February, 1874, to 14 years in prison.

Orton served 10 years of his term. After his release in 1884, he attempted to test his claim again but could not obtain the necessary funds—even after arranging a series of lectures to rekindle public sympathy for his cause. Orton dropped out of the public eye and worked in a music hall, then in a pub, and then in a tobacconist's shop. Finally, desperate for money, he sold his "confession" to the *People* newspaper for $7,500. The money didn't last long. He died in poverty in April, 1898. Orton's death was not without irony, though. On his coffin—donated by a Paddington undertaker who believed Orton's story—was inscribed: "Sir Roger Charles Doughty Tichborne, born 5 January, 1829; died 1 April, 1898."

—J.N.

PEOPLE GONE BUT NOT FORGOTTEN: SEVEN EXTINCT SOCIETIES

ARAWAK OF HISPANIOLA

Their Society: Originally from South America, the Arawak Indians spoke an Amazonian dialect. They had migrated north through the Caribbean island chains to the island of Hispaniola, which today is occupied by the nations of Haiti and the Dominican Republic. This large island lying between Cuba and Puerto Rico was the homeland of 1 million Arawak Indians in the 15th century. The Arawak were primarily farmers; they grew manioc and corn in fields that they cleared by burning off the jungle undergrowth. Arawak men hunted hutias (small rodents) and iguanas and spearfished in the island streams and in the ocean.

The Arawak lived in round or rectangular wood-framed, rattan-and-cane walled houses. The Arawak villages, situated on the sandy shores of Hispaniola, usually had temples to house the tribe's carved stone idols. Every village had its own ceremonial ball court, protected by a stone wall and decorated with petroglyphs. Ruled by *caciques* (chiefs), the Arawak were a peaceful people whose main threat came from their aggressive, cannibalistic neighbors, the Caribs, who raided the Arawak villages and carried off women and children for use as concubines, slaves, sacrifices, and meals.

How and When Destroyed: The Arawak had the rather dubious honor of encountering the first Europeans to visit the Americas. In 1492 Christopher Columbus landed on the north shore of Hispaniola and began trading with the Arawak. On Jan. 14, 1493, in Samana Bay, Columbus's men and an Arawak war party fought a brief skirmish—the first episode in a history of white-Indian wars which would last almost 500 years. During the next decade Spaniards kidnapped Indians and sold them as slaves in Europe and Africa. As Spanish towns sprang up on Hispaniola, the battles increased, and the Europeans, armed with crossbows, muskets, and cannons, invariably won. Also, the Europeans brought typhus, influenza, and smallpox, which took heavy tolls in the Arawak villages.

By 1500 the Arawak had surrendered to Spanish rule, and their chiefs were forced to deliver a regular payment of gold to the Spanish governors. Eventually even gold did not suffice, and the governors ordered the chiefs to turn over men to work as slaves in the Spanish mines.

What finally destroyed the Arawak people was the *repartimiento* system established in 1502, which effectively enslaved the entire Arawak population of Hispaniola. The Spanish governor gave land grants—which included ownership of all Indians living on that land—to Spanish soldiers and settlers. Overworked and undernourished, the Arawak died in scores. Plantation owners complained that suicide by eating the poisonous part of manioc roots was epidemic among their Arawak serfs. So many Arawak died so quickly that by 1508 Spanish plantation owners began importing slaves from Africa to work in the fields and mines.

The Last of the Arawak of Hispaniola: In 1492, when Columbus came ashore, there were 1 million Arawak. Thirteen years later there were only 60,000, and by 1533 these had been reduced to 6,000. By 1548 there were a scant 500, and when Sir Francis Drake visited Hispaniola in 1585 he reported that not one Arawak still lived on the island.

GABRIELINO

Their Society: An American Indian tribe living along the Pacific Ocean, the Gabrielino occupied the Los Angeles Basin area, which today includes Los Angeles County, the northern half of Orange County, and some eastern parts of San Bernardino and Riverside counties. The Gabrielino also inhabited the islands of San Clemente and Santa Catalina. The Gabrielino were a Shoshone people who migrated west from

Jose Salvidea, one of the last of the Gabrielino Indians of southern California.

the regions of Nevada and Utah around 500 B.C. Belonging to the Uto-Aztecan language group, the Gabrielino were related to the Ute, Hopi, and Comanche.

The Gabrielino homeland was a varied region with sandy beaches and coastal marshes, grassy prairies, chaparral-covered foothills, and pine-covered mountains. It is estimated that 100 permanent Gabrielino villages dotted the landscape from the San Bernardino Mountains to Catalina Island. This was a nation of fishermen, hunters, and gatherers. The coastal Gabrielino, who had major villages at what are now Newport Beach, San Pedro, Redondo Beach, Santa Monica, Malibu, and Catalina, fished for shark, rays, abalone, and swordfish. Those on the islands hunted sea otters, seals, and sea lions. Other Gabrielino Indians lived inland in such villages as Cucamongna, Tuhungna, and Yangna. (Yangna, the precursor of modern Los Angeles, lies beneath what is now know as Union Railway Station.) The land-oriented Gabrielino hunted deer, small rodents, and birds. They also moved to temporary mountain camps during certain seasons to gather acorns, sage, yucca, and cacti.

The Gabrielino were one of the most culturally and economically advanced tribes in southern California. On Catalina, Gabrielino mined soapstone—steatite—which they carved into ornaments and eating and cooking utensils. The Gabrielino traded their valuable soapstone products with neighboring tribes. They plied their carved wares as far east as the villages of the Pueblo Indians of Arizona and New Mexico. Since trade was important to the Gabrielino, they eventually developed a monetary system and used strings of various shell beads as legal tender.

The chiefs and their extended families acted as the aristocracy and ruled a village or a confederation of villages. Although a male-oriented society, the Gabrielino sometimes had female chiefs. Often the chief's powers were eclipsed by the village's shaman, or priest. The Gabrielino shamans belonged to the jimsonweed religious cult, which worshiped the god Chingichngish. Supposedly, the shamans, after drinking a jimsonweed (a powerful hallucinogenic drug) and saltwater concoction, could foresee the future and will death on enemies of the village. Often a shaman would fall victim to the evil spirits and turn on his own people, in which case other shamans had to be brought in to strip the malevolent shaman of his power.

In everyday life, the Gabrielino coexisted peacefully with the bountiful land. They had a rigid custom of bathing daily, and they never wore clothes, though the women sometimes wore aprons. They lived in spacious well-ventilated cabins constructed on pole frameworks with tule mats for walls. The Gabrielino were monogamous and made exceptional parents, devoting much of their time to their children. If a man's wife was adulterous, he would beat or kill her and then take her lover's wife as his own.

How and When Destroyed: In 1542 the Gabrielino first encountered Europeans when a Spanish fleet under the command of Juan Rodríguez Cabrillo arrived. Although Spanish explorers frequently visited Gabrielino shores, it was not until 1769 that Spaniards, under Gaspar de Portola, came to establish permanent settlements. Soon thereafter, the

Gabrielino, who had never been exposed to infectious illnesses before, began falling victim to European diseases.

In 1771 Mission San Gabriel was established in the heart of the Gabrielino nation, and the Spanish began herding the Indians into the mission compound. Crowded conditions and continuous contact with Europeans made the Gabrielino even more susceptible to sickness. Within decades, they were nearing extinction. Most of them either became serfs on mission lands or fled to the interior to live with Indian tribes still free of white domination.

When the U.S. took control of California in 1848, the remaining Gabrielino and their problems were simply ignored by the Americans. The survivors turned increasingly to alcohol and this, together with the fact that almost 90% were infected with syphilis, so weakened them constitutionally that they fell easy victims to pneumonia and tuberculosis.

The Last of the Gabrielino: In the late 1700s there remained some 5,000 to 10,000 Gabrielino. A few Gabrielino Indians survived into the 20th century and lived in Los Angeles. Several were interviewed by writer John Harrington, who reported that one Gabrielino told him, "When Indians died, the villages ended. We, all the people, ended." By 1950 the last full-blooded Gabrielino had died.

GUANCHES

Their Society: Inhabiting the Canary Islands, which lie off the coast of northwest Africa in the Atlantic Ocean, the Guanches were a tall, fair or red-haired race of people. It is believed that they were the descendants of Cro-Magnon men who migrated to the islands from southern France and the Iberian Peninsula in oceangoing canoes some 3,000 years ago. The Guanches' own oral history and mythology spoke of 60 men and their families who colonized the uninhabited Canary Islands in prehistory after being driven from Europe, possibly by invading Celts. Later, emigrants arrived from Mauritania in Africa. These newcomers—Berbers and a few black Africans—became a peasant class under the aristocratic Guanches.

The Guanches dominated the large central islands of Tenerife, La Palma, and Gran Canaria. They lived in cave dwellings, which they enlarged into spacious, multilevel residences with wooden floors and partitioned rooms. Many of them are still in use today, the oldest continuously occupied dwellings in the world. The Guanches owned large estates on which they grew wheat and barley and raised sheep and goats with the aid of the African descendants. The Guanches' rulers were known as "overlords." They owned all the land and granted or leased it, almost exclusively, to citizens of Guanches stock. A primitive agricultural people who used stone tools, the Guanches were well suited to their environment. To communicate over the rocky, mountainous regions of their isles, they developed a whistling language that could be heard, according to European accounts, at a distance of 4 mi.

How and When Destroyed: Although the Guanches had contact with ancient Phoenicians, Carthaginians, Greeks, and, probably, Romans, they were isolated from Europe and Africa during the Dark Ages. In the 1300s Genoese and Portuguese slave ships raided the islands in search of human cargo to auction off in European and North African slave markets.

In 1402 a well-organized expedition of French noblemen arrived to conquer the islands. The eastern islands of Lanzarote and Fuerteventura fell to the invaders, but the central Guanches-dominated isles repelled the Frenchmen. Over the next 90 years Spanish generals with thousands of troops invaded the islands, killing the Guanches or capturing them to sell as slaves. The Portuguese slavers and the Spanish soldiers decimated the Guanches population. In 1484 influenza and typhus, introduced by the Europeans, swept through the islands. The Guanches were so reduced in numbers that they could no longer withstand the Spanish onslaught.

The Last of the Guanches: During the early 1500s the last of the Guanches disappeared into slavery, intermarried with their Spanish conquerors, or died of disease. The culture and society of the Guanches ceased to exist.

NATCHEZ

Their Society: The Natchez, an American Indian tribe, lived on the eastern bank of the lower Mississippi River near modern Natchez, Miss. In 1700, some 4,000 Natchez people lived in nine farming communities and grew squash, corn, pumpkins, and beans. They also hunted and were extremely adept at pottery making and textile weaving.

Their government was a despotic theocracy headed by an absolute monarch, who was also the tribe's high priest. The Natchez were sun worshipers; they believed that their king was the descendant of the sun god and revered him as the "Great Sun." Because the Natchez were culturally similar to Indians of central Mexico, and because they used the same building technique in the construction of their temples, it is argued that they may have migrated to the Mississippi region from Mexico.

Unlike most American Indian cultures, Natchez society was stratified into four classes. The Suns, relatives of the Great Sun, formed the highest ranks—rulers and priests. Below the Suns were the Nobles, followed by the Honored Men. Commoners were known as Stinkards and were treated as mere servants of the upper classes. Class structure was not rigid since all people of the upper classes, including the Suns, had to marry commoners.

Natchez society was strongly matriarchal. The mother or sister of a deceased Great Sun chose his successor from among her brothers or sons. The offspring of a female Sun maintained that social status, while the children of a male Sun dropped down one rung on the social ladder. Female Suns lived privileged lives. Their commoner husbands had to wait on them continually and could never disagree with them. If the husband committed an infidelity, the Sun wife could have him beheaded. However, she was allowed as many lovers as she desired.

How and When Destroyed: French explorers led by Robert Cavelier de La Salle initially encountered the Natchez in 1682. By the first decade of the 1700s the French, based in New Orleans, had begun trading with the Natchez and intruding on their lands. A French fort and plantations were established in Natchez territory, and in 1716 and 1723 the French and Natchez engaged in bloody skirmishes. Surprisingly, the Natchez Suns were pro-French and restrained their people from open warfare with the newcomers, at least until 1729, when the arrogant, tyrannical commandant of the French fort on Natchez soil ordered the Indians to vacate their main village so that he could have the land for his personal plantation. The Natchez immediately rose against the invaders, slaughtering 200 Frenchmen, capturing 400 women and children, and burning the fort. The French governor of Louisiana ordered a counterattack by French troops and their Choctaw Indian allies. Overwhelmed by superior numbers and the enemy's artillery, the Natchez were defeated. Approximately 400 Natchez surrendered and were sold into slavery in the West Indies. The rest of the survivors—probably numbering no more than 450—sought refuge among the Chickasaws, Creeks, and Cherokees.

The Last of the Natchez: In 1735 there were still some 700 Natchez alive. Some were slaves in the West Indies; the rest lived with other American Indian tribes. Those in Caribbean bondage soon died, while the remainder gradually lost their tribal identity and language. When the U.S. government forced all Indian nations east of the Mississippi to move to officially designated Indian territory (in present-day Oklahoma) during the 1800s, the remaining Natchez went with them. By 1900 there were only 20 left. In a short time even they had disappeared.

TASMANIANS

Their Society: According to different estimates, 2,000 to 20,000 native inhabitants were living on the island of Tasmania, 150 mi. south of Australia, when English settlers arrived there in 1803. Anthropologists believe the Tasmanians represented a physically distinct race. Unlike the aborigines of Australia, they had woolly black hair and reddish-brown skin. Tasmanian males sharpened sticks and obsidian knives to hunt kangaroo, wallaby, and opossum. The women dived in the ocean for shellfish.

Tasmanians wore no clothes (even in cold weather) but they adorned themselves with grease, feathers, and shells. They fashioned crude shelters from branches and leaves but built no permanent structures. They didn't know how to kindle fire, and they didn't make baskets or pottery. They were a generally peaceful society of primitive hunters and gatherers, divided into eight tribes speaking different dialects. Their basic societal group was the extended family.

How and When Destroyed: In 1803, 49 British settlers, most of whom were convicts from Australia, landed in southern Tasmania. At first the Tasmanians welcomed the British and traded with them. However, on May 3, 1804, an incident occurred which was to cause war. Three

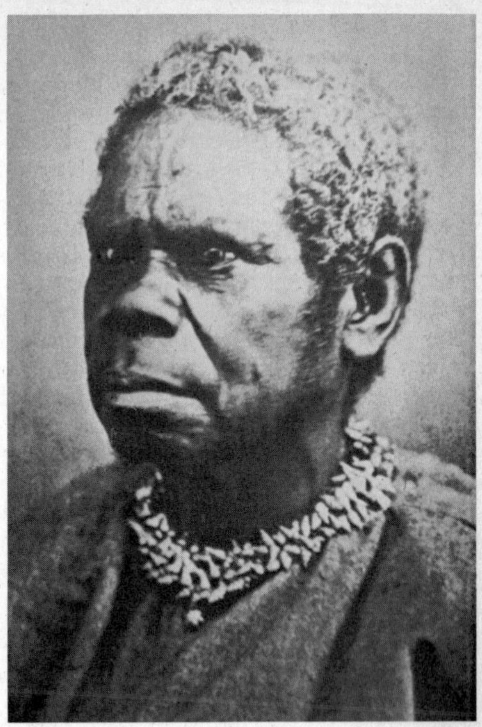

Trucanini, last of the Tasmanians.

hundred Tasmanian hunters were chasing a kangaroo herd, which led them to the outskirts of a small British encampment. A nervous lieutenant by the name of Moore, thinking the Tasmanians were attacking the camp, ordered the cannons to be fired. The dazed and decimated Tasmanians picked up their dead and wounded and departed. In retaliation, they then attacked and killed several British oystermen. That was the beginning of a very one-sided conflict, which resulted in the extermination of the Tasmanians.

By 1820 some 12,000 British settlers and just 1,000 Tasmanians lived on the island. The settlers considered the Tasmanians as mere wild animals and actually organized hunts—complete with hunting jackets, hounds, and horns—to track and kill the natives. Innumerable atrocities were committed against the Tasmanians. Men and boys were castrated; women were gang-raped and murdered; the settlers even shot Tasmanians and fed them to their dogs. An Englishman was once sentenced to 10 lashes for chopping off a Tasmanian's finger, while a servant was given 50 lashes for the much more serious offense of smiling disrespectfully at his mistress.

The Tasmanian population was further reduced by European diseases, especially syphilis, which became epidemic because of the number of sexual assaults by Englishmen on Tasmanian women. In 1838 the remaining 187 Tasmanian people were transported to Flinders Island off the northeast coast of Tasmania. On this barren, almost waterless isle, the Tasmanians were placed under the care of Anglican missionaries, who forced them to wear clothes and learn Western customs. Demoralized, the few surviving Tasmanians lost their will to live and fell easy victims to disease. In one year 50 died of pneumonia.

Finally, in 1847, the survivors were returned to mainland Tasmania and resettled at Oyster Cove, near the capital city of Hobart. Most of the men became alcoholics, and most of the women turned to prostitution.

The Last of the Tasmanians: The last Tasmanian male was William "King Billy" Lanné, who became a local curiosity during the 1860s. An alcoholic, Lanné died of dysentery and cholera in 1869 at the age of 34. The last Tasmanian female was Trucanini, whose fifth husband had been William Lanné. Although a friend and helper to British missionaries, Trucanini had firsthand experience of British violence against her people. When she was a girl, she was captured with a band of Tasmanians, and forced to look on as her companions were hanged. She had also watched white men chop off the hands of one of her husbands and stab her mother to death. During her later life she lived in Hobart on a small pension granted her by the British government. Trucanini died in 1876, and the local citizens hung her skeleton in the town museum.

TIERRA DEL FUEGIANS

Their Society: The large island of Tierra del Fuego with its countless offshore islands and islets was the home of a number of small Indian tribes, including the Ona, Haush, Yahgan, Chono, and Alacaluf. Lying directly south of South America, Tierra del Fuego is the southernmost inhabitated region of the world. It is an inhospitable land with year-round rainfall.

The tribes of this region formed two different cultural and linguistic groups. The Ona and Haush lived on the plains and in the forests of the main island. Land-oriented, they hunted the guanaco, a relative of the llama, and the tuco-tuco, a gopherlike rodent. Organized in loose bands, these Indians observed strict territorial boundaries and lived in branch-framed, skin-covered tents. The other major group, consisting of the Yahgan, Chono, and Alacaluf, inhabited the coastal areas and many small nearby islands. They derived their living from the waters of the Strait of Magellan. Canoe-borne nomads, the men of these tribes caught otter and seal and snared birds, including geese and swans. The women dived into the frigid ocean waters for shellfish. These Indians wore skirts and greased their bodies to protect themselves from the sea and spray and from the continuous rains. Over the centuries they had physically adapted to the cold climate.

How and When Destroyed: The Ona and Haush tribes were decimated shortly after the first permanent European settlement was established in Tierra del Fuego in 1871. Gold miners and sheep ranchers invaded the island and pursued an extermination policy, but it was ultimately measles and smallpox that destroyed the Ona and Haush.

The Yahgan, Chono, and Alacaluf fared better for a time, since the

Europeans had no economic use for their barren homeland. However, during the 1860s, Anglican missionaries settled among them and introduced diseases that proved fatal to the Indians. In 1884 Argentina decided to establish a government station in Yahgan territory and dispatched 20 men to set up the post. The Yahgans welcomed the Argentineans, and seven Indians went aboard their ship. Within hours the seven were infected with measles; when they returned to the land, the disease spread throughout the population because the Yahgan had no natural immunity to it. This first measles epidemic killed over half the population. The well-intentioned missionaries also contributed to the demise of these tribes by insisting that they wear clothes. The grease that the Indians used on their bodies protected them from rain and ocean spray, but their new clothes were perpetually damp; therefore, outbreaks of pneumonia, influenza, and tuberculosis soon became commonplace.

The Last of the Tierra del Fuegians: In 1870 there were roughly 2,500 to 3,000 Ona and Haush, but by 1910 there were only 300 still alive. Fifteen years later, the Ona population had fallen to 100 and the Haush had become extinct. Today, there are two Ona—Pablo Pacheco and Rafaela Ishton—still living in Tierra del Fuego.

Among the coast-dwelling groups, the small tribe of Chono became extinct early in the 20th century. The Alacaluf population has been reduced from around 1,000 in 1870 to the 3 or 4 old people who are still alive today. Their deaths will mark the end of their people. The Yahgan numbered approximately 3,000 in 1881, but three years later only 1,000 still survived. In 1902, 130 Yahgan Indians remained, and that number dwindled to 40 by 1933. Today the Yahgan have been officially classified as "presumed extinct." The last Yahgan may have been an Indian named Domingo, who still lived a nomadic life with his wife and seven children in the mid-20th century.

YAHI

Their Society: The Yahi clan of the Yana Indian nation lived in the Deer Creek and Mill Creek canyons between the Sacramento River and Mt. Lassen in northern California. The Yahi were a small tribe of approximately 300 people. They were hunters and gatherers whose diet consisted of deer, salmon, and acorns. Theirs was a Stone Age society that believed in a sky god and an evil "coyote spirit." They lived in huts made of bark and hide, and were highly protective of their territorial rights—a stance which often caused hostilities with neighboring Indian tribes. Their society was patriarchal; political power was in the hands of chiefs, who were supported by the community and who had the privilege of keeping pet vultures.

How and When Destroyed: During their occupation of California the Spanish and Mexicans had little contact with the Yahi. However, when the U.S. obtained California, settlers blazed a trail to the California gold fields through Yahi lands. From the start, this contact involved bloodshed. Transient gold prospectors and cowboys raped and murdered

Yahi citizens, and the tribe's warriors retaliated by killing local settlers and their families. From 1858 to 1870, Americans and Yahi constantly fought. Since the Yahi were not nomads but lived in permanent villages, they were particularly vulnerable to surprise attack. The battles ended when a force of civilian American "Indian fighters" attacked and butchered the Yahi in Deer Creek Canyon in 1870. Of 300 Yahi, only 12 escaped the massacre.

The Last of the Yahi: The Americans thought they had completely exterminated the Yahi tribe, but the 12 survivors lived on in the wild country around Mt. Lassen in caves and crude huts. The Yahi avoided any contact with the whites, fearing they'd be slaughtered by them, but illness and age reduced their number over the years. By 1908 there were only four Yahi left when a surveying party stumbled into their camp. The Indians fled, and three of them died soon after, leaving one Yahi man alive.

He was 50 years old, and after 40 years of hiding from the Americans, this man decided to seek civilization. He wandered out of the mountains to Oroville, Calif., where the local police put him in jail on Aug. 29, 1911. When news of this "wild Indian" who spoke no English or Spanish reached San Francisco, Thomas Waterman of the University of California's Museum of Art and Anthropology came to his rescue. Waterman took the last of the Yahi to San Francisco and housed him at the Museum of Anthropology. It was taboo for a Yahi to speak his own name, so Waterman named the man Ishi (Yahi for "man"). An amiable and intelligent individual, Ishi became a permanent resident at the museum, where he helped anthropologists in their studies of his people's language, myths, and culture. He acquired a small English vocabulary, and a few of the anthropologists learned some Yahi. Surprisingly, Ishi adjusted to the white man's metropolitan life-style and made a few friends. He rode streetcars and attended Wild West shows and vaudeville performances. He claimed that the white man's greatest inventions were matches and glue. Although often treated like a freak, Ishi maintained his dignity and never surrendered his Yahi beliefs, even though he adopted the dress and other trappings of American culture.

On Mar. 25, 1916, Ishi died of tuberculosis at the University of California Medical School in San Francisco.

—R.J.F.

7

WHODUNIT

UNSOLVED CRIMES: CAN YOU HELP?

Valerie Percy Case (1966)

The Crime: Immersed in the senatorial campaign of 1966, the residents of the Charles H. Percy estate on the shore of Lake Michigan in Chicago's elegant suburb of Kenilworth gave little thought to the possibility of an illegal intruder. The way he entered the 17-room mansion was later obvious. He sliced through a screen and cut a pane from the French door to the music room. Then he climbed to the second floor and entered the room where one of Percy's daughters, a 21-year-old twin, was sleeping. Did he make a noise that wakened her? That isn't known with absolute certainty to this day. What *is* known is that he bashed in the left side of her skull and stabbed her in both breasts, in the neck, twice in the stomach, above the left eye, and in the left cheek, temple, and ear.

The girl managed a long moan, that early morning of Sept. 18, which brought Percy's wife running to the room. The intruder shone his flashlight in the woman's eyes, and as she stood blinded by the light and frozen in horror, he fled. Finally Mrs. Percy screamed, and millionaire Percy woke up and rushed to the room. Too late. Honey-blonde Valerie was dying.

The Investigation: The murder took place in a community that was not used to violent crimes. Suburban Kenilworth led Chicago's 175 suburban communities in median family income ($22,800 a year at the time) and years of schooling (15.3), and it had two churches and no saloons. The village's 11-man police force was more used to investigating hubcap thefts than murder. Therefore, they were augmented by technicians from Chicago's famed crime lab, Cook County investigators, and FBI agents. The doctor who pronounced Valerie dead said, "I am convinced there is some sexual motivation." However, there was no evidence that even indicated whether the killer was a man or a woman. By week's end 150 persons had been questioned, but none was counted a prime suspect.

The Clues: Over the next seven years the list of those questioned grew to 14,000, and 1,317 leads were checked out. Nineteen confessions—all false—were obtained. Number 19 came from a 27-year-old man in

Miami who, for good measure, admitted eliminating John F. Kennedy, Robert Kennedy, and Martin Luther King.

Then, in 1973, the police were certain they had zeroed in on the real killer or killers in the case. It was believed they were members of what authorities called a Mafia-backed band of thieves who specialized in robbing homes of wealthy persons nationwide. Two members of the gang, 46-year-old Francis Leroy Hohimer, who was serving 30 years for armed robbery in the Iowa state penitentiary, and Frederick Malchow, a longtime buddy of Hohimer, who had died in 1967 in a plunge from a railroad trestle after breaking out of a Pennsylvania prison, were considered to have the necessary penchant for violence to have done the job. Hohimer's favorite weapon on heists was a propane blowtorch, which served both as an entry device and as a "convincer" to force reluctant victims to reveal where their valuables were hidden. Hohimer was first fingered by a fatally ill Mafia operative, Leo Rugendorf, who told Chicago *Sun-Times* reporter Art Petacque that Hohimer had informed him: "They'll get me for the Valerie Percy murder. The girl woke up, and I hit her on the top of the head with a pistol." Reporter Petacque, who was to share a Pulitzer Prize for his work, dug up Hohimer's brother Harold, who corroborated Rugendorf's claim, revealing his brother had said that "he had to 'off' a girl." Another witness insisted that Hohimer told him two weeks before the murder that he'd cased the Percy mansion and intended to hit it.

Hohimer finally broke his silence but insisted he hadn't been in on the crime. He accused Malchow, claiming Malchow had come to his apartment on the morning of the murder in clothes soaked with blood. In 1975 Hohimer wrote a book about his years as a cat burglar, *The Home Invaders*, in which he admitted a number of capers—including one at Elvis Presley's Memphis mansion—but held to his version of Malchow's guilt in the Percy job.

Unanswered Questions: Authorities admit there will be no prosecution in the case because physical evidence is weak, failing to link either of the two prime suspects to the mansion. The strongest physical evidence—four palm prints—matched neither Hohimer's nor Malchow's. And what about the vicious nature of the attack, with its repeated stabbings? Such an attack is generally regarded as sexual, and hardly ever the work of professional burglars. Does it indicate that either Malchow or Hohimer was a breed apart from other cat men? Or was one of them cunning enough to disguise the attack as that of a sex maniac? Technically, at least, the failure to prosecute leaves the Percy murder unsolved.

Whom to Notify: Superintendent of Police, Kenilworth, Ill. 60043.

The Zodiac Killer (1966–?)

The Crime: Officially, the oddball but deadly Zodiac case started on Dec. 20, 1968, with the murder of two high school sweethearts, David Faraday, 17, and Bettilou Jensen, 16, who were parked on a lonely road outside Vallejo, Calif., just north of San Francisco. The boy was shot in

WANTED

SAN FRANCISCO POLICE DEPARTMENT

NO. 90-69 WANTED FOR MURDER OCTOBER 18, 1969

ORIGINAL DRAWING AMENDED DRAWING

Supplementing our Bulletin 87-69 of October 13, 1969. Additional information has developed the above amended drawing of murder suspect known as "ZODIAC".

[illegible], 35-45 Years, approximately 5'8", Heavy Build, Short Brown Hair, possibly with Red Tint, Wears Glasses. Armed with 9 [illegible] Automatic.

Available for comparison: Slugs, Casings, Latents, Handwriting.

ANY INFORMATION:
Inspectors Armstrong & Toschi
Homicide Detail
CASE NO. 696314

THOMAS J. CAHILL
CHIEF OF POLICE

the car; the girl was gunned down by five shots when she tried to run away. The killer was never found. The following July 4, however, the killer shot another young couple in a nearby park; the girl died, but the boy survived despite four bullet wounds. The killer had temporarily blinded him with a flashlight, so his description of the assailant was very sketchy. A short while later the Vallejo police got an anonymous phone call. A man said, "I just shot the two kids at the public park. With a 9-mm. automatic. I also killed those two kids Christmas."

On Aug. 1, 1969, the Vallejo newspaper and two San Francisco dailies got letters from the killer, each with a note and one third of a cryptogram—an odd series of letters and signs offering no easy interpretation. The killer signed himself with a circle divided by a cross, his symbol for the zodiac. In subsequent letters he started off: "This is Zodiac speaking."

The Investigation: While newspapers printed Zodiac's taunting letters and promises of more violence, police pressed their hunt for a possible mental case. In addition, San Francisco *Chronicle* reporter Paul Avery discovered that the handwriting in a letter written by the murderer of college coed Cheri Jo Bates in 1966 matched the Zodiac's.

Clues: It took days to crack Zodiac's cryptogram, mainly because his spelling was lousy (perhaps deliberately so). The code did tell something of Zodiac's bizarre motivation. He wrote: "I like killing people because it is more fun than killing wild game in the forrest because man is the moat dangerus anamal of all to kill something gives me the most thrilling expeerence. The best part of it ia thae when I die I will be reborn in paradice and all the I have killed will become my slaves. I will not give you my name because you will trs to sloi down or stop my collecting of slaves for my afterlife."

In September, 1969, Zodiac, wearing a square mask resembling a medieval executioner's hood, captured two college students picnicking near Lake Berryessa and tied them up. He stabbed the boy 6 times and gave the girl a total of 24 knife wounds in the form of a bloody cross. The girl, Cecelia Shepard, died, but the boy, Bryan Hartnell, survived. A few weeks later Zodiac killed a cab driver, but that time he was seen leaving the scene of the crime and the police got their first useful description of him. He was about 25 to 30, 5 ft. 8 in., wore thick glasses, and had short brown (perhaps reddish) hair. It did little good. No arrest was made.

Unanswered Questions: For the next several years the Zodiac played a number game. When the police credited him with 5 murders, he claimed 7. When they upped their figure to 6, he raised it to 17. Eventually Zodiac claimed more than 30 murders, and San Francisco police insisted there hadn't been that many corpses. However, in 1975 Sonoma County Sheriff Don Striepeke came up with a computer study of murder records filed in the state attorney general's office which indicated that 40 murders in five western states could be linked to one killer—possibly Zodiac—because of the similarity in technique. In Washington State, a symbol of two rectangles connected by a line—formed by twigs and with two stones within one of the rectangles—was found by some girls' bodies. Striepeke established that the symbol was a form of witchcraft in England, and that it was once put on the hearth of homes of deceased persons in order to speed the dead to the afterlife. (Zodiac was certainly concerned about his victims' afterlife.)

At least the sheriff's numbers matched Zodiac's fairly well, for in one of his last letters, written in 1974, Zodiac claimed 37 murders. There was one more letter after that, but it proved to be a fake. What happened to Zodiac? Is he out of commission, perhaps dead? Or is he simply killing more and writing less? Sheriff Striepeke at one point came up with the theory that the mass killer was leaving a trail of bodies that trace the letter Z over several Western states.

Whom to Notify: San Francisco Police Dept., 850 Bryant Street, San Francisco, Calif. 94103.

Jimmy Hoffa Disappearance (1975)

The Crime: Officially, Jimmy Hoffa is listed in police files as "Missing Person 75-3425." However, everyone believes that the flamboyant labor leader was murdered. The script of his death has been fairly well authenticated. The 62-year-old Hoffa was released from prison in late 1971 after President Richard Nixon commuted his sentence for jury tampering. (He had served 4 years of the 8-year sentence.) In 1975 Hoffa was preparing to make a bid to regain the presidency of the Teamsters Union when he vanished. On July 30 of that year, Hoffa left his suburban Detroit home and drove alone in his car to the Manchus Red Fox Restaurant in Bloomfield Township. He expected to be picked up there and taken to a meeting with Anthony "Tony Pro" Provenzano, a powerful figure in New Jersey Teamster affairs and a bitter foe of Hoffa's reemergence to power. The meeting had been set up by Detroit gang lieutenant Anthony "Tony Jack" Giacalone, Hoffa's longtime friend.

Hoffa was to meet Giacalone in front of the restaurant at 2:00 P.M. At 2:30 he telephoned his wife. "I wonder where the hell Tony is," Hoffa said. "I'm waiting for him." That was the last anyone heard from Jimmy Hoffa.

The Investigation: Investigators checking the scene of Hoffa's disappearance came up with witnesses who had seen him get into a car with his foster son, 41-year-old "Chuckie" O'Brien, a lower-echelon union official, and two or three other men. Eventually, the car was found, and traces of Hoffa's blood and hair were discovered in the backseat. There was not enough blood for him to have been shot in the car, but he could have been rendered unconscious, or perhaps strangled there and then taken elsewhere and shot.

Clues: The FBI eventually came up with an informer who, on a pledge of secrecy, spilled a story of Hoffa's assassination. His name was "Little Ralph" Picardo, and he was doing 17 to 23 years for procuring a murder. (Picardo's identity was not a mystery for long; Tony Pro learned it right away.) Obviously, Picardo was looking for a reduction of his "heavy time," but he did have an insider's knowledge of affairs in Tony Pro's New Jersey Local 560. Picardo said those involved in Hoffa's death were Tony Pro and several Teamster muscle men, including Gabriel Briguglio, 36, his brother Salvatore, 47, and Thomas Andretta, 38. A man sitting beside Hoffa in the backseat of the car probably hit him over the head, and he was then permanently dispatched either in the car or elsewhere. Hoffa's body, Picardo said, was popped into a 55-gallon oil drum and transported east for disposal in a Jersey City, N.J., garbage dump. An FBI hunt at the dump did not yield Hoffa's body. Finally, the agency assumed the body had never left Michigan, but instead had been disposed of in a large trash shredder, compactor, or incinerator at Central Sanitation Services in Hamtramck—a refuse company owned by two Detroit crime figures, Peter Vitale and Raffael Quasarano.

Unanswered Questions: Unfortunately, the government has failed to get confessions to back up this version. Salvatore Briguglio reportedly started to sing but was murdered in front of a New York restaurant in March, 1978. O'Brien, reputed to be unwaveringly loyal to Hoffa, denied having done anything to hurt him. More importantly, the plot, as expounded by the FBI, had odd aspects. For example, why would Giacalone and Tony Pro link themselves in advance with a meeting where Hoffa was to be assassinated? They risked Hoffa's talking about it—as he did to a number of parties. Not surprisingly, both Giacalone and Tony Pro produced alibis for the time period involved; Giacalone was in a health club, and Tony Pro was in faraway Union City, N.J. The likely explanation is that the pair was carrying out orders of higher-ups and had to proceed with the plan despite being forced to be "up front." An even better question, never raised apparently, is Why, if a rub out was planned, did the hit men arrive 45 minutes late, risking Hoffa's angry departure? Hit men seldom lack the virtue of punctuality.

Still, the FBI version beats a version advanced by another target of the Hoffa inquiry, teamster official Roland McMaster, who said: "Teamsters have professional ethics just like reporters. We don't shoot people and kill people." He theorized that Hoffa "ran off to Brazil with a black go-go dancer" to avoid continued "persecution" by the government. "I hired a soothsayer and asked her where Jimmy was. That's what she told me," said McMaster. With that it seemed clear that Missing Person #75-3425 will stay one for some time to come.

Whom to Notify: Federal Bureau of Investigation, Pennsylvania Avenue between 9th Avenue and 10th Avenue N.W., Washington, D.C. 20535.

Georgi Markov Murder (1978)

The Crime: Six months before he was murdered in September, 1978, Georgi Markov, a Bulgarian defector broadcasting in London for the BBC and the U.S.-funded Radio Free Europe, was informed that he was going to be eliminated. The word came from an anonymous fellow Bulgarian. The Communists planned to make the murder look like a natural death resulting from a very high fever caused by a flu or virus. The real method would be untraceable. Markov didn't laugh off the threat; he just hoped it wouldn't happen. But it did. On Sept. 7, 1978, about 6:30 P.M., the 49-year-old Markov was walking from his car to his night-shift BBC commentator's job when he felt a sharp sting on the back of his right thigh. He turned to see a stranger holding a closed umbrella. "I'm sorry," the man said in a thick accent and disappeared into a taxi.

Markov appeared to be fine for the next 10 hours, but then he complained of a fever to his wife and soon he began vomiting. Taken to the hospital, he told doctors, "I've been poisoned. The umbrella man could have been an assassin." Four days later Markov was dead.

The Investigation: British police, Scotland Yard's antiterrorist squad, and intelligence agents took Markov's dying claim seriously. At first all

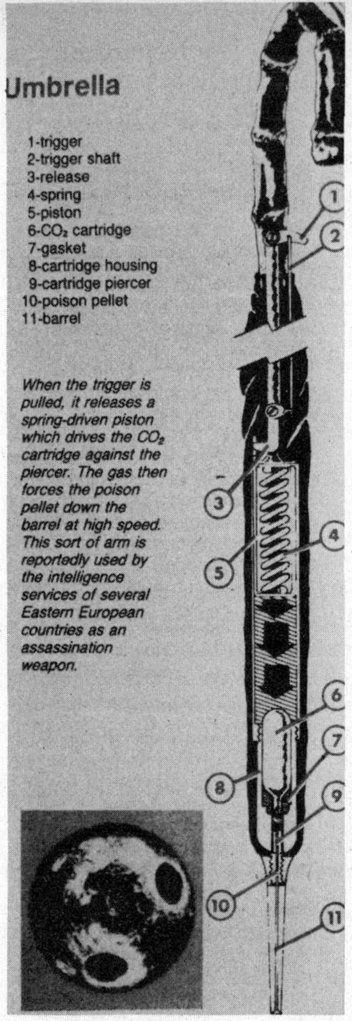
Umbrella
1-trigger
2-trigger shaft
3-release
4-spring
5-piston
6-CO₂ cartridge
7-gasket
8-cartridge housing
9-cartridge piercer
10-poison pellet
11-barrel
When the trigger is pulled, it releases a spring-driven piston which drives the CO₂ cartridge against the piercer. The gas then forces the poison pellet down the barrel at high speed. This sort of arm is reportedly used by the intelligence services of several Eastern European countries as an assassination weapon.
1
2
3
4
5
6
7
8
9
10
11

The killer umbrella.

lab tests failed to explain his death, except to indicate that he had suffered blood poisoning. Microbiological warfare experts finally tested skin tissue from Markov's thigh and found a minuscule platinum-iridium pellet, much smaller than the head of a pin. The pellet had two holes drilled into it at right angles and was proved to have contained a deadly poison. Long periods of testing finally identified the poison as ricin, a derivative of the castor-oil plant. (Most research on ricin has occurred in Eastern Europe.) Scientists injected an equal amount of ricin into a pig, and it died in 25 hours; Markov had lasted four days. Significantly, even if the doctors had known the nature of the poison, they would not have been able to save Markov. There is no known antidote for ricin.

Clues: It was obvious that Markov had been silenced by Communist agents, and it soon became apparent that Markov was not the first to fall prey to the murder-by-umbrella technique. A friend of Markov's, Vladimir Kostov, a defector who had been a French correspondent for the Bulgarian television and radio network, was mysteriously hit in the back the previous August while riding an escalator in a Paris subway station. After Markov's death, Kostov was X-rayed, and a small pellet was found in his back. It was forwarded to London and found to be an exact duplicate of the Markov pellet. Kostov presumably had survived because his pellet had contained a nonlethal amount of poison.

Unanswered Questions: When the poison story broke, the Bulgarian government reacted in anger, first denouncing the tale as James Bondian nonsense and later charging that it was a plot to damage Bulgaria by killing off someone as expendable as Markov and then blaming the episode on the Sofia regime. The Bulgarians said they suspected it was the work of some émigré group in cooperation with a Western intelligence agency. Indeed, many Western observers doubted Bulgarian involvement, claiming that such scientific expertise was beyond their intelligence capabilities and that only SMERSH, the KGB section normally responsible for international murders, could have carried it out. In 1978 the climate of détente and the possibility of the success of the SALT talks required Russian circumspection, and that was possible only if the murder or murders appeared strictly Bulgarian-inspired. Thus, the Russians could send a chilling message to defectors and still maintain friendly diplomatic relations with the West. But aside from such geopolitical considerations, the major unanswered question was, and still is, How many others have been eliminated in the same manner as Markov? All such deaths would almost certainly have been passed off as due to natural causes.

Late in 1980 Markov's widow was informed by Scotland Yard that the file on the Markov case was still open and that the hunt was being pressed.

Whom to Notify: New Scotland Yard, Broadway, London, SW1H OBG.

—C.S.

GREAT DETECTIVES AND THEIR MOST SPECTACULAR CASES

ELLIS PARKER AND THE PICKLED CORPSE CASE (1920)

The Crime

When on Oct. 5, 1920, a 60-year-old bank runner disappeared with a pouch containing $70,000 in cash and another $30,000 in negotiable securities, it was assumed he had absconded. Investigation showed that although considered to be a prim husband, David Paul of Camden, N.J., was quite a wild lover and had taken part in numerous orgies at a cottage some distance outside of town. His sex-oriented friends insisted they had not seen him the night before his disappearance. Then 11 days later Paul's body was found in a shallow grave in a wooded area. He had been shot through the head. Mysteriously, while the ground around the corpse was bone-dry, Paul's overcoat and clothing were sopping wet. The only explanation the police could come up with was that possibly his murderer hadn't been sure whether the bullet had killed him and had therefore "drowned" him in a nearby stream, Bread and Cheese Run. He had been dead, however, according to an autopsy, for only 48 to 72 hours. Thus, either he had absconded with the money and was later killed for it, or he had been kidnapped at the start but kept alive by his abductor for eight or nine days before being eliminated.

Enter the Detective

Ellis Parker was a 5-ft. 6-in., soft-spoken, blue-eyed, gentle-looking man who could have passed for a small-town grocer or almost anything but what he was—the chief of detectives of Burlington County, N.J. Known as the "county detective with a worldwide reputation," Parker was noted for his ability as a crime solver, and other jurisdictions, especially other sheriffs, in the state often called on him for aid. Parker firmly believed that the logical interpretation of facts was almost always the correct one. So far as alibis were concerned, he was convinced that most criminals fabricate an alibi before they commit a crime; therefore, he automatically suspected any person with an alibi. He once nailed a soldier for the murder of a fellow GI at Fort Dix, even though there were over 100 likely suspects. Only one man could provide an alibi for the time the crime was committed. It was illogical for someone to remember what he was doing three months earlier, so the soldier with the alibi headed Parker's suspect list. The shrewd detective soon found incriminating evidence against the murderer and got a confession.

The Chase

Two things about the Paul case struck Parker as illogical. One was that the killer or killers had apparently kept the victim alive for eight or nine days. If they were going to kill him, logic demanded that they do it immediately. The second illogical fact was that the dead man's clothing had been soaking wet. Parker concluded that these two perplexing facts must somehow be related. The more he thought about the case, the more he felt that Paul had been killed at once, regardless of medical findings. Parker would have instantly realized the reason for the victim's wet clothing if Camden County had been his own bailiwick. He would have known about the water in Bread and Cheese Run. As it was, he did not guess the solution until he happened to discover that tanning factories lay upstream. At this point, he filled a bottle with water and took it to a chemist for analysis. Bread and Cheese Run, he discovered, contained a high percentage of tannic acid. And tannic acid is an excellent preservative. A body submerged in this stream would undergo virtually no decomposition in 10 days and would therefore appear to be that of a person dead only a very short time.

The Solution

Once Parker had determined that Paul was killed close to the time of his disappearance, he reexamined alibis. The fact that the killer or killers knew about the chemical properties of the stream meant they were locals. Who had been questioned about the Paul case who didn't have an alibi for the time he disappeared but did have for the "false" period of his murder?

The answer was Frank James and Raymond Schuck, the two men who shared an orgy cottage with Paul. James, a salesman, had been in Detroit for five days at a convention, but that merely proved he couldn't have murdered Paul on the day that he allegedly was killed. Schuck was in the same boat. He had conveniently gone to visit friends downstate during that supposedly critical period. Parker found that while the two men had not spent any large sums of money recently, Schuck, a married man, had given a girl friend who frequented the cottage an expensive fur coat the day after Paul's disappearance.

Separately, Parker broke the two men down, first building up their confidence and then shattering their useless alibis. Each confessed, meanwhile insisting that the other had done the actual killing. Most of the stolen money was found buried in a Camden cemetery in the grave of Schuck's mother. Both men were executed.

Parker managed to carve out an illustrious record in four decades of detective work, during which he solved about 350 crimes, including 118 out of the 124 murder cases submitted to him. Yet he ended up a tragic figure. When news of the Lindbergh kidnapping broke in 1932, Parker was insulted because the law officials who had leaned on him so much in the past failed to contact him. Parker brooded about the case, and after the arrest of Bruno Hauptmann he became convinced that the real culprit was Paul Wendel, a Trenton, N.J., man. Parker virtually kidnapped Wendel and held him captive in various hideaways in Brooklyn and New Jersey until he extracted a so-called confession. In court Wendel effectively repudiated this "confession," and Parker faced a federal charge of abduction. He was sent to prison for six years and died at the penitentiary at Lewisburg, Pa., before he had finished half his sentence.

EDWARD O. HEINRICH AND THE MAIL TRAIN MURDERS (1923)

The Crime

On Oct. 11, 1923, a Southern Pacific mail train, its coaches filled with passengers, was moving slowly through a tunnel in the Siskiyou Mountains in southern Oregon when two men armed with shotguns climbed over the tender (the car behind the engine) and ordered the engineer and fireman to stop as soon as the engine and tender cleared the tunnel. The trainmen could do nothing but comply. They pulled to a halt as the third car, which carried the mail, was also partially clear of the tunnel. As the railroaders watched, immobile in the stare of the shotguns, a man emerged from the woods holding a bulky package, which he placed against the side of the mail car. Running back to a detonator, this third man set off an explosion. The mail car was enveloped in flames. In fact, the charge was so great that the robbers could not even approach the mail car. Their attempt to rob it was therefore a failure; furthermore, they had incinerated the lone clerk inside.

Before the trio could leave, a brakeman who had heard the explosion came running forward through the tunnel. Perhaps out of frustration, perhaps to prevent identification, the bandits shot down the three railroaders in cold blood, bringing the death toll to four, and fled.

Enter the Detective

Immediately after the tragedy, county lawmen, railroad police, postal detectives, and other authorities descended on the scene. They found a detonating device equipped with batteries. Nearby were a revolver and a well-worn and greasy pair of blue denim overalls, as well as some shoe covers made out of burlap soaked in creosote, evidently intended to be worn by the bandits to throw bloodhounds off their scent. It appeared that the criminals had used some alternative false-scent tactic, because posses utilizing canine trackers were stopped cold. After several weeks, all the investigators had come up with was a mechanic from a garage some miles away who, not surprisingly, worked in grease. The grime on his clothes appeared to be similar to the grease found on the overalls. He was questioned at length, but he kept insisting he was innocent. Then someone finally suggested, "Let's see if that fellow Heinrich in Berkeley can help us."

Edward Oscar Heinrich at 42 was a private investigator and handwriting expert who lectured at the University of California on scientific methods of criminal detection. He had already aided police all over the country in hundreds of cases, among them the Fatty Arbuckle manslaughter scandal, and he was commonly known as the "Edison of crime detection." To call him a private detective was indeed a put-down. He was, rolled into one, a geologist, a physicist, a biochemist, a handwriting expert, and an authority on papers and inks. According to Heinrich, the scene of a criminal act always contains many clues, and it is up to a scientific investigator to find and interpret those clues correctly.

The Chase

The first thing Heinrich did was to make a microscopic examination of the overalls and their "contents," such as the dried grease stains and lint from the pockets. He then ordered the mechanic released. "The stains are not auto grease. They're pitch from fir trees. The man you are looking for," he told awed detectives, "is a left-handed lumberjack who's worked the logging camps of the Pacific Northwest. He's thin, has light brown hair, rolls his own cigarettes, is fussy about his appearance. He's 5 ft. 10 in. and is in his early 20s."

None of this was guesswork. Heinrich had found everything out during his laboratory tests. He readily identified the stains as pitch from fir trees, and in the pockets he found bits of Douglas fir needles, common to the forests of the Pacific Northwest. The pockets on the left side of the overalls were worn more than those on the right, and the garment was habitually buttoned from the left side. Hence, the man was left-handed. In the hem of a pocket were two or three fingernail trimmings, carefully cut, indicating that the man was fussy about his appearance. On one button, the scientists found a single light-brown hair. It indicated the man's coloring, of course; even more important, though, through special techniques Heinrich had devised, he was able to compute the man's age by the thickness and character of this single hair.

Heinrich had a final clue, which other investigators had totally overlooked. Wedged at the bottom of the narrow pencil pocket was a small wad of paper, apparently accidentally jammed down by a pencil and washed with the garment several times. The printing on the slip had been blurred past all legibility, but by treating the paper with iodine vapor, Heinrich succeeded in identifying it as registered mail receipt #263-L, issued at Eugene, Ore.

The Solution

Heinrich's work was now completed, and postal and other detectives took over. They found that the mail receipt had been obtained by Roy D'Autremont of Eugene when he sent $50 to his brother in Lakewood, N.M. Authorities located Roy's father in Eugene. It turned out that the elder D'Autremont was worried about his twin sons, Roy and Ray, and another son, Hugh, who had disappeared on Oct. 11, the date of the train holdup. Left-handed Roy fit all the characteristics Heinrich had cited. What followed was one of the most intensive manhunts in American history. Over the next three years and four months, half a million dollars was spent searching for the trio. Circulars were printed in 100 languages and mailed to police departments around the world. Records of the wanted men's teeth, eyeglass prescriptions, and medical records were supplied to dentists, oculists, and doctors. Finally in March, 1927, Hugh was captured in Manila in the Philippines, and a month later the twins were found in Steubenville, O., working in a steel mill under assumed names. Faced with Heinrich's evidence, the three brothers pleaded guilty and were sentenced to life imprisonment.

Edward Heinrich went back to his laboratory. By the time of his death in 1953 he was credited with having solved 2,000 major and minor mysteries for the police, when they had been baffled by what they considered a lack of clues.

MAXIMILIAN LANGSNER AND THE MURDERER'S MIND (1928)

The Crime

On the evening of July 8, 1928, the Royal Canadian Mounted Police received a panicky telephone call from Dr. Harley Heaslip, who reported a mass murder on a farm some 5 mi. outside of Mannville,

Alberta, where the wealthy Booher family lived, along with their hired hands. "Half of them have been murdered," Heaslip said. Constable Fred Olsen went to the scene immediately and found the body of Mrs. Rose Booher slumped over the dining room table. She had been shot in the back of the head. In the kitchen lay the body of her elder son, Fred, shot three times in the face. An inspection of the bunkhouse and barn turned up two more corpses, hired hands who could conceivably have heard the first shots and seen the killer. Since Mrs. Booher was killed while picking stems from a batch of strawberries, she was obviously the first victim, for she would hardly have gone on hulling strawberries if she had heard her son being murdered in the next room. Clearly, Fred had heard a shot and had come to the door to investigate. There the killer had shot him. Then the killer had marched outside and eliminated the two hired hands so that they could never tell what, if anything, they had heard or seen.

Henry Booher and his younger son, Vernon, had spent the afternoon working separately on different parts of the farm, and the two daughters in the family had been in town. Neither of the two male Boohers had paid any attention to the shots because they were common in the country, especially just then when foxes were on the prowl.

Enter the Detective

The police, under Inspector James Hancock, head of the Bureau of Criminal Investigation at Edmonton, and Detective Jim Leslie, arrived the next day to take charge of the case. Nothing had been stolen, and judging by what Mrs. Booher had been doing at the time of the crime, it was also clear the murderer was neither a stranger nor an intruder. Indeed, the fact that the killer had hunted out the men in the barn and bunkhouse confirmed this. The murder weapon was not found, but it was identified as a .303 Lee Enfield rifle, and such a weapon had been reported stolen from the home of a neighboring farmer, Charles Stevenson. The killer obviously knew his way about the Stevenson home as well, since the weapon was always hidden in a closet. Everything pointed back to the surviving Boohers. But which one? Henry Booher appeared totally crushed by the tragedy; however, Vernon seemed strangely unmoved. Police inquiries unearthed the fact that Vernon had recently expressed hatred for his mother because she had broken up his romance with a local girl. Although Vernon was taken into custody, he refused to make a statement, and without the murder weapon the police had no case.

With the investigation still stymied after several weeks of investigation, Inspector Hancock did a strange thing for a professional policeman. He risked public ridicule by bringing in a Vienna-born mind reader who was then demonstrating his art in Vancouver. Maximilian Langsner had studied psychology with Freud in Vienna and later had gone to India, where he researched the way yogis attempted to control the mind. According to Langsner, the human mind, under stress, produces signals that another trained mind can learn to pick up. Newspaper accounts of his career told of the aid he had given European police in solving crimes. For instance, he had assisted the Berlin police in the recovery of some stolen jewels. To do this, he had sat facing the suspect for some time, until he got a "signal" telling him where the jewels were hidden. Following Langsner's instructions, the police found the loot, and the thief confessed. Remarkably, Langsner had recently duplicated this feat in a similar case in Vancouver.

The Chase

Langsner, a dapper little man of 35 who resembled screen actor Adolphe Menjou, arrived in Edmonton a few days later. After being briefed, he was taken by the inspector to confront Vernon Booher. Following a quick, silent meeting with the prisoner, Langsner told Hancock, "The rifle is unimportant. He is guilty. He admitted it to me."

Hancock reminded Langsner that this was not proof, and added that if they could locate the Enfield, they would probably get a confession. Langsner placed a chair outside the suspect's cell and sat there staring at 21-year-old Vernon Booher. He explained to Hancock that the prisoner would know he wanted to determine where the rifle was and so would start thinking of it, thus giving off the proper impulses. Finally, after a five-hour period during which Booher alternately sat quietly and screamed at the mentalist, Langsner left the cell block. He had his information.

The Solution

Langsner sketched a farmhouse, a number of bushes, and some trees. Then he sketched more bushes some 500 yd. from the house and said the rifle was buried there. The building Langsner described was white with red shutters—the Booher place. When Langsner and the officers went to the farm, they quickly located the bushes the mind reader had sketched. Within moments the .303 Enfield was found buried under the soft sod. Brought to the scene and confronted with the rifle, Vernon Booher broke down and confessed, as his tearful father and sisters watched. He had only meant to shoot his mother, but when his brother Fred rushed into the house, Vernon knew he had to kill him too. Vernon expressed remorse only for the death of his brother. He shrugged off the murder of the handymen as merely part of a necessary cover-up.

Vernon Booher—the man who, according to Langsner, could not "escape his own thoughts"—was hanged for quadruple murder on Apr. 26, 1929. As for Maximilian Langsner, whose work in the case was fully reported in the newspapers of the time thanks to a grateful Inspector Hancock, he left Vancouver shortly thereafter to spend the next several years conducting psychic research among the Eskimos. The little Austrian was last heard of in 1939, as he prepared to launch a tour of the Middle East.

TAMEGORO IKII AND THE BANK POISONING MASSACRE (1948)

The Crime

The doors of the Teikoku Bank in the bustling Shiina-machi district of Tokyo, Japan, were about to close at 3:30 P.M. on Jan. 26, 1948, when a thin, distinguished-looking man wearing a loose-fitting white coat with an official-looking armband bearing the word "Sanitation" on it pushed inside. At his urgent request he was ushered into the office of the acting bank manager, Takejiro Yoshida. Once there, he explained that he was a civilian doctor attached to Gen. Douglas MacArthur's staff, and that he had been sent to immunize the bank's employees against amoebic dysentery, which had become rife in the area.

The bank officer had no objection. In postwar Tokyo the drastic shortage of food had resulted in numerous cases of food poisoning; in fact, Yoshida's superior had gone home early that day with an upset stomach. Then, too, civilians were used to following the orders of the occupying powers. At the time, MacArthur was often referred to as Shogun MacArthur.

The "doctor" told the entire staff plus Yoshida to bring their teacups, which he filled with a liquid he said offered better immunization than an injection. He said some of them might find their throats irritated for a moment, and for them he had a second liquid to relieve the discomfort. He instructed everyone to drink quickly, since he had many other places to visit and was pressed for time. As they drank, many were overcome with excruciating pain and dropped to the floor. Only Yoshida, two other men, and one woman would survive.

The bogus doctor stepped over the bodies and went to the tills, picking up 164,400 yen and an uncashed check for 17,405 yen, or a total of just over $500, in exchange for a dozen lives.

Enter the Detective

At 43, Tamegoro Ikii was one of Tokyo's crack investigators, having solved his share of murder and robbery cases. When several weeks of inquiry by teams of investigators turned up only dead ends, Ikii was ordered to drop his other assignments and concentrate on the poison-in-the-teacup affair.

The Chase

At first all the police could discover about the worst crime committed in postwar Japan was that it had been preceded by two apparent "rehearsals" at other banks. During one, the murderer had given the bank manager a card which identified him as Dr. Shigeru Matsui. (He had presented a card imprinted with a different name to the bank official in the fatal robbery, but he had reappropriated it.) These earlier guinea pigs had drunk the proffered liquid and suffered no ill effects. The doctor left, promising that a military health team would check up on the bank later, but none did. Since no crime was apparent, however, no one reported the incident.

The exchange of calling cards has an important meaning in Japan, and custom calls for each party to retain cards so received. When the police tracked down the real Dr. Matsui, he said he had had 100 such cards printed and had only 4 left. He had exchanged about 50 and given the rest to patients. Because he could not remember which patients, the police questioned all of them. Ikii was convinced the solution lay in the 50 calling cards Dr. Matsui had exchanged with businessmen, fellow doctors, and other acquaintances. He questioned and requestioned the recipients and surreptitiously checked the financial condition of each of them. That led eventually to the most likely suspect in Ikii's view, an artist of some renown whom the doctor had met on a ferry. Fifty-year-old Sadamichi Hirasawa, who lived on the Japanese island of Hokkaido, had been interrogated earlier and dropped as a suspect because he was so quiet and mild-mannered. However, Ikii discovered that the artist had actually been in Tokyo at the time of the crime, and a further check of his movements showed that he could have been at the Teikoku Bank at the crucial moment. Ikii also discovered that Hirasawa needed money badly, and that shortly after the robbery 44,500 yen had been deposited in his bank account. Ikii was by then convinced that Hirasawa was his man, because he felt the plot was not only heinous but so bizarre that it would take an artist's mind to conceive it. No one else on the suspect list qualified.

Sadamichi Hirasawa.

The Solution

Although ordered by his superiors to drop the artist as a suspect, Ikii persisted. He believed no murderer could conceal the facts without telling little lies. Hirasawa claimed the money he deposited in the bank came from one of his artistic benefactors—the patronage system was still much in use in Japan—but Ikii learned that actually this man had died two months earlier. During his meetings with the suspect, Ikii treated him with the utmost respect and even asked him for an autographed photo of himself. Hirasawa said he had none, which Ikii knew had to be another lie; all artists used photographs to promote their careers. Before escorting the suspect to a restaurant, the officer phoned the hostess there and asked her to have photos taken as he and his guest said good-bye. But in one the artist dropped his gaze and in the other he distorted his face, so the survivors of the massacre could not identify Hirasawa from the pictures.

Finally, the detective caught Hirasawa in a lie that all of the other investigators had overlooked. He had said he no longer had Dr. Matsui's card because the card had been in the pocket of an overcoat that had been stolen in a Tokyo restaurant the previous May. Ikii pounced on that, charging the artist with a string of deceptions, the supposed theft of the overcoat being the capping one. No one in Tokyo, he pointed out, wore an overcoat in the steamy month of May.

The artist eventually cracked and made a full confession. He also admitted that the so-called rehearsals had been tries at the real thing, but that his mixture of potassium cyanide had been too weak to kill. At his trial Hirasawa retracted his confession, saying the police had not allowed him to sleep until he made a statement. In a Japan mindful of democratic reforms, the defendant's charge was taken seriously, even though few crimes had enraged the public as much as the mass poisoning. Defense leagues were organized for the artist, and they pointed out that some of the survivors were shaky in their identification of Hirasawa. Nonetheless, the artist was found guilty and sentenced to be hanged. Many Japanese, however, fought against any resumption of the death penalty. As a result the case dragged through one appeal after another, and Hirasawa still has not been executed. Now in his 80s, he is the oldest man on death row anywhere in the world. While many people fought to prevent the execution of Hirasawa, many others lionized Officer Ikii. When he retired in 1964, he held the rank of inspector and was often hailed in the streets as a celebrity—a gesture decidedly out of character for the normally reserved Japanese people.

—C.S.

YOU, THE JURY

The Leo Frank Case (1913)

The Murder: At 3:00 A.M. on Sunday morning, Apr. 27, 1913, night watchman Newt Lee was walking through the basement of the National

Pencil Co. in Atlanta, Ga. Suddenly the beam from his lantern, piercing the darkness, fell upon the battered body of a young girl. Appalled, Lee rushed upstairs to phone the police. The investigation that followed determined the identity of the victim: Mary Phagan, a 13-year-old factory employee. Two mysterious notes, hastily scrawled on rough scraps of yellow paper, were also discovered. These notes apparently had been written by the slain girl (later they proved not to be in her handwriting). They accused "that long tall black negro" of sexual misconduct with Mary. A search of the building uncovered what appeared to be bloodstains, as well as strands of Mary Phagan's hair, in a shop on the second floor where pencils were cut. The police, reconstructing the crime, theorized that she had been attacked in this room, that she had fallen and struck her head on a lathe, and that her attacker had gone berserk. The murderer had beaten her first, then strangled her. Afterward, frightened and confused, he had dumped her corpse in the basement.

The Accused: "That long tall black negro" mentioned in the two notes sounded like the night watchman, and he was immediately arrested. However, he withstood a grilling at police headquarters so well that his interrogators concluded that he was not only innocent but the object of an attempted frame-up by the guilty party.

Now the police turned to another suspect. Two days after the discovery of the murder they arrested Leo Frank, a part owner of the pencil factory who also held the position of superintendent. Frank was suspected for several reasons. To begin with, he had an office near the presumed murder room, and his accusers charged that he could not have been unaware of the violent crime committed there at around noon on Apr. 26, the time of the atrocity according to medical experts.

When questioned, a number of Frank's female employees said that he had made "immoral" advances toward them. Moreover, although Frank insisted that he had not known Mary Phagan, it turned out that she had gone to his office to collect her weekly salary on the day she died.

There were other factors in the case against Leo Frank. Originally from New York, he was a Northerner among Southerners. He also ran a factory and was therefore a capitalist among an essentially agrarian people. Moreover, he was a Jew among Protestant fundamentalists. For these reasons, many Georgians disliked him intensely and had found him guilty in their own minds long before he went to trial.

The Prosecution's Points: At Frank's trial, Solicitor General Hugh M. Dorsey directed the prosecution. Having lost some recent cases, Dorsey needed a conviction to restore his reputation, and he went all out to convict Leo Frank. Judge Leonard S. Roan, although presiding impartially, had to struggle to maintain order in the court because of the many unruly anti-Frank spectators. The key prosecution witness was Jim Conley, a black sweeper at the factory. Conley testified under oath that on the day of the murder he had seen Mary Phagan go upstairs and later had heard a scream. After an interval, Frank had summoned him with a whistle and had shown him the girl's dead body. Frank then ordered Conley to help transport the body to the basement in the elevator, and got him to scribble the notes intended to incriminate Newt Lee. Frank had suggested that Conley burn the body in the basement furnace, but Conley refused to do this because Frank would not help him. Conley told the court that he had couched his refusal thus: "Mr. Frank, you are a white man and you done it, and I am not going down there and burn that myself." As a result, the corpse of Mary Phagan remained where the night watchman later found it.

The Defense's Points: The attorney directing Frank's defense was Luther Z. Rosser, an experienced trial lawyer who was generally considered the most astute member of the Georgia bar at cross-examining a witness. Rosser countered charges of the defendant's immorality by calling witnesses who testified to Frank's good character. The lawyer also tried to establish an alibi for his client. Acquaintances verified that Frank was under observation constantly except for a gap of some 20 minutes, scarcely enough time, Rosser told the jury, for him to complete the deed. Most of all, the defense attorney impugned Jim Conley's damaging testimony. For three days Rosser and his assistant put the factory sweeper through a stringent point-by-point cross-examination in an effort to get him to contradict himself. They failed to expose more than minor discrepancies in his story, but they argued that this merely proved that he had memorized it. Taking the stand himself, Frank labeled Conley's accusation "a tissue of lies."

Your Verdict: In summing up for the defense, Rosser denounced the climate of hysteria and bigotry surrounding the trial and accused the prosecution of misrepresenting the evidence. The defense likened the Frank case in Georgia to the Dreyfus case in France, in which, due to anti-Semitism, a Jewish army officer was condemned to Devil's Island as the result of a forged document. The defense's opinion was widely shared by many eminent Americans as the trial drew nationwide attention. The prosecution, in rebuttal, rejected any comparisons between Frank and Dreyfus and emphasized the failure of the defense to shake Conley's testimony. Dorsey ended his summing-up with the intonation: "Guilty, guilty, guilty!" Judge Roan then delivered his charge to the jury, and the jurors retired to decide their verdict. Leo Frank: Guilty or Not Guilty? Now it is up to you, the reader, playing jury, to make up your own mind as to whether or not the defendant killed Mary Phagan. What is your verdict? Does it agree with the real-life verdict below?

The Real-Life Verdict: After deliberating for less than four hours, the jury returned. The foreman rose to his feet and, being asked by the judge for the verdict, replied: "Guilty!" Roan polled the jurors individually. Each answered as had the foreman: "Guilty!" The following day Roan sentenced Frank to be executed for murder. The defendant's lawyers, stigmatizing the proceedings as "a farce," appealed all the way to the Supreme Court. Every appeal failed, but Georgia's Gov. John M. Slaton commuted Frank's sentence to life imprisonment. The governor acted primarily because he learned that the lawyer for Jim Conley (who served a year on a Georgia chain gang as an accessory after the fact in the Phagan murder) considered Conley guilty. Frank was sent to the prison farm at Milledgeville, Ga., where he wrote letters to his partisans proclaiming his faith that one day he would be vindicated and released.

That day never came. On Aug. 16, 1915, a lynch mob broke into the prison farm, overpowered the warden and his staff, and kidnapped Leo Frank. They drove him into the Georgia woods, produced a rope, and called on him to confess his guilt. Instead, he maintained his innocence so strenuously that two members of the lynch mob wanted him to be returned to the prison farm. The rest refused. They summarily hanged their captive from the branch of an oak tree, a crime for which no one was ever punished.

—V.B.

The Hall-Mills Case (1926)

The Murder: On the afternoon of Sept. 16, 1922, a young couple strolling in De Russey's Lane near New Brunswick, N.J., stumbled across the bodies of a man and woman. The man, dressed in a suit and a clerical collar, had been shot once in the head. The woman, who wore a blue polka-dot dress, lay beside him. There was a triangle of bullet holes in her forehead. Her throat had been cut and her tongue, larynx, and trachea had been neatly excised.

The man was identified as the Rev. Edward Wheeler Hall, age 41, pastor of St. John the Evangelist, a fashionable Episcopal church in New Brunswick. The woman was Mrs. Eleanor Mills, 34, wife of the sexton in Reverend Hall's church and a member of the church choir.

Scattered around the bodies were a number of torrid love letters written by Mrs. Mills and addressed to the clergyman. "I know there are girls with more shapely bodies, but I do not care what they have," read one. "I have the greatest of all blessings, the deep, true, and eternal love of a noble man. My heart is his, my life is his, all that I have is his . . . I am his forever."

The Accused: Because of the intimate relationship between the victims, suspicion naturally focused on their families. But the investigation was, according to one observer, "shot through from beginning to end with incompetent bungling." No suspects were indicted during the next four years, and had it not been for the prodding of the New York *Daily Mirror*, the case might have been closed.

In July, 1926, the Hearst paper printed a petition for the annulment of the marriage between Arthur S. Riehl and Louise Geist—a former maid at Reverend Hall's residence. In his petition, Mr. Riehl stated that his wife of 10 months had withheld from him the following information: On the night of the murder, Miss Geist had informed Mrs. Hall that her husband and Mrs. Mills were planning to elope. The Halls' chauffeur then drove Mrs. Hall and her brother Willie, who lived with them, to De Russey's Lane. Louise Geist was paid $5,000 to be quiet.

Although this story was later denied by both Miss Geist and the Halls' chauffeur, other witnesses came forth and the *Mirror* continued to run front-page articles about the unsolved murder. Under public pressure, Gov. A. Harry Moore ordered the case reopened.

Finally, on July 28, the clergyman's widow, the former Francess Noel Stevens, was accused of committing the double murder. The staid

Jane Gibson, the Pig Woman, testifying from her sickbed in court.

daughter of a socially prominent family, she had been seven years older than her philandering husband. Charged with her were her two brothers, Willie and Henry Stevens. Willie, swarthy and bushy-haired, was an eccentric who could find nothing better to do than hang around the firehouse. Henry was prim and respectable, the model of a country-club gentleman. Also arrested—but held over for a separate trial—was their cousin, Henry Carpender, a distinguished New York stockbroker.

The Prosecution's Points: The trial opened on Nov. 3 in the Somerset County Courthouse in rural Somerville and lasted for a month, fueling the tabloid headlines every day. Justice Charles W. Parker, of the state supreme court, presided. He was assisted by a local justice named Frank A. Cleary.

The special prosecutor was Alexander Simpson, an ambitious state senator who made up in melodramatics what he lacked in solid evidence. Early in the trial he established the torrid relationship between the clergyman and the choir singer by calling to the stand the dead woman's 20-year-old daughter, Charlotte, a flapper who reveled in the limelight. She identified the love letters of Reverend Hall and Mrs. Mills, which Mrs. Mills had stored in a crocheted bag in her living room. The bag also held a diary kept by the minister.

Prosecutor Simpson presented one of Reverend Hall's calling cards, found at the scene of the murder, and experts identified the fingerprints on it as those of Willie Stevens. But the prints were later proved to have been fraudulently superimposed.

Then came the most sensational moment of the trial. Simpson called Mrs. Jane Gibson, who claimed to be an eyewitness to the murders. Because she owned a pig farm near the lovers' lane, she had been dubbed "the Pig Woman" in the press. On the first day of the trial she had collapsed of what was diagnosed as a severe stomach ailment and had had to be hospitalized. When she testified on Nov. 18, she was carried into court on a stretcher.

On the night of the murders, she said, while she was looking for a thief who'd been stealing her corn, she heard several people having an argument. First one woman demanded, "Explain these letters." Then there were the sounds of a scuffle. Finally a shot and the voices of two women.

"One said: 'Oh, Henry,' easy, very easy; and the other began to scream, scream, scream so loud, 'Oh my, oh my, oh my.' So terrible loud . . . that woman was screaming, screaming, trying to run away or something; screaming, screaming, and I just about got my foot in the stirrup [of the saddle on her mule] when bang! bang! bang!—three quick shots."

From her stretcher she identified Mrs. Hall, the Stevens brothers, and Henry Carpender as the people she had seen.

The Defense's Points: The defense was headed by Robert H. McCarter, a former state attorney general and a leading light of the New Jersey bar. He was assisted by attorney Clarence Case, who had little trouble pointing out the many contradictions in Mrs. Gibson's account. He even showed that Mrs. Gibson was confused about her own names and marriages.

Nor did it help Mrs. Gibson when her own mother, who had a front-row seat in the courtroom, shouted, "She's a liar, a liar, a liar! That's what she is and what she's always been."

But as she was carried from the court, the Pig Woman propped herself up on the stretcher and shouted to the defendants: "I told the truth, so help me God. And you know it, you know it, you know it!"

The rest of the trial was an anticlimax. Henry Stevens testified that he was fishing miles away on the night of the murders, and three witnesses corroborated his account.

On the 19th day of the trial Mrs. Hall took the stand. McCarter asked her point-blank: "Now, Mrs. Hall, did you kill your husband or Mrs. Mills?"

"I did not."

"Did you play any part in that dreadful tragedy?"

"I did not."

"Were you in the neighborhood of De Russey's Lane or that vicinity on the night of Sept. 14, 1922?"

"I was not."

Willie Stevens's previous testimony agreed with his sister's account of their movements on the night of the murders.

Your Verdict: The closing arguments matched each other in vituperation. The defense intimated that many others could have committed the crime—even the Pig Woman herself!—while Simpson called Mrs. Hall "a Messalina," "a Lucretia Borgia," and "a Bloody Mary."

Guilty or not guilty? It's up to you, the reader, to play jury. What is your verdict? And what was the real-life verdict? Look below.

The Real-Life Verdict: On Dec. 3, 1926, after five hours' deliberation, the jury found all three defendants not guilty. The charges against Carpender were subsequently dropped. Gov. A. Harry Moore summed up popular sentiment when he said: "I think the state has gone far enough. It's prosecution, not persecution, we want."

Although new theories have surfaced from time to time, the case of the minister and the choir singer remains unsolved.

—P.H.

The Jeffrey MacDonald Case (1979)

The Murders: In the early morning hours of Feb. 17, 1970, Mrs. Colette MacDonald, 26, and her two daughters, six-year-old Kimberly and two-year-old Kristen, were brutally murdered in their home at 544 Castle Drive in the junior officers' housing section of Fort Bragg, N.C. Mrs. MacDonald, then five months pregnant, was struck with a club and stabbed repeatedly with a knife and an ice pick. The girls also suffered multiple stab wounds. The word *pig* was scrawled in blood across the headboard of Mrs. MacDonald's bed. Her husband, Capt. Jeffrey MacDonald, also 26, survived a blow on the head and more than a dozen stab wounds—all superficial except for one that grazed his right lung—to telephone the military police at 3:42 A.M. and to describe later in vague terms four drug-crazed hippie intruders who, he said, overpowered him and murdered his family while chanting, "Acid is groovy. Kill the pigs!" Captain MacDonald claimed that one black and two white males and a blond girl holding a candle and wearing a floppy hat and muddy boots committed the crimes. Investigators discovered no evidence of forced entry but found a back door unlocked and two paring knives, an ice pick, an 18-in. club, and a candle about the premises.

The Accused: A native of Patchogue, Long Island, N.Y., Jeffrey MacDonald won a scholarship to Princeton University, which he breezed through in three years. While a student at Princeton he got his childhood sweetheart Colette pregnant; they married in September, 1963, six months before daughter Kimberly's birth. The couple moved to Chicago, where Jeffrey attended Northwestern University Medical School. Graduating in 1968, he interned at Columbia Presbyterian Medical Center in New York and enlisted in the U.S. Army. He served as a narcotics specialist with the Green Berets at Fort Bragg. His marriage to Colette appears to have been a happy one for the first three or four years. But when Colette's mother and stepfather, Mr. and Mrs. Alfred Kassab, visited the MacDonalds at Christmas in 1969, they noticed a palpable strain in the couple's relationship. In addition, shortly before the murders Colette had complained to her mother that she was unhappy about being pregnant again.

On Oct, 28, 1970, following a months-long closed hearing to determine whether sufficient evidence existed to court-martial MacDonald for the murder of his family, the army exonerated him and, at his request, granted him an honorable discharge. MacDonald then moved west to become a highly respected director of emergency surgery at St. Mary Medical Center at Long Beach, Calif., and an honorary member of that city's police association. But while he was busy putting his life back together, his former father-in-law, Alfred Kassab, became suspicious. Kassab had staunchly defended MacDonald during the army hearing, but as he poured over the 2,000-page transcript of the hitherto secret proceedings, he was troubled by certain testimony. For example, MacDonald claimed that he did not own an ice pick, but Kassab had seen one in the MacDonald house. Also, during the hearing MacDonald suggested that a hairbrush which contained hair that did not come from Colette MacDonald's head had been left at the murder scene by the female intruder. The Kassabs, however, recognized the hairbrush as one that Mrs. Kassab forgot to pack at the end of their last visit. With such questions nagging at him, Kassab launched a crusade to bring MacDonald to trial. His efforts touched off a chain of events that in 1975 led a federal grand jury in Raleigh, N.C., to indict MacDonald on three counts of murder. In March, 1979, the U.S. Supreme Court denied MacDonald's second appeal to quash the indictment and ordered him to stand trial in federal court in Raleigh. The trial opened July 16, 1979.

The Prosecution's Points: Federal prosecutors set out to prove that MacDonald had killed his wife during a heated argument and, while still in a rage, murdered their older daughter, perhaps accidentally. When he had calmed down, he concocted the tale of drug-crazed hippie intruders, a fabrication inspired by the Charles Manson cult slayings the previous year. To bolster his story, prosecutors charged, he entered his younger daughter's bedroom and in cold blood stabbed her to death. After scrawling the word *pig* on his wife's headboard, he allegedly drew on his medical knowledge to stab himself repeatedly without inflicting any permanent damage. The prosecution placed on the stand Paul Stombaugh, a former FBI forensic expert, who testified that MacDonald's blue pajama top had been lying over his wife's torso while she was being stabbed and that the number of holes in the pajama top corresponded to the number of stab wounds suffered by Mrs. MacDonald. Investigators testified that a bloody footprint leading from the younger daughter's bedroom could have been that of the defendant. Richard Tevere, one of the military police who responded to MacDonald's emergency call that night, told the court that he had discovered on the scene a bloodstained issue of *Esquire* magazine, which contained an account of the Manson murders, thus encouraging the belief that MacDonald had sought to simulate a cult slaying. During cross-examination prosecutors confronted MacDonald with the club used to strike his wife and scored points with the jury when the accused was unable to offer any explanation as to why threads from his pajama top were found on the club and in the bedrooms.

The Defense's Points: Dr. Jeffrey MacDonald consistently maintained his innocence and stuck to his story that four intruders surprised him as he lay sleeping on the living room sofa. The defense contended that the footprint leading from the younger daughter's bedroom had been made by a careless investigator, not the defendant. As for the pajama top, it had been torn during a brief struggle with the intruders, and MacDonald later placed it over his wife's body to cover her wounds. The jury was impressed with the testimony of James Milne, Jr., who was a neighbor of the MacDonalds' in 1970 and who told the court that he had seen a blond girl with a candle in her hand walking near the MacDonald home about 12:00 A.M. on the night of the killings. Then the defense called a surprise witness, Helena Stoeckley, who testified that she had been high on mescaline on Feb. 17, 1970, and could not account for her whereabouts or actions that evening. She stated further that she vaguely recalled seeing a man sleeping on a couch and admitted owning a blond wig, a hat, and a pair of boots similar to those described by the defendant. With the jury out of the courtroom, six other witnesses testified to the credibility of Stoeckley's story. Each witness had personally talked to Stoeckley about the murders. But the accounts varied greatly. As a result, Judge Franklin T. Dupree, Jr., put restrictions on further testimony concerning Stoeckley's "out-of-court" statements, saying that she was a chronic drug user and a "tragic figure."

Your Verdict: Did Jeffrey MacDonald murder his wife and children and then, in a paroxysm of self-preservation, set the stage to look like a cult slaying? The pajama top, the footprint, and the superficiality of the majority of Dr. MacDonald's wounds all point to his guilt. But what about the blond girl seen lurking about the premises that night? And how could even a surgeon ensure that multiple self-inflicted stab wounds—including one thrust that reached the lungs—would not be fatal? What is your verdict? Does it agree with the jury's verdict below?

The Real-Life Verdict: On Aug. 29, 1979, after deliberating for 6½ hours, the jury found Dr. Jeffrey MacDonald guilty of second-degree murder in the deaths of his wife and older daughter and of first-degree murder in the death of his younger daughter. Judge Dupree sentenced him to three consecutive life terms. MacDonald's motion to remain free pending appeal was denied. He had served less than a year at the Federal Correctional Institution at Terminal Island when, on July 30, 1980, a three-judge panel of the 4th U.S. Circuit Court of Appeals in Richmond, Va., voted 2 to 1 to overturn his conviction on the grounds that the nine-year lapse between the crime and the trial constituted a violation of MacDonald's 6th Amendment right to a speedy trial. MacDonald was freed on Aug. 22, 1980, on $100,000 bond. Asked by reporters whether the court's decision might stigmatize him as a murderer set free on a legal technicality, Dr. MacDonald responded, "I don't think the Bill of Rights is a technicality. The charges are not true . . . I am not guilty, and there is no technicality involved." Prosecutors took the case to the Supreme Court which will render a decision in early 1982.

—W.A.D.

The Theodore Bundy Case (1979)

The Murders: In 1974, eight young women mysteriously disappeared

Ted Bundy acting as his own attorney.

from the streets of Seattle, lured into a beige Volkswagen by a personable man who called himself Ted. The ride always ended in the country, where the raped and bludgeoned corpses were dumped.

Then for a time the killer moved on to Utah, where he struck at random among the largely Mormon population. Young ladies who shunned liquor, coffee, and other vices were nevertheless paid off with the wages of sin—death.

Caryn Campbell, a nurse vacationing in Aspen, Colo., was missing for five weeks before her body was found in a snowbank on Feb. 17, 1975. She had been raped, beaten to death, and left to be gnawed almost beyond recognition by wild animals.

Lisa Levy was likewise gnawed by an animal, in this case her murderer, who left teeth marks on one of her breasts and on her buttocks. In January, 1978, she and Margaret Bowman, sorority sisters at the Chi Omega house in Tallahassee, Fla., were found beaten and strangled to death in their rooms. That same night, six blocks away, actress Cheryl Thomas was bludgeoned and raped in her bed. She lived but could recall nothing about her attacker.

One month after the Chi Omega killings, 12-year-old Kimberly Leach of Lake City, Fla., disappeared from her junior high school in the middle of the day. It was eight weeks before she was found, the victim of "homicidal violence to the neck region."

Police surmised that the same killer was responsible for from 18 to 36 murders spanning about four years and at least four states. The man they finally arrested hardly fitted the stereotype of a homicidal sex maniac.

The Accused: At the time of the Seattle murders, a police computer revealed that there were nearly 3,000 owners of light-colored Volkswagens in that city, and Ted Bundy was among them. A young man of apparently outstanding character, he seemed above suspicion and therefore was not questioned. Bundy had worked as a counselor at a crisis clinic, and while an assistant director of the Seattle Crime Prevention Advisory Commission, he authored a rape-prevention pamphlet for women. He once chased and apprehended a purse snatcher in a shopping mall, a deed which earned him a letter of commendation from the governor of Washington. He was very active in Republican party politics and had been named Mr. Up-and-Coming Republican. According to Ross Davis, a former Washington State Republican party chairman who was well acquainted with Bundy and had used him as an assistant: "If you can't trust someone like Ted Bundy, you can't trust anyone—your parents, your wife, anyone." In late 1974 Bundy moved from Seattle to Salt Lake City, where he attended law school and became a Mormon convert.

Then on Oct. 2, 1975, 19-year-old Carol DaRonch picked Bundy out of a police lineup and identified him as the man who had attempted to handcuff her and force her into his car one night in Murray, U., almost a year earlier. Bundy, who had had a pair of handcuffs in his car when he was stopped for a traffic violation, was adjudged guilty and sentenced to 1 to 15 years in prison. While investigating the DaRonch case, the police became convinced that Bundy was also involved in the murder of Caryn Campbell. In 1977 he was extradited from Utah to Colorado, but before he could be brought to trial in the Campbell case, he executed two daring escapes. The first escape occurred on June 7, when Bundy, left alone in a room in Pitkin County Courthouse in Aspen, jumped out of a second-story window. It took police seven days to capture him. Although he was suspected of committing a heinous crime, the daring fugitive was regarded as a folk hero in some circles, a reputation that endured throughout his future legal battles. On Dec. 30, Bundy again outwitted authorities when he escaped from his jail cell by crawling through a lighting panel in the ceiling. (He had to lose 35 lb. in order to fit into the 18-in. hole.)

Bundy fled cross-country to Tallahassee, Fla., where he moved into the Oak, a rooming house four blocks away from the Chi Omega sorority house. When Levy and Bowman were murdered, several residents of the Oak were suspects, but Bundy was not among them. During this period he became adept at stealing cars and credit cards. His precarious life-style was bound to collapse, and eventually he was arrested while driving a stolen VW in Pensacola. Bundy gave the police a phony name, and it was 36 hours before they realized who their prisoner really was. Five days earlier Ted Bundy had made the FBI's Ten Most Wanted list.

Once he was back in custody, he became a suspect in the Chi Omega killings. In June, 1979, he went on trial for the murders of Lisa Levy and Margaret Bowman. It was a landmark case for two reasons: first, because the state of Florida allowed cameras into the courtroom to record the proceedings; and second, because Bundy, a former law student, took an active part in his own defense. A year later he was tried for the murder of Kimberly Leach.

The Prosecution's Points: The first person to suspect Bundy's involvement in the Seattle murders was his former fiancée, Liz Kloepfer. In 1974 she told police that Bundy resembled a composite drawing of the killer, and that he had once been inspired by the book *The Joy of Sex* to tie her up and nearly strangle her. She added that his sex drive had decreased about the time the murders began. Some of the Seattle victims had reportedly been accosted by a man with a plaster cast on his arm. Kloepfer said that Bundy owned a fake arm cast. But the police considered her accusations merely sour grapes coming from a jilted girl friend. She was never summoned to testify against Bundy.

In speculating about Bundy's motive for the killings, it was observed that most of the victims bore some resemblance to a woman with whom he'd had a stormy, on-and-off relationship. She came from a wealthy California family, often paid for their dates, and was further ahead in college than he was. Bundy felt inferior to her in many ways and once admitted that they were "worlds apart." The killings began shortly after they broke up.

The evidence linking Bundy to the murder of Caryn Campbell was largely circumstantial: a ski brochure with a circle around the names of two lodges, one of them the Wildwood Inn, where Campbell was staying; and credit-card receipts that placed him in Aspen, Colo., at the time of the murder.

Likewise, credit-card receipts revealed that Bundy had spent the night previous to the murder of Kimberly Leach at a Holiday Inn in Lake City, Fla. Also, a stolen van he was driving at the time contained leaves and soil that matched samples taken at the girl's burial site. In addition, bloodstains found in the van matched the dead girl's blood type.

On Feb. 8, 1978, a 14-year-old Jacksonville girl was accosted by a man in a white van, who retreated when the girl's brother approached. The suspicious youngsters had copied down the van's license number, and that plate was found in the Volkswagen Bundy was driving when he was arrested in Pensacola.

In the Chi Omega case, the strongest piece of evidence was the imprint of human teeth on Lisa Levy's body. The marks were made by someone who had very crooked teeth, similar to Bundy's. Also, a hair found in a panty-hose mask left by Cheryl Thomas's assailant was indistinguishable from Bundy's.

The Defense's Points: Unlike fingerprints, bite marks cannot be considered hard evidence. Nor could the hair in the panty-hose mask be so considered, for although it was indistinguishable from Bundy's hair, it was also indistinguishable from the hair of four policemen and medical technicians who arrived at the scene after Thomas was attacked.

Analysis of a semen stain on Thomas's bed sheet and a piece of chewing gum in Levy's hair showed that their attacker was a "nonsecretor"—one whose bodily secretions do not reveal his blood type. Bundy, however, was shown to be a secretor.

The prosecution's mass of circumstantial evidence was further shown to link at least seven other men to some or all of the crimes for which Bundy was blamed. For example, another "Ted," a convicted sex offender, lived in Seattle at the time of the murders there and moved to Aspen before Caryn Campbell was killed. His co-workers at Snowmass, the resort development where Campbell was vacationing, say the man was violent toward women. He was absent from work the day Campbell was murdered; the next day he quit his job and left town. Furthermore, at a pretrial hearing in the Campbell case, before Bundy escaped from jail, an eyewitness who said she saw Bundy at the Wildwood Inn just before Campbell disappeared failed to identify him. Even in the DaRonch case, in which Bundy was convicted, there was another suspect who owned a pair of handcuffs, fit the description of DaRonch's assailant more closely than did Bundy, and later killed a Utah woman.

Throughout his legal ordeal, Bundy repeatedly proclaimed himself innocent of all charges. He accumulated a large following of people who thought likewise, including members of the legal profession and journalists who followed his trials.

Your Verdict: Is it necessarily out of character for a Mormon Republican to commit mass murder? What's your opinion? Was Ted Bundy guilty, or was he just unlucky enough to be caught in a web of circumstantial evidence? For the real-life verdict, read on.

The Real-Life Verdict: Ted Bundy was convicted of killing Lisa Levy, Margaret Bowman, and Kimberly Leach and was given three death sentences. After pronouncing the sentence in the Levy and Bowman cases, in which Bundy had assisted in his own defense, the judge said to him, "Take care of yourself. I say that to you sincerely. It's a tragedy to this court to see such a total waste of humanity. You're a bright young man. You'd have made a good lawyer. I'd have loved to have you practice in front of me." At the time of this writing, Ted Bundy is on death row in Florida, awaiting an appeal of his case.

—M.J.T.

THE GANGSTERS

ARIZONA CLARK "MA" BARKER (1871–1935)

Person: In her younger years "Ma" Barker was a rather dumpy fiddle player and Bible reader. In her 50s she was even dumpier, running to gray hair and fat.

Activities: Despite the usual, almost comic-book concept of her, Ma Barker was never in her life charged with a crime, and there are those who insist that despite FBI propaganda she was nothing more than a dim-witted woman who merely did whatever her sons wanted her to

(L to R) The ferocious Ma Barker and the ill-fated Arthur V. Dunlop.

do. However, it must be said that Ma certainly raised some antisocial sons. The four Barker boys were all vicious criminals.

Born in the Ozark Mountains near Springfield, Mo., Kate was raised in an outlaw tradition. Her greatest thrill as a small girl was seeing Jesse James ride past, and she wept bitterly when Bob Ford shot him in 1882. In 1892 Kate married farm laborer George Barker, who soon begat four monsters: Herman, who committed suicide at 33; Lloyd, who eventually served 25 years and then was killed by his wife; Arthur, who was shot while trying to escape from Alcatraz; and Freddie, the youngest and Ma's favorite. Home for the Barkers was generally a tar-paper shack in some small Missouri town. By 1910 the boys started turning up on police blotters. Sometimes Ma got them off by storming into the station and screaming or weeping, whichever tactic she reckoned would work best.

The boys went on to serious things like bank robberies. The FBI theory was that Ma planned their jobs, taught them getaway routes that she mapped out, and then stayed home and wept and prayed they wouldn't get hurt. Eventually all the boys did time. In 1927 Herman was so badly shot up by the police that he finished himself off with a bullet in the head. This tragedy, according to J. Edgar Hoover, who in the early years of his reign was given to purple prose, changed Ma "from an animal mother of the she-wolf type to a veritable beast of prey." On the other hand, Alvin "Creepy" Karpis—who joined the gang, became its leader, and finally was Public Enemy No. 1,—always insisted that an FBI hype turned Ma into "Bloody Mama" after she was killed. "We'd leave her at home when we were arranging a job, or we'd send her to a movie," he said. "Ma saw a lot of movies."

Leading Crimes: If Ma was a criminal brain, then she was the one who switched the gang from robbery to kidnapping and decided to abduct millionaires William A. Hamm, Jr., and Edward George Bremer, which netted a total of $300,000 in ransom.

Major Victims: If Ma ever killed anyone, it was probably her "loving man" Arthur Dunlop (a billboard painter), who in 1932 ended up ventilated with bullets and dumped in a lake. Then again, maybe the boys did it, unmindful of Ma's feelings, when they suspected Arthur of "ratting to the cops."

How Died: Ma died with Freddie in a famous four-hour shoot-out with the FBI at a hideout cottage in Florida on Jan. 16, 1935. Ma was manning a machine gun and ended up with one to three fatal bullets in her, according to various accounts. That's the FBI and Hollywood story. The counterversion has Ma stopping only one bullet—compared to Freddie's 14—and then committing suicide, while an embarrassed FBI took it from there. George Barker, who had left the family around 1927, buried Ma and Freddie in Welch, Okla. Of his wife and sons Barker later said: "She never would let me do with them what I wanted to."

ALPHONSE CAPONE (1899–1947)

See "Roots and Fruits: A Forest of Family Trees," Chap. 12.

CHARLES ARTHUR "PRETTY BOY" FLOYD (1901–1934)

Person: Floyd was born on a farm in northern Georgia but spent his earliest years in Oklahoma. Tall, heavyset, and handsome in a rugged, scowling sort of way, Floyd was long saddled with a nickname he despised. In Sallisaw, Okla., where he grew up, the hill folk were duly impressed by the fact he was never without a pocket comb. They studied his slick-as-axle-grease pompadour and dubbed him "Pretty Boy." Years later when he was deep in criminality, the nickname resurfaced even though he had tried to keep it secret. The name irritated Floyd right up to the moment he lay dying in an Ohio cornfield. Famed FBI agent Melvin Purvis stood over him and said, "You're Pretty Boy Floyd." The dying gangster flared, "I'm Charles Arthur Floyd."

Activities: Known as the Robin Hood of the Cookson Hills—an area with a long history of honoring the old western outlaws—Floyd, when not busy robbing banks and killing people (at least 10, half of them lawmen), really did give to the poor. He would often sprinkle money out of a car window for the Okies as he and his gang left the scene of a robbery. Unlike his counterparts—Dillinger, the Barker boys, Creepy Karpis, and "Baby Face" Nelson—Floyd had been a hard-working youth and probably never would have become a "public enemy" had he found work in the hard-pressed farm country of Oklahoma, which felt the Depression long before 1929. In the mid-1920s, with a pregnant wife to support, Floyd held up a bank, got caught, and went to prison for three years. When he got out, he gravitated to crime circles in Kansas City and took part in a number of robberies. A machine gun became his trademark. He eventually went "on the road" with a partner, a vicious gangster named Bill "the Killer" Miller. Miller died in a shoot-out in which Floyd killed one officer, wounded another, and escaped. He then hooked up with 40-year-old George Birdwell, an ex–church deacon turned outlaw. They committed a long string of robberies and killings. Today in large parts of Oklahoma Floyd is still revered as a hero. The bad things that happened, including cold-blooded murder, are always attributed to Birdwell. Part of the reason for this adulation of Floyd is that he was an Okie who helped other Okies. When robbing a bank, Floyd tore up all the first mortgages he could find, hoping they had not yet been recorded.

Leading Crimes: Floyd gained fame, not so much from his bank robberies, as for his ability to fight his way out of police traps. In 1930, while en route to the penitentiary by train, he escaped from his guards by plunging through a window and down an embankment.

Major Victims: The FBI always insisted Floyd was one of the machine gunners in the infamous Kansas City Massacre, in which four officers and a prisoner—Frank "Jelly" Nash—were killed. Floyd denied it and even wrote the newspapers protesting his innocence. His favorite victims were Oklahoma lawmen. He once wrote the sheriff in Sallisaw: "I'm coming to see my mother. If you're smart you won't try to stop me." The sheriff was smart.

How Died: On the run, Floyd was cornered by FBI agents in a cornfield near East Liverpool, O., on Oct. 22, 1934, and went down in a hail of gunfire. Asked about the Kansas City Massacre, he said, "I won't tell you nothing." He shut his mouth and died, one of the last men cast in the mold of "the American tradition of the social bandit," according to Prof. Richard Maxwell Brown.

GEORGE R. "MACHINE GUN" KELLY (1895–1954)

Person: This strapping six-footer with a round face and blue eyes seemed to wear a perpetual grin, except when he was talking tough or boasting. Suffering from a bad heart, Kelly was in no shape to do one tenth of the things he claimed he'd done—or were attributed to him by his wife, the law, or the press. Born in Memphis, Tenn., he died while incarcerated in Leavenworth Penitentiary.

Activities: George Kelly met Kathryn Shannon in 1927. Until then Kelly had been no more than an amiable, if less than competent, Oklahoma City bootlegger who spilled more than he delivered. By contrast, Kathryn was a firebrand out of the Mississippi backwoods who dreamed of riches and power and determined to make Kelly a top-flight criminal. Well versed in underworld affairs since her parents ran a ranch where fugitives could hole up for $50 a day, Kathryn began promoting Kelly as a fearless crook who was often "away robbing

The affable Machine Gun Kelly . . . and his press agent–wife Kathryn.

banks." She gave him a shiny machine gun as a present and made him practice shooting walnuts off fence posts. Kathryn, who understood promotion, also passed out cartridge cases in underworld dives, saying, "Have a souvenir of my husband, Machine Gun Kelly."

Kelly eventually made it into some local gangs and took part in a few holdups of small Mississippi and Texas banks. It was as much as he had ever hoped for, but Kathryn, who married Kelly in 1931, insisted they go after the big money in kidnapping. They pulled off only one major job and were promptly caught. A story put out by the FBI stated that when its agents trapped the couple in their Memphis hideout, Kelly cowered in a corner, his hands high, and whimpered: "Don't shoot, G-men, don't shoot." J. Edgar Hoover insisted that that was how his agents got their nickname, but the fact was that the Memphis cops on the raid heard Kelly say nothing of the kind and that employees of the federal government had long been called G-men. Cynics have also challenged the story, suggesting it was part of Hoover's efforts to enhance the image of the FBI and to solidify his own position as a shaky Republican holdover in a Democratic administration.

Leading Crimes: There was only one—the 1933 kidnapping of oilman Charles F. Urschel, from whom the gang collected $200,000. Kathryn opted for "killing the bastard" once they received the ransom, but Kelly, shocked, convinced the rest of the gang that Urschel had to be freed or it would "be bad for future business." As things turned out, Urschel proved to be a human memory machine; although he had been blindfolded, he was able to supply the FBI with so many clues that agents soon pinpointed his place of confinement as Kathryn's parents' ranch in Texas.

Major Victims: None. Machine Gun Kelly never killed anyone—or even fired his weapon in anger.
How Died: Sentenced to life in Alcatraz—and some say happy to be free of Kathryn—Kelly carried on a lengthy and remarkable correspondence with Urschel, once writing: "I must be fair. Being in prison has brought me one positive advantage. It could hardly do less. Its name is comradeship—a rough kindness of man to man; unselfishness; an absence, or diminution, of the tendency to look ahead, at least very far ahead; a carelessness, though it is bred of despair; a clinging to life and the possible happiness it may offer at some future date." Bothered by the Alcatraz climate, Kelly was transferred to Leavenworth, where he died of a heart attack three years later. Kathryn's life sentence was commuted in 1958, and she was released.

CHARLES "LUCKY" LUCIANO (1897–1962)

Person: An immaculate dresser, Luciano nevertheless always looked and talked like a thug. In 1929 he was scarred after being taken for a "ride" by kidnappers—identified by him variously as gangland rivals or rogue cops—who used a knife to sever all the muscles in his right cheek right down to the bone, leaving him with a drooping right eye that thereafter gave him a sinister appearance.
Activities: With the possible exception of Jewish mobster Meyer Lansky, Luciano was perhaps the most criminally intelligent gangster in America. Together they created a national crime syndicate which, despite public misconception, is greater than the Mafia. In fact, Luciano can be said to have killed off the Mafia. Brought to America by his family at the age of 9, Luciano didn't get arrested until he was 10, when he was caught shoplifting. In 1916 he was a full-fledged member of the notorious Five Points gang and was suspected of committing several murders. Early in life Luciano developed a contempt for the "Mustache Petes" who ruled the Mafia gangs, and by the late 1920s he was plotting their elimination. By 1930 Luciano was second-in-command under one of the two top Mafioso, "Joe the Boss" Masseria, who was gunned down in a Coney Island restaurant after Luciano had stepped into the toilet, as he said, "to wash my hands."

Luciano then became number two under Masseria's rival, Salvatore Maranzano, who was now the "boss of bosses." Luciano engineered Maranzano's assassination on Sept. 10, 1931, and in the following 24 hours an estimated 40 other Mustache Petes across the country were reportedly murdered in what became known as "the Night of the Sicilian Vespers." This marked the end of the Mafia, at least as a closed criminal society in America, and signaled its replacement with organized crime, made up of all ethnic elements.

The new crime syndicate included among its directors Meyer Lansky, head of the Bug and Meyer gang, which consisted of Bugsy Siegel, Joe Adonis, Dutch Schultz, Louis "Lepke" Buchalter, Frank Costello, and numerous Mafia crime families, but no boss of bosses. In actual fact, Luciano was the boss in everything but name. The syndicate controlled such operations as bootlegging, gambling, prostitution, narcotics, loansharking, and labor rackets.

Luciano's downfall started in 1936, when special prosecutor Thomas E. Dewey indicted him on charges of compulsory prostitution. Later, the underworld called this a "bum rap," claiming the police case was based on perjured evidence. Handed a 30-to-50-year sentence, Luciano exercised control over syndicate affairs from his cell until he was freed in 1946 and deported to Italy. His controversial release was justified as being a reward for his alleged "war services," especially for his ordering security tightened on the mob-controlled New York waterfront and enlisting the aid of the Mafia in Sicily prior to the Allied invasion. Luciano tried to sneak into Cuba to maintain his reign over American affairs, but he was finally forced back to Italy, where he issued orders and received his cut of racket profits through a stream of gangster couriers.

Leading Crimes: As head of the syndicate, Luciano had his finger in every major underworld murder. His killings were carried out by Albert Anastasia, the chief executioner of Murder, Inc., who worshiped Luciano. Years earlier, when Luciano was plotting the Masseria–Maranzano rubouts, Anastasia was overwhelmed with emotion when he was cut in on the plan. He grabbed Luciano in a bear hug and kissed him on both cheeks, saying, "Charlie, I been waitin' for this day for at least eight years. You're gonna be on top if I have to kill everybody for you."

Major Victims: Ironically, Luciano's most noteworthy crime saved the life of Tom Dewey. When Dewey started making waves, he zeroed in on mobster Dutch Schultz, who demanded that the syndicate "hit" the gangbuster. The idea was rejected on the grounds that Dewey's death would create more problems than it solved. Enraged, Schultz announced he'd carry out his plan alone. For crime's sake, Luciano ordered Schultz killed. Dewey, robbed of his prime target, promptly turned his sights on Luciano.

How Died: Taking a series of mistresses in his later years, the exiled Luciano suffered several heart attacks and was finally ordered by his doctors to refrain from all sexual activity with his current lover, a teenage girl. It is not known whether he followed orders. In 1962 he suffered a fatal heart attack at the Naples airport. Ultimately, Luciano was allowed back into the U.S.—for burial at St. John's Cathedral Cemetery in Queens, N.Y.

ROGER "THE TERRIBLE" TOUHY (1898–1959)

Person: A kinky-haired, hard-eyed tough, Touhy cultivated the appearance of a grim criminal who would as quickly kill an enemy as look at him.

Activities: The bootleg boss of the Chicago suburb of Des Plaines was known as the only gangster to make Al Capone back down in a confrontation. It was a dispute over a mere $1,900, which Capone tried to withhold because, he claimed, 50 out of 800 barrels of beer he'd bought from Touhy had leaks. "Don't chisel me, Al," Touhy said firmly, and Capone backed off. Touhy was always doing things like that as the head of "the Terrible Touhys," six brothers who chose criminality after starting life with a respectable background. Their father was a policeman, and many of their playmates on Chicago's West Side became cops. In the 1920s Touhy went into the trucking business, and when enough legitimate business didn't come along, he started filling his trucks with bootleg liquor.

Touhy's hold on Des Plaines was firm because he produced a beer of very high quality; the kegs—made at his own establishment—never leaked; and the cops and politicians were paid off in bottled beer brewed especially for them. Whenever members of a rival gang made noises about moving in, Touhy would invite them to his headquarters, where they would find the walls lined with submachine guns (borrowed for the occasion from the local cops). Then he would issue "hit" orders on the phone while his visitors listened. The rivals would always pull out, believing his alleged gang of 200 gunmen was too tough to handle. Capone himself got the same treatment when he tried to move other rackets in, noting that Des Plaines was "virgin territory for whorehouses." Touhy gave him a hard-eyed no. Eventually the Capone mob decided that the best way to handle Touhy was to let the law get him. He was framed on a kidnapping charge, and the mob took over.

Leading Crimes: Touhy was convicted for the 1933 kidnapping of Jake "the Barber" Factor, an international con man with ties to the Capone mob. Sentenced to prison for 99 years, Touhy cried frame-up to no avail. In 1942 Touhy escaped from Illinois State Prison in Joliet, but he was recaptured and sentenced to an additional 199 years. Finally, in the 1950s, Touhy won a hearing on his original conviction, and after a 36-day inquiry Judge John P. Barnes concluded that Factor had disappeared "of his own connivance," and rendered his verdict: "The court finds that Roger Touhy did not kidnap John Factor." The judge went on to castigate the Chicago police, the state's attorney, the Capone mob, and the FBI. After serving a quarter of a century for a noncrime, Touhy was freed in 1959.

Major Victims: In a sense Touhy was a victim of his own posturing as an impregnable gang lord. In point of fact he never even made the public-enemies list of the Chicago Crime Commission and, as Judge Barnes noted, was never linked with a capital case.

How Died: Just 23 days after he was freed, Touhy was shotgunned down on a Chicago street by Capone gang member Murray "the Camel" Humphreys, according to general belief. "I've been expecting it," Touhy muttered shortly before dying. "The bastards never forget."

—C.S.

8

THE SKY ABOVE, THE EARTH BELOW

11 PLANETS DISCOVERED BY SCIENCE FICTION WRITERS

1. MESKLIN

Location: Eleven light years from Earth.
Discoverer: None is ever mentioned as a specific discoverer, but Charles Lackland is the first human to spend any time on this highly unusual world. Lackland is a scientist attached to an Earth mission attempting to retrieve a rocket probe that failed to respond to its return signal.
Book: *Mission of Gravity* (1954) by Hal Clement.
Description: Mesklin is shaped like a bowl about six times as wide as it is high, a giant, flattened world spinning so fast that an entire day occupies just 9 min. of Earth time. Gravity at the rim of this toplike structure is about three times that of Earth; at the poles, however, gravitational forces increase to about 700 times Earth normal. The cold atmosphere is hydrogen; the seas are liquefied methane gas. The immense continents are rather featureless and smooth, with a few mountain ranges, extensive plains covered by a tangle of low-lying vine trees, and rivers of flowing methane. The seasons are as peculiar as the planet: Mesklin's erratic orbit around its twin suns provides it with fall and winter seasons just over two Earth months in length; spring and summer, however, each occupy about 830 Earth days, or roughly 26 months. The winter season is marked by extremely violent storms that raise the ocean levels hundreds of feet, literally changing the coastlines of vast portions of the globe within a couple of months. During the spring and summer seasons the storms decrease, and the sea levels gradually drop until the methane "waters" are replenished in the winter rains. In addition to a wide variety of animal and microscopic life suited to the climate, Mesklin has an intelligent race of foot-long caterpillars, whose bodies are well suited to living in the enormous gravitational forces that govern life on this planet. The civilization of these creatures has reached a level comparable to that of the 16th or 17th century on Earth, with seagoing ships, an active commerce, and the beginnings of science.

Lackland persuades the creatures to search for the probe, but when the captain of one of the creatures' ships discovers it, he demands payment before turning over the precious scientific readings to the Earthman. It is not money or riches he wants, but an education for his people.

2. PYRRUS

Location: Somewhere in the galaxy.
Discoverer: Captain Kurkowski, commander of the stellar transport *Pollux Victory*, which settled Pyrrus 300 years before the story.
Book: *Deathworld* (1960) by Harry Harrison.
Description: Pyrrus is a heavy-metal world with a radioactive core surrounded by a shell of lighter materials. It has a large axial tilt, which provides an enormous variation in weather conditions and temperatures from season to season; the weather can vary daily from freezing to tropical, with violent storms, hurricanes, and tornadoes. The radioactive core generates unceasing volcanic activity, plus earthquakes sufficiently violent to sink half a continent within hours. The planet's two moons combine at times to form enormous ocean tides. Gravity is twice Earth normal. The most unusual aspect of this violent world, however, is the animosity shown humankind by the indigenous flora and fauna, all of which are lethal, having either poison fangs, claws, teeth, or other dangerous elements, and all possessing an unreasoning hatred of the human race. Even the plants wage an unceasing war against the lone human settlement. After 300 years of habitation, the human population has dropped from 55,000 to 30,000. Every plant and every animal is telepathic to a degree; the human settlers, not realizing this, in effect attract the enmity of the creatures by their combative and aggressive attitude, an attitude that is instilled through rigorous training from birth. Unless humans can rid themselves of their hatred, there can be only one end to this war against the environment: the death of every human being on Pyrrus.

3. SOROR

Location: Soror is the second planet of the giant red star Betelgeuse, or Alpha Orionis, located about 300 light-years from the planet Earth.
Discovers: Ulysse Mérou, Professor Antelle, and Arthur Levain, who together embark upon the first interstellar voyage in the year 2500. Ulysse is a journalist, Levain a young physician, and Antelle the scientist who funded and constructed the spaceship. With them is Hector the chimp.
Book: *Planet of the Apes* (1963) by Pierre Boulle.
Description: The planet Soror (the name means "sister" in Latin) is virtually a twin of Earth, having similar gravitational pull, atmosphere, plants, animal life, proportion of land mass to oceans, cities and towns, and signs of civilized life. There are minor differences, of course, but physically the two worlds are remarkably alike. Ulysse and his companions are astonished to find upon landing that the humans they encounter, while nearly perfect in outward appearance, seem to react to their overtures with animallike behavior; they possess neither speech nor

Rulers of the planet Soror inspecting a lowly human (Charlton Heston) whom they have captured.

comprehension. Here it is the apes—gorillas, chimpanzees, orangutans—who rule the world, and who look upon humans as mere beasts, brutes to be used for experimental purposes. Ulysse manages to convince several of the younger chimpanzee scientists of his intelligence, but the orangutans, at the center of the bureaucratic establishment, remain unpersuaded. Meanwhile, his companions either have been killed or have gone mad. Finally Ulysse investigates an archaeological site that convinces him that humans once ruled this world, and that the apes took over through a combination of human degeneracy and ape development. When the brute humans begin to show signs of increasing comprehension, the apes sense a threat to their rule, and Ulysse, together with a brute female and their newborn child, must flee Soror with the help of his chimp friends Zira and Cornelius. Returning to Earth after an absence of 700 years, he is greeted at the landing field by two uniformed members of the military establishment—both of them gorillas.

4. ARRAKIS, OR DUNE

Location: Somewhere in the Galactic Empire; Dune is the third planet in the Canopus system.
Discoverer: Unknown. Dr. Pardot Kynes, however, was the world's first planetologist and the first person to study the unique ecology of Dune.

Book: *Dune* (1965) by Frank Herbert, together with its two sequels, *Dune Messiah* and *Children of Dune.*

Description: Dune is a desert world, where water is so precious that the native Fremen—the free tribes of Dune, the dwellers of the void—wear stillsuits to recapture the moisture that their bodies give off, and use stilltents to recapture the moisture in their breaths. Arrakis has no free water as such, although artificial underground catch basins have been built by the Fremen to gather a store of water gradually. Even the water from the dead is squeezed out and returned to the community. The planet is mostly barren, with little plant or animal life; the climate is hot, as might be expected, with blowing sand and dust common climatic conditions. Arrakis is the only source of melange, or spice, mildly addictive when taken in small quantities, severely addictive in larger quantities; spice may produce or enhance telepathic abilities and definitely contributes to long life when taken regularly. Spice is a byproduct of Dune's unusual ecology, at the heart of which are the shai-hulud, or sandworms, immense creatures that grow as long as 1,300 ft. The sandworms prowl the endless waves of sand, feeding on sand plankton and avoiding water, which is poisonous to them. Through a roundabout process, the sand plankton become sandswimmers, which in turn become sandworms, completing the cycle. During the initial stages of the cycle, any existing free water is used up or trapped, and the action of the sandworms creates more sand and grit to add to the mounds already extant. Into this exotic background, Herbert weaves his story of Paul Atreides, later called Muad'Dib by the Fremen, to whom he becomes a prophet and semimythological leader when he overthrows the rule of the empire. Paul, the son of an assassinated nobleman, is accepted by the Fremen as one of their own; his two children attain almost superhuman status in the third book of the series. A fourth novel and a movie are promised in the near future.

5. GOR, OR COUNTER EARTH

Location: Gor occupies the same orbit as Earth but is eternally located on the exact opposite side of our sun; the physical imposition of the sun's bulk between the two planets, as well as deliberate obfuscation on the part of Gor's rulers, prevents Earth's scientists from detecting the presence of another planet in the same orbital plane.

Discoverer: No one can be said to have "discovered" Gor, since Gor's rulers keep their world hidden from Earth's prying eyes; however, Gor's saucer-shaped spacecraft have often abducted men and women from Earth to help populate Gor; one such involuntary voyager is Tarl Cabot, an instructor of English history at a small New Hampshire college, who is kidnapped in the mid-1960s while hiking in the White Mountains.

Book: *Tarnsman of Gor* (1967) by John Norman, together with its 13 sequels.

Description: Gor is a slightly smaller world than Earth, with a lesser gravity; the air, water, and foliage are somewhat similar, however, although the animal life includes giant lizards (tharlarions), leopardlike creatures called larls, huge fighting birds (tarns), intelligent spiders, and

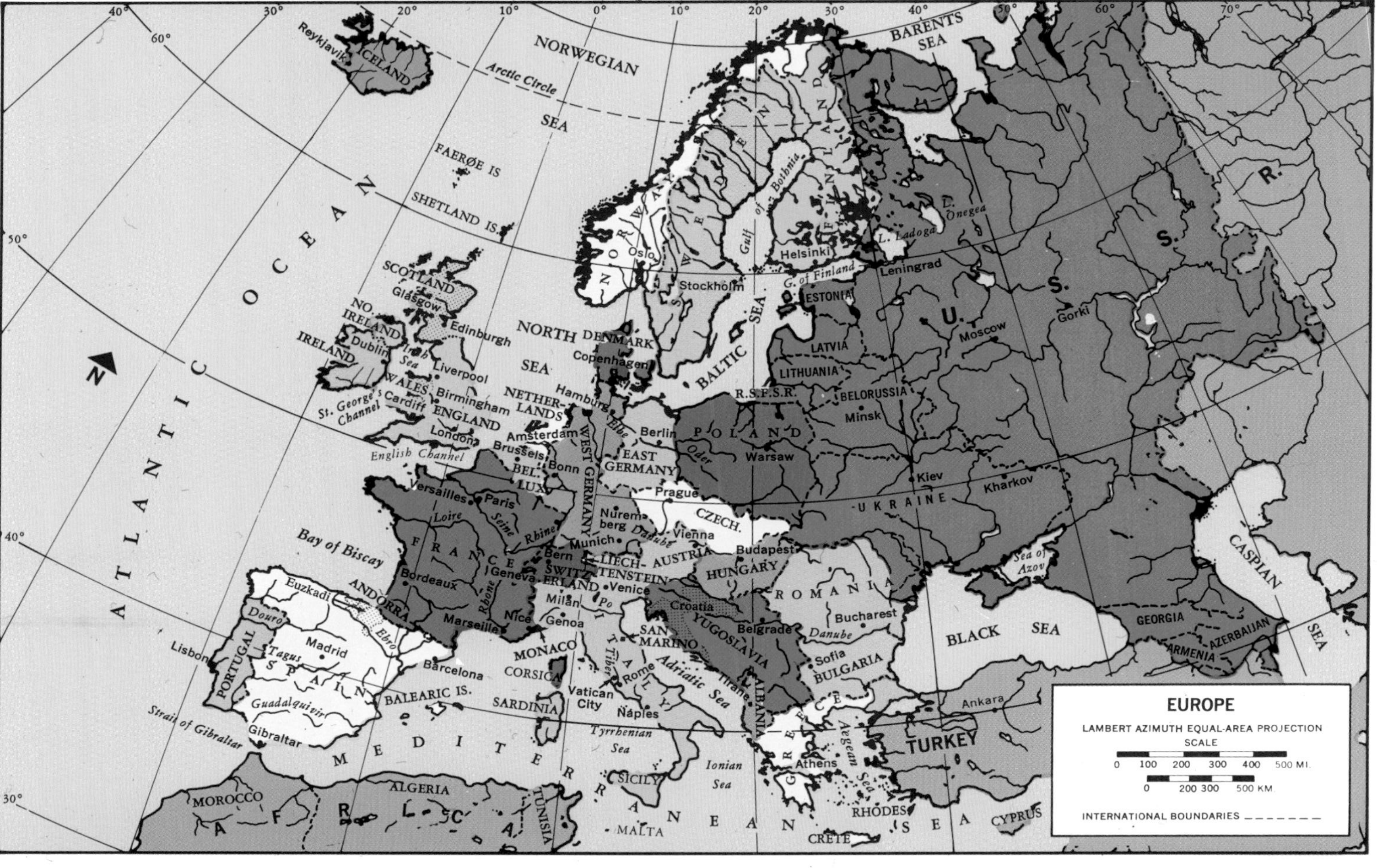
EUROPE
LAMBERT AZIMUTH EQUAL-AREA PROJECTION
SCALE
0 100 200 300 400 500 MI.
0 200 300 500 KM
INTERNATIONAL BOUNDARIES
ATLANTIC OCEAN
NORWEGIAN SEA
Arctic Circle
BARENTS SEA
NORTH SEA
BALTIC SEA
Gulf of Bothnia
G. of Finland
Bay of Biscay
English Channel
St. George's Channel
Irish Sea
MEDITERRANEAN SEA
Tyrrhenian Sea
Ionian Sea
Adriatic Sea
Aegean Sea
BLACK SEA
Sea of Azov
CASPIAN SEA
Strait of Gibraltar
Reykjavik
ICELAND
FAERØE IS
SHETLAND IS.
SCOTLAND
Glasgow
Edinburgh
NO. IRELAND
IRELAND
Dublin
Liverpool
WALES
Birmingham
Cardiff
ENGLAND
London
NORWAY
Oslo
SWEDEN
Stockholm
FINLAND
Helsinki
DENMARK
Copenhagen
NETHERLANDS
Amsterdam
Hamburg
Brussels
BEL.
LUX.
Bonn
WEST GERMANY
EAST GERMANY
Berlin
Elbe
POLAND
Oder
Warsaw
Prague
CZECH.
Nuremberg
Danube
Vienna
Munich
AUSTRIA
Budapest
HUNGARY
LIECHTENSTEIN
Bern
SWITZERLAND
Geneva
Venice
Milan
Po
Genoa
Nice
MONACO
FRANCE
Paris
Versailles
Seine
Loire
Rhine
Rhone
Bordeaux
Marseille
ANDORRA
Euzkadi
Ebro
Douro
Tagus
SPAIN
Madrid
Guadalquivir
Barcelona
BALEARIC IS.
Gibraltar
PORTUGAL
Lisbon
CORSICA
SARDINIA
ITALY
SAN MARINO
Tiber
Rome
Vatican City
Naples
SICILY
MALTA
Croatia
YUGOSLAVIA
Belgrade
Tirane
ALBANIA
GREECE
Athens
CRETE
RHODES
ROMANIA
Bucharest
Danube
Sofia
BULGARIA
TURKEY
Ankara
CYPRUS
MOROCCO
ALGERIA
TUNISIA
AFRICA
ESTONIA
LATVIA
LITHUANIA
R.S.F.S.R.
BELORUSSIA
Minsk
UKRAINE
Kiev
Kharkov
Leningrad
L. Ladoga
L. Onegea
Moscow
Gorki
U. S. S. R.
GEORGIA
ARMENIA
AZERBAIJAN
60°
50°
40°
30°
20°
10°
0°
70°

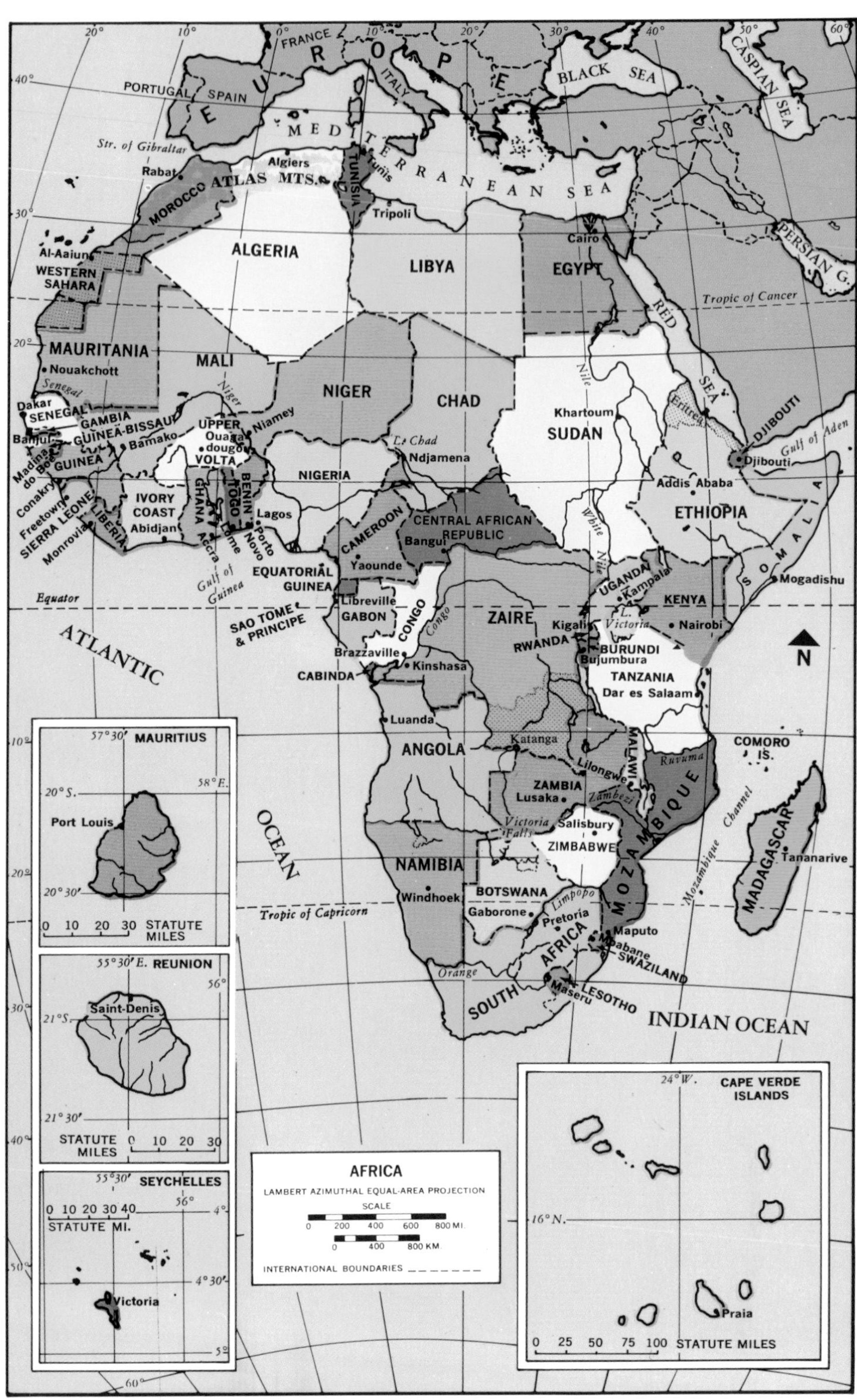

FRANCE
E U R O P E
PORTUGAL
SPAIN
ITALY
BLACK SEA
CASPIAN SEA
MEDITERRANEAN SEA
Str. of Gibraltar
Algiers
Tunis
TUNISIA
Rabat
MOROCCO
ATLAS MTS.
Tripoli
Cairo
PERSIAN G.
Al-Aaiun
WESTERN SAHARA
ALGERIA
LIBYA
EGYPT
Tropic of Cancer
RED SEA
MAURITANIA
Nouakchott
Senegal
MALI
Niger
NIGER
CHAD
Nile
Khartoum
SUDAN
Eritrea
DJIBOUTI
Gulf of Aden
Djibouti
Dakar
SENEGAL
GAMBIA
GUINEA-BISSAU
Banjul
Madina do Boe
GUINEA
Bamako
UPPER VOLTA
Ouagadougou
Niamey
L. Chad
Ndjamena
Conakry
Freetown
SIERRA LEONE
Monrovia
LIBERIA
IVORY COAST
Abidjan
GHANA
Accra
TOGO
Lome
BENIN
Porto Novo
Lagos
NIGERIA
Addis Ababa
ETHIOPIA
CAMEROON
Yaounde
CENTRAL AFRICAN REPUBLIC
Bangui
White Nile
SOMALIA
Mogadishu
Gulf of Guinea
EQUATORIAL GUINEA
Equator
Libreville
GABON
CONGO
Congo
ZAIRE
UGANDA
Kampala
KENYA
L. Victoria
Nairobi
SAO TOME & PRINCIPE
Kigali
RWANDA
BURUNDI
Bujumbura
TANZANIA
Dar es Salaam
ATLANTIC OCEAN
Brazzaville
Kinshasa
CABINDA
N
Luanda
Katanga
ANGOLA
MALAWI
COMORO IS.
Ruvuma
Lilongwe
ZAMBIA
Lusaka
Zambezi
MOZAMBIQUE
Mozambique Channel
MADAGASCAR
Tananarive
Victoria Falls
Salisbury
ZIMBABWE
NAMIBIA
Windhoek
BOTSWANA
Gaborone
Limpopo
Pretoria
Tropic of Capricorn
Maputo
Mbabane
SWAZILAND
Orange
SOUTH AFRICA
Maseru
LESOTHO
INDIAN OCEAN
57°30′ MAURITIUS
58° E.
20° S.
Port Louis
20°30′
0 10 20 30 STATUTE MILES
55°30′ E. REUNION
56°
21° S.
Saint-Denis
21°30′
STATUTE MILES 0 10 20 30
55°30′ SEYCHELLES
56°
4°
0 10 20 30 40
STATUTE MI.
4°30′
Victoria
5°
AFRICA
LAMBERT AZIMUTHAL EQUAL-AREA PROJECTION
SCALE
0 200 400 600 800 MI.
0 400 800 KM.
INTERNATIONAL BOUNDARIES
24° W.
CAPE VERDE ISLANDS
16° N.
Praia
0 25 50 75 100 STATUTE MILES

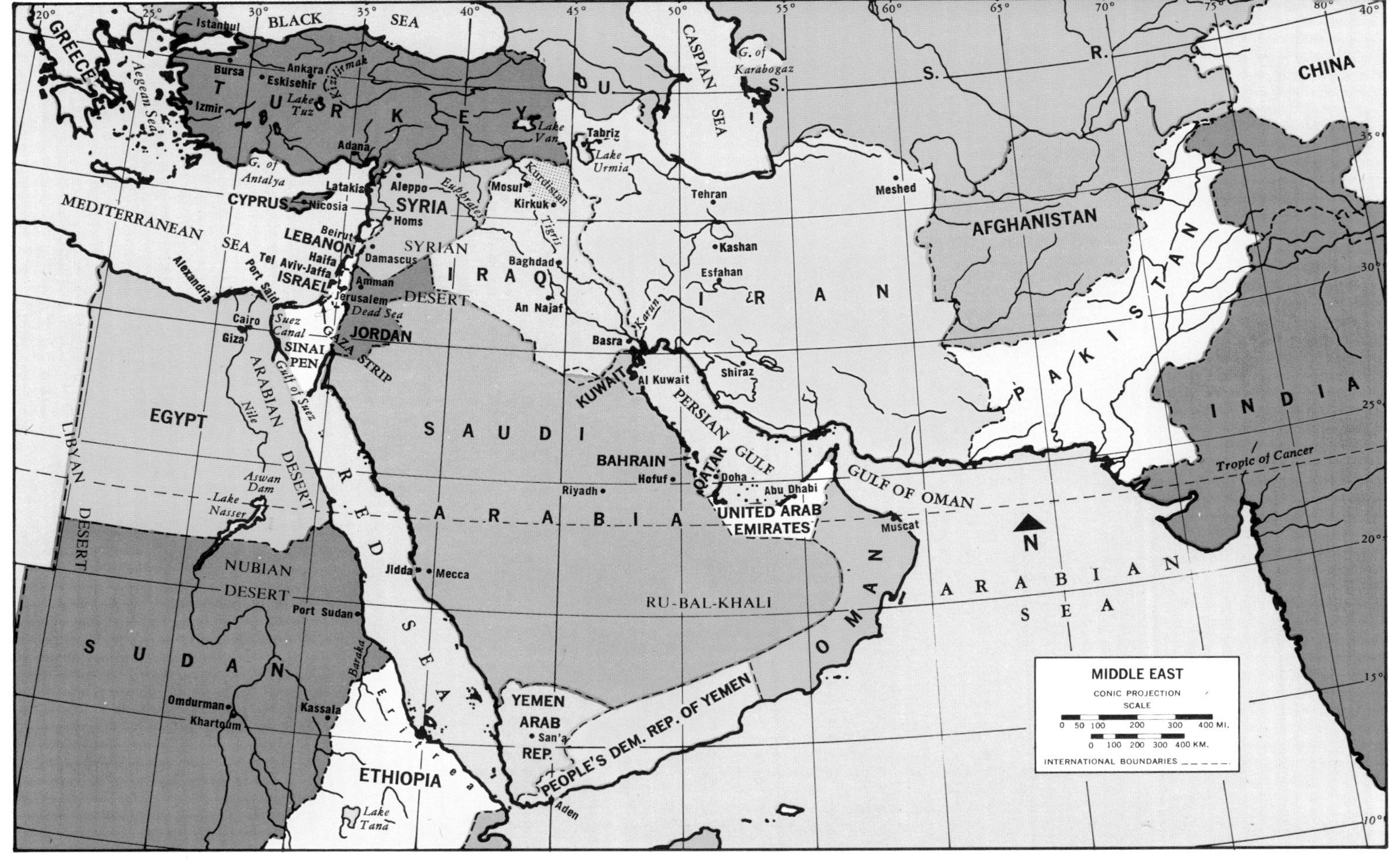
MIDDLE EAST
CONIC PROJECTION
SCALE
0 50 100 200 300 400 MI.
0 100 200 300 400 KM.
INTERNATIONAL BOUNDARIES
GREECE
TURKEY
U.S.S.R.
CHINA
AFGHANISTAN
PAKISTAN
INDIA
IRAN
IRAQ
SYRIA
LEBANON
ISRAEL
JORDAN
CYPRUS
EGYPT
SUDAN
ETHIOPIA
SAUDI ARABIA
KUWAIT
BAHRAIN
QATAR
UNITED ARAB EMIRATES
OMAN
YEMEN ARAB REP.
PEOPLE'S DEM. REP. OF YEMEN
GAZA STRIP
SINAI PEN
BLACK SEA
CASPIAN SEA
MEDITERRANEAN SEA
RED SEA
ARABIAN SEA
PERSIAN GULF
GULF OF OMAN
Aegean Sea
G. of Antalya
G. of Karabogaz
Gulf of Suez
Suez Canal
Dead Sea
Lake Van
Lake Urmia
Lake Tuz
Lake Nasser
Lake Tana
Aswan Dam
Kizilirmak
Euphrates
Tigris
Karun
Nile
Baraka
Eritrea
Kurdistan
SYRIAN DESERT
ARABIAN DESERT
NUBIAN DESERT
LIBYAN DESERT
RU-BAL-KHALI
Tropic of Cancer
Istanbul
Bursa
Izmir
Ankara
Eskisehir
Adana
Latakia
Nicosia
Aleppo
Homs
Beirut
Damascus
Haifa
Tel Aviv-Jaffa
Jerusalem
Amman
Alexandria
Port Said
Cairo
Giza
Mosul
Kirkuk
Baghdad
An Najaf
Basra
Tabriz
Tehran
Kashan
Esfahan
Shiraz
Meshed
Al Kuwait
Hofuf
Riyadh
Doha
Abu Dhabi
Muscat
Jidda
Mecca
Port Sudan
Kassala
Omdurman
Khartoum
San'a
Aden
N

ASIA
LAMBERT AZIMUTHAL EQUAL-AREA PROJECTION
SCALE
0 300 600 900 1200 MI.
0 600 1200 KM.
INTERNATIONAL BOUNDARIES
INTERNAL BOUNDARIES
NORTH POLE
ATLANTIC OCEAN
ARCTIC OCEAN
BERING SEA
SEA OF OKHOTSK
SEA OF JAPAN
ARABIAN SEA
BAY OF BENGAL
SOUTH CHINA SEA
INDIAN OCEAN
PACIFIC OCEAN
UNION OF SOVIET SOCIALIST REPUBLICS
MONGOLIA
CHINA
INDIA
PAKISTAN
AFGHANISTAN
IRAN
NEPAL
BHUTAN
SIKKIM
BANGLADESH
BURMA
THAILAND
LAOS
VIETNAM
CAMBODIA
MALAYSIA
INDONESIA
PHILIPPINES
NO. KOREA
SO. KOREA
TAIWAN
AUSTRALIA
SRI LANKA (CEYLON)
Tropic of Cancer
Tropic of Capricorn
Equator
Arctic Circle

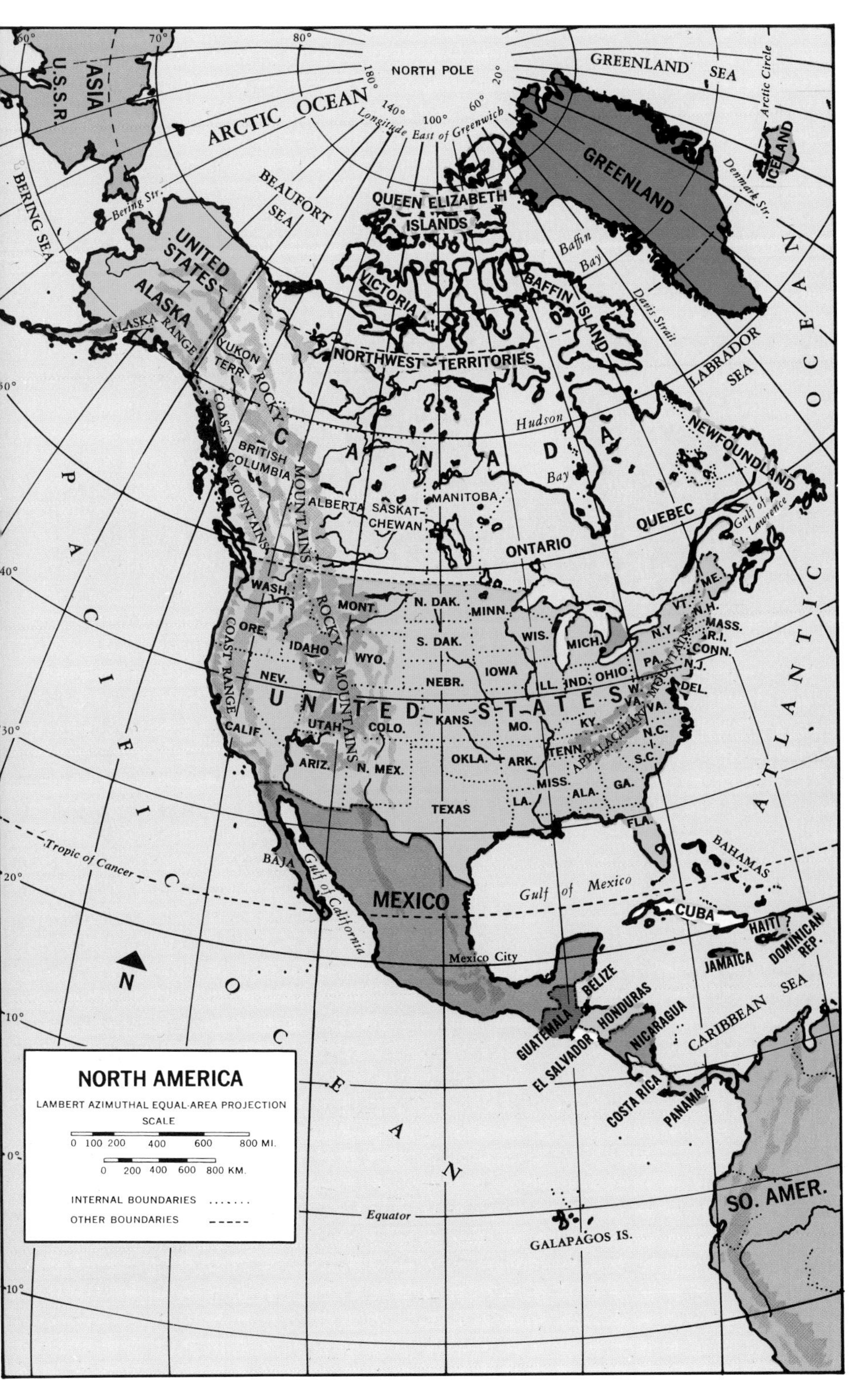

NORTH AMERICA
LAMBERT AZIMUTHAL EQUAL-AREA PROJECTION
SCALE
0 100 200 400 600 800 MI.
0 200 400 600 800 KM.
INTERNAL BOUNDARIES
OTHER BOUNDARIES
NORTH POLE
ARCTIC OCEAN
Longitude East of Greenwich
GREENLAND SEA
GREENLAND
ICELAND
Arctic Circle
Denmark Str.
ASIA
U.S.S.R.
BERING SEA
Bering Str.
BEAUFORT SEA
QUEEN ELIZABETH ISLANDS
VICTORIA I.
BAFFIN ISLAND
Baffin Bay
Davis Strait
UNITED STATES
ALASKA
ALASKA RANGE
YUKON TERR.
NORTHWEST TERRITORIES
LABRADOR SEA
NEWFOUNDLAND
Hudson Bay
CANADA
ROCKY
COAST
BRITISH COLUMBIA
MOUNTAINS
ALBERTA
SASKATCHEWAN
MANITOBA
ONTARIO
QUEBEC
Gulf of St. Lawrence
WASH.
MONT.
N. DAK.
MINN.
ORE.
IDAHO
WYO.
S. DAK.
WIS.
MICH.
N.Y.
VT.
N.H.
ME.
MASS.
R.I.
CONN.
N.J.
PA.
DEL.
NEV.
NEBR.
IOWA
ILL.
IND.
OHIO
W. VA.
VA.
UNITED STATES
COAST RANGE
CALIF.
UTAH
COLO.
KANS.
MO.
KY.
N.C.
TENN.
S.C.
ARIZ.
N. MEX.
OKLA.
ARK.
MISS.
ALA.
GA.
LA.
TEXAS
FLA.
APPALACHIAN MOUNTAINS
PACIFIC OCEAN
ATLANTIC OCEAN
Tropic of Cancer
BAJA
Gulf of California
MEXICO
Mexico City
Gulf of Mexico
BAHAMAS
CUBA
HAITI
DOMINICAN REP.
JAMAICA
BELIZE
HONDURAS
GUATEMALA
EL SALVADOR
NICARAGUA
COSTA RICA
PANAMA
CARIBBEAN SEA
Equator
GALAPAGOS IS.
SO. AMER.
N

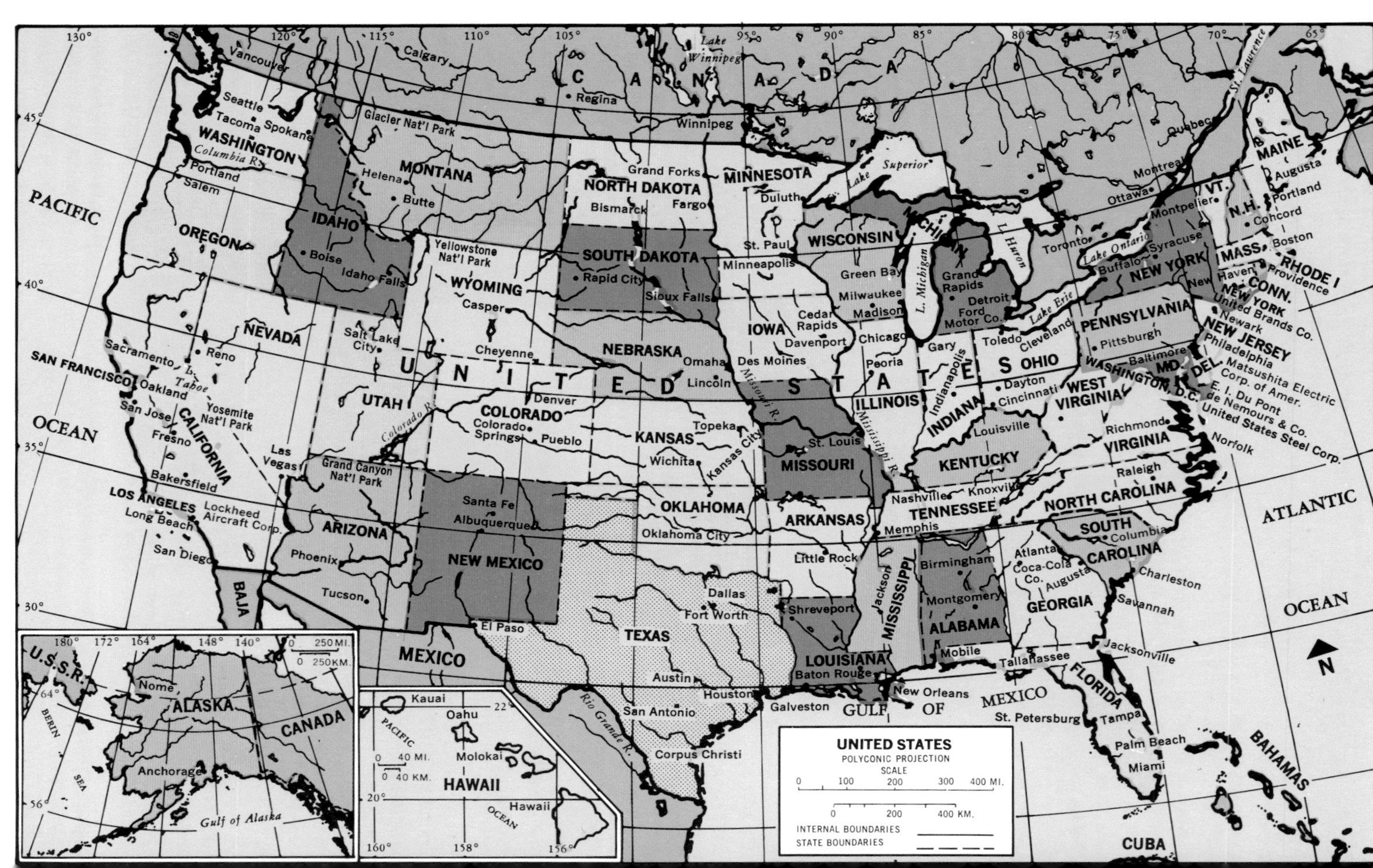
UNITED STATES
POLYCONIC PROJECTION
SCALE
0 100 200 300 400 MI.
0 200 400 KM.
INTERNAL BOUNDARIES
STATE BOUNDARIES
C A N A D A
U N I T E D S T A T E S
PACIFIC OCEAN
ATLANTIC OCEAN
GULF OF MEXICO
MEXICO
BAJA
CUBA
BAHAMAS
WASHINGTON
OREGON
CALIFORNIA
NEVADA
IDAHO
MONTANA
WYOMING
UTAH
ARIZONA
COLORADO
NEW MEXICO
NORTH DAKOTA
SOUTH DAKOTA
NEBRASKA
KANSAS
OKLAHOMA
TEXAS
MINNESOTA
IOWA
MISSOURI
ARKANSAS
LOUISIANA
WISCONSIN
ILLINOIS
MICHIGAN
INDIANA
OHIO
KENTUCKY
TENNESSEE
MISSISSIPPI
ALABAMA
GEORGIA
FLORIDA
SOUTH CAROLINA
NORTH CAROLINA
VIRGINIA
WEST VIRGINIA
PENNSYLVANIA
NEW YORK
NEW JERSEY
DEL.
MD.
WASHINGTON, D.C.
CONN.
RHODE I
MASS.
VT.
N.H.
MAINE
Vancouver
Seattle
Tacoma
Spokane
Portland
Salem
Columbia R.
Boise
Idaho Falls
Helena
Butte
Glacier Nat'l Park
Calgary
Regina
Winnipeg
Lake Winnipeg
Yellowstone Nat'l Park
Casper
Cheyenne
Salt Lake City
Reno
Sacramento
L. Tahoe
San Francisco
Oakland
San Jose
Yosemite Nat'l Park
Fresno
Bakersfield
Las Vegas
Los Angeles
Lockheed Aircraft Corp.
Long Beach
San Diego
Grand Canyon Nat'l Park
Colorado R.
Phoenix
Tucson
Santa Fe
Albuquerque
El Paso
Denver
Colorado Springs
Pueblo
Grand Forks
Bismarck
Fargo
Rapid City
Sioux Falls
Omaha
Lincoln
Topeka
Wichita
Kansas City
Oklahoma City
Dallas
Fort Worth
Austin
San Antonio
Houston
Galveston
Corpus Christi
Rio Grande R.
Duluth
St. Paul
Minneapolis
Des Moines
Cedar Rapids
Davenport
Missouri R.
St. Louis
Mississippi R.
Little Rock
Shreveport
Baton Rouge
New Orleans
Jackson
Memphis
Nashville
Knoxville
Louisville
Green Bay
Milwaukee
Madison
Chicago
Peoria
Gary
Indianapolis
Lake Superior
L. Michigan
L. Huron
Lake Erie
Lake Ontario
Grand Rapids
Detroit
Ford Motor Co.
Toledo
Cleveland
Dayton
Cincinnati
Pittsburgh
Birmingham
Montgomery
Mobile
Atlanta
Coca-Cola Co.
Augusta
Columbia
Charleston
Savannah
Jacksonville
Tallahassee
St. Petersburg
Tampa
Palm Beach
Miami
Raleigh
Richmond
Norfolk
Baltimore
Philadelphia
Matsushita Electric Corp. of Amer.
E. I. Du Pont de Nemours & Co.
United States Steel Corp.
Newark
United Brands Co.
New Haven
Providence
Boston
Concord
Portland
Augusta
Montpelier
Syracuse
Buffalo
Toronto
Ottawa
Montreal
Quebec
St. Lawrence
N
130° 120° 115° 110° 105° 95° 90° 85° 80° 75° 70° 65°
45° 40° 35° 30°
U.S.S.R.
ALASKA
CANADA
Nome
Anchorage
Gulf of Alaska
BERIN SEA
0 250 MI.
0 250 KM.
180° 172° 164° 148° 140°
64° 56°
HAWAII
Kauai
Oahu
Molokai
Hawaii
PACIFIC OCEAN
0 40 MI.
0 40 KM.
160° 158° 156°
22° 20°

CARIBBEAN
SEA
NETHERLAND ANTILLES
TOBAGO
TRINIDAD
Port-of-Spain
Barranquilla
Golfo de Urabá
G. of Venezuela
Maracaibo
L. Maracaibo
Caracas
Orinoco
Georgetown
Paramaribo
Cayenne
ATLANTIC
OCEAN
PANAMA
G. of Panama
ANDES
Magdalena
Medellin
VENEZUELA
GUIANA
GUYANA
Essequibo
SURINAME
FR. GUIANA
Bogota
COLOMBIA
HIGHLANDS
Negro
Equator
Quito
ECUADOR
Guayaquil
Napo
Amazon
R.
Belem
Tapajos
Xingu
PERU
Recife
Tocantins
BRAZIL
BRAZILIAN
Lima
PLANALTO DE
MATO GROSSO
Cuzco
Sao Francisco
Salvador
L. Titicaca
Arequipa
BOLIVIA
La Paz
Brasilia
Cochabamba
Sucre
HIGHLANDS
L. Poopo
Paraguay
Belo Horizonte
PACIFIC
OCEAN
Tropic of Capricorn
PARAGUAY
Rio de Janeiro
Sao Paulo
Asuncion
Encarnacion
CHILE
ARGENTINA
Parana
Uruguay
Porto Alegre
Cordoba
URUGUAY
Rosario
Valparaiso
Santiago
Buenos Aires
Montevideo
La Plata
Rio de la Plata
Concepcion
Bahia Blanca
G. of San Matias
G. of San Jorge
ATLANTIC OCEAN
N
SOUTH AMERICA
LAMBERT AZIMUTHAL EQUAL-AREA PROJECTION
SCALE
0 100 200 400 600 MI.
0 200 400 600 KM.
INTERNATIONAL BOUNDARIES
FALKLAND ISLANDS
Stanley
TIERRA DEL FUEGO
Strait of Magellan
Cape Horn
80°
70°
60°
50°
40°
10°
0°
10°
20°
30°
40°
50°

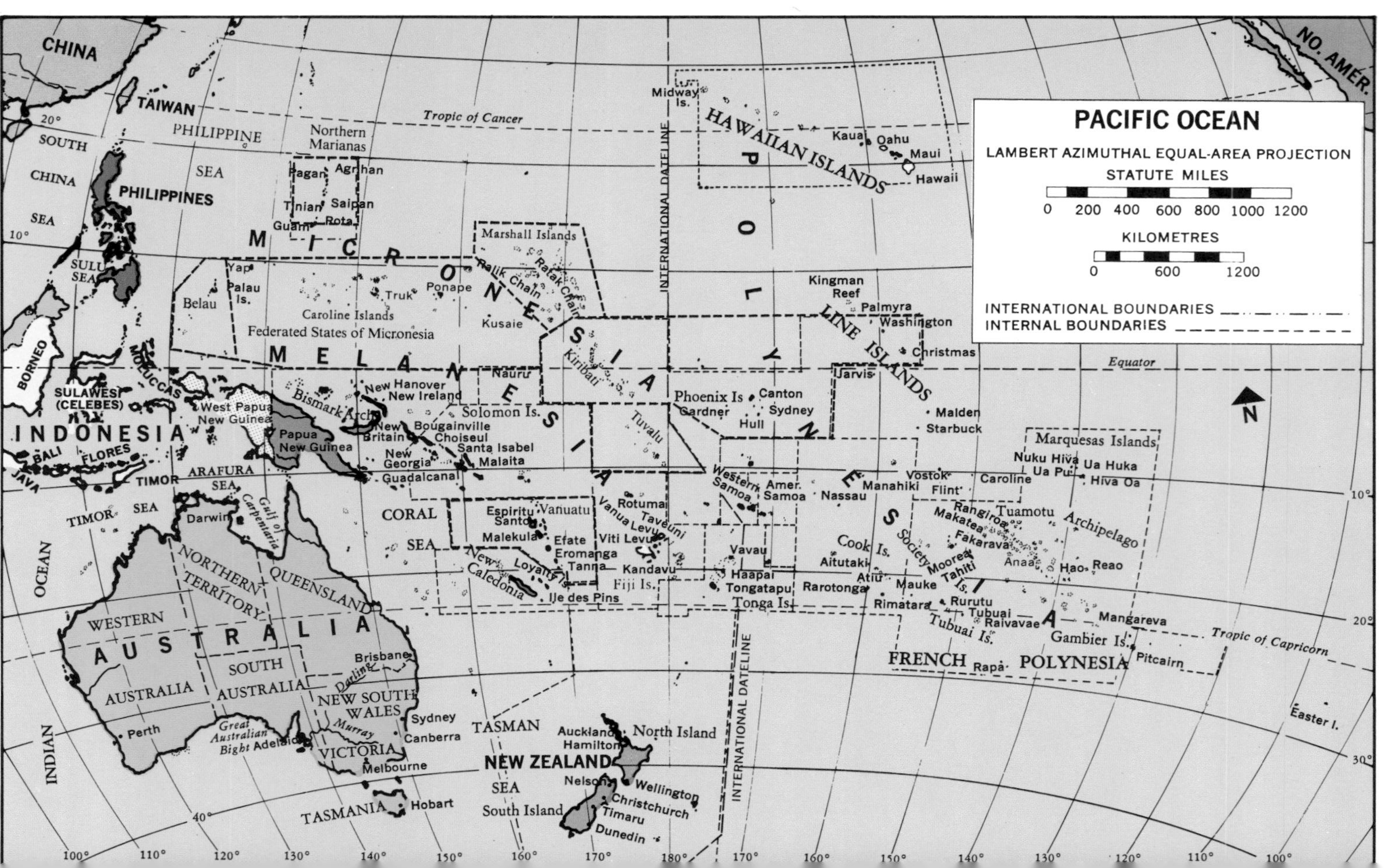
PACIFIC OCEAN
LAMBERT AZIMUTHAL EQUAL-AREA PROJECTION
STATUTE MILES
0 200 400 600 800 1000 1200
KILOMETRES
0 600 1200
INTERNATIONAL BOUNDARIES
INTERNAL BOUNDARIES
N
CHINA
TAIWAN
SOUTH CHINA SEA
PHILIPPINE SEA
PHILIPPINES
SULU SEA
BORNEO
SULAWESI (CELEBES)
MOLUCCAS
INDONESIA
BALI
FLORES
JAVA
TIMOR
TIMOR SEA
ARAFURA SEA
Gulf of Carpentaria
Tropic of Cancer
Northern Marianas
Pagan
Agrihan
Tinian
Saipan
Guam
Rota
MICRONESIA
Yap
Palau Is.
Belau
Caroline Islands
Truk
Ponape
Federated States of Micronesia
Marshall Islands
Ralik Chain
Ratak Chain
Kusaie
MELANESIA
Nauru
Kiribati
Bismarck Arch.
New Hanover
New Ireland
West Papua New Guinea
Papua New Guinea
New Britain
Bougainville
Choiseul
Solomon Is.
Santa Isabel
Malaita
New Georgia
Guadalcanal
CORAL SEA
Espiritu Santo
Vanuatu
Malekula
Efate
Eromanga
Tanna
New Caledonia
Loyalty Is.
Ile des Pins
Tuvalu
Rotuma
Vanua Levu
Taveuni
Viti Levu
Kandavu
Fiji Is.
INTERNATIONAL DATELINE
Midway Is.
HAWAIIAN ISLANDS
Kauai
Oahu
Maui
Hawaii
POLYNESIA
Kingman Reef
Palmyra
Washington
LINE ISLANDS
Christmas
Jarvis
Malden
Starbuck
Equator
Phoenix Is
Canton
Gardner
Sydney
Hull
Western Samoa
Amer. Samoa
Nassau
Manahiki
Vostok
Flint
Caroline
Vavau
Haapai
Tongatapu
Tonga Is.
Cook Is.
Aitutaki
Atiu
Rarotonga
Mauke
Rimatara
Society Is.
Moorea
Tahiti
Rangiroa
Makatea
Fakarava
Tuamotu Archipelago
Anaa
Hao
Reao
Marquesas Islands
Nuku Hiva
Ua Huka
Ua Pu
Hiva Oa
Rurutu
Tubuai
Raivavae
Tubuai Is.
Mangareva
Gambier Is.
Pitcairn
FRENCH POLYNESIA
Rapa
Tropic of Capricorn
Easter I.
NO. AMER.
AUSTRALIA
WESTERN AUSTRALIA
NORTHERN TERRITORY
QUEENSLAND
SOUTH AUSTRALIA
NEW SOUTH WALES
VICTORIA
Darwin
Perth
Brisbane
Darling
Murray
Sydney
Canberra
Melbourne
Great Australian Bight
Adelaide
TASMANIA
Hobart
TASMAN SEA
NEW ZEALAND
North Island
South Island
Auckland
Hamilton
Wellington
Nelson
Christchurch
Timaru
Dunedin
INDIAN OCEAN
10°
20°
30°
40°
100°
110°
120°
130°
140°
150°
160°
170°
180°

other unusual beasts of burden and prey. The human life is similar to that on Earth and may have derived in part or whole from Earth. The men of Gor are a proud people, semibarbaric in nature, with some elements of advanced technology and civilization mixed together with medieval weaponry and social systems. Slavery is endemic, particularly among the female population; the society is heavily male-oriented, and women are kept in subjugation, supposedly much to their liking. The unseen rulers of the planet, the Priest-Kings, limit the technology allowed the Goreans for use in warfare to swords, crossbows, spears, and the like, while permitting sophisticated computer translators, lighting systems, and heating elements. Those who transgress against the Priest-Kings suddenly erupt in blue flame and are consumed within a few moments. The Priest-Kings, who remain eternally secluded in the Sardar Mountains, are large antlike creatures of immense longevity, who have moved the planet to Earth's solar system from its original, distant location, and who nearly destroy themselves in a civil war. The resulting chaos leaves the planet open to an interstellar war with the Beasts, or Kurii, bearlike creatures that are bent on conquering both Gor and Earth. Tarl Cabot becomes a central figure in the developing saga of Gor as he changes from a mild-mannered professor to a fierce barbarian warrior determined to halt the Kurii and maintain the independent life-style of his beloved Earth.

6. PERN

Location: Pern is the third planet of the golden star Rukbat, in the Sagittarian sector, an indeterminate distance from Earth. Rukbat has four other original planets, plus a stray planet that it has attracted and held in recent millennia. The stray has an erratic orbit that brings it close to Pern about every 200 years.

Discoverer: Unknown. Pern was settled by Earthmen during a period of active colonization some hundreds or thousands of years ago; contact with the mother planet was lost during the first encounter with the Red Star, the rogue planet.

Book: *Dragonflight* (1969) by Anne McCaffrey, together with its sequels *Dragonquest, Dragonsong, Dragonsinger, Dragondrums,* and *The White Dragon.*

Description: Pern is similar to Earth in many respects, with temperate weather, breathable air, a gravity of about Earth intensity, and plants and animals that can be used for food and other purposes. The humans on Pern have settled into an agrarian society on a medieval level, with the technology, social system, and political configuration of the Renaissance period. At the top of the social scale, however, are the dragonriders, whose beasts of burden are large, scaled, telepathic reptiles of high intelligence. The dragons can teleport in both time and space nearly instantaneously, carrying their riders with them; the rider must be able to picture the destination clearly in his or her mind before the creature can reach through time or space and transport the person. The dragons are necessary instruments in the fight to preserve humankind against the inroads of the Thread, spores of searing plant life that filter down through the skies of Pern whenever the Red Star is near, during a 10-year period that occurs every 200 "turns," or years. The huge flying creatures use their fiery breath to sear the Thread before it touches Earth, where it burrows and devours any organic matter with which it comes in contact. The dragons were created by the settlers during the first pass of the Red Star, when they realized they were cut off from the help of Earth; the last few technicians used their skills to breed the small, native flying lizards into an effective fighting force. During the course of McCaffrey's saga, the people of Pern fight off a new attack triggered by the Red Star, discover something of their origins, and begin to change their social and political systems through the development of new technology and new ideas.

7. GETHEN, OR WINTER

Location: Somewhere in the galaxy, 17 light-years from Ollul; Ollul is one of the 83 worlds belonging to the Ekumen, a loose organization of planets settled by humans. (The original settlers came from Hain; Terra is one of the members of the Ekumen.)
Discoverer: A team of investigators came to Gethen about 40 years prior to the time of the story; the first extended visitor and representative is Genly Ai, whose duty it is to convince the various nations of Gethen to join their fellow humans in the Ekumen.
Book: *The Left Hand of Darkness* (1969) by Ursula K. Le Guin.
Description: Gethen is a planet of ice and snow; the summer and spring seasons are just bearable by Earth standards, the winter and fall fiercely cold and inhospitable. The planet is divided into several major competing nations and many minor ones; the technological level of the natives has reached the stage where radio, motor vehicles, and sonic guns, among other developments, are common. But Karhide, with its monarchical system of government, resists the intrusion of Ai. Part of the difference between Genly Ai and the natives is sexual; the humans of Winter are neuter most of the time, but periodically enter *kemmer*, during which time they develop either male or female sexual organs. No one can predict which will actually appear during the cycle, so a native of Gethen may be both father and mother during its lifetime. Thus, the Gethenians regard Ai as a pervert, a freak continually in heat. Furthermore, the Gethenian political system is complex, and Ai is caught among various factions struggling for political supremacy. In the end, Genly Ai wins. Karhide and the other Gethenian nations will join the Ekumen, one by one, but only at the cost of a life—the life of Ai's dearest friend.

8. GRAMARYE

Location: Gramarye is the fifth planet of a G-type sun near Capricorn.
Discoverer: The original discoverer is unknown; the rediscoverer of the world is Rodney d'Armand, better known as Rod Gallowglass, an agent for SCENT (the Society for the Conversion of Extraterrestrial Nascent Totalitarianisms), who has been sent by DDT (the Decentralized Democratic Tribunal) to locate the lost Terran colony on Gramarye.

Book: *The Warlock in Spite of Himself* (1969) by Christopher Stasheff, together with its sequel, *King Kobold*.
Description: Gramarye is basically a swamp world filled with amphibians, fish, insects, and very little else of note; its climate corresponds to that of Earth 300 million years ago. One large island has been stocked with Terran plants and animals, the corresponding native life having been exterminated; since the island is flanked by a cold polar current, the temperature is just under Earth normal. The original Terran colony consisted of anachronists and devotees of medieval life who set up a society based on the pattern of romanticized Earth history during the Middle Ages. Hence, no sophisticated technology is allowed; the largest dwellings are castles; the serfs and peasants labor for the aristocratic classes, which consist of a hereditary monarch and assorted noblemen. But Rod finds that all is not quite as ordered as it seems. Witches, werewolves, fairies, elves, warlocks, ghosts, and other figments of medieval imagination really exist on Gramarye and appear to have real magical powers. Rod later determines that the populace has developed psionic powers during its millennium of history; that this isolated colony has produced the only concentrated center of telepaths in the entire galaxy. Gramarye thus becomes the center of a political struggle which transcends time itself, and in which Rod Gallowglass becomes the key to the future of human civilization.

9. RIVERWORLD

Location: Somewhere in the known galaxy.
Discoverers: The 36,006,009,637 men, women, and children who dwelt on Earth during the first several million years of human existence, until about the year 1983 are all resurrected simultaneously on Riverworld by the mysterious aliens known as Ethicals, for purposes only they understand.
Book: *To Your Scattered Bodies Go* (1971) by Philip José Farmer, together with its sequels, *The Fabulous Riverboat, The Dark Design*, and *The Magic Labyrinth*.
Description: The Riverworld has been completely reworked and redesigned from its original configurations, whatever they might have been; now it has Earth-like atmosphere, gravity, and temperature. The terrain has been carved into an extended Rivervalley, perhaps millions of miles long, which crosses and recrosses every square inch of the Riverworld and turns and twists within walls of an impassable 20,000-ft.-high ridge. The River extends from one part of the northern polar sea southward, winds around the world through the southern polar regions, and then winds back as one continuous flowing river 1,000 ft. deep, emptying back into the lone sea at the North Pole. On either side of the River are plains perhaps a mile in width (the width may vary from location to location), another mile or two of foothills, and then a sheer rise of 15,000–20,000 ft. Scavenger fish keep the river clean; otherwise, there is no animal life of any kind save humans. A peculiar kind of interwoven grass grows along the banks; another kind covers the hills,

together with various kinds of trees and shrubs. Every member of the human race who has reached the age of five is resurrected simultaneously along the banks of the River, naked and hairless, with a pitcher in his arm. The pitchers fit into mushroom-shaped facilities that line the River; these flare up daily to fill the pitchers with food and other goods. It is left to Samuel Clemens, Sir Richard Francis Burton, and others of the same ilk to fight the Ethicals with the few tools they have been given and to try to determine why humankind has been resurrected.

10. MIRKHEIM

Location: Somewhere in the galaxy near the inhabited worlds of Babur and Hermes.
Discoverer: David Falkayn, a leading merchant in the Polesotechnic League, a director of the Solar Spice & Liquors Company, a man determined to see that the wealth of Mirkheim is shared by all intelligent races.
Book: *Mirkheim* (1977), by Poul Anderson.
Description: Half a million years ago, a giant sun with an equally giant planet exploded into a supernova, unleashing the unimaginable fury of an overheated stellar furnace, spewing enormous energy and superheavy elements into the surrounding space. Only the size of the planet, 1,500 times bigger than Earth, preserved it from utter destruction; even so, the planet lost most of its mass. There remained only the molten metallic core, which collected some of the stellar material ejected by the star in its death throes. The result was a stark, cold world with no atmosphere, plated over with heavy metals and superheavy atomic elements, a smooth, glittering, featureless ball of enormous value to all the intelligent, space-venturing beings whose need for such minerals has forced them to search the galaxy for mining facilities. The discovery of Mirkheim prompts a war between the various economic and political factions of Earth and the intelligent beings of Babur, who are just venturing out into space. David Falkayn and Nicholas van Rijn must fight to preserve their freebooting way of life, as well as the peace of the galaxy, while making certain no one faction gains control of this treasure world.

11. UNNAMED

Location: Ten months from Earth traveling by faster-than-light spaceship, near Zeta II Reticuli; the planet is one of a number in an uncharted solar system.
Discoverer: Mother, the computer of the interstellar tug *Nostromo*, and the seven crew members: Dallas, Ripley, Kane, Parker, Lambert, Ash, and Brett. The *Nostromo* is towing a petrochemical cargo to Earth when the computer wakens the crew short of their destination to investigate an alien distress signal emanating from the unknown planet.
Book: *Alien* (1979) by Alan Dean Foster, adapted from the screenplay by Dan O'Bannon, which was based on a story by Dan O'Bannon and Ronald Shusett.
Description: The planet is slightly oblate, perhaps 1,200 km. in di-

Crew members of the spaceship Nostromo *exploring a mysterious planet ten months' travel distance from Earth.*

ameter, its gravity .86 that of Earth, making it fairly dense for its size, with a rotation period of 2 hr.; analysis by the computer indicates that it was once molten but is now cooled; composition of the rock is basalt and rhyolite, with occasional lava overlays but with no signs of current volcanic activity. The atmosphere includes inert nitrogen, some oxygen, a high concentration of carbon dioxide, and some methane and ammonia, much of it frozen; the weather is severely cold and windy most of the time; water content is high; vision is obscured by the murky air currents composed of dust, fine bits of rock, and vapor. Only one form of life is evident—an intelligent, highly adaptable, parasitic creature that begins life in a protected egg case, hatches upon contact with other forms of life, attaches itself to another creature, develops inside that creature into a second stage, kills its host and bursts forth into the surrounding atmosphere (of whatever composition), grows in size into a roughly man-shaped killing machine, then lays eggs to begin the cycle anew. In the novel, the crew of the *Nostromo* investigates the ruins of an alien spacecraft found on the planet. Kane is infected by one of the parasites, which terrorizes the *Nostromo* until the last survivor of the crew, Ripley, manages to destroy it. Neither crew nor reader is ever able to determine whether the alien arrived with the derelict craft or whether it was indigenous to the planet.

—R.R.

8 MOTIONS OF THE EARTH

Every passing hour brings the Solar System 43,000 mi. closer to Globular Cluster M13 in Hercules—and still there are some misfits who insist that there is no such thing as progress.

—Kurt Vonnegut, *The Sirens of Titan*

1. CONTINENTAL DRIFT

The continental land masses sit on enormous slabs of rock that slide over the basaltic ocean floor very slowly, at the rate of 1 to 8 in. per year. Many geologists believe that all of earth's land broke away from one supercontinent, called Pangaea, about 230 million years ago. North America is gradually moving westward, away from Europe, at the rate of 3 in. per year. As a result, the Atlantic Ocean is now 120 ft. wider than it was when Columbus sailed it in 1492.

2. EARTH'S ROTATION ON ITS AXIS

Daily rotation is the only motion of the earth that all of us can observe directly, simply by watching the sun or moon rise or set. In each 24-hour rotation, the earth revolves at 1,035 mph, as measured at the equator. However, the friction of the ocean tides against the earth's surface has been slowing our planet's rotation by 1/1,000 second per century. Thus, 2 million years ago, when our distant ancestors were alive, the earth's slightly faster rate of rotation made their day 20 seconds shorter than ours.

3. PRECESSION OF THE EARTH'S AXIS

Because it bulges slightly at the equator, the earth moves like a spinning top as it responds to the gravitational pulls of the sun and the moon. This spinning motion, called precession, causes the North Pole to trace a circular path which takes 26,000 years to complete. As the North Pole moves along this path, the earth's orientation to the stars constantly changes, so that by 14,000 A.D. the star Vega will have replaced Polaris as the North Star.

4. POLAR VARIATION

The earth rocks vary slightly with relation to the North and South poles, making the position of each pole wander in a circle with a 10-to-50-ft. diameter. Called the Chandler Wobble, after the Massachusetts businessman who discovered it, the poles' motion may result from movements of the atmosphere. The Chandler Wobble shifts any given latitude—the imaginary lines measuring the distance toward or away from the equator—by several feet during its cycle of 14 months.

5. EARTH'S REVOLUTION AROUND THE SUN

The earth is following its elliptical orbit around the sun at 19 mi. per sec., or 68,000 mph. Astronomers define various types of years, but our familiar one is the tropical year, based on the seasons. Lasting 365 days, 5 hr., 48 min., and 46 sec., the tropical year is the time between the sun's passage through two spring equinoxes (e.g., Mar. 21, 1981, to Mar. 21, 1982). The fact that the tropical year does not contain an exact number of days has required the invention of leap year.

6. MOTION OF THE SOLAR SYSTEM THROUGH THE GALAXY

With respect to the neighboring stars in this area of the Milky Way galaxy, the sun and its solar system are zooming along at 12.4 mi. per sec. (43,200 mph) in the direction of the star Vega in the constellation Lyra.

7. REVOLUTION AROUND THE CENTER OF THE GALAXY

Our solar system is located in one of the Milky Way's spiral arms, two thirds of the distance from its central core. It is revolving around the galaxy's center at a velocity of 155 to 185 mi. per sec., in the general direction of the constellation Cygnus. Every 225 million years the solar system completes one revolution, called a cosmic year, and thus far the earth has passed through 25 cosmic years. Only one galactic year ago, the first small dinosaurs were evolving.

8. THE GALAXY'S MOTION THROUGH THE UNIVERSE

Recent measurements of variations in the universe's background radiation indicate that the Milky Way galaxy and neighboring galaxies are hurtling through space at 375 mi. per sec., or 1.3 million mph. When the earth's other motions are taken into account, the earth has a net motion of 250 mi. per sec., or 900,000 mph, in the direction of the constellation Leo.

—J.A.

ANIMAL MATING SYSTEMS

3 Animals That Share a Wife (Polyandry)

Examples of animals among which one female is bonded to several males at the same time include these birds.

1. Jacanas
2. Tasmanian hens
3. Tinamous

10 Animals That Share a Husband (Polygyny)

Among these and certain other animals, one male is bonded to several females at once during the breeding season.

1. Elks
2. Fur seals
3. Hamadryas baboons
4. Mountain sheep
5. Pheasants
6. Prairie chickens
7. Red grouse
8. Wild horses
9. Wrens
10. Yellow-bellied marmots

10 Animals That Are Monogamous

Monogamy, a pair-bond between a single male and female, is comparatively rare among mammals. Small songbirds, such as sparrows and warblers, are annually monogamous, forming new bonds each mating season. Perennially monogamous animals include:

1. Ducks
2. Eagles
3. Foxes
4. Geese
5. Gibbons
6. Lynx
7. Marmosets
8. Mountain lions
9. Swans
10. Wolves

10 Animals That Are Promiscuous

Promiscuity is characterized by the absence of even a temporary pair-bond between sexual partners. Mating among the following animals may still be a very selective process, but it is accompanied by no other relationship.

1. Bears
2. Birds of paradise
3. Bustards
4. Chimpanzees
5. Fruit-eating bats
6. Gazelles
7. Grouse
8. Sandpipers
9. Waterbucks
10. Wildebeests

—D.L.

10 ANIMAL SPECIES IN WHICH THE MALE CARES FOR THE YOUNG

1. MARMOSETS

These squirrel-sized monkeys live in the dense jungles of South America. Females typically give birth to twins, which are carried through the trees by the male; he relinquishes them to their mother only briefly, for nursing. When the combined weight of the two youngsters is about equal to his own, the male stops carrying them.

Marmosets—father and child.

2. SIAMANGS

Close relatives of the gibbons, these "lesser apes" inhabit Malaya and Sumatra and are monogamous. Families usually consist of an adult male, an adult female, their infant offspring, and an older juvenile. During the day, while the family forages in the treetops, the male carries the infant; at night he sleeps with the juvenile while the female nurses the infant.

3. SEA HORSES

Among these peculiar-looking fishes, and their close relatives the pipefishes, females deposit up to 200 eggs within the male's brood pouch. The "pregnant" male then carries the eggs around for four to five weeks until they hatch, at which time they are expelled from his body by contractions that closely resemble female labor in mammals.

4. ARROW POISON FROGS

These brilliantly colored orange, red, and yellow frogs are found in South American rain forests. Females deposit their fertilized eggs on the backs of the males, who carry them until they hatch into tadpoles and then release them into the water.

5. JACANAS

These robin-sized wading birds are sometimes called "lily trotters" because their long toes enable them to walk on lily pads. The larger, more brightly colored, and more aggressive females defend territories within which there may be several small, drab, and peaceable males. The female mates with each male, who then incubates and tends the eggs for two weeks without the female's aid.

6. DAMSELFISHES

Males defend individual territories on the bottom of coral reefs. Females swim overhead in small schools, whereupon males perform courtship displays after which a female may detach herself from the school to deposit 20,000 to 25,000 eggs in the chosen male's territory. He fertilizes the eggs, then spends a week or so defending them against predators, until they hatch and the fry become independent. The female, meanwhile, has returned to the school of females and has had nothing to do with her eggs or offspring.

7. MOUTH-BREEDING BETTAS

These small fishes are natives of India. When the female spawns, the male deftly catches the eggs in his anal fin and fertilizes them. The female then gathers the eggs in her mouth and spits them, one by one, at the male, who collects them in his mouth. Occasionally he will return an egg to his mate, and the "ball game" between the two might continue for several throws. The female is adamant about the male's duties, however, and eventually all of the eggs are stuffed into his mouth, where they will incubate for the next four to five days. During this time the male cannot eat. Even after the eggs hatch, the fry will seek refuge in their parents' mouths when they feel threatened.

8. RHEAS

These large flightless birds, relatives of the ostrich, are found in South America. A group of females deposit from 20 to 50 fertilized eggs in the nest of a given male. He incubates the eggs by himself while the females move on to another male, copulate with him, lay eggs in his nest, then abandon him in turn.

9. MALLEE FOWL

These Australian birds are about the size of turkeys. The female lays eggs in a large pile of decaying vegetation, sometimes 3 ft. high and 12 ft. in diameter, gathered by the male. The male assiduously tends these eggs, inspecting them daily to determine their temperature and adjusting the compost pile to keep them neither too hot nor too cold.

10. PHALAROPES

Phalaropes are shore birds about the size of robins, quite abundant in Alaska and the prairie regions of North America. The female, which is larger, more brightly colored, and more aggressive than the male, does the courting. After she lays the eggs, he tends them.

—D.B.

ANIMALS GONE BUT NOT FORGOTTEN

With the assistance of humans, more than 300 species and subspecies of animals have become extinct since the beginning of history. Over three quarters of these creatures have disappeared in the past 300 years. Hunting, the devastation of natural habitats, and a lack of understanding about the complex factors which work together to promote or eliminate life were responsible for the losses, and these forces continue to threaten 1,000 varieties of mammals, birds, reptiles, amphibians, and fishes. Theodore Roosevelt acknowledged the universality of the loss of a unique life form in 1899: "When I hear of the destruction of a species I feel as if all the works of some great writer had perished."

The Great Auk

Physical Description: The Northern Hemisphere's answer to the penguin, the great auk or garefowl, was 2½ ft. tall; its 6-in.-long wings resembled flippers and functioned similarly. Its back was a glossy black, while a white breast and stomach completed the familiar tuxedo look. Unlike its southern counterpart, the auk had a dark brown head and a large white spot between the eye and the beak, which was black and lined with white grooves.

Where and How They Lived: The great auk's original range included

The unforgettable dodo.

Great auk.

Russia, Scandinavia, Spain, Italy, and northern America. Eventually its territory was whittled down to the cold, rocky islands around Iceland and Newfoundland, where the bird's large amount of body fat kept it warm enough to enjoy brisk swims in the Atlantic Ocean. The garefowl's strong wings helped it dive in search of crustaceans and small fish to eat. The female laid one 6-in. black-and-brown spotted egg each season.

How and When Destroyed: Prehistoric men hunted the great auk until it retreated to the north seas. In the late 1400s, after the bird had enjoyed centuries of peace, French, Spanish, and Portuguese fishermen discovered the auk's hiding place and the slaughter began anew. After weeks of monotonous meals aboard ship, the men found the meat delicious, and when it was salted down it could be used to restock their larders for the return journey. The creatures were put to a variety of uses. The feathers were stuffed into beds and pillows; a dried auk could serve as a torch because of its fat content; their collarbones were perfect for fishhooks; and if there was one dead auk too many, it was cut up for fish bait. The birds spent most of their time in the sea, where they could easily outdistance a boat, but in the summer, when they had to come ashore to nest, the killing was incredible. Each butchered female meant one less baby auk to keep the species going. By the mid-1700s, there were too few auks left to make hunting worthwhile, but the local residents started turning a profit by gathering their eggs, which were considered a great delicacy. The desperate auks swam off to an isolated rock outcropping known as Geirfuglasker (Garefowl's Island), where they could finally be safe from humans. Then in 1830 a volcano on the sea floor triggered an earthquake which sank the birds' last refuge. The final count started when museum directors and other collectors entered the picture. Concerned that a species might disappear from earth before they got an egg or a stuffed specimen for their collections, these people spread the word that they would pay big money for assorted aukiana. Some enterprising Icelanders found it easy enough to row out to Eldey Island, where the last 50 auks had congregated, and clobber one or two birds or snatch a few eggs to cash in on. By 1844 only two garefowl remained. A bird collector named Carl Siemsen hired Jon Brandsson, Sigurdr Islefsson, and Ketil Ketilsson to track down some new acquisitions for him. Brandsson and Islefsson killed the last two great auks as they were balancing themselves on the rocks beside their nest, which contained a broken egg that the fishermen shattered on the rocks in disgust. The birds did, however, enjoy posthumous notoriety when an unnamed American businessman began digging for guano on Penguin Island, Newfoundland, in 1863. He discovered a cache of perfectly preserved frozen auks—over 100 of them, enough to supply twice the number of museums that had paid for the bird's extinction.

The Dodo

Physical Description: The dodo was a most improbable-looking bird. Standing 3 ft. tall, it was larger than a turkey and primarily ash gray in color. Its 50-lb. body was fat and lumpy, with a ridiculous tuft of curly feathers serving as a tail. It was flightless but still retained stubby wings from which three or four black feathers protruded. Its huge beak, which ended in a hook, was sometimes as long as 9 in. Its legs and heavy feet were large and yellow, and most of its face lacked feathers.

Where and How They Lived: The dodo and its relative, the solitaire, lived on the three Mascarene Islands in the Indian Ocean. The dodo called volcanic Mauritius home and was content to waddle along undisturbed by predators, snacking on native fruits and vegetation. It nested on the ground, and the female laid one big white egg per year.

How and When Destroyed: The Portuguese discovered Mauritius in 1507, but the explorers were soon off in search of other new lands, and their records fail to mention a large, clumsy bird. The discovery of the dodo fell to a Dutch admiral, Jacob Corneliszoon van Neck, who landed on the island in 1598. Fascinated by the huge flocks of odd birds, one of the admiral's colleagues walked through the dodos' nesting grounds to investigate and was "pecked mighty hard" for his interest. Undaunted, Van Neck left Mauritius with two of the birds, one of which stayed in the Netherlands where it posed for 14 portraits, while the other one traveled to Germany to amuse Emperor Rudolf II. The journal Van Neck kept during his voyage was published in 1601. After his description of the dodo he added: "We called these birds *walghvogels* [disgusting birds] for the reason that the more and the longer they are cooked, the less soft and more unpalatable their flesh becomes." Hungry sailors from the second expedition found the breast meat tasty enough, and their ship left Mauritius with 44 of the birds, enough meat to last them for the rest of the voyage.

Soon Dutch settlers were hopping off ships with their dogs, monkeys, and pigs, and several seasick rats also would scurry ashore at each docking. While the colonists were eating the adult birds, the animals they had brought with them were feasting on the eggs and the young. What could the dodo do? With the exception of its beak, the bird was defenseless. When it tried to run, its big belly scraped on the ground, and it was physically impossible for it to climb a tree to nest out of harm's way. The last dodo on Mauritius was eaten in 1681. By that time a dozen of the birds had made their way to Europe, where one of them became a sideshow attraction in London. Naturalist John Tradescant bought it after its death, had it stuffed, and placed it on the shelf next to his other unusual specimens. The Ashmolean Museum at Oxford acquired the bird in 1683, but during spring cleaning in 1755 the museum's board of directors took one look at the dusty, stupid-looking bird and unanimously voted to discard it. Fortunately, the museum's curator had enough foresight to cut off the head and one foot before he tossed the rest of the world's only stuffed dodo in the trash. The old saying "Out of sight, out of mind" was quite apt in this case.

By 1800 scientists were beginning to doubt that the dodo had really existed. Paintings of it looked ridiculous, and only a foot and a head could be offered as proof the bird had lived. What about those eyewitness accounts from the 17th century? Well, if the scientific community gave credence to every gullible traveler returning from the East, they would have to believe in unicorns, dragons, and many other unlikely creatures. What they needed was something irrefutable, like a skeleton or a stuffed specimen. Finally George Clark, a clever native of Mauritius, figured out that the island's volcanic soil was too hard to accommodate fossils; therefore, some of the dodo bones must have been washed by the rain into the muddy delta near the town of Mahébourg. Sure enough, an excavation of the delta in 1863 yielded a quantity of bones which were assembled into complete dodo skeletons and shipped to the world's museums.

The poor dodo still couldn't rest in peace, however; now the taxonomists had to fit it into the right family of birds. Suggestions abounded, and *Didus ineptus* was no sooner placed in the heron family than it was taken out and put in with the ostriches. A succession of families followed, including the vulture, penguin, snipe, and ibis. When English ornithologist Hugh Strickland declared that the dodo had been a giant dove whose wings had withered away from disuse, his colleagues roared with laughter, but Strickland's theory was proved to be correct. Then the dodo furor died down until 1977, when it came to light that the beautiful calvaria major tree of Mauritius had entrusted the bird with its future and was facing extinction itself as a result of the dodo's demise. The tree's seeds had such thick hulls that they could only sprout after being run through the rigors of the dodo's digestive tract. The calvaria, a long-lived hardwood, had held out for 300 years, but only 13 dying trees remained on the island by 1977. Dr. Stanley Temple, an ornithologist from the University of Wisconsin, came to the trees' rescue with turkeys, whose gastrointestinal systems are capable of wearing down the calvaria seeds so that they can sprout and save the species from the hapless dodo's fate.

The Heath Hen

Physical Description: These plump, 18.-in.-long game birds were light brown with black barring. They had a distinctive tuft of about 10 long pointed feathers on each side of their neck. The male had two orange air sacs on its throat, which it inflated with air during mating season and forcefully emptied to produce a booming call.

Where and How They Lived: The heath hen's original range was the northeast coast of the U.S., from Maine to the Carolinas. It was generally found in the vicinity of oak trees, where its diet consisted of acorns and berries. An occasional foray might be made into an open field to search for tidbits of grain and clover. The hen's nest, an informal arrangement of leaves and grass placed over a hollow in the ground, was usually located at the base of a large stump in the woods. There the female would lay a dozen or more buff-colored eggs.

How and When Destroyed: The timid, defenseless heath hen was doomed from the minute the hungry Pilgrims stepped off the *Mayflower*. The birds were not too intelligent. Hunters needed only to spread ashes on a flock's customary resting ground and wait for the birds to land, beating their wings and raising enough dust to blind themselves in the process. Saving their guns for wilier prey, several men with sticks could finish off the heath hens. For those wastrels who did hunt with rifles, the birds cooperated by rising out of a field one or two at a time and flying off in a straight line. The heath hens weren't alone in their stupidity, however; for while hunters found that the nesting females made easy marks, they apparently never realized that each dead mother meant 8 to 12 fewer birds to fire at the following year.

During colonial times, the heath hen had been found in such abundance that "servants stipulated with their employers not to have Heath Hen brought to the table oftener than a few times a week." By 1791, however, the New York legislature considered "an Act for the preservation of the heath hen and other game," and by 1880 the bird had vanished from even the most remote woods on the mainland, and only 200 heath hens could be found on the island of Martha's Vineyard off the coast of Massachusetts. A forest fire destroyed much of the hens' breeding ground in 1907, reducing their number to 77. The public responded to an appeal for funds, and the Commonwealth of Massachusetts set up a 1,600-acre reserve and hired a warden to stop hunting by both humans and animals. He conscientiously performed his duties, and a count of 2,000 hens in April, 1916, was cause for celebration, but a fire blazed across the breeding grounds a month later. The females refused to leave their nests, even when threatened by flames, so most of the 105 survivors were males. A bone-chilling winter was followed by an invasion of hawks, and the 1917 census of heath hens showed that the total number had dipped below 100. The industrious warden swung into action again, and in 1920 the birds' population hit 600. Then something went wrong. The 1927 count was below 30, and the confused warden started tinkering with every variable that could possibly affect the birds' well-being until it was discovered that most of the males were sterile, and soon the females were similarly afflicted. One male survived until 1932, and he was last seen on Mar. 11. The heath hen colony on Martha's Vineyard had been too small and vulnerable to pull through, even with last-minute assistance from humans.

The Mastodon

Physical Description: This cousin of the mammoth stood 9 to 10 ft. tall at the shoulders and tipped the scales somewhere between 5 and 6 tons. Its legs were short in comparison to the rest of its body, which was entirely covered with a mat of long, thick, dark brown hair. Two large tusks were positioned on either side of its trunk, and the mastodon's teeth were so humanlike in appearance that early settlers in the U.S. believed giant men had once inhabited the continent.

Where and How They Lived: The mastodon originated in Asia and migrated to North America 800,000 years ago, lumbering across a bridge of land which then connected Asia and Alaska. Although these large creatures lived during the Great Ice Age, all evidence indicates that they had no problems avoiding most of the bad weather; in fact, their search for trees and grasses to munch on probably took them into the New World during a time when the route was ice-free. Their passion for birch, willow, and alder leaves led them south from Alaska into Canada, and from there they ate their way into the forests east of the Mississippi. Several of the slower mastodons apparently got lost and made a wrong turn in Canada, and thus discovered the Pacific Ocean long before Vasco Núñez de Balboa.

How and When Destroyed: A present-day panel of experts has pretty much cleared humans of the blame for this extinction even though

Reconstruction of the great mastodon, which died out 10,000 years ago.

Paleo-Indians did occasionally eat mastodons 40,000 years ago, and more recently medicine men used fragments of mastodon tusks to enhance their powers of magic. But why the mastodon died out 10,000 years ago may never be known. Climate changes, scarcity of food and water, and even volcanic eruptions have been put forward as theories to explain the beasts' disappearance.

President Thomas Jefferson was fossil-crazy and hoped that living mastodons and mammoths might be found grazing in the unexplored western regions of the U.S. Charles Willson Peale was a friend of Jefferson who owned the Peale Museum in Philadelphia and painted portraits of famous Americans in his spare time. In 1801 he heard reports that farmers near Newburgh, N.Y., had been pulling mastodon bones out of the area's swamps. Peale resolved his would be the first museum to assemble a mastodon skeleton, and he dashed off to New York to buy the bones from John Masten, who had found the greater part of a skeleton while digging for fertilizer on his farm. In addition to providing a double-barreled gun for Masten's son and city dresses for his daughters, Peale paid the farmer $300 for the heap of bones, but Masten had to agree to allow Peale to excavate until he had a complete set. An exhausted Peale returned to Philadelphia after two months of digging and turned the bones over to his son, Rembrandt, to assemble. Rembrandt did an excellent job except for the tusks, which he placed pointing backwards, but soon he realized his mistake and repositioned them.

On Dec. 25, 1801, the "Mammoth Room" of the museum opened its doors to the public, or at least to those individuals who were willing to pay 50¢ to view "the LARGEST of terrestrial beings—the ninth wonder of the world!!!" The display was an overnight success, and the mastodon's popularity was strangely rewarded when "mammoth" became the most popular adjective of the day. A baker down the street from the museum advertised his "mammoth bread"; a "mammoth eater" in Washington, D.C., gobbled up 42 eggs in 10 min.; and the generous ladies of Cheshire, Mass., sent President Jefferson a "mammoth cheese" weighing 1,230 lb. In 1810 Peale retired and turned the museum over to his son Rubens, who in turn gave it to his half brother Titian in 1842. Realizing the museum business couldn't compete with show business, Titian sold the mastodon display to P. T. Barnum five years later. For 100 years, mastodonists believed the skeleton had been destroyed in a fire that occurred at Barnum's storage building in 1848. Then to everyone's surprise, the American Museum of Natural History received a letter from the Hesse State Museum in Darmstadt, West Germany, in 1954, requesting instructions for mounting a mastodon skeleton. It was Peale's skeleton, a little worse for wear after W.W. II. Barnum had turned a quick profit by selling it to King Louis Philippe of France, who abdicated and left the country before it was delivered. Somehow the bones made their way to London, where they stayed for a few years before being sold at a bargain rate to the German museum in 1854. It had taken the Germans 100 years to ask how to put them together.

Steller's Sea Cow

Physical Description: Resembling huge seals, these slow-moving giants measured 30 ft. from their whiskered noses to their flat tails and weighed an estimated 4 tons. Although they lived in the water, sea cows were warm-blooded mammals like whales. Their wrinkled, warty, blackish-brown skin was an inch thick. The sluggish sea cows could not dive; they supported themselves in shallow water on small forearms which looked like paddles but were bent under so that the animals rested on their "knuckles."

Where and How They Lived: Sea cows lived in herds of 10 to 20 just off Bering Island in the Bering Sea, where their days were spent placidly browsing on kelp. To avoid being beached during low tide, the herds would move out to sea, but they floated back close to shore during high tide. The animals mated in June, and the young were carefully tended by the adults.

How and When Destroyed: German physician-naturalist Georg Wilhelm Steller first saw the animal that would bear his name in 1741, when he took part in a Russian voyage of discovery led by Commander Vitus Bering. Their ship, the *St. Peter*, was shipwrecked on its way back to Siberia when it struck a submerged reef off the shore of an unknown island, which later was named for the expedition's leader. There the sick, starving men spent a cold winter. Thirty-two of them, including Bering, died, but the rest were nursed back to health by Steller, who fed them on sea otter and spectacled cormorant (a bird that is now extinct). When the otters moved out to sea in the spring, the remnants of the crew found seal and sea lion meat unpalatable. In May, 1742, their first attempt to haul in a sea cow with a huge iron hook failed because the animal's skin was too thick. A month later, after the ship's yawl had been repaired, some of the sailors set out in the boat with a harpoon. Steller described the hunt: "As soon as the harpooner had struck one of them the men on the shore gradually pulled it toward the beach; the men in the yawl rushed upon it and by their commotion tired it out further; when it seemed enfeebled they jabbed large knives and bayonets into its body until it had lost almost all its blood, which spurted from the wounds as from a fountain, and could thus be hauled on the beach at high tide and made fast."

The creatures' loyalty to each other was also reported by Steller: "When one of them was hooked, all the others were intent upon saving him. Some tried to prevent the wounded comrade from being drawn on the beach by forming a closed circle around him; some attempted to upset the yawl; others laid themselves over the rope or tried to pull the harpoon out of his body, in which indeed they succeeded several times. We also noticed, not without astonishment, that a male came two days in succession to its female which was lying dead on the beach, as if he would inform himself about her condition." The sea cow provided over 7,000 lb. of meat and fat. The flesh tasted like beef, and when the fat was boiled it had the flavor of olive oil, and the men drank it by the cupful.

Only one more animal was brought in before a new ship built from the remains of the *St. Peter* set sail in August, stocked with plenty of dried sea cow meat.

When the men returned to Russia with the pelts of the sea otters they had eaten during the winter, the Russians, traditionally fur traders, promptly set sail for the Bering Sea and the certain profits this new animal's skin would bring. With its sea cows, Bering Island was a popular stop for provisions. The killing was easy, and the meat was delicious after weeks of dried rations. In 1755 a Russian geologist named Jakovlev visited the island searching for copper-mining sites. He realized that the sea cow was headed for extinction and sent a petition to the authorities in Kamchatka suggesting that legal protection be enacted to save the animals. No response was made by the Russian government. There had been only 1,500 sea cows when the first men came to Bering Island, and 27 years later, in 1768, the final one was harpooned.

The Stephens Island Wren

Physical Description: A flightless bird, the Stephens Island wren measured 4 in. long. The backs of both sexes were dark brown, and the male sported a chrome-yellow breast while the female's underside was tan-gray. Both sexes appeared mottled because each feather was tipped with black.

Where and How They Lived: Not much is known about the daily life of this small wren. It was nocturnal and hopped about on coastal rocks, searching for insects to eat. Stephens Island, New Zealand, is only a mile long, so the wren had the distinction of having the smallest known range of any bird.

How and When Destroyed: In 1894 Mr. D. Lyall went to the island to be the lighthouse keeper, and he took his cat along for companionship. One day Lyall opened the lighthouse door to find that his intrepid cat had brought home a strange bird, which the lighthouse keeper managed to pry out of the feline's mouth and pack off to England. Lord Walter Rothschild, a member of the British Ornithological Club, eventually acquired the specimen, established the wren's classification, and named it *Traversia lyalli*. During the next few weeks Lyall's cat delivered about a dozen more birds, and then the supply was exhausted. Lyall dutifully saved each body, and his diligence is responsible for the number of specimens in the world's museums. This is probably the only case in which a cat was responsible for both the discovery and the extermination of a species of bird.

The Tecopa Pupfish

Physical Description: One of the 12 varieties of pupfish found in the U.S., the Tecopa pupfish was blue with a black vertical streak at the end of its tail. The female could be distinguished by her stripes. The whoppers of this subspecies barely topped 1 in. in length.

Where and How They Lived: The Tecopa pupfish made its home in little salty pools and thermal springs near Death Valley National Monument in eastern California. Thriving in waters up to 108° F, these tiny fish ate blue-green algae and produced anywhere from 2 to 10 generations of offspring in a year's time.

How and When Destroyed: During the 1940s the North and South Tecopa Hot Springs were channeled by the builders of a bathhouse. The pupfish had difficulty adapting to the swift-flowing water; their halcyon days filled with basking and munching greens in gentle, tepid pools were over. Mosquito fish were introduced to the Tecopa waters, where they developed a taste for both the usual pupfish fare and the pupfish themselves. Water pollution from the agricultural and recreational development of the area sounded the final death knell. The last pupfish were spotted in an artificial pond and creek at Jed's Motel in Tecopa Hot Springs. Government biologists have been on the lookout for the Tecopa pupfish since 1970, but it was removed from the endangered animals list in 1978 and declared extinct. "The most depressing thing about this loss of life-form is that it was totally avoidable," said Robert Herbst, the assistant secretary of the interior at the time. The bathhouse has long since gone bankrupt and been deserted.

—L.Sc.

9

EXPLORING THE NEW WORLD

A CHRONOLOGY OF THE EXPLORATION OF THE AMERICAS

THE AMERICAS BEFORE COLUMBUS

The New World was a fabulous and varied human landscape, boasting 22 cultural groups whose people spoke 2,000 languages. Several magnificent civilizations had already risen and waned, yet in places some Stone Age natives still lived simple lives. For example:

- In the Aztec capital city of Tenochtitlán (now Mexico City), with its canals which served as streets, its floating gardens, and its treasure-filled palaces, there was an awe-inspiring temple dedicated to the war god Huitzilopochtli. Near a rack filled with 136,000 skulls, mute evidence of past sacrifices, priests ripped out the hearts of living victims and the long, 114-step temple stairway ran red with blood.
- The Iroquois of North America practiced group therapy and belonged to a politically sophisticated federation known as the Five Nations (later the Six Nations), which influenced the makers of the U.S. Constitution.
- The Incas of Peru built suspension bridges, roads up to 3,000 mi. long, intricate irrigation systems, and, in the capital city of Cuzco, a gold-sheathed Temple of the Sun. Their royal brother-sister marriages resembled those of Egypt's pharaohs. Elaborately knotted strings, *quipus*, formed the basis of their advanced accounting and information systems. However, they were no strangers to barbaric practices; one member of the royal family made a drumhead of the skin of a murdered relative.
- The pueblo-dwelling natives of what is now New Mexico and Arizona, builders of adobe houses, some of which were many stories high, frowned on ambition and had developed an intricate and harmonious religion based on oneness with the universe.
- The Mayas of Yucatán and Guatemala built libraries containing thousands of bark-paper, full-color books written in an as yet undeciphered language. All but three of these were burned in the 1500s by Spanish missionary Diego de Landa because they "contained nothing in which there were not to be seen superstition and lies of the devil." The

Mayas' base-20 number system, which included zero, had been developed a thousand years in advance of its use elsewhere, and their astronomers were capable of astonishing precision in charting the heavens. By the late fifteenth century, when the Europeans came, the Mayas, who had begun to flourish about 350 A.D., were already in decline.

- The gentle Arawaks of the West Indies grew corn and yams, spun and wove cotton. Of them Columbus said, "They invite you to share anything that they possess, and show as much love as if their hearts went with it."
- According to the chronicles of Columbus's second voyage, the Caribs, also indigenous to the West Indies, kept emasculated boy slaves whom they fattened up for feasts at which the babies of female slaves served as appetizers.
- The Chichimecs of northeast Mexico, nomads who played games not only with rubber balls but with arm and leg bones ripped from the bodies of living victims, were so fierce that it took the Spanish 200 years to subdue them.

These and others were the descendants of the Asians who had moved across Siberia and down through Alaska into an unknown continent. The first wave of emigration took place at least 20,000 years ago, and maybe as long as 35,000 years ago. The earliest inhabitants were joined by later waves of Asians coming overland and perhaps by a few boatloads of seafarers from ancient Phoenicia, Africa, and other lands, who had found sailing to the west fairly easy because of the trade winds, but who had learned that getting back home was close to impossible.

POSSIBLE VISITS PREDATING COLUMBUS

C. 450 A.D.—Chinese Buddhist Monk Huishen

The monk's legendary 40-year voyage may have taken him as far as the Americas and back. Recently, controversial evidence of a possible early Chinese visitation came to light when two doughnut-shaped, 80-lb. stone anchors, seemingly of Chinese origin, were discovered off the California coast, one in 1972 and the other in 1975.

6th Century A.D.—Irish Monk St. Brendan the Navigator

St. Brendan, like many other Irish monks, was an expert sailor. According to legend, he traveled for years on a search for an Eden across the Atlantic. The curraghs in which he sailed, boats consisting of a wooden frame covered with oxhide, were very seaworthy. He may have reached Jan Mayen Island north of Iceland and perhaps the mainland of the Americas.

1001—Viking Leif Ericson

Son of hot-tempered Eric the Red, who discovered and colonized Greenland, Leif Ericson was a "temperate, fair-dealing" young man in his 20s when he set sail with a crew of 35 in his *knarr*, a beamy, knockabout cousin of the Viking dragonship. Ericson and his crew made it to Vinland, now identified by archaeologists as Anse aux Meadows, Newfoundland.

CHRISTOPHER COLUMBUS (1451–1506), *"Admiral of the Mosquitoes" and Renaissance Discoverer of the Americas*

Using a plank for a life preserver, a 25-year-old Genoese sailor named Christopher Columbus swam the 6 mi. from his sinking ship to the shores of Portugal. In the next few years, in Lisbon and in Spain, he educated himself and became convinced that the fabulously rich Indies could be reached by sailing west across the Atlantic. From his reading—his marginal notes are still there to be seen in old books—he reached a "big Asia, narrow Atlantic" conclusion and computed the distance from the Canary Islands to "Cipango" (Japan) at only 2,500 nautical mi. The actual distance is more than 10,000 mi. The advisers of Queen Isabella of Spain were right when they told her not to invest in Columbus's venture because his goal was "uncertain and impossible to any educated person." They said, correctly, that the ocean was far too big, although they, and most other educated people, had no quarrel with the theory that the world was round. If Columbus and his crew had not been lucky enough to stumble on the unexpected Americas, they probably would have died of thirst on a seemingly endless sea.

That Columbus was able to obtain financing for and accomplish his "enterprise of the Indies" is attributable to fantastic luck, fanatic persistence, and fortuitous errors. By a chain of events, he was introduced to Queen Isabella, who took an instant liking to him, perhaps because he was a fellow redhead. But she didn't agree to finance him right away, and Columbus single-mindedly trekked from court to court throughout Europe for six years looking for backing before she gave in.

Though he found time to marry an aristocrat, by whom he had his son Diego, and after his wife's death to take a mistress, mother of his son Ferdinand, he thought of very little except doing what he had set out to do—sail west to the Indies. Once he was on his way, he proved to be very good at managing a fleet. He was a genius at dead reckoning, though not at celestial navigation (he did upon occasion "shoot" the wrong star), and his crew, whom he treated well, adored him.

Despite the 475 years since his death, he stands out as startlingly real and human. His feelings as a father are revealed in a diary entry written after a stormy passage at sea: "What gripped me most were the sufferings of my son [Ferdinand]; to think that so young a lad, only 13, should go through so much. But Our Lord lent him such courage that he even heartened the rest, and he worked as though he had been to sea all of a long life. That comforted me."

1492–1493—COLUMBUS'S FIRST VOYAGE

April, 1492 Along with a passport and three letters of introduction, one to the "Grand Khan" and two with a blank space where a salutation could be written in, Columbus was given a grant by the Spanish crown

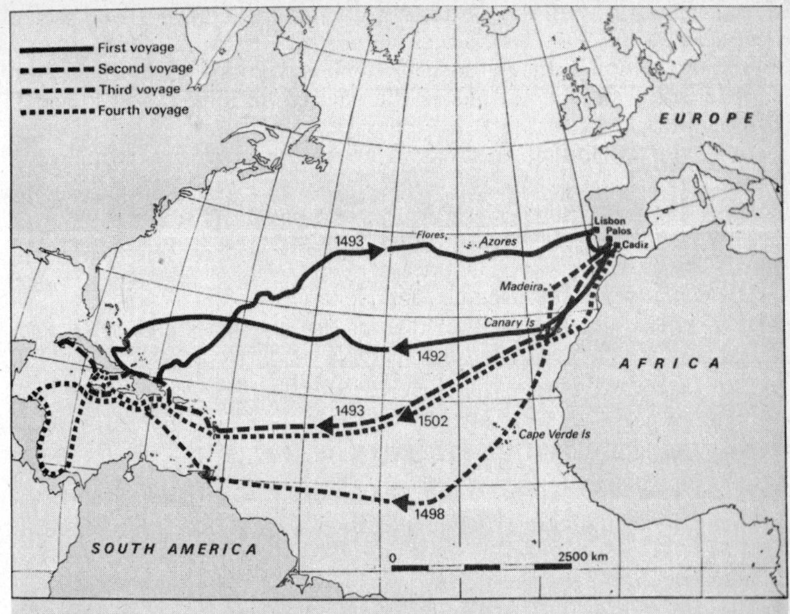

Map of the Atlantic showing the voyages of Columbus, by C. Fisher.

to "discover and acquire certain islands and mainlands in the Ocean Sea."

Aug. 3, 1492 Columbus set sail with his crew of about 90, divided among three ships: the *Santa María* (according to him a "dull sailer"), the *Pinta*, and the *Niña*. After picking up supplies in the Canaries, he noted their course as "west; nothing to the north, nothing to the south." Throughout his voyage, much of it "like April in Andalusia," he kept two logs, one for his true reckoning and a false one to show the crew so that they would not become alarmed at the huge distances they were traversing. However, the false reckoning turned out to be more accurate than the true.

Oct. 9, 1492 Columbus promised a restive crew that if no land was found within three days, they would turn back. He had already seen flocks of birds, and leafy branches were floating by on the waves, which heartened him after he made his promise.

Oct. 12, 1492, 2 A.M. Rodrigo de Triana, the *Pinta's* lookout, shouted "*Tierra! Tierra!*" ("Land! Land!") Landfall was an island (probably Watling Island) in what is now the Bahamas. Columbus thought it to be west of Japan.

October, 1492, to February, 1493 They explored the islands of the Caribbean, including Cuba, where Columbus sent an embassy to meet El Gran Kan, who was actually only the cacique, or chief, of a 50-hut village. The natives wore gold, if not much else. During the return voyage, a storm threatened to sink the *Niña* and the *Pinta* (the *Santa*

Maria had already run aground off Cuba) and the crew vowed that if they were saved, they would seek out a shrine to the Virgin Mary and "go in procession in their shirts." Columbus wrapped his journal of the voyage in a waxed cloth, placed the package in a cask, and tossed it overboard.

Feb. 18, 1493 Landfall, the Azores, where they kept their vow to the Virgin.

Later that year, Columbus, gone gray, presented himself to the Spanish court with six Arawaks and parrots in cases. He wept at the end of the *Te Deum*.

His discoveries: the Bahamas and Cuba.

May 4, 1493 A papal bull allotted lands east of a meridian 318 nautical mi. west of the Azores to Portugal, lands west of it to Spain. West of the boundary, Columbus and others claimed, all lice and fleas miraculously disappeared.

1493–1496—COLUMBUS'S SECOND VOYAGE

Sept. 25, 1493 Columbus set sail. At Gomera, in the Canary Islands, he became *tincto d'amore* ("dyed with love") for a cruel but beautiful widow.

Incidents of the voyage:

- Hispaniola (Haiti): Commander Alonso de Ojeda (1465?–1515), a pirate who had come into the queen's favor by dancing on a 200-ft.-high tower beam in Seville, found three gold nuggets. A settlement, Isabela, was established.
- Jamaica: A bejeweled cacique, his wife in a "little cotton thing no bigger than an orange peel," and their two teenaged daughters went aboard ship and begged to go to Spain, but Columbus sent them home.
- However, Columbus did take 1,500 Indians captive. Of these, 500 were sent to Spain. Then the Spanish colonists at Isabela were allowed as many as they wanted for slaves, and the balance were set free. The latter were so eager to get away from the Spanish that some mothers abandoned their babies during their flight. Only 6,000 Arawak natives out of the original population of about 1 million were alive in Hispaniola in 1533.

Mar. 10–June 11, 1496 During the voyage home, food supplies became so perilously low that the crew suggested they eat the Caribs on board. Columbus refused, saying that they were people too. When they made landfall, the faces of all were "the color of saffron."

- At court, with a cacique in a big gold collar and crown, Columbus presented Ferdinand and Isabella with gold nuggets as big as pigeons' eggs.

1494 The secular Treaty of Tordesillas again divided the undiscovered lands of the world between Portugal and Spain, and moved the boundary line 270 leagues (about 2.5 statute mi.) further west, which was to Portugal's advantage.

1497 John Cabot (1450–1498), a "lower-class Venetian . . . of a fine mind, very expert in navigation," sailed from Bristol, England, under letters of patent issued by Henry VII of England "to seeke out, discover, and finde whatsoever iles, countreyes, regions, or provinces of the heathens and infidelles . . . in what part of the world soever they bee." Cabot—whose name was probably anglicized from Caboto after he and his wife and three sons moved to the seafaring town of Bristol, England, not later than 1495—had one small ship, the *Matthew*, and a crew of 18, including his Italian barber. On June 24 they made their landfall, probably at what is now Belle Isle, off the coast of Labrador. Cabot found fishnets and a red stick pierced at both ends, likely a weaving shuttle, indicating native fishermen. Stone-weighted baskets dropped in the water came up full of cod. This region is now the Grand Bank, a world-renowned fishing ground. Home by August, Cabot, a hero wearing silk clothes bought perhaps with the £10 given him by the king on his return, strutted down Lombard Street while common people ran after him like madmen. He was the first Renaissance explorer to discover North America: Cape Breton Island, possibly Nova Scotia, certainly Newfoundland.

1498 Planning to reach Cipango (Japan), where Cabot thought "all the spices of the world have their origin, as well as the jewels," he left on a second voyage, the first search for a Northwest Passage. He never returned. English historian Polydore Vergil scoffed snidely that Cabot had "found his new lands only on the ocean's bottom."

1498–1500—COLUMBUS'S THIRD VOYAGE

By now the beautiful widow at Gomera was out of the picture. After surviving the doldrums and a tidal wave, Columbus's ships reached Trinidad, where the crew tried to land. To soothe the natives, they played music and danced, but the Indians misinterpreted this sign of European goodwill and let fly with arrows. During this voyage, Columbus became the first Renaissance European to set foot on the American mainland when he went ashore at the Paria Peninsula, in what was to become Venezuela. At first he considered it another island, then feeling the full force of the Orinoco, a mighty freshwater river, he was inspired to write, "I believe that this is a very great continent, until today unknown." Later, however, he reconsidered; it was, he said, actually an extension of China, perhaps paradise, situated on that part of the world that protrudes like a woman's nipple to be closer to heaven. In 1500 crafty and unscrupulous Francisco de Bobadilla, sent by the crown to Santo Domingo, the new capital of Hispaniola, to check up on things, shipped Columbus home in chains. When the ship's captain wanted to free him, Columbus refused; only the king could give the order, he remarked with stiff-necked pride.

1499 Rascally De Ojeda sighted an Indian village built on stilts over water on the northeastern coast of South America and, according to some, named it Venezuela ("Little Venice").

1499–1500 Vicente Yáñez Pinzón (1460?–1524?), the *Niña*'s captain, explored South America and may have reached Brazil and the Amazon. He took 36 painted natives and a monkey back to Spain.

1500 Portuguese nobleman Pedro Álvares Cabral (1460?–1526?), with a crew of 1,200 on 13 ships, reached the southern part of Brazil and claimed it for Portugal. The sailors danced with the Tupi Indians to a tune played by the ship's bagpiper and were so entranced by a native girl who "was so charming that many women of our land, seeing such attractions, would be ashamed that theirs were not like hers" that they didn't notice that the Tupis were cannibals.

1501–1504 Amerigo Vespucci (1454–1512), son of a moneyed, upper-class Florentine family, sailed, in one of several voyages, with Gonçalo Coelho under the flag of Portugal. The expedition may have reached a point near the southern boundary of Brazil. Vespucci became far more famous than Coelho, probably because he wrote such colorful descriptions of what he saw—for example, the women of Brazil, he noted, "being very lustful," applied poison to their mates' genitals to make them swell. Up to this point, the Vespuccis' main claim to fame had been a cousin, Simonetta, who modeled for Botticelli's *Primavera* and *Birth of Venus*.

1502–1504—COLUMBUS'S FOURTH ("HIGH") VOYAGE

He failed to achieve his goal—finding a strait between Cuba (still considered mainland) and South America to the Indian Ocean—but did explore a large part of the Central American coast. Incidents of the voyage:

- Feeling a hurricane in his bones, the old mariner asked for refuge at Santo Domingo, but Governor Nicolás de Ovando, laughing at the bad-weather prediction, refused to let him enter the harbor. Columbus wrote: "What man ever born, not excepting Job, would not have died of despair when in such weather, seeking safety . . . we were forbidden the land and harbor that I, by God's will and sweating blood, won for Spain." However, Columbus rode out the hurricane unscathed, and Ovando got his just deserts: 25 of his ships, with a cargo in gold, sank.
- Trade with the Guaymis of Costa Rica was profitable. For example, three hawk's bells worth 1¢ each bought a gold amulet worth $25.
- Hostile Indians at Santa María de Belén, a trading post set up by Columbus on the Isthmus of Panama, were only temporarily diverted from attack by watching ship's captain Diego Méndez having his hair cut. Later Columbus, trapped on board ship, climbed to the maintop to shout to the men to return to safety. Delirious from malaria, he heard the voice of God, urging him to have faith.
- In June, 1503, the crew of 116 was marooned in Jamaica. The last of their leaky ships had given out. Méndez set off in a dugout canoe to find help. When the Indians on the island refused to give the Spanish food, Columbus warned them that God would evidence his displeasure on Feb. 28, 1504, which he knew was the date of an eclipse of the moon. The trick worked. Terrified by the darkness, which came as predicted, the Indians once again supplied food to the Spanish.

1507 In an appendix to a new edition of Ptolemy's *Cosmographiae introductio*, young geography professor Martin Waldseemüller (1470?–1518?) wrote ". . . and the fourth part of the Globe, which, since Americus discovered it, may be called *Amerige* . . ." and included the word

America in bold letters on a map of South America. By the mid-1500s the name had spread to include North America. Ever since, the naming of the New World for Vespucci has caused controversy. Ralph Waldo Emerson called him a "pickle dealer at Seville who managed in this lying world to suppress Columbus and baptize half the world with his own dishonest name." Actually, he was a ship chandler or dealer in marine supplies.

1508 Juan Ponce de León (1460?–1521) conquered Puerto Rico, where he grew rich on the "labors, blood, and sufferings of his subjects."

1508 Juan Diaz de Solís (1470?–1516) with Vicente Pinzón searched the east coast of South America as far as the Río Negro for a strait to the Pacific, and though they found none, they did prove Cuba to be an island.

1508 Sebastian Cabot (1476?–1557), the son of John Cabot, may have sailed from Newfoundland to Cuba, but we have only his own unreliable word for it. Sebastian was a colorful personage and a great liar. For example, he claimed that Newfoundland codfish, after swimming ashore to eat fallen leaves, were ambushed by bears.

1509 Gone broke, planter Vasco Núñez de Balboa (1475–1519) had himself boxed and shipped in a provision cask with his dog Leoncico from Santo Domingo to the Gulf of Darien, where he ended up in command of a settlement on the western side of the gulf. Later, a cacique's son, watching the Spanish weigh gold and shocked at their greed over it, knocked the scales from a Spaniard's hands and said, "If your hunger of gold bee so insatiable . . . I will shewe you a region flowing with golde, where you may satisfie your ravening appetites." The Indian then pointed toward the southern mountains. Balboa did not forget what he said.

1513 With 190 Spaniards and several hundred Indian guides, Balboa traversed the narrow waist of land at the Isthmus of Panama, 45 mi. of terrible rain forest, swamps, and lakes. On the way Balboa, ordinarily friendly to Indians—after all, he had married one—ordered the gay harem of a cacique they met torn apart by dogs because he hated homosexuality. On either Sept. 25 or 26, in armor and accompanied only by Leoncico, he stood alone on a peak and marveled at the vast Pacific spread before him. Keats's great sonnet "On First Looking into Chapman's Homer" is in fact full of inaccuracies; for example, it wasn't "stout Cortez . . . with eagle eyes" who first saw the Pacific, nor were his men, or even Balboa's, there to "look at each other with a wild surmise." On the 29th, Balboa's expedition reached a bay into which he waded, sword in hand, to take possession for Spain.

1513 On his quest for the Fountain of Youth, which according to legend could miraculously cure *el enflaquecimiento del sexo,* or sexual debility, Ponce de León took an expedition from Puerto Rico to a land he called Pascua Florida (now Florida). Though they found no fountain while cruising the coast, they did discover something else—the Gulf Stream—and on the way back, Yucatán.

1517 With 110 soldiers, Francisco Fernández de Córdoba sailed the

Gulf of Mexico looking for Indians to enslave. In Indian fights, 50 Spaniards were killed and Córdoba himself was struck by 12 arrows. Their discovery: the wealth of Yucatán.

1518 Juan de Grijalva, sailing for his uncle Diego Velásquez, who was governor of the Antilles, further explored the Mexican coast. The crew cut their hair "thinking they would have little leisure time to comb it." Discoveries: the island of Cozumel, site of a Mayan temple, and Tabasco River, now called the Grijalva.

1518 From the Gulf of Mexico, Alonso Álvarez de Pineda sailed up the Mississippi, naming it Espiritu Santo, then traveled south along the Gulf of Mexico to the mouth of the Río Pánuco (present-day Tampico), where he and his crew fought a savage battle with the Aztecs. Many Spaniards, including Pineda, were killed and eaten, and later their skins were hung as trophies in the Aztec temples. One ship, commanded by Diego de Camargo, survived the voyage. He and the crew arrived back in Vera Cruz "ill and very yellow and with swollen bellies."

1519 Balboa was arrested at the order of Pedrarias Dávila, the cruel governor of Darien. As the result of a trumped-up charge of murder and treason, he was beheaded and thrown to the vultures. The arresting officer was Francisco Pizarro, who had accompanied Balboa to the Pacific.

1519 "We Spaniards suffer from a disease that only gold can cure," the Spanish nobleman Hernando Cortes (1485–1547) once said. In 1519, after a career as a planter in Cuba and inspired by tales of Aztec wealth, he set off to conquer the "kingdom to the west." On the way he picked up two interpreters: Jerónimo de Aguilar, who had spent eight years as a Maya captive and knew the language; and Marina, an Indian woman who spoke not only Maya but Nahuatl, or Aztec, and who became the Spanish conqueror's mistress. Cortes landed on the coast of Mexico at the exact time the Aztecs had expected the return of Quetzalcóatl, a white-faced, black-bearded god who was a foil to Huitzilopochtli, then in the ascendancy. Montezuma, the Aztec ruler, sent Cortes gifts, including a huge gold wheel embossed with designs. With his Indian allies and a 400-man Spanish army, Cortes marched to Tenochtitlán, capital of the Aztec empire, maiming and killing hostile Indians along the way. He took Montezuma prisoner and so acquired Mexico for Spain.

1519–1520 Ferdinand Magellan (1480?–1521), a Portuguese navigator sailing for Spain on the first round-the-world voyage, headed down the east coast of South America and discovered the Strait of Magellan, which offered passage to the Pacific. Some events of this part of the voyage:

- At the mouth of the river now known as Rió de Janeiro, the crew dallied with native girls, whose favors were bought from their brothers for the price of a "German knife of the worst quality." Sailor Antonio Pigafetta reported that one beautiful girl, believing herself to be unobserved, filched a nail, valued for its iron, from a cabin. "Picking it up, with great skill and gallantry, she thrust it between the lips of her vagina and bending low, departed, the Captain General and I having witnessed this."

• Sighting a mountain, Magellan cried out, "*Monte video!*" ("I see a mountain!"), and so the capital of Uruguay was named.

• A giant of a man—nearly naked, painted all over, and with huge straw-stuffed shoes on his feet—danced on the shore of a land that Magellan called Patagonia. The word means "land of the big-footed ones."

1520 João Álvarez Fagundes, sailing for Portugal, rounded the south coast of Newfoundland to reach Penguin Island, where flocks of flightless great auks—now extinct—were herded up the gangplanks, killed, and used for fish bait.

1522 Cortes was appointed governor and captain general of the huge territory of New Spain, which included Mexico.

1522 The *Victoria*, commanded by Juan Sebastián del Cano (1487?–1526), reached Seville, its long circumnavigation of the globe as part of the Magellan expedition ended. Magellan himself had been killed in a battle with Philippine natives on Apr. 27, 1521.

1524 Tuscan nobleman Giovanni da Verrazano (1485?–1528?) departed from France, sponsored by the crown and some Lyons bankers, to search for a strait to Cathay. Dark and bearded, with a Roman nose, he had the look of a commander but the personality of a snob; he called his crew *la turba marittima* ("the maritime mob"). Landfall was Cape Fear, off what is now North Carolina. After a brief voyage south, his ship, *La Dauphine*, turned north and proceeded to Newfoundland, with stops at New York Bay and Narragansett Bay. Verrazano wrote the first comprehensive description of the geography and people of the east coast of North America. On the Carolina banks, Verrazano mistook the narrow belt of land for the mainland and the inner bay, apparently limitless, for *el Mare Orientale* ("the Oriental Sea"). For the next century cartographers showed North America as narrow-waisted at this spot, and the bay was known as "Verrazano's Sea." The natives they encountered were friendly—succoring a sailor inadvertently washed ashore and offering peace pipes—and Verrazano waxed rhapsodic about them until the Abnaki, in what is now Maine, shocked him and his crew with their "crudity and evil manners," expressed by "exhibiting their bare behinds and laughing immoderately." In disgust he named their land *Terra Ondi de Mala Gente* ("Land of the Bad People"). Verrazano, immortalized by a bridge named after him that spans the Narrows south of New York Bay, thought he had reached a New World, but his surmise was based on distance miscalculations.

1524 Francisco Pizarro (1470?–1541), son of a Spanish officer, sailed for the Spanish governor of Panama down the Pacific coast of present-day Colombia. With him were 100 men, among them his partner, ugly but likable Diego de Almagro (1475?–1538), and a priest named Hernando de Luque, later nicknamed Hernando el Loco for his propensity to get involved in get-rich-quick schemes.

1526–1528 Pizarro, with two ships and Bartolomé de la Ruiz as navigator, set off down the western coast of Colombia. While Pizarro traveled inland, Ruiz sailed south to a point somewhere below the equator and returned with tales of a great civilization in Peru. He had come upon a native balsa raft carrying finely crafted gold and silver ornaments,

Francisco Pizarro.

rubies, and emeralds. When the governor of Panama refused to let them investigate the new lands, Pizarro drew a line in the sand and said to his men that north of the line was Panama and poverty, south of it Peru and riches. With that dramatic gesture, he began a course that eventually led to the conquest of the Inca empire. He went south to the Inca city of Tumbes and beyond to what is now Trujillo, but made no effort on this expedition to conquer the Incas.

1526–1530 Sebastian Cabot, with a crew of 200 which included the first official "ship's cook," sailed from Seville on what was supposed to be a circumnavigation of the globe. En route to South America Cabot lost his flagship and treated the men so badly that one tried to kill him by "accidentally" dropping a block on his head. Hearing that somewhere in the reaches of the Río de la Plata in South America there was a mountain of solid silver ruled by *el rey blanco* ("the white king"), he scotched his plans to sail around the world and spent three years exploring the Río de la Plata waterways. Sailing upriver, the crew sometimes had to haul the ship with tow ropes. Sometimes they had only snake to eat, sometimes nothing. They didn't find the silver mountain.

1527–1537 The incompetent Pánfilo de Narváez (1480?–1528) sailed from Spain to Florida, where he landed already minus 140 men who had jumped ship and 70 more lost at sea in a storm. He sent his remaining ships to look for a harbor to the west, then set off overland with about 300 men. According to Álvar Núñez Cabeza de Vaca (1490?–1557?), who recorded the journey, which for him was to end more than eight years later, Narváez was extremely cruel to the Indians. For example, after one battle he ordered the cacique's nose cut off and his mother thrown to the dogs to be torn apart alive. The skillful Indian archers, with their 6-ft. bows, retaliated. At the Gulf of Mexico, no ships were waiting. With ingenuity, the Spaniards built five ships out of improvised materials (nails were fashioned from spurs and sails from shirts). One by one these ships were wrecked on a voyage that took Narváez and his men past the mouth of the Mississippi to Galveston Island, where they spent the winter of 1528–1529. Only 15 survived, looking like "pictures of death." Cabeza de Vaca was separated from the others

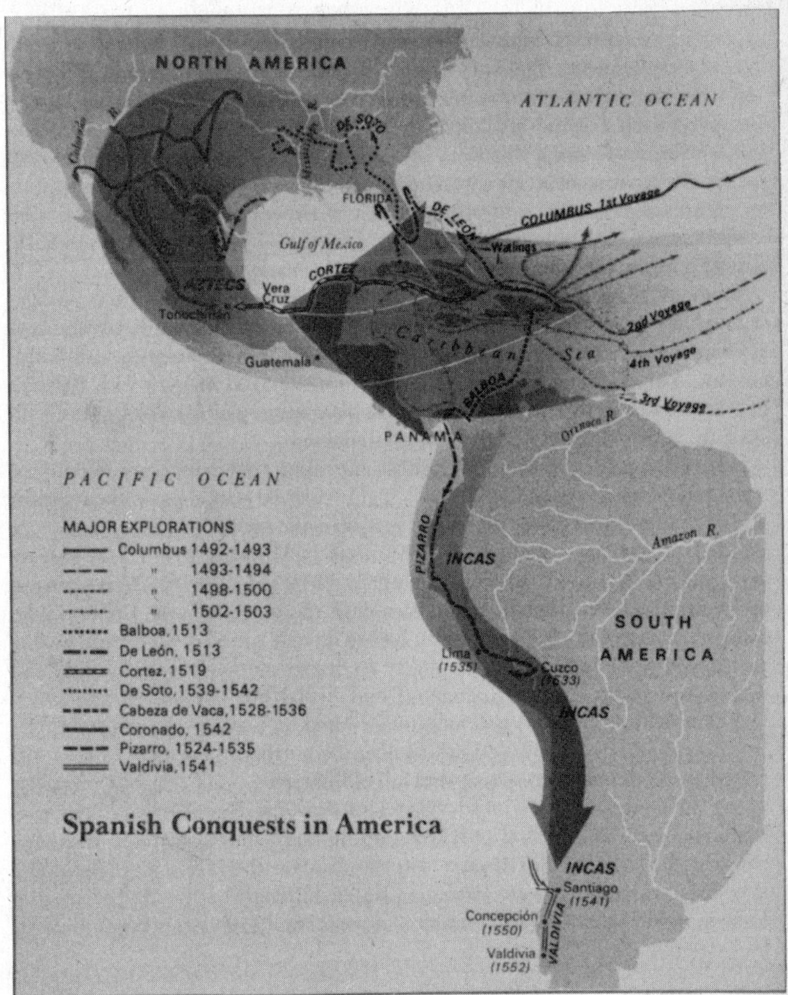

Spanish Conquests in America

until 1533, when he met three survivors at the Colorado River in Texas: Alonso del Castillo, Andrés Dorantes, and Dorantes's black servant Esteban, nicknamed Estebancito by Cabeza de Vaca. With a retinue of thousands of Indians, the four made it through hundreds of miles of territory by acting as faith healers, blessing the sick and reciting prayers over them, and ended up in Mexico City.

1528 Verrazano, looking for a passage to Asia on a third voyage, sailed through the Lesser Antilles and anchored off an island that may have been part of Guadeloupe. He and his brother Girolamo took a longboat to explore the shore. Girolamo sat in the boat while Giovanni waded ashore to be set upon by Caribs, killed, cut up, and eaten raw.

1530 Ambrosio Alfinger, in South America with a German banking group which had been given the right to exploit Venezuela in return for cancellation of Spain's debts to these bankers, searched for El Dorado, a legendary kingdom of incalculable riches, and ended up exploring a large part of Venezuela instead. When several Indian members of his chain gang fell over, Alfinger cut off their heads rather than detach the ring the Indians wore around their necks. He later got what he deserved—death at the hands of angry Indians.

1532–1533 Francisco Pizarro, with 168 men and 3 ships, returned to Peru, where he met with Atahualpa, winner of an Inca civil war, at a sulfur spa in the Andes, 350 mi. southeast of Tumbes. According to one story, a friar greeted the ruler with a Bible and a cross, asking for his allegiance to Spain, whereupon Atahualpa threw the Bible to the ground and, pointing to the sun, said, "My God still lives." Pizarro ambushed Atahualpa and took him prisoner. To gain his freedom, Atahualpa offered treasure enough to fill a room 22 ft. by 17 ft. up to a height of 7 ft., marked by Pizarro with a red line that is still there. He was true to his word, going so far as to strip the gold-sheathed Temple of the Sun in the capital city of Cuzco in order to fill the room. But Pizarro was not so honorable and ordered Atahualpa killed in 1533. Peru was then his.

1534 Jacques Cartier (1491–1557), sailing for the French, voyaged to the Americas on a search for gold and a northwest passage to the Orient. He had two ships and a crew of 61. After arriving at Newfoundland, his crew killed a swimming bear "big as a cow and white as a swan." Cartier was not impressed with much of what he saw, saying of the stony, desolate land, "I am inclined to regard this land as the one God gave to Cain." But L'Île de Bryon cheered him with its "trees, fields of wild wheat, and pease in flower as fair and abundant as I ever saw in Brittany." On the Gaspé Peninsula, the Micmac women showed friendship by rubbing the arms of the French. When Cartier erected a cross to claim the land for France, Huron chief Donnacona, in his old black bearskin, indicated in sign language that the country was his. Cartier placated him with gifts and took him and his two teenaged sons, dressed in French finery, back to France with him. Discoveries: Prince Edward Island, Anticosti Island, the Gaspé Peninsula, Jacques Cartier Passage, Chaleur Bay.

1535–1536 On a second voyage to the Americas, Cartier explored La

Atahualpa, last ruler of the Incas, receiving Pizarro and a friar.

Grande Rivière (today the St. Lawrence) for 1,000 mi. to Hochelaga (now the site of Montreal), until he was finally stopped by rapids. Asked by the Indians to heal the sick, he instead read the Bible and gave the children tin lambs. The French wintered back at Stadacona (which became Quebec City), passing time in an Indian brothel and gaming house. When the crew contracted scurvy, Chief Donnacona's son Domagaya cured the men with arborvitae leaves, rich in vitamin C. (An arborvitae Cartier took back to France was planted at Fontainebleau.) Meanwhile, Donnacona regaled the French with tales of the land of Saguenay, rich in gold and jewels, with European-dressed white natives, one-legged pygmies, and a tribe of anusless people who consumed only liquids. Tricking Donnacona with a false ceremony, Cartier took him and his two sons back to France, where the sons disappeared into the Paris underworld and Donnacona gained fame as a Saguenay expert.

1535–1536 Cortes, sailing north from Mexico, took possession for Spain of Baja California, which he thought was an island, at Bahia de la Paz.

1535–1537 Almagro, by now having lost an eye and several fingers while fighting Indians, explored lands given him south of Peru extending 2,500 mi. below Cuzco. With him were 570 Spaniards and thousands of Indians, many of whom froze to death in the Andes. It has been said that he forced Indians to carry newborn foals on litters. No gold was found. When they got back, Almagro fought Pizarro for possession of Cuzco, but he was captured and executed.

1536–1538 Gonzalo Jiménez de Quesada (1500?–1579?), a Spaniard, explored the interior of Colombia, searching for gold in the rich kingdom of the Chibchas. He founded the city of Santa Fe (now Bogotá) and also uncovered a fortune in gold and emeralds. According to legend, each Chibcha ruler, on ascending the throne, coated his body with resin and gold dust, then paddled a raft out into the center of Lake Guatavita in the firelit night to immerse himself in the waters and watch gold dust shower to the bottom. When the lake was drained in 1912, a treasure worth millions of dollars was found.

1536–1538 Georg Hohemut von Speyer (d. 1520), a Venezuelan German, explored the valleys of the Orinoco and the Amazon.

1538–1543 Hernando de Soto (1500?–1542) landed in Florida after sailing from Spain. With his army of 570 men, he marched for four years through southeastern North America. He was the first to cross the Appalachians, exploring as far as Mobile Bay, the Yazoo Delta, and Oklahoma. During the journey he developed a fever and died. Luis Moscoso de Alvarado took over and led the expedition into the upper Brazos, sailed down the Mississippi, and crossed the Gulf of Mexico to arrive in Río Pánuco with 311 survivors.

1539 Fray Marcos and Estebancito, called "children of the Sun" by the Indians, searched the southwest of North America for the fabulous Seven Cities of Cíbola. Estebancito, dressed in bells and feathers and with an Indian harem, went ahead and sent back a huge cross, indicating he had found the Seven Cities. However, he was put to death as a spy by the Zuñi, and Marcos never found the Seven Cities. He did reach a high point near what is now the Arizona–New Mexico border to view from afar a city of storied pueblos that appeared to his bedazzled eyes and fevered imagination to glitter in the sun with wealth.

1539–1540 Francisco de Ulloa, sponsored by Cortes, explored the Gulf of California, rounded Cabo San Lucas, went north as far as Isla de Cedros, perhaps reached what is now San Diego. He sent one ship back with a report of "ugly and sterile lands" and a notice that Baja California was not an island, but his own ship did not return.

1540–1542 With 300 "vicious young gentlemen" as well as Indians, blacks, and horses, 29-year-old Francisco Vásquez de Coronado, governor of New Spain's New Galicia, began a trek across the Southwest looking for the Seven Cities so glowingly described by Fray Marcos. He found one—an adobe pueblo, but the Spaniards were refused entry by the Zunis, who pelted the invaders with rocks. Melchior Díaz was sent back to locate the expedition's ships, under command of Hernando de Alarcón. Díaz discovered letters buried under a tree where the Colorado and Gila rivers meet stating that Alacrón had given up waiting and had returned to Mexico. Though Díaz started to explore Colorado, he died of a lance wound before he could accomplish much. Another party, led by García López de Cárdenas, discovered the Grand Canyon. Meanwhile, yet another group reached as far inland as Tigeux, which became its winter headquarters, and also Cicúye, an Indian village on the Pecos River. There El Turco, an Indian servant, told them of his hometown to the east, where the inhabitants ate from gold bowls. The Spanish governor followed El Turco all the way to his village in what is now Kansas, but it turned out to be just an ordinary Wichita Indian encampment. El Turco was strangled for his lies. In spite of all the land he explored, Coronado had found no gold, so he received no honors when he arrived back in New Spain.

1541–1542 Cabeza de Vaca, governor of the Río de la Plata territory (parts of present-day Uruguay, Argentina, Paraguay, and Bolivia), led a cross-country expedition into Asunción, governed by Domingo de Irala, who had married the seven daughters of a cacique. There Indian girls had been forced into prostitution by the Spanish. Consequently, Asunción was called "Mohammed's Paradise." The incorruptible Cabeza de Vaca took command and ended such practices.

1541–1542 *'C'est un diamant de Canada!"* ("It's a Canadian diamond!") is an ironic French expression that typifies the fruitless search for Saguenay, continued by Cartier on his third voyage. This time the expedition was under the command of Jean François de la Roque, Sieur de Roberval, who was to follow after Cartier. Cartier established a settlement above Quebec, then set off down the St. Lawrence to look for the fabulous land. At Montreal, some Indians showed him with a map made of sticks that even more rapids lay ahead, so he gave up. When the Indians became hostile in the summer of 1542, Cartier decided to take his group home, but Roberval, whom they found in Newfoundland, ordered them to return to Canada. Cartier refused and sailed back to France.

1541–1542 With one-eyed Francisco de Orellana (1500?–1549), about 200 Spaniards, thousands of chained Indians, and a herd of pigs, Gonzalo Pizarro searched for the "Land of Cinnamon." He headed east from Quito into the Amazon Basin and found the Coca River, which flows into the Napo, a tributary of the Amazon. When supplies ran low, Orellana and 50 men took a boat they had built downriver to look for food, but when they found it, they were unable to sail back against the current and continued on, the first Europeans to navigate the Amazon River as far as the Atlantic. At one point, they ate their belts boiled with herbs to stay alive. They claimed to have seen a tribe of Amazons and certainly did see a cannibal village with dead men's heads affixed to gibbets. Pizarro and his men had turned back and were able to return to Quito—pale, in rags, with rusted swords.

1542–1544 Cabeza de Vaca explored the Paraguay River, then traveled on to Puerto de los Reyes. When he returned to Asunción he was deposed by Domingo Martínez de Irala, chained to a ring bolt on a ship, and sent back to Spain, where he was jailed and finally exiled to Oran, Algeria. Eventually, the banishment was lifted and he returned to Spain, where he died in poverty.

1542–1543 Roberval traveled up the St. Lawrence, having marooned his niece Marguerite de La Roque on an island with her maid for sinning with a young man (who swam to join them). The crew wintered at Cartier's settlement near Quebec. His pilot, Jean Alfonce, in his book *La Cosmographie,* claimed to have explored the Saguenay, where he discovered Cap de Norumbèque, a place inhabited by tall sun-worshipers who spoke a language like Latin and wore sables.

1542–1543 Juan Rodríguez Cabrillo (died 1543), a Portuguese who had soldiered for Cortes, sailed the California coast in two ships, searching for the legendary island of California ruled by the queen of the Amazons and for sources of silver and gold. He reached San Miguel (now San Diego), then went north to Big Sur, where "so great was the swell of the ocean that it was terrifying to see." He went as far as Bodega Bay. After returning to the Santa Barbara Channel Islands, Cabrillo died of complications from a broken arm. His successor, Bartolomé Ferrer, again sailed north and may have reached what is now Klamath, Calif. Besieged by storms and run aground, he and his crew promised to make a pilgrimage to a shrine of Our Lady "en carne" (in their shirts) if they survived, a vow they were happy to fulfill.

1544 A French ship rescued Marguerite de La Roque, whose lover and maid had died (so had her newborn baby) and who had barely survived the rigors of two winters on the island, during which she had killed three bears, one of them a polar bear. Her exploits were immortalized in the *Heptaméron,* a collection of short tales by Marguerite, queen of Navarre.

1545 A Spanish expedition setting out from Peru discovered silver mines in Potosí, Bolivia.

1562 When one of his ships sank and the others became overcrowded, English slaver Sir John Hawkins set some of his sailors ashore on the Gulf Coast of Mexico. Among them was Englishman David Ingram, who walked all the way to Nova Scotia, where he was saved by a French ship. Home in English pubs, he regaled his drinking companions with tales of Norumbega, up the Penobscot River, where people wore jewelry inset with thumb-sized pearls and lived in round houses held up by pillars of crystal, gold, and silver. There were, he said, red sheep and other fabulous beasts, among them one with floppy ears like a bloodhound (a moose?).

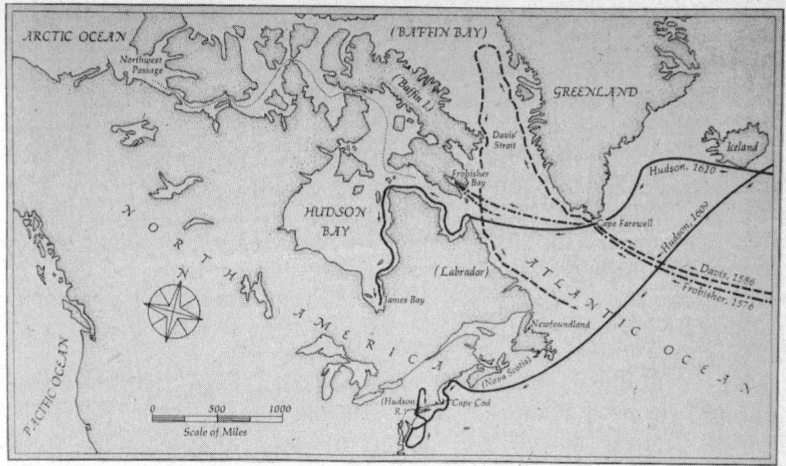

The search for the Northwest Passage.

1576 Martin Frobisher (1535?–1594), a Yorkshireman with a shady past as a pirate, left England searching for the Northwest Passage in two ships, the *Gabriel* and the *Michael*. Both reached Greenland, but the crew of the *Michael*, not trusting the icy seas, returned to England with the erroneous report that the *Gabriel* had been "cast awaye." Frobisher had come close to disaster; at one point he had heroically cut away the mizzenmast in a raging storm to keep the *Gabriel* from foundering. The group may have been the first Europeans in the Renaissance to contact Eskimos, whom Frobisher described as "like unto Tartars, with long black hair, broad faces, and flat noses." Five sailors were kidnapped by the Eskimos. Frobisher brought a piece of black stone (actually iron pyrite, or fool's gold) back to England, where it was falsely assayed as gold-bearing. Before this error was discovered, Frobisher had hauled 1,500 tons of the stone to England. His discoveries: a bay later named for him (Frobisher Bay) and Resolution Island.

1577 On Frobisher's second voyage to the Arctic, he took possession of Baffin Island and his men mined 200 tons of ore. When he and a group tried to capture some Eskimos, the Eskimos turned the tables and chased them, wounding Frobisher in the buttock with an arrow. The English could not discover what had happened to the five sailors kidnapped in 1576. (Nearly 300 years later, explorer Charles F. Hall heard a word-of-mouth story from Arctic Eskimos about five men who had been kidnapped. Later turned loose, they built a boat and froze to death trying to sail away.) On board ship coming home were two Eskimos, an unrelated man and woman, whom the crew watched to observe what form their intercourse took. Although the Eskimos were assigned one bed, they did not have sex, much to the crew's disappointment. In Bristol Harbor, the Eskimo man put on a show in his kayak, spearing ducks on the wing. Frobisher presented a 2-yd.-long narwhal horn (actually a tusk) to Queen Elizabeth, who kept it as a bawdy conversation piece.

1577–1580 Short, ruddy Sir Francis Drake, who was fond of pirating and painting, explored the islands south of Tierra del Fuego and part of the west coast of North America on his circumnavigation of the globe. After passing through the Strait of Magellan, blown south, his fleet reached Henderson Island, where he lay on a grassy slope among wild currants at the edge of the cape, "grovelled on his belly," and stretched his arms toward the South Pole so that no one could claim closer proximity to the bottom of the earth. The ships sailed as far north as Vancouver Island, landed on the coast of North America, perhaps somewhere around San Francisco, and then sailed backed to England via the Philippines.

1578 On his third voyage, with 15 ships, Frobisher sailed up "Mistaken Straits" (Hudson Strait) for 20 days before turning back. Warned by "many straunge Meteors" (the aurora borealis), he decided not to winter in the Arctic and headed home, carrying 1,300 tons of worthless ore. The *Emmanuel,* a small ship called a *buss,* spotted a phantom island southeast of Greenland, which for nearly a century was located on maps as "Island of Buss," but finally was shown as sunken. Except for his discoveries, Frobisher had returned empty-handed, and the Cathay Company, which had backed him to the tune of more than £20,000, went broke.

1583 Sir Humphrey Gilbert (1539?–1583), half brother of Sir Walter Raleigh, left England with 5 ships, 260 men, and a dream—to set up a utopian colony, with free homesteads for the poor, in the Americas. His declared object was to take possession of the coast from Labrador to Florida. On board the flagship *Golden Hind,* according to its captain, Edward Hayes, "for solace of our people and allurement of the Savages, we were provided of Musike in good variety, not omitting the least toyes, as Morris dancers, Hobby horses . . . to delight the Savage people, whom we intended to winne by all faire means possible." Gilbert's men took possession of Newfoundland, where they met men of many nations. Near Sable Island, warned by "strange voyces," one ship the *Delight* struck shoals in a fog, and many aboard drowned. Fifteen sailors then rowed a pinnace, a small boat, with one oar for seven days and were reduced to drinking their own urine to stay alive. Twelve men survived. On the way back to England, Gilbert traveled in the small ship *Squirrel.* In a storm north of the Azores, he was seen with a book in his hand, perhaps Sir Thomas More's *Utopia.* Crew members on board the *Golden Hind* heard him say, "We are as neere to heaven by sea as by land." Shortly thereafter the *Squirrel* was lost at sea.

1585 John Davis (1550?–1605), yeoman neighbor of Gilbert and Raleigh and inventor of Davis's quadrant (a navigational instrument for obtaining latitude), set out in the *Sunshine* and *Mooneshine* with a total crew of 27 on yet another search for the Northwest Passage. On one island, when the Eskimos made "a lamentable noyse . . . with great outcreyes and skreechings," two boat parties danced while the orchestra from the *Sunshine* played, but to no avail; finally a ship's master found the key to calming the Eskimos down when he struck his breast and pointed to the sun several times. The expedition traveled into what became known as Davis Strait (a discovery), then 180 mi. up Cumberland Sound. Because of its deep water and whales, the English thought it might be the Passage (it wasn't). On his second voyage in 1586, Davis found evidence (a cross) that Christian Norsemen had preceded them to the Arctic. The crew wrestled and played a primitive version of football with some Eskimos, fought others with bow and arrow. One ship was sent home because the crew was sick; another was barely saved from foundering during a storm by a single strand of mooring rope; and a third, the *North Starre*, sent to investigate territory "straight over the Pole," was lost.

1587 Davis came close to discovering the Passage on his third voyage when he traveled up Gilbert Sound. On Drum Island, the crew took their hunting dogs ashore for a fox hunt, but the dogs, fat from an easy shipboard life, could not get up any speed. Passing Hudson Strait, the men were awed by "the water whirling and roaring as it were the meeting of the tydes." It was Davis's last voyage to the North.

1587–1590 Sir Walter Raleigh (1552?–1618) set up his elaborate Second Virginia Colony on Roanoke Island. All that remained of it when the rescue party arrived in 1590 was the word *Croatan* carved on a tree.

1595 The dashing and handsome Raleigh, out of favor with Queen Elizabeth since his marriage to her lady-in-waiting Elizabeth Throckmorton in 1594, and having survived an imprisonment in the Tower of London, sailed with four ships and 150 men to the Orinoco on a search for the fabulous—El Dorado, Amazons, men with mouths on their chests and eyes on their shoulders. The river was raging during the rainy season, and though Raleigh brought some gold-bearing ore back to England, the voyage was essentially a failure.

1598–1600 The famous second edition of *The Principal Navigations, Voyages, and Discoveries of the English Nation*—some 1,700,000 words of it—was published. Its author was Richard Hakluyt (1552?–1616), historian, geographer, and promoter of voyages.

1602 The crew of the English bark *Concord*, commanded by Capt. Bartholomew Gosnold (1572–1607), anchored north of what is now Massachusetts Bay, completing the first nonstop transatlantic voyage to the region. They were met by Indians sailing a European shallop, some of them naked, one dressed in European clothes. This was obviously not their first contact with white men, though some things were new to them: mustard, which they "misliked," and a sailor's red beard, which they tried to obtain in trade. The English planted seeds, which grew to the fantastic height of 9 in. in two weeks. They brought back so much sassafras, then popular in Europe as a cure-all for everything from syphilis to plague, that its price dropped from 20 shillings to 3 shillings per pound. Sir Walter Raleigh, who held the charter to Virginia, which included Massachusetts Bay, was angry that they had undertaken the voyage without his permission, and he was not placated by Gosnold's dedication of *A Brief and True Relation of the Discovery of the North Part of Virginia, being a most pleasant, fruitful, and commodious soil,* etc. It didn't matter; by the following year Raleigh was in the Tower of London, accused of conspiracy against the new monarch, James I. The major discovery of Gosnold's voyage was Cape Cod, which he named.

1603 Capt. Martin Pring sailed from England to Penobscot Bay, then south as far as Martha's Vineyard, which Gosnold in 1602 had named for his daughter. The Indians they met danced in a ring to the music of a gittern (a guitarlike instrument) played by a boy from the ship. On a later occasion when the Indians proved less friendly, the ship's mastiffs, Fool and Gallant, managed to frighten them so much with their appearance that "they turned all to a jest and a sport and departed away in a friendly manner."

1603 Visionary Samuel de Champlain (1567?–1635), who had once suggested to Henri IV of France that he build a canal across the Isthmus of Panama, made his first voyage to Canada, where, as the Father of New France, he organized the fur trade and explored vast regions of the northeast section of North America. Though adept at developing friendly relations with the Indians, he encountered the inevitable Catch-22 of the time: By making friends with one tribe, one automatically became the enemy of another. In this case, his friends the Hurons enlisted his help in their battles with the Iroquois.

1604 Champlain explored the coast of Nova Scotia and the Bay of Fundy, where his expedition founded two new settlements, St. Croix and Port Royal, then traveled south to a point below Cape Cod.

1605 The Indians loved sugar candy and raisins, British Capt. George Weymouth noted, and he watched them "stamping" in a dance, which often ended as "they which have wives take them apart and withdraw themselves severally into the wood all night." Weymouth discovered and explored the Kennebec River (in present-day Maine) and shipped back to England five Indians, among them Squanto, who learned English and stayed for several years, acting as public relations agents for the New World.

JOHN SMITH (1580–1631), *A Flamboyant Maverick with a Penchant for Blunt Honesty (Some of the Time)*

At nine, foreshadowing his later adventurous life, the young John Smith and a friend took a not very seaworthy raft out onto the choppy, gray North Sea, but luckily they were rescued before disaster struck (a common occurrence in Smith's life). When he grew up, he became a soldier of fortune who engaged in legendary exploits: He lopped off the head of more than one Turkish soldier while fighting with the Christians in eastern Europe; after being captured and sold into slavery in Constantinople, he bashed in the head of his master, then escaped to Russia, where he fell in love with a blond Russian woman; dressed as a German prince, he rescued English slave Elizabeth Rondee at risk of his life. No wonder such a man was entranced with the New World, where opportunities for exciting experiences were as bountiful as the wildlife.

Yet braggart and swashbuckler though he was, Smith also had a hard-boiled practical side. He realized far ahead of his time that the real

John Smith, creator of the Pocahontas legend.

wealth of the New World lay, not in chimerical gold mines, but in land and resources, in unglamorous cargoes of tar, salted fish, and lumber. The maps Smith drew of the east coast of North America were masterpieces of precise cartography. They were so fine that the dons of Cambridge and Oxford might have offered him academic honors had he not been so flamboyant in his silver armor and full-length fox fur cape, which he wore as he swaggered about London engaging in scandalous open dalliances with young, blond, disreputable ladies.

After spending two years at Jamestown (1607–1609), he returned to England shabby, poor, and scarred from a gunpowder accident. Though his book *A True Relation* (1608) proved popular, he was discredited by his sponsors who hoped the colony would yield gems and gold. They were not impressed that he had kept the colony going by maintaining relatively good relations with the Indians and by forcing colonists to till the soil. His design for an easily defendable star-shaped fort was used by the British until the American Revolution. He spent the rest of his life promoting colonization, exploring New England, organizing fishing expeditions to the North American coast, and writing books. Though his blunt honesty about the difficulties of life in the New World cost him backers, he was nonetheless capable of outrageous lies of self-promotion. For example, the story of how Pocahontas saved his life by offering hers in exchange is a fabrication he created after Pocahontas (then Mrs. John Rolfe) became a favorite of the royal family.

1607–1609 As one of the seven councilors of Jamestown, the first permanent British colony in the New World, Smith traveled inland and traded with Powhatan, an Indian chief who taught him how to plant corn. (Later King James sent Powhatan a crown, a four-poster bed, and a red silk-lined cape, intended to be gifts in exchange for Powhatan's allegiance to Great Britain, which he never gave.) During this time, Smith explored Chesapeake Bay and the Potomac and Rappahannock rivers.

1608–1609 Champlain, after founding Quebec as the center of New France's fur trade, set out with a war party of Hurons and Algonquians down the St. Lawrence and Richelieu rivers and discovered Lake Champlain. His object was to find the Northwest Passage; the Indians' object was to fight the Iroquois. Only the Indians got what they wanted. With Champlain in full armor at their head, they battled 200 Iroquois at the site of Fort Ticonderoga and won. Champlain, appalled at their torture of a prisoner—ripping out his fingernails, burning his penis, scalping him alive, tearing out his arm sinews—persuaded them to kill the man quickly.

1608–1611 Étienne Brulé (1592?–1633), a young French interpreter and protégé of Champlain, lived with the Algonquians (the first European to do so) and explored Lake Huron and its inlet, Georgian Bay.

1609 Using maps given him by his friend John Smith, Henry Hudson, a British subject sailing for the Dutch East India Company in the galleon *Half Moon*, aborted a proposed expedition tu search for a northeast passage to China by following the Russian coastline and headed instead for the New World. Though a skillful navigator, he was a poor leader, prone to vacillation, which exacerbated friction among the mixed Dutch and British crew. After traveling partway up Chesapeake Bay, they went north to New York Harbor, where they traded with the Indians, who were dressed in deerskin and feather mantles and smoked copper pipes. The Europeans exchanged knives and beads for hemp, tobacco, and dried currants. Later the Indians attacked a longboat, killing one man; the survivors were so frightened that they dared not try to land and rowed all night back and forth across the bay. At an anchorage that may have been near present-day 42nd Street, Hudson went ashore on the island Manna-hata. A crew member wrote: "The lands were pleasant, with grass and flowers and goodly trees." In six days, the *Half Moon* sailed up the Hudson to the site of Albany; the longboat went far enough beyond to prove that this route was not the Northwest Passage either. Most relations with the Indians were friendly—a chief broke his arrows to show his love of peace, and Hudson entertained Indians at a drinking party on the ship—but in one incident, an Indian was killed for sneaking on board to steal. Another vandalizing Indian, having lost his hand to the cook's knife, jumped overboard and drowned.

1610 On a return voyage in the *Discovery*, Hudson became the first explorer to sail into Hudson Bay, which he was certain was the gateway to the Pacific. He was forced by ice to winter in James Bay. In the spring, when he wanted to continue his search for a passage west, the crew mutinied. Hudson, his son, and five faithful sailors were overpowered and forced into a boat that was towed into the bay and set adrift among the ice floes. The seven men were never seen again.

1614 After their ship burned in the Hudson River, Capt. Adriaen Block, a sea-going Dutch merchant, and his crew built another. The boat was so rickety that Block was forced to hug the coast sailing north, and thus discovered what the Indians called the Quinnitukut (Connecticut) River.

1614 While in England, John Smith meticulously planned a commercial fishing voyage to the New World; he even got Squanto and another tribesman to teach him Indian dialects in exchange for their return passage to America. In two ships, Smith's party sailed to Newfoundland, and they recorded sighting a mermaid on an iceberg during the trip. Smith then turned south, hauled in 50,000 tuna and cod, and charted the coastline from Nova Scotia to Narragansett Bay. He discovered the Merrimack River and safely deposited his two Indian guides on their native soil. The Pilgrims later survived their first New England winter thanks to Squanto.

1615 On another fishing expedition to the New World, Smith was captured by French pirates. While imprisoned on one of their privateers, he began to write his book *A Description of New England*. (It was he who gave New England its name.) Near the coast of France, he saw a chance to escape, and stuffing his manuscript under his shirt to protect it from the rain, he stole a ship's boat and rowed to safety. A French widow took him in, and the French government gave him a huge reward for information about the pirates.

1615 With a party of Hurons, Champlain traveled into Iroquois territory. Near Lake Oneida (New York) they were defeated by the Oneidas, an Iroquois tribe. Champlain was wounded. Étienne Brulé arrived at their rendezvous at the lake to find Champlain gone, so Brulé explored the Susquehanna River south to Chesapeake Bay, where he lived with the Indians. Later, at Lake Ontario, only a terrible thunderstorm saved Brulé from being tortured to death by the Iroquois.

1615 British explorers Robert Bylot and William Baffin (1584–1622) searched the Foxe Basin above Hudson Bay for a northwest trade route to China.

1616 Baffin and Bylot discovered Baffin Bay in the Arctic Circle and an approach to the Northwest Passage, though they did not recognize it as such.

1616–1617 Free after 13 years in the Tower of London, limping from a stroke and sick with liver disease, Sir Walter Raleigh made his last, ill-fated search for El Dorado. During the trip 42 of the crew died of fever, his son Walter was killed by the Spanish on an exploration up the Orinoco, and his friend Lawrence Keymis committed suicide. No gold was found. Raleigh was executed on the old charge of treason in 1618.

1633 Champlain, captured by the British and sent to England in 1629, returned to New France as its governor. Two years later he died in Quebec, leaving three adopted Indian daughters—Faith, Hope, and Charity.

1633 Brulé was boiled and eaten by a group of unfriendly Huron Indians.

1633–1635 Coureur de bois Jean Nicolet (1598–1642) was sent by Champlain to find a legendary "sweetwater sea," on the shores of which were said to live flat-faced, yellow-skinned Asian tribes. At Green Bay (Wisconsin) on the shore of Lake Michigan, he met the "Asians," who turned out to be Winnebago Indians. In their honor, he wore a fancy Chinese robe and fired two shots from a gun.

1654–1660 Brothers-in-law Médart Chouart, Sieur de Groseilliers (1625?–1697), and Pierre Esprit Radisson (1636?–1710) conducted several expeditions into the North American plains, where they may have been the first to contact Sioux Indians. Radisson's description of exploration is graphic and unromantic: "Sometimes one stands with one's backside in water, has fear in one's belly, an empty stomach, tired bones, and a great desire to sleep possessing one's whole body. And all of it in evil weather which must be borne, for it is an affliction against which there is no protection."

1669 Slightly mad and melancholy, an aristocratic seminarian turned fur trader, Robert Cavelier, Sieur de La Salle (1643–1687) conducted his first New World exploration. He explored the area around the Ohio River.

1669–1670 German John Lederer, a doctor, three times searched for and did not find a pass from the Piedmont through the Appalachians. He said he saw lions and leopards and tree-climbing snakes. When he cut open one of the snakes, he found a squirrel in its stomach.

1673 Père Jacques Marquette (1637–1675), a Jesuit who spoke six Indian languages, joined up with Louis Jolliet, cartographer, organist, businessman and native Canadian, to sail down the Fox and Wisconsin rivers to the Mississippi. Guided by Miami Indians, they cruised nearly 3,000 mi., in spite of heat, hostile tribes, and Indian warnings of "horrible monsters, which devoured men and canoes together." Though they did not reach the Gulf of Mexico, they came close enough to prove that the Mississippi did not empty into the Pacific. Nearly home, Jolliet lost all his records of the journey in a boat accident in the rapids near Montreal.

1678–1680 La Salle built a series of forts for New France, actually centers for the fur trade. He began with Fort Conti on the Niagara River, where his men—working "briskly" in the face of Indian hostility—built the *Griffon*, the first vessel to sail the Great Lakes. With Belgian priest Louis Hennepin (1640–1701?), one-armed Italian Henri de Tonti (1650–1704), and a crew, La Salle sailed the boat to Green Bay through Lake Huron and Lake Michigan, then sent it back with a cargo of furs. On the eastern shore of Lake Michigan they built Fort Miami, then in December, 1796, made a trip up the St. Joseph, portaging to the Kankakee River, which links the Mississippi and the Great Lakes. From Fort Crève Coeur ("Fort Heartbreak"), which they built on the Illinois River, La Salle, leaving "Iron Hand" de Tonti behind, set off with several others on a terrible overland journey to Detroit—during which thickets of thorns bloodied their faces, La Salle later reported—and then on to

Montreal. The journey of 1,000 mi. was completed in 65 days. The *Griffon*, however, was lost. De Tonti, abandoned in the wilderness after a mutiny at the fort, survived by eating garlic, then was captured by the Iroquois, who set him free after sticking a knife to his chest and holding up his hair as if to scalp him. He was reunited with La Salle in 1681. Meanwhile Hennepin, captured by the Sioux and taken to Minnesota, also had a narrow escape; only because the Indians thought his glittering chalice might be inhabited by spirits did they spare his life. After the Sioux let him go, Hennepin accidentally met Daniel Greysolon, Sieur Duluth (De Tonti's cousin), who had been exploring the headwaters of the Mississippi since 1678, and together they traveled back to Montreal.

1682 With De Tonti, La Salle sailed all the way down the Mississippi River. At the mouth of the Arkansas, they heard through the fog the "sound of the tambour" coming from an Indian celebration. In April they reached the Gulf of Mexico, where La Salle took possession of the territory for France, calling it Louisiana in honor of Louis XIV. Then La Salle returned to France.

1684–1687 Back in the Americas, La Salle tried to locate the mouth of the Mississippi again, hoping to establish a colony there, but couldn't find it, so instead he started a settlement on the fever-ridden marshes of the Colorado River. By August, 1686, only 44 of the original 150 settlers were alive and all four of his ships were lost. To save the colony he started marching north on foot, but he was shot to death by his own men near the Brazos River in March, 1687. The survivors of the mutiny—two priests and three soldiers—were led to safety by La Salle's aide, Henri Joutel, who later wrote an account of the experience. De Tonti searched for La Salle's body but never found it.

1687–1711 Eusebius Kino, a German Jesuit explorer and cartographer, made more than 40 expeditions to the north, west, northwest, and southwest of Sonora, Mexico. He drew the earliest map to show the Gila and Colorado rivers and southern Arizona, as they were later named.

1690–1692 "The Boy Henry Kellsey" (1670?–?), "a very active lad, delighting much in Indians' company," was the first to explore the Canadian plains south and west of Lake Winnipeg.

1731 Englishman John Hadley invented the octant, or reflecting quadrant, for determining latitude. It was the precursor of the sextant.

1731–1743 In a family enterprise, Pierre Gaultier de Varennes, Sieur de La Vérendrye (1685–1749), and his sons set up fur-trading posts and explored large parts of the northern U.S. and Canada, including the Saskatchewan River, the Winnipeg Basin, and the upper Missouri River (which they also discovered). In 1736 his eldest son and several friends were murdered by the Sioux. In 1742–1743 two of his sons, traveling on foot and on horseback, may have reached the Black Hills of South Dakota.

CHARLES MARIE DE LA CONDAMINE (1701–1774). ***Is the Earth Shaped Like a Potbellied Man in a Tight Belt or Is It Flat Top and Bottom?***

The French philosopher Voltaire once won 500,000 francs in a lottery because Charles Marie de La Condamine, in order to win the friendship of the great figure, advised him about a miscalculation in the game. The sum of the ticket prices for the lottery happened to be far less than the prize. So Voltaire bought up all the tickets and won. Then it came time to settle a controversy raging in scientific circles: Was the earth an oblate spheroid, flattened at the poles, as Englishman Isaac Newton said, or was it nipped in at the equator "much as a potbellied man might [look if he pulled] in his girth by taking a few notches in his belt," as Frenchman Jacques Dominique de Cassini claimed? Voltaire backed his friend La Condamine as leader of one of the expeditions to measure the earth in order to decide the question once and for all. His choice was a good one, for La Condamine was a scientist as well as an aristocrat, a student of geodesy and an astronomer. Consequently he spent nine years making meticulous measurements at the equator in Ecuador to determine the earth's girth, while another expedition measured the circumference through the North Pole from Lapland. La Condamine's surveys covered a section amounting to 2° of surface in the Andes, and he took rubber back to Europe—he carried his instruments in a bag of cloth waterproofed with rubber by the Indians—as well as quinine from the cinchona tree, and rotenone, which is now used as an insecticide.

1735–1745 After being feted for months at Cartagena, Colombia, La Condamine's expedition finally got under way, traveling toward Quito in Pichincha Province in Ecuador, in February, 1736. In the group were cranky astronomer Pierre Bouguer; botanist Joseph de Jussieu (who later went mad when his plant collection, gathered over five years, was destroyed through the carelessness of servants); astronomer Louis Godin des Odonais; physician Jean Seniergues, (who was subsequently stabbed and stoned to death in Cuenca, Ecuador, by a crowd angry over his intercession in an aristocratic romance); and two Spanish scientists, Don Jorge Juan y Santacilla and Don Antonio de Ulloa. They were later joined by Pedro Vincente Maldonado, mapmaker, mathematician, linguist, and amateur scientist, who led La Condamine to Quito by a little-traveled route up the Río Esmeraldas. During the journey they were plagued by mosquitoes and mouse-sized cockroaches, as they climbed to heights 13,000 ft. above sea level. When mists lifted near the end of their journey, they saw 15 snow-covered volcanoes. After meeting the rest of the group, who had traveled by an easier, longer route, they began their work. Dragging surveying chains up steep slopes and signaling to each other with mirrors from mountain peak to mountain peak, they established the baseline of a triangle, which would yield the arc of the meridian and in turn the length of a degree of longitude. The local inhabitants—both the ignorant and upper-class—were suspicious of them. As one said, "What could move men of decent standing to live so miserable, lonely, and laborious a life, traversing mountains and deserts and observing the stars—unless there was some high payment at stake?" Inca treasure perhaps? These suspicions created such problems with local Spanish officials that La Condamine had to travel the thousand miles to Lima, Peru, to obtain permission to continue this work. Their labors proved Newton right, though the Lapland expedition had come up with the answer first. On the way home La Condamine and Maldonado traveled across South America on the Amazon River, a two-month trip during which they measured the river's depth, width, speed, and other features.

1740–1741 On a search for Gamaland, which Russian Academy of Science cartographers believed to be near Siberia even though no one had ever seen it, the Dane Vitus Bering (1680–1741) in the *St. Peter* and the Russian Alexei Chirikov (1703–1748) in the *St. Paul* left Siberia in early June, 1740, after seven years of preparation for the journey, only to lose each other in the fog. In July the crew of the *St. Peter* sighted 18,000-ft. Mt. Elias on the Alaskan mainland. At Kayak Island, Georg Wilhelm Steller, a German scientist on the ship, went ashore for a few hours, where he identified a new species of jay, later named for him. Many in the crew, including Bering, became ill with scurvy. A violent storm battered their ship, and, desperate, they finally wintered on an uninhabited island (later named Bering Island), living in holes covered with sails. Bering died in December. By spring the 46 men left alive built a ship and sailed to Siberia. Meanwhile Chirikov had lost the *St. Paul*'s two ship's boats. Fourteen of his men trying to go ashore at a landfall sighted Kenai Peninsula and the Aleutian Islands, and finally arrived home. Discoveries: the mainland of Alaska and the Aleutian Islands.

1743–1803 Siberian fur traders explored and exploited Alaska, decimating the furred population as well as the Aleuts.

1762 John Harrison won a £20,000 prize from the British government for his invention of a reliable marine clock, which was necessary for accurate measurement of longitude at sea.

1768–1770 Two Spanish expeditions, one led by Fernando de Rivera y Moncada and the other by Gaspar de Portolá, explored the west coast of North America overland. De Portolá traveled to San Diego with Father Junípero Serra, who founded missions along the coast, then went with 12 soldiers and 44 mission Indians on the first overland trek from southern California to Monterey.

1769–1770 Isabel Godin des Odonais, wife of La Condamine's astronomer, set out from Ecuador down the Amazon to rejoin her husband. Her party's canoe overturned, the natives deserted, and one by one her companions died, until she was left to struggle on alone. She was finally found wandering in the jungle, and met up with her husband in Guiana after a 20-year separation.

1769–1772 Londoner Samuel Hearne (1745–1792), a skilled surveyor and scientific observer, was sent by the Hudson's Bay Company to find a mountain of pure copper, said by the Indians to be in Chippewa territory, and to open up fur trade with the Indians. Two early attempts failed due to Hearne's inexperience and the perfidy of his guides, who robbed and abandoned him. However, the third time, led by a Chippewa chief, he reached a copper deposit (which turned out to be worthless), then went on overland to the shores of the Arctic Ocean, the first European to make such a journey. On the way back he discovered Great Slave Lake.

1769–1775 "I want more elbow room!" was perhaps Daniel Boone's most famous remark. A woodsman since his boyhood, Boone (1734–1820) roamed Kentucky blue-grass country, sometimes alone and sometimes with companions—his brother Squire, brother-in-law John Stuart, and friend John Finley. When they had spare time, they often read *Gulliver's Travels* to each other. In 1773 Boone took his family and a group of other settlers over the Cumberland Gap on the Wilderness Road, with the goal of settling in Kentucky, but Indians ambushed them, killing Boone's son James, 16, and five others. This experience so terrified the group that they refused to go on. Two years later Boone achieved his dream of settling in Kentucky and established the town of Boonesborough, not far from present-day Lexington. In 1778 he was captured and enslaved by the Shawnee, who nicknamed him Big Turtle, but he escaped, traveling 160 mi. on one meal to reach safety. John Filson's book about Boone in 1784 inspired Lord Byron to include seven stanzas about the lengendary woodsman in *Don Juan* (Canto VIII).

1774 The Spanish, alarmed at Russian encroachment from the north (they had built a trading center and fort about 80 mi. north of present-day San Francisco), sent Juan José Pérez in the *Santiago* up the Pacific coast. He discovered Nootka Sound and noticed currents from the Columbia River, but did not investigate because his crew was sick with scurvy.

1776 Father Francisco Garcés found a route from Santa Fe to California. On the way he rode his mule along the rim of the Grand Canyon and visited the Havasupai Indians, who lived in cave dwellings there.

1778 Tall, blue-eyed, with a blunt though kind manner, the British Capt. James Cook (1728–1779) captured the loyalty and admiration of his crews and inspired other mariners who came after him. In 1778, as part of a longer voyage, he explored Alaska, approaching from the west after discovering the Hawaiian Islands. Aboard the *Resolution*, his main officer was the infamous Capt. William Bligh, while a sister ship, the *Discovery*, was commanded by Capt. Charles Clerke. From Drake's New Albion (the Pacific Northwest) they cruised north, mapping the coastline, to the Arctic Circle, where ice 12 ft. thick stopped them. Along the way, Indians stole Cook's watch and sold him oil that turned out to be water. In the far north, according to sailor John Rickman, the crews shot at huge herds of "hideous-looking creatures" (sea lions and other Arctic animals) until not one was to be seen except "such as were killed or so severely wounded as not to be able to crawl to the open sea."

1778 Though contemptuously called "peddlers" by the Hudson's Bay Company men, independent traders like American Peter Pond (1740–1807?) did much to explore North America. In four canoes, with French-Canadian voyageurs, Pond opened up the Northwest as far as 40 mi. south of Lake Athabasca in Canada, mapped it, then tried unsuccessfully to persuade Congress to sponsor an expedition to the Pacific from Lake Athabasca. He was one of the first to recognize the value of Indian pemmican (dried meat mixed with fat) as a practical trail food.

1778–1781 French botanist Joseph Dombey and two Spanish scientists, Hipólito Ruiz Lopez and José Antonio Pavón y Jiménez, were directed by King Carlos III of Spain to explore Peru, their goal to be "the methodical examination and identification of the products of nature of my American dominions . . . not only in order to promote the progress of the physical sciences but also to banish doubts and adulterations that are found in medicine, painting, and the other important arts." One medical remedy the expedition uncovered was boiled shoots of the native plant quiscar to cure colds or, mixed with urine, to alleviate toothache.

1784–1801 Félix de Azara, a Spanish naval officer, conducted seven mapping expeditions to define the region watered by the La Plata, Uruguay, Paraná, and Paraguay rivers. He also became an authority on four-legged animals, propounding a rudimentary evolution theory decades before Charles Darwin.

1785–1787 On a three-year voyage for the French Academy of Science and Medicine, Jean François de Galaup, Count of La Pérouse (1741–1788), an admirer of Capt. James Cook, proved that two mythical continents—Isla Grande in the Atlantic and Drake's Land in the Pacific—were merely small islands off South America. On yet another search for the Northwest Passage, he set out to sail from the Gulf of Alaska south, but was daunted by the irregular coastline and an accident that cost the lives of 21 of his men.

1789–1794 For years, Lombard nobleman Alessandro Malaspina painstakingly mapped the coastlines of South and North America to make precise hydrographic charts, invaluable to seamen. Because he favored the emancipation of Spanish colonies, he was jailed when he returned to Spain, and for 30 years his maps remained in limbo.

1789 After wintering with his mentor, old Peter Pond, at Lake Athabasca, Scots-born Alexander Mackenzie (1764–1820) traveled west to Great Slave Lake. There he discovered a new river, and with several men and three birch-bark canoes he cruised down it to the Beaufort Sea in the Arctic Ocean, a journey of 1,120 mi. He had hoped to reach the Pacific, so he called the new river the River of Disappointment. Today it bears his name.

1791–1794 Trying to prove there was *no* Northwest Passage, Britain's George Vancouver (1757–1798) made three separate mapping expeditions by sea along the northwest coast of America, surveying the network of water in present-day Washington, sailing around Vancouver Island, naming Mt. Rainier and Puget Sound for his associates, but missing the mouth of the Columbia River in bad weather. He proved what he had set out to establish: There was no Northwest Passage from the Bering Strait to the Strait of Magellan.

1792 On a trip to the Pacific Northwest to buy furs from Indians to trade for tea in China, American Robert Gray (1755–1806) discovered the Columbia River, which he named for his ship.

1792–1793 After going back to England to study astronomy and navigation and to buy instruments to calculate position, Alexander Mackenzie returned to Canada in another attempt to find a river route to the Pacific. In a 25-ft.-long canoe Mackenzie and his 10-man party set off on May 9, 1793, down the Peace River from their winter headquarters, Fort Fork, an outpost 200 mi. from Fort Chippewyan. The canoe was "so light that

The only known painting of Alexander Mackenzie.

two men could carry her on a good road 3 or 4 mi. without resting," yet it was able to transport the contingent of men plus 3,000 lb. of supplies. The going was easy until, a few days after sighting the Rockies, they came upon 25 mi. of cascading rapids in the Peace River canyon and were forced to portage and pole their canoe, bailing it out with sponges. On May 31 they reached the fork of the turbulent Parsnip River and the broad Finlay River. In spite of the Finlay's appeal, Mackenzie, remembering the advice given him by a Beaver Indian, chose the Parsnip—correctly. After portaging to the Continental Divide, they continued their travels, once wrecking their canoe in the rapids and patching it up, then moving on at Mackenzie's urging. When hostile Indians threatened to attack, Mackenzie, needing their knowledge of the land, risked his life to walk along the opposite bank of the stream, flashing mirrors and trinkets. His stratagem worked. The group reached the Pacific, where Mackenzie made astronomical observations and wrote on a rock with vermilion dye and grease, "Alex Mackenzie from Canada by land 22 July, 1793." In four weeks they were back in Fort Fork. Mackenzie's plan for a continental, Canadian-based fur-trading company, outlined in his book *Voyages from Montreal* (1801), spurred Thomas Jefferson to thwart Canadian expansion by sending the Lewis and Clark expedition west in 1803.

1797–1811 In 14 years of exploration, Welshman David Thompson, trader-surveyor for the North West Company, covered more than 50,000 mi. of territory in Canada and the U.S. in a canoe, on horseback, or on foot.

1799–1804 German scientist Alexander von Humboldt (1769–1859) had given up on finding other scientists to accompany him on his South American expedition when, on a Paris hotel stairs, he spotted a man carrying what appeared to be a specimen box and introduced himself. It was a serendipitous meeting. The man was Aimé Bonpland (1773–1858), a young French botanist, who accompanied Von Humboldt on his epic 37,000 mi. of exploration, "travelling for the acquisition of knowledge," as Von Humboldt's passport read. On their two trips—the first to the Amazon (1799–1800) and the second to the Andes (1801–1803)—they discovered and surveyed the Casiquiare River, proving that it links the Amazon and Orinoco; made a geological survey of the Andes; set a 30-year men's altitude record by climbing 20,561 ft. up Mt. Chimborazo; collected more than 60,000 plants, 6,300 of them previously unknown to European botanists; took more than 1,500 measurements; found evidence to prove Von Humboldt's theory that volcanoes mark faults in the earth's crust; studied tropical storms; discovered the Humboldt Current in the Pacific; discovered the value of guano (bird droppings), later imported to Europe for fertilizer at Von Humboldt's instigation. Their adventures and near escapes were many. They unknowingly bathed in a mudhole inhabited by electric eels, one of which later zapped Von Humboldt when he stepped on its tail preparatory to dissecting it; Von Humboldt narrowly escaped death when a demented guide tried to poison him with curare; and Bonpland fell in love with Samba, a part-Indian girl who broke his heart by jilting him. Von Humboldt later wrote of the trip: "Every object declares the grandeur of the power, the tenderness of Nature, from the boa constrictor, which can swallow a horse, down to the hummingbird, balancing itself on the chalice of a flower." His 29 books about South America, containing 1,426 maps and illustrations, cost 180,000 francs to publish—a sum he himself paid.

MERIWETHER LEWIS (1774–1809) AND WILLIAM CLARK (1770–1838), ***The Perfect Team***

President Thomas Jefferson's choice of young Meriwether Lewis, who had once been his private secretary, to lead the U.S. Corps of Discovery in the territory beyond the Mississippi was inspired, as was Lewis's choice of his friend William Clark, brother of George Rogers Clark, to share the command. The brilliant but neurotic Lewis and the outgoing, practical Clark balanced each other perfectly, for their differences were complementary. Not that they had nothing in common; both had been soldiers and Indian fighters, and both were poor spellers (examples: "musquiters and knats," "jentle brease"). Clark, accepting Lewis's offer, wrote: "This is an immense undertaking, fraught with numerous difficulties, but my friend I can assure you that no man lives with whom I would prefer to undertake and share the difficulties of such a trip than yourself."

Lewis acted as the expedition's doctor, relying heavily on Rush's Thunderbolts, cure-all pills that he carried in the medicine chest along with 30 other drugs. To his credit, only one man died on the trip, from "biliose chorlick" (probably a ruptured appendix), though several people, including Sacagawea, their female Indian interpreter, became quite ill. There were mishaps, too. Lewis, for instance, was accidentally shot in the buttock by a frontiersman who mistook him for an elk, and for weeks he had to write in his journal standing up. Clark drew the maps and sketches and later prepared the material in their field notebooks for publication. His 1814 report became an American classic.

After the expedition Lewis was made governor of the Louisiana Territory. In October, 1809, on his way to Washington, D.C., 60 mi. from Nashville, he died of a gunshot wound. It is unclear whether he was murdered or committed suicide. Clark became governor of the Missouri Territory, then superintendent of Indian affairs for Louisiana.

1804–1806 Jefferson received only $2,500 from Congress to finance the Lewis and Clark expedition, which was to end up costing $50,000. Its purposes were to look for a water route to the Pacific and to obtain scientific information. Before they left, scientists presented them with a variety of tasks, such as determining the pulse rates of the Louisiana Indians. After wintering on the banks of the Mississippi, they set off in two flat-bottomed boats with a contingent of 45 men (29 of them permanent) up the Missouri in the spring of 1804. The "Big Muddy" was treacherous with its snags and sawyers (sunken trees). They did not come to unknown territory for some time, however. In October they built a winter camp near present-day Bismarck, N.D., 1,600 mi. up the Missouri, where they hired Canadian fur trader Toussaint Charbonneau and his wife, Sacagawea, a Shoshone who had been captured by the Minnetarees when she was 12. Sacagawea, then 16, was a short, squat woman, who wanted to see the monster fish in the Great River. That February she gave birth to her first child, whom she carried on her back throughout the journey. Her presence persuaded tribes along the way of the expedition's peaceful intent; war parties seldom traveled with women and children. On one occasion, when a boat carrying valuable instruments and papers overturned, Sacagawea, thinking quickly, scooped up the articles floating in the water before they were lost, while the others in the party righted the canoe and bailed it out.

In April, 1805, they left Fort Mandan in dugouts, after sending back to St. Louis reports, maps, a painted buffalo robe, Indian herbs, and animal and plant specimens, including a live prairie dog. The way was spiked with dangers: grizzly bears, one 8 ft. tall, and bison, which ran through their camp. On May 26 Lewis sighted the Rockies, and a few days later, in the White Cliff area, he saw sandstone ramparts that looked like "elegant ranges of lofty freestone buildings." At the falls of the upper Missouri, where spray "rose like a column of smoke," Lewis spent four hours, watching in awe. It took them 30 days to negotiate the rapids. When the river split into three streams (which they named Jefferson, Madison, and Gallatin), they chose, on Sacagawea's advice, to follow the Jefferson. After crossing the Continental Divide, they encountered Shoshones and took their chief, Cameahwait, to their camp. Sacagawea, called on to interpret, burst into tears at the sight of him, then ran to him and wrapped him in her blanket. He was her brother.

After a long, cold, hungry journey through mountain trails and the

Bitterroot wilderness, they made their way to the Columbia River, and in dugout canoes they cruised down it to the Pacific. Clark wrote on Nov. 7, 1805, "Ocean in view! Oh! The joy!" By September, 1806, they were back in St. Louis.

1805–1806 As part of his conspiracy with Aaron Burr to take over part of Louisiana, Gen. James Wilkinson sent Zebulon Pike (1779–1813), a young army lieutenant, to search for sites for army posts and the source of the Mississippi. Whether Pike was a spy or unwitting dupe remains a mystery. In a 70-ft. keelboat with 21 soldiers, Pike traveled to present-day Little Falls, Minn., where he set up a winter camp. Then, with a few men, he set off first in a dugout and then by sled to find the Mississippi's source, which he incorrectly identified as Leech Lake. (The true source is Lake Itasca, Minn., discovered in 1832 by geologist and ethnologist Henry Schoolcraft [1793–1864]).

1806–1807 Wilkinson sent Pike to the Southwest to look for the headwaters of the Red River. On Nov. 15, one of Pike's men sighted a "blue cloud," which turned out to be the peak later named for Pike and which gave rise to the pioneers' motto of the 1850s, "Pike's Peak or Bust." On the difficult journey to the river Pike claimed was the Red (it was actually the upper Rio Grande), men froze and horses collapsed from fatigue and hunger. Spanish soldiers appeared to tell Pike he was on the wrong river, and Pike, "feeling low," ordered the American flag taken down. The group was arrested and taken to Santa Fe, where Pike's papers, except those he had safely hidden in gun barrels, were confiscated. Pike and his men were eventually released. Though he brought back valuable new information about the Southwest, his description of the central plains as "incapable of cultivation" and likely to become "as celebrated as the sandy deserts of Africa" gave rise to the myth of the Great American Desert, which slowed settlement of that area for some time.

1807–1808 With a handgun and a 30-lb. pack, mountain man John Colter (1774?–1813), the first European to see the Teton Mountains, traveled alone in a 500-mi. loop from Lisa's Fort through unknown wilderness to discover the seething geysers and bubbling mudholes of "Colter's Hell," now Yellowstone National Park. Later he was captured by Blackfoot Indians, who stripped him, then raced him over sharp stones and prickly pear to bring him down. He outran all but one Indian, whom he killed, then kept running to the Madison River, where he hid under driftwood until the Indians gave up searching for him. He walked 200 mi., naked and with bloody feet, to Lisa's Fort. It took him 11 days.

1811–1812 Guided by Crow Indians, Wilson Price Hunt (1782?–1842), on a harrowing expedition for fur trader John Jacob Astor, took 60 men along what became the western part of the Oregon Trail. At one point they ate moccasins to keep from starving.

CHARLES WATERTON (1782–1865), *The Eccentric Explorer Who Rode a Caiman (Alligator)*

"Squire" Charles Waterton, 27th Lord of Walton Hall (Yorkshire,

Charles Waterton riding an alligator.

England), hated being called an eccentric, but an eccentric he was. He liked to get under the dinner table and bite the legs of his guests like a dog; he walked barefoot in the tropical forests of British Guiana; he climbed the cross of St. Peter's Cathedral in Rome and put his gloves on its lightning conductor; he knocked out a boa constrictor with a mighty punch; he tried to fly from the top of an outhouse ("navigate the atmosphere," he called it), only to land on the ground with a "foul shak"; he fashioned weird monstrosities out of hollow animal skins through his own preserving methods (one, the bearded "Nondescript," made from the skin of a red howler monkey, was probably a caricature of his enemy, Treasury Secretary J. R. Lushington); he bled himself, against doctors' advice, at least 136 times in his life ("tapping my claret"), taking from 16 to 20 oz. of blood each time.

But he was not entirely crazy. He was an enthusiastic field naturalist and conducted valuable expeditions into the South American wild. On 259 acres of the family estate in England, he started the first wild bird sanctuary in history. His book *Wanderings in South America* was a popular best-seller though, according to some naturalists, somewhat short on relevant details.

At age 48 he married a 17-year-old orphan, Anne Edmonstone, granddaughter of an Arawak Indian and descendant of Scottish kings and Lady Godiva. He then described himself as a tall man (5 ft. 11½ in.) with muscular legs, graying hair, and a furrowed face. His wife died shortly after giving birth to their son, Edmund. She was only 18. After her death he slept on the floor, with a block of wood for a pillow.

1812 Charles Waterton explored British Guiana (now Guyana), where he had been managing three family plantations since 1804, in a four-month, 1,000-mi. journey, guided by a Macosi Indian. His purpose was partly to investigate the manufacture and effects of "wourali" (curare), which he thought might be a cure for rabies.

1812–1813 Robert Stuart, a partner in John Jacob Astor's Pacific Fur

Company, discovered the South Pass, a 20-mi. gap wide enough for the passage of wagons, in the Wind River Mountains, as well as the section of the Oregon Trail between St. Louis and eastern Idaho.

1817–1818 On his third South American journey (the second, in 1816, was relatively uneventful), Charles Waterton spent nearly a year in British Guiana. He added to his collection of tropical birds and snakes, investigated the strange habits of the sloth, and studied anteaters. His most famous exploit—capturing a 10½-ft.-long caiman (alligator) by leaping on its back—occurred during this expedition. It was "the first and last time I was ever on a cayman's back," he later wrote.

1822 The first wagon train west was led by Missourian William Becknell (1790?–1832?) from Dodge City to Santa Fe, then on to California, over what became known as the Santa Fe Trail. During the journey, mules dropped from thirst and men drank the animals' blood to stay alive.

1822–1831 An ad placed by St. Louis entrepreneur William Henry Ashley in the *Missouri Gazette* for "enterprising young men" lured young Jedediah Strong Smith (1799–1831) west in 1822. He was to remain for nine years. An encounter with a grizzly bear that nearly tore off his face did not deter him. He explored 16,000 mi. of territory, leading parties that rediscovered the South Pass in Oregon and carved out the Old Spanish Trail. Dubbed the "knight in buckskin," he was a conscientious Bible reader, not at all typical of mountain men. On his expedition of 1826–1827, he and his party followed the Colorado River south to the Mojave Desert, where they ate their horses when they died of hunger and thirst. Then they went on to San Diego—where the Spanish gave them trouble—to board a ship, which they left to sneak back into California. Next they went over the Sierras and into the Great Basin of the Nevada desert, where, after 32 dry days, they were saved by a waterhole and Smith's sense of direction. Smith later escaped massacre by the Indians near Oregon's Umpqua River in 1828. Though he had finally settled down to be a farmer, he decided to take one last trip, leading a wagon train to Santa Fe. It was an unfortunate decision, for while he was out alone scouting for water, he was ambushed and killed by Comanches.

1824 Virginian Jim Bridger (1804–1881), an illiterate frontiersman who roamed the west for 50 years, led a party of trappers down the Bear River (now the Utah). To prove a bet that it flowed into a salt lake or marsh, he canoed down the river's dangerous cascades through Bear Canyon and emerged on Great Salt Lake—its first known white visitor. He thought he had found an arm of the Pacific Ocean.

1831–1836 "The voyage of the *Beagle* has been by far the most important event in my life and has determined my whole career," wrote Charles Darwin (1809–1882), whose trip as *H.M.S. Beagle*'s naturalist along the coasts of Patagonia, Chile, and Peru, as well as to the Galapagos Islands, gave him access to an enormously rich laboratory of plant and animal life. Dramatic evidence of geological change led him, in part, to his theory of evolution through natural selection.

1835–1843 When in 1831 in the British Virgin Islands he saw a slave ship strike an uncharted rock and sink, killing 135 Africans, German-born Robert Hermann Schomburgk (1804–1865) was so appalled that he conducted a survey of nearby waters at his own expense to avert future disasters. Impressed by this, the British government requested that he survey British Guiana, this time for pay, and he agreed. During his exploration, he discovered the source of the Essequibo River, mapped its tributaries, and accurately established boundary lines, which so infuriated the Brazilian and Venezuelan governments that they tore out his boundary posts. Though accurate, his measurements had taken land away from Brazil and Venezuela and given it to Britain.

1842–1845 Having forgiven his handsome son-in-law John Charles Frémont (1813–1890) for eloping with his daughter, Sen. Thomas Hart Benton chose him to lead an expedition to explore Oregon and other Pacific regions in 1842. Frémont found no new territory, but he planted a flag on the highest peak, later named Fremont Peak, in what is now Wyoming. In his next expedition, which began in 1843, Frémont searched for the legendary Buenaventura River, which geographers had fabricated just because it seemed logical that a river should link the Pacific and Great Salt Lake. In January and February of 1844 his party crossed the Sierra Nevada, where the men's feet froze, and some were snow-blinded, and one went crazy before they were finally able to descend into the "perpetual spring" of the Sacramento Valley. Frémont's report on the trip was valuable in that it scotched the myth of the Great American Desert and made a true assessment of the fertility of the Great Plains. On his third trip Frémont opened up a new route from the Great Salt Lake to northern California and participated in the Bear Flag revolt against the Mexican government. Called the "Pathfinder," he was a romantic figure who captured the imagination of Americans. In 1856 he ran unsuccessfully for president as the Republican party's first candidate.

1845–1859 At the age of 59, rotund Sir John Franklin (1786–1847) was chosen by the British government to take a stab at navigating the Northwest Passage in the *Erebus* and the *Terror*, two propeller-driven steamers which could also travel under sail. He and his crew of 129 men disappeared after being sighted in Baffin Bay by a whaler in July, 1845. More than 40 rescue attempts, which included sending out polar foxes with metal message boxes attached to their collars and loosing labeled balloons, failed to turn up any trace of the lost expedition, in spite of the Admiralty's offer of £100,000 reward for its rescue. In searching for Franklin, explorers John Richardson and John Rae explored more than 10,000 mi. of Canadian coastline. In 1859, on King William Island, Francis McClintock, sent on a rescue mission by Lady Franklin, came upon the skeletons of the men and a report of what had happened. Franklin had died in June, 1847. In 1848 the 105 men who had survived two winters decided to abandon ship and head south, where, according to Eskimos they had resorted to cannibaling the dead before the end finally came for them all.

1848–1865 Amateur butterfly collector Henry Walter Bates (1825–1892) and naturalist Alfred Russel Wallace (1823–1913), both self-educated young men from Britain's working class, financed a trip to South America in 1848 with money Wallace had earned as a railroad surveyor. On board ship en route to Brazil, they met botanist Richard Spruce (1817–1893), who decided to join them, as did Wallace's brother Herbert later. Separately and together, they explored the region near Pará (now Belém) at the mouth of the Amazon, the upper Amazon Basin, and Río Negro, collecting specimens and observing wildlife. In 1852, shortly after Herbert died of yellow fever, Alfred Wallace decided to go home. Three weeks from port his ship caught fire, and he watched helplessly from a dinghy as all his specimens burned, including his live birds and monkeys, the last of which clung to the bowsprit before dying in the flames. Wallace's trip was instrumental in his development of the theory of natural selection, which he postulated concurrently with Charles Darwin.

Bates stayed on until 1859, exploring the Tapajós and Solimões river basins, garnering understanding of mimicry in insects (edible species come to resemble nasty-tasting ones in a miracle of self-protection), and gathering a collection of 14,712 species of animals, 8,000 of them new to science. His book, *The Naturalist on the Amazon*, made him famous.

Spruce stayed on until 1865 and went home with 30,000 plant specimens, many previously unknown to science, but he could not get his material published and died in obscurity. He had written, "There . . . grasses are bamboo 60 or more feet high. . . . Violets are the size of apple trees."

1903–1906 When Roald Amundsen (1872–1928) was a boy in Norway, he slept with his window open in the freezing cold to prepare himself for his future explorations. He began to achieve his dream when, with a crew of six men, he sneaked the 47-ton sloop *Gjøa* out of Christiania (now Oslo) in the rain at midnight to escape arrest by one of his creditors, and sailed off to the northeast coast of North America to navigate the Northwest Passage. First, however, he put in two years at King William Island completing the scientific part of his mission—to locate the position of the north magnetic pole. In August, 1905, he began the historic journey from Baffin Bay through Bering Strait to Nome, Alaska. Of the last leg, he wrote: "It seemed the old *Gjøa* knew she had reached a critical moment. She had to tackle two large masses of ice that barred her way . . . and now she charged again into them to force them asunder and slip through. The lads attacked the ice on both sides with boat hooks. . . . The ice yielded a fraction of an inch at a time, but at last it gave way. A wild shout of triumph broke forth as the vessel slipped through." At the end of the trip, the vessel again stuck in ice, so Amundsen traveled 500 mi. by dogsled over a 9,000-ft. mountain range to reach the nearest telegraph office. There, on Dec. 5, 1905, he wired news of his accomplishment to the world. Once home, he made enough by lecturing to pay off his creditors.

1911 "Then I rounded a knoll and almost staggered at the sight I faced. Tier upon tier of Inca terraces rose like a giant flight of stairs." So wrote American archaeologist Hiram Bingham (1875–1956) of his dazzling discovery of the lost city of Machu Picchu, 2,000 ft. above the Uru-

Newly explored Pantiacolla region of southeastern Peru, with arrow pointing to mysterious dots, each almost the size of the Great Pyramid of Egypt.

bamba Valley in the Andes of eastern Peru, whose overhanging ledges had hidden it from Spanish conquistadores.

1914 On a two-month trip, ex-President Theodore Roosevelt (1858–1919), his son Kermit, head of Brazilian Indian Affairs Cândido Rondón, naturalist George K. Cherrie, and a crew of army men and native paddlers explored and mapped 625 mi. of the Río Duvido (River of Doubt) in the Brazilian highlands on the edge of Mato Grosso. Besieged by insects, they nearly encountered hostile natives (who killed their dog), had to lower their dugouts down a 35-ft. waterfall, and faced accident (Kermit almost lost his life in a dugout accident in the rapids which killed one of the natives) and illness (Roosevelt almost died of an infected leg).

1975 to the Present Analyzing a 1975 NASA satellite photograph of the Pantiacolla region of southeastern Peru, Peruvian archaeologist Rodolfo Bragagnini spotted 10 mysterious black dots, in two rows, regular as dots on a domino. In actuality, each dot is only a little smaller than the Great Pyramid in Egypt. As a boy, Bragagnini had heard from Machiguenga Indians of a fabulous fortress in that region, but no one had yet explored the area to search for it. Earlier, the Machiguenga had stoned three explorers to death. Photographs taken from planes have not settled the question of whether the dots represent man-made or geological formations.

—A.E.

10

COMMUNICATIONS

10 TOP-RATED TV SERIES, 1950–1981

The following lists are the 10 top-rated evening television series for every year from 1950 through 1981. The Nielsen rating, television's most important ranking system, is compiled by the market research firm of A. C. Nielsen Co. Their method of audience measurement is based on the percentage of homes that are tuned to a particular program on an average night. For example, a rating of 67.3 would mean that an average of 67.3% of all homes equipped with a television set were tuned to that show.

OCTOBER, 1950–APRIL, 1951

Program	Network	Rating
1. Texaco Star Theater	NBC	61.6
2. Fireside Theatre	NBC	52.6
3. Philco TV Playhouse	NBC	45.3
4. Your Show of Shows	NBC	42.6
5. The Colgate Comedy Hour	NBC	42.0
6. Gillette Cavalcade of Sports	NBC	41.3
7. The Lone Ranger	ABC	41.2
8. Arthur Godfrey's Talent Scouts	CBS	40.6
9. Hopalong Cassidy	NBC	39.9
10. Mama	CBS	39.7

OCTOBER, 1951–APRIL, 1952

Program	Network	Rating
1. Arthur Godfrey's Talent Scouts	CBS	53.8
2. Texaco Star Theater	NBC	52.0
3. I Love Lucy	CBS	50.9
4. The Red Skelton Show	NBC	50.2
5. The Colgate Comedy Hour	NBC	45.3
6. Arthur Godfrey and His Friends	CBS	43.3
7. Fireside Theatre	NBC	43.1
8. Your Show of Shows	NBC	43.0
9. The Jack Benny Show	CBS	42.8
10. You Bet Your Life	NBC	42.1

Lucy and Ethel in I Love Lucy.

OCTOBER, 1952–APRIL, 1953

1.	I Love Lucy	CBS	67.3
2.	Arthur Godfrey's Talent Scouts	CBS	54.7
3.	Arthur Godfrey and His Friends	CBS	47.1
4.	Dragnet	NBC	46.8
5.	Texaco Star Theater	NBC	46.7
6.	The Buick Circus Hour	NBC	46.0
7.	The Colgate Comedy Hour	NBC	44.3
8.	Gangbusters	NBC	42.4
9.	You Bet Your Life	NBC	41.6
10.	Fireside Theatre	NBC	40.6

OCTOBER, 1953–APRIL, 1954

1.	I Love Lucy	CBS	58.8
2.	Dragnet	NBC	53.2
3.	Arthur Godfrey's Talent Scouts	CBS	43.6
4.	You Bet Your Life	NBC	43.6
5.	The Chevy Show (Bob Hope)	NBC	41.4
6.	The Milton Berle Show	NBC	40.2
7.	Arthur Godfrey and His Friends	CBS	38.9
8.	The Ford Show	NBC	38.8
9.	The Jackie Gleason Show	CBS	38.1
10.	Fireside Theatre	NBC	36.4

OCTOBER, 1954–APRIL, 1955

1.	I Love Lucy	CBS	49.3
2.	The Jackie Gleason Show	CBS	42.4
3.	Dragnet	NBC	42.1
4.	You Bet Your Life	NBC	41.0
5.	The Toast of the Town	CBS	39.6
6.	Disneyland	ABC	39.1
7.	The Chevy Show (Bob Hope)	NBC	38.5
8.	The Jack Benny Show	CBS	38.3
9.	The Martha Raye Show	NBC	35.6
10.	The George Gobel Show	NBC	35.2

OCTOBER, 1955–APRIL, 1956

1.	The $64,000 Question	CBS	47.5
2.	I Love Lucy	CBS	46.1
3.	The Ed Sullivan Show	CBS	39.5
4.	Disneyland	ABC	37.4
5.	The Jack Benny Show	CBS	37.2
6.	December Bride	CBS	37.0
7.	You Bet Your Life	NBC	35.4
8.	Dragnet	NBC	35.0
9.	The Millionaire	CBS	33.8
10.	I've Got a Secret	CBS	33.5

OCTOBER, 1956–APRIL, 1957

1.	I Love Lucy	CBS	43.7
2.	The Ed Sullivan Show	CBS	38.4
3.	General Electric Theater	CBS	36.9
4.	The $64,000 Question	CBS	36.4
5.	December Bride	CBS	35.2
6.	Alfred Hitchcock Presents	CBS	33.9
7.	I've Got a Secret	CBS	32.7
8.	Gunsmoke	CBS	32.7
9.	The Perry Como Show	NBC	32.6
10.	The Jack Benny Show	CBS	32.3

OCTOBER, 1957–APRIL, 1958

1.	Gunsmoke	CBS	43.1
2.	The Danny Thomas Show	CBS	35.3
3.	Tales of Wells Fargo	NBC	35.2
4.	Have Gun Will Travel	CBS	33.7
5.	I've Got a Secret	CBS	33.4
6.	The Life and Legend of Wyatt Earp	ABC	32.6
7.	General Electric Theater	CBS	31.5
8.	The Restless Gun	NBC	31.4
9.	December Bride	CBS	30.7
10.	You Bet Your Life	NBC	30.6

OCTOBER, 1958–APRIL, 1959

1.	Gunsmoke	CBS	39.6
2.	Wagon Train	NBC	36.1
3.	Have Gun Will Travel	CBS	34.3
4.	The Rifleman	ABC	33.1
5.	The Danny Thomas Show	CBS	32.8
6.	Maverick	ABC	30.4
7.	Tales of Wells Fargo	NBC	30.2
8.	The Real McCoys	ABC	30.1
9.	I've Got a Secret	CBS	29.8
10.	The Life and Legend of Wyatt Earp	ABC	29.1

OCTOBER, 1959–APRIL, 1960

1.	Gunsmoke	CBS	40.3
2.	Wagon Train	NBC	38.4
3.	Have Gun Will Travel	CBS	34.7
4.	The Danny Thomas Show	CBS	31.1
5.	The Red Skelton Show	CBS	30.8
6.	Father Knows Best	CBS	29.7
7.	77 Sunset Strip	ABC	29.7
8.	The Price Is Right	NBC	29.2
9.	Wanted: Dead or Alive	CBS	28.7
10.	Perry Mason	CBS	28.3

(L to R) James Arness, Amanda Blake, and Milburn Stone in Gunsmoke.

OCTOBER, 1960–APRIL, 1961

1.	Gunsmoke	CBS	37.3
2.	Wagon Train	NBC	34.2
3.	Have Gun Will Travel	CBS	30.9
4.	The Andy Griffith Show	CBS	27.8
5.	The Real McCoys	ABC	27.7
6.	Rawhide	CBS	27.5
7.	Candid Camera	CBS	27.3
8.	The Untouchables	ABC	27.0
9.	The Price Is Right	NBC	27.0
10.	The Jack Benny Show	CBS	26.2

OCTOBER, 1961–APRIL, 1962

1.	Wagon Train	NBC	32.1
2.	Bonanza	NBC	30.0
3.	Gunsmoke	CBS	28.3
4.	Hazel	NBC	27.7
5.	Perry Mason	CBS	27.3
6.	The Red Skelton Show	CBS	27.1
7.	The Andy Griffith Show	CBS	27.0
8.	The Danny Thomas Show	CBS	26.1
9.	Dr. Kildare	NBC	25.6
10.	Candid Camera	CBS	25.5

OCTOBER, 1962–APRIL, 1963

1.	The Beverly Hillbillies	CBS	36.0
2.	Candid Camera	CBS	31.1
3.	The Red Skelton Show	CBS	31.1
4.	Bonanza	NBC	29.8
5.	The Lucy Show	CBS	29.8
6.	The Andy Griffith Show	CBS	29.7
7.	Ben Casey	ABC	28.7
8.	The Danny Thomas Show	CBS	28.7
9.	The Dick Van Dyke Show	CBS	27.1
10.	Gunsmoke	CBS	27.0

OCTOBER, 1963–APRIL, 1964

1.	The Beverly Hillbillies	CBS	39.1
2.	Bonanza	NBC	36.9
3.	The Dick Van Dyke Show	CBS	33.3
4.	Petticoat Junction	CBS	30.3
5.	The Andy Griffith Show	CBS	29.4
6.	The Lucy Show	CBS	28.1
7.	Candid Camera	CBS	27.7
8.	The Ed Sullivan Show	CBS	27.5
9.	The Danny Thomas Show	CBS	26.7
10.	My Favorite Martian	CBS	26.3

OCTOBER, 1964–APRIL, 1965

1.	Bonanza	NBC	36.3
2.	Bewitched	ABC	31.0
3.	Gomer Pyle, U.S.M.C.	CBS	30.7
4.	The Andy Griffith Show	CBS	28.3
5.	The Fugitive	ABC	27.9
6.	The Red Skelton Hour	CBS	27.4
7.	The Dick Van Dyke Show	CBS	27.1
8.	The Lucy Show	CBS	26.6
9.	Peyton Place II	ABC	26.4
10.	Combat	ABC	26.1

OCTOBER, 1965–APRIL, 1966

1.	Bonanza	NBC	31.8
2.	Gomer Pyle, U.S.M.C.	CBS	27.8
3.	The Lucy Show	CBS	27.7
4.	The Red Skelton Hour	CBS	27.6
5.	Batman (Thurs.)	ABC	27.0
6.	The Andy Griffith Show	CBS	26.9
7.	Bewitched	ABC	25.9
8.	The Beverly Hillbillies	CBS	25.9
9.	Hogan's Heroes	CBS	24.9
10.	Batman (Wed.)	ABC	24.7

OCTOBER, 1966–APRIL, 1967

1.	Bonanza	NBC	29.1
2.	The Red Skelton Hour	CBS	28.2
3.	The Andy Griffith Show	CBS	27.4
4.	The Lucy Show	CBS	26.2
5.	The Jackie Gleason Show	CBS	25.3
6.	Green Acres	CBS	24.6
7.	Daktari	CBS	23.4
8.	Bewitched	ABC	23.4
9.	The Beverly Hillbillies	CBS	23.4
10.	Gomer Pyle, U.S.M.C.	CBS	22.8

OCTOBER, 1967–APRIL, 1968

1.	The Andy Griffith Show	CBS	27.6
2.	The Lucy Show	CBS	27.0
3.	Gomer Pyle, U.S.M.C.	CBS	25.6
4.	Gunsmoke	CBS	25.5
5.	Family Affair	CBS	25.5
6.	Bonanza	NBC	25.5
7.	The Red Skelton Show	CBS	25.3
8.	The Dean Martin Show	NBC	24.8
9.	The Jackie Gleason Show	CBS	23.9
10.	Saturday Night at the Movies	NBC	23.6

OCTOBER, 1968–APRIL, 1969

1. Rowan & Martin's Laugh-In	NBC	31.8
2. Gomer Pyle, U.S.M.C.	CBS	27.2
3. Bonanza	NBC	26.6
4. Mayberry R.F.D.	CBS	25.4
5. Family Affair	CBS	25.2
6. Gunsmoke	CBS	24.9
7. Julia	NBC	24.6
8. The Dean Martin Show	NBC	24.1
9. Here's Lucy	CBS	23.8
10. The Beverly Hillbillies	CBS	23.5

OCTOBER, 1969–APRIL, 1970

1. Rowan & Martin's Laugh-In	NBC	26.3
2. Gunsmoke	CBS	25.9
3. Bonanza	NBC	24.8
4. Mayberry R.F.D.	CBS	24.4
5. Family Affair	CBS	24.2
6. Here's Lucy	CBS	23.9
7. The Red Skelton Hour	CBS	23.8
8. Marcus Welby, M.D.	ABC	23.7
9. Walt Disney's Wonderful World of Color	NBC	23.6
10. The Doris Day Show	CBS	22.8

OCTOBER, 1970–APRIL, 1971

1. Marcus Welby, M.D.	ABC	29.6
2. The Flip Wilson Show	NBC	27.9
3. Here's Lucy	CBS	26.1
4. Ironside	NBC	25.7
5. Gunsmoke	CBS	25.5
6. ABC Movie of the Week	ABC	25.1
7. Hawaii Five-O	CBS	25.0
8. Medical Center	CBS	24.5
9. Bonanza	NBC	23.9
10. The F.B.I.	ABC	23.0

OCTOBER, 1971–APRIL, 1972

1. All in the Family	CBS	34.0
2. The Flip Wilson Show	NBC	28.2
3. Marcus Welby, M.D.	ABC	27.8
4. Gunsmoke	CBS	26.0
5. ABC Movie of the Week	ABC	25.6
6. Sanford and Son	NBC	25.2
7. Mannix	CBS	24.8
8. Funny Face	CBS	23.9
9. Adam-12	NBC	23.9
10. The Mary Tyler Moore Show	CBS	23.7

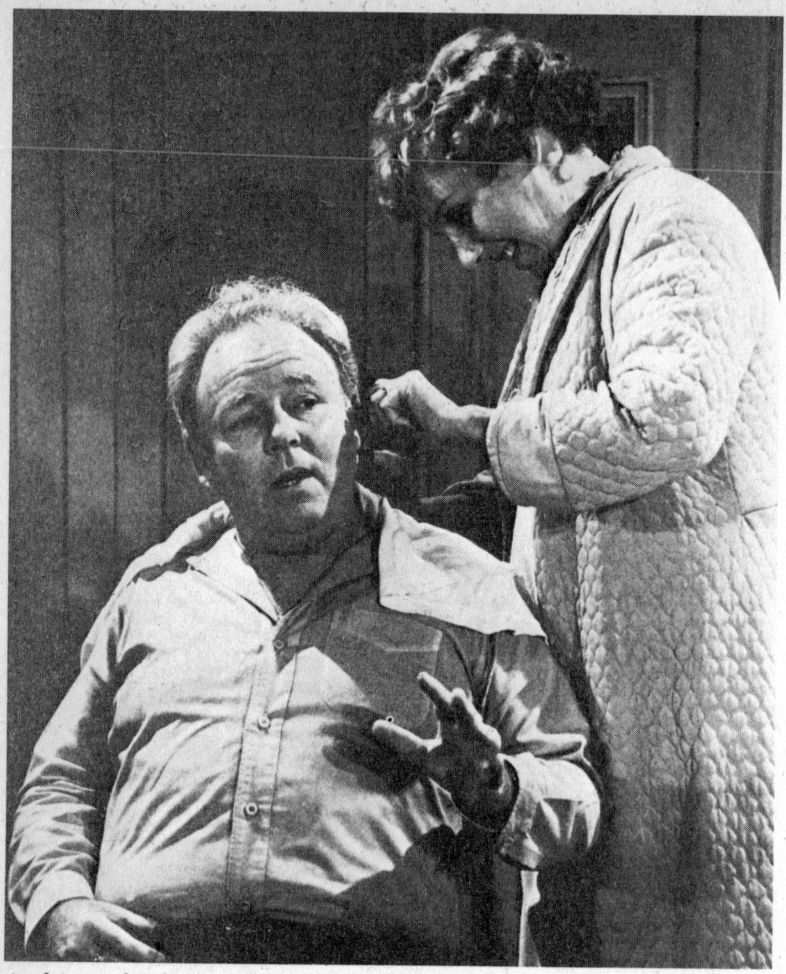

Archie and Edith in All in the Family.

OCTOBER, 1972–APRIL, 1973

1.	All in the Family	CBS	33.3
2.	Sanford and Son	NBC	27.6
3.	Hawaii Five-O	CBS	25.2
4.	Maude	CBS	24.7
5.	Bridget Loves Bernie	CBS	24.2
6.	Sunday Mystery Movie	NBC	24.2
7.	The Mary Tyler Moore Show	CBS	23.6
8.	Gunsmoke	CBS	23.6
9.	The Wonderful World of Disney	NBC	23.5
10.	Ironside	NBC	23.4

SEPTEMBER, 1973–APRIL, 1974

1.	All in the Family	CBS	31.2
2.	The Waltons	CBS	28.1

3. Sanford and Son	NBC	27.5
4. M*A*S*H	CBS	25.7
5. Hawaii Five-O	CBS	24.0
6. Maude	CBS	23.5
7. Kojak	CBS	23.3
8. The Sonny and Cher Comedy Hour	CBS	23.3
9. The Mary Tyler Moore Show	CBS	23.1
10. Cannon	CBS	23.1

SEPTEMBER, 1974–APRIL, 1975

1. All in the Family	CBS	30.2
2. Sanford and Son	NBC	29.6
3. Chico and the Man	NBC	28.5
4. The Jeffersons	CBS	27.6
5. M*A*S*H	CBS	27.4
6. Rhoda	CBS	26.3
7. Good Times	CBS	25.8
8. The Waltons	CBS	25.5
9. Maude	CBS	24.9
10. Hawaii Five-O	CBS	24.8

SEPTEMBER, 1975–APRIL, 1976

1. All in the Family	CBS	30.1
2. Rich Man, Poor Man	ABC	28.0
3. Laverne & Shirley	ABC	27.5
4. Maude	CBS	25.0
5. The Bionic Woman	ABC	24.9
6. Phyllis	CBS	24.5
7. Sanford and Son	NBC	24.4
8. Rhoda	CBS	24.4
9. The Six Million Dollar Man	ABC	24.3
10. ABC Monday Night Movie	ABC	24.2

SEPTEMBER, 1976–APRIL, 1977

1. Happy Days	ABC	31.5
2. Laverne & Shirley	ABC	30.9
3. ABC Monday Night Movie	ABC	26.0
4. M*A*S*H	CBS	25.9
5. Charlie's Angels	ABC	25.8
6. The Big Event	NBC	24.4
7. The Six Million Dollar Man	ABC	24.2
8. ABC Sunday Night Movie	ABC	23.4
9. Baretta	ABC	23.4
10. One Day at a Time	CBS	23.4

SEPTEMBER, 1977–APRIL, 1978

1. Laverne & Shirley	ABC	31.6
2. Happy Days	ABC	31.4
3. Three's Company	ABC	28.3
4. 60 Minutes	CBS	24.4

5. Charlie's Angels	ABC	24.4
6. All in the Family	CBS	24.4
7. Little House on the Prairie	NBC	24.1
8. Alice	CBS	23.2
9. M*A*S*H	CBS	23.2
10. One Day at a Time	CBS	23.0

SEPTEMBER, 1978–APRIL, 1979

1. Three's Company	ABC	30.1
2. Laverne & Shirley	ABC	29.8
3. Mork and Mindy	ABC	28.4
4. Happy Days	ABC	28.3
5. Angie	ABC	26.7
6. 60 Minutes	CBS	25.4
7. M*A*S*H	CBS	25.4
8. The Ropers	ABC	25.2
9. Charlie's Angels	ABC	25.0
10. All in the Family	CBS	24.9

SEPTEMBER, 1979–APRIL, 1980

1. 60 Minutes	CBS	28.1
2. Three's Company	ABC	26.2
3. That's Incredible	ABC	25.6
4. M*A*S*H	CBS	25.3
5. Alice	CBS	25.1
6. Dallas	CBS	24.6
7. Dukes of Hazzard	CBS	24.1
8. The Jeffersons	CBS	24.1
9. Flo	CBS	23.7
10. One Day at a Time	CBS	23.3

OCTOBER 27, 1980–APRIL 19, 1981*

1. Dallas	CBS	33.4
2. 60 Minutes	CBS	27.8
3. Dukes of Hazzard	CBS	26.3
4. M*A*S*H	CBS	24.8
5. Love Boat	ABC	24.3
6. Private Benjamin	CBS	23.9
7. Jeffersons	CBS	23.4
8. Alice	CBS	22.8
9. Three's Company	ABC	22.4
10. House Calls	CBS	22.3

*NBC claims that the season started on Sept. 15, 1980, so their list has the NBC mini-series *Shogun* in first place and differs substantially from this list prepared by CBS and ABC.

Source: A. C. Nielsen

9 MEMORABLE NEWSPAPER STORIES THAT NEVER HAPPENED

1. GREAT ASTRONOMICAL DISCOVERIES New York *Sun*, 1835

The fanciful outpourings of a Dr. Thomas Dick, who claimed that people inhabited the moon, helped to goad Richard Adams Locke, editor of the four-page daily *Sun*, into publishing a series of articles about moon discoveries. The series began with a news item stating that astronomer Sir John Herschel, then studying the heavens at the Cape of Good Hope in Africa, had "made some astronomical discoveries of the most wonderful description, by means of an immense telescope of an entirely new principle." According to later stories, the telescope could magnify an object 42,000 times, stood on 150-ft.-high pillars, and used a method of artificial light "transfusion." Seen through the telescope: moon forests, an amethyst crystal 90 ft. high, a blue goatlike animal with one horn, a beaver that knew how to make fire. But most astonishing were the moon people; short and hairy-bodied, with yellow faces, they had membranous wings reaching from their shoulders to the calves of their legs. These people had built sapphire temples, on whose roofs were designs showing a flaming globe. The *Sun*'s readers, who swelled in number to 19,360, believed the four-installment series. A clergyman talked of getting the Gospel to the moon people. A theater exhibited a huge canvas of moon scenes. Edgar Allan Poe was one of the few to debunk the story for its scientific inaccuracies; e.g., how could birds fly on an airless moon? But Sir John Herschel found the articles amusing.

2. ASTOUNDING NEWS! THE ATLANTIC CROSSED IN THREE DAYS! New York *Sun*, 1844

Edgar Allan Poe, who was morbidly fascinated by death on earth, was equally fascinated by life in the air—namely, ballooning. Moreover, he had a sharp scientific mind and an interest in exploration and discovery. The 1844 New York *Sun* story that told of an Atlantic crossing by balloon was his invention. In the story, which was accompanied by a woodcut showing the balloon, the fictional correspondent interviewed some of the eight people who purportedly took part in the 75-hour crossing from England to South Carolina. Included was a journal entry by one "Herman Ainsworth, British novelist": "God be praised! Who shall say that anything is impossible hereafter?"

3. AWFUL CALAMITY. SAVAGE BRUTES AT LARGE. New York *Herald*, 1874

So read the headlines to an eyewitness account "of the mass escape of the animals in the Central Park Zoo." The alleged toll: 48 people killed (27 identified by name) plus 200 people hurt by beasts that had run amok. Supposedly, some of the animals had been captured when the story went to press, but 12 of them still eluded the searchers—said to include Samuel J. Tilden and Chester A. Arthur—who were checking out churches and businesses on Broadway and Fifth Avenue. The mayor had suggested that people stay home, the article warned. Only the last paragraph revealed that the story was a hoax: "The Moral of the Whole" explained that the managing editor was trying to call the public's attention to the zoo's problems. But readers wanted to believe. Even the owner of the *Herald*, James Gordon Bennett—who should have known better—stayed home in bed. Reporter George W. Hosmer (later associated with Joseph Pulitzer) charged into the newspaper's offices brandishing two revolvers, shouting, "Well, here I am!" And the city editor of *The New York Times*, George F. Williams, went so far as to berate the police for giving the *Herald* an exclusive on the zoo story.

4. GLORIOUS OPPORTUNITY TO GET RICH Associated Press, c. 1875

Willis B. Powell, an Illinois editor, released to the Associated Press a story about a cat-and-rat ranch proposed for his town of Lacon. The story, which was printed throughout the U.S., went as follows: "Glorious Opportunity to Get Rich—We are starting a cat ranch in Lacon with 100,000 cats. Each cat will average 12 kittens a year. The cat skins will sell for 30¢ each. One hundred men can skin 5,000 cats a day. We figure a daily net profit of over $10,000. Now what shall we feed the cats? We will start a rat ranch next door with 1,000,000 rats. The rats will breed 12 times faster than the cats. So we will have four rats to feed each day to each cat. Now what shall we feed the rats? We will feed the rats the carcasses of the cats after they have been skinned. Now Get This! We feed the rats to the cats and the cats to the rats and get the cat skins for nothing." In 1940 *Goldfish Bowl*, published by the National Press Club in Washington, D.C., reported that this prospectus had been a hoax created by Powell.

5. A NEGLECTED ANNIVERSARY New York *Evening Mail*, 1917

Satirist H. L. Mencken, whose acerbic comments frequently jolted the reading public, was the perpetrator of a hoax that lingered on in the media for years. Mencken, incidentally, was a second-generation hoaxer. His father before him was fond of spreading ridiculous rumors; e.g., the collapse of the Brooklyn Bridge, the mass transfer of the entire population of Holland to the U.S., and Otto von Bismarck's giving up his job as chancellor of Germany to start a Milwaukee brewery. H.L.'s newspaper story was supposedly in celebration of the 75th anniversary of the introduction of the bathtub to the U.S. He himself called it a "tissue of absurdities, all of them deliberate and obvious" after it was exposed nearly 10 years later. But no matter how deliberate and obvious the tissue of lies, it was believed, perhaps because of its convincing detail. The story said that one Adam Thompson was the owner of the first bathtub in the U.S.; that the tub was connected to plumbing in Cincinnati in 1842; that physicians denounced the bathtub as a menace to public health; and that the Philadelphia City Council tried to pass an ordinance against its use in winter. Mencken quoted the *Western*

Medical Repository as saying that the bathtub "softens the moral fibre of the Republic." He said President Millard Fillmore had installed the first White House bathtub. The article was taken seriously. At least one Harvard professor quoted it, and its "facts" showed up in scholarly journals. On confessing his hoax, Mencken said, "In the end, no doubt, the thing will simmer down to a general feeling that I have committed some vague and sinister crime against the U.S., and there will be a renewal of the demand that I be deported to Russia."

6. KING TUT'S GOLDEN TYPEWRITER **Toronto *Mail and Empire*, c. 1922**

Charles Langdon Clarke was an old hand at hoaxing readers. He once fooled fundamentalist Christians into believing that the fossil of the whale that might have swallowed Jonah had been unearthed. His best hoax, however, was a serious-looking article headlined KING TUT'S GOLDEN TYPEWRITER. The article appeared after archaeologist Howard Carter discovered the almost untouched tomb of the Egyptian pharaoh Tutankhamen, who lived about 1350 B.C., in the Valley of the Kings. Among the priceless treasures entombed with the monarch, Clarke said, was a miraculous golden typewriter. This ancient and impossible instrument (How to print hieroglyphics with typewriter keys? How to make a typewriter big enough to hold them all?) was so exciting to a rival editor that he sent a reporter to interview Egyptologist C. T. Currelly about the find. At that point Clarke admitted that he had faked the story.

7. KILLER HAWK ATTACKS CHICAGO **Chicago *Journal*, 1927**

When a Chicago reporter sighted a chicken hawk flying above the city streets, a hoax was born. The simple sighting escalated into a thriller portraying the vicious hawk as preying on pigeons around Chicago's Art Institute and downtown elevated-railroad platforms. It became headline news for all Chicago papers. The *Tribune* featured political cartoons, five front-page stories, letters to the editor, and an item by the inquiring reporter—all about the chicken hawk. A newspaper photograph showing a hawk holding a dead pigeon while sitting on top of the Art Institute turned out to be a fake. The Lincoln Park Gun Club appointed a group to gun down the hawk; a banker offered a $50 reward for its death or capture; the Boy Scouts hunted it. Richard J. Finnegan, then editor of the *Journal*, decided to capitalize on the pigeon-and-hawk publicity by running a serial on the subject. Since none of his staff would volunteer, he ended up writing it himself; he called it "trash" and said he was always "just one installment ahead of the composing room." During a social evening, Henry Horner, later governor of Illinois, hearing Finnegan complain about his tight writing schedule, offered to help him prepare the rest of the episodes. He and Finnegan introduced mutual acquaintances into the story under false names.

8. HUNGER MARCHERS STORM BUCKINGHAM PALACE New York *Mirror,* 1932

In the early 1930s, William Randolph Hearst, the colorful newspaper magnate, was pro-labor, and his papers were in the habit of concocting stories that enhanced his stand. An example: In a 1932 issue of the New York *Mirror*, an article described hunger marchers storming Buckingham Palace in London. To back up the story, the paper ran a photograph reputedly showing such a scene. In actuality, the photograph had been taken in 1929 and the crowd of people in it was anxiously waiting for news about the health of ailing King George V.

9. SEVERE CROP FAILURE IN SOVIET UNION Hearst newspapers, 1935

Virulently anti-Soviet, Hearst used his papers to spread propaganda, often based on untruths, against the Russians. For example, in 1935 Hearst papers ran a series of articles about severe crop failures in the U.S.S.R.; these were written by a self-styled reporter using the alias Thomas Walker, who turned out to be an ex-jailbird named Robert Green who had escaped from a Colorado state prison in 1921. Not surprisingly, Walker/Green had been incarcerated for forgery. As was usual with such Hearst campaigns, photographs were used to back up the series, but they were actually of the Volga famine in 1921. Ironically, the same papers carried another series of articles, written by foreign correspondent Lindsay Parrott, which spoke glowingly of the fruitful Russian harvest of 1935. Hearst's other "hoaxes" included atrocity stories that helped foment American intervention in Cuba and the Spanish-American War; faked stories and pictures that helped to create resentment against Mexico in 1927; and photographs of rebel atrocities mislabeled as Loyalist atrocities during the civil war in Spain.

—A.E.

9-DAY WONDERS—ON THE 10TH DAY

Headline—1936: MAX SCHMELING

At the Peak: Even after all these years, it's a name that brings back memories for sports fans of the 1930s. Memories of two boxing matches with bizarre political and racial overtones.

When he was in his prime, German boxer Max Schmeling was hailed by Adolf Hitler as a perfect specimen of the Master Race, particularly after he won the world heavyweight crown in a bout with Jack Sharkey in 1930. Two years later he lost the title to Sharkey, and by 1935 he was considered washed up.

Thus, when he climbed into the ring to face Joe Louis in June of 1936, none of the experts gave the 31-year-old Schmeling a chance. But the beetle-browed veteran went after his younger and heavier opponent with great determination, knocking Louis out in the 12th round for one of the biggest upsets in ring history.

By the time they met for the return match two years later, the world was moving toward war and the press was billing the fight as a clash between the symbols of Nazism and democracy. As it turned out, the fight was no contest. In perhaps the most awesome display of power in his career, the Brown Bomber tore into Schmeling with a devastating series of blows that knocked the German senseless 2:04 min. into the first round.

And Today: After serving as a German paratrooper in W.W. II (he was wounded in the Battle of Crete), losing his first fortune, and retiring from the ring in 1948, the 76-year-old Schmeling lives comfortably on a farm near Hamburg, collects handsome profits from his two Coca-Cola bottling plants, and is still West Germany's most popular sports celebrity.

Any hard feelings toward Louis?

None at all. Schmeling maintains that they've always been friends and that there were never any ideological overtones to their fights. They were just sports contests between two determined men.

Headline—1959: DR. BERNARD FINCH AND CAROLE TREGOFF

At the Peak: Here's one that takes you back to 1959, when automobile tailfins were at their height, Ike was still in the White House, and newspapers were full of stories about the doctor, his girl friend, and his murdered wife.

Finch was a middle-aged Los Angeles–area surgeon who was having a torrid romance with his shapely young receptionist, Carole Tregoff. The only problem was that Finch was already married, and his wealthy and socially prominent wife would clean him out financially in the event of a divorce.

What to do? Murder seemed like the most profitable solution, but a hired assassin failed to get the job done. So the determined lovers were left to do it themselves. In July of 1959, 35-year-old Barbara Finch was found dead in the garage of her home from the combined effects of a bullet in the back and blows that fractured her skull.

At their first two trials, Finch and his paramour beat the rap when the juries failed to agree on a verdict. But after a third sensational trial, during which the prosecutor accused them of "acting out of greed, avarice, lust, and frustration," they were convicted and sentenced to life imprisonment. Tregoff served eight years and was last in the news when she was released on parole in 1969. Finch, who became a fitness addict and kept up with the latest medical literature while behind bars, was released after 12 years and said he wanted to return to the practice of medicine.

And Today: That's just what he's doing in the small, out-of-the-way town of Bolivar on the edge of the Ozark Mountains in Missouri, where he's been licensed to practice by the state medical board and has become an accepted member of the community. At age 63 he's naturally reluctant to discuss the past, though he has said, "It was a terrible thing

I did and I have paid heavily for it and I expect to pay for the rest of my life."

And Carole?

Both her mother and her former lawyer say she's doing well at age 44 as supervisor of medical records at a large southern California hospital, where she has a staff of 12 working under her. She has a new name, remains unmarried, and has had no further contact with Finch.

Headline—1962: SHERRI FINKBINE

At the Peak: It's one of those names from the past that rings a bell, but very faintly. Need a clue? Think back to the thalidomide scares of the early 1960s.

At the center of that tragic emotional storm was Sherri Finkbine, a pregnant TV children's program hostess in Arizona, who for several months had been taking a tranquilizer that her husband had obtained in Europe. Then the news broke that this drug, thalidomide, was responsible for terrible deformities in newborn babies.

The 30-year-old mother of four and her high-school-teacher husband decided she should have an abortion—a decision that provoked worldwide headlines, a condemnation on the Vatican radio, and thousands of critical, as well as a few threatening, letters. Still, Sherri was determined to go ahead. When U.S. medical authorities refused to approve the operation, she flew to Sweden, where the abortion was performed and doctors verified that the baby would indeed have been deformed. After that, the controversy gradually died. Sherri returned to the U.S. and faded from the public eye.

And Today: After losing her TV job, having two more children, and shedding her husband in a 1973 divorce, Sherri moved to La Jolla, Calif., where she worked in a women's center counseling people on abortion issues and other problems.

Mind you, though her name remains synonymous with abortion, she has no shortage of children. Now married to a La Jolla physician, she has at times had 12 children at home—6 from her first marriage plus her 6 stepchildren.

—G.G.

PROBING THE PERIODICALS

THE GUINNESS BOOK OF WORLD RECORDS

History: *The Guinness Book of World Records* was born one bleak fall day in 1954 when Sir Hugh Beaver, while on a shooting expedition in Ireland, aimed at a small flock of golden plover and missed.

Sir Hugh, the managing director of Arthur Guinness, Son and Co., Ltd., had, of course, missed birds before, but it didn't happen often, and he was curious. Clearly the plover were considerably faster than the ducks and geese that he readily bagged. Perhaps, he mentioned to his companions over whiskey and soda that night, the plover was "the fastest game bird we've got." His companions countered with other birds, but the argument ended in frustration because there was nowhere to check. The most erudite encyclopedias, when consulted, proved to have no information on the flight speeds of game birds.

Back in London, Sir Hugh mulled over this deficiency; what modern Britain needed was a book that would tell people quickly and concisely just what was biggest, smallest, fastest, slowest, shortest, longest, etc., about as many things as possible. If such a book did not already exist, one should waste no time creating it; what was more, once created, it could be distributed to the many British pubs where Guinness stout was sold and where it would be useful in settling all those arguments that are peculiar to pubs. But who could put together such a book, considering how difficult the information was to come by? Fortunately, a junior executive at the brewery knew just the man, or in this case, men—identical twins Norris and Ross McWhirter. Sons of a prominent newspaperman, the McWhirters were raised in a house full of periodicals, newspapers, and reference books. As children, they clipped articles of interest and developed such insatiable curiosity about facts and trivia that they compiled their own lists—on subjects like the deepest lakes and the highest mountains. Concerned about the number of discrepancies they found in their sources, the two boys decided that when they grew up they would establish an agency to correct those errors.

In 1951 they started such a business, setting out, in Norris McWhirter's words, "to supply facts and figures to newspapers, yearbooks, encyclopedias, and advertisers." While building up their accounts, they both worked as sports journalists. One of the athletes they knew and covered was runner Christopher Chataway, the employee at Guinness who recommended them to Sir Hugh Beaver. After an interview in which the Guinness directors enjoyed testing the twins' knowledge of records and unusual facts, the brothers agreed to start work on the book. The rest is publishing history. Some four months later the first slim green volume—198 pages long—was at the bookstalls, and in four more months it was England's No. 1 nonfiction best-seller. The whole country, it seemed, was eager to know and pass around such information as the land speed record for a rocket sled (632 mph) and the most prodigious feat of childbearing—an honor claimed by a 19th-century lady, Mrs. Feodor Vassilyev, who bore 69 children (16 sets of twins, 7 of triplets, and 4 of quadruplets).

Once launched, the book acquired momentum as readers by the thousands wrote in with their own facts for inclusion. The McWhirters systematically catalogued them, arranged to have them verified, and sought out more. It was much to their advantage that their thinking processes were so alike; they hardly needed to communicate verbally at all, and if one mislaid a fact, the other one knew where to find it. Inseparable as children, they always shared a room even though their house had seven bedrooms, and they were never apart until they joined the Royal Navy during W.W. II. Norris served on a minesweeper in the Pacific, Ross on one in the Mediterranean, and they saw each other only

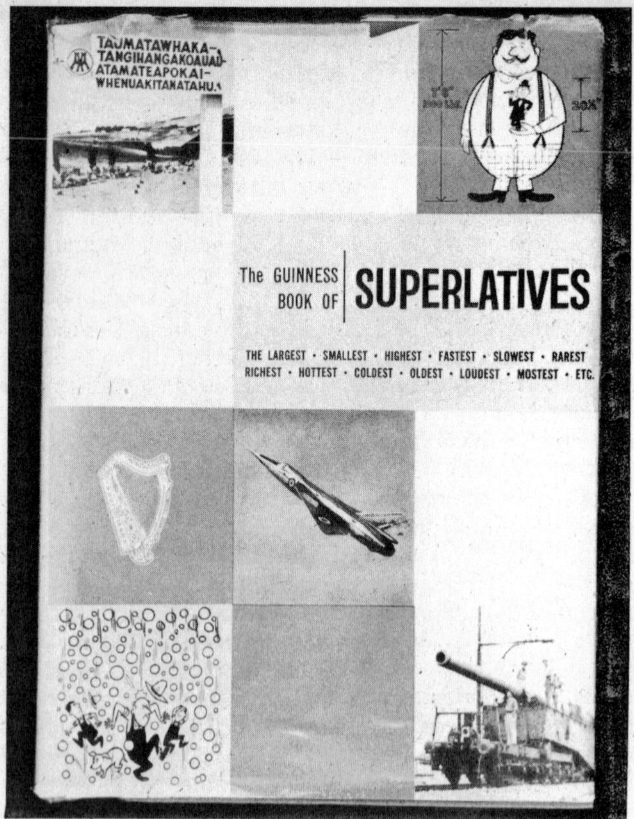

once, when their vessels, making their separate ways to Malta, collided with each other. After the war they went to Oxford together; later married within a few months of each other; ran as Conservatives for Parliament the same year (and lost); and had tastes so similar that Ross, who drank only tea, never ceased to be surprised that Norris occasionally asked for coffee.

TAUMATAWHAKA-
TANGIHANGAKOAUAU-
ATAMATEAPOKAI-
WHENUAKITANATAHU
The GUINNESS BOOK OF
SUPERLATIVES
THE LARGEST · SMALLEST · HIGHEST · FASTEST · SLOWEST · RAREST
RICHEST · HOTTEST · COLDEST · OLDEST · LOUDEST · MOSTEST · ETC.

In 1975 one of their joint political concerns brought their 20-year coeditorship of *Guinness* to an abrupt and tragic conclusion. Both brothers were convinced that the British government was not doing enough to bring to justice the Irish Republican Army terrorist bombers then plaguing London. One day Ross McWhirter announced plans to post a reward for their capture. Three weeks later he was gunned down at his front door, less than a mile from the Guinness office. Since then the entire burden of editorship has rested on the shoulders of Norris McWhirter.

Modern Operation: Guinness Superlatives, the publishing arm of Arthur Guinness, Son and Co., Ltd., operates from the third (and top) floor of a red brick building in the north London suburb of Enfield. In

McWhirter's office every surface—tables, couches, floor—is piled high with the latest of the 20,000 letters he receives each year—letters of inquiry, letters challenging old records with new ones, letters submitting whole new fields of endeavor, all hopeful of inclusion in the next *Guinness*. Since each submission must be accompanied by evidence of verification—photographs, newspaper clippings, corroborations of witnesses—the piles grow even higher. Whatever space remains is occupied by the stacks of books and periodicals from which McWhirter does his own firsthand research. A staff of 14 aids him with the correspondence and verifications.

McWhirter also devises the rules under which the publication operates. This became necessary when people started committing any number of crazy acts for the sole purpose of "getting into *Guinness*." Such activity, commonly known as "Guinnessport," is regularly indulged in both by individuals and groups who organize a kind of Guinness Olympics to establish new fields of endeavor and to set new records in old fields. But McWhirter believes there are limits. "One has to continually preserve the purity of records," he says. "To qualify, something has to be universally competitive, peculiar, or unique." To that end he rules out mere stunts like goldfish swallowing; dangerous activities such as Volkswagen packing or locking oneself into a room with poisonous snakes; alcoholic drinking contests; and sexual feats (the section on "swinging" pertains to playground equipment). He also cautions *Guinness* hopefuls against gargantuan eating contests, although he does list consumption records for certain foods, including prunes, baked beans (eaten one by one with a cocktail stick), and eels. Eating a bicycle, which M. Lotito did in the form of tires and metal filings in 1977, is duly recorded but with the accompanying notation that "no further entries in this category will be accepted."

The American arm of Guinness Superlatives is run by David Boehm, who not only publishes the American hardcover and paperback editions but also—with his staff of three—answers some 10,000 letters a year; produces a television show, *The Guinness Game;* stocks seven Guinness museums around the world; and presides over the mass challenge events in the U.S.

A new edition of *Guinness* appears each year, almost a quarter of it revised and updated from the previous edition. So far there appears to be no decline in the popularity of Guinnessport. As Allen Guttmann, an American Studies professor at Amherst, puts it, holding a record is a "uniquely modern form of immortality."

Size and Distribution of Sales: Although only a few people actually compete for records, a large public avidly reads, absorbs, and delights in quoting those records. With an average sale of 3 million copies a year, *Guinness* has (as of 1981) sold a total of 40 million copies in 23 languages, thus setting its own record as the world's fastest-selling book.

Examples of Typical Material: Mr. and Mrs. Mills Darden were an ordinary American couple except that he weighed 1,020 lb. and she weighed 98 lb., a difference of 922 lb. William J. Cobb thought that his 802 lb. was too much, so he brought it down to 232 lb.—a loss of 570 lb.—in three years. Billy and Benny McCrary, identical twins, had a combined weight of almost 1,500 lb. and had identical 84-in. waists; when Billy died in 1979, he was buried in a square coffin.

Such assorted facts are typical of the "Human Being" section of *Guinness*, which also includes such bizarre cases as Shridhar Chillal, whose fingernails on his left hand total 100 in. in length; Charles Osborne, who started hiccoughing in 1922 while slaughtering a hog and hasn't stopped yet; and Hideaki Tomoyori who has memorized the value of the mathematical symbol π (pi) to 20,000 places. In the "Animal and Plant Kingdom" section, the cheetah is announced to be the fastest mammal and the three-toed sloth the slowest. The female meadow vole breeds when less than a month old and has up to 17 litters of 6 to 8 young each year. The pelts of the sea otter, or Kamchatka beaver, are considered the most valuable, although the coat which Richard Burton purchased for $125,000 in 1970 and gave to his then wife Elizabeth Taylor was a Kojah—a mink-sable cross. A collie named Bobbie, who was lost by his owners in Indiana, found his way back home to Oregon—a journey of almost 2,000 mi., which included crossing the Rockies in the dead of winter. And the world horse population is set at 75 million.

Approximately one quarter of *Guinness* is devoted to sports. The latest Olympic records are, of course, included; but so is New Zealander Paul Wilson's record for running 100 yd. backwards (13.1 sec.). Bowling can be traced back to 5200 B.C. The only heavyweight champion who reigned undefeated throughout his career (1947–1956) was Rocky Marciano. In 1936 English professional golfer Alfred Edward Smith shot 55 on an 18-hole par 70 or more course, the lowest score in history.

Some of the nicest records are those set without Guinnessport in mind at all. Like the 89-ft.-3-in. basket scored by Les Henson, playing for Virginia Tech., in a game against Florida State on Jan. 21, 1980. Or the longest-lasting rainbow—seen for at least three hours in North Wales on Aug. 14, 1979.

Unusual Facts: Perhaps the most unusual fact about *Guinness* is that editor McWhirter has himself memorized most of the 15,000 entries therein, a record not yet challenged, much less bested, and which he explains by saying, "It's the same as a boy memorizing information about baseball. It's a matter of being interested."

Incidently, in case you were wondering what the answer is to Sir Hugh Beaver's original question: the fastest game bird is the red-breasted merganser (*Mergus serrator*) which has a recorded air speed of 80 mph in level flight.

—N.C.S.

PLAYBOY

History: Hugh Marston Hefner (born Apr. 9, 1926) once recounted that his life as a shy introvert altered totally after he read Alfred Kinsey's *Sexual Behavior in the Human Male* while attending the University of Illinois in Urbana. Hefner, who had had a strict Methodist upbringing, suddenly saw puritanism as a farce and recognized the hypocrisy of

American sexual repression. Several years later, this revelation would result in his founding America's greatest magazine-publishing success—*Playboy*.

In 1949 Hefner graduated from college. After completing one semester of postgraduate work in psychology at Northwestern University, he held a number of minor posts in publishing companies, including a job at *Esquire*. Within four years he was ready to launch a new genre of men's magazine. Previously, most of these magazines had been outdoors, macho-oriented publications that featured he-man fiction. Hefner decided to strike out in an entirely different direction, accenting the cosmopolitan and intellectual male (as *Esquire* did), while associating sex, not with a woman standing on a street corner, but with a girl-next-door type. His declared purpose was to break through the stifling sexual attitudes of the 1950s with an unabashed celebration of healthy heterosexuality.

While still on the staff of *Children's Activities* magazine, Hefner, working at the kitchen table in an apartment shared with his wife and infant daughter, put together the first issue of *Playboy*. Although he relied heavily on reprinted material, he also wrote some original articles and fillers. Having raised $10,000 by selling stock to his friends, Hefner bought a series of nudes of Marilyn Monroe for $500 from a Chicago calendar company. With Marilyn on the cover and also featured as the "Sweetheart of the Month"—without her permission—*Playboy* made its debut in December of 1953. Through the years other actresses, including Kim Novak, Ursula Andress, Brigitte Bardot, and Bo Derek, would follow Marilyn on *Playboy*'s pages. The first issue sold 53,991 copies at 50¢ each (collectors now pay as much as $400 for one) and immediately established the magazine and promised financial success.

Those first years saw Hefner working with Ray Russell as editor and Art Paul (who designed the rabbit logo for *Playboy*'s first issue) as art director. Circulation grew, but Hefner continued to rely on article and photograph reprints. When Auguste Spectorsky, a best-selling author, came aboard as editorial director, the magazine began buying original stories and producing its own nude photographs. It also became more sophisticated, and circulation hit the 800,000 mark by the end of 1956, thus surpassing that of the formerly most widely read men's magazine, *Esquire*.

Hefner, while realizing that written content was essential, knew that the photographs of naked women were selling his magazine. During the first few years, *Playboy*'s nudes "had a rather self-conscious fallen look . . . like the girls in other girlie magazines," Hefner admitted. But in 1955 he set a new style by choosing a rather average-looking "girl next door" as a model. "Janet Pilgrim," as she was called, looked "ordinary in a wholesome sort of way." In fact, picture policy during the 1950s was rather tame by today's standards; even photos of bare nipples were usually excluded. Yet problems arose. The post office had to be battled, and occasionally there were charges of obscenity. In 1963 Hefner fought the courts over the printing of a picture showing Jayne Mansfield lying in bed revealing a naked breast. (The case ended in victory for Hefner

because the jury was deadlocked, and after a mistrial was declared, the prosecution did not pursue it.)

Hefner's dedication to *Playboy* cost him his marriage in 1959, but during the 1960s he was consoled by the unparalleled growth of his magazine and by numerous girl friends. In 1964 *Playboy* was selling 2 million copies a month, and by 1968, 5 million. The 1960s were *Playboy*'s golden age. Playboy Enterprises' "private key" clubs, staffed by "bunny" waitresses in skintight costumes complete with ears and tails, opened in major American cities and abroad. The company built hotel-resorts and soon added not only modeling agencies but film, book, and record companies to the empire. Hefner traveled the world in the *Big Bunny*, his private jet, and divided the rest of his time between a mansion in Chicago and one in Los Angeles. By 1972 circulation had hit 7 million copies a month, earning $12 million in profits for the year.

Then, in 1973, disaster struck. The U.S. experienced a recession, and in addition *Playboy* faced stiff competition owing to the proliferation of more explicit men's magazines such as *Penthouse*. Circulation plummeted 2.5 million a month within a year, while Playboy clubs and resorts went seriously into the red. What followed has been nicknamed the "pubic wars." Accustomed to constant success, *Playboy* executives panicked. As Hefner later admitted, "We went through a period when we lost our bearings and started imitating the imitators." The June, 1973, issue featured the first *Playboy* centerfold showing pubic hair. After that, suggestive poses introduced eroticism as standard policy. Two covers in 1975, one implying lesbianism and the other masturbation and both reflecting the new trend, backfired. Conservative advertisers rebelled, and some withdrew their accounts from *Playboy*.

Modern Operations: By 1976 Playboy Enterprises was in trouble. Realizing this, Hefner hired a professional newspaper business manager named Derick Daniels to run the empire. Daniels recognized quickly that Playboy Enterprises' rambling diversification was losing the company millions. He closed several unprofitable Playboy clubs and hotels; reduced budgets, especially those of the film and record companies; and cut the payroll by firing 100 employees—70 in one day—including five vice-presidents. The purges were effective and Daniels led the company back to concentrating on magazine publishing, meanwhile encouraging one other profitable sector: Playboy's London gambling casinos.

With Daniels in charge of Playboy Enterprises, Hefner zeroed in on *Playboy* magazine's problems. Photo essays now are centered on such "wholesome" subjects as the "Girls of the Big Ten," while renewed emphasis has been placed on high-quality written content.

In a few years, the Hefner-Daniels team has successfully revived Playboy Enterprises. Circulation of the magazine has stabilized, and company profits have risen because of increased advertising at higher rates and large profits from the London gambling clubs, 75% of which are petrodollars lost by Arab high rollers. Also, Daniels is approaching *Playboy* with a new business professionalism. Recently he remarked dryly: "I spend more time with balance sheets than with bunnies." The latest Playboy Enterprises innovation is a casino being constructed in Atlantic City, N.J., at a cost of over $50 million.

Examples of Typical Material: Excerpt from an interview with Marlon Brando:

> **Playboy:** What is it that men hate about women?
> **Brando:** I think essentially, men fear women. It comes from a sense of dependence on women. Because men are brought up by women, they're dependent on them. In all societies, they have organizations that exclude women; warrior societies are famous the world over for that. It comes from fear of women. History is full of references to women and how bad they are, how dangerous. There are deprecating references to women all through the Bible. The mere fact that a woman was made out of a man's rib, as a sort of afterthought. Men's egos are frightened by women. We all have made mistakes in that respect. We've all been guilty, most men, of viewing women through prejudice. I always thought of myself not as a prejudiced person, but I find, as I look over it, that I was.

The following is a typical "party joke":

Our Unabashed Dictionary defines *nasty habit* as a nun's outfit by Frederick's of Hollywood.

Size and Distribution of Sales: In 1980 the total annual national circulation was 66,000,000 copies. Presently, *Playboy* guarantees U.S. advertisers a monthly circulation of 5.5 million copies. Each month *Playboy* sells 680,000 copies in Japan, 450,000 in Germany, 300,000 in Brazil, 175,000 in Australia, and 180,000 in France.

Strengths: One of Hefner's earliest goals was to establish *Playboy* as a serious magazine, not just another girlie rag. When he was eventually able to pay high rates to writers, he achieved this goal, especially in the area of fiction. *Playboy* contributors have included John Steinbeck, P. G. Wodehouse, W. Somerset Maugham, Vladimir Nabokov, Ray Bradbury, Gore Vidal, and John Updike.

Another highly acclaimed *Playboy* institution is the *Playboy* interview. Generated by Hefner in 1962, the magazine hired Alex Haley—future author of *Roots*—to do an interview with jazz musician Miles Davis. In subsequent issues, Haley interviewed Malcolm X, Martin Luther King, Jr., and American Nazi leader George Lincoln Rockwell. Over the years, the list of interviewed celebrities has included Fidel Castro, Jimmy Hoffa (Hoffa's last interview before his disappearance), John Lennon, and Gary Gilmore, shortly before his execution. Of course, the most famous interview appeared in the November, 1976, issue, in which Jimmy Carter pronounced: "I've looked on a lot of women with lust. I've committed adultery in my heart many times."

Weaknesses: *Playboy*'s greatest weakness lies in its basic credo, which views sexual freedom, material possessions, financial success, and social status as essential to happiness and the good life. This *Playboy* mentality—an extension of Hefner's own fantasies—has changed little since the magazine's founding in 1953, despite the fact that American society has changed dramatically, if not entirely, since the 1950s. What appeared to be a racy renunciation of sexual oppression in 1953 appears to be sexist exploitation in 1981.

That sexism exists within the Playboy empire is undeniable. A Playboy club bunny manual contains this exhortation: "Your proudest possession is your bunny tail. You must make sure it is always white and fluffy." In *Playboy,* women are treated as proverbial sex objects. This concept is fostered by the photographs of young women frozen into stilted poses. Their every blemish has been removed, and their breasts are sometimes enlarged by the *Playboy* technician's airbrush.

Starting in earnest in the late 1960s, feminists launched their attack on *Playboy*. Germaine Greer remarked that *Playboy* was giving "the illusion that 50-year-old men are entitled to fuck 15-year-old girls . . . [and] displays their girls as if they were a commodity." More recently, when *Playboy* did its photo essay on the "Girls of the Ivy League," the *Harvard Crimson* editorialized that *Playboy* "has played a major role in America's degradation of women."

Faced with the onslaught of the feminists, Hefner reacted strongly and in 1970, in a memo, told his editors, "What I'm interested in is the highly irrational, emotional, kookie trend that feminism has taken. . . . These chicks are our natural enemy. . . . It is time to do battle with them and I think we can do it in a devastating way." Twice Hefner personally confronted feminists on the Dick Cavett Show in the early 1970s. However, he was verbally mauled by his antagonists. On one show, Cavett asked feminist author Susan Brownmiller what sexual equality was. She replied, "When Hugh Hefner comes out here with a cottontail attached to his rear end, then we'll have equality."

To counter the wrath of the feminists, Playboy Enterprises has attempted conciliation during recent years by donating funds to associations supporting the Equal Rights Amendment, abortion, and rape counseling and aid. This seems to have blunted some of the attacks, but Susan Brownmiller referred to the donations as "hush money." Evidence that *Playboy* magazine's "T and A" attitude toward women may be changing comes from Christie Hefner, who, after graduating summa cum laude from Brandeis University, became a Playboy vice-president and the designated successor to her father, Hugh. Ms. Hefner recently noted, "The magazine is changing. It has to deal with more ways of intercourse between the sexes than sexual."

Yet the old colors still fly at *Playboy*, as is evidenced by a recent cartoon showing two little girls talking to each other. The caption: "I'm gonna be a Playboy Bunny when I grow up and out."

Unusual Facts: The international editions of *Playboy* require special editing for certain countries because of local censorship standards. In Japan no pubic hair can be shown, while in Mexico only one bare breast is allowed per page.

In the 1960s Hefner successfully upped subscriptions to the clergy by offering them a special 25% discount. After receiving numerous complaints from seminarians, he extended the offer to them as well.

In 1953 Hefner had decided to call his new magazine *Stag Party*, but his friend Eldon Sellers talked him into calling it *Playboy*.

—R.J.F.

TIME MAGAZINE

History: In the late winter of 1922, two young Yale University graduates, Briton Hadden and Henry Robinson Luce, rented the parlor floor of an old house at 141 East 17th Street in New York for $55 a month, bought some tables and chairs for a total of $48.70, and sat down to write a prospectus for a new weekly newsmagazine to be called, after considerable reflection, *Time*.

Granted, there were already several such periodicals in existence, but the *Literary Digest*, for example, was fat and verbose, and Hadden and Luce were convinced that busy professional men did not have time to pore over it every week. There was a real need for a magazine that would present all the important events of the week in concise and lively prose. As for point of view, well, busy Americans also did not have time

to ruminate over which side of an issue might be the right one, so the editors would do that for them. Surely keeping America informed required presenting not just the news, but what the news *meant*.

Henry R. Luce—Harry to his friends—had been born and brought up in China, where his parents were Presbyterian missionaries. America was a distant homeland of unparalleled promise and beneficence to him, a vision he never relinquished and would insist on perpetrating in varying ways in each of the publications that later emerged from his empire. He and Briton Hadden—Brit to *his* friends—were classmates and rivals at Hotchkiss School and later at Yale, where they held the two top positions on the *Daily News*. When America entered W.W. I, they turned the college paper into a propagandist sheet promoting intense patriotism. By the time they left Yale, both had been tapped for the prestigious senior society Skull and Bones, and Luce had also made Phi Beta Kappa. These achievements were not ends in themselves, but were, along with Yale connections, the keys that would open doors in the world of power and influence for two young men who were long on ideas and ambition, but short on funds.

The first issue of *Time* appeared on Mar. 3, 1923, after more than a year of editorial preparation and attempts to raise $100,000 that had been only partially successful. The staff included as part-timers poets Stephen Vincent Benét and Archibald MacLeish. Volume I, No. 1, was 28 pages long, 6 of which were advertisements, and it dealt with, among other matters, the French occupation of the Ruhr Valley, the famine in Russia, and the pros and cons of Prohibition in America. By the time December rolled around, the magazine was doing well enough that Luce felt he could risk supporting a wife, and he and Lila Ross Hotz, a beautiful Chicagoan, were married.

In the beginning, the editorial responsibilities fell chiefly to Hadden, while Luce was in charge of fiscal affairs. It was Hadden who evolved the famous *Time*-style, reasoning that the way to keep the reader interested was to turn bare fact into embellished fact—not, of course, so embellished as to become fiction, but close. Events recorded in *Time* invariably had beginnings, middles, and ends, with a little suspense woven in wherever possible. People never just *said* something; they always murmured, muttered, or mumbled; buzzed, barked, blared, or boomed; snorted, shrieked, screeched, squealed, or squawked. And they were never just people, either; they were gentle-spirited or sour-visaged, trim-figured or large-paunched, keen-brained or flabby-chinned (which really meant flabby-minded). If *Time* liked them, they marched or strode; if not, they shuffled, straggled, shambled, plodded, lumbered, barged, swaggered, wobbled, or slouched. Their middle names were spelled out in full, particularly when they sounded somewhat amusing. It was all a bit eyebrow-raising, but it was also circulation-raising, so who could argue?

Time was, however, primarily Hadden's creation, and that was a problem for Luce, who did not enjoy being upstaged and who was also creative, but in a different direction. Luce was fascinated by power and the road to it—money. In the late 1920s he began plans for a new magazine, to be centered on the business world, which he planned to call *Power*. Later it emerged as *Fortune*. In December, 1928, Hadden developed influenza and two months later he died. Luce named John Martin managing editor of *Time*, but there was never any doubt about who was in control.

Time retained Hadden's news lingo after his death, but it saw two notable departures in policy: business began to receive considerably more emphasis, all positive, and the Soviet Union more attention, all negative. The tyrannies of Russia and Italy had long been compared on *Time*'s pages, and their leaders were treated very differently; Stalin was always "relentless" and "ruthless," Mussolini, "firm" and "resolute." At *Time* a communist dictatorship was quite another thing from a capitalist one. President Franklin Delano Roosevelt's recognition of Soviet Russia was one battle lost, but the war would go on.

Other events of the 1930s were dealt with in typical Lucean style. The Depression would go away if one worked and prayed hard enough, and if some people starved, well, it was pretty much their own fault. Luce never had any sympathy for losers. The rise of Nazism was clearly a problem, although a "thoroughly misunderstood" one. In any case, we should be rearming faster than we were. That was the one issue on which *Time* and Roosevelt agreed—practically the only one. Then there was the civil war in Spain. The legally elected Popular Front government, being left of center, was by definition insupportable. With Luce's blessings, *Time*'s foreign news editor Laird Goldsborough habitually referred to President Manuel Azaña as "frog-faced," "obese," and "blotchy," while Generalissimo Francisco Franco was a man of "soldierly simplicity," "soft-spoken" and "serious."

Not only its slant but also its subject matter and style increasingly gave the magazine the reputation of existing primarily to call attention to itself. Many editors complained about the overworked word coinages ("tycoon" and "cinemansion" were favorites), the inverted sentence structure, and the recognizable euphemisms ("great and good friend" for mistress or homosexual partner). Sex and scandal, such as the Edward VIII–Wallis Simpson romance and the Mary Astor custody case in which George S. Kaufman figured, were elaborated upon at length. No mention was made, however, of Luce's own romance with Clare Boothe Brokaw, which led to his divorce and remarriage, although these events took him away from *Time* for a good part of 1935. It hardly mattered. The machine was so well oiled by now that it could operate almost independently of him, and effectively did so while he was preoccupied with the founding of *Life*.

The *Time* machine, which was labeled "group journalism" by Luce, generally went like this: Writer-editors would present ideas for news stories at weekly editorial meetings. Acceptable ideas would be passed along to bright young researchers from colleges like Wellesley and Smith, who would gather facts, interview principals, and then give the information to a writer, who would concoct his story, often with more regard for cleverness than for accuracy. From there the story went to an editor for rewriting and then to the managing editor for finishing touches, after which it was returned to the researcher for word-by-word rechecking before it went off to the printer. Considering the preponderance of inaccuracies, the outside world could only wonder where the system broke down, while insiders presumably knew. Some, like Winthrop Sargeant, who was a staff writer for many years, apparently did not mind such abdication of news responsibility, or at least were willing to trade it for the handsome salary that went along with it. Others, like James Agee, openly anguished.

The 1940s and the onset of W.W. II brought about a profound addition to *Time*'s structure—the field correspondent. Before that, war news had come secondhand from the wire services, newspapers, and radio, and had been rewritten in the offices of *Time*, Inc. Beginning with Paris, *Time* opened news bureaus in foreign capitals and staffed them with its own correspondents. Not that the dispatches they sent back to New York were ever published *per se*; they were always subject to extensive rewriting. Articles during this period were invariably anonymous. In 1940 *Time*, always Republican and anti-Roosevelt, did its best to make Wendell Willkie president, and its treatment of the incumbent was usually dishonest. In fact, the manipulation of news and the arrival of "hard line" men like Roy Alexander and Otto Fuerbringer on the staff brought about the gradual departure of many of *Time*'s best writers and editors—Archibald MacLeish, Ralph Ingersoll, T. S. Matthews, John Hersey, Charley Wertenbaker, and Theodore White, to name a few.

Even before America entered the war, *Time* was propagandizing for the country to become involved—not to save democracy or the British, but to establish American dominance in the world. This was to be, Luce said, the "American Century." America must take charge of the world because no one else was worthy. Military supremacy was essential. Aid to one's allies was also important, but only "friendly" allies, which implied that some allies—i.e., the Soviet Union—were not "friendly." In fact, *Time* did its best throughout the war to keep its readers cognizant of the fact that although the Russians were technically on our side, they were still a menace. There was no way, *Time* indicated, that Christian capitalism could truly be allied to communism.

But it was in *Time*'s coverage of China that Luce's anticommunist bias truly got the better of him. He was consumed, obsessed by the land of his birth. His *March of Time* newsreels showed the noble Chinese led by their savior, Chiang Kai-shek, braving the barbarian Japanese invaders. By the mid-1940s, however, those same noble Chinese were braving, not the Japanese, but other, apparently ignoble, Chinese—Chinese Communists, led by one Mao Tse-tung, whose very existence Luce preferred not to recognize. If China was no longer the China of his youth, he didn't want to know about it, and he didn't want *Time* to report it. So *Time* didn't. In its pages China remained identified with Chiang, who somehow, inexplicably, and surely temporarily, had evacuated the mainland and was occupying a small island called Taiwan. The fall of China was not so much mourned as ignored.

China's fall was, of course, the fault of the Democrats: Harry Truman and particularly Dean Acheson, who *Time* reported, was soft on communism. He led those unworthies in the State Dept. who had not lifted a finger to save Chiang. By 1950 *Time* had become almost the house organ of the Republican party, and was instrumental in drafting Eisenhower for its candidate. *Time*'s coverage of the 1952 campaign is remembered as one of its most biased efforts of press innuendo. Ike always "dwelt on" subjects that Stevenson "spouted" about; Ike consistently "rested" while Adlai "loafed." Photographs of the Republican were invariably favorable, while those of the Democrat were unflattering. Staff liberals protested, without recourse. Needless to say, *Time*'s coverage of the eight years of the Eisenhower administration, and especially of John Foster Dulles, was consistently benign.

Otto Fuerbringer, an archconservative, became managing editor of *Time* in 1960, and his impact was such that President Kennedy, who did his best to woo *Time* reporters, said he could always tell when Otto was sick or on vacation because the magazine was different that week. Richard Clurman had gradually upgraded *Time*'s news service until it was one of the best in the world, but Fuerbringer held almost total editorial power. Clurman's reporters might write superbly, but it was Otto who decided whether what they wrote would appear, and how.

This problem became particularly apparent with *Time*'s coverage of the war in Vietnam. At first the magazine loved the war, and so many *Time* dignitaries visited Vietnam in the early 1960s that one reporter, Mert Perry, called it "*Time* Magazine's Disneyland." The editors were euphorically optimistic, and pessimistic dispatches from the field seldom found their way into print. Charles Mohr, assigned to the Saigon office in 1962, soon found himself on a collision course with Fuerbringer, who was convinced that the root of the problem in Saigon was the American press, *Time* included. *Time* employed its "Press" section to attack those critical of the war. When the matter came to a showdown, Mohr and Perry resigned, reviving the old accusations that *Time* was a magazine of preconceptions to which it fitted the facts at will.

In April, 1964, a year after *Time* celebrated its 40th birthday, Luce turned the editorship over to his handpicked successor, Hedley Donovan, who was managing editor of *Fortune* at the time. Donovan, if less colorful than his predecessor, was careful, responsible, and unscarred by the factions of *Time*. Politically, he was more to the center than Luce, but he was cautious. He still believed in the war in Vietnam, and he tended to heed Lyndon Johnson rather than Saigon correspondent Frank McCulloch and didn't print stories that Johnson preferred not to see exposed on the pages of *Time*. By 1967, although Fuerbringer was unchanged, Donovan was slowly moving with the American political center against the war. *Time* did not reflect that shift at once, but in the late summer of that year, when Fuerbringer went on vacation, Donovan came downstairs and edited *Time* for three weeks. For the first time the magazine began to print what its reporters in Saigon had been saying for years—that the war was impossible to win. *Time* never returned to its hard line.

In the 1970s the big story, besides the windup of Vietnam, was Watergate. Considering that Watergate dealt almost entirely with *Time*'s own party, the magazine was less dismayed by events than might have been expected. Richard Nixon never trusted *Time*, and relations between them were not friendly. White House correspondent Hugh Sidey had been allowed into the Oval Office only twice in six years. When the Watergate stories started coming in, Henry Grunwald, who had succeeded Fuerbringer as managing editor, was wary, for practical rather than philosophical reasons. *Time* would go only as far as the evidence would take it, but it would go. Donovan agreed with Grunwald. In Luce's time it would have been unthinkable to share in the exposure of a Republican president, but Nixon was not the usual Republican president, and Luce was dead. He had died on Feb. 28, 1967, of a coronary occlusion. He had been active in all the magazines that made up *Time, Inc.*, until his death. As for his beloved *Time*, he had seen the beginning of the change from a very personal magazine, existing primarily to broadcast the ideals of his own American century, to a magazine that was but one part of a corporate structure, in which the primary motive was profit.

Modern Operation: Traditionally, *Time* has been an editor's magazine, and that fact still holds true. A reporter will put together a "file"—a lengthy, detailed, fact-filled narrative on a particular subject—which is forwarded to New York to be checked by researchers and completely rewritten by a writer, a senior editor, a top-ranking editor, and often the editor in chief or managing editor. It may then stand on its own or be incorporated into a larger story for which many reporters have sent in "files." In stark contrast to the earlier *Time* in which everything was anonymous, not only are critical and feature pieces signed with both the writers' and reporters' names, but many news stories as well. The "Time Essay" represents the editorial that Luce and Hadden vowed they never would have, but then the days when the whole magazine was one large editorial are gone. There is still a bias, but it is less pervasive.

Time (with a small *t*) is a crucial element in a weekly newsmagazine, and not infrequently changes have to be made after the Sunday morning press run has started. Competition with *Newsweek* is especially fierce. *Newsweek* surged ahead of *Time* during the Vietnam War, and in recent years the two have had a kind of seesaw relationship. Both magazines were recently completely redesigned; *Time*'s face-lift was performed quite handsomely by Walter Bernard. The covers of *Time*, which for years have not been the staid portraits Luce favored, are often imaginative portrayals of some aspect of American life or of its pop culture, or representations by such well-known political caricaturists as David Levine, Edward Sorel, or Robert Grossman. Two covers are occasionally done for an issue so that the editors will have a choice. The first issue of each new year features the person or group who most affected, for good or bad, the news of the year just ended. Charles Lindbergh was the first *Time* Man of the Year. President Franklin Roosevelt was selected three times, and Presidents Truman, Eisenhower, Johnson, and Nixon twice. Three women have been chosen "Man of the Year": Wallis Warfield Simpson, Madam Chiang Kai-shek, and Queen Elizabeth II. Occasionally when the choice has been an unpopular one—as with Adolf Hitler for 1938 or Ayatollah Khomeini for 1979—it produced much internal dissension, and subscriptions were canceled.

Size and Distribution of Sales: As of Dec. 31, 1980, more than 5,680,000 copies of *Time* were sold worldwide each week. The magazine has 11 regional editions, 119 supplemental metropolitan editions, 50 state editions, and 8 demographic editions.

Examples of Typical Material: Oct. 1, 1923: "The woodman's axe rings once more among Presidential timber. Industrious politicians prepare with the approach of Winter to sluice their sturdy oaks through the waters of party politics down to the convention sawmill. . . . Calvin Coolidge, President of the U.S., was first of the monarchs of the forest to tremble last week before the insidious chill of the approaching season."

Nov. 20, 1933: "Just as President Roosevelt and Comrade Litvinoff were fraternizing last week . . . the Soviet War Council at Moscow, with blazing indiscretion, issued Order No. 173. Abrupt and militant, it knocked into a Red soldier's turnip-shaped helmet the soothing assertions by Soviet publicists in recent weeks that Russia's leaders have abandoned the objective of her late, great Dictator Nikolai Lenin."

Jan. 8, 1951: "What people thought of Dean Gooderham Acheson ranged from the proposition that he was a fellow traveler, or a wool-brained sower of 'seeds of jackassery,' or an abysmally uncomprehending man, or an appeaser, or a warmonger who was taking the U.S. into a world war, to the warm if not so audible defense that he was a great secretary of state."

Oct. 22, 1965: "Everywhere today South Vietnam bristles with the U.S. presence. Bulldozers by the hundreds carve sandy shore into vast plateaus for tent cities and airstrips. Howitzers and trucks grind through the once-empty green highlands. Wave upon wave of combat-booted Americans—lean, laconic and looking for a fight—pour ashore from armadas of troopships. Day and night, screaming jets and helicopters seek out the enemy. . . . The Viet Cong's once-cocky hunters have become the cowering hunted."

Strengths: With occasional lapses, such as Vietnam, *Time* has understood the nature of its readers. Luce knew that although his staff was made up predominantly of eastern sophisticates, his readership was not, and he periodically insisted that a little more "corn" was needed. He did not, however, talk down to or underestimate the intelligence of his readers. *Time* has always offered intelligent discussions of the latest happenings in economy, business, science, religion, medicine, art, theater, cinema, books, etc., through its many and varied departments. Although the results did not always indicate it, *Time* has hired unusually talented writers and editors from its earliest days.

Weaknesses: Under Luce, truth was often obscured by *Time*'s version of what truth ought to be. Ideology was more important than mere fact, so *Time* often printed Luce's ideology. As Gov. Earl Long of Louisiana once said, "Mister Henry Luce is like a shoe salesman, but all the other shoe-store owners stock all different sizes of shoes, but Mr. Luce, he only sells shoes that fit hisself."

Bias is not so blatant in the current *Time* product, and its style is not so jingoistic as it once was. It is, however, still smug and show-offy and, as the careful reader will detect, not without innuendo. Statements in *Time* are often oversimplified to the extent of being obvious, simplistic, or just plain platitudinous.

Unusual Facts: In a bid for greater accuracy, *Time* regularly circulates to its staff an "Errors Summary Report" listing every mistake in the magazine and pointing out whether it originated with the correspondent, writer, or researcher involved.

A weekly newsmagazine's two greatest difficulties are being current and being accurate. In an attempt at the former, a *Time* music critic was once required to write a fake review of composer Virgil Thomson's 65th birthday concert at Town Hall in New York City five days before the event. The critic did his best to muster up appropriate generalities, but was much embarrassed when the issue with the review appeared on the newsstands the day before the concert.

—N.C.S.

11

IT'S AN ART

GREAT WORKS OF ART WHICH WERE GREETED BY BAD REVIEWS

Keats's *Endymion*

The Work: John Keats published his epic poem *Endymion* in 1818, when he was only 23 years old. The poem is based on the Greek legend of the moon goddess, Cynthia, who loves a mortal, Endymion. Keats's visual, sensuous poem was a dramatic departure from the literary norms of his day. Aware that this opened him to criticism, and that the poem was not perfect, he wrote an unusual preface in which he spoke openly of *Endymion*'s flaws.

The Critics Speak: *Endymion* was the butt of a critical attack so vicious that it was thought to have helped kill Keats, who died three years after the poem was published. The myth was given substance by some verses in Byron's *Don Juan* (Byron despised Keats's writing): "John Keats, who was killed off by one critique, / Just as he really promised something great . . . 'Tis strange the mind, that very fiery particle, / Should let itself be snuffed out by an article."

The first shots were fired by the *British Critic* (after two friendly reviews had appeared in other magazines), which parodied *Endymion* and called its style "monstrously droll."

John Gibson Lockhart, writing under the pen name Z for *Blackwood's Magazine*, brought in the heavy artillery. He was 24, a year older than Keats, and dubbed by his associates "the scorpion who delighteth to sting the faces of men." Lockhart boldly made fun of Keats's "Cockney" poetry, of his background in medicine (he had trained to be an apothecary and a surgeon), and of Keats's friendship with fellow writer Leigh Hunt. He wrote of "the spectacle of an able mind reduced to a state of insanity" because of "a sudden attack" of the poetry-writing bug.

"Whether Mr. John had been sent home with a diuretic or composing draught to some patient far gone in the poetical mania, we have not heard. This much is certain, that he has caught the infection. . . . For some time we were in hopes that he might get off with a violent fit or two, but of late the symptoms are terrible. The frenzy of the *Poems* was bad enough in its way; but it did not alarm us half so seriously as the calm, settled, imperturbable drivelling idiocy of *Endymion*."

Lockhart concluded, "It is a better and easier thing to be a starved apothecary than a starved poet; go back to the shop, Mr. John, back to 'plasters, pills and ointment boxes.' "

The next critique was written by John Wilson Croker in the *Quarterly Review*: "Reviewers have been sometimes accused of not reading the works which they affected to criticise . . . we . . . honestly confess that we have not read his work. Not that we have been wanting in our duty . . . indeed, we have made efforts almost as superhuman as the story itself appears to be, to get through it . . . we have not been able to struggle beyond the first of the four books of which this Poetic Romance consists." Croker ended his review by asking any reader able to finish the work to write to him.

Actually, Keats bore the barrage well, saying that his own self-criticism had pained him more than his reviews. One friend did report that on his deathbed "poor Keats attributed his approaching end to the poisonous pen of Lockhart." Keats only felt this way at the end, when he knew he was dying and would never have the chance to repair his reputation.

History Speaks: Earlier, Keats had said "I think I shall be among the English poets after my death." His prophecy came true; Keats and *Endymion* have withstood the test of time and remained beloved gifts to the English language.

Melville's *Moby Dick*

The Work: *Moby Dick*, written by Herman Melville in 1851, is the story of a demented sea captain's obsession with finding and killing the great white whale that ate his leg years before. It is moreover an immense parable of human life and the quest for identity.

The Critics Speak: *Moby Dick* got mixed reviews, but on the whole they were disappointing to Melville. The critics were particularly annoyed by Melville's departures from the standard structures of novel-writing. All of the following excerpts are from reviews that appeared unsigned.

From the *Athenaeum*: "The opening of this wild book contains some graphic descriptions of a dreariness such as we do not remember to have met with before in marine literature."

From the London *Morning Chronicle*: "Raving and rhapsodizing in chapter after chapter . . . sheer moonstruck lunacy."

From the *Southern Quarterly Review*: "[Aside from the parts where the whale is directly involved] the book is sad stuff, dull and dreary, or ridiculous. Mr. Melville's Quakers are the wretchedest dolts and drivellers, and his Mad Captain . . . is a monstrous bore. . . . His ravings

. . . and the ravings of Mr. Melville himself . . . are such as would justify a writ *de lunatico* for all the parties."
History Speaks: *Moby Dick* is today considered Melville's great masterpiece, as adventure tale, parable, and innovative novel. *Moby Dick* has taken such a permanent place in the body of American literature that it has been required reading for several generations of students.

Verdi's *Rigoletto*

The Work: Giuseppe Verdi's opera *Rigoletto* was first performed at the Fenice theater in Venice, Italy, in 1851. It was based on Victor Hugo's *Le Roi S'Amuse* ("The King Amuses Himself") and it featured distinctive departures from traditional opera. For example, the emphasis is not on the arias but on a series of duets. The most famous melody of the piece is "*La donna è mobile*" ("Woman's a fickle jade"). The opera was considered controversial for political and religious reasons, and its performance was periodically censored altogether, or its text was altered, for a decade.
The Critics Speak: Audiences loved *Rigoletto* from the first, but the critics were not always as generous.

The *Athenaeum* wrote: "The music . . . is puerile and queer—odd modulations being perpetually wrenched out with the vain hope of disguising the meagerness of the ideas."

The Times of London accused Verdi of "imitations and plagiarisms" and concluded by calling *Rigoletto* "the most uninspired, the barest, and the most destitute of ingenious contrivance. To enter into an analysis would be a loss of time and space."

La Gazette Musicale de Paris decided: "*Rigoletto* is the weakest work of Verdi. It lacks melody. This opera has hardly any chance of being kept in the repertoire."
History Speaks: *Rigoletto* gave Rossini cause to exclaim, "In this music I at last recognize Verdi's genius." Critics now consider *Rigoletto* one of Verdi's three greatest works and an operatic masterpiece. The public has never ceased to love it.

Baudelaire's *Les Fleurs du Mal*

The Work: *Les Fleurs du Mal* ("The Flowers of Evil") by French poet Charles Baudelaire, is a collection of poems first published in 1857. The poems deal with decadence and eroticism, and point an uncompromising finger at the reader. The book had barely been published when it was seized for being blasphemous and obscene, and a trial began. Gustave Flaubert had just been tried and acquitted for alleged obscenity in *Madame Bovary*, so Baudelaire felt certain that he would also be found innocent. However, the author, the publisher, and the printers were all found guilty of an offense against public morality and fined. Six of the poems were banned and did not reappear until 1949, almost 100 years after their original publication.
The Critics Speak: It was Baudelaire's belief that the first, scathing

review of *Les Fleurs du Mal* in *Le Figaro* led to his prosecution. It was written by a Mr. Bourdin, who is remembered today only for this piece:

"There are times when one doubts Monsieur Baudelaire's sanity; there are times when there is no longer any doubt . . . the odious is cheek by jowl with the ignoble—and the repulsive joins the disgusting. You have never seen so many bosoms being bitten, chewed even, in so few pages; never has there been such a procession of demons, fetuses, devils, cats, and vermin.

"The book is a hospital open to all forms of mental derangements and emotional putrefaction. . . . If one may understand a poet at the age of 20 allowing his imagination to be carried away by such subjects, nothing can justify a man of over 30 making public such monstrosities in a book."

This next review appeared in the *Journal de Bruxelles:*

"The hideous novel *Madame Bovary* is a work of piety compared to *Les Fleurs du Mal*. . . . Nothing could possibly give you the faintest idea of the heap of filth and horror contained in this book . . . a decent pen cannot even quote. . . ."

J. Habans, a protégé of the minister of the interior, wrote a review which also appeared in *Le Figaro:* "In Monsieur Charles Baudelaire's case we must use the word *nightmare*. . . . All of these coldly displayed charnel-house horrors, these abysses of filth into which both hands are plunged to the elbows, should rot in a drawer."

History Speaks: *Encyclopaedia Britannica* calls Baudelaire "above all others of his age the poet of modern civilization." *Les Fleurs du Mal,* his major work, inspired the Symbolist movement in writing and art, and today can be called nothing less than an enduring classic.

Manet's *Olympia*

The Work: French painter Édouard Manet completed *Olympia* in 1863, and it was exhibited at the Salon of 1865. It depicts an elegant reclining nude, her face turned toward the viewer; behind her is a black servant holding a bouquet of flowers; on her bed is a black cat.

The Critics Speak: The showing of *Olympia* caused an outburst of angry public opinion and critical scorn. Manet's use of color and tone was unusual, which bothered the critics, but far worse was the moral threat his art seemed to pose to 1890s society. As George Hamilton has observed, "Olympia was obviously naked rather than conventionally nude." Further, her head was not averted to indicate she was ashamed, and she was clearly no wood nymph being chased by a satyr (always an acceptable presentation of a nude). *Olympia* was shockingly modern.

Wrote Felix Jahyer: "Such indecency! It seems to me that *Olympia* could have been hung at a height out of range of the eye." Jahyer got his wish, because *Olympia* was eventually moved.

Jules Clarétie's review in *L'Artiste* was equally scathing: "What is this Odalisque with a yellow stomach, a base model picked up I know not where, who represents Olympia? Olympia? What Olympia? A courtesan, no doubt."

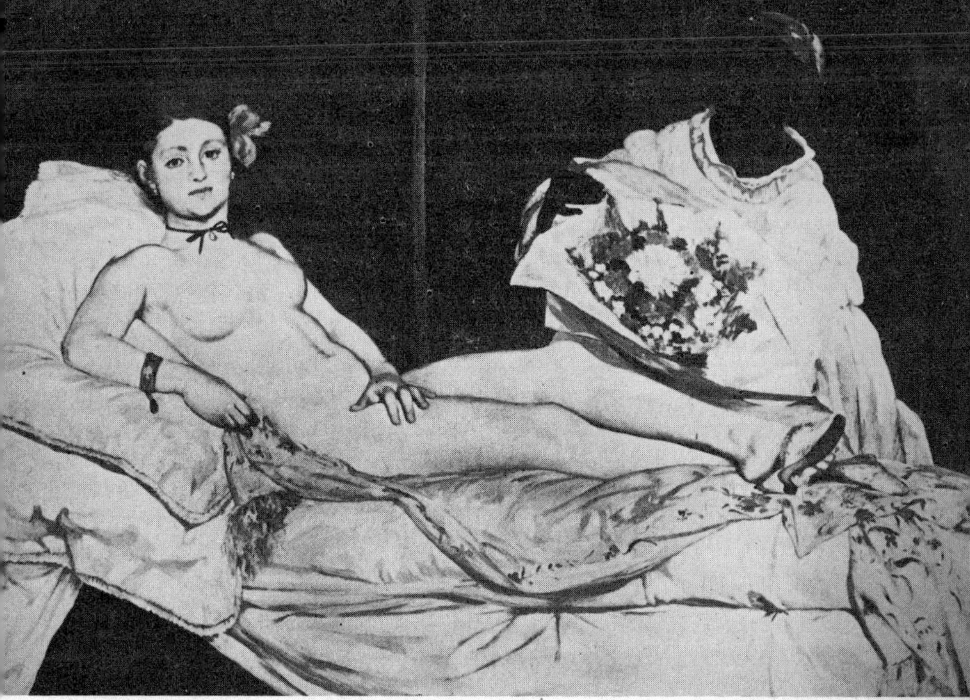

Manet's Olympia*—naked, not nude.*

Even the poet Théophile Gautier had nothing but harsh words for the painting in the *Moniteur*: "*Olympia* can be understood from no point of view, even if you take it for what it is, a puny model stretched out on a sheet. The color of the flesh is dirty, the modeling nonexistent. . . . We would still forgive the ugliness, were it only truthful, carefully studied, heightened by some splendid effect of color. The least beautiful woman has bones, muscles, skin, and some sort of color. Here there is nothing, we are sorry to say, but the desire to attract attention at any price."
History Speaks: Manet, now fully acknowledged as one of the greatest artists of the 19th century, considered *Olympia* his masterpiece. It hangs today in a place of honor in the Louvre.

Cézanne's Paintings

The Works: French painter Paul Cézanne was given a special exhibition at the 1904 Salon d'Automne in Paris, two years before his death. Among the paintings shown were *Mardi Gras* (1888), *The Blue Vase* (1883–1887), and *Portrait of Victor Chocquet* (1879–1882).
The Critics Speak: Cézanne's work, with its thick paint and primitive, impressionistic style, was far from what the critics at the turn of the century admired. Although many young, avant-garde artists regarded Cézanne as their "sage," critics were disgusted with the 1904 exhibition. Even the fact that the salon's catalogue was in alphabetical order caused an uproar, for it meant that Cézanne's name appeared before that of a more "distinguished" colleague, Pierre Puvis de Chavannes.

From *Le Petit Parisien*, by Valensol: "He chooses to daub paint on a canvas and spread it around with a comb or a toothbrush. This process produces landscapes, marines, still lifes, portraits . . . if he is lucky. The procedure somewhat recalls the designs that schoolchildren make by squeezing the heads of flies between the folds of a sheet of paper."

Wrote one nameless critic in *La Lanterne:* "Cézanne is nothing but a lamentable failure. Perhaps he has ideas, but he is incapable of expressing them. He seems not to know even the first principles of his craft."

Sarradin, in *Les Débats,* said: "The impression given by all these clumsily daubed portraits is truly painful; they bear witness to a fatal impotence."

Le Say in *L'Univers* called the paintings "false . . . brutal . . . mad . . . [a] chamber of horrors."

History Speaks: Cézanne's reputation and fame have increased steadily since his death. His work was inspirational to artists such as Picasso in his development of Cubism, and today Cézanne is recognized as a master.

Prokofiev's *Piano Concerto No. 1*

The Work: At the age of 23, Russian musician Sergei Prokofiev gave the first public performance of his *Piano Concerto No. 1 in D-flat Major, Opus 10.* It won him the Anton Rubinstein Prize—a grand piano.

The Critics Speak: Prokofiev's daring, passionate, dynamic concerto caused many critics great consternation, though audiences were charmed by it.

Leonid Sabaneyev wrote in *Golos Moskvy:* "This energetic rhythmic, harsh, coarse primitive cacophony hardly deserves to be called music."

Grigori Prokofiev, a critic for *Russkiye Vedomosti,* complained of "harsh writing and a complete unwillingness to compromise with the listener's taste."

Critic N. Bernstein called it "musical mud."

James Gibbons Huneker wrote in *The New York Times* in 1918: "The first Piano Concerto of Prokofiev was in one movement, but compounded of many rhythms and recondite noises. . . . The composer handled the keyboard—handled is the right word—and the duel that ensued between his 10 flail-like fingers [and the piano was a battle] to the death; the death of euphony . . . the piano all the while shrieking, groaning, howling, fighting back, and in several instances it seemed to rear and bite the hand that chastised it. . . . There were moments when the piano and orchestra made sounds that evoked not only the downfall of empires, but also of fine crockery, the fragments flying in all directions. . . . The Concerto will never be played by anyone on earth . . . Prokofiev wouldn't grant an encore. The Russian heart may be a dark place, but its capacity for mercy is infinite."

For the New York *Tribune,* H. E. Krehbiel wrote, "Mr. Prokofiev's pieces have been contributions not to the art of music, but to national pathology and pharmacopoeia . . . the pianoforte solos . . . invite their own damnation, because there is nothing in them to hold attention. . . . They pursue no aesthetic purpose, strive for no recognizable ideal, proclaim no means for increasing the expressive potency of music. They are simply perverse."

History Speaks: Happily, Prokofiev never worried about bad reviews. When he died in 1953, he had written more than 135 works and had never ceased to be innovative. The First Concerto is now considered a brilliant piece of composing which heralded the arrival of a musical genius.

Keaton's *The General*

The Work: "The Great Stone Face" of silent films, Buster Keaton, directed, starred in, and edited *The General,* first shown in 1926 and put into general release in 1927. This Civil War comedy was expensive to make, containing what was probably the most costly single take in cinema history at that time—a $42,000 shot of a bridge collapsing and a train on it falling into a river.

The Critics Speak: Keaton Called *The General* "my pet," and though he never admitted it, he must have been sorely disappointed by the film's critical and box-office failures.

Norbert Lusk wrote in *Picture/Play Charm* that *The General* was "a one-man show, a mistake in a picture lasting over an hour."

Robert E. Sherwood, who wrote for *Life* magazine, did not approve of a comedy that contained scenes of killing. He complained of Keaton's "woefully bad judgment" and "gruesomely bad taste."

Mordaunt Hall, the regular *New York Times* critic, possessed what one Keaton biographer called "the greatest track record in film history for being wrong." Hall found *The General* inferior to Keaton's previous works, saying Keaton had "bitten off more than he could chew" and that the film "might be described as a mixture of cast iron and jelly."

The *Herald-Tribune* dismissed it as "long and tedious—the least funny thing Buster Keaton has ever done."

The *Daily Mirror* put it down as "slow, very slow," and admonished its creator to "pull yourself together, Buster."

History Speaks: Today *The General* is regarded as an extraordinary, ground-breaking classic. The film has variously been called the best work of a cinematic genius, the silent screen's best, and the first film comedy of epic proportions. Keaton biographer Tom Dardis wrote,

Buster Keaton in The General.

"Many of Keaton's critics have commented on the stunningly convincing look of *The General*, often comparing it with the Civil War photographs of Matthew Brady. In the 50 years since it was made, *The General* has become a piece of American folklore." In a poll taken by *Sight and Sound* magazine in 1972, *The General* was voted one of the 10 greatest films of all time.

Hitchcock's *Vertigo*

The Work: English director Alfred Hitchcock released his most complicated film, *Vertigo*, in 1958. In it James Stewart plays a former detective who gave up his job because of his fear of heights. Kim Novak plays the strange woman he falls in love with.

The Critics Speak: Although French critics appreciated *Vertigo*'s greatness, many American critics gave it a cold reception.

John McCarten wrote in *The New Yorker*: "Alfred Hitchcock, who produced and directed the thing, has never before indulged in such farfetched nonsense."

Arthur Knight wrote in *Saturday Review* that "technical facility is being exploited to gild pure dross," and that the film "pursues its theme of false identity with such plodding persistence that by the time the climactic cat is let out of the bag, the audience has long since had kittens."

Scoffed *Time* magazine: "The old master has turned out another Hitchcock-and-bull story in which the mystery is not so much who done it as who cares."

History Speaks: Many of the early critics have reversed their hostile or indifferent views of *Vertigo*. Many more critics and viewers think of it as Hitchcock's greatest film, and all agree that it is his greatest technical achievement.

—A.W.

10 RENOWNED UNFINISHED WORKS FROM THE ARTS TO ARCHITECTURE

Ah, but a man's reach should exceed his grasp,
Or what's a heaven for?

—Robert Browning

1. LEONARDO DA VINCI: STATUE OF A HORSE (begun 1488)

Leonardo determined to surpass his predecessors when he worked 12 years on the projected sculpture of a bronze horse to be erected at Milan in memory of the father of his patron, Lodovico Sforza. The 23-ft.-high statue would have required the pouring of 200,000 lb. of molten metal into a mold fast enough and at a high enough temperature to allow

Da Vinci's sketches for a never-completed 23-foot-high statue.

uniform cooling. For this purpose Leonardo designed a system of multiple furnaces. In 1493 a clay model of the horse was displayed in Milan and acclaimed as being the most beautiful object ever seen. But war threatened, and the metal ready to be poured for the horse was used for cannon. When the French overwhelmed the Milanese in 1499, Gascon bowmen used Leonardo's model for target practice. Arrow damage allowed water to enter, and after a few seasons the great horse fell apart. Today only sketches of it exist.

2. MICHELANGELO BUONARROTI: TOMB OF POPE JULIUS II (begun 1505)

When Pope Julius II commissioned Michelangelo, 29, to build his papal tomb, the sculptor designed a two-story monument with a sarcophagus surrounded by bronze reliefs and 40 marble statues. A mountain of marble, quarried hundreds of miles away at Carrara, was transported by boat to Rome. The painter Raphael and his relative, the architect Bramante, envious of the glory this opportunity would bring Michelangelo, persuaded the pope that it was bad luck to prepare a tomb during one's own lifetime. They recommended that Michelangelo paint the huge vaulted ceiling of the Sistine Chapel (an impossible task for a sculptor, they thought). Work on the tomb was interrupted for four years while the sculptor completed the greatest single artistic achievement in the history of painting. Although Michelangelo made many attempts to complete the tomb, it remained unfinished at Julius's death, and his successors preempted Michelangelo's time and energy with other assignments. Forty years after beginning his great project, he had completed only a few statues, among them the 10-ft.-high *Moses*, called the greatest example of Renaissance sculpture. In 1545 Michelangelo, now 69, attempted to fulfill his obligation to Julius by improvising a small tomb, with *Moses* at the center, in the church of St. Peter in Chains in Rome.

3. WOLFGANG AMADEUS MOZART: REQUIEM (begun 1791)

In the last year of his life Mozart was approached by a cadaverous stranger who offered him generous payment for the composition of a requiem, at the same time swearing him to secrecy. Seriously ill, Mozart believed the commission was an omen of his own death and began working feverishly to complete what he feared would be his funeral music. Five months later, on his deathbed, Mozart, 36, gave final instructions about the unfinished Requiem to his pupil, Franz Süssmayr, to whom Mozart's wife entrusted the work. Süssmayr arranged the music in accordance with Mozart's intentions, filling in gaps with sections of his own composition. The Requiem was represented to the stranger (who turned out to be the steward of the eccentric Count von Walsegg) as being entirely by Mozart. The deceived nobleman then deceived others by having it performed as his own composition (hence the secrecy). Later Mozart's wife identified the work. Mozart, ironically, had been thrown into an unmarked pauper's grave without benefit of sacred music, but his Requiem was played for Beethoven and Chopin at their funerals.

4. GILBERT STUART: PORTRAIT OF GEORGE WASHINGTON (begun 1796)

America's leading portrait artist made three original portraits of Washington. The last, commissioned by Martha Washington, is undoubtedly the most famous painting by an American artist. It shows Washington uncomfortably clenching a new set of false teeth. To relax the sitter, Stuart chatted about local horse racing as he worked. Stuart deliberately did not finish the portrait so that he could keep it to make copies, which were in great demand in an age without photographs. He sold 70 copies at $100 apiece, calling them his "hundred-dollar bills." Appropriately, this portrait served as a model for the likeness on the dollar bill. Although Washington once went to Stuart's studio to demand his portrait, it remained there—still unfinished—until the artist's death in 1828. Now it is in the Boston Museum of Fine Arts.

5. SAMUEL TAYLOR COLERIDGE: "KUBLA KHAN" (begun 1797)

One of the most beloved fragments in English poetry begins:

> In Xanadu did Kubla Khan
> A stately pleasure dome decree:
> Where Alph, the sacred river, ran
> Through caverns measureless to man
> Down to a sunless sea.

In the summer of 1797, Coleridge, 25, in ill health, stayed at a lonely farmhouse near Porlock in Somersetshire. Laudanum, a form of opium prescribed by his doctor, caused him to fall asleep while reading the following sentence in the book *Purchas's Pilgrimage:* "Here the Khan Kubla commanded a palace to be built, and a stately garden thereunto." He slept about three hours, dreaming that he had effortlessly composed some 300 lines of poetry. Upon awakening, he eagerly wrote down the 50 lines that have been preserved. Then, unfortunately, a "person on business from Porlock" called, detaining him "above an hour." Returning to his room, he found the vision and the poem had "passed away like the images on the surface of a stream." He attempted to finish it, but without success.

6. HONORÉ DE BALZAC: *THE HUMAN COMEDY* (begun 1829)

Balzac's vast picture of the life of his time, *The Human Comedy,* was planned to form a whole comprising three main categories: analytical studies, examining the principles governing human life; philosophical studies, probing causes for human actions; and studies of manners, divided into six types of scenes from life—private, provincial, Parisian, political, military, and rural. The finished work would have contained some 133 volumes. Writing 16 hours at a stretch, usually through the night, Balzac managed to complete more than 100 novels and short stories. The section on analytical studies remained undeveloped, and several other areas were slighted. But no other novelist, it is said, ever conceived such a gigantic scheme. His death at 50 prevented its completion.

7. ANTONIO GAUDÍ: CHURCH OF THE HOLY FAMILY (begun 1882)

This shell of a church, one of the landmarks of Barcelona, Spain, occupied architect Antonio Gaudí throughout his career. He inherited the project from the original architect, Francisco del Villar, in 1883, one year after construction had begun, and transformed the conventional Gothic-style cathedral into a surrealistic forest of imaginative shapes resembling natural objects. After 1910 he abandoned almost all other work, secluding himself on the church site. His work, described as the three-dimensional dreams of a madman, contains bulging facades, swaying pillars, and weird protuberances. In 1926 Gaudí, 73, was run over by a Barcelona streetcar. Only one of the 13 planned tubular towers and one transept of the church were completed when he died five days later. Although the church was brutally damaged during the Spanish Civil War, Gaudí's assistants, friends, and concerned citizens have kept the work going.

8. GIACOMO PUCCINI: *TURANDOT* (begun 1921)

Puccini's last opera, which might have been one of the finest music dramas of the 20th century, was written in a race against death. The composer, dying from cancer of the throat, remarked, "The opera will be given incomplete and somebody will come forward and say: 'At this

The Church of the Holy Family, Barcelona, still under construction after 100 years.

point the composer died.' " A year after the composer's death at 65 his prophecy came true. At the premiere—given at La Scala in Milan on April 25, 1926—the conductor, Arturo Toscanini, turned to the audience halfway through the last act and said, "Here the maestro laid down his pen." So that the work could hold the stage, Puccini's friend and fellow composer Franco Alfano was asked to complete it from sketches Puccini had left. Although Alfano used Puccini's themes, the last scene was unable to fulfill expectations raised by the rest of the opera.

9. F. SCOTT FITZGERALD: *THE LAST TYCOON* (begun 1939)

The author of *The Great Gatsby* had completed only six chapters of his last novel when in December, 1940, he died of a heart attack at age 44. Fitzgerald, who had worked briefly as a Hollywood scriptwriter, modeled his central character after Hollywood producer Irving Thalberg, one of a vanishing breed of gifted, all-powerful movie moguls. Probably aware that his days were numbered, Fitzgerald had stopped drinking shortly before his death, and he spent his last days in bed writing the book. Had Fitzgerald completed it, *The Last Tycoon* could have been a major American novel. The fragment was edited by Edmund Wilson and published in 1941. In 1976 playwright Harold Pinter and director Elia Kazan molded the material into a feature film, which retained the style and mood of the book.

10. JAMES JONES: WORLD WAR II TRILOGY (begun 1951)

When James Jones, considered one of the finest novelists of U.S. Army life, died in 1977 at 55, he had completed all but three chapters of *Whistle*, the last volume of his huge W.W. II trilogy, which included *From Here to Eternity* (1951) and *The Thin Red Line* (1962). The three books form a unified whole as Jones traced the history of the company in which he actually served, following it from Pearl Harbor to Guadalcanal and finally back to U.S. military hospitals. He shows the disintegration of a peacetime army's code of honor under the pressure of trying to survive in combat. By the last volume, the characters no longer know what is honorable or even who the enemy is. Jones worked 10, 12, and 14 hours a day, knowing his fight to complete the book before dying would go down to the wire. His close friend William Morris put together a detailed synopsis of the final missing chapters of *Whistle*, based on the novelist's notes and conversations that they had had.

—M.B.T.

HANK GRANT FILMLORE QUIZ

Hank Grant, daily columnist for *The Hollywood Reporter*, a motion picture and television trade newspaper, and commentator on films for CBS, is a connoisseur of obscure and overlooked movie data.

1. Can you name the late silent screen hero who had a mountain peak named after him?
2. Who played the title role of the bride in *The Bride of Frankenstein* (Universal, 1935)?
3. Can you name one of the two novels, both with hit movie versions, which were buried in a time capsule at the 1939 New York World's Fair?
4. Can you name the female film star who set a record—of sorts—by singing the same song in three separate movies?
5. Marni Nixon, the off-camera singing voice for the likes of Deborah Kerr, Natalie Wood, and Audrey Hepburn, among others, made her on-camera performing debut in what movie?
6. Can you name the famous film star who signed Maj. Clark Gable's discharge papers from the army on June 12, 1944?
7. Can you name a movie in which former First Lady Pat Nixon worked as an extra?
8. What late film star's figure was used without publicity fanfare as Disney's model for Tinker Bell, Peter Pan's fairy companion?

9. Can you name the only female star in Jimmy Cagney's 1940 movie for Warners, *The Fighting 69th?*
10. Can you name the off-camera singer who ghosted Lauren Bacall's songs in the 1944 movie *To Have and Have Not?*
11. Can you name the actor who played the same role in three separate movies over a time span of 28 years?
12. What actress rode Trigger in a movie before the horse became the exclusive property of Roy Rogers?
13. MGM's Leo the Lion trademark first roared for real on the screen in what movie?
14. Who played the role of Babe Ruth in RKO's 1942 movie *Pride of the Yankees?*

Answers

1. One thing Douglas Fairbanks, Sr., cherished above his silent film screen fame was the naming of a mountain peak after him in 1917 in Yosemite National Park.
2. It is usually assumed that Elsa Lanchester played the bride in *The Bride of Frankenstein,* but she played the monster's bride. Valerie Hobson played Dr. Frankenstein's bride.
3. The two novels buried in a time capsule at the 1939 New York World's Fair are Margaret Mitchell's *Gone with the Wind* and Sinclair Lewis's *Arrowsmith.*
4. Doris Day sang "Que Sera Sera" in the 1956 Hitchcock movie *The Man Who Knew Too Much,* reprised it in the 1960 movie *Please Don't Eat the Daisies,* and sang it for a third time in the 1966 movie *The Glass Bottom Boat.*
5. Marni Nixon, ghost singer for the stars, had her first on-camera performance as a singing nun in *The Sound of Music.*
6. Signing Maj. Clark Gable's discharge papers from the army in June of 1944 was his buddy Capt. Ronald Reagan.
7. Former First Lady Pat Nixon, then Thelma Catherine Ryan, worked as an extra in the first full-color technicolor feature film, *Becky Sharp,* in 1931.
8. Marilyn Monroe's body was the model used by Disney animators when they shaped the figure of Peter Pan's fairy companion, Tinker Bell.
9. The only female star in Jimmy Cagney's 1940 movie, *The Fighting 69th,* was Germaine the Mule, who won the American Humane Association's "Best Animal Actor" award for that year. If you remember that much, you may recall that the award was personally presented to Germaine by Humphrey Bogart.
10. The singer warbling Lauren Bacall's songs off-camera in *To Have and Have Not* was none other than Andy Williams.
11. The late Alan Hale, Sr., played the role of Little John opposite Doug Fairbanks, Sr., in the 1922 silent movie *Robin Hood,* played it again opposite Errol Flynn in the 1938 sound version, *The Adventures of Robin Hood,* and for a third time in the 1950 version, *Rogues of Sherwood Forest.*

12. Before Roy Rogers acquired Trigger, the horse—billed as Golden Cloud—was ridden by Olivia de Havilland in *The Adventures of Robin Hood.*
13. Leo the Lion's first roar was heard on the screen on July 31, 1928, in MGM's silent movie *White Shadows of the South Seas.*
14. Though Gary Cooper played the key role of Lou Gehrig in *Pride of the Yankees,* the role of Babe Ruth was played by the Babe himself.

GALLERY OF PROMINENT PERFORMING AND CREATIVE ARTISTS

HUMPHREY BOGART (1899–1957)

Few film stars have achieved the long-standing fame of Humphrey Bogart. The stiff-lipped delivery that eventually became his trademark was the result of a damaged nerve, which he had sustained as a boy of 10 when his angry father punched him in the mouth. For two decades he remained one of Hollywood's top box-office attractions, appearing in more than 60 films and earning upwards of $200,000 per movie.

Best known as "Bogie," he was born Humphrey DeForest Bogart, the son of socially prominent parents. His father, Dr. Belmont DeForest Bogart, conducted a successful medical practice from an office in the family's Manhattan brownstone but spent a lifetime hiding his morphine addiction from his three children and his clients. Bogart's emergence into the public limelight occurred in 1900 when his mother, the well-known illustrator Maude Humphrey Bogart, painted a picture of her one-year-old son playing in his carriage and submitted it to an advertising agency. It was purchased by Mellins Baby Food for use in their ads and on their labels, and soon the "Original Maude Humphrey Baby" became the most popular baby picture of the day.

The Bogarts planned their son's education carefully, hoping that Humphrey would follow in his father's medical footsteps. After attending Trinity School in New York, Bogart was enrolled at the Phillips Academy in Andover, Mass., but his stint at the school was short. During his first year he was expelled for being irreverent to a faculty member.

Naive, 18, with no direction to his life, Bogart decided to join the navy. Following his honorable discharge in 1920, he worked for a year as a runner at a Wall Street investment house and as an office boy for World Films before landing a job as stage manager for an acting group. While with the troupe Bogart had an opportunity to test his skills as director, writer, and stage actor. He failed miserably at the first two, and his initial success at the third was less than spectacular. The 5-ft. 10-in. Bogart appeared in a string of forgettable stage productions, primarily playing juvenile roles in comedies. In 1935 he played the part of the gangster Duke Mantee in the Broadway production of *The Petrified*

Forest, and when the play was made into a movie in 1936, Bogart landed the same role. It was the turning point in his career.

Between 1936 and 1940 Bogart appeared in close to 30 films, carving out a popular public image. Yet, despite his screen image as a snarling, slow-thinking, violent criminal, in private life Bogie maintained the persona of an honest, intelligent, witty iconoclast. In 1947 his fellow actors rallied behind him and converged on Washington to protest the scurrilous investigations of the House Un-American Activities Committee, which was looking into the purported spread of communism within the film community.

When he wasn't playing chess or making a movie, Bogart enjoyed boating. He took sailing seriously, claiming it was more satisfying than acting, and his love for the sea inspired him to call his independent film company Santana Productions, after his yacht, *Santana*. Each year Bogart's popularity grew, but he ignored his large and loyal following, deplored Hollywood critics, and shunned publicity. As a sign of rebellion, Bogart and a handful of stars formed the Holmby Hills Rat Pack. "In order to qualify one had to be addicted to nonconformity—staying up late, drinking, laughing, and not caring what anyone thought or said about us." During the filming of *Dark Passage* (1947), the ruddy-faced actor experienced a sudden loss of hair, and within weeks he was almost entirely bald. Doctors blamed the accelerated hair loss on alopecia areata, a disease caused by vitamin deficiency. The years of drinking heavily and eating erratically had taken their toll.

Continually striving to broaden his scope as an actor, Bogart starred in such memorable movies as *The Maltese Falcon* (1941), *Casablanca* (1942), *The Treasure of the Sierra Madre* (1948), and *The African Queen* (1951), for which he won an Academy Award. However, no film was more meaningful to Bogart than *To Have and Have Not* (1944), since it marked the beginning of a sensational relationship with model-turned-actress Lauren Bacall. They fell in love during the months of filming, at a time when the 44-year-old Bogart was suffering through a deteriorating third marriage. Abiding by his claim that making love was the most fun a person could have without laughing, Bogart engaged in a love affair with his 19-year-old co-star and by the end of 1945 they were married.

Bogart's three previous marriages—to Helen Menken in 1926, to Mary Phillips in 1928, and to Mayo Methot in 1938—had all ended in divorce. However, his flamboyant nightclubbing and frequent drinking bouts never jeopardized his 12-year marriage to the beautiful Bacall. They pursued their individual careers, although it frustrated Bacall to be recognized more as Bogart's wife than as a serious actress.

Bogart lost his two-year battle with cancer of the esophagus and died on Jan. 14, 1957. In addition to wife Lauren, son Stephen, and daughter Leslie, the great actor left behind him the "Bogie" legend—a screen image that has made him a folk hero in American cinema.

—A.K.

RAY CHARLES (b. 1930)

Born to a dirt-poor black Georgia couple during the Depression, he went completely blind at 7, was orphaned at 15, and fought a 20-year battle with heroin addiction which began when he was 16. Yet, despite enough trouble for several lifetimes, the word *self-pity* does not appear in Ray Charles's vocabulary.

As a performing artist alone, his influence on American popular music is inestimable. He has sold over 200 million records in such diverse genres as rhythm and blues, country western, pop, and jazz. Add to this his other successful careers as composer, songwriter, bandleader, producer, and record company executive, and it is no wonder that Frank Sinatra calls him "the only genius in our business."

He was born Ray Charles Robinson in Albany, Ga., on Sept. 23, 1930. (He dropped his last name when he entered show business to avoid confusion with his famous namesake, boxer Sugar Ray Robinson.) Two months after Ray was born, his parents moved to the tiny sawmill town of Greenville, Fla. His father, Bailey, was a railroad man and part-time mechanic; his mother, Areatha, cooked and cleaned for white families and occasionally worked in the sawmill. Their combined income—used to support themselves, Ray, and a younger son—was about $40 a week.

As the Great Depression of the 1930s worsened, so did the Robinson family's luck. In 1935, five-year-old Ray underwent the horrifying experience of watching his little brother drown. He began suffering from glaucoma the same year, and by 1937 he was totally blind.

Ray Charles credits his ferocious independence, his unwillingness to accept blindness as a crippling affliction, to his mother. "You're blind, not stupid," Areatha Robinson told her son. "You've lost your eyes, not your mind." Determined that her boy would never end up begging on a street corner, she assigned him the same chores any normal youngster would do; he chopped wood, swept the house, and scrubbed floors. Later in 1937, Ray was enrolled in Florida's St. Augustine School for Deaf and Blind Children in Orlando, Fla.

Since he demonstrated a talent for music, the school allowed him to study composition and theory. He added Beethoven and Sibelius to the musical influences he had already absorbed—among them gospel singer Alex Bradford, jazzman Art Tatum, and blues shouter Arthur "Big Boy" Crudup.

In 1945 Areatha Robinson died, still in her early 30s. Returning to Greenville in a virtual state of shock, Ray was unable to eat for three weeks. He was force-fed by neighbors, and had scarcely adjusted to this trauma when his father died at age 40.

Charles lived briefly with friends of his family, then struck out on his own, determined to become a professional musician. He played jazz and rhythm-and-blues "juke joints" all over Florida; for example, he played piano briefly for the Florida Playboys, a white hillbilly band. Ray had listened to the country-music radio showcase *Grand Ole Opry* since childhood and loved country-western music as much as he did jazz or R and B. In 1948, desperate for a change but unwilling to move to New York or Chicago and be swallowed up, he asked a friend to draw a line on a map to the U.S. city farthest from Florida. The line ended in Seattle, Wash., and Ray Charles arrived there on a bus shortly thereafter.

He was soon working steadily, fronting a trio who played the smooth "pop" style of his current idol, Nat "King" Cole. He signed a recording contract with a small West Coast label, Swingtime Records, and in 1951 had a Top Ten rhythm-and-blues hit, "Baby, Let Me Hold Your Hand." The next year, Atlantic Records, a larger and more innovative label, bought out his Swingtime contract. According to Atlantic executive Jerry Wexler: "Ray seemed to be just another rhythm-and-blues singer. But suddenly he broke out of a cocoon that we didn't even know he was weaving."

It was one glorious break. Ray Charles completely dropped the "pop" mannerisms and returned—with a vengeance—to the music he had grown up with, gospel and rhythm and blues. His first big hit for Atlantic in 1954, "I Got a Woman," was firmly rooted in gospel music. He forgot about trying to sing like Nat "King" Cole and opened up with both barrels; his voice rasped, growled, and slid up into falsetto. Bluesman Big Bill Broonzy was rather outraged: "He's crying sanctified. He should be singing in church!" (Charles didn't see it that way at all. A few years later, when the president of ABC Records told him he could make a million dollars if he would cut an album of gospel music, the singer refused because he believed that it was improper to "tamper" with religious music. Fortunately, he had no such compunctions about borrowing from the form.)

During the next five years he cut a series of equally remarkable records for Atlantic, culminating in his first million-seller, "What'd I Say," in 1959. It was a landmark performance, with Charles's female backup group, the Raelets, "testifying" gospel-style to his undeniably secular lyrics (so secular, in fact, that the record was banned on a number of radio stations). Charles broke new musical ground by employing the electric piano, an instrument that few musicians took seriously.

Not long after "What'd I Say," Charles left Atlantic for the more commercial ABC-Paramount label. He won greater financial freedom as the result of his contract with ABC, reportedly one of the most lucrative in the industry at that time, which he negotiated himself. He was promised more artistic freedom as well, but ABC executives balked when Charles wanted to do an album of country music in 1962. He ignored them and did it anyway. *Modern Sounds in Country Music* became a million-seller; one single from it, "I Can't Stop Loving You," sold 3 million copies.

Not all of Charles's misery was burned up by his creative pursuits or his aching vocals. Moody, nervous, and unpredictable, he would sometimes show up as much as four hours late for a performance—if he showed up at all. His personal problems were complicated by drugs. In 1955 and 1961 he was arrested for possession and use of heroin. "The daily grind gets to be too much," he said. "A fellow who lives in the dark has to do something." In 1962 a close friend predicted that the singer would be dead within three years. Charles was arrested again in 1964, that time for possession of marijuana. After a well-publicized California heroin bust in 1965, he retired from performing for a year, determined to kick the habit. Apparently he did.

Although Charles is willing to talk in depth about his music and his battle with narcotics, he quickly steers interviewers away from his family life. When pressed, he says, "Just say that I am an extremely happily married man and proud of it." Charles has a daughter from a brief marriage in Seattle. He and his present wife, Della Beatrice Antwine, a former gospel singer, have three sons. During 25 years of marriage Della has learned to accept the fact that her husband is on the road most of the year.

Since Ray Charles has always been unwilling to accept limitations—physical, racial, or musical—he has little patience when they are imposed on others. In 1961, before civil rights became a full-fledged national issue, he refused to play a sold-out concert in Memphis, Tenn., when he learned that the audience would be racially segregated. When the management integrated the audience, Charles gave the concert.

Unlike some performers, Ray Charles has never overtly "committed" himself to social causes. He doesn't need to. It is nearly impossible to listen to his music without feeling empathy for the luckless and stomped-upon people of the world. There is more than a little irony in the fact that his native Georgia adopted Charles's version of "Georgia on My Mind" as its state song.

Today, in his 50s, Ray Charles shows no sign of slowing down. Besides heading up his own record company, he still goes on the road to play concerts. He appeared in a 1980 movie, *The Blues Brothers*, and astounded younger fellow performers with a walloping version of the old rock-and-roll song "Shake a Tail Feather." Summing up his incredible life, he says: "Every experience I've had—good and bad—has taught me something. I was born a poor boy in the South, I'm black, I'm blind, I once fooled around with drugs, but all of it was like going to school—and I've tried to be a good student. I don't regret a damn thing."

—M.S.S.

RUDYARD KIPLING (1865–1936)

The problem with being spokesman for a generation is that the next generation inevitably has its own spokesman, and then one is passé. Out of touch, the new generation says. An anachronism. Rudyard Kipling was the spokesman for the British Empire upon which the sun never set, but imperialism went out of fashion, and his world left him behind.

He was born in Bombay, India, Dec. 30, 1865, and named Joseph Rudyard, the latter after the lake in Staffordshire where his parents became engaged. His father, Lockwood Kipling, was a sculptor and architectural designer, head of the Bombay School of Art and later curator of the Lahore Museum.

Rudyard Kipling.

Like most British children in 19th-century India, Rudyard had his ayah (nursemaid), who pampered and spoiled him, and with whom he spoke Hindustani, the language in which he thought and dreamed for the first three years of his life. At age six, because his parents feared the hazards of the Indian climate and the prevalence of disease more than they did the emotional effects of familial separation, Rudyard and his younger sister, Trix, were sent back to England and "placed" with a family for an undetermined period of time. No adequate explanation was given to the children, who felt abandoned, and no prior investigation was made of the foster family, which turned out to be fanatically religious, mean-spirited, and often brutal, especially to Rudyard. The children did not see their parents for the next six years.

At age 12 Rudyard was enrolled in a new and somewhat inferior boarding school with the unlikely name of United Services College of Westward Ho! in Devonshire. One of his classmates remembered him later as a "cheery, capering, podgy little fellow." He was teased about his thick-lensed glasses (without which he was nearly blind) and bullied in the usual British public-school fashion, but he adapted and eventually made friends with some of the boys. Later he used the experience as raw material for his exuberant *Stalky and Co.* (1899).

Rather than go to university, Rudyard rejoined his parents at Lahore and took a job with the local paper. For the next seven years he worked as a journalist and at the same time observed and wrote about both the Anglo-Indian society and the pageantry and color of the native Indian culture. He published *Departmental Ditties* (satiric verse), *Plain Tales from the Hills,* and six paperback volumes of short stories full of vivid and racy characters from both the civil and military life, which were sold in railroad stations across India and brought their author fame. Gradually the works made their way back to England, where he was hailed as "a rocket out of the magic East."

At 24 Kipling went to London via Japan, San Francisco, and New York, at which time he formed the first of his increasingly negative opinions of America when he discovered that a publishing company had pirated his books (international copyright protection had not yet been established in the U.S.). Although he began his London sojourn in a garret, he managed before the first year was out to publish (or republish) 80 short stories, a volume of verse, and a novel, *The Light That Failed*—all of which captivated the country. Kipling became the interpreter of the lives of the British ruling class in India. He vividly portrayed to those who stayed at home the heat, the disease, and the boredom, as well as the idle frivolity of the English matron and the tedium and brutality of life for the common barracks soldier, in the days before refrigeration and inoculation against tropical diseases.

By 25 Kipling was famous. He was not handsome (short, dark, with a thick mustache and heavy glasses), not the proper gentleman (no Oxford or Cambridge degree), and he had been jilted in love by Florence Garrard, a painter he had first met at the age of 14. It was a one-sided romance; Flo preferred her canvases to the young author's company. He felt himself an outsider in London. Immediately after publication of *Barrack-Room Ballads* in 1892, he set off for a trip around the world. But when news of the death of a close American friend reached him, he changed his mind, and within 10 days of his return to London he had proposed to, been accepted by, and married this friend's sister. From that point on Caroline Balestier managed his life, mothering and protecting him. Some of his best work—*The Jungle Book, The Seven Seas, Captains Courageous*—came out of the early years of their marriage, spent in Brattleboro, Vt., where the Kiplings lived with Caroline's family after Rudyard lost his savings because of a bank failure. The residents of Brattleboro seemed provincial to Kipling, and they viewed his quiet life-style as "secretive and unneighborly." Kipling soon had a quarrel over money with his brother-in-law that culminated in a lawsuit, which was given undue coverage in the American newspapers. Kipling was relieved to leave the U.S. for England in 1896. During another visit three years later, he and his six-year-old daughter, Josephine, were stricken with pneumonia in New York City. People knelt in the street outside his hotel to pray for him. Josephine died and Kipling's recovery took a year. With so many painful memories of America, the Kiplings never returned.

For the rest of their lives they lived in Sussex, England, but they made frequent trips to South Africa. There, as in India, Kipling encountered the white Britishers dutifully spreading enlightenment among the native throngs, unappreciated by either the recipients of their endeavors or their countrymen back home. Again his poems glorified the unsung English hero in far-flung lands. Kipling never doubted the desirability of developing the backward countries; it was, he said, the "white man's burden." But *Kim*, published in 1900, was to be his last work from his east-of-Suez past. The Boer War and American intervention in the Philippines brought a sharp reversal in the public's attitude toward imperialism, and with it a repudiation of one of the British Empire's most admired spokesmen. Suddenly the fickle public found Kipling's philosophy militant, which of course it was, and his poetry jingoistic, which it always had been.

Although Kipling wrote some of his finest stories in the latter half of his life, and although he won the Nobel Prize for literature in 1907, critics who had once praised his work now ridiculed it. He still had his popular following, much of it in America. In Britain schoolboys continued to recite "Gunga Din," "Mandalay," and "If" on prize days. But the poet laureateship went, somewhat inexplicably, to someone else three times, in spite of the fact that in his traits of self-sufficiency, doggedness, and courage no one was more British than Joseph Rudyard Kipling.

—N.C.S.

IGNACE JAN PADEREWSKI (1860–1941)

Among history's great pianists, only Franz Liszt and Anton Rubinstein rank above Ignace Paderewski. No other pianist, however, has ever enjoyed the Polish virtuoso's worldwide popularity and financial success, and few performing artists of any kind have matched his political achievements.

In the pattern of many other musical greats, Paderewski started playing the piano as a young child. However, he struck no one as a prodigy, and some of his early teachers at the Warsaw Conservatory even discouraged him from studying piano. Despite opposition, he was determined to master the instrument and spent long hours practicing. At 15 he was expelled after a fight with the conservatory's orchestra director, whom Paderewski believed was making excessive demands on his study time. The young rebel was eventually reinstated, and by condensing two years of work into six months, he graduated in 1878. Shortly afterward, he married Antonina Korsak, a student at the conservatory. The following year Antonina died in childbirth, but on her deathbed she extracted a promise from Paderewski that he would continue his piano studies.

Leaving his infant son with his mother-in-law, Paderewski continued his musical education in Berlin, where he became acquainted with the foremost musicians of his day. Back home in Poland, while vacationing in the Tatra Mountains, he met actress Helen Modjeska. She was so impressed with his playing that she became his patron and encouraged

him to apply for lessons with Viennese master Theodor Leschetizky. Unimpressed by Paderewski's audition, Leschetizky told him, "It is too late. Your fingers lack discipline. You can never become a great pianist." Paderewski's determination won out, however, and Leschetizky accepted him as a pupil on the condition that he begin his training from scratch. Leschetizky was a notoriously harsh taskmaster. At one point Paderewski fled the old man's studio in such a rage that he had consciously to suppress an impulse to pick up a rock and throw it through Leschetizky's window. But the grueling work was worth the effort. Paderewski later stated that he learned more from Leschetizky in a few lessons than he had learned in all of his previous studies. After three years the master pronounced him ready for the concert stage.

Paderewski scored unexpectedly big successes in a quick series of concerts in Vienna and Paris, then returned to Leschetizky for more study. In 1889 he launched his professional career in earnest. Building his repertory around the works of Bach, Beethoven, Schumann, and, especially, his fellow countryman Chopin, with sprinklings of his own compositions, Paderewski created a sensation in France. Although his first appearance in England met with mixed reactions—one critic claimed that his performance had been like "the march of an abnormally active mammoth across the keyboard"—he soon won widespread praise from the British, too. In late 1891 he began the first of 20 concert tours in the U.S. From that point on, he enjoyed unwaning success as a performer. He commanded several thousand dollars for each concert and earned around $10 million during his career. Characteristically, however, Paderewski gave many benefit concerts and contributed his money to various causes almost as fast as he earned it.

Like Franz Liszt, Paderewski was a charismatic performer whose striking appearance and intense personality combined with his virtuosity to electrify audiences—particularly female audiences. Helen Modjeska described the young Paderewski as resembling "one of Botticelli's or Fra Angelico's angels." He had a delicately handsome face and profuse golden hair, and he maintained a robust figure with regular exercise. Later he proved as impressive an orator as he was a musician, and he combined his talents in the cause of Polish nationalism. Up until his very end, he remained a powerful presence wherever he appeared. (During a brief premiership in Poland, when he was nearly 60, Paderewski personally overwhelmed a knife-wielding would-be assassin.)

Before the arrival of the Beatles, probably no European performer equaled Paderewski's impact on Americans. Crowds mobbed him wherever he went, and his journeys across the continent resembled royal progresses. He traveled in a private train with his own butler, chef, doctor, masseur, piano tuner, and servants. For relaxation, he indulged in his two passions: billiards and bridge. Occasionally he looked further afield for entertainment. While dining in St. Louis with George Johns, editor of the St. Louis *Post-Dispatch*, Paderewski asked him if there was anything unusual to see in the city. Johns responded by taking the pianist to Babe Connors's famous brothel. When they arrived, a large black woman named Mama Lou was belting out "Ta-Ra-Ra-Boom-Der-É," a bawdy song which was to become enormously popular in both the U.S. and England. Paderewski was so taken with the song that he sat down at the piano and had Mama Lou sing it through several times while he learned it.

During the period Paderewski was pursuing his career in America and throughout Europe, his invalid son was being taken care of by the pianist's old friend and admirer, Ladislas Górski, and his wife, Helena. Over the years Paderewski's friendship with Helena ripened into love. With the consent of Ladislas, whom Paderewski praised as "a noble man," the Górski marriage was annulled on a technicality, freeing Helena to wed Paderewski in May, 1899. She accompanied him on an extensive tour of America that same year. He continued his heavy schedule until 1905, when he developed a nervous disorder that made piano playing so painful he had to give up performing. But because his philanthropy kept him ever on the brink of insolvency, he soon resumed his career. Also, the pressing demands of Polish nationalism gave his work an even greater urgency.

Seeing W.W. I as an opportunity to restore independence to his native country, Paderewski rallied support for Poland in the U.S. He personally persuaded President Woodrow Wilson to include Polish independence in his 14 Points for a postwar settlement. After the U.S. entered the war, Paderewski raised a Polish army to fight in France. In January, 1919, he became prime minister and foreign secretary of newly independent Poland and represented Poland at the Versailles Peace Conference. A staggering burden of economic and political problems overwhelmed his government, however, and—smarting from criticism—he resigned the following December. Twenty years later he became the head of Poland's government in exile after Germany reoccupied his country. The 80-year-old pianist and statesman died in the U.S. during yet another campaign to gain support for Poland. Although he was buried in Arlington National Cemetery, his heart was removed from his body before interment. His last request was that it be returned to Poland when his native country was once again free. After spending 12 years in a Brooklyn mortuary, Paderewski's heart was moved to Cypress Hills Abbey Mausoleum in New York City, where it remains to this day.

—R.K.R.

MARCEL PROUST (1871–1922)

A literary genius of the 20th century, French novelist Marcel Proust dedicated his life to one major multivolumed masterpiece, entitled *Remembrance of Things Past.* Twice the length of *War and Peace, Remembrance* is a fictionalized autobiographical account of Proust's life within Parisian society before W.W. I. Proust spent 13 years writing, editing, enriching, and expanding *Remembrance*—a monument to detail and mental analysis. At his death he was still meticulously reworking the novel.

Born at Auteuil, a rural suburb of Paris, Proust was the son of a noted French physician and his extraordinarily beautiful Jewish wife. A frail, asthmatic child, he was spoiled by his overprotective mother. Proust attended school erratically because of his constant ill health. He spent many childhood summers in the country at the village of Illiers and, after it was discovered that the flowers of the region aggravated his allergies, at various oceanside resorts in Normandy. During these vacations, Proust developed a love for nature which he later exhibited in his writing.

After high school Proust served briefly in the army, but because of his poor health he was exempted from any strenuous duty. When he returned home, his father tried to force him into a diplomatic career. The pale, white-skinned youth, with his shag of deep black hair and slight body, compromised by studying law. He completed courses in philosophy and psychology at the Sorbonne and decided, against his father's wishes, to pursue a literary career. Proust was entranced with literature.

His other obsession was Paris's flamboyant aristocratic and literary high society. For the middle-class Proust, entry into the famous salons of this social elite had become his goal in life.

An amusing and ingratiating conversationalist, Proust set out earnestly on his prolonged social climb. His ascent was a calculated undertaking in which he manipulated and fawned on important personages. They included Princess Mathilde, the niece of Napoleon Bonaparte, whose feet Proust would regularly kneel to kiss, and Comte Robert de Montesquiou-Fezensac, a blue-blooded snob, who became Proust's patron and the model for his sexually kinky character the Baron de Charlus.

Proust reached the social pinnacle that he had so desired to attain only to find that the people there were not the mental and cultural giants he had imagined them to be. Disillusioned, he suddenly changed his life completely in 1906 and became a near hermit in his apartment at 102 Boulevard Haussmann, where he dedicated his hours to writing about the elite society that had disappointed him. Over the next six years he wrote *Remembrance* and refined its first volume, *Swann's Way*, which was published at his own expense, after several rejections from publishers, in 1913.

After 1906 Proust no longer hid the fact that he was homosexual, or more accurately, bisexual, with a strong preference for young men. Having had several sexual affairs with women, at the age of 22 he entered his first homosexual affair with Reynaldo Hahn, a 19-year-old musician. The most prominent characteristics of this liaison and later homosexual relationships were Proust's jealousy and his need to dominate his lover. His most involved and intense relationship was with his secretary, Alfred Agostinelli. Oddly enough, Agostinelli, who was a sexual libertine, was not really a homosexual. He allowed Proust his sexual favors but he preferred sex with women. He also refused to be dominated by Proust, and his frequent affairs with women resulted in emotional anguish for the love-struck, jealous novelist. This strange affair finally ended when Agostinelli took up flying and was killed in a plane crash. Proust used Agostinelli as the model for his female character Albertine, who provokes her male lover's jealousy by making love to other women.

For the last ten years of his life Proust refined *Remembrance*, publishing a volume of the serialized novel every few years. During this time Proust became increasingly eccentric. He was highly sensitive to sound, as well as to smells, and insulated his fumigated apartment with cork walls. He worked during the late night hours and went to bed around eight in the morning, sleeping fully clothed, often with gloves on. He helped finance a homosexual brothel, where he went to watch customers being whipped. Yet, even though he was blatant about his string of male lovers, he fought a pistol duel (it resulted in no injuries) with a critic who dared to publish a few snide remarks about his sexual exploits. Despite his homosexuality, Proust had an affair with the beautiful actress Louisa de Mornand, who was also the mistress of one of his friends.

As the years passed, Proust's health deteriorated. On Nov. 18, 1922, at the age of 51, he succumbed to pneumonia. The last volumes of *Remembrance* were published after Proust's death. They served to confirm his literary reputation and to elaborate his philosophy of life—a philosophy that argued the emptiness of life and relationships and the shallowness and vanity of the individual, yet optimistically recorded that people could raise themselves to moments of joy and moral glory. For Proust, *Remembrance* was a study in self-enlightenment and self-realization. It was his effort to bring from his subconscious the reality he believed was buried beneath the daily routines and habits of life.

—R.J.F.

SIDESHOW OF POPULAR AND OFFBEAT PERFORMING AND CREATIVE ARTISTS

Kahlil Gibran (1883–1931)

The author of *The Prophet*—the underground bible quoted at both counterculture weddings and John F. Kennedy's inauguration—was a Lebanese mystic who lived off the labor and love of women who worshiped him as the embodiment of the Second Coming.

"I am indebted for all that I call 'I' to women," admitted Gibran. "Had it not been for the woman-mother, the woman-sister, and the woman-friend, I would have been sleeping among those who seek the tranquillity of the world with their snoring."

He was born near the proverbial cedar forests of Lebanon, high in the mountains of the Turkish-dominated Middle East. His mother, the daughter of a Maronite Christian priest, had emigrated to Brazil with her first husband but had returned to Lebanon after his death. Her second husband, Kahlil Gibran, is usually described as a shepherd, but he was actually the equivalent of a cattle dealer in a culture that substitutes lamb for beef. The name Khalil, meaning "the chosen one," was later changed by his son to Kahlil, since this spelling was more euphonious. But the mystic never ceased to consider himself favored.

Young Kahlil was a difficult, restless child who loved the drama of storms and brooded over the drawings of Leonardo da Vinci. When he was 11, his mother left her second husband to emigrate to the U.S. with Kahlil, his half brother Peter, and his two younger sisters. Settling near Boston's Chinatown, the family went to work so that Kahlil, the chosen one, might study.

After he had had a few years of American schooling, Kahlil was sent back to Beirut to finish his education, possibly because he had fallen into the traps of a "wicked older woman." Spending his summer vacations with relatives in the Lebanese mountains, he met and fell in love with Hala Daher, whose aristocratic family had already arranged a more appropriate marriage for her. This rejection, which he felt as keenly as if he had been expelled from paradise, inspired in Gibran a lifelong mission to free the "children of God" from slavish adherence to tradition.

Kahlil Gibran. *Mary Haskell. Both drawn by Gibran.*

Gibran was recalled to Boston in 1903 because of his sister Sultana's death, and the next year his half brother Peter died of tuberculosis. This was followed by the death of his beloved mother. (*Mother*, he exalted, was "the most beautiful word on the lips of mankind.") There remained only his sister Mariana, who took in needlework to support her brilliant brother while he devoted his time to painting and writing.

At the first exhibition of his mystical paintings, held in Boston in 1904, he acquired a benefactress and a lifelong friend. He was then 21, short and slender, with full lips under his mustache and soulful eyes above it. Mary Haskell, a daughter of impoverished southern gentility, headmistress of her own school in Cambridge, was 31. Gibran described her as "a she-angel who is ushering me toward a splendid future and paving for me the path to intellectual and financial success." Specifically, she offered to support him out of her meager earnings, staking him to two years in Paris and setting him up on his return in a studio in New York's Greenwich Village, where he lived from 1911 until his death. This one-room studio, which he called the Hermitage, became a central gathering place for writers and artists, particularly expatriate Arab literati.

Mary Haskell also served as Gibran's editor, helping crystallize his parables and aphorisms into irreducible "nuggets of wisdom," and as a soul mate for 20 years. Their correspondence, published in *Beloved Prophet* (1972), alternated between ardent passion and burning self-denial. Gibran proposed marriage, either out of guilt or gratitude, but he was refused. ("He who would understand a woman," according to one of Gibran's startling non sequiturs, "is the very man who would wake from a beautiful dream to sit at a breakfast table.") By 1923 the couple had grown apart, and Mary eventually left New York for Savannah, Ga., and marriage to a southern aristocrat, J. Florance Minis.

It was in his New York studio that Gibran found his stride as an artist and writer. In both fields his style was eclectic. His drawings of yearning nudes and his portraits exuding spirituality were influenced by Da Vinci, mystic William Blake, and sculptor Auguste Rodin. His parables and aphorisms derived from such diverse sources as the Bible, La Fontaine, and Nietzsche.

Gibran's first works, which had been inspired by his star-crossed love for Hala Daher, included *Spirits Rebellious* (1908), banned by the Turkish authorities in the Middle East as "revolutionary and poisonous to youth," and *The Broken Wings* (1912), an autobiographical novel of frustrated love and a best-seller in the Arabic-speaking world.

During the years in New York, however, Gibran turned to more universal themes, producing a dozen slender volumes about love and other spiritual strivings. In 1918 he published *The Madman,* a benign, idealistic version of Nietzsche's nihilistic superman. ("Madness in art is creation," Gibran wrote. "Madness in poetry is wisdom.") In 1923 he finished *The Prophet,* 26 minisermons on love, freedom, pain, and sorrow, which he had been polishing for years. This he followed in 1926 with *Sand and Foam,* a collection of aphorisms (example: "An exaggeration is a truth that lost its temper.").

After Mary Haskell's marriage in 1926, Gibran acquired another devotee, or "deathless admirer." Barbara Young was an English teacher who aspired to become a poetess. She was soon content to sit at Gibran's feet and take dictation, for she regarded him as a manifestation of the "Mighty Unnameable Power." After his death she devoted the rest of her life to lecturing and writing about him. Young's biography of Gibran, *This Man from Lebanon,* appeared in 1945.

There was also an affair, carried on by correspondence, between Gibran and May Ziadeh, an expatriate living in Egypt. After an argument over extramarital sex, which Gibran had condoned, May received an envelope containing only a drawing of a burning heart pierced by a dagger.

Gibran died at 48 of cirrhosis of the liver and incipient tuberculosis. According to his will, his "mortal remains"—as well as all future royalties from his books—were to be sent to his native village of Bsherri (population 4,000). His white marble coffin received a hero's welcome in the port of Beirut, and a 50-mi.-long funeral procession wound its way up to the abandoned mountain monastery of Mar Sarkis near Bsherri. Carved into a cliff by monks seeking a safe refuge, inaccessible except by rope or ladder, the monastery was later provided with a path, plastic flowers, and souvenirs for future generations of literary pilgrims.

Over the years Gibran's books enjoyed a continuing vogue, although literary critics often found fault with them. French sculptor Auguste Rodin had declared that Gibran was "the William Blake of the 20th century," but one *Time* magazine critic complained, "Of all the limp, mucid hooey now being sold without a prescription, *The Prophet* is the most blatant and outrageous." Yet young people found in him an expression of their frustrated spirituality, particularly suicide victims, who often left strict instructions to have passages from *The Prophet* read at their funeral. The elderly turned to him for comfort upon bereavement. John F. Kennedy immortalized Gibran's injunction "Ask not what your country can do for you," while hippie weddings were celebrated to the refrains of the prophet Almustafa's advice to "let there be spaces in your togetherness."

In the 50 years after its publication, *The Prophet* sold 4 million copies in English-language editions alone (plain, illustrated, and deluxe), and there were translations in 20 other languages as well. In 1947 Gibran's sister Mariana, by then an old woman, went to court seeking a share of her brother's earnings, but her suit was unsuccessful. And during the 1970s the impoverished villagers of Bsherri were beset by intrigue, embezzlement, even murder, over the division of hundreds of thousands of dollars in annual royalties. The Lebanese government finally intervened, and it now administers this annual windfall from America.

—C.D.

The Marx Brothers

In a 1975 poll of Brown University's freshmen, the third most admired man in world history, after Jesus Christ and Albert Schweitzer, turned out to be comedian Groucho Marx.

Then in his 80s, Groucho was enjoying a renaissance of popularity. A play about the Marx brothers, called *Minnie's Boys*, had been produced on Broadway in 1970. A Carnegie Hall tribute in 1972 attracted a standing-room-only crowd, including dozens of Groucho, Harpo, and Chico look-alikes. Groucho was made a French Commander of the Order of Arts and Letters in 1972 and received a special Oscar in 1974. Marx brothers film festivals and retrospectives created a new generation of fans, some of whom kept a curbside watch outside Groucho's Beverly Hills home, wearing greasepaint mustaches and bushy eyebrows.

The fans may have been new, but the idea was timeless. Nearly 50 years earlier, when the Marx brothers opened on stage in Los Angeles with *The Cocoanuts*, the front row was filled with Hollywood's top stars, all wearing Groucho mustaches and carrying cigars.

It was a long way from East 93rd Street in New York City, where the Marx boys grew up in a noisy, crowded apartment—an extended Jewish family of "castaways," Harpo called them. The household included Grandpa and Grandma Schoenberg from Germany, a former traveling magician and his harp-playing wife; their daughter Minnie, blond and plump, and her husband, "Frenchie" Marx, who came from French-speaking Alsace, an indifferent tailor but a superb cook; Minnie's five sons (a sixth had died in childhood); a homeless cousin; as well as other stray relatives.

"Minnie held us all together while she plotted our rescue," Harpo wrote later. "Minnie was the Outside Man. Frenchie was the Inside Man." With a combination of determination and chicanery, Minnie promoted her various sons, relatives, and friends into vaudeville as "the Three Nightingales," "the Four Nightingales," and "the Six Mascots" (the larger the troupe, the higher the pay in those days), musical acts with pretensions to class.

But Minnie could never quite control her zany sons, not even by hissing "Greenbaum" at them from the wings. (Greenbaum held the mortgage on the first Marx family home.) Once onstage, the boys would begin to roughhouse, compulsively cutting up, demolishing all order and affectation with their nonstop insanity. Soon they evolved a format for their inspired lunacy, variations on a schoolroom theme with Groucho featured as Herr Teacher.

When vaudeville began to decline during W.W. I, the Marx brothers went on tour with *I'll Say She Is*, a musical revue featuring Groucho as Napoleon. "The last time I came home all France was with you," the emperor cried to his Josephine, while she was being passionately pursued by his brothers, "and a slice of Italy too." The show opened to rave reviews on Broadway in 1924, and a triumphant Minnie, having fractured her ankle, arrived at the theater by stretcher. Her dominating passion would thenceforth be playing poker (Frenchie preferred pinochle).

Now the toast of Manhattan, the Marx brothers moved on to two custom-crafted vehicles created by top playwright George S. Kaufman: *The Cocoanuts* (1925), a spoof of the Florida land boom, and *Animal Crackers* (1928), a tropical travesty of the great white hunter. These plays marked the beginning of a 16-year partnership with Margaret Dumont, a woman with a formidable dignity that the Marxes did their utmost to demolish. The brothers did so much ad-libbing and improvising onstage that fans enjoyed seeing the plays over and over again. ("I thought I heard one of the original lines," Kaufman deadpanned one night.) Both plays were filmed in New York.

The 1929 crash put a damper on Broadway just as the advent of the "talkies" was creating a demand for comics who sounded as well as looked funny. So the Marx brothers moved to Hollywood and made 11 films in 12 years—a "soft racket" for the now middle-aged Marxes, who were used to giving up to five performances a day. They went back on the road, however, to polish some gag routines for their two best films, *A Night at the Opera* (1935) and *A Day at the Races* (1937).

Throughout the years in vaudeville, in the legitimate theater, and in films, the Marx brothers had retained their individual identities, which had been forged in the crowded ethnic patchwork of New York City. Leonard "Chico" Marx (1886–1961), the oldest brother and his mother's favorite, was the promoter, the hustler who quit school at 12 to work the streets. He learned a variety of dialects for protection in case he got caught by an Italian or Irish gang, and he learned to play a little piano, at his mother's insistence. But his main interests were gambling and girls, in that order. Chico could "smell money," Harpo insisted, and he had a photographic memory for poker hands. He would later receive his nickname because of his success with the "chickies."

Wearing a pointed hat pulled down over his curly hair, speaking in ice-cream Eye-talian, and "shooting the keys" at the piano, Chico provided a bridge between the acerbic Groucho and the angelic Harpo in the act. He also succeeded Minnie as the brothers' manager, bolstering their confidence and promoting them from vaudeville to the theater by hustling a producer into putting together *I'll Say She Is*. Later, at a card game in Hollywood, Chico discovered Irving Thalberg, who became the producer of the best Marx brothers films. (Anybody that good at bridge must be good at making movies too, Chico reasoned.) Chico was also responsible for their worst films, made after W.W. II primarily to help him pay his gambling debts. He worked intermittently as a bandleader (billed as "Chico Marx and his Ravellis") on the nightclub and county-fair circuit, an unregenerate gambler and Don Juan to the end.

Adolph Arthur "Harpo" Marx (1888–1964) looked like Chico and also inherited his older brother's skill with cards and women, but in temperament he took after his father. A school dropout in the 2nd grade because he was getting beaten up by the Irish boys, he learned German and magic from his grandfather at home. He also taught himself to play the harp, gaining surprising proficiency despite improper tuning and fingering. Onstage, he remained silent except for harp solos, horn beeps, and the clatter of stolen silver dropping from his sleeves.

Alexander Woollcott, the dean of New York critics, hailed Harpo as the star of the Marx brothers plays. Woollcott also introduced Harpo to the celebrated Algonquin Round Table of wits (as the only full-time listener, Harpo joked), invited him to summer with the literati in Vermont and on the Riviera, and persuaded him to tour Soviet Russia as a pantomimist during the 1930s. In California, Harpo was a frequent weekend guest at William Randolph Hearst's "ranch," as Hearst called his castle in San Simeon. He finally married at age 48, adopted four children, and settled into his Palm Springs estate, El Rancho Harpo. "I wanted to have a child at every window, waving to me when I came home," he said.

Julius "Groucho" Marx (1890–1977) was the intellectual of East 93rd Street, the odd man out who preferred books to cards. His nickname has been variously attributed to his moodiness and to the "grouch bag" in which the stingiest Marx kept his money. The most verbally aggressive member of the family—possibly to get a word in edgewise—he developed into a master of the insult, the non sequitur, and the pun. "If you can't get a taxi, you can leave in a huff," he would say. Or "Time wounds all heels." Whenever an attractive young lady asked him to join her, he would reply, "Why, are you coming apart?" With his greasepaint mustache (later real), articulate eyebrows, and predatory leer, he had the most physically distinctive comic persona of the brothers.

Groucho was the only one to develop a successful solo career in show business, as the host of *You Bet Your Life,* a quiz program that endured 4 years on radio, 11 seasons on TV, and went into repeated reruns. Compulsively looking for a laugh, he was able to recall or ad-lib a witty or insulting rejoinder for every statement made by his guests. He was also a voracious reader and the author of several books of his own, including *Memoirs of a Mangy Lover* (1963) and a volume of his correspondence with such luminaries as James Thurber, Harry Truman, and T. S. Eliot—proud accomplishments for a 7th grade dropout. But his caustic wit, exercised on all around him, left him a lonely old man with three ex-wives, three estranged children, and a secretary-companion.

The two younger brothers, Milton "Gummo" Marx (1893–1977), who as a boy wore rubbers to ward off colds, and Herbert "Zeppo" Marx (1901–1979), the dead-end kid of the family, took turns playing straight man in the act. Gummo, who has been described as a cross between Harpo and Groucho, both sweet and funny, had a fair singing voice as the second "nightingale" but suffered from nerves onstage. He left the act to serve in W.W. I, Minnie having allegedly made a deal with the draft board, or so it was said. By volunteering Gummo, Minnie presumably secured exemptions for the others. He was replaced by Zeppo, who wanted to be a comic rather than a straight man. (Standing in once for Groucho, who was in the hospital with appendicitis, Zeppo got a lot of laughs but also got sick on Groucho's cigars.) Zeppo retired from the team after *Duck Soup* was filmed in 1933, became a successful theatrical agent, and later branched out into other fields. Gummo, after failing in business on his own, also became a successful agent with a lucrative piece of Groucho's TV interests.

The camaraderie of Minnie's boys from East 93rd Street survived the years of celebrity and affluence and continued into the years of decline. The brothers always chipped in to bail out a needy relative. Groucho, a sentimentalist despite himself, even supported Chico's ex-wife. As they sang in *Animal Crackers*, by Bert Kalmar and Harry Ruby:

> We're four of the three musketeers.
> We've been together for years.
> Eenie, meenie, minee, (horn),
> . . .
> It's one for all and two for five.
> We're four of the three musketeers.

—C.D.

J.R.R. Tolkien (1892–1973)

He was a typically tweedy, pipe-smoking Oxford professor, an authority on early English languages and literature, with perhaps more than his share of endearing eccentricities. He used to begin his course on *Beowulf* with a commanding solo performance of the epic poem in the original Anglo-Saxon. He also devised crossword puzzles in Anglo-Saxon for the amusement and instruction of his pupils. He was known to have chased a surprised neighbor down the road dressed as an ax-wielding tribal warrior. And in his spare time he composed fables about an imaginary era peopled by small furry creatures called hobbits. Much to his and everyone else's surprise, Tolkien's *The Lord of the Rings* (1954–1956)—described by the London *Times* as having "all the earmarks of a publishing disaster"—became a unique event in world literature, a best-selling fairy tale.

John Ronald Reuel Tolkien (Ronald to his family, "Tollers" to his Oxford cronies) was born in Bloemfontein, South Africa, where his

J.R.R. Tolkien, father of the Hobbits.

father was a banker. He grew up with a strong inner sense of a "lost paradise," cherishing a far better world of memory and imagination. At the age of four he lost his father, who died alone in Africa while the rest of the family was in England on home leave. Tolkien's mother took refuge with her two sons (Hilary was two years younger than Ronald) in a charming cottage in the rural West Midlands; when they had to move to the grim factory town of Birmingham four years later, Tolkien felt as if he had been expelled from heaven. Then, when he was 12, his mother died, leaving her sons under the guardianship of a Catholic priest, Father Francis Morgan.

At the age of 16, while living in a Birmingham boardinghouse, Ronald met another orphan, 19-year-old Edith Bratt, with whom he fell in love. A year passed before Father Francis discovered that Tolkien's attention had been diverted from his schoolwork by the clandestine romance with this "older woman" who was living under the same roof as his ward. The shocked priest moved the Tolkien brothers to new lodgings and forbade Ronald to see or even write to his beloved. Following the highest chivalric ideal, Tolkien remained true to Edith for the next four years and proposed in a letter he wrote to her on his 21st birthday.

When he learned she was engaged to marry another man, Tolkien persuaded her to call it off. They were married after he graduated from Oxford in 1916. It was not an ideal match, however. Tolkien later confided to one of his sons that he and Edith had been able to console one another, but they were never entirely able to overcome their childhood sufferings.

A linguistic genius, Tolkien and his cousin invented a language called Nevbosh, or New Nonsense, in which they wrote limericks. At Oxford, in addition to Latin, Greek, Anglo-Saxon, and other esoteric tongues, he studied Finnish, which he found quite as intoxicating as if it had been alcohol. At various times he kept diaries in an alphabet that resembled a mixture of Hebrew, Greek, and Pitman shorthand.

While serving as a battalion signaling officer in W.W. I, Tolkien found some relief from the horror of trench warfare by scribbling ideas on the backs of envelopes. Convalescing from trench fever, he amused himself by composing a mythology for a Middle-earth—modeled after his beloved West Midlands—where elves, dwarves, goblins, and wizards coexisted with "Big Folk."

After the war Tolkien worked briefly on the *Oxford English Dictionary*. (Later, when his publisher tried to correct the spelling of *elves* and *dwarves*, Tolkien replied, "After all, I *wrote* the *Oxford English Dictionary!*") He taught at the University of Leeds for five years before returning to Oxford in 1925 as professor of Anglo-Saxon. One day, while correcting some dull examination papers, he wrote on a blank page: "In a hole in the ground there lived a hobbit."

By a process of spontaneous generation—"out of the leafmold of the mind"—Tolkien wrote *The Hobbit* (1937), which enjoyed a mild critical and popular success. He continued to write, drawing on his knowledge, experience, and whimsy to create a whole cosmogony, which included a language, geography, and history for Middle-earth. (The Elven language was modeled after Finnish, the dwarves' names were borrowed from the Norse epics, and the cycles of the moon in *The Lord of the Rings* were taken from the 1942 calendar.) Fourteen years after it was begun, *The Lord of the Rings* was published in 1954–1956 as a trilogy. By the mid-1960s it had become a favorite on college campuses all over the world, selling 3 million copies in nine languages and inspiring a network of Tolkien buffs to form clubs, exchange memorabilia of Middle-earth, and write inspired graffiti ("Tolkien is hobbit-forming!").

Wealth and celebrity had little effect on Tolkien, who continued to teach until his mandatory retirement in 1959. He spent his last years wrestling with his literary correspondence. Financially able to indulge himself, he enjoyed an occasional gourmet meal, affected colorful vests, and wrote on a check for his income tax, "Not a penny for Concorde." (Politically, he preferred feudalism to democracy; historically, he detested the French.) And he tried, unsuccessfully, to complete *The Silmarillion*, his story of the creation of Middle-earth begun during W.W. I, long before *The Hobbit* and *The Lord of the Rings* were written. Upon the 81-year-old author's death in 1973, his son, Christopher Tolkien, finished the book, working from a jumble of notes and manuscripts left by his father. *The Silmarillion* made publishing history in 1977 by breaking records for advance publication sales.

Tolkien is buried next to his wife in Oxford. Their tombstones are engraved with the names of Lúthien and Beren, two Middle-earth lovers.

—C.D.

Paul Wittgenstein (1887–1961)

On Nov. 27, 1931, a new concerto by composer Maurice Ravel was premiered in Vienna. The work, a blending of traditional musical forms and modern jazz, was performed by pianist Paul Wittgenstein, whose virtuosity held the audience spellbound. Wittgenstein had personally commissioned the concerto, less to conform to his tastes than to fit his physique. This world-renowned concert pianist had only one arm.

Ravel's *Concerto for the Left Hand* was intended to express the tragedy of wartime sacrifices, something Wittgenstein knew well. In August, 1914, less than a year after he had made his debut on the concert stage, Wittgenstein was leading a patrol near Zamość, Poland, when a sniper's bullet shattered his right arm. The 26-year-old Austrian officer was taken prisoner by the Russians, and in a primitive field hospital his wounded arm was amputated. He was eventually sent to a prisoner-of-war camp in Omsk, Siberia, where he remained until a Red Cross prisoner-exchange program brought about his early release. He was back home in Vienna by Christmas, 1915. Despite his disability, he served as a general's aide on the Italian front until the end of W.W. I and thus displayed the courage and tenacity that would help resurrect his career as a musician.

Wittgenstein grew up in a large, wealthy Viennese household. His father, Karl Wittgenstein, was a successful industrialist known as the "Iron King" of Austria. Paul's father was also a collector of fine paintings, china, and music manuscripts; his mother, Leopoldine, was an accomplished pianist and organist. The Wittgenstein home was a gathering place for noted artists, musicians, and intellectuals of the 19th century. Johannes Brahms, Gustav Mahler, and Clara Schumann were frequent guests, and famed violinist Joseph Joachim was Paul's great-uncle. As a boy, Paul would sometimes accompany Uncle Joseph on the piano, but at that early stage the boy was not particularly accomplished. He had a tendency to pound too hard on the keys.

Karl Wittgenstein pursued the arts as an avocation, but he believed that a man should earn a living in the business world. So he goaded a reluctant Paul into taking a job in a bank. However, Paul soon discovered that he was far better suited to the keyboard than to the balance sheet, and he quit the bank job to devote all his time to music. He studied with both Josef Labor, the blind organ virtuoso, and Theodor Leschetizky, the most respected piano teacher of the day, and his playing improved quickly. It became apparent to all that he did indeed have a gift. In 1913 he faced his first audience in Vienna. Reviews were favorable; an illustrious career was predicted for the young pianist. However, within six months he was drafted.

After the loss of his arm, he did left-handed keyboard exercises to break up the monotony of camp life in Omsk. As he became more accomplished at playing with one hand, he began to envision a return to the concert stage. In fact, he established that as his goal and set about making his remaining five fingers sound like ten. "It was like attempting to scale a mountain," he said. "If you can't climb up from one side, you try another." In 1916 he gave his first one-handed recital to critical acclaim.

Unfortunately, his handicap severely limited his repertoire, since few existing piano pieces could be adapted for a one-handed pianist. Between 1918 and 1921 Wittgenstein dug through musical archives in search of selections that could be arranged for the left hand. He found little, but his wealth enabled him to commission works by some of the foremost composers of his day. In addition to the Ravel concerto, Wittgenstein bought pieces from Richard Strauss, Benjamin Britten, Paul Hindemith, and others, not all of which he found suitable. When Russian composer Sergei Prokofiev sent him a specially written concerto in 1931, Wittgenstein promptly returned it with the following note: "Thank you for the concerto, but I don't understand a note of it, and shall not play it." Wittgenstein and Ravel feuded for a time over alterations the pianist had made in performance of the *Concerto for the Left Hand*, but Wittgenstein eventually conceded that the work should be played as it was written. Wittgenstein's musical tastes ran to 19th-century pieces, which posed some problems for him when he dealt with modern composers.

Special music was the only concession Wittgenstein ever made to his handicap. When a piano company offered to install a custom-made pedal in his instrument, he refused, saying, "People would say the piano was fixed." He constantly struggled to make his recitals more than just a freak show; as *The New York Times* commented in a review in 1934, "His physical handicap was forgotten. Not only this: he showed commanding musicianship and played with an aplomb and gusto thrice admirable."

In 1938 Wittgenstein with his wife, Hilde, and their three children settled permanently in New York. He continued to give concerts, taught piano at the Ralph Wolfe Conservatory in New Rochelle, and opened a studio in New York City for private students. A patient and kind but exacting teacher, Wittgenstein encouraged many one-armed pianists, who found great inspiration in their teacher's stamina and energy. He himself practiced four hours a day until his death in 1961 at age 73.

—M.J.T.

12

DOMESTIC SCENES

FROM BOOK TO BED

The Development of the Sex Manual

***KAMA SUTRA* (100 A.D.–500 A.D.)**

Instructor: Vatsyayana Mallanaga (dates unknown). Mallanaga was a religious student and poet of the Vatsyayana sect in India. During his time rulers had harems, seducing virgins was often an acceptable sport among the male elite and temple walls were polished in order to reflect the beautiful women that passed by. It was a sensual though not licentious age, in which women, appreciated for their orgasmic capacity, were nonetheless subservient to men. Many practices, such as anal intercourse and oral-genital gratification, were considered inferior and were used only by the lower castes. Mallanaga did not create the *Kama Sutra* (verses of Kama, god of love) alone; the book is a compilation of Sanskrit literature from previous centuries combined with contemporary ideas.

Overview: Far more than a sex manual, the *Kama Sutra*, directed at the young Indian *bon vivant*, gives advice on everything from etiquette to house furnishings. Its 64 practices make up a curriculum of arts, skills, and information recommended for the well-bred person: tattooing, calligraphy, fencing, cooking, solving riddles, knowledge of mining, practicing sleight of hand, the science of war, teaching a parrot to talk, and more. It tells how to choose a mate, obtain power and wealth through love, make love, seduce women, use aphrodisiacs and artificial stimulation.

Much is prescriptive. The forbidden is explicated; for example, a man should not make love with a leper, a friend, or a woman who cannot keep a secret. The women of Abhira enjoy oral intercourse, the book states, but it also notes that fellatio and cunnilingus are low-level practices. Though Mallanaga recommends ways of hitting women to achieve sexual pleasure for both partners, he cautions against "dangerous, painful, and barbarous" variations, such as using scissors—once tried by a ruler who accidentally killed his wife in an excess of passion.

The aphrodisiacs of the *Kama Sutra* have questionable efficacy. For example, it is doubtful that throwing vajnasubhi powder mixed with monkey dung over a virgin will keep her from marrying anyone else. Some artificial devices in the book could be downright dangerous (e.g., piercing the penis like an earlobe so that it can hold various adornments).

Advice:

1. To court a woman, go swimming with her. Dive far away, then surface near her, so that your wet bodies touch, as if by accident.
2. Women should never make the first move in sex.
3. To indicate desire, a man may pull at his mustache, stare at the woman meaningfully, click his nails, play with his jewels.
4. Some of the best unions are achieved by matching similar genital sizes, which are designated as follows:

Size	*Woman*	*Man*
Small organ	*Doe*	*Hare*
Medium organ	*Mare*	*Bull*
Large organ	*Elephant*	*Horse*

   According to the *Kama Sutra,* if you're a horse, it's best to stick with an elephant.
5. Scratching and biting arts include the Leap of the Hare (5 nail marks around the nipple) and the Line of Jewels (line of teeth marks). Be careful!
6. One Indian school of thought recommends trying out difficult positions for intercourse in water. (Orthodox Hindu religion prohibits it.)
7. The man should "delicately press and palpitate" the woman's erogenous zones.
8. A recommended embrace is the Tree Climber: The woman puts one foot on the foot of her lover, her other leg around his thigh, one arm around his neck, the other around his loins—while crooning desire.
9. If the man is tired, the couple can assume the woman-astride position (Woman Who Plays the Role of the Man). Some women can turn around and around on the penis while in this position ("Spinning Top"), though, says Mallanaga, in a masterpiece of understatement, "This can only be learned through practice."
10. During the honeymoon, the couple should take 10 days to reach the point of lovemaking.
11. At the end of intercourse, the man should keep his penis in the vagina, thrusting but not removing it (Chasing the Sparrow).
12. An ideal ending for a night of love? The couple should look at the stars while the man gives an astronomy lesson.

THE PERFUMED GARDEN (c. 1500)

Instructor: Shaykh Umar ibn Muhammed al-Nefzawi (probably 16th century). Not much is known about the author of *The Perfumed Garden* except that he lived in Tunis during the 1500s and wrote the book for a minister of the seventeenth ruler of the Hafsid kingdom. Much of his material is derived from ancient Arab books on sex, and after his death other writers modified and added to the work. About 1850, a French officer stationed in Algeria found a manuscript copy of the book and translated it into French, leaving out a chapter on pederasty (homosexuality involving a man with a baby). He ran off 35 copies on official French army printing machines before he was caught. Counterfeit copies floated around Paris, and one was read by noted author Guy de Maupassant, who wrote to a Paris publisher suggesting that the original edition of the book—with its chapter on pederasty—be reprinted. Arabist Richard Burton, who had achieved the fantastic feat of making the trip to Mecca (forbidden to non-Muslims) by disguising himself as an Afghani, translated the book into English from French. In addition, he had started to translate the entire manuscript directly from Arabic, adding his own annotations, before he died. The unfinished work was the "crown" of his life, but unfortunately his wife later burned the manuscript. Another edition, containing the chapter on homosexuality, was published in 1907. On the title page was written: " 'This is no baby's book.' (Sir R. F. Burton)."

Overview: "Praise be given to God, who has placed man's greatest pleasure in the natural parts of woman, and has destined the natural parts of man to afford the greatest enjoyment to woman." So begins *The Perfumed Garden*. It goes on to describe the physiology of foreplay and intercourse, as well as remedies for various sexual difficulties. A large part of the book needs to be taken with a grain of salt. Example: "As to coition with old women, it acts like a fatal poison." And some others:

- Intercourse on an empty stomach may cause the eyesight to weaken, while intercourse on a full stomach may rupture the intestines. (False.)
- Intercourse with a menstruating woman is detrimental to both man and woman: "If the least drop of blood should get into the man's urinary canal, numerous maladies may supervene." (False.)
- A good way to deaden desire is to use a camphor mixture, preferably one used to wash dead bodies. (It might work for obvious reasons.)
- To increase the size of the penis, wrap a piece of leather smeared with hot pitch around it. (Not recommended!)
- Use cow dung as a female deodorant.

Still, *The Perfumed Garden* approaches sex with a lusty and guiltless attitude that must have shocked the Victorians. Anecdotes describe the "deceits and treacheries of women" (hiding their lovers in closets, etc.) and the miracle man who could deflower 80 virgins without ever ejaculating. Terms for the genital organs are almost poetic: for the penis—crowbar, one-eyed, bald one, the rummager, the ransacker; for the vulva—slit, crested one, crusher, bottomless, the delicious.

Advice:

1. Don't make love "only to satisfy the passion of your mistress."
2. "The acme of enjoyment . . . depends on one circumstance . . . that the vulva is furnished with a suction pump [orifice of the uterus], which will clasp the virile member and suck up the sperm with irresistible force."
3. To please a woman, a man's "engine" (penis) must be from 6 to 9 in. long. (False.)

4. Love play and kissing are essential. "A woman is like a fruit, which will not yield its sweetness until you rub it between your hands."
5. Among the positions described are Frog-fashion, Screw of Archimedes, Rainbow Arch. Some are difficult. In the Somersault, the woman lets her pantaloons drop on her feet, then puts her head between her feet so that her neck is caught in the pantaloons, whereupon the man, facing her, grabs her legs and turns her on her back so that she performs a somersault. Then, curving his legs under him, the man inserts his penis in her vagina.
6. A thin man can use a cushion to raise his hip to the right height when having intercourse—side by side—with a fat woman.
7. Try several movements during intercourse, such as Bucket in the Well (alternate pushing movements), Mutual Shock (pushing together and withdrawing), Love's Tailor (several quick moves only partly in the vagina, then plunging in), the Toothpick in the Vulva (up and down, then right and left with the penis), Boxing Up of Love (penis entirely in the vagina, moving hard, never withdrawing).

CREATIVE AND SEXUAL SCIENCE: OR MANHOOD, WOMANHOOD, AND THEIR MUTUAL INTERRELATIONS . . . AS TAUGHT BY PHRENOLOGY AND PHYSIOLOGY (1870)

Instructor: Orson Squire Fowler (1809–1887). Of his "sainted" mother, who died when he was nine, Orson Squire Fowler wrote, "I remember distinctly but two things, laying my head back in her open lap while she kissed, caressed, and fondled me; and her death. Both are indelible." He grew up to concentrate on sex (even "the rap at the door is sexed") and love (he married three times), as revealed by phrenology, the pseudoscience of determining character by the shape of a person's head. Fowler's books and lecture tours (with his brother and brother-in-law) constituted a kind of 19th-century self-help movement, which eventually got him into trouble in the late 1870s, when he was accused of licentiousness for lecturing on sex to women. He was influential in the antilacing (anticorset) and temperance movements, became a vegetarian, and designed and built a 60-room octagonal house with gravel walls ("Fowler's Folly") near Fishkill, N.Y. A handsome, patriarchal-looking man, he had a full beard and intense eyes.

Overview: Though the quaint ideas in this 1,052-page opus reveal its age, the prose remains vigorous: "To the rear, or mate!" cries Fowler, a strong proponent of procreation, who believed that celibates were prone to "dry rot." The subjects in his book are intended to "go straight home to the very heart's core of your inner life!"

Gender is not a dead letter to Fowler, who claims that boys are "boisterous" and girls "fond of doll-babies" and that the male purpose in life is to "establish the most and best life germs." While he advocates equal pay for equal work for women, he believes that "Laying hens alone should cackle."

Phrenology enters the picture, too. He says that the seat of the soul is right under the corpus callosum (fibrous band connecting the hemispheres of the brain) and under that is the seat of love. He talks of

CREATIVE

AND

SEXUAL SCIENCE:

OR

MANHOOD, WOMANHOOD,

AND

THEIR MUTUAL INTERRELATIONS;

LOVE, ITS LAWS, POWER, ETC.;

SELECTION, OR MUTUAL ADAPTATION;

COURTSHIP, MARRIED LIFE,

AND

PERFECT CHILDREN;

THEIR

GENERATION, ENDOWMENT, PATERNITY, MATERNITY, BEARING, NURSING AND REARING; TOGETHER WITH PUBERTY, BOYHOOD, GIRLHOOD, ETC.; **SEXUAL IMPAIRMENTS RESTORED,** MALE VIGOR AND FEMALE HEALTH AND BEAUTY PERPETUATED AND AUGMENTED, ETC.,

AS TAUGHT BY

PHRENOLOGY AND PHYSIOLOGY.

BY PROF. O. S. FOWLER,

PRACTICAL PHRENOLOGIST AND LECTURER; FOUNDER OF FOWLER AND WELLS; AUTHOR OF "HUMAN SCIENCE," "SEXUAL SCIENCE," "SELF-CULTURE," "LOVE AND PARENTAGE," "MATRIMONY," "OFFSPRING, AND THEIR HEREDITARY ENDOWMENT," "MATERNITY," "AMATIVENESS," ETC., ETC.

eugenic mating, of courtship, of love, of raising children. After 644 pages, Fowler reaches the nitty-gritty of the book—diagrams and explanations of the structure and function of the reproductive organs. One omission in his finely detailed graphics is startling: the clitoris is nowhere to be found.

Advice:

1. Be the perfect lady or gentleman. Wives should treat husbands as the fathers of their children; husbands should treat wives as the mothers of their children. Share things and ideas. Cherish each other.
2. Sleep in the same room.
3. Since a "woman lives on love," men should be affectionate.
4. When "uniting in the parental capacity" (the "Holy of Holies"), do it in a pleasant place, when feeling vigorous. The husband should fondle the woman to awaken love in her and be careful not to demand too much. The woman should participate in the "uniting" with reciprocal passion. As Fowler comments, "Not a blush of shame tinges her modest cheek as she interchanges expressions of conjugal affection with the father of her dear babe."
5. Though the man has "rights," he should not force himself on the woman. The time for mating should be chosen by the woman rather than the man.
6. When having intercourse, the couple should try to provoke in each other the qualities wanted in the offspring, for all parental "states" are "stamped" on progeny at this time.

7. If one wants lots of children, one should avoid excessive passion. Girls are conceived within two to three days after menses. (Wrong on both counts. Actually women tend to be in a "safe" period immediately following the menstrual period.)
8. Masturbation is a "secret sin" and "nauseating slime," as sinful as fornication. Those who do it look "mawkish, shamed." (They also have pimples and sunken eyes.) To stop, "Make one desperate struggle. Summon every energy! STOP SHORT!" (Wrong again, as is Fowler's belief, common then, that masturbation could lead to insanity.)
9. Sexuo-maternal and -paternal love is recommended; that is, mothers and sons as well as fathers and daughters should be "lovers" (not in the full sense, of course). Nature prevents the perversion of this love. Regarding a little girl's love for her father, Fowler says, "Burning kisses mount her warm lips, he takes her into his arms. Convulsively she clasps his willing neck. Kiss follows kiss in quick succession, loud, hearty, and free. Impurity there? Then are angels impure?" (Fowler goes overboard on this; incest is not that rare an occurrence.)

THE ANSWER (1911)

Instructor: William James Chidley (1860–1916). An Australian toyshop owner adopted the young Chidley from a foundling home. Chidley's boyhood experiences included slamming a toilet seat on his turgid penis to prevent total erection; it later turned black. As an adolescent, Chidley masturbated while being titillated by French postcards and experienced a great sense of guilt. His first real sexual experience was with a prostitute; later he lived with a woman he met in an Adelaide repertory company. When a doctor diagnosed him as tubercular and gave him two years to live, Chidley went on a regimen of fruit and nuts and abstained from sex in order to cure himself. Evidently the plan worked, for by the late 1880s he was healthy and expounding a new theory—that erection outside the vagina was unnatural. His book, *The Answer*, which details the theory, was published by Chidley himself in 1911, the year the author moved from Melbourne to Sydney. There he paraded about in a thin, neck-to-knee tunic (yes, he wore underpants) and handed out copies of his book from a carpetbag. He was arrested, fined, jailed, and committed to mental institutions several times, in spite of the fact that many sympathizers—including Havelock Ellis—felt he was unjustly persecuted. The last line of Chidley's final public message read: "Mine has been an unhappy life, but it contains a moral, namely, that all my misery comes from that 'erection' in boys and men. Farewell." He died in an insane asylum.

Overview: One day Chidley was lying naked on a bed talking to his girl friend Ada when somehow his flaccid penis "found its way into Ada's vagina." His theory is predicated on his conviction that human intercourse as commonly practiced with the erect penis entering the vagina is unnatural. For proof, he points to animals, among which intercourse "depends on the readiness of the female." Nature, he says, uses forces of gravitation, air pressure, and peristaltic action to draw the penis into the distended vagina. "It should be enough to point this out; the crowbar has no place in physiology." He claims that primitive people had a sexual season similar to that of animals.

The "perverted sex habits of males" cause unhappiness and "stress and strain" in women. Erections are an inherited weakness, and they arise from a lack of muscular tone; after all, he asks, aren't all swellings the result of a loss of tone? Intercourse by the old method causes all kinds of ills, according to Chidley. Among the 50 he mentions: insanity, misery, suicide, epilepsy, crime, opium smoking, obesity, tuberculosis, blindness, pigeon toes, loss of teeth, heart disease, diabetes, and asthma. He points to before-and-after pictures of the famous and not-so-famous, including Edward VII, to show how the accumulated "shocks" of "unnatural coition" cause eyebrows and other features to distort, heads to change shape, eyes to pull closer together. The book ends: "Paradise O Paradise."

Advice:

1. Become a vegetarian if you aren't one already.
2. Be a nudist or at least wear more sensible clothing.
3. Change your sexual habits. Make it a rule never to allow yourself (if a man) to "commence thinking of our present coition with desire. It poisons the mind and paralyzes all better motives. . . . That is the brazen serpent in this wilderness of sin and evil." Instead, enter the woman with a soft penis and be a part of this scenario: "They inhale from each other's lungs, their navels cup with electric thrills, her young vagina becomes erect and waits—like a set trap—until in that fusing embrace his unerect penis touches her clitoris, when her vagina flashes open and his penis is drawn in by pressure of air and secured by its head." It's acceptable for the penis to be erect *inside* the vagina, where a vacuum is formed as the sphincter closes, thus creating suction. *Note:* Chidley's "answer" is hardly in the mainstream of modern thought about sexuality.

IDEAL MARRIAGE: ITS PHYSIOLOGY AND TECHNIQUE (1926)

Instructor: Theodoor Hendrik van de Velde (1873–1937). Van de Velde was a solid Dutch citizen, director of the Haarlem Gynecological Clinic and author of 80 medical papers, when at 36 he left his wife and ran off with a 28-year-old married patient. For the next four years he wandered through Europe in professional and marital limbo. Then, in 1913, his wife granted him a divorce and he was free to marry his lover, who had also obtained a divorce. Information for his book came from his own love life, reports from his patients, and his personal observations of masturbating women (as a scientist, of course).

Overview: "The bridal honeymoon should blossom into the perfect flower of ideal marriage," says Van de Velde, whose sexual advice, daring in its day (as well as popular), now seems curiously old-fashioned. The Sleeping Beauty (unawakened bride) theme underlies a good part of the book, though he asserts that all women are born with the potential for complete sexual response and he urges women to give as well as take sexual pleasure. To Van de Velde, normal intercourse ("communion") is heterosexual, excludes sadomasochism and the use of artificial devices, has consummation as its goal—the ejaculation of semen into the vagina as both man and woman reach climax simultaneously or very close together. The physiology of the male and female are given in great detail, as are erogenous zones and methods of arousing one's partner. While Van de Velde is a strong believer in the "genital kiss," he refuses to use the terms "fellatio" and "cunnilingus" because he feels they have come to connote "pathological practices."

Though he correctly states that vaginal and clitoral orgasms are one and the same because of the interconnections of the nervous system, he is wrong on several other counts—including the possibility of *penis captivus* (locking of the penis in the vagina) and rupturing of the vagina through vigorous thrusting, both rare occurrences.

Advice:

1. Constantly renew your courtship.
2. During the honeymoon, a kind of apprenticeship, the man must play Don Juan to his wife, teaching her to feel "both voluptuous pleasure and actual orgasm." Beginning sex should be conventional.
3. Neglecting love play is stupid.
4. The male should practice the "genital kiss" with "the most delicate reverence."
5. While the wife can give her husband great pleasure by reciprocating with oral-genital sex, Van de Velde warns: *"Is it necessary, however, to emphasize the need for aesthetic delicacy and discretion here?"* Her instincts, however, will keep her from "approaching that treacherous frontier between supreme beauty and base ugliness."
6. If a woman has difficulty achieving orgasm, the man should bring her to climax manually. Orgasm for a woman is important.
7. The "Attitude of Equitation" (woman astride the man) may bring about passivity in the male if used too often, and that is "directly contrary to the natural relationship of the sexes."
8. In kneeling positions, air can get into the vagina and make "only too audible and extraordinarily repulsive noises."
9. During "afterglow" (postcoitus), refrain from genital stimulation.
10. Don't let a wife or husband get used to a pattern of sexual frequency and intensity that can't be maintained.
11. Though a husband should consider the wife's ebb and flow of desire, he should not have to restrict intercourse to the times when she wants it the most.

A MARRIAGE MANUAL: A PRACTICAL GUIDEBOOK TO SEX AND MARRIAGE (1935)

Instructors: Abraham Stone (1890–1959) and Hannah Stone (1894–1941). Abraham Stone was born in Russia and at age 12 was sent to live with an uncle in New York. Years later he met his wife, Hannah, at Bellevue Hospital, where he interned. When Abraham went off to war

(W.W. I), Hannah went on to get her M.D. Both were doctors when they met Margaret Sanger, birth-control pioneer, in 1921. Hannah eventually became director of the Margaret Sanger Research Bureau, a position she held until her death in 1941. Abraham subsequently took over the job. After hearing a series of lectures on marriage at New York's Labor Temple, the couple set up the first marriage counseling service in the U.S. in 1931 at the Community Church in New York City. Their book, first printed in 1935, revised in 1937, was extremely popular. Abraham, an authority on population and birth control, was vice-chairman of the International Union of Family Organizations and vice-president of the Planned Parenthood Federation of America.

Overview: When viewed in its time (pre-W.W. II), this sober-looking book in its biblical black cover seems quietly progressive and controversial. Abortion and sex outside of marriage were then illegal in the U.S., and compulsory sterilization of "defective" people was permitted or ordered in 30 states ("a dangerous social policy," said the Stones). The average sex act lasted less than five minutes, and if the country was "coming out of a puritanical age," it did a lot of looking back.

The book is written as a dialogue between a doctor and a young couple about to be married. Scattered throughout the down-to-earth practical advice and instruction are discussions of the issues of the day (reformation of the moral codes, for example), the possibility of "junior marriage" without children for the immature, and pertinent sexual facts (that a man named Columbus—not Christopher—claimed discovery of the clitoris in 1593 though anatomists had described it earlier). They mention a contraceptive recipe written on an ancient Egyptian papyrus and discuss contemporary anthropological studies by Margaret Mead; in short, the Stones place their advice in a larger framework than the one that surrounded the U.S. of the 1930s. A statement of the relative harmlessness of masturbation opens with typical astringent wit: "Although this attitude [the idea that masturbation is harmful to the mind and the body] has apparently not decreased the practice to any degree. . . ." Some theories they backed up with studies of their own; for instance, they measured the distance from vagina to clitoris (from ½ in. to 2½ in.) in a sample of women.

Forever practical, aware of the mores of the society in which they lived, the couple did not advocate practices like promiscuity which seemed to endanger the "wholesomeness and balance" of their patients. They favor marriage and children. They reject normal intercourse from the rear—as used regularly "only among certain primitive peoples"—and favor the more romantic, face-to-face positions.

Advice:

1. Combine sensuality and sentiment. Understand each other and be in harmony. Cultivate the "art of sex," which blends physical, emotional, and aesthetic factors.
2. Develop your own sexual pattern to make it "a mutual adventure, rather than be guided in every detail by the instructions of a Baedeker in the art of love."
3. Since a woman's sexuality is more diffuse and her arousal slower,

the man should gently and sensitively court her, caressing her and engaging her in love play.

4. Only in the beginning of the relationship should the woman be passive.
5. In many women, "the sexual response can only be evoked by direct stimulation of the clitoris," whereupon it is transferred to the vagina.
6. Having sex during menstruation is not a good idea. (Many would disagree.)
7. Onanism (withdrawal of the penis before ejaculation) is "physiologically and psychologically unsound."
8. The husband's capacity usually determines the frequency of intercourse in marriage. He should not strain his "capacity to the limit."
9. A woman who is indifferent to desire should not "constantly emphasize" that fact to her husband. In fact, say the Stones—but not most modern authorities—she might consider faking interest and "reaction to sexual stimulation," which in turn might "aid in gradually correcting her sexual indifference" as well as "create a greater marital harmony."
10. Ways of awakening a frigid wife include sex education, elimination of fears, birth control, medical and psychiatric help. The husband should acquire delicacy and skill in arousing her and be sensitive to what satisfies her. However, the wife should also play an active part, not lie back and wait for things to be done to her.

THE ART AND SCIENCE OF LOVE (1960)

Instructor: Albert Ellis (b. 1913). Ellis's credentials for writing a marriage manual are impeccable. He holds a Ph.D. in clinical psychology from Columbia University, directs the Institute for Rational Living, and is a fellow of the American Psychological Association. The Ellis school of psychology is highly respected, and its basic tenet—that rational ideas should be substituted for irrational ones—is the foundation for his sexual advice. *The Art and Science of Love* is only one of his many books about sexual matters. Others include *The Psychology of Sex Offenders, The Encyclopedia of Sexual Behavior,* and *The Civilized Couple's Guide to Extramarital Adventure.*

Overview: "Man or woman is far more than penis or clitoris," says Ellis, who believes that only our upbringing keeps us from experiencing the whole spectrum of sexual outlets, from daydreaming to sex with animals. Almost anything goes, and Ellis stresses only one no-no—concentration on any one method; even straight missionary-position intercourse can lead to a fetishistic pattern. "So-called" perversions, he says, are "essential for maximum arousal and satisfaction in millions of individuals in today's world."

The book is grounded in solid research, e.g., the results of studies in psychology and anthropology. Woman's orgasmic capacity is fairly recent in terms of the evolution of humans, Ellis says. When he talks of the quick arousal of men and the diffuse arousal and capacity for multiple orgasms of women, he wonders if these characteristics are innate or cultural. Some of the authorities he quotes tend to be sexist. One, O. H.

Mowrer, claims that women get frigid because they are "imbued with masculine ideals" and have "little or no conception of real womanliness."

Almost everything is included: internal and external human sex organs; ways of arousing a partner; main positions for kissing, caressing, and intercourse; sexual deviations; fertility and birth control.

Advice:

1. Masturbation can help a woman overcome frigidity.
2. If you have an extramarital affair, be loving with all involved. Be discreet but don't lie. Only if both husband and wife agree that extramarital affairs are permissible should either or both participate in them.
3. Tell your partner what your desires are: "If . . . you like your sex with the lights on, with music playing, in front of mirrors, rolling on the floor, slow or fast, orally or manually, by land or sea, for heaven's sake, *say* so. And do your best to discover, by *words* as well as deeds, what your mate likes, too."
4. Using a device like a vibrator or French tickler (fancifully shaped condoms designed to stimulate the female) is no more odd than eating with a spoon or chopsticks.
5. See your partner "as a person rather than a sex machine." Don't equate his or her worth with sexual competence.
6. Agree on a signal indicating readiness for intercourse, a tap on the head, for example.
7. Simultaneous orgasm is not necessary for a satisfactory love life.
8. Favor the partner who has greater sexual difficulty. For example, if a woman is slow to come to orgasm, use a position that also slows the man down.
9. Don't be distracted by thoughts of sexual success when making love.
10. Don't engage in sex when you don't feel like it. But when you do feel like it, don't be guided by anything except your own desires and those of your partner. Averages mean nothing. Age needn't hold you back.

THE JOY OF SEX: A CORDON BLEU GUIDE TO LOVEMAKING (1972)

Instructor: Alexander Comfort (b. 1920). A physician, poet, biochemist, and expert in the aging process among other things, Alex Comfort is and always has been a rebel—a runaway at age seven; a pacifist during W.W. II (when pacifism was a dirty word); an organizer of a ban-the-bomb demonstration in London in 1962; a member of the sexual avant-garde in the 1970s. (He was an active member of Sandstone, a Los Angeles humanistic sex club.) Yet, in his introduction to *The Joy of Sex*, he hid under the cloak of anonymity, attributing authorship of the book, which he wrote himself, to a couple who preferred to remain nameless. His reason: fear of losing his British physician's license.

Overview: It looks like a cookbook in that its main categories are titled "Starters," "Main Courses," "Sauces and Pickles," and "Problems."

Though you could make an infinite variety of sexual meals from its "recipes," it's quite likely that your pickles might be someone else's main course, and vice versa. But the menu is dazzling: horse (which Aristotle liked to play); doing it in a swing; "discipline," including spanking, beating, birching (though, depending on where you live, you may have to "vacation with a chain saw" in order to get the proper birch switches); the tongue bath; underwater sex (which uses up "vast amounts of air because of the overbreathing that goes with orgasm"); paraphernalia, including how to make a G-string; "mouth music," or genital kisses. Not much is frowned upon except the extremely bizarre, such as hard-core sadomasochism, and the undeniably criminal, like rape and child molestation. Comfort recommends sex as play and suggests that both partners read the book and exchange lists of what they would like to try.

The Joy of Sex tells you how to set up a "sexuarium," complete with ceiling mirrors and an array of tools of the trade. It also suggests what kind of bed to buy—with bedposts for bondage and with the top of the mattress level with the man's pubic bone (for certain standing positions). The style is light and humorous, studded with anecdotes like the one about the man who could achieve sexual satisfaction only by having intercourse in a bathtub full of spaghetti. Included in the book are color plates of Indian, Chinese, and Japanese erotic art, as well as explicit drawings of a modern couple making love.

Advice:

1. The two basic rules are "Don't do anything you don't really enjoy" and "Find your partner's needs and don't balk at them if you can help it."
2. Take off your shell along with your clothes.
3. Just before orgasm, try free-associating out loud about your sexual fantasies.
4. Play at psychodrama if it appeals to you, e.g., sultan and concubine; burglar and maiden; "Tonight I'm a virgin."
5. Generally, in oral and manual sex, women tend to use too little pressure to please a man, and men tend to use too much to please a woman.
6. A penis is a fascinating toy for a woman. She can roll it like pastry, among other things. A note to men: If a woman retches when performing fellatio on you, it is not because she doesn't like you, it is just the gag reflex.
7. When a man performs oral or manual sex on a woman's genitals, he should not concentrate too much on the clitoris and should remember that the best point of pressure varies during the act. In a restaurant, a man can take off a shoe and sock and titillate a woman's genitals with his big toe.
8. Decorate your lover with screw-on earrings—on the nipples, clitoris, labia. (Don't screw them on too tightly.)
9. Never blow into a vagina; it can cause an air embolism.
10. Develop your own sexual "meal" of oral and manual sex as well as coitus.

11. Use the woman-on-top position with care. If you're clumsy, you can hurt yourself or your partner.
12. Anal intercourse is illegal in England and in parts of the U.S. If you engage in it, be careful of injury and infection. Wash before switching to a genital-to-genital position.
13. Wear weird clothing if that's what turns your partner on.
14. To alleviate "hair-trigger trouble" (premature ejaculation), thrust only enough to maintain your erection, use the woman-astride position, stop every time orgasm approaches, or see an expert.
15. In the "Birth Control" section, Comfort recommends the use of the pill, which he says "is still the safest and best method [of contraception], and a safer drug than aspirin." Most physicians today, however, recommend the pill with caution because of possible dangerous side effects.

THE TAO OF LOVE AND SEX: THE ANCIENT CHINESE WAY TO ECSTASY (1977)

Instructor: Jolan Chang (or Chang Chung-Lan) (b. 1916). Born in Hangchow, a beautiful seaside city in China, Jolan Chang became interested in women at the age of seven. At 16 he first read of the ancient Tao of loving, which holds as a basic tenet the control of male emissions, but when he began to have sexual relationships with women two years later, he relied on advice in a translation of Van de Velde's *Ideal Marriage* because he wanted to ejaculate every time he made love. For two summer months during W.W. II, he lived with a woman in the ancient walled city of Tsunyi, where Mao had his headquarters during the Long March. Jolan made love to the woman three times a day, ejaculating each time, but she wanted more. Later, at age 30, he began to follow the Tao. Now past 60, he makes love several times a day and claims, "Often on a Sunday, I make love two or three times in the morning, and then go cycling for nearly the whole day, about 20 or 30 mi., and then make love again before going to sleep." He currently lives in Stockholm.

Overview: Jolan's sources for this book are both ancient Chinese and modern international authorities. During the 13th and 14th centuries, Mongols overran China and in 88 years of repression destroyed almost all erotic texts. They did not destroy the *Tao Tê Ching*, however, which fortunately incorporated many earlier works. *The Secrets of the Jade Chamber*, probably written during the Han dynasty (206 B.C. to 219 A.D.), is one of these; it consists of sexual advice given to the probably legendary Emperor Huang Ti by his four advisers (three female and one male). Another of Chang's sources is *Priceless Recipe* by Sun S'sû-Mo, a 7th-century physician who initiated smallpox inoculations. Their advice is compared and incorporated with that of modern sexologists like Alfred Kinsey and Masters and Johnson. What seem to be new discoveries, it turns out, are often rooted in ancient techniques. For example, the squeeze technique to prevent premature ejaculation recommended by the ancient Chinese masters is quite similar to the Masters and Johnson squeeze technique.

The Taoists tied longevity and good health to their lovemaking practices, which were based on the conservation of the male emission, the satisfaction (even satiation) of women, and the harmony of Yin (female essence) and Yang (male essence). Through this process, couples can make love virtually whenever they want to without worry about birth control.

Advice:

1. Determine your optimum frequency for ejaculation. The ancient Chinese were numerical about it; they said a man of 20 should ejaculate once every 4 days, a man of 50 once every 20 days, and so on. Chang recommends keeping track of your reaction to ejaculation. If you are elated and feeling stronger after ejaculating, then you are on the right track.
2. To achieve the ability to refrain from ejaculating, follow a series of steps, according to the ancient Chinese:
   - Don't allow yourself to become too excited. If you start to become overly aroused, stop with your Jade Peak (penis) only 1 in. inside the Jade Gate (vagina) and wait until you are calm.
   - Follow a thrusting pattern of three shallow and one deep at first, then progress to five shallow and one deep, and finally to nine shallow and one deep.

   Chang adds:
   - Spend time with the woman, thinking of her as a person.
   - Avoid fellatio, as it might bring on ejaculation. (Cunnilingus is recommended, both by Chang and the Tao masters, because through it the man obtains precious Yin essence from the woman.)
   - Make love ecstatically and poetically, using all your senses.
3. The ancient Chinese squeeze technique to prevent ejaculation is performed by the man, who puts the fore and middle fingers of his left hand at a point between the scrotum and anus and presses for three or four seconds, while taking a deep breath.
4. Satisfy your partner with the "thousand loving thrusts" which, Chang says, can be accomplished in 1,800 seconds at a slow rhythm.
5. Find the best position for you and your partner as an individual couple.
6. Vary the style and depth of your thrusts; for example, moving up and down "as a wild horse bucking through a stream," pulling in and out "as a group of sea gulls playing on the waves," plunging "low like a huge sailing boat braving the gale."
7. Even though the *Tao* is addressed to men, it stresses the fact that women's sexual needs should be fulfilled. Men are advised to watch for certain female responses, including the following:

   —"If she desires him to enter, her nostrils will be extended and her mouth open."

   —"She raises her legs. It indicates that she wishes closer friction of her clitoris."

   —"She extends her abdomen. It indicates that she wishes shallower thrusts."

   —"She uses her feet like hooks to pull the man. It indicates that she wishes deeper thrusts."

—"Her thighs are moving. It indicates that she is greatly pleased."

SEXUAL SECRETS: THE ALCHEMY OF ECSTASY (1979)

Instructors: Nik Douglas (b. 1944) and Penny Slinger (b. 1947). To discover the inner secrets of Eastern thought about sex and philosophy, Nik Douglas learned Sanskrit and Tibetan and studied in the Himalayas for eight years with Indian physicians adept in the Tantras and with Tibetan lamas.

Penny Slinger, an artist of the erotic, worked from life studies and centuries-old sources to illustrate the book.

Overview: The main theme of *Sexual Secrets* is that "physical love can become the pathway to liberation." Based on 2,000 years of Oriental texts, the book presents the sexual practices of China, Japan, Nepal, Tibet, and India, which are often quite different from one another physically as well as spiritually. A guide to sex and mysticism, *Sexual Secrets* concentrates on the transcendental aspects of the human being as well as the technicalities of intercourse.

The book is divided into "Brahma the Creative," which discusses the "egg" of positive energy, yoga, and other traditional creative arts; "Shiva the Transcendental," a "heart talk" between a man and woman, who become exalted to god and goddess as they make love and discuss archetypical meanings, mystic forms, sexual fantasy and practices, fasting, and other things; and "Vishnu the Preserver," which contains a repertory of ways to make love, including homosexuality and group sex.

Much of the book is complex and detailed. Charts like "Fourfold Evolution of Ecstasy according to the Tantric Tradition" need study before they are useful to the uninitiated. If one wishes to follow Oriental practices for specific days during cycles of erotic passion—aligning the bed and pillows accordingly, using certain positions, making the proper sounds—one must master a wealth of details.

Positions are suggested for reasons other than the purely physical. For example, Tortoise Position—in which the woman sits on the man's lap with her mouth, arms, and legs touching his—circulates and exchanges energy, in addition to holding "the secret of longevity."

Advice:

1. The *Great Moon Elixir* recommends that the man meditate on the yoni (vulva) as he enters it, thinking to himself, "Just as I am now entering this Yoni, so, too, have I emerged numerous times. The Tantric Path which I am following is straight as an arrow, but if I travel along it without knowledge, it becomes the path to countless rebirths. When I enter it with knowledge, it becomes the success of the *Chandamaharosana*, the Great Moon Elixir."
2. Endow the yoni and lingam (penis) with your own personalities and communicate with them affectionately and firmly.
3. According to the Tantric view, every ejaculation should be a conscious act.
4. According to Master Tung, "Sex should be leisurely; smoothly inserting and languorously moving, rarely fast and vigorous."

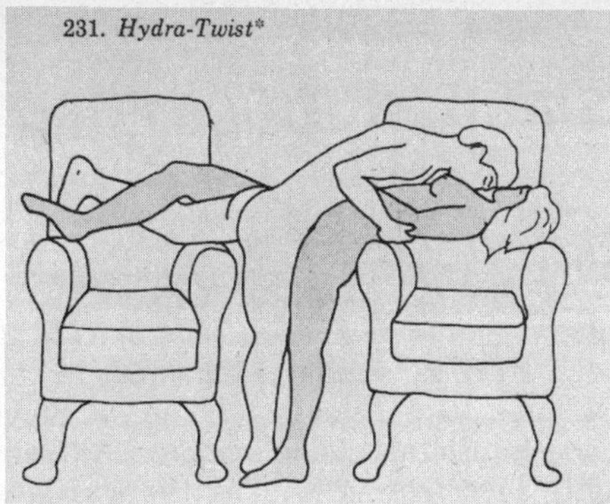
231. *Hydra-Twist**

5. While male homosexuality is frowned upon, female homosexuality is considered acceptable.
6. Anal sex is not a good practice.
7. The woman can learn to contract her urethral sphincter muscles and visualize energy flowing up, then swallow saliva, to achieve the "Diamond Seal," which reserves the energy flow.
8. "In the Temple of Love, there is no *before* or *after*, only the Eternal Now."
9. In the Union of Three (group sex), the third person invited should be "honored equally." This practice should not be engaged in carelessly.
10. "Try to develop a dynamic sense of expectancy, as well as an openness and awareness of both your own and your partner's sexuality."
11. The wisdom of the heart is accessible to those who can "recognize the interrelationship between sexuality and spirituality."
12. When masturbating, "offer the Bliss-waves of orgasm to feed the gods and goddesses within the body. . . . Let the sex energy ascend to the sublime."

A Special Note: 600 Positions

Perhaps the most complete source for positions in sexual intercourse is *The Golden Book of Love* (originally titled *Kinesthesia of Love*), a "recipe book" of 600 ways to do it. The author, Joseph Weckerle, was a founder of the "natural life" cult that flourished in Europe in the early 1900s in rebellion against the puritanical attitudes of the Victorian Age. Though its stance toward sex was hedonistic, the cult sanctioned physical fitness, recommending naked hikes (wearing only a rucksack) and plunges into icy pools. Weckerle was a professor of physical education, a specialist in gymnastics, and many of the positions he describes are only for the athletic (he kindly marks those with a star); some are even planned for the horizontal bars. He is eclectic in his choices of location—horse-drawn hacks, trains, water, pieces of furniture. Each position is fancifully named (for the woman-on-top position, "revenge" or "Ariadne," for example), explained in a concise paragraph or two, and illustrated with a line drawing.

—A.E.

ROOTS AND FRUITS: A FOREST OF FAMILY TREES

NAPOLEON BONAPARTE (1769–1821), French emperor

A natural military genius, Napoleon rose quickly up through the ranks of the French army to become commander in chief in Italy and Egypt. As the result of a coup d'etat in 1799 he was named first consul, and in 1804 he had himself crowned emperor. Although he achieved spectacular military successes as emperor, he was forced to abdicate after his army suffered severe casualties in Russia in 1812, followed by a decisive defeat at Leipzig in 1813. He was removed to Elba in 1814, but he returned to France the following year and attempted to reinstate his empire. After his final defeat at Waterloo in June, 1815, he was exiled to St. Helena, where he died six years later.

His Roots: The mountainous Mediterranean island of Corsica was appropriate ground to nourish the roots of Napoleon Bonaparte, for it had seen centuries of political conflict, having been occupied successively by Romans, Vandals, Byzantines, Lombards, Arabs, Pisans, Genoese, French, and then Genoese and French again by the time of Napoleon's birth in 1769.

Appropriately, too, Napoleon's parents (as he himself said later) saw themselves as the Bourbons of the island, the natural royalty. The Buonaparte family was of ancient Tuscan nobility, having emmigrated to the island in the 16th century. Carlo Maria was a most promising progeny. He was handsome and charming, and before he went to Pisa to study law at age 16, he made his intentions known to Letizia Ramolino, a black-eyed, chestnut-haired beauty, then age 12. Although less aristocratic, the Ramolinos were an even older Corsican family, and Letizia's mother's clan, the Pietra-Santas, were older yet. Families in Corsica were insular and proud. It was merely a matter of course that 14-year-old Letizia was escorted to the Ajaccio Cathedral by more than 50 male cousins on her wedding day, June 2, 1764.

During the 20 years that Carlo and Letizia were married, she bore him 12 children, 8 of whom survived infancy. The beginning of their married life was an exciting period spent at the political capital of Corte, where Carlo's oratorical abilities had placed him second in command to the revolutionary leader Pasquale di Paoli. Genoa had ceded Corsica to France, but when Louis XV sent troops to ensure the purchase, Paoli and his followers resisted. Six months pregnant, Letizia spent the month of May, 1769, crossing and recrossing the Corsican mountains on horseback and hiding out with Carlo and other partisans in the caves. But the French were too strong. The resisters made an honorable peace, and Carlo and Letizia returned to Ajaccio in time for the birth, on the Feast of the Assumption, of their second son, whom they named for Letizia's uncle and fellow partisan, Napoleone.

Letizia Ramolino Bonaparte, mother of Napoleon.

The young revolutionary settled down to practicing law. He became assessor of Ajaccio's Court of Justice, served on the Council of Twelve Nobles, and was selected deputy to represent the Corsican interests at Versailles. He was always charming, if a bit spoiled. His increased importance called, in his opinion, for an expanded wardrobe of embroidered waistcoats and silk stockings that he could not afford, and for enlarging both his house and his library, which, at over 1,000 volumes, was already impressive by Corsican standards. Around Ajaccio he was known as "Buonaparte the Magnificent." He was determined that his children be well educated; otherwise he left their upbringing to their mother. It was Letizia who cared for them, put them on horseback almost before they could walk, insisted that they clean their teeth and bathe daily when to do so regularly was virtually unknown, nursed them when they were ill, disciplined them, and still found time to entertain them with tales from Corsican history with particular emphasis on the part that she and their father had personally experienced.

One by one the older children went off to the Continent to school. Then at age 38, with Letizia carrying their 12th child, Carlo developed stomach cancer and died. Letizia, only 34, was no less beautiful for all the childbearing; she received several proposals but never married again. Her biographers describe her as a one-man woman, but she may just have been tired of always being pregnant. Her *famiglia* was everything to her, and that was large enough already. She early realized that

Napoleon was the son on whom she could depend, and in 1793 she moved the whole family to France to be nearer to him.

Letizia, of course, participated in her son's good fortune. She had her own house in Paris, the Hôtel de Brienne in the Rue St. Dominique, and an allowance of a million francs a year. Later Napoleon also bought her the 17th-century castle of Pont on the Seine outside Paris. She had her own coat of arms and crown and her own ladies-in-waiting, chamberlain, master of horse, equerry, and chaplain. Her full title was *Son Altesse Impériale, Madame la Mère de l'Empereur,* but she was popularly known as "Madame Mère." In spite of such apparent grandeur, she led a quiet life of reading, walks, needlework, cards, and of course chapel. A good part of her allowance she secretly stashed away against the rainy day that, with her typically Corsican sense of the turn of fortune's wheel, she was sure would come.

Madame Mere's fate was predictably affected when Napoleon was exiled to St. Helena. She could not stay in France now that the Bourbons were again in power, and her son would not allow her to accompany him to St. Helena. She was exiled to Rome, where she lived out the rest of her long life hoping for a reversal in the fortunes of her family. Several of her children—including, of course, Napoleon—died before her, to her great grief. Her youngest son, Jérôme, described her in her last years as "thin, with black eyes full of fire, the pure type of Corsican still found in the mountains of the island in families who have never intermarried with other races. She always wore a severe black merino dress and an Empire-style turban. . . . Everything in her palace revealed that one was in the presence of great sorrow, of august memories slowly being transformed into mute and proud resignation."

His Fruits: Napoleon's fruits were less numerous than his parents' had been, and less happy. When he married the beautiful Creole widow Joséphine de Beauharnais, he adopted her two children, Eugène and Hortense. He was extremely fond of them both. When he was creating satellite kingdoms for his brothers and sisters, he made Eugène Duke of Leuchtenberg, a role he performed well, and elevated Hortense to Queen of Holland after marrying her to his brother Louis. Napoleon had been passionately in love with Joséphine, at least at the beginning, but passion does not insure procreation, and since he had proof of his wife's fertility there under his roof, he assumed the incapacity to be his own. He was therefore delighted to receive word that his sister Caroline's young lady-in-waiting, with whom he had carried on an intimate, if short-lived relationship during the late winter and early spring of 1806, had the following December produced a son. He was called Léon, and Napoleon chose as his surname Macon after his friend Gen. Pierre Macon, who had died at Leipzig two months before and was therefore not available to deny parentage.

Napoleon acknowledged Léon as his son, even though he was not all that sure of the monogamous habits of the boy's mother. Léon led an unhappy childhood, separated from his mother and shifted from one nurse to another and then from one boarding school to the next. A settlement was fixed on him and he was liberally supplied with cash during his childhood, but much of that ended with his father's exile. Comte Léon, as he was then known, was extravagant, and by the time he was 30 he was in and out of debtors' prison and the courts, pressing claims for funds. In court his physical resemblance to his father always drew great crowds. He eventually married Françoise "Fanny" Junot, with whom he already had three sons and would soon have a daughter. He continued to live well beyond the pension supplied him by Emperor Louis Napoleon, whom he followed into exile in England. There the family lived on the sale of various family relics to Madame Tussaud's Wax Museum before returning to France, where at the age of 74 he, too, died of stomach cancer.

Napoleon's second son was the result of his love affair with a Polish countess, Marie Walewska, the beautiful young wife of an aged nobleman, who was persuaded to become the emperor's mistress after promises to restore the Polish state. The promises were never kept, but she came to love him anyway, and he was very fond of her, calling her his "Polish wife." He was delighted at news of her pregnancy. It offered even more convincing proof of his own fertility and provided the prime instigation for his divorce from Josephine.

Alexandre Florian Joseph Colonna Walewski was born on May 4, 1810, at Walewice Castle, Poland. He was publicly recognized as Napoleon's son and given a title and handsome settlement. He was also protected by the old nobleman, and he lived a happy childhood in Poland with visits to Paris. Shortly after his fifth birthday he was taken, along with his half brother Léon, to Malmaison to say good-bye to their father for the last time. Comte Alexandre lived mostly in Poland, but when Napoleon III came to power he returned to France and became minister for foreign affairs. He married a beautiful Florentine, Marie-Anne, who claimed descent from Machiavelli. When Napoleon's will drawn at St. Helena was finally executed in 1857, he was the prime beneficiary. He lived, like his half brother Léon, extravagantly. He died in 1868.

Napoleon's only other offspring was the son of plump Marie-Louise of Austria, whom he married in April, 1810, after having repudiated Josephine. The boy's birth was as eagerly anticipated as that of Henry VIII's son, Edward. A layette that included 42 dozen diapers, 26 dozen nightgowns, and 12 dozen nightcaps trimmed with Brussels lace had been prepared; his governess had been selected; and two deputy governesses, three children's nurses, three cradle rockers, two mistresses of the wardrobe, and two maids were held in readiness. The 101-gun salute—it would have been only 21 guns if it had been a girl—began to thunder on Mar. 20, 1811, to the wild excitement of the Parisian populace. Napoleon François Charles Joseph, titular king of Rome, was born.

Because this son was his legitimate heir, Napoleon adored this child above all else. But three years after his birth the empire to which he was heir collapsed, and after Napoleon's abdication his mother took him with her back to Austria where his grandfather, Francis I, took sole charge of the boy. His title King of Rome was replaced by that of Duke of Reichstadt. His tutors received instructions that he was to forget his father, but he knew who he was, and he is said to have wept bitterly at news of Napoleon's death. Napoleon, for his part, had written from St. Helena: "I should wish my son never to forget that he was born a French prince, and never to allow himself to become an instrument in the hands of the triumvirs who are oppressing the peoples of Europe." The boy never had much chance. He became a captain in a Tyrolean regiment, then a colonel, but his health was not good. The Bonapartists continued to place their distant hopes in him, but to no avail. "I die prematurely," Napoleon had written on his deathbed, but in truth it was his son who did so, at age 21 of tuberculosis.

—N.C.S.

ALPHONSE "SCARFACE" CAPONE (1899–1947), U.S. gangster

The most famous U.S. gangster of the 20th century, Capone became head of the Chicago crime syndicate in 1925. Two years later, the 28-year-old gangster was grossing $105 million a year from his operations. He continued to dominate organized crime until 1931, when he was imprisoned for income tax evasion.

His Roots: The land of promise and golden opportunity lured Gabriel Capone (1868–1920)—born Caponi—from his native Italy. Unfortunately, the reality of Brooklyn's Navy Yard district differed drastically from his fantasies. The poor, illiterate immigrant failed miserably in his attempts to adapt to his new country. Working first as a grocer and then as a barber, Al Capone's father could barely pay the monthly rent, averaging between $3 and $4.50 per room in turn-of-the-century New York. Consequently, Teresa (1867–1952), his dour, horse-faced wife, added to the family coffers by working as a dressmaker. Their progeny—seven boys, two girls—were born at the rate of one every three years. Though the father of our country's most famous gangster could not read, write, or speak English, he was able to claim U.S. citizenship in 1906—a month before the laws required these skills.

At the age of 52, in poor health due to the day labor he had been reduced to performing, Gabriel Capone collapsed in a poolroom at 20 Garfield Place, where Al had played profitably in his early days. His heart simply gave out while he was watching the game, and he was dead before the doctor could arrive. Although Gabriel was originally buried in Brooklyn, Al later had his father's remains exhumed and reburied ceremoniously in the family plot he purchased at Mt. Olivet Cemetery in Chicago. And being a loving son, he moved Teresa west to the two-story house he built on Prairie Avenue on Chicago's South Side. From Chicago, Teresa took great pleasure in nostalgic journeys back to her old neighborhood, and Al's cronies always provided her with a bodyguard and a chauffeur-driven Cadillac.

When the tables were turned and Al was in prison, Mama Teresa took care of her boy, cooking his favorite foods and visiting him regularly. Little conversation took place between the pair, though, because she spoke only a few words of English, and foreign languages were strictly forbidden in the prison's visiting area. When Al was transferred to Alcatraz, Teresa baffled prison guards by setting off the alarm during electronic security checks. The cause was eventually found to be the metal straps of her old-fashioned corset! Teresa died at 85, outliving the son who had become Public Enemy No. 1. But until the end she maintained: "Al's a good boy."

More than one gangster emerged from Gabriel and Teresa's nest. Ralph (1893–1974) was so successful at convincing saloonkeepers to use the family's bootlegged whiskey that he was dubbed Bottles. Three other brothers, Frank, John, and Matt, were also involved in this family enterprise.

But there was a white sheep in this dark brood, James (1877–1952), who called himself Richard "Two Gun" Hart and was actually a law-enforcement officer. A teenage runaway, he traveled as a circus roustabout and finally settled down in Homer, Neb. (population 477) in 1919. There he became a government agent for Indian affairs and married a local girl named Kathleen Winch. They had four sons.

Hart's reputation as a man who could not be bribed grew steadily, and he was appointed commander of Homer's American Legion Post as well. A small, rounded man, he presented quite a sight with guns strapped to both hips. But in fact he was a crack shot from either side, which was what earned him his unusual middle name.

Two-Gun Hart served as town marshal, then state sheriff before trouble arose when he was arrested for murdering an Indian in a barroom brawl in Sioux City, Ia., while serving as a special officer for Indian Services. Though he was cleared of the crime, he lost an eye when the dead man's family attempted to even the score. Back in Homer, he was reappointed town marshal and given keys to the town's main-street shops in case he needed to search them during night patrols. This proved the beginning of the end for Hart, who was unable to resist the temptation the opportunity presented. Even his father-in-law's store turned up missing goods, and Richard Hart was relieved of his badge. Next the local Legionnaires asked him for proof of his war record. When he could produce none, he lost his post command. Broke and nearly blind, he asked for and received help from his famous brother Al. Not even Hart's wife of 21 years had been aware of the familial relationship.

His Fruits: The union of Al and Mae Coughlin Capone produced but one offspring, Albert Francis (b. 1919). Nicknamed Sonny, the boy literally had a godfather type for a godfather. Johnny Torrio, Al's early business associate, sent Sonny a $5,000 bond every year for his birthday. Years later, when Torrio formed a partnership with Dutch Schultz, Al instructed his wife from his penitentiary cell to tear up the bonds—by then worth $80,000.

At the age of seven Sonny developed a serious mastoid infection. A high risk factor was attached to the necessary surgery. "I'll give you a hundred thousand dollars if you pull him through," Capone told his doctors, and the boy survived.

Sonny was a shy, introverted child, left partially deaf by his illness. He was quite a contrast to his flamboyant dad. On the boy's 10th birthday, the Capones threw a party for him, inviting 50 of his Catholic school friends. Al, not wanting to offend the already watchful authorities, stipulated that the children must bring signed parental permission slips. Though it may certainly have been curiosity about their infamous neighbor that motivated them, few refused the invitation to this or other Capone gatherings.

Al Capone served only two prison sentences during the course of his illustrious career. During the first, a one-year term for carrying a weapon, Sonny was told that his father was abroad, but throughout the 7½ years Al served for income tax evasion, he was visited regularly by his son in federal prisons at Atlanta and Alcatraz.

Sonny married Diana Ruth Casey, his high school sweetheart, in 1941; they had four children, all girls. He held a variety of jobs, from florist to tire salesman. Both he and Diana were members of the National Pistol Association of America, and she was often a better marksman than her husband.

Basically, Sonny led a straight and lawful life with one noted exception. While shopping in a local supermarket, he had an irresistible urge to steal some transistor radio batteries and two bottles of aspirin, totaling $3.50. "Everybody has a little larceny in him, I guess," said Sonny to the judge, who gave him two years' probation based on his exemplary past.

The following year, 1966, Albert Francis Capone changed his name to Albert Francis.

—S.M.

DOUGLAS FAIRBANKS, SR. (1883–1939), U.S. actor

Fairbanks began his acting career on the stage, but his great athletic ability, immense charm, and suave good looks soon made him the "King of Hollywood." He is known especially for his swashbuckling roles in such films as *The Mark of Zorro, Robin Hood,* and *The Three Musketeers.* Along with Charlie Chaplin, D. W. Griffith, and Mary Pickford, Fairbanks founded the United Artists Corporation in 1919. He was married to Pickford, "America's Sweetheart," from 1920 to 1935.

His Roots: The father of Douglas Fairbanks (born Douglas Elton Ulman) was Hezekiah Charles Douglas Ulman (1833–1915), who was born in Berrysburg, Pa., the fourth child in a relatively well-to-do Jewish family of six sons and four daughters. When he was 17, Charles started a small publishing business in Philadelphia. Two years later he left for New York to study law. He was admitted to the Pennsylvania bar in 1856 and began building a substantial practice. At the onset of the Civil War, Charles joined the Union forces. He engaged in several battles, was wounded, and later became a captain of the reserves. Charles left the service in 1864 and returned to his law practice. Subsequently he founded the U.S. Law Association, a forerunner of the American Bar Association.

Charles met Ella Adelaide Marsh (1847–1915) after she married his friend and client John Fairbanks, a wealthy New Orleans sugar mill and plantation owner. The Fairbankses had a son, John, and shortly thereafter John Senior died of tuberculosis. Ella, born into a wealthy southern

Catholic family, was overprotected and knew little of her husband's business. Consequently, she was swindled out of her fortune by her husband's partners. Even the efforts of Charles Ulman, acting on her behalf, failed to regain any of the family fortune for her. Distraught and lonely, she met and married a courtly Georgian, Edward Wilcox, who turned out to be an alcoholic. After they had a son, Norris, she divorced Wilcox, and Charles acted as her lawyer in the suit. The pretty southern belle soon became romantically involved with Charles and agreed to move to Denver with him to pursue mining investments. They arrived in Denver in 1881 with her son, John. (Norris was left in Georgia with relatives and was never sent for by his mother.) They were married and had a child, Robert, in 1882, and then a second son, Douglas, a year later.

Charles's mining investments went sour, and at the age of 55 he became a campaign speaker for Benjamin Harrison during his presidential bid of 1888. He left for New York and never returned to the family. Several years later Ella divorced him on grounds of desertion and took the name Fairbanks again.

When Douglas was 12, he ran into his father on the streets of Denver. They visited in a bar where Charles had several drinks, and then Douglas talked his father into coming home to see his ex-wife. After Charles left the house, Ella, enraged at her ex-husband's drunken condition, took Douglas downtown and had him sign the W.C.T.U.'s Temperance Pledge, which he kept until the last years of his life. [In *The Book of Lists #1*, we ran Upton Sinclair's list of 15 famous heavy drinkers, which included Douglas Fairbanks. Sinclair, however, was apparently mistaken, for a letter of protest from Douglas Fairbanks, Jr., told us quite the opposite. We have confirmed that the senior Fairbanks was a teetotaler and that he was very dry, indeed.]

Charles was a Shakespearean scholar and had a great love of the theater. He was a friend of Edwin Booth, to whom he bore an uncanny resemblance, and he would often recite long passages from Shakespeare for the benefit of his son Douglas. When he realized that Douglas had inherited some of his own love of the theater, as well as his theatrical temperament, Charles enrolled his son in a local drama school, and there Douglas soon made his stage debut in a production of *Living Pictures*. From his father Douglas also inherited his wanderlust. His mother, who further nurtured Douglas's interest in the theater, was described as selfish, overprotective, and indulgent of her son.

Charles Ulman died the same year Douglas went to Hollywood to make his first film, and his mother died a year later of pneumonia.

His Fruits: Although Douglas Fairbanks, Sr., was married three times, he had but one offspring, by his first wife, Anna Beth Sully. Douglas Fairbanks, Jr., born Dec. 9, 1909, in New York City, was a fat, unathletic child and a disappointment to his father. Moreover, the self-involved Fairbanks Senior was not a particularly good father and paid little attention to his son. "It's just that I was never cut out to be a father," he admitted. "It isn't that I don't like Junior, but I can't feel about him the way I should." Occasionally, though, his fatherly instincts did become aroused, such as the time when Douglas Junior was bitten on the shin by a dog. Fairbanks practically killed the animal. On another occasion, young Fairbanks fell and split open his knee. A bottle of iodine was poured into the gash, and he recalled his father's admiration for his stoic refusal to show any reaction to the pain. "It was one of the proudest moments of my youth," Fairbanks recalled, "as this behavior was remarked on by my father for some weeks afterward." Eventually he grew to be taller and more handsome than his father, though he was never quite as athletic.

Fairbanks's parents were divorced when he was nine, and in order to save money—the generous marital settlement of $500,000 was soon lost through poor investments—mother and son moved to Paris. When Doug was 13, he was approached by the producer Jesse Lasky and talked into making a film. When Fairbanks Senior heard of it, he was livid, perhaps partially due to the fact that he was not anxious to have it known that he had a child in his teens, but also because he felt that his son had been asked to appear in the film simply to trade on the Fairbanks name (true, no doubt). But young Fairbanks persisted, and *Stephen Steps Out* was released in 1923. It was a horrible flop. Nevertheless, because he and his mother needed the money, Fairbanks continued to make films and improve as an actor. In 1927 he appeared in Los Angeles in the play *Young Woodley*, and his father was forced to admit, "He's good; he really *can* act." He subsequently appeared in such film hits as *Gunga Din*, *Little Caesar*, *Sinbad the Sailor*, *The Corsican Brothers*, and *The Prisoner of Zenda*, but he cared little for acting. "I began to be embarrassed that the interpretation was really someone else's creation . . . realizing my own limitations, I became aware that I could never be a creative actor. I would only be an interpretative one or an imitator."

At 19, much to his father's chagrin, Fairbanks married Joan Crawford, who at the time was a struggling, relatively unknown actress. The marriage ended four years later. In 1939 he married Mary Lee Epling.

For most of his childhood Fairbanks was estranged from his aloof father, but as time passed they reconciled and became good friends. His father still had an aversion to being called Dad so his son called him Pete, and he called Douglas "Jayar" (i.e., Jr.). Fairbanks Senior, at the time of his death, was planning to star his son in *The Californian*, a film he was preparing to produce.

The younger Fairbanks was an avowed Anglophile who lobbied tirelessly for British-American cooperation during W.W. II. When the U.S. entered the war, he enlisted in the navy and soon earned the Silver Star, the British Distinguished Service Cross, and the French Legion of Honor. After the war he continued his interest in politics by working for the Marshall Plan, CARE, and the U.N., in addition to starring in several more films and becoming a television and film producer. He was one of the few Americans knighted by the British for his long-standing efforts to promote Anglo-American understanding. By his second wife, Mary Lee Epling, he has three daughters, all of whom are married.

—C.H.S.

HOUSEHOLD HINTS—ROOM BY ROOM

Bathroom

- Wet hands often drop bathroom bottles. "Slipproof" your bottles by wrapping a thin piece of adhesive tape around them.
- Extra shower hooks, placed on the rod inside your shower curtain, are wonderful space savers. The hooks can be used for hanging your shower brush, other toiletries, and hand-washables that can conveniently drip dry.
- Water displacement is the simplest method of saving water in flush toilets. Fill two plastic bottles with pebbles and put them at opposite ends of the toilet tank.
- Make use of leftover soap scraps. Here are three suggestions.
  1. Break soap into very small pieces, place in a blender, add water, and use the "grate" setting to make liquid detergent (ideal for washing nylons or other delicate items).
  2. Make a pocket in a large cellulose sponge by cutting a slot in the longest edge. Insert soap scraps to make an inexpensive sudsy sponge for your bath or shower.
  3. Put soap pieces in an old pan, add water, and slowly melt together on the stove. When you have a firm jelly mixture, pour it into cupcake tins and let it harden into new cakes of soap.

Bedroom

- Forget which garments in your closet need to be mended? Tie ribbons around the hooks of five or six hangers. The next time you are undressing and notice a missing button or ripped seam, put the damaged garment on one of the designated hangers.
- To vacuum beneath dressers that are too heavy to move, simply remove the bottom drawer. The nozzle on your vacuum attachment will easily fit into the empty space you have created.
- Many people stack shoe boxes on top of each other in the closet but hate to get shoes from any of the bottom boxes. Avoid the problem by cutting out one end—not a side—of each box, then restack them. You can see what is in each box and can pull out and replace shoes without toppling the stack of boxes.

Laundry Room

- A scorch mark on a white garment can be removed by placing a cloth moistened with hydrogen peroxide on top of the discoloration and then ironing over the cloth. Remember, this works only for white garments.
- Clothes will wrinkle if they are not immediately removed from the dryer. If this happens, wet a towel, wring it out, and toss it into the dryer

with the clothes. Tumble-dry the load for about 4 min. to get rid of the wrinkles.

• Turn the ironing board around when working on large pieces like curtains or tablecloths. The iron will rest at the pointed end, and the board's larger, wider end will provide more ironing surface for the items.

• Run out of distilled water for your steam iron? One tablespoon of ammonia added to one cup of tap water will result in a fluid that won't clog up the iron.

• Sandpaper, placed under the pleats of a pleated skirt, will hold the pleats in place as you iron the skirt.

Living Room and Dining Room

• To fix a cigarette burn in a wall-to-wall carpet, first cut out damaged fibers with a small pair of scissors. Then cut replacement fibers from a scrap of leftover carpet. Put a little glue into the hole, then press in the new fibers and let dry thoroughly.

• Moving heavy furniture over hardwood floors can be a disastrous experience. To prevent damaging the floor, put crushed plastic milk cartons under furniture legs. The waxed cartons will allow you to slide the furniture across the floor. No scratches—and no injured backs.

• Save money with this homemade furniture wax: Mix one tablespoon of lemon oil (available at drugstores) with one quart of mineral oil (available at hardware stores). Use in a spray bottle if you wish.

• To remove indentation marks left by furniture on rugs, hold a steam iron about 1 or 2 in. over the spot—not *on* the spot. Then brush up the nap.

Kitchen

• If sticky dried fruit—like raisins or dates—clumps together, put it in a warm oven for several minutes. The heat will separate the fruit. Or steam the fruit briefly over boiling water.

• Test the flavor of a new spice by blending a small amount of the spice with two tablespoons of butter or cream cheese. Let the flavor develop for an hour or so, then spread the mixture on a cracker and taste the results.

• To prevent a berry pie from bubbling over: Cut several straws into 2-in. pieces and insert one piece into each slit in the pie's upper crust. The juice will bubble up, not over.

• If you have a lot of similar-sized containers, matching the containers with their correct lids will not be a problem if you "code" them. Use indelible marking pens to put a line of matching color on each top and bottom. Or stick with one color and code with designs (stars, diamonds, or squares), numbers, or letters.

• A method to determine the freshness of an egg: Put the egg on its side in a pan of cold water. A very fresh egg will remain on its side at the bottom of the water. A very old egg will float to the top. Don't use it. If the egg is only a few days old, it will stay underwater but tilt slightly upward. If it is about 1½ weeks old, it will also stay underwater but will tilt to an upright position.

• Garlic skins will come off more easily if the cloves are first held under hot water.

• A mechanic's oilcan (small size) is great for cooking with small portions of oil: no spills. You can buy one at most auto supply stores.

• Bake a two-flavored fruit pie by building a dough wall through the center of your pie crust. Fill each side with a different filling. Just be sure the baking times of the different fillings are the same.

• Rub a piece of lime over a cutting board to kill garlic and onion odors.

• For no-tear onion cutting, put a small square of bread on the tip of your knife. It will absorb the onion fumes.

• To keep eggshells from cracking when eggs are boiling, add a few drops of vinegar to the water.

• To clean a copper-bottomed pan, make a paste of salt, flour, and vinegar. Smear it on, let set for an hour, then wash off.

• Believe it or not, there is a proper way to "cook" water for use in a beverage. Put water into an already warm kettle, then boil it quickly. Remove it immediately for use in tea, coffee, or other drink. If you let boiling water simmer and steam too long, much of the good water will evaporate, leaving behind water with a high percentage of lime, iron, and other "dregs."

• To crack nuts for baking, put them inside a plastic bag and place the bag on a cutting board or other durable surface. Hold the end of the bag closed and crack the nuts with a hammer. Put contents into a bowl and separate the nuts from the shells.

• A good solution to clean crystal glasses and rid them of spots or streaks: one part vinegar to three parts water. Then let them air dry on a clean cloth. The mixture is good for all crystal, but if an item (like a chandelier) is very dirty, it will need several "baths" to get clean.

• To keep pasta from sticking together—or to the pot—while cooking, pour a small amount of cooking oil into the boiling water.

• Hate to reach down into the garbage disposal to retrieve an object? Instead, put floral clay (which you can buy at any florist shop) on the end of a ruler or wooden spoon, then press the clay down on the object and pull it up.

Miscellaneous

• Use colored nail polish to mark quart-measure lines, or dots, on the inside of a cleaning pail or bucket. Takes the guesswork out of mixing cleaning solutions, or plant-food solutions, to the proper strength.

• Bunion pads—cut to proper sizes and placed on the bottoms of chair legs—will prevent scratches on hardwood floors.

• When washing windows, use vertical strokes on one side and horizontal strokes on the other. This technique makes it easy to see on which side any streaks remain.

• Before washing walls, wrap a washcloth around your wrist and secure it with a rubber band. It will stop water from running down your arm.

• Hate paint odors? Cut an onion into large pieces, put them in a bucket of water, and place it in the middle of the room you will be painting. Do this before you start painting. It only takes a few hours for the onion to absorb the odors. Another method to get rid of paint odors: Add a little vanilla extract to the paint—about two teaspoons per quart.

• A patch of luminous tape, placed on light switches, makes them easy to find at night.

• Lost your aglets? (Those are the tips on your shoelaces.) Dip the ends of the lace into a bottle of clear nail polish and twist raveled ends together to create a new, durable casing. Or dip the ends into hot paraffin and follow same procedure.

• An easy way to paint a picture frame: Tack a thin piece of wood to the back of the frame; the piece should extend about 4 in. over the edge of the sides. Use the wood extensions as handles while painting the frame.

• Here's an energy-saving tip: A single 100-watt light bulb gives out as much light as two 60-watt bulbs—and uses only five sixths of the energy. If you have several low-watt bulbs in a lamp, or other fixture, replace them with one higher-watt bulb.

• Losing sleep because of a dripping faucet? For temporary relief, put a sponge under the drip. Or tie a string to the faucet, making sure the string is long enough to reach the sink; the water drops will quietly slide down the string.

• A small, open container of vinegar, hidden in a room before a party, will absorb cigarette odors.

• A pair of pliers can be an invaluable aid in repairing small objects. After gluing a broken object, put it between the jaws of the pliers. Hold the jaws in place by putting a rubber band around the handles. This will hold the item steady until the glue dries.

• If you bathe your dog in the bathtub or sink, put steel wool in the drain openings to catch hairs and prevent a stopped-up drain.

• Extend the life of batteries and photographic film by putting them in plastic bags and storing them in a safe spot in the refrigerator.

• Old shower curtains make excellent drop cloths to use when painting.

• Sharpen scissors by cutting six or seven times into fine sandpaper. This method will not be very effective, however, if the scissors are very dull.

• A system to guarantee that you will always be on time with birthday and anniversary cards: Make a list of all the cards that you will need for six months—or even a year. Buy all of the cards at once, address and sign them. Finally, in the upper right-hand corner—where the stamp will be placed—write in the date that the card should be mailed. Index cards, according to date, and keep in a convenient place.

• Lemon juice is nature's best bleach. A good solution: one cup of 15% alcohol, a drop of glycerin, and the juice of one lemon.

• A scouring pad will last longer if you put it in the freezer. It keeps it rust-free.

- Toothpaste is a great cleaning agent for cuff links and other jewelry. It will also remove small scratches from glass-top tables.
- The inside of a banana skin makes a good emergency shoe polish. Just be sure to follow up by polishing leather shoes with a cloth.
- Don't throw away old lipstick. Instead, put the lipstick tube in a warm place until the contents get soft. Then remove the lipstick and blend it with an equal portion of Vaseline to get homemade lip gloss.
- In the dark, two similar-sized keys on a key chain are hard to distinguish from one another. Alleviate the confusion by filing a notch in the top of one or marking one with a small piece of masking tape so that you can "feel" the difference.
- Before taking a bad-tasting medicine, put an ice cube on your tongue. The ice will temporarily freeze your taste buds.
- In cold weather wash the insides of your windows with alcohol to help prevent frost from forming.
- Salt is a great household cleaner. A nontoxic substance, salt can be used to scour a sink or cutting board. Also, throw a handful or two down a sink drain, then pour in boiling water; this salt-and-hot-water treatment will keep drains from clogging.

—C.O.

13

THE BEST OF HEALTH

A BANQUET OF FAMOUS DIETS

Counting Kal'-o-ries

The Head Woman: In 1918, when Lulu Hunt Peters condensed the state of the art of slenderizing in her best-selling book *Diet and Health,* vitamins were known as vitamines because they were thought to be amine compounds (some are not), and readers had to be taught the pronunciation of an unfamiliar word: kal'-o-ri. An M.D. from the University of California (1909), Dr. Peters was the first woman to intern at Los Angeles County General Hospital. She became chairman of the public health committee of the state Federation of Women's Clubs, wrote a syndicated daily health feature, and spent two years in the Balkans working for the Red Cross. As a woman with a chronic weight problem herself ("my idea of heaven is a place with me and mine on a cloud of whipped cream"), she was naturally interested in diet. Rejecting such contemporary fads as a baked potato and skim milk three times daily, she put together a balanced diet with a mixture of common sense and good humor. Dr. Peters died in 1930, but her book outlived her, going into its 55th edition in 1939.

Overview: The calorie has been around since the 18th century as a unit for measuring heat and energy, but only in this century has it achieved widespread currency as a measure of weight control. Dr. Peters explained that in order to maintain your weight you need to consume 15 calories per pound per day (more if you are unusually active); if your intake is less than that, you will lose weight; if more, you will gain. Suggesting a diet of 1,200 calories a day, she provided menus with caloric equivalents "for those who do not have the desire to compute them." She favored a diet containing 10% to 15% of its calories in the form of protein, with 25% to 30% fats and 60% to 65% carbohydrates as fuel foods. You may eat what you want, provided you count your calories.

Begin your diet with a one-day water fast, Dr. Peters recommended, to "discipline" and shrink your stomach. To get through those moments of temptation, try sucking on dried lemon or orange peel or aromatic breath sweeteners. Moderate calisthenics are advisable so that "you won't be thinking about yourself."

In the belief that "there is a great deal of psychology to reducing," Dr. Peters thought it might be helpful to form a diet club with a public weighing-in ceremony. Anyone failing to lose at least 1 lb. a week (2 to 3 lb. being desirable) would be fined and the proceeds would be donated to charity.

Pro: The basic relationship between calorie intake and weight level is clearly explained by Dr. Peters, and her diet provides a generally sound nutritional program for weight loss.

Con: The diet is deficient in calcium, and adding foods rich in this mineral would bring up its calorie count. A greater variety of foods would eliminate much of the diet's repetitive quality. Fasting, which Peters recommends for weight loss, has been found to be useful only when employed with caution.

Rubinstein's Food for Beauty

The Head Woman: "The ladylike 'vapors' of Victorian days are no longer fashionable," wrote Helena Rubinstein, the Polish-born cosmetics queen who, after W.W. I, became concerned with the effects of diet on health and beauty. Head of an international business built on the cold cream she used to maintain her flawless, milky-white complexion, she also presided over a string of salons offering massages, milk baths, facials, and scalp treatments as well as makeup and coiffures. The search for prolonged youth and heightened beauty led her to the Bircher-Benner Sanatorium in Zurich, which offered a vegetarian diet of *matière vivante* ("living matter," or uncooked fruits and vegetables). Back in New York Rubinstein added a "Zurich Room" to her Fifth Avenue salon; there she experimented with fruit and vegetable combinations attractively arranged for color and pattern on crystal plates. Adding some meat, eggs, and a greater variety of fruit to make the Bircher-Benner diet more palatable to Americans, she presented the revised diet in *Food for Beauty* (1938), such a staple of diet literature that it was reissued in paperback in 1977.

Overview: "The perfect diet for the beauty-hungry woman," Mme. Rubinstein wrote after extensive research, "is composed of raw fruits and vegetables, nuts and whole cereals." She recommended beginning with a few days of "clearance and revitalization," a curative regime in which Bircher-müesli, a raw cereal and fruit mixture moistened with cream, is eaten for breakfast and supper. The main, or "sunlight," meal during the curative phase consists of three types of fresh vegetables and fruit. On the regular maintenance diet, calculated at 2,200 to 2,500 calories daily, the formula is to "select one half of your food from the things your body needs, then select the other half from the things you feel you want terribly." In other words, one half of your diet should consist of fruits and vegetables—up to five or more types per meal. Some meat and even sweets are allowed. Sample meals include a boiled egg, bacon, and buttered toast for breakfast; broiled lamb chops and fruit with whipped cream for dinner. Puddings, pies, and pastries are forbidden, however, and coffee and tea are permitted only reluctantly.

Helena Rubinstein.

Rubinstein advises returning to the curative diet at least twice a year for one to three weeks at a time, and devoting one day weekly to the maintenance diet of "sunlight" nutrition (i.e., fresh vegetables and fruit). The net effect of such a lifelong regime, she claims, will be renewed health, hope, and vitality.

Pro: Rubinstein's maintenance diet provides a generous balance of most vitamins and minerals. It is aesthetically pleasing, and it emphasizes a positive attitude toward diet and respect for the body. An appealing variety of foods makes concessions to American tastes.

Con: The curative diet, though temporary, is nutritionally inadequate. It claims to enable one to shed 2 to 3 lb. per week, but a very sedentary person may not lose any weight at all, given the caloric intake. The maintenance diet, which allows 2,200 to 2,500 calories per day, may not promote weight loss either. Both diets are deficient in calcium, an especially necessary element for growing teenage girls. Eating raw food is beneficial, but the claim that only raw fiber can properly stimulate and clean the digestive tract is false; cooked fiber is perfectly suitable.

Zen Macrobiotics

The Head Man: True believers consider Georges Ohsawa a kind of philosophical Marco Polo, an Easterner who brought the spiritual wealth of the Orient to the West. Born Yukikazu Sakurazawa in Japan in 1893, he traveled extensively abroad and eventually settled in Paris. Ohsawa rejected medication, surgery, and vaccination in favor of a food theory of disease; he believed that cancer was caused by eating sugar and claimed to be able to cure polio, diabetes, kidney disease, asthma, and morning sickness with arcane dietary prescriptions. In 1942 he came up with Zen macrobiotics, a culinary regime based on the ancient Chinese polarities of Yin and Yang. According to Ohsawa, the most perfect food—ideally balanced between Yin (sugar) and Yang (salt)—is brown rice, the staple of the macrobiotic ("large-life") diet. Relying entirely on whole natural foods, locally produced and ritually prepared, the macrobiotic diet is designed to bring the individual into harmony with the seasons, the ecology, and the cosmos. It is not a diet for dilettantes. "Without the guidance of the Philosophy of the Unique Principle [the Yin-Yang concept]," Ohsawa warned, Zen macrobiotic vegetarianism "can descend into mere sentimentalism."

Overview: The macrobiotic diet rejects all "industrialized" food and drink—anything canned, bottled, artificially colored, or adulterated. Animal products also are to be avoided, particularly beef and dairy products, although fish and game are considered relatively free from pollution. Tomatoes, potatoes, and eggplant are taboo, because they are too "yin," and liquids are restricted, with a preference given to green tea. To detoxify and purge the body, the devotee begins with a 10-day rice diet, after which he or she selects a diet from minus three to plus seven on Ohsawa's scale. Minus three is a diet composed of a mixture of meat, vegetables, fruit, and 10% grain. With each step up the ladder, the proportion of grain is increased 10% until the ideal total grain diet is reached at plus seven.

All foods on the macrobiotic diet should be raised organically within a radius of 100 mi. from the consumer, and they should be eaten fresh and whole. (In the case of fish, that means eating the head and tail too.) Refrigeration is discouraged as artificial. The cook should work standing tall in the "kitchen-shrine," preferably completing in the morning all preparations for the whole day. The dining table should be maintained as the center of social life. Macrobiotics is above all a way of life, and only incidentally a way to lose weight.

Pro: A macrobiotic diet is relatively cheap and easy to prepare. There is no calorie counting. Also, it emphasizes fresh vegetables, whole grains, and restricted animal products, insuring high fiber and low cholesterol intake. Processed foods are forbidden as being a source of potentially harmful sugar and chemical additives.

Con: His diet theory of disease notwithstanding, Ohsawa died of cancer in 1966. In November, 1965, a young New Jersey woman on the plus-seven diet wasted away to 70 lb. and died. Following this incident, the Food and Drug Administration closed down the Ohsawa Foundation in New York. A few years later, however, *Newsweek* reported that there were still some 10,000 macrobiotic devotees in this country, primarily in and around Boston, San Francisco, and other centers of the counterculture. Pediatricians have condemned the diet for its effect on children, and in 1971 the American Medical Association warned that a macrobiotic diet can lead to anemia, protein and calcium deficiency, emaciation, kidney malfunction, scurvy, and malnutrition.

Calories Don't Count

The Head Man: The low-calorie diet is a humbug, Dr. Herman Taller declared in his best-selling book, *Calories Don't Count* (1961). A native of Romania, he studied medicine in Italy and became a Brooklyn obstetrician-gynecologist specializing in natural childbirth. He was also a chronically hungry dieter whose weight ballooned up to 265 lb. on a 5-ft. 10-in. frame. In 1955 a cholesterol researcher suggested a mysterious oily substance to help bring down his high cholesterol level.

Taller also found that he was losing weight—65 lb. in 8 months—even while consuming 5,000 calories a day. Researching the process of "lipo-equilibrium," or the "balance between fat formation and fat disposal," he decided that the villain was pyruvic acid, a product of metabolized carbohydrates, an excess of which prevents the body from burning stored fat. The "mystery substance," on the other hand, a polyunsaturated fat, stimulates the body to burn fat. Taller therefore recommended a high-fat diet supplemented by polyunsaturated safflower oil, capsules of which were marketed in conjunction with his book under the brand name CDC, for "calories don't count."

Overview: There is no need to count calories, Taller claimed, as long as you avoid carbohydrates, which produce pyruvic acid, and concentrate on foods that are high in fat and protein. He prohibited all sugar and starches, including high-carbohydrate fruits, vegetables, and juices, and of course cakes, cookies, and bread (except gluten bread). Alcohol is also discouraged. Fish, which is rich in unsaturated fatty acids, should be eaten daily, as well as foods fried in unsaturated oils. Also desirable are meats, cheese, eggs, shell nuts, and low-carbohydrate fruits and vegetables. As for beverages, diet soda, tea, and coffee are permitted, plus one cup of milk daily and plenty of water.

Taller specified three full meals a day, with as much meat, fish, and fats as desired. Overall, the diet should include 2 oz. of corn oil margarine and 3 oz. of highly unsaturated vegetable oil daily. The easiest way to insure that you are getting enough of the vital oils is to take two CDC safflower oil capsules before each meal. This should afford a permanent lifelong solution for 95% of obese people, Taller claimed.

Pro: The attractions of this diet are obvious: lots of fat, countless calories, and a magic mystery capsule that promises to make weight come off quickly. "You have nothing to lose but your girth," Taller joked.

Con: Soon after the publication of *Calories Don't Count*, the Food and Drug Administration filed charges against Taller and the CDC Corporation. Taller's business associates admitted their inability to substantiate the book's claims and pleaded guilty to drug violations, postal fraud, and conspiracy. Taller maintained his innocence, but a jury found him guilty of the same charges in 1967. He was fined and put on probation, his reputation gone along with his girth.

Specifically, Taller's legal difficulties arose from the marketing tie-in of the capsules with the book. It was legal for him to publish his theory of diet and also to market diet capsules, but only so long as he eliminated mention of the pills from the book and vice versa.

Weight Watchers

The Head Woman: Jean Nidetch was a professional dieter, a housewife who tried every conceivable slimming fad, lost weight with each one, then regained it thanks to her habitually "promiscuous" eating habits. In 1961, when she sought help from the obesity clinic run by New York City's Dept. of Health, she was 38 years old and weighed 214 lb. The clinic put her on a diet by Dr. Norman Jolliffe, best known for his "prudent diet." Convinced that she couldn't stick to it alone, Mrs. Nidetch invited some fat friends to form a group and meet weekly to trade horror stories (secret midnight binging in the bathroom) and helpful hints (put that doughnut in the freezer to cool temptation). Established in 1963, Weight Watchers expanded into an international network of clubs, with a product line of diet drinks, sugar substitutes, and publications—the McDonald's of the reducing industry. "My little private club has become an industry," wrote Mrs. Nidetch, amateur nutritionist, in *The Story of Weight Watchers* (1975). In 1978 the organization, with about $50 million in annual revenues and a cumulative membership of close to 2 million, was bought by Heinz Foods.

Overview: The Weight Watchers diet provides for a balance of 25% protein, 40% carbohydrates, and 35% fats. Women are limited to about 1,200 calories daily, men to 1,600, but instead of counting calories you count grams, weighing your food on a postage or kitchen scale. The diet distinguishes between "legal" and "illegal" foods (the latter including butter, sugar, alcohol, and fried foods), and between those items permitted in limited quantities (such as eggs) and those permitted in unlimited quantities (such as coffee, tea, soy sauce, and celery). You must eat fish five times a week, liver once a week. No decisions are required, no substitutions are allowed; all meals are compulsory, with snacks prescribed to ward off temptation. The program offers reducing, "plateau," and maintenance plans. A suggested menu on the reducing plan is as follows: half a grapefruit, 1 oz. hard cheese with toast, and a beverage for breakfast; 4 oz. smoked salmon, tomato salad, a slice of bread, and a beverage for lunch; ham steak, baked squash, and cucumber salad for dinner.

Weight Watchers takes the position that obesity is a problem as insidious as alcoholism or drug addiction, one that can never be cured, merely arrested. Within the Weight Watchers groups, members work together to achieve "behavior modification" for a new way of life. The weekly meetings are structured around lectures, discussions, and a public weighing-in ceremony, each "loser" winning a round of applause.

Pro: According to an in-house study, Weight Watchers members lost an average of 1.6 lb. per week; 15 months later, more than half were close to their weight goals—a respectable showing compared to other diets. Over the years, the program has become increasingly flexible, adapting to new developments in food labeling, testing out members' suggestions, and incorporating an exercise program. But the greatest asset remains the group, where dieters find mutual reinforcement for changing their eating habits permanently.

Con: The Weight Watchers diet, while well balanced nutritionally, is too slow and tedious for dieters with a "crash" mentality. The need to weigh food, in particular, may be burdensome. As for the group approach, it seems to work better for some than for others. Sociologist Joan Rockwell reported in 1977 that club membership is overwhelmingly white, female, and middle-aged, with fewer than 5% men and almost no minorities, whose needs apparently aren't met by the program.

Atkins's Diet Revolution

The Head Man: The skinniest kid on his block in Dayton, O., Robert Atkins developed the largest appetite on campus at the University of Michigan, by his own account, and became a New York cardiologist with two extra chins. Seeking a viable diet that wouldn't leave him chronically hungry, he learned that in the absence of carbohydrates and also during a fast, the body burns its own fat as fuel, somehow assuaging hunger in the process. Disregarding the conventional wisdom that at least 60 grams of carbohydrates are required daily, he discovered that by limiting himself to 35 to 40 grams he could accelerate fat burning and lose weight even while eating constantly. In 1964, while a consultant to the medical department of AT&T, Atkins tried out his ideas with a pilot program of 65 people, who lost an average of 18 lb. the first month.

In 1966 the Atkins diet was presented in *Harper's Bazaar* magazine. As a result of the publicity the former cardiologist soon found himself running a 23-room office complex with a case load of celebrity patients, each of whom received a personally tailored low-carbohydrate diet. Published in 1972, *Dr. Atkins' Diet Revolution* became a best-seller, and the bachelor doctor developed a swinging image as the escort of some of his more svelte patients.

Overview: The Atkins diet begins by reducing carbohydrate consumption to zero in order to convert the body from a "carbohydrate-burning engine" to a "fat-burning engine." The process is monitored by checking the urine with Ketostix, test strips that turn purple to indicate the presence of ketones—a product of fat burning. The dieter progressively adds small amounts of carbohydrates until reaching what Atkins calls the Critical Carbohydrate Level (CCL), when ketosis ceases. Carbohydrates should then be cut back slightly to continue the process of fat burning. Atkins advises dieters to begin with a medical checkup, to consume megadoses of vitamins, and to eat small meals six times a day in order to maintain a constant blood-sugar level. As long as you remain below your CCL, he claims, you can enjoy cheesecake, eggs Benedict, chicken salad with mayonnaise, and other tempting treats. "You can eat this way comfortably, luxuriously, without deprivation, without a single hunger pain, all your life," he writes.

Pro: Many people find it easier to count carbohydrates than calories. Add to this the prospect of gorging on high-calorie, high-fat dishes, and the Atkins diet would seem to be a dream come true for the overweight.

Con: Atkins has been almost universally condemned by the experts. His diet is "essentially a form of planned malnutrition," according to Harvard University nutritionist Frederick Stare; "bizarre" and "without scientific merit," according to the American Medical Association; "unethical and self-aggrandizing," according to the New York County Medical Society. Atkins cited medical research out of context to support his theories, the editors of *Consumer Guide* report. Critics agree that it is illogical if not impossible to stimulate the burning of stored fat by consuming large amounts of new fat. They insist that there is no way to lose weight on a high-calorie diet. Moreover, high fat consumption may cause diarrhea (as well as increased risk of heart disease); ketosis may damage the kidneys; and carbohydrate starvation will lead to fatigue, dehydration, and depression.

Stillman

The Head Man: Irwin Maxwell Stillman (1896–1975) was a family doctor in Brooklyn for 45 years before retiring to Florida in 1960. In the course of treating some 10,000 overweight patients, he found the most expeditious means of losing weight to be a high-protein diet based on Dr. Eugene Dubois's concept of specific dynamic action, or "the cost of digestion." In other words, it takes an extra effort—up to 30% of the calories consumed—to break down protein. By increasing the amount of protein consumed up to 90% of the diet, the "fires of metabolism" are raised and fat is "melted out" of bodily storage centers at a rapid rate. Stillman, who himself lost 50 lb. on his high-protein prescription, wrote *The Doctor's Quick Weight Loss Diet* (1967) in collaboration with author Samm Sinclair Baker, another successful dieter. Their book also contains descriptions of a number of gimmick diets, including a 350-calorie "pilot's diet" and a 40-calorie lettuce and tomato diet.

Stillman subsequently devised a low-protein, almost vegetarian diet—*The Doctor's Inches Off Diet* (1969)—which over a course of six weeks "pulls extra fat from between the muscles." In *The Doctor's Quick Teen-Age Diet* (1971), he offered a compromise between a high-protein and a high-carbohydrate diet specifically geared for adolescents; and he added exercise to his high-protein diet in *14-Day Shape-Up Program* (1974). An estimated 20 million dieters have followed his advice.

Overview: The basic Stillman high-protein diet prescribes unlimited amounts of lean meat, poultry, and sea food, plus eggs and low-fat cheese, preferably consumed in small meals six times a day. No bread, vegetables, fruit, alcohol, or sugar are allowed. You must drink eight glasses of water a day, in order to wash away the ketones, or "ashes left in the furnace," and you can drink as much coffee, tea, and diet soda as you want. Vitamin supplements are required, and in the days before widespread amphetamine abuse Stillman was not averse to a little medication for assistance. He also advised that you consult a physician before embarking on the diet.

Stillman claims you will lose 7 to 15 lb. (or from 5% to 10% of body weight) the first week on the diet and 5 lb. a week thereafter. When you are within 3 lb. of your goal, Stillman advises that you stabilize with his calorie-counting "stay-slim" program before going the last mile. The diet works for 95 out of 100 people, he claims, with no harmful effects, and it can be used again and again.

Pro: The Stillman high-protein diet is clearly defined and easy to follow without calorie counting or menu juggling. You may eat whenever you choose, provided you restrict yourself to the prescribed foods. Weight loss is rapid and dramatic.

Con: A diet composed of 90% protein is necessarily short of other vital substances; should you fail to take a vitamin supplement, you run serious risk of vitamin deficiency. Because this diet is low in roughage, you will probably be constipated, although the daily eight glasses of water will certainly send you to the bathroom frequently. Protein is high in calories, some critics contend, and in principle it is impossible to lose weight on a high-calorie diet. Some of the weight loss is undoubtedly due to water loss, which will be regained as soon as you cease dieting.

The Juice Fast

The Head Man: Americans have been brainwashed by high-protein propaganda and other commercially motivated theories of nutrition, according to Paavo O. Airola. A leading proponent of fasting, he was born in Finland, claimed a Ph.D. in nutrition from the University of Leningrad in 1939, and later moved to the U.S., where he was awarded an N.D. (Doctor of Naturopathy) from the Brantridge Forest School (1966). Europeans satisfy their nutritional needs with a high-natural-carbohydrate, low-animal-protein diet, Airola points out, and they visit popular spas offering two- and three-week courses of fasting. In his books *Are You Confused?* (1971) and *How to Keep Slim, Healthy and Young with Juice Fasting* (1971), Airola makes the case for fasting as a means to cure disease and rejuvenate and revitalize the body, while losing weight in the process. After a few days of fasting, he explains, the body begins to burn and digest its own tissues—a process called autolysis—and to expel accumulated toxins and metabolic wastes. He considers a juice fast preferable to a water fast because juice provides vital nutrients that are absorbed into the bloodstream without interfering with the process of autolysis.

Overview: It is safe to fast for up to 40 days on water alone, according to Airola, and up to 100 days on juice, for therapeutic or healing purposes. For reducing, however, he recommends a series of 7- to 10-day fasts, which are safe to undertake without medical supervision, provided you are in good health. (Vitamin supplements and most drugs should be discontinued while fasting.)

Fasting should begin with a purgative such as castor oil to cleanse the bowels. An enema should be administered at least once daily, in the morning, and preferably twice, to help rid the body of toxic wastes. And since one third of all wastes are eliminated through the skin, Airola recommends dry-brush massage to keep the pores open and stimulate circulation and elimination.

Airola's recommended daily regime consists of herb tea at 9:00 A.M.; a glass of freshly squeezed fruit juice diluted 50-50 with water at 11:00 A.M. and a glass of vegetable juice or broth at 1:00 P.M.; tea again at 4:00 P.M.; and diluted vegetable or fruit juice at 7:00 P.M. Total liquid intake, including water, should be six to eight glasses or more daily. Get plenty of exercise, do some sunbathing if possible, and take hot and cold baths.

It is important to break the fast gradually, beginning with small quantities of fruit and vegetables and adding yogurt, potatoes, and bread on the third day. On the fourth day return to a normal diet. (Airola favors whole grains, fruits, and vegetables, which he calls "the true macrobiotic diet"—not to be confused with the Zen macrobiotic diet.) Vitamin and mineral supplements (especially vitamin C) should be taken daily, Airola claims, both to prevent malnutrition and to combat toxins.

Pro: Hunger actually can be easier to tolerate on a fast than on a restricted diet. Airola's insistence on natural foods for good nutrition provides a diet free of sugar and additives and low in cholesterol. Also, since the diet has minimal animal protein, it is inexpensive to follow.

Con: Fasting without medical supervision can result in liver and kidney damage. Often, weight loss through fasting is temporary, because the dieter soon returns to faulty eating habits. Raw foods, which Airola claims have superior enzyme action to cooked food, are actually no more valuable; the body synthesizes its own enzymes from both cooked and raw foods.

Fiber

The Head Men: During 20 years in Africa, Dr. Denis Burkitt observed that a high-fiber diet seems to protect natives against cancer of the colon and other diseases common in the Western world. Back home in Great Britain, he became known as "the bran man" for advocating more roughage in the diet. In the U.S., the cause was taken up by psychiatrist David Reuben, author of the popular sex manual, *Everything You Always Wanted to Know about Sex (But Were Afraid to Ask)* (1969). Shifting his attention to the intestinal tract, Reuben wrote *Save-Your-Life Diet* in 1975.

According to the current theories popularized by Reuben, fiber, composed largely of cellulose, is indigestible and moves rapidly through the digestive tract. In addition to speeding the process of digestion, it also seems to cause the intestines to excrete rather than absorb fat, in some manner not yet fully understood. Thus, it appears that a high-fiber diet lowers cholesterol, provides protection against diverticulitis and heart disease, and aids in weight control. Other diet gurus who have picked up the fiber theme include Carlton Fredericks and osteopath Sanford Siegal.

Overview: According to Reuben, all low-roughage foods, processed food products, refined sugar, and alcohol should be eliminated from the diet. Instead, you should eat lots of cereals and other grain products, as well as fruits and vegetables, either raw or prepared with a minimum of cooking. Moderate amounts of lean meat, fish, poultry, and oil are allowed. Yogurt is recommended on a daily basis to help maintain favorable intestinal bacteria. Most important, 2 teaspoonfuls of unprocessed miller's bran should be taken three times daily, either with water before each meal or added to cereal, yogurt, soup, and homemade bread. In addition to filling you up, the bran-and-water combination induces what Reuben calls "an internal feeling of calmness and tranquility" and "an indescribable feeling of well-being." Overall, your diet should include 24 grams of fiber daily—enough to produce one or more bowel movements daily that are "large in amount, well-formed, low in odor, and passed without straining," according to Reuben.

Pro: It is nearly universally conceded that the American diet with its reliance on refined and processed foods is deficient in roughage. In correcting that deficiency, a high-fiber diet may also save you money. For example, the recommended allowance of miller's bran costs only 2¢ a day.

Con: Reuben fails to specify the size of portions, relying instead on his "mystical" feeling of fullness to regulate consumption. As critics point out, a calorie is still a calorie regardless of the speed of digestion; should you overeat, you will gain, not lose, weight. The more rapid digestion of fiber, moreover, may result in mineral deficiencies, particularly among younger dieters, and may also produce kidney stones. The sheer bulk of 24 grams of fiber daily may cause flatulence and a constant preoccupation with bowel function. Finally, the scientific verdict on fiber is not yet in. Although Africans have a low incidence of some diseases, they also have a short life expectancy.

U.S. Senate Dietary Guidelines

The Head Man: As chairman of the Senate Select Committee on Nutrition and Human Needs, Sen. George McGovern of South Dakota, former Democratic presidential hopeful and a leading liberal in Congress, saw his role as akin to that of the U.S. surgeon general who condemned smoking as a threat to health. Six out of the leading 10 causes of death in this country, McGovern pointed out, are linked to diet. But when the McGovern committee report came out in January, 1977, after nine years in the making, its conclusions—that cholesterol-rich foods may be as dangerous to health as cigarettes—aroused such a controversy that an amended report was issued 11 months later. The committee was originally conceived as a bridge between health and welfare interests on the one hand and food and farm interests on the other, but its initial recommendations on national nutrition—the first ever by any branch of the U.S. government—seemed to promote the former at the expense of the latter. The revised report made concessions to the meat, dairy, salt, and sugar industries and to the American Medical Association.

Overview: *Dietary Goals for the U.S.* (1977) was intended as a set of guidelines to nutrition rather than as a particular formula for losing weight. As far as dieting is concerned, the committee concluded that calories do count, that caloric intake must be reduced below maintenance needs in order to lose weight, and that no diet yet invented offers a surefire solution to obesity. On the contrary, testimony before the committee indicated that only 10% to 20% of individuals on diet programs actually solve their weight problems. The rest bounce up and down in what nutritionist Jean Mayer calls "the rhythm method of girth control."

In general outline, the McGovern committee recommended increased consumption of complex carbohydrates and naturally occurring sugars, from 28% of caloric intake in the average U.S. diet to 48%; reduction of refined and processed sugar intake by about half, to 10% of total calories; and reduced consumption of fat, from 40% to 30% of intake; with protein making up the final 12%. (The committee's original recommendation to eat less meat was modified in the final report to decreasing consumption of animal and saturated fats.)

More specifically, the committee advised limiting salt consumption to 5 grams daily (up from 3 grams in the original report) and cholesterol to 300 milligrams daily. Senator McGovern also expressed concern over the rapidly growing use of soft drinks, which during the 1970s replaced milk as the second most frequently consumed beverage (after coffee).

Pro: On a national level, lower fat and protein consumption and greater reliance on complex carbohydrates would promote health, reduce medical expenditures, and conserve some of the energy involved in food processing. At the level of the family, cutting back on expensive meat and processed products in favor of fresh vegetables would result in considerable savings.

Con: By the same token, these changes would have a significant negative impact on the meat- and food-processing industries. As far as the advised nutritional balance affects the individual dieter, the editors of *Consumer Guide* point out that in the recommended 1,200 calories you would not be getting enough protein to meet basic needs and should therefore take some of your carbohydrates in the form of high-protein legumes.

The Scarsdale Diet

The Head Man: The son of a successful hat manufacturer, Herman Tarnower became one of the first U.S. cardiologists after receiving his M.D. from Syracuse University in 1933 and pursuing additional studies abroad. He developed a lucrative practice as head of the Scarsdale Medical Center in New York's affluent Westchester County, where he lived on a six-acre estate with its own small lake. Tarnower had been prescribing a two-week crash diet for his patients for many years before collaborating with veteran diet writer Samm Sinclair Baker on *The Complete Scarsdale Medical Diet* (1978), which became an immediate best-seller. House Speaker Tip O'Neill lost 40 lb. on the diet, feminist Gloria Steinem tried it, and even Queen Elizabeth II was said to be on it.

A slender, balding bachelor with an upper-class disdain for celebrity and a dietary preference for truffles, Tarnower was rumored to be a "connoisseur of thoroughbred women." In March, 1980, he was shot to death by Jean Harris, his companion of 14 years and the headmistress of an exclusive girls' prep school, whose help had been prominently acknowledged in the diet book. "I have been through so much hell with him," she told the press, revealing that the 69-year-old diet doctor had an uncontrollable weakness for feminine charms. "He slept with every woman he could," she said. At the murder trial where she was convicted, 10 out of 14 prospective jurors said they had tried the diet.

Overview: The Scarsdale Medical Diet (SMD) is a closely monitored regime designed to rid persons of up to 20 lb. over a two-week period,

Dr. Herman Tarnower.

under medical supervision. (Dieters wishing to lose more than 20 lb. must alternate two weeks on the SMD with two weeks on a more permissive "keep-trim program.") Rapid weight loss is achieved by limiting consumption to around 1,000 calories a day, composed of 43% protein, 34.5% carbohydrates, and 22.5% fats—compared with 40% to 45% fats in the average diet. By eliminating oils, butters, and other fats, the body is encouraged to metabolize existing stores of fat. The SMD also rules out sugar and alcohol but allows a varied menu of lunches and dinners. (Breakfast is set for the duration at half a grapefruit and a piece of dry wheat toast.) Sunday lunch, for example, consists of turkey or chicken with vegetable and fruit, while dinner calls for a broiled steak, salad with lemon juice and vinegar or diet dressing, and brussels sprouts, plus coffee or tea. The SMD can also be modified for vegetarians and gourmets, the latter enjoying Cold Poached Fish Natalia with Mustard Sauce Henri, or Borscht Suzanne.

Pro: If it's Tuesday, successive waves of Scarsdale dieters learned to anticipate, it must be fruit salad; on Friday, it's spinach. The SMD prescribes every meal for a week, which is then repeated for a second week. Thus the dieter is relieved of counting calories and making any confusing or tempting choices. It is also a practical diet in terms of eating out, many restaurants having learned to expect a run on roast lamb on Wednesday night.

Con: The SMD does not specify the size of portions, so a gluttonous dieter could conceivably consume up to 1,400 or 1,600 calories per day and fail to lose much weight. Some of Tarnower's preferences have been criticized—such as cold cuts, which are high in sodium and low in nutrients, or saturated fats (meat) over polyunsaturated oils. But in general the medical profession tends to approve of diets that cut down on fat as the SMD does. At best, however, the SMD is only a temporary solution to the problem of weight control, since most dieters eventually resume their previous overeating habits.

The Pritikin Program

The Head Man: The latest weight-loss vogue in affluent America is Nathan Pritikin's spartan "third-world" diet, composed almost entirely of complex carbohydrates. A University of Chicago dropout who became wealthy by patenting numerous inventions in physics, chemistry, and electronics, Pritikin shifted his attention to nutrition after a diagnosis of coronary insufficiency when he was in his early 40s. Having cured himself with a stringent low-fat and low-cholesterol diet of grains and vegetables plus exercise, he set out to convert the world. Pritikin first established headquarters in Santa Barbara, Calif., in 1976. Then in 1978 the Pritikin Longevity Center, offering a medically supervised 26-day course of diet and exercise for $4,800, opened in Santa Monica, Calif. Pritikin centers were then established as resort spas in Miami and Hawaii, and Pritikin programs were also set up in New York and elsewhere. In 1980 the entire town of Natchitoches, La., which has a rate of heart disease far above the national average, embarked on a do-it-yourself Pritikin diet. Vigorous and rather dogmatic in his 60s, Pritikin became something of a media hound, squaring off with Atkins, the apostle of high fat, in the pages of *People* magazine. His book *The Pritikin Program for Diet and Exercise* was the diet-publishing event of 1979.

Overview: Pritikin rejects the traditional balanced diet, cutting fats to the bare minimum and severely restricting meat and eggs. Sugar and other refined carbohydrates are forbidden altogether, along with coffee and tea, and even cigarettes. The emphasis is on the complex carbohydrates. Every day the dieter is to consume two types of whole grain, two servings of raw vegetables and two of cooked vegetables, one citrus fruit, and three other fresh fruits—a total of 4 lb. of food. Bran may be added as desired, and potatoes are permissible "till kingdom come." A sample day's fare consists of half a grapefruit and cooked whole wheat cereal with banana, skim milk, cinnamon, and bran for breakfast; lentil soup, whole wheat pita bread stuffed with salad, and a glass of water with lemon for lunch; oxtail soup, steamed broccoli and yellow squash, long-grained brown rice, string bean salad, and applesauce mixed with skim-milk yogurt for dinner. On such a regime, supplemented by vigorous exercise twice a day, Pritikin claims you will not only lose weight and live longer but also improve your digestion, regain sexual potency, and sleep better.

Pro: The Pritikin program is highly recommended for diabetics. Coronary cases have also found it an alternative to bypass surgery—a last-chance diet when all else has failed. Since it is basically a vegetarian diet, it is relatively inexpensive to follow at home. It also provides sufficient roughage and nutrients.

Con: Greg Erlandson of *L.A. Weekly* describes the Pritikin program as "a dietary version of a Hanoi reeducation camp." *McCall's* magazine rated it "just too restrictive for the average person," while the AMA and American Heart Association concluded it was "unpalatable and therefore untenable." Archcompetitor Dr. Atkins points out that there is no firm evidence yet that heart disease can be reversed through diet. Others warn of the risk of protein deficiency and of flatulence due to the high consumption of roughage. (The average diet consists of 4 lb. of food weekly, compared to 4 lb. daily on this diet.) Finally, the Pritikin program as administered through the "longevity centers" is prohibitively expensive for all but the wealthy, usually elderly "last chancers." Early results from Natchitoches, La., indicate, however, that while total compliance may be unrealistic, the Pritikin program has succeeded in increasing consciousness of more healthful food alternatives.

—C.D. and L.P.

GREAT PHYSICAL ACHIEVEMENTS AFTER 70

FLOYD PARSONS

At 70, Parsons reluctantly retired from the Canadian Oldtimers' Hockey Association, an organization of 233 teams which holds international tournaments. In the year before his retirement, Parsons, a resident of Omemee, Ontario, played 117 games, but he admits that there comes a time whe one must step aside for the youngsters—the 40- to 60-year-olds.

MAVIS LINDGREN

Born in Manitoba, Canada, where temperatures sometimes plummet to 55° below, Mavis had a history of illnesses—whooping cough, tuberculosis, and chronic chest colds, which often developed into pneumonia.

Then, at 62, Mavis discovered running, and she hasn't stopped since. "After I started running, I never had another cold. I've been sick once in nine years. I had a real bad type of flu. It lasted three hours."

She ran her first marathon at 70, along the Avenue of the Giants in northern California's Humboldt Redwood State Park, and won a trophy for oldest finisher. Six months later she finished the Honolulu Marathon in 4 hr. 45 min. 2 sec., a 19-min. improvement over her first race. She has run two marathons since then, celebrating her 71st birthday with the last one—26 mi. 385 yd. in 5 hr. 10 min. 8 sec.

A. J. PUGLIZEVICH

At 72, A. J. Puglizevich of Merced, Calif., added another medal to his burgeoning collection by winning the 1980 Senior Olympics physique contest for his age group. He also holds 11 world records in the senior division of the National AAU Masters Decathlon Championships.

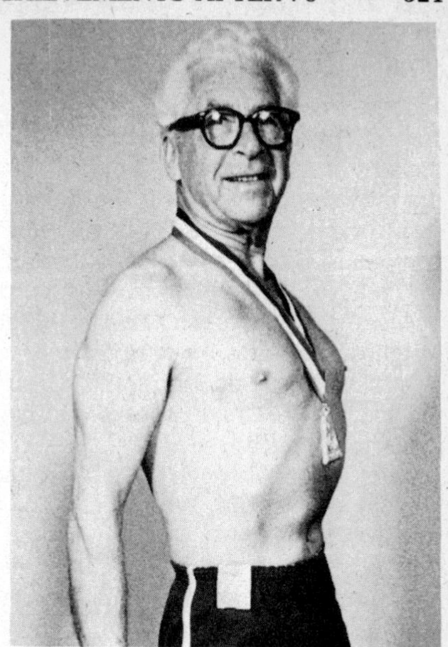

A. J. "Pug" Puglizevich, age 72.

Most mornings about 5:30, Pug can be found running laps at the Merced College track. He's been a firm believer in exercise since the age of 13. Anemic and prone to fainting spells, Pug was diagnosed as having a heart condition. He overheard the doctor tell his mother, "Take him out of school. Let him enjoy life. He's only got about a year to live." Not willing to accept his fate, Pug persuaded his parents to keep him in school and he sent away for body-building equipment. That was the beginning of a lifelong interest in exercise and health.

Even though he has experienced severe hip and knee problems at several times in his life, Puglizevich had always overcome his handicaps. His optimistic philosophy: "When life gives you lemons, make lemonade."

ED DELANO

At 75, "Foxy Grandpa" Ed Delano decided to go all the way from his home in Davis, Calif., to Worcester, Mass., for the 50th reunion of the Worcester Polytechnic Institute. His colleagues might have been concerned that the plane trip would be too tiring for him, but Delano wasn't—because when Foxy Grandpa flies, it's on a bicycle. Delano made the 3,100-mi. journey in 33½ days.

CHARLES STOLFUS

This former heavy-equipment mechanic has, at 75, become a veteran roller skater. He's even come up with a new look in skates—jogging shoes mounted on polyurethane wheels. He skates everywhere he can in his hometown of Lawrence, Kans. "Folks who don't know how to roller-skate," says Stolfus, "don't know what they're missing."

EDWARD PAYSON WESTON

Hundreds of people were gathered at the city limits, bundled up against the winter gales, straining for a glimpse of him. "Here he comes!" came the shout when the great athlete, still only a speck in the distance, came into view. Policemen lined the street in an effort to keep the crowd under control. A mighty cheer arose and the crowd made way for his approach, only to come forward again as an uproarious bodyguard for the remarkable man. A marathon runner? Long-distance cyclist? No. It was Edward Weston, pedestrian.

Always a dandy, the 71-year-old man, who usually wore tight-fitting britches, stout brogans with red tops, a round-top light silk hat, and buff gloves, was dressed a little more heartily for this stage of the trip. Weston had just reached Chicago and had endured a series of storms ever since reaching upstate New York. Trudging through blizzards, sometimes crawling through snowbanks that left his automobile accompaniment hours behind, Weston claimed that the only thing that bothered him was hunger.

This was the third hike that brought Weston to Chicago. Having grown up weak and sickly, he began walking to improve his health. He took his first long walk at 22, covering the 443 mi. from Boston to Washington in 208 hr. His first famous walk was six years later, in 1867, when he hiked from Portland, Me., to Chicago, Ill.—1,326 mi. in 24 days 22 hr. 20 min. After Weston had accomplished several such feats in America, the English, with their great tradition of pedestrianism, invited him to a competition in 1879. He amazed them when he walked 550 mi. in 141 hr. 44 min. and won their prized Astley Belt.

Weston's most famous walk was his first trip across the continent, made in 1910 at the age of 71. He walked 3,895 mi. in 105 days, but due to excessively bad weather he arrived five days later than he had planned and considered it the "most crushing failure" of his career. His last great walk was made when Weston was 75 (he lived to be 90). Invited to lay the cornerstone of the Minneapolis Athletic Club's new clubhouse, he decided to walk the 1,546 mi. from New York City to Minneapolis. It took him exactly 51 days.

Weston spread the gospel of pedestrianism wherever he walked. Doctors who examined him at 70 said that the usual deterioration of men Weston's age was not noticeable.

His secret? "I rise at eight, go to bed at 2 A.M., and invariably nap for an hour and a half after dinner. I eat a simple diet, avoiding rich food, especially pastry, and only indulge in tobacco and alcohol occasionally. And I walk 12 to 15 mi. a day every day except Sunday, when I never take exercise."

FLORRIE BALL

Known as a motorcycle enthusiast, Ball couldn't understand why her insurance company suddenly refused to reinsure her. This cyclist from Lancashire, England, had been riding for 26 years and had never had an accident. At 77 she could still do a 200-mi. trip easily. After a year of trying to get reinsured, Ball finally found an insurance broker who would cover her.

CORINNE LESLIE

While dancing in her disco class, 77-year-old Corinne Leslie noticed that there were many older women like herself with energy to spare. On an inspiration, she formed Leslie's Pompom Squad, a group of cheerleaders who perform at women's fast-pitch games in Sun City, Ariz. The squad dances Rockette-style to disco music; sometimes Leslie stands on her head while another dancer, Foofie Harlan, performs cartwheels, handspins, and splits. The group always receives standing ovations.

FINIS MITCHELL

Finis Mitchell is a 77-year-old explorer and mountain climber. He has climbed 251 peaks in the Wind River Mountains of western Wyoming. He carries 50 lb. of gear on his treks, which last until his food runs out, a maximum of 17 days. Mitchell has named hundreds of mountains, glaciers, and lakes, and is a photographer and the author of *Wind River Trails*. There are only 50 Wind River peaks he hasn't climbed, but that shouldn't present much of a problem for Mitchell, who is sure he'll climb until he's 90.

BILL KANE

Bill Kane was dubbed Vaquero of the Year at the Old Spanish Days Rodeo in Santa Barbara, Calif., when he and his partner, Eldon Tucker, defeated 14 other pairs of competitors in the Old-Time Cowboys Team Roping event. Two years later, at 82, Kane is still riding rodeo. A rancher from the age of 10, he has competed in over 3,000 rodeos. "I expect to be around for some time yet," he says. "I never let anything interfere with my daily workout. You can't stop for a while. If you do, you're a goner."

MARIAN HART

Marian Hart has flown more than 5,000 hr. since she began to fly 30 years ago, at 54. She has made several solo transatlantic flights in a single-engine plane, including one in her 84th year.

BERNARR MACFADDEN

A sickly orphan, Macfadden felt challenged to improve his health after overhearing an aunt whisper that his rasping cough indicated he would soon go the way of his mother—death from tuberculosis. He began lifting weights and soon developed his own philosophy about the human body. By the time Macfadden was 20 he had become the publisher of *Physical Culture*, a magazine that grew to have a circulation of half a million a month. He was now able to familiarize the public with his concept of psychocultopathy—healing diseases by fasting, health foods, and exercise. He purchased several pulp magazines, including *True Detective* and *True Romance*, and built up a fortune estimated at $30 million. He donated $500,000 to the Bernarr Macfadden Founda-

Bernarr Macfadden preparing to parachute 900 feet to celebrate his 84th birthday in 1953.

tion with the hope of perpetuating his efforts toward what he termed "physical culture."

For exercise, Macfadden enjoyed taking long hikes barefoot, often carrying a 40-lb. bag of sand on his back. He was particularly fond of the game leapfrog. He always slept on the floor, even in the most expensive hotels, which led to problems with the maids and sensational stories in the press. His 81st birthday was the occasion for his first parachute jump. He fell 4,000 ft. at N.Y. near the estate of his "physical culture" hotel, and landed unhurt. He told the public that the jump was on the order of leapfrog. On his 83rd birthday Macfadden parachuted 2,500 ft. into the Hudson River, and he jumped again the following year near the Seine. Seven ambulances and 200 reporters stood by in Paris to watch Macfadden, on his 84th birthday, wearing red flannel underwear, fall 900 ft. A good half mile off target, he missed the Seine, as well as the giant police cordon that was meant to protect him from the crowd. He landed on his feet, did a jig, and told the crowd he felt "damn good."

JIM WALDIE

At 88 Waldie, an active member of "the Kids," one of two Florida teams that make up St. Petersburg's Three-Quarter Century Softball

Club, Inc., may possess more ability for his age than any other fielder. He throws out runners, bats .300–.400, and says at 88 he can run the bases like a 75-year-old.

THOMPSON HORAN

The 89-year-old Londoner Horan was furious when the local hang-gliding school refused to continue his lessons because of his age. The veteran of a dozen successful flights, he has lodged a protest with the British Hang Gliding Association.

EULA WEAVER

After a heart attack at 83, Weaver began to walk for exercise and eventually started to jog at a slow pace. At 85 Weaver won the foot race for her age group (she had no competitors) in the 1974 Senior Olympics and became an overnight athletic celebrity. "The Queen of Track and Field," Weaver continued to participate in the Senior Olympics each year, and at 90 she holds the record in her age group for the 1,500-meter walk.

MME. ALEXANDRA BALDINE-KOSLOFF

Former prima ballerina with the Bolshoi Ballet of Moscow, Madame Alexandra toured both Europe and the U.S. Does dancing keep you young? Madame Alexandra seems to think so. At 91 she teaches 90-min. classes with no breaks and demonstrates even the difficult positions to students in her southern California studio.

RALPH FAULKNER

Ronald Colman, Errol Flynn, Douglas Fairbanks, Jr.—to name only a few—all learned their fencing moves from Ralph Faulkner. He has been teaching fencing in Los Angeles since 1929 and, at 91, is still "King of the Swashbucklers."

WALLY LATTIMER

Wally's slowing down at 98. He now rises at 6 A.M. rather than before dawn and works a 12- rather than a 14-hour day. Farmer, philosopher, and traveler, Lattimer has never had a head- or backache and was sick only once—"Got down with the flu in 1918." Having outlived two wives, he now lives alone outside Lyons, Kans., farming 40 acres of wheat and an 11-acre garden. He doesn't wear glasses and he has all his original teeth. How does he do it? "I don't worry and I don't get mad," says Wally.

HENRY GEORGE MILLER

Miller made the *Guinness Book of World Records* and *Ripley's Believe It or Not* when, at 93, he scored a hole-in-one at the 11th hole of an Anaheim, Calif., golf course. He took up the sport in his late 50s and was still golfing at the age of 102.

—J.H.

SENIOR OLYMPIC RECORDS FOR PEOPLE OVER THE AGE OF 70

The Senior Olympics was first held in 1970, ran for four days, and included 200 participants. Only three sports events were represented: diving, swimming, and track and field. Since then the annual games have grown to include over 30 events, and participants number in the thousands. With the addition of winter sports, the Senior Olympics is now held year-round. For further information write to: Senior Olympics, 5670 Wilshire Boulevard, Suite 360, Los Angeles, Calif. 90036.

Event	Age Group	Record	Name	Year
		TRACK AND FIELD (WOMEN)		
100 meters	70–74	18.9	Edith Mendyka (70)	1980
200 meters	70–74	1:01.1	Edith Mendyka (70)	1980
400 meters	70–74	2:33.5	Marilla Salisbury (73)	1980
800 meters	85–89	7:03.0	Eula Weaver (85)	1974
	80–84	5:47.5	Hulda Crooks (82)	1978
	70–74	5:32.3	Marilla Salisbury (73)	1980
1,500 meters	90–94	17:15.0	Eula Weaver (90)	1979
	85–89	13:56.8	Eula Weaver (85)	1974
	80–84	10:59.0	Hulda Crooks (82)	1978
	75–79	9:22.1	Ruth Rothfarb (79)	1980
	70–74	8:38.5	Bess James (71)	1980
5,000 meters	80–84	39:47.7	Hulda Crooks (82)	1978
	75–79	38:08.9	Ruth Rothfarb (79)	1980
	70–74	28:33.8	Bess James (71)	1980
10,000 meters	70–74	1:00:01	Bess James (71)	1980
Marathon		4:37:37	Mavis Lindgren (72)	1979
10,000-meter walk	80–84	1:38:37	Hulda Crooks (81)	1977
Discus	70–74	60′7″	Edith Mendyka (70)	1980
Javelin	70–74	72′0″	Edith Mendyka (70)	1980
Long jump	70–74	7′1″	Edith Mendyka (70)	1980
Shot put	70–74	26′8½″	Edith Mendyka (70)	1980
		TRACK AND FIELD (MEN)		
100 meters	85–89	23.5	Charles Backus (85)	1979

Event	Age Group	Record	Name	Year
	80–84	16.9	Charles Backus (83)	1977
	75–79	15.4	Harold Chapson (76)	1978
	70–74	14.4	Anthony Castro (71)	1980
200 meters	85–89	55.5	Charles Backus (85)	1979
	80–84	40.9	Paul Spangler (80)	1979
	75–79	32.2	Sing Lum (75)	1979
	70–74	29.0	Joseph Packard (74)	1977
400 meters	85–89	2:29.2	Charles Backus (85)	1979
	80–84	2:16.7	Charles Backus (82)	1976
	75–79	1:10.4	Harold Chapson (76)	1978
	70–74	1:05.1	Joseph Packard (74)	1977
800 meters	90–94	8:54.2	Robert Willis (90)	1977
	80–84	3:34.3	Paul Spangler (81)	1980
	75–79	2:43.0	Harold Chapson (76)	1978
	70–74	2:35.8	Harold Chapson (74)	1976
1,500 meters	80–84	6:46.8	Paul Spangler (80)	1979
	75–79	5:39.4	Harold Chapson (76)	1978
	70–74	5:21.5	Harold Chapson (73)	1975
5,000 meters	75–79	23:20.0	Paul Spangler (77)	1976
	70–74	21:12.0	Sidney Madden (72)	1979
10,000 meters	75–79	48:54	Paul Spangler (78)	1977
	70–74	46:15	Lou Gregory	1977
Marathon	75–79	3:52:50	Arthur Lambert (78)	1970
Marathon	70–74	3:07:26	Monty Montgomery (71)	1977
5,000-meter walk	85–89	44:52	Peter Laurino (87)	1980
	75–79	38:34	Robert Boothe (75)	1980
	70–74	30:33	Chesley Unruh (71)	1977
10,000-meter walk	70–74	1:05:16	Chesley Unruh (72)	1978
3,000-meter steeplechase	70–74	15:41.3	Walter Frederick (72)	1980
110-meter hurdles	75–79	26.0	Buell Crane (76)	1975
	70–74	22.0	Stanley Thompson (70)	1980
400-meter hurdles	70–74	1:44.6	Walter Frederick (70)	1978
Discus	85–89	30′2″	Charles Backus (86)	1980
	80–84	74′10″	John Whittemore (80)	1980

Event	Age Group	Record	Name	Year
	75–79	90′10″	Stan Hermann (76)	1980
	70–74	132′4″	Vernon Cheadle (70)	1980
Hammer	80–84	75′9″	John Whittemore (80)	1980
	75–79	73′3″	John Whittemore (76)	1976
	70–74	117′11″	Randolph Hubbell (70)	1979
High jump	80–84	3′8″	Walter Wesbrook (81)	1979
	75–79	4′4¼″	Buell Crane (76)	1975
	70–74	4′4″	Stanley Thompson (70)	1980
Javelin	85–89	19′7″	Charles Backus (86)	1980
	80–84	65′9″	John Whittemore (79)	1979
	75–79	81′9″	Gentry Mowrer	1976
	70–74	132′0″	Robert MacConaghy (70)	1978
Long jump	85–89	5′11½″	Charles Backus (86)	1980
	80–84	11′7″	Walter Wesbrook (80)	1978
	75–79	12′6″	Winfield McFadden (75)	1980
	70–74	13′10¾″	Albert Reiser	1976
Pole vault	80–84	5′6″	Walter Wesbrook (81)	1979
	75–79	6′7″	Walter Wesbrook (77)	1975
	70–74	8′6″	Robert MacConaghy (70)	1978
Shot put	80–84	28′9″	John Whittemore (80)	1979
	75–79	34′10″	Stan Hermann (76)	1980
	70–74	40′6¼″	Vernon Cheadle (70)	1980
Triple jump	80–84	22′7″	Walter Wesbrook (80)	1978
	75–79	26′10¾″	Winfield McFadden (75)	1980
	70–74	29′5″	Winfield McFadden (70)	1975
Decathlon	80–84	596	Walter Wesbrook (80)	1978
	75–79	1,072	John Whittemore (75)	1975
BOWLING				
	80–84	547	Willy Blaska (82)	1978
CYCLING (10 MI.)				
	70–74	28.05	Ed Delano (73)	1978
POWER LIFTING				
181-lb. class	70–74	250 lb.	Joseph Green	1979
198-lb. class	70–74	790 lb.	Henri Soudieres (74)	1979
SPEED SKATING (INDOOR)				
200 meters	85–89	43.0	Horatio Knoll (88)	1977
	75–79	33.1	Frank Knott (77)	1977
400 meters	85–89	1:21.0	Horatio Knoll (88)	1977
	75–79	1:02.4	Frank Knott (76)	1976

Event	Age Group	Record	Name	Year
800 meters	85–89	2:50.0	Horatio Knoll (88)	1977
	75–79	2:05.3	Frank Knott (76)	1976
1,500 meters	85–89	4:55.4	Horatio Knoll (88)	1977
	75–79	3:59.7	Frank Knott (77)	1977
SPEED SKATING (OUTDOOR–WOMEN)				
500 meters	70–74	1:56.0	Dorothy Davis (71)	1979
SPEED SKATING (OUTDOOR–MEN)				
200 meters	85–89	38.2	Horatio Knoll (87)	1976
	80–84	31.5	Johan Hovland (83)	1979
	75–79	27.5	Frank Knott (76)	1976
	70–74	24.8	Oskar Olsrud (74)	1979
500 meters	85–89	1:37.6	Horatio Knoll (87)	1976
	80–84	1:11.8	Johan Hovland (83)	1979
	75–79	1:03.5	Frank Knott (76)	1976
	70–74	58.6	Oskar Olsrud (74)	1979
1,000 meters	85–89	3:25.5	Horatio Knoll (89)	1978
	80–84	2:39.0	Johan Hovland (83)	1979
	75–79	2:26.0	Frank Knott (76)	1976
	70–74	2:12.1	Thomas Anderson (72)	1975
1,500 meters	85–89	4:55.0	Horatio Knoll (87)	1976
	80–84	3:44.0	Johan Hovland (83)	1979
	75–79	3:29.8	Frank Knott (76)	1976
	70–74	3:27.1	Thomas Anderson (72)	1975
SWIMMING (WOMEN)				
50-meter freestyle	80–84	1:21.4	Pearl Miller (80)	1978
	75–79	1:15.1	Pearl Miller (78)	1976
	70–74	1:31.0	Catherine Spees (72)	1980
100-meter freestyle	80–84	4:06.4	Pearl Miller (82)	1980
	75–79	3:06.4	Pearl Miller (79)	1977
	70–74	3:02.1	Pearl Miller (72)	1970
400-meter freestyle	70–74	15:07.0	Catherine Spees (72)	1980
100-meter backstroke	80–84	3:15.5	Pearl Miller (80)	1978
	75–79	3:03.6	Pearl Miller (79)	1977
	70–74	3:10.8	Pearl Miller (72)	1970
200-meter backstroke	80–84	7:10.7	Pearl Miller (82)	1980
	75–79	6:29.6	Pearl Miller (79)	1977

Event	Age Group	Record	Name	Year
		SWIMMING (MEN)		
50-meter freestyle	80–84	1:17.4	Ted Mumby (82)	1979
	75–79	59.4	John Whittemore (76)	1976
	70–74	48.5	Ronald Drummond (72)	1979
100-meter freestyle	80–84	3:14.2	Ted Mumby (80)	1978
	75–79	1:39.8	Sheldon White (75)	1980
	70–74	1:38.0	William Trask	1973
400-meter freestyle	75–79	8:51.7	Sheldon White (75)	1980
	70–74	8:34.9	William Trask	1973
100-meter backstroke	80–84	3:50.5	Ted Mumby (80)	1978
	75–79	3:38.2	Ted Mumby (76)	1974
	70–74	2:19.2	Ronald Drummond (70)	1977
200-meter backstroke	80–84	8:43.5	Ted Mumby (82)	1980
	75–79	5:46.5	Sheldon White (75)	1980
	70–74	5:06.9	Winston Kratz (72)	1978
100-meter breaststroke	70–74	1:15.3	Winston Kratz (70)	1976
200-meter breaststroke	75–79	5:35.4	John Whittemore (77)	1977
	70–74	4:13.9	Winston Kratz (71)	1977
50-meter butterfly	70–74	58.2	Albert Kallunki	1977
100-meter butterfly	70–74	2:12.0	Albert Kallunki	1977
150-meter individual medley	80–84	6:38.6	Ted Mumby (81)	1979
	75–79	5:58.0	Ted Mumby (78)	1976
	70–74	3:04.0	Albert Kallunki	1977
200-meter individual medley	70–74	5:14.8	Ernest Hale (70)	1980

—A.T.

THE GREAT PSYCHOLOGISTS ON THE COUCH

ALFRED ADLER (1870–1937)

Adler spoke of his childhood as an unhappy experience. His early years in Austria were shadowed by the presence of a precocious and respectable elder brother whom Alfred was forever trying to emulate. Even late in life, he said: "My eldest brother is a good industrious fellow—he was always ahead of me—and for the matter of that, he is *still* ahead of me!" Adler's father was a strong-willed man; his mother was dour and nervous. Adler always felt his mother preferred his elder brother to him; his resentment reinforced her natural coldness, and he tended to stay away from home as much as possible. Young Alfred barely survived a case of pneumonia at the age of five; one of his earliest memories was overhearing the doctor telling his father that his son had no chance of survival. "At once a frightful terror came over me, and a few days later when I was well I decided definitely to become a doctor." He was not a good student; like psychologist C. G. Jung, Adler found mathematics a terrifying ordeal, one that left him with recurring nightmares of failure. But he held to his early resolution to study medicine, and soon became interested in psychology. He joined Sigmund Freud's circle but left it after a few years, thus becoming one of the first to break with the master. Unlike Freud and Jung, Adler never claimed that his theories were the only possible explanation of mental illness or neurosis. He seems to have been one of the healthiest figures in the early days of psychology and psychoanalysis.

SIGMUND FREUD (1856–1939)

The father of modern psychoanalysis, Freud was troubled throughout his life by memories of an unhappy childhood. At the age of two or three Sigmund saw his mother nude, an event which aroused his young desires (or so he later claimed) and played a leading role in the formation of his theories on sexuality. He greatly resented the birth of a younger brother, whose unfortunate arrival stole away some of the mother love hitherto reserved exclusively for him; the boy's death eight months later left deep feelings of guilt on Freud's impressionable psyche and provided him with material for his work on family conflicts as the cause of much emotional distress in adults. His love-hate relationship with his father, Jakob, and the hostility he felt as a Jew growing up in German Vienna were reflected throughout his career in his constant struggles with colleagues and disciples. Freud insisted upon complete acceptance of his theories; he could not tolerate even the slightest questioning of his views and would systematically ostracize his major supporters and followers when they inevitably began pointing out inconsistencies in his doctrines. Freud regarded such criticism as a personal attack on him. Like many early psychologists and psychiatrists, Freud became interested in the field through his efforts to analyze his own problems and those of his family. One of his major contributions to the fledgling science was his description of the Oedipus and Electra complexes, in which a boy's desire to mate with his mother, or a girl's desire to mate with her father, can, if carried to extremes, produce severe psychological neuroses and mental aberrations. Freud saw himself as a prime example of a neurotic who had been cured through self-searching; by uncovering the underlying causes of mental problems, he believed, and by understanding them, the patient would surely be freed from his or her bonds. And yet, Freud's own writings and speeches are filled with numerous expressions of inferiority and inadequacy, even late in life. He took an almost masochistic joy in his incessant cigar smoking, although he was warned by swellings and tumors in his throat that the strong fumes were taking their toll. Inevitably, cancer of the mouth developed, and he was forced to suffer through more than 30 operations in 16 years, until he finally died in great pain just prior to W.W. II. Freud's theories live on, a curious reflection of the man who spawned them.

WILLIAM JAMES (1842–1910)

From his teens until his death, philosopher-psychologist William James suffered from "nervous disorders." His father, Henry James, was an eminent philosopher and brilliant conversationalist who had rather unorthodox ideas about child rearing, which were only partially curbed by his more practical but passive wife Mary. While he believed that children should be raised with love, spontaneity, and freedom, he also believed that childhood should be extended as long as possible. This overprotection from life's crueler realities later proved very unhealthy for William.

Henry James wholeheartedly devoted himself to the education of his five children. Unfortunately, he couldn't quite decide upon the best method of teaching. Consequently, the children were dragged back and forth from one school to another in the U.S. and Europe so often that they later claimed they had had a "hotel" childhood. In 1860 the family finally settled in Newport, R.I., so that William could study painting with the respected William M. Hunt. This career decision did not please his tyrannical father, who wanted his eldest son to enter a scientific field. Although William had apparently won the battle of wills, it was during this time that he began to suffer from several psychosomatic illnesses, including severe eyestrain, a nagging backache, and a nervous stomach. Within just a few months he announced that he was giving up painting to enter the Lawrence Scientific School of Harvard University.

Although William James subsequently entered medical school, he continued to wrestle with the many soul-searching philosophical and moral issues that had dominated his family's dinner-table conversations since childhood, often to the extent that he denied himself the pleasures of being a warm, feeling human being. He wrote in his diary, "Nature and life have unfitted me for any affectionate relations with other individuals." He also became obsessed with the idea of suicide. These feelings of inadequacy in relationships, the stifling and overindulgent family atmosphere, and his frustrations in his choice of career finally culminated in a nervous breakdown and a prolonged period of invalidism that lasted nearly three years. He wrote of these times: "If I had not clung to scripture texts like 'The eternal God is my refuge,' etc. . . . I think I should have grown really insane."

In 1872 James began teaching physiology at Harvard and soon became immersed in the new field of psychology. He set up the first laboratory for psychological research in the U.S. and wrote the definitive *Principles of Psychology*. His marriage to Alice Gibbens in 1878 helped to resolve many of his earlier doubts and his depression began to subside. Yet even with a stable personal life and his place in history as one of America's foremost philosophers assured, James continued to suffer the physical effects of a nervous, depressive personality until the day he died. He was not the only member of his family to emerge scarred from their volatile homelife; younger brother Robertson was an alcoholic and sister Alice had several nervous breakdowns and required close supervision throughout her life.

CARL GUSTAV JUNG (1875–1961)

Like his mentor Freud, Jung followed the tortuous road to psychoanalysis through his recollection of traumatic childhood experiences. In his autobiography he says: "I was deeply troubled by my mother's being away [she was ill in the hospital]. From then on, I always felt mistrustful when the word 'love' was spoken. The feeling I associated with 'woman' was for a long time that of innate unreliability. 'Father,' on the other hand, meant reliability and—powerlessness." His mother's illness was apparently psychosomatic in origin, and his parents separated shortly thereafter, while he was still a boy. His first "conscious trauma" was seeing a Catholic priest coming toward him on the road; his father's earlier rantings at the monstrous Jesuits had created a deep-seated fear of clerics in the lad, and he was terrified for days by this "apparition," even going so far as to hide himself for hours on end. "At about the same time . . . I had the earliest dream I can remember, a dream which was to preoccupy me all my life. I was then between three and four years old." What he saw in his mind was a giant phallus 15 ft. tall and 2 ft. thick, perched high on a golden throne. "For many nights afterward I was afraid to go to sleep, because I feared I might have another dream like that." The dream came back to him again and again, and each time it ended with his mother saying: "Yes, just look at him. That is the man-eater." Soon another recurring dream emerged, in which young Carl saw himself suffocated during one of his continual attacks of bronchitis, attacks which he later came to regard as at least partially psychosomatic in origin.

Carl was a lonely child whose life was filled with fear and anxiety stemming from his family problems and from the fact that his fellow students would have nothing to do with him. To avoid school, Jung began to have fainting spells, ostensibly the result of a serious fall; he passed out each time he was returned to school. When he overheard his father speculating on the future of a boy unable to earn his own living, the shock immediately ended the "spells," and he suddenly became a superior student. "That was when I learned what a neurosis is." Jung often thought of himself as "a corrupt and inferior person." Like Freud, he first became a medical doctor and later began studying mental patients; his fascination with psychology and his own childhood problems made him want to learn why and how the patients reacted as they did. Freud took the young doctor under his wing, but after five years Jung broke with the master, believing that the key to most psychoses lay in the interpretation of dreams. Dreams, Jung said, were the key to the patient's unconscious mind, the one section of the brain that reflected the real thoughts and motivations of the individual. By establishing his own school of psychoanalysis, Jung seems to have cured himself, for we hear no more in his writings of his own problems, and he seems to have lived a long and contented life thereafter.

THEODOR REIK (1888–1969)

In his autobiography Reik relates a series of traumatic experiences that occurred during his 18th year. Several days before taking the final examinations for high school graduation, Reik saw his father dying of a heart seizure. As the man lay gasping in his chair, the doctor gave young Reik a prescription to be filled immediately at the local pharmacy, 15 minutes away by foot (no other transportation was available). As he ran through the streets, the image of his father already dead "emerged" in his mind, and he slowed to a walk. Then, realizing that his father's life depended on his speed, he started running again. When he returned home, his father was dead. "The death of my father threw me into an emotional turmoil of the strangest kind. I did not understand then what had happened to me and in me. I was unable to grasp the meaning of the emotions and thoughts which beset me, and I searched in vain for a solution, groping about as does a blind man for the exit from a room." Reik found the answer to his problems in psychology, eventually becoming a disciple of Freud. "When I began to study psychoanalysis a few years later, I recognized how many typical traits were in my attitude and that they had almost the clinical character of an obsessional neurosis. Obsessions and counter-obsessions fought each other in me, and I was for many weeks a victim of those strange thoughts, compulsions, and emotions." Reik, like many of his fellow psychologists, became a compulsive overachiever, submerging his feelings of guilt in his studies and work. "It suddenly occurred to me that I wanted to become famous . . . that I wanted to give honor to his [my father's] name in making my own name well known." It was only much later that Reik realized that nothing could have saved his father—that his death was an accident of fate.

WILHELM STEKEL (1868–1940)

When Stekel was still a young child, he experienced jealousy when his mother paid more attention to his grandmother than to him, and "malignant joy" when his grandmother died. Another early memory was one involving a little girl, with whom he "played house," a game which led naturally into a mutual exploration of their young bodies. "The realization we had done something forbidden came to us both . . . I was probably two-and-a-half years old." Stekel continues: "I know I was not a model child. I was wild, stubborn, defiant; I was a problem child and very difficult to bring up." Stekel outgrew this period, later becoming a physician and then a pupil of Freud. His personality was rather cold and reserved: "My pupils have often complained of finding me unapproachable. . . . Often they have thought that I did not care much for them. . . . I have not tried to win people to my cause or make recruits. I wanted things to come to me spontaneously—as they usually did, publishers, translators, adherents. The fact was that my world had narrow boundaries so that there was no room in it for anyone except myself and my beloved wife. . . . Anyone who wants to win my favor should bring my dog a bone." Stekel had a practice during his early career of antagonizing his friends and supporters, usually just when they expected his support. This almost sadistic urge manifested itself in other ways as well. He quarreled with Freud, divorced his wife after a series of arguments, and drove away many of his acquaintances. Toward the end of his life he was forced to flee Vienna when Hitler invaded Austria, and like so many of his compatriots, he settled temporarily in England. But he was depressed and in ill health, and on June 25, 1940, after carefully planning all the details during the preceding three months, Wilhelm Stekel took his own life.

—R.R. and K.H.J.

WEIRD BEHAVIOR OF FAMOUS PEOPLE

1. When **King Prajadhipok** became ruler of Siam (Thailand) in 1925, his one obsessive fear was that he might someday be overthrown or forced to abdicate and thereby left without income. To alleviate this concern, Prajadhipok became the only known ruler to take out unemployment insurance with British and French insurance companies. The king's fear came true in 1935, when he was forced to abdicate his throne. But he had no material worries. He collected on his insurance policies and dwelt in comfort the remaining six years of his life.
2. **King Otto,** ruler of Bavaria from 1886 to 1913, insisted on starting his day by shooting a peasant every morning. To satisfy their leader's violent whim, two of Otto's more pacifist attendants played a secret game with him. One gave the king a rifle filled with blank bullets, and the other dressed as a peasant, strolled into view, and fell "dead" at the sound of the gunshot.

King Prajadhipok, beneficiary of an unemployment insurance plan.

3. Whenever German composer **Richard Wagner** (1813–1883) conducted music by Felix Mendelssohn, he would wear gloves. After the performance, Wagner would take off the gloves and throw them on the floor to be swept away by a janitor. This behavior was due to the fact that Mendelssohn was a Jew and Wagner was an anti-Semite.
4. Hailed for his 1726 satirical masterpiece, *Gulliver's Travels,* and respected as dean of St. Patrick's Cathedral in Dublin, **Jonathan Swift** suffered through his birthdays. A crusty and embittered bachelor, Swift only wore black attire on his birthdays and rejected all food. He died insane at the age of 78.
5. **Czar Peter the Great,** head of Russia from 1689 to 1725, had one troublesome phobia: He was afraid to cross bridges.
6. American poet **Walt Whitman,** who published *Leaves of Grass* in 1855, wrote much of his free verse in the first person, but he would not read anything written by anyone else in the first person.
7. **Niccolò Paganini,** the flamboyant and romantic Italian violinist and composer, reached the height of his success in Paris and London in 1831. In solo concert performances he often played with frayed violin strings, hoping that all but one would break so that he could show his skill by playing with the single remaining string.
8. Determined to make money to help her impoverished family, **Louisa May Alcott** worked as a teacher, dressmaker, and housekeeper until she finally took up writing books for children. In 1868 she became renowned throughout the U.S. for her best-seller *Little Women.* Yet writing the book bored Alcott. She intensely disliked little girls and only wrote her best-seller at the insistence of her publisher.
9. **Florenz Ziegfeld** (1869–1932), the impresario who produced 24 versions of the Ziegfeld *Follies* on Broadway, rarely communicated by letter. He liked to carry a pad of telegraph blanks with him and dash off wires. He would use up an entire pad of telegraphs in a single day. Even when he sat in the orchestra pit watching his comedians and chorines on stage above him, he would send them telegrams.

10. **King Edward VII,** Victoria's son who became ruler of England in 1901, would allow no one who came into his presence to carry loose change, because the slightest jingling of coins unnerved him.

11. Opera singer **Enrico Caruso,** who died in 1921 at age 48 in Naples, had an Italian peasant's belief in superstitions. He always consulted an astrologer before making an ocean crossing and he never started a journey on Tuesday or Friday.

12. **King Charles II,** ruler of Great Britain from 1660 to 1685 and master of Nell Gwyn, sometimes gathered up powder from the mummies of Egyptian kings and rubbed the powder on himself in the belief that he would acquire "ancient greatness."

13. **Cardinal Richelieu,** prime minister of France in 1624 under King Louis XIII and the real ruler of his country, got his daily exercise by jumping over furniture.

14. **Alphonse Daudet,** French novelist and playwright, made his reputation with the production of his first play, *La Dernière Idole,* in Paris in 1862. He wore his eyeglasses to bed every night and went to sleep with them on.

15. **Eddie Rickenbacker,** the top U.S. flying ace in W.W. I (with 26 victories), made his name as an automobile-racing driver. He became one of America's three leading drivers, yet he never bothered to get a driver's license in his life. He died in 1973.

16. Nothing got the French author **Voltaire** down—not even a month of imprisonment in the Bastille in 1717. Nothing, that is, except the scent of roses. Whenever he smelled roses he fell into a faint.

17. **Baruch Spinoza,** the Portuguese-Jewish philosopher who lived in Holland, worked constantly tutoring, grinding lenses, and writing controversial books (*Ethics,* for one, which he finished in 1674). His favorite form of relaxation was to catch two spiders and watch them fight each other.

18. **Commodore Cornelius Vanderbilt,** the U.S. shipping and railroad tycoon who amassed a fortune of $100 million by the time of his death in 1877, never owned a checkbook. He wrote most of his checks on half sheets of blank writing paper.

19. **Andrew Carnegie** (1835–1919), the benevolent steel magnate, adored his mother and refused to marry as long as she was alive. When she died, Carnegie finally married at age 52 and had his only child at 62. After his mother's death, Carnegie did not mention her name for 15 years.

20. **Hans Christian Andersen,** famous worldwide for such fairy tales as "The Princess and the Pea" and "The Emperor's New Clothes," was terrified of being prematurely declared dead and buried alive. He almost always carried a note in his pocket telling anyone who might find him unconscious that it must not be assumed he was dead unless he was examined again. He often left another note on his bedside table stating, "I only seem dead." But in 1875, when he died of cancer in Copenhagen, he was very dead.

—I.W.

14

MAKING LISTS

TAX BURDEN CARRIED BY PEOPLE IN 22 COUNTRIES

An exhaustive survey of tax revenues in various countries by the Organization for Economic Cooperation and Development (OECD) showed that the total tax burden for individuals in the U.S.—including national, state, and local levies—is smaller than that in most other developed countries. The following figures are measured in cents per dollar of Gross Domestic Product. Sixteen of the 22 developed countries exact a bigger tax bite than the U.S. does, but only in the United Kingdom has the tax rate gone down.

	Cents per Dollar				
	1968–1970				
Country	*Average*	*1979*			
1. Sweden	43.0	52.9	12. Ireland	29.8	33.3
2. Luxembourg	32.4	49.9	13. Italy	30.1	32.8
3. Netherlands	39.7	47.2	14. Switzerland	21.5	31.5
4. Norway	38.4	46.7	15. New Zealand	n.a.*	31.4
5. Denmark	38.7	45.0	16. Canada	30.2	31.2
6. Belgium	33.8	44.5	17. United States	27.9	30.2
7. Austria	35.8	41.2	18. Australia	24.4	28.8
8. France	36.3	41.0	19. Portugal	21.1	25.9
9. Germany	34.0	37.2	20. Japan	19.4	24.1
10. Finland	32.8	35.1	21. Spain	19.2	22.8
11. United Kingdom	36.6	33.8	22. Turkey	20.4	22.5

*Not available.

Source: Revenue Statistics of OECD Member Countries 1965–1979, OECD Paris, 1980.

THE 8 COUNTRIES WITH THE GREATEST NUMBER OF CONTIGUOUS NEIGHBORS

Except for island-nations, every country in the world abuts at least one neighbor; most touch three or four. Five countries—Austria, Mali,

Niger, Yugoslavia, and Zambia—share borders with seven neighbors. The eight countries listed below are the only modern nations with eight or more contiguous neighbors. Their neighbors are listed in clockwise rotation.

1. CHINA (13 neighbors)

1. Mongolia 2. U.S.S.R. 3. North Korea 4. Hong Kong (U.K. dependency) 5. Macao (Portuguese territory) 6. Vietnam 7. Laos 8. Burma 9. India 10. Bhutan 11. Nepal 12. Pakistan 13. Afghanistan

2. U.S.S.R. (12 neighbors)

1. North Korea 2. China 3. Mongolia 4. Afghanistan 5. Iran 6. Turkey 7. Romania 8. Hungary 9. Czechoslovakia 10. Poland 11. Finland 12. Norway

3. BRAZIL (10 neighbors)

1. Uruguay 2. Argentina 3. Paraguay 4. Bolivia 5. Peru 6. Colombia 7. Venezula 8. Guyana 9. Suriname 10. French Guiana

4. WEST GERMANY (9 neighbors)

1. Denmark 2. East Germany 3. Czechoslovakia 4. Austria 5. Switzerland 6. France 7. Luxembourg 8. Belgium 9. Netherlands

5. ZAIRE (9 neighbors)

1. Central African Republic 2. Sudan 3. Uganda 4. Rwanda 5. Burundi 6. Tanzania 7. Zambia 8. Angola (including Cabinda) 9. Congo

6. SAUDI ARABIA (8 neighbors)

1. Iraq 2. Kuwait 3. Qatar 4. United Arab Emirates 5. Oman 6. People's Democratic Republic of Yemen 7. Yemen Arab Republic 8. Jordan

7. SUDAN (8 neighbors)

1. Egypt 2. Ethiopia 3. Kenya 4. Uganda 5. Zaire 6. Central African Republic 7. Chad 8. Libya

8. TANZANIA (8 neighbors)

1. Uganda 2. Kenya 3. Mozambique 4. Malawi 5. Zambia 6. Zaire 7. Burundi 8. Rwanda

—R.K.R.

WHAT 10 DEFEATED NATIONS PLANNED TO DO HAD THEY WON THE WAR

1. GREAT BRITAIN (American War for Independence, 1776–1781)

If Great Britain had defeated the American rebels, it would have restored its authority by assigning a British governor to each of the 13

American colonies and disbanding all revolutionary governments, including the Continental Congress. British Prime Minister Lord Frederick North intended to be lenient with the rebels, granting pardons to all except the most prominent military and congressional leaders. On the issue of taxation, North expected to effect conciliation by offering the colonial legislatures the right to raise their own taxes rather than be taxed directly by Parliament. However, the rebels would have been forced to compensate American Loyalists fully for their losses during the war. If the British had won, they also planned to limit American territorial expansion by giving the Ohio River and Great Lakes region to Canada.

2. FRANCE (Napoleonic Wars, 1796–1815)

Had France conquered Great Britain and Russia, Napoleon Bonaparte would have ruled Europe through his Continental System. Austria, Britain, Prussia, and Russia would have had limited internal autonomy while France retained the right to govern their foreign affairs. The rest of the European nations would have been ruled directly by Napoleon or indirectly through national leaders appointed by him. Among Napoleon's many plans was the unification of conquered Germany and Italy as French satellites. Also, Napoleon intended to create a French colonial empire in the Caribbean, in South America, and in the North American Louisiana Territory. Napoleon's France, if it had won, would have ruled not only Europe but the Americas except for a surrounded U.S.

3. MEXICO (Mexican-American War, 1846–1848)

Initially, a victorious Mexico would have reoccupied Texas, lost in 1836 when American settlers successfully rebelled against the Mexican government and established the Republic of Texas. Then the Mexican government intended to expel a majority of the Americans and outlaw slavery, which had been imported by these Southerners. Officials hoped to march beyond Texas and capture New Orleans and Mobile, with the idea that Louisiana and southern Alabama would ultimately be ceded to Mexico. After defeating the U.S., Mexican leaders would have weakened the American position further by aiding warring Indian tribes and supporting black slave revolts in the South.

4. RUSSIA (Russo-Japanese War, 1904–1905)

By 1904 Nicholas II of Russia had decided to create a Far Eastern empire in Asia. Once the Russo-Japanese War was won, the Russians planned to annex China's immense Manchurian province and incorporate it as part of Siberia. The czar also intended to occupy Korea and eventually make it part of his empire. This would have involved the settlement of Russian and Cossack pioneers in Manchuria and Korea and the building of railroads to link the area with the rest of Russia. Then Russia would have exploited China's weakened political and economic condition and gradually annexed additional chunks of Chinese territory. Had it won the war, Russia, not Japan, would have been the major power in northern Asia in the first half of the 20th century.

5. AUSTRIA-HUNGARY (W.W. I, 1914–1918)

During the war, the Austro-Hungarian Empire's major goal was to stay in existence. A polyglot country comprising the modern nations of Czechoslovakia, Hungary, and Austria—and parts of Poland, Yugoslavia, Romania, and Italy—Austria-Hungary contemplated annexing the Balkan nations of Serbia, Montenegro, and Albania, as well as additional portions of Italy and Romania if the Central Powers were victorious. Allowing Germany to carve off large sections of Russia would have reduced the threat of Russian influence in the Balkans, which then could be dominated by Austria-Hungary from Greece north to Poland. Instead of becoming one nation, this area was splintered into eight unstable countries by the Treaty of Saint-Germain in 1919.

6. GERMANY (W.W. I, 1914–1918)

Germany's primary objective was to become Europe's major military and political power. Had Germany won the war, Kaiser Wilhelm II would have annexed parts of Belgium, including its coastal regions, and made the remainder into a client state. The Germans intended to create a Polish kingdom, dependent on Germany, which would act as a buffer against future Russian aggression. The Germans also wanted to annex the industrial and mining sections of northern France, Russia's Ukrainian and Baltic provinces, and Romania's Black Sea coastline and seaports. In order to become a global naval and colonial power, Germany would have occupied and taken over the Belgian Congo (modern Zaire), the Azores Islands, Senegal, and Tahiti from Belgium, Portugal, and France. While increasing its own might, Germany was going to weaken both France and Russia, making them second-rate powers in Europe.

7. GERMANY (W.W. II, 1939–1945)

Adolf Hitler planned to create a New Order—a united Europe ruled by Nazis for the benefit of Germany. In the Soviet Union, the Nazis were supposed to destroy the major cities and reduce the population so that Russia would become an underpopulated, totally agrarian nation that could be colonized by Germany's excess population. Great Britain was to be occupied and ruled by S.S. Col. Franz Six, whose first move was going to be the arrest of 2,300 political, religious, and intellectual leaders, beginning with Winston Churchill. Then all men between the ages of 17 and 45 were to be deported to continental Europe to work in German industry. Hitler also made tentative plans to occupy the U.S. and Canada from the Atlantic coast to the Rocky Mountains.

8. ITALY (W.W. II, 1939–1943)

Italian dictator Benito Mussolini had visions of recreating the conquests and boundaries of the ancient Roman Empire. The Italian Fascist government was to achieve control of the Mediterranean region of southern Europe and North Africa by annexing and directly ruling Albania, Greece, Tunisia, Egypt, Malta, and possibly Algeria and Morocco. If the Axis Powers had won the war, Mussolini's empire would also have included the Red Sea, the western Indian Ocean, and eastern Africa after his forces occupied the Suez Canal zone, Yemen, the Sudan, and the Horn of Africa, namely, Ethiopia and Somalia. Mussolini made plans to offset his German partner Adolf Hitler's power after the war by creating a "Latin Axis"—an alliance of nations under Italian tutelage—which would include Vichy France, Spain, Portugal, Romania, Hungary, and Finland. Once it was an imperial and colonial power, Italy could have used the natural resources of its client states to become a major industrial and military power as well.

9. JAPAN (W.W. II, 1941–1945)

After victory, Japan expected to eradicate European and American economic and military influence in Asia quickly and establish itself as the political master of that continent. Expansion of the Japanese Empire predicated a direct annexation of Manchuria, Korea, Taiwan, and the southern and central Pacific islands. The rest of Asia—China, Indochina, the Philippines, Thailand, Indonesia, Malaya, Burma, and India—would be controlled through puppet governments belonging to the Japanese Greater East Asia Co-Prosperity Sphere. The Japanese intended to use the Greater East Asia association to feed its expanding industries with raw materials after the war. Japan also expected to defeat the U.S.S.R. and occupy Siberia and Mongolia. At one point, the Japanese tentatively agreed to divide the U.S. and Canada with the Germans after the war was won. Alaska, Hawaii, and the continental U.S. west of the Rocky Mountains were to go to Japan.

10. EGYPT (Israeli War for Independence, 1948)

When the U.N. voted to partition Palestine into separate Arab and Jewish states, Egypt waged war against the Israelis with the intention of destroying the new Jewish country and establishing Arab rule over all of Palestine. Faruk I, the king of Egypt, was determined to dominate Arab Palestine by installing his puppet Mohammed Said Haj Amin el Husseini, the mufti of Jerusalem, as king of the new nation. It is not known what Faruk had in store for the Jews living in Palestine, but his protégé Mohammed Said Haj Amin el Husseini called for "extermination and momentous massacre." Faruk also anticipated seizing the Suez Canal from Britain after defeating the Israelis.

—R.J.F.

6 VICTIMS OF THE FATAL NINTH SYMPHONY

1. LUDWIG VAN BEETHOVEN (1770–1827)

Considered one of history's greatest composers, Beethoven became a professional organist when he was only 11 years old. Some of his most intricate works were created after he became almost totally deaf. He had just completed his Ninth Symphony and had promised the London

Philharmonic Society his tenth when he caught cold on a trip to Vienna. Jaundiced and dropsical, he died a few months later.

2. ANTON BRUCKNER (1824–1896)

As a child, Bruckner was expected to follow in his father's footsteps and become a village schoolmaster in Austria. But after his father's death he became a choirboy at the Monastery of St. Florian near Linz, where he learned to play the organ, bass, and violin. He did not receive recognition as a major composer of sacred music until the end of his life. While working on the final sketches of his Ninth Symphony, Bruckner died. At his request he was buried under the church organ in the village of St. Florian.

Anton Bruckner.

3. ANTON DVOŘÁK (1841–1904)

Dvořák was the first composer of Bohemian ancestry to achieve international acclaim. His exceptional musical ability was first recognized when he played in his father's band at age eight. In 1892 Dvořák accepted the position of director of the National Conservatory of Music in New York. He remained in the U.S. for three years and was extremely successful as a composer, conductor, and teacher. Dvořák's Symphony No. 9 in E Minor, *From the New World,* his final and best-known symphony, was first performed at a Philharmonic Society concert in New York in 1893. He died in Bohemia in 1904, a victim of Bright's disease.

4. ALEKSANDER KONSTANTINOVICH GLAZUNOV (1865–1936)

Glazunov was endowed with an extraordinary musical memory.

Even as a child he could reconstruct a complete piece of music after hearing it only once. His First Symphony was composed at the age of 16. His last complete symphony, the Eighth, was finished in 1906. Two movements of the Ninth Symphony were completed in 1907. Leaving the Soviet Union in 1928, he embarked on a two-year tour of the U.S., which was largely unsuccessful. Subsequently he settled in Paris, where he died at 71.

5. GUSTAV MAHLER (1860–1911)

Mahler was born into a family of Jewish shopkeepers in Bohemia. After discovering the piano in his grandfather's house, the six-year-old genius became oblivious to everything except music. He was taken to a professor at the Vienna Conservatory who, after hearing a few of Mahler's compositions, labeled him a born musician. Throughout his career Mahler set unusually high standards for himself. At one point he even resigned from his position as a conductor in Prague because his musical ideas were not followed fanatically. Suffering from heart disease, he had completed nine symphonies when he collapsed from overwork. Before he died Mahler raised his finger and moved it back and forth as if it were a baton. His last word was *Mozart*. He was buried in Vienna in utter silence—at his request; not a word was uttered, not a note was sung.

6. RALPH VAUGHAN WILLIAMS (1872–1958)

Vaughan Williams was educated at Trinity College in Cambridge and the Royal College of Music in London. His knowledge of English folk music and music from the Tudor period enabled him to create a very individual yet national musical style. His varied compositions include choral and orchestral works, chamber music, and songs. His Ninth Symphony, a rather bleak and desolate piece of music, was completed before his death in 1958.

—D.G.I. and D.B.S.

THE 20 MOST PROLIFIC AUTHORS IN LITERARY HISTORY

1. MARY FAULKNER (1903–1973) 904 books

South African writer Mrs. Mary Faulkner, whom the *Guinness Book of World Records* ranks as history's most prolific novelist, wrote under six pen names, including Kathleen Lindsay. Her novels include *There Is No Yesterday, Wind of Desire,* and *Harvest of Deceit.*

2. LAURAN PAINE (b. 1916) 850+ books

American paperback novelist using 70 pen names. Paine has written mostly westerns, such as *The Man from Wells Fargo* (1961), and some mysteries and romances.

3. PRENTISS INGRAHAM (1843–1904) 600+ books

American dime novelist who occasionally wrote a 35,000-word book overnight. He wrote 200 books on Buffalo Bill alone.

3. JÓZEF IGNACY KRASZEWSKI (1812–1887) 600+ books

Polish writer of novels, plays, poetry, essays, biographies, history, memoirs, and political sketches. His novels included *Szalona (The Crazy Woman).*

5. ENID MARY BLYTON (1900?–1968) 600 books

English children's writer whose books are popular worldwide. Her best-known series are the Noddy, Famous Five, and Secret Seven ones.

6. JOHN CREASEY (1908–1973) 564 books

Gordon Ashe, Michael Halliday, and J. J. Maric were among this English mystery writer's many pen names. His Inspector West and Gideon series are the most popular.

7. SUYUTI (1445–1505) 561 books

Arab encyclopedist who wrote on almost every aspect of science and literature. His best-known works are commentaries on the Koran.

8. URSULA BLOOM (b. 1898?) 520+ books

English romance novelist with many pen names. Her books include *Doctor on Call* and *The Flying Nurse*. She also has written some nonfiction under her own name.

9. GEORGES SIMENON (b. 1903) 500+ books

Belgian-born mystery writer with more than 200 books published under his own name and over 300 published under 17 pen names. His most famous character is Inspector Maigret.

10. HOWARD ROGER GARIS (1873–1962) 500+ books

American children's writer, best known as the creator of Uncle Wiggily. Garis also contributed books to Edward L. Stratemeyer's many series (see below).

11. ARTHUR WILLIAM GROOM (1898–1964) 400+ books

British writer of children's books and adult fiction and nonfiction under many different pen names. A specialist in westerns, he wrote "novelizations" about real people such as Roy Rogers and Davy Crockett as well as books about fictional heroes like Hopalong Cassidy.

11. EDWARD ZANE CARROLL JUDSON (1823–1886) 400+ books

American dime novelist and magazine writer, better known as Ned Buntline. Judson gave William F. Cody the nickname Buffalo Bill and wrote the first stories about him.

11. EDWARD L. STRATEMEYER (1862–1930) 400 + books

American founder of the publishing syndicate that puts out the Nancy Drew and Hardy Boys and other popular children's series. Using many pen names, he wrote more than 400 novels himself and outlined hundreds more for staff writers. His daughter, Harriet S. Adams, succeeded him.

14. BAKIN (1767–1848) 300 + books

Japanese novelist. One of the most popular writers of his day, Bakin is best known for his 106-volume novel, *Hakkenden (Tale of Eight Dogs).*

14. EVELYN EVERETT GREEN (1856–1932) 300 + books

British author of both adult and children's books, often writing as "Cecil Adair." Her last book was *The Imprudence of Carol.*

14. NIGEL MORLAND (b. 1905) 300 + books

British mystery writer with several pen names. His best-known character is Mrs. Pym of Scotland Yard.

17. D. S. ROWLAND (b. 1928) 286 + books

British paperback novelist who uses more than 50 pen names. His output includes westerns, science fiction, and such romances as *Highland Nurse* and *Wayward Nurse.*

18. BARBARA CARTLAND (b. 1902) 280 ± books

British writer of historical fiction who also uses the name Barbara McCorquodale. In recent years she has published over 20 books per year, including *The Curse of the Clan* and *I Seek the Miraculous.*

19. ALEXANDRE DUMAS père (1802–1870) 277 books

The famous French author of *The Three Musketeers* and *The Count of Monte Cristo* said to Napoleon III that he had written 1,200 volumes, but that, of course, was in the days of multivolume novels. (*Musketeers* originally filled eight volumes.) His complete works were collected in 277 volumes, most of which he wrote with collaborators.

20. L. T. MEADE (1854–1914) 258 ± books

British writer of stories for girls of all ages. Her most popular books include *The Autocrat of the Nursery* and *A World of Girls.*

—R.K.R.

20 ILLUSTRIOUS PEOPLE WHO WERE ONCE SCHOOLTEACHERS

1. Louisa May Alcott (1832–1888), U.S. author
2. Clara Barton (1821–1912), U.S. founder of the American Red Cross

3. Clarence Darrow (1857–1938), U.S. lawyer
4. Havelock Ellis (1859–1939), British sexologist
5. Roberta Flack (1940–), U.S. singer
6. John Fowles (1926–), British author
7. Art Garfunkel (1941–), U.S. singer
8. Vo Nguyen Giap (1910?–), Vietnamese army chief
9. W. C. Handy (1873–1958), U.S. blues composer
10. John Wesley Hardin (1853–1895), U.S. outlaw
11. Edith Head (1907–), U.S. costume designer
12. Lyndon B. Johnson (1908–1973), U.S. president
13. D. H. Lawrence (1885–1930), British author
14. Albert Luthuli (1898–1967), South African political leader
15. Benito Mussolini (1883–1945), Italian dictator
16. Carry Nation (1846–1911), U.S. temperance leader
17. Pat Nixon (1912–), U.S. first lady
18. George Orwell (1903–1950), British author
19. Thomas Paine (1737–1809), U.S. patriot
20. Lydia Pinkham (1819–1883), U.S. patent-medicine manufacturer

—The Eds.

10 CHILDREN WHO SUPPORTED THEIR PARENT(S)

1. WOLFGANG AMADEUS MOZART (1756–1791), Austrian composer

When the young Mozart was six—and already an accomplished pianist and neophyte composer—his father, Leopold Mozart, took his children on the first of several moneymaking tours of Europe, during which Wolfgang and his sister performed for royalty. Leopold's stipend as Kapellmeister to the Austrian court was cut off in 1769 because of his frequent lengthy absences from Salzburg. Until his father's income was restored, Wolfgang supported the family.

2. GIOACCHINO ROSSINI (1792–1868), Italian composer

By 1804, when his mother's chronic throat ailment ended her singing career, young Gioacchino had made his operatic debut, and a year later he was singing professionally—sometimes for only three lire a night—and writing sonatas. His father, also a musician, was not earning much, and Gioacchino became the main support of the family. His singing voice was so beautiful that there was talk of making him a castrato, but his mother vetoed the idea.

3. CHANG and ENG BUNKER (1811–1874), Siamese twins

After their father died in the cholera epidemic of 1819, the boys—joined chest to chest by a 6-in. ligament—struggled to support the family of five by working first as fishermen and then as merchants, from the age of 8 until they were 13. Later they became famous when they were exhibited around the world as the original "Siamese Twins."

4. JAMES KEIR HARDIE (1856–1915), British labor leader

Employed as a messenger boy, he became his family's sole support at the age of 10 when his father had no work during a shipyard lockout. Later the same year, young James went to work in the mines. It was owing to his experiences as a child that Hardie became a labor agitator and founded the British Labour party.

5. ANNIE JONES (1865–1902), U.S. circus star

When she was only nine months old, the infant—already sprouting hair on her face—was signed up for display as a freak in P. T. Barnum's circus. Her $150-a-week salary went to support her family. By the age of five she had a mustache and sideburns and was known as the "Bearded Girl."

6. WILLIAM RICHARD MORRIS (1877–1963), British industrialist

Though it was his ambition to become a surgeon, 15-year-old William Morris had to go to work repairing bicycles to support the family when his father got sick. This job eventually led to his later career as developer of Morris Motors, Ltd., and other enterprises.

7. UPTON SINCLAIR (1878–1968), U.S. author

Sinclair's father, who came from a long line of southern aristocrats, was a heavy drinker and consequently was unable to provide for his family. At age 15, Sinclair became the family's financial mainstay by selling short stories to *Argosy* magazine and jokes to pulp magazines. At 17 he moved away from home but continued to support his parents.

8. DAVID SARNOFF (1891–1971), U.S. radio executive

A recent chairman of the board of RCA, Sarnoff became the sole support for his poverty-stricken Russian immigrant family when he began selling newspapers at age 10. He supplemented this income by jobbing out to other newsboys and singing in the synagogue choir. When he was 13 he bought his own newsstand with the help of a $200 gift from a wealthy patron, selling it four years later for a profit.

9. RUTH SLENCZYNSKA (b. 1925), U.S. pianist

Ruth's father was so anxious to sire a musician that he chose his wife partly for her well-shaped hands. He started teaching Ruth piano when she was three, and soon was forcing her to practice as much as nine hours a day. At four she was playing in public, earning $1,100 per performance. It was this money that took the family to Europe and enabled them to live comfortably. She ended her career at 15, though she later made a comeback.

10. DARLA HOOD (1933–1979), U.S. movie actress

From the time she was 5 until she was 10, Darla Hood—billed as the "little sweetheart"—made 48 *Our Gang* comedies at a salary of $750 a week. The money went to support her family.

—A.E.

28 COUNTRIES WITHOUT TELEVISION

1. Andorra
2. Bhutan
3. Botswana
4. Burundi
5. Cameroon
6. Cape Verde Islands
7. Comoro Islands
8. Fiji
9. Gambia
10. Guyana
11. Kampuchea
12. Kiribati
13. Laos
14. Lesotho
15. Liechtenstein
16. Malawi
17. Mali
18. Namibia
19. Nauru
20. Nepal
21. Papua New Guinea (TV service expected to begin 1982)
22. Rwanda
23. San Marino
24. Seychelles
25. Solomon Islands
26. Tonga
27. Tuvalu
28. Vatican City

—W.J.C. and the Eds.

20 ATHLETES WHO OVERCAME HANDICAPS

1. ROCKY BLEIER—football

Drafted during his rookie season with the Pittsburgh Steelers and sent to Vietnam, where his right foot and leg were severely injured (40% disability) by an exploding grenade. After years of a self-imposed regime of exercise and struggle against seemingly insurmountable odds, Bleier became a regular in the Steeler backfield after distinguishing himself on special teams. His superb blocking and running helped carry Pittsburgh to four Super Bowls.

2. CHARLEY BOSWELL—golf

Blinded during W.W. II while rescuing a buddy from a tank that was under fire. A gifted athlete and pro baseball prospect, he took up golf, a sport he had never before attempted. In 1947 won the National Blind Golf tournament, a feat that he repeated 13 times. Received the Ben Hogan Award (1958) and the Distinguished American Award (1965).

3. LOU BRISSIE—baseball

Both legs badly mangled in W.W. II, requiring 23 operations over a two-year period. Made it to the majors as a pitcher. Was 14–10 for the Philadelphia A's in 1948.

4. HAROLD CONNOLLY—track and field

Born with slightly withered left arm; took up hammer throw to strengthen it. Won the gold medal in the hammer in the 1956 Olympics; held the world record until 1960.

5. GLENN CUNNINGHAM—track and field

Both legs severely burned in schoolhouse fire at age 8. Became the NCAA and AAU champion in the mile. Won the Sullivan Trophy for athletic achievements and sportsmanship. Despite a toeless left foot, he set world record in the mile in 1934 with 4:06.7. Took silver medal in the 1,500 meters in the 1936 Olympics.

6. WALTER DAVIS—track and field

Polio victim at age 9; used athletics for rehabilitation. Excelled in high school and college basketball. Won the gold medal in the high jump in the 1952 Olympics with 6 ft. 8¼ in.; set world record in 1953 with 6 ft. 11½ in.

7. RAY EWRY—track and field

Stricken with a form of paralysis in childhood. Confined to bed, then a wheelchair. Regained use of legs through daily exercises. Won Olympic gold medals in various standing jumps in 1900, 1904, 1906, and 1908. Still holds the record for the most medals won in Olympic competition (10).

8. PETER GRAY—baseball

The only one-armed major leaguer in history, Gray lost his right arm in an accident at age 6. In 1944 the Southern League voted him Most Valuable Player, and the following season he was signed by the St. Louis Browns. He played 77 games with the Browns and batted .218.

9. LIS HARTEL—equestrian

The Danish riding champion contracted a severe case of polio in her mid-20s. Was finally able to walk on crutches after months of grueling daily exercises. Three years after illness, took second in the women's dressage in the Scandinavian riding championships, though she was still paralyzed below the knees. Took the silver medal in the dressage in 1952 and 1956 Olympics.

10. JOHN HILLER—baseball

The ace reliever for the Detroit Tigers suffered a heart attack in January, 1971. Rejoined the team midway in 1972 season. Set record in 1973 with 38 saves. Won the Fireman of the Year award, Comeback

Player of the Year, Tiger of the Year, and the Hutchinson Award, given to the player exhibiting extraordinary courage.

11. BEN HOGAN—golf

Golf career appeared to be ended by a near-fatal accident in 1949. Received numerous injuries; surgery for blood clots in legs left circulation impaired. Came back to dominate major tournaments. Won U.S. Open in 1950; Masters and U.S. Open in 1951; Masters, U.S. Open, and British Open in 1953, a theretofore unequaled achievement. Named to PGA Hall of Fame in 1953.

12. JOHN KONRADS—swimming

Became a world champion despite having had polio as a youngster. Discovered by a swimming coach at age 12. Won the gold medal for Australia in the 1,500-meter freestyle in the 1960 Olympics.

13. GENE LITTLER—golf

A consistent tournament winner, one of the few golfers to win both the U.S. Amateur and the U.S. Open (1953 and 1961, respectively). Underwent surgery for cancer of the lymph glands in the spring of 1972; was back on the tour in October. Won over $95,000 in 1973. Received Golf Writers' Award for courageous comeback and the Ben Hogan Award, given by the USGA for distinguished sportsmanship.

14. JACK PARDEE—football

Distinguished career as linebacker for the Los Angeles Rams interrupted in 1964 by skin cancer on the arm. Came back to the Rams in 1966. Was later traded to the Washington Redskins, for whom he became head coach in 1978.

15. RICK RHODEN—baseball

Crippled with osteomyelitis as a youngster. Wore a brace on his right leg for three years, then walked with a cane. Drafted as a pitcher by the Los Angeles Dodgers. Came up in 1974; earned a place in the starting rotation in 1976.

16. WILMA RUDOLPH—track

Stricken with scarlet fever and double pneumonia at age 4, lost use of left leg. Learned to walk at age 7; took up track at 12. Won three gold medals in the sprints in the 1960 Olympics, setting an Olympic record in the 100-meter dash.

17. O. J. SIMPSON—football

As a youth, suffered from rickets, a calcium deficiency. Wore braces for several years; disease left legs bowed. Won the Heisman Trophy in 1968 after outstanding career at the University of Southern California. Holds all-time pro rushing record of 2,003 yd. in single season.

18. DAVE STALLWORTH—basketball

A two-time All-American and first-round draft choice of the New York Knicks. Suffered a heart attack at end of second pro season. Came back after two years; played all 82 games for the Knicks in 1970.

19. KÁROLY TÁKACS—pistol shooting

The champion Hungarian marksman lost his right hand in 1938; learned to shoot with his left. Won gold medals in 1948 and 1952 Olympics.

20. BILL TALBERT—tennis

Diagnosed as diabetic at age 9 in 1928, when prescribed treatment was total inactivity to conserve energy. At age 13 took up tennis after he convinced his father and his doctors to allow him to participate in active sports. Won a total of 33 national championships, 30 of them in doubles.

—L.Ch.

15

THE PEOPLE'S DIRECTORY

UNUSUAL AND SPECIALIZED MAGAZINES AND PERIODICALS

THE ALLERGY SHOT

Subscription: Quarterly; $10 per annum; Allergy Information Association, Room 7, 25 Poynter Drive, Weston, Ontario M9R 1K8, Canada; circulation 3,500.
Subject Matter: Tips on the practical management of allergies. Includes hints on special foods, cooking, fabrics, cleaning products, plus medical news, research, and book reviews.
Sample Articles: "Label Reading"; "Flame-retardant Sleepwear—U.S.A."; "Heart Attacks Fewer for Breast-fed Babies."
Sample Materials: "It is now estimated that we all eat 9 lb. of additives a year, unless we make a real effort to avoid them. In 1970, the estimated figure was 5 lb. per annum per person. Despite the increased use and interest in natural food, we are still consuming more additives every year. We are all aware of the possibility of toxicity of additives. . . . It is difficult enough to buy pure fruit juices, so many 'juices' offered are only sugar, water, and additives. Substitute eggs, claimed to be equal in nutrition to eggs, failed a rat feeding test."

"Wine has been prescribed as a medication for centuries. Researchers with the Department of Health and Welfare know why. Wine reduces the activity of several viruses that infect the human stomach. For example, wine kills herpes simplex virus—a cause of cold sores. The chemicals contained in the skin of grapes are the source of the benefits of wine. Red wine is better than white wine for this action. Pure grape juice is the best source of all."

"The principal ingredient of deodorant is a highly allergenic substance, aluminum chlorhydrate. . . . [Researchers] have discovered that rats exposed to aluminum chlorhydrate via spray developed chronic lung inflammation. . . . Asthmatics have been cautioned by AIA and their physicians not to use spray products of any kind."

ALTERNATIVE SOURCES OF ENERGY

Subscription: Bimonthly; $15 a year, $20 a year to businesses and institutions; 107 S. Central Avenue, Milaca, Minn. 56353; circulation 6,000.
Subject Matter: The magazine covers how-to articles and current innovative trends in practical application of alternative forms of energy—solar, wind, wood, water, alcohol, biomass, etc.
Sample Articles: "Architecture Is People"; "Envelope Homes: A Climate Study"; "Earth Shelter 2: A Conference Report."
Sample Material: "On Tuesday, Mar. 28 [1980], alcohol-powered cars went on sale in Brazil. Brazilians are buying alcohol-powered cars from Volkswagen, Fiat, Ford, General Motors, and Chrysler. 'We and the other manufacturers agree that the alcohol car is now a reality for Brazil,' Ford's director of manufacturing and engineering, Mauro Borghetti, told *Business Week* magazine. . . . The Brazilian government expects that, within a few years, all private cars will be required to use only alcohol, not just gasohol."

ANABIOSIS

Subscription: Triannually; $15 per year, overseas $20 per year; P.O. Box 2309, East Peoria, Ill. 61611; circulation 243.
Subject Matter: *Anabiosis*, subtitled "A Regular Digest of News for the Membership of the Association for the Scientific Study of Near-Death Phenomena, Inc.," contains information about the latest developments in the field of near-death research, personal accounts of near-death experiences, life-after-death themes in historical art, news briefs, and book reviews.
Sample Material: "No mode of nearly dying has occasioned more interest than that of the suicide attempt. What does the individual who attempts to take his own life experience when he reaches the threshold of death? . . . it appears that suicide-related NDEs [near-death experiences] are not different in any significant way from those which occur in conjunction with illness or accident. Exactly the same features are disclosed by suicide survivors who have come close to death in finding themselves out of their body, being able to view their physical body as though a spectator to it, floating through a dark space, becoming aware of a golden light and a 'presence' with which they communicate, and so on."

THE APBA JOURNAL

Subscription: Monthly; $9.50 a year; 5705 Williamsburg Way, Durham, N.C. 27713; circulation 2,500.
Subject Matter: *The APBA Journal* is devoted exclusively to fans of APBA table-top sports games produced by the APBA Game Company, Lancaster, Pa.
Sample Materials: "I recently visited the APBA Game Company . . . and had the pleasure to interview Mr. Fritz Light, APBA's master card maker.

AJ: Who are your favorite teams?

FRITZ: The Phillies, I'm sorry to say, and the Eagles.

AJ: When did you start to play APBA?

FRITZ: I started with the 1952 set . . . let's see, that would be in 1953, when I was seven years old.

AJ: Which is your favorite APBA game?

FRITZ: Baseball, since it is my favorite sport.

AJ: Do you play the master or the regular game?

FRITZ: I like both. I like the managerial challenge involved in the master game, but I guess I prefer the basic game for solitaire since I grew up playing it."

"Here's a trivia oddity. The 1975 Mets were playing the 1973 Yankees. Matty Alou of the Yanks was on second base with one out. Ron Blomberg, Roy White, and Graig Nettles were the next three hitters. My next three dice rolls were 11, 66, 11 and you know how many runs I got out of it? None! That's right! Nobody! . . . Here's how it happened. With Blomberg at the plate, I rolled an 11 but one die rolled off my dining room table for a foul ball. The next dice roll was a 66 but one die was on the floor after once again rolling off my table. So, then I rolled another 11. This time it remained on the table. Blomberg has a five there. Homer, right? Wrong! Tug McGraw was pitching and his Master Game rating is an 11. Blomberg loses five points against the lefthander McGraw."

THE BAKER STREET JOURNAL

Subscription: Quarterly; $10 a year, $11 overseas; Fordham University Press, University Box L, Bronx, N.Y. 10458; circulation 2,000.
Subject Matter: The *Journal* is the official organ of the Baker Street Irregulars, the American Sherlock Holmes society. It is devoted to articles on Sherlock Holmes and the Sherlockian scene.
Sample Articles: "The Theology of Sherlock Holmes"; "Sherlock Holmes was a Bastard!"; "Sherlock Holmes: Victorian Archetype."
Sample Material: "In no way have Victorians been more frequently exemplified than by their treatment of the delicate subject of sex. Discretion and decorum were everything to Victorians. Their affairs were conducted discreetly, and for the sake of appearances, they prudently refrained from referring to sex in polite conversation or in print. Here Holmes was the perfect Victorian. Like Lord Kitchener, another idol of the British public, Holmes's sexual instincts were entirely sublimated. . . . Women interested the great detective only as clients or as specimens to be studied. Irene Adler, who was always *the* woman in Holmes's life, was the exception. But Watson observed that Holmes felt no emotion akin to love for Miss Adler. He admired her for her mind and because she was among the three persons who had succeeded in outwitting him."

BARE IN MIND

Subscription: Monthly; $10 a year; Box 697, Perris, Calif. 92370; circulation 2,200.
Subject Matter: *Bare in Mind,* subtitled "A Nudist News Service," publishes news of naturist clubs as well as free-beach and other clothing-optional news.
Sample Materials: "The annual San Carlos High School nude relays came off a success as teenagers from various high schools joined in on the festivities. . . . Twenty boys and two girls disrobed and ran 50 yd. forward and back again a couple of times and called it quits for the evening. The Redwood City police helped direct the traffic to the relay site. Various traffic citations were issued during the event that goes back to 1964."

"[Bill] Marino will represent the U.S. later this year [1980] in Las Vegas in the Mr. Nude International final against entrants from several other countries (including Mr. Nude Yugoslavia). The Soviet Union is boycotting the event, as usual."

BOXCAR

Subscription: Irregularly; $5 a lifetime; P.O. Box 14437, San Francisco, Calif. 94114; circulation 2,000.
Subject Matter: *Boxcar,* subtitled "A Journal of the Women's Itinerant Hobos' Union," publishes stories overheard along the road. It prints fiction and poetry that in some way show an "intimate sense of motion."
Sample Articles: "The Overalls Brigade"; "Boxcar Bertha."
Sample Materials: "Every different mode of long-distance travel in America can be likened to a different cause of death. Jet travel is heart attack, the quick killer; automobiles are cancer, prolonged and remorseless. Buses are murder, a messy and painful death. Hitchhiking is clearly suicidal nowadays. And trains; trains are that most romantic of terminal illnesses, tuberculosis. Like T.B., train travel is generally thought, in America, to have been eliminated."

"It was September, 1972. We were riding freights to the thirty-second General Convention of the Industrial Workers of the World in Chicago, inspired by a famous episode in 1908 when 20 'Wobblies' from Portland had beat their way via 'sidecar Pullman' to that year's conclave. . . . Midnight found us in the Western Pacific railyards of West Oakland, under bright stars, listening to boxcars being slammed back and forth like rounds of heavy artillery coming in from the explosion of light that was San Francisco across the bay."

THE BULLETIN OF THE TYCHONIAN SOCIETY

Subscription: Five issues yearly; free, donations accepted; 14813 Harris Road, R.R. #1, Pitt Meadows, British Columbia V0M 1P0, Canada; circulation 200.

Subject Matter: The *Bulletin* is dedicated to the defense of a geocentric universe. It publishes papers by international scientists who either accept the view that the earth is the center of the observable cosmos or want to discuss the possibility that such is true.

Sample Material: "The Bible, therefore, enables us to interpret scientific experiments properly. For example, the Michelson-Morley experiment, which Einstein tried to explain away, actually indicates that the earth is not travelling in space but is stationary. In other words, the earth cannot be removed out of its place (Psalms 104:5). It has an absolute inertia which cannot be overcome. This absolute inertia of the earth, combined with the earth's gravity, probably guides the motion of the sun and moon. It would not control the movements of the planets, however, since these are governed by the gravity of the sun. Hence it is possible that the sun, like the moon, revolves about the earth, while the planets revolve about the sun."

CHOCOLATE NEWS

Subscription: Bimonthly; $9.95 per annum; P.O. Box 1745, F.D.R. Station, New York, N.Y. 10150; circulation figure not available.

Subject Matter: Subtitled "The World's Favorite Flavor Newsletter," *Chocolate News* deals with things chocolate—recipes, how-tos, tips on the latest items, trivia, and historical and service features for the chocolate lover. Printed on cocoa-colored stock scented like chocolate.

Sample Articles: "Mother Fudge"; "Interview: James Coco"; "Chocolate-Covered Cherry Cordials"; "Chocolate Aphrodisia."

Sample Materials: "Just picture a dainty French courtesan popping a chocolate bonbon between her freshly painted cherry lips. Chocolate smacks of luxury and decadence and sensual gratification carried, most often, to the brink of overindulgence. But does our favorite sweet deserve its reputation, or has chocolate, like so many other good things, derived its legendary power from sinful associations?"

"It is claimed that Christopher Columbus was the first European to encounter chocolate, when he arrived in Nicaragua in 1502. The natives were using the beans as currency and drinking chocolate as a common beverage."

THE CHRISTIAN RANCHMAN

Subscription: Monthly; free upon request; P.O. Box 7557, Fort Worth, Tex. 76111; circulation 16,000.

Subject Matter: Published by Cowboys For Christ, the message of *The Christian Ranchman* is about the saving grace of Jesus Christ.

Sample Materials: "Thank the Lord we have Cowboys For Christ now! I'm just hoping and praying that the barrel racers and their families will become Christians like all of us here, too. It breaks my heart when I go to rodeos or barrel racing things and see and hear them drinking, cussing, and doing other things! If they only knew that if they'd let God into their hearts and let Him take everything over, they wouldn't have so much trouble with their lives! Maybe some day we will have Cowgirls For Christ too."

"We had very little money and not many things, but I had a registered horse that was just starting to show promise in several events and I know how important he was to me; too important. My dream was to have several horses and in particular raise a few foals and have a good stallion, but as this seemed out of the question, I attached even more importance to the one I had, who was even a gelding. God spoke to me about it time and time again, but I just couldn't bring myself to give him to Him because I knew if I did, He would take him and then I'd have nothing and I couldn't live without horses."

CO-OP MAGAZINE

Subscription: Bimonthly; $10.50 yearly; P.O. Box 7293, Ann Arbor, Mich. 48107; circulation 3,000.
Subject Matter: *Co-op* provides analysis, description, and comment on cooperative enterprises in the U.S. and Canada. It is published by the North American Students of Cooperation, which provides technical assistance to cooperatives.
Sample Materials: "You've heard of the corny Tate family. They pervade every organization. There is Dick Tate, who wants to run everything. Ro Tate tries to change everything; Agi Tate stirs up trouble whenever possible (and Irri Tate always lends him a hand). Whenever new ideas are suggested, Hesi Tate and Vegi Tate pour cold water on them. Imi Tate tries to mimic everyone; Devas Tate loves to be disruptive; and Poten Tate wants to be a big shot. But it's Facili Tate, Cogi Tate, and Medi Tate who always save the day, and get everyone pulling together."

From "Ralph Nader on Co-ops":

"[Q.] *Should Chrysler solve its problems by becoming a cooperative?* [A.] Co-ops would be the answer to Chrysler if you had auto consumer co-ops that looked at the Chrysler scene and said, look, you want an infusion of capital in sales, here is the kind of car we want to see you produce in the next two years. Then they would deliver."

COUNTER SPY

Subscription: Quarterly; $10 per year; P.O. Box 647, Ben Franklin Station, Washington, D.C. 20044; circulation figure not available.
Subject Matter: *Counter Spy* publishes well-documented articles that deal with the crimes and abuses of intelligence agencies.
Sample Articles: "CIA–IMF–World Bank–Aid: Counterinsurgency in Thailand"; "CIA's Chamber of Commerce in Argentina"; "New CIA Bill: Death to the First Amendment."
Sample Material: "The recent uprisings in Iran and South Korea share two exacerbating causes: a CIA-created, euphemistically-entitled intelligence agency and an exploiting Gulf Oil Corporation. In Iran, the secret intelligence agency was the illegal, brutal SAVAK. In South Korea, it is the equally brutal Korean Central Intelligence Agency (KCIA). Gulf, of course, was one of the U.S. oil corporations which, along with the CIA,

installed the shah and his 26 years of repression that meant untold profits for Gulf. Appropriately enough, Gulf later hired as a vice-president, Kermit Roosevelt, who engineered the CIA's coup and installation of oppression in Iran in 1953. . . . Gulf is also in South Korea. . . . During Roosevelt's vice-presidency, Gulf made illegal payments to the Democratic Republican Party of Park Chung Hee. . . . Gulf later channeled $3 million to Park's 1971 presidential campaign."

CULTURAL SURVIVAL NEWSLETTER

Subscription: Quarterly; $15 for membership; 11 Divinity Avenue, Cambridge, Mass. 02138; circulation 8,000.
Subject Matter: Cultural Survival is a center for information on indigenous people and threatened cultures. Its newsletter is designed to expose urgent problems facing indigenous people everywhere and to publicize and mitigate against the more violent infringements of human rights as well as the more subtle ongoing ones.
Sample Materials: "The government of Guyana is still attempting to finance the large-scale, hydroelectric scheme on the Upper Mazaruni River that would flood the homes of some 4,500 Akawaio Indians."

"Cultural Survival will assist the Cubeo [Indians] in converting a local food source into a cash crop. This project will support the production, development, and international distribution of powdered chili peppers (aji), a hot and spicy seasoning. The Cubeo are not presently involved in the large-scale coca production for use in cocaine, although the production of coca is spreading through much of the Colombian Amazonia."

EDSELETTER

Subscription: Monthly; $8 per year; P.O. Box 86, Polo, Ill. 61064; circulation 800.
Subject Matter: The *Edseletter* carries news and folklore about the Edsel.
Sample Material: "Featured at the Saturday night banquet was C. Gayle Warnock, one of the top echelon officials in the development of the Edsel, and his speech was very interesting. (Of course, he is also the author of *The Edsel Affair*, a must book for every Edsel fan. After reading it, the reason the Edsel failed is not nearly the mystery it once was.) Although Mr. Warnock disclaimed any heroes right at the very outset, I took Richard Krafve as worthy of hero status. Others seemed to opt for Larry Doyle. One thing for sure, though, Robert McNamara must have used his Edsel experience as basic training for the Vietnam War."

ELECTRIC VEHICLE NEWS

Subscription: Quarterly; $12 a year, $18 outside of U.S.; P.O. Box 350, Westport, Conn. 06881; circulation 14,000.
Subject Matter: *Electric Vehicle News* is concerned with the engineering, research, design, manufacture, marketing, and useful application of electric vehicles.
Sample Material: "We are not ready for small nuclear plants in our

road vehicles. We are not ready for coal-stoked power for vehicles either. But we are ready for stored electric power to drive massive numbers of cars, buses, trucks and other vehicles that are so essential in our society."

FIRESIDE CHATS

Subscription: Bimonthly; $6 per year; 154 Laguna Court, St. Augustine, Fla. 32084; circulation 420.
Subject Matter: Contains philatelic and historic information on Franklin D. Roosevelt and Eleanor Roosevelt, as well as the Roosevelt era; plus information on stamps issued by over 60 countries featuring the Roosevelts; and a trading post for the buying, selling, and trading of Roosevelt stamps.
Sample Material: "Are Roosevelt stamps a good investment? This question is occasionally being asked and in all frankness we have to answer that we do not know. It is a fact that catalog values hardly change from year to year. . . . Yet, there are some of us who feel that as interest in Roosevelt issues grows, the demand will also effect the prices."

FLAT EARTH NEWS

Subscription: Quarterly; $10 per year; Box 2533, Lancaster, Calif. 93539; circulation 1,800.
Subject Matter: Published by fundamentalist Christians Charles and Marjory Johnson, the *News is* dedicated to proving that the earth is flat and that there is hardly one word of truth in modern astronomy and physics. (Skylab was a hoax; the sun and moon are each 32 mi. across and 3,000 mi. from earth.)
Sample Article: "Charles Lindbergh Proved Earth Flat."
Sample Material: "The river Nile in its long course flows for 1,000 mi. with only a fall of one foot. This would be an impossibility if the supposed curvature of the earth's surface were a reality. Thus we see how irrefutable facts directly controvert the theories and assumptions of modern astronomy, and how persistently these facts are ignored."

Flat Earth News

International Flat Earth Research Society
$7.00 yearly to Associate Members only.
Box 2533, Lancaster, California 93534
Phone: (805) 946-1595
Quarterly
RESTORING THE WORLD TO SANITY
May 1978
Charles K. Johnson, President
Marjory Waugh Johnson, Secretary

AUSTRALIA
NOT DOWN UNDER

A Compass Always Points North

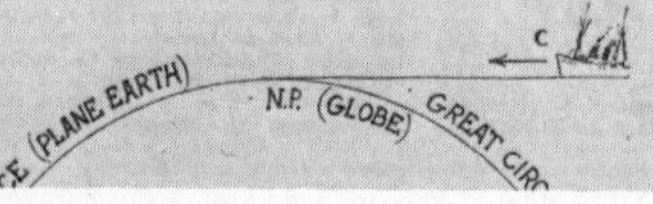

Australia...

AUSTRALIA could very well be the Key or the catylist to the DESTINY of the human race and the Future of the World! The answer could be my friend in this IF, so much hinges on this little word as Kipling has so well said.... "If you can keep you sanity, when all about you are losing theirs..." If Aussies could as a people overcome their natural reticence and their deference to Crazy English Scientists... who have kept them "down under" you, for so very long, come out of the closet and Lift up their voice and speak up with one voice and state what they all know to be true, they are not hanging

FLOWER ESSENCE QUARTERLY

Subscription: Quarterly; $10 per year; P.O. Box 586, Nevada City, Calif. 95959; circulation 2,400.
Subject Matter: The *Quarterly* is devoted to the subject of flower essences and how they can be used as healing aids.
Sample Material: "Case #2: Boy, age 7. He has cerebral palsy and was born hydroencephalic. A shunt in his head drains the water from his brain, leaving his intelligence intact. He could not speak nor could he nod, for his head was stuck in one position. . . . In the first session, the boy was given deep tissue therapy and energy modification using sound and laying-on-of-hands. At the end of the session, flower essences were selected with the pendulum by carefully balancing the essence bottles on his abdomen. The indicated essences were Pentstemon for overcoming hopelessness and adversity, Iris for transforming feelings of frustration and Morning Glory for breaking out of stuck behavior patterns."

F.Y.E.O.

Subscription: Biweekly; $50 per annum; 257 Park Avenue South, New York, N.Y. 10010; circulation figure not available.
Subject Matter: *F.Y.E.O.* (For Your Eyes Only), subtitled "An Open Intelligence Summary of Current Military Affairs," features articles gleaned from some 60 defense and military-oriented periodicals.
Sample Materials: "Dateline: 25 September [1980]—The U.S. detonated two nuclear devices under the Nevada desert, each yielding a blast equivalent to 20,000 to 150,000 tons of TNT."

"Dateline: 26 September—Radioactive Xenon 131 and 132 was found to be leaking from Nevada Test Site where two nuclear devices were detonated yesterday. The gas remains confined within a 3,000-ft. radius of ground zero on the Nevada Test Site 90 mi. northwest of Las Vegas. Officials had previously announced that there had been no leakage from the underground tests but EPA planes detected the gas 12 hours after the test had occurred."

GADGET

Subscription: Monthly; $15 a year; 116 W. 14th Street, New York, N.Y. 10011; circulation 45,000.
Subject Matter: Known as "The Newsletter for Grown-Up Kids," *Gadget* previews and reviews the latest consumer gadgets, machines, and things, from revolving corn holders to state-of-the-arts videocassette recorders and videodisc players.
Sample Materials: "What's bigger than a contact lens but smaller than a dime? Give up? It's the world's smallest quartz watch movement from the Citizens Watch Co. (1099 Wall Street, Lyndhurst, N.J. 07071). Designed in the analog style, this timepiece measures only 120 cubic millimeters including the battery. The *Citizens Quartz 1500* represents a new breakthrough in microminiaturization. . . . There will be three styles available. Two are bracelet-types in 18K yellow gold, one with

154 diamonds. The movement will also be incorporated into an 18K gold ring. Price: around $10,000."

"Recently, Americans have embraced the sport of soccer with a zest resulting in a meteoric rise in popularity. New players and long-time enthusiasts alike will love the *Lighted Soccer Ball*. It's great for night games. Distributed by Soccer International, Inc. (P.O. Box 7222, Dept. GWL, Arlington, Va. 22207) . . . the ball is illuminated by a light stick which fits into a cavity molded into the ball. The light stick, which lasts 10–12 hours, can be stored in the freezer when not in use. Price: $18.00 (plus $1.50 postage and handling)."

GNOME NEWS

Subscription: Three times annually; £2.50 in Great Britain, £3.50 abroad; The Gnome Reserve, West Putford, Devon EX22 7XE, England; circulation 600.
Subject Matter: *Gnome News,* sent to members of the Gnome Club, contains a wide variety of articles about Gnomes and related subjects, some serious (ecology, metaphysics), others humorous. *Gnome News* is really the publication of the 1,500 model Gnomes that live on the Gnome Reserve. It links Gnomes around the world via their human friends.
Sample Materials: "It makes me happy to think about Gnomes. It makes me happy to be making Gnomes in concrete or in pottery or to be writing or speaking about them. For it makes me happiest when I can share Gnomes and the land in which the Gnomes live with other people. For Gnomes live in the inner earth, where the sun never rises and never sets, but always shines. . . . Every male Gnome looks very old—perhaps as old as the earth—and simultaneously as young as a small child. While every female Gnome is created with and never loses eternal beauty. All Gnomes therefore combine the wisdom of the ages with the innocence of a child. It makes me happy to think about this."

Advertisement: "Secretary Wanted—The Fairy Investigation Society (first founded in 1927) is in need of a dedicated Hon. Sec. Any offers? Please contact Leslie Shepard, County Dublin, Irish Republic."

GROWING WITHOUT SCHOOLING

Subscription: Bimonthly; $15 for 6 issues, $24 for 12, $30 for 18; 308 Boylston Street, Boston, Mass. 02116; circulation 3,000.
Subject Matter: For people who have taken or would like to take their children out of school and have them learn at home, and for anyone interested in alternative ways of learning and growing. Also includes a mail-order booklist.
Sample Materials: "Walt Disney Educational Media Co., a division of Walt Disney Productions, has prepared a series of educational materials in the form of four filmstrips. [Example] Filmstrip #3, 'Is Natural Healthy?' refers to health food faddists as being overly excited about chemical fertilizers, pesticides, and food additives, and says these are not only necessary but actually beneficial. . . .

"Throughout the entire four filmstrips, the media company goes to great lengths to justify white bread, white sugar, chemical colorings and additives, preservatives, chemical pesticides and fertilizers . . . and offers an unfavorable depiction of health food stores and of products from vitamin and supplement companies."

"We are printing a list of school districts that are willingly and happily cooperating with home schoolers . . . to encourage and reassure school officials who may be hesitant about approving home schooling, and let them know that there are other districts enjoying good relationships with their home schooling families."

KITE LINES

Subscription: Quarterly; $9 a year; 7106 Campfield Road, Baltimore, Md. 21207; circulation 5,000.
Subject Matter: Kite plans, flying techniques, reviews of books about kites, profiles of kiting personalities, and in-depth feature articles fill the pages of *Kite Lines*.
Sample Articles: "How to Bridle a Giant Japanese Kite (without getting tied up in its 48 lines)"; "Kites and the Cambodian Spirit."
Sample Material: "Kitefliers from as far away as Cocoa, Fla., maneuvered their craft through fickle winds and even through ocean waves in competition for 22 ribbons and prizes at the First Annual Wright Kite Festival in July, 1979. The occasion at Kill Devil Hills, N.C., continued the tradition of the Nags Head, N.C., kite contests of summers past.

"A modified box kite shaped and painted like a crab was awarded 'best in show' and 'most unusual aerodynamic design (novice class),' but not until its designer, Charles Dunton of Richmond, Va., had fished it from the sea. . . . G. William Tyrrell of Huntingdon Valley, Pa., was performing barrel rolls with a 200-plus square-foot Sutton Flow Form Parafoil, which ended up draped over the power lines and was awarded the special prize on the spot."

LAST MONTH'S NEWSLETTER

Subscription: Every so often; free to members of the Procrastinators' Club of America; 1111 Broad-Locust Building, Philadelphia, Pa. 19102; circulation 3,600.
Subject Matter: *Last Month's Newsletter* publishes the "late" news of the Procrastinators' Club, including information on upcoming events, cartoons, essays, and poems emphasizing the procrastination philosophy, and advice on how to procrastinate beneficially.
Sample Materials: "Every year we pay homage to one specific person or thing who warrants the famed 'Procrastinator of the Year Award.' When you get around to it, why not submit a nominee you consider worthy? Past honors include—

A Topless Dancer (for putting things off, of course)
Methodist Hospital (for not placing their cornerstone, dated 1968, until 1972)

Illinois Central (for the latest of trains—left in 1903 and hasn't arrived yet!)"

" 'President's Message': Please forgive us this one time, but the president's message, which was planned to appear in this space, missed our late deadline, and we promise to make every effort to get a message prepared in time for our next issue if and when it comes out, provided we're not pushed or rushed into it and end up with a message as inferior as this one would have been if we had more time and space."

"Get your votes in for your choice of Miss Procrastinator of 1966. Soon, please. The girls are getting old."

THE LAST ? RESORT

Subscription: Bimonthly; $10 per year; 977 Keeler Avenue, Berkeley, Calif. 94708; circulation 1,000.
Subject Matter: Subtitled "Newsletter of the Committee to End Violence Against the Next Generation," *The Last ? Resort* prints news of corporal punishment in schools and strategies for abolishing it.
Sample Materials: "Public records and court 'findings of fact' reveal that for several years during the 1970s the Kate School staff:
—Slapped children on the hands, about the head, on the back, chest, legs and buttocks.
—Pulled children's hair and ears, pinched them and poked them, sometimes with a closed fist.
—Forced one child to eat regurgitated food by holding his mouth and nose closed, force-fed other children or deprived them of food.
—Electrically shocked children with a cattle prod, until the state ordered the practice stopped in 1972."

"It may take a while before spanking with a paddle returns to Los Angeles city schools, but when it does, school board member Bobbi Fiedler said she would be the first one to 'bend over.'

" 'I not only want to see what these paddles look like,' Fiedler said . . . 'I want to experience it.'

"Fiedler explained that being paddled will help her 'gather empirical evidence' on what kind of paddle should be used in spanking."

LIFE LINES

Subscription: Quarterly; free to members; P.O. Box 696, San Marcos, Calif. 92069; circulation 10,000.
Subject Matter: *Life Lines* is a digest of information on research in the field of aging. It is the official organ of the Committee for an Extended Lifespan, a nonprofit association dedicated to the subject of longevity.
Sample Materials: "You may be interested in my experience in extending life. At age 36 I supposedly had four more years to live. Through the use of electronic medicine I have extended my life to 85 and still expect another 15 years.

"I have learned that diseased body tissues are, in principle and effect, minute broadcasting stations. Every type of disease, therefore, has its characteristic and specific wavelength and frequency.

"Electronic treatment machines are designed to detect the imbalances of body energies manifested in disease and to apply delicate and finely-tuned electromagnetic waves of low intensity for their correction, thereby affording nature an opportunity to clear up the disease and restore the patient to health."

"Sue Willie Reid celebrated her century mark last February [1980], in Omaha, Neb. She attributes her long life to 'the grace of God and an ounce of 100-proof Kentucky bourbon daily as a "toddy for the body." ' . . . Centenarian Alice M. Loomis is busily engaged in research in the prevention of senility. The Lincoln, Neb., Ph.D., who never married, attributes her long and healthy life to constructive activity, insatiable curiosity, and a continuing desire for education."

LOWRIDER MAGAZINE

Subscription: Monthly; $15 per year; P.O. Box 28365, San Jose, Calif. 95159; circulation 102,000.

Subject Matter: *Lowrider* features articles and photos about customized cars with elaborate paint jobs, lots of chrome, tiny chain steering wheels, and hydraulic lifts for raising and lowering the body.

Sample Material: "It was a great day for LRM's Second Annual Lowrider Happening at Ventura as cars were hopping. . . . Coming out on top in the Zoot Suit Contest was Dino Zarate of Colonia Chiques, followed by the entries of El Pachuco Fashions for Fullerton. . . . Added excitement was seeing vehicles featured in LRM, such as Steve Gonzales's famous chopped-top '50 Merc with accent lights."

Lowrider *special*.

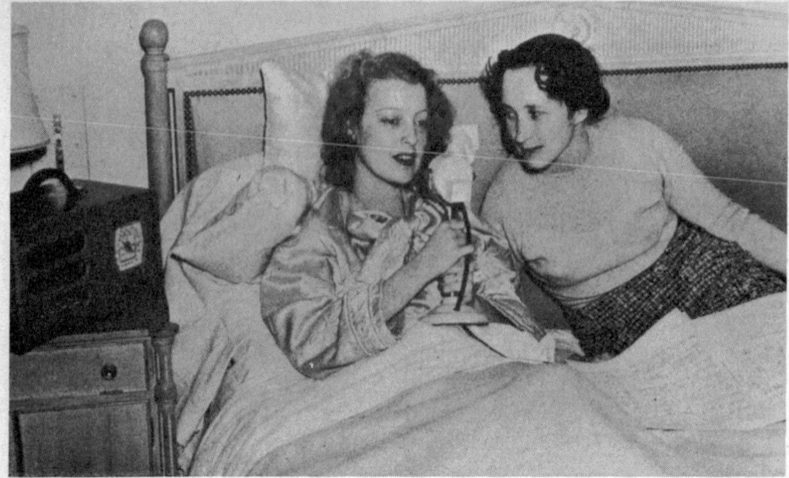

Jeanette MacDonald recuperating after hearing the news of Nelson Eddy's marriage.

MAC/EDDY TODAY

Subscription: Quarterly; $15 annual membership, $5 per issue; P.O. Box 1915, Burbank, Calif. 91507; circulation figure not available.
Subject Matter: Published by the Jeanette MacDonald/Nelson Eddy Friendship Club, Inc., *Mac/Eddy Today* prints photos of and articles about the famous film couple.
Sample Material: "Nelson himself never had any recollection of what occurred on Jan. 19, 1939. Only from his mother did he learn how they [Eddy and Ann Franklin] had driven to Las Vegas, where he had somehow stood before the judge to receive his sentence. . . . To the day he died, Nelson always believed the judge had been paid off, for no one could ethically marry someone in the condition Nelson had been in. . . . According to Jeanette, Nelson's first instinct, when he finally realized what had happened, was to get the marriage annulled. However, it seems the very night they were married, Ann and her cohorts had taken Nelson to a hotel, where he passed out on the bed. Some incriminating photos were taken to prove the marriage had been consummated. . . . Nelson, in later years, said, 'I never have had a head for drinking.' "

MADNESS NETWORK NEWS

Subscription: Quarterly; $5 for six issues; P.O. Box 684, San Francisco, Calif. 94101; circulation 1,500.
Subject Matter: MNN is a national journal of the antipsychiatry movement. It reports personal experiences of former mental patients, institution workers, and others opposed to coercive psychiatric treatment.
Sample Material: "The two most dangerous attributes of the psychiatrists I have known are their power vis-à-vis their 'patients' and their reactionary and individualistic world view. My therapists decided

which problems to discuss; they chose the labels to brand me with; they told me whom to blame and what to do about it . . . keeping the control over my life in my own hands means that I decide what I want to work on. I choose which problems I feel I can face and which ones I don't want to deal with (yet?). It also means I trust my perceptions, my feelings and my intuition."

MALEDICTA

Subscription: Semiannually; $15 a year, $20 for institutions; 331 South Greenfield Avenue, Waukesha, Wis. 53186; circulation 2,000.
Subject Matter: Subtitled "The International Journal of Verbal Aggression," *Maledicta* provides scholarly, uncensored studies of insults and "dirty" or "offensive" words and expressions.
Sample Articles: "Putting Obscene Words into the Dictionary"; "In a Pig's Eye and Related Expressions"; "Racial and Ethnic Slurs: Regional Awareness and Variations."
Sample Materials: From the regular column "Elite Maledicta," which features "bad words" used by or against famous people:

"Among the angry reactions about the hostages taken by Iran's Khomeini, a bumper sticker seen in Washington, D.C., Feb. 3, 1980: *KHOMEINI is a Shi'ite Head.*"

"Wisconsin's funny governor, Lee Dreyfus, recently upset the Honey Producers Association by telling the State Honey Queen, Lynn Ludack, that he ate honey, but his wife did not because she considers it *bee poop.*"

MEDICAL SELF-CARE

Subscription: Quarterly; $15 per year; P.O. Box 717, Inverness, Calif. 94937; circulation 15,000.
Subject Matter: Features articles that teach paramedical skills and offer guidelines on effective use of doctors and the health care system, gives news of the growing self-care classes and resource centers, and reviews health books.
Sample Articles: "Why Doctors Don't Speak Your Language"; "Are Cigarettes Radioactive?"; "In My Mind's Eye, I'm Shirley MacLaine."
Sample Material: "American cigarette consumption may be slowly leveling off, but in the Third World sales are booming as never before. Third World peoples see smoking as an emblem of national progress, and smoking American cigarettes is often considered a status symbol. . . The health risks of smoking are also less widely known."

MOTC'S NOTEBOOK

Subscription: Quarterly; $5 a year; 5402 Amberwood Lane, Rockville, Md. 20853; circulation 10,000.
Subject Matter: The National Organization of Mothers of Twins Clubs publishes this journal, which is devoted to the family and the special problems of rearing twins.

Sample Materials: "More and more doctors are beginning to listen to expectant mothers when the mother says she is having two. Studies are now being done on symptoms of twin pregnancies. Perhaps these will aid in early testing and diagnosis for the future. It does help to be prepared for the arrival of twins."

"Because the special bond between twins is so strong—and especially strong between identical twins—it is important to provide time apart from one another, as well as time to be together and enjoy the specialness of being a twin."

NESS INFORMATION SERVICE

Subscription: Bimonthly; $8 a year; Huntshieldford, St. Johns Chapel, Bishop Auckland, Co. Durham, DL13 iRQ, England; circulation 200.
Subject Matter: This is an informal newsletter sent to N.I.S. members, dealing mainly with the activities at Loch Ness but also containing news from any other location in the world that reports strange water creatures.
Sample Material: "Lake Bala: The Sunday Express of Oct. 14, 1979, had an article about the Welsh Lake Bala. . . . There have been sightings reported at regular intervals over the past 12 years. In September, 1979, Mrs. Jones, from Llanuwchllyn two miles from the lake, was being driven along the lakeside road when the water was suddenly disturbed and she saw for a short time a large, dark, humped shape. This submerged smoothly just leaving the waves behind. When she told neighbours what she had seen, she was apprehensive that they would laugh at her. But she found others had had similar experiences with 'Anghenfil,' the Welsh name for the monster."

OLE HOMEGROWN QUARTERLY

Subscription: Quarterly; $6.50 per annum; Aeon Products, Inc., 7 Commercial Boulevard, Ignacio, Calif. 94947; circulation 4,000.
Subject Matter: This journal deals with the growing of marijuana, particularly indoors and in hydroponics. It includes news of interest to growers and helpful growing tips.
Sample Materials: "It seems that a lady in St. Louis was arrested for growing pot. The claim was that she had 624 marijuana plants in her back yard, not a shabby crop. This worthy 54-year-old citizen was acquitted because she stated quite simply that she thought the plants were tomatoes."

"One worried person wanted to know why the bottom leaves are turning brown and drying off. Very simple, that is the natural cycle of the plant. The lower leaves and branches mature first, which is why you start pruning at the bottom and work your way up."

PRIVACY JOURNAL

Subscription: Monthly; $25 a year; P.O. Box 8844, Washington, D.C. 20003; circulation 2,000.
Subject Matter: Known as "an independent monthly on privacy in a

computer age," *Privacy Journal* covers credit, medical and bank records, wiretapping, polygraphs, new technology, new legislation, and court decisions affecting privacy.
Sample Materials: "Using the Privacy Act, a Los Angeles man discovered a reason why he could not find work in the film industry for many years. The FBI had falsely branded him a Communist."

"The list of materials you've borrowed from the library may be more interesting to some investigators than the library's books and films themselves: 1980—In Texas, police officers asked a public library to provide the names of all persons who had borrowed chemistry manuals found at the site of an illegal drug lab. 1979—State criminal investigators in Iowa asked the Des Moines Public Library to provide the names of borrowers of books on occult practices. The officers were investigating cattle mutilations thought to be the results of cult rites. In Connecticut, police investigating the burning of a cross asked the local library for names of persons using materials on the Ku Klux Klan."

"The Church of Scientology has more than 20 lawsuits against federal agencies including one for as much as $750 million. But in a letter to the FBI, church attorneys have now complained of an invasion of members' privacy and demanded from the FBI damages of just $6. The Scientologists said they caught two FBI agents sneaking into a church movie presentation through a kitchen at the Los Angeles Hilton Hotel. And they want to recover the $3 admission charge for each intruder."

QUARTERLY REVIEW OF DOUBLESPEAK

Subscription: Four times per year; $3 per year; NCTE, 1111 Kenyon Road, Urbana, Ill. 61801; circulation 800.
Subject Matter: Features articles, book reviews, and notices dealing with doublespeak. Included also are examples of current doublespeak, as well as resources to combat its spread.
Sample Materials: "A report on the results of a program designed to attack functionary illiteracy among adults which was prepared by the National Testing Service Research Corporation of Durham, N.C., said in part: 'The conceptual framework for this evaluation posits a set of determinants of implementation which explains variations in the level of implementation of the Comprehensive Project . . . .' "

"The New Jersey Division of Gaming Enforcement in a report to the Casino Control Commission did not use the term 'Mob,' 'Syndicate,' 'Mafia,' or 'Cosa Nostra.' Instead, the report refers to a 'member of a career offender-cartel.' "

QUILTER'S NEWSLETTER MAGAZINE

Subscription: Ten issues per year; $8.50 a year; Box 394, 6700 W. 44th Avenue, Wheat Ridge, Colo. 80033; circulation 110,000.
Subject Matter: For quilters of all ages, *Quilter's* contents include articles on design and technique, history, new and old quilt patterns,

museum quilts, current events in quilts, and personal profiles of quilt-makers.

Sample Material: "During those times Fannie [Shaw] and her family sat close to the radio late at night to hear Herbert Hoover tell them over and over that 'prosperity is just around the corner.' . . . 'It troubled and tossed me so. Then one morning I woke just knowin' what I could do to picture it out. A quilt just come to me like a light one night in what was kindly like a dream. "Prosperity Is Just Around the Corner." Hoover said it so many times, and we needed bad to believe it. So . . . I made my quilt.' "

ROBOTICS AGE

Subscription: Quarterly; $8.50 per year; P.O. Box 801, La Canada, Calif. 91011; circulation 9,170.

Subject Matter: *Robotics Age* features articles dealing with the basic principles and capabilities of robots and related equipment, industrial robot applications, and advanced robot research.

Sample Material: "Robots and other intelligent machines will certainly help improve America's productivity. But, these are only tools and will play a limited role in our recovery. The future depends on how well we apply these new tools. Many changes are needed on the manufacturing floor before computers and robots can be successfully integrated into our industrial processes."

SOYFOODS MAGAZINE

Subscription: Quarterly; $15 a year; Sunrise Farm, 100 Heath Road, Colrain, Mass. 01340; circulation 12,000.

Subject Matter: *Soyfoods Magazine* is the production, marketing, research, and consumer-interest journal for the worldwide soyfoods industry. It publishes articles on all soyfoods (tofu, tempeh, miso, soynuts, and secondary products), soyfoods pioneers, soybean agriculture, nutrition, and cooking.

Sample Articles: "How to Grow Soy Sprouts in a Commercial Shop"; "In Search of the Real Tamari"; "The Ohio Miso Company."

Sample Material: "Not only can tofu give people on restricted diets the much sought after inexpensive alternative, but it can also provide a totally flexible and delicious food that supplies many nutritional requirements.

"Both [heart disease and atherosclerosis] call for . . . restrictions in diet. (1) Protein, vitamins, and minerals are needed to maintain satisfactory nutrition. Tofu (firm, 3 oz.) supplies 12 gm. protein, 36 gm. calcium, 120 gm. phosphorous, 2.7 gm. iron, .068 gm. thiamine, .026 gm. riboflavin. (2) A low-calorie diet should be used if obesity is a problem. Tofu (67.5 calories for 3 oz.) has less calories than cottage cheese (127.2). (3) Cholesterol intake should be restricted; tofu has no cholesterol. (4) Intake of saturated fat is reduced to a minimum. Tofu has the lowest fat count of any other source of protein, and only 15% of that fat is saturated."

THE STAR

Subscription: Bimonthly; $1 per annum; Box 325, Carville, La. 70721; circulation 74,000.
Subject Matter: The primary objective of the magazine, published by patients at the National Hansen's Disease Center, Carville, La., is to "Radiate the Light of Truth on Hansen's Disease" (as the subtitle suggests). HD is erroneously associated with biblical "leprosy." Each issue contains articles on care and treatment of HD patients, articles on research, and human interest stories at Carville and throughout the world.
Sample Material: "I was on a bus on my way to Carville. The man sitting next to me started to talk to me. . . . He seemed surprised that there was a Public Health Service hospital at Carville. I explained that it was a specialty hospital, and that its specialty is Hansen's disease (HD). . . . I went on to explain that it is a skin disease that produces skin lesions that sometimes become anesthetic. . . . Trauma due to lack of sensation often causes injury to hands and feet. I also mentioned that it is only slightly contagious. . . . He said he was surprised that he'd never heard of the disease before. I said, 'You probably have, it's also known as "leprosy." ' . . . He inched over to the edge of his seat and looked around the bus (probably to find another seat, but the bus was full)."

STRATEGY & TACTICS MAGAZINE

Subscription: Bimonthly; $18 a year, $34 for two years; 257 Park Avenue South, New York, N.Y. 10010; circulation 34,000.
Subject Matter: The magazine of conflict simulation, *Strategy & Tactics* features a complete military conflict simulation (adventure game) in every issue, as well as articles on military history, brief items of interest to the military historian-gamer, and reviews of games and books.
Sample Articles: "The Central Front: The Status of Forces in Europe and the Potential for Conflict"; "Fifth Corps: The Soviet Breakthrough at Fulda, Exclusive Rules."
Sample Materials: "A U.S. Navy pilot flying a Grumman Flll Tiger fighter actually managed to shoot himself down when, during air gunnery practice, he fired a burst from his 20mm cannon, executed a shallow dive (thus picking up speed) and pulled up—directly into the path of his own cannon shot! (He ejected safely.)"

"How to Play the Game—*Central Front* is a two-player game. One player controls the NATO forces, while the other player controls the Warsaw Pact forces. The players agree on a scenario they wish to play, and playing pieces are placed on the game-map in accordance with the scenario instructions. . . . The game-map portrays an area of West Germany where the hypothetical confrontation occurs, and is based on current military maps at . . . scale."

Advertisement: "Computer Ambush (TM) . . . The sweat and death of war. In our first three months, nearly 2,000 of you bought the '$2,160 wargame,' Computer Bismarck (TM). . . . The second $2,160 wargame, Computer Ambush (TM), is more gut-wrenching than mind-stretching."

TAP

Subscription: Bimonthly; $5 per year bulk, $7 first-class; Room 603, 147 W. 42nd Street, New York, N.Y. 10036; circulation 2,000.
Subject Matter: *Tap* is a newsletter for the exchange of antisystem technical information. Includes information on ways to rip off Ma Bell, Con Ed, and other utilities; also material on lockpicking, getting your money's worth from vending machines, phoney ID schemes, phone phreaking, TWX (teletype) and computer phreaking.
Sample Material: "A meeting of phone phreaks, fancying themselves as 'Communications Hobbyists,' met on a quiet afternoon in January in the Los Angeles area to discuss the future of access to the telephone network by the hobbyists (phreaks). Speakers sent from as far as the Midwest and the East Coast to attend the gathering . . . Captain Centrex, a Midwest-based phone phreak, hosted the conference. He discussed new Pell switching computers which are putting the phreaks out of the 'free fones' arena of calling around the world for a dime (and getting the dime back)."

TECHQUA IKACHI

Subscription: Frequency depends on funds collected from donations; P.O. Box 174, Hotevilla, Ariz. 86030; circulation 3,000.
Subject Matter: Short stories and profiles on the problems in the land of the Hopi Indians.
Sample Materials: "You will now enter the world of Bahanna (white race). The period when the first Bahanna planted the curse in Hopi land. . . . From your uncle's lips you have been hearing a lot about the Bahanna. . . . You often wondered what he looks like and when he will come. You did not know that you will have a chance to witness the historical event until the village crier announced that strange people are coming up to the mesa. . . . They seem to be harmless and want to be friends. With the other children you go out to explore what the first Bahannas are like. . . . By and by you come nearer to get a better look. You hear them speaking a strange tongue. 'Look,' you say excitedly, awed by such strange creatures, 'look, their clothing is different.' 'Look, they have hairs on their faces like dogs!' . . . One of the Bahannas takes out a piece of cloth. Another pulls off the top of his head and replaces it without a show of blood. 'They must be witches,' you think to yourself."

TRANSITION

Subscription: Published from time to time; $10 for 10 issues; Box 56, Tappan, N.Y. 10983; circulation 1,000.
Subject Matter: *Transition* contains news and analysis of medical, legal, governmental, and other developments of interest to transsexuals, transvestites, and the professionals serving them.
Sample Materials: "Tall girls don't look graceful in short jackets. Overweight girls shouldn't wear pleats; pleats are lines too and add to your width. Sheath or straight skirts make you look slimmer. Large prints are

for tall people. Loud prints should never be worn by small men or women. Patch pockets are for tall girls, slit pockets for shorties. Bouffant sleeves are for tallies and slimmies."

"Nancy (36 and two years post-op) had some reassurance to offer on this point (insecurity). 'I still felt that I was masquerading as a woman for quite a while after the surgery. But as I kept changing and becoming more feminine, the feeling of falseness went away.' "

WICA NEWSLETTER

Subscription: Ten times per year; $4 per year; Dr. Leo Louis Martello, Suite 1B, 153 W. 80th Street, New York, N.Y. 10024; circulation 6,300.
Subject Matter: The newsletter of the Witches Anti-Defamation League and the Witches Liberation Movement presents articles on the pre-Judeo-Christian Pagan religion and news of the current Pagan (nature-oriented) Movement around the world.
Sample Materials: From an interview with Dr. Leo Louis Martello:

"Q. Why were witches associated with the devil?

"A. . . . The association of witches with the devil came about because of the horned goat-god of the witches. The Sabbatical Goat shown in symbols, drawings, and images became the scapegoat of Christian fanatics. Witches didn't believe in Satan which is a Christian concept. The Old Religion was based on nature worship and identification with natural law.

"Q. Does psychic power have anything to do with sex?

"A. Yes. Poltergeists (literally means 'noisy ghosts' from German) are caused by the repressed sexuality of an adolescent. Cases where objects fly around room, glasses break, clocks fall off the walls, etc., are usually caused by the presence of a teenager. Young virgin boys or girls were often used as mediums to gaze into a crystal ball or a glass of water . . . the developing but unexpressed sexuality gave power and clear vision (clairvoyance)."

WORLD AFFAIRS REPORT

Subscription: Quarterly; $12 annually; Asian Languages Building, Room 250, Stanford University, Stanford, Calif. 94305; circulation 700.
Subject Matter: The *World Affairs Report* provides a detailed analysis of what the U.S.S.R. is doing and saying about world affairs, based primarily on Russian and other non-English sources, translated into English. In this way it is able to define the polarity between the U.S. and the U.S.S.R. and to indicate where all other countries stand in relation to this pattern.
Sample Materials: "The Soviet Union's European spy network was dealt a severe blow by the defection to Great Britain of former Tass correspondent Ilya Djirkelov, bringing important documents. Moscow immediately recalled large numbers of its agents in Europe. Djirkelov was press attaché to the World Health Organization in Geneva, which the *Daily Mail* (London) described as the nerve center of Soviet espionage in Europe."

"*Pravda* spoke of serious discontent, especially among housewives unable to find common necessities, and demanded that managers produce more consumer goods."

"Poland: April is the month of national memory, devoted to recalling the horrors of Nazi occupation. Soviet propaganda harped on this, but without a word about the Hitler-Stalin pact, the partition of Poland, and Soviet annihilation of anti-Communists. It referred to the vicious, neofascist propaganda, apparently a reference to those who wish to raise the issue."

THE WORLD OF DARK SHADOWS

Subscription: Quarterly; $8 per year; c/o Kathleen Resch, P.O. Box 2262, Mission Station, Santa Clara, Calif. 95051; circulation 300.
Subject Matter: This publication is dedicated to the ABC Television serial *Dark Shadows*, which ran from 1966 to 1971. Typical contents include a biography of one or more of the actors, summaries of the episodes, articles exploring aspects of plot and characterization, photographs, original fiction, and art.
Sample Material: "Christmas 1978, at the Maine house of Collinwood: a relentless snow continues to pelt the great estate on this tumultuous night—a night of imminent horror which has disturbed the very spirit of the 1795 matriarch, Naomi Collins. The phantom of Barnabas Collins' mother appeared to him at David's bedside to warn Barnabas of the two deaths which are destined to occur tonight—one at the hands of the mad werewolf, Marvin Gibson; the other due to the unholy thirst of the vampiress, Ruth Venn."

ZYMURGY

Subscription: Quarterly; $8 per year; Box 287, Boulder, Colo. 80306; circulation 2,000.
Subject Matter: *Zymurgy* is the Journal of the American Homebrewers Association. Readers share tips and techniques about brewing. Also includes stories, lore, anecdotes, editorials, and product and book reviews.
Sample Materials: "Now that you have decided to start your own brewery, you don't have to take out a loan from the bank for equipment. The entire hardware can be purchased for under $50, if you shop around."

"Many seasoned homebrewers have avoided the use of domestic malt extract because they have felt that beer brewed with it tastes cidery and possesses a 'big bubble' feeling when drunk. Whimmy Diddle Brown Lager is a brew concocted especially for dealing with these detributes in mind."

—V.S.

16

ALL GOD'S CHILDREN

56 WELL-KNOWN SONS AND DAUGHTERS OF MINISTERS

Anglican

1. Louis Leakey (1903–1972), British anthropologist.
2. Sir Bernard Montgomery (1887–1976), British soldier known as Montgomery of Alamein for driving Nazi Gen. Erwin Rommel's forces from Egypt at El Alamein in 1942.
3. Sir Laurence Olivier (1907–   ), British stage and screen actor.
4. Virginia Wade (1945–   ), British professional tennis player and winner of the 1977 Wimbledon women's singles championship.

Baptist

5. Rita Coolidge (1944–   ), U.S. singer.
6. Aretha Franklin (1942–   ), U.S. gospel and rock singer.
7. Barbara Jordan (1936–   ), U.S. congresswoman from Texas.
8. Martin Luther King, Jr. (1929–1968), U.S. clergyman and civil rights leader awarded the Nobel Peace Prize in 1964.
9. Elijah Muhammad (1897–1975), U.S. Black Muslim leader.
10. Huey Newton (1942–   ), U.S. cofounder of the Black Panther party.
11. Maury Wills (1932–   ), U.S. professional baseball player.
12. Malcolm X (1925–1965), U.S. black militant leader and founder of the Organization of Afro-American Unity and the Muslim Mosque, Inc.

Lutheran

13. Ingmar Bergman (1918–   ), Swedish film director and writer.
14. Rudolf Bultmann (1884–1976), German theologian known for his writings which "demythologize" the New Testament.
15. Carolus Linnaeus (1707–1778), Swedish botanist whose work laid the foundation for the modern system of botanical nomenclature.
16. Martin Niemöller (1892–   ), German theologian who became an anti-Nazi leader and opposed state control of German churches.
17. Friedrich Nietzsche (1844–1900), German philosopher.
18. Albert Schweitzer (1875–1965), French clergyman, physician, and

musician who received the Nobel Peace Prize in 1952 for his missionary work in French Equatorial Africa.

19. Paul Tillich (1886–1965), German philosopher and Protestant theologian.

Methodist

20. Alistair Cooke (1908–), British author and journalist.
21. Stephen Crane (1871–1900), U.S. writer.
22. David Frost (1939–), British television personality.
23. George McGovern (1922–), U.S. senator from South Dakota.
24. Walter Mondale (1928–), U.S. politician and vice-president.
25. Norman Vincent Peale (1898–), U.S. Methodist minister and author.
26. Paul Robeson (1898–1976), U.S. singer and actor.
27. Nina Simone (1933–), U.S. singer, composer, and pianist.
28. Fran Tarkenton (1940–), U.S. professional football player.
29. Dorothy Thompson (1894–1961), U.S. journalist.
30. John Tower (1925–), U.S. senator from Texas.

Presbyterian

31. Henry Ward Beecher (1813–1887), U.S. clergyman known for his outspoken views favoring suffrage for women and the abolition of slavery.
32. Pearl S. Buck (1892–1973), U.S. novelist who won the Pulitzer Prize for literature in 1932 and the Nobel Prize for literature in 1938.
33. Aaron Burr (1756–1836), U.S. political leader and third vice-president.
34. Erskine Caldwell (1903–), U.S. author.
35. Grover Cleveland (1837–1908), 22nd and 24th president of the U.S.
36. William O. Douglas (1898–1980), U.S. Supreme Court justice.
37. John Foster Dulles (1888–1959), U.S. lawyer and secretary of state during the Eisenhower administration.
38. Robinson Jeffers (1887–1962), U.S. poet.
39. Kenneth Kaunda (1924–), president of Zambia.
40. Melvin Laird (1922–), U.S. secretary of defense during the Nixon administration.
41. Henry Luce (1898–1967), U.S. editor and magazine publisher who founded *Time, Fortune,* and *Life.*
42. Carl McIntire (1906–), U.S. clergyman known for his ultra-conservative political views.
43. Agnes Moorehead (1906–1974), U.S. screen actress.
44. Sir John Reith (1889–1971), British engineer, government official, and founder of the BBC.
45. Dean Rusk (1909–), U.S. secretary of state during the Kennedy and Johnson administrations.
46. William Saroyan (1908–1981), U.S. playwright and author.

47. Harriet Beecher Stowe (1811–1896), U.S. author best known for *Uncle Tom's Cabin* and her abolitionist views.
48. Norman Thomas (1884–1968), U.S. social reformer who ran for president in six consecutive races from 1928 to 1948 on the Socialist party ticket. He was also an ordained Presbyterian minister until he resigned in 1931.
49. DeWitt Wallace (1889–1981), U.S. publisher and founder of *Reader's Digest*.
50. Woodrow Wilson (1856–1924), 28th president of the U.S.

Unitarian

51. Horatio Alger (1832–1899), U.S. author and Unitarian minister.
52. Frank Lloyd Wright (1869–1959), U.S. architect.

United Brethren

53–54. Orville and Wilbur Wright (1871–1948; 1867–1912), U.S. inventors and pioneers in aviation.

Evangelical

55. Leon Jaworski (1905–), U.S. lawyer and government investigator.
56. Carl Jung (1875–1961), Swiss psychiatrist.

—J.H.W.

7 WELL-KNOWN SONS OF RABBIS

1. Shmuel Yosef Agnon (1888–1970), Israeli author awarded the Nobel Prize in literature in 1966.
2. Shalom Aleichem (1859–1916), Yiddish humorist who emigrated from Russia to the U.S. in 1906.
3. Levi Eshkol (1895–1969), Israeli prime minister from 1963 to 1969.
4. Harry Houdini (1874–1926), U.S. magician.
5. Erich Segal (1937–), U.S. novelist.
6. Isaac Bashevis Singer (1904–), U.S. writer awarded the Nobel Prize in literature in 1978.
7. Stephen S. Wise (1874–1949), U.S. rabbi who founded the Free Synagogue in New York City and led the American Jewish Congress at the Paris Peace Conference in 1919.

—J.H.W.

THERE IS NO EVIDENCE . . .

That Jesus Was Born in 4 B.C.
That He Was Born in a Manger.
That He Was a Carpenter.
That He Was Crucified on Mt. Calvary.

HERE ARE THE FACTS.

WHEN WAS JESUS BORN?

The exact date of the birth of Jesus has never been determined for certain and probably never can be. There is not a single contemporaneous reference to Jesus in existence, either in or out of the Bible, and all specific and definite conclusions on the subject of the date of his birth rest upon a pyramid of presumptions. The Gospels, probably written between 50 and 100 years after the birth of Jesus, are vague and general in their references to historical persons, events, and facts. Attempts to determine the date of Jesus' birth from historical, archaeological, and astronomical data have resulted in doubtful success. The Jews and Romans had different methods of reckoning time and dating historical events. In all the Bible there is not one single date in the modern sense of the word.

The solution of the problem of the birth date of Jesus hinges on a very few events in the Gospels that can be determined with a fair measure of certainty. From Matt. 2:1 we learn that "Jesus was born in Bethlehem of Judaea in the days of Herod the king." History tells us that this Herod, surnamed the Great, died sometime in 4 B.C., according to our present calendar. Therefore Jesus must have been born in or before that year. The year of his birth has been placed by different authorities all the way from 4 B.C. to 20 B.C. Many suppose that Jesus was born at least two years before Herod's death. This is based on Matt. 2:16, which says that Herod, in his attempt to destroy Jesus, slew all the children "from two years old and under," indicating that the king thought that Jesus might be as much as two years of age at that time. We have no way of knowing, however, that this incident occurred during the last year of Herod's life. In Luke 2:1–2 we are told that in the days when Jesus was born "there went out a decree from Caesar Augustus, that all the world should be taxed" and that "this taxing was first made when Cyrenius was governor of Syria." This Cyrenius is generally believed to have been Publius Sulpicius Quirinius, who, we learn from Roman history, occupied important positions in Syria, which included Judaea, three different times—6–4 B.C., 3–2 B.C., and 6–9 A.D. It is known that Augustus Caesar in 23 B.C. started the practice of making an enrollment of the taxpayers every 14 years. Accordingly, such an enrollment would have been due in Syria in 9 B.C. Such enrollments, however, probably required more than one year, and in some cases they may have been postponed a year or two for various reasons. Probably an enrollment took place sometime between 9 B.C. and 6 B.C., possibly the first year that Quirinius was proconsul of "Asia," which suggests 6 B.C. as the year of the birth of Jesus. There is not enough evidence to justify a definite conclusion. The best that can be said is that Jesus was probably born before 4 B.C., and very likely several years earlier. There is no evidence whatever to indicate what time of the year, month, or day he was born.

WAS JESUS BORN IN A MANGER?

There is nothing in the Bible to justify the popular belief that Jesus was actually born in a manger. Allusions to the place of the nativity of Jesus are few and obscure in the Scriptures. Matt. 2:11 says that when the wise men "were come into the *house*, they saw the young child with Mary his mother, and fell down, and worshipped him." *Manger* is used three times in Luke. In Chapter 2, Verse 7, we read: "And she brought forth her first-born son, and wrapped him in swaddling clothes, and laid him in a manger; because there was no room for them in the inn." According to Luke 2:12 the angel said to the shepherds: "Ye shall find the babe wrapped in swaddling clothes, lying in a manger." Luke 2:16 says: "And they came with haste, and found Mary, and Joseph, and the babe lying in a manger." A manger, properly speaking, is a trough or box from which domestic animals eat. The Greek word rendered *manger* in the passages quoted above is derived from a verb meaning "to eat" and literally means "feeding-place." Some authorities suppose that the manger in which Mary laid her child was in the court of an inn or caravansary. The typical Near Eastern inn of that day consisted of a rude, unfurnished shelter surrounding a court in which the camels, horses, and other beasts of burden were picketed. It should be noted that the Bible nowhere mentions a stable in this connection. Pictures representing the wise men worshiping Jesus in a stable surrounded by cattle and horses are not based on Scripture. A local tradition dating back at least to the 2nd century places the manger and nativity in a grotto or cave near Bethlehem. In 165 A.D. St. Justin wrote: "Having failed to find any lodging in the town, Joseph sought shelter in a neighboring cavern of Bethlehem." About half a century later the celebrated ecclesiastical writer Origen declared that "at Bethlehem is shown the grotto where he first saw the light." This grotto, it is supposed, was used as a shelter by the shepherds and their flocks. St. Helena, mother of Constantine the Great, identified a grotto near Bethlehem as the birthplace of Jesus and had it converted into a chapel. Later a basilica was erected over the grotto.

SOURCE: *A Book About the Bible* by George Stimpson. Copyright 1945 by Harper & Row, Publishers, Inc. Reprinted by permission of the publisher.

FALSE MESSIAHS

Throughout the ages there have been many pretenders to the role of Messiah. In Judaism, the Messiah is the awaited king and deliverer of the Jewish people. In Christianity, he was Jesus, who is to appear again in a second coming at the end of the world. Those who have claimed to be this redeemer have been labeled heretics or lunatics, but to the believers who pin their faith on them, they give, if just for a short time, hope and inspiration.

ABRAHAM BEN SAMUEL ABULAFIA (1240–1291?)

Born in Saragossa, Spain, in 1240, Abulafia left his native land in

1260 to search for a mythical river in Israel, but because of the ongoing Crusades he was turned back at Acre. He returned to Europe, where he began to study the works of cabalists—those who rely on an esoteric and mystical ciphering method to interpret the Scriptures. He soon developed his own cabala by transposing the four Hebrew letters in the holy name of God to form different words and by assigning number values to those letters. Through this technique, meditation, and an ascetic life-style, he claimed to be able to receive God's prophecies. Arriving back at his homeland, he began to preach about his discovery, but finding few disciples there, he embarked on an odyssey through Italy, Sicily, and Greece. By 1273 he had a small following. In 1280 he set out for Rome determined to convert Pope Nicholas III to Judaism. Not quite ready to accept the gospel according to Abulafia, Pope Nicholas ordered him arrested and put to death. Only the pontiff's own death soon thereafter saved Abulafia from being burned at the stake. After stewing in jail for a month, he was released. Abulafia returned to Sicily, where in 1284 he elevated himself from prophet to Messiah. God, he said, had communicated with him, and based on that communication Abulafia proclaimed the year 1290 as the dawn of a great messianic era. Through his boldness and charisma, he gained a large following eager to believe that redemption was at hand. These believers, however, were largely Christians. Jewish leaders condemned him as a charlatan or a mental case. He retorted that "whilst the Christians believe in my words, the Jews eschew them, and absolutely refuse to know anything of the calculations of God's name, but prefer the calculation of their money." Needless to say, Abulafia was hounded out of Sicily for that statement, and he spent his last years in seclusion on the tiny island of Comino in the Malta group. There he wrote many volumes on prophecy, and his works eventually gained wide circulation, significantly influencing later cabalists, most notably those of Safed, a renowned Israeli center of cabalism in the 16th century.

JAN BOCKELSON (JOHN OF LEIDEN) (1509–1536)

The son of a Leiden merchant, Bockelson was a tailor by trade before joining the radical Dutch Anabaptist movement as a disciple of Jan Matthyson. In 1534 the two engineered a revolt against civil and religious authorities in Münster, Westphalia, and they and their followers expelled the city's ruler, Prince-Bishop Francis Von Waldeck. They set about persecuting Catholics and Lutherans, and proclaimed the city a new Jerusalem. Upon the death of Matthyson shortly thereafter, Bockelson assumed command. Very persuasive and especially attractive to women, he told his followers that God had chosen him to be the new Messiah. With the city continuously under siege by troops representing outraged Protestants, several German princes, and disenfranchised Münster merchants, he roused his people to build a communist theocracy directed by his word alone. He decreed that men could now take multiple wives and that women must, under penalty of death, submit to whichever men chose them. For his part, Bockelson chose 16 wives and used a pegboard system to keep track of whom he was sleeping with each night. He tore down church steeples, communized all property, and minted fresh coins bearing his likeness and the legend "The Word Was Made Flesh." He staged lavish banquets while the people of the city were starving under the effects of the siege. In June, 1535, troops under the aegis of the former prince-bishop recaptured the city. Bockelson was taken into captivity and, like Christ on the cross, was ridiculed by his captors for not saving himself if he was really the Messiah. Sentenced to death, in 1536 he was shackled to a stake, scorched with heated pincers, and detongued. The *coup de grâce* was a hot knife through the heart. His body was then displayed in a cage at St. Lambert's Church. Other Anabaptist leaders in the city were similarly tortured to death.

SABBATAI ZEBI (1626–1676)

The central figure in the largest messianic movement in Jewish history, Sabbatai Zebi was born in Smyrna in 1626, the son of a poultry man turned rich merchant. Sabbatai, a manic-depressive, was plagued all his life by wild mood swings, but was said to be very charming and possessed of a mellifluous voice. During one of his manic moods in 1648, he announced to the community that he was the Messiah and dared to speak the full name of God, a forbidden practice. His persistence in such blasphemy led to his expulsion from Smyrna in 1651. In a similar incident in Salonika, Sabbatai took the Torah as his "bride," with full Jewish ceremony—an act that got him kicked out of that city, too. He spurned his first two wives, divorcing them because, he said, he was waiting for God to send him a bride. That bride was Sarah, a Polish prostitute who had long maintained that she was destined to marry the Messiah. Just how they met is unclear, but the two wed in Cairo in 1664. An even more fateful meeting, however, was that between Sabbatai and Nathan ben Elisha Hayyim Ashkenazi, a young visionary. Nathan listened to Sabbatai's messianic claims in Jerusalem, became convinced that he was genuine, and announced to the people of the city that Sabbatai was the long-awaited redeemer, offering as proof a prophecy he claimed had been written long before, which clearly named Sabbatai as the Messiah. Word of Sabbatai's mission quickly spread from Jerusalem throughout Palestine and eventually across Europe. Even many Christians, including some as far away as England, came to believe in him. Returning to Smyrna, Sabbatai was mobbed by thousands of frenzied worshipers. Elsewhere, believers clogged the synagogues to hear the latest news. Many gave up their worldly goods and forgave debts to prepare for Judgment Day.

Sabbatai's message was anything but orthodox. He did not chastise the faithful for their sinful ways. On the contrary, he urged them to free themselves of all inhibitions and revel in life's pleasures. Sexual promiscuity and nudity were suddenly in fashion as virtues. Because equal rights for women were a basic tenet of the new faith, Jewish women became the movement's most ardent supporters. Of course, traditionalists denounced Sabbatai as a charlatan, often paying for their outspokenness with a beating from pro-Sabbatai mobs. But Sabbatai's time of glory was brief. In 1666, while sailing from Smyrna to Constantinople, he was arrested at sea by Turkish authorities who had heard rumors that he was conspiring to overthrow the sultan. While in Turkish custody, he was visited by Nehemiah ha-Kohen, a cabalist who pronounced Sabbatai a fake and told the Turks that Sabbatai had indeed planned to topple the sultan. Summoned before the sultan and ordered to choose between death by torture or conversion to Islam, Sabbatai, without batting an eye, renounced Judaism for the faith of Mohammed and took the name Mehmed Effendi. He was made royal doorkeeper and lived well for a time, but his wanton sexual activity and erratic behavior eventually drew fire from Muslim authorities, who exiled him to the remote Albanian seaport of Dulcigno (now Ulcinj, Yugoslavia), where he died on September 17, the Day of Atonement, in 1676. Although his conversion to Islam had taken the steam out of the movement he had created, many of his worshipers, including Nathan, remained faithful. But during the 18th century Sabbataianism fragmented into numerous sects; the last of these to survive, the Doenmeh in Turkey, petered out in the mid-20th century.

JEMIMA WILKENSON (1752–1820)

According to Wilkenson, the daughter of a Quaker farmer in Rhode Island, she "died" when she was 20. Before her family could bury her, however, she arose as a reincarnation of Christ, sent on a divine mission to found the Church and prepare the Chosen Few for the Second Coming, scheduled to occur, she said, in her lifetime. A tall, persuasive woman, often clad in kilts and the broad hat worn by men of her time, she won fierce loyalty from her congregation of "Universal Friends," who numbered about 250 and of whom she demanded strict celibacy. She once announced that, like Jesus, she could walk on water. Just as she was about to demonstrate this miracle, she turned to her followers and asked if they believed she could do it. When they all shouted "Yes!" she decided there was no point in actually doing it and walked home on land. Wilkenson preached in Rhode Island, Massachusetts, Connecticut, and Pennsylvania, and by 1790 she had carved out a religious settlement in the wilderness of the Finger Lakes region of western New York. The community befriended the local Indian population and prospered until 1820, when Jemima Wilkenson died. In keeping with her instructions, members did not bury her but instead waited anxiously for her to rise once again. As her body decomposed, the faith of many of the Universal Friends declined. Their numbers dwindled rapidly, and in 1874 the last believer died.

HENRY JAMES PRINCE (1811–1899)

Born in Bath, England, Prince was ordained an Anglican minister in 1840. Within just three years after his ordination he became convinced of his own divinity, and in 1849 he established the Abode of Love, or

Agapemone, whose congregation lived and worshiped on a 200-acre commune near Spaxton in Somerset. The estate included a chapel equipped with a billiard table. "Look on me," he told the faithful of his newly created sect. "I am one in the flesh with Christ. By me, and in me, God has redeemed all flesh from death, and brought the bodies of breathing men into the resurrection state." About 50 believers, mostly middle-aged, middle-income folk, were charter members of the Abode of Love. In the late 1850s Prince the Messiah—who was already married to a woman old enough to be his mother—took a virgin bride, claiming it was his religious destiny. It was supposedly a purely spiritual union, and his followers were shocked when the young woman became pregnant. The baby, a girl, was denounced as the devil's offspring and grew up in the Abode as an outcast and an example of Satan's work. This incident led to rumors of orgies at Spaxton that caused a sensation in the press, and outside contributions quickly dried up. But a wealthy benefactor came forth in time to save the Messiah from bankruptcy. Despite his claims of immortality, Prince died in 1899. A few years later a second Messiah, John Hugh Smyth-Pigott, took up the fallen scepter at Spaxton, which continued to serve as the spiritual home of about 100 worshipers, virtually all women by then. After Smyth-Pigott died in 1927, the Abode of Love gradually flickered out with the deaths of its members. In 1962 the estate was sold.

HUNG HSIU-CH'ÜAN (1812–1864)

Born in Fu-yüan-shui village, Kwantung Province, China, Hung repeatedly failed the national civil service examinations and grew so frustrated over his inability to land a government job that he suffered a nervous breakdown in 1837. Shortly after Hung had once again failed the exams in 1843, his cousin gave him a Christian pamphlet entitled "Good Words for Exhorting the Age." After reading the pamphlet, Hung believed he finally understood the meaning of the hallucinations he had suffered during his breakdown six years earlier. It became clear to him that he was Jesus Christ's younger brother, sent by his father, God, to save China. He became further acquainted with Christianity through study with an American missionary in China and soon began to promulgate a doctrine that relied mainly on the Old Testament with its emphasis on a vengeful God. Together with his disciple Feng Yün-shan, he engineered the T'ai P'ing Rebellion (1850-1865), a revolt against the ruling Ch'ing (of the Manchu) dynasty. The extreme poverty, crowded conditions, widespread xenophobia, and general discontent under the alien Manchus attracted legions of followers to Hung, who promoted a kind of primitive egalitarianism. His armies captured hundreds of cities, most notably Nanking in 1853, which became their capital. Hung ordered the destruction of non-Christian temples and promoted women's rights while clamping down on such traditional vices as adultery, drug abuse, drinking, smoking, and gambling. However, as time passed, the movement was weakened by corruption, political infighting, and moral decadence among the leaders, who maintained enormous harems. The disaffected left in hordes. With the tide of the war clearly turning against him and his support crumbling, Hung swallowed poison in June, 1864, six weeks before the fall of Nanking to Manchu forces. Some rebels continued the struggle for a few more years. Hung's T'ai P'ing Rebellion cost millions of lives but contributed to the ultimate overthrow of the Manchus in 1911.

ORIC BOVAR (1917–1977)

A quiet, charismatic figure who drifted from astrology to mysticism, Bovar by the mid-1970s had attracted some 200 followers in New York and California. His accurate astrological readings coupled with instruction in meditation and clean living—no drinking, smoking, drugs, or extramarital sex—appealed to such people as Carol Burnett and Bernadette Peters. However, he alienated many when he announced that he was Jesus Christ and began celebrating Christmas with the faithful on August 29, his own birthday. His personality is said to have been so mesmerizing that at times he would introduce strangers to each other with the words "This is your husband, you must marry him"—and be obeyed. He also ordered his followers to refuse medical treatment from doctors and increasingly sought to control their lives. Several former adherents attribute Bovar's change from a benevolent spiritual leader to a mad Messiah to a nervous breakdown he is said to have suffered while living in Italy in the early 1970s. In New York in 1976 he convinced five followers—a Wall Street clerk, a college speech teacher, a writer, an Evelyn Wood speed-reading instructor, and an Amtrak employee—to join him in a continuous two-month vigil over the decomposing corpse of Stephanos Hatzitheodorou, a Bovarite who had died of cancer. Arrested for failing to report a death, Bovar told police (who, responding to a tip, raided the apartment where the vigil was being held) that he was trying to raise his disciple from the dead. On Apr. 14, 1977, shortly before he was scheduled to appear in court to respond to the charge, the slim, white-haired Bovar jumped from his 10th-floor apartment, leaving behind a confused and dwindling flock.

—W.A.D.

THE AFTERLIFE IN DIFFERENT RELIGIONS

CHRISTIANITY

Christian afterlife beliefs have never been precisely formulated. Doctrines accepted at various times and by different denominations allow wide variation in imagery and content. Probably at no time were all the elements here described accepted universally or uniformly interpreted.

When a person dies, the physical body is separated from the soul, and the soul must now be judged to be in a state of grace or a state of sin.

This is the Immediate Judgment, which determines where the person will spend eternity. If the soul is in a state of grace, it goes to Heaven to await the Last Judgment. Heaven, the abode of God, is located beyond the skies. Here, amid choirs of angels, blissful souls enter gates of pearl and walk golden streets.

However, condemned souls await the Last Judgment in Hell, located in the Earth's center or—on a vaster scale—beneath the visible cosmos. Here the leader of the fallen angels, Satan, dwells in exile from Heaven, flapping vast bat wings. (Occasionally he visits Earth to attempt to seduce humankind in defiance of his Maker.) Hell is a pit of visible darkness where the damned are punished in fiery heat or intense cold. For purposes of torment, their spirits are as tangible as physical bodies. They may be lashed by horned demons, rolled over sharp stones, or made to lie naked beneath swarms of snowflakes. Above all, they suffer the "worm of conscience," which reminds them incessantly how easily in life they might have earned the eternal bliss of God's presence. In a special compartment of Hell called Limbo the souls of unbaptized children and morally righteous people who lived before Christ's coming are confined, not in torment, but forever excluded from bliss.

In a variation, some souls, probably the vast majority, who die in a state of grace but with some taint of sin as yet unpaid for, will be sentenced to a term in Purgatory, a place or state in which the soul can be purified until it is ready to dwell with God. In Purgatory suffering is intense; souls are deprived of God's presence and suffer the sensations of physical tortures. They may be steeped in mud, eaten by worms, immured in stone, seared by fire, or have their eyes sewn closed with iron thread.

On the day of the Last Judgment, four angels standing at Earth's four corners (the points of the compass) will sound trumpets to initiate cataclysmic events. Christ will descend from Heaven in triumph to judge all people and nations in the presence of one another. (The Immediate Judgment is private.) Then the dead bodies will rise from their tombs in a glorified state and be reunited with their departed souls. The throne of judgment will be set, and Christ, robed in white and assisted by the archangel Michael, will separate the saved from the damned, as a shepherd separates the sheep from the goats. The Elect among the faithful (those who suffered martryrdom on Earth for Christ) will act as cojudges. Christ will have a great book in which details of each life are recorded; He will have another book (the Book of Life) in which the names of the saved are already written down. Archangel Michael may at this time perform a ritual weighing of each person's good and evil actions on a huge balance scale.

Now the damned souls are cast back into Hell to suffer eternal torment in indestructible physical bodies which can feel more intense pain than could their spiritual selves. Or alternatively, they may undergo complete annihilation. Satan, too, will be cast into fire and brimstone, his oppression of humans forever terminated. Now a new Heaven and a new Earth will appear. The saved will take their places amid joy and feasting in the Kingdom of God. Their state will be one of eternal

Some of the unpleasantness of Christian Hell.

beatitude, as they sing hymns of praise to God everlastingly. The Earth itself will be transformed into a paradise, without sorrow, pain, or death. In its midst will be a transfigured city, the New Jerusalem. There will be no more nations, no more war; the lion and the lamb will lie down together.

In another version, at some time prior to the Last Judgment the faithful will reign on Earth for a thousand years (the millennium) with Christ at his Second Coming. At this time only Christians will be resurrected (i.e., reunited with their bodies) to share in the reign. Afterward there will be a time of universal strife on Earth until Satan is thrown permanently into a lake of fire preparatory to the final resurrection of all the dead and the Last Judgment.

EGYPTIAN

The god Atum, or Ra, Lord of the Universe, was the first of a divine line that produced two couples: Osiris and Isis, and Seth and Nephthys. Osiris and his sister-wife Isis ruled Egypt during a golden age, taking humanity under their protection. Seth, their brother, married to their sister Nephthys, became insanely jealous of Osiris and sought to destroy him. He lured Osiris into an open coffin, nailed it shut, and cast it into the Nile. Distraught, Isis searched everywhere for the coffin, finally finding it hidden in a sycamore tree in Phoenicia. When she returned with the coffin to Egypt, Seth seized the body of Osiris, cut it up into 14 pieces, and scattered the fragments. Isis, however, found them and, with the help of Anubis, the jackal god, put them back together, thus creating the first mummy.

Osiris's posthumous son, Horus, was hidden from Seth by Isis. After he grew up, he avenged the death of his father by emasculating Seth but lost an eye in the struggle. Thoth, the ibis-headed god of wisdom and writing, intervened to heal both opponents, who were then summoned before a tribunal of gods to determine their guilt or innocence. The deities found Horus in the right and ordered Seth to return his eye. Horus gave the eye to Osiris, who was then magically restored to life. Osiris, the first being to undergo death and resurrection, bequeathed the crown of Egypt to Horus and retired to the underworld, Amenthe, to rule over the dead. Spirits of the dead, who have been mummified after the example of Osiris, also may live eternally beyond the grave of Amenthe. The entrance lies in the extreme west beyond the sea where the sun descends under the earth.

Before arriving at Amenthe, the soul must successfully complete a perilous journey. The Book of the Dead, which relatives leave in the tomb along with food and other necessities, will guide the soul and ward off evil. With its help the deceased may elude demons and monstrous monkeys that lie in wait with nets to catch traveling souls. The dead must cross snake-infested plains and a body of water stretching to Amenthe. To reach Amenthe he must ask the taciturn ferryman Face-Behind (so called because he always faces backwards) to row him across the water.

At Amenthe's gate sits a hybrid monster, part crocodile, part lion, part hippopotamus, who warns that he will tear out the heart of sinful travelers. Inside the gates, the soul wanders through magnificent halls until it comes to a place where there are 42 assessors, who initially hear its case. To them the soul must make the Declaration of Innocence, saying, "I have not blasphemed, I have not killed any man, I have not robbed, I am pure, I am pure, I am pure," etc. Then comes the awesome final trial in the Hall of the Two Truths (approving and condemning) before Osiris and a tribunal of deities. Here three deities, Horus, Anubis, and Thoth, supervise the weighing of the heart of the deceased on a scale balanced against a feather, symbol of Maat, goddess of truth. Anubis adjusts the balance carefully while Thoth, inventor of writing, sits ready to record the result. If the heart and Maat exactly balance, it proves the sincerity of the dead person's Declaration of Innocence. Thoth's report is then given to the divine tribunal, and the deceased advances to the throne of Osiris to receive verdict and sentence.

If the soul is condemned, it is either scourged back to earth to be reincarnated as a vile animal or plunged into the tortures of fire and devils. Alternatively, it might be driven up into the atmosphere to be tossed by violent storms until its sins are expiated. The ruler of this zone is Pooh, overseer of souls in penance. After their purgation in this region, the souls are granted probation through another life in human form.

The blessed soul lives eternally with the gods in Amenthe, where it may encounter its parents, offspring, friends, and lovers. The deceased's servants may accompany him to Amenthe, for there is work to be done. The blessed hunts and fishes, plows and sows, reaps and gathers in the Field of the Sun on the banks of the Heavenly Nile. He will receive his reward in inexhaustible crops of beans and wheat, with bread from divine granaries and figs and grapes to eat. And if in life he has been a pharaoh, he may join the blissful company of the sun-god Ra as he sails on the celestial Nile in his radiant barque.

ESKIMO

HEAVEN AND HELL

by Nalungiaq

And when we die at last,
we really know very little about what happens then.
But people who dream
have often seen the dead appear to them
just as they were in life.
Therefore we believe life does not end here on earth.

We have heard of three places where men go after death:
There is the Land of the Sky, a good place
where there is no sorrow and fear.
There have been wise men who went there
and came back to tell us about it:
They saw people playing ball, happy people
who did nothing but laugh and amuse themselves.
What we see from down here in the form of stars
are the lighted windows of the villages of the dead
in the Land of the Sky.

Then there are other worlds of the dead underground:
Way down deep is a place just like here
except on earth you starve
and down there they live in plenty.
The caribou graze in great herds
and there are endless plains
with juicy berries that are nice to eat.
Down there too, everything
is happiness and fun for the dead.

But there is another place, the Land of the Miserable,
right under the surface of the earth we walk on.
There go all the lazy men who were poor hunters,
and all women who refused to be tattooed,
not caring to suffer a little to become beautiful.
They had no life in them when they lived

so now after death they must squat on their haunches
with hanging heads, bad-tempered and silent,
and live in hunger and idleness
because they wasted their lives.
Only when a butterfly comes flying by
do they lift their heads
(as young birds open pink mouths uselessly after a gnat)
and when they snap at it, a puff of dust
comes out of their dry throats.

SOURCE: *Songs and Stories of the Netsilik Eskimos,* translated by Edward Field from texts collected by Knud Rasmussen, courtesy Education Development Center, Newton, Mass.

GREEK

Hades, son of Cronus and brother of Zeus, was given Hades, the land of the dead, as his inheritance. He was notorious for having abducted Persephone, daughter of Demeter, goddess of agriculture. As Persephone gathered flowers in a field, he carried her away in his chariot to be queen of his underground realm. Her distraught mother had to accept the gods' edict that Persephone would be returned to her for only half the year. It is summer when Persephone is with her mother, winter when she rules in Hades.

When the Fates fix the hour of a person's death, red-robed infernal deities (called "dogs of Hades") seize the dying mortal, deliver him a decisive blow, and carry him to the land of shadows. Entrances to the underworld are to be found in certain caverns and subterranean watercourses. The shade, or ghost, wanders across a bleak region of black poplars called the Grove of Persephone until it reaches the gate of the Kingdom of Hades. Here it encounters Cerberus, the three-headed watchdog, whose mouth dribbles black venom. The terrible beast will wag its tail and ears if appeased by honey cakes, and then the shade will be permitted to proceed.

Now the shade must cross Acheron, one of the five underground rivers. (The other four are Cocytus, Lethe, Phlegethon, and Styx.) Souls are taken to and fro over the river by old Charon, the official ferryman, who demands an obol (a small coin) for this service. If the dead person has not been buried with an obol in his mouth, Charon will pitilessly drive him away. He will have to wander the deserted shore and never find refuge.

After crossing the river, the soul is handed over to a tribunal in order to be assigned to an eternal home. This tribunal consists of Hades and his three assessors, Aeacus, Minos, and Rhadamanthus, all sons of Zeus and highly qualified judges. The tribunal examines the soul and assigns it to the type of afterlife it deserves. If the soul is of the ordinary sort, it remains in a neutral region of Hades reserved for people who deserve neither reward nor punishment. This is a dull, drab place where the sun never shines and few things grow other than asphodel, a plant that thrives on ruins and in cemeteries. Here the shade wanders joylessly among the shadows, a pale reflection of its former self. Many such souls go to the river Acheron, mount whatever conveyances they can get, and travel to the Acherusian Lake. Here they dwell and are purified of any evil deeds in order that they may receive the reward of good deeds according to their deserts.

If the dead person has committed a great crime, he will be cast into Tartarus, a somber place with gates of bronze, surrounded by a triple wall, situated on the river Phlegethon. Here are held the rebel Titans, gods who warred with Zeus. Here Tantalus, who killed his son and served him to the gods as food, is condemned to stand in water that recedes when he tries to drink it, and is tempted with fruit hanging above him that recedes when he reaches for it. Cruel Sisyphus must roll a rock up a steep hill without respite. Ixion, who made love to Zeus's wife, is bound to a flaming wheel, and the Danaids, who murdered their bridegrooms, eternally fill a bottomless barrel with water. If crimes are attended by extenuating circumstances, the shade remains in Tartarus for only one year. It then goes to the shores of the Acherusian Lake, where it must seek forgiveness of those it has wronged.

If the soul is among the blessed, the fortunate few who have led pure lives, it is conducted to the Elysian Fields, also called the Islands of the Blest. Here the dead can indulge in pleasures they enjoyed on earth, such as gaming, minstrelsy, and chariot driving, amid sunlight and flower-filled meadows.

HINDU

Brahman, the Absolute, inhabits and totally permeates the universe, which it brought forth from its own substance. Sometimes the Absolute is not manifest; then no worlds exist because the One has not become multiple. Sometimes the Absolute is manifested, as now, in the creation of the many worlds of gods, demons, and people. What appears as many is but the one existent soul distributed among all things. The appearance and disappearance of the universes is cyclic. In a future stage of creation, following the dissolution of the present universe of struggle and opposition, there will be a universe in which all things cooperate and complement one another.

All space is located within the Cosmic Egg, which contains the seven heavens (realms of gods and deceased ancestors) and the seven netherworlds (where demons, serpent deities, and other spirit entities dwell). Between these two regions lies the earth. In addition, there are as many as 8,400,000 hells, located in a lower realm.

The individual soul can never die but must constantly be reborn. A human soul evolves gradually from lower forms, starting with minerals and vegetables, then progressing upward through lower animals and then higher animals before attaining the human state. This state, highest of all, is the only one that allows escape from the everlasting round of births and deaths. When the soul can eliminate desire and become

One of apsaras *who gratify the sexual needs of men in Hindu paradises.*

aware of the unity of the self with Brahman, rebirth will cease. This is not the end of being, but perfect bliss. All will attain it in time.

When a person dies, the soul goes to the land of the dead, ruled over by Yama, the first of mortals to die and enter that other world. Yama is green in color, wears red robes, and has a flower in his hair. He rides a buffalo and carries a lasso. Yama does not judge; he is merely an executor who assigns the region in the hells or heavens where the soul is to stay for varying lengths of time and where the fruits of its past actions (karma) will determine its state or situation. It is karma itself which constitutes an unceasing judgment within each person.

The soul assigned to a heaven may reap the rewards of its good actions, but many sages, given a choice, refuse to enter heavens because they are mere way stations on the path to the Infinite. Eventually the soul will return to the earthly plane to resume its spiritual labors.

If the soul needs to be punished for evil actions (such as neglect of family obligations, lack of respect for teachers, and incorrect bodily habits, as well as murder, theft, and lying), it may be assigned to one of the various hells. Punishments may include being boiled in oil, devoured by worms, pecked at by birds, encircled by snakes, frightened by tigers, or forced to ingest spit, pus, feces, and urine. After the required time in hell, the soul returns to earth in a lowlier status than before. If its crimes were serious, it is sent back to be reincarnated as a worm, insect, cockroach, rat, or bird. If it has committed a crime causing defilement, it returns as an untouchable. If it has been a criminal of the worst sort, it must return as a plant.

ISLAM

Allah, a supreme, personal, and inscrutable God, will punish those who turn to other gods and fail to recognize His chosen messenger, Mohammed. A drop of blood shed in the cause of Allah, a night spent in His defense, is of more avail than praying and fasting. Whoever falls in battle will be forgiven for his sins.

At death the soul in the tomb is visited by the Examiners, Munkar and Nakir, two black angels with breath like violent storms and eyes like lightning flashes. They question the terrified soul concerning its faith. If its answers are satisfactory, sweet breezes from Paradise will blow upon the soul and its tomb will be filled with light until the Final Judgment. (Souls of prophets and martyrs are admitted to Paradise directly.) But if its answers are unsatisfactory, the walls of the tomb will close in to crush the soul; it shall await the Final Judgment while being stung by scorpions and beaten with an iron mace.

On the day of the Final Judgment the angel Israfil will blow a warning blast upon his trumpet. At a second blast all creatures will die and the material world will melt. At a third blast the souls of all humankind will issue from his trumpet like a swarm of bees to be reunited with their bodies made new. They will stand before the divine tribunal, waiting in silence before Allah as He sits in judgment, for no one may speak without Allah's permission. Mohammed, advancing immediately to the front of the assemblage, will be permitted to speak for those who profess Islam.

The angel Gabriel will hold up an enormous scale, half of it covering Paradise, the other half covering Hell. Every person's deeds will be weighed, and exact justice will be done. To each person will be given a book, the record of his or her life. Those whose books are placed in their right hands are blessed, while those whose books are placed in their left hands are damned. They await sentencing in shoes of fire, their skulls boiling like pots. At last (after 50,000 years or in the twinkle of an eye), Allah passes sentence upon the righteous and the wicked.

Now all the souls must cross the Bridge of Sirat, which spans the distance from Earth to Paradise, passing directly over Hell. Although this bridge is hair-thin and razor-sharp, it will broaden out beneath the steps of the faithful. Infidels will lose their balance and topple into the abyss.

Hell has seven levels. The first and mildest is for sinners among the true believers, who will enter Paradise after purification. The second is for Jews, the third for Christians, the fourth for Sabians, the fifth for Magians, the sixth for abandoned idolators, and the seventh and worst for hypocrites of all religions. In Hell the damned will be broiled, beaten with red-hot iron maces, suspended by their tongues, forced to drink boiling water and molten copper, and will have their brains boiled and their flesh cut with scissors of fire. True believers, lying on couches in Paradise, will see the damned suffer and laugh at them scornfully.

Dividing Hell and Heaven is an impassable wall, al Araf, covered with contemptible beings whose good works exactly cancel out their evil ones, thus fitting them for neither place.

In Paradise every desire of soul and body shall be satisfied. Whoever drinks the fragrant milk-white waters of Mohammed's Pond, which is a month's journey in circumference, will never again be thirsty. Other refreshments will include milk, wine, dates, honey, manna, fattened birds, and beef from cattle that graze in the Garden of Eden. Body wastes will be eliminated through perspiration. All male inhabitants will become fair, beardless, curly-haired, 90 ft. tall, and 33 years old. Black-eyed houris, or nymphs, of perfect beauty, free from excretions of any kind, await them in pavilions of green cushions. Other beautiful damsels will refrain from beholding any but their own spouses. Every man in Paradise will marry 500 houris, 4,000 virgins, and 8,000 nonvirgins.

JUDAISM

The soul may have difficulty separating from the physical body at death and may experience a loss of identity. To prevent this from happening, Dumah (Silence), guardian angel of the dead, asks each soul for its Hebrew name. If the soul in life has learned a Torah verse that begins with its first initial and ends with the last letter of its name, it will remember its name in death, for the Torah is eternal.

The newly dead soul may be unable to silence all the sensory images and noise that cling to it from this world. Two angels stand at each end of the world and toss the soul back and forth to get rid of this earthly static. Otherwise, the lost soul would wander in the world of Tohu (Confusion and Emptiness), perhaps for hundreds of years.

After death the impure soul goes to Gehenna (Gehinnom). It is located beneath the land and the sea and has entrances in both places. It is immeasurably large, dark, and cold, but within it are rivers of fire. Here the soul is purged of all defilement that it has accumulated during its lifetime. Punishments may consist of being cast into fire and snow or being hanged from different limbs of the spirit body. The thoroughly wicked remain here in everlasting disgrace. The ordinary soul need stay no more than 12 months, during which time it can be helped by prayers and sacrifices made by the living. (It is an insult to recite prayers for more than 11 months, because it implies that the deceased would be required to serve the full term.) Gehenna is emptied on the Sabbath, and the souls are given a glimpse of the light of Paradise. Without this respite, they would be unable to endure the anguish of the other six days in Gehenna.

Now the soul is ready to enter Gan Eden (Paradise, or the Garden of Eden) where it will be bathed in a River of Light to cleanse away all lingering earthly illusions. First it goes to the lower Gan Eden, the heaven of emotional fervor. It will revel in benign emotions extended toward God and other souls. Souls with interests in common form heavenly societies in which they serve God according to their area of specialization. Each group has its own leader, or rabbi, to help it progress in celestial attainments.

Ascending to the higher Gan Eden, the soul will once again bathe in the River of Light, this time to forget the tumultuous emotions of the lower Eden. Here the goal is to gain understanding of the divine mind, for which purpose groups of souls are organized into schools. Each midnight God Himself visits upper Gan Eden to share His wisdom with those who have attained it.

Once the soul has gained all the understanding of which it is capable in heaven, it will be permitted to strive for further perfection on earth through reincarnation, a process which is repeated until the soul has built a complete spiritual body through good deeds.

After the number of souls meant to be created has been achieved, God will bring about the reunion of souls and bodies. At this time, the Messiah, an ideal ruler of an earthly Kingdom of God, will summon all humankind to dwell in peace and righteousness under divine sovereignty. The resurrection of the dead will take place; the spiritual body will be reunited with the physical body it formerly inhabited. Or, alternatively, the resurrection will be a materialization of the level of spiritual body that the soul has attained through many incarnations. These materialized souls will then perform the remaining deeds required of them to complete their spiritual bodies in a world free of death and evil.

After a time the earthly rule of the Messiah will end and the Last Judgment will take place. God, "ancient of days," garbed in white raiment, with hair like pure wool, will sit upon a throne of fiery flames to judge all people in one another's presence. The wicked will be doomed and the righteous will be transported to a newly created heavenly or earthly paradise.

KALAPALO (Brazilian Indians)

The Kalapalo believe a person's shadow travels upon death to a village located in the sky, far to the east near the point where the sun rises. After the body has been buried, that night the shadow visits the grieving family for the last time in their house and consumes food that the family has prepared for him. The next day he leaves the village and travels to the east (in the direction of the sunrise) until he reaches the sky. Still traveling east, the shadow approaches the entrance path to the village of the dead. Here he first encounters a side path leading to a smaller settlement. The shadows who live in this village always try to persuade the newly deceased to join them, and if the traveling shadow turns to look at them as they call to him, he is compelled to live in their village without ever seeing the main one.

If he is successful in avoiding this detour, the shadow then comes to a stream over which are placed logs covered with a thick layer of moss. The shadow has difficulty walking over this slippery bridge and must be met by a deceased relative (frequently a parent or a sibling) who assists in the crossing. Finally, the shadow is conducted to the plaza of the village of the dead, where he is seated on a stool and presented to Sakufenu, out of whose body all men originally came. Sakufenu has one breast swollen with milk (some say she has only one breast, the other having been cut off by her creator, Kwatini). The newly arrived shadow drinks from her breast or from a gourd dipper into which the milk has been squeezed. Then a seclusion chamber is built, and the shadow enters for as long as it takes to grow strong again. During this period of isolation, the male shadows are visited by Sakufenu, who has sexual relations with them. Female shadows are visited by the men of the village. Finally, when the soul is strong once more, he or she joins the rest of the community in continual ceremonial dancing and singing. Sakufenu, rejecting the newly strengthened shadow, takes as her lover the next newly deceased man who arrives. The people of the village of the dead are able to spend all their time singing and dancing in ceremonies, for they do not have to cultivate manioc. In the center of the village is a large manioc silo, filled with flour, which never becomes empty. Although the village is very large, consisting of several concentric rings of houses, no one ever goes hungry because of this magical silo.

SOURCE: *Kalapalo Indians of Central Brazil* by Ellen B. Basso. Copyright 1973 by Holt, Rinehart, and Winston.

SOCIETY ISLANDS

At death the soul lingers near its familiar home, inhabiting small wooden carvings of male and female figures placed for this purpose about the burial ground. But sooner or later it is led away by other spirits to the land of *po*, or Night, thought by some to be located in the crater of a volcano. When the spirit arrives, the souls of ancestors or relatives, who now rank among the gods, scrape it with a serrated shell prior to eating it. When a soul has been eaten and digested three times, it becomes a deified spirit and may revisit the earthly world. Sometimes the soul is baked in an earth oven like a pig, then placed in a basket of coconut leaves to be served to the favorite god of the deceased. Now the soul, rendered immortal by this union with the god, issues from the body of the god purified for entrance into a state of bliss. A man who remains pure by avoiding sexual relations with women (abstinence need last only a few months before death) can pass immediately into bliss without being eaten.

Even after purification, souls feel human passions. Former enemies, now invulnerable, renew rivalries in the spirit world. Dead wives renew relationships with their husbands and may have offspring without ever embracing their spouses.

In Bora Bora kings are threatened with being converted after death into hat stands made from tree branches. These hat stands, upon which headgear, clothing, and baskets may be hung, are for the convenience of more fortunate ghosts in the other world. A king who wishes to avoid becoming a hat stand has to give expensive presents (like fat hogs or canoes) to priests, who then pray for him daily until he dies. After his death his relatives must continue to take presents to the priests to assure his escape from the utilitarian fate. Souls are assigned different degrees of happiness or misery in the spirit world according to the rank they held in life, irrespective of vice or virtue. The best places are reserved for chiefs and great men, while souls of a lower order lodge in inferior places. The only punishable sins are the neglect of religious rites and the failure to provide offerings.

TIBETAN BUDDHISM

Everyone has returned from death. Many persons do not believe this because they cannot remember it, yet although they have no memory of their birth, they do not doubt that they were born. The supreme goal is to be born no more. This can be accomplished when one understands that the world is an illusion, a mental construct. This knowledge, plus a willingness to understand that the self is likewise an illusion, liberates one to merge with the Universal Mind, the divine mind of Buddha, in the state of enlightenment known as Nirvana.

At the moment of death the deceased enters the Bardo state, the afterdeath plane, lasting about 49 days between death and rebirth. The Bardo has three stages: the Chikhai Bardo, the Chonyid Bardo, and the Sidpa Bardo. The Chikhai Bardo begins at the moment of death, when the deceased has a supreme vision of the liberating Truth. But the dead person, unless trained in yoga or meditation, will not be able to remain in this transcendental state. Only those who have come close to negating the self can seize this opportunity to enter Nirvana. The great majority pass through the brilliantly intense divine light, unwilling to be absorbed into it. In this Bardo the deceased person may remain several days in a trancelike state, unaware that he has separated from his physical body.

In the second stage, the Chonyid Bardo, the deceased encounters the dreamlike state of karmic illusion. (Karma is the psychic residue of our previous existence.) Thought forms generated by the deceased person's own mental content take on terrifying reality. The deceased involuntarily fabricates encounters with good and evil powers, peaceful and angry deities. Buddhas (enlightened ones) and Bodhisattvas (semidivine beings who have deferred their own Nirvanic state in order to help others achieve it) appear majestic and awesome. Their radiance will cause the impure deceased person to shrink back so as to preserve his insignificant selfhood. Many lights and colors will bewilder the dead person. Evil karma may produce thought forms of flesh-eating demons making a frightful tumult, competing with each other to seize the deceased. In this Bardo the deceased will experience a vision of judgment and punishment. Dharma-Raja, King of the Dead, holds a balance scale on which are placed black pebbles (evil deeds) and white pebbles (good deeds) to be weighed. Supervising the weighing is the monkey-headed god Shinje. Also present is a jury of gods, some with animal heads, some with human heads. Dharma-Raja holds up the Mirror of Karma, in which the naked deceased person is reflected. Devils await the deceased who is an evildoer to conduct him to the hell-world of purgation. He will imagine himself to have a physical body which can feel intense pain as demons gnaw his flesh, drink his blood, and pull out his intestines. None of these deities or demons have any real existence; they are thought forms. If the deceased could realize this, he would enter the Nirvanic state.

In the third stage, the Sidpa Bardo, the deceased descends into the ultimate degradation of a new physical birth, having been unable to profit from experiencing the two previous Bardo states. He falls prey to sexual fantasies and is attracted by a vision of mating couples. He is caught by a womb and born into the earthly world again. Although the deceased might have taken rebirth in a nonhuman world or one of the Paradise realms, human life alone generates the karma that makes it possible to end the rebirth cycle.

SCIENTIFIC

There is no scientific proof of an afterlife, but recent studies (such as those of Doctors Raymond Moody, Karlis Osis, Elisabeth Kübler-Ross, and Kenneth Ring) describe fascinating experiences. Thousands of interviews with the dying, the "clinically dead," and their physicians reveal a consistent pattern in the accounts of near-death experience. Not every nearly dead person remembers such an experience; one study indicates that about half do. Not all the elements of the "core experience" occur in each instance, nor are they in the same sequence. But in each case the same journey is described, with different people encountering different segments of the whole. The vast majority of people travel along the initial stages of the journey; only about one fourth go most or all of the way. Neither religiousness nor prior acquaintance with near-death research affects the likelihood of a person's having such experiences. However, brain impairment, drugs, and alcohol are inhibiting factors. What follows is a generalized description of the "round trip," based on the studies of Moody and Ring.

The person near death is filled with a sense of peace and well-being, which soon turns into happiness or overwhelming joy. There may be a windlike sound or ringing in the ears, but usually all is quiet and there is no pain. He may be aware that he is dying or already "dead." Next he finds himself at a distance from his physical body, looking at it from above or from a corner of the room. All this seems real, not dreamlike: hearing and vision are sharp, the mind is alert, thoughts are logical and coherent. He can hear the conversations and watch the actions of doctors and nurses, friends and relatives as they grieve or try to resuscitate him. He notices that he still has a body but of a different kind from the one he has left. It is weightless and without sensation.

He soon becomes aware of "another reality" into which he is gradually drawn. He enters a dark void, beyond time and space. Sometimes the darkness is perceived as a tunnel, narrow at the entry and getting wider as the physical world recedes. He may experience feelings of loneliness but not of fear. Serenity and peace continue to fill his consciousness. He floats through the still darkness toward a bright light. It emits vibrations of love, warmth, strength, and security. The light becomes identified with an unseen presence, a godlike being, perhaps God himself, who emphasizes the importance of acquiring knowledge and loving one another. The presence speaks to the person in a masculine tone or simply projects thoughts directly into his mind.

He knows he has reached a boundary or threshold. The presence communicates to the person that he must choose whether to proceed towards the unknown destination or return to physical life. He is shown, as if on a movie screen, a rapid replay of the events of his past. He may be given some information about his future life in case he decides to return (e.g., that he will have children or suffer more pain). His mind rationally considers the alternatives, then decides to return because of obligations to the living or unfinished earthly business.

Sometimes the person may catch a glimpse of the ineffably beautiful "world of light," where there are unforgettable colors, crystalline blue lakes, golden grass, fields and meadows with music and singing birds. In this world there are structures which resemble nothing on earth. Here he is temporarily reunited with deceased friends and relatives, who greet him and urge him to return to life. The person feels great joy in the reunion and is reluctant to leave.

Once the decision to leave is made, the experience terminates abruptly. Now the person is wrenched or jolted back to life, reentering the physical body as if through the head. Or he may be unaware of how he returned. Afterwards he can find no words adequate to express his experience and is reticent about discussing it for fear of being misunderstood or ridiculed. However, he is convinced that life after death is not merely probable, but "a veritable certainty."

—M.B.T.

A Tale of the Sands

A stream, from its source in far-off mountains, passing through every kind and description of countryside, at last reached the sands of the desert. Just as it had crossed every other barrier, the stream tried to cross this one, but it found that as fast as it ran into the sand, its waters disappeared.

It was convinced, however, that its destiny was to cross this desert, and yet there was no way. Now a hidden voice, coming from the desert itself, whispered: "The wind crosses the desert, and so can the stream."

The stream objected that it was dashing itself against the sand, and only getting absorbed; that the wind could fly, and this was why it could cross a desert.

"By hurtling in your own accustomed way you cannot get across. You will either disappear or become a marsh. You must allow the wind to carry you over, to your destination."

But how could this happen? "By allowing yourself to be absorbed in the wind."

This idea was not acceptable to the stream. After all, it had never been absorbed before. It did not want to lose its individuality. And, once having lost it, how was one to know that it could ever be regained?

"The wind," said the sand, "performs this function. It takes up water, carries it over the desert, and then lets it fall again. Falling as rain, the water again becomes a river."

"How can I know that this is true?"

"It is so, and if you do not believe it, you cannot become more than a quagmire, and even that could take many, many years; and it certainly is not the same as a stream."

"But can I not remain the same stream that I am today?"

"You cannot in either case remain so," the whisper said. "Your essential part is carried away and forms a stream again. You are called what you are even today because you do not know which part of you is the essential one."

When he heard this, certain echoes began to arise in the thoughts of the stream. Dimly, he remembered a state in which he—or some part of him, was it?—had been held in the arms of a wind. He also remembered—or did he?—that this was the real thing, not necessarily the obvious thing, to do.

And the stream raised his vapour into the welcoming arms of the wind, which gently and easily bore it upwards and along, letting it fall softly as soon as they reached the roof of a mountain, many, many miles away. And because he had had his doubts, the stream was able to remember and record more strongly in his mind the details of the experience. He reflected, "Yes, now I have learned my true identity."

The stream was learning. But the sands whispered: "We know, because we see it happen day after day, and because we, the sands, extend from the riverside all the way to the mountain."

And that is why it is said that the way in which the Stream of Life is to continue on its journey is written in the Sands.

17

MOVING ON

FINAL DAYS

AUBREY BEARDSLEY, English illustrator

Died: Hôtel Cosmopolitain, Menton, France, Mar. 16, 1898, early morning.

Beardsley's last day, like the weeks of days preceding it, was spent in a morphine stupor. The artist was suffering the terminal stage of tuberculosis. The disease, contracted when he was six, had allowed some years of remission, but from 1896 until his death at 25 it sapped his already wraithlike constitution and made him a total invalid. During those last two years, however, he illustrated numerous works, including Alexander Pope's *Rape of the Lock.* When he died, Beardsley was working desperately to finish some ornate lettering for an edition of Ben Jonson's *Volpone.* Although a member of the homosexual clique that included Oscar Wilde and the English aesthetes, Beardsley was basically heterosexual—though perhaps his only female partner had been his adored elder sister, Mabel (who may also have borne his miscarried child). Some biographers suggest that Wilde's celebrated downfall and the public revulsion that followed it may have precipitated Beardsley's final illness. In March, 1897, after converting to Roman Catholicism, he and his mother traveled to Paris. Doctors advised against spending the winter in the city, so in November they went to southern France. There, ravaged by chills and weakness, Beardsley took to bed and never left his room after a bad lung hemorrhage on Jan. 26. Thoughts of religion and guilt about the frank eroticism of his past work haunted him, and he spent hours reading about the lives of Roman Catholic saints. Nine days before he died, he scribbled a note to his London publisher with the heading "Jesus is our Lord & Judge." The note read: "I implore you to destroy *all* copies of *Lysistrata.* . . . By all that is holy—*all* obscene drawings." (Since the book had already been published, however, posterity was not deprived of these most original and openly suggestive illustrations.) Unable to manage the delicate penwork for *Volpone,* he resorted to pencil. Early in the morning on Mar. 16, when his mother and Mabel were out of the room, the artist apparently tried to draw, for when Ellen Beardsley returned, her son was dead and his favorite gold pen—either thrown or dropped on the floor—was standing upright like

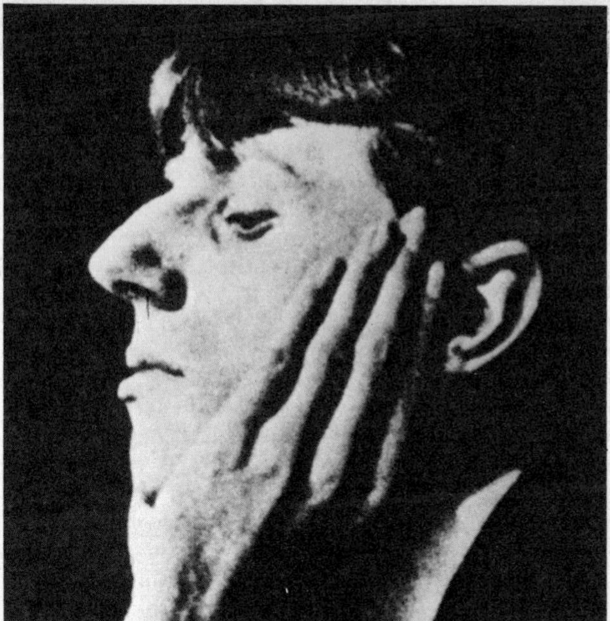

Aubrey Beardsley.

an arrow. *The New York Times* for Apr. 2, 1898, condescendingly recognized his originality but prophesied that "a coming age will wonder why there was any brief interest taken in Beardsley's work. It was a passing fad, a little sign of decadence, and nothing more."

ANNE BOLEYN, English queen, consort of Henry VIII

Died: Tower Green, London, May 19, 1536, about noon.

Condemned to death, Anne Boleyn, second wife of Henry VIII and mother of Elizabeth I, spent her last day praying in her chamber at the Tower of London. Twice in two days her beheading had been postponed. This time, however, the executioner would end her life for the supposedly witnessed crimes of incest with her brother and adultery with four other men. In addition, she had been convicted of high treason. In a gesture of macabre concern, Henry had declared that Anne should die by a "merciful" sword rather than by the conventional burning at the stake. For the job he had summoned an expert headsman from Calais. Anne was to have died on May 18, three days after her trial, but her queenly bearing throughout the plainly unjust proceedings had brought a large sympathetic crowd to Tower Green. Lord Thomas Cromwell, who was in charge of the execution, hoped the throngs of people would disperse if Anne's death were delayed a day. He also lowered the scaffold in order to obscure the view of the spectators. The tactics didn't work, and on the morning of May 19 the time was changed again—from 9:00 A.M. to noon. Anne complained to jailer Sir William Kingston, "I thought to be dead by this time and past my pain." Kingston replied, "It is no pain, it is so subtle." He was astonished at her sudden burst of laughter as she commented: "I heard the executioner is very good, and I have a little neck." Kingston uncomfortably concluded that "this lady hath much joy and pleasure in death." Anne experienced rapidly shifting moods, but she never lost control. "The people will have no difficulty in finding a nickname for me; I shall be Queen Anne Lack-Head," she told her hovering ladies-in-waiting.

Escorted from her cell to the Tower Green, she mounted the scaffold and faced the crowd still gathered despite Cromwell's precautions. In perfect composure she addressed the people, saying nothing about her guilt or innocence but telling them: "I pray God to save the king, and send him long to reign over you—for a gentler nor a more merciful prince was there never; and to me he was ever a good, a gentle and sovereign lord. And if any person will meddle with my cause, I require them to judge the best. And thus I take my leave of the world, and of you all, and I heartily desire you all to pray for me." An embroidered handkerchief was tied over her eyes, and a linen cap held up her hair. "Madame," spoke the masked headsman, "I beg you to kneel, and say your prayers." "To Jesus Christ I commit my soul. O Lord, have mercy on me," she repeated over and over until one fierce chop of the heavy blade interrupted her voice and severed her from life. As the executioner lifted her head from the blood-soaked straw, some witnesses said that her lips still prayed.

CHARLOTTE BRONTË, English author

Died: Haworth parsonage, Haworth, England, Mar. 31, 1855, at night.

"I always told you, Martha," said old Rev. Patrick Brontë to a servant, "that there was no sense in Charlotte marrying at all, for she was not strong enough for marriage." Charlotte Brontë was the last survivor of the widower's six children and the nine-month wife of Rev. Arthur Nicholls, who was curate at Haworth under Reverend Brontë. The brilliant, well-known author of *Jane Eyre* was a frail sparrow of a lady, standing only 4 ft. 9 in. tall. She had wed the kindly but stolid Arthur after a long, painful process of gaining her father's reluctant consent; the best she had hoped for, at 38, was "congeniality" in marriage. Both partners were intimidated—he by her fame, she by the loss of independence imposed upon a wife. But her affection for Arthur grew after marriage. A drenching walk with him on the moors in late November, 1854, thoroughly chilled her, and she was unable to shake the cold that followed. In January she discovered that she was pregnant, and thus suffered the agonies of "morning sickness." The condition worsened and confined her to bed. Food was nauseating to her, and she vomited for hours at a time. Soon her flesh wasted to skeleton hollows. "A wren would have starved on what she ate during those last six weeks," said a family friend. In early March, however, she rallied and developed a ravenous appetite. But when the screaming winds of the vernal equinox whipped across the moors, Charlotte—always physically sensitive to weather changes—immediately relapsed into delirium. She begged for food but was unable to swallow. Arthur knew a week beforehand that she was dying. As he prayed beside her bed near the end, she awoke to whisper in surprise: "Oh, I am not going to die, am I? He will not separate us, we have been so happy." Her last hours faded out in coma, and she died early on a Saturday night. Arthur said that she died "of exhaustion," but young Dr. Dugdale ascribed death to "phthisis" with no mention of pregnancy—though decades later he said that of all the babies he ever lost, the one he regretted most was Charlotte Brontë's child. Modern medicine has diagnosed her illness as "hyperemesis gravidarum," a kind of runaway morning sickness that today is easily treated.

ELIZABETH BARRETT BROWNING, English poet

Died: Casa Guidi, Florence, Italy, June 29, 1861, about 4:30 A.M.

"Ba," as her devoted husband of 16 years called her, was used to being sick, and Robert Browning was used to having her sick. She was, in fact, a semi-invalid from the age of 15, when she suffered a spinal injury. Years of pain and drug dependence had turned her, at 55, into a frail, hollow-eyed, increasingly lethargic woman overcome by weakness at the slightest exertion. Her life had become an unbroken succession of physical and emotional crises. In November, 1860, Elizabeth's sister Henrietta died. Devastated by grief, the distraught poet wrote to a friend, "It is a great privilege to be able to talk and cry; but I cannot, you know. I have suffered very much, and feel tired and beaten." She sympathized deeply with the cause of Italian independence in her *Casa Guidi Windows* (1851), and she was also shattered by the death of Count Camillo Cavour in the spring of 1861. She dreaded raising herself from her sofa for so much as a short walk on the terrace near Casa Guidi, the Brownings' home of 14 years. Her decline had been so gradual over so many years, however, that nobody suspected that she was dying. Elizabeth was, as she said, "always dying and it makes no difference." An attack of lung congestion on June 22 alarmed her, but she insisted that previous attacks had been worse. Speaking in a croaking whisper, she seemed curiously lighthearted, almost gay. While nothing indicated that she was nearing death, Robert Browning felt vaguely apprehensive.

During Elizabeth's last afternoon, she and her husband sat in the drawing room and discussed moving from Casa Guidi to a cooler villa outside Florence. Their 11-year-old son, Pen, seemed disturbed and asked, "Are you really better?" "*Much* better," his mother assured him. She drank her prescribed asses' milk that evening and ate a little bread and butter. "I not only have asses' milk but asses' thoughts," she whispered, then added, "I am so troubled with silly political nonsense." Robert Browning sat by her bedside as he had for the past several evenings. At 4:00 A.M. she seemed half delirious, and her hands and feet were icy cold. Robert held her in a sitting position on the edge of the bed and put her feet in a basin of hot water. "Well, you *are* making a fuss about nothing!" she said, almost laughing. Then he fed her some consommé and a "glass of lemonade, not a quarter of an hour before the end," he later wrote. "Do you know me?" he asked. "Know *you*. My

Robert—my heavens, my beloved!" she exclaimed as she kissed him passionately. "Our lives are held by God," she said and embraced him, "kissing me with such vehemence," said Browning, "that when I laid her down she continued to kiss the air with her lips. . . . Her last word was when I asked 'How do you feel?'—'Beautiful.' " Still anxious, he raised her and felt her struggle to cough. She slumped in his arms and was gone. Her face seemed transfigured, he reported, with "all traces of disease effaced." Elizabeth died with a tranquil smile on her lips, and as Robert said, "She looked like a young girl."

EDITH CAVELL, English nurse

Died: Tir National, Brussels, Oct. 12, 1915, shortly after 6:00 A.M.

Ten weeks after her arrest for using her Brussels clinic to help about 200 Allied soldiers escape German-occupied Belgium, 49-year-old Edith Cavell heard her death sentence pronounced on the afternoon of Oct. 11. "How long will they give me?" the diminutive nurse asked German Lutheran prison chaplain Paul le Seur in St. Gilles Prison. "Unfortunately only until the morning," he replied. Urged to appeal for mercy, she placidly answered, "No, I am English. It is useless. They want my life." The extremely harsh penalty for her readily confessed "treason" was, however, kept secret from all outside the prison, and Allied diplomatic officials who had followed the trial proceedings met with repeated German denials that the sentence had been handed down. Her own Anglican pastor in Brussels, Stirling Gahan, arrived at 8:30 P.M. and found the prisoner "her bright, gentle, cheerful self, as always, quietly smiling, calm and collected." Cavell told him that the sentence was what she had expected under the circumstances, and that she was grateful for the weeks of rest that her imprisonment had provided. "I have seen death so often that it is not strange or fearful to me . . . in view of God and Eternity, I realize that patriotism is not enough," said this daughter of a country vicar. She then added, "I must have no hatred or bitterness towards anyone." After taking communion in her cell, she softly repeated with Pastor Gahan the words of "Abide with Me." Word of her impending death leaked out on the eve of the execution.

A concerted diplomatic effort to secure a reprieve—involving American ambassador Brand Whitlock, Spanish ambassador Marquis de Villalobar, and others—continued unavailing into the night. Prime responsibility for the execution lay with German military governor General von Sauberzweig, who angrily dismissed all frantic appeals for clemency. By midnight it was evident that all hope was lost. The prisoner in cell 23 wrote last letters to her nursing staff, friends, and her mother in England. Her last visitor that night was probably a friend, Ada Bodart, who had bribed a guard with 10 francs for a few minutes of farewell. At about 6:00 A.M. an army car carried Cavell and Brussels architect Philippe Baucq, also condemned for aiding the enemy, to the Tir National, the Brussels rifle range. The officer commanding the two eight-man firing squads reassured his men that they need not hesitate to shoot a woman whose crimes had been so heinous. "I am glad to die for my country," she told Pastor le Seur, who led her to the execution post, where her tear-filled eyes were bandaged. From six paces, the shots rang out on command, and Edith Cavell sank to the ground, made several reflex movements as if to rise, then lay bloody and still. Her execution, a gratuitous act of hatred toward England, raised an Allied furor and greatly increased English enlistment rates.

GERONIMO, U.S. Chiricahua Apache warrior

Died: Apache hospital, Fort Sill, Okla., Feb. 17, 1909, 6:15 A.M.

The rugged old guerrilla fighter, confined with his tribespeople under longtime "house arrest," had lived on the army post at Fort Sill for 15 years. Here he became a prosperous farmer with a sizable bank account but also took advantage of his notoriety by selling handicrafts and photos of himself. Although he grew increasingly absentminded in his 80th year, never far from his mind was the futile hope that the U.S. government would let him return to his Arizona homeland to die. A week before his death, Geronimo rode to a store in Lawton, Okla., that sold bows and arrows and paid a soldier to buy him some illegal whiskey. The next morning neighbors found the intoxicated Apache lying partly in a creek, where he had fallen from his horse while riding home during the night. The severe cold that resulted turned to pneumonia on Feb. 15, but Geronimo's wife and the old women who cared for him at first refused to let an army ambulance take him to the Apache hospital on the post because too many Apaches had never returned from that "death house." However, he was finally escorted by an army scout to the hospital, where he held out for two more days, waiting for the arrival of his son and daughter, who attended Chilocco Indian School. In a state of delirium, the old warrior relived the brutal 1858 Mexican massacre of his first wife, mother, and small children. He also seemed tormented by guilt over his refusal to embrace Christianity, which had been drummed at him for years by Dutch Reformed Church missionaries. Now it was too late for conversion. By the evening of Feb. 16, Geronimo's children had still not arrived. Tribesmen sat by his bed through the night as he sank rapidly; "I was sitting beside him holding his hand when he died," said his devoted friend Asa Daklugie. Summoned by letter instead of telegraph by a thoughtless officer, his children arrived the next day.

JOHN F. KENNEDY, 35th U.S. president

Died: Dallas, Tex., Nov. 22, 1963. Death certificate stated 1:00 P.M. at the request of Mrs. Kennedy, who desired that he receive Roman Catholic rites before being pronounced dead. Death actually occurred within seconds after the bullets struck him at 12:30 P.M. at Dealey Plaza.

On the afternoon of Nov. 21 Kennedy was traveling on a political peace mission high above mid-America on Air Force One headed for Texas, where a feud between Sen. Ralph Yarborough's liberal faction and Gov. John Connally's right-leaning followers threatened to split Texas Democrats. The President was accompanied by First Lady Jacqueline Kennedy—always a great political asset. Early that afternoon at San Antonio, the presidential motorcade passed 125,000 people jammed along the route to Brooks Medical Center, where Kennedy gave a speech. Later at Houston, the party settled into the Rice Hotel, where Kennedy stripped to his shorts and worked on his evening speech. After dinner the President had a tense meeting with Vice-President Lyndon Johnson—their final conference—about the Texas political feuding, and Johnson angrily stomped out of the Kennedy suite. At the Coliseum later that evening, Kennedy inserted a mock blooper into his speech that delighted his Houston audience. This was an area that depended on military contracts, and the nation was about to launch the space program's biggest booster, rocketing "the largest payroll—payload," Kennedy corrected himself, "into space." Landing at Fort Worth after 11:00 P.M., the exhausted couple retired to a drab suite at the Hotel Texas.

The next morning Kennedy was pleased and excited to see that a crowd had gathered outside despite a gray drizzle. "There are no faint hearts in Fort Worth!" he greeted them. "Mrs. Kennedy is organizing herself. It takes her a little longer, but, of course, she looks much better than we do when she does it," he added. Back inside the hotel, he growled at Senator Yarborough, who was balking at riding in the same car with the Vice-President. "For Christ's sake cut it out, Ralph," the President ordered, then told the senator to ride in the motorcade with Johnson or walk. Surveying the morning edition of the *Dallas News*, Kennedy disgustedly noted a black-bordered, full-page ad headed "Welcome Mr. Kennedy to Dallas." It challenged the President to answer 12 loaded questions written from an archconservative viewpoint. "We're really in nut country now," he remarked to Jackie. "Last night would have been a hell of a night to assassinate a president." He reflected that "anyone perched above the crowd with a rifle could do it." Air Force One took the entourage on the 13-minute flight from Carswell Field in Fort Worth to Love Field, Dallas, landing at 11:39 A.M. in brilliant weather. Kennedy strolled the crowded airport fence longer than usual, "showing he is not afraid," noted one reporter. By noon the motorcade was headed for the Dallas Trade Mart, where he intended to lace into right-wing fanaticism. Sidewalk crowds were thin but friendly as SS 100 X, the blue Lincoln convertible, eased down Main Street. The sun was bright and Jackie slipped on her sunglasses. The President glanced at her and said, "Jackie, take your glasses off." He explained that people had come to see her and that the glasses masked her face. A few minutes later she absentmindedly put them back on, and again he admonished her to remove them. Traveling at 11.2 mph, the convertible approached the Texas School Book Depository Building on Dealey Plaza. People continued to clap as the motorcade moved along. Delighted at the reception the President was receiving, Nellie Connally, wife of Governor Connally, turned toward the back seat and said, "You sure can't say Dallas doesn't love you, Mr. President." Kennedy smiled and said, "No, you can't." One minute later, at 12:30 P.M., the first 6.5 mm bullet struck the President in the neck. "My God, I'm hit!" agent Roy Kellerman in the front seat heard him cry, and Kennedy lurched forward. Five seconds later, a second or third bullet tore off his right upper skull as brain tissue spattered the limousine. JFK belonged to the ages.

Last picture of Margaret Mitchell, summer, 1949.

MARGARET MITCHELL, U.S. author

Died: Grady Memorial Hospital, Atlanta, Ga., Aug. 16, 1949, 11:59 A.M.

The runaway success of *Gone with the Wind,* Mitchell's only book, turned into a full-time job for the 48-year-old novelist; a heavy schedule of meeting visitors, filling engagements, and answering mail left her little time to write another book. Thirteen years after publication of her novel, wrote biographer Finis Farr, "Margaret had come to one of those pauses in life, when a mature person can draw a breath, look ahead, and see some kind of order in the next few years." The day of the auto accident that took her life was more inactive for her than most. The hot Atlanta sun baked the city, and she stayed inside all day. In the cooler evening, Margaret and her ailing second husband of 24 years, John R. Marsh, decided to go to a movie at the Arts Theater on Peachtree Street, where the British film *A Canterbury Tale* was showing. Shortly after 8:00 P.M., they left their apartment on Piedmont Avenue, Margaret driving, and parked on Peachtree across from the theater. At 8:20 they started to walk across the street. When they were little more than halfway across, a car suddenly barreled around the corner from the south at about 50 mph (in a 25-mph zone). Margaret pulled away from her husband and ran back toward the curb they had just left. The car, brakes screeching, skidded and swerved violently for 67 ft. It seemed to pursue her, finally smashing her against the curb. Embraced by her unharmed husband until the ambulance arrived, Mitchell lay in critical condition with blood trickling from her left ear. She never fully regained consciousness. Police arrested a 29-year-old off-duty cab driver, Hugh D. Gravitt, on charges of drunken driving, speeding, and driving on the wrong side of the road. Until the author's death five days later, crowds kept an anxious vigil outside Grady Hospital. Her injuries were massive: two pelvic fractures and a skull split from crown to spine. On Aug. 15 her condition worsened, and her doctors in desperation tried brain surgery early on Aug. 16. Shortly after 11:00 A.M. she began sinking rapidly and died within the hour. Gravitt, a driving menace who had been cited 28 times in 10 years, was sentenced to 18 months for involuntary manslaughter. Before beginning his sentence, he ran his car into a truck, injuring himself and his wife.

O. HENRY (WILLIAM SYDNEY PORTER), U.S. author

Died: New York Polyclinic Hospital, New York City, June 5, 1910, 7:06 A.M.

Back in his room at the Caledonia Hotel in New York City after a "rest cure" winter in Asheville, N.C.—where he reunited briefly with his second wife, Sara, and quit drinking—a pale and haggard Porter couldn't get started on his proposed play *The World and the Door.* He had been unproductive for months, scraping by on small advances from publishers for promised material that, uncharacteristically, he was unable to deliver. "New York doesn't seem to agree with me as it used to," he remarked. In wretched shape owing to years of alcoholism and neglect of a diabetic condition, O. Henry wrote to a friend on Apr. 15: "I thought I was much better and came back to New York about a month ago and have been in bed most of the time. . . . There was too much scenery and fresh air [in North Carolina]. What I need is a steam-heated flat with no ventilation or exercise." He stayed in his room, worked painfully and sporadically on his last short story ("The Snow Man"), and solitarily drank whiskey to keep going. On June 3, three months before his 48th birthday, the author collapsed and was taken (by taxi, at his insistence) to the Polyclinic Hospital. Despite spasms of pain, he also insisted on walking in himself and emptied his change pocket at the reception desk. "I've heard of people being worth thirty cents," he said, "and here I am going to die and only worth twenty-three cents." Maintaining his favorite "front" as a castaway from Broadway's underground, he signed himself in as "Will S. Parker" (his real identity wasn't disclosed to hospital personnel until after his death). Dr. Charles R. Hancock found advanced diabetes, cirrhosis of the liver, and a greatly enlarged heart. Porter grew steadily weaker. As a nurse dimmed the lights at midnight on June 4, he murmured, "Turn up the lights. I don't want to go home in the dark" (paraphrasing a popular song of 1907). He survived the night, and the next morning sunlight blazed into the room when he spoke his last words: "Send for Mr. Hall" [Gilman Hall, one of his editors]. "He was perfectly conscious until within two minutes of his death," reported Dr. Hancock, "and knew that the end was approaching. . . . Nothing appeared to worry him at the last." Beneath his bed at the Caledonia nine empty whiskey bottles were found.

NELSON ROCKEFELLER, U.S. political leader, vice-president

Died: 13 West 54th Street, New York City, Jan. 26, 1979, 11:15 P.M.? Since retiring from politics in 1977 after a long public career, the 70-year-old Rockefeller had devoted himself to his huge art collection, producing books and selling reproductions of the masterpieces he owned. He spent most of his last day working on his latest book in his Rockefeller Center office. In the late afternoon, he went to Buckley School on 73rd Street, where his two young sons were students, to introduce former secretary of state Henry Kissinger to a class. Following Kissinger's speech, he returned to his duplex apartment at 812 Fifth Avenue and dined with his family. His chauffeur then drove him and Andrew Hoffman, a security aide, to the brownstone town house he had maintained for 30 years on 54th Street. From there he called 31-year-old Megan Marshack, his staff assistant, shortly before 9:00 P.M. She arrived a few minutes later wearing a long black evening gown, and they sat down to work on the art book. There are several confusing versions of the events that followed. At about 11:15 P.M., according to the revised account given by family spokesman Hugh Morrow, Rockefeller suffered a heart attack and collapsed on the floor. "Megan made a quick effort at artificial respiration, and Hoffman tried, too," said Morrow; then Megan called 911, the emergency number. The two policemen who arrived first on the scene found Rockefeller in a suit and tie lying on the floor. Officer George Frangos reported that "he was still warm. His face was reddish, not kind of polka-dot blotches or bluish, the way they get a little later." They could find no pulse. Ambulance and paramedic teams, which arrived a few minutes later, failed to revive him. At Lenox Hill Hospital, Dr. Ernest Esakof, Rockefeller's physician, officially pronounced him dead at 12:20 A.M.

Morrow had first stated that Rockefeller died almost instantly at 10:15 P.M. in his Rockefeller Center office, but the first call received by police was at 11:16 P.M. Morrow then corrected the address and explained that Marshack—whose presence was previously undisclosed—had, in her shock, simply given an erroneous time. On Feb. 10 further confusion was created when journalist Ponchitta Pierce, a friend of Marshack's, revealed that Marshack had phoned her on Jan. 26 between 10:50 and 11:00 P.M. and told her that "Governor Rockefeller had suffered a heart attack." Pierce said she went to the town house and found Rockefeller on a couch with Megan trying to revive him. Pierce stated that she herself dialed 911 for help; then, inexplicably, she left before the police arrived. Police analysis of the taped, frantic call verified that the woman caller was not Marshack. All of the witnesses—including security aide William Keogh and chauffeur Lonnie Wilcher—have since remained silent. Because no autopsy was performed, even Dr. Esakof's judgment that death resulted from a heart attack was, at best, an educated guess.

GEORGE BERNARD SHAW, Irish playwright

Died: Shaw's corner, Ayot St. Lawrence, England, Nov. 2, 1950, 4:59 A.M.

At 94, Shaw had slowed physically, but his mind was sharp and his wit still caustic. He was also still writing plays; his last play, unfinished, was *Why She Would Not,* published in 1956. He had just finished a rhyming guide to the village of Ayot St. Lawrence, his home since 1906, which he had illustrated with his own photos. One of his favorite pastimes was puttering in his yard, and on September 10 he decided to prune some trees. Missing his step at one point, he fell and fractured his thigh. In an operation next day at Luton Hospital, the bone was set; having little use for doctors and nurses, he characteristically proceeded to give them a hard time. "Already he has demanded of his nurse a certificate proving that he has had his bed bath," reported *The New York Times* on Sept. 13, "because 'otherwise someone will come along in five minutes and give me another one.' " The hip knitted very well, but Shaw's fall had aggravated a latent kidney and bladder infection, so he underwent two more operations, which weakened him. "When Shaw guessed that he might live only to become a bedridden invalid," reported *Time,* "he lost interest in the business." He was taken home, to his immense relief, where he sat huddled and blanketed in a wheelchair in his garden, serenely declining food and moving deliberately toward death. Lady Nancy Astor visited him in late October. "Oh, Nancy, I want to sleep, to sleep," he told her. To nurse Gwendoline Howell he said, "You're trying to keep me alive as an old curiosity, but I'm done, I'm finished, I'm going to die." Just before he lapsed into a final, 26-hour coma on Nov. 1, he told visitor Eileen O'Casey, "Well, it will be a new experience, anyway." The two nurses who were with him at the end said that he seemed to smile quizzically before he died. Rev. R. G. Davies, the Anglican clergyman who visited the self-styled communist and atheist in his last hours, remarked that "Mr. Shaw was not really an atheist. I would call him rather an Irishman."

ADLAI STEVENSON, U.S. political leader, diplomat

Died: En route to St. George's Hospital, London, July 14, 1965, about 5:30 P.M.

Close friends were uncertain as to how many of Stevenson's doubts about American Vietnam policy were only his "normal grousing," the chronic qualms of a man given to much agonizing self-examination. Though publicly supportive of U.S. policy, he seemed increasingly skeptical and frustrated in his own role as U.N. ambassador during his last days. Newsman Eric Sevareid, who conversed with him on July 12, said that Stevenson at 65 was on the brink of retirement: "He said he had to decide that very week." "For a while," he told Sevareid, "I'd really just like to sit in the shade with a glass of wine in my hand and watch the people dance." He had been in London since July 10, and his last 24 hours were full of typical activities. Though he had suffered a brief dizzy spell about a week earlier, "he was as gay as ever" at an evening embassy party on July 13, reported Anthony Lewis, "and he looked a little leaner and more fit, if anything, than in recent years." Next morning he saw a British diplomat, then lunched at Claridge's with William Benton, who was trying to persuade Stevenson to join

Adlai Stevenson 45 minutes before his death.

Encyclopaedia Britannica when he quit his U.N. post. At the U.S. Embassy in the afternoon, he taped a brief interview with a BBC reporter for broadcast that evening, again defending American Vietnam policy. Then at 4:00 P.M. he asked Marietta Tree, an old friend and U.N. colleague, to take a walk with him. They strolled to the nearby site of his 1945 residence, only to find it replaced by a modern building. "That makes me feel very old," he remarked. As they walked toward Hyde Park, he complained of not being able to line up a tennis match. They turned onto Upper Grosvenor Street, where he told Mrs. Tree, "You're going too fast for me," and said he felt very tired. At about 5:10 P.M. he unaccountably said to her, "Keep your head high." Then he remarked, "I am going to faint." "He looked ghastly," recalled Mrs. Tree. While she looked around for something he could sit on, she felt his hand hit against her, and he fell backward, his head striking the pavement with a heavy thud. "His eyes were open, but he was unconscious," said Mrs. Tree. People brought blankets, a doctor who happened to be passing by massaged his heart, while Mrs. Tree gave mouth-to-mouth resuscitation. He began to breathe raggedly, and though still alive when the ambulance sped away, he was dead on arrival, of an apparent heart attack, at St. George's Hospital a few blocks away.

SPENCER TRACY, U.S. actor

Died: Beverly Hills, Calif., June 10, 1967, shortly after 6:00 A.M.

On May 26 Tracy had finished work on what he and everyone else knew would be his last film, *Guess Who's Coming to Dinner?*, with Katharine Hepburn and Sidney Poitier. There was much emotion on the set. "We shook hands," Tracy told Garson Kanin, "and [director Stanley Kramer] started to cry and so did I and I figured the hell with it and came home." The film, his 74th but the first in four years of declining health, had exhilarated but also weakened him. Years of hard living and drinking had caught up with him at 67, emphysema and heart disease plagued him, and he was often feeble and breathless. Once the toughest of Hollywood tough guys, he became increasingly cantankerous and difficult as he aged, yet he continued to command enormous respect and affection from the film colony for his talent and intense commitment to his craft. "You only live once," was his favorite saying, "and if you work it right, once is *enough*." After finishing the film, he retired to his cottage on director George Cukor's estate and rested. Tracy lived by himself; long and amicably separated from his wife, he was closest to Katharine Hepburn, his companion of 26 years and frequent co-star. Cukor reported him as "very, very happy, and very, very tired"; most friends stayed away, knowing he needed rest. A few hours before he died, he told Kanin that he felt "okay, but all in." Though Charles Higham stated in his biography of Katharine Hepburn that she was in the house with him when he died, most accounts agree that she was not present when he suffered a heart attack after rising in the early morning of June 10. He was still alive when his housekeeper, Ida Gheczy, found him a few minutes after 6:00 A.M., but he died before his brother Carroll Tracy arrived with a physician.

ALEXANDER WOOLLCOTT, U.S. journalist, raconteur

Died: Roosevelt Hospital, New York City, Jan. 23, 1943, 11:46 P.M.

The physically and emotionally gross Woollcott more closely resembled Faruk than Falstaff. Woollcott was not only "The Man Who Came to Dinner" in the play that George S. Kaufman wrote satirizing him, but also a man who, in real life, stayed for four helpings. Critic Percy Hammond described him as "a mountainous jelly of hips, jowls and torso [but with] brains sinewy and athletic." His self-dramatics were legendary, as were his gifts for spontaneous invective and studied insult; many viewed him as a petulant, 230-lb. exhibitionist who made enemies for effect and never climbed offstage. His compulsive role of everyman's intellectual made him a middlebrow favorite, however, and his books and broadcasts gained popularity for their engaging style if thin substance. A survivor at 56 of two previous heart attacks (the first in 1940), Woollcott lunched on his last day with DeWitt and Lila Wallace, editors of *Reader's Digest.* He napped at his Gotham Hotel suite and made plans to attend the theater that evening after a CBS broadcast commitment. He was hardly an expert on Nazi Germany, but because he could be relied upon to opinionate about anything, he had been invited to discuss the subject "Is Germany Incurable?" on the program *People's Platform.* Fellow panelists were novelists Marcia Davenport and Rex Stout and two college presidents, Dr. George N. Shuster and Harry D. Gideonse.

Woollcott arrived at 5:30 P.M., ate what was for him an unusually light dinner in the studio with the other panelists, and exchanged bitter remarks with Marcia Davenport, resuming an ancient feud between them. On the 7:00 P.M. broadcast, he opined that Germany "might be cured by the process of time as the Vikings were." His last words on the air, at about 7:15, were typical of him: "The people of Germany are just as responsible for Hitler as the people of Chicago are for the Chicago *Tribune*. . . . I do think it's a fallacy to think that Hitler was the cause of the world's present woes. Germany was the cause of Hitler." Then he flushed, bent over his microphone, and printed on a slip of paper "I AM SICK." "I knew something was radically wrong with Aleck," said panelist Stout later. "A healthier Woollcott would have printed: I AM ILL." Moderator Gideonse signaled for the others to continue and helped the stricken man to a sofa in an outside corridor. "I am dying," he gasped. "Get my glycerin tablets." In a matter of minutes his body seemed to self-destruct; the massive heart attack had fused a sudden cerebral hemorrhage with left-side paralysis. His physician, a police emergency squad, and a coronary specialist administered oxygen before taking him to Roosevelt Hospital at 9:20 P.M. There he rallied briefly, then failed rapidly until he died. Most listeners to the broadcast were not aware that anything was wrong until his obituary appeared the next day.

—J.E.

CURIOUS WILLS

S. SANBORN, American hatter, died 1871

Last Will: Sanborn left his body to science, bequeathing it to Oliver Wendell Holmes, Sr.—then professor of anatomy at Harvard Medical School—and to one of Holmes's colleagues. He stipulated, however, that two drums were to be made out of his skin and presented to his friend Warren Simpson, provided that every June 17th at dawn he would drum out the tune "Yankee Doodle" at Bunker's Hill. After he had been skinned and carved for anatomy class, the useless residue, he instructed, was "to be composited for a fertilizer to contribute to the growth of an American elm, to be planted in some rural thoroughfare."

JONATHAN JACKSON, Columbus, O., animal lover, died about 1880

Last Will: "It is man's duty as lord of animals to watch over and protect the lesser and feebler," he wrote in his will. To do his part, he left money for the creation of a cat house—that is, a place where cats were to enjoy such creature comforts as sleeping quarters, a dining hall, a conversation room, an auditorium where they could listen to live accordion music, an exercise area, and specially designed roofs for easy climbing.

JOHN BOWMAN, Vermont tanner, died 1891

Last Will: Predeceased by his wife and two daughters, he became convinced that after his death the family eventually would be reincarnated together. Therefore, he left a $50,000 trust fund for the maintenance of his 21-room mansion and a mausoleum in Cuttingsville, Vt. The will instructed servants to prepare dinner nightly in case the Bowmans came back on an empty stomach. This procedure was carried out until the trust was depleted in 1950.

HENRY DURRELL, Bermuda tycoon; will executed 1921

Last Will: Equally fond of his three nephews, this prominent Bermudan stipulated that a game of dice should determine which one was to inherit his grand estate overlooking Hamilton Harbor. After his death the trio dutifully rolled dice for the inheritance, and Richard Durrell won.

T. M. ZINK, Iowa lawyer, died 1930

Last Will: He left some $50,000 in trust for 75 years, at the end of which time he hoped the fund would have swelled to $3 million, enough to found the Zink Womanless Library. The words *No Women Admitted* were to mark each entrance. No books, works of art, or decorations by women were to be permitted in or about the premises. "My intense hatred of women," he explained in the will, "is not of recent origin or development nor based upon any personal differences I ever had with them but is the result of my experiences with women, observations of them, and study of all literatures and philosophical works." His family successfully challenged the will.

HERMAN OBERWEISS, Texas farmer; will probated 1934

Last Will: In his own hand, he wrote, in part, "i don't want my brother Oscar to get a god dam thing i got . . . i want it that Hilda my sister she gets the north sixtie akers . . . i bet she don't get that loafer husband of hers to brake twenty akers next plowing . . . Mama should the rest get . . . I want it that mine brother Adolph be my executor and i want it that the judge should please make Adolph plenty bond put up and watch him like hell."

MARGARET "DAISY" ALEXANDER, British heiress, died 1939

Last Will: Two years before her death, the daughter of sewing machine magnate Isaac Singer placed her will in a bottle and cast it out to sea from England. In 1949 Jack J. Wurm, a jobless restaurant employee, found the bottle on a San Francisco, Calif., beach. The will read: "I leave my entire estate to the lucky person who finds this bottle and to my attorney, Barry Cohen, share and share alike." Wurm and Cohen stood to split a $12 million estate and a $160,000 annual income from Singer stock. However, the Singer Co. has not paid out any funds, apparently because the will was not witnessed.

WILLA CATHER, American author, died 1947

Last Will: Angered over the way Hollywood had butchered her novel *A Lost Lady* while bringing it to the silent—and later the talking—screen, she stipulated in her will that no work of hers was ever to be adapted for stage, screen, radio, or television, or otherwise mechanically reproduced "whether by means now in existence or which hereafter may be discovered or perfected." However, she did authorize the transcription of her work into braille.

GEORGE HARRIS, Canadian farmer, died 1948

Last Will: While Harris was working alone in his fields, his tractor accidentally backed up over him, slicing and pinning his legs. As he lay bleeding to death, he scratched into the fender of the tractor with his penknife: "In case I die in this mess, I leave all to the wife." The fender itself was later probated and is on file at the District of Kerrobert (Saskatchewan) Surrogate Court.

McNAIR ILGENFRITZ, American pianist and composer, died 1953

Last Will: He left the bulk of his estate, $150,000, to New York's Metropolitan Opera provided that within four years the Met stage one of his operas, either *Le Passant* or *Phèdre*. Hard pressed for funds, Met officials nearly capitulated but, accused of prostituting the vocal arts, they ultimately rejected the bequest.

JAMES KIDD, Arizona hermit and miner, declared dead 1956

Last Will: Having disappeared in 1949, he was declared legally dead after seven years, and in 1963 his handwritten will was discovered. In it he said that the bulk of his $275,000 estate should "go in a research for some scientific proof of a soul of a human body which leaves at death." Arizona courts dismissed more than 100 petitions—including one from Beaulah Miller, an elderly woman who claimed to have spent 35 years studying the nature of the soul—and in 1971 awarded the legacy to the American Society for Psychical Research in New York City. However, a study of deathbed experiences conducted by this organization failed to prove the soul's existence.

MARY MURPHY, California widow, died 1979

Last Will: A San Francisco resident, she left the bulk of her estimated $200,000 estate to Pets Unlimited, a nonprofit animal shelter, but her will's most controversial clause ordered the immediate destruction of her collie–sheep dog Sido. The Society for the Prevention of Cruelty to Animals (SPCA) challenged this clause in court. Meanwhile, California Gov. Jerry Brown hurriedly signed into law a special bill sparing the dog's life. After that, Sido's fate was no longer debatable, and Probate Judge Jay Pfotenhauer further upheld the SPCA challenge on the grounds that animals, although regarded as property, have limited rights, too—a precedent in California law. Sido remained with Richard Avanzino, the SPCA director who had taken the dog into his home and his heart as he led the campaign to save it.

—W.A.D.

POSTHUMOUS FAME

JOHANN SEBASTIAN BACH (1685–1750), German composer

Bach achieved a fairly wide musical reputation in Germany while he lived, but it centered mainly on his virtuoso ability as an organist. During his career as church musician in several German cities and as court musician to German princes and the Elector of Saxony, his more than 1,000 compositions for instruments and voice—written against Sunday deadlines for provincial choirs, as keyboard exercises for his students, or for the ears of a princeling he thought important to flatter—attracted only condescending notice. This was because he wrote outmoded music; the polyphonic forms of fugue, cantata, and motet had become anachronisms. He realized this—yet his attitude was that of a craftsman rather than the later Romantic view of the artist as a heroic "creator." He wrote most of his music in order to fulfill the practical demands of his job. "Whoever is equally industrious will succeed just equally as well," he said. "You have only to hit the right notes at the right time, and the instrument plays itself." Even his gifted sons regarded "the old Wig" as a quaint practitioner of dead music, and they lost many of his scores after his death. For 80 years Bach was quite forgotten except by a few opinionated musicians (who included Mozart and Beethoven). Then, in 1829, Felix Mendelssohn conducted a butchered version of the *St. Matthew Passion,* which awoke a new musical public to Bach's transcendent sounds. Though rarely performed well for 80 more years, his works achieved increasing stature. The definitive 60-volume edition of his scores was published in 1900, only six years after his lost grave was discovered in Leipzig. Albert Schweitzer's *J. S. Bach* (1905) was the first modern study of the musician, and interpreters Wanda Landowska, Pablo Casals, and Andrés Segovia gave his music wide public performance. Today Bach appeals to fans of both classical and popular music, and the Baroque instruments of his own time vie with modern choirs, orchestrations, and electronic synthesizers to explore the seemingly limitless riches of his music.

KARL VON CLAUSEWITZ (1780–1831), Prussian military strategist

Far from the stiff, monocled stereotype of the Prussian martinet, his portraits reveal the high forehead and sensitive face of a romantic intellectual—which, in many ways, Clausewitz was. After learning military science under Gerhard von Scharnhorst and studying literature and philosophy, he embarked on a military career that included nearly two years as a French war prisoner and distinguished service as a Russian staff officer during Napoleon's 1812 invasion. Promoted to general in 1818, he was appointed director of the War College in Berlin, where ample leisure for the next 12 years gave him time to write histories of the Napoleonic campaigns and military philosophy—none of them published in his lifetime. He was almost finished with the rough draft for *On War*, the three-volume treatise for which he is remembered, when he was transferred to Poland and died there at age 51. His widow edited his papers, which were published in 10 volumes from 1832 to 1837. Almost immediately his strategic concepts began to influence European military thought. In formulating his theory of warfare, Clausewitz originated the modern concept of standard military goals: to conquer and destroy the enemy's armed forces, to acquire or immobilize his material resources, and to gain the support of public opinion. "Surprise," he emphasized, "is the most powerful element of victory," and a commander must find and destroy the enemy's center of gravity. Bismarck was the first to implement Clausewitz's theories, during the period of German unification; and German military planning was guided by Clausewitz during both World Wars, Hitler's *Blitzkrieg* being a direct outgrowth. (Marx, Engels, and Lenin also studied Clausewitz, and their theories on the nature of war were largely influenced by him.) Since the advent of nuclear weapons, a neo-Clausewitzian school of thought has grown up—represented by Herman Kahn and Henry Kissinger, among others—which argues that warfare is still a permissible act of policy and that a "rational" nuclear strategy is therefore necessary. Clausewitzian thought has also highly influenced war games theory and modern management, peace research, and conflict studies. But the world can only hope that the presumed validity of warfare so scientifically legitimized by the mild soldier-professor of Berlin will never be pursued to its nightmarish "logical" conclusions.

FRANZ SCHUBERT (1797–1828), Austrian composer

Called "the most poetic of all musicians" by Franz Liszt, Schubert was a short, dumpy, rather ugly, but extremely sociable man who was not musically well trained. He was, however, amazingly prolific in his short lifetime, turning out a constant stream of piano and ensemble pieces, operas, symphonies, and songs—some 634 of them, set to any sort of verse, much of it bad. A failed schoolteacher, Schubert was unable to gain a livelihood from his compositions, most of which he never heard performed. Complications of the syphilis he contracted in 1822 led to a long decline in health, and he died of typhoid at age 31 in Vienna, leaving hundreds of musical manuscripts with his brother and scattered among friends. Over the next 50 years Schubert's work was published in a slow trickle. One Viennese music critic wrote in 1862 that "it is as though he continued to work invisibly. One can hardly keep up with him." Though highly admired by a small circle of devotees, his work remained largely unknown to the public until 1838, when German composer Robert Schumann discovered Schubert's Symphony in C Major (the *Great*) in the black polished chest where Ferdinand Schubert kept his brother's manuscripts. Franz Liszt also began performing arrangements of Schubert's songs on the piano in 1838, but there was still no large public response. Schubert had given the score of his *Unfinished* symphony, for which he is probably best known, to a close friend, Josef Hüttenbrenner, in 1823. Josef's pianist brother Anselm acquired it in 1827 and hoarded it among other Schubert manuscripts as a private "treasure" for 40 years, until he reluctantly permitted its first performance in 1865. The first complete edition of Schubert's works was finally published in the years 1884 to 1897. Then, about 1900, he was commercially "discovered," and the haunting melodies that had gone largely unnoticed for years became a veritable gold mine. Biographer Joseph Wechsberg noted that "unscrupulous people . . . made more money out of him in a month than Schubert earned in his whole life"—less than the equivalent of $3,000. Today his immortality and genius stand secure, and occasionally another long-forgotten piece is discovered. A new German edition of his works, begun in 1969, is attempting to correct much of the distortion of the past 150 years.

HENRY DAVID THOREAU (1817–1862), U.S. naturalist, philosopher

"The country knows not yet, or in the least part, how great a son it has lost," spoke Ralph Waldo Emerson at Thoreau's funeral in Concord, Mass. The thorny, Harvard-educated Thoreau, who supported himself by pencil-making, surveying, and tutoring, openly defied the work ethic and conventional morality, though his own character was puritanical in the extreme. At his death, he had authored two obscure books, and his influence extended only to a scattered circle of admirers. His *A Week on the Concord and Merrimack Rivers* (1849), whose publication he paid for out of his own pocket, was a dismal failure: "I have now a library of nearly 900 volumes, over 700 of which I wrote myself," he recorded. *Walden* (1854) sold out its first printing of 2,000 by 1859 and has never been out of print since. Probably his most influential work, however, was an essay entitled *Resistance to Civil Government,* written after he had been jailed for refusing to pay his poll tax to a proslavery government. Retitled *Civil Disobedience,* it became the classic statement of anarchist political doctrine, which deeply impressed such activists as Mahatma Gandhi and Martin Luther King, Jr. Thoreau was mainly considered a somewhat eccentric nature writer until the late 1920s, and first wide recognition of his literary and political value came from abroad. The early British Labour party used *Walden* as a manual. Today his published works number more than 20 volumes, including his 24-year *Journal.* As a prose stylist, he has few equals in American literature. Yet even Emerson shortsightedly saw Thoreau as an unfulfilled man: "I cannot help counting it a fault in him that he had no ambition . . . instead of engineering for all America, he was the captain of a huckleberry party."

GREGOR JOHANN MENDEL (1822–1884), Austrian monk, scientist

Many of the truly epochal scientific discoveries have resulted from the work of gifted generalists or amateurs. Such was the founder of the science of genetics, who lived in the Augustinian monastery of Brno (now in Czechoslovakia) for most of his life. A quiet scholar, vulnerable to psychological breakdowns, and without a strong religious vocation, Mendel devoted himself to teaching natural science and pursuing his private but highly sophisticated research in botany and meteorology. Between 1856 and 1863 he cultivated and tested at least 28,000 pea plants in the monastery garden. He focused on single, easily observed traits, then cross-pollinated the plants with great care and noted the types and frequency of traits in their progeny. His results, presented in 1865 before the local Natural Science Society, gave the first scientific description of the mechanism of heredity, and his summarized interpretations are today known as Mendel's Laws. These laws define the basic behavior and relationships of genes (though Mendel used the word *factors*) in the transmission of hereditary traits. Charles Darwin never learned of Mendel's work, which would have provided the missing key he needed to account for the process of natural selection. With no ties to the international scientific community, the monk's work sank into oblivion. In 1900, however, three European botanists independently discovered the same principles—and were astonished to learn they had only repeated the findings recorded in Mendel's obscure monograph.

EMILY DICKINSON (1830–1886), U.S. poet

Visitors to the rambling mansion in Amherst, Mass., caught only fleeting glimpses of a slight figure dressed in white, usually disappearing down a hallway. Her neighbors knew her as "gifted but queer," an eccentric oddity who habitually frustrated her own impulses: She loved music but would not enter the parlor where it was played; she wrote letters but refused to send them; and she spent most of her adult years in her second-story bedroom. Yet this brilliant, painfully shy woman wrote some of the most haunting lines of American poetry. Several biographers believe that she suffered a psychotic episode following an aborted love affair (details of which remain highly speculative), and that her intensely personal verse became the sublimated focus of her emotional life. Life itself, to Emily Dickinson, was the inconvenient vestibule to eternity, and she anticipated the grave as the gateway to freedom. In the meantime, she composed hundreds of verses, including "The Soul Selects Her Own Society," "Because I Could Not Stop for Death," and "Pain Has an Element of Blank." Only seven of her poems were published during her lifetime. Yet she seemed aware of her work's value, for she kept her poems in boxes and bureau drawers. After Emily's death, her sister Lavinia enlisted two literary friends to edit and publish her work. They discovered that Emily had even supplied lists of alternate words to substitute in certain poems. The first collection of her poetry appeared in 1890. While some critics scoffed, her lines received immediate popular acclaim. Later editions followed, then interest faded until 1924, when she was enthusiastically rediscovered. Her work has been praised ever since. Today many critics would agree with Conrad Aiken that her poetry was "perhaps the finest by a woman in the English language."

PAUL GAUGUIN (1848–1903), French painter

One of Gauguin's last letters sold in 1957 for 600,000 francs. The letter stated: "I am now down and out, defeated by poverty." For the gregarious ex-stockbroker from Paris who deserted home and family to live and paint in the South Pacific, the idealistic paradise he sought never materialized. Nor did artistic success come during his lifetime, though he achieved recognition from a few European painters who were mostly as "down and out" as he was. Yet Gauguin's rebellion against "pretended rules," his efforts to convey emotional essence through painting technique, and his embrace of native culture as a fit subject of art revolutionized Impressionist painting. "His end was his beginning," as one biographer stated. A small Gauguin Memorial Exhibition in the fall of 1903 laid the basis for his future reputation, even though the first Post-Impressionist Exhibition of 1910 in London—which included works by Gauguin, Van Gogh, and Matisse—evoked ridicule from *The Times*. Appreciation for Gauguin increased gradually by means of occasional exhibitions until 1942—a year which coincided with the appearance of the film *The Moon and Sixpence,* based on W. Somerset Maugham's 1919 novel about Gauguin. Since then, prices of his paintings have risen dramatically until today his works number among the world's most expensive modern art.

VINCENT VAN GOGH (1853–1890), Dutch painter

The greatest Dutch painter after Rembrandt was a minister's son who felt an intense calling to help the poor. He prepared for the ministry but lost his religious faith when church authorities disciplined him for practicing Christianity too literally by giving away everything he had. As a young man he worked for an art dealer in London and Paris, but he had no formal art training and his own artistic career was concentrated within only the last 10 of his 37 years. In this time he produced almost 600 still lifes, landscapes, and portraits, not including drawings and watercolors, painting at a furious speed in order to capture an effect or mood while it possessed him. He considered his vibrantly pulsating canvases as a simple extension of his preaching vocation. "In a picture I

Vincent van Gogh.

should like to say something as consoling as music," he wrote, aiming to "express hope with a star." Dreading failure but even more terrified of success—"about the worst thing that can happen," he believed—he signed few of his paintings and rejected even the few favorable notices that came his way during his last year. A masochist, he often wallowed helplessly in his sense of his own shortcomings. The psychotic episode in which he spitefully cut off part of his left ear occurred in 1888 while he lived with Paul Gauguin at Arles. These episodes became increasingly frequent and severe, and in 1889 he committed himself to an asylum for a year, where he continued to paint. His name was virtually unknown when, despondent at the prospect of old age and continuing failure, he shot himself at Auvers. Only one painting—*The Red Orchard*—was ever sold in his lifetime. One-man shows began to exhibit his work in 1892, but his fame dates from the early years of the 20th century, when German Expressionists recognized his entirely new conception of art as a revelation of inner truth.

CASEY JONES (1864–1900), U.S. railroad engineer

John Luther Jones was born near Cayce, Ky., and carried the nickname Casey throughout his life. He began work on the Illinois Central Railroad as a fireman in 1888, soon graduated to engineer, and thereafter drove express freights in the South and Midwest. On the night of Apr. 29, 1900, when he ended his New Orleans–Memphis run on the Cannonball Express, he learned that the engineer scheduled for the return trip was ill. Casey needed the money, so he took the throttle of the "Old 382" again. At 4:00 A.M. near Vaughan, Miss., he saw a stalled freight train on the track ahead, tried to brake his hurtling locomotive, but knew he couldn't stop it in time. "Jump, Sim!" he shouted to his fireman, and Casey rode his engine alone into the collision. He was the only casualty; workmen found his mangled body with one hand on the whistle cord, the other on the brake. Newspapers spread an account of the incident throughout the country, and engine wiper Wallace Saunders, a black friend of Jones's, wrote "The Ballad of Casey Jones." The song immortalized Casey's name and made him a legendary folk figure. Casey's home in Jackson, Tenn., is now a railroad museum.

SCOTT JOPLIN (1868–1917), U.S. composer

Precocious son of a former slave, Joplin taught himself to play the guitar, bugle, and piano before he was seven. In his native Texarkana, he received expert training in harmony, counterpoint, and classical music. Joplin left home at age 14, played honky-tonk piano in Texas and Louisiana, attended college in Sedalia, Mo., and worked in St. Louis and Chicago nightclubs. By the time he moved to New York he had begun to publish numerous ragtime compositions in sheet-music form. The syncopated "ragged time" had evolved from an improvised mating of black folk music with the European march. Played in Southern saloons and red-light districts, it was a grandparent of American jazz. Joplin treated the music as a serious art form, maintaining that "what is scurrilously called ragtime is an invention that is here to

Scott Joplin.

stay. . . . Syncopations are no indication of light or trashy music, and to shy bricks at 'hateful ragtime' no longer passes for musical culture." He structured and formalized the pattern in his own compositions, best known of which was the 1899 *Maple Leaf Rag*. Joplin achieved recognition and a measure of prosperity within Harlem, but his name never traveled far beyond this cultural underground during his lifetime. In 1911 he completed his ragtime opera *Treemonisha*, exhausting his physical and emotional resources in staging a single Harlem performance in 1915. Interest in ragtime music faded with the new rhythms of Tin Pan Alley, and Joplin, sick and disillusioned at 48, died in Manhattan State Hospital. The Joplin revival started in 1970, when Nonesuch Records issued a Joplin series played by classical pianists. Republication of his rags soon followed, and the 1973 film *The Sting* made Joplin's *The Entertainer* rag a national hit. Joplin's grave finally received a permanent marker; and *Treemonisha*, with elaborate orchestration, arrived on Broadway in 1975.

ROBERT HUTCHINGS GODDARD (1882–1945), U.S. physicist, rocketry pioneer

Goddard taught physics for most of his career at Clark University in Worcester, Mass. His now classic paper "A Method of Reaching Extreme Altitudes" (1919) predicted the development of spacecraft and their possibility of reaching the moon and beyond. Over the next 25 years he experimented, plotted trajectories, and tested several fuel and guidance systems, anticipating much of the later progress in rocketry. *The New York Times*, in a 1920 editorial, ridiculed his claim that rockets could fly to the moon, even though Goddard had clearly demonstrated that they could operate in a vacuum. He was called "moon mad" and his insights were ignored by both the general public and the government—although the German V-2 production of W.W. II adopted many of his ideas. Almost 15 years after his death, the Soviet Sputnik 1 orbiter vindicated Goddard's theories. Since U.S. research could not proceed without infringing on many of his 214 patents, the government paid $1 million to the Guggenheim Foundation, which had supported his work. In belated recognition of Goddard's skill and foresight, the NASA research facility at Greenbelt, Md., was named the Goddard Space Flight Center. And, as the Apollo 11 astronauts prepared to walk on the moon on July 17, 1969, *The New York Times* printed a formal retraction of its 1920 editorial.

FRANZ KAFKA (1883–1924), Austrian author

Kafka, said poet W. H. Auden, bears the same relation to our age that Dante, Shakespeare, and Goethe bore to theirs. His novels *Amerika*, *The Trial*, and *The Castle* pose the spiritual and artistic problems that have occupied most serious 20th-century writers and thinkers. The author was a typical victim of the urban rat race. As a harassed functionary of the Workers' Accident Insurance Institute in Prague, he struggled for free time from his job and domineering family to write. He was the most sedentary of men, lonely, untraveled, and inexperienced except in business. Five slim volumes appeared and sank out of sight during his lifetime, and only a few friends knew that he was writing the novels that would help form the core of 20th-century literature. These works remained incomplete and unpublished when tuberculosis killed him at age 40. After years of tortuous efforts to "begin my real life" and to describe a precise statement of his soul, Kafka considered his efforts a failure. In a last request, he asked his friend Max Brod to burn all of his papers and manuscripts. Brod indignantly refused, saying that if Kafka had really wanted them destroyed, he would not have given the task to the one person he knew would never consent to it. Thus Kafka's best-known novels, prophetic of the nightmare state of fascism, were first published in Germany in 1925 through 1927. Although the Nazis soon banned the books, translated editions surfaced in other countries. Kafka's reputation has steadily increased since the 1940s, and today the works of his critics and interpreters far outnumber his own.

LEON "BIX" BEIDERBECKE (1902–1931), U.S. jazz musician

No jazz lover who has heard Bix Beiderbecke's pure cornet has ever forgotten it. Though he came from a musical family and studied classical music on his own, he never took a cornet lesson in his life but taught himself at age 14 by playing along with Dixieland records. The shy, inarticulate boy from Davenport, Ia., dropped out of school, and a succession of jobs with vagrant musical groups finally landed him his first steady work with Frank Trumbauer's band in 1925. He soon moved into Jean Goldkette's orchestra, where he often alternated between cornet and piano. In 1927 he joined Paul Whiteman's band, where he made $200 per week—the financial high point of his career. "Proud of his recordings with Whiteman," wrote Dan Morgenstern, "Bix religiously sent each record to his family; he was deeply hurt when by chance he looked into a closet at home and found it filled with his unopened packages." Whiteman often featured Beiderbecke's cornet solos, which attracted a devoted circle of fans, but the stress of the big band's commercial pace increased his already severe alcohol problem. By 1929 Beiderbecke was no longer dependable on the stand, and Whiteman had to let him go. He played a few odd jobs for a while before he died of pneumonia at age 28. Beiderbecke remained forgotten until 1938, when Dorothy Baker published her *Young Man with a Horn*, a sentimental novel based on his life. The 1950 film of the same title, starring Kirk Douglas, was an even more romanticized version. Yet the novel marked the beginning of the Beiderbecke cult, and in time the true story of his life proved far more intriguing than the fictional one. In Beiderbecke's integration of Impressionist composers, especially Debussy, his style and tone had lasting influence on jazz, and such recordings as "Singin' the Blues" and "In a Mist" have become classics. Today he is recognized as the first important jazz innovator among white musicians.

ANNE FRANK (1929–1945), German diarist

Among the many persons driven underground by Hitler was a young Jewish girl who wanted to be an author and died at the age of 15 in Bergen-Belsen Concentration Camp. She fled Germany with her parents and settled in Amsterdam shortly after the Nazis took over in 1933. When the Nazi occupiers began to round up Dutch Jews for extermination in 1941, the Franks and four neighbors went into hiding on the top floor of an obscure row house on the Prinsengracht Canal. Here they lived for two years, and here Anne confided in a notebook an account of daily existence, family activities, and her own feelings. Finally betrayed by a Dutch informer on Aug. 4, 1944, the group was arrested by the Gestapo. Only Anne's father, Otto Frank, survived the war. He retrieved the diary where it had fallen on the tenement floor the day of the arrest. Its publication and theater adaptation caused an immediate sensation. One of the most literate and engaging prison logs in history, *The Diary of Anne Frank* is a profoundly moving document of the triumph of the human spirit over circumstance. It has been translated into 32 languages, and the Amsterdam hideaway in which it was written continues to attract visitors from all over the world.

—J.E.

18

STRANGER THAN FICTION

THE PEOPLE'S ALMANAC ODDITY QUIZ

Questions

1. What do the letters in Mafia stand for?
2. In 1910 King Edward VII of England, son of Queen Victoria, endorsed a product. What was it?
3. Iran was formerly called Persia. What was it called before that?
4. Did William Shakespeare have any siblings?
5. Did any white men ever play basketball on the Harlem Globetrotters?
6. How many teeth does your run-of-the-mill mosquito have?
7. Who created the Invisible Man?
8. Who was Ebenezer Scrooge's onetime partner in Charles Dickens's *A Christmas Carol?*
9. What infamous politician was Lt. John F. Kennedy's commanding officer in the Solomon Islands during W.W. II?
10. How many people must live in a community before the U.S. government calls it a city?
11. In the 1934 All-Star baseball game, left-hander Carl Hubbell of the New York Giants successively struck out the five greatest hitters in the American League. Who were they?
12. During W.W. II, the head of Hitler's Luftwaffe, Hermann Göring, offered a $5,000 reward to anyone who could kill or capture a famous American airman. Who was this airman?
13. Is being "busy as a bee" very busy?
14. Do you know the names of two well-known Americans who were buried in the Kremlin?
15. Anyone who knows anything about American football knows the playing field is 100 yd. in length. What is its width?
16. How much time a year does an American man spend tying his necktie?
17. What phobia are you suffering from if you are afraid of the number 13?
18. What famous journalist fought on both sides in the U.S. Civil War?
19. When you lick a postage stamp, how many calories do you consume?

20. In what sports do you win going backwards?
21. What number do you mean when you say "a few"?
22. The average person's IQ is 90 to 110. What is the IQ of a moron?
23. Of what country was Charlie Chaplin the dictator in his film *The Great Dictator?*
24. What would a dog see if he sat through a Technicolor movie?
25. Her name was based on the words *Arab Death*. Who was she?
26. In 1972 astronaut Buzz Aldrin did a TV commercial comparing a certain car to a spacecraft. What was the car?
27. What two words in English, used as one word, spell the same forwards and backwards?
28. Two of President Nixon's henchmen once worked at Disneyland in Anaheim, Calif. Can you guess which two?
29. Which is the only Middle Eastern country without a desert?
30. If you were flashed a secret code reading "Climb Mt. Nitaka," what would you do?
31. Who was the monarch who reigned in the famous fictional kingdom of Ruritania in *The Prisoner of Zenda?*
32. What young man, who was to become a world-famous aviator in 1938, was one of the workers who helped build Charles Lindbergh's single-engined airplane *The Spirit of St. Louis* in San Diego, Calif.?

Answers

1. *Morte Alla Francia Italia Anela* ("Death to the French Is Italy's Cry").
2. Angelus Player Pianos.
3. Iran.
4. Shakespeare had seven brothers and sisters. Two sisters were older than he—Joan, six years older, who died before the playwright was born; and Margaret, two years his senior. He also had two younger sisters and three younger brothers: another Joan, two years younger; Anne, seven years younger; Gilbert, a haberdasher, two years younger; Richard, 10 years younger; and Edmund, who may have become an actor, 16 years his junior.
5. Yes, three whites at various times played on the Globetrotters—Bob Karstens, Harold "Bunny" Levitt, and Abe Saperstein. Levitt, who had never been to college, was only 5 ft. 4 in., too small for competitive basketball. But he became the greatest free-throw artist in court history. He also sank 499 successive free throws. The Globetrotters offered $1,000 to anyone who could beat him at the line. No one ever did. Saperstein, London-born, founded the Globetrotters in 1927. At first he had only five players. Whenever someone was injured, Saperstein, though only 5 ft., would substitute for him. He was, if nothing else, a great dribbler. He died in 1966.
6. Isaac Asimov tells us a mosquito has 47 teeth.
7. H. G. Wells.
8. Jacob Marley. He died on a Christmas Eve and comes back to haunt Scrooge on a Christmas Eve.

9. None other than President Nixon's attorney general, John Mitchell, who served a prison term for his involvement in the Watergate scandal.
10. About 8,000 people.
11. Babe Ruth, Lou Gehrig, Jimmy Foxx, Al Simmons, and Joe Cronin all went down swinging.
12. He was a tail gunner and aerial photographer on B-17's. His name was Clark Gable.
13. You bet. To gather and store 2 lb. of honey, 60,000 worker bees visit 3 million flowers in one hour.
14. One was John Reed, an author-adventurer, and the other was William D. "Big Bill" Haywood, a radical labor leader. Reed, who came from a wealthy Portland, Ore., family, was a Harvard graduate who wrote for *The Masses*, a socialist magazine. Covering W.W. I as a correspondent, Reed became a friend of Lenin. In 1919 Reed headed the Communist Labor party in the U.S. Indicted for treason, he escaped to Russia. Before his "exile," he produced his best book, *Ten Days That Shook the World*, an eyewitness account of the Russian Revolution. In 1920, three days short of his 33rd birthday, he died in Moscow of typhus. He was buried inside the Kremlin. William Haywood, leader of the Industrial Workers of the World, the radical IWW, or Wobblies, was charged with being accessory to a murder in Idaho. Clarence Darrow defended him and he was acquitted. In 1918, under the new U.S. wartime laws, Haywood was tried for sedition in a 138-day Chicago trial, found guilty, sentenced to 20 years' imprisonment and a $10,000 fine. When the U.S. Supreme Court rejected his appeal, he jumped bail and found a haven in the Soviet Union. He never became a Communist. In Moscow he explained that as a Wobbly he knew "how to sock scabs and mine guards and policemen . . . but wasn't as long on the ideological stuff as the Russians." Homesick and lonely, he died in Moscow in 1928. The Soviets respected him and buried him inside the Kremlin.
15. The field is 53⅓ yd. wide.
16. Four hours a year.
17. Triskaidekaphobia.
18. Henry Morton Stanley enlisted with the Confederates, was taken prisoner, then joined the Union. Seven years after that he went to Africa to find Dr. David Livingstone.
19. One tenth of one calorie.
20. Tug-of-war, rowing, swimming the backstroke.
21. St. Peter in the New Testament says a few means 8: "the days of Noah while the ark was being constructed, in which a few, that is, eight souls were being conveyed safely through water." The Koran says a few means 3 to 10. *Webster's Third New International Dictionary* says, "consisting of a small number . . . not many but some." Expert George Stimpson says, "It is relative in respect to the number to which it is compared. If 10 persons attend a meeting where 100 are expected, 10 are a few; on the other hand, if 100 attend when several thousand are expected, 100 are a few."

22. 50 to 70.
23. Tomania.
24. He would see a movie in shades of gray. Dogs can't distinguish colors. Next time, take a bird. Most birds can see colors.
25. Theda Bara, the celebrated screen vamp of silent picture days. Theda was derived from an anagram of Death. Bara is merely Arab spelled backwards.
26. A Volkswagen.
27. Race car.
28. H. R. Haldeman and Ron Ziegler had been employees of Disneyland.
29. The half-Christian, half-Muslim nation of Lebanon, where the official language is Arabic.
30. If you were Japanese and the calendar read "Dec. 7, 1941," you would start the attack on Pearl Harbor.
31. King Rudolf V.
32. Douglas Corrigan. In 1938 he said he was flying (in an old plane with a faulty compass and no radio) from New York to San Diego, then pretended to get mixed up and flew across the Atlantic Ocean to Ireland—to become renowned as "Wrongway" Corrigan.

—I.W.

MYSTERIOUS HAPPENINGS

The Event: The Disappearance of Raoul Wallenberg
When: Jan. 17, 1945
Where: En route from Budapest to Debrecen, Hungary
The Mystery: Raoul Wallenberg, a 32-year-old architect from a prominent banking family in Sweden, had completed his mission in Budapest at the close of W.W. II. He had saved literally tens of thousands of Hungarian Jews from Adolf Eichmann and the Nazi crematoriums. Attached to the neutral Swedish mission in Budapest, he had handed out protective Swedish passports to thousands of Jews, whom he then hid in 32 safe houses protected by diplomatic immunity. He once saved 70,000 Jews in one evening, through sheer force of intimidation: Having heard that Hungarian Nazis and German soldiers were about to slaughter the entire population of the city's walled ghetto, he informed the commanding officer, Gen. August Schmidhuber, that if the pogrom took place he personally would see that the German commander was tried as a war criminal after Hungary's liberation. Permission for the raid was withdrawn.

On Jan. 16, 1945, with the German surrender now a foregone conclusion and the Russian forces laying siege to Budapest, Wallenberg decided to seek out Marshal Malinovsky, the Russian commander headquartered at Debrecen, 120 mi. east of the capital. He wanted to discuss plans for his proposed Wallenberg Institution for Rescue and Reconstruction, an agency that would restore to Hungarian Jews property confiscated from them during the war. Wallenberg made his intention known to Soviet forces fighting in Budapest, and the next day he was

Raoul Wallenberg—still alive in a Soviet prison?

picked up by two officers of the Russian secret police, who said they would escort him safely to Debrecen. Thus on Jan. 17, 1945, Wallenberg and his Hungarian driver, Vilmos Langfelder, set out for Debrecen with the two Russians. Making a final stop at his Budapest office before leaving the city, Wallenberg whispered to his aides, "I am going to Marshal Malinovsky's headquarters, whether as a guest or a prisoner I do not know yet." The four then drove east towards Debrecen. Neither Wallenberg nor his driver was ever heard from again.

Possible Solutions: On Mar. 7, 1945, Radio Kossuth, the Soviet station in liberated Budapest, announced that the Gestapo had ambushed and murdered Wallenberg and his driver en route to Debrecen. It sounded reasonable. After all, the Swede had been on Eichmann's hit list for a long time. But no body was ever produced, and with the release of German and Italian prisoners of war from Russian camps came reports of a Swede held captive in a Moscow prison. Asked by Swedish officials for an explanation, the Soviets insisted that Wallenberg had never been held captive in Russia. Then, on Feb. 7, 1957, Moscow issued a correction. Yes, Wallenberg had been a prisoner at Lubyanka Prison in Moscow, Soviet authorities admitted, but, alas, he had died of an apparent heart attack on July 17, 1947. They blamed his wrongful detention on Viktor S. Abakumov, former minister of state security, one of Stalin's henchmen who had recently been executed during the period of destalinization. The Soviets expressed their regrets and considered the matter closed.

But the Wallenberg file kept popping open. In 1961 a Russian physician, Dr. Aleksandr Myashnikov, confided to a Swedish colleague, Dr. Nana Svartz, that Wallenberg was alive and incarcerated in a mental asylum near Moscow. Again pressed by Sweden to investigate the matter, Soviet officials produced Dr. Myashnikov, who in an understandable attempt to protect himself, denied having said any such thing. In 1979 Jan Kaplan, a Soviet Jew recently released from prison, wrote his daughter in Tel Aviv that, while in the Butyrka prison hospital in Moscow recuperating from a heart attack in 1975, he had met a 63-year-old Swede who claimed to have been in prison for 30 years. When this news became public, Kaplan was immediately rearrested.

Wallenberg's family continues to believe that he is still alive, vegetating in some Russian prison. In May, 1980, his half sister, Mrs. Nina Lagergren, and his half brother, Guy von Dardel, joined with human rights advocates from around the world to marshal public opinion against Soviet silence on Wallenberg's fate. The cause célèbre has reached such proportions in Sweden in recent years that Stockholm has abandoned its traditional obsequious attitude toward Moscow and has begun to demand full disclosure.

But why? Why would the Soviet Union go to such lengths to hold a Swedish humanitarian who posed no apparent threat to them whatever? One answer may be that the Russian army of occupation in Hungary simply could not believe that a Scandinavian gentile from a capitalist family would risk his life to save a clutch of East European Jews without an ulterior motive. Russian authorities interrogated Wallenberg's associates in Hungary and learned that his rescue operation had been funded entirely by the U.S. Was the Swede, then, an American spy? Would his campaign to restore confiscated property threaten Soviet plans to impose communism on Hungary? And how did Wallenberg survive so long as a highly visible champion of Jews in a Nazi-controlled country? Why did the Germans tolerate him? The Russians may have suspected that he collaborated with the Germans against the Russians in exchange for more tolerant treatment of the Jews. But if the Soviets had taken Wallenberg prisoner in 1945, why did they not release him in 1957 when they acknowledged his imprisonment? Since they blamed his wrongful detention on Stalinist excesses, why would it have been necessary to say that he had died if in fact he was still alive? That is the hardest question to answer. As for why Soviet authorities do not release him now in the face of intensifying international criticism, those who believe that he is still alive argue that perhaps after 36 years in the brutal Russian prison system the 68-year-old might be an emotional basket case. To release the hero of Sweden and world Jewry in such a condition after maintaining that he was dead all these years would deliver a devastating propaganda defeat to the Soviets.

In January, 1981, the Swedish Raoul Wallenberg Association held an international conference in Stockholm. In attendance were lawyers, politicians, and scientists from eight Western nations. After listening to testimony from former Soviet prisoners, the association issued this statement: "There is every reason to believe that Raoul Wallenberg is still alive. The hearing requests the Soviet authorities to reexamine the case promptly and to return Raoul Wallenberg to his family."

—W.A.D.

The Event: The Disappearance of James Thompson
When: Mar. 26, 1967
Where: Malaysia
The Mystery: On a warm Easter Sunday, 61-year-old American millionaire James Thompson was vacationing with friends at the Malaysian resort of Cameron Highlands. With his companion Mrs. Connie Mangskau, an English-Thai businesswoman, and his hosts, Dr. and Mrs. T. G. Ling of Singapore, Thompson went to church that morning and then on a picnic. About two-thirty in the afternoon, the group returned to the Lings' resort home, Moonlight Cottage. The Lings and Mrs. Mangskau went to their rooms for a siesta, but Thompson, who seemed restless, went out on the veranda to sun himself. About three-thirty the Lings, who were resting but not sleeping, heard someone walking down the gravel road leading from the cottage to the resort's golf course. They assumed it was Thompson.

When the Lings and Mrs. Mangskau awoke from their naps, they couldn't find Thompson but were not concerned. Thompson had visited Moonlight Cottage before and had frequently gone for walks and hikes on nearby trails. Besides, Thompson, a former officer in the OSS—the predecessor of the CIA—had had intensive training in jungle warfare and survival during W.W. II and since then had become an avid jungle hiker and explorer in Thailand.

As dusk approached, the vacationers became slightly concerned, especially after they discovered that Thompson must not have planned a very long walk, for he was a chain-smoker and had left his cigarettes and lighter on the veranda. Also, the pills that he always carried to combat his occasional but extremely painful gallstone attacks were left behind. They were perplexed. Thompson could not have intended to go far without cigarettes and pills, and he knew that darkness came early, about six-thirty. He also knew quite well that it was cold and dangerous at night in the mountain jungles.

As night fell, the Lings called the local police. People at the resort and the local inhabitants were questioned, but nobody had seen the American that afternoon. Searchers went out with flashlights, but no trace was found of the millionaire. Thompson's friends continued to hope for his safe return; they knew he had been temporarily lost before during his jungle excursions in even wilder country. Except for the gallstones, Thompson was in good physical condition and was accustomed to outdoor hardships. However, morning came and Thompson did not return. In fact, he never returned, and no clue to his fate—no footprints, no personal articles, no body—has ever been found. Thompson had taken an Easter stroll into total oblivion.

A man of inherited wealth and a Princeton graduate, Thompson had been introduced to Southeast Asia during W.W. II, while serving in the OSS. After W.W. II he remained in Bangkok, Thailand, where he revitalized and organized the Thai silk industry and became known as the "silk king." By 1967 his Thai Silk Company had $1.5 million in annual revenues. The disappearance of this man, who was recognized as an economic and political power in Southeast Asia, generated a massive manhunt. Malaysian and British troops with helicopters and bloodhounds searched the jungle surrounding the resort. Local tribesmen were also pressed into service, as well as a local Boy Scout troop. Gen. Edwin Black, commander of the U.S. support forces in Thailand and a friend of Thompson, led an American search mission. Even psychics and local tribal medicine men—called bomahs—were enlisted in the effort to find Thompson. Richard Noone, renowned British jungle fighter and explorer, who was hired by executives of Thompson's Thai Silk Company to hunt for him, stated categorically, "I am fully convinced that Mr. Thompson is not lost in the jungle."

Possible Solutions: Although there is no concrete evidence, there are many theories about what happened to Thompson. One of the simplest explanations is that Thompson was attacked and eaten by one of the tigers known to roam the Malay Peninsula jungles. Another theory holds that he had an accident and fell from a trail into a jungle ravine, where his body still remains. Yet another conjecture is that Thompson, an adventurous man, was bored with his routine life and committed suicide. These theories lack credence because trackers never found a trace of his body.

Other theories suggest kidnapping. Bandit gangs were known to operate in that area of Malaya, and they often kidnapped wealthy businessmen for ransom. However, a $25,000 reward was offered—together with an offer of immunity from prosecution—for Thompson's return, but nobody responded. Some argue that Thompson was kidnapped for political reasons. Proponents of this theory infer, without proof, that Thompson, the former colonel in the OSS, was still active as a CIA operative in Thailand. He was supposedly abducted by Communist agents who whisked him away to one of the numerous abandoned airfields that the British had constructed during their war against Communist insurgents during the 1950s. From there he was flown to Laos or Cambodia, where he was forced to reveal information on CIA operations in Southeast Asia. Or, possibly, his captors tried to brainwash him for later use as a propaganda tool by the North Vietnamese, who were then battling the U.S. in South Vietnam.

A related hypothesis is that Thompson went voluntarily with foreign agents to Cambodia, there to meet with Vietnamese Communists, whom he had known as OSS allies during the war against the Japanese, in order to open lines of communication for a peaceful settlement to the Vietnam War. Opponents of the theory that Thompson left voluntarily point to the fact that he left both his cigarettes and pills at the Ling cottage. This group of theories assumes that Thompson was either executed by the Communists or is still being held in either Vietnam or China.

At this time, the riddle of Thompson's disappearance is no closer to being solved than it was in 1967.

—R.J.F.

The Event: Cattle Mutilations
When: 1963 to the present
Where: United States
The Mystery: Although incidents of cattle mutilations have been noted as far back as 1810, in the area of the Scotch-English border, the real story doesn't begin until November, 1963. That was when cattle near Gallipolis, O., were discovered after having been carved up with "surgical precision." All the blood had been drained from their bodies, and the brains and other organs had been removed. This strange discovery remained an isolated episode until Sept. 9, 1967, when a gelding named Snippy was found on the Harry King Ranch near Alamosa, Colo., with organs missing and blood drained. Since Snippy's death, over 8,000 cattle mutilations have been reported.

Basic patterns have emerged from the study of these mutilations. In a classic mutilation case, the deed is done at night, with no witnesses. No footprints or vehicle tracks can be found and there are no signs of struggle. The victimized cow is devoid of blood, but there are no traces of blood nearby. Several organs may be missing, usually the sex organs. The rectum has been cut out cleanly, and sometimes miscellaneous body parts, such as the tongue or patches of skin, are gone. Occasionally, mysterious lights have been reported in the area just before a mutilation.

During the early 1970s incidents of cattle mutilations occurred sporadically. Then in 1973 there was a dramatic increase in mutilation cases. During a six-week period beginning on Nov. 30, 44 cows were mutilated in north-central Kansas alone. Over 100 mutilations took place during the summer of 1974 in South Dakota, Nebraska, and Iowa. In the fall, activity centered in Minnesota. In 1975 reports of cattle mutilations moved south. By February mutilated cows were being discovered all over Texas and Oklahoma. On Feb. 21 the Oklahoma Cattlemen's Association offered a cash reward for information leading to the arrest and conviction of persons responsible for the mutilations. In March and April, Kansas was hit again. In June, the Elbert County Colorado Livestock Association offered a reward after that county experienced 36 mutilations in four months. Before the year was out, the Elbert County total had risen to 80. The situation had also reached epidemic proportions in Montana, Idaho, and parts of Wyoming. Between August, 1975, and May, 1976, authorities in Cascade County, Montana, received reports of more than 100 cattle mutilations as well as 130 sightings of mysterious craft in the sky.

The cattle mutilations phenomena peaked in 1975 but has continued at a steady rate since then, with noteworthy flare-ups in 1978 and 1979 in Arkansas and New Mexico.

Possible Solutions: Unidentified flying objects, a satanic cult, the CIA, military experimenters, uranium companies, pranksters, predators, blackleg disease, vampire bats. Take your pick. The UFO theory was the first to gain a substantial following because it explained the lack of tracks and the reports of mysterious lights in the sky. But some ranchers who had lost cattle to mutilators claimed that the flying objects they had observed were quite identifiable. They were, in fact, helicopters. But whose helicopters? In 1973 there was much talk of airborne cattle rustlers, but suspicion soon shifted to the military, which has access to more helicopters than anyone else. Cascade County, Montana, site of the 1975–1976 rash of mutilations, is the home of Malmstrom Air Force Base. Many other mutilations, particularly in Colorado, have occurred near military bases.

One theory has it that the cattle are picked up at one spot, operated on at a second spot, and then lowered to the ground somewhere else. No tracks, no footprints, and no traces of blood. The culprits could be military or CIA operatives studying the effects of nerve gas or radioactivity. A related theory, propounded in New Mexico in 1979, has it that the mutilations are part of a modern-day range war in which a group of powerful ranchers have gotten together to intimidate smaller ranchers and scare them into selling their land.

In early 1975 investigators in Gregg County, Texas, uncovered evidence of a satanic cult, the Sons of Satan, and allegations were made that these devil worshipers were using the blood and body parts of animals in their predawn rituals. Elsewhere in Texas, similar accusations were made against a motorcycle gang called the Devil's Disciples. Public sentiment turned against the satanists. Rev. Robert King, minister of the Church of Satan in Fort Worth, Tex., defended the members of his congregation, or "grotto," in a statement to the press in April, 1975. "Satanists are getting the blame for everything," King complained, "just like the Communists did in the 1950s. Well, my family's got a lot of investments in cattle. Why should I want to see cattle killed?" In fact, no positive connection has ever been proved between satanic cults and cattle mutilations.

From the very beginning there have been those who believed that reports of cattle mutilations were nothing but mass hysteria, that there really is no such thing as a cattle mutilation. These people say that every gruesome detail can be attributed to the work of predators—wolves, coyotes, dog packs, weasels, skunks, birds, buzzards. The predator theory received a big boost in October, 1979, when the sheriff's department of Washington County, Arkansas, released the results of an experiment they had performed six weeks earlier. On Sept. 4, a sick cow was deliberately killed and left in a field to be observed and photographed by two Arkansas State Police officers, Sgt. Rick O'Kelley and Sgt. Doug Fogley. After 33 hours the bovine corpse displayed all the characteristics of a classic mutilation case. The eyes were gone and so were the sex organs and so was the blood. The rectum was neatly cored. But the only visitors to attack the cow had been buzzards and blowflies. The blowflies were given credit for creating the appearance of "surgical precision" when swarms of them cleaned up the rectum and eyes after the buzzards had had their fill. Sergeant Fogley claimed that 95% of cattle mutilations could be attributed to predators and that the other 5% were probably the work of copycat killers.

In 1979 the state of New Mexico and the federal Law Enforcement

Assistance Administration (LEAA) spent $50,000 on a study of cattle mutilations. Former FBI agent Kenneth Rommel was put in charge of the investigation. His report, released the following year, supported the conclusions of the Arkansas police: predators and nothing but predators.

But many ranchers and others remain unconvinced. They say that Rommel studied only 15 dead cows and that none of them was a classic mutilation case. And they challenge the validity of any study done under the auspices of the LEAA, a notoriously wasteful and inefficient agency. Meanwhile the mutilations continue to be reported.

—D.W.

THE CONTINUING SEARCH FOR . . .

THE CONTINUING SEARCH FOR SHAMBHALA

Background

Is there really a hidden galaxy of minds living in seclusion in an inaccessible part of Asia, or is it merely a myth? Shambhala, the "Hidden Kingdom," is thought of in Tibet as a community where perfect and semiperfect beings live and are guiding the evolution of humankind. Shambhala is considered to be the source of the Kalacakra, which is the highest and most esoteric branch of Tibetan mysticism. The Buddha preached the teachings of the Kalacakra to an assembly of holy men in southern India. Afterwards the teachings remained hidden for 1,000 years, until an Indian yogi-scholar went in search of Shambhala and was initiated into the teachings by a holy man he met along the way. The Kalacakra then remained in India until it made its way to Tibet in 1026. Since then the concept of Shambhala has been widely known in Tibet, and Tibetans have been studying the Kalacakra for the last 900 years, learning its science, practicing its meditation, and using its system of astrology to guide their lives. As one Tibetan lama put it, how could Shambhala be the source of something which has affected so many areas of Tibetan life for so long and yet not exist?

Tibetan religious texts describe the physical makeup of the hidden land in detail. It is thought to look like an eight-petaled lotus blossom because it is made up of eight regions, each surrounded by a ring of mountains. In the center of the innermost ring lies Kalapa, the capital, and the king's palace, which is composed of gold, diamonds, coral, and precious gems. The capital is surrounded by mountains made of ice, which shine with a crystalline light. The technology of Shambhala is supposed to be highly advanced; the palace contains special skylights made of lenses which serve as high-powered telescopes to study extraterrestrial life, and for hundreds of years Shambhala's inhabitants have been using aircraft and cars that shuttle through a network of underground tunnels. On the way to enlightenment, Shambhalans acquire such powers as clairvoyance, the ability to move at great speeds, and the ability to materialize and disappear at will.

The kingdom of Shambhala.

The prophecy of Shambhala states that each of its kings will rule for 100 years. There will be 32 in all, and as their reigns pass, conditions in the outside world will deteriorate. Men will become more warlike and pursue power for its own sake, and an ideology of materialism will spread over the earth. When the "barbarians" who follow this ideology are united under an evil king and think there is nothing left to conquer, the mists will lift to reveal the icy mountains of Shambhala. The barbarians will attack Shambhala with a huge army equipped with terrible weapons. Then the 32nd king of Shambhala, Rudra Cakrin, will lead a mighty host against the invaders. In a last great battle, the evil king and his followers will be destroyed.

By definition Shambhala is hidden. It is thought to exist somewhere between the Gobi Desert and the Himalayas, but it is protected by a psychic barrier so that no one can find the kingdom who is not meant to. Tibetan lamas spend a great deal of their lives in spiritual development before attempting the journey to Shambhala. Those who try to get there who are not wanted are swallowed by crevasses or caught in avalanches. People and animals tremble at its borders as if bombarded by invisible rays. There are guidebooks to Shambhala, but they describe the route in terms so vague that only those already initiated into the teachings of the Kalacakra can understand them.

Clues for the Hunt

The first known Western reference to Shambhala comes from two Catholic missionaries who left Europe in the 17th century to convert the Tibetans and Chinese. They were looking for a way to China through Tibet from India and heard about a land called Xembala. Thinking it was China, they headed in its direction and did not discover their mistake until they reached the major monastery for lamas interested in Shambhala. About 1627 they mentioned the kingdom in their letters home. But the spiritualist Elena Petrovna Blavatsky was the first to present Shambhala seriously to the public eye in the West. She believed that she received secret teachings from spiritual masters living somewhere beyond the Himalayas, and that the highest of these masters was from Shambhala. The followers of the Theosophical Society, which she and Henry Steel Olcott founded in 1875, familiarized the public with their notion that the society's secret doctrines came from Shambhala, which they considered the world's spiritual center.

Strange sightings in the area where Shambhala is thought to be seem to provide evidence of its existence. Tibetans believe that the land is guarded by beings with superhuman powers. In the early 1900s an article in an Indian newspaper, the *Statesman*, told of a British major who, camping in the Himalayas, saw a very tall, lightly clad man with long hair. Apparently noticing that he was being watched, the man leaped down the vertical slope and disappeared. To the major's astonishment, the Tibetans with whom he was camping showed no surprise at his story; they calmly explained that he had seen one of the snowmen who guard the sacred land.

A more detailed account of these "snowmen" guardians was given by Alexandra David-Neel, an explorer who spent 14 years in Tibet. While traveling through the Himalayas she saw a man moving with extraordinary speed and described him as follows: "I could clearly see his perfectly calm impassive face and wide-open eyes with their gaze fixed on some invisible distant object situated somewhere high up in space. The man did not run. He seemed to lift himself from the ground, proceeding by leaps. It looked as if he had been endowed with the elasticity of a ball, and rebounded each time his feet touched the ground. His steps had the regularity of a pendulum."

There have been a number of strange aircraft sightings in these areas. During Nicholas Roerich's expedition through central Asia in 1925–1926, his party suddenly noticed a huge disk in the sky. Three men with binoculars watched a large spheroid body moving very fast, suddenly changing direction and disappearing behind the Humboldt mountain chain. The Tibetan lamas accompanying Roerich exclaimed, "The sign of Shambhala!" Two airships were also observed by British mountaineer Frank Smythe while on Mt. Everest in 1933. He recorded having seen two dark objects, one with squat wings and the other with a sort of beak, surrounded by a pulsating aura, at an altitude of 26,000 ft. The most recent sighting was made near Shillong, Assam, in India in 1967. A whirling disk hovered 650 ft. above the ground and then dived into a river, creating a huge vortex and a lot of noise. It then reappeared, ascended, and flew in a zigzag pattern over the jungle until it disappeared.

The Search

While people (especially Tibetan lamas) have been searching for Shambhala for centuries, those who seek the kingdom often never return, either because they have found the hidden country and have remained there or because they have been destroyed in the attempt. Of the Westerners on record, Nicholas Roerich's expeditions in search of Shambhala are the most famous. In 1925 Roerich, a Russian poet and artist who designed scenes for Diaghilev's ballets, made an expedition from Kashmir to Khotan, where he and his group resided from October, 1925, to January, 1926. Upon his return to Russia in June, 1926, the commissar of foreign affairs and the commissar of education asked to see him. A new social order was then being established in Russia, and Roerich presented the commissar with a message from the Mahatmas (great souls) of the Himalayas. The message, now in the state archives of the U.S.S.R., reads:

> In the Himalayas we know what you are accomplishing. . . . You perceived the evolution of society. You indicated the significance of knowledge. You bowed your head before beauty. To the children you brought all the might of the cosmos. . . . We stopped a revolt in India as it was considered to be premature. But at the same time we recognized the timeliness of your movement. Greetings to you who are seeking the common good!

Roerich made another expedition in 1934, backed by Henry Wallace, the U.S. secretary of agriculture. Roerich ostensibly was sent to look for "drought-resistant grasses," although *Newsweek* magazine reported that "around the Department of Agriculture the Secretary's assistants freely admitted that he also wanted Roerich to look for the signs of the Second Coming." From Roerich's writings it is clear that he discovered signs of Shambhala all over central Asia, along with the widespread belief that its golden age was on the way. But whether or not he actually ever made it to that land is unknown.

Conclusions

Tibetan texts containing what appear to be historical facts about Shambhala, such as the names and dates of its kings and records of corresponding events occurring in the outside world, give Tibetans additional reason for believing that the kingdom exists. Recent events that seem to correspond to the predictions of the mythic kingdom add strength to their belief. The disintegration of Buddhism in Tibet and the growth of materialism throughout the world, coupled with the wars and turmoil of the 20th century, all fit in with the prophecy of Shambhala.

Edwin Bernbaum, the Western scholar who has published the most recent and thorough work on the subject, feels that of all the regions of central Asia the Tarim Basin southwest of Turfan in China comes closest in size and shape to Tibetan descriptions of Shambhala. For nearly 800 years before the Kalacakra had reached India and Tibet, Buddhism had been flourishing in this basin. Bernbaum also points out that some scholars have singled out Khotan, the largest and most fertile oasis on the southern rim of the basin, as the most likely location of Shambhala. (This is the area where Roerich and his expedition spent four months before returning to Russia.) But Bernbaum also points out, in detail, the many ways in which the guidebooks to Shambhala may be taken as directions for an inner journey, the arrival point—Shambhala—being the equivalent of enlightenment. Of the Tibetan lamas Bernbaum interviewed, many think that the only way to reach Shambhala is via death and rebirth in that country, that it is no longer possible to develop the superhuman powers necessary to get there via the guidebooks. Other lamas believe that although Shambhala is invisible to most people, it is still possible to attain the heightened awareness necessary to perceive it. Bernbaum points out that Shambhala could exist on another planet or at the outer edge of our physical reality, but he believes that the most likely explanation is that Shambhala was once a real kingdom which has now faded into the realm of myth.

—J.H.

THE CONTINUING SEARCH FOR PERCY H. FAWCETT

Background

During his "forest experience" in South America, British army explorer and surveyor Percy Harrison Fawcett (1867–1925?) heard stories of red-haired, blue-eyed tribes descended from colonists from the East, who brought with them a written language resembling Sanskrit and who built magnificent stone cities surrounded by walls. The stories, along with other "scraps of information," drew him into the obsessive belief that the cities were built at sea level by pioneers from the legendary lost continent of Atlantis. Then in 11,000 B.C. they were heaved to mountain heights by the same worldwide cataclysm that submerged Atlantis. Most had been deserted long ago, but one or two, among them a city he called Z, were still inhabited by a white, timid, clothed people, whose glory was gone, but who knew how to write and had an arcane knowledge of electricity. Guarding them were fierce Morcegos Indians—referred to as bats because they came out only at night—who lived in holes and caves covered with wicker.

Fawcett was a highly competent surveyor, who explored much new territory on his trips to South America between 1906 and 1914 in an effort, sponsored by the Royal Geographical Society, to settle a boundary dispute involving Bolivia, Peru, and Brazil. In his relations with Indians, who were often armed with poisoned darts, he strove to be peaceful. Once, as hostile Guarayos shot at his party, who were canoeing down the wild Heath River, he and his group sang an assortment of songs, including "Swanee River" and "A Bicycle Built for Two," until the astonished Indians lowered their weapons in perplexity—a pretty picture of nonviolence.

Though Fawcett had given up his army commission in 1910, he returned to England to fight in W.W. I, emerging with a DSO and the rank of colonel. But his dream of searching for lost cities was still very much alive, and by 1920 he was back in South America. His trip netted little except the discovery in the archives of Rio de Janeiro of a 1753 Portuguese account of a trip to a stone city apparently destroyed long before by an earthquake. By 1922 he was back in England, scheming to return to South America before he was too old (he was then in his 50s) and attempting to prove his theory through various means, including psychometry (a psychic he consulted held a small ancient statue and "saw" a continent stretching from North Africa to South America and a city destroyed by cataclysm).

He decided on 1925 for his expedition. A friend went to New York with an initial $1,500 to raise more funds, while Fawcett planned the trip with his son Jack and Jack's friend Raleigh Rimell, whom he was to take with him. Jack was a handsome athlete, who on a sojourn in California had been a cowhand and had tried to become a movie actor. (Mary Pickford used Jack's cricket bat in *Little Lord Fauntleroy*.) Raleigh was a "born clown," "keen as mustard" for the trip.

It began badly. In New York they found that their money-raising friend had spent the $1,500 in a drunken binge and had collected no more funds. Living on the cheap, they scrounged for other financing and finally found it: the North American Newspaper Alliance agreed to back them for rights to their story. By the spring of 1925 they were in Cuiabá, on the edge of the Mato Grosso, that huge, swampy Brazilian wilderness inhabited by snakes, insects, and hostile Indians. Their route would take them to Dead Horse Camp, where Fawcett's horse had died in 1921, then northeast to the Xingu River, on past an eternally lit "fat tower of stone," then through the forest and north to present-day Conceição do Araguaia, across to the Rio Tocantins, where Z was, to the Rio São Francisco, to the city mentioned in the 1753 account, and out by rail to Bahia City.

May 19 was son Jack's 22nd birthday. On May 29, from Dead Horse Camp, Fawcett wrote a letter to his wife, his last communication, in which he complained of insects, noted that Raleigh had a sore leg, and assured her, "You have no fear of any failure."

Clues for the Hunt

After the disappearance of the party, several individuals claimed to have seen Fawcett. In 1927 French engineer Roger Courteville said he had met a feverish, ragged man claiming to be Fawcett on a road in Minas Gerais, Brazil. Five years later Swiss trapper Stefan Rattin, on a visit to an Indian camp north of the Bomfin River, managed to talk with an old man, a captive, with bright blue eyes, a yellow-white beard, and long hair, who told him he was an English colonel and that his son was with him, but was sleeping. The story was discredited because Fawcett was bald and gray-eyed.

In the following year, a woman from a Nafaqua village at the junction of the Kuluene and Tanguro rivers (not on Fawcett's route) said that three white men had come to their village in a canoe, then gone to live with the Aruvudu Indians. The old man was made chief of the tribe, and the son married a chief's daughter by whom he had a blue-eyed child. They were unable to escape because of hostile tribes, she said.

Other stories, mostly disproven, placed them at the Xingu River, and it was reported at least twice that Indians had killed the party.

A compass, issued to Fawcett in 1913, was found near a tribe of Bacairy Indians in 1933. It was in perfect condition. A dog that accompanied the expedition later returned home, skinny and without a message.

The Search

Compounding the difficulty of searching for the Fawcett party were Fawcett's secretiveness concerning their specific route and his claim that they would be unable to get word to the outside for at least two years.

It was not until 1928 that the North American Newspaper Alliance sent a search party led by George Dyott into the Mato Grosso. In the hut of the chief of the Nafaquas, Aloique, who was wearing European pants (Fawcett's?), Dyott spotted a metal uniform case and heard the story of three white men who, Aloique said, had been taken to a Kalapalo village on the Kuluene, then had headed east. Smoke from their fires was seen for five days, then no more. Dyott reached the conclusion that perhaps Aloique had killed the group.

In 1930 Albert de Winton, a journalist, disappeared on a search for Fawcett, somewhere near the Kalapalo village.

Irish writer and paranormal practitioner Geraldine Cummins supposedly heard from Fawcett through automatic writing in 1935. He was, he wrote, in the jungle, where he had found Egyptian-looking pyramids and taken a drug-induced trip back in time.

In 1951 the chief of the Kalapalos confessed on his deathbed that he had clubbed the three men to death because father and son had fornicated with one of his wives and because Fawcett had slapped him for refusing to lend carriers and canoes. This story did not jibe with Fawcett's attitude toward Indians or Jack's pristine attitude toward sex. A later chief took a search party to the alleged Fawcett grave; the bones were exhumed and sent to England, where they were proven to be of a small man, probably not European.

In 1952 and 1955 Fawcett's other son, Brian, led aerial searches over the Mato Grosso to look for the party. Results: zero. Other searchers have proved that the legendary city is nothing but peculiar rock formations.

Conclusion

For some reason—illness, a spectacular find, Indian trouble—the party probably headed back toward civilization by a river route that took them to the Nafaqua village. Sometime after that, it is very likely that they died of fever or were killed by Indians. Still, it is pleasant to entertain the thought that they found Z after all and were so entranced by its cultured inhabitants that they decided to stay forever.

—A.E.

THE CONTINUING SEARCH FOR THE ELUSIVE FORMULA FOR COCA-COLA

Background

Coca-Cola is by far the most popular soft drink in the world; at present over 190 million drinks a day are sold, in 135 countries. A product so well known would hardly seem to be the stuff of which mysteries are made, yet since 1886, when the first batch of Coca-Cola was concocted by Atlanta pharmacist John S. Pemberton, the exact ingredients and their proportions have remained a closely guarded secret.

Even though the drink is available worldwide, the syrup from which it is made is blended only in the U.S. It is then shipped to the various bottling plants, where it is mixed with local water. Thus, the recipe remains safely at home, entrusted to fewer than 10 people. For years the secret recipe existed only in the memories of the select few who mixed it. Today it is also on paper in a safe-deposit vault at the Trust Company of Georgia, a bank that controls nearly $70 million worth of Coca-Cola stock. The vault containing the formula can be opened only after a vote by the board of directors.

In 1977 Coca-Cola, Inc., showed how much it would sacrifice in order to protect its secret formula. The drink was selling well in India, especially since the Dalai Lama, exiled there after the Communist takeover of Tibet, was photographed enthusiastically quaffing a Coke. However, the company chose to shut down 22 bottling plants rather than divulge the recipe to the Indian government, which wanted to "Indianize" the beverage business. Presently, Coke is available in India only on the black market.

The Search

It might seem that the Coca-Cola company is a bit overcautious in guarding a recipe that has been so closely imitated. All cola drinks have the same basic ingredients—sugar, water, caffeine, and caramel for coloring—but differ in what the Coke people call "essential oils and flavors." Cola connoisseurs will attest that Pepsi, RC, Shasta, and the rest do not taste like Coke or match the original in other properties. One man, so the story goes, claimed his wife douched with Coca-Cola for years as a method of birth control and became pregnant only after switching to Pepsi.

Although Coke is not recommended as a family-planning aid, it was originally sold as a patent medicine, an elixir said to relieve headaches, sluggishness, indigestion, and hangovers. Its proprietor, Asa G. Candler, made a weekly batch of Coca-Cola in the same copper kettle he used to brew his Botanic Blood Balm. (He made Coke on Saturdays and Balm on weekdays.) At the turn of the century, the drink's refreshing qualities stemmed in part from the inclusion of cocaine derived from coca leaves used in the recipe. The amount of the drug was miniscule, but it was enough to raise a furor when rumors spread that black "dope fiends" high on cocaine were apt to rape and pillage. The New York *Tribune* thundered against Coca-Cola, and by 1903 the state of Virginia considered banning it altogether. However, the company quietly switched from unprocessed coca leaves to "spent" ones.

Nowadays, the lift one gets from Coke is due to its high content of caffeine and sugar. A 12-oz. can of Coca-Cola contains about the same amount of caffeine as a 5-oz. cup of instant or freeze-dried coffee. Because caffeine is extremely bitter, a lot of sugar is needed to make the drink palatable; the Coca-Cola company purchases 10% of all the processed sugar sold in the U.S. (It has been demonstrated that rat's teeth dropped into a glass of Coke will completely dissolve in six months. Company spokesmen counter that anyone who soaks his teeth in Coca-Cola for six months deserves tooth decay.)

In Coke's case, there are at least 14 syrup ingredients, which the company calls "merchandises" and refers to by number. Some of them are known: Merchandise number 1 is sugar, number 2 is caramel, number 3 is caffeine, number 4 is phosphoric acid, and number 5 is an extract of "decocainized" coca leaves and cola nuts. Beyond that, various chemical analysts have identified the following: cinnamon, nutmeg, vanilla, glycerine, lavender, fluid extract of guarana, lime juice, and other citrus oils.

Then there is a supersecret ingredient known as Merchandise 7X, which no outsider has yet succeeded in identifying. Merchandise 7X comprises less than 1 percent of the formula. Asa Candler's son, Charles Howard Candler, summed up the Coca-Cola mystique in these words: "One of the proudest moments of my life came when my father . . . initiated me into the mysteries of the secret flavoring formula, inducting me . . . into the 'Holy of Holies.' No written formulae were shown. Containers of ingredients, from which the labels had been removed, were identified only by sight, smell, and remembering where each was put on the shelf. To be safe, Father stood by me several times while I compounded these distinctive flavors . . . with particular reference to the order in which they should be measured out and mixed . . . and I thereupon experienced the thrill of making up with his guidance a batch of merchandise 7X."

In 1954 a rumor spread through Morocco that Coca-Cola contained pig's blood, which would have made it taboo among Muslims. The beverage remained under suspicion until the sultan's son publicly drank a Coke. The company eagerly publicizes one fact about its ingredients—that the glycerine used is extracted from vegetable matter, not pork.

Conclusions

The inclusion of secret ingredients in a food product might seem on the surface to violate some government standard. To be sure, Coke has had a few legal problems concerning the drink's ingredients, but the company always succeeded in keeping its recipe hidden from both the FDA and the public. In a roundabout attempt at forcing disclosure of Coke's mysterious contents, the government took the company to court in a celebrated 1909 case—*The U.S. v. Forty Barrels and Twenty Kegs of Coca-Cola*—that tested the strength of the new Pure Food and Drug Act. After nine years of litigation, the government's case simply fizzled out. Since then, Coke's secret recipe has been further insulated by a "standard of identity" ruling by the FDA, which exempts beverage makers from having to identify on the label certain essential ingredients, among them the mysterious Merchandise 7X.

—M.S.

THE RAINMAKER

Nothing much distinguished the 39-year-old man who stood before the San Diego City Council on Dec. 13, 1915—except his occupation. Although he modestly preferred to call himself a "moisture accelerator," Charles Mallory Hatfield always would be known as "the rainmaker." The Minnesota-born pluviculturist had been "persuading moisture to come down" in thirsty southern California since 1902, when he perfected his technique on his father's ranch near Bonsall. His credentials were impressive. In 1904 he raised the level of the Lake Hemet Land and Water Company's reservoir by 22 ft., and he collected $1,000 from the Los Angeles Chamber of Commerce for producing 18 in. of rain during the first four months of 1905. He traveled to the Klondike the following year to fill the streams around Dawson City so the miners could pan for gold. And the farmers in California's San Joaquin Valley were so impressed with his work that he was invited to return for eight successive years. However, only the urging of the Wide Awake Improvement Club had induced the skeptical San Diego councilmen to request Hatfield's professional services. The city's population had doubled in four years, and an adequate water supply was necessary for continued growth. While the year's total rainfall had been average, it had been too intermittent to replenish the depleted reservoirs. The new 13 billion–gallon Morena Reservoir had never been more than half full, and on Dec. 10 it held a scant 5 billion gallons of water. For $10,000 Hatfield promised he would fill this reservoir to overflowing before the end of 1916, and agreed that if he failed the city would owe him nothing.

Hatfield immediately set out for the Morena Reservoir, located 60 mi. east of San Diego in the lower elevations of the Laguna Mountains,

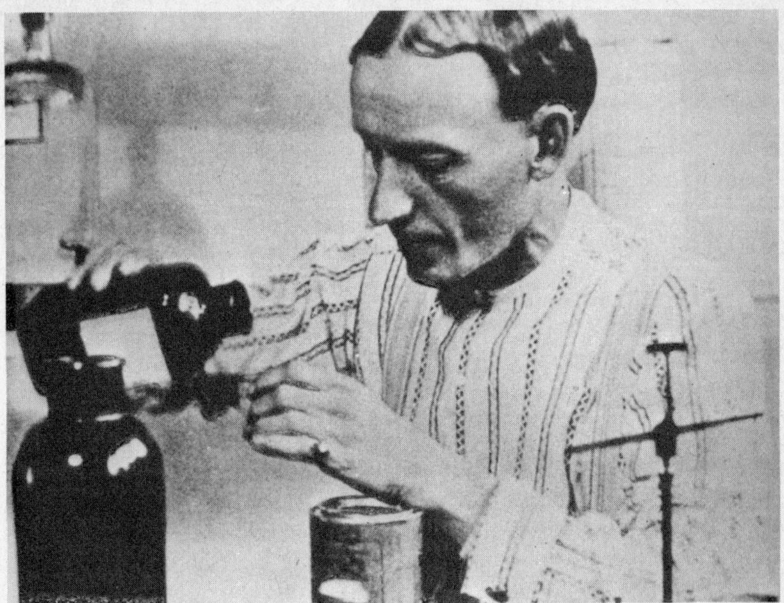

Charles Hatfield, the Rainmaker.

where, with the assistance of his brother Paul, he built a "rain attraction and precipitation plant"—a 24-ft. wooden tower topped with a fenced 12-ft.-square platform to hold the vats from which his secret chemicals were dissipated into the atmosphere. Three dry days passed, but 1.02 in. of rain fell on Dec. 30. Using a formula that was "300% stronger . . . than ever before," the Hatfields worked around the clock. There were only a few showers during the next two weeks, but then a six-day storm that began on Jan. 14 delivered 4.23 in. of rain to San Diego. DOWNPOUR LAYS MANTLE OF WEALTH ON SAN DIEGO and COUNTY RAIN RECORDS SMASHED read the headlines. By the time the rainmaker telephoned city hall on the 17th, 12.73 in. of rain had fallen at Morena. With a "loud, clear, and confident" voice, he explained, "Within the next few days I expect to make it rain right. . . . Just hold your horses until I show you a real rain."

The sky cleared on Jan. 20, but another six-day storm rolled in four days later and brought 2.85 in. of rain to add to "Hatfield's Hatful." Since the ground was still saturated from the previous rains, disaster was inevitable. The San Diego River jumped its banks, and several houses floated out into San Diego Bay. Police in rowboats rescued stranded home owners and motorists, and one man, wiping the water from his eyes as he was hauled on board, suggested, "Let's pay Hatfield $100,000 to stop." Ironically, the rain cut off the city's water supply, forcing people to seek out water holes. A variety of animals, including hundreds of snakes, appeared in the city's streets. The coastal highway to Los Angeles was impassable, boats were swept from their moorings in the bay, telegraph and telephone lines were felled, rail service to the area was discontinued because stretches of track had vanished, and 110 of the county's 112 bridges were washed away. Except for the arrival of an occasional relief steamer loaded with food, the city was completely isolated for a week.

Winds blowing up to 62 mph were clocked on the morning of the 26th, and the north abutment of the Sweetwater Dam collapsed 24 hours later. On the evening of the 27th, the Lower Otay Dam burst "like the crack of doom," releasing 13 billion gallons of water. A 50-ft. wall of water drowned approximately 20 people and scoured the Otay Valley on its 7-mi. journey to the San Diego Bay.

At Morena the Hatfields were oblivious to the destruction the rain had wreaked upon the rest of the county. When a band of farmers gathered at the base of their tower and yelled up at them to stop the rain, the brothers thought they were joking and continued their efforts to fill the reservoir. Charles explained, "I had a year to do the job, but I thought I'd might as well wind it up right away." By the end of January, 44 in. of rain had fallen at Morena, and the water flowing over the top of the dam was 4 ft. deep. Only when the brothers started into San Diego to claim their fee did they realize the magnitude of the storm damages. Since the road was gone, they had to walk, and they posed as the "Benson boys" to avoid being lynched by angry ranchers.

When Hatfield arrived in the city after four days of hiking, the city council refused to pay him. The rainmaker had been so eager to start to work that he had left San Diego before the contract was signed. When he threatened to sue the city for his fee, the council agreed to pay him only if he would assume responsibility for the $3.5 million in damage suits that had been filed against the city for hiring a rainmaker. (The rains were later judged to be "an act of God, not . . . of Hatfield," and the city settled for 5¢ on the dollar.) Hatfield was philosophical about the loss and said, "It was worth the publicity, anyhow."

The rainmaker's reputation spread around the world after his feat in San Diego. In 1922 he was called to Naples by the Italian government to end a drought, and his last contract took him in 1930 to Honduras, where he doused a raging forest fire in 10 days and produced a total of 15 in. of rain in two months.

David Hatfield, Paul's son, claimed the brothers' greatest achievement occurred in 1922, on the California desert in unpopulated Sand Canyon, when they decided to "shoot the works." They hauled in barrels of chemicals, set up a tower, and waited two days for the rain. "It rained for about a day, but in one hour the weather bureau recorded 250 in. of rain," David reported. (The current Guinness record is 73.62 in. in 24 hr.) The canyon was destroyed, the Southern Pacific tracks were washed out for 30 mi., and a man living 20 mi. away was "running for his very life."

After 503 successful rainmaking attempts, Charles retired from the business and settled in Eagle Rock, a suburb of Los Angeles, where he sold sewing machines. Although rain aggravated his varicose veins in his later years, he was ready to return to San Diego to fill the reservoirs once again. In 1956 the 81-year-old Hatfield attended the Hollywood premiere of *The Rainmaker*, a film that had been inspired by his career.

The Hatfields were offered large sums for their rainmaking process on several occasions. After Sand Canyon, Charles and Paul decided their formula was "too devastating a force to unleash to any one individual, or to a group of bureaucrats who might misuse it," David reported. "They looked around and they saw very few people of integrity, men who stood by their words at all costs, and they said, 'Well, the secret will die with us.' And that's what happened."

—L.Sc. and J.W.B.

THE SPIRITUAL THUNDERBOLT

Lying in a hotel room on the French Riviera, Louis Pasteur was dying. Neither the famous French medical researcher nor the dozen doctors who visited and tested him could diagnose what the strange malady was that was destroying his body. Several hundred miles away in London, another doctor, Anna Kingsford, knew exactly why Pasteur was dying. His bodily functions were rapidly degenerating because she had willed his death. Anna Kingsford believed that her will could generate what she called a "spiritual thunderbolt"—a modern rendition of the evil eye—which could strike and kill her victims. If he had known of it, Pasteur would have dismissed Anna Kingsford's curse as preposterous, as his two colleagues, Dr. Paul Bert and Dr. Claude Bernard—both of whom had also been targets of her thunderbolts—would have done had they not died recently from sudden afflictions brought on by Anna's will. For Anna Kingsford, these spiritual assassinations were reasonable and just. She was ridding the world of men who tortured animals, which she knew had souls.

Born in Stratford, England, on Sept. 16, 1846, Anna Bonus was the small, sickly, beautiful daughter of a wealthy London merchant and his domineering wife. Throughout her youth, Anna learned to be the graceful and proper young lady that Victorian society demanded she be, but she also developed in two other ways: as an intellectual and as a spiritualist. She possessed a fine mind, which she used in pursuit of academic, literary, and scientific interests, but more interesting were her occult talents, which came to light and developed as she grew older.

At the age of 21 the tall, slender, golden-haired Anna married her cousin, Algernon Kingsford, who became an Anglican clergyman during the first years of their marriage. Their honeymoon ended almost before it began when Anna was stricken with a severe asthma attack. Thereafter, their marriage was largely one of convenience, though they did have a daughter. Kingsford allowed his wife to follow her own interests, and soon she had purchased a magazine and was serving as its editor. She was already a published writer of theological essays, short stories, and poems.

In 1873 Anna met Edward Maitland, who was to be her platonic

Anna Kingsford.

companion in spiritualism for the remainder of her life. With Maitland she moved to Paris to study medicine. She graduated in 1880 as a medical doctor and returned to London to practice. In Great Britain she was a leader in the Theosophical Society, and with Maitland she established the Hermetic Society. Through these organizations she tried to reconcile her own mystic experiences with her belief in Christ and with Eastern religions and to publicize what she referred to as the restoration of esoteric Christianity.

The bedrock of Anna's personality was her belief in the mystical. As a girl she had exhibited psychic gifts and claimed to have met fairies. She had uncannily accurate premonitions of deaths within her family and had dream encounters with ghosts, genies, and angels, as well as with such historical characters as Mary Magdalene and John the Baptist. Late in life she claimed she had extensive trance contact with the Swedish philosopher Emanuel Swedenborg. Also, she believed in reincarnation and visited herself in past lives spent as Anne Boleyn, Joan of Arc, and Faustina, the wife of Roman emperor Marcus Aurelius. Another of her talents was the ability to leave her body and travel through the universe.

With Maitland, and aided by a personal genie named Salathiel, Anna Kingsford communicated with the spirit realm in séances by means of an automatic writing machine called a planchette. During these séances she sometimes communicated with the spirits of animals. Confirmed in her belief that animals had souls, she was a vegetarian and refused to wear or use anything made from dead animals, including furs and leather shoes and belts.

As a medical student in Paris, Anna was sitting in the library one day when she heard weird screams coming from a nearby laboratory. She learned from an attendant that one of her instructors, Dr. Claude Bernard, was dissecting a live dog in one of his medical experiments. Revolted by this example of what she considered hideous murder, she became an ardent and vocal opponent of vivisection, the surgical use of live animals in medical studies. She wrote pamphlets and articles and debated at the university to stop the practice, but without success since most people believed vivisection was necessary for the advancement of science. Holding her pet guinea pig Rufus, Anna would emotionally debate the problem with Maitland, and she once offered herself for vivisection if the professors would stop experimenting on animals.

In December of 1877, while listening to Dr. Bernard lecture on his latest experiments, in which he had slowly baked animals to death in a specially constructed oven in order to study body heat, Anna jumped up and screamed, "Murderer!" There followed an argument between Anna and Bernard over the morality of his "torturing of defenseless animals." After storming out of the classroom, Anna stopped in the hall and summoned all of her powers. Feeling as though she were a "spiritual thunderbolt," she launched her occult self against Bernard, cursing his existence, and then she collapsed. Soon after that Bernard fell ill. Six weeks later, when Anna arrived at his classroom, she found a note tacked to the door announcing his funeral.

Anna exultantly told Maitland of her part in Bernard's death with these words: "Woe be to the torturers. . . . I will make it dangerous, nay, deadly, to be a vivisector. It is the only argument that will affect them. Meanwhile, thank God the head of the gang is dead." In 1886 her attention turned to Dr. Paul Bert and Dr. Louis Pasteur. She labeled Dr. Bert, a noted medical researcher, "the most notorious of the vivisecting fraternity." Occupants of buildings near Bert's Parisian laboratory frequently complained about his habit of leaving partially dissected animals alive overnight. Their cries of agony made it impossible for these neighbors to sleep. Anna again hurled her thunderbolt, and Bert slowly but surely fell ill and wasted away until he died in November, 1886. Anna noted in her diary: "I have killed Paul Bert, as I killed Claude Bernard; as I will kill Louis Pasteur if I live long enough . . . it is a magnificent power to have, and one that transcends all vulgar methods of dealing out justice to tyrants."

The thunderbolt directed at Pasteur struck a couple of months after Bert's death, in February, 1887. Although the ailment took Pasteur to the brink of death, he swiftly recovered within the month. A year later, on Feb. 22, 1888, Anna Kingsford died in London. A cold she had caught while investigating Pasteur's laboratory, aggravated by her asthma, turned into tuberculosis, which killed her.

—R.J.F.

ALLIGATORS IN THE SEWERS

One of the most persistent urban rumors is that alligators live in the sewers of various major American cities. Alligators and crocodiles have materialized in cotton bins in Texas, express trains in West Germany, hot water ditches in Illinois, and basements in Kansas, and there is good reason why reports of them slithering and slinking through the New York City sewer system should not be dismissed.

Many people believe the alligator stories originated in the 1950s when baby alligators became a popular gift item, only to be flushed down the toilet when they grew too big. However, alligator sightings in New York actually go back to the 1930s. On June 28, 1932, several alligators were seen in the Bronx River, and a dead three-footer washed up on the bank. On Mar. 7, 1935, a 3-ft. 'gator was captured alive in North Yonkers. A barge captain at Pier 9 on the East River brought in a 4-ft.-long alligator on June 1, 1937. Five days later a commuter bagged a two-footer at the Brooklyn Museum subway station.

Perhaps the most exciting alligator story from the 1930s is the one that appeared in *The New York Times* on Feb. 10, 1935:

ALLIGATOR FOUND IN UPTOWN SEWER
Youths Shoveling Snow Into Manhole
See The Animal Churning In Icy Water.
SNARE IT AND DRAG IT OUT
Reptile Slain By Rescuers When It Gets Vicious—
Whence It Came Is Mystery.

According to the *Times*, the alligator was discovered by three teen-aged boys shoveling snow on East 123rd Street, near the Harlem River. It was sundown, and they had almost finished dumping the accumulated snow down a manhole into the sewer below.

Salvatore Condulucci, 16, noticed that the sewer was clogging up with slush and bent down to take a look. In the fading light he could barely see the icy mass. But it was moving, and a dark shape seemed to be trying to break through. Salvatore could hardly believe it. He sprang to his feet, yelling something about an alligator. Jimmy Mireno, 19, looked skeptical. He moved closer, peered down the dark hole, and had to admit that he, too, saw an alligator. Frank Lonzo, 18, was next. Soon there was a crowd of curious onlookers around the manhole, straining to get a glimpse of the strange reptile thrashing around in the slush.

The boys thought of pulling the creature out and sent someone down the street to the Lehigh Stove and Repair Shop for some rope. Then Salvatore Condulucci (who had learned such things watching western movies) devised a noose of clothesline and managed to rope the 'gator around the neck. Pulling hard, he heard the grating of skin and claws against the broken ice, but he couldn't get the animal out. Several people offered to help. They finally hoisted the alligator out of the sewer and up onto the street. It looked dazed, probably as much from the cold as from the clothesline ordeal.

One of the boys moved closer to loosen the line, and the alligator feebly opened its long, tooth-lined jaws. Clearly this was an alligator in a bad mood. The boys jumped out of the way, and the crowd seized snow shovels and started to bludgeon the animal. The alligator lashed its tail weakly a few times, but already half frozen, it died without much of a fight.

Though their conquest was tinged with regret at killing such an impressive creature, the boys took the alligator's carcass to the Lehigh Stove and Repair Shop. It weighed 125 lb. and measured nearly 8 ft. The store had never before been the center of so much activity.

Eventually someone called the police. When they arrived, there was nothing much for them to do except calm the excited neighborhood people who were milling about the store.

No one could figure out where the alligator had come from. There were no pet shops nearby, and no other source of alligators seemed reasonable. Perhaps a steamship from Florida, passing the 123rd Street sewer conduit in the Harlem River, had been harboring an alligator. Maybe the alligator fell overboard and swam toward land to get out of the cold water. Entering the sewer outlet, it may have swum through the system until it reached the slushy snow under the open manhole.

Half-dead from cold, the alligator was rescued only to be killed by those in awe of its last fearsome display of teeth. By 9:00 P.M. the Dept. of Sanitation had picked up the carcass and taken it to an incinerator.

Teddy May, the superintendent of the New York City sewers during the 1930s, then began getting reports from sanitation inspectors who claimed to have seen more alligators, but he did not believe them. He even refused to approve reports which had inspectors' notations about alligators. May went as far as hiring men to spy on the inspectors and tell him how they were managing to get drunk down in the sewers. The word came back that his men weren't drinking, and the reports of narrow escapes from alligators persisted. Determined to lay the claims to rest, Teddy May decided to go down and have a look for himself.

A few hours later, he returned to his office shaken. His own flashlight, according to Robert Daley in *The World Beneath the City,* had illuminated the truth behind the rumors—alligators 2 ft. and longer. To avoid the dangerously fast currents in the main sewer lines under the major avenues, the alligators had gravitated to smaller pipes in quiet areas of the city. May now was faced with the job of removing them. Within a few months he had accomplished that task by using rat poison on them and by forcing them into the main trunk lines, where they either drowned or washed out to sea. Or so he thought. For in 1938 five alligators were caught in New Rochelle, N.Y., and sightings of others in New York City sewers were recorded in 1948 and again in 1966.

Alligators in sewers are neither rumors nor myths, but real dangers in the world underneath some of the large cities in the U.S. In addition to the New York sightings, recent accounts indicate that alligators are to be found in the sewers of Atlanta, Ga. and St. Paul, Minn. How widespread this phenomenon is remains to be seen.

—L.C.

19

SURVIVORS

BUSTING LOOSE—INCREDIBLE ESCAPES

Jack Sheppard

As criminals go, Sheppard was strictly run-of-the-mill. In his brief life—ended by the hangman's noose in London's Tyburn Prison at age 22—he failed to achieve lasting notoriety. His real talent, which made his name known in high-society drawing rooms in 1723–1724, was his ability to escape from all but one of the prisons in which he was incarcerated. He was written up in pamphlets and books, gossiped over in pubs and on the seamy London streets, sung about in doggerels and ditties, and even excoriated by zealous vicars as an unrepentant backslider. The Drury Lane Theater catapulted him to even greater fame through a short pantomime called *Harlequin Sheppard* and a three-act comedy that described his vocation more accurately: *The Prison-Breaker*. Newgate Prison made its own contribution by allowing Sir James Thornhill, the famous painter responsible for the dome work of St. Paul's Cathedral, to do a portrait of the skinny, callow escape artist.

Sheppard began his chosen career humbly, as a nimble pickpocket working London's foggy streets. Apprenticed to a carpenter for four years, Sheppard quickly saw an easier way to make a living. Once inside a house he was to remodel or repair, he mentally inventoried the owner's valuables as he worked, eyeballing the easiest way to gain access when he surreptitiously returned. The stolen articles were passed along to two female fences, "Edgeworth" Bess and Poll Maggott. The arrangement nearly caused Sheppard's undoing when Poll urged him to rob a merchant named Bains. Sheppard broke into Bains's shop at midnight and selected a quantity of dry goods, after he had emptied the till. Unable to carry all of his booty away, he hid a piece of fustian—a velveteenlike fabric—in his toolbox, intending to retrieve it the next morning. Unfortunately, Bains was suspicious, checked the box, and found the damaging evidence. But before the merchant could press charges, Sheppard had restolen the fustian, thus saving his neck.

The cocky youth next took in his brother Tom as an accomplice, but the partnership was brief. Caught with stolen goods on him, Tom—hoping for leniency from the crown—squealed on not only Jack but Bess as well, an act that started Jack on his path to fame. Remanded to

St. Giles's Roundhouse, Jack soon eeled his way out of a hole in the jailhouse roof. His liberty lasted only a few days. Picked up for a momentary lapse into pickpocketing, Sheppard was hustled to Newgate Prison, along with Bess. Allowed to share a common bed as husband and wife, the two thieves passed their time by using tools slipped in by friendly visitors to file off their leg chains. Once mobile, Jack went to work on the bars in the window and soon took Bess along with him to freedom, escaping from what had been thought to be the "safest" cell in the prison.

Sheppard joined forces with a new associate in crime, a notorious housebreaker known as Blueskin because of his swarthy complexion. They operated out of a stable in London's Westminster section for months, storing their stolen merchandise with William Field. Field was to sell it for them but, greedy for a larger share of the profit, went them one better. He not only restole the goods from Sheppard and Blueskin but also passed on incriminating evidence against them to Jonathan Wild, an infamous highwayman with whom Sheppard had recently quarreled. Wild promptly ingratiated himself with the crown by informing on his two enemies. They were both convicted of capital offenses for their robberies and sentenced to death. The unfortunate Blueskin, unable to break out, died on the gallows.

But Sheppard had other plans. Lodged in Newgate's condemned hold, an underground death-row chamber that sported only a hatch for access, Sheppard managed to file through a hatch bar so that it could be broken off by hand at the right moment. His chance came on Aug. 30, 1724. Huddling with two female friends who ostensibly had come for a final visit before he was to hang, the puny lad snapped off the weakened iron spike, wriggled his scrawny body through the narrow hatchway, and disappeared from custody, hidden by the ladies' petticoats as they left. His freedom lasted one week. He was picked up by Newgate guards acting on a tip and rejailed in the prison.

This time the keepers added auxiliary confinements. Sheppard was moved to a Newgate high-security room called "the Castle." Handcuffed, he was further immobilized by cumbersome leg irons anchored to the floor. To obviate any help from the thousands of people who—attracted by Sheppard's notoriety—now flocked to see him, no one was allowed within arm's reach. The precautions were but a small inconvenience to the escape artist. He picked the handcuffs and the prison's strongest padlocks, and as darkness fell on his last night there he shinnied up the chimney. Stopped by an iron bar embedded across the flue, he painstakingly chipped out the mortar around it, went through the prison chapel, wrenched the hinges off one barred door, unlocked another, and scrambled onto the prison roof. Once outside, finding the distance to the ground too far to jump, he coolly returned to "the Castle" to get his sleeping blanket for use as a rope. The escape was further impeded by the heavy leg irons, which he had been unable to remove, but he hobbled off through the steady rain that was now falling and hid in a barn in the fields. Within a few days, by fabricating a story that he had been jailed for fathering a bastard child, Sheppard had conned a shoemaker into striking off the chains. Freed, he hurried to a tavern to listen, unrecognized, as the drinkers toasted his escape in song.

By November, 1724, Sheppard's notoriety had become almost legendary. Caught again, he now became a celebrity. Commoners and noblemen alike came to hear the prison recitals in which he boasted of his numerous crimes. On Nov. 10 he was again sentenced to death, and six days later he was hanged publicly before a large crowd.

Until the moment the rope ended his short life by a slow strangulation, Sheppard's final thoughts had been of escape. Managing to hide a small knife in his pocket, he fully intended to cut his bonds on the way to the scaffold and make a quick leap into the friendly crowd. He didn't get the chance, but curiously he had yet another scheme. Told that bleeding a corpse after putting it into a warm bed could restore it to life, Sheppard entreated his cronies to give the idea a try. Instead, they carried his remains to a pub for an all-out wake before they put the legend of Jack Sheppard to its final rest in the burial ground of St. Martin's-in-the-Fields.

Rufin Pietrowski

Like thousands of other Poles, Pietrowski fled into a self-imposed Parisian exile after the Polish defeat by the Russians at Ostroleka in 1831. Twelve years later the homesick Pole, armed with a forged passport identifying him as Joseph Catharo, a native of Malta, slipped secretly across the Ukrainian frontier. He was going back to his beloved Kamenets-Podolski, a small river town some 220 mi. southwest of Kiev. Well versed in French and Italian, with a fair command of English and German, Pietrowski taught languages in the Podolian capital for nine months. Unfortunately, his habit of confiding to intimate friends that he was Polish, not Maltese, led to his downfall. Arrested and tried as a war criminal, Pietrowski was sentenced to death. The order was commuted to life imprisonment in a Siberian labor camp, and he was assigned to Ekaterinski-Zavod, a government distillery 180 mi. north of Omsk.

Beginning his sentence on July 29, 1844, Pietrowski elected to become a model prisoner. A year later his captors rewarded the obedient Pole by removing his leg chains and giving him an easier job in the factory countinghouse. This inside position brought Pietrowski into daily contact with visitors who came from all over Siberia to purchase liquor and grain. Stealthfully, he queried them in detail, acquiring a firsthand knowledge of possible escape routes. Well aware that recapture would mean instant death, or at best a lingering torture, Pietrowski made his final preparations. He forged two passports, the usual one needed by peasants to go from village to village, the other a rarer document, which bore the czar's official seal and permitted the bearer to make long journeys. He let his beard grow and fabricated a sheepskin wig to protect his head against the piercing, 60-below Siberian winter.

At the end of December, 1845, Pietrowski got his chance. Finally allowed to live outside the camp barracks—a privilege granted only to the most trustworthy prisoners—he moved in with two fellow Poles who had built a small wooden hut for themselves. On the night of Feb. 8, 1846, Pietrowski put on three woolen shirts and a pair of heavy cloth trousers, wrapped a long fur cloak about his shoulders, and disappeared into a howling blizzard. He also carried a bag containing a spare pair of boots, another shirt, and blue trousers—the standard costume for a Siberian summer. For provisions he had a few crusts of bread and some dried fish, saved from his meager rations.

Struggling through hip-deep snow, the weary Pole did not stop until he reached the nearby village of Soldatskaya, where he paused briefly to warm himself at an inn. The rest was costly. A pickpocket stole nearly all his money and both passports, a loss that meant immediate arrest if he were asked for identification. Nevertheless, he pushed on for Irbit, a regional capital famous for centuries because of its annual trade fair. Joining hundreds of other strangers heading for the festivities, Pietrowski continued on past the town and into the forested, snow-covered foothills. As a general rule, he circled the few villages he saw, keeping to the dense woods and scooping out holes in the snow for sleeping at night.

By March he had crossed the Urals and had come back down into the western foothills at Solikamsk. Two months later he walked into Veliki-Ustyug, a tiny river town clogged with pilgrims waiting for the ice to break so that they could travel downstream to the holy convent of Solovetsk. Pietrowski joined them, assuming the role of a "worshiper of God" and hoping the new disguise would give him protective coloration. The ruse succeeded. When the spring thaw on the Dvina made river travel possible, Pietrowski joined with the other pilgrims, singing religious chants, carrying lighted tapers, and praying with local priests. His lack of money was no problem. According to custom each pilgrim was given free passsage and arrived in Solovetsk with a bonus of 15 rubles paid for pulling an oar.

Arkhangelsk, however, brought a new danger. The harbor port was swarming with soldiers, all busily checking passports at the docks. Dismayed, Pietrowski plunged again into the desolate wastelands, skirting the marshes to the south, and reached the village of Vytegra. Here he found a ship captain willing to carry him to St. Petersburg, the summer capital of Czar Nicholas I. Once more he risked capture, but he reasoned that he would be less noticeable in city crowds. Loitering around the docks on the Neva, he surreptitiously read the red and yellow notices that advertised steamer departures. (As a "peasant," he was expected to be illiterate.) Eventually, a willing captain transported him to Riga, where he transformed himself into a buyer of hog bristles. This disguise let him openly ask directions to the Prussian frontier, which he crossed in broad daylight.

Elated, he now became a "French cotton spinner returning to France." On July 27 the bogus Frenchman arrived in Königsberg and immediately celebrated by getting drunk. He was found sleeping in an abandoned house and taken into custody. Unable to convince the police that he was French, Pietrowski confessed his true identity and asked for asylum. The request placed the authorities in a dilemma since a new extradition treaty, just signed, required them to return him to Russia. Unable to ignore the fact that he had also become a national cause célèbre once the story of his unparalleled escape had become known, the Berlin ministers issued a unique order to the Königsberg police: Send him back—in one week. They took the hint and, releasing him from custody, suggested to Pietrowski that he use the time to good advantage. The Pole fled for Danzig (Gdańsk) in the morning, and on Sept. 22, 1846, he returned to Paris, completing a 1,500-mi. odyssey that had taken eight months. The exploit made him the first man to escape from a 19th-century Siberian exile.

Winston Churchill

In 1806 the British expanded their colonial empire by acquiring the Cape Province territory of South Africa. To escape from British rule, many Boer farmers migrated northeast during the Great Trek of 1835–1838, founding the republics of the Orange Free State, Natal, and the Transvaal. British settlers continued to pour in, taking over not only commerce but the gold mines as well. The Boer government retaliated by refusing citizenship to the unwanted *Uitlanders* and taxing them so heavily that Britain sent troops to protect the rights of its nationals. When Great Britain refused to withdraw the soldiers, both Transvaal and the Orange Free State declared war on Britain on Oct. 12, 1899.

Churchill, then a 24-year-old journalist for the London *Morning Post*, was assigned as war correspondent and immediately dispatched to South Africa. Landing at Durban, the young reporter joined infantry companies based at the tiny mining community of Estcourt, 70 mi. away. They were engaged in making reconnaissance forays toward Boer-occupied territory aboard an armored train nicknamed Wilson's Death Trap. Shortly after Churchill's arrival, the train was ambushed and he was taken prisoner.

Prior to his capture Churchill had actively taken part in the futile efforts by the British troops to break free of the barricades the Boers had placed on the rails. Consequently, the Boers flatly ignored his vigorous protests that he was just a civilian noncombatant. Sent to a holding compound for prisoners of war at the State Model Schools in Pretoria, Churchill continued to claim he was being unjustly held, but to no avail. Three weeks later, on Dec. 11, the still indignant Churchill drafted a unique letter addressed to the Transvaal government. In it he tersely promised them he would be leaving "hastily and unceremoniously," and at the same time he expressed his deepest appreciation for the kindness his captors had shown him during his brief imprisonment. On the following night, true to his promise, he escaped.

During his captivity Churchill had carefully studied the Boer security precautions for the enclosure. On two sides of the school grounds a 10-ft.-high corrugated iron fence had been erected, and the other two sides were protected by a solid wall topped with ornamental ironwork. Inside this perimeter, Boer sentries were posted 50 yd. apart. Powerful

£25.–.–

(vijf en twintig pond stg.)
belooning uitgeloofd voor
de Sub-Commissie van Wijk V
voor den Specialen Constabel
dezer wijk, die den ontvluchte
Krijgsgevangene
Churchill
levend of dood te dezen kantore
aflevert.

Namens de Sub-Comm.
Wijk V
Lodk. de Haas
Sec.

Translation.

£25

(Twenty-five Pounds stg.) REWARD is offered by the Sub-Commission of the fifth division, on behalf of the Special Constable of the said division, to anyone who brings the escaped prisioner of war

CHURCHILL,

dead or alive to this office.

For the Sub-Commission of the fifth division.
(Signed) LODK. de HAAS, Sec.

NOTE.–The Original Reward for the arrest of Winston Churchill on his escape from Pretoria, posted on the Government House at Pretoria, brought to England by the Hon. Henry Masham, and is now the property of W. R. Burton.

Winston Churchill—Dead or Alive.

floodlights illuminated every building and the entire area inside the perimeter—except at one point, spotted by the sharp-eyed Churchill. Near one wall, a short section lay in partial shadow cast by a circular lavatory. Choosing the precise moment when both sentries simultaneously turned their backs on him, Churchill scaled the wall, scrambling down into the garden of the villa next door. With a confident nonchalance, he walked out through the garden gate, passing within 15 ft. of the nearest camp sentry, and entered the suburbs of Pretoria. Shortly after his escape a £25 reward was posted for his recapture—dead or alive.

Ahead, Churchill faced 300 mi. of hostile Boer country before he would reach neutral ground at Delagoa Bay in Portuguese East Africa. It was a journey he planned to complete without map or compass, at night, and unable to speak a word of either Dutch or the native dialect (Xhosa). A half mile south of the camp, Churchill came to a railroad track. Blindly, he elected to turn left. Evading the Boer pickets who had been placed at the bridge trestles, he stumbled along for two hours until he reached a station. He hid near its platform for another hour, then jumped aboard a train that stopped momentarily to unload goods. Once inside, he went to sleep on a pile of coal sacks. At the first light, aware that he would be retaken if he waited until the train reached its destination and was unloaded, he leaped off and struck out to the east, in the direction of the sunrise.

Sleeping by day, Churchill went on at night through the swamps, the high grasses, and across the shallow streams paralleling the rail line. With dogged determination he plodded along until he finally saw lights, which turned out to be the furnace fires from the Transvaal Collieries, a coal mine. He knocked boldly on the door of a house at the minehead. Churchill was reluctantly allowed in by the occupant, who was somewhat startled by his unannounced caller. At first claiming he had fallen from the train, Churchill finally confessed that he was an escaped prisoner and asked for help. He was amazed to learn that he had chosen the only British-occupied house for 20 mi. around. The mine's manager, John Howard, agreed to hide Churchill, although it meant he would be shot for treason if he were caught. Quickly, he hustled Churchill down the main shaft of the mine and left him there for two days, providing him from time to time with food and water.

Further arrangements were made with a Dutchman named Charles A. Burnham—sympathetic to the British—to transport Churchill to Delagoa Bay, hidden amidst the bales of wool being loaded on a freight car. The train eventually chugged into Komatipoort, the Boer frontier station, then on to Lourenço Marques, in Portuguese territory. After three days Churchill left his hiding place on the train and followed Burnham (who was waiting for him) to the British consulate.

There he overcame his final obstacle—the consulate secretary. Advised by the irritated civil servant to come back later, at a more appropriate hour, Churchill lost his temper and demanded to see the consul. One mention of his name was enough to gain an immediate audience. By the time Churchill returned to Durban he had become a popular hero. The escape brought him instant recognition, embarking him upon the illustrious political career that eventually led to his fame as one of the 20th century's greatest statesmen-politicians.

Donald Woods

A fifth-generation South African, Donald Woods became editor of the *East London Daily Dispatch* at age 31 and held the position for 12 years. (The South African city of East London is about 150 mi. northeast of Port Elizabeth.) Initially his views were those of a white liberal. He strongly opposed, in his widely read editorials, the Black Consciousness Movement founded by Stephen Biko, urging his black readers not to support an activist group that appeared to advocate racism in reverse. Equally, he tried to convince blacks that not all whites were racist. Biko, aware that the *Dispatch* articles were stunting BCM growth, arranged a private meeting with the journalist to explain his nationalist philosophy. Biko's arguments were so persuasive that the newspaperman soon joined him in confronting the government's segregationalist policy of apartheid. This radical stance angered Prime Minister Vorster, and Woods was totally ostracized by his fellow whites as a direct result of his new alliance.

With Biko's death under suspicious circumstances on Sept. 12, 1977, while in the Pretoria jail, Woods began a highly visible campaign throughout the Union of South Africa, making speeches that demanded a full inquest and criticizing the Union's police-state tactics. Allegedly Biko had been savagely beaten by the police in Port Elizabeth, then transported—naked, unconscious, and shackled—600 mi. by Land Rover to the Pretoria jail, where he had died just after arrival. Woods's angry denunciations were silenced one month later. He was "banned" by government decree for five years, an order that effectively ended his journalistic career in South Africa. Under the terms of the ban, Woods was not allowed to write, publish, or be quoted. He could not attend social functions and he was prohibited from talking to, or even being in the presence of, more than one person at a time. The order magnanimously made an exception for his wife, Wendy, and their five children, considering them to be all "one person." Woods's home and car were bugged openly and placed under 24-hour surveillance. To complete the humiliation, the East London security-police chief, Colonel van der Merwe, curtly informed him that he could expect unannounced break-ins at any time of the day or night, should someone believe the conditions of the ban were being violated.

Ten days after the decree took effect, Woods secretly began writing a biography of Stephen Biko and the cause he had died for. Titled *The Indictment*, the 175,000-word manuscript, finished in two months, was smuggled out of South Africa in sections by friends who risked their own freedom to do so. Because the completed book expressed opinions that made Woods liable to charges of treason under the Terrorism Act and therefore subject to the death penalty, he realized that he and his entire family would have to leave South Africa before its publication in England.

The attempt to escape from the Pretoria regime's jurisdiction was originally planned for May 1978, but two unforeseen events caused Woods to move up the date. First, a national election overwhelmingly reaffirmed approval by white voters of the apartheid policy, dashing his hopes that the Vorster administration might ease its inflexible position. Second, his five-year-old daughter, Mary, became the innocent victim of the continual harassment that had plagued the family. The child had been given a T-shirt with a likeness of the dead Biko on it. As she pulled the garment over her head, she screamed in agony, instantly burned by a chemical that had been sprayed inside the shirt. Later analysis showed that the corrosive agent was Ninhydrin, an acid-based powder used by the police to bring out fingerprint traces. To prevent further attacks on his family, Woods decided to escape from South Africa on Dec. 31, 1977, five months earlier than originally planned. He resolved to flee northward by car to reach the independent kingdom of Lesotho, a land totally surrounded by the Union of South Africa but with charter flights to Botswana, Zambia, and other African countries.

During November and December, Woods and his wife made their final preparations. He acquired a fake passport, one good enough to pass a quick scrutiny by upcountry officials. He bought black hair dye, a false mustache, and some white cloth to make a Catholic priest's Roman collar. By chance, in laying out the escape route, Woods had picked a border crossing that was just a few miles away from an obscure Catholic mission. He reasoned that—disguised as a priest—he could claim to be headed for St. Theresa's Mission, which was nearby, if stopped for questioning. Wendy quietly made multiple visits to their East London bank, withdrawing small sums each time until she had amassed a miserly 800 rands (approximately $800 in U.S. money). To have taken more of their life savings might have aroused suspicion. Simultaneously, Wendy and the children rehearsed their own roles. They were to go in the family car to visit Wendy's parents at Umtata and wait there for a phone call from Woods at precisely 10:00 A.M. If he verified that he was safe in Lesotho, they were to dash for the border and, posing as tourists, cross over for their reunion at Maseru, the capital.

At 6:00 P.M. on Dec. 31, the plan was put into action. Huddled under a blanket on the floor of the Mercedes, Woods lay inert as his wife carefully drove past the bored security guard at the street corner and headed for the city limits. Woods got out, kissed her good-bye, and hiked quickly down the dark road to the prearranged rendezvous spot where his friend, Drew Court, was waiting with two cars that had been hidden earlier. For the 185-mi. ride across the veldt, Court had provided two-way radios for both vehicles. Driving the lead car, he could thus warn Woods of the roadblocks that police often set up at night to intercept marijuana smugglers. Trouble, however, came from an unexpected direction. As they drove through low-lying areas, the special-frequency radios sputtered, then died entirely, reviving only after the road climbed into higher altitudes. Near Cathcart, Woods's battery gave out, a nerve-racking setback until he found that Court had brought along a spare. At Queenstown, a police van edged in between their cars for long, anxious minutes, but finally sped past. In Jamestown at midnight, a second patrol car pulled alongside Woods at a traffic light, but he ignored it. Just before dawn the two men reached the Telle River where it served as the boundary between South Africa and Lesotho. Abandoning the cars, they plunged into the scrub bush for the long walk to the normally narrow and shallow stream. To their dismay, they found that heavy rains had eroded the sandy soil of the riverbed into a series of parallel gulches 10 ft. deep. As they helped each other across the mini-ravines, Woods grimly kept reminding himself of the truism voiced by the African National Congress leader Nelson Mandela, "There is no easy walk to freedom." On three occasions a powerful searchlight of unknown origin swept toward them, giving them the impression that they had been seen. But their luck held. On the Lesotho side, a brisk 5-mi. walk took them to where a third friend, Robin Walker, waited with another car. He jubilantly carried them to the offices of the British High Commission, where they asked for political asylum. The next morning the Woodses were united once again—and free.

Donald Woods has since settled in Great Britain where he and his wife have established the Information Service on South Africa to counter the propaganda efforts of the South African government.

—W.K.

REAL-LIFE ROBINSON CRUSOES

The Castaway: Pedro Serrano
Year Marooned: 1528

After many months of bare subsistence on a sandy island off the coast of Peru, Pedro Serrano—a Spanish sailor shipwrecked in the Caribbean in 1528—awoke one morning to find himself plagued by devils. Clearly, there could be no other explanation for the sudden appearance of the two strange creatures who trailed him about the island. The demons of hell had finally arrived, reasoned Serrano, adding one final misery to an already desolate and interminable plight. Serrano fled, after warning his lone island companion—a young boy, also shipwrecked—and crying out for mercy to the good Lord.

The apparitions were not demons; they were sailors recently washed ashore at a nearby shoal. After one look at Serrano, they, too, feared that the devil was occupying this barren cay. After months of thirst, hunger, exposure to the elements, and isolated despair, Pedro Serrano truly looked the part of a demon. His hair and beard were unnaturally long, baked dry like thistles, stiffened and filthy from numerous showers of salt and spray. But upon hearing Serrano's religious plea, the strangers immediately declared their own allegiance to the Christian God. As proof, one of them recited the Apostles' Creed. Serrano rejoiced. He had two additional companions to help him endure the island hardships and to share what small hope of rescue remained.

Unlike Serrano, the newcomers had been the sole survivors aboard their vessel. Serrano's fate, and that of his companions, had been painfully prolonged. Following the shipwreck, Serrano and some of his crew members made their way to shore and existed for nearly two months on cockles, turtles, and seal blood. Unwilling to continue in this manner, half of the survivors fashioned a raft from their ship's wreckage and pushed out to sea with little hope of survival. Serrano stayed behind with a boy and two other men. Within a few days, one of the men began raving. Soon he began eating his own arms, and then he quickly died. A short time later the intense heat from the sun and the harsh living conditions on the island took the life of the other man. Serrano and the boy, fearing that they too would die, hastily worked to insure their mutual survival. They fashioned water basins out of turtle shells and made sealskin-lined storage pits for food and liquids. In addition, they hunted sea cows and birds and burrowed for roots that tasted somewhat like fresh greens. Serrano built a small raft and returned to the scene of the shipwreck, where he dived in search of flint. Successful, he returned to the island. He and the boy could now make fires quickly to alert any passing ships of their presence. However, while many ships sailed near, none were able, or willing, to risk the dangerous coral that barricaded the island.

After the arrival of the two sailors, new plans for an escape effort commenced. Diving at the site of the sailors' recent wreck, Serrano and his companions salvaged some iron parts to use as nails and tools. They constructed a crude forge and fashioned a bellows from dried and tightened sealskin. In time they had a small vessel in which two people could cross the sea. It was decided that Serrano and the boy would travel to Jamaica, where they would organize a rescue party for the others.

However, on a test run Serrano realized that the boy would never stand the punishment of the sea. Serrano therefore abandoned his own hopes of a timely deliverance. The boy and one of the other men, however, finally insisted on risking the journey—in foul weather—and were never heard from again.

A full three years later—and eight years after Serrano had first come to the island—a ship finally appeared in the distance, apparently roused by smoke signals. As the rescue boat approached, its crew members saw two men, rather, two great, hairy, sun-baked bodies, who flailed their arms about like monsters and cried out in a most desperate fashion. The rescue boat turned back. Once again, Serrano and his companion yelled out in the name of Jesus, asserting their own true brotherhood with any Christians at sea. Realizing then that these men were not devils, the seamen returned and rescued the two unfortunates.

Upon arriving in Havana, Serrano's companion promptly died. Serrano was taken to Spain. He later toured the courts of Europe, where his sealskin garments, knee-length hair and beard, and adventurous tales made him a celebrity. Supported in grand fashion for many years by curious and wealthy patrons, Serrano died a very rich man in 1564. As a final tribute, his name became immortal when a group of shoals in the Caribbean Sea, some 200 mi. off the coast of Nicaragua, was named the Serrana Bank.

The Castaway: Philip Quarll
Year Marooned: 1675

The sea stood remarkably calm. Seizing this opportunity, though acting against his better judgment, Edward Dorrington—an 18th-century trader from Bristol, England—ordered a small rowboat to be lowered from his anchored ship. He and a small crew pointed the boat toward the shining gem of a Pacific island that beckoned him. Dorrington had a special feeling about this island; he was willing to risk the dangers imposed by its craggy, irregular shoreline and its hazardous ledges in order to prove his instincts correct.

Once ashore, Dorrington was quickly vindicated. On the lush, beautiful island—supposedly uninhabited—was a single, hand-fashioned thatched abode situated near a deep forest. Soon the island's sole resident appeared. He was an old man, an old Englishman to be precise, and his flowing white beard and trailing locks covered his shoulders and naked belly. At his side stood a most companionable monkey, who looked on as the old man prepared dinner for welcome guests—soup, meat, and fish—all set out on a tablecloth made of a ship's sail and served up in plates of gleaming seashell. Later, Dorrington remarked that the meal surpassed anything he had ever eaten in his native England. It was a masterpiece of simplicity, created by a man keenly in touch with his environment.

The island's inhabitant was Philip Quarll, a former sailor, trader, husband, vagabond. Shipwrecked in 1675, Quarll presided for 50 years as solitary monarch over this tiny island of monkeys and pomegranate fields far off the coast of Mexico. However, lonely as Quarll's life could be, he made it clear to his guests that he had long since ceased to think of himself as a victim. Now, presumably rescued, Quarll carefully explained that he had no intention of abandoning his island cell. In the slow course of a half-century, the shipwrecked stranger had become a self-sufficient hermit.

This evolution from desolate isolation to regal solitude was not easily understood by Dorrington and crew. Quarll explained: "I was shipwrecked, thanks to my Maker, and was cast away. Were I made emperor of the universe, I would not be concerned with the world again, nor would you require me, did you but know the happiness I enjoy out of it." As proof of his sincerity (and sound mind), Quarll handed Dorrington his "memorial"—a tidy bundle of rolled parchment diaries. This was Quarll's paean to self-reliance and faith in the Lord, a message to the world of men and events from a former participant now happily residing in a remote and marginal corner of existence.

Dorrington returned to England on Jan. 3, 1725, and there devoted himself to a careful study of Quarll's lengthy diaries. They began with the story of a poor boy born into the parish of St. Giles, falsely imprisoned for robbery, and turned by necessity to the sailor's profession. The diaries chronicled the disappointments of Quarll's early life. Often, after "having lost the rudder of their reason," Quarll and his drunken shipmates found themselves in the company of women, and Quarll was soon a married man. Then followed the sickness and early death of his young bride, his equally impetuous second marriage, and the couple's ill-fated voyage around Cape Horn, which resulted in a disastrous shipwreck that left Quarll the sole survivor and resident of a deserted isle.

Quarll soon recognized that he had entered an island paradise. "Heaven be praised!" he reasoned, "Here is my dream: right where Providence rescued my life from the grim jaws of death, there it has provided me wherewithal to support it." Indeed, Quarll's new home came amply stocked with mussels, oysters, exotic birds, and codfish nearly 6 ft. in length. For a home, he lashed together branches, twigs, and plants "in the manner sheep-pens are made." For furniture he wove grass mats and turned shellfish and tortoise shells into various kitchen utensils. His writing implements arrived by courtesy of the sea; all of his needs washed ashore one day, bound tight and dry inside a storage chest that belonged to yet another unlucky traveler.

The absence of companionship was the one problem Quarll had to overcome. Although he did have "visitors" from time to time, they were not of an abiding or hospitable temperament. Like rascals in paradise, these visitors—the monkeys of the island—often plundered Quarll's modest collection of hand-hewn tools and foodstocks. However, one red monkey, who was very good-natured, became Quarll's friend and constant companion. Named Beaufidelle, the monkey died after a brutal beating administered by other monkeys in a pomegranate field, and Quarll felt a great sense of loss—strangely equal to human losses he had experienced. Perhaps this experience helps to explain Quarll's reluctance to accept Dorrington's offer of assistance and return passage to England. After 50 years, Quarll's idea of "home" had changed too radically for him to be able to adjust once again to the patterns of his past.

Quarll's island has never been located by modern mapmakers or sailors.

The Castaway: Bruce Gordon
Year Marooned: 1757

Captained by a drunkard, the whaler *Anne Forbes* left Scotland in 1757 and several months later became trapped in ice somewhere in the polar seas north of Greenland. Seaman Bruce Gordon was ordered to the masthead seconds before two ice fields crushed the wooden ship between them. Thirty minutes later the ship sank and all hands on board were killed—except for Gordon, who was thrown onto one of the ice fields as the *Forbes* rolled on its side.

His prospects for remaining the sole survivor were grim. Floating on an ice field in an uncharted ocean without food, shelter, or adequate clothing, Gordon's only comfort was the Old Testament—given to him by his mother—which was tucked in his pocket. Then came a lucky break. The day after the disaster, the *Forbes* resurfaced some distance away and became imbedded, upside down, in the ice.

Gordon realized that his life depended on reaching the wreck. He climbed ice mountains and sank neck-deep into slush pools before finally arriving at the ship. However, he couldn't go inside because the keel was uppermost, and it provided no entrance. As thirsty and hungry as he was exhausted, Gordon searched the area and eventually discovered an ice mountain made of fresh water. With his thirst quenched but his hunger renewed, he foraged through the debris looking for tools. Using a small boat hook and a harpoon, he managed to dig through the ice and reach a cabin window. Upon entering, he made a beeline for the bread locker, ate his fill of biscuits, washed them down with rum and brandy, and fell into a deep, long sleep.

During the ensuing weeks Gordon drank liquor daily in order to keep warm. Unaccustomed to alcohol, he slept a lot, sometimes 24 hours at a time, while lying on a pile of frozen blankets inside the captain's closet. For water he drank frost, which was sometimes 2 in. thick.

Gordon found various utensils, such as knives and forks, in the cabin, but he knew that without a fire for warmth and additional food, he probably would not survive the winter. He had to reach the ship's stores, but with everything upside down and frozen that proved to be a Herculean task. After many days, he forced his way to the hold, only to be frustrated because the weight of the cargo rested against it and prevented him from entering. Further effort brought him to the coal bin, however, and he started a fire with the coal and flint—after jerry-rigging a smoke flue through the keel. During these journeys through the ship, he also located clothes, tools, and other useful supplies.

The long, dark Arctic night set in, and Gordon remained quietly ensconced in the cabin. One night, in the middle of a blizzard, a polar bear broke in. Gordon killed it with a carving knife, sliced the meat, laid it on ice below decks to freeze, and spread out the skin for a rug. He now had at least 100 lb. of good meat. Settling down again, he heard odd, plaintive cries outside and discovered the bear's cub. He fed the animal, named it Nancy after a girl back home, and became its constant companion.

Shortly after Nancy joined him, Gordon discovered an alternate route into the hold. He emerged with freshwater ice, coal, whale meat, beef, ham, whiskey, pipes, tobacco, and blubber for Nancy. They were now well provisioned for the duration of the winter. Gordon and Nancy spent their time sleeping, reading from the Old Testament, and playing. Sometimes they'd stroll on the ice, with Gordon dressed in the captain's Sunday best escorting Nancy, whom he had taught to walk upright beside him, her paw on his arm.

When the sun began to reappear, Gordon cut steps into the crest of a giant mountain of ice and used it as an observation post. He knew that when the ice fields began to melt in the spring they could be carried farther north, and his only hope for rescue was to find land. But where? Figuring that the iceberg itself was too large to melt or sink, he used a bar of pig iron to carve a couple of chambers. He stocked the new "apartment with a view" with supplies and lived there for the next two months, hoping to spot land. Nancy was always at his side, and when the ice began breaking up, she kept them well supplied with fish. Eventually their iceberg, including the imbedded hulk of the ship, broke free of the ice field, causing them to drift around the northern seas for another six months. Bruce once sighted a headland and several mountains, and even floated close enough to see a woman on the shore, but the iceberg did not stop moving until a second Arctic winter descended, and once again they became bound by the ice.

One day the sound of gunshots inspired Gordon to pack some supplies and look for land. Attacked by a huge male polar bear, Gordon's life was saved because Nancy aided him in fighting the beast. Both were badly wounded before they killed the bear. The two bleeding friends abandoned their search and struggled weakly back to the ship.

The next winter was much stormier than the last. When spring arrived, Gordon and Nancy again set out. This time they located some hunters, who welcomed Gordon and his muzzled pet. The twosome lived with the villagers for several months. In time, though, Nancy became dissatisfied with tribal life and disappeared one night. Gordon searched for her, but he never saw her again. That summer word reached the village that ships had been sighted to the south. Gordon took a canoe and reached a ship that eventually returned him to Scotland. He had been gone for seven years and one month.

The Castaway: Daniel Foss
Year Marooned: 1810

In the early fall of 1809, mariner Daniel Foss set sail for the Friendly Islands (now called the Tonga Islands) by way of the Cape of Good Hope. It was the beginning of a six-year ordeal that would lead him through disaster at sea, near starvation, cannibalism, years of enforced solitude, and, finally, a well-earned though long-delayed rescue.

On Nov. 25, Foss's ship, the *Negociator*, encountered a storm and hit a growler (a nearly submerged iceberg). Within five minutes the brig had completely sunk. Foss climbed aboard a small open boat along with 20 of his shipmates. Immediately, they set a southerly course, praying that their modest provisions—beef, pork, water, and beer—would sustain them until they could find land or be rescued at sea. But the food and water stocks were meager and the bad weather continued. Within nine days the 21-man crew had been reduced to eight. By Jan. 10, Foss and two others were the only survivors; starvation seemed imminent. The three men were forced to eat their own shoes after soaking them in fresh water; Foss later remembered that the shoes were "devoured with the keenest appetite." Finally the men decided to draw lots to determine who would be sacrificed for the survival of the remaining two. The ship's surgeon lost. He opened an artery in his left arm, and Foss and his fellow survivor nourished themselves on their companion's warm blood as he quietly expired.

For 12 days Foss and his shipmate subsisted on the decaying carcass, and on Mar. 5 they finally sighted land. Here Foss's plight took a new, although equally agonizing turn. Thrown against a line of rocks barring the island, the boat quickly capsized and plunged the two men into rough surf. Foss seized an oar and fought his way to shore. His companion was lost in the breakers.

Resisting an overwhelming urge to panic, Foss proceeded to explore his new island domain. His findings brought little cheer. The island was terribly small, no more than a half-mile long and a quarter-mile wide, and there was no sign of animal, fowl, or accessible sea life, excepting a few shellfish. Foss had been without food for three days; his body was bloated and scratched raw from the wind, sea, and rocks. He knew that he would soon die, and thinking about his home, he was plunged into a deep melancholy. However, the next morning the sturdy man awoke resolved to continue his struggle. By noon he discovered the body of a dead seal in a rocky crevice. Several days later he awoke to what must have sounded like the roar of an open kennel. Rushing to the shore, Foss found, not a pack of dogs, but thousands of living seals. He tore into their ranks, swinging his oar with a vengeance. By the end of the day he had slaughtered more than 100 of them.

The problem of food having been solved, Foss set to work on perfecting a water supply system. Up to then, lacking suitable containers, Foss had had to drink from a few mucky pits that filled during frequent rainstorms. Now he fashioned a bucket from a large rock by grinding away at its center with a smaller, harder stone. Within five weeks he had a 14-lb. stone bucket that held two quarts of water. Over the next few months he capped the island's natural water-catching holes with flat-rock lids. As a result, Foss had 200 gallons of fresh water at his disposal at all times.

By his second year on the island Foss had done much to overcome the hardships of his captivity. He erected a stone hut, surrounding it with a 10-ft.-high barricade to protect him from the sea spray and high winds. At the highest point on the island he built a 30-ft. pillar and adorned it with his own bright and tattered flannel shirt—a distress signal for passing ships. He gave his isolated existence order and conventional discipline by creating a crude calendar on the only piece of flat wood on the island—his oar. Foss's oar became his all-purpose tool—weapon, flagstaff, cane, and prodder—and Foss guarded it jealously, protecting it from the elements with a sealskin blanket. In later years the oar also served as a hymnal: Foss cut into the wood a short verse which he chanted to himself every Sabbath. Inspired by this feat, he later utilized the broad end of the oar as a kind of journal, setting down the story of his wreck and subsequent life in exile. At best he could engrave 12 letters per day—all this so that upon his death he would not be forever forgotten.

Appropriately enough, it was the oar which finally secured Foss's rescue in the sixth year of his confinement. Sighting a ship within shouting range of his encampment—and its small landing boat trying desperately to pierce the rough, rock-strewn coast—Foss dived headlong into the perilous surf and paddled toward the smaller vessel. After he was safely aboard the larger ship, Foss, and his oar, were regarded with great curiosity and admiration by the astonished sailors. Foss subsequently returned to his home in Elkton, Md. His much-regarded oar was presented to the curator of the Peal Museum in Philadelphia. Unfortunately, the museum no longer exists, and the oar has disappeared.

—F.S. and P.A.R.

THE GREAT SURVIVOR—P'U-YI

His titles were auspicious—the Son of Heaven, He Who Is Above, the Enthroned One, the Lord of Ten Thousand Years, the Lord of Myriad Years, the One Who Faces South, the Celestial Emperor, the Last Emperor of Cathay, of the Middle Kingdom, of China.

In reality he was a puppet, a quintessential political puppet, never to know a day of total autonomy in his life.

In 1908 Tzu Hsi, the aging empress dowager of the Manchu dynasty, anticipating her own death and fearful that her exiled nephew, Kuang Hsü, would return to the Dragon Throne, named Aisin-Gioro P'u-Yi, her two-year-old grandnephew, emperor of China. As child-emperor, P'u-Yi led an absolutely preposterous life behind the walls of the Forbidden City. He was separated from his mother, his siblings, and other children until the age of ten. He saw his father, Prince Ch'un, who served as regent, only once every two months. He was attended by 100 physicians, 200 chefs, and 1,000 eunuchs, some of whom he had flogged for his own simple amusement. He ordered 25-course meals at will, never wore the same clothing twice, and believed the color yellow was his alone.

At age six he abdicated. Republican forces led by Sun Yat-sen, a former adviser to P'u-Yi's late uncle and predecessor, Kuang Hsü, had gathered strength in China. When Yüan Shih-k'ai, a general in the imperial army, threw his support to the republicans, the Manchu dynasty collapsed. China's royal family was spared the bloodbath that usually accompanies such revolutions because the republicans did not want to alienate the empire's Manchu populace and because Yüan Shih-k'ai, who became president of the new republic, entertained dynastic ambitions of his own and therefore wished to maintain the trappings of royalty. So P'u-Yi and his family were offered the Articles of Favorable Treatment, an extraordinary document which permitted the emperor to retain his title, his home in the Forbidden City, his bodyguards, and a sizable annuity.

For five years, from 1912 to 1917, P'u-Yi lived inside the walls of the Forbidden City, blissfully ignorant of the crosscurrents of political change blowing through China. In 1915, when President Yüan tried to solidify his power by trading Chinese sovereignty to the Japanese in exchange for their support of his regime, the republican armies revolted, throwing China into a state of chaos and thrusting P'u-Yi onto center stage again. A Chinese warlord named Chang Hsun attempted to restore order by reinstating the monarchy with himself as chief adviser to the boy emperor. But P'u-Yi's Manchu advisers objected to allowing a Chinese into their inner circle. The republicans meanwhile rallied around President Yüan's successor, Li Yüan-hung, and with the aid of China's only warplane attacked Peking and routed Chang Hsun's troops. In his memoirs P'u-Yi recalled hearing bombs burst over his school, the Palace for the Cultivation of Happiness, and seeing the streets littered with pigtails—those plaited symbols of Manchu loyalty which Chang Hsun's army had cut off and thrown away in retreat.

On July 12, 1917, less than two weeks after the restoration, P'u-Yi abdicated the dragon throne for the second time in his young life. Again his life was spared by the republican armies, still eager to maintain Manchu support in the face of growing external threats from Japan.

With the sudden end of the restoration P'u-Yi returned to the role he was born to—that of hollow emperor. Through his teenage years he was

Emperor P'u-Yi of China.

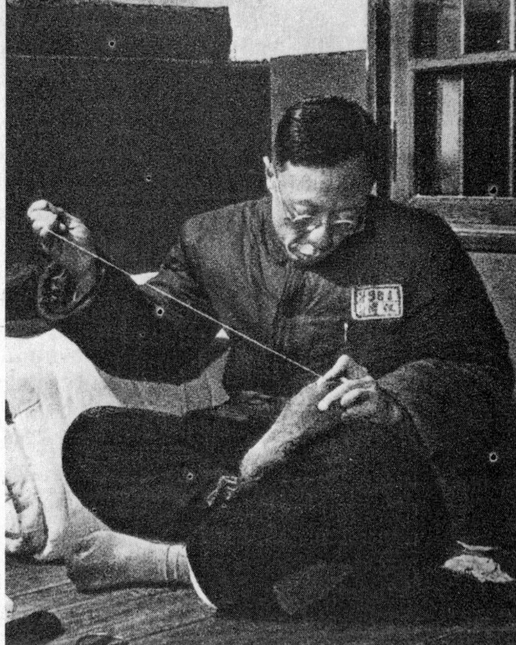

Comrade P'u-Yi of China.

tutored by a Britisher named Reginald Johnston, who succeeded to a great degree in westernizing the boy. He persuaded him to cut off his own queue, send the eunuchs out of the Forbidden City, and take on the name of Henry, after King Henry VIII of England.

In 1922, sensing that his son was getting bored and restless with his life, Prince Ch'un arranged to have the emperor take a wife. Since the republic had changed things from the days when the most beautiful women in the land were brought before the emperor for his selection, P'u-Yi had to make his choice from photographs. He picked a woman named Wen Hsiu, but she was rejected by his court, which chose Wan Jung (or Elizabeth Yuang), the daughter of a rich and powerful family. Because the emperor had already looked favorably upon Wen Hsiu, it was determined that no other man would be worthy of her, so she was given to P'u-Yi as a consort. His wedding night with Wan Jung was a disaster. P'u-Yi's biographer, Arnold C. Brackman, suggests that his political impotency reflected sexual impotency as well. All those years in the company of eunuchs and the womanless Johnston, says Brackman, encouraged homosexual tendencies in the young emperor.

Outside the bedchamber things didn't fare much better for the Manchu dynasty. In 1924 another round of civil war erupted in China, this time with an antimonarchist general gaining the upper hand and driving P'u-Yi and his family out of the Forbidden City and into the welcoming arms of the Japanese. The Japanese protected the royal family until they overran Manchuria in 1931. They renamed it Manchukuo and tried to legitimize their blatant aggression by installing P'u-Yi as emperor.

Chiang Kai-shek, who was battling Mao Tse-tung for control of China at this time, offered P'u-Yi the chance to return to the Forbidden City under the Articles of Favorable Treatment if he would not accept the Japanese scheme. But P'u-Yi, who was bitter at Chiang because a renegade group of his soldiers had desecrated the Manchu ancestral tombs, refused the offer and became a Japanese pawn. They forced him to attend his coronation in a Japanese army officer's uniform; they made him bow before their gods; and they exploited Manchukuo to aid their invasion of China. To add to the humiliation, his consort Wen Hsiu left him; his wife had an affair with a palace guard and—upon banishment to her quarters—became an opium addict; his second wife died mysteriously; and his third wife, a Japanese-educated Manchurian, was foisted upon him by his "benefactors."

Fortunately for him Japan lost the war. The day before the official surrender, P'u-Yi took the opportunity to abdicate one more time. He was captured by Russian troops at the Manchurian border and spent the next 14 years of his life as a prisoner, first of Stalin and then of Mao. In 1959 he was released from Mao's thought-control camp as a dedicated Communist. "I owe more to Mao Tse-tung than any subject ever owed to any emperor," he claimed. He returned to Peking, where he was greeted by his relatives—most of whom he had not seen in 25 years—and a host of newspaper, magazine, and radio interviewers. P'u-Yi was a celebrity of sorts, a curious anomaly of the 20th century.

Because of his interest in horticulture, P'u-Yi was assigned to work in the botanical gardens of the Chinese Academy of Sciences' Institute of Botany. He joined the local militia and demonstrated in the streets against the ratification of the Japanese-American Security Treaty. On Nov. 22, 1960, the former emperor was given full rights as a citizen of the People's Republic of China, and soon after he was elected to the National Committee of the People's Political Consultative Conference of the National People's Congress. He married a Chinese woman, thus ending once and for all any chance of a Manchu restoration. Throughout these years, P'u-Yi was also at work on the story of his astonishing life, *From Emperor to Citizen*, which was published by Peking's Foreign Language Press in 1964.

In 1967 he died. There are those who claim he was a victim of China's Cultural Revolution, but those who had respect for his talents as a survivor say the Lord of Ten Thousand Years simply died of heart disease.

—D.R.

20

THE VOICE OF THE PEOPLE

READERS WRITE

In *The People's Almanac 1* and *The People's Almanac 2*, we invited readers to participate in the making of *The People's Almanac 3*. The response was exciting and gratifying. During a period of six years, an avalanche of mail has descended upon us. Readers in every corner of the U.S. as well as in foreign lands have sent us ideas and fascinating facts that they have read about or heard about or witnessed. And many have sent clippings and suggested that we reprint them. Although some of the contributions from these letters appear in other chapters, what follows is a representative selection of the varied material we received. Readers, thank you one and all.

Facts about the Deaf

Reader: JOHN HUEY (Sunnyvale, Calif.)

John Huey is a 28-year-old data terminals assembler. Deaf since birth, John attended the California School for the Deaf in Berkeley, Calif., from 1961 to 1972 and then attended Gallaudet College in Washington, D.C., the leading deaf college in the world. In 1978 he wrote a series of articles about the deaf in the *Daily Midway Driller* and sent us a copy. The following are excerpts from those articles.

Generally, people I have met have accepted my deafness, but some people have strange ideas about the deaf. Years ago it was thought that the deaf were mentally retarded. Even now we are asked silly questions like "Do you drive?" Deaf people make the best drivers. We're not distracted by noise.

If you can't speak, you can still read. There's nothing wrong with your mind just because you can't hear. Terms like "deaf and dumb" and "deaf mute" are outmoded.

Most people aid the blind. Likewise, the disabled. But when a deaf man asks for help, the story is often different. There is widespread vocational, psychological, and educational stereotyping of deaf people. They simply ignore the psychology of individual differences. The deaf struggle to relate to society. The deaf person is aware of his limits and has increased his other sensory awareness accordingly.

Some other facts about the deaf world:

- The deaf can't serve on juries. In a recent case in Los Angeles where a deaf woman was being considered as a juror, the court ruled that a prospective juror must have the normal senses.
- Edison, a deaf man, gave the world electricity, and almost nothing in jobs from the electrical power companies was given to the deaf in return.
- Civic clubs should ask the deaf to be guest speakers. They can always speak through interpreters.
- The National Association of the Deaf near Washington, D.C., was founded in 1880 to protect the rights of the deaf.
- The odds against the deaf borrowing money to start a business are great.
- There is a life insurance agency, the National Fraternal Society of the Deaf, headquartered in Oak Park, Ill.
- U.S. presidents did nothing for the deaf except in the field of education. What good is education if the deaf adult can't find a job?
- At times deaf job-seekers have sought the aid of the state rehabilitation office, but it's often a fruitless effort.
- The deaf are accepted into employment more readily in Ohio than elsewhere.
- Abilities, Inc., in Long Island, N.Y., hires only the handicapped. I believe it is a tool plant.
- West Virginia has a deaf miner.
- There have been deaf newspaper columnists and editors, deaf lathe operators, airplane mechanics, truckers, and pilots.
- Some deaf persons have been shot by police officers by mistake because they could not hear a policeman's command.
- The deaf live mostly in big cities.
- The most frustrating thing about deafness is the inability to talk on the phone.
- The deaf can talk to each other by a special telephone. The portable, battery-powered Manual Communication Module looks like a small typewriter. Its message is printed electronically. The MCM costs about $600 and weighs about 6 lb. It can be attached to any phone and even used in a phone booth.
- There are three categories of deafness: the congenital deaf (born deaf), adventitiously deaf (became deaf through accident or illness), and hard of hearing.
- Sign language classes are popping up everywhere because more people are helping the deaf.
- When you first start using sign language, you really feel awkward. If a word has no sign, you spell it. There are two different kinds of sign language. Signing Exact English (SEE) is taught to young children because the signing is in complete sentences. The shorter "real deaf language" is American Sign Language (ASL or ameslan). It's a picturesque language.

• Sign language can also be used as a "secret code."
• The estimated number of formal signs is 1,500–2,000.
• Sign language is the third-largest foreign language in the U.S., outranked only by Spanish and Italian.
• The World Federation of the Deaf at Gallaudet College in Washington, D.C., developed GESTUNO, the International Sign Language.
• Presidents Ford and Carter used the "I love you" sign in the 1976 presidential campaign.
• There are 13.8 million hearing-impaired people in the U.S. Of those, 1.8 million are deaf.
• Annually, 3,500 people are born very profoundly deaf.
• Today 22 states require competent interpreters for deaf clients in court.
• Some deaf people have a special light-bulb doorbell that alerts them to callers.
• I know of some successful deaf-hearing marriages. Marriage demands 100% from each other all the time.
• *Spiritus surdus* is "deaf pride" in Latin.
• The best deaf high school senior is two to three years behind a hearing one.
• A typical deaf adult is one who attended a residential school for the deaf; works at a skilled trade but earns less; attends a deaf club regularly; reads English on a fifth grade level; writes English on a third or fourth grade level; and associates socially with deaf people.
• The average deaf person is an avid movie watcher. There is a captioned film loan service for the deaf.
• Cobras can't hear the snake charmers.
• The snake, the turtle, the housefly, and the starfish are all deaf.
• Juliette Low, founder of the Girl Scouts of America, was deaf.
• We have four deaf lawyers in the U.S., and the first deaf doctor lives in San Francisco.
• Some deaf people "love" music!

Houdini's Secret

Harry Houdini (1874–1926) was the best-known magician of the 20th century. He was famous, said *Encyclopaedia Britannica*, for his "daring feats of extrication from shackles, ropes, and handcuffs and from various locked containers. . . . In a typical act he was shackled with irons and placed in a box that was locked, roped, and weighted. The box was submerged from a boat, to which he returned after freeing himself underwater."

The big mystery, in all of Houdini's stunts, was how did he free himself? How did he escape every time?

Suffering an accident that would lead to his death, Houdini was rushed to a hospital in Detroit. One of our readers was present. She may have the solution to the great Houdini mystery. Here is her contribution.

From: LOU NITZBERG (Pleasant Ridge, Mich.)

I was the scrub nurse for Dr. J. B. Kennedy when he operated on Houdini. Then, after the surgery, I was the floor nurse. Mr. Houdini had very thick black hair and in it he kept a long metal spindle. Another one fitted into the callous part of his foot. They were probably used to help open locks, etc.

Kilroy's Christmas Trolley

From: NICHOLAS EVOSEVIC (Pittsburgh, Pa.)

I have been doing research on W.W. II for several years. This is one of the tidbits that I uncovered about two years ago. I believe the article best explains the enigma of "Kilroy Was Here." Until a better explanation is offered, I'll settle for this one. As a youngster, I grew up in the Kilroy era. Who the heck was Kilroy? It took a long time . . .

Everybody knew the man by name. American servicemen in W.W. II had carried his name to remote corners of the world. He was Kilroy, whose name G.I.s scrawled almost everywhere they went in the catch phrase, "Kilroy Was Here."

Was there really a Kilroy?

Well, one fall evening in the late 1940s, James J. Kilroy, a 47-year-old shipyard worker from Halifax, Mass., was trying to figure out how to scrape up enough money to buy Christmas presents for his nine children. No matter how hard or how long a day a man may work, there never seems to be enough money around at Christmas when there are nine children in the house.

"We'll be pinching pennies again this Christmas, Margaret," Kilroy remarked to his wife that evening. They were sipping cocoa and listening to the kitchen radio after the children had been put to bed. "We'll only be able to come up with one small gift for each of the children. Money's tight."

Then over the radio came the coaxing voice of an announcer with still another commercial. "Are you Kilroy?" the radio voice asked. "If you are the man responsible for the slogan, 'Kilroy Was Here,' and can prove it, we have a wonderful prize waiting for you."

Both Kilroys beamed when they heard the announcement. That "wonderful prize" might be cold cash. And with Christmas so close at hand, it certainly would come in handy. At least, Jim and Margaret thought the prize would be "something sensible." Alas, that was *not* the case in this contest—sponsored by the Transit Company of America.

James Kilroy is dead now. He died in 1962. His widow resides in Plympton, a town only a few miles from Halifax. "My Jim," she recalls, "was too old for the Second World War. And he was too young for the First World War. But he was very proud of the tribute our American servicemen paid to him when they adopted his 'Kilroy Was Here' slogan as their very own."

Kilroy is here.

After the broadcast that night, she remembers, Kilroy sat down and penned a letter to the Transit Company of America, proving he indeed was the Kilroy who was "here."

"Jim was a checker at the Fore River Shipyard in Quincy, just south of Boston," says Mrs. Kilroy. "He started to work there in 1941 shortly before Pearl Harbor. His job was to go around and count the number of holes a riveter had filled. The riveters were on piece work and got paid so much for each rivet. After he had counted the rivets, he'd put a check mark in chalk, so the rivets wouldn't be counted twice.

"Now, some riveters would wait until the checker went off duty and erase the last mark. Another checker would come through and count the rivets a second time, and the riveters would get paid twice. Just as he was going off duty one day, Jim heard his boss ask a riveter if Kilroy had been by checking rivets. The riveter said no. When Jim heard that, he got angry because he had just checked those particular rivets. He took some chalk, went over to where the two men were standing, and wrote, 'Kilroy Was Here,' in big letters over the rivets. That was the start of it. After that, every time he checked the rivets, he scrawled, 'Kilroy Was Here,' in big letters next to the check mark."

Ordinarily, the rivets and chalk marks would have been covered up by paint. But there was a war on, and ships were leaving the Quincy yard so fast there wasn't time enough to paint them. And so they arrived at their destinations with the now mysterious inscriptions still on them.

Kilroy's prize in that Transit Company contest turned out to be a 2-ton trolley car. It was 25 ft. long and 7 ft. high. Exactly what the Transit Company of America figured Kilroy, or anybody else, was supposed to do with a vintage trolley—it had been built in 1910—must remain a moot point.

Jim Kilroy, however, was not about to be overwhelmed by a mere streetcar. He gathered his children around him. When Peggy, 15; James, 13; Mary Ann, 12; Robert, 10; Ellen, 9; Ann, 6; Kathleen, 4; Larry, 3; and Judy, six months, were all together, he asked them: "How would you like Santa Claus to bring you a trolley car for Christmas?" They were overjoyed. After all, what child wouldn't want a real trolley car for Christmas?

On Dec. 23 the old trolley was loaded aboard a 75-ton low bed trailer to be lugged over the road to Halifax. That king-size truck may not have looked much like a sleigh as it grunted and groaned its way out of the Boston Elevated trolley yard in Everett, about 35 mi. from Halifax, but to the Kilroys, it was just that.

The trolley was escorted by a crew of nine men, and their assignment was to make certain it didn't get caught under any low bridge or in any street lights during the long, slow trip to Halifax. The first day, the trolley traveled about 20 mi. It was just about halfway home. That night, it was parked in a vacant lot in the town of Canton. Overnight, tiny flakes of snow drifted slowly down from the sky. A few at first. Then more and more of them. By daybreak, it was a blizzard. It was going to be a white Christmas after all.

White Christmases may be what most people want, but at the Kilroys' in Halifax, a couple of nervous parents did a lot of fingernail nibbling. To them, it seemed the entire family was destined to endure a gloomy Christmas thanks to all that white stuff outside. With so much of it on the ground, how was Santa going to be able to make his special Christmas delivery at their house?

During the afternoon, the snow stopped. And in the evening, a crowd of neighbors and friends, and even the local Board of Selectmen, were on hand to welcome the trolley—if it ever showed up. It didn't. After a reasonable wait in the snow, everybody went home.

The Kilroy children hung their stockings by the fireplace with care and headed up to bed. The older ones prayed the trolley would be there in the morning. The younger ones knew it would be there. Such is the power of Santa.

Christmas morning dawned. Like children all over, the children were up early that day at the Kilroy home. In fact, they were all dressed and out in the backyard playing when their parents awoke. In the yard, amid all that snow, was the bright orange trolley. It was parked by the side of the house, and though it lacked tracks, the vintage vehicle was destined to make countless journeys to wonderlands even modern-day trolleys, with all their complex gadgets, have never been privileged to visit.

There may have been a blizzard that Christmas Eve. But St. Nick was not about to disappoint those nine Kilroy children. Chalked on the ceiling of the trolley was the message: "Santa Was Here." There was no doubt about that.

SOURCE: By Richard Pritchett. Reprinted with permission from the *NRTA Journal*. Copyright 1976 by the National Retired Teachers Association.

Seeing Is Believing

From: MARIE RILEY (Enfield, Conn.)

In the summer of 1979, I stopped at a neighborhood store and went directly to the deli section for my purchases. I was astounded to see a young lady and young man standing among the fine foods smiling, but with tears streaming down their faces. Needless to say, I did not know what to make of this, so I waited for one of them to explain.

"Ma'am, did you see the lady in the green suit that just passed you?" he finally asked.

I replied that I had. He went on to share with me what in Webster's terms could be described as a "miracle." The lovely lady had just ventured her first trip to the store after having an eye transplant. She had been blind since birth.

"She has a daughter *my age* and has *never* seen her," said the young lady. "I cannot imagine my mother never being able to see me."

I too shed tears for this lovely event. Upon leaving the store, I saw the green-suited lady was smiling, still observing life for the first time. She was a little confused, though. It appears she and her dearest friend, her beautiful, trusting dog, had made this adventure without money to purchase the items she wanted. Gently, a woman offered her a dime and explained where the phone was so she could call her husband.

It was a beautiful sight to share. Perhaps you the reader, too, can enjoy God's true gifts to mankind. Seeing is indeed believing.

Diversion #1

From: TOM DAVIS (Bellingham, Wash.)

Can you move only one match and make the equation equal?

Answer: Move one match from the right side to make a square-root sign.

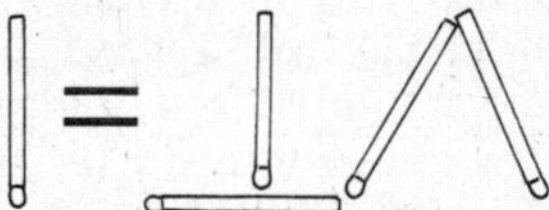

The Dream

From: ELIZABETH BEHR (Rochester, N.Y.)

My dreams are unusual, I think, judging from comparison with other people and assorted articles on the subject. They are very realistic. I live them. Occasionally I watch them; that is, I, as myself, do not appear in them. They are always in color. I hear sounds as I would if I were awake. In fact, all of my senses seem to function in a normal manner.

Frequently, I have what I call "dream hangovers." A dream hangover results from a deep involvement in the dream and lasts until the dream is explained or the emotions wear themselves out. I have had dream hangovers which last five minutes, and others which last as long as three weeks. One of my longest hangovers was from the following dream:

I am in a ladies' room, somewhere in the world. There is an old woman who came in with me. I think I carried her suitcase. She walked with her head lowered, and her legs were wrapped in ragged bandages. They were wound from the tops of her dusty black shoes to the frayed hem of her polka-dot dress. There was only one receptacle in this ladies' room. The old woman entered it. She was in there for close to 30 min. Soundlessly. As soon as I became aware of the silence, I began hearing strange sounds. Tearing, shredding, slapping, mushy sounds. I suddenly realized what I was hearing. She was unwrapping the bandages. These noises continued for close to an hour. Very abruptly they stopped. I found myself wondering if she was all right. Finally I called to her, asking if she needed anything, asking if she needed help. There was no response. I waited about 15 min. before repeating my questions. As before, there was no answer. I thought she might be dead. I told her that if she did not answer me, I would have to open the door. I waited for an answer, and when I got none I pushed open the door. I awoke sweating, with a scream stifled in my throat.

I had this exact same dream recur two or three times a year for about three years before it happened. Yes, it happened.

Two years ago, at the age of 25, I chanced to be in a Greyhound bus station in Long Beach, Calif. It was the first time I had ever been west of Chicago. I arrived at the station at approximately 5:15 A.M. My cash assets consisted of one quarter. My plan was to call my uncle, who lived in the area, but it was just a little too early. I saved a dime for the telephone and splurged on a cup of coffee. I started to drink the coffee and decided to take it up to the ladies' room and relax, smoke, wash up, and change clothes.

I reentered the lobby from the coffee shop. As I headed for the stairs at the end of the room, I noticed an old woman who seemed to be struggling with her luggage. She had two suitcases and was carrying a sheaf of cardboards. She looked around 85 years old, give or take a few years. She was pushing one bag ahead of her with her foot and towing the other with the handle of her umbrella. I went around a row of seats and offered my assistance. I noticed that her legs were completely bandaged and wondered if it was for support or because of a disease.

The old woman said yes, I could take her suitcases, but she did not look up at me. She appeared to be concentrating on her luggage. She told me to take them to the ladies' room. As I reached for the smaller bag to put under the arm that was carrying my coffee, she abruptly stopped me. "No," she said, "you'll have to put that down. These are my sister's suitcases and I can't have anything happen to them." I told her to wait while I took my coffee upstairs. When I returned, she was exactly as I had left her, waiting patiently. Since she did not look up, I announced my return and picked up her bags. She clung protectively to the cardboards. I started off in front of her, but in a rather alarmed voice she told me to stop. I turned to see her staring at my feet. "I can't lift my head more than this, so you must stay where I can see your feet." In this fashion, we made our way to the end of the room and on up the stairs.

There was only one free toilet in the restroom and that had no catch on the door. She told me to put her suitcases in the stall. She followed them in, closed the door, and rearranged the bags so that the door did not swing open. Since my financial situation forced me to wait for her, I washed, changed my clothes, smoked a couple of cigarettes, and drank my coffee. I sat down to do my nails. Then it started!

The noises! Suddenly that nightmare was with me. My first reaction was that it couldn't be happening. I went over every little detail that I could remember. The top of her bowed gray head, her shoes, her dress, her voice, and of course, the core of the dream—the bandages! It was all too obvious; my dream was happening before my very eyes. More than anything, I was amused at the events which seemed so meaningless by themselves, but which were necessary to bring me to this time and place.

I knew, of course, what the ripping and tearing sounds were. In fact, I felt privileged to know. Removal of the bandages lasted almost 30 min. Then there was a period of complete silence. It was shattered by a voice on a loudspeaker. "Miss ________. Miss ________, there is a message for you at the ticket counter." The old woman called to me, "Are you there?" I said I was. She told me they were paging her and to go down and tell them where she was, but under no circumstances was I to ask what the message was.

I relayed the information to the man at the desk and turned to go back. I had taken three steps when he called to me, "We just want to know what we are to do with all these cartons." He gestured towards the baggage room, and I couldn't help following his hand. There, not 30 ft. away, was a pile of cartons on a forklift. The pile was about five boxes wide, five deep, and seven high. They were not in the best of condition. They were frayed and torn, and desperately needed the strings they were tied with in order to stay together. Peeking out of sides and corners were nothing but rags and crumpled newspaper.

When I returned to the ladies' room, I told the old woman that I had done what she requested, and asked her if she would be much longer. Again, she did not answer me. It was now almost 6:30.

After a few minutes, I remembered—from my dream—what I was supposed to do. I thought I might as well get it over with. I called, "Miss ________, are you all right?" No response. Again, "Miss ________, can you answer me?" Not only was there no answer, there was no sound of any kind. I knew she was alive, and yet I couldn't keep from thinking she might be dead. I forced myself to wait another 15 min. Finally, positioning myself in front of the toilet door, I said, "Miss ________, I know what I'm supposed to do. I know what you want me to do. But I'm not going to open that door. So if you don't let me know that you are all right, I will have to get the manager." After a moment's hesitation, she flushed the toilet.

So that was my answer. Shortly, the slapping sounds of reapplying the bandages began. This operation lasted close to 45 min. During this time, it occurred to me that her dressings were not made by Johnson & Johnson. I knew that the paper-strewn floor of the receptacle would be neater when she left it. I was right.

When at last she emerged, shuffling her suitcases, her head held a trifle higher, she bore her old brown eyes into my blue ones. Her expression was smug and secretive. She pointed to her luggage and we made our way down the stairs and to the desk. I set her bags down and said good-bye. She didn't say a word.

I have not had that nightmare since then; almost two years have passed. There has been no suggestion of it. And yet, I still have a slight hangover. Should I have discovered what frightened me in the dreams? Or was I spared a more horrible nightmare? I'll never know. Because, I do believe, that was the end of the dream.

SOLUTIONS—PRACTICAL PROPOSALS AND BRAND-NEW APPROACHES TO A MULTITUDE OF PROBLEMS

Human civilization has advanced because people have faced problems as challenges and sought solutions. What follows is a series of plans, programs, and ideas the purpose of which is to help us live a better life. In the interests of encouraging the exchange of ideas, we ask you to share with us your practical solutions to problems that all of us or some of us face in our daily lives. Please send your solutions to:

SOLUTIONS
The People's Almanac
P.O. Box 49699
Los Angeles, Calif. 90049

GOVERNMENT

The Other Candidates

The 1980 presidential election was pretty dreary. I think that the tradition of "the lesser of two (or more) evils" hit a new low. Voter participation continued to drop. Ronald Reagan's "landslide" victory meant that 27% of the voting-age population voted for him. If the campaign had gone on for another month, I don't think anyone would have voted. What really bothered me, though, was that when I went into the voting booth, there were not three candidates on the ballot, but seven! I had never heard of four of them. All I knew about were Reagan, Carter, and Anderson—the ones who debated and were covered by the news.

There should be a law that requires all TV networks and all newspapers to give equal time to every candidate who is on the ballot. Newspapers should be forced to print a chart showing the views of all candidates on each of the major issues. And the TV networks should present *all* the candidates at once, answering the same questions. The candidates would be required by law to participate.

William Corman
Denver, Colo.

Why We Have Poor Presidents—An End to Party Politics

Because our system of representative democracy is so promising, it deserves our most serious effort to make it better. Surely the twinkle of time since independence from Britain should not delude us into thinking we have shaped a system that cannot be improved.

Many people feel unable to do anything that will significantly influence their destiny. The trauma of detachment, which for many people results from living in oversized cities, where they perform depersonalized and highly specialized work while being serviced by apathetic government bureaucracies and profit-oriented business monoliths, is made worse by the operation of the party system; parties increase the individual's feeling of isolation and ineffectiveness.

My proposal for revitalizing our electoral process is offered out of a deep conviction that party politics is passé and in the hope that this will provoke additional recommendations for worthwhile reform.

Americans do elect representatives to Congress, and every voter has a chance to judge the legislators and, if satisfied, can reward them with a new term. But the people rarely have the opportunity to elect delegates to national party conventions.

This reinforces my conviction that the congressional caucus, the method used to nominate presidential candidates before the rise of party politics, was essentially the correct one. It produced a generally fine group of candidates, utilized an already existing apparatus, and ultimately was accountable to the electorate.

However, rather than having congressmen of like political persuasion retreat into private meetings to negotiate a caucus nominee, I propose that Congress openly exercise its power to nominate.

Every four years, after summer recess, all members of the Senate and House would sign one petition for any American they think should be president. Any person receiving 5% of these signatures would be considered nominated.

At this point there might be as many as 20 candidates reflecting all shades of opinion. Most voters would find in this group a candidate whose opinions somewhat closely represented their viewpoint, a situation so rare in recent elections that a majority of citizens have been forced to cast their ballot for the one of two men they distrusted least.

The campaign in which this multitude of nominees would run would last six weeks, a week longer than the British elections. It would be conducted exclusively on television and radio, since almost everyone can be reached directly by those media. The exhausting tedium of frenetic travel and the wastefulness of rote speeches to restless crowds would be ended.

All costs would be paid by the U.S. Treasury. Private contributions would be outlawed.

The election would take place, as is now customary, at the beginning of November. There would no party labels camouflaging the names of this legion of candidates.

Central to the election is the appearance on the ballot of two identical lists of nominees. You'd first vote for president by pulling a lever under List #1. The computerized voting machines would automatically block out that candidate's name from List #2. You'd then pick someone else for vice-president from List #2.

In effect, this first election would be equivalent to a national primary; it would differ from the present presidential primaries, which take place in only 37 states, because it would be held on one day, would involve all candidates, and would not be dominated by parties.

If no candidate wins a majority in the first election—equivalent to a national primary—a presidential runoff would take place the following week. Although the field would be narrowed to, say, the top five candidates, most citizens would find one candidate whose position still somewhat approximates their own. If this election proved inconclusive, a final vote between the top two candidates would be held the next week.

On the state and local levels, governors and mayors would be elected in much the same manner. This way all elected executive officials in the U.S. would be nominated by legislative bodies and then finally chosen by the people. There would be no qualifying conventions or primaries controlled by party organizations. Such a polling process could conceivably revitalize voter interest and turnout.

This is not a call for the end of politics or an outline for a country without a political system. Every social group must have its political arrangements. It is a plea for Americans to recognize that their political system has been taken over by two parties. The parties' basic function is to perpetuate their own power—thus excluding the people from the process of selecting leaders—while giving the impression that the entire system exists only to respond to the people's wishes.

It is also a call for change, and as such, it may disturb those who perceive of their existence as immutable, reliable, and the product of natural laws with which one cannot tamper.

Our common liberty and good sense must be allowed to mold the form of our political institutions. We are a free, responsible people who have proved we are capable of accomplishing wonders. Among these can be the construction of an election system that will honor reason and, hopefully, lead us further from the cave and the club toward a time when party taskmasters will no longer be in a position of determining to whom we give our precious gift of leadership.

Leonard Lurie
New York, N.Y.

SOURCE: Copyright 1980 by Leonard Lurie. From the book *Party Politics: Why We Have Poor Presidents*. Reprinted with permission of Stein and Day Publishers.

The Three-Person Presidency

The problem with the U.S. presidency is that it is too much work. Modern presidents have tended to become exhausted or power-hungry. President Carter suggested that each president be elected to one 6-year term. This is a good idea, except that there should be three presidents with overlapping terms. Every two years we would elect a new one.

For the first two years, a newly elected president would be known as the junior president and he would mostly be in charge of ceremonial duties, while he learned the job from the two more experienced presidents. For the second two years, he would be known as the national president and would be responsible for domestic affairs. During the last two years of his term, each president would be called the senior president and he would be responsible for international relations. Naturally, the three presidents would be expected to meet regularly to coordinate their activities.

(Sp. 4) Steven Spelman
Frankfurt, West Germany

Support Democracy: End Elections

In *The People's Almanac #2*, Russell E. Simmons of Raton, N.M., suggested that candidates for legislative offices be chosen at random instead of by political parties. I support the premise of this proposal but would like to take it further.

I propose that congressional elections be eliminated entirely and that the members of Congress be selected instead by lottery, much the way that juries are selected now. The current system doesn't work because the voters of most districts are forced to choose between two candidates they don't want. Also, 83% of congressional elections are won by the candidate who spends the most money. The winner then sets out on his path towards becoming a professional politician, selling his soul to wealthy campaign donors, lobbyists, and political action groups.

The Founding Fathers may have conceived the present form of government as a representative democracy, but it hasn't worked out that way. Members of Congress are overwhelmingly upper-class, white males. Half of them are lawyers and another third are businessmen. Some may argue that lawyers and businessmen are, more often than not, the most qualified people in our society to make laws, but I disagree. Just as it is the role of generals to *fight* wars, not declare them, so it should be the role of lawyers to *write* laws, not make them. The making of laws is a moral task, and right morality is not limited to lawyers, to say the least. Likewise, successful businessmen may have proven themselves adept at turning a profit in private life, but their extensive participation in government has done nothing to prevent the country from going $1 trillion into debt.

Some may argue that the average citizen does not have the specialized knowledge that is needed to evaluate budget requirements, allocate funds, and vote on issues dealing with international relations. But not very many of our present members of Congress are qualified to handle these issues either. That is what congressional staffs are for. These staffs, particularly committee staffs, have been growing steadily since the 1890s and have been mushrooming since 1947. There are currently 44 staff members for each congressional representative. These are the people who research issues, provide statistics and alternatives, and actually prepare bills, leaving the 535 members of Congress free to concentrate on voting, attending committee meetings, and wielding power.

Some may argue that a Congress of random Americans would allow greedy, unsophisticated people to abuse their years in office by taking bribes, getting drunk, and partying. But take a look at recent, and even not so recent, history. Alcoholism is twice as common among members of Congress as it is in the population at large. Corruption and womanizing are also already painfully commonplace in Washington. Could it really be any worse?

So how would such a new system work? If the entire House of Representatives and one third of the Senate were replaced every two years, it would cause chaos. A better method would be for four congressional districts to change representatives each week. That way there would be a complete turnover every two years without serious disruption or discontinuity. Senators would still serve six-year terms, but there would be one new senator every three weeks.

As the end of a congressperson's term of office neared completion, back in his or her district a successor would be chosen by lottery from the list of registered voters (who would still be voting for propositions, state offices, and the U.S. presidency). This new person would be required to pass a test dealing with the Constitution. Those who failed would then receive six weeks of instruction from a tutor. Anyone failing the test a second time would be replaced by an alternate, already waiting in the wings. The new senator or representative would serve an apprenticeship of 8 to 10 weeks, learning the job from the outgoing officeholder.

I realize that many problems would develop during the transition to a nonelected Congress, but I believe that the basic honesty and ingenuity of the American people would allow such a system to succeed.

David Wallechinsky
Santa Monica, Calif.

P.S. In case you are wondering how the composition of Congress would change if the members were chosen at random instead of elected, here is a chart that compares the two systems.

	Current Congress	Typical New Congress
Women	17	268
Blacks	16	67
Poor people	0	60
Lawyers	270	2
Businessmen	156	22
Teachers	34	12
FBI agents	6	0
Clergy	5	1
Athletes	4	0
Secretaries	1	13
Housewives	0	110
Unemployed	0	37
Salesclerks	0	9
Truck drivers	0	7
Carpenters	0	5
Registered nurses	0	4
Auto mechanics	0	4
Waitresses	0	4
Farm workers	0	3
Cosmetologists	0	2
Maids	0	2
Plumbers	0	1
Firemen	0	1

MONEY

Ecological Tax Incentives

I don't understand why the government doesn't use tax incentives to clean up our environment. Instead of giving tax breaks to the oil industry, they should be given to the solar and wind energy industries. Companies engaged in recycling of waste products shouldn't have to pay taxes at all. In the last *People's Almanac* you talked about businesses owned by the employees. These could receive tax breaks too.

Suzi Belknap
Toronto, Ontario

Picture Credit Cards

I am presently considering getting a credit card. I have no need for credit, but often, when I want to cash a check, salespeople will ask to see a credit card. I told this to a friend of mine and she advised me not to; if I lost the card someone could use it (although only up to $50 would be charged to me).

I have an idea. Why not put the person's picture on his or her credit card? This way, if a person lost his credit card, anyone who found it couldn't charge things to the owner's name (unless he was a good look-alike). This would cost more than issuing a plastic card. The company could simply charge the person a fee for the picture (rather than charge indirectly through service charges).

Gary De Jong
Pella, Ia.

COMMUNICATING

A Universal Language

In the article "Toward a Universal Language" (pp. 748–751, *The People's Almanac #1*), the writer points out the necessity of a universal language and the stumbling blocks which heretofore have stood in the way of success; namely, politics and provincialism that demanded that either the root words or the pronunciation be based on a particular language.

The solution with which the article inspired me is, simply, a hand sign language based not on words, but on concepts. No spelling or pronunciation or knowledge of anything but universal hand signs would be involved. Since most of the civilized world has the same physical needs and emotional responses, about the only subject matters that would be ruled out would be those of a scientific, technical, philosophical, or religious nature. Nor could conversations be conducted by phone. Certainly, the means of implementation are gargantuan. The hand language would have to be taught in the early grades of school all over the world (but that would hold true for any universal language). The benefits to mankind would be tremendous if we could all communicate with each other.

Ruth Shapiro
Houston, Tex.

The Alphabet Reformed

In the late 1700s, English spelling was very disorderly; the written language was decades behind the development of the spoken language. Children who were learning to read had to recognize what was almost an ancient dialect as far as spelling was concerned; what they read did not jibe with what they heard.

American author, inventor, and statesman Benjamin Franklin decided that speech should indicate spelling and attempted to reform the alphabet. He wanted to drop the following letters because he saw them as unnecessary and superfluous: C, J, Q, W, X, and Y. Franklin also designed some new characters and reassigned limited uses for standard ones. His alphabet, which was never completed, is as follows:

Names of Letters as expressed in the reformed Sounds and Characters.	Characters.	Sounded respectively, as in the words in the column below.
o	*o*	Old.
a	*a*	John, folly; awl, ball.
a	*a*	Man, can.
e	*e*	Men, lend, name, lane.
i	*i*	Did, sin, deed, seen.
u	*u*	Tool, fool, rule.
ɥ	*ɥ*	um, un; as in umbrage, unto, &c., and as in *er*.
huh	*h*	Hunter, happy, high.
gi	*g*	Give, gather.
ki	*k*	Keep, kick.
ish	*ſh*	(sh) Ship, wish.
ing	*ŋ*	(ng) ing, repeating, among.
en	*n*	End.
r	*r*	Art.
ti	*t*	Teeth.
di	*d*	Deed.
el	*l*	Ell, tell.
es	*s*	Essence.
ez	*z*	(ez) Wages.
eh	*h*	(th) Think.
eh	*h*	(dh) Thy.
ef	*f*	Effect.
ev	*v*	Ever.
b	*b*	Bees.
pi	*p*	Peep.
em	*m*	Ember.

Franklin wished to see the order of the letters of the alphabet patterned on phonetics. In arguing for an end to A-B-C, he proposed:

o to *huh*	It is endeavoured to give the alphabet a *more natural order;* beginning first with the simple sounds formed by the breath, with none or very little help of tongue, teeth, and lips, and produced chiefly in the windpipe.
g k	Then coming forward to those, formed by the roof of the tongue next to the windpipe.
r n *t d*	Then to those, formed more forward, by the fore part of the tongue against the roof of the mouth.
l *s z*	Then those, formed still more forward, in the mouth, by the tip of the tongue applied first to the roots of the upper teeth.
h *h*	Then to those, formed by the tip of the tongue applied to the ends or edges of the upper teeth.

f / *v* — Then to those, formed still more forward, by the under lip applied to the upper teeth.

b / *p* — Then to those, formed yet more forward, by the upper and under lip opening to let out the sounding breath.

m — And lastly, ending with the shutting up of the mouth, or closing the lips, while any vowel is sounding.

A Letter from Mary Stevenson to Benjamin Franklin in His New Alphabet

FROM MISS MARY STEVENSON TO B. FRANKLIN.

Kensiŋtyn, 26 *Septembyr*, 1768.

Diir Syr,

yi hav transkryib'd iur alfabet, &c., huitʃi yi ɧink myit bi av syrvis tu ɧoz, hu uiʃi to akuyir an akiuret pronynsieʃyn, if ɧat kuld bi fiks'd; byt yi si meni inkanviiniensis, az uel az difikyltis, ɧat uuld atend ɧi briŋiŋ iur letyrs and arɧagrafi intu kamyn ius. aal avr etimalodʒiiz uuld be last, kansikuentli ui kuld nat asyrteen ɧi miiniŋ av meni uyrds; ɧi distinkʃyn, tu, bituiin uyrds av difyrent miiniŋ and similar saund uuld bi iusles, ynles ui liviŋ ryiters pybliʃi nu iidiʃyns. In ʃiart yi biliiv ui myst let piipil spel an in ɧeer old ue, and (az ui fyind it iisiiest) du ɧi seem aurselves. With ease and with sincerity I can, in the old way, subscribe myself,

Dear Sir,

Your faithful and affectionate servant,

M. S.

—The Eds.

HEALTH AND FAMILY

Legalize Heroin

It may seem strange to suggest that a drug as evil as heroin be legalized, but please hear me out. If I had my way, no one would take heroin. But in reality, lots and lots of people use it and many of them become addicts. And these addicts need large amounts of money, every day, to support their habits. To get this money, many heroin addicts become thieves, preying on innocent people in order to afford the outrageous prices which pushers are able to charge since they are dealing in an illegal, underground substance which they sell to customers who have to have it.

If heroin were legal, the price would go way down, addicts wouldn't have to steal to support their habit, and the rest of us wouldn't be victimized. Who would lose if heroin were legal? Only the pushers and the crime syndicates. It makes you wonder why politicians have allowed the heroin trade to go on as long as they have. If heroin were legal, the police would have more time to deal with other crimes. I have heard that in New York City over 50% of the crime is committed by heroin addicts.

The victims of heroin addicts are both rich and poor. Last summer, three blocks from my suburban house, two darling teenagers were shot to death when they came home from school and surprised a burglar. That burglar turned out to be a heroin addict with a $300-a-day habit. Four days later my housekeeper came to work crying because her brother was in critical condition in the hospital, having been stabbed by an intruder. Fortunately he survived, but this intruder too was a heroin addict.

Perhaps it is true that legalized heroin would cause there to be more addicts, but those addicts would commit far less crimes than the addicts in the system we have now. When I told my friends about my idea to make heroin legal, one of them said that she had heard the idea before on the radio. And she said that some well-known lawyers and even judges supported it. If this is so, then why is heroin still illegal? Are the politicians afraid that if they support legal heroin, then people will think they are pro-drugs? Or is organized crime so strong that they can buy off the politicians or otherwise convince them not to act?

(Mrs.) Marsha Phillips
Silver Spring, Md.

A Safer Cigarette

A self-extinguishing cigarette could save 2,000 lives, prevent 4,000 injuries, and avoid $180 million in property losses which occur each year in the U.S. as a result of 70,000 smoking-related fires. Four bills have been introduced in Congress during the past five years which would require cigarettes to be self-extinguishing. The Tobacco Institute, which represents the American cigarette industry, can't seem to make up its mind on the issue. In 1980 spokeswoman Ann Browder said these bills were "based on untested and highly questionable assumptions that such a cigarette can even be produced." At approximately the same time, Sen. Alan Cranston (D-Calif.), who sponsored one of the bills, was told by representatives of the institute and the Philip Morris Company that "manufacturing self-extinguishing cigarettes would be a relatively easy thing to start doing." The problem, according to another institute spokesman, Walker Merryman, is that the output of tar, nicotine, and carbon monoxide is boosted in this type of cigarette, and in

Charles Cohn and his self-extinguishing cigarette.

saving "an insignificant number" of lives, the industry "would be increasing the number of people who could contract lung and heart disease." None of the institute's spokespersons has mentioned that a business whose profits are tied into billions of "idling" cigarettes stands to lose money marketing one that will last longer because it won't burn continuously for up to 45 min.

Enter 78-year-old Charles Cohn, a New Jersey inventor who has patented a cigarette that puts itself out in two to three minutes, releases 25% less tar and nicotine with each drag than ordinary cigarettes, is smokeless between draws, and has fewer ashes to fall on clothing and furniture. In addition, Cohn's cigarette delivers extra puffs and satisfies even the most discriminating smoker. Nonsmokers will be happy to hear that this amazing cigarette produces 65% less of the harmful side-stream smoke that is the primary component of the traditional smoke-filled room.

Cohn paints the paper of his "safe" cigarettes with three strips of a compound he calls Colite, commonly known as water glass (sodium silicate). Chemically inert Colite is "clear, nontoxic, noncarcinogenic, nonirritating, nonallergenic, tasteless, odorless, and inexpensive," costing only 3/100 of a cent to coat a pack. When a treated cigarette is lit, the Colite melts and forms a cage which insulates the ash and makes the tobacco burn cooler and slower.

Charles Cohn started inventing when he was fresh out of high school and has received 34 patents, most of them in the field of metallurgy. Twenty years of research devoted to making cigarettes less dangerous began "when my son went to private school and took up the habit. Neither my wife nor I smoke, but he was smoking like a chimney. I said to myself, 'My goodness, here's a boy who might be doing himself harm.' " After designing a better filter, Cohn began considering the safety angle. None of his patents, including the seven related to cigarettes, has made him a millionaire, and he and his wife Rose continue to live in the Atlantic City row house that has been their home since 1952. Cohn can't understand why the cigarette industry isn't interested in his self-extinguishing model, which has been tested and praised by several government agencies, including the National Bureau of Standards and the U.S. Dept. of Health, Education, and Welfare. When he approached the six major companies with his concept, "they said they have their own research departments to do things like this." Undaunted, the self-made scientist went back to his drawing board. His latest idea? The childproof match.

—L.Sc.

Alcohol and Vitamin B_1

I sit by the woman's bed.

"Mrs. Miller, where are you?"

Cold sober, she looks at me, then at my white coat, at the monitors, at the nurse passing by.

"I'm in a hotel."

"No, Mrs. Miller, you're in a hospital. How long have you been here?"

"Two hours."

She has been in the hospital for three weeks, ever since her family brought her to the emergency room in an alcoholic stupor. Though she has drunk no alcohol since checking in, she remains confused and cannot remember from minute to minute what is happening.

Five minutes later, I ask again, "Where are you, Mrs. Miller?"

She hesitates, puzzled. "I think I'm in a hotel."

Mrs. Miller (not her real name) has Wernicke-Korsakoff syndrome. When she is discharged, she will spend the rest of her life in a nursing home. She is 42 years old.

Wernicke-Korsakoff syndrome is partial destruction of the brain caused by a lack of thiamine (vitamin B_1). It usually occurs in severe alcoholics who do not eat even minimally nutritious food. Even among alcoholics the disease is rare—but devastating. There is no treatment; the victims frequently die.

Yet this disease can easily be prevented—simply by adding thiamine to all liquor, wine, and beer.

Almost 40 years ago there was a call to supplement alcoholic beverages with vitamins because of the frequency of vitamin-deficiency diseases in alcoholics. But the proposal was killed by a curious Catch-22: By law, all food additives must be listed on the label. And by law nothing can be printed on the labels of alcoholic beverages which implies that drinking alcohol is healthy. Thus vitamins, which are good for you, cannot be listed as ingredients—and therefore cannot be added.

This antiquated ruling should be modified to exempt the listing of vitamins. Indeed, appropriate additions of thiamine to alcohol should be federally mandated since alcohol is controlled by the U.S. Bureau of Alcohol, Tobacco, and Firearms.

Since the public pays for the care of many alcoholics suffering from Wernicke-Korsakoff syndrome and other ailments, adding thiamine to alcohol—once the technical problems of doing so are resolved—would save millions of dollars. For every dollar's worth of thiamine added to alcoholic beverages, the public would save about $7 in nursing home costs—not a bad return in this era of cost-consciousness.

Public interest in the proposal has grown, yet the alcoholic beverage industry has remained cool to the idea of a thiamine additive. The Distilled Spirits Council of the U.S. takes the position that preventing Wernicke-Korsakoff syndrome would give "false encouragement" to alcoholics—a curious statement from an industry that spends millions each year to encourage drinking.

Cynics accuse the industry of avoiding responsibility for alcoholism; adding thiamine to their product would constitute implicit admission that alcoholics drink it. To avoid such an implication, the industry apparently prefers to avoid adding thiamine. More charitably, the industry may be hesitant to promote vitamins in alcohol because doing so would violate the present laws governing additives.

Even so, the alcoholic beverage industry should take an active interest in the health of alcoholics. In Sweden, Dr. Leonard Goldberg has demonstrated that although alcoholics make up only 5% of the adult population, they consume fully half of all alcoholic beverages sold there. Many suspect that the industry sustains alcoholism, but few realize that the reverse is also true—alcoholism sustains the industry.

Doubtless some, unimpressed by the economic arguments, will ask, "Why bother to protect alcoholics from a rare disease?" In 1915 pellagra—a destroyer of thousands of lives—was traced to a dietary deficiency of niacin. For 25 years (during which 10,000 pellagra victims died) this discovery was ignored because the disease occurred mainly among the poor: Jewish and Italian immigrants, blacks, and "white trash." Today most states mandate niacin fortification of cereals and bread.

Alcoholics are a group with little influence who are victimized by a specific vitamin deficiency. Indifference to their needs is no excuse for not preventing Wernicke-Korsakoff syndrome.

But even if the syndrome were eradicated, alcoholism would remain a menace to American life—vast, destructive, and lethal. Can we prevent alcoholism itself? By a pill or vaccination, no. But we can help to prevent it by education and by alleviating the stresses that lead to alcoholism.

Why is alcohol heavily taxed? Presumably because our society considers it a social evil that should be discouraged. Each year the federal government collects $5.5 billion in alcohol taxes—paid, of course, by the public. Each year it disburses about $140 million for alcoholism treatment and prevention programs—less than 3% of what it takes in. Clearly the federal government is more interested in alcohol as a source of revenue than as a cause of disease, poverty, and death.

Alcoholism costs the U.S. $44 billion each year in lost income. If taxes on alcohol are to be justified, they should be used to defray the damage drinking does. Programs for the prevention of alcoholism should have primary claim on alcohol-tax dollars.

An extravagant proposal? Perhaps, but alcoholism, even apart from Wernicke-Korsakoff syndrome, is an extravagantly costly disease. Just ask Mrs. Miller's family.

Brandon Centerwall
N. Hollywood, Calif.

NEW CALENDARS

The Liberty Calendar

A calendar is simply a system of reckoning time. There have been many different forms and several are still in use. The form we are using is most favored, yet both scientists and studious business persons have for many years claimed that it is exceedingly cumbersome and very poorly adapted to the needs of this strenuous age. This is because there is so little regularity in its construction. The months are of uneven length; not one of them contains any given number of complete weeks, and one of them has an additional day tacked on each fourth year. The calendar is an outgrowth, or evolution, of forms which previously were in use. One more evolution of the right sort will make it entirely satisfactory.

Many people suppose the months are regulated by changes of the moon, or by movements of some of the planets, but this is a mistake. The use of lunar months was discontinued even before our present calendar came into use. Neither the number nor the length of the months is governed by any of nature's laws; hence, there is no good reason why they cannot be changed as the welfare of society may require.

Various plans for an improvement of the calendar have been suggested; but on January 1, 1917, Joseph U. Barnes of Minneapolis, Minn., evolved a plan which is conceded to be by far the best yet proposed. Under this plan, our present complicated and inconvenient arrangement can easily be made so simple and convenient that printed calendars would soon be unknown. Only three simple changes are required. They are as follows:

First, make New Year's Day an independent legal holiday. Have it fall between the last day of December and the first day of January. Do *not* include it in any week or month.

Second, provide another independent legal holiday for Leap Year. Have it fall between the last day of one month and the first day of the next. Do *not* include it in any week or month.

Third, divide the remaining 364 days into 13 months of exactly four weeks each, making Monday the first day of every month and Saturday the last workday of every month. The days of the week would then be permanently fixed as follows:

The 1st, 8th, 15th, and 22nd days of every month would always be on Monday.

The 2nd, 9th, 16th, and 23rd days of every month would always be on Tuesday.

The 3rd, 10th, 17th, and 24th days of every month would always be on Wednesday.

The 4th, 11th, 18th, and 25th days of every month would always be on Thursday.

The 5th, 12th, 19th, and 26th days of every month would always be on Friday.

The 6th, 13th, 20th, and 27th days of every month would always be on Saturday.

The 7th, 14th, 21st, and 28th days of every month would always be on Sunday.

While making the change, Good Friday and Easter Sunday should be placed on certain fixed dates. According to history, the placing of these on fixed dates was seriously considered at the time that our present calendar was adopted. This change would secure a much-desired regularity and would be especially appreciated by members of the mercantile trade.

This simplified calendar could be adopted by Congress to take effect on Sunday, the first day of next year, and the change would cause scarcely a ripple in our business or social life. Six months' experience under this simplified form would make us wonder why we put up with the inconvenience of our present form so long.

The name chosen for the new month is Liberty. Barnes had, early in 1917, chosen the word *Gregory*, but the stirring events of 1917 and 1918 made the word *Liberty* so prominent that, when the president of a Minneapolis bank suggested it as a name for the new month, the suggestion was immediately adopted.

The new month is placed immediately after February, so in the new plan the months read: January, February, Liberty, March, etc. The independent legal holiday provided for Leap Year will be called Correction Day.

The advantages of this simplified calendar cannot be overestimated. The savings of time and mental effort in making calculations for the future would be beyond all comprehension. These advantages would arise from the fact that all the months in the entire year would be just alike. Every month would have exactly four weeks and every month would commence with Monday and end with Sunday. All holidays and anniversaries would always fall on the same day of the week. Every day in all the months would receive an absolutely fixed place in the four weeks. Our present exasperating system of four and a fraction weeks to the month would be done away with, and there would be no more five Sundays in a month to upset all our calculations.

People are called upon every day of the year to set dates for future occurrences. Dates for meetings, payments, commencement of employment, quitting employment, occupancy or vacancy of property, legislation, etc., would be consistent. This simplified calendar would enable anyone to tell at once on what day of the week any future day of the month would fall.

Under this equal-month calendar, exactly the same length of time would elapse between all regular paydays, which is not now the case when paydays are monthly or semimonthly. This would very greatly simplify terms of employment and be a great convenience to both employers and employees.

As another simple illustration of the inconvenience of our present calendar, it might be stated that millions of people in this country alone ask every year on what day of the week Christmas will fall. Under this new form of calendar, everyone would know that as Christmas comes on the 25th day of the month, it would always fall on Thursday. The same question asked with reference to any future holiday, or any anniversary, or any date whatsoever, could be as easily answered.

The positive convenience of the proposed new calendar may be tested in every conceivable way, and there need be no fear that the arrangement will not stand the test. All the fundamentals of the present calendar are retained, even to the extent that Correction Day is omitted from the last year of any number of centuries not evenly divisible by the number 400. This is necessary because the calendar is unavoidably 34 seconds per annum out of exact correspondence with the sun.

Probably the only objection of consequence to a division of the year into 13 months would be the fact that the year could not then be as easily divided into quarters. However, little business is done on the basis of quarters, and if one should want to divide the year into quarters, he would know that each quarter would contain exactly 13 weeks, or 3¼ months, and that each quarter would begin on Monday and end on Sunday. The superstition that 13 is an unlucky number is too silly to be considered.

As the new form provides that Monday shall be the first day of every month, it naturally follows that it should also become the first day of every week. There should be no serious objection to this change, and there is a certain fitness in the Sunday of rest following the six days of toil. Again, this change would in a way be a return to the original Sabbath as it stood before the change to the first day of the week.

Regarding the new month of Liberty—the use of this name will, of course, seem strange for a time, but we will soon become accustomed to it, and we will surely indulge in a feeling of joy and proprietorship throughout the month because of what the word *liberty* means to the world.

On November 25th of each year, Thanksgiving will occur. It will be on Thursday as usual, but we will have the satisfaction of knowing that hereafter it will always come on November 25th, as the last Thursday in every month will be the 25th.

On December 25th, Christmas day will come—also on Thursday. The last day of the year will be Sunday, December 28th, and we will have passed through the whole year without any friction and with scarcely any inconvenience whatsoever. Of course, we will have noticed that a few people have been somewhat annoyed because, in their particular cases, the anniversary of their birthdays has always come after the 28th of the month, and they had to change to the 28th or set their birthdays forward a day or two, the same as a few people have always had to do whose birthdays were on February 29th.

The day following Sunday, December 28th, will be New Year's Day. It will be the first day of the New Year, but it will not be Monday, nor will it be January 1st. Again, we will remember to date our letters "New Year's Day." The day following New Year's Day will be Monday and that will be January 1st. We will then start over again and live exactly the same routine as in the year before.

Under the new equal-month calendar, it seems absolutely certain that we shall agree that the new form has given splendid satisfaction. It will surely be a wonderful relief to feel that through every year thereafter, and for all time to come, the same positive regularity will continue, and that henceforth we will be able to make calculations for future dates without any reference whatever to printed calendars, which will already have gone entirely out of use.

SOURCE: Joseph U. Barnes, *The Liberty Calendar and the First Year under the New Calendar*, Minneapolis, Minn., 1918.

The Barlow Calendar

Down through the ages man has tried to make adjustments to the solar calendar invented by the Egyptians in 4236 B.C. Such historical heavyweights as Moses, Julius Caesar, and Pope Gregory XIII all made some minor changes, but the calendar we use today is virtually identical to the one used by the pharaohs 23 centuries ago.

To some, this would suggest that the calendar started by the Egyptians must have been a good one to have lasted so long effectively intact. To others, such as Wallace Barlow, an engineer in Washington, D.C., the fact that the calendar is still being used is more a testament to man's fear of change. Mr. Barlow believes the calendar should be changed, or updated, if you will. And if he has his way, the U.S. Congress will adopt the Barlow Calendar as our official way of keeping track of the days.

At first glance, the Barlow Calendar does not appear radically different from the one we use today. There are still 12 months, and each retains its order and name. What makes the Barlow Calendar different is the way it assigns the days and holidays to those months. Each month, according to Mr. Barlow, should have 28 days, or exactly four weeks, and should begin on a Monday and end on a Sunday. Of course, if you could split up 365 days as evenly as that, the Egyptians would have figured it out long ago.

What remains is 29 days. All of these remaining days would be national holidays, or festival days, as Barlow refers to them. The festival days would begin at the end of each month and would not be called Monday or Friday, but rather the first day of festival, the second day of festival, and so on. Some months would have only one festival day

The Barlow Calendar

following them, but since the month ends on a Sunday, the least you could expect each month would be a three-day (weekend) festival. Others, such as May, would be followed by a seven-day festival on leap year and a six-day festival normally. In addition, with the Barlow Calendar, everyone would have a week off for Christmas.

Christmas, however, would fall on December 30, which points up one of the problems Barlow has been having selling his calendar idea to Congress. There was a minor uproar from some corners when Congress adopted the Monday holiday system and took some important dates in history and arbitrarily set observance of those dates at the nearest Monday. Changing Christmas from December 25th or moving the observance of the 4th of July to the three festival days following July might be more than the legislators can stand, despite Barlow's argument that the 62-century-old calendar should be reformed to meet the recreational and working needs of 20th-century men and women.

John Parker
Beltsville, Md.

SOURCE: Calendar page 697, Calendar Reform Foundation, 6210 Massachusetts Ave., Washington, D.C. 20016.

MISCELLANEOUS

No More Report Cards

I am 17 years old and a senior in high school and I propose that tests and report cards be eliminated. I know. You've heard it before. But I think I've got some new reasons. First of all, let me make it clear that I have benefited from the tests-and-report-cards game. I learned early (from my older brother) that the purpose of school is not to acquire knowledge, but to get good grades. And you can get good grades by using certain tricks—special ways to take tests and to play up to the teachers. I have a very high grade average and I get to go to the college of my choice. Teachers love me. They look right at me when they lecture and they give me A's. I feel sorry for some of the other students: the slow learners, the poor test-takers, the intimidated. As soon as they get an F or a D or even a C on a test, most teachers forget about them, preferring to concentrate on those of us who will "go far."

How stupid! The other students deserve just as much attention as I do, maybe more. But the teachers are too busy giving tests, weeding us out, creating hierarchies so that employers will know whom to hire. Which brings me to my point: schools exist not to provide education, but to pre-sort prospective employees for the business "community." You out there! You taxpayers! You are giving corporations a free ride by providing services that they should be paying for. Let the corporations do the testing and training. If there were no tests and no report cards, school would be more relaxed, more people would receive a good education, and our society would be better for it.

I would also like to add that I, personally, have spent over 1,000 hours taking tests and I haven't even graduated from high school yet. Instead of classes and schools having "exit" exams, universities and businesses should have "entrance" exams. Have I made myself clear? Have I learned to communicate my thoughts? It doesn't really matter because I've gotten straight A's in my English classes.

"4.0 Freddie"
Kettering, O.

Coping with Bureaucracy

We need better tools for coping with bureaucracy. Bureaucracies cause everyone trouble; and there is good reason to believe that they always will, no matter how well they are operated or how they are staffed. This is because bureaucracies are *group*-oriented. A ticket clerk needs to sell all auditorium tickets as quickly as possible. You, standing in the back of the line, want only one ticket, and you want it now; you are *individual*-oriented. These goals may be closely related, but they are not identical. Therefore, there is inevitable conflict. Many consumer-conscious bureaucracies are trying to reduce these problems by changing their antiquated methods. For instance, many banks have eliminated the old system of one line for each teller (which puts some people in very slow lines) and have replaced it with the new single-feeder line, which allows the head of the line to take the first available teller. We, as consumers, can also take some steps to reduce bureaucratic headaches.

1. The first words you speak to a bureaucrat, whether to a clerk or to a president, should be brief and to the point. Don't burden your listener with a long story. Let them do the talking and questioning while you direct the conversation to your problem.

2. Make a phone call first. Is the organization open? Are they the right group to speak to? Whom should you see? What should you bring with you? How long are the lines? A phone call may make your trip unnecessary.

3. Use a basic checklist for all bureaucratic encounters. Make a note (mental or otherwise) of the name of the person to whom you are talking, the job title, what he or she said, when, and where and why it was said. A record will remind you of exactly what you have done and help you verify your claims later.

4. Know exactly what you want. Bureaucrats are confused enough as it is. Don't expect them to find out what your problem is *and* solve it. Do some research. Rehearse to yourself so that your request will be clear and to the point.

5. Get out of the runaround quickly. Finding the right person in a bureaucracy means *knowledgeable persistence*. Don't be pushed along to another person until you have found out all you can about finding a solution to your problem. Be sure that the person you are speaking to knows if the next person can really help you. If persistence isn't working, consult your list and go back to the most knowledgeable person you have run across. Explain that you aren't getting the help you need. When it is clear that you are not going away, someone will usually try to solve your problem just to get rid of you.

6. Motivate the bureaucrat. When you have found the person you need, have a good explanation regarding why you need assistance. Demonstrate that you aren't just a troublemaker and that you have a real problem. Doc Ricketts, in John Steinbeck's novel *Cannery Row*, wanted a beer milk-shake but knew he couldn't just ask for one without being

considered a lunatic. So he told the waitress that he was under a doctor's orders to drink one every day. She served it to him and inquired kindly about his health.

7. When buying products or services, set limits. Specify *in advance* exactly when the service will be done, how much it will cost, and how it will be paid for. If you are suspicious, set an absolute time limit when all work must be completed (or cease at no cost to you). You can also agree to pay half of the total cost on completion of the job and half in 60 days. You may have to go to another individual who will provide your product or service, but you won't get burned.

8. Don't ask for special favors, if at all possible. Bureaucracies are set up to do a *few* things for *many* people. If you want egg in your beer, or sequins on your pajamas, you are going to have a lot of trouble. Personal experience has taught me that you can get special favors if you are persistent and clever, but it is seldom worth the effort.

9. Keep your cool. Demanding to see the manager or writing a nasty letter to the company president may get the revenge you want. However, that probably won't solve your problem any quicker than a clerk with whom you have been firm, clear, and persistent.

Usually, the worst communication breakdowns occur when a highly specialized front-line bureaucrat meets an unprepared customer. Bureaucrats are not necessarily vicious, but they are always single-minded and orderly. I once saw a man applying for automobile registration. "What was the date of purchase?" asked the clerk. "I don't know," replied the man. "I can't issue you the registration unless I know the date of purchase," the clerk explained. "I don't know," the man replied. They repeated this routine five or six times. Finally the clerk leaned forward and whispered, "Guess." The man did and got his registration. Bureaucracies exist to serve you, but you have to do things their way.

Thomas Gray
Monterey, Calif.

INVITATION TO THE READER

We hope that you have found *The People's Almanac #3* to be of interest and value, and we hope that your minds and emotions have been stimulated. But now, if we have our wish, it is your turn to stimulate us to help make the fourth edition of *The People's Almanac* better and even more comprehensive than the first, second, and third.

If there is any subject you missed that you would like to read about in the next *Almanac*, tell us what it is and we will try to include it. If you or your friends have written something that you think belongs in a future *Almanac*, please send us a copy. Our address is:

The People's Almanac
P.O. Box 49699
Los Angeles, Calif. 90049

We will pay for anything we publish. If you want your material returned, or a reply to your letter, please include a stamped, self-addressed envelope with your letter and be patient. We do read every letter that comes our way.

Further, if you have a specialty, an observation, an experience, or an unusual or inside bit of knowledge, please let us know about it. If you have books to recommend, recipes or household hints to share, utopias to discuss, or general knowledge to pass on, please write us about it—and through us let people everywhere be informed and entertained.

As to the present *Almanac,* if there is anything in it that confused you, please ask us to explain. We shall be happy to do so. If you have found any misinformation or discovered any major omissions, please let us know. We will eagerly correct the errors or fill in what is missing in editions to follow. Too, we will be interested to know what you liked most in *The People's Almanac #3,* as well as what you disliked most.

Above all, we visualize this as a participatory *Almanac,* one in which people will involve themselves by collaborating to make it the perfect reference book to be read for pleasure. We hope the pages in editions to come will reflect your interests as well as our own. It is only through airing and sharing ideas that new solutions can be found to deal with the many problems of modern society. So let us know what you have learned up to this point in your lives, and together we can try to transform our dreams into reality.

David Wallechinsky
Irving Wallace

INDEX

S

PHOTO CREDITS

Aerofilms, Elstree, England, p. 152; Anchor Press/Doubleday, p. 636; American Museum of Natural History, p. 359 (L); Archives de la Indias, p. 378; ASCAP, p. 622; A.T.M. Communications, Inc., p. 565; Avon Books, p. 607; Bantam Books, p. 518; Bild-Archiv ver Osterreichischen Nationalbibliothek, Wien, p. 543; Black Star, p. 283, 524; The Leigh B. Block Collection, Chicago, p. 620; The Bodley Head Ltd., p. 601; Bunch Books, London, p. 4; Cassell Australia Ltd., p. 294; CBS Television, p. 410; Chalermnit, Bangkok, p. 536; Flora Chavez, p. 190; David & Charles Ltd., p. 51; Delacorte Press, p. 385; Duell, Sloan and Pearce, p. 402; Elicson Photography, p. 265; Reproduced by gracious permission of Her Majesty Queen Elizabeth II, p. 272; Foreign Language Press, Peking, p. 669 (2); Werner Forman, p. 591; Fuji Seihan Printing Co. Ltd., p. 223; Gryphon Books, p. 586; Copyright James Hansen, 1979, p. 315; Harper & Row, p. 7 (B); Paul Hatfield Collection, Pearblossom, p. 645; The Robert F. Heizer Estate, p. 300; Houghton Mifflin Co., p. 362 (R); Bruce Humphries, Inc., p. 143; International Flat Earth Research Society, p. 560; Jeanette MacDonald/Nelson Eddy Fan Club, p. 566; Raymond Juschkus, Courtesy Chase Manhattan Bank, p. 92; Gary Keever, *Merced Sun Star*, p. 521; Alfred A. Knopf, p. 466 (2); Kyodo News Enterprise, p. 324; Land's End Press, p. 491; *Life* Magazine, p. 166; Little, Brown & Co., p. 379; Louvre, Paris, p. 443; Michael Lyster, Zoological Society of London, p. 356; Richard Marek Publishers, Inc., p. 408; William Morrow & Co., p. 329; National Archives, p. 268; National Gallery of Canada, Ottawa, The Canadian War Memorials Collection, p. 398; Courtesy of the National Trust, Bakman's Burwash England, p. 458; Jawaharlal Nehru Memorial Fund, p. 278; Courtesy of the New York Public Library Picture Collection, p. 291; Oresko Books Ltd., London, p. 450; Paddington Press Ltd., pp. 145, 498; Peebles Press International, Inc., p. 63; People's Almanac Photographic Archives, pp. 26, 101, 110, 363, 389, 428, 432, 445, 461, 472, 480; Perskor Publishers, p. 242; *Philadelphia Inquirer*, p. 690; Phoebus Publishing Co., p. 648; Clarkson N. Potter, Inc., p. 13; Prentice-Hall, Inc., p. 657; Richard Pritchett, New Hampshire, p. 675; Courtesy of the Rockefeller Archives, p. 70; Jimmy and Fay Rodolfos, p. 173; Royal Library of Copenhagen, p. 381; Royal Library, Windsor, p. 447; John Seelye, p. 724; Charles Scribner Sons, p. 7(T); The Karen Silkwood Fund, p. 16 (2); Hans Silvester, The Viking Press, p. 184; Smithsonian Institution, p. 24; South American Explorers Club, p. 406; Sovfoto, pp. 45, 59; Superlatives, Inc., p. 424; Sussex at the University Press, p. 80; TAT/Tandem Productions, p. 414; *Time* Magazine, p. 137 (L); 20th Century-Fox Film Corp., pp. 347, 356; UPI, pp. 40, 41, 122, 125, 158, 311, 338, 341 (2), 611; The Viking Press, p. 371; Votava, p. 53; A. Watkins, Inc., p. 508; Wide World Photos, pp. 137 (R), 334; Yad Vashem Archives, Jerusalem, p. 629

Vol. II.] THE [No. II.

PEOPLE'S ALMANAC

Containing Five Sets of Calculations, **1840** embracing the whole U. States and the Canadas

Of Useful and Entertaining Knowledge.

BOSTON--PRINTED AND PUBLISHED BY S. N. DICKINSON, AND FOR SALE BY THE TRADE.

"Value-packed, accurate, and comprehensive . . ."
—*Los Angeles Times*

"Unbeatable . . ."
—*The Washington Post*

LET'S GO:
EUROPE

is the best book for anyone traveling on a budget. Here's why:

No other guidebook has as many budget listings.

In Barcelona we found dozens of hotels for less than $12 a night. In Florence we found 19 under $15. In the countryside we found hundreds more. We tell you how to get there the cheapest way, whether by bus, plane, or thumb, and where to get an inexpensive and satisfying meal once you've arrived. There are hundreds of money-saving tips for everyone plus lots of information on student discounts.

LET'S GO researchers have to make it on their own.

Our Harvard-Radcliffe researchers travel on budgets as tight as your own—no expense accounts, no free hotel rooms.

LET'S GO is completely revised every year.

We don't just update the prices, we go back to the places. If a charming restaurant has become an overpriced tourist trap, we'll replace the listing with a new and better one.

No other budget guidebook includes all this:

Coverage of both the cities and the countryside; directions, addresses, phone numbers, and hours to get you there and back; in-depth information on culture, history, and the people; listings on transportation between and within regions and cities; tips on work, study, sights, nightlife, and special splurges; city and regional maps; and much, much more.

LET'S GO is for anyone who wants to see Europe on a budget.

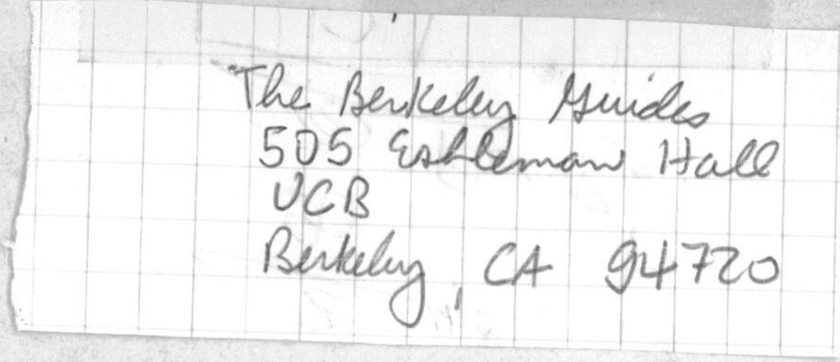

Books by Harvard Student Agencies, Inc.

Let's Go: London
Let's Go: New York City
Let's Go: Washington, D.C.

Let's Go: Europe
Let's Go: Britain & Ireland
Let's Go: France
Let's Go: Germany, Austria & Switzerland
Let's Go: Greece & Turkey
Let's Go: Italy
Let's Go: Spain & Portugal
Let's Go: Israel & Egypt

Let's Go: USA
Let's Go: California & Hawaii
Let's Go: The Pacific Northwest, Western Canada & Alaska
Let's Go: Mexico

LET'S GO:

The Budget Guide to

EUROPE

1992

Ian Watson
Editor

Christopher Capozzola
Laura Kay Rosen
Assistant Editors

Written by Harvard Student Agencies, Inc.

ST. MARTIN'S PRESS
New York

Helping Let's Go

If you have suggestions or corrections, or just want to share your discoveries, drop us a line. We read every piece of correspondence, whether a 10-page letter, a tacky Elvis postcard, or, as in one case, a collage. All suggestions are passed along to our researcher/writers. Please note that mail received after May 5, 1992 will probably be too late for the 1993 book, but will be retained for the following edition. **Address mail to: *Let's Go: Europe;* Harvard Student Agencies, Inc.; Thayer Hall-B; Harvard University; Cambridge, MA 02138; USA.**

In addition to the invaluable travel advice our readers share with us, many are kind enough to offer their services as researchers or editors. Unfortunately, the charter of Harvard Student Agencies, Inc. enables us to employ only currently enrolled Harvard students.

Distributed outside the U.S. and Canada by Pan Books Ltd.

ISBN: 0-312-06391-1

First Edition
10 9 8 7 6 5 4 3 2 1

Let's Go: Europe is written by Harvard Student Agencies, Inc., Harvard University, Thayer Hall-B, Cambridge, Mass. 02138.

Editor	Ian Watson
Assistant Editors	Christopher Capozzola
	Laura Kay Rozen
Managing Editor	Jamie Rosen
Publishing Director	Zanley F. Galton III
Production Manager	Christopher Williams Cowell
Office Coordinator	Hilary Holmquest
Researcher/Writers	
Iceland, Norway, Murmansk, Southern Sweden	Erik Bækkeskov
USSR	Jeremy Bransten
Central Germany, Eastern Germany, Northern Germany	Amy Sarah Davidson
Northern Italy, Southern Italy, Tuscany and Umbria	Andria L. Derstine
Northern Italy, Tuscany and Umbria	Carla Deykin
Castile	Simon Doubleday
Brittany, Loire Valley, Périgord-Quercy	Calysta Drake
Eastern Germany	Edward Drew Dutton
Baden-Württemberg, Bavaria	LeeAnn Einert
Brittany, Paris	Hannah Feldman
Northern Italy	Nara T. Garber
Malta, Sicily	Scott C. E. Gelormino
Estonia, Finland, Latvia, Lithuania, Northern Germany, Sweden	Matthew Gordon
Balearic Islands, Catalonia, Mediterranean Coast	José A. Guerra
Faroe Islands, Scotland	Seth S. Harkness
Burgundy, Corsica, French Alps	Sarah-Anne Henning
London, southern England	Maura A. Henry
Andorra, Southwestern France	Douglas J. Herbert
London	Nick Hoffman
Berlin	Daniel Horch
Northern France, Rome, Sardinia, Southern Italy	Katherine Insalata
Belgium, French Switzerland, Luxembourg, Netherlands	Mary Louise Kelly
Bulgaria, Romania, Yugoslavia	Steven J. Kolias
Portugal	Matthew A. Light

Austria, Bavaria	Virginia W. Lunsford
Alsace and Lorraine, Brittany, Champagne, Channel Islands, Normandy, northern France	Adrienne M. MacMillan
French Riviera, Provence	Brian Martin
Liechtenstein, Switzerland	Heidi Meinz
Andalusia	Alec Milam
Poland, Slovakia	Nina Nowak
Catalonia, Northern Spain	Edward Owen
Glasgow, Ireland, Northern England, Northern Ireland	Courtney T. Pyle
Albania, Hungary, Transylvania	Charles Reiss
Baden-Württemberg, Central Germany	Geoffrey Rodkey
Adriatic Ports	Gil Rosenthal
Bohemia, Moravia	Laura Kay Rozen
Denmark, Northern England	Zachary M. Schrag
Galicia, León	Kenneth A. Smith
Wales, West Country	Abigail N. Sosland
London	Jonathan Taylor
Ireland	Woden Teachout
Hannover and Braunschweig	Brian R. Trelstad

Sales Group Manager	Michael L. Campbell
Sales Group Representatives	Julie Barclay Cotler
	Robert J. Hutter
President	Robert Frost
C.E.O.	Michele Ponti

ACKNOWLEDGMENTS

To all forty-two researchers who are the soul of this book. Jeremy Bransten is a Russian and Soviet Studies concentrator from Geneva, Switzerland and Norwood, Massachusetts. Erik Bækkeskov is a half-Icelandic Social Studies concentrator from Copenhagen, Denmark. Matt Gordon is a Linguistics concentrator from Arlington, Massachusetts. Seth Harkness is a Social Studies concentrator from Suncook, New Hampshire. Steve Kolias is an Economics concentrator from Vestal, New York. Nina Nowak is an English concentrator from Springfield, Massachusetts. Charles Reiss is a graduate student in Indo-European linguistics from New York City. Laura Rozen, from Shawnee Mission, Kansas, is now a graduate student in the comparative literature department at the University of Iowa. Zach Schrag, from Washington D.C., plans to study Mongolian history next semester. Each regional-book researcher is equally deserving of a bonus.

To the rest of the office staff for endless consultation and help: Jamie Rosen and Zan Galton; Lorraine Chao; Michael Armstrong Roche, Steve Blyth, Boris Dolgonos, Jessica Goldberg, John Larew, Marlies Morsink; Hilary Holmquest; Joe Hayashi and Chris Cowell; Pete Deemer, Andrew Kaplan, and Laurent Ruseckas; Atissa Banuazizi, July Belber, Steve Burt, Lev Grossman, Tara Kelly, Dennis King, Mark Templeton, and Steve Voss.

To previous staff who shared enthusiasm and experience, including Jessica Avery, Charlotte Chiu, Ravi Desai, Steve Glick, Lara Goitein, Anne Gowen, Linda Haverty, Karen Kim, Mike Krivan, Brian Palmer, Matt Steinglass, Bruce Stevenson, John Thompson, and Darcy Tromanhauser.

Invaluable logistic assistance came from Edwin Aoki, Andrej Benedejčič, Connie Christo, Maria Conte, Breda Gros, Stephanie Horton, Pat Hoy, Daiva Izbickis, Andrzej Klonecki and Marek Kordylewski, Kathy Kutrubes, Bill Mackie, Bill Poist, Peeter Rebane, Kamenna Rindova, Juta Ritsoo, Joshua Rubinstein, Vita Terauds, Egils and Rasma Veverbrants, og Stefán Wathne.

Chris thanks David Javerbaum, Michael Grunwald, Melissa Hart, the folks at *Let's Go* and his denim shirt. He spent last year hitchhiking in Africa (hint, hint).

Laura thanks the Québecers, especially John; Miranda Spieler; Danae Wright, Daniel Trantham, Wendy Feng, Rachel Vile, Marian St. Onge, and Kevin Young, who let her write about all the coffee houses she could find.

Ian thanks Carl Carlson, Edna Deutsch, Sigríður Dúna Kristmundsdóttir, and Simon Williams. He'd rather be hitchhiking, anywhere in northern Europe.

We all thank our families (including Ian's cat Whiskers, Laura's cat Tom, and all nine of Chris's siblings).

CONTENTS

0
400 miles
0
400 kilometers
Reykjavik
ICELAND
Norwegian Sea
Faroe Islands
ATLANTIC OCEAN
Shetland Islands
NORWAY
Orkney Islands
Oslo
Stock
SCOTLAND
North Sea
Glasgow
Edinburgh
Belfast
IRELAND
DENMARK
Dublin
UNITED KINGDOM
Copenh
WALES
Hamburg
Cardiff
NETHERLANDS
Amsterdam
Berlin
London
N
Brussels
GERMANY
BELGIUM
Bonn
LUXEMBOURG
Pra
Rennes
Paris
CZECH
LIECHTENSTEIN
Munich
Vienna
Bay of Biscay
SWITZERLAND
Bern
AUSTRIA
Lyon
Bordeaux
Milan
Venice
Zagreb
FRANCE
Marseilles
Florence
Nice
Adriatic Sea
PORTUGAL
ANDORRA
MONACO
Madrid
SAN MARINO
Corsica (Fr.)
Lisbon
Barcelona
Rome
SPAIN
Valencia
ITALY
Naples
Malaga
Balearic Islands (Sp.)
Sardinia (It.)
Tyrrhenian Sea
GIBRALTAR
Mediterranean
Sicily
Rabat
Tunis
MOROCCO
MALTA
TUNISIA
ALGERIA

Murmansk
Gulf of Bothnia
FINLAND
RUSSIA
L. Onega
L. Ladoga
Helsinki
St. Petersburg
Tallinn
ESTONIA
Volga R.
Nizhnii
Novgorod
(Gor'ky)
Riga
Moscow
LATVIA
LITHUANIA
Vilnius
SOVIET UNION
(U.S.S.R.)
Minsk
KAZAKHSTAN
BYELORUSSIA
Volgograd
Kiev
Khar'kov
Kraków
Dnieper River
L'viv
UKRAINE
Caspian
Sea
MOLDAVIA
Sea of
Azov
Budapest
Odessa
ROMANIA
Yalta
GEORGIA
Bucharest
Black Sea
ARMENIA
BULGARIA
Sofia
Skopje
Istanbul
IRAN
Ankara
TURKEY
Aegean
Sea
Athens
IRAQ
SYRIA
GREECE
Sea of Crete
LEBANON
CYPRUS
Crete

LIST OF MAPS

About Let's Go

A generation ago, Harvard Student Agencies, a three-year-old nonprofit corporation dedicated to providing employment to students, was doing a booming business booking charter flights to Europe. One of the extras offered to passengers on these flights was a 20-page mimeographed pamphlet entitled *1960 European Guide,* a collection of tips on continental travel compiled by the HSA staff. The following year, students traveling to Europe researched the first full-fledged edition of *Let's Go: Europe,* a pocket-sized book with tips on budget accommodations, irreverent write-ups of sights, and a decidedly youthful slant.

Throughout the 60s, the series reflected its era: a section of the 1968 *Let's Go: Europe* was entitled "Street Singing in Europe on No Dollars a Day." During the 70s *Let's Go* gradually became a large-scale operation, adding regional European guides and expanding coverage into North Africa and Asia. Now in its 32nd year, *Let's Go* publishes 15 titles covering more than 40 countries. This year *Let's Go* proudly introduces two new guides: *Let's Go: Germany, Austria & Switzerland* and *Let's Go: Washington, D.C.*

Each spring 80 Harvard-Radcliffe students are hired as researcher-writers for the summer months. They train intensively during April and May for their summer tour of duty. Each researcher-writer then hits the road on a shoestring budget for seven weeks, researching six days per week, and overcoming countless obstacles in a glorious quest for better bargains.

Back in a basement deep below Harvard Yard, an editorial staff of 30, a management team of six, and countless typists and proofreaders—all students—spend four months poring over more than 70,000 pages of manuscript as they push the copy through a rigorous editing process. High tech has recently landed in the dungeon: some of the guides are now typeset in-house using sleek black desktop workstations.

And even before the books hit the stands, next year's editions are well underway.

A Note to our Readers

The information for this book is gathered by Harvard Student Agencies' researchers during the late spring and summer months. Each listing is derived from the assigned researcher's opinion based upon his or her visit at a particular time. The opinions are expressed in a candid and forthright manner. Other travelers might disagree. Those traveling at a different time may have different experiences since prices, dates, hours, and conditions are always subject to change. You are urged to check beforehand to avoid inconvenience and surprises. Travel always involves a certain degree of risk, especially in low-cost areas. When traveling, especially on a budget, you should always take particular care to ensure your safety.

LET'S GO: EUROPE

General Introduction

Let's Go is a helpful companion that introduces the budget traveler to every country in Europe. Our researchers travel on a shoestring budget, so their concerns are the same as yours: how to travel, eat, drink in the sights, enjoy evenings, and sleep in the most economical way possible. We list the best of the least expensive accommodations and restaurants in each town. We suggest ways to cut costs at every corner and corners from every cost.

Let's Go: Europe is organized by country; this year in particular, it's been hard to decide what's a country and what isn't. Estonia, Latvia, and Lithuania are listed separately; Slovenia is not, though it may be independent by the time you read this. Russia and Ukraine are still part of a USSR section. As the eastern countries reembrace their national identities, the nations of western Europe are poised to transcend their own and form the European Community (EC). And one by one, the Alpine and Nordic members of the European Free Trade Association (EFTA) are coming in from the cold and signing on with the EC. Yet these events are likely to have much less effect on the budget traveler than the upheaval in the east, which in 1991 had cracked open Albania and the Baltic states, flooded Prague and Budapest with English- and German-speaking tourists, and made chaos of the main train route from Western Europe through Yugoslavia to Greece, Turkey and the Middle East.

Each country section begins with an introduction that tries to capture the flavor of its cities and the texture of the countryside. Brief guides to transportation, accommodations, and food follow. City sections follow the same layout, starting with an introduction to the city and an orientation to its geography. Practical Information listings supply just that, to prepare you not only for the poetry but also for the prose of your destination. With your purse in mind, a ranked list of accommodations follows, succeeded by a similar list of restaurants. Finally, each city section concludes with a write-up of sights, festivals, and nightlife, and a description of possible daytrips in the countryside nearby.

Let's Go also guides you through the maze of tasks that need to be performed before you go. This General Introduction gives details about applying for passports, visas, and student IDs; what to pack; how to secure an inexpensive flight; and procedures for sending mail and money overseas. We help you decide what kind of trip to take and whether to invest in a railpass or hostel card. Read the General Introduction as carefully as you can, since the information in it won't be repeated every time it is applicable. The same is true for each country introduction.

For more in-depth coverage, look through our seven regional guides: *Let's Go: Britain & Ireland, Let's Go: France, Let's Go: Spain and Portugal, Let's Go: Italy, Let's Go: Greece and Turkey, Let's Go: Germany, Austria, and Switzerland,* and *Let's Go: London.* But use our guides as a starting point for your own explorations; the best discoveries may be those you make yourself. If *Let's Go* is indeed the Bible of the budget traveler, healthy skepticism may serve you better than blind faith.

A Note on Prices and Currency

Remember that the exchange rates and prices listed here were compiled in the summer of 1991, when our researcher/writers were in the field. Inflation and currency fluctuations will skew them. Since we revise every year, though, our prices should be closer to reality than those from any other source. More importantly, comparisons will still be valid. Check the financial pages of a large newspaper for current exchange rates.

Planning Your Trip

It's difficult to predict—especially the future.
—*Lenin*

Europe's a big place. Fortunately, there are big industries devoted to helping travelers tackle it. The organizations listed below and the national tourist offices at the end of this chapter will send you a mound of literature which is perhaps equally daunting. Dive in and plan a trip tailored to your specific interests. The urge to see and do *everything*—blitzing Rome in two days, or Scandinavia in a week—is perhaps encouraged by the scope of this book. Curb it. A madcap schedule will only detract from your enjoyment.

Give careful consideration to those with whom you travel. It is amazing how rapidly organized becomes bossy, relaxed becomes slothful, and fun becomes downright annoying when traveling. Friends can also insulate you from local culture. On the other hand, they share in food and lodging costs, provide extra safety in numbers, and are an invaluable source of energy and comfort. If you choose to travel with others, discuss your trip in detail before you leave to make sure your general interests are compatible.

Going solo can be the best way to travel and the worst. Freedom of movement is counterbalanced by the danger of loneliness. However, the budget travel subculture that this book is a part of fills all Europe's hostels, and ensures that you will be only as lonely as you want to be. Other travelers you meet along the way will seem your best friends after a day or two of travel together.

In the late summer, tourists flock into European cities and natives leave; prices go up, vacant accommodations are more difficult to find, and hot, angry crowds detract from the ambiance. On the other hand, during the off-season, museum hours may be abbreviated and some hostels closed. June is perhaps the best of both worlds.

Useful Travel Organizations

The following student- and youth-oriented travel organizations provide so many services that we will refer to them over and over throughout the General Introduction. Many of the same services (including railpasses, ISIC and IYHF cards, and budget flights) are also available through **Let's Go Travel,** Harvard Student Agencies, Thayer Hall-B, Harvard University, Cambridge, MA 02138 (tel. (617) 495-9649 or (800) 553-8746), run by the same students who write these books.

Council on International Educational Exchange (CIEE), 205 E. 42nd St., New York, NY 10017 (tel. (212) 661-1414). Information on academic, work, voluntary service, and professional opportunities abroad. Administers ISIC, FIYTO, and ITIC cards. Write for their free *Student Travel Catalog* and their pamphlet *Work Abroad.* Also available are *Work, Study, Travel Abroad: The Whole World Handbook* (USD12.95); *The Teenager's Guide to Study, Travel and Adventures Abroad* (USD11.95); *Volunteer! The Comprehensive Guide to Voluntary Service in the U.S. and Abroad* (USD8.95); *Summer Jobs in Britain* (USD13.95); and *Emplois d'Eté en France* (USD13.95). Postage USD1 per book. **Council Travel,** a subsidiary of CIEE, operates 34 offices throughout the U.S., Europe and Asia, selling railpasses, guidebooks, IYHF cards, student identification, and (best deals for students and those under 26) budget airfares. Offices include 205 E. 42nd St., New York, NY 10017 (tel. (212) 661-1450); 28A Portland St., London W1V 3DB; 729 Boylston St., #201, Boston, MA 02116 (tel. (617) 266-1926); 1093 Broxton Ave., #220, Los Angeles, CA 90024 (tel. (213) 208-3551); 1153 N. Dearborn St., Chicago, IL 60610 (tel. (312) 951-0585); 919 Irving St., #102, San Francisco, CA 94122 (tel. (415) 566-6222); and 2000 Guadalupe St., Austin, TX 78705 (tel. (512) 472-4931). **Council Charter** (tel. (800) 800-8222), another CIEE division, sells charter flights, which can also be purchased through Council Travel offices.

STA Travel, 222 Faraday St., Melbourne, Victoria 3053, Australia (tel. (03) 347 69 11); 64 High St., Auckland, New Zealand (tel. (09) 39 04 58); 48 E. 11th St., New York, NY 10003 (tel. (800) 777-0112 or (212) 986-9470); 7202 Melrose Ave., Los Angeles, CA 90046 (tel. (213) 934-8722); 74 and 86 Old Brompton Rd., London SW7 3LQ, England (tel. (071) 937 9921 for European travel, (071) 937 9971 for North America, (071) 938 4362 for Israel, Egypt

& Turkey, and (071) 937 9962 for the rest of the world). Offers bargain flights, accommodations, tours, railpasses, insurance, and ISIC cards.

Travel CUTS (Canadian Universities Travel Service), 187 College St., Toronto, Ont. M5T 1P7 (tel. (416) 979-2406). Branches in Burnaby, Calgary, Edmonton, Halifax, Montréal, Ottawa, Québec, Saskatoon, Sudbury, Victoria, Waterloo, and Winnipeg. In England, 295A Regent St., London W1R 7YA (tel. (071) 255 1944). Discount transatlantic flights from Canadian cities; student rail tickets; ISIC, FIYTO, and hostel cards; information on working abroad for Canadian students.

Documents

Passports

You must have a valid passport to enter any European country and to reenter your own. Applying for a passport is complicated, and we don't have room for all the gory details. Make sure you get questions answered in advance—don't wait two hours in a passport office to be told you'll have to come back later because you weren't prepared. For instance, personal checks are not always accepted, and U.S. citizens applying in person and paying with cash must bring exact change. Apply in autumn or winter for fastest processing.

U.S. citizens may apply for a passport at any office of the U.S. Passport Agency or at selected federal and state courthouses and post offices. If you are over 18, have been issued a passport before, and own a passport which is not more than 12 years old and which was issued after your 16th birthday, you may renew it by mail (USD35). If you do not meet these conditions, you must apply in person and pay USD42 (USD27 if under 18). Parents must apply for children under age 13, and parental permission is required for those aged 13-17. Processing usually takes two weeks if you apply in person at the Passport Agency, and longer if you apply at a courthouse or post office. The Passport Agency will rush your application if you have proof of dire need (such as plane tickets with an early departure); you can pay for an express-mail return of the passport. For a 24-hour recording that gives complete information including agency locations and hours, call (202) 647-0518.

For yet more detailed information, write to the Passport Office at 1425 K St. NW, Washington, DC 20522-1705.

Canadian citizens may apply by mail for their passports to the Passport Office, Department of External Affairs, Ottawa 1, Ontario K1A 0G3. You may also apply in person at one of 21 regional offices. Expect a three- to five-day wait if applying in person, two weeks if applying by mail. The fee is CAD25. More information can be found in the free brochure *Bon Voyage, But . . . ;* write to the Passport Office for a copy. **British citizens** may pick up an application from main post office branches (except in Northern Ireland) or from six regional passport offices. Passports cost £15 and generally take about four weeks to process. **Australian citizens** must apply in person at the local post office or at a passport office (usually located in the provincial capital) and will pay AUD76 (AUD31 if under 18). Australians are also required to purchase a **departure tax stamp** (AUD20) at a post office or airport before leaving home. **New Zealanders** must visit or write to the Department of Internal Affairs in Wellington (or the local district office) for an application. Apply at one of the passport offices listed on the application. Passports cost NZD50.

Replacing a stolen or lost passport in a foreign country is a hassle. Notify the local police, and go to your nearest consulate or embassy as soon as possible; they'll bitch and moan, and make you pay lots of money and sign sworn documents, but will replace it within a day or two—*if* you can prove your identity and citizenship. Keep photocopies of your passport and important identification in multiple places (perhaps with a traveling companion). The U.S. Passport Office recommends that you carry a birth certificate (don't take the original; have another issued by the Bureau of Vital Statistics of your state or province) or an expired passport in a location apart from your other documents.

Visas

A visa is a stamp placed in your passport by a country's government, permitting you to visit for a specified purpose and period of time. Most Western European nations do not require visas of American, Canadian, British, Australian or New Zealand citizens staying for less than three months; the major exception is France, which requires a visa from Australians. Eastern European countries' visa requirements have been eroding steadily since 1989, but vary for citizens of different countries: Americans need no visa for Poland, Czechoslovakia, Hungary, Yugoslavia, and Bulgaria, but the only country where Australians don't need one is Yugoslavia. We list specific visa requirements and consulate addresses in the "Getting There" section of each Eastern European country introduction.

Most visas cost USD10-30, and allow you to spend about a month in the country, within six months to a year from the date of issue. Transit visas, valid for just enough time to get through a country on your way to somewhere else, are usually cheaper than a regular visa. Unless it costs a lot more, get a visa valid for as long as possible (else you'll have to go to the local police station to get an extension—bothersome, and not always possible at the last minute).

To get a visa by mail, apply to the embassies or consulates of your destination countries; you'll usually have to fill out a form they supply, and send it along with two to four photographs, the fee, and your passport (which they faithfully return). The process takes several weeks. Alternatively, most countries will issue a visa on the spot or within a few days if you visit a consulate in person (either in Europe or in your home country). In emergency situations and for a hefty fee, you can sometimes procure visas at the border, but don't count on it (especially coming by train). Agencies in capital cities will get your visas for you for a fee, an especially useful service if you need them quickly. Check the phone book; in the USA, try **Visa Center, Inc.,** 507 Fifth Ave., #904, New York, NY 10017 (tel. (212) 986-0924), or **World Visa and Document Services,** 1413 K St. N.W., Washington, DC (tel. (202) 289-6251), among many others.

Some visas are incompatible: for example, Greece won't let you in if you have a passport stamp from Northern Cyprus, Morocco turns away those with Israeli stamps, and South Africans have been denied entry to Scandinavia. Occasionally,

you may insist that these visa or entry stamps be placed on a removable page in your passport.

The U.S. Department of State publishes a helpful pamphlet for American citizens called *Foreign Visa Requirements.* Send a check for 50¢ per pamphlet to the Consumer Information Center, Department 459X, Pueblo, CO 81009 (tel. (719) 948-3334). Another helpful, regionally specific publication, **Tips for Travelers,** is available for USD1 from the Superintendent of Documents, U.S. Government Printing Office, Washington, D.C. 20402 (tel. (202) 783-3238).

Youth and Student Identification

International Student Identification Card (ISIC), the most widely accepted form of student identification. Entitles those of student age to over 8000 discounts on museum admissions, local transportation, theater tickets, and other services worldwide. When issued in the U.S., the card includes limited sickness and accident insurance. Apply in person or by mail through any of the places listed in Useful Travel Organizations above or in the Budget Travel listings for European cities, or contact the umbrella **International Student Travel Confederation (ISTC),** Gothersgade 30, 1123 Copenhagen K, Denmark (tel. +45 33 93 93 03) for a location nearer you.Applications must include: (1) current, dated proof of full-time student status (e.g., a letter on school stationery signed and sealed by the registrar or a photocopied transcript, grade report or bursar's receipt with your name printed); (2) a 1½-inch by 2-inch photo with your name printed on the back; (3) proof of age (12 or over); (4) proof of nationality; (5) name and address of beneficiary (for insurance purposes); (6) a certified check or money order for USD14. Cards are valid from September until December of the next year. The **International Teacher Identification Card (ITIC),** available through much the same channels as the ISIC, in theory gives similar discounts, but in practice is not yet well recognized.

International Youth Card, available to anyone under age 26. Provides discounts similar to those available to ISIC holders. Available from most of the same agencies (send proof of birthdate, a 1½-inch by 2-inch photograph, and USD10). Often referred to as the FIYTO card after its parent organization, the **Federation of International Youth Travel Organizations,** Islands Brygge 81, DK-2300 Copenhagen S, Denmark (tel. +45 31 54 60 80).

Money

If you stay in hostels and prepare your own food, expect to spend anywhere from USD12-40 per day, depending on the local cost of living and on how much you eat. Transportation will increase these figures. Spend and enjoy; saving all your money for two years to live like a beast is no fun.

Many Western European countries charge 10-20% **sales tax** (VAT); most of these will refund the tax on large purchases (say, over USD100) that are being taken out of the country, if you present your receipts (and sometimes a special form) at the border. Check with a national tourist office for the correct procedure.

European **tipping** customs vary, but are rarely as generous as North American ones. In Scandinavia it's rare to tip at all; as you move east and south it becomes more and more common to add 5-10% to the bill or simply round it up. In Eastern Europe this will often be done for you.

American Express offices across Europe perform all sorts of useful financial services: they'll cash cardholders' personal checks, sell and replace traveler's checks, hold mail for cardholders and checkholders, send and receive wired money, and exchange cash and traveler's checks. When we list the name of a travel agency in boldface in an American Express listing, this indicates an American Express representative, which may not offer as many services as a full-fledged office.

Currency and Exchange

Banks usually offer the best exchange rates, though they also generally charge a commission per check or per transaction. To minimize your losses, convert fairly large sums (or large-denomination traveler's checks) at one time. American Express offices usually have no commission, but sometimes slightly poorer rates. Tote bills or checks in small denominations, especially for those moments when you are forced to exchange money at train stations or, worse yet, at luxury hotels or restaurants.

Banks in Europe often use a three-letter code based on the name of the country and the name of the currency (for example, New Zealand dollars are NZD and Norwegian kroner are NOK); we list this code at the beginning of each country section.

Avoid carrying Australian and New Zealand dollars; in some countries they're impossible to exchange. Keep some U.S. dollars or German marks handy when heading into the Eastern bloc; one crisp, clean George Washington can facilitate some sticky situations, and western currency is often the preferred payment in hotels.

Purchase no more of one currency than you'll need, since you lose money whenever you convert. Save transaction receipts; some countries will not let you reconvert local currency to your own without them. Exchanging your old currency *before* moving on to a new country is good insurance against arriving after hours in a bankless town. Coins become souvenirs when leaving a country; buy an ice cream at the station or drop them in an airport donation jar. Familiarize yourself with a country's currency before arriving; swindlers at train stations have been known to quote travelers a fictional exchange rate.

Traveler's Checks

Traveler's checks are the safest and most convenient way to carry money. They are accepted for exchange at banks throughout Europe and at some stores and restaurants. The major brands are eagerly sold by agencies and banks everywhere, usually for a 1-2% commission, or for a set fee.

American Express: (tel. (800) 221-7282 in U.S. and Canada (0800) 52 13 13 in the U.K.; (02) 886 19 21 in Australia; elsewhere call England collect at +44 (273) 57 16 00). Although all traveler's checks are basically the same, American Express offices cash their own checks commission-free (except in countries whose government requires otherwise), and offers additional conveniences, such as a multitude of European offices and a mail-holding service (see Keeping in Touch). Checks in 7 currencies, available commission-free to American Automobile Association members at AAA offices. Call and ask for their cute booklet, *Traveler's Companion,* which gives full addresses for all their travel offices, as well as stolen check hotlines for each European country.

Bank Of America: (tel. (800) 221-2426 from U.S., from Canada and elsewhere call Canada collect (415) 624-5400). Commission 1%. Checks only in USD.

Barclays Bank: (tel. (800) 221-2426 from U.S. and Canada, (071) 937 8091 in the U.K.; from elsewhere call New York collect (212) 406-4200). Many branches throughout Britain. Commission 1%. Checks in GBP, USD, and CAD.

Citicorp: (tel. (800) 645-6556 in U.S. and Canada; from elsewhere call U.S. collect (813) 623-1709). Commission 1%. Checks in USD, JPY, GBP, and DM.

Thomas Cook: (tel. (800) 223-7373 in U.S.; from elsewhere call New York collect (212) 974-5696). Services MasterCard traveler's cheques. Commission 1%; banks may charge an additional fee. Checks in 11 currencies.

Visa: (tel. (800) 227-6811 in US and Canada; (071) 937 8091 in London; call Canada collect (415) 574-7111 from elsewhere. Checks in 13 currencies. Commission depends on individual bank.

Each agency provides refunds for lost or stolen checks and many dole out additional services. Inquire about refund hotlines, message relaying, and emergency assistance when you purchase your checks. Unless you are only visiting one or two countries, buy traveler's checks in your own currency, since you will usually get fatter exchange rates abroad.

Refunds on lost or stolen checks are snail-paced. To accelerate the process, keep check receipts in a separate place. Record check numbers as you cash them to help sniff out exactly which checks are missing, and leave a xerox of check numbers with someone sensible at home. Most importantly, always stow some cash for emergencies when you can't exchange checks.

Credit Cards and Cash Cards

Credit and charge cards are becoming increasingly functional for the budget traveler. Major credit cards instantly extract cash advances from banks and teller machines throughout Western Europe, in local currency (and with hefty interest charges). Credit cards are invaluable in an emergency—an unexpected hospital bill or a ticket home—and constitute proof of funds to immigration officials afraid you'll become a pox on their nation. Try to pay for large purchases abroad by credit card; the credit card company gets a better exchange rate than you would have. Credit cards also offer an array of other services, from insurance to emergency assistance; these depend completely on the issuer. Some even cover car rental collision insurance. If a family member has a credit card, an additional card can be effortlessly issued in your name, with bills going to your loved ones. **American Express, MasterCard,** and **Visa** are the most welcomed cards in Europe. Keep in mind that MasterCard and Visa have aliases in Europe (Eurocard and Carte Bleue, respectively); some cashiers may not know this until they check their manual. Find out where your credit card is accepted (especially the location of teller machines) in the regions you visit before you get there, and remember your personal identification number (which must be no longer than four digits to work in European machines). VISA cash machines are everywhere; American Express's cash machines tend to stay near their offices.

Cash cards—popularly called ATM cards—are widespread within Europe, but their electronic impulses haven't made the transatlantic connection well. Major North American cash card networks such as Cirrus and Plus have big plans for expansion in Europe, but in summer 1991 few of them were realized. One intrepid *Let's Go* researcher had their card munched while testing a machine in France. Things should improve soon—fortunately so, since overseas cash-card withdrawals get the same good exchange rates as credit cards without the ruinous interest charges.

Sending Money Abroad

The easiest way to get money from home is to bring an **American Express card;** AmEx allows green-card holders to draw cash from their checking accounts (checkbook welcomed but not required) at any of its full-fledged offices and many of its

representatives' offices, up to USD1000 every 21 days (no service charge, no interest). With someone feeding money into your account back home, you'll be set. The next best approach is to wire money through the instant international money transfer services operated by **Western Union** (tel. (800) 225-5227) or **American Express** (tel. (800) 926-9400). The sender visits one of their offices or calls and charges it to a credit card; the receiver can pick up the cash at any overseas office within minutes (fee about USD25-35 to send USD250, USD70 for USD1000). American Express is slightly cheaper and serves more countries than Western Union. To pick up the money, you'll need either ID or the answer to a test question. The simplest and stodgiest route is to **cable money** from bank to bank. Find a local bank big enough to have an international department; bring the address of the receiving bank and the destination account number. Both sender and receiver must usually have accounts at the respective institutions. Transfer can take up to a few days; the fee is usually a flat USD20-30. Outside an American Express office, avoid trying to cash checks in foreign currencies; they usually take weeks and a USD30 fee to clear.

If you are an American and suddenly find yourself in big trouble, you can have money sent to you via the Department of State's **Citizens Emergency Center** (tel. (202) 647-5225). This service will get you cash fast but is considered an extreme imposition, so use it only in life or death situations. Citizens of other countries might check if their own government provides a similar service.

Health

The standard advice—eat well and get plenty of rest—is as true in Europe as it is at home, just more difficult to follow. The water in southern and eastern Europe is home to bacteria you may not have met yet; drink it cautiously, until you are sure you can handle it. In the northern parts of Eastern Europe in particular, bottled beverages are a better idea. Avoid eating under-cooked meat ("well-done" in France is "rare" to most Americans), and for God's sake don't subsist on bread and cheese for your whole trip. If you are traveling in hot weather or doing a lot of walking, swig plenty of liquid to avoid dehydration (bring a plastic water bottle with a no-leak top). Resist the temptation of madcap tourism . . . don't press for those extra 100km on your Eurailpass or that last obscure museum when you are too tired to enjoy yourself. Exhaustion can be as debilitating as illness.

Pack a small first aid kit: bandages, tweezers, aspirin, and antiseptic, a thermometer in a sturdy case, a Swiss Army knife (with as many gizmos as possible) and sunscreen. Some hardware stores sell ready-made kits. Ask your doctor for a general antibiotic to take with you on your trip in case you come down with something really awful. While Europe has much to offer, European bathrooms are not worth an extensive tour—bring something for diarrhea. You may want to pack remedies from motion sickness. Contraceptives are available in Europe, but purchase them at home where you have a greater knowledge of their reliability. Travelers to the Balkans and the USSR may want to consider a gamma globulin shot, which gives temporary protection against certain forms of hepatitis. Ask your doctor.

Women taking the pill and diabetics taking insulin should remember to take time zone changes into account and to make the necessary adjustments in their medication schedules. All travelers on medication should bring an ample supply since it may be difficult to match prescriptions. If you will be carrying insulin, syringes, or any narcotic drugs, get a statement or prescription from your doctor displaying the medication's trade name, manufacturer, chemical name, and dosage.

Any traveler with a medical condition that cannot be easily recognized (e.g. diabetes, allergies to antibiotics, heart conditions) should seriously consider obtaining a **Medic Alert Identification Tag.** In an emergency, this internationally recognized tag indicates the nature of the bearer's problem and provides the number of Medic Alert's 24-hr. hotline, through which attending medical personnel can obtain information about the member's medical history. Lifetime membership and the tag cost USD25; write to Medic Alert Foundation International, P.O. Box 1009, Turlock,

CA 95381-1009, or call (800) 432-5378. Diabetics may receive an ID card and reprinted documents by contacting their local American Diabetes Association office.

After years of unmonitored pollution, Eastern Europe is now home to some of the world's foulest air. Travelers with asthma or similar respiratory problems should beware the smog on muggy, cloudy days.

In the event of sudden illness or an accident, call the local emergency number, listed in country and city Practical Information sections. At least one pharmacy in many European cities stays open around the clock. Many first-aid centers and hospitals *Let's Go* lists in major cities can provide you with medical care from an English-speaking doctor (although getting sick in a foreign country can do wonders for one's language skills). A membership in the **International Association for Medical Assistance to Travelers (IAMAT)** entitles you to a worldwide directory of English-speaking physicians, plus an I.D. card, and immunization and infectious disease charts. There is no charge for membership, but IAMAT depends solely on voluntary contributions, and USD25 gets you an excellent set of climate charts. Contact IAMAT at 417 Center St., Lewiston, NY 14092 (tel. (716) 754-4883); 40 Regal Rd., Guelph, Ont. N1K 1B5 (tel. (519) 836-0102); or P.O. Box 5049, Christchurch 5, New Zealand.

Check at a bookstore for more information on health concerns: Dr. W. Robert Lange's *International Health Guide for Senior Citizen Travelers* (USD4.95) or Dr. Richard Dawood's *How to Stay Healthy Abroad*may be helpful. The USD5 booklet *Health Information for International Travelers* is available from the **Superintendent of Documents,** U.S. Government Printing Office, Washington, DC 20402-9325 (tel. (202) 783-3238); call (202) 647-5225 for more information on U.S. government travel publications.

Safety and Security

Common sense will serve you through better than twitching paranoia. Avoid looking like a tourist; the gawking camera-toter is much easier prey than the casual local look-alike. Stash your valuables in a money belt or neck pouch and make it your Siamese twin for the entire trip. Carry your bag on the side away from the street and dress modestly; expensive jewelry will, if it's not stolen, only attract unwanted attention, and insurance companies are not renowned for speedy replacements. Pickpockets come in all shapes and sizes and frequently lurk in front of stations and other heavily-touristed areas. Their fingers are fast, practiced, and professional. Watch for bands of benign-looking gypsy children, who use especially vulpine schemes to distract and rob luggage-laden tourists. Choose train compartments with care, especially at night, and bail out if you feel threatened. *Let's Go* lists locker availability in hostels and stations. Train station lockers are useful if you plan on sleeping outdoors or don't want to lug everything with you, but not for storing valuables; you'll often need your own padlock for hostel lockers. Never leave your belongings unattended; even the most demure-looking hostel may be a hive of thieves. Make photocopies of all important documents, your passport, IDs, credit cards, and the numbers of your traveler's checks. Keep one set of copies and receipts in a secure place in your luggage, separate from the originals, and leave another set at home. Although copies can seldom substitute for originals, you won't have to rely on memory if trying to reconstruct essential information. Finally, make sure you know where the fire exits are in your hostel and who to dial in an emergency.

Insurance

Insurance is like a contraceptive: you only *really* want it when it's too late. Avoid unnecessary coverage, though. Many travel insurance programs simply duplicate medical or household policies you may already have and then only reimburse what your existing policy won't, which in most cases amounts to very little. Most household policies cover damage, loss or theft of belongings when you're abroad and some even cover documents such as passports and rail tickets. Most medical insurance also pays for treatment worldwide (although Medicare covers you only in the U.S.). University term-time medical plans often thoughtfully include insurance for summer travel. Canadians are usually protected under their home province insurance plan; check with local officials. When purchased in the U.S., the International Student Identification Card (ISIC), Teacher's International Card or the Youth Identification Card (see Documents) provide insurance. CIEE also has a *Trip Safe Package,* which doubles card-holders' insurance and provides coverage for travelers ineligible for the cards.

The other perks bundled into travel insurance packages are often not worth the expense, or can be found elsewhere. Referral to physicians and lawyers (but not payment) can be obtained through a consulate. A major credit card will get you cash in a flash in case of theft. Buying travel insurance for the accidental death and dismemberment is paranoia gone wild.

Still, if you have less than perfect faith in your travel plans, trip cancellation or interruption insurance which protects you in case your airline or tour operator strands you at the final hour, may be useful. Check the yellow pages, newspapers and with your travel agent and major credit card companies. Expect to pay USD2-5 per USD100 coverage for cancellation and interruption insurance. Remember that claims can usually only be filed in your home country and must be accompanied by proper documentation; a copy of the police report in the case of theft or receipts and a doctor's statement in case of medical expenses.

Drugs

The penalties for illegal possession of drugs in Europe range from severe to horrific. Every year thousands of travelers are arrested for trafficking, possession, or for simply being in the company of a suspected user. Even reputedly lenient countries such as Denmark and the Netherlands take a dim view of drugged-out travelers. It is not uncommon for a pusher to increase profits by first selling drugs to tourists and then turning them into the authorities for a reward. In many countries police may legally stop and search anyone on the street. If you are arrested, you are entirely subject to local law; all your home country's consulate can do is visit you, provide a list of attorneys and inform family and friends. The London-based organization **Release** (tel. +44 (71) 377 5905 or 603 8654) advises people who have been arrested on drug charges, but is hardly a life raft. If you think extradition is the worst possible fate of a convicted traveler, try a foreign jail.

Make sure you get a statement and prescription from your doctor if you'll be carrying insulin, syringes, or any narcotic medications. Leave all medicines in original labelled containers. What is legal at home may not necessarily be legal abroad; check with the appropriate foreign consulate before leaving to avoid being innocently arrested. Politely refuse to carry even a nun's excess luggage onto a plane; you're more likely to wind up in jail for possession of drugs than in heaven for your goodwill.

Packing

Your backpack or suitcase may be light as a feather when you buy it or drag it out of storage, as buoyant as your enthusiasm all the way to the airport, but as soon as the airplane wheels bounce on European asphalt, it will become a ponderous, hot, itchy monster. Before you leave, pack your bag and take it for a walk. Try to convince it that you're in Europe already. At the slightest sign of heaviness, curb vanity and hedonism and unpack something. A good general rule is to set out what you think you'll need, then eliminate half of it and take more money.

If you plan to cover a lot of ground by foot, a sturdy **backpack** with several external compartments is hard to beat. Internal frames stand up to airline baggage handlers and can often be disguised as shoulder bags; external frames distribute weight more evenly and lift the pack off your back. Whichever style you choose to buy, avoid extremely low economy prices (good packs usually cost at least USD100). If checking a backpack on your flight, tape down loose straps which can catch in the conveyer belt and rip your bag apart. Take a light **suitcase** or a large **shoulder bag** if you will not be doing much walking. A plastic bag or lightweight duffel packed inside your luggage will be useful for dirty laundry, while a small **daypack** is also indispensable for plane flights, sightseeing, carrying a camera, and/or keeping some of your valuables with you.

Guard your money, passport, and other important articles in a **moneybelt** or **neck pouch** and keep it with you at *all times.* The best combination of convenience and invulnerability is the nylon, zippered pouch with belt that can sit either outside or inside the waist of your pants or skirt. Moneybelts are available at any good camping store or through Let's Go Travel.

Bare shoulders and shorts above the knee are forbidden in places of worship all over Europe, even when simply making a short visit. Women (and adventurous men) may wish to avoid the heat and hassle of tugging on jeans in church doors by packing a long, easily thrown on wrap-around skirt.

Comfortable shoes are essential. In sunny climates, sandals or other light shoes serve well. For heavy-duty hiking, sturdy lace-up walking boots are necessary. Make sure they have good ventilation. The new leather-reinforced nylon hiking boots are particularly good for hiking and for walking in general: they're lightweight, rugged, and dry quickly. The light hiking boots that look like souped-up sneakers are also good. A double pair of socks—light absorbent cotton inside and thick wool outside—will cushion feet, keep them dry, and help prevent blisters. Bring a pair of light flip-flops for protection against the foliage inhabiting the bottom of some station and hostel showers.

In such wet regions as the U.K., raingear is essential. Shoot for a system that will cover you *and* your pack at a moment's notice. A fold-up umbrella plus a waterproof Gore-Tex jacket plus a backpack rain cover does nicely; a rain poncho is more cumbersome but sometimes less bulky.

Also consider taking a pocketknife (with all the gizmos), tweezers, a flashlight, needle and thread, string, waterproof trick matches, a sturdy plastic water bottle, clothespins and clothesline, a pencil with some electrical tape wound around it for patching tears, a small notebook, a traveler's alarm clock, earplugs, rubber bands,

sturdy plastic containers (for soap and detergent, for example), zip-lock baggies, and a padlock. It is wise to carry extra toiletries such as aspirin, razor blades, and tampons in Eastern Europe or North Africa. The toilet paper in some areas of Europe is notoriously rough on tender Western bottoms—if this is yours, bring your own.

In most European countries, electricity is 220 volts AC, enough to fry any 110V North American appliance. Visit a hardware store for an adaptor (which changes the shape of the plug) and a converter (which changes the voltage). Travelers who heat-disinfect their contact lenses should consider switching temporarily to a chemical disinfection system. Check with the respective national tourist office for further details, or contact **Franzus,** Murtha Industrial Park, P.O. Box 142, Railroad Ave., Beacon Falls, CT 06403 (tel. (203) 723-6664) for their free pamphlet, *Foreign Electricity is No Deep Dark Secret.*

Alternatives to Tourism

Study

Foreign study beckons to the average student as a fail-proof good time. Be warned, though: programs vary tremendously in expense, academic quality, living conditions, degree of contact with local students, and exposure to the local culture and language. Most American undergraduates enroll in programs sponsored by domestic universities, and many colleges staff offices to give advice and information on study abroad. Take advantage of these counselors and put in some hours in their libraries. Ask for the names of recent participants in the programs, and impose on them.

If you have extensive language ability, consider enrolling directly in a European university. European universities are much cheaper that North American ones (which is why study-abroad programs are so popular, since American universities charge you more than they pay the European institution but less than you'd pay for a term in America). Contact the embassy of the country you're interested in; many have literature describing their national university systems.

American Field Service, International and Intercultural Programs, 313 E. 43rd St., New York, NY 10017 (tel. (800) 237-4636 or (212) 949-4242). High school exchange program. Half of participants receive financial aid.

American Institute for Foreign Study/American Council for International Studies, 102 Greenwich Ave., Greenwich, CT 06830 (tel. (800) 727-2437; Boston (617) 421-9575; San Francisco (800) 222-6379). Organizes study at European universities. Separate division for high school students. Summer programs last 3-12 weeks. Fees vary widely; government loans are recommended and a deferred payment plan for summer programs is offered.

Association of Commonwealth Universities, John Foster House, 36 Gordon Square, London, WC1H 0PF, Great Britain (tel. (071) 387-8572).

Central Bureau for Educational Visits and Exchanges, Seymour Mews House, Seymour Mews, London W1H 9PE, England (tel. (071) 486 5101). Publishes *Study Holidays* (£10.75, postage included) which gives basic information on over 600 language study programs in 25 European countries. Distributed in North America by IIE (see below).

Council on International Educational Exchange (CIEE), 205 E. 42nd St., New York, NY 10017 (tel. (212) 661-1414). Publishes *Work, Study, Travel Abroad: The Whole World Handbook* every two years (USD12.95 plus USD1 postage), describing over 1000 study programs during both the academic year and the summer and their application procedures. Also publishes *The Teenager's Guide to Study, Travel, and Adventure Abroad* (USD11.95 plus USD1 postage), describing over 200 programs primarily for high school students.

The Experiment in International Living (EIL), School for International Training, College Semester Abroad Admissions, Kipling Road, Box 676, Brattelboro, VT 05302 (tel. (800) 451-4465 or (802) 257-7751). Offers sophomores, juniors, and seniors 15-week programs. Often, U.S. colleges will transfer credit from SIT. Minimal financial aid from SIT, but some home institutions will provide aid. USD7300-11,500 inc. room and board.

Institute of International Education (IIE), 809 United Nations Plaza, New York, NY 10017-3580 (tel. (212) 883-8200). Offers a variety of resources on study abroad. Their free pamphlet, *Basic Facts on Foreign Study,* will help you get started. Annually publishes *Academic Year Abroad* (USD31.95, USD3.80 postage), describing over 1300 semester and year-long study programs. *Vacation Study Abroad* (USD26.95, USD3 postage) details over 1600 summer and short-term study programs offered by U.S. colleges and by foreign and private sponsors. Also publishes *Financial Resources for International Study* (USD36.95, postage USD5.75), available from Peterson's Guides, P.O. Box 2123, Princeton, NJ, 08543-2123 (tel. (800) 338-3282). Lists 630 foundations. Though some foundations offer assistance to undergrads, most are available to grad and post-grad study only.

Unipub Co., 4611-F Assembly Dr., Lanham, MD 20706-4391 (tel. (800) 274-4888). Distributes *International Agency Publications* including UNESCO's *Study Abroad* (USD18.50, postage USD2.50). International scholarships and courses for students of various ages. Unwieldy but excellent book.

Work

There is no better way to submerge yourself in a foreign culture than to become part of its economy. The good news is that it's very easy to find a temporary job in Europe; the bad news is that unless you have connections, it will rarely be glamorous and may not even pay for your plane ticket over.

Officially, you can hold a job in European countries only with a work permit, applied for by your prospective employer (or by you, with supporting papers from the employer). Many countries are tight-fisted with work permits, especially with thousands of Eastern Europeans pounding on their borders; often, an employer must demonstrate that a potential employee has skills locals lack. The real Catch-22 is that normally you must physically enter the country in order to have immigration officials validate your work permit papers and note your status in your passport. This means that if you can't set up a job from afar (which requires contacts and time) and have the work permit sent to you, you must enter the country to look for a job, find an employer and have them start the permit process, then *leave* the country until the permit is sent to you (up to six weeks), and finally reenter the country and start work.

In practice, it's rarely so complicated. Friends in Europe can help expedite work permits or arrange informal work-for-accommodations swaps at their uncle's grocery store or their cousin's farm. Many permitless agricultural workers go untroubled by local authorities, who recognize the need for seasonal manpower. European Community citizens can work in any other EC country without working papers, and if your parents or grandparents were born in an EC country (hear ye, Australians and New Zealanders), you may be able to claim dual citizenship or at least the right to a work permit. (Beware of countries where claiming citizenship obligates you to do military service.) Students can check with their universities' foreign language departments, which may have official or unofficial connections to job openings abroad.

If you are a full-time student at a U.S. or Canadian university, the cleanest, simplest way to get a job abroad is through work permit programs run by **CIEE** and its member organizations (see Useful Travel Organizations above for addresses). For a USD96 application fee, CIEE can procure three- to six-month work permits (and a handbook to help you find work and housing) for Britain, France, Germany, Ireland, and some non-European countries. You just hop on the plane, land, and start job-hunting. The French and German positions require evidence of language skills; the British program is the best for neophytes, since an entire work-abroad subculture absorbs thousands of summer participants into the job market in London, where a special CIEE office even helps with finding openings and making friends. Travel CUTS's Canadian program is similar, but does not include Germany.

The number of books listing work abroad opportunities has ballooned in the past couple years. Start with CIEE's free booklet *Work Abroad,* then graduate to the excellent publications put out by **Vacation Work,** 9 Park End St., Oxford OX1 1HJ, England (tel. (0865) 24 19 78), including *Directory of Summer Jobs Abroad* (£6.95);

Work Your Way Around the World (£7.95); *Working in Ski Resorts: Europe* (£5.95); and *The Au Pair and Nanny's Guide to Working Abroad* (£5.95). Postage costs £1 (£2 outside the U.K.). Many of these books are available in bookstores in the United States, through CIEE or Travel CUTS, or from **Peterson's Guides,** 202 Carnegie Center, P.O. Box 2123, Princeton, NJ 08543-2123 (tel. (800) EDU-DATA or (609) 243-9111). CIEE also publishes *Work, Study, Travel Abroad: The Whole World Handbook* (USD12.95 plus USD1 postage). Ask **InterExchange Program,** 356 W. 34th St.; 2nd floor, New York, NY 10001 (tel. (212) 947-9533) for their pamphlets describing international and *au pair* work. **World Trade Academy Press,** 50 East 42nd St. Suite 509, New York, NY 10017 (tel. (212) 697-4999) publishes *Looking for Employment in Foreign Countries* (USD16.50) which gives information on federal, commercial, and volunteer jobs abroad and advice on resumes and interviews. However, remember that many of the organizations listed in books like these have very few jobs available, and have very specific requirements (like a degree in forestry or fluency in Finnish).

The best tips on jobs for foreigners come from other travelers, so be alert and inquisitive in hostels and other youth hangouts. Hikers who merely asked to sleep in a barn have found work on dairy or sheep farms in Great Britain. Many travelers follow the grape harvest in the fall—mostly in France, but also in Switzerland and Germany's Mosel Valley. More or less menial jobs can be found anywhere in Europe; for instance, Swiss ski resorts leave much of the gruntwork to foreigners. Ask at pubs, cafés, restaurants, and hotels. Youth hostels frequently provide room and board to travelers willing to stay a while and help run the place. You can also earn room and board as an *au pair.* These baby-sitting and household jobs abound in Great Britain, France, and, to some extent, in Germany and Scandinavia. Look for newspaper ads and bulletin board notices.

In non-English-speaking countries, consider **teaching English.** Post a sign in markets or learning centers stating that you are a native speaker, and scan the classifieds of local newspapers, where residents often advertise for language instruction. Teaching English may be your only option in Eastern Europe; various organizations in the U.S. will place you in a (low-paying) teaching job in Czechoslovakia, but we aren't listing them because the market is approaching the saturation point. Professional English-teaching positions are harder to get; most European schools require at least a bachelor's degree and most often training in teaching English as a foreign language.

Volunteering

Volunteer jobs are readily available almost everywhere; in some countries, they're your only hope. You may receive room and board in exchange for your labor, and the work can be fascinating. Opportunities include kibbutz work, archaeological digs, and community and workcamp projects. The following organizations and publications can help you to explore the range of possibilities. Keep in mind that organizations which arrange placement sometimes charge high application fees, in addition to the workcamps' charges for room and board. You can avoid this extra fee by contacting the individual workcamps directly, though it's a hassle. Listings in Vacation Work's *International Directory of Voluntary Work* (£6.95; see ordering information under Work above) or UNESCO's *Workcamp Organizers* (contact CCIVS, 1, rue Miollis, 75015 Paris) can be helpful.

Archaeological Institute of America, 675 Commonwealth Ave., Boston, MA 02215 (tel. (617) 353-9361). Ask for their *Archaeological Fieldwork Opportunities Bulletin,* available in January. Lists field projects in the Middle East and throughout the world.

Council on International Educational Exchange (CIEE), 205 East 42nd St., New York, N.Y. 10017 (tel. (212) 661-1414). Arranges workcamps in Belgium, Bulgaria, Czechoslovakia, Denmark, France, Germany, Hungary, Morocco, the Netherlands, Poland, Portugal, Spain, Turkey, the USSR, Wales, Yugoslavia, and other non-European countries. Projects generally involve social work, construction or renovation, environmental conservation, archeology, or work with children, the disabled, and the elderly. Minimum age 18 (16 in Germany); language ability sometimes required. Call or write for materials.

Service Civil International/USA, Rte. 2, Box 506, Innisfree Village, Crozet, VA 22932 (tel. (804) 823-1826). Arranges placement in workcamps in Europe, U.S., USSR, Turkey, Greenland, Canada, Asia and Africa. You must be 16 to work in U.S. camps, 18 in European camps, and 20 to work in Asia or Africa. Registration fees for the placement service range from USD25-70.

Volunteers for Peace, 43 Tiffany Rd., Belmont, VT 05730 (tel. (802) 259-2759). Arranges placement in workcamps in 34 countries, primarily in Europe. Opportunities as diverse as reclaiming an abandoned island near Venice, repairing bicycles in Belgium for export to South African refugees, and excavating concentration camps in Germany. Gives perhaps the most complete and up-to-date listings in the annual *International Workcamp Directory* (USD10 postpaid). Registration fee USD90-100.

Additional Concerns

Women Travelers

Women traveling in Europe should exercise caution, particularly when traveling alone. In many areas of Europe there is a fine line between flirtation and harassment. Memorize the emergency numbers of the countries you visit, and keep change for the phone and cab money with you at all times. When waiting in stations and public places, stay in shouting range of police, and do not hesitate to ask them for assistance. Choose train compartments occupied by other women or couples. In general, ask your questions of women or couples—in some areas, asking a man for the time will get you a date instead. Walk confidently as if you know exactly where you are going, even if it means walking around the block twice. Wearing a wedding ring or walking arm in arm with another woman can discourage potential suitors. And, of course, the less you wear the more unwanted attention you will invite, particularly in southern Europe. Women traveling alone may wish to do the bulk of their travel in the north to minimize harassment, which is, though often not dangerous, exhausting. The *Handbook for Women Travelers* (£4.95), by Maggie and Gemma Ross, offers further tips for women travelers. Write to Judy Piatkus Publishers, 5 Windmill St., London W1, England (tel. (071) 631 0710).

Senior Travelers

Proof of senior citizen status is required for many of the discounts listed below, so be prepared to be carded.

American Association of Retired Persons (AARP), Special Services Dept., 1909 K St. NW, Washington, DC 20049 (tel. (800) 227-7737 or (202) 662-4850). U.S. residents over 50 and their spouses receive benefits which include travel programs and discounts for groups and individuals, as well as discounts on lodging, car and RV rental, air arrangements, and sightseeing. USD5 annual fee.

Elderhostel, 75 Federal St., 3rd floor, Boston, MA 02110 (tel. (617) 426-7788). You must be 60 or over, and may bring a spouse who is over 50. Programs at colleges and universities in over 40 countries focus on varied subjects and generally last 2-4 weeks.

Gateway Books, 13 Bedford Cove, San Rafael, CA 94901 (tel. (415) 454-5215). Publishes Gene and Adele Malott's *Get Up and Go: A Guide for the Mature Traveler* (USD10.95). Offers recommendations of places to go and general hints for the budget-conscious senior.

National Council of Senior Citizens, 1331 F St. NW, Washington, DC 20004 (tel. (202) 347-8800). For USD12 a year or USD150 for a lifetime an individual or couple of any age can receive hotel and auto rental discounts, a senior citizen newspaper, use of a discount travel agency, and supplemental Medicare insurance (the insurance is only for those over 65).

Pilot Books, 103 Cooper St., Babylon, NY 11702 (tel. (516) 422-2255). Publishes *The International Health Guide for Senior Citizens* (USD4.95) and *The Senior Citizens' Guide to Budget Travel in Europe* (USD4.95).

Travelers With Children

Lonely Planet Publications, 112 Linden St., Oakland, CA 94607 (tel. (415) 893-8555); also P.O. Box 617, Hawthorn, Victoria 3122, Australia. Publishes Maureen Wheeler's *Travel with Children* (USD10.95, postage USD1.50 in the U.S.).

Disabled Travelers

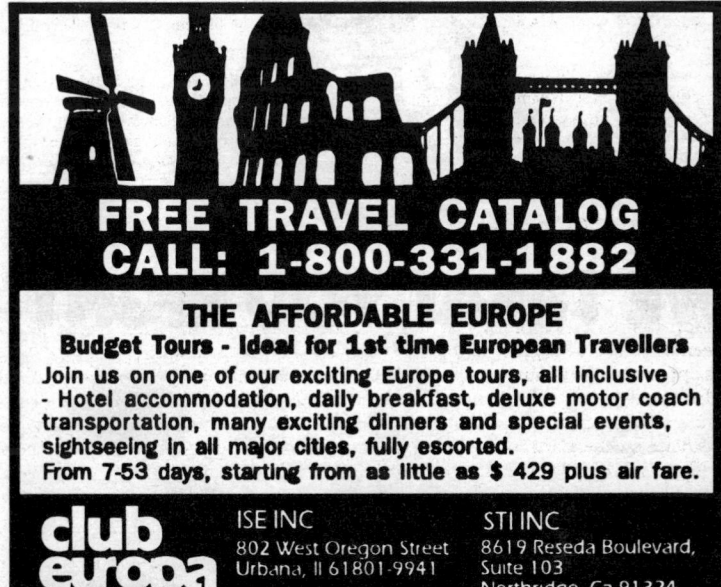

European countries vary in their general accessibility to disabled travelers. The British, Dutch, French, and Italian national tourist boards provide directories on the accessibility of various accommodations and transportation services. In other nations, contact the various institutions directly rather than relying upon travel agents. The amount of information about travel for the disabled is small, so if you are disabled, please send us information about your traveling experiences.

Rail is probably the most convenient form of travel. British Rail offers a discount card, conveys guide dogs free of charge, and (if you let them know in advance) will assure a comfortable spot for a wheelchair. The French national railroad offers a guide to stations equipped for wheelchairs; all TGV (high speed) trains accommodate wheelchairs, and guide dogs travel free. Other trains have a special compartment and an escalator for boarding. Contact your destination's station in advance. In Italy, the law requires that wheelchairs be transported free. However, the chair will be packed away with your luggage.

Most countries require a six-month quarantine for all animals, including guide dogs. To obtain an import license, owners must supply current certification of the animal's rabies, distemper, and contagious hepatitis inoculations and a veterinarian's letter attesting to its health.

American Foundation for the Blind, 15 W. 16th St., New York, NY 10011 (tel. (800) 232-5463 or (212) 620-2147). ID cards (USD6) and information on discounts; write for an application.

Directions Unlimited, 720 North Bedford Rd., Bedford Hills, NY 10507 (tel. 800) 533-5343; in Westchester Country (914) 241-1700). Specializes in arranging individual and group vacations, tours, and cruises for the disabled.

Disability Press, Ltd., Applemarket House, 17 Union St., Kingston-upon-Thames, Surrey KT1 1RP, England (tel. (081) 549 6399). Publishes the *Disabled Traveler's International Phrasebook,* including French, German, Italian, Spanish, Portuguese, Swedish, and Dutch phrases (£1.75). Supplements also available in Norwegian, Hungarian, and Serbo-Croatian (60p each).

Evergreen Travel Service, 4114 198th St. SW, Suite #13, Lynnwood, WA 98036-6742 (tel. (800) 435-2288 or (206) 776-1184). Its "Wings on Wheels" tours provide charter buses worldwide with wheelchair accessible facilities. Other services include tours for the blind, deaf, and "lazy bones" tours for those not wanting a fast-paced tour.

Flying Wheels Travel, 143 West Bridge St., P.O. Box 382, Owantonna, MN 55060 (tel. (800) 535-6790). Arranges domestic and international trips for groups and individuals.

The Guided Tour, 555 Ashbourne Road, Elkins Park, PA 19117 (tel. (215) 782-1370). Year-round travel programs for physically handicapped and learning-disabled adults.

Mobility International, USA (MIUSA), P.O. Box 3551, Eugene, OR 97403 (tel. (503) 343-1284). Membership costs USD20 per year, newsletter USD10. Sells updated and expanded *A World of Options: A Guide to International Educational Exchange, Community Service, and Travel for Persons with Disabilities* (USD14 for members, USD16 for non-members, postpaid). Special exchanges to the USSR, China, and Mexico.

Pauline Hephaistos Survey Projects Group, 39 Bradley Gardens, West Ealing, London W13 8HE, England (tel. (071) 997 70 55). Distributes access guides to London, Israel, Paris, and Jersey (£4 each).

Royal Association for Disability and Rehabilitation (RADAR), 25 Mortimer St., London W1N 8AB, England (tel. (071) 637 5400). Information on travel in Britain; publishes *Holidays for Disabled People* (£6, postpaid).

Society for the Advancement of Travel for the Handicapped, 347 Fifth Ave., Suite 610, New York, N.Y. 10016 (tel. (212) 447-7284). Publishes quarterly travel newsletter *SATH News* and information booklets (free for members, USD2 for non-members). Advice on trip planning for the disabled. Annual membership is USD40; students and seniors USD25.

Travel Information Service, Moss Rehabilitation Hospital, 1200 W. Tabor Rd., Philadelphia, PA 19141 (tel. (215) 329-5715). Send USD5 for their brochures on tourist sights, accommodations, transportation and travel accessibility services mailed for nominal fee.

Twin Peaks Press, P.O. Box 129, Vancouver, WA 98666 (tel. (206) 694-2462). *Travel for the Disabled* lists tips and resources for disabled travelers (USD14.95). Also available are the *Directory for Travel Agencies for the Disabled* (USD19.95) and *Wheelchair Vagabond* (USD9.95). Postage USD2 for first book, USD1 for each additional.

Gay and Lesbian Travelers

Are You Two Together?, published by Random House, available at bookstores (USD18). A new gay and lesbian guide to spots in Europe.

Ferrari Publications, P.O. Box 37887, Phoenix, AZ 85069 (tel. (602) 863-2408). Publishes *Places of Interest* (USD12.50), *Places for Men* (USD12.50), *Places of Interest to Women* (USD10), and *Inn Places: USA and Worldwide Gay Accommodations* (USD14.95). Also available from Giovanni's Room (see below).

Gaia's Guide, 9-11 Kensington High St., London W8, England. Annually revised "international guide for traveling women" lists lesbian and gay information numbers, publications, cultural centers and resources, hotels, and meeting places (USD11.95). Also available from Giovanni's Room (see below) and from **Open Leaves,** 71 Cardigan St., Carlton, Victoria 3053, Australia.

Gay's the Word, 66 Marchmont St., London WCIN 1AB, England (tel. (071) 278 7654). Tube: Russel Square. open Mon.-Sat. 11am-7pm, Sun. and holidays 2-6pm. Information for gay and lesbian travelers. Noticeboard and coffee area. Mail order service available.

Giovanni's Room, 345 S. 12th St., Philadelphia, PA 19107 (tel. (800) 222-6996; in PA (215) 923-2960). International feminist, lesbian, and gay bookstore with mail-order service.

Spartacus International Gay Guide, (USD27.95). Order from 100 East Biddle St., Baltimore, MD 21202 (tel. (301) 727-5677) or c/o Bruno Lützowstraße, PO Box 30 13 45, D-1000, Berlin 30, Germany; also available from Giovanni's Room (see above) and from Renaissance House, P.O. Box 292 Village Station, New York, NY 10014 (tel. (212) 674-0120). Extensive list of gay bars, restaurants, hotels, bookstores, and hotlines throughout the world. Very specifically for men.

Kosher, Vegetarian, and Diabetic Travelers

National tourist offices often publish lists of kosher and vegetarian restaurants.

Jewish Chronicle Publications, London EC4A 1JT, England. Publishes the *Jewish Travel Guide.* Available in the U.S. from Sepher-Hermon Press, 1265 46th St., Brooklyn, NY 11219 (tel. (718) 972-9010) for USD11.50, postage USD1.75. In England, order from Jewish Chronicle Publications, 25 Furnival St., London EC4A England. Lists Jewish synagogues, kosher restaurants and institutions in over 80 countries.

North American Vegetarian Society, P.O. Box 72, Dolgeville, NY 13329 (tel. (518) 568-7970); also the Vegetarian Society of the U.K., Parkdale, Dunham Rd., Altrincham, Cheshire WA14 4QG, England (tel. 06 19 28 07 03). Ask for their *International Vegetarian Travel Guide* (USD15.95, postage USD2).

Miscellaneous Books and Maps

European Association of Music Festivals, 122, rue de Lausanne, 1202 Geneva, Switzerland (tel. +41 (22) 732 28 03). Their booklet *Festivals* lists dates and programs of major music galas. Student rates are often available.

Forsyth Travel Library, P.O. Box 2975, Shawnee Mission, KS 66201 (tel. (800) 367-7984). Call or write for their catalog of maps, guidebooks, railpasses, and timetables.

Harmony Books, 400 Hahn Road, Westminster, MD 21157 (tel. (800) 733-3000). Yes, someone has compiled *The World Guide to Nude Beaches and Recreation* (USD18.45, postpaid). *Let's Go* wishes we'd thought of it first.

Hippocrene Books, Inc. 171 Madison Ave., New York, NY 10016 (orders: tel. (718) 454-2360). Strong concentration on Eastern Europe.

Michelin Maps and Guides, Davy House, Lyon Rd., Harrow, Middlesex HA1 2DQ, England (tel. +44 (18) 61 21 21). Their famous Green Guides can't be matched for historical and cultural background. Guides for most regions of western Europe. Visit your bookstore or, in the U.S., call or write P.O. Box 3305, Spartanburg, SC 29304 (tel. (803) 599-0850).

Travelling Books, PO Box 77114, Seattle, WA 98177 publishes a catalogue of travel guides which will make the armchair traveler weep with wanderlust.

Wide World Books and Maps, 1991 45th St. N, Seattle, WA 98103 (tel. (206) 634-3453). Write to them for hard-to-find maps.

Getting There

The airline industry manipulates their computerized reservation systems to squeeze every dollar from customers; finding a cheap airfare in this jungle will be easier if you understand the airlines' systems better than they think you do. Call every toll-free number and don't be afraid to ask about discounts. Have a knowledgeable travel agent guide you through the options; better yet, have several knowledgeable travel agents guide you, as some may turn out to be more knowledgeable than others. Remember that travel agents may not want to do the legwork to find the cheapest fares (for which they receive the lowest commissions). Students and young people under 26 should never need to pay full price for a ticket (see below for details). Seniors can also get mint deals; many airlines offer senior traveler club deals or airline passes, and discounts for seniors' companions as well. Sunday newspapers have travel sections that often list bargain fares from the local airport. Outfox airline reps with the phone book-sized *Official Airline Guide* (at large libraries); this monthly guide lists every scheduled flight in the world (including prices). George Brown's *The Airline Passenger's Guerilla Handbook* (USD14.95) is a more renegade resource.

Most airlines maintain a fare structure that peaks between mid-June and early September. "Midweek" (Mon.-Thurs.) flights run about USD30 cheaper each way than on weekends. If possible, leave from a travel hub; cities like New York, Atlanta, Dallas, Chicago, Los Angeles, San Francisco, Seattle, Vancouver, Toronto, and Montréal offer more competitive fares. A similar flexibility in destination is also advisable. Flying to London is usually the cheapest way across the Atlantic, though special fares to other cities—such as Amsterdam or Brussels—can cost even less. Return-date flexibility is usually not an option for the budget traveler; except on

youth fares purchased through the airlines, traveling with an "open return" ticket can be pricier than fixing a return date and paying to change it. Avoid one-ways too: the flight from North America to Europe may be economical, but the return fares are outrageous.

Whenever flying internationally, avoid last-minute problems by picking up your ticket in advance of the departure date and arriving at the airport several hours before your flight.

Commercial Airlines

Even if you pay an airline's lowest published fare, you may waste hundreds of dollars. The commercial airlines' lowest regular offer is the **APEX** (Advance Purchase Excursion Fare); specials advertised in newspapers may be cheaper, but have correspondingly more restrictions and fewer available seats. APEX fares provide you with confirmed reservations and allow "open-jaw" tickets (landing in and returning from different cities). Reservations must usually be made at least 21 days in advance, with 7 to 14 day minimum and 60 to 90 day maximum stay limitations, and hefty cancellation and change-of-reservation penalties. For summer travel, book APEX fares early; by May you will have difficulty getting the departure date you want.

Most airlines no longer offer standby fares, once a staple of the budget traveler. Standby has given way to the **three-day-advance-purchase youth fare,** a cousin of the one-day variety prevalent in Europe. It's available only to those under 25 (sometimes 24), and only within three days of departure—a gamble that often pays off. Return dates are open, but you must come back within a year, and once again can book your return seat no more than three days ahead. Youth fares in summer aren't really cheaper than APEX (in 1991, USD800-900 round-trip to Western Europe), but off-season prices drop deliciously.

A few renegade airlines offer other miscellaneous discounts. **Icelandair** (tel. (800) 223-5500) offers a "get-up-and-go" fare from New York to Luxembourg (round-trip from USD612, peak season). Reservations can be made no more than three days before departure, and your reservation must coincide with ticket purchase. After arrival, Icelandair offers discounts on trains and buses from Luxembourg to other parts of Europe. **Virgin Atlantic Airways** (tel. (800) 862-8621) offers an Instant Purchase Plan; you can reserve tickets to Europe only ten days in advance (New York to London USD349, one way) and peak season competition for seats is fierce.

Student Travel Agencies

Students and people under 26, with proper ID (see Youth and Student Identification under Documents above), qualify for sparklingly reduced airfares. These are rarely available from airlines or travel agents, but instead from student travel agencies like **Let's Go Travel, STA, Travel CUTS,** and CIEE's **Council Travel** (see under Useful Travel Organizations at the beginning of the book). These agencies negotiate special reduced-rate bulk purchases with the airlines, then resell them to the youth market; in 1991, peak season round-trip rates from the east coast of North America to even the offbeat corners of Europe rarely topped USD700, and off-season rates can be under USD400. Return date change fees tend to be low (USD25-50). Most of their flights are on major scheduled airlines, though in peak season some seats may be on less reliable chartered aircraft. Student travel agencies can also help non-students and people over 26, but may not be able to get the same low fares.

Charter Flights and Ticket Consolidators

Ticket consolidators (often known as "bucket shops") resell unsold tickets on commercial and charter airlines that might otherwise have gone begging. Look for their tiny ads in weekend papers (in the U.S., the Sunday *New York Times* is best), and just start calling them all. There is rarely a maximum age; tickets are also heavily discounted, and may offer extra flexibility or bypass advance purchase requirements, since you are not tangled in airline bureaucracy. But unlike tickets bought through an airline, you won't be able to use your tickets on another flight if you miss yours, and you will have to go back to the consolidator to get a refund, rather than the airline. Phone around and pay with a credit card if you can; you can't stop a cash payment if you never receive your tickets. Ask also about accommodation and car rental discounts; some consolidators have fingers in many pies. Insist on a receipt that gives full details about the tickets, refunds and restrictions. It is best to buy from a major organization that has experience in placing individuals on charter flights. One of the most reputable is the CIEE-affiliated **Council Charter,** 205 E. 42nd St., New York, NY 10017 (tel. (800) 223-7400; their flights can also be booked through Council Travel offices (see Useful Travel Organizations at the beginning of the book).

Consolidators sell a mixture of tickets: some are on scheduled airlines, some on **charter flights.** Once an entire system of its own, the charter business has shriveled, and effectively merged with the ticket consolidator network. The theory behind a charter is that a tour operator contracts with an airline (usually a fairly obscure one that specializes in charters) to use their planes to fly extra loads of passengers to peak-season destinations. Charter flights thus fly less frequently than major airlines, and have correspondingly more restrictions. They are also almost always fully booked, schedules and itineraries may change at the last moment, and flights may be traumatically cancelled. Shoot for a scheduled air ticket if you can.

And then there's **Airhitch,** 2790 Broadway #100, New York NY 10025 (tel. (212) 864-2000); you choose a date range in which to travel and a list of preferred European destinations, and they try to place you in a vacant spot on a flight in your date range to one of those destinations. (Airhitch is not for the clueless; be sure to read *all* the fine print they send you.) Absolute flexibility is necessary, but can pay off: flights to Europe from the East Coast have cost USD160 for years.

Courier Flights

Those who travel light should consider flying to Europe as a courier. The company hiring you will use your checked luggage space for freight; you're left with the carry-on allowance. Restrictions to watch for: most flights are round-trip only with fixed-length stays (usually short); you may not be able to fit your sweetie into your carry-on (single tickets only); and most flights are from New York (including a scenic visit to the courier office in the 'burbs). Round-trip fares to Western Europe from the U.S. range from USD175 to USD400. **NOW Voyager,** 74 Varick St., #307, New York, NY 10013 (tel. (212) 431-1616), acts as an agent for many courier flights worldwide from New York, as does **Courier Travel Service,** 560 Central Avenue, Cedarhurst, N.Y. 11516 (tel. (800) 922-2359 or (516) 374-2299). You can also go directly through courier companies in New York, such as World Courier and Halbart Express, or check your bookstore for handbooks such as *The Insider's Guide to Air Courier Bargains* (USD12.95) or the *Courier Air Travel Handbook* (USD8.95).

By Boat

While the idea of cruising to Europe may evoke images of the *Love Boat,* the *Titanic* or *Anything Goes,* sea passage is a potentially viable option. The **Queen Elizabeth 2,** the jewel of the Cunard line, offers a standby fare from New York to London starting from USD1129, including a return trip ticket on British Airways. (You can take your return trip on the faster, more environmentally-incorrect **Concorde** for an additional USD700, a rare opportunity.) Contact Cunard Ships, 555 Fifth Ave., New York, NY 10017 (tel. (800) 221-4770). **Polish Ocean Lines** offers limited spaces on 8-14 day one-way voyages from New York and other East Coast cities to Le Havre, Rotterdam and Bremerhaven (about USD1100). Contact Gdynia America Line Inc., 39 Broadway, 14th floor, New York, NY 10006 (tel. (212) 952-1280).

Once There

Getting Around

By Train

European trains retain the charm and romance their North American counterparts lost long ago. In western Europe, second-class travel is pleasant, and compartments, which seat six , are excellent places to meet folks of all ages and nationalities. In eastern Europe, first class may be worth it, though second class (compartments seat eight) is bearable. Bring some food and buy a plastic water bottle which you can refill at your hotel or hostel and take with you on all train trips, as the train café is often expensive, and train water, nasty. Trains are never very robber-proof; lock the door of your compartment if you can, and keep your valuables on your person at all times.

Many train stations have different counters for domestic tickets, international tickets, seat reservations, and information; check before lining up. On major lines, reservations are always advisable, and often required, even if you have a railpass; make them at least a few hours in advance at the train station (usually less than USD3). Faster trains, such as France's famed TGV, require a special supplement (about USD4-5). Sometimes you can pay for your supplement on board, but it'll cost a little more.

You may be tempted to save on accommodations by taking an overnight train in a regular coach seat, but it's a temptation well worth resisting; *if* you get to sleep you are sure to wake up exhausted and aching, and if you spread yourself over several seats in an empty compartment, someone is sure to come in at 2am and claim one of them. A sleeping berth in a bunkbedded couchette car, with linen provided, is an affordable luxury (about USD10; reserve at the station at least several days in advance). Very few countries give students or young people discounts on regular domestic rail tickets, but many will sell a student or youth card valid for one-half

or one-third off all fares for an entire year. Check the Practical Information section of each country chapter for details.

Buying a **railpass** remains the most popular way of touring Europe, and it is indeed a sensible option under many circumstances. Ideally conceived, a railpass allows you to jump on any train in Europe, go wherever you want whenever you want, and change your plans at will. The handbook that comes with your railpass is designed to tell you everything you need to know, including a timetable for major routes, a map, and details on ferry discounts. In practice, of course, it's not so simple. You still must stand in line to pay for seat reservations (the only guarantee you have against standing up), for supplements, and for couchette reservations, and to have your pass validated when you first use it. Passes are only valid on state-run railways, not on private lines (though there are few of these). More importantly, railpasses don't always pay off. Find a travel agent with a copy of the *Eurailtariff* manual (or call Rail Europe at (800) 345-1990), add up the second-class fares for the major routes you plan to cover, deduct 5% (the listed price includes a commission), deduct a rough 30% if you're under 26 and eligible for BIJ (see below), and compare. You may find it difficult to make your railpass pay for itself in Belgium, Greece, Ireland, Italy, Luxembourg, the Netherlands, Portugal, Spain, and all of Eastern Europe, where train fares are reasonable or distances short. If, however, the total cost of all your trips comes close to the price of the pass, the convenience of avoiding ticket lines will be worth the difference. Avoid an obsession with making the pass pay for itself; you may come home with only blurred memories of train stations.

The **InterRail** pass (about USD250) is the best railpass around, entitling travelers under age 26 to one month of free travel in every country in Europe (including Morocco and Turkey), except Iceland (which has no trains), Albania (where they're gross beyond description), the Baltic states and the Soviet Union, and the country you buy it in (where you only get 50% off). Passes for those 26 and over cost about USD380. However, you can only buy the pass in a European country where you have resided for six months (ideal for visiting students traveling after a year abroad). Any train conductor can demand to inspect your passport if they suspect you misrepresented the date you entered Europe.

The various **Eurailpasses** are also excellent for extensive international travel. The passes are valid in all the countries covered by InterRail except Morocco, Turkey, Yugoslavia, Bulgaria, Romania, Czechoslovakia, Poland, and Great Britain. The first-class **Eurailpass** is very rarely profitable (15 days for USD390, 2 months for USD840, 21-day and 1- and 3-month versions too). If you are traveling in a group of two or more, you might prefer the **Eurail Saverpass,** which allows unlimited first-class travel for 15 days for USD298 per person. Only travelers under age 26 can buy the **Eurail Youthpass,** good for one or two months of second-class travel (USD425 and USD560, respectively). The one-month pass is tough to make pay off; the two-monther is better. First-class Eurail **Flexipasses** allow limited travel within a longer period (for example, five days of travel within a 15-day period for USD230). Second-class youth Flexipasses are also available (e.g. 30 days within 3 months for USD540). You write in the days of validity yourself; if you start an overnight trip after 7pm, you only need to write down the next day's date on your pass. Despite their name, Flexipasses only pay off with careful planning; for instance, if you buy the five-day pass mentioned above, you should know exactly which trains you're going to take, and exactly how much they would have cost otherwise.

You'll almost certainly find it easiest to buy a Eurailpass before you arrive in Europe; contact Council Travel, Travel CUTS, or Let's Go Travel (see Useful Travel Organizations above), among many other travel agents. A few major train stations in Europe sell them too (though American agents usually deny this). If you're stuck in Europe, ineligible for InterRail but unable to find someone to sell you a Eurail, make a transatlantic call to an American railpass agent, which should be able to send a pass to you by express mail. Although Eurailpasses are not refundable once validated, you will be able to get a replacement if you lose one. When you get the pass, sign it immediately and detach the validation slip. This slip and a receipt from the sales agent confirming issuance will permit reissue for USD5 in the event of loss.

If you plan to focus your travels in one country, consider a national railpass, available in many countries including Austria, Britain, Finland, France, Germany, Greece, Hungary, Ireland, Italy, Poland, Portugal, Spain, and Switzerland. Also look into regional passes such as the ScanRail and Nordturist passes in Scandinavia, the BritFrance pass, the Benelux Pass, and the EastRail or European East pass, which covers Poland, Czechoslovakia, Hungary, and Austria. Some of these passes can be purchased only in Europe, some only outside of Europe, and for some it doesn't matter; check with a railpass agent or with national tourist offices.

Those country passes that can be bought in Europe are usually cheaper in Europe. Travel professionals, who must rely on information control to make money, rarely tell you this. For instance, one version of the ScanRail pass, available in America, costs USD239 for all ages and allows nine days of train travel in Scandinavia within a 21-day period. Purchased at a train station in Denmark, the equivalent Nordturist pass costs the equivalent of USD252 (USD184 for ages 12-25), but allows travel on all 21 of those 21 days.

For those under 26, **BIJ** tickets (Billets Internationals de Jeunesse, sold under the **Wasteels, Transalpino, Eurotrain,** and **Route 26** names) are an excellent alternative to railpasses. Available for international trips within Europe and Morocco and for travel within France, they save 10-40% of regular second-class fares. Tickets are sold from point to point, with free and unlimited stopovers along the way. However, you cannot take longer than two months to complete your trip, and you can stop only at points along the specific route of your ticket. In 1991, for instance, Wasteel's London office (tel. (071) 834 6744) offered round-trip tickets to Berlin for USD143, and a London-Berlin-Prague-Budapest-Vienna-London ticket for USD239—less than half the cost of a 2-month youth railpass. You can always buy BIJ tickets at Wasteels, Transalpino, or Eurotrain offices (usually in or near train stations). In some countries (Denmark, Germany and Switzerland, for example), BIJ tickets are also available from regular ticket counters. Some travel agencies also sell BIJ (such as ORBIS in Poland). In the U.S., contact Wasteels at (407) 351-2537.

Check bookstores for Lenore Baken's *Camp Europe by Train* (USD15.95), which covers nearly all aspects of train travel and includes sections on railpasses, packing, and the specifics of rail travel in each country. **The Eurail Guide** (USD14.95) lists train schedules and brief cultural information for almost every country on earth. The *ultimate* reference is the *Thomas Cook European Timetable* (USD23.95), updated monthly, which covers all major and many minor train routes in Europe. In the U.S., order it from **Forsyth Travel Library,** P.O. Box 2975, Shawnee Mission, KS 66201 (tel. (800) 367-7984 or (913) 384-3440).

By Bus

European trains and European railpasses are extremely popular, but the bright light can be deceptive. In Britain, Ireland, Portugal, Yugoslavia, Morocco, Turkey, and Greece, long-distance bus networks are more extensive, efficient, and often more comfortable than train services; in Spain, Hungary, Albania, and northern Scandinavia, the bus and train systems are on a par. In the rest of Europe bus travel is more of a crapshot, with scattered offerings from private companies—often cheap, but really hard to plan. All over Europe, short-haul buses wind into rural areas inaccessible by train.

Bus travel in Europe is significantly more comfortable than in North America, though you can never really have a true non-smoking section (a problem in southern and eastern Europe), and some companies force you to watch bleary videos or listen to the radio. The biggest problem is deregulation; bus routes are not as permanent as train tracks, there is little pan-European organization, and it can be difficult to understand fares and schedules unless you know the territory.

Amsterdam, Athens, Istanbul, London, Munich, and Oslo are centers for private lines that offer long-distance rides across Europe and, from time to time, all the way to India; see the Buses listings under those cities.

By Car and Van

Yes, Virginia, there really is no speed limit on the Autobahn. Cars offer great speed, great freedom, access to the countryside, and an escape from trains' town-to-town mentality. Unfortunately, they also insulate you from the *esprit de corps* of European rail travelers. Although a single traveler will almost never save by renting a car, four usually will; groups of two or three may also find renting cheaper than a railpass, unless planning on traveling unusually long distances. (Gas in Europe costs USD3-4 per gallon.) If you can't decide between train and car travel, you may relish a combination of the two; rail and car packages offered by Avis and Hertz are often economical for two or more people traveling together, and Rail Europe and other railpass vendors (see above) offer economical "Euraildrive" passes.

You can **rent** a car from either a U.S.-based multinational (Avis, Budget or Hertz) with its own European offices, from a European based company with local representatives (National and American International represent Europcar and Ansa respectively), or from a tour operator (Europe by Car, Auto Europe, Foremost, Kemwel, and Wheels International), which will arrange a rental for you from a European company at its own rates. Not surprisingly, the multinationals offer greater flexibility, but shop around, since the tour operators often strike good deals and may have lower rates. Rentals vary considerably; expect to pay at least USD120 a week, plus tax, for a teensy car. Reserve well before leaving for Europe and pay in advance if you can; rates within Europe are harsh. When quoted a price, always check if it includes tax and collision insurance; some credit card companies will cover this automatically if you pay with their plastic. This may be a substantial saving, but ask if a credit hold will be put on your account and if so, how much. Ask about student and other discounts and be flexible in your itinerary; picking up your car in Brussels or Luxembourg is usually cheaper than renting from Paris. Ask your airline about special packages; sometimes you can get up to a week of free rental. Minimum age restrictions vary by country; rarely, if ever, is it below 21. Try **Auto Europe,** (tel. (800) 223-5555); **Avis Rent a Car,** (tel. (800) 331-1084); **Budget Rent a Car,** (tel. (800) 472-3325); **Europe by Car,** (tel. (800) 223-1516, (800) 252-9401

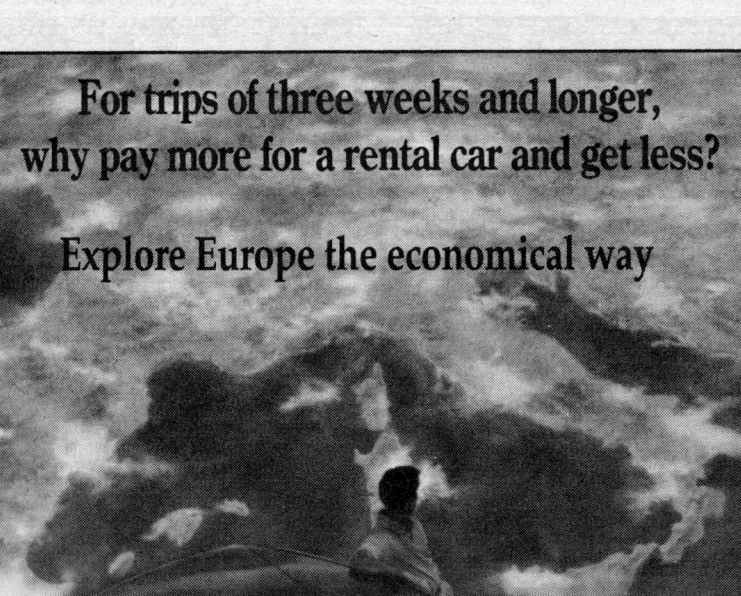

in CA); **Foremost Euro-Car,** (tel. (800) 423-3111; (800) 272-3299 in CA); **France Auto Vacances,** (tel. (800) 234-1426); **Hertz Rent a Car,** (tel. (800) 654-3001); **The Kemwel Group,** (tel. (800) 678-0678).

For longer than three weeks, **leasing** can be cheaper than renting; it is sometimes the only option for those aged 18-20. The cheapest leases are actually agreements where you buy the car, drive it, and then sell it back to the car manufacturer at a pre-agreed price. As far as you're concerned, though, its a simple lease and doesn't entail galactic financial transactions. Leases include full insurance coverage and are not taxed. The most affordable leases usually originate in Belgium and France and start at USD1000 for 60 days. Contact Foremost, Europe by Car and Auto Europe. You will need to make arrangements well ahead of time.

If you're brave or know what you're doing, buying a used car or van in Europe and selling it just before you leave can provide the cheapest wheels on the Continent. Check with consulates for different countries' import/export laws concerning used vehicles, registration, and safety and emission standards. David Shore and Patty Campbell's *Europe Free!: The Car, Van & RV Travel Guide* (USD5.95 postpaid) may be helpful. To order, write to 1842 Santa Margarita Dr., Fallbrook, CA 92028 (tel. (619) 723-6184). Gil Friedman promises that his book *How to Buy and Sell a Used Car in Europe* (Yara Press, USD4.95, postage 75¢) is like no other. Write to Box 1063, Arcada, CA 95521 (tel. (707) 826-2121).

Caravanning, which encompasses car and trailer and outfitted bus arrangements, gives the advantages of car rental without the hassle of finding lodgings or cramming six friends in a Renault. You'll need those six friends to split the gasoline bills, however. Caravans are less convenient than you may think; European roads are really, really, narrow and parking in major cities is totally hellish. Prices vary even more than for cars, but for the outdoor-oriented group trip, caravanning can be a dream. Contact car rental firms (above). Shore/Campbell's *Europe by Van and Motorhome* (USD13.95, outside U.S. USD16.95) available from the above address, may also have some snappy ideas.

Before setting off, be sure you know the laws of the country you're driving in (for instance, both seat belts *and* headlights must be on at all times in Scandinavia), and parking. (Oh, and by the way, keep left in Ireland and the U.K.) Scandinavians and Western Europeans use unleaded gas almost exclusively; unleaded is essentially invisible in Eastern Europe and North Africa. Rental companies will often tell you that you only need an U.S. license to rent anywhere; this may be true, but *driving* is another matter. Only a few European countries will accept a foreign driver's license, so it's wise to purchase an **International Driver's Permit** in your home country, valid for one year. The permit is available from any AAA branch in the U.S. or by mail from the American Automobile Association (AAA), 1000 AAA Drive, Heathrow, FL 32746-5063 (tel. (800) 556-1166); in Canada, contact the Canadian Automobile Association (CAA), 2 Carlton St., Toronto, Ont. MFB 1K4 (tel. (416) 964-3170). Applicants need a completed application form, driver's license, two passport-sized photos, proof of age (18 or older) and USD10.The **International Insurance Certificate,** sometimes called the "green card," is standard auto insurance. Get it from an insurance company or rental agency.

By Airplane

Unless you're under 25, flying across Europe on regularly scheduled flights will eat through your budget; nearly all airlines cater to business travelers and set prices accordingly. If you are 24 or under, special fares on most European airlines requiring ticket purchase either the day before or the day of departure are a happy exception to this rule (London-Berlin USD153, Copenhagen-Rome USD230). These are often cheaper than the corresponding regular train fare (Copenhagen-Bergen USD108 by plane, USD150 by train), though not always as cheap as student rail tickets or railpasses. Student travel agencies in Europe and America also sell cheap tickets (a London-Paris flight bought through one of the agencies in the Budget Travel listing in the London section will usually be no more expensive than the train). Budget fares are also frequently available in the spring and summer on high-volume routes between northern Europe and resort areas in Spain, Italy, and Greece. Consult budget travel agents and local newspapers and magazines. The **Air Travel Advisory Bureau,** Morley House, 320 Regent St., London WI, England (tel. (071) 636 50 00), can put you in touch with discount flights to worldwide destinations, for free.

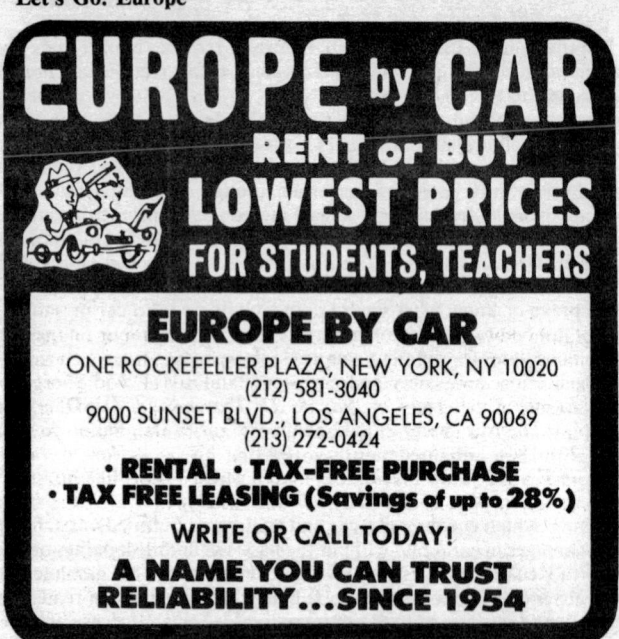

By Boat

Travel by boat is a bewitching alternative much favored by Europeans but overlooked by most foreigners. Most European ferries are straightforward, comfortable, and well-equipped, and the cheapest fare class sometimes includes use of a reclining chair or couchette where you can sleep the trip away (otherwise, you'll probably wind up crashing on the lounge room couch). You should check in early for a prime spot, at least two hours in advance; allow plenty of time for late trains and to get to the port. It's a good idea to bring your own food to avoid the mushy, astronomically priced cafeteria cuisine. Fares jump sharply in July and August. Always ask for discounts; ISIC holders can often get student fares and Eurail and InterRail passholders get many reductions and free trips (check the brochure that comes with your railpass). You'll occasionally have to pay a small port tax too (under USD10). Advance planning and reserved ticket purchases through a travel agency can spare you several tedious days of waiting in dreary ports for the next sailing. The best American source for European ferry information and tickets is **Eurocruises,** 303 W. 13th St., New York, NY 10014 (tel. (212) 691-2099 or (800) 688-3876).

Ferries in Europe divide into four major groups. The **Mediterranean** offers a carnival array of routes: from Genoa or Marseille to Tunisia, from Venice to the Yugoslav coast or Greece, throughout the Greek islands, from Brindisi to Greece, and from Greece to Turkey and Cyprus are just some of the most lively. Mediterranean ferries may be the most glamorous, but they're also the most treacherous. Reservations are recommended, especially in July and August, when ships are insufferably crowded and expensive (stash some toilet paper). Ferries run on erratic schedules, with similar routes and varying prices; shop around, and watch out for dinky, unreliable companies which will often not accept reservations. Ferries across the **English**

Channel from Ireland or Britain to France, Belgium, or the Netherlands are steely and workaday; see the United Kingdom Getting There section for more details. Ferries in the **North Sea** and the **Baltic Sea** are prized by Scandinavians for their duty-free shops' candy and alcohol selections; they also offer student and youth discounts, are universally reliable, and go everywhere (in summer, it's possible to go from St. Petersburg to Iceland or Scotland without once using land transport). Those content with deck passage rarely need to book ahead, though it can't hurt. **Riverboats** acquaint you with many towns that trains can only wink at. Most popular are the Moselle, Rhine, and Danube steamers, but these have been overrun by gaudy tourists; the least animated-looking lines are usually the most seductive.

By Bicycle

Imaging gliding down a deserted country road in the cool morning air. Imagine sitting on something smaller than you've ever sat on for five hours at a time. Biking can bring elements to your trip like no other form of travel. Today, biking is one of the key elements of the classic student budget Eurovoyage. Everyone else in the youth hostel is doing it, and with the proliferation of mountain bikes, you can combine biking with some serious natural sightseeing.

For information about touring routes, consult national tourist offices or any of the numerous books available. *Bicycle Touring In Europe,* by Karen and Gary Hawkins (USD11.95, Pantheon Books, Random House, New York, 1980), is a helpful guide to outfitting yourself and your bike, while *Europe By Bike,* by Karen and Terry Whitehill (USD10.95, The Mountaineers Press, Seattle, 1987), is a great source of specific area tours. Michelin road maps are clear and detailed guides.

Touring is not the same as the old ten-minute ride to school. You will be pedaling not only yourself but also whatever you store in the panniers (bags which strap to your bike). Take some reasonably challenging day-long rides before you leave, both to get in shape and to assure yourself that you are not in over your head. Have your bike tuned up by a reputable shop. Wear visible clothing, drink plenty of water (even if you're not thirsty), and ride on the *same* side as the traffic. Learn the international signals for turns and use them. Although you may not be able to build a frame or spoke a wheel, almost anyone can fix a modern derailleur-equipped mount and change a tire with a few simple but specialized tools and the help of a good bike manual.

Most airlines will count your bicycle as your second free piece of luggage (you're usually allowed two pieces of checked baggage and a carry-on piece). As an additional piece, it will cost about USD50 each way. Policies on charters and budget flights vary; check with the airline before buying your ticket. The safest way to send your bike is in a box, with the handlebars, pedals, and the front wheel detached. Within Europe, most ferries let you take your bike for free. You can always ship your bike on trains, though the cost varies from a small fixed fee to a substantial fraction of the ticket price.

Riding a bike with a frame pack strapped on it or on your back is about as safe as pedaling blindfolded over a sheet of ice; panniers are essential. The first thing to buy, however, is a suitable **bike helmet.** At about USD30-100, the best helmets are much cheaper and more pleasant than critical head surgery or a well-appointed funeral. To lessen the odds of theft, buy a U-shaped **Citadel** or **Kryptonite** lock. These are expensive (about USD20-49), but the companies insure their locks against theft of your bike for one or two years. *Bicycling* magazine has the lowest sale prices. **Bike Nashbar,** 4112 Simon Rd., Youngstown, OH 44512 (tel. (800) 627-4227), has generally excellent prices; they cheerfully beat competitors' prices by 5¢.

Renting a bike is preferable to bringing your own if your touring will be confined to one or two regions. A sturdy if unexciting one-speed model will cost USD6-8 per day; be prepared to lay down a sizable deposit. *Let's Go* lists bike rental shops in most cities and towns. Some youth hostels (especially in France) rent bicycles for low prices. In many countries (including France and Belgium), train stations rent bikes and often allow you to drop them off elsewhere in the country without charge.

By Moped and Motorcycle

Motorized bikes have long spiced southern European roads with their flashy colors and perpetual buzz. They offer an enjoyable, relatively inexpensive way to tour coastal areas and countryside, particularly when there are few cars. They don't use much gas and can be put on trains and ferries, and are a good compromise between the high cost of car travel and the limited range of bicycles. However, long distances become never-ending when sitting upright and cruising at only 40km/h. Mopeds are also dangerous in the rain and unpredictable on rough roads or gravel. Always wear a helmet and never ride wearing a backpack. If you've never been on a moped before, a twisting Alpine road is not the place to start. In general expect to pay USD15-35 per day; try auto repair shops and remember to bargain. Motorcycles are faster and more expensive but normally require a license. Before renting, ask if the quoted price includes tax and insurance or you may be hit for an unexpected additional fee. Avoid handing your passport over as a deposit; if you have an accident or mechanical failure you may not get it back until you cover all repairs. Pay ahead of time instead.

By Thumb

Some swear they'll never do it, some swear it's the only way. Many Americans, used to considering hitchers as drugged-out roadkill unfit to be looked at without rubber gloves, are surprised to find hitchhikers much more common and much less socially stigmatized in Europe. Many of those who choose to hitch report making good time, conserving global oil resources, and meeting heaps of congenial Europeans. Yet hitching (called "autostop" in much of Europe) is not something to do without careful thought to the risks involved. Not everyone can be an airplane pilot, but most every bozo can drive a car, and hitching means entrusting your life to a randomly selected person who happens to stop beside you on the road. In light of this, *Let's Go* does not recommend hitching, and the information presented below and throughout the rest of the book is not intended to do so.

If you do choose to hitch, here are some factors that will determine your success. First of all, *who you're with.* Two women get around quickly, and a man and a woman are also a speedy combination. Two men usually wait, and three go nowhere. Women should avoid hitching alone.

Next, consider *where you are.* Britain and Ireland are probably the easiest places in Western Europe to get a lift. Hitching in Scandinavia is slow but steady. Long-distance hitching in the developed countries of northwestern Europe demands close attention to expressway junctions and rest stop locations, and often a destination sign. Hitching in southern Europe is generally mediocre; France is the worst. Hitching remains common in Eastern Europe, though the increase in crime there since the demise of authoritarian rule may make it slightly less safe than it used to be. In the USSR, the Baltic states, and some other Eastern European countries, there is no clear difference between hitchhiking and hailing a taxi, and hitchers are supposed to pay (though locals often refuse money from foreigners).

Where you stand is also vital. Experienced hitchers pick a spot outside of built-up areas, where drivers can stop, return to the road without causing an accident, and have time to look over potential passengers as they approach. Hitching on hills or curves is hazardous and unsuccessful. Hitching (or even standing) on superhighways is generally illegal: you may only thumb at rest stops, or at the entrance ramps to highways—*in front* of the cute blue and white superhighway pictograph (a bridge over a road). In the Practical Information section of many cities, we list the tram or bus lines that will take you to strategic points for hitching out.

Finally, your success will depend on *what you look like.* Successful hitchers travel light, and stack their belongings in a compact but visible cluster. Most Europeans signal with an open hand, rather than a thumb; many write their destination on a sign in large, bold letters, and draw a smiley-face under it. Drivers like hitchers who are neat and wholesome, yet dynamic, who stand up, plead, smile, and dance.

No one stops for a grump, or for anyone wearing sunglasses. When a car does pull up, don't dawdle, and be friendly.

Although hitchhiking in Europe is seldom hazardous, don't tempt fate. A wedding ring or conservative dress will often ward off prospective suitors. Avoid getting in the back of a two-door car, and never let go of your backpack. Hitchhiking at night can be dangerous; stand in a well-lighted place and expect drivers to be leery of nocturnal thumbers. When you get into a car, make sure you know how to get out again in a hurry. Couples may avoid hassles with male drivers if the woman sits in the back or next to the door. If you ever feel threatened, insist on being let off, regardless of where you are. If the driver refuses to stop, try acting as though you're going to open the car door or vomit on the upholstery.

Several organizations pair drivers with riders, with a fee to both agency (about USD25) and driver (per km). **Eurostop International** (called **Verband der Deutschen Mitfahrzentralen** in Germany; **Allostop** in France) is one of the largest in Europe. Look them up in any large city. *Europe: A Manual for Hitchhikers* gives directions for hitching out of hundreds of cities, rates rest areas and entrance ramps, and deciphers national highway and license plate systems. It's available in bookstores or from **Vacation Work Publications,** 9 Park End St., Oxford OX1 1HJ, England (tel. (0865) 24 19 78).

By Foot

Europe's grandest scenery can often be seen only by foot: Crete's Samaria Gorge, the Italian Alps, and Yorkshire's Pennine Way are but a few examples. *Let's Go* describes many daytrips for those who want to hoof it, but native inhabitants (Europeans are fervent, almost obsessive, hikers), hostel proprietors, and fellow travelers are the best source of tips. Many European countries have hiking and mountaineering organizations; alpine clubs in Germany, Austria, Switzerland, and Italy, as well as tourist organizations in Scandinavia, provide inexpensive, simple accommodations in splendid settings. Facilities are usually open to all. Good books include J. Sydney Jones's *Tramping in Europe: A Walking Guide* (USD7.95), and Brian Spenser's *Walking in the Alps* (USD9.95).

Accommodations

If you arrive in a town without an advance reservation, your first stop should be the nearest bank of phone booths or the local tourist office. Tourist offices across Europe distribute extensive accommodations listings free of charge and will also reserve a room for a small fee (though some favor their friends' establishments). National tourist offices will also supply more complete lists of campsites and hotels. *Let's Go* is not an exhaustive guide to budget accommodations, but most of the places we list will be happy to refer you to somewhere else when full. Unless otherwise noted, we list hostel prices per person, prices elswhere per room. (Expect them all to rise in January.)

Often, hostel proprietors or locals with rooms to rent will approach you in ports or train stations. This may seem dangerous, but it is a custom in many areas. However, there is no guarantee of the quality of the accommodations they offer. Carry your own baggage and ask the proprietor to write down the offered price; otherwise, you may find that the price has mysteriously increased while you've been walking across town.

Hotels, Guesthouses, and Private Homes

Hotels are quite expensive in Britain, Switzerland, Austria, and northern Europe, where even the dignified stay in youth hostels: rock bottom for singles is USD14-17, for doubles USD18-22. In the rest of Europe, couples can usually get by fairly well (rooms with a double bed are generally cheaper than those with two twin beds), as can groups of three or four. Inexpensive European hotels may come as a rude shock to pampered North American travelers. You'll share a bathroom down the hall; one of your own is a rarity, and costs extra when provided. Hot showers may also cost extra. Be careful of the bidet (that thing next to the toilet); there's a difference. Continental breakfast, often included, consists of a roll, jam, coffee, or tea, and maybe an egg; in Britain and Ireland a larger meal is served. Some hotels offer "full pension" (all meals) and "half pension" (breakfast and lunch). Unmarried couples will generally have no trouble getting a room together, although couples under age 21 may occasionally encounter resistance (in Ireland and Belgium, for example).

Smaller, family-run **guesthouses** and **pensions** are usually a little cheaper than the cheapest hotels. Even less expensive are rooms in **private homes,** of which the local tourist office usually has a good list. If you're traveling alone, this is an economical way to get your own room and get in touch with real Europeans. The British **bed and breakfast** is a self-conscious type of private room that's extra heavy on the bacon and eggs. Private rooms are an excellent option in Eastern Europe, where youth hostels are primitive and hotels in flux; in the absence of good tourist offices, travel agencies book most private rooms in the east, and proprietors flag down tourists at the train station (try not to get stuck in a distant, vapid suburb).

If you write ahead for reservations, indicate your night of arrival and the number of nights you plan to stay. The hotel will send you a confirmation and may request payment for the first night. Not all hotels accept reservations, and few accept checks in foreign currency. Enclosing two International Reply Coupons (available at any post office) will ensure a prompt reply (but will cost as much as a short transatlantic phone call).

Hostels

Especially in the summer, Europe is overrun by young, budget-conscious travelers. Hostels are the hub of this gigantic subculture, providing innumerable opportunities to meet students from all over the world, find new traveling partners, trade stories, and learn about places to visit. At USD7-14 per night, prices are extraordinarily low; only camping is cheaper. Guests tend to be in their teens and twenties, but most hostels welcome travelers of all ages. In northern Europe, where hotel prices are astronomical, hostels have special family rooms, a higher standard of cleanliness and service, and correspondingly less of a student atmosphere. In the average hostel, though, you and anywhere from one to fifty roommates will sleep in a sex-segregated room full of bunk beds, with common bathrooms and a lounge down the hall. The hostel warden may be a laid-back student earning money during summer vacation, a hippie dropout, or a crotchety disciplinarian. Most hostels have well-equipped kitchens; some will serve you hot meals.

The basic disadvantage of hostels is their regimentation. Most have an early curfew—fine if you're climbing a mountain the next morning, but a distinct cramp in your style if you plan to rage in Paris or Copenhagen. There is also usually a lockout from morning to mid-afternoon. Conditions are generally spartan and cramped, there's little privacy, and you may run into more screaming pre-teen tour groups than you care to remember. Hostel quality also varies dramatically. Some are set in strikingly beautiful castles, others in run-down barracks miles from the town center. Rural hostels are generally more appealing than those in large cities. Hostels usually prohibit sleeping bags for sanitary reasons, instead providing blankets and requiring so-called **sleepsacks.** You can make your own sack by folding a sheet and sewing it shut on two sides. The lazier and less domestic can order one (about USD14) from Let's Go Travel or your youth hostel federation.

Large hostels are reluctant to hold advance telephone reservations because of the high no-show rate; citing an exact train arrival time or promising to call again and confirm can sometimes help. In large city hostels in Western Europe, take advantage of hostel-to-hostel fax booking services where the hostel you're staying at faxes another to see if there's space, then charges you the overnight fee plus a booking fee (less than USD1), and finally issues you a confirmation slip which you present to the other hostel.

Prospective hostelers should become a member of the official youth hostel association in their country; all national hostel associations are part of the **International Youth Hostel Federation (IYHF).** You don't absolutely have to become a member in advance, though: if you show up at an IYHF hostel but have not joined a national youth hostel organization, the hostel should give you a blank membership card with space for six validation stamps. Each night you'll then pay a nonmember supplement (equal to one-sixth the membership fee) and earn one Guest Stamp; get six stamps and you're a member. This system works well in most of Western Europe, though in some countries you may need to remind the hostel reception to issue you a guest card. In Eastern Europe, though, many hostels don't care whether you're a member or not; if they do, they'll just charge a small supplement but not issue a guest card. Some hostels in Germany and Austria will not accept nonmembers under any circumstances. Most student travel agencies sell IYHF cards on the spot, or contact one of the national hostel organizations listed below. Ask them about the *International Youth Hostel Handbook, Volume I,* which provides up-to-date listings on all IYHF hostels in Europe and the Mediterranean countries (about USD11).

International Youth Hostel Federation headquarters, 9 Guessens Rd., Welwyn Garden City, Herts, AL8 6QW, England (tel. (0707) 33 24 87). National member associations include **American Youth Hostels (AYH),** P.O. Box 37613, Washington, DC 20013-7613 (tel. (202) 783-6161). Cards cost USD25 (renewals and ages under 18 and over 54 USD15); family cards USD31. Other countries' card prices are often lower. **Canadian Hostelling Association (CHA),** National Office, 1600 James Naismith Dr. #608, Gloucester, Ont. K1B 5N4 (tel. (613) 748-5638). **Youth Hostels Association of England and Wales (YHA),** 14 Southampton St., Covent Garden, London WC2E 7HY (tel. (071) 836 1036). **Australian Youth Hostels Association (AYHA),** Level 3, 10 Mallett St., Camperdown, N.S.W. 2050 (tel. (02) 565 1699). **Youth Hostels Association of New Zealand,** P.O. Box 436, corner of Manchester and Gloucester St., Christchurch 1 (tel. (03) 79 99 70).

Privately owned hostels are found in major tourist centers and throughout some countries (most notably Ireland). No membership is required, and you won't always have to contend with early curfews or daytime lockouts, but they vary more widely in quality. The YMCA runs 29 **Interpoint** hostels in major northern European cities in July and August; membership cards are available at each location.

Camping

Camping in Europe is the best and the worst of worlds. Some nights you will pitch your tent against an ancient standing stone and fade into sleep under the infinite violet sky, amid the watchful silence of nature. Other nights you will be surrounded by gas-belching motor homes, obnoxious children, pot-bellied families beating their domestic animals, and the ethereal blue haze of television sets. **Organized campgrounds** exist in almost every European city, most accessible by foot or by public transportation, more easily by car. Showers, bathrooms, and a small restaurant or store are common; some sites have more elaborate facilities. Prices range from USD1-10 per person with an additional charge for a tent. Money and time expended in getting to the campsite may eat away at your budget and your patience; if you're doing the Eurail thing, hostels are probably more pleasant. Camping in the countryside is far more attractive (often in breathtaking and deliciously empty sites), and equally inconvenient.

Hit tourist offices or national camping organizations for comprehensive campground listings. *Europa Camping and Caravanning* (USD11), an annually updated catalog of campsites in Europe, is available through Recreational Equipment, Inc. (see below). Lenore Baken's excellent book *Camp Europe by Train* (USD12.95) offers general camping tips and suggests camping areas along Eurail lines. An **International Camping Carnet** (membership card) is required by some European campgrounds but can usually be purchased on the spot. In the U.S., it's available for USD23 through the National Campers and Hikers Association, 4804 Transit Rd., Bldg. #2, Depew, NY 14043 (tel. (716) 668-6242). Ask for their magazine *Camping Today.*

Freelance camping may be more your style. Sweden, Finland, and Norway permit you to camp for one night anywhere except on fenced land. In many other countries, you can camp where you please in the countryside, as long as you are discreet, polite, and ask permission.

Prospective campers will need to invest a lot of money in good camping equipment and a lot of energy in stuffing it all into a backpack and carrying it on their shoulders. Spend some time skimming catalogs and questioning knowledgeable salespeople before buying anything. Use the many reputable mail-order firms to gauge prices; order from them if you can't do as well locally. In the fall, last year's merchandise may be reduced by as much as 50%. **Campmor,** 810 Rte. 17N, P.O. Box 997-P, Paramus, NJ 07653-0997 (tel. (800) 526-4784), has a monstrous selection of equipment at low prices. **Cabela's,** 812 13th Ave., Sidney, NE 69160 (tel. (800) 237-8888), offers great prices on quality equipment. **Recreational Equipment, Inc. (REI),** P.O. Box C-88126, Seattle, WA 98188 (tel. (800) 426-4840 or (206) 431-5804), stocks a wide range of the latest in camping gear and holds great seasonal sales. And 24 hours a day, 365 days a year, **L.L. Bean,** 1 Casco St., Freeport, ME 04033 (tel. (800) 341-4341), supplies its own equipment and national-brand merchandise.

Most of the better **sleeping bags**—down (lightweight and warm, but slow to dry) or synthetic (cheaper, heavier, and more durable)—have ratings for specific minimum temperatures. Anticipate the most severe conditions you may encounter and subtract a few degrees. Expect to pay at least USD70 for a synthetic bag and up to USD200 for a down bag suitable for use in sub-freezing temperatures. Avoid the tapered, mummy-shaped model, which will restrict your leg movement and enlist you in the frazzled ranks of claustrophobiacs. **Sleeping bag pads** start at USD12 for simple Ensolite pads to about USD65 for the best air mattresses. The best **tents** are free-standing, with their own frames and suspension systems. They set up quickly and require no staking. The tent should have a protective rain fly; remember to seal the seams to protect against water seepage. Backpackers and cyclists may wish to pay a bit more for a sophisticated lightweight tent—some two-person models weigh only two pounds. Expect to pay at least USD100 for a good two-person tent.

Other basics include a battery-operated **lantern** *(never* gas) for use inside the tent and a simple plastic **groundcloth** to protect the tent floor. When camping in autumn, winter or spring, bring along a "space blanket," a technological masterpiece that will keep you warm by retaining your own body heat. Large, collapsible **water sacks** will significantly improve your lot in primitive campgrounds and weigh practically nothing when empty. **Campstoves** come in all sizes, weights, and fuel types, but none are truly cheap (USD40-125). Consider GAZ, a form of bottled propane gas that is easy to use and widely available in Europe.

Alternative Accommodations

In university and college towns, ask whether **student dormitories** are open to travelers when school is not in session. Prices are usually comparable to youth hostel prices, and you usually won't have to share a room with strangers or endure stringent curfew and eviction regulations. Many **monasteries** and **convents** will open their doors to those seeking corporeal or spiritual relief, particularly in Italy. A letter of introduction from a clergyperson could facilitate matters.

A number of host networks will help you find accommodations with families throughout Europe. **Servas** is an organization devoted to promoting world peace and understanding among people of different cultures. Traveling members may stay free in other members' homes in 80 countries. You are asked to contact hosts in advance, and you must be willing to fit into the household routine. Stays are limited to two nights, unless you are invited to stay longer. Find your hosts on a map before you agree to it; they may be far out of town. Membership is USD45, and for a USD15 deposit you receive a directory with short self-descriptions of each member. Write the U.S. Servas Committee, 11 John St., #407, New York, NY 10038 (tel. (212) 267-0252).

Sleeping in European train stations is a time-honored tradition. However, the romance of being "down and out" is overshadowed by reality. While it *is* free and often tolerated by local authorities, it is neither comfortable nor safe. Spending the night in an urban park is also cheap, but only do so if you ascribe a similarly low value to your life.

ACCOMMODATION

Keeping in Touch

Mail

Regular airmail between North America and Western Europe averages a week to 10 days. Allow at least two weeks for Australia and New Zealand. Surface mail takes six to eight weeks, up to ten for Australia and New Zealand. Parts of Eastern Europe are another story; air mail can take four to six weeks and surface mail may have diminished by its nuclear half-life before it gets to you.

You can have your mail sent to you through **Poste Restante** (the international phrase for General Delivery) in any city or town. Poste Restante is well worth using, and much more reliable than you might think. Mark the envelope "HOLD" and address it, for example, "Joanne CRAWFORD, Poste Restante, City, Country." The last name should be underlined and capitalized. Unless you specify a specific post office by street address or postal code, it will wind up at a special desk in the central post office. In eastern Europe, put a "1" after the city name to make sure this happens. Some countries appreciate it if you use their word for Poste Restante *(Lista de Correos* in Spain and *Postlagernde Briefe* in German-speaking lands). When picking up your mail, bring your passport or other ID with you. If the clerk insists that there is nothing for you, try checking under your first name as well. In a few countries you will have to pay a minimal fee (50¢) per item received. *Let's Go* lists post offices in the Practical Information section for each city and most towns.

Sending mail c/o American Express offices is quite reliable; offices will hold your mail for free if you have American Express traveler's checks or a card. Even if you buy another brand of traveler's checks, you may want to buy some American Express checks in order to use this service. Mail will automatically be held 30 days; to have it held longer, just write "Hold for x days" on the envelope. Again the sender should underline and capitalize your last name, marking the envelope "Client Letter Service." We list in most large cities. A complete list is available for free; call (800) 528-4800 in the U.S. and ask for the booklet *Traveler's Companion.*

Express mail services provide the fastest, most reliable service between the U.S., Canada, Australia, New Zealand, and Europe. By **Federal Express** (tel. (800) 238-5355 in the U.S.), an express letter from North America to Western Europe costs USD20-25 and takes 2-3 days; service to Eastern Europe costs much more and is often limited to cities. **DHL** (tel. (800) 225-5345 in the U.S.) covers every country in this book except Albania; packages under 8 oz. from North America to Europe cost USD36 and take one to three days.

Telephones

International direct dial is simple. First you dial the **international dialing prefix** for the country you are in, then the **country code** for the country you are calling (both listed at the beginning of each country section). Next punch in the **area code** or **city code** (listed in parentheses, or in the Practical Information listings for large cities). Finally, dial the **local number.** In most countries (the U.S., Canada, the Soviet Union, and Hungary are exceptions) the first digit of the city code is the **domestic long-distance prefix** (usually 0, 1, or 9); omit it when calling from abroad, but use it when dialing another region in the same country.

Some countries in Eastern Europe do not have an international dialing code; you must go through the operator. In some other countries you must wait for a tone after the international dialing code. Denmark, Luxembourg, and most of Europe's microstates have neither city codes nor domestic long-distance prefixes; just skip the relevant step. For more information, see each country's Practical Information section. Note that we sometimes cite numbers in the standard international format, which prefixes the country code with a + and lists the city code in parentheses with the first digit dropped. Country codes and international dialing codes are 1 and 011 respectively for both the USA and Canada; for Australia, 61 and 0011; for New Zealand, 64 and 00.

In Europe, you can usually make direct international calls from a pay phone, but you may need a companion to feed it as you speak. Countries with card-operated telephones are better, since you can just buy a large-denomination card. Some countries also have phones that accept major credit cards. Never dial from a hotel and pay later; you'll be charged sky high international rates plus a fat commission tacked on by the grinning proprietor.

Operators in most European countries will place **collect calls** for you. It may be cheaper to find a pay phone and deposit just enough money to be able to say "Call me" and give your number (though some pay phones in Europe can't receive incoming calls). A better alternative is AT&T's **USA Direct** service, which allows you to dial a number in Europe (either toll-free or charged as a local call), and connect instantly to an operator in the U.S. Rates run about USD1.75-2 for the first minute plus about USD1 per additional minute. Calls must be either collect (USD5.75 surcharge) or billed to an AT&T calling card (USD2.50); the people you are calling need not subscribe to AT&T service. In summer 1991, USA Direct service was available from every country in Europe (though not always every region within that country) except Iceland, Bulgaria, Romania, Albania, Estonia, Latvia, Lithuania, and the Soviet Union. We list USA Direct numbers in each country's Practical Information section; for more information, call (800) 874-4000. **Canada Direct, Australia Direct,** and **New Zealand Direct** are similar to USA Direct, though not as extensive. For information in Canada, call (800) 561-8868; in Australia, dial 0102; and in New Zealand, dial 018. In the USA, **MCI** offers a similar program for its customers only, which is slightly cheaper than AT&T's USA Direct but covers fewer countries (for information, call (800) 444-4444).

Remember **time differences** when you call. Britain and Ireland, Portugal, Morocco, Iceland, and the Faroe Islands are on Greenwich Mean Time (GMT), five hours ahead of New York. Finland, Estonia, Latvia, Lithuania, the western Soviet Union, Romania, Bulgaria, Greece, and Turkey are two hours ahead of GMT and seven hours ahead of New York. Everywhere else in this book is one hour ahead of GMT and six ahead of New York. Some countries (like Iceland) ignore daylight savings time, and fall and spring switchover times are not entirely standardized between those countries which do use it.

In Eastern Europe **telegrams** are faster and cheaper, both domestically and internationally, than the antiquated, overloaded phone systems. Show up at any post or telephone office and fill out a form; cables to North America take a couple days to arrive. In Western Europe, telegrams are slower, more expensive, and not half as much fun as a short overseas phone call. Stop. Major cities across Europe have bureaus where you can pay to send and receive **faxes.** If you're spending a year abroad and want to keep in touch with your friends back at the university, try using an **electronic mail** ("e-mail") system. It takes only a minimum of computer knowledge and a little pre-arranged planning, and your messages will be beamed instantly across the seas for free. That's right. For free.

Several companies offer answering services for travelers in Europe, though as transatlantic phone rates drop, you should use them for convenience rather than to save money. Among others, contact **EurAide,** P.O. Box 2375, Naperville, IL 60567 (tel. (708) 420-2343).

Weights and Measures

1 centimeter (cm) = 0.4 inches	**1 inch = 2.54cm**
1 meter (m) = 3.28 feet	**1 foot = 0.31m**
1 kilometer (km) = 0.62 miles	**1 mile = 1.61km**
1 gram (g) = 0.04 ounces	**1 ounce = 28g**
1 kilogram (kg) = 2.2 pounds	**1 pound = 0.45kg**
1 liter (ℓ) = 0.26 gallons	**1 gallon = 3.76ℓ**

Customs: Returning Home

Customs is not the nightmare you've been led to believe. Unless you're bringing back a BMW or a barnyard animal, you'll go straight through the "green line" and on to the baggage claim. The rules and regulations of customs and duties may appear the height of bureaucratic bullshit, but they pose little threat to the budget traveler; many don't waste time collecting receipts. Go to the customs officer whose belly shakes when he laughs like a bowl full of jelly. Keep these real rules in mind:

U.S. citizens returning home may bring USD400 worth of goods duty-free; you pay 10% on the next USD1000 worth. You must declare all purchases; have sales slips ready. Duty-free goods must be for personal or household use (this includes gifts) and cannot include more than 100 cigars, 200 cigarettes (1 carton), and one liter of wine or liquor (you must be 21 or older to bring liquor into the U.S.). You must have remained abroad for at least 48 hours and cannot have used this exemption or any part of it within the preceding 30 days to be eligible. If you registered with customs valuables you took out of the U.S. as you left, you'll have an easier time returning. You can mail unsolicited gifts duty-free if they're worth less than USD50. However, you may not mail liquor, tobacco, or perfume. Spot checks are occasionally made on parcels; mark the price and nature of the gift on the package. If you send back a parcel worth over USD50, the Postal Service will collect the duty plus a handling charge when it is delivered. If you mail home personal goods of U.S. origin, mark the package "American goods returned" in order to avoid duty charges. For more information, check the brochure *Know Before You Go,* available from the **U.S. Customs Service,** 1301 Constitution Ave., Washington, DC 20229 (tel. (202) 566-8195). Foreign nationals living in the U.S. are subject to different regulations; ask for the leaflet *Customs Hints for Visitors (Nonresidents).*

Canadian citizens face similar regulations. Any number of times per year, after you have been abroad at least 48 hours, you may bring home up to CAD100 worth of goods; once every year, after you have been abroad at least seven days, you may bring in up to CAD300 worth of goods. The duty-free goods can include no more than 50 cigars, 200 cigarettes (1 carton), 1 kg of tobacco, or 1.1 liters of alcohol.

You must be at least age 16 to bring tobacco products into Canada, and you may import liquor only if you meet the legal age of the province of your port of return. Anything above the duty-free allowance is taxed: 20% for goods which accompany you, more for shipped items. You can send gifts up to a value of CAD40 duty-free, but again, no alcohol or tobacco. The pamphlets *I Declare/Je Déclare* and *Bon Voyage, But . . .* are available from the **Revenue Canada Customs and Excise Department,** Communications Branch, MacKenzie Ave., Ottawa, Ont. K1A 0L5 (tel. (613) 957-0275).

Australian citizens are allowed 200 cigarettes (1 carton), 250 grams of cigars or 250 grams of tobacco, and one liter of alcohol upon returning home. You may bring in up to AUD 400 worth of goods duty-free; if you are under age 18, your allowance is AUD200. You can mail back personal property as long as it's at least 12 months old (i.e., no infants). You may mail unsolicited gifts duty-free as long as they legitimately look like gifts. For further information, see the brochure "Customs Information for All Travellers," available from local offices of the Collector of Customs or from Australian consulates.

New Zealanders face extensive and zealously enforced customs regulations. Only those aged 17 and older may bring tobacco or alcohol into the country. The concession is 200 cigarettes (1 carton) or 250 grams of tobacco or 50 cigars or a combination of all three not weighing more than 250 grams. You may also bring in 4.5 liters of beer or wine and 1.125 liters of spirits or liqueurs. Each person may bring in up to NZD500 worth of goods duty-free. However, goods must be intended for personal use or as unsolicited gifts. Persons traveling together may not combine individual concessions. *New Zealand Customs Guide for Travelers,* and *If You're Not Sure About It, DECLARE IT,* are both available from any customs office.

The U.S., U.K., Canada, Australia, and New Zealand prohibit or restrict the importation of firearms, explosives, ammunition, fireworks, controlled drugs, most plants and animals, lottery tickets, teenage mutant ninja turtles and obscene literature and films. To avoid problems in carrying prescription drugs, make sure the bottles are clearly marked and have a copy of the prescription to show the customs officer (see Health above).

National Tourist Offices

Andorran Delegation

U.K.: 63 Westover Rd., London SW18. Tel. (081) 874 4806.

Austrian National Tourist Office

U.S.: 500 Fifth Ave., #2009-2022, New York, NY 10110. Tel. (212) 944-6880.
Canada: 2 Bloor St. East, Toronto, Ont. M4W 1A8. Tel. (416) 967-3381.
U.K.: 30 St. George St., London W1R 0AL. Tel. (071) 629 0461.
Australia: 36 Carrington St., 1st flr., Sydney NSW 2000. Tel. (02) 241 19 16.

Belgian National Tourist Office

U.S.: 745 Fifth Ave., #714, New York, NY 10151. Tel. (212) 758-8130.
U.K.: Premier House, 2 Gayton Rd., Harrow, Middlesex HA1 2XU. Tel. (081) 861 3300.

Balkan Holidays (Bulgaria)

U.S.: 41 E. 42nd St. #606, New York, NY 10017. Tel. (212) 573-5530.
U.K.: Sofia House, 19 Conduit St., London W1R 9TD. (081) 491 4499.

Čedok (Czechoslovak Travel Bureau)

U.S.: 10 E. 40th St., #1902, New York, NY 10016. Tel. (212) 689-9720.
U.K.: 17-18 Old Bond St., London W1X 4RB. Tel. (071) 491 9180.

Danish Tourist Board

U.S.: 655 Third Ave., New York, NY 10017. Tel. (212) 949-2333.
Canada: P.O. Box 115, Station N, Toronto, Ont. M8V 3S4. Tel. (416) 823-9620.
U.K.: Sceptre House, 169-173 Regent St., London W1R 8PY. Tel. (071) 734 2637.

Finnish Tourist Board

U.S.: 655 Third Ave., New York, NY 10017. Tel. (212) 949-2333.
U.K.: 66-68 Haymarket, London SW1Y 4RF. Tel. (071) 839 4048.

French Government Tourist Office

U.S.: 610 Fifth Ave., New York, NY 10020-2452. Tel. (900) 420-2003.
Canada: 1 Dundas St. West, #2405, P.O. Box 8, Toronto, Ont. M5G 1Z3. Tel. (416) 593-4723.
U.K.: 178 Piccadilly, London W1V OAL. Tel. (071) 491 7622.
Australia: B&P Building, 12th floor, 12 Castlereagh St., Sydney NSW 2000. Tel. (02) 231 52 44.

German National Tourist Office

U.S.: 747 Third Ave., 33rd floor, New York, NY 10017. Tel. (212) 308-3300.
Canada: 175 Bloor St. E, North Tower #604, Toronto, Ont. M4W 3R8. Tel. (416) 968-1570.
U.K.: Nightingale House, 65 Curzon St., London W1Y 7PE. Tel. (071) 495 3990.
Australia: Lufthansa House, 12th floor, 143 Macquarie St., Sydney NSW 2000. Tel. (02) 367 38 90.

Gibraltar Tourist Office

U.S.: 1134 15th St. NW, Ste. 710, Washington, DC 20005. Tel. (202) 452-1108.

Greek National Tourist Organization

U.S.: Olympic Tower, 645 Fifth Ave., 5th Floor, New York, NY 10022. Tel. (212) 421-5777.
Canada: 1233 rue de la Montagne, #101, Montréal, Québec H3G 1Z2. Tel. (514) 871-1535.
U.K.: 4 Conduit St., London W1R DOJ. Tel. (071) 734 59 97.
Australia: 51-57 Pitt St., P.O. Box R203, Royal Exchange, Sydney NSW 2000. Tel. (02) 241 16 63

IBUSZ (Hungary)

U.S.: 1 Parker Plaza, #1104, Fort Lee, NJ 07024. Tel. (201) 592-8585.
U.K.: Danube Travel, 6 Conduit St., London W1R 9TG. Tel. (071) 493 0263.

Icelandic Tourist Board

U.S.: 655 Third Ave., New York, NY 10017. Tel. (212) 949-2333.

Irish Tourist Board

U.S.: 757 Third Ave., 19th floor, New York, NY 10017. Tel. (212) 418-0800 or (800) 223-6470.

Canada: 160 Bloor St. East, #934, Toronto, Ont. M4W 1B9. Tel. (416) 929-2777.
U.K.: 150 New Bond St., London W1Y 0AQ. Tel. (071) 493 3201.
Australia: MLC Centre, 38th Level, Martin Place, Sydney NSW 2000. Tel. (02) 232 71 77.

Italian Government Travel Office
U.S.: 630 Fifth Ave., #1565, Rockefeller Center, New York, NY 10111. Tel. (212) 245-4822.
Canada: 1 Place Ville Marie, #1914, Montréal, Québec. H3B 3M9. Tel. (514) 866-7667.
U.K.: 1 Princes St., London W1R 8AY. Tel. (071) 408 1254.

Luxembourg National Tourist Office
U.S.: 801 Second Ave., New York, NY 10017. Tel. (212) 370-9850.
U.K.: 36-37 Piccadilly, London W1V 9PA. Tel. (071) 434 2800.

Malta Tourist Information
U.S.: 249 E. 35th St., New York, NY 10016. Tel. (212) 725-2345.
Canada: 1 St. Johns Rd. Ste. 305, Toronto, Ont. M6P 4C7. Tel. (416) 767-4902.
U.K.: 16 Kensington Square, London W8 5HH. Tel. (071) 938 1712.

Monaco Tourist Information
U.S.: 845 Third Ave., New York, NY. Tel. (212) 759-5227.
U.K.: Chelsea Garden Market, Chelsea Harbour, London SW10 0XE. Tel. (071) 352 9962.

Moroccan National Tourist Office
U.S.: 20 E. 46th St., #1201, New York, NY 10017. Tel. (212) 557-2520.
Canada: 2001 rue Université, #1460, Montréal, Quebec PO H3A 2A6. Tel. (514) 842-8111.
U.K.: 205 Regent St., London W1R GHB. Tel. (071) 437 0073.

Netherlands Board of Tourism
U.S.: 355 Lexington Ave., 21st floor, New York, NY 10017. Tel. (212) 370-7360.
Canada: 25 Adelaide St. East, #710, Toronto, Ont. M5C 1Y2. Tel. (416) 363-1577.
U.K.: 25-28 Buckingham Gate, London SW1E 6LD. Tel. (071) 630 0451.

Norwegian Tourist Board
U.S.: 655 Third Ave., 18th floor, New York, NY 10017. Tel. (212) 949-2333.
U.K.: Charles House, 5-11 Lower Regent St., London SW1Y 4LR. Tel. (071) 839 6255.

Polish National Tourist Office
U.S.: 333 N. Michigan Ave., Ste. 228, Chicago, IL, 60601. Tel. (312) 236-9013.
U.K.: 82 Mortimer St., London W1N 7DE. Tel. (071) 637 4971.

Portuguese National Tourist Office
U.S.: 590 Fifth Ave., New York, NY 10036. Tel. (212) 354-4403 or (800) PORTUGAL ((800) 767-8842).
Canada: 4120 Yonge St., #414, Willowdale, Ont. M2P 2B8. Tel. (416) 250-7575.
U.K.: New Bond St. House, 1-5 New Bond St., London, W1Y ONP. Tel. (071) 493 3873.

Romanian National Tourist Office
U.S.: 573 Third Ave., New York, NY 10016. Tel. (212) 697-6971.
U.K.: 17 Nottingham St., London W1M 3RD. Tel. (071) 224 3692.

Consulate General of San Marino
U.S.: 1899 L St. NW, Suite 500, Washington, DC 20036. Tel. (202) 223-3517.

Tourist Office of Spain
U.S.: 665 Fifth Ave., New York, NY 10022. Tel. (212) 759-8822.
Canada: 102 Bloor St. West, 14th floor, Toronto, Ont. N5S 1M8. Tel. (416) 961-3131.
U.K.: 57-58 St. James St., London SW1A 1LD. Tel. (071) 499 1169.
Australia: 203 Castlereagh St., Suite 21A, P.O. Box A675, Sydney NSW 2000. (02) 264 79 66.

Swedish National Tourist Office
U.S.: 655 Third Ave., New York, NY 10017. Tel. (212) 949-2333.
U.K.: 29-31 Oxford St. London W1R 1RE Tel. (071) 437 5816.

Swiss National Tourist Office (including Liechtenstein)
U.S.: 608 Fifth Ave., New York, NY 10020. Tel. (212) 757-5944.
Canada: 154 University Ave., Suite 610, Toronto, Ont. M5H 3Z4. Tel. (416) 971-9734.

U.K.: Swiss Centre, 1 New Coventry St., London W1V 8EE. Tel. (071) 734 1921.
Australia: 203-233 New South Head Rd., P.O. Box 193, Edgecliffe, Sydney NSW 2027. Tel. (02) 326 17 99.

Turkish Government Information Office

U.S.: 821 United Nations Plaza, New York, NY 10017. Tel. (212) 687-2194.
U.K.: 170-173 Piccadilly, 1st floor, London W1 V 9DD. Tel. (071) 734 8681.

Intourist (USSR) Travel Information Office

U.S.: 630 Fifth Ave., #868, New York, NY 10111. Tel. (212) 757-3884.
Canada: 1801 McGill College Ave. #630, Montréal, Québec H3A 2N4. Tel. (514) 849-6394.
U.K.: 219 Marsh Wall, Isle of Dogs, London E14 9FJ. Tel. (071) 538 8600.

British Tourist Authority

U.S.: 40 W. 57th St., 3rd floor, New York, NY 10019. Tel. (212) 581-4700.
Canada: 94 Cumberland St., 6th floor, Toronto, Ont. M5R 3N3. Tel. (416) 925-6326.
Australia: 171 Clarence St., 4th floor, Sydney NSW 2000. Tel. (02) 29 86 27.

Yugoslav National Tourist Office

U.S.: 630 Fifth Ave., #280, New York, NY 10111. Tel. (212) 757-2801.
U.K.: 143 Regent St., London W1R 8AE. Tel. (071) 734 5243.

Parting Words

The best way to sample a new culture is to dissolve discreetly in it; there's no faster way to learn about new people than to let them think you're one of them. As a foreigner, you'll probably be conspicuous—but you will be welcomed as a superstar if you make a real effort to fit in without being rude or obnoxious. An afternoon of quiet relaxation at a park in Prague or a café in Colmar (cafés are *made* for people-watching) will often teach you more about a country and its people than a museum. Take the time to actually meet people. A photo of Hans and Gisela Kriege who put you up for the night in Munich will contain many more memories than a postcard of the Eiffel Tower. Europeans are earnestly interested in other lands and cultures, but have a very strong sense of their own cultural history; if you insult or belittle it you'll only seem ignorant. Don't expect things to work the way they do at home; half the fun is untangling a new system. Culture shock can really happen, but unless you're very homesick, skip the McDonalds and Pizza Hut for the *paté* and goulash.

The myth that "they all speak English" is manifestly false; every time you address a European in English, you're asking a favor that you probably couldn't return were they to visit your home town. Humbly ask "Do you speak English?" before launching into a question. Better yet, try to learn a little about the foreign languages you'll be encountering and don't be afraid of trying them out (they're laughing with you, not at you). Except for Finnish, Estonian, and Hungarian (related to each other), Turkish (related to Central Asian tongues), Maltese (related to Arabic), and Basque (related to nothing in particular), all the languages in Europe are part of the Indo-European language family (whose branches include the Celtic, Germanic, Baltic, Slavic, Romance, Greek, and Albanian groups). Indo-European languages are remarkably similar: for instance, the words for "three" in Albanian, French, Lithuanian, Norwegian, and Polish are *tre, trois, trys, tre,* and *trzy* respectively. You can learn any pronunciation system, plus the words for yes, no, where is, how much, and the numbers up to ten, in about fifteen minutes. Really. At least learn one phrase: thank you.

Albanian	faleminderit	fah-leh-meen-DARE-eet
Arabic	shukran	shoo-krahn
Basque	eskerrik asko	ess-kare-eek ahs-ko
Breton	trugarez	troo-GAHR-ay
Bulgarian	благодаря	blah-goh-dahr-YAH

Catalan	gràcies	GRAH-see-ahs
Czech	děkuji	DYEH-koo-yee
Danish	tak	tack
Dutch	dank u	DAHNK ü
Estonian	aitäh	EYE-teh
Faroese	takk	tahk
Finnish	kiitos	KEE-tohs
French	merci	MARE-see
German	danke	DAHNK-uh
Greek	efharisto	eff-hah-ree-STOE
Hungarian	köszönöm	KUR-sur-nurm
Icelandic	takk	tahk
Irish	go raibh maith agat	Please tell us!
Italian	grazie	GRAHT-syeh
Latvian	paldies	PAHL-dyess
Lithuanian	ačiū	AH-choo
Macedonian	hvala	KHVAH-lah
Norwegian	takk	tahk
Polish	dziękuję	jeng-KOO-yeh
Portuguese (to women)	obrigada	oh-bree-GAH-dah
Portuguese (to men)	obrigado	oh-bree-GAH-doo
Romanian	mulţumesc	mool-TSOO-mesk
Russian	спасибо	spah-SEE-bah
Scottish Gaelic	tapadh leat	TAH-pah lett
Serbo-Croatian	hvala	KHVAH-lah
Slovak	d'akujem	DYAH-koo-yemm
Slovene	hvala	KHVAH-lah
Spanish	gracias	GRAH-see-ahs
Swedish	tack	tahk
Turkish	teşekkur	TEH-shek-koor
Ukrainian	дякую	DYAH-koo-yoo
Welsh	diolch	DEE-olkh

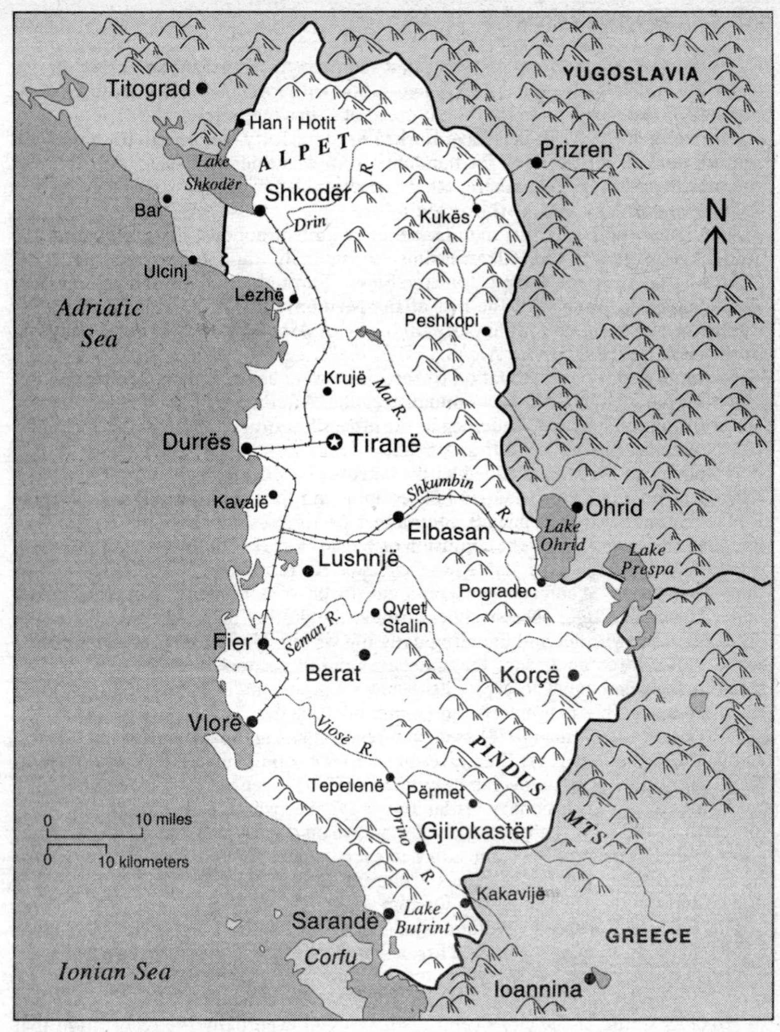

ALBANIA

USD$1 = 10.0 leks (ALL)	**1 lek = USD$0.10**
CAD$1 = 8.69 leks	**1 lek = CAD$0.12**
GBP£1 = 17.1 leks	**1 lek = GBP£0.06**
AUD$1 = 7.87 leks	**1 lek = AUD$0.13**
NZD$1 = 5.70 leks	**1 lek = NZD$0.18**
Country Code: 355	**International Dialing Prefix: N/A**

After decades of isolationism and obscurity, Albania (Shqipërië) was a regular feature on the front pages of western newspapers throughout 1991. Unfortunately Albania's fame was mostly due to heart-wrenching reports of mass exodus from an impoverished country in the throes of political and economic transformation.

As its citizens emerge from a system that required them to steal and cheat merely to survive, yet forbade even casual conversation with foreigners, they are often disillusioned by the obstacles to the development of a thriving, democratic society. Many people feel as if the Albanians have worked hard for forty-five years with no reward and are now entitled to look for handouts from wealthier nations, or to run away and seek their fortunes elsewhere; others are dismayed by this pessimism and exhort their people to stay and work for the future.

Albanians stubbornly maintain that they're autochthonous, descended from the Stone Age settlers of the Balkan peninsula. Basically, though, they just want you to know that they got there before the Slavs. Throughout ancient times the area was involved in trade with the rest of the Mediterranean, as Greek, Roman and Byzantine ruins attest; you may be familiar with Albania's ancient name of Illyria from Shakespeare's *Twelfth Night.*

Albania's history of domination by foreign powers helps explain the extreme isolationism pursued by the late communist regime. After a brief period of sovereignty under the national hero Skënderbeg in the fifteenth century, Albania plunged under Ottoman rule for four centuries; a fleeting democratic government under Bishop Fan Noli in the 1920s soon ended with a takeover by Zog, a chieftain from northern Albania, who quickly proclaimed himself king and then sold the country off to the Italian Fascists. The indigenous communist partisans—*not* the Red Army—who liberated the country after the confusion of World War II actually brought the country its first ever period of stable independence. Determined to go their own way, they made Albanian communism a nationalistic beast rather than an agent of Soviet imperialism. The state obsessively controlled the destiny of its citizens by filtering influence from without and dictating daily life within. Unwritten laws and a brutal secret police force made sure that sideburns didn't get too long and hemlines too short in their campaign to create "the new man and the new woman." Albania's leaders successively denounced the Communist parties in Yugoslavia (1948), the USSR (1961) and China (1978) as craven revisionists, and proclaimed that Albanians would rather eat grass than give up their communist ideals. The new government banned religion—a decree only lifted in 1991—yet nearly replaced it with a hero-cult of the revolutionary leader Enver Hoxha, who ruled as a dictator until his death in 1985. Hoxha's personal effects were on display in a giant pyramid (now a disco) in Tiranë, and his name adorned every other mountainside in letters large enough to distract passing Martians. Comrade Enver's portrait was found in every home, and children wrote poems for him, their fear twisted perversely into love.

The Eastern European revolutions of 1989—especially the removal of Nicolae Ceauşescu in Romania—prompted first a softening of the Communist line and eventually its utter collapse. Protests ignited by student hunger-strikers in 1991, the removal of the deceased dictator's name from the university in Tiranë, the toppling of Hoxha's statue in the city's central square, and eventually the recognition that the totalitarian regime was losing its monopoly on power. In the summer of 1991 President Ramiz Alia, the hand-picked successor of Enver Hoxha, and the Socialist Party, the thinly veiled successor of the communist Party of Labor, were still nominally in control, but the country was essentially a lawless free-for-all.

Though the international media have discussed only Albania's desperation and poverty, the country sits on hefty oil reserves and is the world's third largest exporter of chromium, a metal that is essential for more than just bumpers. Limited but fertile farmland, virgin forests and a tourist-starved Adriatic coastline are also part of Albania's endowment. With technical assistance from abroad these resources could be exploited more cleanly and more lucratively than the antiquated equipment currently allows; accordingly, developers and sleazy venture capitalists have been pouring into Tiranë all through 1991. Tourism in Albania, however, is still in the realm of adventure travel. Yet an eventual return to the calmness of the Communist days—when Swiss tourists sipped mint juleps on the terrace of the Hotel Adriatiku in Durrës—is not unimaginable.

Albania divides into two ethnic and to some extent geographic zones. Speakers of the Gheg dialect live in the more mountainous north, have preserved more of the customs that the country is known for, and long for unification with their Gheg brethren across the border in the Yugoslavia's autonomous Albanian province, Kosovë. Speakers of the Tosk dialect, from Tiranë on south, are anything but eager to see the balance of power shifted towards the mountain men; they remain more loyal to Hoxha (born in the southern town of Gjirokastër) and his visions. Two-thirds of the Albanian population still lives among the donkey-carts, fig trees, and hillside villages of the stunning Albanian countryside, though you may only get a chance to see it if your bus breaks down in the middle of nowhere. To familiarize yourself with Albanian history and culture read Edith Durham's cult classic, *High Albania,* an entertaining account of turn-of-the-century Albanian highland customs, or any of the novels by national hero and recent defector Ismail Kadare.

Getting There

As we go to press, Americans (and presumably citizens of Canada, Australia, New Zealand, and the U.K.) of Albanian descent do not need visas to enter Albania, but must present evidence of Albanian descent at the border (e.g. a parent's baptismal certificate). No joke. For the time being, other travelers need a visa from an Albanian embassy abroad: try the one in Paris (131, rue de la Pompe, Paris, France 75116, tel. +33 (1) 45 53 51 32), the embassy in Washington (as soon as they run enough bake sales to buy a building—call directory information to see if it's opened), or the ones in Athens, Budapest, Belgrade, and Rome (see Embassies and Consulates in those cities). In September 1991, some reports indicated that visas were issued painlessly within two to three weeks, while others suggested that you need to find someone in Albania organized to put together an official invitation for you. If current trends continue, visa requirements for Americans, at least, may atrophy entirely by 1992; call ahead to check. If you absolutely *must* go individually and there is no other way, contact Kutrubes Travel or Regent Holidays (see below), who can arrange your stay through Albturist (the Albanian state travel agency) for an outrageous USD180 per day (which does include accommodations, full board, and a car and driver).

Travelers with a valid individual visa should be able to enter through any border crossing. The major ones are at Han i Hotit in the north (on the road from Titograd in Yugoslavia), at Qafë Thane in the east (on the road from Ohrid in Yugoslavia), and at Kakavijë in the south (on the road from Ioannina and Athens in Greece). Public transport from Yugoslavia is nonexistent right now, but there is rumored to be bus service through Kakavijë from Athens and Ioannina twice weekly, and **Deryatur,** Meşrutiyet 131, 1st floor, İstanbul, Turkey (tel. +90 (1) 144 99 94; open daily 8:30am-6pm) runs a weekly bus between İstanbul and the Albanian city of Korçë, via Greece and Kakavijë (leaves Topkapı bus terminal in İstanbul Fri. at 5pm, leaves Korçë Sun. at noon; 16 hr.; USD30; reservations recommended). Durrës (Durazzo in Italian) is Albania's main port, and **Adriatica Navigazione** runs a ferry on the 7th, 17th, and 27th of each month from Trieste in Italy to Durres (25 hr., deck passage a hefty L110,000). They may run a much more convenient ferry from Bari to Durrës next year; contact their head office in Venice at +39 (41) 78 16 11 or 78 16 53). Flying to Tiranë is a simpler option; there are one to three flights per week on Swissair from Zürich, Air France from Paris, Alitalia from Rome and Bari, TAROM from Bucharest, Olympia from Ioannina and Athens, and Malév from Budapest; flights from Greece and Budapest are cheapest.

Travelers unable to get an individual visa can easily go on a group tour (the tour operator will handle visa matters). In the U.S., **Kutrubes Travel,** 328a Tremont St., Boston MA 02116 (tel. (617) 426-5668 or (800) 878-8566) is America's most experienced specialist in both individual and group travel to Albania, and will be running one- to two-week Boston-based tours in 1992. In Britain, **Regent Holidays,** 15 John St., Bristol BS1 2HR (tel. (0272) 21 17 11), has organized excellent tours to Albania since 1970, and can also handle individual travel. In both cases, prices run USD1000 and up. If you're already in Europe, it will be cheaper and simpler to go on a short tour from Greece. **Kalami Turist Service,** in Kalami on the island of Corfu (tel.

+30 (663) 913 69) runs one-day boat tours (every Wed., Fri., Sat., and Sun.) from Corfu town with an overnight in Sarandë, a lovely city on the Adriatic in southern Albania; book by phone at least four days in advance (4900dr plus USD20). In Athens, **Albturist-Planitis,** Akademias 3 (tel. +30 (1) 364 25 26) has six-day bus tours every week throughout southern Albania (13000dr plus USD200). Other tours are rumored to be leaving from Ioannina. Short, inexpensive bus tours from Yugoslavia will probably resume as soon as Yugoslavia quiets down enough for tourists to return. Contact **Putnik** across from the bus station in Ohrid (tel. +38 (96) 224 77; 3-day tours to Tiranë USD150-200), **Atlas Tours,** Pile 1, in Dubrovnik (tel. +38 (50) 273 33, or Suntours, ul. Oktobarske Revolucije 52, in Titograd (tel. +38 (81) 323 33).

If you can't make it to Albania, at least go to the **Albanian Shop,** 3 Betterton St., London WC2H 9BP (tel. (071) 836-0976; Tube: Covent Garden; open Tues., Thurs., and Fri. 10am-1pm and 2-6pm, Sat. 11am-4pm; may move, so call ahead), which stocks more Albanian music, literature, and crafts than any other store inside or outside the country.

Getting Around

Political unrest and random vandalism have been the kiss of death to Albania's already dilapidated public transportation system. Most buses and trains have only the skeletons of seats; all upholstery has been torn out—even foam rubber is in short supply here. Albanians will try to convince you that public transport is "not suitable" for you, the honored guest. However, both rail and bus systems promise vast improvement in coming years—the former with the formation of international partnerships, the latter with the introduction of competition from the private sector.

Durrës, Albania's main port, is also the hub of the **rail** system, with connections south to Ballsh (just below Fier), inland to Tiranë and Pogradec, and north to Shkodër. Other major cities such as Gjirokastër and Korçë are reachable by connecting bus service. In the 1980s, a rail track was laid from Shkodër north across the Yugoslav border to Titograd, but it has yet to see passenger traffic. Contracts have also been negotiated to extend the system southwards into Greece, but this project also may take several years.

The **bus** system has already received a boost from independent operators who ofter regular service in relative comfort to major destinations; see the listings in the Tiranë section. **Public buses,** both between and within towns, are usually retirees from the fleets of German and French cities. The only route information may be placards left over from one of these past lives ("Place des Invalides," for example). A native's help is usually necessary.

Many Albanians bicycle, and just as many hitchhike rides—mostly on the back of government-owned flatbed trucks. If you join them, you'll be expected to pay about the same price as the bus fare.

Practical Information

Unless you play Albturist's game at USD180 a day, there is no organized source of travel information in Albania. Available guidebooks are poor on logistics, though still good for sights; *Nagel's Albania* covers the country village by village and includes a rare street map of Tiranë.

Like Greek, the Albanian language is an isolated descendant of Indo-European. Buy a textbook or phrasebook before you go; just learning a few dozen words will flatter every Albanian you meet and open up enormous possibilities. Place names change slightly when inflected: Tirana and Durrësi are the definite forms of Tiranë and Durrës, respectively. Surprisingly many educated Albanians speak English or French; almost everyone understands some Italian after years of watching Italian television—their link to the outside world. As in Bulgaria, Albanian head movements for yes *(po)* and no *(jo)* are the reverse of Western European ones.

The Albanian monetary unit is the lek, divided into 100 qindarkas. Many Albanians still quote prices in old leks (phased out in 1964): 10 old leks to one new lek. Bring foreign cash in small bills and coins for unround prices in hard currency shops. Any major Western currency will do. The best way to change money is with an Albanian acquaintance. Agree on a rate which is favorable to both of you. In banks the price for buying hard currency is three times the selling rate, so most natives are keen to work out a deal. The rate may vary greatly between hotels and the bank, so check both before changing any large amounts. Albturist hotels and hard currency shops accept only American Express traveler's checks. The State Bank in Tiranë will dispense wired money and change any traveler's check or Eurocheque into hard currency for a 1% commission (see below).

The runt of Ma Bell's litter, Albania has the fewest phones per capita in Europe. Pay phones on the street are hardly worth mentioning. Call from hotels and post offices. Both international and domestic long distance calls can be dialed directly only to numbers in Tiranë, Durrës, Elbasan, Shkodër and Gjirokastër. For all other locations you must call through an exchange in Tiranë; give the name of the district you want to reach and the local number. From abroad this is done by dialing the Tiranë operator number after the country code and Tiranë city code (i.e. +355 (42) 07). Outgoing calls can be made at post offices (18 leks per minute to the U.S.) or from snazzier tourist hotels (USD1.80 per minute). Albanians feel no compunction about ripping off international service, which is fully subsidized by the Italian government—one of the most popular methods involves safety pins. It is currently impossible to make collect calls from Albania.

Until the situation stabilizes, postal rates will vary according to the whim of the clerk behind the counter. A few Albanian phrases and some smiles may help secure a favorable rate. *Par Avion* or *Air Mail* on your letter will usually produce the desired effect. Normal hours of operation for larger post offices are 7am to 9pm, though the telephones may be open later at the main post office in a larger city. In summer 1991, one American, to his utter amazement, received mail addressed to Poste Restante in Tiranë. Albanians express considerable skepticism about the survival rates of both incoming and outgoing packages.

Accommodations

There are no longer any restrictions on where you may stay though you may be required to pay for a hotel in dollars where an Albanian can pay in leks. In hard times basic services such as running water might only be available at the more expensive facilities. Many of Albturist's hotels are being bought and renovated by private companies—the money usually comes from Albanians in Kosovë, Yugoslavia. The **Hotel Tiranë**, the second-most expensive in Tiranë, charges USD60 per night for a double with bath. Singles are rare and go for USD45. Cheaper hotels exist, but you will likely find them sickening. It is possible, and preferable, to stay in private homes (toilet paper and hot water not generally available). By summer 1992 there are bound to be agencies finding rooms in private homes, and police registration requirements seem to be on the verge of dissolving. Check with agencies in the nearest Albanian community in your country. Of course, the ideal Albanian experience is to travel between farms and hilltop *kulas* (stone fortress-homes) and experience the Albanians' legendary hospitality towards guests.

Until the privatization and publicization of more rural resort facilities progresses, the best serviced areas will be those typically visited by Albturist tours: Korçë, Pogradec, Berat, Gjirokastër, Durrës, Krujë and the isolated beaches between Vlorë and Sarandë. Shkodër serves as a good base for trips into the northern mountains.

Food, Drink and Customs

Unless people start to work again there will be no food in the country when you arrive. Even if there are shortages, however, you should avoid the hard-currency restaurants and try your luck in a restaurant frequented by natives. There may be only one dish available and it will usually incorporate meat and potatoes. Any tip will be appreciated (10-15% is generous), though service may be slow. In a private home you will be served milk, yogurt, feta cheese, tomato and onion salads and hearty public-bakery bread, if your host can find it all. More and more food is available from private merchants but at a cost prohibitive to Albanians. Wonderful trout are available in some regions, fresh from the mountain streams. In the northern mountains try *oriz më tamel,* a delicious sheep's-milk rice pudding. Follow the customs of your native companions—for instance, in the north it is considered a sign of dissatisfaction if you wipe your plate with bread at the end of a meal. In cities, stands on the street sell various incarnations of pulverized, grilled meat and bottled drinks, but many Albanians are dubious about this prototypical fast food in the absence of any sanitary licensing procedures.

Albanian tap water tastes surprisingly good—it's straight from the high mountains—but *Glina* mineral water is often available for fussier stomachs. The table wines supplied with every meal are a little rough, but generally cheap and cheerful. The local firewater is *raki,* made from grapes or other fruit; it stars in some of Albania's most powerful folk songs. Fancier hotels have a hard-currency shop, which often sells Western soft drinks and alcohol as well as souvenirs.

You probably don't belong in Albania if you are not comfortable with caffeine, nicotine, alcohol and meat. Albanian traditions of hospitality, still influenced by the ancient law of the *Kanun*—the legendary code of the medieval lawgiver Lek Dukagjini—will even override obligations for revenge, so that a house will shelter and feed a man who has killed one of its members. (The *Kanun* is now available in English translation, with prescriptions on all aspects of life from vendetta etiquette to the ritual of the first haircut.) Assuming things don't get so dramatic you will still be served coffee and *raki* and offered a smoke whenever you enter a home. In the north the exchange of cigarettes is elevated to the status of a greeting ritual—like shaking hands. In more formal situations it is best to accept graciously. You may find yourself smoking a butt, holding a pack of your own, wearing one behind the ear, and yet being offered greeting cigarettes by three strangers simultaneously. Reciprocation with Marlboros will work wonders. The same cancer sticks are useful for everything from ingratiating yourself with waiters to getting past the guards at the police and military officers' mess hall.

Even in Tiranë you may meet people who have never spoken to a foreigner before. If you are unable to communicate they are happy enough to shake their head side-to-side repeating *mirë* ("good") and to drape an arm over your shoulders with Queequegian fondness. A two-sided kiss, which seems to have evolved from the forehead tap observed in the north, is the normal greeting and farewell between members of the same sex. A man and a woman will usually just shake hands.

Under no circumstance should you turn down an invitation to an Albanian wedding. In rural areas, where many of the guests will have arrived in the back of farm trucks, the plentiful food, drink and dancing may even give way to the discharge of firearms, the quintessential Albanian expression of joy.

In general Albanian women are relegated to a secondary role in social situations, despite the fact that they perform the brunt of the physical labor in the country. It is claimed that among the educated classes women are extremely liberated, but what this means in daily life is not so clear. A foreign woman traveling alone is sure to attract an overwhelming amount of attention from Albanian men, but her safety is perhaps guaranteed by the all-pervading respect for foreigners.

As tourism increases it is inevitable that the Albanian hospitality, which leads natives to buy your meals and even your bus tickets, will erode. Get there soon.

Tiranë

With the recent lifting of the ban on private cars, Tiranë is no longer the bikers' and walkers' paradise it used to be. The city's most attractive architecture dates from the period of the Italian occupation, which ended with WWII. Food and drink shortages as well as general poverty may keep western-style nightlife to a minimum, but late-night strolling, gossiping and now political debate make Tiranë, with 300,000 inhabitants, look like other small Mediterranean cities. In 1991, open manholes and other effects of a crumbled infrastructure seemed to pose a greater threat to night-time promenades than actively hostile forces. Emerging from an era of central planning in all spheres it is only natural that Albania's capital also serves as its cultural and intellectual center.

Orientation and Practical Information

Except in *Nagel's Albania,* it's impossible to find a map of Tiranë and there are no street signs. Bring a compass. Fortunately, everything centers around Skënderbeg Square. Imagine if you will, that the Hotel Tiranë—at 15 stories the tallest building in the country—is on the north side of the square (it's actually more to the northeast). One main street goes due south behind Skënderbeg's statue and crosses the river, bringing you to the park, the university, the embassies and the Darth Vaderesque Hoxha pyramid. Another goes east towards the market. Another goes west towards the airport and Durrës. A fourth street goes due north to the railroad station. A fifth street goes northwest toward Shkodër. If you can't find something, just ask; you'll probably be escorted there.

Tourist Office: Albturist, the state travel authority, has offices in the lobby of Hotel Tiranë. The desks at Hotel Tiranë and Hotel Dajti have a paltry supply of maps and brochures.

Embassies: The American embassy was expected to open in October 1991; until it does, there will be a consul in the Hotel Dajti.

Currency Exchange: Banka e Shtetit Shqiptar (State Bank of Albania), in the southwest corner of Skënderbeg Sq. Changes any traveler's check or Eurocheque into hard currency for a 1% commission. Dispenses wired money in hard currency; their American correspondent is Crédit Lyonnais in New York. Open Mon.-Sat. 7:30-11:30am. The two main hotels (Tiranë and Dajti) may offer the same rate—check beforehand.

Post Office: Behind the State Bank. Open daily 7am-9pm, some services only til 6pm.

Telephones: Pay in hard currency at the two main hotels or in leks at the main post office. Open regular hours for international calls. Open 24 hrs. for domestic calls. **City Code:** 42.

Flights: Rinas Airport, 26km from town. A taxi should cost about USD10. Flights are usually also met by a bus to the city center. The bus leaves for the airport about 2 hrs. before each flight from the international airlines' city office, which is just west of Skënderbeg Sq. on the right side of the street. **Swissair's** office is in the Hotel Dajti.

Trains: Face the Hotel Tiranë; go due north along the street that runs on the left side of the hotel, which dead-ends into the station after 4-5 blocks. The burned-out, pissed-on ticket windows are to the right of the snack stand. Yum. Schedules are posted nearby. To: Durrës (9 per day, 1 hr., 4.50 leks); Shkodër (2 per day, 3-3½ hr., 10 leks). Service from Durrës continues to Pogradec (2 per day, 6 hr.), Fier (4 per day, 3½ hr.) and Vlorë (2 per day, 5 hr.)

Buses: Dardania Transport sends daily buses from behind the History Museum in Tiranë, which were just starting in summer 1991 (expect schedule changes). Buy tickets on board. To: Durrës (every 2 hr. from 6:15am, 40 min., 6 leks); Vlorë (at 5:30am, 3½ hr., returning from Vlorë at 1pm; 25 leks); Shkodër (at 9am, 3 hr., returning from Shkodër at 2pm; 20 leks); Kakavijë with connections to Athens (Wed. and Sat. at 4:30am, stopping in Gjirokastër). For public buses, ask a native; there are rarely any signs either at bus stops or on buses.

Public Transportation: City bus tickets normally cost 30q. In summer 1991 the ticket kiosks had closed and fares were collected on board.

Taxis: Beat-up Albanian taxis are cheaper than the bright red ones recently bought with money from Kosovë. Both haunt the Hotels Dajti and Tiranë; another stand is near the market. Agree on a price beforehand. Drivers will happily take payment in dollars.

Laundry: Hotels Dajti and Tiranë offer expensive, slow laundry service. Better to bring a sink plug.

Bookstore: Take the street that runs from the southeast corner of Skënderbeg Square; a small bookstore on the left after the street starts to curve sells some literature on Albania in English and other foreign languages.

Emergencies: Contact a foreign embassy.

Accommodations and Food

The **Hotel Tiranë** in Skënderbeg Square and the **Hotel Dajti,** a couple blocks south of the square on the left, are the only places where you are guaranteed basic services such as food, electricity and running water. Albturist has grossly inflated prices at both—at the Tiranë, the cheaper of the two, a double room with bath now costs USD60. Some of the other hotels in town have plumbing, though the water wasn't on in 1991. The **Hotel Arbëria** is the nicest of these; it's a few blocks north of Skënderbeg Square on your left. The **Hotel Drini** is behind the mosque. The **Hotel Peza** is about a block behind the Hotel Tiranë. Private rooms will probably start to sprout soon; their hawkers will find you.

Hotel Tiranë has an overpriced lek restaurant and a hard-currency bar downstairs, which should have food. **Hotel Arbëria,** on the left down the street towards the train station, is also reasonably well supplied (for leks). Behind the mosque, the **Restorant Drini** is a mess, but the waiters are friendly (ask for Gjergj and Gëzim and tell 'em Charles sent you). The restaurant at the top of the hill in the park, overlooking the artificial lake, had food in summer 1991. Behind the post office is one of many restaurants, open only for breakfast, which will weigh you out a piece of bread and a piece of cheese. Head straight east from Skënderbeg Square and look to the left for the **free market,** where home-grown vegetables, butter churns, tobacco and various and sundry chotchkies go on sale beside the empty stalls of government shops.

Sights and Entertainment

You may be driven to the conclusion that you, the tourist, are the most interesting sight in Tiranë. Meeting people who are thrilled to talk and show you around takes no effort at all. Many Albanians, mostly men, spend lots of time in one of Tiranë's many cafes or bars. In the midday heat, order a lemonade if you can find a waiter, if he can find a glass, if the water is running, if there's a table free (sharing is fine)—and sit back and observe the most exotic society in Europe.

Again, the simplest way to find your way around Tiranë is to disregard reality, treat the front of Hotel Tiranë as the northern edge of the square and orient yourself accordingly. Across the street to the west of the hotel sits the **National Historical Museum,** where knowledgeable, multilingual guides will fill you in on Albania from the Stone Age to the present beside case after case of historical displays. Be sure to look at both sides of the Apollo bust—also known as the Goddess of Butrint—which seems to change genders depending on the observer's position. (Most Tiranë museums open Fri.-Wed. 9am-noon and 5-8pm, Thurs. 5-8pm.) One block north, behind the museum, is the **variety show hall,** open several evenings a week, and a block further north is a **one-ring circus.** Cheer extra loud for Elastic Boy, the 10-year-old darling of the acrobats and star of the Albanian silver screen. One of the circus spotters is an Olympic weight-lifting champion from the 1972 Olympic Games in Munich.

The multicolumned **Palace of Culture,** where opera and concert tickets go for a mere five leks, forms the eastern edge of Skënderbeg Square. You may still see broken windows and burn marks from the 1991 demonstrations that brought down the statue of Enver Hoxha on the other side of the fountains in the square. There's a movement afoot to replace it with a statue of another famous Albanian, Mother Teresa.

Leaving the square eastwards along the Hotel Tiranë, a quick left turn will bring you to a **cinema.** Your neighborhood video shop back home will probably not carry a large supply of Albanian films; get a glimpse of this creative closed system before foreign influence creeps in. A few blocks further east leads once more to the free market; shop here for cheap souvenirs at better prices than the hotel shops.

Tiranë's main **mosque** rises on the southeast corner of Skënderbeg Square. The southern edge of Skënderbeg Square is marked by the bodacious equestrian **statue of Skënderbeg** himself. On the street behind the statue, the **Puppet Theater** is located 30 paces west, amid the yellow ministry buildings. Continuing south on the main street you'll pass more ministries and government buildings, then the main art gallery, behind which is a drama theater and the **palace of King Zog,** who betrayed the country to the Italian fascists and fled with his riches just before the outbreak of WWII. A new monarchist party, the National Democrats, has recently formed around Zog's son, Prince Leka, who now lives in South Africa but (as some theorize) could return to Albania bearing hard currency. On the right side of the main street, across from the Hotel Dajti, is a **park** where the leaders of tomorrow's Albania hang out in the evening to watch people and cars and to listen to western music when they can get their hands on some batteries. A few minutes' walk to the right along the river will bring you to the **Shqiperië Sot** (Albania Today) exhibition, renovated in 1991, where the marvels of Albanian mining, food processing and farming are on display. The souvenir shop has decent prices (in dollars).

With the demise of the **Enver Hoxha Museum** in 1991, Albania can now claim to have the world's most architecturally outrageous discotheque—the glass pyramid built at a cost of USD70 million to preserve the dictator's belongings after his death in 1985. Head south of Skënderbeg Sq. and then to the east.

Durrës

The resort and port town of **Durrës** is under an hour away from Tiranë by bus (public or private) and train. Hopefully, **ferry service** from Bari, Italy will by 1992 no longer consist of the forced repatriation of Albanian refugees. Durrës is the hub of Albania's tattered train system, with daily service to Tiranë, Pogradec, Shkodër, Vlorë and Fier. From the **train station** you can walk into town or take a bus to the beach area. **Buses** from Tiranë should stop either at the beach or in town. Durrës's main sight is a semi-excavated **Roman amphitheater** with early Christian chapels incorporated into the foundations. Leaving the amphitheater, walk towards the Adriatic past the cigarette factory where soldiers loiter, looking for freebies tossed out the windows by sympathetic workers. Turn right on the street along the shore for the small **sculpture museum.** Numerous hotels of varying grades line the beachfront; try to get a native to point out the different ones formerly reserved for foreign tourists, party officials, secret police and the like. Who knows—you might even be able to get a room.

True to the stereotype of port cities, Durrës has its mean side. During the chaos of summer 1991 violent gangs were rampaging through the town and beaches, destroying property and attacking bystanders. Albanians consider it inconceivable that a foreigner would ever be attacked, but it's not worth testing their faith in Albanian hospitality.

Northern Albania

Shkodër, in the northwest corner of Albania, is a dusty city, partially rebuilt after a 1979 earthquake. Home to one of the branches of the national university, the city was a hotbed of activity during the democratization of the last two years, and the site of the infamous massacre of Democratic Party leaders in March 1991. The insistence of the northerners on a continued investigation into the incident should continue to make waves at the highest levels of Albanian politics.

Shkodër can serve as a launching pad for forays into the mountains of the north, where archaic customs thrive, as does Albanian nationalism (manifested in the longing for unification with ethnic Albanians across the Yugoslav border in the autonomous region of Kosovë). The districts *(rrethi)* of Tropojë, Kukës and Dibrë are all known for their wild beauty. Car travelers can cut down on harrowing mountain drives by taking ferries along the Drin River, which has been dammed for hydroelectric purposes into an extensive and breathtaking system of hydroelectric lakes. Service can fluctuate with water levels so check regularly. Use the district centers as bases for day trips to more remote mountain villages. In the near future there may be guide services available for treks along ancient sheep trails into the wolf-infested mountains.

Lezhë, on the road between Shkodër and Tiranë, is the birthplace of Albanian nationalism. In 1444 Gjergj Kastrioti rebelled against the Turks who had trained him and given him the honorary name of Skënderbeg, and united the Albanian people in the League of Lezhë. See the restored hilltop castle and Skënderbeg's presumed tomb (uncovered by an earthquake in 1979) and have lunch at the nearby hunting lodge-*cum*-restaurant, which belonged to Mussolini's son-in-law before he was executed.

Southern Albania

Within a few hours' drive south of Tiranë, the hillside "museum cities" of Gjirokastër and **Berat** preserve beautiful, brown-shingled houses along narrow, dusty streets. Enver Hoxha's reconstructed boyhood home may still be standing in Gjirokastër, while the Muzeu Onufri in the fortress at Berat has an unforgettable collection of Greek Orthodox icons by medieval Albanian painters. **Sarandë,** visited by tours from Corfu, is a seaside town with warm breezes; under the Communist regime, a searchlight swept the narrow straight between it and Corfu to prevent defectors. The swimming's even better from the red beaches at **Ksamil,** just south of Sarandë. The road along the so-called "Albanian Riviera" from Sarandë to **Vlorë** is actually Albania's highest pass, with grey scrub-covered peaks above and the Adriatic far below. Most group tours visit Albania's two major classical sites, **Butrint** (south of Sarandë by the Greek border) and **Apolonia** (near Fier); although Apolonia suffers from too much reconstruction and not enough excavation, Butrint is agreeably explorable and unmolested. Further inland, many foreigners call **Korçë** Albania's most beautiful city, perhaps because the greatest concentration of Albanian immigrants trace their roots back to it; to the north, **Pogradec** is an agreeable town by the shores of Lake Ohrid.

ANDORRA

Andorra uses Spanish currency and the French telephone system. Its city code is 682.

Embracing fewer than 250km^2 between France and Spain in the hermetic confines of the Pyrenees, grape-sized Andorra (pop. 50,000) is unabashedly Europe's greatest anomaly. Despite vestiges of self-rule and autonomy in the guise of a 28-member General Assembly, Andorra remains subject to her French and Spanish overseers—respectively, the president of France and the erstwhile Count of Urgell. A mountain stronghold for the contraband trade during the Spanish Civil War and WWII, Andorra is now seeking integration with the EEC. Though many maps fail to acknowledge the country's existence, European tourists overrun the capital in search of bargains in the duty-free perfumeries and electronics shops lining the main avenue of **Andorra la Vella.** Beyond the capital's madcap consumerism, you'll discover the country of unadulterated bucolic charm that Napoleon wanted to preserve as a museum piece.

The mountains around Andorra limit access routes. All traffic from France hairpins over the **Pas de la Casa** on the eastern side of the country. Base yourself along the train line that chugs a few times per day from Toulouse south through **Ax-les-Thermes** and **L'Hospitalet** to **La Tour de Carol** on the Spanish border, connecting to Barcelona in Spain. The **Société Franco-Andorrane de Transports (SFAT)** (tel. 21 3 72 in Andorra) climbs from L'Hospitalet to Andorra la Vella (daily at 7:40am, 22F), and from May to October, directly from Ax-les-Thermes (1 per day at 4:12pm; July 15-Sept. 15 also daily at 11:56am). **Autos Pujol Huguet** sends buses from La Tour de Carol to Andorra la Vella year-round (daily at 10:45am and 6:10pm; Oct.-June daily at 10:45am). The Spanish border crossing is on the other side of Andorra, south of Sant Julià de Lòria. **Alsina Graells,** located at 34, rue Prat de la Creu in Andorra la Vella (tel. 27 3 79) makes two runs per day from Andorra-la-Vella to Barcelona and back (from Barcelona at 6:30pm and 2:45pm; 1805ptas, Sun. 2060ptas). Plan carefully, since buses are few and far between; in winter, many consider hitching.

The main **tourist office** in Andorra la Vella (tel. 20 2 14), on Avenue Docteur Villanova at the foot of the **Barri Antic** (Old Quarter), dispenses an annually updated list of the country's hotels and restaurants, but makes no reservations. (Open daily 9am-1pm and 3-7pm; Sept.-June Mon.-Sat. 10am-1pm and 3-7pm, Sun. 10am-1pm). The **youth office** in Area del Jovent, at the base of a flight of stairs to the left of a bar, informs on lodgings and cultural and sporting activities. (Open Mon.-Fri. 9am-1pm and 3-7pm.) Don't let the patina of glitzy hotels along Andorra la Vella's Avinguda Meritxell fool you; cheap *residència* make up for a lack of hostels, offering reasonable rooms without breakfast. The affable mother-daughter team that oversees the simple, clean rooms at **Residència Benazet,** 19, Carrer La Llacuna, speaks no English, but will make a valiant effort to bridge the language gap. (Singles 1000ptas. Doubles 2000ptas. Triples 3000ptas.) Camp at **St-Coloma** (tel. 28 8 99), just off the main road in Santa Coloma (5 min. by bus from the capital). (300ptas per person and per tent. No kitchen, but cheap food nearby.) Tear yourself away from the shopping fray to visit the centerpiece of Andorra la Vella's old quarter: the **Casa de la Vall** (House of the Valleys). Built in the 16th century and graced with mini-Barbican towers, the edifice serves at once as Andorra's official parliament and palace of justice.

AUSTRIA

USD$1 = 12.3 schilling (AS, or ATS)	**10AS = USD$0.81**
CAD$1 = 10.8AS	**10AS = CAD$0.93**
GBP£1 = 20.6AS	**10AS = GBP£0.49**
AUD$1 = 9.59AS	**10AS = AUD$1.04**
NZD$1 = 7.02AS	**10AS = NZD$1.42**
Country Code: 43	**International Dialing Prefix: 900**

Culturally, politically, and geographically, Austria (Österreich) binds together Eastern and Western Europe. For centuries, the Austro-Hungarian empire kept Magyars, Germans, Italians and myriad other ethnic groups united under a common political order. Even today, neutral but Western-oriented Austria serves as a commercial bridge between the industrial democracies of Western Europe and the fledgling market economies to the east. More mountainous than even Switzerland, this nation of glorious scenery and historical cities nurtured the ineffable brilliance of Mozart, Schönberg, Beethoven, Brahms, Strauß, Freud, Klimt, Kokoschka and Wittgenstein—as well as the maniacal evil of Adolf Hitler.

The once-sprawling Austrian empire is now a tiny fragment of its imperial self. Despite its lack of prior democratic tradition, post-war Austria has seen a successful, stable blend of social welfarism and democratic pragmatism. Although shaken by disputes between coalition partners, Austria's marriage of socialism-with-a-brain and conservatism-with-a-heart will probably endure. For more information on the country, pick up a copy of *Let's Go: Germany, Austria and Switzerland.*

Getting There and Getting Around

Rail travel in Austria is extraordinarily reliable and efficient, but it can be expensive (Vienna-Innsbruck 5½ hr., 620AS; Vienna-Salzburg 3½ hr., 360AS). Eurail and InterRail are valid. Austrian rail deals include the **Rabbit Card,** giving four days of unlimited travel over a ten-day period (2nd-class 1070AS; Juniors (under 27) 660AS). The **Bundes-Netzkarte** provides unlimited travel on Austrian trains for one month and scores a 50% discount on railway-operated boats and Danube steamers (2nd-class 3400AS). Seniors (men over 65, women over 60) are entitled to **half-price tickets** *(Umweltticket für Senioren)* on trains, long-distance buses, Danube steamers, and many cable cars; you must show an official **Reduction Card** *(Ermässigungsausweis),* valid for one year (220AS). All cards are available at major post offices and train stations.

The Austrian **bus** system consists of orange **Bundesbahn buses** and yellow **Post buses.** Both are efficient and cover mountain areas inaccessible by train. They usually cost a bit more than trains, and railpasses are not valid. For river **steamers** and **hydrofoils,** see the Danube section.

Austria is a hitchhiker's nightmare—Austrians rarely pick them up, and many mountain roads are all but deserted. The thumb signal is recognized, but signs with a destination and the word *bitte* (please) are just as common. For longer, inter-city routes, you could make things easier on yourself by contacting a *Mitfahrzentrale,* which charges roughly half the going rail fare to connect you with somebody traveling by car in your direction.

About 160 Austrian rail stations rent bikes. They can be returned to any participating station and cost 80AS per day—half-price if you have a train ticket *to* the station from which you are renting, and have arrived on the day of rental. Look for signs with a bicycle and the word *Verleih.* Pick up the list **(Fahrrad am Bahnhof)** of participating stations at any station. Tourist offices provide regional bike route maps. It costs 40AS to take your bike aboard a train; look for the *Gepäckbeforderung* symbol on departure schedules to see if bikes are permitted. Most Austrian train stations offer luggage storage (up to several months) for 15AS per piece; many offer lockers as well (10-20AS, depending on size).

Practical Information

The Austrian government operates a network of chipper and clued-in tourist offices *(Verkehrsamt* or *Verkehrsverein);* even the smallest towns have them. Most tourist offices will reserve private rooms, usually for free.

Western Austria is one of the world's best skiing regions. The areas around Innsbruck and Kitzbühel in the Tyrol are saturated with lifts and runs. There's good skiing year-round on several glaciers, including the Stubaital near Innsbruck and the Dachstein in the Salzkammergut. High season runs from mid-December to mid-January, from February to March, and from July to August. Local tourist offices provide information on regional skiing and can point you to budget travel agencies that offer ski packages. Lift tickets generally run 250-300AS per day.

Communication should not be a tremendous problem; English is the most common second language. Any effort, however incompetent, to use the mother tongue will win you loads of fans. See the Germany section for helpful words; "Grüß Gott" (God bless) is the typical Austrian greeting.

Banks throughout Austria are usually open weekdays 7:45am-12:30pm and 2:15-4pm. In Vienna, most banks are open Monday to Wednesday and Friday 8am-3pm, Thursday 8am-5:30pm; branch offices close from 12:30-1:30pm. Many banks offer cash advances to Visa holders (the **Zentralsparkasse und Kommerzialbank** does this at most branches). The town's main post office is usually the best place to exchange money. All banks are legally required to charge a commission for cashing foreign traveler's checks. Stores in Austria close Saturday afternoons and Sunday, and many museums take Monday off. Stores in many small towns take most of the afternoon off for lunch (usually noon-3pm). Everything closes on Austrian National Day (Oct. 26) and on religious holidays, which include Epiphany (Jan. 6), Whit Monday (occuring in May or June), Corpus Christi (June), Assumption (Aug. 15), All Saints' (Nov. 1) and Immaculate Conception (Dec. 8).

You can make international phone calls at telephone centers (usually only in the larger cities), in most post offices, and from pay phones. **Telephone cards** *(Wertkarten),* available in post offices, train stations and some stores, come in 50AS and 100AS denominations. For the operator, dial 00. For AT&T's **USA Direct,** dial 022 903 011. For directory assistance, dial 08. For the police anywhere in Austria, dial 133; for an ambulance, dial 144; for a fire, dial 122. When using an older pay-phone, you must push the red button when your party answers.

Accommodations and Camping

Rooms in Austria are usually spotless and comfortable. Even the most odious of Austria's 107 **youth hostels** *(Jugendherberge)* are, by international standards, quite tolerable. Most charge about 100AS per night (130AS in larger cities), breakfast included. Nonmembers are normally charged an extra 20AS, and sometimes turned away completely. For information about Austria's hostels or for a membership card (160AS, under 26 90AS), contact the **Österreichischer Jugendherbergsverband** (Austrian Youth Hostel Association), Schottenring 28, Wien (tel. (0222) 533 53 53); and the **Österreichisches Jugendherbergswerk,** Helferstorferstr. 4, Wien (tel. (0222) 533 18 33 or 533 18 34).

Hotels are expensive, but smaller pensions and *Gasthäuser* are often within the budget traveler's range. Local tourist offices will help set you up, and also give advice on camping. Otherwise, look for *Zimmer Frei* or *Privat Zimmer* signs; they advertise usually-inexpensive rooms in private houses (110-170AS per person). Campgrounds are the cheapest option, charging about 25-50AS per person, per tent, and per car.

The various Alpine associations in Austria currently maintain more than 1100 huts *(Schuzhütten),* which provide accommodations, cooking facilities, and occasionally, hot meals. Prices for an overnight stay are 50-150AS and no reservations are necessary; if they're crowded, you may end up sleeping on a cot, but you won't be turned away. Topographic maps *(Alpenvereinskarten),* available in most bookstores, show hut locations. If you plan carefully, you can undertake week-long hikes that bring you to a hut every night, thus freeing yourself from the burden of carrying a tent and cooking gear. Several guidebooks plot out such hikes for you. *Walking Austria's Alps Hut to Hut* by Jonathon Hurdle is excellent (USD11). Those planning extensive walking tours of the Austrian Alps may want to purchase membership in the largest of the Alpine associations, the **Österreichischer Alpenverein** (395AS, under 26 270AS, one time fee 70AS). This will entitle you to a 30-60% discount at their refuges, all of which have beds, as well as discounts on some cable car rides and organized hikes. Their main office is at Wilhelm-Greil-Str. 15, Innsbruck 6020 (tel. (05222) 58 41 07).

Even if you're going for only a day hike, check terrain and weather conditions. Weather patterns in the Alps change instantaneously. A bright blue sky can become rain—or even snow—before you can chatter "hypothermia." *Always* carry waterproof clothing and some high-energy food; wear durable footwear and tell someone where you're going. If you get into serious trouble, use the *Alpinenotsignal* (Alpine Distress Signal)—six audible or visual signals spaced evenly over one minute and followed by a break of one minute before repetition. Paths marked "Für Geübte" are for experienced climbers only. Finally, remember that those gorgeous Alpine meadows are extremely fragile habitats. Leave trails and campsites exactly as you found them.

Food and Drink

One of life's great enigmas is how a country with such unremarkable cuisine can produce such heavenly desserts. In mid-afternoon, Austrians flock to *Café-Konditoreien* to nurse the national sweet tooth with *Kaffe und Kuchen* (coffee and cake). Try *Sachertorte,* a rich chocolate pastry layered with marmalade. Staple foods include *Schweinfleisch* (pork), *Kalbsfleisch* (veal), *Wurst* (sausage), *Ei* (egg), *Käse* (cheese), *Brot* (bread) and *Kartoffeln* (potatoes). Austria's most renowned dish is *Schnitzel,* a meat cutlet (usually veal or pork) fried in butter with bread crumbs. Most butchers sell a hefty *Wurstsemmel* (sliced sausage on a bulkie roll) for under 10AS. The best discount supermarkets in Austria are **Billa, Sparmarkt, Hofer** and **Konsum.** Most Austrian restaurants expect you to seat yourself. And don't wait around for the check when you're finished; it would be a crude insult for a waiter to bring the bill without first being asked. Say *bezahle* (be-TSAHL-ah) to settle your accounts.

Imbibing in Austria is trouble-free—beer is sold more commonly than soda, and anyone old enough to see over the counter can buy it (although those under 18 will have trouble purchasing liquor and getting into nightclubs). Eastern Austria is famous for its white wine. Both reasonably priced and dry is Grüner Veltliner's *Klosterneuburger.* Austrian beers are outstanding; try *Stiegl Bier,* a Salzburg brew, *Zipfer Bier* from upper Austria, and *Gösser Bier* from Graz. Austria imports lots of Budweiser beer, a.k.a. *Budwar*—the original Czech variety, not the American imitation. For a more potent potable, try *Loköre* (liqueurs) and *Schnäpse* (schnapps); every region has a local specialty.

Vienna (Wien)

"The city was a dream," Hermann Broch once said of Vienna. The city of Mahler, Beethoven, Brahms, and Schubert—home to Sigmund Freud and Karl Kraus, birthplace of modern music and modernist architecture—has been both dream and nightmare in recent times. Its imposing palaces and cathedrals resurrect the vast Habsburg Empire, while the vigor of Kärntner Straße attests to the prosperity of the post-war Austrian welfare state. At the turn of the century, Vienna flitted between elegance and decadence, waltzing in the shadows of world war. A young Adolf Hitler was enraged by the carefree aestheticism of the *fin-de-siècle* city, rejected by its art-school jurors, and intrigued by the provincial anti-Semitism of mayor Karl Lueger. Hitler's Nazi regime, with the Austrians by and large in collaboration, sent 200,000 people to perish in Mauthausen concentration camp. Amid the pleasant cafés, elegant theater and efficient trams, the traveler can scarcely discern the tragedies of the past.

Orientation and Practical Information

Vienna is in eastern Austria, within 40km of the Hungarian and Czechoslovakian borders. The core of historic Vienna is the area south of the old Danube within the Ring, bound by the roughly circular belt of *Ring*-roads. *Bezirk* (district) numbers precede each street address. Generally, district 1 is everything inside the Ring; districts 2-9 are arranged clockwise around it inside the *Gürtel* (a major thoroughfare that surrounds the *Ring)* and any number above 9 is more distant. District numbers hide in postal codes: 1010 is district 1, 1020 is district 2, 1100 is district 10, etc. A 15-minute walk will take you between any two points in any given district. *U-Bahn* (subway) stops are indicated by U-number (subway line number) and the name of the stop.

Epicenter of Viennese life, the intersection of the Opernring, Kärntner Ring and Kärntner Straße is home to the Opera House, tourist office, and the **Karlsplatz** U-Bahn stop.

Tourist Offices: 1010 Kärntner Str. 38 (tel. 51 38 82), behind the Opera House. Pick up excellent free city map. Books rooms (350-400AS plus) for 35AS fee. Open daily 9am-7pm. Other offices at Westbahnhof (open daily 6:15am-11pm) and Südbahnhof (open daily 6:30am-10pm), at the ship station by the Reichsbrücke (open May-Sept. daily 7:30am-8pm), and at the airport (open June-Sept. daily 9am-11pm; Oct.-May 9am-10pm). Also on the A1 and A2 *Autobahns* (will book rooms). Information stands also at the following U-Bahn stations: Karlsplatz, Stephansplatz, Praterstein, Philadelphiabrücke, Landstraße and Volkstheater. All open Mon.-Fri. 8am-6pm; Karlsplatz and Stephansplatz stands also open Sat.-Sun. 8:30am-4pm. English-speaking city information office in the *Rathaus* (tel. 428 00 20 85) provides information on events. Open Mon.-Fri. 8am-6pm. Tickets sold Mon.-Fri. 10am-6pm. **Jugend-Info Wien** (Youth Information Service), Bellariapassage (tel. 526 46 37), in the underground passage at the Bellaria intersection. Entrance at the Dr.-Karl-Renner-Ring/Bellaria tram stop (on lines 1, 2, 46, 49, D, and J). Additional entrance from the Volkstheater U-Bahn station. Staffed by young, knowledgeable hipsters. Lots of info on cultural events, and sells tickets at bargain prices. Get the indispensible *Youth Scene* brochure here. Receives daily

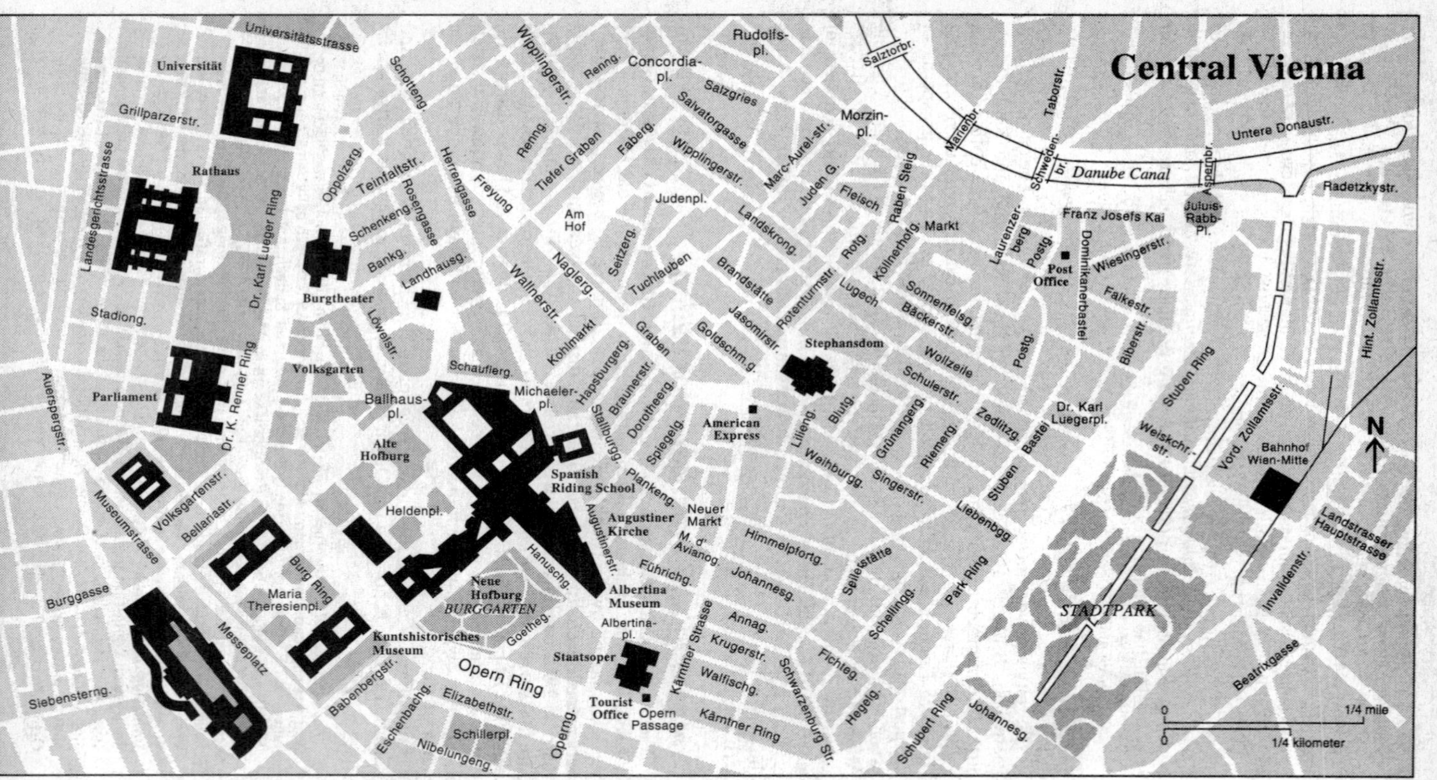
Central Vienna
Danube Canal
N
1/4 mile
1/4 kilometer
Hint. Zollamtsstr.
Radetzkystr.
Untere Donaustr.
Landstrasser Hauptstrasse
Bahnhof Wien-Mitte
Vord. Zollamtsstr.
Invalidenstr.
Beatrixgasse
Julius-Raab-Pl.
Aspernbr.
Stuben Ring
Weiskchr.-str.
STADTPARK
Franz Josefs Kai
Wiesingerstr.
Falkestr.
Biberstr.
Dominikanerbastei
Post Office
Schweden-br.
Taborstr.
Dr. Karl Luegerpl.
Postg.
Laurenzer-berg
Marienbr.
Salztorbr.
Bastei
Stuben
Zedlitzg.
Liebenbgg.
Park Ring
Johannesg.
Schubert Ring
Sonnenfelsg.
Bäckerstr.
Wollzeile
Schulerstr.
Riemerg.
Grünangerg.
Singerstr.
Raben Steig
Köllnerhofg.
Markt
Fleisch
Rotg.
Lugech
Morzin-pl.
Juden G.
Marc-Aurel-str.
Rotenturmstr.
Stephansdom
Blutg.
Weihburgg.
Seilerstätte
Schellingg.
Hegelg.
Fichteg.
Lilieng.
Rudolfs-pl.
Salzgries
Landskrong.
Brandstätte
Jasomirstr.
Goldschm.g.
American Express
Himmelpfortg.
Johannesg.
Schwarzenburg Str.
Annag.
Krugerstr.
Walfischg.
Kärntner Ring
Kärntner Strasse
Concordia-pl.
Salvatorgasse
Wipplingerstr.
Judenpl.
Tuchlauben
Graben
Spiegelg.
Dorotheerg.
Neuer Markt
M. d' Avianog.
Führichg.
Albertina Museum
Albertina-pl.
Tourist Office
Opern Passage
Staatsoper
Renng.
Faberg.
Seitzerg.
Am Hof
Naglerg.
Kohlmarkt
Braunerstr.
Hapsburgerg.
Stallburgg.
Plankeng.
Augustiner Kirche
Augustinerstr.
Spanish Riding School
Operng.
Wipplingerstr.
Tiefer Graben
Renng.
Freyung
Wallnerstr.
Michaeler-pl.
Hanuschg.
Goetheg.
BURGGARTEN
Neue Hofburg
Opern Ring
Elizabethstr.
Schillerpl.
Nibelungeng.
Herrengasse
Schotteng.
Schauflerg.
Landhausg.
Bankg.
Rosengasse
Schenkeng.
Teinfaltstr.
Oppolzerg.
Löwelstr.
Ballhaus-pl.
Alte Hofburg
Heldenpl.
Kuntshistorisches Museum
Eschenbachg.
Babenbergstr.
Universitätsstrasse
Burgtheater
Volksgarten
Dr. Karl Lueger Ring
Burg Ring
Maria Theresienpl.
Messeplatz
Universität
Rathaus
Dr. K. Renner Ring
Bellariastr.
Volksgartenstr.
Grillparzerstr.
Landesgerichtsstrasse
Stadiong.
Parliament
Museumstrasse
Auerspergstr.
Burggasse
Siebensterng.

fax from hostels detailing available openings. Open Mon.-Fri. noon-7pm, Sat. 10am-7pm. **Austrian National Information:** 4 Margarentenstr. 1 (tel. 587 20 00). Open Mon.-Fri. 9am-5:30pm. **Wiener Stadtinformation** (tel. 43 89 89) is a phone number to call (Mon.-Fri. 8am-4pm) for an answer to any question about the city.

Budget Travel: ÖKISTA, 1090 Türkenstr. 4-6 (tel. 347 52 60). Discount flight and BIJ tickets; newsy bulletin boards with personal ads. Open Mon.-Fri. 9:30am-5:30pm. Branch at 1040 Karlsgasse 3 (tel. 65 01 28) offers the same services and shorter lines. **ÖS Reisen** (Austrian Student Travel), 1010 Reichstratstr. 13 (tel. 42 15 61), sells cheap train, flight, and bus tickets. Open Mon.-Fri. 9:30am-5:30pm. **Österreichisches Verkehrsbüro** (Austrian National Travel Office), 1010 Operngasse 3-4 (tel. 588 62 38), opposite the Opera House; patient English-speaking staff sells BIJ tickets, the *Thomas Cook Timetable* (240AS) and train timetables for Eastern European countries (100AS). Open Mon.-Fri. 9am-5:30pm, Sat. 9am-noon.

Embassies: U.S., 1010 Gartenbaupromenade 2 (tel. 31 55 11), off Parkring. Open Mon.-Fri. 8:30am-noon and 1-4:30pm. **Canada,** 1010 Dr.-Karl-Lueger-Ring 10 (tel. 533 36 91). Open Mon.-Fri. 8:30am-12:30pm and 1:30-3:30pm. **U.K.,** 1030 Jauresgasse 10 (tel. 75 61 17; for after-hours emergencies 713 15 75). Open Mon.-Fri. 9:15am-noon. **Australia,** 1040 Mattiellistr. 2-4 (tel. 512 85 80 164). Open Mon.-Fri. 8:45am-1pm and 2-5pm. **New Zealand,** 1010 Lugeck 1 (tel. 52 66 36). Open Mon.-Fri. 8:30am-5pm. **Bulgaria,** 1040 Schwindgasse 8 (tel. 65 64 44). Open Mon.-Tues. and Thurs.-Fri. 9am-noon. **Czechoslovakia,** 1140 Penzingerstr. 11-13 (tel. 894 31 11 or 894 62 36). Open Mon., Wed., and Fri. 9am-noon. **Hungary,** 1 Bankgasse 4-6 (tel. 533 26 31). Open Mon.-Fri. 8:30am-12:30pm. **Poland,** 1130 Heitzinger-Haupstr. 42c (tel. 82 74 44). Open Mon.-Tues. and Thurs.-Fri. 9am-1pm. **Romania,** Prinz-Eugen-Str. 60 (tel. 505 23 43 or 505 32 27). Open Mon.-Fri. 8-11am. **Yugoslavia,** 1030 Salmgasse 4 (tel. 712 12 05). Open Mon.-Wed. and Fri. 8am-1pm, Thurs. 8am-noon.

Currency Exchange: Banks are open Mon.-Wed. and Fri. 8am-3pm, Thurs. 8am-5:30pm. Bank and airport exchanges use same official rates (minimum commission of 65AS for traveler's checks, 10AS for cash). Longer hours and lighter commission at train stations. (Daily opening hours: Opernpassage 9am-7pm, Westbahnhof 7am-10pm, Südbahnhof 6:30am-10pm, the City Air Terminal 8am-12:30pm and 2-6pm, and Schwechat airport 6:30am-11pm.) Cash advance with VISA at numerous banks, including the **Zentralersparkasse,** 1010 Kärntner Str. 32. Open Mon.-Wed. 8:30am-12:30pm and 1:30-3pm, Thurs. 8:30-12:30pm and 1:30-5:30pm.

American Express: 1010 Kärntner Str. 21-23 (tel. 515 40), down the street from main tourist office. More convenient than post office for receiving mail. Lower commission on traveler's checks than banks. Open Mon.-Fri. 9am-5:30pm, Sat. 9am-noon.

Post Office: 1010 Fleischmarkt 19 at Postgasse, in the big yellow building. During renovations, office will operate at the corner of Barbaragasse and Postgasse. Open 24 hrs., as are branches at Westbahnhof and Franz-Josefs-Bahnhof. All main branches change currency.

Telephones: At Franz-Josefs-Bahnhof, Westbahnhof, and 1010 Barbaragasse 2. Open 24 hrs. Also 1010 Börseplatz 1, near the Schottenring, and at Südbahnhof. Open daily 6am-midnight. Push red button on pay phones to connect. Deposit 1AS and up for local calls, 9AS for long-distance calls. **City Code:** 0222.

Flights: Wien Schwechat airport (tel. 77 70 22 32), 19km from the city center, is linked by regular buses (50AS) to Westbahnhof, Südbahnhof, and the City Air Terminal (next to the Hilton Hotel in 3rd district; take U-Bahn to Landstr. or train to Wien-Mitte). *Schnell-Bahn* metropolitan railway also runs to the airport each hour from Wien Mitte or Wien Nord stations (20-21AS one-way; Eurail valid; Vienna public transport passes valid). Buses leave for the airport from Westbahnhof 6am-7:15pm (every hr., 35 min.) and from Südbahnhof 6:15am-7:30pm (every hr., 20 min.). Buses leave hourly for Westbahnhof and Südbahnhof from the airport 7am-7:15pm.

Trains: Tel. 17 17, 24 hrs. English spoken. There are 4 principal stations in Vienna. **Wien-Mitte,** in the center, handles commuter trains. **Franz-Josefs-Bahnhof** handles local trains, and trains to Berlin via Prague; tram D (direction "Südbahnhof") runs to the Ring. **Westbahnhof** sends trains to France, western Germany, Switzerland, the Netherlands, Belgium, the U.K., Bulgaria, Romania, Hungary and western Austria; U-Bahn line 3 and trams #52 and 58 run to the Ring. **Südbahnhof** has trains to Italy, Yugoslavia, Greece, Czechoslovakia via Bratislava, and (June-Sept.) Bulgaria and Hungary; take tram D (direction "Nußdorf") to the Ring. To: Prague (2 per day, 5-6 hr., 400AS); Berlin (2 per day, 15 hr., 796AS); Warsaw (1 per day, 11 hr., 600AS); Budapest (3 per day, 4-5 hr., 380AS plus 80AS InterCity supplement); Kraków (1 per day, 8 hr., 500AS). Showers and baths available in the Westbahnhof at **Friseursalon Navratil,** on the ground floor. 40AS per ½-hr. shower; 60AS per ½-hr. bath. Open Mon.-Sat. 7am-8pm, Sun. 8am-1pm.

Buses: City bus terminal at **Wien-Mitte** rail station. Post and Bundesbahn buses to points all over Austria; private buses to many European cities. Currency exchange and lockers available. Domestic ticket desk open daily 6:15am-6pm; international private lines maintain travel agencies in the station. Call 711 01 for bus information (daily 6am-9pm).

Public Transportation: The **U-Bahn** (subway), bus, and tram systems are excellent. Tickets 20AS, block of 5 tickets 75AS, 24-hr. pass 45AS, 72-hr. pass 115AS. The 8-day ticket (235AS) must be stamped for each ride; with this card, 4 people can ride for 2 days, 8 for 1, etc. Week pass 125AS (requires passport-sized photo). All passes allow unlimited travel on system during period of validity; to validate, punch your ticket in the machine on board. Purchase tickets from *Tabak* kiosks or machines in major U-Bahn stations. The system closes shortly before midnight. Special night buses (25AS one-way, passes not valid) run Fri. and Sat. nights 12:30-4am between the city center (at Schwedenplatz) and various outlying districts; stops are designated by "N." signs. Tram lines and U-Bahn stops are listed on the tourist office's free city map.

Ferries: Cruise with **DDSG** to Budapest for 790AS, 1200AS round-trip. (Apr. 26-Sept. 21 Thurs.-Tues.; Sept. 22-Oct. 28 Mon., Wed., Sat.; 4½ hr.) Buy tickets at tourist offices. Boats dock at the Reichsbrücke on the New Danube (U-1: Reichsbrücke).

Taxis: Tel. 17 12; 313 00; 401 00; 601 60; 910 11. Base charge 22AS. 10AS surcharge for taxis called by radiophone, for trips on Sun. and holidays 11pm-6am and for luggage over 20kg. 20AS surcharge for luggage over 50kg.

Bike Rental: Best bargain at **Wien Nord** and **Westbahnhof** train stations. 80AS per day, 40AS with train ticket. Elsewhere in the city rental averages 30AS per hour. Pick up the *Vienna By Bike* brochure at tourist office.

Hitchhiking: Those who choose to hitch to Salzburg take the tram to the end of the line at Hütteldorf station and walk over to the beginning of the Autobahn. Those hitching south try the traffic circle near Laaerberg (tram #67 to the last stop). **Mitfahrzentrale Wien,** 5 Franzensgasse 11 (tel. 56 41 74), pairs drivers and riders (Salzburg 190AS, Innsbruck 240AS). Open Mon.-Fri. 9am-1pm and 3-6pm, Sat. 10am-2pm; off-season Mon.-Fri. 9am-1pm and 3-6pm, Sat. 10am-1pm.

Luggage Storage: Lockers at all train stations (20AS for 24 hrs.). Adequate for sizable backpacks. Left luggage office charges 15AS. Open 4am-midnight.

Lost Property: Central Lost Property Office, 1090 Wasagasse 22 (tel. 313 44 92 11). Open Mon.-Fri. 8am-midnight. For objects lost on public transport system, call 50 13 00 within 3 days.

Bookstores: British Bookshop, 1010 Weihburggasse 8. Open Mon.-Fri. 9am-6pm, Sat. 9am-noon.

Laundromat: Münzwäscherei Kalksburger & Co., 1030 Schlachthausgasse 19 (tel. 78 81 91). 90AS per 6kg. Soap 10AS. Dry 10AS. Open Mon.-Fri. 7:30am-6:30pm, Sat. 7:30am-1pm. **Münzwäscherei Margaretenstraße,** 1040 Margaretenstr. 52 (tel. 587 04 73). 85AS per 6kg, soap included. Dry 10AS. Open Mon.-Fri. 7am-6pm, Sat. 8am-noon.

Crisis Hotline: House for Threatened and Battered Women, emergency hotline 31 56 56 or 48 38 80. Open 24 hrs. **Rape Crisis Hotline,** tel. 93 22 22. Answered Mon. 9am-midnight, Tues. and Thurs. 6-9pm.

Medical Assistance: General Hospital, 1090 Alserstr. 4 (tel. 48 00).

Emergencies: Police (tel. 133); *Fremdenpolizei* (foreign police) headquarters at Bäckerstr. 13 (tel. 63 06 71). **Ambulance** (tel. 144). **Fire** (tel. 122).

Accommodations and Camping

The only unpleasant aspect of Vienna is the hunt for cheap rooms. The June crunch abates slightly from July to September, when university dorms metamorphose into hostels. Write ahead or call the day before for reservations, and make sure to pick up the lists of hostels and hotels from tourist information. During the summer, arrive between 6am and 9am, and start calling hotels from the station (most proprietors speak English). If they're full, ask for suggestions—don't waste time tramping around. Beware of offers made at the station, and shady talk of *Studentenzimmer* (student rooms), which are often weensy. Tourist offices handle private homes (3-day min. stay) in the 180-250AS range, but many of these are in the suburbs. **ÖKISTA** (see Budget Travel) finds cheaper rooms and charges no commission. The office is at 9 Türkenstr. 4-6 #314 (tel. 34 75 26 23), adjacent to the budget travel office. (Open Mon.-Wed. and Fri. 9:30am-4pm, Thurs. 9:30am-5:30pm.) In summer, the **Mitwohnzentrale** at Laudongasse 7 (tel. 402 60 61) will find you a room or apartment for 150AS per night, apartments from 500AS per day; for a stay of a month or longer, rooms from 2500AS (book 4 weeks in advance). Bring your passport. (Open Mon.-Thurs. 10am-5pm, Fri. 10am-1pm.)

Hostels

Myrthengasse (IYHF), 1070 Myrthengasse 7 (tel. 936 31 60 or 939 42 90). From Westbahnhof, take U-6 to Burggasse, then bus #48A to Neubaugasse; walk back about 50m, and take the 1st road on the right. About 15 min. by bus to city center or Westbahnhof. Sparkling rooms in historic building contain 2-4 beds, washroom and big lockers. Enthusiastic management, pleasant courtyard, gameroom, and unique lounge. 123 beds. Reception open 7:30am-1am. Lockout 9am-noon. Curfew midnight. Disabled access. Members only, 130AS. Breakfast included. Laundry 50AS per load. Call ahead and make reservations.

Neustiftgasse (IYHF), 1070 Neustiftgasse 85 (tel. 936 31 30 or 939 42 90). Around the corner from Myrthengasse and managed by the same friendly folks. 90 beds and a laundry service (50AS per load). Reception open 7:30am-1am. Lockout 9am-noon. Curfew midnight. Members only, 130AS. Breakfast included. Disabled access. Reservations recommended.

Jugendgästehaus Hütteldorf-Hacking (IYHF), 1130 Schloßberggasse 8 (tel. 877 02 63). From Südbahnhof, take U-1 to Karlsplatz, then U-4 to its terminus at Hütteldorf; cross footbridge and follow signs. From Westbahnhof, take S-50 train (Eurail valid) to Hütteldorf (last train 10:15pm; all international trains bound for Westbahnhof stop here). Great views and a huge, sunny yard. 277 beds. Reception open 7am-11:45pm (arrival before 10pm requested). Lockout 9am-4pm. Curfew 11:45pm. Members only, 130AS. 1-night guest card 30AS. Sheets, showers, and breakfast included. Laundry 60AS per load.

Jugendgästehaus Wien Brigittenau (IYHF), 1200 Friedrich-Engels-Platz 24 (tel. 338 29 40). Efficient and helpful management oversees brigades of high-school kids. Take subway to Schwedenplatz and then tram N to Floridsdorfer Brücke/Friedrich-Engels-Platz. 334 beds. Reception open 24 hrs. Lockout 9am-4pm. Flexible midnight curfew. Members only, 130AS, breakfast included.

Schloßherberge am Wilhelminenberg (IYHF), 1160 Savoyenstr. 2 (tel. 458 50 37 00—yes, all 9 digits). Always a pleasure to sleep in a castle. Out in the woods, but beautiful. From Westbahnhof, take U-6 (direction "Friedensbrücke") to Thaliastraße stop, then take tram #46 to bus #46B or 146B at Maroltingerstraße stop. 164 beds in comfortable quads, all with shower and WC. Disabled access. Reception open 7am-midnight. 170AS, breakfast included. Open March-Oct.

Hostel Ruthensteiner, 1150 Robert-Hamerling-Gasse 24 (tel. 83 46 93 or 830 82 65), 3 min. walk from Westbahnhof. Walk down Mariahilferstr., take 1st left at Palmgasse, then 1st right. Small, sunny rooms. Pop in and say hi to Neil and Angelica in the Presidential Suite. 76 beds. Reception open 24 hrs. Courtyard and kitchen. Dorm bed (bring sheet or sleeping-bag) 119AS. Singles 199AS. Doubles 358AS. 100AS for extra bed. Breakfast 22AS. 50AS key deposit for big lockers. Bicycle rental 78AS per day. Call before arriving.

Turmherberge "Don Bosco" (IYHF), 1030 Lechnerstr. 12 (tel. 713 14 94). U-4 to Landstr., then bus #75 to Lechnerstr. 50 beds. Reception open 6am-noon and 5-11:30pm. Lockout 9:30am-5pm. Curfew 11:30pm. Hours and location are inconvenient, but at 58AS (breakfast included) it's the cheapest in town. Catholic management provides dulcet 8am wake-up call by loudspeaker. Open March-Nov.

Hostel Zöhrer, 1080 Skodagasse 26 (tel. 43 07 30), just off Alserstr. Take bus #13A from Südbahnhof, tram #5 from Westbahnhof, tram #43 or 44 from along the Ring. 30 beds. Hospitable owner tends garden courtyard, furnished kitchen and front-door key. Reception open 8am-10pm. 150AS per person. Sheets, showers, breakfast and kitchen facilities included.

Believe-It-Or-Not, 1070 Myrthengasse 10, #14 (tel. 526 46 58 or 96 46 58), at Neustiftgasse off Burgring. From Südbahnhof, take bus #13A to Kellermanngasse or walk 15 min. from Westbahnhof. Camaraderie flourishes in cramped quarters. Wonderful, fully-equipped kitchen. Buckets o' hot water. Thoughtful owner. Lockout 10:30am-12:30pm. 160AS per person. Sheets and showers included. Call ahead.

University Dormitories

The following dorms become summer hostels generally from July to September. Expect mass-produced university cubicles.

City Hostel, 1010 Seilerstätte 30 (tel. 512 84 63 or 512 79 23), 2 blocks from the main tourist office. As central as they come. 170 beds. Reception open 24 hrs. Singles 260AS; doubles 180AS per person; after 1st night 220AS and 165AS. Breakfast included. Bring IYHF card or student ID.

Porzellaneum der Wiener Universität, 9 Porzellangasse 30 (tel. 34 72 82). From Südbahnhof, take tram D towards Nußdorf and get off at the Fürstengasse stop. From Westbahnhof, take tram #5 to Franz-Josefs-Bahnhof, then tram D (direction "Südbahnhof") to Fürstengasse. Renovated singles and doubles 145AS per person, 160AS for one-night stands. Sheets and showers included. Make a reservation.

Haus Pfeilheim, 1080 Pfeilgasse 6 (tel. 438 47 62), in the Hotel Avis. From Südbahnhof, take bus #13A up Strozzigasse. From Westbahnhof, take the U-Bahn to Thaliastr., then walk a block north to Pfeilgasse and take a right (15-20 min.). Spartan rooms, but clean and more than adequate. 400 beds. Reception open 24 hrs. Singles 220AS. Doubles 190AS per person. Breakfast included.

Katholisches Studentenhaus, 1190 Peter-Jordan-Str. 29 (tel. 34 92 64), From Westbahnhof, take tram #38 to the Hardtgasse stop, then turn left onto Peter-Jordan-Str. From Südbahnhof, take tram D to Schottentor, then #38 to Hardtgasse. The reception's on the 2nd floor. Singles and doubles 140AS per person. An affiliated dorm (with doubles only) is at 1210 Zaunschertgasse 4 (tel. 38 21 97).

Sommerhotel Josefstadt, 1080 Buchfeldgasse 16 (tel. 43 52 11), behind the *Rathaus*. Take tram J from the Dr.-Karl-Lueger-Ring stop. Great location, cushy rooms, lots of hot water, and a mongo breakfast. Doubles 250-275AS per person.

Hotels and Pensions

Irmgard Lauria, 1070 Kaiserstr. 77, apt. 8 (tel. 93 41 52), a 10-min. walk down Kaiserstr. from Westbahnhof, or take tram #5 during the day to Burggasse. From Südbahnhof, take #13A to Kellermahngasse, then #45A to Kaiserstr. Enchanting, custom-designed rooms. Owner and staff are warm and thoughtful. Billowy down quilts, color TVs, refrigerators, hot pots, and front door keys provided. 2-night min. stay on advance bookings. Dorms 160AS. Doubles 460-500AS, with bath 660AS. Triples 660AS, with bath 750AS. Quads 800AS, with bath 880AS.

Pension Kraml, 1060 Brauergasse 5 (tel. 587 85 88), off Gumpendorferstr. From Westbahnhof, walk down Mariahilferstr., take the 3rd right onto Otto-Bauer-Str., make the 1st left, then the 1st right (15 min.). From Südbahnhof, take bus #13A. Tidy, comfortable, new, and run by a cordial family. The hallways and larger rooms outshine the singles. Singles 230AS. Doubles from 520AS, with shower 620AS. Triples 840AS. Quads 1040AS. Breakfast included. Call ahead.

Privatzimmer Hedwig Gally, 1150 Arnsteingasse 25 (tel. 812 90 73 or 830 42 44). 10-min. walk from Westbahnhof. Incredibly cozy, clean, and comfortable. All rooms sport a hot plate; some have elegant chandeliers. Singles 210AS. Doubles 360AS, with shower 440AS. Triples 510AS, with shower 570AS. Breakfast 40AS. Extra bed 100AS. Call ahead.

Camping

Wien-West I and **II,** at Hüttelbergstr. 40 and 80 (tel. 94 14 49 and 94 23 14), respectively, are the most convenient (both in the 14th *Bezirk* about 6km out of the city center; both 52AS per person, 50AS per tent/car, 30AS per child). I is open from late June to early September; II year-round. II also rents four-person bungalows (360AS). For either, take U-4 to the end, then switch to bus #52B. Both offer laundry and cooking facilities, grocery stores and more.

Food

Viennese cuisine was born of the city's imperial position, and its specialties betray the influence of Eastern Europe; try *Serbische Bohnensuppe* (Serbian bean soup) and *Goulash* (spicy beef stew). Even the vaunted *Wiener Schnitzel* (fried pork or veal with bread crumbs) originated in Milan. *Wurst* stands vend tasty and inexpensive fare. Vienna's sublime desserts are impossibly rich, although you may not be after paying for them.

The restaurants in the touristy **Kärntnerstraße** area are generally overpriced. A better bet is the neighborhood just north of the university where **Universitätsstraße** and **Währingerstraße** meet; reasonably priced *Gaststätten, Kneipen* (bars), and restaurants are easy to find. Otherwise, nibble the aromatic delicacies at the open-air **Naschmarkt** at Linke Wienzeile and Getreidemarkt and other places scattered throughout Vienna. (Open Mon.-Fri. 7am-6pm, Sat. 7am-1pm.) For discount supermarket fare, try the ubiquitous *Billa.* Except at train stations, all grocery stores close from Saturday afternoon to Monday morning. To avoid starving on Sunday or a holiday, try shops in and around train stations. Vegetarians can always find a meal like *Gemüsestrudel* (vegetable strudel) at the **Wienerwald** restaurant chain, and should check out the two **Wrenkh** restaurants as well. The **Pizzaparadies** and **Pizzaland** franchises offer pizzas from 51AS and 54AS respectively. Eat early, for few restaurants serve after 10pm. Two succulent flavors of ice cream from the fancy *Eissalons* cost only 10AS.

Restaurants

Schnitzelwirt Schmidt, 1070 Neubaugasse 52. From the Burgring, take bus #49 until it stops at Neubaugasse (5 min.). The bigger-than-your-plate *Schnitzel* (55AS), *Knoblauchschnitzel* (schnitzel with garlic, 73AS), and *Mohr im Hemd* (pancake with chocolate and whipped cream, 38AS) will sate your desires and spare your budget. Portions big enough for 2. Open Mon.-Fri. 11am-10pm, Sat. 11am-2:30pm and 5-10pm. Closed 3 weeks in Aug. and Dec. 24-Jan. 6.

Tunnel, 1080 Florianigasse 39. Take the U-2 to Landesgerichtstr., and walk opposite the *Rathaus.* A popular young pub serving pizza, pasta, and *Schnitzel* (35-98AS).

Trześniewski, 1010 Dorotheergasse 1, 3 blocks from Stephansdom. A famous stand-up sandwich restaurant—they've been serving open-face delicacies for over 75 years. Franz Kafka used to stuff his face here. Small sandwiches (¼ slice of bread) about 7AS. Open Mon.-Fri. 9am-7:30pm, Sat. 9am-1pm. Another branch at 1070 Mariahilferstr. 26-30, in the Herzmansky department store. Open Mon.-Fri. 9am-6pm, Sat. 8:30am-1pm.

University Mensa, 1090 Universitätsstr. 7, on the 7th floor of the university building, midway between U-2 stops Rathaus and Schottentor. Open to all. Ride the groovy old-fashioned elevator (no doors and it never stops; you have to jump in and out). Typical university meals in the dining hall 20-50AS; open Mon.-Fri. 11am-2pm. An adjacent snack bar open Mon.-Fri. 8am-7pm. There are other inexpensive student cafeterias throughout the city.

Sobieski, 1070 Burggasse 83, 5 min. by bus #48 from the Burgring. Superb Polish specialties in a friendly, romantic atmosphere. 70-128AS, lunch special 52AS. Open Mon.-Fri. 11am-3pm and 6-11pm.

Blue Lotus, 1070 Burggasse 123, at Neubaugürtel. 8-min. on bus #48A from Burgring, or 2 stops from Westbahnhof on tram #8. A Chinese restaurant with specialties from Singapore. Large lunch *menus* 52-55AS. A la carte meals 68-88AS. Open daily 11:30am-3pm and 5:30pm-midnight.

Cafés and Konditoreien

The café is a centerpiece of Vienna's unhurried charm. Choose a piece of cake at the counter before sitting down; often you'll pay for it immediately and give your receipt to the server when you order beverages. With any luck, the server then returns with your pastry. Coffee can be ordered *schwarzer* (black), *brauner* (a little milk), *melange* (light), and *mazagron* (iced with rum).

Demel, 1010 Kohlmarkt 14. Walk ten minutes from Stephansdom or Imperial Palace. Deservedly the most famous bakery in Austria. Heavenly cakes (35-45AS) arranged like jewels in glass cases. Consume them in *fin-de-siècle* elegance. Open daily 10am-6pm.

Hotel Sacher, 1010 Philharmonikerstr. 4 (tel. 512 14 87), around the corner from the main tourist information office. This historic sight has been serving its world-famous *Sacher Torte* (a delicious chocolate-peach cake, 45AS) in red velvet elegance for years. Open daily 6:30am-midnight.

Café Hawelka, 1010 Dorotheergasse 6, 3 blocks from Stephansdom. The artists, intellectuals and radicals hang out here, devouring the irresistible *warme Büchteln,* sweet rolls filled with preserves (available only after 10pm). Coffee 30-40AS. Open Wed.-Sat. and Mon. 8am-2am, Sun. 4pm-2am.

Sperl, 1060 Gumpendorferstr. 11, 5 min. from Westbahnhof. The *fin-de-siècle* Vienna art nouveau circle gathered here long before the usurping tourists. Billiards every morning and evening at 9:30. Coffee 20-33AS, cake 28AS. Open Mon.-Sat. 7am-11pm; July-Aug. also Sun. 3-11pm.

Sights

Vienna from A to Z (30AS from the tourist office, more in bookstores) gives all you need for a self-created tour. The free *Museums Vienna* brochure from the tourist office lists all opening hours and admission prices. Individual museum tickets usually cost 15AS; 150AS will buy you a book of 14. It also distinguishes municipal museums (admission free on Fri. mornings) from national museums (admission free the first Sun. of the month).

Start your odyssey at the Gothic **Stephansdom,** in the city center at the Stephansplatz U-1 stop. The smoothly tapering stone lace spiral of this magnificent cathedral has become Vienna's emblem, appearing on every second postcard. (Tours in English Mon.-Sat. 10:30am and 3pm, Sun. and holidays 3pm. Also June-Sept. Sat. 7pm, and July-Aug. Fri. 7pm.) View Vienna from the **Nordturm** (North Tower; elevator ride 30AS, open daily 9am-5:30pm). Next to the elevator, descend to the catacombs, the final resting place of the Habsburgs. The marvelous **Kärntner Straße** connects Stephansdom to the **Staatsoper** (State Opera House). During the summer, street music fills the air with everything from Bolivian mountain music to Dylan to Schubert. If you miss the shows (standing room tickets 15AS) at the Opera House, tour the glittering gold, crystal, and red velvet interior (featured in the movie *Amadeus* and once conducted in by Mahler). (Tours July-Aug. daily 11am-3pm on the hour; Sept.-June on request.)

From the Opera House, follow the Opernring around to the **Hofburg** (Imperial Palace). *Vienna from A to Z* will get you around this monstrous complex, home to the Habsburg emperors until 1918, and currently the Austrian president's offices. Wander through the *Schweizerhof* (Swiss Courtyard), the *Schatzkammer* (treasuries), the *Burgkapelle* (chapel, where the Vienna Boys' Choir sings mass on Sundays and religious holidays), the *Schauräume* (state rooms), the *Neue Burg* (New Palace), built from 1881-1913, and the *Kaiser Appartment.* (Open Mon.-Sat. 8:30am-noon and 12:30pm-4pm, Sun. 8:30am-12:30pm; tours 25AS, students 10AS.) Between Josefsplatz and Michaelerplatz sit the Palace Stables *(Stallburg),* home to the Royal Lipizzaner stallions of the **Spanische Reitschule** (Spanish Riding School). Their equine performances (March and Nov. to mid-Dec. Sun. at 10:45am; April-June and Sept. Sun. at 10:45am and Wed. at 7pm) are always sold out; you must reserve tickets six months in advance. (Write to Spanische Reitschule, Hofburg, A-1010 Wien (tel. 533 90 32). If you reserve through a travel agency, you pay a 22% surcharge. Write only for reservations; no money will be accepted. Tickets 200-600AS, standing room 150AS.) Watching the horses train is much cheaper. (March-June and Nov. to mid-Dec. Tues.-Sat. 10am-noon; Feb. Mon.-Sat. 10am-noon, except when the horses tour. Tickets sold at the door at Josefsplatz, Gate 2, from about 8:30am. Admission 50AS, children 15AS. No reservations.)

Across the street on the other side of Burgring is the world-famous **Kunsthistorisches Museum,** home to one of the world's best art collections, including entire rooms of prime Brueghels, Vermeer's *Allegory of Painting* and numerous works by Rembrandt, Rubens, Titian, Dürer and Velázquez. Cellini's famous golden salt cellar is here, along with a superb collection of ancient art and a transplanted Egyptian burial chamber. (Open Tues.-Fri. 10am-6pm, Sat.-Sun. 9am-6pm; Nov.-March Tues.-Fri. 10am-4pm, Sat.-Sun. 9am-4pm. Admission 95AS, seniors and students 45AS.)

Follow Burgring west through the **Volksgarten's** hundreds of varieties of roses to reach the impressive, sculpture-adorned **Parliament** building—a gilded lily of neoclassical architecture adorned with scads of sculpture. Just up Dr.-Karl-Renner-Ring is the **Rathaus,** an intriguing remnant of late 19th-century neo-Gothic with Victorian mansard roofs and red geraniums in the windows. The **Burgtheater** opposite contains frescoes by Klimt. Immediately to the north on Dr.-Karl-Lueger-Ring is the **Universität.** The surrounding sidestreets gush cafés, bookstores, and bars. Here also is the meager **Sigmund Freud Haus Museum,** Berggasse 19, where Freud lived from 1891 to 1938. (Open daily 9am-3pm. Admission 30AS, students 15AS.)

If your appetite for art is still only whetted, take tram D to the **Museum Moderner Kunst** (Museum of Modern Art) in Liechtenstein Palace at 1090 Fürstengasse 1, which displays Klimt's *Portrait of Adele Block-Bauer,* Schiele's *Portrait of Eduard Kosmack,* a Picasso Harlequin, and various Magrittes, Légers, and Ernsts. (Open Wed.-Mon. 10am-6pm. Admission 28AS.) The **Albertina,** 1010 Augustinerstr. 1, is one of the world's finest collections of graphic art, with 200,000 original etchings and prints and 20,000 drawings and watercolors, including works by Dürer, Michelangelo, Rembrandt, and Rubens—though only facsimiles of the real treasures are displayed. (Open Mon.-Tues. and Thurs. 10am-4pm, Wed. 10am-6pm, Fri. 10am-2pm, Sat.-Sun. 10am-1pm; July-Aug. Mon.-Sat. only. Admission 28AS.) Vienna's Old Masters repose in the **Akademie der Bildenden Künste** (Academy of Fine Arts), 1010 Schillerplatz 3, which contains Hieronymus Bosch's oh-so-spooky *Last Judgment* and works by a score of Dutch painters. (Open Tues., Thurs. and Fri. 10am-2pm, Wed. 10am-1pm and 3-6pm, Sat.-Sun. 9am-1pm. Admission 15AS, students 5AS.)

The greatest monument of *fin-de-siècle* Vienna is the **Secession Building,** Friedrichstr. 12, built just before the turn of this century when some artists broke with the uptight Vienna art establishment. Joseph Olbrich designed this extraordinary ivory-and-gold edifice as a reaction to the overblown neoclassicism of the Ring museums. Exhibits by contemporary artists adorn the walls, as does Gustav Klimt's bodacious *Beethoven Frieze.* (Open Tues.-Fri. 10am-6pm, Sat.-Sun. 10am-4pm. Admission 20AS, 10AS if you're just friezing.) Those interested in Klimt and his fellow radicals Egon Schiele and Oskar Kokoschka should try to visit the **Austrian Gallery,** in the **Belvedere Palace,** entrance at Prinz-Eugen-Str. 27. Also check out the *Biedermeier*-era paintings and the breathtaking view of the city from the upper floors. (Open Tues.-Sun. 10am-4pm. Admission 60AS, students 30AS.)

For more of the art nouveau movement, visit the **Österreichisches Museum für Angewandte Kunst** (Museum of Applied Art), 1010 Stubenring 5 (tel. 711 36), the oldest museum of applied arts in Europe. Otto Wagner furniture and Klimt sketches sit amidst crystal, china, furniture, and rugs from the Middle Ages to the present. (Open Wed.-Mon. 11am-6pm. Last entry 5:30pm. Admission 30AS, students 15AS.) *Art Nouveau in Vienna* is an excellent pamphlet prepared by the tourist office, with color photos and a discussion of the style's top addresses in town. Request the *Jugendstil* map as well. Unmissable creations are Otto Wagner's **Pavilion** at Karlsplatz, the major U-Bahn station, his **Kirche am Steinhof,** 1140 Baumgartner Höhe 1 (take bus #48A to the end of the line) and his **Postsparkassenamt** (Post Office Savings Bank), on the Postgasse.

Music lovers might also trek out to the **Zentralfriedhof** (Central Cemetery), 11 Simmeringer Hauptstr. 234, where Beethoven, Brahms, Wolf, Schubert, the Straußes, Schönberg, Schmidt, Pfitzner, Lotte Lehmann, Bösendorfer, Salieri, Mozart, and Jim Morrison are buried. Take tram #71. (Open daily May-Aug. 7am-7pm; March-April and Sept.-Oct. 7am-6pm; Nov.-Feb. 8am-5pm.) The **Prater** is an amusement park and forest between the city and the Danube where you can spin on the *Riesenrad,* a colossal ancient ferris wheel cherished as a symbol of the city.

Entertainment

Music and Theater

You can enjoy Viennese opera in the imperial splendor of the **Staatsoper** (State Opera House) for a mere 15-35AS. Get in line on the west side early (about 4:30-

5:30pm) for standing room *(Stehplätze,* sold only on day of performance). Go early to get tickets for the center because you see nothing standing at the side. Bring a scarf to tie on the rail to save your place during the show. Costlier advance tickets (100-600AS) are on sale at the **Bundestheaterkassen,** 1010 Goethegasse (tel. 514 44 22 18; open Mon.-Fri. 8am-6pm, Sat. 9am-2pm, Sun. 9am-noon). They also sell tickets for Vienna's other public theaters, the **Volksoper, Burgtheater,** and **Akademietheater.** Discount tickets for these theaters go at the door an hour before performances (50-400AS); students must have a non-ISIC student ID *(Studentenausweise;* standing room is 15AS and up). Vienna's musical glory is, however, the **Vienna Philharmonic Orchestra,** which performs in the **Musikverein.** For tickets, write to the Gesellschaft der Musikfreunde, Dumbastr. 20, A-1010.

Vienna, most musical of cities, wanes somewhat in summer—the **Staatsoper** and the **Wiener Sängerknaben** (Vienna Boys' Choir) vacation during July and August. During the rest of the year the Sängerknaben sing 9:15am mass each Sunday at the **Burgkapelle** (Royal Chapel) of the Hofburg. Reserve tickets at least two months in advance; write to Verwaltung der Hofmusikkapelle, Hofburg, Schweizerhof, A-1010 Wien. Do not enclose money. Unreserved seats are sold starting at 5pm on the preceding Friday. Standing room is free. Sunday High Masses in the major churches (Augustinerkirche, Michaelerkirche, Stephansdom) are accompanied by choral or organ music that approaches the celestial.

The **Theater an der Wien,** 1060 Linke Wienzeile 6, opens with musicals in July (entrance to box office at Lehárgasse 5; tickets 170-500AS), and the **Wiener Kammeroper** performs during the summer in Schloß Schönbrunn (tickets 50-350AS). The **Arkadenhofkonzerte** are fine orchestral concerts held in the courtyard of the *Rathaus.* The setting is memorable, the programs familiar, and the tickets reasonable, but buy them at the *Rathaus* to avoid a service charge. (July-Aug. Tues.-Thurs. at 8pm. Admission 120AS.) On Wednesday and Saturday summer evenings, there are combined tours/concerts at Schönbrunn; be there at 7:15pm for the tour, 8:15pm for the music (150AS). During the summer, free tidbits of music by all the famous Viennese composers are performed in front of the *Rathaus* (Tues. and Fri. at 5pm). See the pamphlets *Wien Monats Programm* and *Wiener Musiksommer* for more ideas.

English theater is offered at **Vienna's English Theatre,** 1080 Josefsgasse 12 (tel. 42 12 60 or 42 82 84; box office open Mon.-Sat. 10am-6pm, evening box office opens at 7pm; tickets 150-420AS, students 100AS on night of performance), and at the **International Theater,** 1090 Porzellangasse 8 (tel. 31 62 72; tickets 220AS, seniors and students under 26 120AS). Check the *Youth Scene* for a list of English-language films playing in Vienna.

Heurigen and Nightlife

Vienna is almost as famous for its *Heurigen* (outside seating at picnic tables, with mugs of wine and a sprig of pine hung over the door) as for its art and music. Unique to Vienna, *Heurigen* began when Empress Maria Theresa, in a fit of largesse, allowed the local wine-growers to sell and serve their wine in their homes at certain times of the year. The mood is festive and informal; in most places, you can carry out food served inside or bring a picnic. Only wine produced on the property is served. After the feast of Martinas on November 11, the wine remaining from last year's crop becomes "old" wine—no longer authentic *Heurigen*—so Viennese mount a huge effort to spare the wine this fate by consuming it. You might want to know (since Austrian wine can be sickly sweet) that the word for "dry" is *trocken.*

Heurigen freckle the northern, western, and southern suburbs, where grapes are grown. **Grinzing** is the largest *Heurigen* area, but the atmosphere and the wine are better in **Nußdorf** (tram D from the Ring), in **Sievering** (tram #38 and change to a bus), and in **Salmannsdorf** (tram #38 and change to #35). One of the best *Heurigen* is in Beethoven's home in **Heiligenstadt** (open Jan. 11-Dec. 19). Take tram #37 to the last stop, walk down Wollergasse and through the park, take a right, then take your first left on Pfarrplatz. Ask the tourist office for its extensive list of *Heurigen.* Most are open daily from 4pm to 11pm; wine is about 120AS per liter.

There are some wonderful *Weinkeller* (wine cellars) downtown as well. **Zwölf Apostelkeller,** 1010 Sonnenfelsgasse 3, like Hell, has many levels—the lowest is the liveliest. This is one of the best Viennese cellars, with much atmosphere and lots of locals. (Open Aug.-June daily 4:30pm-midnight.) **Esterházykeller,** 1010 Haarhof, off Naglergasse, is the cheapest and perhaps the best *Weinkeller* in Vienna; a ¼ liter is 18-22AS, and food is inexpensive. Try the *Grüner Veltliner* wine from Burgenland. (Open Mon.-Fri. 10am-1pm and 4-9pm, Sat.-Sun. and holidays 4-9pm.)

Vienna has a fast-paced, cutting-edge nightlife. *Falter-Zeitschrift,* a local newspaper, is the best source of information on the scene. In summer it provides partial English coverage in the entertainment section. The 8th district is renowned for its student-oriented establishments, such as **The Tunnel,** featuring good music and a casual atmosphere. (Open 10am-2am; live music daily from 8:30pm. Cover 30-90AS, Mon. free. See restaurant listing.) Loved by all, the **Schwelzerhaus,** 1020 Str. des 1 Mai 116, in the Prater, serves daily specials and beer beneath leafy trees. (Open March-Nov. daily 10am-midnight.) Nightlife centers around the **Bermuda Dreieck,** just north of Stephansdom. For disco, a major rager is **P1,** 1010 Rotgasse 3, 2 blocks north of Stephansdom (tel. 535 99 95; open Mon.-Thurs. 9pm-4am, Fri.-Sat. 9pm-5am). For jazz, try **Jazzland,** 1010 Franz-Josefs-Kai 29 (tel. 533 25 75; open Tues.-Sat. 7pm-2am), and **Opus One,** 7 Mahlerstr. 11 (tel. 513 20 75; open daily 8:30pm-4am; cover varies). **Manhattan,** Laimgrubengasse 3 (tel. 587 44 78), is a relaxed bar for gay men. Ring the doorbell to be let in. (Open daily 8pm-4am. No cover.) **Why Not?,** 1 Tiefer Graben (tel. 66 11 58), is a plush disco and bar for gay people. Keep up with the latest through the *Youth Scene* brochure.

The Danube (Donau)

The "Blue Danube" is largely the invention of Johann Strauss's ¾ imagination, but this mighty, muddy-green river still merits a cruise. The **Erste Donau Dampfschiffahrts-Gesellschaft (DDSG)** runs ships daily from May to late October. They operate offices in Vienna (Handelskai 265, by the Reichsbrücke; tel. (0222) 21 75 00), Linz (Nibelungenbrücke; tel. (0732) 27 00 11) and Passau (Im Ort 14a, Dreiflußeck; tel. (0851) 330 35). Cruises run from Vienna to Grein and between Linz and Passau, Germany. East of Vienna, hydrofoils run to Bratislava, Czechoslovakia, and Budapest, Hungary. Fortunately, Eurailpasses are valid, while InterRail merits a 50% discount. Everyone pays full fare for the eastbound hydrofoils.

Between Krems and Melk along the Vienna-Grein route, ruined castles stand as crumbling testimony to Austria's glorious past. Ships run from Vienna upstream to Krems (5 hr. upstream, 3¾ hr. downstream, 294AS, round-trip 442AS) and from Krems further along to Melk (3 hr. upstream, 1¾ hr. downstream, 220AS, round-trip 330AS). You can also sail from Vienna to Melk (8 hr. upstream, 5½ hr. downstream, 490AS, round-trip 736AS). Few make the full Vienna-Grein run (11¼ hr. upstream, 8¼ hr. downstream, 686AS, round-trip 1030AS). Bikes can be brought on board for 35AS, but call in advance to make arrangements. Check with tourist office for a variety of reduced fares, as well as train-ship and bus-ship combinations (from Vienna by train to Krems takes 1 hr., to Melk 2 hr.).

Like a feudal princess, **Krems an der Donau** is beautiful and virtually silent. Find window shopping paradise along Krem's **Obere Landstraße** and **Untere Landstraße.** Climb the covered stairway to the 15th-century **Piaristenkirche,** a light Gothic structure with baroque altars. The pedestrian zone was renovated in medieval style, with pastel 17th-century houses lining the tranquil Steiner Landestraße. The **tourist office,** Undstr. 6 (tel. (02732) 826 76), just down Wichnerstr. (which becomes Schillerstr.) from Südtirolerplatz, finds affordable rooms. (Open Mon.-Fri. 9am-noon and 2-6pm, Sat. 10am-1pm and 2-6pm; Nov.-April Mon.-Fri. 8:30am-noon and 1:30-5pm.) Train service connects Krems to the outside world; the station (tel. (02732) 825 36) sits off the thoroughfare of Ringstr. The **Jugendherberge (IYHF),** Kasenstr. 6 (tel. (02732) 842 17), near Südtirolerplatz, resembles an army barracks. (Reception open 5-10pm. Lockout 9am-5pm. Curfew 10pm. 100AS, sheets and breakfast included. Members only.) A second **Jugendherberge (IYHF)** at Ringstr. 77 (tel. (02732) 834 52) accommodates 52 in 4-6 bed rooms amidst a leafy yard. (Reception open 5-10pm. Lockout 9am-5pm. Curfew 10pm. Members only, 145AS, sheets and breakfast included. 140AS for additional nights.) Right by the marina is **Donau Camping,** Wiedengasse 7 (tel. (02732) 44 55), on the Danube. (35AS per person, 10-30AS per tent, 30AS per car; warm showers included; open mid-April to Oct. daily 7:30-10:30am and 4:30-7:30pm.) Bargain eats are scarce in Krems. **Gasthaus Neuwirth,** Wienerstr. 3 (tel. (02732) 841 34), just off the Ringstr., serves local Austrian dishes to a local clientele. (Open daily 8am-10pm.)

Melk, sprawled along the south bank of the Danube upstream from Krems, boasts the recently restored **Benediktinerstift,** a monastery adorned with gold-leaf angels. (Open Palm Sunday-Nov. 1 daily 9am-5pm; Nov. 2-Palm Sunday by obligatory tours at 11am and 2pm. Admission 40AS, 50AS with tour; students (under 26, with ID) and children 20AS, 30AS with tour. Hourly tours in German; check with the admission desk for English tours.) You might also bike (some hitch) 5km out of town to visit the **Schallaburg,** one of the most magnificent Renaissance castles in central Europe. Take Kirschengraben (off Lindestr., itself off Bahnhofstr.) out of town and turn right under the *Autobahn.* Or hop the "Taxi Bus" (30AS each way) that travels to the castle from in front of the train station daily at 10:30am and 3:10pm. (Open May 18-Oct. Mon.-Fri. 9am-5pm, Sat.-Sun. and holidays 9am-6pm. Admission to castle, thematic art exhibits and tranquil grounds 50AS, students and children 15AS, seniors 30AS, families 80AS. Guided tour additional 20AS. Combined admission to Melk Abbey 72AS.) The genial **tourist office,** Rathauspl. 11 (tel. (02752) 23 07), is in the center of town. (Open July to mid-Aug. daily 9am-6pm; mid-April to mid-June and mid-Aug. to mid-Oct. Mon.-Sat. 9am-noon and 3-7pm, Sun. and holidays 9am-noon; mid-Oct. to mid-April Mon.-Fri. 7am-noon and 1-4pm.) Single private rooms start at 150AS, pension rooms at 160AS. The Melk **train station** (tel. (02752) 23 21) is on Bahnhofstr., a 10-min. walk from the tourist office. Buses serving the local area pick up here too. Melk's **Jugendherberge (IYHF),** Abt-Karl-Str. 42 (tel. (02752) 26 81), a 15-min. walk from the station (walk down Bahnhofstr. and turn right on Abt-Karl-Str.), has cramped quarters but amiable hosts. (Reception open 5-9pm. Lockout 10am-5pm. Curfew 10pm. 111AS, sheets, showers and breakfast included.) **Gasthof Goldener Stern,** Sterngasse 17 (tel. (02752) 22 14) has respectable rooms and hearty Austrian fare at the restaurant downstairs. (Singles 200-230AS. Doubles 320-390AS. Breakfast included. Restaurant open Wed.-Mon. 7am-1am; off-season Sun.-Fri. 7am-11pm.) **Camping Melk** overlooks the Danube near the ship station (tel. (02752) 32 91; reception open 8am-midnight; 30AS per person, 30AS per tent, 25AS per car, 15AS per shower).

The trip between industrial but attractive **Linz** and Passau in Germany is not terribly exciting, but then it isn't especially expensive (6 hr. upstream, 5 hr. downstream; 180AS, round-trip 210AS). Travelers can also arrive by rail or bus. Both the main **train station** (tel. (0732) 17 17) and **bus station** *(Postaustelle)* (tel. (0732) 21 60 or 16 71) are on Bahnhofstr. The main **tourist office** (tel. (0732) 23 93 or 17 77) awaits at Hauptplatz 34. (Open Mon.-Fri. 8am-6pm, Sat., Sun. and holidays 8-11:30am and 12:30-6pm; Oct.-May Mon.-Sat. 8am-6pm). Linz has three **IYHF youth hostels.** The **Linz Jugendherberge,** Kapuzinerstr. 14 (tel. (0732) 28 27 20), offers the cheapest bed and the best location in town. (Reception open 7-10am and 5-8pm. 36 beds. No curfew if you get a key from front desk. Students under 27 and everyone under 18 75AS. All others 90AS. Nonmembers 15AS extra. Sheets 15AS.) **Landesjugendherberge Lentia,** Blütenstr. 23 (tel. (0732) 23 70 78), a skyscraperesque structure across the river from the Hauptplatz, may be infested with ecstatic *Kinder.* (106 beds. Reception open 5-7pm. Curfew 10pm. 105-130AS, sheets and breakfast included.) The **Jugendgästehaus,** Stanglhofweg 3 (tel. (0732) 66 44 34) presents a soulless exterior but a liveable interior. 152 beds. (Reception open 5-7pm. 150-180AS, breakfast and sheets included. Call ahead.) At Promenade 16, near the *Altstadt,* patrons of **Café Traxlmayr** bask in the lofty, genteel sophistication of a "Viennese café." After strolling around, catch a view of the *Altstadt* from the 537m **Pöstlingberg,** accessible in an old-fashioned trolley car (28AS round-trip).

Austrians take no pride in the main tourist attraction of **Mauthausen,** about a half-hour down the river from Linz—a forced-labor camp where thousands perished under the Nazis. The museum does its best to underplay Austria's enthusiasm for Hitler in the late 1930s. From Linz, take a train to Mauthausen (58AS round-trip); buses travel there as well. No smiling tour guide will meet you at the station, and there are no buses. The camp is a 5km walk away. Follow signs to "KZ Mauthausen." (Open Feb.-Dec. 15 daily 8am-4pm. Admission 15AS, students and children 5AS.)

Salzburg

Protected by forested mountains, Salzburg is a city of castles, horse-drawn carriages, majestic church towers and enchantment, whose voice is the sublime music of favorite son Wolfgang Amadeus Mozart. Salzburg's adulation of the composer crescendoes during its annual summer music festival, the Salzburger Festspiele. For those wishing to pay homage to moviedom's sweetly-trilling Von Trapp family singers, Salzburg is the place to be; *The Sound of Music* was largely filmed here, as the tour guides won't let you forget.

Orientation and Practical Information

Salzburg straddles the **Salzach River** a few miles from the German border. The expensive old town clusters around **Residenzplatz** on the east side of the river. The train station is in the (relatively) new town, which centers around **Mirabellplatz** and **Marktplatz,** west of the Salzach. Both towns are a 15-20 minute walk down **Rainerstraße** from the train station. You can also get to either by taking bus #1, 5, 6, or 55 from the bus stop across the street from the station.

Tourist Office: Mozartplatz 5 (tel. 84 75 68 or 80 72 34 62), in the old town. Open July-Aug. daily 8am-10pm; April-June and Sept.-Oct. 9am-7pm; Nov.-March Mon.-Sat. 9am-6pm. Hours may vary in spring and autumn. Free hotel map is almost the same as the 5AS city map. Youth-oriented pamphlet is excellent but dated. Other branches at train station, Bahnsteig 10 (open Mon.-Sat. 8:45am-8:30pm) and all major approach roads.

Budget Travel: ÖKISTA, Wolf-Dietrich-Str. 31 (tel. 84 67 69). InterRail information and service. Open Mon.-Fri. 9:30am-5:30pm. **Activ,** Kaigasse 21 (tel. 89 11 48) just off Mozartplatz. Open daily 8am-8pm; Sept.-May Mon.-Fri. 9am-6pm, Sat. 9am-noon. **Young Austria,** Alpenstr. 108a (tel. 25 75 80), behind the McDonalds. Open Mon.-Fri. 9am-6pm, Sat. 9am-noon. All three have discounts, especially for students under 35 and anyone under 26.

Currency Exchange: Banking hrs. are Mon.-Fri. 8am-noon and 2-4:30pm. Currency exchange at the station open daily 8am-10pm. Best rates at post offices.

American Express: Mozartplatz 5 (tel. 84 25 01). Open Mon.-Fri. 9am-5:30pm, Sat. 9am-noon.

Consulates: U.S., Giselakai 51 (tel. 286 01). Open Mon.-Fri. 9-11am and 2-4pm. **U.K.,** Alter Markt 4 (tel. 84 81 33). Open Mon.-Fri. 9am-noon.

Post Office: Mail your brown paper packages tied up in strings in the train station. Office open 24 hrs. Poste Restante defaults to the office in town, Residenzplatz 9. Open Mon.-Fri. 7am-7pm, Sat. 8-10am. **Postal Code:** A-5010.

Telephones: At the train station post office. Open 24 hrs. Also at Residenzplatz post office. Open Mon.-Fri. 7am-7pm, Sat. 8-10am. **City Code:** 0662.

Trains: Hauptbahnhof (tel. 804 85 50) on Südtirolerpl. in the new city.

Buses: across from the train station on Südtirolerpl. (tel. 167). Ticket window open Mon.-Fri. 7-9:25am, 9:45am-2:30pm and 2:50-6:20pm, Sat. 7-9:25am and 9:45am-2:20pm.

Flights: Flughafen Salzburg, a few km west of the city center (tel. 85 20 91). Take bus #77 between airport and train station.

Public Transportation: Information at Griesgasse 21 (tel. 205 51). Buses are excellent (routes traced on all maps). 17AS per ride, 14AS if purchased at a *Tabak Trafik,* 13AS if purchased from an automatic vendor, 60AS for a book of 5. A 24-hr. pass costs 20AS but you must buy at least 5; a 24-hr. pass that includes the cable car to the castle, the Mönchsberglift, and the tramway as far as Bergheim costs 44AS, and you may buy only 1.

Luggage Storage: At the train station. Large lockers 20AS per 48 hrs. Small ones 10AS. Luggage check 15AS. Open 24 hrs.

Bike Rental: At the station (tel. 71 54 13 37). 80AS per day, with train ticket 40AS. **Activ** (see Budget Travel). Bikes 80AS per day, mountain bikes 150AS per day.

Hitchhiking: To Innsbruck, Munich, Italy (except Venice), hitchers go first to the German border then take bus #77 from the train station. To Vienna or Venice they take bus #2 from the train station to Mirabellplatz, cross the street and take bus #4 (direction "Liefering") to the *Autobahn* entrance. Bus #4 can also be picked up in other parts of town. **Mitfahrzentrale,** Wiener-Philharmoniker-Gasse 2 (tel. 84 13 27), in the Studentenhaus Katholische Hochschulgemeinde. Open Mon.-Thurs. 9am-noon and 2-5pm, Fri. 9am-noon. May close its doors soon.

Bookstores: Bücher Schneid, Rainerstr. 24 (tel. 717 05). Open Mon.-Fri. 8am-6pm, Sat. 8am-noon. Sells *Let's Go,* as well as other less seminal English literature.

Laundromat: Wäscherei Constructa, Kaiserschützenstr. 10, opposite the station. Wash and dry 92AS. Open Mon.-Fri. 7:30am-6:30pm, Sat. 8am-noon. **Wasch Salon,** Südtiroler Pl., across from the train station. Wash 67AS, dry 20AS. Open Mon.-Fri. 6:30am-8pm, Sat. 6:30am-1pm.

Pharmacy: Elisabeth-Apotheke, Elisabethstr. 1 (tel. 714 84), a few blocks left of the train station. Open Mon.-Fri. 8am-12:30pm and 2:30-6pm, Sat. 8am-noon. Check the door of any closed pharmacy to find an open one.

Medical Assistance: When the dog bites, when the bee stings, when you're feeling sad, call the **Hospital,** Müllner Hauptstr. 48 (tel. 315 81).

Emergencies: Police (tel. 133). Headquarters at Alpenstr. 90 (tel. 295 11). **Ambulance** (tel. 144). **Fire** (tel. 122).

Accommodations and Camping

Ask for the tourist office's list of private rooms *(not* the hotel map). During the summer festival (late July-Aug.) hostels fill by mid-afternoon; call ahead. The youth pamphlet provides information on hostels in the suburbs. The tourist office charges 25AS to reserve accommodations, plus a 50AS deposit.

Institut St. Sebastian, Linzergasse 41 (tel. 87 13 86). Primarily a residence for female university students, this elegant, spotless dormitory opens its doors to travelers of both genders. Friendly clerks speak excellent English. Part of a church, so expect tolling bells, especially on Sundays. Cable TV with CNN. Reception open Mon.-Fri. 8am-noon and 3-10pm, Sat.-Sun. 8-10am and 6-10pm. No lockout or curfew. Dorms 110AS. Doubles 360AS. Triples 480AS. Showers and lockers included. Sheets 20AS. Open May-Oct.

Naturfreundehaus, Mönchsberg 19c (tel. 84 17 29), towering over the Old Town from the top of the Mönchsberg. Take bus #1 to Gstättengasse or Mönchbergaufzug, then the elevator built into the cliff (round-trip 19AS). From the elevator, turn right and head down the path. When you spot the stone arch of the old fortress, take the small path to the immediate left; it's about 50m ahead on the right. Or hike up the stairs at Toscaninihof, take the right path at the top, and it's on the right. Staggering views. Run by a charming, hospitable couple. Dorms 100AS. Sheets 5AS. Quick, warm showers 10AS. Breakfast 45AS. Open May to mid-Oct.

International Youth Hotel, Paracelcusstr. 9 (tel. 796 49), off Franz-Josef-Str. Full of Americans finding joy in a sub-21 drinking age. Very social, but also clean and comfortable. Action-packed until 1am. No curfew. Quiet time 10pm (not!). Dorms 110AS. Doubles 300AS. Quads 480AS. Showers 10AS. Adequate dinners 40-60AS. Lockers 10AS. Sheets 15AS, zippy stylish sheetsacks 20AS. Key deposit 100AS. *Sound of Music* tours 250AS.

Haunspergstraße (IYHF), Haunspergstr. 27 (tel. 750 30), near the train station. Staff occasionally disappears from the office; just wait. Reception open 7am-2pm and 5-11pm, but hostel fills by late afternoon. Curfew 11pm. 110AS. Sheets and breakfast included. Laundry 50AS per load. Arcane IYHF booking vouchers necessary for reservations. Open July-Aug.

Jugendgästehaus Salzburg (IYHF), Josef-Preis-Allee 18 (tel. 84 26 70 or 84 68 57), just southeast of the Old Town. Take bus #5 or 55. Decor crosses McDonald's and an elementary school. Often overrun with school groups. Reception open Mon.-Fri. 7-9am, 11-11:30am, noon-1pm, 3:30-5:30pm, 6-9:30pm, and 10pm-midnight; Sat.-Sun. 7-9am, 11-11:30am, noon-1pm, 4:30-7:30pm, and 10pm-midnight. You must memorize and recite these each time you enter. Curfew midnight. Dorms 110AS per person. Doubles 440AS per room. Quads with showers 660AS. Sheets and showers included. Lunches, bag lunches, and dinners 55AS. No reservations; come by 11am to get a place.

Aigen (IYHF), at Aignerstr. 34 (tel. 232 48). Take bus #5 to Mozartsteg, then bus #49 to Aignerstr. and walk for 10 min. Sunny rooms with lots of wood. A long, long way to run, but clean and comfortable. Pretty, parklike neighborhood. Reception open 7-9am and 5-11pm. Curfew 11pm. 100AS, nonmembers 115AS. Breakfast, shower and sheets included.

Glockengasse (IYHF), at Glockengasse 8 (tel. 762 41). Walk to the foot of the Kapuzinerberg (mountain) from the train station. Chaotic labyrinth of dormitories with few showers. If it's full, ask to sleep on the floor. Reception open 5pm-midnight. Curfew midnight. 98AS, breakfast, showers and sheets included. Lockers 10AS. Open April-Sept.

Haus Moser, Kasern Berg 59 (tel. 53 32 33). A few km from the city, with mountainwards views. Take bus #15 from Mirabellpl. to Kasern, or any northbound train from the main train station to the first stop, Salzburg-Maria Plain, and walk up. The hills are alive with Frau Moser's affection for her guests. Mountainside, dark-timbered home with cozy rooms, 160-220AS per person (250AS with balcony). Fortifying breakfast and shower included.

Hans Kernstock, Karolingerstr. 29 (tel. 82 74 69). Take bus #27 or 77 from the train station. Commodious rooms and an ample breakfast. Warm and energetic hostess. 2-4-bed rooms 220AS per person, including breakfast.

Camping Stadtblick, Rauchenbichlerstr. 21 (tel. 506 52). Take bus #51 from the station to Itzling-Pflanzmann, then walk 5 min. up the hill on the gravel road. Thick grass and a sweeping view of the city. 50AS per person, 15AS per tent, 15AS per car. Showers included. Owners also operate an adjacent **pension** with handsome, spacious rooms. 220AS per person. Breakfast and showers included. **Stadtcamping Salzburg,** Bayerhamerstr. 14 (tel. 711 69). Expensive, but the closest to the city. Reception open 8am-noon and 3-8pm. 60AS per person (including tent), 35AS per car.

Food

Blessed with fantastic **beer gardens** and innumerable **Konditoreien** (pastry shops), Salzburg begs its guests to eat outdoors. *Knoblauchsuppe,* a Salzburger specialty—rich cream soup loaded with croutons and pungent garlic—shouldn't daunt the confident (or the asocial). **Hofer,** at Schallmooser Hauptstr. and Franz-Josef-Str., is a discount supermarket (open Mon.-Fri. 8am-6pm, Sat. 7:30am-noon); **KGM,** Karl-Wurmb-Str. 3, across from the train station, is also well-stocked and reasonable (open Mon.-Fri. 8am-6pm, Sat. 8am-12:30pm). Open-air markets bloom daily on in the old town's squares.

Michael Haydn Stube, Mirabellplatz 1, in the Aicher Passage. A student hangout run by the Salzburg College of Music. Best deal in town. Vegetarian, fish, *Schnitzl,* and *Wurst* dishes 35-68AS. Continental breakfast 38AS. Open Mon.-Fri. 8am-8pm. Hot food 11am-7:30pm.

Fischmarkt, facing the river on a path parallel to Müllner Haupstr., between the Staatsbrücke and the Markatsteg. Succulent, inexpensive, and fresh seafood. Very casual—you may have to stand. Two mammoth trees reach through the roof of the building. Open Mon.-Fri. 9am-6pm, Sat. 9am-12:30pm.

Gast-Garten Happy Chinese, Linzergasse 47. Calm, homey restaurant with fresh-cut flowers and a garden covered by a sheltering arbor and thick, leafy vines and roses. Extremely generous servings, lots of veggies. Fried rice 80AS, chicken with cashews 90AS, beef with broccoli 88AS. Open daily until 10pm.

Restaurant Zur Bürgerwehr-Einkehr, Mönchsberg 19 (follow the directions for Gasthof Naturfreundhaus in the Accommodations section). Perhaps the most delightful café and restaurant in Salzburg—certainly boasts the most splendid setting. Sandwiches 30-40AS. *Gulasch mit Brot* 35AS. Mouthwatering tortes 27AS. Freshly grilled meats on summer weekends. Open daily 11am-11pm. Meals served until 8:30pm.

Sights

Salzburg sprang up under the protective watch of the hilltop fortress **Hohensalzburg,** Mönchsberg 34, built between 1077 and the 17th century by the ruling Archbishops. The first-rate tours wind through medieval torture chambers and the castle's impressive staterooms, and pregnate its impregnable watchtower. (Tours every 40 min., 45AS, students 25AS. Admission to fortress without tour 20AS, students and children 10AS.) **The Rainer Museum,** inside the fortress, displays more medieval weapons and instruments of torture. (Admission free with tour. Otherwise 10AS, students and children 5AS.) The cable car from Festungsgasse runs every 10 minutes (17AS, round-trip 27AS; children 8.50AS, round-trip 13.50AS).

For splendor of another sort, visit the **Schloß Mirabell** and its delicately manicured **Gardens,** in the new town on Rainerstr. Prince-Archbishop Wolf Dietrich built this wonder in 1606 for his mistress Salome Alt; it was embellished in the 1720s by architect Lukas von Hildebrandt. You can wander around the extravagant rosebeds and lawns of the **Zwerglgarten.** The tourist office provides a pamphlet listing dates of chamber music concerts in the Schloß. Back in the old town lies the archbishop's own palace, the **Residenz,** Residenzplatz 1, which features baroque staterooms and a gallery filled with works by Rembrandt, Rubens, Brueghel, and Kliont. (Stateroom tours 30AS, students 20AS, under 15 free. Gallery open daily 10am-5pm.)

The powerful monks and bishops who ruled Salzburg and its environs for centuries left behind some jaw-dropping ecclesiastical architecture. The **Dom,** completed by the Italian Santino Solari in 1628, was the first standard baroque edifice of its kind north of the Alps. The western front has witnessed performances of Hugo von Hofmannstahl's play *Jederman* (Everyman) since 1920 (with an unpleasant hiatus during the *Hitlerzeit)*—it is now enacted during the Festival. Johann Bernhard Fischer von Erlach's simple concave façade of his **Dreifaltigkeitskirche** (Trinity Church) hides a glorious altar of gilded clouds and cherubim. The larger **Universitätskirche** on Universitätsplatz is generally considered Fischer von Erlach's masterpiece.

A slightly different brand of baroque graces the elaborate interior of **St. Peter's.** Behind this Benedictine church is the entrance to the **Katakomben** (catacombs), St.-Peter-Bezirk 1, where Christians worshiped in secret as early as 250 AD. (Open May-Sept. daily 10am-5pm. Tours in English every ½ hr. (minimum 5 people); Oct.-April Mon.-Fri. 11am-noon and 1:30-3:30pm every hr. Admission 10AS, seniors and students 7AS.)

Wolfgang Amadeus Mozart was unleashed upon the world from what is now called **Mozarts Geburtshaus** (birthplace) at Getreidegasse 9. The street itself is worth a look; the guild signs and painted walls remain as they were when Mozart was a wee tyke. The house exhibits pictures, letters, stage sets for Mozart's operas, and the Hammerklavier on which he composed *The Magic Flute.* (Open daily 9am-7pm; Oct.-April 9am-6pm. Admission 50AS, students 35AS, ages 15-18 20AS, ages 6-14 15AS.) Mozart's **Wohnhaus** (residence), Marktplatz 8, was badly damaged in World War II air raids, and is now the site of a museum relating to his 1773-1780 work. (Open June-Sept. daily 10am-5pm. Admission 35AS, students 25AS. Admission to both houss 60AS, students 35AS, ages 15-18 20AS, ages 6-14 10AS.)

For silence and a ripping view of the city, wander the footpaths of the Mönchsberg, the hill next to the old city. You can either descend by the elevator built into the mountain, or go the long way and emerge at **Hildmannplatz** or **Toscaninihof**—a great 15-minute walk. The elevator is at Gstättengasse 13. (Open daily 7am-3am; 11AS, round-trip 19AS; ages 6-15 5.50AS and 9.50AS.)

Just south of the city lies the unforgettable **Schloß Hellbrunn,** a one-time pleasure palace for the tricky Archbishop Markus Sittikus. Markus amused himself with his booby-trapped table, which could spout water on his drunken guests, and his elaborate water-powered figurines. (Open daily July-Aug. 9am-6pm; May and Sept. 9am-5pm; June 9am-6pm; April and Oct. 9am-4:30pm. Admission to the park and fountains 48AS, seniors and students 43AS, under 16 24AS.)

Entertainment

The renowned **Salzburger Festspiele** (Summer Music Festivals) run from late July to the beginning of September. Detailed programs are available in December from Direktion der Salzburger Festspiele, Festspielhaus, Hofstallgasse 1, A-5010 Salzburg, or from an Austrian national tourist office. The few tickets still available in summer are sold at the Festspielhaus box office (tel. 84 25 41; open March-June Mon.-Thurs. 9am-12:30pm, Fri. 9am-12:30pm and 3-5pm; July Mon.-Sat. 9:30am-5pm; Aug. daily 9:30am-5pm). Travel agencies in Salzburg add a 20% service charge to the ticket price. Opera seats cost 350-3300AS, concert seats 150-1700AS. Standing room is available for 50AS and up. At **Marionetten Theater,** Schwarzstr. 24 (tel. 724 06), a lighthearted show is accompanied by tapes of past festival opera performances (tickets 250-350AS).

The **Stadtkino,** Anton-Neumayr-Pl. 2 (tel. 84 03 49 13) has everything from jazz and rock concerts to postmodern dance. Every summer, the **Szene** sponsors an international theater and dance festival which coincides with the **Festspiele** (tel. 84 34 48; tickets 120-160AS; open Mon.-Fri. 10am-5pm, in summer also Sat. 10am-noon).

For an evening of steinhoisting and general *Gemütlichkeit,* go to **Augustiner Bräustüble,** Augustinergasse 4-6 (tel. 312 46), home of Salzburg's first brewery. Grab a stein, rinse it out in the tub, then have it filled by the enormous man who rolls out the wooden beer barrels and taps them with a brass bung and a massive mallet. (1 liter 408AS. ½ liter 20AS, but only tourists and little kids drink ½ liters. Open daily 3-11pm.) The **Felsenkeller,** in the Toscaninihof, near St. Peter's graveyard, dispenses wine in a damp, coin-studded cellar built right into the cliff. Look for the huge iron door 5m into the mountain; the crowd inside is mainly local. (Open Sun.-Fri. 2:30-11pm, Sat. 10am-1pm and 3-11pm.)

Panorama Tours (tel. 740 29) offers "The Original *Sound of Music* Tour," departing daily at 9:30am and 2pm from the Mirabellplatz bus terminal. *Sound of Music* fans will find the thorough 3½-hour English tour (250AS) positively orgasmic. For those who saw the movie as a tragic tale of a deviant family of incestuous children and a wimpy, deserting father who had a disturbing nun fetish, the tour is probably a loss.

Near Salzburg

It was the Salzburgers, not the Columbians, who first coined the phrase "white gold," and the **Salzbergwerke** (salt mines) around the Salzkammergut explain why. The tremendous wealth provided by the region's colossal resources long buttressed the political hegemony of the ruling bishops. The closest mines, at **Bad Dürrnberg** near Hallein, are quite an experience. On the 1½-hour tour you wear traditional miner's clothes, slide down passages in the dark, take a miniature train ride, and sometimes a raft ride on the salt lakes. The Salzbergbahn cable car ride to the entrance provides an outstanding view. (Open April 27-Sept. 30 8:50am-5:50pm; Oct. 1-14 11am-4:50pm. Admission 155AS, students 145AS, children 80AS, including round-trip cable car, tour, and museum.) For more information, call (06245) 27 37 or 51 39. You can reach the mines at Bad Dürrnberg by bus (from Salzburg's train station, take the bus headed for Hallein or Gölling) or rail (7 trains per day from Salzburg station 8:45am-2:33pm; 7-10 per day return to Salzburg 8:56am-1:09am; 15-20 min., 28AS, round-trip 48AS). Then take a cable car from Hallein to Bad Dürrnberg (10 min., round-trip 75AS, students 65AS, children 37.50AS).

Salzkammergut

East of Salzburg, the landscape swells into towering mountains pockmarked with frigid, unfathomably deep lakes. The Salzkammergut takes its name from the long-abandoned salt mines which, in their glory days, paid for Salzburg's architectural treasures.

The Vienna-Salzburg rail line skirts the northern edge of the Salzkammergut. At Attnang-Puchheim, 50km east of Salzburg, a spur line begins its way south through Gmunden, Ebensee, Bad Ischl, Hallstatt, and Bad Aussee to Steinbach. If you're traveling by bus, or have your own wheels, you can enter directly from Salzburg along Highway 158. Within the region there is a dense network of **post buses;** most run four to 12 times per day. Ask at the Salzburg kiosk for a comprehensive schedule, or call for information: Salzburg (0662) 167; Gmunden (07612) 46 13; Mondsee (06232) 26 69; St. Gilgen (06227) 425; Bad Ischl (06132) 31 13; Bad Aussee (06152) 20 50. The pamphlet *Wandern mit dem Postauto* (Hiking with the Post Bus), available at the main bus stations in these towns, details hikes that coincide with the Post Bus network. There is also a less complete network of **Bahnbuses;** their schedule is available at local rail stations. If hitching from Salzburg, take bus #29 to Gnigl, and come into the Salzkammergut at Bad Ischl. The lake district itself is one of the rare, refreshing Austrian regions in which hitchhikers make good time. Most of the train stations in the region rent bikes. Reasonably-priced ferries serve each of the larger lakes. The **Wolfgangsee** line is operated by the Austrian railroad, so railpasses are valid; on the **Attersee** and **Traunsee** lines, Eurailpass holders receive a discount.

Cheap beds abound in the Salzkammergut. You'll find IYHF hostels in Bad Aussee, Bad Ischl, Gosau, Hallstatt, Mondsee, Obertraun, Weißenbach and St. Gilgen. Often, however, locals offer far superior rooms in private homes and pensions at just-above-hostel prices. **Campgrounds** dot the region, but many are trailer-oriented; away from large towns, you can camp discreetly almost anywhere without trouble. Hikers can capitalize on dozens of **cable cars** in the area to gain altitude before setting out on their own, and almost every community has a local trail map publicly posted and/or available at the tourist office. At higher elevations there are **alpine huts**—check carefully at the tourist office for their opening hours.

A winsome playground of a town in the western Salzkammergut, **St. Gilgen** is squeezed between the placid waters of the **Wolfgangsee** and the **Schafberg** summit. The **IYHF youth hostel** in St. Gilgen, Mondseerstr. 7 (tel. (06227) 365), is positively luxurious (especially the singles and doubles), and sits right on the lake. (Reception open 5-7pm. Curfew 11pm. Members only. Singles 158AS. Doubles 138-158AS. Triples 118-138AS. Quads and quints 108-118AS. Breakfast, shower and sheets included.) The **Verkehrsverein** (tel. (06227) 348), in the *Rathaus,* details alternative budget accommodations. (Open 8:30am-noon and 2-6pm, Sat. 8:30am-noon; Sept.-June Mon.-Fri. 8:30am-noon and 2-6pm.) For a heart-stopping ride, ascend the 1783m Schafberg on the cog-wheeled **Schafbergbahn.** The hike back takes three hours. (Open early May to early Oct. Up 98AS, down 80AS, round-trip 178AS. Railpass holders free.) A steamer runs from St. Gilgen to the base of the railway in nearby St. Wolfgang (April-Oct., 40AS one-way, Eurail valid); ask for the schedule at the Verkehrsverein. The lovely lakeside village of **St. Wolfgang** is itself worthy of exploration. The delicate and intricate carved wooden altar, fashioned by Michael Pacher in 1481 and now a world-renowned masterpiece, still sits in the dainty **parish church.**

Across the Schafberg from St. Gilgen in the tiny village of **Weißenbach** on the **Attersee** lake, proletarians and capitalists alike are welcomed at the **Europa-Camp (IYHF)** owned by the Austrian Young Socialists (tel. (07663) 220). Here, a campground, a psychedelic hostel, and a modest disco are run with an efficiency worthy of the free market. (Reception open 8am-12:30pm and 2-6pm. Dorms 80AS per person, showers included. Breakfast 15AS. Call ahead.) A ferry service links the small villages around the Attersee, which is easily accessible from Mondsee, St. Gilgen, Bad Ischl, and Gmunden.

The cultural and geographic center of the Salzkammergut, **Bad Ischl** is best known for its purportedly curative mineral baths and mud packs. Skeptical visitors can still enjoy the free outdoor concerts (mid-May to Sept. 2-3 per day) and the Ischl Operetta Festival, which recalls the town's heyday as a rest home for stressed-out composers such as Brahms, Bruckner and Lehár. (July-Aug. 130-420AS.) Traffic and crowds can create a sort of quiet/frenzied feeling in Bad Ischl, but a stroll along the town esplanade comforts with New Age music and the swish of rushing water. The **tourist office** *(Kurdirektion),* Bahnhofstr. 6 (tel. (06132) 35 20), finds rooms in private homes (from 130AS) and *pensionen* (from 160AS) for no charge. (Open Mon.-Fri. 8am-6pm, Sat. 8am-4pm, Sun. 9-11:30am; Oct.-May Mon.-Fri. 8am-noon and 1-5:30pm, Sat. 8am-noon.) Bad Ischl's roomy **Jugendgästehaus (IYHF)** (tel. (06132) 65 77) is at Am Rechensteg 5, in the town center. Show up at 5pm if you want a spot. (Reception allegedly open 5-9:45pm. Flexible curfew 10pm. 110AS. Sheets, showers, and breakfast included. Lunch and dinner available.) **Pfarrheim (IYHF),** Auböckplatz (tel. (06132) 34 83), beside the post office, is a basement hostel with two 20-bed rooms. (Reception open 5:30-10pm. Curfew 10pm. 50AS. Showers included. Sheets 10AS. Open mid-June to mid-Sept.) **Pension Stadlmann Josefa,** just outside town at 21 Mastaliergasse (tel. (06132) 31 04), has rooms ranging from cozy to cramped for 130-170AS, breakfast included. Near Bad Ischl, Austria's last emperor, Kaiser Franz-Josef, built the **Kaiservilla,** his summer getaway palace, and stuffed it full of expensive decorations that he mistakenly thought were tasteful. (Open May-Oct. daily 9am-noon and 1-5pm. Admission 59AS, 55AS with guest card, children 28AS. Admission to the estate grounds and surrounding park 25AS.) The **Katrin Cable Car** runs to the top of 1500m Mt. Katrin, laced with fine hiking trails. (Open daily 9am-4pm. Closed Nov. 5-Dec. 7. Up 110AS, down 80AS, roundtrip 130AS, 115AS with guest card.) **Bike rental** and **luggage check** at the station are open daily 5am-8:10pm.

South of Bad Ischl poses **Hallstatt,** small, isolated and breathtaking in its austere, mountainous setting. If you arrive by train, alight at the Hallstatt station, across the lake from the village itself. Ferries cross the lake after each train's arrival (18AS). Post buses also make the journey from Bad Ischl (38AS round-trip). The Hallstatt **tourist office** (tel. (06134) 208), in the **Kultur- und Kongresshaus,** off Seestr., finds cheap rooms (there are plenty). (Open Mon.-Fri. 9am-noon and 3-5pm; Oct.-May Mon.-Fri. 8am-noon.) Site of one of the richest archeological finds in Europe, Hallstatt was once a center of Iron Age civilization. The **Prähistorisches Museum** exhibits some of the relics unearthed in the area. (Open daily 10am-6pm; Oct.-April 10am-4pm. Admission 30AS, with guest card 25AS, children 20AS.) Take the **Salzbergbahn** to the site of the dig. (Open daily 9am-6pm; mid-Sept. to June 1 9am-4pm. One-way 45AS, children 30AS; round-trip 80AS, with guest card 65AS, children 45AS.) The **Salzbergwerk** (saltworks) just up the path from the ancient groves, are the oldest still-operating ones in the world (2500 years). (Open June to mid-Sept. daily 9:30am-4:30pm; mid-Sept. to mid-Oct. and May daily 9:30am-3pm. Admission 110AS, with guest card 95AS, children 35-55AS.) Paths lead back to Hallstatt at the foot of the mountain.

The **IYHF Hallstatt hostel** at Salzbergstr. 50, 10 min. from the town center, offers basic, inexpensive lodgings in a tidy, flower-bedecked house. (Reception open 6-10pm. Lockout 10am-6pm. Curfew 10pm. 72AS. Sheets 25AS. Breakfast 25AS. Coffee or tea 10AS. Key deposit 51AS. Kitchen facilities.) There's also a sparkling IYHF hostel in nearby Obertraun (tel. (06131) 360). **TVN Naturfreunde Herberge,** Kirchenweg 36 (tel. (06134) 318), is a poser hostel with very cheap rooms. (Curfew midnight. 145AS. Half and full board available. Sheets 10AS.) Equally cheap *Privat Zimmer* speckle the town. **Camping Höll** is at Lahnstr. 6 (tel. (06134) 329), near the bus stop. (32AS per person, 27AS per tent, 23AS per car, 3.50AS tax.) The charming **Franziska Zimmerman,** Gosaumühlstr. 69 (tel. (01043) 309) offers cozy rooms in her beautiful lakeside home, built in 1599. (150AS. Breakfast on the leafy terrace included. Showers 10AS.) The **Bräu-Gasthof** restaurant, Seestr. 120-121, can be expensive, but stick to the delicious 50AS omelettes and other lower-priced far and you too can enjoy their waterside terrace, friendly ducks and swans, big leafy trees and trellis-climbing roses.

The prodigious **Dachstein Ice Caves,** though marred by cheeseball names like "Cave Venus" and "Hall of Oblivion," give eloquent testimony to the geological hyperactivity that forged the region's natural beauty. (Open May to Oct. daily 9am-4pm. Admission to Giant Ice Cave 64AS, to Mammoth Cave 59AS, combined 88AS.) To enter, take the Dachstein cable car, an eye-exciter in itself, up 1350m to Schönbergalm (round-trip 128AS). For information on winter and summer skiing, contact the **Skischule Zauner,** in Hallstatt at Markt 51 (tel. (06134) 246) or the Hallstatt tourist office.

Kitzbühel

Little over an hour by train from Innsbruck, Kitzbühel is the St. Moritz of Austria, where wealthy visitors pump enough Deutschmarks and dollars into the local economy to keep the cobblestone streets in good repair and sidewalk cafés flourishing. Site of the first cable car in Austria, Kitzbühel challenges skiers and hikers with an ever-ascending network of lifts and runs. At night, the international playchildren gather in tiny pubs to squander their parents' money.

Tiny Kitzbühel has two train stations, one at either side of the lazy U-curve that the railroad makes around the town. From Salzburg, you arrive first at Hauptbahnhof; from Innsbruck or Wörgl, at Hahnenkamm. Hahnenkamm is more convenient to town, but not all trains stop there. The Hauptbahnhof rents out bikes. The **Verkehrsbüro** (tourist office), Hinterstadt 18 (tel. (05356) 22 72 or 21 55) finds rooms for no fee and has a complimentary reservations phone outside the front door. From the main train station, walk straight up Bahnhof-Str. as you exit the station. Turn left on Josef-Pirchl-Str. and follow it until you go right on Hinterstadt. From Hahnenkamm, walk down J.-Herold-Str., make a left on Vorderstadt and another, immediate left on Hinterstadt. Ask them about the free discount-bearing guest card. (Open July-Sept. Mon.-Sat. 8:30am-7:30pm, Sun. 10am-5pm; May-June Mon.-Fri. 8:30am-noon and 3-6pm, Sat. 8:30am-noon; Oct.-April Mon.-Fri. 9:30am-noon and 3-6pm.) Opposite the Verkehrsbüro, **Reisebüro Eurotours** (tel. (05356) 313 10) exchanges money at bank rates. (Open Mon.-Fri. 8am-12:30pm and 3-6:30pm, Sat. 8am-12:30pm and 4:30-6:30pm, Sun. 10am-noon and 4:30-6:30pm.)

You won't break a sweat finding a place to stay during the off-season—Kitzbühel has more guest beds (10,000) than inhabitants (8070). **Schmidinger-Rupinger Pension,** Ehrenbachgasse 13 (tel. (05356) 31 34), pampers with down comforters, commodious rooms, and the hospitality of a gracious lady who sympathizes with students. From the town center, take Bichlstr. until you see Ehrenbachgasse on the right. The pension is set off from the street about 20m on the left. (Singles and doubles 150-180AS. Breakfast and showers included. Reservations welcomed.) If a 15-minute walk from the center of town is no worry, stay at the tranquil **Haus Wieser,** Malernweg 56 (tel. (05356) 51 25 55) set among a cluster of family farms. (Watch street signs closely. Balconies in all rooms. 150AS, breakfast, hall shower and small kitchen included.) Fill up on meat, *Knödel,* and sauerkraut for 65-96AS at **Huberbräu Stüberl Restaurant,** Vorderstadt 18, right in the city's hub. (Open daily 8am-midnight.) Grocery shoppers can hit the SPAR Markt on the corner of Ehrengasse and Bichlstr. (open Mon.-Fri. 8am-12:30pm and 2-6:30pm, Sat. also 7:30pm-12:30am). A Tyrolean market with fresh cheese, eggs, schnapps, fruit and more takes place every Wednesday and Saturday in front of the tourist office. At the **post office,** 11 Josef-Pirchl-Str., you can also make international calls and change money. (Open Mon.-Fri. 8am-noon and 2-7pm, Sat. 8-11am.)

An extensive network of hiking trails snakes up the mountains surrounding Kitzbühel. To reach some of the lower trails and meadow walks, ride the **Hahnenkammbahn** from Hahnenkamm station (130AS, with guest card 110AS, children 65AS; Nov.-April 120AS, with guest card 100AS, children 60AS; open daily 8am-noon and 1-5:30pm). Or climb up yourself; the descent is free on all area cable cars. The **Kitzbüheler Hornbahn** cable cars will take you up to the **Alpen Blumen Garten,** where over 120 different types of Alpine flowers blossom each season. (Cable cars same prices; mid-Oct. to April 60AS for each of three sections. Garden free.) Those with guest cards can take advantage of the tourist office's *wunderbar* free mountain hiking program. Guided hikes begin daily at 9am at the office. The out-of-hand Kitzbühel ski area boasts some of the world's best steep and deep. Fifty-six lifts and the shuttle buses that connect them are yours with a one-day ski pass (300-

320AS in early morning, less as the day progresses; children under 15 160AS). Downhill ski rental runs 95-140AS for the first day, and lessons run 340AS per day. Ask at the tourist office about ski packages—one week of lodging, ski instruction, and ski passes (available before Christmas and after Easter; rock bottom 2900AS without instruction). For a snow report (in German) call (05356) 181 or 182.

Innsbruck

Thrust into the international limelight by the Winter Olympic games of 1964 and 1976, the ancient capital of the Tyrol is a city of over-laden rose bushes, snow-topped mountains, music festivals, Baroque façades, museums and universities. More than 150 cable cars and chairlifts and an extensive network of mountain paths radiate from Innsbruck, making the Alps surrounding the city accessible to winter skiers and summer hikers alike.

Orientation and Practical Information

Many of Innsbruck's sights and attractions are within easy walking distance of the city's historic center, the *Altstadt.* From the main station, take tram #1 or 3 or any of a dozen buses, or walk 10 minutes on Museumstr., on the right as you emerge from the station. For help with directions, the straight dope on what's going on in Innsbruck, a message board and general calm, stop by the **Jugendwarterraum** (youth waiting room) in the station, where amiable, English-speaking receptionists are at your service. (Open Mon.-Fri. 1-5pm; Sept.-June 11am-7pm.) At the Jugendwarterraum or at any tourist office you can get a copy of the indispensable *Innsbruck Information,* with a city map. You can join **Club Innsbruck** at no charge if you have registered at any Innsbruck accommodation for three or more nights: enjoy discounts on cable cars and museums, free bike tours, and the option to participate in the club's fine hiking program, run from June through September (ask at the tourist information office).

Tourist Office: Fremdenverkehrsverband Innsbruck-Igls, Burggraben 3, 2nd floor (tel. 598 50), on the edge of the *Altstadt,* just off the end of Museumstr. A kindly face, free brochures and city map, lots of ski info and an ultra-valuable list of private room accommodations in Innsbruck and Igls. Open daily 8am-7pm. The **Jugendwarterraum,** in the Hauptbahnhof (tel. 58 63 62), near the lockers. Brochures, maps, free accommodation service, and mutual understanding. **Innsbruck Information,** Burggraben 3, 1st floor (tel. 53 56). Same building as the *Fremdenverkehrsverband.* The place to come to arrange tours, buy concert tickets, etc. Not really budget-minded in the accommodations department; room reservations 25AS. Message board. Open daily 8am-7pm. Branches at the Hauptbahnhof (tel. 58 37 66; open daily 9am-10pm. and all main approach roads. **Tirol Information Office,** Bozer Platz 7 (tel. 598 85). Open Mon.-Fri. 9am-12:30pm and 2-6pm.

Budget Travel: ÖKISTA, Josef-Hirn-Str. 7-2 (tel. 58 89 97). Open Mon.-Fri. 9:30am-5:30pm. **Tiroler Landesreisebüro,** on Wilhelm-Greil-Str. at Boznerpl. (tel. 598 85). Open Mon.-Fri. 8:30am-12:30pm and 2-6pm. Both have discounts on international train, plane, and bus tickets.

Consulates: U.K. Mathias-Schmidt-Str. 12-I (tel. 58 83 20). Open Mon.-Fri. 9am-noon.

Currency Exchange: Poor rates at the station. Open daily 7:30am-noon, 12:45-6pm, and 6:30-8pm. Best option is to go to the main (tel. 50 00) or Bahnhof post offices. Innsbruck banks are open Mon.-Fri. 7:45am-12:30pm and 2:15-4pm.

American Express: Brixnerstr. 3 (tel. 58 24 91), in front of the main train station. Open Mon.-Fri. 9am-5:30pm, Sat. 9am-noon.

Post Office: Maximilianstr. 2, down from the Triumph Arch. Open 24 hrs. Poste Restante (postal code: 6020). Branch next to the train station. Open Mon.-Sat. 7am-9pm, Sun. 9am-noon.

Telephones: At either of the above post offices. **City Code:** 0512.

Trains: The **Hauptbahnhof** on Südtiroler Pl. (tel. 17 17) has lockers, luggage storage, currency exchange, restaurant, bike rental and showers (15AS).

Buses: Next to the train station on Sterzinger Str. Post buses to all areas of the Tyrol. Open Mon.-Fri. 7am-5:30pm, Sat. 7am-1pm. For information call 57 66 00.

Public Transportation: The excellent tram and bus system is almost unnecessary in this compact city. One ride 15AS, available from driver. 5 one-ride tickets for 47AS, 1-day tickets for 50AS, and 5 one-day tickets for 95AS, available from Innsbruck-Information.

Taxis: Innsbruck Funktaxi (tel. 53 11).

Bike Rental: At the main train station. 80AS per day, 40AS per day with Eurail, InterRail, or train ticket on the day(s) for which it is valid. Return to any train station in Austria. Open April-early Nov.

Hitchhiking: Mitfahrzentrale, Brixnerstr. 3 (tel. 57 23 43). Pairs drivers and riders. Open Mon.-Fri. 9am-noon and 3-6pm. Otherwise, hitchers go to the Shell gas station by the DEZ store off Geyrstr. near Amras; bus K delivers to Geyrstr. Most cars leaving Innsbruck take this exit.

Luggage Storage: 10-20AS per 48 hr. at the train station. **Gepaäckaufbewahrung** at the station 15AS. Open 24 hrs.; Nov.-April 7am-midnight.

Laundromat: Waltraud Hell, Amraserstr. 15, behind the station. Wash and dry 80AS. If busy, the attendant will hold your stuff and heave it into the first free machine for no charge. (Open Mon.-Fri. 8am-6pm, Sat. 8am-1pm.)

Medical Assistance: University Hospital, Anichstr. 35 (tel. 50 40).

Emergencies: Police (tel. 133). Headquarters at Kaiserjägerstr. 8 (tel. 590 00). **Ambulance** (tel. 144 or 594 44). **Fire** (tel. 122). Police precinct adjacent to the main train station.

Accommodations and Camping

Beds are scarce during June, when only three hostels are open. Every kind of bed is scarce in July and August—book in advance. The **Jugendwarterraum** at the main train station will aid you in your search for accommodations and will telephone hostels to check availability and reserve beds. The **Fremdenverkehrsverband** (tourist office) will cheerfully hand out a list of families renting rooms in the city (120-222AS, including breakfast and shower). Beware: nonwhites may experience discrimination in Innsbruck.

Jugendherberge Innsbruck (IYHF), Reichenauerstr. 147 (tel. 461 79 or 461 80). Take bus R or O to Campingplatz-Jugendherberge. A large concrete edifice resembling an office building inside and out. Lots of Americans. Often crowded. No phone reservations; also evasive about making reservations in person—be assertive. 190 beds in 4-6 bed rooms. Open year-round except Christmastime. Reception open 5-10pm. Lockout 10am-5pm. Laundry (45AS) and kitchen facilities, but you must notify the desk of your intention to do laundry at exactly 5pm. No one knows why. Members only. 1st night 121AS, 91AS subsequently. Breakfast and sheets included. In July and Aug., the **Innsbruck Studentheim (IYHF)** next door (same management) adds 96 beds in singles and doubles.

Volkshaus Innsbruck (IYHF), Radetzkystr. 41 (tel. 46 66 82), right around the corner from Jugendherberge Innsbruck and Jugendzentrum St. Paulus. Radetzkystr. is off Reichenaustr., before the Campingplatz. Spartan and modern. 52 beds in 2-5 bed rooms. Open all year. 80AS, sheets and shower included. Breakfast 40AS.

Jugendzentrum St. Paulus, Reichenauerstr. 72 (tel. 442 91). Take bus R to Pauluskirche. Cheapest in town. Helpful staff. Cavernous 16-bed dorms. 3-night max. stay. Reception open 7-9am and 5-10pm. Lockout 10am-5pm. Curfew 10pm. 75AS, breakfast 20AS, sheets 20AS. No reservations. Open mid-June to mid-Aug.

Hostel Torsten-Arneus Schwedenhaus (IYHF), Rennweg 17b (tel. 58 58 14), along the river. Guests rave about this spotless, warm and fuzzy hostel. Great location—take bus C from the station to the Handelsakademie stop, or walk for about 15 min. 75 beds in 2-4 bed rooms. Reception open 5-7pm. Lockout 8am-4pm. Curfew 10pm. Members only, 75AS. Breakfast 40AS. Sheets 20AS. Open July-Aug.

MK (IYHF), Sillgasse 8a (tel. 57 13 11), near the station. Bare rooms, friendly management, and a delirious café next door. Reception 5-11pm. Lockout 9:30am-5pm. Curfew 11pm. 1st night 120AS; subsequently 90AS, nonmembers 110AS. Breakfast and shower included. Sheets 10AS. Open July to mid-Sept.

Haus Wolf, Dorfstr. 48 in the pretty suburb of Mutters (tel. 58 40 88). Take STB (Stubaibahn) tram to Mutters, walk toward the church steeple, and take a right on Dorfstr. The inimitable Frau Wolf will pick you up at the station, and may even drive you back if you eat all your breakfast. Cozy rooms with soft beds and a zombie-like German shepherd to cuddle. Exquisite in winter; near to ski shuttle. Singles, doubles and triples 150AS per person. Breakfast and shower included.

Camping: Camping Seewint, Amras, Geyrstr. 25 (tel. 461 53). From Hauptbahnhof, turn right on Amrasser Str., left on Amrasser See Str., right on Geyr Str. Or take bus K. Restaurant and warm showers. Open all year. 50AS per person; 35AS per tent.

Food

An indoor **market** takes place in the Markthalle along the Inn behind the *Altstadt* (Mon.-Fri. 8am-6pm, Sat. 8am-noon). The **M-Preis** grocery store is near 4 hostels, on the corner of Reichenauerstr. and Andechsstr. (Open Mon.-Fri. 8am-6pm, Sat. 8am-noon.)

University Mensa, Herzog-Siegmund-Ufer 15, on the 2nd floor of the new university between Markthalle and Blasius-Hueber-Str. Fabulous lunches (30-50AS) and crisp salads. Student ID unnecessary. Open Mon.-Fri. 11am-2pm.

Hörtnagl, Burggraben 4-6, just outside the *Altstadt.* This sprawling deli-restaurant-café complex serves gigantic portions of *Schnitzel*-and-potatoes fare at the downstairs self-serve café for 38-74AS. (Open Mon.-Fri. 10:30am-6pm, Sat. 10:30am-1pm.)

Philippine Vegetarische Küche, Müllerstr. 9, at Templstr. 1 block from post office. Glossy vegetarian nirvana. Polish off the meatless *schnitzel,* 85AS, with *Erdbeeren "Grossmutterart"* (sauce-dipped strawberries), 38AS. English menus. Entrees 82-130AS. Open Mon.-Sat. 11:30am-2:30pm and 7:30-10:30pm, Sun. 6pm-midnight.

Vegetarisches Restaurant Country-Life, 9 Maria-Theresien-Str. An air-conditioned oasis in the midst of the flash and dash of downtown Innsbruck. Crunchy salads and smooth, cool fruit soups 28-45AS. Daily special menus 95AS. Main restaurant open Mon.-Fri. 11:30am-3pm; buffet open Mon.-Thurs. 11:30am-7pm, Fri. 11:30am-3pm.

Hafele, on the corner of Innrain and Rehengasse, in the midst of Innsbruck University. Finger-lickin' good baked half-chicken 30AS. Grilled cutlet with fries 48AS. Fresh daily menus and salads. Open Mon.-Fri. 7am-6pm, Sat. 8am-noon.

Sights and Entertainment

The *Altstadt* is the center of Innsbruck, and the **Goldenes Dachl** (Golden Roof) is both the center of the *Altstadt* and the city's emblem. It once served as a vantage point for spectators during the medieval tournaments held in the square below. Inside the building is the **Olympiamuseum,** which commemorates the 1964 and 1976 Winter Games with relics and films. (Open daily 9:30am-5:30pm. Admission 20AS, children 15AS, seniors and students 10AS.) The **Goldenes Dachl** sits amidst a number of splendid 15th and 16th-century buildings. Take a look at the elaborate stuccowork on the **Heiligenhaus,** and don't miss the adjacent **Stadtturm,** the 14th-century city tower. Combined tickets to the city tower and Olympiamuseum are available. (Open daily July-Aug. 10am-6pm; March-June and Sept.-Oct. 10am-5pm. Combined admission 30AS; tower alone 16AS, children 8AS.) From the Goldenes Dachl, look to your left on the Herzog-Friedrich-Str. to see the 16th-century **Goldener Adler** Inn. Countless dignitaries and artists—among them Goethe, Heine, and Sartre—have stayed or dined here. The area immediately behind the Goldenes Dachl houses the stunning baroque **Dom of St. Jakob,** with its superb *trompe l'oeil* ceiling and an altar decorated with Cranach's *Intercession of the Virgin.*

At **Rennweg** and **Hofgasse** stands the grand **Hofburg** (Imperial Palace) and **Hofkirche** (Imperial Church). Built between the 16th and 18th centuries, the **Hofburg** is filled with portraits of its one-time royal residents. Empress Maria Theresia glowers over nearly every room; a portrait of Maria's youngest daughter, Marie Antoinette (with head) is in the palace's main hall. (Open daily 9am-4pm; mid-Oct. to mid-May Mon.-Sat. 9am-4pm. Admission 20AS, students 5AS. English guidebook 5AS.) The nearby **Hofkirche** also houses aristocrats, conquerors, and monarchs—this time, as mammoth bronze statues. (Open daily 9am-5pm; Oct.-April 9am-noon and 2-5pm. Admission 20AS, students 14AS.) A combined ticket (30AS) will also admit you to the collection of the **Tiroler Volkskunstmuseum** (Tyrolian Handicrafts Museum), next door. Dusty implements, peasant costumes, and furnished period rooms give a brief introduction to Tyrolean culture. (Open Mon.-Sat. 9am-5pm; Oct.-April Mon.-Sat. 9am-noon and 2-5pm. Museum also open Sun. 9am-noon. Admission to museum alone 15AS, students 10AS.) The collection of the **Tiroler Landesmuseum Ferdinandeum,** Museumstr. 15, several blocks from the main train station, includes exquisitely colored, delicately etched stained-glass windows and several outstanding medieval altars and paintings. (Open May-Sept. Tues.-Wed. 10am-5pm, Thurs. 10am-5pm and 7-9pm, Fri.-Sat. 10am-5pm, Sun. 9am-noon. Admission 20AS, students 14AS.)

From the **Triumphbogen** (Triumphal Arch), stroll down broad Maria-Theresien-Str. and savor the power panorama of the **Nordkette** (Northern Range). Other attractions in Innsbruck include the famed **Alpenzoo,** where you can see every vertebrate species indigenous to the Alps in their natural habitat and enjoy a bird's eye view of the city. Don't miss the zoo's network of scenic trails weaving through the hillside. (Open 9am-6pm; mid-Nov. to March 9am-5pm. Admission 50AS, students 25AS.) To reach the zoo, take bus K to St. Nikolaus and walk 25 min. up the hill, or catch the Alpenzoo bus (Linie Z) at 45 Maria-Theresien-Str. or at the Hofburg on Renweg (mid-May to Sept. every hr. 10am-5pm, 19AS, round-trip 30AS). Archduke Ferdinand left behind heaps of armor and paintings at **Schloß Ambras** (open May-Sept. Wed.-Mon. 10am-5pm). To reach Ambras, take tram #3 or 6 towards Pradl. If you ever suspected that ski jumpers have a few screws loose, a trip out to the **Olympische Schischanze** jump will convince you. Take tram #1 to Bergisel.

During July and August, Innsbruck hosts the **Festival of Early Music,** featuring concerts at the **Schloß Ambras** on period instruments and organ recitals in the Hofkirche on the 16th-century Ebert organ. (Concerts at the castle every Tues. at 8pm; tickets 100-220AS; bus to castle leaves from Landesreisebüro on Bozner Platz at 7:30pm. Check with Innsbruck-Information for other prices and times.) The **Tiroler Laudestheater** (tel. 52 07 44), across from the Hofburg on Rennweg, is the finest theater in the region. (All performances in German. Tickets available Mon.-Sat. 8:30am-8:30pm or an hour before the performance at the door, 40-250AS.)

Treibhaus (tel. 58 68 74), Angerzellgasse 8, hidden in an alley to the right of China Restaurant is Innsbruck's favorite student hangout. Left-wing protest music serenades the young crowd in the evening. Jazz on Sunday mornings. During the summer, the Treibhaus presents its "Sommergarten" series, which includes concerts every Saturday evening, a June Blues festival, a June Jazz festival and other hip events. For general goings-on about town, saunter over to Innsbruck University and read the various announcements on the kiosks or check the monthly arts calendar published by the city and available at tourist offices.

Near Innsbruck

A few ice ages ago, a gargantuan glacier scooped out the **Stubai Valley,** south of Innsbruck. The mountain villages of **Fulpmes** and **Neustift** make good camps from which to set out on foot. Take the STB (Stubaibahn) tram from Innsbruck station to Fulpmes (54AS, round-trip 98AS). Innsbruck buses leave from the train station to Neustift (44AS, round-trip 80AS) and Fulpmes (36AS, round-trip 65AS). At the very top of the valley, you can ski year-round (except June) on the magnificent **Stubaigletscher.** Many private groups and pensions in Innsbruck offer package deals for a day's skiing; decide whether the convenience they offer is worth paying a little more (usually about 100AS). Also, know that many packages are reluctant to refund your money if your plans change. For the most reliable operation, turn to Innsbruck Information's offices at the train station or the *Altstadt.* They offer ski packages that include round-trip bus fare to the glacier, all-day lift ticket, and equipment for 590AS. Three day packages run 835AS, 680AS in low season. To go it alone, take the Omnibus Stubaital bus (leaves the bus station from platform #1 at 7:25 and 9:45am) to the Mutterbergalm-Talstation stop (80 min., round-trip 150AS). Here, buy a daypass (230-295AS) and ride the gondola to the top station, where you can rent equipment (140AS per day). Four lifts are always open, with many more running in winter. A self-service restaurant on the summit serves meals for 60-100AS. For a glacier weather report in German, call (05226) 81 51.

The Arlberg

Nestled between the cosmopolitan conurbation of Innsbruck and the rollicking gaiety of the Bodensee (Lake Constance) festival towns, the tiny mountain settlements of the Arlberg attract swarms of outdoor adventurers. On the eastern side of the Arlberg tunnel are the region's two cheapest towns, **St. Anton** and the cheaper **St. Jakob.** Farther north, the classy resorts of **Lech, Zürs,** and **St. Christoph** become more expensive in that order. Trains run to St. Anton from Bregenz (round-trip 134AS), Innsbruck (round-trip 140AS), and Zürich, and buses connect the town to nearby villages (St. Christoph 22AS; Zurs 37AS; Lech 41AS).

The comprehensive **Arlberg Ski pass** scores 77 lifts, 200km of pistes and 180km of powder, but unfortunately, no busing between the resorts it covers (besides the five above, tiny **Stuben,** south of St. Christoph; 380AS per day, 2110AS per week; off-season 340AS and 1900AS). Many hotels and pensions also participate in the **Arlberg Special,** which blesses visitors with more special discounts (1950AS, off-season 1750AS). For a weather and snow report, call (05583) 18 (Lech) or (05446) 25 65 (St. Anton). For more info on hiking as well as skiing, contact the tourist offices in Lech (tel. (05583) 216 10), or better yet, in St. Anton (tel. (05446) 226 90; open July-Aug. Mon.-Fri. 8am-noon and 2-6pm, Sat.-Sun. 10am-noon; Sept. to mid-Dec. and mid-April to June Mon.-Fri. 8am-noon and 2-6pm; mid-Dec. to mid-April Mon.-Fri. 8am-noon and 2:30-6:30pm, Sat. 9am-noon and 1-7pm, Sun. 10am-noon and 3-6pm.)

Shun hotels and hole up at a cozy B&B (180-300AS per person in summer, 400-600AS per person in winter). There are no campgrounds nearby, but outside of Lech roosts the sprawling yet down-home **Jugendheim Stubenach** (tel. (05583) 24 19). From the post office, head out of town, take the right fork at the Stubenach sign, and follow the main road for 10 minutes. (Reception open 5-9pm. Curfew 10pm. 130AS, with dinner 205AS. Open mid-Dec. to Nov.) Housing *anywhere* fills fast; in high season, book rooms 1½ to 2 months in advance, in the off-season, two weeks in advance.

Lienz

No less rich in mountain attractions than its neighbors to the north, Lienz is quietly captivating, unhurried in its charm. In the jagged Dolomites of the eastern Tyrol, the city is approximately three hours by train from Innsbruck or Salzburg. Lienz boasts not one but two **tourist offices** *(Verkehrsämter):* one at Hauptpl. 9 (open Mon.-Fri. 8am-7pm, Sat. 10am-1pm), the other a 10-min. walk west of the train station at Albin-Egger Str. 17 (tel. (04852) 652 65; open Mon.-Fri. 8am-noon and 2-6pm; mid-Sept. to June daily 8am-6pm). Ask about discount-oriented "guest cards" and the winter ski package, *Schipauschale.*

Lienz has a wonderful **Jugendherberge (IYHF)**—spotless, rustic, and directly on the fierce River Isel at Linker Iselweg 22 (tel. (04852) 633 10). From the station, cross the river and walk 10-15 min. upstream. (Reception open 6-10pm. Curfew 10pm. 85AS per night. Ages over 18 7AS more. Sheets and breakfast included. Open July-Aug.) Both tourist offices find rooms (starting at 100AS) for free, or wander away from the center and look for *Zimmerfrei* signs. **Gasthof Goldener Stern,** Schweizergasse 40 (tel. (04852) 621 92), gives a warm welcome and offers spacious rooms in a rustic house. (English spoken. 160-240AS per person, Dec. 2-22 and Jan. 6-Feb. 2 180-255AS, Dec. 22-Jan. 5 280-355AS. Showers 20-25AS. Single room supplement 15AS. Breakfast included.) Down the street at Schweizergasse 3 is one of the best bars this side of the Alps, **Café Wha** (open daily 3pm-1am). For inexpensive meals (60-80AS), try **China Restaurant Sehcuan** on Marcherstr. off Linker Iselweg., just a jaunt from the hostel. Open daily 11:30am-2:30pm and 5:30-11:30pm.

Above Lienz is the **Schloß Bruck,** home of the **East Tyrolian Regional Museum,** which houses everything from Roman remains and local artifacts to carved Christmas *crèches.* Buses run from the train station (12AS; take the Matrei bus), or foot it for 15-20 minutes. (Open June-Sept. daily 10am-6pm; April 8-May and Oct. Tues.-Sun. 10am-5pm. Admission 28AS, students 20AS, children 9AS.) For a moderate four- to five-hour hike, take the Hochsteinbahnen chairlift, which starts near the castle (40AS), then climb **Hochstein** (2057m), and descend to the valley (55AS). Open daily 9:30am-5:15pm. The **Zettersfeld** chairlift (one way 55AS) provides access to hiking on the Zettersfeld peak (1930m). And from Boznerstr. 2, buses run to another good hiking base, the **Lienzer Dolomitenhütte** in the mountains above town. (June-Sept. daily at 8am, 1pm, and 4:30pm, 1 hr., round-trip 90AS.)

Some 14 ski lifts operate between November and April. Full-day ski passes cost 230AS (seniors 190AS, ages under 15 115AS); successively cheaper ones let you start at 11am, noon, or 2pm. Prices descend after the first day. The **Lienzer Dolomiten Skischule,** at the Zettersfeld lift (tel. (04852) 656 90), gives private lessons for 310AS (each additional person 120AS). Cross-country ski rental is also available.

Outside Lienz begins the scenic **Großglocknerstraße,** one of the highest mountain roads in Europe. At 3797m, **Großglockner** peak is the highest mountain in Austria. Buses depart from Lienz twice daily for Zell am See (the other end of the Großglocknerstraße; buy a ticket from the driver for 185AS). You may choose to break up the trip by stopping in **Heiligenblut** (4 buses daily; 58AS). A comfortable, ever-popular **IYHF youth hostel** in Heiligenblut, Hof 36 (tel. (04824) 22 59) accommodates 84 in dorm rooms and offers bed, sheets and breakfast for 115AS per night; half-board 160AS, full board 200AS. (Reception open 5-10pm. Open Jan. 1-Sept. 30 and Dec. 12-Dec. 31. Absolutely reserve ahead.) Stop at Franz-Josefs-Höhe, at the foot of Großglockner, and take the **Gletscherbahn** (round-trip 70AS) for a stunning view of the glacier. For information on hiking on the mountain, call the special information bureau at (04824) 22 12 or 22 13. The road often closes in the winter and visibility can be poor at any time of year. Those hitchhiking or driving to Innsbruck might take the **Gerlosstraße** past the **Krimmler Waterfalls** and the Tyrol's **Ziller Valley.**

Graz

Centuries after Charlemagne claimed this strategic crossroads for the Germanic empire, Graz retains the flavor of southeastern Europe. The celebrated castles, military museum and clocktower recall Graz's long history as a political and military battleground. Despite the city's charm, its ancient streets remain unclogged by Anglophone tourists.

The **Hauptplatz** is the heart of the city. An easy 2-3 min. jaunt away is the **tourist office,** at Herrengasse 16 (tel. 83 52 41; open daily 9am-7pm), with a free room-finding service and more than enough information about Graz. You can change money at any of the banks along Herrengasse, but rely on the **main post office** at Neutorgasse 46 (open Mon.-Fri. 8am-6pm, Sat. 8am-4pm; on Sun., go to the post office booth at the train station). To reach the Hauptplatz from the main train station, walk straight down Keplergasse across the Mur River on the Keplerbrücke and right on Kaiser-Franz-Josef-Kai to the left on Sackstr.

Worth exploring is the Renaissance **Landhaus** (state capitol) and **Zeughaus** (military museum) on Herrengasse. Five floors of spears, muskets, and pistols—enough, in fact, for 28,000 mercenaries—are on display in this former armory of the Styrian estates. (Open April-Oct. Mon.-Fri. 9am-5pm, Sat.-Sun. 9am-1pm. Admission 25AS, students free.) Appropriately, Napoleon once spent the night across the street at 13 Herrengasse.

From high atop the **Schloßberg,** a hill overlooking the city that for centuries served as a military vantage point, looms the 16th-century bell tower, the city's symbol. Take the cable car from Schloßberg Platz. (Open May-Sept. 10am-8pm; 15AS, round-trip 20AS, children 7AS and 10AS). The 15-20 minute hike to the top is more exhilarating than exhausting, with excellent views of the city all along the well-marked paths. The **Schloß Eggenberg** (Eggenberg Castle), at Schloß-Str., houses a diverse collection of 17th-century artifacts. To see the castle's elegant **Prunkräume,** you must join one of the six free tours. (Open April-Oct. Tours every hour on the hour from 10am-4pm except 1pm. Admission to the entire complex 25AS, students free.) Roam with the peacocks through an enchanting game preserve adjacent to the castle. (Open daily 8am-7pm. Admission 2AS.)

Accommodations in Graz are generally affordable and easy to find, except in July and August. The cheapest bed in town is at the **youth hostel (IYHF)** at Idlhofgasse 74 (tel. 91 48 76), a 20-minute walk from the train station. Head south on Bahnhofgürtel, take a left at Josef-Hubergasse, then a right at Idlhofgasse. Its reasonable dorms (110AS, nonmembers 120AS, breakfast and sheets included) are overrun by jubilant East Européans. Escape to the hostel's tranquil garden, featuring swaying poplars, a lily pond, flowers, and picnic tables. (Reception open 5-10pm. Lockout 9am-5pm. Curfew 10pm.) A more comfortable and expensive option is the **Hotel Strasser,** Eggenbergergürtel 11 (tel. 91 39 77), a short walk from the train station, with big rooms on a busy street. (Singles 240-265AS, with shower 300-330AS. Doubles 380-480AS, with showers 480-590AS. Breakfast included.) 30,000 students sustain a blitz of cheap eateries in Graz (and vice versa). The best deal in town is the **Mensa** of the University of Graz, just east of the Stadtpark at Zinzendorfgasse and Schuberstr. (Full meals 30-60AS.) **Zotter,** Glacisstr. 25, also just east of the Stadtpark, has an ornate interior, friendly service, and succulent desserts. (Breakfast 25-58AS, sandwiches 17-22AS, salads 25-48AS. Open Tues.-Fri. 7:15am-8pm, Sat.-Sun. 9am-8pm.) Escape this land of sausage and beer at **Margolds Vollwert Restaurant,** Griesgasse 11. Scenically set right on the Mur, Margolds offers a cafeteria and café serving vegetable salads, juices and desserts (12-45AS; open Mon.-Sat. 11am-8pm).

Graz's remarkable **Operhaus** (opera house) at Opernring and Burgasse, sells student tickets (33-150AS) at the door an hour before curtain, as does the **Schauspielhaus** (theater) at Hofgasse and Burgring (33-130AS). Regular tickets and performance schedules are available at **Theaterringemeinde,** Herrengasse 2 (tel. 83 02 74; open Mon.-Fri. 9am-12:30pm and 4-6:30pm).

Burggasse and **Bürgergasse,** just north of the Opera House, are littered with tiny pubs where you can quaff a liter or two of Gösser, the local brew. For a bargain night on the town, stroll down Herrengasse and let the street musicians serenade you.

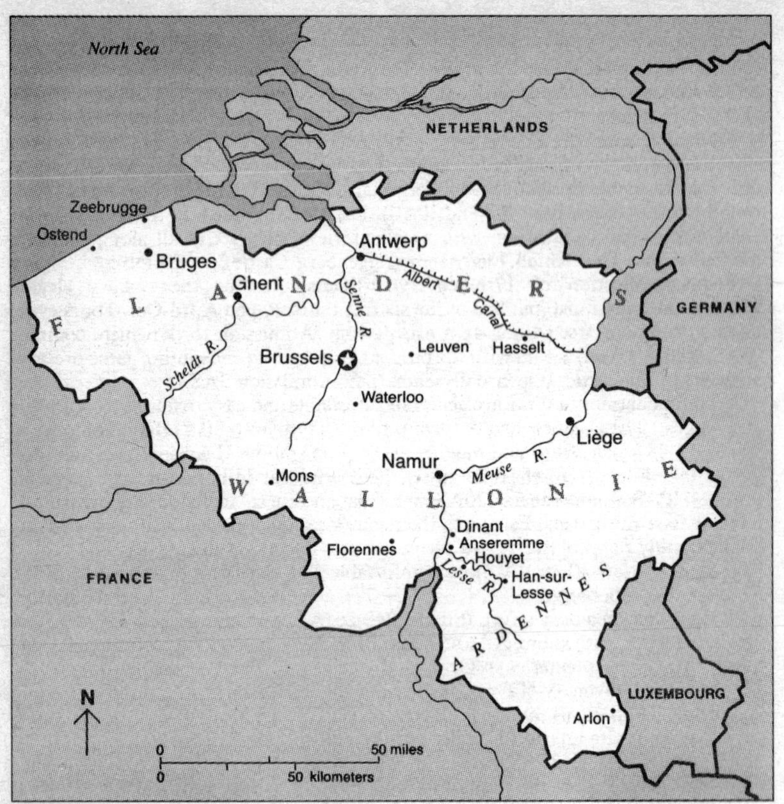

BELGIUM

USD$1 = 36.1 francs (BF, or BEF) | **10BF = USD$0.28**
CAD$1 = 31.5BF | **10BF = CAD$0.32**
GBP£1 = 60.2BF | **10BF = GBP£0.17**
AUD$1 = 28.1BF | **10BF = AUD$0.36**
NZD$1 = 20.5BF | **10BF = NZD$0.49**
Country Code: 32 | **International Dialing Prefix: 00**

Despite its status as one of Europe's "little countries," the appeal of Belgium (Belgique, België) is wide and varied. In the south, the wooded Ardennes lolligag over gentle hills; near the North Sea, Bruges and Ghent bask in guildhoused medieval splendour; centrally located Brussels revels in decorous frenzy and in its new status as a European power broker.

The vast graveyards around Ypres left behind by the massive conflicts of this century fit congruously into the chaotic course of Belgian history. Until it gained independence in 1830, Belgium served as a perennial battleground for larger continental powers, whose partitions gave rise to the nation's present cultural dichotomy between the Flemish in the north, who speak a Dutch dialect, and the French-speaking Walloons in the south. The Roman Empire extended as far north as modern-day Brussels, while Germanic Franks conquered the lands of Flanders to the north. Ages later, after centuries of campaigns on the part of France's rulers and the Hapsburg Empire to secure Belgium's strategic ports and fertile lands, the ancient division was reinforced when the revolt of the United Netherlands against the Spanish crown stalled at the present-day border with Wallonie. The cultural split is today reinforced by economics; Flanders relies on industry and commerce, while Wallonie is primarily agricultural. Language remains a point of contention; after centuries of French as the only official language, the Flemish today defiantly cling to their own tongue. It is diplomatic to approach people in the north with English rather than French.

Getting There and Getting Around

Belgium's train network is the densest in the world and one of the most reliable in Europe. Prices are low (Namur-Brussels 195BF; Brussels-Bruges 310BF; Bruges-Ghent 145BF), if only because the country is small (only four rail hours across at its widest point). Both Eurail and InterRail are valid on intercity buses as well as trains. Many natives scam trips to the beach or countryside to take advantage of low weekend fares: if your round-trip ticket leaves between noon Friday and noon Sunday and returns between noon Saturday and noon Monday, you save 40%. Each additional person with you saves 60%. The **B-Tourrail "5/17" Pass** (5 days of travel during a 17-day period) is very hard to make pay off (1700BF, under 26 1300BF). So is the **TTB** (Train, Tramway, Bus) pass, good for 5 days during a 17-day period on both intercity and municipal transportation (2200BF, under 26 1700BF). The **Benelux Tourrail Pass** is a better deal, covering five days' travel in Belgium, the Netherlands, and Luxembourg during a 17-day period (2770BF, ages under 26 1990BF; available April-Oct.). A **Half-Fare Card** (550BF for 1 month) is also available.

Like the Netherlands, Belgium—especially Flanders—is a **cyclist's** nirvana. The land is flat, intercity distances are short, and roads have bicycle lanes. When you see two sidepaths next to the street, the inner one is for bicycles and mopeds; the outer one is for pedestrians. Sixty of Belgium's 150 train stations rent bikes; you can return a bike to any of 75 designated stations. Bikes cost 120BF per day, 100BF per day for three or more days (200BF per day without a rail ticket); tandems cost 300BF and 250BF (425BF). Pick up the brochure *Train et Vélo/Trein en Fiets* at any station.

Hitching on secondary roads in Belgium is generally auspicious. Use a bilingual sign: "please" is *s.v.p.* in French, *a.u.b.* in Flemish. **Taxi Stop** has offices in major cities and matches travelers with Belgian drivers to destinations all over Europe. (2BF per km, 150-500BF per trip.) Call 512 10 15 for information. **Ferries** from Zeebrugge and Oostende, both near Bruges, cross the Channel to Dover and other British ports.

Practical Information

Belgium's dense network of efficient tourist offices is supplemented by **Infor-Jeunes/Info-Jeugd,** a nationwide information service that caters to young people, helping with medical or legal problems, work or study in Belgium, and short- or long-term accommodations. The English-language weekly *Bulletin,* (75BF at most newsstands), lists everything from movies in English to job opportunities.

Major national holidays in Belgium are Ascension Day (the 6th Thurs. after Easter), Whit Monday (the 7th Mon. after Easter), July 21 (Belgian National Day), and August 15.

Public telephones (which can't receive incoming calls) take two 5BF coins. A 200BF **phonecard** from PTT (telephone and telegraph) offices in larger cities may be more convenient. To reach AT&T's **USA Direct,** call 11 00 10. In an emergency anywhere in Belgium, dial 100 for medical service and the fire brigade, and 101 for the police. To reach the domestic operator, dial 1307; the European operator, 1304; the international operator, 1322.

Accommodations, Camping, and Food

Hotels in Belgium are expensive, with trench-bottom prices of 600BF for a single and 900-1000BF for a double. Avoid bankruptcy by staying in any of the 31 IYHF hostels, which charge 280-320BF per night (350-550BF in Oostende and Brussels). Pick up *Budget Holidays* at any tourist office for complete hostel listings. Campgrounds charge about 100BF per night. The pamphlet *Camping*, with complete listings and prices, is available free at tourist offices.

Belgian cuisine just isn't very good. Godiva chocolates and other less famous and cheaper brands (always marked *pralinen),* brighten the gastronomic scene, however, and you will surely appreciate Belgium's brewing process. Choose from 30 to 45 different beers in any saloon—the country produces a total of 355 varieties. Regular beer or quirky *blonde* pils cost as little as 30BF, and dark beers cost about 50BF. *Gueuze* beer is made from local wheat and ferments in the bottle, while the marvelously sweet (and very potent) *Kriek* is made from cherries.

Brussels (Bruxelles, Brussel)

A city with a lineage of leadership, Brussels aspires to become "capital of Europe" as the vaunted 1992 reforms unfold. Previously the city has served as headquarters for the Spanish Low Countries, the Dutch Kingdom, and more recently the European Community, NATO, and countless international firms. Building cranes abound and property values are soaring. Although Brussels' post-war growth has taken a toll on the city's ancient beauty, the Grand-Place acts as an ornate and mighty aesthetic anchor.

Orientation and Practical Information

Tourist Brussels is roughly bounded by Gare du Nord in the north, Brussels Park in the east, the Palais de Justice in the south, and the Bourse (stock exchange) in the west. Gare Centrale and the Grand-Place share the center.

Brussels and its suburbs are officially bilingual, existing since 1980 as a third region in this federal state, separate from Flanders and Wallonie. Since most Bruxellians speak French (the city is estimated to be 75% Walloon), and since French is more familiar to most travelers than Flemish, *Let's Go* uses French.

Tourist Offices: National, 61, rue du Marché aux Herbes (tel. 512 30 30). From the Grand-Place, walk north (away from town hall) 1 block to Marché aux Herbes. Books rooms throughout Belgium. Pick up the exhaustive *What's On* brochure. Open June-Sept. daily 9am-8pm; Oct. and March-May daily 9am-6pm; Nov.-Feb. Mon.-Sat. 9am-6pm, Sun. 1-5pm. Branch office at the airport (tel. 722 30 00). Open daily 6am-10pm. **TIB (Tourist Information Brussels),** in the town hall on the Grand-Place (tel. 513 89 40). Brochures and free room reservations. *Brussels Guide and Map* (50BF). Theater, opera, and ballet tickets sold 11am-5pm. Open daily 9am-6pm; Oct.-March Mon.-Sat. 9am-6pm.

Tours: Le Bus Bavard/De Babbelbus. An escape from the aimless wanderer syndrome. Walking tour of the old city, then a bus to attractions on the outskirts, capped off by a snack and a chat in a café. Tours leave daily June-Sept. 15 at 10am from 90, rue Marché aux Herbes (at the entrance to the St.-Hubert Galleries). 3hr.; 250BF, 220BF if staying in a youth hostel.

Budget Travel: Acotra World, 51, rue de la Madeleine (tel. 512 55 40). Room-finding service (free), budget flights. Open Mon.-Wed. and Fri. 10am-6pm, Thurs. 10am-7pm, Sat. 10am-1pm. Also check out **Infor-Jeunes,** 27, rue du Marché aux Herbes (tel. 512 32 74), a bonanza for budget travelers. Open Mon.-Fri. noon-5:45pm. Also at Gare du Midi (tel. 522 58 56) March-Oct.

Embassies: U.S., 27, bd. du Régent (tel. 513 38 30). **Canada,** 2, av. Telvurel (tel. 735 60 40). **U.K.,** 28, rue Joseph II (tel. 217 90 00). **Australia,** 6, rue Guimard (tel. 231 05 00). **New Zealand,** 47-48, bd. du Régent (tel. 512 10 40). **France,** 65, Rue du Cale (tel. 512 17 15).

Currency Exchange: At Gare du Nord (open daily 7am-11pm), Gare Centrale (open Mon.-Sun. 8am-9pm), and Gare du Midi (open daily 7am-11pm). No commission but mediocre rates. Banks are the way to go—all have good rates, and some (Crédit Communale is one) ask no commission. "Change" booths mushrooming near tourist sites give abysmal rates; beware.

American Express: 2, pl. Louise (tel. 512 17 40). Long waits; bring a book. Decent exchange rates. Open Mon.-Fri. 9am-5pm, Sat. 9:30am-noon.

Post Office: Main office on the 2nd floor of the Centre Monnaie, the tall building on pl. de la Monnaie. Open Mon.-Thurs. 9am-6pm, Fri. 9am-7pm, Sat. 9am-noon. Branch office at Gare du Midi, 48a, av. Fonsny, is inconvenient, but open 24 hrs.

Telephones: 17, bd. de l'Impératrice, near Gare Centrale. Open daily 8am-10pm. Private office at 30a, rue de Lombard, charges the same and is more pleasant. Open daily 10am-8pm. For operator assistance within Brussels, dial 12 80. **City Code:** 02.

Flights: Tel. 720 71 67. Trains to **Brussels International Airport** (75BF) leave from Gare Centrale at 14, 39, and 55 min. past the hr., from 5:39am to 11:14pm; all stop at Gare du Nord.

Trains: Tel. 219 28 80. Most trains stop at **Gare Centrale,** and many stop at either **Gare du Nord** or **Gare du Midi** as well. Gare Centrale is near the Grand-Place and the tourist office, but a 15-min. walk from most budget accommodations. Gare du Nord is in a lean neighborhood, convenient to several hostels and little else. 15 min. southeast of the center, Traffic to**Gare du Quartier Leopold,** 15 min. southeast of the center, generally passes through one of the main stations.

Buses: STIB (Société des Transports Intercommunaux Bruxellois) has offices in Gare du Midi (open Mon.-Fri. 8:30am-12:30pm and 1:30-6pm, Sat. 10am-12:30pm and 1:30-5:30pm), and in town at 20, Galeries de la Toison d'Or, 6th floor (tel. 515 30 64).

Luggage Storage: Lockers and offices at the 3 major train stations; each 15BF per day.

Public Transportation: The **Métro** (Mo.) covers most of the city. Buses, Métros, and trams all cost 40BF. Tickets available at any Métro or train station, or on the bus. Forgo the many passes; the city is most walkable. Public transportation runs 6am-midnight.

Hitchhiking: Those hitching to Antwerp and Amsterdam take tram #52 from Gare du Midi or Gare du Nord to Heysel, the terminus. About 300m from the terminus, they fork right for Antwerp. Those going to Liège and Cologne take tram #90 from the Gare du Nord to Mo. Diamant to reach the E40. Those headed to Ghent, Bruges and Oostende take bus #85 from the Bourse to one stop before the terminus and follow the E40 signs. Those going to Paris take tram #52 (direction: "Gare du Midi") to rue de Stalle and walk toward the E19.

Bookstore: Replace stolen *Let's Gos* at **W.H. Smith,** 71-75, bd. Adolphe Max (tel. 219 50 34), a vast and expensive English bookstore. Open Sat.-Thurs. 9am-6pm, Fri. 9am-7pm.

Laundromat: Salon Lavoir, 5, rue Haute, around the corner from Breugel's youth hostel. Wash and dry 210BF. Open Mon.-Fri. 8am-6pm.

Crises: SOS-Jeunes, 27, rue Mercellis (tel. 512 90 20, 24 hrs.).

Pharmacies: Pharma-Congrès, 56, rue du Congrès, at rue du Nord, near the Jacques Brel hostel. Open Mon.-Fri. 8:30am-1pm and 1:30-5:30pm. **Neos-Bourse Pharmacie,** boulevard Anspach at rue du Marché aux Polets (open Mon.-Fri. 8:30am-6:30pm, Sat. 9am-6:30pm).

Medical Assistance: Free Clinic, 154a, chaussée de Wavre (tel. 512 13 14). Open Mon.-Fri. 9am-6pm. 24-hr. medical services (tel. 479 18 18 or 648 80 00).

Emergencies: Police (tel. 101). **Ambulances** or **First Aid** (tel. 100).

Accommodations and Camping

Brussels has a gaggle of hostels. The tourist office in the Grand-Place and Acotra will help you find other places.

Centre Jacques Brel (IYHF), 30, rue de la Sablonnière (tel. 218 01 87), on the pl. des Barricades; a 10-min. walk from Gare du Nord, 15 min. from Gare Centrale. Mo. Madou. Institutional rooms, each with its own shower. Myriad services, bar and outdoor terrace. Reception open 8:30am-6:30pm. Lockout 10am-2pm. Curfew 1am. Dorms 350BF. Singles 570BF. Doubles 940BF. Triples and quads 395BF per person. Showers and breakfast included. Sheets 100BF. Fills up quickly.

Sleep Well, 27, rue de la Blanchisserie (tel. 218 50 50). Mo. Rogier. From Gare du Nord, walk to pl. Rogier and continue straight to rue Neuve, then take the 1st left. Friendly and relaxed, bedecked with funky murals. Lockout 10am-5pm, but lounge and small lockers (30BF) open. Curfew 1am. "Sleep-ins" (huge dorms) 220BF (July-Aug.). Dorms 290BF. Singles 450BF. Doubles 790BF. 4- to 6-bed rooms 345BF per person. 25% off if your passport number has "27" anywhere in it. Free on your birthday. Showers and breakfast included. Sheets 80BF. Restaurant and bar open Mon.-Sat. 6-11pm. 2-hr. walking tour only 50BF.

Maison Internationale, 205, chausée de Wavre (tel. 648 85 29 or 648 97 87). Take bus #37 or 38 from Gare du Nord, bus #38 from Gare Centrale (stop "Throne;" they run infrequently), or catch a train from either station to the Gare du Quartier Leopold, 5 min. away. If you're alone, this place rules. Roomy singles with sinks, for regular hostel prices. Flexible 3-day max. stay. Reception open 7am-12:30am. Lockout 9:30am-4pm. Curfew 12:30am. Singles 350BF. Doubles 580BF. Showers and breakfast included. Laundry 150BF. For 220BF, you can pitch a tent in their garden.

CHAB, 8, rue Traversière (tel. 217 01 58). Mo. Botanique. From Gare du Nord, take bus #61 to rue Traversière or walk 10 min. From Gare Centrale, take bus #65 or 66, and get off at rue du Méridien. Spotless echo-chambers and a grassy courtyard. Lots of fun. Kitchen facilities. Lockout 10am-4pm. Curfew 2am. Co-ed "sleep-ins" 280BF. Smaller dorms 340BF. Singles 580BF. Doubles 960BF. Triples and quads 400BF per person. Showers and breakfast included. Large lockers (100BF padlock deposit). Sheets 80BF. Laundry 150BF.

Bruegel (IYHF), 2, rue du St. Esprit (tel. 511 04 36), in an alley behind Notre-Dame-de-la-Chapelle. Noisy teen-tour groups. Lockout 10am-2pm. Curfew midnight. Dorms 360BF. Singles 590BF. Doubles 960BF. Quads 1620BF. Hot showers and breakfast included. Dinner 220BF. Free lockers with deposit. Sheets 100BF. Reservations recommended in summer.

Hôtel Pacific, 57, rue Antoine Dansaert (tel. 511 84 59). Fine location, a *Let's Go* library and finger paintings on the walls. Curfew midnight. Singles 800BF. Doubles 1250BF. Showers 100BF. Breakfast—including yummy bacon-and-cheese omelette—included.

Pension Bosquet, 70, rue Bosquet (tel. 538 52 30). Mo. Hotel des Monnaies. Squeaky-clean. English-speaking owner. Some rooms have small terraces. Reception open 8am-11pm. Singles 800BF, with shower 1000BF. Doubles 1200BF, with shower 1600BF. Quads 2400BF, with shower only. Hall showers 100BF. Free breakfast on the gracious patio. Across the street is a similar hotel with the same owners and prices, the **Résidence Osborne,** 67, rue Bosquet (tel. 537 92 51). Reserve during high-season.

Camping: Besides the camping option at the Maison Internationale, all sites are outside Brussels. Definite first choice is **Paul Rosmant,** Warandeberg 52 (tel. 782 10 09), in Wezembeck-Oppem. Reception open 9am-12:30pm and 2-10pm. 65BF per person, 65BF per tent; municipality tax 30BF. Open April-Sept. Just north of Brussels in Grimbergen is **Veldkant,** 64 Veldkantstr. (tel. 269 25 97). Take bus G or H from Gare du Nord; alight at Grimbergen. 70BF per person, 100BF per tent, 10BF per bike. Open April-Oct.

Food

Brussels restaurants look really nice, but range from expensive to very expensive. Inexplicably renowned in this landlocked city are the seafood establishments along the rue des Bouchers. You'll do best at the city's plentiful *frites* stands and snack bars, supplemented with an occasional and ever-so-scrumptious Belgian waffle. There are daily **markets** at pl. Ste. Catherine (7am-5pm), pl. Emile Bockstael (7am-2pm), and pl. de la Chapelle (7am-2pm). **GB** supermarkets are at 248, rue Vierge Noire (open Sat.-Thurs. 9am-8pm, Fri. 9am-9pm) and in the "City 2" shopping center, 50m from the Sleep Well. Restaurants usually have a *plat du jour* for 300-400BF. Try the open-air cafés on rue des Bouchers.

Chez Léon, 18-20, rue des Bouchers, just off the Grand-Place. Deep in the tourist maelstrom, but fun. Hamburgers and Brussels' famed mussels (large portions 290-595BF). Spaghetti bolognese 225BF. Open daily noon-midnight.

Falstaff, 17-27, rue Henri Maus, next to the *Bourse.* Stop in at 3am after a late night of dancing to enjoy fat and jolly pastries (60-70BF), coffee (55BF), and *menus du jour* (325BF) amid antique chandeliers and stained-glass. Open daily 9am-5am.

Le Grand Café, 78, bd. Anspach, on the other side of the *Bourse.* Generous menu with appetizer, main course and dessert 470BF. Open Sun.-Mon. 7am-midnight, Fri.-Sat. 7am-1pm.

La Mort Subite, 7, rue Montagne-aux-Herbes-Potagères. One of Brussels' oldest and best-known cafés, complete with worn marble floors, heavy oak tables and snooty waiters. Open daily 7am-1am. (3x!)

Sights and Entertainment

Victor Hugo dubbed the **Grand-Place** "the most beautiful square in the world." This magnificent collection of guildhalls and public buildings teems with visitors day and night. The 15th-century **Town Hall** on the *place* is open to visitors. (Open Tues.-Fri. 9:30am-5pm, Sun. 10am-4pm. Tour in English at 10:45am. Admission 75BF.) Three blocks behind the town hall on rue de l'Etuve at rue du Chêne is Brussels's most giggled-at sight, the **Mannekin-Pis,** a fountain of a small boy urinating. The story goes that a 17th-century mayor of Brussels promised to build a statue in the position that his lost son was found; another says the statue commemorates a boy who saved the city by ingeniously extinguishing the fuse which had been lit to blow up the Town Hall.

The **Musée d'Art Ancien,** 3, rue de la Régence, displays a huge collection of early Flemish masters, including Pieter Brueghel the Elder's *Fall of Icarus* and *Census in Bethlehem.* (Open Tues.-Sun. 10am-noon and 1-5pm. Free.) Next door is the spruced-up **Musée d'Art Moderne,** 1, pl. Royale. This huge, eight-level underground museum houses the best of 19th and 20th-century Belgian modernists, along with Dalí's *Temptation of St. Anthony* and Bacon's *Pope with Owls.* (Open Tues.-Sun. 10am-1pm and 2-5pm. Free.) The **Musées Royaux d'Art et d'Histoire,** 10, parc du Cinquantenaire, cover a wide variety of periods and genres—Roman torsos missing their heads, Syrian heads missing their torsos, and colorful Egyptian caskets with protruding wooden feet. (Mo. Merode. Open Tues.-Fri. 9:30am-12:30pm and 1:30-4:45pm, Sat.-Sun. and holidays 10am-4:45pm. Free.) **Autoworld,** next door at # 11, houses the largest collection of automobiles in Europe, with vintage cars dating from 1894. (Open 10am-6pm; Nov.-March 10am-5pm. Admission 200BF.)

Brussels—known informally as the "Comic Strip Capital of the World"—recently opened the **Belgian Comic Strip Centre,** in the art nouveau Waucquez Warehouse, 20, rue des Sables, near the well-endowed rue de St. Laurent. It contains originals of the most famous Belgian comic strips and many Tintin comics. (Open Tues.-Sun. 10am-6pm. 120BF.) Like Barcelona, Brussels is one of Europe's top addresses for art nouveau architecture. For a taste, visit the classy café and dance hall **De Ultieme Hallucinatie,** 316, rue Royale (tel. 217 06 14). (Restaurant open Mon.-Fri. noon-2:30pm and 7:30-10:30pm, Sat. 7:30-10:30pm. Take tram #92 or 94.) Baron Victor Horta is the style's greatest representative; his house, the **Musée Horta,** is at 25, rue Américaine; take tram #81 or 92. (Open Tues.-Sun. 2-5:30pm. Admission 100BF.) The neighborhood around ave. Louise and rue de Livourne flaunts several other impressive examples. **St. Michael's Cathedral,** is the city's most impressive Gothic edifice; **Galerie St. Hubert** is Europe's oldest shopping arcade.

The **Cinema Museum,** 9, rue Baron Horta (tel. 513 41 55) near Gare Centrale, shows two silent movies per night with piano accompaniment, and three talkies, sometimes in English, with French subtitles. (Open 5:30-10:30pm. 80BF for a 2-hr. stay.) For more frenzy for your franc, string along the nightclubs, discos, and bars in the streets surrounding ave. Louise and rue de Livourne. **Minim,** 57, rue des Minimes, specializes in rock, new wave and blues (open Wed.-Sun. from 11pm), while **L'Ecume des Nuits,** 122a Galerie Louise, at pl. Stéphanie, spins black funk (open Thurs.-Sun. 11pm-dawn). For live jazz try **Travers,** 11, rue Traversière (tel. 218 40 86; open Mon.-Sat. 9pm-1am; weekly concerts 300BF, students 250BF, beers 40BF), or **The Brussels Jazz Club,** 13, Grand-Place (tel. 512 40 93; open Tues.-Sat., featured performer 11pm-2am; cover charge 200BF). From June through September, concerts frequently pop up on the **Grand-Place,** pl. de la Monnaie, and in the **Parc de Bruxelles.** For more events information, pick up a calendar at the tourist office, or call **BBB Agenda** (tel. 512 82 77).

Near Brussels

Twenty minutes away by train, you can find relief from Bruxellian brick and bustle in medieval **Leuven's** charming and spotless sidestreets, lined with wrought-iron balconies, colorful stained-glass windows, and windowbox flowers. Trains leave hourly from each of Brussels' three major stations (30 min., 115BF). Pedestrians rule the streets of this town, home to Belgium's oldest and largest university, and nearly every corner sports a bookshop or café. From the station, walk straight down Bondgenotenlaan to the town square. There you can pick up a map (10BF) at the **tourist office,** Naamsestr. 1a (tel. (016) 21 15 39; open Mon.-Fri. 8am-5pm, Sat.-Sun. 10am-5pm). You can cover most of Leuven in a day. If you must spend the night, try the university residences at **Zomerverblijen.** K.U. Leuven, Van Dalecollege, Naamsestr. 80 (tel. (016) 28 43 70; 500BF, breakfast included; open Aug.-Sept., students only). Otherwise, check into **Hôtel Mille Colonnes,** Martelarenplein 5 (tel. (016) 22 86 21), just across from the station. (Singles 550-800BF. Doubles 950-1000BF.)

Start your ramblings in the square, where the **Stadhuis** (Town Hall) is perhaps the most sculpture-burdened Gothic edifice in Europe (the statues are a 19th-century afterthought). Visit by guided tour only. (Daily at 3pm. 20BF.) Across from the Stadhuis is **St-Pieterskerk,** a 15th-century church with a collection of paintings by Dirk Bouts, including his *Last Supper.* (Open Tues.-Sat. 10am-noon and 2-5pm, Sun. 2-5pm; Oct.-March Tues.-Sat. 10am-noon and 2-5pm. Admission 50BF.) Several blocks down Naamsestr. is the **Groot Begijnhof,** a lovely "city within a city." Built with brick and sandstone during the 17th and 18th centuries, the buildings once housed "Beguines," women thought to be heretics because they led religious lives but insisted on keeping their own property and supporting themselves *(mon dieu,* what brazenness!) University students now frolic in the restored houses and narrow streets of this former convent. Shotgun beers with them in the plentiful pubs clustering around the **Oude Market** (Old Market); **Café de Rector** and **De Weerelt** do an especially booming business pouring Belgium's finest brews. **Kruidtuin,** a bountiful botanical garden at the end of Minderbroederstr., offers a quiet respite from the hustle and bustle of the town.

Napoleon was finally caught with both hands in his shirt at **Waterloo,** south of Brussels. Climb the **Lion Mound** for a superb view of the plains where he was defeated. (Open April-Oct. 9:30am-6:30pm; Nov.-March 10:30am-4pm. Last entry ½ hr. before closing. Admission 40BF. The **Musée Wellington** traces European political developments before and after Napoleon's conquests and eventual defeat, as well as hour-by-hour descriptions of the battles themselves. (Open daily 9:30am-6:30pm; mid-Nov. to March daily 10:30am-5pm. Admission 60BF, students 50BF, children 40BF.) To reach Waterloo, board a train from Gare Centrale to nearby Nivelle, and then a bus; or take bus W directly to Waterloo (every ½ hr.; 40BF each way) from pl. Rouppe in Brussels (itself accessible via tram #90).

Bruges (Brugge)

Bruges, the capital of Flanders, is Europe's sleeping beauty. Five hundred years ago, this wealthy Renaissance town lapsed from greatness as accumulating silt from the River Zwin cut it off from the sea and its livelihood. Antwerp quickly took up the role of economic capital, and Bruges was pronounced dead and cryogenically frozen. But in 1907, a second seaport—Zeebrugge—was attached to the town, and Bruges awoke from its time-warping nap. The result: northern Renaissance architecture is better preserved here than anywhere in Europe. Remarkable façades reflect in romantic canals, horse-drawn carriages clop over cobblestones, swans glide over the serene Minnewater; the overall impression is of a living museum.

Orientation and Practical Information

Many make Bruges a daytrip from Antwerp or Brussels, but it's almost wiser to make Brussels a daytrip from Bruges. A highway and canal encircle Bruges; several other canals flow through the town. All converge at the **Markt,** a handsome square presided over by the magnificent **belfort** (belfry). The train station lies just outside the ring, due south of the Markt.

Tourist Office: Burg 11 (tel. 44 86 86), just east of the Markt, in the town's other main square. Turn left out of the station, pass the crazy fountain and enter 't Zand Sq., then turn right on Zuid-Zangaltonstr. Books rooms, and sells a good map for 20BF. Open Mon.-Fri. 9:30am-6:30pm, Sat.-Sun. 10am-noon and 2-6:30pm; Oct.-March Mon.-Fri. 9:30am-12:45pm and 2-5:45pm, Sat. 10am-12:45pm and 2-5:45pm. Smaller office at the train station also sells maps and books hotels (open Mon.-Sat. 2:45-9pm; Nov.-Feb. 1:45-8pm). **Youth Information Center: JAC,** Kleine Hertsbergestr. 1 (tel. 33 83 06). Information on cheap accommodations, meals, travel, and youth clubs. Also serves as a youth crisis center. Open Mon. and Wed. 9am-noon and 1:30-8pm, Tues. 1:30-8pm, Fri. 9am-noon and 1:30-6pm, and Sat. 10am-12:30pm.

Post Office: Markt 5. Poste Restante. Open Mon.-Fri. 9am-6pm. **Postal Code:** 8000.

Telephones: City Code: 050.

Trains: Tel. 38 23 82 daily 6:30am-10:30pm. On Stationsplein, a 15-min. walk south of the city center.

Bike Rental: Standard prices at the train station. **Koffieboontje,** Hallestr. 4 (tel. 33 80 27), off the Markt next to the belfry, charges 250BF 1st day, 150BF thereafter, students 110BF, 750BF per week. **Eric Popelier,** Hallestr. 14, rents similar quality bikes at the same prices.

Hitchhiking: Those hitching to Brussels take bus #7 to St. Michiels or pick up the highway behind the station.

Luggage Storage: At bike rental section of train station. Lockers (15BF) at the tourist office.

Laundromat: Belfort, Ezelstr. 51, next to Snuffel's Traveller's Inn. Wash 'n' dry 120BF. Open daily 7am-10pm.

Emergencies: Police or **Ambulance,** tel. 100. Police headquarters at Hauwerstr. 3 (tel. 44 88 44), off 't Zand Sq.

Accommodations, Camping, and Food

While the official hostel offers slightly better basics, the private hostels are central and heaps more fun. Arrive before noon in July and August.

Bauhaus International Youth Hotel, Langestr. 135-137 (tel. 33 61 75), a 10-min. walk from the Markt. Bus #6 from the station (30BF). Infamous throughout backpacker culture as one of the most happening hostels in Europe; with your beer goggles on, you probably won't see the gnats. Art-deco bar downstairs. Co-ed dorms 295BF. Singles 550BF. Doubles 900BF. Triples 1140BF. Quads 1280BF. Showers and breakfast included.

Bruno's Passage, Dweersstr. 26 (tel. 34 02 32), 1 block from 't Zand. Respectable rooms above a rollicking bar. Attain your species-being on the house piano, guitar, or horn. Free **Bruno's card** good for discounts at several area shops. No lockout or curfew. Dorms 310-375BF. Showers and breakfast included. Show your *Let's Go* for a 5% discount off more expensive rooms.

Snuffel's Traveller's Inn, Ezelstr. 49 (tel. 33 31 33), a 10-min. walk from the Markt; follow Sint-Jakobstr., which turns into Ezelstr. Bus #3, 8, 9, or 13 from the station. A funhouse. Hip bar and café downstairs. Long trek to the bathroom. No lockout or curfew. Coed dorms 320BF. Doubles 900BF. Showers and breakfast included. In July and Aug., ask about doing chores in exchange for a free night's stay.

Europa Jeugdherberg (IYHF), Baron Ruzettelaan 143 (tel. 35 26 79), a 25-min. walk south from the Markt; take bus #2 to Steenbrugge. Very clean and slick, but comparatively dull. Reception open Mon.-Sat. 8-10am and 1-11pm, Sun. 8-10am and 5-11pm. Lockout 10am-1pm. No curfew. Dorms 320BF. 4-bed rooms with shower 1620BF. Nonmembers add 80BF. Showers and breakfast included. Dinner 220BF. Free lockers. Sheets 120BF. Bar open 6pm-midnight (beer 25BF). Reserve ahead.

Hotel Lybeer, Korte Vulersstr. 31 (tel. 33 43 55), just off 't Zand Sq. Fresh and pretty rooms, each with their own window box of flowers. Singles 800BF. Doubles 1350BF. Triples 1900BF. Breakfast and showers included.

Camping: St. Michiel, Tillegemstr. 55 (tel. 38 08 19), southwest of town off the road to the *autoroute.* Bus #7 from the station. Endless and crowded but well kept. Reception open 9am-10pm. 85BF per person, 100BF per tent. Hot showers 50BF. Well-stocked store and a restaurant.

The Lotus, near the Markt at Wapenmakerstr. 5, dishes out super soup (40BF) and vegetarian plates (175-190BF) in a mellow atmosphere. (Open mid-Aug. to July noon-1:30pm.) Non-guests and guests alike squeeze into the **Bauhaus** hostel for their pizzas and pastas, among the cheapest and cheesiest in town. Forage through the **Nopri Supermarket** at Noordzanstr. 4, near the Markt (open Mon.-Thurs. and Sat. 9am-6:30pm, Fri. 9am-5pm). Markets take over 't Zand Sq. every Saturday morning and the Burg every Wednesday morning until 1pm.

Sights and Entertainment

Bruges is best seen on foot; the tourist office suggests excellent walking tours. You can't miss the Markt's grand architectural flagship, the **belfort,** subtly luminous by night. Climb its 366 steps for a stupefying panorama—even better in leap years—but go early to enjoy it alone. (Open daily 9:30am-6pm; Nov.-March 9:30am-12:30pm and 1:30-5pm. Admission 80BF, students 60BF.) The 14th-century **Stadhuis** (Town Hall), on nearby Burg Sq., is flamboyantly Gothic. (Open daily 9:30am-6pm; Oct.-March 9:30am-noon and 2-5pm. Admission 40BF.)

Many Flemish masters fulminated in Bruges; masterpieces of van Eyck and Gerard David remain in the splendid **Groeninge Museum** on Dijverstr. (Open daily 9:30am-6pm; Oct.-March Wed.-Sun. 9:30am-noon and 2-5pm. Admission 70BF, students 50BF.) Next door is the **Gruuthuse Museum,** in the 15th-century residence of wealthy beer magnates. The museum today hosts a collection of historic weapons, musical instruments, pottery, lace, and coins. (Open daily 9:30am-6pm; Oct.-March Wed.-Mon. 9:30am-noon and 2-5pm. Admission 100BF, students 70BF.) The **Church of Our Lady** contains the only Michelangelo to leave Italy during the master's lifetime, a touching *Madonna and Child.* Pay 30BF to inspect a collection of stately mausoleums and a fantastically ornate wood pulpit. (Open Mon.-Fri. 10-11:30am and 2:30-5pm, Sat.-Sun. 2:30-5pm; Oct.-March Mon.-Sat. 10-11:30am and 3-4:30pm, Sun. 2:30-4:30pm.)

Though not nuns proper, some young women in medieval Belgium resided in citadels of celibacy called *beguinages.* Benedictine sisters now occupy Bruge's tranquil **begijnhof,** but you can still visit its verdant courtyard and tour one of the old homes. If cycling is more your speed, join the droves of backpackers scouting out Bruges *en vélo,* or, if you will, *op een fiets.* Excellent **bike tours** of the city depart every two hours from the Markt (Mar.-Oct. daily 9am-7pm, 1½ hr., 300BF). The longer countryside tour meanders through sleepy villages and an 18th-century traditional farm (Mar.-Oct. daily departure 1pm, 4 hr., 450BF). Buy tickets at the Reyghere Bookshop, 12 Markt, or by calling 33 12 36 from 8-9am or 9-10pm. **Boat tours** along Bruges's picturesque and winding canals leave every half-hour (10am-6pm) from five different points on the main canal; check the map (130BF).

If you yearn for nightlife, go no further than your hostel bar—the Bauhaus's late-night hilarity is particularly wild. Serious beer-drinkers will go nuts in **Brugs Beertje,** Kemelstr. 5, where proprietor Jan De Bruyne bubbles with enthusiasm about the proper way to serve and drink the 300-plus brands he stocks (open Thurs.-Tues. 4pm-1am). **De Versteende Nacht,** Langestr. 11, has live jazz (Tues.-Thurs. and Sun. 7pm-2am, Fri.-Sat. 7pm-4am; closed for 2 weeks in early July). **Cactus,** Langestr. 127, draws an artsy local crowd into its hazy, smoke-filled chambers (open Mon.-Fri. noon-2pm and 7:30pm-1am, Sat.-Sun. 3pm-1am). Bruges's major-rager dance club, **Vila Dzava,** Langerei 98, is so hip that it's only open once a week (Sat. 10pm-6am; cover 100BF).

A wonderful evening awaits at the **Marionette Theater,** Sint-Jakobstr. 36 (tel. 33 47 60), which stages seven full-blown puppet operas through the summer. (Open July-Aug. Mon.-Sat.; April-June and Sept. Thurs.-Sat. All performances at 8pm. Admission 400BF, students and seniors 350BF. Tickets available from tourist office.) During the **Festival van Vlaanderen** (late July-early Aug.), the entire town pulses with the **International Fortnight of Music.** Snatch the monthly program *Agenda Brugge* at the tourist office for a schedule of local events.

Near Bruges

An informative **Quasimodo** tour (tel. (050) 31 86 57 or 37 04 70) is one way to explore Flanders while keeping Bruges as a base. There are three flavors: one somberly patrols the battlefields of the World Wars (Mon. and sometimes Sat., 850BF); another giddily hops through Flemish breweries (Tues. and Thurs., 950BF—samples included); a third checks out the North Sea coast, stopping in Damme and Zeebrugge (Wed. and Fri., 850BF). Conducted in English, these tours leave various hostels around 9am, return around 5pm, and include brunch.

A scenic 30-km bike trip runs along Canal Brugge-Sluis to **Damme;** according to legend, this is the birthplace of Tijl Uilenspiegel, the inspiration of Richard Strauß's symphonic poem. You can **camp** in Damme at **Hoecke,** Damse Vaart Oost 10 (tel. (050) 50 04 96; 65BF per person, 65BF per night; open March-Nov. 15). From April through September, an **excursion boat** putts between Bruges and Damme. Take bus #4 to Dampoort, where the *W.S. Lamme Goedzak* (tel. (052) 33 37 62) sails from Noorweegse Kaai 31 (leaves every 2 hr. 10am-6pm; return every 2 hr. 9:15am-5:20pm. 120BF, ages 3-12 and over 65 80BF; round-trip 180BF and 65 120BF.)

Towns on the North Sea coast of Belgium win fans largely for their beaches. Ferries chug daily from Zeebrugge and Oostende to the U.K. Daily ships and jetfoils leave for England from **Oostende** and **Zeebrugge,** easily accessible by train from Bruges. Get tickets from travel agencies, at the ports, or in the Oostende train station. **P&O European Ferries** (tel. Brussels (02) 231 19 37; Oostende (059) 70 76 01; Zeebrugge (050) 54 22 22) sails between Oostende and Dover (7 per day), Zeebrugge and Dover (6 per day), and Zeebrugge and Felixstowe (2 per day). (One-way 1370BF, 60-hr. round-trip 1370BF, 5-day round-trip 2000BF.) In Oostende, the **De Ploate youth hostel (IYHF),** Langestr. 82 (tel. (059) 80 52 97), is only five minutes from the station. Campgrounds freckle the coast. **De Vuurtoren,** Heistlaan 168, in Knokke (tel. (050) 51 17 82; 75BF per person, 85BF per tent; open mid-March to mid-Oct.), and **Jamboree,** Polderlaan 55, in Blankenberge (tel. (050) 41 45 45; 105BF per person, 100BF per tent), are two options; both towns are trainable from Bruges.

Ghent (Gent)

A raging textile industry lifted 14th-century Ghent into the ranks of Europe's great cities. On the continent, only Paris exceeded it in size and splendor. The modern city has lost some of its Renaissance glory, but it still challenges the beauty of Bruges and the *savoir-faire* of Antwerp.

Practical Information

Tourist Office: Municipal Tourist Office, in the crypt of the town hall on Botermarkt (tel. 24 15 55). Take tram #1 from the train station to the main post office. Maps (25BF) and informative walking-tour booklets (30BF). Open daily 9:30am-6:30pm; Nov.-March 9:30am-4:30pm.

Budget Travel: JOKER/Acotra, Overpoorstr. 58 (tel. 21 97 94). BIJ tickets and helpful advice. Open Mon.-Fri. 10am-1:15pm and 2-6pm; May-Aug. Mon.-Fri. 10am-1:15pm and 2-6pm, Sat. 10am-1pm. **Taxi-Stop,** Onderbergen 51, (tel. 23 23 10). Matches drivers with riders

(2BF per km), books cheap last-minute flights and sells **Eurolines** bus tickets for points across Europe. Open Mon.-Fri. 9am-6pm.

Post Office: Korenmarkt 16 (tel. 25 20 34). Poste Restante. Open Mon.-Thurs. 9am-6pm, Fri. 9am-7pm, Sat. 9am-noon.

Telephones: Keizer Karelstr. 1. Buy telephone cards here. Open Mon.-Fri. 8am-8pm, Sat. 8am-noon and 12:30-4:15pm, Sun. 11:15am-7:15pm. **City Code:** 091.

Trains: Tel. 22 44 44. Trams #1, 10, 11, and 12 run between **Sint-Pieters Station** on the southern edge of the city, and Korenmarkt, the center of the old city. Frequent trains to Bruges, Brussels, and Antwerp.

Hitchhiking: Ghent lies at the intersection of the E40, connecting Brussels and Germany with Oostende, and the E17, linking Paris and Amsterdam. Hitchers turn right out of the station onto Clementinalaan, which becomes Burggravenlaan, and continue until they reach the E17.

Laundromat: St. Jacobsnieuwstr. 85. Open daily 8am-10pm. Wash and dry 140BF; bring plenty o' 20BF coins.

Emergencies: Police or **Ambulance** (tel. 100; free). Police headquarters (tel. 24 61 11).

Accommodations, Camping, and Food

Travelers can often find a free bed in the dorms of Ghent's university; rooms are available all year (in much greater abundance mid-July to Sept.). A single with sink costs 400BF (breakfast and shower included). Call the office at Stalhof 6 (tel. 22 09 11) for information and reservations. Otherwise, try **De IJzer,** Vlaanderenstr. 117 (tel. 25 98 73), near Woodrow Wilsanplein. (Singles 600BF. Doubles 700-900BF. Showers and breakfast included.) Hotels near the station tend to levy high prices for low-quality rooms, but just to the right of the train station, **La Lanterne,** Prinses Clementinalaan 140 (tel. 20 13 18) touts comfortable rooms at comfortable prices. (Singles 900-1000BF. Doubles 1200-1300BF. Breakfast 125BF.) **Camping Blaarmeersen,** Zuiderlaan 12 (tel. 21 53 99), is 15 blocks or a bus ride (#38) northwest of Sint-Pietersstation. (100BF per person, 110BF per tent. Open March to mid-Oct.)

When bread and cheese just won't do it anymore, treat yourself to a meal at **De Appelier,** Citadellaan 47 (tel. 21 67 33), near the Museum of Fine Arts. Their vegetarian plates (185-260BF) are a scrumptious bargain. Ask to sit in the rose garden in back. (Open Sun.-Fri. 11:30am-2pm and 5:30-8pm.) At the student cafeteria **Overpoort,** in the Restaurant Rijksuniversiteit Gent building on Overpoortstr., near Citadellaan, you'll find typical student subsistence: macaroni, spaghetti and hamburgers (100-200BF). Sweets-lovers will die and go to heaven when they enter the **Bloch Alsacienne Patisserie,** Veldstr. 60-62, a bakery shop stuffed with sinful, dripping platters of honey, nuts and dough. There is a **Unic** grocery store at St. Jacobsnieuwstr. 119 (open Mon.-Sat. 9am-6:30pm), but snare your fruits and vegetables at the **Groentenmarkt** (open Mon.-Fri. 7am-1pm, Sat. 7am-7pm).

Sights and Entertainment

Ghent has more than its share of medieval edifices. The forbidding medieval fortress **Gravensteen** (Castle of the Counts of Flanders) stands on the Canal Sint-Veerleplein. (Open daily 9am-6pm; Oct.-March 9am-5pm. Admission 80BF, students 40BF.) The august **belfort** (belfry) offers a 15th-century cloth hall, a bronze dragon, and an excellent audio-visual introduction to the city's past and present. (Belfry open daily 10am-12:30pm and 2-5:30pm, admission 100BF. Guided tours 2:30pm daily from the tourist office next door, 2 hrs., 150BF. Video shown in English Easter-Oct. 11:35am and 3:20pm, 80BF.) Also appealing is the **Stadhuis** (Town Hall) on the corner, an arresting juxtaposition of Gothic and Renaissance architecture. Another block down on Limburgstr. lies **Sint-Baafskathedraal,** built over the 14th, 15th, and 16th centuries. The real pearl here is Jan van Eyck's *Adoration of the Mystic Lamb,* an imposing polyptych on wood panels. (Open Mon.-Sat. 9:30am-noon and 2-6pm, Sun. 1-6pm; Oct.-March Mon.-Sat. 10:30am-noon and 2:30-4pm,

Sun. 2-5pm. Admission to cathedral free; 50BF to see the *Mystic Lamb.)* Rap from the pulpit of **Bijloke Abbey,** Godshuizenlaan 2, a 10-minute walk from the center just across the river Leie. Also worth a visit is the **Museum voor Schone Kunsten** (Museum of Fine Arts), in the arboriferous Citadel park, which lodges a strong Flemish collection and an outstanding exhibit of avant-garde contemporary art. (Open Tues.-Sun. 9am-12:30pm and 1:30-5:30pm. Admission 180BF, students 90BF.)

Ghent's nightlife lives and dies by its university students—from October to July 15, you're in luck. Students cavort in the cafés and discos near the university restaurant on Overpoortstr. **Dulle Griet,** Vrijdagmarkt 50, serves 250 brands of beer and often features live jazz (open Mon. noon-4:30pm and Tues.-Sun. noon-1am).

Antwerp (Antwerpen)

Predecessor of Amsterdam as the early commercial capital of Europe, Antwerp rode to the center of the Northern Renaissance behind the painting of the Flemish Old Masters, most notably favorite son Rubens. Today commerce still rules; Antwerp's port is an international hub for the garment and diamond trade. Be sure to venture out of the *oude stat* to explore the mind-boggling art-deco mansions lining Cogels Osylei and the Orthodox Jewish quarter.

Orientation and Practical Information

Antwerp rests 40km north of Brussels on the Amsterdam-Brussels-Paris rail line. **Centraal Station,** true to its name, sits in the city center. The **Meir,** a wide avenue lined with shops and eateries, connects it to the **Grote Markt** and **Groenplaats,** Antwerp's two major squares.

Tourist Offices: Municipal Tourist Office, Grote Markt 15 (tel. 232 01 03). From the train station, turn left onto DeKeyserlei, which becomes Meir, and follow it to Groenplaats; turn right past the cathedral. Hotel list, free reservations and city maps (10-20BF). Open Mon.-Fri. 9am-6pm, Sat. 9am-5pm.

Budget Travel: VTB, St. Jacobsmarkt 45-7 (tel. 234 34 34). General travel information and youth tickets. Open Mon.-Fri. 9am-5:30pm, Sat. 9am-12:30pm. **Jeugd-Info-Antwerpen,** Apostelstr. 20-22 (tel. 232 27 28), provides a friendly ear. (Open Mon.-Fri. 10am-7:30pm, Sat. 2-5pm.)

Consulates: U.S., Nationalestr. 5 (tel. 225 00 71). **U.K.,** Korte Klarenstr. 7 (tel. 232 69 40).

Currency Exchange: Both bureaus at Centraal Station have poor rates, but one is open daily 8am-11pm. Best rates at American Express, and at the **Thomas Cook** bureau on Koningen Astridplein, in front of the train station.

American Express: Frankrijklei 21 (tel. 232 59 20). Open Mon.-Fri. 9am-5:30pm (but exchange and mail desk closes noon-2pm), Sat. 9:30am-noon.

Post Office: Main office and Poste Restante on Groenplaats. Open Mon.-Fri. 9am-6pm, Sat. 9am-noon. Branch across from Centraal Station on Pelikaanstr. 16. Open Mon.-Fri. 9am-6pm. **Postal Code:** 2000.

Telephones: Jezusstr. 1. Open daily 8am-8pm. Also at Centraal Station. Open Mon.-Fri. 9am-noon and 12:30-5:15pm. **City Code:** 03.

Trains: Centraal Station is a 15-min. walk from the Grote Markt and most of the sights. 20 trains per day to Rotterdam and Amsterdam, 4 per hr. to Brussels. Lockers here (15BF) are cheaper than checking your bags (60BF).

Public Transportation: Trams and buses cost 35BF; purchase an 8-ride ticket for 154BF at Centraal Station and in underground tram and subway stops. The tourist offices also offer a 24-hr. pass good for all municipal transportation in Belgium (140BF). Open 6am-midnight.

Pharmacy: Apoteek devollesmacht, Nationalestr. 119. Open Mon.-Fri. 9am-12:30pm and 2-6:30pm. Closed pharmacies direct you to open ones.

Hitchhiking: Those heading to Germany, the Netherlands, and Ghent take bus #20 from the train station to the big interchange (Plantin en Moretuslei) outside town. Those going to Brussels and points south take tram #2 to the intersection of Jan Devoslei and Jan van Rijswijklaan.

Laundromat: Wassalon Soeki, Van Den Nest Lei 5, 1 block from the New International Youth Home. Wash 60BF. Dry 5BF.

Medical Assistance: Stuivenberg Hospital, Lange Beeldekenstr. 267 (tel. 217 71 11).

Emergencies: Police or **Ambulance** (tel. 100). Police headquarters, Oudaan 5 (tel. 231 68 80).

Accommodations, Camping, and Food

Budget accommodations possibilities are less than spectacular. Some of the cafés around the train station advertising "rooms for tourists" rent lodgings by the hour.

Jeugdherberg Op-Sinjoorke (IYHF), Eric Sasselaan 2 (tel. 238 02 73). Take tram #2 (direction "Hoboken") to Bouwcentrum or bus #27 to Camille Huysmanslaan and follow the signs. A hike, but handsome and modern. Kitchen, laundry, lockers, and game room. Work 3 hours and stay free, or work 5 and get a free bed and 3 square meals. Lockout 10am-5pm, but you can leave your stuff. Curfew midnight. 310BF, nonmembers 400BF. Breakfast included. Lunch 105BF. Dinner 220BF. Sheets 120BF. Bar open 5-11:30pm.

Boomerang Youth Hostel, Volkstr. 49 (tel. 238 47 82), a block from the Royal Art Gallery. From Centraal Station, take bus #23 to the Museum stop, or walk 25 min. Vagabonds keep coming for the mellow, post-Amsterdam aura of friendliness. Long on character, short on spic-and-span. Free lockers take padlocks. Movie every night at 8pm, terrace with barbecue. Dorms 340BF. Breakfast included. Sheets 90BF.

New International Youth Home, Provinciestr. 256 (tel. 230 05 22). Take tram #11 from Centraal Station or walk left down Pelikaanstr., and take another left onto Provinciestr., the 5th underpass under the railroad tracks (10 min.). Rooms are squeaky clean, and not far from the station. Changes money and sells maps. No lockout. Curfew 11pm, but you can get a night key. Singles 650BF. Doubles 930-990BF. Triples 1350BF. Quads 1760BF. Dorms 340BF. Dinner at 7:30pm, 300BF. Sheets 100BF. Reserve ahead in summer.

Camping: Jan van Rijswijcklaan, on Vogelzanglaan (tel. 238 57 17), and **De Molen,** on St. Annastrand (tel. 219 60 90). Both 35BF per person, 35BF per tent, and open April-Sept.

The old city cooks up all sorts of cuisine; many of the Italian restaurants and pizzerias around the Groenplaats and the Grote Markt spoon out surprisingly tasty and cheap pasta. Try a "brown pub" such as **De Ware Jacob,** Vlasmarkt 19; the moniker derives from their oak interiors. (Menu 350BF; open Mon.-Sat. noon-2am.) Cheap Greek restaurants line Oudekoornmarkt (filled pitas about 140BF). A sage budget choice is the vegetarian **Atlantis,** Korte Nieuwstr. 6; dishes like omelettes, pasta and cheese toast cost 125-220BF. (Open Mon. and Wed.-Fri. noon-2pm and 5-10pm, Sat.-Sun. 5-10pm.) Wander south down Pelikaanstr. to the **Jewish District** for fine kosher shops and restaurants. A huge supermarket weighs down Schoenmarkt just off the Groenplaats.

Sights and Entertainment

Start with a walk through the **oude stad** (old city), beginning at Grote Markt, where the **Stadhuis** (Town Hall) is a noble example of Renaissance architecture. (Open Mon. 9am-noon, Tues.-Thurs. 9am-3pm, Fri.-Sat. noon-3pm. Admission 30BF.) The nearby **Kathedraal van Onze-Lieve-Vrouw,** Groenplaats 21, has a showy Gothic tower. Its interior is richly decorated with stained glass and Flemish masterpieces, notably Rubens's *Descent from the Cross* and *Exaltation of the Cross.* (Open Mon.-Fri. 10am-5pm, Sat. 10am-3pm, Sun. 1-4pm. Admission 30BF.) Few tourists get to **Cogels Osylei,** an avenue in the southeastern part of Antwerp with an uninterrupted procession of eclectic art nouveau mansions, each outshining the one before it. Transvaalstraat and Pretoriastraat, twin streets running parallel to Cogels Osylei on either side, boast similarly dazzling homes. Plantin, an Antwerp native who raised printing to an art during the 16th century, left behind many of his tools and presses; they're on display in his former home, now the **Plantin-**

Moretus Museum, Vrijdagmarkt 22, three blocks south of Groenplaats. (Open daily 10am-5pm. Admission 75BF, students 30BF.) The little-known **Mayer van den Bergh Museum** at Lange Gasthuisstr. 19 harbors Brueghel's *Mad Meg* and other works. (Open Tues.-Sun. 10am-5pm. Admission 75BF, students 30BF.)

Antwerp is nuts about Peter Paul Rubens, who built **Rubens Huis,** Wapper 9 (off Meir) himself, and filled it with a trove of art. (Open daily 10am-5pm. Admission 75BF, students 30BF.) The **Royal Art Gallery,** Leopold De Waelplaats 1-9, showcases one of the best collections of Old Flemish Masters (from the 14th to 17th centuries) in the world, especially Memlinc, van Eyck, and van der Weydens, as well as some monumental Rubens canvases. Natural lighting and the originality of its exhibit designs have made this gallery a model for many others. (Open Tues.-Sun. 10am-5pm. Free.)

The zestiest bars in Antwerp huddle around Grote Markt. The **Pelgrom,** Pelgrimsstr. 15, is a converted 16th-century wine cellar specializing in Belgian ale. Contemplate the baseness of the outside world while gorging on a cheese or meat plate (250BF). (Open daily 11:30am-late.) **Bierland,** Korte Nieuwstr. 28, offers over 200 varieties of Belgian beer, and 250 or so imported labels. (Open Mon.-Thurs. noon-midnight, Fri. noon-3am, Sat. 5pm-3am, Sun. 1-10pm.) For movie listings or a list of events, pick up the monthly guide *Antwerpen* at the tourist office.

Namur and the Ardennes

Heart of Wallonie and gateway to the Ardennes Forest, Namur is an ideal base for exploring the Belgian provinces of Namur, Liège, and Luxembourg (not the independent country); castles, caves, and kayaks greet those who forge beyond the city. Trains link the larger towns, and buses, though infrequent, cover the rest.

Not quite an hour's train ride from Brussels, Namur itself deserves exploration. The scars of 20 sieges have faded, but the city's immense **citadel** remains, glowering from its rocky perch. Start the steep climb or ride the *téléférique* (cable car) from Grognon, a hill on the southern edge of the city. (130BF, round-trip 150BF). Once atop the citadel, a two-hour visit includes an informative film, a museum, a guided tour through underground passages and a train ride around the fort (180BF). Of Namur's 13 museums (including a strawberry museum (tel. (081) 46 01 13) in nearby Wepion), perhaps the best is the **Musée de Croix,** 3, rue J. Saintraint, a handsome 18th-century mansion and former refuge for sickly monks. (Tours daily 10am-noon and 2-5pm. Admission 50BF.)

For all the info a traveler could possibly want, visit the **provincial tourist office,** 3, rue Notre Dame (tel. (081) 22 29 98; open Mon.-Fri. 8am-5pm), which has a list of farms amenable to campers (usually 120BF per person, 25BF per tent), or the city's own **tourist office,** pl. Leopold (tel. (081) 22 28 59), in the pavilion—300m up av. de la Gare, to the left as you leave the train station. (Open July-Aug. 9am-6pm; April-June and Sept. 9am-12:30pm and 1:30-6pm; Oct.-March Mon.-Fri. 9am-5pm.) For youth travel information, consult **Infor-Jeunes,** Beffroi 4 (tel. (081) 22 38 12), in Namur's medieval belfry. (Open daily 11:30am-6pm.)

The newly renovated **Auberge Félicien Rops (IYHF),** 8, av. Félicien Rops (tel. (081) 22 36 88), may well rank among the classiest youth hostels ever to hit the budget traveler scene. The snazzy facility comes equipped with laundry service (100BF), kitchen facilities (20BF), bountiful meals, and bargain brew (30BF). (320BF, nonmembers 420BF. Breakfast included. Lunch 170BF; packed lunch 100BF; dinner 220BF. Sheets 100BF.) To reach the hostel, take bus #3 from across the street from the station, to La Plante. **Camping des Quatre Fils Aymon,** the nearest campground, is 12km away at 5, chaussée de Liège (tel. (081) 58 83 13), in Lives-sur-Meuse. (36BF per person and per site. Open April-Sept.) **Les Trieux,** 99, rue des Tris (tel. 44 55 83), in Malonne, is another "wilderness" option. (6km from the city; take bus #6 to Malonne. 65BF per person; 40BF per site. Open April-Oct.) There's a 340BF *ménu du jour* at **Le Rimbaud,** 58, rue de la Croix. (Open Mon.-Sat. noon-2pm and 6pm-midnight.)

Don't whiff the opportunity to scout the countryside surrounding Namur. Rent a bike at the train station (100BF) and pedal 10km along Route 90 (also known as Chausée du Charles-Roi) to **Floreffe,** which has a miraculously well-preserved 12th-century abbey (open Mon.-Fri. 11am-6pm, Sat.-Sun. 11am-8pm; admission 60BF, children 40BF), and perpetually cool caves. Bus #10 (60BF) and trains also run to Floreffe. At **Dinant** (a ½-hr. train ride south of Namur) you can meander through the extensive **grottoes.** (Open July-Aug. daily 10am-6pm, April-June and Sept. 11am-4pm; accessible only via 50-min. tours. Admission 140BF, under 14 90BF, seniors 120BF.) The region's most striking architectural feature is a bizarre, Kremlinesque bulb atop a late-Gothic church. Dinant's **tourist office** is at 37, rue Grande (tel. (082) 22 28 70).

Southeast of Dinant, back-country adventurers can travel the **River Lesse** by kayak from Houyet to Anseremme (11-21km); the river winds through the Ardennes and passes some spiffy cliffs and a massive château just before Anseremme. Same-day reservations usually float during the week, but call a few days in advance for weekend jaunts. For kayak rental, try **Ansiaux** (tel. (082) 22 23 25) or **Lessé-Kayaks** (tel. (082) 22 43 97). (Both open April-Oct., trips 250-600BF. Arrive in Houyet before 11am, and bring a change of clothes.) Further up the river at **Han-sur-Lesse,** tour boats ply the subterranean river that courses through caves below the town. (Open April-Oct. 9:30am-5pm, March and Nov. 9:30am-3:30pm. 265BF, children 185BF.) The 45km cycle from Namur to Han-sur-Lesse is flat and scenic; otherwise, take the train to Jemelle (40 min.), then a bus.

12/04/92 ANKUNFT IN BRÜSSEL <20:51>

12/05/92 BRÜSSEL

12/06/92 MECHELEN / BRÜSSEL

12/07/92 GHENT / BRUGS

12/08/92 BRÜSSEL

22:52 <ABFAHRT NACH BERLIN>

GELD: REISE 176 RÜCKFAHRKARTE
(BERLIN ↔ BRUSSEL)
+6 (ZUSCHLAG)

182 DM
110 DM BAHNKARTE

TÄGLICHE KOSTEN: 130DM

4 TAGE ⇝ 32.50 DM/TAG

BULGARIA

USD$1 = 18.3 leva (Lv, or BGL)	**10Lv = USD$0.54**
CAD$1 = 16.0Lv	**10Lv = CAD$0.63**
GBP£1 = 30.5Lv	**10Lv = GBP£0.33**
AUD$1 = 14.2Lv	**10Lv = AUD$0.70**
NZD$1 = 10.4Lv	**10Lv = NZD$0.96**
Country Code: 359	**International Dialing Prefix: N/A**

During the early Middle Ages, the powerful Bulgarian Kingdom stretched from the Black Sea to the Aegean and the Adriatic, bridging the intellectually and artistically vibrant Byzantine Empire and the more northern Slavic nations. Flowering Slavic Orthodox monasticism produced the Cyrillic alphabet and great literature before the country was crushed by Byzantine, Serbian, and finally Turkish invaders in the 14th century. The Ottomans valued this region solely for its agricultural output; for over five centuries they ruthlessly kept Bulgaria a nation of peasants. The 19th century witnessed a "National Revival" of Slavic identity, and a struggle for independence from the Ottoman Empire's yoke. Russia was the only European power that sympathized; tied to Russia by Eastern Orthodox Christianity and a similar Slavic language, Bulgaria (България) became the Soviet Union's closest ally in the Eastern Bloc.

In 1989, Bulgaria again followed the Soviet Union's urgings toward reform. The Bulgarian Communist Party retired Todor Zhivkov, the unpopular, conservative leader, changed its name to the Socialist Party, and held elections. The Socialists, who advocated a gradual shift to social democracy, have held the leadership ever since. Although personal freedoms have bounded ahead, many Bulgarians are starting to feel the chokehold of financial limitations and skyrocketing inflation. For tourists, some of the onerous regulations, such as visa requirements, have been relaxed, while others, like the statistical card issued at the border, remain.

Bulgaria's landscape varies from proud mountains to yawning plains and valleys. The Stara Planina mountain range bisects Bulgaria horizontally from Sofia to Varna, sloping down towards the Danube in the north. The Rila and Pirin Mountains are south of Sofia, and the Rhodopi Mountains center around the resort of Pamporovo, south of Plovdiv. Between the Rhodopis and the Stara Planina nestles the famous Valley of Roses.

Getting There

As of September 1991, American citizens could visit Bulgaria visa-free for up to 30 days, but Canadians, Australians, New Zealanders, and U.K. citizens need either a 30-day tourist visa (USD23) or a 30-hour transit visa (USD12). Even in European capitals, visas can take a week or more to process, so try and get yours in your home country. Bulgarian embassies are at 100 Adelaide St. W., Suite 1410, Toronto, Ont. F5H 1S3 (tel. (416) 363-7307), at 187 Queen's Gate, London SW7 (tel. (071) 584 9400), and at 1-4 Carlotta Rd., Double Bay, Sydney, NSW 2028. (tel. (02) 36 75 81). It is sometimes possible to shortcut the visa application process by buying accommodations vouchers from travel agencies—ask at embassies in Europe. Bulgaria has no minimum daily exchange requirements, but you will need to produce an exchange receipt that shows that you've obtained leva legally to pay for accommodations or international train tickets.

When you cross the border you will be given a **statistical card.** While you are in Bulgaria, this document will serve as your passport. If you lose it, you will be unable to get a hotel room. The establishment in which you stay each night will add its stamp to the card. It used to be that if you didn't have a stamp for each night you've spent in Bulgaria, you'd have to pay a fine when you left the country. With the new openness, Bulgaria border officials tend to be much less strict; any card with at least a couple stamps on it should suffice.

Getting Around

Public transportation in Bulgaria costs about 10Lv per 100km. The **train** system is quite comprehensive; direct trains run between Sofia and all major towns. Service is especially frequent to Plovdiv, Burgas, and Varna. Trains come in three flavors: express (експрес), fast (бързи), and slow (пътнически). Couchettes are an option (10Lv on most trains); purchase spots on the train. To buy an international ticket, you must go to the appropriate office, usually in the town center; you must pay for international tickets in Western currency or be able to produce a receipt showing you have exchanged your leva legitimately. You can buy only domestic tickets at the station. Buying a ticket on the train doubles the cost but enables you to bypass the lines. Stations are poorly marked, and signs are often only in Cyrillic. Try to find out the exact time you are due at your destination or take along a good map which shows your route. If you miss your stop, even on a main line, you can blow an entire day trying to get back. Some useful words are влак *(vlak,* train), автобус *(avtobus,* bus), гара *(gara,* station), перон *(peron,* platform), коловоз *(kolovoz,* track), билет *(bilet,* ticket), заминаващи *(zaminavashti,* departure), and пристигащи *(pristigashti,* arrival). **Buses** usually cover distances of less than 100km and are perfect for taking you into rural, undiscovered Bulgaria. Check at the bus station (автогара) for fares and timetables. For longer distances, once-cheap **Balkan Air** shuttle fares have swollen enormously over the past year—a one-way from Sofia to Varna or Burgas weighs in at USD45. Book seats at Balkan Air Offices up to 30 days in advance and at the airport on the day of travel.

Hitchhiking, once popular and reliable in Bulgaria, has subsided a bit with the recent severe rise in gasoline prices. Expect to wait about half an hour for a ride. Many drivers have space for only one passenger.

Practical Information

Balkantourist, the national tourist bureau, maintains offices throughout the country. The staff changes money, books hotel rooms and, in Sofia, will book private accommodations. Hotels throughout the country, now in charge of their own finances, often maintain tourist offices which can be of great help. One leva (Lv), the standard monetary unit, is divided into 100 stotinki (st), but we list most prices in U.S. dollars (USD). Though the official exchange rate is USD1 to approximately 18Lv, there are private banks which use different rates. When paying in leva for accommodations, you must show an exchange receipt, proving you have exchanged your money legally. The black market is largely useless in Bulgaria; you won't get more than 20Lv per dollar, and you risk being swindled. Any Bulgarian bill not dated 1962 or 1974 is worthless—check carefully.

Language poses great problems in Bulgaria. Unless you learn rudiments of the Cyrillic alphabet, signs will be incomprehensible. See the Cyrillic transliteration table in the USSR section; Bulgarian is much the same, except that x is *h,* щ is *sht,* and ъ is *ŭ,* sometimes transliterated *â* (pronounced as in English b*u*g). Key phrases include добър ден (DO-bur den, "hello"), кога (ko-GA, "when"), къде (kuh-DEH, "where"), колко (KOL-ko, "how much"). Russian is the most useful foreign language; many Bulgarians are learning English, but it is still not widely spoken, especially in the countryside. Bulgarian-English phrasebooks are sold in bookstands and bookstores for about 30Lv. Since Bulgarian head movements for "yes" and "no" are the reverse of the West's, try to confirm everything with *da* (yes) or *ne* (no). Also be aware that many street names will be changed as the country decommunizes. Distrust any map that isn't from 1992.

Making international calls from Bulgaria requires the patience of a dead person. There is no direct dial and no USA Direct. A five-minute call to the U.S. will run USD10 from the telephone office, USD20 from the less-crowded Sheraton Hotel. Expect a half-hour wait. To call collect, dial 0123 for an international operator. In an emergency (such as visa complications or urgent phone calls) go to your embassy, to one of the big Western hotels in Sofia (the Sheraton, tel. 87 65 41, or the English-speaking Novotel). Postage (including packages) is very cheap in Bulgaria; international postcards require only 80st. Bulgaria is situated in the same time zone as Greece and Romania, one hour ahead of Yugoslavia.

Accommodations, Camping, and Food

ORBITA runs **youth hostels,** but they are open to Westerners by reservation only. Groups of five or more may be able to book them in advance from Sofia. If you show up at a hostel without reservations, you will likely find that it has been filled by a Bulgarian or Russian student group. **Hotels** in Bulgaria are classed by stars. The rooms in one-star hotels are identical to those in two- and three-star hotels but have no private bath; they run about USD18 for singles and USD32 for doubles. Private rooms are easily found only in Sofia (USD8-10). Outside of major towns, **campgrounds** give you a chance to meet Eastern European backpackers (USD1.80-USD3.10 per person). Spartan wooden bungalows await at nearly every site, but are often full. During the past year, a large number of campgrounds have been shut down due to lack of visitors. Freelance camping is popular, but you risk a fine.

Food from kiosks is cheap (5Lv for a sandwich and a Coke), and restaurants average 30Lv per meal. Kiosks sell *kebabcheta* (small hamburgers, 1.30Lv), salami sandwiches (1.20Lv), and cheese-filled breads (1Lv). In 1991 stores stocked bread, cheese, sausage, and *kisselo mlyako* (yogurt), and a few fruits and vegetables. Bulgarians work wonders with vegetables. *Shopska salata* is a widely available, addictive salad of tomatoes, peppers, and cucumbers, covered in *sirene* (a feta-like cheese). *Appetit* is a hot pepper salad. *Kiopolou* and *imam bayalda* are eggplant dishes. A *gjuvetch* is a mixed vegetable stew with onion, eggplant, peppers, beans, and peas. Also try *tarator*—a cold soup made with yogurt, cucumber, and garlic. Eat carefully. Don't drink the unpasteurized milk unless it's been very well heated. Eschew sour yogurt and resist rare hamburgers. Do not fear the water; it's probably purer than the stuff you are used to drinking back home. The fountains and taps scattered throughout the cities and countryside will save your life on more than one day under the hot Balkan sun. Bring a water bottle and a hearty spirit.

Sofia София

Depending on their point of view, those arriving in Sofia may either be astonished to find a dusty, doctrinaire Paris, or relieved to find a manageable, well-planned metropolis right in the heart of the Balkans. The center of town, with its grid of enormously wide *bulevards* paved with yellow bricks, may make you feel like you've arrived in the Land of Oz. Most of the sights are within walking distance of the city center and easily found with the aid of a good map. Sofia is for the most part a new city—only a few medieval churches and two mosques survive. National Revival architecture from the turn of the century rears up in small enclaves north of pl. Lenin. Watch for small palaces and public buildings that look like a cross between the German baroque and Russian Imperial styles—the Sheraton Hotel building, for example. Most of these are surrounded by massive modern monuments, and Sofia is in fact a carnival of socialist architecture: the party house, facing what used to be Lenin's statue across Lenin Square is one of the best Stalinist monsters outside Moscow. Outside the city center, the Emerald City ends and Sofia rapidly turns into an aesthetic nightmare of run-down neighborhoods and shoddy new highrises.

Orientation and Practical Information

Sofia, situated right in the center of the Balkan peninsula, lies in far western Bulgaria, 50km from the Yugoslav border and 500km southeast of Belgrade. International trains run to Belgrade, Thessaloniki, Athens, İstanbul, and Bucharest. Buses shuttling back and forth between İstanbul and northern Europe will let you off here. Lenin Square (ploshtad Lenin, площад Ленин) is the center of Sofia. The central district is ringed by a road that changes names as it circles the city. Incoming roads intersect this ring; the most important starts life as bul. Vitosha (бул. Витоша) and runs north through pl. Lenin, where it changes its name to bul. Georgi Dimitrov (бул. Георги Димитров) and bends around to reach the train station at the northern end of the city. Perpendicular to bul. Georgi Dimitrov, **bul. Stamboliiski** (бул. Стамболийски) and bul. Dondukov (бул. Дондуков) are two other major thoroughfares. Get a street map in the Roman alphabet from Balkantourist or a newsstand and practice transliterating the Cyrillic signs; bus and tram routes all appear on city maps.

Tourist Offices: Balkantourist, bul. Dondukov 37 (tel. 88 44 30). Take tram #1, 7, or 15 from the train station to pl. Lenin, walk up the boulevard to the left of the Sheraton Hotel, and go left at the fork onto bul. Dondukov. Accommodations and maps. The train station office is basically just an exchange booth, but the tellers speak English. **The new office** at bul. Vitosha 1 (tel. 433 31) and the office at the airport, in the International Arrivals Building, arrange accommodation. All offices open daily 7am-10pm, but often open late and close early. Arrive early for private rooms.

Budget Travel: ORBITA, bul. Stamboliiski 45a (tel. 87 95 52), 5 blocks from pl. Lenin, in the opposite direction from the party house. ISIC cards. Branch office in the ORBITA Hotel: take tram #9 south past the Palace of Culture to the intersection with bul. Anton Ivanov and look behind Hotel Vitosha. Open Mon.-Fri. 10am-noon and 1-9pm. May be able to find you a private room.

Embassies: U.S., bul. Stamboliiski 1a (tel. 88 48 01), 3 blocks from pl. Lenin. Library. Periodicals and TV tapes. Open Mon.-Fri. 11:30am-4:30pm. (Duty officer available 24 hrs.) **U.K.,** bul. Marshal F. Tolbuhin 65 (tel. 88 53 61), 3 blocks northwest of the Palace of Culture. Open Mon.-Thurs. 8:30am-12:30pm and 1:30-5pm, Fri. 8:30am-1pm. Both embassies hold mail. Travelers from **Canada, Australia,** and **New Zealand** should contact the British embassy. **Romania,** ul. Sitnjakavo 4 (tel. 70 70 67).

Currency Exchange: At Balkantourist offices and all large hotels. All open daily 7am-10pm. Be sure to hold on to your receipt to prove you exchanged legally. Otherwise, hotels will demand hard currency. There is no **American Express** office in Sofia.

Post Office: ul. General Gurko 2, at the park east of pl. Lenin. Poste Restante here, but embassies are much more reliable. Generally open 7am-8:30pm. Many hotels provide postal services as well.

Telephones: Across from the post office. Open 24 hrs. Expect long lines. To avoid them, call from the Hotel Sheraton's lobby phones, but be prepared to pay nearly twice the rate. For local calls, use 20st coins. **City code:** 02.

Flights: Aeroport Sofiya (tel. 45 11 13 for domestic flights; 72 24 14 for international). Municipal buses #84 and 284 run regularly. **Bulgarian Balkan Airlines,** pl. Narodno Sŭbranie 12 (tel. 87 57 24). Another office 2 blocks west of pl. Lenin, at ul. Lege 19 (tel. 88 41 92). Open Mon.-Fri. 7:30am-7:30pm, Sat. 8am-4pm. To Varna or Burgas (USD45), Moscow (USD267), and Warsaw (USD210). Also try the comprehensive ticket office under the Palace of Culture (tel. 59 79 95) for plane tickets.

Trains: Sofia's central train station is north of the center on G. Dimitrov. Trams #1, 7, and 15 travel to pl. Lenin. The windows at the station sell domestic tickets only; cop couchettes on board. For information, international tickets, and couchette reservations, visit the **Rila travel office** at ul. General Gurko 5 (tel. 87 07 77). Domestic tickets can also be bought at the nearby ticket office at pl. Slaveikov 5 (tel. 87 57 42). Both offices open daily 8-11:30am and noon-4pm though mid-afternoon hours are capricious. To Athens (USD46), Belgrade (USD29), Bucharest (USD7), Budapest (USD51), İstanbul (USD36). 20% discount on international rail travel for ISIC cardholders at Rila travel office. Also try the comprehensive ticket office under the Palace of Culture (tel. 59 31 06) for rail tickets.

Buses: Terminal at bul. Gen. H. Mihailov 23 (tel. 52 50 04) handles tickets for sales on international routes.

Public Transportation: The system of trams, trolley buses and buses is gleefully cheap (70st). Purchase tickets at kiosks near stops or from the driver. Operating hours: officially 4am-1am (although many routes stop before midnight).

Hitchhiking: Those hitching to Rila Monastery take tram #5 to highway E79. Those headed to Koprivshtitsa take tram #3 from Sofia. Leave early to return the same day.

Laundromats: There aren't any per se in Bulgaria. The larger hotels have laundry service but are often unwilling to wash non-guests' clothing, even for hard currency. Don't despair; the hot Balkan sun dries hand-washed clothes faster than a cheetah.

Pharmacy: ul. Alabin 29 (tel. 87 90 29). Open 24 hrs.

Medical Assistance: In a medical emergency, contact a hotel receptionist, who will get you help ASAP. Emergency aid for foreigners is free of charge in Bulgaria.

Hospital: bul. Patriarh Evtimii 35 (tel. 87 95 32).

Emergencies: Police (tel. 166), **Ambulance** (tel. 150).

Accommodations, Camping, and Food

Balkantourist and ORBITA (see above) arrange all types of private rooms for USD8-10 per night. So do our friends at the train station—don't call them, they'll call you. (Remember that these "cheap private room" pushers may not stamp your statistical card.) If you arrive in Sofia after Balkantourist closes, you're on your own.

Hotel Iskŭr (Хотел Искър) (tel. 83 58 11), on ul. Iskŭr, just a block behind the Balkantourist on bul. Dondukov. Centrally located, but not much else. Sinks in rooms. Scary communal bathrooms and showers. Singles USD11, breakfast included.

Hotel Sevastopol (Севастопол), on ul. Rakovski (ул. Раковски), near ul. General Gurko (tel. 87 59 41). Take the boulevard on the left of the Sheraton 5 blocks, then turn right onto ul. Rakovski. Caters largely to students. Sink in room. Mildly usable communal bathroom with shower. Singles USD19, doubles slightly more. Breakfast included.

Hotel Hemus (Хемус), bul. Traikov 31, past the Palace of Culture at the southern extreme of downtown (tel. 66 14 15). Take trams #1, 7, or 15 to Palace of Culture, then head straight for the high-rise further down bul. Traikov. Benign, in-room bathrooms with shower, not to mention a capital view of the city. Clean and friendly, although a bit far from the center. Singles USD27.50. Doubles USD47. Breakfast included.

Camping: Cherniya Kos, 11km southeast of city center (tel. 57 34 79). Take tram #5 from behind Museum of History, then a bus. Set on a wooded slope near the base of the Vitosha and Lyulin Mountains, this campground offers bungalows for USD13 per person. 2-person bungalows USD16. Open May-Oct.

Food

Inexpensive meals are easy to come by in Sofia, but finding variety is a different story.

Bulgarska Gozba (Българска Гозба), bul. Vitosha 34 (tel. 87 91 62), a few blocks south of pl. Lenin. Intimate, folksy setting. Excellent place to sample Bulgarian cuisine. Meals are as cheap as USD4. Have some fun and ask when they are open, which might resemble Mon.-Fri. 10:30am-3:30pm and 5-10pm, Sat. 10:30am-3:30pm and 4:30-9pm, Sun. 10am-3pm.

Melnik Grill, in the side of the Sheraton Hotel (enter from the street). Named after quaint Bulgarian town in the Pirin Mountains. Sheratonesque interior. Often has live traditional music. Uncommonly wide variety of steaks, salads, soups, and desserts. Full meal about USD8. Menus in English. Peerlessly clean restrooms. Open noon-4pm and 7-11:30pm; in winter noon-4pm and 6-11:30pm. Last orders at 3pm and 10:45pm.

Rubin (Рубин) restaurant complex, pl. Lenin (tel. 87 47 04). Prime location but at a premium. Skip the gaudy "business club" and go to the more affordable café/disco-club on the opposite side. Café open 8am-10pm. Disco open 11pm-4am ("convenient appearance desired").

Kiosk/Snack Bar ("Снек Бар") in front of Rubin on pl. Lenin. Sofia's ideal eating spot. Espy bustling Bulgarians while downing a sandwich and a soft drink for under 5 leva. Plenty of tables and chairs protected by a pavilion.

Havana (Хавана), bul. Vitosha 27 (tel. 80 05 44). Take your pick: a restaurant, a café, and a cocktail bar are available in this complex resembling an indoor Cuban city. Know what you are ordering unless you enjoy living dangerously. The spicy fare from the restaurant downstairs might give even Castro heartburn. Café open 7am-11pm. Restaurant open noon-3pm, 7-11pm.

Budapest (Будапешт) ul. Rakovski 145 (tel. 87 27 50). Hungarian cuisine. Full meals USD3. Menu in Bulgarian only. Open 10am-11pm.

Sights and Entertainment

Sofia's two most venerable churches, the late Roman **St. George's Rotunda** and the early Byzantine **St. Sophia** sprang up in the 4th and 6th centuries, respectively. St. George's hides in the courtyard of the Sheraton Hotel while St. Sophia, the city's namesake, lurks several blocks behind the Party house. Both are closed for restoration but worth seeing from the outside. St. Sophia is flanked by the **Tomb of the Unknown Soldier** with its eternal flame. Across the square from St. Sophia looms the massive, gold-domed **St. Alexander Nevsky Cathedral,** erected in the early 20th century in memory of the 200,000 Russians who died in the 1877-78 Russo-Turkish War. The icons by the altar offer an interesting comparison of the styles of different Eastern European and Russian painters, but the main attraction is downstairs in the **crypt,** a monstrous collection of painted icons and religious artifacts from the past 1000 years. (Crypt open Wed.-Mon.) In an underpass in pl. Lenin is the tiny 14th-century **Church of Saint Petka Samardzhiiska,** which contains some eye-grabbing frescoes; despite its size, this is one of Sofia's finest churches. (Theoretically open Tues.-Sat. 10:30am-1pm and 3-5:30pm. Free admission.)

The former **Georgi Dimitrov Mausoleum,** on pl. 9 Septemvri, deserves perusal if it's still standing in 1992. This memorial to Stalin's former right-hand man, long hated and now officially vilified, is closed. His remains have been evicted and buried, and debate rages over the fate of the building. If you're lucky, you may catch an anti-government protest outside. Unless you understand the labels (Bulgarian only), the **National Museum of History** off pl. Lenin is an excellent opportunity to flounder among relics of Bulgarian history with nary a clue about their meaning. (Open Tues.-Thurs. and Sat.-Sun. 10:30am-6pm, Fri. 2:30-6:30pm. Admission 1.20Lv.) The **Archeological Museum,** at bul. Vitosha and pl. Lenin, houses relics from the Thracian, Greek, Roman, and Turkish settlements in Bulgaria. (Open Tues.-Sun. 10am-noon and 2-6pm.) On the other side of pl. Lenin is the 16th-century **Banya Bashi Mosque** (now a museum), worth a look for those whose itineraries don't include Turkey. At the **Sofia Municipal Art Gallery,** ul. General Gurko 1, near ul. Sofiiska Komuna, you can taste Bulgarian impressionism and modern art. (Open Wed.-Sun. 10:30am-7pm. Free.) For a look at traditional Bulgaria, be sure to check out the National Ethnographic Museum at pl. 9 Septemvri. (Open Wed.-Sun. 10am-noon and 1:30-6pm.)

Even a quiet city like Sofia can sweeten the social life. Try the **disco** underneath the Palace of Culture (open 7pm-4am, cover 5Lv) or the more congested **Yalta** club near the Hotel Sofia in pl. Narodno Sŭbranie. **Bul. Vitosha,** down towards the Palace of Culture, is a popular hangout on summer nights; some of its cafés stay open until 1am. You can also purchase tickets to see one of Bulgaria's fine performing arts companies. Arrange these through Balkantourist or any of the fancy hotels north of pl. Lenin.

Rila Monastery Рилски Манастир

The **Rila Monastery,** 120km south of Sofia, is the largest and most famous monastery in Bulgaria. Founded by the hermit Ivan Rilski in the 10th century, it maintained the arts of icon painting and manuscript copying during the Turkish occupation. The Kurdalis destroyed the monastery in the 18th century, but it was rebuilt during the National Revival period and is now considered the finest architectural monument of that era. The 1200 frescoes on the central chapel and surrounding walls form an outdoor art gallery. Try to make one of the services at 6:30am or 5pm. To reach the monastery from Sofia, take the lone (6:30am) train to the Kocherinovo (Кочериново) station (12km from Kocherinovo town); buses run to the monastery every half-hour. Alternatively, hop a bus from the Ovcha Kupel (овча Купел) station in Sofia (take tram #5). Those hitching, take tram #5 to Highway E79. **Camping Bor** is 1km beyond the monastery (USD2.50 per person, USD2.50 per tent; 3-person bungalows 16Lv; open early June-late Sept.).

Koprivshtitsa Копривщица

Allow yourself even the smallest lapse in sanity and Koprivshtitsa will take you back in time. With its picturesque wood-and-stone cottages and its proud history of revolt, Koprivshtitsa is one of the most enchanting villages in Bulgaria. The sound of disciplined hoofbeats periodically interrupts Koprivshtitsa's tranquility, and one senses that this is one of the few functioning Balkan villages remaining, a place where horses cart more than a histrionic duty.

One hundred years ago in this quaint little village, Todor Kableshkov pricked his own finger and drafted his momentous "letter of blood" announcing the April uprising against Ottoman rule, the most passionately glorified event in Bulgarian history. The Turks savagely crushed the insurgency, but their brutality sparked an international furor that led to the Russo-Turkish War of 1877 and Bulgarian independence.

Koprivshtitsa flaunts some brilliant examples of National Revival architecture. Several houses now serve as museums of Bulgarian handicrafts. You can buy an informative book about the town at the bookstore in the town center (open 8am-noon and 3-5:30pm). You will see two types of cottages here. The first are the sturdy, half-timbered houses from the early 19th century, with open porches, high stone walls, and sparse ornamentation; the **Benkovsky House,** the eminent poet **Dimcho Debelyanov's House,** and the building of the restaurant **Diado Liben,** are good examples. The second, more common type features enclosed verandas and delicate woodwork. The **Oleskov** and **Doganov Houses** exemplify this style. (Generally open 7:30am-noon and 1:30-5:30pm.)

Trains from Sofia to Varna stop at Koprivshtitsa station (6 per day, 2 hr., 10Lv), 8km away from the town. Koprivshtitsa is the station after Антон. A bus awaits to take you into town (10 min.). If hitchhiking, take tram #3 out of Sofia; the last 12km from the highway to Koprivshtitsa see few cars during the week. Rooms for Westerners are scarce here, especially on weekends. Strongly consider seeing the village in a daytrip from Sofia, which is possible if you leave early. **Balkantourist** is in the brown house facing the river behind the restaurant enclave in the center. The staff here speaks little English. (Open Mon.-Fri. 8am-5pm.) **Hotel Koprivshtitsa** (tel. 21 82) offers singles for USD10 and doubles for USD15. Cross the second stone bridge from the center and ascend the steps. If they are full ask about rooms in the charming **Shuleva Kŭshta.** Some devious maps show a nonexistent campground. The picturesque **Restaurant Diado Liben,** in the blue house across the river from the town center, serves grilled specialties including *sirene po trakiiski* (cheese with sausage). There is an excellent **cafeteria** inside the restaurant complex in the town center where a hearty meal costs no more than 5Lv.

Valley of Roses

Two and a half hours east from Sofia along the Sofia-Varna rail line is **Karlovo** (Карлово), a small town huddled at the foot of the Stara Planina. Expect to uncover a piece of Bulgaria not obsessed with the blind mimicry of the West; few speak English here. If at all possible, travelers should visit this region from late May to early June, during the annual **rose festival** (Празник На Розата). This week-long welcome to the rose-picking season punctuates performances by traditional Bulgarian song-and-dance troupes with comedians, soccer matches, bazaars, and the like. Ask Balkantourist for details of when and where you go to catch the many events. As you face away from the train station, take a 10-15 minute walk up ul. Stamboliiski (ул. Стамболийски) toward the mountains until you arrive at pl. 20 Juli (площад 20 юли). During the Rose Festival, this square accommodates a delightful show of traditional Bulgarian song and dance with snow-capped mountains in the background; people from the world over come to appreciate the beautifully resonant voices which have made Bulgarian folk music internationally famous.

For a grand view of the square, book a room in the **Rosova Dolina Hotel.** (Singles USD30. Doubles USD40.) Karlovo's **Balkantourist** office occupies the lobby of this hotel. Be sure also to visit the home of Bulgarian revolutionary martyr Vasil Levski (Васил Левски).

Trains connect Karlovo with **Kazanlŭk** (Казанлък) several times a day (1½ hr., USD0.50). Kazanlŭk, the largest city in the valley, houses the Rose Museum, an ethnographic museum, and the famous Kazanlŭk Tomb, which dates back to the late 4th century BC. Two of the cheaper hotels are the **Somiza** and the **Rosa.** (Singles at both USD11.50. Doubles USD20.) Or try the **Campground Kazanlŭshka Roza** 4km north of Kazanlŭk (open May-Oct.) Ten km south of Kazanlŭk (USD4 by taxi) is Lake Georgi Dimitrov, a scenic, brownish lake complete with beach and campground (open May-Oct.).

At the northern extreme of the Valley of Roses looms the legendary **Shipka Pass,** sight of the bloody and pivotal battle where Russian and Bulgarian forces prevented the Turks from advancing beyond the Balkan Mountains.

Plovdiv Пловдив

You may wonder why you came at first, as most of Bulgaria's second city seems to be the worst sprawl of gray apartment complexes and exhaust-ridden boulevards the country has to offer. Hold your disappointment until you stroll up the **Trimontsium** (Three Hills) into the rambling stairway-streets of the **Old Town.** Here Bulgarian Revival houses hang their beamed, protuding upper stories over the cobblestones, windows stare down into alleyways at impossible angles, and churches and mosques hide in secluded corners. To see the old town, start at the **Dzhumaya Mosque** (Джумая джамия) on ul. Vasil Kolarov (ул. Васил Коларов), and wander up ul. Maksim Gorki (ул. Максим Горки). Turn to find the second-century **Amphitheater of Philippopolis,** at the entrance to the tunnel that runs under the old town. If at all possible, try to see a performance in the amphitheater; a panoramic view of the modern metropolis creates an awe-inspiring contrast to the elaborate, ancient proscenium. Back on Maksim Gorki, continue a bit farther to the **National Ethnographic Museum** (Етнографски мызей). Housed in an exquisite townhouse characteristic of the National Revival, it contains a well-presented collection of artifacts from this period. (Open Tues.-Sun. 9am-noon and 2-5pm.) The most interesting and colorful baroque houses are down the hill from here, through the Roman gate. The **Georgiadi House** (къща Д Георгиади) displays exhibits from the War of Liberation. Plovdiv's **Archaeological Museum** (Археологически музей) in a square off bul. 6 Septemvri (бул. 6 Септември) near the river, is worth visiting only for its collection of gold goblets from the 4th century BC. (Open Tues.-Sun. 9am-12:30pm and 2-5:30pm.)

From the train station, take bus #28 or 102 to the town center (5 stops away). The **Balkantourist** office, bul. Moskva 34 (бул. Москва) (tel. (032) 55 38 48; open daily 7am-9pm), is gracious and English-speaking. Pick up a copy of their colorful brochure with a city map and inquire about tickets to the **Plovdiv Chamber Music Festival** (June-July) or to many diverse performances in the city's two theaters. To reach the office from the train station, take tram #102 to bul. Moskva (the 9th stop). Walk back one block—it's on your right. **Hotel Bulgaria,** ul. Patriarh Eftimii 13 (tel. (032) 260 64), is the cheapest hotel in town. (Singles USD25. Doubles USD36.) You will probably have to settle for **Trakia Camping** (tel. (032) 55 13 60), 4km west of town, or **Maritsa Camping** (tel. (032) 23 34 23), 5km farther. For Trakia, take bus #4 to the end of the line, about 1km from the campground. Take a taxi to Maritsa.

Be sure to visit **Taverna Pŭldin** (Пълдин) in the heart of the Old Town, built right into the Roman walls at ul. Knjaz Tsereteli 1 (Кнез Церетели); here you can sample Bulgarian fare in an arabesque setting as masses dance under the watchful eye of Dionysus. Also in the Old Town, try the **Restaurant Alafrangite** (Алаф рангите) on ul. Kiril Nektariev, in an eye-catching National Revival house that appeared in a *National Geographic* article on Bulgaria some years back. On a cool evening, head to the fountainside café in the Public Garden (formerly the Garden of King Boris), within walking distance from the Old Town. Multi-colored strobes illuminate the fountain—the most popular hangout in town—to the rhythm of Western music, and you can rent rowboats to splash your way around the small lake. For a cheaper meal, try the kiosks or self-service cafeterias around town.

Trains from Sofia to İstanbul stop in Plovdiv, as do most Sofia-Burgas trains. Sofia-Plovdiv service runs about every two hours (2½ hr., USD1). A system of faster, private buses has also opened up (1½ hr., twice a day).

About 28km north of Plovdiv is the **Bachkovo Monastery,** second largest in the country after Rila. Take a bus from the main bus station to Asenovgrad, where you can catch a bus to the monastery.

Veliko Tŭrnovo Велико Търново

Veliko Tŭrnovo, set dramatically on the steep banks of the River Jantra, was once the capital of the powerful Second Bulgarian Kingdom. Amid the ruins of the palaces of Bulgarian czars and patriarchs are fragments of mural paintings and mosaics that proudly testify to the vibrancy of this center of medieval culture.

Veliko Turnovo is half an hour by train or bus south of Gorna Oryahovitsa (Горна оряховица), which is on the main rail line connecting Sofia and Varna. From the Gorna Oryahovitsa train station, walk straight ahead to the first main street and take the bus. From the Veliko Tŭrnovo train station 1km from the center, take the bus up the steep bank to the town center and walk 15 minutes down ul. Vasil Levski (ул. Васил Левски) to Balkantourist. Buses run from Balkantourist and the town center to the old town. The ruins of the fortress **Tsarevetz,** which once housed the royal palace and patriarchate, litter the top of a large hill. There's enough here to keep the summer youth brigades employed in restoration work for decades. As you wander to or from the fortress, stop at the **Archeological Museum,** off ul. Ivan Vasov, which contains wonderful Thracian pottery, a fine collection of medieval crafts from the Tŭrnovo ruins, and copies of the most famous Bulgarian religious frescoes. You can see 20th-century depictions of Veliko Tŭrnovo over the ages at the municipal **art museum,** situated on the peninsula within the river's bend (Open daily 10am-6pm). The Saints Cyril and Methodius University (Унив ерситет Кирил и Методии), perched on the mountainside, commands a princely view of Tsarevetz and offers a youthful environment. **Balkantourist,** on ul. Vasil Levski near ul. Hristo Botev (tel. (062) 281 65 or 218 14), provides useful brochures. There is now an excellent **youth hostel** in the Hotel Edelvais (Хотел Еделвайс) at ul. Blagoev 79 with private toilets and hot showers. Cheap lodging is also available at **Motel Sveta Gora** (tel. (062) 204 72), 2km west of town. Take the bus across from Balkantourist. **Hotel Etŭr** (tel. (062) 220 41) is centrally located on ul. Hristo Botev just before the park. The cafés and restaurants of ul. Blagoev are nothing to write home about, but try to get a window seat at the **Balkan Restaurant. Restaurant Bulgaria,** in the basement across the street from Balkantourist, serves hearty meals. (Open Sun.-Fri. 11:30am-11pm.) The **Mehana** (Механа), in the small square where ul. Dimitrov becomes ul. Blagoev, is a fine place to sample *shishlik* (lamb kebab) and a loaf of homemade bread, accompanied by live Bulgarian music. (Open Wed.-Mon. 4-11:30pm.) There's a **market** at ul. Vasil Levski and ul. Dimitŭr Ivanov.

The village of **Arbanassi,** 4km northeast of Veliko Tŭrnovo, has several merchant houses dating from the 17th and 18th centuries, when the town was a flourishing commercial center; take a bus from the old bus station, just uphill from the main one. About 50km southwest of Veliko Tŭrnovo lies the ethnographic museum park of **Etŭra,** established in the 1960s to preserve the awareness of arts and crafts from the National Revival period; here you can watch the authentic production of flour, sheets, gold jewelry, wool carpets, and much more. It is a bit out of the way, but well worth a half-day's visit; take the train west from Gorna Oryahovitsa, get off in Gabrovo, and Etura is just on the outskirts of town.

Black Sea Coast

In summer, the crowded Black Sea coast reveals more about Eastern European swimsuit fashion than Bulgarian culture. Much of the erstwhile socialist bloc and a growing contingent of Western Europeans come here to bronze themselves in July and August. Varna and Burgas are the principal transportation centers. Strewn between the largest resorts are tiny villages where you can escape the crowds. Train travel from Sofia is excruciatingly crowded and slow, yet still a bargain at under USD4. Flying, once a viable alternative, now costs USD45. Along the coast, frequent yet crowded buses run between most points of interest. Hydrofoils run between Varna, Nesebŭr, Burgas, Pomorie, and Sozopol. Service is infrequent but fast; tickets go on sale one hour before departure. Inquire at the portside. Hitching to the coast from Sofia can often be a multi-day ordeal.

Varna Варна

Varna, the third largest city in Bulgaria, grows decidedly crowded in summer. On the bright side, it sports an alluring old town with well-preserved Roman baths, seaside gardens, and a beach complete with roller-skating young Bulgarians. **Balkantourist,** ul. Avram Gachev 33 (Аврам Гачев) (tel. (052) 22 23 89), is on the other side of the underpass from the train station. (Open daily 8am-6pm). If you hitchhike in, take bus #48 from the intersection of ul. Karl Marx (Маркс) and ul. Dimitŭr Blagoev (Благоев). A few stops later is the hydrofoil port. **Hotel Musala,** ul. Musala 3 (tel. (052) 22 39 25), is the cheapest in town. (Singles USD9. Doubles USD14.) To get there, walk up A. Gachev from Balkantourist until you reach pl. 9 Septemvri (пл. 9 Септември), make a sharp right on ul. Vaptsarov (ул. Вапцаров), then cut across the small park on your left. During the summer getting a room without reservations can be arduous. **Balkantourist** will book you a private room for USD8 per night (min. 4 nights). It is sometimes worth paying for the extra night or two even if you bail out early. The **Cape Galata campground,** 6km away, has bungalows. (Open mid-June to mid-Sept.) In summer, everything is booked and travelers crash in the park next to the train station; check your luggage at the *Garderob* across from the train station. (Open 5:30am—10:30pm.) Restaurants (meals average USD2) and nightlife center around pl. 9 Septemvri and along ul. Lenin. As you stroll along Varna's **seaside gardens,** have a look inside the **Marine Museum** (open 8am-4pm; free) and check out the щука in the **Aquarium** (Аквариум; open Mon. 2-10pm, Tues.-Sat. 8am-10pm; admission 2Lv, students 1Lv). Varna's beach charges an appropriately nominal 1.50Lv entrance fee. For serious sunbathing, head out to Varna's renowned resort, **Golden Sands** (Златни Пясъци). While there, you can go parasailing (180Lv) high above the Black Sea Coast and then plunge into a hearty seaside meal (often less than 30Lv). To get there, hop on bus #9, which leaves every half-hour and stops near the center (by the cathedral) and by the Cherno More Hotel (2.40Lv each way). Just up the coast, **Albena** is popular among the more youthful multitudes. Both Albena and Golden Sands offer a prestigious number of watersports, nightclubs, and tourists. For more seclusion, seek out some of the smaller resorts farther up the coast.

Burgas Бургас

The Black Sea coast's other transportation hub, Burgas offers easy access to nearby villages and beaches. Burgas is Bulgaria's fourth-largest city and main coastal industrial center. It is not without its own charm, however, as testify the playful seagulls which greet you upon arrival. **Balkantourist,** at ul. Pŭrvi Mai (ул. Първи Май) and bul. Vazov (Бул. Вазов), can't offer you private rooms unless you stay at least five days (open Mon.-Sat. 11am-10pm). That's OK: the **Hotel Primoretz** (tel. (056) 441 17) is a steal at 63Lv per night for a single with private bathroom, telephone, and balcony overlooking the snazzily-paved parking lot. (With your back to the hydrofoil port, take a right onto the mainroad until the seaside gardens.) Walking along the beach, seek out the Triumph Fretata (Триумф-Фретата), a restaurant built inside a ship commanding a charming view of the sea. (Open 9am-4pm and 6-11pm.) Six buses per day (14.50Lv) connect Burgas with Varna's main bus station (in the northwest of town). In July and August, three **hydrofoils** per day run from Burgas to Varna with a stop in Nesebŭr. Another runs to Sozopol and a third to Pomorie. (Less frequent service May-June and Sept.)

The area south of Burgas has rapidly become one of the ragingest resorts for students and families celebrating the fall of communism. Poles, East Germans, Russians, and many others occupy no less than 15 campgrounds along the stretch between Burgas and Ahtopol. In summer all cheap accommodations, including campgrounds, may be clogged with these visitors. Make reservations a few days in advance, preferably from Sofia. **Sozopol,** 45 minutes south of Bourgas by bus, is one of the most enticing coastal towns, resting on the site of an ancient Greek harbor for the moment occupied by the Soviet Navy. The **Balkantourist** office, ul. Ropotamo 28, is helpful, but you may have trouble finding someone who speaks English. Face the park in front of the bus stop, go right on the road until it ends and then make a left. When the street forks, keep left until you approach the water. (Open 7am-midnight.) Their private rooms are available only for stays of at least five nights. There are campgrounds a few km away. One, the **Zlatna Ribka,** sprawls on the beach and is linked by bus to Burgas. There are no hotels. For a delicious meal and a romantic view of the sea, follow the East Europeans to the **Vyatŭrna Melnitsa** on ul. Morski Skali. (Open 7am-11:30pm.) Sozopol is an easy daytrip from Burgas (every hr., 3.50Lv).

The area north of Burgas caters to family and package-vacation crowds, making it grueling to find cheap lodgings. The big resort here is the crowded **Sunny Beach** (Слънчев Бряг). Show up at any Balkantourist office and you will be ushered to one of the more expensive hotels. **Nesebŭr** (Несебър), a touristy fishing village perched atop the peninsula at the southern end of Sunny Beach, brandishes Byzantine churches and traditional tavernas. Reach Sunny Beach and Nesebŭr from Burgas (every 20 min., 6Lv).

CZECHOSLOVAKIA

USD$1 = 30.4 koruny (kčs, or CSK)	**10kčs = USD$0.33**
CAD$1 = 26.6kčs	**10kčs = CAD$0.38**
GBP£1 = 50.8kčs	**10kčs = GBP£0.20**
AUD$1 = 23.7kčs	**10kčs = AUD$0.42**
NZD$1 = 17.3kčs	**10kčs = NZD$0.58**
Country Code: 42	**International Dialing Prefix: 00**

An uneasy federation of two distinct societies, Czechoslovakia (Československo) is the classic example of Eastern European regionalist tensions. To the west, in Bohemia and Moravia, the Czechs have historically balanced their own language with a German-speaking intellectual culture that nurtured artists such as Rilke, Kafka and Mozart. In the mountainous east, the Slovaks speak a closely related but significantly different language, and have spent much of their time as an Austro-Hungarian fiefdom. The rapid Communist industrialization of previously agricultural Slovakia made the region tragically dependent on outdated and ecologically unsound factories and heavy industry, and the continuing Prague-o-centrism of Czechoslovakia's intellectual and political life has left Slovaks feeling underrepresented and underappreciated. Some question the alliance, but secession seems unlikely.

The notion of self-determination in Czechoslovakia is a fairly new thing; from the Holy Roman Empire to the Nazis and the Soviets, foreign powers have driven the country's internal affairs. The 1960s witnessed a flourishing of democratic socialism under Alexander Dubček, which culminated in the so-called "Prague Spring." In 1968 the Soviet Union put an end to the thaw with the iron rumble of tanks. After a twenty-one year winter under the Soviet puppet government of Gustav Husák, Czechoslovakia blossomed quietly and exuberantly in the Velvet Revolution of 1989, so dubbed for its smooth and peaceful nature and its Velvet Underground of artistic angst. Prompted by the changes sweeping Poland and Hungary, Czechs and Slovaks rallied in gigantic demonstrations against the Communist government, which stepped down seemingly under the force of their sentiment.

The natural successor was political activist and playwright Václav Havel, who had led the anti-communist dissident movement, founded the human-rights group

Charter 77, and then came out of prison to stage manage the revolution from Prague's Magic Lantern theater before stepping in to assume the mantle of president in a fittingly ironic twist. Though his dramas speak passionately against totalitarianism, Havel-as-president has been questioned by his constituency for his soft approach—in April 1991, 200,000 people filled Wenceslas Square to protest his considered leniency toward former Party members and the secret police, and the tentativeness of his moves toward a market-oriented economy, which are hampered by Czech-Slovak infighting.

The sheer beauty of the countryside and its several thousand castles should take your mind off politics. Glorious Prague is one of the great Gothic and Baroque cities of Europe. A Victorian ambience pervades the spas of Karlovy Vary and Mariánské Lázně. And Bratislava, only a few dozen kilometers east of Vienna, welcomes travelers with medieval castles and monuments.

Getting There and Getting Around

Visa requirements for visitors to Czechoslovakia have been eroding steadily since the revolution. In September 1991, Americans did not need visas for stays up to 30 days; U.K. citizens could stay visa-free for 180 days. Canadians, Australians, and New Zealanders still needed either a 30-day tourist visa or a 48-hour transit visa. Visit embassies in Europe, or at 1305 Pine Avenue West, Montréal, Canada H3G 1B2 (tel. (514) 849-4495) or 47 Culgoa Circuit, O'Malley, Canberra, ACT 2606, Australia (tel. (02) 90 15 16).

InterRail became valid in Czechoslovakia in 1990, EastRail in 1991, and Eurail may by 1993, but since rail travel is still so cheap (only 16-30kčs per 100km), they may not be such a great deal. The fastest trains are the *expresný;* the *rychlík* (fast) trains cost as much as the express, while the few *spěšný* (semi-fast) trains cost less; avoid *osobný* (slow) trains. The monster *Jízdní Řád* (national train schedule, 75kčs) is helpful if only for its two-page English explanation in front. As in other European countries, *odjezd* (departures) are on yellow posters, *prijezd* (arrivals) on white.

Čedok gives ISIC holders a 50% discount off domestic tickets bought at their offices, and up to 35% off international tickets. The train station may or may not. If you are heading to Austria or Germany, buy a ticket to the border, and use a railpass or buy a ticket from there. Seat reservations *(místenka,* 6kčs) are required on almost all express and international trains; snag them at the counter with a boxed "R" above it. A slip of paper with the destination, time, date, and an "R" expedites the transaction.

Buses are significantly faster and only slightly more expensive than trains, especially near Prague and for shorter distances. **ČSAD,** the national bus company, also services international routes. From Prague, buses run a few times per week to Munich, Milan, Dubrovnik, etc. and there is frequent service from Bratislava to Vienna and Budapest, and from Brno to Linz, Austria. Consult the bus timetables posted at stations or buy your own (25kčs) alongside the train timetables at *Svobodný Slovo* ("the free word") bookstore/newstands, around the country.

Hitchhiking is popular in Czechoslovakia, especially during the morning commuting hours (6-8am). Roads throughout Czechoslovakia love cyclists. Unfortunately there are no bicycles available for rent; you may, however, bring your own across the border.

Practical Information

The importance of **Čedok,** the official state tourist company and relic of centralized communist bureaucracy, has been seriously diminished by the crop of private tourist agencies which have sprung up since the 1989 revolution. **CKM,** its junior affiliate, remains helpful for the student and budget traveler, by acting as a clearinghouse for youth hostel beds and issuing ISIC and IYHF cards. The problem with private agencies is that their quality and trustworthiness vary; use your instinct. **Information offices** in major cities provide heaps of printed matter on sights and cultural events as well as lists of hostels and hotels. Even in post-revolution Eastern Europe, luxury hotels remain tourist oases, equipped with English speakers, currency-exchange desks, international telephones, fax machines, foreign-currency (Tuzex) shops, bars, cafés, and swanky restaurants.

The Czech and Slovak languages are mutually understandable Slavic tongues, but differ significantly. Russian *was* every student's mandatory second language, but English first will win you more friends. A few German phrases go even further. English-Czech dictionaries are indispensible and in high demand in Czechoslovakia. Before you leave home, pick up a *Say it in Czech* phrasebook. Published by the government and available in Prague, the godsend *Olympia Guidebook* has pages of useful Czech phrases and fine city maps, but is hard to find in English. Even better city maps *(plán města)* are available for almost all tourist destinations (15-35kčs).

There is no longer any mandatory foreign currency exchange requirement. However, keep a couple of exchange receipts in order to change money back upon leaving. Though still operating, the black market is graying around the temples, and since the official exchange rate has almost reached street levels, it is hardly worth the risk. Bring western currency in small denominations, as it greatly facilitates certain transactions (such as bribes) and is often preferred as payment in hotels. Souvenirs of a few DM or USD can render difficult train conductors and hotel managers more accommodating.

Travelers with initiative can hook positions as English teachers, especially if willing to teach outside of Prague. The message board at the **American Hospitality Center** (see Prague: Tourist Offices) posts requests, as do the classifieds of the English-language newpaper, *Prognosis.* Terms of employment vary, from monthly stipends plus housing, to lunch money and Czech lessons. Organizations which recruit volunteers include **Education for Democracy/USA,** P.O. Box 40514, Mobile, Alabama 36640-0514 (tel. (205) 434-3889) and the **Charter 77 Foundation,** 888 Seventh Ave., Suite 3301, New York, NY 10106 (tel. (212) 397-5563). Another means of visiting Czechoslovakia is to participate in one of the **Volunteers for Peace** international work camps. Two-to three-week programs of archaeological work, castle restoration, trail maintenance, and the like take place in July and August. Make arrangements several months in advance through Volunteers for Peace (see the General Introduction) or through **Service Civil International/USA,** Rte. 2, Box 506, Innisfree Village, Crozet, VA 22932.

Bring your own film, batteries, and feminine hygiene supplies. The mail works fine. International phone calls are quite possible, though finding a grey pay phone that works can be challenging. Look for a phone with a globe above it; most in post offices work. Inserting the coin at the precise time in Czech phones is an art. In the grey phones, drop the coin in the holding slot and dial; as soon as the other party answers, push in the coin. In the orange boxes, the coin will fall automatically when you are connected. Local calls cost 1kčs regardless of length. For AT&T's **USA Direct,** dial 00 42 00 01 01; divine instant connection.

Crime has climbed dramatically since the 1989 revolution, and the subsequent less-velvet economic revolutions. Be especially aware of snatch-and-run and pick-pocketing. In emergencies, make use of your country's embassy; local police may flounder in English (and tend to flounder in Czech as well). The **emergency phone number** throughout Czechoslovakia is **158.** National holidays include New Year's Day (Jan. 1), Easter Sunday and Monday, the now-ironic Anniversary of Soviet Liberation (May 9), and Christmas (Dec. 25-26).

Accommodations and Camping

A converted university dorm is your cheapest option in July and August. Comfortable two-to-four-bed rooms go for 100-180kčs per person; either go there directly or check at CKM for the address. CKM also runs **Junior Hotels** (year-round hostels loosely affiliated with the IYHF, which give discounts to both IYHF and ISIC cardholders); these are comfortable but often full. Wildcat hostel operations have usurped CKM's monopoly on youth accommodations, but not necessarily surpassed its reliability. Scan train stations for "hostel," "zimmer," or "accommodations" ads, or head to one of the private agencies we list.

Across the country, **private homes** have become a legal and feasible accommodations opportunity. In Prague, hawkers offer expensive rooms (USD10-25), sometimes including breakfast. Quality varies wildly. Make sure anything you accept is easily accessible by public transport. Outside of Prague, Čedok handles most private room booking, although private agencies are burgeoning around train and bus stations. Be prepared for a healthy commute to the center of town.

If you're sticking to **hotels,** consider reserving ahead of time from June to September in Prague, Bratislava, and Brno, even if it requires pre-payment. Otherwise you might become an intimate of the train station floor. Outside these cities, it's easier to find space. Hotels come in five flavors: A-star, A, B-star, B and C. The C hotels often provide the greatest opportunity to fraternize with Eastern Europeans, but a B might be all you can stand. In 1991, a single in a B hotel averaged 350kčs, a double 650kčs.

Inexpensive **camping** is available everywhere (most sites open only mid-May to Sept.). The book *Ubytování ČSR,* in decodable Czech, comprehensively lists the hotels, inns, hostels, huts, and campgrounds in Bohemia and Moravia. Bookstores also sell a fine hiking map of the country, *Soubor Turistických Map,* with an English key.

Food and Drink

Schnitzel (breaded cutlets, often accompanied by *knedliki*—filling flour dumplings) appears with almost miraculous consistency in Czechoslovak restaurants, and its innards are anyone's guess. Contemplation of the genus and species of the schnitzelled item is a national pastime. In fact, it has been theorized that it is this dietary influence which has contributed to the Germanic and East European preoccupation with national and ethnic roots; it is a metaphor for the desire to know what it is they eat.

In any case, you can eat (and certainly drink) almost recklessly in Czechoslovakia for very little money. Signs which should command your salivary attention are *bufet, samoobsluha* (self-service), and *občerstveni,* all variations on the stand-up snack bar, and usually vending sausages, beer, and soda very cheaply. A *hostinec* caters to a steady clientele of beer drinkers and is one of the best places to meet people. *Kavárny* and *cukrárny* serve coffee and exquisite pastry. Note that *káva* (coffee) in Czechoslovakia is often a thick layer of grounds topped with boiling water. A *pivnice* is a beer hall and a *vinárna* a wine bar, usually specializing in fine Slovak wines; both are good places to eat. Czech beers are among the world's best. The most famous are *plzeňský Prazdroj* (Pilsner Urquell) and *Budvar* (the original Budweiser). At just 7-14kčs per half-liter, it'll keep a silly grin on your face for next to nothing. *Slivovice* (plum brandy) is at its best here in the country that invented it. Other popular liquors are *Borovička* (made of juniper berries), *becherovka* (a nuclear yellow herbal potion), and *myslivec,* very popular with students. From Saturday noon to Sunday morning, all grocery stores and most restaurants close.

It is customary to round up the bill a few kčs, and often it will be done for you. At finer eateries, give a 10% tip as you pay; do not leave it on the table.

Vegetarians can supplement an otherwise highly satisfactory liquid diet with *smíselny sýr* (fried cheese), a scrumptious Czech specialty sold at some "sausage" stands, and produce from *ovoce zelenina* (greengrocers). Smuggling in a jar of peanut butter is not a bad idea.

The Czech Republic

Prague (Praha)

The Princess Libuše stood atop one of seven hills overlooking the River Vltava and declared, "I see a city whose glory will touch the stars; it shall be called *Praha* (threshold)." Indeed, from its mythological inception to the present, benefactors have always placed Prague on the cusp of the divine. Karel IV, King of Bohemia and 14th-century Holy Roman Emperor, envisioned a royal seat worthy of his rank and rebuilt Prague into the "city of a hundred spires" it is today. Artists and musicians have always been drawn here; Mozart himself felt that only in Prague was he fully understood (and he didn't even speak Czech). The city has waltzed through the 20th century as if charmed; Czechoslovakia was not of major strategic importance in either of the world wars, and the capital escaped the ravages suffered by comparable cities such as Dresden.

Orientation and Practical Information

Prague straddles the River Vltava (German Moldau) in western Czechoslovakia. Direct rail and bus service links it with Vienna, Berlin, Munich, and Warsaw. All train and bus terminals are on or near the Metro; the **nám. Republiky** Metro station is closest to the principal tourist offices and accommodations agencies. Free maps are scarce at the train station; instead, go to a *tabak* stand or bookstore and buy an indexed *plán města.* Pick up a copy of Prague's English language newspaper, *Prognosis,* at newsstands; it has a helpful Visitor's Guide and timely political and cultural discussion.

At the top of the western bank of the Vltava lies **Hradčany,** Prague's castle district and principal landmark. Below it is the lovely **Malá Strana,** originally built and populated by Prague's urban gentry. From Malá Strana, the pedestrian-only **Karlův Most** (Charles Bridge) crosses over the Vltava into **Staré Město** (Old Town), at the center of which is the huge, architecturally pristine plaza, **Staroměstké náměstí.** North of Staroměstké náměstí lies **Josefov,** the old Jewish quarter. South of Staré Město is **Nové Město** (New Town), established in 1348 by Karel IV. South of Nové Město is **Vyšehrad,** a former seat of royalty. Most of Prague's architectural monuments are in the castle district and the Old Town. Nové Město, to the south, is busier and more commercial.

The center of Prague is dominated by 3 streets which form a *T.* The base of the *T,* separating Old and New Towns, is **Václavské náměstí** (Wenceslas Square—but more of a boulevard); at its lower end begins the major shopping street **Na příkopě,** which forms the right arm. 28 října on the left becomes Národní and leads to the river. Small streets lead to Staroměstské nám. two blocks above the *T.*

The streets and the Metro are generally safe at night, though travelers should exercise regular caution; Prague holds many unlit nooks and crannies.

Tourist Offices: Čedok, Na příkopě 18 (tel. 212 71 11). No longer essential, but can be a convenient place to buy train and bus tickets. Processing tickets can take over an hour in high season. Open June-Sept. Mon.-Fri. 8:15am-4:15pm, Sat. 8:15am-2pm; Oct.-March Mon.-Fri. 8:15am-4:15pm; April-May Mon.-Fri. 8:15am-4:15pm, Sat. 8am-noon. Train tickets sold Mon.-Fri. 8:15am-3pm. Next door at **Pražska Informační Služba** (Prague Information Service), Na příkopě 20 (tel. 54 44 44), grab a handful of brochures on upcoming concerts and city sights. Open Mon.-Fri. 8am-8:30pm, Sat.-Sun. 9am-3pm; Oct.-May Mon.-Fri. 8am-7pm, Sat. 8am-noon. **CKM,** in Junior Hotel Praha, Žitná 12 (tel. 29 85 89). Information, IYHF, and ISIC cards. Open Mon.-Fri. 8-10am and 1-4:30pm. Branch office at Jindřisská 28 (tel. 26 85 07). Open Mon. and Wed. 10am-noon and 2-6pm, Tues. and Thurs-Fri. 10am-noon and 1-5pm. Come to the **American Hospitality Center,** Malé náměstí 14 (tel. 236 74 86) not so much for the city info as the message board, posted with requests for English tutors, cycling companions, notes to friends, and the like. CNN, MTV, and great popcorn. Open daily 10am-6pm.

Embassies: U.S., Tržište 15, Praha 12548 (tel. 53 66 41, ext. 229 for consular services), 10 minutes from Metro Malá Strana, in the former Colloredo Schönborn Palace, where Kafka worked as a librarian. Open 8am-1pm and 2-4:30pm. The newly remodeled library, with books and current periodicals, is open Mon.-Thurs. 11am-6pm, Fri. 11am-3pm. **Canada,** Hradčany, Mickiewiczova 6 (tel. 32 69 41). Open Mon.-Fri. 8am-noon and 2-4pm. **U.K.,** Thunovská 14 (tel. 53 33 47). Open daily 9am-12pm and 2:45-4pm. Travelers from **Australia** and **New Zealand** should contact the British embassy. All Western embassies will hold mail. **Hungary,** Mičurinova 1 (tel. 36 50 41). Same-day visa USD20 plus 2 photos. Open Mon.-Wed. and Fri. 10am-1pm. **Poland,** Valdštejnská 8 (tel. 53 69 51); consular section Václavské nám. 19 (tel. 26 54 41). Usually same day visa service. Citizens of Australia and New Zealand pay USD35 plus 2 photos; less for students. Open Mon.-Fri. 8:30am-12:30pm. **USSR,** Pod kaštany 1 (tel. 38 19 41). Visas USD10 with proper preparation.

Currency Exchange: 1% commission at state banks, 2% at Čedok and Interhotels. The several Interhotels on Václavské nám. will change money day and night. The state bank at Na příkopě 20 (a stone's throw from Čedok) will cash traveler's checks for USD or DM. Open Mon.-Fri. 8am-6pm. The black marketeers who hang out in Staroměstké nám. would cheat their own grandmothers.

American Express: Čedok, Na příkopě 18 (tel. 222 42 51). Mail held at the U.S. visitors counter. Cardholders' personal checks cashed for kčs only. Visa and Mastercard advances.

Post Office: Jindřišská 14. Poste Restante at window 17, but embassies are more reliable. Open 24 hrs. Mail parcels under 2kg from the office in the main train station. Open Mon.-Fri. 8am-8pm, Sat. 8am-1pm. **Parcels** over 2kg can be mailed only at Pošta-Celnice (TSELL-neats-uh), Plzeňská 129. Take tram #9 westbound, and ask where to get off. A royal bureaucratic pain. Airmail it, and it should arrive within 10 days. Open Mon.-Tues. and Thurs.-Fri. 7am-3pm, Wed. 7am-6pm, Sat. 8am-noon.

Telephones: At the post office. Open 24 hrs. Counter on the left handles international direct calls (70kčs per min. to U.S.). No minimum charge. **City Code:** 02.

Flights: Ruzyně Airport (tel. 36 78 16 or 36 78 14), 12 mi. northwest of city center. The Czechoslovak airline ČSA (tel. 36 78 14) runs buses from Revoluční 25 (around back), 5 blocks from the nám. Republiky metro stop, to the airport every 20-30 minutes from 6am-7pm daily (8kčs).

Trains: There are 4 train stations in Prague. Always ask about your point of departure—the information may not be volunteered. The main station, **Praha hlavní nádraží** (a.k.a. Woodrow Wilson station; Metro: hlavní nádraží), figures in most international routes and many domestic ones. The basement has baggage storage (15kg max., 4kčs per day, open 24 hrs.), lockers (2kčs, usually full), and clean showers (8kčs). **Masarykovo nádraží,** formerly Praha střed, is on Hybernská 700m away around the corner and serves only domestic routes. **Praha-smíchov** (Metro: Praha-smíchov) and **Praha-Holešovice** (Metro: Praha-Holešovice) are across the river. If you speak Czech or know someone who does, call train information (tel. 24 44 41 or 26 49 30).

Buses: ČSAD has 3 terminals *(Autobusové nádraží)* in town. The central one is **Praha-Florenc,** on Křižíkova (tel. 22 14 45), behind the Masarykovo nádraží railway station. Metro: Praha-Florenc. The staff at the *Informace* desk does not speak English, but the posted schedules are legible and extensive. Open Mon.-Fri. 6am-8pm, Sat. 6am-2pm, Sun. 6am-4pm. Buy tickets at least a day in advance, as they often sell out. Thrice weekly to Milan, Venice, Vienna, Dubrovnik, Budapest, Munich, and other international destinations, and extensive service throughout Czechoslovakia.

Public Transportation: Tel. 22 95 52. The **Metro,** tram, and bus systems serve the city well. Bus routes frequently shift for street repairs. Tickets, good for all forms of transportation, cost 4kčs; stock up at newspaper stands and *tabak* shops as the orange *automat* machines in Metro stations require exact change. Red ticket machines sell books of 24 for 25kčs. *Tabak* stores in Metro stations also sell 2-3 day tourist passes for 40-50kčs. Punch your ticket when boarding, and when switching vehicles—except in the Metro, where your ticket is valid for 90 minutes after punching on all lines. If you're caught without a punched ticket when exiting, you'll be fined 100kčs. Metro runs daily 5am-midnight. Night trams 51-58 and buses 500-510 run after midnight (every 40 min.); look for their midnight blue signs at transport stops.

Hitchhiking: Travelers going east take tram #9, 13, or 16 to the last stop. To points south, they take Metro C to Pražskeho povstáni, then go left 100m, crossing náměstí hrdinů to 5 Květná, also known as highway D1. To Munichbound, they take tram #4 or 9 until the intersection of Plzeňská and Kukulova/Bucharova, then start hitching to the south. Those going north take a tram or bus to Kobyliské nám., then bus #175 up Horňátecká.

Luggage Storage: Lockers (2kčs) in every train and bus station. Beware of those who might relieve you of heavy baggage by watching while you set your 4-digit code.

Laundromat: If you stay in a private flat, you might ask if your laundry could be included with the family's. Often it will come back darned and ironed, even your underwear. If you're on your own, the *prádelna* (cleaners) **Jitřenka,** inside the arcade at Václavské nám. 17 (tel. 26 13 12), will launder your pants (20kčs), shirts (15kčs), and underwear (10kčs) in 24 hrs. Open Mon.-Fri. 6am-9pm. At **Čistěni,** Pařížská 12 (tel. 232 69 77), prices are a few *koruny* lower, but it takes 3 days. Open Mon.-Fri. 8am-noon and 2-6pm. Next door they wash shirts for 2.20kčs, but it takes 5 days.

Bookstore: Zahraniční Literatura, Vodičkova 41, off Václavské nám., sells a staple supply of English language tour guides, Agatha Christies, the essential *Sun Sign Personality Guide,* and classics you managed to avoid in college (150-500kčs). Open Mon.-Fri. 9:30am-1pm and 2-6pm. A diminutive version of itself exists in the "Alfa" complex at Václavské nám. 28.

Pharmacy (Lékárna): Na příkopě 7 (tel. 22 00 81). Open 24 hrs.

Emergencies: (tel. 158). **Ambulance** (tel. 333 or 37 33 33). **Medical Emergency Aid** in English and German: (tel. 29 93 81). No English spoken; try calling your embassy. **Police** headquarters at Olšanská 2 (tel. 21 21 11 11). Metro: Flora, then walk down Jičinská and right onto Olšanská; the station is about 200m on your right. Or take tram #9, 10, or 13. Come here to get a visa extension. Open Mon.-Tues. and Thurs.-Fri. 8am-noon and 12:30-3:30pm, Wed. 8am-noon.

Accommodations

Finding a bed in Prague is less Kafkaesque now, thanks to the burgeoning supply of agencies renting rooms in private flats. Basically, budget travelers have four options: a room in a private flat (see Private Agencies or Pragotur below), a bed in a youth hostel or dorm (see CKM), a class B or C hotel room, or a campground. Hotel space is the tightest and most expensive of these options. In late June, when vast hordes of tourists begin to make the train station floor look tempting, enormous university dorms begin to empty for the summer, freeing up hundreds of cheap rooms. In July and August, bypass agencies and head directly there. At other times of the year, see the agencies below armed with Kafka's *Complete Works* and ample patience; you'll need both to deal with the absurdities of the system.

Accommodations Services

Official Agencies

CKM, Žitná 12 (tel. 229 65 26). Metro: nám. I.P. Pavlova, then backtrack on street, or walk down Štěpánská from Václavské nám. If you want youth hostel-type accommodations, plant yourself here when you arrive. Lists dormitories and youth hostels around town that currently have beds available (110-350kčs) and provides exact directions on the metro and trams. Havel himself couldn't get a room at the Junior Hotel Praha next door.

Pragotur, U Obecního domu 2 (tel. 231 72 81), a side street off nám. Republiky, across the street from the Hotel Paříž. Metro: nám. Republiky. Handles C-class hotels and private homes. Rooms are often far from the center of town. Doubling or tripling up with other people waiting may speed things up. 3-day min. stay for private rooms. Doubles 450-650kčs; 60kčs commission per person. Open Mon.-Fri. 7:30am-9pm, Sat. 8am-8pm, Sun. 8am-2:15pm; Dec.-Feb. Mon.-Fri. 8am-8:30pm, Sat. 9:15am-6:30pm.

Čedok, Panská 5 (tel. 22 56 57 or 22 70 04). Coming out of the main office at Na příkopě 18, go left, and take the first left. The only branch handling accommodations; will try to put you in the Ritz. Why tempt yourself? Go to CKM. Singles 365-720kčs, but you'll have to fight tooth and nail for these prices. Doubles 600-1200kčs. Open Mon.-Fri. 9am-10pm, Sat. 8:30am-6pm, Sun. 8:30am-4:30pm; Dec.-March Mon.-Fri. 9am-8pm, Sat.-Sun. 8:30am-2pm.

Private Agencies

Agencies which offer rooms in private flats set up shop seemingly overnight in prominent areas of town. Keep your eyes open. Again, make sure any rooms you accept are easily reachable by public transportation. Payment in American dollars or Deutschmarks is usually preferred, often required.

Top Tour, Rybná 3 (tel. 229 65 26, 232 10 77 or 232 08 60), one block west of nám. Republiky. Books dorm hostels (150-300kčs) and private rooms (USD15-25). Open Mon.-Fri. 9am-8pm, Sat.-Sun. 11am-7pm.

AVE Ltd., Wilsonova 80 (tel. 236 25 60), two offices on the top floor of the main train station. Office at the airport as well (tel. 236 25 41). Make sure you understand just what sort of accommodations you are paying for here; in fact, make them write it down. Rooms in private apartments run about USD20 per night (hard currency only).

KONVEX, Kamzíková 4 (tel. 236 67 60), on a side street off Staroměstské nám., near the town hall and the astronomical clock. Rooms in private flats (USD15-20) and whole flats for rent near the center of town (USD25-35). Open daily 10am-7pm.

Hello Ltd., Gorkého-Senovážná 3 (tel. 22 42 83). From nám. Republiky, walk down Hybernská, then take a right on Dlážděná. Choose rooms you like from photographs (USD15-20). Open daily 9am-10 or 11pm.

Hostels (Studentska Kolej)

It is better to book a bed at the following hostels through **CKM** (see Accommodations: Official Agencies), although in July and August, you can check into some of the university dorms directly. An enormous cluster of hostels (open July-Aug.) is west of the old town and the river in the Strahov neighborhood, near the Olympic stadium. From Metro: Dejvická, take bus #217 (every ½ hr.) Ask backpacking vagabonds on the bus about their hostel. All prices listed below are per bed, per night.

TJ Slavoj, V náklích (tel. 46 00 70). Take tram #3, 17, or 21 to last stop. 34 beds available in the sleeping quarters of a boathouse down by the riverside, 4-bed rooms. 170kčs. Breakfast available.

Domov Mládeže, Dykova 20. Take tram #16 from Ječná to 4th stop, or the Metro to nám. Miru, and then tram #16 to 2nd stop. Hall showers. 2-night max. stay. 150kčs.

Zimní Stadion Vokovice, Zalany. Metro: Dejvická, then tram #2, 26, or 20 to 4th stop, Horoměřická. Old building 100kčs, new 170kčs.

Akademie Výtvanvych Umění (AVU), U Starého Vystaviště 188. Metro: Fučíkova, then tram #12. Houses Czech fine art students during school year; sculpture studios downstairs. One bed in a dorm room 160kčs; in doubles 180kčs, with shower 200kčs.

Koleje VŠCHT—VOLHA, Kosmonautů 950. Metro: Chodov, then bus #154, 122, or 145. 300 beds. Double with shower, kitchen in hall 280kčs. Open July 5-Aug. 4. Beds also available at **Koleje VŠCHT—VLTAVA,** Chemická 953.

TJ Dolní Měcholupy, Na paloučku 223. Metro: Želivského, then bus #228 or 229 to Měcholupska. Or Metro: Skalka, then bus #268, 265, or 111 to Měcholupska. Singles 160kčs, with breakfast 190kčs. Open year-round.

ESTEC Students House, Kolej Strahov, Spartakiádní, blok (building) 5 (tel. 463 75 84). Metro: Dejvická, then 6th stop on bus #217. Friendly student staff speaks beautiful English. 3-hr. student-led walking tours 10kčs. Reception (and bar) open 24 hrs. Snack bar. Doubles 200kčs per person. 400 beds from July to mid-Sept. Limited space available mid-Sept. to June.

TJ Dukla Karlin, Malého (tel. 22 20 09), behind the Praha-Florenc bus station. Metro: Sokolovská. Bunk beds for the 1st 10 arrivals; cots in a gymnasium for the rest. Not elegant, but there's usually room. Reception open 6pm-midnight. Check-out 7am. 70kčs.

Hotels

A few dollars' tip can sometimes free up a room in an unyielding situation. Beware that hotels might sometimes try to bill you for a room substantially more expensive than the one you stayed in. Come prepared with pen, paper, and receipts to give them a lesson in arithmetic.

Savoy, Keplerova 6 (tel. 53 74 50), behind the castle district. Take tram #22 from Národní. B-category. Slightly worn, but should soon be renovated, and the location is beautiful. Singles 320kčs. Doubles 640kčs. Reservations recommended.

Národní dům, Bořivojova 53 (tel. 27 53 65; C-category). Take tram #9 (from Štěpánská) or tram #26 to Sladkovského nám. and walk south 1 block. C-category. Dorms (often filled by groups) 400kčs. Doubles 500kčs. Triples 600kčs. Quads 800kčs.

Hybernia, Hybernská 24 (tel. 22 04 31), across the street from Masarykovo nádraží station and around the corner from the main train station and Praha-Florenc busport. B-category. Only in a late-arrival pinch. Singles 610kčs. Doubles 850kčs. Bath down the hall.

Hotel Opera, Těšnov 13 (tel. 231 56 09 or 231 57 35), just down the street from the Praha-Florenc bus station. Metro: Sokolovská. Can arrange laundry and dry cleaning. Singles 533kčs. Doubles 900kčs, including breakfast. Restaurant open daily 7am-9pm.

Camping

Theoretically, Pragotur lists the city's seven campgrounds, but they may tell you they have no space or that they no longer have the brochure *(Praha Camping).* Be insistent, ask for the addresses, and call the campgrounds yourself—German is always spoken, English sometimes. The closest to the center is **Sokol Troja,** Trojská 171 (tel. 84 28 33). Take bus #112 from Metro: Fučikova: get off at Kazanka, and walk 100m. (60kčs per person and per tent. Bungalows 180kčs per bed. Reservations recommended; English spoken on the phone.) Or try **Sokol Dolní Počernice,** Dolní Počernice, Nad rybníkem (tel. 71 80 34). Take tram #9 to the end of the line, then bus #109 and ask for the campground.

Food

Restaurants in Prague eat foreigners alive. The more manipulative ones will even try to conceal the menu from you and generously serve you only the most expensive items. Fight back or try to adopt slightly irregular meal hours to beat the tourist crowds. For a light snack or a quick lunch, the numerous window stands selling tasty *párek y rohliku* (sausage in a small roll with mustard) for 15kčs are a bargain. In many squares half the people are eating sausages and the other half are waiting to buy them. Many an outlying Metro stop becomes an impromptu marketplace during the summer. The best *cukrárny* (bakeries) are on Vodičkova, 2 to 4 blocks off Václavské nám. The salad bar at the Palace Hotel, Panská 12, in the Nové Město, can tide vegetarians over until they reach a less carnivorous country. Ice cream *(zmrzlina)* is a virtual food group in Czechoslovakia; crowds flock to the **Italská Zmrzlina** (Italian ice cream) shop at Vodičkova 4, near Karlovo nám.

U Schnellů, Tomášská 2, in Malá Strana. Clean and cheery, and around the corner from the best beer in town. *Zbojnický gulyás* with the ubiquitous *knedliki* is authentic and tasty (30kčs). *Däbelské* toasties will fill you for 9kčs. Open daily 11am-3pm and 4:30-11pm.

Vegetárka, upstairs at Celetná 3, beside Týn Church, in Staroměstské nám. Vegetarian for Prague, which means some of the dishes are available without meat. A meal of fried cheese, rice, and an egg, 25kčs. Open daily 11am-2:30pm.

Automat Koruna, at the corner of Na příkopě and Václavské nám. A food factory. Serves everything from pastries to pickled herring, all cheap. Open Mon.-Fri. 6am-10pm (food until 8pm), Sat. 9am-7:30pm, Sun. 8am-7pm.

Peking Čínská (Chinese) Restaurace, Vodičkova 19, Praha 1 (tel. 26 26 97). Good *moo shu* and duck—yes, in Prague. Open Mon.-Sat. noon-3pm and 6-11pm (dinner seatings at 6 and 8pm).

St. Matthew's Cukrárna, Na příkopě 30, next to the Kino Sevastopol. Serves strawberries topped with chocolate mousse and whipped cream, even for breakfast. Open daily 10am-8pm.

Sights

Prague grew up as five independent towns and was not united by central administration until 1784. The **Staré Město** (Old Town) was the first and most important, but the Jewish village **Josefov** was not far behind, winning its own banner and government in 1358. **Hradčany,** across the river, was the royal city, crowned by the sprawling Gothic castle. Beneath it **Malá Strana** (Lesser Town) rose on the 17th-century ambitions of the local gentry; Italian architects built its splendid palaces and gardens. Once the Hussite stronghold, **Nové Město** was repeatedly destroyed in religious wars. Its rich 19th-century façades and echoing squares are now the commercial center of Prague. The central boulevard of **Václavské náměstí,** a favorite meeting place of students and activists in the days of liberation, saw mass demonstrations in both 1968-69 and November 1989.

Staroměstské náměstí is the city's most famous square, dominated by the **Old Town Hall,** which expanded from the original 14th-century tower to include several neighboring buildings. Townspeople as well as tourists gather on the hour to see its famous clock, with 12 peering apostles and a bell-ringing skeleton, representing death. The clockmaker had his eyes put out by the man who commissioned the work, so that he could not craft another one. A statue of martyred Czech theologian and leader **Jan Hus** occupies the place of honor in the center of the square. Across from the Town Hall is **Týn Church,** once a center of the Hussite movement. The difference between the two towers is intentional: one represents Adam, the other Eve. Between Maislova and the church is Franz Kafka's former home, marked with a plaque. (Hard-core Kafka devotees can visit the writer's final resting place at the Jewish Graveyard right outside Metro: Želivského.) A short detour down Jilská will bring you to the **Bethlehem Chapel,** where Jan Hus preached to his loyal congregation from 1402 until he was burnt at the stake.

Walk up Václavské nám. to reach the **National Museum.** Its mammoth collection includes meteorites, textiles, precious stones, and skeletons still on the ground as they were discovered—don't miss the horse and rider. (Open Wed.-Thurs. and Sat.-Sun. 9am-5pm, Mon. and Fri. 9am-4pm. Admission 5kčs, students 2.50kčs.)

Josefov, the traditional Jewish quarter around Pařížská and U starého hřbitova, lost much of its population to Nazi death camps during World War II, when it was emptied and used for storage. What remains can be seen in the scattered buildings of the **Státní Židovské Muzeum** (State Jewish Museum), Jáchymova 3, which includes five synagogues, a cemetery, and a collection of Jewish artifacts from Bohemia and Moravia. Hitler ordered that these relics of Judaica be preserved for an intended museum of the extinct Jewish race, whose exhibits would have been complete with Slavic museum guides dressed up as Jews. A unique collection of children's drawings and poems from the wartime Terezin ghetto also survives. (Open in summer Sun.-Fri. 9am-5pm; off-season 9am-4:30pm. Admission 5kčs, students 3kčs.) The fascinating underground **Staronová Synagogue** is the oldest in Europe; parts date from 1270. Succeeding generations have added up to twelve layers to the nearby **Jewish cemetery,** which now ripples with the layering of the 20,000 tombstones crowded within in its walls. Tours to **Terezin** concentration camp depart every Sunday and Thursday at 10am from the Jewish Town Hall, Maislova 18, and return at 3pm.

Karlův most (Charles Bridge) has been declared the best bridge in Europe, and it certainly rivals the most festive. Tourists, artisans, classical guitarists and other street musicians fill the bridge day and night and overlook a bevy of swans. Look for the legendary hero Jan Nepomuk, arrested in marble as he is thrown from the bridge for guarding his queen's confidences, and for the French noblemen frozen in the act of rescuing despondent Christians from the Turks. Climb the Gothic **defense tower,** on the Malá Strana side, for the best view of Prague's red roofs, the bridge, and the river. (Open daily 10am-6pm. Admission 2kčs, students 1kčs.) **Slovanský ostrov** (island) and the larger **Střelecky ostrov** (accessible from most 1 Máje) offer soothing shade. On the Old Town side of the bridge, you can see where to rent rowboats on the Vltava (15kčs per ½ hr.).

The **Malá Strana** (Lesser Town) is rich in palaces, ornate gardens, and grand baroque churches. The grandest of all is certainly **St. Nicholas's Church,** built by the Jesuits in the 18th century and considered the highest achievement of Czech baroque art. Mozart played the church organ here. (Open daily 9am-6pm.) Nearby on Karmelitská rises the more modest **Church of Our Lady Victorious,** repository of the world-famous statue of the Infant Jesus of Prague. The statue is reputed to have miraculous powers, and has been replicated the world over. A modest gate on Letenská (off Malostranské nám.) opens onto the **Valdštejnská zahrada** (Wallenstein Garden), one of Prague's best-kept secrets. This tranquil 17th-century baroque garden, adorned with frescoes and statues, is enclosed by old buildings that glow golden on sunny afternoons. Concerts are held here during the summer. (Open May-Sept. daily 9am-7pm.) If you poke around, you'll come upon still more hidden gardens. Five are open to the public in this part of town. Venture, for example, through the gate at Karmelitská 25 into petal paradise.

You can spend entire days wandering about the edifices that comprise the **Pražský hrad** (Prague Castle), on Nerudova. All the styles of architecture that have made Prague so astonishingly beautiful are well represented here. The castle itself houses the **Národní Galerie** (National Gallery), which contains an excellent collection of woodcuts and paintings, including works by Dürer and Breughel. (Open Tues.-Sun. 10am-6pm.) The **Katedrála sv. Vita** (St. Vitus' Cathedral) took 600 years to build; it was not completed until the 1930s. The brilliance and purity of the massive stained-glass windows are astounding, and the tombstones inside are nothing short of mesmerizing. To the right of the high altar stand Christ and four angels, a 3m-high baroque bonanza of glistening silver. Nearby, the **Starý královský palác** (Old Royal Palace) offers a bodacious buffet of Gothic design. Higher up is a tiny street carved into the fortified wall, **Zlatá ulička** (Golden Lane), where the court alchemists supposedly toiled. Kafka wrote for a time in 1917 at #21, now a tiny bookstore. (Buildings open Tues.-Sun. 9am-5pm; Oct.-March Tues.-Sun. 9am-4pm. Admission to each building 2kčs, students 1kčs. Golden Lane free. For more information on the entire complex, go to the Informační středisko behind the cathedral.)

The **Petřínské sady,** gardens on the hills to the south, are dominated by a model of the Eiffel Tower (admission 1kčs). A funicular to the top (1kčs) leaves from just above the intersection of Vítězná and Újezd. Not far from the station at the top is a wacky little castle offering juvenile bliss—a hall of mirrors. (Open daily 9am-6pm. Admission 2kčs, students 1kčs.) Just east of the park lies **Strahov Stadium,** the world's largest. Take on Central Europe's best on the tennis and basketball courts. The **Múzeum Mozart,** Mozartova 169, is housed in Villa Bertramka, an old but beautifully restored farmhouse where Mozart lived in 1787. (Open Tues.-Fri. 2-5pm, Sat.-Sun. 10am-noon and 2-5pm.)

A half-hour walk south of Nové Město is the quiet fortress **Vyšehrad,** Czechoslovakia's most revered landmark, delightfully free of tourists, and the view of Prague is extraordinary. On the mount above the river, the fortress encompasses a Neo-Gothic church, a Romanesque rotunda, and the Vyšehrad Cemetery. (Complex open 24 hr.) Take tram #3, 17, or 21, or Metro C to Vyšehrad. The subway stop is a sight itself, with a movie-sweep vista of Prague.

Entertainment

Václavské náměstí thumps with numerous dancespots, but the best way to enjoy Prague at night is to head to a *pivnice* or a *vinárna.* Prague is especially sweet when merrily stumbled through. Not that *Let's Go* condones that sort of thign. Thing.

U sv. Tomáše, Letenská 12. Around the corner from the U Schnellů restaurant. Originally founded as a brewery in 1358 by swinging monks on the grounds of their monastary, this *pivnice* serves possibly Prague's best beer—no small feat.

U Fleků, Křemencova 11. Look for the huge clock at the entrance. Another contender for the title of Prague's best brew; also Prague's answer to the German beer house, with live music, an outdoor garden, homebrewed brown ale, and intimate seating for 1000. It's amazing how quickly strangers become friends here. Open daily 9am-11pm.

Scene A, under the weeping willow tree on the Old Town side of Charles Bridge. With its West European sophistication and expensive drinks (gin and tonic 20kčs), resembles Paris more than Prague. Good jazz in the back theatre, but Mozart takes over on Sunday nights in spring.

Reduta, Národní 20. A good jazz club with live music nightly and a clientele of artists drowning in tourists. Cover 25kčs. Open daily 9pm-midnight.

Rock Club, next to the Reduta. Live music every night until 3am. Cover 20kčs.

Café Slavia, Národní and Smetanovo nábřeží, opposite the National Theatre. Smoky hangout of literati, punks, and the theater crowd. Open daily 8am-midnight.

U Kalicha, Na bojišti 12. Serves 1st-rate Pilsner Urquell beer. This classic Czech pub is immortalized in Jaroslav Hašek's *The Good Soldier Schweik.* Open daily 11am-11pm.

Every year from mid-May to early June, the **Prague Spring Festival** draws musicians from all over the world; outdoor concerts animate courtyards all over the city. Tickets (15-80kčs) can be bought at **Sluna,** Panská 4, Černá ruže Arcade (tel. 22 12 06). For a list of exhibits, concerts, museums, and films, pick up a copy of *The Month in Prague* at Prague Information Service or Pragotur, and, in summer, the monthly brochure *Prague Cultural Summer.* The star tourist attraction is the **Laterna Magika,** Národní 40 (tel. 26 00 33). The clever integration of film, drama, and dance might be a little too cute for some, but the show regularly attracts a large international audience. (Performances Mon.-Fri. at 8pm, Sat. at 5pm and 8pm. Tickets 25-35kčs. Box office open Mon.-Fri. 10am-noon and 2-6pm, Sat. 2-6pm. Often sold out in summer 2 weeks in advance.)

Near Prague

The Central Bohemian hills surrounding Prague backdrop 14 castles, some built as early as the 13th century. A 45-minute train ride from Prague brings you to **Karlštejn,** a walled and turreted fortress built by the inestimable Charles IV to house his crown jewels and holy relics. The **Chapel of the Holy Cross** is decorated with over 2000 inlaid precious stones and 128 apocalyptic paintings by medieval artist Master Theodorik. Trains cart gawkers half-hourly from Praha-Smíchov station (Metro: Smíchovské nádraži). Or horseback ride here (DM35); contact the Hucul Club Riding Centre (tel. 52 83 13; open Fri.-Wed. 9am-5pm). There is a campground nearby, on the left bank of the River Berounka.

Animal-rights activists might wish to avoid **Konopiště,** in Benešov (bus from Praha-Florenc station), a Renaissance palace with a luxurious interior preserved from the days when Archduke Franz Ferdinand bagged game here—over 300,000 animals. Fittingly, the **Weapons Hall** contains one of the finest collections of 16th- through 18th-century European arms.

An hour and a half southeast of Prague by bus is the former mining town of **Kutná Hora.** Soon after a silver vein was struck here in the 13th century, a royal mint—**Vlašský dvůr**—was established to produce the Prague groschen (silver coin). The mint itself contains an uninteresting coin museum with commentary written entirely in Czech, but up the stairs from the courtyard is a magnificent **Gothic Hall** with frescoes and lovely carved wooden tryptychs. The most convincing evidence of the wealth that once flowed through the town is the fantastic, begargoyled **Cathedral of St. Barbara,** built to rival St. Vitus' in Prague. Buses leave nearly hourly from Prague's Metro: Želivského, platform #2.

Western Bohemia

Bohemia, comprising the western third of Czechoslovakia with Prague at its center, is the traditional homeland of the Czech people. But common Slav heritage and a shared enemy in the Slovaks to the south have done little to prevent the Bohemians from squabbling amongst themselves, as the hundreds of prickly castles guarding former feudal principalities attest. Essential to a Bohemian itinerary are the springs of **Karlovy Vary** (Karlsbad in German), whose guest list is a roster of the 19th-century poor and misunderstood. Goethe, Schiller, Tolstoy, Gogol, Beethoven, Metternich, and even Marx sampled the waters here. Its fabled origin is traceable to Charles IV who, on a hunting expedition in 1347, discovered the spring of Vřídlo when his dog fell in and was scalded. Charles, an aficionado of Italian health cures, constructed baths on the spot. People still throng to the town to attempt to cure their ailments and to enjoy the air of Victorian luxury and grandeur. Every little tappet draws from a different spring, each with its own documented, supposedly curative minerals. To be safe, try them all, or better yet, fill your canteen. Libation from the "thirteenth spring" is a potent liqueur with a pastoral aftertaste called *Becherovka,* made from herbs and Karlovy Vary water. A fitting accompaninment to all Karlovy Vary ritual are the circular *oplatký* wafers which resemble 7" beer coasters; they taste divine plain or chocolate-covered.

The river Teplá winds through the town like an upside-down question mark. On the banks behind the modern thermal sanatorium is a public thermal pool (open daily 2-9pm). The many-pillared **Colonnade of Czechoslovak-Soviet Friendship** (known as the **Mill Colonnade)** contains a few thermal faucets. BYO cup, or buy one in a souvenir shop. The heart of Karlovy Vary is the **Yuri Gagarin Colonnade,** with its gushing 12-meter fountain. Try the faucet's scalding water. The **Baroque Church of Mary Magdalene** overlooks the colonnade. The **Diana Funicular Railway** zooms hourly up to **Diana Tower** and an inexpensive restaurant at the top, as do hiking paths. Trails appear on the Karlovy Vary city map, available in bookstores. The **White Russian Orthodox Church** on Gottwaldova glitters with gold.

The cheapest place to stay in Karlovy Vary is the attractive **Junior Hotel Alice (IYHF)** at ul. Pětiletky 147 (tel. (017) 248 48). Set amid the oaks and squirrels, the hotel is a 3km hike out of town, but the walk is lovely. From the city bus station (near the market), take bus #7 about nine stops. Reserve in advance. (Members and ISIC holders in 3-bed rooms 180kčs, nonmembers in singles 480kčs.) For B hotels, Čedok recommends reserving three to four months in advance, although the hotels listed below often have rooms available. One **Čedok** is 3 blocks east of the bus station at the corner of Dimitrovova and Moskevská. The **Čedok** closest to the waters, at Karla IV 1 (tel. (017) 261 10; take bus #13) books private rooms (doubles 400kčs). (Open Mon.-Fri. 9am-5pm, Sat. 9am-noon; Oct. to mid-May Mon.-Fri. 9am-4pm, Sat. 9am-noon.) **"W"** (tel. (017) 277 68), on nám. Republiky, near the bus station, also books private rooms (DM20-30; open Mon.-Sat. 10am-6pm).

Four hotels huddle within five minutes of the main bus station. Around the corner is **Hotel Adria,** Koněvova 1 (tel. (017) 237 65; singles DM27, doubles DM39; hard currency only). **Hotel Turist,** Dimitrovova 18 (tel. (017) 268 37), toward the town center, is the cheapest. (Doubles 400kčs.) **Down** the street, **Hotel Jizena,** Dimitrovova 7, (tel. (017) 250 20) charges DM38 **per** person. On the street parallel to the north is **Hotel Národní dům,** Československé armády 24 (tel. (017) 233 86; singles DM21, doubles DM31). The milk bar and the restaurant across from Čedok on Tržiště serve tasty, inexpensive food, as does the Fortuna Restaurant at Zámecký vrch 14.

Five hours speedier than the train, the bus is your ticket from Prague to Karlovy Vary (2½ hr., 48kčs). Buses leave Praha-Florenc every few hours, but buy the tickets, which sell out, 2 or 3 days in advance. In Karlovy Vary, hop off at the city bus center, near the farmers' market.

Mariánské Lázně (Marienbad in German), 40km south of Karlovy Vary (2 hr. by mountain train, 8kčs), is another spa popular among ailing European gentry and their raucous offspring. The town is a stately park, designed and landscaped by the ingenious Václav Skalník. It was here also that Goethe expressed his love for the beautiful Ulrika von Levetzow in the *Marienbader Elegie.* At the Maxim Gorki Colonnade, the faucets go on and off magically when you wave your hand over them. There is a fountain concert every hour.

The **Čedok** office is located in the Hotel Evropa on Třesbílského (tel. (0165) 25 00), in the center of town; take bus #5 from the station and get off at the sixth stop. Easily the finest pad is CKM's beautiful **Junior Hotel Krakonoš (IYHF)** (tel. (0165) 26 24), 5km southeast of town in a gorgeous wooded location. From the train station, take bus #5 six stops to the Hotel Excelsior and then bus #12 to the top of the mountain (Members and ISIC holders 180kčs, nonmembers 480kčs; reserve in advance). There is camping beside the Junior Hotel (May-Sept.). Several B-category hotels line the main street (singles 350-400kčs, doubles 500-600kčs). You'll have the most luck securing lodgings either early in the morning or shortly after 5pm (sometimes 6pm), when people with reservations don't show up. Picnic fixings and hotel restaurants are fairly similar in price and setting (full meals 60-100kčs).

The restaurant **Koliba,** on the corner of the corner of Dusíkova and Karlovarská, serves Orson Welles-sized portions for 60-80kčs. Mariánské Lázně is on the Prague-Nuremberg rail line. Express trains come hither from Prague's main station (3 per day, 3½ hr., 100kčs).

Plzeň, 80km southwest of Prague, is immortalized as the birthplace of beer and as the source of *Plzeňsky Prazdroj* (Pilsner Urquell), arguably the best brew in the world. If you find beer compelling, reserve accommodations well in advance, as 1992 is Plzeň's 700th birthday. Improve the industrial view with several rounds of the town's best at the **Pivnice Prazdroj,** U Prazdroja 1 (tel. (019) 356 08), right outside the brewery gates. Say "Prazdroj" and people will point you in the right direction. To spend the night (in a hotel, not a bar), contact **Čedok,** at the corner of Sedláckova and Arešovská (tel. (019) 366 48; open Mon.-Fri. 9am-noon and 1-6pm, Sat. 9am-noon.) The **Hotel Plzeň,** Žižkova 66 (tel. (019) 27 26 56), offers doubles for 746kčs. Take streetcar #1 or 4 from the center of town. The **Bíla Hora autocamping** (tel. (019) 356 11) has bungalows for 450kčs per person. Take bus #20 5km north of town. (Open May-Sept.) Plzeň lies conveniently on the Prague-Munich line; alternatively, it's two hours and 48kčs from Mariánské Lázně.

Southern Bohemia

České Budějovice, the cultural and administrative center of South Bohemia, earned its fame as the original home of **Budvar** (Budweiser) beer. Founded in 1265 as a royal town at the confluence of the rivers Vltava and Malše, České Budějovice grew fat in the 16th century and then thinned out during the Thirty Years War. The Budějovice to Linz horse-drawn railway was the first in Europe.

The center is **nám. Jana Žižky,** one of the largest squares in Europe, flanked by pastel Renaissance and Baroque houses and overlooked by the 72m **Black Tower,** which rewards a hefty climb with a nifty view (open Tues.-Sun. 10am-6pm). Once Gothic, St. Nicholas's Cathedral received a baroque facelift during 1641-1649.

Čedok, in the southwest corner of nám. Jana Žižky (tel. (038) 380 56), changes money, but does little else. (Open Mon.-Fri. 9am-5pm, Sat. 9am-noon.) **CKM,** Osvobození 14, may book hostels in July and Aug. With your back to Čedok, walk straight up 5 Května to **Švermovo nám.** past the river; the information kiosk in a red trailer across the road imparts detailed information in English (open Mon.-Fri. 9-11am and 2-6pm, Sat.-Sun. 9am-noon and 1-6pm). Midway you pass **Srba International Travel Service** at 5 Května 1 (tel. (038) 250 61). They sell a map (15kčs) and book private rooms all over South Bohemia. (Doubles 400-680kčs. Open Mon.-Fri. 2-8pm, Sat.-Sun. 9am-8pm.)

Lannova Tř. connects nám. Jana Žižky to the train station, across Nádražni from the bus station. **Hotel Malše** (tel. (038) 276 31; B-category), across from the station at Nádražní 31, charges Western prices for Eastern quality, although its wine cellar saves starving late arrivals. (Singles 380kčs. Doubles 500kčs. Showers 46kčs.) **Hotel Zvon,** nám. Jana Žižky 28 (tel. (038) 353 61; category A-B) requires hard currency. (Singles USD18.30. Doubles USD28.20.) The famous **Masné Kramy beer hall** crams tables into former Renaissance meat shops and is the most interesting spot in town for people-watching (open daily 9am-10pm). On the other end of 5 Května, **U Železne Panny** offers as much ambience and far better food, including fish specialties. (Entrees 13-25kčs. Open Mon.-Sat. 9am-10pm.)

From Prague, buses run almost hourly to České Budějovice (3 hr., 48kčs). České Budějovice makes a superb springboard for visits to nearby towns such as becastled Český Krumlov, Tábor, Jindřichuv Hradec, and Třeboň. Many Czechs come to České Budějovice to visit the fairy-tale palace of **Hluboká nad Vltavou,** 12km to the north. Several buses per day make the trip. (Open Tues.-Sun. 8am-noon and 1-5pm.)

Brno

Midway between Prague and Bratislava on the rail line, Brno is the third-largest city in Czechoslovakia and the political and cultural capital of Moravia, the wine-making eastern half of the Czech Republic. If you can only squeeze in one Czecho-slovak metropolis besides Prague, make it this one.

To find the principal sights, simply look up. The **Cathedral of Sts. Peter and Paul and Mary** rears above the city in a kaleidoscope of stained-glass. Atop the hill, the **Špilberk Castle** fell to both Napoleon and Hitler; the latter used it as SS headquarters and executed over 80,000 prisoners in the castle's dungeons. The 41 mummified bodies of the **Capuchin Cloisters** repose in Kapucínské nám. downhill from the cathedral. (Admission 4kčs, students 2kčs.) Across the street is the **Reduta Theater,** where the 11-year-old Mozart conducted in 1767. **Nám. Zelný trh** hosts the daily **produce market** and the **Dietrichstein Palace,** which holds the Moravian History Museum (admission 8kčs, students 4kčs). Buy theater tickets (19-30kčs) at Předprodej, Dvořáka 11, I. Poshodi.

The Čedok office across the street from the train station sells maps (15kčs) but refers inquiries to the **Čedok** office for foreigners, Divadelní 3 (tel. (05) 231 79; open Mon.-Fri. 9am-6pm, Sat. 9am-noon). To reach this office from the train station, walk across the street and up **Masarykova,** the main street which bisects the old city. When you see **nám. Zelný trh,** head right onto Orli and walk to the end. (Masarykova continues ahead to **nám. Svobody,** the main square.) The office books hotels and private accommodations (3-day min. stay; singles 300kčs, doubles 500-700kčs). If you arrive during July or August, inquire at **CKM,** Česká 11, on a major street running from the northeastern corner of nám. Svobody. Their four summer **hostels** probably have room (70-90kčs; office open Mon.-Fri. 10am-noon and 2pm-6pm, Sat. 10am-noon). The cheapest hotel is the C-category **Společenský dům,** Horova 30, (tel. (05) 74 41 85). Coast about 8 stops on tram #10 from Husova street, which comprises the western boundary of old town. (Singles 340kčs. Doubles 570kčs.) More central is **Hotel Evropa** (tel. (05) 266 21; B-category), one block before nám. Svobody at the intersection of Jánská and Masarykova. (Singles 365kčs. Doubles 730kčs. Breakfast included.) **Hotel Astoria** is at Novobranska 3, near Čedok's office for foreigners. (Singles 540kčs. Doubles 770kčs.) For big food, sample from ubiquitous stand-up buffets such as **Pipi Grill** on nám. Svobody. The popular **M-klub,** at Pekařská 3 beneath the cathedral, is an ultra-swanky establishment with bar and wine cellar. (Open Tues.-Thurs. and Sat. noon-11pm, Fri. noon-midnight.) A pizzeria by day, the **Galerie Grill,** on Smetanova off Veverí, metamorphoses into a major student hang-out and *vinárna* at night. (Personal pizza, glass of wine, and a coffee 40-50kčs).

Just 20km from Brno are the stalagmites and stalactites of the **Moravian Kras** (caves), and the Macacha Abyss (take the bus to Blansko).

The Slovak Republic

While political tensions rose to the boiling point in Yugoslavia in July 1991, the world watched Czechoslovakia out of the corner of its eye. Slovakia, always under the rule of such outside powers as Hungary and the USSR, has never been an independent state save for a brief period as a Nazi protectorate in WWII. Impatient nationalistic rumblings often sound in Bratislava, tired of being outshadowed by Prague. Such discontent fades as one approaches the lush green forests and jagged rock faces of northern Slovakia. The region shares its most spectacular gem, the Tatry Mountains, with Poland, its neighbor to the north, and a little bit of Polish goes a long way in Slovakia.

Bratislava

The view from Castle Hill says it all. An old city, sliced in half by a multi-lane highway and marred by an industrial skyline, Bratislava is the victim of rampant modernization at the hands of the Communists. Row after row of identical apartment blocks crams the opposite bank of the Danube river in Petržalka, yet another suburban vision gone sour. Despite such scars, Bratislava clings to its heritage. Capital of Hungary for three centuries, the city now serves as the capital of the Slovak Federal Republic and is Czechoslovakia's second largest city. Slovak nationalism thrives here, doing its best to take the Czech out of Czechoslovakia.

Orientation and Practical Information

Bratislava lies on the banks of the Danube, a proverbial stone's throw from the Austrian and Hungarian borders. Trains and buses connect the city with Budapest (143km) and Vienna (64km), with hydrofoils also serving Vienna. Traveling by rail to Prague (6 hr.), sometimes requires a change at Brno. Avoid debarking at the Nové Mesto train station, which is much farther from the center than Bratislava's *hlavná stanica* (main station).

The Danube runs west-to-east across Bratislava. The old town, with its cluster of tourist offices and restaurants, sits just north of the river bank, bordered by the **Staromestská** highway to the west, **námestie SNP** to the north, **Štúrova** to the east, and **Hviezdoslavovo námestie** to the south. To reach the old town from the train station, take tram #13. Buy a batch of tickets (3kčs) for the tram from the orange automat machines (strewn throughout town near tram stops). The green-and-orange *mapa mesta* (27kčs), explicates Bratislava's tram routes and tourist destinations in five languages.

Tourist Offices: BIPS, Laurinská 1 (tel. 33 37 15, 33 43 25, or 33 43 70). Speaks excellent English and provides information on youth hostels and cultural events. Open Mon.-Fri. 8am-6pm, Sat. 8am-1pm; Oct.-May Mon.-Fri. 8am-4:30pm, Sat. 8am-1pm. **Čedok,** Jesenského 5 (tel. 526 45 or 526 24). The only Čedok serving foreigners. Currency exhange, help with accommodations (but no private rooms), international tickets, and general information. Take tram #13 from the train station. Open Mon.-Fri. 9am-6pm, Sat. 9am-noon. Train tickets Mon.-Fri. 9am-4pm.

Currency Exchange: At any Čedok, fancy hotel, or at the **VÚB** (Všeobecna Úverová Bank).

Post Office: At nám. SNP 35. Poste Restante. Enter by the side door. Open Mon.-Fri. 7am-9pm, Sat. 7am-5pm, Sun. 9am-2pm.

Telephones: Kolárska 12. Open 24 hrs. **City Code:** 07.

Trains: Tel. 469 45. **ČSD Hlavná stanica,** the main station, is at the northern end of town off Malinovského. To Prague (4 per day, 6 hr., 122 kčs), Budapest (6 per day, 3 hr., 237 kčs), and Vienna (4 per day, 1 hr., 203kčs). International tickets at counter #8 or 9.

Buses: ČSAD Autobusová stanica, at Mlynské nivy (tel. 632 13 or 21 22 22). Take bus #215 or 220 to the town center. To Prague (11 per day, 124kčs), Budapest (1 per day), and Vienna (4 per day, USD6). Check Vienna ticket for bus number *(č. aut.)*, since a whole fleet leaves simultaneously at departure time.

Hydrofoils: ČSPD, on the river bank next to Slovak National Musem. To Vienna (7am daily, 1¼ hr., USD14).

Hitchhiking: Those hitching to Vienna cross the SNP bridge and walk down Viedenská cesta. The same road takes you to Hungary via Györ, though fewer cars head in that direction. Those headed to Prague take bus #104 from the center up Pražská to the Patronka stop.

Pharmacy (Lekárĕn): 3 Špitálska 3. Open 24 hrs.

Emergencies: Police (tel. 158). Station at Mestskásprava VB, Špitálska 14 (tel. 593 41 or 531 71). **Ambulance** (tel. 155).

Accommodations and Camping

Bratislava is hopping with student accommodations, largely due to the Vienna-bound crowds in the summer. **Uniatour,** on Leškova 5 (tel. 439 67), an infant tourist company run by Slovak students, books the cheapest rooms, from July to August, at the **Mladá Garda** hostel at Račianska cesta 103 (70 kčs, students 60kčs). BIPS and **CKM,** at Hviezdoslavovo nám. 16 (tel. 33 16 07; Mon. and Wed. 9am-6pm, Tues., Thurs., and Fri. 9am-4pm, Sat. 9:30am-12:30pm) also direct you to inexpensive summer dorms, with maps to boot.

Youth Hostel Bernolak (BIPS), Bernolákova 1 (tel. 580 18). Look for the posters at the bus and train stations; from either, take trolleybus #210 to Račianske mýto intersection and follow the posters. High-rise student dorm only 15 min. walk from old town. Doubles 280kčs, with ISIC 240kčs. Triples 360kčs, with ISIC 285kčs. Open July-Aug.

Mladost (BIPS), Asmolovova 53 (tel. 72 12 03). Take bus #39 from Račianske mýto or downtown to last stop, then follow the red footprints marked "elam" to the main dorm. 140kčs; 90kčs after staying three nights. Open July-Aug.

YMCA na Slovensku, Karpatska 2 (tel. 49 73 42). Call for directions. Reception open 8am-11pm. DM5. Open mid-July to mid-Aug.

Ustav vzdelávania ve stavebnictve, Bárdošova 33 (tel. 37 52 12). Ride tram #44 three stops from train station to Bárdošova; hike up to the 3-story white and glass building with the hotel name on top. This academic residence moonlights as a hotel, providing cheap, comfortable beds in the suburbs. Uphill climb and it may be full, so park your bags first. Doubles with bath 300kčs. Triples 450kčs.

Youth Hostel CKM (IYHF), Ružinovská 1 (tel. 22 04 41, ext. 56). Has maps plastered all over bus and train stations. Take bus #22 or 24 to Račianske mýto, then bus #54 to sixth stop. Drab grey dorm with simple rooms but eager management. 150kčs; for nonmembers, singles 410kčs, doubles 600kčs, triples 780kčs.

Juniorhotel Sputnik CKM (IYHF), ul. Drieňová 14 (tel. 23 43 40). Take tram #8 from the train station to the 8th or 9th stop and look for a small lake on your left. Across it lies the hotel. Deluxe student lodging year-round with disco, café, and restaurant. Members and ISIC holders 180kčs per person. For nonmembers, singles 570kčs, doubles 900kčs. Reservations recommended. English spoken.**Hotel Krym,** Šafárikovo nám. 6 (tel. 554 71; B-category). Off Štúrova, three blocks north of the Danube.

Motel Zlaté Piesky, ul. Vajnorská (tel. 651 70 or 660 28), in suburban Trnávka. Take tram #2, 4, or 10, then bus #32 for three stops. Campground and bungalows down by the lakeside, way out of town. Try hotels instead.

Food

Bratislavans grow up on grilled meats and Slovak wine. Denný bars, offering an array of salads, sandwiches, and other ready-to-eat foods, are everywhere. For groceries, go to the huge **Prior** department store complex downtown.

Slovanské Reštauracie, Štúrova 3. In the arcade next to the large "Luxor" self-service restaurant sign. Dandy food and delicious soups (5-12kčs). The heaping Slovak platters for two are a steal (96-158kčs). Ask for the English menu. Open Mon.-Fri. 11am-3pm and 5:30-10pm, Sat. 11am-4pm.

Perugia Reštauracie, Ventúrska, in the old town. A pleasantly airy dining room serving more-than-affordable dishes (16-40kčs). Open Mon.-Sat. 11am-10pm.

Čajovňa-Bistro Flauta, next door to Perugia. Mediterranean tearoom with a feel for wicker, palms, and railed balconies in the courtyard. Open daily.

Stará Sladovňa, Cintorínska 32. 15 minutes northeast of old town. An old malt house reincarnated as a boisterous beer hall. Occasional live music and dancing on the top floor. Meals from 60kčs. Open daily 10am-10pm.

Arkadia, Beblavého 3 (tel. 33 56 50), next to the castle gate. Top drawer elegance on the top of Castle Hill. Open noon-3pm and 4-11pm.

Sights and Entertainment

The imperial residences of the **Bratislavský hrad** (Bratislava Castle) burned during the Napoleonic Wars and were resurrected only after World War II. The castle now houses the Slovak National Assembly and the principal branch of the **Mestské Múzeum** (City Museum). For a crash course in 20th-century Slovak history, art and culture, visit the third floor. (Open Tues.-Sun. 9am-5pm. Admission 40kčs, students with ISIC 6kčs.) From Castle Hill, **ul. Zámocká** leads across the highway to the **Staré Mesto** (Old Town) and **St. Martin's Cathedral,** the early Gothic coronation site of Hungarian monarchs, and publisher of early Crusader editions of *Let's Go: The Holy Land.* The **Mirbach Palace,** at Františkánske nám. 11, houses the Municipal Art Gallery, with temporary exhibits of modern Slovak paintings and a beautiful series of 17th-century English tapestries. Take time to listen to the recorded description of the tapestries' mysterious appearance in Bratislava. (Open Tues.-Sun. 9am-5pm. Admission 6kčs, students 2kčs.) The baroque **Old Town Hall,** at Primalciálne nám. 1, hosts a museum of Bratislava's history. The best-preserved section of the town wall is the **Michalská veža,** a baroque tower metalled with weapons. The **Franciscan Church,** at Františkánske nám. 1, is an impossibly harmonious hybrid of Gothic, Renaissance, and baroque styles.

For concert and theatre schedules, pick up a copy of *Kám* (3kčs) at BIPS. Although not in English, the information is easy enough to decipher.

The High Tatras (Vysoké Tatry)

Mountains throw their powerful shadows over much of Czechoslovakia's frontier. Rearing over the **Nízké Tatry** (Low Tatras) to the south, the **Malá Fatra** (Little Fatra) to the west, and the Matras Mountains across the Hungarian border is the **Vysoké Tatry** (High Tatras) range. A scant 26km long, it is the most compact high mountain range in the world. The dizzying ridges conceal a hundred and fifty glacial lakes *(pleso),* and the forests harbor deer, bear, and edelweiss. Two indispensable maps are *Vysoké Tatry 21* (10kčs), indicating hiking trails, and the street map *Tatranské Strediská* (Centers of the High Tatras, 7kčs).

Poprad-Tatry is the springboard for the main rail system to the High Tatras. The city is a frequent stop for trains running from Košice to Prague (3 per day, 8 hr.) or Bratislava (10 per day, 5 hr.). The same trains also stop in Žilina, 2 hr. west of Poprad-Tatry.

Right outside the train and bus stations, across from the Hotel Europa, the narrow-gauge Tatras Electric Railway (TEŽ) train runs to **Starý Smokovec,** the administrative and transportation center of the Tatras (6am-5:30pm 2 per hr., 2-6am and 5:30-10:30pm 1 per hr.; ½hr.; 7kčs). The bright red trains also connect Starý Smokovec with woodsier **Tatranská Lomnica** (10 min., 4kčs) and the swankier ski resort of **Štrbské Pleso** (50 min., 7kčs) every half hour (5am-10:30pm). If travelling directly from Poprad-Tatry, buy a through ticket even if you change at Starý Smokovec. Save coins to use the automat machines when ticket windows close.

Starý Smokovec

A thriving Tatras settlement for 200 years, Starý Smokovec is a tourist hub for every season. A prodigious funicular (from 6am-7:45pm, 2 per hr., 10kčs) leads up to the ski resort **Hrebienok** (1285m), where a ski path wends its way along the green trail back to town. An easy 20-minute hike from Hrebienok leads to the foaming *Studenovodské vodopada* (waterfall). Continue downhill along the blue trail through towering pines to Tatranská Lomnica (1½hr.), or face the challenge of the 6km **Vel'ka Studená dolina** (Big Cold Valley) leading to the **Zbojnicka Chalet** (3 hr.) in the opposite direction on the blue trail. The green trail passes through **Malá Studená dolina** (Little Cold Valley) and rises in steep terraces to Téryho Chalet (3 hr.). The region's principal trail, the red *Magistrála* route, also winds past Hrebienok along the southern face of the High Tatras, reaching its highest point at a mountain saddle below Mt. Svišt'ovka (2020m).

Back in town just above the train station, **Čedok** provides hiking information, books hotels, and can do it in English. (Open Mon.-Fri. 8am-6pm, Sat. 8-12:30pm.) Any private rooms (100-150kčs) are in Nová Lesná, near Poprad, and not worth the hassle. Čedok books beds at their four mountain chalets (205-240kčs). The other four mountain huts and **Hotel Bystrina** (near the ski lift) are handled exclusively by **Slovakoturist,** down the main road and past Hotel Sport. The cheapest accommodation is the **CKM Juniorhotel Vysoké Tatry (IYHF)** in Horný Smokovec, two stops on the way to Tatranská Lomnica (tel. (0969) 26 61; ISIC and IYHF cardholders 100kčs, nonmembers 140kčs per person). Reservations two months in advance are recommended. The B-category **Tatra Hotel** (formerly Udernik, as the maps on every street refer to it) is next to the Bistro beyond Čedok. (Singles 392kčs. Doubles 588kčs.) The nearest campground is **Tatracamp,** 3km away down the road or rail line to Poprad, but it may be full, so try the camps near Tatranská Lomnica instead.

The **grocery store** next to Čedok (open Mon.-Fri. 8am-6pm, Sat. 8am-1pm) and department store sell hiking paraphernalia. The stand-up **bistro** next to Čedok vends sandwiches, tasty salads, and milk. (Open Mon.-Fri. 7am-1pm and 2-5pm, Sat. 7am-1pm.) Get out of the woods and into elegance at the 4-star **Grand Hotel,** a remnant of turn-of-the-century majesty.

Tatranská Lomnica

High above Tatranská Lomnica, a monster ski-lift runs like a prickly spine up Lomnický Štít (2632m), the runner-up peak in Czechoslovakia. From the train station, plow straight ahead and follow the signs for 15 minutes to "Kabinova lanovka Skalnaté Pleso." (Open Tues.-Sun. 7am-8pm. 25kčs.) Beat the line stretching out to the parking lot and get there early. A less convenient option is to walk 20 minutes to the 4-star **Grandhotel Prague** and take the 30-seat banana tram (Wed.-Mon. 7am-10pm every 20 min.). At Skalnaté Pleso, perambulate around pondlike Glacia Lake, or continue on the chairlift to Lomnický Sedla for a jaw-dropping view of the Tatra range (20kčs round-trip; open Tues.-Sun. 8am-5:30pm). A gutsier option is to take the impossibly vertical cabin lift to the top of the rocky peak itself (50kčs round-trip; open Tues.-Sun. 7:30am-5:30pm). Hikers can follow the red (Magistrála) or blue trail across the mountains. Back in town, the **Tatras National Park Museum** has exhibits on the natural history and human settlements of the area. (Open Mon.-Fri. 8am-noon and 1-5pm, Sat.-Sun. 8am-noon. Admission 6kčs.) **Mountain bike rental** is available at the Hotel Slovakia on the main road (full day 99kčs, ½ day 60kčs).

In 1991, **Hotel Lomnica** (tel. (0969) 96 72 51), across the tracks from the train station to the right, was the accommodations aficionado in town. (Doubles 581kčs, with bath 776kčs. Breakfast included.) The reception also books rooms at **Hotel Mier** (C-category), five minutes away in a venerable house with heaps of character (doubles 507kčs), and at the bare-bones, rustic **Chaty Kysuce** off the main road near the ski jumps (205kčs per person, breakfast included). **Čedok** is on the ground floor next to Hotel Lomnica. (Open Mon.-Fri. 9am-noon and 1-4pm.) Campers can catch a bus at the parking lot next to Hotel Lomnica to the humongous **Eurocamp FICC** (tel. (0969) 967 74 15; 55kčs per person and per tent; 4-person bungalows 1240kčs). The cheaper, but less fancy **Tatranec** is one bus stop earlier (tel. (0969) 96 77 04; 33kčs per person, 42kčs per tent; 6-person bungalow 677kčs).

The restaurant in the Hotel Lomnica serves inexpensive entrees (23-60kčs). **Piccolo Pizza,** near the train station, has developed a small American cult following. The **grocery store** across from the station stocks fresh bread and other essentials.

If you want to cross into Poland from the High Tatras, the only way is to take a bus from either Starý Smokovec or Tatranská Lomnica north to Łysa Polana (15 per day, 12kčs). The bus will drop you off in a parking lot right before the border. Walk across the bridge to have your passport stamped, then wait at the bus stop on the main road for either a private "mini-bus" (30 min., 6000zł), or a PKS bus (only every other hr.) to Zakopane, Poland. You won't mind the shuffle when you see the gorgeous mountain scenery along the way.

Malá Fatra

Smaller peaks and smaller crowds await just to the east of the High Tatras in the Malá Fatra (Little Fatra), where the Vrátna Valley wanders through an imposing canyon flanked by towering rock, and tiny villages cling to their lifeline, a road which winds up to the valley and its hiking trails.

The place for accommodations is Žilina, a drab but convenient pit-stop of a town. Looking from right to left with your back to the train station, you will spy the pricey **Hotel Polom** (B-star category; singles with bath 364kčs, doubles with bath 557kčs), **Hotel Metropol** (B-category; doubles 320kčs, showers 40kčs), and the bus station. The only restaurant in sight is also at the Hotel Polom (entrees 20-60kčs; open daily 6am-2am). To reach the old town from the train station, trudge 15 minutes on Slov. Nar. Povstania and up the steps past the cathedral to **nám. Dukla. CKM** (tel. (089) 235 18) is in the corner of the square on the right with no sign. (Open Mon., Wed., and Fri. 8:30am-4pm; Tues. and Thurs. 9am-5pm; Sat. 9am-noon.) With CKM on your right, turn left and walk across the square out of old town to **Čedok** (tel. (089) 230 93) on nám. V.I. Lenina. (Open Mon.-Fri. 9am-6pm, Sat. 9am-noon.)

Buses to the Vrátna valley leave from platform #10 in the bus station (16 per day, 6am-6:30pm; 1 hr.; 14kčs). Most buses stop in the village of Štefanová in the national park and are labeled "Vrátna ces Štefanová." The bus hits all the worthwhile stops within the park. The chairlift to Grúň Peak (989m; open 8:30am-7pm; 16kčs round-trip) floats through the green-tipped pines to a mountain chalet on a sleepy slope. The bus also stops at a large sign marking the road to the **Hotel Boboty,** and passes a campsite (16kčs per person and per tent). The end of the road in the park is the **Chata Vrátna** chalet and ski lift to Chleb Peak (1647m; open 7:30am-7pm; 22kčs round-trip; min. 20 people per run). Helpful rangers at the **Mountain Rescue Service** near the Grúň Peak lift struggle valiantly to explain the hiking options in English (tel. (089) 952 32; open daily 7am-7:30pm). Pick up the *Malá Fatra Vrátna 12* trail map and *Vrátna-Martinské hole* ski map here, at Chata Vrátna, or in metropolitan bookstores.

Košice

Capital of the country's easternmost provice (East Slovakia), faded Košice nevertheless boasts an old town studded with 460 historic buildings. Archeological finds in Košice document uninterrupted settlement back to the Paleolithic Age. In 1347, Košice became a free royal city and peaked in the 15th century as the third largest town in what was then Hungary; a gypsy flavor lingers today.

The old town stretches like an oval, bisected by what in 1991 was still called **Leninova.** From the train station (next to the bus station) cruise straight through the park onto Gen. Petrova to the **Cathedral of St. Elizabeth,** which dominates the center of the old town. This Gothic church has a peaceful, easy feeling; special stone from Ukraine makes it warm, too. Turn right (northwards on Leninova) for more points of interest. The **Art History Museum** on Leninova 40 exhibits works ranging from Romanesque to contemporary, and on nám. Maratonu Mieru at the northern end of the old town, the **East Slovak Museum** devotes itself to archaeology, prehistory, and precious gold coins. (Museums open Tues.-Sat. 9am-5pm, Sun. 9am-1pm; about 2kčs.) Concerts resonate in the **State Theater,** which was undergoing cosmetic surgery in 1991.

On the south end of Leninova, snuggling up to the 4-star Slovan Hotel, **Čedok** speaks English and changes money fluently. (Open Mon.-Fri. 9am-5pm, Sat. 9am-noon.) The comfy **Hotel Europa** is near the park on Protifašistických Bojovníkov

1 (B-category; tel. (095) 238 97). One block down on the right is **Hotel Imperial** (tel. (095) 221 46; B-star category; singles 419kčs, with bath 605kčs; doubles with bath 877kčs). **Hotel Centrum** beyond Slovan is not so steep (doubles 554kčs). For **Auto Camping Salas Barca,** take a streetcar south on trieda Sovietskej Armady from the Slovan Hotel to the overpass and walk west 500m. (Open April-Sept.) Treat yourself right in the 4-star **Hotel Slovan Restaurant,** where dozens of resplendent entrees are reasonably priced from 20-100kčs. (Open daily noon-3pm and 6-10pm.) Across from the State Theater, the **Kaviareň Stávia** on Leninova enhances its pub atmosphere with wooden booths, plush olive upholstery and a well-stocked bar. (Open Tues.-Sun. noon-10pm.) Take a left off Mlynská from the train station to **Ajvega,** Orlia 10, where vegetarians munch pear soup, soy entrees, and seed and coconut desserts (open daily 10am-midnight). The **open-air market** unfolds 1 block west of the cathedral at Dimitrovovo nám., near Hotel Imperial.

Košice is Eastern Europe's sleeper train hub, along most routes from Poland to Bulgaria and Romania, and near the halfway point of the 13-hr. Kraków-Budapest slog. Other connections to Budapest require a change at Miskolc. Two trains per day from Prague cross the Ukrainian border to L'viv (8 hr.) and Kiev (17 hr.) in Ukraine, and ultimately Moscow. Domestic service rolls to Prague (6 per day, 9 hr.); Bratislava (7 per day, 6 hr.); Poprad-Tatry (1½ hr.); and Žilina (2½ hr).

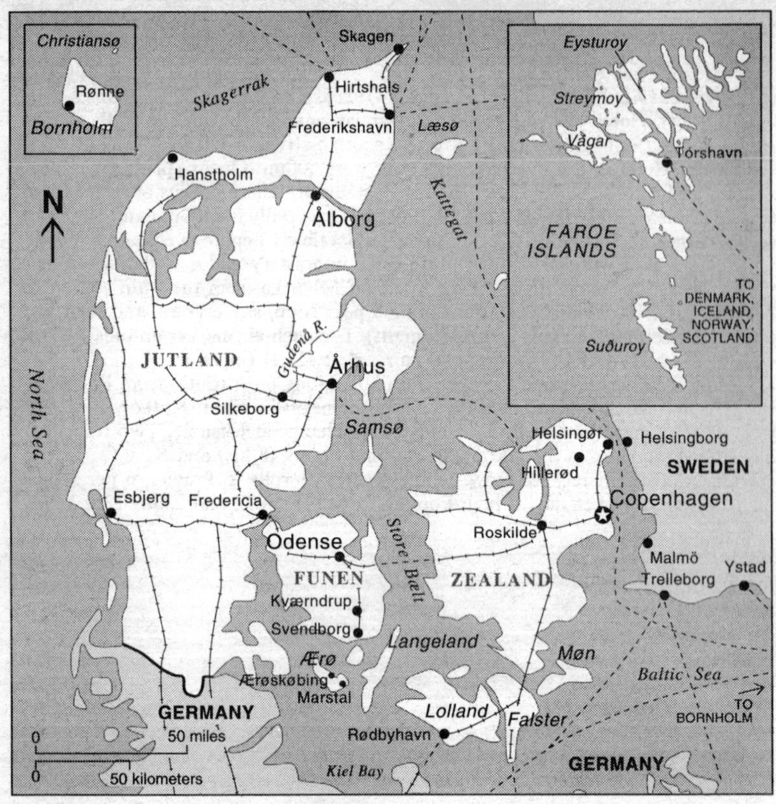

DENMARK

USD$1 = 6.77 kroner (kr, or DKK) — **1kr = USD$0.15**
CAD$1 = 5.92kr — **1kr = CAD$0.17**
GBP£1 = 11.3kr — **1kr = GBP£0.09**
AUD$1 = 5.27kr — **1kr = AUD$0.19**
NZD$1 = 3.86kr — **1kr = NZD$0.26**
Country Code: 45 — **International Dialing Prefix: 009**

The word "Dane" once struck fear into hearts all over Europe, but today the Vikings live only in tourist shops and brochures. On a short visit, Denmark (Danmark) seems such an overwhelmingly *good* country: the Danes (who rarely jaywalk) saved their Jews from the Nazis, invented Lego, spend tons of money on education, and make such wonderful ice cream. The only threat Denmark poses is its cuteness. To immunize yourself against the onslaught of Hans Christian Andersen knickknacks, peruse *The Present Age* by the wry Danish philosopher Søren Kierkegaard, and note that the conservative Danish government has curtailed the vast spending of the social-paradise days of the 1960s and 1970s. Denmark's foreign debt has stopped growing for the first time, but unemployment is rising (and the Social Democrats again say they're the only ones who know how to deal with it).

Under the Kalmar Union, lasting into the 16th century, the Danish crown ruled an empire of the northern sea, which united Norway, Sweden, Iceland, and parts of Germany. Strategically positioned at the northern tip of continental Europe,

Denmark was the bridge across which first Christianity, then the Protestant Reformation, and then the socialist movements of the late 19th century crossed into Scandinavia. Now Denmark's membership in the EC is infecting Sweden and Finland; cheap Euroimports have already made Denmark by far the least expensive country in Scandinavia.

Danes joke that if you stand on a carton of beer you can see from one end of the country to the other, but Denmark is neither quite that flat nor quite that small—especially when you consider that Greenland, the world's largest island, is Danish territory. Though Copenhagen may be Denmark at its most festive, save time for the sea breezes and snug farmhouses of the countryside, where Danes often enjoy their annual five-week vacations.

Getting There and Getting Around

Flat terrain, bike paths in the countryside and bike lanes in the towns and cities make Denmark a cyclist's paradise. Bicycles can be rented for 35-50kr per day from some tourist offices (not Copenhagen's), ubiquitous bicycle rental shops, and a few railway stations in North Zealand (Copenhagen, Helsingør, Hillerød, Klampenborg, and Lyngby). A 200kr deposit is ordinarily required. A system of free use of public bicycles within Copenhagen is planned for January 1992—check at the tourist office to see if it has gone into effect. For quality maps and tour information, contact the **Dansk Cyklist Forbund** (Danish Cycle Federation), Rømersgade 7, 1362 Copenhagen K (tel. 33 32 31 21; open May-July Mon.-Wed. and Fri. 9:30am-5pm, Thurs. 9:30am-7pm; Aug.-April Wed. 9:30am-3pm, Thurs. 9:30am-5pm). It's often possible to tote bicycles on the train; DSB, the national rail company, publishes a pamphlet with rules and prices.

A reliable network of trains *(tog),* buses, and ferries neatly links most points in Denmark. Eurail and InterRail passes are valid on all state-run DSB routes. The **Nordturist** pass, available at rail stations and DSB travel agencies, allows 21 days of unlimited rail travel throughout Denmark, Sweden, Norway, and Finland (second class 1690kr, ages 12-25 1260kr, under 12 845kr). It's much cheaper than the similar ScanRail pass sold in the USA. Seat reservations are compulsory on some trains, including the plush IC (Intercity) and all trains that cross on the ferries over the Store Bælt (the channel between the islands of Funen and Zealand). They cost 20-30kr and may require long waits, so you may want to stick to the seat-yourself IR and Re trains. Towns not on rail lines are often served by regional buses that stop at the nearest train station.

To reach Copenhagen by train from the rest of Denmark or from any other country you'll need to use at least one **ferry;** however, you may barely notice, since these ships are specially equipped with rails, and the trains just drive on and off. Trains from Odense cross from Nyborg to Kørsor, trains from Hamburg cross from Puttgarden to Rødby Færge, trains from Berlin from Warnemünde to Gedser, and trains from Stockholm from Helsingborg to Helsingør. Railpasses are also valid on the ferries from Hirtshals to Kristiansand in Norway, and Frederikshavn to Gothenburg in Sweden. The *Danmark Ferry Guide,* available at tourist offices, can help you sort out the dozens of smaller ferries that serve Denmark's outlying islands.

Practical Information

Stacks of helpful and free tourist information, published in English by local national and tourist boards, are an extra bonus when visiting Denmark. Good street maps are waiting at almost every tourist office, as are comprehensive city guides. If you're planning well in advance, you can get this info from tourist offices outside of Denmark.

Danish phone numbers are all eight digits long, and you must dial the whole thing regardless of where you're calling from (no city codes). The emergency number is 000 throughout Denmark. No coins are required. From pay phones, local calls require a minimum of 1kr, often 2kr. For information on how to use the phones, dial

0030. For directory information, dial 0033 (free from pay phones). For international information, dial 0039. For AT&T's **USA Direct,** dial 80 01 00 10.

While Denmark is not an English-speaking country in the literal sense, most every Dane speaks English, and a simple "Pardon?" will generally prompt a switch. As for Danish, it is much easier to read than to pronounce, so don't even try. The Danish alphabet adds *Æ, Ø,* and *Å* (still sometimes written as *Aa)* at the end; thus Aalborg and Århus would follow Viborg in an alphabetical listing of cities. One particularly useful word to know is *ikke* ("not"), which will help you to figure out such signs as "No smoking" and "Don't walk on the grass."

Accommodations and Camping

The 105 **IYHF youth hostels** *(vandrerhjem)* throughout Denmark are well-equipped and well-run, have no age limit, and generally include rooms for families. All charge 52-67kr per bed; nonmembers pay 22kr extra for a guest stamp. Tykes under 2 are free. Children under 10 sometimes win a discount. You can generally feast on an unlimited breakfast for 35kr. Reception desks normally close between noon and 4pm and close for the day at 9 or 11pm. Reservations are required from September to mid-May and recommended in summer. They can be made by phone without a deposit, but you will be asked to show up by 5pm on the first night of the reservation or call that day to confirm. Cards (112kr) and an official hostel guide (free and available in English) are available at **Danmarks Vandrerhjem,** Vesterbrogade 39, 1620 Copenhagen V (tel. 31 31 36 12). (Open Mon and Wed. 9am-4pm, Tues. 9am-5pm, Thurs. 9am-6pm, Fri. 9am-3pm; Sept.-March Mon.-Thurs. 9am-4pm, Fri. 9am-3pm.)

Other options are hotels, the cheapest of which run about 200kr for a single without shower, and cheaper rooms in private homes, which can often be arranged through tourist offices.

Before you pitch a tent in Denmark, you must get the landowner's OK. You can also stay at one of the many official campgrounds (about 35-37kr per person per night). Campgrounds rank from one star (basic facilities) to three (the works). You'll need a camping pass; the Danish version is available at all campgrounds (24kr; family pass 48kr) and expires in January; one-time guest passes are 6kr (families 12kr), and international passes are accepted, too. The **Dansk Camping Union,** Gammel Kongevej 74d, Copenhagen (tel. 31 21 06 04), will sell you passes and a campground handbook (65kr; also available in bookstores; open Mon.-Fri. 10am-5pm; May 15-July 15 Mon. and Wed.-Fri. 10am-5pm, Tues. 10am-6:30pm). Sleeping in train stations, parks, and streets is illegal. You can fraternize with youthful Danes by joining a **workcamp;** contact **Mellemfolkeligt Samvirke** at Borgergade 10-14, 1300 København K (tel. 33 32 62 44). For a fee of USD25, **Friends Overseas** will connect you with families along your itinerary in Denmark, Sweden, Norway and Finland who are eager to introduce you to their families and their communities; send a self-addressed, stamped envelope to 68-04 Dartmouth Street, Forest Hills, NY 11375, for more information.

Food

Danish? Pastry. Right, but don't let it stop there. Beyond the "Danish," called *wienerbrød* by the Danes, are myriad other baked goodies: flaky *kringle,* syrupy *brunsvigerkage,* and more. Try them all. Then there is ice cream. While Danish ice cream, especially nut flavors like pistachio, is generally quite good, better still are the cones it comes in, fresh-baked waffle cones with pointy bottoms filled with whipped cream, then three or four flavors of ice cream, plus more cream and jam on top. And remember: ice cream doesn't have any calories if you eat it in a foreign country. For more substantial fare, Danes favor *smørrebrød,* small, open-faced sandwiches with such toppings as cheese, smoked salmon, pickled herring or raw beef (moo!). Wash these down with the national brews, Carlsberg and Tuborg. The many varieties of *akvavit,* a distilled liquor, are so expensive that they are served one shot (0.2 liter) at a time.

Menus and restaurant checks include both tax and service; what you see is what you pay. Everything is much cheaper if purchased as take-out. All-you-can-eat buffets are very popular in Denmark. Youth hostels offer unlimited breakfasts of cereal, rolls, cheese and meat for around 36kr; restaurants may have buffets of pizza, herring or Mongolian barbeque. Unfortunately, *Let's Go* has yet to locate a bakery offering all-you-can-eat pastries. But perhaps if one leads a virtuous life . . .

Copenhagen (København)

A savory buffet of parks, waterways, and teeming pedestrian streets, the Danish capital may be the most sensuous and exuberant city in northern Europe—at least in summer. Copenhagen's countless street performers, outdoor cafés, ice cream vendors and all-night discos epitomize Nordic *joie de vivre.* In winter, the outdoor seating is packed away and the harsh realities of life above the 55th parallel set in.

Orientation and Practical Information

Copenhagen lies on the east coast of the Danish island of **Zealand** (Sjælland). Malmö, in Sweden, is just across the sound (Øresund). Copenhagen's **Hovedbanegården** (Central Station) lies close to the city's heart. One block north of the station, **Vesterbrogade** passes **Tivoli** and **Rådhuspladsen** (the city's central square, where most bus lines originate) and then leads into **Strøget** (STROY-yet), the longest pedestrian thoroughfare in the world. The districts of Vesterbro, Nørrebro, Østerbro, and Christianshavn fan out from this central area.

Tourist Offices: Danmarks Turistråd, H. C. Andersens Blvd. 22, 1553 København V (tel. 33 11 13 25), in the Rådhuspladsen Tivoli entrance, in the corner of the square nearest the train station. Everything you need to know about Copenhagen and the rest of Denmark (much of it hidden behind the counter), plus a free map and the helpful *Copenhagen This Week.* Open June to mid-Sept. daily 9am-6pm; mid-Sept. to April Mon.-Fri. 9am-5pm, Sat. 9am-noon; May Mon.-Fri. 9am-5pm, Sat. 9am-2pm, Sun. 9am-1pm. **Use It,** Rådhusstræde 13 (tel. 33 15 65 18), in the Huset complex 2 blocks east of Rådhuspladsen. A youth-oriented travel office with heaps of free assistance, from bed-finding to passport retrieval. Mail held, ride boards, message boards, flash reports on the availability of accommodations (list posted after-hours) and free baggage storage (50kr deposit). Publishes three helpful guides: *Copenhagen By Bike, Copenhagen By Foot* and *Copenhagen By Bus.* Get their map (superior to the Turistråd's) and a copy of their guide *Playtime.* Open daily 9am-7pm; mid-Sept. to mid-June Mon.-Fri. 10am-4pm.

Budget Travel: Transalpino sells tickets at Skoubogade 6 (tel. 33 14 46 33). Open Mon.-Fri. 10am-5pm. Similarly reduced train and plane fares also at **DIS,** Skindergade 28 (tel. 33 11 00 44). Open Mon.-Wed. and Fri. 10am-5pm, Thurs. 10am-7pm; mid-May to mid-July also Sat. 10am-1pm. **Spies,** Nyropsgade 41 (tel. 33 32 15 00), arranges cheap charters to southern Europe. Open daily 6am-midnight.

Embassies: U.S., Dag Hammarskjölds Allé 24 (tel. 31 42 31 44; bus #1 or 6). **Canada,** Kristen Bernikowsgade 1 (tel. 33 12 22 99; bus #28 or 41). **U.K.,** Kastelsvej 36-40 (tel. 31 26 46 00; bus #1, 14 or 40). **Australia,** Kristianiagade 21 (tel. 31 26 22 44; bus #1, 6 or 9). Travelers from **New Zealand** should contact the British embassy. **Estonia** (tel. 33 93 34 62), **Latvia** (tel. 33 93 18 67) and **Lithuania** (tel. 33 93 48 17) all at H.C. Andersens Blvd. 38. **Poland,** Richelieusallé 10 (tel. 31 62 77 02).

Currency Exchange: At Central Station (daily 6:45am-10pm; Oct. to mid-April 7am-9pm), the Tivoli office (in summer daily noon-11pm), or the airport (daily 6:30am-10pm; traveler's checks and cash only). Many banks on Vesterbrogade, between the train station and Rådhuspladsen, and in the pedestrian district. Regular bank hours Mon.-Wed. and Fri. 9:30am-4pm, Thurs. 9:30am-6pm. Commissions on traveler's checks are high (30-35kr min.), except at American Express.

American Express: Amagertorv 18, on the Strøget (tel. 33 12 23 01). Open Mon.-Fri. 9am-5pm, Sat. 9am-noon.

Post Office: Tietgensgade 37-39, behind Central Station. Poste Restante. Open Mon.-Fri. 10am-6pm, Sat. 9am-1pm. **Postal Code:** 1500 København V. Branch office at Central Station. Open Mon.-Fri. 8am-10pm, Sat. 9am-4pm, Sun. and holidays 10am-5pm.

Flights: Tel. 31 54 17 01. Bus #32 (32 min., 12kr or 1 stamp on yellow stripcard), from Rådhuspladsen, and the SAS bus (20 min., 26kr), from Central Station, run to and from **Kastrup Airport.** SAS buses run to the airport 5:40am-9:45pm every 10-15 min. and from the airport 6:30am-11:10pm every 10-15 min.

Trains: All trains stop at **Hovedbanegården** (Central Station, København H) in the center of town. For information, call 33 14 17 01. To: Stockholm (495kr, Transalpino 365kr); Oslo (595kr, Transalpino 475kr). The **InterRail Center** in the station, for all holders of BIJ, InterRail, Nordturist or Eurailpasses, is one of Copenhagen's most useful and friendly assets. Relax in a special lounge, wait for late-night connections, make phone calls, get information and take showers (10kr per 10 min.). Open mid-June to mid-Sept. daily 6:30am-midnight.

Public Transportation: Buses and S-trains (a cross between subways and suburban trains) operate on a shared zone system. Three zones cover all of central Copenhagen, while 11 zones gets you all the way to Helsingør. You can buy tickets (9kr for journeys within 3 zones, 4.50kr each additional zone) or, better, a yellow *rabatkort* (rebate card), which gets you 11 "clips" for 80kr, each clip being good for 1 ride within 3 zones; more zones require more clips. These cards can be purchased at kiosks or from bus drivers and must be clipped in the machines provided each time you begin a journey. Children under 12 ride for half-price; under 5s are free. Once you have purchased a ticket or clipped a clip, you have an hour of unlimited transfers on both buses and trains. All railpasses allow free travel on S-trains but not on buses. Another option is the **Copenhagen Card,** which allows unlimited free travel throughout North Zealand, discounts on ferries to Sweden, and free admission to most sights (including Tivoli); it's available for one day (105kr), two days (170kr) or three (215kr), with 50% discounts for children 5-11, at hotels, travel agencies, tourist offices, and large train stations. The free maps issued by the tourist office and Use It both show bus routes and include S-train network maps; for more detailed info, check the maps posted in Rådhuspladsen, the point of convergence for many bus lines. Buses and trains run approximately Mon.-Sat. 5am-12:30am, Sun. 6am-12:30am; night buses cost an extra 4kr and run through the night, but less frequently and on fewer routes. Bus information, tel. 31 95 17 01. Train information, tel. 33 14 17 01.

Ferries: The variety and number of ferry services from Copenhagen boggle the mind; consult the tourist office for more complete details. There are four basic groups. To **Norway:** DFDS/Scandinavian Seaways sails daily, year-round, departing at 5pm from Copenhagen to Oslo (16 hr., 500kr, 20% Eurail discount, 50% InterRail discount, bigger student discounts through DIS—see Budget Travel above); for bookings call 33 11 22 55. To **Sweden:** trains from Copenhagen to the rest of Scandinavia cross over the Helsingør-Helsingborg DSB ferry at no extra charge to passengers or railpass holders. Hydrofoils cross hourly all day and evening between Havnegade at the end of Nyhavn in Copenhagen and Malmö, Sweden (tel. 33 12 80 88; 45 min., 80kr, 60kr with railpasses). To **Poland:** Polferries sails year-round Mon. and Wed.-Sat., at 11pm from Nordre Toldbod off Esplanaden in Copenhagen to Świnoujście in the northwest corner of Poland, where there are rail connections to the rest of the country (tel. 33 11 46 45; 9½-10½ hr., 260kr, 210kr with ISIC). To **Bornholm:** See the Bornholm section.

Taxis: Tel. 31 35 35 35. Expensive. Central station to Kastrup Airport, 110kr.

Bike Rental: Dan Wheel, Colbjørnsensgade 3 (tel. 31 21 22 27). From 40kr per day, 190kr per week. Deposit 200kr. Open Mon.-Fri. 9am-5:30pm, Sat.-Sun. 9am-2pm. **DSB Cykelcenter,** Reventlowsgade 11 (tel. 33 14 07 17), in the same building as the train station. From 40kr per day, 185kr per week. Deposit 200kr. Repairs too. Open Mon.-Fri. 7am-7pm, Sat. 9am-5pm, Sun. noon-6pm.

Hitchhiking: Those hitching to Helsingør or Sweden take bus #1, 6, 24, or 84 to Vibenshus Runddel. Those heading to the rest of Denmark and Germany take the S-train to Ellebjerg Station or bus #16 to Gammel Køgevej, and hitch west on Folehaven (Ring 11). Hitching is weak; try **Use It's** ride boards (see Tourist Offices above).

Luggage Storage: Free at **Use It** (50kr deposit), but they have limited hours (see Budget Travel above). In **Central Station,** the luggage lockers are accessible daily 5:30am-1am (10-20kr per 24 hrs.), and the DSB Garderobe is open daily 6:30am-12:15am (suitcases 10kr, backpacks 15kr per 24 hrs.).

Bookstores: Atheneum, Nørregade 6 (tel. 33 12 69 70), serves the university community. **The Book Trader,** Skindergade 23 (tel. 33 12 06 69), sells second-hand English books. Open Mon.-Thurs. 11am-5:30pm, Fri. 11am-7pm, Sat. 10am-1pm.

Laundromats: Just about everywhere; look for the sign *"møntvask."* At Borgergade 2, Nansensgade 39, and Istedgade 45. Facilities at the two main IYHF hostels.

Disabled Services: Contact the Danish Tourist Board (tel. 33 11 13 25) for a free copy of *Access in Denmark: A Travel Guide for the Disabled.*

Women's Centers: Kvindehuset, Gothersgade 37 (tel. 33 14 28 04), runs a bookstore-café. **Kvindecentret Dannerhuset,** Nansensgade 1 (tel. 33 14 16 76), is an overnight shelter for women who have been attacked. (Open all night.)

Gay Services: National Organization for Gay Women and Men, Knabrostræde 3 (tel. 33 13 19 48), provides information and advice, as well as a bookstore.

Pharmacy: Steno Apotek, Vesterbrogade 6c (tel. 33 14 82 66). Open 24 hrs. From 8pm-8am Mon.-Fri., 2pm-8am Sat., and all day Sunday, you must ring for entrance and pay a 10kr fee on purchases except for prescriptions written that day.

Medical Assistance: (tel. 0041). 24 hrs.; free.

Hospital: Rigshospitalet (tel. 31 39 66 33) at Blegdamsvej 9. Denmark offers free medical care to visitors lacking health insurance (except pre-existing afflictions).

Emergencies: Police or **Ambulance** or **Fire** (tel. 000). No coins needed for public phones. **Police Station** is at Nyropsgade 20 (tel. 33 91 14 48).

Accommodations

Though rich in hostels and campgrounds, Copenhagen, like all of Scandinavia, is poor in budget hotels. In summer, the three IYHF hostels fill early, despite their remote locations. Reservations are especially advisable during Karneval (mid-May), the Roskilde Festival (late June) and the Copenhagen Jazz Festival (early July). Failing that, consult **Use It** (see above under Tourist Offices) or Værelseanvisning, a hotel reservation booth in Central Station (open May to Aug. daily 9am-midnight; Sept. daily 9am-10pm; Oct. daily 9am-5pm; Nov.-March Mon.-Fri. 9am-5pm; Sat. 9am-noon; April Mon.-Sat. 9am-5pm). Both give a listing of hostels. Slumbering in a park or the station is never a good idea.

Hostels

Københavns Vandrerhjem (IYHF), Herbergvejen 8, in Bellahøj (tel. 31 28 97 15). In a park with a small lake, 15-min. bus or bike ride from Rådhuspladsen. Take bus #2 (direction "Bronshøj") to Fuglsang Allé, or night bus *(natbus)* #902. The Godthåbsvej S-train stop is about a 15-min. walk away, but you'll have to transfer at Ryparken to get downtown. Copenhagen's best. 295 beds (in 4-8 bed dorms) fill quickly. Lobby and reception open 24 hrs., rooms open 1pm-10am. No curfew, despite a trilingual sign to the contrary. 52kr, nonmembers 74kr. Breakfast 34kr. Backpack-size lockers, optional lock rental 5kr, deposit 20kr. Sheets 25kr. Laundry 25kr per load. Open mid-Dec. to mid-Nov.

Copenhagen Youth Hostel (IYHF), Sjællandsbroen 55 (tel. 32 52 29 08). Take bus #46 (Mon.-Fri. 6am-5pm) from Central Station or #37 (destination Valby Station) from Holmens Bro (across the street from the front of Christiansborg Castle) to Sjællandsbroen, or take the S-train to Valby station and bus #37 from there. More comfortable than the one in Bellahøj—the varnished pine will let you know you're in Scandinavia—but a longer bus ride. 528 beds. Hotel-like, lockable 2-bed (ideal for trysts) and 5-bed rooms. Reception open 1pm-10am, bathrooms closed 9am-1pm. No curfew. 57kr, nonmembers 79kr. Breakfast 34kr. Dinner 34-54kr. Sheets 30kr. Laundry 25kr per load. Kitchen. Free use of safe. Handicapped accessible. Open Jan. 2-Dec. 20.

YMCA Inter Point, KFUK, Store Kannikestræde 19 (tel. 33 11 30 31). Super-central location. 60 beds in a ballroom divided into 5-bed cubicles. You'll need an Inter Point pass, which costs 25kr and is good for one calendar year throughout Europe. Reception open daily 8am-noon and 2:30pm-12:30am. Lockout 10am-2:30pm. Curfew 12:30am. 50kr. Breakfast 20kr. Sheets 20kr. Open July to mid-Aug. Also at Vesterbros KFUM, Valdemarsgade 15 (tel. 31 31 15 74). Approx. 40 beds, open mid-July to mid-Aug.

City Public Hostel, Absalonsgade 8, in the Vesterbro Ungdomsgård (tel. 31 31 20 70). Central location makes it worth the price. Despite its name, it's not run by the city and it's non-IYHF. Mellow and messy. 210 beds. Rooms vary in quality; the largest has 60 beds (men only). Reception open 24 hrs. Lockout 10am-noon. 85kr, with all-you-can-eat breakfast 100kr. No kitchen, but there is a patio with a charcoal grill. Small unlocked lockers free, locks sold for 30kr. Optional sheet rental 30kr. Open early May-Aug.

Sleep-In, Per Henrik Lings Allé 6 (tel. 31 26 50 59). Take bus #1 or night bus #953 to Per Henrik Lings Allé, or bus #6 or 14 or nightbus #914 to Ved Idrætsparken; you can also take the S-train to Nordhavn, but it's a serious haul from there. 450 beds in a festive but noisy ice rink (it's not cold) partitioned into 2-4-bed cubicles. The best last-minute place; they'll virtually always find you a spot to crash. Lockout noon-4pm. 75kr. Continental breakfast included. Free lockers, deposit 30kr. Sheets 20kr, deposit 40kr, but best to bring your own. Open late June-Aug. During the highest of the high season, another 320 beds open up down the street.

Lyngby Vandrerhjem (IYHF), Rådvad 1 (tel. 42 80 30 74). Take the S-train (lines A, B, or L) to Lyngby station, then bus #182 or 183 to Lundtoftevej and Hjortekærsvej, and follow the signs to Rådvad (3km). Bus #187 goes all the way from the station to the hostel, but only 4 times a day. Bucolic spot, but impractical if you want to frequent town by public transportation. 94 beds in 2-14 bed rooms. No laundry or lockers. Reception open 7am-noon and 4-9pm. Curfew 11pm, key on request. 52-57kr, nonmembers 74-79kr. Breakfast 38kr. Sheets 30kr. Reservations necessary. Family rooms available. Open Jan. to mid-Dec.

Private Homes and Hotels

Central Station's Værelseanvisning will find you a room in a hotel or private home (often a haul from the center of town) for a booking fee of 13kr per bed. Private home prices start at 120kr per person. Use It can often beat these prices, and does not charge a fee.

Søfolkenes Mindehotel, Peder Skramsgade 19 (tel. 33 13 48 82), conveniently located near Nyhavn. A seafarer's hotel with clean, simply furnished rooms and an earnest, affable staff. Reception open 24 hrs. Singles 215kr. Doubles 380kr. Breakfast included.

Hotel Jørgensen, Rømersgade 11 (tel. 33 13 81 86), in a quiet area about 20 min. from Central Station. Cramped but clean. Reception open until 2am. Co-ed basement dorm 65kr, with breakfast 80kr (June-Aug. only). Singles 250-350kr. Doubles 400-575kr. Lockers free (deposit 20kr). Sheets 30kr.

Cab Inn, Danasvej 32-24 (tel. 31 21 04 00), 10 blocks west of the city center. A high-tech pleasure palace. Magnetic cards open compact rooms with TVs, VCRs, showers and fold-up bunkbeds. Two rooms handicapped accessible. Glitzy silver reception lounge open 24 hrs. Singles 375kr. Quads possibly worth it at 600kr.

Camping

Bellahøj Camping, Hvidkildevej (tel. 31 10 11 50), 5km from the center. Take bus #2 (direction "Bellahøj") or nightbus #902 from Rådhuspladsen. Reception open 24 hrs. 34kr, ages 2-13 17kr. Open June-Aug.

Absalon Camping, Korsdalsvej 132 (tel. 31 41 06 00), 9km away. Take S-train line B or L to Brøndbyøster, then walk 10 min. north through the housing projects (ask for directions at the station). 35kr, ages 2-13 18kr; mid-Aug. to late June 29kr and 15kr. Cabins, store, laundry.

Food

In Copenhagen, food is a party. Stroll down the Strøget with an ice cream cone in your hand and peach juice dripping down your chin, munch pickled herring by the waterfront and sample the goodies staring out of every bakery window. All this comes cheaply if you avoid the touristy sit-down restaurants, especially in the pedestrian district and Tivoli. Picnic in a park or by the harbor on take-out *smørrebrød* (from 10kr), or shop for your own in the supermarkets **Netto, Irma** and **Brugsen;** all operate several stores in the town center. Supermarkets—except the one in Central Station (open daily 8am-midnight)—are closed Sundays. An open **market** occurs on weekdays in Israels Plads near Nørreport Station for much of the year, and scads of fruit stalls line **Strøget.** For cheap hot meals, your best bet will be pizza or pasta at one of the many Italian joints that line the city's open spaces, some with outdoor seating.

Centrum Smørrebrød, Vesterbrogade 6c, near Scala and Tivoli. Scrumptious take-out sandwiches from 10.50kr. Open 24 hrs. The affiliated **City Smørrebrød** at Gothersgade 10 is open Mon.-Fri. noon-8pm.

Nyhavns Færgekro, Nyhavn 5. Sit indoors or along the canal. Lunch consists of all-you-can-eat herring (65kr), over a dozen varieties. You can't get much more Danish than that. Dinners around 130kr. Open daily 11:30am-4pm and 5-11:30pm.

Riz Raz, Kompagnistræde 20. Savorous all-you-can-eat vegetarian Mediterranean buffet, 39kr before 4pm, 59kr therafter. Kebabs 90-100kr. Open daily 11:30am-midnight.

Pasta Basta, Valkendorfsgade 22. Classy establishment with a cold pasta buffet for 69kr, entrees 56-200kr. Open Sun.-Wed. 11:30am-3pm, Thurs.-Sat. 11:30am-5am.

ReeF N' BeeF, Landemarket 27, near Kultorvet. It turns out the Australians do have a distinctive cuisine beyond shrimps on the barbie. Try the red snapper in mango sauce (125kr). Mostly steak and seafood, as the name implies. Lunch until 3pm 50-60kr, dinner entrees 80-160kr. Open Mon.-Sat. 11:30am-10pm, Sun. 5-10pm.

Alexander's Original Pizza House, Lille Kannikestræde 5. All-you-can-eat pizza and salad 49kr. Open daily noon-11:30pm.

Café Smukke Marie, Knabrostræde 19, near Nytorv. An example of the Danish tendency to do one thing and do it well. Here the one thing is crêpes, for dinner (90kr) or dessert (20-50kr). Kitchen open Sun.-Fri. 4-10pm, Sat. noon-10pm. Open for drinks Mon.-Sat. noon-midnight, Sun. 5pm-midnight.

Sights

A fairly compact city, Copenhagen is best seen on foot or by bike. First, pick up *Copenhagen This Week,* a list of sights, prices, and hours, available free from Use It or the tourist office.

Founded in 1843, **Tivoli,** Copenhagen's celebrated amusement park, doesn't have the most thrilling rides in the world, but parts of it are awfully pretty. The wild swans—each painted differently—give a terrific, spinning panorama of the city's skyline. Most people go in the evening, when the park becomes a spectacle of schmaltzy illuminated ponds, outdoor concerts and closing fireworks (Wed., Fri., Sat., Sun.). (Open late April to mid-Sept. daily 10am-midnight. Rides from 11am. Admission 30kr, under 12 15kr, under 4 free; discount before 1pm. Single ride tickets 8kr, 10 for 70kr; rides cost 1-2 tickets. Ride-pass 125kr.)

Next to Tivoli, the **Ny Carlsberg Glyptotek,** funded by the Carlsberg beer empire, displays ancient, classical, and impressionist art, including a fine collection of Roman portrait busts. The museum centers on a glass-domed tropical plant conservatory. (Open Tues.-Sun. 10am-4pm; Sept.-April Tues.-Sat. noon-3pm, Sun. 10am-4pm. 15kr, free to under 12, ISIC holders, and everyone on Sun. and Wed.) Nearby, the **National Museum,** at Frederiksholms Kanal 12, contains Danish and European archeological discoveries, including two rooms full of massive runestones. (Open Tues.-Sun. 10am-4pm; mid-Sept. to mid-June Tues.-Fri. 11am-3pm, Sat.-Sun. noon-4pm. Free.) Across the canals on Slotsholmen Island is **Christiansborg Palace,** the meeting place of the *Folketing* (parliament). (Hourly tours Sun.-Fri. 10am-4pm; Oct.-May Sun. 10am-4pm. Free.)

Continuing north, one reaches **Kongens Nytorv,** the departure point for harbor and canal boat tours. (July-Aug. every ½ hr. 10am-6pm; May-June and Sept. hourly 10am-6pm; 50 min., 24-36kr depending on guide and length, children ½-price.) Boats also leave from Gammel Strand across the canal from Thorvaldsens Museum. (Information office at Gammel Strand, tel. 33 13 31 05.) Kongens Nytorv marks the ritzy endpoint of **Strøget,** the pedestrian street; the **Royal Theatre** here is home to the world-famous Royal Danish Ballet. East of the square is **Nyhavn,** a picturesque canal crammed with yachts and lined with restaurants, where Hans Christian Andersen wrote his first fairy tale. Farther north is **Amalienborg Palace,** a group of four rococo mansions that serves as the official royal residence. The Changing of the Guard takes place at noon on the brick plaza. The western approach to the plaza frames a view of the impressive dome of the **Marmorkirken** (marble church). The inside of the dome is almost as elaborate. (Open Mon.-Sat. 11am-2pm. Sunday mass 10:30am. Free.) A few blocks north of Amalienborg is the intriguing **Frihedsmuseet** (Resistance Museum), Churchillparken, which chronicles the Nazi occupation of 1940-1945. While proudly documenting Denmark's heroic rescue of almost all its Jews, the museum also examines the intial period of resigned acceptance of German "protection," when the Danish government arrested anti-Nazi saboteurs. (Open Tues.-Sat. 10am-4pm, Sun. 10am-5pm; mid-Sept. to April Tues.-Sat. 11am-3pm, Sun. 11am-4pm. Free.) On the other side of **Kastellet,** a 17th-century fortress-turned-park (open daily 6am-dusk) is Edvard Eriksen's statue of **Den Lille Havfrue** (The Little Mermaid), the model for all those souvenir paperweights you've been seeing. Behind her is the narrow, shallow strait where, in 1801, Horatio Nelson literally turned a blind eye to a signal to withdraw, and went on to destroy the Danish fleet.

The area around Østervoldgade and Sølvgade houses Copenhagen's finest parks and gardens. The **Botanisk Have** (Botanical Gardens) flower daily 8:30am-6pm; Sept.-late March 8:30am-4pm. The palm house is open daily 10am-3pm; the cactus house Sat.-Sun. 1-3pm. Across the street is **Rosenborg Palace and Gardens;** the palace (entrance on Østervoldgade) houses a collection of royal treasures. (Open June to mid-Oct. daily 10am-4pm; late Oct.-April Tues., Fri. and Sun. 11am-2pm; May daily 11am-3pm. Admission to both 30kr, children 5kr.) Nearby, at Rømersgade 22, the gripping **Arbejdermuseet** (Workers' Museum) graphically portrays the lives of those who could not afford royal treasures. (Open Tues.-Fri. 10am-3pm, Sat.-Sun. 11am-4pm. Admission 20kr, children 10kr.) Three blocks north, at Østervoldgade and Sølvgade—in yet another garden—is the **Statens Museum for Kunst** (State Museum of Fine Arts), not as grand as its name, but worth a visit for its Matisses and Dutch masters. (Open Tues.-Sun. 10am-4:30pm. Admission 20kr, students and seniors 10kr, children free.)

Back in the pedestrian district, climb the unique spiral ramp of the **Rundetårn** (round tower) for a good view of many of the city's spires. Halfway up, an art gallery gives you a chance to rest. (Open June-Aug. daily 10am-8pm; April-May and Sept.-Oct. Mon.-Sat. 10am-5pm, Sun. noon-4pm; Nov.-March Mon.-Sat. 10am-4pm, Sun. noon-4pm. Admission 12kr, children 5kr.)

Southeast of downtown, in the Christianshavn district, lies **Christiania** (entrances on Prinsessegade). This utopian "free city" was founded in 1971 by youthful squatters in abandoned military barracks. A source of continuing controversy, Christiania accepts visitors, and you can wander among its houses, workshops and meadows. With lots of hash and pot and mess, it's not everyone's cup of tea. Always ask before taking pictures.

Beer enthusiasts should tour the city's breweries: **Carlsberg,** Ny Carlsbergvej 140 (take bus #6 west from Rådhuspladsen; tours Mon.-Fri. at 11am and 2pm), and **Tuborg,** Strandvejen 54 (take bus #6 north from Rådhuspladsen; tours Mon.-Fri. at 10am, 12:30pm, and 2:30pm). Both offer free beer (about 2 bottles per person) and soda at the end of the tour. Near the Tuborg brewery, the **Eksperimentarium,** Tuborg Havnevej 7, has plenty of science toys to play with. (Open Mon., Wed. and Fri. 9am-6pm, Tues. and Thurs. 9am-9pm, Sat.-Sun. 11am-6pm. Admission 50kr, children 35kr, reduced admission on Mon. and Tues.-Fri. after 1pm.)

Entertainment

Jocularity in Copenhagen knows no bounds; weekends often begin on Wednesday, and nights of jollity roll until 5am. The central pedestrian district reverberates with populous bars and discos, while Kongens Nytorv contains fancier joints and Nyhavn exudes the salty charisma of moored ships. For current events listings, consult *Copenhagen This Week* or contact **Use It** (see Tourist Offices above), which also distributes a lesbian and gay guide to the city.

Huset, Rådhusstræde 13. A relaxed, unpretentious cultural center. Use It is on the 2nd floor. On the ground floor, **Kafé pår Zalü** overflows into a student-filled courtyard. Coffee 10kr, beer 17kr. Open daily noon-2am. Upstairs, **Græshoppen** screens American and Danish films (with English subtitles) for 35kr, Mon. 20kr. Open 5:30pm-midnight.

Din's, Lille Kannikestræde 3. A stuffed goose watches over the loose goose crowd. Rock played everyday, stand-up comedy some Thursdays. Open Mon.-Wed. 4pm-1am, Thurs. 4pm-2am, Fri. 4pm-4am, Sat. 1pm-4am. Fri.-Sat. 20kr cover.

Rådhuskroen, Løngangstræde 21. A jamming spot for blues. Open Mon.-Sat. 8pm-4:30am, Sun. 3pm-4:30am. Cover generally Thurs.-Sat. 40-50kr.

Pan Café, Knabrostræde 3. A popular lesbian and gay center. Open Mon.-Tues. 1pm-3am, Wed.-Thurs. noon-4am, Fri.-Sat. 1pm-5am, Sun. 1pm-3am. Dancing nightly after 10pm (with a 20-50kr cover charge Wed.-Sat.). Cafe and disco for women only on Thurs.

hos Simon, Løngangstræde 37. A cozy pub with live, folky rock after 11pm. 20kr Fri.-Sat. cover might be waived when you tell Giora that *Let's Go* sent you. Open Mon.-Thurs. 4pm-4am, Fri. 4pm-5am, Sat. 9pm-5am.

International Jazz Montmartre, Nørregade 41. A stomping jazz club. Open Tues.-Sat. 8pm-midnight (music from 9pm). Cover 50-250kr. Disco Fri.-Sat. midnight-5am. Cover 50kr.

The world-famous **Copenhagen Jazz Festival** begins the first Friday in July and lasts 10 days; make accommodations reservations early. **Karneval,** a Brazilian dance extravaganza, is slated for Whitsund—salsa ho!

Near Copenhagen

Royal castles, scenic beaches and the stunning Louisiana Museum of Modern Art are all within easy reach of Copenhagen by train. Two rail lines go north from Copenhagen: a more or less coastal line up to Helsingør (paralleled by the very coastal and more scenic bus #388), and an S-train line to Hillerød. Close in on the coastal line (alternatively, at the end of S-train line C), **Klampenborg** offers a pleasant beach to those who prefer their blondes topless, and the **Bakken** amusement park, where there are more thrills (magnified by untranslated warning signs and unknown safety codes) but far less ornament than at Tivoli. (Open late March-late Aug. daily 2pm-midnight. Just north from the train station, turn left, cross the bridge over the road and head along the avenue through the park. Admission free.)

Up the coast from Klampenborg in **Rungsted,** the recently-opened **Karen Blixen Museum,** Rungsted Strandvej 111, occupies the home of the late author, who is known to the world as Isak Dinesen and was portrayed with a charming Danish accent by Meryl Streep in the film *Out of Africa.* Many of her Gothic Tales paint a sweeping picture of 19th-century Denmark. (Open daily 10am-5pm; Oct.-April Wed.-Mon. 1-4pm. Admission 30kr.) Farther up in Humlebæk is the spectacular **Louisiana Museum of Modern Art,** an absolutely first-rate complex. Named after the three wives of the estate's original owner, all called Louisa, the museum contains works by Picasso, Warhol, Giacometti, Lichtenstein, and other 20th-century deities. Stretched along a knoll overlooking the sea and the Swedish coast, the remarkable building and its sculpture-studded grounds are themselves well worth the trip. Follow the signs 1½km north from the Humlebæk station or snag bus #388. Evening concerts on summer Wednesdays cost 70kr, including museum admission. (Open Thurs.-Tues. 10am-5pm, Wed. 10am-10pm. Admission 40kr, seniors and students with ID 32kr, children under 16 free.)

Farther north, three castles give evidence of the Danish monarchy's fondness for lavish architecture. **Helsingør**—Elsinore in Shakespeare's *Hamlet*—is at the end of the coastal rail line (from Central Station 3 per hr., 50 min., 11 zones). This is the major ferry departure point for Sweden and its many liquor stores cater to Swedes seeking to avoid Sweden's steep alcohol tax. **Kronborg Slot** was built in the 15th century to collect tolls from passing merchant ships. While smaller, simpler, and more tourist-ridden than Frederiksborg in Hillerød, the castle is certainly nothing to sneeze at. Viking chief and Danish national hero **Holger Danske** sleeps in the castle's dungeon. Legend has it that he arises to face menaces to Denmark. The royal apartments boast some impressive furnishings—a pair of renaissance globes will certainly appeal to cartographers. (Open daily May-Sept. 10:30am-5pm; April and Oct. Tues.-Sun. 11am-4pm; Nov.-March Tues.-Sun. 11am-3pm. Admission 10-34kr, depending on how much you want to see. Children 5-17kr.) The **tourist office** in Helsingør is to the left of the train station as you exit (tel. 49 21 13 33; open Mon.-Sat. 9am-7pm; mid-Aug. to mid-June Mon.-Fri. 9am-5pm, Sat. 9am-1pm). An **IYHF youth hostel** (tel. 49 21 16 40) stands by the beach at Ndr. Strandvej 24. (Open Feb.-Nov.) The famous **Brostræde Ice Cream Shop,** on Brostræde, serves top-notch cones filled with medium-notch ice cream.

Moated **Frederiksborg Slot** in **Hillerød** is the most impressive of the castles north of Copenhagen, featuring exquisite gardens and brick ramparts. Built in 1560 but given its present form in the early 17th century by the indefatigable Christian IV, the castle now houses the National Historical Museum, which consists mainly of portraits of hundreds of prominent Danes from several centuries. Concerts are given on the famous **Esaias Compenius organ** in the chapel Sundays at 5pm. Call 42 26 13 31 for information. (Castle open daily 10am-5pm; Oct. 10am-4pm; Nov.-March 11am-3pm; April 10am-4pm. Admission 25kr, children 5kr, students 10kr with ID.) Featuring exquisite gardens and brick ramparts, Hillerød is at the end of S-train lines A and E from Copenhagen (40 min., via Lyngby; 32kr or three clips on the yellow *rabatkort)* and also accessible direct from Helsingør by train (30 min.). Along the train line halfway between Hillerød and Helsingør is **Fredensborg Castle,** built in 1722 and still in use as the spring and autumn royal residence. When Queen Margrethe is in, there is a colorful changing of the guard. The park is free and open year-round, while the castle tour gives some idea of what it's like to be a regular royal queen. (Castle open July daily 1-5pm. Admission 7.50kr, children 3kr.) You can peek into the palace gardens from the **Fredensborg Vandrerhjem,** Østrupvej 3 (tel. 42 28 03 15), 1km from the train station (70kr per night).

Roskilde, 25-30 min. west of Copenhagen (32kr or 3 clips on the yellow *rabatkort),* is home to much Danish history; King Harald Bluetooth built the first Christian church in Denmark here in 980. The **Viking Ship Museum,** down on the shore of Roskilde Fjord, houses the dinosaur-like remains of five vessels. The ships were sunk about 1000 AD to bar the passage of enemy fleets through the fjord and are somewhat worse for the wear, but the reconstructions moored in the harbor outside aid the imagination. (Open daily 9am-5pm; Nov.-March 10am-4pm. Admission 25kr, children 16kr, includes 15-min. film.) Thirty-eight Danish monarchs repose in the **Roskilde Domkirke** (cathedral); their tombs vary from lavish white marble baroque monuments to austere modernist structures. Raphaëlis's organ, vintage 1554 AD, cranks up for concerts most Thursdays at 8pm. (Open May-Aug. Mon.-Sat. 9am-5:45pm, Sun. 12:30-5:45pm; April and Sept. Mon.-Fri. 9am-5:45pm, Sat. 11:30am-5:45pm, Sun. 12:30-3:45pm; Oct.-March Mon.-Fri. 10am-3:45pm, Sat. 11:30am-3:45pm, Sun. 12:30-3:45pm. Closed during church services. Admission 3kr, children 1kr.) Between the museum and cathedral is the city park, which in July erupts into a dazzling field of poppies and periwinkles. The **tourist office** (tel. 42 35 27 00), near the cathedral, can suggest walking tours around the enchanting old quarter. Roskilde's **IYHF youth hostel** is at Hørhusene 61 (tel. 42 35 21 84; bus #601 or 604), and you can camp by the beach at Vigen Strandpark, Baunehøjvej 7-9, 4km north of town on bus #602 (tel. 46 75 79 96; adults 31kr, children 16kr; open early April to mid-Sept.). A vegetable, fruit, flea and flower **market** transforms Roskilde. (Wed. and Sat. 8am-2pm.) In late June, Roskilde hosts one of northern Europe's largest music festivals, with rock, jazz and folk bands from all over the planet.

Bornholm

East of Denmark proper and south of Sweden, the gorgeous island of Bornholm lures vacationers to its expansive sand beaches, cozy fishing villages and winding bicycle paths. The sun, sand, and red-roofed cliffside villas may remind you of southern Europe, but the rolling fields and woods, flowers, and tidy half-timbered houses are irretrievably Danish.

From Copenhagen, the fastest way here is the **Bornholmerpilen** service that leaves Kastrup Havn near Copenhagen's airport three times a day, with bus connections to Central Station (2½ hr.; early May to mid-Sept. only; adults 165-195kr, seniors and children 85-100kr, same day return 225-265kr, seniors and children 150-175kr; fares higher from late June to mid-Aug.; tel. 56 95 95 95 daily 8:30am-6:30pm). Slower, smoother and cheaper are the **Bornholmstraffiken** car ferries (tel. 33 13 18 66), which sail overnight daily from Kvæsthusbroen 2 in Copenhagen (leaving at 11:30pm; morning departures also in summer Thurs.-Mon. 8:30am; 7 hr., 164kr) and two to five times daily from Ystad in Sweden (2½ hr., 90kr). The #866 **Bornholmerbussen** service runs twice daily in summer and once a day the rest of the year from Central Station in Copenhagen to the Ystad ferry, cutting travel time to 5½ hrs. (Copenhagen-Bornholm 160kr, children 80kr; for reservations call 44 68 44 00). All run to the harbor in Rønne, Bornholm's main city. An efficient local BAT bus service connects most points in Bornholm, and there are numerous cycling paths.

Rønne, on Bornholm's western coast, is part workaday port and part festive resort town. Its **tourist office** (tel. 56 95 08 10), by the Bornholmstraffiken terminal, can help you plan your stay on the island and will book you a room in a private home. Rønne's **vandrerhjem (IYHF),** Sdr. Allé (tel. 56 95 13 40), is in a quiet, woodsy area. (52-57kr. Open April-Oct.) There are **campgrounds** at Strandvejen 4 (tel. 56 95 23 20; open May 15-Aug.) and Antoinettevej 2 (tel. 56 95 22 81; open April-Sept.). Bikes can be rented at Søndergade 7 and at Havnegade 11 (near the tourist office) for 50kr per day.

Dueodde, on Bornholm's southeastern tip, is lined with capacious beaches swept with sand almost as fine as talc. The beach, the hostel, and four ice cream stands are indeed Dueodde's *raison d'être.* Bronze beach bums pack the **Dueodde Vandrerhjem (IYHF),** Skrokkegårdsvej 17 (tel. 56 48 81 19; 57-67kr; kitchen and laundry; open May-Sept.).

Three robust towns anchor Bornholm's spectacular north coast: Svaneke, Gudhjem, and the Siamese community of Sandvig-Allinge. Each has a hostel, a tourist office, bus connections, and campgrounds. Just outside of **Sandvig** is the **Vandrerhjem Sjøljan (IYHF),** Hammershusvej 94 (tel. 56 48 03 62; 57-67kr; kitchen; open June-Oct.). Another kilometer down the same road sulks **Hammershus,** a thrilling heap of stone perched above the sea. Free and always open, it is northern Europe's largest castle ruin. In the middle of the north coast, **Gudhjem's** harbor appeared in the agonizing film *Pelle the Conqueror.* Its popular **Vandrerhjem Sct. Jørgens Gård (IYHF)** (tel. 56 48 50 35), right by the harbor and across from the bus stop, has a kitchen of greatness. (52-57kr. Open year-round.) A small beach is about 1km away, to the right of the harbor.

Far off Bornholm's north coast is the **Ertholmene** island group, where a little over a hundred people maintain a small fishing community. There are daily sailings in summer from Allinge, Gudhjem, and Svaneke to Christiansø, the main island, where you can poke around for a few hours (round-trip from 100kr).

Funen (Fyn)

Funen is Denmark's garden. Colorful flowerbeds grace nearly every house, and diverse wildflowers carpet coastal areas. A bridge connects Funen to Jutland on the east, and regular ferry service shuttles between Funen and Zealand. Hourly trains from Copenhagen to Odense and points beyond cross on the ferry from Korsør on Zealand to Nyborg on Funen, and require seat reservations; railpass holders can get around this by taking one of two-four slightly slower local trains to Korsør, getting off the train and onto the ferry, and then back onto another train when the ferry reaches Funen. Going from Funen to Zealand, get off at "Nyborg FGH" and walk to the ferry.

Birthplace of Hans Christian Andersen, the old manufacturing metropolis of Odense (OH-then-sa) has grown to become Denmark's third largest city. Seek out its cobblestoned alleyways, pedestrian zones, town gardens, and waterways. The **tourist office** (tel. 66 12 75 20), in the City Hall, a few blocks south of the train station, spews free maps, exchanges currency when banks are closed, and books rooms in private homes (100kr per person). They also have a **Meet the Danes** program: with two days' advance notice, they arrange an intriguing evening of tea and conversation with a Danish family who shares your interests. Follow Jernbanegade, to the right of the station, all the way to Vestergade, and turn left. (Open Mon.-Sat. 9am-7pm, Sun. 11am-7pm; Sept. to mid-June Mon.-Fri. 9am-5pm, Sat. 10am-1pm.) Bus routes radiate from Klingenberg, south of the city hall; board at the rear of the bus and pay your fare when you disembark (9kr, children 5kr). Regional buses to elsewhere on Funen stop behind the train station.

Vandrerhjem Kragsbjerggården (IYHF), Kragsbjergvej 121 (tel. 66 13 04 25), inhabits a pastoral yellow building enclosing a courtyard, about 2km from the town center. Take bus #62 or 63 from Klingenberg or the train station. (Reception open 8am-noon and 4-8pm. 57kr. Kitchen. Open mid-Feb. to Nov.)

Odense's sights begin at the train station. The **Railway Museum,** Dannebrogsgade 24, just across the tracks, has locomotives and coaches from various periods, plus a model railway elaborate enough to make any tot drool. An English-language brochure is available. (Open daily 10am-4pm; Oct.-April Sun. 10am-3pm. Admission 15kr, children 5kr. Free to railpass holders.) At **H.C. Andersens Hus,** Hans Jensens Stræde 39-43, you can learn about the author's eccentricities and listen to recordings of his stories in English. (Open daily June-Aug. 9am-6pm; April-May and Sept. 10am-5pm; Oct.-March 10am-3pm. Admission 15kr, children 5kr.) At the other end of the pedestrian district, **Brandts Klædefabrik,** Brandts Passage 37, Odense's cloth-factory-*cum*-art-and-culture center, hosts street performers and exhibits, including a graphic museum, an art gallery and a photography museum. Don't miss the rainbow **Butik Salam** at Brandts Passage 34, with its dazzling menagerie of Third World crafts. Cheap eateries line the nearby pedestrian streets; when in doubt, hit the low wood tables of **Franck-A** at Vestergade 19. **Madhuset,** Albanigade 53 (tel. 66 12 16 12) serves light three-course dinners for 80kr. (Open Mon.-Sat. 5-9:30pm.)

Just south of **Fruens Bøge,** the enticing park in the south part of Odense which accommodated Andersen in his weirder moods, is **Den Fynske Landsby** (Funen Village), Sejerskovvej 20, a pleasant collection of old rural buildings brought here by pillaging curators from towns all around the island. Take bus #25 or 26. (Open June-Aug. daily 10am-7:30pm; Sept.-Oct. and April-May daily 10am-4pm; Nov.-March Sun. 10am-4pm. Admission 15kr, children 5kr.) You can **camp** next to Fruens Bøge at Odensevej 102 (tel. 66 11 47 02). Take bus #13. (32kr per person. Also rents cottages. Open late-March to mid-Oct.). The Fruens Bøge train stop just out of town on the Odense-Svendborg train line is convenient to both museum and campsite.

About 45 minutes south of Odense on the Svendborg rail line is **Egeskov Slot,** a stunning 16th-century castle that appears to float on the lake that surrounds it—it's actually supported by 12,000 oak piles. The castle itself houses some old furnishings and an assortment of hunting trophies accumulated by a keen-eyed owner. The surrounding grounds include formal gardens, a bamboo labyrinth, and museums housing dozens of vintage vehicles—autos, motorcycles, horse-drawn carriages, military aircraft and (what the hell) a Sherman tank. On summer Sundays at 5pm, classical concerts resound in the castle's great hall (free with admission to castle and grounds). (Grounds open daily June-Aug. daily 9am-6pm; May and Sept. daily 10am-5pm. Castle open May-Sept. daily 10am-5pm. Admission to grounds 40kr, children 20kr. Admission to castle itself an additional 40kr, children 20kr, which may or may not be worth it.) To get to Egeskov, get off the Svendborg-bound train at **Kværndrup;** exit the station and turn right, until you reach the Bøjdenvej, the main road. You can then wait for an hourly bus, or turn right on the road and walk the 2km to the castle.

Svendborg, on Funen's south coast an hour from Odense by rail, makes the best base for longer stays on Funen and for bicycle trips to the islands just south of it.

The 17th-century estate of **Valdemars Slot,** across the bridge on the island of Tåsinge, was built by Christian IV for his son Valdemar. (Admission 30kr, children 10kr. Take bus #200 or buy a boat ticket at the Svendborg tourist office. Open May-Sept. daily 10am-5pm; Easter to the end of April and Oct. Sat.-Sun. and holidays 10am-5pm.) Outdoor cafés rim the *torvet* (town square), which lies between a 16th-century farmhouse and a brick church, just up the hill from the train station. The **tourist office** (tel. 62 21 09 80) is on this square; it provides a map of comely beaches and finds rooms in private homes. (Open mid-June to mid-Aug. Mon.-Fri. 9am-5:30pm, Sat. 9am-1pm, Sun. 10am-noon; mid-Aug. to mid-June Mon.-Fri. 9am-5pm; mid-March to mid-June and mid-Aug. to mid-Sept. also Sat. 9am-noon.) On the other side of the train station is the dock for ferries to Ærø. Svendborg's newly-minted **youth hostel** (tel. 62 21 66 99), at Vestergade 45, has 2-4 beds per room (67kr). **Carlsberg Camping,** Sundbrovej 19 (tel. 62 22 53 84), is across the sound on Tåsinge. (36kr. Open mid-April to mid-Sept.) Rent a **bike** at Havnegade 4 (tel. 62 21 31 28).

Ærø and other islands

All around Funen lie smaller islands where the open sea frames venerable villages, hardy farmhouses, and wind-blown wild flowers. Ærø, south of Funen, is the most accessible to rail travelers, since certain trains from Odense to Svendborg are timed to meet the ferry from Svendborg to Ærø's principal town, Ærøskøbing. (Ferry 38kr, seniors 23kr, children 19kr; round-trip 75kr, 45kr, and 38kr allows return on other ferries to Ærø. Call 62 52 10 18 for schedule information.)

Ærø's farmland rolls gently, its little towns speckled with old churches and windmills. The water is shallower, and the beaches calmer than those of Denmark's west coast, making windsurfing auspicious. In Ærøskøbing, cobbled lanes, hollyhocks, and tiny half-timbered houses attract yachtspeople from Denmark and Germany. The **tourist office** (tel. 62 52 13 00), near the church on the *torv* (main square), arranges rooms in private homes. (Singles 85kr. Doubles 150kr. 7kr fee. Open June-Aug. Mon.-Fri. 9am-5pm, Sat. 9am-1pm, Sun. 10am-noon; Sept.-May Mon.-Fri. 9am-4pm.) The gracious **IYHF youth hostel,** Smedevejen 13 (tel. 62 52 10 44), lies 1km from town on a former farm. (57kr. Open April-Sept.) **Ærøskøbing Camping,** Sygehusvejen 40b (tel. 62 52 18 54), is 10 minutes to the right as you leave the ferry on the waterfront. (35kr per person, 4-person bungalows 76kr. Open May to mid-Sept.) You can rent a bike at the hostel (35kr per day, 60kr for 2 days), the campground, or the gas station at Pilebækken 7. Restaurants line up along Vestergade, the primary street leading into town from the ferry port. The most impressive establishment on the row is **Vaffelbageriet,** Vestergade 21, an ice cream stand whose "Ærø Special" consists of superb walnut ice cream, topped with whipped cream and maple syrup and served in a home-baked cone that is excellent even by Danish standards. (13-27kr, depending on the scoops.)

Marstal, 13km away on Ærø's east coast, is similarly picturesque. The **tourist office,** Kirkestræde 29 (tel. 62 53 19 60), on the *torv,* rents bikes and finds rooms in private homes. (Open June-Aug. Mon.-Fri. 9am-5pm, Sat. 10am-3pm; July also Sun. 10am-noon; Sept.-May Mon.-Fri. 9am-4pm.) The **IYHF youth hostel,** Færgestræde 29 (tel. 62 53 10 64), is by the harbor, a 10-min. walk to the left of the ferry. (57kr. Kitchen. Open May-Aug.) Down Havnegaden, past the hotel, you can **camp** steps away from the town's best beach (tel. 62 53 19 60; 30kr, children 15kr; open mid-May to Aug.). Reach Marstal by bus #990 from Ærøskøbing, or by ferry from Rudkøbing on the island of Langeland.

Jutland (Jylland)

Homeland of the Jutes (who made history when they hooked up with the Angles and Saxons and conquered England), the Jutland peninsula is Denmark's largest land lump and the only link to continental Europe. Low hills and occasional forests make for a slightly more variegated topography than that of the islands, while numerous beaches and countless campgrounds mark the peninsula as prime summer vacation territory. Because nature and relaxation are the top attractions, Jutland may not be suitable for a whirlwind tour.

Scandinavian Seaways runs ferries from **Esbjerg,** on Jutland's west coast, to Harwich, England six to eight times a week (mid-June to mid-Aug; 1100kr, round-trip 1700kr; lower fares off-season). From mid-June to mid-August there's also service to Newcastle, England (2 per week), and Tórshavn in the Faroe Islands (1 per week). (Some reductions for railpass holders; call for information in Esbjerg, tel. 75 12 48 00, or Copenhagen, tel. 33 11 22 55.) There are rail connections to Esbjerg and a youth hostel 3km from town at Gammel Vardevej 80 (tel. 75 12 42 58; 57kr; open Feb. to mid-Dec.). In northern Jutland, ferries also travel to the Faroes from **Hanstholm** (tel. 33 93 90 97; bus connections to Århus and Copenhagen) and to Norway from **Hirtshals** (tel. 98 94 19 66; accessible by train, changing at Hjørring).

Fredericia

Situated across the Lillebælt from Funen and on the Århus-Copenhagen rail line, Fredericia is not at all flashy, but quite picturesque. The **Fredericia Ramparts,** built in the 17th century, reflect the town's origins as a military stronghold. Today the bastions are covered with grass, and water lilies grow in the moats, but neither disguises the engineered precision of the zig-zagging works. Near the southern end of the ramparts and the train station, the **Fredericia Museum,** Jernbanegade 10 (tel. 75 02 65 68), functions as the town's attic, with a barn full of old tools and exhibits on the town's military history. (Open daily 10am-5pm; mid-Aug. to mid-June Tues.-Sat. noon-4pm, Sun. 11am-4pm.) The south and east edges of the town are defended by the sea—the south edge is the port, while the east has a beach.

The **tourist office,** on Jyllandsgade at Axeltorv (tel. 75 92 13 77), is aflurry with printed matter, including the subtle *Fredericia is the Town for Everyone.* (Open July to mid-Aug. Mon.-Fri. 9am-6pm, Sat. 9am-2pm; May-June and late Aug. Mon.-Fri. 9am-5pm, Sat. 9am-1pm; Sept.-April Mon.-Fri. 9am-5pm.) The **IYHF Youth Hostel,** Skovløberværnget 9 (tel. 75 92 12 87), is 2km outside the ramparts and also 2km from the train station; bus #2 runs from the station to within a few blocks of the hostel. (Reception open 8am-noon, 4-6pm and 8-9pm. 52-67kr. Breakfast 38kr. Hostel open early Jan.-late Dec.) In town, **Café Jasmin,** Jyllandsgade 25 (tel. 75 93 25 22), serves an interesting variety of pizzas (44kr), as well as sandwiches and meat dishes, and the menus are in English. (Open Mon.-Sat. 11am-10pm.)

Northwest of Fredericia, **Legoland,** a huge amusement park built out of 33 million Legos, celebrates Denmark's national toy with Lego versions of the space shuttle *Columbia,* Mt. Rushmore, and an Amsterdam canal. Take the train from Fredericia north to Vejle (1 per hr., 17 min.), then a bus to **Billund.** (Open May-3rd Sun. of Sept. daily 10am-8pm. Admission 44kr, children 22kr.)

Århus

Århus, Denmark's second city, is the cultural and student center of Jutland, the closest thing Denmark has to a college town. Thanks to the city's rivalry with Copenhagen, its residents are the traditional butt of Danish jokes. Two milennia ago the people living near Århus sacrificed some of their own and threw them into nearby bogs, whose antiseptic acidity preserved the hideous squished bodies. Take bus #6 from the train station to the **Moesgård Museum** at the end of the line to see one of the creatures. (Open daily 10am-5pm; mid-Sept. to March Tues.-Sun. 10am-4pm. Admission 20kr, students and seniors 10kr, ages under 15 free.) From behind the museum, the open-air **Prehistoric Trail** leads through mock prehistoric settings all the way down to a splendiferous sand beach (3km). Bus #19 returns you from the beach to the Århus station (summer only). To enter the more recent past, visit **Den Gamle By,** a unique cultural history museum with more than 60 original buildings from the 16th through 19th centuries. Take bus #3 to the Den Gamle By stop. (Open daily 9am-6pm; Sept.-May reduced hrs. Admission 25-30kr, under 12 free.) For a fuller perspective, you can drop by the **Women's Museum** and its café behind the cathedral at Domkirkeplads 5. (Open Tues.-Sun. 10am-4pm. Admission 10kr, seniors and children 5kr.)

The annual **Århus Festuge,**—a rollicking week of theater and music—begins on the first Saturday in September. The **tourist office** is in the town hall (tel. 86 12 16 00), one block down Park Allé from the train station. As always, get your grubby little hands on a free map and city guide. Contact them a day or two in advance if you'd like to reconnoiter with a Danish family through the **Meet the Danes** program. The office also books accommodations (around 100kr per bed) for 20kr. (Open mid-June to early Aug. daily 9am-8pm; early Aug. to mid-Sept. daily 9am-7pm; mid Sept. to mid-June Mon.-Fri. 9am-4:30pm, Sat. 9am-1pm.) Århus's **IYHF youth hostel** rests peacefully 3km from the city center and five minutes from the beach at Marienlundsvej 10 (tel. 86 16 72 98), in the Risskov forest. Take bus #1 or 2 to the Marienlund terminus and follow the signs to the hostel. (Curfew 11pm. 55kr. Breakfast 36kr. Kitchen and laundry. Lockers. Open mid-Jan. to mid-Dec.) The area's campgrounds include beauteous **Blommehaven,** located near a beach in the Marselisborg Forest at Ørneredevej 35 (tel. 86 27 02 07). Take bus #19 (summer only) from the rail station directly to the grounds, or bus #6 to Hørhavevej. (Open late April-early Sept.) Forage for food along the pedestrianized Søndergade, where cafés and stands are clustered.

Silkeborg

Less than an hour west of Århus by train, Silkeborg resplends amidst Jutland's lake and canal country. The town makes a fine launchpad for canoeing and hiking; pick up a map at the **tourist office** on the main square at Torvet 9 (tel. 86 82 19 11). From the train station, turn right, take the first left onto Hostrupsgade, then turn right at the first four-way traffic light; Vestergade leads through the pedestrian zone to the square. (Open July-early Aug. Mon.-Fri. 9am-5pm, Sat. 9am-3pm; April-June and mid-Aug. to Sept. Mon.-Fri. 9am-5pm, Sat. 9am-noon; Oct. and March Mon.-Fri. 10am-4pm, Sat. 9am-noon; Nov.-Feb. Mon.-Fri. 10am-4pm.) The **Silkeborg Museum** in Hovedgården houses the Tollund Man, another bog person (see Århus above). (Open daily 10am-5pm; mid-Oct. to mid-April Wed. and Sat.-Sun. noon-4pm. Admission 15kr, children 5kr.) The **Silkeborg Museum of Art,** Gudenåvej 7-9, contains an arresting array of paintings and ceramics by Asger Jorn and the COBRA (COpenhagen BRussels Amsterdam) group he founded. (Open Tues.-Sun. 10am-5pm; Nov.-March Tues.-Fri. noon-4pm, Sat.-Sun. 10am-4pm. Admission 20kr, children free with adult.)

For marine exploration, rent a boat at **Silkeborg Kanofart,** Remstrupvej 41 (tel. 86 82 35 43). **Cyclecompagniet,** Vestergade 18, rents bikes for 35kr per day (deposit 100kr). Beside a duck-filled canal stretches the grassy lawn of **Vandrerhjemmet Åbo (IYHF),** Åhavevej 55 (tel. 86 82 36 42). Walk to the right from the train station to the end of the street, turn left, then take the first right. (Reception open 8am-noon and 4-8pm. No curfew. 57-67kr. Kitchen and laundry. Open March-Nov.) For camping, **Indelukket** (tel. (06) 82 22 01) is a bit closer, but **Århusbakkens** (tel. 86 82 28 24) is more appealing.

Frederikshavn and Skagen

The self-proclaimed busiest ferry terminal in the world, **Frederikshavn** is truly drab. **Stena Line** ferries (tel. 98 42 43 66) leave here for Gothenburg, Sweden (4-8 per day; 3¼ hr.; 90kr, a mere 2kr for all railpass holders except the trains-only version of InterRail, which provides a 50% discount), as well as for Oslo and other points in Norway (1-2 per day, 224-324kr). Ferries are rarer and cheaper off-season. Frederikshavn's **tourist office** is near the Stena Line terminal, 400m south of the rail station at Brotorvet 1 (tel. 98 42 32 66; open mid-June to mid-Aug. Mon.-Sat.

8:30am-8:30pm, Sun. 11am-6pm; mid-Aug. to Sept. and April-early June Mon.-Fri. 9am-5pm, Sat. 11am-2pm; Oct.-March Mon.-Fri. 9am-4pm). The **IYHF youth hostel,** Buhlsvej 6 (tel. 98 42 14 75), jovial but packed in summer, is a 15-min. walk from the station and harbor. (Reception open 7am-noon and 4-9pm. 52-67kr. Kitchen. Open Feb. to mid-Dec.) You might enjoy the ferry trip from Frederikshavn to the island of **Læsø** (4 per day, 1½ hr.), where you can stay in an **IYHF hostel** near the dock at Vesterø Havn (tel. 98 49 91 95; 57kr; open Feb.-Nov.).

More majestic is **Skagen,** which lies among the dunes at Denmark's northernmost tip. The town is well known for its 19th-century artists' colony. Works of the Skagen painters are on display in the **Skagen Museum,** in **Anchers Hus,** and in **Drachmanns Hus.** Get information on these sights and the area's many fine beaches at the **tourist office** at Sct. Laurentiivej 22 (tel. 98 44 13 77; open June-Aug. Mon.-Fri. 9am-5:30pm, Sun. 11am-2pm; Sept.-Oct. and May Mon.-Fri. 9am-4pm, Sat. 10am-noon; Nov.-April Mon.-Fri. 9am-4pm). **Nordjyllands Trafikselskab** runs both buses and private trains from Frederikshavn to Skagen as Route #79 (28kr each way, railpasses not valid). The **IYHF youth hostel,** Højensvej 32 (tel. 98 44 13 56), in Gammel Skagen, 4km west of Skagen, is somewhat inconvenient. The #79 bus stops right in front of it, or it's a 20-minute walk from the Højen train stop (the last stop before Skagen). Reserve ahead. (57-67kr. Kitchen. Open mid-March to Oct.) Most campgrounds around Skagen are open late April to mid-September; try **Grenen** (tel. 98 44 25 46), **Poul Eegs** (tel. 98 44 14 70), or **Østerklit** (tel. 98 44 31 23).

Faroe Islands

The Faroe Islands print their own paper money, but use Danish coins and accept Danish bills.

Country Code: 298 **International Dialing Prefix: 009**

Flung out in the middle of the North Atlantic between Norway and Iceland, the 18 Faroe Islands are a handful of emerald mountains where colorful fishing villages cluster beside grassy slopes that give way to towering sea cliffs. Though the Faroes are a self-governing member of the Danish Commonwealth, the 47,000 Faroese prefer to identify themselves by their linguistic, cultural and geographical proximity to Iceland and Norway. This anomalous political and geographic situation has helped prevent the onslaught of tourism that would take place if the Faroes were any more accessible. Furrowed with fjords and valleys and covered with birds, sheep and fog, the islands are surpassingly beautiful. The efficient exploitation of nearby fishing banks has allowed the islanders to attain a Scandinavianly high standard of living in just one generation, and their excellent infrastructure of roads and tunnels continues to expand on a daily basis.

The Faroes are accessible by ferry during the summer and by air all year round. From June to August, **Smyril Line,** J. Broncksgøta 37, P.O. Box 370, FR-110 Tórshavn, Faroe Islands (tel. 15900) runs a car ferry stopping at Hanstholm (Denmark) Sat. at 4pm; Tórshavn (Faroes) Mon. at 6am; Lerwick (Shetland) Mon. at 10pm; Bergen (Norway) Tues. at noon; Lerwick again Wed. at 1:30am; Tórshavn again Wed. at 3pm; Seyðisfjörður (Iceland) Thurs. at 8am; and Tórshavn again Fri. at 6am. The one-way fare (no round-trip reduction) from Lerwick to the Faroes is 680kr (£60), from Bergen 1040kr, from Seyðisfjörður 1150kr, from Hanstholm 1320kr (25% discount for students under 26; another 25% off early June and late Aug. sailings.) You can also book via Eurocruises, their American agent (tel. (800) 688-3876) or their British agent, P&O Ferries, P.O. Box 5, P&O Terminal, Aberdeen, Scotland AB9 8DL (tel. (0224) 57 26 15). Weekly summer service (late June to mid-Aug.) also connects Scrabster (Scotland) with Tórshavn (13-14 hr.; leaves Tórshavn Fri. 11:59pm, Scrabster Sat. 6:30pm; from £72 one-way, £144 return,

25% off with ISIC). Contact either P&O Ferries or **Strandfaraskip Landsins,** Yviri við Strond 6, FR-100 Tórshavn, Faroe Islands (tel. 14550). **DFDS/Scandinavian Seaways** (tel. in Denmark 33 11 22 55, in North America (800) 533-3755) runs a weekly car ferry from Esbjerg, Denmark to Tórshavn (mid-June to mid-Aug.; 33hr.; leaves Esbjerg Mon. 9pm, Tórshavn Wed. 9:30am; 990-1300kr one-way, 1690-2300kr round-trip, 20% off with ISIC). Flying is a trifle more expensive and is much less hassle. **Danair** (part of SAS) and **Atlantic Airways** fly 2-4 times daily between Copenhagen and the Faroes (one-way 1920kr, 25% off if under 25, advance purchase round-trip 2800kr). From mid-June to August, Atlantic Airways also jets to the Faroes from Billund, Denmark. **Icelandair** flies 2-3 times per week from Reykjavík to the Faroes.

Take advantage of the Faroes' top-notch transportation and hostel network to explore even the remotest fringes of the islands. Students save 10% on bus and ferry rides. Many find hitchhiking simply dreamy, but hitchers should avoid the unventilated tunnels. You can stay in private homes, official campsites, or at any of seven hostels (which also offer camping facilities). **Tórshavn** (pop. 15,000), on the island of Streymoy, is the Faroes' capital and transportation center; all international ferries dock in its harbor, while the airport is a two-hour, 90kr bus-and-ferry ride away. There are two hostels in town. The independent hostel at Skrivaragøta 3 (tel. 10310; open mid-May to early Sept.) is far more comfortable than the cavernous official hostel on Gundadalsvegur by the soccer stadium (tel. 18900; open March-Aug.) You'll pay 80kr at either abode. Looking out over Tórshavn from beneath its sod roof, the **Nordic House** (tel. 17900) is a triumph of Scandinavian design and a busy venue with cultural events almost every evening of the summer. The **Faroe Islands Tourist Board** office, Reynagøta 17, FR-100 Tórshavn (tel. 16055) opens for all ferry arrivals; write ahead for comprehensive sights and accommodations brochures, or pick them up on arrival.

The overwhelmingly scenic village of **Gjógv,** on northern Eysturoy, is nestled in a valley at the mouth of a sea loch. Behind the hostel (tel. 23171 or 23175; open all year), grassy slopes rise to the crest of a colossal ocean-side precipice. (2 buses per day from Tórshavn, 2 hr., 50kr.) **Kirkjubøur,** 12km over the ridge from Tórshavn, was the islands' religious and cultural center in the Middle Ages. A 900-year old farmhouse converted into a **museum** and an unfinished 14th-century **cathedral** invite exploration. (2-5 buses per day from Tórshavn, 30 min., 20kr.)

ESTONIA

As we went to press, Estonia was still using the Soviet Union's currency and telephone systems; however, we expect this to change by early 1992.

The northernmost of the Baltic states, Estonia (Eesti) stands only 80km from its linguistic and cultural relatives in Finland. Split between the Germans and the Danes in the 13th century, Estonia later spent a century under Swedish rule, broken in the 18th century by Russian annexation. On February 24, 1918, Estonia declared independence from a Bolshevik Russia weakened by civil war, and after a two-year struggle with the Russians and Germans, was recognized by the Soviet Union in February 1920. In June 1940 the USSR annexed the country, outlawed the blue, black, and white Estonian flag, and began deporting tens of thousands of Estonians. Even under Soviet occupation, though, Estonia's linguistic and geographical proximity to Finland made it the most Scandinavian of the Baltic states. Estonians tend to dress in brighter, more Western clothes, Finnish joint ventures are everywhere, and Estonia seems positioned for quick economic success now that independence has returned.

Like the other Baltic states, Estonia is very small; you can drive from the Gulf of Finland to the southern border in a couple hours. Tallinn (Estonia's capital and main port), the university town of Tartu, and the town of Pärnu on the Gulf of Riga are the three main centers. The islands of Saaremaa and Hiiumaa in the west, which shelter the Gulf of Riga from the Baltic Sea, are well worth visiting as they become more accessible.

Getting There and Getting Around

As we went to press in September 1991, Estonian visas were being issued on arrival at the border; bring one photograph and some evidence that someone in Estonia is planning to take care of you (like a personal invitation or a confirmed hotel reservation). Visas are also available from the consulates in Helsinki and Stockholm under the same conditions (show up in person and allow a few days). The companies listed in the Tallinn accommodations section can book rooms in advance and issue a confirmation slip to present at the border. The hope is that the accommodations system in Estonia will become sufficiently flexible by early 1992 to allow the visa system to be eliminated entirely. Check ahead with a ferry company, or contact the Estonian consulate at 9 Rockefeller Plaza, Suite 1421, New York, N.Y. 10020 (tel. (212) 247-1450); also see the listings in Helsinki, Stockholm, and Copenhagen.

The easiest way to reach Estonia is by sea from Helsinki. **Saimaa Lines,** Fabianinkatu 14, 00100 Helsinki (tel. +358 (0) 65 10 11 or 65 87 33) are agents for the Soviet ship *Georg Ots,* which sails from Helsinki to Tallinn (Fri.-Wed. at 10:30am, returning from Tallinn Thurs.-Tues. at 6:30pm; Feb.-March 3 per week). Look for the ship with the hammer and sickle on the funnel. The more Western **Tallink** (tel. +358 (0) 60 28 22) leaves Helsinki in the evenings (Mon.-Sat. at 3pm or 5pm, returning from Tallinn Tues.-Sun. at 9:30am, 11am, or 1pm; mid-Aug. to May from Helsinki Mon.-Tues. and Thurs.-Sat., from Tallinn Tues.-Wed. and Fri.-Sun.). Both ferries take 3½ to 4 hours and cost 120mk each way. **Helta,** Eteläranta 7, Helsinki (tel. +358 (0) 64 47 33) also plows its hydrofoil through the 80km of Baltic waves (late April-Oct. 1-2 per day each way; 2 hr.; 150mk one-way, 250mk round-trip; often canceled). Buy a round-trip ticket to avoid lines at the Tallinn terminal, and pick up one of the ferry brochures in Helsinki that has a small Tallinn map.

Travel from Sweden is also an option. **Estline's** *Nord Estonia,* Estlineterminalen i Frihamnen, 11556 Stockholm (tel. +46 (8) 667 00 01) skims from Stockholm to Tallinn and back (3-4 per week at 5:30pm from Stockholm, returning from Tallinn at 7pm; 13½-14½ hr.; 335-420kr, students 255-315kr). Most of the ferry companies run short cruises which allow you to spend the night on the ferry and the day walking around Tallinn (1-day cruise on the Georg Ots 175-190mk); any of the ferry companies will arrange this.

Finnair flies from Helsinki to Tallinn (5 per week, from 620mk round-trip); SAS from Stockholm (1-2 per week); Aeroflot from Helsinki (3 per week), Stockholm (2 per week), Frankfurt (1 per week), and Budapest (1 per week).

Buses and trains radiate from Tallinn out across Estonia, with connections to Russia, Latvia, and Lithuania. In 1991, a good schedule (the *sõiduplaan)* was sporadically available in Tallinn; ask around. Taxis will take you anywhere you want for hard currency, although it is cheaper to pay in rubles.

Practical Information

Tourist offices per se don't yet exist in Estonia, but the country is more and more used to foreign visitors; by Baltic standards, there's a veritable profusion (by Baltic standards) of maps, schedules, and tourist brochures (most of which betray Scandinavian influence). Inroads' *Guide to the Baltic States* (USD18) is useful, but distinctly weaker on Estonia than on Latvia and Lithuania.

Estonian is a Balto-Fennic language, closely related to Finnish. *Aitäh* (EYE-taa) means "thank you"; *palun* (PALL-oon), "please" or "here you are." Yes is *ja* and no is *ei* (rhymes with "hay"). Finns and Estonians can understand each other with a little effort and a few days of adjustment. Of the three Baltic states, Estonians speak the poorest Russian; first try English, which few speak well, though most have studied.

Tallinn

A bustling port city 80km across the Gulf of Finland from Helsinki, Tallinn and its old city are so beautiful that the Danes, the Germans, the Swedes, and the Russians have all laid claim to the town. In the last 30 years, immigrants have almost doubled the city's population to half a million, leaving 47% of it Russian-speaking.

Orientation and Practical Information

Tallinn centers on the **Vanalinn** (Old City), an egg-shaped maze of streets which peaks in the fortress-rock of **Toompea,** whose 13th-century streets are level with the church steeples in the lower parts of the Old City. To get to the Old City from the harbor, walk up to the intersection and take tram #2; or walk west on Sadama tn., which turns into Põhja pst., then go left on Suur-Rannavärav. From the train station, cross Toompuiestee and the old city is straight ahead of you on Nunne tn.; the stairway up Patkuli trepp, on the right side of Nunne tn., is a shortcut direct to Toompea.

Under Finnish influence, Tallinn's tourist literature is rapidly approaching Scandinavian standards. The 22-story Hotel Viru on Narva mnt., just east of the Old City and a short walk up Mere pst. from the harbor, sells *Tallinn This Week* and *Estonia—Tallinn—A Practical Guide,* two very good city guides; for rubles they have the *Tallinn City Paper* (5.50R) and a drab city map (2.88R). The reception desk at the Hotel Sport, Regati pst. 1, five kilometers northeast of the Old City, sells a much better color map with a street index (USD5). The booklet *Tallinn, Capital of Estonia: The Traveler's Guide* contains self-guided tours, maps, and pictures.

Tourist Offices: Hotel desks can give *brief* answers to *specific* questions and book train and bus connections. **Intourist** in the Hotel Viru can also book hotel rooms, and purchase train and bus tickets for you at a slightly higher cost than at the train station.

Currency Exchange: At the Hotel Viru. Open daily 9am-1pm, 2-5pm and 5:30-9pm. Also at other hotels, the seaport, the airport, and banks. For the best rates in town, call **Travel Bureau "Rare"** (tel. 59 33 76 or 66 60 87).

Post Office: Main office at Narva mnt. 1, across from the Hotel Viru. Poste Restante. Open Mon.-Sat. 8am-8pm.

Telephones: It is possible to call Tallinn from Helsinki and vice versa; in Helsinki, ask the operator for the correct code, and in Tallinn, use Finnish marks in the special phones at the air terminal and the port. Otherwise, calls out of the Baltics must be made from the main post office. Open Mon.-Sat. 8am-8pm, Sun. 8am-3pm. **City Code:** 0142.

Trains: From the **Balti jaam** station on Toompuiestee. To: Moscow (4 per day, 14 hr.), Leningrad (4 per day, 7 hr.), Tartu (2 per day, 3½ hr.), Rīga (2 per day, 8 hr.), Vilnius (1 per day).

Buses: From the **Autobussijaam** (station) on Masina tn., 1.5km southeast of the old town. To: Rīga (10 per day, 6½ hr.); Leningrad (6 per day, 8 hr.); Kaliningrad (1 per day, 13 hr.); Vilnius (1 per day, 12 hr.); and other destinations.

Public Transportation: Many trams and buses stop at the station in front of the Hotel Viru. Most lines run until about midnight. Special minibuses take you away to various points in the city (3pm-2am) from in front of the hotel, leaving when full.

Emergencies: Police: (tel. 01). **Ambulance:** (tel. 03).

Accommodations and Food

As we went to press, the accommodations scene in Tallinn was totally up for grabs. Will there be private rooms? Bed-and-breakfasts? Youth hostels? Probably—the demand is there—but no one knows yet. **Tallinn Technical University,** Ehitajate tee 5, Tallinn 200108, Estonia (tel. 53 29 61; fax 53 24 46; telex 64 17 31 01) may be able to help with rooms in student dorms. Rooms at the **Hotel Sport,** Regati pst. 1 (tel. 23 85 98) or the Hotel **Olympia,** Kingissepa pst. 33 (tel. 60 24 38)—the cheapest of Tallinn's major hotels—should run about USD40, though **Estlands Resor** in Stockholm (tel. +46 (8) 11 05 69) can reserve doubles in the Hotel Sport for SEK300 per night. In Helsinki **Estoom,** Vuorimiehenkatu 23a (tel. +358 (0) 62 92 99) can book hotels in Tallinn as little as one day in advance, and may be able to help with private rooms and camping in summer. For reservations in a private home or hotel, call the **Travel Bureau "Rare"** in Tallinn (tel. 59 33 76 or 66 60 87) a day in advance (try to call from Helsinki).

Tallinn is loaded with good restaurants, though getting in may be difficult and many things may not be available. **Restaurant Astoria,** Vabaduse väljak 5, has excellent meals for 40-50R, excluding drinks. (Open 9am-2am, but go and make a reservation between 3-5pm; you'll pay 10R for a ticket.) The joint-venture Italian restaurant **Bistro,** on Narva mnt. at the corner of Maneeži tn., with another branch on Estonia pst. in front of Tammsaare park, serves lunch for about 10R. **Reeder,** Vene tn. 33, in the Old Town, serves hearty meat and soup dishes for rubles (open daily noon-midnight). **Gnoom,** Viru tn. 2, in the old town, also proffers drinks and food for rubles (open daily 9am-9pm). The **Palace Pizzeria** at Vabaduse väljak 1 has excellent pizzas and the best desserts in town, and serves alcohol (about 25R); just nearby on Pärnu mnt., **Peetri Pizza** is cheaper. Or try the Indian restaurant **Maharaja,**Raekoja pl. 13, near the **Penguin** ice-cream shop. Check *Tallinn This Week* and the *Tallinn City Paper* for more suggestions.

Sights

Most of the sights in Tallinn are packed in the **Old City,** particularly within **Toompea's** walls. Climbing the stairs on Komandandi tee, you'll come to the tremendous **Neitsi Torn** (Virgin Tower), built by the Danes in the 14th century as a wartime refuge; it's now a haven for students, who gather in the multiple-story, oak-tabled café and bar, which winds up through medieval levels of narrow spiral staircases. Head for the murky basement to sample from the huge vat of Estonian *hõõgvein* (HUG-vane, or hot wine). (Open daily 11am-10pm.) Nearby stands the **Kiek in de Kök** (Peek in the Kitchen), a fat tower originally built in 1475, but renovated in the 17th century; it now houses a museum with exhibits on Tallinn's history. Check out the cannonballs packed into the 50m high structure. (Open Tues.-

Fri. 10:30am-5:30pm, Sat.-Sun. 11am-4:30pm.) Right in the heart of Toompea, off Kohtu tn., is the spot with the best view of the orange-roofed houses of the Old City and the rusty cranes of the harbor. Just in front of you, on top of the Town Hall, sits **Vana Toomas** (Old Toomas), the legendary defender of Tallinn; in the distance beyond him rise the gray apartment blocks where most of Tallinn's Russian population lives. As you walk through the Old Town's narrow cobblestone streets, listen carefully; you might hear some old Russian woman singing about better days and nights at home in St. Petersburg.

On the other, lower side of the Old City, near its Suurtüki tn. entrance and the Hotel Viru, is the **Loodusmuseum** (Museum of Natural History), Laborätooriumi tn. 29. A former merchant's house, it was built in the 15th century. On the street parallel to Laborätooriumi tn. towers the **Oleviste Kirik** (St. Olav's Church), the world's tallest building (in the 16th century). At Vene tn. 24 stands Tallinn's **Russian Orthodox church** and its ice-cream-cone-shaped spires. In front of the **Raekoda** (Town Hall) on Raekoja plats is a star-shaped spot from where you can see steeples from five different churches without moving, provided you're over 5'5" (165cm). Look closely; one of the steeples is barely visible behind another building. One of the most interesting churches in Tallinn is the **Niguliste kirik** (St. Nicholas's Church), just a minute from Raekoja pl. on Harju tn. It houses concerts, exhibits, and a famous fragment saved from the canvas *Dance Macabre,* by the Lübeck artist Bernt Notke.

About 2½km west of the Hotel Viru on Narva mnt. is the clam-shaped amphitheater **Lauluväljak,** home of an annual music festival, which attracts Western performers as well as native musicals; the Song of Estonia Day in 1988 drew a crowd of 300,000—almost one-third of the entire population of Estonia.

Pärnu

One hundred and thirty kilometers south of Tallinn on Estonia's western coast, the 19th-century beach and retirement resort of Pärnu has suffered greatly under Soviet occupation, which heavily industrialized and polluted the city. Now too dirty to swim in, a new cleanup campaign may make Pärnu Bay (an arm of the Gulf of Riga) safe for swimmers and fish by 1992. A museum in town honors **Lydia Koidula,** a poet during Estonia's 19th-century national awakening. Pärnu also boasts the restaurant **Postipoiss,** which makes an especially scrumptious type of fried cheese *(juust)* from an ancient secret recipe. Pärnu is reachable from Tallinn by taxi (approximately 180R if you can find a driver willing to accept rubles), by train (4 per day, 3 hr.) or by bus.

Tartu

The most remarkable sight in Tartu—Estonia's second-largest city—is definitely **Tartu University,** whose remarkable architechture and long history attract many visitors every year. Founded in 1632, it's the oldest operating university in northern Europe. Reach Tartu from Tallinn by train (2 per day, 3-4 hr.), or by bus (frequently, 3 hr.); many Estonians hitchhike. Look for a guidebook to the city before you leave Tallinn.

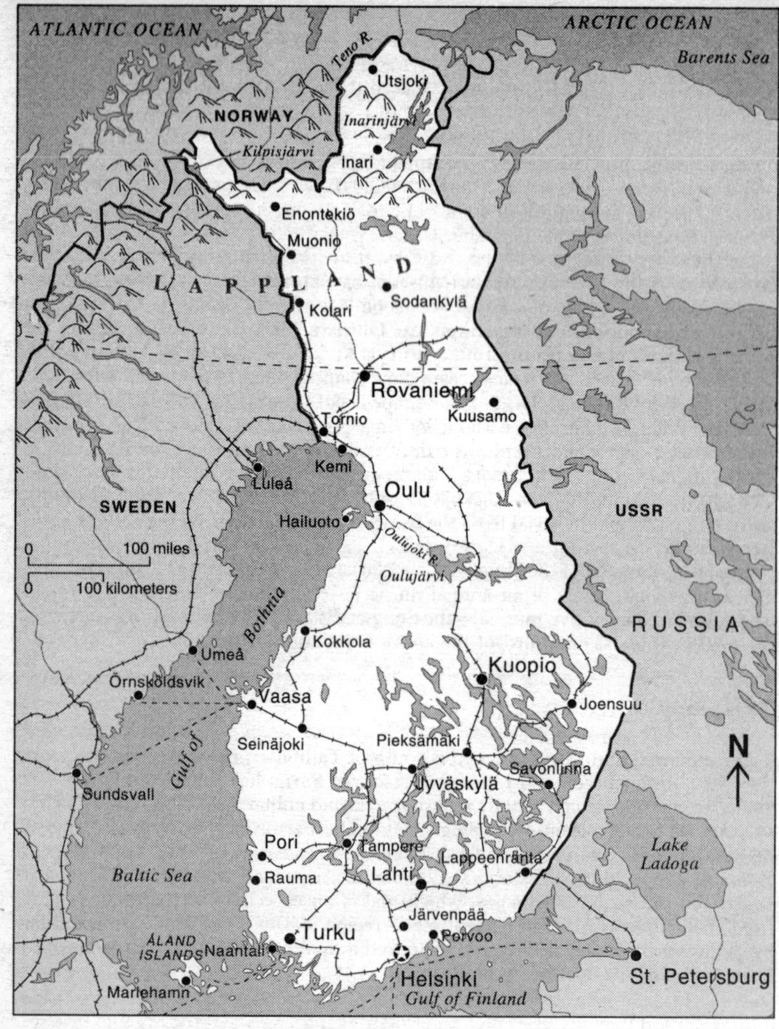

FINLAND

USD$1 = 4.26 markka (mk, or FIM)	**1mk = USD$0.23**
CAD$1 = 3.72mk	**1mk = CAD$0.27**
GBP£1 = 7.11mk	**1mk = GBP£0.14**
AUD$1 = 3.32mk	**1mk = AUD$0.30**
NZD$1 = 2.43mk	**1mk = NZD$0.41**
Country Code: 358	**International Dialing Prefix: 990**

Between the Scandinavian peninsula and the Soviet wilderness lies a long-suffering land of coniferous trees and five million taciturn souls. After enduring seven centuries between the warring Swedish and Russian empires, Finland (Suomi) experienced a romantic nationalism in the 19th century, nurtured by the *Kalevala* folk epic, Jean Sibelius's rousing patriotic symphonies, and Akseli Gallen-Kallela's mythic paintings. Once free of Russian domination in 1917, the Finns turned on themselves in a bitter civil war that saw the right, under Mannerheim, slaughter the Social Democrats. On the principle that the enemy of my enemy is my friend, Finland joined the Nazis in their war against the USSR.

With its painfully checkered past somewhat put to rest by Mikhail Gorbachev's October 1989 acceptance of Finnish neutrality, Finland today incarnates a confident Scandinavian egalitarianism. The country is a legal pioneer, tying speeding penalties to the offender's annual income—a businessman was recently fined USD11,400 for driving too fast. In this first European nation to enfranchise women (1906), mothers and fathers are now paid substantially for their childrearing work. Trains often have children's cars complete with baby bottle warmers and parents receive a chest of free supplies when their baby is born. Internationally, Finland leads the world in participation in the U.N. Peacekeeping Forces. The nation's acclaimed mediation efforts are memorialized in Namibia, where hundreds of children are named Ahtisaari after the Finnish diplomat who supervised the Namibian independence process.

From the west, Finland appears a Nordic anomaly, an Eastern-influenced culture whose language has almost as many grammatical cases as letters in the alphabet. But travelers discover plenty of Western postmodernity—no other country manufactures as many cellular telephones. Outside the Helsinki metropolitan area, undisturbed nature predominates. The east coast of Finland is dotted with old wooden shacks and the Swedish-speaking Åland Islands are a green biker's paradise. For the avid sailor, the Lake District in southeastern Finland is the place to be. Lappland, in the north, sports rugged if rather flat terrain, street-wandering reindeer, and Finland's several thousand indigenous Sami people.

Getting There

The titanic vessels of **Silja Line** and **Viking Line** resemble ostentatious floating shopping malls jammed with hundreds of partying Scandinavians. Silja (Helsinki tel. (90) 180 44 22, Stockholm tel. (08) 22 21 40) sails twice daily from Stockholm to Turku (8:15am (except Mon.) and 8pm; 10-11 hr.; 136mk, students, InterRailers, and YIEE holders 94mk) and once a day from Stockholm to Helsinki (260mk and 195mk, 15 hr., breakfast included). Eurailpass holders ride free on Silja while Nordturist holders get 50% off the adult price. Silja also jets thrice weekly from Travemünde, Germany to Helsinki (360-660mk, depending on the day, students 300-600mk, with InterRail 50% off).

Viking line (tel. Helsinki (90) 123 51, Stockholm tel. (08) 44 07 65) also steams from Stockholm to Helsinki (80-195mk, 30% off for students and InterRailers). and from Stockholm to Turku via Mariehamn (66-132mk). Viking gives a 30% discount to students and InterRailers, but nothing off for Eurail or Nordturist. Avoid Fridays from May to mid-June and mid-August to September, when prices balloon (Stockholm-Helsinki 275-300mk).

Wasa line (tel. Vaasa (61) 26 06 00, Sundsvall tel. (060) 12 93 10) travels five times a week from Sundsvall, Örnsköldsvik and Umeå, Sweden to Vaasa on Finland's east coast (75-125mk, 50% discount with Nordturist). **Polferries** connect Gdańsk, Poland with Helsinki (Helsinki tel. (90) 680 96 78) for 230-330mk (with ISIC or InterRail 120mk), and various ferries connect Helsinki with Tallinn, Estonia (see under Baltic States).

Finnair (tel. (90) 81 88 00) flies economically to points abroad as well as within Finland if you're under 25 and book one day in advance (Copenhagen 650mk, London or Paris 895mk). Buses and trains connect Helsinki to St. Petersburg via Lahti (see Helsinki Practical Information).

Getting Around

Efficient trains zip as far north as Kemijärvi at the usual painful Nordic prices (Turku to Helsinki 82mk); railpasses are valid. The **Nordturist** pass (Pohjola Junalla in Finnish) gives 21 days of boundless travel in Sweden, Denmark, Norway, and Finland for 1104mk (ages under 26 812mk). A **Finnrail Pass** offers free transit and free seat reservations throughout Finland (8 days for 470mk; 15 days, 730mk; 22 days, 920mk). Seat reservations (12-25mk) are necessary on certain express trains. Couchettes (in triples) cost 60mk from Monday to Thursday, 90mk from Friday to Sunday.

Buses cost about what trains do, though expresses demand an 8mk surcharge. The **Bussilomalippu** pass offers 1000km of travel over two weeks for 280mk. For bus information anywhere in Finland, call 97 00 40 00. Students often receive a 30% discount on bus tickets for distances over 75km; the word for student is *opiskelija* (OH-pees-KAY-lee-yah). Railpasses are valid on some buses that follow disused train routes, so give it a try. **Finnair** takes 40% off domestic fares for ages under 25; the regular Helsinki-Rovaniemi fare is 655mk. A **Finnair Holiday Ticket** puts you in the air for 15 days of boundless travel for USD 300, ages 12-24 USD 250. Steamers and motorboats link up many cities in the lake district.

Hitchhikers will find more rides in Finland than elsewhere in Scandinavia, while **cyclists** may long for Denmark's shorter distances. Campgrounds often rent bikes, as do some youth hostels and tourist offices. Rates average 40-50mk per day, 180mk per week with 140mk or a passport as a deposit.

Practical Information

Most shops close at 5pm weekdays and around 1pm Saturday, but urban supermarkets often stay awake until 8pm (Sat. 4-6pm). Kiosks sell basic food, snacks, and toiletries until 9 or 10pm. Banks are open weekdays 9:15am-4:15pm. Local calls usually cost 2mk, and most pay phones take 1mk and 5mk coins. Call 020 for domestic information, 920 20 for international information, 920 23 for price estimates, 920 22 to place a collect call, and 000 in emergencies. For AT&T's **USA Direct,** call 980 01 00 10.

In 1992, Finns will celebrate May Day and Eve on April 30 and May 1, Whitsun on June 7, Midsummer Eve and Day on June 19-20 and Independence Day on December 6. Many stores and all banks and post offices are closed on these days as well as on Easter, Christmas, New Year's Day, and the like.

Not an Indo-European language, Finnish is virtually impenetrable to foreigners. Watch out for town names that modify their form on train schedules. Swedish, often seen on signs, is the official second language; many Finns speak English too. The pride of Finland is the *sauna.* Don't be surprised if a strange Finn asks you to throw away all inhibitions and partake in Finland's chief export. "M" and "N" on bathroom and sauna doors designate men and women, respectively.

Disabled travelers can contact the Finnish Tourist Board and the Helsinki City Tourist Office as well as **Rullaten Ry** (Vartiokyläntie 9, 00950 Helsinki; tel. (90) 32 20 69), an organization which assists the handicapped with travel planning.

Accommodations, Camping, and Food

Finland shelters 165 *retkeilymaja* (youth hostels, pronounced RET-kay-LOO-mah-yah), 60 of which shelter travelers year-round. Prices are based on a four-star system and range from 30mk to 90mk; most charge 40-65mk. Some include saunas, and most prohibit sleeping bags. Hotels are generally exorbitant (over 200mk) and private room booking is not as common as in Sweden, but local tourist offices will help you find the cheapest accommodations. The **Finnish Youth Hostel Association** (Suomen Retkeilymajajärjestö) is located at Yrjönkatu 38b, Helsinki (tel. (90) 694 03 77). As in much of the rest of Scandinavia, you may camp anywhere as long as you respect fauna and flora and stay a polite distance away from homes. Well-equipped official campgrounds dapple the country, some offering saunas; they cost 20-50mk per night. Various **workcamps** take place in Finland; to participate make advance arrangements with Kansainvälinen Vapaaehtoinen Työleirijärjestö in Helsinki at (90) 14 44 08.

A Finnish *baari* is not a bar, but a café that serves food, coffee, and occasionally beer. *Kahvilat* also serve food and are often a bit classier, while *grillit* are fast food stands. A *ravintola* is a restaurant; some evolve into dance-spots or bars toward the end of the evening (cover charge 10mk and up; doorkeeper is often tipped a few markkas). The standard minimum age is 18, but it can be as high as 24, and alcohol is no bargain. You need not tip servers (the bill is often rounded up). Beer *(olut)* is classified into three groups. Olut IV is the strongest and most expensive (at least 20-25mk per ½-liter), while olut III is slightly weaker and cheaper. Olut II doesn't exist, and if you're thinking of having an olut I, just reach for a glass of tap water instead.

Among the cheaper supermarkets are Alepa and Valintatalo. Many large hotels offer bargain breakfasts open to outsiders. Short of that, lunch is the best deal, often incarnated as an all-you-can-eat buffet (35-60mk). Fish ranges from *silli* (Baltic herring) to *lohi* (salmon). Finnish dietary staples include robust *ruisleipä* rye bread, malodorous cheeses, and squirming yogurt-like *viili.* In July and August, the land blossoms with blueberries, lingonberries, cranberries, and, in the far north, Arctic cloudberries.

Åland Islands (Ahvenanmaa)

The Åland (OH-land) Islands have long been a cultural and geographic bridge between Sweden and Finland. Swedish for many centuries, they became part of Finland in 1807. Since 1921, Åland has been an autonomous territory within Finland, with its own flag and parliament. The Ålanders are entirely Swedish-speaking and they vigilantly minimize Finnish influence. Political controversy seems out of place here; the gentle landscape more befits leisurely hikes, bike rides, and sun-soaking. Most establishments on Åland accept both Finnish marks and Swedish kronor.

Viking Line (tel. in Mariehamn (928) 260 11) sails daily between the capital city of Mariehamn and Stockholm (34mk), Turku (40mk), and Naantali; students and InterRail holders may subtract 30%. **Birka Lines'** *Princess* sails daily between Stockholm and Mariehamn (26mk, 50% off with InterRail; tel. in Marienhamn (928) 270 27, in Stockholm (08) 714 55 20), and **Eckerö Line** (tel. in Grisslehamn (0175) 309 20, in Mariehamn (928) 280 00) travels from Eckerö on the west coast of Åland, to Grisslehamn, Sweden (33mk) with bus connections to both Mariehamn and Stockholm (26mk). Inter-island ferries are generally free (though there is a 40mk entry fee for the Turku archipelago).

Home to 10,000 of Åland's 22,000 inhabitants, **Mariehamn,** on the south coast of the large main island, is the hub of activity on Åland. Local artwork and history springs to life at the **Åland Museum** at Stadshusparken off Storagatan, (open Wed.-Sun. 10am-4pm, Tues. 10am-8pm). Just ½km north of the ferry terminal, the **Sjöfartsmuseum** displays navigational instruments in a cleverly constructed land-bound ship (open daily 9am-5pm; admission 13mk). In the water next to it is the real thing, the **Pommern,** built in 1903 (open daily 9am-5pm; admission 10mk). For maps of Åland and an *Åland Guide,* head to the **tourist office** at Storagatan 11 (tel. (928) 273 00), five minutes from the Viking Line terminal. (Open daily 9am-6pm; Sept.-May Mon.-Sat. 10am-4pm). **Botel Alida** on Österleden on the other side of the Marienhamn peninsula, 2km from the ferry terminal, offers sardine-like doubles on a ship for 60mk. Otherwise, **Ålandsresor,** Storagatan 9 (tel. (928) 280 40), books accommodations for all the islands. (Singles in private homes 120mk. Doubles 150mk. Open Mon.-Fri. 9am-5pm; harbor office open June to mid-Aug. daily noon-4:30pm.) **Campground Gröna Udden** (tel. (928) 110 41) relaxes by the water, 10 minutes down Skillnadagatan from the town center. (10mk per tent. Open May-Aug.)

Mariehamn's restaurant prices make **supermarket** food suddenly alluring; try the one at Ålandsvägen 42 on the corner of Norragatan (open Mon.-Fri. 9am-7pm, Sat. 9am-4pm, Sun. 11am-4pm). **Cha Shao,** Nyagatan 10, across from the Hotel Savoy, has a popular terrace, and Chinese food and pizza (meals 33mk; open Mon.-Fri.

10am-8pm, Sat.-Sun. 1-8pm.) Taste-test Swedish and Finnish foods in the town's cafés; Swedish wins if you bite into *Ålands pannkakor,* covered with marmalade and whipped cream. Try **Amanda Kaffestuga,** Norragatan 15 (open Mon.-Sat. 10am-6pm, Sun. 11am-6pm) or **Varmas Coffee Bar** at Torgatan, near the supermarket (open Mon.-Fri. 8:30am-5:30pm, Sat. 8:30am-3pm).

The rest of the main island is best explored by bike, but short bus trips work too. Pick up the *Ålandstrafiken* bus schedule from the tourist office in Mariehamn. For bike rental, **RoNo Rent** (tel. (928) 128 20), across from the ferry terminal in Mariehamn, is the most convenient. (Bikes 25mk per day, 125mk per week. Mopeds, windsurfers, and boats too. Open June-Aug. daily 9am-noon and 1-6pm; May and Sept. reduced hrs.)

Deep bays and cliffs predominate in the hilly northern districts of **Geta** (take bus #2 from Mariehamn; Mon.-Fri. 3 per day, 23mk) and **Saltvik** (bus #3; Mon.-Fri. 6 per day, 15mk). Just east of Saltvik is **Sund,** home to three attractions located only meters from each other. Once you've gotten on bus #4 (7 per day, 15mk), get off at the Kastelholm stop and follow the sign to the 13th-century **Kastelholm Castle** (May-Aug. 6 tours per day, 10mk). Right nearby sits Finland's only prison museum, **Vita Björn,** which features prison cells from various centuries. (Open daily 10am-5pm. Free.) At nearby **Bomarsund** (also on the bus #4 route) are the ruins of an ancient Russian fortress blown up by the British and French in the Crimean War. Two **bicycle ferries** (Skarpnätö-Hällö (20mk) in the north, and Långnäs-Bomarsund (40mk) in the southeast) run twice daily, creating manageable loops for daytrips.

In **Djurvik,** on the way to Eckerö in the west, there is an easy-to-afford but hard-to-reach guesthouse called **Djurviks Gästgård** (tel. (928) 324 33) on a secluded inlet full of fish and bluish swimmers. Take bus #1 to Gottby (9km), then walk the 4-5km to the guesthouse; the light traffic hinders hitching. (1-2 person room 140-180mk. Breakfast 25mk. Sheets 15mk. Call ahead or contact Ålandsresor). Farther east, on Eckerö, **Hummelvik** (tel. (928) 383 11) charges only 8mk per tent; take the bus to Handelslagan and walk 2km. A free wilderness hut with a wood stove, four bunks, and a portrait of Åland's first prime minister stands proudly atop **Orrdals klint,** Åland's highest peak (a Himalayan 129m). To get there, many take the bus to Saltvik-Kvarnbo, hitch towards Långbergsöda, and hike for an hour from the Orrdals junction by the logging road and trail (follow the signs). Freelance camping is forbidden without the landowner's permission, but the 10 campgrounds are quite cheap. Campgrounds often rent cottages (2 persons 170mk, 3 persons 195mk, 4 persons 220mk). On islands without campgrounds, a courteous request usually wins permission to freelance.

Ever lonelier and tinier island clusters ring Åland's outer edges; many ferries to these depart from Hummelvik on Vårdö (accessible by bus #4 (26mk)) or from Långnäs.

Turku

From meek beginnings as a trading outpost, the old city of Turku became Finland's first capital and premier town. It lost that preeminence in 1812, when Czar Alexander I snatched Finland from Sweden and reined the capital Russiawards to Helsinki. Shortly thereafter, Scandinavia's worst fire devoured 2500 of Turku's wooden buildings. Despite these losses, Turku today remains a flourishing cultural and academic center. Reflecting the city's rich Swedish inheritance, one of its two universities, **Åbo Akademi,** operates in Swedish. Near the campus, the massive, white-vaulted **cathedral,** completed in 1300, speaks of a time when Turku was a center for the spiritual and commercial colonization of the Finnish hinterland. (Open Mon.-Fri. 9am-7pm, Sat. 9am-3pm, Sun. 11:30am-4:30pm; Sept.-May Mon.-Fri. 10am-4pm, Sat. 10am-3pm, Sun. 11:30am-4:30pm. Concerts in summer Tues. at 8pm. Free.)

Sheltered from the ferry ports by a screen of trees, 700-year-old **Turku Castle,** along the river Aura about 3km from the center of town, owes its impressive proportions to the town's days under the Swedish crown. Its restored interiors tastefully combine sleek lines, medieval artifacts, and an intriguing **historical museum.** (Open daily 10am-6pm; Oct.-April 10am-3pm. Admission 10mk, children 5mk.) Anchored on the river midway between these sites is the **Suomen Joutsen,** "Swan of Finland," a three-masted frigate which brought supplies to World War II submarines (open mid-May to mid-Aug daily 10am-6pm; admission 5mk). **Luostarinmäki,** the only part of Turku to survive the 1827 fire, now hums as an open-air **handicrafts museum** recalling workaday life (open daily 10am-6pm; Oct.-April 10am-3pm; admission 10mk, children 5mk). Across the river in Puolalan puisto park, under the granite spires of the bite-sized **Turku Art Museum,** hang some of Akseli Gallen-Kallela's vibrant *Kalevala* paintings. (Open Mon.-Wed. and Fri.-Sat. 10am-4pm, Thurs. 10am-4pm and 6-8pm, Sun. 10am-6pm. Admission 15mk, children 10mk.) The perplexing **Wäinö Aaltonen Museum,** Itäinen Rantakatu 38, houses the artist's ponderous sculptures (open daily 10am-6pm; Sept. to mid-June Mon.-Fri. 10am-4pm and 6-8pm, Sat. 10am-4pm, Sun. 10am-6pm; admission 5mk, some exhibits cost extra).

In summer, open-air rock concerts rattle the park surrounding the Turku Art Museum (schedules at the tourist office), including **Ruisrock** in the last weekend of June. The **Down by the Laituri** music festival transplants chunks of 1950s Americana to the river's banks in late June, and street dancing erupts at 6pm on most summer Tuesdays by the Auransilta Bridge.

One of Finland's best-appointed youth hostels, **Turun Kaupungin Retkeilymaja (IYHF),** Linnankatu 39 (tel. (921) 31 65 78) beckons 20 minutes up Linnankatu from the ferry terminals, or take bus #1. (Reception open 6-10am and 3pm-midnight. Dorms 40mk. Singles 80mk. Doubles 50mk per person. Nonmembers 15mk extra.) **Kåren Youth Hostel (IYHF),** Hämeenkatu 22 (tel. (921) 32 04 21 or 51 75 57 in winter) costs more but has more doubles for hopelessly infatuated couples. (Lockout noon-3pm. 40mk, doubles 55mk, nonmembers 15mk extra. Kitchen, laundry, and sauna.) For quiet, commodious and immaculate singles (180mk) and doubles (260mk), try the **St. Birgittas Convent Guesthouse,** Ursininkatu 15a (tel. (921) 50 19 10). If it's sybarism you seek, **Ruissalo Camping** (tel. (921) 58 92 49) comes complete with sauna, water slide, and nude beach. Take bus #8 (2 per hr., 6mk) for 10km from Market Sq. (25mk, families 50mk, open June-Aug.). Ruissalo Island also makes a refreshing day trip, with lush forests, sunbathing (bare or not), and boat rental at Saaronniemi Beach.

There's no shortage of Turku tourist offices: a train station branch (open June to mid-Sept. Mon.-Fri. 9am-9pm, Sat.-Sun. 9am-3:30pm) supplements the main branch at Käsityöläiskatu 3 (tel. (921) 33 63 66) in the town center (open Mon.-Fri. 8am-4pm; Sept.-May 8:30am-4pm). The **InterRail Center,** Läntinen Rantakatu 47-49 (tel. (921) 30 45 51) offers snacks, free luggage storage, bike rental (10mk per day, 40mk deposit), and free showers (open late June to mid-Aug. Mon.-Sat. 8am-10pm).

For groceries, hop directly over the river from the Kaupungin hostel. **Market Square** peddles produce, while just southwest on Eerikinkatu the red-brick **Market Hall** vends pricey pastries (open Mon.-Thurs. 8am-5pm, Fri. 8am-5:30pm, Sat. 8am-2pm). **Verso,** upstairs at Linnankatu 3, is a riverside veggie bistro extraordinaire. Lunches run 30mk; any student ID shaves off 10% (open Mon.-Fri. 11am-5pm; Sept.-May also Sat. noon-5pm). At the same address (enter by the iron gate), **Pizzeria Italia** serves daily specials (30mk) at outdoor tables (open Mon.-Thurs. 10:30am-10pm, Fri. 10:30am-11pm, Sat. 11am-11pm, Sun. 1-10pm). For cheap breakfasts and lunches, head for bright, modern **Gadolinia,** the Swedish-speaking students' café, in back and upstairs at Piispankatu 14, behind the cathedral (open Mon.-Fri. 9am-2:30pm, Sat. 10:30am-2pm).

Festive Turku swims in cafés and riverside beer gardens. Stone-walled **Pinella,** by Tuomiokirkko bridge, exchanges a beer for 25mk, while **Erik XIV,** Eerikinkatu 6, is a popular and expansive indoor beer farm (23mk a mug). All these nightspots are generally open until midnight, on weekends 1am. The youthful, student-run **Kåren** disco throbulates at Hämeenkatu 22 (open Wed. and Fri.-Sat. 7pm-1am during the school year).

Turku is accessible from Helsinki (several trains daily), and from points northward via Pieksämäki. From the ferry terminal 4km from the train station, daily ferries ply to Mariehamn in the Åland Islands and beyond to Stockholm. (See Getting There.)

Near Turku

Rauma, 92km north of Turku, is one of Finland's best-preserved medieval communities, lauded for seafaring, lace making, and an incomprehensible dialect. The easiest access from Turku is by bus (10 per day, 1½ hr., 50mk) though hitching also does the trick. The **Rauma Museum** in the Market Place resuscitates the region's rich history (open mid-May to mid-Aug. daily 10am-5pm). The **Rauma Lace Festival,** held in late July, celebrates the fabric with exhibits, music, and plays. The **tourist office,** Eteläkatu 7 (tel. (938) 22 45 55), is down Nortamonkatu from the bus station. (Open Mon.-Fri. 8am-4pm.) There is also tourist information on the Market Square during the summer (open June-Aug. 8am-3:15pm). A less-than-lavish **IYHF youth hostel** with a **campground** (tel. (938) 22 46 66) sprawls around a beach 1km from town (hostel 30-45mk, camping 25mk per person; open mid-May to Aug.).

Helsinki

Less festive than Copenhagen and less affluent than Stockholm, lonely Helsinki has long seen itself as a meeting point of West and East, a place where Lutheran and Russian Orthodox cathedrals stand almost face to face. The city's southeast corner is a nest of diplomats and spies, and Helsinki has become a synonym for human rights and international cooperation. Planned streets and neoclassical buildings lend an august aura to this city of half a million, while aggressive traffic and plentiful drunks bespeak the pathos of workaday life.

Orientation and Practical Information

Helsinki, "daughter of the Baltic" and "white city of the North," sits on a peninsula on the southern edge of Finland. The central city's layout resembles a "V" with a large, bulbous point and several smaller peninsul-ettes. The train station lies just north of the vertex from which the Mannerheimintie and Unioninkatu thoroughfares radiate. The harbor and most sights are south of the train station. All street signs have both Finnish and Swedish names. For candid and practical information, the free youthful paper *Exploring Helsinki* is unbeatable, while *Helsinki This Week* lists current happenings (as does an English recorded message line, tel. 058). The tourist office also publishes *This Summer in Helsinki,* which gives very detailed sights and activities listings. The **Oranssi Organization,** Väinö Auerinkatu 6, also offers info on current happenings and might open a youth hostel in 1992.

Tourist Offices: City Tourist Office, Pohjoisesplanadi 19 (tel. 169 37 57), near the market square. From the train station, walk 2 blocks south on Keskuskatu and turn left on Pohjoisesplanadi. Free phone for local calls. Open Mon.-Fri. 8:30am-6pm, Sat. 8:30am-1pm; mid-Sept. to mid-May Mon. 8:30am-4:30pm, Tues.-Fri. 8:30am-4pm. **Hotellikeskus** (Hotel Booking Center), Asema-aukio 3 (tel. 17 11 33), between the post office and the train station. Primarily room-finding (10mk fee; hostel beds 5mk), but also has city maps, youth hostel lists and useful brochures. Open Mon.-Fri. 9am-9pm, Sat. 9am-7pm, Sun. 10am-6pm; mid-Sept. to mid-May Mon.-Fri. 9am-6pm. Both offices sell the **Helsinki Card,** offering unlimited local transportation, museum discounts, and other treats (1 day 70mk, 2 days 100mk, 3 days 120mk, children under 17 half price). **Finnish Tourist Board,** Unioninkatu 26 (tel. 17 46 31), covers the whole country, including campgrounds. Open Mon.-Fri. 9am-5pm, Sat. 9am-1pm; Sept.-May Mon.-Fri. 9am-4pm.) **Finnish Youth Hostel Association,** Yrjönkatu 38b (tel. 694 03 77), on the south side of the bus station, lists hostels nationwide and arranges Lappland accommodations for hikers. Open Mon.-Fri. 9am-4pm.

Budget Travel: Travela, Mannerheimintie 5 (tel. 62 41 01). Sells BIJ/Eurotrain tickets and IUS student cards. Open Mon.-Fri. 9am-5pm.

Embassies: U.S., Itäinen Puistotie 14b (tel. 17 19 31). Open Mon.-Fri. 9am-noon. **Canada,** Pohjoiesplanadi 25b (tel. 17 11 41), at Fabianinkatu. Open Mon.-Thurs. 8am-4:30pm, Fri. 8am-1:30pm. **U.K.,** Itäinen Puistotie 17 (tel. 66 12 93). Travelers from **Australia** and **New Zealand** should contact the British Embassy. **Estonia,** Vyokatu 9 (tel. 66 14 49 or 63 35 48). Open Mon.-Fri. 9:30am-noon. **Lithuania,** Hameentie 54 (tel. 753 02 62). **USSR,** Vuorimiehenkatu 6 (tel. 66 18 76). **Poland,** Armas Lindgrenintie 21 (tel. 684 80 77).

Currency Exchange: Rates are generally identical, with a minimum 20mk commission on traveler's checks. Most banks are open Mon.-Fri. 9:15am-4:15pm. Same rates and fees at the handy Poste Restante office 50m west of the train station. Open Mon.-Fri. 8am-9pm, Sat. 9am-6pm, Sun. 11am-9pm. The airport terminal has money exchange (cash only) open from 6:30am-11pm daily. Credit card advances on Visa are available from **STS** bank automats 24 hrs.

American Express: Area Travel, Pohjoisesplanadi 2 (tel. 185 51), at Mannerheimintie. As of 1991, waiting for permission to offer full American Express service. Open Mon.-Fri. 9am-5pm.

Post Office: Mannerheimintie 11 (tel. 195 51 17), next to the station. Open Mon.-Fri. 9am-5pm. Poste Restante office sells stamps and exchanges money; open Mon.-Fri. 8am-9pm, Sat. 9am-6pm, Sun. 11am-9pm. **Postal Code:** 00100.

Telephones: In the same building as the post office. Open Mon.-Fri. 9am-10pm, Sat.-Sun. 9am-9pm. **Telecom Center,** Mannerheimintie 5. Open Mon.-Fri. 9am-11pm, Sat.-Sun. 9am-10pm. **City Code:** 90.

Flights: Tel. 818 79 80. Sirola Company bus #615 runs frequently 5:25am-11:50pm between the **Helsinki-Vantaa** airport and train station platform #12 (13mk). Bus #614 from platform #45 at the bus station does the same. The Finnair bus shuttles between the airport and the Finnair building at Asema-aukio 3, next to the train station (daily 5:05am-midnight, 18mk).

Trains: For information, call 101 01 15; for trains to St. Petersburg (8 hr., 238mk) and Moscow (16 hr., 437mk), dial 62 52 16. The station has lockers (10mk) and luggage service (10mk). Open 6:30am-11pm.

Buses: Tel. 97 00 40 00. The long-distance station, with routes throughout Finland (approx. 1mk per 2km) and to St. Petersburg via Lahti (9 hr.; approx. 270mk) sits just west of the post office, between Salomonkatu and Simonkatu. Buy tickets there, on board, or at the train station.

Ferries: For voyage details, see "Getting There" in the Finland introduction. Take tram #4 from Mannerheimintie, near the train station, towards Kauppatori until you see the port. **Viking Line** (tel. 123 51), **Polferries** (tel. 17 76 61) and **Finnjet** (contact Silja Line) terminals are east along the shore from the market square; **Silja Line** (tel. 180 44 55), the **Georg Ots,** and **Tallink** lie to the south.

Public Transportation: The Metro and most trams and buses run approximately 6am-11pm (though certain bus and tram lines, including the indispensible tram 3T, continue to 1:30am). On the weekend, trains run until 2:30am. 7.50mk per hour of travel, transfers free; children 2.50mk. 10-trip tickets cost 65mk at R-Kiosks and City Transport offices. Punch your ticket on board. The **Tourist Ticket** provides boundless transit in Helsinki, Espoo, and Vantaa (1 day 48mk, 3 days 96mk, 5 days 144mk); available at City Transport and tourist offices. For transit information, tel. 472 24 54 or 101 01 11.

Bike Rental: Cheapest at the **Olympic Stadium youth hostel** (tel 49 60 71). 40-50mk per day, 100mk deposit. Also at **Cat Sport Oy,** Pohjoiskaari 9 (tel. 692 36 76).

Bookstore: Academia Bookstore, Keskuskatu 1. Dazzling selection of books in English. Open Mon.-Fri. 9am-8pm, Sat. 9am-5pm.

Laundromat: Look for the words *Itsepalvelu Pesula.* Try Suonionkatu 1 (40mk per load; open Mon.-Fri. 8am-5pm, Sat. 8am-2pm) or Punavuorenkatu 3 (open Mon.-Fri. 7am-8pm, Sat. 9am-6pm).

Women's Center: The Union of Feminist Women runs **Naisten huone,** Bulevardi 11a (tel. 64 24 61), a cultivated social center and café. Open Aug.-June Mon.-Fri. 4-9pm; Sept.-April also Sat. noon-6pm.

Gay and Lesbian Information: Contact the **Organization for Sexual Equality,** Mäkelänkatu 36a5 (tel. 76 96 41 or 76 96 32; open Tues. and Fri. 10am-2pm, Wed. 2-9pm, Thurs. 2-6pm).

Disabled Travelers: For information on facilities and transport, contact **Helsinki Invalidien Yhdistys** (tel. 63 01 24) or **Rullaten Ry** (tel. 32 20 69).

Sauna and Pool: Uimastadion, Hammarskjöldintie (tel. 402 93 84), behind the Olympic Stadium. Built for the 1952 Olympics. 7mk, children 2mk, water-slide 10mk. Open June-late Aug. Mon.-Sat. 7am-8pm, Sun. 9am-8pm; May and early Sept. reduced hrs. If you can't stand the heat, get out of the **Sauna Society** (tel. 67 86 77) in Lauttasaari.

Medical Assistance: Helsinki University's **Meilahti Hospital,** Haartmaninkatu 4 (tel. 47 11) receives and refers foreigners. Take tram #4 north on Mannerheimintie to Nordenskiöldinkatu, then left up Messeniuksenkatu. Buses #14 and 18 go direct.

Emergencies: (tel. 000). **Police** (tel. 002). Stations at Olavinkatu 1a, Kasarmikatu 25b, P. Roobertinkatu 1-3 and at the train station near platform #11 (tel. 18 91 for switchboard).

Accommodations

Kallio Youth Hostel, Porthaninkatu 2 (tel. 70 99 25 90). From the train station, walk 15 min. north on Unioninkatu, or take the Metro to Hakaniemi. Cozy 30-bed hostel, exceptionally amicable staff. TV room and kitchen. Reception open 7:30-11am and 3-11pm. Lockout 11am-3pm. Curfew 2am. 50mk, sheets included. Free small lockers. Sheets 10mk. Laundry 15mk. Open mid-May to Aug.

Stadionin Youth Hostel (IYHF), Pohj. Stadiontie 3b (tel. 49 60 71), in the Olympic Stadium complex. Take tram #3T or 7A, or walk 25 min. from the train station. Enormous (200 beds), crowded, and a touch grungy, but cheap. Kitchen, TV, bicycles (see Bike Rental above). Reception open 7am-11pm. Lockout from rooms 10am-4pm. Curfew 2am (2mk fee after 11pm). Doubles 50mk. Dorms 35mk, nonmembers 15mk extra. Breakfast 20mk. Backpack-sized lockers. Sheets 20mk. Laundry 15mk. Open all year.

YWCA InterPoint, at Raumantie 5 in 1991 (tel. 55 78 49). 5km north of the city center. Take bus #18 to the last stop and up Raumantie. May grant emergency floorspace when all others are full. Music, TV, kitchen. Reception open 8-11am and 4pm-midnight. Lockout 11am-4pm. Curfew 12:30am. 40mk. Sheets 7mk. Breakfast 10mk. Open July to mid-Aug. Call Minna Muukkonen at 44 80 66 for 1992 location.

Hotel Satakuntatalo, Lapinrinne 1 (tel. 69 58 57). Less than 1km southwest of the train station. Student dorm used as a summer hotel; clean and well-run. Phones in most rooms, sauna (25mk, 40mk for groups), laundry. Singles 200mk. Doubles 290mk. Students 20-50% off. Breakfast included. Open June-Aug.

Hotel Academica, Hietaniemenkatu 14 (tel. 402 02 06), 1km west of the train station. Another transmogrified university dorm, complete with refrigerators, sauna, pool, and disco. Singles 195-245mk (160mk with ISIC or YIEE). Doubles 240-290mk (200mk). Breakfast 25mk. Open June-Aug.

Matkakoti, Uudenmaankatu 9 (tel. 64 21 69), less than 1km from the train station. Go south on Mannerheimtie to Erottajanpuisto, then right on Uudenmaankatu. TV in every room, microwave, showers and toilets in the corridor. Reception open 24 hrs. Singles 190mk. Doubles 240mk. Triples 270mk. Quads 340mk. Breakfast 25mk. Open all year.

Eurohostel, Linnankatu 9 (tel. 66 44 52), 2km west of the train station. Take tram #4 past the port. Brand spankin' new in 1991. Huge (approx. 250 beds) with clean rooms. Kitchen on every floor. Reception open 24 hrs. Singles 140mk. Doubles 220mk. Triples 240mk. Extra bed 80mk. Breakfast 15mk. Laundry. Open all year.

Camping: Rastila Camping (tel. 31 65 51), 14km from the center. Take the Metro to Itäkeskus and then catch bus #90, 90A, or 96. Vast, cheap, municipal campground with washing, cooking, and abluting facilities. 20mk; cabins 100mk. Open mid-May to mid-Sept.

Food

Corporate monopolies make even groceries expensive; seek refuge in the **Alepa** chain (the one in the tunnel under the train station is open Mon.-Sat. 10am-10pm,

Sun. noon-10pm). **Stockman** and cheaper **Sokos** department stores (both on Mannerheimintie near the train station) also harbor supermarkets (open Mon.-Fri. 9am-8pm, Sat. 9am-5pm). Energetic epicures can dive into **Market Square,** by the port (open mid-May to early Sept. Mon.-Fri. 6:30am-2pm and 3:30-8pm; early Sept. to mid-May Mon.-Fri. 6:30am-2pm) and the nearby **Market Hall** (open Mon.-Fri. 8am-5pm, Sat. 8am-2pm).

Aurinkotuuli, Lapinlahdenkatu 25, 1km southwest of the train station. Vegetarian meals in a botanical atmosphere (32-40mk). Open Mon.-Fri. 11am-6pm, Sat. noon-4pm.

University cafeterias: Humanists relate in the convivial main building, Fabianinkatu 33, while technocrats exchange impulses in outdoor-terraced Porthania, Hallituskatu 6 at Fabianinkatu (both open in summer Mon.-Fri. 8am-3:30pm, longer hrs. rest of year). Money-lovers gorge at the economics school, Runeberginkatu 14 at Arkadiankatu, 1km west of the train station (open Mon.-Fri. 8:30am-2:30pm; Sept.-May Mon.-Fri. 8am-5:30pm). Nearby prowls the Museum of Zoology cafeteria, Pohjoinen Rautatiekatu 13. All four offer entrées from 14mk.

Kasvis, Korkeavuorenkatu 3, 10 min. south of Eteläesplanadi. Popular vegetarian wood-and-fern restaurant. A hearty soup and salad 35mk, all-you-can-eat meals 50mk. 25% discount with YIEE card. Open Mon.-Fri. 11am-5pm, Sat.-Sun. noon-5pm.

Palace Café, Eteläranta 10, 2nd floor, next to the Palace Hotel. A homely cafeteria with harborscape and complete lunches (10:30am-1:30pm) for 32mk. Open Mon.-Fri. 7:30am-5pm.

Bulevardin Kahvisalonki, Bulevardi 1. A cozy, genteel parlor; self-service makes the atmosphere affordable. Fruit pastry 8-14mk, coffee 6mk. Open Mon.-Fri. 8am-10pm, Sat. 10am-10pm, Sun. from Sept.-May 10am-9pm.

Sights

Tram 3T is the city's cheapest tour (pick up its free itinerary on board). Or just walk—most sights are packed within 2km of the train station. The tourist office will give you the booklet "See Helsinki on Foot"; their only serious omission is the **Temppeliaukio Church**—a modern masterpiece built into a hill of rock. From the train station, head west on Arkadian Katu and then right on Fredrikinkatu to the square where the temple's buried. (Open Mon.-Sat. 10am-8pm, Sun. noon-1:45pm, 3:30-3:45pm, 5-6pm and 7-8pm.) The striking **Jean Sibelius Monument,** 750m north of the church in Sibelius Park on Mechelininkatu, was dedicated to one of the 20th century's greatest composers by sculptor Eila Hiltunen. It looks like a cloud of organ pipes blasted into outer space. (Take bus #18 from the train station.) The **Kansallismuseo** (National Museum), 500m northwest of the train station on Mannerheimintie 34, sets out intriguing displays of Finnish culture, from Gypsy and Lapp costumes to *ryijyt* (rugs), along with a splendid exegesis of the country's tortuous history. (Open Wed.-Mon. 11am-4pm, Tues. 11am-4pm and 6-9pm; Oct.-April Wed.-Mon. 11am-3pm, Tues. 11am-3pm and 6-9pm. Admission 10mk, children 5mk, Tues. free.) Across from the train station sprawls Finland's largest art museum, the **Art Museum of the Ateneum,** Kaivokatu 2-4. (Open Tues. and Fri. 9am-5pm, Wed.-Thurs. 9am-9pm, Sat.-Sun. 11am-5pm. Admission 10mk, special exhibits 25mk.) Finnish finesse in graphic and industrial design is well documented at the **Museum of Applied Arts,** Korkeavuorenkatu 23, south of Eteläesplanadi. (Open Tues.-Fri. 11am-5pm, Sat.-Sun. 11am-4pm. English tours Sat. 2pm. Admission 20mk, students and children 15mk.) The handsome neoclassical buildings surrounding **Senate Square** on the corner of Unioninkato and Aleksanterinkatu were conceived almost singlehandedly by German architect Carl Ludwig Engel in the early 19th century, just after Helsinki replaced Turku as Finland's capital. The crowning glory is the **Lutheran Cathedral.** (Open Mon.-Sat. 9am-7pm, Sun. noon-7pm.) Elsewhere in the city, the boldly simple creations of the city's great 20th-century architects—notably Aalto and Saarinen—blend with slick neoclassical lines. Aalto has said of Finland that "architecture is our form of expression because our language is so impossible." The southern tip of the peninsula, from the shady paths of **Kaivopuisto** to the winding streets of **Eira,** makes for pleasant strolling.

Helsinki's relaxed surrounding islands counterweigh the bustling center of town. Ferries from the market leave hourly (15mk round-trip) for the now-demilitarized fortress island of **Suomenlinna.** The military museum here displays equipment and photographs, primarily from the 1939-40 Russo-Finnish War. (Open mid-May to Aug. daily 10am-5pm; Sept. to mid-May Sat.-Sun. 11am-3pm. Admission 5mk, students and children 2.50mk.) The same ticket includes admission to the submarine **Vessiko,** a WWII veteran. (Open mid-May to Aug. daily 10am-5pm; Sept. daily 11am-3pm.) When museumed-out, relax on the rocky beach. (Open mid-June to mid-Aug. 10am-6pm.) **Seurasaari,** connected to the mainland by a causeway, is a peaceful place to picnic, swim, or saunter. Its open-air museum contains churches and farmsteads transplanted from the Finnish countryside. (Open June-Aug. Thurs.-Tues. 11am-5pm, Wed. 11am-7pm; May and Sept. Mon.-Fri. 9am-3pm, Sat.-Sun. 11am-5pm. Admission 10mk, children and students 5mk, Wed. free.) Take bus #24 from inside the Swedish Theater to the last stop. There's also boat service from Market Sq. in summer.

Entertainment

Much of Helsinki nods off early. Sway to afternoon street music in the leafy **Esplanadi** or party on warm nights at **Hietaniemi beach. Kaivopuisto** park hosts open-air rock concerts on Sundays in July, while **Hakanementori** offers waterside beer gardens. Consult *Helsinki This Week* for current happenings and *Exploring Helsinki* for more bars and nightclubs. In late August, the two-week **Helsinki Festival** cobbles together a mélange of arts events.

Finland is one of the few European countries where the drinking age—18 for beer and wine, and 20 for hard alcohol—is usually enforced. Both bouncers and cover charges usually relax on weeknights. Tickets to some discos sell out before the evening begins; the super-cautious can buy in advance at **Tiketti** in the Forum mall at Keskuskatu 7 or **Lippupalvelu,** Mannerheimintie 5. If discos leave you lonely and poor, the cheapest place to drink yourself into a stupor is the state-run liquor store **Alko** (branches at Eteläesplanadi 22, Mannerheimintie 1 and Salomonkatu 1; open Mon.-Thurs. 10am-5pm, Fri. 10am-6pm, Sat. 9am-2pm).

Cantina West, Kasarminkatu 23 (tel. 63 98 60), south of the train station on Keskuskatu, then east on Etaläesplanadi. Tex-Mex restaurant and bar with cacti on the tables. *The* happening place in Helsinki. 3 floors, live music. Min. age 22. Cover 15mk on weekends. Open Mon.-Fri. noon-2am, Sat.-Sun. 11am-2am.

Old Students' House, Mannerheimintie 3 (tel. 66 73 76). Neoclassical building with pubs, dance floors, restaurant, beer patio, and sociable students. Beer only 19.50mk, 20mk cover for live bands. Open daily 11am-1am.

Café Metropol, Kaivopiha plaza (tel. 66 69 66), off Mannerheimintie near the Old Students' House. A high-tech behemoth of loud rock music and posing yuppies. Beer 25mk. Min. age 18. Cover 25-35mk. Open Mon.-Sat. 4pm-2am, Sun. 9pm-2am.

Gambrini, Iso Roobertinkatu 3 (tel. 64 43 91), 3 blocks south of Esplanadi. Helsinki's happening gay and lesbian bar and restaurant. 30mk cover Fri.-Sat. after 7pm, otherwise free. Open Tues.-Thurs. and Sun. 6pm-1am, Fri.-Sat. 6pm-2am.

Near Helsinki

The cobblestone streets of **Porvoo,** Finland's oldest town after Turku, lie 50km east of Helsinki. Sights include the **J.L. Runeberg Home,** Aleksanterinkatu 3, where the national poet burned the midnight oil. (Open Mon.-Sat. 9:30am-4pm, Sun. 10:30am-5pm; Sept.-April Mon.-Sat. 10am-4pm, Sun. 11am-5pm. Admission 10mk, free on Mon.) The **Historical Museum,** Vanha Raatihuoneentori, houses an impressive collection of historical items from the Porvoo area. (Open daily 11am-4pm; Sept.-April Wed.-Sun. noon-4pm. Admission 10mk.) The main **tourist office,** Rauhankatu 20 (tel. (915) 17 01 45), 50m from the bus station, can direct you to more museums (open Mon.-Fri. 8am-4pm, Sat. 10am-2pm). You can end a day's meanderings at the splendid **Youth Hostel (IYHF)** Linnakoskenkatu 1 (tel. (915) 13 00

12; 35mk; open early Jan.-late Dec.). Buses for Porvoo (30-38mk) leave the Helsinki bus station about every 15 minutes, while the *J.L. Runeberg* (tel. (90) 62 59 44) goes by sea (May-Aug. Fri.-Sun. and Wed. 10am; 3 hr., 90mk, round-trip 130mk).

Jean Sibelius tormented himself for 43 years in **Järvenpää.** At his placid home, **Ainola,** the composer brooded and drank and drank and brooded; his perfectionism was so exacting that he destroyed much of his late work. *Let's Go* often follows a similarly excruciating regime, except for the destruction and the brooding. (Open May-Sept. Tues.-Wed. and Sat.-Sun. 11am-5pm; admission 15mk, children 3mk.) Buses to Tuusula pass this sad site (every ½ hr. from platform #9, 11 or 12 in the Helsinki bus station, 18mk).

Lake District

The vast Lake District of southeastern Finland is a sylvan fest of canoeing, hiking, biking and cross-country skiing amidst boundless stretches of water and forest. The major centers strain under the burden of tourism, so make a point of escaping to the pine-shaded waters in a canoe or a sailboat and staying at one of the area's isolated youth hostels. Tourist offices can arrange rooms in farmhouses and point out free wilderness huts.

Savonlinna

The czarist aristocracy turned Savonlinna into a fashionable resort 150 years ago, and it has balanced on the thin edge of fashion ever since. With its attractive harbor, pleasurable islands and ancient fortress, Savonlinna is the most alluring of the Lake District towns. While the others merely border lakes, Savonlinna is almost completely surrounded by the region's crystal water.

The renowned **Opera Festival** (July 2-31 in 1992) forms the centerpiece of a host of highbrow cultural events. Divas come from all over the world to perform each evening in the courtyard of Olavinlinna Castle. (Tickets to performances cost 200-500mk and should be ordered as early as the preceding Oct. Write to Opera Festival, Olavinkatu 35, SF-57130 Savonlinna, or contact the tourist office (see below). Unclaimed tickets are sold at 4pm the day of the show at the same address (tel. (957) 514 700); be there at 2pm to beat the crowds.) The **Retretti Arts Center** takes culture to new depths; a summer concert series resounds in the wonderful acoustics of a deep cave. (Tickets 90mk, students 45mk. Inquire at the Opera Festival Ticket Office.) The 1½km of caverns feature paintings and sculpture amid shimmering reflecting pools, worth visiting even without a concert. From Helsinki, take the train toward Savonlinna. (Open May-June 10am-7pm; July 10am-8pm; Aug.-Sept. 10am-7pm; Feb.-April Tues., Thurs., and Sun. 11am-7pm. Admission 60mk.)

Head east from the bus and train stations on Olavinkatu and cross the bridge to reach the lakefront **market,** where you can buy fresh produce and hand-crafted souvenirs. When you're bored watching the sightseeing boats chug by, hug Linnankatu along the south shore until you reach the moat. Looming on the other side of the wooden footbridge is **Olavinlinna Castle,** a weatherworn but intact medieval fortress. High up the castle walls, jutting out over the water, are the ventholes of the medieval toilets (free-fall flush). A guided tour sallies through steep defense passages, winding stairways and three 16th-century towers. (Open daily 10am-5pm. Admission 15mk.) For some peace and sun, island-hop north via the two footbridges to **Sulosaari,** a pine-covered isle dotted with boulders.

The most bestest **tourist office** in Finland occupies the yellow building across the bridge from the market at Puistokatu 1 off Olavinkatu (tel. (957) 134 92). They will hold your baggage, help you find accommodations, and change money when banks are closed. (Open early June and Aug. daily 8am-6pm, late June-July daily 8am-10pm; Sept. and May daily 9am-6pm; Oct.-April Mon.-Fri. 9am-4pm.) Lake and bake at the shoreside sauna of the **Savonlinna Hospits,** Linnankatu 20 (tel. (957) 224 43), conveniently wedged between the castle and the market square. (Kitchen facilities. Dorms 40mk. Breakfast 20mk.) **Retkeilymaja Malakias (IYHF),** Pihlajavedenkuja 6 (tel. (957) 232 83), is 1½km from town. Going up Tulliportinkatu, veer right on Savonkatu, or take bus #2, 3, or 4. (50mk, nonmembers 65mk. Open June to mid-Aug.) **Vuohimäki Camping** (tel. (957) 53 73 53) is 7km out, but bus #3 runs twice per hour. (35mk per site. Open late May-late Aug.)

Eating and imbibing here centers around Olavinkatu. For a great breakfast deal, visit **Pietari Kylliäinen** at Olivinkatu 15, on the castle side of town. (All-you-can-eat 17mk; open Mon. and Sat. 7-9:30am, Tues.-Fri. 6:30-9:30am, Sun. 7-10am). For lunch or dinner, try **Pizzeria Capero,** Olavinkatu 51, with pizza and salad for 29-36mk (open Mon.-Fri. 10:30am-10:30pm, Sat. 11am-10:30pm, Sun. noon-10:30pm). Across Olavinkatu from the market, throw back a few 11mk beers at **Happy Time Pub,** Kauppatori 1 (open Mon.-Fri. 24 hrs., Sat.-Sun. 10am-midnight).

Savonlinna is yours by train from Helsinki (3-4 per day, 62mk, express 70mk) or bus from Pieksämäki (3-4 per day, 56mk, railpasses valid). The train stops first at Savonlinna-Kauppatori in the center of town and near the tourist office, and continues to the Savonlinna stop by the train station. Water travel costs a pretty *penni* but provides the best access to the pristine regions of the lakes; motorboats shuttle daily between Savonlinna and Kuopio (depart Tues.-Sun. 10am, 220mk).

Near Savonlinna

The stretch of land and water between Savonlinna and Kuopio includes many worthwhile stops. One of the best is the isolated farmhouse **Pohjataival (IYHF)** (tel. (972) 664 19), 18km from Heinävesi, with its own steamboat pier. Unwind with the cows, ducks, and dogs, bloat yourself with glorious homecooked meals (20mk) and debauch in the sauna. (Dorms 45mk. Rowboats available.) The Savonlinna-Kuopio motorboat will drop you literally at the doorstep; otherwise take the bus to Pieksämäki, the train to Heinävesi, and then call the farmhouse for a 25mk lift.

At the handsome **Valamo Monastery,** (tel. (972) 619 59), 35km from Heinävesi along the Savonlinna-Kuopio boat route, guests often outnumber monks 20 to one. Stay in the guest house for 50mk per night, and chow at the restaurant for 35-50mk. (No shorts or photographs or photographs of shorts.) Some young Finns complete their compulsory period of social service here. A more worldly retreat is **Rauhalinna,** a wooden palace built in the 19th century by a Russian commander for his wife. Cruises to this elegant island, where you can stroll the grounds and sip tea in an atmosphere of czarist romance, leave the market square in Savonlinna several times daily (30mk).

Jyväskylä

Right in the middle of Finland's lake district, Jyväskylä is famous as the home of architect Alvar Aalto. The otherwise drab city is sprinkled with Aalto's buildings, which, if you can't pick them out yourself, are presented in a guide (5mk) offered by the **tourist office,** Vapaudenkatu 38 (tel. (941) 62 49 03), up Asemakatu (the street perpendicular to the train station) one block and left one block. (Open Mon.-Fri. 8am-6pm, Sat.-Sun. 10am-6pm; Sept.-May Mon.-Fri. 8am-5pm.) The **Aalto Museum,** at Alvar Aallon Katu 7, left on Vapaudenkatu to the end, will help you follow the development of Aalto's style. The building itself is his spawn. (Open Wed.-Sun. noon-6pm, Tues. noon-9pm. Admission 10mk; free on Sat.) The nearby **University of Jyväskylä,** largely designed by Aalto, occupies an isolated campus in piney woods near the museum.

Sporty **Laajari (IYHF)** (tel. (941) 25 33 55), has a ski-slope and skateboard ramp in its backyard, and a free sauna in the basement. Take bus #25 (7mk) from the park across from the tourist office. (Dorms 30mk. Kitchen.) The hostel occupies a brown building 200m from reception. Lakeside **Tuomiojärvi Camping** (tel (941) 62 40 85) lies 2km north of town by bus #32. (25mk per person. Cabins 170mk for 4 persons. Open Jun.-Aug.) **Pikantti,** in Citymarket on Asemakatu, offers Finnish cuisine for lunch; 24-38mk includes bread, salad and a dessert. (Open Mon.-Sat. 11:30am-1:30pm.) Trains from Turku (3 per day) and Helsinki (7 per day) plus bus connections to towns throughout the Lake District make Jyväskylä a regional transport hub.

Kuopio

Strategically situated in central Finland at the northern edge of the Lake District, Kuopio was originally established in 1782 to boost the maritime trade industry in the eastern Finnish province of Savo. Now, 200 years later, Kuopio is playing up its ideal location again as Finland's lakeside cruise hub. Steamers sail daily to Heinävesi (5 hr.; 105mk) and Savonlinna (11½ hr.; 220mk); you can find out more about lunchtime, afternoon, and sunset cruises and the rest of this burgeoning business at the **tourist office,** Haapaniemenkatu 17 (tel. (971) 18 25 84 or 18 25 85), next to the market square and the town hall. (Open Mon.-Fri. 8am-5pm, Sat. 9am-1pm; mid-Aug. to May Mon.-Fri. 8:30am-4pm.) The branch at the train station (tel. (971) 16 62 06) has less information, but longer hours. (Open daily 9:30am-7:30pm.)

The **Orthodox Church Museum,** Karjalankatu 1, is the only one of its kind in Scandinavia, with a remarkable collection of icons, illustrated bibles, and music books brought from Soviet territories after WWII. (Open Tues.-Sun. 10am-4pm; Sept.-April Mon.-Fri. 10am-2pm, Sat.-Sun. noon-5pm. Admission 15mk.) Kuopio's **Open-Air Museum,** Kirkkokatu 22, replicates 1780-1930 living quarters and trade exhibits. Walk up Puijonkatu away from the station and turn left. (Open Thurs.-Tues. 10am-5pm, Wed. 10am-7pm; mid-Sept. to mid-May Tues.-Sun. 10am-3pm. Free.)

Retkeilymaja Tekma is the closest hostel to the train station (2½km), easily accessible by buses #3 and 5 (every 20 min., 7mk). (Singles 100mk. Triples 40mk per person. Nonmembers add 15mk.) **Rauhalahti Camping** (tel. (971) 31 22 44), 7km from town, has Kuopio's best beach; take bus #20 (2 per hr., 7mk). They also rent bikes, mopeds, canoes, and boats. (55mk. Open mid-May to Aug.) Kuopio's **marketplace** is lively and colorful, with crafts, flowers, and delicious traditional foods. This is the place to sample *kalakukko,* a Finnish fish bread (fish in the middle). Finicky cats agree—it's yummy. At 7am you can buy hot *munkki* pastries for 3mk, and then sit in one of the outdoor cafés. At 3pm, the show moves to **Matkustajasatama,** the passenger harbor along the waterfront. Lining the market square, several grocery stores keep late hours on weekdays (open until 8pm Mon.-Fri.).

Four daily trains link Kuopio to Helsinki; two also run to Jyväskylä, and there are connections to Kajaani and Oulu in the north.

Oulu

Oulu's flower-bordered streets lend a Mediterranean grace that belies its history as one of Finland's busiest ports and the world's leading tar exporter during the 19th century. Biking along its well-tended paths is the best way to explore this expansive city. Hidden in the northeast corner of the Gulf of Bothnia, all trains between northern and southern Finland pass through Oulu's clutches.

The **municipal tourist office,** at Torikatu 10 (tel. (981) 24 12 94) will greet you with good-natured help. Take Hallishatu, the broad avenue perpendicular to the train station, and then a left on Torikatu. (Open Mon.-Sat. 9am-6pm, Sun. 9am-4pm; Sept.-May Mon.-Fri. 9am-4pm.) **Retkeilymaja Välkkylä (IYHF),** Kajaanintie 36 (tel. (981) 22 77 07), offers the only inexpensive lodgings in town; roomy quads, without heinous bunkbeds, make for a comfy stay. (Kitchen facilities. 65mk, nonmembers 80k. Open June-July.)

Nallikari, Finland's Côte d'Azur, rims an island 5km northwest of town. The largely untouristed and splendiferous beach is the best place in Northern Finland to enjoy the Bothnian waters, despite its tacky amusement park. You can camp here at **Nallikari Camping** by the beach (tents 25mk per person; 4-person cabins 250mk).

Take bus #5 from Kajaanintie outside the hostel heading toward the center of the city, after you've stopped by the **Ainola Museo,** the local history museum that overlooks the mouth of the river off Kasarmintie. (Open Mon.-Tues. and Thurs. 10am-6pm, Wed. 10am-7pm, Sat. 10am-3pm, Sun. 11am-6pm. Admission 3mk, students 1mk.)

You can see and sniff exotic flora from around the world at the University of Oulu's **Botanical Gardens,** 7km north of the center along bus route #4, 6, or 23. Twin glass pyramids, named Romeo and Julia, house citrus, olive, and cocoa trees. (Pyramids open Tues.-Sun. 10am-5pm. Open-air gardens open daily 7am-10pm. Free.) Finland's rock musicians congregate here for a weekend in mid-July at the annual **Kuus Rock Festival.** For a panoramic overview of the city, take bus #13 or 19 (7mk) to the **observation tower,** 4km from the city center (admission 5mk). A bizarre cultural phenomenon awaits at the shopping center between the rail station and the youth hostel: hundreds of Finnish teens drive imported cars back and forth for hours on end, with friends jumping in and out of backseats, in an unusual form of "cruising." Those unlucky souls without a car can drown their sorrows in a glass of beer at **Café Lillemor** at Pakkahuoneenkatu 19 (open Mon.-Tues. and Thurs. 1-10pm, Wed. and Fri. 1pm-midnight, Sun. 10am-10pm). Four to five trains per day leave south to Helsinki and north to Rovaniemi.

Kuusamo and the Karhunkierros

For foaming rapids and bottomless gorges, lace up your hiking boots and head for the **Karhunkierros** (The Bear's Ring), a 75km hiking trail through untainted landscape near the Soviet-Finnish border. To get started, head to Kuusamo from either Oulu (6 per day, 3½ hr., about 100mk), Kajaani (1 bus per day, 4 hr., 114mk), or Rovaniemi (1 per day, 4 hr., about 100mk). In Kuusamo, stay at **Kuusamon Kansanopisto (IYHF)** (tel. (989) 221 32), a yellow house across from the bus station. (Open June to mid-Aug. Doubles 50mk.) Stock up on food at **Kitkan Viisas** in the same building as the bus station (open Mon.-Fri. 9am-8pm, Sat. 9am-6pm).The Kuusamo **tourist office,** Torangintie 2 (tel. (989) 204 29 10), 2km from town at the corner of highways 20 (Ouluntie) and 5, peddles maps (47mk) and proffers information about the trail, which takes 4-6 days, depending on your condition. If you want to hike just part of the trail, they'll show you which buses to catch. (Open Mon.-Fri. 9am-8pm; Sept.-May Mon.-Fri. 9am-5pm, Sat. 9am-4pm.) There are free 10-20 person cabins every 10km or so along the way, but bring a tent during the summer in case they are full. You may want rubber boots for the boggy stretches. Bring food and mosquito repellent—there are only two supply stations on the trail and billions of pesky pests ready to eat you alive. To fish, you need a local license (50mk per day) and a state license (30mk), both available at the tourist office in Kuusamo.

Lappland (Lappi)

For a different sense of space and time, for untouched fells rising against a clean northern sky, for vast swarms of reindeer and herds of mosquitoes . . . visit Lappland, Europe's most desolate wilderness. In the south, near Tornio on the Swedish border, you'll find crashing river rapids and whitefish. To the north lies 80-kilometer-long *Inarinjärvi* (Lake Inari) and its countless islands, and, even farther north, the steep tundra slopes of the Teno River Valley. Continue beyond Kolari and Sodankylä to the true fell-and-bog of northern Lappland. The highest mountains rise in the northwest.

The hot sun never sets on Lappland during the two-to three-month summer. In winter, temperatures hit the opposite extreme and the sun rises for only a few hours a day. Yet, clear sky, moonlight, and white snow produce an eerie blue glow, and in December and January, the green, red, and yellow streaks of the Northern Lights illuminate a surreal snowscape. Skiing is ideal from March to mid-May, with facilities and rental outlets at almost every tourist center (Saariselkä, Pallas, Ylläs, and Ounasvaara, near Rovaniemi). In summer, guides lead hiking expeditions from the same places. Only experienced groups should undertake independent excursions. Hikers should plan their routes around the mountain huts run by the Finnish Youth Hostel Association. Information on these huts is available at most tourist offices, notably the Rovaniemi tourist office.

Most of the Sami (Finnish Lapps) and Kolttas (originally Russian Lapps) live in the four northernmost parishes of Sodankylä, Enontekiö, Inari, and Utsjoki. About three-fourths of the Finnish Sami population still speak their own language; at least 800 families still make their living from reindeer herding. Local delicacies include *poro* (reindeer meat), *lohi* (salmon), *siika* (whitefish), and liqueurs and desserts made from Arctic *lakat* (cloudberries).

Rovaniemi

Tucked 8km south of the Arctic Circle, Rovaniemi is the capital of Finnish Lappland and, more importantly, yet another of Santa Claus's home towns. Rovaniemi is easily accessible by trains coming northward through Kemi and by southbound buses from Inari, Muonio, Enontekiö and Karasjok, Norway. Finnair also flies here from Helsinki (youth fare 420mk). Take bus #8 from the train station (on the hour, 8.50mk) to **Santa's Residence,** from where destinations around the world are served by reindeer shuttle (departures yearly in late December; youth fare free if you've been good). Yes, you can meet the elves and pet the reindeer too; in fact, Mr. and Mrs. Claus's home is one of the nicest in this drab metropolis.

If you are staying to see more than St. Nick, check out the **tourist office** at Aallonkatu 1 (tel. (960) 162 70; open Mon.-Fri. 8am-7pm, Sat.-Sun. 10am-7pm; Sept.-May Mon.-Fri. 8am-4pm). From the train station, head right on Ratakatu, go up the hill and turn right on Hallituskatu; follow Hallituskatu to the end, where you go left on Valtakatu, which becomes Aallonkatu after 3 blocks. They find rooms in private homes (about 100mk), and dish up a weekly events listing comically called *Let's Go,* as well as information on boat (90-550mk) and snowmobile safaris (220-530mk), complete with English-speaking guides. Another branch is at the train station (tel. (960) 222 18; open June-Aug. Mon.-Sat. 7:30-noon and 2-5:30pm, Sun. 7:30am-noon). Rovaniemi's **IYHF youth hostel,** Hallituskatu 16 (tel. (960) 146 44), lacks kitchen facilities. Turn right from the station, go up the hill, through the large intersection, and down Hallituskatu. (Reception open 6:30-10am and 5-10pm. 39mk, nonmembers 54mk. Small breakfast 23mk). Across the river from the town center, **Ounaskoski Camping** (tel. (960) 153 04) has a prime location and river swimming. (32.50mk per person, families 69mk. Open June to mid-Aug.) The tourist office has a list of restaurants and prices. Not far from the station, **Ravintola Lapinpaula,** Hallituskatu 24, serves a mean buffet lunch for 34mk. (Open daily 10am-1am.) **Rinnemarket** is the closest market to the station, with a huge selection including several types of *lapinleipä* (Lappish bread). (Open Mon.-Fri. 9am-8pm, Sat. 8am-6pm.)

The main thing you'll want from Rovaniemi is connections north and east. Roughly 3 buses daily head north to Inari (5-6 hr., 155mk) and continue to Norway. A bus a day crosses to Kuusamo (4 hr.).

Northern Lappland

The areas north of Rovaniemi exceed even the most rapturous visions of boundless tundra, perpetual summer sun, and endless forests; only the *ilmavoimat* of mosquitoes detracts. If you set out for northern Lappland, plan ahead; connections will be difficult. From Rovaniemi, there are two hitching/bus routes to the north: Highway 79 leads towards Muonio and Enontekiö in the northwest; Highway 4 to Inari due north. At the information office in the Rovaniemi train station, pick up timetables for Lappland's three bus companies: the **Postilinjat** (postal buses), **J.M. Eskelisen Lapin Linjat Oy,** and **Pikavuoro.** Prices and times are fairly similar, although the postal line is slightly slower. Students: remember to flaunt your studenthood; it could earn you a discount.

Next to Lake Inari, the minute town of **Inari** is both a tourist spot and an old Lapp center. Seaplanes roar off the lake, and befuddled reindeer wander the streets, occasionally chased back into the pines by children on bicycles. A well-kept and friendly (but small) **retkeilymaja (IYHF)** (tel. (9697) 512 44) welcomes travelers. It's a few hundred meters north from the center of town; turn left at the gas station. (Doubles 50mk, nonmembers 65mk. Open June-Sept.) **Inari Opisto** (tel. (997) 510 24) operates as a summer hotel (100mk). Six official **campgrounds** punctuate the wilderness. The tiny **tourist office** (open mid-June to mid-Sept. Mon.-Sat. 9am-8pm) sits in the shadow of the giant **Näkkäläjärvi** souvenir shop in the town center. Head to the island **Ukko** in Lake Inari, lorded over by the Sami god of fishing. Two-hour boat tours leave daily at 2pm across from the tourist office (50mk). The secrets of Sami life (including the magic rings to help the reindeer urinate) are divulged at the **open-air museum,** 200m north of the center of Inari. (Open June to mid-Aug. 8am-10pm; mid-Aug. to Sept. 8am-8pm; Sept. 1-20 9am-3:30pm. Admission 12mk, students and children 5mk.) From here you can hike 7km to the **Pielppajärvi Wilderness Church,** built in 1760. People used to come from miles around to worship here, but now there is screaming nothingness. Travelers may stay in the two huts at the church site. Ask the Inari tourist office about the **Lemmenjoki River** hiking area about 40km from Inari (daily bus connection). The **Ravadasköngäs Falls** resound for kilometers; make day-hikes and return to Inari, or crash out in the wilderness huts along the trails. A few professional gold-panners still work claims along the river.

North of Inari, the River Teno winds along the Norwegian border below dwarf birches and tundra-covered fells. Most Rovaniemi-Inari buses continue another couple hours to the river at either Karigasniemi (to the west) or Utsjoki (to the north), then cross the border and connect with the main Norwegian bus line at Karasjok or Skipagurra, respectively.. **Karigasniemi,** a classic outland of desolation, has a **retkeilymaja (IYHF)** (tel. (9697) 611 88) right in the center of "town" (30-60mk).

The western route from Rovaniemi passes through forgotten Lappish villages in the "arm" of Finland. Buses run north from Rovaniemi to **Muonio,** then continue either north to Kautokeino in Norwegian Lappland (7½ hr. from Rovaniemi), or northwest through **Kilpisjärvi** in Finland's most mountainous region (7 hr.) before emerging an hour later at Skibotn on the Norwegian coast and connecting with the bus to Tromsø. You can also reach Muonio via the eye-popping Highway E78 from Tornio (on the Gulf of Bothnia and the rail line to Sweden). Hiking in this part of the world is neato, but this is the brink of uninhabited wilderness; carry a map and compass at all times. Muonio has two hostels, while in Kilpisjärvi you can stay at the **Retkeilykeskus (IYHF)** (tel. (9696) 26 59; 35-50mk); the path to the top of **Saana Fell** (1029m) begins right behind Kilpisjärvi's Excursion Center (4 hr.). Another hike leads from Kilpisjärvi across the gently rounded peaks of the **Malla Nature Reserve** and the **Three Countries Frontier,** where Finland, Norway, and Sweden meet on the shores of a lonely lake.

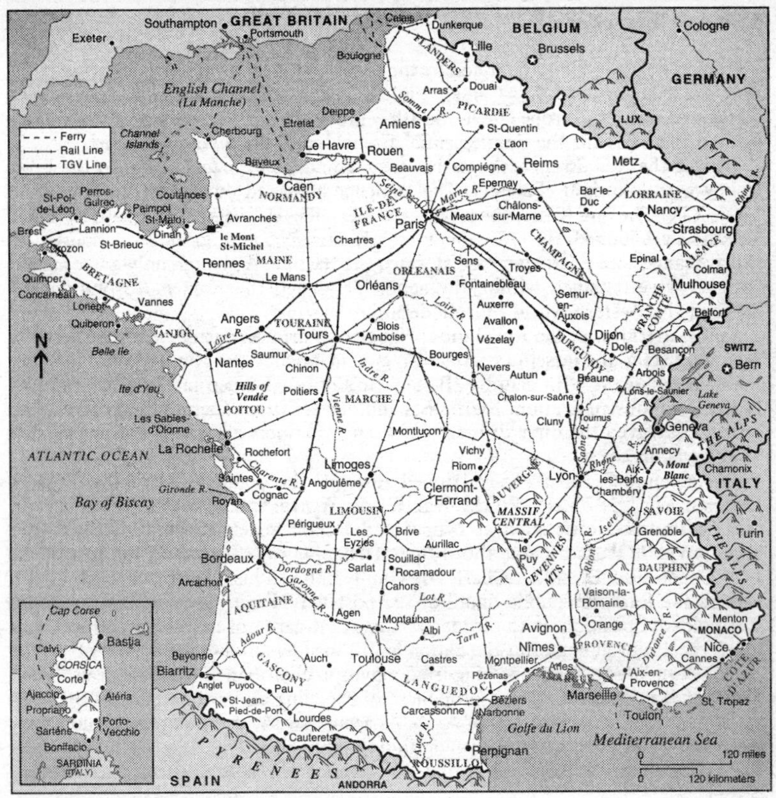

FRANCE

USD$1 = 5.95 francs (F, or FRF) — **1F = USD$0.17**
CAD$1 = 5.20F — **1F = CAD$0.19**
GBP£1 = 9.94F — **1F = GBP£0.10**
AUD$1 = 4.63F — **1F = AUD$0.22**
NZD$ = 3.39F — **1F = NZD$0.29**
Country Code: 33 — **International Dialing Prefix: 19**

Monolith of culture, cuisine, fashion, snobbery, and cheese, France comprises an extraordinary mosaic of tiny villages, walled medieval cities, seamy ports, and sophisticated Paris. The politically astute Charles de Gaulle, WWII Resistance hero and French president during much of the post-war era summed up the French spirit with the words, "France cannot be France without greatness." Galling as this statement may be, it testifies to the pride which the French feel for their land. In the center of all this splendor, the crowded brilliance of Paris presents only one of France's many faces. In the north, the industry of Lille hangs close by the bubbly of the Champagne region. The cliffs and fertile countryside of Normandy posed for the Impressionists and embraced an Anglo-American liberation, while Brittany and Corsica have clung passionately to distinct cultural identities. The Loire Valley blossoms with the architecture of the French Renaissance; the snowcapped Alps illustrate the architecture of God. The Dordogne River valley shelters 20,000-year-old cave paintings, while the Côte d'Azur is so glorious it has nearly ruined itself.

France was originally inhabited by the Gauls, a Celtic people who eventually fell prey to the legions of Julius Caesar. Violent feudal strife ensued until Charlemagne conquered most of Europe late in the 8th century. The exploits of one of his knights formed the basis for the quintessential French epic, the *Song of Roland.*

During the Renaissance, the nation grew grand, as François I planted the Loire Valley with luxuriant châteaux. The opulence climaxed during the noon years of Louis XIV, The Sun King, whose palace at Versailles still sets the standard by which all others are judged. By 1789, the wretched citizens could no longer support such extravagance, and a Parisian mob stormed the Bastille. Although only a few mental patients were detained within, the action detonated the French Revolution and dragged the western world into modernity.

In the afterglow of the Revolution, Napoleon's armies mastered Europe, and the marching song of Marseille's tattered regiment became the country's national anthem. Later in the 19th century, Bonaparte's bravado faded into a grim and gray process of industrialization. Journalists and literary titans such as Hugo, Zola, and Balzac portrayed the dirty drudgery of France's miners and the indulgences of its wealthy bourgeoisie.

French and German armies ripped through the countryside in the Franco-Prussian War (1870-71), World War I, and World War II. After the first war, French Impressionists such as Monet and Renoir redefined painting, and after World War I, Paris became the shrine of Hemingway, Stein, and the rest of the Lost Generation. President Charles de Gaulle pursued his claims to French Greatness as the foremost public figure of the post-WWII era. Comtemporary France still holds its position as the leader in the avant-garde of aesthetic, cultural, and intellectual movements. But the nation is still torn by an undying xenophobia. The popular candidacy (for everything from mayor to chairman of the European Parliament) of Jean-Marie Le Pen—proponent of expelling all immigrants and their offspring—and paranoid rumors of Arab, African, Jewish, and homosexual conspiracies supply the sad proof of this continuing prejudice.

Pick up a copy of *Let's Go: France* for detailed coverage of the country's every corner.

Getting There and Getting Around

France does not require visas of U.S., Canadian, New Zealand, or EC passport holders. Australians *do* need visas; we apologize for the mix-up in last year's edition. Contact consulates in Europe or at St. Martin's Tower, 31 Market St., Sydney, NSW 2000 (tel. (02) 261 57 79).

The **Société Nationale de Chemins de Fer (SNCF)** is one of Europe's most efficient and extensive rail networks. A train ticket is not valid until you insert it in the orange machine at the entrance to the platforms. Seat reservations are especially recommended for international trips. The SNCF's premier offering, the **France Railpass,** comes in two varieties: four days of travel within a 15-day period (USD119) or nine days within a month (USD209). The pass must be purchased outside France; contact a travel agent for details. Other special tickets apply during specified periods. "Blue periods" are periods of minimum train traffic, usually Monday afternoon through Friday morning and Saturday afternoon to Sunday afternoon; "white periods" coincide with heavier train use (most other times), while holidays are "red periods." The **Carissimo** (180F for 4 trips, 360F for 8 trips) allows you and up to seven friends (under 26) discounts of 20% during white periods and 50% during blue periods. A **Carte Vermeille** (100F) entitles travelers over 60 to essentially the same discounts. These passes are available from most large train stations. Bring a photo when you make your purchase.

French **buses,** usually slow and cheap, are useful for filling the gaps in the rail network. The bus station, usually near the train station, is called the *gare routière.*

France is among the worst countries in Europe for **hitching.** The larger the city, the more difficult it will be to get a ride. **Allostop** is a nationwide service that pairs drivers and riders. They charge 65F per trip, plus 17 centimes per km over 500km, and 150F per one year's membership. Their main office (84, passage Brady, 75010 Paris; tel. 42 46 00 66) can give you the addresses of offices throughout the country.

French roads, with a wealth of well-paved minor routes, are terrific for **cycling.** Prime regions include the Loire Valley, Normandy, Provence, the Dordogne River Valley, Alsace-Lorraine, and Burgundy. SNCF's pamphlet *Guide du train et du vélo* offers details on combining cycling and railroading in France. Bikes cost 48F to transport on trains, and they often take three days to arrive. Many train stations rent bikes (around 50F per day); you may sometimes return it to another station.

Practical Information

The extensive French tourism support network revolves around **syndicats d'initiative** and **offices de tourisme,** both of which *Let's Go* labels "tourist office." Either will help you find accommodations (for about 10F), distribute maps, and suggest excursions to the countryside.

Everything you've heard about the rudeness of the French may prove true if you address people in English without a prefatory *"Parlez-vous anglais, Madame/Monsieur?"* Contrary to popular opinion, even the most flailing efforts to speak French will often be appreciated, especially in urban areas. Be lavish with your *Monsieurs, Madames,* and *Mademoiselles,* and greet people with a friendly *bonjour (bonsoir* after 6pm).

Just about everything snoozes in France from noon to 2pm, and closes on Sundays. Many provincial areas shut down on Mondays, too. Food stores remain open on Sunday mornings. Most museums close for at least one day per week.

France's telephone system splits into two halves: Paris (city code 1) and everything else (no city code). To dial the provinces from Paris, preface the eight-digit number with 16; in reverse, dial 161, then the eight-digit Paris number. To operate payphones, you'll be best off buying a *télécarte,* or telephone credit card. Available at train stations, post offices, and *tabacs,* they cost 40F *(petite)* or 96F *(grande).* To call collect, tell the operator *"en PCV"* (on-pay-say-vay). For AT&T's **USA Direct,** dial 19, wait for the tone, then dial 0011. Anywhere in France, dial 10 for an operator, 12 for directory assistance, 15 for medical emergencies, 17 for police assistance, and 18 for the fire department. Dial 19 33 11 for the international operator, and be prepared to wait for up to one hour.

Accommodations and Camping

Auberges de jeunesse (youth hostels) cover France, ranging from well-kept, centrally located castles to run-down barracks. Most are affiliated with IYHF; they charge nonmembers slightly more, and sometimes remember to stamp their guest cards. Hostels run 40-80F per person, with breakfast about 15F (usually not obligatory).

The quality of hotels in France generally matches their standardized rating, a scale of zero to four stars. Rock-bottom hotels start at about 60-90F for singles, 80-100F for doubles, without private bath or breakfast. Rates are often the same for single- and double-occupancy. Showers are usually not included in the price of the room and can run 15-25F. Inquire whether the breakfast or meals at the hotel are *obligatoire.* Breakfast (12-22F) almost always means bread, jam, and coffee or hot chocolate. Reservations (confirmed with one night's deposit) are highly recommended for the larger cities in summer.

Campgrounds, plentiful in France, are also rated on a four-star system. *Michelin's Camping and Caravanning in France* details the best sites. The **Club Alpin Français** maintains a network of mountain huts in upland regions. For further information, contact the office at 9, rue de la Boëtie, 75008 Paris (tel. 47 42 38 46).

Tourist offices list local *gîtes d'étape* (shelters forbidden to motorists) and *chambres d'hôte* (rustic farmhouse accommodations). Most tourist offices in rural areas have a list of *campings à la ferme*—small campsites located on private farms.

Food and Drink

The French love affair with food is as renowned as the less fortunate relationships between Romeo and Juliet, Antony and Cleopatra, or Julia and Kiefer. In restaurants, fixed-price three-course meals (called *menus)* begin at 45F. Service is always included; tips are only in order for sensational treatment, which is rare. Exert caution when ordering *à la carte; l'addition* (the check) may exceed your weekly budget. You can buy *sandwiches* at most French cafés; for 8-20F you get a foot-long baguette with cheese or meat inside. Cafés are a forum for continuous conversation, but you pay for the right to sit and watch the world go by. Drinks and food are often 10-30% more if served in the dining room *(salle)* or outside *(sur la terrasse)* than at the bar *(comptoir).*

Traditionally, the complete French dinner includes an *apéritif,* an *entrée* (appetizer), *plat* (main course), salad, cheese, dessert, fruits, coffee, and a *digestif* (after-dinner drink), and takes several hours to complete. A meal to tell your grandchildren about will run about 150F. The French *always* take wine with their meals. You might hear the story of how Woody Allen was kicked out of a French restaurant for ordering a Coke with his meal. Of him, it was said, "*Il manque du savoir vivre*" ("He doesn't know how to live").

Boulangeries, pâtisseries, and *confisseries* tempt with bread, pastries, and candy. *Fromageries* and *cremeries* present an astonishing array of cheeses. *Charcuteries* sell salads and meats. For supermarket shopping, look for **Félix Potin, Uniprix, Prisunic,** or **Monoprix.** Local markets *(marchés)* are picturesque, animated, and often offer better quality. Smaller towns hold them once or twice per week; they are a fixed feature in larger cities, coloring the streets every morning except Sunday and Monday.

Paris

Paris slakes the human thirst for perfection. If Paris did not exist, we would have to invent it. If we did not exist, Paris wouldn't care. Walter Benjamin proclaimed Paris the capital of the nineteenth century, and to modern Parisians, Paris remains no less than the nucleus of human civilization, an incarnation of the mythological longing for luxury, indulgence, romance, and beauty. Thousands world-wide have left their native lands to come to Paris in search of an allegorical contentment denied them at home. Think of Wilde and Joyce, the Hemingways and the Fitzgeralds, Gertrude Stein and Milan Kundera. Because everyone dreams about Paris before actually coming here, no one is at a loss for words to speak of it, but few have anything original to say. And yet, its heartbreaking beauty is entirely artificial, composed of monuments to order, improve, please, and transcend. Your own first visit to Paris may feel like an odd sort of homecoming. Or still, it may be filled with a nostalgic longing; for a myth, like a dream, never fully comes true. Place aside your expectations and discover a Paris of your own creation.

Hemingway called Paris a moveable feast, a city with a foretaste so irresistible that once you swallow, you will carry memories of the experience around with you forever after. It is also something of a giant all-night *patisserie,* a collection of delights able to satisfy individuals of every inclination. Seductive and addictive, arch and sassy, Paris exudes a *joie de vivre* that seems to jet from the Seine into the city's famous sewers and infect everything it passes. But don't let intimidation keep you from seeing and doing what you want. A surrender to Paris can be the sweetest of all possible defeats.

Orientation and Practical Information

Paris is in northern France, 200km and two to three rail hours from the English Channel *(La Manche),* a similar distance from Brussels, and no more than 12 hours from any major city in France. The city is divided into 20 *arrondissements,* or districts. The numbers rise clockwise in a rough spiral from the first or *premier* district around the Louvre to outer *arrondissements* near the periphery. *Let's Go* gives the *arrondissement* with every address: 5*ème* means *cinquième* or fifth. The River Seine, which flows from east to west, splits the city; **Rive Gauche** (Left Bank) lies to the south, and **Rive Droite** (Right Bank) to the north. If you stay in Paris for more than a few days, buy the *Plan de Paris par Arrondissements* (45-120F from kiosks), with maps of each *arrondissement* and a complete street index. Paris's efficient Métro (abbreviated here as "Mo.") will whisk you from one quarter to the next (see Public Transportation below).

Tourist Offices: Bureau d'Accueil Central, 127, av. des Champs-Elysées, 8*ème* (tel. 47 23 61 72). Mo. Etoile. Helpful, English-speaking, and packed. Reserves rooms (15F commission on 1-star hotels, 5F for hostels). Not the best way to get a cheap room. Can also reserve in 40 other French cities, though not more than 1 week in advance (23F). Open daily 9am-8pm. Also, branches at Gare de Lyon (tel. 43 43 33 24), major train stations and Eiffel Tower. **Maison de la France,** 8, av. de l'Opéra, 1*er* (tel. 42 96 10 23). Mo. Palais-Royal. Information on other regions of France. Open Mon.-Fri. 9am-7pm. **Tourist Information:** Tel. 47 20 88 98. A taped message in English gives the week's major events.

Budget Travel: Accueil des Jeunes en France (AJF), 119, rue St-Martin, 4*ème* (tel. 42 77 87 80), in front of the Pompidou Center. Mo. Rambuteau. Commission-free room-finding and maps. Open Mon.-Sat. 9:30am-6pm. Another office at Gare du Nord. **Centre Franco-Américain Odéon,** pl. de l'Odéon, 6*ème* (tel. 46 34 16 10.) Mo. Odéon. CIEE's work and study center for American students in Paris. Open Mon.-Fri. 9am-6:30pm. **Council Travel,** 51, rue Dauphine, 6*ème* (tel. 43 26 79 65). Mo. Odéon. Sells cheap charter flights, BIJ tickets, and ISICs (45F). All open Mon.-Fri. 11am-1pm and 2-6:30pm, Sat. 10am-1pm and 2:30-5pm. **Office de Tourisme Universitaire,** 39, ave. G. Bernanos, 5*ème* (tel. 43 36 80 27). Mo. Port-Royal. A CIEE-esque French student travel agency. Open Mon. 11am-6:45pm, Tues.-Fri. 10am-6:45pm. **CROUS** next door (tel. 40 51 36 00) has pamphlets on student housing, employment, university restaurants, and health care.

Embassies and Consulates: U.S.: 2, av. Gabriel, 8*ème* (tel. 42 96 12 02). Mo. Concorde. **Consulate,** 2, rue St-Florentin (tel. 42 96 12 02, ext. 2613), 3 blocks away. Open Mon.-Fri. 9am-4pm. **Canada:** 35, av. Montaigne, 8*ème* (tel. 47 23 01 01). Mo. Franklin Roosevelt. Open Mon.-Fri. 9-11:30am and 2-4pm. **U.K.:** 35, rue du Faubourg-St-Honoré, 8*ème* (tel. 42 66 91 42). Mo. Concorde/Madeleine. **Consulate,** 16, rue d'Anjou. Open Mon.-Fri. 9am-1pm and 2:30-6pm. **Australia:** 4, rue Jean Rey, 15*ème* (tel. 40 59 33 00). Mo. Bir-Hakeim. Open Mon.-Fri. 9:15am-noon and 2-5pm. **New Zealand:** 7ter, rue Léonard-de-Vinci, 16*ème* (tel. 45 00 24 11). Mo. Victor-Hugo. Open Mon.-Fri. 9am-1pm and 2:30-6pm.

Currency Exchange: Banks usually give the best rates; try the 9th *arrondissement.* **Change Automatique,** 66, av. des Champs-Elysées, 8*ème.* ATM machine accepting USD5, 10 and 20 bills. Poor rates. Open 24 hrs. All **train stations** (except Gare Montparnasse) have currency exchanges with mediocre rates (open daily 7am-9pm). Most cash machines will give you *francs* off your MasterCard or Visa.

American Express: 11, rue Scribe, 9*ème* (tel. 47 77 77 07), across from the Opéra. Mo. Opéra/Auber. Mediocre exchange rates. Open Mon.-Fri. 9am-5:30pm.

Post Office: 52, rue de Louvre, 1*er* (tel. 40 28 20 00), by the Bourse de Commerce. Mo. Châtelet-Les-Halles. Poste Restante. Only urgent telegrams, and no mailings over 2kg, outside normal business hours. Open 24 hrs.

Telephones: At the main post office. Open 24 hrs. No collect calls to the U.S. on Sun. Buy a *télécarte* (40 or 98F) at any rail station ticket window, post office, or *tabac,* as coin-operated phones are scarce. For calls outside Paris, dial 16. To Paris from the provinces, dial 161. From abroad, use the **city code:** 1.

Flights: Most international flights land at **Aéroport Roissy-Charles de Gaulle** (tel. 48 62 22 80), 23km northeast of Paris. The cheapest, fastest way to get into town is by Roissy Rail, a bus-train combination to central Paris. Take the free shuttle bus from Aérofare 1, arrival gate 28; Aérofare 2A, gate 5; Aérofare 2B, gate 6; or Aérofare 2D, gate 6 to the Roissy train station, where you can ride the RER B3 to the city (45 min., 29F). **Aéroport Orly,** 12km south of Paris, handles charters and many European flights. From Orly Sud, gate H or Orly Ouest, Gate F, you can take the free shuttle bus to Orly train station, and the RER C2 to central Paris (35 min., 23F).

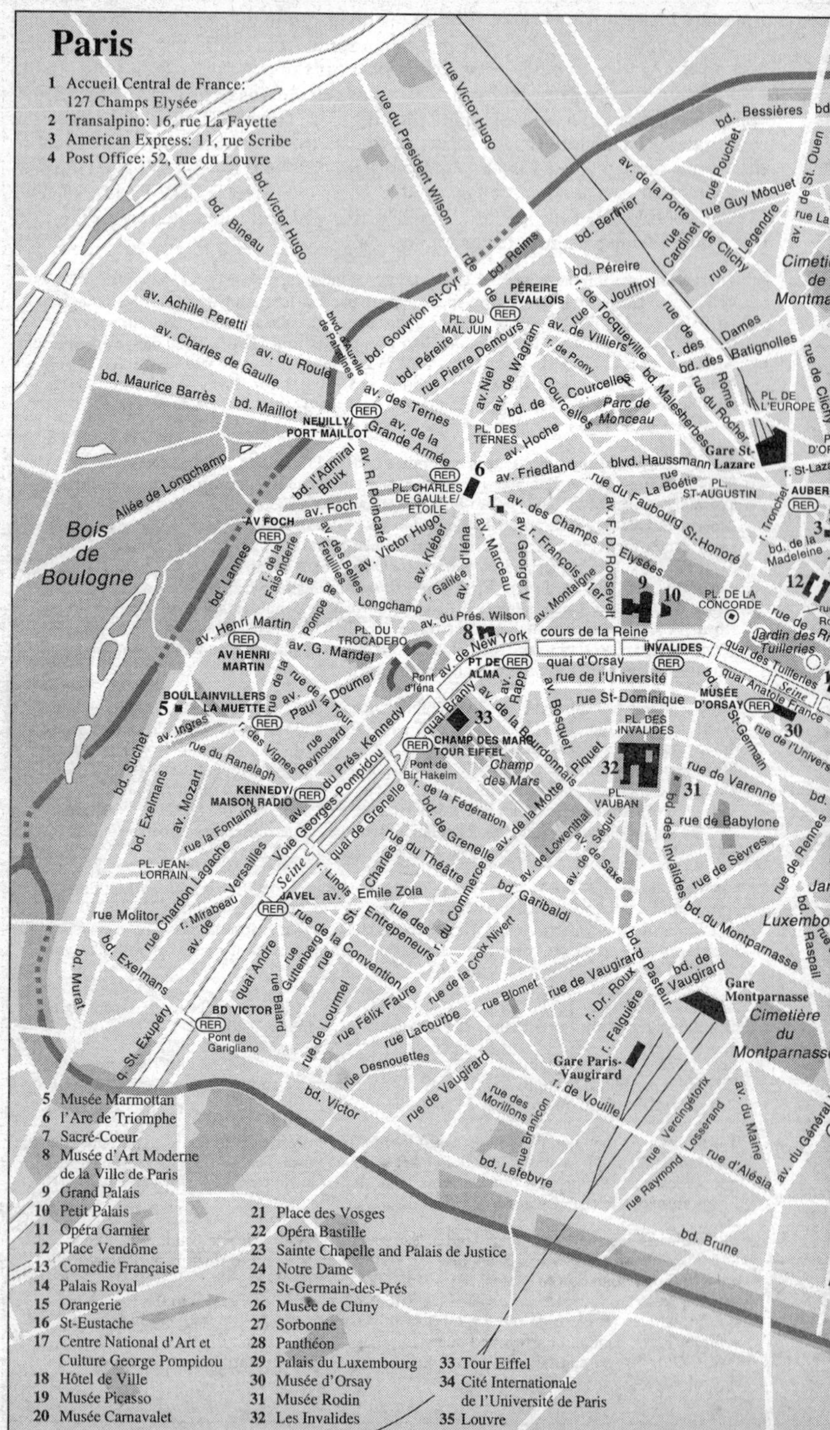
Paris
1 Accueil Central de France: 127 Champs Elysée
2 Transalpino: 16, rue La Fayette
3 American Express: 11, rue Scribe
4 Post Office: 52, rue du Louvre
Bois de Boulogne
Allée de Longchamp
av. Achille Peretti
av. Charles de Gaulle
bd. Maurice Barrès
bd. Maillot
av. du Roule
bd. Bineau
bd. Victor Hugo
rue du President Wilson
rue Victor Hugo
bd. Bessières
rue Pouchet
rue Guy Môquet
av. de St. Ouen
av. de la Porte de Clichy
rue Cardinet
rue Legendre
bd. Berthier
bd. Péreire
PÉREIRE LEVALLOIS
bd. Reims
bd. Gouvion St-Cyr
PL. DU MAL JUIN
rue Pierre Demours
r. de Tocqueville
rue Jouffroy
av. de Villiers
r. de Prony
rue des Dames
bd. des Batignolles
rue de Rome
rue du Rocher
PL. DE L'EUROPE
rue de Clichy
NEUILLY/PORT MAILLOT
av. des Ternes
av. de la Grande Armée
av. Niel
av. de Wagram
bd. de Courcelles
rue de Courcelles
Parc de Monceau
bd. Malesherbes
PL. DES TERNES
av. Hoche
blvd. Haussmann
Gare St-Lazare
av. Friedland
rue La Boétie
PL. ST-AUGUSTIN
AUBER
r. Tronchet
bd. de la Madeleine
rue du Faubourg St-Honoré
PL. CHARLES DE GAULLE/ETOILE
bd. l'Admiral Bruix
av. Foch
AV FOCH
av. R. Poincaré
av. Victor Hugo
av. Kléber
av. d'Iéna
av. Marceau
av. George V
av. des Champs Elysées
r. François 1er
av. F. D. Roosevelt
PL. DE LA CONCORDE
Jardin des Tuilleries
bd. Lannes
r. de la Faisanderie
rue de la Pompe
av. des Belles Feuillies
rue de Longchamp
r. Galilée
av. Montaigne
av. du Prés. Wilson
cours de la Reine
av. Henri Martin
AV HENRI MARTIN
PL. DU TROCADERO
av. G. Mandel
av. de New York
PT DE ALMA
quai d'Orsay
INVALIDES
quai des Tuilleries
quai Anatole France
Seine
rue de l'Université
rue St-Dominique
MUSÉE D'ORSAY
bd. St-Germain
BOULLAINVILLERS LA MUETTE
av. Paul Doumer
rue de la Tour
Pont d'Iéna
quai Branly
av. Rapp
av. Bosquet
av. de la Bourdonnais
PL. DES INVALIDES
rue de l'Univers
av. Ingres
rue des Vignes
rue Reynouard
av. du Prés. Kennedy
CHAMP DES MARS TOUR EIFFEL
Champ des Mars
Pont de Bir Hakeim
av. de la Motte Piquet
PL. VAUBAN
rue de Varenne
bd. des Invalides
rue de Babylone
rue de Sèvres
rue de Rennes
bd. Suchet
rue du Ranelagh
bd. Exelmans
av. Mozart
KENNEDY/MAISON RADIO
Voie Georges Pompidou
quai de Grenelle
r. de la Fédération
bd. de Grenelle
av. de Lowenthal
av. de Ségur
av. de Saxe
rue la Fontaine
PL. JEAN-LORRAIN
rue Chardon Lagache
av. de Versailles
r. Linois
rue Charles
rue du Théâtre
av. du Commerce
bd. Garibaldi
bd. du Montparnasse
Luxembourg
bd. Raspail
rue Molitor
r. Mirabeau
JAVEL
av. Emile Zola
rue St. Entrepeneurs
rue de la Convention
rue de la Croix Nivert
rue de Vaugirard
bd. Pasteur
bd. de Vaugirard
Gare Montparnasse
Cimetière du Montparnasse
bd. Murat
quai André
rue Guttenberg
rue Balard
rue de Lourmel
rue Félix Faure
rue Blomet
r. Dr. Roux
r. Falguière
rue Lacourbe
BD VICTOR
Pont de Garigliano
q. St. Exupéry
rue Desnouettes
Gare Paris-Vaugirard
r. de Vouille
av. du Maine
rue Vercingétorix
rue Losserand
rue d'Alésia
rue Raymond Losserand
rue des Morillons
rue Brancion
bd. Victor
bd. Lefebvre
bd. Brune
5 Musée Marmottan
6 l'Arc de Triomphe
7 Sacré-Coeur
8 Musée d'Art Moderne de la Ville de Paris
9 Grand Palais
10 Petit Palais
11 Opéra Garnier
12 Place Vendôme
13 Comedie Française
14 Palais Royal
15 Orangerie
16 St-Eustache
17 Centre National d'Art et Culture George Pompidou
18 Hôtel de Ville
19 Musée Picasso
20 Musée Carnavalet
21 Place des Vosges
22 Opéra Bastille
23 Sainte Chapelle and Palais de Justice
24 Notre Dame
25 St-Germain-des-Prés
26 Musée de Cluny
27 Sorbonne
28 Panthéon
29 Palais du Luxembourg
30 Musée d'Orsay
31 Musée Rodin
32 Les Invalides
33 Tour Eiffel
34 Cité Internationale de l'Université de Paris
35 Louvre

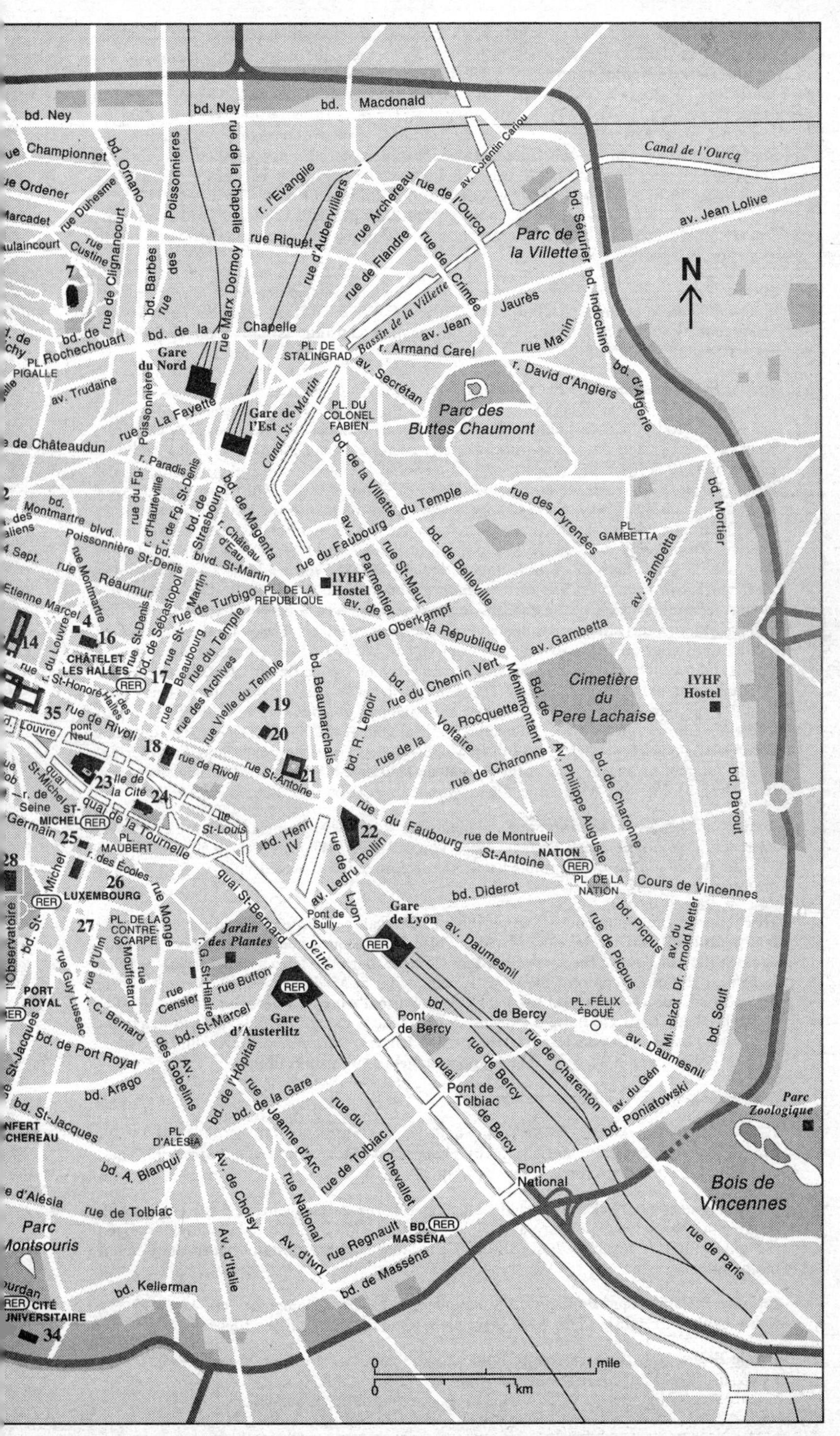
bd. Ney
bd. Macdonald
Canal de l'Ourcq
rue de la Chapelle
rue Marx Dormoy
rue Riquet
rue d'Aubervilliers
rue de Flandre
rue de l'Ourcq
av. Jean Lolive
Parc de la Villette
bd. Sérurier
bd. Indochine
bd. d'Algérie
N
Bassin de la Villette
PL. DE STALINGRAD
av. Jean Jaurès
r. Armand Carel
rue Manin
r. David d'Angiers
av. Secrétan
Parc des Buttes Chaumont
PL. DU COLONEL FABIEN
Gare du Nord
Gare de l'Est
Canal St-Martin
PL. PIGALLE
av. Trudaine
rue La Fayette
bd. de Magenta
bd. de la Villette
bd. de Strasbourg
rue du Faubourg du Temple
rue des Pyrenées
PL. GAMBETTA
bd. Mortier
bd. de Belleville
rue St-Maur
av. Parmentier
IYHF Hostel
PL. DE LA REPUBLIQUE
rue Oberkampf
av. de la République
av. Gambetta
Cimetière du Pere Lachaise
rue du Chemin Vert
bd. Voltaire
rue de Charonne
bd. Beaumarchais
rue de Rivoli
CHÂTELET LES HALLES
RER
Louvre
pont Neuf
Ile de la Cité
Ile St-Louis
rue St-Antoine
bd. Henri IV
rue du Faubourg St-Antoine
rue de Montrueil
NATION
PL. DE LA NATION
Cours de Vincennes
bd. Davout
bd. Diderot
Gare de Lyon
av. Daumesnil
Jardin des Plantes
Seine
quai St-Bernard
Gare d'Austerlitz
LUXEMBOURG
PL. DE LA CONTRE SCARPE
rue Mouffetard
rue Monge
PORT ROYAL
bd. de Port Royal
bd. St-Marcel
bd. de l'Hôpital
Av. des Gobelins
Pont de Bercy
bd. de Bercy
rue de Charenton
PL. FÉLIX ÉBOUÉ
bd. Soult
bd. Poniatowski
Parc Zoologique
Bois de Vincennes
Pont National
PL. D'ALESIA
bd. Arago
bd. St-Jacques
DENFERT ROCHEREAU
bd. A. Blanqui
rue de Tolbiac
Parc Montsouris
Av. de Choisy
Av. d'Italie
rue National
Av. d'Ivry
rue Regnault
BD. MASSÉNA
bd. de Masséna
bd. Kellerman
CITÉ UNIVERSITAIRE
rue de Paris
0 1 mile
0 1 km

Trains: Tel. 45 82 50 50 for information; 45 65 60 60 for reservations. Guard your valuables, and don't buy train or Métro tickets from anyone except the uniformed personnel in the booths. **Gare du Nord** for northern France, Belgium, Netherlands, Scandinavia, and northern Germany. To: Brussels (10 per day, 3 hr., 182F); Amsterdam (6 per day, 5-6 hr., 295F); Cologne (6 per day, 5-6 hr., 295F); Copenhagen (4 per day, 15 hr., 954F). **Gare de l'Est** for eastern France, Luxembourg, northern Switzerland, southern Germany, and Austria. To: Zürich (7 per day, 6 hr., 344F). **Gare de Lyon** for southeastern France, southern Switzerland, Italy, and Greece. To: Geneva (10 per day; 8 hr. by night, 4 hr. by TGV; 295-359F); Rome (4 per day, 16 hr., 558F). **Gare d'Austerlitz** for southwestern France, Spain, and Portugal. To: Barcelona (6 per day, 11-14 hr., 460F); Madrid (5 per day, 12-16 hr., 556F). **Gare St-Lazare** for Normandy. **Gare de Montparnasse** for Brittany. All train stations are also Métro stops for at least two lines.

Buses: Many international buses arrive at **Gare Routière Internationale,** 3, av. Porte de la Vilette, 19*ème,* in northeastern Paris. Mo. Porte de la Vilette. Check with your company for the precise location. For international bus information, call **International Express Eurolines Coach Station** (tel. 40 38 93 93).

Public Transportation: The Paris subway, **Métropolitain** or **Métro** (Mo.), is quick and efficient. It is said that no point in the city is more than 5 min. from the nearest stop. Lines are referred to by final destination *(direction),* not by number. Connections are called *correspondances.* Tickets anywhere within the city cost 5.50F, but it's more practical to buy a *carnet* of 5 (17.50F) or 10 (34.50F). Several passes allow unlimited travel on the Métro and buses. *Formule 1* is valid for one day (23F). *Carte Jaune* is valid Mon.-Sun., regardless of what day you buy it (54F). *Carte Orange* is valid from the first to the last day of the month (190F). Bring a picture for the *cartes,* which you can get from automatic machines in many stations. First class service on the Métro has been discontinued. Hold onto your ticket until you pass the point marked "*Limite de Validité des Billets;*" you could be asked for it by a uniformed *contrôleur.* Also, any *correspondances* you make to the **RER** (Réseau Express Régional—commuter train to the suburbs, express subway within central Paris) require that you insert into a turnstile your validated (and uncrumpled) ticket. Buses use the same tickets as the Métro, but on trips crossing 2 zones (refer to the route map on buses) you'll need 2 tickets, both of which must be validated in the machine by the driver's seat. Métro service runs approximately 5:30am-12:15am (check the *Principes de Tarification* poster on every platform for specifics on each line). Buses run until 8:30pm, *autobus du soir* until 12:30am, and a few *Noctambus* run all night. Schedules are available at the RATP office, 53ter, quai des Grands-Augustus, 6*ème* (tel. 43 46 14 14). Mo. St-Michel. Open daily 6am-9pm. For information about public transport, ask at the **Bureau de Tourisme RATP,** pl. de la Madeleine, 8*ème* (tel. 42 65 31 18). Mo. Madeleine. Open Mon.-Sat. 7:30am-7pm, Sun. 6:30am-6pm.

Taxis: Cab stands near train stations and major bus stops. 3 person max. Taxis are expensive, especially if you don't speak French. When you call (47 39 47 39, 42 41 50 50, or 42 70 41 41), the meter starts running immediately (i.e. before you are picked up). A 12-15% tip is customary.

Hitchhiking: Thumbing out of Paris is difficult and can be unsafe. Toward the east (Strasbourg, Munich), hitchers take the Métro to Porte de Charenton and walk along bd. Massena to catch the A4. Toward the north (Brussels, Cologne, Berlin), Métro to Porte de la Chapelle, right next to the A1. Toward the west (Rouen, Mont St-Michel, St-Malo), Métro to Porte de St-Cloud, and up bd. Murat toward pl. de la Porte d'Auteuil, where the A13 begins. Toward the south, Métro to Porte d'Orléans, down av. de la Porte d'Orléans, and left to a number of *autoroutes:* A16 goes to Lyon, the French Riviera, Switzerland, Italy, and Barcelona; A10 to Bordeaux and Madrid; A11 branches off A10 towards Brittany.

Luggage Lockers: At all train stations. 15F.

Lost Property: Bureau des Objets Trouvés, 36, rue des Morillons, 15*ème* (tel. 45 31 14 80). Mo. Convention. No information given by phone. Open Mon. and Wed. 8:30am-5pm, Tues. and Thurs. 8:30am-8pm, Fri. 8:30am-5:30pm.

English Bookstore: Shakespeare and Company, 37, rue de la Bûcherie, 5*ème* (no phone), across from Notre Dame. A Paris and New York institution. In 1922, Sylvia Beach arranged the publication of Joyce's *Ulysses* through her store. Library upstairs. Open daily noon-midnight.

Libraries: Bibliothèque Publique Information, at the Centre Pompidou (tel. 42 77 12 33). Many books in English. Open Mon.-Fri. noon-10pm, Sat.-Sun. 10am-10pm.

Public Baths: Beat the high cost of hotel showers at 8, rue des Deux Ponts, 4*ème* (tel. 43 54 47 40). Mo. Pont-Marie. Showers, soap, and towel 4.60F. Check under *Bains Douches*

Municipaux in the phone book for other addresses. All open Thurs. noon-7pm, Fri. 8am-7pm, Sat. 7am-7pm, Sun. 8am-noon.

Crises: SOS Friendship (tel. 47 23 80 80). Crisis help line staffed daily 3-11pm. Assistance in English. **Rape: SOS Viol** (tel. 05 05 95 95). Call free from anywhere in France. Open Mon.-Fri. 10am-7pm; July-Aug. irregular hours, but they have an answering service. **Drug Problems** (tel. 45 74 00 14). Open 24 hrs. **Alcoholics Anonymous** (tel. 46 34 59 65). A recorded message in English refers you for help. **SOS Racisme,** 64, rue de la Folie Mérincourt, 11*ème* (tel. 48 06 40 00). Mo. Oberkampf. Defends minority rights. Open 10am-7pm.

Pharmacy: Les Champs Elysées, 84, av. des Champs Elysées, 8*ème* (tel. 45 62 02 41). Mo. George V. Open 24 hrs.

Medical Assistance: Hôpital Franco-Britannique de Paris, 48, rue de Villiers, Levallois-Perret (tel. 47 58 13 12). Mo. Anatole France. Consultations with English-speaking doctors. **Hôpital American,** 63, bd. Victor Hugo, Neuilly (tel. 46 41 25 25). Mo. Sablons. More Expensive. Blue Cross-Blue Shield accepted as long as you fill out the forms first.

Emergencies: Police (tel. 17). **Ambulance: SOS Médécins** (tel. 15). **Fire** (tel. 18). Police station in every *arrondissement.*

Accommodations

If you arrive in Paris in high season (December and January and the end of June to August) without a reservation, you will probably spend most of your first day looking for accommodations, ruin your initial impression of this luminous city, and end up settling for something mediocre either too far from the city center or priced beyond your daily budget. If life delivers you in Paris with this unfortunate fate, don't waste your time by visiting random hotels. Find a payphone and begin the local tourist version of a telethon. The task will be infinitely easier if you search early in the day (9-11am). Better yet, search earlier in the year; many of the best places book up months in advance. To reserve before you leave, write to the hotel of choice and specify date of arrival, length of stay, and type of room desired. Enclose two international reply coupons, available at post offices. The hotel will send a confirmation, usually requesting one night's deposit. The whole process should take no more than a month, but emphasize to the hotel that you must receive confirmation before leaving. Phone reservations are often accepted with deposits; otherwise improve your chances by proposing a time, before noon, by which you'll arrive. The several room finding services in Paris (see "Tourist Offices" under "Practical Information") can be of invaluable help if you arrive without a reservation. In summer, don't be picky. Snag the first room you can afford.

Hostels

Parisian hostels lack the strict rules and regulations of other IYHF hostels; there is no curfew, no lockout, and no peace. If you are unable to reserve ahead (with deposit), arrive as early as possible, since any free beds will be gone by noon. Non-IYHF members pay an 18F surcharge per night.

Auberge de Jeunesse "Le d'Artagnan" (IYHF), 80, rue Vitruve (tel. 43 61 08 75). Mo. Porte de Montreuil or Porte de Bagnolet. A 420-bed behemoth. Luggage storage, sinks, and sometimes a shower swirl behind closets to maximize space utilization. Bar, laundromat, TV room, and kitchen facilities. Three-night max. stay. Reception open 24 hrs. Comfortable 3- to 8-berth rooms 82F. Showers and breakfast included. Sheets 16F. No reservations accepted for individuals; arrive early.

Auberge de Jeunesse "Jules-Ferry" (IYHF), 8, bd. Jules Ferry (tel. 435 75 56 00). Mo. République. Smaller (100 beds) and more central. Party atmosphere and jovial management. Line forms at 7am. 4-night max. stay. Two- to 6-bunk rooms 72F. Showers and breakfast included. Sheets 14F. Reservations accepted with IYHF voucher. Also books rooms in hostels around France, runs sightseeing tours of Paris, and sponsors group excursions to cities around Europe. (Call 43 57 02 60, fax 40 21 79 92 for information.)

Foyers

Foyers are independently run dormitory-like accommodations that are usually less hectic than hostels and less expensive than hotels. They vary in size from small boarding houses with singles to huge high-rises that welcome families as well as backpackers. Breakfast, showers, and linen are usually included in the price, and many *foyers* have kitchen facilities. **Accueil des Jeunes en France (AJF)** (see "Budget Travel" under "Practical Information") will find you a room in a *foyer* for free in one of their foyers, 10F elsewhere. You must pay the full price of the room when you make your reservation, before seeing it. AJF can also help you find a hotel room without commission. Be sure to remind the agent of this policy if you are asked to pay for the service. Often, however, they cannot find you a room for the full duration of your stay; you may have to return. All prices listed below are per person.

Hôtels de Jeunes (AJF): Le Fauconnier, 11, rue du Fauconnier, *4ème* (tel. 42 74 23 45), Mo. St-Paul or Pont-Marie. **Le Fourcy,** 6, rue de Fourcy, *4ème* (tel. 42 74 23 45), Mo. St-Paul; and **Maubisson,** 12, rue des Barres, *4ème* (tel. 42 72 72 09), Mo. Pont-Marie. These *foyers* are all located in elegant historic buildings in the Marais district, close to the sights. Though they vary in size (Fauconnier is the largest and Maubisson the smallest), rooms are spacious and comfortable. Groups and a young clientele dominate the scene. No reservations accepted, so arrive early. Lockout noon-4pm. 85F. Showers and breakfast included. AJF also runs the **Résidence Bastille,** 151, av. Lédru Rollin, *11ème* (tel. 43 79 53 86), slightly pricier with a few singles. Mo. Voltaire. Reception open 8am-10:30pm. Lockout noon-2pm. 2- to 4-bed rooms 80F, showers and breakfast included. **Résidence Luxembourg,** 270, rue St-Jacques, *5ème* (tel. 43 25 06 20). Mo. Luxembourg. Open July-Sept. only, and has the same prices. Both are more tranquil than the older, more established *foyers,* and rooms are just as comfortable.

Centre International de Paris (BVJ), Paris Louvre, 20, rue Jean-Jacques Rousseau, *1er* (tel. 42 36 88 18), Mo. Louvre; **Paris Opéra,** 11, rue Thérèse, *1er* (tel. 42 60 77 23), Mo. Pyramides; **Paris Les Halles,** 5, rue du Pélican, *1er* (tel. 40 26 92 45), Mo. Palais Royal; **Paris Quartier Latin,** 44, rue des Bernardins, *5ème* (tel. 43 29 34 80), Mo. Maubert. In the center of things, these 4 *foyers* cater to youthful crowds. No individual reservations accepted; arrive by 9am. Crowded, small, but spotlessly clean multi-bedded rooms and a few singles. 90F. Showers and breakfast included. Quartier Latin has the most singles and limited kitchen facilities. Three-night max. at all centers.

Centre International de Séjour de Paris (CISP). Ravel, 6, av. Maurice Ravel, *12ème* (tel. 43 43 19 01), Mo. Porte de Vincennes; and **CISP Kellerman,** 17, bd. Kellerman, *13ème* (tel. 45 80 70 76), in a park, Mo. Porte d'Italie. Both on the edge of the city. Lots of groups. Full by late morning. Large, comfortable rooms with showers and breakfast included. Reception open daily 6:30am-1:30am. Two- to 5-bed rooms 100F. 12-bed dorms 84F. Singles 127F.

Association des Etudiants Protestants de Paris (AEPP), 46, rue de Vaugirard, *6ème* (tel. 46 33 23 30 or 43 54 31 49). Mo. Luxembourg or Odéon. Ideally located across from the Jardin du Luxembourg, this *foyer* has a warm, international atmosphere. Ages 18-25. TV room, full kitchen, and table tennis. Reception open Mon.-Fri. 9am-noon and 3-7pm, Sat. 9am-noon and 4-8pm, Sun. 10am-noon. Dorms 63F. Singles 82F. Doubles 75F.

3 Ducks Hostel, 6, pl. E. Pernet, *15ème* (tel. 48 42 04 05), to the left of Eglise Jean Baptiste de Grenelle. Mo. Commerce. Renowned for revelry and the manager's distinctive wake-up call. Rooms way crowded, so everyone hangs out in the courtyard. Reception open 9-11am and 5pm-1am. Lockout 11am-5pm. Curfew 1am. 75F. Limited kitchen facilities. Reservations accepted with one night's payment.

Aloha Hostel, 42, rue Borromée, *15ème* (tel. 42 73 03 03; Mo. Volontaires), on a tiny street off 243, rue de Vaugirard. Brand new *foyer* with 1-, 2-, 4-, and 6-bed rooms. Showers and cooking facilities included. All rooms 75F per person. Curfew 1am. Reservations accepted with 1 night's deposit.

Maison des Clubs UNESCO, 43, rue de la Glacière, *13ème* (tel. 43 36 00 63). Mo. Glacière. Helpful staff. Small, simple rooms, some with facilities for the disabled. Three-night max. Singles 120-135F. Two- to 4-bed dorms 110F. Reservations accepted only for groups. Show up at 9:30-10am.

Foyer International des Etudiantes, 93, bd. St-Michel, *6ème* (tel. 43 54 49 63), across from the Jardin du Luxembourg. Mo. Luxembourg. Accepts women only Oct.-June. Kitchenettes on each floor, laundry rooms, and library. Reception open Sun.-Fri. 6am-1:30am, Sat. 24 hours. Singles 140F. Doubles 190F. Reserve in writing 2 months ahead. Try calling or visiting around 9:30am to check for no-shows.

Foyer International d'Accueil de Paris, 30, rue Cabanis, *14ème* (tel. 45 89 89 15). Mo. Glacière. Monolithic, modern, and immaculate. Some rooms with facilities for the disabled. Singles 120F, with shower 160F. Doubles 105F, with shower 120F. Meals 46F. Written reservations accepted 1 month in advance.

Maison Internationale des Jeunes, 4, rue Titon, 11*ème* (tel. 43 71 99 21). Mo. Faidherbe-Chaligny. Spartan, tranquil rooms and garden out back. Ages 18-30, but exceptions can be made. 3-day max. stay. Reception open 8am-2am. Lockout 10am-5pm. 90F. Sheets 12F. Reservations accepted in writing.

Y&H Hostel, 80, rue Mouffetard, 5*ème* (tel. 45 35 09 53; Mo. Monge). Ideally located. Reception open daily 8-11am and 5pm-1am. Curfew 1am. 79F. 490F per week. Sheets 10F. Reserve with 1 night's payment or arrive early.

Cité Universitaire, 15, bd. Jourdain, 14*ème* (tel. 45 89 35 79). Mo. Cité Universitaire. In summer you can stay in any of the houses. (Canadian, Swiss, and Norwegian are recommended; the Moroccan house is likely to have space.) For reservations, write to: M le Délégué Général de Cité Universitaire de Paris, 19, bd. Jourdain, 75690 Paris, CEDEX 14, or ask in person for the *secrétariat.* Pay in advance to book. Seven- to 10-night min. stay in summer. Reception open Mon.-Fri. 8am-noon and 4-7pm. Singles 80-110F. Doubles 70-80F.

Foyer Franco-Libannais, 15, rue d'Ulm (tel. 43 29 47 60). Mo. Cardinal-Lemoine or Luxembourg. Excellent location. Reception open 8am-midnight. No curfew. Singles 100F, with shower 110F. Doubles 80F, with shower 100F. Triples with shower 80F.

Hotels

Of the three classes of Parisian budget accommodations, hotels may be the most practical for the majority of travelers. There are no curfews, no school groups, total privacy, and often concerned managers—features hostels and *foyers* usually can't offer. Budget hotels in Paris are not significantly more expensive than their hostel/foyer counterparts. Larger groups (of 3 and 4) may actually find it more economical to stay in a hotel. Parisian law forbids hanging laundry from windows or over balconies to dry. Proprietors will remind you that food in the rooms breeds mice.

Expect to pay at least 110-160F for a single, but only 40-60F more for a single-bedded double; two-bed doubles are rare and cost considerably more. In less expensive hotels, few rooms come with private bath, though most have *bidets* (a toilet-like apparatus used for cleansing the more private of body parts) and sinks with hot and cold water. Showers are usually available for 15-25F extra. No matter how desperate you are, do not use your *bidet* as a toilet. You will cause yourself much embarrassment and force an unfortunate proprietor to spend a few hours bleaching the bowl and cleaning out the pipes.

Rooms disappear quickly after morning check-out (generally 10am-noon), so try to arrive early or reserve ahead; all hotels accept reservations unless otherwise noted. Instead of parading yourself and your bags around town all morning, call first.

The Left Bank (Rive Gauche)

Myths about the Left Bank's bohemia often fall flat in the face of inflated prices and neighborhood gentrification. Nonetheless, the plethora of inexpensive restaurants, chic cafés, and lively bars still make this area, especially the centrally located 5th and 6th *arrondissements* (the Latin Quarter and St-Germain-des-Prés), among the most popular in Paris.

Hôtel Marignan, 13, rue du Sommerard, 5*ème* (tel. 43 54 63 81). Mo. Maubert. Spacious, spotless hotel run by a Franco-American couple. 3-night min. stay in summer. Strict noise limit after 10pm. Singles 140F. Doubles 220F. Triples 290-310F. Quads 350-380F. Showers and breakfast 20F.

Hôtel du Progrès, 50, rue Gay-Lussac, 5*ème* (tel. 43 54 53 18). Mo. Luxembourg. Simply decorated rooms are always clean. Top floors with charming garret-like rooms. Singles 124F. Doubles up to 285F. Triples 300F. Breakfast 25F.

Hôtel Nesle, 7, rue de Nesle, 6*ème* (tel. 43 54 62 41), off rue Dauphine. Mo. Odéon. Rooms are bright and spacious, and the psychedelic murals chronicle French history. A rose garden and Turkish bath inhabited by two quarrelsome ducks complete the spread. Primarily a young crowd; families would be happier elsewhere. Doubles 110-120F per person. If you come alone you may be paired with others. Showers and breakfast included.

Grand Hôtel Oriental, 2, rue d'Arras, *5ème* (tel. 43 54 38 12). Mo. Cardinal Lemoine. Cavernous rooms with firm mattresses. Singles and doubles 212F, with shower 272F. Showers 15F. Breakfast 25F.

Hôtel St-Jacques, 35, rue des Ecoles, *5ème* (tel. 43 26 82 53). Mo. Maubert. Big, scrubbed-down rooms. Singles 96-160F. Doubles 160-350F.

Hôtel Gay-Lussac, 29, rue Gay-Lussac, *5ème* (tel. 43 54 23 96). Mo. Luxembourg. Large rooms with sculpted ceilings. Singles and doubles 265F, with shower 300F. Triples with shower and toilet 450F. Showers 10F. Breakfast included.

Hôtel St-Michel, 17, rue Gît-le-Cœur, *6ème* (tel. 43 26 98 70). Mo. St-Michel. Large, comfortable rooms with strawberry carpets and curtains. Singles 175F. Doubles 284F, with shower 319F. Showers 15F. Breakfast included.

Hôtel le Home Latin, 15-17, rue Sommerard, *5ème* (tel. 43 26 25 21). Mo. Maubert or St-Michel. Nothing extraordinary, but quite accommodating. Singles and doubles 200F. Showers 10F. Breakfast included.

Hôtel Stella, 41, rue Monsieur-le-Prince, *6ème* (tel. 43 26 43 49). Mo. Odéon or Luxembourg. Little Tokyo. Friendly managers. Ready for renovation. Singles with shower and toilet 158F. Doubles with shower and toilet 198F. No reservations.

Hôtel des Alliés, 20, rue Berthollet, *5ème* (tel. 43 31 47 52). Mo. Censier-Daubenton. Comfortable, well-kept rooms, and a no-nonsense proprietor. Singles 100F. Doubles 140F, with bath 240F. Showers 10F. Breakfast 20F (in bed if you wish).

Hôtel des Carmes, 5, rue des Carmes, *5ème* (tel. 43 29 78 40). Mo. Maubert. Shocking yellow decor brings life (and blindness) to otherwise dull, clean rooms. Singles and doubles 260F. Breakfast included.

Hôtel le Petit Trianon, 2, rue de l'Ancienne Comédie (tel. 43 54 94 64). Mo. St-Germain-des-Prés. Tucked away into a busy corner. Somewhat sagging. Singles 120F. Doubles 200F. Triples 300F.

Hôtel de Nevers, 3, rue de l'Abbé-de-l'Epée, *5ème* (tel. 43 26 81 83). Mo. Luxembourg. Slightly worn, but clean enough. Singles 110F, with shower 210F. Doubles with shower 260-350F. Breakfast 20F. Confirm reservations 1 day before arrival.

Hôtel le Centrale, 6, rue Descartes, *5ème* (tel. 46 33 57 93). Mo. Maubert or Cardinal Lemoine. Dark rooms on a lovely café-filled square. Singles 130-150F. Doubles 190F. Triples 220F. Showers in every room.

Hôtel de Médicis, 214, rue St-Jacques, *5ème* (tel. 43 29 53 64 or 43 54 14 66). Mo. Luxembourg. Loyal patrons excuse the peeling paint and leaky faucets for the admittedly genial atmosphere. 3-day min. stay when busy. Singles 70-110F. Doubles 140F. Showers 10F.

Once the center of expatriate Paris, **Montparnasse** (*14ème)* retains its glamor around the bd. du Montparnasse, while the northern end of av. du Maine (Mo. Gaîté) is overrun with sex shops.

Hôtel de Blois, 5, rue des Plantes, *14ème* (tel. 45 40 99 48). Mo. Mouton-Duvernet or Alésia. Carpeted rooms with huge bathrooms. Concerned management and glamorous mirror-lined halls. Singles with shower 190F. Doubles with bathroom 240F. Triples with shower 320F. Breakfast 25F.

Ouest Hôtel, 27, rue Gergovie, *14ème* (tel. 45 42 64 99). Mo. Pernety or Plaisance. Large rooms in a sleepy neighborhood. Homey atmosphere. Singles 120F. Doubles with toilet 160F, with shower 220F. Showers 20F. Breakfast included.

Plaisance Hôtel, 53, rue Gergovie, *14ème* (tel. 45 42 11 39 or 45 42 20 33). Mo. Pernety. Mellow manager peddles large rooms with firm beds. Singles 130F, with bathroom 220F. Doubles 140F, with bathroom 270F. Showers 20F. Breakfast 20F.

Ile de la Cité

Since Roman times, budget accommodations on the Ile de la Citeé have been hard to find. Fear not, ye adamant and determined traveler; one exception remains.

Hôtel Henri IV, 25, pl. Dauphine, 1*er* (tel. 43 54 44 53). Mo. Pont-Neuf or Cité. Family management offers clean rooms. Drawbacks are faded walls, and bathrooms accessible only by a little staircase that curls around the building. Singles 150F. Doubles 150-180F. Showers 17F. Breakfast included.

The Right Bank (Rive Droite)

The **Right Bank** calls to mind *grands boulevards, grands musées, grands magasins,* and *grands prix.* Unexpected bargains still lurk behind the tourist-ridden 1*er* arrondissement. The 2*ème,* 3*ème,* and 4*ème arrondissements,* engulf one of Paris's trendiest areas as well as one of its most culturally and ethnically diverse.

Hôtel Picard, 26, rue de Picardie, 3*ème* (tel. 48 87 53 82). Mo. Filles du Calvaire or République. Wondrously generous proprietor and his daughter offer a 10% discount to *Let's Go* travelers in this fabulous 2-star hotel. Singles 170F. Doubles 250F, with shower and toilet 300-380F. Showers 15F. Breakfast 25F.

Hôtel de Nice, 42bis, rue de Rivoli, 4*ème* (tel. 42 78 55 29). Mo. Hôtel-de-Ville. Tasteful decor and friendly manager makes this clean hotel an excellent choice. Only the noisy street detracts. Singles and doubles 190-220F, with showers 290-330F. Triples 270F. Showers 20F. Breakfast 25F.

Tiquetonne Hotel, 6, rue Tiquetonne, 2*ème* (tel. 42 36 94 58). Mo. Etienne Marcel. Sweet and dandy. You can decide if the red light district around the corner is a pro or a con. Singles and doubles 110F, with shower and toilet 200F. Showers and breakfast 20F.

Grand Hôtel des Arts-et-Métiers, 4, rue Borda, 3*ème* (tel. 48 87 73 89). Mo. Arts-et-Métiers. A popular, sedate family hotel. Singles and doubles 140-170F. Showers 15F. Breakfast 15F.

Hôtel Loiret, 8, rue des Mauvais-Garçons, 4*ème* (tel. 48 87 77 00). Mo. Hôtel de Ville. Rundown but well-placed. Singles and doubles 140F, with shower 200F. Showers 20F. Breakfast 25F.

Hôtel Moderne, 3, rue Caron, 4*ème* (tel. 48 87 97 05). Mo. St-Paul. Attentive management but spartan quarters. Singles and doubles 110-120F, with shower 160F, with bathroom 190F.

Grand Hôtel Malher, 5, rue Malher, 4*ème* (tel. 42 72 60 92). Mo. St-Paul. On a street between rue des Francs-Bourgeois and rue St-Antoine. Mongo, comfortable rooms in this family hotel. Singles and doubles 120-150F, with shower 275F. Showers 15F. Breakfast 20F.

The **Tenth Arrondissement** (10*ème)* holds an interesting if somewhat unsafe mixture of *émigrés,* bohemian artists, and blue-collar workers.

Cambria Hôtel, 129bis, bd. de Magenta, 10*ème* (tel. 98 78 32 13). Mo. Gare du Nord. Large, immaculate rooms with comfortable beds and high ceilings. Singles 105F, with shower 198F. Showers 20F. Breakfast included.

Palace Hôtel, 9, rue Bouchardon, 10*ème* (tel. 40 40 09 456). Mo. Strasbourg-St-Denis. Somewhat unkempt but big. More attractive than many others in this area. Singles 90F. Doubles 120F. Triples 280F. Showers 18F. Breakfast 18F. No reservations.

Hôtel Métropole Lafayette, 204, rue Lafayette, 10*ème* (tel. 46 07 72 69). Mo. Louis Blanc. Luscious reception area gives way to worn but well-lit rooms. Singles and doubles 130-160F, with shower 180-190F, with bathroom 210F. Showers 25F. Breakfast 15F.

Montmartre (18*ème)* and the **Ninth Arrondissement** are filled with many hotels which cater to the proverbial oldest profession. The ones listed below attract tourists and don't rent by the hour. Pigalle is filled with pickpockets during the day, and should be avoided by lone travelers at night. Avoid Anvers, Pigalle, and Barbes-Rochechouart Métro stops; use Abbesses instead.

Hôtel des Trois Poussins, 15, rue Clauzel, 9*ème* (tel. 48 74 38 20). Mo. St-Georges. M and Mme. Desforges love *Let's Go*-ers. Large tidy rooms. Singles 140F. Doubles with shower 220F. Showers 15F. Breakfast 20F.

Hôtel Tholozé, 24, rue Tholozé, 18*ème* (tel. 46 06 74 83). Mo. Abbesses. Warm family operation offers spacious, sunny rooms. Singles 165F. Doubles with shower 240F. Triples 250F. Showers 18F. Breakfast 18F.

Hôtel du Delta, 89, rue Rochechouart, *9ème* (tel. 48 78 56 99). Mo. Cadet. Rooms are small and dark, but quite clean. Laid back, congenial proprietor. Singles 140F. Doubles 200F, with shower and toilet 280F. Triples 300F. Showers 15F. Breakfast included.

Hôtel Idéal, 3, rue des Trois-Frères, *18ème* (tel. 46 06 63 63). Mo. Abbesses. Stylish rooms with creaky beds. Singles 80-120F. Doubles 150F, with shower 200F. Showers 20F.

Food

The world's first restaurant was born in Paris over 200 years ago. Ironically its purpose was not to indulge its clientèle with delicious foods and wines, but rather to restore (from the French verb *restorer)* over-fed party-goers (most of Parisian high society throughout history) to a state of physical health. Restaurants were a social respite from the high-calorie world of soirées, balls, and private diner parties. Here, one could be in a social atmosphere and eat nothing. Instead, one was served a single glass of a ghastly brew made from concentrated meat and vegetable products.

Over the centuries, dining has become the center of culture in this, the most cultured of all cities. Even on a budget you can partake in this culinary bonanza. In a city with some of the world's most fabulous restaurants, you can spend as much as you care to, but even Parisians seldom dole out more than 100F on a meal. You can eat satisfactorily for 50F, enjoyably for 65F, superbly for 90F, and unforgettably for 130F. Dabble in more authentic French tastes. *Tripes* (stomach lining of a cow) cooked in herbs is well-loved by many; the sausage version is called *andouille* or *andouillette. Raie* (skate) is an unusual fish that is sometimes bland and tough but can be delectable *au beurre noir* (in black butter). The infamous *escargots* (snails) are a French delicacy unapproached by almost any other. *Pigeon* (pigeon) is a hearty and succulent form of fowl often served in a casserole or pastry shell. Try to understand what it is exactly that makes the French love eating so much . . . surely it cannot be Cheez-Whiz and Oreos.

Cafés serve light meals such as soups, salads, sandwiches, and omelettes all day long, although for the money, you might be better off chasing away the hunger with a 3.20F *baguette* and waiting until dinner. **Markets** color every *arrondissement,* offering a kaleidoscopic array of produce, cheese, sausage, and bread. (Open Mon.-Sat. 8am-noon and 3-7pm.) Prices often plunge before closing, but otherwise are similar to those in stores. In most markets and specialty shops, you point (never touch), and the salesperson fetches. *Epiceries, boulangeries,* and other small stores seldom close before 7pm.

At university restaurants (some closed on weekends and in summer), you can get an institutional three-course meal for a mere 19.20F in the company of oodles of French youth; you will ordinarily be asked to show a student ID. A complete list of *restaurants universitaires* ("Resto-U") is available from **CROUS,** 39, av. Georges Bernanos, *5ème.* (Mo. Port Royal; open Mon.-Fri. 9am-5pm.) The most popular are **Albert Châtelet,** 10, rue Jean Calvin, *5ème* (Mo. Censier-Daubenton) and **Mabillon,** rue Mabillon (Mo. Mabillon; open Mon.-Fri. 11:30am-2pm and 6:30-8:25pm. For summer hours, consult CROUS.)

The listings below include exceptional *crêpe,* sandwich, and salad options, restaurants with affordable *menus,* traditional French stalwarts, and the occasional treat to send you to heaven. Vegetarians may be dismayed by the dearth of strictly vegetarian restaurants in Paris. True die-hards may want to ask if their vegetable entrée has been cooked with meat stock. Ethnic cuisine, especially Vietnamese and North African, often provide excellent vegetarian options. Kosher travelers and anyone else looking for a good deli should stroll through the Jewish neighborhood around rue des Rosiers. Whatever your taste, don't be scared of adventure. Parisian dining is not for the timid; if you can afford to, do it right: pick an atmosphere suiting your mood and company and make your meal an evening.

Hungarian restaurants, American bars, Tunisian *patisseries,* Breton *crêperies,* and eateries of seemingly every other variety pack the ancient streets of the **5th arrondissement.** Look past the ubiquitous tourist traps on the bd. St-Michel to find some terrific bargains on **rue de la Harpe** and **rue Mouffetard.** If in doubt, do what the French might do—stock up on picnic supplies and head for the Jardin de Luxembourg. Every *arrondissement* has at least one outdoor market (most last Mon.-Sat. 7am-noon). Ask at your hotel for the nearest one.

The Left Bank (Rive Gauche)

Restaurant Perraudin, 157, rue St-Jacques, *5ème.* Mo. Luxembourg. Archetypal bistro. The delightful owners sate their patrons with specialties from around the country. *La caille aux raisins* (quail with grapes) 48F. Open Mon.-Fri. noon-2:15pm and 7:30-10:15pm.

Restaurant Chez Léna et Mimille, 32, rue Tournefort, *5ème* (tel. 47 07 72 47). Mo. Censier-Daubenton. True elegance, overlooking a pretty tree-lined *place.* Fabulous 88F lunch and 170F dinner *menus* offer delicious French selections. *Apéritif* and wine included. Good choice for that special dinner. Open Tues.-Fri. noon-2pm and 7-11pm, Mon. and Sat. 7-11pm. Reservations suggested.

La Mosquée, 39, rue Geoffroy-St-Hilaire, across from the Jardin des Plantes. Mo. Censier-Daubenton. Enter behind traditional mosque walls and experience the Middle East. Eat and drink (no alcohol) in the exquisite courtyard. Or indulge in the healing powers of a Turkish bath *(hammam).* 90F *menu* includes salad, *brik à oeuf* (a thin dough with a fried egg inside), and a huge helping of lamb *couscous.* Women, especially traveling alone, should note that the Middle Eastern experience here is complete, and single women may receive unwanted attention. Tea room open Sept.-July 11am-9pm. Restaurant open 11am-8pm. Bath times vary for men and women; call for details.

In the neighboring **6th arrondissement,** a myriad of restaurants jostle for street-front between **place de l'Odéon** and **place St-Sulpice.** The daily market on **rue de Seine** (Mon.-Sat. mornings) is an expensive stop for fresh fruit, fish, and cheese.

Restaurant des Beaux-Arts, 11, rue Bonaparte, *6ème,* across from the Ecole des Beaux Arts. Mo. St-Germain-des-Prés. Delicious fare and prompt service are venerable traditions in this gourmand's delight. The 63F *menu* includes unusual offerings like *maquereau aux pommes à l'huile* (mackerel with apples in oil) and a daily vegetarian special. Open daily noon-2:30pm and 7-10:45pm.

Le Petit Vatel, 5, rue Lobineau, *6ème,* between rue de la Seine and rue Mabillon. Mo. Odéon or Mabillon. An institution among students and artists. Informal atmosphere and excellent cuisine. Try the *lapin au vin blanc* (rabbit in white wine). Vegetarian dish nightly. Main dishes 30-50F. Open Mon.-Sat. noon-3pm and 7pm-midnight, Sun. 7pm-midnight. Closed 1 week in Aug.

Montparnasse comprises that area where the fashionable 6th *arrondissement* meets the busy, less residential 14th. Center of expatriate life in the 20s, it provided a surplus of cafés and restaurants for the Hemingway/Stein crowd. In recent years, however, the area has become a favorite of tourists rather than artists. Avoid the inauthentic tourist restaurants—betrayed by their multingual menus. The shadow of the **Tour Montparnasse** falls on the 13th to the east and the 15th to the west, pointing the way towards less expensive dining. Chinatown around av. de Choisy and rue de Tolbiac in the 13th, and Frenchville in the 15th offer cheaper eating and better food.

La Coupole, 102, bd. du Montparnasse, *14ème.* Mo. Vavin. A world unto itself, this huge restaurant was once a second home for the expats of the 20s. Inhale the elegance of the cavernous dining hall. Centered around a dazzling bouquet Gladioli is Paris's most complete dining crowd—tourists, stars, and students. Appetizers 40-100F, entrées 60-120F, desserts 45F. Or just come and watch it all with a coffee on the terrace café. Restaurant and café open daily 8am-2am.

Sampieru Corsu, 12, rue de l'Amiral-Roussin, *15ème.* Mo. Cambronne. Corsican separatist and Marxist family ask 36F for each meal, although you are asked to pay according to your means. On some nights there is entertainment; add 10F for the performer. Open Mon.-Fri. 11:45am-1:45pm and 7-9:30pm.

Le Jérobaum, 72, rue Didot, *14ème.* Mo. Pernety. Wonderfully comfy authentic French restaurant. To-die-for lunch buffet 49F. Dinner *menu* 89F. Tues.-Sat. noon-2pm and 7-10pm, Mon. noon-2pm.

The Right Bank (Rive Droite)

Most Right Bank restaurants attract the kind of diner who enters a restaurant because it looks elegant, not because it is cheap. As a result, these quarters shelter an unfortunate number of obscenely overpriced restaurants catering to the flood of tourists and businesspeople who wash over the area. Rue des Rosiers in the Marais (4th *arrondissement)* is the nucleus of Paris's Jewish neighborhood. Come here for kosher delis and *patisseries,* many of which remain open on Sunday, when much else in Paris is closed. The 8th *arrondissement* is the *Michelin* diner's dream come true: many of Paris's finest and most famous restaurants have assembled in this posh neighborhood. Farther east, however, the 9th and 10th sequester phenomenal Middle Eastern and North African bargains in colorful multiethnic neighborhoods. In the streets radiating from the Bastille (11th *arrondissement),* Paris's young and trendy brush elbows with the old-fashioned French working class, creating a vibrant interaction of social backgrounds.

Lescure, 7, rue de Mondovi, 1*ere* Mo. Concorde. Lively ambience has accompanied hearty French cuisine for over 60 years in this popular restaurant. 90F (wine included) *menu* offers a wide selection and huge servings. Open Sept.-July Mon.-Fri. noon-2:30pm and 7-10pm., Sat.-Sun. noon-2:30pm.

Country Life, 6, rue Daunou, 2*ème* Mo. Opéra. Vegetarian *haute cuisine* in a charming wooded health food store. Crowded 55F buffet includes soups and salads as well as hot and cold entrées. Mon.-Fri. 11:30am-2:30pm. Store open Mon.-Thurs. 10am-6:30pm, Fri. 10am-3pm.

The Front Page, 56-58, rue St-Denis, 1*er.* Mo. Châtelet-Les-Halles. Paris's sole tribute to Americana. Expensive but lively, offering warm memories of the New World—hamburgers 42-55F; salads 35-44F; cocktails 35-40F. Open daily 11:30am-5am.

Le Trumilou, 84, Quai de l'Hôtel de Ville, 4*ème.* Mo. Hôtel de Ville. Charming old bistro facing the Seine. An old Parisian favorite. 58F and 76F *menus.* Open Mon.-Fri. 11:30am-2:30pm and 6:30-9:30pm.

Chez Jo Goldenberg, 7, rue des Rosiers, 4*ème* (tel. 48 87 20 16). Mo. St-Paul. Established in 1920, this is everyone's favorite kosher deli. Fills daily with regulars who love the delicious cold cuts (60F) and courteous service. Also take-out counter with home-cooked *borscht,* sauerkraut, pickles, and pastries. Deli open daily 9am-1pm and 2:30-6pm. Tea room open 2:30-6pm.

Chez Marianne, 2, rue des Hospitaliers St-Gervais 4*ème,* at rue des Rosiers. Mo. St. Paul. Israeli specialties in a popular and social establishment. Falafel, *blini, perogi,* and strudel. Open Sun.-Thurs. 11am-midnight.

Le Chartier, 7, rue Faubourg-Montmartre, 9*ème.* Mo. Montmartre. Housed in an splendid, mirrored salon straight from the 18th century, Le Chartier offers a wide selection of delicious, inexpensive, traditional French delights. Try such endearing favorites as *tendron du veau grand-mère* (tender veal just like grandma used to make, 41F). Not the place for a leisurely meal. **Le Drouot,** 103, rue de Richelieu, 2*ème.* (Mo. Richelieu-Drouot); and **Le Commerce,** 51, rue de Commerce, 15*ème* (Mo. Lamotte-Picquet), are both under the same management but less crowded. Each open daily 11am-3pm and 6-11:30pm.

Casa Miguel, 48, rue St-Georges, 9*ème* Mo. St-Georges. Proudly displaying its certificate for being the cheapest restaurant in the western world, this restaurant proves that unlike *Let's Go* researchers, *Guinness Book* researchers didn't stop to sample the food. Though your complete meal (entrée, main dish, dessert, wine, bread, and service) will come to 5F, you get what you pay for. Arrive early. Open Mon.-Sat. noon-1pm and 7-8pm, Sun. noon-1pm. Closed for 1 week at the end of July and the beginning of Aug.

Chez Paul, 13, rue de Charonne, 11*ème.* Mo. Ledru-Molin or Bastille. Always packed with a fun-loving, wine-drinking crowd, this restaurant restores the memory of *gai Paris.* Appetizers 18-55F. Main course 58-72F. Open daily 11:45am-2pm and 7:30pm-2am.

Au Grain Folie, 24, rue de la Vieuville, 18*ème* (tel. 42 58 15 57). Mo. Abbesses. A wee vegetarian restaurant featuring a 65F *menu* with delicious salads and quiches. Open Tues.-Sun. noon-2:30pm and 7-9:30pm, Mon. 7-9:30pm.

Refuge des Fondus, 19, rue des Trois-Frères, 18*ème* (tel. 42 55 22 65). Mo. Abbesses. Food isn't fantastic, but a goofy gimmick makes this restaurant overwhelmingly popular: the 70F *menu* includes a full baby bottle of wine. Open daily 7pm-2am.

Sights

The whole city is a sight. Even its design deserves your attention. Commissioned by Napoleon III to make the city more resistant to attack, urban planner and architect Baron Georges-Eugène Haussmann widened the major streets in order to facilitate movement of the military, changing Paris from an intimate medieval city to a bustling modern metropolis. His "assaults" on the city included leveling hills (there were seven before Haussmann; now only Montmartre and Parc des Buttes Chaumont remain), expanding the system of sewers, widening existing streets, and building new thoroughfares to make the city both more accessible and more monumental. Catering to the decadent 19th-century bourgeoisie, his grandiose projects left thousands homeless as beautiful new streets were blasted through existing dwellings. The entire area surrounding today's place de l'Opéra was a tranquil residential neighborhood before 1850. As its name implies, Montparnasse was a hill. Note that the façades on one side of some streets date back to the 18th century while the other side was built after Haussmann widened the avenue, obliterating the buildings on one side while keeping the other intact. There are historians who maintain that without Baron Haussmann, Paris would still be the world's largest medieval city.

Paris is not a museum, but you could certainly spend all your time going from one to the next. Every institution, artistic movement, ethnic group, and custom seems to have a museum devoted to its history, art, and memorabilia. For listings of temporary exhibits, consult the bimonthly *Le Bulletin des Musées et Monuments Historiques,* available at the tourist office. *Musées et Monuments, Paris,* published by the tourist office, describes the museums and indexes them by theme and *arrondissement. Pariscope, 7 à Paris,* and *L'Officiel des spectacles* also list museums with hours and temporary exhibits.

Frequent museum-goers, especially those ineligible for discounts, may want to invest in a **Carte 60,** which grants entry into 60 Parisian museums as well as in the suburbs and environs. The card is available at major museums and Métro stations (1 day 50F, 3 days 100F, 5 days 150F).

Although pre-Celtic peoples may have settled in this area as early as the third millennium BC, the existing city wasn't founded until the third century BC when the Parisii, a tribe of hunters, sailors, and fishing folk, built huts on the Ile de la Cité and began collecting tolls. Although Paris has expanded considerably over the past 23 centuries, the **Ile de la Cité** and neighboring **Ile St-Louis** remain at its physical and sentimental heart. Interestingly, these are only two of the eight islands the Parisii initially populated. The other six were destroyed by Henry IV, Paris's first city planner, to make room for ships navigating the Seine.

In 1163, Pope Alexander III laid the cornerstone for the **Cathédrale de Notre Dame de Paris** (tel. 43 26 07 39; Mo. Cité) over the remains of a Roman temple to Jupiter. During the Revolution, it was renamed the *Temple du Raison* and dedicated to the Cult of Reason. The resplendent 700-year-old rose windows inside are widely considered the most exquisite in the world. For a view of Paris made famous by Victor Hugo's *Notre-Dame de Paris (The Hunchback of Notre-Dame),* climb the stairs to the bell tower. In a supreme act of sacrilege, people have been known to commit suicide by jumping off the tower. (Open Aug. daily 10am-6:30pm; April-July and Sept. 9:30am-11:30am, 2pm-5:30pm; Oct.-March 10am-4:30pm. Admission 30F, students 16F.) Outside the west door in the courtyard, a star marks the spot from which all distances from Paris are measured.

Behind the cathedral, across from pl. Jean XXIII and down a narrow flight of steps, is the **Mémorial de la Déportation,** a haunting memorial erected in remembrance of the 200,000 French victims of Nazi concentration camps. Two hundred thousand flickering lights represent the dead, and an eternal flame burns over the tomb of an unknown victim.

Just east of the **Pont Neuf** (New Bridge), ironically Paris's oldest, lies the massive **Palais de Justice.** Since 52 BC, various forms of the French judiciary have been housed in a building occupying this location. All trials are open to the general public, but don't expect a *France v. Dreyfus* every day. A small church inside the courtyard of the Palais de Justice, **Ste-Chapelle,** bd. du Palais, 4*ème* (tel. 43 54 30 09; Mo. Cité), is one of the oldest structures in the city. Begun in 1246 to house the highest symbols in the Christian faith—Christ's Crown of Thorns, Jesus's swaddling clothes, and a bottle of the Virgin's milk—the Ste-Chapelle is perhaps the supreme achievement of Gothic architecture. (The Crown—minus the thorns St-Louis gave away as political favors—now rests in Notre-Dame.) The domed roof looms cavernously over brilliant red, blue, and gold stained glass windows, which suck in enough light to bleach a priest's cassock. (Open daily 9:30am-6:30pm; Oct.-March 10am-5pm. Admission 24F, ages 18-25 and over 60 13F, ages 7-18 5F. Combined ticket for the chapel and the Conciergerie (see below) 40F.) During the French Revolution, Marie Antoinette, Robespierre, and many other guillotine-bound *ennemies de l'Etat* spent their last capitated moments in the **Conciergerie,** located in the same complex of buildings (enter from quai de l'Horloge). Here, Robespierre spoke his prophetic last words: "I leave you my memory. It will be dear to you, and you will defend it." (Open daily 9:30am-6pm; Oct.-March 10am-5pm. Admission 24F, students 13F, ages 7-18 5F.)

Just upstream and connected by a foot bridge, the residential **Ile St-Louis** has always lived in the shadow of the grand, public buildings of its westerly neighbor. Constantly ignored, the inhabitants grew tired of the lack of press and whimsically proclaimed the island an independent republic in the 1930s. Some of the most privileged of Paris's exceedingly privileged elite, including the Rothschilds and Pompidou's widow, now call this scrap of land home. Although the Ile St-Louis lacks the tourist attractions of the Cité, the *hôtels particuliers* (aristocratic mansions) along quai d'Anjou are particularly beautiful. Most importantly, Paris's best ice cream (to Parisians, that means the *world's* best ice cream) is served, albeit in painfully small scoops, at **Berthillon,** 31, rue St-Louis-en-l'Ile.

A preposterously enormous residence for the French royalty until the construction of Versailles, the **Palais du Louvre** (tel. 40 20 50 50, Mo. Palais-Royal/Musée du Louvre) is Paris's single largest building, the largest palace in Europe, and probably the most recognized symbol of art and culture in all history. As early as 1214, a fortress was built here to defend the city's west side. François I transformed it into a splendid Renaissance palace in 1546, and Catherine de Médicis, Henry IV, Louis XII, Louis XIV, and Napoleon III all added their own "improvements" in the style of the day. Not until 1793 did the palace assume its present function. The debate on exactly which of the world's museums is actually the richest is not likely to be resolved in the near future, but few will dispute that the **Musée du Louvre** is a strong contender. Unlike every other museum in Paris, the collection in the Louvre represents no overarching theme. In and amongst a sprawling array of minor works appear the staggering masterpieces for which the museum is famous: the *Mona Lisa,* the *Venus de Milo, Slaves* by Michelangelo, and *Winged Victory of Samothrace.* Frequent tours (in French and English) or a rented cassette recorder can give an excellent introduction to the museum, but the exploring and the appreciating are up to you. Try to bring a guide book or a well-read friend. The Louvre is always beautiful, but with some good inside dope it can be simply divine. (Museum open Thurs.-Sun. 9am-5:15pm, Mon. and Wed. 9am-9pm. The I.M. Pei-designed pyramid is open Wed.-Mon. 9am-10pm. Principal entrance through the pyramid, but students and seniors can skip the lines by entering through the gate opposite the Métro station. Advice to anyone paying the full admission fee: save up to ½ hr. by using one of the automatic ticket machines; most tourists are scared of them. Admission 30F, ages 18-25 and over 60 15F, under 18 free. Sun. 15F. Tours in English every 20 min. 25F. Recorded tours of 25 masterpieces (available in English) 25F.)

At the western foot of the Louvre, geometry prevails over nature in the **Jardin des Tuileries,** probably the most famous of Paris's parks. Catherine de Médici, missing the public promenades of her native Italy, had the gardens built in 1564; in 1649 André le Nôtre (designer of the gardens at Versailles) imposed his preference for straight lines and sculptured trees. The western end of the Tuileries gives way to the **place de la Concorde,** where Louis XVI, Marie Antoinette, Robespierre, and 1300 others lost their heads during the Reign of Terror (1793-1794). Two museums stand at the far end of the gardens. To the south, the **Musée de l'Orangerie** houses a small but distinguished collection of Impressionist and early 20th-century art. The gem of the collection is Claude Monet's *Les Nymphéas* (The Water Lilies), occupying two rooms in the underground level. Each is paneled with three large curved murals of the most sublime representation of nature on canvas. (Open Wed.-Mon. 9am-5:15pm. Admission 25F, students and seniors 13F, Sun. 13F.) To the north, the newly reopened **Jeu de Paume** used to house Paris's Impressionist collections until they moved to the Musée d'Orsay. The Jeu de Paume recently reopened with a brand-new exhibit of contemporary art.

Follow the **avenue des Champs-Elysées,** whose chic reputation is besmirched by rampant tourism, to the Place de Charles de Gaulle, from which 12 tree-lined *grands boulevards* radiate. In the center of this place, the **Arc de Triomphe,** ordered by Napoleon to honor his *grande Armée* and completed in 1836, is the world's largest triumphal arch. Climb to the top for a grand view. (Open daily 10am-5:30pm. Admission 27F, ages under 25 15F). The Tomb of the Unknown Soldier has rested under the arch since November 11, 1920; the eternal flame is rekindled every evening at 6:30pm, when veterans and small children lay wreaths decorated with blue, white, and red. North of the Concorde is the severe **Madeleine Church.** Completed as a church in 1842, the structure stands alone in the medley of Parisian churches, distinguished by its four ceiling domes, 52 exterior Corinthian columns, and the absence of even one cross.

Charles Garnier's **Opéra** (tel. 42 66 50 22; Mo. Opéra) towers high above the *grands boulevards* of the 9th *arrondissement,* lording its opulence over contemporary Paris. The most important of Haussmann's projects, this grand building epitomizes the Second Empire's obsession with canonized ostentation. The interior of the Opéra demonstrates the fabric of 19th-century bourgeois social life with its grand staircase, enormous golden foyer, vestibule, and five-tiered auditorium, all designed so that the audience could watch each other as much as the action on stage. Although Garnier incorporated iron, the latest technological innovation, into the framework, he purposely hid all traces of iron to satisfy a bourgeoisie so intent on classicism that it eradicated all evidence of modernity. (Open daily 11am-5pm. Admission 25F, ages 10-16 13F.)

Following rue de la Paix, you'll encounter **place Vendôme,** dignified and elegant, with its stodgy banks, *parfumeries,* and jewelers. The story goes that Baron Rothschild, instead of lending his friends money, would allow them to parade around pl. Vendôme with him for a few minutes past onlooking financiers—on the morrow the fortunate souls would be certain of credit at the most prestigious banks.

The **Bois de Boulogne** spreads its leafy umbrella just beyond the 16*ème arrondissement.* The Bois is livened by prostitutes at night, but a fashionable place to be seen strolling during the day. Nearby, the **Musée Marmottan,** 2, rue Louis-Boilly, 16*ème* (tel. 42 24 07 02; Mo. La Muette), is Paris's third museum of Impressionist painting. The collection includes a large array of Italian Renaissance painting and a colossal showcase of Monet canvases. *Impression: Soleil Levant,* the crown jewel of the museum and the painting from which the term "Impressionism" was stolen, was itself stolen last year. (Open Tues.-Sun. 10am-5:30pm. Admission 25F, students and seniors 10F.)

Some of Paris's finest treasures glow in quiet removal from the hurly-burly of the city in the **Marais,** a district that harbors elegant fragments of the past and vigorous communities (ethnic, intellectual) of the present. **Place des Vosges** (Mo. St-Paul), Paris's oldest square, was designed by Henry IV, who yearned for the opportunity to promenade himself in courtly opulence. Unfortunately, Henri never got to see the completion of his plans; he lost a duel in 1610. The square was completed in 1612 and inaugurated with the marriage of Louis XIII to Anne d'Autriche, an event which drew 10,000 spectators to Paris's largest empty space. At #6, the **Maison de Victor Hugo** displays a collection of Hugo memorabilia, including the original sketch of Cosette later used as a logo for *Les Misérables.* (Open Wed.-Mon. 10am-5:40pm. Admission 12F, students 6.50F.) The **Musée Carnavalet,** 23, rue de Sévigné, *3ème* (Mo. St-Paul), tells the history of Paris from prehistoric times to the present through painting, sculpture, documents, and reproductions of typical homes from various periods. (Open Tues.-Sun. 10am-5:40pm. Admission 16F, students 10F.) Housed in the Archives Nationales, the *Musée de l'Histoire de France,* 60, rue des Francs-Bourgeois, *3ème* (Mo. Rambateau), displays the wills of Napoleon and Louis XIV and the Declaration of the Rights of Man among other venerable documents. (Open Wed.-Mon. 1:45-5:45pm. Admission 15F, students and seniors 6F.) In the Hôtel Salé, the **Musée Picasso,** 5, rue de Thorigny, *3ème* (Mo. St-Paul), arranges its collection according to stages in the artist's career. Note Picasso's telling mutilation of women's bodies and faces—the man was a beastly misogynist. (Open Thurs.-Mon. 9:15am-5:15pm, Wed. 9:15am-9:15pm. Admission 25F, ages under 25 and over 60 13F.) Nearby, the **place de la Bastille** was the site of a riot on July 14, 1789; the French Revolution followed. The new **Bastille Opéra,** inaugurated July 14, 1989 amidst tremendous hoopla, now stages all opera in Paris, leaving the old Garnier Opera only with ballet.

Next to the Marais in the old market and artisan neighborhood of Les Halles, the **Centre National d'Art et de Culture Georges Pompidou** (Mo. Rambuteau), or **Beaubourg,** looms over a sloping square animated by artists and street performers. The structure itself is a building turned inside out—the pipes and the support beams are on the outside. Inside, the **Musée National d'Art Moderne** houses Paris's greatest modern art collection. (Open Mon. and Wed.-Fri. noon-10pm, Sat.-Sun. 10am-10pm. Admission to the complex is free. Separate admission to major exhibits. Museum 27F, students and seniors 18F. Day pass to all exhibits 55F.) A few hundred yards away is the **Forum des Halles** (Mo. Les Halles), an immense subterranean shopping extravaganza. Avoid the area at night; police with terrifying dogs patrol and drug addicts abound. Les Halles and the surrounding streets lodge a number of chic restaurants, popular bars, fashionable cafés and clothing stores.

The quasi-Byzantine **Sacré-Coeur** perches atop **Montmartre** in the 18th *arrondissement.* Sit on its steps at dusk for an enchanting panorama of the City of Light. For an even better view, ascend the dome. (Church and dome open daily 11am-6pm. Dome 25F, students 15F. Crypt 15F, students 8F.)

No visit to Paris is complete without a pilgrimage to the **Père-Lachaise Cemetery** in the *20ème* (Mo. Père Lachaise), the resting place of Molière, Chopin, Oscar Wilde, Gertrude Stein, Proust, and Colette. The most adored and adorned grave on the site belongs to a pure-blooded American boy named Jim Morrison (the Lizard King is buried here, really). (Open Mon.-Sat. 7:30am-6pm; Nov. 6-March 15 Mon.-Sat. 8am-5pm.)

The **Cité des Sciences et de l'Industrie,** 30, av. Corentin-Cariou, *19ème* (tel. 40 05 70 00; Mo. Porte de la Villete), is the best science museum in France, with innovative hands-on exhibits and excellent audiovisual presentations. (Open Tues.-Sat. 10am-6pm. Admission 35F, students and seniors 25F. Planetarium 15F extra.)

Across the river, the **Musée d'Orsay,** 62, rue de Lille, *7ème* (RER Musée d'Orsay), houses the greatest collection of Impressionism in the world. The Orsay has arranged its exhibits in a way which highlights the development of contrasting artistic styles throughout the second half of the 19th and the early years of the 20th centuries. The museum itself is housed in a former train station, the *Gare d'Orsay,* which, when finished in 1840, was as shocking an example of the new "modernism" as the Eiffel tower was a half-century later. To emphasize the contrast between traditional works (such as those by Ingres and Delacroix) and modern works (such as Monet and Manet), the Orsay museographers placed the traditional works on the right side of the ground floor in the central hall and the early modern works on the left. The most influential painting in the museum, Manet's *Olympia* (1863), smashed the bourgeoisie's self-confidence with a nude prostitute's accusing stare.

(Open Tues.-Wed. and Fri.-Sat. 10am-6pm, Thurs. 10am-9:45pm, Sun. 9am-6pm. Admission 30F, 18-25 and over 60, and on Sun. 15F, under 18 free.)

The **Musée Rodin,** 77, rue de Varenne, *7ème* (Mo. Varenne), shelters *The Kiss, The Thinker,* and other sensational Rodin sculptures in an 18th-century mansion. (Open Wed.-Sun. 10am-5:30pm, Tues. 10am-7:30pm. Admission 20F, ages 18-25 and over 60, and Sun. 10F.) In the Latin Quarter, the **Musée de Cluny,** 24, rue du Sommerard, *5ème* (Mo. Odéon or St-Michel), is Paris's museum of medieval artifacts, lodged in a former 15th-century edifice next to the ruins of the Roman *thermes* (baths). (Open Wed.-Mon. 9:45am-5:15pm. Admission 15F, under 18 free.)

Upon completion of his impressive iron monument, Eiffel proudly declared in 1889 that "France will be the only country in the world with a 300m flagpole." An internationally recognized symbol of Paris, the **Tour Eiffel** (Mo. Bir Hakeim), still pierces through the Parisian skyline. Emile Zola denounced it as a Tower of Babel. Maupassant liked to eat his lunch in the two-and-a-half acre expanse beneath the tower, supposedly because this was the only place in Paris he could avoid seeing it. Loving centennial renovations have made the tower look sparkling new, and Parisians and tourists alike have reclaimed it. (Admission 2nd level by foot 8F; by elevator 1st level 17F, 2nd level 32F, 3rd level 49F.)

The imposing **Panthéon** (Mo. Luxembourg) in the 5th *arrondissement* holds the tombs of Hugo, Voltaire, Rousseau, Zola and others. (Open daily 10am-5pm. Admission 25F, seniors and students 12F.) The impressive **Hôtel des Invalides,** 2, av. de Tourville, *7ème* (Mo. Invalides), contains Napoleon's remains, tucked into seven coffins sitting one inside the other—a riot of bombast that delighted Adolf Hitler when he toured Paris in 1940. The complex includes the **Musée de l'Armée,** with a monotonous collection of weaponry, armor, uniforms, and memorabilia. (Open daily 10am-6pm; Oct.-March 10am-5pm. Admission 27F, 7-18 14F.)

When Parisian culture and architecture begin to wear you down, head to one of Paris's beautiful and relaxing splotches of green—the **Jardin du Luxembourg** in the 6th, the **Jardin des Plantes** in the 5th, or the affluent **Parc Monceau** in the 8th are all fine temporary resting places for the weary sightseer.

Entertainment

Paris after dark: you've heard a lot about it, but where to begin? Check the weekly magazines *Pariscope, l'Officiel des Spectacles,* or *7 à Paris,* for complete listings of dance, theater, concerts, and more. The tourist office has a list of current festivals. The student organization, **COPAR,** 39, av. Georges Brenanos, *5ème* (tel. 43 29 12 43; Mo. Port-Royal), offers discounted student tickets for plays and many concerts. (Open Sept.-July Mon.-Fri. 9am-4:30pm.) You can snag tickets for plays, festivals, and a slew of concerts at **Alpha FNAC: Spectacles,** with three offices: 136, rue de Rennes, *6ème* (tel. 45 44 39 12; Mo. Montparnasse-Bienvenue); 26, av. de Wagram, *8ème* (tel. 47 66 52 50; Mo. Charles de Gaulle-Etoile); and Forum des Halles, 1-7, rue Pierre Lescot, *1er* (tel. 42 61 81 18; Mo. Châtelet-Les Halles).

While throngs on the Left Bank ensure that the streets are relatively safe, elsewhere nighttime Paris should be approached with caution. Steer clear of the *quais* and the Bois de Boulogne at night. Also avoid the Gare du Nord, Les Halles, and Pigalle, especially if solo. Métro trains and stations are usually safe if you don't linger.

Classical Music, Opera, and Dance

The **Orchestre de Paris,** Salle Pleyel, 252, rue du Faubourg-St-Honoré, *8ème* (tel. 45 63 07 40; Mo. Termes), delivers first-class performances from September through April (50-250F). Call the **Théâtre Musical de Paris,** pl. de Châtelet, *1er* (tel. 42 33 00 00; Mo. Châtelet) for information on visiting orchestras and musicals (60-336F). Opera in Paris's new **Bastille Opéra,** pl. de la Bastille (tel. 43 43 96 96) and ballet in the old **Opéra Garnier,** pl. de l'Opéra (tel. 47 42 53 71) beguile and astound. Most churches and cathedrals host free weekend concerts. Call 43 29 68 68 for info, or look for ubiquitous posters throughout the city.

Jazz

Though no longer the jazz mecca that it once was, Paris still nourishes a string of first-rate clubs. The variety of music—including African, Antillean, Brazilian—is dizzying and the atmosphere vibrant. For complete listings, pick up a copy of *Jazz Magazine.*

Caveau de la Huchette, 5, rue de la Huchette, *5ème* (tel. 43 26 65 05). Mo. St-Michel. In a 300-year-old building that functioned as a Revolutionary tribunal, prison, and execution site. Maxim Saury has whistled dixie here since the jazz bar opened. Students often flood the joint. Cover with 1st drink Sun.-Thurs. 50F, students 45F; Fri.-Sat. 60F. Drinks from 20F. Open Sun.-Thurs. 9:30pm-2:30am, Fri. 9:30pm-3am, Sat. 9:30pm-4am.

New Morning, 7-9, rue des Petites-Ecuries, *10ème* (tel. 45 23 51 41). Mo. Château d'Eau. Immense hall (500 seats) with gigs by jazz greats. Around 110F. Open Sept.-July Tues.-Sat. from 9:30pm.

Discos and Rock Clubs

The stable of nightclubs and discos that are "in" (or even in business) changes as quickly as champagne goes flat. The area along the Seine between **rue St-Jacques** and **rue Bonaparte** (Left Bank) is the old standby, especially for mellower clubs and bars. The elephant-sized discos vibrate on the Right Bank, around Pigalle. Go in groups to this treacherous, lecherous red-light district. Solo women are salaciously welcomed, while solo men may be refused at the door. In general, dress cool, and expect to sweat with wall-to-wall people after midnight weekdays and after 11pm weekends.

7, rue de Bourg l'Abbée, *3ème.* Ultra-selective to say the least but worth the ego bashing. Hipper than hip, cooler than cool, this *is* the place. Open Tues.-Sun. midnight-5am. First drink 120F. Second drink 100F.

La Locomotive, 90, bd. Clichy, *18ème.* Mo. Blanche. Shaped like a huge locomotive. Bump and grind. Open Tues.-Sun. 11pm-5am, Tues.-Thurs. and Sun. 60F, Fri.-Sat. 100F. 2nd drink 50F. Gay tea dance Sun. 5-10pm.

Le Palace, 8, rue du faubourg Montmartre, *9ème* (tel. 42 46 10 87). Mo. Montmartre. The funkiest disco in Paris and the most architecturally impressive, with swoon-room for a few thousand on multi-level dance floors. Top 40 music. Dancing teas and rollerskating afternoons. Occasional rock concerts. Cover Tues.-Thurs. 85F; Fri.-Sat. 130F; Sun. men 130F, women free. Gay tea dances Sun. 5-10pm. Open Tues.-Thurs. and Sun. 11pm-6am, Fri.-Sat. 11pm-11am. The British owners also run **Le Centrale,** 102, av. des Champs Elysées, *8ème.* Mo. George V. Same hrs. and prices.

La Plantation, 45, rue Montpensier, *1er.* Mo. Palais-Royal. Salsa and African beats in a friendly bar whose owner is concerned with improving race relations. Open Tues.-Sun. 11pm-dawn. Cover and first drink 80F, 2nd drink 50F.

Cafés

The hours I have spent in cafés are the only ones I call living, apart from writing.

—Anaïs Nin

Cultivate the correct etiquette. Learn to nurse a tiny espresso for hours. Stare at passers-by without lowering your eyes if they stare back. Flaunt the title of an intimidating tome while pretending to read. Buy round after round of 40F beers as a lively conversation spins off into the night.

La Coupole, 102, bd. du Montparnasse, *14ème* (tel. 43 27 09 22). Mo. Vavin. **Le Séléct,** 99, bd. du Montparnasse, *14ème* (tel. 45 48 38 29), Mo. Vavin. Once brimming with political exiles (Lenin and Trotsky), musicians (Stravinsky and Satie), writers (Hemingway, Breton, Cocteau), artists (Picasso and Eisenstein), Paris's star cafés continue to draw hordes of Beautiful People. Both open daily 8am-2am.

Les Deux Magots, 6, pl. St-Germain-des-Prés, *6ème* (tel. 45 48 55 25). Mo. St-Germain-des-Prés. A favorite of Jean-Paul Sartre. Open daily 7:30am-2am.

Le Flore, 172, bd. St-Germain, *6ème* (tel. 45 48 55 26), next door to Les Deux Magots. Sartre's 2nd choice and poet Guillaume Apollinaire's first. Open daily 7:30am-1:30am.

Bars

Pub St-Germain-des-Prés, 17, rue de l'Ancien Comédie, *6ème.* Mo. Odéon. Overrated and overpriced, this huge, three floor bar is where *all* the visiting Americans flock. Beers and mixed drinks start at a dizzying 72F. Open daily 11:30am-5am.

Le Bar sans Nom, *11ème.* Mo. Bastille. One of the coolest of the cool bars in Paris: small, deep red, intimate, and wild. Now if it only had a name. . . Beer 18F. Drinks 42F. Open daily 8pm-2am.

Cinema and Theater

Paris may well be the film capital of the world, screening international classics, avant-garde and political films, and little-known or dusty works in countless theaters. Ever since the New Wave crested, French interest in American movies has soared; American films play here that have not rolled in U.S. cinemas for years. Entertainment weeklies list showtimes and theaters. The notation "V.O." (for *version originale)* indicates the film is in its original language with French subtitles. Many cinemas offer students a 10F discount off their regular 30-45F admission on weekdays. Look to bd. Montparnasse, bd. St-Germain and the Champs-Elysées for the most concentrated offerings.

Supported by the French Government, **national theaters** are the stars of Parisian theater and usually stage classics. Founded by Molière, the oldest of these is **La Comédie Française,** 2, rue de Richelieu, *1er* (tel. 40 15 00 15) Mo. Palais-Royal. Though private theaters lack the histories or reputations of national theaters, some are as reliable for staging superb productions. Look to the entertainment weeklies for complete listings.

Near Paris

Versailles, the resplendent palace of the Sun King, Louis XIV, embodies his absolute power and abuse of wealth. Disliking Paris for its association with the power struggles of his youth, Louis XIV transformed his father's humble hunting cottage into a royal residence and shining capital. The court was the center of French noble life, pomp, and circumstance, but ostentatious Versailles quickly climaxed the Régime's economic drain on its citizens. Be sure to see the **Grand Trianon,** a royal guesthouse; the **Petit Trianon,** Marie Antoinette's toy palace; and **Le Hameau,** the hamlet where the Queen amused herself by playing shepherdess. It was here that she supposedly uttered the unforgettable "Let them eat cake" *(brioche* actually). Sally out to Versailles by RER line C (4 per hr., 35 min., round-trip 24F). (Main palace open Tues.-Sun. 9am-7pm. Admission 30F, students and Sun. 15F. Grand Trianon open 11am-6:30pm. Admission 16F and 8F, respectively. Petit Trianon open Tues.-Sun. 11am-6pm. Admission 11F and 6F.)

The hypnotic **Cathédrale de Chartres,** spared by bureaucratic inefficiency after condemnation during the Revolution, survives today as one of man's most sublime creations. The dark vault glows with rich "Chartres blue" stained glass, chronicling human history from Adam and Eve to the Last Judgment. Malcolm Miller—the man who, for the last 34 years, has animated the cathedral for English-speaking visitors—gives introductory tours. (Open daily 7:30am-7:30pm; Oct.-March 7:30am-7pm. Tours at noon and 2:45pm; a donation—about 20F—is expected.) Also of interest at Chartres is the **Centre International du Vitrail** (Stained Glass Center), 5, rue Cardinal Pie. (Open Tues.-Sun. 10am-12:30pm and 1:30-6pm. Admission 15F, students 12F.) Stop by the **tourist office** in front of the cathedral (tel. 37 21 54 03; open Mon.-Sat. 9:30am-12:30pm and 2-6:30pm, Sun. 9:30am-12:30pm and 1:45-6:15pm; Nov.-April Mon.-Sat. 9:30am-12:30pm and 2-5pm.) The pleasing **auberge de jeunesse (IYHF),** 23, av. Neigre (tel. 37 34 27 64), is 2km north of the station—past the cathedral, and over the river by the Eglise St-André (follow the signs). (Curfew 11pm. 54F.) Trains run from Gare Montparnasse to Chartres (every hr. 7:19am-8:30pm, 1 hr., round-trip 114F).

Fontainebleau is older than Versailles, and less mobbed by camera-clickers. For eight centuries, sovereigns contributed to the grandeur of what started out as a medieval castle, adding a room here or a wing there. Napoleon dubbed it *La Maison des Siècles* (the house of centuries), a wry allusion to its haphazard stew of styles. Take the train from Gare de Lyon (hourly 10am-midnight, 40 min., 59F round-trip). (Palace open Wed.-Mon. 9:30am-12:30pm and 2-5pm. Admission 23F, Sun. 12F.)

Compiègne, one hour and 55F from Paris's Gare du Nord, seems to have a knack for resolving conflicts. Joan of Arc was taken prisoner here by the English in 1429, and the armistice ending World War I was signed in a local field on November 11, 1918. Trying to rewrite history, Adolf Hitler forced the French to surrender at the same spot in 1940. During the war, the town became an important departure point for Nazi concentration camps. Today, Compiègne is a bustling town with three unusual museums. The **Palais National,** originally built as a summer cottage for Louis XV and used by Napoléon, contains accoutrements from the 18th century and is surrounded by formal gardens. (Tours Wed.-Mon. 9:30am-noon and 1:30-5pm. Admission 25F, students 15F.) Your ticket also admits you to the adjoining **Musée de la Voiture,** which displays an amusing collection of ostentatious horse-drawn carriages, including several used by Napoléon and Josephine for naughty jaunts. The **Musée de la Figurine Historique,** in the Hôtel de Ville (tel. 44 40 72 55), contains a precious collection of toy kings and soldiers depicting episodes from 1500 years of French history. (Open Tues.-Sun. 9am-noon and 2-6pm; Nov.-Feb. Tues.-Sun. 9am-noon and 2-5pm. Admission 10F, students 5F). The **auberge de jeunesse (IYHF),** 6, rue Pasteur (tel. 44 40 72 64), with large dormitories and kitchen facilities, hides behind a church just outside the cobblestoned pedestrian district (33F).

Normandy (Normandie)

Inspiration to impressionists and generals, fertile Normandy is a land of gently undulating, unkempt farmland, tiny fishing villages, gray skies, and soaring cathedrals. Vikings, or Norsemen (a term later corrupted to "Normans"), seized the region in the 9th century, and invasions have twice secured Normany's place in military history: in 1066, when William of Normandy conquered England, and on D-Day, June 6, 1944, when Allied armies landed on the Norman beaches and began the liberation of Europe.

Normandy supplies a fat percentage of France's butter. Try the creamy, pungent *Camembert* cheese, but be sure it's ripe (soft in the middle). Eating *tripes à la Normandaise* (made from cow guts) requires intestinal fortitude. The province's traditional drink, *cidre,* is fermented apple juice that comes both dry *(brut)* and sweet *(doux).* A harder cousin is *Calvados,* apple brandy aged 12-15 years, whose fumes alone are lethal.

Rouen

Joan of Arc burned here, Emma Bovary was bored here, and the Germans bombed here. Victor Hugo dubbed Rouen the city of 100 spires, the most famous of which are the needles, gargoyles, and gables of the **cathedral.** The now-grimy Gothic façade so obsessed Monet that he painted it over and over again. (Open daily 10am-noon and 2-6pm.) Behind the cathedral lies **Eglise St-Maclou,** a fine example of the later, flamboyant Gothic style. Its charnel house, **Aitre St-Maclou** (turn left into 186, rue de Martinville), with its cloister of macabre wood carvings, has also been preserved. (Open daily 9am-noon and 2-6pm.) Joan of Arc burned at the stake on **place du Vieux Marché,** east of the center of town; a cross near the modern, boat-shaped **Eglise Jeanne d'Arc** marks the spot. (Open daily 9am-noon and 2-6pm.) Pedestrian precincts full of cafés and restaurants radiate from the charmingly imprecise **Gros Horloge,** a 14th-century clock tower and Renaissance gatehouse. The **Musée Flaubert et d'Histoire de la Médecine,** 51, rue de Lecat, houses an awesome but gruesome array of pre-anesthesia medical instruments, including gallstone crushers, a primitive spiked enema machine, and a battlefield amputation kit. (Open Tues.-Sat. 10am-noon and 2-6pm. Free.)

From Rouen's train station (lockers 15-30F), walk straight down rue Jeanne d'Arc and turn left on rue Gros Horloge for pl. de la Cathédrale and the **tourist office** (tel. 35 71 41 77). (Books rooms for 11F. Open Mon.-Sat. 9am-7pm, Sun. 9:30am-12:30pm and 2:30-6pm; Nov.-Easter Mon.-Sat. 9am-12:30pm and 2-6:30pm.) Rouen's modern, cacophonous **auberge de jeunesse (IYHF)** is at 17, rue Diderot (tel. 35 72 06 45), 2km from the train station on the left bank of the Seine. Take bus #12 to rue Diderot or walk straight from the station down rue Jeanne d'Arc across the bridge, and turn left on av. de Caen to rue Diderot. (Curfew 11pm. 51.50F. Breakfast and linen included.) From June through September, you can get a single for 41F at the **Cité Universitaire,** in Mont St-Aignan, well out of town. Take bus #10 from the center. You will need a student ID and an extra photo; contact **CROUS,** 3, rue d'Herbouville (tel. 35 98 44 50) for details. **Hôtel Normandya,** 32, rue du Cordier (tel. 35 71 46 15), offers attractive rooms only 10 minutes from the train station. (Singles and doubles 80-100F, with shower 130F. Breakfast 18F.)

A **market** enlivens pl. du Vieux Marché from Tuesday through Saturday, and gourmet *traiteurs* line the streets. You'll find a host of costly and cost-effective restaurants on the streets in back of the Vieux Marché. **La Pétite Flambée,** on the corner of the market and rue Chauchoise, flips super *crêpes* and *galettes* (whole-wheat crêpes) from 10-28F. (Open Mon.-Sat. noon-3pm and 7-10pm.) Near the cathedral, **Natural Vital,** 3, rue du Petit Salut, serves delicious hot vegetarian *plats du jour* (38F) and other healthful options. (Open Tues.-Sat. noon-3pm. Well-stocked health food store open Tues.-Sun. 8am-7pm.)

Rouen is easily accessible from Paris's Gare St-Lazare (1 per hour, 70 min., 90F) and from Dieppe (every 1-2 hr., 1 hr., 44F). It is a convenient stopover for those traveling between Paris and London via either Dieppe or Calais.

Norman Coast

The coast from Dieppe to Le Havre meanders past white cliffs, startling blue green water, and the half-wild green farmlands of the interior. With its vibrant quays, boardwalk, and faded Victorian hotels,**Dieppe** mirrors Dover, across the channel. Steep white cliffs rise above the western edge of the port city, completing the image. The dismal **auberge de jeunesse (IYHF)** is a 25-minute hike from the station on rue Louis Fromager (tel. 35 84 85 73). Take bus #1 to "Javie" (every 20 min.). If you walk, turn left from the station, then right four blocks later on rue de la République, then sharply left onto rue Gambetta, right onto av. Jean Jaurès, and finally, left on Fromager (you still have a ways to go). (No lockout. Members only, 39F. Breakfast 15F. Kitchen facilities.)

Fécamp, an deep-sea fishing port, is famous for its massive **Abbatiale de la Trinité,** with a nave matching that of Paris's Notre Dame. (Open May-Oct. Mon.-Sat. 11am-5pm. Free.) An **auberge de jeunesse (IYHF)** overlooks town from rue du Commandant Roquigny. (Tel. 35 29 75 79. Members only, 39F. Camping 19F. Rents bikes for 40F per day. Open July-Aug.) Buses and trains service Fécamp frequently from both Le Havre and Dieppe.

Claude Monet was aroused by the two natural arches hewn out of the cliffs that frame the harbor at **Etretat,** the next coastal resort. The **tourist office** pl. de la Mairie (tel. 35 27 05 21), can help you with accommodations. Etretat has no hostel but is accessible by bus from Le Havre and Fécamp.

The country's largest transatlantic port, **Le Havre,** connects France with Rosslare and Cork in Ireland and Southampton and Portsmouth in England. **P&O European Ferries,** quai de Southampton (tel. 35 21 36 50), serves Portsmouth year-round. Take bus #3 from the train station or the Hôtel de Ville. **Irish Ferries,** route du Môle Central (tel. 35 53 28 83), serves Rosslare year-round and Cork in summer; already the most convenient way to Ireland from the Continent, these ferries are free with Eurail or InterRail. Take bus #4 from the train station or the Hôtel de Ville to the Marceau stop. If you must stay overnight, avoid the areas near the port and the train station. Try the hostel-like **Union Chrétienne de Jeunes Gens,** 153, bd. de Strasbourg (tel. 35 42 47 86), with 43F singles and an appetizing cafeteria *(plat du jour* 15-25F) or the pleasant **Hôtels St-Pierre and Jeanne d'Arc,** 91, rue Emile-Zola (tel. 35 41 26 83), centrally located off rue du Paris. (Singles 98F. Doubles from 108F. Breakfast 15F.) The English-speaking **tourist office** is across the bridge inside the **Hôtel de Ville.** (Open Mon.-Sat. 9am-12:15pm and 2-7pm.)

Bus Verts du Calvados bus #20 serves the coast west of Le Havre all the way to Cabourg and then on to Caen.

Caen, Bayeux, and the D-Day Beaches

Despite a punishing Allied bombardment during World War II, the Romanesque churches of **Caen** recall the prosperous 11th century, when the town was William the Conqueror's ducal seat. In the town center, the powerful ruins of William's **château** enclose two notable museums, the **Musée des Beaux Arts,** with paintings by Monet, Rubens, van der Weyden, and Perugino, and the **Musée de Normandie.** (Both open Wed.-Mon. 10am-noon and 2-6pm; Nov.-Feb. Wed.-Mon. 10am-noon and 2-5pm. Admission 6F, students 3F, combination ticket 7F, Sun. free.) Beneath the château, the 13th-century **Eglise St-Pierre** features a majestic bell tower and an ornate Renaissance façade. Perched above the city center, the **Abbaye-aux-Dames** and its twin church, the **Abbaye-aux-Hommes,** were built by William and his cousin, Matilda, to expiate their sin of their incestuous marriage. North of the center, the excellent **Mémorial: Un Musée Pour la Paix** (tel. 31 06 06 44) makes a cogent plea for world peace using a unique combination of hi-tech audio-visual aids and actual WWII footage. Take bus #12 from *centre ville* (every 20 min., 20 min., 5.50F). (Open daily 9am-10pm; Sept.-May daily 9am-7pm. Adults 42F, students 17F.) The well-informed, English-speaking **tourist office,** pl. St-Pierre (tel. 31 86 27 65), finds rooms (10F fee) and exchanges money from June to September. (Open Mon.-Sat. 9am-7pm, Sun. 10am-12:30pm and 3-6pm; mid-Sept. to May Mon. 10am-noon and 2-7pm, Tues.-Sat. 9am-noon and 2-7pm.)

Caen's **auberge de jeunesse foyer Robert Rème (IYHF),** 68bis, rue Restout (tel. 31 52 19 96), is lively and modern. Take bus #3 towards Grace de Dieu from the train and bus station to the Armand Marie stop. (Reception open daily June-Sept. 7-10am and 5-10pm. 55F. Breakfast included.) The more conveniently located **Hôtel de la Paix,** 14, rue Neuve-St-Jean (tel. 31 86 18 99), near the château, likes *Let's Go* readers and offers comfortable rooms. From the tourist office, take a left onto rue St-Pierre, then a right through the underpass. (Singles and doubles 100F, with shower 140-150F. Breakfast 20F. Shower 20F.) The clean and modern rooms of the **Hôtel St-Jean,** 20, rue des Martyrs (tel. 31 86 23 35), near pl. de la Résistance are run by a history-buff owner. (Singles and doubles 110F, with shower 140F. Breakfast 17F. Private parking.) Several inexpensive *crêperies* and *brasseries,* as well as a smattering of ethnic restaurants, can be found around rue du Vaugeux and av. de la Libération, near the château. **Restaurant Kouba,** 6, rue du Vaugueux (tel. 31 93 68 47), serves hearty *couscous* from 48F. (Open daily noon-2pm and 7-11pm.)

Castles, spectacular views, museums, and wine tastings got you down? Jump off a bridge at France's first **Bungy Jumping** facility (tel. 31 67 37 38). A worker attaches your ankles to a 90m rubber band (also attached to the bridge), and you plunge into the gorgeous valley. After a most bodacious two minutes of upside-down bouncing, you're lowered to the ground and think to yourself, "Whoa! Better than lawn darts!" (Take one of the frequent buses from Caen to Vire, and call to be picked up. 400F per jump and worth it, students 300F. Reservations recommended a day in advance, but not required. Open daily noon-8pm.)

Beautiful and ancient **Bayeux** is an ideal launching point for the D-Day beaches, and is itself renowned for the **Bayeux Tapestry,** which recounts the Norman Conquest of Britain in 1066. The captions are in Latin, but the audio-visual exhibition interprets the tapestry and the history of the Battle of Hastings in both French and English. The linen embroidery, probably commissioned for Bayeux's cathedral, is now housed in a seminary on rue de Nesmond. (Open daily 9am-7pm; Oct. to mid-March 9:30am-12:30pm and 2-6pm; mid-March to May 9am-12:30pm and 2-6:30pm. Admission 25F, students 12F.) Nearby is the splendid **Cathédrale.** Outside, Gothic spires crown older Romanesque towers; inside, light pours through Gothic stained glass to illuminate Romanesque arches a century older. (Open daily 8am-7:30pm; Sept.-June 8am-noon and 2:30-7pm.)

The superhuman **tourist office,** 1, rue des Cuisiniers (tel. 31 92 16 26), makes hotel reservations for the price of a phone call, hunts down rooms in private homes, and changes money when banks are closed in a single transaction. (Open Mon.-Sat. 9:30am-12:30pm and 2-6:30pm, Sun. 10am-12:30pm and 3-6:30pm; mid-Sept. to May Mon.-Sat. only.) The coziest place to stay is **Family Home (IYHF),** 39, rue Général-de-Dais (tel. 31 92 15 22), off rue de la Juridiction, with billowing quilts and a rural ambience. (Open daily 7am-7pm. 71F, nonmembers 98F. Breakfast included. Rusty bikes for rent, 50F per day. Make reservations.) Dinner is sublime—countless dishes and unlimited wine (55F). The **Centre d'Accueil,** chemin de Boulogne (tel. 31 92 08 19), has modern singles (75F for IYHF members, showers and breakfast included). Weary travelers may opt for the friendly reception and spacious rooms at **Hôtel de la Gare,** pl. de la Gare (tel. 31 92 10 70; singles 85-90F; doubles 100F; students 50F; breakfast 20F). For authentic and delicious Norman cuisine, try **Le Petit Normand,** 35, rue Larcher (tel. 31 22 88 66), overlooking the cathedral (menus start at 47F).

Nine km north of Bayeux on the D516 is **Arromanches,** easternmost of the **D-Day beaches.** Its fascinating **Musée du Débarquement** displays miniature models of the artificial harbor constructed after the Allied invasion. (Open daily 9am-6:30pm; Sept.-June 9-11:30am and 2-5:30pm. Admission 20F, students 10F.) The high cliffs of **Omaha Beach,** scaled by invading American troops, lie to the west. The **American Cemetery** is in Colleville-St-Laurent; the **Canadian Cemetery** is at Bény-sur-Mer-Reviers, near Courseulles. English-speaking tours based in Bayeux are more convenient than buses: **Normandy Tours** (tel. 31 92 10 70 or contact Hôtel de la Gare) gives small, flexible tours for one to eight people (2 per day, 100F, students 90F), while **Bus Fly,** 24, rue Montfiquet (tel. 31 22 00 08) leaves twice daily from the Family Home (120F).

Northwest of Bayeux at the northern tip of the Cotentin peninsula, **Cherbourg 's** port shuttles passengers to and from Portsmouth, Poole, and Southhampton, England. **Irish Ferries** (tel. 33 44 28 96) run to Rosslare, Ireland three times per week; Eurail and InterRail are valid. The train station is just a 10-minute walk from the ferry terminal; trains run frequently to Paris (6 per day, 3½hr., 192F), Rouen (3 per day), Caen (6 per day), Bayeux (9 per day), and points south in Normandy and Brittany. If you stay overnight in this city of concrete blockhouses, try the dorm-like **Auberge de Jeunesse** (tel. 33 44 26 31) on av. Louis Lumière, 1½km from the train station. Take bus #2 (direction "Tourlaville") from behind the station to the Fleming stop, or walk: take a right on the highway towards Tourlaville, hang a right at the first light (after 1km) on av. Maréchal de Latte, and the hostel is one block up on the left corner. (Members only, 38F. Sheets 14F. Breakfast 15F. Lockout 10am-6pm. Reception open daily 8-10am and 6-11pm.)

Mont Saint-Michel

Viewing Mont St-Michel for the first time, your dropping jaw may bruise your knees. A venerable abbey and exquisite cloister balance precariously on the jutting rock, surrounded by military fortifications and a *ville basse* built to serve medieval pilgrims. Pack a lunch and make the Mont a day trip; ignore its tourist swarms. You can pay to visit just limited parts of the abbey on your own, or take a one-hour guided tour to see more. (French tours every 20 min.; English tours daily at 10am, 11am, noon, 1:30pm, 2:30pm, 3:30pm, 4:30pm, and 5:30pm. Admission 31F, ages 18-25 17F, under 18 5F; Sun. half-price.) The two-hour *visites conférences* (French only) are a special treat; they allow you to walk atop a flying buttress and creep inside the pre-Roman crypts. (Tours daily at 10am and 2:30pm. Admission 39F, ages 18-25 and over 60 31F, under 18 21F.) The tide rushes in to envelop the Mont at 2m per second—an extraordinary sight. Try to time your visit with the highest tides—36 to 48 hours after the new and full moons respectively (especially in March, April, Sept., and Oct.). You must be on the Mont two hours ahead of time, as the causeway becomes impassable. Mont St-Michel is as stunningly illuminated at night as it is during the day (nightly; Oct.-June high-tide nights and during festivals).

To get to Mont St-Michel, take a train to **Pontorson;** from Paris, change at Folligny (2 per day, 5½ hr., 192F) or take the TGV to Rennes and change there (3-4 per day, 3¼ hr., 224F plus min. 32F required reservation). Conquer the remaining 9km to the Mont by boarding the STN bus outside the Pontorson station (4 per day, 10 min., round-trip 19.20F) or by renting a **bike** at the station (open daily 8am-noon and 2-8pm; 50F per day). Locker your baggage at the station (3F) or with the gracious toilet attendant at the Mont's entrance (10F per day). Most hotels and restaurants on the Mont blow away a *Let's Go* budget, although the **Hôtel de la Croix Blanche,** rue Grande Pontorson (tel. 33 60 14 04), has small rooms with panoramic views of the coastline. (Singles and doubles 120-210F. Open Feb.-Nov. Call several weeks in advance.) In Pontorson, stay in the cheery rooms of the **Hôtel de l'Arrivée,** pl. de la Gare (tel. 33 60 01 57; singles and doubles 67-135F). The **Hôtel de France,** 2, rue de Rennes (tel. 33 60 29 17), has worn but inexpensive rooms and a friendly proprietor. (Singles and doubles 65-95F.) The **Centre Duguesclin (IYHF)** (tel. 33 60 18 65), on rue Gén. Patton in Pontorson, is a 10-minute walk from the station and has good facilities (38F). For night views of the Mont, stay across the bay in Avranches at the **auberge de jeunesse** at 15, rue du Jardin des Plantes (tel. 33 58 06 54), accessible by train from Pontorson (2 per day, 20 min., 19F). (48F. Breakfast included.)

Brittany (Bretagne)

This sea-battered peninsula stands apart from the rest of France, intent on its own direction. Linguistically and ethnically Celtic, Brittany fought off affiliation with France until the 16th century, and to a certain extent, still seems to now. Language, food, extremist politics and religion still mark out this province, despite its growing popularity with tourists. While there are plenty of summer resorts and soft sandy beaches here, a wilder beauty is never distant. The wave-beaten cliffs of the Northern Coast are spectacular; farther west, ancient *menhirs* (prehistoric stone obelisks) dot the high, windy headlands of the Côte Sauvage on the Quiberon peninsula. Retreat to the wooded Argoat interior for a respite from coastal crowds.

Reservations are essential in July and August. Hotel prices can rise (or fall) dramatically in good or bad weather. The **Association Bretonne des Relais et Itinéraires (ABRI)** or any of the larger tourist offices can supply you with a list of area *gîtes d'étape,* shelters in rural settings where travelers can spend the night for only 26F (off-limits to motorists). Many towns shutter up for long stretches during the winter, though a number of IYHF *auberges de jeunesse* in the region remain open most of the year.

Bretons make *crêpes* of ground wheat flour *(froment)* with sweet fillings and *galettes* of darker buckwheat *(sarasin),* wrap them around eggs, cheese, or sausage, and chase them with *cidre bouché,* hard cider, or the sweeter *cidre doux.* Delectable seafood meals like *coquilles St-Jacques* (scallops), *saumon fumé* (smoked salmon), and *moules marinières* (mussels in a white wine sauce), are served with *Muscadet,* a dry white wine from the vineyards around Nantes. With the exception of the flan-like *far breton,* Breton desserts are best left unsampled.

Rennes, Quimper, and Brest are connected to Paris by TGV. The main rail lines are Rennes-Brest in the north, Rennes-Redon-Quimper in the south, and Redon-Nantes in the southeast. Private bus lines connect other towns, but service is infrequent and expensive. Cycling is the best and most common means of travel. Many youth hostels, including those at Dinan, St-Brieuc, Lannion, and Quimper, rent bikes to IYHF members for about 30F per day. As in the rest of France, some train stations rent bikes for around 50F per day. Many find hitching a little easier in Brittany than in the rest of France; they stick to the major roads, such as the D786. The quickest hitching to Paris is via Avranches in the north and Nantes, Angers, and Le Mans in the south.

Rennes

In 1720, a drunken carpenter knocked over his lamp and set Rennes ablaze, destroying most of the medieval town. Today, a constant flow of young university students lights up the city. If you're tired of nightlife, introduce yourself to Breton history at the **Musée de Bretagne** and the **Musée des Beaux-Arts,** 20, quai Emile Zola. (Both open Wed.-Mon. 10am-noon and 2-6pm. Admission 11F, to both museums 17F; ½ price with student ID.) In the first week of July, Rennes celebrates summer with **Les Tombées de la Nuit,** a spectacular music, dance, and theater festival.

The **tourist office** on Pont de Nemours (tel. 99 79 01 98) lists all the youth hostels, hotels, and campgrounds in Brittany and has maps of most of the larger cities. From the train station, follow rue Jean Janvier to the canal and turn left; the office is two blocks down on your right. You can also visit **ABRI,** 9, rue des Portes Mordelaises (tel. 99 31 59 44), which provides lists of travel shelters, bike routes, and the like. (Open Tues.-Fri. 9:30am-12:30pm and 2-5:30pm, Sat. 10am-12:30pm and 2-5pm.) The **Centre d'Information Jeunesse Bretagne,** in the Maison du Champ de Mars (tel. 99 31 47 48) has myriad leaflets (open during school vacations and July-Aug. daily 10am-6pm; other times 2-6pm). A **post office** on pl. de la République (tel. 99 79 50 71) exchanges currency (open Mon.-Fri. 8am-7pm, Sat. 8am-noon). **Provoya,** Maison du Champ de Mars, 6, cours des Alliés (tel. 99 30 98 87), pairs riders with drivers. (Open Mon.-Fri. 1:30-5pm, Sat. 9am-noon; Sept.-June Mon.-Fri. 2-6:30pm, Sat. 9am-noon.)

Rennes's renovated **auberge de jeunesse (IYHF)** is at 10-12, Canal St-Martin (tel. 99 33 22 33). From the station, walk or take bus #20 or 22. (Reception open Mon.-Fri. 7:45am-11pm, Sat.-Sun. 8-10am and 6-11pm. 1-2 bed rooms 64.50F; 3-4 bed rooms 50F. Showers in every room.) **Hôtel de Léon,** 15 rue de Léon (tel. 99 30 55 28), near the Vilaine River off quai de Richemont, has commodious quarters and winsome owners. (Singles 105-160F. Doubles 174-184F.) Ask at the tourist office for the location of the **market** (Tues.-Sat. 7am-6pm). For a sit-down meal, try the *crêperies* in the old quarter and on rue St-Melaine; **Le Boulingrain,** at #25, is a particularly good value. (Open daily 11:30am-2pm and 6:30-11pm.)

Trains from Rennes run throughout Brittany, to Paris (3 per day, 3½ hr., 200F; by TGV 9 per day, 2 hr., 200F plus min. 32F required reservation), to Nantes (8 per day, 2 hr., 95F), and to Tours via Le Mans (8 per day, 3½ hr., 153F). Call 99 65 50 50 for information. Cheaper (but slower and less frequent) buses leave from the train station and bus station (three blocks up on the bd. Magenta) for Mont

St-Michel (1-5 per day, 1 hr., 51F), Nantes (3 per day, 3 hr., 86F), and Vannes (2 per day, 2¾ hr., 83F).

St-Malo and Dinan

Once a town of privateers and merchants, **St-Malo** is now a fashionable summer resort, especially electric at night. High granite walls separate the postcard-perfect beaches outside the *vieille ville* from the chic boutiques and seafood restaurants within. At low tide, stroll over to the **Fort National** on the **Ile du Grand Bé** to see the lonely grave of the Romantic *écrivain* Châteaubriand. To tour the ramparts—and you must—look for the sign "Accès aux Ramparts" next to any of the gates, such as **Porte St-Vincent,** the main gate to the old town. The few original, unreconstructed houses along the **rue Pelicot,** which ends at the **cour la Houssaye** and the 17th-century house of Duchesse Anne de Bretagne, queen to two successive kings of France, evoke St-Malo's history.

St-Malo's **tourist office** is located on Esplanade St-Vincent, just outside Porte St-Vincent (tel. 99 56 64 48; open Mon.-Sat. 8:30am-8pm, Sun. 10am-6:30pm; Sept.-June Mon.-Sat. 9am-noon and 2-6:30pm). To reach the tourist office and the old city, turn right as you exit the train station, cross bd. de la République, and head straight down av. Louis-Martin (10-15 min.). Red buses #2 and 3 and purple bus #4 run from bd. de la République (turn right and right again from the station) to St-Vincent, near the center (every 20 min., 6.2F until 7:30).

Finding a hotel room in St-Malo in July and August can prove impossible. Even the lively **auberge de jeunesse (IYHF),** 37, av. du Père Umbricht (tel. 99 40 29 80), fills up, although the **Foyer des Jeunes Travailleurs** may take on the overflow. To get to the hostel take red bus #2 or blue #1 from av. Jean Jaurès (3 per hr., 6F, last bus 7:30pm) to Courtoisville, or walk down av. Jean Jaurès, take a left on bd. Gambetta and a right on av. du Père Umbricht, and the hostel is on your left (5 min. from the beach, and 25 min. from the station). (Reception open Mon.-Fri. 7:30am-noon and 2-7pm and 7:30pm-5:30am, Sat.-Sun. 24 hrs. Members only, 57F.) With a little luck (or a reservation), you might find a room at **L'Auberge Au Gai Bec,** 4, rue des Lauriers (tel. 99 40 82 16). (Singles and doubles 95-150F. Breakfast 20F.)

All train journeys from Paris to St-Malo require a change at Rennes (from Gare Montparnasse, 12 per day, 5 hr., 222F; by TGV 3½ hr., 222F plus min. 32F reservation fee). The pavilion on Esplanade St-Vincent houses the helpful offices of almost all bus and ferry services; inquire about sailings to the Channel Islands (see under United Kingdom), and daytrips to Mont St-Michel (87F; see Normandy).

Dinan, 35km southwest of St-Malo, has more to see—and fewer people trying to see it—than its neighbor to the north. Dinan rightly prides itself as Brittany's best-preserved medieval town. The precipitous, cobblestoned streets and gabled 15th- and 16th-century houses of the *vieille ville* stand 66m above the Rance Valley. The splendid **Château de Dinan** is a short and scenic jaunt from the post office along **Promenade des Petits-Fossés.** The heavily fortified 14th-century **donjon** houses an excellent museum displaying polychromatic religious statuettes and medieval weapons. A collection of *gisants* (tomb sculptures) resides in the chilly dungeon of the **Tour de Coëtquen** next door. (Château and museum open daily June-Aug. 10am-6pm; Sept.-Oct. and March-May 10am-noon and 2-6pm; Nov.-Feb. Wed.-Mon. 1:30-5:30pm. Admission 15F, students 10F.)

The well-stocked **tourist office,** 6, rue de l'Horloge (tel. 96 39 75 40), is 10 minutes from the station. Bear left across pl. du 11 Novembre 1918 onto rue Carnot, then right onto rue Thiers, which brings you to pl. Duclos. Head up the hill to the left on rue du Marchix and turn left at the sign for the *office de tourisme.* Cross the square and take rue Ste-Claire to rue de l'Horloge. (Open Mon.-Sat. 9am-7pm, Sun. 10am-1pm and 2-7pm; Oct.-April daily 8:30am-12:30pm and 2-6pm.) The **auberge de jeunesse (IYHF),** in a forest a half-hour's walk downhill from the train station (tel. 96 39 10 83), is a peaceful place with excellent facilities. From the main exit of the train station, turn left, left again across the tracks, and follow the signs (members only, 42F). **Hôtel du Théâtre,** 2, rue Ste-Claire (tel. 96 39 06 91), in the heart of the *vieille ville,* has cozy rooms. Follow directions for the tourist office above. (Singles and doubles 115-140F.) **Hôtel-Restaurant de l'Océan,** pl. du 11 Novembre 1918 (tel. 96 39 21 51), opposite the station, has clean rooms and friendly owners. (Singles and doubles 100-130F.) Camping is possible outside the youth hostel in a hidden spot near a stream (20F per person). Closer is the **Camping Municipal,** 103, rue Châteaubriand (tel. 96 39 11 96). If you're facing the post office and pl. Duclos, find rue Châteaubriand to your right.

The *vieille ville* shadows a variety of Breton restaurants; don't miss the **Crêperie des Artisans,** 6, rue du Petit Fort, with fabulous four-course *menus* (crêpes and *galettes)* for 42-57F. (Open Tues.-Sun. noon-10:30pm, Oct.-March daily noon-10:30pm.) An outdoor **market** awakens Thursday from 8am to noon in pl. du Champ, at pl. Duguesclin.

Dinan is accessible by train (change at Dol) from Rennes (6 per day, 2 hr., 57F) and St-Malo (7 per day, 1¼ hr., 39F). From July to September, buses between Dinan and St-Malo run three times per day (1 hr., 28F).

Northern Brittany

Brittany's northern coast is compelling, sweeping around rugged cliffs and jagged rocks to serene coves and sandy beaches. Adventurers will love the windswept splendor of **Cap Fréhel,** on the Côte d'Emeraude. The **auberge de jeunesse Plévenon (IYHF)** (tel. 96 41 48 98), a rugged tent camp 4km from the Cap, offers cots for 32F (open June-Aug.). From St-Brieuc (45-55 min. by Brestwards train from Rennes), CAT runs buses to Le Vieux-Bourg (2 per day, 38F); from here you're on your own—the Cap is 5km northeast on the D34A. Reach **St-Cast** by bus-train combo from St-Brieuc, via Lambale (2 per day, 28F); **Pointe de St-Cast** is 2km north of the bus stop in St-Cast, with fine photo opportunities of the Breton coast. Mme. Grouazel, the friendly director of **Camping de la Ferme de Pen-Guen** (tel. 96 41 92 18), will fetch you from the bus stop for the price of gas (about 10F; 8F per person; 4.30F per tent, 6F per car, bikes free.)

To the west, the secluded beaches of the **Ceinture Dorée** provoke interest with their geological oddities, like the Côte de Granite Rose and the rocks of Trégastel. The touristy town of **Paimpol** makes an excellent launch pad for daytrips to the pastoral **Ile de Bréhat.** Take a bus from the Paimpol train station to Arcouest (10 per day, 15 min., 13F), where boats leave for Ile de Bréhat (every hr., Sept.-May about every 2 hr.; 10 min.; round-trip 48F). The unforgettable **auberge de jeunesse (IYHF)** in Paimpol (tel. 96 20 83 60) is an old castle 25 minutes by foot from the station; turn left on av. Général de Gaulle, right at the first light, left at the next light, and then follow the signs for "Keraoul." (39F. Nightly feast 47F.)

Follow the stretch of coast from **Perros-Guirec** to **Trébeurden** for beaches and brilliant seascape. A tremendous cliff path, the **Sentier des Douaniers,** leads from Perros's beach to the Pors Rollnd at Ploumanach. Nearby **Morlaix,** 100 minutes by train from Rennes, has an adequate **auberge de jeunesse (IYHF)** at 3, route de Paris (tel. 98 88 13 63), 20 minutes from the station; from Morlaix, trains (30-45 min.) and buses run north to the coast at **Roscoff,** a small resort and the departure point for ferries to Cork, Ireland, and Plymouth, England. **Brittany Ferries** (tel. 98 29 28 28) sends boats to both. In Roscoff, **Hôtel les Arcades,** 15, rue Admiral Réveillère (tel. 98 69 70 45), has doubles for 110-230F. (Open April to mid-Oct.) Rocky coast, virgin beaches, and emerald-green seascape hide on the **Ile de Batz.** The island's remarkable **auberge de jeunesse (IYHF)** (tel. 98 61 77 69) is straight up the hill from the dock. (Beds 39F. Cots in tent 33F.) Ferries serve the island regularly from Roscoff. (8am-8pm 1 per hr.; Oct.-June 8am-8pm every 1½ hr. Round-trip 25F, no bicycles.)

Inland, **Huelgoat** is a refreshing town on a sparkling lake. *Menhirs* dot this corner of the Argoat. Stroll along cool paths through hilly forests, or bicycle to tiny Breton-speaking villages. Within walking distance of Huelgoat are the **Roche Tremblante,** a 137-metric-ton boulder that can be moved if you know the secret, the **Grotte du Diable,** more a space between heaps of boulders than a cave, and the **menhir de Kerampeulven.** In town, the tourist office is off pl. Aristide-Briand (tel. 98 99 72 32; open June 15-Sept. 15 Mon.-Sat. 10am-noon and 2-4pm). **Hôtel de l'Armorique,** 1, pl. Aristide-Briand (tel. 98 99 71 24), has simple rooms with divine mattresses. (Singles and doubles 80-110F. Triples 160F.) **Camping Municipal du Lac,** rue Général de Gaulle, sprawls conveniently and attractively along the lake, but is often crowded. Two to three SNCF buses per day run from Morlaix to Huelgoat. The one-hour trip (28F, railpasses valid) ends at pl. Aristide-Briand.

At the tip of the Breton peninsula hunkers **Brest,** an industrial and military port and the terminus for trains from Rennes (2-2½ hr.). The **IYHF hostel** is at Le Moulin Blanc, rue de Kerbriant (tel. 98 41 90 41), about 4km from the station. Take bus #72 from the train station (last bus 7:10pm) to Port de Plaisance; the hostel has superb facilities next to a vast, sandy beach. (37F. Bike rental 35F per day.) Rue de Siam, which becomes rue Jean Jaurès, is the place to stock up on supplies. From Brest, a 2½-hour boat ride brings you to **Ile d'Ouessant,** a rugged island where sheep outnumber people. Its inhabitants evolved Breton traditions found nowhere else, such as elaborate ceremonies for folk lost at sea and a custom where women proposed to men. Boats dock at **Port du Stiff,** where you can rent bikes; across the island in the main town of **Lampaul,** the **tourist office** (tel. 98 48 85 83) will give you a map and information on the four hotels in town. (Boats run daily, late March-early July Sat.-Thurs.; 69F, round-trip 112F.)

Voyage easily from Brest to the **Crozon Peninsula,** with its steep, jagged cliffs, ancient *menhirs,* and splendid beaches. Boats run from Brest's port of commerce to Le Fret three times per day, with connecting buses to Camaret, Crozon, and Morgat (tel. 98 44 77 04; 44F, round-trip 80F). **Autocars Douguet** runs buses from Brest to Crozon and Camaret (Mon.-Fri. in the morning and afternoon, Sat. morning only; to Camaret 42F). Four SNCF buses per day (railpasses valid) run from Quimper to Camaret via Crozon and Morgat (42F). Prices on the peninsula are often as steep as the cliffs, but the scenery is worth it. **Camaret** is a good base for the peninsula; the small and simple **IYHF youth hostel** (tel. 98 27 98 24) on rte. de Toulinguet has 38F beds and an astonishing view. (Open mid-June to Sept. Call first.) **Camping Municipal de Lannic** (tel. 98 27 91 31) is close to the center of Camaret, off rue du Grounach. (8F per person, 5.50F per tent. Showers 6F. Open mid-June to mid-Sept.) Inquire about other lodgings at Camaret's **tourist office** on quai Toudouze (tel. 98 27 93 60), near the bus stop (open mid-June to mid-Sept. Tues.-Sat. 10am-noon and 2-5pm; otherwise, call the mayor's office at 98 27 94 22). In **Crozon,** ask about two nearby *gîtes d'etape* at the well-appointed Crozon **tourist office** (tel. 98 26 17 18) on rue St-Yves at the bus stop. (Open Mon.-Sat. 9am-8pm; Sept.-June Tues.-Sun. 9am-12:30pm and 2-6pm.) Close to Crozon's SNCF station is the three-star **Camping Pen-Ar-Ménez** (tel. 98 27 12 36), off noisy rue de la Marne. (13F per person, 7F per tent, 7F per car. Showers included. Open April-Sept.)

Southern Brittany

Quimper presides over the Breton homeland of **La Cornouaille,** whose inhabitants originally came from Cornwall in England. Its grand cathedral, famous traditional *faïencerie* (porcelain) and bustling *vieille ville* attract crowds in the summer. An internationally renowned folk festival, the **Festival de la Cornouaille,** is held between the third and fourth Sundays in July.

Quimper is readily accessible by TGV from Paris (7-10 per day, 5 hr., 283F plus 30F reservation), Rennes (139F), or Nantes (144F). From the train station, turn right and follow av. de la Gare to the river; cross the bridge and turn left on bd. Admiral de Kerguélen, then right on rue du Rois Gradlon for the **Cathédrale St-Corentin** and the *vieille ville.* The **tourist office** (tel. 98 53 04 05) is at Place de la

Résistance. From the station, follow av. de la Gare, which becomes bd. Dupleix. (Open Mon.-Sat. 8:30am-8pm, Sun. 9:30am-12:30pm, later during festival week; Sept.-June Mon.-Sat. 9am-noon and 1:30-6:30pm.)

Quimper's newly remodeled **auberge de jeunesse (IYHF),** 6, av. des Oiseaux (tel. 98 55 41 67) is in a woodsy area 2km outside of town; take bus #1 from across the street from the tourist office to the Chaptal stop (39F per person). The two-star **municipal campground** is next door. Call the *Mairie* (tel. 98 98 89 89) for info (6F per person, 1.70F per tent). Near the train station, **Hôtel de l'Ouest,** 63, rue le Déan (tel. 98 90 28 35), has cheery rooms and a delightful owner. (Singles 95-160F. Showers 13F. Breakfast 20F.)

A number of private bus lines connect Quimper to surrounding towns, such as **Concarneau,** a seafaring town 22km to the south with a memorable waterfront hostel (tel. 98 97 03 47), and the **Pointe du Raz,** the westernmost point in France, which has unremittingly glorious cliffs. Ask the tourist office for information.

The **Presqu'île de Quiberon** is a long, narrow peninsula, flanked on its western side by the 10km, magnificently craggy **Côte Sauvage,** and capped by the expensive and modern beach resort of **Quiberon.** Tourists invade in July and August, grabbing spots on the long and clean **Grande Plàge** in Quiberon, and setting sail for startling Belle-Ile.

Quiberon is accessible by rail in July and August only, when trains run from Auray on the Quimper-Rennes line (6 per day, 40 min., 25F). Buses also run from Auray (5-7 per day, 1½-2 hr., 30-31.50F). The **tourist office,** 7, rue de Verdun (tel. 97 50 07 84), provides complete bus and ferry schedules. (Open Mon.-Sat. 9am-8pm, Sun. 10am-noon and 5-8pm; Sept.-June Mon.-Sat. 9am-12:30pm and 2-6:30pm.)

There are a few decent, inexpensive hotels in Quiberon. Perhaps **Hôtel de L'Océan,** 7, quai de L'Océan (tel. 97 50 07 58), with bright rooms overlooking the harbor, can put you up. (Call ahead July-Aug. Singles and doubles 145F, with shower 180-210F.) Ask the tourist office about one of the dozen or so campgrounds that speckle the peninsula. Let loose at the new **Le Gun** disco, just off pl. Hoche on rue du Phare. (Open daily 11pm-4am, Oct.-March weekends only).

Ferries leave year-round for wild **Belle-Ile** from Port-Maria, a small port just next to the Grande Plage (tel. 97 31 80 01; 10-12 per day, Sept.-June 5-7 per day; 45 min.; 74F round-trip, bikes 32F). When you land at **Le Palais** on the island, you can rent bikes from a number of stores on the boardwalk. Ask the **tourist office** (tel. 97 31 81 93) at the end of the quay in Le Palais about various hiking and biking circuits that take you past the picturesque fishing port of **Sauzon,** the rock formations at **Pointe des Poulains,** and the caves of the **Grotte de l'Apothicaire,** all three surrounded by high cliffs, small creeks, and flowered pastures. The clean and convenient **auberge de jeunesse (IYHF)** is just up the hill from Le Palais's port (42F, breakfast 15F).

Tour the **Côte Sauvage** by following the D186 along the west side of the Quiberon Peninsula. Don't swim along the western coast, even where *baignades interdites* (swimming prohibited) signs are not posted. The waters are genuinely treacherous, with a fierce undertow and monster waves. The beaches on the eastern side of the island, notably **Port Andro,** are calm and alluring.

Nantes

"*Nantes, ça bouge!*" is the slogan here, and even a short stay proves that this is indeed a city on the move. Nantes resembles Paris on a smaller scale: wide boulevards mark the boundaries between its various medieval, 18th, and 19th-century districts, interspersed with oversized *places* where the not-too-uptight *Nantais* hang out in cafés.

The Gothic vaults of Nantes's **Cathédrale St-Pierre,** which soar higher above mortals' heads than the arches of Notre-Dame, transport you to a sort of heaven on earth. (Open daily 8:45am-noon and 2-7pm.) Just down rue Mathelin Rodier looms Nantes's heavily fortified 15th-century **château,** surrounded by a moat and an emerald-green strip of lawn. Built by François II, and the birthplace of Duchesse Anne de Bretagne, it now houses three museums. The **Musée des Arts Populaires Régionaux** displays an excellent collection of colorful Breton costumes, period rooms, and fine carved-oak furniture. The **Musée des Salorges** recounts Nantes's commercial history since the 18th century, while the **Musée des Arts Décoratifs** sponsors temporary exhibits of international contemporary art. (Château and museums open Wed.-Mon. 10am-7pm; Sept.-June Wed.-Mon. 10am-noon and 2-6pm. Entry to courtyard and ramparts free. Ticket to all museums 15F, students 7F, free Sun.)

Two blocks from the cathedral on rue Clemenceau is Nantes's extensive **Musée des Beaux Arts,** with paintings by Rubens, Courbet, de la Tour, Ingres, early Italian painters, and various contemporary artists. (Open Wed.-Sat. and Mon. 10am-noon and 1-5:45pm, Sun. 11am-5pm. Admission 5F, students 2.50F, Sun. free.) The **Musée d'Histoire Naturelle,** 12, rue Voltaire (tel. 40 73 30 03), bursts with a mind-boggling array of thousands of species. You name it, they got it. (Open Tues.-Sat. 10am-noon and 2-6pm. Admission 5F, students 2.50F. Take bus #1 to stop "Jean V.") The **Musée Jules Verne,** 3, rue de l'Hermitage (tel. 40 69 72 52), near the river in square M. Schwob, recreates the fantasy world of Captain Nemo and other characters of this Nantes native. (Open Wed.-Sat. 10am-noon and 2-5pm, Sun. 2-5pm. Admission 5F, Sun. free.) The nearby **planetarium** is at 8, rue des Acadiens (tel. 40 73 99 23), off pl. Moysan. (Showings Tues.-Sat. at 10:30am, 2:15pm, and 3:45pm, Sun. at 2:15pm and 3:45pm.)

Ile Feydeau, between allée Turenne and allée Tuouin, was once an island where wealthy sea merchants spent their slave-trade spoils on lavish houses—in 1930 the surrounding waters were filled in with earth. Walk down **rue Kervegan** for the best vista. Even more stately are 18th-century **place Royale** and **rue Crébillon,** leading to **place Graslin.** Corbu-buffs can make a pilgrimage to Le Corbusier's **Cité Radieuse,** an ingeniously conceived apartment complex. Take bus #31 from the Commerce stop on cours Franklin Roosevelt. Although the **Université de Nantes** is strewn across the city, students gravitate to the area north of rue Crébillon in the evening, and rue Scribe has a multitude of late-night bars and cafés. Catch live jazz every evening at 10pm at **The Tie Break Club,** 1, rue des Petites Ecuries. (Open Mon.-Sat. 10pm-3:30am.) In the first two weeks of July, Nantes hosts **Les Fêtes d'Eté,** an artistic extravaganza of 1000 dance, music, and theater groups. Contact the tourist office for more information.

The **tourist office** (tel. 40 47 04 51) is on pl. du Commerce; go left down cours John Kennedy 10 minutes from the station, or take the tram to pl. du Commerce. (Open Mon.-Fri. 9:30am-7pm, Sat. 10am-6pm.) For budget travel information, visit **CRIJ,** 28, rue du Calvaire (tel. 40 48 68 25; open Mon. noon-7pm, Tues.-Fri. 10am-7pm).

To reach the modern **auberge de jeunesse (IYHF),** 2, pl. de la Manufacture (tel. 40 20 57 25), take a right onto bd. de Stalingrad as you leave the station, then a left into the Manufacture complex (15 min.), or take the tram from the station to the Manufacture stop. Facilities include a kitchen and TV room. (45F. Breakfast 15F. Sheets 15F. Open July-Aug. daily 7-10am and 6-11pm.) The **Centre Jean Macé,** 90, rue du Préfet Bonnefoy (tel. 40 74 55 74), at rue Sully, rents clean, dimly lit two-, three-, and four-bed rooms. Take bus #12 from the SNCF station to pl. Maréchal Foch, or walk down bd. Stalingrad, which becomes cours J. Kennedy. Go right at pl. de la Duchesse Anne onto rue Henri VI which becomes rue Sully and intersects with rue de Préfet Bonnefoy at the center. (49F per person, 11F supplement for every empty bed in your room. Breakfast 15F, other meals about 32F). Camp at **Camping du Val de Cens,** 21, bd. du Petit Port (tel. 40 74 47 94), 3km from town. Buses #51 and 53 run from pl. du Commerce to "Marhonnière" stop. (8.10F per person, 12F per site.)

The Nantes outdoor **market** sprouts Tuesday through Saturday in pl. du Bouffay (9am-1pm). For hot food, join the students at laid-back **Crêperie Jaune,** 1, rue des Echevins, off pl. du Bouffay, for the *pavé nantais,* a double-decker *galette* extravaganza (37-45F). The ethnic **Chez Rémy-La Brasserie des Sportifs,** rue de la Bâclerie (tel. 40 47 98 68), also off pl. du Bouffay, has an outdoor *terrasse* and delicious *cous-cous* and seafood dishes (50-95F; open Tues.-Sat. noon-2pm and 7-11pm).

Many a train links Nantes to Paris (4-5 per day, 207F; 12-14 TGVs per day, 2 hr., 239F), Bordeaux (5-8 per day, 4 hr., 200F), Quimper (7-10 per day, 3½ hr., 150F), Poitiers (5 per day, 169F), and Quiberon (July-Aug. only 4 per day, 102F).

Near Nantes, **La Baule** boasts that it has the most beautiful beach in Europe. A smooth curve of sand stretches for miles along the coast, washed by gentle, warm waves. Leisure seems to be the town's main industry, making it expensive and busy in summer. Cheap hotels are scarce, but you might try **Hôtel Marini,** right across the street from the train station. The laid-back, welcoming owner rents clean, modern singles and doubles from 150-185F. Trains connect Nantes to La Baule (6 per day, Oct.-June 8-10 per day; 1 hr.; 52F). There are two **train stations:** La Baule les Pins, east of the center in a quiet area close to camping, and La Baule Escoublac, close to the busy center. Avenue Georges Clemenceau runs from the train station to pl. de la Victoire, where you will find the **tourist office** (tel. 40 24 34 44; open daily 9am-7:30pm, Sept.-June Mon.-Sat. 9am-12:30pm and 2:15-6:30pm). From here, av. du Général-de-Gaulle runs down to the beach.

Loire Valley (Pays de la Loire)

The châteaux of the Loire mark the zenith of French power. Medieval fortresses were transformed into magnificent playgrounds; nobility entertained in mirrored halls, seduced each other in gaudy apartments, and hunted on endless grounds. If you could write a book about each one, flamboyant Chambord might appear in an adventure novel, graceful Chenonceau in a romance, and fairy-tale Villandry in a Renaissance classic. Blois and Cheverny merit a visit for their gilded interiors, Azay-le-Rideau for its perfectly-manicured gardens, Angers for its episodic tapestries. Seeing all the major ones will take five or six days. With major train lines running from Paris through Orléans, Blois, and Amboise to Tours, and from Nantes through Angers, Saumur, Tours, and Chenonceaux, the region is ideal for train travelers. Four of the most spectacular châteaux, though—Ussé, Villandry, Cheverny, and Chambord—can be reached only by bike, tour bus, or thumb. Bus tours leave Tours to tour two to four castles (80-175F). In Blois you can buy a bus pass (½ day 50F, students 35F; full day 100F, students 70F) and visit up to three castles on your own itinerary. Visit the tourist offices in Tours and Blois for information.

Unquestionably the best way to see the valley is by bike. Distances are relatively short, and the terrain is flat and lush. Train stations at Amboise, Blois, Chinon, Langeais, and Tours rent bikes for 50F per day, with a 500F deposit, and you can often drop a bike off at a different station (inquire when you rent). SNCF's *Train plus Vélo* brochure has extremely helpful information on rail/bike itineraries. Hitching to the isolated châteaux, such as Chambord and Chenonceau, is difficult. Fortunately, many châteaux lie near well-traveled roads; snaring a ride to these spots is easier.

The Loire Valley caches particularly pleasing **IYHF auberges de jeunesse** in Saumur, Blois, Chinon, Orléans, and Beaugency. Those in Tours, Amboise, and Angers are less distinguished. Ask any tourist office for the blue book listing hours and prices for all the region's attractions and the green book listing the area's many campgrounds. Blois, Amboise, and Chinon make comfortable bases for daytrips; Tours is the most convenient but the least appealing, due to its modern feel.

Orléans

In 1429, Joan of Arc wrested Orléans, then the most important city in France after Paris, from the English. Today, the city proudly sports her name on restaurants, cafés, and hotels. Though an industrial center now, its cathedral and museums distract agreeably on the way to château country. **Cathédrale Ste-Croix** will knock your tattered socks off with its lacy spires, stained-glass windows and Carolingian floor mosaic. (Open daily 9am-noon and 2-6pm.) The **Maison de Jeanne d'Arc,** 3, pl. de Gaulle, features period costumes and an audio-visual re-creation of the siege of Orléans. (Open Tues.-Sun. 10am-noon and 2-6pm; Nov.-April Tues.-Sun. 2-6pm. Admission 8F, students 4F.) When you tire of churches and museums, take bus S from place Albert 1*er* to the **Parc Floral,** a peaceful garden of purple irises and tulips. (Open daily 9am-7pm; Nov. 12-March 2-5pm. Admission 16F, students 8F.)

The tourist office, pl. Albert 1*er* (tel. 38 53 05 95), next to the train station, sponsors walking tours and books accommodations for 6F (open daily 9am-7pm; Sept.-June Mon.-Sat. 9am-7pm). One of the brightest spots in Orléans is the homey, well-appointed **auberge de jeunesse** at 14, rue Faubourg Madeleine (tel. 38 62 45 75), on the west side of town; take bus B (direction "Paul-Bert") from in front of the train station, or walk—about 15 min. (Reception open 7-9:30am and 5:30-10pm. 34F.) The owner of the **Hôtel de Paris,** 29, rue du Faubourg Bannier, likes to speak English and keeps clean rooms with firm, new mattresses. (Singles 90F. Doubles 110F. Showers 10F. Breakfast 17F.) **Hôtel Coligny,** 80, rue de la Gare, (tel. 38 53 61 60) about 15 minutes from the station, has bright, spotless rooms. (Singles and doubles 95-120F, all with shower. Breakfast 16F.)

Blois

Though Blois's château is right in the middle of town, diehard Eurail users should still head to Tours, from where more châteaux are accessible by rail. The **Château de Blois** was constructed over four centuries, which explains the almost absurd juxtaposition of different architectural styles. The spiral staircase crawls with King François I's stone salamanders. (Open daily 9am-6pm; Oct.-May 9:30am-noon and 2-5pm. Admission 27F, students 15F.) A medium-sized city bursting at its seams, Blois wedges in attractive churches and gardens. The **Abbaye St-Lomer** impresses inside and out, a tinted hodgepodge of Renaissance and Gothic. Don't miss the old quarter around the **Cathédrale St-Louis.**

The **tourist office,** 3, av. Jean Laigret (tel. 54 74 06 49 or 54 78 23 21), will change money (22F commission) and book rooms (5F fee). (Open Mon.-Sat. 9am-7pm, Sun. 10am-1pm and 4-7pm; Oct.-March Mon.-Sat. 9am-noon and 2-6pm.) Ask here about bus passes to create your own itinerary to colossal Chambord, refined Cheverny, graceful Chenonceau, and lofty Amboise. (Half-day pass 50F, students 35F; one-day pass 100F, students 70F.) Accommodations in Blois fill up fast. The homey and rustic **auberge de jeunesse (IYHF),** 18, rue de l'Hôtel Pasquier (tel. 54 78 27 21), is 5km from the station, surrounded by forest. Take bus #4 from pl. Valin by the river. (Lockout 10am-6pm. 39F. Open March to mid-Nov.) **Hôtel St. Nicolas,** 2, rue de Sermon (tel. 54 78 05 85) has correct, quiet rooms near the church. (Singles 95F. Doubles 125F. Showers 12F. Breakfast 19F). **Le Pavillon,** 2, av. Wilson (tel. 54 74 23 27), on the edge of the Loire across the bridge, has bright, spacious rooms. (1-3 bed rooms 85-150F. Showers 15F. Breakfast 25F.) You'll receive a warm welcome to Blois near the train station at the **Hôtel St-Jacques,** 7, rue Ducoux (tel. 54 78 04 15). (Singles and doubles 130F. Bath 15F. Particularly good breakfast 22F.)

Eating is most blissful on lively, restaurant- and bar-lined rue Foulerie; try **La Tosca,** at #36 with bubbling fondues from 68F in a cozy ambience. (Open daily noon-2pm and 7-11:30pm.) **Le Maidi,** 42, rue St-Lubin, serves traditional 50 and

70F *menus* as well as *couscous* (38-65F), all in the shadow of the château. (Open Fri.-Wed. 11:30am-2:30pm and 7-10pm.)

Blois to Tours

Built by François I for his frequent hunting trips and orgiastic fêtes, **Chambord** is the largest and most extravagant of the Loire châteaux, the peak of French Renaissance culture. Access to the expansive grounds and surrounding wildlife preserve is free and unlimited. Seven hundred of François I's calling-card stone salamanders, symbols of bravery, lurk on Chambord's walls, ceilings and ingenious double-helix staircase. 365 fireplaces scattered throughout the 400 rooms create a miniature rooftop city of decorated chimneys. (Open daily 9:30am-6:45pm; Sept.-June 9:30-11:45am and 2-4:45pm. Admission 30F, students 16F, children 5F.) Chambord is accessible by bus, bike, or thumb from Blois: take the D956 south for 2-3km and turn left onto the D33 for 11km.

Cheverny, also served by bus from Blois, soothes with stately classical lines and the most elegant interior of all the châteaux. A compound on the ground houses 70 bloodhounds; watch them ravenously devour their dinner. (Mon-Sat. at 5pm; Sept. 16-March Mon. and Wed.-Fri. at 3pm. Château open daily 9:15am-6:45pm; Sept. 16-May 9:30am-noon and 2:15-5pm. Admission 25F, students 18F.) Those hitching to Cheverny from Blois follow the D956 south.

Turreted, moated, and drawbridged **Chaumont-sur-Loire** serves as a reminder that castles were first built to defend kingdoms, not to star in TV specials. The château is also known for its luxurious *écuries* (stables). (Château open daily 9am-6pm; Oct.-May 9:15-11:35am and 1:45-3:50pm. Admission 23F, students 12F.) Take a train from Blois (5 per day, 10 min., 15F) or Tours to Onzain, across the river 2km north of Chaumont.

The château at **Amboise** marks the beginning of the decorative Renaissance style which later inspired Blois and Chambord. Much of the castle has decayed through neglect over the years, but what remains is richly decorated. Leonardo da Vinci spent the last three years of his life in the nearby Clos Lucé, and his bones are said to rest in the flamboyant **Chapelle St-Hubert,** the gem of the château's remaining structures. The required tour (French or English) includes the chapel, the Logis du Roi, and the Tours des Minimes, a giant five-story spiral ramp for bringing horses and carriages to the château. (Open daily 9am-6:30pm; Sept.-June 9am-noon and 2-5pm. Admission 27F, students 17F.) You can also visit the **Clos-Lucé,** where Leonardo painted, pondered and invented; IBM has made models from his sketches, which include inventions that presaged the modern paddle steam boat, the airplane and the stick-shift car. (Open daily Feb.-Dec. 9am-7pm. Adults 30F, students 22F.) Amboise has a comfortable **auberge de jeunesse** (tel. 47 57 06 36) on the delightful Ile d'Or. (44F, sheets 26F. May close for Sun. and Mon. arrivals; call ahead.) About half the trains on the Blois-Tours route stop midway at Amboise.

The graceful château of **Chenonceau** arches effortlessly over the languid river Cher. Three women overlooked and influenced the construction of this romantic palace: Catherine Briçonnet, Diane de Poitiers (Henri II's mistress), and Catherine de Médicis (Henri's wife). (Ms. Médicis forcefully evicted Diane from the château after Henri's death.) You can walk through the well-renovated rooms on your own, soothed by soft Renaissance music, or row under the arches of the gallery that spans the river. During WWII, the Cher marked the division between German-annexed France and the puppet state of Vichy France, and Chenonceau served as an escape passageway for thousands of refugees fleeing the Nazis. (Château open daily in summer 9am-7pm; in off-season 9am-noon and 2-4:30pm. Admission 30F, students 20F.) The only reasonable accommodation in town is the two-star **Hostel du Roy,** near the château (tel. 47 23 90 17; singles and doubles 140F). From Tours, three trains per day (towards Vierzon, not Blois) travel to town (¾ hr., 28.50F); the castle is 2km from the station.

Tours

Tours is an island of industry in a sea of lush farmland and vineyards. The city offers visitors frequent bus and train links to nearby châteaux, an energetic student crowd, a glitzy pedestrian zone, cheap hotels, and an attractive *vieille ville.* From the two remaining massive towers of the **Basilique St-Martin,** walk along rue du Change to pl. Plumereau, lined with 15th-century wooden houses where the student population hangs out. To the east, **Cathédrale St-Gatien** looms on lofty buttresses. (Open daily 8:30am-noon and 2-8pm; in off-season until 5pm.) Tours's **tourist office** (tel. 47 05 58 08) is in the Hôtel de Ville, straight out of the station and to the left on the bd. Heurteloup. The staff provides a supermarket of services and speaks English. (Open Mon.-Sat. 8:30am-8pm, Sun. 10am-noon and 3-6pm; in off-season Mon.-Sat. 9am-noon and 2-6pm.)

Tours's **auberge de jeunesse (IYHF)** (tel. 47 25 14 45), 5km from town and accessible via buses #2 and 6 from pl. Jean Jaurès (turn left as you exit the station), is cavernous and comfortable with kitchen facilities and a lively crowd. (Lockout 10:30am-5pm. Curfew 11pm, but the last bus leaves town at 8:30pm. 54F, includes breakfast.) **Hôtel Vendôme,** 24, rue Roger-Salengro (tel. 47 64 33 54), is a splendid crash-pad one block off av. Grammont. (Singles 90F. Doubles 95F.) Or try **Mon Hôtel,** 40, rue de la Préfecture (tel. 47 05 67 53; singles and doubles 80-130F). Rue Blaise Pascal near the station has a string of slightly seedy hotels. Better than most of them, **Hôtel de Lys d'Or,** 21-23 rue de la Vendée, has spic 'n' span rooms; the owner will give you a 3% discount upon presentation of your *Let's Go* book. (Singles and doubles 83-130F.)

Tasty feasts are yours around rue Colbert and the old quarter around pl. de la Lamproie. **Aux Trois Canards,** 16, rue de la Rotisserie, serves elegant dinners for 45-70F, and a three-course 45F *menu,* wine included. Join the local proletariat at **Le Foyer,** 16, rue Palissy, where the student discount cuts the price of four courses to 35.50F. (Open Mon.-Fri. 11am-1:30pm and 7-8pm, Sat.-Sun. 11:45am-1:30pm; Aug. Mon.-Fri. 11:45am-1:30pm and 7-8pm, Sat. 11:45am-1:30pm.)

Tours to Anger

Easily accessible by train from Tours is the pastoral **Azay-le-Rideau,** a graceful château on the River Indre. Trees and a picturesque moat surround the castle's white stone towers, fairytale battlements, and Renaissance *loggia.* (Château open daily July-Aug. 9:45am-6:45pm; April-June 9:30am-6pm, Sept. 9:30am-12:30pm and 2-5:45pm; Jan.-March and Oct.-Dec. 10am-12:15pm and 2-4:45pm. Admission 24F, students 13F.) In Azay-le-Rideau, rent a 10-speed steed at **Le Provost,** 13, rue Carnot (tel. 47 45 40 94), to make the peaceful half-hour ride to green **Villandry** . (Bicycles 36F per day. Shop open Tues.-Sat. 8am-noon.) At Villandry, the star attractions are the magnificent formal gardens, three terraces of sculpted shrubs, flowers, and vegetables; the château is interesting, but pales in comparison. (Open mid-March to Nov. 15 daily 9am-6pm; gardens open year-round 9am-7pm. Admission 34F, students 26F; 12F less if you skip the château.)

Ussé, engulfed by the thick woods of the Forêt de Chinon, is also an easy bike trip from Azay. Its pointed towers, white turrets and chimneys inspired *Sleeping Beauty;* you don't have to take the tour to see the models of the story, in 18th- and 19th-century French costume. Today the château is still home to a marquis. (Open March-Nov. daily 9am-noon and 2-7pm. Admission 44F.) Just west of Tours and connected to Ussé by a pastoral cyclist's dream-road (the D16) is the feudal and forbidding **Langeais.** Notice the stone slabs along the upper fortifications, which, when drawn back, reveal holes for hurling boiling oil at attackers. Trains run from Saumur (24F) and Tours (21F).

Farther from Tours is delightful **Chinon.** Its ruined château will nudge your mind into the past while the wine-tasting establishments in the *vieille ville* brighten (or blur) the present. Relatively unmolested by tourists, Chinon also has a fantastic **auberge de jeunesse** on rue Descartes (tel. 47 93 10 48), a five-minute walk from the station. (Reception open 6-10:30pm. Lockout 2-6pm. 42F, sheets 15F.)

About 30km northwest of Chinon, a massive 14th-century wedding cake of a château cuts an imposing profile above the town of **Saumur.** (Open June 15-Sept. 15 daily 9am-6:30pm; Sept. 16-30 and April-June 14 9am-noon and 2-6pm, Oct.-March Wed.-Mon. 10am-noon and 2-5pm. Admission 23F, students 13F, 2F extra July-Aug.) France's elite equestrian order, the Cadre Noir, resides here. Many wine and mushroom caves surround Saumur, where locals produce a famous sparkling wine and cultivate 70% of France's mushrooms. Ask at the **tourist office,** pl. Bilange (tel. 41 51 03 06) for information about horse exhibitions, wine *dégustations,* and fungus tours. An excellent, modern **auberge de jeunesse** (tel. 41 67 45 00) is on Ile d'Offard, between the station and town center, with a free swimming pool and an inspiring view of the château. (Reception open 8-10am and 5-10pm. 39F per night. Sheets 21F. Breakfast 16F.) Saumur is towards the Angers end of the Tours-Angers rail line.

Angers

Angers's massive stone walls, guarding the western gateway to the château region, once daunted Norman hordes; today they remain imposing despite a stifling urban onslaught. Yet since their construction, the 17 formidable towers have been truncated and toppled, and the deep moat's waters replaced with formal gardens and a deer park. Inside, the priceless **Tapestries of the Apocalypse** depict the Book of Revelations. Spun in gold thread, this tour de force of medieval art is large enough to carpet a small street. (Château open 9am-7pm; Sept. 16- May 9am-12:30pm and 2-6pm. Admission 24F, students 13F.)

Angers's **tourist office** (tel. 41 88 69 93), across from the château, organizes castle trips and changes money when banks are closed. (Open Mon.-Sat. 9am-7pm, Sun. 10:30am-6:30pm; Oct.-May Mon.-Sat. 9am-12:30pm and 2-6:30pm.) There is a **Foyer des Jeunes Travailleurs** on rue Darwin (tel. 41 48 14 55), 4km from the station. Take bus #8, direction "Beaucouzé" to "CFA." (Curfew 11pm. 40F per person.) Excellent accommodation awaits at the **Centre d'Accueil du Lac du Maine,** (tel. 41 48 57 01), rte. des Pruviers; take bus #6 from the station. (54F per night; breakfast 16F.) The cordial, clean **La Coupe d'Or,** 5, rue de la Gare (tel. 41 88 45 02), is one of the best deals near the train station (100-150F).

Appetizing eateries garnish the pedestrian district around pl. Romaine. **Le Petit Mâchon,** 43, rue Bressigny, serves wonderfully French fare to typically French people. (57F *menu* features specialties like pig's feet, *escargots,* or French onion soup.) **Le Spirit Factory,** 14-16, rue Bressigny, serves mussels (47-59F) any which way but loose in a fun factory interior, where the owner displays the Dr. Seuss-like machinery in which he brews the house beer and ferments stray mussels.

Southwestern France

Comfortably beyond Paris's outstretched metropolitan tentacles, southwestern France enjoys a spiritual and cultural independence of which the northern regions can only dream. Bordeaux's vineyards provide wine for the world, while Biarritz, the Monte-Carlo of western France, is an arrogant old-style resort that has raised the *grande promenade* to a decadent art form. Nearby Bayonne, the political center of France's Basques, is home to a pleasing collection of French, Italian, and Spanish art. Thronged with tourists, though, none of these larger towns give any hint of the whitewashed farmhouses of the Basque interior or the sheepy Pyrenean villages further on. Punch onward (and inland) to the misty mountains, thick with memories of Cathar heretics who pitted the entire region against the papacy in the 13th century, and come down from the hills to the medieval fortress at Carcassonne and the Romanesque cathedrals of Toulouse.

Périgord-Quercy

This region's forested hills, serene river valleys, and dramatic cliffs first attracted paleolithic man 150,000 years ago. The cave paintings and engravings, skeletons, and other artifacts that these ancient civilizations left behind have revealed more about prehistory than any other region on earth. Today, the Dordogne, Vézère, Isle and Lot rivers snake past more modern vestiges: 12th-century Byzantine-Romanesque churches, chapels clinging to the rocks in the pilgrimage town of Rocamadour, *bastides* (fortified mountaintop towns) built during the Hundred Years War, and the pastoral villages near Sarlat and Périgueux. Périgord-Quercy also boasts some of the finest gastronomy in France. Though *foie gras* (fat liver) and *cèpes* and *truffes* (mushrooms sniffed out by pigs) are beyond the budgeteer's range, *confit de canard* (potted duck leg cooked in its own fat) is not. Canoe rentals abound throughout the region, as do *chambres d'hôtes* (farmhouse accommodation).

The capital of Périgord, **Périgueux** is a good base for the caves. The town receives several trains a day from Bordeaux (1½ hr., 82F), Limoges (1 hr., 65F, with connections to Paris), and Toulouse (161F; change at Agen). In town, modern façades mask the labyrinthine *vieille ville* and the multiply-domed **Cathédrale St-Front.** Ask the **tourist office,** 26, pl. Francheville (tel. 53 53 10 63), about buses to the bucolic village of **Brantôme,** and pick up the indispensable brochure *La Fête en Périgord.* (Open Mon.-Fri. 8:30am-noon and 1-7pm, Sat. 9am-noon and 2-5pm.) The cramped and poorly marked **Foyer des Jeunes Travailleurs** (Résidence Lakanal; tel. 53 53 52 05), just behind the Club Municipal de Loisirs et Culture at the end of rue des Thèmes, won't thrill you, but it's darn cheap. From the station (20 min.), turn right and follow the tracks; when you reach bd. Lakanal, turn right to find the tracks, and look to your right for the *foyer.* (Reception open Mon.-Fri. 4-8pm, Sat.-Sun. noon-1pm and 7-8pm. 4-bed rooms 55F per person. Singles 70F. Showers and breakfast included.) On rue Denis-Papin, the lower the numbers, the higher the prices and quality. The **Hôtel des Voyageurs** (tel. 53 53 17 44), opposite the train station, at #22, replaces showers with plenty of space. (Singles and doubles 65-90F.) There's always camping 1½km away in Boulazac at **Barnabé-Plage,** 80 rue des Bains (tel. 53 53 41 45). Hop the city bus (direction "Cité Belaire") from the station or from cours Montaigne. (11.50F per person, 10.50F per tent.)

Febus, 11, rue Notre-Dame, attracts a young, local crowd with daily 28-32F *plats du jour* and chili (32F). **La Grignotière,** rue du Ruy Limogeanne, serves hearty salads in a quiet courtyard. Try the *salade de Périgord,* topped with duck, walnuts, and *foie gras.* (Open Mon.-Sat. noon-2pm and 7:15-9pm.)

Four trains per day from Périgueux (30-45 min., 33F; on the Toulouse line) make **Les Eyzies-de-Tayac** a perfect daytrip. Prehistoric caves—crowded to the bursting point from July to mid-September—conceal fascinating paintings and carvings, and spectacular stalagmites and stalactites. Get here by 8am (on the 7:14 train from Périgueux) to buy a ticket; prepare to kill time before your guided visit starts. The best paintings near town are at the **Grotte de Font de Gaume** (tel. 53 06 97 48), just outside of town, where 20,000-year-old horses, bison, reindeer, and woolly mammoth cavort along the walls of the cave. (Open Wed.-Mon. 9-11:15am and 2-5:15pm; Oct.-March Wed.-Mon. 10-11:15am and 2-3:15pm. Admission 24F, ages 18-25 and over 60 13F, artists and art students free. Tickets go *fast.)* In town, the **Musée National de La Préhistoire** has an excellent collection of paintings, carvings, skeletons, and other fascinating artifacts. (Open Wed.-Mon. 9:30am-6pm, Sept.-June Wed.-Mon. 9:30am-noon and 2-5pm. Admission 16F, ages 18-25 and over 60 8F.)

Rent bikes at Les Eyzies station or at the **tourist office** in pl. de la Mairie (tel. 53 06 97 05; open July-Aug. Mon.-Sat. 9am-7pm, Sun. 10am-noon and 2-6pm;

March-June and Sept.-Nov. Mon.-Sat. 9am-noon and 2-6pm; Jan.-Feb. Tues. and Thurs. 9am-noon and 2-6pm). Hotels in Les Eyzies are booked solid in summer, try the idyllic *gîte d'étape* at **Ferme des Eymaries,** route de St-Cirq (tel. 53 06 94 73). From the center of town, head out route de Périgueux, cross the train tracks and the River Vézère, and take route de St-Cirq on your left; after 1½km, turn right just before more tracks, and follow the signs for 1km. (32F. Breakfast 17F. Open April-Oct. daily 6pm-10am.)

Despite the dense mobs that swarm **Sarlat** each summer, its remarkable *vieille ville,* a sculpture of golden sandstone with an uncommon medieval atmosphere, is worth the visit, and its Saturday market is renowned throughout France. One or two buses per day (½ hr., 18.50F) run north to **Montignac,** where the nearby man-made **Lascaux II** cave convincingly impersonates **Lascaux,** the largest cave paintings on earth—themselves closed to the public since 1963 due to devastating deterioration. (Open July-Aug. daily 9:30am-7pm; Feb.-June and mid-Sept. to mid-Dec. Tues.-Sun. 10am-noon and 2-5pm. Buy tickets at 9am on pl. Tourny. Admission 35F.) Stop by Sarlat's **tourist office,** pl. de la Liberté (tel. 53 59 27 67) for the crucial *Guide Pratique* (open Mon.-Sat. 9am-7pm, Sun. 10am-noon and 3-6pm; Sept. 16-June 14 Mon.-Sat. 9am-noon and 2-6pm) and information on **Hep! Excursions** daytrips to nearby towns (including Lascaux II; 100-140F).

Sarlat's **auberge de jeunesse (IYHF),** 15 bis, av. de Selves (tel. 53 59 47 59), 30 min. from the train station but only 10 min. from the *centre ville,* has an easy-going atmosphere and outdoor showers and toilets. (Lockout 10:30am-6pm. 39F per person. Sheets 14F. Camping site 20F. Open July-Oct. 15.) **Hôtel des Rêcollets,** 4, rue Jean-Jacques Rousseau (tel. 53 59 00 49), has spotless rooms in the quiet half of the *vieille ville.* (Singles and doubles 150F, with shower 175F. Breakfast 30F.) Camp at **Les Acacias** (tel. 53 59 29 30) on the D47, 2½km from town. (16F per person, 15F per tent. Electricity 12F. Open Easter-Oct. 15.) **Restaurant du Commerce,** 4, rue Albérie Cahuet, has a filling and typical 50F *menu* (including *confit de canard)* on one of the liveliest terraces in town. Rent bikes (50F per day) or mopeds (85F per day) at **Garage Matigot,** 52, av. Gambetta (tel. 53 59 03 60; open Tues.-Sat. 9am-noon and 2-6:30pm). The train station also rents bikes (50F per day). Trains run to Périgueux (63F) and Bordeaux, and inconveniently timed **Transpérigord** buses (railpasses not valid) connect Sarlat to Souillac on the Paris-Toulouse train line (3-4 per day, 50 min., 23.50F).

Another dramatic collaboration of nature and artifact, the town of **Rocamadour** hangs off a cliff in the Alzou Canyon. The miraculous setting befits a town famous for centuries as a pilgrims' destination. **Le Grand Escalier** climbs from the town's one street; some devouts still journey here to kneel at each of its 216 steps. At the top hovers the **Cité Religieuse,** a complex of chapels including the **Chapelle de Notre-Dame,** home to the venerated Black Virgin and the **Chapelle St-Michel** (tip the guide 1-2F), where the supposed sword of Roland and the rock it's stuck in hang above the door. Female and single? Legend holds that if you touch this sword you'll find your prince within the year. (Cité open June-Sept. 9am-noon and 2-6pm. Call 65 33 63 29 in the off-season.) Perched precariously at the top of the cliff—and more zigzagging steps—is the 14th-century **château.** Its ramparts are open to the public and command exceptional views of the valley. (Open July-Aug. 9am-7pm; April-June and Sept.-Oct. 9am-noon and 1:30-8pm. Admission 6F, under 18 4F.) Elevators ascend to both *Cité* and château every three minutes (24F). Rocamadour is most easily reached via Brive-la-Gaillarde, to the north on the Paris-Toulouse line; trains run 5 times per day (45 min., 35F). Coming from Sarlat or Souillac, take a bus to St-Denis-Près-Martel, then a train. A taxi (tel. 65 33 62 12) will shuttle you the 5km from the Rocamadour train station to **L'Hospitalet,** just above Rocamadour proper, for a steep 30F. Vans (min. 8 people) charge 9F per person. Walking or renting a bike (50F per day at the station) is easy and oh-so-scenic.

Bordeaux

Like many of the fine vintage reds for which it is renowned, Bordeaux has grown noticeably darker with age, an apparent victim of its own success. The thin layer of grime which coats the city's once-resplendent high Gothic cathedrals bespeaks a rapid, post-haste industrialization. Historically, Eleanor of Aquitaine's 12th-century marriage to Henry Platagenet resulted in a then much cleaner port city falling under English hegemony. In ensuing years, the British weakness for smooth *vin rouge* followed the rising star of the *bordelais* merchants, until the town's ultimate annexation to France in 1453. Though naysayers may tell you otherwise, Bordeaux's twinkle is far from defunct: the *bordelais* are scrubbing down their monuments, and city planners are in the midst of expanding this globally acclaimed wine center.

Orientation and Practical Information

Bordeaux is 40km inland from France's Atlantic coast, about 200km north of the Spanish border. The city is crawling with tourists in the summer and pickpockets all year; watch your valuables. **Rue Ste-Catherine** connects **place de la Victoire** and **place de la Comédie,** the city's two main squares. Buses #7 and 8 connect the train station with the *centre ville.*

Tourist Office: 12, cours du 30 Juillet (tel. 56 44 28 41). Take bus #7 or 8 from the train station and get off at pl. de la Comédie. Office is 50m ahead on the right. Sells Carte Jeune (100F) and 1-day bus tickets (18F). Take the wine-tasting tour of nearby vineyards (mid-May to mid-Oct. daily at 1:45pm; 100F, students 85F). Open Mon.-Sat. 9am-7pm, Sun. and holidays 9am-3pm; Oct.-May Mon.-Sat. 9am-6:30pm. Info booth at train station open Mon.-Sat. 9am-12:30pm and 1:30-6pm; Sun. 9am-3pm. Oct.-May closed Sun. **Centre d'Information Jeunesse d'Aquitaine,** 5, rue Duffour-Dubergier (tel. 56 48 55 50). Reams of info on campgrounds, hostels, and activities. BIJ and other train tickets, *cartes jeunes.* Job-related enquiries must be made in person. Open Mon.-Fri. 9am-6pm.

Currency Exchange: Thomas Cook, at the train station (tel. 56 91 58 80). Open daily 8am-8pm. On Sat. try the main **post office** (open 8am-noon).

American Express: 14, cours de l'Intendance (tel. 56 81 70 02). Sweet rates and 10F commission fee. Open Mon.-Fri. and Sun. 8:45am-noon and 1:30-6pm.

Post Office: 52, rue Georges Bonnac (tel. 56 48 87 48). Open Mon.-Fri. 8am-7pm, Sat. 8am-noon. Branch office on cours de la Marne, 5 blocks from the station. **Postal Code:** 33000.

Trains: Gare St-Jean, rue Charles Domercq (tel. 56 92 50 50). To: Paris (10-14 per day, 4½-5½ hr., 260F); Poitiers (10-14 per day, 2½ hr., 133F); Nantes (5-8 per day, 4 hr., 187F); Angoulême (8-12 per day, 1 hr., 79F); Bayonne (6 per day, 2 hr., 110F). Showers in station 15F. Information office open daily 8am-8pm.

Buses: Citram, 14, rue Fondaudege (tel. 56 81 18 18), in the center. The principal regional carrier. To: Libourne (Mon.-Sat. 15-18 per day, 45 min., 30F); St-Emilion (5-7 per day, 1¼ hr., 32F); and most nearby towns. Open Mon.-Sat. 9am-noon and 2-6:15pm. Urban buses, **CGFTE,** 25, rue du Commandant Marchand (tel. 56 24 23 23), cost 7F. Ask for a schedule at the tourist office, and snag your Carte Bordeaux Decouverte, good for 1 day of travel (18F; 3 days 43F, with Carte Jeune 21.50F). Also available at train station.

Bookstore: Bradley's Bookshop, 32, pl. Gambetta. Wide selection of regional travel guides, dictionaries, and more. Open Mon. 2-7pm, Tues.-Sat. 9:30am-12:30pm and 2-7pm.

Laundromat: cours de la Marne, 3 min. from station. Wash 15-16F, dry 2F per 5 min. Open daily 7am-10pm.

Medical Assistance: Hospital/Clinic St-André, 1, rue Jean Burguet (tel. 56 79 56 79) or **SAMU** ambulance service (tel. 56 96 70 70).

Accommodations, Camping, and Food

The *accueil* bureau *(quai* #1 in the train station) provides maps and accommodation listings. Call ahead in July and August.

Auberge de Jeunesse Foyer Barbey (IYHF), 22, cours Barbey (tel. 56 91 59 51). From station (10 min.), bear right diagonally, then turn left onto cours de la Marne, then left again onto cours Barbey. Business-like management, well-eqiupped kitchen, bright bathrooms, commodious 8-bed quarters, Reception open 7-9:30am and 6-11pm. 9:30am-6pm lockout, 11pm curfew. 37F, nonmembers 42F. 5F beers and sandwiches in main-floor lounge.

Maison des Etudiants, 50, rue Ligier (tel. 56 96 48 30). Take bus #7 or 8 from the train station to Bourse du Travail (7F), then continue in the same direction on cours de la Libération to rue Ligier, on the right. Or walk right from the station onto cours de la Marne to pl. de la Victoire; pick up cours Aristide-Briand (straight across the *place),* which becomes cours de la Libération; look to your right for rue Ligier (30 min.). The auberge is fine, but this is finer. Women only Oct.-June, but open to men as well July-Aug. TV and kitchen facilities. Singles 45F, non-students 55F. Showers and sheets included.

Hôtel la Boëtie, 4, rue de la Boëtie (tel. 56 81 76 68), on a quiet street between pl. Gambetta and the Musée des Beaux Arts. Attentive management lends personal touch to spacious, comfortable rooms with bedside TV, mini-bar and telephone. 24-hr. video rental. Singles 95-110F. Doubles 120-145F. Triples 160F. All rooms with shower. Breakfast 18F, English-style (with green eggs and ham) 15F extra.

Hôtel-Bar-Club Les 2 Mondes, 10, rue St-Vincent-de-Paul (tel. 56 91 63 09). One block from train station. Immaculate rooms well-maintained by English proprietor. Daily happy hour at adjoining bar (beers 8F from 7-8pm). Singles 82F, with shower 100F. Doubles 98F, with shower 120-130F. Triples 180F. No hall showers. Breakfast 17F. Reservations held until 6pm.

Hôtel d'Amboise, 22, rue de la Vieille Tour (tel. 56 81 62 67), in *centre ville.* Tempting, clean, bright rooms overlooking a busy side-street. A few singles 70F. Doubles 75-85F, with shower 100-110F. Showers 8F. Breakfast 18F. Open 7am-9:30pm.

Camping: Camping les Gravières, Pont-de-la-Maye (tel. 56 87 00 36), in Villeneuve D'Ornon. In a riverside forest. 16F per person, 15F per tent. Open 8am-11pm.

Bordeaux, known in France as *la région de bien manger et de bien vivre* (the region of fine eating and living), has some of the most affordable restaurants in France, especially in pl. St-Michel, between *centre ville* and the station. **Café les Arts,** 138, cours Victor Hugo, at the intersection with rue Ste-Catherine, is a perpetually busy sidewalk *brasserie* with lamb or chicken *basquaise* for 42F (bar at rear; open daily 9am-1am). **L'Athenée** is a small, intimate retreat one block east of the cathedral with mouth-watering three-course menus starting at 41F. (Open Mon.-Fri. noon-2pm and 8-10:30pm, Sat. noon-2pm). Call CROUS at 56 91 98 80 for information on university cafeterias, where you can eat for 25F. (Open Oct.-Aug. Sun.-Fri. 11:40am-1:30pm and 6:40-8:10pm.)

Sights

Nine hundred years after its consecration by Pope Urban II, **Cathédrale St-André** remains the grandfather of Bordeaux's high Gothic masterpieces. Amble in for free organ concerts every other Tuesday evening from mid-June to mid-September. Adjacent to the **Church of St-Michel** is the equally elegant, free-standing bell tower; if you ever wondered what flamboyant Gothic was all about, just look up. Bordeaux's Romanesque **Church of Ste-Croix** has a richly ornamented façade. The **Musée d'Aquitaine,** 20, cours Pasteur, houses a comprehensive collection of *bordelais* agricultural, maritime, and commercial treasures. During a recent initiation of new archaeological exhibits, the museum brought the French minister of culture to Bordeaux. (Open Wed.-Mon. 10am-6pm. Admission 13F, students 6F. Wed. free.) The small **Musée des Beaux Arts** (near the cathedral) houses works by Delacroix, Corot, Renoir, and Matisse. (Open Wed.-Mon. 10am-noon and 2-6pm. Admission 13F, students 6F, Wed. free.) The **Maison du Vin,** 1, cours du 30 Juillet (tel. 56 52 82 82), pours free tastings of regional labels, answers any wine questions, and distributes a list of smaller châteaux in the area. Inquire about screening times for their 15-minute film on *bordelais* wines. (Open Mon.-Fri. 8:30am-6pm, Sat. 9am-12:30pm and 1:30-5pm.)

Near Bordeaux

Visiting the major wine-producing châteaux requires an advance phone call; only some smaller châteaux allow impromptu visits. Few offer free samples. **Château Haut-Briand,** the largest winery near Bordeaux, tends to cater to a high-falutin clientele for whom reservations are immeasurably easier to come by. Contact the tourist office in **St-Emilion** (tel. 57 24 72 03) for tours of the surrounding châteaux or the village's spectacular **Eglise Monolithe,** an underground behemoth painstakingly carved from a single, massive rock. Wine tours may also be arranged by enlisting the help of the Bordeaux tourist office. Trains connect St-Emilion with Bordeaux (2 per day, 45 min., 39F).

Trains leave Bordeaux's Gare St-Jean for **Arcachon** (24 per day, 45 min., 39F), the first leg of a daytrip to the **Dune du Pilat.** A mountain of sand that brings out the acrobat in everyone, the Dune is possibly the most sublime beach in the world. Its 60 sandy tons, 104-114m high, pose an encroaching threat to the homes lying at its base. Rent bikes at the Arcachon station (40F per ½ day, 50F per day, deposit 500F). Buses leave from the Arcachon station for Pyla-sur-Mer (about 20 per day, last return around 7:45pm, 40 min., 7.50F), which is a 10- to 15-minute walk from the Dune; continue in the direction the bus was traveling, climbing to the left.

Toulouse

Known to natives as *"La Ville Rose,"* an epithet honoring the city's red-brick architecture and alluding to its leftist poltical tendencies, the heart of Languedoc palpitates with youthful vitality and the spicy influences of Spanish and North African immigrants. Against this full-throttle backdrop, Toulouse earnestly strives to maintain dominance as France's aeronautics research center *par excellence,* the hometown of Ariane rockets and the Airbus jumbo jet.

Perenially a bastion of Catholicism in a Protestant region, Toulouse boasts an assemblage of distinctive churches, inimitable in style and grace. The **Basilique St-Sernin,** on rue du Taur, is France's largest and most prodigious Romanesque cathedral. (Open Mon.-Sat. 8-11:45am and 2-5:45pm, Sun. 2-5:45pm. Admission 8F. Subterranean crypt open 10-11:30am and 2:30-5pm. Admission 8F.) The **Eglise Notre-Dame-du-Taur,** named for Toulouse's first priest, Saturnin, who was tied to a bull's tail and dragged to martyrdom, also looms down the rue du Taur. In the austere interior of **Les Jacobins,** rue Lakanal, amber colonettes run up a row of thin columns and from the vaults, creating a dazzling rainbow effect against the pale stone. (Church open Mon.-Sat. 10am-noon and 2-6pm, Sun. 2:30-6pm. Admission to cloisters 7F.) The **Musée des Augustins,** rue de Metz, near rue Alsace-Lorraine, exhibits exquisite Romanesque and Gothic sculpture. (Open Mon. and Thurs.-Sat. 10am-noon and 2-6pm, Wed. 10am-noon and 2-10pm, Sun. 2-6pm. Admission 6.50F, Sun. free.) Next to St-Sernin, the **Musée St-Raymond** houses an impressive collection of regional archaeological finds; check out the sculpture gallery of Roman emperors on the entry level. (Open Wed.-Mon. 10am-noon and 2-6pm, Tues. 2-6pm. Admission 7F. Students free.) Many *hôtels particuliers* (mansions) near the Garonne River shelter 17th-century courtyards open to the public; try the opulent **Hôtel d'Assezat** or the gaudy **Hôtel de Pierre.** Stroll down **rue St-Rome's** cobbled walkway past fashionable boutiques and nightclubs as well as the signature towers of the 13th-century governing bourgeoisie, the Capitouls. Place du Capitôle fuses with the student-thronged pl. St-Georges and the cinema-filled pl. Wilson and animates the city day and night. Pick up the free *Regard* magazine for a list of effervescent nightlife hubs.

The **tourist office,** pl. du Capitôle (tel. 61 23 32 00), in the Donjon, changes money when banks are closed and books rooms. (Open daily 9am-7pm; Oct.-April Mon.-Sat. 9am-6pm. Currency exchange May-Sept. Sat.-Sun. and holidays 11am-1pm and 2-4:30pm.) The **auberge de jeunesse Villa des Rosiers,** 125, rue Jean Rieux (tel. 61 80 49 93), is friendly, but remote and a bit rundown. (Pit toilets. 39F. Breakfast

15F. Sheets 14F.) **Hôtel des Arts,** 1bis, rue Cantegrol (tel. 61 23 36 21), at rue des Arts, off pl. St-Georges, is the best of the town's cheap hotels, run by a delightful, English-speaking young couple who'll help find rooms when they're full. (Singles 80F, with shower 120-135F. Doubles 120F, with shower 140-160F. Breakfast 22F.) Room 32 at the **Hôtel du Grand Balcon,** 8, rue Romiguières (tel. 61 21 48 08), at a corner of the pl. du Capitôle, sheltered St-Exupéry (best known for his book *Le Petit Prince)* and his buddies, who piloted mailplanes from Toulouse to Rio and Algiers. (Singles 100F. Doubles 120F, with shower 170F. Quads with shower 185F. Breakfast 20F. Open Sept.-July.)

Daily **markets** line bd. Victor Hugo and bd. Strasbourg (Tues.-Sun. 9am-1pm), and food stands spill over the ground floor of the Parking Victor Hugo, Les Halles. **CROUS,** 7, rue des Salenques (tel. 61 21 13 61) sells university cafeteria meal tickets (10.50F; open Mon.-Fri. 2-4pm, or at the university *guichet,* 11:30am-12:45pm). Inexpensive restaurants stand shoulder-to-shoulder around rue St-Rome, its extension rue des Filatiers, and toward the university on rue du Taur. **Auberge Louis XIII,** 1bis, rue Tripière, with shaded terrace and country cuisine, is a sage choice. *(Menus* 40F and 55F. Open Mon.-Fri. noon-2pm and 7-9:45pm.) **La Tantina de Bourgos,** 27, av. de la Garonnette, is a worthy but lengthy walk from the center. Hearty Spanish specialties include sizzling *paëlla* (60F) and a *bar à tapas* in an unwinding atmosphere. (48F lunch menu. Open Tues.-Sat. noon-1:30pm and 7:30pm-midnight.)

Near Toulouse

Albi (1 rail hr. northeast of Toulouse) has settled into graceful serenity; the bellicose days of Cathar heresy are now a distant memory. The town, which derived its name from the bloody 13th-century Albigensian crusade initiated by the Pope against its population, presides over culture rather than carnage today. The grandiose **Musée de Toulouse-Lautrec,** in the Palais de la Berbie houses a stunning collection of the controversial artist's work—bequeathed by his mother in 1922—including the lithographs which earned him his international reputation. (Open daily 9am-noon and 2-6pm; Oct.-Easter Wed.-Mon. 10am-noon and 2-5pm. Admission 18F, students 9F.) Across from the museum, the enormous **Basilique Ste-Cécile** hides rich Italian frescoes and Burgundian and Gothic statuary. The nearby **Eglise** and **Cloître St-Salvy** provide a fragrant garden and an intimate contrast to the imposing basilica.

The **tourist office,** 19, pl. Ste-Cécile (tel. 63 54 22 30), provides accommodations information (open daily 10am-noon and 2-6pm; Sept.-May Mon.-Fri. 10am-noon and 2-5pm, Sun. 2-5pm). The **Maison des Jeunes et de la Culture,** 13, rue de la République (tel. 63 54 20 67), offers dorm bunks for 22F. **Hôtel la Régence,** 27 av. Maréchal-Joffre (tel. 63 54 01 42), opposite the station, has tasteful rooms and cable TV from 90-100F. Camp at **Parc de Caussels** (tel. 63 54 38 87), 2km east of Albi, on the route de Millan (37F per 2 people). **Le Petit Bouchon,** 77, rue Croix Verte, offers a 52F *menu* featuring a choice of several *plats du jour.* Mention *Let's Go* and get 10% off. (Open Mon.-Fri. 8am-10pm, Sat. 8am-4pm.)

Set on a hillside overlooking the patchwork farmland of the Cerou River Valley, **Cordes** beckons to approaching visitors much as it has since serving as a vigilant sentinel on the Cathar frontier. A flux of lesser artists and artisans have followed Jean-Paul Sartre and Albert Camus here; the double-walled, 13th-century bastide features Gothic houses flanking steep, cobblestoned walkways in a flawlessly-preserved medieval setting. Unique in France, the **Musée de l'Art du Sucre,** on the Grande Rue, presents a highly caloric display of sculptures crafted entirely of sugar, and, in a few instances, chocolate—the private efforts of Yves Thuriès, a two-time French champion *patissier,* and his assistants. (Open daily 10am-noon and 2-6pm; Oct.-April Tues.-Sun. 3-5pm. Admission 5F.) Hotels here are exorbitant: day-trip from Albi, but plan ahead. From pl. Jean Jaurès in Albi, SNCF mini-vans depart for Cordes (Mon., Wed., and Fri. 8:45am; Tues. and Thurs. 11:45am; 26F; returns to Albi normally at 4:50pm.) Alternatively, take the train to Vindrac-Cordes and walk the remaining 4km to town, or call for a minibus a day in advance (18F; 26F at night; tel. 63 56 14 80).

Carcassonne

The Cité de Carcassonne is a child's toy castle grown to adult proportions, a thirteenth-century Disneyland: a double-walled, fortified city with towers and turrets rising from a precipitous plateau in the Garonne valley. Begun in Gallo-Roman times, the **Cité** played an important role in Languedoc's unsuccessful effort, lasting until 1209, to remain independent of northern France. By the mid-19th century, villagers had so thoroughly pillaged the walls for building materials that only truncated ruins remained. But rising interest in medieval France spurred the rebuilding of the Cité, directed by architect/restorer Viollet-le-Duc.

Black bus #4 serves the medieval Cité from both the train station and pl. Gambetta (every ½ hr., 4.40F), or hike 25 min. up the hill. Originally constructed as a palace, the **Château Comtal** fortress overlooks the south side of the Cité. Admission is by guided tour (in French every 20-30 min. from 9am; in English July-Aug. 2 per day; all start inside the château's gates. Open July-Aug. 9:30am-12:30pm and 2-7:30pm, May-June and Sept. 1-15 9:30am-12:30pm and 2-5pm. Admission 40F, ages 18-25 and over 60 13F.) The **Basilique St-Nazaire,** adjacent to the château on rue Dame Carcas, has stained its glass with great finesse. The entire Cité medievalizes during the **Médiévales** festival in August.

To reach the **tourist office,** 15, bd. Camille-Pelletan (tel. 68 25 07 04), off pl. Gambetta, turn left onto bd. Omer Sarraut (a block in front of the train station) and walk two blocks, then follow bd. Jean Jaurès up to the right. (Changes currency when banks close. Open July-Aug. Mon.-Sat. 9am-7pm, Sun. 10am-noon; Sept. and April-June Mon.-Sat. 9am-noon and 2-7pm; Oct.-March Mon.-Sat. 9am-noon and 2-6:30pm.) There is an annex in the *porte narbonnaise,* within the Cité. (Open July-Aug. 9am-7pm; April-June and Sept.-Oct. 9am-12:30pm and 1:20-6pm.) The immaculate **auberge de jeunesse (IYHF)** is on rue Vicomte Trencavel in the Cité. (Tel. 68 25 23 16. 59F. Curfew midnight, in off-season 10-11pm. Open Feb.-Nov.) In the *basse ville,* the warm owners of the **Hôtel de l'Octroi,** 106, av. Général Leclerc (tel. 68 25 29 08), provide comely rooms. (Doubles 95-105F, with shower and toilet 180F. Triples 135F. Showers 14F. Breakfast 20F.)

Cassoulet, the local specialty, is a hearty stew with white beans, herbs, and usually lamb or pork. Sample a succulent rendition at **Au Bon Pasteur,** 29, rue Armagnac, in the Cité. (60F *menu.* Open Feb.-Dec. 23 Tues.-Sat. noon-2pm and 7-9pm.) **L'Ostal des Troubadours,** 5, rue Viollet-le-Duc, posts the cheapest *menus* (39F and 59F *service non compris)* and remains animated all year with live performers nightly. (Open daily noon-midnight; *menus* served noon-2pm and 6-10pm.) **L'Hippocampe,** 38, rue du 4 Septembre, is a relaxed, countertop restaurant with inexpensive local fare in the *basse ville.* (Pizza 26F. Tables in rear. Open Mon.-Sat. 11:30am-2pm and 6:45-10pm.) For provisions, visit the **market** in pl. Carnot (Tues., Thurs., and Sat. mornings).

Provence

When the Romans came to this region in 6 BC, they found looming mountains covered in lavender and rosemary and a fertile river valley sprinkled with sage. By the end of the Empire, they had left behind lush olive groves and vineyards, amphitheaters and a rich tradition of festivals; some of the best-preserved Roman structures in the world now crumble here. Situated midway between Spain and Italy, the sweetness and light of the region inspired Cézanne, Picasso, and Van Gogh. Summer brings bullfights, festivals, and concerts, often staged in old arenas and palaces. Provence is also an ideal place to delight in French wine. Do as the Romans did and spend a few centuries here.

Avignon

Nestled among the lush vineyards of the Rhône Valley, the walled city of Avignon sparkles with artistic brilliance. Film festivals, street musicians, and the famed **Festival d'Avignon** keep this university town shining, even in the shadow of Mt. Ventoux.

Sitting atop the city's highest point is the grandiose **Palais des Papes.** Built in the 14th century when the popes moved from Rome to Avignon, this palatial medieval fortress recalls that Avignon was once the center of the Christian world. (Open July-Sept. daily 9am-7pm; April-June and Oct. daily 9am-12:15pm and 2-6pm; Nov.-March daily 9am-noon and 2-5pm. Admission 22F, students 15F. English guided tours daily 10am and 3pm; 30F, students 23F.) Next to the Palais, the popes' expansive garden, **Le Rocher des Doms** overlooks the 12th-century **Pont St-Bénezet,** the "Pont d'Avignon" of nursery-rhyme fame, and the Rhône Valley. The bridge, which now ends abruptly mid-stream, affords a great view of the sunset over Avignon, but is not worth the 7F admission fee. For a free and equally spectacular view of the bridge, watch the sunset from the more modern Pont Daladier.

From early July through early August, the **Festival d'Avignon** puts on everything from avant-garde plays to all-night readings of the *Odyssey.* (Tickets 50-135F. Reserve through the Bureau du Festival, 8bis, rue de Mons, 84000 Avignon (tel. 90 82 67 08).) The inevitable "fringe" festival occurs in tiny basements and theaters. (Tickets 50-100F, available at the door. Look for a 60F card that gives a 30% discount.)

The **tourist office,** 41, cours Jean Jaurès (tel. 90 82 65 11), three blocks from the train station, dishes out a list of all accommodations and changes money when the banks are closed. (Open Mon.-Fri. 9am-6pm, Sat. 9am-noon and 2-6pm. During the festival, the office is open daily 9am-7pm.) Avignon lacks an official youth hostel, but claims four habitable *foyers,* the best of which is **Foyer Bagatelle** (tel. 90 86 30 39), Ile de Barthelasse, across the river (take bus #10 (5.50F) from the post office, or simply cross the Pont Daladier; it'll be on your right). (No curfew. No lockout. 46F in 10-bed rooms.) The **Foyer YMCA,** 7bis, bd. de la Justice (tel. 90 25 46 20) is also across the Pont Daladier in Villeneuve (take bus #10), but is more difficult to walk to. (Lockout 10am-5pm. Curfew midnight. 48F. Breakfast 15F.) **Hotel Mignon,** 12, rue Joseph Vernet (tel. 90 82 17 30) has carpeted rooms, TVs, and telephones. (Doubles 115F, with shower 160F. Triples 290F. Breakfast 18F.) Also recommended is the popular **Hôtel le Parc,** 18, rue Perdigurer (tel. 90 82 71 55), off cours Jean Jaurès near the tourist office. (Singles and doubles 100F, with shower 134F. Triples with shower 170F. Breakfast 16F.) For camping, the best site is **Camping Bagatelle** (tel. 90 86 30 39), a big ol' three-star site just beside the Foyer Bagatelle, with hot showers, a cafeteria, laundromat, and supermarket. (18F per person, 8F per tent.)

The tourist office's *A Comme Avignon* lists restaurants serving meals under 80F. The restaurants and cafés on shaded rue des Teinturiers are popular during the festival. The area around rue Thiers and rue Philonarde has several inexpensive places, but women might not want to dally here alone at night. Tuesday through Sunday mornings, a huge indoor **market** convenes in **Les Halles** on pl. Pie (7am-1pm). **Cafétéria Flunch,** 11, bd. Raspail, off rue de la République, piles on the food and then practically gives it away. (Roast chicken with 2 vegetables 17F. Open daily 11am-10pm.) The **Restaurant l'Arlequin,** 84, rue Bonneterie (tel. 90 85 79 56) is a bit more pricey, but serves tasty *provençale* cuisine. (55F menu includes salad, main course, and dessert. Open daily noon-2pm and 7-9pm.)

Near Avignon

Fifteen minutes north of Avignon by train (24F), **Orange** has a pair of famous monuments from its days as the Roman city of Aurasio—an imposing **triumphal arch** and the best preserved **Roman theater** in France (the only one in Europe with an original stage). Concerts, theater, and opera spring up regularly here throughout July and August. The **tourist office** on the cours Aristide Briand (tel. 90 34 70 88) has a list of events. The **Hôtel Freau,** 3, rue Ancien-College (tel. 90 34 06 26) has comfortable beds and kind managers. (Singles and doubles 95F, with shower 120F. Breakfast 20F). Or for a real treat, stay at the *incredible* **auberge de jeunesse (IYHF)** in nearby Séguret (see below). For a creative French meal that you'll remember, try **La Roselière,** 4, rue du Renoyer, off pl. Clemenceau. (60F lunch *menu.* Open daily noon-2pm and 7-11pm.)

Vaison-la-Romaine, a village in the heart of the Rhône wine valley, features partially excavated Roman villas, a medieval city, and a hillside castle. The **tourist office** is on pl. du Chanoine Santel (tel. 90 36 02 11) and has guided tours (30F, students 15F, under 19 10F) of the region and free wine tasting. (Open daily 9am-12:30pm and 2-7pm; Sept.-June 9am-12:30pm.) The amazing **auberge de jeunesse (IYHF)** in nearby **Séguret** (tel. 90 46 93 31) should not be missed. Proprietors Henri and Line will serve you a four-star *provençale* meal amidst idyllic vineyards. Take the bus from Orange (20 min.) or Vaison (15 min.) (Comfy dorm with cozy beds 60F. Breakfast included. Fabulous dinner with wine from the valley 58F.) Back in Vaison, the **Centre Culturel à Coeur Joie,** about 1km down av. César Geoffrey (tel. 90 36 00 78), rents bare but spotless singles (110F, with shower 135F) and doubles (155F, with shower 175F), with breakfast included. **Les Voconces,** pl. Montfort (tel. 90 36 00 94), is a small hotel with big rooms. (Singles and doubles 110F, with shower 150F. Breakfast 25F.) Vaison is 80 minutes and 37F from Avignon.

Arles

Roman grandeur haunts the sun-baked remnants of Arles' **Roman baths,** lingers in the beautiful **Arènes** (now used for bullfights), and endures in the city's **Théâtre Antique** (now used for frequent summer concerts). Proudly Provençal, Arles inscribes plaques in the regional tongue and celebrates the **Fête de la Tradition** (the last weekend in June) in local costume, with bonfires blazing in the streets. Arles' beautiful monuments and vistas drew both Picasso and Van Gogh (who lost an ear here) to its festive streets.

The **Musée Réattu,** rue du Grand Prieuré, exhibits contemporary art, 57 Picasso drawings (donated by the master himself) and paintings by Van Gogh. (Open June-Sept. daily 9am-12:30pm and 2-7pm. Admission 15F, students 7.50F). The July **Rencontres Internationales de la Photographie** (exhibits 20F each, global ticket 120F, students 100F) is followed by a dance and music **Festival,** with international performances in the Théâtre Antique. The **tourist office,** bd. des Lices (tel. 90 96 29 35), has festival information, currency exchange, and an accommodations service (4F). From the train station, enter the city and follow rue de la Cavalerie and then rue de l'Hôtel de Ville to bd. des Lices. (Open Mon.-Sat. 9am-8pm, Sun. 9am-1pm; Oct.-March Mon.-Sat. 9am-6pm.)

Inexpensive hotels cluster around pl. du Forum and pl. Voltaire, filling fast in July and August. The sleek **auberge de jeunesse (IYHF)** is on av. Foch (tel. 90 96 18 25), a few blocks behind the tourist office. (Reception open daily 7-10am and 5pm-midnight. 63F 1st night, 50F thereafter. Breakfast and showers included. Sheets 13F.) The **Hôtel de Studio,** 6 rue Réattu, has bright flowery rooms and a great restaurant below. (Singles 80F. Doubles with shower 120F. Breakfast 20F.)

A busy **market** is held Wednesdays along bd. Combes, and Saturdays along bd. des Lices (both open 7am-12:30pm). The largest supermarket is the **Monoprix,** off pl. Lamartine. The popular **Lou Gardian,** 70, rue 4 du Septembre (tel. 90 96 76 15), at the end of rue d'Hôtel de Ville, is run by a proud *provençale* family. The food is incredible and the servings plentiful. *(Menu* 53F. Open Mon.-Sat. noon-2pm and 7-9:30pm.) Other cheap restaurants can be found near pl. Voltaire.

Frequent buses run from the *gare routière* (next to the train station) to the **Camargue,** an enormous natural reserve where flamingoes and wild horses run free (8 per day, 1 hr., 32F) and the **beaches** at nearby Stes.-Marie-de-la-Mer (same bus). Trains roll from the **train station,** av. Tallabot, to Avignon (every hr., 20 min., 39F), Marseille (16 per day, 1 hr., 68F) and Aix-en-Provence (10 per day, 1¾ hr., 82F).

Aix-en-Provence

A major university town and artistic center, Aix-en-Provence (pronounced "Ex") attracts thousands of intellectuals, painters, and musicians. Pass the afternoon sitting in a café on the **cours Mirabeau,** or walk along the **chemin de Cézanne** and check out the original studios of Aix's own Paul Cézanne.

Aix hosts an internationally renowned **Music Festival** in July and August (for info call 42 63 06 75) and supports several museums of note. The **Musée Granet** pl. St-Jean de Matte (tel. 42 38 14 70) displays a striking collection of Roman sculpture, bushels of Dutch and French works, and eight small paintings by Cézanne. (Open Wed.-Mon. 10am-noon and 2-6pm. Admission 13F, students 7F.) The **Musée des Tapisseries,** pl. des Martyrs de la Résistance (tel. 42 21 05 78) houses a lovely collection of 17th- and 18th-century tapestries. (Open Wed.-Mon. 10am-noon and 2-6pm. Admission 11F, students 5F.) The **Fondations Vasarely,** 1, av. Marcel Pagnol, next to the youth hostel, is worth a trip for its modern art experiments-in-color. (Open Wed.-Sun. 9:30am-12:30pm and 2-5:30pm. Admission 30F, students 15F.)

The **tourist office,** 2, pl. du Général de Gaulle (tel. 42 26 02 93), can help with free hotel reservations. From the train station, bear left up av. Victor Hugo for the tourist office and the central city bus terminus. The crowded **auberge de jeunesse (IYHF)** at 3, av. Marcel Pagnol (tel. 42 20 15 99), is 2km from the station; take bus #8 or walk down av. de l'Europe for 25 minutes (look for the black-and-white Vasarely building). (Curfew 11pm. 69F first night, 59F thereafter. Breakfast included. Sheets 10F.) During summer the **Hôtel Vigoroux,** 27, rue Cardinale (tel. 42 38 26 42), near pl. des Dauphins, offers singles for 120F and doubles for 140F (breakfast 26F). The friendly **Hôtel du Casino,** 38, rue Victor Leydet (tel. 42 26 06 88) has comfy rooms and a great location. (Singles 110F. Doubles 170F. Breakfast 25F.)

Several inexpensive restaurants cluster near pl. des Augustins and pl. des Prêcheurs. **Hacienda,** 7, rue Mérindot, in the pl. des Fontêtes, is an excellent value, with a delicious 55F *menu* including wine. (Open Sept. 4-Aug. 5 Mon.-Sat. noon-2pm and 7-10:30pm.) **Djerba,** 8bis, rue Rifle-Rafle, serves French and North African specialities. *(Couscous* 46-70F. Open daily 9am-3pm and 6pm-midnight.) Buy a picnic lunch at the fresh **market** at pl. de Verdun (Tues., Thurs., Sat. 7am-1pm) or stock up at **Supermarché Casino,** 1, av. de Lattre de Tassigny (open Mon.-Sat. 9am-8pm). Be sure to sample Aix's famed almonds, used in cakes and cookies, at one of the numerous *pâtisseries* or *salons de thé* along rue d'Italie or rue Espanàt.

To get virtually anywhere by train from Aix, one must first go to Marseille by train (every hr. by train, 40 min., 34F) or on cheaper buses (every 15 min.; 45 min.; 20F, students 23F round-trip). Six buses per day run to Avignon (1½ hr., 75F).

French Riviera (Côte d'Azur)

Paradises are made to be lost. The Côte d'Azur fell from its seductive grace as shrewd developers obscured its dazzling horizon with condominiums and transformed its sun-blessed pleasures into profit. Yet the Riviera's elysian waters and topless beaches still work their seductions. Centers like Nice make inexpensive bases for daytrips to less-infested beaches. If you arrive early in the season or trek to less-frequented centers such as Antibes, Cap d'Ail, or the coastal islands, you may catch a glimpse of the Côte of yesteryear, unobscured by cars or people. An uncommonly beautiful area, its colors alone are spectacular. Dazzling white villas rim a blue sea, while olive trees shadow fragrant rose and mimosa. Away from the coast, an exquisitely varied hinterland nourishes both wooded ridges and expanses of flat farmland. Traces of the Roman rule established by Caesar remain at Fréjus, Antibes, and Digne. Nearly every town along the eastern part of the Riviera takes pride in a local edifice decorated by Matisse or Chagall, and excellent museums and festivals abound.

Accommodations, restaurants, and roads become hellishly jammed as summer wears on. Youth hostels are often booked months in advance, forcing roving bands of travelers to the stations and the pebbly beaches. If you join them, stay close to others and guard your valuables, or, better yet, lock them up at a bus or train station. Organized campsites are well equipped and near the beaches.

The Côte d'Azur is conveniently compressed—all the towns lie on a straight line from Marseille northeastwards to Menton and the Italian border, and both trains and buses connect coastal resorts frequently, quickly, and inexpensively. Hitching in July and August is awful.

Marseille

Steaming hot, full of spice, and a stew of residents from all over the Mediterranean, Marseille is a lot like the *bouillabaisse* for which its restaurants are famed. France's third largest city, Marseille has a mean, not entirely unmerited, reputation; watch yourself at night. The center of town is the **Vieux Port,** which hums with life from the first throaty calls of the morning fish sellers to the final inebriated good-byes just before dawn. Running straight out of the port is Marseille's main artery, **La Canebière,** a turbulent, crowded thoroughfare affectionately known by English sailors as "Can o' beer." Between La Canebière and the station twist the narrow, dusty streets of the North African quarter.

Rising high above the city, the 19th-century **Basilique de Notre Dame de la Garde** keeps watch over Marseille and its attendant isles and mountains. (Admission free. No shorts. Take bus #60.) Motorboats run from quai des Belges (tel. 91 55 50 09) to **Château d'If** (20 min., round-trip 40F), immortalized by Alexandre Dumas in *The Count of Monte Cristo.* See our scaly friends at Marseille's **Aquarium del Prado,** pl. Admiral Muselier (tel. 91 71 00 46), where 8000 fish of 350 different species boogie all night long. (Open Sun.-Thurs. 10am-7pm, Fri.-Sat. 10am-midnight. Admission 35F, students 25F. Take bus #19 or 72.)

The **tourist office,** 4, La Canebière (tel. 91 54 91 11), on the Vieux Port, has a free accommodations service. Turn left from the station steps, walk along bd. d'Athènes, and take a left onto La Canebière at McDonald's. (Open daily 8am-8pm; Oct.-June Mon.-Sat. 9am-7:30pm, Sun. 10am-5:30pm.) The **U.S.** (12, bd. Paul Peytral; tel. 91 54 92 00) and the the **U.K.** (24, av. du Prado; tel. 91 77 54 01) maintain consulates.

FOR A FREE BROCHURE CALL TOLL FREE
1•800•755•8755
FROM THE UNITED STATES AND CANADA

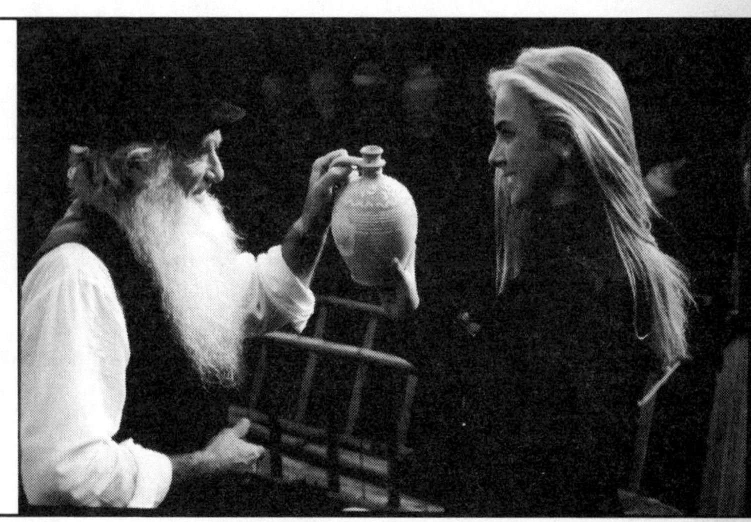

Are you 20-40 years old? Then join us and discover a care-free, fun way of all-inclusive European Travel. Come alone (like a third of all people traveling with us) or bring a friend. What ever you choose, we've planned the best time of your life; just for you. Stay in selected hotels, tour in luxurious buses and try delicious cuisine. Travel with a group of 30-40 persons, and you'll always have friends joining you in exploring culture, art and spectacular nightlife. There's plenty of free time and in the end you'll say "I had a ball and the price was right."

amadeus
international tours

FOR A FREE BROCHURE PACKED WITH GREAT VACATION VALUES CALL TOLL FREE

1•800•755•8755

FROM THE UNITED STATES AND CANADA OR FILL OUT THIS CARD AND MAIL TODAY.

NAME

ADDRESS

CITY

STATE ZIP CODE

PLEASE TELL US ABOUT YOUR SPECIAL INTERESTS:

PHOTO OTHER SIDE: POTTERY SELLER IN AUSTRIA

PLACE STAMP HERE

amadeus
international tours

23564 Calabasas Rd.
Suite 208
Calabasas, CA 91302
U.S.A.

Take bus #6 or 8 (7F) from cours Joseph Thierry to the **auberge de jeunesse de Bois-Luzy (IYHF),** 76, av. de Bois-Luzy (tel. 91 49 06 18), Marseille's most convenient hostel, in a relaxing old château. (Curfew 11pm. 39F.) Inexpensive hotels overflow place des Marseillaises, bd. Maurice Bourdet, and rue Breteuil. The best bargain is probably **Hôtel Moderne,** 30, rue Breteuil, off La Canebière (tel. 91 53 29 03). (Singles 85F. Doubles with shower and TV 180F. Breakfast 22F.) Enjoy a bowl of *bouillabaisse* (a fish and seafood stew flavored with saffron and bay leaves) at **Racasse-Dauphin,** 6, quai de Rive-neuve, on the Vieux Port. (56F. Open Fri.-Wed. noon-2pm and 7-11pm.) The area around cours Julien is also good for a cheap bite.

Marseille is a transport hub, with trains to Paris (4 per day, 4¾ hr., 380F), Toulouse, Barcelona, and Nice. Nastier but cheaper buses run along the coast. **SNCM,** 61, bd. des Dames (tel. 91 56 62 05), has information on ferries to Corsica and North Africa. (Open Mon.-Fri. 9am-5pm, Sat. 8am-noon.)

St-Tropez

A stroll down the streets of St-Tropez is like an episode of *Lifestyles of the Rich and Famous.* In this tiny port town, Hermès goes to bathe with Yves St-Laurent, Lamborghinis pull away from Mercedes, small cafés post four-star menus and *everybody's* had a rough day at the beach.

Unless you've brought your Gold Card and your butler, don't plan to stay in St-Trop' (as the Pierre Cardin-clad locals affectionately say). Do a daytrip; take the bus (but don't admit it) from St-Raphaël (2 hr., 41F) or Toulon (3 hr., 80F; call 94 92 62 82 for more information). The faster and more scenic boat ride to St-Raphaël is much more suave and not that much more expensive (47F; call 94 95 17 46 for more information).

Buses also run to St-Tropez's distant beaches (8F), the Plage des Salins (4km) and the oh-so-chic Plage de Tahiti (4km). Be prepared to have your body (and your tanline, if you must have one) critically assessed. Hitching is poor (you'd soil the upholstery). Rent your own wheels at **Louis Mas,** 5, rue Joseph Quaranta (tel. 94 97 00 60; bicycles 50F per day, deposit 500F; mopeds 87F per day, gas 25F, deposit 2000F; open April-Oct. 15 Mon.-Sat. 9am-7:30pm, Sun. 9am-12:30pm).

Most hotels are light years out of the budget range and usually full anyway. Call ahead or hope for the best at **Hotel Mediterranée,** bd. Louis Blanc (tel. 94 97 00 44; singles and doubles 150F, with shower 270F; breakfast 25F). Camping is a lesser evil: the **tourist offices** on quai Jean Jaurès and at the *gare routière,* off av. du Général Leclerc (tel. 94 97 41 21), have a list of appallingly expensive sites. (Offices open daily 9am-8pm; Oct.-June 15 Mon.-Sat. 9am-12:30pm and 2-6:30pm.) **La Croix du Sud,** rte. de Pampelonne (tel. 94 79 80 84; 25F per person, 36F per tent; open Easter-Sept.) and **Les Tournels,** rte. du Phare de Camarat (tel. 94 79 81 38; 40F per person, tent included) are large sites, but reserve in summer. The nearest **youth hostel (IYHF),** in Fréjus (tel. 94 52 18 75), is only a short boat or bus ride away. (Lockout 10am-6pm. Curfew 11pm. 40F per night. Breakfast 15F.) To assemble your own meals, shop at **Prisunic supermarket,** 7, av. du Général Leclerc (open Mon.-Sat. 8am-8pm, Sun. 8am-1pm) or try the *grand marché* at pl. des Lices every Tues. and Sat. 6:30am-1pm. Restaurants are expensive, but try the 38F *spaghetti carbonara* at **Trattoria di Roma,** av. du Général Leclerc (open daily noon-2:30pm and 7-10:30pm); **Mario,** 9, rue Aire du Chemin at rue de la Miséricorde, serves French and Italian dishes (65F *menu)* on a lavender terrace (open daily noon-7pm).

In St-Tropez, attitude is everything. Strike a pose and have a *café* (10F) at the popular **Café des Arts,** on pl. des Lices. Anyone who's *anyone* will be there, darling, and you owe it to yourself. You've had a rough day at the beach.

Cannes

Sister city to Beverly Hills, Cannes has all the glitz and glamour of St-Tropez, but is slightly less exclusive. Here you can tan on the same beach with the Rockefellers and shoplift from the same shops as the Trumps, and never spend a dime. You'll still be terribly underdressed, but Armani and Hermès will forgive you. Tickets for the Cannes Film Festival are not available to the general public (that's you), but the sidewalk circus is absolutely free.

By day, most folks tan on the sandy public beaches next to the Palais des Festivals. By night, everyone boogies in Cannes' hot clubs. Check out the scene at **Jane's,** at the Hôtel Grand d'Albion (tel. 93 99 04 94), for dancing and scamming from 11pm 'til dawn (cover 60F). The super-popular **Mogambo Palm Beach,** at pointe de la Croisette (tel. 93 43 91 12) keeps rocking from 11pm 'til 7am (cover 50F). **Les 3 Cloches** (tel. 93 68 32 92) is Cannes' hottest gay club (open 11pm-dawn; cover 50F). The gay scene can also be found voguing at the **Club 7 Disco,** 7, rue Rouguière, near the port. (Open nightly 11pm-6am. Cover 90F. Drinks 25-35F.) Cannes's **Le Casino Croisette,** 1, get. Albert Edoef (tel. 93 38 12 11), near the Palais des Festivals, has slots, blackjack, and roulette. (Gambling daily 5pm-4am, open for slots at 11am. No shorts. Must be 18. Free.)

The helpful **tourist office** (tel. 93 39 24 53), next to the Vieux Port in the modern Palais des Festivals, makes hotel reservations for free (open daily 9am-8pm; Sept.-June Mon.-Sat. 9am-6pm). A branch office (tel. 93 99 19 77), in the station, can also find you a bed. (Open Mon.-Sat. 9am-12:30pm and 2-6:30pm.) Although there is no youth hostel in Cannes, the exemplary **Auberge de St-Raphaël-Fréjus (IYHF)** (tel. 94 52 18 75) is just 20 minutes away by train (31F), and the **Relais International de la Jeunesse** (tel. 93 61 34 40) is only 15 minutes away (11F) in sunny Antibes. **Hôtel Chanteclair,** 12 rue Forville (tel. 93 39 68 88), a few streets from rue Félix-Faure, is the loveliest and cheapest place in town (singles 150F; doubles 200F, with shower 210F; breakfast 18F). **Le Florian Hôtel,** 8, rue du Commandant André (tel. 93 39 24 82), off rue d'Antibes, has clean rooms, all with showers and telephones. (Singles 120-160F. Doubles 150-240F. Breakfast 20F.) **Hôtel de Bourgogne,** 13, rue du 24 Août (tel. 93 38 36 73), has spotless rooms, with telephones and carpeting, in a sweet location near the station. (Singles 120-200F. Doubles 150-250F. Breakfast 22F.) Take bus #10 to **Ranch Camping,** Chemin St-Joseph (tel. 93 46 00 11), in Rochville, 2km from town. (2 people and tent 60F, weekends 70F.) **Caravaning Bellevue,** 67, av. M. Chevalier (tel. 93 47 28 97), in Cannes-La-Bocca, is only one train stop away. (69F per person, tent included. Open Jan.-Oct.)

The small cafés and restaurants on the pedestrian walkway, rue Meynadier, are lovely and affordable. Check out **Chez Mamichette,** 11, rue St-Antoinne, off the western end of the rue Meynadier and rue Félix-Faure. This cozy place proposes fondue (50F) and a rib-sticking *raclette* for 89F. (Open Mon.-Sat. noon-3pm and 7-11pm.) **La Sangria,** 76, rue Meynadier, serves a filling *paëlla gitane* (95F) and tasty *crêpes fruits de mer maison* (32-45F). (Open Mon.-Sat. 11am-2pm and 7-11pm.)

Near Cannes

The secluded beaches and pine forest of the **Iles de Lérins** make a great get-away from the mainland. Both the Ile St-Honorat and the Ile Ste-Marguerite can be reached by boat from Cannes's *gare maritime,* next to the Palais des Festivals (to St-Honorat ½ hr., round-trip 40F; to Ste-Marguerite 15 min., round-trip 35F).

The small hillside town of **Grasse** (15km away) is the perfume capital of the world. Visit the **Parfumerie Fragonard** (tel. 93 36 45 65) for a whiff of Grasse's many concoctions (open daily 9am-6pm). Buses run daily from Cannes' *gare routière* (tel. 93 39 31 37; 45 min., 18F).

Antibes's beautiful beaches and Picasso museum make it one of the hottest new spots on the Riviera for the budget backpacker. The extraordinary **Musée Picasso,** pl. Grimaldi Château (tel. 93 34 91 91), exhibits works Picasso produced in the area, as well as art by his contemporaries. Set above the sea in a restored castle, the museum is a work of art in itself. (Open Wed.-Mon. 10am-noon and 2-6pm; Sept.-June 14 Wed.-Mon. 10am-noon and 2-7pm. Admission 22F, students 12F.)

Chow on the filling, homemade ravioli (42F) and pasta (60-80F) at **La Famiglia,** 34, av. Thiers (tel. 93 34 60 82). The **Relais International de la Jeunesse,** bd. de la Garoupe (tel. 93 61 34 40), is in an old villa by the ocean at Cap d'Antibes. If you speak French to the old woman in charge, she may supply you with 8F bottles of wine (but watch out for her flying monkeys). The lighthouse above the hostel is an inspired place to drain them. Take the "Garoupe bus" from Hôtel des Postes in Antibes or the train station (5F), or walk on bd. de la Garoupe. (Curfew midnight. 55F. Breakfast included. Meals 48F. Sheets 10F. Open June-Sept.)

Nice

Blessed with a beautiful beach and all the nightlife, arts, entertainment, and laundromats of a large city, Nice is popularly known as the capital of the French Riviera. Every spring, on Fat Tuesday, Nice erupts into song and dance during the annual **Carnaval** (grandmother of New Orleans' famed Mardi Gras), and the carnival spirit lasts all summer long. Unfortunately, big-city thrill is coupled increasingly with big-city crime. Beware of purse-snatchers around the train station, rue Masséna and the old section of town, Vieux Nice.

Orientation and Practical Information

Nice spells "daytrip base"—well-linked to all parts of the Côte d'Azur, and one of the few spots on the Riviera with reasonably priced accommodations. The city also receives trains from Paris, Bordeaux, Italy (only 45 min. away), Barcelona, and other major centers.

Two main drags, **av. Jean Médecin** and **bd. Gambetta,** lead from the station down to the majestic **promenade des Anglais,** which sweeps along the coast. The pedestrian zone west of **place Masséna** swarms with boutiques, restaurants, and tourists. **Vieux Nice,** tucked into the southeastern pocket of the city, is charming by the day, but best avoided after dark.

Tourist Office: av. Thiers (tel. 93 87 07 07), beside the station. Free map. Makes hotel reservations (10F fee) only after 10am. Open Mon.-Sat. 8:45am-6:30pm, Sun. 8:45am-12:15pm and 2-5:45pm; Oct.-May Mon.-Sat. 8:45am-12:30pm and 2-6pm. **Branch office** at 5. av. Gustave V (tel. 93 87 60 60), near pl. Masséna. Open same hours.

Currency Exchange: Cambio, 17, av. Thiers (tel. 93 88 56 80), across from the train station. Fair rates and no commission. Open daily 7am-midnight.

American Express: 11, promenade des Anglais (tel. 93 87 29 82), at the corner of rue de Congrès. Eternal lines in summer. Open daily 9am-6pm; Oct.-April Mon.-Fri. 9am-noon and 2-6pm.

Post Office: Main office, 23, av. Thiers (tel. 93 88 52 52), near the train station. Poste Restante and telephones. Open Mon.-Fri. 8am-6pm, Sat. 8am-noon. **Postal Code:** 06000.

Trains: Gare SNCF, av. Thiers (tel. 93 87 50 50). To: Cannes (35 min., 28F); Monaco (25F); and Paris via Marseille (about 11 per day, 7½ hr., 465F). Lockers 12F for 72 hrs. Showers at the station 12F, towels 3F, soap 1F. Toilets 2F. Open daily 7am-7pm. Information office open Mon.-Sat. 8am-7pm, Sun. 8am-noon and 2-6pm.

Buses: Gare Routière, promenade du Paillon (tel. 93 85 61 81), off av. Jean Jaurès. Frequent buses along the coast, slightly more expensive and slower than trains. To: Monaco (19F); Antibes (24F); Cannes (29F). Open Mon.-Sat. 8am-6:30pm.

Public Transportation: Frequent buses connect all locations within the city. **Station Centrale,** 10, av. Félix Faure (tel. 93 62 08 08), near pl. Masséna. Individual tickets 8F. *Carnet* of 5 tickets 27.40F. Day pass 20F.

Bike Rental: Nicea Location Rent, 9, av. Thiers (tel. 93 82 42 71), near the station. Bikes 120F per day, deposit 2000F (credit cards accepted). Open daily 9am-6:30pm. **Cycles Arnaud,**

4, pl. Grimaldi (tel. 93 87 88 55), near the pedestrian zone behind Hôtel Meridien. Bikes 85F per day; the longer the cheaper. Credit card required as deposit. Open Mon.-Fri. 8am-noon and 2-7pm.

Laundromats: Lavomatique, 11, rue du Pont Vieux (tel. 93 85 88 14), near the *gare routière.* Wash 20F. Dry 5F per 6 min. Open Mon.-Sat. 8am-8pm. **Quicklar,** 4, rue Gioffredo (tel. 93 53 62 22). Wash 9F. Dry 5F per 6 min. Open daily 8am-10pm.

Hospital: St-Roch, 5, av. Pierre Devulny (tel. 93 13 33 00).

Pharmacy: 7, rue Masséna (tel. 93 87 14 29). Open daily 9am-noon and 2-6pm.

Emergencies: Police (tel. 17). **Stolen property** (tel. 93 92 62 22). **Ambulance** (tel. 93 53 03 03).

Accommodations

Rooms in summer are like Marlboros in Russia: gone as soon as they're on sale. Arrive at the av. Thiers tourist office early for help in finding a room, or call individual hotels in advance. The largest concentration of nice, clean, and affordable ones clusters around Notre Dame on rue de Russie. Nice's two youth hostels and two summer *résidences* (temporary hostels set up in vacant university dorms) are all great, but far away from it all and often full. Arrive super-early, or book ahead. Sleeping on the beach is illegal, but some people put everything they own in a locker at the station, hide the key, and stay in groups. Sleeping at the train station is perilous.

Auberge de Jeunesse (IYHF), rte. Forestière du Mont-Alban (tel. 93 89 23 64), Too far-flung to walk, but worth the 4km commute. Take bus #5 from the train station to pl. Masséna, then bus #14 (both cost 8F and run until 7:30pm). Lockout 10am-5pm. Curfew midnight. 65F, breakfast included. Laundry and kitchen facilities.

Relais International de la Jeunesse "Clairvallon," 26, av. Scudéri (tel. 93 81 27 63), in Cimiez, 10km out of town. Take bus #15 from pl. Masséna. A large, unofficial hostel in an old villa with a free swimming pool. Curfew midnight. Bed and breakfast 60F.

Résidence Les Colinettes, 3, av. Robert Schumann (tel. 94 21 11 86; 93 97 10 33 after June 6). Near the train station, this temporary summer hostel provides beds for 90F per night. Great location. Midnight curfew. Open July-Aug.

Espace Magnan, 31 rue de Coppet (tel. 93 86 28 75). Right near the promenade des Anglais and the beach. From the station, take bus #23 and ask the driver to drop you off. Clean and efficient, if somewhat impersonal. Baggage room 10F. Café, restaurant, and nearby pool. Lockout 10am-6pm. 45F. Open June-Sept.

Hôtel Belle Meunière, 21, av. Durante (tel. 93 88 66 15), a 2-min. walk from the station. Quasi-villa with a large garden, once a gift from one of Napoleon's generals to his mistress. Friendly managers. Dorms 75F. Singles 90F. Doubles 140F, with shower 170F. Triples 220F, with shower 310F. Showers 15F. Breakfast included. Open Feb.-Dec.

Hôtel Novelty, 26, rue d'Angleterre (tel. 93 87 51 73), also close to the station. Clean rooms and comfy beds. Dorms 60F. Singles 90-110F, with shower 120-150F. Doubles 130F, with shower 180F. Hall showers 10F. Breakfast 20F. In summer, waves of American students make this and the Belle Meunière "Frat Nice."

Hôtel St-François, 3, rue St-François (tel. 93 85 88 69), in Vieux Nice near the morning fish market and across from the *gare routière.* Clean, quiet, but tiny rooms. Singles 75F. Doubles 110F, with shower and toilet 190F. Breakfast 13F.

Hôtel Idéal Bristol, 22, rue Paganini (tel. 93 88 60 72), off rue Alsace-Lorraine. Ideal hotel in an ideal spot, run by a conversable couple from the north of France. Squeaky clean rooms. Splendid TV room. Dorm rooms with kitchenette and refrigerator 75F. Singles 100F. Doubles 115F, with shower 125-150F. Triples 165F, with shower 210F.

Food

The Mediterranean, the North African connection, and the nearby Italian border have made Nice's cuisine heavy on the seafood, *couscous,* and olive oil. The area around the train station provides inexpensive but mediocre food. Try the pedestrian streets of Vieux Nice for a more interesting meal. *Spécialités niçoises* include creamy *bouillabaisse* (fish stew), *couscous* and lamb, *pissaladière* (an olive, onion, and anchovy pizza) and of course, the *salade niçoise* (chef's salad). Those low on cash should hit the large **Supermarché Prisunic,** 42, av. Jean Médecin (open Mon.-Thurs. and Sat. 8:30am-7pm, Fri. 8:30am-8pm) or **Supermarché Casino,** rue Deudor, near av. Jean Médecin (open Mon.-Sat. 8:30am-8pm).

Le Saëtone, 8, rue d'Alsace-Lorraine. 45-70F *menus* featuring regional dishes such as *soupe au pistou, salade aux fruits de mer* and *mousse au café. Plat du jour* 35F. Open Tues.-Sat. 11:30am-2pm and 6-10pm.

Restaurant de Paris, 28, rue d'Angleterre, near the train station. Tasty 35-52F *menus.* Yummy beef fondue (with fries or salad, 45F) and *tarte aux pommes chantilly* (22F). Open Dec.-Oct. daily 11:30am-2:30pm and 7:30pm-midnight.

Chez Annie, 6 rue Delille (tel. 93 62 59 52), near the pedestrian walkway *(rue piétonne)* Masséna. Wonderful *niçoise* specialties such as *raviolis niçoise* (45F), and *aïoli* (vegetables with garlic and mayonnaise sauce, 32F). Great pasta and lasagna dishes (30-45F). Open Mon.-Sat. 11:30am-2pm and 7-11pm.

Cafétéria Flunch, av. Thiers, next to the train station. Good food, monster portions, and what a bargain. Half roast chicken with 2 vegetables 19F. Open daily 11am-10pm.

Le Pacific Pizzeria, 18, rue Miron, 5 min. from the station. Munch on the largest 35-55F pizzas in Nice amidst 1950s-60s American decor. Open daily noon-2pm and 7-11pm.

Sights

Though Nice focuses on its long thin beach, the most enticing sands lie elsewhere on the Riviera; **Villefranche-sur-Mer** and **Cap d'Ail** are only 10 minutes away by train (6F and 10F, respectively). Despite the temporary closing of the **Musée Matisse**—which *may* reopen in March 1992—Nice's fabulous museums will dazzle you with the shapes and colors of their impressionist, surreal, and contemporary collections. The **Musée National Marc Chagall,** av. du Docteur (tel. 93 81 75 75) houses paintings, mosaics, sculptures, and tapestries by the master himself. (Open Wed.-Mon. 10am-7pm; Oct.-June Wed.-Mon. 10am-12:30pm and 2-5:30pm. Admission 16F; students, seniors, and everyone on Sun. 8F.) **The Musée des Beaux Arts,** 33, av. Baumettes (tel. 93 44 50 72), displays an excellent collection of Degas, Monet, Sisley, and Renoir. Take bus #38 or 40 (8F) to the Cheret stop. (Open Tues.-Sun. 10am-noon and 3-6pm; Oct.-April Tues.-Sun. 10am-noon and 2-5pm. Free.) The new **Musée d'Art Moderne et d'Art Cotemporain,** promenade des Arts (tel. 93 62 61 62), at the intersection of av. St-Jean Baptiste and Traverse Garibaldi, is housed in a funky building with four marble towers connected by transparent footbridges. The collection counts over 400 French and American pieces dating from 1960 to the present, including works by Andy Warhol, Roy Lichtenstein, and Kenneth Noland. (Open Sat.-Mon. and Wed.-Thurs. 11am-6pm, Fri. 11am-10pm. Free.) If you're sick of France's dark Gothic and Romanesque churches, visit the magnificent **Cathédrale Orthodoxe Russe St-Nicolas,** 17, bd. du Tsarévitch, off bd. Gambetta. This beautifully tiled church has six Yaroslav domes that sparkle in the summer sun. (Open daily 9am-noon and 2:30-5pm. Admission 12F. No shorts.)

Nice's boulevards of sun-baked façades are broken by a number of secluded parks and gardens. The most central is the **Jardin Albert 1er,** at the junction of promenade des Anglais and quai des Etats-Unis. The **Esplanade du Paillon,** near pl. Masséna, has a spectacular central fountain and lots of green and scented places.

Spilling out of the southeast corner of the city, **Vieux Nice** is quite a mélange, alternating between touristy cafés and charming old *niçois* architecture. Climb to the top of the **château** for a spectacular Rivierorama. (Gates close at 8pm.)

Entertainment

Nice's party crowd keeps swingin' long after the folks in St-Tropez and Antibes have gone home for the night. The bars and nightclubs around rue Masséna and

Vieux Nice are constantly hoppin' with jazz, snazz and rock 'n' roll. The area around the clubs in Vieux Nice can be dangerous at night and should not be visited alone. Most backpackers show up ready to dance around 10pm (when crowds are low, streets are safer, and women get in free) and then go home on the bus before it stops running (around midnight).

The **Jok Club,** 1, promenade des Anglais (tel. 93 87 95 87) is Nice's latest hot-spot. Dance 'til you drop and then cool off with the sea breeze on the promenade des Anglais. (Open daily 10pm-3am. Cover 60F.) **Ruby's,** along bd. Jean Jaurès opposite the Promenade de Paillon, is a local calypso club. (Cover 60F, Sat. 75F. All drinks 50F. Open nightly 11:30pm-6am). **Le Centre Ville Discothèque,** 1, pl. Masséna, attracts a young crowd with pop, funk, rap, and new wave. (Cover and 1st drink 75F, Sat. 100F. Women dance for free on Wed., Thurs., and Sun. Open Wed.-Sun. 11pm-6am; every night in July). The **Quartz Discothèque,** 18, rue Congrès (tel. 93 88 88 87) attracts a mixed gay and straight crowd to its long bar and small dance floor. (Open 11pm-dawn; cover 70F). Nice's bar and pub scene can also be lots of fun, but again, take care of yourself. **The Hole in the Wall,** 3, rue de l'Abbaye, in Vieux Nice about 1 block from rue de la Préfecture, has a lively British pub flavor with live pop and rock every night at 9pm. (Open Tues.-Sun. 8pm-midnight.) **Scarlet O'Hara's,** 22, rue Droite (tel. 93 80 43 22) off rue Rosetti in Vieux Nice, attracts a predominantly French crowd (open Mon.-Sat. 7pm-12:30am).

Nice's **Parade du Jazz** in mid-July at the parc and arènes de Cimiez (tel. 93 21 22 01) attracts some of the most successful European and American jazz musicians to its stages. Greats like B.B. King and Miles Davis perform simultaneously on three stages for seven hours every night (tickets 120F). If you happen to be on the Côte in February, don't miss Nice's **Carnaval,** with fireworks and parades up the wazoo. For more information on annual events, call the **Comité des Fêtes,** 5, promenade des Anglais (tel. 93 87 16 28).

Near Nice

Several great daytrips await you just beyond Nice. Buses roll regularly to **St-Paul-de-Vence,** a cobblestoned artists' colony northwest of Nice (every ½ hr., 50 min., 21F). St-Paul is the proud home of the **Fondation Maeght,** an outdoor museum displaying modern sculpture in a natural setting by artists such as Chagall, Calder, and Matisse. If you can go to only one museum in the whole Riviera, make this the one. (Open daily 10am-7pm; Oct.-June 10am-noon and 3-6pm. Admission 45F, students 30F, and worth every centime.) **Cap d'Ail,** on the rail line east of Nice, has a sheltered beach and seaside walkway that winds along the coast all the way to Monaco. There is a glorious **Relais International de la Jeunesse** (tel. 93 78 18 58) at Cap d'Ail in an old villa overlooking the Mediterranean. (Lockout 10am-5pm. Curfew midnight. Dorms 60F first night, 50F each subsequent night. Large bed in a tent with electric lights 50F. Breakfast included.)

Monaco

Legendary Monaco is Robin Leach's dream come true. The lifestyles of the rich are perpetrated by the darkly tanned and tuxedo-clad who play and gamble the night away at Monte-Carlo's famed Casino, while the lifestyles of the famous bring the noteworthy to the **Royal Palace** to party with the royal family. A young and lovely actress named Grace Kelly once came and ended up staying with Prince Rainier of Monaco until death did her part.

The **Casino** at Monte-Carlo is free but will usually refuse you admission if you wear shorts or sneakers, or are under 21. (Slot machines open at noon; the *salle américaine's* blackjack, craps, and roulette tables open at 4pm. Admission to the *salons privés,* where the big people play, is 50F.) When you leave the train station, head right and then uphill on av. de La Porte Neuve to see the **palace** (changing of the guard 11:55am) and narrow streets of **Monaco-ville;** take rue Grimaldi to the casino. Next to the palace is the stately **Cathédrale de Monaco,** 4, rue Colonel B. de Castro, where Grace Kelly married Prince Rainier and is now buried. (Open Mon.-Sat. 10am-6pm, Sun. 2-6pm.) The work of another legend, Jacques Cousteau, is inside the **Musée de l'Océanographie,** av. St-Martin. Monaco's international money-fondlers come here to monger the equally international fish collection. (Open daily 9am-9pm; Sept.-June 9am-7pm. Admission 50F, students 20F.)

Most of Monaco's restaurants and hotels are beyond the budget traveler's means. If you're lucky, you can stay at the excellent **Centre de Jeunesse Princess Stéphanie,** 24, av. Prince Pierre (tel. 93 50 83 20), a bright, converted villa. (3-day max. stay, 1 day in summer. Reception open 7-10am and 2pm-12:30am. 50F. Breakfast included. No reservations. Get there before 7:30am to sign up for a bed. Open July-Aug.) Buy your supplies at the **Codec Supermarket,** 30, bd. Princesse Charlotte, by the tourist office. (Open Mon.-Fri. 8:30am-noon and 3-7pm, Sat. 8:30am-7pm.) Frequent trains link Nice and Monaco (25 min., 21F).

Corsica (Corse)

The Mediterranean island of Corsica is covered with charming coastal and mountain villages amid stunning rock formations, fine white beaches, and sweet-smelling scrub. Though officially a part of France, it maintains its own language (an Italian dialect) and cultural traditions honed by centuries of discomforting Genoese and French domination. The island relies heavily on the tourist industry, welcoming half its visitors in July and August—when prices rise and ferry and hotel reservations are essential.

The **Société National Maritime Corse Méditerranée (SNCM)** operates car ferries from Marseille, Toulon, and Nice on the mainland to Ajaccio, Bastia, Calvi, Ile Rousse, and Propriano on Corsica (220F from Marseille and Toulon, 245F from Nice; mid-Sept. to mid-June 30-50% reductions for ages under 25 and over 60). Not every city is served every day; call in advance for schedule information. On the mainland, SNCM offices are located in Nice (quai du Commerce; tel. 93 13 66 66), Marseille (61, bd. des Dames; tel. 91 56 80 20), and Toulon (21, av. de l'Infanterie de Marine; tel. 94 41 25 76). **Corsica Ferries** provides frequent service from the Italian ports of Genoa, Livorno, and La Spezia to Bastia, Ajaccio, and Calvi. In Genoa, the office is located at Piazza Dante, 1 (tel. (010) 59 33 01). **NAVARMA** provides regular service between Bonifacio, in southern Corsica, and Sardinia (60F); in Bonifacio their office is at port de Bonifacio (tel. 95 73 00 29). Flying isn't much more expensive, especially since youth, family, and senior citizen reductions are available year-round. **Air France** and **Air Inter** fly to Bastia, Ajaccio and Calvi from Paris (791F, 501-621F with discount), Nice (377F, 261F) and Marseille (424F, 300F). Reservations are essential. In Paris, the Air France office is at 74, bd. Auguste-Blanqui (tel. 45 35 61 61) and Air Inter at 54, rue du Père-Corentin (tel. 145 39 25 25).

When you arrive, visit any tourist office for free, comprehensive transportation and accommodations information. Eurailpasses are not accepted on Corsica's trains, which link Ajaccio, Calvi, Bastia, and Corte; InterRail gets 50% off. Buses connect most towns on the island, but are expensive and infrequent. Consider renting a car. **Calvi,** a beautiful north coast port and resort, has Corsica's only official IYHF hostel, the **BVJ Corsotel** (av. de la République; tel. 95 65 14 15; open March-Oct.; 100F per person, including breakfast) and a tourist office at Port de Plaisance (tel. 95 65 16 67). On the west coast, **Ajaccio,** Corsica's capital and Napoleon's birthplace, wildly celebrates the birthday of its diminutive native son each August 15. Stay at the small **Hôtel Colomba,** 8, av. de Paris (tel. 95 21 12 66; singles 130-150F, doubles and triples 160F), and visit the **tourist office** at pl. Foch (tel. 95 21 40 87). The **Parc Naturel Régional de la Corse** office on rue Général Fiorella in Ajaccio will fill you in on Corsica's spectacular, well-marked hiking trails.

The Alps (Savoie-Dauphiné)

After the humdrum undulations and urban blight of much of France's geography, the Alps are a majestic aspirin. Snow-capped crests, tumbling waterfalls, and rich pastures exhilarate the weary traveling soul, and crystal-clear air will make Paris smog seem just a distant memory.

The region is divided into **Savoie,** including the Mont Blanc massif, and **Dauphiné.** Trains link Grenoble, Chamonix, Chambéry, Aix-les-Bains, and Annecy to each other and to other parts of France, Italy, and Switzerland; a thorough bus system services even the most remote villages. When trains stop at the base of the mountains, cable cars continue. Many towns maintain chalet dormitories, as well as hostels and campgrounds; in less accessible spots, the **Club Alpin Français** runs refuges. Get a list at one of their offices: 136, av. Michel-Croz, Chamonix (tel. 50 53 16 03); 38, av. du Parmelan, Annecy (tel. 50 45 52 76); av. Félix Vialet, 32, Grenoble (tel. 76 87 03 73).

Sample rainbow trout from cold, Alpine streams, raw hams from the Vercors, and sweet *eau de vie,* distilled from wild berries. A warm pot of *fondue savoyarde* (made from local cheese, white wine, and garlic) or a round of *raclette* (grated from the gourd of a grilled swiss cheese, and served with potatoes and gherkins) are both heart-attackingly rich.

The Winter Olympics, based in Albertville, will take place February 8-23, 1992, at ten different ski resorts in Savoie. In France, call 79 92 92 92 for tickets; residents of other countries should go through a designated agency (in Australia, tel. (03) 521 19 10; in Canada, tel. (514) 285-8543; in Great Britain, tel. (0235) 55 48 44; in the U.S., tel. (800) 538-0999).

Annecy

With its winding cobblestone streets, overstuffed flowerboxes, turreted castle, and clear mountain lake, Annecy is reminiscent of those high school homecoming queens that everyone resented for their perfection but fell in love with anyway. Hordes of vacationers, French and otherwise, come to enjoy the lakeside beaches and stroll along the flower-dotted canals around the **Palais d'Ile.** Climb up to the **Château d'Annecy,** also a museum, for a splendid view of the lake. (Open July-Aug. daily 10am-noon and 2-6pm; June and Sept. Wed.-Mon. 10am-noon and 2-6pm. Admission 15F, students 10F.) Boats and windsurfers (45-85F per hr.) cover the transparent waters of the **Lac d'Annecy,** reputedly the purest in Europe.

In mid-July, the **Festival de la Vieille Ville** draws mobs to Annecy for a slew of indoor and outdoor concerts and performances. On the first Saturday in August, Annecy holds a fireworks and watershow extravaganza, the **Fête du Lac** (tickets 45-190F).

Reservations are vital throughout the summer, particularly during July and August. The **tourist office,** pl. de la Libération (tel. 50 45 00 33), in the Bonlieu mall, dispenses a list of hotels and a bevy of brochures on both Annecy and the quieter towns on the upper part of the lake. (Open daily 9am-6:30pm; Oct.-May 9am-noon and 1:45-6:30pm.) With a gorgeous view of the lake, the **Maison des Jeunes (MJC),** 52, rue des Marquisats (tel. 50 45 08 80), is comfortable and modern. Take bus #1 from the station, or walk along the lake from the tourist office. (Reception open 24 hrs. Dorms 55F. Doubles with showers 75F. Call Mon.-Fri. 9am-3pm for reservations.) The **Auberge de Jeunesse La Grande Jeanne (IYHF),** rte. de Semnoz (tel. 50 45 33 19), is in a quiet, wooded area, but requires a 45-minute uphill haul (follow the signs from the tourist office) or a ride on the infrequent bus marked "Semnoz" across the street from the Hôtel de Ville (6F). (Reception open 5-10pm. 50F, breakfast included.) On the road to the youth hostel is the oft-mobbed **Camping Le Belvedere** (tel. 50 45 48 30; open March to mid-Oct.). The five lakeside campgrounds in Albigny help absorb the overflow. (Take a Voyages Crolard bus from Annecy's *gare routière,* connected to the train station.) **Hôtel Savoyard,** 41, av. de Cran (tel. 50 57 08 08), in a residential area 10 minutes from the train station, is comfortable and cheery. (Singles and doubles 100F. Triples 140F. Showers 10F. Breakfast 18F.)

The *vieille ville* has plenty of affordable restaurants serving delicious regional specialties (most *menus* 50-75F). Try the *savoyard* (50F) and *raclette* (55F) at **Taverne du Freti,** 12, rue Ste-Claire (open Tues.-Sun. 7-11:30pm). Bustling open-air markets are held on pl. Ste-Claire (Tues., Fri., and Sun. mornings) and on bd. de Taine (Sat. mornings). A mammoth **Prisunic supermarket** is on pl. Notre-Dame. (Open Mon.-Sat. 8:45am-12:15pm and 2:15-7pm.)

From Annecy's train station, take a Voyages Crolard bus (6 per day, 45 min., 27.50F) to St-Jean-de-Sixt; from the cozy chalet **Les Lucioles** (tel. 50 02 25 04), you can hike, mountain bike or ski without the crowds of the larger resort towns. (Refreshingly comfortable doubles 200F. Triples 250F. Huge, delicious breakfast included. Call ahead to reserve.)

Chamonix

Maybe the Himalayas or the Andes have more mountains per square meter, but only in Chamonix do so many mechanical conveniences move you around them (including **Mont Blanc,** Europe's highest) with so little effort. The cog railway from St-Gervais prepares you for spectacular scenery as it winds over gorges and waterfalls, past forests, and towards the peaks. The valley of Chamonix embraces a number of villages, accessible by foot or bus. Directions and location are often expressed in altitudes—Chamonix is at 1035m, and most everything else is up from there.

Chamonix has some of the most breathtaking *téléphériques* anywhere. Get under way as early as you can—crowds and clouds usually gather by late morning. The dazzling **Aiguille du Midi** is one of the highest in the world. The simplest trip takes you to Plan de l'Aiguille (47F, round-trip 60F), but most continue to Aiguille du Midi (106F, round-trip 140F). Summer skiers (rentals available throughout Chamonix) can go to the next stop, Gare Helbronner, in Italy (153F, round-trip 210F; bring your passport). Bring warm clothes and lunch, and remember that so much in the mountains depends on the weather. The huge **Mer de Glace** glacier can be reached by a special cog railway next to the train station (38F, round-trip 50F) or a slightly strenuous (but safe) one-hour hike.

The **tourist office** at pl. de l'Eglise (tel. 50 53 00 24) has a free room-reservation service as well as information on camping, climbing, and weather conditions; they also sell good 20F maps with trails clearly marked. (Open daily 8:30am-7:30pm; Sept.-June 8:30am-12:30pm and 2-7pm.) Across the street, the **Maison de la Montagne** houses the **Compagnie des Guides** (tel. 50 53 00 88) and a ski school. Upstairs in the **Office de Haute Montagne** (tel. 50 53 22 08), you can get specific, vital information on trails and mountain refuges.

In summer, it's easier to find rooms here than in other resort towns. Hotels in town will flatten your wallet; fortunately, chalets on the periphery are friendly and affordable. A prime choice is the **auberge de jeunesse (IYHF)** in Les Pélerins (tel. 50 53 14 52). Take the bus from pl. de l'Eglise in Chamonix towards Les Houches; get off at the Les Pélerins: école stop, and cross the highway. If coming by train, get off at Les Pélerins, and follow the signs up the hill for 600m. (Reception open 8-10am and 5-10pm. 63F, nonmembers 81F. Breakfast included. Open Dec.-Sept.) The **Chalet Ski Station,** 6, rte. des Moussoux (tel. 50 53 20 25), left of the *téléphérique du Brévent,* up the hill from the tourist office, has large dorm rooms. (Reception open 8am-11pm. 45F. Showers 5F. Sheets 15F.) **Chalet le Chamoniard Volant,** 45, route de la Frasse (tel. 50 53 14 09), provides homey 4-6 bed co-ed rooms and kitchen facilities. (Reception open 10am-10pm. 50F. Breakfast 22F.) The tourist office dispenses a map marked with campsites; **L'Ile des Barrats,** route des Pélerins (tel. 50 53 11 75), near the base of the Aiguille du Midi *téléphérique* is the closest. (16F per person, 14F per tent. Open June 15-Sept. 15.) It is illegal to pitch tents in the Bois du Bouchet.

Le Fer à Cheval, 118, rue Whymper, serves an aromatic fondue for 55F per person. (Open noon-10:30pm.) Several of the restaurants on **rue Joseph Vallot** serve filling 60F *menus.* Restaurant prices will soon drive you to **Supermarché Payot Pertin,** 117, rue Vallot. (Open Mon.-Sat. 8:15am-12:30pm and 2:30-7:30pm, Sun. 8:30am-12:15pm.)

One of Chamonix's most rewarding hikes is to **Lac Blanc,** a turquoise pool encircled by jagged peaks and Alpine flowers. To get there, take a 25-minute walk along the Bois du Bouchet to les Praz, and then board the *téléphérique* for La Flégère (30F, round-trip 43F). From there you can hike the two hours to the lake, often ice-covered even in July.

Grenoble

The largest city in the French Alps and capital of the Dauphiné region, Grenoble combines cultural excellence and an active nightlife with plenty of opportunities to enjoy the surrounding mountains. Take the bubble-shaped cable car (the *téléphérique de la Bastille)* up to the **Bastille** for a spectacular view of the city and the landscape which inspired the likes of Percy Bysshe Shelley to ethereal free verse. Several mountain hikes begin here. *(Téléphérique* open June 15-Sept. 15 daily 9am-midnight; April-June 14 and Sept. 16-Oct. Sun.-Mon. 10am-7:30pm, Tues.-Sat. 9am-midnight; Nov.-March daily 10am-6pm. 17.50F one-way, 28F round-trip; students 9.50F, 14.50F.) A path down will take you through two pretty parks. In the center of town are several interesting museums, including the **Musée de Peinture et de Sculpture,** pl. Verdun (open Wed.-Sun. 10am-noon and 2-6pm; admission 9F, students 5F) and the **Musée de la Résistance et de la Déportation,** 14, rue J-J Rousseau (open Wed.-Sat. 3-6pm; free).

The **tourist office,** 14, rue de la République (tel. 76 54 34 36) has maps (2F), accommodation service (20F), and brochures on hiking and skiing in the region. (Open Mon.-Fri. 9am-6:30pm, Sat. 9am-12:30pm and 1:30-6:30pm.) To reach the **auberge de jeunesse (IYHF),** 18, av. du Grésivaudan (tel. 76 09 33 52), 4km out of town, take bus #8 (6F) from cours Jean Jaurès (one block from the station) to La Quinzaine. (Dorm rooms 65F. Reception open daily 7:30am-11pm.) In the center of town, **Hôtel de la Poste,** 25, rue de la Poste (tel. 76 46 67 25) has friendly management and large rooms. (Singles 100F. Doubles 120-160F. Triples 150-180F.) Wander through the immigrant neighborhood on **rue Chenoise** for cheap North African restaurants, or try the regional specialties at **Bleu Nuit,** 9, pl. de Metz (open Mon. 11:30am-2pm, Tues.-Sat. 11:30am-2pm and 7:30-10:30pm). There's a **Prisunic supermarket** next to the tourist office (open Mon.-Sat. 8:30am-7pm).

Lyon

Capital of Roman Gaul, a free city when France was a monarchy, and now the second-largest city in France, Lyon is known for wealth, food, and its mascot, a marionette named Guignol who has been disparaging kings, ministers, and presidents since 1808. Interesting neighborhoods, 26 museums, energetic nightlife and reasonably priced accommodations make Lyon a fine place to visit. The Saône and the Rhône cleave Lyon into three parts. The heart of Lyon lies between the two rivers, split by rue Victor Hugo, which runs from Perrache (Lyon's main train station) to place Bellecour, and then continues as rue de la République to Terreaux. East of the Rhône are the modern financial district of Part-Dieu, the Part-Dieu train station, and Lyon's large botanical gardens. **Vieux Lyon** (the old city), on the west bank, is a neighborhood of cobblestoned lanes and restored homes, some dating from the Renaissance. Many of the houses sport intriguing architectural quirks: the wincing gargoyle on the top of 11, pl. Neuve St-Jean, or the *traboule* (a passageway from one house to another) from 1, rue de Boeuf to 24, rue St-Jean, are but a few examples. For a walking tour of the old town, pick up the pamphlet at the tourist office.

Best scoped from across the Saône, the **Cathédrale St-Jean** rises amid red tiles and gray stone. The building is noted for its strongly articulated nave, flamboyant rose window, and 14th-century astronomical clock in the north transept. From pl. St-Jean, take the cable car up to the **Fourvière esplanade,** from which you can gaze down onto the urban sprawl. On the summit of the hill rises the extravagant 19th-century **Basilique de Fourvière.** (Open daily 8am-noon and 2-6pm. Free.)

The **Musée des Beaux Arts,** in the Palais St-Pierre at pl. des Terraux, is known chiefly for its Spanish and Dutch Masters, impressionists, and early moderns. (Open Wed.-Sun. 10:30am-6pm. Admission 20F, students 15F, under 18 free.) The **Musée d'Art Contemporain,** located in the same building, houses some excellent temporary exhibits of contemporary artists. (Open Wed.-Mon. noon-6pm. Admission 20F, students 15F, under 18 free.) The **Musée des Marionettes** at pl. de Petit Collège (tel. 78 42 03 61) in the Hôtel Gadagne displays the beloved Lyonnais Guignol (Open Wed.-Mon. 10:45am-6pm. Admission 20F, students 15F). The tourist office can supply you with a list of additional museums, and a 30F day pass to all of them. When museumitis strikes, leave the city noise behind for the roses and fawns of the **Parc de la Tête d'Or,** Lyon's botanical and zoological garden. (Open daily in summer 6am-10pm; in off-season 8am-8pm.)

The **tourist office** is on pl. Bellecour (tel. 78 42 25 75), two metro stops or a 10-minute walk down rue Victor Hugo from the Perrache train station. (Open Mon.-Fri. 9am-7pm, Sat. 9am-6pm, Sun. 10am-6pm; Sept.-June Mon.-Fri. 9am-6pm, Sat. 9am-5pm, Sun. 10am-5pm.) An additional office is in Gare Perrache itself (tel. 78 42 22 07; open Mon.-Sat. 9am-12:30pm and 2-6pm). Lyon's **auberge de jeunesse (IYHF),** 51, rue Roger Salengro (tel. 78 76 39 23), is a sociable place with excellent kitchen facilities, a TV room, and a snack bar upstairs. Take the metro to Bellecour and bus #35 to Georges Lévy; after 9pm, take bus #53 from Perrache to Etats-Unis Viviani, and walk ½km along the train tracks. From Part-Dieu station, take bus #36 to Viviani Juliot-Curie. Look for grape-picking jobs here in September. (Reception closed noon-5pm. Curfew 11:30pm. 42F, nonmembers 60F. Breakfast 15F.) The **Residence Benjamin Delessert,** 145, av. Jean Jaurès (tel. 78 61 41 41), is a dormitory with comfortable beds. From Perrache, take any bus that goes to J. Macé and walk under the train tracks for five to 10 minutes; from Part-Dieu, take the subway to Macé. (Singles 70F. Doubles 112F. Open July-Aug. only.) **Hôtel Croix-Pâquet,** 11, pl. Croix-Pâquet (tel. 78 28 51 49), in Terreaux, has simple and comfortable rooms. Take the subway from either station to the Croix-Pâquet. (Singles 90-100F. Doubles 100F, with shower 130-160F. Showers 15F. Breakfast 18F.) For **camping,** try huge **Dardilly** (tel. 78 35 64 55). Take bus #19 from the Hôtel de Ville (direction "Ecully-Dardilly") to the Parc d'Affaires stop. (45F, tent and car included; 17F each extra person. Open March-Oct.)

Meals climax a sojourn in Lyon. Though the world's best chefs charge more than you can afford, there are still plenty of great budget options. Chocolate lovers should not miss the museum-like *pâtisserie* **Bernachon,** 42, cours Franklin Roosevelt, on the east bank of the Rhône with beautifully-presented pastries that taste even better than they look. Some say their *palets d'or* are made of the world's best chocolate (open Tues.-Sat. 8am-7pm, Sun. 8am-5pm). The **Café Jura,** 25, rue Tupin, six blocks north of Hôtel Dieu, is one of Lyon's 20 remaining *bouchons* (inns specializing in local cuisine; entrées change daily (35-72F; open Mon.-Fri. from 7:30am; lunch noon-2pm, dinner 7:30-10:30pm). **L'Eau Vive,** 65, rue Victor Hugo, serves health food galore, cafeteria-style. *(Plats du jour* and salad bar 24-30F. Open Mon.-Sat. 11:30am-2:30pm.) Check the rue St-Jean, in Vieux Lyon, for more restaurants.

Lyon is a major rail center, with frequent connections to Paris, Switzerland, Italy, Germany, the Côte d'Azur, and Spain. Gare Perrache is the more convenient of Lyon's two train stations; Gare Part-Dieu is in the center of the city's commercial district. BIJ tickets are sold at **Voyage Wasteels** (tel. 78 37 80 17) at Gare Perrache. (Open Mon.-Fri. 9am-6:30pm, Sat. 9am-5:30pm.) Hitching is utterly dismal; if you choose to hitch to Paris, take bus #2, 5, 19, 21, 22, or 31 to Pont Monton and the N6.

Burgundy (Bourgogne)

Burgundy's ambassadors to the outer world are its annual 40 million bottles of wine, which graciously represent a grand, sparse landscape of monasteries, cathedrals, and châteaux. Burgundy was an ecclesiastical center in medieval times, and the religious orders that constructed the monumental abbeys at Tournus, Cluny, and Vézelay also planted the green vineyards which now carpet the hills. Their wines were originally reserved for liturgical celebrations, but are now an integral part of the region's gastronomy, imparting flavor to *boeuf bourguignon, coq au vin,* and Dijon's famous mustard. Other regional specialties include *gougère* (a soft pastry with cheese), *escargots,* and *quenelles* (dumplings of fish or veal). Go to Dijon and the smaller cities for culture and excitement, but leave time to explore the charming villages of the surrounding countryside, with its winding rivers and rolling hills.

Dijon

Dijon's grace persists from its days as a ducal city that rivaled even the French crown in wealth and influence. On a cool summer night, when the streets are deserted, the rows of elegant *hôtels particuliers* (mansions) silhouetted against the darkening sky seem frozen in the 17th century. Yet Dijon is an animated, vibrant city: its festive and tastefully restored *vieille ville* lends itself to wandering and people-watching, and its prominent university keeps the ancient city young.

Dijon's greatest attraction is undoubtedly the **Musée des Beaux Arts,** occupying a wing of the splendid **Palais des Ducs de Bourgogne.** Second only to the Louvre among French museums, it houses the impressive tombs of Philippe le Hardi and Jean sans Peur. (Open Wed.-Mon. 10am-6pm. Admission 10F, free Sun. A 12.60F card will admit you to all of Dijon's museums.) Gargoyles leer from the front of the **Eglise de Notre Dame,** while **Cathédrale St-Benigne's** austere façade remains an excellent example of Burgundy's early Gothic. The fine Gallo-Roman collection of the **Musée Archéologique** is housed under the 13th-century arches of the adjacent monastery.

For a complete list of the more than 50 *hôtels particuliers* still standing, including those at 38 and 40, rue des Forges and 8 and 10, rue de la Chouette, visit the **tourist office,** pl. Darcy (tel. 80 43 42 12), a five-minute walk down av. Maréchal-Foch from the train station (open July-Aug. 8am-9pm; mid-April to June and Sept. to mid-Nov. 9am-noon and 2-9pm; mid-Nov. to mid-April 9am-noon and 2-7pm). The cheapest beds in Dijon are at the **auberge de jeunesse (IYHF),** 1, bd. Champollion (tel. 80 71 32 12), a classic mega-hostel with bar, disco, and screaming school groups (dorms 58F). To reach it, take bus #5 from the "Bar Bleu," pl. Grangier to Epirey, the terminus. The **Foyer International d'Etudiants,** 1, av. Maréchal Leclerc (tel. 80 71 51 01; take bus #4 (direction "St. Apollinaire") to Parc des Sports) is a cheerful dormitory. (Singles 51F.) Hotels in the center fill quickly in summer. Try **Hôtel Monge,** 20, rue Monge (tel. 80 30 55 41) near Eglise St-Jean. (Singles and doubles off a courtyard 115-125F, with shower 150-160F. Triples and quads 180-250F.) **Hôtel Montchapet,** 26-28, rue Jacques Cellerier (tel. 80 55 33 31), on a quiet, residential street a 10-minute walk from the center, has luxurious singles and doubles for 120-175F (with shower 150-220F; triples and quads 260-290F). **Camping du Lac** (tel. 80 43 54 72), 1km behind the train station via av. Albert 1*er*, is clean and near a pretty lake (10.50F per person; open April-Nov. 15).

The most elegant way to sample Burgundy's fabulous wines is with a gourmet meal—easy to come by in Dijon. **Au Bec Fin,** 47, rue Jeannin, is outstanding, with a 49F *menu* at lunch, and 69F and 89F *menus* at dinner. (Open Mon.-Fri. noon-1:30pm and 7:30-10:30pm, Sat. 7:30-10:30pm.) Otherwise, pick up vital vittles at any of the food shops along rue de la Liberté.

From June to November, Dijon becomes a festival town; the brochure *Un Petit Guide de la Vie Musicale en Bourgogne* lists the concerts played during the **Festival des Nuits de Bourgogne** and during **Un Eté Musical.** The latter attracts internationally renowned groups. On a Sunday in early September, the weeklong **Festival International de Folklore** culminates in Dijon's traditional **Fête de la Vigne,** a festival honoring Burgundy's grapes.

Near Dijon

The proud and prosperous town of **Beaune,** 20 minutes south of Dijon on the Lyon rail line (12 per day, 30F) has disgorged wine for centuries. Beaune is famous for its ancient *caves* (wine cellars) and *dégustation* (tasting) of local wines. Visit the **Marché aux Vins,** near the Hôtel-Dieu. For 40F, plus 10F for a cup, you can drink an unlimited quantity of 37 of Burgundy's finest wines (the best of which come last, so don't get too rocked on the early labels). (Open Feb.-Nov. daily 9:30am-noon and 2:30-6:30pm.) Busloads of tourists arrive by late morning, so hit the *caves* early. The **Hôtel-Dieu,** built by the tax-collector Nicholas Rollin in the 15th century as a hospital for the poor, is a landmark of Burgundian architecture with its colorful roof tiles. (Open daily 9am-6:30pm; Jan.-March and Nov. 18-Dec. 9-11:30am and 2-5:30pm. Admission 30F, students 20F.) The **tourist office,** opposite the Hôtel-Dieu (tel. 80 22 24 51), provides a list of *caves* in Beaune and the surrounding area. (Open June-Sept. daily 9am-midnight; March-May and Oct-Nov. daily 9am-10pm; Dec.-Feb. daily 9am-7:15pm.) The **Transco** bus company (tel. 80 71 40 34) stops at all the important wine centers on the **Côte d'Or;** a schedule is available at the tourist office.

Twenty minutes and 25F south of Beaune on the Dijon-Lyon train line, the small city of **Chalon-sur-Saône** merits a visit for its convenient location and excellent photography museum. The **Musée Nicéphore-Nièpce,** 28, quai des Messageries, named after the Chalon native who invented photography in 1816, has a fascinating permanent collection, including the first camera ever made. (Open Wed.-Mon. 9:30-11:30am and 2:30-5:30pm. Admission 10F, students 5F, Wed. free.) The basic **auberge de jeunesse (IYHF),** rue d'Amsterdam (tel. 85 46 62 77), on the river, has dorm rooms for 38F. (Office open 7-9:30am and 5:30-10:30pm.) Pick up a map and information on Chalon's many festivals at the **tourist office** (tel. 85 48 37 97) in pl. Chabas on bd. de la République (open Mon.-Sat. 9am-12:30pm and 1:30-7pm).

Once the center of Western Christendom, with its largest church until St. Peter's was built in Rome, the abbey at **Cluny** is an ultimate Romanesque masterpiece. Founded in 910 AD, most of the abbey was destroyed during the French Revolution, but you can still be awed by the grandeur of its remnants by taking the informative tour that leaves from the Musée Ochier. **Cluny Séjour** (tel. 85 59 08 83), behind the bus stop, is hostel living at its finest in a renovated 18th-century building. (Singles 105F, doubles, triples or quads 60F per person. Reception open 7-11am and 5:30-10pm.) SNCF buses run to Cluny 4 to 6 times per day from Macon and Chalon-sur-Saône, both on the main rail line. The Cluny **tourist office,** 6, rue Mercière (tel. 85 59 05 34), explicates local sights and wines. (Open daily 10am-7pm, April-June and Oct. Mon.-Sat. 10am-noon and 2-6pm; Nov.-March Tues.-Sat. 2-4:40pm.)

Perched high atop a hill overlooking a lush checkerboard of forest and fertile pastures, **Vézelay** is famous for its 12th-century Romanesque **Basilique de la Made-**

leine. The prominent tympanum over the central portal inside the church depicts Christ inspiring his apostles to convert the peoples of the world. To reach Vézelay from Paris or Dijon, take the train to Laroche-Migenne and change for Avallon. Buses run from Avallon and Sermizelles (Mon.-Sat. 2 per day, 1 on Sun.) The Avallon and Vézelay tourist offices have schedules, or call Cars de la Madeleine (tel. 86 33 25 67). Hitchhiking is fairly easy as well. Stay at the friendly and rustic **Centre de Rencontres Internationales Pax Christi,** rue des Ecoles (tel. 86 33 26 73), off the main street (45F; open July-Sept. 5) or the **auberge de jeunesse (IYHF),** route de l'Etang (tel. 86 33 24 18 or 86 33 25 57), 600m out of town. (Lockout 10am-6pm. Curfew 10:30pm. 39F. Camping next door 10F per person. Open June-Sept.)

Alsace and Lorraine

Acrimoniously disputed during the 19th and early 20th centuries, Alsace and Lorraine figured prominently in three modern wars between France and Germany; the cultural battle has never stopped. The Route du Vin, a ribbon of wine-producing villages, threads through the lakes, valleys, and wooded slopes of the Vosges region. Dividing the provinces, the Vosges make for ideal hiking, camping, and cross-country skiing, with hundreds of miles of marked trails and overnight shelters along the way. Club Vosgien dispenses maps and guides to the region (4, rue de la Douane in Strasbourg; tel. 88 32 57 96).

Sophisticated and elegant, **Strasbourg** impressed both Goethe and Rousseau. Home of the Council of Europe and one of three bases of the European Parliament, the city today is a symbol of international cooperation. Unlike many bland diplomatic centers, it retains a distinctive local flavor with half-timbered houses, covered bridges, and flower-lined canals.

Start a tour at the **cathedral,** whose airy spire soars 160m above the historic center. While you wait for the tuneful tinkle of the **horloge astronomique** (astrological clock) at 12:30pm, take a gander at the **Pilier des Anges** (Angels' Pillar), a masterpiece of Gothic sculpture; both are in the south transept (4F to see the tiny apostles parade around and the rooster crow). Across from the cathedral is the gilded 18th-century **Palais Rohan,** housing porcelain, archeological artifacts, and fine arts museums, and the **Maison de l'Oeuvre Notre-Dame,** a huge collection of medieval and Renaissance art. For folklore, visit the **Musée Alsacien,** 23, quai St-Nicolas. The **Musée d'Art Moderne,** also across from the cathedral, holds a collection of paintings and sculpture by Chagall, Arp, Klee, and the usual lineup of impressionists. Many of the more famous works are in storage, awaiting the opening of a new museum in 1994. (All museums open Wed.-Mon. 10am-noon and 2-6pm; Oct.-March Mon. and Wed.-Sat. 2-6pm, Sun. 10am-noon and 2-6pm. Admission to the Palais Rohan 15F, students 8F. Admission to all other museums 10F, students 5F.) In early June, Strasbourg hosts an **International Festival of Music.**

The main **tourist office** on pl. Gutenberg (tel. 88 32 57 07), in the kernel of the old city, dispenses guides to entertainment and 2F city maps. (Open June-Sept. daily 8am-7pm; April-May and Oct. 9am-6pm; Nov.-March Mon.-Sat. 9am-12:30pm and 1:45-6pm.) They'll find you a room for 6F, as will the **annex** at the train station (tel. 88 32 51 49). Winsome budget hotels flourish in Strasbourg, but reserve one to two days ahead in summer. The **Auberge de Jeunesse René Cassin (IYHF),** 9, rue de l'Auberge de Jeunesse (tel. 88 30 26 46), 2km from the station, has one of the best hostel bars in France, a game room, good meals, and a campground. Take bus #3, 13, or 23 from rue du Vieux-Marché-aux-Vins. (Reception open 7am-12:30pm and 2pm-midnight. Members only. Dorms 59F. Singles 130F. Doubles and triples 83F. Breakfast included. Camping 33F per person; breakfast included. Midnight curfew. No lockout.) The sparkling **CIARUS (Centre International d'Accueil de Strasbourg),** 7, rue Finkmatt (tel. 88 32 12 12), flags terrific rooms just 15 minutes from the train station. Take rue du Maire-Kuss to the canal, turn left, then make a left onto rue Finkmatt. (Dorms 65-70F. Singles 165F. Breakfast included. Lunch or dinner 45F. No lockout. Curfew 1am.) **Hôtel de la Cruche d'Or,** 6, rue des Tonneliers (tel. 88 32 11 23) is near the cathedral and has spacious, impeccable rooms. (Singles and doubles 100F, with shower 145-165F. Extra bed 40F. Breakfast 20F.)

Sample succulent, calorie-laden Alsatian cuisine in the bevy of restaurants around rue de la Douane and pl. St-Etienne. **Pizzaria Aldo,** 8, rue du Faisan, is a wildly popular pizza joint where you decorate sundaes (29F) and pizzas (39F) with toppings galore. Around the corner, France's one and only milk bar, **Lait's Go,** 27, rue des Frères, misses a trademark violation by just two letters, but hits the target with exotic milky cocktails (25F) and a 41F luncheon *menu.*

Strasbourg is a major European rail junction; trains go to Paris (every 2 hr., 4½ hr., 247F), Luxembourg (4 per day, 2½ hr., 136F), Frankfurt (every hr., 2½ hr., 188F), and Zurich (6 per day, 3 hr., 188F).

Ringed by vineyards and overshadowed by the craggy Vosges, **Colmar** slices Alsatian life more authentically. The recently restored tanners' lodgings and **La Petite Venise** preserve the feeling of a medieval town. Don't miss the extraordinary **Musée Unterlinden,** on pl. Unterlinden, a Dominican convent housing medieval religious art, including Matthias Grünewald's gruesome and beautiful *Isenheim Altarpiece.* (Open daily 9am-6pm; Nov.-March Wed.-Mon. 10am-noon and 2-5pm. Admission 25F, students 15F.) The annual **Alsatian Wine Festival** is held here in August, with kegs of beer and free wine tasting. Early September brings the **Jours Choucroute** (Sauerkraut Days), two weeks of feasting, dancing, wine and beer, and plenty of you-know-what. A five-minute walk from the station, the **Maison des Jeunes (Centre Internationale de Séjour),** 17, rue Camille Schlumberger (tel. 89 41 26 87) occupies a wealthy residential neighborhood close to the town center. (Reception open 8am-noon and 2-11pm. Curfew 11pm. Dorms 35F.) Colmar is 30 minutes south of Strasbourg by frequent train.

In neighboring Lorraine, the public buildings of **Metz** are all constructed of a special regional stone, *pierre de jaumont,* which lends the city its glowing mustard overtone. The **Cathédrale St-Etienne** is a veritable gallery of stained glass, with four tiered windows including masterpieces by Chagall. Nearby, Metz's fascinating **Musée de l'Art et de l'Histoire,** built over ruins of Roman baths, reconstructs medieval and Renaissance home interiors. (Open Wed.-Mon. 10am-noon and 2-6pm; Oct.-May Wed.-Mon. 10am-noon and 2-5pm. Admission 15F, students 7.50F.) The fantastic **Auberge de Jeunesse,** allée de Metz Plage (tel. 87 30 44 02), is on the river across town from the station. Hop bus #3 or #11 from the station to Pontiffroy. (Free bike rental. Lockout 10am-5pm. No curfew. 6-bed dorms 55F per person. Singles 80F. Doubles 140F. Breakfast included.) Metz lies on the main rail line between Strasbourg and Luxembourg; trains run to Strasbourg (every 2 hr., 1½ hr., 42F) and Basel in Switzerland (3 per day, 3 hr., 162F).

Champagne

Champagne, the region between Lorraine and Paris, is under French law the only source of real champagne, which must be vinted according to the rigorous *méthode champenoise.* The best way to see and tase the results of this painstaking procedure is to visit the underground **caves** of Reims and Epernay, both a little over an hour from Paris's Gare de l'Est, where prestigious champagne houses carefully guard their precious troves.

Pounded to rubble during World War I, **Reims** has been tenaciously reconstructed and the modern city gracefully combines contemporary structures (such as funky egg-shaped fountains) with a restored fleet of Gothic and Roman buildings. The **Cathédrale de Notre Dame** on pl. du Cardinal Luçon is a Gothic fantasy ornamented with dreamlike Chagall windows. From Clovis to Charles X, 25 kings of France were crowned beneath its vaulted roof. The **Palais du Tau** next door, once the Episcopalian archbishop's palace, houses medieval sculptures and cathedral treasures. (Open daily 9:30am-6:30pm; Sept.-June daily 9:30am-noon and 2-6pm. Admission 23F, students 12F.) To the east lies the **Basilique St-Remi,** reputed resting place of France's earliest kings. The **Musée St-Denis,** once an ancient abbey, has a fine Corot collection and some impressionist works. (Open Mon.-Fri. 2-6:30pm, Sat.-Sun. 2-7pm. Admission 8F, students free.) Snag a brochure with maps and hours of Reims's underground city of **champagne caves** from the tourist office. Most offer free tours in French and English. The most engaging *caves* (and perhaps the best wines) belong to **Pommery,** 5, pl. du Gén. Gouraid (tel. 26 49 59 70).

The **tourist office** (tel. 26 47 25 69) is in the ruins of the old chapterhouse, next to the cathedral, at 2, rue Guillaume de Machault. (Open Mon.-Sat. 9am-7:30pm, Sun. 9:30am-6:30pm; Oct.-March Mon.-Sat. 9:30am-6:30pm, Sun. 9:30am-5:30pm.) Stay at the spruce, spritely **Centre International de Séjour (IYHF),** 1, chaussée Bocquaine (tel. 26 40 52 60), opposite parc Leo Lagrange, a 15-minute walk from the station. Turn right on bd. Général Leclerc on the far side of the gardens in front of the station, cross the bridge (rue de Vesle), and take the first left. (Members only. Singles 67F. Doubles and triples 61F per person. Breakfast 11F.) If you have a student ID, **CROUS,** 34, bd. Henri Vasnier (tel. 26 85 50 16) can set you up with cheaper though more distant singles in vacant university dorms during July and August (40F; open Mon.-Fri. 8:30am-noon and 1:30-5pm; call 3-4 wks. ahead). The agreeable **Hôtel d'Alsace,** 6, rue Général-Sarrail (tel. 26 47 44 08), is but steps away from both the station and the sights. (Singles 90-105F, doubles 115F, with shower 145F. Breakfast 20F.) With a bonsai tree, stained glass and fireplaces in many rooms, **Hôtel Linguet,** 14, rue Linguet (tel. 26 47 31 89), lets singles and doubles for 70-90F (with shower 110-120F; breakfast 18F).

Place Drouet d'Erlon is crammed with *brasseries* serving *menus* for around 55F. **Les Brisants,** 13, rue de Chativesle, is on a side street off pl. d'Erlon and has a filling, four-course, 69F *menu* served in a refreshing dining room. (Open Mon.-Fri. noon-2pm and 7:30-10pm, Sat. 7-11pm.)

There are no great cathedrals in **Epernay,** but the golden *caves* under avenue de Champagne inspire worship of a different sort. Several firms offer free samples. The most popular tour is at **Moët et Chandon,** 20, av. de Champagne, home of James Bond's preferred vintage, *Dom Perignon.* For information about other *caves* and about lodging, consult the **tourist office** 7, av. de Champagne (tel. 26 55 33 00), off pl. de la République. The **Foyer des Jeunes Travailleurs,** 2, rue Pupin (tel. 26 51 62 51) often has space in huge modern rooms three minutes from the station off rue de Reims. (Ages 18-25 only. Singles and dorm rooms 62F. Breakfast and sheets included. Decent institutional meals 36F.) **Hôtel St-Pierre,** 1, rue Jeanne d'Arc (tel. 25 54 40 80), seduces guests with elegant rooms and sweetheart management (singles and doubles 84-89F, with shower 120F. Breakfast 21F).

The North

The North remains the final frontier of tourist-free France, probably because ferry passengers from England are so disheartened by the dreary port cities of Calais and Dunkerque that they flee directly to Paris. Head inland to the grand cathedral towns and dodge the coast entirely; although the dearth of English-speaking tourist officials may cause snags, the region's authenticity richly rewards the discomfort. The world's battlefronts have swept across northern France four times in this century alone, and nearly every town bears scars from the wanton bombing of World War II.

The Channel Ports

Ever since Richard the Lion-Hearted and his crusaders passed through *en route* to Jerusalem, **Calais** has been the Continent's primary portal to Britain. The cranes in town are working on the **Channel Tunnel,** which, upon completion in 1993, will finally connect England to Europe by rail. For now, Calais is the most frequently used transfer point for **Sealink** (tel. 21 96 70 70) and **P&O** (tel. 21 97 21 21) ferries to Dover, England (1½ hr., 210F). The **Hoverport** (tel. 21 96 67 10) fires its space-age craft to Dover every hour (35 min., 220F, 5-day round-trip 330F). A free shuttle bus connects you from port to train station; from there it's a three- to four-hour trip to Paris Nord. Ferry tickets can be purchased in advance from travel agencies in London and Paris. There are 24-hour **currency exchanges** at both the ferry terminals and the Hoverport. The town's **tourist office,** 12, bd. Clemenceau, provides information on much of France (open Mon.-Sat. 9am-12:30pm and 2:30-6:30pm). Should you have the dubious pleasure of staying the night here, try the **Maison Pour Tous,** 81, bd. Jacquard (tel. 21 34 69 53; reception open 5-10pm; 35F; open July-Aug.), or drop your bags at **Hôtel le Littoral,** 71, rue Aristide Briand (tel. 21 34 47 28), with huge, comfy rooms. (Singles 90F. Doubles 100-130F.) The large, friendly **Taverne Kronenbourg,** 46, rue Royale, has a 68F three-course menu. (Open daily 9am-10pm.)

In 636, a pilotless boat carrying a statue of the Virgin Mary washed up on the beach at **Boulogne,** and the town immediately became a magnet for pilgrims. Towering over the *vieille ville* (old city) is the 19th-century **Basilique de Notre Dame.** Beneath it are crypts containing the remains of a Roman temple (open Tues.-Sun. 2-5pm; admission 8F, children 4F). Next to the cathedral stands the **belfry,** a 13th-century tower that surveys the port. (Open Mon.-Sat. 8am-noon and 2:30-6pm. Free.) Hovercrafts zoom from the **Hoverport** (tel. 21 30 27 26) for Dover (every 2 hr., 40 min., 220F); **Sealink** (tel. 21 30 25 11) ferries run to Folkestone (every 3 hr., 1½ hrs., 210F; 15% student discount); and **P&O Ferries** ships passengers to Dover (every 3 hr., 1½ hr., 210F; 15% student discount). The town has a convivial **tourist office** at pl. Frédéric Sauvage (tel. 21 31 68 38; open daily 10am-7pm, Oct.-May Tues.-Sat. 9am-noon and 2-6pm). Boulogne's **auberge de jeunesse (IYHF),** 36, rue de la Port Gayole (tel. 21 31 48 22), offers cramped but polished dormitories. (Reception open 8-10am and 5-11pm. 55F. Sheets 14F.) The **Hôtel Hamiot,** 1, rue Faidherbe, across the bridge from the ferries (tel. 21 31 44 20), has spotless, sun-drenched rooms. (Singles 103F. Doubles 116F. Breakfast 18F.) Restaurants, bistros, and their quintalingual menus line rue de Lille in the *vieille ville.*

A fishing town since the 10th century, **Dunkerque,** now the third largest port in France, went through Flemish, Spanish, and English rule before being sold to the French in 1662, and still remains unaffected by the waves of foreigners washing over its tiled sidewalks and clean beaches. The **tourist office,** pl. du Beffroi (tel. 28 66 79 21), has an excellent free map of the city, locates accommodations for the desperate, and changes cash after banks close. (Open Mon.-Sat. 9am-6:30pm; Sept.-June Mon.-Sat. 9am-noon and 2-6:30pm.) The town's **auberge de jeunesse (IYHF),** pl. Paul Asseman (tel. 28 63 36 34), by the beach, is crowded but clean (42F, breakfast 15F). **Hôtel le Moderne,** 2, rue Nationale (tel. 28 66 80 24), provides pleasant, spacious rooms above a lively café. (Singles 100F. Doubles from 105F.) The intimate **Tête d'Ail,** 26, rue Terquem, serves a marvelous *menu* for 89F, lunch only 45F. (Open Mon.-Fri. noon-1:30pm and 7pm-2am, Sat. 7pm-2am, Sun. noon-1:30pm and 7-11pm.) The **Musée d'Art Contemporain,** rue des Bains, across from the hostel (tel. 28 59 21 65) has a fine contemporary art collection and is enclosed by the **Jardin des Sculptures.** (Museum open Wed.-Mon. 10am-7pm. Admission 6F, students 3F.) Also worth a peek is the **Musée des Beaux Arts,** pl. du Général de Gaulle (tel. 28 66 21 57), which houses copious 17th- and 18th-century paintings by French and Flemish painters. (Open Wed.-Mon. 10am-noon and 2-6pm. Admission 6F, students 3F, free Sunday.)

Lille

Founded in the 11th century as a way-station for trade boats on the river Deûle, once-industrial Lille is now the fifth-largest city in France. A quarter of its residents are students, and despite their socialist leanings the birthplace of General de Gaulle at 9, rue Princess, has been converted to a museum. (Open Wed.-Sun. 10am-noon and 2-5pm. 7F.) Among French museums, the town's **Musée des Beaux-Arts,** on pl. de la République, is second only to the Louvre, but is closed until May 1993 for restorations. You should savor the town's ultra-modern, fully computerized, and conductor-less **métro** at least once. The **tourist office,** pl. Rihour (tel. 20 30 81 00), haunts a 15th-century castle (open Mon.-Sat. 9am-12:15pm and 1:30-6pm). Five minutes away, the **post office** is at 7, pl. de la République (open Mon.-Fri. 8am-7pm, Sat. 8am-noon). The **auberge de jeunesse (IYHF)** at 1, av. Julien Destrée (tel. 20 52 98 94), is newly renovated, and 10 minutes from the train station by foot. (Strict 11pm curfew. 53F. Sheets and breakfast included.) Conveniently in the pedestrian district, **Hôtel Constantin,** 5, rue des Fossés (tel. 20 54 32 26), proffers agreeable singles and doubles for 80F. **La Chicorée,** 15, pl. Rihour, serves fantastic seafood and Flemish specialties around the clock to *lillois* in the know. (Menu 60F. Open daily 10am-6am.) After dinner, Lille's young set packs into **Bar de L'Echo,** 20, pl. Charles de Gaulle, for Irish-style pints (12-14F; open Mon.-Sat. 5pm-2am).

From Lille to Paris

The route from Lille to Paris hides some of northern France's best-kept secrets, largely uncompromised by tourists. **Arras** is built above underground tunnels *(les Boves)* that housed first medieval chalk miners, then British soldiers in World War II. The **tourist office** (tel. 21 51 26 95), in the 15th-century **Hôtel de Ville,** lists accommodations and restaurants, as well as times of tours of the tunnels (17F). (Open Mon.-Fri. 9am-12:15pm and 1:30-6pm, Sat. 9am-noon and 2-5pm.) Arras's **Grand'Place** and **Place des Héros** feature façades in the Flemish style after the Grand'Place in Brussels. The town has a central **auberge de jeunesse (IYHF),** 59, Grand'Place (tel. 21 25 54 53), with firm beds and a culinary bonanza (even a microwave). (Open daily 7:30-10:30am and 6-11pm. 39F. Shower and sheets included.) Try the pizza with mussels at **Restaurant Montesilvano,** 55, Grand'Place (pizzas 27-36F). Eight kilometers north of Arras lie the somber tunnels and monument of **Vimy,** a memorial to the 75,000 Canadians killed in World War I. (Open daily 10am-6pm. Free.) Trains run three times per day from Arras (13 min., 24F round-trip). It's a healthy hike from the station to the memorial.

The stately Gothic **Cathédrale de Notre Dame** in **Amiens,** begun in 1220, was intended to provide suitable housing for a piece of St. John the Baptist's skull, and perhaps indirectly to cast the great cathedrals of Paris and Laon in its shadow. The highly ornate west façade and detailed interior together display some 4000 figures tracing episodes from the Old and New Testaments. Of interest to science fiction fans is the home of **Jules Verne,** at the corner of bd. Jules Verne and rue Charles Dubois (tel. 22 45 37 84; open Tues.-Sat. 9:30am-noon and 2-6pm; free), and his tomb in the **Cimetière de la Madeleine.** Amiens has no hostel, but the inexpensive **Hôtel de la Renaissance,** 8bis, rue André (tel. 22 91 70 23) will cheerfully put you up in rooms near the cathedral. (Singles 80-100F. Doubles 90-110F. Breakfast 15F.)

Laon, a dramatic town perched on an upstart butte in the middle of flat prairie, huddles under its tremendous **Cathédrale de Notre Dame,** the first of the great Gothic cathedrals. The cathedral's five towers sport the heads of oxen, in memory of the ox who mysteriously appeared to help bring building materials to the top of the hill. Ask at the **tourist office** (tel. 23 20 28 62), beside the cathedral (in what was France's first hospital), for the full story and a list of budget accommodations and restaurants. Or stay in the pumpkin-orange interior of the **Maison des Jeunes**

20, rue du Cloître (tel. 23 20 27 64), near the cathedral. (No curfew. 65F, breakfast and sheets included. Call ahead.)

GERMANY

USD$1 = 1.75 Deutschmarks (DM, or DEM) — DM1 = USD$0.57
CAD$1 = DM1.53 — DM1 = CAD$0.65
GBP£1 = DM2.92 — DM1 = GBP£0.34
AUD$1 = DM1.36 — DM1 = AUD$0.73
NZD$1 = DM1.00 — DM1 = NZD$1.00
Country Code (West): 49 — International Dialing Prefix: 00
Country Code (East): 37 — International Dialing Prefix: 06

For decades, being German meant being divided. Two years after the firestorm of massive popular demonstrations that spelled East Germany's simultaneous liberation and collapse in October, 1989, Germany (Deutschland) is whole again. East

Germany formally withered away completely on October 2, 1990, and the last of its non-convertible *Ostmark* coins were carted away for scrap metal in July 1991. But while the Wall has become an old memory, destroyed by bulldozers and tourists' chisels, investment in infrastucture, from transportation to telecommunications, is sorely needed in the east, and Germany now faces the harder task of reconstructing a common, borderless consciousness in the hearts, minds and laws of the people.

Unable to compete with the west, the east's old state socialist firms have been hit with wholesale bankruptcy, and the popularity of Chancellor Helmut Kohl is eroding in the face of this increasingly obvious economic crisis. In the summer of 1991, over one million so-called *Ossis* (easterners) were unemployed, despite a rash of new buildings and bright paint jobs. Meanwhile, their richer *Wessi* cousins, after the euphoria of greeting lost relatives, have begun to taunt them for supposed capitalist backwardness and naive consumerism. There's much confusion, but no real regret: Germans are committed to a common future as Europe's largest and most powerful nation. Some see this as a historically tragic situation, but this time Germany is politically anchored in the European Community, whose vision of a united Europe it has consistently supported. Still, eyebrows are rising at home and abroad about the hotly contested decision in July 1991 to return the *Bundestag* (parliament) from quiet Bonn to its old imperial seat in giant, belligerent Berlin—a city fast regaining its place among the great metropolises of Europe.

Language and culture have always united Germans much more than politics; when present-day Germany was no more than a hodgepodge of fortified principalities, the poets, musicians and architects gave the nation an idea of itself. Here eastern Germany takes pride of place. From its cities sprang Luther, Bach, Händel, Goethe, Schiller, Hegel and Nietzsche, shooting stars of human intellectual and artistic achievement. Today, the nation has a more diverse face than many of its own citizens recognize. Decades of immigration have made the myth of a homogenous blond nation falser than ever. One test for modern Germany lies in the fate of its so-called *Ausländer* (foreigners) and *Gastarbeiter* (guest workers), brought in during labor shortages from countries like Yugoslavia and Turkey; their children are now Germany's as well, but many remain unrecognized, subject to distrust and (especially in the east) resurgent xenophobia. Still, Germans have plenty to celebrate. From the rubble of wartime destruction, Germany has built the richest, most humane society its people have ever known.

Both east and west are lands of great cities, from the arched cathedral of Cologne to the stubborn Bavarian independence of vivacious Munich and the moodiness of united Berlin, while letters and music gush from Dresden, Leipzig and Weimar. But away from the modern metropolises, the old image of Germany as a land of half-timbered villages survives. The towns on the Romantic Road and the *Märchenstraße* (Fairy Tale Road, by the Weser River) have preserved much of their late medieval appearance. The old cities of Heidelberg, Tübingen and Freiburg in the southwest have long contributed to Germany's illustrious university tradition, while the rural villages of the Thuringian Forest, Elbe River valley and sunny Baltic coast belie eastern Germany's stark reputation. Span the old border across Goethe's haunted Harz Mountains, wander the hills of the Black Forest, sail down the Rhine, or satisfy your *Wanderlust* in the lofty Bavarian Alps.

Flip to the Eastern Germany regional introduction for a guide to the peculiarities of traveling in the east. For serious expeditions, *Let's Go: Germany, Austria and Switzerland* will open any door.

Getting There and Getting Around

"Ein Land, zwei Bahnen" is the new German motto to travel by: one country with two railroads, the western **Deutsche Bundesbahn** (DB) and old eastern **Reichsbahn** (DR). Averaging over 120km per hour including stops, the DB network is one of Europe's best (and most expensive). Both DB and DR lines run cross-country, but in 1991, eastern train travel did not match up to its western counterpart. The main problem is complex connections; on an indirect route, allow about twice as much time as you would in the west. A hook-up with the DB's now invaluable computerized reservation and connection information system won't be complete until 1993. On the bright side, low regional fares and dirt-cheap public transportation in the east should persist through 1991. Commuter trains, marked "City-Bahn" (CB), "S-Bahn" or "Nahverkehrszug" (N), are very slow; "D" and "E" (Eilzug) trains are slightly faster and "FD" trains are faster still. "Interregio" (IR) trains, between neighboring cities, are speedy and comfortable. From metropolis to metropolis, "IC" (inter-city) trains approach the luxury and speed of an airplane. Unless you have a full-fare railpass, you must purchase a supplementary "IC Zuschlag" to ride an "IC" or "EC" train (DM6 when bought in the station, DM7 on the train). Even the IC yields to the brandy-dandy-new super-sleek InterCity Express (ICE), which fairly zooms along (with its own exorbitant pricing system).

The **German Railpass** gives unlimited travel to all parts of the country (5 days DM270; 10 days DM410; 15 days DM520). One-month second-class passes for the DB (including ICE) cost DM965 (DM1240 includes the DR). Anyone under age 23 and students under age 27 can buy a one-month domestic **Tramper-Monats Ticket,** good for unlimited second-class travel on all DB trains except the ICE, the railroad-run buses (Bahnbusse) and the local S-Bahn, for DM290; a combined DB/DR ticket is DM320. Add DM100 to both prices to include the ICE. (Bring proof of age and a student ID.) International train stations (Frankfurt's, for example) may not sell the Tramper-Monats-Ticket to foreigners over 23 who are not students at a German university; go to a nearby, smaller station and try again. The **Junior-Paß,** available to travelers aged 18-22 and students under 27, is valid for one year and gets you a 50% discount on all rail tickets, DB and DR alike (DM110). The **Taschengeld-Paß** has the same deal for everyone between 12 and 17 (DM40), and the **Familien-Paß** offers the same discount for families, single parents with children under 18, and married couples (DM130). Anyone over age 60 can purchase either a **Senioren-Paß A,** valid one year for a 50% discount on all fares for travel Monday-Thursday and Saturday (DM75), or **Senioren-Paß B,** good every day of the week (DM110). All passes are available at major train stations throughout Germany, and all require a small photo.

Eurail and InterRail passholders get free passage on the S-Bahn (commuter rail) and on DB bus lines (marked *Bahn.)* Passholders also get free rides and discounts on the Romantic Road buses and on some Rhine steamers, and railpasses are valid for the ferries from Puttgarden, Warnemünde, and Saßnitz to Denmark and Sweden, although most trains drive right onto the ferry anyway.

Regional **bus** systems are, at least in the west, a blessing. Long-distance bus travel is more of a crap-shot, with scattered offerings from private companies.

Frankfurt International Airport, Europe's second-largest, is the German hub, though the international terminals at Hamburg and Munich are also busy. Within Germany, **air travel** is uniformly expensive; the few student discounts around tend to be restricted to the natives.

Anyone with a railpass or ticket can rent a **bicycle** at over 270 rail stations throughout western Germany for DM5 per day (regularly DM10; generally April-Oct. only). Occasionally, you can return the bicycle to any train station that rents. The brochure *Fahrrad am Bahnhof,* from any train station, includes regional bike routes and a list of stations that rent. Bikes can be brought on any train that has a **Gepäckwagen,** indicated by a bicycle icon on the schedule. Otherwise, ship it two days in advance. (Prices vary with distance.) In most towns, bike paths are built *into* the sidewalks, with their own crossings. The DB offers special combined bike/rail trip discount packages; check out the deal of the month at major stations.

Germans drive *fast;* before venturing on the road, be *very* familiar with traffic rules and especially signs and symbols. It is permitted and quite common to **hitch** on the German autobahns (expressways), but, as elsewhere, hitchers may stand only at **Raststätten** (rest stops), **Tankstellen** (gas stations), and in front of the "Autobahn" signs on on-ramps. Autobahn hitchers will need a good map to navigate the tangled interchanges in the Rhine valley. If hitching, pay attention to license plates:

B—Berlin, M—Munich, F—Frankfurt, HH—Hamburg. Hitching is also common on the heavily traveled *Bundesstraßen,* scenic secondary roads marked by signs with a yellow diamond.

Mitfahrzentralen are offices in many cities that pair drivers and riders. For a fee of DM10-20, the MFZ will give you the telephone number of the driver, whom you can then call to make arrangements and set a price (usually determined by splitting gas costs). Check in the white and yellow pages *(Gelbe Seiten)* under "Mitfahrzentrale."

Urban public transit is excellent in the west and fair to middling in the east. You'll see four types: the **Straßenbahn** (trams), the **S-Bahn** (above-ground commuter rail), the **U-Bahn** (subways), and regular **buses.** Consider purchasing a day card *(Tagesnetzkarte)* or multiple-ride ticket *(Mehrfahrkarte),* which will usually pay for itself by the third ride. Often you must get your ticket beforehand at an automat and then validate *(entwerten)* it in one of the little boxes either in the station or on board.

Practical Information

Every city in western Germany has a tourist office, usually located near the main train station *(Hauptbahnhof)* or in the central market square *(Marktplatz)* of each town's old city *(Altstadt),* and marked with signs reading *"Verkehrsamt"* or *"Verkehrsverein."* They provide city maps and book rooms (usually for a small fee).

The German mark is divided into 100 pfennigs; currency exchange *(Wechsel)* is found in all large train stations and in virtually all banks (open Mon.-Fri. 9am-noon and 2-4pm). The best rates are often at post offices (in major cities usually open Sat.-Sun.), which will cash American Express checks for DM3 per check. Credit card acceptance is markedly less common in Germany than in the U.S. or U.K., though many banks—including the **DUKB Wechselstube,** found in many train stations—provide cash advances with VISA.

In the west, most post offices are open Monday through Friday from 8am to 6pm, Saturday from 8am to noon; all accept Poste Restante *(Postlagernde Briefe).* In western phone booths, a local call costs 30pf. Deposit coins first, even for toll-free calls. Change will not be returned; however, if you hang up, then quickly pick up the receiver again, you can make another call. The *Kartentelefon* accepts cards sold at the post office in DM12 and DM50 denominations; it saves loose change and time in line, and is displacing coin-ops in many cities. Only phones marked "international" can be used for international calls. Dial 01188 for information, 00118 for international information, and 0114 for an operator. For international collect calls, go to the post office; for AT&T's **USA Direct,** dial 01 30 01 00. Call 110 for police and 112 for fires or medical emergency.

Shops are generally open weekdays from 8:30am to 6pm, and Saturday until 1pm. In some smaller towns, stores close from noon to 3pm for *Mittagspause.* In larger cities, stores stay open later on the first Saturday of each month *(langer Samstag).* English language ability preserves Germany's divisions; crisp BBC accents in the west contrast with the stumbling of the easterners, who only recently threw out their Russian textbooks. In all cases, introduce yourself with a polite, universally applicable *bitte* (please, excuse me, thanks, help), the even politer *bitte schön,* or the definitive *Entschuldigung* (excuse me, sorry I bumped into you, help me *now,* or get the #!@%& out of my way). The letter *ß* is equivalent to a double *s.*

Accommodations and Camping

Local tourist offices can usually find you a bed for a DM2-6 fee. Hotels are uniformly expensive. In the west, *Pensionen,* their less elegant but equally comfortable counterpart, are more reasonably priced. Smaller western towns have *Gasthäuser,* cozy family-run establishments. Rooms in a private home *(Zimmer Frei)* are usually a few marks less, but are often unavailable (or more expensive) for one-night stays; the same holds true for many rural pensions. **Mitwohnzentralen** offices in large cities can help find lodging for both short and long stays. Living in the cheaper suburbs of a town may be false economy, as public transportation is often costly.

A German schoolteacher founded the world's first youth hostel in 1909, and there are now 537 hostels *(Jugendherberge)* in Germany—Europe's most extensive system. Signs for hostels read "DJH." In June 1990, the **Deutsches Jugendhergewerk** festively engulfed its eastern counterpart, but inconsistencies remain; western hostels are still more convenient. Beds in the west normally cost DM10-15 for "juniors" (ages under 27) and 2 or 3 marks more for "seniors" (ages 27 and over). Bavarian hostels accept *only* juniors; elsewhere, they are given priority (until 7pm). Curfews at western hostels are normally early, between 9:45pm and 11pm. A small breakfast is almost always included (not always in the east). Sheetless guests must rent bed linen (DM3.50-5); sleeping bags are often unacceptable. All hostels are required to hold extra beds for unannounced individual travelers, although these can fill quickly. In some western cities, the new-generation **Jugendgästehaus** is displacing the hostel, with higher prices (DM21.50 and up, sheets included) and a later curfew, catering more to young adults than schoolchildren.

Campgrounds are everywhere, and usually cost only DM4-7 per person, DM3-4 per tent; ask at the local tourist office for the most convenient sites. Freelance camping has been made illegal in order to protect the environment.

Food and Drink

Though German cuisine does not enjoy international popularity and is generally fatty and ponderous, a visit here need not torture your taste buds. Some of the more savory German dishes include *Schnitzel* (a thin cutlet of veal lightly fried in butter), *Spätzle* (noodles from the South), and almost anything that swims (from the North Sea). Pork and potatoes in all forms are staples of the German diet. Vegetarians will have a tough time with sit-down meals, although most eateries offer a salad plate *(Salatteller)*, and Germany's palette of home-baked breads and cheeses puts the baguette to shame. The fresh rolls *(Brötchen* or *Semmeln)* sold at any bakery are unforgettable. Supermarkets are open Monday to Friday from 8am to 1pm and 3 to 6:30pm, and on Saturday from 9am to 1pm. **Aldi, Plus,** and **Penny Markt** are popular and very cheap discount chains.

German breakfasts *(Frühstück)* are simple, consisting of coffee and buttered rolls with cheese or salami, and the occasional hard-boiled egg. The main meal, *Mittagessen,* is served at noon. At about 4pm, you may notice Germans with sweet tooths and coffee addictions heading to the *Konditorei* for *Kaffee und Kuchen* (coffee and cake) or to the ubiquitous *eis cafés.* The evening meal, *Abendbrot* or *Abendessen,* is traditionally a repeat performance of breakfast—bread, cheese, and cold cuts.

In a restaurant or *Gaststätte* (a simpler, less expensive restaurant), order from the *Tageskarte* (daily menu). All restaurant prices include tax and service *(Mehrwertsteuer und Bedienung).* If you wish to tip, simply round up the bill a mark or two. For inexpensive food, go to a department-store cafeteria or *Mensa* (dining halls located at most universities). Most *Mensas* are only *supposed* to admit only their own students. Stop at an **Imbiss** for anything fast; they dot the pedestrian zones. Most German towns have relatively inexpensive Greek, Yugoslavian and especially Turkish restaurants. Italian restaurants, almost as common as BMWs, generally offer a decent, low-priced plate of pasta.

In good weather, stein-hoisters flock to the ubiquitous open-air *Biergarten.* The classic beer type is called *Pilsner* or *Pils;* other types include *Weizen* (wheat) and *Alt* (old). A few German brands merit special mention. In the north, look for *Flensburger;* in the west, *Veltins;* in the southwest, *Rothaus;* and everywhere else, the Czech *Budweiser* (the original, a.k.a. *Budvar).* Try also German wine, especially the sweet *(lieblich* or *süß)* whites of the Rhine and Mosel valleys and the comparatively unknown dry *(trocken)* whites of southwestern Baden.

Eastern Germany

Harrowing border crossings, intimidating searches, travel restrictions, and East Germany itself have all dissolved like a bad nightmare. Those visiting the former G.D.R. for the first time will be surprised to find that the lion's share of Germany's cultural and historic monuments lie in the east—though careless industrialization and sloppy power production have decimated much of the environment, casting whole regions a depressing, sooty gray. Those who have been here before will marvel at how quickly things are changing, how much cleaner the air is already, and the difference that a little paint can make. Socialism's demise means rechristening for streets, hospitals, universities, and entire towns, as well as museums closed for historical "updating." For travelers, the confusion takes its toll, but no one is more frustrated than the people who live here. Freedom of choice is also the freedom to make mistakes: eager East Germans jumped at the newer, slicker products of the West and deprived their domestic economy of capital. Few doubt that East Germany is being rebuilt to have the best and most modern infrastructure available, but the payoff is yet to come. The eastern economy is in shambles and millions of East Germans have lost their jobs; the unpredictability of life has translated into anger and fear. If you've come expecting to dance on the wall, you're a little late.

The new provinces are slowly being integrated into the West's transportation system. Eastern trains (and service personnel) are sluggish, but tickets and passes are now essentially interchangeable. Buses to smaller towns run from main train stations; purchase tickets on the bus or from the crabby clerks on the platform. (Ask if they accept your railpass, though chances are they'll look at you as if you asked for their firstborn.) Hitchhiking is common in the south; the Prussians farther north are slightly less generous.

The old East German state travel authority offices now perform much the same functions as western tourist offices, and often have indispensable indexes of changed street names. Major West German banks have opened offices in the east, though getting a traveler's check cashed in a small town may become a half-hour training lesson for the whole staff. Bring a phrasebook; eastern Germans are pretty bad at English, and failure to learn Russian was a subtle and widely practiced form of political protest. A merger of mail systems has left eastern Germany with the worst of both worlds: western prices but old-time inefficiency. The postal system may be slow, but the phones are the real problem. The biggest nightmare is the *Vorwahl,* or city code; a town's prefix differs depending on whether the call is east to east or west to east. Many are being changed altogether, and the codes are notoriously hard to find out. (Call information.) To call east-to-west (about DM1 per minute), dial 07, then the western city code (minus the zero). USA Direct doesn't work in the east; dial 00114 for operator assisted collect and credit card calls, and let it ring until an operator answers (10-15 min.). Fight for the bright yellow pay phone boxes with digital connections to the west.

The German youth hostel federation has absorbed hundreds of Eastern hostels with remarkable efficiency, though many of the most luxurious ones have been converted to costly hotels and pensions. For hotels and private rooms, check with the town information office; since demand is high and supply low, expect to pay western prices for eastern standards. Campgrounds are empty (newly-unshackled East German vacationers have fled to Italy).

A last word of advice: due to the rise in right-wing terrorism, visible minorities should be careful alone at night in the larger cities, particularly Dresden, Frankfurt an der Oder, Leipzig and Halle.

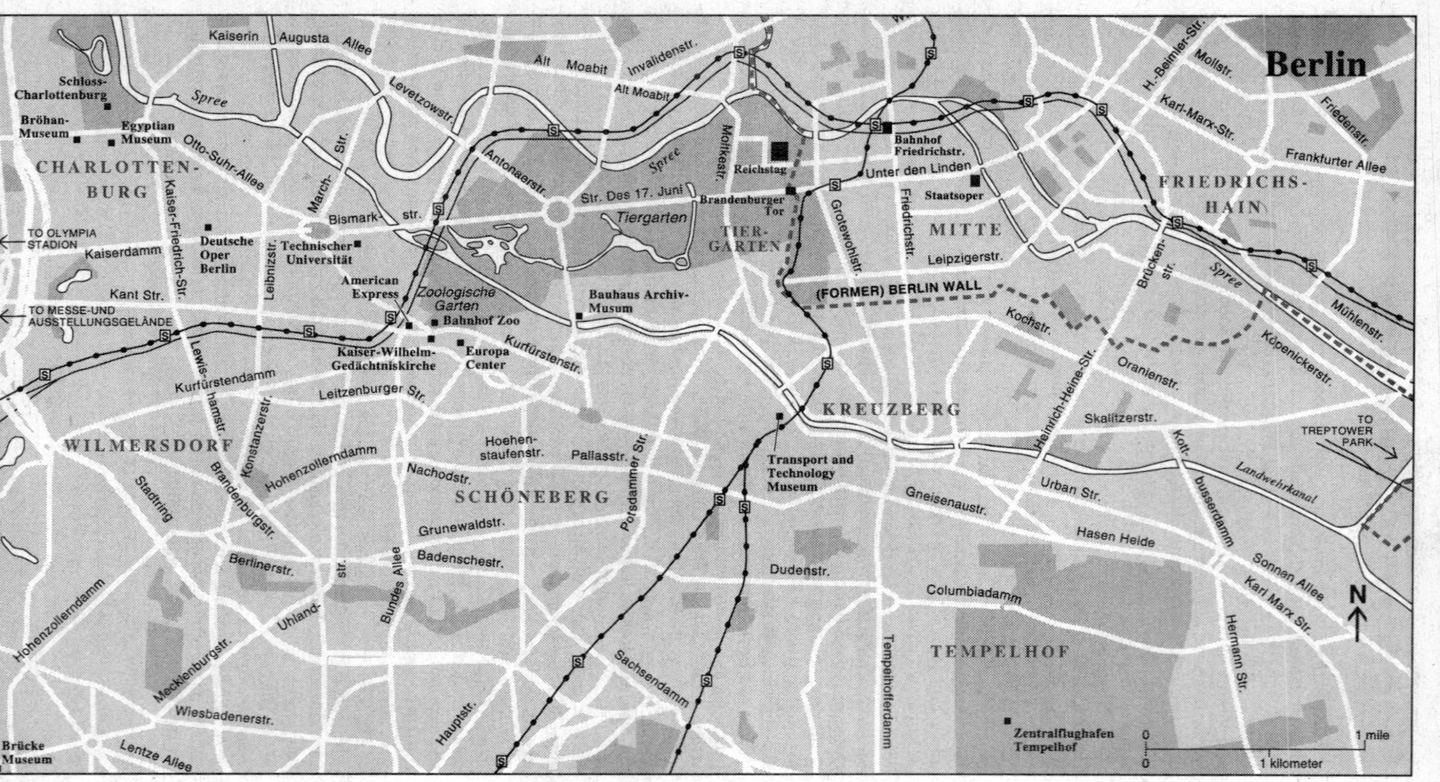
Berlin
FRIEDRICHS-HAIN
MITTE
KREUZBERG
TEMPELHOF
TIER-GARTEN
CHARLOTTEN-BURG
SCHÖNEBERG
WILMERSDORF
(FORMER) BERLIN WALL
Friedenstr.
Frankfurter Allee
Mühlenstr.
Köpenickerstr.
Mollstr.
Karl-Marx-Str.
H.-Beimler-Str.
Spree
Brücken-str.
Oranienstr.
Heinrich-Heine-Str.
Skalitzerstr.
Kott-busserdamm
Landwehrkanal
Sonnen Allee
Karl Marx Str.
Hermann Str.
Hasen Heide
Urban Str.
Gneisenaustr.
Columbiadamm
Zentralflughafen Tempelhof
Tempelhofferdamm
Dudenstr.
Sachsendamm
Transport and Technology Museum
Kochstr.
Leipzigerstr.
Staatsoper
Unter den Linden
Bahnhof Friedrichstr.
Friedrichstr.
Grotewohlstr.
Reichstag
Brandenburger Tor
Moltkestr.
Str. Des 17. Juni
Tiergarten
Bauhaus Archiv-Musum
Potsdammer Str.
Pallasstr.
Hohen-staufenstr.
Alt Moabit
Invalidenstr.
Antonaerstr.
Kurfürstenstr.
Europa Center
Bahnhof Zoo
Zoologische Garten
Kaiser-Wilhelm-Gedächtniskirche
American Express
Leitzenburger Str.
Nachodstr.
Grunewaldstr.
Badenschestr.
Bundes Allee
Hauptstr.
Levetzowstr.
Bismarck-str.
March-str.
Technischer Universität
Leibnizstr.
Augusta Allee
Kaiserin
Otto-Suhr-Allee
Deutsche Oper Berlin
Kaiser-Friedrich-Str.
Lewis-hamstr.
Kurfürstendamm
Konstanzerstr.
Hohenzollerndamm
Brandenburgstr.
Berlinerstr.
Uhland-str.
Mecklenburgstr.
Wiesbadenerstr.
Stadtring
Lentzze Allee
Brücke Museum
Schloss-Charlottenburg
Bröhan-Museum
Egyptian Museum
Kaiserdamm
Kant Str.
TO OLYMPIA STADION
TO MESSE-UND AUSSTELLUNGSGELÄNDE
TO TREPTOWER PARK
N
1 mile
1 kilometer
0

Berlin

Reanointed as capital of the new Germany in June 1991, Berlin today is synonymous with apocalyptic energy, a riotous artistic avant-garde, and seething East-West conflicts. The Wall came down on November 9, 1989 and official reunification followed on October 3, 1990, bringing two very different societies together. For the next few years visitors will be able to see both side by side, united by an extraordinary cultural life and overwhelming nightlife. The former **West Berlin** is *the* city of decadence and counter-culture, fed for years by generous subsidies for the arts and city residents' exemption from the military draft. Students in West Berlin never heard that the spirit of '68 ended, and the annual May 1 demonstrations are always riotous. **East Berlin** boasts magnificent museums but carries the scars of a totalitarian past. It suffers from the same overwhelming economic problems as the rest of the former East Germany, and never faced up to its Nazi past the way West Germany did. Now that the initial euphoria has faded, West and East Berliners have discovered that they don't like each other much. The city has become a microcosm of modern Europe's problems: a poor East and a rich West, unhappily coexisting. Although Berlin is the most international city in Germany, with huge Asian and Eastern European populations, the economic depression in the Eastern half has led to xenophobic, neo-Nazi movements: Africans, Asians and other conspicuous non-Germans should avoid East Berlin at night. But Berlin's dark side is small in comparison with the exhilaration of being on the cutting edge of history.

Orientation and Practical Information

Berlin surveys the Prussian plain in the northeastern corner of reunited Germany. It is about four rail hours southeast of Hamburg and double that time north of Munich, with excellent rail and air connections to numerous European capitals. Ten hours by train from Warsaw and six from Prague, Berlin serves as an excellent springboard for exploration to the east.

The western and eastern halves of unified Berlin are two worn puzzle pieces that no longer fit together smoothly. For forty years, the western half sat amidst communism like a rejected heart, and the brusque fusion with its poorer, drabber eastern half has created a challenge for any traveler. Today Berlin is *immense,* the agglomeration of a national capital and what for decades functioned as a small, isolated democratic state. A city map *(Stadtplan),* available at any kiosk for DM6, will be worth its weight in gold. Collectively, the major points of interest form a lollipop on the city map. The stick is a frenzied corridor in the western section between Bismarckstr., becoming Straße des 17 Juni, and the renowned **Kurfürstendamm** or **Ku'damm,** modern Berlin's great commercial boulevard. East Berlin represents the candied disc, which centers at **Marx-Engels Platz** and **Alexanderplatz.** Although the region around the junction of the stick and the disc, near the Brandenburg Gate, now represents the geographical center of a tremendous metropolis, for forty years it was fringe neighborhood, with its back against the Wall. Accordingly, it remains rather dead.

The commercial district of West Berlin centers around **Bahnhof Zoo** and **Breitscheidplatz,** site of the bombed Kaiser-Wilhelm-Gedächtniskirche, the boxy tower of Europa Center, and the main tourist office. **Bahnhof Zoo** is Berlin's major train station and the central point of Berlin's subway and surface rail systems. A star of streets radiates from Breitscheidplatz. Toward the west run **Hardenbergstraße, Kantstraße,** and the Ku'damm. Half a mile down Hardenbergstr. is Steinplatz and the enormous Berlin Technical University. Half a mile down Kantstr. is **Savignyplatz,** home to cafés, restaurants, and pensions. The first place to see what remains (almost nothing in many areas) of the **Berlin Wall** is by the Reichstag building and the Brandenburg gate, at the eastern end of Berlin's large urban park, **Tiergarten.** The central artery of East Berlin is **Unter den Linden,** which flows from the Brandenburg Gate to the heart of the eastern section, Marx-Engels Platz and the neighboring Alexanderplatz. As you cross the city, you might pause to remember the hundreds of people who died in the last forty years trying to get from one side to the other.

Many spots besides the **Tiergarten** shelter a measure of tranquility from the chaos of the twin downtowns. The **Landwehrkanal,** the **Havel,** and its various lakes—from the popular Wansee in the south to the Teglersee in the north—form a crescent around the western edge of the city. The Landwehrkanal runs from Tiergarten, by the Nationalgalerie, then through the length of seedy Kreuzberg.

In newly united Berlin, many municipal services are still divided between East and West, although they are gradually being joined. When services are duplicated in both parts of the city, *Let's Go* lists those in West Berlin, and then their Eastern counterparts. The phone system is far from unified: there are different area codes for the different parts of the city and it's difficult to call from one part to another. The busy signal you'll hear when you try does not mean that the line is occupied, but that all circuits between the two halves of the city are full. Keep on redialing until you get through. *Let's Go* lists the Eastern numbers with the area code (9) before them, but omits the area code for calling from East to West (849) before the Western numbers.

Tourist Offices: Verkehrsamt Berlin, in the Europa Center at Budapesterstr. 45 (tel. 262 60 31). From Bahnhof Zoo, walk along Budapesterstr. toward and then past the Kaiser-Wilhelm-Gedächtniskirche, about five minutes. Open daily 8am-10:30pm. Branch offices at Bahnhof Zoo (tel. 313 90 63 or 313 90 64) and Tegel Airport (tel. 41 01 31 45) open daily 8am-11pm. Branch at Dreilinden autobahn control point (tel. 803 90 57) open daily 8am-8pm. All offices provide a simple city map, *Berlin von A bis Z,* and the exhaustive *Berlin Programm* (DM2.50). Their leaflet *Tips für Jugendliche* lists inexpensive accommodations. All offices have a room finding service (see Accommodations section). **Informationszentrum Berlin,** Hardenbergstr. 20, 3rd floor (tel. 31 00 40), across from the train station. Mainly historical and political information, but also *Berlin for Young People,* an invaluable, free booklet in English. Open Mon.-Fri. 8am-7pm, Sat. 8am-4pm. **In East Berlin: Informationszentrum am Fernsehturm,** Panaramastr. 1, under the radio tower in Alexanderplatz (tel. (9) 212 46 75 or (9) 212 45 12). Theoretically provides the same services as its Western counterparts. In reality, should be used only as a last resort.

Budget Travel: ARTU Reisebüro, Hardenbergstr. 9 (tel. 31 04 66), down the street from Bahnhof Zoo. Branch offices at Takustr. 47 (U-Bahn: Dahlem-Dorf, tel. 831 50 94), Nollendorfpl. 7 (U-Bahn: Nollendorf Platz, tel. 216 30 91), and in Kreuzberg, at Mariannenstr. 7 (U-Bahn: Kottbusser Tor, tel. 614 68 22). Issues IUS, the student card for erstwhile socialist countries, and sells Transalpino. Hardenbergstr. branch open Mon.-Tues. and Thurs.-Fri. 10am-6pm, Wed. 11am-6pm, Sat. 10am-1pm. Other branches open same hours, but closed an hour for lunch. Transalpino also sold at the Bahnhof Zoo and at Budapesterstr. 44 (open Mon.-Fri. 10am-6pm, Sat. 10am-1pm). Better deals are often to be found flipping through the ads in the magazines *Zitty* or *Tip.* **In East Berlin: Europäisches Reisebüro,** Alexanderplatz 5 (tel. (9) 215 44 15). Also called **Haus des Reisens.** Building says "Reisebüro" in big blue letters. Books private accommodations with families for DM15-25 per night, sells tickets for cultural events (10% markup), bus tours and *Weiße Flotte* boat excursions. Open Mon.-Fri. 10am-6pm, Sat. 10am-5pm.

Embassies and Consulates: U.S., Clayallee 170 (tel. 819 74 19). Open Mon.-Fri. 8:30am-10:30am. **Canada,** Europa Center, 12th floor (tel. 261 11 61). Open Mon.-Fri. 9am-12:30pm and 2-4:30pm. **U.K.,** Uhlandstr. 7-8 (tel. 309 52 92). Open Mon. Fri. 9am-noon and 2-4pm. Travelers from **Australia** and **New Zealand** should contact the British consulate until the Bonn-to-Berlin move takes effect. **Czechoslovakia,** Otto-Grotewohl-Str. 21. Visa section open Mon. and Wed.-Fri. 10-11:30am and 1-2:30pm. **Poland,** Unter den Linden 72 (tel. (9) 220 25 51). Visa section open Mon. and Wed.-Fri. 9am-1pm.

Currency Exchange: Deutsche Verkehrs-Kredit Bank at Bahnhof Zoo, on Hardenbergstr. Open Mon.-Sat. 8am-9pm, Sun. 10am-6pm. Charges the typical DM5 fee. **Berliner Bank** in Tegel Airport is open daily 8am-10pm. Branches of commercial banks are sprouting in East Berlin. You can also change money at most West Berlin post offices.

American Express: Kurfürstendamm 11, 2nd floor (tel. 882 75 75). The usual. Open Mon.-Fri. 9am-5:30pm, Sat. 9am-noon.

Post Office: In Bahnhof Zoo, D-1000 Berlin 12 (tel. 313 97 99). Open 24 hrs. Poste Restante (held at window #9) should be addressed: Poste Restante/Hauptpostlagernd, Postamt Bahnhof Zoo, D-1000 Berlin 12. Branch office at Tegel Airport (tel. 430 85 23) open daily 6:30am-

9pm. **In East Berlin:** Postamt Berlin 17, Str. der Pariser Kommune 8-10, Berlin 1017 in the Hauptbahnhof. Open 24 hrs.

Telephones: At Bahnhof Zoo. Open 24 hrs. From West Berlin, dial (9) for East Berlin, (037) for the old East Germany. To dial West Berlin from East Berlin, use area code (849). **City Code** for West Berlin: 30.

Flights: Flughafen Tegel (tel. 410 11) is West Berlin's main airport, connected to Bahnhof Zoo by bus #109. **Flughafen Tempelhof** (tel. 690 91) was the site of a 19-minute flight by the Wright Brothers in 1908. **Flughafen Schönefeld** (tel. (9) 67 20), in East Berlin, is connected by S-Bahn to the city.

Trains: Routings into Berlin were changing throughout 1991. Check ahead, but the latest word was that trains to the West leave from **Bahnhof Zoo,** West Berlin's principal station. Trains to Dresden, Leipzig, Prague, and other southern destinations leave from **Bahnhof Lichtenberg,** in East Berlin some distance east of the center, stopping also at **Schönefeld.** Trains to Poland leave only from Lichtenberg. Through trains may stop at several stations. All stations are connected by S-Bahn and/or U-Bahn (Zoo-Lichtenberg about 1 hr.). Student fares to: Munich (9 hr., DM87); Frankfurt am Main (9 hr., DM87); Hamburg (3½ hr., DM37); Vienna (11 hr., DM70); Zürich (11 hr., DM133); Paris (13½ hr., DM135); Amsterdam (9 hr., DM135); Warsaw (10 hr., DM30); Budapest (14 hr., DM67); Prague (6 hr., DM37); London (many, many hr., DM177). **Bundesbahn Information,** tel. 194 19. For recorded information (in German) on departures, call 115 31; for arrivals 115 32.

Buses: ZOB, the central bus station (tel. 301 80 28), is by the Funkturm near Kaiserdamm. U-Bahn: Kaiserdamm. Check *Zitty* and *Tip* for deals on long-distance buses (often only slightly cheaper than the train or plane).

Luggage Storage: In the Bahnhof Zoo train station. Lockers DM2, larger ones DM3. 24-hr. limit. **In East Berlin:** at Ostbahnhof, Bahnhof Lichtenberg, and S-Bahnhof Alexanderplatz. Lockers DM0.50. 24-hr. max.

Public Transportation: The transit system is as indispensable and efficient as it is expensive. The **U-Bahn** (subway) and **S-Bahn** (commuter rail) systems of East and West Berlin now operate as one complete system. U-Bahn, S-Bahn, and the extensive **bus system** all cost DM2.70 *(Einzelfahrschein Normaltarif)* per ride. A 5-ride *Sammelkarte* (Multiple Ticket) costs DM11.50. Each ticket entitles you to 2 hrs. travel on all 3 networks. Eurail holders can ride the S-Bahn (but not the U-Bahn) for free. You can also buy an *Einzelfahrschein Kurzstreckentarif* (short-trip fare) for DM1.70 (5-ride Multiple Ticket DM7). This allows travel up to 6 bus stops or 3 train stations, with one transfer (not valid on airport bus lines). You can buy single tickets from machines, bus drivers, or ticket windows in the U- and S-bahn stations. When an *Einzelfahrschein* is bought from a transportation official, you must stamp it in the *Entwerter* as soon as you board. *Sammelkarten* cannot be bought from drivers; they must be stamped in the machine at the station entrance or in the *entwerter* behind the bus driver. The **"Berlin Ticket"** (DM9, ages 6-14 DM5) is a 24-hr. pass on the bus, U- and S-bahn. A **6-day Berlin Ticket** (Mon.-Sat.) costs DM26 (DM19 for 1-fare area). Children under 6 travel free. If you're planning to use the transportation system extensively, buy a *Liniennetz* map, which shows the bus and subway routes in detail (DM2); otherwise, the free map distributed at tourist offices suffices. U- and S-Bahn do not run from 1-4am (except the U-1 and U-9, which run all night Fri.-Sat.). There is an extensive system of night buses, stopping every ½hr.

Lost Property: BVG Fundbüro, Potsdamerstr. 184 (tel. 216 14 13). For items lost on public transportation. Open Mon.-Tues. and Thurs. 9am-3pm, Wed. 9am-6pm, Fri. 9am-2pm. Closed on holidays. See also Police headquarters below. **In East Berlin: Zentrales Fundbüro,** Wilhelm-Pieck-Str. 164 (tel. (9) 282 61 35). Open Tues. and Thurs. 10am-1pm and 2-6pm, Fri. 10am-1pm. **BVB Fundbüro,** at Bahnhof Friedrichstr. (tel. (9) 492 23 46). For items lost on East Berlin public transportation. Open Mon.-Tues. and Thurs.-Fri. 8am-3pm, Wed. 10am-6pm.

Bike Rental: Fahrradbüro Berlin, Hauptstr. 146 (tel. 784 55 62). U-Bahn: Kleistpark. DM12 per day, DM50 per week. Tandems DM25 per day. Deposit DM50; bring ID. Open Mon.-Fri. 10am-6pm, Sat. 10am-2pm.

Hitchhiking: If you decide to hitch west or south (Hannover, Munich, Weimar, Leipzig) take the S-Bahn to Wannsee, then bus #211 to the Autobahn entrance ramp. To hitch north (Hamburg, Rostock) take the U-Bahn to Tegel, then take bus #224; ask the driver to let you out at the *Trampenplatz.* Both have huge crowds, but someone gets picked up every few minutes. **Mitfahrzentrale** has offices at Kurfürstendamm 227 (tel. 882 76 04; open Mon.-Sat. 8am-9pm, Sun. 10am-6pm) and Südstem. 14 (tel. 693 60 95). Berlin has numerous other Mitfahrzentrale not belonging to the national chain; see *Zitty* or *Tip* magazines for addresses and phone numbers. There are also Mitfahrzentralen exclusively for women (tel. 215 31 65 or 215 38 77). The Mitfahrzentrale in U-Bahnhof Alexanderplatz specializes in the East (tel. (9) 246 31 51). Open Mon.-Fri. 8am-9pm, Sat. 8am-6pm, Sun. 10am-6pm.)

Pharmacies: Europa-apotheke, Tauentzienstr. 9-12 (tel. 261 41 42), by Europa Center (close to main train station). Open 9am-9pm. Closed *Apotheken* post signs directing you to the nearest open one. **In East Berlin: Apotheke am Alexanderplatz,** Hans-Beimler-Str. 70-72 (tel. 212 57 66). **Emergency phone number:** 160.

Bookstores: Marga Schoeller Bücherstube, Knesebeckstr. 34 (tel. 881 11 12), at Mommsenstr., between Savignyplatz and the Ku'damm. Mongo selection of books in English. Open Sun.-Fri. 9am-6:30pm, Sat. 9am-2pm, 1st Sat. of month 9am-6pm.

Laundromat: Wasch Centers at Leibnizstr. 72, Wexstr. 34, Rheinstr. 62, Markstr. 4, Behmstr. 12 and (in East Berlin's Prenzlauer Berg) Jablonskistr. 21. All open daily 6am-midnight. Wash DM8 per 6kg, soap included. Dry DM2.

Crisis Lines: Sexual Assault Hotline (tel. 251 28 28). Open Tues. and Thurs. 6-9pm, Sun. noon-2pm. **AIDS Hotline** (tel. 783 24 56).

Medical Assistance: The tourist office has a list of English-speaking doctors. **Emergency Doctor,** tel. 31 00 31 (West), 12 59 (East). **Emergency Dentist,** tel. 11 41. If stranded in East Berlin try the emergency room of **Rettungsamt Berlin,** Marienburgerstr. 41-46 (tel. 282 05 61).

Emergencies: Police (tel. 110). Headquarters at Platz der Luftbrücke 6 (tel. 69 90; lost and found 69 93 64 44). **Ambulance and Fire** (tel. 112). **In East Berlin: Police** (tel. 110). **Ambulance** (tel. 115). **Fire** (tel. 112).

Accommodations and Camping

Since the Wall came down, Berlin has been bursting at the seams. You can almost always find a room somewhere, but in summer it's best to book ahead or at least arrive early in the day. East Berlin has few budget hotels; if you want to stay in the East, your best bet is private accommodation booked through the **Europäisches Reisebüro** (see Budget Travel above).

For pensions and hotels, go straight to one of the tourist offices. For a DM3 commission they'll save you the trouble of calling tens of pensions before you find one with a vacancy. Count on spending at least DM50 for a single, DM90 for a double. They also have private accommodations from DM35 per person with breakfast (two-night minimum). The office prefers to fill up the pensions first, so you may have to ask for private rooms. Reserve a room by writing directly to a pension or to the Verkehrsamt Berlin, Martin-Luther-Str. 105, 1000 Berlin 62. The Verkehrsamt requires that you state precisely how much you want to spend (minimum DM60 for a single, DM95 for a double). Write at least four weeks in advance.

For longer visits (more than two days) the various *Mitwohnzentralen* will arrange for you to housesit or sublet someone's apartment. Prices start at DM35 per night, and go down the longer you stay. The **Mitwohnzentrale** in Ku'damm Eck (Kurfürstendamm 227/228, 2nd floor) is the biggest. Open Mon.-Fri. 10am-7pm, Sat.-Sun. 11am-4pm. Tel. 883 051. **Wohnagentur Q-3-A** specializes in (often cheaper) apartments in East Berlin. Prenzlauer Allee 17, tel. (9) 437 15 15. Open Mon.-Fri. 10am-7pm, Sat 11am-4pm.

Hostels and Dormitories

Hostels quickly fill with German school groups (especially in summer and on weekends); call ahead. All are for members only, but some hostels will give nonmembers a guest stamp for DM4. To buy an IYHF card, head to Tempelhofer Ufer 32 (tel. 262 30 24; open Mon., Wed., and Fri. 10am-3pm, Tues. and Thurs. 2-5:30pm.).

Jugendgästehaus am Zoo, Hardenbergstr. 9a, 1000 Berlin 12 (tel. 312 94 10). Bus #145, or a short walk from the Zoo. Worth the extra cost for the older, international crowd and central location. No curfew. Singles DM40, doubles DM70, small dorms DM26.

Jugendgästehaus (IYHF), Kluckstr. 3, 1000 Berlin 30 (tel. 261 10 97). Bus #129 from Kurfürstendamm toward Oranienplatz or Hermannplatz. Central location, many school groups. Lockout 9am-noon. If you arrange in advance, you can sometimes stay out an hour past the midnight curfew. Juniors DM20. Seniors DM26. Sheets included. Lockers in rooms. Key deposit DM10. Reservations strongly recommended.

Jugendgästehaus Wannsee (IYHF), Kronprinzessinnenweg 27, 1000 Berlin 38 (tel. 803 20 34). Near the Strand Bad Wannsee beach. Take the S-Bahn to Nikolassee station and walk 10 min. toward the beach. Far from the center, likely to have space. Loud and fun. Curfew midnight. Juniors DM20. Seniors DM26. Sheets included. Key deposit DM20.

Jugendherberge Ernst Reuter (IYHF), Hermsdorfer Damm 48, 1000 Berlin 28 (tel. 404 16 10). U-Bahn #6: Tegel, then bus #125 headed for Frohnau; get off at the 4th stop. Similarly remote, so also likely to have space. Curfew midnight. Juniors DM20. Seniors DM26. Sheets included. Dinner from DM5.20. Key deposit DM10.

Studentenhotel Berlin, Meiningerstr. 10, 1000 Berlin 62 (tel. 784 67 20). U-Bahn: Rathaus Schöneberg. From Bahnhof Zoo, hop on bus #146, get off at Rathaus Schöneberg, and walk across Martin-Luther-Str. Decent dormitory accommodations in a green, quiet neighborhood. Doubles DM62. Quads DM116. Showers and breakfast included. Reservations recommended.

Jugendhotel am Tierpark, Franz-Mett-Str. 7 (tel. (9) 510 01 14). In East Berlin. Take the U-Bahn to Tierpark and follow the signs for 150m. A monster of a youth hostel, with 770 beds and a restaurant and nightclub in residence. DM28, breakfast included. Arrive between 3-9pm.

Internationales Jugendcamp, Ziekowstr. 161, 1000 Berlin 27 (tel. 433 86 40). U-Bahn: Tegel. Open only June 21-Aug. 31. Far away, but DM7 gets you a mat under a giant tent with shower facilities. Lockout 9am-5pm. No written reservations accepted.

Jugendgästehaus Central, Nikolsburgstr. 2-4, 1000 Berlin 31 (tel. 870 188). U-Bahn: Güntzelstr. Looks like a high school, with puke-green walls, but worth it if you can get a double. Curfew 1am. DM30 per person, including breakfast, in 2-8 bed rooms, many with shower and WC. Full pension DM4 extra.

Jugendgästehaus Feurigstraße, Feurigstr. 63, 1000 Berlin 62 (tel. 781 52 11). U-Bahn: Kleistpark. Good location for the bars and clubs of Schöneberg. DM30, including sheets and breakfast.

Studentenwohnheim Hubertusallee, Delbrückstr. 24, 1000 Berlin 33 (tel. 891 97 18), at the corner of Hubertusallee. Bus #129. Way out, but a pretty area. Singles DM40. Doubles DM60. Triples DM70. Bring ISIC (higher prices for non-students). All rooms have shower and WC. Breakfast included. Open April-Oct. only.

Hotels and Pensions

Berlin prices are shooting up; the good old days of singles for DM40 are, for the most part, gone forever. A few bargains still exist—the area around Savignyplatz is a good place to look. The tourist office's *Tips für Jugendliche* has a long list of budget accommodations, but the prices tend to be out of date.

Hotelpension Bialas, Carmerstr. 16 (tel. 312 50 25). Bus #149 to Steinplatz. The best location in Berlin, and the comfy rooms have sculptured ceilings. Singles DM55, with shower DM120. Small dorms from DM30 per person. Breakfast included.

Pension Molthan, Lietzenburgerstr. 76 (tel. 881 47 17). Bus #219. Homey pension in house with four other pensions. Singles DM50, doubles DM80. Small dorms DM35 per person. Breakfast DM8.

Hotelpension Domino, Neue Kanstr. 14 (tel. 321 69 06). Bus #149 to Kuno-Fischerstr. Small rooms, but each has shower and WC. Singles DM40, doubles DM80. Prices may rise April-June and Sept.-Oct.; call first.

Pension Kreuzberg, Grossbeerenstr. 64 (tel. 251 13 62). U-Bahn: Mehringdamm, or bus #119. Near the bars and clubs of Kreuzberg. Singles DM40, doubles DM65, triples DM80, quads DM100. Breakfast DM7.

Hotelpension Gloria, Wielandstr. 27 (tel. 881 80 60). Bus #119 to Bleibtreustr. Just off the Ku'damm. Singles DM45, with shower DM65. Doubles with shower DM100. Breakfast included.

Centrum Pension Berlin, Kantstr. 31 (tel. 316 153). Bus #149. Convenient location, but lots of street noise. Singles DM41. Doubles DM75. Triples DM90. Quads DM120. Breakfast DM7.

Hotelpension Cortina, Kantstr. 140 (tel. 313 90 59). Bus #149. Across the street from Centrum; slightly better rooms. Doubles DM95 (with breakfast). Singles (only when business is slow) DM60. Extra beds in room upon agreement.

Pension Knesebeck, Knesebeckstr. 86 (tel. 31 72 55). Just north of Savignyplatz. Large rooms with running water. Singles DM57. Doubles DM90. Triples DM114. Quads DM152. Breakfast included.

Pension Fischer, Nürnbergerstr. 24a (tel. 24 68 08). Across from U-Bahn: Augsburgerstr. Comfy rooms with clashing decor. Singles DM35-40. Doubles DM55. Mongo rooms: doubles DM60, triples DM80, quads DM100. Showers included. Breakfast DM6.

Hotel Transit, Hagelbergerstr. 53-54 (tel. 785 50 51). U-Bahn: Mehringdamm, or night bus #19 (every 10-15 min., 24 hrs.). In a newly renovated factory in Kreuzberg. Don't be intimidated by the exterior; rooms are airy, well lit, clean, and have high ceilings. Small dorms DM30. Singles DM55. Doubles DM85. Triples DM115. Showers in all rooms. Breakfast included.

Hamburger Hof, Kinkelstr. 6 (tel. 333 46 02), in the old quarter of Spandau. Easily accessible, next to U-Bahn #7: Altstadt Spandau. A tiny, comfortable hotel with only 15 beds, but so far from the action that they usually have room. Singles DM45. Doubles DM90. Showers and breakfast included.

Charlottenburger Hof, Stuttgarterplatz 14 (tel. 324 48 19). Across the street from S-Bahn: Charlottenburg. Pleasant rooms, some with balconies. Open 24 hrs. Singles from DM65. Doubles DM85, with shower DM120. Triples DM135. Quads DM180. Small breakfast DM5, large breakfast DM8.

Camping

Of the four major campgrounds in Berlin, three are adjacent to the former Berlin Wall. **Kladow,** Krampnitzer Weg 111/117 (tel. 365 27 97) is in Spandau; take U-Bahn to Rathaus Spandau, then bus #135 to the end, then follow Krampnitzer Weg another ½km. Closer to the center of Spandau is **Haselhorst,** Pulvermühlenweg (tel. 334 59 55; take U-Bahn to Haselhorst, then head north on Daumster to Pulvermühlenweg). Perhaps the most unusual is **Dreilinden** (tel. 805 12 01; U-Bahn to Oskar-Helene Heim, then bus #118, then follow Kremnitzufer to Albrechts-Teergfen about 20 min.), which is surrounded on three sides by the vestiges of the Berlin Wall. All charge juniors DM1.70, seniors DM6, ages under 8 free. All are open year round. Make reservations with **Deutscher Camping Club,** Geisbergstr. 11, 1000 Berlin 30 (tel. 24 60 71).

Food

Berlin's restaurant scene is as international as its population; German cuisine should not be a priority here. *Berliner Weißbier* is one exception; natives swear by this concoction of beer and fruit syrup. But typical Berlin food is Turkish: almost every street in the city has its own Turkish imbiss or restaurant. The *Döner Kepab,* a sandwich of lamb and salad, has cornered the fast food market, with *falafel* running a close second. For DM3-4 either makes a small meal. You should also try slower Turkish food; **Meyhane,** at Bleibtreustr. 50, is an inexpensive restaurant. The second wave of immigrants has brought quality Indian restaurants to Berlin, and Italian is always a safe choice.

Forty years of bargain gastronomy in East Berlin ended with currency conversion in the summer of 1990. Although budget eateries are scarce in this portion of the city, street vendors with all shapes, sizes and flavors of cheap food fill **Alexanderplatz** every day.

Like all big cities, Berlin has numerous supermarkets. **Aldi** and **Penny Markt** are the cheapest, but can be unpleasant shopping experiences, especially Aldi. Supermarkets in the East are called *Kaufhalle.* (Markets open Mon.-Fri. 9am-6pm, Sat. 9am-1pm.) The best open air market is Saturday mornings in Winterfeldplatz.

West Berlin

Mensa of the Freie Universität, in the huge complex at Habelschwerdter Allee 45. U-Bahn: Thielplatz. Surely some of the best university food in Germany. Meals from DM2, ISIC required. Open Mon.-Fri. 11:15am-2:30pm.

Mensa TU, Hardenbergstr. 34. Bus #145 to Steinplatz. Hard to miss: says "MENSA" in big letters on the building. More conveniently located, but slightly worse food than the above. Meals from DM2. Open Mon.-Fri. 11:15am-2:30pm.

Tiergartenquelle, Stadtbahnhogen 482, under the S-Bahn bridge at S-Bahn Tiergarten. Huge portions of food in friendly, student-filled atmosphere. Most entrees under DM12. Open 6pm-midnight.

Cafe Hardenberg, Hardenbergstr. 10, opposite the TU mensa. Cheap food, lots of students. Also good for a few drinks. Open 7am-midnight.

Ashoka, Grolmanstr. 22, just off Savignyplatz. Really cheap Indian food; you can easily have a meal for DM10. Order at the counter. Open noon-midnight.

Rogacki, Wilmersdorferstr. 145. A huge delicatessen, with every sort of hot and cold food imaginable. Something good in every price range (lobster only DM50). Take out, or stand up and eat your winnings at the counters in the back. Open Mon.-Fri. 9am-6pm, Sat. 9am-1pm.

Schwarzes Café, Kantstr. 148, near Savignyplatz. A hopping café with loads of young people and hip music. Serves breakfast: omelettes start at DM7. Great tortellini (DM10). For a real jolt of caffeine try its namesake (DM7). Closed from 3am on Mon. to 11am on Wed.; otherwise open 24 hrs.

Die Rote Harfe, Oranienstr. 13, in Heinrichplatz, the center of Kreuzberg. Young leftists eating solid German food. The *Schweizer Schnitzel* (DM15.90) and the *Algauer Kässpatzle* (DM9.90) are both treats.

Rani, Goltzstr. 32. Good Indian food, strategically located near the bars and clubs of Schöneberg. Order at the counter. Most entrees under DM12. Open noon-1am.

Rococco, Knesebeckstr. 92. When you want to treat yourself; fantastic Italian food for DM20-30. Open Mon.-Sat. noon-midnight, Sun. 7pm-midnight.

Cour Carré, Savignyplatz 5. A marvelous little French café in ivy-bedecked surroundings. Meals DM20-40. Best on a sunny day. Open noon-2am.

Tegernseer Tönnchen, Mommsenstr. 34, near Wilmersdorferstr. A delightful Bavarian restaurant. For a mountain of food, order the *Grosse Schlachtplatte,* an assortment of Bavarian *Wurst* (DM13.50). Three-course daily *menus* DM10.50-17.90. The *Zigeunerschnitzel* (pork chop with peppers and spicy sauce) feeds a monster (DM14.50). Wide selection of beers (DM2.20-4). Open daily 11am-midnight.

Dicke Wirtin, Carmerstr. 9, around the corner from Cour Carré. Huge bowls of thick soup and stew for DM2-5. Open daily noon-4am.

Café Voltaire, Stuttgarterplatz 14. Trendy but inexpensive café. Great breakfasts (5am-3pm, DM6-8); warm meals noon-5am. Open 24 hrs.

Bistro Am Wittenbergplatz, located across the street from U-bahn: Wittenbergplatz. Fun café with a view of the *platz.* English menu available. Open Mon.-Sat. 9am-1am, Sun. 10am-midnight. Meals DM15-25.

Café Mövenpick, located in Breitscheidplatz between the Kaiser-Wilhelm-Gedächtnis-Kirche and the Europa Center. Great location matched by a great view of the fountain. Specializes in Italian food. Meals DM10-20. Tasty ice cream specialties DM10-15. Cocktails DM5-10. Open daily 8am-midnight.

East Berlin

Zur Rippe, Poststr. 17, is a pleasing café around the corner from the Nikolaikirche, near the Mühlendammbrücke. Tasty meals DM10-14. The *Berlin Weiße mit Rippenshosse* (DM3.80), a bizarre red cocktail, is delicious.

Zur Letzten Instanz, Waisenstr. 16, is an historic old-Berlin restaurant, dating back to the 16th century. Located near the Supreme Court, its name means "the last appeal." Brimming with atmosphere. Meals run DM9-12, drinks DM2-6. Open daily 11am-midnight.

Morava,Rathauspassage 5, at Alexanderplatz. This popular Czech restaurant was closed for renovation during the summer of 1991. Worth checking out if in the area.

Gastmahl des Meers, Spandauerstr. 4, at the intersection of Karl-Liebknecht-Str. A seafood restaurant with a late-night bar and disco. Meals DM10-25. Restaurant open Mon.-Sat. 11am-11pm, Sun. 11am-4pm. Bar and disco open Mon.-Thurs. 4pm-midnight, Fri. 7pm-3am, Sat. 11am-3pm, Sun. 11am-midnight.

Sights

The difference between the two halves of this formerly divided city strikes most trenchantly after dark, when all the tourists and hucksters have vanished. Take a ride across the city in the evening and compare the throbbing neon of the Ku'damm to the stately, almost deserted avenues of East Berlin, with their floodlit monuments.

West Berlin

A sobering reminder of the devastation caused by World War II, the shattered **Kaiser-Wilhelm-Gedächtniskirche** now houses an exhibit dedicated to peace. (Open Tues.-Sat. 10am-6pm, Sun. 11am-6pm.) It has, however, lost some of its didactic force amidst the giddy neon of the Ku'damm and the Europa Center. To the north and east, toward what was the center of old Berlin, spreads Berlin's lush **Tiergarten,** a vast landscaped park formerly used by the Prussian monarchs as a hunting ground. In the heart of the Tiergarten, the **Siegessäule** victory column celebrates Prussia's campaign against France in 1870; note that it faces toward France. The base of the monument was added by the Nazis, who wanted to increase its height to make it more impressive. (Open April-Nov. Mon. 1-5:45pm, Tues.-Sun. 9am-5:45pm. Admission DM1.20, students DM0.70.) Climb to the top for a sweeping view of the monuments beyond the wall. The **Soviet Army Memorial** (yes, you're still in West Berlin) stands at the end of Straße des 17. Juni, right near the **Brandenburger Tor** (Brandenburg Gate). The Tor is next to the former East-West border. Built during the reign of Frederick Wilhelm II as a symbol of peace, this is the spot where East Germans pranced the night away on December 22, 1989.

Built overnight on August 13, 1961, the 99-mile-long **Berlin Wall** arbitrarily separated families and friends, sometimes even running through people's homes. At various places along the remnants, small crosses mark where East Germans were killed fleeing to the West. Claiming that the Wall was constructed to "secure the border" with the West and to permit the "systematic and undisturbed reconstruction of the city," the East German government nonetheless had to force its citizens—often at gunpoint—to build it. Tourists have already chiseled away all that there is to be had. The "pieces of the Wall" sold by the nearby hawkers have as much relation to the Wall as any rock has to another: it's not the real thing.

No trip to Berlin is complete without a visit to the **Haus am Checkpoint Charlie,** Friedrichstr. 44 (U-bahn: Kochstr., or bus #129). Through film and photo, the museum narrates the history of the Wall, including numerous harrowing escape attempts. Upstairs there are general exhibits on human rights, as well as artistic representations of the Wall. Films and documentaries in German are shown daily from 9am to 5:30pm. (Open daily 9am-10pm. Admission DM5, students DM3.50.) Just to the north of the Brandenburger Tor sits the **Reichstag** building, once and future seat of unified Germany's parliament. In August 1914, Karl Liebknecht's famous "Nein!" was one of a few votes in its halls against the impending First World War. In 1918, after Kaiser Wilhelm II had abdicated, Philip Scheidemann, much to the surprise of his superiors in the Social Democratic Party, proclaimed the German Republic from one of its windows. His move turned out to be wise, since two hours later Karl Liebknecht announced a German Socialist Republic in the Imperial Palace down the street. Civil war conditions in Berlin and much of the rest of Germany resulted. In February 1933, just one month after Hitler became chancellor, the building mysteriously burnt down. The Nazis blamed the Communists and later outlawed the Communist party and terrorized other opponents. Hitler used the Reichstag fire to woo support for the infamous Enabling Act. He managed to convince the "moderate" parties in parliament to help him pass the Act, which made him legal dictator of Germany. In 1991, the Reichstag (no longer a government building) held only an exhibit of German history, though this will change as Parliament returns to Berlin.

Indispensable for a sense of Berlin's counter-culture (or "alternative" scene, as West Berliners call it) is a visit to **Kreuzberg,** an area loaded with cafés and bars. For its more respectable face, get off at U-Bahn #6 or 7: Mehringdamm, and wander around anywhere—Bergmannstraße features an especially large proportion of old buildings and second-hand shops. At night many bohemian and punk clubs overflow onto Yorckstraße, which heads west from its intersection with Mehringdamm. Other good streets are the more radical Oranienstraße (U-Bahn: Kottbusser Tor) and the east end of Kreuzberg, near the old Wall (U-Bahn: Schlesisches Tor), which boasts Balkan and Turkish neighborhoods (half of West Berlin's foreigners are Turkish).

Schloss Charlottenburg, the vast baroque palace built by Friedrich I for his second wife Sophie-Charlotte, stands on the outskirts of town amid spacious landscaped gardens. Seek out the gardens behind the palace, with their carefully planted rows of trees, small lake, footbridge, and fountains. The ornate **Knobelsdorff Wing** is the most lavish of the palace suites. From Ernst-Reuter-Platz, take Otto-Suhr-Allee northwest to Spandauer Damm, or take bus #145 from Bahnhof Zoo. (Open Tues.-Sun. 9am-5pm. Admission to the entire palace complex *(Sammelkarte)* DM6, students DM3, ages under 14 free. Knobelsdorff Wing alone DM2.50, students DM1.50, ages under 14 free.) **The Palace Gardens** (open Tues.-Sun. 6am-9pm) surround the **Royal Mausoleum** (open April-Oct. 9am-noon and 1-5pm); **Belvedere,** an 18th-century residence housing a porcelain exhibit; and the **Schinkel Pavilion,** with furniture designed by Schinkel (open Tues.-Sun. 9am-5pm).

A somber monument to the victims of Nazism, the **Gedenkstätte Plötzensee Memorial** exhibits documents recording death sentences of "enemies of the people" (including the officers who attempted to assassinate Hitler in 1944) in the former execution chambers of the Third Reich. The stone urn in front of the memorial contains soil from Nazi concentration camps. Literature on the monument is available in English at the office. Take bus #123 from S-Bahn: Tiergarten to Goerdelerdamm, and follow Hüttingpfad 200m away from the Kanal, along a tall brick wall. (Open daily March-Sept. 8am-6pm; Feb. and Oct. 8:30am-5:30pm; Nov. and Jan. 8:30am-4:30pm; Dec. 8:30am-4pm. Free.)

Southeast of the city center and south of Nollendorfplatz is the **Rathaus Schöneberg,** where West Berlin's city government convened. On June 26, 1963, 1½ million Berliners swarmed the streets to hear John F. Kennedy reassure them of the Allies' continued commitment to the city (in 1948, Allied airlift had provided the Western sectors of Berlin with supplies during the 11-month Berlin Airlift, after Soviet forces closed off land routes between Berlin and West Germany). Kennedy's speech ended with the now-famous words, "*Ich bin ein Berliner.*" Although the phrase literally translates as "I am a jelly doughnut," everyone understood that he meant to say "I am a Berliner." Not too far away is Fehrbelliner Platz (U-Bahn: Fehrbelliner Platz), an excellent example of Nazi architecture. These huge, prison-like blocks were meant to be model apartment houses; try to imagine a city full of them.

In the southern suburb of Dahlem, Berlin's **Botanischer Garten,** Königin-Luise-Str. 6-8, is a delight, especially the tropical greenhouses. Take bus #19 from the Ku'damm to Potsdamerstr., then bus #48 south. (Open daily 9am-sunset. Admission DM2.50, students DM1.20.) The renowned **Zoo,** entrance at Budapesterstr. 34 (the Elephant Gate), across from the tourist office in the Europa Center, houses an exotic collection of fauna as well as the spectacular **Aquarium,** Budapesterstr. 32. (Zoo open daily March-April 9am-5pm; May-Oct. 15 9am-6pm; Oct. 16-Feb. 9am-4:45pm. Aquarium open daily 9am-6pm. Admission to zoo DM7.50, students DM6.50, ages 3-15 DM4. Admission to aquarium DM7, ages 3-15 DM3.50. Comprehensive admission DM11.50, students DM10, ages 3-15 DM6.)

East Berlin

Walking through the Brandenburger Tor brings you onto **Unter den Linden,** once one of the ritziest streets in Europe and the most famous boulevard of old Berlin. All but the most famous buildings have been destroyed, but farther down many 18th century buildings have been restored to their original splendor, hinting at the incredible pomposity of Wilhelmine architecture while the famous statue of Frederick the Great atop his horse looks on. Past Friedrichstraße, the first massive building on your left is the **Deutsche Staatsbibliothek** (Library), with a pleasant café inside. Beyond the library is the **Humboldt Universität** once one of the finest in the world (Hegel and Fichte worked there); the university's fate is up for grabs today. Next door, the old **Neue Wache** (New Guard House), designed by the renowned Prussian architect Friedrich Schinkel, is today the somber **Monument to the Victims of Fascism and Militarism.** Buried inside are urns filled with earth from the Nazi concentration camps of Buchenwald and Mauthausen and from the battlefields of Stalingrad, El Alamein and Normandy. The honor guard in front changes on the hour, with the full ceremony on Wednesday at 2:30pm. Across the way is **Bebelplatz,** the site of Nazi book burnings, now named for the old Social Democratic Party leader August Bebel. The building with the curved façade is the **Alte Bibliothek.** On the other side of the square is the handsome **Deutsche Staatsoper,** fully rebuilt from original sketches by Knobelsdorf. The most striking of the monumental buildings is the **Zeughaus,** now the **Museum of German History.** From the museum you can enter the courtyard and see the tormented faces of Andreas Schlüter's "Dying Warriors."

Berlin's most impressive ensemble of 18th-century buildings is a few blocks south of Unter den Linden at **Platz der Akademie,** graced by the twin cathedrals of the **Deutscher Dom** and the **Französischer Dom.** Enclosing the far end of the square, the classical **Schauspielhaus,** designed by Schinkel, is Berlin's most elegant concert space and hosts many international orchestras and classical performers. Destroyed by an air attack in 1945, it was painstakingly reconstructed and reopened in 1984.

Unter den Linden, as it crosses the bridge, opens out onto Marx-Engels-Platz. To the left is the **Altes Museum,** with a big polished granite bowl in front, and the multiple domed **Berliner Dom** (Berlin Cathedral). Severly damaged by an air raid in 1944, the cathedral's interior is being restored. (Open Mon.-Sat. 10am-noon and 1-5pm, Sun. noon-5pm. Last entry 4:45pm. Admission DM2, seniors and students DM1.) Behind the Altes Museum lie three other enormous museums and the ruins (now being restored) of a fourth. The ensemble, a spectacular jungle of pediments, porticoes, and colonnades, is known as **Museumsinsel** (Museum Island; see museum listings below).

Crossing another bridge brings you to the **Marx-Engels-Forum** (not Platz), a park and "conceptual memorial" consisting of steel tablets engraved with images of worker struggle and protest surrounding a twin statue of Marx and Engels. Behind the forum you'll see the the single tower of the **Rotes Rathaus,** Berlin's famous town hall and the twin spires of the **Nikolaikirche,** Berlin's oldest building. A small museum inside the latter has exhibits of the early history of the city. (Open Tues.-Sun. 10am-6pm. Admission DM2, students DM1.) The reconstructed city kernel around the church is very popular and crowded; among the historic buildings are the Knoblauchhaus and Ephraim-Palais. Another early church, the 15th-century **Marienkirche,** stands on the wide open plaza before the **Fernsehturm** (television tower), which offers fabulous views of both Berlins and a revolving telecafé with very expensive food. (Open daily 9am-11pm; open the 2nd and 4th Tues. of each month 1-11pm only. Last entrance to observation tower 10:30pm, to telecafé 9:45pm. Expect a 1-hr. wait. Tower admission DM5, seniors, students, and children DM3. Admission to telecafé DM5 and DM3.) The tower, which bears a startling resemblance to the Death Star, is the tallest structure in Berlin. Just beyond the tower is the sterile **Alexanderplatz.** This atrociously ugly square was meant to be a showpiece for socialism, a fact which becomes understandable after one sees the even more hideous housing projects in the outer boroughs of East Berlin. Today the square hums daily with con artists (three-card monte is especially popular) and enterprising street vendors, peddling everything from food processors to fast food. Friends from both Germanies often meet at the plaza's **Weltzeituhr,** the international clock.

An excellent and easy way to get a quick overview of most of the above sights is by **bus #100.** It takes the scenic route from Zoo to Alexanderplatz, going down Unter den Linden. (Standard Berlin rapid transit ticket valid.)

Northwest of Alexanderplatz is the **Scheuenviertel,** the former ghetto of Berlin. It was later home to the Jews who fled the Eastern European pogroms only to end up in Hitler's concentration camps, and it contains many reminders of Berlin's former Jewish community, once the most emancipated and cultured in the world. It later became a showpiece for the East German government; many old buildings have been restored, and some of the new constructions have a flair unusual for Berlin, West or East. The area has also become a center of the squatter scene, with a corresponding amount of cultural and café life. Down Oranienburgerstr. at #30 is the burnt-out shell of Berlin's major **synagogue;** this huge temple was once the center of West European Judaism. Torched by Nazis on *Kristallnacht* (November 9, 1938) the restoration work has been delayed by lack of funds. The façade is nonetheless gorgeous. A sign on the side of the building reads "Never forget this."

Take Oranienburgerstr. all the way to Friedrichstr. and bear left to reach the **Brecht-Haus Berlin,** Chausseestr. 125, where Bertolt Brecht lived and worked from 1953 to 1956. If you understand German you should take the guided tour, given in a flamboyant Brechtian style. (Open Tues.-Wed. and Fri. 10am-noon, Thurs. 10am-noon and 5-7pm, Sat. 9:30am-noon and 12:30-2pm. Tours every ½-hr.) Just before Brecht's house, the **Dorotheenstädtischer Friedhof** contains the graves of a host of German luminaries, including Brecht, Fichte and Hegel. (Open 10am-7pm.)

From Oranienburgerstr. you might want to wander east into **Penzlauer Berg,** a former working-class district largely neglected by East Germany's reconstruction efforts. Many of its old buildings are falling apart; others still have shell holes and embedded bullets from WWII. The result is the charm of age and graceful decay. The especially nice (and restored) **Husemannstraße,** home to cafés, restaurants and several museums. The area's population belies the aging architecture; heaps of students, artists, cafés, clubs and communes have given it the reputation of "Kreuzberg of the East," but the city government's anti-commune policy is in danger of destroying this (counter-)cultural renaissance. The nearby **Volkspark Friedrichshain** is a pretty little park containing a **Märchenbrunnen** (fairy-tale fountain).

The powerful **Soviet War Memorial,** at S-Bahn Treptower Park, is a mammoth promenade built with marble taken from Hitler's Chancellery. The Soviets dedicated the site in 1948, honoring the soldiers of the Red Army who fell in the "Great Patriotic War." The memorial sits in the middle of **Treptower Park,** a spacious wood ideal for morbid picnics. The neighborhood adjoining the park is known for its pleasant waterside cafés and handsome suburban mansions.

An enjoyable way to take in the city is by boat. The **Weiße Flotte ship service** follows the city's waterways (DM3.50 for 3 hr.). For reservations, check with the **Verkehrspavillion Treptow** at the dock (tel. 271 23 27), by the Treptower Park S-Bahn station. (Open March-Sept. Mon. and Wed.-Fri. 9-11:30am and 12:30-5pm, Tues. 9-11:30am and 12:30-6pm; Oct.-Dec. 15 Mon.-Fri. 8-11:30am and 12:30-4pm.)

Museums

The collections of the three museums on the Museumsinsel (S-Bahn: Marx-Engels-Platz) in East Berlin are astoundingly broad. When buying tickets, students should always ask for the student price. Standard university IDs and the ISIC card are usually valid.

Pergamonmuseum, Kupfergraben (tel. (9) 20 35 50), Museumsinsel. One of the world's great museums. The scale of its exhibits is mind-boggling: the Babylonian Ishtar Gate (575 BC), the Roman Market Gate of Miletus, and one of the ancient wonders of the world, the majestic Pergamon Altar of Zeus (180 BC). The altar's great frieze (400 ft. long and 7-8 ft. high), depicting the victory of the gods over the giants, symbolizes the triumphs of Attalus I. The museum also houses extensive collections of Greek, Assyrian, Islamic, and Far Eastern art. Open Wed.-Sun. 10am-6pm; architecture halls (including altar) open Mon.-Tues. also. Last entry 30 min. before closing. Tours of Pergamon Altar at 11am and 3pm. Admission DM1.05, seniors and students DM0.50. Mandatory baggage check DM0.20.

Alte Nationalgalerie, Bodestr. 1020 (tel. 220 03 81), Museumsinsel. Good collection of expressionism, including Feininger, Kokoschka, and the Brücke school. Open Wed.-Sun. 10am-6pm. Admission DM1.05, students DM0.50.

Bodemuseum, Monbijoubrücke (tel. (9) 203 550), Museumsinsel. A world-class exhibit of Egyptian art, as well as late Gothic wood sculptures, early Christian art, 15th-18th century paintings, and an exhibit on ancient history. Open Wed.-Sun. 10am-6pm. Admission DM1.05, seniors and students DM0.50.

Dahlem Museum, Arnimallee 23-27 and Lansstr. 8. U-Bahn: Dahlem-Dorf. A huge complex of 7 museums, each one worth a half-day visit. Particularly superb are the **Gemäldegalerie,** a fantastic collection of Italian, German, Dutch, and Flemish Old Masters (including 26 Rembrandts); the **Museum für Ostasiatische Kunst,** housing Japanese, Korean, and Chinese art; the **Museum für Völkerkunde** (Ethnography), with magnificent Mayan and Incan treasures; and the **Museum für Indische und Islamische Kunst.** All open Tues.-Fri. 9am-5pm, Sat.-Sun. 10am-5pm. Free.

Schloss Charlottenburg (U-Bahn 2: Sophie-Charlotte-Platz or bus #145) contains several museums. The **Ägyptisches Museum,** across Spandauer Damm from the main entrance to the castle, houses a fascinating collection of ancient Egyptian art, including the 3300-year-old bust of Queen Nefertiti (1350 BC). Also check out the **Antiken Museum** and the **Galerie der Romantiks.** All open Mon.-Thurs. 9am-5pm, Sat.-Sun. 10am-5pm. Free.

Martin-Gropius Bau, Stresemannstr. 110 (tel. 254 860). S-Bahn: Anhalter Bahnhof. Numerous museums and exhibits including the world-famous **Metropolis** exhibition of modern art, the **Topographie des Terrors,** which describes the development of fascism in Germany, and **Juden in Berlin,** with documents, pictures and paintings about and by Berlin's Jewish community. Most exhibits open Tues.-Sun. 10am-10pm. Admission DM8, students DM4. Topographie des Terrors open Tues.-Sun. 10am-6pm. Free.

Nationalgalerie, Potsdamerstr. 50. Take bus #129 from the Ku'damm. This handsome building, designed by Mies van der Rohe, houses a remarkable collection of expressionist works, as well as exhibits of contemporary art. Open Tues.-Fri. 9am-5pm, Sat.-Sun. 10am-5pm. Free.

Bauhaus Archiv-Museum für Gestaltung, Klingelhöferstr. 13-14. Take bus #129 to Lützowplatz. The shimmering modern building designed by Walter Gropius, founder of the famous school, displays exemplary works by Bauhaus members (among them, Kandinsky and Klee). Open Wed.-Mon. 11am-6pm. Admission DM3, students DM1.

Brücke Museum, Bussardsteig 9. From the Zoo, take bus #115 to Clayallee at Pücklerstr. An impressive collection of works by the German expressionist Brücke school, which flourished in Dresden and Berlin from 1909 to 1913. Open Wed.-Mon. 11am-5pm. Admission DM3.50, students DM1.50.

Entertainment

Berlin is *wild,* all night, every night. The best guides to theater, cinema, nightlife, and the extremely active musical scene are the biweekly magazines *Tip* (DM3.40) and the more "alternative" *Zitty* (DM3). Listings are usually comprehensible to non-German speakers. Both are available at newsstands and are issued in alternate weeks. The monthly *Berlin Program* (DM2.50) lists more "cultural" events and includes good theater information. *Berlin von hinten* (Berlin from the rear) is the best guide to gay life.

Nightlife

No place in the German-speaking world shakes and shouts at night like Berlin; residents and visitors party until 4am every night with a vengeance that is a matter of municipal pride. Mainstream activity centers around two areas to the north and south of the Ku'damm. The north is a bit more inviting to the youthful: the middle point is Savignyplatz and it includes Grolmanstr., Knesebeckstr., Bleibtreustr., and Schlütterstr., as well as Steinplatz, along Carmerstr. to the north. Café Hardenberg and Schwarzes Café, listed as restaurants, are both also excellent for a drink. The area to the south of Ku'damm centers on Ludwigkirchplatz, and is roughly bordered by the Ku'damm, Fasanenstr., and Pariserstr. up to Adenauerplatz. The **"alternative" scene** is what Berlin is good for (if you want beer halls, go to Munich). Head to Kleiststr. between Wittenberg Platz and Nollendorfstr., or to Potsdamerstr., one of the toughest streets in Berlin. Another non-mainstream area is Kreuzberg near Viktoria Park, along Yorckstr. and Gneisenaustr. Use caution in this area at night; it could be dangerous for females or people alone. Check the listings in *Berlin for Young People* and *Tip* for information on specific nightspots.

East Berlin can't compete with the chic bars of the West, but for those in the know, the center of Berlin's alternative and underground music scene has moved to the East. Prenzlauer Berg and the old Scheuenviertel are the best places to look.

Metropol, Nollendorfplatz 5 (tel. 216 41 22). U-Bahn: Nollendorfplatz, or night buses #19, 29, or 85. Still *the* place to go. Nude male and female statues fraternize on the gray façade. Live band or disco music. Cover about DM10. Music usually lasts until 4am. Open Wed.-Sat. from 10pm.

Ku'dorf, Joachimstalerstr. 15 (tel. 883 66 66), near the Ku'damm. A group of 22 *kneipen* adjoining each other below street level, serving 16 different kinds of beer (from DM3.50). The best of the bunch is the Musik-Laden. Cover DM5. Open Mon.-Sat. from 8pm. Upstairs is **Chaplin's Garden,** a disco with cover Sun.-Thurs. DM3, Fri.-Sat. DM5.

Loretta im Garten, Lietzenburgerstr. 89 (tel. 882 34 48), near Knesebeckstr. A lively German beer garden, complete with ferris wheel, disco, outdoor food stands, and all kinds of people guzzling all kinds of beer. Beer DM3.50. Open daily 7pm-1am.

Go In, Bleibtreustr. 17 (tel. 881 72 18). Live folk, blues, cabaret. Opens at 8pm, concerts start at 9:30pm. Cover varies according to the performer; sometimes free.

Quasimodo, Kantstr. 12a (tel. 312 80 86). A basement pub, with live jazz and rock (frequent big names) and a lively crowd. Open daily from 8pm, concerts usually begin at 10pm. Cover free to DM30. Concert tickets available daily from 8pm or at Kant Kasse ticket service (tel. 313 45 54).

Ex, Mehringhof, Gneisenaustr. 2a. A typical Kreuzberg kneipe and hangout for the people from the "alternative scene." Average *Let's Go*-er might be freaked out. Piped-in music and punk. Occasional concerts. Open Tues.-Thurs. 11am-1am, Fri. from 8pm, Sun. 8pm-1am, Mon. from 11am.

Yorck-Schlößchen, Yorckstr. 15 (tel. 215 80 70). Enjoyable pub sometimes with live music late in the evening. Now and then a punky crowd. In an old Kreuzberg tenement. Pleasant garden in front. Open daily 9am-3am.

Wu Wu, Kleiststr. 4 (tel. 213 63 92). U-bahn: Nollendorfplatz. A gay bar and disco; men only. No cover. Open daily 10pm-7am.

Knaack-Klub, Greifswalderstr. 224 (tel. (9) 436 23 51). S-Bahn: Marx-Engels-Platz, then tram #24 or 28. Probably the most "normal" place in Berlin. Different types of music each night; Sat. is disco night. Popular among local Prenzlauer Berg crowd. Cover DM4.

Tacheles, Oranienburgerstr. 53-56 (tel. (9) 282 61 85). U-Bahn: Oranienburger Tor. In a squatter's commune, so most people there seem to know each other. Live music nightly on ground floor, performance art, drama or film above, and occasionally a disco below. Cover DM5 per floor.

Klub 29, Rosa-Luxemburg-Str. 27. U-Bahn: Rosa-Luxemburg-Platz. Live bands nightly. Cover DM3.

Homo Bar, Oranienstr. 168. U-Bahn: Kottbusser Tor. Relaxed gay and lesbian bar in Kreuzberg.

Quartier Latin, Potsdamerstr. 96 (tel. 262 90 16). U-Bahn: Kufurstenstr. Aims to recreate the feel of Berlin in the 20's. Disco supposedly has the best DJ in Berlin. Also has Sunday tea dances, Varieté shows and occasional bands. Cover varies; usually DM12-18.

Concerts, Opera and Dance

Berlin reaches its musical zenith during the fabulous **Berliner Festwochen,** lasting almost the entire month of September and drawing the world's best orchestras and soloists, and the **Berliner Jazztage** in November. For more information on all these events (and tickets for the last two, which sell out far in advance), write to Berliner Festspiele, Budapesterstr. 48-50, 1000 Berlin 30 (tel. 25 48 92 50; open daily noon-6pm). In mid-July, **Bachtage** (Bach Days) offer an intense week of classical music; every Saturday night in August **Sommer Festspiele** turns the Ku'damm into a multi-faceted concert hall with punk, steel drum, and folk groups competing for attention.

In the the monthly pamphlet *Kultur in Berlin,* as well as the biweekly magazines *Tip* and *Zitty,* you'll find notice of concerts in the courtyard of the old Arsenal, on the Schloßinsel Köpenick (Castle Island), or in the parks. Many tickets are available at the **Europäisches Reisebüro** (see Budget Travel above). If you know what you want, call or visit the auditorium yourself and evade the 10% commission charged by these offices. Unfortunately, most theaters close from at least mid-July to late August. Always ask about student discounts. Theater box offices (see below) also often sell concert tickets.

Philharmonie, Matthäikirchstr. 1 (tel. 25 48 80). Take bus #129 from Ku'damm to Potsdamerstr. and walk 3 blocks north. The big yellow building is as acoustically perfect within as it is unconventional without, and the Berliner Philharmoniker, led for decades by the late Herbert von Karajan, is perhaps the finest orchestra in the world. It's nigh impossible to get a seat; check an hour before concert time or write far in advance. Here and at the Oper, you can also stand out front just before the performance with a small sign saying *"Suche Karte"* (Ticket wanted); invariably a few people can't come at the last moment. Sadly, the Philharmonie is often closed during the summer months. Ticket office open Mon.-Fri. 3:30-6pm, Sat.-Sun. and holidays 11am-2pm.

Deutsche Staatsoper, Unter den Linden 7 (tel. (9) 200 47 66). Berlin's leading opera company. Ballet and classical music, too. Box office open Mon.-Sat. noon-6pm, Sun. 4-6pm. Tickets DM18-35.

Deutsche Oper Berlin, Bismarckstr. 35 (tel. 343 81). U-Bahn #1: Deutsche Oper. Berlin's best opera. Box office open Mon.-Fri. 2-8pm, Sat.-Sun. 10am-2pm and 1 hr. before performances. Ten min. before performances, you can get student discounts of up to 50% off depending on the price of the ticket. Tickets DM10-125.

Tanzfabrik, Möckernstr. 68 (tel. 786 58 61). U-Bahn #1 or 7: Möckernbrücke. Modern dance performances and a general center for dance workshops. Ticket office open Mon.-Thurs. 10am-1pm and 5-8pm. Down the alley and to your left, up three flights of stairs. Tickets DM15. Occasional weekend performances starting at either 8 or 8:30pm.

Theater and Film

Theater listings are available in the monthly pamphlet *Kultur in Berlin,* the *Berlin Programm, Tip* and *Zitty.* They are also posted in most U-Bahn stations; look for the yellow posters. You can reserve tickets by calling the theater directly; most theaters have student discounts of up to 50%, but only if you buy just before the performance begins. Numerous box offices charge commission and do not offer student discounts. The main box office is **Theaterkasse Centrum,** Meinekestr. 25 (tel. 882 76 11). Berlin has a lively English-language theater scene; look for listings in *Tip* or *Zitty* that say *"in englischer Sprache"* (in English) next to them.

On any night in Berlin you can choose from 100 different films, many in the original language. ("O. F." next to a movie listing means "original version"; "O.m.U." means original with German subtitles. Everything else is dubbed.) Check *Tip, Zitty,* or the subway posters. There is an international **Film Festival** (late Feb.-March) and a **Theater Festival** (May).

Das Schiller Theater, Bismarckstr. 110 (tel. 319 52 36). U-Bahn: Ernst-Reuter-Platz. The most respected theater in the country; sometimes it's hard to see why. Tickets DM10-45.

Deutsches Theater, Schumannstr. 13a (tel. (9) 287 12 25). U- or S-Bahn: Friedrichstr. The best theater in the country. Innovative productions of both classics and newer works. The Kammerspiel des Deutschen Theaters (tel. (9) 287 12 26) has smaller productions. Tickets DM10-32; 50% student discount often available.

Berliner Ensemble, Berthold-Brecht-Platz (tel. (9) 282 31 60). U- or S-Bahn: Friedrichstr. Competent but rather listless performances, mostly of Brecht. Box office open Tues.-Fri. 11am-1:30 pm and 2-6pm, Mon. 11am-5pm, and 1hr. before performances. Tickets DM4-25.

Maxim Gorki Theater, Am Festungsgraben 2 (tel. (9) 208 27 83), just off Unter den Linden. Excellent contemporary theater. Box office open Mon.-Fri. 2-8pm, Sat. 4-8pm. Tickets DM3-20.

Die Distle, Degnerstr. 9 (tel. 376 51 74) and Friedrichstr. 101 (tel. 207 12 91). A cabaret of political satire. Box office opens Wed. at 5pm, Thurs. at 3pm, and Fri. at 11am.

Filmtheater Babylon, Rosa-Luxemburg-Str. 30. Screens German oldies and silent movies.

Near Berlin: Potsdam

Potsdam, city of Frederick the Great and palatial seat of the Prussian empire, is an essential foray from Berlin. Take bus #113 from S-Bahn: Wannsee (45 min.; leaves every 20 min.). You can also take an S-Bahn from Wannsee to Potsdam (20 min.; leaves every hour). Berlin rapid transit tickets are valid on the bus, the S-Bahn, and public transportation within Potsdam.

The 600-acre **Sanssouci Park** houses four baroque palaces and countless exotic pavilions. The largest of this royal quartet, the **Neues Palais,** was originally built by Frederick the Great while pouting after several unsuccessful wars. Inside is the 19th-century Grottensaal, a reception room whose ribbed walls glitter with seashells and semi-precious stones. The palace also houses a luxurious café. (Open Mon.-Sat. 10am-7pm. Admission to palace DM2, students and seniors DM1. Closed 2nd Mon. of month.) At the opposite end of the park stands **Schloß Sanssouci,** where Fred used to escape his wife and other troubles *(sanssouci* means "without a care"). Next door, the fabulous **Bildergalerie** houses works by Caravaggio, van Dyck, and Rubens beneath its gilded ceiling. Exemplar of early Romanticism, **Schloß Charlottenhof** melts into its landscaped gardens and grape arbors; the **Römische Bäder** lie nearby. Overlooking the park from the north, the pseudo-Italian **Orangerie-Schloß** is famous for its 67 dubious Raphael imitations. The most bizarre of the park's pavilions are its "oriental" houses: the **Chinesisches Teehaus** is a gold-plated opium dream, complete with rooftop Buddha (a.k.a. Neptune with a parasol). The **Drachenhaus** is around the corner from the Orangerie. (All palaces open daily April-Sept. 9am-5pm; Oct. and Feb.-March 9am-4pm; Nov.-Jan. 9am-3pm. Closed 1st Mon. of month and daily for 30-60 min. between noon and 1:30pm.)

The **Brandenburger Tor,** Potsdam's monumental arch, rises above regal Platz der Nationen. From here, **Brandenburgerstraße,** a cobbled street flanked by restaurants and shops, leads down to the 19th-century **Peter-Pauls-Kirche.** 1 block before the church, Friedrich-Ebertstr. heads left to the red-brick **Dutch Quarter.** The sumptuous if somewhat decrepit mansions along **Hegelallee** hint at Potsdam's bygone grandeur.

The **tourist office,** Friedrich-Ebertstr. 5 (tel. 211 00) is near the Platz der Einheit tram station and closer to the Alter Markt station. All trams from the bus or train station go to one of the two stops. From the bus station it's a 10 min. walk: right on Wilhelm-Pieck-Str., then left onto Friedrich-Ebert-Str. The office provides information on local events, a modest map, and private accommodations (Separate tel. for accommodations 233 85. Rooms DM15-20 per person. Private bungalows DM35 per person. Office open Mon.-Fri. 9am-8pm, Sat.-Sun. 9am-6pm.) The main campground is **Intercamping-platz Riegelspitze am Glindower See,** 5km outside of the village of Werder, on the other side of Lake Havel from Potsdam (DM7.50 per person, DM6 per tent). Bus #631 runs from the main bus station and Potsdam Hauptbahnhof to the campground. The **Jugendherberge** at Eisenhardtstr. 5 (tel. 225 15) offers beds in high-ceilinged quads and quints. (Juniors DM9.50, seniors DM12.50. Breakfast DM4.50. Dinner DM5.50.) Take tram #95 to Behlerstr., walk a few feet down Behlerstr. and turn left onto Eisenhardtstr. It's almost always full in summer, so call ahead.

Brandenburgerstraße is filled with restaurants, including (thanks to capitalism) *döner kepab* stands and Mexican fast food. Near the head of the street at Brandenburger Tor, the elegant main salon of **Restaurant Am Stadttor** is usually booked solid, but the upstairs **Speisebar** has entrees for DM9-13. (Both open daily 11am-9pm. Restaurant closed 3rd Mon. of month; Speisebar closed 2nd Mon. of month.)

Across the street, **Gastmahl des Meeres,** Brandenburgerstr. 72, serves seafood for DM10-19. (Open Mon.-Fri. 10am-8pm, Sat.-Sun. 11am-3pm.) In the Sanssouci area, the only hot food is at **Gaststätte Charlottenhof,** Geschwister-Schollstr. (Entrees DM10-14. Open Mon.-Fri. 12:30-11pm, Sat.-Sun. 10am-11pm.)

Tangermünde

In 1373, Kaiser Karl IV gave up the spires of Prague to lay out a new capital on the banks of the Elbe, about 30km downstream from Magdeburg. For five years, Tangermünde became *the* place in Germany to see and be seen. When the emperor died, however, the capital was moved and Tangermünde retreated to provincial status (sound familiar, Bonn?). Today, all that remains of those heady days is the **Kanzlei,** the emperor's disco, and Tangermünde's *Altstadt,* filled with towering glazed brickwork and crowded with wood-frame houses. Plan connections carefully. **Stendal,** on the main train line between Berlin and Amsterdam, is the main link to Tangermünde. Trains and buses leave about every two hours from Stendal's main station, but the schedules suffer from some erratic suprises. Basically, transportation here sucks.

The great gates of **Hühnerdorfer Tor** and **Neustadter Tor,** as well as the **Rathaus** and the **St. Stephankirche,** all date from the 15th century when the city was a loaded customs port. Most of the homes however, were constructed after a disastrous fire in 1617 (sound familiar, Chicago?). At the time, irate villagers found a scapegoat in a young woman who was burnt as a witch (sound familiar, Salem?) for her part in the fire.

The closest thing to an **information office** is at the town hall, Rathaus Stadtverwaltung, rm. 20 (tel. 29 71; open Mon.-Fri. 9am-noon and 1-5pm). Stores and hotels inside the walls also shower guests with info. Both hotels are way out of line, but **Pension am Schrotturm** offers tiny, tidy rooms (sound familiar, Canaday?) and an expansive breakfast for DM25.

Schwerin

Built as a way station for Henry the Lion's 12th-century march through the east, Schwerin makes a restorative stop on the way to the swarming Baltic coast. In October 1990, Schwerin regained its prewar status as capital of Mecklenburg-Pomerania, a province of fallen Junkers, rye bread, tall brick churches and seagulls borne in by Baltic breezes. With an *Altstadt* still untouched by evil western capitalists, Schwerin has an old-fashioned look of shabby gentility.

From the station, head up zum Bahnhof and go right on Wismarschestr. and left on Martinstr. for the *Altstadt.* Its most fanciful structure is the **Märchenschloß** (Fairy Tale Castle), a majestic old arsenal in the center of town. Its white turrets are supposedly haunted by the long-suffering **Petermännchen,** Schwerin's patron ghost. Schwerin's **Schloß,** a solid baroque castle with intricate cupolas, presides over its own fairy-tale island fiefdom just south of the center, over the Lennestr. bridge at the end of Schloßstr. Inside, the throne room and banquet hall have been lavishly restored, under and above a first-floor archeological museum. (Open Tues.-Sun. 10am-5pm.) Across from the castle, the **Alter Garden** square was the site of mass demonstrations against the old regime in October 1989. In peacetime, visitors come for the **Staatliche Museum** and its **Gemäldgalerie,** which an 18th-century Duke with an unhealthy relationship with the Dutch Renaissance endowed with one of the best Old Masters collections in Germany, in addition to German glass and porcelain. (Painting gallery and gardens open Tues. and Thurs.-Sun. 10am-5pm, Wed. 9am-6pm.) The **Mahn-und Gedenkstätte der Jüdischen Landesgemeinde Mecklenburg,** Schlachterstr. 3 (tel. 81 29 97), is a long name for a simple set of exhibits in tribute to the region's erstwhile Jewish communities. (Open Tues.-Wed. 2-4pm.)

Schwerin **information,** at Am Markt 11 (tel. 81 23 14), sells maps and books private rooms (from DM20). From the station, head up zum Bahnhof, right on Wismarschestr., left on Arsenal, and right on Bischofstr. (Open Mon.-Fri. 10am-6pm, Sat. 10am-3pm.) The less formal **Zimmervermittlung** at Körnerstr. 18 is open daily from 4pm "until the rooms are gone." From the Markt, take Schmiedestr. one block to Pushkinstr. and left to Körnerstr. **Jugendherberge Schwerin,** Waldschulerweg 3 (tel. 21 30 05), lies south of town in a woodsy setting oversmelling the zoo and overlooking the lake. From the station, take tram #1 to Platz der Jugend and change for bus #15, or take bus #15 directly from the bus station on Hermann-Matern-Str. to the last stop. (Juniors DM13.50. Seniors DM16. Sometimes full; call ahead.) The brightly refurbished **Reichshof Hotel,** Am Gunthalplatz 15-17 (tel. 86 40 45), has a classic façade and an excellent, across-from-the-station location. (Singles DM50, with shower DM60. Doubles DM85, with shower DM90, with shower and bath DM100.) The superest supermarket is **Kaisers** on Schmiedestr., while cafés line the streets around the old *Markt.* Eat on red-and-white checkered tablecloths at the colorful **Alt Schweriner Schankstuben,** on the well-preserved *Fachwerk* Schlachtermarkt behind the *Markt.* (Entrees DM10. Open daily 11am-midnight.) There is squat to do in the evening except stroll along the lake shores or the narrow pedestrian streets, and sip something at the umbrella-topped tables beside the Pfaffer Teich fountains, serviced by a kiosk. (Open daily 9:30am-10pm.) Rent a rowboat at the docks to test the more troubled waters of the **Schweriner See** (around the Schloßinsel and to the west) or take a cruise; ferries depart from the Weiße Flote dock near the Lennestr. bridge (daily 10am-5pm).

Rostock

The largest and most active port in eastern Germany since the 14th century, Rostock went into the textbooks as socialist Germany's "gateway to the world." In practice, however, the port was closed to all but a chosen few. Since reunification, Rostock's booming business has all but disappeared. With open borders and hard currency prices, western ships stop in Hamburg while eastern customers stay home. However, sun-seeking tourists continue to flock to the beaches of nearby Warnemünde during the summer.

The city's main architectural landmark is the 13th-century **St. Mary's Church,** a monster brick edifice near the main square at the end of pedestrian Kröplinerstr. Enter and behold a towering organ. (Open Tues.-Sat. 10am-noon and 3-5pm, Sun. 11am-noon.) In the final weeks of the 1989 revolution the services here overflowed with political protesters who came to hear the inspiring messages of Pastor Gauck. In one of the more heroic gestures of the revolution, the pastor began to publicly and personally chastise three members of the *Stasi* (secret police) who were in the audience making notes on their disruptive comrades. In an ironic twist, Gauck is now the only man in Germany trusted enough to guard the old East German secret police files from embarrassing public exposure. Near the church is the rosy Renaissance **Rathaus,** topped by seven striped Gothic towers.

Rostock Information, at Schnickmannstr. 13-14 (tel. 252 60), just off Langestr., three stops west on any tram from the train station, will direct forlorn tourists to the office booking private accommodations (open Mon.-Fri. 9am-7pm). Otherwise, the closest **youth hostel** is on a great old ship in the harbor, about 20 minutes from the Lutten Klein station. Follow Warnowallee down to the harbor and around to the left. The hostel is at the end of the road. Near the tourist information office in Rostock, on the water's edge, is **Zur Krogge,** Wokrenter Str. 27. The model ships hanging from the ceiling and the patron's Low German dialect make this place a must. The catch of the day costs DM6-8.

Rostock may no longer be the East's gateway to the world, but it is still a convenient link to Denmark. The main port and beach are at **Warnemünde** on the Baltic, 25 minutes away by S-Bahn (DM1). Ferries make the two-hour crossing to Gedser at least five times daily; the Berlin-Copenhagen train drives onto the ferry and crosses too. To reserve a seat, contact **Europa Linien** (tel. 812 23 21 or 36 63 10 30).

Stralsund and Rügen

A Swedish possession until 1815, the red-brick Baltic port of **Stralsund** looks northward metaphorically as well as physically. The only Baltic city to make it through the Thirty Years War unscathed, Stralsund wasn't so lucky under the communist regime—many buildings betray the years of neglect. The **Alter Markt** in the center is surrounded by several of Stralsund's oldest buildings. The Gothic **Rathaus,** built in the 13th century, shows off a spectacular 14th-century façade that towers high above the main structure. From the Alter Markt, Ossenreyerstr. (turn right at the end) takes you to **Marienkirche,** the city's largest. (Open Mon.-Fri. 10am-5pm, Sat. 10am-12:30pm and 2:30-5pm, Sun. 2:30-5pm. Church admission free; tower DM1.) Stralsund's **tourist office,** Alter Markt 15 (tel. 24 39), distributes free maps in English and helps hunt down vacant rooms. (Open Mon. 2-5pm, Tues. 9am-12:30pm and 2-6pm, Wed.-Thurs. 9am-12:30pm and 2-5pm, Fri. 9am-12:30pm and 2-4pm, Sat. 8:30-11am; Oct.-May 5 closed Sat.) Stralsund is about three hours north of Berlin by train.

If the tourist office's service fails you, try the **Zimmerbörse,** Ossenreyerstr. 28, which has the biggest selection of rooms (most of them private) in the city. **Jugendherberge "Grete Walter" (IYHF),** Am Küter Tor 1 (tel. 21 60), is located in the town wall with a courtyard and a convenient location. Arrive by 3pm at the latest. From the front of the train station, turn right onto Iribseer Damm and go straight to the Hauptbahnhof bus stop. Take bus #4 or 5 to Küter Tor (the second stop), turn right and take the first left; the hotel is just before the big gate on the left. (Reception open 3-10pm. Lockout 9am-3pm. Curfew 1am. DM13; over 26, DM15.50. Choice of breakfast included.) **Gastmahl des Meeres,** Ossenreyerstr. 4, in the pedestrian zone, serves only fish, but in every imaginable variety. (Full meals DM7 and up. Open Mon.-Fri. 11am-9pm, Sat.-Sun. 11am-3pm.)

Sitting in the Baltic Sea north of Stralsund, **Rügen** is Germany's largest island, encompassing a dazzling array of natural wonders: white beaches and rugged chalk cliffs, farmland and beech forests, heaths and swamps. At the northern end of the island, the resort town of **Saßnitz** is at the end of the rail line from Berlin, an hour past Stralsund. The **room-finding service,** Hauptstr. 50, is down Bahnhofstr. from the station. (Open Mon.-Fri. 10am-1pm and 3-6pm.) **Ferries** leave Saßnitz for Trelleborg, Sweden (5 per day, 4 hr., DM26-32, free with railpasses) and Rønne on the Danish island of Bornholm. Tickets for the Saßnitz-Trelleborg and Saßnitz-Rønne runs are sold through the **Deutsche Reichsbahn,** at Trelleborgstr. (tel. 222 67).

Accessible by train from Saßnitz, the town of **Binz** is a once-fashionable spa town with a 4km beach. There you can hop on the ironically named **Rassender Roland** (Racing Roland), an old-fashioned narrow-gauge train that hurtles along at the dizzying speed of 30km per hour (single fare DM3.60). Binz has Rügen's only **Jugendherberge (IYHF),** Strandpromenade 35 (tel. 24 23), directly on the beach. (DM9.50; over 26, DM12.50. Call ahead.) The highlight of Rügen is the spectacular chalk cliffs of the **Große Stubbenkammer,** where a crowded lookout offers a fabulous view over the Baltic Sea (admission DM1, students DM0.50).

The Spreewald

About 100km southeast of Berlin, on the train line to Cottbus and Görlitz, the Spree River breaks apart and spreads itself over the countryside in a maze of streams and canals over 1000km long. This is the land of the *Irrlichter,* a sort of Saxon leprechaun that (for a price) lights the waterways for those who lose their way and leads astray those who refuse to pay. Here folklore, tradition and wildlife have survived in remarkable harmony. Farmers still row to their fields and children paddle home from school. Hire a gondola, rent a paddle boat or take to the trails by foot.

Lübben is a good starting point for the forests of the **Unter-Spreewald** (Lower Spreewald), which stretches north toward Leibsch. The **tourist office,** Lindenstr. 14 (tel. 30 90) is right on the harbor (open Mon.-Fri. 8am-6pm). They'll help with rooms (rare as hens' teeth here) or guide you to the pre-WWII **Jugendherberge Lübben,** Zum Wendenfürst (tel. 30 46), which is right on the Spree about 20 min. from the Hauptbahnhof (paddle boat rental DM3). The Spreewald has long been famous for its pickles, preserves and fresh vegetables. Someone should let the local restaurants in on this; they stick largely to pork, pork and pork. The hunters in Lübben gather at the **Gaststätte "Kinoklause"** across from the church on Poststr. (tel. 33 28). Join them for tasty, cheap schnitzel and fries (DM 5.85; open 8am-midnight). The town's newest, most Western and only foreign restaurant, **Ristorante La Laguna,** is ironically on Karl-Marx-Str., near the train station. (Open Tues.-Sun. noon-11pm.) Lübben's elevated Hauptstraße has guided the armies of Napoleon, Peter the Great and Hitler back and forth to Russia, but its canals should lead you north to **Straupitz,** where master German architect Karl Friedrich Sinkel erected a classic Prussian church in the middle of nowhere. (No one knows why, but rumor has it that Jim Morrison is buried nearby.)

If you are more a village-and-meadow person, head straight for **Lübbenau,** gateway to the **Ober-Spreewald.** There's no hostel here; for private rooms (expect to pay at least DM20) drop by the **tourist office** (tel. 22 36), a 5 min. walk straight down Ernst-Thälmann-Str. to #25. (Open Mon., Wed., Fri. 7am-3pm, Tues. and Thurs. 7am-5pm.) Or try the enterprising fellows at the **Spreewaldbüro,** Groucho-Marx-Str. (tel. 30 07); they guarantee rooms and speak English. The **Gasthaus Spreewaldeck,** Maxim-Gorki-Str. 31 (tel. 28 21) offers chicken dishes (about DM9) and vegetarian food. Enjoy exploring Lübbenau's old city before setting off for Lehde, the most romantic village in these parts. Here homes and farms hang precariously over the water's edge. **Burg,** farther east and harder to reach, is most impressive from the **Bismarkturm,** which offers a great view over the surrounding forests. The easiest way to get around is on foot, but many stores rent bikes, and gondolas with a German guide leave the harbor for 2, 4 or (ouch!) 10-hr. tours most mornings from March to October. If you set out in a paddle boat (rentable in both Lübben and Lübbenau for DM10), take a map and pay attention; the *Irrlichter* aren't all that dependable.

About 45 minutes outside of Berlin, the *Personenzüge* (slow trains) that chug between the capital and the Spreewald stop briefly in the unobtrusive village of **Halbe.** A five-minute walk due south of the train station will bring you to the edge of the forest and the mass graves of the **Gedenkstätte Waldfriedhof.** On April 19 and 20, 1945, in the final days of the Third Reich, these woods witnessed the last great European battle of WWII. Two hundred thousand war-weary German soldiers awaiting reinforcement met the advancing Soviet front; surrounded and outgunned, some 40,000 of them perished. Today, their gray tombstones stretch across the forest floor. Also buried here are victims of labor camps set up by the Soviet occupation from 1945 to 1949. For forty years this tiny reminder of both German fascism and the Soviet socialist "liberation" was a thorn in the side of the East German government, a symbol of everything the communists in Berlin wanted to forget about German history.

Dresden

No matter where you go in Dresden, you will not not be able to forget the fact that this city of minimal military importance but incredible cultural value was incinerated by U.S., Canadian and British bombers in the final months of WWII. Nor will you escape the fact that the fires that burned here for weeks claimed some 35,000 lives—more victims than the atomic bomb in Nagasaki. A wave of Deutschmarks swept over the city after German reunification in October 1991, muffling the ruins with the busy sounds of reconstruction. This economic instability has fueled a skinhead movement that recognizes Dresden as its capital; if you are a member of a visible minority, be particularly careful here at night.

Orientation and Practical Information

The capital of Saxony, Dresden stands magnificently on the Elbe River about 80km northwest of Czechoslovakia and 180km south of Berlin on the train line to Prague. As usual in eastern Germany, watch for name changes: Georgi-Dimitroff-Brücke is now Augustus Brücke and Straße der Befreiung is often referred to as Hauptstraße. Watch for future changes and avoid older maps.

Tourist Office: Fremdenverkehrsbüro, Pragerstr. 10/11 (tel. 495 50 25). Turn left out of the front door of the Hauptbahnhof, cross Leninplatz and walk straight down Pragerstr. 5 min.; the office is on the right hand side. Rooms, maps, theater tickets and tours. Open April-Sept. Mon.-Sat. 9am-8pm, Sun. 9am-1pm; Oct.-March Mon.-Fri. 9am-8pm, Sat. 9am-2pm, Sun. 9am-1pm.

Currency Exchange: Deutsche Verkehrs Bank, in the Hauptbahnhof. Open Mon.-Fri. 7am-7:30pm, Sat. 8am-4pm.

American Express: Köpckestr. 15, (tel. 56 62 865), in the Bellevue Hotel across the Elbe from the Opera.

Post Office: Hauptpostamt, Dr. Otto-Nuschke-Str. 2, (tel. 484 80). Near Zwingergallery, follow Fenskestr. from Postplatz for 3 min. (Open Mon.-Fri. 7am-7pm, Sat. 11am-noon.) **Postal code:** 8010.

Telephones: For western Germany, dial (07) from any pay phone, drop the first (0) from the city code, and dial the number, still a very frustrating game. For other countries dial (00114) for operator-assisted (i.e., collect and credit card) calls. Have a thick book to read and let it ring ring ring (usually a 15-min. wait). **City code:** 051.

Trains: From **Dresden Hauptbahnhof** (the main station) travelers shoot off to Warsaw, Paris, Kraków, Berlin, Budapest, Copenhagen, Munich, and Frankfurt. Trams #3 and #11 connect it to **Dresden Neustadt** station on the other side of the Elbe. Watch out: the two stations look exactly the same. Both stations have lockers.

Public Transportation: Affectionately dubbed "Dubček's Revenge," the noisy streetcars came from Czechoslovakia shortly after the 1968 Prague Spring. Punch tickets (which expire after 30 min.) as you board the train (adults DM0.50; package of 11 DM2.50; day pass DM2).

Hitchhiking: Mitfahrzentrale Dresden, Bischofsweg 66 (tel. 534 39). Open Mon.-Fri. 10am-7pm, Sat. noon-2pm.

Emergencies: Ambulance (tel. 115). **Fire** (tel. 112). **Police** (tel. 110).

Accommodations, Camping and Food

Arrive early and expect a struggle. Contact the tourist office for private rooms (singles DM20-30; doubles DM30-80).

Jugendherberge Rudi Ardnt, Hübnerstr. 11 (tel. 47 06 67) in a mansion built by the sewing machine magnate Singer. Take Juri-Gagarin-Str. from the Hauptbahnhof, walk down 2 blocks, turn right on Reichenbach (which becomes Altenzellerstr.) for about 4 blocks and turn left; or take S-Bahn line #3 to the end station Südvorstadt, walk in the direction you have come from and turn right onto Hübnerstr. Go in person; the friendly manager is slow to commit himself to new guests, but softens by suppertime. 73 beds. DM17.50, under 26 DM14.

Jugendherberge Oberloschwitz, Sierksstr. 33 (tel. 366 72). Beautiful location worth the hour-long trip. Phone first. Take tram #6 from the Neustadt station (direction "Niedersedlitz"); at about the 13th stop (Schillerplatz and Loschwitzerbrücke), get off and cross the Elbe to Körnerplatz. From Körnerplatz ride the Schwebebahn (hill train; *not* the Standseilbahn) up to Sierksstr. and turn right out of the station for 5 min. 50 beds. DM16.50, under 26 DM13.50.

Camping: Campingplatz Moritzburg Borderitzer Str. 8 (tel. 17 82 26). From the Hauptbahnhof, take the Moritzburg or Moritzburg/Radeburg bus and get off at Sonnenland (1-hr. ride). DM10 per person, DM10 per tent.

Food

Restaurants are opening and closing daily in Dresden, as the new market mentality shuffles the status quo. **Straße der Befreiung (Hauptstraße)** is a good place to track down chow, but the *Gaststätte* of the back streets are often your cheapest bet.

Restaurant am Zwinger, across from the Zwinger Gallery on Postplatz. Pure DDR preunification decor. Rock bottom prices. Macaroni and wieners for DM4.50. Open Mon.-Sat. 7am-7pm, Sun. 10am-6pm.

Bierbar "Am Thor," Str. der Befreiung 35 (tel. 513 72), across from Platz der Einheit (Albertplatz) in the *Neustadt.* Smoky, but clean; tasty German fare for Easties and Westies DM9-12. Open daily noon-2am.

Restaurant 7 Schwaben, An der Augustenbrücke (Georgi Dimitroff Brücke) (tel. 511 38). On the Neustadt side of the Elbe; turn right immediately after crossing over. Heavy Germans enjoying heavy fare in early-beer-hall-baroque. Beef stew with beans and potatoes (DM8.90). Open daily 10am-midnight.

Sights

The extravagant collection of Augustus the Strong, and the magnificent private gallery he built to house it, the **Zwinger,** once rivalled the Louvre in Paris. Today the collection, centered around Raphael's Sistine Madonna, remains by far the best in Germany. The **Alte Meister** collection normally housed in the Zwinger's **Semper Gallery** is under the weather in summer 1991, but will reopen in 1992. Until then, some of the Gemäldegalerie Alte Meister's collection poses at the Albertinum; see below. The **Porzellansammlung** traces the history of Dresden's famous porcelain. (Open Mon.-Thurs. 9:30am-4pm, Sat.-Sun. 9am-4pm. No entrance 11:30am-noon and after 3:45pm. Admission DM1.05, students and seniors DM0.50.) Inside the palace courtyard, the sky-blue porcelain bells of the *Glockenspiel* gate chime the hour. The northern wing of the palace, a later addition, was designed by Gottfried Semper, revolutionary activist and master architect. Semper's famed Opera House, the **Semper-Oper,** echoes the robust style of the palace wing. Its painstaking restoration, both inside and out, has made it Dresden's major attraction. Near the Zwinger lie the ruins of the **Palace of Saxony's Electors and Kings,** levelled by firebombing on February 13, 1945. The lighter stonework is all spanking new, evidence of the speed with which restoration has been proceeding since reunification. A private walkway connects the palace to the **Katholische Hofkirche** (Catholic Cathedral), originally the royal family's private chapel. Nearby the first Protestant celebration of communion took place in the **Protestant Kreuzkirche** on the Altmarkt. With a little luck you may even catch a performance by the **Kreuzchor,** one of the world's most famous boys' choirs. Adorning the alley leading to the main entrance of the Catholic cathedral, the *Fürstenzug* (Procession of Kings), a pictorial in porcelain tiles tracing the history of Saxony since the Middle Ages.

From the Catholic cathedral, the 16th-century **Brühlsche Terrasse** offers a prime photo opportunity of the River Elbe (best at sunset). Turn right at the end of the terrace to reach the **Albertinum,** another of Dresden's fabulous museum complexes. The **Gemäldegalerie der Neuen Meister** presents a banquet of 19th- and 20th-century works, including Gauguins and Monets. (Open Tues. and Thurs.-Sun. 9am-5pm, Wed. 9am-6pm. Admission DM5, seniors and students DM2.50; consider an all-day pass to the Albertinum's several galleries.) The **Grünes Gewölbe** dazzles with priceless coins and gem-studded treasures. At the end of WWII, the Soviet Union snatched the collection for "cataloging," and only returned it in 1955, after West German protests. In all fairness, considerable restoration was done. (Open Fri.-Mon. and Wed. 9am-5pm, Tues. 9am-6pm; Oct.-May Fri.-Wed. 10am-4pm. Often humongous lines, so come early. Admission DM5, students and seniors DM2.50. Photo permit DM2.) From the Albertinum, a walk to the Neumarkt will take you to what was once Germany's most splendid Protestant church. The ruins of the **Frauenkirche,** now overscored by trees and vegetation, were to remain as a memorial to the destroyed city, but West German money has convinced the city fathers to rebuild. Jog south to the beginning of Ernst-Thälmann-Str., where the 18th-century neoclassical **Landhaus,** houses the **Museum für Geschichte der Stadt Dresden.** The exhibit contains some numbing photos of the city from 1945. (Open Mon.-Thurs. and Sat. 10am-6pm, Sun. 10am-4pm. Admission DM1.05, students DM0.40, seniors DM0.50.)

Paradoxically, Dresden's **Neustadt** is now the oldest part of the city, for it escaped the worst of the bombing. In front of the Catholic church, the picturesque Georgij-Dimitroff Brücke spans the Elbe to the **Goldener Ritter,** a gold-plated statue of Friedrich August II with a very healthy glow (after fathering over 365 children, he was renamed Augustus the Strong). The pedestrian **Straße der Befreiung** (Hauptstraße), a cobbled, tree-lined avenue of shops and restaurants, promenades from the river bank to **Platz der Einheit,** still surrounded by handsome 19th-century mansions. Vonnegut aficionados can take tram #15 from the Hauptbahnhof to the last stop to reach the **Schlachthofringe** *(slaughterhouses),* little-changed since they were pressed into service as a camp for prisoners of war. North of the Platz der Einheit (Albertplatz), **Böhimischestraße** and **Louisenstraße** all offer a taste of the city's run-down, but stubbornly beautiful pre-war residential blocks.

Entertainment

For centuries, Dresden has been a focal point for theater, opera and music. The incredible **Semper Oper** has premiered many of Strauß and Wagner's greatest. Buy, beg, or borrow your way to a show here. Tickets are usually available at the door 1 hr. before the performance for about DM5-10. Book ahead if you like, but expect to pay at least DM40. For German speakers, Dresden offers excellent drama, from the classics at the **Schauspielhaus,** Ostraallee 1 (tel. 484 20) to satirical cabaret at the **Dresdener Brettl,** Maternistr. 17 (tel. 495 41 23). For those who don't speak, the **Podium,** Str. der Befreiung (tel. 532 66) offers good mime a few times each week. Phone for dates and times. **Die Tonne,** Tzschirnerplatz 3 (tel. 495 13 54) grooves to great jazz. Those aiming for the alternative scene might want to catch **Cholera,** Schaufußstr. 35 (tel. 303 89). Open daily 7pm-4am. The new local magazine **SAX,** available at any newsstand, gives a run-down on what's hot and what's not.

Near Dresden

Dresden lies in the fertile Elbe River valley, which produces the frabjous grapes of Meissner wines. The striking, hilly landscape around the resort city **Bad Schandau,** upriver from Dresden, is known as **Sächsische Schweiz** (Saxon Switzerland). Take the train (or a Weiße Flotte boat) from Dresden toward Bad Schandau and Prague and alight at the town of **Königstein.** The spectacular medieval fortress on the cliff was used by the Nazis as a stash for stolen art. It now houses museums of everything from weaponry to porcelain. (Open 8am-8pm, Oct.-April 9am-5pm. Admission DM5, students and seniors DM3.50; Oct.-April DM3.50, students and seniors DM2.) The Königstein tourist office, Dresdner Str. 1, may convince you to spend weeks exploring. (Open Mon.-Tues. and Fri. 9am-6pm, Wed. 9am-11pm, Thurs. 9am-3pm, Sat. 9am-noon; Oct.-March Tues. 9am-6pm, Fri. 9am-noon.) Take the ferry across to the **Lilienstein** for a spectacular view of the Saxon countryside. The gem of this area is Germany's newest national park, the **Bastei,** a breathtaking stretch of gigantic sandstone boulders and sharp ravines. The quickest way to get there is to alight at **Rathen.** Also worth a visit is the **Schloß Pillnitz,** built as a weekend retreat by Augustus the Strong (perhaps to escape his 365 children). The lush gardens overlook the river; inquire about tours of the castle and its art. (Open April-Oct. Tues.-Sun. 9:30am-10:50pm. Admission DM5, students DM2.50). The boat ride from Dresden takes about an hour and costs 4DM each way.

Trains (50 min., DM1) and boats (2 hr.) run downstream from Dresden to **Meißen.** Crowded with narrow, hilly streets and teetering 16th- and 17th-century homes, Meißen brims with treasures from the last milennium. Towering above the city is the **Albrechtsburg,** Domplatz 1, a grand fortress, palace, and cathedral that spiritually and physically guarded this royal Saxon city. (Open Feb.-Dec. daily 9am-5pm. Last entrance 4pm. Admission DM2, seniors and students DM1.) The cathedral is open only to tours, which leave from the front of the church about every 30 minutes. Back down in the village, the porcelain bells of the **Frauenkirche** will lead you to the **tourist office,** An der Frauenkirche 3 (tel. 44 70), which arranges rooms and guides wayward tourists to the **Jugendherberge (IYHF)** at 25 Wilsduffer Str. (Tel. 30 65. Juniors DM10. Seniors DM11.) Seize the chance to try (or at least look at) Meißen's famous wines. The wine cellars at **Vincenz Richter,** An der Frauenkirche (tel. 32 85) offer samples by the glass, bottle or case. Though deservedly famous for its architecture, its Elbe-side real estate, and its grapes, Meißen is best known for its precious porcelain. Augustus the Strong, Elector of Saxony, King of Poland and renowned stud, built Europe's first porcelain factory here, the source of Dresden china. Tour the **Staatliche Porzellanmanufaktur,** at Talstr. 9. (Open April-Oct. Tues.-Sun. 8am-noon and 1-4pm. Admission DM2, students and seniors DM1.)

Between Dresden and the Polish border roll the hills of the **Oberlausitz.** This is the infamous Valley Of The Clueless: the only territory of former East Germany that was unable to receive West German television or radio transmissions. While their compatriots tuned in to West Berlin's evening news, the people here were left to interpret the political signifance of the communists' latest steel production statistics. Flanked by three socialist neighbors, the Oberlausitz was a region seldom visited by Westerners. Consequently the Politburo left the region's cities to rot almost beyond repair. But as the homeland of the **Sorbs** (a.k.a. the Wends and the Lusatians), Germany's Slavic-speaking minority, the area is rich in traditions and customs long abandoned elsewhere. **Bautzen,** an hour east of Dresden by frequent trains, is both the gateway to the Oberlausitz and cultural center of the Sorbian community of about 75,000 people. The **Sorbisches Museum,** Ortenburg 3 (tel. 424 03) is great, but those hoping for a live glimpse of the rapidly assimilating Sorbs will have to leave the city: the villagers of **Panschwitz-Kukau** and **Neschwitz** still sport the ornate traditional *Trachten* and speak the language on a day to day basis. Bautzen itself is a fascinating hodgepodge of Gothic, medieval, Renaissance and Baroque architecture. The **Dom St. Petri** (Cathedral of St. Peter) is Germany's only **Simultankirche,** divided straight down the middle to accommodate both Catholics and Protestants. Near the church stands the **Nikolaiturm** in which the citizens entombed (alive) a treacherous 16th century mayor. Yum. Otherwise give yourself a few hours to wander the **Osterweg** and the city's back streets. The **tourist office,** next to the cathedral at Fleischmarkt 2-4 (tel. 420 16), now has pamphlets and assistance in English. (Open Mon. 9am-1pm, Tues.-Fri. 9am-5pm; May-Sept. also open 9am-noon.) They will arrange rooms (for free) and guide you to the defense tower-*cum*-**youth hostel** (tel. 440 45) in the city center at Am Zwinger 1. (Juniors DM12. Seniors DM14.)

Wittenberg

The Protestant Reformation, which threw Europe into centuries of convulsive upheaval, began quietly in **Lutherstadt Wittenberg** on October 13, 1517, when Martin Luther, a local professor, nailed his 95 theses to the wooden door of the castle church (Schloßkirche). This small town on the Leipzig-Berlin train route makes for a relaxing and Luther-filled daytrip from either city. As you exit the train station, head straight and swing right under the tracks onto **Collegien Straße.** On your right, note the sickly elm tree; under it Luther proudly burned a papal order of excommunication. At #54 stands the **Lutherhalle,** where Martin moved in 1508. (Open Tues.-Sun. 9am-5pm. Admission DM4.) Make sure you grab an English guide from the ticket desk; the exhibition follows the course of the Reformation and of Luther's groundbreaking Bible translation. The family living room has been preserved intact, as has obnoxious tourist Peter the Great's signature, scribbled on the door when he stopped by in 1702. Farther down the street is **St. Marienkirche** (St. Mary's Church); its distinctive altar, painted by Incas Cranach the Elder, incorporates Luther and several other town notables in the biblical scene. Nearby rises the town's **Rathaus,** with an imposing Renaissance façade and statues to Luther and the philosopher-humanist Melancthon. Also in the square is the **Jungfernröhrwasser** (fountain of youth), a 16th century well whose refreshing and drinkable waters still flow through the original wooden pipes, proof that East German infrastructure was once quite reliable. Farther down the street, a sumptuous Baroque cupola crowns the tower of the **Schloß.** It was here that Luther nailed his theses to the door; a copy of his original draft is inside.

There are some really great doubles at the **youth hostel** in the castle. **Wittenberg Information** (tel. 511 44), at Collegianstr. 29 just off the market, will help finding rooms. (Open April-Oct. Mon.-Fri. 9am-6pm, Sat.-Sun. 10am-2pm; Nov.-March Mon.-Fri. 9am-5pm.)

Leipzig

Badly bruised in WWII, Eastern Germany's second-largest city compensates for its lack of beauty with one of Europe's most brilliant political and cultural pedigrees. Originally, Leipzig gained its fame through music and letters. The university, founded in 1409, upholds an illustrious tradition of learning that embraces the names of Leibniz, Lessing, and Nietzsche, among others. Book merchants have translated this home-grown genius into a thriving industry; the *Altstadt* gushes bookstores, and three major international book fairs take place here annually. Leipzig's musical heritage began in 1723 when Johann Sebastian Bach settled here, filling local churches with his early works. A century later, Felix Mendelssohn founded the *Leipzig Gewandhaus Orchester,* still a superb ensemble. When the orchestra performs at home in the **Gewandhaus,** Augustus Platz (tel. 77 96), tickets go fast. (Ticket office open Tues.-Wed. 2-6pm, Thurs.-Fri. 9am-1pm.)

The **Museum der Bildenen Künste,** Georg-Dimitroff-Platz 1, has a ponderous collection of over 2500 paintings and sculptures, including a particularly extensive Dutch collection. (Open Tues. and Thurs.-Sun. 9am-5pm, Wed. 1-7:30pm. Admission DM3, students and seniors DM1.) The fortified towers of the **Neues Rathaus** dominate the *Altstadt* in the south. Just off the Marktplatz is the **Thomaskirche** where J.S. Bach served as cantor; his grave lies just in front of the altar. Mozart and Mendelssohn also performed in this church, and composer Richard Wagner was baptized here in 1813. Next door, the **Johann-Sebastian-Bach-Museum,** Thomaskirchof 16, chronicles Bach's work and years in Leipzig (1723-1750). (Open Tues.-Sun. 9am-5pm. Last entry 4:30pm. Box office opens at 7:30pm for concerts in the Bachsaal.) The heart of the city centers on the **Marktplatz,** a colorful, cobbled square guarded by the charming **Altes Rathaus.** Inside, the **Museum für Geschichte der Stadt Leipzig** is being purged of its socialist interpretation of the city's history; the exorcism should be complete by late 1991. Continuing away from the Marktplatz, take Universitätsstr. to the modern **Universität Leipzig** (formerly Karl-Marx-Universität). Small morsels of the pre-war university, studded like raisins in the modern campus, are all that remain of the original institution. Just off the campus lies the **Moritzbastei,** Universitätsstr. (tel. 29 29 32), a group of great student nightclubs in the underground ruins of the old city wall. The university's **Musikinstrumenten-Museum,** Taibchenweg 2, contains over 3500 instruments, some dating back to the 16th century. (Open Tues.-Thurs. 2-5pm, Fri. and Sun. 10am-1pm, Sat. 10am-3pm.) The **Völkerschlachtdenkmal** on the Sudfriedhof east of town commemorates those who helped turn the tide against Napoleon in the 1813 Battle of Nations. Another revolutionary victory began at the **Nikolaikirche,** down from the university on Nikolaistr., the site of the "Monday meetings" which eventually led to the collapse of Erich Honecker's Communist regime.

Leipzig's **tourist office,** Sachsenplatz 1 (tel. 795 90), books private rooms (DM40-50). From the train station, walk through Platz der Republik and bear right past the Interhotel "Stadt Leipzig." Walk one block down Nikolaistr., then turn right onto Brühl. (Open Mon.-Fri. 9am-7pm, Sat. 9:30am-2pm.) The **Jugendherberge (IYHF),** is at Käthe-Kollwitz-Str. 62-66 (tel. 47 58 88). Take tram #1 or 2 west for four stops. Two other good bets are the spot-sized but spotless **Haus Ingeborg Hotel,** Nordstr. 58, two blocks up from the tall Interhotel Merkur, or the **Pension Am Zoo,** next to the zoo at Dr.-Kurt-Fischer-Str. 23 (both DM40).

Leipzig's oldest restaurant, the **Burgkeller,** at Naschmarkt 1-3 next to the *Altes Rathaus,* has meals for less than DM12. The upstairs dining hall serves the best food, but it's usually either packed or closed. The downstairs sction is less crowded and great for breakfast (served 9-11am). There's also a boisterous bar (open daily 7-10:30pm). **Auerbachs Keller,** Mädlerpassage, across the street, appears in *Faust;* in the play, Mephisto manages to bring forth free wine. Try your luck. (¼ chicken DM10. Open daily 10am-midnight.) For a quick lunch, grab some *bratwurst* at a street stand (DM2), or stop by the **Buffet Am Hallischer Tor,** a cafeteria on the corner of Wagnerstr. (No tourists here. Main dishes DM5-9. Open Mon.-Fri. 7:30am-7pm, Sat. 8am-7pm.) **Leipzig University Student Mensa** off Universitätsstr. runs a really reasonable student cafeteria (DM3-4) from 11am-2pm and 4-9pm.

To the north, about 30 min. by train from Leipzig on the way to Berlin, lies Germany's dirtiest city: **Bitterfeld,** whose highly appropriate name means "bitter fields." Thousands have made a pilgrimage here to see for themselves what humans can do to the environment. Particularly disturbing is nearby **Wolfen,** where the lakes have a chlorine content 600 times that of the Rhine and high concentrations of cyanide, arsenic and chrome.

Halle

Halle an der Saale was one of the few German metropolises to emerge from WWII more or less unscathed, but three months after the war's end, as the people of Halle thanked the heavens for their good fortune, the occupying Americans traded the city to the Soviets for a piece of Berlin. From that point on, pollution and neglect devastated what the war had spared. Yet even in despair, Halle's streets, collapsing apartment blocks and screeching trams still provide a glimpse of what this historic German city must have been. Halle is a quick half-hour by train from Leipzig.

Halle has two favorite sons: composer Georg Friedrich Händel and political *Wunder* Hans Dietrich Genscher, Germany's current foreign minister. Fans of Händel can visit the museum here, while those looking for Genscher need only scout the marketplace at election time. The market itself buzzes with activity and streetcars. The **Rote Turm,** a strange red tower, rises in the center of the town square. Across from the tower lies the **Pfarrkirche St. Marien,** with the organ where little Händel began his studies. (Open Mon.-Wed. and Fri. 3-6pm, Thurs. 4-5pm, Sat. 9am-noon, Sun. 11am-noon. Half-hour organ concerts Tues. 4:30pm and Fri. 5:30pm.) The **Händelhaus,** the composer's family home at Große Nikolaistr. 5 (tel. 246 06), houses one of the best museums in eastern Germany. High quality stereo soundtracks in 19 languages guide pilgrims through Händel's career in Germany, Italy and England. (Open Tues.-Wed. and Fri.-Sun. 9:30am-5:30pm, Thurs. 9am-7pm.) Afterwards, grab a drink in the cheap courtyard café downstairs.

From Händel's home to the **Dom** (cathedral) is a five-minute walk down Nikolaistr. Just a few steps from the *Dom* lies the **Moritzburg fortress.** One of the fortress towers hosts the city's **Studentenclub.** Most of the remaining building is reserved for the **Staatliche Galerie Moritzburg-Halle,** a mid-size art museum focusing mostly on 19th- and 20th-century German painters. Much of the museum's extensive expressionist collection was deemed "degenerate" and burned or sold by the Nazis.

The **tourist office,** in the *Rote Turm* on the marketplace, sells maps and books rooms (DM40 and up). From the main train station, cross under the underpass to the left and take tram #4 (direction "Heide/Hubertusplatz") or tram #7 (direction "Kröllwitz") four stops to the market. The **Jugendherberge (IYHF),** August-Bebel-Str. 48a (tel. 247 16), is in a newly restored mansion north of the market. Take tram #7 (direction "Kröllwitz") to Pushkinstr., six stops from the train station or two from the market. Follow Pushkinstr. and turn right onto August-Bebel-Str. Budget accommodations in Halle are bloody rare, but at least they're friendly when they tell you they're full. **Christliches Hospiz Martha-Haus,** Adam Kuckhoff-str. 5 (tel. 244 11), is a tidy, friendly, Christian establishment with singles for DM35. Cheap pasta awaits on the marketplace in **Mario's Pizzeria und Delicatessen,** Markt 11 (tel. 25 15 24), a brand-new restaurant with minimal atmosphere but tasty fare. (Pizza DM5, lasagna DM8.) Those who just can't tear themselves from filling German *Schnitzel* can stuff themselves at **Gaststätte Casino,** Leipzigerstr. 18. (Open Mon.-Thurs. 11am-11pm, Fri. 11am-3pm.)

Weimar

Weimar epitomizes the wild oscillations of German history, encompassing both the lofty peaks of its humanism and the darkest elements of its barbarism; it is the birthplace of the Bauhaus art school, site of the Buchenwald concentration camp and the city where Germany's first republic was founded. Goethe, Schiller, Herder, Liszt and Nietzsche have all called Weimar home.

In the city center, the shadows of the Third Reich virtually disappear under the brilliance of Johann Wolfgang Goethe, Germany's very own Renaissance man, who still presides over these streets 150 years after his death. Given the poet's ego, such immortality would likely not surprise him. His estate is fascinating; especially impressive are his flawless manuscripts and private chambers in the **Goethe Haus,** Frauenplan 1. A stalwart English guide, *Goethe's House on the Frauenplan at Weimar,* will guide you through the rooms where Goethe entertained, wrote, studied and ultimately, like Faust himself, died and was scurried away to the netherworld.

The cobbled **Marktplatz** stretches beneath the pseudo-Gothic **Rathaus** and the colorful Renaissance façade of the **Lucas Cranach Haus.** Adjoining the Marktplatz is the handsome **Stadtkirche St. Peter und Paul,** with Lucas Cranach's last spectacular triptych altar. The church is also called the *Herderkirche,* after philosopher Johan Gottfried von Herder, who once preached here regularly; the **Kirms-Krackow Haus,** Jakobstr. 10, documents Herder's life and times, but was closed for historical reinterpretation in the summer of 1991. Retrace your steps to the Marktplatz, crossing over Frauentorstr.; **Schillerstraße,** a pedestrian zone crammed with antique shops and bookstores, materializes on your right one block up. At the end of the street, **Schillerhaus,** Schillerstr. 12, the former residence of the playwright, displays original drafts, early editions of plays, and a biographical chronicle of the life of Goethe's friend and rival. (Open Wed.-Mon. 9am-5pm. Admission DM3, students DM2.) Around the corner, the pair are reconciled in stone before the **Deutsches Nationaltheater,** which first breathed life into their works, and from whose balcony the doomed Weimar Republic was proclaimed in 1919. The contemporary repertoire varies but still features performances of the classic works.

Modern architecture fans will want to check out the birthplace of the **Bauhaus,** now the **Hochschule für Architektur und Bauwesen** (College of Architecture and Construction). Founded here in 1919, Walter Gropius's school of aesthetic design for the modern age taxed the finances and patience of the municipality before moving onto Dessau in 1925. The neighboring **Park an der Ilm,** landscaped by Goethe, sprouts numerous 18th-century pavilions and shelters grazing sheep and goats. Of particular note are Goethe's fake ruins and the statue of William Shakespeare, still bearing the scars of a coat of black paint applied by the Nazis in 1939. On the park's slopes rests **Goethes Gartenhaus,** Corona-Schröter-Str., the poet's first home in Weimar, and later his retreat from the city. (Open Tues.-Sun. 9am-noon and 1-5pm.) At the edge of the park is the **Franz Liszt Haus,** Marienstr. 17, where the composer spent his last years. The instruments and furnishings are supposedly original, but given Liszt's torrid love life, the small single bed seems unlikely. (Open Tues.-Sun. 9am-5pm.)

Also south of the town center, the **Historischer Friedhof** contains, among other notable memorabilia, the **Goethe-und-Schiller-Gruft** (tombs of Goethe and Schiller) and the **Denkmal der Märzgefallenen,** designed by Bauhausmeister Gropius to honor those killed in the 1919 revolution (between WWI and the Weimar Republic, when Germany almost became independently socialist). The monument's completion in 1923 led to the Bauhaus's expulsion from Weimar. (Tombs open Tues.-Sun. 9am-1pm and 2-5pm.)

Bus #4 links Weimar's train station with Goetheplatz in the center of town (from the station 45 min. past every hr.). From there, the **tourist office,** Marktstr. 4 (tel. 21 73), is but steps away. Walk out Geleitstr. and continue down Eisfeld until you come to the Herderkirche, then walk right along Dimitroffstr. to the marketplace; the office is around the block to your right. (Open Mon. 10am-6pm, Tues.-Fri. 9am-6pm, Sat. 9am-4pm. Accommodations help Mon.-Fri. 10am-7pm, Sat. 9am-4pm.)

The city's youth hostels have been bashed about by reunification: two are gone and one is an endangered species, victims of Western Germans who have returned to claim private property. Try **Maxim Gorki (IYHF),** Zum Wilden Graben 12 (tel. 34 71), or the superconvenient **Jugenherberge Germania,** (tel. 20 76), 5 minutes from the train station straight down Carl August Allee (formerly Leninstr.) to #13. (Both charge juniors DM13.50, seniors DM17.) The former hostel at **Buchenwald** is presently continuing under the foggy status of a **Begegnungstätte Buchenwald** (youth meeting place) (tel. 672 16), but has yet to join the IYHF flock. Otherwise the **Hotel International,** Carl August Allee 17 (tel. 21 62), across the street from the train station, offers doubles from DM50.

The **Weimarhalle,** Karl-Liebknecht-Str. 3 (tel. 23 41), is tucked away, so mostly locals go there. (Meals DM10-13. Open daily 9am-11pm.) The **Scharfe Ecke,** Eisfeld 2 (tel. 24 30), offers sturdy fare (schnitzel and potatoes DM10; open 5pm-1am). Potato salad, pizza and beer are cheap at the student club/tower **Kasseturm** on Karlsstr. (Open most evenings. Student ID necessary.)

Near Weimar

Goethe and Schiller chose to spend their last days in Weimar, but 65,000 nameless men, women and children did so against their will at the Nazi concentration camp in nearby **Buchenwald.** Reach Buchenwald by bus from the Weimar train station (departures Tues.-Sun. 8:15am, 9:15am, 10:15am, noon, 2pm and 3pm). At the memorial, signs point to the **KZ Lager** and the **Gedenkstätte.** The former refers to the remains of the camp; the latter is an impressive monument overlooking the valley. (Monument open dawn to dusk; camp open Tues.-Sun. 9am-4pm.) Everywhere you turn at Buchenwald there are reminders of the dead. In the summer of 1991, displays were still fudging history here, claiming that the camp held only political prisoners after WWII and ignoring Buchenwald's use as a Stalinist work camp in which 17,000 Germans lost their lives between 1945 and 1949. Only a small memorial to the "Russian Revenge" lies at the end of the gravel path behind the crematorium.

In **Naumburg** on the Leipzig-Weimar train line towers the stupendous **Naumburger Dom,** a phenomenal cathedral begun in 1042, but spectacularized two centuries later when the nameless sculptor known as the Master of Naumburg stopped in and chiseled 12 lifelike figures out of the cathedral walls. The church once crowned a grand city, but if you climb the **Wenzelkirche** tower, the ruins will convince you that this city is in big trouble. So is the local **tourist information office,** which is so broke that they even charge for photocopied maps. They will, however, book rooms in private homes for DM1. Or try **Haus des Handwerks,** Salzstr. 15-16 (tel. 23 80), with cheap rooms (DM20) and delicious, inexpensive and hearty fare in the restaurant downstairs.

Goethe and Schiller met for the first time in **Rudolstadt,** a pleasant city that serves as the gateway to the Schwarza-Tal. Before you take to the steep valleys in and around **Schwarzburg,** check with the **information office,** Ernst-Thälmann-Str. 32a (tel. 236 33; open Mon.-Fri. 9am-12:30pm and 1:30-4pm, until 5pm on Mon. and Fri. and until 6pm on Thurs., Sat. 10am-1pm). The **Jugendherberge** here is in a manor house on the forest's edge, and anyone who comes from afar bearing Deutschemarks, frankincense and *Let's Go* is promised a phenomenal welcome (no myrrh, thanks). Goethe and his lover Charlotte von Stein met many times in the woods 8km north of Rudolstadt. While Charlotte's husband stayed in Weimar with the kids, the intellectual pair contemplated the world's problems in the enchanted, moated palace of **Schloß Kochberg.** (Open Tues.-Sun. 9am-noon and 1-5pm; Sept.-April. Wed.-Sun. same hours. Admission DM3, students DM2.) To check out their romantic love shack, take the bus or hike to the tiny village of **Groß Kochberg.**

Erfurt

A visit to the new capital of Thüringen is without question one of the high points of a trip to eastern Germany. Erfurt's towering cathedral and lavish patrician houses give the city a style and flair all its own, all too rare among the gray cities of the East.

Martin Luther liked Erfurt so much that he spent ten years here as a monk. **Augustiner Kloster** on Augustinerstr., the cloister where Brother Martin chanted, is in great shape and now functions as a Protestant college. (Open Tues.-Sat. 10am-4pm with tours on the hour; Nov.-March Tues.-Sat. with tours at 10am, noon and 2pm.) A brief glance at Luther's regime (up at midnight, prayers until dawn, begging until noon, studies and chants until 8pm, then four hours of sleep) may give you an indication of what might have turned him against the Catholic Church. At the magnificent **cathedral,** Luther interrupted his ordination to throw a Bible across the altar (he claimed later he was aiming at Satan). Visitors to the cathedral will be left breathless by the complex, including both the **Dom** and the early Gothic **Severikirche** (open Mon.-Sat. 9-11:30am and 12:30-5pm, Sun. 2-4pm).

Take time to explore Erfurt's marketplaces and streets as well. **Angerstraße,** the main shopping street, **Fischmarkt,** with the ornate **Rathaus,** and the **Krämerbrücke,** a medieval bridge teeming with small shops, are all nifty areas in admirable condition. Those in the mood for a touch of socialist reality might want to wander down **Pergamentergasse** north of the Fischmarkt.

The **information office,** Bahnhofstr. 37 (tel. 262 67), is five minutes straight out from the train station. They hawk maps and book rooms in private homes (DM30-50 per night). (Open Mon. 10am-noon and 1-6pm, Tues.-Fri. 9am-noon and 1-6pm, Sat. 9am-12:30pm.) Erfurt's hotel scene is particularly chaotic. Get a list of pensions from the tourist office. The **youth hostel** is in a great old mansion at Hochheimerstr. 12 (tel. 267 05). Take tram #5 from the train station (direction "Steigerstraße"), get off at the Steigerstraße stop and turn right down Straße der Einheit; the hostel is on the left corner at the first intersection. (Juniors DM14. Seniors DM17.) Weimar's three hostels are only a 15-minute train ride away. Try the *Thüringer Rostbrätt* (DM10) at the **Gaststätte Feuerkugel** (tel. 631 97), just off the Fischmarkt and next to the Krämerbrücke.

Near Erfurt

South of Erfurt stretch the time-worn mountains and peaceful pine woods of the **Thüringer Forest.** Two centuries ago, Goethe and Schiller scribbled some of their best poetry on these slopes. More recently, the East German Politburo kept a number of luxury hotels here for the party's "hunting holidays." Foreigners are now free to wander the famous **Rennsteig** and other trails here. The Erfurt tourist office will prepare you with guides and maps for an extended jaunt. Pack plenty of time and patience: foreigners are rare here, English is seldom understood and buses have an unfortunate, un-German habit of running late.

Ilmenau, 40 minutes by train or bus south of Erfurt, is a good starting point for the denser forests. The **information office** is at Straße des Friedens 28 or Lindenstr. 12, both just off the main shopping strip. The trails south of here were some of Goethe's favorites and the places he hung out are now open to visitors. The huts on the **Kickelhahn** and **Jagdhaus Gabelbach** (tel. 26 26) are interesting breaks from the trails. (Open Tues.-Sun. 9am-noon and 1-5pm, Nov.-April Wed.-Sun. 9am-noon and 1-4pm.) Those looking for a real live nasty Politburo hotel can check out **Gabelbach Hotel** nearby. Today the guards and dogs are gone and it is the prices that keep the proletariat away. At Stützerbach, south of Ilmenau, trains run back to the city or south to the idyllic **youth hostel** at Rennsteig 5 (tel. 464; seniors DM16, juniors DM13.50).

Eisenach

Marx and Engels called the Eisenacher faction "our party"; Hitler called the town's **Wartburg Schloß,** where Goethe came on pilgrimages, "the most German of all German castles." Eisenach has been a partisan in many struggles for Germany; now, as Wartburg takes its place as a symbol of national unity, it has entered the fray again. Wartburg sits on the south side of industrial Eisenach, down Bahnhofstr. and Wartburg Allee. From there, there are two ways to reach the castle—take the cheesy **Wartburg Express** (DM1) like any tourist, or go on foot like a pilgrim (30 wooded minutes). The castle's halls, immortalized in Richard Wagner's opera *Tannheuser,* sheltered Martin Luther after his papal excommunication. He used his solitude to translate the Bible into German, and, working too late one night, had a visit and struggle with the devil himself. Sightseers are legion; arrive early on a weekday. (Open daily 8:30am-4pm; in winter 9am-3:30pm. Admission DM1 for courtyard and tower; for the inner rooms and museum DM5, students DM3.) Johann-Sebastian Bach stormed into the world in 1685 in the **Bachhaus,** Frauenplan 21 (tel. 22 84), down Gimmlestr. off Wartburg Allee, which now recreates the family's living quarters. Downstairs are period instruments, on which some guides perform. (Open daily 9am-4:30pm. Admission DM4, seniors and students DM3.) Eisenach's **information office,** Bahnhofstr. 3-5 (tel. 61 61, for rooms 48 95), to the right of the station, runs tours (DM2) and books private accommodations. Singles range from DM15-25. (Open Mon. 10am-5pm, Tues.-Fri. 9am-5pm, Sat. 9am-1pm. Accommodations phone line answered Mon. 10am-7pm, Tues.-Fri. 9am-5pm, Sat. 9am-6pm.) An old villa past the castle is home to Eisenach's **Jugendherberge (IYHF),** Marientalstr. 24 (tel. 36 13). From the station, take Bahnhofstr. to Wartburg Allee, which runs into Marientalstr. (Reception open 9am-8pm. Curfew 10pm. Juniors DM13.50. Seniors DM16.50.) Town life centers on the pastel **Markt,** bounded by a tilting dollhouse of a **Rathaus.**

Eisenach's medieval rainbow houses ornament the northwestern slope of the Thüringer Forest; the easiest train connections are through Erfurt and Bebra.

Bavaria (Bayern)

From the tiny, hidden villages of the Bavarian Forest and the glittering baroque cities along the Danube to the medieval churches punctuating the Romantic Road and the turreted fantasy castles in the Alps, Bavaria is the Germany most travelers seek. The oom-pah bands, *Lederhosen,* and beer halls of modern myth are all quintessentially Bavarian. A kingdom unto itself until the late 19th century, Bavaria was ruled for most of recorded history by the Dukes of Wittelsbach, and the fiercely independent local residents have always been Bavarians first and Germans second. It took wars, with France and Austria, to pull the region into Bismarck's orbit. Though largely rural, predominantly Catholic, and (save Munich) staunchly con-

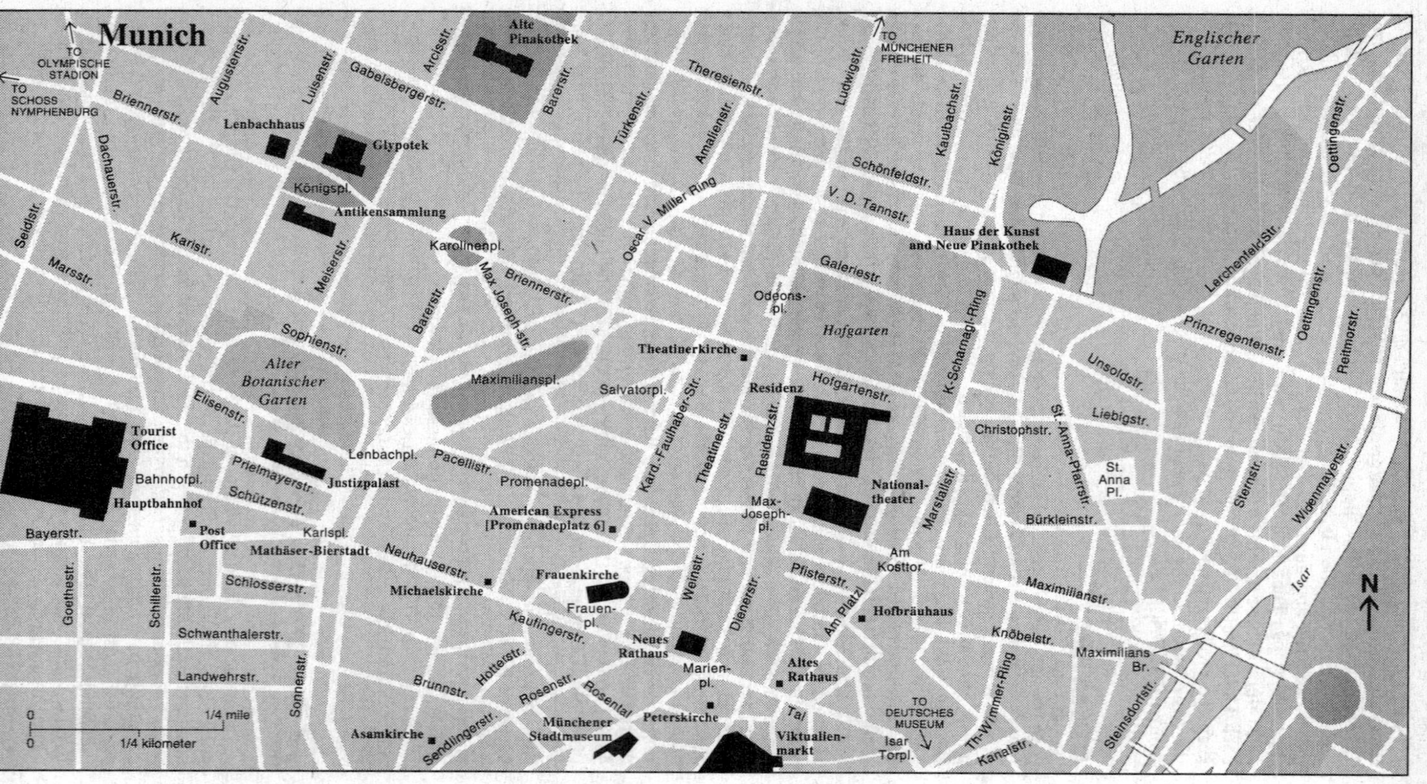
Munich
TO OLYMPISCHE STADION
TO SCHOSS NYMPHENBURG
Augustenstr.
Luisenstr.
Arcisstr.
Alte Pinakothek
Gabelsbergerstr.
Barerstr.
Theresienstr.
Ludwigstr.
TO MÜNCHENER FREIHEIT
Englischer Garten
Briennerstr.
Dachauerstr.
Lenbachhaus
Glypotek
Türkenstr.
Amalienstr.
Kaulbachstr.
Königinstr.
Oettingenstr.
Königspl.
Antikensammlung
Schönfeldstr.
V. D. Tannstr.
Oscar V. Miller Ring
Seidlstr.
Karlstr.
Karolinenpl.
Haus der Kunst and Neue Pinakothek
Marsstr.
Meiserstr.
Max Joseph-str.
Briennerstr.
Galeriestr.
Lerchenfeldstr.
Barerstr.
Odeons-pl.
Hofgarten
K-Scharnagl-Ring
Prinzregentenstr.
Oettingenstr.
Reitmorstr.
Sophienstr.
Theatinerkirche
Alter Botanischer Garten
Maximilianspl.
Salvatorpl.
Residenz
Hofgartenstr.
Unsoldstr.
Elisenstr.
Kard.-Faulhaber-Str.
Theatinerstr.
Residenzstr.
Liebigstr.
Christophstr.
St.-Anna-Pfarrstr.
Tourist Office
Lenbachpl.
Pacellistr.
Prielmayerstr.
Justizpalast
Promenadepl.
Bahnhofpl.
St. Anna Pl.
National-theater
Sternstr.
Widenmayerstr.
Schützenstr.
Hauptbahnhof
American Express [Promenadeplatz 6]
Max-Joseph-pl.
Marstallstr.
Bürkleinstr.
Bayerstr.
Post Office
Karlspl.
Mathäser-Bierstadt
Neuhauserstr.
Am Kosttor
Frauenkirche
Weinstr.
Dienerstr.
Pfisterstr.
Maximilianstr.
Isar
N
Schlosserstr.
Michaelskirche
Frauen-pl.
Am Platzl
Hofbräuhaus
Goethestr.
Schillerstr.
Kaufingerstr.
Schwanthalerstr.
Neues Rathaus
Knöbelstr.
Maximilians Br.
Hotterstr.
Marien-pl.
Altes Rathaus
Landwehrstr.
Brunnstr.
Rosenstr.
Rosental
Tal
TO DEUTSCHES MUSEUM
Th-Wimmer-Ring
Steinsdorfstr.
Sonnenstr.
Peterskirche
0
1/4 mile
Sendlingerstr.
Münchener Stadtmuseum
Viktualien-markt
Isar Torpl.
Kanalstr.
Asamkirche
0
1/4 kilometer

servative, this largest of Germany's federal states harbors some of the highest of high-tech companies within its borders, including Kugel-Fischer, Siemens, and BMW. Keep in mind that Bavarian youth hostels only accept those 26 and under.

Munich (München)

A glamorous, cosmopolitan sprawl amidst the bucolic Bavarian heartland and the solidly conservative southern German population, Munich breathes with the vitality of Germany's post-war economic boom. World-class museums, stately parks and architecture, a thriving theater and art scene and a jubilant mix of avant-garde *haute* pop culture and hearty Bavarian *Gemütlichkeit* collude to keep the city awake around the clock—with particular relish during *Fasching,* Germany's equivalent of *Mardi Gras* or *Carneval* (early Jan.-mid-Feb.), and the famous *Oktoberfest,* which lasts from the third Saturday in September through the first Sunday in October.

Orientation and Practical Infomation

Touring by foot is easy in Munich's compact center. Straight ahead from the Hauptbahnhof, Schützenstr. leads towards **Karlplatz am Stachus** and the famed **Marienplatz.** Neuhauser-Str., which connects the two squares, is the main pedestrian shopping area. Keeping straight ahead, first Im Tal and then Zweibrückenstr. lead to the Isar River. North of Marienplatz, the pedestrian zone ranges past magnificent **Odeonplatz,** next to the Residenz, to glittering Ludwigstr. Further north lie the University and **Schwabing,** Munich's student district. To the east, the enormous **Englischer Garten** sprawls along the Isar. West of Schwabing lies genteel **Nymphenburg,** surrounding **Nymphenburg Palace.** Southwest of Marienplatz, well-preserved **Sendlingerstraße** heads towards Sendlingertor, from which Lindwurmstr. leads to Goetheplatz. Mozartstr. proceeds onwards to **Theresienwiese,** site of the annual Oktoberfest.

Radius Touristik (tel. 59 47 14), across from track #35 in the main train station, offers a two-hour walking tour of the old city (DM12.50) daily at 10am, a tram-hopping tour (DM18, DM14 with own *Tageskarte)* daily at 11am and 2:30pm, and a three-hr. bicycle tour (DM28, DM20 with own bike) Mon., Wed. and Fri. at 10:30am.

Tourist Office: Fremdenverkehrsamt (tel. 239 12 56 or 239 12 57), across from track #11 in the main train station. A must, but a 15-30 min. wait in summer (**EurAide,** listed below, is faster and also helpful). Books rooms (DM5) and sells accommodations lists (DM0.50). Adequate free map and the invaluable *Munich for Young People* (DM1). Open daily 8am-10pm. The encyclopedic *Monatsprogramm* (German only, DM1.80) lists museum hours, cultural events, and *almost* everything you may need to know. *Munich Found* has much the same information in English for DM2.50 (available at Internationale Presse at the station or the Anglia English Bookshop). Branch office at **Munich Riem Airport** (tel. 90 72 56), in the arrival lounge. Open Mon.-Sat. 8:30am-10pm, Sun. 1-9pm. The **Fremdenverkehrsband München-Oberbayern,** Sonnenstr. 10 (tel. 59 73 47), has brochures, maps and information on Munich's environs. **Euraide in English** (tel. 59 38 89), in the station next to track #11. Come here before waiting in any lines. Provides free train information, finds accommodations (DM6), and generally facilitates passage through the tourist bureaucracy. Their *Inside Track* (free) available at their office and in the *Reisezentrum.* Thomas Cook timetables sold (DM37) and Eurailpasses validated. Open daily June-Oct. 7:30-11:30am and 1-4:30pm.

Budget Travel: ASTA Reisen, Amalienstr. 73 (tel. 50 06 05 40), near the university. Open Mon.-Fri. 9am-6pm. Sells FIYTO and ISIC cards Mon.-Fri. 10am-2pm. **Budget Reisen Transalpino Tourismus,** Dachauer Str. 149 (tel. 129 53 53) and Sonnenstr. 8 (tel. 55 71 65), has reduced train tickets for those under 26.

Consulates: U.S., Königinstr. 5 (tel. 288 81). **Canada,** Tal 29 (tel. 22 26 61). **U.K.,** Amalienstr. 62 (tel. 381 62 80). **Czechoslovakia,** Karlsplatz 3 (tel. 59 74 76).

Currency Exchange: Go to the post office across from the station to exchange large denomination traveler's checks (DM3 per check). The bank at the station also changes currency and checks, and gives advances with Visa and MasterCard. Open daily 6am-11:30pm. **Euraide**

often strikes a deal with a local bank—low rates for customers with the *Inside Track*—so drop in and ask before changing money.

American Express: Promenadepl. 6 (tel. 219 90). From the train station, walk straight through Karlspl. to Neuhauserstr. and turn left on Ettstr. Open Mon.-Fri. 9am-5:30pm, Sat. 9am-noon.

Post Office: Bahnhofstr. 1 (tel. 53 88 27 32). Poste Restante open daily 7am-11pm. All other services 24 hrs. **Postal code:** 8000.

Telephones: Make credit card and collect calls from the post office on the 2nd level of the train station or across the street. **City code:** 089.

Flights: Riem Airport (tel. 92 11 21 27). Take the S-Bahn to the Riem stop (DM2.40), and a free shuttle bus will whisk you to the airport (3-5 min.). Buses also run from the train station every 15 min. (DM5.50; from station 4:15am-9pm, from airport terminal #1 or 2, 5:45am-9:10pm). A new airport, also accessible by S-Bahn, will open in May of 1992.

Trains: Munich's **Hauptbahnhof** is the transportation *omphalos* of southern Germany. For schedules, dial 194 19; fare info, 55 41 41; reservations, 128 59 94. (In German only.) Station open daily 5am-12:30am. To: Frankfurt (45 per day, 3½ hr., DM93); Berlin (25 per day, 9½ hr., DM117); Prague (7 per day, 6½ hr., DM90.30); Vienna (19 per day, 5½ hr., DM83.60); Zürich (5 per day, 4½ hr., DM88).

Public Transportation: Runs from about 5am-12:30am on weekdays, and until 1:30am on weekends. Eurail and InterRail passes are valid on any S-Bahn (suburban) train. Single rides on the U-Bahn, on Straßenbahn (trams) and on buses cost DM2.40. The *Innere Tageskarte* (inner-city day pass) is valid on all public transport in Munich proper until 4am (DM7.50). Cancel your ticket in the boxes marked with an "E" *before* you go to the platform. Transit maps can be had at the tourist office, Euraide, and the MVV counters near the subway entrance in the train station.

Bike Rental: Most convenient to town center is English-speaking **Radius Touristik** (tel. 59 61 13), near platform #35 at the station. Bikes DM3.20-5 per hour, DM16-27 per day. DM50 deposit. 10% discount for students, 5% for Eurailpass holders. Friendly owners loan rain gear to bikers in inclement weather. Open daily 8:30am-6:30pm.

Hitchhiking: Mitfahrzentrale, Lämmerstr. 4 (tel. 59 45 61), near the train station, and **Känguruh,** Amalienstr. 87 (tel. 28 01 24), Amalienpassage, both match drivers and passengers. Open Mon.-Fri. 8am-7:30pm, Sat. 9am-3pm, Sun. 10am-3pm. **Frauenmitfahrzentrale,** Klenzestr. 57b (tel. 201 6 10), matches women passengers with women drivers. Open Mon.-Fri. 9am-1pm and 3-7pm. Also scan the bulletin boards in the *mensa* at Leopoldstr. 13. If you choose to thumb it, head for autobahn on-ramps. For Autobahn E11 (direction Salzburg-Vienna/Brenner-Italy), take U-Bahn #1 or 2 to Karl-Preis-Platz. For E11 in the opposite direction (Stuttgart/France), take U-1 to Rotkreuzplatz and tram #12 to Amalienburgstr. *or* S-2 to Obermenzing. Either way, you then take bus #73 or 75 to Blutenburg. For all points north, take Autobahn E6; ride the U-6 to Sudetenstadt and walk 500 yards to the Frankfurter Ring. For the Autobahn to Lake Constance and Switzerland, take U-4 or U-5 to Heimeranplatz, then bus #33 to Siegenburgerstr. For Garmisch-Partenkirchen, take the Autobahn E6 to the south, ride the U-3 or U-6 to Westpark, (and from bus #33) to Luise-Kesselbach-Platz.

Bookstores: The gloriously chaotic **Anglia English Bookshop,** Schellingstr. 3 in Schwabing (tel. 28 36 42), has most *Let's Go* books. Open Mon.-Fri. 9am-8:30pm, Sat. 9am-2pm.

Pharmacy: Bahnhof Apotheke (tel. 59 41 19), on the outside corner of the station. Open Mon.-Fri. 8am-6:30pm, Sat. 8am-2pm. 24-hr. service rotates.

Medical Assistance: Tel. 55 86 61. The main **university clinic** is across the river on Ismaningerstr.

Emergencies: Police (tel. 110). **Ambulance** (tel. 192 22).

Accommodations and Camping

Accommodations in Munich fall into one of three categories: slimy, expensive or booked solid. Everything should be reserved in advance in summer and during *Oktoberfest.* At several of Munich's hostels you can check in all day—start your search well before 5pm. Sleeping in the Englischer Garten is unsafe and illegal; the police sometimes patrol. If you have a railpass, Augsburg's hostel (30-45 min. by train) is a viable option, but check the curfew. Remember, Bavarian IYHF hostels do not accept guests over age 26.

Hostels

Jugendlage Kapuzinerhölzl ("the Tent"), Frank-Schrank-Str. (tel. 141 43 00). Take U-1 to Rotkreuzplatz, then tram #12 (direction "Amalienburgstr."), and hop off at Botanischer Garten (ticket inspectors are especially rigorous on this route). Austere lodging in 2 circus tents. DM6 gets you a foam pad, blankets, a dry spot on the floor, bathrooms, a shower, hot tea, and enthusiastic management. 3-night max. stay. Reception open 5pm-9am. No lockers. To be safe, leave anything you hope to see again at the station. No reservations. Ages under 24 only (sometimes flexible). Open late June-early Sept.

Jugendgästehaus München (IYHF), Miesingstr. 4 (tel. 723 65 50). Take U-1 or 2 to Sendlinger Tor, then U-3 to Thalkirchen (Tierpark) stop, walk south on Pognerstr. and turn left onto Frauenbergstr. Cross Plinganserstr., walk 2 blocks, and turn right onto Miesingerstr. (30 min.). Ample and immaculate, but distant. Reception open 7am-1am; rooms available after 3pm. Curfew 1am. 8-15 bed dorms DM21. Singles DM29. Doubles DM50. Triples DM69. Quads DM88. Ages under 27 only.

Jugendherberge (IYHF), Wendl-Dietrich-Str. 20 (tel. 13 11 56). Take U-1 to Rotkreuzplatz; enter on Winthirplatz. Central, with noise, crowds. It's a good idea to leave your valuables in a locker at the station. Wait in line before noon in the summer. Reception open noon-1am. Lockout 8:30am-6pm. Curfew 1am. DM17.80-19. Ages under 27 only.

Haus International Youth Hotel, Elisabethstr. 87 (tel. 12 00 60). Take U-2 to Hohenzollernplatz (direction "Olympia Zentrum"), then tram #12 or bus #33 to Barbarastr. Spacious, stark rooms. Singles DM44. Doubles DM84. Triples DM38.50 per person. Quads DM36.50 per person. Quints DM35 per person. Prices slightly lower mid-Nov. to late Feb.

CVJM (YMCA) Jugendgästehaus, Landwehrstr. 13 (tel. 552 14 10), 2 blocks south of the station. Frill-less, pristine rooms in a shabby neighborhood. Reception open 8am-12:30am. Curfew 1am. Singles DM39. Doubles DM68. Triples DM93. Ages over 27 add 14% tax. Prices go down after 2nd night. Breakfast and showers included.

Jugendhotel Marienberge, Goethestr. 9 (tel. 55 58 91), less than a block below the train station. Catholic hostel open only to women 25 and under. Rough neighborhood but secure building; the rooms are spotless. Reception open 5-9pm. Curfew midnight. Singles DM31. Giant 6-bed dorms DM27 per person. Kitchen and showers included.

Hotels and Pensions

When the city is full, finding singles under DM50-60 or doubles under DM80-100 is nearly impossible. The tourist office charges DM5 to find lodgings. When they say they have nothing available under DM60, believe them. Euraide, Inc. at the train station also finds quarters (DM6).

Hotel-Pension Am Markt, Heiliggeiststr. 6 (tel. 22 50 14), between Viktualienmarkt and Im Tal, next to Heiliggeist Kirche. Aging photographs recall the celebrities who have graced the hotel's sparsely furnished though immaculate rooms. Singles DM54, with shower DM80. Doubles DM90-98, with shower DM110-130. Breakfast included.

Hotel Helvetia, Schillerstr. 6 (tel. 55 47 45), around the corner from the train station. Safe and smiling rooms. Singles DM55-60. Doubles DM85-100. Hall showers and breakfast included.

Pension Clara, Wilhelmstr. 25 (tel. 34 83 74). Take U-3 or 6 to Münchener Freiheit, take the escalator to Herzogstr., and follow it to Wilhelmstr. A small pension with simple rooms and a doting host. Singles DM55. Doubles DM80-98. Hall showers and breakfast included.

Pension am Kaiserplatz, Kaiserplatz 12 (tel. 34 91 90). Directions as above to Herzogstr.; follow it until you take a left onto Viktoriastr., then walk to Kaiserplatz. Charming hostess has carefully decorated each of the elegant, high-ceilinged rooms to recall the splendor of years past. Singles DM39. Doubles DM67-75. Hall showers and breakfast included. Call ahead.

Pension Frank, Schellingstr. 24 (tel. 28 14 51). Take U-3 or 6 to Universität. Relaxed, friendly staff, clean rooms, and a backpacker clientele. Singles DM55. Doubles DM70-85. Share a room wherever a bed is available for DM40. Showers and breakfast included. Book ahead June-Aug.

Camping

Campingplatz Thalkirchen, Zentralländstr. 49 (tel. 723 17 07), in the Isar River Valley Conservation Area. Take U-1 or 2 to Sendlinger Tor, then U-3 to Thalkirchen. Large and crowded. Curfew 11pm. DM5.20 per person, DM3-4.50 per tent, DM4 per car. Showers DM1. Laundry facilities and a cheap restaurant (meals DM2-6). Open mid-March to Oct.

Food

Munich's gastronomic center is the vibrant **Viktualienmarkt,** two minutes south of Marienplatz, with a rainbow array of bread, fruit, meat, pastry, cheese, wine, vegetable and sandwich shops. (Open Mon.-Fri. 6am-6:30pm, Sat. 6am-noon.) Try the *Leberkäse* (a mixture of beef and bacon) and *Weißwürst* (veal sausage), Munich's most famous specialties.

University Mensas, Arcisstr. 17 (near the Pinakotheks), Leopoldstr. 13, Dachauer-Str. 98b, and Helene-Mayer-Ring (in the former Olympic village). Cheapest edible meals in town; large portions only DM2.40-3.50. Open Nov.-July Mon.-Fri. 11am-1:45pm. At Leopoldstr. 15, there's also a student café with sandwiches (DM2-3; open Mon.-Fri. 9am-5pm). Student ID required.

Weißes Brauhaus (Schneider), Im Tal 10, between Isartor and Marienplatz. Loud, rude, and very Bavarian—since 1490. Grab a free seat and throw back a shot of schnapps with the locals. Local specialties DM10.50-21.90. Open 9am-midnight.

Zum Bögner, Im Tal 72, near the Heiligengeist Kirche. Big and bustling with every Bavarian specialty under the sun. Excellent pork and beef dishes DM9-21.70. Try the *Bauernschmaus* for a little of everything (DM20). Accepts credit cards. Open daily 9am-midnight.

Lehrer Lämpl, Amalienstr. 81, right behind the university. Student hangout with light meals and vegetarian dishes (DM7-12). Open Mon.-Fri. 10am-1am, Sat. 6pm-1am.

Türkenhof, Türkenstr. 78, west of the university. Try a pendulous plate of *Käsespätzle* (delicious cheese noodles, DM9.50). Open daily 11am-1am.

Schmalznudel Café, Prälat-Zistl-Str. 8, just off the Viktualienmarkt. *The* breakfast place in central Munich for early risers and late-night convalescents. Try a *Schmalznudel* (doughnut-like fried pastry, a Munich specialty) with coffee (DM3.75). Open Mon.-Fri. 5am-2pm, Sat 5am-1pm.

Cafe Bayou, Amalienstr. 36, near the University. A smoky student hangout with sandwiches (DM4-5). Open Mon.-Fri. 10am-10pm.

Sights

The 15th-century **Frauenkirche,** one of the city's most beloved landmarks, dominates Munich's skyline. At the **Neues Rathaus,** the famous **Glockenspiel** steals the show with an elaborate mechanized display of jousting knights and dancing coopers. At 9pm, a mechanical watchman marches out and the Guardian Angel escorts the Münchner Kindl, the little monk who is the symbol of Munich, to bed. (Daily performances 11am. May-Oct. also at noon and 5pm.) Munich's ritual past is represented on Petersplatz by the 11th-century **Peterskirche,** whose tower has been affectionately christened "der Alter Peter" (Old Peter) by locals. (Open Mon.-Sat. 9am-6pm, Sun. and holidays 10am-6pm. Admission to tower DM2, students DM1, children DM0.50. Admission to church free.)

The magnificent **Residenz,** Max-Joseph-Platz 3, with dozens of richly decorated rooms built from the 14th to the 19th centuries, testifies to the power and wealth of the Wittelsbach family. The Residenz houses several museums, including the state collection of coins and the state treasury. (U-3, 4, 5 or 6 to Odeonsplatz. Residence complex open Tues.-Sun. 10am-4:30pm. Admission DM3.50.) Even posher is **Schloß Nymphenburg,** the royal summer residence. A baroque wonder set in a winsome park, the palace hides unexpected treasures, including a two-story granite marble hall seasoned with stucco and frescoes and a Chinese lacquer cabinet. Check out crazy King Ludwig's "Gallery of Beauties;" whenever a woman caught his fancy, he would have her portrait commissioned (a particularly scandalous habit as most were mere commoners). Take U-1 to Rotkreuzplatz, and then tram #12 (direction "Amalienburgstr."). (Main palace open Tues.-Sun. 9am-12:30pm and 1:30-5pm; Oct.-March Tues.-Sun. 10am-12:30pm and 1:30-4pm. The pagodas and palaces have similar hours. Admission to main palace DM2.50, to entire complex DM5, students DM1.50. Wander the grounds for free.)

Munich is a superb museum city. Take tram #18 to Isartor, where the **Deutsches Museum,** one of the world's most important museums of science and technology, fills a not-so-small island in the River Isar with displays on just about anything ever invented on this planet. The planetarium (DM1.50) and the daily electrical show will warm the cockles of any young Einstein. (Open daily 9am-5pm. Admission DM8, students DM4.) The **Alte Pinakothek,** Barerstr. 27, and the **Neue Pinakothek,** just across the street, rank with the world's finest art museums. Take U-8 to Königsplatz or tram #18. The older museum holds an extensive collection of masterpieces from the 13th to the 17th centuries, including a number of Dürers and Rubenses, and Albrecht Altdorfer's mind-occludingly detailed *Battle of Alexander.* The sleek quarters of the newer museum house an array of 18th- and 19th-century works. (Both Pinakotheks open Wed. and Fri.-Sun. 9:15am-4:30pm, Tues. and Thurs. 9:15am-4:30pm and 7-9pm. Admission to either DM4, students DM2; to both DM7, students DM3; Sun. free.) In the Haus der Kunst, Prinzregentenstr. 1, right below the Englischer Garten, the impressive **Staatsgallerie Moderner Kunst** showcases works by Beckmann, Kandinsky, Picasso, and Nolde, among others. (Open Tues.-Wed. and Fri.-Sun. 9:15am-4:30pm, Thurs. 9:15am-4:30pm and 7-9pm. Admission DM3.50, students DM1.80; Sun. free.)

Facing one another on the Königsplatz, the **Glypothek,** Königsplatz 3, and the **Antikensammlung,** Königsplatz 1, hold Germany's best collections of antiquities, particularly Greek, Etruscan, and Roman sculpture. (Glypothek open Tues.-Wed. and Fri.-Sun. 10am-4:30pm, Thurs. noon-8:30pm. Antikensammlung open Tues.-Wed. and Fri.-Sun. 10am-4:30pm, Thurs. noon-8:30pm. Admission to one DM3.50, students DM1.80; to both DM6, students DM3; Sun. free.)

If the decadence of art has destroyed your morals and lowered your inhibitions, head to the **Englischer Garten,** one of Europe's oldest landscaped public parks, to sunbathe. The further one goes in the direction of Schwabing, the less one is expected to wear.

Entertainment

Munich's streets erupt with bawdy beer halls, rowdy discos, trendy movie theaters, and cliquish cafés, every night of the week. Pick up the *Young People's Guide to Munich,* or buy a copy of the biweekly **Münchener Stadtmagazin** at any newsstand to find out what's up.

To most visitors, Munich means beer. The six great city labels are *Augustiner, Hacker-Pschorr, Hofbräu, Löwenbräu, Paulaner-Thomasbräu,* and *Spaten-Franzinskaner.* Each brand supplies its own beer halls. (Most open daily until 11pm or midnight. Beer is served by the *Maß,* which is about a quart or liter, DM7-8.) *Weißbier,* a Bavarian specialty which comes in both light and dark versions, is traditionally served in tall glasses rather than mugs. This smooth, potent brew makes addicts of many visitors, but the real gourmands know that the light, cloudy *Weizenbier* is the beer to end all beers. A few points of beer hall and beer garden etiquette: Before seating yourself at one of the long tables, ask *"Ist hier noch frei?"* (ist here knock fry, "Is this place free?"). When ordering "ein Bier" (one beer), hold up your thumb (not your index finger, which is German body language for "please wait"). Finally, when toasting, clink only the bottoms of the glasses, and then pound them once on the table. Prost!

Munich's world-famous **Hofbräuhaus am Platzl,** Platzl 9, two blocks from Marienplatz, has been tapping barrels since 1859, though it now caters primarily to tourists. *(Maß* DM7.20. Open daily 10am-midnight. Brass band after 7pm.) To sample great suds with Germans, head to one of Munich's other brewery-sponsored beerhalls: **Hacker-Pschorr,** Theresienhöhe 4 and 7; **Augustinerkeller,** Neuhauserstr. 16; **Löwenbräu,** Nymphenburgerstr. 2 (U-1 to Stiglmaierplatz); or **Spatenhof-Keller,** Neuhauserstr. 26. The **Mathäser-Bierstadt,** Bayerstr. 5 near Karlsplatz, is, with 5000 seats, the world's largest "beer city." Several distinct "districts," each with its own atmosphere, spread out over acres of ground. *(Maß* DM7.60. Open daily 8am-midnight.) For outdoor Stein-hoisting, nothing rivals the **Chinesischer Turm** beer garden, hidden away in the Englischer Garten. (Take the U-3 or 6 to Giselastr., follow Giselastr. into the park and then take any one of the paths to the right and look for the pagoda, or take bus #54 from Sudbahnhof to the Chinesischer Turm stop. Open daily in balmy weather 10am-11pm. Beers DM7-7.50.)

Beer is a mere fanfare to nightlife in Munich. The **Schwabing** district, especially **Ludwigstraße** and **Leopoldstraße,** is littered with bars, cafés, cabarets, discos, and galleries. This is the beating heart of Munich's trendy nightlife. The area in Schwabing around **Münchener Freiheit** is the most touristy, but you'll also find the most serious partying and loudest discos here. More low-key is the southwestern section of Schwabing, directly behind the university on Amalienstr. and Türkenstr.; this area is drowned in student cafés, cheap restaurants, and mellow bars. The blocks between Viktualienmarkt and Gärtnerplatz are the center of the city's gay nightlife.

The **Wirtshaus im Schlachthof,** Zenettistr. 9 (tel. 76 54 48), features frequent live concerts (generally rock or jazz; cover DM15-28), cheap food, and beer. Take U-3 or 6 to Poccistr. (Beers DM3.30. Open nightly 9pm-1am.) Listen to free (for the price of a beer, that is) classical music Monday through Friday at the **Gaststätte Mariandl,** Goethestr. 51, right off Beethovenplatz south of the train station. Get there just before 8pm; Mondays are open microphone. At night, raucous revelers of many sexual orientations gather at the **Villanis Café-Bistro,** Kreuzstr. 3b (tel. 260 79 72), in the passage *(Asamhof)* between Sendlinger Str. and Kreuzstr. (Beers DM3.30. Open Mon.-Sat. 10am-1am, Sun. and holidays 11am-1am. Sunday is gay night.) The city's rompingest gay disco, the **New York,** Sonnenstr. 25, flaunts fantastic laser lighting. (Strictly male. Cover DM10.20. Beers DM6. Open daily 11pm-4am.) **Oly,** Helene-Meyer-Ring (tel. 351 77 33), is a slick and loud student dance spot.

Munich's cultural offerings rank with the world's best. The tourist office's monthly program and the magazine *Munich Found* provide thorough schedule and ticket information for concerts and theater performances. Standing-room (DM9) and reduced-rate student tickets to the operas and ballets of the **Bavarian State Opera** are sold at Maximillianstr. 11 (tel. 22 13 16), behind the Opera House or one hour before the performance at the opera itself. (Box office open Mon.-Fri. 9am-1pm and 3-5:30pm, Sat. 10am-noon.) The **Staatstheater,** Gärtnerplatz 3 (tel. 201 67 67), stages comic opera and musicals; standing room tickets start at DM5. Take U-1 or 2 to Frauenhoferstr., tram #18 or 20, or bus #52 or 56. (Open Mon.-Fri. 10am-1pm and 3:30-5:30pm, Sat. 10am-12:30pm.) Munich's **Opera Festival** runs throughout July as does a concert series in the Nymphenburg and Schleißheim palaces. English-language films screen at the **Europa-Kino,** Schwanthalerstr. 2-6 (tel. 55 56 70).

Near Munich

"Once they burn books, they'll end up burning people," wrote the 19th-century German poet Heinrich Heine. This eerily prophetic statement is posted at **Dachau,** Germany's first concentration camp, next to a photograph of one of Hitler's book burnings. Though most of the buildings were destroyed in 1962, the walls, gates, guard towers and crematoria remain. The terrifying legacy of Dachau lives in photographs and on film in the museum, the two reconstructed barracks and the several memorials and chapels on the grounds. Take S-2 toward Petershausen, get off at Dachau and catch bus #722 (DM2) in front of the station to the *KZ Gedenkstätte* (Memorial), a 20-minute ride. (Open Tues.-Sun. 9am-5pm. 22-min. English film at 11:30am and 3:30pm. Free.) Euraide, Inc. offers a guided tour in English that leaves from the Munich *Hauptbahnhof.* (June-Aug. Tues. and Thurs. 9:30am. DM25, DM17 for railpass holders.)

The monastery at **Andechs** combines Bavaria's two most acclaimed attributes—Catholicism and beer gardens—on a gorgeous mountaintop. The monks brew up a tasty light beer and a strong *Bockbier* which, piously, is not served on Sundays *(Maß* DM5.40). The adjacent **Klosterkirche Heiliger Berg** houses more than 250 centuries-old votive candles—giant, ornate candles commemorating departed brothers. (Beer hall open Mon.-Sat. 10am-8:45pm. Church open daily 10am-7pm.) To get to Andechs, take S-5 to Herrsching, then switch to the private bus line Omnibus-Verkehr Rauner (runs Mon.-Sat. 7-10 times daily 7am-6:30pm, returning 9-12 times, last return 6:45pm; Sun. 11 times 7:56am-6:33pm, returning 9:30am-6:45pm), or work up a thirst on the 3km hiking trail up the mountain. Follow signs marked "Fußweg nach Andechs" and stick to the trail; a sign reminds hikers of 11 people who met their death short-cutting down the precipitous slope.

Further south, on the cusp of the Alps, lies the breathtakingly beautiful **Chiemsee,** Bavaria's largest lake and a favorite German holiday spot. Ludwig II of Bavaria built the third and last of his extravagant castles, **Herrenchiemsee,** on the **Herreninsel,** the largest of the lake's islands. The dozen completed rooms are replicas of rooms at Versailles, only more fabulously decorated. (Obligatory tours every 10 min. available in English. Admission DM5. Students and seniors DM2.50. Open daily 9am-5pm. Nov.-March daily 10am-4pm.) To reach Chiemsee and Herrenchiemsee, take the train from Munich to **Prien,** the main town on the lake. A steam-driven train runs between the Prien train station and the lake (DM2.50). Ferries connect Prien with the islands and the other towns on the lake. (DM7 round-trip to the Herreninsel.) Once on the island, follow the wooded path from the ferry to the castle, or ride in a horse-drawn carriage (every 15 min., DM3.50).

Nuremberg (Nürnberg)

In 1332, Nuremberg was declared a "free city" by the Holy Roman Emperor—meaning that its citizens answered only to the authority of the Emperor and no other master—and the Reichstag (parliament) was held here until 1543. It was this long connection with the empire that first attracted Hitler to Nuremberg, where he established the Reichsparteitag of the Nazi Party in 1927. The racial purity laws, which came to be known as the "Nuremberg Laws," were passed here in 1935. These events and the 1945-1949 Nuremberg war criminal trials have left the city indelibly tainted by the memory of Nazism, a taint that other German cities have cloaked in high-tech, well-engineered affluence.

From the station, walk straight down Königstr. to the **Lorenzkirche,** which houses an exquisite 20m tabernacle and the **Engelsgruß,** a large free-hanging wooden carving, over the main altar. (Open Mon.-Sat. 9am-5pm, Sun. 2-4pm.) Across the Pegnitz River on the Marktplatz is the **Frauenkirche,** a Gothic churchlet with beautiful stained-glass windows. (Open Mon.-Sat. 9am-5pm, Sun. 12:30-6pm.) Every day at noon you can watch the antics of Emperor Karl IV and his seven elector-princes on the church clock. On the other side of the square is the pastel and gold **Schöner Brunnen** (beautiful fountain). In December, the marketplace is the sight of the world-famous **Christkindlmarkt.** The **Kaiserburg** (Emperor's castle), begun in 1040, dominates the city below. Obligatory tours of the interior (in German) are offered every 10 minutes. (Open daily 9am-noon and 12:45-5pm; Oct.-March 9:30am-noon and 12:45-4pm. Admission DM3, students DM2.) Below the castle is the **Dürer House,** a perfectly preserved monument to the 15th-century painter. (Open Tues. and Thurs.-Sun. 10am-5pm, Wed. 10am-7pm. Admission DM3, students and children DM1.)

Germany's uglier contributions to modern civilization are on display at the **Dutzendteich Park.** Site of the *Parteitage* rallies in the 1930s, the park still envelops the **New Congress Hall** and broad **Great Road.** To get there, take any train to Dutzendteich or tram #9 (direction: "Luitpoldhain") to the last stop. On the other side of town on Fürtherstr., many of the Nazi leaders faced a less enthusiastic audience of Allied military judges in Room 600 of the **Justizgebände.** The building still serves as a busy courthouse. Take U-Bahn #1 to Bärenschanze and continue walking away from the old town on Fürtherstr.

Nuremberg's two **tourist offices** (tel. (0911) 233 60) are located in the main train station (open Mon.-Fri. 9am-8pm, Sat. 9am-7pm) and downtown on Marktplatz (open Mon.-Sat. 9am-1pm and 2-6pm, Sun. 10am-1pm and 2-4pm). The **Mitfahrzentrale** office is a 10-minute walk from behind the station at Allerbergerstr. 31a (tel. (0911) 446 96 66; open Mon.-Fri. 9am-6pm, Sat. 8:30am-1pm, Sun. 11am-2pm). **American Express** (tel. (0911) 23 23 97) has an office at Alderstr. 2 (open Mon.-Fri. 9am-5:30pm, Sat. 9am-noon). The comfortable and well-run **Jugendherberge Kaiserstallung (IYHF),** Burg 2 (tel. (0911) 22 10 24), is in the imperial castle. (Juniors only, DM22. Sheets included. Curfew 1am.) Take tram #9 (direction "Thon") to the Krelingstr. stop, take a left on Krelingstr. and walk through the Kaiserburg to the other side of the castle. The **Jugendhotel,** Rathsbergstr. 300 (tel. (0911) 521 60 92), is 25 minutes north of town (DM19-24, breakfast included). Take tram #3 to the last stop, then bus #41 to Felsenkeller. Close behind the train station, **Pension Vater Jahn,** Jahnstr. 13 (tel. (0911) 44 45 07) offers comfortable, tidy rooms. (Singles DM32-35. Doubles DM60-65. Breakfast included.) **Pension Fischer,** Brunnengasse (tel. (0911) 22 61 89), has singles for DM35 and doubles for DM65. Breakfast is included. **Pension Alt-Nürnberg,** Breitegasse 40 (tel. (0911) 22 41 29) is 1½ blocks away. (Singles DM30-35. Doubles DM50-60. Breakfast included. Call ahead.) **Camping,** Haus-Kalb-Str. 56 (tel. (0911) 81 11 22), is behind the soccer stadium; take the U-Bahn south to Messenzentrum. (DM6 per person, DM5 per tent, DM5 per car. Open May-Sept. Call ahead.) *Rostbratwurst,* a mild sausage, is the thing to eat in Nuremberg, and the place to do so is beneath the smoking chimney of tiny **Bratwurst-Häusle,** below St. Sebalduskirche *(Rostbratwurst* with sauerkraut or potato salad DM8-15; open Mon.-Sat. 9:30am-10pm). The **Mensa** of the Erlangen-Nürnberg university is located in the historic Weinstadel building, at 8 Maxplatz near the river. (Open daily 11:30am-2pm. Lunch DM3.20. Student ID required.)

Romantic Road (Romantische Stra ßē»

Beautful, gently rolling countryside stretches between Würzburg, nestled among the Franconian vineyards, and Füssen, in the Alpine Lech valley. Sensing opportunity, the German tourist industry christened these bucolic backwaters and ancient artifacts the Romantic Road in 1950. The world has responded—this is the most visited region in Germany, so be prepared.

Deutschebahn's **Europabus** runs along the Romantic Road from Würzburg through Rothenburg, Nördlingen, Dinkelsbühl, and Augsburg to Füssen (11 hr., DM81) from mid-March to late October (only 1 bus per day March-May). The trip can also be done in segments, priced appropriately, or you can stop anywhere along the line and catch the bus the next day (this must be specified in your reservations). Eurail and all Deutschebahn passes cover the charge. InterRail gets a 50% discount. Students under 26 receive a 10% discount. Leave the stickers on your luggage to avoid paying DM3 when switching buses. Reservations (free) need to be made at least three days in advance through Frankfurt's **Touring Büro,** am Römerhof 17 (tel. (069) 790 32 40). For a more leisurely, less crowded tour, Deutschebahn's identically priced regular *Linien* buses go to all the towns on the Europabus route and then some. The same railpass discounts apply. Schedules are posted in all train stations or, in towns with no train station, in the tourist office. The Romantic Road can also be easily biked. Any tourist office in the area will provide detailed maps and lists of camping sites, hostels and pensions along the route. Campsites tend to be 10-20km apart, towns with hostels or pensions much closer. Many travelers also hitch the route quite successfully. For general information about transportation, facilities and sights, contact the **Romantische Straße Arbeitsgemeinschaft,** Marktplatz, D-8804 Dinkelsbühl (tel. (09851) 902 71).

Straddling the Main river and surrounded by vineyards, **Würzburg** sports an expansive baroque palace, a muscular fortress, and numerous alcohol-centered festivals. In front of the train station, a **tourist office** (tel. (0931) 374 36) provides excellent tour maps (DM.50) and helps find rooms (DM30-38 per person) for a DM3 fee. (Open Mon.-Sat. 8am-8pm.) Another tourist office is in the Falkenhaus, at the Marktplatz (tel. (0931) 373 98; open Mon.-Fri. 9am-6pm, Sat. 9am-2pm). In March, the **Kulturamt,** also in the Falkenhaus, will begin selling tickets for June 5th's **Mozartfest.** Würzburg's answer to Oktoberfest—the **Kiliani Festival**—is held in July, and an annual **Wine Festival** takes place in late September. The striking 13th-century **Marienburg Fortress** stands vigil from high upon a hillside over the Main. Masochists can climb (40 min.). Otherwise take bus #9 (DM1.60), which runs every half-hour (May to mid-Oct. 9:43am-5:43pm) from the Spitäle bus stop at the western end of the Alte Mainbrücke bridge. (Open Tues.-Sun. 9am-noon and 1-5pm; Oct.-March Tues.-Sun. 10am-noon and 1-4pm. Admission DM3, students DM2, under 15 free.) The fortress also houses the **Mainfränkisches Museum,** with a large collection of Riemenschneiders. (Open daily 10am-5pm; Nov.-April 10am-4pm. Admission DM3, students DM1.50.) Neumann's masterpiece, the **Residenz** (ecclesiastical palace), containing the largest ceiling fresco in the world, lies in **Residenzplatz.** (Open Tues.-Sun. 9am-5pm; Oct.-March Tues.-Sun. 10am-4pm. Admission DM4.50, students DM3.) The **Residenzhofkirche** church is astounding. (Open Tues.-Sun. 9am-noon and 1-5pm; Oct.-March Tues.-Sun. 10am-noon and 1-4pm. Free.) In front of the Residenz stands the 900-year-old **Dom,** or **Cathedral of St. Kilian,** rebuilt in the mid-1960s after obliteration in 1945. (Open Mon.-Sat. 10am-5pm, Sun. 1-6pm; Nov. 1-Easter Mon.-Sat. 10am-noon and 2-5pm, Sun. 12:30-1:30 and 2:30-6pm. Tours April-Oct. Mon.-Sat. at noon, Sun. at 12:30pm. Admission DM2.) Würzburg's **Jugendherberge (IYHF),** Burkarderstr. 44.(tel. (0931) 425 90) is tucked in the lee of St. Burkard's Basilica, across the river from downtown. Take tram #3 from the station (direction "Heidingsfeld") to the Ludwigsbrücke stop. (Reception open 2-5:15pm and 6:30-10pm. Juniors only, DM22. Sheets included.) **Weinhaus Schnabel,** Hagerpfarrgasse 10 (tel. (0931) 533 14), has clean, simple singles (DM30) and doubles (DM60; breakfast included for both). Campers should take tram #3 (direction "Heidingsfeld") and get off at Judenbühlweg for **Camping Kann Club,** Mergentheimerstr. 13b (tel. (0931) 725 36; DM4 per person, DM4 per tent).

For a bargain standup meal, head to the **Metzgermeister Grill,** Kaiserstr. 12, where *Schnitzel mit Pommes* costs a mere DM8.50. (Open Mon.-Sat. 10am-6pm.) Behind the Marktplatz at Domstr. 14, **Sternbäck** hawks baked potatoes with more than 20 available toppings for DM3. (Open Mon.-Sat. 8am-1am, Sun. 10am-1am.) Europabuses cruise down the Romantic Road daily at 9am and 10:15am, departing from beside the station. The 10:15 bus fills quickly (see above for reservations information).

If you can visit only one town on the Romantic Road, make it **Rothenburg ob der Tauber.** This place invented quaint; though it is undoubtedly the most touristed spot in Germany, it may be your only chance to ever see a completely intact walled medieval city. The **tourist office,** Marktplatz 1 (tel. (09861) 404 92) next to the Rathaus, supplies handy maps and books rooms (usually no fee, DM2 in peak times; open Mon.-Fri. 9am-noon and 2-6pm, Sat. 9am-noon and 2-4pm). Housed in medieval buildings, Rothenburg's two youth hostels stand just blocks apart. At the **Jugendherberge Rossmühle (IYHF)** (tel. (09861) 404 92), Rossmühleweg, the worn stone exterior belies immaculate, carpeted rooms. From the station, turn left and then right onto Ausbacher-Str., go through the wall and turn left at the Marktplatz; the hostel is four blocks down on the right. (Reception open 7-9am, 5-7pm and 8-10pm. Curfew 11:30pm. Juniors only DM15.50. Showers, breakfast, and lockers free.) One block farther is the cheaper, mustier **Jugendherberge Spitalhof (IYHF)** (tel. (09861) 78 89). (Same reception and curfew. Juniors only, DM12.)

Not as pre-packaged as Rothenburg, **Dinkelsbühl,** 40km south, maintains a full complement of half-timbered houses. Visit the **St. Georgskirche,** complete with Riemenschneider School wood carvings, and walk down **Nördlingerstraße,** where none of the old houses are perfectly rectangular—medieval superstition correctly held that houses with 90° angles were homes of demons. The **tourist office** (tel. (09851) 902 40) in Marktplatz can help you with accommodations. (Open Mon.-Fri. 9am-1pm and 2-6pm, Sat.-Sun. 10am-noon and 2-4pm; Nov.-March Mon.-Fri. 9am-1pm and 2-6pm, Sat. 10am-1pm.) The **IYHF youth hostel,** Koppengasse 10 (tel. (09851) 509), is an old half-timbered house three blocks from the town center. (Juniors only, DM13.50. Open March-Oct.)

The walled city of **Nördlingen,** 35km south of Dinkelsbühl, sits near the center of a circular meteor crater, the **Ries,** nearly 12km in diameter. The crater and the town can be viewed from **Der Daniel,** the tower of the lovely 15th-century **St. Georgskirche** (DM2). The 14th-century wall, the only completely preserved city wall in Germany, is nearly 3km long and can be walked in its entirety. The **tourist office** (tel. (09081) 841 16), next door to the Rathaus, provides a list of pensions in town and books rooms for a few marks. (Rooms from DM25. Open Mon.-Fri. 8am-6pm, Sat.-Sun. 9:30am-12:30pm; Oct.-March Mon.-Fri. 8am-5pm.) Try the pleasant **IYHF youth hostel,** Kaiserwiese 1 (09081) 841 09; juniors only, DM13.50; open March-Oct.).

Founded by Caesar Augustus in 15 BC, **Augsburg** became the financial center of the Holy Roman Empire through the industry of the Fugger banking dynasty, later the personal financiers to the Habsburgs. Augsburg's medieval period unfolds at the brightly colored **Guildhouse,** down Bgm.-Fischer-Str. from the train station, and the **Fuggerei,** founded by Jakob Fugger the Rich as the world's first welfare housing, a capacity in which it still serves. (Museum open March-Sept. daily 9am-6pm. Admission DM1.) The **Brechthaus** at Auf dem Raim 7 is the birthplace of influential 20th-century playwright Bertolt Brecht, and now tells the story of his life through photos and letters. (Open Tues.-Sun. 10am-5pm; Nov.-April Tues.-Sun. 10am-4pm. Admission DM2, students DM1.)

Augsburg's resourceful **tourist office,** Bahnhofstr. 7 (tel. (0821) 50 20 70), is about 300m in front of the station. For DM1.50, they will find you a single from DM30 or a double from DM55. (Open Mon.-Fri. 10am-6pm, Sat. 9am-1pm.) Another tiny tourist office is in front of the station. To find the **IYHF youth hostel,** Beim Pfaffenkeller 3 (tel. (0821) 339 03), take tram #2 (DM1.60) from the Bahnhof to the Stadtwerke stop. They are often full in summer, so call ahead. (Reception open 5-7pm. Juniors only, DM14. Open Jan. 1-Dec. 11.) The Romantic Road's **Europabus** stops in Augsburg on its way south to Füssen. The **Mitfahrzentrale** is at Barthof 3 (tel. (0821) 15 70 19; open Mon.-Sat. 10am-9pm, Sun. 1-9pm).

Bavarian Alps (Bayerische Alpen)

South of Munich, the land buckles into a series of dramatic peaks and valleys which keeps on tossing through Austria into Italy. Rail lines are scarce in this magical terrain; buses fill the gaps. For regional info, contact the **Fremdenverkehrsverband** (you've gotta love those German nouns) **Oberbayern,** Sonnenstr. 10, 8000 München, (tel. (089) 59 73 47).

At the southern terminus of the Romantic Road, **Füssen** draws an inordinate number of visitors because it's near the **Königschlösser** (royal castles), two extravagant architectural concoctions of the fading Bavarian monarchy. Coming from Munich, take a train to Buchloe or Kaufbeuren and transfer to the regional train to Füssen. (Entire trip about 2 hr., DM28.) Turn left from the station to reach the town center, dominated by the **Hohes Schloß** (High Castle), former summer residence of Augsburg's bishops. Inside is the **Gemäldegalerie,** a collection of regional late-Gothic and Renaissance art. (Admission DM3. Open Mon.-Sat. 10am-noon and 2-4pm; Sun. 10am-noon; Dec.-March Thurs. 2-4pm.) The baroque **St. Mangkirche,** just below the castle, contains the 10th-century subterranean crypt of St.

Magnus. The adjacent **Chapel of St. Anne** harbors the skeleton-bedecked "Totentanz" (Death Dance), a mural depicting the misfortunes that death bestows upon the living.

The Füssen **tourist office,** Augsburger-Tor-Platz (tel. (08362) 70 77), a three-minute walk from the station toward the center of town, gives advice on hiking and finds rooms for free. Budget singles in *Gasthäuser* run DM25-40; in *Pensionen,* DM30-40. Private rooms are considerably cheaper (DM18-25), but rent only for three or more nights. (Tourist office open Mon.-Fri. 8am-noon and 1-7pm, Sat. 10am-noon and 4-6pm, Sun. 10am-noon; Sept.-June Mon.-Fri. 8am-noon and 2-6pm, Sat. 10am-noon.) Though decaying, Füssen's **Jugendherberge (IYHF),** Mariahilfstr. 5 (tel. (08362) 77 54), is generally packed. Turn right from the station and follow the railroad tracks. (Reception open 5-7pm (or later, if you ask nicely). Lockout 9-11:30am. Curfew 10pm. Juniors only, DM14.50. Use of kitchen facilities DM1; one load of laundry, wash and dry DM4. Open mid-Dec. to Oct.)

Both of the Königschlösser are about 5km from Füssen and accessible by the bus marked "Königschlösser," which departs more or less hourly from the train station (Eurail valid). It was in neo-Gothic **Hohenschwangau,** built by Maximilian II, that Ludwig II, Bavaria's "crazy king," spent his childhood. Though lacking that lived-in look, **Neuschwanstein,** inspiration for the Disney World "Fantasyland" castle and pinnacle of Ludwig's desperate building spree across Upper Bavaria, is by far more impressive in its excesses. The lines tend to be endless for the obligatory tours, which are brisk (20 min.) and heavily accented. Consider taking the tour first thing in the morning and spending the rest of the day hiking around the castle environs, which are spectacular, particularly from the Pöllat Gorge behind Neuschwanstein. (Both castles open 9am-5:30pm; Nov.-March 10am-4pm. Admission to Hohenschwangau DM7, students and seniors DM4; to Newschwanstein DM8, students and seniors DM5.) Other buses to the castles depart from the Garmisch train station and stop directly in Hohenschwangau village (3 per day at 8am, 12:10pm, 4:50pm; 2 hr.; DM12.80, round-trip DM21, free with Eurail; return at 1:13pm and 5:24pm). If coming from Munich, consider the Königschlösser tours run by **Euraide.** (June 5-Aug. 10 Wed. and Sat. 9am. DM55, DM45 with a railpass.) Reserve your seat a day in advance at the Euraide office in Munich. All tours leave from the Munich main train station.

Site of the world-famous Passion Play every ten years since 1634, **Oberammergau** is a charming little Alpine village. The next performances will be in the summer of 2000. Book years ahead. The **tourist office,** Eugen-Papst-Str. 9a (tel. (08822) 10 21), has free maps and finds rooms for DM1. The loud, kiddie-group-infested **Jugendherberge (IYHF),** Malensteinweg 10 (tel. (08822) 41 14), is across the river from the tourist office. (Juniors only, DM14.50. Curfew 10pm. Open Dec. 27 to mid-March and April to mid-Nov.) Between Oberammergau and Garmisch-Partenkirchen stands **Schloß Linderhof,** Ludwig II's small hunting palace, surrounded by an elegant, manicured park with a 25m high fountain. (Open daily 9am-12:15pm and 12:45-5:30pm. Admission DM7, students DM4.) Buses (round-trip DM7) run from Oberammergau 7 times per day (10am-7:02pm) and return 7 times daily (last bus leaves Linderhof at 5:40pm). Get to Oberammergau by bus from Garmisch-Partenkirchen (round-trip DM11), Schongau (round-trip DM12.60), or Füssen (round-trip DM18). Railpasses are valid on all of these routes. Trains from Munich run to Oberammergau 11 times per day, switching at Murnau (1 ¾ hr., DM20.60).

The two small resort villages of **Garmisch** and **Partenkirchen** united in 1935 in anticipation of the following year's Winter Olympics, and today Garmisch-Partenkirchen, in the shadow of the **Zugspitze,** Germany's highest mountain, is a thriving ski-paradise. There are two ways up the peak: the first is to take a cog railway from the Zugspitzbahnhof (50m behind the Garmisch main station) to the Hotel Schneefernerhaus stop, then a cable car, "Gipfelseilbahn," to the top; the trip lasts 80 minutes, 65 min. to the ski area. (Round-trip DM50, DM45 in winter.) Another cable car, "Eibseeseilbahn," runs from Eibsee to the summit (DM50). Tickets are interchangeable and include the cog railway between the two base stations. Hiking trails of every grade radiate from town. A map of local paths, *Spazierwege rund um Garmisch-Partenkirchen,* costs only DM1 at the tourist office, **Verkehrsamt der Kuverwaltung,** Richard-Strauss-Platz (tel. (08821) 18 06); turn left from the train station, then left down Von-Brug-Str. The tourist office finds lodgings but does not make reservations. (Open Mon.-Sat. 8am-6pm, Sun. and holidays 10am-noon.) When the office is closed, check out the automat in front of the building (DM18-30, generally a 3-night min.). The less-than-immaculate **IYHF youth hostel,** Jochstr. 10 (tel. (08821) 29 80), is 4km from town in Burgrain; take bus #6 or 7. (Reception open 7-10am and 5-10pm. Juniors only, DM13.50. Open late Dec.-Oct.) **Camping Zugspitze** (tel. (08821) 31 80) is on highway B24 at the base of the Zugspitze; take the blue-and-white bus from the station towards Eibsee/Grainau and get off at Schmölzabzweigung. (DM5.70 per person, DM8.50 per tent. In winter, DM6.50 and DM9.50, and call ahead.) The cheapest **ski equipment rental** is at **Sepp Hohenleitner's,** at the Zugespitzbahnhof (tel. (08821) 506 10), a 20-min. walk to the slopes. Procure **mountain bikes** at **Mountain-Bike-Schule Garmisch-Partenkirchen,** Wildenauerstr. 8 (tel. (08821) 712 48). (Half day DM16, full day DM25.)

At the easternmost point of the Bavarian Alps, near Salzburg and the Austrian border, **Berchtesgaden** profits from Hitler's **Kehlsteinhaus,** a mountaintop retreat christened the "Eagle's Nest" by occupying American troops. Tourists fascinated by Hitler's private life journey in droves to witness a slice of "up close and personal" WWII history—expect crowds even in this small village, stashed away in the Alpine boondocks. In fact, there's no museum at the Kehlsteinhaus, simply a restaurant, souvenir shop and fantastic view. If you're still up for it, marked buses depart every 30-45 min. from the Berchtesgaden train station to Obersalzberg-Hintereck. There you switch to a special bus (every 30-45 min. 8:45am-5pm) that winds summitwards along a stomach-wrenching one-lane road, hewn into solid rock by an army of 3,000 unfortunate men excused from military service for health reasons. An elevator jets you up the last 150m; else walk 20 min. (Open late-May to early Oct. Admission runs DM22.50 for buses and elevator, children DM14.) You may prefer the more wholesome **salt mines** *(Salzbergwerk)* a bus ride from town, where you can dress up in an old salt miner's outfit, slide down snaking passages in the dark, and go on a raft ride on a salt lake. (Tour 1½ hr. Open May to mid-Oct. daily 8:30am-5pm; mid-Oct. to April Mon.-Sat. 12:30-3:30pm. Admission DM13.50, children DM7.)

Berchtesgaden's **tourist office** (tel. (08652) 50 11) is opposite the train station on Königsseer Str. (Open Mon.-Fri. 8am-6pm, Sat. 8am-5pm, Sun. 9am-3pm; in off-season Mon.-Fri. 8am-5pm, Sat. 9am-noon.) The beguiling **IYHF youth hostel,** Gebirgsjägerstr. 52 (tel. (08652) 21 90), is in the neighboring village of Strub, half an hour down the road to the right as you emerge from the train station; take the first right, and follow the hill path up to the left, or take bus #9539 (direction "Strub Kaserne," 25 min., DM2). (Reception open 5-7pm. DM15 per night. Flexible curfew 10pm. Reception open 5-7pm.) **Gästehaus Alpina,** is right next to the Berchtesgaden station at Ramsauer Str. 6 (tel. (08652) 25 17). All rooms include toilet, shower, and fat down comforters—many boast balconies too. (DM23-24, breakfast included.) The most convenient **camping** sites are **Grafenlehen** (tel. (08652) 41 40; DM6.50 per person, DM7 per tent including car) and **Mülleiten** (tel. (08652) 45 84; DM8.50 per person, DM6 per tent), both near the Königsee, a lake so extraordinarily calm that its surface almost perfectly mirrors the surrounding Alpine cliffs. Shop at the *Edeka Markt* on Dr.-Imhof-Str. (open Mon.-Fri. 8am-6pm, Sat. 8am-noon).

Reach Berchtesgaden by frequent train (1½ hr., round-trip 145AS or DM20.40) or bus (1 per hr., 35 min., round-trip DM10) from the train station in Salzburg, Austria. From Munich, transfer in Freilassing (3 hr., round-trip DM76, DM46 same-day return available Tues.-Thurs. and Sat.-Sun.)

The Danube

Northeast of Munich, the Danube valley, with baroque Passau and Gothic Regensburg, is every bit as inviting as the Romantic Road. Rolling hills and lovely riverscapes attract visitors year-round—Germans themselves summer in cottages here.

Regensburg was once the capital of Bavaria, and later the administrative seat of the Holy Roman Empire. The halls where the Imperial Congress met live on in the **Reichstags Museum,** housed in the Gothic **Altes Rathaus.** (Obligatory tours Mon.-Sat. 9:30am-4pm every 30 min. (in English at 3:15pm), Sun. 10am, 11am, and noon; Nov.-March Mon.-Sat. 9:30am, 10:30am, 11:30am, 2pm, 3pm, and 4pm, Sun. 10am, 11am and noon. Admission DM3, students DM1.) The splendid Gothic **Cathedral of St. Peter** towers over the city. (Open daily 6:30am-6pm; Nov.-March 6:30am-4pm.) The **Fremdenverkehrsamt** (tourist office), on Rathauspl. (tel. (0941) 507 21 41) finds rooms, provides a free map, and sells tickets to city events. From the station, walk down Maximlianstr. and take a left on Grasgasse. Take a right onto Obere Bachgasse and follow it to Rathauspl. The **Jugendherberge (IYHF),** Wöhrdstr. 60 (tel. (0941) 574 02), is partially renovated and hopefully will be finished by summer 1992. (Reception open 7am-11:30pm. Lockout 9am-1am. Curfew 11:30pm. DM14.50. Reservations encouraged.) Other inexpensive pensions peer down the alleys and side streets of the central pedestrian zone (DM32-40), or the tourist office can try to find you a room in a private home. Campers should head for the **Campingplatz** (tel. (0941) 268 39) on Weinweg 40 outside of town. Take bus #6. (DM5, children DM3; car and tent DM6.50, tent alone DM3.50. Open March-Oct.) Trains depart to Munich 11-13 times per day (1-1½ hr., DM28), usually transferring at Landshut. Trains to Passau (50 min., DM26) run every ½-1 hr.

Northeast of Regensburg and Passau along the Czech border, the **Bavarian Forest** (Bayerischer Wald) is Central Europe's largest range of wooded mountains. Germans and Austrians (and now Czechs and Hungarians) go to the **Bavarian Forest National Park** for nature walks, mountain climbing and cross-country skiing. For news of the Forest, contact the **Fremdenverkehrsverband Ostbayern,** Landshuterstr. 13 (tel. (0941) 571 86), 10 minutes by foot from the train station in Regensburg. Alternatively, contact the **Bayerischer Wald Park Verwaltung,** Freyunger Str. 2, 8352 Grafenau (tel. (08552) 20 85). The park's thick, cool woods conceal glass factories and 17 **IYHF youth hostels,** some an easy bus or train ride from Regensburg and Passau; take a bus from Passau to the hostel at **Mauth,** Jugendherbergstr. 11 (tel. (08557) 289). (Juniors only, DM14.50.)

Elegant, baroque **Passau** spans two peninsulas formed by the confluence of the Danube, Inn and Ilz rivers. A center of trade and both sacred and profane power for centuries, Passau teems with beautiful churches, palaces and cloisters. Its beautiful baroque architecture reaches a pinnacle in the sublime **St. Stephen's Cathedral.** Hundreds of chubby, wingèd cherubs splatter the ceiling, and the world's largest church organ, gilded and filigreed, rests weightily above the choir. (Cathedral open Mon.-Sat. 8-11am and 12:30-6pm. Free. Organ concerts May 2-Oct. 31 Mon.-Fri. noon, Thurs. 8pm. Noon concerts DM3, students, seniors and disabled DM1. Evening concerts DM6 and DM3.) Nearby are the **Residenz,** former home of the bishops of Passau, and the 14th-century Gothic **Rathaus.** The **Domschatz** (cathedral treasury), in the Residenz, testifies to the wealth and power of the German church. (Rathaus open Easter-Oct. Mon.-Fri. 10am-noon and 1:30-4pm, Sat.-Sun. 10am-4pm. DM1. Domschatz open May-Oct., Christmas-early Jan. and the week after Easter Mon.-Sat. 10am-4pm. DM2, children DM1.)

The ominous 13th-century military complex of **Veste Oberhaus** now houses a regional **Cultural History Museum** (open March-Jan. Tues.-Sun. 9am-5pm. Admission DM3, students DM1.50. Bus runs Tues.-Sun. 10am-5pm), as well as the noisy **Jugendherberge (IYHF)** (tel. (0851) 413 51), an aging hostel redeemed only by a fantastic view of Austria through the windows. (Take the Pendel-Bus-Verkehr bus from Rathausplatz, or take bus #1, 2, or 3 from the train station to Ilzbrücke and make the punishing 30 min. ascent to the fortress. Reception open 1:30-11pm. Curfew 11:30pm. Juniors only, DM14. Lockers require your lock. Sheets DM4.50.) If you prefer to sleep in the *Altstadt,* try **Gasthof Blauer Bock,** on the Fritz-Schäffer-Promenade (tel. (0851) 346 37). Try to get a room with a view of the Danube. (Singles with WC DM30. Doubles with WC DM60.) The tourist office can find you a room for a DM1.50 fee. Bikes rent at the train station for DM10 (DM5 for train patrons), and can be returned in Austria. The "Three-Rivers Round Trip" tour of Passau is well worth DM7 (children DM3; March-early Nov.; boats leave whenever enough people show). The **tourist office** is at Rathauspl. 3 (tel. (0851) 334 21), and has free maps, schedules, and hiking and camping information (open Mon.-Fri. 8:30am-noon and 1-5pm). Trains to Munich switch at Landshut, Plattling, or Regensburg (6-9 per day, 2-2½ hr., DM43). Danube steamers cruise to Linz, Austria from May to late October (5 hr., round-trip DM52).

Bayreuth and Bamberg

When composer Richard Wagner first moved to Bayreuth in 1872, he saw in the small provincial town the perfect setting for his music, and the perfect wealthy patroness, the Margravine Wilhelmina, to support him. Every year in late summer (around July 25-Aug. 28), thousands of visitors pour in for the **Bayreuth Festspiele,** a vast and bombastic celebration of Wagner's works in the **Festspielhaus,** the theater Wagner built for his "music of the future." Tickets (DM17-230) go on sale a year in advance and sell out almost immediately. For the 1992 festival, you must order tickets in writing by November 15, 1991 at the latest. Write to Postbox 100262, D-8580 Bayreuth 1, Germany. Reserve a room as soon as you get tickets. Ticketless visitors can console themselves with a tour of Wagner's house, **Villa Wahnfried,** Richard-Wagner-Str. 48. Snippets from Wagner's compositions are performed daily here at 10am, noon, and 2pm. (Open daily 9am-5pm. Admission DM3.50, students DM1; Sept.-June DM2.50, students DM2.)

Except during the Festspiele, accommodations in Bayreuth are abundant and reasonable. To reach the roomy and modern **IYHF youth hostel,** Universitätsstr. 28 (tel. (0921) 252 62), take bus #4 (DM1.60) from the Marktplatz to the last stop, Universität. (Curfew 10pm. Juniors only, DM14.50. Open Feb. to mid-Dec.) **Gasthof Vogel,** Friedrichstr. 13 (tel. (0921) 682 68), is very centrally located and offers clean, pleasant rooms. (Singles DM28. Doubles DM56.) The **Schützenhaus,** Am Schießhaus 2 (tel. (0921) 221 90) offers authentic Franconian delights in a large beer garden. (Open Tues.-Sat. 9:30am-midnight. Kitchen open Tues.-Sun. 9:30am-2pm and 5-10pm.) The **tourist office,** Luitpoldplatz 9 (tel. (0921) 885 88), in the Reisebüro, to the left and about 4 blocks from the train station, provides a free map of the city, a list of hotels, and information about surrounding areas. (Open Mon.-Fri. 9am-6pm, Sat. 9am-noon.) Bayreuth lies off the beaten track, but frequent trains and buses connect it to Nuremberg (DM20) and Bamberg (DM18).

In contrast to Bayreuth's secular excesses and thriving tourist trade, few travelers know enough to explore the treasures of the Franconian cathedral city of Bamberg. The **Altes Rathaus,** half *Fachwerk* (timber and plaster) and half baroque fresco, guards the middle of the Regnitz River like an anchored ship. Up Dominikanerstr. is the **Domplatz,** the center of ancient Bamberg. The **Dom** itself, dating from 1004, began Romanesque and ended up Gothic. Rounded choirs cap both ends of the church. Inside is the mysterious horse-and-rider statue called the *Bamberger Reiter* and a wooden Christmas altar by the master carver Veit Stoss. (Open daily 9am-6pm, except during services. Half-hour organ concerts Sat. at noon. Free.) Across the square, the **Neue Residenz,** Bamberg's former episcopal residence, poses baroquely; from its **rose garden,** the town is a sea of roofs. (Palace open daily 9am-noon and 1:30-5pm; Oct.-March daily 9am-noon and 1:30-4pm. Admission DM2.50, students DM1.50.) The tourist office at Geyerwörthstr. 3 (tel. (0951) 210 40) is a short jaunt from the train station. (Open Mon.-Fri. 9am-6pm, Sat. 9am-5pm.) Bamberg's hostels are far from the center of town, but both are unusually clean and pleasant. To reach **Wolfsschlucht (IYHF),** Oberer Leinritt 70 (tel. (0951) 560 02), take bus #18 from Promenade to Bug; get off at "Am Regnitzufer." (Reception open 3-5pm. Curfew 10pm. Juniors only, DM14. Open Feb. to mid-Dec.) **Stadion (IYHF),** Pödeldorferstr. 178 (tel. (0951) 123 77), is a newer hostel near the stadium. Take bus #2 to Stadion. (Reception open 4-7pm. Lockout 9am-4pm. Curfew 10pm. Juniors only, DM13.50. Open April-Sept. Call ahead.) The **Maiselbräustübl,** Obere Königstr. 38 (tel. (0951) 255 03) has large rooms overlooking a serene courtyard. (Singles DM30. Doubles DM55, with shower DM65. Breakfast included, delectable dinners from DM9.) The university **mensa,** centrally located at Ausstr. 37, off Grüner Markt, serves the cheapest edible meals in town at DM8. Any student ID will do. (Open Nov.-July 11:30am-2pm.) Vegetarians will connipt with joy at the all-you-can-eat salad bar at **Hofbräustübl "La Bamba",** Geyerswörthplatz 1, every Wednesday and Thursday after 6pm.

Frequent trains connect Bamberg to Würzburg (DM21) and Nuremberg (DM14.40).

Baden-Württemberg

Two of the most prominent German stereotypes—the brooding, romantic one put forth by the Brothers Grimm and the more modern economic variety engendered by Mercedes-Benz—both come to a head in Baden-Württemburg. Rural custom and tradition still persist in the hinterlands of the Black Forest and the Swabian Jura—home of cuckoo clocks and pretzels—while the modern capital city of Stuttgart helps make Baden-Württemberg the richest German province, the healthiest steed in Germany's economic Ride of the Valkyries. The region also hosts the ancient university towns of Freiburg, Tübingen and Heidelberg—as well as the snooty millionaires' resort of Baden-Baden, whose vaunted edifices form a stereotype all their own.

Stuttgart

Perhaps more than the tri-colored flag, Stuttgart symbolizes the prosperous, stable, and democratic "New Germany" that rose from the ashes of the Third Reich to pump post-war Europe's economic heart. Many of the flashy cars and high-tech appliances that grace German kitchens are designed and produced here. Though it lacks architectural monuments, Stuttgart's refined cultural offerings and refreshingly laid-back vitality make the city a lively and enjoyable stop.

Stuttgart's few historically notable buildings and a wealth of excellent museums span the massive gardens and stately plazas of the **Schloßgarten** and **Schloßplatz,** accessible through the Arnulf-Klett-Passage to the right of the train station. Lie on the grass in the sun or wander over to the superb **Staatsgalerie,** across from the Schloßgarten at Adenauer-Str. 30, which contains an excellent modern collection including works by Picasso, Kandinsky, Beckmann and Dalí. (Open Wed. and Fri.-Sun. 10am-5pm, Tues. and Thurs. 10am-8pm. Free.) The imposing baroque **Neues Schloß** (new palace) is now an office building, but the 16th-century **Altes Schloß** (old palace) houses the **Landesmuseum,** a collection of regional art and artifacts. (Open Tues. and Thurs.-Sun. 10am-5pm, Wed. 10am-7pm. Free.)

Stuttgart's most popular museums display expensive art works of a wholly different sort. The **Gottlieb Daimler Museum** is housed in the workshop where Herr Daimler, the inventor of the automobile, built the first generation of Mercedes-Benzes. (Open Tues.-Sun. 9am-5pm. Free. Take bus #56 to the Stadion stop, or S-Bahn #1 to Neckarstadion.) Not to be outdone, Dr. Porsche created the **Porsche-Museum.** (Open Mon.-Fri. 9am-noon and 1:30-5pm. Free. Take S-Bahn #6 to

"Neuwirkshaus," direction "Wiel der Stadt.") For more high value-added exhibitions, visit the **Haus der Wirtschaft,** Willi-Bleicher-Str. 19, which showcases the region's contributions to technology and product innovation. (Take U-Bahn #4 to Berlinerplatz. Open Tues.-Sun. 11am-6pm. Free.)

The **tourist office,** Königstr. 1 (tel. (0711) 222 80), directly next to the escalator up from the Arnulf-Klett-Passage, finds rooms for free and provides the useful brochure *Übernachtung in Stuttgart.* With this and a series of free pamphlets on services and entertainment for young travelers, courtesy of *Jugendinformation Stuttgart,* you should be set. The bilingual *Monatsspiegel* (DM1.90) lists museum hours, cultural events and musical performances and includes a guide to restaurants and nightlife. Maps (DM1), bus and train schedules are also available. (Open May-Oct. Mon.-Sat. 8:30am-10pm, Sun. 11am-6pm; Nov.-Dec. Mon.-Sat. 8:30am-10pm, Sun. 1-6pm; Jan.-April Mon.-Sat. 8:30am-10pm.) Exchange money, make international phone calls and pick up Poste Restante at the main **Post Office** on Bolzstr., a few blocks south of the main station (open Mon.-Fri. 8am-6pm, Sat. 8:30am-12:30pm, Sun. 11am-noon). The **American Express** office, Lautenschlagerstr. 3 (tel. (0711) 208 90), is one block south of the station. (Open Mon.-Fri. 9am-5:30pm, Sat. 9am-noon.) Tickets for Stuttgart's public transportation are a hefty DM2.20; a *Tageskarte*—valid for all trains and buses for 24 hours—is DM11. Railpasses are valid on S-Bahn suburban commuter trains.

Accommodations around the pedestrian zone and train station cater to customers used to paying top-mark for creature comforts, while most of Stuttgart's budget beds are located on the ridges surrounding the city and are easily accessible by tram. The **Jugendherberge (IYHF),** Haußmannstr. 27 (tel. (0711) 24 15 83; entrance on Kernerstr.), is left of the station on Schillerstr. and up the hill; otherwise take U-Bahn #15 or #16 (direction "Heumaden"), and get off at Eugensplatz. (Reception open noon-11pm. Curfew 11:30pm. Juniors DM15. Seniors DM18.) If the hostel is packed with rampaging school groups, head to the quiet, delightful **Jugendgästehaus Stuttgart,** Richard-Wagner-Str. 2 (tel. (0711) 24 11 32). Take U-Bahn #15 (direction "Heumaden") to Bubenbad. (Reception open Mon.-Fri. 8:30am-6pm and 6:30-10:30pm, Sat.-Sun. 11am-noon and 6:30-10pm. Spotless singles with plenty of elbow room DM35. Doubles and triples DM30 per person. Breakfast, showers and lockers included. Key deposit DM20.) Camp at **Campingplatz Stuggart,** Mercedesstr. 40 (tel. (0711) 55 66 96), Cannstatter Wasen, on the river. (DM5.50 per person, DM4-5 per tent, DM3 per car. Showers DM2.) Take S-Bahn #1 or 2 (direction "Obere Ziegelei" or "Fellbach").

At the **University Mensa,** Holzgartenstr. 9-11, quantity compensates for quality (meals DM3-4). You must get a Mensa credit card at the entrance and leave a deposit. (Open 11:15am-2pm; Aug.-Sept. 11:15am-1:30pm. Student ID required.) Eberhardstraße, dotted with restaurants, bars and **Gaststätten,** is the place to go for inexpensive cuisine of all kinds. **Iden,** Eberhardstr. 1 (tel. (0711) 23 59 89), serves cheap, good vegetarian food, cafeteria-style. (Open Mon.-Fri. 11am-9pm, Sat. 10am-4pm.)

The **Staatstheater,** just across the plaza from the *Neues Schloß,* is Stuttgart's most famous theater (tickets available Mon.-Fri. 9am-1pm and 2-5pm; DM10-90). There are at least 25 other local theaters, and tickets for them are usually much cheaper (DM10-25, students DM5-15). The tourist office provides schedules and sells tickets. Local bands provide live music of all sorts at **Life,** a music bar at Bolzstr. 10 near the post office. (Cover varies. Open Sun.-Thurs. 5pm-2am, Fri.-Sat. 5pm-5am.) The walls sweat and the music blasts at **OZ,** a popular hard-rock dance spot at Büchenstr. 10 (entrance on Kronprinzstr.; open Fri. 8pm-5am, Sat. 8pm-8am, Sun. 6pm-midnight). **Roxy,** Königstr. 51 at the corner of Breitestr., plays lighter disco and pop music for a crowd of all sexual orientations. (Open Sun.-Thurs. 8pm-4am, Fri.-Sat. 8pm-5am.)

Southwestern Germany's transport hub, Stuttgart has direct rail links to most major German cities. Trains roll out to Munich 30 times per day.

Tübingen

Left-wing graffiti smeared across 15th-century public buildings leaves no doubt that Tübingen is one of Germany's renowned ancient academic towns. Because nearly one third of the city's residents are affiliated with its 500-year-old university, Tübingen has retained the graceful aloofness of its intellectual origins. The students leave in August and September, but at other times you will find Tübingen buzzing with young people and short on tourists.

The hilly, twisting alleys and gabled houses of the town center surround the 15th-century **Stiftskirche** (open daily 9am-5pm). The church's **chancel** contains the ornate tombs of 14 members of the House of Württemberg, and the rickety stairs of the adjacent **tower** can be climbed for a broad view in all directions (chancel and tower admission DM1 each, students DM0.50 each). The ornate, painted façade of the **Rathaus** faces the old market square in the middle of the old city. On top of the hill that rudely separates the university from most of the city stands the **Hohentübingen Castle,** which can be visited only on weekends. (Open April-Oct. Tours only, Sat. at 5pm, Sun. at 11am and 3pm. Admission DM3.) Without a tour, you can still go out on the balcony for a view of the old town. From the Rathaus, follow signs marked "Schloß" leading up to the left in order to reach the castle. One block north of the Rathaus on Kornhausstr. is the half-timbered **Kornhaus,** which houses the newly-opened **Stadtmuseum** (open Tues.-Sat. 3-6pm, Sun. 11am-1pm and 3-6pm. Free.) Along the river, the tree-lined path of the **Platanenallee**—which runs the length of a man-made island on the Neckar—makes for a pleasant walk with a scenic view of the *Altstadt.* On the northern riverbank is the **Hölderlinturm,** a tower where the 18th-century poet Friederich Hölderlin lived out the final 36 years of his life in a state of clinical insanity. The tower now houses a memorial museum (open Tues.-Fri. 10am-noon and 3-5pm, Sat.-Sun. 2-5pm. Admission DM2, students DM1). For dreamily romantic sightseeing, rent a boat from **Bootsvermietung Tübingen,** on the river under the tourist office. (Tel. (07071) 315 29; rowboats for 1 to 3 people; DM9 per hour. Open mid-April to Sept. daily 10am-8pm.) Those pining for that other university in England can rent punts; inquire at the tourist office.

Tübingen's small but well-staffed **tourist office** (tel. (07071) 350 11) is located on the south side of the Eberhardsbrücke (bridge). From the front of the train station, turn right and walk to Karlstr., then turn left and walk to the river. The building is on the right side of the bridge. The office books hotel lodgings for DM4.50 and lodgings in private homes for DM3. (Open May-Oct. Mon.-Fri. 9am-6:30pm, Sat. 9am-5pm, Sun. 2-5pm; Nov.-April Mon.-Fri. 9am-6:30pm, Sat. 9am-5pm). A kiosk in front of the station offers city maps (open Mon.-Fri. 7am-6:30pm, Sat. 8am-3pm). **Mitfahrzentrale** (tel. (07071) 267 89) is inside a photocopy center at Mühlstr. 12 (open Mon.-Fri. 9am-6:30pm, Sat. 9am-1pm, Sun. 10am-1pm).

The large, worn **Jugendherberge (IYHF),** Gartenstr. 22-2 (tel. (07071) 230 02), overlooks the River Neckar just downstream from the bridge at the tourist office. Take bus #11 from the station (DM2.50) to the Jugendherberge stop. (Reception open 7:30-9am, 5-8pm, and 9:30-9:45pm. Strict curfew 11:30pm. Members only. Juniors DM14.50. Seniors DM17.) The only affordable private lodgings near the old city are the clean, commodious rooms at the somewhat scruffy-looking **Gasthof zum Ritter,** am Stadtgraben 25 (tel. (07071) 225 02). After crossing the bridge, continue for 10 minutes, then turn left. (Singles DM45. Doubles DM85.) Most of the other accommodations in the city are not priced to please, except for rooms rented out by private families (listed at the tourist office.) **Camp** at **Rappernberghalde,** on the river (tel. (07071) 431 45); go upstream from the town or left from the station, cross the river on the Alleenbrücke, then turn left again (DM6 per person, DM4-5 per tent; open April-mid-Oct. daily 8am-1pm and 3-10pm).

Tübingen's students keep a number of superb yet inexpensive restaurants busy. The student-run **Marquardtei,** Herrenbergerstr. 34, (tel. (07071) 433 86) serves whole-wheat pizza and a vast selection of vegetarian and meat dishes in a politically liberal, wood-paneled environment (open Sun.-Fri. 11:30am-1am, Sat. 6pm-1am. Entrees DM6-15). In the *Altstadt,* **Restaurant beim Hölderlinturm** at Bursagasse 4 (tel. (07071) 512 27) cooks up Swabian specialties for DM9.50-24. (Beer DM3-4. Open daily 11am-2pm and 5:30-10:30pm.) During weekdays, **Zum alten Fritz,** at Gartenstr. 13 (tel. (07071) 279 74) just up the street from the youth hostel, serves lunch for under DM10 (Open Sun.-Fri. 11am-2:30pm and 5pm-midnight. Dinners DM15-25).

Nightlife isn't hard to find in Tübingen; nearly every block claims one or two student pubs. The **Zentrum-Zoo** disco, popular with students but occasionally overrun by a younger crowd, brings down the house nightly on Schliefmühleweg 86, in the heart of the new city. (Beer DM3.50-4. Cover varies, usually DM4.) **Jazzkeller,** Haaggasse 15, caters to a more refined musical palate nightly between 9pm and 2am (cover varies). Just down the street at Haaggasse 24 is **Alter Simpel,** a typical student pub proffering beer, drinks and beer for DM3-4.

Black Forest (Schwarzwald)

Stretching west of the Rhine from Karlsruhe to Basel, the Black Forest looms large in the German cultural consciousness. Fairy tales, storybooks and romantic lyrical poetry owe their inspiration to the tangled expanse of evergreens where Hansel and Gretel were left to stew; the forest received its name from the eerie, pine-shadowed darkness that led the dear kiddies astray. The area remained remarkably isolated from the rest of the world until early in this century: venerable farm houses sporting trademark straw roofs appear around every turn in the road, as do venerable farmers sporting traditional rural garb. The cuckoo clock originated here too, as the numerous souvenir shops attest. Hiking is a favorite activity; trails are frequent and well-marked, and many are used in winter for cross-country skiing.

The main entry points to the Black Forest are Freiburg to the southwest, Baden-Baden to the northwest, and Stuttgart to the east. Public transportation is thin in this mountain region; rail lines run along the perimeter from Baden-Baden to Freiburg and east from Freiburg to Donaueschingen and Stuttgart, but many of the innermost regions are accessible only by often-infrequent bus service (check return connection times in advance before setting off on day trips). Many of the bus lines are privately owned, so railpasses may not be valid.

The undisputed metropolis of the Black Forest, **Freiburg** was accidentally bombed in 1940 by bungling *Luftwaffe* pilots who mistook the city for a French border town. Historically and culturally at least, this is a relatively easy mistake to make. A political football that has spent most of its 800-odd years under Austrian or French control, modern Freiburg maintains a more relaxed and multicultural atmosphere than perhaps any other German city. The **tourist office** at Rotteckring 14 (tel. (0761) 368 90 90), 2 blocks down Eisenbahnstr. from the train station, will find rooms for DM3 and distributes the wonderfully comprehensive *Freiburg Official Guide* (DM3, in German or English). (Open May-Oct. Mon.-Sat. 9am-9:30pm, Sun. 10am-2pm; Nov.-April Mon.-Fri. 9am-6pm, Sat. 9am-3pm, Sun. 10am-noon.)

The pride of Freiburg is the **Münster,** a tremendous stone cathedral built at intervals between the 13th and 16th centuries. Its 116m tower can be climbed for DM1.50, offering dizzying views of the city and the forest beyond. A stroll through the surrounding *Altstadt* is certain to uncover several of the **Bächle,** narrow open streams of swift-flowing water that run throughout the city. In medieval times, these open gutters were used to water cattle and protect against fires; today, they exist only to soak the shoes of unwary tourists. Two medieval towers—the **Schwabentor** and the **Martinstor**—still stand within a few blocks of one another in the southeast corner of the *Altstadt.* From the Schwabentor, take the pedestrian overpass across the heavily trafficked Schloßbergring and climb the **Schloßberg** for an excellent view of the city. Four city museums in the blocks between the two towers and the cathedrals cater to many tastes. The **Augustiner Museum** on Augustinerplatz contains a hefty collection, mostly of medieval religious artifacts. Across the square, the **Mu-**

seum of Natural History and the **Museum of Ethnology** share a building at Gerberau 32; the ethnology museum's displays of North and South American Indian culture are worth sampling. Two blocks to the south at Marienstr. 10a is the **Museum of Modern Art,** hung with a modest collection of 20th-century German artists. (All museums open Tues.-Fri. 9:30am-5pm, Sat.-Sun. 10:30am-5pm. Free.)

Accommodations in Freiburg tend toward the expensive; the tourist office has a list of cheaper private rooms (DM20-30), but most require a stay of at least 3 nights. The **Jugendherberge (IYHF),** Kartäuserstr. 151 (tel. (0761) 676 56), offers modern accommodation in an arboreal setting. Take tram #1 (direction "Littenweiler") to the Römerhof stop, walk down Fritz-Geiges-Str., cross the stream, and turn right. (Reception open 7am-11:30pm. Curfew 11:30pm. Members only. Juniors DM15.50, seniors DM18.50.) Take tram #1 (direction "Littenweiler") to the end, then bus #17 to **Haus Lydia Kalchtaler,** Peterhof 11 (tel. (0761) 671 19), where doubles are only DM36 (showers DM2). **Hotel Schemmer,** Eschholzstr. 63 (tel. (0761) 27 24 24), has friendly management and a central location. From the train station, take the overpass that crosses over the tracks, then go past the church and turn left. (Singles DM40. Doubles with shower DM70.) **Camp** at **Hirzberg,** Kartäuserstr. 99 (tel. (0761) 350 54). Take tram #1 (direction "Littenweiler") to Messplatz. (DM5 per person, DM3.50 per tent. Open April to mid-Oct.)

A truly unique culinary experience awaits at **Toast Reich,** at Münsterplatz 14 next to the cathedral. Europe's first—and possibly only—toasteria, it features an eclectic menu of open-faced combinations for DM7-15 (open daily 9am-midnight). For inexpensive Italian food, try **Milano** at Schusterstr. 7 in the *Altstadt* (open daily 11am-midnight). Enjoy a beer (DM4) or a local vintage (DM5.30) on a hillside terrace overlooking the city at **Greiffenegg-Schlößle** at Schloßbergring 3 (open Tues.-Sun. 10am-midnight).

Thirty km east of Freiburg is the resort town of **Titisee,** along the lake of the same name. The train line between Freiburg and Titisee runs through the **Höllental** (Hell's Valley), which nearly lives up to the dramatism of its name—the ride is one of the most scenic in all of Germany. The Titisee is an attractive lake set against a backdrop of dark pine-forested ridges that were cruelly bludgeoned some time ago by a massive influx of consumer tourism. At the very least, no other locale in the Black Forest combines natural beauty with so many modern conveniences. **Tourist information** is in the **Kurhaus** on Jägerstr. (tel. (07651) 81 01); to reach the building, turn right in front of the station and walk to the first intersection, then turn right at the entrance to the pedestrian zone and look for the flagpoles that dot the Kurhaus lawn. The office will book rooms for DM4 and provides a map for DM6.80 that details all of the 130-plus km of trails in the vicinity of the lake (summer hours Mon.-Fri. 8am-6pm, Sat. 10am-noon and 3-5pm, Sun. 10am-noon). Paddleboats can be rented along the shore by Seestr. for DM8-12 per hr., and guided boat tours depart regularly from the same place (approx. 25 min., DM5). **Jugendherberge Veltishof (IYHF),** Bruderhalde 27 (tel. (07652) 238), is comfortable but out in the boonies at the far end of the lake. Catch one of the elusive Bundesbahn buses (direction Todtnau) from the main station to the "Feuerwehrheim" stop, or brave the 30-min. walk along the main road from the Kurhaus. (Reception open 5-6pm and 7:30-8pm. Curfew 10pm. Juniors DM14.50, seniors DM17.) Wake up by the water at **Campingplatz Weiherhof** (tel. (07652) 14 68), around the corner from the hostel (sites DM8.50, DM5-6 per person).

Thirty minutes south of Titisee by train is the larger, less touristed **Schluchsee,** whose sprightly **Jugendherberge (IYHF),** Im Wolfsgrund 28, has rooms named after wildflowers and an ideal location right on the lake. From the station, turn left and follow the tracks across the bridge. (Tel. (07656) 329. Reception opens at 5pm. Juniors DM15, seniors DM18).

At the center of the Hochschwarzwald (High Black Forest) is **Triberg,** a hiker's paradise that boasts over 200km of trails in its surrounding hills. From the train station, the city center is a 10-15 min. walk uphill; turn right in front of the station, head down the stairs at the overpass and follow the road up past the large post office building. Triberg's prime attraction is the highest waterfall in Germany, located at the top of Hauptstr. Mobs of sightseers shell out DM2 (students DM1) to see the waterfall plunge 162m in 7 separate drops (open daily 9am-7pm). Triberg's **tourist office** is in the Kurhaus at Luisenstr. 10 (tel. (07722) 812 30), 1½ blocks to the left of the waterfall's entrance. The office books rooms and sells city maps in English and German for DM1 and detailed hiking maps in German for DM6. (Open Mon.-Fri. 8am-noon and 2-5pm, Sat. 10am-noon.) One block from the waterfall in the opposite direction, the **Schwarzwald Museum** details the art, culture and day-to-day life of Black Forest denizens both past and present. (Open daily 9am-6pm. Admission DM4, students DM2.) Triberg's **Jugendherberge (IYHF)** (tel. (07722) 41 10) is situated in a scenic location on Rohrbacherstr. 35, but the journey there—a grueling 20 min. walk uphill from the waterfall or 40 min. from the station—may dismay the heavily laden. (Reception open 5-7pm. Curfew 10pm. Members only. Juniors DM15, seniors DM17.50.)

The dark, meandering valleys of the Northern Black Forest, spanned by an extensive network of trails, are a hiker's dream. The region's transportation hub is **Freudenstadt,** a town of quiet residential neighborhoods that makes a good base for excursions into the heart of the surrounding darkness. The town's spacious **Marktplatz** is lined by arcaded storefronts that are reproductions of older buildings torched to the ground by French troops in 1945. The southwest corner of the square is dominated by the copper-domed **Stadtkirche,** whose unique construction—the two aisles stand at right angles, with the altar in the middle—reveals the moral fiber of its founders, who planned segregated services that both men and women could attend without any temptation to make eyes during lengthy sermons (open daily 10am-noon and 2-4pm). If long hours on the train or the trails have left you feeling tacky, head for the **Panorama Bad** on Ludwig-John-Str. (tel. (07441) 576 20), a swimming pool and hot tub complex with eight holes to choose from. (Open Mon.-Fri. 9am-10pm, Sat.-Sun. 9am-8pm. Last entry 1½ hr. before closing. Admission DM8, students DM6.)

Freudenstadt's **tourist office** *(Kurverwaltung)* is in the modern-looking *Kurhaus* complex at Promenade Platz 1 (tel. (07441) 86 40). From the main train station, it's a 15-minute walk uphill; bear left and take Bahnhofstr. to Turnhallestr., then turn left and keep walking to the first large intersection. The office will book rooms at no charge (open Mon.-Fri. 9am-6pm, Sat. 9am-noon, Sun. 9:30am-12:30pm). The **Jugendherberge (IYHF),** Eugen-Nägele-Str. 69 (tel. (07441) 77 20), is a tile-and-concrete edifice constructed in the Early Boredom style. (Reception at 5-7pm, 9pm and 10pm. Curfew 10pm. Members only. Juniors DM14.50, seniors DM17.) **Gasthaus am Dobel,** Gottlieb-Daimler-Str. 71 (tel. (07441) 68 18), is a student house with soccer-happy management. (Reception open 9:30am-midnight. Singles, doubles and quads DM25 per person).

Lake Constance (Bodensee)

Ancient castles, manicured islands and endless opportunities to tan to a crisp draw Germans, Austrians, Swiss, and whatever you call people from Liechtenstein to the vast Bodensee all summer long. The entire northern (German) bank harbors lovely lakeside towns like Meersburg and Lindau, and enjoys dramatic panoramas of the Alps on the other side. The southern banks belong to Austria and Switzerland.

Spanning the Rhine's exit from the lake, the elegant university city of **Konstanz** numbers among the few German cities never struck by a bomb. The narrow streets wind around painted façades in the center of town, while promenades and gabled and turreted 19th-century houses create an aura of undeniable elegance along the river. When the sun shines, Konstanz's three free public beaches overflow. **Strandbad Horn** is the largest and most popular (take bus #5). The university's beach is where the cool people frolic, suits optional. (Take bus #4 to Egg and walk past the playing fields.) In inclement weather, people head next door to **Freizeitbad Jakob,** Wilhelm-von-Scholz-Weg 2 (tel. (07531) 611 63), an ultra-modern indoor-outdoor pool complex with thermal baths and fake-and-bake sun-lamps north of the Rhine, about a 30-minute walk along the waterfront from the train station. (Open daily 9am-9pm. Admission DM7, students DM4.) Boats run every hour from behind the train station to the Freizeitbad and the Freibad Horn. (DM5. Boats run June-Aug. daily 10:50am-5:50pm; May and Sept. Sun. only.) The **tourist office** (tel. (07531) 28 43 76), in the arcade to the right of the train station, finds rooms (DM40-60) for a DM5 fee and provides an excellent walking map. (Open Mon.-Fri. 8am-8pm, Sat. 9:30am-1:30pm and 4-7pm, Sun. 10am-1pm; Nov.-April Mon.-Fri. 8:45am-noon and 2-6pm.) Konstanz has two **IYHF youth hostels.** The one in Konstanz proper, at Allmannshohe 18 (tel. (07531) 332 60), juts out of the ground like a vast concrete grain elevator, with decaying quarters and clean bathrooms. Take bus #4 (DM1.80) from the Marktstätte stop, just around the corner from the post office in front of the station, to the Jugendherberge stop. (Reception open 5-7pm. Curfew 11:30pm. Juniors DM15. Seniors DM17.50.) The other hostel is in a lovely old house on the water in Kreuzlingen, a Swiss suburb of Konstanz. Take bus #8 to the Kreuzlingen train station, and walk toward the waterfront, following the signs.

Fill up on Konstanz's cheapest grub at the **University Mensa,** where lunches, including dessert and a view of the lake, cost just DM2.50. Take bus #9 from the station. (Open Mon.-Fri. 8am-7pm, Sat. 8am-1pm. No student ID required.) Stroll through the area around **Rheingasse,** the oldest part of Konstanz, and now the center of its vibrant alternative scene—complete with health food stores, leftist graffiti and student cafés.

Ships depart about once per hour from behind the train station to all the ports on the Bodensee. Consider the cruise that stops at Meersburg, Mainau (a flora-carpeted island), Unteruhldigen, and Überlingen. (Daily June-late Sept. Round-trip DM13.20, half price with railpasses.) For more information and schedules, contact the **Weiße Bodenseeflotte** counter (tel. (07531) 28 13 89) in the harbor behind the train station.

Central Germany

Frankfurt am Main

A city of skyscrapers and investment bankers, Frankfurt belongs more properly to the Germany of the future than the Germany of the past. It has the reputation—among both non-Germans and Germans alike—of being the most Americanized city in Europe, a dubious distinction given its recent coronation as the crime capital of Germany. However, it's still a kindergarten compared to Manhattan. Not much of historical Frankfurt survived the carpet bombings of WWII, but the treasures of the surviving *Altstadt,* coupled with an extraordinary variety of museums and one of the best zoos in the world, reward a few days' stay.

The train station is in the middle of Frankfurt's moderately sleazy red-light district; the rest of the city is considerably more amenable. What's left of old Frankfurt is in the **Römerberg** district, a 15-minute walk down Münchener Str. from the station. At the east end stands the **Römer,** a distinctly gabled red sandstone structure that's served as Frankfurt's city hall since 1405. The upper floors contain the **Kaisersaal,** a former imperial banquet hall whose walls are adorned with portraits of the 52 German emperors from Charlemagne to Franz II (open Mon.-Sat. 9am-6pm, Sun. 10am-1pm; admission DM1). The west end of Römerberg is dominated by the Gothic **Dom,** a huge cathedral that was the site of coronation ceremonies for German emperors from 1562 to 1792. The view from the Dom's tower is well worth the climb to the top (open April-Oct. 9am-12:30pm and 2:30-6:30pm; admission DM1). Near the Römer at Saalgasse 19 is the **Historisches Museum,** which contains a first-rate series of exhibitions on the history of the city and the larger German nation. (Open Tues.-Sun. 10am-5pm, Wed. 10am-8pm. Free.) A few blocks northwest of the Römer at Großer Hirschgraben 23-25 stands the **Goethe Haus,** birthplace of Germany's premier man of letters and now a carefully preserved museum whose comfortable and spacious interior proves you don't have to suffer to produce great art. (Open Mon.-Sat. 9am-6pm, Sun. 10am-1pm. Admission DM3, students DM2).

From Römerberg, it's an easy 10-minute walk across the Eiserner Steg footbridge to the **Museumsufer,** a string of seven museums along Schaumainkai on the left bank of the Main. There's something for everyone here, including collections devoted to ethnography, architecture, filmmaking, and a postal museum; the highlight is the **Städel,** one of the top art galleries in Europe. (All museums open Tues.-Sun. 10am-5pm, Wed. 10am-8pm. All free except the Städel, which costs DM6, students DM3, free on Sun.). For less cerebral entertainment, head to Frankfurt's four-star **Zoo** on the eastern side of town (U-Bahn #6 or 7 to the Zoo stop). Feeding time for the apes (daily at 4pm) is a must-see—if you ever questioned the theory of evolution, this should erase all doubt (open daily 8am-7pm; Oct. to mid-March 8am-5pm; admission DM9.50, students DM4.50).

The **Alt Sachsenhausen** district between Dreieichstr. and Brückenstr. is crawling with pubs, patio bars and restaurants. Frankfurt's renowned jazz scene centers around Kleine Bockenheimer Str.—also known as Jazzgasse—in the city center. The most famous of the venues is **Der Jazzkeller,** Kleine Bockenheimer Str. 18a. (Tel. (069) 28 85 37. Open Tues.-Sun. 9pm-3am. Cover varies.) Gay nightlife flourishes in the area between Zeil and Bleichstr.

Frankfurt's airport and train station are among the busiest in Europe. From the airport, S-Bahn lines #14 and 15 travel every 10 min. to the train station (DM3.80 from a blue automat, Eurail and InterRail valid). Direct and frequent trains leave the station for all the other major cities in Germany and the rest of central Europe. Those hitchhiking to Munich should take bus #36 or 960 from Konstablerwache south to the *Autobahn.* For all other directions, take tram #13 or 61 to Stadion, and continue in the same direction along Mörfelder Landstr. **Mitfahrzentrale,** Baselerstr. 7 (tel. 23 64 44), is located 200m from the Hauptbahnhof (open Mon.-Fri. 8am-6pm, Sat. 8am-noon).

The **tourist office** (tel. (069) 21 23 88 49) in the train station across from track 23 will book rooms for DM3 (open Mon.-Sat. 8am-10pm, Sun. 9:30am-8pm; Nov.-March Mon.-Sat. 8am-9pm, Sun. 9:30am-8pm). A second office is in the airport Halle B (open daily 7am-10pm). **American Express** (tel. (069) 21 05 48) is at Kaiserstr. 8 (open Mon.-Fri. 9:30am-5:30pm, Sat. 9am-noon). There's a 24-hr. **post office** on the second floor of the train station; fetch Poste Restante at counter 6 or 7 of the main branch at Zeil 110 (U-Bahn: Hauptwache; open Mon.-Fri. 8am-6pm, Sat. 8am-noon). Exchange currency in the airport Halle B (open daily 7:30am-9pm) or in the train station (open daily 6:30am-10pm).

The **IYHF youth hostel,** Deutschherrnufer 12 (tel. (069) 61 90 58) is clean and conveniently located near the Sachsenhausen pubs. From the station, take bus #46 (DM1.80, DM2.40 during morning and evening rush hours) to Frankensteinerplatz. The hostel is 50m west in the large yellow building. After 7:30pm, take tram #16 to Textorstr., then walk north to Deutschherrnufer. (Reception open 1-10pm. Lockout 9am-1pm. Curfew midnight. Juniors (here under 20) DM17.50, seniors DM21. Security deposit DM10.) **Pension Brukner,** Stuttgarter Str. 9 (tel. (069) 25 35 45), 3 blocks behind the station to the right, has clean rooms and pleasant management. (Reception open until 3 or 4pm. Singles DM49. Doubles DM82.) **Pension Lohmann,** Stuttgarter Str. 31 (tel. (069) 23 25 34), is roomy and located even closer to the station. (Closed in July. Singles DM36. Doubles DM64.) **Pension Backer,** Mendelssohnstr. 92 (tel. (069) 74 79 92), is in a nice location near the university. Take the U-Bahn to Westend or tram #19 (direction "Ginnheim") to the Siesmayer/Mendelssohnstr. stop. (Singles DM40. Doubles DM60.)

Marburg

The Brothers Grimm spun their fairy tales in the rolling hills around Marburg; from a distance the town seems more of their world than ours. The first Protestant university was founded here in 1527, and is the life of Marburg today. Its alumni list reads like a syllabus for an intellectual history course: Martin Heidegger, Boris Pasternak, T.S. Eliot, and Robert Bunsen (as in the burners) are but a few. Climb the endless narrow staircases of the *Altstadt* to the **Landgrafenschloß,** former haunt of the infamous Teutonic Knights and scene of a 1529 tiff between Martin Luther and Ulrich Zwingli; an epidemic in the town infected their dispute over communication with a fear of contagion as well as the fear of God, and the rival reformers irrevocably split. (Open Tues.-Sun. 11am-1pm and 2-5pm. Free.) **Elisabethkirche,** the oldest Gothic church in Germany (1283), commemorates the town's patron, a countess-and-widowed-child-bride-turned-altruist (and you thought German had long words). Her reliquary is so overdone, it's glorious. (Open April-Sept. daily 9am-6pm; Oct. daily 9am-5pm; Nov.-March Mon.-Sat. 10am-4pm, Sun. 11am-4pm. Admission DM2, students DM1.) To get there, cross the bridge opposite the train station and take a left at Elisabethstr. Built on the banks of the Lahn, Marburg is served by frequent trains from Frankfurt (1 hr.) and Kassel (1-1½ hr.). The **tourist office** (tel. (06421) 20 12 62), to the right of the train station, finds rooms from DM30, free of charge. (Open Mon.-Fri. 8am-12:30pm and 2-5:30pm, Sat. 9:30am-noon; Nov.-March Mon.-Fri. 8:30am-12:30pm and 2-5pm.) A hospitable riverside **Jugendherberge (IYHF),** Jahnstr. 1 (tel. (06421) 234 61), keeps watch over the *Altstadt* and the castle above. City buses run from the station to Rudolfsplatz; from there follow Am Grün to An der Weide, turn left and cross both bridges. (Reception open 3-8pm. Curfew 11:30pm, Nov.-March 10pm. Juniors DM16. Seniors DM19.) Call (06421) 194 14 at any hour for recorded information on vacant hotel rooms. **Camping Lahnaue** (tel. (06421) 213 31) is on the Lahn River; take bus #1 toward Sommerbad (DM4 per person. DM3 per tent). The brilliant **Blaue Welle** laundromat shares its quarters with **Bistro Waschbreft,** at the corner of Jäger and Güttenbergstr.; have a beer and *brötchen* while the dryer spins. (Laundry open Mon.-Sat. 8am-11pm, Sun. 5-11pm. Bistro open Mon.-Fri. 9am-1pm, Sat. 9am-midnight, Sun. 5pm-midnight.) The *Altstadt's* nighttime crowds drop by **Café Bartuß,** Bartußstr. 5, for Teuer on tap, bottled Guinness and a late-night vegetarian dinner (DM8-10; open daily 10am-1am). On the first Sunday in July, Marburgers drink an early-morning beer at the Frühschopper Fest, on the Markt. (Open 11am-dusk.)

Local trains from Marburg follow the Eder River through **Waldeck Forest**and Ederbergland. Regional information and excellent bike maps are available in the 1200-year-old garrison town of **Frankenberg,** 40 minutes away, at Bahnhofstr. 8-12 (tel. (06451) 521 69; open Mon.-Fri. 7:30am-3:30pm).

Heidelberg

In 1386, the sages of Heidelberg turned from illuminating manuscripts to illuminating young German minds. This, the oldest of Germany's university towns, is perhaps also the most quintessentially German. Set against a backdrop of wooded hills along an ancient river, the crumbling edifices of the once-majestic Schloß and the cobblestone streets of the *Altstadt* have a powerful magnetism that draws thousands of shutter-clicking, beer-swilling tourists every year.

Orientation and Practical Information

To get in to, out of, and around the city, buy a 36-hour Multi-ticket for the streetcars and buses (DM6) at the **HSB Verkauf-Stelle,** opposite the side entrance to the station; single rides are a ridiculous DM1.70.

Tourist Office: directly in front of the station (tel. 277 35). Rooms reserved for DM2 fee. Open March-Oct. Mon.-Sat. 9am-7pm, Sun. 10am-6pm; Nov.-Dec. Mon.-Sat. 9am-7pm, Sun. 10am-3pm.

Budget Travel: HS Reisebüros, am Bismarckplatz (tel. 271 51). Special student deals; any student ID will do. Open Mon.-Fri. 9am-12:30pm and 2-4pm, Sat. 9am-noon.

American Express: Friedrich-Ebert Anlage 16 (tel. 290 01). Open Mon.-Fri. 9am-5pm, Sat. 9am-noon. Banking services closed noon-2pm.

Post Office: Diagonally to the right across from the station. Open Mon.-Fri. 8am-6pm, Sat. 8am-noon. **Postal Code:** 6900.

Telephones: At the post office. Open Mon.-Fri. 8am-9pm, Sat. 8am-3pm, Sun. 10am-3pm. **City code:** 06221.

Trains: From the station, take tram #1 to Bismarckplatz, bus #33 to Kornmarkt, or bus #11 to Universitätsplatz.

Bike Rental: At the station. DM10, with railpass DM5. Open April-Sept. Mon.-Fri. 6:30am-7pm, Sat. 7:30am-5pm, Sun. 10am-5pm.

Hitchhiking: If you decide to hitch, walk to the western end of Bergheimerstr. for all directions. **Mitfahrzentrale,** Kurfürstenanlage 57 (tel. 246 46), 200m in front of the station. Open Mon.-Fri. 9am-5:30pm, Sat. 10am-2pm, Sun. 11am-2pm.

Laundromat: Wasch Salon SB, Post. Str. 49, next to Kurfürst Hotel. Wash DM6, dry DM1. Open Mon.-Sat. 7am-11pm.

Emergencies: Tel. 110 for all emergencies.

Police, Rohrbacherstr. 11 (tel. 52 00).

Accommodations, Camping, and Food

Heidelberg's cheap beds get snatched up in a flash; as usual, arrive early in summer. If Heidelberg fills up, the tourist office's listings in nearby Kirchheim (a 20-min. bus trip) may be worth investigating.

Jugendherberge (IYHF), Tiergartenstr. 5 (tel. 41 20 66). Take bus #33 from Bismarckplatz or the station; after 8pm, take tram #1 to the Chirurgisches Klinik, and then bus #330. The hostel is the first stop after the zoo. Reception open 7:30-9am and 3-11pm. Curfew 11:30pm. Lockout 9am-1pm. Juniors DM15.50. Seniors DM18.50.

Jeske Hotel, Mittelbadgasse 2 (tel. 237 33). From the station, take bus #33 to the Kornmarkt. Central location and sprightly, efficient management attract many students. 2- to 5-bed rooms DM20 per person. Showers DM2.

Hotel-Pension Schmitt, Blumenstr. 54. (tel. 272 96) A 10-min. walk from the station, just off Kurfürsten-Anlage. Large rooms, central location. Singles DM50. Doubles with shower DM100.

Pension Elite, Bunsenstr. 15 (tel. 257 34), between the station and the town center. Ample yet cozy rooms. Singles DM50. Doubles DM75-85. Book ahead.

Hotel Weisser Bock, Grosse Mantelgasse 24 (tel. 222 31). Fantastic location with peachy rooms. Singles DM50. Doubles with shower DM98. Breakfast included.

Camping: Haide (tel. (06223) 21 11) is between Ziegelhausen and Kleingemünd. Take bus #35, get off at the Orthopedic Clinic, and cross the river. DM5 per person and per tent.

Heidelberg's restaurants will flatten your wallet. Eschew the heavily touristed and wildly priced pedestrian area around Hauptstr. Many pubs and restaurants catering to students await you just beyond the pedestrian zone. Groceries are yours at **Handelshof,** Kurfürsten-Anlage 62, 200m in front of the train station on the right. (Open Mon.-Wed. and Fri. 8am-6:30pm, Thurs. 8am-8:30pm, Sat. 8am-2pm.)

Goldener Hecht, Steingasse 2, Am Brückenker, by the Alte Brücke. A 270-year-old Wagnerian pub. Filling meals DM20, appetizers DM7. Credit cards accepted.

Roter Ochsen, Hauptstr. 217. A student hangout family-owned for over a century. Bismarck and Mark Twain dissipated themselves, and so can you for DM4 per 0.4 liter. Meals 4.50-25DM. Open Mon.-Sat. 5pm-midnight.

Zum Sepp'l, Hauptstr. 213. Next door to Roter Ochsen with a similarly loud crowd. Meals 6-20DM, beer 4.30DM. Open daily 11am-midnight.

Sudpfanne, Hauptstr. 223. Door shaped like a keg. Excellent, filling meals DM7-25 and a menu (German only) the size of the Gutenberg Bible. Open Mon.-Fri. 4pm-midnight, Sat.-Sun. 11:30am-midnight.

Abel's Cafe and Weinstube, Hauptstr. 133, on Universitätsplatz. Winsome open-air café next to the old university. Beers DM4, meals 6-10DM. Open daily 10am-11pm, Sat. until 1am.

Higher Taste, Kornmarkt 9. Vegetarian meals for DM2-5. Open daily 10:45am-6:30pm.

Sights

The **Heidelberger Schloß,** first built in the early 13th century and laid waste by French troops in 1689, exists today in a state of partial ruin that conveys a sense of tragic beauty. It's easily reached by foot or by cable car *(Bergbahn),* which runs from Kornmarkt to the castle (round-trip DM3.50) and farther up to Königstuhl (from the base every 20 min. 9am-6:20pm, round-trip DM5.50). Fireworks light up the skies surrounding the castle on the first Saturday evening in June, July and September. (Castle open daily 9am-5pm. Tours 9am-noon and 1:30-4pm. Admission DM4, students DM2.) The obligatory tour includes a visit to the **Fass,** reputedly Germany's largest wine barrel. (Admission DM1, students DM0.50.) One of the princes who lived in the palace reportedly quaffed 30 liters of wine per day; he was also president of the German anti-alcoholism society. The **Apothekenmuseum,** also in the castle, features a 17th-century pharmacy and alchemist's laboratory. (Open daily 10am-5pm; Nov.-March Sat.-Sun. 11am-5pm. Admission DM2, students DM1.)

In town, most sights are clustered near the **Marktplatz,** a cobbled square surrounded by picturesque buildings. Notice **Hercules' Fountain,** where witches and heretics were burned in the 15th century. Here stand the two oldest structures in Heidelberg: the 15th-century **Heiliggeistkirche** and the 16th-century **Haus zum Ritter,** a charming Renaissance mansion that is now a fancy hotel. The stately **Rathaus** presides over the far end of the square. From the Marktplatz take Hauptstr. west for more camera-clinching; 5 blocks down, the **Universitätsplatz,** centered about a stone lion fountain, is the former headquarters of the Alte Universität. Between 1778 and 1914, naughty students were jailed in the Student Prison, Augustinergasse. (Open Mon.-Sat. 9am-5pm. Admission DM1, under 14 DM0.70.) At Hauptstr. 97, the **Kurpfälzisches Museum** is crammed with artifacts such as the jawbone of "Heidelberg man" (one of the oldest humans yet unearthed), works of art by Van der Weyden and Dürer, and a spectacular Gothic altarpiece by 15th-century sculptor Tilman Riemenschneider. (Open Tues.-Wed. and Fri.-Sun. 10am-5pm, Thurs. 10am-9pm. Admission DM1, students free.) Between Hauptstr. and the river is the new **Friedrich-Ebert Gedenkstätte,** 18 Pfaffengasse, in the birthplace of Germany's first president. The exhibit details Ebert's rise from saddle-maker to Social Democratic agitator to President of the ill-fated Weimar Republic. (Open Tues.-Wed. and Fri.-Sun. 10am-6pm, Thurs. 10am-8pm. Free.)

Along the river stand the handsome **Kongresshaus** and the turreted **Marstall,** a former prison that now houses a student mensa. Survey these façades from across the river. A stroll across the elegant **Karl-Theodor-Brücke** reveals the statue of Karl-Theodor himself, which he commissioned as a symbol of his modesty. From the far end of the bridge clamber up the **Schlangenweg,** a winding stone stairway, to the **Philosophenweg,** a famous pedestrian walkway where Hegel indulged in afternoon promenades. The path traverses one side of the 400m **Heiligenberg** and affords pretty pictures of the town, especially at sunset. Atop the Heiligenberg lie ruins of the 12th-century **St. Michael Basilika,** the 13th-century **St. Stephan Kloster,** and an **amphitheater** built under Hitler in 1934 on the site of an ancient Celtic gathering place. From May through September, the **Rhein-Neckar-Fahrgastschiffahrt,** in front of the Kongresshaus, runs cruises up and down the Neckar. You might want to cruise to **Neckarsteinach** and its four hilltop castle ruins. (7 cruises per day 9:30am-3:30pm, 1¼ hr. each way, round-trip DM15.) You can also rent boats on the Neckar near the Kongesshaus (6-10DM for ½hr., 10-16DM for 1 hr.).

Heidelberg's **Faschings Parade** struts through the city on Mardi Gras, the day before Ash Wednesday. The two-week **Spring Festival** begins at the end of May. A **wine festival** is held in mid-September, and the **Christmas market** runs from late November to December 22.

Near Heidelberg

The cathedral sites of Speyer and Worms to the west and the ancient castles of the green Neckar Valley to the east are both simple day trips from Heidelberg. Passenger cruises run daily along the Neckar between Heidelberg and Neckarsteinach (see above). Or view the valley from the Heidelberg-Heilbronn rail line, which follows the river with frequent stops in the medieval towns of **Neckarsteinach** and **Hirschhorn.** Along a slightly different Heidelberg-Heilbronn line lies the picture-perfect hamlet of **Bad Wimpfen,** whose quaint *Altstadt*—shadowed by an ancient castle ruin high above the Neckar—is worth a journey by itself. To the west of Heidelberg, the fabulous gardens of **Schwetzingen Palace** are also worth a detour. Designed by the Palatine Electors in the 18th century, the gardens conglomerate statues, fountains, moats and elaborate scaled-down replicas of Roman temples, Egyptian ruins and even a mosque—all of which must be seen to be believed (open daily 8am-8pm; DM2.50, students DM1.50). From Heidelberg, bus #7007 (leaves approx. every 30 min. from the train station at stop #2, Eurail and InterRail valid) reaches **Schwetzingen** in about 30 min. and deposits passengers just across the street from the castle.

Bus #7007 continues on to **Speyer** (1hr.), which can also be reached by train via Mannheim. Speyer's gargantuan 11th century **Dom** dominates the town center and harbors a spooky **crypt** at its far eastern end, where eight Roman emperors from the 11th through the 14th centuries are buried. The bus from Heidelberg stops just outside the Dom; from the train station, take the city shuttle (DM1 for an all-day ticket) to the Maximilianstr. stop. Just south of the cathedral is the **Historisches Museum der Pfalz,** which proudly displays the world's oldest bottle of wine: Rome, 300 AD. It costs a lot and probably tastes nasty (museum open daily 9am-5pm. Admission DM2, students DM1). The **Verkehrsamt** (tel. (06232) 143 95) is located on Maximilianstr. 11, straight ahead of the main entrance to the cathedral (open Mon.-Fri. 9am-5pm, Sat. 10am-noon).

The site of Martin Luther's brave stand before the Imperial Diet in 1521 (an act that sent him promptly into exile), **Worms** is now home to seven pre-1900 churches, all located within a stone's throw in the *Altstadt.* The grandaddy of them all is the **Dom St. Peter,** a Romanesque cathedral whose vaulted interior is both eerie and awe-inspiring. Across from the Dom to the east on Neumarkt 14, **Stadtinformation** (tel. (06241) 250 45) provides maps of the town highlighting Worms's six other churches. (Open Mon.-Fri. 9am-noon and 2-5pm, Sat. 9am-noon.) The thousand-year legacy of Worms's Jewish community survives today in the **Heiliger Sand** cemetery on Andreasring west of the Dom, and in the former Jewish quarter around **Judengasse** at the north end of the *Altstadt.* Just off the Judengasse are the **synagogue,** which houses the yeshiva of the famous Talmudic commentator Rabbi ben Yitzhak Shlomo (Rashi), and the **Rashi-Haus Museum,** which traces the history of the community (open Tues.-Sun. 10am-noon and 2-5pm).

Mainz to Koblenz

The Rhine may run all the way from Switzerland to the North Sea, but in the popular imagination it exists only in the 80km of the Rhine Gorge that stretches from Bonn to just north of Mainz. This is the Rhine of legend, a sailor's nightmare and a poet's dream, where robber-baron castles overlook treacherous whirlpools and craggy riverbanks. From the Loreley Cliff above St. Goarshausen fair sirens once lured passing sailors to their death on the sharp rocks below, and the Rhine wines from the hillside vineyards have been the source of many lesser tragedies.

The Mainz-Koblenz train affords excellent views, but the best way to see the Rhine is by boat. The **Köln-Düsseldorfer (KD) Line** makes the complete Mainz-Koblenz run thrice daily in summer, and along shorter stretches more frequently. (Fewer sailings off-season. Mainz-Koblenz one-way DM69, round-trip DM85.60, free with Eurail.) English copies of the schedule are available at local tourist offices or along the docks; for more information call (0221) 208 83 18 or 208 83 19. Seniors (over 60) ride for half-price Mondays and Fridays, and everyone gets a free ride on their birthday.

An easy 30 min. by S-Bahn (line 14) from Frankfurt, **Mainz** makes a convenient starting point for Rhine tours; KD ships depart from the docks across from the postmodern façade of the **Rathaus.** As the capital of the Rhineland-Palatinate region, Mainz has better things to do than cater to tourists. Mainz's most famous son, Johannes Gutenberg—the father of modern printing—is immortalized along with his most important creations in the **Gutenberg Museum** on Liebfrauenpl. (open Tues.-Sat. 10am-6pm, Sun. 10am-1pm; free). Across the square stands the colossal 11th-century red sandstone **Martinsdom,** one of the most impressive cathedrals in Germany and the final resting place of several Archbishops of Mainz, where extravagant tombs line the walls. (Open Mon.-Fri. 9am-6:30pm, Sat. 9am-4pm, Sun. 1-2:45pm and 4-6:30pm; Oct.-March Mon.-Fri. 9am-5pm, Sat. 9am-4pm, Sun. 1-5pm.) The adjacent **Dom Museum** houses sculptural artifacts dating from the early years of the Holy Roman Empire. (Open Mon.-Wed. and Fri. 10am-4pm, Thurs. 10am-6:30pm, Sat. 10am-2pm. Free.)

To make the maze of Mainz more maneuverable, streets running parallel to the Rhine have blue nameplates and streets running toward the river have red nameplates. The **tourist office,** Bahnhofstr. 15 (tel. (06131) 23 37 41), down the street opposite the train station, reserves rooms for DM2; unfortunately, the town offers few inexpensive ones. (Open Mon.-Fri. 9am-6pm, Sat. 9am-1pm.) Mainz's well-run **IYHF youth hostel** (tel. (06131) 853 32) is in the Volkspark in Weisenau. From the train station, take bus #1 to the Jugendherberge stop (DM2) or #22 to the Viktorstiff stop. (Reception open 5-10pm. Curfew 11:30pm. Juniors DM15.50, seniors DM18.50.) Camp at **Camping Maarave,** (tel. (06134) 43 83), across the river. (Reception open 8am-1pm and 3-8:30pm. DM5.50 per person, DM4.50 per tent, DM4 per car.) For reasonably cheap eats, head to the *Altstadt* in the streets behind the Dom; **Weinstube Hof Ehrenfels,** Grebenstr. 5-7, satisfies locals with delectable **Käseschnitzel** (cheese-fried pork) with salad and fries (DM14.80) and smooth wines (DM2.40-3.80 per 0.2 liter; open Tues.-Sun. from 4pm).

On the west bank of the Rhine between Mainz and Koblenz is the cozy village of **Bacharach,** whose many **Weinkeller** (wine cellars) and **Weinstuben** (wine pubs) do their best to live up to the town's name (which means "altar to Bacchus"). The **tourist office,** a 3-minute walk up to the right from the train station at Oberstr. 1 (tel. (06743) 12 97), has a detailed listing of local wine purveyors, including Anglophonic ones (open Mon.-Fri. 8:30am-12:30pm and 1:30-5pm). **Burg Stahleck,** a 12th-century castle set on a steep hill above town, now houses a **youth hostel** (tel. (06743) 12 66), whose management will bowl you over with friendliness. The view of the Rhine Gorge from the terrace is incomparable. (Curfew 10pm. Juniors DM13.80. Seniors DM16.80.)

At the north end of the Rhine Gorge stands **Koblenz,** whose location at the confluence of the Rhine and the Mosel has ensured prosperity since Roman days. Koblenz turns 2000 years young in 1992, promising celebrations all year; the annual **Rhein in Flammen** festival on the second weekend in August should see more than its usual share of pyrotechnics.

Koblenz is a popular jumping-off point for Rhine and Mosel cruises. Bus line #1 connects the train station to the main docks at the Rheinfähre stop (one-way

DM2.40); on foot, it's a 25-min. walk from the station down Markenbildchen Weg and then left along the river. Cruises lasting anywhere from one hour to all day depart frequently from the docks. The **tourist office** (tel. (0261) 313 04), across the street from the station, gladly gives away boat schedules and city maps complete with hotel, restaurant and pub listings. (Open mid-June to mid-Oct. Mon.-Thurs. 8:30am-8:30pm, Fri.-Sat. 8:30am-8:15pm, Sun. 2-5pm; mid-late Oct. and May to mid-June Mon.-Fri. 8:30am-6pm, Sat. 11:30am-6pm; Nov.-April Mon.-Fri. 8:30am-1pm and 2:15-5pm.)

The focal point of the city is the **Deutsches Eck** (German Corner), the peninsula at the confluence of the Rhine and Mosel that supposedly saw the birth of the German nation when the Teutonic Order of Knights settled there in 1216. The monumental **Mahnmal Der Deutschen Einheit** (Monument to German Unity) now dominates this little corner of history; first erected in 1897 in honor of Kaiser Wilhelm I for his dubious role in unifying the German Empire, the 14m equestrian statue of Kaiser Bill that once crowned the monument was destroyed in 1945. Today the 100-odd steps of the base are pompous enough in themselves. Most of the nearby *Altstadt* was flattened during WWII, but the most important buildings have been carefully restored and merit at least a cursory tour. The **Mittel Rhein Museum,** Florinsmarkt 15-17, contains a reputable collection of German art and antiquities (open Tues.-Sun. 10am-4:30pm; free). From the boat docks on the Rhine, a frequent ferry (DM1.20) runs across the river to **Ehrenbreitstein** and the giant **Festung,** an extensive fortress first occupied by the archbishops of Trier and rebuilt by the Prussians in the early 19th century. The 20-min. climb to the battlements is worth it for the view; a chairlift *(Sesselbahn)* also makes the trip (May-Oct. 9am-5:50pm; one-way DM4, round-trip DM7). Inside the fortress are the **Landesmuseum,** a ho-hum collection of early industrial exhibits (open mid-March to Oct. daily 9am-12:30pm and 1-5pm; free), and the recently renovated **Jugendherberge (IYHF),** which may well have the most scenic location of any hostel in Germany (tel. (0261) 737 37). From the train station take bus line #8,9 or 10 to the Kapuzinerpl. stop, then take the chairlift or follow the main road along the train tracks to the road leading up to the castle. (Curfew 11:30pm. Juniors DM15.50, seniors DM18.50.) **Campingplatz Rhein-Mosel** is across the Mosel from the *Deutsches Eck;* a smaller ferry makes the journey across the river during the day (tel. (0261) 80 24 89; open April to mid-Oct. DM3.75 per person, DM3.75 per tent). Most of the hotels and restaurants in Koblenz are priced to bleed tourists dry, with only a few exceptions. **Gasthaus Christ,** Schützenstr. 32 (tel. 377 02), has extremely friendly management and cozy rooms. From the station, turn right and follow the road around the post office and along the tracks, then head through the underpass and take the first left (DM30 per person).

The Mosel Valley (Moseltal)

An arresting landscape, a comparable number of ancient castles, even more vineyards, and a lot fewer tourists than the Rhine to the east make the Mosel Valley as intriguing as its legendary counterpart. The river meanders northeasterly across more than 200km of German territory from Trier on the Luxembourg border to Koblenz, where it flows into the Rhine. The valley's slopes aren't quite as steep as the Rhine's narrow gorge, and the countless vineyards that crowd the gentle hillsides have been producing quality vintages since the days of the Romans. See the valley's splendid scenery by boat, bus or bicycle, since the train line between Koblenz and Trier strays frequently from the river into considerably duller countryside. Some train stations will rent you a sturdy, heavy one-speed for DM10 per day, or DM5 per day if you have a train ticket, Bundesbahn bus ticket, or railpass. You can drop off the bike at another train station at no extra charge and have your cabbage sent ahead. Although passenger boats no longer make the complete Koblenz-Trier run, several companies run daily summer trips along shorter stretches; local tourist offices will provide details.

Nestled in a bend in the river 35 minutes from Koblenz, a third of the way to Trier, is the town of **Cochem.** Cochem appears to exist solely to produce wine and coddle tourists—and that's exactly what it does. High on a vineyard-blanketed hill above the town, the majestic turrets of the **Reichsburg** castle dominate the setting. Originally built in the 11th century, the castle—like much of the Palatinate—was destroyed in 1689 by French troops under King Louis XIV. In 1868, it was rebuilt in neo-Gothic style by a wealthy Berlin merchant. The interior can be seen today only on a guided tour. (Open March 15-Oct. 31 daily 9am-5pm. Tours on the hour. Written English translation avaiable. Admission DM3.50, students DM1.50.) Even if you bag the tour, the view from the castle grounds alone is worth the 20-min. uphill climb along Schloßstr. from the Marktpl. Cochem itself is a maze of twisting streets and tourist establishments. The flower-lined **promenade** along the river offers some respite from the endless succession of beer steins and postcard trees.

The **tourist office** (tel. (02671) 39 71) is on Enderplatz right next to the bridge; from the train station, go to the river and turn right. The office will book rooms free of charge (open Mon.-Fri. 9am-1pm and 2-5pm, Sat. 10am-3pm; Nov.-May Mon.-Fri. 9am-1pm and 2-5pm). Cochem's friendly but minimalist **Jugendherberge (IYHF)** is 30 minutes from the station on the opposite shore at Klottener Str. 9 (tel. (02671) 86 33). Walk across the Mosel bridge and turn left on Burgstr., which turns into Klottener Str. (Reception open 12:30-1, 5-6:30 and 9:45-10pm. Curfew 10pm. Juniors DM14.30, seniors DM17.30.) Camp at **Campingplatz am Freizeitzentrum** (tel. (02671) 12 12) on Stadionstr. just below the youth hostel (open April-Oct. 8am-10pm) or at **Schausten-Reif** on Enderstr. 124 (tel. (02671) 75 28) slightly farther from town.

Ten km upstream from Cochem lies **Beilstein,** a tiny hamlet with more attractive and less touristed half-timbered houses and crooked cobblestone streets. A private bus line (railpasses not valid) makes several trips a day between Cochem (stopping at the train station and on Endertplatz), and Beilstein (15 min., DM3.30 one-way); the passenger boats of **Personenschiffahrt Kolb** (tel. (02673) 15 15) make four round trips per day (1 hr. each way, DM15 round-trip, railpasses not valid). Wine cellars abound in Beilstein; get drunk with one of the full-bodied local whites. Not to be missed here are the ruins of **Burg Metternich,** another casualty of the pyromaniacal French tourists of 1689; the view from its broken-down edifices sweeps the valley (open daily April-Oct. 8:30am-7pm; admission DM2, students DM1).

The ancient city of **Trier** dominates the western reaches of the German Mosel. Now just a shade over 2000 years old, Trier had its heyday in the 4th century as the capital of the Western Empire and residence of Emperor Constantine. From there, it's been a long, slow 1600-year decline, but a graceful one; today, some of the most extensive Roman ruins outside Italy and an *Altstadt* that's as attractive and well-preserved as they come combine to make Trier more than worth your time.

A short five- to ten-minute walk down Theodor-Heuss-Allee from the train station brings you to the 2nd-century **Porta Nigra** (Black Gate), named for the centuries of grime that have turned its sandstone face varying shades of gloom (all Roman ruins open daily 9am-6pm; Oct.-March 9am-5pm; admission DM2, students DM1). In the shadow of the Porta Nigra is Trier's **tourist office** (tel. (0651) 480 71; open Mon.-Sat. 9am-6:45pm, Sun. 9am-3:30pm; Nov.-March Mon.-Sat. 9am-6pm, Sun. 9am-1pm). From there, stroll down Simeonstr. to the **Hauptmarkt;** this busy street is the northern leg of Trier's remarkably large, bustling, and attractive pedestrian shopping district. A left onto Sternstr. brings you to the impressive interiors of the 11th-century **Dom.** (Open daily 6am-6pm; Nov.-March 6am-noon and 2-5:30pm.) From the Dom, Liebfrauenstr. leads to the **Konstantin Basilika,** Constantine's 4th-century throne room, now about as exciting as an airplane hangar. Nearby are the ruins of the **Kaiserthermen,** baths where the emperor washed and put on his new clothes. From here, it's a five-minute walk uphill along Olewiger Str. to the remains of the 2nd-century **ampitheater.** If the Rolling Stones had toured in 169, this 20,000-seat venue—one of the largest in the Roman Empire—would definitely have been on the itinerary. Marxists and poststructuralist neo-socialists should check out the **Karl-Marx Haus,** Brückenstr. 10, the birthplace of the bearded philosopher, which now houses a slightly dry account of his life and work. (Open Mon. 1-6pm, Tues.-Sun. 10am-6pm; Nov.-March Mon. 1-6pm, Tues.-Sun. 10am-1pm and 3-6pm. Admission DM3, students DM2.)

Trier's **Jugendherberge (IYHF),** Maarstr. 156 (tel. (0651) 292 92), has all the comforts of home. From the station, it's a 30-minute walk; take Theodor-Heuss-Allee to the Porta Nigra, turn right on Paulinstr., take the first left onto the narrow, poorly marked Maarstr. and follow it until it ends. Or take bus #2 or 8 (direction: "Trierweilerweg" or "Pfalzel/Quint") to Georg-Schmidt-Pl., then walk five minutes downstream on the path along the top of the embankment. (Lockout 9:30am-1pm. Curfew midnight. Juniors DM15.50, seniors DM21. Accepts credit cards.) Camp at **Schloß Monaise,** at Monaiser Str. (tel. (0651) 862 10) on the grounds of an 18th-century castle. From the station, take bus #40 toward Zewen to the Flugplatz stop (DM5 per person, DM6 per car). The **Jugendhostel Kolpinghaus** and the adjacent **Hotel Kolpinghaus,** for those under and over 25 respectively, are clean, friendly and well-located, one block off the Hauptmarkt at Dietrichstr. 42 (tel. (0651) 751 31; reception open 8am-11pm; juniors DM22, seniors DM30; call ahead). **Astarix,** Karl-Marx-Str. 11, serves ridiculously inexpensive meals in a casual student-dominated environment. (Open Mon.-Sat. 11am-1am, Sun. 6pm-1am.)

Several trains a day make both the 90-minute trip from Trier to Koblenz in the east and the one-hour jaunt from nearby Luxembourg to the west. From May to October, one boat per day departs for Bernkastel-Kues in the Mosel Valley (9:15am, DM38).

Cologne (Köln)

Cologne began as a Roman colony ("colonia," hence "Cologne") and gained fame and fortune as a medieval crossroads rich in academic life, its eight bridges straddling the Rhine just north of Bonn. The city pulled itself up by its bootstraps after WWII, which left 90% of its inner parts in ruins. Cologne is the city of novelist Heinrich Böll; his classic *The Lost Honor of Katherine Blum,* set here, tells a story of rumors and corruption appropriate to Germany's fourth-largest city and modern media and arts capital.

Practical Information

Tourist Office: Unter Fettenhennen 19 (tel. 221 33 45), across from the main entrance to the cathedral. City maps (free) and rooms booked (fee DM3). Open Mon.-Sat. 8am-10:30pm, Sun. 9am-10:30pm; mid-Oct. to April Mon.-Sat. 8am-9pm, Sun. 9:30am-7pm.

Currency Exchange: At the train station daily 7am-9pm, or at any bank until 4pm.

American Express: Burgmauerstr. 14, near the Dom. ATM outside for cardholders. Open Mon.-Fri. 9am-5:30pm, Sat. 9am-noon.

Post Office: Main office, An den Dominikankern. Poste Restante at windows 3 and 4. **Postal Code:** W-5000.

Telephones: City code: 0221.

Flights: Take bus #117 from the Bus-Bahnhof to the Köln-Bonn Flughafen. Call (02203) 40 40 01 for flight information.

Trains: Hauptbahnhof, next to the cathedral. To: Düsseldorf (frequently, 25 min.); Hamburg (every hr., 4 hr.); Frankfurt (every hr., 2 hr.); Brussels (12 per day, 2½-3 hr.); Amsterdam (11 per day, 2¾ hr.). The auxiliary **Köln-Deutz** is across the river.

Public Transportation: For schedule information on DB and S-Bahn lines #6, 11, 12, call 14 11. Day card for Cologne's bus, S-Bahn and U-Bahn lines DM8.

Hitchhiking: Mitfahr-Büro, Saarstr. 22, tel. 21 99 91. Open Mon.-Sat. 9am-7pm; or try **Mitfahr-Treff,** Beethovenstr. 16-18 (tel. 21 09 67 or 68 or 69), near the university. Open Mon.-Sat. 9am-7pm.

Laundry: Wasch Center, Brüsselerstr. 62. Wash DM6, soap included. Dry DM2 for ½ hr. Open Mon.-Sat. 6am-11pm. Free laundry at the Deutz hostel for guests.

Pharmacy: Dom-Apotheke, Komodienstr. 5, near the station, offers advice in English. A list of late-night pharmacies is posted outside.

Accommodations

Cologne has two hostels, separated by the city center and the Rhine. Just over the Hohenzollernbrücke, **Jugendherberge Köln-Deutz (IYHF),** Siegesstr. 5a (tel. 81 47 11), has cramped rooms but a prime location and a great jukebox. From the Deutz station, go one stop on DB or S-Bahn 6, 11, or 12; head left and up Neuhöfferstr. and right on Siegesstr. The hostel's 374 beds fill up quick; the best time to check in is 6-9am. Riskier reception after 12:30pm. (Curfew 12:30am. Juniors DM19.20. Seniors DM22.70. Sheets included. AmEx and Visa accepted.) More luxurious and rather less full, but also less convenient is the **Jugendgästehaus Köln-Riehl (IYHF),** An der Schanze 14 (tel. 76 70 81), on the Rhine north of the zoo. From the station, take S-Bahn #5 (Mon.-Fri. until 7pm) or U-Bahn #16 or 18 (direction "Eberplatz/Mülheim") to the Boltonsternstr. stop, or walk (40 min.) along the Rhine on Konrad-Adenauer-Uferstr., which turns into Niederländerstr. and finally An der Schanze. The hostel's first floor **Köln-Treff Café** is busy with thirsty hostelers from 8pm-12:30am daily. (Reception open 11am-midnight. Curfew 1am. DM26.20, DM24.20 for 2 or more nights. Sheets included.) The tidy **Hotel Flintsch,** Moselstr. 16-20 (tel. 23 21 42), is close by the university scene. From the station, take U-Bahn #9, 12, 16, 17 or 18 to Barbarossa Platz, head down Luxemburger and left on Mosel. (Singles with shower DM60. Doubles with shower DM85. Call ahead.) Camp on the Rhine at **Campingplatz Poll** (tel. 83 19 66), southeast of the *Altstadt.* Take U-Bahn #16 to Marienburg, and cross the Rodenkirchener Bridge. (DM5.50 per person, DM5 per tent. Open May-Sept.) One warning—if you're thinking of a last-minute room anywhere near Carneval, forget it (though the tourist office takes on hopeless cases).

Food and Entertainment

Cafés and restaurants line **Am Bollwerk,** along the Rhine between the Hohenzollernbrücke and Deutzelbrücke. The best corner of this strip is the cobbled **Fischmarkt.** A night-time student scene takes over the streets around Zülpicher Platz in the **Quartier Lateng,** near the university; take S-Bahn #7 to Zülpicher Platz, or U-Bahn 6, 10, 12, 15, 16, 17 or 18 to Barbarossa Platz.

Inexpensive food, Laura Ashley curtains, slinky red teddies and more is yours along **Hohe Straße,** the main pedestrian shopping thoroughfare by the cathedral. Buy groceries in **Karstadt's** basement here or at the huge, salad bar-equipped **Deutsche Supermarkt** off of Zülpicher Platz. **Apfelmuß** completes Cologne's own *Rievekochen* (potato pancake); a stand between the cathedral and station fries them late. The **Bergisches Viertel,** around Bismarckstr., is your headquarters for gay bars and dance clubs. **Papa Joe's Bierlokal,** Buttermarkt 37 (tel. 21 79 50), near the Fischmarkt in the *Altstadt,* features live jazz nightly (from 8:30pm) that's as good as it gets in these parts. Check out *Jazzfrüschoppen,* morning drinking with a Dixieland band, every Saturday from 11am. (Open daily 7pm-1:30am. No cover.) Sistership **Papa Joe's Biersalon,** Alter Markt 52, is a boisterous old-time pub, complete with saloon-style piano. Half-liter of *sion* beer, DM5.50. (Open daily 11am-1am.) At either *lokal,* grab *Papa Joe's Kunst und Bier Blatt,* with a monthly list of performers. **Peppermint,** Hohenstaufenring 23, on Zülpicher Platz, is a wood-paneled café with a sing-song Cantina Mexicana upstairs. Low-priced specials after midnight (taco/enchilada plate DM8). Intriguing specialties. (Café with breakfast menu open Mon.-Sat. 10am-3am, Sun. 6pm-2am; restaurant open daily 7:30pm-2am.) Brewheads will gravitate to **Bier Museum,** Rote-Funken Plätzchen, in the *Altstadt.* A regular collection: 18 beers on tap, 15 more in bottles. Tables for open-air exhibits. Surely this is enough. (Open daily 2pm-3am.)

Sights

No structure speaks more effectively for a reborn Germany than the spectacular Gothic **Kölner Dom.** Struck by no less than 14 bombs during WWII, the cathedral was still intact in 1945 and became the nation's most powerful icon in the years that followed. Over 500 years in the making, the smoke-colored cathedral stands over the train station, keeping watch on the Rhine; the giant wooden construction crane, still kept inside, was as much Cologne's landmark as the Dom's two towers. The view from the **Südturm** (509 steep steps up) leaves the modern city in the dust. A **Glockenstube,** on the way up the tower, clangs with the world's heaviest swinging bell. (Open daily 6am-7:30pm. Organ concerts mid-June to Sept. Tues. at 8pm. Free. Cathedral tower open daily May-Sept. 9am-5:30pm; March-April and Oct. 9am-4:30pm; Nov.-Feb. 9am-3:30pm. Admission DM2, students DM1.)

Half of Cologne crosses the **Domvorplatz** daily, amid jugglers, agitators and tourists lying flat on their backs for that all-encompassing cathedral view. Click, click. On the other side of the cathedral from the station, the **Römisch-Germanisches Museum,** Roncallipl. 4 (tel. 221 44 38), displays artifacts from the city's Roman days. Imperial mementos include the risqué **Dionysos-Mosaik,** a nearly complete tile floor. (Open Tues. and Fri.-Sun. 10am-5pm, Wed.-Thurs. 10am-8pm. Admission DM3, students DM1.) On the riverside Heinrich-Böll-Platz, near the station, the unusual building housing both the **Wallraf-Richartz** and **Ludwig-Museum** provides a maximum of indirect, natural light. The museum's early modern and very modern collections are integrated, so it's only a few steps from the sublime to the ridiculous. (Open Tues.-Thurs. 10am-8pm, Fri.-Sun. 10am-6pm. Admission DM3, students DM1, with additional charge for special exhibits.) Smaller museums hide in every *Kölsch* corner. A one-day **Museumspaß** (DM6), with list (available at the tourist office) gets you into as many as your heart desires.

The cathedral doesn't exhaust the religious trip; twelve Romanesque churches still attest to Cologne's glory days. Most striking, despite extensive wartime damage, are the four spires of the 12th-century **Groß St. Martin,** south of the museums on the Rhine (open Mon.-Fri. 10am-6pm, Sat. 10am-12:30pm and 1:30-6pm, Sun. 2-4pm).

The departure point for **Rhein Rundfahrten's** one-hour river cruises (DM10) is just north of the Hohenzollern Bridge. (Daily April-Oct. 8:15am-10:30pm.) With trips from a few hours to a few days, the **Köln-Düsseldorfer** (KD) line's many Rhine and Mösel boats dock a bit to the south; Eurail holders sail free, and InterRail gets 50% off. For schedule information, call or visit the Rheingarten office (tel. 21 28 64). You can also enjoy the Rhine on your own; a walk across the panoramic **Hohenzollernbrücke** is absolutely a required journey.

Cologne becomes a living spectacle during the **Carneval,** celebrated in the opulent spirit of the city's Latin past. For the dancing-in-the-street **Rosemontag** procession on the last Monday before Lent (March 2, 1992), everyone's in costume and gets a couple of dozen *Bützchen*—Kölsch for a kiss on a stranger's cheek. Arrive early; this is Cologne's specialty, and half of Germany wants in.

Bonn

Poor Bonn. Founded by the Romans, a historical nonentity for most of its 2000 years, the so-called *Hauptdorf* (capital village) made it big by chance. Since Konrad Adenauer, the revered post-war chancellor, had a house in its suburbs, the ever-considerate occupying powers promoted humble Bonn to capital status. Easy come, easty go: newly resurgent Berlin is poised to become what it always really was, Germany's capital. Snide Berliners like to say that Bonn is "half the size of a Chicago cemetery and twice as dead," though decades of internationalism have made this "small town in Germany" rich in culture and the nostalgia of power.

Before the Bundestag, Bonn had Beethoven. Ludwig wailed his first notes in what is now called **Beethovens Geburtshaus,** Bonngasse 20, a museum that only a mother could love. (Open Mon.-Sat. 10am-5pm, Sun. 10am-1pm; Oct.-March Mon.-Sat. 10:30am-4pm, Sun. 10am-1pm. Last entrance ½ hr. before closing. Admission DM5, students DM1.50.) The next **Beethoven Fest** is set to grip Bonn in the summer of 1992. At the first scandal-ridden fête in 1845, the composer himself snubbed Queen Victoria, and Lola Montez—the King of Bavaria's illicit lover—danced on the tables.

The station's front exit opens on to the pedestrian zone. On the **Markt,** the 18th-century pink and blue party-cake **Rathaus** is one of the most ludicrously pastel Baroque buildings around. Nearby stands the **Kurfürstliches Schloß,** an 18th-century palace later converted into the central building of Bonn's university. Just behind the train station is the **Rheinisches Landesmuseum Bonn,** Colmantstr. 14-16, showcasing the absolutely best works by dozens of absolutely mediocre Rhenish artists, plus cosmopolitan visiting shows. (Open Tues. and Thurs. 9am-5pm, Wed. 9am-8pm, Fri. 9am-4pm, Sat.-Sun. 11am-5pm. Admission DM4, students DM2.) **Poppelsdorfer Allee's** broad promenade runs straight from the station to **Poppelsdorfer Schloß,** baroque centerpiece to the **Botanic Gardens.** (Open Mon.-Fri. 9am-6pm, Sun. 9am-1pm; Oct.-April Mon.-Fri. 9am-4pm.) South along the river, the **Bundeshaus,** Görrestr. 5, is known far and wide as the least prepossessing parliamentary building in Europe. Take tram #16, 63 or 66 to Heussallee/Bundeshaus. (Obligatory tours depart every hour mid-March to Dec. Mon.-Fri. 9am-4pm, Sat.-Sun. 10am-4pm; Jan. to mid-March Mon.-Fri. 9am-4pm. Closed holidays.)

Bonn's **tourist office,** which books hotels for a DM3-5 fee, is in a passageway at Münsterstr. 20 (tel. (0228) 77 34 66), just off the station. Use the "Stadtmitte" exit, walk 60m up Poststr., turn left at Münsterstr., and left again. (Open Mon.-Sat. 8am-9pm, Sun. 9:30am-12:30pm; Nov.-March Mon.-Sat. 8am-7pm, Sun. 9:30am-12:30pm.) Bonn has an embarrassment of consular riches. Highlights: **U.S.,** Deichman Ave. 29 (tel. (0228) 339 20 53; open Mon.-Fri. 8:30-11:30am); **Australia,** Godesberger Allee 107 (tel. (0228) 810 30; open Mon.-Fri. 9am-noon); **Canada,** Godesberger Allee 119 (tel. (0228) 81 00 60; open Mon.-Fri. 8am-4pm). The best public transport option is the 3-day unlimited pass (DM13).

Cocooned in renovations in 1991, the **Jugendgästehaus Bonn-Venusberg (IYHF),** Haager Weg 42 (tel. (0228) 28 12 00), will take wing in 1992. Take bus #621 to suburban, wooded Venusberg. (Curfew 1am. DM26.20 per person, DM24.20 if staying 2 or more nights. Sheets included.) The more central **Jugendgästehaus Bonn-Bad Godesberg (IYHF),** Horianstr. 60 (tel. (0228) 31 75 16) is just as spiffy. Take tram #63 or 616 from the main station, or bus #625 from the Bad Godesberg station to the Jugendherberge stop. (Reception open 4:30-10pm. Curfew 1am. Same prices and perks.) Back in town, the homestyle **Hotel Deutsches Haus,** Kaernerstr. 19-21 (tel. (0228) 63 37 77), near the Beethovenhaus, is a base for the **Bonner Schubert Chor.** Take tram #61 to Landgericht, then go one block east on Oxfordstr. and left on Kasernen, or walk through the pedestrian zone (bearing left) onto Kasernerstr. (Singles DM45, with shower DM55. Doubles DM75, with shower DM85, with shower and bath DM95.)

Young Bonners stomach inexpensive but barely palatable meals (DM2.20-3.90, DM1 extra without student ID) at the **University Mensa,** Nassestr. 11, a 15-min. walk from the train station along Kaiserstr., with a ridiculously cheap (DM5 per kg) salad bar upstairs. (Open Mon.-Fri. 11:30am-2pm; late Sept. to mid-July Mon.-Thurs. 11:30am-2:15pm and 5:30-8pm, Fri. 11:30am-2pm, Sat. noon-1:45pm.) The better buffet is at **Cassius Garten,** Maximilianstr. 28d, at the edge of the pedestrian zone facing the station, which fulfills your wildest vegetarian fantasies (DM1.26-1.96 per 100g. Open Mon.-Wed. and Fri. 11am-8pm; Thurs. 11am-9pm, Sat. 11am-3pm.) Vendors shout out bargains at the produce market on Münsterpl. (Mon.-Fri. 8am-6:30pm.)

Aachen

Tramping across 8th-century Europe, Charlemagne fell in love with Aachen (then Aix-la-Chapelle) and made it the capital of the nascent Frankish empire. Charlemagne unpacked his memories of the east in Aachen, building an octagonal neo-Byzantine **Dom,** one of the world's immortal cathedrals, in its center. The emperor's successors added a Gothic choir with stained glass windows. (Open daily 7am-7pm.) Charlie cuts more of a figure in the **Schatzkammer** (treasury) around the corner to the right from the Dom exit; the solid gold *Karlsbüste,* the best known likeness of the emperor, shines here. (Open Mon. 10am-2pm, Tues.-Sat. 10am-6pm, Sun. 10:30am-5pm; late Oct.-early April Mon. 10am-2pm, Tues.-Sat. 10am-5pm, Sun. 10:30am-5pm. Last entrance ½ hr. before closing. Admission DM3, students DM2.) Cathedral tours, the only way to get close to the imperial throne, begin at the treasury (DM2). On the northern façade of the 14th-century **Rathaus,** over the Marktplatz beside the cathedral, stand 50 statues of former German sovereigns, 31 of whom were crowned in Aachen. (Open Mon.-Fri. 8am-1pm and 2-5pm, Sat.-Sun. 10am-1pm and 2-5pm. Admission DM1, students DM0.50.) In a converted Bauhaus umbrella factory, the **Ludwig Forum für Internationales Kunst,** Jülicherstr. 97-108, brings new artists in from the cold. The timing couldn't be better—the newly opened (May 1991) museum had the space, money and access to invest in a stunning Eastern European collection. Warhol looks stodgy by comparison. (Open Tues.-Wed. and Fri.-Sun. 11am-7pm, Thurs. 11am-10pm. Admission DM4, students DM2.)

Aachen is a way-station between Germany and Belgium, and an inexpensive departure point for trains to France. Düsseldorf and Cologne are both a good hour away. Aachen's central **tourist office** (tel. (0241) 180 29 65) is in the Atrium Eliserbrunnen on Friedrich-Wilhelm-Platz. Another office is at Bahnhofpl. 4 (tel. (0241) 253 12), opposite the train station. Both book rooms for a DM3 fee. (Open Mon.-Fri. 9am-6:30pm, Sat. 9am-1pm.) Walk through the Pont Tor to find a ride at the **Mitfahrzentrale,** Roermonderstr. 4 (tel. (0241) 15 54 00). A **Sammelnkarte** for five city bus rides is DM7.50. Aachen's whitewashed brick **Jugendherberge Colynshof (IYHF),** Maria-Theresia-Allee 260 (tel. (0241) 711 01), sits on the fringe of a forest south of the city. From the station, walk left on Lagerhausstr. to the Finanzamt stop, at the corner of Mozartstr.; from Finanzamt, take bus #2 (direction "Preusswald") to Ronheider or bus #12 (direction "Dierperberden") to the slightly nearer Colynshof stop. (Reception open until 10pm. Curfew 11:30pm. Juniors DM15.30. Seniors DM17.80.) A high-ceilinged pre-war building is home to **Hotel Klenkes,** Heinrichs Allee 46 (tel. (0241) 50 90 34), near Hansemann Platz. From the station, take bus #1, 3, 11, 13 or 21. (Personable singles DM55, with shower DM65. Doubles DM85, with shower DM95.) From the edge of the pedestrian zone to medieval **Pont Tor,** Pontstraße, near Aachen's university, is lined with restaurants and student pubs. **Katakomben Studentenzentrum,** Pontstr. 74-76, a student cafeteria, serves good, inexpensive food (breakfast 9-11:30am; lunch 11:30am-3pm, DM4.20-7.50; dinner 7-10:30pm). The colorful *Salatteller* is a healthy DM4.20. Nonstudents pay DM1-2 more. Pocket some *Aachen Printen,* trademark nut-studded ginger cookies, at local bakeries.

Düsseldorf

Germany's fashionable advertising center and multinational corporate base, stately Düsseldorf runneth over with German patricians and poser aristocrats. Residents have a maxim that Düsseldorf isn't on the Rhine, it's on the posh *Königsallee* (a.k.a. "the Kö"), a kilometer-long fashion runway 10 minutes by foot down Graf-Adolf-Str. from the station. At the other end of this see-and-be-seen *Belle Epoque* promenade, the **Hofgarten** park adds a spot of green, with open air concerts in the summer. Between the park and the river, Düsseldorf's *Altstadt* is home to over 500 pubs and restaurants and much of the city's history. Heinrich Heine was born on the brewery-packed Bölkerstr.; the writer's life and Düsseldorf career are documented farther south in the **Heinrich Heine Institut,** Bilkerstr. 12-14, in the quieter Karlstadt quarter, the south end of the *Altstadt.* The author's death mask, cast from still-warm features, is on display. Yum! (Open Tues.-Sun. 11am-5pm.) At the upper end between the Hofgarten and the river stands the black-glass **Kunstsammlung Nordrhein-Westfalen,** Grabbeplatz 5, an exceptional modern art museum, with *the* definitive Paul Klee collection. Take U-Bahn #70, 76 or 78 to Heinrich-Heine-Allee and walk north two blocks. (Open Tues.-Sun. 10am-6pm. Admission DM5, students DM3.) Medieval and early modern art finds refuge in the grand old **Kunstmuseum Düsseldorf,** Ehrenhof 5, north on the Rhine. (Open Tues.-Sun. 11am-6pm. Admission DM5, students DM2.50.) Even farther north on the Rhine, but still in Düsseldorf, are the well-preserved ruins of Emperor Friedrich's palace in the tiny district of **Kaiserswerth.** Built in 1184, the palace was destroyed in 1702 during the War of Spanish Succession. From the station take U-Bahn #79 to the Klemenzsplatz stop. Then follow Kaiserwerther Markt to the Rhine and walk left another 150m. In the late afternoon, the pubs and streets of the *Altstadt* begin to fill with people enjoying Düsseldorf's trademark *Altbier,* served in small 0.2 liter glasses (usually DM2 a shot) designed to help you lose count. It's quite a sight. Far to the south of town, **Schloß Benrath,** Benrather Schloßallee 104, is a princely 18th-century mansion surrounded by a baroque park. From the station, take S-Bahn #6 to the Benrath. (Open Tues.-Sun. 10am-5pm. Last tour at 4pm. Admission DM2, students DM1.) The Rhine was Düsseldorf's road to riches—don't forget it. Walk on the trademark wiry bridges (**Oberkasseler Brücke** empties into the *Altstadt)* or cruise down. The **Köln-Düsseldorfer** line, which accepts Eurailpasses and offers 50% off to InterRail holders, sails from the **Rheinterrasse,** above the city center just west of the Hofgarten.

Düsseldorf is 25 minutes by frequent train from Köln. The prime **tourist office** is on Konrad-Adenauer-Platz (tel. (0211) 35 05 05), down Immermannhof 50m to the right of the train station. Their free monthly *Düsseldorf Monatsprogram* is packed with information. (Ticket sales and general services Mon.-Fri. 8:30am-6pm, Sat. 9am-12:30pm; accommodations advice (DM3) Mon.-Sat. 8am-10pm, Sun. 4-10pm.) A second office at Heinrich-Heine-Allee 24 (tel. (0211) 899 23 46) specializes in culture. (Open Mon.-Fri. 9am-5pm; Oct.-March Mon.-Thurs. 9am-5pm, Fri. 9am-1pm.) Brits in need can head to the **U.K. Consulate,** Yorckstr. 19 (tel. (0211) 944 80). The more worldly **American Express** office is at Heinrich-Heine-Allee 14 (tel. (0211) 802 22; open Mon.-Fri. 9am-5:30pm, Sat. 9am-noon). The newly constructed central **post office** is on Konrad-Adenauer-Platz.

Frequent S-Bahns travel from the station to Düsseldorf's airport; *Tagesnetzkarten* day transport passes (DM8.50) are good until 3am. Call (0211) 42 12 23 from 6am-midnight for domestic and international flight information. **Change money** at the airport (daily 6am-10pm) or at Deutsche Verkehrs Credit Bank in the Hauptbahnhof. (Open daily 7:30am-8pm.) The **Mitfahrzentrale** is at Konrad-Adenauer-Platz 13 (tel. (0211) 37 60 81). The *Rheinbahn* includes subways, trams, buses and the S-Bahn. Single rides cost DM1.50-2.60, depending on distance.

Düsseldorf is a convention city, and during fairs crowds make rooms costly; if you're after a reasonable hotel, get a convention *(Messe)* schedule or call the tourist office for dates; come in the lull. Most rooms go for DM40 per person even in the off-season. The conjoined **Jugendherberge und Jugendgästehaus Düsseldorf (IYHF),** Düsseldorf Str. 1 (tel. (0211) 57 40 41), is an all-around better deal, just over the Rheinkniebrücke from the *Altstadt.* From the station, take bus #835 to Jugendherberge or U-Bahn #76, 705 or 717 to the Lugeplatz stop and walk 500m. (At both, reception open 7-9:30am, 12:30-5:30pm and 6-10:30pm; curfew 1am; open early Jan. to mid-Dec. At the Jugendherberge, juniors DM17; seniors DM20. In the Jugendgästehaus, singles DM26.20 per person, DM24.20 for 2 or more nights; sheets included). Bible literature is the only frill at the standard **CVJM-Hotel,** Graf-Adolf-Str. 102 (tel. (0211) 36 07 64), down the street to the left of the train station. (Singles DM46. Doubles DM76.) **Hotel Bristol,** Aderstr. 8 (tel. (0211) 37 07 50), is a friendlier sort of place, one block south of Graf-Adolf-Str. at the bottom tip of the Kö. Call ahead. (Singles DM55, with shower DM85. Doubles DM90, with shower DM120-140.) Stake out **Campingplatz Lörick,** Niederkasseler Deich 305 (tel. (0211) 59 14 01), across the Rhine from the Nordpark. From the station, take U-Bahn #76, 705 or 717 to the Belsenplatz stop, then bus #828 to Strandbad Lörick. (DM4 per person, DM6 per tent. Open April-Sept.)

Düsseldorf's specialty is "eating while shopping," but for most of the spots on the Kö, if you have to ask, you probably can't afford it. One exception is the **Marché,** in the Kö-galerie mall at Königsallee 60. Jejune herbivores can pick from the *Gemüse Buffet* (DM7.50 per plate) and fresh juice bar. Grill meals start at DM9.50. (Open Mon.-Thurs. and Sun. 8am-11pm, Fri.-Sat. 8am-11:30pm.) Or try the basement food stands in the **Carschhaus,** Heinrich-Heine-Pl., off Heinrich-Heine-Allee. The **breweries** in the *Altstadt* sell cheap meals as well as the inevitable *Alt.* Sausage-steaming crowds cry up the central old town; **Hausbrauerei zum Schlüssel,** Bolkerstr., is distinguished from its neighbors by a huge copper vat at the back of its cavernous hall and a menu (meals from DM8.50) in dialect. (Open daily 10am-midnight. Hot food until 10:30pm.) The more clubbish, "alternative" quarter is in the upper *Altstadt* between Mühler and Ratingerstr. **Zum Goldenen Einhorn,** Ratingerstr. 18, stocks imported Coronas in addition to Schlösser shots (DM2). An open air **market** adds color to Karlsplatz Monday to Saturday. In good weather, Düsseldorfers pack the **Burghof** beer garden in Kaiserwerth, next to Friedrich's ruins on the Rhine. Take U-Bahn #79 to the Klemensplatz stop.

Near Düsseldorf

Düsseldorf owes a good deal of its modern prosperity to the wealth of the **Ruhr Valley** *(Das Ruhrgebiet),* a sprawling conglomeration of cities joined by the densest concentration of rail lines in the world. Between the 1850s and the 1970s, riverside coal deposits were mined to feed Germany's breakneck industrialization. Infamous 19th-century railroad and armaments mogul Alfred Krupp perfected steel-casting in industrial **Essen.** The **Villa Hügel,** for decades the Krupp family home, was given to the city in the 1950s in an attempt to brighten the company's image, sooted by questionable wartime activities. Take S-Bahn #6 from the Essen train station. (Park open daily 8am-8pm. Villa open Tues.-Sun. 10am-6pm. Admission DM1.50.) Near the station at Steelerstr. 29, Essen's **Alte Synagogue,** now a museum, evokes different memories. Nearby **Dortmund** is the grudgingly undisputed beer capital of Germany, at least in terms of volume. South along the Wupper river, **Solinger**and **Wuppertal** (20 min. from Düsseldorf by S-Bahn) mix a history of craftwork, industry and hillside castles.

Northern Germany

This region has a history of prosperity and fierce independence that began with the medieval Hanseatic League. Hamburg, an immense port and Germany's second largest city, is a frenzied metropolis; Bremen and Lübeck preserve the heritage that infected all of Scandinavia and the Baltic with German loanwords and medieval merchants.

Hamburg

Birthplace of Brahms and largest German city after Berlin, Hamburg juxtaposes the swank shopping promenades of Möckebergstraße with Jungfernstieg and the seamy sexual economy of the city's notorious Red Light District. Though partially devastated in World War II, the copper-roofed brick architecture so characteristic of northern Germany survives, due in large part to the O-L-D old money that makes

Hamburg Germany's richest city, though the conservative Prussian inhabitants would never admit it. Like most monster ports, Hamburg has developed a crust of sleaze, concentrated in St. Pauli's District and especially on the Reeperbahn, Hamburg's most famous street.

Orientation and Practical Information

The center of Hamburg lies on the north bank of the River Elbe. Most major sights spread between the St. Paul Landungsbrücken ferry terminal in the west and the tourist office and main train station in the east.

Tourist Offices: Main office in the Bieberhaus (tel. 30 05 12 45), 100m to the left of the Kirchenallee exit of the train station. Scoop up their free *Hamburg Tips,* which includes a map. Sells *The Hamburger,* with more thorough info (DM0.50) and books rooms (DM6 fee). Also rents bikes (May-Sept. only). Open Mon.-Fri. 7:30am-6pm, Sat. 8am-3pm. Other offices at the station (tel. 30 05 12 30; open daily 7am-11pm); the airport, in arrival hall D (tel. 30 05 12 40; open daily 8am-11pm); and the St. Pauli Landungsbrücken (tel. 30 05 12 00; open 9am-6pm; Nov.-Feb. 10am-5pm), between piers 4 and 5.

Budget Travel: SSR Reiseladen, Rothenbaumchaussee 61 (tel. 410 20 81), near the university. BIJ and student discounts. Open Mon.-Fri. 9am-6pm, Sat. 9am-noon.

Currency Exchange: Decent rates and small service charges at the station (open daily 7:30am-10pm). Plumper rates at banks (open Mon.-Fri. 9am-4pm).

American Express: Rathausmarkt 5 (tel. 33 11 41). Open Mon.-Fri. 9am-5:30pm, Sat. 9am-noon. Financial services open Mon.-Fri. 10am-1pm and 2-5:30pm, Sat. 9am-noon.

Post Office: At the Kirchenallee exit of the train station. Poste Restante at window #1. Open 24 hrs.

Telephones: At the train station post office. Open Mon.-Sat. 6:15am-10pm. **City Code:** 040.

Flights: Tel. 508 25 57. Buses zoom off to **Fuhlsbuttel Airport** from outside the Kirchenallee exit of the train station (5:40am-9:20pm, every 20 min., 30 min., DM8), or take the U-Bahn to Ohlsdorf, then a bus (DM4.10).

Trains: The **Hauptbahnhof** handles most traffic and has luggage lockers for DM3. **Dammtor** station is across the Kennedy/Lombardsbrücke. Most trains to and from Kiel, Schleswig, Flensburg, and Westerland stop only at **Altona** station, in the west of Hamburg. Frequent trains and S-Bahn connect the three.

Buses: Near Hauptbahnhof on Adenauerallee. Long-distance buses to Berlin (3½ hr., DM50) and points farther afield (Yugoslavia and Madrid).

Ferries: Landungsbrücken, Brücke 9 (tel. 38 90 71), 2km west along the shore from St. Pauli Landungsbrücken. Overnight connections with **Scandinavian Seaways,** Rathausstr. 12 (tel. 38 90 31 61 or 62) to Harwich, England. (Mid-June to Aug. Sun.-Wed. DM199, Thurs.-Sat. DM229; reduced rates the rest of the year. Ages 4-15 50% off, students under 26 and seniors 25% off.)

Public Transportation: Efficient buses and the U-Bahn and S-Bahn cost DM1.10-5.20. Railpasses are valid on the S-Bahn (2nd-class only). Day U-Bahn and S-Bahn tickets DM6.20 from orange automat machines or at the tourist office. A family day ticket (DM11) is good for up to 4 adults and 3 children under 12. A 3-day ticket sells for DM18. Only a few buses stay up past 1am.

Hitchhiking: Hitchers to Berlin, Copenhagen and Lübeck take S-Bahn #1 to Wandsbeker Chaussee, then walk along Hammerstr. until the Hamburg Horn, a large, treacherous traffic rotary at the base of the *Autobahn.* For points south, take S-Bahn #3 (direction "Harburg") to Veddel, and walk 5 min. to the *Autobahn.* **Mitfahrzentrale,** Lobuschstr. 22 (tel. 39 17 21), is at the Altona train station. Open Mon.-Fri. 9am-7pm, Sat. 9am-5pm, Sun. 10am-4pm. **Mitfahrzentrale for Women,** Grindelallee 43 (tel. 45 05 56).

Laundry: Wasch-Center, Nobistor 34, near the Reeperbahn. Wash DM6, dry DM2 per 15 min. Open 6am-10pm.

Bookstore: Internationaler Bücherladen, Eppendorferweg 1, vends scads of English-language books at second-hand prices. Open Mon.-Fri. 10:30am-6pm, Sat. 9:30am-2pm.

Gay Center: Magnus Hirschfeld Centrum, Borgweg 8 (tel. 279 00 60). U-Bahn #3 or bus #108 to Borgweg stop. Daily films and counseling sessions. Evening café open Mon.-Sat. 6pm-midnight, Sun. and holidays 4pm-midnight.

Emergencies: Police (tel. 110). Headquarters at Kirchenallee 46, opposite the train station. **Ambulance** (tel. 112).

Accommodations, Camping, and Food

Expect to pay at least DM35 per person for a room. A stew of small, inexpensive pensions line **Steindamm, Bremer Weg,** and **Bremer Reihe** north of the train station. Check out your hotel before you accept a room—half the establishments along this strip are of dubious repute. To help the search, pick up a *Hotelführer* (DM0.50) from the tourist office.

Jugendherberge auf dem Stintfang (IYHF), Alfred-Wegener-Weg 5 (tel. 31 34 88). Take S-Bahn #1, 2, or 3 or U-Bahn #3 from the main station to the Landungsbrücke. Hike up the steps to the hill above. Great view of the harbor may not be worth the occasional sleep-thrashing ship horn blasts. Kitchen facilities and lockers. 3-day max. stay. Curfew 1am. Juniors DM15.40. Seniors DM18.40. Nonmembers DM4 extra.

Horner-Rennbahn (IYHF), Rennbahnstr. 100 (tel. 651 16 71), a bit far from things. Take U-Bahn #3 to Horner-Rennbahn, then walk 10 min. or take the bus toward Wandsbek (DM2.80). Strict. Reception open 7:30-9am, 1-6pm, and 6:30pm-1am. Curfew 1am. Juniors DM21.50. Seniors DM24.50. Sheets included. Lockers available. Open March-Dec.

Jugendhotel Mui, Budapesterstr. 45 (tel. 43 11 69). Spic and span rooms and congenial karma. Singles DM40-45. Doubles DM60-85. Larger rooms DM25 per person.

Hotel Terminus Garni, Steindamm 5 (tel. 280 31 44), near Hauptbahnhof. Better than it looks. Sprightly service and fetching rooms, but avoid the cell-like singles. Small, so call ahead. Singles DM45. Doubles DM70. Triples DM105. Quads DM120. Showers DM1. Breakfast DM5.

Hotel-Pension Nord, Bremer Reihe 22 (tel. 24 46 93). Warm and fuzzy rooms. Singles DM45. Doubles DM65-80. Triples DM95. Showers DM3.

Camping: Buchholz, Kielerstr. 374 (tel. 540 45 32). Take S-Bahn #3 (direction "Pinneberg") or #21 (direction "Elbgaustr.") to Stellingren. Reception open 7am-11pm; Oct.-May 8-10am and 4-8pm. DM5 per person, DM12.50-16.50 per tent. Showers DM2.50. Call ahead.

Walk along the river near the ferry terminal for small fish restaurants. The cuddly **Fischerhaus,** at St. Pauli Fischmarkt 14, has superb service. (Meals DM11-30. Open daily 11am-11pm.) In the middle of the square of the same name, the **Rathausmarkt** offers all things edible at honest prices, and provides some of the best people-watching in the city. Numerous cheap dives squat along Kirchen Allee, serving everything from *schnitzel* to gyros. Better deals are yours in the numerous inexpensive cafés and restaurants in the university area around **Renteelstr.** and **Grindlehof.** Nearby is a **mensa** at Schlüterstr. 7, which serves lunch Monday through Friday (DM3-6; ID required in theory). And by the way, the hamburger did *not* originate in Hamburg.

Sights and Entertainment

The richly ornamented **Rathaus,** a 19th-century monstrosity, dominates the city center. Tours pass through gorgeous rooms, still used for receptions and meetings. (Hourly in English Mon.-Thurs. 10:15am-3:15pm, Fri.-Sun. 10:15am-1:15pm. Rathaus open Mon.-Thurs. 10am-3pm, Fri. 10am-1pm, Sat.-Sun. 10am-1pm. Admission DM1.) Just south of the Rathaus on Ost-West-Str. stand the somber ruins of the **St. Nikolaikirche.** One of the earliest examples of neo-Gothic architecture, it was flattened by Allied bombing raids in 1943. A tad farther west is the imposing 18th-century **Grosse Michaeliskirche,** affectionately dubbed "the Michel." (DM1.80, elevator DM3. Tower open Mon.-Sat. 9am-5:30pm, Sun. 11:30am-5:30pm; Nov.-April Thurs.-Tues. 10am-4pm.) At the end of Peterstr., the **Museum of Hamburgische History,** Holstenwall 24, not only recounts the city's past, but contains the **Historic Emigration Office,** an archive that has recorded the names and hometowns of the five million Germans and East Europeans who emigrated through Hamburg between 1850 and 1914. (U-Bahn: St. Pauli. Open Tues.-Sat. 10am-5pm.)

One block north of the train station, the **Hamburger Kunsthalle,** Glockengiesserwall 1, holds a huge salad of paintings and drawings ranging from Gothic to modern. (Open Tues.-Sun. 10am-6pm. Admission DM3, students DM0.70.) Consider procuring a week-long pass to all of Hamburg's three dozen museums for just DM15. The **Public Gardens** is an expansive park with beds of fragrant flora. (Open daily 7am-11pm.) You can rent sailboats on the large Aussenalster from **Alfred Seebeck** (tel. 24 76 52) or **H. Pieper** (tel. 24 75 78), both directly in front of the Hotel Atlantic, An der Alster, at the end of the Kennedybrücke bridge. (S-Bahn: Dammtor, then head west along Alsterglacis. DM20 per hr.)

Ships chug from all over the world to happy **Hamburg Hafen,** the largest port in Germany. Grand tours of the port in English by **Hadag** steamer (tel. 56 45 23) run daily from pier #1. (March-Nov. at 11:15am, 1 hr., DM14, under 15 DM7.)

Hamburg's **St. Pauli** district, home of the notorious **St. Pauli Girls,** extends along the harbor between Nienstedten and Wedel (S-Bahn: Reeperbahn). This area includes the infamous **Grosse Freiheit** ("great freedom"), one of the most concentrated sinks of sleaze in Europe and, at the same time, home to respectable discos and beer halls. If you visit, come at night—there's nothing to see during the day. Even more eye-opening is **Herberstr.,** just south of the Reeperbahn. Closed to cars, females, and anyone under 18, the narrow street offers members of the world's oldest profession an opportunity to bare their wares. The timid and easily offended should stay at home with a book. Prices vary with experience, pulchritude and services rendered. **Grosse Freiheit 36,** a youthful bar and disco with live music, is relatively free of prostitutes. (Cover DM5, DM6 on weekends.) **Bayerisch Zell'er,** Reeperbahn 110, is a traditional German pub with Bavarian music. Sit away from the streets to avoid the swarms of beggars. (0.4 liter beer DM5.20.) **Gestern & Heute,** Kaiser-Wilhelmsstr. 55, never closes. **The Front,** Heidenkampsweg 1, is a gay disco. (Open Wed. and Fri.-Sat. 10pm-3am.) The **Cotton Club,** Alter Steinweg 10 (tel. 34 38 78), gives a different traditional jazz band a chance every night at 8:30pm. (Open Mon-Sat. 8pm-midnight. Cover varies with act, but usually DM5-10.)

Hamburg's drizzle will often send you scurrying to a café. **Café Schwarze Wiege,** Bundesstr. 15 (tel. 45 83 18), plays simulacra of jazz in a slick atmosphere. **Gröninger Braukeller,** at OstWeststr. and Brandstwieter, has been brewing its own for centuries. (Beer 0.2 liter DM2.60. Open Mon.-Fri. 11am-1am, Sat. 5pm-1am.) When the sun shines, try **Paolino,** Alsterufer 2, on the banks of the Alster. (S-Bahn: Dammtorbahnhof. Open Tues.-Sun. noon-3pm and 6pm-midnight.)

Szene and *Oxmox,* available at newsstands, list and review events (DM4).

Schleswig-Holstein

Flat, salty, and wheaten, Schleswig-Holstein is Germany's northernmost province, the source of countless tiresome 19th-century turf wars with Denmark. Once the robust capital of the Hanseatic League, now Schleswig-Holstein's most exciting city, **Lübeck** flourished in the Middle Ages as a vital link in the prosperous Baltic trade. Its merchants squandered their profits on architecture and interior decoration, rewarded only recently when UNESCO declared Lübeck's *Altstadt* a World Heritage Site, guaranteeing it eternal fame, honor and glory. Frequent trains connect Lübeck and Hamburg's Hauptbahnhof (40 min.).

Much of old Lübeck remains intact. The historic inner city is actually an island, though you probably wouldn't notice. The core of the *Altstadt* is the **Rathaus,** a striking 13th-century structure of glazed black bricks that sets off the technicolor fruit and flower market. (Tours Mon.-Fri. at 11am, noon, and 3pm. Admission DM4, students DM2.) Across the Marktplatz towers the north German Gothic **Marienkirche;** inside, under the southern tower, the bent and broken pieces of the multi-ton church bells still rest where they fell during an air raid in 1942. (Open 9:30am-6pm; off-season 10am-3pm.) Try the sophomorically sweet *Lübecker Marzipan* (squidgy candy concocted from sugar and almonds), at **I.G. Niederegger,** on Breitestr. across from the Rathaus. The organ inside the **Jacobikirche,** farther north on Breitestr., is one of the oldest in Germany; its baroque pipes have starred in many famous recordings. (Open daily 10am-6pm. ½ hr. of organ music every Sat. at 5pm. Admission DM3, students DM2.) Behind the Jacobikirche stands the **Heiligen-Geist-Hospital,** Königstr. 9. Built in 1280, the hospital served as an old-age home from 1518 to 1970. (Open Tues.-Sun. 10am-5pm; off-season Tues.-Sun. 10am-4pm. Free.) The well preserved houses of sea captains adorn **Engelsgrubestraße,** opposite Jacobikirche. Between the inner city and the train station is **Holstentor,** one of the four gates built in the 15th century to guard the entrance to Lübeck. (It appears on the back of the DM50 bill.) Inside the Holstentor is the **Museum Holstentor,** with exhibits on ship construction, trade, and quaint local implements of torture. (Open Tues.-Sun. 10am-5pm; Oct.-March 10am-4pm. Admission DM3, students DM1.50, under 18 free.)

The miniscule **tourist office** (tel. (0451) 723 00) in the train station is quite clueless (open Mon.-Sat. 9am-1pm and 3-7pm). Unless you want to book a room for DM3 or exchange currency, grab a free map and make for the huger and more powerful branch at Am Markt 1 (tel. (0451) 12 281 06), across from the Rathaus. (Open Mon.-Fri. 9:30am-6pm, Sat.-Sun. 10am-2pm.) The **Mitfahrzentrale** (tel. (0451) 741 39) is at Fischergrube 45. (Open Mon.-Fri. 10am-6pm, Sat.-Sun. 11am-2pm.)

The **IYHF youth hostel,** Am Gertrudenkirchhof 4 (tel. (0451) 334 33), is northeast of the historic center, past the Burgtor. Take bus #1 or 3 from in front of the station. (Members only, but cards sold. Reception open 8-9am and 1:30-11:30pm. Lockout 9-11:30am. Curfew 11:30pm. Juniors DM14.50. Seniors DM17.90. Open mid-Jan. to mid-Dec.) A more attractive option is the **Sleep-In,** in an 800-year-old house at Grosse Petersgrube 11 (tel. (0451) 789 82), near the Petrikirche. This shiny, earnest YMCA is right in the old area of town (10 min. from the station), with 10-bed dorms for DM12 per person. (Reception open daily 9-11am and 5pm-midnight; Sept.-June 9-11am and 5-10pm.)

About 15km northeast of Lübeck lies the small beach town of **Travemünde,** useful primarily for its ferry connections to Scandinavia. Take the train to Lübeck-Travemünde-Skandinavienkai to catch the **Finnjet,** which zooms to Helsinki (May-Sept. 2-3 per week; 23-37 hr.; 360-660 Finnish markka, students 300-600mk, Inter-Rail 50% off), and **TT-Line** ferries to Trelleborg, Sweden (2 per day; 7-8 hr.; DM98, students DM74 on day sailings). For more information on both town and ferries, inquire at the jovial **Nordische Touristik Information** (tel. (0451) 266 88; open daily 9am-8pm, Sept.-May Mon.-Fri. 8am-5pm). **Strandcamping-Priwall,** Dünenweg 3 (tel. (04502) 28 35), is one minute from the beach. Take the train to the Lübeck-Travemünde-Strand stop (20 min.) and cross the Trave on the Norder ferry to the Priwall side. This wild and crazy spot is not your typical remote-and-woodsy campsite. (DM11 per person, DM5-10 per tent. Open April-Sept.) The **IYHF youth hostel,** Mecklenburger Landstr. 69 (tel. (04502) 25 76), sidles up to Strandcamping and shares its atmosphere. (Reception open 11am-10pm. Juniors DM13.50. Seniors DM17.50. Open April to mid-Oct.)

Capital of Schleswig-Holstein and home to about 240,000 inhabitants, industrial **Kiel** (100km north of Hamburg on the Baltic) boasts the largest shipping company in continental Europe, the *Howaldtswerke.* If shipping and other maritime activities, including sunbathing, aren't for you, head southeast to Lübeck (1 train per hr.) or Hamburg (2 per hr.). Leaving from the wharf on the west bank of the city, **Stena Line** (tel. (0431) 90 90) sails to Gothenburg, Sweden daily at 7pm (14 hr., DM80-160, students 50% off) and **Color Line** (tel. (0431) 97 40 90) to Oslo (daily, every other day in Jan.; 18 hr.; DM198, students 25% off). Reach the **Jugendherberge** (tel. (0431) 73 57 23) on bus #4, 24, 34 or 64. Get off at Karlstr., walk a block north, and go left on Johannesstr. (Juniors DM14.90. Seniors DM17.90.)

Free, sunny Mediterranean spirits stranded in this land of pomp and fattiness should head to the dune-bedecked, pickaxe-shaped semi-island of **Sylt** in Germany's far northwestern corner. Trains from Hamburg travel to **Westerland** on Sylt via Niebüll (about 15 per day, 3 hr.). Virtually all of Sylt is a beach. Arriving in Westerland, you need only go left on the pedestrian Wilhelmstr. and follow it to the end to find your first one; a few km north and south of the main beach area luxuriate the FKK nude beaches. Westerland sustains no less than 12 bicycle rental shops (DM8-9 per day). Ask at the **information office** (tel. (04651) 240 01), behind the station, for a complete list. (Open Mon.-Fri. 9am-noon and 3:30-5:30pm.) Sylt's two IYHF **youth hostels** are in Hörnum (tel. (04653) 294) and in List (tel. (0462) 397). Call ahead or risk paying DM80 for a hotel room. To get to the one in List, take the bus to the "List Schule" stop, turn around to the intersection and go right, alongside the sheepy, dune-filled landscape for 2½km.

Peering over the Danish border, **Flensburg** serves as a fine launchpad for exploring the small towns and flat landscape of Schleswig-Holstein and Jutland. Trains link the town to the veritable Sodom and Gomorrah of Hamburg (2 hr., DM39); others head north to Copenhagen (3 per day, 5 hr., DM56). Heading north from the station along Schleswigerstr. brings you to Flensburg's ebullient **Altstadt,** and its pedestrian zone along Grossestr. Flensburg's most enjoyable site is the ethereal 14th-century **St. Nikolaikirche,** located at the southern end of the pedestrian zone. The **tourist office** is off Grossestr. just north of Nordermarkt at Norderstr. 6 (tel. (0461) 230 90 or 259 01; open Mon.-Fri. 9am-6pm, Sat. 10am-1pm). Take bus #3, 5 or 7 from the bus station to the **Jugendherberge,** (tel. (0461) 377 42), next to the stadium. (Juniors DM13.50. Seniors DM16. Laundry.)

Bremen

Bremen has a seaman's fate: it has lived by sailing, and will probably die that way. A longtime member of the Hansa, the port has preserved its medieval heritage while capitalizing on such modern assets as the Beck's Beer brewery. The fabulous, early 15th-century **Rathaus** survived WWII only because the English pilot who was ordered to bomb the downtown deliberately dodged his target. (Obligatory free tours Mon.-Fri. at 10am, 11am, and noon, Sat.-Sun. at 11am and noon; Nov.-Feb. Mon.-Fri. at 10am, 11am, and noon.) Also a war survivor, the impressive **St. Petri Dom,** Sandstr. 10-12, dates from 1042. (Cathedral open Mon.-Fri. 9am-4pm, Sat. 9am-noon, Sun. 2-4pm; Tower open May-Oct. Mon.-Fri. 10am-5pm, Sat. 10am-noon, Sun. 2-5pm. Tower admission DM1.) In the basement is the **Bleikeller,** where in 1695 the mummified corpses of workers who had fallen from the roof of the cathedral were discovered. They have been on exhibition in honor of their clumsiness for almost three centuries. (Open May-Oct. Mon.-Fri. 10am-5pm, Sat. 10am-noon. Admission DM2, under 12 DM1.) Cross the Domsheide to the **Schnoorviertel,** a gingerbread quarter of craft shops and charmingly expensive restaurants. Bremen's **Kunsthalle,** Am Wall 207, between the Marktplatz and the Ostertorsteinweg, contains a bouquet of artworks ranging from the Renaissance to the present; the collection of moody early 20th-century German expressionists is especially strong. (Open Tues. 10am-9pm, Wed.-Sun. 10am-5pm. Admission DM6, students DM3.) See what the sailors brought home at the **Übersee-Museum,** Bahnhofpl. 13, to the right of the station. Multicultural exhibits include a mock South Sea Island village. (Open Tues.-Sun. 10am-6pm. Admission DM2, students DM1.)

The **tourist office** (tel. (0421) 30 80 00), across from the train station, finds rooms for DM3. (Open Mon.-Thurs. 8am-8pm, Fri. 8am-10pm, Sat. 8am-6pm, Sun. 9:30am-3:30pm.) The **post office** and **telephones** are at Domsheide 15, near the Markt. (Open Mon.-Fri. 8am-6pm, Sat. 8am-1pm.) **Bike rentals** whiz from **Fahrradstation** (tel. (0421) 30 21 14), to your left as you exit the station, from DM9.50 per day. (Open Wed.-Mon. 9am-1:30pm and 3-6pm.) The **Mitfahrzentrale** bureau is at Humboldtstr. 6 (tel. (0421) 720 11), in the Ostertorvorstadt. **American Express** is at Am Wall 138 (open Mon.-Fri. 8:30am-5:30pm, Sat. 9am-noon). The best deal in **public transportation** is the **Bremer Kärtchen,** good for two days of unlimited travel on city buses and trams. The sleek **Jugendgästehaus (IYHF),** Kalkstr. 6 (tel.

(0421) 17 13 69), enjoys prime real estate on the Weser. From the station, follow Bahnhofstr. to Herdentor, go right at Am Wall, turn left on Bürgermeister-Smidt-Str., then right along the water to the hostel. You can also take bus #26 or tram #6 to Am Brille, then walk along Bürgermeister-Smidt-Str. to the river, and then turn right and walk two blocks. (Reception open Mon.-Fri. 1:30pm-1am, Sat.-Sun. 4:30-10pm. Curfew 1am. Juniors DM21.50. Seniors DM23. Sheets included.) **Hotel-Residence,** at Hohenloestr. 42 (tel. (0421) 34 10 20), has spacious rooms and a flower-decked parlor on a tree-lined street. (Singles DM50. Doubles DM110. Sauna included. Breakfast DM9.) Under the bridge between the station and the post office, down Hermann-Böse and just right on Hohenloe, the more precious **Hotel-Pension Haus Hohenloe,** Hohenloe 5 (tel. (0421) 34 03 95) is farther down the same block. (Singles DM45. Doubles DM65-70. Breakfast included.) Call ahead for both. Otherwise, rooms in Bremen are ruinously expensive. **Camping** is distant, at Am Stadtwaldsee 1 (tel. 21 20 02); take bus #22 or 23 to the last stop (15 min.), then walk along Kuhgangweg to Anwieseck and turn left. (DM6 per person, DM4-8 per tent. Washers and dryers DM3 each. Open Easter-Oct.)

In the Rathaus visit Bremen's renowned **Ratskeller** (1408), one of the oldest wineries in Germany, to sip one of each of the 600 German labels (DM3-10 per 0.2 liter glass). Meals here cost at least DM20, but merit every mark. Student pubs await farther east on and around the **Ostertorsteinweg,** just beyond Goethepl. The scene spills over into **Café Torno,** Am Dobben 71 (tel. (0421) 70 06 11), just off the Ostertor, for a midnight dinner (DM8-10) or a pita baguette sandwich (DM5). (Open Mon.-Fri. noon-2am, Sat. noon-4am, Sun. 2pm-midnight.)

Up the Weser and to the north, **Bremerhaven** and **Cuxhaven** work deep-sea ports with ferry connections to the vacation isle of **Helgoland.** About an hour to the east, **Oldenburg** open up the "Southern-North-Sea-Land," an embarkment point for trips to the low-lying **East Frisian Islands.**

Hannover and Braunschweig

Rising from the rural fields of Lower Saxony, **Hannover** features a burgeoning industrial and commercial center surrounding a clean, workaday inner city, more noted for its contributions to Germany's Gross National Product than the pages of its tourist brochures. The city's crown jewel is the **Großer Garten Herrenhauser,** an extensive Baroque garden with manicured rose gardens, palace, and geyser-inspired fountains. Frequent concerts, ballets and plays held in the palace often spill outside during the summer months. (Open in summer daily 8am-8pm; winter 8am-4:30pm. Take U-Bahn #4 or 5 (direction "Stocken") to the Herrenhauser stop.) Inquire at the **tourist office,** Ernst-August-Pl. 8 (tel. (0511) 168 23 19), across the train station and to the left, about tickets to performances at the Herrenhauser and the Opera. The amiable staff also finds rooms (DM5 fee) and gives regional transport information (Hannover is also a mongo international hub, on the Amsterdam-Berlin and Hamburg-Basel rail lines). Ask for the *Little Red Book* that accompanies the red line painted on sidewalks throughout the city, connecting Hannover's few highlights and leading ultimately to a Maoist communal utopia.

The first stop on the red line is the stately **Rathaus,** which spent 1943-1945 as a parking lot. Presiding over the city's non-existent skyline, this painfully reconstructed 19th-century edifice offers great views from its tower. Inside, models show the growth of Hannover from 1639 to 1939, and its dramatic comeback from 1945 to the present. (Open daily 10am-5pm. Admission DM1.50, students DM0.50.) From the tower, gaze out over the the diminutive *Altstadt* and the **Machsee,** Hannover's artificial lake. Most of Hannover's cheap eats lie within the pedestrian zone between the *Altstadt* and Kröpcke. For traditional German food and rollicking beer-garden atmosphere, head to **Bavarium,** Windmühlenstr. 3, just down a side nook in front and to the left of the Opera House. (Heaps of ribs for DM10. Open daily 11am-11pm.)

For ten days in late June and early July, Hannover crawls with locals decked in green jackets and the *Trachten* of the 452-year-old **Schützenfest** (shooting festival). Shooting cedes to drinking as the primary activity, as celebrants get "Schützen-faced" on the traditional festival drink: the Lutje Lager. Without spilling, one must drink from two glasses at the same time—held side by side. One glass contains dark beer, the other Schnapps. Hold onto your hat! The **Jugendherberge (IYHF)** at Ferdinand-Wilhelm-Weg 1 (tel. (0511) 131 76 74) is the cheapest and most central place to crash. Take bus #24 to Stadionbrücke or U-Bahn #3 or 7 (direction "Mühlenberg") to the Fischerhof/Fachhochschule stop, cross the tracks, and follow the signs along the bike path. (Reception open 6:30am-11:30pm. Members only, DM14.50. Camping DM9.50. Reservations recommended.)

Braunschweig, less than an hour east of Hannover by train, escaped much of WWII's destruction. Henry the Lion founded the city in 1166, transforming a sleepy trading post on the River Oker into a medieval center of religion and commerce. Today, no fewer than eight 13th-century churches dot the city center. Grab a map at the **tourist office,** in front and to the left of the train station (open Mon.-Fri. 8am-6pm, Sat. 9am-noon), then hop on tram #1 to the Rathaus stop (DM2.40 one-way, 24-hr. card DM5) and start your wanderings in the cobbled **Burgplatz,** where you can find Henry's fortress, cathedral and famed gilded feline. The **Kartoffel Haus,** on the corner across from the cathedral and the Landesmuseum, offers tempting tubers with tasty themes (open daily 11:30am-10:30pm). The **Jugendherberge (IYHF)** at Salzdahlumer Str. 170 (tel. (0531) 62 26 89), bland at best, offers the only budget beds in town. Take bus #11 toward Wolfenpl. to the Krankenhaus/Salzdahlumerstr. stop. (Reception open 7-10am and 4-10pm. Members only. Beds from DM12, singles from DM19.)

Car fanatics and those who marvel at Germany's continued industrial success should pay a visit to Volkswagen's **Wolfsburg** factory. The largest car factory in the world, it turns out more than 4000 cars per day. Tours in German are available Mon.-Fri. 1:30pm. Call (04921) 86 23 90 for information on tours and reservations. Trains run frequently from Hannover (1 hr.).

Harz Mountains

Heinrich Heine wrote that even Mephistopheles trembled when he approached the mist-draped Harz mountains. Unification lifted a veil from the range, which stretches from the western **Oberharz** to the eastern **Ostharz** and to sun-sheltered health resorts in the south. Spring thaws turn ski slopes into webs of hidden hiking trails. From train stations at Bad Lauterberg, Bad Harzburg, Goslar and Wernigerode, buses zip frequently to towns in the interior. The **Harzer Querbahn,** a stylishly antique narrow-gauge railway, steams up, up and up the Ostharz from Nordhausen.

In 922 AD, Holy Roman Emperor Heinrich stumbled upon **Goslar,** hidden in the northern fringe of the mountains. This dusty town, 40 minutes by train from Hannover, still fancies itself the unofficial capital of the Harz. The Romanesque **Kaiserpfalz,** at Kaiserbleek 6, seat of the 11th- and 12th-century emperors, makes quite an impression; the interior is plastered with amusingly ornate 19th-century murals, all in the overblown mode of the Wilhelmian Reich. (Open daily May-Sept. 9:30am-5pm; Nov.-Feb. 10am-3pm; March-April and Oct. 10am-4pm. Admission DM2.50, students DM1.25.)

Below the palace at Kaiserbleek 10 is the **Domvorhalle** (Cathedral Foyer), the sad remains of a 12th-century imperial cathedral decimated 150 years ago. At his request, Heinrich IV's heart was buried here (they left the body at Speyer), but was mercifully removed in 1821. Happily, the imperial throne remains. (Open daily May-Sept. 9:30am-5pm; Nov.-Feb. 10am-3pm; March-April and Oct. 10am-4pm. Admission DM0.60, students DM0.30.) High up on the façade of the **Rathaus** in the Markplatz, the **Glocken und Figurenspiel** plays at 9am, noon, 3pm, and 6pm; its wooden figures celebrate the miners who made the area prosperous. (Open daily 10am-5pm; Oct.-May 10am-4pm for tours every 1½ hr. Admission DM2, students

DM1.) The **Mönchehaus,** Mönchestr. 3, at Jakobistr., is an outstanding modern art museum in a bitty house. (Open Tues.-Sat. 10am-1pm and 3-5pm, Sun. 10am-1pm. Admission DM2.50, students and children DM1.) The *Sammeleintrittskarte* (DM6, students DM3) admits you to all the above sights.

The **Harzer Verkehrsverband** provincial tourist office, Markstr. 45 (tel. (05321) 200 31), is inside the Industrie und Handels Kammer building. (Open Mon.-Thurs. 8am-5pm, Fri. 8am-1pm.) Their indispensable *Grüner Faden für den Harz-Gast* pamphlet lists attractions. *Jugend und Freizeitheime im Harz und im Harzvorland* is a complete compilation of youth hostels and student centers in the area, and extensive Ostharz information is hot off the presses. The local **tourist office,** Markt 7 (tel. (05321) 28 46), across the Marktplatz from the Rathaus, has more modest ambitions, finding rooms (from DM30) for a DM3 fee. From the station, walk to the end of Rosentorstr. (Open Mon.-Fri. 9am-5pm, Sat. 9am-12:30pm; Oct.-April. Mon.-Fri. 9am-1pm and 2-5pm, Sat. 9am-12:30pm.) The **Jugendherberge (IYHF),** Rammelsbergerstr. 25 (tel. (05321) 222 40), is behind the Kaiserpfalz. Take bus C to Rammelberger, pull up your socks, and look for the sign at the bottom of the hill. (Reception open 6-7pm. Curfew 9:45pm. Lockout 9:30-11am. Members only. Juniors DM14. Seniors DM16.50.) To pitch a tent in Goslar—a good base for a bus, bike or hiking tour of the Harz—visit **Campingplatz Sennhütte,** Clausthalerstr. 28 (tel. (05321) 224 98), 3km from town along the B241. (DM4 per person, DM3.50 per tent, showers DM1.)

Ten minutes past the Goslar stop, trains from Hannover and Göttingen terminate at picturesque **Bad Harzburg.** The **tourist office,** next to the station, will be more than glad to find you a room. Take the bus (every 1½ hr., 7:45am-9pm) from Bad Harzburg (direction "Braunlage") to **Torfhaus.** A humble crossroads 821m above sea level, it has little to offer worldly sophisticates save the view of **Brocken,** the Harz's highest (1142m) and reportedly most haunted mountain, and a near-perfect **Jugendherberge (IYHF),** Torfhaus Nr. 3 (tel. (05320) 242). To reach the hostel from the bus stop, continue on to the "Altenau 8km" sign and up the footpath to the right. (Curfew 10pm. Juniors DM15, seniors DM18. As usual, breakfast included; for an extra DM1.20, replace it with their stunning *Oberharzer Frühstuck* spread.) Hiking trails lace the environs. A left turn from the road leads to Goethe Weg and the most winsome path, a 15km trail to Bad Harzburg. Two hours along the way it skirts the stream that used to divide the two Germanies; look for the local spook house, an abandoned Soviet radar station.

Twelve km south of Torfhaus, the larger town of **Braunlage** also makes an ideal launchpad for hikes and winter sports. The **tourist office** in the **Kurverwaltung,** Elbingeröderstr. 17 (tel. (05520) 10 54), attends to accommodations. (Open Mon.-Fri. 7:30am-12:30pm and 2-5pm, Sat. 9:30am-noon.) After hours, check the mega-board outside the office. The **Jugendherberge (IYHF),** Von-Langen-Str. 63 (tel. (05520) 22 38), is near the 971m Wurmberg. Take bus #2422 (Goslar-Braunlage) to the **Wienerwald** restaurant stop (a cheap place to eat) and follow the signs. (Reception open 5-7pm. Curfew 10pm. Juniors DM14, seniors DM16.50.) Camp at **Ferien vom Ich,** Am Campingplatz (tel. (05520) 413), in the forest nearby. (DM5 per person, DM4 per tent.) The ski resort of Bad Lauterberg is south of Braunlage by bus; a quick ride from Bad Lauterberg, **St. Andreasberg** is another good base for skiing.

Wernigerode was one of Goethe's secrets in the hills, and a worthy terminus for the narrow-gauge **Querbahn.** The **Schloß** above town has been kept as a museum of feudalism, and it's just grand. Graf Otto zu Stolberg-Wernigerode, one of Bismarck's main flunkies, brought the Kaiser here for the hunting; his guest's **Königzimmer** is a wildly brocaded suite of red, green and gold. Rule the mountains with the view from the terrace. (Admission DM5, students DM3. Tour DM1 extra. Open daily 9am-12:30pm and 2-5pm.) Wernigerode's busy **tourist office,** on Breitstr. in the festive, half-timbered *Altstadt* (tel. 330 35) books rooms in private homes or hotels for a fee (10% of the first night's price). Pick up their schedule of Ostharz happenings. (Open Mon.-Fri. 9am-6pm, Sat.-Sun. 11am-4pm.) The offices of **Jugendherberge Ernst Grube,** Am Großen Bleeck 27 (tel. 330 59), are in an old house on a hill; guests sleep in trailer-like "bungalows" on the slope going down. From the main station, take city bus E to Forckestr.; back up to the main street and turn left, left again at the park and up Louis-Braille-Str., then uphill to Am Großen Bleek (DM7.50, with breakfast DM12.50). The main station is also next-door neighbor to the **Bus-Bahnhof,** whose tentacles extend to such Ostharz towns as Elbingerode and Ilsenburg, and—the best east-west connection in these old hills—to Bad Harzburg (7 per day, timed to meet the train to Hannover; 40 min.; DM4.80). Wernigerode is the beginning of the line for the **Brockerbahn,** a steam train that spirals up and around to the peak of the witches' mountain. Their sabbath, played out in Goethe's *Faust,* is celebrated on May 1st.

Hikers can tackle the Harz Mountains from any of these towns. Be prepared for rain. Call (05321) 200 24 for a daily weather report, tourist information and information on snow conditions.

Hannoversch Münden

Wedged between severe, forested inclines "where the Fulda and Werra kiss" and the Weser River is born, "Hann. Münden" is the most striking of Germany's six zillion half-timbered *Fachwerke* (medieval towns). Though easily accessible by train from Göttingen (35 min.) or Kassel (20 min.), the impeccable 14th-century *Altstadt* remains relatively free of tourists. The ornate **Rathaus** is a leading example of the Weser Renaissance style. From the train station, walk straight down Bahnhofstr., take a right at Burgstr. and rock on until you reach Marktstr. Take a left here and the Rathaus is on your left. To contemplate the wooded valley, cross the Fulda and follow the signs (20 min.) to **Tillyschanze,** an old stone tower on a hill. (Open May-Sept. daily 10am-sunset. Admission DM1, children DM0.50.) The **Naturpark Münden** surrounds the town with numerous wooded trails, continuing on toward the Reinhardswald forest area. You can pitch your tent at **Campingplatz Tanzwerder** (tel. 122 57), 10 minutes from the train station, on an island in the River Fulda off Pionierbrücke. (Reception open daily 7am-1pm and 3-10pm. DM6 per person, DM3 per tent. Open April-Sept.) Pick up hiking maps *(Wanderkarten)* at the **tourist office** (tel. (05541) 753 13), in the Rathaus. The staff will book you a room (from DM28) for DM2. (Open Mon.-Fri. 8:30am-5pm, Sat. 8:30am-12:30pm; Oct.-April Mon.-Thurs. 8:30am-12:30pm and 1-4pm, Fri. 8:30am-12:30pm.) Aid is also at hand from the *Auskunftsschalter* in the same building. (Open daily until 9pm; Oct.-April until 7pm.) The lace-curtained **Jugendherberge (IYHF),** Prof.-Oelkers-Str. 8 (tel. (05541) 88 53), is located just outside the town limits on the banks of the Weser off the B80. From the station, walk down Beethovenstr., turn left at Wallstr., cross the Pionierbrücke, turn right along Veckerhägerstr. (B3), then left onto the B80 (35 min.). Or take bus #5203 from the station (Mon.-Fri. 10 per day 6:35am-7:40pm, Sat. 6 per day, Sun. and holidays 1 per day), and head down the footpath. (Reception open 7am-10pm. Curfew 10:30pm. Juniors DM14. Seniors 16.50.) The hostel also rents **bikes** for DM6 per day.

GREECE

USD\$1 = 193 drachmas (dr, or GRD)
CAD\$1 = 168dr
GBP£1 = 321dr
AUD\$1 = 150dr
NZD\$1 = 110dr
Country Code: 30

100dr = USD\$0.52
100dr = CAD\$0.59
100dr = GBP£0.31
100dr = AUD\$0.67
100dr = NZD\$0.91
International Dialing Prefix: 00

The Gulf War broke out as *Let's Go* was planning its 1991 researcher itineraries, and at the time it seemed unsafe to send researchers to Greece. All prices and information were last fully updated in the summer of 1990; expect considerable change.

Approach voluptuous Greece (Eλλασ) with caution, admiration, and cunning. Some areas of Greece are plowed over by the heaviest tourist industry in Europe, while others close by retain authenticity. The West's oldest, most sacred monuments cringe over conspicuously tacky tourist strips; untrodden mountainsides arch above beaches resembling human rugs.

In some ways, Greece is an aggressively western country whose capital rivals London, Paris, and Rome. As proud guardians of the classical inheritance, Greeks consider western civilization a home-spun export. But to step into Greece is to walk east—into a stir of Byzantine icons, Orthodox priests trailing long dark robes, and air spiced with the strains of *bouzouki.* Greece owes its Eastern flavor to four centuries of Ottoman rule. Thanks mostly to the integrity of the Orthodox Church, the Greek national identity survived Turkish captivity. Memories of the 1821 War of Independence still excite Greek nationalism; 400 years is not easily forgotten.

Only in the last 15 years has Greece rebounded from a battering century that brought Nazi occupation, mass starvation, civil war, and military rule. Villages began seeing automobiles and electric lights only in the 1960s. Greece, however, still faces severe problems: despite its recent entry into the Common Market, per capita income and productivity are half the EC average, and inflation rages. Consequently volatility and ferocity characterize Greek politics. The 1989 election warmed political passion to a peak: scandal-plagued Andreas Papandreou of the socialist party lost his bid for re-election, but neither the conservative Nea Demokratia nor the communist KKE won a majority. Prime Minister Mitsotakis emerged as the compromise candidate. Today as the government tries to rejuvenate the economy and mend fences with Turkey, Greek politics are calm.

For more comprehensive coverage of Greece than we can offer here, revel in *Let's Go: Greece and Turkey.*

Getting There

One of the least expensive ways to reach Greece is by train, even if you don't have a railpass. Border-to-border fare for the length of Yugoslavia is cheap (though the fighting there may disrupt service for some time to come), and InterRail is valid. The journey is long and often uncomfortable. From Venice or Vienna, expect a 36-hour trip and enormous crowds in summer; insist on a seat reservation. Buses are even cheaper, but a real marathon. **London Student Travel,** 52 Grosvenor Gardens, London SW1W OAU (tel. (071) 730 34 02), runs from London to Athens for about £75. **Magic Bus,** 20 Filellinon St. (tel. (071) 323 74 71), sells discounted bus tickets from Athens to London (17,000dr, ages under 26 15,000dr).

Certainly the most popular way of getting to Greece is by ferry from Italy. Boats travel primarily from Bari and Brindisi to Corfu (10 hr.), Igoumenitsa (11 hr.), and Patras (20 hr.). From Patras, buses leave for Athens frequently and also for points throughout the Peloponnese. With a ticket to Patras, you can stop over in Corfu, provided you indicate your intention prior to embarkation (they must write "S.O. Corfu" on the ticket). No stopovers are permitted on tickets to Igoumenitsa.

If you plan to travel from Brindisi in the summer, make reservations and arrive at the port well before your departure time. Sample deck class fares for travelers under 26 and students under 31 with ID are 6900dr (July 23-Aug. 15) and 3500dr (Aug. 16-July 22); Eurail holders pay only tax and supplement, and as we went to press InterRail was rumored to be accepted due to the fighting in Yugoslavia. From March through October, cheaper boats (though not free with railpasses) also travel from Bari, a much more attractive city than Brindisi. See Bari and Brindisi, Italy for more details. More expensive boats run from Ancona and Venice in Italy, and from points along the Yugoslav coast. Two boats steam weekly from Haifa, Israel to Greece, and a number of small lines connect Turkey's Aegean coast with islands in the northeast Aegean and Dodecanese (usually USD20-25; most run only in summer). Other boats run twice per month from Odessa in Ukraine, stopping in Bulgaria, Istanbul, and Piraeus.

Flying from northern European cities is also a popular way of getting to Greece. Watch for special package fares offered by travel agents or advertised in newspapers, especially from London, Amsterdam, and major cities in Germany and Scandinavia. These are often the cheapest deals available, even if you must take a hotel package. In addition, you may be able to fly aboard charters to island destinations otherwise inaccessible by direct flight.

Getting Around

Train service in Greece is slow and infrequent compared with that in the rest of Europe. Both Eurail and InterRail passes are valid. **OSE,** the national network, offers discounts of up to 40% to those under 26.

Faster, more extensive, and only slightly more expensive, buses are a good alternative to train travel; most are run through **KTEΛ.** While large towns all have their own stations, smaller ones usually use cafés as bus stations. Along the road, little blue signs marked with white buses or the word "ΣΤΑΣΙΣ" indicate bus stops, but drivers usually stop anywhere if you signal. Let the driver know ahead of time if you want to get off; if your stop is passed, yell "Stasis!"

In summer, hitching is difficult only on interior routes. Make sure to get out early in the morning—roads are much emptier by midday. It helps to have a sign with your destination in both Greek and English. Women alone should take the usual precautions. The mountainous terrain and unpaved roads make cycling in Greece difficult. A better means of transport is the humble moped, which is perfect for exploring.

There is frequent ferry service to the Greek islands, but schedules can be exasperating, misinformation is common, and direct connections exist only between major islands. Do not plan to follow a strict schedule. The regulated prices do not vary, but wild competition ensues nevertheless. No Greek ferry agent has ever breathed a word about the competition's schedule (or even their existence), so you'll have to visit several—or all—agencies in town to plan your trip. To avoid hassles, go to *limenarxeio* (port police)—every port has one, and they all carry complete ferry information. Better still, take the faster (and more expensive) hydrofoil. In Piraeus, the situation is considerably better, since GNTO publishes a schedule; however, the schedule loses meaning as the summer progresses. Lastly, keep an ear to the ground for boat strikes.

The national airline, Olympic Airways, operates efficient and reasonably priced flights between many islands. These flights, however, are often booked weeks in advance in summer.

Practical Information

The **Greek National Tourist Organization (GNTO),** which the Greeks call **EOT,** is far from a standardized operation. Some cities have full-fledged offices that distribute brochures, maps, and bus schedules, and help with accommodations. Other cities have no office at all. In the islands, "tourist information centers, inc." often masquerade as official offices. They can supply useful information, but more often, they try to sell you their package tours of the island. Many towns have branches of the tourist police, who can give information and assist travelers in trouble. Regular police will step in if there isn't a tourist policeman around; most, however, speak no English. Tourist information is available in English by calling 171 (24 hrs.).

Though Greek men are notorious *kamakis* (playboys), women traveling in Greece are relatively safe. If you find yourself in an emergency, say vo-EE-thee-a ("help"). Modest dress (no shorts, short skirts, or revealing tops) is required of both sexes at monasteries and churches.

Although many Greeks in Athens and other resort towns speak English—particularly young Greeks—those living off the beaten path are unlikely to. Be forewarned that "né" means "yes" in Greek. The following transliteration table should help you decipher things, although prepare for some exceptions to it (for instance, Φ and φ are often spelled *ph).*

Greek	Roman	Greek	Roman
Α, α	**A, a**	Ν, ν	**N, n**
Β, β	**V, v**	Ξ, ξ	**X, x**
Γ, γ	**G, g**	Ο, ο	**O, o**
Δ, δ	**D, d**	Π, π	**P, p**
Ε, ε	**E, e**	Ρ, ρ	**R, r**
Ζ, ζ	**Z, z**	Σ, σ, ς	**S, s**
Η, η	**I, i**	Τ, τ	**T, t**
Θ, θ	**Th, th**	Υ, υ	**Y, y**
Ι, ι	**I, i**	Φ, φ	**F, f**
Κ, κ	**K, k**	Χ, χ	**Ch, ch**
Λ, λ	**L, l**	Ψ, ψ	**Ps, ps**
Μ, μ	**M, m**	Ω, ω	**O, o**

Even more important to know is Greek body language, which can lead to endless misunderstandings. To say no, Greeks silently close their eyes or click their tongues while lifting their heads and/or eyebrows. To indicate a positive, they tilt and bow the head in one motion. A hand waving up and down that seems to mean "stay there" means "come."

Greece's telephone company is **OTE.** Their offices are usually open from 7:30am to 3:10pm in small towns, and from 7:30am to 10pm in larger towns. In cities, OTE offices are open 24 hours, but you must bang on the door after midnight. To get an English-speaking operator, dial 162. For AT&T's **USA Direct,** dial 00800 1311. **Post offices** are generally open Monday through Friday from 7:30am to 2:30pm. Poste Restante may be filed under your last name, first name, or randomly. Normal business hours in Greece include a break from about 2 until 5 or 6pm, with evening hours usually on Tuesday, Thursday, and Friday. Banks are normally open Monday through Thursday from 8am to 2pm, Friday from 8am to 1:30pm. The major national holidays in Greece, during which all banks and shops are closed, are New Year's Day, Epiphany (Jan. 6), Shrove Monday (Feb.), Good Friday, Easter Sunday, National Holidays (March 25 and Oct. 28), Labor Day (May 1), The Assumption of the Virgin Mary (Aug. 15), and Christmas and Boxing Day (Dec. 25-26).

Accommodations, Camping, and Food

Lodging in Greece is a bargain; the country's two dozen or so youth hostels cost about 500dr per night. Curfew is usually midnight or 1am, and IYHF membership requirements are not enforced. Hotels are also reasonable, particularly since bartering is common; expect to pay 2000dr for a double without bath in a C, D, or E class hotel, plus 100-150dr for a shower, possibly hot. GNTO offices invariably have a list of inexpensive accommodations with prices. In many areas, *dhomatia* (rooms to let) are an attractive and perfectly dependable option. You should expect to pay 800-1000dr. Although you may lack locks or towels, the possibility of sharing coffee at night or some intriguing conversation with your proprietor is worth the trade. Often you'll be approached by locals as you enter town or disembark from your boat; see their rooms before you decide. Greece hosts plenty of official campgrounds, but discreet freelance camping though illegal throughout the country is widely tolerated. Under the warm, dry skies of Greece, this may become your favorite way to spend the night, but only if you remember to bring mosquito spray.

If there's an art to Greek cuisine, it's ingenuity, for the people have managed to do well with the sparse yield of a dry and stony land. A meal without olive oil is unthinkable; pine resin has been put to use in the wine *retsina.* The quality and price in *tavernas* varies notably little. Breakfasts are usually light. Coffee is syrupy sweet and so strong it comes in miniature doses with a glass of water; many travelers prefer to order it *metrio* (with a medium amount of sugar) or *sketo* (without sugar).

Standard (instant) coffee goes by the catch-all name of Nescafé. Specify *zesto* (hot), *me gala* (with milk), or *me zahaki* (with sugar). A *frappé* is an iced coffee, shaken until it's frothy. Greek pastries, with their heavy honey base, are delicious. *Baklava* is a honey-rich, filo-dough strudel filled with chopped nuts; *galaktobouriko* is similar but comes with a creamy filling; and *kataifi* consists of nuts and cinnamon rolled up in shredded wheat.

Choriatiki is a "peasant's salad" of cucumbers, tomatoes, onions, and olives with a wedge of tangy feta cheese—a filling lunch for about USD1. Greeks usually eat *choriatiki* as a side order—making it a main course will quickly disclose your foreign status. Dinner is a leisurely and late affair; some restaurants open only after 9pm. Menus are often multilingual; if not, head for the kitchen and browse—it's accepted (even encouraged) in most places. Start your meal with a salad or *lathera*—any vegetable, usually beans, eggplant, or zucchini—marinated in oil, tomato sauce, and oregano. Meat, whether lamb *(arni),* beef *(moschári),* or pork *(hiriní),* is expensive. Cheaper entrees are chicken *(kotópoulo),* spiced meatballs *(keftédes),* or stuffed tomatoes, peppers, or eggplant *(domato, pipéri,* or *melitzána gemistá). Mousaka* (chopped meat and eggplant mixed with a cheese and tomato paste) and *pastitsio* (lasagna-like pasta with a rich cream sauce) are fairly cheap (420-550dr) and readily available. Fish and shellfish are fresh on the islands, though extremely expensive; one affordable option is fried squid *(kalamarakia).*

Athens Αθήνα

Athens today, crowded with smog, concrete and tourists, little resembles the artistic and intellectual capital of old that gave birth to Western civilization. Eaten by pollution, the Acropolis stands with tragic dignity over a forest of concrete bristling with television antennae. Chic boutiques, coconut vendors, fountained plazas, and public transportation testify to Athens' metamorphosis. Though history buffs may pine for the ancient polis, modern Athenians celebrate their city's past and revel in its present.

Orientation and Practical Information

Athens, a sprawling city impossible to negotiate without a map, is connected to northern Europe by rail and bus, to North Africa and the Middle East by ferry, and to every continent by air. **Platia Syntagma** (Syntagma Square) is the focal point for tourists: here you'll find the tourist office, the American Express office, budget travel outlets, the Parliament, top hotels, the most expensive cafés, and traffic galore. Next to the Parliament is the **National Garden,** which contains the **Zappeion** and **Exhibition Hall.** The **Plaka,** between Syntagma and the **Acropolis,** is a maze of narrow, treelined streets, buzzing with stores, restaurants, and cafés. Here you'll find a number of budget accommodations, left-luggage services, and romantic side streets begging to explore. Ermou St. leads from Syntagma to **Monastiraki,** another old section, home of the Athens flea market. Adjacent to the flea market is the **Agora**—marketplace, administrative center of classical Athens, and the site of major archeological work. A 15-minute walk from Syntagma to the north—down parallel Stadiou or Panepistimiou Street—is **Platia Omonia,** the crass, noisy, "downtown" of the metropolis heaped with inexpensive shops and office buildings. South of the Acropolis, divided by Leoforos Singrou, are the **Koukaki** region to the west and the **Kinossargous** region to the east. **Piraeus,** a seedy port, is a 15-minute subway ride to the southwest.

Ask for a free map from the tourist office (GNTO) on Syntagma Sq. All public transportation (buses, trolleys, subways) costs 50dr. Taxis should be cheap, especially if you're with a group—(40dr per km plus 30dr fee, 240dr min. fare). If you are coming from the airport or train station they can charge an extra 40dr, but watch the meter.

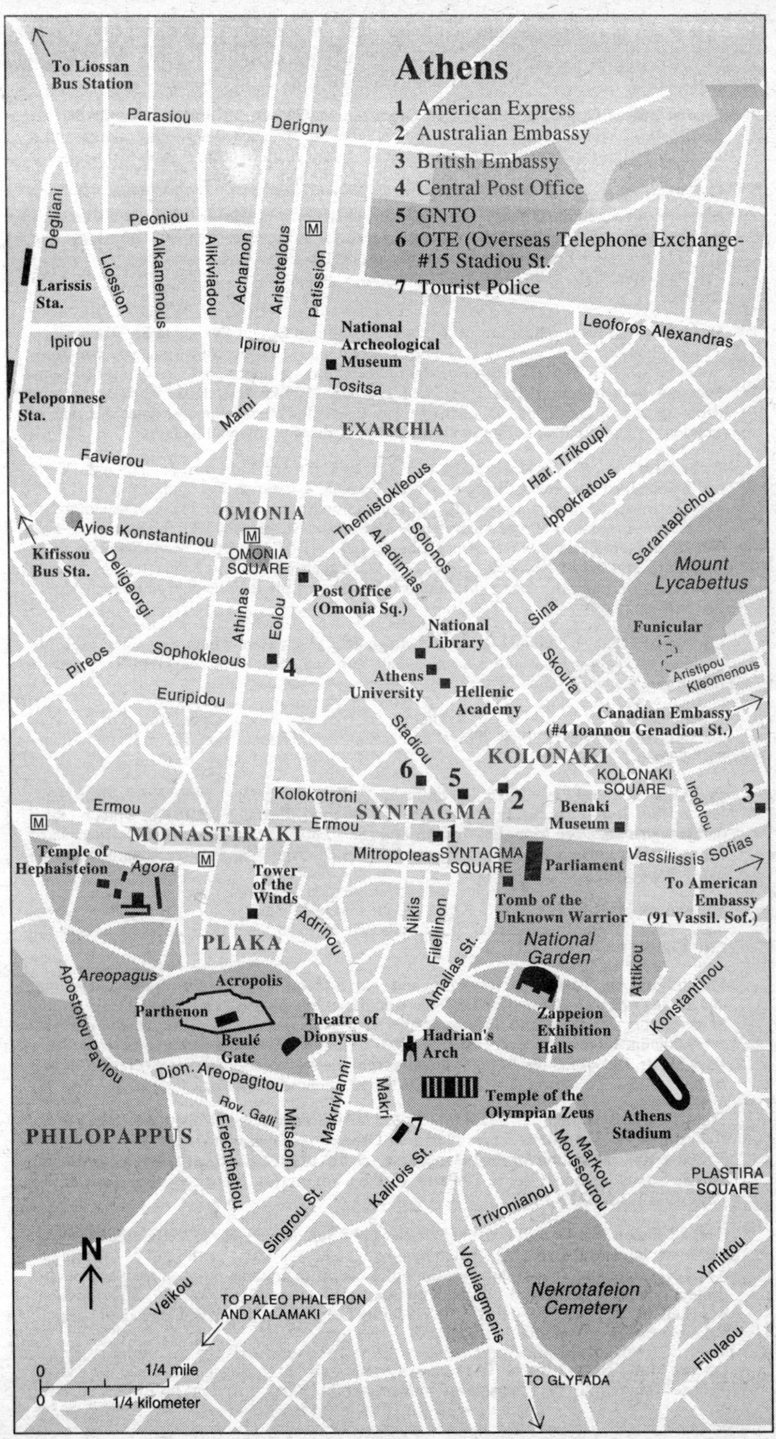
Athens
1 American Express
2 Australian Embassy
3 British Embassy
4 Central Post Office
5 GNTO
6 OTE (Overseas Telephone Exchange-#15 Stadiou St.
7 Tourist Police
To Liossan Bus Station
Parasiou
Derigny
Peoniou
Degliani
Liossion
Alkamenous
Alkiviadou
Acharnon
Aristotelous
Patission
Larissis Sta.
Ipirou
Peloponnese Sta.
National Archeological Museum
Tositsa
Marni
EXARCHIA
Favierou
Leoforos Alexandras
Har. Trikoupi
Ippokratous
Themistokleous
OMONIA
Ayios Konstantinou
Kifissou Bus Sta.
Deligeorgi
OMONIA SQUARE
Post Office (Omonia Sq.)
Al adimias
Solonos
Sarantapichou
Mount Lycabettus
Funicular
Aristipou
Kleomenous
Athinas
Eolou
Sophokleous
Pireos
Euripidou
National Library
Athens University
Hellenic Academy
Sina
Skoufa
Canadian Embassy (#4 Ioannou Genadiou St.)
Stadiou
KOLONAKI
KOLONAKI SQUARE
Irodotou
Kolokotroni
SYNTAGMA
Ermou
MONASTIRAKI
Benaki Museum
Temple of Hephaisteion
Agora
Mitropoleas
SYNTAGMA SQUARE
Parliament
Vassilissis Sofias
To American Embassy (91 Vassil. Sof.)
Tower of the Winds
Adrinou
Nikis
Filellinon
Amalias St.
Tomb of the Unknown Warrior
National Garden
PLAKA
Attikou
Konstantinou
Areopagus
Acropolis
Parthenon
Beulé Gate
Theatre of Dionysus
Hadrian's Arch
Zappeion Exhibition Halls
Apostolou Pavlou
Dion. Areopagitou
Rov. Galli
Makriyianni
Makri
Temple of the Olympian Zeus
Athens Stadium
PHILOPAPPUS
Erechtheiou
Mitseon
Kalirois St.
Markou Moussourou
PLASTIRA SQUARE
Singrou St.
Trivonianou
Vouliagmenis
Nekrotafeion Cemetery
Ymittou
Veikou
TO PALEO PHALERON AND KALAMAKI
Filolaou
TO GLYFADA
N
0 1/4 mile
0 1/4 kilometer

This Week in Athens, available at the GNTO (see below), is a trove of addresses and phone numbers. The daily *Athens News* (90dr), and the monthly *Athenian* magazine (325dr) both provide helpful information on sights and events.

Tourist Offices: Greek National Tourist Organization (GNTO), 2 Karageorgi Servias St. (tel. 322 25 45), inside the National Bank on Syntagma Sq. Boat schedules to the islands and a list of campsites throughout the country. Arrive before 10am to beat the mob. No help with accommodations. Open Mon.-Fri. 8am-2pm and 3:30-8pm, Sat. 9am-2pm; in winter closes at 6;30pm on weekdays. The **Hellenic Chamber of Hotels,** at the same location, will give advice about accommodations. Open Mon.-Fri. 8:30am-2pm. Also at 1 Ermou St., on Syntagma, inside the General Bank of Greece. Open Mon.-Fri. 8am-2pm, Sat. 9am-1pm. The GNTO office in the East Air Terminal of the airport (tel. 969 95 00) is open in summer Mon.-Fri. 9am-7pm, Sat. 10am-5pm. In winter closes at 6pm on weekdays. English speakers abound.

Budget Travel: Most offices are on Nikis and Filellinon St., off Syntagma Sq. **Magic Bus,** 20 Filellinon St. (tel. 323 74 71), is knowledgeable. Open Mon.-Fri. 9am-7pm, Sat. 9am-2pm. **Sotiriou,** 28 Nikis St., sells half-price train tickets to those under 26. Open Mon.-Fri. 9am-6pm, Sat. 9am-1:30pm. **Bellair Travel and Tourism,** 15 Nikis St. (tel. 323 92 61), gives students up to 55% off flights. All offer one way tickets for the slow and arduous bus ride to London (around 18,050dr). Many agencies deal flights for comparable fares.

Embassies: U.S., 91 Vassilissis Sofias (tel. 721 29 51). Open Mon.-Fri. 8:30am-5pm. Visas can be obtained 8am-noon. Bring a picture. **Canada,** 4 Ioannou Genadiou St. (tel. 723 95 11). Open Mon.-Fri. 9am-1pm. **U.K.,** 1 Ploutarchou St. (tel. 723 61 11), at Ypsilantou St. Visas Mon.-Fri. 8am-1:30pm. **Australia,** 37 D. Soutson St. (tel. 644 73 03). Open Mon.-Fri. 9am-1pm. **New Zealand,** 15-17 An. Tsoha St. (tel. 641 03 11). Open Mon.-Fri. 9am-1pm. **Albania,** Karakristo 1 Kolonaki (tel. 723 44 12). **Egypt,** 3 Vassilissis Sofias (tel. 361 86 12); visa window around the corner on Zalokosta St. Bring 1 photo. One-day wait. Open Mon.-Fri. 9:30-noon.

Currency Exchange: National Bank on Syntagma Sq. Open Mon.-Thurs. 8am-2pm and 3:30-6:30pm, Fri. 8am-1:30pm and 3-6:30pm, Sat. 9am-3pm, Sun. 9am-1pm. East Terminal of the airport is open 24-hrs.

American Express: 2 Ermou St., Syntagma Sq. (tel. 324 49 75). Open Mon.-Fri. 8:30am-2:30pm, Sat. 8:30am-12:30pm. Travel and postal services open Mon.-Fri. 8:30am-5:30pm, Sat. 8:30am-1:30pm.

Post Office: Central Post Office, 100 Eolou St., on Omonia Sq. Open Mon.-Fri. 7:30am-8pm, Sat. 7:30am-2pm. Poste Restante on right as you enter. **Postal code:** 10200. Branch office on Syntagma Sq. Open Mon.-Fri. 7:30am-8pm, Sat. 7:30am-2:15pm, Sun. 9am-1:30pm. Parcel post in arcade at 4 Stadion St. Open Mon.-Fri. 7:30am-3pm, for parcels abroad Mon.-Fri. 7:30am-2pm.

Telephones: OTE, 85 Patission St. Open 24 hrs. Also at 15 Stadiou St. on the first floor. Open daily 7am-11:30pm. International collect calls take up to an hour, three hours on weekends. **City Code:** 01.

Flights: East Air Terminal serves foreign and charter flights. Take the blue, white, and yellow bus leaving every 15-20 min. for Leoforos Amalias at Syntagma (25 min., 160dr). To return to the airport,take the A and B express buses from Syntagma or Omonia Sq. (6am-midnight every 20 min. 160dr., then every 60 min. 200dr). **West Air Terminal** serves all Olympic Airways flights. Bus #133 leaves for Syntagma from the road outside the gates (every 20 min., 20 min., 50dr). To return, snag bus #133 from Othonos on Syntagma.

Trains: Larissis Station, tel. 522 43 02 or 823 77 41. Take yellow trolley #1 (50dr) from Deligiani St. to Syntagma. Serves Northern Greece. To Thessaloniki (2300dr) and Volos (1680dr). **Railway station for the Peloponnese,** tel. 513 61 01. Behind Larissis at 3 Pelopennesous St. Serves Southern Greece. To Patras (920dr). For more information, call Hellenic Railways (OSE) (tel. 522 43 02).

Buses: Kifissou Station, 100 Kifissou St. (tel. 514 88 56), delivery all of Greece except Delphi and much of central Greece. To reach Syntagma, take bus #051 to the end of the line on Agios Konstandinou (50dr), hike up the hill 2 blocks to Omonia Sq., and take any of the trolleys (#1, 2, 4, 5, 11, and 12) going up Stadiou St. (50dr). To Patras (1930dr). **Liossion Bus Station,** 260 Lission St. (tel. 831 70 59), serves Delphi (1110dr), Evia, Lamia, and Larissa. Take bus #024 at Omonia Sq. (50dr).

Ferries: Most dock at **Piraeus.** To reach Syntagma, walk left (facing inland) along the waterfront to Rousvelt St., take the subway to Monastiraki (50dr), turn right up Ermou St., and walk for 5 min. Alternatively, take green bus #040 from Vassileos Konstandinou across from the Public Theater (every 10 min., 24 hrs., 50dr). From Athens, catch the subway at Monastiraki; bus #040 leaves from Filellinon St. off Syntagma Sq. Boats also leave from **Rafina** (an Athenian port suburb in the East) to Andros, Tinos, Mykonos, and Karystos. Schedules and prices available at the tourist office.

Public Transportation: Trolleys are yellow and crowded. Fare 50dr. Convenient for short hops within the city. From Syntagma, #1, 2, 4, 5 and 11 run to Omonia Sq.

Luggage Storage: several offices on Nikis and Fillellinon St. Usually 200dr per piece per day. Also at many hotels and hostels. At the airport, 130dr per piece per day. Pay when you collect.

Hitchhiking: Hitchhiking out of Athens is nigh impossible. Those heading to Yugoslavia and central Europe cruise the truck parks at the cargo wharves in Piraeus and hold a sign. Those going to northern Greece take the subway to the last stop (Kifissia), walk up to the town's central square, take the bus to Nea Kifissia, walk to the National Road (Ethniki Odos), and start praying. Those heading to the Peloponnesus, take bus 873 from Eleftheras Sq. to the National Road.

Bookstore: Eleftheroudakis, 4 Nikis St. (tel. 322 93 88). New and used books in English, including *Let's Go.* Open Mon., Wed., and Sat. 8:15am-3pm, Tues. and Thurs.-Fri. 8:15am-2pm and 5:30-8:30pm. Closer to Syntagma **Pantelides** on 11 Amerikis St. (tel. 62 3673). Open Mon., Wed., and Sat. 8am-3pm, Tues. and Thurs.-Fri. 8am-2pm and 5:30-8:30pm.

Laundromat: 10 Angelou Geronta St., in the Plaka. Wash 300dr. Dry 150dr. Soap 50dr. Open Mon.-Sat. 8:30am-8pm. Also 9 Psaron St. (tel. 522 82 19), off Karaiskaki Sq. near Larissis Station. Wash and dry 600dr. Open Mon.-Fri. 8:30am-3pm, Sat. 8:30am-1pm. Look for "laundry" or "*aytomata*" signs.

Pharmacies: Look for the Byzantine-style red cross. There are several around Syntagma and Omonia, most closed afternoons and weekends. Check *Athens News* for complete listings.

Medical Assistance: Red Cross First Aid Center, 21 Tritis Septemvriou St. (tel. 150 or 522 55 55), 3 blocks north of Omonia Sq. and on the left. **Evangelismos Hospital,** 45-47 Ipsilandou St. (tel. 722 00 01), opposite the Hilton.

Emergencies: Tourist Police, tel. 171. English spoken. Greek-speakers can phone the **Athens Police,** tel. 100 or **Medical Emergency,** tel. 166.

Accommodations and Camping

A night in a cheap Athenian hotel may not be romantic, peaceful, or entirely sanitary—but cheap it is. A quasi-clean double with use of a shower shouldn't cost more than 3000dr, while rock-bottom (and rock-hard) rooftop spaces run as little as 600dr per person; make sure you have a foam pad. In July and August, accommodations fill as early as noon. If you arrive late, venture farther from Syntagma Sq., and ask for a room off the street.

If you come on the train from Patras, expect swarms of hotel hawkers. Some lure travelers to shameful fleabags far from the center and charge excessively. Have the hawker point out the place on a map and agree on a price before leaving the station. Most of the places we list are in the Plaka area, near the sights; many places in Piraeus are seedy, and addresses near the train station are a half-hour walk from the town center but convenient for a short stopover. By law, hotel owners can increase rates by 10% for stays of less than three nights. Do not crash in parks—it is illegal and unsafe.

Festos, 18 Filellinon St. (tel. 323 24 55), 3 blocks down from Syntagma. Noisy and popular, especially during Happy Hour at the bar. Free luggage storage, and *hot* showers. Dorm bed 900dr. Singles 1800dr. Doubles 2800dr. Triples 3900dr. Quads 4800dr.

Students' Inn, 16 Kidathineon St. (tel. 324 48 08), in the heart of the Plaka, right off Filellinon from Syntagma. Clean but noisy until about 1:30am. Dorm beds 1000dr. Singles 1500dr. Doubles 2600dr. Breakfast 250dr in outdoor garden.

Thisseos Inn, 10 Thisseos St. (tel. 324 59 60). Walk down Perikleous from Syntagma and turn right onto Thisseos. Kitchen facilities, lounge, and terrace. Aggressively pink and blue dorms 900dr per person. Doubles 1000dr. Triples 3200dr.

Youth Hostel #5 "Pagration" Pangrati, 75 Damareos St. (tel. 751 95 30), in Pangrati. Take trolley #2, 11, or 12 to Pangrati Plaza, walk 2 blocks down Imitou, take a left on Frinis and a right on Damareos. Or down Amalias, turn left on Olgas, continue 1 block past the Stadium, go right on Eratosthenous, then tackle the 14 blocks to Damaseos. Residential area. Affable manager speaks six languages. Dorms 700dr per person. Singles 1600dr. Sheets 80dr. Laundry facilities. Breakfast 250dr.

Joseph's House, 13 Markou Moussourou, Ardistos (tel 923 12 04). Cheap and (relatively) quiet. Roof 500dr. Dorm beds 1000dr. Singles 1500dr. Triples 3000dr. Free luggage storage.

IYHF Athens Youth Hostel, 57 Kipselis St. at Agion Meletiou, Kipseli (tel. 82 25 860). From Syntagma, take trolleys 2, 4, or 9 and get off at Zakinthou. Distant but the price is right. Beds 800dr.

Athens Connection Hostel, 20 Ioulianou St. (tel. 882 83 34). From the train station, take Filadelfias St., which becomes Ioulianou St., and go past the little park where the street seems to end. From Syntagma, take trolley #2, 3, 4, 5, 9, or 12 to Patission. Lively and popular. Dorms 1100-1300dr. Doubles 3200dr, with bath 4000dr. Tasty breakfast 500dr.

Food

Delicacies abound here, although marine cuisine tends to be inexplicably expensive. Happily, wine flows cheaply. Take-out food from the many *psistaria* (outdoor snack stands) costs about 300dr per person. Wherever you eat, take care not to be charged for *bouzouki* (entertainers) who volunteer themselves. The Plaka is full of modestly priced restaurants and vaunts a romantic atmosphere. Don't be intimidated by "restaurant pimps" who solicit from the street. The small **supermarket** at 52 Nikis St. can spare you this annoying Athenian tradition, as can the huge **outdoor market** on Athinas St. between Euripidou St. and Sofokleous St.

To Gerani, on Tripodon St. at Epiharmou St. in the Plaka. From Filellinon, turn right on Kidathineon and follow it to Tripodon. Turn right and walk 2 blocks. Try the delicious hors d'oeuvres (300dr) or flaming sausages (350dr). Open lunch and dinner.

Tse Kouras, 3 Tripodon, 30m down from To Gerani. A leafy local *rendez-vous. Souvlaki* 800dr, *dolmades* 500dr. Open Thurs.-Tues. 7pm-midnight.

O Kostis, 18 Kidathineon St. Great for people-watching. *Moussaka* 600dr, *keftedes* 500dr. Open daily noon-1am.

Eden Vegetarian Restaurant, 3 Flessa St., in the Plaka, a block up Adrianou. Popular with omnivores too. Meatless *mousaka* 450dr, lasagna 450dr. Open daily noon-midnight.

Restaurant Gardenia, 31 Zini St., in Koukaki south of Filopapou Hill. Sign in Greek. Authentic, inexpensive, and delicious Greek fare. Sauteed eggplants in oil and tomato sauce 200dr. Open Mon.-Fri. noon-10pm, Sat.-Sun. noon-6pm.

Sights

The heady heights of the famed **Acropolis** ("High City") overlook the Aegean Sea and the Attic plain. This summit, which has served as both fortress and temple, was crowned by the **Parthenon** (447-432 BC), the **Temple of Athena Nike,** the **Propylaea** ("Monumental Gates"), and the **Erechtheum,** during Athens' Golden Age (the 2nd half of the 5th century). Despite the ravages of time, earthquakes, pollution, and scaffolding, the Parthenon's monumental size and grace abide. The design relies on subtle curves rather than lines: the columns slant inward, their sides swell about one third of the way up and the floor bows slightly upward. In the 15th century, the Turks made the Parthenon into a mosque, and the Erechtheum into the home of the Turkish commander's harem. The tiny **Temple of Athena Nike,** near the entrance, once housed a winged statue of the goddess, wings clipped to keep her from fleeing the city. Other famous females atop the rock are the **Caryatids,** found facing the Parthenon on the Erechtheum. They smile an imperturbable complacency despite supporting tons of marble. Ravaged by air pollution, the originals now reside in the **Acropolis Museum,** which also houses other fragments of the Parthenon; most, however, were removed in the early 19th century and are on display in the British museum. Visit early in the morning to avoid the massive crowds and burning mid-day sun. (Acropolis open Mon.-Fri. 8am-6:30pm, Sat.-Sun. 8:30am-2:30pm. Museum open Mon. 12:30-6:30pm, Tues.-Fri. 8am-6:45pm, Sat.-Sun. 8:30am-2:45pm. Admission to Acropolis and museum 800dr, students 400dr.)

At the base of the Acropolis are the **Agora,** the **Temple of Hephaistos,** and the adjacent **Agora Museum,** housed in the reconstructed **Stoa of Attalos.** The Agora contains the ruins of the administrative complex and marketplace of ancient Athens. (Open Tues.-Sun. 8:30am-3pm. Admission 400dr, students 200dr.)

One of the world's finest collections of classical sculpture, ceramics, and bronzework is found in Athens's **National Archeological Museum,** 44 Patission St. Pieces that would shine elsewhere impact only dimly amid the general magnificence. The "Mask of Agamemnon," from Heinrich Schliemann's Mycenae digs, is a must-see. (Museum open Mon. 12:30-7pm, Tues.-Fri. 8am-7pm, Sat.-Sun. 8:30am-3pm. Admission 600dr, students 300dr. Coin collection open Tues.-Sun. 8am-2pm.)

A precious collection of simple marble figurines can be seen at the air-conditioned **Goulandris Museum of Cycladic and Ancient Greek Art,** 4 Neophytou Douka St., near Kolonaki. (Open Mon. and Wed.-Fri. 10am-4pm, Sat. 10am-3pm. Admission 200dr, students 100dr). The Byzantine period is also represented in Athens by the numerous churches that perch in unlikely corners of the Plaka. **Kapnikaria Church** on Ermou St. at Eolou St. is exemplary.

Entertainment

For live entertainment, watch the pomp-laden guards strut their stuff every hour on the hour in the **Changing of the Guard** by the Tomb of the Unknown Soldier on Syntagma Sq. The **Monastiraki** region is wonderful for browsing or shopping; the indoor and outdoor market sells all the food you could possibly desire. The **National Garden** is the easiest escape from the noise and fumes of the city, and singers, comedians, and acrobats appear nightly at its **Zappeion Exhibition Hall.**

The best summertime alternative to café relaxation is the **Athens Festival.** Concerts and classical theater productions animate the **Odeon of Herodes Atticus,** a restored Roman amphitheatre dating from 170 AD. The festival office is at 4 Stadiou St.The **Wine Festival** in nearby Daphni runs its Bacchanalian revelry from the end of July to early September, nightly from 7:45pm-midnight (tel. 32 27 944 for more information).

The **Funicular** on Lycabettus Hill offers an eye-popping view of Athens and the Acropolis and a refreshing respite from the bust and dust below. (200dr round-trip. The station is at the top of Ploutarchou St.)

Near Athens

The dazzling flash of the Aegean from the **Temple of Poseidon** makes a visit here a spiritual experience even for those who don't chew Trident. The 16 remaining Doric columns of this sanctuary, built by Pericles in 440 BC, sit on a promontory high above the coast at Cape Sounion, 65km from Athens. Visit before the 2pm tour bus deluge. (Open Mon.-Sat. 9am-sunset. Admission 300dr, students 150dr. Last bus to Athens departs at 9:30pm.) Buses leave every half-hour from the depot at 14 Mavromateon St., next to Areos Park, but you can also snag them on Filellinon St. at Xenofondos St., 20 min. before the hour (2 hr., 400dr). Don't forget water and a lunch.

The masterful mosaics in the monastery at **Daphni** (tel. 581 15 58) deserve a visit. The monastery has served as both an army camp and a lunatic asylum, which may explain the pronounced scowl on Christ's face as he stares down from the dome. (Open Tues.-Fri. 8am-5pm, Sun. 8:30am-3pm. Admission 200dr, students 100dr.) Daphni also hosts an indulgent all-you-can-drink bash. (Late June-early Sept. Nightly 7:45pm-12:30am. Admission 300dr, students 150dr.) **Camping Daphni** (tel. 581 15 63) is on the road to the monastery (600dr per person, 600dr per large tent). Buses travel to Daphni from Eleftherias Sq. (25 min., 50dr).

The oracle at **Delphi** (Δελφί), where an old woman called a *Pythia* ruled the rulers of the ancient world, maintains its stature as a pilgrimage site. Tourist billions seek the sanctuary so visit early in the morning. There are several buses a day from 260 Liossion St. in Athens (3hr., 1400dr). Take city bus #024 from Omonia Sq. or from Amalias Ave. at the National Garden entrance to get to the Liossion St. station. If you have a railpass, take the train to Levadia and catch the Delphi bus from there (340dr). For more mosaics, hop off between Levadia and Delphi at the turn-off to Distomo, and beg, borrow, or steal a ride to the monastery of **Ossios Loukas.** (From the turn-off it's 3km to Distomo, whence it's 9km to the monastery.) From the Liossion station, there is also a daily bus to the monastery (10:30am, 3½ hrs., 1300dr). The multicolored stone buildings look like gingerbread cake and are decorated with rich Byzantine mosaics. Delphi's delightful **IYHF youth hostel** (tel. 822 68) charges 680dr, and has wonderfully hot showers. There is **camping** 3km away (tel. 289 44; 300dr per tent, 500dr per person). Delphi's best food for the drach is at **Taverna Vakhos,** next to the hostel.

Northern Greece

The northern provinces of **Macedonia** (Μακεδονία), **Thessaly** (Θεσσαλία), **Thrace** (Θράκι), and **Epirus** (Ηπειρος) adamantly cling to the hospitality and charm that the Greek Islands long ago relinquished. Although Northern Greece has its quota of teeming beaches and ostentatious resorts, the glitz quickly fades as you travel through the unspoiled landscape and ancient villages of the interior.

The capital of Macedonia and the second largest city in Greece, **Thessaloniki** (Θεσσαλονίκη) vibrates with a tumultuous ambiance similar to that of Athens. Historically a crucial cultural center of the Byzantine Empire, it is situated on the crossroads of important trade routes and is thus buzzing with extensive commerce; it's also the halfway point for the daily 18-hour marathon train from Athens to Sofia, Bulgaria. Amongst the numerous churches filled with mosaics and frescoes, the superlative **archeological museum** houses opulent artifacts from the significant Macedonian finds at Vergina. (Open July-Sept. Mon. 12:30-7pm, Tues.-Fri. 8:30am-7pm, Sat.-Sun. 8:30am-3pm;Oct.-June Mon.-Fri. 8am-3pm, Sun. 9am-2pm. Admission 400dr, students 150dr.) The least expensive lodgings are clustered at the western end of Egnatia St., near the railway station. The **IYHF youth hostel** (tel. 22 59 46) is at 44 Alex. Sivolov St. (June-Sept. 864dr, Oct.-May 700dr) and the **YWCA** ("Xen" in Greek) is at 11 Agias Sophia St. (tel. 27 61 44; women only; 800dr for 5-bed room). Restaurants downtown, located within the market area (Aristotelous, Irakliou, Egnatia, and Dragoumi Streets) will gratify a ravenous body and pacify an anxious wallet.

Pella (Πέλλα) was the capital of ancient Macedonia and the birthplace of Peter the Great. The ruins, including remarkably creative mosaic floors, are hurled from the road along which Edessa-Thessaloniki buses pass every hour. To the east are the gorgeous sandy beaches of the **Sithonia** (Σιθωνία) peninsula—try coastal towns of **Vourvourou, Kalamitsi,** and the aptly named **Paradissos.**

Greece's loftiest peak, **Mt. Olympus** (Ορος Ολυμπος), lords over **Thessaly** as the gods who lived there ruled Greece in ancient times. The mountain's eight eerily beautiful summits require two days of challenging hiking but no special equipment. Get an early start from the town of **Lithohoro,** at the foot of the mountain and stay at one of two hostel-like refuges (SEO and EOS) along the ascent (1000dr per person). In town, the **GNTO,** Ag. Nickalou 15, in the town hall (tel. 831 00) can give you a rundown on the trails. The manager of the **IYHF youth hostel** (tel. 813 11), uphill from the main square, is equally helpful, although sardine-can dorms (650dr) may tempt you to stay at the spotless **Park Hotel,** on the main drag (tel. 822 52, doubles with bath 2821dr). Climbing season, when hostels and refuges are open, runs from late May to September.

Southwest of Olympus is **Meteora** (Μετέωρα), where Orthodox monasteries grip the tops of 600m-high rock formations. From the 11th century AD, monks created Byzantine cloisters to escape the secular world and its marauding infidels. Today the few monks and nuns who remain spend much of their time shepherding crowds of visitors. The most popular base for exploring Meteora is the town of **Kalambaka** (Καλαμβάκα) (eponymous origin of the clambake), where the **Hotel Astoria** (tel. 222 13), near the train station, has bright clean singles for 1600dr. The town also has abundant *dhomatia* (rooms to let) for 1000-1500dr per person; call **Georgios Totis** (tel. 222 51) to find one. Closer to Meteora, the village of **Kastraki** has the **Hotel Kastraki** (tel. 222 86) and two swell campgrounds. (Singles 2000dr. Doubles 3000dr.) The swimming pool at **Camping Vrachos** provides welcome relief from the parching sun (450dr per person, 500dr per tent). The five monasteries accessible by bus from Kalambaka (5 per day; in winter, 1 per day; 100dr) are open 9am-1pm and 3-6pm. The regulations against picture-taking and revealing dress are enforced with severity.

West of Kalambaka, in the mountainous province of Epirus, the ancient village of **Metsovo** (Μέτσοβο) clutches its old-world charm despite being hawked as a "traditional settlement." Fill up on the village's renowned goat-milk cheese before hiking to the nearby **Katara Pass.** A room at the Hotel Athenai (tel. 417 25), downhill from the main square, insulates against the year-round mountain chill. (Doubles with bath 2750dr.)

Farther west is **Ioannina** (Ιωάννινα), now Greece's major launchpad for bus trips to Albania, with a mosque and a museum housing remnants of the town's Ottoman rulers. Just north of Ioannina, the spectacular **Vicos-Aoos National Park** encompasses the canyons of the Vicos and Aoos Rivers and the remote villages of **Zagoria,** built entirely of gray stone and slate and regarded as a national treasure. Infrequent buses make the torturous trip from Ioannina to **Papingo** and **Monodendri,** the two most convenient gateways to the Vicos Gorge. The main road past Monodendri runs for 7km through strange rock formations before reaching a precipice overlooking the Vicos. Most visitors to the area pitch tents in the woods, but each village has a few *dhomatia* (1500-2000dr). The most convenient base for this area is **Konitsa** (4 buses per day from Ioannina, 1hr., 550dr). Here you can stock up on provisions and stay in the hotel **Egnatia.** (Singles 1300dr. Doubles 2800dr. Big, old-fashioned bathtubs.) From Konitsa, a footpath leads through the Aoos River Gorge to a monastery where you can lodge (1½-2 hr. hike).

The Peloponnese Πελοπόννησος

The Peloponnese, a divine union of *vouna* (mountains) and *thalassa* (sea), is the Greece of legend. History slumbers in the ruins at Mycenae, Epidavros, and Corinth, the Byzantine remains at Mystra and Monemvassia, and the Turko-Venetian castle-fortresses at Methoni, Koroni, and Pylos. Stay in the serene mountain villages in Arcadia, the lively port towns of Gythion and Nafplion, or the bland but central modern cities of Sparta, Tripolis, Patras, Kalamata, and Corinth. The rugged should explore barren but fascinating Mani with its dramatic tower houses. Most enter the Peloponnese by sea from Italy to Patras, or by land from Athens to Corinth. The train system is limited, but buses run almost everywhere. Service to villages may be available only once or twice a day. Many find hitching is easy in summer, especially around popular ancient sites. Tourists are catching on to the Peloponnese, but away from sights you should be able to find solitude and ample opportunity to see Greek life oblivious to your presence.

Argolis and Corinthia Αργόλλα και Κόρινθά

This mountainous region of the Peloponnese is doused with some of the ancient world's grandest ruins. Corinth, Mycenae, and Epidavros recall more than the heyday of the Greek city states; at their fringes whisper the legends of Oedipus Rex and the House of Atreus.

The first stop for most visitors to the Peloponnese from Athens is **Corinth** (Κορίνθος), a town twice crumpled by earthquakes and once rebuilt with squat, concrete houses. The ruins of Ancient Corinth are 7km from town; follow either the road to Patras or the one to Argos and look for signs. The elaborate **Fountain of Peirene** still gurgles, and the 6th-century BC **Temple of Apollo** keeps a quiet vigil over the city's Roman ruins. Also worth a peek are the mosaics from the site, found now in the **museum.** Votive offerings of cured **body parts** from the Asklepion testify to Ancient Corinth's tradition of healing. (Site open Mon.-Sat. 8am-7pm, Sun. 8am-3pm. Admission 500dr, students 250dr.) The Turko-Venetian fortress of Acrocorinth towers 575m over the classical site; you can take a taxi directly from Corinth, or make the tough one-hour hike up for a truly spectacular view. Buses leave on the hour for Ancient Corinth from Corinth's main station on Koliatsou at Ermou St. (100dr), returning on the half-hour. If you must stay in Corinth, try the **Hotel Belle-vue** (tel. 220 88) on the waterfront. (Doubles 2800dr.) Literati will want to patronize Corinth's cheapest, the **Hotel Byron** (tel. 22631), across from the train station (Doubles 1600dr). Buses to Corinth from Athens leave from 100 Kifissou St. (5:30am-9:30pm, every ½ hr., 750dr). Returns are from Ermou St. at Koliatsou St.

Nafplion (Ναύπλιο), one hour from Corinth by bus (from the station at Aratou and Ethnikis Anistassis St. 550dr), is the best for launching off to see the northeast Peloponnese. Nafplion's lone **IYHF youth hostel,** Neon Vyzantion St. (tel. 277 54), in the new part of town, is clean and social. Usually members only. (11pm curfew. 500dr. Dinner 600dr.) From the bus station, walk down 25 Martiou St. with the Palmidi fortress on your right, and turn left on the road to Argos. After walking 10 min., turn right 2 blocks after Hotel Argolis and before the Texaco station. Reasonably priced hotels dapple Nafplion's older, finer half. Try the **Hotel Amymoni** (tel. 272 19), in the Ionian Bank building at the end of Amalias St. near Syntagma Sq. (Singles 1500dr. Doubles 2000dr. Triples 2700dr.) **Hotel Epidavros** (tel. 275 41) offers clean rooms on Ipsilandou St., 1 block below Amalias St. (Doubles 3200dr, 5200dr with private bath.)

Evenings in Nafplion are made for sitting in a waterfront café and watching the *volta* (promenade). At the corner of Bouboulinas and Singrou streets, **Kanaris** serves delicious fish dishes. Soften your arteries on the nearly 900 steps to the **Palamidi Fortress.** (Open Mon.-Fri. 8am-6:30pm, Sat.-Sun. 8:30am-2:45pm. Admission 200dr, students 100dr.)

From Nafplion the bus rambles daily to Mycenae (250dr), Tiryns (Argos bus; every ½ hr., 100dr.), and Epidavros (3 per day, 270dr). **Mycenae,** the supreme city in Greece from 1600 to 1100 BC, was once ruled by Agammemnon, commander of the Greek forces during the Trojan War. His wife Clytemnestra and her fatal attraction Aegisthus axed him in a bathtub. Most of the treasures from the excavation are in the Athens Museum, but the **Lion's Gate** and the **Beehive Tombs** number among the most celebrated archeological finds in modern history. (Site open Mon.-Fri. 8am-7pm, Sat.-Sun. 8:30am-2:45pm. Admission 500dr, students 250dr.) Arrive ahead of the mid-day heat and tourist swarms, and hold on to your ticket so you won't have to pay twice. Mycenae has a sunny **IYHF youth hostel** (tel. 662 24; 600dr). Another imposing Mycenaean fortress sits at **Tiryns,** 4km north of Nafplion. (Open Mon.-Fri. 8am-7pm, Sat.-Sun. 8:30am-3pm. Admission 300dr, students 150dr.)

In **Epidavros** (Επιδαυρος), visit the ruins of the **Sanctuary of Asclepius** as well as the wowingly well-preserved theater, which once seated 12,000. You can see classical drama (in Greek) at the theater on Friday and Saturday evenings in July and August. Tickets for shows start at 500dr for seats and may be purchased at the theater four hours before the performance (usually at 9:30pm), or at travel agencies including Olympic Airways (2 Bouboulinas St., Nafplion) and Bourtzi Tours (near the bus station in Nafplion).

Patras Πάτρας

Don't jump ship in Patras. Get in, get out, travel light, stay on the move. Everything you need is on the waterfront. Leaving the customs house, make a right for the bus station and continue (with the water on your right) to the train station. The youth hostel is 1½km in the other direction. **Trains** roll with glacial speed to Athens (5-6 per day, 5 hr., 970dr), stopping in Corinth (670dr). Trains head south to Kalamata (4 per day, 6 hr., 990dr) and Olympia via Pirgos (7 per day, 2 hr., 480dr). For Delphi take the train to Ceradia. You can leave baggage at the train station (95dr per day). **Buses** run to Athens (every hr., 4 hr., 2050dr) and Kalamata (2 per day, 4 hr., 1950dr). There is an **OTE** at the Customs House (open Mon.-Sat. 8am-10pm, Sun. 4-10pm) as well as a **post office** (open Mon.-Fri. 7:30am-8pm, Sat. 7:30am-2pm and Sun. 9am-1:30pm). The staff at the **GNTO information office** at the Customs House (tel. 42 03 05) knows the ferry schedules cold. The **tourist police** (tel. 22 09 02) are located on Patreos Korinthon St. and are helpful but remote. For **ferry tickets,** go to one of the general ticketing offices such as **Bimaras travel** (tel. 27 77 83), 14 Orthonos Amalias St., or look for agencies with signs offering discount fares. To Brindisi, deck fare is 5500dr; Eurailpass 1300dr and with Inter-Rail (or if you're a student or under 28) 4500dr. Everyone shells out a 1000dr port tax. In summer, boats depart at 6pm and 10pm; in off-season at 10pm only. Get to the port two hours early. Boats sail to Corfu at 9:30pm (10 hr., 2300dr), and to Cephalonia and Ithaca (1:30pm and 9pm; off-season 1:30pm, 4-5 hr., 1500dr).

Stay at the crowded but adequate **IYHF youth hostel,** 68 Iroon Polytechniou St. (tel. 42 72 78; beds 800dr; no curfew). Other inexpensive lodgings hole up in the shabby buildings on Agiou Andreou St., 1 block from the waterfront along the main square. Or try **Hotel Parthenon** (tel. 27 34 21), 25 Erma St., with huge rooms and pungent bathrooms. (Singles 1100dr. Doubles 1800dr. Triples 2100dr.) For general tourist services and a restaurant and showers, go to the rosy **Europa Centre** at the corner of Othonos Amalias St. and Karolou (tel. 43 48 01). The **Achaia Clauss Winery,** 9km from town, has a free tour and tasting. Take bus #7 from Kolokotroni and Kanakari St. While waiting to get out of town, climb the stairs to the Venetian *kastro,* on the street leading from the long pier by the train station. If you're stuck in Patras overnight in the summer, the **Patras International Arts Festival** (tel. 27 87 30) is the only way to pass the time.

Western Peloponnese

From Pirgos, trains (5 per day, 45 min., 100dr) or buses (every hr., 45 min., 190dr) will take you to **Olympia** (Ολυμπία), the religious sanctuary that hosted the ancient Olympics. The site is scattered and poorly labelled, but nonetheless lovely; the museum is excellent. (Site open Mon.-Fri. 8am-7pm, Sat.-Sun. 8:30am-3pm. Admission 500dr, students 250dr. Museum open Mon. 12:30-7pm, Tues.-Fri. 8am-7pm, Sat.-Sun. 8:30am-3pm. Admission 500dr, students 250dr.) Inside is Praxiteles' statue of Hermes, whose subtle expression changes from each viewing angle. The modern town is touristed but tasteful. In the center of town is a 50-bed **youth hostel** (tel. 225 80; 500dr per night, breakfast 200dr, sheets 100dr). **Camping Diana** (tel. 223 14), just above town, costs 550dr per person plus 400dr per tent. Otherwise find one of the scores of rooms to let, or stay at the **Hereon** (tel. 225 49), with singles 1000dr, doubles 1500dr (try bargaining). **Hotel Pelops** can be an incredible bargain when business is slow. Most rooms to let roost on Spiliopoulou St., parallel to the main road.

To the south, **Pylos** (Πύλος) beckons with its fecund environs and low prices. Take the bus (120dr) to the Mycenaean remains of Nestor's Palace. Nearby is **Chora,** which has a good museum. In Pylos, stay at the **Navarino** (tel. 222 91), with singles for 1500dr and doubles for 2500dr. A search should yield doubles along the outer streets for 1500dr. Quieter and more beautiful is a trio of towns to the south—**Methoni** (Μεθώνη), with the ultimate Venetian fortress sprawled lazily beside sandy stretches (stay at the **Iladision** (tel. 312 25; doubles 2000dr) or in a private house); **Koroni,** farther to the east, where you can stay at the **Diana** (tel. 223 12); and, in the middle, the tiny fishing village of **Finikoundas** (Φίνικούντας). All can be reached from **Kalamata** (Καλαμάτα), the frenetic capital of Messenia—stay at **Hotel Nevada** (tel. 824 29) or at **Hotel Avra** (tel. 827 59); from the bus or train station, grab a #1 city bus and get off when it turns left by the water. Bus #1 also ports you to Kalamata's **camping** spots. Try **Camping Patista** (tel. 295 25).

Laconia Λακωνία

Sparta (Σπάρτη) might rightly be portrayed as the Baron Scarpia of the classical world—a savage hawk divebombing the democratic doves of civilized Athens. Great ruins are lacking here; the Spartans considered monumental architecture a luxury that made strong citizens weak. They would have been scandalized by the Byzantine opulence 5km away in **Mystra** (Μυστρά), where three tiers of tiled churches and ghostly palaces grope up a steep hillside. (Site open Mon.-Fri. 8am-7pm, Sat.-Sun. 8:30am-3pm. Admission 400dr, students 200dr.) You can camp at **Camping Mystra** (tel. (0731) 227 24) between Sparta and Mystra. (500dr per person, 250dr per tent.) The new **Camping Castleview** is also near Mystra (tel. (0731) 933 84; 500dr per person; 250dr per tent). Sparta is a convenient, if bland, place to stay—find cheap lodgings close to the bus station. **Hotel Anessis** (tel. (0731) 210 88), across from the stop for buses to Mystra, is run by a kind woman and has coincidentally spartan rooms. (Singles 1800dr. Doubles 2500dr. Discounts for large groups.) One street beyond, **Hotel Cyprus** (tel. 265 90) is probably your best bet. The proprietor is a veritable fount of Spartan trivia. (Doubles 2400dr. Triples 3300dr.) To reach either hotel, turn left out of the main bus station onto Paleologou St. and then right onto Lykourgou. **Dhiethnes** is in a corner of the main square across from the **GNTO** office in the town hall. Good spaghetti (450dr) and standard *taverna* fare. Buses connect with Argos (2½ hr., 950dr), Tripolis (1¼ hr., 480dr), and Kalamata (2 hr., 290dr).

The bold can plunge south into the lower reaches of the **Mani** (Μάνη), the middle peninsula of the southern Peloponnese, known for a bloody past of family feuds and savage piracy. The entire region is stark. Bald mountains drop to a jagged coast, and forbidding, hooded towers guard the abandoned towns. Rooms can be rented in the nearby town of **Kardamili.** From **Areopolis,** you can make daytrips to **Gerolimenas** and to the spectacular **Glyfatha Lake Caves** of **Pirgos Dirou,** known as *Ta Spilia.* (Open daily June-Sept. 8am-6pm; Oct.-May 8am-3pm. Admission 1000dr.) The ticket includes a 30-minute boat ride and walk through this dense forest of stalactites and stalagmites. When the site is crowded, visitors are admitted according to the number on their ticket; you may have to wait up to two hours (if you arrive after 4pm, you won't get in). Buses come here from Gythion, Areopolis, and sometimes Sparta; allow a full day for the expedition. For a bed in Areopolis, take Kapetan Matapa St. off the main square and scout a sign for rooms to rent dangling off a balcony, or hang a left at the church on the main drag to find other rooms to rent (tel. 513 01).

From Gerolimenas, hike the 11km to the deserted, dramatic tower houses of **Vathia.** In an effort to increase tourism, the town has been uglified with modernity. Continue through stupendous countryside to **Porto Kagio,** in the extreme south. On the east coast, **Kotronas** is a pretty port with a **pension** (doubles 1500dr).

The capital of the Mani is the picturesque port of **Gythion** (Γύθειο). Swim off the wooded islet nearby or in many of the desolate rocky coves to the southeast. Lodge on the far right as you face the sea and on the street above. Try the comfortable, super-clean rooms of **Xenia Karlaftis** (tel. 227 19) at the end of the causeway. (Doubles 2500dr, with private bath 3500dr; ask about the *veranda).* The gloomy **Aktaio** (tel. 224 08) is right on the waterfront. (Doubles 2500dr with balconies.) There are four splendid campgrounds: **Gytheio Beach** (tel. (0733) 255 22), **Mani Beach** (tel. (0733) 234 50), **Melteni** (tel. 228 33), and **Kronos** (tel. (0733) 241 24). The first is cheapest. Boats from Gythion connect with Piraeus (via Kythera and Monemvassia) on Saturday at 3:45pm and with Crete on Monday, Wednesday, and

Friday. Contact **Rozakis Travel Agency** (tel. (0733) 222 29) on the waterfront for schedules.

Off the easternmost peninsula of the Peloponnese is **Monemvassia** (Μονεμβágaσια), a ruined city atop a huge rock rearing straight from the sea. A charming medieval village, still inhabited, clings to the rock by the church at the summit. Stay in the new town on the mainland at the **Akrogiali** (tel. (0732) 612 02; singles 1600dr, doubles 2350dr). Rooms to let hover along the water, beyond the bridge to the island. Buses connect Monemvassia with Sparta (4-5 per day, 850dr) and Gythion (1 per day, 650dr). Flying Dolphin hydrofoils link the town with Piraeus (1 per day, 2 on Sun., 4 hr., 4200dr).

Ionian Islands Νησιά τού ιονίου

This archipelago melds Byzantine tradition with Renaissance culture, hoary South European mountains and beaches with crass North European tourism. It's possible to hop from Cephalonia to Ithaka to Corfu, but Zakinthos is reached only by ferry from Killini on the Peloponnese. You can stop in Corfu en route between Brindisi, Italy and Patras or Igoumenitsa, Greece.

Corfu (Kerkyra) Κέρκυρα

In Corfu Town, British palaces sit on an esplanade modeled after Rue de Rivoli in Paris. Behind are shuttered alleyways of an ersatz Venice. Such a pastiche only makes sense on this island of extremes—shimmering seascapes and ruined beaches, dense olive groves and rudely commercialized villages. Throughout the town, the smell of stewing lobster and veal mingles with the stench of raw sewage drifting from the street grates.

Ferries from Patras and Italy dock in Corfu Town's new port. Follow the water to your left to get to the old town, where you'll find an informative **GNTO** in the palace (tel. 305 20; open daily 7am-8pm; mid-Sept. to April 7am-2:30pm). As you disembark from your ferry, you'll be besieged by hoteliers. Agree on a price before you leave the dock area, and find out exactly where the room is located—Corfu is a big island, and some accommodations are remote. Corfu's isolated and crowded **IYHF youth hostel** (tel. (0661) 912 02) is 4½km north on the main road from the port; take bus #7 (2 per hr., 20 min., 75dr) from Platia San Rocco to Kontokali. (Rooms 715dr, cold showers included.) The friendliest and most welcoming place to stay in Corfu Town is the difficult to find, immaculate **Hotel Cyprus,** 13 Agion Pateron (tel. (0661) 300 32), near the National Bank on Voulgareos St. (Doubles 3500dr. Triples 4800dr.) Nearly all the cheap hotels and restaurants in town cluster around N. Theotoki, which runs from the Esplanader through the old town. **Hotel Elpis,** 4, 5H Parados N. Theotoki St. (tel. (0661) 302 89), in an alleyway opposite 128 N. Theotoki St. in the Old Port, offers clean, quiet, and basic rooms. (Singles 1200dr. Doubles 2000dr. Triples 2500dr. Hot showers 100dr.) Closer to the new port is **Hotel Europa** (tel. 393 04), popular among backpackers. (Doubles 3000dr.) The hotel rents mopeds for 800dr, motorcycles for 1800dr. **Pizza Pete,** 19 Arseniou St., serves excellent vegetarian and pizza specials for 600-1100dr. (Open April-Oct. daily 9am-midnight.)

KTEL buses leave frequently from New Fortress Sq. in Corfu Town for most of the island's major spots (some are reached by city buses from Platia San Rocco); it's easier but more dangerous to travel by moped. You can rent one almost anywhere for 1400-1800dr per day. A trip west takes you to **Paleokastritsa** and its whitewashed mountaintop monastery. Ask for the *monopati* (footpath) to the bella vista promontory. Also here are the knee-weakening beaches of **Glyfada** and Pelekas and the nearby nude beach **Moni Mirtidon.** (Retro topless sunbathing is the rule on just about all of Corfu.) Pelekas swings at night and has several inexpensive pensions, notably **Nikos Hotel,** 5 minutes down the road to the beach (1500dr per person). Nearby are the stunning cliffs of **Agios Gordios,** arguably Corfu's most spectacular beach, and the site of the **Pink Palace,** a summer camp/frat/hotel, amazingly popular with North Americans. (2100dr per person. Laundry 1000dr. Breakfast, dinner, showers, and disco included.)

A trip north will take you to the great sand beaches at **Roda, Kharoussades,** and **Sidari.** These are crowded near towns, but in between are much quieter stretches. There is a clean **campground** at Roda. You can camp freely on Sidari beach's sandstone cliffs. From Sidari, walk the 3½km west to catch the sunset in Peroulades. For relatively secluded shores, head down the southwest coast of Corfu to the beaches of **Vitalades** and **Agios Giorgios.**

Ithaca ιθάκη

The placid beauty of the island's northern villages explain to a degree Odysseus' compulsive homesickness for this small, steep, rocky place. **Ferries** run from Nidri on Lefkas via Fiskardo on Cephalonia. There is also a ferry from Patras on the mainland to Vathi on Ithaca via Sami on Cephalonia. Another ferry departs from Astakos on the mainland for Vathi, and continues to Agia Efemia on Cephalonia. You can also catch that ferry on its way back to Vathi from Agia Efemia. Check boat schedules with travel agencies at your port of embarking.

The main town of **Vathi** is an amiable cluster of shops and houses in the center of a horseshoe harbor. All hotels here are expensive. Walk up Odysseus St. away from the water to find a simple room. (Doubles around 2000dr.) Some travelers camp illegally on the nearby beach. The **Taverna To Trescantin,** 1 block from the water, is a cheap local hangout. For travel information, try Polyctor Tours on the main square.

Those of poetic imagination and adequate footwear will want to climb up to the **Cave of the Nymphs,** where, it is said, Odysseus hid his treasure when he returned home; bring a flashlight or you'll see only the entrance. The site of Odysseus's palace is farther north in Stavros. Ask for the village schoolteacher's wife; she has the key to a museum (free) erected on the alleged site. Swim in the tingling waters of the gentle pebble coves of the east coast between charming Friker and Kioni. Kioni's only bar is the island's best. An exhilirating bus route serves these villages from Vathi.

Cephalonia Κεφαλλωνιά

If Corfu whets your appetite for islands, visit rugged Cephalonia, larger and far less touristed. In summer, **Ionian Lines** links Patras and Cephalonia non-stop (2 per day, 4 hr., 1490dr). Boats from Corfu and Brindisi stop here daily in July and August on their way to Patras. All boats leave you on the east coast of the island in **Sami,** a tranquil port town. Though smaller and duller than the capital town, Sami has a beach and is closer to the beauty of the island's northern part. Stay at the **Hotel Kyma** (tel. (0674) 220 64; doubles 3700dr; off-season, doubles 2500dr; showers 180dr). Or, in August, take a cot on the roof of the **Hotel Melissani** (tel. 224 64) for 1000dr per person. Otherwise head for the main town of **Argostoli,** the island's transportation center. A **GNTO** is on the waterfront by the customs house. (Open Mon.-Fri. 8am-3pm, 5-10pm, Sat. 5-10pm; in winter Mon.-Fri. 8am-3pm.) The surprisingly interesting and eclectic **Historical and Cultural Museum** shows pictures of the town before it was wiped out by the 1953 earthquake. (Open Tues.-Sun. 8:30am-3pm. Admission 100dr.) Hotels here are expensive. There are cheaper rooms to let: **Emilia Dionisatou** (tel. 287 76) and **Denis Vassilatos** (tel. 286 05), across from each other at 18 and 16 Avilhou St., rent immaculate doubles with terraces, free showers, and kitchen facilities (3000dr; off-season 2000-2500dr). Both Sami and Argostoli have superb **campgrounds** (640dr per person, 410dr per tent, 320dr per car); Sami's is right by the town's uncomfortable pebble beach; Argostoli is a 3km trek.

Take the trip north to the fishing town of **Fiskardo,** the only village left intact after the 1953 earthquake. On the way are the sensational beaches at **Agia Kyriaki** and **Myrtos,** as well as the little town of **Assos,** joined by a narrow isthmus to an island with a Venetian fortress. You can stay here at the **Assos Snack Bar** (doubles 1600dr). There are only two buses per day, but mopeds are yours for 1200dr in either Argostoli or Sami.

Saronic Gulf Islands Σαρονικός

No matter how many Hellenes thronged the shores of the Saronic Gulf Islands in ancient times, the high rocky interiors remained gloriously quiet. Accordingly, historic sanctuaries were built as far from the inundated shore as possible. The hills are ideal for serene hikes to temples and monasteries that wink at rocky beaches and scores of tourists below. The cheapest lodgings are upland from busy centers. Search the streets and alleys on the hills above the main towns for *dhomatia* and "rooms to let" signs. (Singles 1500dr. Doubles 2500-3000dr.) Consult the tourist police and larger tourist agencies for assistance, but also query the Greek children, who often serve as roving *hôteliers* on behalf of their parents. Freelance camping is illegal but common in the hills and atop quiet sands. If you arrive on a weekend, you'll have a tough time finding lodgings.

The **Argosaronicos Line** regularly runs ferries from Piraeus to each of the islands, pausing at points in between. They also run the "Flying Dolphin" hydrofoils from Zea Marina in Piraeus (sexy but 30% more expensive). For information on hydrofoils, call 452 71 07; on regular boats, call the Port Authority of Piraeus at 451 13 11 or 417 26 57.

Only 1½ hours by ferry from Piraeus, **Aegina** (Αιγινα) is the busiest of the islands. Port hotels and back street "rooms to let" in Aegina town are convenient places to stay. Bus routes radiate from Aegina Town. On the other side of the island stands the magnificently-preserved Doric **Temple of Aphaea.** (Open Mon.-Fri. 8:15am-5pm, weekends and holidays 8:30am-3pm. Admission 300dr, students 150dr. Take the Agia Marina bus.)

Poros (Πόρος) is more appealing island with toothesome beaches and spirited visitors, who, during July and August, outnumber the native population of 5000. **Family Tours** and **Takis Travel,** both on the waterfront, can help you find accommodations, mostly private doubles, for about 3000dr, but pension owners will probably accost you before you get to either of these places. The **tourist police** are on Agio Nikolaou (tel. 224 62), 100m to the right of the main ferry landing. (Open mid-June to Sept. Mon.-Fri. 8am-2:30pm.) **Neorion Beach** is 3km to the left as you face inland; small boats travel back and forth frequently. The main sight on Poros is the **Monastery of Zoodochos Pigis,** a scenic bus or boat ride from town (20 min., 60dr). History buffs should rent mopeds (from 1800dr) and buzz up to the scant ruins of the **Temple of Poseidon** at the top of the mountain. A short caïque ride (20dr) across to the Peloponnese brings you to **Galatas** and the sandy beaches of **Plaka** and **Aliki.** Walk 1km to **Lemonodassos** and its dense lemon groves, where **Cardassi Taverna** serves fresh-squeezed lemonade. In the opposite direction from Galatas and Oz lies a spacious plain of manicured flowers. Poros offers the best bargain eats in the Gulf; try **Caravella** and its neighbor **Lagoudera,** a short walk to the right along the wharf. **Ferries** shuttle between Poros and Piraeus daily (3 hr., 900dr).

To sail into **Hydra** to enter a painting. The artist has created a perfect port town whose Venetian-style houses are colored every blue, white, and red. In a stroke of brilliance, the artist omitted automobiles and motorbikes. Walk up the street beside the marble clock tower to find the **tourist police** (tel. 522 05; open 24-hr.). The **Sophia Hotel** on the harbor has the cheapest beds. (Doubles 3315dr. Triples 4420dr.) There are many "Rooms for Rent" signs, but Hydra's accommodations fill quickly. The village of **Vlihos** has a prime pebble beach. **Ferries** run between Hydra and Piraeus daily (4 hr., 965dr).

In the southernmost currents of the Saronic Gulf is **Spetses** (Σπέτσες), almost completely covered with pines. John Fowles taught English here and made it the setting for his novel *The Magus.* Unfortunately, the once sleepy isle has recently been discovered, by raucous Brits especially. From the harbor you can see the tourist bureaus; **Takis Travel** (tel. 728 88), at the left of the wharf, has most of the rooms in town at its disposal. (Singles rarely available. Doubles about 3000dr.) The **tourist police** (tel. 731 00), straight up from the dock on Botassi St., are open 24 hrs. and can help with accommodations. The **bank** and **OTE** are adjacent facing the water on Santou St. (Bank open in summer Mon.-Thurs. 8am-2pm and 7-9pm, Fri. 8am-1:30pm. OTE open Mon.-Fri. 7:30am-11pm, Sat.-Sun. 9am-3pm and 6-9:30pm.)

A bus leaves three times per day for the excellent beaches of **Anargyri** and **Paraskevi** (round-trip 280dr; boats to Anargyri round-trip 400dr). Why the best caves remain empty is a mystery—they're yours for the price of a moped tour. (You can also hike the island's 28km perimeter.) **Ferry** service between Spetses and Piraeus is often offered only once per day (5 hr., 1200dr).

Cyclades Κυκλάδες

Once upon a time, the Cyclades were remote Greek isles with lovely secluded beaches and yawning port towns. Then travel magazines (and budget travel guides) began advertising them as such. Now, the Cyclades hemorrhage tourists each summer. But in spite of the crowds, the Cyclades are still the quintessential Greek islands. Traditionalists extol the villages where webs of winding cobblestone streets and whitewashed homes drape the mountainsides, and the blue-green shutters and doors welcome expanses of sky and sea. If you want a taste of authentic Greek culture, ypu should travel in the off-season, but nothing in all Europe can match the Cyclades nightlife in summer. Accommodations in July and August are, however, often scarce; on the more popular islands, be prepared to either camp or sleep on roofs.

Pick up a ferry schedule from the GNTO in Athens. The main islands are served frequently in summer; islands mentioned in this chapter are connected to each other at least three times per day. In off-season, service dwindles; even in summer, bad weather makes the ferry system a capricious beast.

One *caveat:* although mopeds are the best way to ramble over these islands, roads are often rocky, unpaved and winding, and donkey and goat jams are frequent at rush hour. Many happy-go-lucky people maul themselves each year. Inspect your bike before zooming off, and drive defensively.

Mykonos and Delos Μύκονος και Δήλος

Narcissus survives on the island of Mykonos as more than just a soporific flower, but as an attitude which inculcates all who come to this isle of the chic-and-sleek. The social life, gay and straight, is pricey on this favorite among the Cyclades islands—you'd need a wallet thicker than your *Let's Go* to enjoy all the flash. But you needn't pay to savor the beaches and the labyrinthine streets of Mykonos Town, dotted with the odd confused mule and pompous pink pelican.

Mykonos is five hours on the ferry from Rafina (1900dr), with daily connections in summer to all the other major Cyclades. Most D-class hotels are rip-offs in high season (May-Oct.), charging about 3500dr for singles and 4500dr for doubles; prices drop at least 20% in off-season. In high season, grab the first person who tries to rent you a room, as accommodations are scarce and get scarcer as the day goes on. Freelance camping is popular on the larger beaches, but it's also illegal. There is an official **campground** on Paradise Beach (tel. 221 29), whose complimentary van meets all boats. (400dr per person, 200dr per tent.) Try **Angela's Rooms** in Taxi Sq. (tel. 229 67); roof space 700dr), or try the old white house at **13 Mitropoleos St.** (Doubles 2200dr. Triples 2800dr.)

For dinner, descend on any of the restaurants clustering behind the **tourist office,** at the far right of the waterfront (facing inland). **Taverna Antonini** (chicken 780dr, *mousaka* 700dr) and **Alexi's** *(souvlaki* with pita 250dr, Hawaiian-style hamburger 250dr) are in busy Taxi Sq.

The **National Bank of Greece** (open Mon.-Thurs. 8am-2pm, Fri. 8am-1:30pm; special exchange window open Mon.-Fri. 6-8:30pm, Sat.-Sun. 5-8pm) is on the south side of the waterfront. The **tourist office** (tel. 239 90; open daily 9am-9pm) is a few blocks past the bank, on the far right side of the waterfront (facing inland). To find the **police** (tel. 224 82 tourist info, 222 35 general info; open 24 hrs.), follow the "Bus to Plati Yialos" signs and turn left on Plateia Dim. Koutsi.

The **post office** is at the edge of the town beach, next to **Olympic Airways,** and the **OTE** is uphill from the far left of the waterfront (facing inland). **Buses** are the best way to cover the island. The "North Station" next to the beach serves the northern and eastern beaches; "South Station," oddly enough, serves the south. (Open Mon.-Sat. 9am-1pm and 5-9pm.)

If you can afford a hotel, your best bets are the **Apollon Hotel** (tel. 232 71), a traditional house which overlooks the harbor. (Singles 4000dr. Doubles 4500dr. Triples 6800dr.) The **Hotel Phillippi,** 32 Kolagera St. (tel. 222 94), its neighbors all have similar prices.

For most visitors, "beach" is synonymous with the renowned nakedness of **Paradise Beach,** and the far superior, largely gay, nude **Super Paradise Beach** nearby. Take a bus to Plati Yialos (90dr) and a boat from there (150dr to Paradise, 200dr to Super Paradise). The beaches at **Megali Ammos, St. Stephanos,** and **Psarou** are closer to town and have less of a meat-market atmosphere. At night, the sprawling **Scandinavian Bar** is always packed. (Beers 170dr, cocktails 500dr.) The popular, slick **Windmill Disco** next door growls when thought of as cute. (Beers 300dr, cocktails 600dr.) And neighboring that, at the **City Disco,** don't miss the duo Zanman drag/strip show nightly at 1am. Ho! **Montparnasse,** in "Little Venice," has a stately bay window and classical music. (Wine 300dr.) At **Pierro's** on Matogianni St., the mainly gay crowd spills out into the square. (Brews 600dr, mixed drinks 1000dr.) For the party after the party (3-8am), head to **The Yacht Club** on the south side of the waterfront (beers 200dr).

The nearby island of **Delos,** legendary birthplace of Apollo and his twin sister Artemis, was one of the great spiritual centers of the ancient world. Extensive ruins cover the island, but they can only be visited on a daytrip from Mykonos or Naxos, as overnight stays are forbidden. Boats leave the dock by the tourist information office. (Tues.-Sun. 8:50am, return 1pm; 3 hr. visit; round-trip 740dr; admission to site 500dr, students 250dr.)

Paros and Naxos Πάρος και Νάξος

Paros has joined Santorini, Mykonos, and Ios as one of the Cyclades' most coveted islands. Its role as hub for Aegean ferries only fattens the crowd. **Parikia,** the main port of the island, has two redeeming features: a healthy nightlife and the wonderful Byzantine church of **Panagia Ekatontapiliani.** Nearby is the aptly named **Valley of the Butterflies. Hotel Dina** (tel. 213 25) is quiet, immaculate, and right off the main street. (Doubles with showers 4000dr; reserve ahead.) **Rooms Mimikos** (tel. 214 37), past the National Bank, has airy rooms in a tame waterfront neighborhood. (Singles 1700dr. Doubles 2200dr. Triples 2850dr.) **Pensions** east of town generally charge 2200dr for doubles and 2800dr for triples. Since accommodations are an endangered species from late July to mid-August, sleeping on the island's beaches is quite common and, though illegal, is tolerated by police everywhere but in Parikia. There are also official campgrounds such as **Koula** (tel. 220 82), near town; **Parasporas** (tel. 219 44), 2km south of Koula; and new **Krios Camping** (tel. 217 05) on Krios Beach across the harbor. (All charge 500dr per person, 200dr per tent.) The **tourist information** office (tel. 220 79) occupies the converted windmill on the dock. A **laundromat** is off the waterfront just before the bus stop. (Wash and dry 1350dr. Open Mon.-Sat. 9am-3pm and 5-9pm.)

Beautiful **Chryssi Akti** (Golden Beach) is a short bus or windsurf jaunt from town. Also worth a visit is the adjacent island of **Antiparos** and its ancient stalactite caves, with graffiti from as far back as 1776. **Piso Livadi** and **Naoussa** are quieter towns in which to base a stay on Paros. **Camping Naoussa** (tel. 515 95) charges 500dr per person, 200dr per tent. Paros is six ferry hours from Piraeus (5-6 per day, 1876dr) and in summer is linked to all the neighboring islands by frequent service. Olympic Airways has flights between Paros and Athens (10 per day, 8600dr).

Naxos is the land of Ariadne, daughter of King Minos of Crete. After she saved Theseus from her father's labyrinth, he expressed his gratitude by abandoning her. You too might wish to maroon yourself from spoilt demi-gods on this largest and least spoiled of the major Cyclades. The twining streets of **Naxos Town,** also called the "chora," dazzle with flashes of blue ocean behind ice white walls.

On the waterfront across from the boat dock is a **tourist office** (tel. (0285) 245 25 or 243 58; open daily 8am-9:30pm; July-Aug. 8am-12:30am) where you can store luggage (150dr), change money, make phone calls, and trade used books. There are numerous **pensions** on the small hill behind the OTE office. (Doubles 2500-2800dr.) In the old market section, near the Venetian *kastro* and directly uphill from the port (look for painted red hands pointing the way), is the **Hotel Dionyssos** (tel. 223 31). (Depressing dorm beds in basement 500dr. Singles 1000dr. Doubles 1500dr. Triples 2000dr. Roof 400dr. Cold showers included.) **Hotel Okeanis** (tel. (0285) 224 36), across from the docks, offers doubles for 2000dr. **Naxos Camping** (tel. (0285) 235 00), off Agios Giorgios Beach, charges 400dr per person, 200dr per tent. Walk all the way down to the southern end of the waterfront for the **National Bank of Greece.** (Open Mon.-Thurs. 8am-2pm, Fri. 8am-1:30pm.) Opposite the bank is the **OTE** (open June-Sept. daily 7:30am-midnight; Oct.-May, daily 7:30am-10pm). The **telephone code** is 0285. Around the corner and up the hill is the **post office** (open Mon.-Fri. 7:30am-2:15pm; in summer also Sat. 8am-2:30pm, Sun. 9am-1:30pm), with **Pro Wash Laundry** (open daily 9am-9:30pm) nearby. To find the **police** (tel. (0285) 221 00 or 232 80), turn left after the tourist office, take a right, and then a left (on the 2nd floor, open 24 hrs.). You can rent mopeds from **Theoharis** (tel. 239 00), a patient man with fluent English and endless knowledge about Naxos; turn left after the tourist office (open daily 8am-2pm and 5-9pm; mopeds 1400dr, including third party insurance and helmets).

Naxos's bewitching interior is easily traversed by bus or, with some difficulty, by moped. **Buses** (just behind the ferry dock) are cheap and frequent. The main road across the island passes through the resplendent **Tragea,** a vast arcadian olive grove. Along the way visit the tranquil terraced towns of **Chalki** and **Apiranthos.** Near Chalki, on the road to Moni, the 8th-century church **Panagia Drossiani** is well worth a sidetrip. In Aperanthos, vist the **Folkart** and **Michael Bardani** (Cycladic Art) **museums** (open in the mornings, free), which lie in the shadows of the two castles commanding the town. The road ends at the enticing beach town of **Apollon** on the west coast. Don't miss the 10m-high *kouros* (sculpture of an idealized male figure) outside of town.

Naxos Town is also worthwhile. Begging to be strolled, the *Kastro* includes a **museum** where Nikos Kazantzakis, author of *The Last Temptation of Christ* and *Zorba the Greek* studied. (Open Tues.-Sun. 8:30am-3pm. Admission 200dr, students 100dr.) The **Palatia,** an impressive 6th-century marble archway on the hilltop peninsula near the port, is a perfect photo and picnic spot.

Solitude-seekers should head east of Naxos to rugged **Amorgos,** home of the cliff-hanging **Khozoviotissa Monastery.** (Daily ferries.) The tiny islands of **Shinoussa, Koufonissa, Iraklia,** and **Donoussa** have ferry service every couple of days and rarely see visitors.

Ios Ιος

Everything that you've heard about Ios from the staggering and exhausted is true. Dionysian revelry is reborn here; if your idea of paradise is to beach-wallow all day and prance in stupor all night, this is your island. Bottles, trash, and unmentionable substances litter the streets of this, Europe's premium pick-up spot. On Ios, life is simple: until midnight, bar-hop in the village (where the drinks are cheaper)—try **Disco 69, The Slammer Bar, Caro d'Oro,** or get some at **Satisfaction;** then migrate with sloshed peers to the row of discos on the main road that heads to Milopatos Beach—**Scorpion's** is the most popular with a terrace overlooking the sea (if you can still see). Make sure to try Ios's native drink, the "Slammer" (a mixture of tequila, Tia Maria, and carbonated lemonade).

You can take care of business in Ios within a 3-block radius of the bus stop. In front of the stop is the **tourist office** (open daily 9am-3pm and 4:30-10pm) and the **police station.** The **bank** is behind the big church. (Open Mon.-Thurs. 8am-2pm, Fri. 8am-1:30pm.) **Buses** shuttle between the port, the village, and the beach every 15 minutes.

Ios gushes cheap lodgings (doubles 1800-2200dr), which fill quickly in July and August. First try your luck at the row of pension clones behind the bus stop; if there are no vacancies, seek out the rooms to rent beneath the windmills in the village. **Francesco's** (tel. 912 23), uphill from the bank with a lively patio, and **The Wind,** (tel. 911 39) below Hotel George Irene, both have doubles for 2000-2500dr. **Marko's Pension** (tel. 910 60), to the left of the Wind, is newer and shinier, (doubles 3200dr).

You mayn't camp on any of the town beaches in Ios; this perturbs the police patrols. Backpackers freelance camp on the quieter beaches (such as **Manganari** or **Koumbara).** Dandy **Milopatos Beach,** the center of all daytime activity, is the home of **Camping Stars** (tel. 413 92; 500dr per person) at the far end of the strand. If you arrive late, go to **Camping Ios** (tel. 913 29), next to the port (500dr per person). For great Greek fare, try **Pithari,** near the bank *(mousaka* or stuffed tomatoes 500dr) or feast on shark (420dr) at **Saïni's,** on the village's main road.

Santorini (Thira) Θήρα

Santorini's accentuated landscape, with dark cliffs salted with sparkling white buildings, burning black-sand beaches, and hills punctuated by deep gashes, is as wildly beautiful and dramatic as the cataclysm that carved it. This striking island of the Aegean was formed by a massive volcanic eruption that gave rise to the Atlantis legend and is believed by many to have destroyed the Minoan civilization on Crete. The island is actually the outer eastern rim of a sunken volcano, its entire western coast a succession of small towns perched on high cliffs. Santorini's glitz rivals that of Mykonos and its nightlife that of Paros; the finished product outclasses both islands.

Larger ferries land at **Athinios** harbor, where you can strike a deal for a room with the homeowners who meet each boat. Try for one of the small towns near **Thira,** the island's dramatically situated capital, or near beautiful **Perissa Beach.** In Thira, the **tourist police** station is at 25 March St. (tel. 226 49), north of the square. The **Commercial Bank** and the **National Bank** in the square exchange money (open Mon.-Thurs. 8am-2pm, Fri. 8am-1:30pm). **American Express** is located in the square at the X-Ray Kilo Travel and Shipping Agency (open daily in summer 8am-11pm). You can stay at the 100-bed **IYHF youth hostel,** 400m north of town; look for the blue and white signs. (700dr per person. Roof 600dr. Breakfast 200dr.) For more privacy, amble over to the Delfini (tel. 712 72) where doubles go for 3000dr. You can also camp right on the beach at **Perissa Camping** (600dr per person, 300-400dr per tent). The drove of travel agents in Thira's town square books rooms and excursions, stores baggage, and exchanges currency. **Santorama Travel** (tel. 231 80, 231 21, or 231 77) and **Pelikan Travel** (tel. 222 20, 224 78, or 229 40) are especially good.

If other tourists cramp your style, camp at uncrowded but dirty **Monolithos.** Dividing Perissa from Kamari is a small mountain topped by the remains of **Ancient Thira,** Greek and Roman ruins and a thunderous view. (Open Tues.-Sun. 9am-3pm. Free.) More fascinating are the excavations at **Akrotiri,** a late Minoan city preserved virtually intact under layers of volcanic rock. (Open Tues.-Sat., 8:30am-noon. Admission 500dr, students 250dr.) Unfortunately, the famed frescoes of Akrotiri are in the Archeological Museum in Athens. Guided bus tours and twelve public buses per day will take you to most of these sights, or you can hike to Ancient Thira from Kamari or Perissa. A three-hour trek from **Pyrgos** via the hilltop **Monastery of Profitis Ilias** will pay off when you catch the calling and the view. Even more stunning is **Oia,** a small village clinging to the rocky promontory at the island's northern tip, 300m above the sea—a prime spot for appreciating the sunset. Afterwards, go for it at **Mama Africa's Bar,** on the ridge overlooking Thira town and the volcano. Music funky, crowd real spunky.

Western Cyclades δυτικές Κυκλάδες

A more laid-back scene filters the western Cyclades: **Milos, Sifnos, Serifos,** and **Kea,** where many Greeks vacation. Don't plan on finding a room here in summer; prepare to sleep beneath fragrant cedars on a pampering beach. The police let sleeping tourists lie, and public showers are usually easy to find. In Sifnos **The Dionysos,** on the waterfront, has hot showers (150dr) and in Serifos, showers are to be had at the **Relax Café** (150dr), above Livadakia Beach. Tent freelance at Boubarda Beach, near the dock. Kea has an official campground near the beach at Poiessa (tel. 222 32; 400dr per person, 350dr per tent). There's ferry service between the eastern islands **(Ios** and **Santorini)** and the western isles. For Kea, take the ferry from Larrion on the mainland or from Kithnos.

Sporades Σπορδες

The thickly wooded interiors and pronounced cliffs of the Sporades are calmer and generally less touristed than the famed Cyclades. No one would call the Sporades undiscovered, though, and July and August invite droves of tourists, most notably to Skiathos and Skopelos. Frequent hydrofoils link these two islands with Alonissos.

Stop at **Alkyon Travel,** 98 Akadimias St., Athens (tel. 362 20 93) to pin down the best way to reach the islands. For Skiathos (Σκιάθος), Skopelos, and Alonissos it's easiest to travel by bus from Athens to Agios Konstantinos (2½ hr., 1350dr), and from there by ferry (to Skiathos, 3½hr., 1639 dr; to Skopelos, 4½ hr., 1944dr; to Alonissos, 5 hr., 2165dr). Skyros is linked to the charming town of **Kimi,** on Evia (5 buses per day from Liossion Station, 3½ hr., 1400dr). The **Kimi Hotel** (tel. (0222) 224 08) is cheap and comfortable. (Singles 1500dr. Doubles 2200dr.) Most buses going to Kimi should continue on to the port area, Paralia Kimi. From there a ferry travels daily to Skyros (1100dr). Infrequent boats leave Kimi for Skiathos (4½ hr., 2559dr), Skopelos (3¾ hr., 2276dr), Alonissos (3 hr., 2806dr), and Volos (9 hr., 3938dr) Monday at 6:30pm and Friday at 11am; in summer boats run four times per week. There are also twice-weekly ferries to Limnos (7 hr., 1601dr) and Kavala (14 hr., 2595dr). Ferries arrive in Skopelos from Skiathos three times per day (1½ hr., 614dr) and continue on to Alonissos (½ hr., 717dr). Hydrofoils also connect the Sporades with Agios Konstantinos and Volos for 60% more.

Cosmopolitan and expensive, **Skiathos** earns the title "Mykonos of the Sporades." Single rooms are scarce in late July and August; homes advertising "rooms to let" *(dhomatia)* have the cheapest rates. Try the home of **Yolanda Constantinidou,** a task to find. Follow the signs off Evangelistrias St. for Taven Ilias. Call first. (Singles 2000dr. Doubles 2200dr. Also triples and quads). **Hadula Tsourou,** 17 Mitrop. Ananiou St. (tel. (0427) 223 64), and **Maria Papagiorgiou,** just off Grigoriou before Christina's Bar (tel. (0427) 215 74) also have pleasant rooms. Solo travelers, here and elsewhere, must double up or convince the proprietor to set up a cot (usually 900dr). For dinner, try the lamb dishes at **Taverna Stavros** on Evangelistrias. Skiathos bursts with drink and dance. The **Bourtzi,** a prominent club on its own promontory, lets you swim by day and dance 'til dawn (open 24 hrs). Calmer folk gently simmer the midnight oil at the **Adagio,** a classical music bar on Evanpelistrias St (150dr).

A bus runs every half-hour along Skiathos's only paved road to the 60 beaches on the southern coast. The same bus route also passes the island's two campgrounds; **Aselinos Camping,** a 20-minute walk from the road, is the nicer. (500dr per person, 300dr per tent.) At the end of this line, **Koukounaries** beach and nearby, nudist **Banana** beach feature pine trees, golden sand, and big crowds. Head north to **Mandraki,** or east to the coves for pines, sand, freelance camping, and solitude.

Skopelos (Σκόπελος), Skiathos' most immediate neighbor, weathers fewer tourists. During the summer crush, more travelers discover Skopelos—sometimes out of necessity, as there are accommodations here. For the lowest prices, bargain with the *dhomatia* owners who will meet you at the ferry.

Consider making the four-hour round-trip hike from Glossa, on the opposite side of the island, accessible by bus from town, to **Agios Ioannis,** a chapel topping a sheer cliff. The best beaches are the sometimes-nude **Velanio,** reached by bus from either Glossa or Skopelos to Agnondas, and then by a small boat.

Alonissos is the most tranquil of the four major islands, though the majestic mountain scenery, ravishing beaches, and graceful "Chora" (Old Town) may soon begin to draw more foreigners to this earthly paradise. The ferry drops you in **Patitiri,** where **Ikos Travel** will help with rooms and information and exchange money. Ask at Boutique Mary, on Pelagson Ave., about rooms at **Dimakis Pension** (singles 1500dr, doubles 2100dr). Make the uphill hike to the old town of Alonissos (45 min.; ask a local for directions). Among the myriad beaches kissing the Aegean, **Chrismilia** is the best.

Skyros (Σκύρος) is the most beautiful of the Sporades, and its hardy island culture outlasts increasing tourism. Try to get a room in a traditional home (singles 1800dr, doubles 2500dr); home improvement has been a major folk art here since the island's upper class began purchasing decorative items from pirates. **Campers** sack out 1km out of the village at Molos, near one of the best beaches in the Sporades; the local bugs will welcome you as zestily as the manager. (Tel. 919 55. 500dr per person, tent included.)

Skyros Travel runs boat and bus excursions around the island (800dr). In town, visit the **Monastery of St. George** and the **Venetian/Byzantine Fortress** which surrounds it, the **Archeological Museum,** and the **Faltaits Museum,** whose interior is a model of a traditional Skyrian home. The two museums are located near the **Rupert Brooke Statue,** which commemorates the English poet who perished here of fever en route to Gallipoli. Rent a moped (1500dr per day with gas) at either the **Trahanas** house, the third right from the bus stop, or **Cosmos,** across from the bank. Maps are available at Skyros Travel. The island ignites several night-spots in town; **Skyropoula** and **On The Rocks** are beachside alternatives.

Crete (Kriti) Κρήτη

The people of Crete are Cretans first, then Greeks—perhaps because they became Greek only in 1913. Due to the island's strategic location, Cretans have spent centuries repelling invaders, including Romans, Byzantines, Venetians, Turks, and, most recently, Nazis. Luckily for today's invading armies of tourists, Cretans today have the reputation for being proud, impulsive, effusive, and inviting. Most of the visitors stick to the eastern half of the easily accessible north coast. Don't make this mistake. Explore the rugged mountains, specked with olive groves, tiny blue ports, and ruins of bygone civilizations.

Iraklion, the port of entry for most visitors, is connected by ferry with Piraeus (2 per day at 6:30 and 7pm, 2800dr) and Santorini (mid-July to mid-Sept. 1 per day, off-season 3-5 per week; 5 hr., 1429dr). Ferries also leave Piraeus daily at 7pm for Hania (11 hr., 2580dr). A boat from Piraeus passes through Gythion (on the Peloponnese) and Kythera en route to Kastelli at the western end of the island (2 per week, 7 hr., 1945dr). Three ferries also connect Agios Nikolaos on Crete with Kassos, Karpathos, Halki, Rhodes, Milos, Folegandros, Anafi, and Santorini; the *Vergina* and the *Silver Paloma* sail weekly via Iraklion from Athens to Cyprus and

Israel. (Iraklion-Cyprus 8600dr. Iraklion-Israel 13,400dr. 20% student/youth discount. 2500dr port tax.)

Central Crete

Many visitors' first impression of Crete is the ungainly, ugly, and overdeveloped mess of **Iraklion (Χράκλειο).** All that is impressive in this town is its past: the superb museum and spectacular ruins will explain why Crete is considered the cradle of Western civilization. The **Archeological Museum** off Eleftherias Sq. houses colorful Minoan frescoes, as well as what may be the world's first board game. (Open Mon. 12:30-7pm, Tues.-Sun. 8am-7pm. Admission 500dr, students 250dr.) Across the street is an office of the **Greek National Tourist Organization (GNTO)** (tel. 22 82 03), with maps of the city, hotel lists, and schedules. (Open Mon.-Fri. 7:30am-2:30pm.) A branch office is at the airport (tel. 22 56 36; open daily 9am-9pm). The main **post office,** 10 Gianari St., near Eleftherias Sq., has Poste Restante. You can make international calls at the **OTE,** next to El Greco Park. (Open daily 7am-11:30pm.)

Most of Iraklion's cheap accommodations cluster around **Handakos Street,** which runs from the waterfront to Venizelou Sq. Turn right after disembarking at the port and right again at the old city walls, then walk along the waterfront about 700m until you pass the Xenia Hotel; Handakos is to your left. The cheapest bed is at the clean and quiet **IYHF youth hostel,** 5 Vironos St. (tel. 28 62 81). Walk down 25th of August St. toward the water and turn left onto Vironos. (Curfew 11:30pm, open for late ferries 650dr.) **Hotel Rea,** Kalimeraki St. (tel. 22 36 38), off Handakos St. near the Historical Museum, has spotless pastel-colored doubles for 2500dr and rents cars for 28,000dr per week. **Rent a Room Vergina,** 32 Chortatson St. (tel. 24 27 39), rents rooms near Handakos St. Clean and homey with a few English books. (Doubles 2500dr. Triples 3200dr.) For food, head to the open **market** on 1866 St., just off Venizelou Sq. There you can either amass a picnic or sample one of 10 colorful *tavernas* on **Theodosaki Street,** the first left as you enter the market. **Tavern Rizes,** Handakos St., near the water, serves cheap, tasty food in an intimate setting. (Open daily 5:30pm-midnight. **Skala,** 24 Bofor St., is Iraklion's trendiest after-hours magnet. (Open daily 10pm-3am.)

Bus #2 travels from Venizelou Sq. to **Knossos,** 6km south. Here the mythohistorical palace of King Minos and the ancient capital of the Minoan civilization have been imaginatively reconstructed. (Open daily Mon.-Fri. 8am-7pm, Sat.-Sun. 8:30am-3pm. Admission 500dr, students 250dr.) Nine buses per day travel from Hania Gate in Iraklion to the Greco-Roman ruins at **Gortys,** where a stone wall is inscribed with one of the earliest records of Greek law. (Open Mon.-Sat. 8:45am-3pm, Sun. 9:30am-2:30pm. Admission 200dr, students 100dr.) The same bus continues to the Minoan ruins at **Phaestos** (2 hr., 440dr). Purists will appreciate this site; the various layers of palaces from four successive periods have been left more or less unmolested. (Open Mon.-Sat. 8am-7pm. Admission 300dr, students 150dr.) At the end of this route are the sandy beach and spacious caves of **Matala.** The grottos surrounding the town were cut by the Romans, used by the Nazis as hideouts, and became summer homes for 1960s flower children. The caves above the central harbor are now fenced off, but those above the town to the south aren't. Most budget travelers stay legally at **Matala Camping** (200dr per person, tent, car, or motorcycle), or at one of Matala's few pensions. Flash your ***Let's Go*** at **Rent Rooms Dimitris** and snag posh 3500dr doubles for 2500dr. (Inquire at Matala Travel in the center of town.)

Western Crete

Rethymnon (Ρέθυμνο), 81km west of Iraklion, is an enchanting slice of Crete's past spiced with vestiges of Turkish and Venetian occupation. The **IYHF youth hostel,** 41 Tombasi St. (tel. (0831) 228 48), is cheerful, relaxed, and crammed in summer. (No curfew. 600dr. Hostel cards not necessary.) **Vrisinas,** 10 Chereti St.

(tel. (0831) 260 92), is a blur of plants and petals. (Doubles 2000dr.) **Olga's Pension,** 57 Souliou St. (tel. (0831) 298 51), is an eternal party, with homemade wine (50dr) at the **Terrarium Café.** (Singles 1800dr. Doubles 2600dr. Triples 3000dr. Quads 3600dr. Full bath included. Roof dorms 500dr, hot shower included.) **Elizabeth Camping** (tel. (0831) 286 94), 3km east of town, charges 600dr per person, 400dr per tent; buses run frequently from the bus station. The **tourist office** (tel. (0831) 291 48), on the waterfront, supplies maps and bus and ferry schedules.

South of Rhethymon are the coastal towns of **Agia Galani** and **Plakias.** The former is riddled with tourists, but the latter is friendly and inexpensive. The **youth hostel** (tel. 313 06), all the way up the road from the beach, is clean and sociable. (600dr. Open March-Dec.) The equally superb but more sedate **youth hostel** (tel. 31302), in the village of **Myrthios,** a 40-minute walk up the hill from Plakias, glories in a great view (600dr per person). Both welcome non-members.

Ottoman and Venetian architecture coagulates at the lively harbor town of **Hania** (Ξανιά). The **tourist office** (tel. 433 00) is in a converted mosque at the harbor's eastern end. (Open Mon.-Sat. 8:30am-2pm and 3-8:30pm, Sun. 9am-3pm.) The **IYHF youth hostel,** 33 Drakonianou St. (tel. (0821) 535 65), is far from the center of town; take the Agios Ioannis bus from Platia 1866 and ask the driver to let you off at the *xenónas néon* (600dr; baggage storage 50dr per day; open March-Nov.). You can't walk two steps in Hania without knocking at an inexpensive pension. **Hotel Piraeus,** on Zambeliou St., has superb rooms and fairy-godmother management. (Singles 1200dr. Doubles 2000dr. Triples 2700dr.) The fine seafood restaurants coating the waterfront are about as distinctive as blades of grass, so naturally pick the one with the prettiest tablecloths. The **municipal market** on Gianari St., behind the bus stop, is a good place to provision for the Samaria Gorge. Discos and live music enliven at the eastern end of the harbor beyond the tourist office.

One of the "musts" in Crete is a hike through the **Samaria Gorge**, a spectacular ravine that cuts through heavy forests and sheer granite cliffs. (Open officially May-Oct.) Buses run from Hania via Omalos to **Xyloskalo** at the mouth of the gorge daily at 7:30am, 8:30am, and 4:30pm (1½ hr., 450dr, round-trip 1150dr). The 18km route ends at the nasty tourist hamlet of **Agia Roumeli.** From there you can take a ferry to Chora Sfakion (1¼ hr., 800dr), where buses stop on the way back to Hania. Energetic hikers should explore Crete's unspoiled southwest coast. Peaceful **Loutro,** accessible only by ferry from Agia Roumeli or Chora Sfakion, holds the distinction of being the only town in Crete where you cannot buy postcards of naked women. From there, another path continues east past two coves to the nudist colony at **Sweetwater Beach** (2 hr.) (the clad are tolerated but pitied for their inhibitions) and to Chora Sfakion. **Sougia** and **Paleochora,** to the west of Agia Roumeli, are likewise beautiful, though more crowded.

Eastern Crete

European package tours have rapidly stripped Crete's northeastern coast of its natural appeal. Visit the overpriced resort town of **Malia** (Μαλιά) for the ruins of the **Palace of Malia,** one of the three great cities of Minoan Crete (admission 200dr), or for the brain-melting boogie-orgies of Malia's many hip discos. The **IYHF youth hostel** is about 200m past the OTE on the road to Iraklion. (No curfew. 650dr. Bring mosquito repellent.) Campers should try **Camping Creta** in Gouvres (tel. (0897) 414 00) or **Camping Karavan** in Limera Hersonissos (tel. (0897) 220 25).

The harbor town of **Agios Nikolaos** (Αγιος Νικόλαος) is eastern Crete's most scenic resort. The **tourist office** (tel. (0841) 223 57), at the bridge between the "bottomless lake" and the port, changes currency and makes room reservations. The bursting **IYHF youth hostel,** 3 Stratigou Koraka St. (tel. (0841) 228 23), situated up the concrete steps from the harbor bridge, is grungy, but the management is very friendly. To save, offer to clean the place. The harbor nightlife is Agios Nikolaos's best attraction. Dance to funkitude at **Scorpio's** until dawn pokes with rosy fingers. (Open daily 8pm-3am. No cover.)

In the Lassithi Plateau's main village, **Tzermiado,** stay at **Lassithi** (tel. 221 94; doubles with bath 2600dr) or the **Hotel Kri-Kri** (doubles 1500dr). Near Tzermiado at **Psychro** is the **Dikteon Cave,** where Rhea stashed the baby Zeus from hungry papa Kronos. (Admission 200dr, students 100dr.) Infrequent buses connect Lassithi with Iraklion, Malia and Agios Nikolaos.

Sitia (Σητεία), at the eastern end of the island, is a hospitable harbor town with a good **IYHF youth hostel,** 4 Therissou St. (tel. (0843) 226 93; no curfew; 550dr). A pelican crash-landed here a few years ago, and the locals adopted him as their own. For ferry tickets to the Dodecanese and Piraeus, ply **Spanoudakis Travel** (tel. (0843) 284 66 or 228 14) on Papanastasiou St., next to the main post office. From Sitia, it's an easy trip to the fortified monastery of **Toplou.** Notice the holes above the gate where gentle monks poured boiling oil on the heads of pirate invaders. Also nearby are the ravishing beaches of **Zakros** and **Vai.** Vai's main beach is bronzed with tour groups, but you can camp and sunbathe *au naturel* in the somewhat less-crowded coves to either side.

Crete's southeast coast is an unattractive smattering of concrete hotels and tourist shops. One notable exception is the town of **Myrtos,** with its 5km span of black sand. You can best reach the southeast coast by bus from **Ierapetra,** the drab resort. **Cretan Villa** (tel. (0842) 285 22), 16 Lakerda St., northeast of Venizelou Sq., has lovely, high-ceilinged rooms in a 200-year-old structure. (Doubles 2500dr. Triples 3500dr.) The **tourist office** (tel. (0842) 286 58) is at the base of Kostoula on the waterfront.

Northeast Aegean and Dodecanese Islands Βορειοανατολικά Νησιά τόυ Αιγίου και Δωδεκάνησα

Strung along the coast of Turkey, Lesvos, Chios, and Samos lead the Northeastern Aegean group. Once home of the sensual poetess Sappho, **Lesbos** (Λέσβος) was inhabited by only women for a time, this according to legend. **Plomari,** in the south, and **Molyvos,** in the north (dominated by a Genoese fortress) are two destinations of choice. Coming from the main port of Mitilini, the bus stops at Molyvos's **tourist office** (tel. (0253) 713 47), which finds private rooms for about 1800dr per person. But **Petra,** 5km to the south, is calmer and as scenic. Settle in at the **Women's Agricultural-Tourist Cooperative,** (tel.(0253) 412 38) by the bus stop, and partake of daily family life (doubles 2500dr). International lesbian travelers make their pilgrimage to the western villages of **Eressos** and **Skala Eressos,** and camp along the fine sands of the Aegean. Boats run daily to Lesvos via Chios from Piraeus (15 hr., 2871dr), as do several flights from Athens (9100dr) and Thessaloniki (13700dr).

When the mythical Orion drove the wild beasts off Chios, the vegetation had a field day. Tall pines, graceful mastic trees, and brown prickly shrubs dapple valleys and cloak mountainsides. Bizarre, ornamental architecture in the well-preserved southern towns of **Pirgi** and **Mesta,** and the impressive **Monastery of Nea Moni** (16km from Chios Town, accessible by bus Wed. mornings only), lend the island a medieval aura. The **tourist office** (tel. (0271) 242 17) on 18 Kanari St. in Chios Town between the main square and the waterfront helps find rooms (open Mon.-Fri. 7am-2:30pm). The **Hatzelenis Travel Agency** (tel. (0271) 267 43) provides the same service, and stays open for the 4am ferries from Piraeus. They also rent mopeds, better than a donkey for seeing the island (2-seaters 2000dr per day). The closest beach, sandy **Karfas,** is clogged by tourists in summer and is serviced by frequent buses. Instead, seek the stunning black volcanic beach at **Emborio,** which

American Youth Hostels Office Locations

To get the most out of your hostelling experience, contact the American Youth Hostels office nearest you. All offices provide American Youth Hostels cards, international hostel guidebooks and sheet sleeping sacks. Some even offer railpasses, travel gear and more.

Alaska
P.O. Box 240347
Anchorage, AK 99524

Arizona
1046 E. Lemon St.
Tempe, AZ 85281
602-894-5128
M-F noon-6 pm Mountain

California
P.O. Box 3645
Merced, CA 95344
209-383-0686
M-F noon-4 pm Pacific

425 Divisadero #301
San Francisco, CA 94117
415-863-9939
M-F noon-6 pm Pacific

1434 Second St.
Santa Monica, CA 90401
310-393-3413
Tu-Sa 10 am-5 pm Pacific

335 W. Beech St.
San Diego, CA 92101
619-239-2444
M-F 10 am-6 pm;
Sa 10 am-5 pm Pacific

Colorado
P.O. Box 2370
Boulder, CO 80306
303-442-1166
M, Tu, W 10 am-4 pm;
Th noon-7 pm Mountain

Connecticut
118 Oak Street
Hartford, CT 06106
203-247-6356
M-F 1-4 pm Eastern

D. C.
1017 K St. N.W.
Washington, D.C. 20001
202-783-4943
M-Sa 10 am-6 pm Eastern

Florida
P.O. Box 533097
Orlando, FL 32853-3097
407-649-8761
M-F 9 am-5 pm Eastern

Georgia
223 Ponce De Leon Ave.
Atlanta, GA 30308

Illinois
3036 N. Ashland Ave.
Chicago, IL 60657
312-327-8114
M-W, F 9 am-5 pm;
Th noon-8 pm;
Sa 9 am-1 pm Central

Indiana
8231 Lakeshore Drive
Gary, IN 46403-0016

Iowa
Box 10
Postville, IA 52162
319-864-3923
M-F 8 am-5 pm Central

Maryland
17 W. Mulberry St.
Baltimore, MD 21201
410-576-8880
M-Sa 10 am-6pm Eastern

7420 1/2 Baltimore Blvd.
College Park, MD 20740
301-209-8544
M-Sa 10 am-6 pm Eastern

Massachusetts
1020 Commonwealth Ave.
Boston, MA 02215
617-731-6692
M-W, F noon-6 pm;
Th noon-8 pm Eastern

Michigan
3024 Coolidge
Berkley, MI 48072
313-545-0511
M-F 10 am-5 pm;
W 10 am-8pm Eastern

Minnesota
795 Raymond Ave.
St. Paul, MN 55114-1522
612-659-0407
M-F noon-6 pm Central

Missouri
7187 Manchester Road
St. Louis, MO 63143
314-644-4660
M, Tu, Th, F noon-5 pm;
W 4-7 pm Central

Nebraska
1237 R St. #102
Lincoln, NE 68588
402-472-3265
M-F 8 am-5 pm Central

New Mexico
517 Adams N.W. #4
Albuquerque, NM 87108

New York
P.O. Box 6343
Albany, NY 12206

P.O. Box 1110
Ellicott Station
Buffalo, NY 14203

891 Amsterdam Ave.
New York, NY 10025
212-866-3226
M-F 9 am-5 pm

535 Oak St.
Syracuse, NY 13203
315-472-5788
Daily 5-9 pm Eastern

North Carolina
714 Ninth St. #207
Durham, NC 27705

P.O. Box 10766
Winston-Salem, NC 27103

Ohio
P.O. Box 141015
Cincinnati, OH 45250

P.O. Box 14384
Columbus, OH 43214
614-447-1006
M-W 9:30 am-6 pm;
Th 11 am-7 pm
F 9:30 am-4 pm Eastern

P.O. Box 173
Lima, OH 45802

6093 Stanford Road
Peninsula, OH 44264
216-467-8711
Daily after 5 pm Eastern

6206 Pembridge Drive
Toldedo, OH 43615

Oregon
311 E. 11th Ave.
Eugene, OR 97401
503-683-3685
M-F 11 am-5 pm Pacific

3031 S.E. Hawthorne Blvd.
Portland, OR 97214
503-236-3380
Tu-Sa noon-5 pm Pacific

Pennsylvania
38 S. Third St.
Philadelphia, PA 19106
215-925-6004
M-F noon-6 pm;
Sa 11 am-3 pm Eastern

6300 Fifth Ave.
Pittsburgh, PA 15232-2922

Tennessee
P.O. Box 242108
Memphis, TN 38124

Texas
2200 S. Lakeshore Blvd.
Austin, TX 78741
512-444-2294
Daily 8-11 am,
7-10 pm Central

3530 Forest Lane #127
Dallas, TX 75234
214-350-4294
M-F 3-6 pm Central

5302 Crawford
Houston, TX 77004
713-523-1009
Daily 7-10 am,
5-11 pm Central

Washington
419 Queen Anne Ave. N.
#101
Seattle, WA 98109
206-281-7306
M, Tu, Th, F noon-4 pm;
W 3-7 pm Pacific

Wisconsin
2224 W. Wisconsin Ave.
Milwaukee, WI 53233
414-933-1170
M 5-7 pm;
Tu-F 9 am-1 pm Central

National Office
P.O. Box 37613
Washington, D.C.
20013-7613
202-783-6161
M-F 9 am-6 pm Eastern

is relatively untouched by the scourge. Blue buses lumber from main square in Chios Town to Karfas and also to the nearby rocky beaches at **Vrondados** and **Daskalopetra** (every ½ hr., 100dr). Green buses wheeze from the square to Emborio, Pirgi, and Mesta (4-8 per day, 200-350dr). Boats leave daily for Piraeus, (at 8pm, 10hr., 2364dr), Lesvos (at 4:30am, 4hr., 1500dr), and also for Çeşme, Turkey (July-Aug. 1 per day, Sept.-June 2-4 per week, one way 5000dr, round-trip 7000dr).

Samos is perhaps the most beautiful and certainly the most touristed island in the area, although it's quiet compared to most of the Dodecanese and the Cyclades. Ferries run from **Samos Town** to Piraeus (daily, 12 hr., 2731 dr), Chios (2 per week, 3-5 hr., 1085 dr) and Paros (4 per week, 1720dr) and less frequently to Lesvos, Mykonos, and Syros.

Ferries leave from equally touristy **Pythagorion** for Patmos (4 per week, 4 hr., 910dr) and points south. Most boats serving Samos Town also stop at **Karlovassi,** the island's pimpled western port. In Samos Town, **Samos Tours** (tel. (0273) 277 15), right at the end of the ferry dock, has all the information you'll need (open daily 6am-3pm and 5:30-11pm and usually when boats arrive). The **tourist office** (tel. (0273) 285 30), further down the waterfront is helpful, but opens whimsically. Accommodations are scarce in July and August. The best place to stay is the clean, cheap **Pension Ionia** (tel. (0273) 287 82; singles 1500dr, doubles 2200dr). Phone ahead; if they can't squeeze you in, they'll direct you elsewhere. Similarly priced is the pleasant **Pension Avli** (tel. (0273) 229 39), in a renovated convent.

Beaches rimming the northern coast are numerous and beautiful, and excepting picturesque **Kokkari,** uncrowded. **Psili Ammos** on the southern coast is especially nice after 4pm, when the excursion buses return to Samos Town. At Pythagorion you can see the magnificent remains of Polykrates' 6th-century BC engineering projects: the **Tunnel of Eupalinos,** a rock pier built in 40m of water, and the **Temple of Hera,** one of the seven wonders of the ancient world.

Samos is the main transit point to **Ephesus** on the Turkish coast, the site of perhaps the most extensive classical ruins in the Mediterranean (see Turkey). Ferries leave twice daily in summer (8am and 5pm) to Kuşadası (4000dr one-way, 5500dr round-trip). The Turkish port tax (not included) is USD8 or 1500dr; if you stay overnight you have to pay the tax again. Charter flyers should check with their companies to make sure crossing into Turkey will not pose problems.

An aura of legends permeates **Rhodes** Ροδός, despite the absence of the Colossus (toppled by the devastating earthquake in 226 BC) and the annual inundation of tourists in both the capital city and Lindos. The island is famous for its unparalleled medieval architecture, impressive ancient ruins, and splendid beaches and coves. The best beaches stretch along the east coast towards Lindos, at **Faliraki, Tsambika,** and **Haraki.** Five km north of Faliraki is **Kalithea,** once an exclusive spa for European aristocrats and one of the few places in the island's north where you can camp in peace. On the northern coast are the ruins of an ancient town at **Kamiros,** and farther west, the majestic hilltop castle at **Monolithos.** The interior and southern half of the island are quieter, subsisting on agriculture rather than tourism.

The city of **Rhodes** is dominated by the massive and beautifully restored **Crusader Castle** of the Knights of St. John. Commence an exploration of the medieval city from the **Hospital of The Knights** on Argykastrou Sq., an imposing fortress that contains the **Archeological Museum.** (Open Mon. 12:30-7pm, Tues.-Fri. 8am-7pm, Sat.-Sun. 8:30am-3pm. Admission 300dr, students 150dr.) **Ipotou Street,** which ascends from the square, is the historic **Avenue of The Knights** on which different national orders of the Crusaders kept their "Inns." At the top of the street stands the castle itself, an impregnable fortress complete with moats, drawbridges, and colossal battlements. Also let the **Chora** awe you; from Kleovolou Sq. as you leave the palace, turn left onto Orfeos St. Plane trees form a canopy over the street. The exclusive reserve of Turks and Jews during Ottoman rule, the Chora harbors the **Mosque of Süleyman** (closed to the public) and the **Turkish baths** on Arionos Sq. (Open daily 5am-7pm. Baths Mon., Wed., and Sat. 50dr, Thurs.-Fri. and Sun. 150dr. Bring soap.)

Though the modern **new town** is crammed with hotels and expensive shops and restaurants, the **old town** of Rhodes welcomes budget travelers with its small pensions and inexpensive restaurants. The **City of Rhodes tourist office** (tel. 359 45) is on Rimini Sq. near Mandraki (the port area). The **GNTO** (tel. 232 55) is a few blocks up the street. Stay at the friendly and international **Steve Kefalas's Pension,** 60 Omirou St. (tel. 243 57; cots on roof 500dr, dorms 900dr). Alternatively, try **Pension Apollon,** 28c Omirou St. (tel. 320 03), near Steve's, or the **Dionisos Pension,** 75 Platanos St. (tel. 220 35). Both have rooms for 750-800dr per person. The cheapest foodlet is the **Belmore Inn,** 46 Amerikis St. (tel. 323 64), in the new town. The place is small, but portions are large and worth the trek.

The Crusader fortress, ancient acropolis, steep whitewashed streets, and sandy beach of **Lindos** attract huge crowds and warrant high prices. Vacant rooms during high season are elusive—either make Lindos a day trip or camp with mosquitoes and other backpackers on the beach, where there are free showers. The walk up to the acropolis will tax your legs not nearly as much as the donkey ride up will tax your wallet. If you head down the other side of the hill, you can toast in relative solitude on the rocks by the sea.

There are **ferries** from Rhodes to all of the Dodecanese islands, to Athens (Piraeus; 4000dr), and to Marmaris in Turkey (4000dr). Rhodes lies on the route of boats traveling from Piraeus to Cyprus and the Middle East. These run four times per week, docking in Cyprus one day later and Haifa or other Middle East destinations 12 hours after that. For tickets and schedules, go to **Triton Tours,** 25-27 Plastira St. (tel. 306 57; open Mon.-Fri. 8am-2pm and 4-9pm, Sat. 9am-1:30pm and 4-8pm). Regular flights in summer leave from Rhodes to Athens, Crete, Kos, Santorini, Mykonos, Karpathos, and Kassos. Various European charters also fly into Rhodes's airport.

Keeping the island of **Kos** (Κως) a secret from travel agents is like hiding truffles from a pig. In summer visitors throng to the classical and Hellenic ruins, carpet the wide, sandy beaches, and frisk about bars. The most popular beach is at **Tingaki,** 10km west of **Kos Town,** notable only for a boisterous nightlife. **Paradise Beach,** about 50km south of Kos Town, is Kos's most unspoiled sand. For accommodations, inquire at the **tourist office** (tel. 287 24) on the waterfront. Try **Pension Alexis,** 9 Irodotou and Omirou St. (tel. 287 98), the first right off Megalou Alexandrou St. (Doubles 3000dr. Triples 3500dr.) The main archeological sites are in town and at **Asclepion,** Hippocrates' school of medicine, 5km away. The five mountain villages of **Asfendiou** and the surrounding hills beg to be hiked. For a quieter beach town than Kos itself, try **Mastihari** on the northern coast or petite **Kamari,** near the southern tip of the island. Two boats per day travel from Kos to Bodrum, Turkey (3500dr one way).

The rest of the Dodecanese are substantially more subdued. For gracious islands as yet unmolested, try **Nissiros,** with the dormant volcano of Polyvotis, or **Tilos,** even quieter, with long empty beaches at **Livadia,** the port, and on the other side of the island at Erestos. Both Nissiors and Tilos welcome two or three ferries a week from Rhodes and Kos. **Kalymnos** and **Leros** are on the main ferry route to Piraeus and are hence a little busier.

Patmos (Πάτμος), northernmost of the Dodecanese islands, is where St. John is said to have written the Book of Revelations in a hillside cave. The sprawling **monastery** dedicated to him, just above the charming and labyrinthine hilltop village of **Chora,** presides over the austere beauty of the island. Stay in the pleasant port of **Skala;** though accommodations can be scarce, you can rent a room from the welcome wagon at the dock or camp for 500dr per person at the well-appointed site at **Meloi Beach** (tel. 318 91), 1½km from Skala.

Karpathos (Κάρπαθος), south of Rhodes, is more isolated and features **Olymbos,** a traditional town with two working windmills, women in traditional garb, and the pretty, stony beach at **Vananda.** Both are accessible from the small port of **Diafani** in the northern part of the island; the main administrative port is **Karpathos** in the south. In Karpathos Town, stay at the family-run, English-speaking **Harry's Pension** (tel. 221 88), just up the hill and to the left of the Arva Hotel. (Singles

1229dr. Doubles 1800dr. Open April-Dec.) The beautiful, nearly deserted beaches of **Ahata** and **Amopi** are perfect for camping and nude bathing. The island is served by boats sailing from Rhodes to Crete; departures are infrequent in winter, and always at the mercy of the weather in this, the roughest stretch of the Aegean.

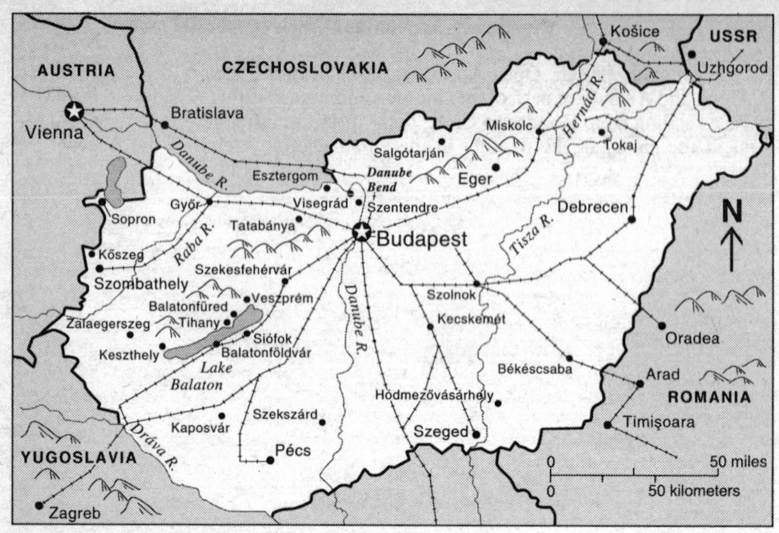

HUNGARY

USD$1 = 76.8 forints (Ft, or HUF) | **10Ft = USD$0.13**
CAD$1 = 67.2Ft | **10Ft = CAD$0.15**
GBP£1 = 128Ft | **10Ft = GBP£0.08**
AUD$1 = 59.8Ft | **10Ft = AUD$0.17**
NZD$1 = 43.8Ft | **10Ft = NZD$0.22**
Country Code: 36 | **International Dialing Prefix: 00**

The people of Hungary (Magyarország) combine the best of what are generally considered typical northern and southern European characteristics. Exacting attention to detail, resulting in an admirable level of efficiency, complements a Mediterranean type of affability—all of which miraculously survived the apathy associated with the late communist system. More academic minds will be content to marvel at the result of the centuries-old tension between Magyar ethnicity and foreign domination. From the 16th to the 18th century, the Turks and Hapsburgs plundered the country; in the 20th century, World War I redistributed two thirds of it and after World War II, the Soviet Union transformed Hungary into a buffer state with a puppet government. In 1956, Hungarian patriots led by the moderate communist Imre Nagy rose up against Soviet control with a passion that was only crushed by Soviet tanks and Nagy's execution.

In the fall of 1990, urged on by the death rattle of the command economy and a massive national tribute to the martyrs of 1956, the Hungarian people fulfilled the aspirations of the previous generation and broke away from the Soviet orbit in a bloodless revolution. Eager to further privatize Hungary's hybrid economy, the ruling party relinquished its monopoly on power and, as a dubious symbol of progress, renamed the People's Republic of Hungary the Republic of Hungary. Elections have since transferred power to the Hungarian Democratic Forum. Change continues at a dizzying pace; the last Soviet troops went home in June, 1991.

Although still aglow with their political triumphs, Hungarians are beginning to experience a vicious economic hangover. Inflation estimated at 20-50% is rapidly reducing one quarter of the population to poverty. Many are exhausted by the second jobs necessary to maintain a satisfactory standard of living. High prices for daily necessities, widespread unemployment, and yawning inequities in wealth harshly remind Hungarians of the desperate side of liberty. Realizing that there are no quick solutions, most Hungarians are resigning themselves to a painful but necessary decade of transition.

Hungarian culture has flourished throughout the country's tumultuous history. Hungary's contribution to the music world includes 19th-century composer Ferenc (Franz) Liszt, as well as 20th-century geniuses Zoltán Kodály and Béla Bartók. Many current musical groups enjoy worldwide respect, and theater and film also thrive under the direction of such luminaries as Miklós Jancsó. Modern artist Victor Vasarely is also one of Hungary's children. Folk music collectors should look for tapes by Sebestyén Márta.

With a fifth of Hungary's population and loads to see and do, Budapest dominates the country. The capital does not, however, have a monopoly on cultural attractions. None of the provincial centers is more than a three-hour train ride through fertile farmland from Budapest, making daytrips feasible. Wander around the medieval streets of Sopron, or the art museums of Pécs, or stop off in the eastern city of Debrecen on your way to the Soviet Union. A castle, wine cellars, and baroque houses greet the visitor to Eger; or just relax on the shores of Lake Balaton.

Getting There and Getting Around

In September 1991, visas were necessary for citizens of Australia and New Zealand, who should contact Hungarian missions in Europe or the embassy at Unit 6, 351A Edgecliff Rd., Sydney, NSW 2027 (tel. (02) 328 78 59; USD15 for a 30-day tourist visa, 48-hr. transit visas also available). Citizens of the U.S. and Canada did not need a visa for visits up to 90 days. For U.K. citizens, the limit was 180 days. After 30 days in the country, all visitors must register with the police or at the KEOKH, Foreign Nationals Office, Andrassy út 12, Budapest (tel. 118 08 00).

More than you could ever want to know about every mode of travel to, from, and within Hungary is contained in the helpful and, believe it or not, entertaining booklet *Travel in Hungary,* available from Tourinform and travel agencies. All modes are trying to expand in step with growing business and tourism demands, but the basic plan remains. Budapest's Ferihegy airport handles all international traffic, including MALÉV, the national airline. Hungary's domestic transportation network resembles a wheel, with Budapest again at the hub. The spokes represent rail lines, and no point on the perimeter is more than three hours by express train from Budapest. It usually makes sense to use buses to travel around the rim of the wheel, or else to come back into Budapest to make connections.

Hungarian trains are reliable and inexpensive; Eurail and InterRail passes are both valid. *Személyvonat* are excruciatingly slow; *gyorsvonat* cost the same and move at least twice as fast. All of the larger provincial towns are accessible by the express rail lines *(sebesvonat).* The express fare from Budapest to any of the provincial cities should cost little more than 300-400Ft each way, including a seat reservation (required on trains marked with an "R" on schedules). Express trains wear red signs reading "gyors," not to be confused with the city Györ. Hungarian train terms include *indúlás* (departure), *vágány* (track), and *pályaudvar* (station, abbreviated *pu.)* In 1991 student discounts on domestic trains were available only to those with Hungarian student cards; train conductors check IDs. The ISIC commands discounts on international tickets from IBUSZ, Express and station ticket counters. (Book several days in advance.) International tickets are no longer the bargain they used to be (Budapest-Vienna one-way in second class USD17, Prague USD12, Warsaw USD50). A trans-Siberian ticket, once USD48, now runs about USD300. Between socialist countries, buying a ticket to the border and then another one on the train sometimes works out cheaper.

The extensive bus system is cheap but crowded. Most routes between provincial cities pass through Budapest. The main bus station at Erzsébet tér in Budapest posts schedules and fares. Inter-city bus tickets can generally be bought on the bus, while tickets for local city buses must be bought in advance from a newsstand (about 14Ft) and punched on board.

The Danube hydrofoil is the most enjoyable (and most expensive) way to go to Vienna, but no longer runs to Bratislava. The trip between Vienna and Budapest costs about USD70 one-way, USD100 round-trip. Tickets are cheaper at the IBUSZ travel bureau (Kärntnerstraße 26 in Vienna) than at the dock. Some travelers cross the Austrian border by hitchhiking on the main highway between Vienna and Budapest (E5). It's a five-hour drive capital-to-capital. Avoid crossing the border on foot.

Either IBUSZ or Tourinform can provide a guide to cycling in Hungary, which includes maps, suggested tours, repair shops, and recommended border crossing points. Write to the **Hungarian Nature-Lovers' Federation (MTSZ),** 1065 Budapest, Bajcsy-Zsilinszky út 31, or the **Hungarian Cycling Federation,** 1146 Budapest, Szabó J. u. 3, for more information. Some rail stations rent bicycles to passengers. Hungarians who hitchhike use the main roads and wave their hands to flag down approaching cars.

Practical Information

Perhaps the best word for foreigners to know is **IBUSZ,** the Hungarian national travel bureau, with offices throughout the country. They can make room arrangements, change money, sell train tickets, and charter tours. Snare the pamphlet *Tourist Information Hungary,* and the monthly entertainment guide *Programme in Hungary* (both free and written in English). **Express,** the national student travel bureau, handles student accommodations and tours and changes money. In most towns, Express handles youth hostel accommodations. The main Express office sells Inter-Rail cards to those who qualify. Regional travel agencies are almost always more helpful than IBUSZ and Express in outlying areas. **Tourinform** is a fantastically helpful information service with one central location in Budapest. They answer questions about Budapest and the rest of Hungary, often serving as interpreters.

Change money only as you need it. If you save your exchange receipts, you can convert 50% back into Western currency. Make sure to save some Western cash, necessary for some purchases (e.g. visas and international train tickets). All exchange desks offer the same official rate. Clearly marked exchange windows freckle major cities. The maximum commission for exchange is 1%. Exchange away from official desks is illegal yet very common, but the rates offered are usually not favorable enough to risk the large chance of being ripped off, and undercover cops keep tabs on moneychangers even outside of Budapest. The entire question will be moot as soon as the forint becomes convertible (perhaps in the near future).

Many addresses are changing in the wake of the 1989 revolution. Tourist brochures, maps, subway station signs and even street signs may not reflect the latest purges, so it's advisable to get new maps for all areas. Hungarian addresses usually involve one of the following: *utca,* abbreviated *u.* (street); *út* and the related *útya/útja* (avenue); *tér* and the related *tere* (square); and *körút,* abbreviated *krt.* (ring-boulevard). A single name such as Baross may be associated with several of these in completely separate parts of a city—i.e. Baross út, Baross u., Baross tér, etc. Numbers on the two sides of a street are not always in sync.

Western newspapers and magazines are available in many newsstands and in large hotels. Hungary's English-language paper, *Daily News* is supposed to be resuscitated soon. Used bookstores, called *antikvárium,* often sell English books at firesale prices. English language radio and TV programming is found most easily in the English language *Budapest Week.*

Learning a bit of the Hungarians' Finno-Ugric language will not only make you a better person, but also endear you to the natives. A few starters for pronunciation: the letter *c* is pronounced ts as in ca*ts;* *cs,* ch as in cat*ch;* *gy,* dy as in the French a*di*eu; and *ly,* as in *y*am; *s,* sh as in *sh*ovel; *sz,* s as in *s*ink; *zs,* s as in mea*s*ure; *a,* as in "*aw* shucks." The first syllable in a word usually gets the emphasis. Some useful tidbits: hello—jó napot *(YOH naw-pot);* thank you—köszönöm *(KUR-sur-nurm);* when?—mikor? *(MI-kor?);* where?—hol? In personal names, the family name precedes the given name.

The half of Hungary's pay phones that work require a 5Ft piece every three minutes. Wait for the dial tone before putting your money in. Dial slowly. For long distance, dial 06 before the area code (two digits long, except in Budapest). International calls require red phones or new, digital-display blue ones, found at large post offices and sometimes on the street and in metro stations. At 200Ft per minute to the U.S., the phone sucks money so fast you need a companion to feed it. Direct calls can also be made from the telephone office in Budapest, with a 3-minute minimum to the U.S. To call collect, dial 09 for the international operator. For AT&T's **USA Direct,** put in a 20Ft coin, dial 00, wait for the second dial tone, then dial 36 01 11.

The mail works fine (airmail to U.S. 5-10 days). Airmail is *légiposta;* whether it's faster than something called *expressz* is unclear. Because Hungary's per capita telephone rate is the second lowest in Europe (Albania wins) it is very common to send telegrams, even across town. Ask for a telegram form *(távirati ürlapot)* and fill it out before returning to the counter.

General business hours in Hungary are Monday to Wednesday and Friday from 10am to 6pm (7pm for food stores), Thursday from 10am to 8pm. Banks close around 2pm on Friday, and on Saturday many businesses close after 1pm, but hours keep expanding as businesses privatize and Marx gives way to Mammon. Post offices are open weekdays 8am to 6pm, and Saturday from 8am to 2pm. Nothing is open on national holidays, the Christian holidays, May 1 and August 20. The upheaval in 1989 produced two new holidays, March 15 and Oct. 23, and pitched two Soviet-inspired ones (April 4 and November 7).

Should you get sick, contact your embassy for lists of English-speaking doctors in Budapest. Some travelers have supported themselves in Budapest for years by teaching English at an English-language school or in private tutoring. Contracts run for a semester. For more information, contact the English Teachers' Center through the American Embassy, or look for listings in the libraries of the American and British embassies. You can also try calling the myriad private schools that advertise in *Budapest Week* or on posters.

Accommodations and Camping

In the past, most travelers stayed in private homes booked through a tourist agency. (Singles 600-1000Ft. Doubles 800-1400Ft.) If you stay less than four nights, you must pay a surcharge (30% of one night's stay). Singles are scarce, so it's worth finding a roommate. Insist on a cheap room (but with a good location). Otherwise the agency may try to foist off their most expensive quarters on you. Outside of Budapest, the best and cheapest office is usually the regional one, such as Balatontourist in Balatonfüred, or Egertourist in Eger. You can also ditch the agencies and find your own room where there is a sign for *szoba kiadó* or *Zimmer frei.* As competition and demand increase, new tourist agencies keep opening up to book rooms.

Unfortunately, renting a private room is less an introduction to Hungarian life than a business transaction. Many owners keep their quarters and lives walled off from the traveler. You receive a front-door key and sometimes access to the kitchen. Others, however, will offer a gracious welcome.

Some towns have cheap hotels (doubles 800-1100Ft). As the hotel system develops and room prices rise, hosteling will become more attractive. Many can be booked at **Express** or sometimes the regional tourist office after you arrive (200-600Ft). From late June through August, university dorms metamorphose into hostels. Locations change annually, but registration is always through an **Express** office. The staff at Express generally speak German, sometimes English. They cannot book hostels in another city. Hostels are usually large enough to accommodate peak-season crowds. In 1991 hostels did not require an IYHF card, though that may change as Hungary's tourist industry integrates with Western Europe's. Nor are sleep sacks needed.

Over 100 campgrounds are sprinkled throughout Hungary, charging about 400Ft per day for two people. You can often rent four-person bungalows for 1400Ft, but you must pay for every space, whether or not it is filled. Most sites are open from May through September. Tourist offices offer the comprehensive booklet *Camping Hungary,* which is being revised for 1992. For more information and maps, contact the **Hungarian Camping and Caravanning Club** in Budapest, or Tourinform.

Food and Drink

With its fantastic concoctions of meat, spices, and fresh vegetables, many find Magyar cuisine among the finest in Europe. Paprika, Hungary's chief agricultural export, is the predominant spice, and many Hungarian meals run red with it. In Hungarian restaurants, called *vendéglö* or *étterem,* you might begin your meal with *gulyás,* a beef soup seasoned with paprika, or with the addictive *meggyleves* (sour cherry soup). Close to what we call goulash is *pörkölt,* a pork or beef stew, again with paprika. Vegetarians can find the tasty *rántott sajt* (fried cheese), *rántott gombafejek* (fried mushrooms), and *gombapörkölt* (mushroom stew) on most menus. *Túrós táska* is a chewy pastry pocket filled with a sweetened cottage cheese (called *túró,* often translated as "curd"). *Somlói galuska,* Hungarian sponge cake, is a fantastically rich and delicious concoction of chocolate, nuts, and cream, topped with a chocolate-rum sauce. Crescent-shaped *bürkiffli,* with a walnut-and-powdered-sugar topping and a nut paste filling, are easy to tote. Hungarians claim that the Austrians stole the recipe for *rétes* and called it *strudel.*

Formal restaurants *(étterem)* come in class I and II; gypsy music spells tourist trap. Class I restaurants will often bring and charge for items you did not order, such as bread, potatoes, and mineral water. Check your bill meticulously. It's customary to tip 10%, even if the bill includes a service charge (which goes to the management). Give the money to the waiter when you pay. A gypsy musician expects about 150Ft from your table, depending on the number of listeners. A *csárda* is a traditional inn, and a *bistró* an inexpensive restaurant. A *kifözde* rarely offers more than 10 dishes; tables are always shared. To see what you order, try an *ön kiszolgáló étterem,* or cheap cafeteria. Since precious few menus are in English, a dictionary is handy. For pastry and coffee, look for a *cukrászdák. Kávé* means espresso. **Salátabárs** vend not fresh salads, but deli concoctions. Restaurants outside of Budapest offer higher quality, lower prices, and wider services.

Vegetarians may have trouble filling up in Hungarian restaurants, but fresh fruit and vegetables flower on small stands and produce markets. Supermarkets (ABC) sell dry goods and dairy products. The fresh milk is delectable but goes bad within 48 hours. With the exception of "non-stops," most shops close from 1pm on Saturday to Sunday morning.

Hungarians are justly proud of their wines. Most famous are the red *Egri Bikavér* ("Bull's Blood of Eger"), the white *Tokaji* wines, and the whites of the Balaton region. Most go down well (150Ft per bottle at a store, 300Ft at a restaurant). Fruit schnapps *(pálinka),* most notably apricot *(barack),* cherry *(cserszny),* and pear *(körte),* are a national specialty; you can try them in most cafés and bars. Local beers are good; the most common is *Dreher.*

Budapest

At once a cosmopolitan European capital as well as the stronghold of Magyar nationalism, Budapest's intellectual and cultural scene has often been compared to that of Paris. Like Vienna, Budapest bears the architectural stamp of Hapsburg rule. But unlike its fastidious western neighbor, Budapest retains a worn-at-the-elbows charm in its squares and cafés. World War II punished the city; from the rubble, Hungarians rebuilt with the same pride that weathered the 1956 Soviet invasion, and subsequent decades of socialist subservience. Today, the city manages to maintain its charm, even under siege from capitalism's inevitable glitzification.

Orientation and Practical Information

Budapest is in northwestern Hungary, about 250km downstream from Vienna. Regular trains and excursion boats connect the two cities. Budapest also has direct rail links to Belgrade to the southeast, Prague to the northwest, and other mega-metropolises throughout Eastern Europe. The city forms a circle, split by the River Danube. Medieval Buda lies on the west bank. On the east side buzzes Pest, the commercial heart of the modern city. Three central bridges bind the two halves together. The **Széchényi lánc híd** (Chain Bridge) connects Roosevelt tér to the cable car, which leads to the Royal Palace. To the south, the white **Erzsébet híd** (Elizabeth Bridge) runs from near Petőfi tér. Further south, the green **Szabadság híd** joins Dimitrov tér to Gellért Hill, topped by the Liberation Monument.

Budapest's metro runs on three color-coded, numbered lines: yellow (#1), red (#2), and blue (#3). An "M" indicates a stop. The three lines converge at **Deák tér,** which is beside the main international bus terminal at Erzsébet tér. Deák tér serves as the hub of Pest's loose arrangement of concentric ring boulevards and spoke-like avenues. Walk two blocks or take the yellow metro one stop to Vörösmarty tér. If you face the main statue, then **Váci utca,** the main pedestrian shopping zone, extends to the right.

Addresses in Budapest include a Roman numeral representing the district number. Central Buda is I, and downtown Pest is V. In mailing addresses, the middle two digits of the zip code correspond to the district number. Many street names repeat; always refer to districts as well. Because many street names have changed recently, a new map is essential. (The American Express office has an excellent, free tourist map.) Anyone planning an exhaustive visit to Budapest should find a copy of András Török's *Budapest: A Critical Guide.*

Tourist Offices: Tourinform, V, Sütöút. 2 (tel. 117 98 00). Located off Deák tér (M: Deák tér) around the corner from Porsche Hungaria. This multilingual national tourist office provides information ranging from sightseeing tours to opera performances to the location of Aikido dojos. Open daily 8am-8pm. Sightseeing, accommodation bookings, travel services available at **IBUSZ, Cooptourist** and **Budapest Tourist** (offices in train stations and tourist centers).

Budget Travel: Express, V, Zoltán u. 10 (tel. 111 64 18). M: Kossuth Lajos or Arany Janós. Some reduced international plane fares for under-26 crowd. Also youth and ISIC reductions on certain international rail fares to Eastern European destinations (but same reductions also available at station ticket offices). Open Mon.-Thurs. 8:30am-12:30pm and 1:30-4:30pm; Fri. 8:30am-12:30pm and 1:30-3:30pm. Around the corner at the Express main office, V, Szabadság tér 16 (tel. 131 77 77), pick up your FIYTO card (200Ft) or ISIC card (165Ft). Open Sat.-Mon. and Wed. 9am-4pm, Tues. 9am-5pm, Fri. 9am-2pm. The Express accommodations office in Keleti station may be licensed to sell reduced travel tickets by 1992. (Open daily 8am-9pm; tel. 14 27 72). For both domestic and international budget travel, the bus is often the best deal.

Embassies: U.S., V, Szabadság tér 12 (tel. 112 64 50, after hours 153 05 66). **Canada,** II, Budakeszi u. 32 (tel. 176 76 86). Take bus #22 from Moszkva tér. **U.K.,** V, Harmincad u. 6 (M: Vörösmarty tér, near Gerbaud; tel. 218 28 88). **Australia,** VI, Délibáb u. 30 (tel. 153 42 33). **New Zealanders** should contact the British embassy. **Albania,** VI, Bajza u. 26 (tel. 122 92 78). **Czechoslovakia,** XIV, Népstadion út 22 (tel. 163 66 00). Open Mon.-Fri. 8:30am-1pm. **Romania,** XIV, Tökölyi út. 72 (tel. 142 69 44). **USSR,** VI, Bajza út 35 (tel. 131 89 85). **Yugoslavia,** VI, Dozsa György út 92b (tel. 142 05 66). Open Tues. and Thurs.-Fri. 10am-noon.

Currency Exchange: A bushel of offices cash traveler's checks and change money. IBUSZ at V, Petőfi tér 3, just north of Elizabeth (Erzsébet) Bridge, is open 24 hrs. All exchange offices give the same rate. Only a few (large hotels, train stations) charge the maximum 1% commission. If you save your receipts, you can change 50% of your remaining forints back into hard currency. Larger exchange offices will turn hard currency traveler's cheques into hard currency for 6% commission. **Visa cash advances** in forints only from Foreign Trade Bank (Külker Bank), V, Szent István tér 11 (all open Mon.-Fri. 8am-6pm).

American Express: V, Deák Ferenc u. 10, next to the new Kampinski Hotel, visible from southeast corner of Vörösmarty tér. Sells traveler's cheques for hard cash, Moneygrams, or cardholders' personal checks. Cash advances only in forints. Open Mon.-Fri. 9am-5pm, Sat. 9am-1pm. The 24-hr. IBUSZ also performs AmEx services.

Post Office: Poste Restante at V, Városház u. 18 (tel. 118 48 11). Open Mon.-Fri. 8am-8pm, Sat. 8am-3pm. 24-hrs. branches at Nyugati (VI, Teréz krt. 105-107) and Keleti (VIII, Baross tér 11c) train stations. After-hours staff no speak English. Have mail sent to American Express.

Telephones: V, Petöfi Sándor u. 17. English-speaking staff. Open Mon.-Fri. 8am-9pm, Sat. 8am-3pm. At other times, try post office. All Budapest numbers begin with 1 or 2. Local operator: 01. **City Code:** 1.

Flights: Ferihegy Airport (tel. 157 00 86). Easily reached by Volán bus, which runs every half hour daily 5am-9pm to and from Erzsébet tér (M: Deák tér; ½ hr., 100Ft). Youth (under 26) as well as standby (under 25) tickets at the Malév office (V, Dorottya u. 2, on Vörösmarty tér; open Mon.-Fri. 8am-5pm) or at any travel agent. Other airlines also offer discounts. Express runs a hostel at the airport for those catching early flights.

Trains: Tel. 122 78 60 for domestic trains, 22 40 52 for international trains. The word for train station is *pályaudvar,* often abbreviated *pu.* The three main stations (Keleti pu., Nyugati pu., and Déli pu.) are also metro stops. Trains to and from a given location do not necessarily stop at the same station; for example, trains from Prague may stop at Nyugati or Keleti, trains from Vienna at Déli or Keleti. Each station has schedules for the others; go and check. 2nd class to Vienna (7 per day, USD17), Prague (7 per day, USD12), Warsaw (3 per day, USD50), Berlin (4 per day, USD32), Belgrade (3 per day) and Bucharest (1 per day). There are domestic ticket counters downstairs at the metro entrances in Keleti and Nyugati stations. International and domestic tickets may be purchased at IBUSZ (see above) or at **MÁV Hungarian Railways,** VI, Andrássy út 35 (tel. 22 80 49 or 22 80 56). Open Mon.-Sat. 9am-5pm. Any discount available at Express should also be available at the station. Be insistent and whip out all your student/youth IDs. Several days' advance purchase may be necessary for international tickets. **Wagons-lits,** V, Dorottya u. 3, near Vörösmarty tér, sells InterRail and discounts for seniors, but no discounted youth rail tickets.

Buses: Tel. 117 29 66 for domestic service, 117 25 62 for international service. **Main Station,** V, Erzsébet tér (M: Deák tér). Luggage storage. Several buses per week to Bucharest, Istanbul ($50), and Venice ($55). Domestic buses are usually a little cheaper than trains but take much longer. Buses to the Danube Bend leave from the Árpád Híd station.

Public Transportation: The metro is rapid and orderly; it and the extensive bus and tram service take you almost anywhere. All Trafik Shops and occasional sidewalk vendors sell yellow tram and metro tickets *(villamos jegy)* for 12Ft and blue bus tickets for 15Ft. Punch a ticket when you enter and a new ticket every time you change subway lines. Day pass good for bus, trams, and metro costs 120Ft. If staying a week or more, consider a monthly pass (1 photo necessary; metro and tram pass 450Ft, bus pass 660Ft. Both valid from the 1st of one month through the 5th of the next.) Some buses follow the metro lines after subway (open 4:30am-11:10pm) shuts down. Metro stops peddle excellent maps (24Ft) showing metro and train routes.

Hydrofoils: For information and ticketing, **MAHART International Boat Station,** V, Belgrád rakpart 2 (tel. 18 17 58; open Mon.-Fri. 8am-4pm, Sat.-Sun. 8am-noon), near the Erzsébet bridge; or **IBUSZ** office, Felszabadulás tér 5 (tel. 118 68 66). Arrive 1 hr. before departure for customs and passport control.

Taxis: Fötaxi (tel. 122 22 22) or **Volántaxi** (tel. 166 66 66). 40Ft plus 25Ft per km. Better off staying away from other companies.

Hitchhiking: Thoe going south to Szeged and Belgrade (M5 and E75) take tram #2 out Soroksári út to the end of the line; they then switch to bus #23, then bus #4. To go west to Györ and Vienna or southwest to Lake Balaton and Zagreb, they take bus #12 from Moszkva tér out to Budaörsi út, then switch to bus #72. The highway splits a few kilometers outside Budapest, with M1 heading west and M7 going south.

Bookstore: Kossuth Könyvesbolt, V, Vörösmarty tér 4, to the right of Gerbeaud Café. Sells English tourist books and paperback novels. Leaving this store, turn left and walk straight down Váci u. where three bookstores beckon within two blocks on the left, stocked with international news and some novels not so fit to print.

Zipper Surgeon: Wossala György, I, Károlyi Mihály u. 4, in the courtyard next to the store with jigsaw puzzles of the Pope in the window (cross-shaped pieces!). A tiny shop with lovely people performing a miraculous service. Open Mon.-Fri. 11am-6pm.

Laundromat: Mosószalon, V, József Nádor tér 9, and V, Városház u. 3. Bigger shops with ordinary people performing a mundane service. Both open Mon.-Fri. 7am-7pm, Sat. 7am-3pm.

Emergencies: Police (Rendörség), Tel. 112 34 56. Call or visit **KEOKH,** the Foreign Nationals Office, VI, Andrássy út 12.

Accommodations and Camping

Private Accommodations Services

Although the Hungarian tourism boom of the last few years has levelled off, accommodations remain in short supply. In fact, Budapest is currently unable to house all its own inhabitants; summer 1991 saw students demonstrate for affordable housing in Vörösmarty tér. New accommodation services, and new branches of established ones, are springing up like wildflower after a spring rain. The rates are about the same at all of them (singles and doubles 600-1400Ft). Three of the most established are **IBUSZ** (at all train stations and tourist centers; 24-hr. accommodation office at V, Petöfi tér 3, tel. 118 39 25), **Budapest Tourist,** V, Roosevelt tér 5 (on the Danube across the street from the Forum Hotel and 10 minutes from Deák tér; tel. 117 35 55; open Mon.-Sat. 8am-8pm, Sun. 9am-3pm) and **Cooptourist,** VI, Bajcsy-Zsilinszky út 17 (tel. 111 70 34). The *Express* office at Keleti station also books private rooms.

The sweetest deals are at IBUSZ. By booking one or more days ahead at their local office (Mon.-Fri. only), you can hope for a cheaper room, ideally near a metro stop. Be dogged about securing the lowest possible price. If you arrive early (8am) you may be lucky enough to get a single for 600Ft or a double for 800Ft. IBUSZ sometimes enforces a 3-night minimum rule. If the IBUSZ at the train stations are closed or fully booked, head for the 24-hr. office. At the end of a day, the only thing left may be doubles for 1400Ft. The IBUSZ offices swarm with Hungarians pushing "bargain" rooms; these are often far away and dingier than IBUSZ rooms, but they may be fine and are perfectly legal. If you find a Magyar grandma attached to your elbow cajoling, "Sleep,sleep!" find out the location and price, as well as if there will be any roommates. It's possible to get a good deal this way, and you can always check in immediately.

Hostels

Most hostel-type accommodations, including university dorm rooms, are handled by Express. You must register at an Express office before proceeding to the hostel. Try V, Semmelweis u. 4 (tel. 117 66 34 or 117 86 00; leave Deák tér on Tanács krt., go right on Gerlóczy u., first left is Sammelweis u.) or V, Szabadság tér 16 (between M: Arany János and Kossuth Lajos). Individual hostels advertise in the Budapest train stations on billboards and small photocopied notices. Any hostel publicly advertised is a legal *Kollegium.* You may also see the standard IYHF symbol outside buildings. Private hostels began springing up in 1990, wedging many people into diminutive 2-room apartments. Before accepting lodging at the rail station, make sure you're not being brought to one of these cattlecars. For hostel beds atop Gellért Hill see Hotel Citadella, below.

For hostel rates with the convenience of a locked room, consider the **Diáksport Hotel,** XIII, Dózsa György út 152 (tel. 140 85 85). From M: Dózsa György, exit towards Hotel Volga on Dózsa György út; then walk one short block, cross Dózsa György út, and the entrance is on a side street, Angyalföldi út. Its tiny, plain rooms (sometimes filled by schoolgroups) afford travelers a genuine taste of Eastern Europe; a hostel cafeteria is nearby. (Singles 250Ft. Doubles 400Ft, with shower 600Ft.)

Hotels

Budapest still has a few inexpensive hotels, frequently clogged with groups. Call ahead. Proprietors generally speak English over the phone. All are registered with Tourinform.

Hotel Kandó, III, Bécsi út 104-108 (tel. 168 20 32). Take bus #60 from Batthyáni tér. Doubles 900Ft. Triples 1150Ft. Quads 1350Ft.

Hala dás Motel, IV, Üdülö Sor 7 (tel. 189 11 14). Bus #104. Doubles 650Ft.

Turistaszálló, III, Pusztakúti út 3 (tel. 168 40 12). HÉV from Batthyány tér for 15 min. to Csillaghegy. Doubles 1120Ft.

Hotel Citadella, atop Gellért Hill (tel. 166 57 94). Dorm beds 140Ft. Doubles 1200Ft. Quads 1600. Take tram #47 or 49 three stops into Buda to Móricz Zsigmond Körtér, catch bus #27 to Citadella.

Camping

Camping Hungary, available at tourist offices, describes Budapest's campgrounds.

Zugligeta Niche Camping, Zugligeti út 101. Take bus #158 from Moszkva tér. Chairlift at campground entrance ascends the Buda Hills. English spoken. 200Ft per person. Open March 15-Oct. 15.

Hárs-hegy, II, Hárs-hegy út 5 (tel. 115 14 82). Take bus #22 from Moszkva tér. Good cheap restaurant. 400Ft for 2 people. 4-person bungalows. Open Easter-Oct. 20.

Római Camping, III, Szentendrei út 189 (tel. 188 71 67). M: Batthyány tér, then HÉV tram to Rómaifürdö. A whopping 1300-person capacity. Disco, pool, and clean squat toilets. Reception open 6am-10pm. 220Ft per person, 90Ft per tent. Bungalows: 2 persons 1150Ft, 4 persons 1600Ft.

Food

Even the most expensive restaurants in Budapest may be within your budget, although they are not necessarily the best. Class I restaurants target clueless tourists, seduce them with gypsy music and stab them with outrageous prices. (Full meal with tip about 600Ft.) Many restaurants have menus in German, a few in English. Keep your eye out for Class II restaurants with Hungarian-only menus, and bring a dictionary. An average meal runs 150-250Ft. Cafeterias lurk under **Önikiszolgáló Étterem** signs (vegetable entrees 18Ft, meat entrees 70-120Ft). The listings below are just a nibble of what Budapest has to offer. Try out the *kifözde* or *kisvendéglö* in your neighborhood for a taste of Hungarian life.

Travelers may also rely on markets and raisin-sized 24-hr. stores labeled "Non-Stop" for staples. Loot the **produce market,** IX, Tolbuhin krt. 1-3 at Dmitrov Tér (open Mon. 6am-3pm), the **ABC Food Hall,** I, Batthyányi tér 5-7 (open Sun. 7am-1pm) or the **Non-Stops** at V, Oktober 6 u. 5 and at V, Régi Posta u. off Váci u., past McDonald's.

Vegetárium, V, Cukor u. 3, a block and a half from M: Ferenciek tér: walk up Károlyi M. u. to Irány u. on the right, and a quick left puts you on Cukor u. Vegetarian and macrobiotic dishes (macrobiotic tempura dinner 280Ft). A good place to detox after a week of Wild Boar Transylvanian Style. Algae plate available. Classical guitar in the evening. Open daily noon-10pm.

Megálló ("Busstop"), VII, Tanács krt. 23, two doors to the left of IBUSZ's Tanács krt. office. M: Deák tér. Look beyond the ratty bearskin on the wall to the 130-item menu (available in English) which includes such temptations as "rumpsteak with gizzard in red vine." Dinner about 200Ft. Open Mon.-Sat. 11am-11pm.

Centrál, V, Tanács krt. 7, 50m from IBUSZ and down the street from Megálló above. M: Deák Tér. The largest cafeteria in Budapest. Cheap and greasy survival food for low, low budgets. Some outdoor seating. Open daily 8:30am-9pm.

Claudia, V, Bástya u., off of Kecskeméti u. M: Kálvin tér. Below-ground polyglot family restaurant with hearty, cheap food. Open daily about 11am-11pm.

Marcello's, XI, Bartók Béla út 40 (tel. 166 62 31). Only pizzeria in Budapest to use tomato sauce rather than ketchup. Pizzas 120-170Ft, salad bar too. Reservations suggested. Open Mon.-Sat. noon-10pm.

Mézes Mackó, V, Kigyó u. 4-6. Central. M: Ferenciek tér, northwest exit. A popular, representative salátabár. Sandwiches and deli delights about 50Ft. Open Mon.-Fri. 7am-8pm, Sat. 8am-4pm.

Budapest University of Economics, IX, Dimitrov tér 8, facing Szabadság bridge. A student cafeteria in a basement, open to all. The site of some of the earliest student protests leading to the end of communist rule. Open Aug.-June Mon.-Fri. for lunch.

Paprika, Harmincad u. 4, just north of Vörösmarty tér, at the big red pepper. Hungarian fast food and a picture menu to help speed word-food coordination. Entrees 62-68Ft. Open Mon.-Sat. 10am-9:30pm, Sun. 10am-4:30pm.

Szindbád, V, Markó út 33 (tel. 132 29 66), at the corner of Bajcsy-Zsilinszky. Two blocks from M: Nyugati tér. Indulge in impeccable elegance and stupendous desserts. Class I. Book 2 days ahead and look hot. Open Mon.-Fri. noon-midnight; Sat.-Sun. 6pm-midnight.

Toldi Etkezde, I, Batthyány u. 14. M: Battyány tér. A *kifözde* restaurant. Entrees 75-170Ft. *Töltött* (stuffed pepper) 109Ft. Open Mon.-Fri. 10am-5pm.

Apostolok, Kigoyó u. 4-6 (tel. 118 37 04). Visible from M: Ferenciek tér. An eclectic, expensive evening of gothic ambience and superb food in an old beer hall. Entrees 200-700Ft. Open daily 10am-midnight.

Restaurant Hanna, VII, Dob u. 35, a 10-min. walk from Deák tér. Wholesome kosher food won't leave you kvetching in this Orthodox Jewish time-warp. Dress conservatively. Open Sun.-Fri. noon-4pm.

Wine and Pastry

Wiener (Vienna) Kaffeehaus, inside the Forum Hotel on the Danube. Budapest's *crème de la cake* tantalize from glass cases, with prices around 75Ft. Eszterházy torte, *somlói galuska* and everything else served by pink-clad Magyar maidens. Open 9am-9pm daily.

Vörösmarty (Gerbeaud) Cukrászda, V, Vörösmarty tér 7. M: Vörösmarty tér. Formerly the meeting place of Budapest's literary elite, this café retains a 19th-century elegance. Service is haphazard; go to the counter. Around 80Ft. Open daily 7am-9pm.

Ruszwurm, I, Szentháromság u. 3. Confecting since 1827 and strewn with period furniture. Open daily 10am-8pm. Stop by when you tour Mátyás Cathedral down the street. This baroque coffeehouse was once so renowned that couriers came from Vienna to select from its delectables. Best ice cream in Budapest 10Ft. Cakes 30-40Ft. Open daily 10am-8pm.

Café New York, VII, Erzsébet krt. 9-11 (tel. 122 38 49). This remarkably ornate café was a favorite hangout of artists, writers, and journalists at the turn of the century. Neat gold ceilings. The adjoining restaurant is wildly extravagant and overpriced, but fun. Open daily 11:30am-3pm and 6:30pm-midnight.

Lukács cukrászda, VI, Andrássy út 70, near Hösök tere. The most beautiful café in Budapest. Open 8:30am-9:30pm.

Sights

Strategically perched a hundred yards above the Danube, Budapest's Castle District sits atop the mile-long block known as Castle Hill (Várhegy). Cross the Széchenyi Lánchíd (chain bridge) and ride the *sikló* (cable car) to the top of the hill (40Ft). At the top, turn right and walk five minutes to **Trinity Square,** the site of the Disneyesque **Fisherman's Bastion,** a group of stone towers offering fantastic views across the river. Behind the towers stands the neo-Gothic **Matthias Church** (Mátyás templom); here High Mass is celebrated at 10am Sundays with orchestra and choir (come early for a seat), and organ concerts deafen all on Friday or Saturday evenings during the summer. Next door sits the **Budapest Hilton Hotel,** which has incorporated the remains of Castle Hill's oldest church, an abbey built in the 13th century by Dominican Friars. Intricate door-knockers and balconies adorn the Castle District's historic buildings; wander through the quaint **Fortuna utca,** lined with baroque townhouses, or along **Táncsics Mihály utca** in the old Jewish commercial sector (the excavated foundation of the old **synagogue** is at #26). By **Vienna Gate** at the northern tip of the Castle District, frequent minibuses run to Moszkva tér. Bus #16 runs to Erzsébet tér across the bridge. From Moszkva tér you can reach the suburban Buda Hills and the *Vadaspark* (Game Park), where boars and deer roam free. (Take bus #56 up Szilagyi Erzsébet fasor from Moszkva tér.) The **cog railway,** in front of the round Hotel Budapest, will take you to the top of Szabadság-hegy, where you can catch the **Pioneer Railway,** run (for now) entirely by Pioneers, the socialist equivalent of the Boy Scouts. Ask where to get off for the János-hegy **chairlift** *(libegö),* which takes you back down the hill. (Runs 9am-5pm; mid-Sept.to mid-May 9:30am-4pm.) To complete the tour of the Castle District, ascend by cable car to the uppermost grounds of the **Royal Palace** and its museums. Built in the 13th century, the castle has endured sieges by Tatars, Turks, Nazis, and the Red Army. The Germans made their last stand here in 1944-45, leaving it and Castle Hill in ruins; the bullet holes in the façades recall the 1956 uprising. During post-war reconstruction, extensive excavations revealed artifacts from even the earliest palace; these can be seen in the **Budapest History Museum** in wing E of the palace. The **Hungarian National Gallery** (Wings B, C, and D) contains work of Hungarian artists from the 11th century to the present.

Further south in Buda, atop Gellért Hill, looms the **Liberation,** a.k.a. **Reoccupation Monument,** portraying in bronze a woman blessing the Soviets for "saving" Hungary from the Nazis. Hike up to the **Citadella** from beside Gellért Hotel at the base of the hill, or take bus #27 from Móricz Zs. körtér, two bus stops beyond the hotel. The views from the top are spectacular at night. (Try to get a hostel bed in the Hotel Citadella, located near the statue—see Accommodations).

Pest, commercial center of the capital across the river, throbs with activity. Its heart is the **Inner City,** an old section once surrounded by walls, now centered in the popular pedestrian zone of Váci u. and Vörösmarty tér. Near the pedestrian zone, step from Kossuth Lajos u. onto Petöfi Sandor u. and look up to your left at the twenty bronze torsos detachedly watching the bustle below. Pest's river bank sports a string of modern luxury hotels, leading up to the 19th-century neo-Gothic **Parliament** building at Kossuth tér (arrange tours at IBUSZ). Just north of Parliament, the Margit híd (bridge) crosses to the lovely island of **Margitsziget,** a municipal park, off-limits to private cars, with thermal baths and shaded terraces. (Take bus #26 from Szt. István krt.)

On Hösök tere (Heroes' Square), the **Szépmuveszeti muzeum** (Museum of Fine Arts), displays a fine collection of European drawings, one of the best collections of Spanish painting outside Spain, and works by Italian and Flemish masters. Across the square lies the **Mücsarnok** (Art Gallery), where temporary exhibits of Hungarian and international art are presented. Some of these excel; check with Tourinform or IBUSZ to see what's on. The **Millenium monument** on Hösök tere shows off 1000 years of Hungarian leaders and national heroes. The **Városliget** (City Park), behind the monument, contains a permanent circus, an amusement park, and the tremendous Széchenyi Baths and Vajdahunyad Castle, part of which is modeled after a Transylvanian original.

If you are at all interested in Hungarian history, the **National Museum,** Muzeum körút 14-16, is a must-see (invest in the 25Ft English guidebook). Set majestically in a huge chamber are the crown, scepter, and orb of the Hungarian kings (returned to Hungary from the U.S. in 1978).

The Budapest **Synagogue,** on the corner of Dohány and Wesselény streets, is the largest active synagogue in Europe. Notice around back all the gravestones planted in the forties. (Five minutes' walk from IBUSZ on Tanács körút.) The ethereal harmonies of organ and mixed choir float through the enormous chamber during Friday evening services from 6-7pm. Next-door, the **Jewish Museum** devotes one haunting room to photos and documents from the Holocaust. (Open April-Oct. Mon. and Thurs. 2-6pm, Tues. and Fri. 10am-1pm.)

Entertainment

Budapest is a city of concerts: the monthly *Program in Hungary,* available free at tourist offices, lists all performances. The new English-language **Budapest Weekly** (48Ft) also lists events. If you arrive in mid-June, you might catch one of the season finales. A performance in the gilded, Italian Renaissance **State Opera House** costs as little as 200Ft, and ushers sell latecomers tickets at scalper's prices.

(VI, Andrássy út 2; tel. 153 01 70. M: Opera. Ticket office open Tues.-Sun. 10am-7pm.)

The city's **Philharmonic Orchestra** is also world famous (tickets about 200Ft). Performances resound in Budapest almost every evening from September through June. During the summer season, there are still plenty of opportunities to see a concert, theater, or rock performance, especially in one of the many open-air arenas. Summer theaters include the **Hilton Hotel Courtyard** (opera); **Margitsziget Theater** (opera and Hungarian music concerts); **Zichy Mansion Courtyard,** III, Fö tér 1 (orchestral concerts); and the **Mátyás Cathedral** (organ and other recitals). Folk-dancers stomp across the stage at the **Buda Park Theater,** XI, Kosztolányi Dezsö tér. Brochures and concert tickets flood from the ticket office at Vörösmarty tér 1. (70-250Ft; tel. 117 62 22. Open Mon.-Fri. 11am-6pm. Little English spoken.) The central theater booking office is next to the Opera House at Andrássy út #18 (tel. 112 00 00; open Mon.-Fri. 10am-2pm and 2:30-7pm). You can also buy tickets at theater offices or discreetly from ushers. The **Budapest Spring Festival,** in late March, provides an excellent chance to see the best in Hungarian art and music. The autumn **Budapest Arts Weeks** is another major festival.

Hungary has an outstanding cinematic tradition; most notable among its directors are Miklós Jancsó *(The Round-Up, The Red and the White)* and István Szabó *(Mephisto, Colonel Redl).* Cinemas abound in Budapest, screening the latest Hungarian and foreign films. The English-language *Daily News* lists movies with an English soundtrack; also check the kiosks around town. If *szinkronizált* or *magyarul beszélö* appears next to the title, the movie has been dubbed. Tickets are a bargain (70Ft).

Nightlife

Budapest's citizens are rapidly catching up on 35 years of foregone revelry. **Vén Diak** (Old Student), V, Egyetem tér (tel. 119 46 03) gets hot around 2am. (M: Kálvin tér, then walk up Kecskeméti u..) Gyrate with abandon at the **Rock Café,** Dohány u. 20. (M: Astoria. Live music every night at 9:30 and 11:30pm. Entrance 100Ft. Open daily 6pm-4am.) **Fregatt** (on Molnár u., one street away from the Danube; M: Ferenciek tér) is full of anglophonic Magyars and magyarophilic Anglos in search of an English pub (open until midnight). All the universities maintain clubs, such as **KEK,** the club of Eötvös Loránt University, V, Károlyi Mihály u. 9 (tel. 117 49 67; M: Ferenciek tér; July and Aug. open only Tues. 6-10pm and Thurs. 7pm-midnight.) **Fiatal Müvész Klubja** (Young Artists' Club), Andrássy út 112, installs one band upstairs and another in the restaurant downstairs. (Open Tues.-Sun. 6pm-2am. Entrance 100Ft.) Punk music rocks the **Fekete Lynk** (Black Hole), several rooms in the basement of a factory. (Golgota u. 3. M: Népliget, then tram #23 one stop; cross Könyves Körút, walk down Vajda Péter út (away from the park) and take the first right, then the first left. (Open Wed.-Thurs. and Sun. 8pm-2am, Fri and Sat. 8pm-4am.) Nearer downtown in Mikszáth tér is **Tilos az Á** ("A" is forbidden). This cryptic Magyar name should strike a chord with hard-core Winnie the Pooh fans. (M: Kálvin tér; then exit to Baross u. and bear left off of Baross for one block. Open daily 8pm-4am.) Stomp with Transylvanians at **Táncház,** an itinerant folk-dancing club. They invariably have a beginners' circle and an instructor. Locate them in *Pesti Mušor* (Budapest's weekly entertainment guide, in Hungarian) or ask at Tourinform. The exclusive gay club **Local** at the intersection of Dob u. and Kartász u. just off Erzsébet körút (district VII) admits only people they like.

To soak away weeks of city grime, crowded trains and yammering camera-clickers, sink into a thermal bath, a constitutive part of the Budapest experience. The post-bath massages vary widely from a quick 3-minute slap to a royal half-hour indulgence. The **Király** baths, II, Fö u. 84 (tel. 115 30 00) date from the Turkish times. (Open Mon.-Sat. 6:30am-6pm; Mon., Wed., Fri. for men, Thurs. and Sat. for women.) The Gellért baths are conveniently located inside Gellért Hotel at the base of Gellért Hill, but the Gellért service can be Gellértly curt. (Women and men frolic in the buff in separate baths. Bath entrance 150Ft. 100Ft more for an alleged 10-minute massage. Open Mon.-Sat. 6am-7pm, Sun. 6am-4pm.)

Danube Bend (Dunakanyar)

North of Budapest, the Danube sweeps in a dramatic arc known as the Danube Bend as it flows down from Vienna along the Czechoslavakian border. Roman ruins from settlements of the first century dapple the countryside, and medieval palaces gaze upon the river in **Esztergom** and **Visegrád.** An artist colony thrives today amidst the museums and churches of **Szentendre.** Lying within thirty miles of Budapest, the region makes for winsome day trips from the capital.

If the region were a clock face, Budapest would sit at 5 o'clock, Esztergom at 10, Visegrád at 12, and Szentendre at 1. Hourly buses from Budapest's Árpád Híd metro station link the three towns with the capital. If you're going directly to Esztergom, take the bus that travels through Pilisszentlíels; the 1½-hr. ride is more than an hour shorter than the route winding along the river through Visegrád. The suburban railway (HÉV) to Szentendre (45 min., 35Ft) starts from Batthyány tér in Budapest, by the metro stop of the same name. The river boats from Budapest are a pleasurable, if painstaking, way to visit the region. Boats cast off from Budapest's Vigadó tér dock at 7am, 7:30am, 10am, and 2pm daily and steam upriver to Visegrád (3 hr., 90Ft) and Esztergom (5 hr., 95Ft), making short stops along the way. Not all boats stop at Szentendre (1 hr., 60Ft). **Dunatours,** V, Bajcsy-Zsilinszky út. 17 (tel. 131 45 33), in Budapest, will book private rooms in Szentendre. (Open Mon.-Fri. 8am-4pm; Sat. 9am-1pm.)

Twelve miles north of Budapest, **Szentendre** draws rampaging legions of tourists to its cobblestone streets lined with art galleries. In the 17th century the town was settled by Serbian merchants whose Orthodox heritage is still alive. From the HÉV and bus station, use the underpass and walk ten minutes up Kossuth Lajos u. to the center of the old town, Fö tér. Branching off at the top of the square to the right is Bogdányi u. The **IBUSZ** office, Bogdányi u. 11 (tel. (26) 103 15; open Mon.-Fri. 9am-5pm, in summer also Sat. 10am-6pm and Sun.10am-2pm) finds rooms (doubles 1000Ft) and rents bicycles (500Ft per day). **Dunatours,** Bogdányi u. 1 (tel. (26) 113 11), speaks rough-hewn English but can usually secure you a comparably priced room should IBUSZ fail. (Open June-Aug. Mon.-Fri. 8am-4pm, Sat. 9am-7pm, Sun. 10am-4pm.) Fans of *film noir* might prefer to spend the night at the *Márka Fugado* tourist-motel-*cum*-bowling-alley down by the train tracks. Out of the railroad station, take a left through the small shop area, then a left onto Vasúti villasor; pass about six streets on right, then take the first left onto Szabadkai u. and follow it across one set of train tracks. The sign is 30m along on your left; enter 30m further at the office and 2-lane bowling alley. (Five beds and a bath in each room; 250Ft per person.) Camping is available at **Pap-szigeti Camping** (tel. (26) 106 97; open May-Sept.), a half mile north of Fö tér.

On **Templomdomb** (Church Hill) above Fö tér is Szentendre's first stone church, built in the 13th century. (Open 10am-noon and 3-5pm, subject to astrological influences.) Across Alkotmány u. is the rival **Orthodox Cathedral** with an exquisite Serbian icon screen. The church is open only for Sunday services but the grounds house a museum of 18th-century religious art (open Wed.-Sun. 10am-4pm). The third big church on Fö tér is the 18th-century **Blagovestenska Church.** The most impressive of Szentendre's museums are the **Kovács Margit Múzeum,** at Vastagh György u. 1, which exhibits ceramic sculptures and tiles by the 20th-century Hungarian artist Margit Kovács (the works include *Pound Cake Madonna* and *Angels After Work)* and the **Czóbel Museum,** atop Church Hill, which exhibits the works of Hungary's foremost impressionist, Béla Czóbel. (Museums open Tues.-Sun. 10am-5:30pm. Admission 30-40Ft, some free to students.)

Eight miles upriver between the Pilis and Börsöny mountains, **Visegrád** was once the high-water mark of the Roman Empire. After suffering one too many Mongol invasions, King Béla IV built a stone **citadel** on the hilltop in 1259—hike up to

"Fellegvár" from the King Matthias statue near the wharf (40 min.). For nearly two centuries, Visegrád and Buda rotated as the capital of Hungary. Below the citadel, **Solomon's Tower** once formed part of a lower castle for regulating river traffic. The museum inside holds relics from the royal palace. (Open May-Sept. Tues.-Sun.) From the tower, cavort towards Esztergom on Fö u. several hundred meters to the terraced ruins of the fourteenth century **palace** of King Charles Robert. (Open Tues.-Sun. 9am-5pm, Nov.-March 8am-4pm. Admission 30Ft.) Rubble somewhat obscures the former grandeur of its two elegant marble fountains and its ornate carvings.

Few tourists sleep in Visegrád, which consists of only two major streets. The **tourist office,** Fö u. 3a (tel. (26) 283 30), is across the street from the wharf at the base of the hill below the citadel. (Open Mon.-Thurs. 8am-4pm, Fri. 8am-4pm, Sat.-Sun. 10am-4pm. Rooms in private homes are expensive at around 1000Ft per person). Get off at the bus at the first stop in town when coming from Szentendre. The second of the bus's three stops in town will put you just south of a new private campground along the river road (2 people plus tent 250Ft). Or else walk into town away from the river and take the first right after the green-tipped church for the Széchenyi u. campground and hostel. (2 people and tent, 240Ft; hostel bed 250Ft.) Show your ISIC at both sites for small discounts. Fö u. runs parallel to the Danube and the main road to the cathedral at the other end of town. Near the green-tipped church at about Fö u. 100, several houses rent private rooms. **Diofa Kisvendéglö,** Fö u. 46, serves excellent, home-style dishes. (Entrees 100-200Ft.)

Thirteen miles beyond Visegrád lies **Esztergom,** a former royal capital of Hungary where Hungary's first king, Saint István (Stephen), was born and crowned in 1000 AD. Strategically located at the western entrance of the Danube Bend, Esztergom has been invaded and occupied by everyone—most notably Mongols, Turks, and the Austrian Habsburgs. Today it is most famous as a stronghold of the Catholic church.

Esztergom Cathedral, the fattest church in Hungary, crowns **Várhegy** (Castle Hill) to the north. Franz Liszt composed and conducted the consecration mass for this colossal structure, which was begun in 1010 AD and completed in 1856. Enter and be engulfed. The **treasure room** contains the coronation cross upon which all the kings of Hungary (the last in 1916) took their oath (admission 15Ft). From the cupola you can look across the river into Czechoslovakia. The **Christian Museum,** at the foot of the hill, houses an exceptional collection of Hungarian and Italian religious artwork. Experience the country-town atmosphere of this one-time capital at the early-morning **market** on Zalka Máté.

IBUSZ, Mártirok u. 1 (tel. (33) 125 52) has doubles for 1400Ft. (Open Mon.-Fri. 8am-11:50am and 12:30-4pm, Sat. 8-11am.) From the bus station, walk up Zalka Máté u. (or the main street Kossuth Lajos, parallel to it one block to the west) to the center, where those streets and Mártírok útja meet in Széchenyi tér. Up the street at Mártirok u. 6, **Komtourist** (tel. (33) 120 82), has cheaper rooms than IBUSZ. Ask them about hostels. (Open Mon.-Fri. 9am-5pm, Sat. 9am-noon.) **Express** is nearby at Széchenyi tér 7. **Vadvirág Camping** (tel. (33) 122 34), one of the three in town, is 10 bus minutes outside the city (take the **Visegrád** bus which leaves 5 min. before the hour from the station and passes through the center of town). From IBUSZ, walk down Mártírok u. to the Danube and turn right. (Doubles 630Ft.) And for fish specialties, continue on Mártirok u. across the bridge and look left: **Halászcsárda** serves *Fogas molnárné* (pike-perch) under a straw roof. (Open daily noon-10pm.)

Eger

A thousand years of invasions and Bacchanalian revelry have made Eger one of the most beguiling towns in Hungary. Two hours by train northeast of Budapest, Eger deserves at least a daytrip, and serves as a launch pad for exploring the Baradla caves in Aggtelek and the Bükk and Mátra Mountains, the loftiest in the country.

Trains from Budapest-Keleti go directly to Eger, or make a tight six-minute connection in Füzesabony (about every 3 hr., 2 hr., 304Ft). Trains split in Hatran, so beware. From the train station take the #3 bus two stops or walk to the right on Deák Ferenc út, to the banana yellow cathedral on Eszterházy tér. (The bus station is one block to the northwest on the other side of the cathedral in Pyrker tér.) Turn right on Kossuth Lajos u., then take a quick left along Eszterházy tér to reach Széchenyi István u. **Express,** Széchenyi István u. 28 (tel. (36) 107 27 or 118 65) spurts information about summer youth hostels in university dorms (open Mon.-Fri. 8am-4pm). It is possible to go directly to the dormitories, whose rates range from about 200-400Ft. Consider **Sas Hotel,** Sas u. 92 (4-bed rooms 800Ft); **Mátyás Hotel,** Mátyás Király u. 140; **Katonai Kollégium,** Bem u. 3; **Kun B. Kollégium,** Leányka u. 6; **Berzeviczy Kollégium,** Leányka u. 2; **Középiskolai Kollégium,** Dobó tér 25; or **Mezögazdasági Kollégium,** Mátyás Király u. 132-134. Bajcsy-Zsilinsky u. starts right at the beginning of Széchenyi u. **Egertourist,** Bajcsy-Zsilinszky u. 9 (tel. (36) 117 24) finds private rooms (singles from 400Ft, doubles from 800Ft; open Mon.-Sat. 8am-6pm.) They also run **Egercamping** at Rákóczi u. 59-79 (tel. (36) 105 58), ¾ mi. out of town. Go directly there on city buses #5, 10, 11, or 12. In a courtyard behind Egertourist is IBUSZ, Bajcsy-tömb belsö (tel. (36) 114 51) where doubles fetch 800Ft. (Open Mon.-Fri. 8am-noon.) Follow Bajcsy-Zsilinszky two minutes further to Dobó István tér where **Cooptourist,** Dobó tér 3 (tel. (36) 119 98), has doubles from 600Ft. (Open Mon.-Fri. 9am-4:30pm, Sat. 9am-noon.) A new private campground, **Virág,** sits at the edge of town in the Valley of Beautiful Women (see below). The 20Ft, street-indexed map is less misleading than the free photocopied tourist map.

Eger's most venerable buildings date from the baroque and Turkish periods. At medieval **Eger Castle,** István Dobó and his fighters temporarily rebuffed the Turkish invasion. Hungarians still revere it as a symbol of national pride. The intelligent **István Dobó Museum** displays excavated doorways, weapons, and pottery. (Open Tues.-Sun. 9am-4pm. Admission 30Ft, students free.) The castle innards include subterranean barracks, catacombs, and a crypt. Reach the castle from Kossuth u. The other end of Kossuth u. leads to the yellow classical cathedral, the second-largest church in Hungary, on Eszterházy. (Open daily 9am-6pm. Free.) Skillful painters have made it nigh impossible to distinguish real marble from the painted illusions. Opposite the cathedral, the rococo, 18th-century college stages operettas and other performances (80Ft). Sixteen forints admits you to the frescoed **library** in room #48 (Open Tues.-Sun. 9:30am-12:30pm), the **Museum of Astronomy** on the 6th floor (open Tues.-Sun. 10am-1pm), and the periscope on the 9th floor. Have another Kodak moment of Eger from the **Turkish minaret,** the northernmost Turkish monument in Europe. Claustrophiliacs will relish the opportunity to pump up their quads climbing up the vertiginous 97-step spiral tower.

The potent **Egri Bikavér** (Bull's Blood) flows from Eger, the red-wine capital of Hungary. The **Szépasszonyvölgy** (Valley of Beautiful Women) in the southwestern part of the town shelters hundreds of wine cellars, of which **Ködmön,** is the most famous. (From Deák tér and Eszterházy út, go west away from the center on Telekessy István, which becomes Bacsó Béla u. and eventually Szépasszonyvölgy u. Keep walking straight for 20 min. until you reach the bottom of the hill; it's the first restaurant on your left.) Rowdy Hungarians here drink and sing along with gypsy violinists in the candlelight, and the inexpensive food is as fine as the atmosphere. (Entrees 100-200Ft. Bottle of Egri Bikavér 200Ft. Open daily noon-10pm, but kitchen closes around 8pm.) Back in town in the shadow of the cathedral, **Kazamata** restaurant is a mass of round tables in a concrete cave. (Stuffed meat pancakes 90Ft. Entrees 100-400Ft. Open daily 10am-11pm. Disco/bar 10pm-4am). Country women hawk produce and flowers in the cavernous **indoor market** near Centrum Áruház department store in the center. (Open Mon.-Fri. 10am-6pm, Sat. 6am-2pm, Sun. 6-10am.) Upstairs, fabulous barbeque ribs sell for a paltry 85Ft. (Open Mon.-Fri. 8am-7:30pm, Sat.-Sun. 8:30am-7:30pm).

Near Eger

Eger's charm derives partly from its proximity to the **Bükk Mountains,** a small, densely forested range with a national park and numerous hiking trails. Szilvásvárad, a small town 27km north of Eger in the beautiful Szalajka Valley, is an excellent base for mountain merriment. A bus makes the 1-hr. trip from Eger nearly every hour. Szilvásvárad's camping romps over Eger's. Try **Hegyi Camping** at Egri út (tel. (36) 552 07; open May-Sept.) Or reserve a hostel bed at Eger's Express office.

Beyond the Bükks, near the Czechoslovak border, is the village of **Aggtelek.** Beneath the venerable houses stretch the **Baradla Caves,** among the most spectacular in Europe. Tours start from Aggtelek and Jósvafo, about 6km east. With stalagmites reaching 25m and lakes 2km in length, the caves will knock your socks off. They're accessible by bus from the bus station in Pyrker tér (at 8:50am daily, returns at 3:15pm, 1½ hr; this bus actually originates in Budapest). The only place to stay, **Hotel Cseppkö,** (tel. (36) 117 24) is at the caves, 3km from the Jósvafo-Aggtelek train station, accessible via Miskolc. (Doubles 700Ft. Book ahead at Express in Eger.)

Györ

Though usually associated with heavy industries such as the Rába truck factory, Györ, with its well-preserved **Belváros** (Inner City) is not without charm: it is still possible to see a horse-drawn firewood cart slowing down rush-hour traffic. The city proudly plays up the fact that it is the third largest tourist town in Hungary, due no doubt to a fortuitous position on the Vienna-Budapest rail line, but boosted by a rich cultural atmosphere. Györ is two hours from Budapest's Keleti station (6 per day, 266Ft) and an easy day-trip from Sopron (6 per day, 1 hr.).

From the bus station, take the underpass to the train station (signs say Belváros) and emerge 40m to the right of the train station's main entrance. Straight ahead is Aradi Vértanúk u. and the city bus stop. Bus #8 stops at Ciklámen Camping, Kiskút-liget (tel. (96) 189 86; camping and bungalows open April 15-Oct. 15, motel open year-round). One block up Aradi Vértanúk u., at the intersection with Szent István út, is **Ciklámen Tourist,** Aradi u. 22 (tel. (96) 115 57 or (96) 167 01), where doubles go for 600Ft. (Open Mon.-Thurs. 8am-4pm, Fri. 8am-3pm, Sat. 8-11am.) Otherwise, a right from Aradi onto Szent István for two blocks will bring you to Szent István út 29-31, where **IBUSZ** rents singles from 360Ft and doubles from 500Ft in a germ-free environment. (Open Mon.-Fri. 8am-4pm, Sat. 8am-1pm.) Two blocks into the tourist area, take a right to Bajcsy-Zsilinszky út where **Express** offers service-*sans*-clue and no youth hostels (tel.(96) 288 33; open Mon.-Fri. 7:30am-noon and 12:40-3:30pm). There is a post office down the street at Bajcsy-Zsilinszky út 46.

About 10 minutes up Aradi vértanúk from the stations is **Köztársaság tér** (Republic Sq.) site of the strikingly orange **Carmelite Church** and the remains of a medieval castle. Further north the **Cathedral** which houses the **Reliquary** of the canonized **King Ladislas** is visible atop **Káptalandomb.** Follow Alkotmány u. away from the river to Széchenyi tér, the old town center, to drink *kávé* and people-watch. The marketplace on the river transmogrifies into a bazaar on Wednesday, Friday, and Saturday mornings. Györ frolics away its **summer festival** in late June and early July with theater, ballet, and concerts.

Vaskakas (Iron Rooster) Tavern, in the dungeon of the castle on Köztársaság tér, has music, a great location and a 24-hr. schedule (platters 100-500Ft). **Várkapu,** at Köztársaság tér 7, serves excellent paprika garnished lightly with food. (Open daily 11am-11pm.) The inexpensive **Korzo Cafeteria,** at Baross u. 13 in the center of a pedestrian zone, serves entrees from 25-90Ft. (Open Mon.-Fri. 7am-7pm, Sat.-Sun. 7am-5pm.) Share a table with local, indigenous natives at **Széchenyi tér** (open Tues.-Sat. 11am-9pm, Sun. 11am-3pm; soup, meat, and side dish 140Ft) or another *vendéglö,* **Kuckó** just up the street at #33.

Sopron

One of Hungary's most alluring medieval towns, Sopron rises from fecund farmland only a few rail hours from Budapest's Déli station (5 per day, 3 hr.) and Vienna's Südbahnhof (7-9 per day, 1½ hr.). The pillaging Turks bypassed Sopron, leaving its medieval buildings and Roman foundations intact. **Fö tér** is the old town, an oval oozing museums and aged houses and bounded by Várkerület. Enter under the tall green fire tower *(tüztorony)* which presides over the shingled roofs of the old town. (Sights open Tues.-Sun. 10am-6pm. Museums free with ISIC.) On the right, **Storno-Ház,** an ex-Renaissance palace, holds a marvelous collection of baroque thingamabobs. Across the street on the right is the **Bencés Templom** (Goat Church), built by a happy herder whose goats found gold. The **Mining Museum,** once the Esterházy City Palace, faces the church. Next door at 6 Fö tér, **Fabricius House** holds Roman sculpture in its Gothic cellar. Walk down Új u. to two rare 14th-century **synagogues** at #11 (under renovation in 1991) and #22, which evoke life in the Jewish community, expelled in 1526 (open Wed.-Mon.). Ten minutes outside of the old town at the intersection of Május 1 and Csatkai Endre is the **Liszt Ferenc Muzeum** (Franz Liszt Museum). During the **Sopron Festival Weeks** (June-July), the town hosts a profusion of opera, ballet, and concerts, some set in the nearby **Fertörákos Quarry** caverns. (10km, 1 bus per hr. from main bus terminal. Admission to quarry 10Ft for students. Concerts 300-400Ft. Tickets for all events from Liszt Ferenc Culture House on Széchenyi tér.)

From **Gysev pu.,** the terminus for all trains from Vienna, walk north on Mátyás Király út for ten minutes to reach Várkerület. (Or take bus #1, 2, or 12 for 3 stops. All local buses 4Ft. Buy tickets from newstands.) On the left side of the street is **Lokomotiv,** Várkerület 90 (tel. (99) 111 11) where you can get doubles for 450-800Ft or a whole apartment for 1000-1200Ft. (Open Mon.-Fri. 8am-4:30pm, Sat. 8am-1pm.) The **IBUSZ** office is at Várkerület 41. (Tel. (99) 124 55. Singles and doubles around 600Ft. Open Mon.-Fri. 8am-4pm, Sat. 8am-noon.) An accommodations resource with some character is **Ciklámen Tourist,** Ógabona tér 8 (tel. (99) 120 40). At the northern end of the Várkerület oval, jog left for 2 blocks to the major intersection with Lackner Kristóf. (In summer, singles 350-400Ft, doubles 700Ft. Open Mon.-Sat. 8am-8pm, Sun. 8am-1pm; in winter Mon.-Thurs. 7:30am-4pm, Fri. 7:30am-7:30pm, Sat. 8am-8pm, and Sun. 8am-1pm.) Lövér Campground (tel. (99) 117 15) on Köszegi u. at the south end of town, is often crammed. (Bungalows 670Ft for double, 970Ft for triple.) Take bus #12 from Várkerület, and ask the driver to let you off at the campground. (One bus per hour, 14Ft, last bus 9:50pm.) The bus station is a short hop north of Ciklámen Tourist on Lackner Kristóf. A **post office** is on Széchenyi tér, at the southern end of the old town. There is a **Non-Stop** grocery store on the corner of Móricz Zsigmond u. and Magyar u.

For authentic Hungarian cuisine in a candid atmosphere, try **Szélmalom** (Windmill Restaurant), set on a hilltop with a view (mushroom soup 22Ft, entrees 84-412Ft; live music after 8pm). From Várkerület, walk 10 minutes down Otvös u., which becomes Magyar u., turn left at Köfargo tér, before the gas station, then take a quick right to Fraknói út 4. (Open Tues.-Fri. 10am-10pm, Sat. 10am-2am, Sun. 10am-10pm.) In the old town, pork aficionados will not want to miss the wurst at **Cézár Pince,** Hátsókapu út 2, a wine cellar that specializes in homemade sausages with sweat-breaking horseradish. Walk to the end of Szent György u. and turn left; it's on the right. For tasty, inexpensive, down-Hungarian cooking, drop into the cafeteria **Onkiszolgáló Etterem** at the south end of the old town on Széchenyi tér (50-75Ft; open daily 7am-3pm). The **City Grill** on Várkerület, across from Hotel Pannonia, performs fast-food renditions of wurst and strudel. (Open Mon.-Fri. 8am-8pm, Sat. 7am-7pm, Sun. 9am-7pm.)

Near Sopron

Twenty-seven kilometers east of Sopron in the small town of **Fertöd** stands the magnificent rococo **Eszterházy Palace,** easily the finest in Hungary. Miklós Eszterházy, a.k.a. Miklós the Sumptuous, built the palace in 1766 to hold his multi-day orgiastic feasts. Court composer Franz Joseph Haydn wrote and conducted here; stellar concerts still resound within. (Open Tues.-Sun. 8am-4pm.) Buses leave hourly for Fertöd from stage 5 in the station on Lackner Kristóf in Sopron (45 min., 58Ft). Fertöd has dorm beds and a few doubles, but groups often fill them. (Book with Ciklámen Tourist in Sopron.)

Roadside shrines and thriving farm villages lie along the bus route from Sopron to **Köszeg** (take the Szombathely line; 6 per day, 1½ hr., 118Ft). Köszeg is also served by trains from Szombathely (about 15 per day; ½ hr.; 34Ft). The town saw its heyday in the Middle Ages, when its castle helped battle Turkish invaders. Today, Köszeg's central Jurisics tér retains its medieval cityscape; **St. James Church** is one of the country's most significant Gothic treasures. The bus from Sopron stops first at the train station and then closer to the center. Step off the bus to the corner and turn right on Kossuth Lajos u.; one block up is **Várkör** (Castle Ring), the ovoid main street. From the train station, cross the little bridge and bear right up Rákóczi u. about ¾ mile into the center. At Várkör 69 sits **Savaria Tourist** (tel. (94) 602 38) with doubles in private homes (or in the castle at Rajnis u. 6, in Jurisics tér) for 800Ft. At the corner of Városház u. is an **Express** office (tel. (94) 602 47) with hotel rooms (double with breakfast 1160Ft, 10% off with IYHF card), and 20m further, **IBUSZ,** Városhaz 3 (tel. (94) 603 76) has doubles from 750Ft. (All tourist offices open Mon.-Fri. roughly 8am-4pm, Sat. 8am-noon.) There is also a campground in town. **Irottkö Restaurant,** Köztársaság tér 4, is good, and the costlier **Kulacs Restaurant,** Várkör 14, 1½ blocks from Irottkö, is better yet.

If you need to stop in **Szombathely** (4 hours from Budapest by train), check out the **Bartók Concert Hall** and the ruins of the **Isis temple.** For accommodations, walk straight out of the train station several blocks and turn left on Bajcsy-Zsilinszky to **Savaria Tourist** on Mártirok tere. (Open Mon.-Fri. 8am-5pm, Sat. 8:30am-12:30pm.)

Lake Balaton

Shallow Balaton is the largest lake and one of the most coveted vacation spots in Central Europe. Settlements germinated here in the Iron Age, and the first villas appeared during the Roman Empire. When a railroad linked Lake Balaton to the surrounding population in the 1860's, it mushroomed into a favorite summer playground. Today, mobs of Germans, Austrians and Hungarians invade the region less for the muddy waters or the rocky shores than for the rich scenery and comparatively low price tag.

Long and narrow, Lake Balaton is easily accessible from Budapest through Balatonfüred on the northern shore or Siófok on the southern shore. These two centers sate vacationers with discos and bars, but leave little for rainy days. Quiet Tihany, 11km west of Balatonfüred, offers hiking trails and an empty beach. Buses run from Balatonfüred to Tihany (6am-10pm 1 per hr.), while ferries link the three towns approximately once per hour from mid-April to mid-Oct. (from Siófok to Balatonfüred 1 hr., to Tihany 1½ hr., 66Ft). A bundle of tourist agencies book private rooms at the bus and train stations, and there are numerous signs for rooms for rent on the street.

Balatonfüred

Established as an elegant resort in 1772, Balatonfüred has since updated its leafy, lakefront promenade with a string of discos and casinos. Invalids from around the world crowd into its curative spring waters. From the train tracks, go downstairs to reach the combination **train** and **bus station. MÁVtours,** in the station, proposes doubles from 800Ft. (Open daily 8am-5pm.) Also in the station, **Volán Tours** (tel. (86) 427 00) claims to have singles for 500Ft and doubles for 1000Ft. **IBUSZ** is 10 minutes away at Petöfi Sándor u. 4/a. (Leave the station parking lot and turn left on Horváth Mihály, then right on Jókai Mór, which intersects with Petöfi Sándor u.; IBUSZ is one block to the right. Doubles 800-1000Ft. Open June daily 8am-6pm, July-Aug. daily 8am-10pm, Sept.-May 8am-6pm.) **Balatontourist,** Blaha Lujza u. 5 (tel. (86) 428 23), is 2 blocks east of Jókai and five minutes uphill from the ferry terminal. (Singles 350-400Ft. Doubles 800-1500Ft. Open Mon.-Sat. 8:30am-6:30pm, Sun. 8:30am-12:30pm; Sept.-May Mon.-Fri. 8:30am-4pm.) They also rent scooters (300Ft per hr., 2000Ft per day). Buses headed on to Tihany stop at the humongous lakefront **FICC Rally Camping,** 3km from the train station. (Open mid-April to mid-Oct.)

More a park than a beach, the lakeside is packed with children reveling on swings and seesaws, aboard pedal boats (150Ft per hr.), or in the chilly, 3-ft. deep water. The beach (40Ft) and a string of fast-food stalls are open daily from 7am to 7pm during the summer. In town at Jókai 22 at the intersection of Petöfi Sándor u., **Füred Bisztro** (tel. (86) 802 50) resounds with live music 6pm-midnight. (No cover. Meals 100-300Ft. Open daily 9am-midnight.) Observe nascent capitalism at the open-air market in the parking lot between Huray u. and Petöfi Sándor, where budding entrepeneurs wheel and deal in produce, clothing, bearskin rugs, and cheesy souvenirs. (Open daily in summer 8am-6pm, several bistros open 7am-9pm.)

Tihany

Perched on a peninsular hilltop, Tihany is the most luscious spot on Balaton Lake. The discos of the lowlands give way to the town's venerable baroque church, and further up to the hiking trails which lace the rolling hills. The price of peace is predictably high, and Tihany's isolation means fewer hedonistic diversions.

Distinguish between the two ferry landings, Tihany and (to the southwest) Tihanyi-rév. The village is at the top of the hill, marked by the twin-towered church. Take the bus (local ones leave frequently from both ferry wharves, or stay on the bus from Balatonfüred) up to town, or hike up the winding paths toward the church. Lording it over the peninsula and visible from Balatonfüred, the magnificent 1754 **Abbey Church** has baroque altars, pulpit, and organ. (Open Tues.-Sun. 10am-5:30pm. Admission 20Ft.) Buried in the crypt at the front of the church is Andrew I, one of Hungary's first kings. His grant establishing the first church on the site in 1055 is one of the oldest extant texts in Hungarian. Ask about the occasional organ concerts during the summer. Next door, an 18th-century monastery has been reincarnated as the **Tihany Museum** (open Tues.-Sun. 10am-6pm; admission 30Ft), whose eclecticism encompasses psychedelic dreamscapes, colorized etchings, and Roman inscriptions displayed in a cool, subterranean lapidarium. Far more unique and a bit removed from the madding crowd is the bizarre garage-gallery of "painter artist, writer, professor" Gergely Koós-Hutás, at Füdötelep 43, a five-minute climb from the Tihany wharf. Works include massive canvases of a didactic Lenin as well as several of the artist himself in front of famous edifices around the world, such as Grauman's Chinese Restaurant in Hollywood. Signed photos of the artist are a steal at 20Ft.

Balatontourist, the **post office,** and the church all huddle next to the bus stop. Balatontourist, Kossuth u. 20 (tel. (86) 485 19) arranges private rooms in the village. (Doubles 900Ft. Open in summer Mon.-Sat. 9am-6:30pm, Sun. 9am-1pm.) Set up your own accommodations at the numerous houses posting *zimmer* signs. A room close to the lake (4000-5000Ft) is not worth it, since the village is but a hop, skip and a jump away from through the path in the woods. A campsite is near the Tihanyi-rév wharf and beach. The promenade behind the church also leads to the beach (follow the "strand" signs). **Sport Rest** restaurant on the beach comes complete with violinists, but the atmosphere transcends the food. (Open daily 9am-9pm.) For an indoor panorama, choose **Echo Rest,** the round building at the end of the promenade. (Open daily 10am-10pm.) Next to the abbey, **Rege Presso** (Panorama Teraze) has a more restricted view, but the best pastries on the peninsula. (35Ft. Open daily 9am-8pm.) The beach is open daily 7am-7pm (40Ft), though the sidegate remains unlocked after hours.

Siófok

Located on Lake Balaton's less scenic southern shore as well as the Budapest-Zagreb rail line, Siófok is better suited than Balatonfüred to those seeking a Hungarian facsimile of Florida Spring Break. Turn left from the rail and bus stations onto Fö u.; **IBUSZ,** Fö u. 174 (tel. (84) 110 66), has doubles for around 900Ft. Fö u. runs into Szabadság tér where **Siótour,** Szabadság tér 6 (tel. (84) 108 00) offers doubles from 800Ft. Finagle a room near the beach, since some others are ½ hr. away. Bus #2 runs 4km from the Siófok station to **Strand Camping,** Fürdötelep (tel. (84) 118 04), which has a most happy beachfront location. Five other huge campgrounds share in lodging the masses.

Fare from the food stalls, clustered at the ferry landing, is cheap and tasty. On Wednesdays at 9pm during the summer, **folk dancing** fills the large open-air theater in Dimitrov Park. You need to stay in Siófok to attend, since ferries will retire earlier than you.

Pécs

Spiced with minarets by the Ottoman occupation, graced by historic monuments dating from Roman times, and home to over a dozen museums and galleries, Pécs (rhymes with *h)* is the cultural capital of Hungary. Located three hours south of Budapest in warm and sunny southern Transdanubia, a visit to Pécs is *de rigeur* for anyone who wants to get to know Hungarian culture. Several trains per day chug Pécswards from Budapest's Déli station (444Ft). Direct train service between Pécs and Yugoslavia has ceased; instead change at Nagykanisza, or take the bus. The bus and train stations are about half a mile apart at the bottom of the town's historic district. Bus #34 connects both with Széchenyi tér, the town's tourist center.

The cultural syncretism around Pécs is worth your attention, on both the synchronic and diachronic planes. The town's name cryptically derives from the Slavic word for "five," explained by its German name Fünfkirchen (Five Churches). Magyar and Gypsy elements are present as well, and the local cuisine models in miniature the multi-ethnic contact which takes place at the region's international folk festival each autumn. Remnants of the Turkish period in Pécs linger in the city's erstwhile **mosques,** long reconverted to Christianity, while an impressive **synagogue** recalls a once-thriving Jewish community. The inspiring, four-towered **Cathedral,** whose earliest parts date back to the 4th century, was restored in Romanesque style from 1881-92. Cycles of neglect and regeneration, traced in the building's different styles, mirror the city's schizophrenic history. Museums include an **Archaeological Museum** with Roman ruins, as well as the **Zsolnay Porcelain Museum.** Not to be missed is the **Csontváry Museum,** which houses the works of Tivadar Csontváry Koszka (1853-1919), Hungary's two-eared answer to Van Gogh.

Rent a private room at the MÁV travel office in the railway station, or take any bus that goes to Széchenyi tér (including #30 and #34) and head into one of the many tourist offices on or just below the square. **IBUSZ,** Széchenyi tér 8 (tel. (72) 121 76) has single rooms for 400-500Ft and doubles for 500-700Ft. (Open Mon.-Thurs. 8am-5pm, Fri. 8am-2pm, Sat. 8am-noon.) **Mecsek Tourist,** just uphill from IBUSZ at #9 (tel. (72) 133 00) speaks more English, has singles for 360Ft and doubles for 600Ft, and runs three campgrounds in the area. For hostel beds, catch bus #30 from the train station; at the turnaround at the last stop, look for the sign for Hotel Nyár pointing to one of the nearby university dormitories at Jakabhegyi út 6. (Summer only.) The **Express** office, Bajcsy-Zsilinszky u. 6, on the other side of the indoor market from the bus station, also runs a hostel on Universitas u. (office open Mon.-Thurs. 8am-4pm, Fri. 8:15am-2pm). Early in the day, or outside of peak season, take bus #34 directly to the **campground** in the hills above the city, where tent sites (400Ft per 2 persons), 3-bed bungalows (1000Ft), and singles and doubles (1000Ft and 1350Ft) in a one-star hotel are located at the entrance to hiking trails into the Mecsek Hills. Call the campsite for same-day reservations, (tel. (72) 159 81); in advance, call Mecsek Tourist (see above).

Near Pécs

From Pécs, consider a daytrip to the incredible sculpture park in **Nagyharsány,** hard by the Yugoslav border 37km to the south. Located in and around a former quarry, the park contains pieces by artists from around the world. Facing the quarry, follow the path on the right for a climb to even better views of the town and the fruited plains below. First take a train to Villány (several per day, round-trip 128Ft); from the station, turn left and follow the main road (towards Siklós) about 4km. There is a map across from the ABC supermarket 1km along, or just ask for the *szaborpark.*

Szeged

Arriving in Szeged, you may feel you've stumbled on the hippest town in Hungary outside of Budapest. Szeged's easy-going charm belies the fact that it is Hungary's only planned city and the economic and cultural dynamo of the great southeastern plain. The savory scent of sweet paprika and spicy fish soup *(halászlé),* for which Szeged is famous, perfumes the city.

In 1879, the river **Tisza** burst its banks, destroying almost everything in town. Survivors of the flood constructed the neo-Romanesque **Votive Church** in Dóm tér, whose dome and twin towers dominate the city's skyline. One of the largest churches in Hungary, its organ has over 10,000 pipes. (Open daily 8am-6pm.) Behind the Votive Church is the less imposing **Serbian Church,** with its precious Orthodox icons. Kissing the church is the 12th-century **Demetrius Tower,** Szeged's oldest monument. Note the sculptures of great Hungarian heroes in front of the cathedral. In the center of town is **Széchenyi tér,** where the yellow **Town Hall,** was restored after the deluge to its present eclectic form. Walk along the Vörösmarty u. side of the square to see the lavish, art nouveau **gyógyszertár** (pharmacy) building. Just southwest of Széchenyi tér, in Aradi Vértanúk tere, stands **Hösök Kapuja** (Heroes' Gate), guarded by stone likenesses of the fascist soldiers it was originally meant to honor. From July 20 to August 20 every year, the country's largest open-air theater, the **Szeged Weeks** in Dóm tér, tickles tens of thousands of visitors with operas, ballets, and folklore performances (Fri.-Sun. at 8pm).

With your back to the train station, follow the tracks outside the front entrance (going right) for 15 minutes, or take tram #1 to Széchenyi tér. One block back, on the other side of Híd u., is Klauzál tér, the pedestrian center where **tourist agencies** live. **Szeged Tourist,** Klauzál tér 7 (tel. (62) 218 00), arranges private rooms, and has an English-speaking staff. (Singles 300Ft. Doubles 600Ft. Open Mon.-Fri. 9am-5:30pm, Sat. 8am-noon; in July- Aug. daily 8am-7pm.) The street map (31Ft here, 38Ft at IBUSZ) is worth the investment. Across the street, **IBUSZ,** Klauzál tér 2 (tel. (62) 265 33) sells train tickets and finds rooms but speaks weaker English (and has longer lines) than Szeged Tourist. (Doubles 600-800Ft. Open Mon.-Fri. 8am-4pm, Sat. 8am-1pm.) At Kígyó u. 3 (1 block from the northwest corner of Klauzál tér), **Express** does hostels in July and August. (About 360Ft per person. Open Mon.-Fri. 8am-4pm.)

Two cafeteria-style establishments have low-priced food: **Festival** (open daily 10am-10pm), on Oskola u. across the street from the Votive Church, is a little snazzier than **Boszorkány Gyors Büfé** (The Witch's Snack Express), just off Széchenyi tér at Híd u. 8. For an upscale evening, try **Alabárdás,** Iskola u. 11, two blocks from Klauzal tér at the other end of Oroszlán. (120-590Ft. Open Mon.-Fri. 6pm-midnight, Sat. 6pm-2am.) Terraces overlook Széchenyi tér from **Szeged Restaurant** (95-300Ft; open Mon.-Fri. 9am-midnight, Sat. 9am-2am, food from 11:30am.)

A brutal day trip from Budapest, Szeged is worth a stop for those spending a longer stretch in Hungary. When going to Budapest-Nyugati from Szeged, make sure to board the right car since the train splits midway (6 expresses per day, 2½ hr., 380Ft). Buses serve Belgrade and other cities in Yugoslavia, and Romania-bound trains pass through Békéscsaba, which has regular connections with Szeged.

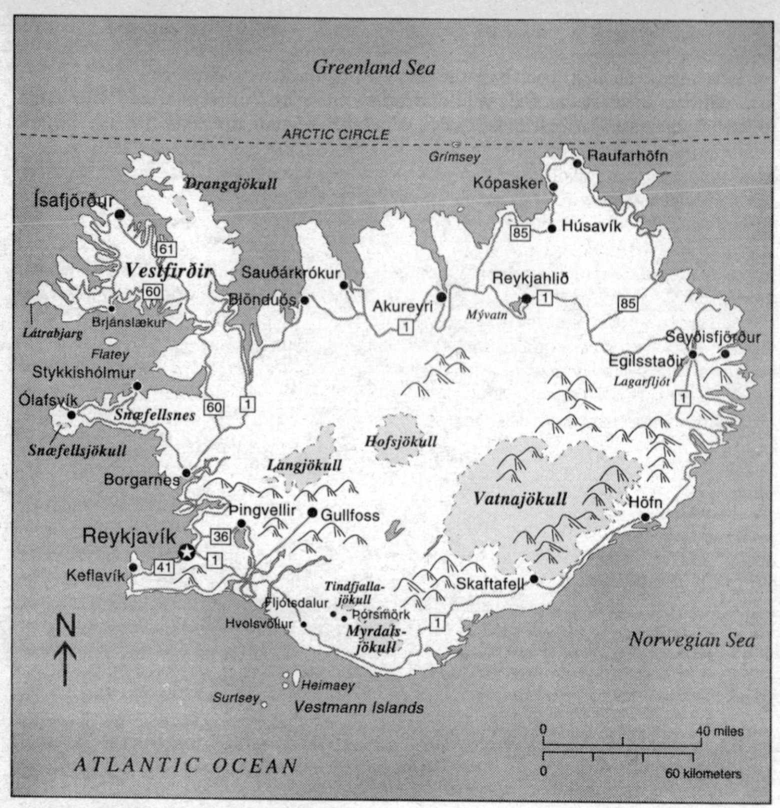

ICELAND

USD$1 = 65.6 krónur (kr, or ISK)	**10kr = USD$0.15**
CAD$1 = 57.4kr	**10kr = CAD$0.17**
GBP£1 = 110kr	**10kr = GBP£0.09**
AUD$1 = 51.0kr	**10kr = AUD$0.20**
NZD$1 = 37.4kr	**10kr = NZD$0.27**
Country Code: 354	**International Dialing Prefix: 90**

Land at Iceland's Keflavík Airport and you'll think you're on another planet, or at least on the moon. As the airport bus brings you towards Reykjavík past inland mountains and plumes of geothermal steam, you may begin to notice that the country is more than the level fields of brown, crumbled lava that surround the terminal. Further afield rages a topographical riot of lava and moss, birch shrubs and glacier-tipped valleys, torrential rivers and spawning salmon, harsh winds and sheltered coves, green hillsides and spitting volcanoes. Iceland (Ísland) isn't the word for it, since the Gulf Stream keeps winters warmer than New York's.

In fact, Iceland pushes social frontiers even more than geological and geographic ones. First off, Icelanders are liberal about ignoring European convention: 55% of children are born out of wedlock, people don't frown on using friendships to get lower prices and better service, and everyone loves their president, who, incidentally, is a woman. At the same time, Icelanders are fervent homogenizers and traditionalists. Women keep their maiden names, a language committee systematically banishes foreign words, most roads are still unpaved, city teenagers still do farm work during summer vacation, milk and meat imports are banned, and one of the greatest delicacies is singed sheep's head *(svið;* the tongue is the best part). Despite near-Japanese prices and rampant consumerism (cellular phones are everywhere, and the per capita consumption of Coke is surpassed only by Mexico's), Icelanders have figured out how to live with nature. 80% of all households are geothermally heated, hydroelectric power makes fossil fuels redundant, the sea supplies Iceland with 70% of its exports, and trash is nowhere in sight.

In fact, the fierce, independent, exiled Norwegian noblemen who settled here with their Irish slaves in the 9th century started Iceland's tradition of internal democracy when the country's first parliament (the *Alþingi)* met at Þingvellir in 930 AD. Today, it's worth a case of chronic sticker shock to join Iceland's 250,000 residents, who still consider themselves privileged to live half-apart from the rest of Europe—even though they must work the longest week in the world (54-56 hours) to maintain this paradoxical modern life on an island in the middle of the North Atlantic.

Getting There

From North America, flying is the only option. **Icelandair** (tel. (800) 223-5500) flies from New York all year (Thurs.-Tues. in summer), from Orlando (early Sept.-late May 1-2 per week), and from Baltimore (April-late Oct. 3-4 per week). These planes connect each morning with flights to Icelandair's European destinations; Luxembourg is the most popular (New York-Luxembourg round-trip APEX fare $778; 3-day-advance-reserve youth fare $306 one-way). The only non-Icelandair flights to Iceland are on **SAS** from Copenhagen (3 per week).

The only opportunity to feel the sea wind as you travel to Iceland's rugged shores is on the ferry *Norröna,* which circles the North Atlantic via Seyðisfjörður (East Iceland), Tórshavn (Faroe Islands), Lerwick (Shetland Islands), Bergen (Norway), and Hanstholm (Denmark); see the East Iceland section for more information.

Getting Around

Icelanders make it very easy to travel in their country. One and only one operator runs every bus and ferry route, and most air routes. There are no trains. Free schedules are available in hostels and tourist offices wherever you go. For buses, pick up the essential and entirely comprehensive **(Leiðabók)** (timetable), or the *Iceland 1992* brochure, which lists selected bus schedules as well as tours and ferry routes (available everywhere).

Though flying is by far more comfortable, **bus travel** is much cheaper. Land travel focuses on the 1411km **Highway #1,** completed in 1974, which circles the island. (Only partially paved, it often has just one lane.) Plan on at least a week in Iceland if you want to circle the country on the ring road; buses do it in four five- to nine-hour stages (Reykjavík to Akureyri to Egilsstaðir to Höfn and back to Reykjavík, and vice versa), with daily service on each leg from mid-June through August. Frequency drops dramatically off-season; snow and tourist shortages curtail bus service entirely on the eastern half of the ring (Akureyri-Egilsstaðir-Höfn) from October to mid-May. You can buy tickets in the stations *(umferðarmiðstöð)* in Reykjavík and Akureyri, or from the driver. The national bus cooperative, **BSÍ,** based in the Reykjavík bus station, sells two passes that simplify bus travel greatly. The **Full Circle Passport** (10,500kr) allows you to circle the island at your own pace. The **Omnibus Passport** entitles you to a period of unlimited travel on all scheduled bus routes (1 week 12,300kr, 2 weeks 16,200kr, 3 weeks 20,900kr, 4 weeks 23,400kr). Both passes are sold from mid-May through September, and entitle users to 10% discounts on many ferries, camping grounds, farms, and *hótel edda* sleeping-bag accommodations. In the off-season, one-week Omnibus Passports are sold at a lower price, since fewer routes are available. With all bus passes and tickets, children 9-12 receive 50% off, those 4-8 get 75% off, and under 4's travel free.

The only quick way to travel in Iceland is by air; flights are on propeller planes with stellar views over glaciers, mountains and lava fields. **Flugleiðir** (Icelandair's domestic service) flies primarily between Reykjavík and major towns, **Flugfélag Norðurlands** between Akureyri and other towns, **Flugfélag Austurlands** between towns in the east, and several smaller airlines on miscellaneous other routes. Flugleiðir offers three great package deals. The **Air Rover** ticket (15,700kr) lets you fly the circuit Reykjavík-Ísafjörður-Akureyri-Egilsstaðir-Höfn-Reykjavík, in that order. The **Air/Bus Rover** (fly one way, bus the other) is also a deal. Another option is the **Iceland Airpass**—four flight coupons for USD190, but purchasable only outside Iceland. (Passes often have family discounts.) If you're between 12 and 20 or over 67, you can get **40% standby discounts** on all Flugleiðir flights (available one hour before takeoff); this makes flying cheaper than the bus. Flugfélag Norðurlands offers 25% student discounts on all flights. Iceland's bizarre weather can ground flights on short notice for several days; *do not* plan to fly back to Reykjavík the day before your plane leaves Iceland.

Seeing the country by **car** (preferably four-wheel-drive) allows you the most freedom. Car rental *(bílaleiga)* is everywhere, starting at about 3000kr per day and 30kr per km (always ask about special package deals). **Hitching** is possible on the busiest roads in the summer, if you are patient. The traffic is sparse and the weather unpredictable. Bring a tent and a map and be aware of recent road closings. **Cycling** is becoming increasingly popular, but ferocious winds, non-existent road shoulders, and thousands of aimless sheep conspire to make the going difficult.

The cheapest and most rewarding way to see Iceland is on foot. Well-marked trails are rare, but many areas of the country are suitable for walking. (See The Interior for more information.)

Practical Information

The tourist season in Iceland lasts from June through August. Most accommodations, transport, and tourist information offices hibernate until June 1. The summer *is* the best time to travel here. Though the sun technically dips beneath the horizon for a few hours each night, it never gets really dark, there's no snow, and it's warm enough to camp and hike. The Gulf Stream keeps temperatures moderate: the mercury rarely gets above 60°F (16°C) in summer, or below 20°F (-6°C) in winter. Bring watertight, lightweight clothing that can be layered. A rain jacket, woolen sweaters, and sturdy shoes are a must any time of the year.

Seek out the tourist information offices in large and important towns for mounds of schedules and brochures. Must-haves are the free brochures **Around Iceland,** with accommodations, restaurant, and museum listings for every town, and **Iceland A-Z,** which gives relevant practical information.

Iceland's hot water wells spawn an extensive outdoor bathing culture. Every town has comfortable pools with special hot pools on the side.

The Icelandic language has changed little from Old Norse, but fortunately most Icelanders speak English. Icelandic's two extra letters need not confuse: *Þ* (lower-case *þ)* is pronounced as in *th*orn, *Ð* (lower-case *ð)* as in *th*e.

On June 17, Independence Day festivals are held all over Iceland, the best of them in Reykjavík. Regular business hours are weekdays from 9am to 6pm (beware exceptions). Banking hours are weekdays from 9:15am to 4pm. Currency exchange commissions vary only slightly from bank to bank (except at the airport), and the exchange rates are set by the government. Post *(póstur)* offices are generally open on weekdays from 8:30am to 4:30pm, as are telephone *(sími)* offices (often in the same building). Post offices and hostels normally hold mail. Pay phones take 5, 10 and 50kr pieces; local calls cost 10kr. Iceland does not have USA Direct. For assisted international calls, dial 09. **Emergency numbers** vary across the country; they are listed in the inside front cover of the *símaskrá* (phone book), or you can call the operator 24 hrs. by dialing 03. Since Icelandic surnames are simply the father's name plus "son" or "dóttir," the phone book lists people by first name. Iceland does not observe daylight savings time, so it is even with London in winter but stays an hour behind in summer.

Accommodations and Camping

Iceland has 18 **IYHF youth hostels** (get the *Hostelling in Iceland* brochure at the tourist office for a complete listing) which charge 960kr (nonmembers 1200kr) and are generally clean, with kitchens and common rooms. **Sleeping-bag accommodations** *(svefnpokapláss),* widely available on farms, at summer hotels, and in guest houses *(gistiheimili),* are a viable and competitively-priced alternative (most often you get at least a mattress); consult the *Around Iceland* and *Icelandic Farm Holidays* brochures (the latter lists about 100 farms nationwide). Starting in late June, many schoolhouses become *hótel eddas,* which offer sleeping-bag accommodations. Most of these places also offer breakfast and made-up beds (both of which will blow your budget out of the water). Be warned: while staying in a tiny farm or hostel may be the highlight of your Icelandic trip, the nearest bus may be 20km away and run once a week. Check out the bus schedules *very* carefully and try not to hurry through your trip. Many remote lodgings offer to pick up car-less tourists at the nearest town, sometimes free, sometimes for a small fee.

In cities and nature reserves **camping** is permitted only at designated campsites. Outside of official sites, camping is free, but discouraged by the authorities; watch out for *Tjaldstæði bönnuð* (No Camping) signs and *always* ask in the nearest farm before you camp anywhere else. Use gas burners; Iceland has no firewood and it is illegal to burn the sparse vegetation. Always bring your waste with you to the nearest disposal. **Official campsites** (open in summer only) range from rocky fields with cold water taps to the sumptuous facilities in Reykjavík. Upper-crust sites run 350kr per person, more basic ones about 250kr. Rent camping gear suited to Iceland's climate from **Sportleigan,** at Vatnsmýrarvegur 9 (tel. (91) 130 72), across from the Reykjavík bus station (one week's sleeping bag rental 1800kr, 2-3 man tent rental 4800kr; summer hours Mon.-Fri. 9am-6pm, Sat. 10am-2pm). For smaller camping items, go to **Skátabúðin** in Reykjavík at Snorrabraut 60 (tel. (91) 120 45), between Egilsgata and Bergþórugata (open Mon.-Fri. 9am-6pm, Sat. 10am-2pm).

Food and Drink

Grocery stores are the basic hunting grounds for travelers in Iceland; most every town has a **Kaupfélag** (cooperative grocery store) and usually a fast-food kiosk. Gas stations, usually open until 10 or 11pm, sell snacks too. Grocery stores in many small towns are closed for an hour at lunch (noon-1pm). Larger towns commonly have supermarkets: the best deals are the comprehensive **Hagkaup** and the discount **Bónus** markets. Most larger towns also have restaurants which serve fish and meat courses. Remember that food is extremely expensive in Iceland; a *cheap* meal at a restaurant will cost you no less than 700kr. There's no tipping in Iceland.

Virtually unknown outside the North Atlantic, Icelandic cuisine celebrates animals you might normally have considered wonderful and exotic pets. Check supermarkets or ask around for traditional Icelandic foods such as *lundar* (puffins), *rjúpa* (ptarmigan), *selshreifar* (seal flippers), *hrútspungar* (rams' testicles), or the various dishes soured in *mysa* (whey). More normal options include *skyr,* a sort of nonfat yogurt thinned with milk or cream and eaten with fruit or sugar, and *mysingur* and *mysuostur,* respectively spreadable and sliceable lowfat whey cheeses. Outlandish Icelandic breads, available everywhere, include thick rye *flatbrauð* and deep brown *seytt rúgbrauð,* a swooningly aromatic rye steamed in a hot spring for 24 hours. Conservative eaters can stick to the excellent fish and lamb. Pick up *The Shopper's Guide to Icelandic Food* at the tourist office; it explains (and illustrates) everything.

Icelanders drink in spurts, mostly on weekends. Alcoholic beverages are sold only in state-run monopoly outlets (located in few places and open very few hours), and in pubs and restaurants. A beer in a pub costs more than 400kr. The drinking age is 20, but poorly enforced; driving under the influence is, however, severely punished.

Reykjavík

Home to only a hundred thousand people, Reykjavík's cosmopolitan frenzy belies its small size. Heavy traffic races along the main streets, noisy schoolboys run through the city hawking the daily papers, and expensive foreign goods shine in shop windows. Nevertheless, the snow-striped inland peaks, visible when not shrouded in persistent rain clouds, serve as a silent reminder that the world's northernmost capital still belongs to the wilderness.

Orientation and Practical Information

Lækjartorg, the main square in Reykjavík's old center, sits on the northern side of a stubby peninsula on Iceland's southwest coast. To the north and across the harbor and the fjord looms Mount Esja. Roughly south of Lækjartorg are the lake, the long-distance bus station, and finally Reykjavík Airport on the peninsula's south shore. The pedestrian street, Austurstræti, runs west from Lækjartorg, and across the street Bankastræti runs east and turns into Laugavegur after a block.

All international flights arrive at **Keflavík Airport,** 55km from Reykjavík. 45 min. after each arrival, a "Flybus" (tel. (91) 62 10 11; USD8 or 460kr) shuttles to 5 hotels in Reykjavík. The bus terminal and the domestic **Reykjavík Airport** are closest to Hótel Loftleiðir (the first stop), the Laufásvegur hostel and the Salvation Army Guest House are closes to Hótel Holt (the fourth stop), while the campsite and the Sundlaugarvegur hostel are closer to the Holiday Inn (the fifth stop). Outgoing Flybuses leave the Holiday Inn 2½ hours and Hótel Loftleiðir 2 hours before each departure from Keflavík. Many flights depart before city buses run, so leave plenty of time for walking to the Flybus stops, or book a cab in advance. From Hótel Loftleiðir's Reykjavík Excursions desk (open 24 hrs.), which runs the Flybus and many tours, you can pick up a free city map and a free copy of *What's on in Reykjavík.* After-hours currency exchange is cheapest at the hotel's **Landsbanki Íslands** branch (open Mon.-Fri. 8:15am-4pm and 5-7:15pm, Sat. 8:15am-7:15pm, Sun. 2-6pm; commissions substantially higher on weekends and holidays).

Tourist Office: Upplýsingamiðstöð Ferðamála á Íslandi, Bankastræti 2 (tel. 62 30 45), at the end of the small courtyard immediately to your right as you walk uphill from Lækjartorg. Free maps, tons of brochures, extensive information on tours, accommodations, cultural events, weather conditions, etc. Open Mon.-Fri. 8:30am-6pm, Sat. 8:30am-2pm, Sun. 10am-2pm; Sept.-May Mon.-Fri. 10am-4pm, Sat. 10am-2pm. Sunday hours on holidays.

Budget Travel: Ferðaskrifstofa Stúdenta, Hringbraut (tel. 61 56 56), next to the National Museum. Same building as the university bookshop. Discounts on international travel only; sells ISIC and InterRail. Open Mon.-Fri. 9am-5pm.

Embassies: U.S., Laufásvegur 21 (tel. 291 00). Open Mon.-Fri. 8am-12:30pm and 1:30-5pm. **Canadian consulate,** Suðurlandsbraut 10, 3rd floor (tel. 68 08 20). Open Mon.-Fri. 8am-4pm. **U.K.,** Laufásvegur 49 (tel. 158 83). Open Mon.-Fri. 9am-noon, phones answered until 5pm.

Currency Exchange: Banks open Mon.-Fri. 9:15am-4pm; there are many on Austurstræti and Laugavegur. After-hours exchange at the Hótel Loftleiðir bank (see above). Also at the tourist office (Mon.-Fri. 4:30-6pm, Sat. 9am-1pm).

American Express: Úrval-Útsýn Travel, Pósthússtræti 13, P.O. Box 9180 (tel. 269 00). Traveler's checks not cashed; no wired money accepted.

Post Office: Póstur, Pósthússtræti 5 (tel. 63 60 00), in the town center. Open Mon.-Fri. 8am-4:30pm. Branch at **BSÍ** bus station is open Mon.-Fri. 8:30am-6pm, Sat. 8:30am-2pm.

Telephones: Póstur og Sími Afgreiðsla, across from Kirkjustræti 8 in the city center. Open Mon.-Fri. 8:15am-7:30pm, Sat. 9am-7pm, Sun. 11am-7pm; Sept.-May. Mon.-Fri. 8:15am-7:30pm. **City Code:** 91.

Flights: Keflavík Airport, for international flights. (See above.) The Icelandair ticket office is at Lækjargata 2 (open Mon.-Fri. 9am-5pm; information tel. 69 03 00). Domestic **Reykjavík Airport,** just south of town, has two distinct halves. On the *western* side of the runways, **Flugleiðir** (tel. 69 02 00) services Iceland, Greenland, and the Faroe Islands. Take bus #5 from Lækjartorg or Sundlaugarvegur, or walk (15 min. along the short-cut dirt road near the bus station, at the junction of Hringbraut and Vatnsmýrarvegur). From the *east* side of the airport, next to Hótel Loftleiðir, **Arnarflug** (tel. 61 60 60) flies to several small towns in Iceland, including Vestmannaeyjar. Take bus #17 or walk (15 min. from the bus station).

Buses: Umferðarmiðstöð, Vatnsmýrarvegur 10 (tel. 223 00), near the Laufásvegur hostel and Reykjavík Airport. Terminal open daily 7am-midnight, tickets sold from 7:30am. Go to BSÍ Travel upstairs for bus passes and schedules (open June-Aug. Mon-Fri. 7:30am-7pm, Sat. 7am-2pm, Sun. 7am-1pm and 5-7pm).

Public Transportation: Strætisvagnar Reykjavíkur (SVR) runs yellow city buses (tel. 127 00). Fare 65kr, 6 tickets for 360kr. Ask the driver for a free transfer ticket *(skiptimiði)*, good for 45 min. Kiosks at four terminals sell sheaves of schedules and bunches of tickets; the two main ones are at Lækjartorg (in the building on the north side of the square) and at "Hlemmur" (in the building between Hverfisgata and Laugavegur at Rauðarárstígur). Buses run Mon.-Sat. 7am-midnight, Sun. and holidays 10am-midnight.

Taxis: BSR, Lækjargata 4b (tel. 117 20). 24-hr. service. About 500kr from Lækjartorg to Hótel Loftleiðir.

Bike Rental: Reiðhjólaverkstæðið Borgarhjól, Hverfisgata 50 (tel. 156 53). Three-speed, 100kr per hr. and 600kr per 24 hrs.; mountain bikes 120kr per hr. and 840kr per 24 hrs. Open Mon-Fri. 8am-6pm, Sat. 10am-2pm. Both hostels also rent out bikes from this shop (same prices).

Hitchhiking: Those hitching take buses #15a, 15b, 10, or 100 to the east edge of town; they stand on Vesturlandsvegur for the north, Suðurlandsvegur to go southeast. Be warned: you risk exposure if you are not picked up quickly.

Luggage Storage: At the Laufásvegur and Sundlaugarvegur hostels. 50kr per day, even for non-guests. Also at the BSÍ terminal (open Mon.-Fri. 7:30am-11:30pm, Sat. 7:30am-2:30pm; 100kr per day, 310kr per week).

Weather: Daily radio broadcasts in English on FM 92.4 and FM 93.5, June-Aug. 7:30am. Also available at the tourist office or by calling an English recording (tel. 69 36 90).

Laundromat: Ask your hostel about special arrangements with nearby cleaners. Otherwise, visit **Þvoið Sjálf,** Barónsstígur 3, below Hverfisgata (tel. 274 49). Wash 350kr, dry 250kr. Open Mon.-Fri. 8am-7pm, Sat. 10am-4pm, until 6pm on Sat. from June-Aug.

Medical Assistance: Borgarspítalinn (City Hospital), on Sléttuvegur. Take bus #6, 7, 8, or 9. Or call 69 66 00 (Mon.-Fri. 8am-5pm); at other times 212 30.

Emergencies: Police (tel. 111 66). **Fire** and **ambulance** (tel. 111 00).

Accommodations and Camping

The tourist office has complete listings of guesthouses that offer sleeping-bag accommodations.

Reykjavík Youth Hostel (IYHF), Sundlaugarvegur 34 (tel. 381 10). Stay on the Flybus to the Holiday Inn, or take bus #5 from Lækjargata to Sundlaugarvegur. Modernized. 115 beds in 2-8 bed rooms, with special rooms for handicapped. Large kitchen and common area. Shopping and swimming nearby. Reception open daily 8am-11am and 4pm-midnight. Lockout 11am-4pm. Curfew midnight. Sells bus and air tickets and stores baggage (50kr per day). 960kr, nonmembers 1200kr. No sleeping bags; sheets 240kr. Reservations (recommended mid-June to mid-Aug.) held until 7pm or later with advance notice.

Reykjavík Youth Hostel (IYHF), Laufásvegur 41 (tel. 249 50), between the BSÍ bus station and the center of town, a 5-10 min. walk from Hótel Holt. 60 beds, old and cozy. Same services, hours, and prices as Sundlaugarvegur. No handicapped facilities. Open June-Aug. **Please note: this hostel may close by 1992.**

Hjálpræðisherinn Gesta- og Sjómannaheimili (Salvation Army Guest and Seamens' Home), Kirkjustræti 2 (tel. 61 32 03), a pale yellow house in the city center on the same street as the House of Parliament. Well located and cheap, crowded with travelers and the hard-up.

2-5 beds per room. Sleeping-bag accommodations 900kr, sheets 200kr. Open daily 7am-1am, doorbell answered all night.

Camping: Tel. 68 69 44. Next to the youth hostel at Sundlaugarvegur 34; take bus #5. The only spot in town. Showers, laundry, and cooking facilities. 175kr per tent, 175kr per person. Open June-Aug.; reservations recommended July-Aug.

Food

Coffee shops, hot-dog stands and kiosks abound, usually open until 10 or 11pm but variable in price and quality. Many inexpensive restaurants cluster on Tryggvagata by the harbor. The cheapest supermarkets are **Bónus** (a discount deal with limited selection), **Hagkaup** (with a branch at Laugavegur 72) and **Miklugarður.** The Bónus nearest the Sundlaugarvegur hostel is off Skeifan (open Mon.-Fri. noon-6:30pm).

Múlakaffi Cafeteria, on Hallarmúli. Don't be discouraged by the tattered black-and-white sign or the Icelandic menu; walk straight in and enjoy a traditional Icelandic meal. Fish 640kr. Beef with vegetables 860kr. Open daily 11:30am-2pm and 5:30-9pm.

Thailandi, just by Laugavegur 11 on Smiðustígur. Step off the monochromatic streets of Reykjavík into a crowded, bright orange, green and blue Bangkok alley with parkometer and mirrors. 8 Thai dishes of varying hotness; large servings 440kr, rice included. Open daily 11:30am-10pm.

Á Næstu Grösum, Laugavegur 20b, entrance on Klapparstígur (the first door on your right coming from Laugavegur). Simple 2nd-floor macrobiotic restaurant done in light colors; the aroma of boiled lentils and wild rice meets your nostrils as you enter. Iceland's only vegetarian restaurant. Limited selection. Limitless refills 700kr; small portion without refills 350kr. Open Mon.-Fri. 11:30am-2pm and 6-8pm.

Svarta Pannan, Tryggvagata, at Pósthússtræti, near Lækjartorg, under the black-and-white sign. Americanized fast food. Light wood interior. Tasty fried fish 310kr. ½ chicken 695kr. Lamb with potatoes 970kr. Open daily 11am-11:30pm.

Sights and Entertainment

For a better idea of the layout of the city, hike up Skólavörðustígur to the audacious, organ-shaped **Hallgrímskirkja** (Hallgrímur's Church), visible from almost anywhere in town. The observation deck in the church steeple lets you appreciate how miniscule Reykjavík is compared to Mount Esja across the fjord (open Tues.-Sun. 10am-6pm; 100kr to ascend). For the destructive at heart and anyone curious about the brute forces that shaped Iceland, the **Volcano Show** at Hellusund 6a (almost a continuation of Skothúsvegur as you walk from the lake; tel. 299 75) offers over two hours of seismographic delight. Vilhjálmur Knudsen and his father Ósvaldur sniff out all volcanic activity on the island; they've filmed the eruptions at Mývatn continuously for 16 years. (Shows June-Aug. daily at 10am, 3pm, and 8pm; Sept.-May Tues., Thurs., and Sat. at 8pm. 750kr.)

The **Þjóðminjasafn Íslands** (National Museum of Iceland) at Hringbraut and Suðurgata beside the university, packs a millennium of history into a few well-arranged rooms on two floors—from the disintegrating iron swords of the 10th-century Norse settlers to models of 19th-century fishing boats. (Open mid-May to mid-Sept. Tues.-Sun. 11am-4pm; mid-Sept. to mid-May Tues., Thurs., Sat., and Sun. 11am-4pm. Free.) The bright, modern **Listasafn Íslands** (National Gallery of Iceland), by the lake at Fríkirkjuvegur 7 (entrance on Skálholtsstígur) shows Icelandic paintings and frequent international shows. (Open Jan. to mid-Dec. Tues.-Sun. noon-6pm. Free admission, 300kr for special exhibits.) The **Kjarvalsstaðir Art Gallery** on Flókagata (buses #1 and 17 run straight to the door) has changing exhibits amid arboreal surroundings. (Open daily 11am-6pm; 200-300kr, occasional student discounts.) **Árbæjarsafn,** a collection of old buildings from all over the country, traces the history of daily life in Iceland. (Take bus #10 or 100 to Rofabær and walk back to the end of the street and through the underpass. Open June-Aug. Tues.-Sun. 10am-6pm; 250kr, seniors and under 16 free.) **Light Nights,** by the lake at Tjarnargata 10e, is a multi-media show based on Icelandic history and sagas. (Performances mid-June to Aug. Thurs.-Sun. at 9pm. 1350kr, ages 4-11 700kr.) A bi-annual **Listahátíð** (Art Festival) will grace the museums, theaters, and streets of Reykjavík during the first half of June 1992. Icelandic and international artists of all kinds will crowd the streets, showing their abilities.

You haven't experienced Iceland without a plunge into one of Reykjavík's geothermally heated pools. The outdoor **Laugardalslaug,** on Sundlaugarvegur next to the campground, is the largest. (100kr, children 5-13 50kr, under 5 free. Open Mon.-Fri. 7am-8:30pm, Sat. 7:30am-5:30pm, Sun. 8am-5:30pm. Closed holidays.)

Weekends bring busy but expensive gaiety and drunken 15-year-olds to downtown Reykjavík's streets, and mixed older crowds to the pubs and nightclubs, Most pubs are on Laugavegur, Austurstræti and the vicinity thereof; consult *What's On in Reykjavík* for addresses and entertainment info. Pubs with cover charges usually have live music. **Glaumbær,** Tryggvagata 20, is a popular spot with beers (400kr) amid a mixed, cosmopolitan crowd (open Sun.-Thurs. 6pm-1am, Fri.-Sat. 6pm-3am). **22,** Laugavegur 22, is an artsy, black-white-and-mirrors hangout (gay club upstairs) where life begins around midnight.

Near Reykjavík

Warm lakes full of fish and bathers, birches growing in sheltered ravines, historical sites and steaming geysers are all within a few hours' travel across the lava fields that spread across southeastern Iceland. Most travel agents, tourist offices, and hostel wardens arrange one-day tours for the convenience of the wealthy traveler only (seldom less than 2000kr). Check the regular BSÍ bus schedule for cheaper "tours" (really scheduled buses) to the same places.

Þingvellir National Park, 50km east of Reykjavík, is both the junction of the European and American tectonic plates and the site of the world's first parliament. The *Alþingi* first met in 930 on the cliffs of the Almannagjá ravine, which runs north to south through the park. Crossing the ravine and then emptying into Þingvallavatn (Iceland's largest lake), the river Öxará separates the Lögberg (law rock) from the church on the site where the Icelanders traded paganism for Christianity in 1000 AD. Rowboat rentals (500kr for 30 min.) are available on the lake, which sinks 2mm per year into the Atlantic Fault. (Buses from Reykjavík to Þingvellir daily at 2pm, July-Aug. also at 10:30am; 400kr).

One of the more popular day trips from Reykjavík takes you to the twin attractions of **Gullfoss** (Golden Falls) and **Geysir** (the etymological parent of geysers worldwide). (Scheduled buses from Reykjavík daily in summer at 9am and 11:30am; 1900kr round-trip.) Geysir, which can shoot as high as 80m, is roped off and has been inactive for years, but is sometimes made to spout through the addition of large quantities of soap, which breaks the surface tension of the water. These eruptions are announced in the papers and tourist offices; there is always an attempt on Iceland's Labor Day (August 2 in 1992). A few steps away, the smaller **Strokkur** makes up for its size with the energetic frequency of its eruptions (every 5-10 min.). Across the road, **Hotel Geysir** (tel. (98) 689 15) offers sleeping-bag accommodations (1000kr) and camping (200kr per person, no charge per tent). (Open approx. April-Oct.; camping open mid-May to mid-Sept. Call ahead. Canteen sells basic staples.) 9km uproad lies torrential Gullfoss, golden-hued from the vast amounts of mud it carries downriver, and surrounded by a steady mist; bring raingear if you're planning to go close (bus leaves once more at 12:45pm and 3:30pm).

If you long to bathe in steaming water white with diatomite, surrounded by lava (and tourists) on all sides, visit the **Bláa Lónið** (Blue Lagoon), 40 min. east of Reykjavík. (Take the Grindavík bus from Reykjavík; daily at 1pm and 9pm, July-Aug. also 5pm; round-trip 760kr. Lagoon open daily 10am-10pm; shower and enter for 300kr.)

Snæfellsnes and the West Fjords

Clawing into the Greenland Sea like the gnarled hand of a fisherman, the Snæfellsnes peninsula and the West Fjords (Vestfirðir) together form Iceland's most isolated coastal region and the heart of its vital fishing industry. At the western tip of Snæfellsnes, the extinct glacier-capped volcano **Snæfellsjökull** opens the way to the inner world (or so claims Jules Verne in *Journey to the Center of the Earth.)* To the north, separated from Snæfellsnes by the island-strewn **Breiðafjörður,** lie the magnificent **West Fjords,** whose deep and narrow inlets mirror towering snow-veined mountain slopes.

Only 150km north of Reykjavík, Snæfellsnes is best reached by road. Daily bus departures from Reykjavík (Mon.-Fri. 9am, Sat. 1pm, Fri. and Sun. 7pm) serve the entire peninsula. To see Snæfellsjökull, connect to Ólafsvík (4 hr., 1700kr) or Hellisandur (4½ hr.); ask the Reykjavík tourist office about sleeping-bag accommodations and glacier tours. Otherwise, stay on the bus to Stykkishólmur (4 hr., 1550kr). Daily buses return to Reykjavík from Ólafsvík (Sun.-Fri. 5:30pm, Sat. 8am; Hellisandur ½ hr. earlier) and from Stykkishólmur (Sun.-Fri. 6pm, Sat. 8:30am).

Stykkishólmur is the principal port and major town of the peninsula. The main street, Aðalgata, is the continuation of the intercity road. As you arrive in town, you'll pass the **campsite** on your right, just before the gas station. **Hótel Egilshús** (tel. (93) 814 50), in the red and white wooden building at the end of Aðalgata at the harbor, offers sleeping-bag accommodations (25 beds, 1150kr; singles 1650kr). Uphill from Egilshús and overlooking the harbor lies the newly extended and renovated **IYHF hostel,** Höfðagata 1 (tel. (93) 810 95; 50 beds; 960kr, nonmembers 1200kr, sheets 240kr). Ask the Reykjavík tourist office or the boat office (tel. (93) 814 50) beside Egilshús about tours of Breiðafjörður on the speedboat *Eyjafirðir.*

The ferry *Baldur* from Stykkishólmur is the most convenient, scenic, and economical way to the West Fjords; it runs twice daily across Breiðafjörður to **Brjánslækur** in the southern West Fjords (mid-May to Aug. leaves Stykkishólmur daily at 10am and 4:30pm, returns from Brjánslækur at 1pm and 7:30pm; 1200kr, 10% discount with bus passes). On Mondays, Wednesdays, and Fridays (mid-June to Aug. only) buses run from Ísafjörður to Brjánslækur and back (1½ hr. each way, 850kr), meeting the *Baldur's* 1pm arrival and departure; Tuesdays, Thursdays, and Saturdays see similar service to the cliffs of **Látrabjarg,** Europe's westernmost point, where daring cragsmen gather thousands of bird eggs each June (3½ hr., 1080kr). The *Baldur* also stops mid-journey at the gorgeous island of **Flatey,** where you can gambol over coastal dales among shocked sheep and underneath thousands of sibilant seabirds. **Café Vogur** on Flatey stocks some food and has space for sleeping-baggers (tel. (93) 814 13; 800kr).

Walled in by the cliffs of Eyrarfjall and Ernir, **Ísafjörður** is the center of all things in the West Fjords, and in many peoples' humble opinion the most beautiful town in Iceland. From mid-June through August, direct buses connect it to Reykjavík (12 hr.; from Reykjavík Tues. 10am and Thurs. 8am; from Ísafjörður Wed. and Fri. at 8am and July-Aug. Sun. 10am). Flugleiðir has daily flights from Reykjavík to Ísafjörður while Árnarflug (tel. (94) 41 50), Flugfélagið Ernir (tel. (94) 42 00), and Flugfélagið Norðurlands (tel. (94) 30 00) provide regular service between Ísafjörður and other Icelandic cities. Still, the *Baldur* is the cheapest transportation option to the area. The only way to get from Ísafjörður to Akureyri is by plane (1 per day); by bus, you must backtrack to Reykjavík or Borgarnes.

The main part of Ísafjörður rests on a spit of land that curves out into Skutulsfjörður, forming a natural harbor. As you approach Ísafjörður from the bottom of the fjord, its **Summer Hostel** is on your left as you enter the main part of town, in the Menntaskólinn á Ísafirði, a two-story white building with red trim and roof (tel. (94) 38 76; sleeping-bag accommodations 750kr, beds 1200kr; open mid-June to Aug.). Beside it is a **campsite** (300kr per tent, 100kr per person; open mid-June to Aug.) There is one **guest house** in town (Austurstræti 7, tel. (94) 38 68); sleeping-bag accommodations 1100kr, singles 1500kr). The **tourist office** is at Aðalstræti

11, on your right past the hotel in the center of town and the post and telephone offices (tel. (94) 35 57; open Mon.-Fri. 8am-6pm, Sat. 10am-2pm, Sun. 9am-1:30pm). Follow the waterfront past the trawlers (look for a big sign on a red wall pointing the way) to the second-floor **Sjómannastofan,** a fishermen's cafeteria offering huge meals (fish 800kr, meat 1000kr). Further out towards the point of the town, the **Sjóminjasafn Ísfirðinga** (Maritime Museum) gives a sense of rough seamens' life. (Open June-Aug. Tues.-Sun. Free.) If Ísafjörður's harmonious beauty tires you, there are two ways to tour the Ísafjarðardjúp (the West Fjords' main inlet) and the fjords branching off it: the regular ferry *Fagranes* (tel. (94) 31 55; full-day tour 1000kr, reservations necessary) and the speedboat *Eyjalín* (2500kr; talk to the tourist office).

North Iceland (Norðurland)

Basking in the glow of the midnight sun and sheltered from the polar winds by snow-capped mountains lining the Eyjafjörður, **Akureyri** is the hub of the north. Iceland's second city and Reykjavík's alter-ego, temperate summers make Akureyri a welcome respite from Reykjavík's incessant clouds. It is also a launch pad for exploring the lunar landscape near **Lake Mývatn,** 100km to the east, and the village-strewn fjords along the north coast.

Daily buses connect Reykjavík and Akureyri all year, leaving Reykjavík at 8am and Akureyri at 9:30am (8 hr., 3200kr); summer brings extra evening buses in both directions (2-4 per week at 5pm). 8:15am buses depart Akureyri for Lake Mývatn (May-Sept. daily, 3 hr., 950kr) and Egilsstaðir (3-4 per week mid-May to mid-June and Sept., daily mid-June to Aug.; 6 hr., 2500kr). Flugleiðir flies five times daily to and from Reykjavík (50 min., 5550kr), while Flugfélag Norðurlands flies direct from Keflavík to Akureyri (5 per week) and from Akureyri to smaller Icelandic towns.

The helpful **tourist office** (tel. (96) 277 33) and the **bus station** (tel. (96) 244 42) share a building at Hafnarstræti 82 in the center of town. (Tourist office open June-Aug. Mon.-Fri. 7:30am-9:30pm, Sat.-Sun. 7:30-11:30am and 2:30-6:30pm; Sept. Mon.-Fri. 8:30am-5pm.) Pick up one of their **SVA** city bus schedules (65kr per ride). The **post office** is also on Hafnarstræti, farther north. (Open Mon.-Fri. 9am-4:30pm.) **Phones** are in the same building. (Open Mon.-Fri. 9am-6pm, Sat. 10am-3pm.)

Akureyri's two **IYHF hostels** are somewhat further from town than you need to be. The hostel on the second floor of Stórholt 1 (tel. (96) 236 57) is a 20-minute trudge from the bus station: go north on Drottningarbraut, the busy street along the shore; it changes its name to Glerárgata after the town center, and Stórholt is on the right. (900kr, nonmembers 1000kr. Sheets 100kr.) A second hostel is 3km north of town in Lónsá; if you call (tel. (96) 250 37), the owners will pick you up. (Same prices.) Clean guesthouses right in the center of town offer sleeping-bag accommodation for 1000kr (minimum 2 people); the tourist office has an exhaustive list. Try **Salka,** Skipagata 1, 3rd floor (tel. (96) 226 97) or **Ás,** Skipagata 4 (tel. (96) 261 10). The **campsite** is near downtown on Þórunnarstræti, beside the outdoor swimming pool (350kr per person). For plain but filling meals, head to **Bautinn,** at the corner of Kaupvangsstræti and Hafnarstræti across from the pedestrian district, which serves tasty meals with endless bread and salad (from 900kr including salad bar and soup; open daily 9am-11pm) or to **Súlnaberg cafeteria,** across the street, which does mediocre (but very full) traditional meals (fish from 700kr, meat from 900kr, sandwiches from 300kr). The cheapest food store is the **Hagkaup** supermarket at Norðurgata 42 (red, orange, and purple line buses go straight to the door).

Wander through Akureyri's **Lystigarður** (Botanical Garden), on Eyrarlandsvegur, to see how life persists in the far north: you too will have to hunker down to the ground to read the labels on the garden's fascinating collection of Arctic plants. (Open daily; free.) Not far away, the **Minjasafn Akureyrar** (Akureyri Museum), at Aðalstræti 58, gives insight into the town's history. (Open June-Aug. daily 11am-5pm. Admission 200kr.)

Iceland's ongoing geological tumult explodes into view in the region surrounding **Mývatn,** a shallow lake shaped by 2000 years of volcanic eruptions. Trails lead through strange lava formations known as "black castles" which fill a jagged area called **Dimmuborgir;** pyramids of ash rise nearby, and in the **Devil's Kitchen** the ground steams madly while sulfurous pits burp and spit blue sludge. When exploring this last area, take heed of the many warning signs and stick to the brown soil, or you may drop through the thin crust to the boiling sulfur pit below (destroying the surface and ruining your day).

Regular one-day bus tours of the Mývatn area leave the Akureyri bus station daily from mid-May to September at 8:15am (3400kr, 50% off with either bus pass). Buses stop at the small communities of Skútustaðir (on Mývatn's south shore) and Reykjahlíð (on the northeast side), which from June to August host camping (Reykjahlíð tel. (96) 441 03, Skútustaðir tel. (96) 442 79) and sleeping-bag accommodations (Reykjahlíð tel. (96) 442 20, Skútustaðir tel. (96) 442 79 or 442 12).

Akureyri makes a fine base for exploring northern Iceland's other attractions; ask about getting to the islands of **Hrísey,** in the fjord north of Akureyri, and **Grímsey,** Iceland's only territory north of the Arctic Circle (by bus and ferry from Akureyri), or to Europe's most powerful waterfall at **Dettifoss** and the cliffs of **Ásbyrgi** and **Hljóðaklettar** (by bus).

East Iceland (Austurland)

Iceland's eastern fjords are unjustly overlooked; small, quiet fishing villages and bristling fjordside peaks make the east well worth an unhurried stay. The main town in the east is land-locked **Egilsstaðir,** at the northern tip of the narrow lake **Lagarfljót.** The Kaupfélag Héraðsbúa supermarket and its parking lot make a good reference point; just uphill are the post office and bank, while the **tourist office** (open Mon.-Fri. 9am-5pm) and **campsite** (300kr per person) are at the far end of the parking lot. Looking lakewards from the Kaupfélag, you can easily spot white-walled, red-roofed **Egilsstaðir Farm,** a 10-15 min. walk away, which has sleeping-bag accommodations for 1110kr (tel. (97) 111 14; open all year). Egilsstaðir is the opposite node of the bus ring from Reykjavík, with service to Akureyri (see under North Country) and Höfn (5-6 hr.; leaves Höfn 9am, Egilsstaðir 4pm; mid-May to mid-June and Sept. 3-4 per week, mid-June to Aug. daily.) Planes arrive from Reykjavík (3-4 per day) and Akureyri (1 per day).

Twenty-six km from Egilsstaðir, **Seyðisfjörður's** curving, sheltered fjord harbors Iceland's only international car and passenger ferry, the *Norröna* (tel. (97) 211 11, in Reykjavík (91) 62 63 62; bookings in U.S. through Eurocruises, tel. (800) 688-3876). Service is to Tórshavn in the Faroe Islands (16 hr., about USD190, with 25% student discounts and another 25% off early and late in the season), continuing from there to Bergen (Norway), Hanstholm (Denmark), and Lerwick in the Shetland Islands. (Arrives Seyðisfjörður June-Aug. Thurs. 8am, departing at noon.) Seyðisfjörður's excellent **IYHF hostel** (tel. (97) 214 10) is in the pink house out on the north shore of the fjord. (28 beds. 960kr, nonmembers 1200kr, sheets 240kr. Open all year. Make reservations on nights before and after the ferry.) Buses connect Egilsstaðir and Seyðisfjörður over a fogbound pass that sometimes stays snowy all summer (Mon.-Fri. leaving Seyðisfjörður at 9:45am, Egilsstaðir at 11am, late June-late Aug. additionally Sat.-Sun. at 2:45pm and 4:15pm; extra service Wed.-Thurs.)

The eastern coast between Egilsstaðir and Höfn will make you glad you came east. Buses that stop at Reyðarfjörður take Highway #96, which meanders through small fjord villages before rejoining Highway #1 at Breiðdalsvík. From there, the route miraculously clings to steep, dark seaside cliffs with dramatic mountain landscapes at every turn. There are two isolated hostels along the way, at Berunes and Stafafell.

The Southern Coast (Suðurland)

Flatter and gentler than the east or the north, Iceland's southern coast would nevertheless be the star attraction of most countries. Sandy glacial outwash gives way to hilly sheep-filled pastures and steep green cliffs, beyond which waterfalls, lava fields, glaciers, and volcanoes provide exhilarating hiking.

The run-of-the-mill town of **Höfn** links the southern coast to the eastern fjords; it's the terminating point for buses from both Egilsstaðir (see above) and Reykjavík (June to mid-Sept. leaves Reykjavík daily 8:30am, Höfn 9am; mid-Sept. to May Sun., Tues., and Fri. leaves Reykjavík 8:30am, Höfn 10am; 9-10 hr., 3400kr), as well as the launching point for tours to **Vatnajökull** (Europe's largest glacier), which dwarfs the town and shimmers a robust gold at sunset. Reconstruction at the **campsite** (on your left as you come into town), which doubles as a **tourist office,** should be finished by 1992. Look on your right for cheap sleeping-bag accommodation in the local theater-cum-ballroom-and-cinema at Hafnarbraut 17 (tel. (97) 811 61; June to mid-Sept. Sun.-Thurs. only, 650kr). Further along the street is the **IYHF youth hostel,** Hafnarbraut 8 (tel. (97) 817 36; reception open 7:30-11:30am and 5-11:30pm; 960kr, nonmembers 1200kr, sheets 240kr; open mid-May to mid-Sept.; 27 beds). Intercity buses let people off wherever they want in town, but depart only from the **Hótel Höfn** at Víkurbraut 30, a short walk from either the campsite or the hostel.

The best way to appreciate the vast, rolling mass of Vatnajökull is to day-hike amid the dense shrubbery, tumbling rivers, and icy alpine vistas in **Skaftafell National Park,** on Highway #1 three hours west of Höfn (bus fare from Reykjavík 2440kr, from Höfn 960kr). An excellent **campsite** serves as a good hiking base (tel. (97) 816 27; 350kr, 100kr per shower); an information center with maps and a grocery store complete this handicapped-accessible facility. The farmhouse **Bolti** (tel. (97) 816 26) offers year-round sleeping-bag accommodations (from 1200kr) and kitchen facilities. Buses between Skaftafell and Höfn stop briefly at **Jökulsárlón,** a glacial lake with floating blue icebergs that makes a visit to Greenland redundant. (Boat rides available.)

The coastline between Skaftafell and Reykjavík is mostly owned by farmers who let their sheep graze freely on the grassy slopes. The Reykjavík-Höfn coastal bus stops at every little town; ask about hostels and sleeping-bag accommodations in **Vík** or in the farm country around **Selfoss,** center of Iceland's dairy industry.

The Interior

The interior of Iceland is Europe's most forbidding wilderness, a vast expanse of lava fields, volcanos, glaciers, and swift-flowing unbridged rivers. Traveling here is safest and easiest by bus. In summer, special buses (with huge tires) run over the glacier-bordered, black-sanded **Sprengisandur** in the heart of the island; to the luscious valleys of **Þórsmörk** (where much of *Njáls Saga* took place), west of Mýrdalsjökull; to summer skiing at **Kerlingarfjöll;** and to the warm rivers of **Landmannalaugar** north of Mýrdalsjökull. Some trips continue across the island to Akureyri, an interesting alternative to the Reykjavík-Akureyri coastal bus. Consult **BSÍ Travel** at the Reykjavík bus station (tel. (91) 223 00) for times, prices, and reservations.

Several companies offer guided hiking trips in the interior, of varying duration and difficulty. You might try **Útivist,** Grófin 1, 101 Reykjavík (tel. (91) 146 06), **Dick Phillips,** Whitehall House, Nenthead, Alston, Cumbria CA9 3PS England (tel. +44 (498) 814 40), or **Austurland Travel,** P.O. Box 9088, 109 Reykjavík (tel. (91) 67 85 45). Without professional guidance, prepare well. The **Ferðafélag Íslands** (Icelandic Touring Club), at Öldugata 3 in Reykjavík (tel. (91) 195 33), can give you more information. Never venture out without a four-season sleeping bag, a sturdy, wind resistant, waterproof tent, a compass, a detailed map, and more provisions than you think you'll need. **Landmælingar Íslands** (the Iceland Geodetic Survey) runs a map shop with the most complete and up-to-date selection, at Laugavegur 178 in Reykjavík (tel. (91) 68 09 99; open Mon.-Fri. 9am-6pm). Before departing Reykjavík, leave an itinerary with the **Landssamband Hjálparsveita Skáta** (Association of Icelandic Rescue Teams), at Snorrabraut 60 above the Skátabúðin camping store (tel. (91) 62 14 00: 24-hr. hotline (91) 68 60 68; open Mon.-Fri. 9am-5pm). Be certain to pick up a copy of the brochure *How To Travel in the Interior of Iceland* at any of the above locations. There are many huts in the interior (marked on good maps), and popular places like Þórsmörk and Landmannalaugar have campsites.

Vestmann Islands (Vestmannaeyjar)

Rising steeply from the ocean floor, this group of 15 islands is inhabited mostly by birds, and only barely by humans: the one town, also called Vestmannaeyjar, spreads over the island of **Heimaey.** In 1973, Heimaey threw open its vaults and sent molten lava from the volcano **Eldfell** flowing through the town streets. Luckily, Vestmannaeyjar's whole fishing fleet was in port and everyone was rescued, but the harbor was saved only as Icelandic civil engineers pumped billions of gallons of seawater onto the lava to harden it and prevent it from plugging the entrance channel. Vestmannaeyjar stands modernized and rebuilt today, surrounded by cooling lava and jagged green mountains which enclose the town and separate the harbor from the sea.

The airport sits below Eldfell's twin peak **Helgafell,** a short uphill walk from town. Five Flugleiðir flights per day arrive from Reykjavík (20 min., 7320kr roundtrip), but prepare for cancellations in bad weather. Sailing is slower but cheaper; connecting buses (1½ hr., 430kr) link Reykjavík to **Þorlákshöfn,** meeting the *M.S. Herjólfur,* which continues to Vestmannaeyjar. (4 hr., 1150kr, students and ages 6-12 460kr, under 6 free. From Þorlákshöfn Tues.-Thurs. 12:30pm, Fri. and Sun. 12:30pm and 9pm, Mon. and Sat. 2pm; June-July Thurs. 9pm. From Vestmannaeyjar Tues.-Thurs. 7:30am, Fri. and Sun. 7:30am and 5pm, Mon. and Sat. 10am, and June-July Thurs. 5pm.) For information in Reykjavík, call (91) 686 464; in Vestmannaeyjar (98) 117 92.

Vestmannaeyjar's **tourist office** is the reception desk at Hótel Gestgjafinn (on Heiðarvegur; open 24 hrs.). Signposts point from both the harbor and airport to the **IYHF hostel,** Faxastígur 38 (tel. (98) 129 15), a fairly new place which can house 40 people in 4 rooms and a dorm (960kr, nonmembers 1200kr, sheets 240kr; open June to mid-Sept.; no laundry facilities available). The hostel runs clearly-signposted **camping,** 1km along Dalvegur (175kr per person; open June-Aug.) **Eyjakaup,** the largest supermarket (open Mon.-Fri. 9am-6pm, Sat. 10am-2pm) is right next to the hostel.

Get face-to-face with Iceland's strange sea creatures at the country's only **aquarium,** on Heiðarvegur (open 11am-5pm; admission 200kr). From the harbor, guided boat tours show you the rest of the islands in the archipelago daily at 11am and 4pm (Páll Helgason Travel Service, tel. (98) 115 15; 1½ hr., 1300kr). Better yet, follow the dirt tracks which lead safely through the still-warm gray-brown lava desert around Eldfell, and save on cooking expenses by letting nature boil an egg or potato for you. (Dig into a steamy patch and bury your food; the deeper you go, the quicker it's done. Eggs take approximately 1-1½ hr. to boil.)

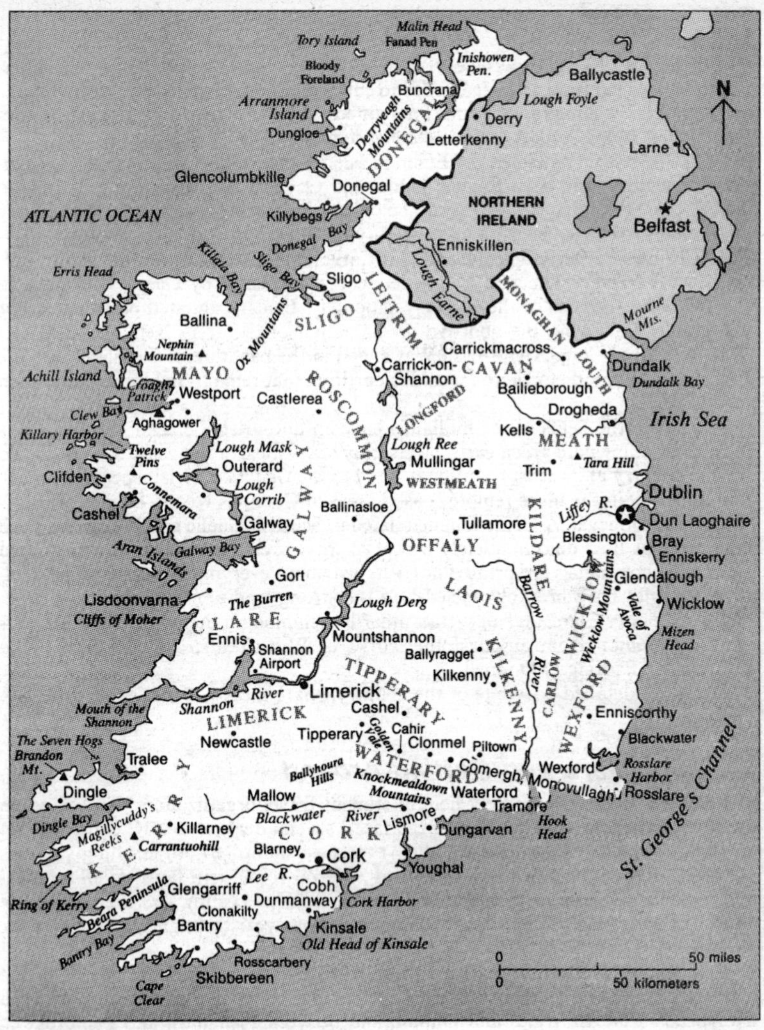

IRELAND

USD$1 = 0.65 pounds (£, or IEP)	**£1 = USD$1.53**
CAD$1 = £0.57	**£1 = CAD$1.75**
GBP£1 = £1.09	**£1 = GBP£0.91**
AUD$1 = £0.51	**£1 = AUD$1.96**
NZD$1 = £0.37	**£1 = NZD$2.68**
Country Code: 353	**International Dialing Prefix: 16**

For centuries, Ireland (Éire) was the mysterious western fringe of what Europeans knew of the world. The abruptly rising mountains in the southwest, bleak wind-swept sheets of Connemara stone, and the rocky crags of the Wicklow Mountains offered few comforts to Ireland's early settlers. St. Patrick's 5th-century arrival ended the era of virgin sacrifices and heralded the great age of Irish monasteries; pilgrims voyaged from all over Europe to enlighten themselves in the "land of saints and scholars." Viking raiders came for a different reason—to pillage monastic settlements—but many settled and were converted from their evil ways.

In 1170, Henry II claimed the Emerald Isle for the English throne in a less-than-decisive victory, and both English feudal and Gaelic Irish influences split Ireland during the Middle Ages. As Britain colonized inexorably westwards, the tragedy of Ireland's existence became its proximity to its eastern neighbor. Protestant settlers, Cromwell's Puritan army, and anti-Catholic Penal Laws typified English policy toward Ireland. The trail to independence was blazed by Daniel O'Connell in the 1830s; by the turn of the century, nationalist Fenians agitated passionately for home rule. Following the abortive proclamation of the Irish Republic in Easter 1916, a five-year-long Anglo-Irish War ended in the partition of the island into the Irish Free State and Northern Ireland, a partition that remains in bloody contention to this day.

The flat fertile fields of the midlands have an untouristed charm, but Ireland is most dramatic where green earth meets gray sea—stick to the coast if you can. To see the country at its most traditional, head to the *Gaeltacht* (Irish-speaking areas), found mainly in the more remote coastal areas of Counties Kerry, Dingle, Galway, Mayo, and Donegal. A Celtic tongue related to Scottish Gaelic and Welsh, the Irish language has died out completely except in these areas; even here, although road signs and shop names are printed in Irish, just about everyone speaks English. Cultural energies have been channeled into the strong traditional music scene, especially in County Clare, and an extraordinarily rich modern literature; choose a traveling companion from amongst the works of W.B. Yeats, James Joyce, Flann O'Brien, or Padraig O'Donnell.

For more detailed coverage of the country, snare a copy of *Let's Go: Britain & Ireland.*

Getting There and Getting Around

USIT is Ireland's extremely helpful student travel organization, with offices in London and Paris: they provide cheap fares, special deals and ISIC cards (£5.50) to those under 26. They also sell the **Travelsave** stamp (£7.50) entitling students to a 50% discount on one-way fares and 30% on round-trip fares on all national rail and bus services in Ireland (except on local runs costing less than £2). Like the ISIC, the stamp is valid from September of one year through December of the next.

You can get to Ireland by air or by sea; sea is cheaper. Trains and buses connect with all the ferries. **B&I** and **Sealink** ferries make several runs per day between Holyhead in North Wales and Dublin, and between Fishguard and Pembroke in South Wales and Rosslare. Fares are IR£16-22, round-trip IR£32-44, with a 25% discount for IYHF members. B&I gives a 25% discount for ISIC and 50% for the Travelsave stamp, but these are valid only during certain parts of the week—check when you buy your ticket. **Irish Ferries** sail between Rosslare Harbor and Le Havre and Cherbourg in France, leaving from both ports between 5 and 10:30pm and taking the better part of a day (mid-July to Aug. £80, mid-June to mid-July £65, Sept. to mid-June £50-55; 50% off with InterRail, free passage with Eurailpass or InterRail plus Ship). **Swansea Cork Ferries** leaves daily (9am from Cork, 9pm from Swansea) during the summer months and less frequently during winter, costing £18-22. The daily **Supabus,** a combined bus and ferry charge, costs £28-36 from London to Dublin. From Great Britain north of Manchester, the cheapest way to Ireland is usually to cross from Stranraer, Scotland to Larne, Northern Ireland, and then take a train or bus to Dublin. (See Northern Ireland in the United Kingdom section.) Flights from London to Dublin are reasonable after a recent price war between Aer Lingus and Ryan Air (about £70, £50 through USIT). Direct flights from North America to Ireland are available, but it's usually cheaper to fly to London and take a ferry or plane to Ireland.

Expensive **trains** connect most large cities to Dublin but not to one another. **Buses,** run by **Bus Éireann,** cover most of the country; Eurailpass holders get free passage on **Expressway** buses to most sizable towns; local Bus Éireann and private buses serve the more rural areas. **Rambler tickets** for eight days (within a period of 15) of second-class rail or bus travel (£58) or eight days of rail *and* bus travel (£75) don't pay off unless you sprint instead of ramble.

Cycling is one of the best ways to explore remote areas. Tourist offices have a national listing of bicycle rental locations (about £7 per day), and you are allowed to bring bikes on trains. Youth hostels frequently lie within 20 scenic miles of each other. **Hitchhiking** proves harder now than 20 years ago, but is still an accepted method of getting around. Sundays and very rural areas can leave you by the side of the road for hours; on main roads competition can be stiff, but progress is usually steady. As always, consider the risks.

Practical Information

The **Irish Tourist Board (Bord Fáilte)** operates a nationwide network of offices, selling maps (including £3 survey maps for hikers) and detailed local guidebooks, and handing out the free *Calendar of Events* in Ireland. Their accommodations booking service (locally £1, nationwide £2, 10% deposit) can be helpful, but do extra homework: many fine hostels and **B&Bs** are not "approved" (which involves paying a regular cut to Bord Fáilte), so the tourist office can't tell you about them.

Weather in Ireland is both temperate (summer temperatures 10-27°C—50-80°F) and temperamental. Keep a rain poncho or umbrella handy and carry a warm sweater, as warm sunshine often suddenly yields to chilly dampness.

Ireland has nine annual bank holidays: New Year's Day, St. Patrick's Day (March 17), Good Friday, Easter Monday, the first Mondays in June and August, the last Monday in October, Christmas Day, and St. Stephen's Day (Dec. 26). Also check for local half-day holidays, when banks and stores close down. Banks open from Monday to Friday 10am-12:30pm and 1:30-3pm. In Dublin, banks are open until 5pm on Thursdays. The Bank of Ireland has offices throughout the country, but no standardized exchange rates, so do your business in larger towns. English coins (though not the £1 coin) are accepted in Ireland, but not vice versa (pounds sterling are worth more than Irish "punts").

The green-fronted post offices are labeled in Irish—*Oifig an Phoist.* Most phones have a miniature rampway on top; line up your coins, and they'll automatically feed into the phone as needed. Press the "FC" button on newer phones (follow-on-call) before hanging up if you want to make another call. Dial 10 for the operator and 190 for international directory assistance. The AT&T **USA Direct** number is 1800 550 000. Dial 999 anywhere in the country in an emergency.

Accommodations, Camping, and Food

Hosteling is the way to go in Ireland. **An Óige,** the Irish IYHF association, runs 50 hostels throughout the country, which are generally clean, friendly, and relaxed by IYHF standards. IYHF hostels charge £3.50-6 per night (ages under 18 £2.50-5); nonmembers pay an extra £1.25. The hostels in Dublin, Cork, Limerick, and Killarney offer special train fares (£13.95 for a one-way ticket between cities including one overnight at an IYHF hostel). All IYHF hostels will call ahead for you to reserve a bed at another IYHF hostel (no booking charge). In addition to the IYHF hostels, there are scores of independent hostels, most costing £4-5 and lacking the institutional atmosphere, curfews, membership requirements, and daytime lockouts that can make hosteling a drag. For information of the **Independent Hostel Owners (IHO)** association, contact Patrick O'Donnell, Dooey Hostel, Glencolumcille, Co. Donegal (tel. (073) 301 30), or pick up their booklet for £1 at any member hostel. The **Irish Budget Hostels,** all of which are "approved" by the tourist board, can be reached through Josephine Moloney, Doolin Hostel, Doolin Village, Co. Clare (tel. (065) 740 06). B&Bs are a wonderful, luxurious break from hosteling and occasionally the only option. Expect to pay £10-13 for a bed and a sizzling morning meal of cereal, toast, eggs, bacon, sausage, tomato, and tea or coffee.

Camping can be a soggy proposition on the Emerald Isle. *Caravan and Camping Parks* (£1.50, available at most tourist offices) lists all approved sites; most charge £3-5 per tent. Some independent hostels will let you camp outside and use their facilities for about £2.50, and farmers often permit short-term camping for free, but ask first and tread lightly on the earth.

Irish food should be appreciated for what it is: hearty, wholesome, simple fare. Homemade soup and brown bread are available nearly everywhere for about £1; shepherd's pie, Irish stew and potatoes in many forms are yours in pubs for £2-3. Delicious cheeses, yogurt and the addictive sodabread keeps you alive and kicking for very little money; sidewalk markets overflow with vegetables in season, and you can buy (or catch) fresh fish along the coast.

Ireland's wonderful pubs prove true the saying "there's more friendship in a glass of spirits than in a barrel of buttermilk." Travelers who stop in for a nip will find themselves engaged in an intimate conversation three or four nips later. The standard Irish beer is Guinness, a rich dark brown stout (it grows on you). Irish coffee—strong, laced with Irish whiskey, sweetened with brown sugar and dolloped with whipped cream—can make you jocose, bellicose, lachrymose, and comatose, all in a single afternoon. Pubs close at 11:30pm (11pm on Sun. and in the winter) and also for "holy hour" during the afternoon in Dublin and usually from 2-4pm in most places on Sunday. Many pubs feature live music, planned or spontaneous; besides rock and jazz, you can hear traditional Irish music, or, if you're lucky, see the set dancing.

Dublin

Dublin's troubled history is filled with conquest and colonization—first the Vikings, then the British for 800 years. In response, city dwellers have a fierce attachment to Irish independence and Gaelic culture, celebrating the glorious Easter Uprising of 1916, literary heroes like Swift, Wilde, Yeats, Joyce and Beckett, and their traditional music, which can be heard nightly in pubs around the city. Despite its friendly, parochial atmosphere, hard economic times plague modern Dublin, and Dickensian street urchins scuttle into alleyways with bags and wallets.

Orientation and Practical Information

The river Liffey bisects the city: the more glittery, affluent south centers around Trinity College and the Grafton St. shopping area, while in the north, streets lead off the main O'Connell St. into working-class neighborhoods and abandoned housing. Most city buses leave from O'Connell and along the quays, fanning out to the suburbs. Connolly Train Station lies in the north, and also provides DART (commuter train) service; Heuston Train Station is along the Liffey west of the city (take bus #90 to city center, 55p).

Tourist Office: 14 Upper O'Connell St. (tel. 74 77 33). From Connolly Station follow Talbot St. Free maps. Accommodations service £1. RYANAIR desk. Open mid-June to July Mon.-Sat. 8:30am-6pm; July-Aug. Mon.-Sat. 8:30am-8pm, Sun. 10:30am-3pm; Sept. Mon.-Fri. 9am-5pm; Oct. Mon.-Fri. 9am-5pm, Sat. 9am-1:30pm. **Dublin Airport** branch (tel. 37 63 87) open daily May 8am-8pm; June-Sept. 8am-10:30pm; Sept.-Dec. 8am-6:30pm; Jan.-April 8am-6pm. **North Wall Ferryport** (B&I Terminal) branch, on Alexander Road, is open late June-early Sept.

Budget Travel: USIT, 19-21 Aston Quay (tel. 77 81 17), near the O'Connell Bridge. ISIC, IYHF cards. USIT card (£5.50) scores discounts on transportation plus. Travelsave stamp (£7.50). Open July Mon. 10am-5:30pm and 7:30-9pm, Tues.-Fri. 10am-5:30pm, Sat. 10am-12:30pm; Aug.-June Mon. 10am-2pm, Tues.-Fri. 10am-5:30pm.

Embassies: U.S., 43 Elgin Rd., Ballsbridge (tel. 68 87 77). Open Mon.-Fri. 8:30am-4pm. **Canada,** 65 St. Stephen's Green South (tel. 78 19 88). Open Mon.-Wed. 8:30am-12:30pm and 2-4pm, Thurs.-Fri. 8:30am-12:30pm. **U.K.,** 33 Merrion Rd. (tel. 69 51 11). Open Mon.-Fri.

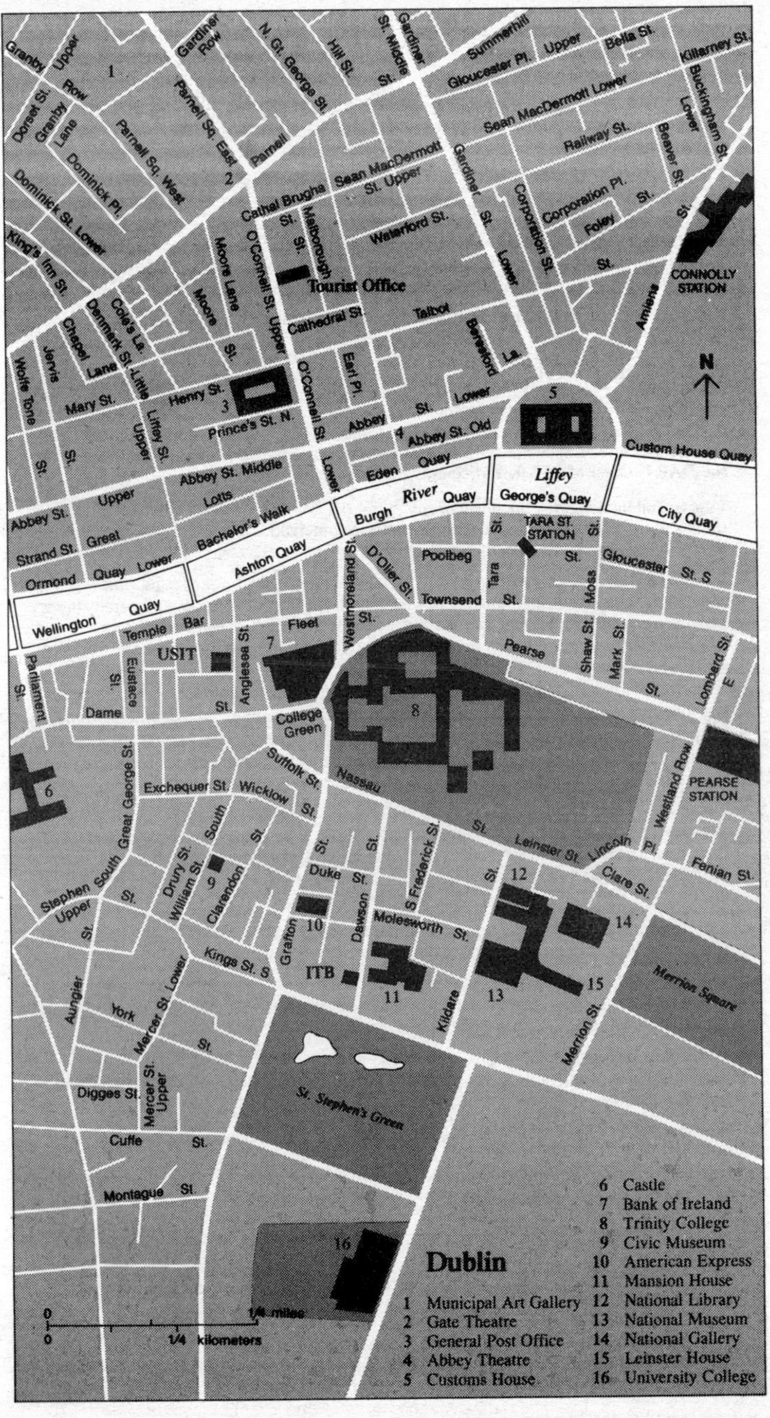

Dublin
1 Municipal Art Gallery
2 Gate Theatre
3 General Post Office
4 Abbey Theatre
5 Customs House
6 Castle
7 Bank of Ireland
8 Trinity College
9 Civic Museum
10 American Express
11 Mansion House
12 National Library
13 National Museum
14 National Gallery
15 Leinster House
16 University College
Tourist Office
USIT
ITB
CONNOLLY STATION
TARA ST. STATION
PEARSE STATION
River Liffey
St. Stephen's Green
Merrion Square
N
0 1/4 miles
0 1/4 kilometers

10am-noon and 2-4pm. **Australia,** Fitzwilton House, Wilton Terr. (tel. 76 15 17). Open Mon.-Thurs. 8:30am-1pm and 2-5:20pm, Fri. 8:30am-1:45pm. **New Zealanders** should contact the British Embassy.

Currency Exchange: Best rates at **banks,** with 1% commission. Otherwise, try the *Bureau de Change* in the **General Post Office** (1% commission; open Mon.-Sat. 8am-8pm), or the **Bank of Ireland** at Dublin Airport (open in summer daily 6:45am-10pm; in winter daily 6:45am-9pm.)

American Express: 116 Grafton St., Dublin 2 (tel. 77 28 74), up the street from Trinity Gates. Open Mon.-Fri. 9am-5pm, Sat. 9am-noon.

Post Office: General Post Office, O'Connell St. (tel. 72 88 88), near the tourist office. Site of the 1916 rebellion, now a pickpockets' haunt. Open Mon.-Sat. 8am-8pm (packages 8am-7pm), Sun. 10:30am-6:30pm (no packages). Postal code for Poste Restante: Dublin 1.

Telephones: In the post office. Open same hours. **City Code:** 01.

Trains: Heuston Station (tel. 36 62 22) is Dublin's main station, with service to Cork, Limerick, Waterford, Tralee (County Kerry), Galway, and Westport. Bus #90 connects it with the city center. **Connolly Station** (tel. 74 29 41), just behind Busáras and the Customs House on Amiens Rd. Service to Belfast, Sligo, Wexford, and Rosslare. **Pearse Station** (tel. 77 65 81), on Westland Row directly behind Trinity College, serves suburban lines. **Irish Rail Information,** 35 Lower Abbey St. (tel. 72 42 22 or 36 33 33) handles questions on all trains plus the DART. Open Mon.-Sat. 9am-5pm.

Flights: Dublin Airport, 7 mi. north of city center (tel. 37 99 00). Flights primarily to Europe (flights to the U.S. leave from Shannon Airport in Limerick). Take bus #41A or 41C (95p) to city center, or express airport coach (£2.30).

Buses: Busáras, Store St. (tel. 36 61 11), directly behind the Customs House (down to the right of O'Connell St. Bridge, looking from the south side). Central station for intercity buses. Day lockers available. For bus information, go to 59 Upper O'Connell St. (tel. 36 61 11 and 73 42 22 after hrs.), opposite the tourist office. Provides information on Expressway, Provincial, Bus Eíreann, and Dublin City buses. Open Mon. 8:30am-5:30pm, Tues.-Fri. 9am-5:30pm, Sat. 9am-1pm. **Lost property:** Tel. 72 00 00. Mon.-Fri. 9am-5:30pm.

Public Transportation: Buses run 6am-11:30pm. Buy tickets from the bus driver (50-95p). Unlimited travel for 1 week £11.50 (£9 with ISIC). One-day bus ticket £2.90. One-day bus and train £3.50. (Buy these at 59 Upper O'Connell St.) The *Dublin District Timetable* (50p) gives schedules. **Dublin Area Rapid Transit (DART)** trains cost the same as buses and run from Howth to Bray.

Ferries: B&I (tel. 79 79 77) or **Sealink** (tel. 80 77 77) ferries from Liverpool or Holyhead. Both have offices on Westmoreland St. Arriving by B&I ferry, catch bus #53 to the center. Buses #7, 7A, and 8 as well as the DART provide citybound service from the Sealink ferry dock in **Dun Laoghaire.** Exact change not required.

Bike Rental: Rent-A-Bike, 58 Lower Gardiner St. (tel. 72 59 31). Bikes from £4-6 per day, £22-25 per week, £30-50 deposit. You can return bikes to any office (Roseclark, Cork, Sligo, Galway, Westport, Killarney or Limerick). Open Mon.-Sat. 9am-6pm.

Laundromat: Nova Laundrette, Belvidere Rd., just off Dorset St. Washers £1.60. Dryers £1.50. Open Mon.-Sat. 8:30am-8pm, Sun. 11am-6pm.

Youth Information Centre, at Sackville House, Sackville Pl. (tel. 78 68 44), behind Clery's on O'Connell St. Bulletin boards advertising youth and special-needs groups. Open Mon.-Wed. 9:30am-6pm, Thurs.-Sat. 9:30am-5pm.

Rape Crisis, 70 Lower Leeson St. (tel. 61 49 11 or 61 45 64). Open Mon.-Fri. 9am-5pm.

Gay Centers: Gay Switchboard Dublin, Old Doctor's Residence, Richmond Hospital (tel. 72 10 55). Open Mon.-Fri. 8-10pm, Sat. 3:30-6pm, Sun. 7-9pm.

Hospitals: Mater Hospital, Eccles St. (tel. 30 11 22) just off Berkeley St. **Adelaide,** Peter St. (tel. 75 89 71) near White Friar St. Take bus #16, 19 or 22.

Emergencies: Police (Garda) or **Ambulance** (tel. 999; free). Police station at Harcourt Sq. (tel. 73 22 22).

Accommodations and Camping

Most hostels in the Dublin area are on the depressed side of town, a 10-minute walk north of the center. Watch your belongings.

Hostels

Dublin Tourist Hostel (Isaac's), 2-4 Frenchman's Lane (tel. 74 93 21), near Busáras under the railway line. Free music Wed. nights in this low-ceilinged, wood-raftered grotto. Reception open 24 hrs. Kitchen facilities. No curfew. Lockout 11am-5pm. Dorms £4.75 per person. Singles £12. Doubles £15. Café, lockers, baggage storage.

Kinlay House, 2-12 Lord Edward St. (tel. 79 66 44), near Christ Church Cathedral. Dark wood bannisters in lofty entrance hall; comfy beds and soft couches. Very convenient to city center. Kitchen facilities. No curfew or lockout. 40 dorms £7.50-9.50. Doubles £12.50, with bath £14. Breakfast included. Lockers and laundry.

M.E.C., 43 North Great George St. (tel. 72 63 01) off Parnell St. Light, airy huge Georgian building was once a convent. Still heavenly. Reception open 24 hrs. Dorms £6.50. Singles (in old nun's cells) £12. Doubles £9 per person. Breakfast and sheets included. Parking lot. Cheaper weekly rates.

Goin' My Way/Cardijn House, 15 Talbot St. (tel. 78 84 84 or 74 17 20), over Tiffany's Shoe Shop. A good deal, but not for giants. Coffee bar. Lockout 10am-5pm. Midnight curfew. Beds £5. Sheets and breakfast included.

Dublin International Youth Hostel (IYHF), Mountjoy St. (tel. 30 17 66) off Dorset St. Phones are in confessional boxes, free breakfast in the old chapel. Large and comfortable. Reception (with currency exchange) open 24hr. No lockout. Flexible midnight curfew. Courtesy bus meets the ferries. Sept.-June members £8.50, nonmembers £9; July-Aug. members£9, nonmembers £9.50. Sheets 50p. Kitchen facilites. Free lockers. Parking lot with security guards.

Young Traveller, St. Mary's Pl. (tel. 30 50 00), off Dorset St. Standard hostel decor and an extensive notice board encourage you out into the city for entertainment. A bit dark. Reception open 24 hrs. £8.50. Breakfast included. Laundry facilities. No lockers, but a safe in the baggage room.

Bed and Breakfast

Dublin's many B&Bs range from £9-25. The tourist office has a complete list (£2) or will call for you. Suburban B&Bs tend to be private homes, offering special attention and that grandmotherly touch. City B&Bs are more hotel-ish. You'll find lots of them on Upper and Lower Gardiner Streets, as well as the Parnell Square area.

Camping

Shankill Caravan and Camping Park (tel. 82 00 11), near Cromlech, in Shankill, Take bus #45, 45a, 84, or the DART from Connolly Station. 50p per person, £3.50-4.50 per tent. 8-min. shower 50p. Stay a week and get one night free. Open Easter-Oct.

Food

Dublin's open-air **Moore Street Market** provides fresh and cheap fruits and vegetables, but keep your hand on your wallet. (Open Mon.-Sat. 9am-5pm.) The **Runner Bean** grocery store at 4 Nassau St. (open Mon.-Fri. 7:30am-6pm; reduced hours Sat.) sells healthy wholefoods. **Dunne's Stores,** a cheap supermarket chain, has a branch on N. Earl St. off O'Connell St. (Open Mon.-Wed. 9am-6pm, Thurs. 9am-8pm, Fri. 9am-7pm, and Sat. 9am-6pm.) Fast, greasy take-out places distribute fish and chips (and coronary surgery) throughout the city. "Pub grub" means sandwiches, chicken and pints (meals £3-4, pints around £1.70).

Bewley's Café, Grafton St., Westmoreland St. and South Great George's St. *The* classic Dublin 19th-century coffeeshop. Pastries (95p) and lunch. The Westmoreland St. branch was James Joyce's all-time favorite (open Mon.-Sat. 8am-7pm, Sun. 10am-5pm). The Grafton St. branch is larger (open Mon.-Fri. 8am-8pm, Sat. 8am-7pm). South Great George's St. café open Mon.-Sat. 8:15am-4pm.

Beshoff's, 14 Westmoreland St. and 7 O'Connell St. Chips and 17 different varieties of fish. Luxurious fake plants. Your mackerel and chips (£1.90) come in a box. Open Mon.-Thurs. 11:30am-11pm, Fri.-Sat. 11:30am-1am, Sun. 12:30-11pm.

Bad Ass Café, Crown Alley off Dame St. (tel. 71 25 96 for pizza). Huge Dublin warehouse inexplicably converted into a loud Viewmaster snapshot of "Born in the USA" American culture. Lunch £3-5. Student menu (with ISIC). Open daily 9am-10pm.

Cornucopia, 20 Wicklow St. Peaceful longbeards munch whole grains and vegetables on high stools. Meals £1.30-3. Open Mon.-Sat. 8-11am and noon-8pm, until 9pm on Thurs.

Sights

The best way to explore Dublin's 18th-century Georgian architecture is to use the walking guides available from the tourist office (£1 each) or take the two-hour **guided tour** offered by the students of Trinity College. This crash course in Irish history meets at Trinity's front gate, daily at 11am, noon, 2pm and 3pm from June-August only (£3.50). **Trinity College,** the alma mater of Swift, Moore, Beckett, Wilde and Burke, holds the 8th century **Book of Kells** in its wood-vaulted **Long Room.** Written by Irish monks around 800 AD, this dizzyingly intricate illuminated manuscript was found buried in 1007. (Open Mon.-Fri. 9:30am-4:45pm, Sat. 9:30am-12:45pm. Admission charged April-Oct. only, £1.75, seniors and students £1.50, under 18 free; Nov.-March free.) The witty, caustic ½-hr. **Trinity College Tour** concentrates on the University itself and includes admission to the Book of Kells. (Tours every 15 min. from inside the front gate June-Sept. 9am-4:30pm.) Many of Dublin's museums cluster just behind the university, between Kildare St. and Merrion St. Particularly interesting is the **National Museum,** Kildare St. (tel. 61 88 11), which houses the world's best collection of Irish cultural artifacts, including Celtic goldwork, the Tara brooch, a stirring exhibit on the 1916 uprising, and a live leprechaun. (Open Tues.-Sat. 10am-5pm, Sun. 2-5pm. Free except for the Treasury: £1, students 50p, children 30p, families £2, free Tues.) Down the street on Merrion Sq. is the **National Gallery,** which houses works by Spanish, Flemish, and Dutch masters. The walls of the four-story winding staircase are hung with portraits of Irish greats including Lady Gregory, Jonathan Swift, James Joyce, Daniel O'Connell, and George Bernard Shaw. (Open Mon.-Sat. 10am-6pm, Thurs. 10am-9pm, Sun. 2-5pm. Free.)

Christchurch Cathedral, at the end of Dame St., and **St. Patrick's,** down Patrick St., are beautifully historical churches boasting artifacts and tombs. (Christchurch open daily 10am-5pm; 50p donation. St. Patrick's open Mon.-Fri. 8:30am-6:15pm, Sat. 8:30am-5pm, Sun. 10am-4pm; 50p donation, students 30p.) The corpses in the vaults of **St. Michan's Church** (including a 700-year-old Crusader) have been effectively mummified by the dry atmosphere. (Open Mon.-Fri. 10am-12:45pm and 2-4:45pm, Sat. 10am-12:45pm. Admission £1.50, students and seniors £1, under 16 50p.)

No visit to Dublin is complete without seeing the **Guinness Brewery,** the world's largest. The motto "Guinness is good for you" echoes from the film and museum walls; after this indoctrination, visitors may sample the legendary dark brew. (Open Mon.-Fri. 10am-3pm. Admission £2, children 50p.) Take bus #21A, 78, 78A, or 78B west along the Liffey, to St. James Gate, where the scent of Guinness is strong and the murky river curiously resembles the beverage.

Entertainment

Pints of Guinness (around £1.70) and chatty camaraderie make Dublin's pubs congenial. Most open at 10:30am (12:30pm on Sun.), and all close at 11:30pm (11pm on Sun.). Within city limits pubs must also obey the "holy hour" from 2:30 to 3:30pm. James Joyce notorized **Mulligan's,** 8 Poolbeg St., **Davy Byrne's,** 21 Duke St., and the **Bailey,** also on Duke St. The music scene centers around these gathering places, where every night musicians play rock, jazz, country and Irish music in exchange for free beer, and Dubliners and foreigners alike clap hands and stamp feet to the drone of the pipe and the roll of the *bodhrán* (BOW-rawn) drum. There is sometimes a cover charge of £2-3. For these nightly sessions, also try **O'Shea's Merchant** and the **Brazen Head** (both on Lower Bridge St. off Merchant's Quay) and **O'Donaghue's,** 15 Merrion Row, near Baggot St. The fortnightly *In Dublin* has complete listings of all events (£1.30).

Theater provides a cultural alternative to bar-hopping. In addition to mainstream plays, theaters often produce experimental or new Irish shows. Curtains rise at 8pm. For information on the **Dublin Theatre Festival,** which takes place in late September and early October, call the Festival Booking Office, 47 Nassau St. (tel. 77 84 39). **The Abbey,** 26 Lower Abbey St. (tel. 78 72 22), is the national theater of Ireland. (Box office open Mon.-Sat. 10:30am-7pm. Tickets £8-13, student standby discounts from 7pm.) You can also try **The Gate,** 1 Cavendish Row (tel. 74 40 45; box office open Mon.-Sat. 10am-7pm; tickets £8-13). For alternative shows, try the **Project Arts Centre,** 39 East Essex St. (tel. 71 23 21).

On **Bloomsday** (June 16), Joyce aficionados commemorate the hero of *Ulysses* and his 19-hour cross-city "odd-yssey." Recharting his course, with a helpful map (50p) and appropriate drinking and debauchery, actually takes 30 hours. Check with the tourist office for ways to join.

Rugby season starts in October; home games shake the turf in **Lansdowne Stadium.** Gaelic football and hurling (the national sport of Ireland) championships abound on summer Sundays. The **All-Ireland Finals** are played in early September in **Croke Park,** Phibsborough Rd. For more information, contact the G.A.A. (tel. 36 32 22).

Southeastern Ireland

The southeast is the self-professed sunniest part of Ireland. Sandy beaches line the coast, good for swimming and buying fresh fish (**Brittes Bay,** between Wicklow and Arklow, is especially popular), and roadsides swarm with strawberry stands in summer. For the beaches, take the train to Wicklow, Arklow or Rosslare, and local buses from there. **Rosslare Harbour** is a major transportation point, with daily ferries for Britain and France. Buses and trains meet ferries, connecting to Dublin (4 per day, 3 hr.; bus £7, £5.50 with ISIC and Travelsave stamp; train £18, £9 with ISIC and Travelsave stamp); to Cork (2 per day); to Wexford (7 per day, 20 min., £2.30, £1.60 with ISIC and Travelsave stamp); to Limerick and Waterford (3 per day); and to Galway, Killarney and Tralee (1 per day).

The **Youth Hostel (IYHF)** (tel. (053) 333 90) offers a friendly welcome and delicious bread and soup (£1) just up the steps from the harbor. (Check-in 5:30pm. Lockout 9:30am-5:30pm. Curfew 11:30pm. £6. Kitchen. Reserve ahead in summer.) Rosslare is forested with B&Bs; the best of the lot is **Mrs. O'Leary's** 100-acre farm (tel. (053) 331 34), with a private beach. (Singles £13.50. Doubles £11-12.50 per person.)

Inland from the east coast, the **Wicklow Mountains'** lofty granite summits and verdant valleys, enclosing waterfalls and gorse glens, have an ancient and spellbinding allure. The 70-mile **Wicklow Way** hiking trail passes through the range, stopping at hostels; would-be hikers should contact the main tourist office in Dublin or the tourist office in the Bray Town Hall (tel. (01) 86 71 28; open late June-late Aug.). **Glendalough,** the area's geographical and spiritual center, a spectacularly scenic uninhabited valley, cradles two lakes, a pine forest and the best-preserved of Ireland's ruined monastic settlements. Stay in the **Glendalough Youth Hostel (IYHF)** (tel. (04040) 453 42; £4.50-6.50) or the **Old Mill Hostel** (tel. (0404) 451 43) in the town of Laragh, one mile away (£4.80, camping for £2.50). **St. Kevin's Bus Service** (tel. (01) 81 81 19) shuttles between Dublin and Glendalough twice daily in the summer.

The area around **Kilkenny,** farther west, bursts with castles, abbeys and other ruins. Kilkenny itself boasts the splendidly preserved 14th-century **Kilkenny Castle** (open daily 10am-7pm; Oct. to mid-June daily Tues.-Sun. 11am-5pm; admission

£1, students 40p) and the 13th-century **St. Canice's Cathedral** (open daily 9am-1pm and 2-6pm; admission £1, students 30p). The **Kilkenny Tourist Hostel,** 35 Parliament St. (tel. (056) 635 41) costs £5 nightly (kitchen facilities; no lockout or curfew). The 16th century **Foulksrath Castle Hostel (IYHF)** (tel. (056) 676 74) lies 8 mi. north in Jenkinstown. Take Buggy's buses from the Parade in Kilkenny, twice daily in summer. (Open March-Oct. Kitchen facilities. £4-4.50.) Good pubs are the **Kilford Arms** and **O'Gormans,** both on John St. Do the B&B thing on Waterford and Castlecomer Rds. Trains running from Waterford to Dublin stop in Kilkenny; buses leave for Cork (3 per day) and Dublin (2 per day, £8).

Nearby **Cashel** is hard to reach from Kilkenny, but easy from Dublin or Cork (4 Expressway buses daily; hitchhiker's delight on a major truck route between the two cities). The **Rock of Cashel** makes the whole trip worthwhile: it's a fairy-like complex of medieval buildings rising out of the plains, but unfortunately mobbed with tourists in summer. (Open daily 9am-7:30pm; in winter 9:30am-4:30pm. £1.50, students 60p.) Try the B&Bs on **Moor Lane,** and the pub grub (£2-3) or the supermarket along Main St.

Cork City

Cork has few historical wonders, but that doesn't distract from the charm of the modern city (pop. 140,000). Two branches of the River Lee surround the city center, where tiny streets filled with coffeeshops and eateries stretch across like strings on a harp. Historical Cork, such as it is, clusters around the southern Lee; the vibrant commercial center and music-ringing pubs lie between the two; and north finds most of the hostels, and the train station (the immediate vicinity of which can be dangerous at night). Favorite activities include spectator sports and drinking the local **Murphy's,** a sweeter stout than Guinness.

St. Fin Barre's Cathedral, a limestone gingerbread house incorporating angels, saints and griffins, stands where the saint founded his School of Cork in 606. (Open Mon.-Sat. 10am-1pm and 2-5:30pm; Oct.-April 10am-1pm and 2-5pm. Admission 50p.) **Shandon Church's** red and white, three-tiered pepperpot tower affords a Corkian panorama. (Open Mon.-Sat. 10am-4:30pm; in winter Mon.-Sat. 10am-4pm. Admission £1; the whole kit 'n' kaboodle of church, tower and bells for £1.50.) Both the wide-ranging **Crawford Municipal Gallery,** Emmet Place (open Mon.-Fri. 10am-5pm, Sat. 9:30am-4:30pm) and the modernist-oriented **Triskal Arts Center,** off South Main St. (open Tues.-Fri. 10:30am-5:30pm, Sat. 11am-5pm) offer free exhibits by Irish artists. The **Opera House,** Emmet Pl. (tel. (021) 27 00 22; box office open Mon.-Sat. 10am-5pm; tickets £8-16) and the less expensive **Everyman's Theatre,** MacCurtain St. (tel. (021) 50 30 77; box office open Mon.-Sat. 11am-7pm; tickets £4-6) stage productions year-round. Regular festivals enliven the city: the **International Film Festival** (mostly documentaries) in late September, the **Guinness Jazz Festival** (late October), and in neighboring Cobh, the **International Folk Dance Festival** (second week in July). Summer games of hurling and Gaelic football are played at **Pairc Ui Chaoimh,** Marina.

In the southern part of the city, the **tourist office** (tel. (021) 27 32 51), on Grand Parade, has an accommodation service (£1) and a 50p map. (Open June Mon.-Sat. 9am-6pm; July-Aug. Mon.-Sat. 9am-7pm; Sept.-May Mon.-Fri. 9:15am-5:30pm, Sat. 9:15am-1pm.) Just around the corner, the **Bank of Ireland,** 32 South Mall, changes money (open Mon. 10am-12:30pm and 1:30-5pm, Tues.-Fri. 10am-12:30pm and 1:30-3pm). The nearby **American Express** at Casey Travel Ltd., 60 South Mall, does not cash travelers checks, but cardholders can go here for emergency check cashing. (Open Mon.-Fri. 9am-5:30pm.) Oliver Plunkett St., which spines through the city, holds the **post office** (open Mon.-Sat. 9am-5:30pm), while **USIT,** the student travel office (tel. (021) 27 09 00), is in a small arcade off the perpendicular Grand Parade (open Mon.-Fri. 9:30am-5:30pm, Sat. 10am-2pm). **Buses** stop at the station on Parnell Pl. (tel. (021) 50 33 99; schedules 80 81 88), on the Lee in the northern part of city center, while over the river and through the warehouses Kent Station (tel. (021) 50 44 22) on Lower Glanmire Rd. shuffles trains to major destinations. **Carroll's Cycles,** Dillon's Cross (tel. (021) 50 89 23) rents bikes northeast of the station (mountain bikes £4 per day).

The **Raging Red Hag,** 8 Pembroke St., slaps together tremendous sandwiches to go (£1.25-1.50; open Mon.-Sat. 10am-6pm). At 40 Paul St., **Bully's** serves hot and hearty Italian fare from its roaring oven at the back (£3-6). Sit at the **Quay Co-op,** 24 Sullivans Quay, and watch the world change. (Meals £3-4. Open Mon.-Tues. 10am-6:30pm, Wed.-Sat. 10am-6pm.) Traditional music mavens should try **An Bodhrán** (#42) and **DeLacey's** (#74) on Oliver Plunkett St. Union Quay is a great pub corner: **The Lobby** and **An Phoenix** are the cream of the crop.

Hostels congregate north of the Lee. **Isaacs,** on MacCurtain St. (tel. (021) 50 00 11) features live music and light rooms in a newly renovated furniture warehouse. (Reception open 24 hrs. £4.75. Sheets 50p.) Sheila's **Cork Tourist Hotel** (tel. (021) 50 55 62), 10 Belgrave Pl., by the intersection of York St. and Wellington St., is convenient to both the bus and train stations, has laundry facilities (£2.50 per load), sauna (£1), snooker and video. (Reception open 8am-10pm. No lockout or curfew. £4.75. Sheets 50p. Key deposit £2. Kitchen.) The **Cork City Hostel** (tel. (021) 50 90 89), on 100 Lower Glanmire Rd. near the train station, is a little creaky at the knees, but has a lot of character. (No lockout or curfew. £4.50. Sheets 50p. Kitchen facilities.) **Kinlay House,** Bob & Joan Walk (tel. (021) 50 89 66), down the alley to the right of Shandon Church, is a maze-like configuration of rooms with all the amenities. (Reception open 24 hrs. No lockout or curfew. £7, sheets and breakfast included. Kitchen.) On Western Rd., due west of the Grand Parade (15-min. walk; take bus #8 from Patrick St.), the small and luxurious **Campus House,** 3 Woodland View (tel. (021) 34 35 31) costs £4.75. The **IYHF youth hostel** on Western Rd. (tel. (021) 54 32 89), several doors down, has bike rental, kitchen and bus service to Blarney (£2 return) and a bureau de change. (Curfew 11:55pm. Lock-out 10am-5pm. £4.30-5.90. Sheets 50p.) Cork B&Bs cost £10-13; the less pretentious variety line Lower Glanmire Rd., while those on Western Rd. are more upscale.

Five miles outside Cork is the ultimate camera-clicker shrine, the **Blarney Castle,** where with some acrobatics (you have to lean upside down over the parapet wall) you can kiss the **Blarney Stone** and acquire the gift of eloquence. Give it a little tongue for the ultimate in loquaciousness. Check at the tourist office for the castle's hours. (Admission £2.50, students and seniors £1.50, children £1.) Frequent buses run to Blarney from Cork's central bus station (round-trip £2).

Western Cork

Southwest of Cork, the roads narrow, the population thins, the landscape roughens, and the air freshens. **Kinsale,** beautiful seaside resort and gourmet capital of Ireland, lies about 15 miles directly south. The **tourist office** is on Pier Rd. (tel. (021) 77 22 34; open mid-May to mid-Oct. Mon.-Sat. 9:30am-5:30pm, Sun. 11:30am-5:30pm). **Dempsey's Hostel,** about a 5-min. walk from town on the Cork Rd. (tel. (021) 77 21 24) costs £4 for no-frills accommodation. (Shower 50p. Kitchen.) The **Kinsale Youth Hostel (IYHF)** in Summer Cove (tel. (021) 77 23 09), 2 mi. out of town, with fluffy comforters, squats next to the one-time British stronghold of **Charles Fort** (open mid-June to Sept. daily 9am-6:30pm; mid-March to mid-June Tues.-Sat. 9am-5pm, Sun. 2-5pm; £1, students 50p). **The Anchor Bar** and **Cuckoo's Nest,** both on Main St., offer beds for £7-9 (breakfast £3 extra). There is a **SuperValu Market** on Pearse St., but Kinsale is the place to blow money on food: try **The Copper Grill,** Pearse St. (around £3) or **Piazzetta Pizzeria,** Market Sq. (huge pizzas from £4). Unwind with a pint and some music at **The Anchor Bar** or **The Shanakee,** both on Main St. At least four buses run to Cork daily from the Esso station (£3.50, return £4.70).

Baltimore and the islands, south and west of Cork, make another good trip. A bus runs from Cork to **Skibbereen,** whose **tourist office** is on North St. (tel. (028) 217 66; open late June-Aug. Mon.-Sat. 9am-6pm). Head from Skibbereen southwest to **Baltimore,** an 8-mi. bus ride (Mon.-Fri. 3 per day; also 4 per day on Sat., £1.75). Baltimore is a tiny fishing village, and home to **Rolf's Hostel** (tel. (028) 202 89), in a wonderful cozy stone cottage. (No lockout or curfew. £4.50.) **Casey's Cabin,** on the road to Skibbereen, serves great seafood (£2-3) and **Declan McCarthy's** is the place for music. Ask at the hostel about boats to nearby **Sherkin Island** (15 min., round-trip £3) and the slightly more distant **Cape Clear Island** (45 min., round-trip £7), where you can camp near almost deserted beaches and the pubs stay open until the wee hours. The **Sherkin Island Youth Hostel** (tel. (028) 203 02) is a family home with a magnificent view (£4.50); the **Cape Clear Youth Hostel (IYHF)** (tel. (028) 391 44) feels a little barren, but has a fire. (Open April-Oct. Flexible curfew. No lockout. £4.30-5.50.)

The **Beara Peninsula,** the longest in West Cork, extends peace, quiet and beaches. Stay in Castletown Bere, the principal town, at the chicken-soup-cooking **Beara Hostel** (tel. (027) 701 84; £4.50, camping £3; kitchen) and rent a bike in town (£7 per day, £30 per week at the SuperValu supermarket); public transport is rare and the rain will wash hitchhikers' bones clean before a car even passes. The rugged **Allihies Youth Hostel (IYHF)** (tel. (027) 730 14) near the famed **Ballydonegan Strand** at the end of the peninsula, will relieve you of £4-4.50 for a night's stay. (Open April-Sept. Kitchen. Midnight curfew.)

County Kerry

Kerry's vast coastline and stark peaks may instill a profound conviction of the insignificance and pettiness of human beings; so too may the packs of tourists. **Killarney** is the classic springboard for exploring the Ring of Kerry, a 112-mi. road that encircles the **Iveragh Peninsula.** The Ring presents ethereal chiseled cliffs, misty mountains, and deep-blue lakes. Public buses leave from the station (tel. (064) 310 67) on East Avenue Rd. (1 per day, £9); for commentary and camera-clicking, book a coach tour at the tourist office (£10). You can bike the Ring in three days, but mind the region's frequent downpours. Hitchhiking is extraordinarily difficult; luckily frequent youth hostels mean you won't have to walk further than 10 miles. B&Bs ring the Ring like hungry buzzards.

Killarney, tourist mecca that it is, provides expensive meals and lots of hostels. Eat lunch at the herbivore **Súgán Kitchen,** Lewis Rd. (open daily noon-9pm; Sept.-June 6-9pm) or along **High St.,** or buy groceries at the **Dunne's Supermarket** there. The nicest hostels are the clean and cozy **Súgán Kitchen Hostel,** Lewis Rd. (tel. (064) 331 04), at Michael Collins' Pl. (£5; sheets 50p) and the laid-back **Bunrower House Hostel** (tel. (064) 339 14), a 15-min. walk out Ross Rd. (£5. Sheets 50p. Free shuttle from the Súgán.) Walk down Cork Rd. to the peaceful yellow villaed **Park Hostel** (tel. (064) 321 19), off Cork Rd., up the hill across from the Texaco station (£5; showers 50p; kitchen, laundry, and sports facilities). The **IYHF youth hostel** (tel. (064) 312 40) in Aghadoe, 3 mi. west of town, is a mansion with magnificent views of the surrounding mountains. Free vans shuttle hostelers to and from the bus and train stations. (Curfew midnight. £4.30-5.90. Kitchen and laundry facilities. Bikes £4 per day.) Just past the youth hostel is the **Fossa Caravan and Camping Park** (tel. (064) 314 97; units £5.50-7 plus 50p per adult and 25p per child; hikers and bikers £2; use of kitchen, laundry, and tennis court included; open mid-March to Sept.). Hikers and mountain bikers delight in the many trails leading out of Killarney's dramatic **Gap of Dunloe,** several miles west (head out Killorglin Rd., then turn left following signs). The nearby **Macgillycuddy's Reeks** present some of Ireland's most challenging climbs. A network of hostels makes it all accessible; get maps (50p) from the tourist office.

On the Ring of Kerry's northern coast, **Glenbeigh** ("The Valley of the Cows") offers terrific sands, oft frequented by bovine beach bums. Nearby is the **Hillside House Hostel** (tel. (066) 682 28; £4; showers 50p). Three hostels on **Valenia Island,** and the **IYHF youth hostel** in **Ballinskelligs** (tel. (0667) 92 29; £4.30-5.50; open April-Sept.) provide good bases for a venture to the **Skellig Rocks,** a cluster of steep offshore crags crowned by an ancient monastic settlement (ask locally; trip £15). You can also get there from **Waterville,** once the summer roost of Charlie Chaplin, where the Bob Dylan-playing 15-bed **Peter's Place** (tel. (0667) 41 61) provides an alternative to the athletic-mad **Waterville Leisure Center** (tel. (0667) 44 00; £5, showers 50p; weights; climbing wall). Hostels dot the rockily scenic route along the southern coast back to **Kenmare,** famous for its stone circle (50p, always open). Kenmare's **tourist office** (tel. (064) 412 33; open late June to early Sept. Mon.-Sat. 10am-6pm, closed 1 hr. for lunch), banks, and restaurants are all along its wide Main St. Henry St. is chock full of grocery stores and intimate pubs. Opposite the **post office** on Henry St. (open Mon.-Fri. 9am-1pm and 2-5:30pm, Sat. 9am-1pm) is the warm and comfortable **Fáilte Hostel** (tel. (064) 410 83), a well-groomed independent hostel. (Kitchen facilities. No lockout or curfew. Dorms £4. Private rooms £5.50 per person. Showers 50p.) **Finnegan's,** several doors down, rents bikes for £6 per day; £3 per half-day; £30 per week (bring ID as deposit).

North of Killarney, it's an easy bus ride to **Tralee,** a town whose redeeming features are its **Siamsa Tíre Theatre,** Godfrey Pl. (tel. (066) 230 55), Ireland's national folk theater (shows May-Sept., tickets £4-6) and bus links to **Dingle Town,** in the heart of the Dingle Peninsula. (Hitching is weak.) Despite ladles of tourists, Dingle retains charm, crafts and outstanding traditional music: try **O'Flaherty's** (Bridge St.) and **An Droichead Beag** (Lower Main St.). Unless you want to shell out £10 for one of the B&Bs on **Dykegate Street,** head out Strand St. to the crowded **Westlodge/Westgate Hostel** (tel. (066) 514 76; curfew 2am; £4.30; camping £2; kitchen), or the much nicer **Rainbow Hostel** (½ mi. west, £5). Rent a bike at **Moriarty's** on Main St. (tel. (066) 513 16; £4 per day, £20 per week, £7 deposit) to see the historical site-studded western tip of the Irish-speaking peninsula. On the road to **Dunquin** landowners charge 50-75p to see **Dunbeg Fort** and **beehive huts** built by early Christian monks. From Dunquin Pier, summer ferries (round-trip £7) shuttle to the **Blasket Islands,** uninhabited for much of the year. Dunquin's **IYHF youth hostel** (tel. (066) 561 21) lies opposite the pier. (£3.80-5.50. Sheets 60p. Kitchen. Curfew midnight.) The narrow **Conor Pass** between Tralee and Dingle Town is often shrouded in clouds, but almost overly dramatic on a sunny day.

Counties Limerick and Clare

County Limerick's monotonous farmlands and dullsville capital will quicken your pace either north to Clare or south to captivating Kerry. Limerick City's **tourist office** is on Arthur's Quay (tel. (061) 31 75 22; open Mon.-Fri. 9am-6:30pm, Sat.-Sun. 9:30am-5:30pm). The bus and train station is off Parnell St.; buy your Expressway bus ticket inside. (For train info, call (061) 31 55 55; bus info, call (061) 31 33 33.) **Limerick Hostel,** George's Quay (tel. (061) 452 22), though understaffed, offers spacious double rooms for £4.50. (No curfew. Kitchen.) The **IYHF youth hostel,** at 1 Pery Sq. (tel. (061) 31 46 72), just around the corner from the station, diagonally opposite the People's Park, is often crammed. (Curfew midnight. £4.30-5.90. Sheets 50p. Kitchen. Bike rental £5 per day, £25 per week.) Otherwise peruse the B&Bs (£10-12) on Ennis Rd. across the River Shannon.

County Clare has a stunning coastline and a thriving traditional music scene. The 700-ft. **Cliffs of Moher** plunge dramatically into the choppy, cold Atlantic; the observation point bristles with tourists, but you can roam along the cliffs for miles. Tiny **Doolin,** 5 mi. north, merits its universal accolades for its traditional music: both **O'Connor's** and **McGann's** pubs have won awards. The large whitewashed **Doolin Hostel** (tel. (065) 740 06), runs its own shop, currency exchange and bike rental (£5 per day, £10 deposit). (No curfew. £4.95. Kitchen and laundry.) Alternatively, try the small, cheery **Rainbow Hostel** (tel. (065) 744 15) or the stone-floored **Aille River Hostel** (tel. (065) 742 60; open mid-March to mid-Jan.). Both charge £4.50. The **campsite** (tel. (065) 741 27) at the harbor costs £1.50 per tent plus £1 per person (showers 50p; kitchen and laundry).

North of Doolin, the **Burren** is a 100 sq. mile lunar landscape of tortured limestone formations and rare wildflowers. The **Burren Tourist Hostel,** (tel. 743 00), situated in Lisdoonvarna, ranks among Ireland's best hostels, with exquisite woodwork and a pub on the premises featuring good food (£3-5) and nightly set dancing in summer (£4; doubles £5; kitchen). **Johnston's Hostel** (tel. (091) 371 64), Main St., Kinvara, on the northeastern edge of the Burren, also serves as a springboard to **Coole Park** (on the N18), the erstwhile home of W.B. Yeats. (Open May-Sept. 10am-6pm. £2.50, students £2.)

Transportation in the area is scanty. Buses wheeze from Galway, Limerick, and Ennis to Doolin, Lisdoonvarna and Kinvara (3 per day in summer, one on Sun.); an often-full post bus leaves the Ennis post office to Liscannor and Doolin (1 per day Mon.-Sat.; £1). Hitching drags its heels; rent a bike at the Doolin Hostel or Burke's Garage, Lisdoonvarna (£7 per day).

Galway City

Coastal Galway shines in Irish drama and music; perched at the edge of part o' the *Gaeltacht* (Irish-speaking area), it provides a good base for trips to Ireland's wild west. Crafts, wholefood cafés, leprechauns and other assorted characters abound in the cobblestoned **Quay St.** area; take in a show (£2-6) at the **Druid Theatre Company** (tel. 686 17) or the **Punchbag Theatre** (tel. (091) 654 22), both off Quay St., or make merry to Irish music at **Quays Pub** and **Seaghan Ua Neachtain,** both *on* Quay St. Dance knaughtily at **Kno-Kno's Knite Klub,** Eglinton St. (opens at 10pm; £2 cover). Art lovers pour into the city for the two-week **Galway Arts Festival,** which attracts Ireland's finest performers, and the carnival-like **Busking Festival** (July or August).

Grassy, fountained Eyre Sq. centers the town. The **tourist office,** Victoria Pl., off Eyre Sq. (tel. (091) 630 81), does bookings (£1 fee) and plans voyages to the Aran Islands. (Open Mon.-Sat. 9am-6:45pm; Sept.-June Mon.-Sat. 9am-5:45pm., Sun. 1:30-4:30pm). One block away is the **train and bus station** (tel. (091) 621 41; office open July-Aug. Mon.-Fri. 8:30am-8pm, Sat. 8:30am-6pm, Sun. 10am-6pm; Sept.-June Mon.-Sat. 9am-6pm). Change money at the **Bank of Ireland,** 43 Eyre Sq. (open Mon.-Fri. 10am-12:30pm and 1:30-3pm, Thurs. until 5pm); mail letters at the **post office** on Eglinton St. (open Mon.-Sat. 9am-5:30pm, Wed. from 9:30am). Rent bikes on the ramp under the station for £5 per day, £25 per week. (Open daily 9am-6pm; free panniers.)

Hostels multiply daily in Galway. The aging but roomy **Corrib Villa,** 4 Waterside (tel. (091) 628 92), down Eglinton St. past the courthouse, costs £4.50. (No curfew. Showers 20p. Kitchen.) Upper Dominick St. has two lively ones: the carpeted **Arch View Hostel,** 1 Upper Dominick St. (tel. (091) 666 61), across from Monroe's Tavern (£5.50; Oct.-May £4.50) and the shabbily spontaneous **Owens** (tel. (091) 662 11, but no phone reservations; no curfew; £5; kitchen). Or try the disco- and youth-packed suburb of Salthill, 1½ mi. southwest of Galway (take bus #1) for the well-vacuumed **The Grand,** Promenade (tel. (091) 211 50; no curfew; £5; kitchen) and the dusky mirror-lined **Stella Maris Hostel,** 151 Upper Salthill. (No curfew. July-Sept. £6. Oct.-June £5. Kitchen.) B&Bs fester in Salthill; **Mrs. S. O'Kelly,** Grianan, 12 Glenard Ave., Salthill (tel. (091) 221 51), a fairy godmother, beds you and then feeds you a continental breakfast for £6; £9 for full fry. Fortify dwindling supplies at the **Roches Stores** supermarket at the northwestern corner of Eyre Sq. (open Mon.-Thurs. and Sat. 9am-5:30pm, Fri. 9am-9pm), but do your eating on Quay St.: at the cheap (under £3) and filling **Hungry Grass** (just around the corner on Cross St.; open Mon.-Wed. 8:30am-6pm, Thurs.-Sat. 8:30am-9pm, Sun. noon-6pm) or **Sev'nth Heav'n,** where out-of-this-world chowder and brown bread costs a mere £1.50 (open daily noon-midnight).

Connemara and the Aran Islands

West of Galway, the unmolested coastline rises into the flowing mountains of **Connemara.** From Galway to Clifden, take the public bus that goes via Cong and behold Connemara's most exquisite meadows and lakes. In **Clifden,** at Connemara's Atlantic edge, rent a bike at **Mannions** to probe the beckoning environs. (£6 per day, £30 per week; open Mon.-Sat. 9:30am-7pm.) Stay at **Leo's Hostel,** Beach Rd. (tel. (095) 214 29) for £4.50, or choose a B&B on Main St. or Bridge St. over the musty, dirty **Clifden Hostel and Camping** (tel. (095) 212 19; also £4.50, camping £2). The **tourist office** (tel. (095) 211 63; open June to mid-Sept. Mon.-Sat. 9am-7pm, Sun. 10am-6pm), on Market St., will send you north to Cleggan for ferry trips (£10 return) to the glorious white strands of the island of **Inishbofin.**

Sleep in the **Old Monastery Hostel,** (tel. (095) 411 32), in Letterfrack (£5), 11 mi. from Clifden at the entrance to the **Connemara National Park** (open May-Sept. daily 10am-6:30pm; admission £1, families £3, students and children 40p), or continue 2½ mi. east to **Kylemore Abbey,** a multi-turreted 19th-century castle from which Benedictine nuns chastely admire the lakes and towering hills. Camp on any of the coast **beaches,** or continue to Ireland's only fjord, where the **Killary Harbour Youth Hostel (IYHF)** (tel. (095) 434 17) appreciates the dramatic vista. (£3.80-5.50. Open March-Oct.) A daily bus traverses the Clifden-Westport route past these treasures; thumbing produces better results on the main road than on tiny byways.

The southern coast of Connemara cradles Galway's **Gaeltacht,** the epicenter of Irish language, music, and folk traditions. **Spiddal,** 14 mi. west of Galway, hosts **currach races** (small boats made from wicker rods and covered with cowskin), small festivals, and nightly performances of traditional music and dance at the **Ceol na Mara** (cultural entertainment center). Stay at the **Spiddal Village hostel** (tel. (091) 835 55) for £5 or venture 8 mi. west to the **Indreabhán (Inverin) Youth Hostel (IYHF)** (tel. (091) 931 54), which will relieve you of £4.30-5.90 for a night's stay.

Plan your trip to the **Aran Islands** at the Galway tourist office. The quickest crossings leave from Rossaveal (25 min., £12 return, bikes free, shuttle bus from Galway to Rossaveal £3 return). The rugged granite of ancient cliffside fortresses and miles of crisscrossing stone walls share the islands with an Irish-speaking fishing community and a warm tradition of knitwear; increasingly, tourism plays a role. On **Inishmore,** the largest of the islands, the **tourist office** (tel. (099) 612 63) will find you a room in one of many B&Bs. (Open June-Sept. daily 10:30am-6pm.) Book ahead in the spacious, convivial **Mainstir House Hostel** (tel. (099) 611 99; £6.50 with breakfast) to avoid the stuffed-to-the-gills **Aran Islands Hostel** (tel. (099) 612 55), on the pier (£5). Hop a boat to **Inishmaan** (most culturally active of the Arans) or beach-blessed **Inisheer,** where the **Bru Hostel** (tel. (099) 750 24) organizes currach trips. (£5.50. Open all year.)

County Mayo

Mostly a flat, barren peat bog buffeted by Atlantic tempests, Mayo rises towards its southern border into Connemara's dramatic hills. The two lakes of Lough Mask and Lough Corrib stretch between Counties Mayo and Galway; stay in the **Lough Corrib Hostel** (tel. (091) 826 34) in **Oughterard** for trips to the murder hole in **Aughnanure Castle** (open June-Sept. 10am-6pm; 80p; students 30p) or take the hostel-run boat trips (£5) to **Inchagoill Island** with its early Christian **Stone of Lugna,** ancient tombstone of St. Patrick's nephew and navigator. Stuck between the two lakes, the village of **Cong** boasts a 12th-century abbey open to the public, and **Ashford Castle,** where the Guinness family once reigned as King of Cong, now a luxury hotel from which the *Corrib Queen* departs for Inchagoill Island (£7). The spacious **Quiet Man Hostel,** Abbey St. (tel. (092) 465 11), shows the John Wayne flick, filmed locally, every night. (June-Sept. £5.50, April-May £4.95. Bike rental £5. Open April-Sept.) *Get to Know Cong,* a free guide detailing limestone caves, early Christian churches, Oscar Wilde's childhood home, and other local wonders, is available at the **tourist office,** Abbey St. (Open June-Sept. daily 9am-6pm.)

At the end of the train line from Dublin (1-3 per day, 3¾ hr.), the pretty 18th-century planned town of **Westport** sits at the base of island-speckled **Clew Bay.** On the last Sunday in July, over 60,000 pilgrims (many barefoot) hike up the holy mountain of **Croagh Patrick,** 6 mi. west of Westport, where St. Patrick supposedly fasted, prayed and banished snakes. Across from the train station, the large **Club Atlantic,** Altamount St. (tel. (098) 266 44) has all the amenities (£4.30-5.90); Louisburg Rd. leads to the spartan **Granary Hostel** (tel. (098) 259 03), one mile from town with outdoor showers (£4 per night), and the Georgian **Summerville Hostel,** which features a soul-calming atmosphere and a Kodak moment of Clew Bay, two mi. from town (tel. (098) 259 48; £4.50 per person. Open mid-March to mid-Oct.). The **tourist office,** North Mall (tel. (098) 257 11; open Mon.-Fri. 9am-7pm, Sat. 10am-1pm; off-season Mon.-Fri. 9am-1pm and 2-5:15pm) will fill you in on Westport's wonders, including musical **Matt Molloy's** pub, and the vegetarian-satisfying **Crockery Pot,** both on Bridge St. Westport sends several buses daily west to the wild beaches, mountains and cliffs of **Achill Island. Wild Haven Hostel** (tel. (098) 453 92) in **Achill Sound,** is the island's finest. (£5 per person, light breakfast £2; kitchen facilities.)

County Sligo

William Butler Yeats spent his youthful summers in Sligo and landscaped his poetry with its countryside. But this was an area rich in mythic tales long before Yeats' time; the remains of early warfare between Connaught and Ulster—cairns, dolmens, passage graves, and ring forts—pockmark Carrowmore, near serene **Sligo town.** The River Garavogue lollygags through the town itself, whose most prominent ruin is the **Dominican Abbey** (c. 1250), Abbey St., with a well-preserved cloister and pillars. The **County Museum,** Stephen St., contains one of the finest collections of modern Irish art in the country and numerous Yeats first editions. (Open Tues.-Sat. 10:30am-12:30pm and 2:30-4:30pm. Free.) The writer's simple grave lies 4 mi. north of town in Drumcliffe Churchyard. Take the Donegal bus. In town, the **White House Hostel,** Markievicz Rd. (tel. (071) 451 60) offers a hip, happening ambience and a "mystical" breakfast of toast and iffy coffee (£5). Farther out, the **Eden Hill Hostel,** Pearse Rd. (tel. (071) 432 04), opposite the second Esso station, has great facilities (laundry and bikes for rent), but sagging beds and untidy bathrooms (£5). For accommodations bookings (£1), free city maps, and information on the area, visit the **tourist office** on Temple St. (tel. (071) 612 01; open July-Aug. Mon.-Sat. 9am-8pm, Sun. 10am-2pm; June Mon.-Sat. 9am-6pm; Sept.-May Mon.-Fri. 9am-5pm). **Kate's Kitchen** on Market St. has fantastic choose-your-makings sandwiches (£1.50-2.50) and quiche (£2; open Mon.-Sat. 9am-6pm).

During the **Yeats International Summer School's** two-week August session, Sligo comes alive with Yeats plays, poetry readings, and traditional Irish music. Try to see a show at the **Hawk's Well Theatre,** beneath the tourist office (tel. (071) 615 26), which has rapidly become the drama center of the northwest. (Box office open Mon.-Sat. 2-6pm; tickets sold at the tourist office Mon.-Sat. 10am-2pm. Tickets around £5, students £3.) **T.D.'s Lounge** has an enthusiastic crowd and synthesizer-saddled sound. For slightly beefier tunes, try **McLynn's** on Market St., **Feehily's** on Bridge St., or the Tuesday night meetings at the **Sligo Trades Club** on Castle St. (£2 cover). Post-pubbing generally goes on at the **Clarence** on Wine St., with live bands and dancing.

County Donegal

Mountainous and barren even by Irish standards, this northernmost Irish county is a land of silent peat bogs, fierce sea winds, and cliffs of biblical proportions. Tourists do visit, but outside the main towns of Donegal and Letterkenny the vastness of the elements easily digests them. Brave the wind-driven rain and spend some time hiking or fishing in this primitive wilderness.

The **tourist office** (tel. (073) 211 48), on the Sligo road just south off the Diamond, the main square in Donegal Town, books accommodations for £1. (Open July-Aug. Mon.-Sat. 9am-8pm, Sun. 10am-2pm; May-June and Sept. Mon.-Sat. 10am-6pm.) The **Peter Feely Hostel** (tel. (073) 220 30), a two-minute walk from the Diamond on the Killybegs road, has jam-packed rooms and a witty warden. (£4.50. Free shower. Kitchen facilities.) The commodious **Ball Hill Youth Hostel (IYHF)** (tel. (073) 211 74), 3 mi. away (continue down the Killybegs road and turn left at the signpost), commands a rowboat as well as a great view of the harbor. (£4.50; under 18 £3.50. Camping £3. Kitchen facilities.) Restaurants in town are puny and weak, but try the respectable **Errigal's Restaurant,** on Main St. (open daily 10am-11pm). Stock up on basics at the **Foodland** supermarket in the Diamond (open Mon.-Fri. 9am-7pm, Sat. 9am-6:30pm). **Schooners** on Upper Main St. is a hopping pub with live music most nights.

From Donegal buses run west to **Killybegs,** a well-worn port with exceptionally amiable inhabitants (wave back). (Mon.-Sat. 5 per day; late Aug.-early July Mon.-Sat. 3 per day). The **Hollybush Hostel** (tel. (073) 311 18) is 1 mi. east of Killybegs on the main Donegal road, attached to a pub (£4, showers 50p, camping £2; kitchen facilities open all year). Buses from Killybegs continue westwards to **Glencolumbkille** (Mon.-Sat. 2 per day); the comfortable **Derrylahan Hostel** (tel. (073) 380 79) lies on the coast road between Kilcar (8 mi. west of Killybegs) and Carrick (several miles farther on). (£3.50, showers 50p, camping £2. Laundry facilities and well-stocked shop.) From **Carrick,** journey up to the 325m cliffs of **Slieve League.** The path marked "Bunglass" affords even better views than the one to Slieve League and gets you to the summit just the same. A 5-mi. walk southwest of Glencolumbkille will bring you to **Malibeg,** a happy hamlet on the edge of a sandy cove. A 1-mi. walk up the hill behind the folk museum in Glencolumbkille leads to the **Dooey Hostel** (tel. (073) 301 30; £4.50) set into the craggy hillside, run by a pair of wonderful wardens who've seen it all.

The **Glengesh Pass,** the road from Glencolumbkille northeast to Ardara, makes a truly lusty bike ride. Hikers might want to stick to the coast of the peninsula; every headland reveals another helping of Ireland's most tragic coastal scenery. North of Ardara rise the **Derryveagh Mountains,** completely unspoiled hiking territory with **IYHF youth hostels** at **Crohy Head** (tel. (075) 213 30), 5 mi. west of Dungloe (£3.80, under 18 £3; open April-Oct.); **Aranmore Island** (no phone; £3.50, under 18 £3; open May-Sept.), 10 mi. north of Crohy Head; and **Errigal** (tel. (075) 311 80), 1 mi. west of the village of Dunlewy (£4.30, under 18 £3.50; open March-Oct.).

Letterkenny is the proverbial college town of the north. The **tourist office** (tel. (074) 211 60) is a little out of town on the Donegal road. The independent hostel on High Rd. (tel. (074) 252 38) has spacious accommodations and bedrooms you'd actually want to spend time in. (£3.50. No curfew. No lockout.) The **Swilly** bus service (6 per day) connects Letterkenny to Derry in Northern Ireland.

ITALY

USD\$1 = 1311 lire (L, or ITL)
CAD\$1 = L1147
GBP£1 = L2190
AUD\$1 = L1021
NZD\$1 = L747
Country Code: 39

L1000 = USD\$0.76
L1000 = CAD\$0.87
L1000 = GBP£0.46
L1000 = AUD\$0.98
L1000 = NZD\$1.34
International Dialing Prefix: 00

You may have the universe if I may have Italy.
—Giuseppe Verdi

Massive, rough-hewn medieval walls still encircle many of Italy's cities. In past centuries they insulated communities from the mayhem of the outside world, encouraging the development of highly original artistic and architectural styles, dialects, and customs. Though the asphalt and steel of the 20th century have long since broken the rough stone seal, a proud individualism persists in each city, expressing itself in political and regional particularities. If it's not politics, it's soccer, and if not soccer, then wine which provokes lusty disagreement. Since the fall of Mussolini and the fascists, Italy (Italia) has seen no less than 47 governments, the result of an electoral system that gives power to even the smallest of parties, necessitating unwieldy and fractured coalitions. Regionalism persists: the blue-eyed, Alpine North speaks with a German-forked tongue, while the Southern olive-growing regions have hearty, Latin spirits. The culturally cosmpolitan, fashion-oriented Romans and Florentines deny fraternity with either set.

A trip through the history of Italy (Italia) begins beneath the grassy hills of Tarquinia, in the brightly painted tombs of the Etruscans; this highly developed civilization ruled central Italy centuries before the beginning of the Common Era. In Sicily, the Greeks honored their gods with soaring temples in white marble. Traces of the vast Roman Empire define the landscape, from the monumental amphitheaters of Rome and Verona to the volcanically embalmed towns of Pompeii and Herculaneum. Somber early Christian churches, sparkling with Byzantine frescoes, distinguish Ravenna as a treasure house of early medieval culture, while San Gimignano bristles with the forbidding towers of the later Middle Ages, a time when perceptive potentates from emperors to popes grappled for their share of prime Mediterranean beachfront property. Florence preserves the Italian Renaissance at its most intoxicating.

For more detailed coverage than can be offered here, turn to *Let's Go: Italy.*

Getting There and Getting Around

Italian **trains** run on time, more or less, and the rail network is comprehensive. A *locale* stops at nearly every station; the *diretto* is rather more direct, while the *espresso* is considerably faster. The *rapido* zooms along, but requires a *supplemento* (Eurailpass and InterRail holders exempt); this should be purchased ahead of time along with your ticket. The price may quadruple if you board the train without a supplement. The *Biglietto Chilometrico* is good for 20 trips amounting to 3000km and can be used for two months by as many as five people. The ticket can be purchased for L120,000 at any Italian rail station. If you have no railpass and are under 26, the **cartaverde,** only L10,000, is a must. Showing this card entitles you to a 20-30% discount on rail tickets. The *Nuovo Orario delle Ferrovie* lists state train lines, hours, and prices (L3500 at newsstands).

Intercity **buses** are often preferable to trains on shorter hauls off the main rail lines, especially when the geography—the hills of Umbria and Tuscany, for example—prevents trains from pulling directly into town. For **city buses,** buy tickets in *tabacchi* stores, or most newsstands, and validate them on board. The *autostrade* (super-highways) are gorgeous celebrations of engineering and relatively uncrowded (except in Aug.), but gas and tolls are prohibitive, and Italian drivers crazed speed demons. **Mopeds** can be a great way to see the islands and the more rural areas of Italy, but are potentially disastrous and stressful in unknown major cities, where you should stick to public transportation. **Bicycling** is a popular national sport but not always pleasant. Bike trails are rare, drivers often reckless, and except in the Po Valley, the terrain challenges even the fittest. **Touring Club Italiano** maps are invaluable for drivers, hitchers and bikers. Detailed regional maps are available free in most tourist offices.

Practical Information

Italian tourist offices come in two varieties: the bureaucratic **Ente Provinciale per il Turismo (EPT),** in the largest cities, and the fuzzier **Azienda Autonoma di Turismo** nearly everywhere else. Most offices can usually help you find a room.

Any knowledge of Spanish, French, Portuguese, or Latin will help you understand Italian. Most tourist office staff speak at least some English. If your conversation partner speaks Italian too quickly, kindly ask them to *rallenta* (rah-LEN-ta, slow down).

Italy's cathedrals are religious institutions and not museums. Don't visit during mass, and cover your legs and shoulders; the more neatly and conservatively you dress, the better you'll be treated.

Italian men have a tarnished reputation, well-deserved. Women may encounter unwanted attention; no response at all is often more effective than a show of anger or disgust.

Festivals are a significant aspect of life in Italy. Events such as **il Palio** in Siena (July 2 and Aug. 16), the **Carnevale** in Venice (early March), and the bizarre **Corsa dei Ceri** in Gubbio (May 15) have age-old histories and rituals. August, especially the weeks around the 15th, is vacation month for most Italians; the cities are closed up and empty. Summers are humid and hot in the north, drier and hotter with every step south. In general, early afternoon is good for nothing but a *siesta* (snooze). Winters are ferocious in the Alps and cold and damp in Venice, Florence, and Rome, but Sicilian waters are swimmable year-round.

Just about everything closes from 1 to 3 or 4pm. Museum hours vary, but most are open from 9am to 1pm and some again from 4 to 7pm. Monday is the *giorno di chiusura* (day of closure) for most museums. In general, banks are open from 8:30am to 12:30pm and 2:30 to 4pm.

Many of Italy's pay phones demand *gettoni,* L200 tokens sold in bars and *tabacchi,* and are also accepted as L200 change, but most take coins and cards. Magnetic phone cards are more convenient (sold in L5000 and L10,000 units from *tabacchi* and SIP agencies). For AT&T's **USA Direct,** use your phone card or deposit L200 (which will be returned), then dial 172 10 11. **SIP** and **ASST,** the state phone companies, as well as some post offices, allow you to talk first and pay later *(telefono a scatte).* Many bars also have this option. **Fermo posta** is the Italian for Poste Restante.

Accommodations and Camping

The Italian hostel federation **(AIG)** operates dozens of youth hostels *(ostelli della gioventù)* across the country, especially in the north. A complete list is available from most EPT and CTS offices and from many hostels. Prices average about L12,000 or 13,000 per night, including breakfast. The hostels that require IYHF cards charge L5000 extra for nonmembers. Cards can be purchased at many hostels for L30,000. Hostels are the best option for solo travelers (single rooms are relatively scarce in hotels), but curfews, lockouts, and out-of-the-way locations detract from their charm. Two or more people can often stay almost as cheaply in a hotel. Convents are an alternative to hostels. Singles are quiet, clean, and cost about L15,000; doubles L20,000. Their curfews are even earlier than the hostels, usually around 10pm. No Twister in the buff, either.

The hotel industry is rigorously controlled in Italy; the prices of all rooms are set not by private owners but by the state. Under Italian law all guests must be registered by passport on a special form, so check the room *first,* and then don't be afraid to hand it over for a while (usually overnight). One-star *pensioni* are the best budget option. Prices fluctuate by region, but singles usually start at L19,000; doubles, at L30,000. By law, the price must be posted on the door of each room; if it isn't, get it in writing from the management. It is illegal to charge more than what's posted. Always check to see if tax (IVA), breakfast, and shower privileges are included and/or mandatory. For doubles, specify *doppia* (2 beds) or a *letto matrimoniale* (double bed). A triple should cost no more than 135% the price of a double. A private bath *(con bagno)* usually costs at least L5000 extra. *Affitta camere* (rooms to let in private residences) sometimes cost significantly less. An even better value in most large cities are the **Protezione della Giovane,** dorms run by religious orders for women travelers only. Quality is high, and beds average only L10,000, but there are usually curfews. Try to reach your destination and begin looking for accommodations before noon, especially during the summer. If you must arrive late, call and reserve the day before.

Camping sites tend to be loud and modern and may run as high as L12,000 per person plus L6000 per tent, even higher in big cities. No all-inclusive guide to Italian campsites exists, but the *Euro Camping* guide to Italy and Corsica is a good start and widely available (L9500), as are tourist office lists.

Food and Drink

"*Mangia, mangia!*" The production, preparation, and loving consumption of food are all close to the core of Italian culture. For simple, hearty, and inexpensive eating, try *alimentari* stores; they often whip up *panini* (sandwiches), with fresh local salami and slices of excellent Italian cheese—*groviera, Bel Paese, provolone,* or the divinely rich *parmigiano* (parmesan). *Rosticerie* sell hot foods to take out, and often are the cheapest option for a filling dinner. Local markets *(mercati)* also offer these delicacies, along with the freshest produce, although supermarkets are often cheaper. A *tavola calda* is a cheap, sit-down option, as is the student *mensa* in every university town. *Osterie, trattorie,* and *ristoranti* are, in roughly ascending order, fancier and more expensive. They are usually open from 12:30 to 2pm and 7 to 11pm (later in the south). Menus in smaller restaurants are often incomplete or nonexistent; ask for the *piatti del giorno* (daily specials). A *menù turistico,* when offered, might run only L13,000-16,000 for a full meal, but variety is limited. Sit-down establishments charge *pane e coperto* (a bread and cover charge), with luck not far above L1500-2500. Check whether service is included *(servizio compreso).*

A full meal consists of an *antipasto* (appetizer); a *primo piatto,* pasta or soup; a *secondo piatto,* meat or fish with a vegetable *(contorno);* and usually salad, fruit, and/or cheese. As one travels south, spice and tomatoes play an increasingly significant role. By the time you reach Naples, the standard pasta dish beads the brow with sweat. Pastries also get progressively sweeter, reaching an all-time glucose high in the sinfully sugary *marzipan* of Sicily.

Coffee is also a focus of Italian life. *Espresso* is meant to be quaffed quickly. *Cappucino,* a mixture of *espresso* and hot, frothy milk, is the normal breakfast beverage. *Caffè macchiato* (literally, "spotted coffee") is *espresso* with a touch of milk, while *latte macchiato* is milk with a splash of coffee. Perhaps the best finish to a delicious meal is a *caffè corretto* ("corrected coffee"), *espresso* spiked with your favorite liqueur. Beginning with the delicate white *Asti Spumante* from Piedmont and *Soave* from Verona, Italian local wines get rougher and earthier on the way south, although there are numerous exceptions. Italian beer leaves something to be desired. Drink Peroni or Wührer only if there are no imports in sight.

Bars are a good place to sample wines, eat breakfast, and stop for snacks. They also serve a colorful collection of Italian liqueurs. Try *grappa,* the gut-wrenching liqueur of the Veneto flavored with various fruits, and *sambuca,* a sweet Roman concoction served with coffee beans in it. Sitting down at a table doubles the price of anything you order. In almost every Italian town you can find numerous shops selling Italy's greatest contribution to civilization save *Aida: gelato.* Look for the *produzione propria* (homemade) sign. Also delicious on hot summer days are *granite* ("Italian ices") and *frullati* (cool fruit shakes), guaranteed to drop your temperature.

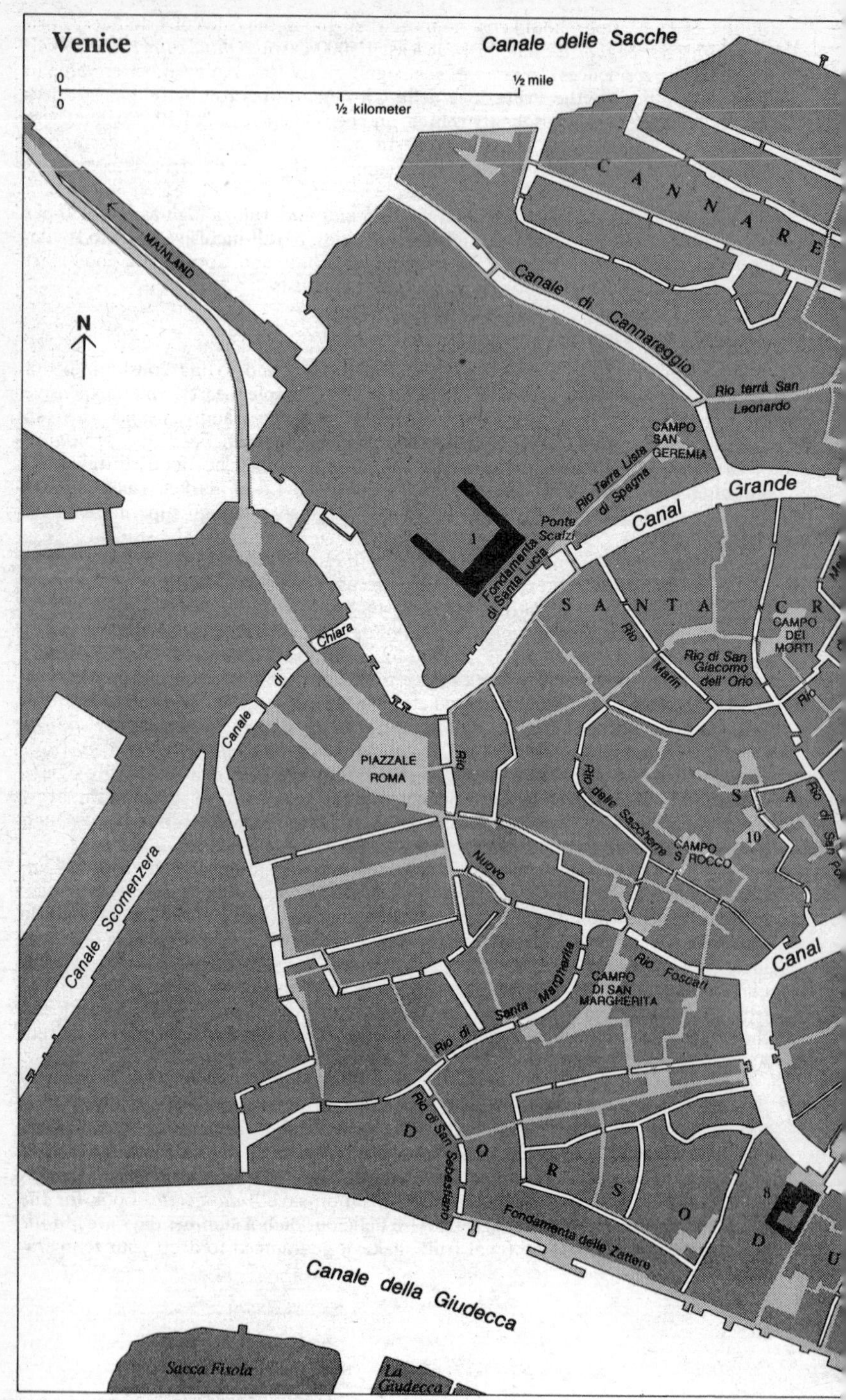
Venice
Canale delle Sacche
0 ½ mile
0 ½ kilometer
MAINLAND
N
CANNARE
Canale di Cannareggio
Rio terrà San Leonardo
CAMPO SAN GEREMIA
Rio Terra Lista di Spagna
Ponte Scalzi
Fondamenta di Santa Lucia
Canal Grande
1
SANTA CR
Rio Marin
Rio di San Giacomo dell' Orio
CAMPO DEI MORTI
Chiara
Canale di
PIAZZALE ROMA
Rio Nuovo
Rio delle Sacchere
CAMPO S. ROCCO
10
S A
Canal
Rio Foscari
CAMPO DI SAN MARGHERITA
Rio di Santa Margherita
Canale Scomenzera
Rio di San Sebastiano
D O R S O D U
8
Fondamenta delle Zattere
Canale della Giudecca
Sacca Fisola
La Giudecca

1 Train Station
2 Post Office
3 Amex
4 IYHF
5 Piazza San Marco
6 Palazzo Ducale (Doge's Palace)
7 Campo San Salvatore
8 Gallerie dell'Accademia
9 Church of S. Maria Della Salute
10 Campo dei Frari
11 Church of San Zaccaria
12 Campo S. Giorgio
13 Campo SS. Giovanni e Paolo
14 Church of S. Maria Formosa
15 Teatro Goldoni
Canale delle Navi
Sacca della Misericordia
MURANO
Cimitero San Michele
Strada Nova
Rio di Noale
Rio di San Felica
CAMPO DEI S.S. APOSTOLI
Rio dei Mendicanti
Rio di San Marina
Barbaria delle Tole
Rio delle due Torri
Rio di San Cassiano
Ponte Rialto
CAMPO DI SAN POLO
POLO
Rio delle Madonnetta
Grande
Rio di San Salvador
Calle dei Fabbri
Rio della Guerra
Rio di Palazzo o della Paglina
CASTELLO
Rio San Lorenzo
Rio dei Greci
Rio di San Luca
CAMPO MANIN
CAMPO SAN ANGELO
SAN MARCO
CAMPO SAN STEFANO
Rio dei Barcaroli
Rio delle Ostreghe
Rio di San Moise
Molo
Riva degli Schiavoni
Canale di S. Marco
LIDO
San Giorgio Maggiore

Northern Italy

If the regionally chauvinistic Northern Italians weren't forced to give money to the South, they might renovate and beautify themselves into another Switzerland. There's little grime here in Italy's knee-cuff, only the snow-capped heights of the Valle d'Aosta's 4000m glaciers and the icy name-dropping of Milan's fashion-conscious elite. Along the western border fluency in French is *de rigeur,* while all things Germanic thrive in the neighborhood of the Brenner Pass. To the east, the dialects and Slavic affinities of Fruili-Venezia Giulia's pastoral backwaters fade into the fertile expanses of the Po Valley and the much-touristed sophistication of Venice's *piazze* and *palazzi.*

Venice (Venezia)

In Italo Calvino's *Invisible Cities,* Marco Polo admits to Kubla Khan that all his descriptions of fabulous cities are but feeble attempts to capture one city—Venice. The inner islands of the Venetian lagoon were originally settled by Roman citizens fleeing the wrath of Atilla, and the slap-dab community of refugees achieved economic stability by exporting salt. Young Venice gained a proper patron when its wily sailors smuggled the remains of St. Mark out of Alexandria, and proper ornamentation when it sent the impecunious soldiers of the fourth Crusade to sack Constantinople; by the 15th century, the clever Republic controlled much of the Roman overseas empire. The Venice of today has little to do with such humble origins or loftier days of glory. The modern Venetian economy is entirely dependent upon tourism, and judging from the 10 million that flock yearly to the island of canals, an army of Huns brandishing swords on the mainland could hardly increase the city's appeal. From the universally recognized domes of San Marco to the automobile-free silences of the more remote *piazze,* Venice's artistic and cultural merits are legitimate, and cannot be tarnished by the superficiality of the tourist trade.

Orientation and Practical Information

Situated at the northern tip of the Adriatic, Venice is linked by ferry to Yugoslavia, Greece, and the Middle East, and by rail to major European cities. If arriving by train, get off at **Santa Lucia** train station *(Venezia S.L.).* The Santa Lucia stop is at the northwest corner of the Venetian islands and just across the Grand Canal from **piazzale Roma.** To get to **San Marco** (and the central tourist office) directly, take *vaporetto* (canal boat) #2 from the station or piazzale Roma. For a splendid introduction to the *palazzi* along the stately **Canal Grande,** take #1 or 34. You can easily walk to San Marco—just follow the signs. The city is a confusing maze, but the tourist office in the train station and ACTV information office in p. Roma distribute free maps to minimize disorientation.

The main part of Venice is divided into six *sestieri,* or districts: **San Marco, Castello, San Polo, Santa Croce, Cannaregio,** and **Dorsoduro.** Within each section, there are no individual street numbers, but one long sequence of numbers (roughly 6000 per *sestiere)* that wind their way haphazardly through the district. Every building is also located on a "street"—*fondamenta, salizzada, calle, via, campo, piazza, piazzale*—and *Let's Go* also lists these wherever possible. Always be sure you're looking in the proper *sestiere;* some street names are duplicated and no *sestiere* boundaries are marked. Yellow signs posted all over town will direct you to and from piazza San Marco (at the border of San Marco and Castello), the Rialto Bridge (linking San Marco to San Polo), the train station *(ferrovia;* in Cannaregio), piazzale Roma (in Santa Croce) and the Accademia (in Dorsoduro). Boats plow across the lagoon regularly to Venice's two principal islands, **Giudecca** and the **Lido.**

The **Canale Grande,** Venice's main artery, is shaped like an inverted *S,* with the train station at one end and **piazza San Marco** at the other. It can be crossed on foot at only three points. The **Ponte degli Scalzi,** just outside the train station, links the sestiere of Cannaregio with San Polo and Santa Croce. **Ponte Rialto** links the northern end of San Marco with San Polo. The **Ponte Accademia** links the districts of San Marco and Dorsoduro. The remaining district, Castello, extends east of the piazza San Marco.

For current information on nightlife, events, museums, *vaporetti,* and transportation schedules, pick up the free booklet *Un Ospite di Venezia* at any tourist office, or shell out L5000 for the more comprehensive monthly *Marco Polo,* sold at newsstands.

Tourist Offices: APT (tel. 71 90 78), at the train station. Open Mon.-Fri. 9am-noon and 3-6pm, Sat. 8am-2pm. The central office is at **p. San Marco,** Ascensione, 71/F (tel. 522 63 56), under the left arcade at the opposite end of the piazza from the basilica. Open Mon.-Sat. 8:30am-7pm. A third is on the *Lido* at Gran Viale, 6/A (tel. 526 57 21). Open Mon.-Sat. 9am-2pm. All three offices distribute free maps and, for those between 15 and 26, the *Carta Giovanine* (a discount-earning youth pass; get a passport photo taken in the station). For accommodations services, go to **AVA,** p. Roma, 540d (tel. 522 74 02; smaller branch in station, tel. 71 50 16). Reservations made in one and two-star hotels with a L10,000 deposit per person.

Budget Travel: Centro Turistico Studentesco (CTS), Dorsoduro, 3252 (tel. 520 56 60), on the fondamenta Tagliapietra near campiello Squellini due west of campo Santa Margherita. Vaporetto: S. Tomà. Budget tickets available. Open Mon.-Fri. 9am-12:30pm and 3:30-6:30pm, Sat. 9am-12:30pm. Also a **Transalpino** booth (tel. 71 66 00) outside the station.

Consulates: U.K., Dorsoduro, 1051 (tel. 522 72 07), near the Accademia bridge. Open Mon.-Fri. 9am-noon and 2-4pm. The closest **U.S., Canadian,** and **Australian** consulates are in Milan. **Kiwis** should head to Rome.

Currency Exchange: Banco Ambrosiano Veneto, San Marco, 2378, across the bridge from American Express on calle Largo XXII Marza. Open Mon.-Fri. 8:20am-1pm and 2:35-4:05pm. **Banca d'America e d'Italia,** San Marco, 2217, on same street gives cash advances on Visa cards. Open Mon.-Fri. 8:30am-1:30pm and 2:45-3:45pm. If you exchange at the station, avoid the long lines and get the same extortionary rates at the Alitalia travel office outside to the left.

American Express: San Marco, 1471 (tel. 520 08 44), on salizzada San Moisè, a few blocks west of p. San Marco. Cash machine outside for cardholders. Exchange services open Mon.-Sat. 8am-8pm. All other services Mon.-Fri. 9am-5:30pm, Sat. 9am-12:30pm.

Post Office: Main branch, San Marco, 5554, at salizzada Fontego dei Tedeschi, near the eastern end of the Rialto bridge off Campo S. Bartolomeo. Poste Restante *(Fermo Posta)* here. Open Mon.-Sat. 8:15am-7pm. Another office is just through the arcades at the end of p. San Marco. Open Mon.-Fri. 8:15am-1:30pm, Sat. 8:15am-12:10pm. **Postal code:** 30124.

Telephones: ASST, in the train station. Open Mon.-Fri. 8am-7:45pm, Sat. 8am-1:45pm. Also next door to the main post office at San Marco, 5551. Open daily 8am-7:45pm. **SIP,** p. Roma. Open daily 8am-9:30pm. **City code:** 041.

Trains: Stazione di Santa Lucia (tel. 71 55 55). To: Florence (4½ hr., L16,500); Milan (3½ hr., L16,700); Bologna (2 hr., L10,800); Rome (L35,900). **Luggage storage** L1500.

Buses: ACTV, p. Roma (tel. 528 78 86). Frequent service to the villas on the Riviera del Brenta, and links to the Dolomites.

Public Transportation: The only motorized vehicles in Venice travel on water. Efficient *vaporetti* ply the Canale Grande and travel to the outlying islands. Slower boats *(accelerati)* L1800. Faster ones L2500, plus a L500 surcharge if you buy your ticket on board. Many maps, including the tourist office's, include all *vaporetto* lines and stops. Line #5 circumnavigates the city both clockwise *(destra)* and counterclockwise *(sinistra);* lines #1 and 2 both sail the Grand Canal out to the Lido. A 24-hr. pass costs L10,000; a three-day pass L17,000. Neither is a bargain unless you plan on boating all day. More practical is the *Youth Pass;* holders pay a mere L13,000 (see Tourist Offices). Valid for 3 years, a **Carta Venezia** (L10,000) entitles you to 60% discounts on all lines. Bring a passport photo to the ACTV office at the S. Angelo *vaporetto* stop. (Open Mon.-Sat. 8:30am-1pm.) Listen for news of frequent strikes *(scioperi).*

Hitchhiking: Hikers begin their odysseys in the parking lots near p. Roma 6, planting themselves (and their signs) just before the bridge that leads from the *piazzale* to the mainland. A better beginning is the entrance of the *autostrada* in Mestre.

Bookstore: Il Libraio a San Barnabà, Dorsoduro, 2835a (tel. 522 87 37), on fondamenta Gherardini, off campo San Barnabà. A broad selection of classics (including *Let's Go)* as well as Venice guides. Open unreliably Mon.-Tues. and Thurs.-Fri. 10:15am-1pm and 3:15-8pm, Wed. and Sat. 10:15am-1pm.

Laundry: Lavaget, Cannaregio, 1269, on fondamenta Pescaria next to the Ponte Guglie bridge. Open Mon.-Fri. 8:15am-12:30pm and 3-7pm. L11,000 for 3kg.

Public Baths: Albergo Diurno, San Marco, 1266, at the west end of p. San Marco. Showers L1000 (with towel L4000), toilets L500. Long lines. Luggage storage L1000. Showers open daily 8am-6:30pm. Toilets open daily 7am-8pm. More toilets near the Rialto (L200) on either side.

Pharmacy: Call 192 to find out who's on 24-hr. duty, or look in *Un Ospite di Venezia.*

Hospital: Ospedali Civili Riuniti di Venezia, campo SS. Giovanni e Paolo (tel. 529 45 17).

Medical Emergency: Ambulance, tel. 52 00 00.

Police: Headquarters *(questura),* fondamenta San Lorenzo (tel. 52 32 22). **Ufficio Stranieri** (Foreigners Office), tel. 52 07 54. **Emergencies:** tel. 113.

Accommodations and Camping

Venice is a squirming mass of tourists in summer, and expensive to boot. Make a reservation by phone at least one night before you get to Venice and be on the doorstep well before the time you agreed to arrive. By mail, a letter in English with a one-night deposit is standard. Most proprietors are reluctant to hold a cheap room; expect to be offered a room with private bath (L7000 or more extra) and mandatory breakfast (at least L5000 per person).

The tourist office at the train station is also a good place to begin your quest for a bed—as always, arrive early. You might consider bypassing Venice altogether the first day; stay in Padua, Treviso, Vicenza or Verona, and spend your first afternoon looking for accommodations in Venice. Only Padua (½ hr. by train) is close enough to stay in during your entire visit to Venice.

Hostels and dorms run by religious orders are often cheaper and invariably more vacant than cheap hotels. Women will almost always find a place at one of the dormitories run by nuns. As a last resort, try looking in the ugly bedroom community of Mestre (5 min. by train). Unofficial camping on the steps of the train station is technically prohibited.

Hostels and Dormitories

Ostello Venezia (IYHF), fondamente di Zitelle, 86C (tel. 523 82 11), on the Giudecca. Take *motoscafo* #5 *(sinistra)* from the station, #5 *(destra),* or #8 from S. Zaccaria, near S. Marco. Get off at Zitelle and walk to your right. A respectable and renovated *palazzo.* The 4- to 30-bed rooms can get hectic. Curfew 11pm. Members only; IYHF cards sold. L14,000. Sheets and breakfast included. Meals L10,000. Ask here to find out if any of the other defunct hostels are back in service for '92. Reserve ahead in summer; often fills up in the morning.

Suore Cannosiano, fondamente del ponte Piccolo, 428 (tel. 522 21 57), also on the Giudecca. Take boat #5 to Sant' Eufemia, and walk to your left. Women only. Kind nuns and a restorative garden. Flexible lockout 8:30am-4pm. Curfew 10:30pm. L13,000.

Foresteria Valdese, Castello, 5170 (tel. 528 68 97). *Vaporetto* stop: S. Zaccharia. From campo S. Maria Formosa take calle lunga S.M. Formosa and go over the first bridge. Engaging frescoes and ebullient management. Reception open 9:30am-1pm and 6-8:30pm (occasionally 1-6pm as well). Lockout 10am-1pm. No curfew. L20,000 in small (8-16 people) dorm rooms. Breakfast included. Call for information on their kitchen apartments, available in 1992.

Domus Civica, S. Polo, 3082 (tel. 522 71 39), at calle Chiovere and calle Campazzo, between the Frari Church and p. Roma. Women only. Great management. Great TV. Great ping-pong table. Curfew 11:30pm. Singles L25,000. Doubles L40,000. Open June-July and Sept. to mid-Oct.

Istituto San Giuseppe, Castello, 5402 (tel. 522 53 52). From p. dei Leoncini (to the left of S. Marco), take calle dei Specchieri to campo S. Zulian, then go right on campo de la Guerra over the bridge; turn left immediately. Reserved for families. In summer, write a month ahead with a 1-night deposit. Curfew 11pm. L25,000 per person. Call ahead; sometimes closed in the middle of the day. Closed Easter and Christmas.

Hotels

Locanda Ca' Foscari, Dorsoduro, 3887B (tel. 522 58 17), at the foot of the calle Crosera just east of calle Larga Foscari on Calle della Frescata *(vaporetto)* #1 or 34 to S. Tomà). The small sign is easy to miss. Airy rooms. Singles L31,000. Doubles L46,000, with bath L52,000. Showers L1000. Breakfast L5000. Phone reservations honored until noon. Open Feb.-early Nov.

Hotel Caneva, Castello, 5515 (tel. 522 81 18), a 2 minute walk from the Rialto, in a turn-off from campo della Fava. 17 of the 23 attractive rooms overlook a canal. Singles L25,000, with bath and breakfast L50,000. Doubles L40,000, with bath and breakfast L70,000. Triples L56,000. Quads L68,000. Breakfast L8000.

Locanda Montin, Dorsoduro, 1147 (tel. 522 71 51), on a sunny canal. From campo S. Barnaba, go south through the passageway Casin dei Nobili, across the bridge, right on fondamenta Lombardo, and then around the corner onto fondamenta di Borgo. Modern paintings and restored antiques all around. Singles L30,000. Doubles L44,000. Showers included. Breakfast L4000. Closed 10 days in Jan. and 10 days in Aug.

Villa Rosa, Cannaregio, 389 (tel. 71 65 69), on corner of calle della Misericordia and calle Pesaro. Turn left before crossing the Ponte della Guglie and left again to the end. A comfortable hide-out in a residential quarter. Singles L35,000, with bath L50,000. Doubles L55,000, with bath L85,000. Breakfast included.

Casa Petrarca, San Marco, 4386 (tel. 520 04 30). From campo San Luca, go south on calle dei Fuseri, take the 2nd left, then turn right onto calle Schiavone. All is sweetness, from the wicker furniture to the hospitality of the English-speaking proprietor. Singles L29,000, with bath L39,000. Doubles L54,000, showers included. Triples L74,000. Call to reserve.

Locanda Antica Casa Carettoni, Cannaregio, 130 (tel. 71 62 31), down the lista di Spagna to the left of the station. Cozy, with a cobweb or two. Singles L25,000. Doubles L45,000. Triples L60,000. Showers included. Open March-June.

Casa/Pensione de Stefani, Dorsoduro, 2786 (tel. 522 33 37), on calle del Traghetto off S. Barnabà. Converted from a 16th-century *palazzo;* try to get one of the large rooms with a frescoed ceiling. Singles L33,000. Doubles L50,000, with bath L60,000.

Locanda Sant' Anna, Castello, 269 (tel. 528 64 66). Take via Garibaldi east of P. San Marco along the banks of Canale della Giudecca, which becomes Fondamenta Sant' Anna (on the right side of the canal), left across the bridge at calle Crociera, and then right at corte del Bianco. Take *vaporetto* #1 or 4 to Giardini near via Garibaldi. Spotless rooms and an accommodating family are well worth the hike. Singles L35,000. Doubles L44,000, with bath L74,000. Showers L2500. Optional breakfast L8000. Sometimes closed in Nov. or Jan.

Pensione Smeraldo, Cannaregio, 1333 (tel. 71 78 38). Right over the Ponte Guglie bridge on Rio Terà S. Leonardo. A *principessa* lived in this old palace until 1940. Once regal, now rickety. Still, a high ceiling provides blessed coolness. Beds in 4 person dorms L20,000. Doubles L50,000. Quad L80,000. Will haggle.

Albergo Bernardi—Semenzato, Cannaregio, 4363 (tel. 522 72 57). From Strada Nova, take calle del Duca, then take first right on calle dell'Osa. Clean, simple rooms. Proprietor's wife speaks English. Singles L26,000. Doubles L42,000. Triples L57,000. Breakfast L3000.

Camping

Prices are outrageous—unless you're with two or more companions, go with a hotel. The **Litorale del cavallino**—one long row of campgrounds on the beach—is a penisula about 25 minutes southeast of p. San Marco, by *vaporetto* #15. Try **Marina di Venezia,** via Hermada (tel. 96 61 46) and **Ca' Pasqualli,** via Fausta (tel. 96 61 10). Marina charges about L7000 (depending on the season) per person, L20,000 per tent (open year-round); Pasqualli is pennies cheaper (open mid-May to mid-Sept.). Another option is **Camping Fusina,** via Moranzani, in Fusina (tel. 547 00 55). From p. Roma, take bus #4 (L700) to Mestre, change to bus #13 (across from Supermarket Pam), and ride to last stop (1 hr., last bus at 10pm). Or, take *vaporetto* #5 left to Zattere and #16 (L2500) for 20 minutes to Fusina. (English spoken. L5000 per person and L25,000 per tent. Call ahead.)

Food

Most restaurants in Venice are laughably expensive. Venetians subsist on frequent snacks of *panini* (sandwiches), *tramezzini* (triangles of soft-as-wonder white bread with meat and vegetable fillings), and other yummy bar food, consumed standing (prices triple if you sit down). Avoid restaurants along major routes in favor of the Dorsoduro quarter between the Accademia and the Frari, and relatively untouristed Castello. Cover *(coperto)* charges are twice as high in Venice as elsewhere in Italy; L3000 per person is not unusual. Restaurants rarely close in August.

For fresh produce and fish, try **open-air markets** (Mon.-Sat. on campo Santa Margherita and every morning at the bustling **Rialto** market). One of the best deals in town is the nameless **supermarket** on fondamenta Zattere, 1492, near the S. Basilio *vaporetto* stop on the way to Fusina. (Open Mon.-Tues. and Thurs.-Sat. 8:30am-12:30pm and 3:30-7:30pm, Wed. 8:30am-12:30pm.) The best *gelato* in Venice springs from **Nico,** Dorsoduro, 922, on fondamenta Zattere, near the *vaporetto* stop of the same name; the rich chocolate and whipped cream *gianduiotto* (L2700) is a Venetian specialty. (Open Fri.-Wed. until 11pm—earlier in winter.) Flashy **Il Doge** in campo Santa Margherita is a competing favorite among locals.

Mensa DLF, Cannaregio, to your right as you exit the train station. This cafeteria for train station employees is open to the hungry public, but you may have to let the train workers have dibs on the hearty, inexpensive self-service fare. Pasta L3000. Main courses L5000. Open 12:30-1:30pm, 6:30-9pm. Expect arbitrary schedule changes.

Mensa Universitaria di Cà Foscari, S. Polo, 2480 (tel. 520 44 96) on calle del Magazen near p. Santa Margherita. Full meals including drink and dessert only L4000 with Carta Giovani. Open Mon.-Sat. noon-2pm and 6:30-8pm, Sun. noon-2pm.

El Chef, Dorsoduro, 2765 (tel. 522 28 15), under the archway from campo San Barnabà. If a dish of local fish is not your wish, go elsewhere. Open Tues.-Sun. noon-3pm and 6-10:30pm.

Osteria al Mascaron, Castello, 5225, on calle longa Santa Maria Formosa east of the *campo* of the same name. Older Venetians linger here all afternoon to play inscrutable card games; the young and hip hang out after dark. House wine L8000 per liter. Watch the wandering chef whip something up from scratch and order accordingly, or try the **spaghetti alle vangole vera** (L12,000). Cover L2000. Open mid-Jan. to mid.-Dec. Mon.-Sat. 10:30am-3pm and 7-10:30pm. Closed 1 week in Aug.

Cantina Do Spade, San Polo, 860, on the sottoportego delle Do Spade. Tucked under an archway before the Do Spade bridge (the first one south of campo Beccarie). A winery (L500-1600 per glass) with sumptuous sandwiches (L2000-3500). Open Sept.-July Mon.-Sat. 9am-1pm and 5-8pm. **Cantina Do Mori** is a similar place down the street at #429 with wine from L800-5200 per glass and *tramezzini* for L1500. Open mid-Aug. to July Mon.-Tues. and Thurs.-Sat. 8:30am-1:30pm and 5-8:30pm, Wed. 8:30am-1:30pm.

Vino, Vino, S. Marco, 2007a, on calle del Cafetier, just off calle Largo XXII Marzo (which runs from the Ponte Moisè bridge). This small and distinctive eatery lays on the Venetian culinary charm. Plate of the day (L10,000) is always fresh and delicious. Wines galore, L800-9000 per glass. Cover L1000. Open Wed.-Mon. for drinks 10am-1am, for meals noon-3pm and 7-11:30pm.

Sights

To wander aimlessly is to be seduced by Venice. Take *vaporetto* #1 down the Grand Canal for an introduction to Venetian architecture and the loop of its main waterway. Without a map, you'll soon be blundering through the city's serpentine *sestieri* (quarters) without a glimmer of direction. Getting lost in Venice is a joyous thing, but those with trains to catch will only dead-end against unbridged canals.

Venice revolves around **piazza San Marco,** called by Napoleon "the most magnificent entry in the world." Housing the body of an evangelist was the last word in civic prestige during the Middle Ages, so the Republic set about acquiring one. Two patriotic merchants smuggled the body of St. Mark out of Alexandria by burying it under a consignment of pork, which they gambled (correctly) would put off the Muslim customs officials—and thus the purloined St. Mark became the patron saint of Venice. His remains remain beneath the main altar of the mosaic-covered **Basilica di San Marco** (tel. 522 56 97). The masterpiece of the basilica is the **Pala D'Oro,** a glittering gold Byzantine bas-relief. (Open Mon.-Sat. 10am-5pm, Sun. 1:30-5pm. Admission L2000. Shorts and sleeveless shirts prohibited.) The same ticket admits you to the **Tesoro** (treasury), a dazzling collection of gold and bones. Upstairs in the **Galleria della Basilica** stand four musclebound bronze horses that Venice snagged from Constantinople; those standing on the *loggia* are reproductions. (Open daily 9:30am-5pm. Admission L2000.) The **Torre dell' Orologio** (clock tower), left of San Marco, is an attractive arrangement of sculpture and sundials. The two bronze Moors on top still strike the hour (closed for restoration in 1991). You can ascend the brick **Campanile** in front of San Marco for a Kodak moment of the whole city. Built in 902 AD, the bell tower crumbled into a pile of rubble in 1900, just before its 1000th birthday. The stairs in the original tower were wide enough for nobles on horseback to ascend, but modern Venetians have overcome the inconvenience of the 99m equine climb by installing an elevator. (Open daily 9:30am-8pm. Admission L3000.)

Toward the sea, the *piazza* opens into the **piazzetta San Marco,** with the two symbolic columns of Venice at the far end, topped with the winged lion and Neptune. The **Palazzo Ducale** (Doge's Palace), next to San Marco, faces Sansovino's exquisite **Libreria** across the open space. Visit the palace for an exhaustive display of Titians, Veroneses and Tintorettos, as well as the armor museum and the ominous **Ponte dei Sospiri** (Bridge of Sighs), leading out to the prison. Its bathrooms—rare in p. San Marco—are clean and located near the exit; save your ticket for access. (Open daily 8:30am-7pm. Admission L8000, seniors and children L5000.)

The **Accademia** in Dorsoduro displays the best of Venetian painting. The world-class collection includes a superb Bellini *Madonna,* Giorgione's enigmatic *Tempest,* and Tintoretto's magnificent cycle depicting the life of St. Mark. Go early to get your money's worth. (Open Mon.-Sat. 9am-2pm, Sun. 9am-1pm. Admission L8000.) For a very different art, visit the **Collezione Peggy Guggenheim,** Dorsoduro, 701, in her magnificent canalside *palazzo* east of the Accademia off fondamenta Venier. All the major names in modern art are here. (Open Wed.-Fri. and Sun.-Mon. 11am-6pm, Sat. noon-9pm. Admission L5000, seniors, children, and students with pass L3000, Sat. 6-9pm free.)

Another art-filled area surrounds the Gothic **Basilica dei Frari** (1340-1443); in San Polo *(vaporetto:* San Tomà). The basilica houses a moving wooden sculpture of St. John by Donatello, Bellini's *Madonna and Saints,* and Titian's dramatic *Assumption.* (Open Mon.-Sat. 9am-noon and 2:30-6pm. Admission L1000, free Sun. and holidays 3-5pm.) The *scuole* of Venice were a cross between guilds and fraternities. In addition to providing welfare services, the *scuole* battled each other with their decorators; their "clubhouses" became some of the most ornate edifices in a city known for its opulence. The richest *scuola* of all was the **Scuola Grande di San Rocco** (across the campo at the end of the Frari), which gloats over 56 Tintorettos. Tintoretto set out to out-Titian Titian, by, in his own words, "combining the color of Titian with the drawing of Michelangelo." The *Crucifixion* panel takes in so large a scene that half the people in the painting are oblivious to the central event. (Open daily 9am-1pm and 3:30-6:30pm; in off-season Mon.-Fri. 10am-1pm and 3:30-6pm. Admission L6000, holders of youth pass L5000.)

Across the Giudecca canal, on the island of Giudecca, stand two churches designed by the great late Renaissance architect Palladio—**San Giorgio Maggiore,** on the Isola di San Giorgio, and the **Chiesa del Redentore,** on Giudecca itself and built after one of the many Venetian plagues. Both can be viewed from the **Church of Santa Maria della Salute,** a baroque extravaganza commemorating yet another plague savior, at the tip of Dorsoduro. Take *vaporetto* #5 or 8 from p. San Marco.

North of Venice stretches the **lagoon.** With a *vaporetto* ticket (L1800-L2500), you can visit the glass museum at the island of **Murano** (#5); the fishing village of **Bu-**

rano (#12); and **Torcello,** an island with an enchanting Byzantine cathedral and some of the finest mosaics in Italy. The mudflats *(barreme)* that the ocean reveals at low tide give you some idea of the very real sweat that went into the construction of the Ethereal City. The **Lido** separates the Venice lagoon from the Adriatic. Its long sandy beach is as popular as its water is polluted.

For a more thorough treatment of this maze of stone and color, try a copy of Mary McCarthy's *Venice Observed.*

Entertainment

Perhaps the most entertaining evening activity in Venice is a tour of the Grand Canal at twilight; board a slow *vaporetto* at either end. **Gondolas** are indeed romantic, but probably out of reach—the official rate begins at L70,000 per hour, increasing to L90,000 after sundown. To make them affordable, assemble a group of six (the maximum capacity), and split the fare. For cheaper water travel, join residents and use the *traghetti* (water buses) that cross the Grand Canal between bridges. Look for a street that dead-ends onto the canal (marked "calle del traghetto") and pay L400 for a 90-second ride.

To get acquainted with Venetian life and times, attend Steven Wolf's talk, **Venice in English: The Art and History of Venice,** given Mon.-Fri. 8:45pm, on calle delle Botteghe near campo S. Stefano at the Nuova Acropoli, S. Marco, 2965. (Admission L10,000, students L7000. The third talk is free.)

Concerts and exhibitions take place in the city's beautiful *palazzi.* Check *Un Ospite di Venezia,* the magazine *Marco Polo,* or the APT for details. At night, cafés and strolling are much more popular than dancing, but if you have the fever the **Nuova Acropoli** at lungomare Marconi, 22, on the Lido, is a good disco.

Venice's most kaleidoscopic festival is the **Festa del Redentore,** a transplendent, hour-long orgasm of fireworks on the third Saturday of July and a gondola race the next day at the Chiesa del Redetore. Venice's annual **International Film Festival** brings the world's best cinema and glitteriest *glamorati* to the **Lido** for the last week of August and the first week of September. (The APT has schedules. Tickets from L8000.) On the first Sunday in September, the city holds its **Regata Storica,** a procession of elegantly decorated boats down the Grand Canal, followed pell-mell by a series of cut-throat gondola races. Grandstands are erected along the canal; seats cost about L20,000. **Carnevale,** a touristy delirium of costumed celebration and dancing in the streets, takes place during the 10 days prior to the onset of Lent (the last week of February through March 3rd in 1992).

Trieste

Although geographically as marginal as international borders will allow, this cosmopolitan city is the intellectual and cultural capital of the Friuli-Venezia Giulia region. James Joyce and Ernest Hemingway both contributed to the city's literary heritage, while Trieste displays a wealth of Hapsburg and Nationalist architecture—legacies of various periods in its war-riddled past. The city presently owes much of its vitality to its transporation resources. Ferry service along the Istrian Peninsula and frequent trains to Ljubljana (Yugoslavia) make Trieste a logical connection point for Yugoslavs heading west or Europeans seeking Slavic lands.

The **train station,** in the p. della Libertà (tel. (040) 41 87 07), serves Venice (2 hr., L12,000), Milan (7½ hr., L27,000), and Ljubljana (3½ hr., L18,000). **Agemar Viaggi,** p. Duca degli Abruzzi, 7/A (tel. (040) 36 37 37) will arrange ferry bookings with **Adriatica Navigazione** to Novigrad (3½ hr., L11,700) and Pula (4½ hr., L19,100) in Yugoslavia and to Durrës, Albania (31 hr., L110,000-L145,000). The **Ostello Tegeste (IYHF),** viale Miramare, 331 (tel. (040) 22 41 01) stacks only members in its bunks. Take bus #6 from *across* the street from the tourist office to the last stop, then bus #36 to the hostel. (Registration noon-11:30pm; L15,000 includes showers and breakfast.)

Padua (Padova)

A university town for some 800 years, Padua has nurtured numerous Italian intellects. Dante, Petrarch, and Galileo are just three of the illustrious predecessors to the 40,000 students who enliven this small city. Padua's proximity to Venice and efficient transportation networks make it an ideal camp for Venicewards forays.

The center of town lies down corso Garibaldi from the train station (bus #3 or 8, or 10 min. on foot). On the way you'll pass the **Cappella degli Scrovegni,** the unmarred masterpiece of the medieval innovator Giotto. The 36 panels on the Redemption theme are the painter's only fresco cycles to have escaped even partial deterioration. Their unprecedented portrayal of space marked the transition to Renaissance realism, and influenced Giotto's successors for centuries to come. (Open daily 9am-7pm; Oct.-March Tues.-Sun. 9am-6pm, Mon. 9:30am-12:30pm. Admission L8000, students L5000. Tickets are sold (and also valid) at the **Museo Civico.** Consider investing in a museum pass (L10,000; students L7000) which wins a year's unlimited entrance to all of Padua's museums.)

Piazza delle Erbe and piazza della Frutta surround Padua's famous food market, the **Salone.** Take via Antenore, then turn down via del Santo to get to the **Basilica di Sant' Antonio,** a delicious salad of medieval architectural styles. The tongue and jaw of St. Anthony (patron saint of lost and found) are preserved in a heart-shaped reliquary in the apse of the church; most Catholics who make the pilgrimage to Padua incline to kiss the more appealing toe of his sarcophagus. (Open daily 6:30am-7:45pm; Oct.-March 6:30am-7pm.) Padua erupts in celebration during the weeklong **Festa di Sant' Antonio** in late June. On the piazza del Santo, don't miss Donatello's imposing equestrian statue of *Gattemelata,* a mercenary general. Cast in the same pose as the famous *Marcus Aurelius,* this was the first great equestrian bronze cast since antiquity. Across the *piazza* is the **Oratorio di San Giorgio,** where Giotto's students studied and decorated the walls, and the **Scuola del Santo,** which contains a 16th-century tribute to the saint in frescoes, and includes four early Titians. (Both open daily 8:30am-12:30pm and 2:30-6:30pm; Oct.-Nov. and Feb.-March 9am-12:30pm and 2:30-4:30pm; Dec.-Jan. 9am-12:30pm. Admission to each L1000.)

The **APT** (tel. 875 20 77) in the train station provides free maps and listings of Padua's myriad, identically priced one-star hotels. During the summer, however, these fill up with refugees from nearby Venice (1 per ½ hr.; ½ hr.; L2800, roundtrip L4800). It's wise to call ahead. If you arrive in town late, check the vacancy board outside the tourist office. The friendly, crowded **Ostello Città di Padova,** via Aleardi, 30 (tel. 875 22 19), has kempt rooms and seemingly eternal renovations. From the station, take bus #3, 8, or 18. (Curfew 11pm. L13,500. Breakfast included.) **Albergo Pace,** #3 via Papafava (tel. 875 15 66), just across the canal north of the hostel, has a maze of spacious quarters and bike storage. (Extremely popular. Singles L24,000. Doubles L30,500.) The friendly family at **Albergo Pavia,** a few doors down at #11, will give you rooms (and clothesline space) for the same price. Quasi-institutional **Casa del Pellegrino,** via Cesarotti, 21 (tel. 875 21 00), along the northern side of Sant' Antonio, features ascetic rooms—pink or brown and crucifix-filled. (Flexible midnight curfew. Singles L26,000. Doubles L41,000, with bath L61,000. Open Feb-Dec. 10.) Reserve a week in advance. Also try the one-star places around the piazza del Santo, where singles are L24,000 and doubles L30,500.

Padua has several **university mensas,** but during the summer only the larger ones, at via San Francesco, 122, and at the top of via Marzolo, are likely to be open. (Full meals L8000, ISIC not necessary. Open noon-2pm and 7-9pm.) **BREK,** in p. Cavour, 20, is centrally situated self-service with a touch of style. (*Primi* begin at L2500. Open Sat.-Thurs. 11:30am-3pm and 6:30-10:30pm.) **Al Pero,** via Santa Lucia, 72, is an appealing *trattoria* with irresistable prices; concoct your own menu for under L15,000. (Open Sept.-July Mon.-Sat. noon-2:20pm and 7-10pm.) Padua's **city code** is 049; **postal code,** 35100.

Verona

Shakespeare immortalized Verona when he appropriated the local story of Romeo and Giulietta, but a cursory glance at the city's opulent *palazzi* shows that greater names than the Montagues or Capulets have resided here. The wealth of Roman ruins reveals the classical origins of the modern metropolis, and in July and August, the Colosseum-like **Arena** (built in 100 AD) comes to life for the summer opera season. Even the cheap seats are L17,000, but it's your only opportunity to hear Verdi amidst the ruckus of a ballgame. Bring food and a cushion—the pageantry lasts as long as a double-header. (Tickets available under arches #8 and #9, tel. (045) 59 65 17. Open Mon.-Fri. 8:40am-12:20pm and 3-5:50pm, Sat. 8:40am-12:20pm.) The **Teatro Romano** across the river welcomes jazz, ballet, and Shakespearean drama—in Italian—to its recently excavated stage (tel. (045) 59 00 89; tickets from L12,000). The train station, on both the Milan-Venice and Bologna-Brenner Pass lines, is a 20-minute walk on corso Porto Nuovo or a L1000 ride on bus #2 from Verona's center, **piazza Brà.** Up via Mazzini from the arena resides **piazza delle Erbe,** where vendors hawk fruit and hokey trinkets amid the Renaissance *palazzi* constructed by Veronese merchants. Through an arch on the right are **piazza dei Signori** and the **Tombs of the Scaligeri,** the peculiar Gothic remnants of the della Scala, Verona's medieval bosses. The equestrian statue of the Cangrande della Scala, a glorification of raw power, rides in the museum of the **Castelvecchio.** (Open Tues.-Sun. 8am-7pm. Admission L5000.) Along the south riverbank stands **Chiesa di San Zeno Maggiore,** a Romanesque church noted for the 11th-century bronze panels of its door and its Mantegna altarpiece. Mantegna's spatial composition still draws the viewer into the scene; pay L500 to have the altarpiece lit. The first chapel to the left of the **duomo,** behind p. Erbe, houses Titian's *The Assumption of the Virgin,* an ethereal work that marks the zenith of the Venetian Renaissance. Die-hard romantics can shell out a small fortune for a moment of disillusionment at **Juliet's House,** via Cappello, 23; you'll get to stand on a diminutive balcony and thrill to a view of camera-happy tourists. (Open Tues.-Sun. 8am-6:45pm. Admission L3500.) What the Veronese call **Romeo's House,** via Arche Scaligere, 2, is now a bar.

The **tourist office,** behind the arena at via Dietro Anfineatro, 6 (tel. (045) 59 28 28; open Mon.-Sat. 8am-8pm, Sun. 9am-2pm) has a busy but good-natured staff. To get to the heavenly **Ostello Verona (IYHF),** salita Fontana del Ferro, 15 (tel. (045) 59 03 60), take bus #2 across Ponte Nuovo to p. Isolo, turn right at via Ponte Pignolo, walk 3 blocks, turn left, then right, and left again. The best hostel in Italy combines the best of both worlds—15th-century frescoes and superspotless bathrooms. (Curfew 11pm, later if you're at the opera. L13,000. Camping in a shady garden L7000. Breakfast included. 3-course dinner L10,000.) Women might try **Casa della Giovane,** via Pigna, 7 (tel. (045) 59 68 80; L15,000-L22,000; 10:30pm curfew, extended for opera-goers). On the hotel front, clean and cheerful **Locanda Catullo,** via Catullo, 1 (tel. (045) 800 27 86), is a bargain with singles for L21,000, doubles for L30,300. **Camp** at **Camping Castel S. Pietro,** via Castel S. Pietro, 2 (tel. (045) 59 20 37).

For zesty pizza (L5000-7500) and refuge from the crowded main thoroughfares, go to **Pizzeria Corte Farina,** corte Farina, 4, down via Pelliciai from p. Erbe, through the galleria to the left. (Open Tues.-Sun. 9am-3pm and 6pm-midnight.) Across the river is **Trattoria al Cacciatore,** via Seminario, 4, with a fine *menù* for L13,500. (Open Mon.-Fri. noon-2pm and 7-9:30pm, Sat. noon-2pm.) **Ristorante Nuova Gvottina** has proven itself with Verona's student body at via Interrato dell'Acqua Morta, 38. (Hearty *menù* only L12,000. Open Fri.-Wed. noon-3pm and 6pm-1am.) **Supermarket PAM** is at via Teatro Filarmonico, 3, off corso Porta Nuova. (Open Mon.-Tues. and Thurs.-Sat. 8:30am-7:30pm, Wed. 8:30am-noon.)

Mantua (Mantova)

Mantua basks in the afterglow of its heyday as court of the embarrassingly extravagant Gonzaga dynasty. During their 400-year reign, the Gonzaga loaded the center of town with palaces, churches, and towers, and attracted some of the most important artists of the Renaissance to their court. Mantua is about two hours southeast of Milan by train; the train station lies a 10-minute walk up via Solferino e S. Martino and via Fratelli Banchiera from the center of town.

Mantua's **Church of Sant'Andrea** is acclaimed as the most brilliant creation of Florentine architect Leon Battista Alberti. Its ensemble of single barrel-vaulted nave, perpendicular side chapels, and domed crossing set the pace for European church-building for the next 300 years. The immensity of its interior seems even more staggering when compared to the intimate *piazza* in front and the small houses along the side. In nearby p. Sordello rises the **Palazzo Ducale,** one of the largest and most sumptuously decorated palaces in Europe. Its more than 500 rooms include a series of miniature chambers designed for court dwarves. Displayed in the *Camera degli Sposi* (marriage chamber) are Andrea Mantegna's famed frescoes of the Gonzaga family (1474). His use of vanishing perspective lines makes the frescoes appear to be an extension of the space of the room; this was the first Renaissance decoration to exploit this optical illusion. (Open Tues.-Sat. 9am-1pm and 2:30-5pm, Sun.-Mon. 9am-1pm. Admission L10,000.)

At the southern end of town is the **Palazzo del Tè,** built in the early 16th century as the Gonzaga family's suburban villa. Romano decorated the rooms of the palace with an extraordinary cycle of frescoes based on classical themes. The frescoes in the giant's room depict *Jove's Victory Over the Mad Presumption of the Giants,* a terrifying apocalypse of billowing clouds and falling columns. Before leaving the palace grounds, visit the **Casino della Grotta,** to the left at the end of the garden. The palace is on viale delle Aquile, off viale Risorgimento. (Open Tues.-Sun. 10am-6pm. Admission L5000, children under 12 L2000.)

The friendly, well-informed **APT** (tourist office) is on p. Mantegna (tel. (0376) 35 06 81; open Mon.-Sat. 9am-noon and 3-6pm). Mantua's youth hostel, **Ostello Sparfucile (IYHF)** is superb—a 16th-century castle on the outskirts (tel. (0376) 37 24 65). Take bus #2, 6, or 9 from p. Cavallotti. (L10,500 per person, with breakfast. Open April to mid-Oct. Camping available July-Aug.) Otherwise try the cordial **Locanda La Rinascita,** via Concezione, 4 (tel. (0376) 32 06 07; Singles L22,000, doubles L34,000.) The **Albergo Roma Vecchia,** via Corridoni, 20 (tel. (0376) 32 21 00), off p. Belfiore, provides minimalist but spacious accommodations. (Singles L22,000. Doubles L34,000.) For cheap sit-down meals go to the **Self-Service Virgiliana,** p. Virgiliana, 57; this *mensa* has a *menù* for L11,000. (Open Mon.-Fri. noon-2pm.) For spicier, pricier fare, try **Al Quadrato,** right around the corner in p. Virgiliana. Huge pizzas run L5000-9000; pasta's in the same range. (Cover L2000. Open Tues.-Sun. noon-3:30pm and 7pm-1am.)

The Lakes and the Dolomites

In Italy, the land of monuments and museums, even the most avid art fanatic can experience a lapse in their *duomo*-discernment abilities. Time for a change of scenery—which is what Italy's lakes and mountains are all about. The Dolomites dominate the landscape in the province of Trentino-Alto Adige, rising from Austrian-influenced valley communities to lofty peaks equipped for skiing, hiking, or dumbfounded admiration. The lake country, by contrast, has long attracted a less athletic breed of tourist to its restorative breezes and indolent repose, though a new generation of windsurfers is challenging the sedentary stereotype. Contemplate the meaning of life in the shade of lakeside verdure or the isolation of a mountain hut before descending upon Italy's man-made wonders with renewed enthusiasm.

An oddly shaped amalgam of three lesser lakes, **Lake Como** (Lago di Como) is a half-hour north of Milan en route to the nearby Swiss border. The **tourist office** in the city of **Como,** the lake's largest urban outpost, is near the waterfront at p. Cavour, 16 (tel. (031) 27 40 64), and distributes information on the rest of the lake (open Mon.-Sat. 9am-12:30pm and 2:30-6pm). The **ferry landing** (tel. (031) 27 33 24) is across lungo Larro Trieste from p. Cavour, and frequent service runs to all the other lake villages (tickets L1200-9900). In Como, stay in the **youth hostel** behind imposing Villa Olmo, via Bellinzona, 6 (tel. (031) 57 38 00); there are privately run hostels in **Menaggio** (tel. (0344) 323 56) and **Domaso** (tel. (0344) 960 94). All three charge L11,500 per person. Como's stately *duomo,* a combination of Gothic and Renaissance elements with an impressive array of stained glass, is the lake's most notable Christian edifice, but a multitude of luxurious *ville* overlook the dreamy waters amidst the secular splendor of shoreside parks and gardens. Contact the tourist office for a list of these and their visiting hours.

Lake Garda (Lago di Garda) is the largest and most popular of the lakes, a fact which has unfortunately led to intensive and extensive development efforts, particularly on the southern shores. **Riva del Garda,** at the northern end in the Trentino region, has thus far escaped complete commercialization, but **Sirmione,** the southern peninsula, once praised for its unspoiled vegetation, becomes a zoo with summer tourists. The peaceful eastern shore is serviced by local buses. Pick up a list of lakeside campgrounds at the tourist office in Riva (tel. (0464) 55 44 44) or Sirmione (tel. (030) 91 61 14), or choose the indoor economy option at Riva's **Ostello Benacus,** p. Cavour, 9 (tel. (0464) 55 49 11, L12,000 per person). The lake's impressive castles include the **Rocca** at Riva and an equivalent at Sirmione, most of which owe their existence to Verona's Scaligeri clan, who evidently knew how to appreciate the wetter things in life. Garda is an easy bus trip from Verona. The nearest train stations are at Desenzano on the south end and Rovereto to the north.

Trent (Trento, Trient) is an hour north of Verona on the Bologna-Brenner train line. Italian prevails culturally and linguistically, but you'll see Austrian influence in the local cuisine and the local interest in all things mountainous. The city's **tourist office** is across the park from the train station at via Alfieri, 4 (tel. (0461) 98 38 80), but head to the regional office at corso III Novembre, 134 (tel. (0461) 98 00 00) for hiking and skiing info, and for listings of Trentino's *rifugi* (mountain huts for those who prefer to linger in the hills after sundown). Stay at the luxurious, hotel-like **Ostello Giovane Europa,** via Manzoni (tel. (0461) 23 45 67) for L13,500 per person. Pay a visit to the sprawling, Gothic-Renaissance *duomo* and the *Castello di Buonconsiglio,* the fortified residence that once housed Trent's royalty. Take advantage of Trent's proximity to **Monte Bondone** and explore nearby sporting options, or the mountains of the **Brenta Group** (easily reached by bus).

Only an hour and a half north of Trento, also en route to the Brenner Pass, **Bolzano** (Bozen) seems to be a world apart. Austrian architecture shapes the romantic city streets, and you may hear an occasional yodel if you catch the blue-aproned natives off guard. Stout, stone-walled castles replace Renaissance *palazzi,* and würstel and schnitzel plaster the local menus. Bolzano is an ideal place to acclimate to **Südtiroliën** valley culture and stock up on essentials for a mountain escape. The **tourist office** at p. Walther, 8 (tel. (0471) 97 56 56) has local information including some easy hiking recommendations in the neighboring hillsides. For serious mountaineering preparation, go to the **Provincial Tourist Office for South Tyrol,** p. Parracchia, 11 (tel. (0471) 99 38 09), and talk to the resident Alpine guru, Dr. Hanns-jörg Hager. Also pick up their volume of regional accommodations services. For housing in Bolzano itself, run for the hills (you'll find great views and lower prices). **Magdalena Weinstube,** St. Magdalena, 22 (tel. (0471) 97 43 80) offers bed and breakfast for L20,000 per person as do a number of other guesthouses on the same street. Return to nature an hour and a half's bus ride away in the **Alpe di Suisi.**

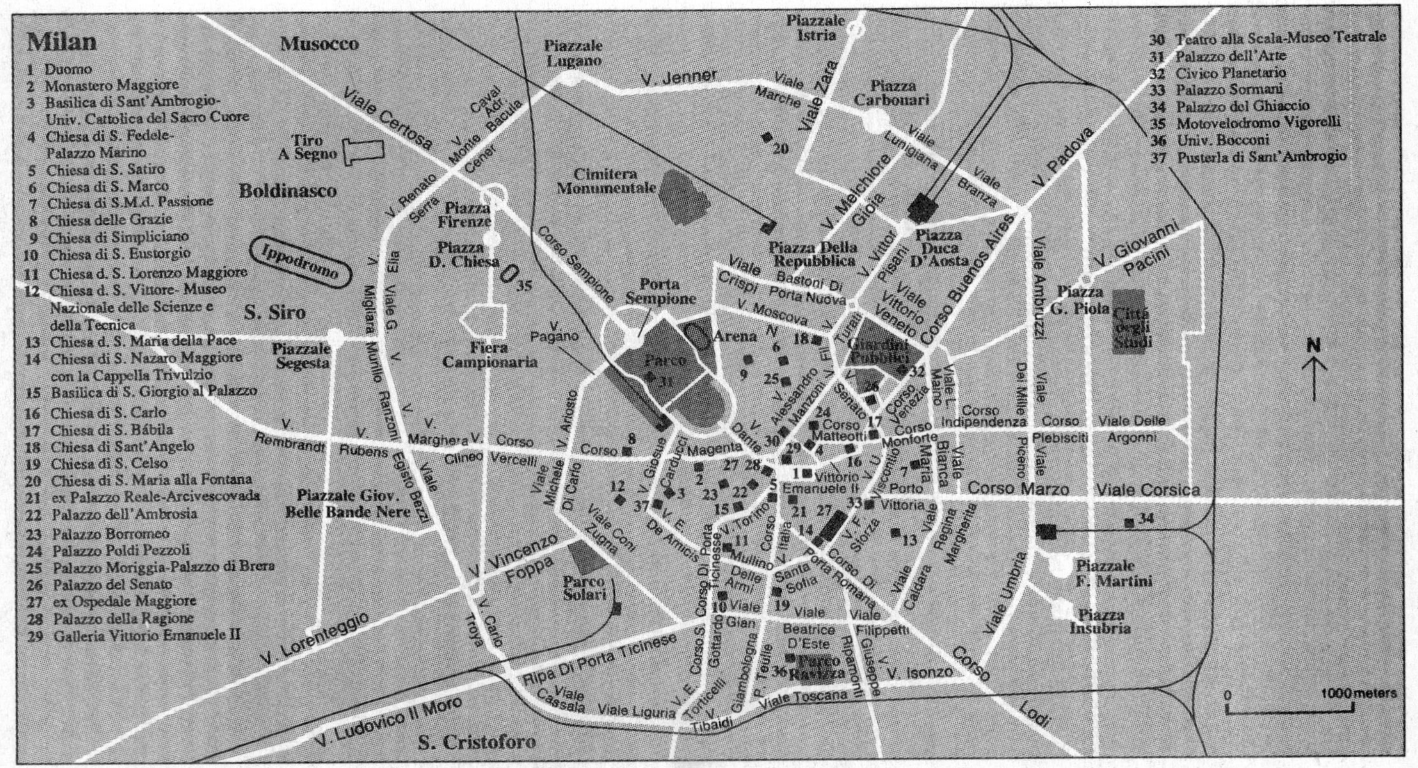
Milan
1 Duomo
2 Monastero Maggiore
3 Basilica di Sant'Ambrogio-Univ. Cattolica del Sacro Cuore
4 Chiesa di S. Fedele-Palazzo Marino
5 Chiesa di S. Satiro
6 Chiesa di S. Marco
7 Chiesa di S.M.d. Passione
8 Chiesa delle Grazie
9 Chiesa di Simpliciano
10 Chiesa di S. Eustorgio
11 Chiesa d. S. Lorenzo Maggiore
12 Chiesa d. S. Vittore- Museo Nazionale delle Scienze e della Tecnica
13 Chiesa d. S. Maria della Pace
14 Chiesa di S. Nazaro Maggiore con la Cappella Trivulzio
15 Basilica di S. Giorgio al Palazzo
16 Chiesa di S. Carlo
17 Chiesa di S. Bábila
18 Chiesa di Sant'Angelo
19 Chiesa di S. Celso
20 Chiesa di S. Maria alla Fontana
21 ex Palazzo Reale-Arcivescovada
22 Palazzo dell'Ambrosia
23 Palazzo Borromeo
24 Palazzo Poldi Pezzoli
25 Palazzo Moriggia-Palazzo di Brera
26 Palazzo del Senato
27 ex Ospedale Maggiore
28 Palazzo della Ragione
29 Galleria Vittorio Emanuele II
30 Teatro alla Scala-Museo Teatrale
31 Palazzo dell'Arte
32 Civico Planetario
33 Palazzo Sormani
34 Palazzo del Ghiaccio
35 Motovelodromo Vigorelli
36 Univ. Bocconi
37 Pusterla di Sant'Ambrogio
Musocco
Piazzale Lugano
Piazzale Istria
V. Jenner
Viale Zara
Piazza Carbonari
Viale Certosa
Tiro A Segno
Boldinasco
Cimitera Monumentale
Piazza Firenze
Piazza D. Chiesa
Ippodromo
S. Siro
Piazzale Segesta
Fiera Campionaria
Porta Sempione
Corso Sempione
Parco
Arena
Piazza Della Repubblica
Piazza Duca D'Aosta
Corso Buenos Aires
V. Padova
Viale Ambruzzi
Piazza G. Piola
Città degli Studi
Giardini Pubblici
Corso Indipendenza
Corso Plebisciti
Viale Delle Argonni
Corso Marzo
Viale Corsica
Piazzale Giov. Belle Bande Nere
V. Vincenzo Foppa
Parco Solari
Piazzale F. Martini
Piazza Insubria
Viale Umbria
Corso Lodi
Corso Di Porta Romana
Ripa Di Porta Ticinese
Parco Ravizza
V. Isonzo
Viale Toscana
V. Lorenteggio
V. Ludovico Il Moro
S. Cristoforo
N
0
1000 meters

Milan (Milano)

It is said that for every church in Rome, there is a bank in Milan. Lest one should think Milan one-dimensional, however, it is important to note that this wealthy metropolis has other pressing concerns. Such as fashion. The prestige question depends not so much on what you do or who you did it with, as on what you are wearing when whatever it was was done. Thus, Milan's adolescent youth without a cause can pass hours astride their Vespas with the engines off, complacent in the knowledge that they look *maahgnifico.* In August, the clothing boutiques shut down, causing a mass exodus which strands many non-natives in an empty city, bereft of food, entertainment and outfits.

Orientation and Practical Information

Milan lies in the heart of northern Italy and is linked by rail to all major cities in Italy and Europe. The city is huge but manageable if you familiarize yourself with the historic center and the concentric rings of streets which surround it like a giant bullseye. On a radial street to the northeast is the huge **Stazione Centrale,** a frightening collusion of art deco and Fascist bombast. The center of the city is the unmistakable and equally frightening Gothic **duomo** (cathedral), and its elegant commercial counterpart, the lofty **Galleria Vittorio Emanuele II.** Like most *Milanesi,* you probably won't be able to afford lodgings in this area, but the **Metropolitana Milano (MM)** makes getting around easy.

Tourist Offices: APT, at 2 locations, all with free city maps and cultural brochures. **Stazione Centrale** (tel. 669 05 32) and **Piazza del Duomo** (tel. 80 96 62), open in summer Mon.-Sat. 8am-8pm, Sun. 9am-12:30pm and 1:30-5pm. To reserve a hotel room, call **Hotel Reservation Milano** (tel. 76 00 60 95).

Budget Travel: Centro Turistico Studentesco, via S. Antonio, 2 (tel. 58 30 41 21). Open Mon.-Fri. 9:30am-6pm, Sat. 9:30am-noon. Non-student travelers should head to **CIT,** in the middle of the Galleria Vittorio Emanuele II (tel. 86 66 61).

Consulates: U.S., largo Donegani, 1 (tel. 29 00 18 41). **Canada,** via Vittor Piana, 19 (tel. 669 74 51). **U.K.,** via San Paolo, 7 (tel. 869 34 42). **Australia,** via Borgogna, 2 (tel. 76 01 33 30). **New Zealand** citizens should contact the embassy in Rome.

Currency Exchange: Banca Nazionale delle Comunicazioni, at Stazione Centrale (tel. 669 02 53). Standard rates. Open Mon.-Fri. 8am-8pm, Sat. 8am-6:30pm, Sun. 9am-1:30pm.

American Express: via Brera, 3 (tel. 855 71), beyond p. Scala. Open Mon.-Fri. 9am-5:30pm.

Post Office: via Cordusio, 4, between the castle and the *duomo.* Stamps at counters 1 and 2. Poste Restante at CAI-POST office to the left after entering. Open Mon.-Sat. 8:15am-7:40pm. **Postal Code:** 20100.

Telephones: SIP, in the Galleria Vittorio Emanuele II. Open daily 7am-midnight. **City code:** 02.

Flights: Tel. 74 85 22 00 for both airports servicing Milan. Buses to and from intercontinental **Malpensa Airport** run every 45 min. (1 hr., L8500). If you're on a charter, check a day or two in advance with the **Doria Agency** (tel. 669 08 36) in Stazione Centrale about reserving a seat; buses leave just outside. They can also tell you about scheduled buses (5:50am-9pm, every 20 min., L2900, children L1500) to and from **Linate Airport,** where domestic and European flights land; it's cheaper and just as convenient to take city bus #73 (L1000) from p. S. Babila (on MM1).

Trains: Stazione Centrale, p. Duca d'Aosta (tel. 675 00), on MM2. International service to France via Turin, and Switzerland via the lake country.

Buses: Intercity, at p. Castello and the streets nearby. For points throughout Italy, the largest company is **Autostradale,** p. Castello, 1 (tel. 80 11 61).

Public Transportation: The 3 efficient lines of the **Metropolitana Milano** serve much of the city; buses fill the gaps. Information at the MM stop at p. Duomo (tel. 87 54 95). A L1000 ticket is good for 75 min. of surface travel and 1 subway ride. Day passes available at major stations (L3900).

Hitchhiking: Those hitching to Bologna, Rome or Florence take tram #13 from via Mazzini, near p. del Duomo, to p. Corvetto. Those going north take tram #14 from largo Cairoli (on MM1) to viale Certosa or go to pl. Kennedy (MM1: Lampugnano). Those destined for the Riviera and Genoa begin at p. Belfanti, near the Romolo end-station of MM2.

Luggage Storage: In the train station. Open daily 4am-2am.

Laundromat: Lavanderia Automatica, east on via Botticelli, 7 (tel. 266 33 00). Open Sept. to mid-July.

Pharmacy: Go to Stazione Centrale (tel. 669 07 35; open 24 hrs.) or call 192 to find out about rotating 24-hr. pharmacies.

Medical Assistance: Ospedale Maggiore Policlinico, via Francesco Sforza, 35 (tel. 551 16 55).

Emergencies: Police or Ambulance tel. 113. *Questura* (headquarters) at via Fatebenefratelli, 11 (tel. 622 61, ext. 327).

Accommodations

Staying in Milan flattens wallets in a hurry. Cheap*er* rooms lurk south of the station, along corso Buenos Aires and viale Tunisia.

Ostello Piero Rotta (IYHF), viale Salmoiraghi, 2 (tel. 36 70 95), ½ hr. from the station. MM1: QT8. Concrete, modern. Flexible 3-day max. stay. Reception open 7-9am and 5-11pm. Strict daytime lockout. Curfew 11:30pm. Members only, L15,000. IYHF cards L30,000. Sheets, padlock-accepting lockers, and breakfast included. Open Jan. 13-Dec. 20.

Albergo Canna, viale Tunisia, 6, 5th floor (tel. 29 52 02 19). MM1: Porta Venezia. Ample rooms and an obliging proprietor. Singles L28,000. Doubles L38,000. Hall showers included. **Hotel Kennedy,** on the 6th floor (tel. 29 40 09 34), has spotless rooms and dreamworld décor. Singles L40,000. Doubles L55,000. Some English spoken at both.

Due Giardini, via Settala, 46 (tel. 29 52 10 93). From the station, turn left on via Scarlatti, then 3rd right on Settala. A welcome respite from the dusty streets. Singles L34,000. Doubles L49,000. No reservations; show up in the morning.

Hotel Valley, via Soperga, 19 (tel. 669 27 77), 2 blocks from the station. English spoken. Reserve ahead, but make sure the price is established. Singles with shower L37,000. Doubles with shower L62,500.

Food

Milanese specialties include *riso gallo* (rice with saffron) and *cazzoeula* (a mixture of pork and cabbage). Restaurants are uniformly overpriced, especially around the *duomo* and near the station. Haggle in the **markets** around via Fauché or viale Papiniano on Saturdays and Tuesdays, and along via Santa Croce on Thursdays. The raucous **Fiera di Sinigallia,** Milan's oldest market, fills via Calatafini all day Saturday. After dinner, indulge in one of the exotic flavors at **Viel Gelati,** Milan's most famous *gelateria,* on via Luca Beltrami, off largo Cairoli. (Open Thurs.-Tues. until 2am.)

Spaghetteria Enoteca, via Solferino, 3. Amazing variations on spaghetti. Daily specials. Try the *assagini,* 5 "little tastes" of spaghetti in different sauces for L8500. Open Sept.-July Mon.-Sat. 7:30pm-midnight.

Flash, via Bergamini, 1, at p. Santo Stefano. Scrumptious sandwiches (including vegetarian) and pizza, just south of the Duomo. Soup and *panini* (L2000-4000) bar open Mon.-Sat. 7am-6:30pm. Restaurant open Tues.-Sun. noon-2:15pm and 7pm-midnight.

Brek, via Lepetit, 24. Classy, dependable self-service. Near the station, but you could be anywhere. *Primi* L4100. *Secondi* L7500. Open Sun.-Fri. 11:30am-3pm and 6:30-10:30pm.

Ciao, p. del Duomo. Pioneer of the Brek concept. Wholesome food, with a view of the cathedral if you can grab a window seat. Open daily noon-2:30pm and 6:30-11pm.

Sights

The *duomo* is a tribute to Milanese extravagance and six centuries of swirling cultural *mélange.* The flamboyant façade contrasts starkly with the darker Gothic interior. After a look at the stained glass and rose windows, ascend to the roof and stroll among pinnacles and marbleized citizenry. (Cathedral open daily 7am-7pm. Roof open daily 9am-5pm; Oct.-May 9am-4:30pm. Admission for the stairs L3000, elevator L5000.)

Beside the *duomo* is the true center of Milan, the colossal neo-classical **Galleria Vittorio Emanuele II,** a colossal iron-and-glass arcade that houses cafés and shops. As you enter the far *piazza,* **La Scala,** the world-famous opera house, lies to your left. Here, innumerable opera titans, from Caruso to Pavarotti, made their international debuts. To see the lavish, red-velvet hall, you must enter through the **Museo alla Scala** (tel. 805 34 18), which houses operatic and theatrical memorabilia. (Open Mon.-Sat. 9am-noon and 2:30-6pm. Admission L5000.)

Via Verdi leads to via Brera and the **Pinacoteca di Brera,** one of Italy's finest museums. This 17th-century *palazzo* has a horde of canvases by Caravaggio, Bellini, and Raphael. (Usually open Tues.-Thurs. 9am-6:30pm, Fri.-Sat. 9am-1:30pm, Sun. 9am-12:30pm. Admission L4000.) The **Museo Poldi Pezzoli,** at via Manzoni, 12, houses an outstanding private art collection and a dazzling trousseau of silverware, embroideries, and china. (Open Tues.-Fri. and Sun. 9:30am-12:15pm and 2:30-5:20pm, Sat. 9:30am-12:15pm and 2:30-7:30pm. Closed Sun. afternoons April-Sept. Admission L5000.)

The **Castello Sforzesco** (MM1: Cairoli) is the huge 15th-century castle of the Sforza, Milan's Renaissance dukes. The felicitously arranged sculpture collection includes Michelangelo's *Pietà Rondanini.* (Open Tues.-Sun. 9:30am-12:15pm and 2:30-5:30pm. Free.) Behind the castle is the vast **Parco Sempione,** the site of free open-air concerts in summer and a prime picnic spot.

Leonardo da Vinci created his *Last Supper* for the refectory wall of the **Basilica di Santa Maria delle Grazie** (MM1: Sant'Ambrogio). View Leonardo's characters and use of perspective through the blur of flooding, bombing and natural decay and scaffolding, likely to be up until the turn of the millenium. (Open daily 9am-1:15pm. Admission—splutter—L10,000.)

Entertainment and Shopping

Milan's pace doesn't let up at night: immerse yourself in the local culture, which isn't always so very *haute.* Pick up the tourist office's *What's on in Milan.* Every Thursday Milan's two leading papers, *Corriere della Sera* and *La Repubblica,* sum up the city's cultural offerings in slick magazine-type inserts that include information about performances at **La Scala** (tel. 72 00 37 44; regular season Dec.-June, fewer shows in summer and Sept.). Gallery seats are available from L12,000—you won't see much, but the sound is magnificent. (Box office open Tues.-Sun. 10am-1pm and 3:30-5:30pm; on performance days unsold gallery seats and standing room available after 5:30pm.)

Cinema Anteo, via Milazzo, 9, and **Cinema Mexico,** via Savona, 57, show films in English. Two established rock clubs are **Prego,** via Besenzanica, 3 (open Thurs.-Mon. until 2am; L15,000), and **Rolling Stone,** corso XXII Marzo, 32 (open Thurs.-Sun. 8pm-2am; cover L10,000, more on live-music nights). For jazz, Milan's leading venue remains **Le Scimmie,** via Ascanio Sforza, 49 (tel. 89 40 28 74; open Wed.-Mon. nights until 2am). If you want dance action, prepare to drop L15,000-20,000 at a major rager such as **USA,** via B. Cellini, 2 (open Wed.-Sun. 11:30pm-3am). Of Milan's gay discos, **Nuova Idea,** via de Castillia, 30 is the largest and best-known (L8000-10,000; open Tues. and Thurs.-Sun. 9:30pm-2 or 3am).

Fashion—designing it, buying it, and flaunting it—is Milan's lifeblood. Reasonably priced, high-quality clothing is sold in the shops along **corso Buenos Aires.** The **Fiera di Sinigallia** market (Sat. on via Calatafini; MM2: Sant' Agostino) will reward the assiduous shopper with the best bargains in Milan. Even if you don't want (can't afford) to buy, stroll down via Monte Napoleone and peek into the headquarters of greats like Armani and Versace. Trendy types can pay homage at **Fiorucci's** original shop at Galleria Passarella, 1 (tel. 70 00 80 33), at corso Vittorio Emanuele (MM1: San Babila). Open Tues.-Sat. 10am-7pm.

Genoa (Genova)

Descended from a proud and piratical maritime republic, Genoa's citizens still sail the seas and its sailors still swagger down the streets. In 1992, Genoa celebrates the 500th anniversary of native son Christopher Columbus's stumbling upon America, which should bring exhibitions, tall ships, and Americans themselves, along with a little more recognition for this somewhat cleaned-up port city.

Genoa is easily accessible by rail from Milan, Turin, and Pisa (each 2-2½ hr., L10,800). The French border lies only two hours westwards. There are two main train stations: **Stazione Principe,** p. Acquaverde (tel. (010) 26 24 55) to the west near the port, and **Stazione Brignole,** p. Verdi (tel. (010) 58 63 50) farther east. From Principe, **via Balbi** leads to piazza Nunziata, while via Fiume connects Brignole to **via XX Settembre,** which eventually leads into **piazza de Ferrari,** the center of town. South and southwest lies the town's historical center. Explore it during the day; at night, not even the police venture here. North of p. de Ferrari is p. Fontane Marose, off of which runs **via Garibaldi,** where the splendid *palazzi* **Bianco, Rosso, Municipale, Potestà,** and **Paroti** house many of the Flemish and Dutch masterpieces amassed by the merchant Genovese. Two other musts are the **Palazzo Ducale** in p. Matteotti, and **Villetta di Negro** with its **Museo d'Arte Orientale** off p. Corvetto. (Museum open Tues.-Sat. 9am-1:15pm and 3-6pm, Sun. 9:15am-12:45pm. Admission L4000.)

There are helpful **tourist offices** in both Principe (tel. (010) 26 26 23) and Brignole (tel. (010) 56 20 56) train stations. (Both open daily 8am-8pm.) Genoa has a **U.S. consulate,** p. Portobello, 6 (tel. (010) 28 27 41), and a **U.K.** one, via XII Ottobre, 2 (tel. (010) 56 48 33).

The city is constructing a youth hostel for the '92 celebrations on via Constanzi, overlooking the city; talk to the tourist office for details. Women should take advantage of the **Casa della Giovane,** p. Santa Sabina, 4 (tel. (010) 20 66 32), near p. Nunziate. Clean rooms cost L11,000-15,000, shower and breakfast included. (Curfew 10:30pm.) The neighborhood near Stazione Brignole is a tad more expensive, but far more pleasant. From the station walk down via de Amicis to your right; at the first intersection (p. Brignole) go right again, cross the tracks, and head up via Gropallo. The large, ornate building on the left at #4 houses several *pensioni;* **Mirella** is the best value. (Singles L25,000. Doubles L35,000.) Avoid the hotels in the *centro storico,* which rent rooms by the hour.

Genoa claims *pesto,* an otherworldly pasta sauce made from basil, cheese, pine nuts, garlic and olive oil—anywhere else it is *not* the same. Try *pansotti,* ravioli filled with cheese and herbs served with a walnut sauce. **Borgo Incrociati,** behind Stazione Brignole, crawls with inexpensive *trattoria* serving Genoese specialties; **Osteria du Colombo e Bruno,** at #44r, offers delicious full meals for L10,000. (Open Mon.-Sat. 12:30-2:30pm and 7:30-9:30pm.) In the *centro storico,* **Sa Pesta,** via Giustiniani 16r, knows its pesto, and it's cheap. (*Primi* L3000-4000, *secondi* L5000-6000. Open Mon.-Sat. noon-2:30pm. Avoid this neighborhood at night.) On summer nights, people escape the city to nearby **Nervi** (minutes by bus or train) where they barhop along the *lungomare* (beachfront promenade).

Italian Riviera

The Italian Riviera neatly divides at Genoa into two halves—the **Riviera di Ponente** (the Riviera of the Setting Sun) to the west, and the **Riviera di Levante** (the Riviera of the Rising Sun) to the east. **Liguria,** the crescent-shaped coastal strip encompassing both halves, differs greatly from the French Riviera; here you'll find elegance, not arrogance, and much less hype. While you're here, don't miss the *pasta alla genovese,* more commmonly known as "al pesto," or *focaccia,* delicious oily bread topped with onions or tomato sauce.

Finale Ligure marks the perfect spot for a *grand finale,* or grand beginning, to any Italian jaunt. West of Genoa on the Riviera di Ponente, it is the most pleasant of the Ponente resorts. The beaches are expansive, and the Gucci-garbed tourist menace keeps its distance. Trains leave hourly for Genoa (L4400), Ventimiglia (L5700), and Santa Margherita Ligure (L6300). Outside the train station on v. Torino, SAR **buses** run to neighboring beachside towns. Loquacious Luisa at the **AAST** tourist office, via S. Pietro, 14 (tel. (019) 69 25 81), on the street parallel to the waterfront, provides a free map and hotel listings. (Open Mon.-Fri. 8am-1:15pm and 3:30-6pm, Sat. 8am-12:45pm and 3:30-6:30pm, Sun. 9am-12:30pm.) Orange city buses go to the historic town, Finalborgo (L800). Rent **bikes** at Oddone, via Colombe, 20 (tel. (019) 69 42 15), on the street behind the tourist office.

The **IYHF youth hostel,** via Generale Caviglia (tel. (019) 69 05 15), is set in a turreted castle overlooking the sea. From the station, walk straight ahead and take the second left onto via Torino, following it all the way to the Esso station, then turn left and head up the 321-step staircase. (Lockout 9:30am-5pm. Curfew 11:30pm. L12,500 per night, sheets, showers and breakfast included. Dinner L11,000.) Try via Rossi and via Roma, inland from the waterfront, for food. Eat great *panini* and listen to rock at **Paninoteca Pilade,** via Garibaldi, 67 (open June-Aug. daily 10am-1am; Sept.-May Thurs.-Tues. 10am-2:30pm and 4-8pm). **Spaghetteria Il Posto,** via Porro, 19, is an elegant locale for a pasta-fest. Try *penne zar* (with salmon and caviar) for L7500. (Open Tues.-Sun. 7:30-10:30pm.)

The Riviera di Levante, east from Genoa, is the most splendid stretch of the Ligurian coast, where charming hamlets and colorful fishing villages gaze at themselves in clear turquoise water. Most beautiful are the Portofino peninsula (about ½ hr. by train east of Genoa) and the Cinque Terre area (immediately west of La Spezia). In July and August, only reservations or amazingly good fortune will find you a place for the night.

Base your exploration of the **Portofino peninsula** in **Santa Margherita Ligure;** frequent trains run from Genoa (L2100). Keep an eye out for the flowering white Margherita bush: in full bloom it appears to be covered with giant snowballs. The English-speaking **tourist office** is at via XXV Aprile, 2b (tel. (0185) 28 74 85). Turn right from the train station onto via Roma and when you arrive at largo Giusti, turn right again. Get maps, assistance in finding rooms, and change money here. (Open Mon.-Sat. 8:30am-noon and 3-6pm.) If your budget permits, the upscale but underpriced **Hotel Fasce,** via Luigi Bozzo, 3 (tel. (0185) 28 64 35), off corso Matteotti, is probably the only hotel listed in *Let's Go* to offer rooms with safes, private phones, color satellite TV, free parking, laundry service and rooftop sundeck with bar service. (L30,000 per person, with private bath L40,000 per person. Breakfast included. Half-pension required in Aug., L65,000 per person. Show them your *Let's Go.)* The **Famiglia Moras,** via Roma, 18 (tel. (0185) 28 67 58) rents homey, spotless rooms just down the street from the station. (Singles L25,000. Doubles L45,000.) The less attractive and slightly cheaper **Corallo,** via XXV Aprile, 20 (tel. (0185) 28 67 74), is about 3 blocks from the tourist office. (L20,000 per person. Showers L5000. Breakfast L5000.) Buy bread, cheese, meat, and produce along corso Matteotti; on Fridays from 8am to 1pm, the shops spill out onto the corso. For a night out, try the Giavanuzzi family's **Trattoria Baicin,** via Algeria, 9, off p. Martiri della Libertà. Mamma's *Trofie alla Genovese* (L5500) is delightful. (Open Tues.-Sun. 12:15-2pm and 6:45-11pm.) **Trattoria da Pezzi,** via Lavour, 21, has yummy rotating specials. (Open Sun.-Fri. 11:30am-2:15pm and 6-9:30pm. Take-out service 10am-2:45pm and 5-9:20pm). The best beaches are a 10-minute train trip east in Lavagna.

Camogli, a contraction of *casa moglie* (wives' house), is a name coined when all the husbands of this spectacular hamlet were out fishing. You can see Camogli's daily catch being landed from 4 to 6pm at the port. Reach Camogli by train (L1000) or bus (L1400) from Santa Margherita. The **tourist office** is at via XX Settembre, across from the bus stop and to your right as you exit the station. (Open Mon.-Sat. 9am-12:30pm and 3:30-6:30pm, Sun. 9am-12:30pm.) Stay at **Pensione La Camogliese,** via Garibaldi, 55 (tel. (0185) 77 14 02), down the stairway across the street from the train station. The wonderful owner offers his "Let's Go *amici*" discounts on his luxurious rooms (discounted singles with bath L35,000; doubles with bath L55,000) and finds them other spots when his are full. Don't miss the joy of eating a *camogliese*—a chocolate-covered rum cream puff—at **Revello,** via Garibaldi, 183, where they were conceived. (Open daily 8am-1pm and 3:30-8pm.)

Gorgeous yacht- and boutique-filled **Portofino** merits a day-trip from Santa Margherita. Though you won't be able to afford to stay or eat, the sight of the harbor will lull you into quiescence. **Buses** leave every 20 minutes to and from Santa Margherita (L1100)—get off at Portofino Mare, not Portofino Vetta. Make the well-marked trek up to the **castel** and **church** of San Giorgio overlooking the bay for matchless vistas, or take the path to the **lighthouse** (20 min. from the castle) for a bit more seclusion. More isolated than either Camogli or Portofino is **San Fruttuoso,** a green gem of a village at the western corner of the peninsula. Only boats run here (about 1 per hr.) from Camogli (L6000 round-trip). Intrepid trekkers can make the pretty, not terribly strenuous three-hour hike from Camogli or the 90-minute hike from Portofino.

Tripping down the coast, don't miss a visit to the **Cinque Terre,** a group of five isolated villages lost in time along the Ligurian coast. Renowned for limpid blue water and unforgettable scenery along the goat-paths that connect the towns, the Cinque Terre are also easily accessible by rail from Genoa, Pisa, Livorno, and Rome. Monterosso, largest of the five, hails farthest west; next come Vernazza, Corniglia, Manarola and Riomaggiore. The **tourist office** is next to the train station in Monterosso (tel. (0187) 81 75 06; open daily 10am-noon and 5-7pm) with accommodations service and currency exchange. Sojourn at **Hostel Momma Rosa,** p. Unità 2, Riomaggiore (tel. (0187) 92 00 50), an ultra-mellow establishment to the left of the train station (L15,000; 4 bathrooms for 60 beds) or check out the ubiquitous *affittacamere* (private rooms) signs in Corniglia. Munch happily on any of the seafood dishes that abound in the Cinque Terre, and be sure to wash them down with gulps of the excellent local white wine, *sciacchetrà.*

La Spezia is newer, more crowded, and less pleasant than the smaller towns to the immediate west, but is a good jumping-off point for the Cinque Terre. The nearest **IYHF youth hostel,** splendidly set and friendly, is on viale delle Pinete, 89 (tel. (0585) 78 00 34), in **Marina di Massa,** about 33km south of La Spezia. Take a train from La Spezia to Carrara; from here the hostel is 3km away by bus (get off at viale Avenzare). (L10,000, breakfast L2000, showers L500. Open 7am-11:30pm.) The most accessible **campground** is Campeggio Maralunga, v. Carpanini, 61 (tel. (0187) 96 65 89), off via Tagliata in **Lerici.** Take bus L from the La Spezia train station. Back in La Spezia, you can check in at **Hotel Terminus,** via Paleocapa, 21 (tel. (0187) 372 04) on your left as you exit the station. (Singles L23,000. Doubles L34,000). **Osteria del Prione,** via Prione, 270, will satisfy your every culinary whim. (Pasta from L6000, pizza from L4500. Open Mon.-Sat. 6-11pm.) La Spezia's **tourist office** lurks at viale Mazzini, 45, near the water. (Open Mon.-Fri. 9am-12:30pm and 4-7pm, Sat. 8am-1:30pm.)

Parma

Parma, so elegant, so intelligent, so conveniently located on the Bologna-Milan rail line, is one of the most fabulous stops in Italy. Parma rivals Bologna as Italy's food capital, and is home to the most refined *prosciutto* ham and fragrant *parmigiano* cheese on the peninsula, as well as *Lambrusco,* a deliciously intoxicating sparkling red wine. Plan to arrive famished.

Parma's harmonious **duomo** contains two medieval masterpieces: the moving *Descent from the Cross,* precursor of several Renaissance versions, and the *Episcopal Throne* by Benedetto Antelami, Parma's medieval master sculptor. Correggio painted the interior of the cathedral's dome of the **Church of San Giovanni Evangelista,** while Antelami festooned the exterior of the **battistero** (baptistry) with bas-reliefs of fantastic animals and biblical allegories. (Churches open daily 7:30am-noon and 3-7pm.) Nearby, the **Palazzo Pilotta** houses the **Galleria Nazionale di Parma,** with works by Correggio, da Vinci, the Holbeins, and van Dyck. (Open Tues.-Sat. 9am-2pm and Sun. 9am-1pm. Admission L6000.)

Via Garibaldi, Parma's main street, runs from the station to the center of town. The **Azienda Promozione Turistica,** p. Duomo, 5 (tel. (0521) 23 47 35), gives fine maps and counsel. (Open Mon.-Fri. 9am-12:30pm and 3:30-6:30pm, Sat. 9am-12:30pm.) The **Ostello Cittadella (IYHF),** via Passo Buole (tel. (0521) 58 15 46), lodges in a 17th-century fortress; take bus #9 in front of station. (Reception open 24 hrs. Curfew 11pm. L10,000. Open April-Oct.) The **Albergo Leon D'Oro,** viale A. Fratti, 4 (tel. (0521) 77 31 81), off via Trento, 2 blocks left from the station, has functional if uninspiring rooms. (Singles L21,000. Doubles L29,000.) **Casa Della Giovane,** via del Conservatorio, 11 (tel. (0521) 23 93 94), in the heart of the *centro storico* lets beautifully clean rooms to women (L15,000).

Don't hold back on your food budget while in Parma. The elderly **Sorelle Pachini** (Pachini Sisters), Bogo Farini 27, near p. Garibaldi, hide the best *trattorio* in town under the cover of a salami shop. Homemade *ravioli* galore only L6500. (Open Mon.-Sat. noon-2:30pm.) For dinner, hit the **Trattoria Corrieri,** via Conservatorio, 1 (tel. (0521) 23 44 26). The chef takes pride in the hams he slings from the rafters. Exceptional *tortellini di zucca* (ravioli made with sweet squash in a parmigiano sauce) are L6000; wash them down with L5000 carafes of *Lambrusco* wine. (Open Mon.-Sat. noon-2:30pm and 7:30-10pm.) Replenish staples at **Supermarket 22,** via XXII Luglio 27c (open 8:30am-1pm and 4-8pm, Thurs. 8:30am-1pm and 4-8pm).

Bologna

A savory plate of Bologna's *tortellini* aptly expresses this city's refinement and grace. The same high style radiates from its 900-year-old university, the oldest in Europe. The principled activism of its prominent student population makes Bologna the national bastion of left wing, if hardly proletarian, politics. In the town, alternately elegant and funky Bolognese gad about among endless porticoed walks and towering *palazzi.*

From the train station, walk down the galleries of via dell'Indipendenza to the main east-west street, **via Ugo Bassi.** Straight ahead are p. Nettuno and Maggiore, where the crowd gathers under the Corinthian columns of the **Palazzo del Podestà.** Follow the afternoon shade to the steps of the **Basilica of San Petronio,** a huge Gothic structure that some claim would have been bigger than St. Peter's had the Pope not meddled. The bronze *Neptune and Attendants* (by Giambologna) splash happily in the fountain outside. The two towers to the west on **piazza di Porta Ravegnana** attest to a time when Bologna's neighborhoods were organized around towers built by the most powerful families. You can climb the less tipsy one. (Open daily 9am-6pm. Admission L3000.)

Down via Santo Stefano, the triangular **piazza Santo Stefano** opens into a complex of Romanesque churches of austere beauty. The grandest is the round **Santo Sepolcro,** where San Petronio, patron of Bologna, rests under a carved pulpit. In the courtyard behind is the **Basin of Pilate,** in which Pontius supposedly washed his hands. Don't miss the cloisters behind the **Church of the Crucifixion** next to Santo Sepolcro, or the arches of the **Church of San Vitale,** the oldest in the group. A few blocks away in the **Church of San Domenico,** the saintly founder of the Dominican order is buried under a marble monument with statuettes by Michelangelo and Nicolò dell'Arca and four softly molded reliefs by Nicola Pisano. (Most churches open early morning-noon and 4-6pm.)

The **Pinacoteca Nazionale,** via delle Belle Arti, 56 (tel. (051) 22 37 74), one of Italy's major galleries, contains a beguiling bevy of Bolognese paintings and a spread of Renaissance masterpieces. (Open Mon.-Sat. 9am-2pm, Sun. 9am-1pm. Admission L6000.)

Bologna's **Informazione Azienda Turistica (IAT),** in the train station (tel. (051) 24 65 41), spews maps, up-to-the-minute information on vacant rooms, and posts a list of accommodations after hours. (Open Mon.-Sat. 9:30am-12:30pm and 2:30-6:30pm, Sun. 9:30am-12:30pm.) The main office in Palazzo Comunale at p. Maggiore (tel. (051) 23 96 60) is more exhaustive. Poste Restante goes to the **post office** at p. Minghetti, southeast of p. Maggiore. (Open Mon.-Fri. 8:15am-6:40pm, Sat. 8:15am-12:30pm.) One of Italy's biggest rail hubs, the **train station** is in p. delle Medaglio d'Oro at the northernmost end of town, a 20-minute walk from the center (or hop bus #25 or 30 for L1000).

Bologna's clean, congenial **Ostello (IYHF),** via Viadagola, 14 (tel. (051) 51 92 02), overlooks fecund farmland 6km from town. Take bus #93 east on V. Irnerio, off via dell'Indipendenza not far from the station (Mon.-Sat. until 8:15pm, L800) or bus #301 or 20 (Sun. and Aug. 1-24). (Reception open 7-9am and 5-11:30pm. L11,000, nonmembers L16,000. Breakfast included.) Hotels are expensive (singles L31,000, doubles L53,000) and vacancies rare; it's best to book (no fee) through the tourist office at the station. In the heart of town, try **Albergo Panorama,** via Livraghi 1 (tel. (051) 22 18 02; singles L31,000; doubles L53,000; view is free). Closer to the station, **Albergo Minerva,** via de Monani, 3 (tel. (051) 29 96 52), offers a convenient location and complaisant management. (Doubles L47,000, with bath L58,000.)

Bologna's rich cuisine commands some of the highest restaurant prices in Italy. The university district provides the best deals. **Antica Trattoria Roberto Spiga,** v. Broccaindosso 21/A, off strada Maggiore about 500m down from the two towers, makes its own *gnocchi* and serves full meals for a miraculous L15,000. (Open Sept.-July Mon.-Fri. noon-2pm and 7-10pm.) **Pizza Altero,** via dell'Indipendenza, 33, is crowded, delicious, and strictly take-out. (Slices only, L2000; open Thurs.-Tues. 8:30am-1am.) **Ristorante Clorofilla,** strada Maggiore 64, serves up innovative vegetarian specialties. (Open Mon.-Sat. 11am-3pm and 7pm-midnight.) Or mingle with the student crowd at the university **Mensa** (cafeteria), piazza Putoni, 1, where you can load up on a full meal for only L3000 (show any student ID to buy a ticket; open Sept.-July Mon.-Sat. 11:45am-2:30pm and 6:45-9pm.)

The university guarantees classical concerts and happening nightlife during the academic year. Get *Bologna Spettacolo* from the tourist office for listings and times. Bar-hop the university quarter around p. Verdi, and keep an eye out for posters trumpeting smaller performances.

Tuscany and Umbria

In these archetypical Italian provinces, the people are warm, the food of the highest caliber, and the medieval villages from another time. Tuscany has been congratulating itself for its civic spirit, food, wine, and, above all, its art, for 700 years. Its landscape is the classic background of much of Italian painting, and Tuscan, the language of Dante, Petrarch, and Machiavelli, is today's textbook Italian.

Umbria is the self-proclaimed green heart of Italy, carelessly bypassed by kamikaze tourists who stick slavishly to the Florence-Rome rail and roadways. Its marvelously preserved medieval hill towns preside over misty fields and olive groves, inspiring 20th-century travelers much as they did St. Francis, Perugino, Giotto, and Signorelli.

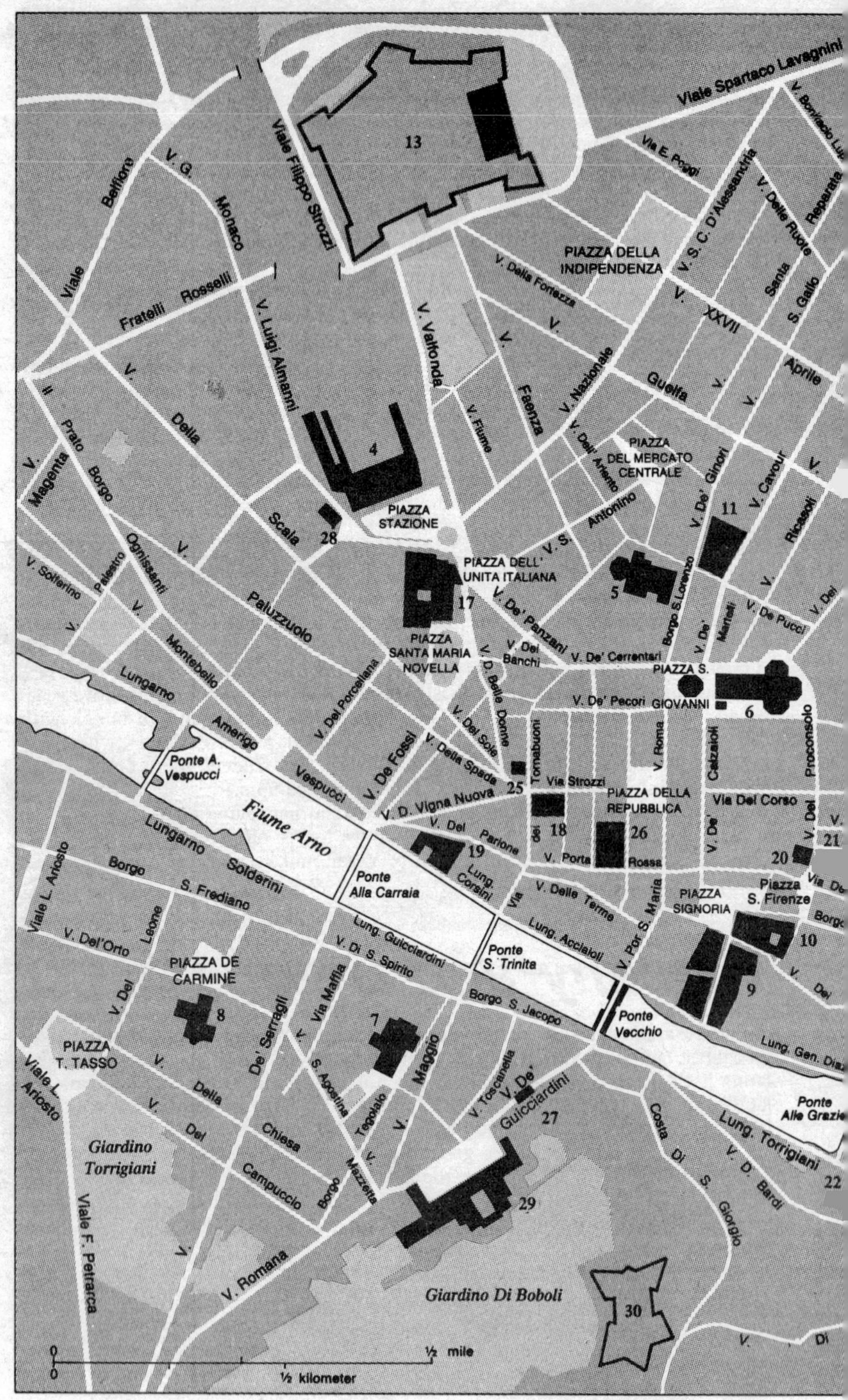
13
Viale Spartaco Lavagnini
V. Bonifacio Lupi
Via E. Poggi
V. S. C. D'Alessandria
V. Delle Ruote
Reparata
Santa
S. Gallo
PIAZZA DELLA INDIPENDENZA
V. XXVII Aprile
V. Della Fortezza
Viale Filippo Strozzi
V. G. Monaco
Viale Belfiore
Viale Fratelli Rosselli
V. Luigi Alamanni
V. Valfonda
V. Faenza
V. Nazionale
Guelfa
V. Fiume
V. Dell' Ariento
PIAZZA DEL MERCATO CENTRALE
V. De' Ginori
V. Cavour
V. Ricasoli
V. Della Scala
V. Il Prato
Borgo Ognissanti
V. Magenta
4
PIAZZA STAZIONE
28
V. Palazzuolo
V. Solferino
V. Palestro
V. Montebello
V. S. Antonino
11
PIAZZA DELL' UNITA ITALIANA
17
5
V. De' Panzani
Borgo S.Lorenzo
V. De' Martelli
V. De Pucci
V. Dei
PIAZZA SANTA MARIA NOVELLA
V. Dei Banchi
V. De' Cerretani
PIAZZA S. GIOVANNI
6
Lungarno Amerigo Vespucci
V. Del Porcellana
V. D. Belle Donne
V. Dei Sole
V. Della Spada
V. De' Pecori
V. De' Tornabuoni
V. Roma
V. Calzaioli
V. Del Proconsolo
Ponte A. Vespucci
V. De Fossi
25
Via Strozzi
PIAZZA DELLA REPUBBLICA
Via Del Corso
V. D. Vigna Nuova
Fiume Arno
V. Del Parione
18
26
21
Lungarno Soderini
19
V. Porta Rossa
20
Viale L. Ariosto
Borgo S. Frediano
Ponte Alla Carraia
Lung. Corsini
Via V. Delle Terme
PIAZZA SIGNORIA
Piazza S. Firenze
Via De
Borgo
10
V. Dell'Orto
V. Del Leone
Lung. Guicciardini
V. Di S. Spirito
Lung. Acciaioli
Ponte S. Trinita
V. Por. S. Maria
PIAZZA DE CARMINE
8
Via Maffia
9
V. Dei
Borgo S. Jacopo
Ponte Vecchio
7
PIAZZA T. TASSO
V. De' Serragli
V. S. Agostino
V. Maggio
Lung. Gen. Diaz
V. Della Chiesa
V. Del Campuccio
V. Toscanella
V. De' Guicciardini
27
Costa Di S. Giorgio
Ponte Alle Grazie
Viale L. Ariosto
Giardino Torrigiani
Tegolaio
Borgo
V. Mazzetta
Lung. Torrigiani
V. D. Bardi
22
29
Viale F. Petrarca
V. Romana
Giardino Di Boboli
30
V. Di
0
½ mile
½ kilometer

Florence
1 Piazza M. D'Azeglio
2 Giardino Della Gherardesca
3 Giardino Dei Semplici
4 S. Maria Novella Station
5 San Lorenzo
6 Duomo
7 S. Spirito
8 S. M. Del Carmine
9 Uffizi Gallery
10 Palazzo Vecchio
11 Palazzo Riccardi
12 S. Marco Università
13 Fortezza Da Basso
14 Pal. Pandolfini
15 S. Croce
16 S. S. Annunziata
17 S. Maria Novella
18 Palazzo Strozzi
19 Palazzo Corsini
20 Badia
21 Bargello
22 Museo Bardini
23 Youth Hostel
24 Camping
25 Azienda Autonoma di Turismo
26 Post Office
27 American Express
28 Bus Station
29 Palazzo Pitti
30 Forte Belvedere
N
PIAZZA SAVONAROLA
V. Giacomo Matteotti
V. A. Lamarmora
V. Giorgio La Pira
Giardino Della Gherardesca
V. Giuseppe Giusti
Borgo Pinti
V. Della Colonna
Degli Alfani
Viale Antonio Gramsci
V. Degli Artisti
Via Dei Della Robbia
V. Giambologna
V. L. C. Farini
Masaccio
V. G. Carducci
V. G. B. Niccolini
Mattonaia
V. Dell'Orivolo
Fiesolana
Via Dei Pilastri
V. Di Mezzo
Borgo Degli Albizi
V. Pietrapiana
Borgo La Croce
V. G. Verdi
PIAZZA BECCARIA
V. F. Paolieri
Via Dell' Agnolo
Ghibellina
Via Allegri
Borgo
P. S. Croce
Via S. Giuseppe
Corso Dei Tintori
Via Tripoli
Lung. Della Zecca Vecchia
Viale Gionanni Amendola
Fiume Arno
Lung. Serristori
Di S. Niccolo
Ponte San Niccolo
Via Dei Bastioni
Viale Michelangelo
PIAZZA F. FERRUCCI
Belvedere
PIAZZALE MICHAELANGELO

Florence (Firenze)

Epicenter of the Renaissance, Florence retains its beauty and vitality. Florentines such as Michelangelo, Machiavelli, and Cellini presided over Italy's cultural rebirth, and the Medici court became Italy's political and economic standard-bearer. The fruits of this period are still evident in the city's seemingly endless array of museums, churches, and *palazzi.* Florence preserves its wool town beginnings in small churches and family *trattorie* even as it upholds the Renaissance ideal of progress with a flair for fashion, finance and food.

Orientation and Practical Information

In Florence, all roads lead to the **duomo,** its giant profile an unmistakable reference point. The historic center of town lies between the *duomo* and the **Ponte Vecchio,** the principal bridge across the **River Arno.** The **Oltrarno,** the residential section of Florence on the opposite bank of the Old City, oozes major sights and loads of amazingly cheap and untouristed restaurants. The main train station, **Santa Maria Novella,** lies down via de' Cerretani (which becomes via de' Panzani), off the *duomo's* piazza. The hub of street nightlife is car-free via Calzaivoli, which links the *duomo* with **piazza della Signoria.** Forgo compact Florence's public transit system unless you're camping or hosteling; most pensions and sights are within a 15-minute walk of the *duomo.* But beware of the lightning-fast *Vespa*-borne mopedeers, who run wild in the streets and concede right-of-way to no one; they eat tourists for lunch.

Florence has two entirely independent sequences of street numbers: red indicates a commercial building, and blue or black a residential one (including most *pensioni).*

Tourist Offices: Azienda Promozionale di Turismo, via Manzoni, 16 (tel. 247 81 41 or 234 62 80), off p. Beccaria in the east end of town. Cultural information, free maps. No accommodations service. Open Mon.-Sat. 8:30am-1:30pm. **Branch offices** are at via Cavour 1r, (tel. 276 03 82), between the *duomo* and p. San Marco. Also at Chiasso Baroncelli, 19r (tel. 230 21 24), off p. della Signoria. (Both offices open Mon.-Sat. 8am-2pm.) **Consorgio ITA,** (tel. 28 35 00), in the train station by track 16 next to the pharmacy. An accommodations service. Come in person and they'll find you a room for an L2800 fee. Open daily 8:40am-8:30pm; mid-Nov. to mid-April 9am-8:45pm.

Budget Travel: STS (Student Travel Service), via Zanetti 18r (tel. 29 20 88 or 29 60 67), near the *duomo.* Discounts on rail and airplane tickets. Open Mon.-Fri. 9:30am-12:30pm and 3:30-6:30pm, Sat. 9:30am-12:30pm.

Consulates: U.S., lungarno Vespucci, 38 (tel. 239 82 76 or 21 76 05). Open Mon.-Fri. 8:30am-noon and 2-4pm. **U.K.,** lungarno Corsini, 2 (tel. 28 41 33). Open Mon.-Fri. 9:30am-12:30pm and 2:30-4:30pm. Citizens of **Canada, Australia** and **New Zealand** should contact their consulates in Rome.

Currency Exchange: Banks have the best rates. Open Mon.-Fri. 8:20am-1:20pm and 2:45-3:45pm. Banks open on Saturday mornings close by 11:20am. Many have 24-hr. ATMs. Try the Banca di Toscana, near the train station at the corner of via Nazionale.

American Express: via Guicciardini, 49r (tel. 27 87 51), across the Ponte Vecchio from the old city, on the left. If you pass the Palazzo Pitti, you've gone too far. Open Mon.-Fri. 9am-5:30pm, Sat. 9am-12:30pm.

Post Office: via Pellicceria, off p. della Repubblica. *Fermo Posta* at windows #23 and 24. Open Mon.-Fri. 8:15am-7pm, Sat. 8:15am-noon. **Postal Code:** 50100.

Telephones: ASST, in the post office and at via Cavour, 21r. Open 24 hrs. Shorter lines at **SIP** in the train station. One booth available for international calls. Open daily 7:30am-9:30pm. **City Code:** 055.

Trains: Most trains arrive at **Santa Maria Novella** station, near the center of town, though some to Rome stop only at **Campo di Marte** station, on Florence's east side; bus #19 links the two stations (24 hrs.). Information (tel. 27 87 85) open daily 7am-9pm.

Buses: LAZZI, via della Stazione, 1-6r (tel. 21 51 54). To Lucca (L6400), Pisa (L8700), and Pistoia (L4200). **SITA,** via Caterina da Siena, 15r (tel. 21 14 87), outside the train station. To Siena (L7000), San Gimignano (L6700), and Arezzo.

Public Transportation: ATAF information booth in the station outside the exit by track #5; also at p. del Duomo, 57r. Buy tickets (L800 for 70 min.) at *tabacchi* or at ticket machines by stops. Buy a ticket before you get on the bus and validate it once aboard.

Taxis: tel. 47 98, 43 90, or 436 19 04.

Moped Rental: Motorent, via S. Ganobi 9r (tel. 49 01 13). L5000 per hour, L30,000 per day, L180,000 per week.

Hitchhiking: Expect all the usual hazards. Those going on the A-1 to Bologna and Milan or the A-11 to the Riviera and Genoa take bus #29, 30, or 35 from the train station to the feeder near Peretola. Those desiring the A-1 to Rome and for the Siena extension take bus #31 or 32 from the station to exit 23. For information on hooking up with someone going your way, try the **Agenzia Autostop,** corso Tintori, 39 (tel. 28 06 21). Open Mon.-Sat. 9am-7:30pm, Sun. noon-3pm.

Bookstores: Paperback Exchange, via Fiesolana, 31*r.* Buy, trade, or sell. Open Mon.-Sat. 9am-1pm and 3:30-7:30pm; Dec.-Feb. Tues.-Sat. 9am-1pm and 3:30-7:30pm. **BM Bookshop,** Borgognissanti, 4r (tel. 29 45 75). Hugest selection of English language books in Florence. Open Mon.-Sat. 9am-1pm and 3:30-7:30pm, Sun. 9am-1pm; Nov.-Feb. closed Sun.

Laundromat: Lavanderia Manfred, via S. Antonio, 66r, across from the mercato centrale. L10,000 per 5kg load. **Lavanderia Automatica,** via degli Alfani, 44r. L11,000 per 5kg load. Open Mon.-Fri. 8am-1pm and 3-7:30pm.

Public Baths: Bagno S. Agostino, via S. Agostino, 8, off p. Santo Spirito. Open Tues. and Thurs. 3:30-6:45pm, Sat. 8:30am-noon and 3:30-6:45pm.

Pharmacy: Farmacia Comunale, by track #16 in the station (tel. 26 34 35). **Molteni,** via Calzaiuoli, 7r (tel. 26 34 90). Both open 24 hrs.

Medical Assistance: Misericordia, p. del Duomo, 20 (tel. 21 22 22). **Tourist Medical Services,** via Lorenzo il Magnifico, 59 (tel. 47 54 11). 24-hr. house calls.

Emergencies: Police, tel. 113. **Ufficio Stranieri,** via Zara, 2 (tel. 497 71), for foreigners (English-speaking personnel 9am-2pm).

Accommodations and Camping

Travelers with strong attachments to breakfast in bed will adore Florence; most hotels will enthusiastically provide this service. . .for only L10,000 per person, thrice the price and half the quality of a bar breakfast. Unfortunately, during the summer months, no one has much choice in the matter. Proprietors by and large will deny rooms to those who don't want breakfast; ask first if breakfast is mandatory. Reservations are wise at any rate. Florence abounds with lodgings, but the clean and convenient ones are booked far in advance, or fill up in the early morning. To reserve, send a one-night deposit by postal money order (dollars are generally OK). If you don't have a reservation, begin looking early, or reconcile yourself to the offerings of the tourist offices. If you arrive much later than noon, consider taking whatever they give you and shopping around later. *Do* eyeball the room before you relinquish your passport. If you are overcharged, or have complaints, talk first to the proprietor, and then to the tourist office (APT) on via Manzoni.

In past years, the city has run an *area di sosta* at Villa Favard (6km out of town), which provides a canopied spot to sling a sleeping bag, plus showers and toilets—all for free. Avoid camping or parking in secluded areas.

Hostels

Ostello della Gioventù Europa Villa Camerata (IYHF), viale Augusto Righi, 2-4 (tel. 60 14 51). In an old building on the northeast of town, 30 min. from the station on bus #17B (exit by track #5), or take the bus from the *duomo.* Open Mon.-Fri. 9am-1pm and 3-7pm. Members only. L16,000. Sheets and breakfast included. Reserve by mail only.

Instituto Gould, via de' Serragli, 49 (tel. 21 25 76). Near p. Santo Spirito in the Oltrarno. Take bus #36 or 37 from p. Santa Maria Novella to the 1st stop across the river. Or walk down via de' Fossi, cross the Ponte alla Carraia, and continue on via de' Serragli. Sunny, cheerful hotel with outgoing management. No curfew—they give out keys. No check-in or check-out on Sun. Open Mon.-Fri. 9am-1pm and 3-7pm; Sat. 9am-1pm. Singles L27,000, with bath L30,000. Doubles L44,000, with bath L48,000. Triples L54,000, with bath L72,000. Beds in a quad L17,000. No breakfast. Phone ahead.

Pensionato Pio X, via de' Serragli, 106 (tel. 22 50 44), a couple blocks beyond Instituto Gould. Gets an award for the four C's: clean, comfortable, cheerful and *cheap.* Hot showers are no problem. 2-day min. stay, but if you stay one night, you'll want to stay another. Curfew midnight. L15,000. No breakfast. No reservations, so arrive early.

Ostella Santa Monaca, via Santa Monaca, 6 (tel. 26 83 38), near the Carmine Church in the Oltrarno. Cramped bedrooms in an overcrowded and over-used hostel. The narrow staircase could use a good cleaning. Lack of toilets for women makes meeting morning necessities an interesting endeavor. L15,000. Sheets L2500. *Strict* midnight curfew. Daytime lockout. Arrive 9:30am-1pm, sign the list if there are still slots available (empty slot means empty bed). Drop any ID in the box, then return between 4 and 4:30pm to register.

Hotels: Near the Railroad Station

Leaving the station by track #16, the *piazza* and church of Santa Maria Novella are a five-minute walk to the right and then straight ahead. **Via Nazionale** and **via Faenza** also lie about five minutes from the station; as you exit track #16, turn right, and then this area will be on your left (look for the **Banca Toscana** at the beginning). Via Faenza has a lot of cheap beds in its noisy touristy streets; **Santa Maria Novella** is more tranquil and centrally located, but has fewer beds.

Pensione Ausonia/Pensione Kursaal, via Nazionale, 24 (tel. 49 65 47). Gregarious proprietors provide respite from chaos, spotless and sunny rooms, and tons of advice for anyone feeling a little lost. Singles L29,500, with bath L37,500. Doubles L43,500, with bath L54,500. *Let's Go* discount: March-Oct. 5% off, Nov.-Feb. 10% off. Breakfast L7000. Curfew 1am.

Pensione La Mia Casa, p. Santa Maria Novella, 23 (tel. 21 30 61). Make this your *casa* away from home. Large quarters in a 17th-century *palazzo.* Free nightly movies in English. Curfew midnight. Singles L26,000. Doubles L39,000, with bath L48,000. Breakfast L8000. Phone reservations held until noon.

Locanda Romagnola/Soggiorno Gigliola, via della Scala, 40 (tel. 21 15 97), 2 blocks from the train station, exiting by track #5. Plenty of comfortable, clean rooms and amiable management. Singles L29,500. Doubles L43,500, with bath L54,500. Showers L1300. Breakfast included. Curfew midnight. Phone reservations accepted.

Via Faenza 56: Six different *pensione* reside here; find the one you like best. **Pensione Azzi** (tel. 21 38 06). Curfew 1am. Singles L29,500. Doubles L46,000. Hostel-ish beds L17,000. Breakfast L7000. **Pensione Merlini** (tel. 21 28 48). Curfew 1am. Singles L29,500. Doubles L43,500-L54,500. Breakfast L9000. **Pensione Armonia** (tel. 21 14 46). No curfew. Singles L29,500. Doubles L43,500. Breakfast L9000. **Pensione Anna** (tel. 239 83 22). No curfew. Singles L29,500. Doubles L43,500. Breakfast L11,000. **Albergo Marini** (tel. 28 48 24). Curfew 1am. Singles L29,500. Doubles L43,500-L54,500. Breakfast L9000. **Albergo Paola** (tel. 21 36 82). No curfew. Doubles L40,000. Breakfast L5000. Showers L5000.

Albergo Nazionale, via Nazionale 22 (tel. 26 22 03), near p. dell'Indipendenza. Sunny rooms and friendly management. Breakfast served in your room. Singles L29,500, with bath L37,500. Doubles L43,500, with bath L54,500. Breakfast L9000.

Locanda Marcella, via Faenza 58 (tel. 21 32 32). Spacious rooms, some with a view of a colorful garden. Singles L29,500. Doubles L43,500, with bath L50,000.

Pensione Ottaviani, p. Ottaviani, 1 (tel. 29 62 23), on the corner of p. Santa Maria Novella. Overlooking the *piazza.* Clean and airy rooms. Singles L25,000. Doubles L43,500, with bath L54,500. Breakfast L7000.

Universo Hotel, p. Santa Maria Novella, 40 (tel. 21 14 84). Your spotless room will have a beautiful view of the *piazza* and *chiesa.* Singles L29,500, with bath L37,500. Doubles L42,000, with bath L52,000. Breakfast L9000.

Hotel Elite, via della Scale, 12 (tel. 21 53 95). Homey establishment with kindly, outgoing proprietor. Well-lit and comfortably furnished rooms worth slight extra expense. Singles L38,000. Doubles with bath L70,000. Breakfast L8000. No curfew. Reserve ahead if possible.

Locanda Nella, via Faenza, 59 (tel. 28 42 56). Kindly older proprietress takes care of you. Singles L29,500. Doubles L45,000. No breakfast.

Pensione Daniel, via Nazionale, 22 (tel. 21 12 93), near p. dell'Indipendenza. Small and dark, with Easter-egg walls. Curfew midnight. Doubles L26,000. Triples L39,000. Showers L1500. Curfew midnight. No reservations—show up early.

Hotels: In the University Quarter

Hotel Colomba, via Cavour 21 (tel. 28 91 39). Immaculately clean and fantastically spacious rooms. Singles L28,000. Doubles L41,000, with bath L51,000. Breakfast L10,000.

Albergo Casci, via Cavour, 13 (tel. 21 16 86; fax 239 64 61). Twenty-six charming rooms, some overlooking a gorgeous garden. Frescoed living room ceiling. Helpful management. All-you-can-eat breakfast, including O.J. Singles L37,500. Doubles L54,500. Breakfast L10,000. 10% *Let's Go* discount. Curfew 1am.

Albergo Sanpaoli, via San Gallo, 14 (tel. 28 48 34). Relax on your own private *terazzo* at this peaceful, sunny hotel. Refrigerators on each floor. No curfew. Singles L29,000. Doubles L43,000, with bath L52,000. No breakfast.

Hotels: Near the Duomo

Farther from the station, prices fall, with good deals between the *duomo* and the river. The daily tourist deluge misses many of these establishments, improving their atmosphere. None of the following is more than a 15-minute walk from the station, but park your pack or call first.

Locanda Orchidea, borgo degli Albizi, 11 (tel. 248 03 46). Seven large rooms surround a charming garden. Dante's wife was born in this 12th-century palazzo. Singles L28,000. Doubles L42,000. No curfew. One of the best buys in Florence, so reserve ahead.

Maria Luisa de' Medici, via del Corso, 1 (tel. 28 00 48). Old furniture meets funky art deco. Doubles L43,500, with bath L54,500. Hearty breakfast L12,000. Curfew midnight.

Hotel Colore, via dei Calzaivoli, 13 (tel. 21 03 01). Conveniently-located near *duomo.* Some rooms have view. Singles L29,000, with bath L32,000. Doubles L40,000, with bath L45,000. Breakfast included.

Albergo Firenze, p. Donati 4 (tel. 21 42 03), off il Corso. Clean, friendly, and centrally located. Singles L29,000. Doubles L43,500, with bath L54,000. Breakfast L8000.

Hotel Maxim, via Calzaivoli, 11 (tel. 21 74 74). Friendly owner proffers clean-and-sunny rooms near the *duomo.* Doubles L60,000, with bath L78,000. Breakfast L13,000. Laundry L12,000 per load.

Camping

Camping Italiani e Stranieri, viale Michelangelo, 80 (tel. 681 19 77), near piazzale Michelangelo. Take bus #13 from the station. An invigorating view, one you'll share with *many* others. May tell you they're full on the phone, but if you show up with your pack, they'll probably cough up a space. 500 campsites for tents. L5500 per person, L6000 per tent. Open April-Oct. 6am-midnight. Also try the slightly cheaper **Camping Villa Camerata,** viale A. Righi, 2-4 (tel. 61 03 00), near the youth hostel. L4500 per person, L5600 per tent.

Food

Like all things Florentine, food comes with style. The bizarre rumor that you can no longer get an excellent meal at excellent prices is only that. Stick to *trattorie* for the best bargains. Try the city's numerous *rosticcerie* and *gastronomie* to defray costs without sacrificing Tuscan delights like *lampredotta* (tripe), *pecorino* (sheep's milk cheese), or white *piattellini* beans. Forage through the enormous *Mercato Centrale,* near San Lorenzo, for picnic fixings. (Open Mon.-Sat. 6:30am-1pm and 4-8:30pm; Oct.-May Mon.-Sat. 6:30am-1pm.) *Supermarket Standa,* via Pietrapiana, 1r, serves all your needs. (Open Mon. 3-8pm, Tues.-Sat. 8:30am-8pm; Oct.-May Mon.-Sat. 6:30am-1pm.)

A daily dose of *gelato* is mandatory in Florence. Look for signs saying *produzione propria* to ensure that a store is vending a homemade product. A couple *gelaterie* in Florence are truly outstanding: **Vivoli's,** via della Stinche, 7, behind the Bargello (open Wed.-Mon. 8am-midnight); **Gelateria Green Eyes,** via dei Neri 20-22r (open daily 10:30am-midnight); and **Perchè No?,** via Tavolini, 19r, off via Calzaiuoli (open Wed.-Mon. 8am-1pm).

Acqua al Due, via dell'Acqua, 2r, behind the Bargello. A favorite with young Italians. Pasta sampler *assaggio* is an array of 5 delicious dishes (L8000). Open Tues.-Sun. noon-3pm and 7:30pm-1am.

Trattoria da Benvenuto, via dei Neri, 47r. Locals crowd it for lunch. Load up on a hefty plate of *gnocchi* (dumplings) for only L4500. Open Mon.-Tues. and Thurs.-Sat. noon-3pm and 7:15-10pm.

Amon, on via Palazzuolo. Some of the best Middle Eastern food to be found on any continent. Cool and crunchy cucumber salad L2500. Take-out only. Open Mon.-Sat. noon-3pm and 7-11pm.

Trattoria du Giorgio, via Palazzuolo 100r. Not fancy, but serves up delicious down-home Florentine meals for L13,000, including pasta, meat, salad, water, and wine. Open Mon.-Sat. noon-3:30pm and 6:30-10pm.

Trattoria Casalinga, via Michelozzi 9r, near p. Sante Spirite. Hearty Tuscan meals in a relaxed family-run establishment. Go for the *ravioli* made with spinach and ricotta (L4000). Menu changes daily. Open Mon.-Sat. noon-2pm and 7:30-10pm.

Car Lie's American Bakery, via Brache, 12r. The one and only true outpost of America. Wax nostalgic over their deathly fudge brownies and gooey chocolate chip cookies (L1000-L2000). Owners give out tons of advice. Open Mon.-Sat. 10:30am-1:30pm and 3:30-7:30pm. Open Sept.-July 15.

Sights

Florence has entranced intellectuals for centuries, and the same spell that bewitched Goethe and Camus may overcome you. Pick up the photocopied museum list at the tourist office for up-to-date information. An excellent warm-up for the sights of Florence is the series of **Renaissance Art Talks** given by Kirk von Dürer in the Penthouse Galleria at borgo San Lorenzo, 20 (tel. 28 54 37; April-Oct. Sun.-Thurs. at 8:30pm; lecture with slides L9000, students L7000).

The Accademia, Medici Chapel, Pitti Palace, Bargello, Museo Nazionale, Museo di San Marco, and Galleria Palatina close at 2pm; the Uffizi, Accademia, Medici Chapel, and Museo di San Marco are closed on Monday. See below for specific hours. Remember that during summer many of the most popular sights—the *duomo,* the Uffizi, the Accademia, and the Bargello—are as crowded as cattle cars. Moo. Arrive early.

Begin your exploration of Florence with the incomparable **Uffizi,** a complex built between 1559 and 1580 to house the Florentine public offices, guilds, and court artists. Today it houses the prime of the Italian Renaissance: Giotto, Cimabue, Filippo Lippi, Paolo Uccello, Piero della Francesca, Botticelli, Leonardo da Vinci, Michelangelo, Raphael, and Titian, along with some superb examples of northern art—works by Rubens, Rembrandt, and Dürer. (Open Tues.-Sat. 9am-7pm, Sun. 9am-1pm. Admission L10,000.) Vasari designed the Uffizi, and incorporated a **secret corridor** between Palazzo Vecchio and Palazzo Pitti in the Oltrarno; the corridor containing a portrait gallery runs through the Uffizi and over the Ponte Vecchio.

The **Palazzo Vecchio,** which replaced the Bargello as the seat of Florentine government upon the completion of its construction in 1314, dominates **Piazza della Signoria.** (Open Mon.-Fri. 9am-7pm, Sun. 8am-1pm. Admission L8000.) A vast space by medieval standards, the area around the *piazza* forms the city's civic center. Symbolic sculptures grace the area, including an awkward Neptune statue to whose sculptor Michelangelo quipped: "Oh Ammannato, Ammannato, what lovely marble you have ruined!"

More recently, excavations under the piazza have disfigured the original setting of Michelangelo's **David,** now housed in the **Accademia,** via Ricasoli, 60 (tel. 21 43 75; open Tues.-Sat. 9am-2pm, Sun. 9am-1pm; admission L10,000). Near the

Palazzo Vecchio on via del Proconsolo lies the **Museo Nazionale,** containing pinnacles of Florentine sculpture. Housed in the **Bargello**—the medieval palace of the chiefs of police—the collection includes Donatello's delicate *David* (an effeminate flower child compared to Michelangelo's) and the *Sacrifices of Abraham* sculpted by Ghiberti and Brunelleschi. (Open Tues.-Sat. 9am-2pm, Sun. 9am-1pm. Admission L6000.)

Symbol of Florence for centuries, the **duomo** stands at the heart of the city, down via del Proconsolo from p. della Signoria. Begun in 1299, the huge bath towel-colored building has always spoken more for Florentines' civic pride than for their piety. Climb the dome (L4000), the marvel of the 15th century, for the romantic view and examine firsthand the ingenious double shells that Brunelleschi employed to raise medieval Italy's tallest structure. The *duomo* is a house of worship, and those in immodest attire (bare shoulders or legs) will be rebuffed. *(Duomo* open to tourists daily 10am-5pm. Masses held 7-10am and 5-7pm. Free. Dome (tel. 21 32 29) open 10am-5:40pm, last entrance 5pm.) The much older **Battistero** (Baptistery), just in front of the *duomo,* is famous for its bronze doors (the southern set by Andrea Pisano, the others by Ghiberti). Entering the cool, cavernous interior, note the mosaics in the cupola—the devils beneath Christ's feet and the intricate tortures of Hell are worthy of Dante, who was baptized here. (Interior open Mon.-Sat. 1-6pm, Sun. 9:30am-12:30pm and 2:30-5:30pm. Free.)

Next to the *duomo* stands the brightly-colored **Campanile,** or "Giotto's Tower." (Open daily 8:30am-7:30pm; in off-season 9am-5pm; last entry 40 min. before closing. Admission L4000.) Most of the *duomo's* sculpture is housed in the nearby **Museo dell'Opera del Duomo.** The collection includes an unfinished *Pietà* by Michelangelo, nearly destroyed by the frustrated sculptor. Here also are the panels of the baptistry east doors, the "Gates of Paradise," restored after the 1966 flood. (Open Mon.-Sat. 9am-7:30pm; Nov.-Feb. Mon.-Sat. 9am-6pm. Admission L4000.)

In many ways, the churches of Florence are museums. Lorenzo il Magnifico, the great Medici political boss and patron of the arts, is buried in Brunelleschi's **Basilica di San Lorenzo** (tel. 21 66 34; open daily 7am-noon and 3:30-7pm). The neighboring **Biblioteca Laurenziana** (tel. 21 07 60), its rooms designed by Michelangelo, was a wellspring of mannerist architecture. (Open Mon.-Sat. 8am-2pm. Free.) Michelangelo's simple, unfinished **New Sacristy,** the final resting place of Lorenzo and Giuliano de' Medici, stands in sharp contrast to the gaudy, ornate chapel that shelters it. The dubious look of the female figures *Dawn* and *Night* may derive from Michelangelo's refusal to employ female models. (Open Tues.-Sat. 9am-2pm, Sun. 9am-1pm. Admission L8000.) Michelangelo used the walls of a basement room beneath the New Sacristy as a sketch pad. To see it, ask for a supplementary ticket (free) to *la sala di Michelangelo.*

Near the Accademia, the **Museo di San Marco** has a series of monks' cells decorated by Fra Angelico, who was nearly canonized for his unique shade of blue. (Open Tues.-Sat. 9am-2pm, Sun. 9am-1pm. Admission L6000.) Masaccio's *Holy Trinity* may be seen in the Dominican **Basilica di Santa Maria Novella** (tel. 21 01 13; open daily 7-11:30am and 3:30-5pm). To see Giotto's epoch-making frescoes, visit the **Church of Santa Croce,** far and away the most lavish in the city. Among the famous Florentines buried here are Michelangelo, Machiavelli, Rossini, and Galileo. Dante was supposed to be buried here, and his empty sarcophagus stands waiting; instead the people of Ravenna, the city which took him in after Florence banished him, clung to the remains. (Open daily 8am-12:30pm and 3-6:30pm.)

Florence's grandest frescoes are those by Masaccio, Masolino and Filippino Lippi in the **Brancacci Chapel** of the **Church of Santa Maria del Carmine.** The finest panels, entirely by Masaccio, depict *The Tribute Money* and *The Expulsion from Paradise.* (Open Mon.-Sat. 10am-5pm, Sun. 1-5pm. Admission L5000.)

Strewn about the city in all their outsized glory are various *palazzi,* grand palaces reflecting the architectural magnificence of the Renaissance. The **Palazzo Medici** (tel. 276 01), just around the corner from the *duomo,* was one of the first of the type. (Closed indefinitely for restoration in 1990.) Where the Medici led, others quickly followed: products of the ensuing building boom include the huge **Palazzo**

Strozzi, the quintessential Tuscan *palazzo*, with its rusticated stonework and carefully articulated façade. (Open Mon., Wed., and Fri. 4-7pm. Free.) The façade of the **Palazzo Rucellai** was Alberti's characteristically unique contribution. (Open Tues.-Sun. 10am-7:30pm. Admission L3000.) Across the Ponte Vecchio, paved with expensive jewelers, souvenir stands, and international flotsam, is the **Palazzo Pitti**, another onetime Medici stronghold. It contains five fine and not-so-fine museums, most notably the **Galleria Palatina.** (Open Tues.-Sat. 9am-2pm, Sun. 9am-1pm. Admission L8000.)

Entertainment

Florentines and tourists alike congregate on the steps of the *duomo*, along via Calzaiuoli, on p. della Signoria, on the Ponte Vecchio, and on piazzale Michelangelo. Major ragers will enjoy dancing at **Yab Yum**, via dei Sassetti (tel. 28 20 18), off p. della Repubblica. (Open nightly 11pm-4:30am. Cover with first drink L15,000.) Their clientele makes a yearly summer exodus to **La Capitale**, in parco delle Cascine, to party out under the stars. Also try **Space Electronic** (tel. 29 30 82), via Palazzuolo, 37, which attracts a young, international crowd and has a fish-tank bar filled with piranhas (open nightly 9:30pm-1:30am, in winter Tues.-Sun.; cover L15,000). American infiltration is still limited at the new **Rockcafé**, borgo Albizi, 66. (Open Tues.-Sun. 10pm-4am. Cover L15,000.) **Tabasco**, p. S. Cecilia, 3*r*, (tel. 21 30 00) near p. della Signoria, is Florence's most popular gay disco. (Open Tues.-Sat. 9:30pm-2:30am. Cover Tues.-Thurs. L12,000, Fri.-Sun. L15,000.) For live jazz and a slick scene, try the **Jazz Club**, via Nuova de' Caccini, 3 (disregard the "members only" sign; open Sept. 21-July 14). **Last Exit**, down the street at Borgo Pinti, 17*r*, is a more "cultured" hangout, where art meets dancing. (Open Sept.-June.) The **Astro Cinema**, opposite Gelateria Vivoli on p. S. Simeone, shows films in English (admission L6500; closed in summer).

After warming up with the **Scoppio del Carro** festival on Easter Sunday, Florence indulges in another fireworks-filled celebration on June 24, the **Feast of St. John**, the city's patron saint. The last week of June also brings the traditional games of **Calcio Storico in Costume**, an archaic, hilarious form of soccer, played in historical dress. Contact the tourist office for ticket information. The **Florence Film Festival** is usually held in December at the Forte Belvedere. In summer the **Estate Fiesolana** fills the old Roman theater in **Fiesole** with concerts, opera, theater, ballet and movies (early June, July, and Aug.). Tickets are reasonable (L15,000 and up); pick up the schedule from the EPT in Florence. Bus #7 runs to Fiesole from Florence's train station (30 min.). In July the **Teatro Comunale** offers ballet and concerts in the courtyard of the Palazzo Pitti, and the international music festival, **Maggio Musicale Fiorentino**, takes place in May and June. For tickets, visit the box office at corso Italia, 16. (Open Tues.-Sun. 9am-1pm. Seats L15,000-40,000.)

Siena

A flourishing center of trade during the 13th and 14th centuries, Siena became Florence's deadliest rival during the medieval wars between the Guelphs and Ghibbelines, equalling and even surpassing its nemesis as a city of wealth, power and culture. The city remains a living masterpiece; even in Italy, few places are as aesthetically harmonious. Its visual consonance encompasses even the backlying red clay hills, source of the burnt Siena hue that tints the buildings of the historic center. Siena is at its spectacular best in July and August, when the entire populace wildly celebrates its medieval heritage during the *Palio* horse races.

Siena lies off the main Florence-Rome rail line. From Florence, change at Empoli (L4400); from Rome, at Chiusi (L16,700). Take any bus passing across the street from the station to the center of town (L700), or prepare for a 45-min. uphill trek. Express **SITA** buses, often faster than the train, link Siena with Florence (1 hr.,

L6800) and Rome (3½ hr., L14,800). Siena's **city code** is 0577, and its **postal code** is 53100.

The striking, shell-shaped **piazza del Campo** is the focus of Sienese life, day and night. At the bottom of the shell is the **Palazzo Pubblico,** an elegant Gothic palace over which soars the **Torre del Mangia,** nicknamed for the dock's gluttonous bell-ringer. Inside, the **Museo Civico** contains some of the fines of Siena's Gothic painting; don't miss the *Allegories of Good and Bad Government* by brothers Pietro and Ambrogio Lorenzetti. (Open Mon.-Sat. 9am-6:45pm, Sun. 9:30am-12:45pm; Nov.-March daily 9am-12:45pm. Admission L5500, students L3000. Tower open June-Oct. daily 10am-7pm; Nov.-Feb. Sun. 10am-6pm; March-May daily 10am-6pm. Admission L4000.)

Siena's zebra-striped **duomo** is meticulously crafted, and one of the few entirely completed duomos in Italy. The **pulpit,** with scenes from the life of Christ, is one of Nicola Pisano's finest, remarkably expressive for the period. Pay L1500 to enter **Libreria Piccolomini,** off the left aisle, which holds frescoes by Pinturicchio and some lavish 15th-century illuminated musical scores. (Both open daily 9am-7:30pm; Nov.-March 8am-5pm.) One of the duomo's greatest treasures, the **Font,** lies in the baptistry at the back of the church. With brass relief panels by Ghiberti, della Quercia and Donatello, this font marks the transition from International Gothic to Renaissance sculpture with Donatello's careful attention to detail and perspective.

The **Museo dell'Opera della Metropolitana,** next to the cathedral, displays some incredible Gothic sculpture by Giovanni Pisano, as well as Duccio's splendid *Maestà.* (Open daily 9am-7:30pm; off-season 9am-1:30pm. Admission L5000.) For more of this school, take in the exceptional collection of the **Pinacoteca,** via San Pietro, 29. (Open Tues.-Sat. 8:30am-2pm and 4-7pm, Sun. 8:30am-2pm. Admission L8000.)

Try to visit Siena on July 2 or August 16 for **il Palio,** a day-long celebration and colorful procession in 15th-century costume. The central event is a traditional horse race around the p. del Campo, jammed with tens of thousands of people. Get there three days before the race to watch the rambunctious horse selection in the campo and to pick a *contrada* to root for. The best seats for the 7pm race are at the top of the *piazza* near the fountain, but these cost about L150,000. Infield standing-room is free, but unless you arrive early in the day you will be far from the track. The winning district holds a torch-lit procession through the city the night after the race. For tickets and a list of hotels and *pensioni,* write to the tourist office by March; arrive without a reservation and you'll be sleepin' on the streets. Train tickets should be bought well in advance.

The **tourist office** (tel. 28 05 51), p. del Campo, 56, provides maps and deciphers transportation schedules. (Open Mon.-Fri. 9am-12:30pm and 3:30-7pm, Sat. 9am-12:30pm.) Siena is extremely popular in summer, with a limited number of inexpensive rooms and precious few singles; arrive by noon or book ahead. The somewhat inconveniently located **Ostello della Gioventù "Guidoriccio" (IYHF),** via Fiorentina 89 (tel. 522 12), in localita lo Stellino, is about a 25 min. bus ride from the center. (Members only. Curfew 11pm. L15,000, breakfast included. Dinner L10,000.) Take bus #4 or 15 across from the station or p. Matteoti; if coming from Florence by bus, get off at the stop just after the large black and white sign announcing that you've entered Siena. The **Casa del Pellegrino,** via Camporegio, 3 (tel. 441 77), behind p. San Demonico, is a spotless establishment run by nuns; the rooms have fantastic views of the *duomo.* (Curfew 11pm. Singles with bath L36,000. Doubles with bath L50,000. Triples with bath L70,000.) The **Albergo Continentale,** via Banchi di Sopca, 85 (tel. 414 51) is a good bargain in a central location, near p. Matteoti. (Singles L30,000. Doubles L52,000.) Truly a pearl, **Albergo la Perla,** via delle Terme, 25 (tel. 471 44) has sufficient rooms and a central location. Singles with bath L34,000. Doubles L45,000, with bath L53,000. The newly renovated **Hotel Etruria,** via Donazelle, 1-3 (tel. 28 80 88) offers comfortable rooms and easy access to the *Campo.* (Singles with bath L45,000. Doubles with bath L65,000.)

Siena's bakeries offer a wide selection of sinfully rich pastries, most notably a concoction of honey, almonds, and candied fruit called *panforte.* Sample them at **Bar**

Pasticceria Nannini, via Banchi di Sopra, 22-24. Hang out with the student crowd at the **Mensa Universitaria,** via Sant' Agata, 1, in a courtyard beneath Sant' Agostino. (Meals L8500. Open Mon.-Sat. noon-2pm and 6:45-9pm.) **Il Barbero,** p. del Campo, 80-81, purveys cheap cafeteria grub and grog, with a wide selection of *primi* (L6000) and *secondi* (L13,000). (Open daily noon-3pm and 7-9:30pm). Hearty Tuscan specialties in a homey atmosphere are yours at **Trattoria "Titti,"** on via Camollia, 193 (open 12:30-2:30pm and 7:30-10:30pm). Popular **La Grotta del Gallo Nero,** via del Porrione, 65-67 (tel. 22 04 46) also serves Tuscan specialties at unbeatable prices and has a heady selection of area *chianti.* (Open daily noon-3pm and 7-10:30pm.) For cheap foodstuffs, check out the well-stocked grocery **Consorzio Agrario,** via Pianigiani, 5, off p. Salimberi or the **COOP** by the train station.

Near Siena

Like a hedgehog against the rolling Tuscan landscape, the medieval towers of **San Gimignano** bristle skywards only an hour away by bus from Siena (approx. 8 Tra-In buses daily, L5200). The towers and the perfectly preserved walled *centro* recall 13th-century struggles between San Gimignano's two wealthiest families, the Ardinghellis and the Salvuccis, who competed to construct these fortified stalks. Of the original 72, 14 remain. Scale the **Torre Grossa,** the tallest of the remaining towers, attached to **Palazzo del Popolo,** for a 360° panorama of Tuscany. San Gimignano hosts one of the cleanest and friendliest hostels in central Italy, **Ostello della Gioventù,** via della Fonti, 1 (tel. (0577) 94 09 91; only L13,500 per night, including sheets, shower, and breakfast). **Chiribiris'** osticceria offers the best deal in this overpriced town; pick up copious portions of pasta (L4500) or *secondi* like roast chicken (L7000). (No service, but you can eat at the tables in the store.)

If you've had it with the chaos of city hopping, a few day's respite of sun and swimming on the island of **Elba,** just off the coast of Tuscany, is definitely what you're hankering for. Take the train to Montepescali and change for Piombino Maritima (L12,200), where you can hop a Torremar ferry to Elba (about 8 per day, 1 hr., L6000). Avoid Elba in July and August, when chaos reigns as half of Italy and two-thirds of Germany cram onto the tiny island and snatch all the beds.

Pisa

No plastic model or commemorative ashtray can even begin to capture the mad splendor of Pisa's crazily tilting tower. Pisa bubbles with pride not only for its tower, but for its lesser known but unsurpassable *duomo* and its intellectually effervescent ancient university. As a young medieval republic, it rivaled Genoa and Venice for maritime supremacy, Padua and Bologna for scholarly brilliance, and permanently laid its claim to architectural fame. Today Pisa subsists largely on the daily tide of tourists from Florence (1 hr. by train) and other neighboring cities, who come to ogle the tipping tower—which is now closed to the public.

Pisa's most revered monuments lie in the **Campo dei Miracoli,** a grassy field on the northern side of the river Arno. A L12,000 ticket lets you into all of the Campo's sights. The dazzling **Duomo** is chock full of art, including Giovanni Pisano's elaborate pulpit and its burlesque Gothic reliefs. The swinging motions of the lamp over the center aisle supposedly sparked Galileo's discovery of pendulum motion in 1581—although the lamp was not finished until 1587. (Open daily 7:45am-12:45pm and 3-6:45pm; off-season 7:45am-12:45pm and 3-4:45pm.) Next door in the **baptistry,** ask the custodian for a demonstration of the acoustics—a sung note resounds for minutes. (Open same times as Duomo. Admission L5000.)

The adjoining **camposanto,** a long white-walled cemetery, has many classical sarcophagi admired by Renaissance artists, and a series of haunting frescoes by the so-called "Master of the Triumph of Death." (Open daily 8am-7pm; off-season 9am-5pm. Admission L5000.) The **Museo delle Sinopie,** across the street, displays the elegant underdrawings that Nicola Pisano inscribed into the wall to guide him as he painted. (Open daily 9am-1pm and 3-7pm; off-season 9am-12:45pm and 3-5pm. Admission L5000.) The **Museo dell'Opera del Duomo,** behind the Tower, displays works by Pisano and Guardi, alongside archaeological finds. (Open daily 8am-8pm; off-season 9am-5pm. Admission L5000.) One hidden treasure is the church of **Santa Maria della Spina,** on lungarno Gambacorti, on the south side of the river. (Open daily 8am-12:30pm and 3-7pm.)

The **tourist office** at the station (to the left as you exit) doles out maps with directions to the tower (tel. (050) 422 91; open daily 9am-1pm and 3-7pm). The branch office off the Campo dei Miracoli, in p. del Duomo, has more detailed information. (tel. (050) 56 04 64; open daily 9am-1pm and 4-6pm).

The **Albergo Gronchi,** p. Archivescovado, 1 (tel. (050) 56 18 23), is just off p. del Duomo. (Singles L25,000. Doubles L38,000.) **Albergo Helvetia,** via Don G. Boschi, 31 (tel. (050) 412 32), around the block from Gronchi, is simple and clean. (Singles L26,000. Doubles L38,000, with bath L42,000.) Both have midnight curfews. The **Casa della Giovane,** via Corridoni, 31 (tel. (050) 227 32), a 10-minute walk from the station (turn right immediately), offers beds to women (L15,000, breakfast included; reception closes midnight). **Camping Torre Pendente** is just outside the gates at viale delle Cascine, 86 (tel. (050) 56 06 65; L6000 per person, L3000 per tent).

Pisa's cheapest (and most well-rounded) meals cost L3000 at the **Mensa Universitaria** on via Martiri off p. dei Cavalieri. Buy tickets during lunchtime (no student ID necessary) or hit up passing students, who might sell extras at dinner. (Open mid-Sept. to mid-July Mon.-Fri. noon-2:30pm and 7-9pm, Sat.-Sun. noon-2:30pm.)

Perugia

The exquisitely polite population of Perugia seems to be making up for several millenia of exquisite nastiness, during which they regularly stoned each other for fun and even threw tree-hugging St. Francis of Assisi into a dungeon. Perugia, once home to the masochistic Flagellant cultists, is now the center of the Italian chocolate world, a university town which hosts a popular world-class jazz festival from late June to early July. City buses (L600) regularly connect the station, in the valley, with p. Italia and p. Matteotti, in the center of town. Perugia is a three-hour train ride from either Rome or Florence (most often changing at Terontola and Foligno), and is also close to Assisi (by bus 40 min., by train 25 min.), the excruciatingly cute **Gubbio** (an hour by bus), and 1½ hr. by bus from other Umbrian hilltop delights like **Orvieto** (which has arguably the best cathedral façade in Italy), and **Spoleto** (home of Italy's biggest modern arts festival, the *Festival dei Due Mondi* in June and July).

The towering fountain of **Piazza IV Novembre,** at the opposite end of corso Vannucci from p. d'Italia, is adorned with sculptures and bas-reliefs by Nicola and Giovanni Pisano. The **Palazzo dei Priori,** with its colored marble and widening steps, adds drama to the setting. The palace houses the frescoed **Sala dei Notari** and the **Galleria Nazionale dell'Umbria,** with works by Perugino, Duccio, Piero della Francesca, and Fra Angelico. (Open Tues.-Sat. 8:45am-1:45pm and 3-7pm, Sun. 9am-1pm. Admission L8000.) Next door are the delicate frescoes of the **Collegio del Cambio,** painted by Perugino in collaboration with his pupil Raphael. Further towards the piazza, visit the **Collegio della Mercanzia,** a richly paneled room still home to Perugia's merchant guild. (Both open Tues.-Sat. 9am-12:30pm and 3-6pm, Sun. 9am-12:30pm. Admission for both L2000.) The **Museo Archeologico Nazionale dell'Umbria,** next to the Church of San Domenico near via Cavour, emphasizes Perugia's Etruscan heritage. (Open Tues.-Sat. 9am-1pm and 3-7pm, Sun. 9am-1pm. Admission L4000.) **Rocca Paolina,** by via Marzia, is a 16th-century fortress which now houses modern art exhibits and shelters the city's *scala mobile* (escalator) leading to p. Partigiani. Above, the geometric **Giardini Carducci** is *the* place to love-clutch your *amore,* as famous lovers Nicola and Corolien did centuries ago. Off via della Prone, near the University for Foreigners, is the **Arch of Augustus,** the largest piece of Etruscan stonework in existence.

The **Azienda di Promozione Turistica,** at p. IV Novembre (tel. (075) 233 27) in the corner across from the *duomo,* provides regional information, accommodations listings, a map, and a detailed walking guide. (Open Mon.-Sat. 8:30am-1:30pm and 4-7pm, Sun. 9am-1pm.) **Laundromat GR** is at c. Garibaldi, 34, near the University for Foreigners (open Mon.-Fri. 8:30am-1pm and 3:30-7:30pm, Sat. 8:30am-1pm; L3000 per kg). For a cheap, clean bed, ply the independent youth hostel, **Centro Internazionale di Accoglienza per la Gioventù,** at via Bontempi, 13. (Tel. (075) 228 80. Lockout 9:30am-4pm. Strict midnight curfew. Dorms L10,000. Sheets L1000.) Rooms in **Albergo Anna,** via del Priori, 48, 4th floor (tel. (075) 663 04), are clean, cool and 17th-century. **Pensione Lory,** corso Vannucci 10 (tel. (075) 242 66) has an optimal location and a homey atmosphere. Both offer singles for L26,000 and doubles for L33,000-36,000. **Albergo Etruria,** via della Luna, 21 (tel. (075) 237 30) has a beautiful 12th-century sitting room (comparable prices).

Dining in Perugia is at once tasty and cheap. *The* place to sample simple Italian cooking is at the **Trattoria Calzoni,** via Cesare Caporali 12, off p. Repubblica. The saintly *signora* creates complete meals nightly for about L12,000. **Ristorante dal Mi Cocco,** c. Garibaldi, 12, offers what may be the best deal in Italy. A full six-course meal including two types of wine runs L17,000. The **Tavola Calda** on p. Danti offers up self-service repasts for about L10,000. Cleanse your palate at the excellent **Gelateria 2000,** via Luigi Bonazzi, 3, off the main drag.

Assisi

Assisi has emerged as the center of a religious renaissance among Catholic youth, thanks in part to those oh-so-hip friars, often sporting jeans and Birkenstocks under their black frocks, who order their lives according to St. Francis, a poetic Dr. Doolittle-type monk who preached poverty, obedience and love over eight centuries ago. After St. Francis's death in 1226, the greatest Florentine and Sienese painters decorated the **Basilica di San Francesco** with a spectacular concentration of frescoes illustrating his life. The Basilica is actually three churches in one—the sumptuously-decorated and well-lit Upper Church, the more subdued and pious Lower Church, and the Crypt, which houses St. Francis' tomb as its altar. (Open daily in summer 6:30am-7pm, closed to tourists Sun. mornings and holy days. English-language Mass Sun. at 8:30am. English tours Mon.-Sat. 10am and 3pm. Modest dress; no photography.) A one-hour uphill hike through Porta di San Francesco takes you to the **Eremo delle Carceri,** the hermitage where St. Francis got away from it all. (Open daily dawn to dusk.) Towering above town, the imposing **Rocca Maggiore** provides Italy's best hide-n-seek location. Climb around in this fortress and let your imagination run wild. (Open daily 9am-8pm; in winter daily 10am-4pm. Admission L3000, students with ID L1500.)

Check with **Azienda di Promozione Turistica,** p. del Comune, 12 (tel. (075) 81 25 34), for help with lodgings and for schedules of summer festivities; ask about stays in private homes or religious institutions. (Open Mon.-Fri. 8am-2pm and 3-7pm, Sat. 9am-1pm and 4-7pm, Sun. 9am-1pm.) The well-appointed private **hostel and campground** (tel. (075) 81 36 36) is about 1km from Assisi, in the hamlet of Fontemaggio (L12,000, sheets included); take the bus from the station to Matteotti, and take the road from there towards Eremo delle Carceri. Several houses off p. Matteotti offer *camere* (rooms) for about L18,000 per person. Try **Camere Maria Bocchini,** via dell'Acquario, 3 (tel. (075) 81 31 82) with clean and cool rooms for L20,000 per person; ask about surprise discounts. Nearby, **Camere Maria Fortini,** via Villamena, 19 (tel. (075) 81 27 15) has cozy singles for L20,000 (doubles L24,000).

To experience Umbrian country cuisine, try **Trattoria Da Ermenio,** via Montecarallo, 19, near Matteotti (open Fri.-Wed. noon-2pm and 7-9pm). For scrumptious *pizza al taglio* baked by the friendliest Neapolitan in Italy, see Vincenzo at his **pizzeria** on via S. Rufino just off p. Comune (open daily 8am-2pm and 4-8:30pm).

Assisi sits on the Foligno-Terontola rail line, about 30 minutes from Perugia (L2100). From Florence (L12,200), change at Terontola; from Rome (L12,200) or Ancona (L9300), change at Foligno. Orange city buses (L600) make the 5km trek between station and city every 10-15 min. Buses run to Perugia and other Umbrian towns.

Rome (Roma)

Rome has been home and playground to Caesars, popes and artists, but rather than linger in its bygone glory, the Eternal City lustily embraces the present. Concerts rock among the ruins, movies and soccer games screen in the piazze, and laundry flaps dry on Bernini statues. Rome showers the visitor with delightful surprises; the Pantheon happens quite suddenly as you wind your way through the narrow streets of this urban planner's nightmare. Relish the lonely piazza and the surprise outdoor market at the end of every wrong turn.

Orientation and Practical Information

No longer defined by its Seven Hills, Rome sprawls haphazardly between the hills of the Castelli Romani and the beach at Ostia. Even so, from **Termini** (the main train station), almost everything you'll want to see is in a compact area to the west (straight ahead as you leave the station). To the northwest is the plush home of sumptuous shops and sauntering tourists around **piazza di Spagna** and **via Veneto,** and to the north of them is Rome's largest park, the **Villa Borghese.** Southwest are most of the Roman ruins, including the Forum, Palatine, and Colosseum. Due west is the **old city** surrounding **piazza Navona** and the **Pantheon;** and across the **River Tiber** are **Vatican City** and the colorful **Trastevere** quarter.

When it comes to schedules, Rome is mystifying and frustrating. Go with the flow. The *pennichella* (Rome's mid-afternoon siesta) and long meals always take precedence over business. Generally, shops and offices are open weekdays from 9am to 1pm and 3:30 to 7:30pm, and often Saturday mornings. On Monday mornings in winter, most shops are closed, and food stores close early on Thursdays. And, as an added hassle, Rome shuts down in August; by *Ferragosto* (Aug. 15), the big summer holiday, the Romans have vanished. Although important sights stay open, just about everything else—including restaurants—is shut tight.

Violent crime is extremely rare here, but pickpocketing, purse-snatching, con-artistry, and car theft are not. Keep constant guard of your valuables, and be particularly careful on crowded city buses (especially #64 to the Vatican), subways, train stations, and any place crowded with tourists. Overnight trains into Rome are notorious, as are the *zingarelli,* children with tiny, wandering hands. *Always* keep your valuables in a well-concealed moneybelt.

Tourist Offices: Ente Provinciale per il Turismo (EPT), in Stazione Termini (tel. 487 12 70 or 482 40 78 or 46 54 61), between tracks 1 and 2. Open daily 8:15am-7pm. EPT headquarters 10 min. away at via Parigi, 5 (tel. 488 37 48). Go straight from the station on viale L. Einaudi, crossing p. della Repubblica and turning right at via G. Gomita. Open Mon.-Sat. 8:15am-7:15pm. Interminable lines and rushed service at the station make the jaunt to the central office worthwhile. Both find rooms, but are reluctant in the busy summer months: reservations are imperative. Pick up free maps and copies of the excellent brochures *Here's Rome* and *Romamor* at the **Vatican Information Office,** p. San Pietro (tel. 698 44 66), on the left of the piazza as you face the Basilica. Open Mon.-Sat. 8:30am-6:30pm. **Italian Youth Hostels Assocation (AIG),** via Cavour, 44 (tel. 46 23 42 or 474 12 56). No beds here, but plenty of advice and a list of hostels throughout Italy. Open Mon.-Fri. 8am-3pm. **Ente Nazionale per il Turismo (ENIT),** via Marghera, 2/6 (tel. 497 12 82), distributes information on Italy outside Rome. Open Mon.-Tues. and Thurs.-Fri. 9am-1pm, Wed. 4-6pm.

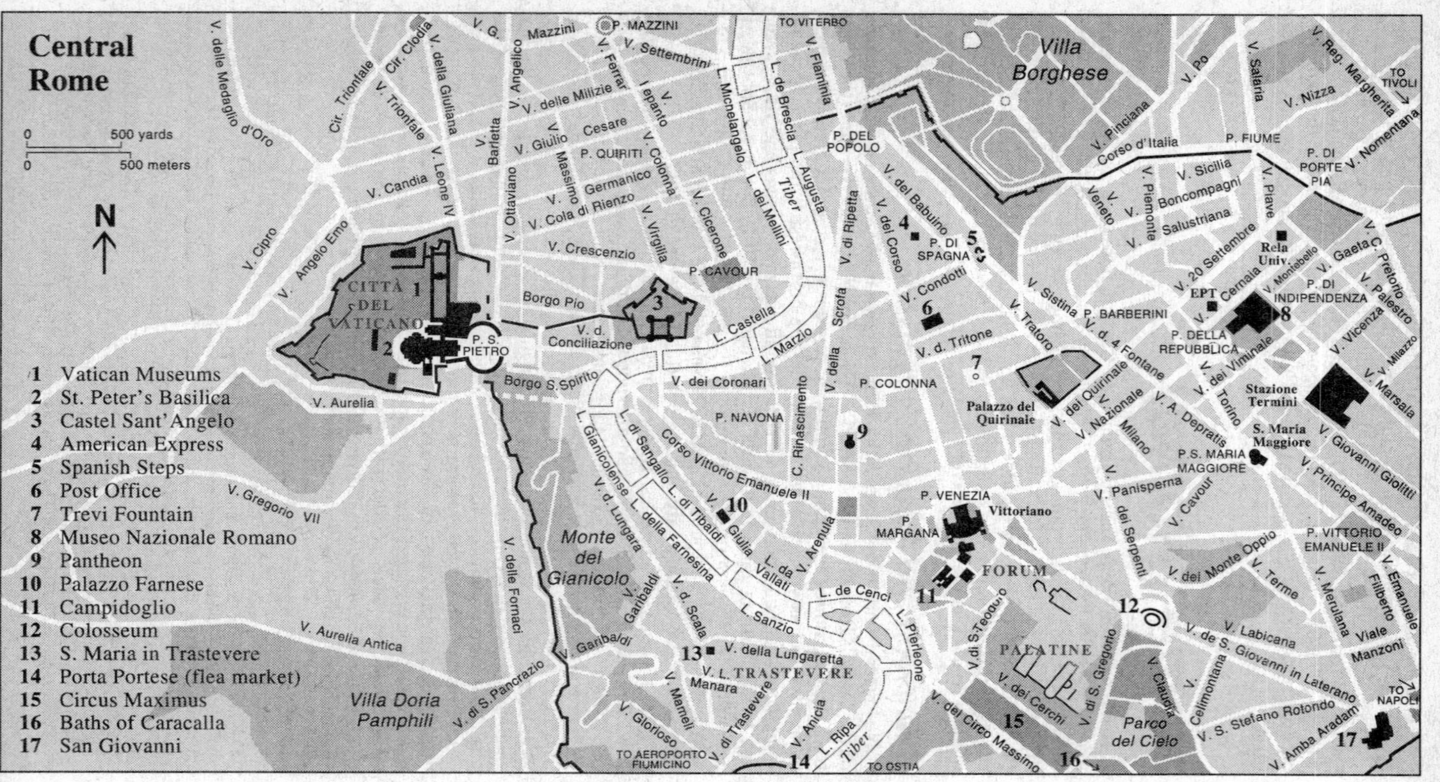

Central Rome
0 500 yards
0 500 meters
N
1 Vatican Museums
2 St. Peter's Basilica
3 Castel Sant' Angelo
4 American Express
5 Spanish Steps
6 Post Office
7 Trevi Fountain
8 Museo Nazionale Romano
9 Pantheon
10 Palazzo Farnese
11 Campidoglio
12 Colosseum
13 S. Maria in Trastevere
14 Porta Portese (flea market)
15 Circus Maximus
16 Baths of Caracalla
17 San Giovanni
Villa Borghese
CITTÀ DEL VATICANO
P. S. PIETRO
Tiber
Monte del Gianicolo
Villa Doria Pamphili
V. L. TRASTEVERE
FORUM
PALATINE
Parco del Cielo
Stazione Termini
Palazzo del Quirinale
Vittoriano
S. Maria Maggiore
EPT
Rela Univ.
P. DEL POPOLO
P. DI SPAGNA
P. BARBERINI
P. DELLA REPUBBLICA
P. DI INDIPENDENZA
P. VENEZIA
P. NAVONA
P. COLONNA
P. CAVOUR
P. MAZZINI
P. FIUME
P. DI PORTE PIA
P. VITTORIO EMANUELE II
P.S. MARIA MAGGIORE
P. MARGANA
P. QUIRITI
TO VITERBO
TO TIVOLI
TO NAPOLI
TO OSTIA
TO AEROPORTO FIUMICINO
V. del Corso
V. del Babuino
V. di Ripetta
V. Flaminia
V. Veneto
V. Sistina
V. d. Tritone
V. Nazionale
V. Cavour
V. dei Serpenti
V. Merulana
V. Labicana
V. dei Cerchi
V. del Circo Massimo
V. Salaria
V. Piave
V. 20 Settembre
V. Marsala
V. Giovanni Giolitti
V. Principe Amadeo
V. Cola di Rienzo
V. Crescenzio
V. d. Conciliazione
Borgo S. Spirito
Borgo Pio
V. Ottaviano
V. delle Fornaci
V. Aurelia
V. Aurelia Antica
V. Gregorio VII
V. Leone IV
V. Trionfale
Cir. Trionfale
Cir. Clodia
V. della Giuliana
V. delle Medaglie d'Oro
V. Cipro
V. Angelo Emo
V. Candia
V. Barletta
V. Angelico
V. G. Mazzini
V. Settembrini
V. Ferrar
V. delle Milizie
V. Giulio Cesare
V. Lepanto
V. Massimo
V. Germanico
V. Colonna
V. Virgilia
V. Cicerone
Corso Vittorio Emanuele II
Corso d'Italia
C. Rinascimento
V. della Scrofa
V. Condotti
V. Tratoro
V. d. 4 Fontane
V. del Quirinale
V. Milano
V. A. Depretis
V. Torino
V. del Viminale
V. Cernaia
V. Montebello
V. Gaeta
V. C. Pretorio
V. Palestro
V. Vicenza
V. Milazzo
V. Po
V. Pinciana
V. Nizza
V. Reg. Margherita
V. Nomentana
V. Sicilia
V. Piemonte
V. Boncompagni
V. Salustriana
V. Panisperna
V. dei Monte Oppio
V. Terme
V. Emanuele Filiberto
Viale Manzoni
V. de S. Giovanni in Laterano
V. Celimontana
V. S. Stefano Rotondo
V. Amba Aradam
V. Claudia
V. di S. Gregorio
V. di S. Teodoro
V. Giulia
V. Arenula
V. dei Coronari
L. di Sangallo
L. di Tibaldi
L. da Vallati
L. Gianicolense
L. della Farnesina
V. d. Lungara
V. d. Scala
L. Sanzio
L. de Cenci
L. Pierleone
L. Michelangelo
L. de Brescia
L. Augusta
L. dei Mellini
L. Castella
L. Marzio
L. Ripa
V. della Lungaretta
V. di Trastevere
V. Anicia
V. Manara
V. Garibaldi
V. Mameli
V. Glorioso
V. di S. Pancrazio

Budget Travel: Centro Turistico Studentesco (CTS), via Genova, 16 (tel. 44 67 91). Discounts, BIJ tickets, and room-hunting in Rome and other Italian cities, and a currency exchange. Some cheap long-distance bus tickets. Open Mon.-Fri. 9am-1pm and 4-7pm, Sat. 9am-1pm. BIJ tickets also sold from the **Transalpino** booth at Termini aisle #6 (tel. 46 05 36). Open daily 8:30am-9:30pm. **Compagnia Italiana di Turismo (CIT),** in Terminito (tel. 475 14 36), to the left of the info booth. Bus, train, and plane tickets. Open Mon.-Fri. 9am-1pm and 2:30-6pm.

Embassies: U.S., via Veneto, 119a (tel. 467 41). Open Mon.-Fri. 8:30am-4:30pm. **Canada,** via G.B. De Rossi, 27 (tel. 844 24 00). **U.K.,** via XX Settembre, 80a (tel. 475 54 41). Open Mon.-Fri. 9:30am-12:30pm and 2-4pm. **Australia,** via Alessandria, 215 (tel. 83 27 21). Open Mon.-Thurs. 9am-noon and 1-4pm, Fri. 9am-noon. **New Zealand,** via Zara, 28 (tel. 440 29 28). Open Mon.-Fri. 8:30am-12:45pm and 1:45-5pm. All maintain a 24-hr. referral service. **Albania,** via Asmara, 9 (tel. 838 07 25). **Yugoslavia,** via Monti Parioli, 20 (tel. 320 07 96).

Currency Exchange: Many *cambios* inside Termini; the one by the train information booth is open daily 8am-8pm. **Frana,** on via Torino 21B (tel. 475 76 32) off via Nazionale, near Termini, is open Mon.-Fri. 8:30am-7pm, Sat. 9am-1:30pm, with a branch at corso Rinascimento, 73/75 (tel. 654 84 06), near p. Navona. No commission. 24-hr. automatic change machine at via Veneto, 74-76.

American Express: p. di Spagna, 38 (tel. 72 28 02). Fairly efficient, but long lines and high commission. Open Mon.-Fri. 9am-5:30pm, Sat. 9am-12:30pm. For lost or stolen cards, call 722 81; for lost or stolen checks, call toll-free 24 hrs. 167 87 20 00.

Post Office: p. San Silvestro, 19 (tel. 67 71). Open Mon.-Fri. 8:25am-9:40pm, Sat. 8:25-11:30am. *Fermo Posta* (Poste Restante) held here (L250 per letter). **Postal Code:** 00100. To mail packages heavier than 1kg, go to p. dei Caprettari near the Pantheon. The **Vatican post office,** p. San Pietro, is faster and much more reliable, but has no *Fermo Posta.* Open Mon.-Fri. 8:30am-7pm, Sat. 8:30am-6pm.

Telephones: ASST, next to the main post office. Open Mon.-Sat. 8am-midnight. Also 2 offices at Termini (upstairs and downstairs). Upstairs open 24 hrs. **City Code:** 06.

Flights: International and domestic flights touch down at Aeroporto Leonardo da Vinci, usually referred to as **Fiumicino.** The metro line whisks you from Fiumicino to the Piramide/Ostiense stop on the B line; Termini and other destinations are just a transfer away (L5000). Many charters arrive at **Ciampino;** take the Acotral bus (1 per hr., L700) to the Anagnina stop on Metro line A.

Trains: All trains come and go from **Stazione Termini,** the center of all Rome's transportation and practically a city itself, with information, money exchange, ticket agencies, bars, overpriced restaurants, hotels, barber shops, and even an aquarium. Beware of pickpockets. To: Florence (frequently, 2 hr., L19,600 plus L7000 *rapido* supplement) on the Naples-Milan, Rome-Verona, or Rome-Trieste lines; Venice (9 per day, 4-5 hr., L35,900, *rapido* supplement L13,800) on the Rome-Trieste line; Naples (frequently, 2-3 hr., L13,700 plus L5300) on the Rome-Naples, Rome-Bari, and Rome-Syracuse lines; Brindisi (4 per day, 5-6 hr., L38,900 plus L14,000). International service to: Paris (L118,800); Vienna (L110,000); Athens (via Brindisi, L184,300). BIJ agents can sell you a Greece ticket, as can **Hellenic Mediterranean Lines,** via Umbria, 21 (tel. 474 01 41), near via Veneto or in the American Express office.

Buses: ACOTRAL, via Ostierse, 131 (tel. 575 31, information 591 55 51). Local service in Lazio region.

Public Transportation: Buses and 2 subway lines are complex and crowded during rush hour, but cheap and efficient. Buy **bus** tickets (L800) at *tabacchi* or terminal bus stops. 24-hrs. BIG ticket good on all bus networks and subway lines L2800. 8-day tourist bus pass (L6000) sold at silver **ATAC** booth outside Termini. Open daily 7:30am-7:30pm. Consult bus routes marked in blue on the tourist office map, or pick up an ATAC map with a table giving directions to and from major sights (L1000). Regular service until midnight with infrequent service on certain key routes until 5:30am. The **subway** *(metropolitana)* has 2 lines intersecting at Termini. Line A runs until 11:30pm; line B until 9pm, 11:30pm on weekends. L700 per ticket, L6000 for 10.

Taxis: Tel. 49 94, 35 70, or 84 33 (24 hrs.). Can also be flagged down. Expensive, plus hefty surcharges for night and airport service. Make sure your taxi is official and has a meter or you will be hornswoggled.

Scooter and Bicycle Rental: Rome's many hills, cobbled streets, and dense traffic (both pedestrian and vehicular) dim the appeal of 2-wheeled transport. In summer, cyclists might try the unmarked stands at various piazzas throughout the city (especially along via del Corso) which tend to stay open until 1am. (Generally L4000 per hour, L10,000 per half-day, L15,000 per day.) Near the Vatican, **St. Peter Rent,** via Porta Castello, 43 (tel. 687 57 14), has bikes, mopeds, and scooters. Open daily 9am-7pm. **Scoot-a-long,** via Cavour, 302 (tel. 678 02 06). Scooters run around L55,000 per day. Open 9am-7pm.

Hitchhiking: Those hitching north toward Florence try the entrance of Autostrada A1 (Roma-Firenze) in the Salaria region. Those going south toward Naples head to the entrance of Autostrada A2 (Roma-Napoli).

Luggage Storage: At Termini off track #1. L2000 per piece per day. Open daily 5am-1am.

Bookstores: Economy Book and Video Center, via Torino, 136 (tel. 474 68 77), off via Nazionale, has Italy's largest selection of English language books, new and used. Accepts trade-ins. Open Mon. 3-7:30pm, Tues.-Fri. 9am-7:30pm, Sat. 9am-1pm; Sept.-June Mon. 3-7:30pm, Tues.-Sat. 9am-1pm and 3:30-7:30pm. **American Book Shop,** via della Vite, 57 (tel. 679 52 22). Open Mon. 4:30-8pm, Tues.-Fri. 9am-1:30pm and 3:30-7:30pm, Sat. 9am-1pm. In July Sat. 9am-1pm only. Both carry *Let's Go.*

Laundry: Lavaservice, via Montebello, 11, east of Termini. Open Mon.-Fri. 9am-7pm, Sat. 9am-1pm. **Lavasecco a Gettone,** p. Carpodei Fiori, 38. Open Sept. to mid-Aug. Mon.-Fri. 9am-8pm. L4000-L6000 per kilo.

Public Baths: Albergo Diurno Stazione Termini (tel. 474 28 83), underground in the station. Showers L9000. Towels L1000. Soap L1500. Shampoo L1200. Open daily 7:20am-8:30pm.

Crises: Samaritans, in the Chiesa di San Silvestro on p. San Silvestro (tel. 678 92 27). English-speaking. Open 1:30-10:30pm. Leave a message at other times.

Pharmacies: Inside Termini (tel. 46 07 66). Open Sept.-July 7am-11:30pm. **24-hr. pharmacy: Farmacia Internazionale Antonucci,** p. Barberini, 49 (tel. 46 29 96).

Medical Assistance: International Medical Center (tel. 46 23 71 or 475 15 75). English-speaking; will even send doctor to your hotel. Open 24 hrs. **Hospital: Policlinico Umberto I,** viale de Policlinico, 255 (tel. 499 71). Free and closest to the station. **V.D. Clinic: San Gallicano,** via dei Fratte di Trastevere, 52A (tel. 58 48 31). Open daily 8-11am.

Emergencies: (tel. 113). First Aid: **(tel. 115). Police: Foreigners Bureau** (Ufficio Stranieri), via Genova, 2 (tel. 46 86 29 87). English spoken. Open 24 hrs. **Train station police,** for things lost or stolen on trains, at far end of track #1.

Accommodations and Camping

The good news: Rome has ample *alberghi, pensioni* and *locande.* The bad: prices are not always posted, the best places are usually full, proprietors can play hard-to-get, and singles are rare. Reservations ensure the best bargains with the least hassle, especially during the summer overload. Write ahead with a deposit, or try booking a few nights ahead by phone. Otherwise, *arrive early.* Tourist offices and budget travel agents usually do not book bargain nooks.

Hostels and Dormitories

Roman hostels are not much cheaper than private accommodations, and their early curfews and daytime lockouts may cramp your style. Many *pensioni* near the station are more convenient and rent by the bed just like hostels.

Ostello del Foro Italico (IYHF), viale delle Olimpiadi, 61 (tel. 396 47 09), miles from town. Take Metro line A to Ottaviano and transfer to bus #32. Not worth the trip. 3-night max. stay when full. Lockout 9am. Curfew 11pm. Members only, L16,500.

YWCA, via Cesare Balbo, 4 (tel. 46 04 60), west of Termini. Women only. Safe but no bargain. Curfew midnight. Singles L36,000. Doubles L58,000. Triples L69,000.

University Housing, via Cesare de Lollis, 24-B, and viale del Ministro degli Affari Esteri, 6. Rooms available late July to mid-Sept. Contact EPT (tel. 46 37 48) or AIG (tel. 359 92 95) for more information. Max. stay 1 week. L20,000 for B&B.

Hotels and Pensions

The area around the station overflows with inexpensive hotels. Though the *pensioni* themselves are often clean, comfortable, and friendly, the neighborhood can be unsafe at night. Some hotels and restaurants rocket their prices at the whisper of a foreign voice; always ask to see the official EPT price statement that all hotels must post. The area north of Stazione Termini, surrounding via Montebello, is quieter and less shabby, but farther from the major sights.

Rome becomes more expensive as you migrate from the station, but the extra *lire* deliver you from the backpackers' ghetto to a more truly Roman holiday.

Hotels and Pensions: Near the Station

Pensione Tizi, via Collina, 48 (tel. 474 32 66 or 482 01 28). From p. Independenza, take via Goito, cross over via XX Settembre onto via Piave, and turn left on via Flavia, which leads to via Collina. Or take bus #3 or 4 from Termini. Named after the proprietor's eldest daughter, this family pensione has welcomed students for years into its clean and comfortable rooms. Singles L30,000. Doubles L43,000, with shower L50,000. Triples L20,000 per person. **Pensione Ercoli** (tel. 474 54 54), on the third floor. Young, personable English-speaking Sardinian management. Rooms and bathrooms in perfect order. Singles L25,000. Doubles L38,000, with shower L44,000. Triples L60,000.

Pensione Papà Germano, via Calatafimi, 14a (tel. 48 69 19), off via Volturno. Clean rooms, great showers, and some of the lowest prices in Rome have made Mamma and Papà Germano something of a legend among backpackers. Excellent English. Singles L30,000. Doubles L45,000, with bath L50,000. Triples L20,000 per person. 10% cheaper Nov.-Feb.

Pensione Monaco, via Flavia, 84 (tel. 481 56 49 or 474 43 35), around the corner from Tizi and Ercoli. Wonderful motherly management takes special care of you. Check out 9am; curfew midnight. Singles L23,000. Doubles L35,000. Triples L17,000 per person.

Hotel Hane Michele, via Palestro, 35 (tel. 444 12 04). Pleasant management makes this inexpensive pensione a real pleasure. Singles L25,000. Doubles L45,000. Triples L15,000 per person.

Pensione Bolognese, via Palestro, 15 (tel. 49 00 45). Large, clean, comfortable rooms. Singles L30,000-L35,000, with bath L45,000. Doubles L45,000, with bath L60,000. Triples L70,000, with bath L90,000.

Hotel Gexim, via Palestro, 34 (tel. 44 41 31 or 446 02 11). Upbeat rooms freshly painted every year in bright pastels. No curfew. Singles L32,000. Doubles L46,000, with shower L59,000. Triples L22,000 per person. Laundry done for L13,000 a load.

Pensione Cervia, via Palestro, 55 (tel. 49 10 57). Meticulously maintained but weathered. Curfew 2am. Singles L30,000. Doubles L45,000, with bath L55,000. Triples L20,000 per person. Quads L19,000 per person.

Pensione Eureka/Arrivederci, p. della Repubblica, 47 (tel. 46 03 34 or 488 03 34). Statues and murals in the entry make you feel right at Rome. Singles L33,000, with shower L36,000. Doubles L56,000, with shower L64,000. Triples L77,000, with shower L88,000. Breakfast included.

Pensione Esedra, next door (tel. 488 39 12). Comparable in every way to Eureka. Curfew 1am. Singles L33,000. Doubles L62,000. Triples L83,000. Quads L108,000. Quints L132,000.

Pensione Pezzotti, via Principe Amadeo, 79D (tel. 446 69 04 or 446 68 75). Also runs higher-priced hotel. Singles L40,000. Doubles L55,000. Triples L73,000.

Pensione Orlanda, via Principe Amadeo, 76 (tel. 488 06 37). Tony and Dawn would probably stay here. Clean and spacious at a good price. Singles L36,500. Doubles L47,000, with bath L60,000. Triples L65,000. Showers L6000.

Hotel Milo, same building (tel. 474 01 00 or 474 53 60). The renovations are still coming along. Singles L40,000, with bath L55,000. Doubles L70,000, with bath L90,000.

Hotel Castelfidardo, via Castelfidardo, 31 (tel. 474 28 94 or 494 13 78). Completely new rooms. Singles L36,000. Doubles L46,000. Triples L22,000 per person. Credit cards accepted.

Pensione Piave, via Piave, 14 (tel. 474 34 47 or 487 33 60). Worth every lira. Phones, TVs, carpeting, fireplaces, and private bath in every room. Big-bedded singles L44,500. Doubles L60,000.

Albergo California, via Principe Amadeo, 47 (tel. 482 20 02), 100m from station—and all that entails—but cheap. L20,000-L25,000 per person.

Hotels and Pensions: Near the Spanish Steps

Pensione Fiorella, via del Babuino, 196 (tel. 361 05 97). A spruce set-up with an obliging management. Curfew 1am. Singles L33,000. Doubles L58,000. First breakfast included.

Hotel-Pensione Parlamento, via delle Convertile, 5 (tel. 679 20 82 or 684 16 97), off p. San Silvestro. Beautiful, flowered roof-top terrace, high ceilings, and amiable management. Singles L46,000. Doubles L65,000. Triples L90,000.

Hotels and Pensions: Near the Piazza Navona

Albergo della Lunetta, p. del Paradiso, 68 (tel. 686 10 80), first right off via Chiavari. Economic Eden in the heart of Old Rome. Singles L30,000. Doubles L55,000. Triples L75,000.

Pensione Mimosa, via S. Chiara, 61 (tel. 654 17 53), off p. di Minerva, off the Pantheon. Matronly owner presides over cozy, kitschy, and clean rooms. Singles L40,000. Doubles L70,000. Triples L95,000. Shower and breakfast included.

Albergo Panezia, via dei Chiavari, 12 (tel. 686 13 71). A speck of oatmeal in a sea of chili. Colorful neighborhood counters bland, clean rooms. Singles L40,000. Doubles L60,000. Triples L80,000. Less Nov.-Feb.

Albergo Abruzzi, p. della Rotonda, 69 (tel. 679 20 21). In front of the Pantheon, a humble abode amidst greatness. Singles L40,000. Doubles L64,000. Triples L86,000.

Hotels and Pensiones: Ottaviano and Trastevere

Pensione Zurigo/Pensione Nautilus, via Germanico, 198 (tel. 372 01 39 or 31 55 49). Both run by same English-speaking management. Safe, spacious, spic-and-span. Doubles L55,000. Triples L23,000 per person. **Residence Guiggioli,** (tel. 31 52 09), same bldg. Five of the best rooms in Rome. Gorgeous antiques. Doubles L47,000. Matrimonial suite with bath L60,000. **Pensione Lady,** (tel. 31 49 38), on the 4th floor. 1960s mod decor, mellow management. Singles L37,000. Doubles L47,000. Triples L65,000.

Pensione Manare, via Luciano Manara, 25, 2nd and 5th floors (tel. 581 47 13). Take a right off viale Trastevere to via delle Fratte di Trastevere to via Manare. A haven for the insecure. 24-hr. desk person; intercom in every room. Doubles L46,500. Triples L62,775. Quads L79,050. Showers L3000.

Pensione Ottaviano, via Ottaviano, 6 (tel. 38 39 56), off p. del Risorgimento near Vatican City. English-speaking manager keeps crowded dorms. L20,000 per person.

Camping

The closest campground is **Nomentano,** via della Cesarina (tel. 610 02 96), at via Nomentana. (L8100 per person, L4000 per tent. Open March-Oct.) Take bus #36 from Termini and transfer to bus #337 at p. Sempione. Those who value their lives shouldn't sleep rough in Rome; if this is unavoidable, store your bags and sleep in the train station, with your money stowed under your clothes, or in the hourly hotel in Termini downstairs (L8000 for two hours).

Food

Meals in Rome are prolonged affairs (breakfast—a quick gulp of caffeine—is the exception); each course seems a mere fanfare to the next. When selecting a restaurant, avoid hotels, main streets, English-language menus, anything near the station, and anywhere that recruits. The most authentic food can be found in **San Lorenzo,** a university area 10 minutes west of Termini on bus #71 or 492, and in **Testaccio,** south of the center on the eastern banks of the Tiber, reached by bus #27 from Termini. Restaurants near the **Spanish Steps** are generally atrocious in price and quality. The areas around **Piazza Navona, Campo di Fiori,** and across the river in **Trastevere** abound with flavor—edible and cultural. For daytime snacks try any of the numerous places that sell *pizza rustica* (the cruder square pizza, sold by weight) or *panini* (bulging sandwiches). For provisions, invade the *alimentari,* the numerous outdoor markets throughout the city (generally open Mon.-Sat. 6am-1pm). Try p. Vittorio, near the station, or Campo di Fiori. *Gelato* (ice cream) rarely disappoints at any place that has a *produzione propria* (homemade) sign, but two

Roman legends prevail: **Giolitti,** via degli Uffici del Vicario, 40, near the Pantheon, and **Fassi Palazzo del Freddo,** via Principe Eugenio, 65/67, west of Termini. Also don't miss out on the numerous cafés supplying Rome with its leading fuel—coffee.

La Cantinola da Livia, via Calabria, 26, near Termini. Take via Piave off via XX Settembre, then take your fourth left onto via Calabria. Stellar cuisine and impeccable service with a smile. *Scampi* (shrimp) L15,000. Open Mon.-Sat. 12:30-3pm and 7:30pm-1:30am.

Ristorante Tudini, via Filippo Turata, 5. One block south of Termini on corner with via Gioberti. Appetizing respite from Termini fare. Lovely, modern marble tables and greenery. *Pennette alla vodka* (pasta) L7000. Veal scallopine L10,000. Credit cards accepted. Open Mon.-Sat. 12:30pm-11:30pm.

Restaurant Monte Arci, via Castelfidaro, 33, east of Termini. A bit pricey, but the scrumptious food and boisterous waiters make it the best choice near the station. Try the *paglia e fieno al Monte Arci* (gnocchi with mushrooms and asparagus, L7000). Open Thurs.-Tues. noon-3pm and 7-11:30pm. Credit cards accepted.

Pizzeria L'Economica, via Tiburtina, 46, on the main road of San Lorenzo on bus route #71. Swamped with student devotees. Bubbling pizza from L3500. Antipasti L4500. Open Sept.-July Mon.-Sat. 6:30-11pm.

Ristorante Del Pallaro, largo del Pallaro, near piazza Navona. Worthwhile L24,000 for a humongous full-course meal, including wine and dessert. At this Homesick Restaurant, there are no choices—you get whatever they're inspired to make. Pleasant outdoor tables. Open Tues.-Sun. 12:30-3pm and 8pm-midnight.

Il Gardinetto, via del Governo Vecchio, 125, amidst the hard, dusty cobblestones of Piazza Navona. Try the pasta primavera (L7000), accompanied by *verdure all'agro* (cooked greens, L4000). Credit cards accepted. Open Tues.-Sun. 12:30-3pm and 7:30pm-midnight.

La Crêperie di St-Eustachio, p. St-Eustachio, 50. Salted crêpes with cheese and/or prosciutto (L7000-L9000) and dessert crêpes (L7000), more creative than their French counterparts. Eat in or take out—same price. Open Mon.-Sat. noon-3pm and 7-11pm.

Palladini, via del Governo Vecchio, 29. The lack of signs or seating doesn't deter Roman crowds hungry for splendiferous sandwiches on fresh pizza bread (large L3500). *Prosciutto e fichi* (cured ham and figs) is the rave. Open Sept.-July Mon.-Fri. 7am-2pm and 5-8pm, Sat. 7am-2pm.

Ristorante da Ugo al Gran Sasso, via di Ripetta, 32, near the Spanish Steps. Ugo's a great guy, and he serves up a great dish of spaghetti *alle vongole* (with clam sauce, L8000). Pasta Carbonara L6000. Cover and service L2000. Open Sun.-Fri. noon-3pm and 7-11pm. Closed Aug. 1-20.

Pizzerio Ivo, via San Francesco a Ripa, 157-158. Take via delle Fratte di Trastevere off viale Trastevere. Soccer theme and sporty waiters in a spacious but thronged interior. Legendary pizzas from L7000. Cover L1000. Open Sept.-July Wed.-Mon. 6pm-1am.

Birreria della Scala, p. della Scala, 58-60, also in Trastevere. Rowdy would-be Dionysi, live music, and vast pasta selection (L5500-8000). Drinks L7500-L8000. Open Thurs.-Tues. 7:30pm-2am.

Sights

Roma non basta una vita—"For Rome, one life is not enough." Plan your day carefully, as opening times are a source of endless frustration. Churches are usually open from early morning until noon, and many reopen for several hours in the afternoon. With the exception of the Vatican, all museums are closed Mondays. When visiting churches, dress modestly—those in shorts, short skirts, sleeveless dresses or sleeveless shirts will not be welcome.

Rome is not so much one city as many cities, built on top of and in the midst of one another. The result is both cluttered and grandiose. Get lost—many of Rome's greatest treasures lie hidden in the maelstrom of side streets, and Rome's charm lies in its ability to astonish. The builders, artists, and architects whose masterpieces adorn this city worked not so much with stone and paint as with space itself, and some of the most beautiful sights are not buildings but the streets and piazzas they line—piazza Navona, the Campidoglio, piazza del Popolo, piazza di Spagna, and piazza San Pietro, to name but a few.

Occupying 109 acres entirely within Italy's capital, the **Vatican City** is the last territorial toehold of a Catholic church that once flipped the levers of power all over Europe. Under the Lateran Treaty of 1929, the Pope remains supreme monarch of this tiny theocracy, exercising all legislative, judicial, and executive powers over the 300 souls who hold Vatican citizenship. The state maintains an army of Swiss Guards—all descended from 16th-century mercenaries hired by Pope Julius II. Michelangelo designed their resplendent costumes.

The entrance to the **Vatican Museums** is at the end of via Tunisi, a 10-minute walk from the Ottaviano stop on line A. Select one of the four tour routes—"D" winds past Egyptian mummies and through miles of extravagantly decorated corridors full of treasures. Classical sculpture, including the *Laocoön* and *Apollo Belvedere,* decorates the elegant **Belvedere Courtyard.** Sculpted from a single piece of marble, the first-century *Laocoön* depicts the Trojan priest Laocoön and his two sons struggling in terror to free themselves from serpents set upon them by Athena.

All routes in the museum lead through the breathtakingly frescoed **Raphael Stanze** (rooms) and ultimately to the **Sistine Chapel.** The serene beauty and genius of Michelangelo's partially restored, partially-visible ceiling arches far above mobs of Minolta-manacled morons. In the *Creation of Adam,* its eight Old Testament scenes climax in the electric touch of God's and Adam's fingers. On the end wall, the haunting *Last Judgement* is still closed for restoration. The newly resplendent colors of the chapel have raised the consciousness of many and the eyebrows of some; art historians who once hailed Michelangelo for his dark tones and ominous shadows are rapidly rewording their praise. Once out of the Sistine Chapel, linger at the **Pinacoteca;** Raphael's *Transfiguration* alone is worth the stop. (Museums and Sistine Chapel open Easter week and June-Aug. Mon.-Fri. 9am-5pm, Sat. 9am-2pm; Sept.-May Mon.-Fri. 9am-2pm. Admission L10,000, with ISIC L7000. Open, free, and mobbed on the last Sun. of every month 9am-2pm. Last visitors admitted 1 hr. before closing.)

Outside, you can approach the **Basilica di San Pietro** (St. Peter's), the largest cathedral in the world, through Bernini's peerless baroque colonnades. (To appreciate Bernini's genius, stand on either of the round, dark stones next to the piazza's twin fountains. The three rows of columns line up so perfectly that they appear as a single row.) Begun on the reputed site of St. Peter's tomb by Bramante, under Julius II the project was carried on by da Sangallo, Michelangelo, Raphael, and finally Maderna, who added the present façade. Michelangelo's sorrowful *Pietà* now sits in grace on the ground level behind bullet-proof glass (a maniac attacked the sculpture with an ax in 1978). Downstairs, the **grottoes** harbor the tombs of St. Peter and his successors. The **dome** of St. Peter's, for centuries the world's largest, was Michelangelo's final opus. To enjoy a matchless view of Rome, make the strenuous climb to the top. (St. Peter's open daily 7am-7pm; off-season 7am-6pm. Flash photography prohibited. Free. Grottoes (free) and dome (L2000, elevator halfway L1000) close 1 hr. before the Basilica.) **Mass** is conducted several times per day, with a particularly beautiful vespers service Sunday at 5pm. When in town, the Pope grants **public audiences** in p. San Pietro on Wednesdays (Sept.-May 10am, June-Aug. 11am). Get free tickets (Mon.-Tues. 9am-1pm) at St. Peter's Gate (bronze doors to right of Basilica).

Across the River Tiber from the Vatican lie the few tangible remnants of ancient Rome. The same Church which erected so many beautiful buildings destroyed the monuments left by its pagan predecessors. Enter the Roman **Forum** (Metro: Colloseo), once the center of the Empire and now under restoration, from via dei Fori Imperiali, just behind the neoclassical horror of the Vittoriano monument. The Forum houses dozens of significant monuments, including the **Curia,** where the Senate met; the reputed **Tomb of Romulus,** one of Rome's legendary founders; the **Imperial Rostra,** from which politicians orated; and the **Arch of Titus,** which features the famous frieze of Roman legionnaires making off with the great Menorah from the Temple of Jerusalem. At the far end of the Forum, the **Palatine Hill** houses a complex of imperial palaces surrounded by parks and gardens. The largest and most impressive structure here is the **Palace of Domitian,** divided into the Domus Flavia (official palace), the Domus Augustana (private residence), and the Stadium. (Forum and Palatine open Mon. and Wed.-Sat. 9am-1 hr. before sunset, Tues. and Sun. 9am-1pm. Admission L10,000.) At the southern base of the Palatine is the **Circus Maximus;** you can still see the start and finish lines for the chariot races once held here. To the east stands the **Domus Aurea,** the splendid dwelling built for Emperor Nero (closed for restoration).

Dominating the heart of ancient Rome, the **Colosseum** (Metro: Colloseo), erected in 80 AD by Emperor Flavius, stands as the city's grandest symbol. Although used as a quarry by popes through the 18th century, it was hallowed as a site where Christian martyrs perished (actually, only pagan gladiators died in the games). In its heyday, the Colosseum accommodated more than 50,000 spectators, was equipped with an awning rolled out on a wooden frame by agile sailors, and could be filled with water for mock naval battles. (Open Mon., Tues., and Thurs.-Sat. 9am-1 hr. before sunset, Sun. and Wed. 9am-1pm. Free, ascent to upper levels L6000.) Recently unveiled after much buffing, the **Arch of Constantine,** to the side of the Colosseum, is the celebrated 4th-century structure that triumphs over all other triumphal arches. The **Museo Nazionale Romano della Terme,** on via delle Terme di Diocleziano, near Termini, exhibits some of the most striking classical scupture in Rome. (Open Tues.-Sat. 9am-2pm, Sun. 9am-1pm. Admission L3000.)

The best preserved monument of the ancient city is the **Pantheon,** erected in 120 AD in honor of all the gods; it survives because it was consecrated as a church in 609. The only source of light is the central hole of the famous cupola—an unprecedented and once inimitable structural feat. The Pantheon lies between piazza Navona and via del Corso. (Open Mon.-Sat. 9am-2pm, Sun. 9am-1pm; July-Sept. Mon.-Sat. 9am-5pm, Sun. 9am-1pm. Free.) Only a short walk away, **piazza Navona** is the finest baroque space in Rome, and home to three Bernini fountains, most notably the **Fountain of the Four Rivers.** This centerpiece represents the Nile, Ganges, Danube, and Rio de la Plata (all identifiable by representative flora and fauna). According to 17th-century paintings, the *piazza* was sometimes blocked off at the ends and flooded for mock naval battles. At night, it is one of the most electric spots in the city.

Michelangelo left his mark on Rome's secular face in his masterful redesign of the **Campidoglio** (Capitoline Hill), off piazza Venezia. Once the political and religious center of ancient Rome, the hill has been the seat of the city's civic government since the 11th century. Piazza Venezia is easily recognizable by the adjacent **Vittoriano,** the huge, white 19th-century monument King Victor Emanuel II erected to himself. From the back of piazza del Campidoglio, behind Rome's City Hall (the central building), there's a great daytime view of the Forum. On Campidoglio's piazza are the **Musei Capitolini,** home to an extraordinary collection of classical sculpture and Renaissance painting. An Etruscan bronze, the *Capitoline She-Wolf* represents Romulus and Remus, the twins suckled by the She-Wolf, who founded Rome in 753 BC. The two children were tacked onto the statue only during the Renaissance. (Museums open April-Sept. Tues.-Sat. 9am-1:30pm, Tues. also 5-8pm and Sat. also 8-11pm, Sun. 9am-1pm; Oct.-March same hrs. except Sat. evening 5-8pm. Last admission ½ hr. before closing. Admission L4500, students L2500.)

Renaissance Rome is at its enigmatic finest in **Vecchia Roma** (Old Rome), which surrounds the **campo di Fiori.** (Buses #64 and 62 from Termini run along corso Vittorio Emanuele.) The baroque **Gesù,** on nearby corso Vittorio Emanuele, is the parent church of the Jesuit order. Back toward the station, at the intersection of via Barberini and via XX Settembre, the **Church of Santa Maria della Vittoria** houses Bernini's *St. Theresa in Ecstasy.* The rendition of the saint swooning with physical and spiritual delight is unforgettable. (Open daily 6:30am-noon and 4:30-7:30pm.) **The Church of San Pietro in Vincoli,** on via Cavour near the Colosseum, contains Michelangelo's statue of Moses. The goat horns protruding from Moses's head arise from a mistranslation of the Hebrew Bible; when Moses emerged from the Sinai with the Ten Commandments, according to scriptures, "rays" (similar to "horns" in Hebrew) shone from his brow. (Open 7am-12:30pm and 3:30-7pm.)

Many of the Renaissance and baroque **palazzi** (mansions), some built by papal "nephews" (read sons), today serve as galleries. On the grounds of Rome's largest park, the **Villa Borghese** (Metro: Piazza di Spagna), the **Museo Borghese** houses Bernini's greatest early sculpture (including *Apollo and Daphne* and *David)* plus a large collection of Titians and Caravaggios. (Visits are limited to groups of 25 leaving every ½ hr. Tues.-Sat. 9am-1:30pm, Sun. 9am-12:30pm. Free while undergoing restoration.) While at the park, also visit the **Museo di Villa Giola,** a vast trove of Etruscan art discovered in burial grounds north of Rome. The Etruscans, speakers of a mysterious, half-deciphered non-Indo-European language, dominated the Italian peninsula in the 7th to 5th centuries BC, before the meteoric rise of the Romans. (Open Tues.-Sat. 9am-7:30pm, Sun. 9am-1pm; mid-Aug. to April Tues.-Sat. 9am-2pm, Sun. 9am-1pm. Admission L8000.)

The **Palazzo Barberini's Galleria Nazionale d'Arte Antica** in via Quattro Fontane, near the Barberini Fountain, houses a superb collection of paintings from the 13th to the 18th centuries. (Open Mon.-Sat. 9am-2pm, Sun. 9am-1pm. Admission L6000.) The most important of the other palazzi-*cum*-galleries are the **Spada,** near the campo di Fiori in piazza Capo di Ferro (open Mon.-Sat. 9am-2pm, Sun. 9am-1pm; admission L4000), and the **Doria Pamphili** at p. del Collegio Romano, 1a, near the Pantheon (open Tues. and Fri.-Sun. 10am-1pm; admission L4000, L3000 more for a tour of the private apartments).

The **catacombs** are mysterious monuments to Christianity, built before the conversion of Rome under Constantine. Thousands of Christians are buried in 20km of underground labyrinths. The greatest concentration rests along the Appian Way, one of the oldest Roman roads still in use. Take bus #118 from via Claudia, near the Colosseum, down via Appia Antica. The catacombs of **San Sebastiano, Santa Domitilla,** and **San Callisto** are next to each other (open 8:30am-noon and 2:30-5pm; San Sebastiano closed Thurs., Santa Domitilla closed Tues., San Callisto closed Wed.; required tour L4000.) The **Protestant Cemetery** lies off the Piramide stop on Metro line B. Behind Roman tribune Caius Cestius's tomb—a marble pyramid jutting out of the medieval city wall—are the graves of Keats and Shelley, carefully tended in the garden-like cemetery. (Open daily 8-11:30am and 3:20-5:30pm; Oct.-March 8-11:30am and 2:20-4:30pm. Donation requested.)

Designed by an Italian, paid for by the French, occupied by the British, and now haunted by Americans, the **Spanish Steps** (Metro: Spagna) have a truly international atmosphere. Ideal for people-watching, the Spanish Steps and **piazza di Spagna** take their names from the Spanish Embassy, located since 1647 in the hourglass-shaped *piazza.* The **Trevi fountain** is another focus for the flirtatious and flippant. It depicts the chariot of Neptune drawn by two Tritons. Try to visit the fountain at night, as water pressure droops during the day. (The fountain is currently under the weather, and disappointingly drained dry.) **Trastevere,** (bus #170 from Termini) on the far bank of the River Tiber, is a quarter of meandering streets, innumerable *trattoria,* and impromptu celebrations in its many *piazze.* Perched above Trastevere sits **San Pietro in Montorio,** home of one of Italy's smallest and most exquisite buildings, the **Tempietto.** With this circular jewel Bramante awakened his contemporaries to the meaning of Roman architecture.

Entertainment

Roman entertainment is a public affair—concerts under the stars, street fairs with acrobats and fire-eaters, and Fellini-esque crowds of hopeful Romeos, gypsy accordionists, and dazzled foreigners all flooding the *piazze.* Check *La Repubblica* or other newspapers for specific events; the tourist office is a good source for event calendars (many in English) such as the *Carnet di Roma.* Of special note are the operas in the ancient **Baths of Caracalla** in July and August; the extravagant productions are great fun. *Aida,* Verdi's Egyptian masterpiece, with a cast of over 200 complete with chariots and horses, is a perennial favorite. Buy tickets two days in advance (L20,000-60,000) at the **Teatro dell'Opera,** p. Beniamino Gigli, 1 (tel. 488 17 55).

In late July, Trastevere hosts the **Festa Noantri.** Every night for 10 days, viale Trastevere closes to traffic and becomes a gaudy avenue of food and junk stalls, with jugglers and fun fairs. Perhaps the best time to appreciate the vigor of Christianity in Rome is during **Holy Week,** when every church hosts concerts and High Mass; the Pope traditionally conducts the Way of the Cross in the Colosseum on Good Friday. Also in spring are the antique and art festivals of via del Coronari and via Margutta, and the flower festival on the Spanish Steps (when they take the photos for the postcards).

The one Roman cinema which does not dub out English is **Cinema Pasquino** (tel. 580 36 22), on vicolo del Piede off p. S. Maria in Trastevere; movies change every few days with four showings per day and cost L7000. (Open Sept.-July.) Roman discos are outrageous only in price; less expensive and less formal clubs are more worthwhile. Try **Yes Brasil,** via S. Francesco a Ripa, 103 (drinks L8000-L10,000), or **Alexanderplatz,** via Ostia, 9, off Largo Trianfale near the Vatican. (No cover; restaurant attached. Open Tues.-Sun.) The hard-drinking set should check out the **Druid's Den,** via San Martino ai Monti, 28, just south of Santa Maria Maggiore, the Irish hangout where Romans get to be tourists (Guinness L4500). **L'Esperimento,** via Rasella, 5, is Rome's "alternative" subterranean rock club with live bands nightly. If your feet have got to meet the beat no matter what price, point your toes towards **Opera,** via della Purificazione, 9, or via Giovanni Schiapparelli, 29/31 (tel. 87 05 04), but expect to pay L15,000-25,000. Gay clubs include **Angelo Azzurro,** via Cardinal Merry del Val, 13, in Trastevere, **L'Alibi,** via Monte Testaccio, 44, and the women's option in Trastevere, **Fruellandia,** vicolo del Piede, 18. Like everything else in Rome, many clubs close in August.

Near Rome

The fascinating remnants of an archetypal Roman city, **Ostia Antica,** are beyond the hills of the modern metropolis. Considered by many the near equal of Pompeii, these extensive ruins effortlessly and eerily recall the yester-millenia. Ostia's restored amphitheater makes a prime picnic spot. Trains (L1000) leave from the Magliana stop on Metro line B. (Admission L8000. Open daily 9am-1 hr. before sunset.)

Do as the (ancient) Romans did to escape the urban commotion; retreat to **Tivoli,** summer resort for such archaic big-wigs as Horace and Hadrian, only an hour outside the city. Three buses per hour pull out from via Gaeta near p. Cinquecento (round-trip L3400). The 16th-century **Villa d'Este** is a dazzling, splashy park overflowing with fountains and waterfalls, some trickling, others torrential. (Open Tues.-Sun. 9am-1 hr. before sunset. Admission L10,000.) Just outside of Tivoli is the **Villa Adriana,** where the Emperor Hadrian reconstructed the architectural wonders of his far-flung empire. (Open Tues.-Sun. 9am-1 hr. before sunset. Admission L8000.)

The Roman countryside is a far cry from the din and disorder of the city proper; just outside the road that rings the city lie peaceful towns such as **Frascati,** renowned for its white wine. Acotral buses run from the Anagnina stop on Metro line A (every ½ hr., L1000). Up the hill lie the Roman ruins at Tusculum, while down the other side rests the hamlet of **Grottaferrata,** 3km from Frascati. This town's handsome Romanesque 11th-century **abbey** is inhabited by the Greek Orthodox monks of St. Niles, whose pious ranks run an ancient winery. Here you can catch the bus back to Rome (last one at 9pm, L1000).

Southern Italy

South of Rome, the sun gets brighter, the meals longer, the marginal product of labor lower, and the passions more intense. Though Southern Italy has long been subject to the negative stereotypes and prejudices of the more industrialized North, the so-called "Mezzogiorno" (midday) region remains justly proud of its open-hearted and generous populace, strong traditions, classical ruins, and enchanting beaches and islands. Adorned with the Amalfi coast and a troupe of paradisical islands, Campania (the area around Naples) gets the most press. The most genuine *Italia* is further south and east in Calabria, Apulia, and Basilicata.

Naples (Napoli)

Greeting the world with haggling market crowds, hell-bent and honking cars, and packs of screaming youngsters, Naples has never bothered to groom itself. Below the surface, however, flourishes one of Europe's most cultured and convivial cities, where grand *palazzi* and rich museums mesh with humble artisans' shops and the sounds of twanging mandolins. The *Camorra* mafia has earned the city its infamous reputation, but a tourist has yet to receive an offer he couldn't refuse. Theft is a problem, so take care not to flaunt your valuables. Leave your watch, camera and valuables at the hotel (preferably under lock and key), and wear your daypack on both shoulders.

Orientation and Practical Information

Naples is on the west coast of Italy, two hours south of Rome. The city is an important port, with regular sailings to Sicily, Tunisia, and Sardinia, and a hub for rail lines, with service to and from Rome, Calabria, Sicily, and the Adriatic.

Tourist Office: Ente Provinciale per il Turismo (EPT), in the train station (tel. 26 87 79). Calls hotels. Pick up the invaluable *Qui Napoli* (Here's Naples) and a city map. Open Mon.-Sat. 9am-8pm, Sun. 9am-1pm. Main office, p. Martiri, 59, scala B, 2nd floor (tel. 40 53 11). Take bus #150. Open Mon.-Fri. 8:30am-2:30pm. Other booths open irregularly at Stazione Mergellina (tel. 761 21 02) and the airport (tel. 780 57 61). For info on city sights, go to the **Information Office,** p. Gesù Nuovo (tel. 552 33 28), in the heart of the old city. (Open Mon.-Sat. 9am-7pm, Sun. 9am-2pm.)

Consulates: U.S., p. della Repubblica (p. Principi di Napoli on some maps; tel. 761 43 03). Open Mon.-Fri. 8am-noon and 2-4pm. **U.K.,** via Francesco Crispi, 122 (tel. 65 35 11). Open Mon.-Fri. 8am-1:30pm; mid-Sept. to June Mon.-Fri. 9am-12:30pm and 3-5:30pm.

Currency Exchange: Neapolitan banks charge high commissions. Change money before arriving. If you're heading to Capri, change there. If you have to, the exchange office at Stazione Centrale is open daily 8am-1:30pm and 2:30-8pm.

American Express: Ashiba Travel, p. Municipio, 1 (tel. 551 53 03). Mail held 1 month. Checks and cards replaced. Open Mon.-Fri. 9am-1pm and 3:30-7:30pm, Sat. 9am-1pm.

Post Office: p. Matteotti (tel. 551 14 56), off via Toledo on via Diaz. *Fermo Posta.* Open Mon.-Fri. 8:15am-7:20pm, Sat.-Sun. 8:15am-1pm. **Postal code:** 80100.

Telephones: At the train station. Less crowded office at via Depretis, 40, off p. Bovio at the end of corso Umberto. Both open 24 hrs. **City code:** 081.

Trains: Lines and booths open daily 7am-9pm. **Digiplan** machines in the station have English print-outs of prices and schedules; or call 553 41 88. To: Rome (1-2 per hr., 2½ hr., L13,700); Syracuse (10 hr., L41,900); and Brindisi for ferries to Greece (6½ hr., L27,100).

Ferries: Caremar, Molo Beverello. To: Capri (6 per day, 70 min., L7300); Ischia (7 per day, 70 min., L7300); Procida (5 per day, 60 min., L6100). **Tirrenia,** Molo Angioino. To: Palermo (10½ hr., L58,900 plus L2000 port tax); Cagliari (16 hr., L45,400); and Malta (25 hr., L134,600).

Medical Assistance: (tel. 752 06 96).

Emergencies: Police (tel. 794 11 11). English-speaking *ufficio stranieri* (foreigners' office) at the *Questura* (police station), via Medina, 75, at via Diaz.

Accommodations and Food

Naples's only youth hostel is the expensive **Ostello Salita della Grotta (IYHF),** salita della Grotta, 23 (tel. 761 23 46), two quick rights from the Mergellina metro stop. (Lockout 9:30am-4pm. Curfew 11:30pm. L15,000. Sheets and breakfast included.) Naples has plenty of cheap, grungy hotels. Consider spending a little more for more comfort and safety. Neapolitan hotel owners often play with the room prices: agree on a rate before unpacking or surrendering up your passport. Call the EPT (tel. 41 98 88) if you have complaints. The Mergellina area (on the far end of the bay) is one of the nicer, if rather distant, places to stay. **Pensione Teresita,** via Santa Lucia, 90 (tel. 41 21 05), has cozy, secure rooms. (Singles 20,000. Doubles 30,000. Showers included.) **Albergo Astoria,** downstairs (tel. 41 89 03) has similar prices. Cheaper and convenient accommodations can be found in the noisy and occasionally dangerous university district near p. Dante. Take bus #185, CS, or CD from p. Garibaldi. **Soggiorno Imperia,** p. Miraglia, 386 (tel. 45 93 47), has large, well-furnished rooms and the most charming and helpful proprietress in Southern Italy. (Singles L20,000. Doubles L32,000. Showers included.) Make the area around the train station your last choice. **Albergo Zara,** via Firenze, 81 (tel. 28 71 25), has clean rooms with peeling neoclassical ceilings. Hang a right out of the station on corso Novaro, then your 1st left. (Singles L22,000. Monster doubles 40,000.) The **Casanova Hotel,** via Venezia, 2 (tel. 26 82 87) has a relaxing rooftop terrace. (Singles L18,000. Doubles L38,500.)

Pizza, of course, is what put Naples on the map. **Antica Pizzeria da Michele,** via Cesare Sersale, 1/3, off corso Umberto not far from the train station, is a Neapolitan tradition. Try their L3000 *Marinara.* (Open Mon.-Sat. 8am-10pm.) Spaghetti was also first cooked up by Neapolitan chefs. Seek it out *alle vongole* (with clams), *alle cozze* (with mussels), and *alla puttanesca* (with tomatos, olives, and capers). Neapolitan snacks include *crocchè* (a tubular, deep-fried, potato knish) and *sfogliatelle* (ricotta-filled pastries). Some of the best eateries are near p. Dante and down by the bay in Mergellina. **Osteria Canterbury,** via Ascensione, 6 (tel. 41 35 84), left off via Vittoria Colonna, right down the stairs, right again, then a quick left. Home to the best meal in the area, and an exquisite *insalata caprese* (a salad of sliced tomato, fresh mozzarella and basil leaves). Huddling under the Dante clock tower, **Pizzeria Port'Alba,** via Port'Alba, 18, is Naples's oldest *pizzeria.* Try the *vecchia Port-Alba* for a tasty treat (L8000). **Sorbillo's,** via Tribunali, 35, is testimony to Neapolitan pizza-making culture, with sawdust from the wood oven everywhere (pizza from L2500). In Mergellina, enjoy a large bowl of *zuppa di cozze* (mussel soup) in any of the outdoor restaurants that fill p. Sannazzaro or hike over to **Antica Trattoria al Vicoletto,** via C. Cucca, 52 (tel. 66 92 90) for excellent *tagliatelle* (L7000).

Sights

Begin with the world-famous **Museo Nazionale Archeologico** (Metro: Cavour) and its collection of frescoes and jewelry excavated from Pompeii and Herculaneum. (Open Tues.-Sat. 9am-2pm, Sun. 9am-1pm. Admission L8000.) On a hill overlooking the city, beside a large park, stands the **Museo di Capodimonte;** take bus #110 or 127. The highlight of the museum is the fabulous **Galleria Nazionale,** which features the art of Simone Martini, Massacio, Raphael, and other notables. (Open Tues.-Sat. Admission L8000.) The **Museo San Martino,** in a Carthusian monastery on the hill of San Elmo, explicates the art and history of Naples since the 16th century. Take the cable car from via Toledo near Galleria Umberto. (Open Tues.-Sat. 9am-2pm, Sun. 9am-1pm. Admission L6000.) The ornate **Palazzo Reale,** on p. del Plebiscito, illustrates the lifestyle of the city in a more glorious era. (Open daily 9am-1pm. Admission L6000.) The neighboring **Galleria Umberto,** on via Roma, is an exquisite iron-and-glass arcade of shops, offices, and cafés. For a little semi-fresh air, head to the **Villa Floridiana,** on a knoll overlooking the bay. Here you'll find a lovely park and the **Ducia di Martina Museum,** with local pottery. (Open Tues.-Sat. 9am-2pm, Sun. 9am-1pm. Admission L4000.)

Journey into the heart of the **old city,** known as **Spaccanapoli;** it's sketched out by the streets of via Benedetto Croce, via San Biagio dei Librai, and via Vicaria Vecchia, running east to west off via Roma. Here is traditional Naples: narrow streets, venerable shops, and workaday Italians (but strip yourself of valuables before the workaday Italian thieves strip you). But don't skip a visit to Naples' best-kept secret, the **Cappella di San Severo,** via de Sanctis, which houses Sammartino's incredible *Veiled Christ* sculpture, as well as two leering and grisly corpses. (Open Mon. and Wed.-Sat. 10am-1:30pm and 5-7pm, Tues. and Sun. 10am-1:30pm. Admission L3000.) Off p. Gesù Nuovo, step into the **Chiesa del Gesù** and more serene *Chiesa di Santa Chiara* for a few moments of tranquility. For more information on sights, consult the *Qui Napoli* guide from the tourist office.

Near Naples

Adumbrated by the immense, dormant **Mount Vesuvius,** the area surrounding Naples has spectacular offerings: Roman ruins, Greek temples, and the Amalfi Coast. The eruption of the great volcano in 79 AD buried the nearby Roman city of Herculaneum (Ercolano) in mud, and its neighbor Pompeii (Pompei), in ashes. Ongoing excavation continues to uncover the lives of the ancients with frightening precision. Both sites are accessible by the Circumvesuviana train running from the lower floor of Naples's Stazione Centrale toward Sorrento. In **Pompeii** you can wind your way around the streets and alleys radiating from the main thoroughfare, via dell'Abondanza, stopping at the amphitheater (near the east entrance), the *teatro grande,* and the forum (at the western end of the via). To reach the site, take the train to the Pompeii-Villa dei Misteri stop (round-trip L3600), walk straight to the Church of the Madonna of Pompeii, and turn right on via Roma, which leads to the east entrance. The remains at **Herculaneum** (round-trip L1200) is smaller, but better preserved. (Both sites open daily 9am-1 hr. before sunset. Admission L10,000 each.)

South of Naples on the far side of the Amalfi Peninsula, windy and narrow cliff-side roads and tiled towns that cling to the cliffs (and occasionally slide into the water) make the **Amalfi Coast** the most beautiful stretch of shoreline in Italy. Both **Sorrento,** at the western end of the peninsula (1½ hr. and L2700 by Circumvesuviana train), and **Salerno** at its eastern base (1 hr. and L3200 by regular rail) are an easy trip from Naples; buses between them (every 2 hr.) go through all the coastal towns. The towns to see are Positano, Amalfi and Ravello; but only Praiano and Atrani have affordable beds. To fully grasp the coast's beauty, rent a moped in Sorrento from **Ciro's,** via degli Aranci, 93b-c (tel. (081) 878 25 22; L25,000 per day plus 19% tax and gas). In **Praiano,** between Sorrento and Amalfi, enjoy the coastal views from **La Tranquilità,** via Roma, 10 (tel. (089) 87 40 84; bungalows L25,000 per person; campsites L12,000 per person, Sept.-Nov. and March-June L10,000.) Above the Tranquilità is the open-air **Ristorante Continental,** whose conspiracy of mountain air, endless views, and exquisite L15,000 meals will leave you in Amalfi Coast bliss. Saturday is pizza night. (Open March-Nov. daily noon-3pm and 8pm-midnight.) In **Atrani**—a 10-minute walk from Amalfi—stay in **A Scalinatella,** p. Umberto I (tel. (089) 87 14 92), in the town's main *piazza.* It has accommodating hostel-type rooms and laundry machines (L5000 per load; open Sept.-July L10,000 per person, plus L2500 if you stay 2-3 days without your own bedding; Aug. L15,000 per person.)

Since imperial times, the divine landscapes and azure waters of the island of **Capri** have beckoned wayfarers from the Italian mainland. The **Grotta Azzura** (Blue Grotto) is the island's symbol, but avoid the ripoff motorboat tours; instead take a bus (L300 from Anacapri) to this fluorescent cave, and don't swim. Ferries to Capri leave several times per day from Naples; others leave from Sorrento and

Amalfi. On the island, ships dock at Marina Grande; take the bus up to **Anacapri** (L1500), where rooms are most agreeable. **Villa Eva,** via della Fabbrica, 8 (tel. (081) 837 20 40), is splendidly isolated. Mamma Eva and Papà Vincenzo will pick you up from Anacapri center (L30,000 per person). **Hotel Biancamaria,** via G. Orlandi, 54 (tel. (081) 837 10 00), is near the bus stop in Anacapri's p. Vittoria (with *Let's Go,* L25,000 per person; in shared rooms of 3 or more people, L20,000 per person). Dine in style in Anacapri at **Trattoria il Solitario,** via G. Orlandi, 54 (tel. (081) 837 13 82), an outdoor flower-filled hideaway serving hand-prepared *ravioli caprese* for L6000. (Cover L1500. Open daily in summer 12:15-3pm and 7pm-midnight; off-season Tues-Sun.) In July and August, when Capri swarms with humanity, consider fleeing to the larger island of **Ischia** or smaller **Procida.**

Adriatic Ports

The three major cities of Ancona, Bari, and Brindisi, all on the Bologna-Lecce train line, are Italy's principal departure points for Yugoslavia, Greece, Cyprus, and Albania. Ancona is a bustling maritime city with an appealing, if slightly seedy, urban landscape. Bari is the South's most vibrant city, with easy daytrips to dozens of picturesque, architecturally distinct villages. Brindisi is quite possibly the most disgusting town on the face of the earth, but, human cruelty being what it is, it offers the cheapest travel to Greece for Eurailpass holders.

From **Ancona,** the northernmost, **Jadrolinija** (tel. (071) 20 20 34) sails to Yugoslavia; **Karageorgis** (tel. (071) 20 10 80) and **Strintzis**(tel. (071) 500 62) to Greece and Cyprus; and **Minoan Lines** (tel. (071) 567 89) to Greece and Turkey. To get to the ferries from the train station, take municipal bus #1 (L800) to the **Stazione Marittima** (at least two hours before departure). The **tourist office** in both the station and the *stazione* offer free museum tickets and food vouchers. Don't miss the **Museo Archeologico,** with two life-size bronze statues of Roman emperors, or the **Galleria Comunale** with Titian's *Apparition of the Virgin.* Stay at **Pensione Milano,** via Montebello, 1/A (tel. (071) 20 11 47), in the town center (singles L20,000; doubles L30,000) or **Hotel Cavour,** viale della Vittoria, 7 (tel. (071) 20 03 74), one block from the eponymous *piazza.* (Singles L23,000. Doubles L33,500).

Yes, Virginia, there is a Santa Claus, and he's dead. The burial place of St. Nicholas, **Bari** continues in the spirit of generosity with a miraculous program designed to *attract* scruffy backpackers. From mid-June to mid-September, the **Stop-Over in Bari Program** (24-hr. hotline (080) 44 11 86) will cater to your every need—if you're under 30. Stop over at Stop-Over **information offices** in the train station and ferry station for information on free concerts, discounts, and other goodies (open daily 8am-8pm); pick up their daily English newsletter, or tune into 102FM. Stop-Over offers free camping (if you've got a sleeping bag), pasta and cooking instructions. If you're sackless, Stop-Over's English-speaking student types will put you up in a private home for two nights for only L25,000. Rejoice: you needn't patronize Bari's overpriced fleabag hotels, unless it's winter or you're too old. In the *medina*-like **old town,** stop in at the **Church of St. Nicholas** to view the remains of the Nickster himself. **Adriatica** (tel. (080) 33 15 55) runs ferries to Split in Croatia; **Jadrolinija** (tel. (080) 521 28 40) plies to Dubrovnik; and **Morfimare** (tel. (080) 521 00 22) serves Bar. **Ventouris Ferries** (tel. (080) 521 05 04) is Greece or bust.

Brindisi, 1½ hr. by train from Bari, has exactly one redeeming features: its ferries to Greece are semi-free for Eurailpass holders, discounted 50% for *cartaverde* bearers, and normally discounted 30% for InterRail holders (though InterRail may be made fully valid due to the fighting in Yugoslavia). If you have no railpass, the Bari ferries are cheaper. **Adriatica,** Stazione Marittima (tel. (0831) 52 38 25), or c/o Pattimare, p. E. Dionisi, 11 (tel. (0831) 265 48); **Hellenic Mediterranean Lines,** corso Garibaldi, 8 (tel. (0831) 285 31); and **Fragline,** corso Garibaldi, 88 (tel. (0831) 56 82 32) all run to Corfu, Igoumenitsa, and Patras in Greece. Eurailers sail free on

Adriatica and Hellenic Mediterranean, except for L10,000 in port taxes and a L14,000 high season supplement. There is no reason to spend money on anything more plush than deck class; in summer you'll actually be more comfortable on deck than in an airplane-style seat in a large, smoke-filled cabin. Advance reservations are best, but you can also buy your tickets at any of the travel agencies between the train station and the port, or from the ticket offices at the port itself (where you must go anyway to get a boarding pass and pay port taxes, and where they will double-check all your ID). Bypass the "representatives" hanging around the train station. Bicycles travel free on most lines. Makeshift groups of 20-25 people working through a travel agent can sometimes secure a 10-15% discount per person, plus a free trip for the enterprising leader. Check in at the embarkation office at least two hours before departure or lose your reservation and ticket. Allow plenty of time for late trains, and for the 1km station-to-port walk. Trains leave Rome for Brindisi five times per day. The **EPT tourist office,** lungomare Régina Margherita, 5 (tel. (0831) 219 44), is edifying. If you need to change money, avoid the rip-off artists at the *stazione marittima,* and the many *drachma*-wielding places along corso Garibaldi.

Two Brindisi restaurants offer special discounts for *Let's Go* carriers. **Trattoria Da Emilia,** vilo del Raimondo, 11, off corso Garibaldi, offers fresh pasta, salad, and beverage for L7000. (Open daily 9am-10pm.) **Spaghetti House-Osteria Cucina Casalinga,** via Mazzini, 57, not far from the station, serves excellent, filling meals from L6000. Flash your attractive orange *Let's Go* for special discounts. (Open Mon.-Sat. 11am-2:30pm and 4-8:30pm.) A venture off the main drag and onto via Pisanelli will reward you with *focaccia* at much cheaper prices. Try the *alimentari* at via Pisanelli, 22. The supermarket at the end of corso Garibaldi is convenient for boat-ride provisions. (Open daily 9am-1pm and 4-8pm.) Sleep with Stop-Over in Bari and take the train if you can help it. If you're absolutely stuck in Brindisi and suicide is not a viable option, try **Hotel Altair,** via Tunisia (tel. (081) 52 49 11), off corso Garibaldi. Call ahead. (Singles L25,000. Doubles L40,000.)

Sicily (Sicilia)

Smack in the heart of the Mediterranean, Sicily is an island apart from the Europe most travelers meet. Irrepressible invasions by Mediterranean civilizations over the past 2500 years have left their marks—the ancient Greeks left temples and theaters, the Romans bridges and aqueducts, the Saracens mosques and towers, and the Normans churches and castles. Negligent northern European rule inspired the Sicilians to take the law into their own hands, hence the success of one of Italy's most enduring institutions—the Mafia. Earthquakes and the eruptions of Mt. Etna, Europe's largest active volcano, are equally destructive.

Trains to Sicily from the mainland meet their ferries (no extra charge) at Villa San Giovanni or, less frequently, at Reggio di Calabria. **Tirrenia** sails from Naples to Palermo (1 per day, 10½ hr., L48,000-63,000). FS trains run from Messina (across from Villa San Giovanni) to Palermo, Palermo to Trapani, and Syracuse to Messina via Catania. Buses link tinier towns and fill gaps in the interior. Some major sights can be reached only by private trains and buses. Expects delays and confusion. Hitching is onerous—there are simply not enough cars on major roads. There are only two hostels on the island and campgrounds are expensive. Although authorities frown on freelance camping, it may be an option; check with the tourist office for the local policy.

Palermo

Although the dreaded Mafia has ceased to be an acknowledged presence, Palermo retains a flavor of intrigue. Sicily's capital and cultural center, its brightly lit avenues mask a labyrinth of dark, older streets, and a port brimming with rusty sculls. Despite the city's overpopulation and lack of restoration, the *palazzi* strewn about the town contain some of the most wondrous courtyards in Italy. To reach the exuberant *duomo* from the stadium, head straight from the exit on via Roma, bearing left on corso Vittorio Emanuele. (Open daily 7am-noon and 5-7pm.) Close by, the **Palazzo dei Normanni** exhibits an impressive fusion of artistic styles, while the **Church of San Giovanni degli Eremiti,** while in shambles, dons some pink Arab domes covering an exotic cloistered garden. (Palazzo open Mon. and Fri.-Sat. 9am-noon unless the Sicilian parliament is in session; church open Mon.-Sat. 9am-2pm and 3-10pm, Sun. 9am-1pm and 3-10pm.) The **Museo Archeologico,** off via Roma at p. Olivella, just a block from via Cavour, contains the panels of a famous Doric frieze from the Greek temple of Selinunte. (Open Mon., Wed.-Thurs., and Sat. 9am-1:30pm, Tues. and Fri. 9am-1:30pm and 3-6pm, Sun. 9am-1pm. Admission L2000.) If you like mosaics, try not to pass up the opportunity to visit nearby **Monreale,** where the cathedral mixes Norman architecture with Sicilian and Arabian motifs. (Take bus #9 (L800) from via Lincoln, across from the train station and to the left. Open daily 8am-12:30pm and 3:30-6:30pm.) The **Benedictine Cloister** next door frames a garden with fanciful medieval columns. (Open daily 9am-7pm. Admission L2000.)

For maps and information, visit the **APT** office (tel. (091) 58 38 47) in the train station; the staff speaks decent English (generally open Mon.-Sat. 8am-8pm). **Pensione Sud** via Maqueda 8, (tel. (091) 617 57 00) is two blocks from the station, with cool, comparatively spacious, and extremely affordable rooms. (Singles L16,000. Doubles L26,000. Triples L33,000. Showers L2000.) **Albergo Rosalia Conca d'Oro,** via Santa Rosalia, 7 (tel. (091) 616 45 43), is also close to the station. Turn left off via Roma as you head toward town. Come in summer and get free tickets to the beach. (Singles L20,000. Doubles L32,000. Triples L45,000.) **Albergo Letizia,** via Bottai, 30, off corso Vittorio Emanuele (tel. (091) 58 91 10), is in Palermo's hippest neighborhood. The owner loves Americans and collects rainwater in his spare time. (Singles L20,000. Doubles L32,000, with bath L38,000. Extra bed L13,000.)

Despite its Chinese name, the food at **Trattoria Shanghai,** vicolo de Mezzani, 34, overlooking piazza Caracciolo just a few blocks from the intersection of via Roma and corso Vittorio Emanuele, is pure Palermo with great *gambieri* (shrimp); a meal costs about L8000. (Open daily for lunch and dinner.) After dinner, hike up town to Frankie's **Bar Fiore,** via Principe di Belmonte, 84, where Palermo's biggest extrovert will give ya a *frullato* (a frothy Italian milkshake) for only L3500. Most of Palermo's nightlife is outside the city proper in nearby **Mondello;** take bus #6, 14, or 15 from via della Libertà or the station, and get off at Mondello Paese to join the crowds of young Italians sampling *gelato* and fish from seaside stalls.

Agrigento

Among Sicily's classical remains, the **Valley of Temples** at Agrigento shares top honors with those at Syracuse: **Concordia,** one of the world's best-preserved Greek temples, owes its survival to its consecration by early Christians. On the road to the archeological park from the city center lies the **Museo Archeologico Nazionale,** which houses the sole surviving colossal statue from the Temple of Olympian Zeus. (Open Tues.-Sun. 9am-2pm and 3-7pm. Free.)

The **tourist office** is in the underground passage near the station. (Open daily 8:30am-1:30pm and 4:30-7:30pm.) Bus #10 leaves p. Marconi (in the underground passage) every half-hour for both the Valley of Temples and the buxom **beach** at S. Leone (L600).

Although Agrigento can be seen as a daytrip from Palermo (2½ hr. by train, L9300), **Bella Napoli,** p. Lena, 6 (tel. (0922) 204 35), at the north end of via Atenea, has friendly owners, a terrace overlooking the valley, and biblical rains. (Singles L25,000. Doubles L35,000.) Closer to the train station is **Concordia,** via San Francesco, 11 (tel. (0922) 59 62 66), a clean modern place on a dirty street. (Singles L23,000, with bath L25,000. Doubles L33,000, with bath L39,000.) **Paninoteca Manhattan,** Salita M. Angel, 9, up the steps to the right off via Atenea coming up from p. Moro, serves hearty sandwiches. Try the "Rockhfeller" with tuna, pepper, lettuce, tabasco, *insalata russa,* and a dousing of whiskey (L3500). (Open Mon.-Sat. 8:30am-3pm and 5:30pm-midnight.)

Syracuse (Siracusa)

Founded in 734 BC by Corinthians who fancied its splendid harbor and natural spring water, the Hellenic city of Syracuse stood eye to eye with Athens; during the 5th to 3rd centuries BC, when it produced Pindar, Archimedes, and the world's first cookbook, it looked down. Cross the bridge on corso Umberto to the island of **Ortigia** to pay homage to the Temples of **Apollo** and **Athena.** The latter, now part of the city's cathedral, has a richly embellished baroque façade, added in the 18th century. Wander through Ortigia's mazelike sidestreets, unchanged since medieval times, to the southern coast of the isle. A park there contains the splendid **Spring of Arethusa,** whose waters are said to emanate from the Alpheus River in Greece.

Most sights, including the **Archeological Park** and the **Museo Paolo Orsi,** lie across town. The park contains the world's largest **Greek Theater** (5th century BC), where Aeschylus's *Persians* premiered, along with the **Paradise Quarry,** now a shady park. (Park open Mon.-Sat. 9am to 2 hrs. before sunset, Sun. 9am-1pm. Admission L2000.) The most impressive feature of the area is the **Orecchio di Dionisio** (Ear of Dionysius), a giant artificial grotto with an earlobe-shaped entrance. The cave's acoustics reputedly allowed the tyrant Dionysius to overhear prisoners talking in the lower room. Nearby is the covered **Roman Amphitheater** (2nd century AD), and the monstrous **Altar of Hieron II** (241-215 BC), once used for public sacrifices. The elegant **Palazzo Bellomo,** on via Capodieci, has a superb collection of painting and sculpture, including Antonella da Messina's *Annunciation* (1474). (Open daily 9am-1pm.)

Opposite the **Catacombs of San Giovanni** (L2000 for a whirlwind tour of a labyrinth of frescoed passages; March-Nov. Thurs.-Tues. hourly 10am-noon and 4-6pm) the **EPT** office at lungo Paradiso finds accommodations and has decent maps. (Open daily 8am-2pm, Tues.-Fri. and Sun. also 3-6pm.) There is a **youth hostel** at via Epipoli, 45 (tel. (0931) 71 11 18), near the Castello Eurialo, about 8km from Syracuse. Take bus #9, 10, or 11 to Belvedere. (Curfew 11pm. L13,500. Call ahead.) **Hotel Bel Sit,** via Oglio, 5 (tel. (0931) 602 45), on the 5th floor, has caring proprietors and is near the station and high above the bustle. (Singles L17,500, with bath L20,500. Doubles L27,000.) The city's grandest supermarket is **Supermercato Linguanti,** corso Umberto, 186, to the left of the train station. (Open Mon.-Tues. and Thurs.-Sat. 7am-1pm and 3-8pm, Wed. 7am-1pm.) **Tuttopizza,** Lungomare Alfeo, 12 (tel. (0931) 677 56), combats Syracuse's high-priced tourist menus (pizzas L3000-8000, cover L1000; open Wed.-Mon. 9pm-1am).

Venture 18km on bus #34 from Foro Siracusano park to the long, sandy beach of **Fontane Bianche,** or ride the 8km on bus #21 or 22 to the hipper **Arenella** beach. Southwest of Syracuse by SAIS or AST bus is the baroque village of **Noto,** overshadowed by anomalously huge palaces and churches. Take a walk down corso Vittorio Emanuele for a sampling of fine structures hewn from soft golden rock.

Aeolian Islands (Isole Eolie)

Home of the smithy god Hephaistos, of the Sirens, and of Aeolus of the winds, the Lìpari or Aeolian Islands are an enchanting volcanic archipelago off northern Sicily. On **Lìpari,** the largest and most central of the islands, the pastel-colored houses of the town of Lìpari hug a small peninsula crowned by the walls of a medieval *castello.* The comely **Ostello Lìpari (IYHF)** (tel. (090) 981 15 40) is inside the castle walls (L9000. Breakfast L2500. Full meals L10,000. Kitchen facilities, blankets, sheets, and cold showers provided. Open March-Oct.) Reach Lìpari by ferry (L8600) from the city of **Milazzo,** on the Messina-Palermo train line (from Messina L3500; from Palermo L12,200). Ferries and hydrofoils fan out from Lìpari to the other islands; the closer islands (Vulcano, Salina, and Panarea) merit the quicker, more expensive hydrofoils, but for Stromboli, Filicudi, and Alicudi you're better off taking a ferry and using your savings to rent a boat when you arrive.

The island of **Vulcano,** only 15 minutes from Lìpari by hydrofoil (L3700), has thermal springs and bubbling mud baths. From the dock at Porto di Levante, head to the left up the snaking path to the crater around the sulfur fumaroles for a breathtaking view of the other isles. **Stromboli** (½ hr. and L17,000 from Lìpari) is the most dramatic and enticing of the islands, with an active volcano, stream o' lava, voluptuous vegetation and alluring beaches. Make a point of staying overnight; an evening spent at the summit watching red-hot lava against pitch-black sky is unforgettable. (Nights are crisp and windy at the crater, so bring a plastic groundsheet and sleeping bag, a heavy sweater, plenty of food, two liters of water per person, and a flashlight with an extra set of batteries, as the path isn't lit. Always stay within the rocky enclosures.) The hike takes three hours up, two hours down. Although not required, guides are available to escort you on a day trip; they leave daily in summer from in front of Il Gabbiano restaurant by the Ficogrande beach at 6:30pm (L18,000 per person). Get away from it all on **Filicudi** or **Alicudi;** neither supports more than 400 people, and electricity only came recently. The beautiful beaches and crystal-clear waters of **Panarea** and **Salina** are expensive and best seen as daytrips from Lìpari.

Sardinia (Sardegna)

The 200km crossing between Sardinia and Italy belies the greater gulf that separates this island from the mainland. Mountainous, barren, and wild, Sardinia has never been completely civilized or conquered. Waves of Phoenicians, Byzantines, Pisans, Genoans and Aragones have tried to bring the island into step with the rest of Europe, but to no avail. Sardinia proudly proclaims its autonomy, flying its own flag despite Italian sovereignty and clinging to its own dialect, food, and customs. Sardinia's beaches rival any others in Europe, and the island is still a refuge for marine seals and pink flamingoes. Tourism has been its only conquerer, vanquishing the northeastern **Costa Smeralda;** stick to the stunning beaches and ancient ruins further south.

Tirrenia (via Bissolati, 41 in Rome; tel. (06) 474 22 42) runs the most extensive ferry service, plying from Civitavecchia (frequent trains from Rome, 1 hr.) to Olbia (two per day, 7 hr., L21,200); Civitavecchia to Cagliari (daily, 13 hr., L44,700); Genoa to Olbia (daily, 13 hr., L50,500); Genoa to Cagliari (3 per week, 20½ hr., L74,200); Naples to Cagliari (3 per week, 16 hr., L45,400); and Tunisia to Cagliari (Tues. at 8pm, 21 hr., L97,400). **Flights** arrive in Olbia and Cagliari (Rome-Olbia about L122,500 one-way). On the island, **ARST** buses link to regional towns; **PANI** buses, to other major cities. **Trains** are picturesque and inexpensive but slow; most ignore railpasses. Car or moped rental is not a bad idea. Ask at any tourist office for the *Annuarii degli Albergi and Campeggi,* which lists all Sardinian hotels, *pensione* and campsites.

Olbia is an overpriced port town to pass through; **Cagliari,** at the very southern tip of the island, is the island's delightful capital city, near beautiful beaches, ancient ruins and flamingoed lagoons. Stay at the **Albergo Firenze,** corso Vittorio Emanuele, 50 (tel. (070) 65 36 78; singles L18,000; doubles L20,000), or **Albergo Centrale,** via Sardegna, 4 (tel. (070) 65 47 83; singles L22,000; doubles L35,000). Try the nearby **Trattoria Gennargentu,** via Sardegna, 60 (tel. (070) 65 82 47) for a traditional Sard menu (L14,000). **Sassari** is the second largest city in Sardinia and a great homebase for daytrips. Try **Pensione Famidia,** viale Umberto, 65 (tel. (070) 23 95 43; huge doubles L20,000). **Alghero** is a charming seaside town near Sássari with a well-preserved medieval quarter and pretty port and beach. **Nuoro** is an authentic Sardinian town in the heart of the island, largely unblemished by tourism. From Nuoro, a one-hour bus trip will connect you with **Cala Gonore,** a beautiful beach and jumping-off point for boat trips to **Bue Marino** where seals still romp at night.

LATVIA

As we went to press, Latvia was still using the Soviet Union's currency and telephone systems; however, expect this to change in the next year.

As Latvia (Latvija) gained independence in 1991, its autonomy seemed more fraught with difficulty than in Estonia or Lithuania. Latvia is the most industrialized of the Baltic states, but also the most statistically Russified; little more than fifty percent of its 2.6 million residents are native Latvians. The situation dates back to the 1950s, when Russians flooded the country, assigned to work in Latvia's strategic military bases and comparatively modern factories; retired officers still own retirement homes along the seashore near Rīga.

Latvia is no exception to the Baltic states' history of foreign domination; Germany, Poland, Sweden, and tsarist Russia all laid claim to its gentle landscape and five thousand lakes. After Lenin's Bolsheviks failed to maintain control of the country, Latvia enjoyed a taste of freedom until 1940, when the Soviet Union demanded free troop passage through Latvian territory; a brief, but terrifying occupation by Nazi Germany. As the shrapnel of the Second World War began to rust along the Baltic shore, Latvia found itself war booty, a newly-christened Soviet Socialist Republic. Now Latvia hopes to build on its relative prosperity while righting the colossal social and ecological wrongs of the Soviet period.

Getting There and Getting Around

In September 1991, visas were issued at the border; it is advisable to present some evidence (a letter of invitation, or a confirmed hotel reservation) that someone in Latvia will be looking after you. Journalists and government officials required visas in advance, obtainable from the Latvian embassy at 4325 17th St. N.W., Washington DC 20011 (tel. (202) 726-8213); the only European representation issuing visas was in Stockholm. If you arrive in Latvia from Estonia or Lithuania, you may not need as much advance preparation. These policies, however, were *very* temporary, and will be changed as soon as new legislation is passed in Latvia. The trend seems to be towards eliminating visas altogether, at least for certain nationalities. Check ahead before you go.

From approximately May to September, **Lettline** (tel. +46 (11) 12 33 39) runs a hydrofoil from Norrköping in Sweden to Rīga (leaves Norrköping Tues.and Fri. 8am; leaves Rīga Mon. and Thurs. 9am; 10 hr.; 600kr, 980kr round-trip, breakfast and lunch included; students and seniors 10% off). Check ahead, since the hydrofoil is canceled in high winds. Norrköping is an easy train ride from Stockholm (1 per hr., 2 hr.)

SAS flies from Copenhagen to Rīga (2 per week, from 1600kr round-trip); **Aeroflot** flies from Copenhagen (2 per week), Stockholm (3 per week), and Helsinki (2 per week). **Baltia Airlines,** which began in a Brooklyn immigrant's apartment and miraculously beat out major carriers for the FAA's Baltic rights, expects to have five flights per week (Wed.-Sun.) from JFK Airport in New York to Rīga by spring 1992, with connections to Tbilisi, Minsk, and Kiev. Call (800) 555-1212 to get their current number.

Two suffocating trains daily cover the Tallinn-Rīga and Rīga-Vilnius legs (about 8-10 hr.). The overnight trains are probably your best option, unless you prefer to do your sweating (or freezing) in the heat of the day. Note that Rīga is Riia in Estonian. Buses also cover the same connections and are slightly faster, but more cramped and slightly more expensive.

Practical Information

Tourist information and maps are still difficult to come by in Latvia. The major tourist hotels can answer specific questions, but probably won't be frothing with helpful tips. Inroads' *Guide to the Baltic States* (USD18), however, has a particularly comprehensive chapter on Latvia.

Latvian is a Baltic language, whose closest relative is Lithuanian. Key words include *lūdzu* ("please") and *paldies* ("thank you"). Virtually everyone speaks Russian too, especially in Rīga, where Russians are in the majority. Still, you should start off in your native language and break into Russian only after they clearly have no idea what you're talking about. Most young people have studied English as a third language, but few speak it well.

Latvian currency should start circulating in 1992; the phone system will become independent over the next couple years, and mail is currently being routed both through Moscow and Scandinavia.

Accommodations, Camping, and Food

As in Estonia and Lithuania, finding a room in Latvia was a chaotic process as we went to press, with establishments adjusting to walk-in customers instead of preprogrammed Intourist tours. The situation may have calmed slightly by summer 1992. Contact one of the following groups in advance, or on your arrival in Rīga; some can help with cheap airfares.

LUTK—Latvian University Tourist Club, Raiņa bulv. 19, Rīga 226098, Latvia (tel. 22 31 14). Can arrange accommodations and trips in Rīga and other cities.

Baltic Environmental Tours, Ecological Center, University of Latvia, Raiņa bulv. 19, Rīga 226098, Latvia (tel. 22 53 04; fax 22 50 39). Sponsors work and study camps, primarily for groups of seven to fifteen people (7-14 days, DM600-900).

Celotājs, Tallinas iela 88/24, 226009 Rīga, Latvia (tel. and fax 33 22 76). U.S. partner is **Chips Travel,** Middleburg Plaza, 15330 E. Bagley Rd., Middleburg Heights, OH 44130 (tel. (216) 845-9090).

Inroads, Inc., P.O. Box 3197, Merrifield, VA 22116-3197 (tel. (703) 641-9118). Sponsors home stays with private families for USD225 per week, primarily in Rīga, and sells *A Guide to the Baltic States* (USD18).

Livonija Ltd. Co., Jauniela 14, 226050 Rīga, Latvia (tel. 28 05 34 or 21 35 09; fax 21 35 09). German partner is Reisebüro Alainis, Revalweg 4, 8940 Memminger (tel. (08331) 35 82).

Union Tours, 79 Madison Ave., New York NY 10016 (tel. (212) 683-9500).

Riga

Avant-garde art and film thrive in Rīga, whose residents also bemoan the pollution in the Daugava River—they joke that it's safer to drink than to swim in. Yet, a relatively high standard of living has combined with Rīga's strategic importance as a Soviet military and shipping center to attract thousands of Russian settlers in the past fifty years; now barely 40% of the city's inhabitants are Latvian.

Orientation and Practical Information

Cozy bars and restaurants speckle the old town, a box of densely packed building blocks on the right bank of the river, split down the middle by Kalku iela (formerly Leņina iela). From the train station, go two blocks riverwards on Suvorova iela and the old town will be just to your right. The **Bastejkalna** park and its cute canal divide the old town from the university. You can purchase a map in Latvian or Russian at **Hotel Rīga,** just off Aspāzijas bulv. (formerly Padomju bulv.) between Kalku iela and Teātra iela. A new, improved map with updated street names is expected out by 1992.

Tourist Office: Hotel reception desks (see below) can answer specific questions about the city. The **Intourist** office is one block southeast of **Hotel Latvija** on Elizabetes iela, but often mobbed with people screaming for train tickets.

Currency Exchange: At the Hotel Latvija.

Post Office: Near the Freedom Monument on Brīvības bulv.

Telephones: Best to make calls at tourist hotels. **City Code:** 0132.

Trains: Rīgas centrālā dzelzceļa stacija, Stacijas laukums, off Suvorova iela. To: Tallinn (2 per day, 8 hr.); Vilnius (2 per day, 8 hr.); Leningrad, Moscow, and Minsk, and to points within Latvia: Jūrmala (every 10 min.) and Sigulda.

Buses: Autoosta, Pragas iela 1, near the train station. To: Tallinn (10 per day, 6½ hr.), Leningrad, Moscow, Minsk, and other cities.

Public Transportation: Many buses and mini-vans depart from the lot across from the train station. Connections to Jūrmala (every 8-15 min.).

Emergencies: Police: (tel. 01). **Ambulance:** (tel. 03).

Accommodations and Food

The three best hotels are the **Hotel Rīga,** Aspāzijas bulv. 22; **Hotel Latvija,** Elizabetes iela 55 (formerly Kirova iela), at the corner of Kalku iela three blocks northeast of the old town; and the **Hotel Ridzene,**reached from the old town by walking up Kalku iela, turning left on Raiņa bulv., then taking your first right; it's on the right. The Rīdzene still has bullet holes in the glass staircase from January 1991 battles between the Latvian home guard and Soviet troops. They cost from between USD80-125 per night, if you book yourself; tourist groups can swing you a lower rate. There is a big dropoff in cost to the next level of hotels, most often frequented by Soviet citizens.

Clustered in the old city are a number of fine ruble restaurants. The **Pi Kristapa,** Jauniela 25-29, serves large green ceramic pitchers of beer (12R) and traditional Latvian entrees (4-10R) in a smoke-filled cellar. The **Rīga Restaurant** in the Hotel Rīga serves elegant meals, if you can get in (entrees 6-10R). **Café Arhitekts,** nestled in a courtyard off Amatu iela, offers entrees at similar prices, as well as alcohol and coffee. **Café Forums,** Kalku iela 26, serves food and alcohol, often to live music. A "dry" hangout, popular among young people for its Pepsi, is **Café Možums,** Šķūņu iela 19, in the southeast corner of the Doma laukums (a square). If you feel like shelling out hard currency for Western surroundings, head to **Café Jever** at the corner of Skarņu iela and Kalku iela (imported beers DM3, entrees DM15-20).

Sights

In the square between the Old City and the university, where Kalku iela meets Brīvības iela, rises the **Brīvības piemineklis** (Freedom Monument), built when Latvia declared independence in 1918 and left strangely untouched by the Soviet occupation. Only five years ago, any attempt to place flowers on the monument resulted in arrest and prosecution for anti-Soviet activities. Today, the base of the monument is filled with flowers, and the monument is a focus of Latvian pride.

The **Doma Church** on Doma laukums is the largest in the Baltic states, built in 1226; its pipe organ is world-renowned. Two blocks away, on Torņa iela just east of Komjaunautnes iela, the **Arsenāls Museum** changes exhibits monthly; avant-garde art is usually on the menu. (Open Mon. and Wed.-Fri. noon-6pm, Sat.-Sun. 11am-6pm.) By the river, near the corner of Krīsjāna Valdemāra iela (formerly Gorkija iela) and Komjaunautnes krastmala, is the **Garden of Sculpture,** featuring the latest works of Latvian sculptors, including Indulis Ranka's intriguing, bulbous human figures. (Open daily 10am-7pm). The entrance on the left side of the garden leads to a building which houses more sculptures; the next building houses the **History Museum** and the **Literature and Arts Museums,** named after the national poet, Raiņa. (All open approx. Mon.-Tues. and Thurs.-Sat. 11am-5pm, Wed. 1-7pm.)

Across from the Garden of Sculpture and near the sculpture museum is the **Monument of Pēteris Stučka,** a Latvian communist who sent many Latvians to death in the struggle for independence between 1918 and 1920. Stučka's popularity among Latvian independence circles rivals that of Lenin, who as of August, 1991, still had his own monument on the corner of Elizabetes iela and Brīvības iela, but had lost his street.

Two blocks outside the Old City stands the two-story **Latvijas PSR Mākslas muzejs** (National Fine Arts Museum), Krišjāna Valdemāra iela 10a. Exhibits include brilliantly colored works by Rerich and other Soviet painters as well as 20th century avant-garde art by Latvian painters. (Open Mon. and Wed.-Fri. noon-6pm, Sat.-Sun. 11am-6pm.) A few kilometers west of the city center on S. Eizenšteina iela is a **Car Museum,** with Stalin's chauffeured automobile; a mannekin of Joe himself sits in the back seat.

Near Riga

Thirty kilometers west of Rīga is the sandy-beached coastal **Jūrmala,** famous throughout the Soviet Union as a rest and resort village. Many Latvians come here on vacation, although the water is too polluted to swim in. There is even a Western-style amusement park (open daily 11am-7pm) as well as a concert hall. Musicians play western songs on the main street, two blocks from the train station, while street vendors proffer the traditional Latvian souvenir, amber. Jūrmala is yours from Rīga by train (every 10 min.) or by bus vans (every 8-15 min.).

Every Latvian has a painted wooden cane from **Sigulda,** fifty kilometers east of Rīga in the **Gauja National Park,** which sports cliffs, streams, and caves full of ancient writings. Numerous trains link Rīga with Sigulda; from there, a car or a patient taxi driver is advisable. Two kilometers from the train station is the world-class **bobsled track,** training ground for the medal-winning Latvian bobsledders of the 1988 Winter Olympics in Calgary. Ride the elevator to the lookout tower for a complete view of the track. The museum alongside the ruins of **Sigulda Castle** features Latvian currency from the independence days and exhibitions about the Liven, a tribe of Balto-Fennic people with less than 100 members, who still live on the Latvian coast.

LIECHTENSTEIN

Liechtenstein uses Swiss currency and the Swiss phone system; its city code is 075.

Famous chiefly for its postage stamps, wines and royal family, Liechtenstein's minute size renders the principality its own main tourist attraction. Though its people have enjoyed the status of a sovereign territory since 1806, a customs agreement with Switzerland makes border passage hassle-free. **Postal buses** speed visitors to the capital city **Vaduz,** from Buchs (1SFr) or Sargans (2SFr) in Switzerland or Feldkirch (1.40SFr) in Austria (all on rail lines). Liechtenstein's national **tourist office** (tel. 214 43), a few paces from the Vaduz bus stop, snags rooms at no charge and distributes a list of hiking routes and a map of bike routes; trusty rusty steeds can be rented around the corner at **Hans Melliger** (tel. 216 06), Kirchstr. 10, for 20SFr per day. Although biking is a dream in this flat, green principality, one can also opt for the efficient and cheap postal bus system that links all 11 villages (most trips 1SFr). Botticelli and Bellini headline Vaduz's **Staatliche Kunstsammlung,** Städtle 37, next to the tourist office, which exhibits paintings collected by the princes of Liechtenstein over the last 400 years. (Open daily 10am-noon and 1:30-5:30pm; Nov.-March 10am-noon and 2-5:30pm. Admission 3SFr, students 1.50SFr.) The **Walser Heimatmuseum** in nearby **Triesenberg** chronicles the simple lifestyle of an oppressed people driven from their homeland. (Open Tues.-Sat. 1:30-5:30pm; June-Aug. also Sun. 2-5pm. Admission 2SFr, students 1SFr.) The Triesenberg **tourist office** (tel. 219 26) is in the same building as the museum and has the same hours. Winter sports breathe life into the mountain communities of **Malbun** and **Steg;** ski passes range from 22SFr (per day) to 80SFr (per week). Lift and lodging packages are available at many hotels (450-620SFr per week); contact the Malbun **Verkehrsbüro** (tel. 265 77) for specifics. (Open Mon.-Wed. and Fri.-Sat. 9am-noon and 1:30-5pm. Closed Nov. to mid-Dec. and mid-April to June.)

Liechtenstein's lone **youth hostel (IYHF),** is in **Schaan.** Take the "Schaan" bus from the bus stop in Vaduz and request the Hotel Mühle stop; from there, turn on Marianumstr., and follow the signs. A 90s kind of place, this pink and blue wonderland offers all the amenities of home. (Reception open 7-9:30am and 5-10pm, Sun. 6-10pm. Members only, 16.20SFr. Sheets, showers, and breakfast included. Dinner 7SFr. Lockers and laundry facilities. Open Jan.-Nov. 15.)

If the hostel is full, head for rural comfort at the friendly **Pension Schönblick,** Winkel 617, in Triesenberg (tel. 219 05). Rock-bottom prices justify the 10-min. ride. (Singles 25-30SFr. Doubles 50-60SFr. Breakfast and showers included.) Of the two **campgrounds** in Liechtenstein, the more convenient is in **Bendern** (tel. 314 65), with cooking facilities, accessible by bus. (4SFr per person, 2-4SFr per tent, 3SFr per car.) Eating in Liechtenstein is an absolute nightmare; shop at **Denner Superdiscount,** Aulestr. 20, in Vaduz, and find a shady tree. (Open Mon.-Fri. 8:30am-1pm and 1:30-6:30pm, Sat. 8am-4pm.)

See *Let's Go: Germany, Austria, and Switzerland (including Liechtenstein)* for in-depth coverage of this little country.

LITHUANIA

As we went to press, Lithuania was still using the Soviet Union's currency and telephone systems; however, this may change during 1992.

In October 1990, Lithuania (Lietuva) shocked the world by declaring itself independent. Nobody (except Iceland) took them seriously. The international community reacted uneasily, and Moscow immediately began reprisals, starting with a crippling shutoff of all oil supplies and culminating in an assault on Vilnius's radio and TV center in January 1991 that left 13 dead. Yet the Lithuanian declaration crucially focused world attention on the Baltics; the freedom that came in the wake of the failed putsch of August 1991 vindicated Lithuanian radicalism, and a goal that had seemed so improbable for 51 years suddenly became a reality.

Today, Lithuanian President Vytautas Landsbergis's nationalistic belligerence is in danger of alienating the country's Russian and Polish minorities and scaring away foreign investors. Such nationalism, however, has deep historical roots. Under the redheaded Vytautas the Great, the medieval Grand Duchy of Lithuania extended deep into Russia and clear to the Black Sea. Subsumed into Poland by the 16th century, the 19th century saw it come under the rule of tsarist Russia. Twenty years of independence after World War I gave way in 1940 to Soviet rule, interrupted for three years by a bloody Nazi occupation that destroyed Lithuania's sizeable Jewish population. Still, the Communist quislings in the republican government never entirely abandoned Lithuanian nationalism, slyly helping to temper the influx of Russians engineered by the Soviet authorities: 80% of Lithuania's 3.5 million people are ethnically Lithuanian.

Independent Lithuania hopes to be a popular tourist stop. *Let's Go* brings you only Vilnius, the capital, which lies only 21 miles from the Byelorussian border. We will have mo' better coverage next year, hopefully including **Kaunas,** Lithuania's second city, and the Baltic seaside resort of **Palanga.** In southern Lithuania, the endless rolling Baltic hills break out into swampland and dark, witchy forests. Also accessible from Vilnius is the awkwardly separated Kaliningrad oblast of the Russian Republic, the birthplace of Immanuel Kant, known as Königsberg during its centuries as part of East Prussia.

Getting There and Getting Around

As we went to press, it was possible to just get a visa at the border, but the trend is towards requiring travelers to get a visa in advance at a Lithuanian consulate. In September 1991, the Lithuanian Legation at 2622 16th St., N.W., Washington DC 20009 (tel. (202) 234-5860) was issuing visas; send them USD25, an application form, and your passport (no photographs). Alternatively, contact the Lithuanian representatives at 17, Essex Villas, London W8 7BP (tel. (071) 937 1588), at 235 Yorkland Blvd., Suite 1011, Willowdale, Ont. M2J 4Y8 (tel. (416) 494-4099), or in European capitals. Visas were valid at all Lithuanian border points, which include the Vilnius airport, the Baltic port of Klaipėda, the crossings for trains from Rīga and Tallinn, the Polish road border at Lazdijai, and all crossings between Lithuania and Russia and Byelorussia. Note that train travel from Warsaw is not an easy option since the train transits Grodno in Byelorussia on its way to Vilnius, making a Soviet visa necessary on top of the already difficult-to-get reservation. However, a new rail link may be built across the Polish border north of Suwałki.

As we went to press, Aeroflot was the only airline flying to Vilnius—from Berlin (2 per week), Frankfurt (1 per week), and Warsaw (2 per week). Service to Copenhagen on an undetermined airline should begin by January 1992. Icelandair may soon begin service from New York via Reykjavík; call them. Trains run to Vilnius from Tallinn (1 per day, 13 hr.), Rīga (2 per day, 8 hr.), Warsaw, and cities in Russia and Byelorussia. **Greif Reisen,** Universitätsstr. 2, 5810 Witten-Heven, Germany (tel. +49 (2302) 240 44), has information about bus tours from Germany and reservations on the ferry from Mukran (near Saßnitz on the island of Rügen in northeastern Germany) to Klaipėda (1 per day, 16-20 hr.)

Within Lithuania, a reasonable network of trains and buses connects Vilnius to Kaunas, Klaipēda, and other cities; taxis will take you anywhere too.

Practical Information

Of the three Baltic states, Lithuania is the least used to tourism. In 1991, for instance, the only available map of Vilnius was in Cyrillic, but this will certainly change (most of the street names have already been Lithuanianized). Remember to pick up a copy of Inroads' impressively comprehensive *Guide to the Baltic States* (USD18).

Lithuanian is a Baltic language, related to Latvian and more distantly to the Slavic tongues. It is of particular interest to Indo-Europeanists because of its splendidly intact case system. *Ačiū* (AH-choo) means "thank you" and *prašom* (PRAH-shom) means "please." Virtually everyone speaks Russian too, but don't begin a conversation in it. The small Polish minority speaks their own language. Some young people have studied English or German as a third language.

There is no news on the reinstatement of Lithuanian currency (the *litas).* A Lithuanian telephone country code is expected soon, and direct mail routing (bypassing Moscow) has already begun.

On bathroom doors, a triangle with the point facing the infernal depths means "men;" with the point facing up, "women."

Vilnius

Though it's been Lithuania's capital since 1323, Vilnius has historically been an international crossroads. The nineteenth-century aristocracy spoke Polish, and, as far as they were concerned, lived in Wilno. As Vilna, the city was the center of turn-of-the-century Eastern Europe's Yiddish literary and cultural life, and half its population was Jewish. Even now, Vilnius is half Russian, Polish, and Byelorussian, though firmly Catholic. The outskirts are full of faceless Khrushchev-era apartment buildings; come for the timeless old town.

Orientation and Practical Info

The River Neris winds through the city's center; most of the old town is on the left bank. The railway and bus stations are only a few steps from the heart of the old city. The **Hotel Lietuva** stands just across the Neris from the old town. They sell a map of Vilnius, but only Cyrillic was available in 1991; there were plans for a new, improved, Roman map in 1992. Street names may change before your very eyes.

Tourist Offices: The front desk at the **Hotel Lietuva** can answer questions.

Currency Exchange: at Hotel Lietuva, or at the bank on Totorių g. (open Mon.-Fri. 9am-1pm).

Post Office: Main post office on Gedimino g. between Vrublevskio g. and Vilniaus g. Open daily 9am-8pm.

Telephones: At the post office. **City Code:** 0122.

Trains: Station on Geležinkelio g., on the southern edge of the old town. To Kaunas (100 min.), Rīga (8 hr.), Kaliningrad (4½-5 hr.), Moscow, and Minsk.

Buses: Connections from the bus station, north of the train station on Pylimo g. To Kaunas (3 per hr., 2 hr.) and to major Russian and Byelorussian cities.

Public Transportation: Most buses stop at the railway station.

Emergency Numbers: Police: (tel. 02). **Ambulance:** (tel. 03).

Accommodations and Food

The accommodations system should be adjusting to walk-in visitors in 1992. In the summer, check with the **Vilnius University Student Union,** Universiteto 3, Vilnius 232734, Lithuania (tel. 61 44 14 or 61 79 20; fax 61 79 20) about rooms in student dorms. **GT International Travel,** 9525 S. 79th Ave. Hickory Hills, IL 60457 (tel. (708) 430-7272) can book hotel rooms through their office in Vilnius for about USD45 a night including breakfast. Under the Soviet system, western tourists have typically stayed in **Hotel Lietuva,** Ukmergės g. 20 (tel. 73 60 16). There is no shortage of fine restaurants in the old town. One of the tastiest is the privately run ruble restaurant **Stiklių Café,** on Dominikonu g.; try their cold *šaltibarščiai* (bright pink beet soup).

Sights

Vilnius's old town is the largest in the Baltics. The **Gediminas Tower** and **castle ruins** are in the park between Vrublevskio g. and Sventaragio g. Built in the 14th century, the tower houses an historical museum. Climb on top of it for a matchless view of the city and the Neri River. Nearby, at the corner of Maironio g. and Sventaragio g., stands the intricate brick **Church of St. Anne.** Further west on the corner of Kosciuškos g. and Olandų g., the baroque **Peter and Paul Church,** built by the nobleman Pacas in the 17th century, stands open for worship. If you look up just inside the entryway, you'll see the heads of whores, drunkards, and other outcasts from society. Pacas had their likenesses sculpted into the foyer to discourage the entrance of their real-life counterparts.

On a more sober note, the **TV tower** taken over by Soviet soldiers during the infamous January 1991 events stands on C. Konarskio g., near Žemaites g. on the western edge of the old town. Further north on Poželos g. stands the **Parliament building,** which Lithuanians risked their lives to encircle in anticipation of further violence that January evening, and again during the failed coup attempt in August 1991.

Costumed musicians and folk dancers from all three of the Baltic states and parts of Scandinavia will gather in Vilnius in mid-July 1992 for the **Baltica Festival,** which alternates between the three Baltics capitals.

Near Vilnius

Take a bus or train from Vilnius to the peaceful lakeside village of **Trakai,** thirty kilometers to the south. Trakai was the first capital of Lithuania in the 13th century, and the site of biannual fairs in the Middle Ages. Destroyed by Crusaders in the 13th century, **Trakai Castle** was rebuilt and fortified in the 14th century by Duke Vytautas as he extended Lithuania's power. Now it houses a historical museum. The castle is on an island in Lake Galvė, accessible by bridges (watch out for snapping alligators beneath the moat, which eat Teutonic knights for brunch). Another island in Lake Galvė was the site of tortures and executions after the Soviets arrived in 1940. In a bizarre version of Groundhog Day, Lake Galvė's medieval residents used to tell whether the lake would freeze come winter by throwing someone in during the autumn and seeing if they sank. Boatmen offer trips around the lake (about 30R per ½ hr.)

LUXEMBOURG

USD$1 = 36.1 francs (LF, or LUF)	**10LF = USD$0.28**
CAD$1 = 31.5LF	**10LF = CAD$0.32**
GBP£1 = 60.2LF	**10LF = GBP£0.17**
AUD$1 = 28.1LF	**10LF = AUD$0.36**
NZD$1 = 20.5LF	**10LF = NZD$0.49**
Country Code: 352	**International Dialing Code: 00**

The Grand Duchy of Luxembourg has been a pawn on the European chessboard for centuries. Founded in 963, it was first named Luclinburhuc, or "little castle." By the time successive waves of Burgundians, Spaniards, French, Austrians, and Germans had receded, the little castle had become a bristling armored mountain and the countryside was saturated with fortresses. Only after the last French soldier returned home in 1867 and the Treaty of London restored its neutrality did Luxembourg begin to cultivate its current image of peacefulness and independence. Today Luxembourg is an independent constitutional monarchy, a member of the European Community, and a tax-haven for investors from around the globe, with the Grand Duke and his Cabinet of 12 ministers still wielding supreme executive power over the country's 370,000 residents.

Luxembourg's embattled history shows in the scarred fortifications of its capital and in the steep citadels and fortresses that dot the landscape. From the wooded and hilly Ardennes in the north to the fertile vineyards of the Moselle Valley in the south, its unspoilt countryside strikes a marked contrast with the bustling banking industry of its capital city.

Transportation and Practical Information

Luxembourg is only 2600km square, so there's not far to go. Both Eurail and InterRail will whisk you across the country; you pay about 3-4LF per km without passes. All train and bus stations sell **Billets Reseaux** good for unlimited second-class train and bus travel (not valid for buses running within the capital). A one-day ticket—worthwhile only on long round-trips—is 120LF. A **Benelux Pass,** good for unlimited travel any five days in a 17-day period in Belgium, the Netherlands, and Luxembourg, costs only 1990LF, ages over 26 2770LF. (This is a good deal—it's not that much more expensive than a one-way ticket from Luxembourg to Amsterdam.) Bicycles are permitted on any train for 30LF, regardless of distance. Hitching is fair—distances are short, but traffic is light.

The tourist office network in Luxembourg is exhaustive and highly skilled at ferreting out hidden bargain rooms across the countryside. Nearly every town out of three thousand has an office that provides local and national information (smaller ones open Mon-Sat. 10am-noon and 2-6pm). Youth hostels are also great sources of information, and frequently offer discounts on guided tours. The hostel association maintains trails (marked with white triangles) between each of their houses. The longest distance between any two hostels is 30km.

While the official languages of Luxembourg are French and German, at home and on the streets the most commonly spoken language is Letzebuergesch, a German dialect with a slew of French loanwords. Many Luxembourgers shine in all three languages, though their French or German may be a bit shaky depending on which part of the country they live in. English is widely, though by no means universally, spoken.

Most banks are open Monday through Friday from 8:30am to 4:30pm; most shops Tuesday through Saturday from 9:30am to 6pm and Monday from 2 to 6pm. However, many shops close at noon for two hours, especially in the countryside, where even the post offices shutter up and only the taverns may be open after 6pm. Luxembourg francs are worth as much as Belgian francs; you can use Belgian money in Luxembourg, and Luxembourg bills (but not coins) are valid in Belgium. The AT&T **USA Direct** number for Luxembourg is 08 00 01 11.

Accommodations, Camping, and Food

There are 12 IYHF youth hostels in Luxembourg, charging 250LF, ages over 25 290LF (both 40LF higher in the capital). Breakfasts are included, packed lunches 100LF, and dinners with dessert 210LF; eating at least one meal in the hostel wins a 15LF discount. Nonmembers pay 90LF extra. Sheets are 100LF. Members over 35 have last priority on vacancies. Lockers require a 200LF deposit. All hostels (except the one in Grevenmacher) have kitchen facilities.

One night in a Luxembourg hotel runs between 900 and 1300LF. The more tourist-clogged towns tend to have cheaper rooms. Campgrounds abound; the amenities offered vary drastically, but almost all have hot showers (some for a small charge). Two people with their own tent can expect to pay 200-300LF. Luxembourg cuisine is closely linked to that of the neighboring Lorraine region of France, with paper-thin sliced Ardennes ham standing out as a national specialty.

Luxembourg

Rising triumphantly on both sides of the steep gorge that divides it, the city of Luxembourg is one of the most physically dramatic capitals of Europe. To the north of the gorge lie the heart of the old city and the youth hostel, while to the south lie the train station and the vast majority of budget hotels. Home to international firms and the European Court of Justice, Luxembourg adds a dollop of cosmopolitanism to the overwhelmingly rural, provincial Grand Duchy.

Practical Information

Tourist Offices: Grand Duchy National Tourist Office, pl. de la Gare (tel. 48 11 99), in the Luxair office. Turn right as you leave the train station. Indispensible map, hotel listings, and reservations service—all free. Open daily July to mid-Sept. 9am-7:30pm; mid-Sept. to Nov. and April-June 9am-noon and 2-6:30pm; Dec.-March Mon.-Sat. 9am-noon and 2-6:30pm. Branch office at **airport** (tel. 40 08 08). Open daily 10am-6:30pm. The **Municipal Tourist Office,** pl. d'Armes (tel. 228 09), in the center of town, offers information on and services for the city only. Open Mon.-Fri. 9am-7pm, Sat. 9am-1pm and 2-7pm, Sun. 10am-noon and 2-6pm; mid-Sept. to mid-June Mon.-Sat. 9am-1pm and 2-6pm.

Budget Travel: SOTOUR, 17, pl. du Théâtre (tel. 226 73 or 46 15 14). BIJ and other discount tickets. Open Mon.-Fri. 9am-6pm, Sat. 9am-noon.

Embassies: U.S., 22, bd. E. Servais (tel. 46 01 23). **U.K.,** 14, bd. Roosevelt (tel. 298 64). Open Mon.-Fri. 10am-noon and 2-5pm. Answering machine gives a 24-hr. emergency number. Travelers from **Canada, Australia,** and **New Zealand** should contact the British embassy.

Currency Exchange: At the train station. Mediocre rates. Open Mon.-Sat. 8:30am-9pm, Sun. 9am-9pm. It's best to change money at the banks; all have nearly the same rates. Many banks operate out of offices on the square in front of the train station.

American Express: 6-8, rue Origer (tel. 49 60 41), a short walk from the train and bus station. Mail held. Traveler's checks cashed, sold, and replaced, but no wired money accepted. Decent exchange rates. Open Mon.-Fri. 9am-1pm and 2-5pm, Sat. 9:30am-noon.

Post Office: Main office, 38, pl. de la Gare, across the street and to the left of the train station. Poste Restante office open daily 6am-8pm. Branch office, 25, rue Aldringern, 2 blocks from place d'Armes. Open Mon.-Fri. 7am-8pm, Sat. 7am-7pm.

Telephones: At both post offices. Main office open Mon.-Fri. 8am-7:45pm, Sat. noon-8pm. Phones at the branch on rue Aldringern have the same hours as the post.

Flights: Bus #9 (30LF plus 25LF for baggage) is cheaper than the Luxair bus (120LF), and runs the same airport-hostel-train station route.

Trains: Gare CFL, (tel. 49 24 24), av. de la Gare, near the foot of av. de la Liberté. In the southern part of the city, a somewhat seedy area, 10 min. away from the city center. Bus #9 runs between the railway station, the hostel, and the airport. Pick it up on your right as you leave the station, in front of the Luxair office. Luxembourg lies on major train routes from Brussels to Basel, and from Amsterdam to Milan.

Buses: Buy a punch card at banks or the bakery around the corner from the tourist office. Single rides 30LF; 10 municipal bus rides 240LF.

Luggage Storage: At the station. Check your bags for 60LF (open 6am-10pm) or use the lockers (60LF).

Laundromat: Quick Wash, 3, pl. Strasbourg, near the station. Wash 210LF, dry 20LF for 7 min. Open Mon.-Fri. 8am-7pm, Sat. 8am-6pm.

Pharmacy: Pharmacie du Globe, 12, rue Jean Origier (tel. 48 70 09), near the station. Open Mon.-Fri. 7:40am-noon and 1:30-6pm. Dial 012 on weekends for the location of an open pharmacy.

Medical Assistance: Tel. 012. A 24-hr. number for physicians and pharmacists (English spoken).

Emergencies: Police 58-60, rue Glesner (tel. 40 94 01). **Ambulance** (tel. 012).

Accommodations, Camping, and Food

Mounds of inexpensive hotels jam the streets around the train station. Several of these establishments offer quite pleasant rooms, despite the shabby neighborhood around them. Hotels become increasingly more pricey and posh as you move north of the ravine and into the older and more scenic portion of the city. The tourist office offers a free room-finding service.

Auberge de Jeunesse (IYHF), 2, rue du Fort Olizy (tel. 268 89). Take bus #9 from the airport or the train station to the Vallée d'Alzette below rue Sigefroi in the northeast section of town. Sweet and dandy, with an exceptionally friendly staff. 3-day max. stay if the hostel is full. Reception open 7:30-9:30am and 3-11pm. Lockout 9:30am-2pm. No curfew. Lockers require 300LF deposit. Bike rental 300LF, 150LF for each additional day.

Hotel Carlton, 9, rue de Strasbourg (tel. 48 48 02), near the station. Dirt-cheapest rooms in the city. Ornate lobby with stained-glass windows, clean rooms, cheerful management. Reception open 24 hrs. Singles 650-850LF, with shower 1100-1250LF. Doubles 1500LF. Breakfast 150LF.

Hotel Paradiso, 23, rue de Strasbourg (tel. 48 48 01). A cute hotel with a TV room. Managed by a Sicilian and his dog. Singles 850-1000LF. Doubles 1350-1450LF, with shower 1650-1950LF. Breakfast 175LF.

Hotel Axe, 34, rue Joseph Junck (tel. 49 09 53), near the station. Spruce rooms over a fugly street. Singles 900LF. Doubles 1400LF, with shower 1800LF. Triples 2100LF.

Camping: Kockelscheuer (tel. 47 18 15). 90LF, children 50LF. 100LF per tent. Disabled access. Open Easter-Oct. Take bus #2 4km southwest from the station.

If you eat in restaurants, Luxembourgeois food will quickly devour your budget. **EMS,** 30, pl. de la Gare, packs in locals with their inexpensive specialties like smoked Ardennes ham and fish. Shop at the huge and modern **supermarket** at 47, ave. de la Gare; go to the back of the shopping center and descend the stairs.

Sights and Entertainment

To cover the city in a day, follow the tourist office's well-organized walking route. The **Bock-Casemates,** the oldest remnant of Luxembourg's ancient complex of fortresses and tunnels, looms imposingly over the Alzette valley. A network of subterranean passages and storerooms, the Bock sheltered 35,000 people from bombs during WWII. From the entrance at rue Sigefroi, near chemin de la Corniche, explore its corkscrew staircases and catch tremendous views through the loopholes. (Open March-Oct. 10am-5pm. Admission 50LF, ages under 12 30LF.) The nearby streets and buildings are the oldest in town; devout laborers laid the first stones of **St. Michael's Church** in 987. The earliest section of the façade of the **Grand-Ducal Palace** was built in Spanish Renaissance style and is all you're likely to see. The magnificant interior is open to the peasantry only during the Grand Duke's six-week summer vacation from mid-July to August. (Tickets 100LF at the tourist office at place d'Armes. Open mid-July to Aug. English tours given Mon.-Tues. and Thurs.- Fri. at 4pm.) The **Musées de l'Etat** is a salad of ancient and contemporary art, natural history, and local history. (Open Tues.-Fri. 10am-noon and 1-5pm, Sat. 2-6pm, Sun. 10am-noon and 2-6pm. Free.) When you tire of the crowded old city, head for the parks along the shaded River Pétrusse. You can hear mellow live music from outside tables in the pl. d'Armes. *La Semaine à Luxembourg,* available at the tourist office, lists the week's events.

Foreigners and locals alike sip brews at **Scott's Pub and Restaurant,** 4 Bisserweg (tel. 2 64 74). Scott serves up beer, snacks, and English cheer. Take the lift from Rue St-Unic, then walk across the bridge. (Open daily noon-1am.)

The Countryside

In 1944 the frozen and bloody Battle of the Bulge raged through the wooded Ardennes, flattening the forests into slime and mud. Nature has recovered, though, and today the revived forests and shallow rivers of Luxembourg's countryside will quickly entice you away from the city. Trains grind regularly between Luxembourg and Ettelbrück (hourly, 30min. 90LF), and from the Luxembourg and Ettelbrück stations you can take the brown CFL buses to smaller towns (Luxembourg-Echternach 1 per hr., 1 hr., 130LF; Ettelbrück-Echternach 2 per hr., 30 min., 130LF; Echternach-Vianden 2 per day, 50 min., 130LF; Vianden-Ettelbrück 9 per day, 30 min., 80LF). Railpasses are valid.

Though there is nothing much to do in **Ettelbrück** itself, it is perhaps the best base for exploring the countryside because its train and bus stations serve as a central hub for the rest of the country. The station's **tourist office,** 1, place de la Gare (tel. 820 68), is open daily 8:30am-noon and 1:30-5pm; Sept.-June Mon.-Fri. 8:30am-noon and 1:30-5pm. The **IYHF youth hostel,** rue Grande-Duchesse Josephine-Charlotte (tel. 822 69), often has room when nearby hostels are booked. (Reception open 5-11pm, but baggage can be left from 2pm. Open mid-March to mid-Oct. and early Dec. to mid-Feb. Closed several weekends.) **Camp** in Ettelbrück at **Kalkesdelt** (tel. 821 85) for 100LF per person, 100LF per site. (Open April-Sept.)

Deeper into the countryside, hostels lurk in the woods at **Beaufort,** 6, rue de l'Auberge (tel. 860 75); **Bourglinster,** 2, rue de Gonderange (tel. 781 46); **Eisenborn,** 5, rue de la Forêt (tel. 783 55); **Grevenmacher,** Gruewereck (tel. 752 22); **Hollenfels,** 2, rue du Château (tel. 30 70 37); **Lultzhausen,** (tel. 894 24); **Troisvièrges,** 24, rue de la Gare (tel. 980 18); and **Wiltz,** rue de la Montagne (tel. 95 80 39). Most tourist offices have a brochure with all hostels, their addresses, and a brief description of their facilities. Most hostels open at 5pm and close at 11pm.

Echternach

The great, the old, and the ossified form the trinity tourists seek in Echternach. The month-long **Festival Internationale** begins in late May and showcases opera, orchestra and organ performances. Buy student tickets from the tourist office (150LF); regular tickets run 300-1500LF. Concerts are held in the **Basilica** and the **Eglise Sts-Pierre-et-Paul.** Nearby, the **Benedictine Abbey,** founded in honor of St. Willibrord, houses his bones in the crypt. The **tourist office** (tel. 722 30) in the Basilica coolly coordinates it all. (Open daily 9am-noon and 2-6pm; Sept.-June Mon.-Fri. 9am-noon and 1-5pm. From the bus station head left through the pedestrian zone and follow the signs.) The **IYHF youth hostel,** 9, rue Andre Duchscher (tel. 721 58), packs rustic charm only 350m from the bus stop. (Reception open 5-11pm.) The cheapest alternative to the hostel, also near the bus stop, is **Bon Accueil,** 3, rue des Merciers (tel. 720 52). (Singles 750LF. Doubles 1000LF. Triples 1400-1700LF. Showers and breakfast included.) The cheapest of the town's campgrounds is near the bus station: **Camp Officiel,** rue de Diekirch (tel. 722 72), charges 90LF per person, 100LF per site (open March 25-Oct. 20).

Near Echternach lies the region ever-so-cutely dubbed Little Switzerland. To explore its hills or the River Sûre, pick up the tourist office map (60LF); it describes 12 walks (3-30km) in the vicinity. Another alternative is to wind through forested ravines and the rugged **Gorge du Loup,** from Echternach to the small farming town of **Berdorf** (6km, route number "B1" or "G" on the map), then take the CFL bus back.

Vianden

After Victor Hugo fled his native France he happened upon Vianden, and finding it "consoling and magnificent," stayed. The village spills down a steep hill beneath a slickly renovated 9th-century **château,** which contains an exhibit on its own history and a grape-sized art gallery. Dutch tourists crowd the riverside parades, and Dutch dishes are served in the restaurants, all because Vianden is the ancestral home of the formidable Orange-Nassau dynasty, rulers of Holland and (in the person of William III) England as well. (Château open May-Aug. daily 9am-7pm; Sept.-Dec. 10am-5pm; Jan.-Feb. Sat.-Sun. and holidays 11am-5pm; March daily 10am-4pm; April daily 10am-6pm. Admission 100LF, students 70LF.) The **tourist office** (tel. 842 57) is in the **Victor Hugo House,** on rue de la Gare, beside the bridge over the River Our. (Open June to mid-Sept. 10am-noon and 1:30-5:30pm; May to mid-Sept. Thurs.-Tues. 9:30am-noon and 2-6pm.) Ride Vianden's *télésiège* (chairlift) from rue de Sanatorium, 500m upstream from the tourist office (round-trip 140LF; open daily Oct.-March Sat.-Thurs.). The ascent affords a phenomenal photo opportunity of both the château and Europe's largest hydroelectric plant, the **Barrage.** The

IYHF youth hostel, 3, Montée du Château (tel. 841 77), is neat and cheery. Cross the bridge from the tourist office and follow the Grande Rue until it curves left and ends. (Reception open 5-11pm, but you can leave your bags before—enter from the side.) Numerous cheap hotels litter the Grande Rue; the tourist office lists rooms in private homes (300-500LF). Vianden presents three camping options, all on the River Our: **Camp op dem Deich** (tel. 843 75) costs 100LF per person and per site (open Easter-Oct. 15); **Camp du Moulin** (tel. 845 01) costs the same (open May 17-Aug.); and **Camp de l'Our** (tel. 845 05) costs 90LF per person, 90LF per site, plus 30LF for showers (open Easter-Sept.). A short bus ride delivers you to any of them.

MALTA

USD$1 = 0.33 lira (Lm, or MTL) **1Lm = USD$3.01**
CAD$1 = 0.29Lm **1Lm = CAD$3.44**
GBP£1 = 0.56Lm **1Lm = GBP£1.80**
AUD$1 = 0.26Lm **1Lm = AUD$3.86**
NZD$1 = 0.19Lm **1Lm = NZD$5.27**
Country Code: 356 **International Dialing Prefix: 01**

In the crossroads between Sicily and Libya, Malta is an independent state of three tiny islands—Malta, Gozo, and Comino—struggling as hard as it can to endure the throes of tourism. Come quick: its eclectic mix of cultures and people may soon drown under waves of Northern Europeans. The Maltese language is related to Arabic, but English and Italian are ubiquitous; 150 years of British colonialism ended only in 1964.

Malta is most easily reached by **ferry** from Sicily to **Valletta,** the main town of both Malta the country and Malta the island. **Tirrenia,** 311 Republic St. in Valletta (tel. 23 22 11), is the most inexpensive and practical company. (From Catania and Syracuse at 1pm and 4:30pm, respectively, each Tues., Fri., and Sun.; 8 hr.; L78,100). **Catamarans** make the trip in half the time for double the price. Ferries generally arrive at night; change money before you leave. **Air Malta** often has youth and student specials; ask a travel agent.

Boats drop all visitors at the base of Valletta's fortress, right by the **Grand Harbour.** From the port, an uphill walk leads to the **City Gate** and the **bus terminal.** The **tourist office** (tel. 22 77 47) is through the City Gate and to the right. The **Malta Youth Hostel Association** has four dorms (1.25-1.75Lm) in Paola (17 Tal-Borġ St.), Paceville (30B Triq Wilġa), Senglea (190 Two Gates St.), and on Gozo (21A Triq Cordína). Before going anywhere, call or drop by the central office (tel. 69 39 57) in Paola (an easy 7 min. from Valletta on bus #5, 11, or 26; get off near the Mid-Med Bank).

Start off a tour of Valletta with a trot down **Republic Street** from the city gate. Old Theater Street leads right to the **Grand Master's Palace,** the historic residence of Malta's rulers, while **St. John's Co-Cathedral** (1573-1577) flaunts an intricate interior paralleled only by Italy's many *duomo.* Going all the way to Republic Square, hang two consecutive lefts for Maltese food at Maltese prices at the **Happy Return Restaurant,** 55 Strait St. (rabbit stew 75ċ; open Thurs.-Tues. 11:30am-10:30pm, Wed. 11:30am-3pm). Join Malta's hedonistic nightlife in Sliema and Paceville, across Marsamxett Harbor from Valletta and accessible by ferry and bus. **Axis,** on St. George's Road, hops every night of the week.

Bus #80 takes you to catacombs, awesome villas, and the city of **Rabat** in central Malta. Take bus #53 to Mosta, where the **Mosta Dome** survived a WWII German bomb that crashed through the marble shell and slid across the floor, but still hasn't exploded. It's on display in the sacristy. (Church open daily 9am-noon.) Bus #45 leaves Valletta every hour or so for Arkewwa Bay, connecting with ferries to the smaller island of **Gozo,** just west of Malta. From **Victoria,** Gozo's central town, take bus #64 to the awesome Ġgantija temples and the caves at Xagħra. Between Malta and Gozo, the ferry passes **Comino,** Malta's third island—really a glorified rock, home only to an expensive hotel.

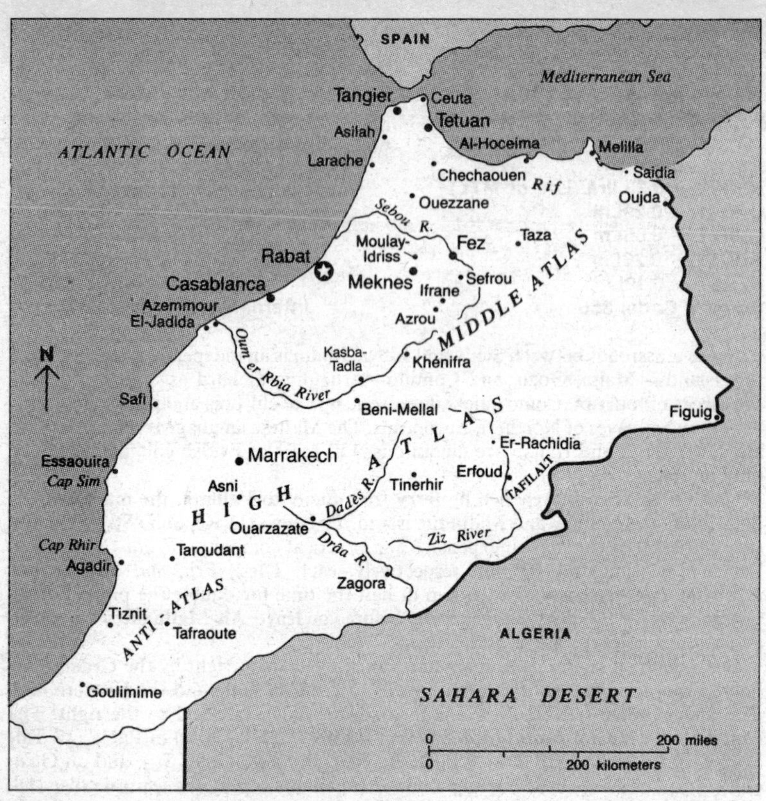

MOROCCO

USD$1 = 8.75 dirhams (dh, or MAD) | **1dh = USD$0.11**
CAD$1 = 7.66dh | **1dh = CAD$0.13**
GBP£1 = 14.6dh | **1dh = GBP£0.07**
AUD$1 = 6.81dh | **1dh = AUD$0.15**
NZD$1 = 4.99dh | **1dh = NZD$0.20**
Country Code: 212 | **International Dialing Prefix: 00**

The Gulf War broke out as *Let's Go* was planning its 1991 researcher itineraries, and at the time it seemed unsafe to send researchers to Morocco. All prices and information were last fully updated in the summer of 1990; expect some change.

Every step in Morocco barrages your senses. The crowds, the animals, the wailing prayers, the pounding desert sun: all are routine to Moroccans, confounding to most Westerners. Hashish is everywhere, yet alcohol is taboo even to less devout Muslims. Hustlers threaten to form a barrier from other natives, who are at once infinitely curious, deeply sincere and unnervingly timid. The hoods and veils, the smells, songs and smoke, the abject poverty and the abandoned wealth of colonialism—all conspire to inspire in this paradise of paradox.

The mountains and high plateaus of Morocco have been settled since time immemorial by Berber tribesmen, but the coastal towns have seen a parade of foreign rulers, including Phoenicians, Carthaginians and Romans. After the Romans dispersed, Idris Ibn Abdullah founded an Islamic empire that was to stretch far north into Spain. Europeans reconquered the Iberian peninsula in the 15th century, and by the 19th had completely turned the tables: Morocco was divided into two protectorates, one Spanish, the other French. A nationalist movement rallied around Sultan Mohammed V after WWII, and French Morocco won independence in 1956. Spanish Morocco did not win independence until 1969, and relations between Morocco and Spain still sour over the issue of anti-Muslim discrimination in the Spanish sovereign enclaves at Ceuta and Melilla. Sultan Hassan II (Mohammed's successor) has bigger problems, however; a 13-year-old war against Algerian-backed Polisario guerrillas in the western Sahara rages unabated to this day despite the peaceful reestablishment of diplomatic relations with Algeria. The regions affected are in the arid southwest of the country, far from the itinerary of any traveler.

Getting There

You can enter the country through either Tangier or Ceuta ("Sebta" in Arabic). From Algeciras, there are four ferries per day to Tangier in summer (2½ hr., 2300ptas, Eurail 20% off, InterRail 30% off) and three per day in winter. The ferries from Algeciras to Ceuta are more frequent (Mon.-Sat. 6-12 per day, Sun. 3-5, 1¼hr., 1250ptas). Tangier is the most convenient port of entry; Ceuta may be less shocking to a Westerner, but getting across the border here can be a nightmare. If you have trouble at the border, wait until the nettlesome official goes off duty. To make the customs officer happy, look respectable, speak softly and carry a fat wallet. Bearers of passports with Israeli or South African stamps are refused entry in theory only.

Getting Around

Trains are faster, more expensive, and more comfortable than buses, but the **ONCF** train network runs only two routes: Tangier-Rabat-Casablanca-Marrakech and Casablanca-Rabat-Meknes-Fes-Oujda. Train tickets come in three classes: 1st (nominally better than 2nd), 2nd (the most popular) and E (for cattle, corpses, and the most thrifty of travellers). InterRail is valid in Morocco; Eurail is not. Buses are more frequent and less expensive than trains, and connect the smaller villages and all cities, but are much less comfortable on long hauls. **CTM,** the national bus line, is best, charging about 15dh per 100km (2nd-class train tickets are about 20% more). Countless other private lines are cheaper and nastier. Baggage too big for the overhead shelf goes on the roof of the bus (about 2dh per bag). Many routes, especially in the south, run only once or twice per day, and you may find yourself stranded if you get off during the journey. If your bus line does not originate in the city where you board, you may be delayed hours waiting for a bus with space.

Collective taxis and *grands taxis* are often the only option for traveling between cities, and usually cost only 15% more than CTM bus fares. Most cut-rate car rental agencies are based in Casablanca and Agadir. Hitching is onerous, even on well-traveled roads, and sometimes dangerous. Moreover, truck drivers often demand more money than buses traveling the same route.

Within cities, *buses urbaines* never cost more than 2.20dh, and *petits taxis* are cheap—fares average 4-10dh. Always ask the driver to use the meter. If it's broken (as they often are) fix a price beforehand. Taxis are prohibited by law from carrying more than three people, and there is a 50% surcharge after 8pm.

Practical Information

Many towns have both a state-run tourist office and a semi-private *syndicat d'initiative.* Many are nothing more than staffed brochure stands, but some will change money for you when banks are closed. Black-market money transactions are seldom any more profitable than official exchanges and are often risky—hustlers have a bag of tricks with which to bleed you dry.

Morocco's brief term as a French protectorate left a lasting imprint; French remains the official commercial language and wafts through every city. Arabic is very helpful in rural areas and any attempt to use the language will win you friends. Start off with *salaamu 'aleikum* (hello). *Na'am* means "yes," and *lah* means "no." Finish off with *shukran* (thank you) and *baslamah* as a farewell. *Imshee* means "go away."

Morocco has staggering unemployment, which has given rise to a bevy of informal "jobs." When a service is performed for you, a small tip is always appreciated and may be the key required to open locked gates. At every tourist spot in Morocco, you will be approached and told that you need a guide. Such unofficial guides are illegal and often incompetent—fend for yourself with a guidebook and a map. If you do hire a guide, be sure to set the price beforehand (10-20dh is fair for 2-3 hr.) and make it clear that you want to go sight-seeing—not shopping, smoking or anything else. Keep track of where you and your belongings are at all times. Never go shopping with a guide—they make a healthy commission on anything you buy.

In large cities, "guides" whose services you refuse will often wish you a good vacation and move on; in more rural areas they may be more persistent. Your attitude in refusing the guide's offers has a great deal to do with the way you are received. Do not become frightened or adamant without provocation. A simple question or compliment on the city can transform the person from a predator into your impromptu protector. If you want an official guide, head to the local *syndicat d'initiative* or tourist office. Expect to pay 30dh for a half-day, 50dh for a full day. Although less personable than unofficial guides, the extra 10-20dh is worth the assurance that you won't get lost or swindled. The guides who work with the tourist office have numbered bronze badges and can only be engaged through the office.

Solo travelers of both sexes may encounter the challenge of their lives in Morocco. Those unfamiliar with the language and culture may sorely miss the cultural buffer a travel companion can provide, as well as the assurance found in numbers. Very few women travel alone here. Common sense and cultural sensitivity are the best means of coping with unpleasant situations and avoiding threatening ones. If you dress like the local women you'll be treated with more respect. An air of confidence and composure works wonders. If a situation becomes genuinely threatening, a tirade (in any language), especially in the presence of onlookers, is often effective. **Women should not venture into dark sidestreets or isolated parts of town alone, and never onto beaches without companions.** Unmarried couples will be accepted and given hotel rooms together, but public displays of affection should be avoided.

Although **marijuana** *(kif)* and **hashish** ("chocolate") abound and are often openly smoked, drugs are *not* legal. If you are caught with drugs, your government can do little, if anything to extricate you (see General Introduction). In the north, especially around the Rif Mountains, there are road checks. As you walk down the street, you'll be surrounded by hustlers murmuring "hashish, hashish." Many Moroccan dealers double as police officers; admit to nothing.

Morocco has been described as "a cold country with a hot sun." Most visitors prepare for the blistering heat but blanch at the chilly nights, ocean breezes and snow-covered mountains. Pack a sweater and a warm sleeping bag along with your sandals and shorts. Inland areas are generally warmer than the coast, and the southern region and the Sahara are suffocating during the summer. Bring adequate bottled water wherever you go in these areas, and concentrate your energy in the early morning and late evening, resting in the hot afternoon.

Most Moroccan cities have two parts: the **medina,** which usually is the ancient, walled portion of the city, and the *ville nouvelle.* The medina is often the only area of interest to the tourist: here one finds artisans' shops, cultural attractions and the most inexpensive accommodations and food. The medina's narrow, winding alleyways are often more intimidating than the streets of the *ville nouvelle,* but both areas are equally dangerous late at night.

During the monthlong Islamic holiday of Ramadan, pious Muslims do not smoke, eat, or drink between sunrise and sunset. Travel during the day becomes easier since there are fewer people about, but abstain from public displays of consumption. Each evening of Ramadan is marked by a flurry of activity in cafés, restaurants, and streets. Ramadan in 1992 runs approximately from March 5 to April 3.

International telephones are located at the main post offices (PTT), and most major cities have new orange pay phones from which you can direct dial abroad. Calling collect (P.C.V. in French) requires intestinal fortitude. Give a slip of paper with the complete number you're calling, the city and country, and your name to the individual in charge of telephones. You will then have to wait (sometimes 1-2 hrs.) until your name is called. The connections in Casablanca are very good and the connections in Marrakech are very bad. For **emergency assistance** in any city, call the police (tel. 19).

Accommodations, Camping and Food

Travel in Morocco is a bargain. Inflation is negligible; after a good year, prices may even go down. Camping may not be worth the trouble of lugging your gear around; charges are generally 7dh per person plus 5dh per tent. The nine Moroccan IYHF youth hostels charge 12-26dh but vary tremendously in quality. There are two major divisions in Moroccan hotels: *classé* and *non-classé. Classé* hotels are government-regulated, price-fixed, and rated by stars. Each rating is subdivided into A and B. (For example, 1-star B is lower than 1-star A; 5-star A is the highest rating.) *Non-classé* hotels are unregulated and unrated, not as classy, and cheaper. *Classé* hotels are listed in the *Royaume du Maroc: Guide des Hôtels,* free at any Moroccan tourist office.

As a rule, the cheapest hotels are in the medina; 20-30dh per person is typical. An extra 15-20dh may get you a large, comfortable room in a modern hotel, often in a newer part of town. Showers cost 2-5dh; in cheaper places hot water is often available only at certain times, if at all. *Hammam* (public Turkish baths) or *bain-douches* (public showers) run 2.50-3dh and are a good source of hot water. Carry toilet paper with you; getting used to the holes-in-the-ground that prevail in holes-in-the-wall will be trouble enough. Neat dress and an obvious camera might gain you admission to the cleaner restrooms of modern hotels.

Couscous is the national dish, consisting of semolina grain covered with saffron-flavored chicken, beef, lamb or fish, and cooked with onions, fruits, beans and nuts. Local restaurants invariably serve meats roasted or smothered in a *tajine* (a fruit and vegetable stew with olives, prunes or artichokes). A "complete" or "standard" restaurant meal will include an entree, salad or soup, vegetables and an orange or yogurt for dessert. If tip is not included, 10% is plenty.

Although introduced only in the 18th century by the English, the ritual of tea preparation, using sprigs of fresh mint and great quantities of sugar, dominates the daily routine of contemporary Moroccan life (1.50-2dh per glass and 3dh per pot). You may find that a glass of tea will quench your thirst better than any cold drink. If you're lucky enough to be invited to a traditional rural feast, scoop up mouthfuls of food with pieces of bread, or shovel with the middle three fingers of your *right* hand (never the left, which tends to a later stage of the digestive process).

For the sake of your health, drink Sidi Ali or Sidi Harazem, heavily chlorinated mineral waters sold everywhere at 3-5dh per 1½-liter bottle. If the bottle isn't completely sealed, it's tap water. Although the water is reputedly safe in the north, unpurified water and uncooked vegetables are likely to wreak havoc on your bowels. Eat only fruit you can peel yourself. A one-day fast generally helps to cure diarrhea; local remedies (yogurt, or lemon or lime juice) can be effective. Over-the-counter remedies are also common. Drink much boiled or bottled water to avoid dehydration during recovery.

Tangier

Mark Twain's epithet, of "that African perdition called Tangier," is undeserved. Though present-day Tangier retains only a skeleton of its more romantic past as an international outpost of lawlessness, the city is not entirely unappealing: drums throbbing in the *kasbah* conjure up remote oases in the deepest Sahara, while Parisian-style cafés around the corner add a cosmopolitan twist.

Orientation and Practical Information

Hustling freshly arrived foreigners has become a formidable industry in Tangier. Be polite but firm when discussing guides, and be particularly cautious if you venture into the medina or *kasbah* at night. Unwelcome—and dangerous—incidents do occur with alarming frequency in Tangier, and many of them begin under seemingly innocent circumstances.

From the port, the train station is the large, white building to the left; buses leave from the chaotic square in front of it. Don't be "guided" onto the wrong bus; confirm the destination with the driver. For long distances, take the CTM bus or the train. Give your baggage to no one but the ticket-taker, and offer a 1-2dh tip.

Tourist Office: 29, bd. Pasteur (tel. 329 96). Turn left onto av. d'Espagne from the port, take rue Salah Eddine el-Ayoubi, turn left on rue Anoual, and follow it as it curves sharply to the right; at the end of the street, make 2 left turns onto bd. Pasteur. It may be best to take a *petit taxi* from the port (3dh). English spoken. Sketchy maps. Train, bus, car and ferry information. Open in summer and Ramadan Mon.-Fri. 9am-3pm; in off-season Mon.-Fri. 8:30am-noon and 2:30-6:30pm.

Consulates: U.S., 29, rue el-Achouak (tel. 359 04). Open Mon.-Fri. 7am-noon and 1:30-5:30pm. **U.K.,** 9, rue Amérique du Sud (tel. 358 95). **France,** pl. de France (tel. 320 39). Open Mon.-Fri. 9am-noon and 1-6pm.

Currency Exchange: Banks (open at 8:30am) will change at official rates with no commission. Travel agencies near the port are required to change money at official rates. If they don't, demand a receipt. Black market transactions aren't worth it.

American Express: Voyages Schwartz, 54, bd. Pasteur (tel. 334 59). Mail held and checks replaced; no check-cashing but cardholders can buy traveler's checks with personal checks. Open Mon.-Fri. 9am-12:30pm and 3-7pm, Sat. 9am-12:30pm; Ramadan closes at 6pm on weekdays.

Post Office: 33, bd. Mohammed V (tel. 356 57), the continuation of bd. Pasteur. Open Mon.-Fri. 8:30am-12:15pm and 2:30-5:45pm.

Telephones: In the post office. Open 24 hrs. **City Code:** 099.

Trains: Av. d'Espagne (tel. 312 01), to the left as you leave the port. Express to Rabat (72dh) and Casablanca (93dh) at 4:22pm and 5:22pm, respectively. Non-express to Rabat (58dh) and Casablanca (75dh) at 8:50pm. To continue to Marrakech (135dh), change at Casablanca. Direct to Meknes (52dh) and Fes (64dh) at 8:12pm.

Buses: At the intersection between rue de Fes and rue de Lisbon, roughly 3km from the port. **CMT** runs 5 departures per day to Rabat (6½ hr., 59dh) and Casablanca (7½ hr., 79dh), and points in between. Two departures per day to Fes (6 hr., 55dh). CTM and private companies provide buses that leave hourly for Tetuan and Cevta (2hr., 15dh).

Ferries: Voyages Hispamaroc, at the corner of bd. Pasteur and rue el-Jabha el-Quatania (tel. 359 07). To Algeciras daily at 7:30am, 12:30pm, and 3:30pm (2½ hr., Class A 235dh, Class B 196dh). **Gibiline Catamaran** to Gibraltar Mon. at 9am and 5:30pm, Wed. 2:30pm, Fri. 2:30 and 6:30pm, Sun. 5:30pm (2½ hr., 210dh). Ferry to Tarifa daily at 2:30pm (1½ hr., 160dh).

Bookstore: Librairie des Colonnes, 54, bd. Pasteur (tel. 369 55). Maps and guidebooks, mostly in French. Open Mon.-Fri. 10am-1pm and 4-7pm, Sat. 10am-1pm.

Car Rental: Hertz, 36 av. Mohammed V (tel. 333 22). A Renault 4 for 3 days with unlimited mileage is 1329dh.

Medical Assistance: Hôpital Al-Kortobi, rue Al-Kortobi (tel. 324 44, in emergencies 342 42).

Emergencies: Police (tel. 19). **Ambulance** (tel. 15).

Accommodations and Food

Accommodations in the medina, while cheaper and closer to the port, are not as comfortable and safe as those in the new city. There's a good range of places in the medina along **rue Mokhtar Ahardan** (a.k.a. rue des Postes) off the Petit Socco. From the port, make a U-turn around the CTM office and head west along rue de Cadiz. Mount the stairs on the left, just before the lower gate to the *kasbah.* **Pension Palace,** at #2 (tel. 392 48), has gracious management and fresh, airy rooms around a tiled courtyard. (30dh, hot shower included.) **Hotel Mamora,** at #19 (tel. 341 05), by far the most enticing in the medina, has laundered rooms and obliging staff. (Singles with shower 94dh, with full bath 119dh. Doubles with shower 110dh, with full bath 138dh.)

In the new city, look for the strip of hotels along **rue Salah Eddine el-Ayoubi** (formerly rue de la Plage). From the train station, head east along av. d'Espagne and take the first right. The often full **Pension Miami,** at #126 (tel. 329 00), has bright, snug rooms. (Singles 30dh. Doubles 50dh. Triples 80dh.) **Hôtel de Paris,** 42, bd. Pasteur (tel. 381 26), is easily the smartest snag in the new city. Many of the marshmallowy rooms have balconies. (Singles 45dh, with shower 66dh. Doubles 61dh, with shower 85dh.)

The least budget-blowing meals grace the one-person stalls of the medina. Frugal meals can be found at the restaurants on rue du Commerce, an alley off rue Jamaa Kebir at the junction of the Petit Socco and rue Mokhtar Ahardan. **Restaurant Ahlen,** 8, rue Mokhtar Ahardan, is more comfortable, with athletic portions and a wide selection; try the lamb *couscous* (15dh). In the new city, rue Salah Eddine el-Ayoubi breathes with bargain eateries. **Restaurant Africa,** at #83, is a breezy spot serving excellent *tajine* and *couscous* dishes for 12-13dh. For a treat, try **Palace Mamounia,** just inside the medina at 6, rue Semmarine (tel. 350 99), between the Grand Socco and the Petit Socco. Waiters in traditional garb present a variety of dishes off the *menu touristique* (100dh). Acrobats balancing trays of burning candles on their heads season the scene. (Open daily 11am-11pm.) Frugal diners can amass fruit, bread, and canned goods in and around the **Grand Socco** (see Sights).

Sights

As any hustler will tell you, the **medina** (old city) is Tangier's most interesting sight. Limit yourself to window-shopping though—you'll get better deals elsewhere. Never buy anything when accompanied by a guide, hustler or "friend"; a 30% commission will be tacked onto the already inflated price.

Once the city's market, the **Grand Socco** is today a noisy square oozing fruit and honey-drenched parsley stands. Go through the **Bab Fahs** to rue d'Italie and its steeper continuation, rue de la Kasbah. At the top, a right through the **Porte de la Kasbah** brings you to rue Riad Sultan. Along it are the **Jardins du Sultan,** where artisans weave carpets. (Open Mon.-Sat. 8am-2pm; in off-season 8:30am-noon and 2:30-6pm.) To the right as you exit the garden is **place de la Kasbah,** whose promontory overlooks the Spanish and Moroccan coasts. Walk back from the promontory and then to the right toward the towering octagonal minaret of the **Mosquée de la Kasbah.** Directly opposite the mosque is the entrance to **Darel-Makhzen,** a palace begun during the reign of Moulay Ismail and later enlarged. It now houses the nifty **Musée des Arts Marocains,** as well as the **Musée des Antiquités.** The Moroccan arts exhibit presents Fes ceramics, Berber and Arabic carpets, copper and silver jewelry, and the star, the Roman mosaic, *The Navigation of Venus,* excavated at Volubilis. (Entire complex open in summer Wed.-Mon. 9am-noon and 3-6pm. Admission 3dh per museum.) Just southwest of the Grand Socco is the **New Mosque.** Made possible through the aid of Kuwait, this is the largest house of worship in North Africa. Like all Moroccan mosques, the interior is closed to non-Muslims.

Near Tangier

Asilah spells relief. Only 46km south of Tangier's tangle, the golden beach and polished Portuguese-style medina make this the perfect place to slip gently into Morocco. Though not without handicraft shops and self-appointed guides, the town remains a snoozy base from which to explore the beaches and ruins of the northwest coast.

The zippiest deal for accommodations is at **Hotel Marhaba,** 9, rue Zakallah (tel. 71 44), outside the entrance to the medina, with well-washed rooms and bathrooms. (All rooms 50dh.) The **Hotel Asilah,** 79, av. Hassan II (tel. (091) 72 86), has clean, spartan rooms, and sunning-roof. From rue Zakallah, turn left and follow the halls of the medina. (Singles 60dh. Doubles 76dh.) **Camping Sahara.** is 1km north of the train station. Sleepy and on the beach, it has an on-site restaurant and bar. (5dh per person, 7dh per tent. Bungalows 120-140dh.) The tiny restaurants that freckle avenue Hassan II along the walls of the medina will satiate you for 12-15dh.

Asilah is served by hourly buses from Tangier (70 min., 6.50dh). Collective taxis to Tangier are 10dh. The train station is 2km out of town (Tangier 9dh).

Tetuan

In the local Berber dialect, "*Tetuan*" means "Open your eyes." Keep them peeled for both the charms and the wiles of Morocco's second gateway. Tetuan's neo-Andalusian architecture and the widely spoken *castellano* recall centuries of Spanish domination that extended well into the 20th century. Though the pace of life is somewhat less hectic and the medina more enchanting than in Tangier, Tetuan is by no means a typical Moroccan town.

Orientation and Practical Information

To reach Tetuan from Spain, traverse **Ceuta,** a Spanish community north of Tetuan where ferries from Algeciras unload their intrepid cargo. The **tourist office** (tel. 51 13 79; open Mon.-Fri. 9am-2pm and 4-6pm, Sat. 9am-2pm) is at the end of Muelle Cañonero Dato as you leave the port complex to enter downtown. To reach the border from Ceuta, take local bus #7 from Plaza de la Constitución (45ptas). Customs can squander 90 minutes. Team up with four other travelers to share a *grand taxi* from the border to Tetuan (15-20dh per person).

Tourist Office: 30, av. Mohammed V (tel. 70 09). Turn left as you exit the upper floor of the bus station, then right onto bd. Sidi Mandri. Three right turns up is av. Mohammed V; the office is a few blocks to the left. No maps, but you can photocopy the one on display. Friendly counsel in French. Open Mon.-Fri. 8am-3pm; Sept.-June Mon.-Thurs. 8:30am-noon and 2:30-6:30pm, Fri. 8:30-11:30am and 3-6:30pm; Ramadan Mon.-Fri. 9am-3pm.

Currency Exchange: Banque Marocaine Change (BMCE), pl. Moulay el-Mehdi. Open Mon.-Fri. 8am-9pm, Sat.-Sun. 9am-1pm and 3-8pm.

Post Office: pl. Moulay el-Mehdi (tel. 67 98), just above av. Mohammed V. Service is best before 11am. Open Mon.-Sat. 8:30am-3:30pm; Sept.-June Mon.-Sat. 8:30am-12:15pm and 2:30-6:45pm; Ramadan Mon.-Sat. 9am-4pm.

Telephones: Along the far wall in the post office. Open daily 8:30am-9pm. Public phones outside entrance for international calls. **Telephone Code:** 096.

Buses: Long-distance, bd. Ouadi al-Makhazine, near bd. Sidi Mandri. Service by several bus companies. Buy your ticket early, ask for a numbered seat and don't pay extra for baggage. **CTM** (tel. 62 63) runs buses to Rabat (1 per day, 6 hr., 65dh) and Casablanca (2 per day, 80dh). Other companies serve many more destinations, including Ceuta (1 per hr., 1 hr., 6dh) and Tangier (1 per hr., 1½ hr., 14dh). A special **shuttle service** (2dh) to the beaches at Cabo Negro, Mdiq, Restinga-Smir and Martil leaves July-Aug. about every 15 min. from the main station and from behind an old green and white palace on the road to Ceuta, a few blocks from the main bus station.

Taxis: The best way to reach Ceuta or Tangier (and one which beats the flesh-press of a bus). **Collective grand taxis** to Ceuta (10-15dh per person) at a taxi stop on bd. Maarakah Annoual, 1 block above the bus station; to Tangier (15-20dh per person) at the gas station across the street from the lower level of the bus station.

Medical Assistance: Hospital, bd. Sidi Mandri at bd. Generalissimo Franco (tel. 19), 1 block above av. Mohammed V.

Emergencies: Police, bd. Sidi Mandri at bd. Generalissimo Franco (tel. 19), below the hospital.

Accommodations and Food

There are scads of cheap hotels (12dh per person) in and around the medina, but most are crawling with cockroaches and hustlers. **Pensión Iberia,** 12, pl. Moulay el-Mehdi (tel. 36 79), at the head of av. Mohammed V, just above the BMCE bank, is clean and airy. (Singles 25dh. Doubles 50dh. Showers 4dh.) **Hotel Regina,** 8, bd. Sidi Mandri (tel. 21 13), left and then right from the upper level of the bus station, has clean rooms. (Singles with shower 62dh, with full bath 92dh. Doubles with shower 110dh, with full bath 132dh.) Also above par is pleasant, airy **Hotel Nacional,** 8, rue Mohammed Torres (tel. 32 90), 2 blocks up from the bus station. (Singles 45dh, with shower 66dh, with full bath 85dh. Doubles 61dh, with shower 85dh, with bath 98dh.)

Wander the medina for the cheapest food. Pass through the entrance across from Pensión Central on pl. Hassan II, and take the first left to find a series of small places. Back in the new city, the cheapest and fastest meals await at **Bocadillas Chatt,** av. Mohammed Torres, the corner opposite Restaurant Zarhoun. Their 5dh sandwiches are well-stuffed. (Open daily 5am-11pm.) **Sandwich Ali Baba,** 19, rue Marrakuh, 1 street downhill from bd. Sidi Mandri, serves what you would expect (5dh; open daily 9am-11pm.) The best deal in town is at **Restaurante Moderno,** 1, pasaje Achach, between av. Mohammed V and av. Mohammed Torres (through the marble-tiled alley from pl. Hassan II). Try the house specialty, *tajine de kefta,* a popular meatball-and-egg concoction (16dh; open daily 9am-9pm). The **Café la Unión,** across the *pasaje,* is a good place to meet Moroccans or play *parchisi.* (Open daily until midnight.)

Sights and Entertainment

Tetuan's **medina** is alluring mayhem. Official guides from the tourist office cost 30dh per half-day, but tend to be jaded. If you hire an unofficial guide, agree in advance on a 10-20dh fee and buy nothing while accompanied. The main access to the medina is at pl. Hassan II, but if you go through **Bab el Rouah** near Moulay el-Mehdi, you'll find yourself in the teeming market area. Worth a gander are the flea market and the various *souks* where Berbers from the Rif Mountains sell their crafts. Before leaving, visit the ornate **Brisha Palace** or the **Mellah el-Bali** (the old Jewish quarter) and the "new" (300-year-old) quarter on **rue Msallah,** where a few Jewish Moroccans remain. The palace lies just beyond pl. Hassan II. Nearby, the small, two-story **Museo Arqueológico,** on 1, bd. Aljazaer, displays prehistoric, Phoenician, and Roman bric-a-brac excavated from Lixus and Tamuda. (Open Mon., Wed. and Thurs. 8:30am-noon and 2:30-6:30pm, Fri. 8:30-11:30am and 3-6:30pm. Admission 10dh.)

Outside the walls of the medina, across the street from the Bab el-Okla, is the **Escuela de Arte,** which houses a worthwhile museum of history and folklore. (Open Mon.-Fri. 8:30am-noon and 2:30-5:30pm, Sat. 8:30am-noon. Admission 10dh.) Potters, coppersmiths, tile-makers and other artisans craft away on the patio outside.

In the evenings, strollers gravitate toward **place Hassan II.** Drink tea at the tables in the square or wander into a café, where locals can be found sampling the hash harvest from the nearby mountains.

Near Tetuan

Chechaouen (Chaouen), a beautiful mountain town 80km (2 hr.) south of Tetuan, has long been popular with young folk who all completely ignore its proximity to the plentiful *kif* (hashish) fields of the Rif Mountains. Whether you prefer rolling hills or rolling your own, Chechaouen's fresh mountain air makes a great escape from the hassle of Tetuan and Tangier. Stay at **Hotel Rif,** 49, rue Tarik Ibn Ziad (tel. 62 07). Corteous proprietor tends comfy rooms and banishes the hustlers. (Singles 38dh, with shower and toilet 40dh. Doubles 40dh, with shower and toilet 60dh.) In the medina, try **Pension Mauritania,** 20, rue Kadi Alami (tel. 62 39). Follow the signs from **pl. Uta el-Hamman** at the top of the medina. Small rooms sparkle. (Singles 25dh. Doubles 45dh. Breakfast and common shower included. Chechaouen is easily accessible by bus from Tetuan (every hr. 7am-6pm, 2 hr., 11dh).

Meknes

Meknes is sprawling, lazy and warmly provincial. The monumental mosques and *madrasa* (koranic schools) of the old city peer suspiciously over the valley at the brutal concrete columns of the new, while the medina, a smaller, tamer version of its eastern cousin at Fes, hustles, reeks and buzzes away.

Meknes's primary attraction is the **Dar el-Kebira** (Great Palace), the largest palace in the world. It was the residence of dictator Moulay Ismail, who chose the city as his capital in 1672; the scale of the ruins testifies to his megalomania. Storm the palace from **Bab El Mansour;** once inside, keep to the right and turn left just before the next gate. To the right is the emerald-green roof of the **Salle des Ambassadeurs.** Ask the guard to unlock the door leading to the **Christian Dungeon** and descend to the dark chamber where the sultans stored the 60,000 slaves who built the palace. (Open Sat.-Thurs. 8:30am-noon and 3-6pm. Admission 10dh.) As you leave the dungeon, walk through the arch ahead to the left. This is the mega-mosque housing the **Tomb of Moulay Ismail,** the only mosque in Morocco open to visitors. Dress modestly. Visitors cannot enter the tomb itself; proceed to the adjacent prayer area bedecked with straw mats. (Open Sat.-Thurs. 9am-noon and 3-6pm. Tip the custodian-guide.)

In the medina stay at the **Hôtel Maroc,** 103 av. Benbrahim (tel. (05) 307 05), just off av. Roumazine, which leads from the bridge toward Bab El Mansour. Well-kept, friendly and safe, the rooms overlook an idyllic garden. (Singles 30dh. Doubles 50dh.) For more comfort and less action, head to the *ville nouvelle.* **Hotel Excelsior,** 57 av. des F.A.R. (tel. 219 00), around the corner from the CTM station, has fresh and capacious rooms. (Singles 45dh, with shower 66dh, with full bath 85dh. Doubles 61dh, with shower 85dh, with full bath 87dh.)

The cheapest food issues from the one-person stalls along **rue Dar Smen,** in front of Bab El Mansour. The plush *salon marocain* in the touristy but tasty **Rotisserie Oumnia,** across av. Roumazine from the Apollo Cinema, serves a 30dh *menu.* In the *ville nouvelle,* **Rotisserie Karam,** 2 av. Ghannah (tel. 224 75), offers a 22dh *menu* with hamburger or chicken. Their 26dh *menu* features excellent *tajinade viande hachée.*

The old town is separated from the *ville nouvelle* by the **Oued Bouffekane,** a long river valley about ½km wide. You can cross it on foot along av. Moulay Ismail, or catch a city bus (#5, 7, or 9) from the **CTM bus station,** 47, bd. Mohammed V (tel. (05) 225 83), to Bab El Mansour. (5 per day to Rabat, 3 hr., 3dh.) Near the CTM terminal is the small **el-Amir Abdelkader train station** on rue d'Alger, 2 blocks from bd. Mohammed V. (8 per day to Fes, 50 min., 14dh.) Do not get off at the bigger station on av. de la Basse. **Private buses** to the Middle Atlas and other destinations leave from the rosy stone building at the foot of the hill below Bab El Mansour. The **tourist office** on pl. Administrative (tel. (05) 212 86) supplies a decent map. (Open Mon.-Fri. 8am-3pm; mid-Sept. to late June Mon.-Fri. 8:30am-noon and 2:30-6:30pm; Ramadan Mon.-Fri. 9am-3pm.) The **post office** is next door (same hrs. as the tourist office).

Fes

Here is the medina of medinas: hammers ring on sheets of brass, chickens hung by their feet squawk their alarm, throaty voices battle in perpetual skirmish, prayers drone from countless minarets, bodies squeeze in needle-narrow streets and the mouth-watering aroma of brochettes on open grills, whiffs of hash, the stench of tanning lye and donkey droppings, the sweet wafts of cedar shavings and freshly-cut mint leaves drive the scene deep into your memory. The medieval **medina** and *fondouks* are cool refuges from the chaos outside, as the modern boulevards of the *ville nouvelle* stretch coolly detached from the maelstrom of the medina.

Orientation and Practical Information

The insipid *ville nouvelle* is a long walk from the old city. Take a *petit taxi* (8dh) or a bus (#2 or 9, 1.20dh) that connects the private bus station at **Bab Boujeloud,** the main entrance to the medina, with the junction of av. Hassan II and av. Mohammed V in the *ville nouvelle.* The older city is splits into two discrete fortified sections. **Fes-el-Bali** (Old Fes) can be traversed along rue Talaa Kebira, which runs southwest-northwest from Bab Boujeloud to the Karaouyine Mosque. As you leave the medina through Bab Boujeloud, you meet avenue des Français, which leads to the entrance to **Fes-el-Jdid** (New Fes)—not to be confused with the *ville nouvelle.* South of this entrance is the grande rue de Fes-Jdid, a grande dead end. Here, rue Bou Ksissat bends right to the **Royal Palace** at pl. des Alaouites.

Tourist Offices: Office National de Tourisme, av. Hassan II (tel. 234 60), at pl. de la Résistance. From the CTM terminal, walk down bd. Mohammed V and turn right onto av. Hassan II. From the train station, walk along rue Chenguit, bear left at pl. Kennedy, then turn left onto av. Hassan II. English spoken. Open Mon.-Fri. 7am-2pm; Oct.-June Mon.-Fri. 8:30am-noon and 2:30-6:30pm; Ramadan Mon.-Sat. 9am-3pm. **Syndicat d'Initiative,** pl. Mohammed V (tel. 247 64), in the BMCE building. Not as well stocked. Open Mon.-Fri. 8am-3pm; mid-Sept. to June Mon.-Fri. 8:30am-noon and 2:30-6:30pm; Ramadan Mon.-Fri. 10am-3pm.

Currency Exchange: BMCE, pl. Mohammed V beneath the tourist office. Open 8:30-12pm and 3-5pm. **Les Merinides,** in the Borj Nord (tel. 425 25). Open daily 5-10pm.

Post Office: At av. Hassan II and bd. Mohammed V in the *ville nouvelle.* Open Mon.-Fri. 7am-2:30pm; Sept. 16-June Mon.-Fri. 8:30am-6:45pm. Stamps sold on Sat. at av. Hassan II entrance 8:30-11:30am; off-season 8-11am.

Telephones: In the main post office. Open daily 8:30am-9pm. Enter from the side on bd. Mohammed V. **City Code:** 06.

Trains: Av. des Almohades (tel. 250 01), at rue Chenguit. To Casablanca (10 per day, change for Marrakech, 72dh), Rabat (10 per day, 52dh), Meknes (10 per day, 14dh), Tangier (5 per day, only direct connection at 5am, 70dh).

Buses: CTM, bd. Mohammad V (tel. 220 41), at rue Ksar el-Kebir. To Rabat (6 per day, 44dh), Casablanca (6 per day, 60dh), Marrakech (2 per day, 41dh), Meknes (8 per day, 13dh), Tangier (2 per day, 60dh), and Tetuan (1 per day, 41dh). **Private buses** leave from the **Gare Routière,** Bab Boujeloud (tel. 335 29).

Taxis: Key stands for *petit taxis* are at the post office, pl. Mohammed V, tourist office, Bab Boujeloud, and Bab Guissa. After 8:30pm (Sept. 16-June after 8pm), rides cost 50% more than the meter shows.

Bookstore: English Bookstore of Fes, 68 av. Hassan II, near pl. de la Résistance. Novels, guidebooks, phrasebooks, maps. English spoken. It is illegal for bookstores in Morocco to sell *Let's Go* books because of a territorial dispute. Open Mon.-Fri. 8:30am-12:30pm and 3-7pm.

Accommodations and Camping

In the *ville nouvelle,* the best inexpensive accommodations are on or just off the western side of bd. Mohammed V between av. Slaoui, near the CTM station, and av. Hassan II, near the post office. Accommodations in Old Fes cluster around Bab Boujeloud. Though rooms are cheaper here, hustlers outnumber even the cockroaches and bargaining is an ordeal.

Auberge de Jeunesse (IYHF), 18, bd. Mohammed el Hansale (tel. 240 85). From the tourist office, walk 4 blocks along bd. Chefchaouni, turn left to the street below and look for the whitewashed walls and the sign. Reasonably clean rooms, toilets, showers and a small kitchen. Hot water in winter only. Reception open daily 8-9am, noon-3pm, and 6-10pm. 15dh, nonmembers 17.50dh. IYHF cards 75dh (bring 2 photos).

Hotel Excelsior, 107, rue Larbi el-Kaghat (tel. 256 02). From the main post office, walk 3 blocks up bd. Mohammad V and look to your right. Respectable rooms, toilets and showers. Singles with shower 62dh. Doubles with shower 78dh, with full bath 92dh.

Hotel Central, 50, rue Nador (tel. 223 33), 3 blocks toward the CTM station from Hotel Excelsior (above). Neat if plain rooms. Helpful management. Singles 50dh, with shower 71dh, with full bath 95dh. Doubles 71dh, with shower 95dh, with full bath 105dh.

Hotel Renaissance, 47, rue Abdekrim el-Khattabi (tel. 221 93), near pl. Mohammed V. Passably clean rooms; those with balconies overlooking the street are least musty. Pit toilets and no showers. Singles 25dh. Doubles 40dh.

Hotel du Jardin Public, 153, Kasbah Boujeloud (tel. 330 86), an alley as you approach Bab Boujeloud from outside the medina. Winding hallways surround a small, cool lobby. So-so showers and pit toilets. Singles 35dh. Doubles 60dh. Hot water 4dh (winter only).

Hotel du Commerce, pl. des Alaouites in Fes el-Jdid. Right now the cleanest place in the area. Singles 30dh, with *terrace* 50dh. Doubles 60dh. Showers 4dh.

Food

In the *ville nouvelle,* restaurants chatter on the little streets to either side of bd. Mohammed V. Rue Kaid Ahmed, a few blocks from the post office, has a number of finds, including snackbars where a meal of brochettes or liver is 15dh. Old Fes eateries are just inside Bab Boujeloud. If no menu is posted, haggle before you hoover.

Restaurant des Voyageurs, 41, bd. Mohammed V (tel. 255 37), near the CTM station. Try the *menu touristique:* lamb *tajine almondine* with *pastilla* and dessert, all delicious and a bargain, 45dh. Service 10% Open daily noon-4pm and 6pm-midnight.

Restaurant CTM, rue Ksar el-Kbir, under Hotel CTM. Tasty, cut-rate food. *Tajine Marocaine,* salad, and bread 32dh. Open daily 9am-11pm.

Rotisserie La Rotonde, rue Nader (tel. 205 89), down the street from Hotel Central. Clean enough to wear to a party and friendly enough to let out around the mailman. Excellent ¼-chicken, tomato sauce, bread, and rice 10dh; ½-chicken 18dh. Open daily 11am-11pm.

Restaurant Bouayad, 26, rue Serrajine (tel. 362 78), on your right after you pass through Bab Boujeloud. Gushing locals and tourists. Good *tajine* or *couscous* 15dh. Open 24 hrs., even during Ramadan.

Sights

The enormous maze that is the **medina** (15km in circumference) is the largest and roughest to navigate in Morocco. Hire an official guide before noon at either tourist office; a morning tour costs 30dh for up to 10 people *(not* per person). The greatest attraction of a guide is the guarantee that the other guides and hustlers will stay away for the rest of the day. Tell your guide you wish to see the sights and refuse to enter any shops, for his commission boosts prices 30%. Don't allow your camera or other valuables to be carried, and never tour after sunset. Try to have an idea of where you are at all times; one of the hustlers' stand-bys is to threaten to abandon you if a large wad of dirhams is not forthcoming. Children make cheaper (albeit less-informed) guides. If a sense of adventure impels you to strike out on your own, prepare yourself for constant harassment by hustlers inside and outside the medina. Arm yourself with a good map, and consider saving Bab Boujeloud until the end of your visit to avoid dragging its swarm of hustlers with you throughout your excursion. Get off the bus just before Bab Boujeloud and enter the medina from a side entrance, or descend through Bab Boujeloud on the heels of a tour group and blend in until you leave the hustlers behind. Alternatively, grab a piece of large shrubbery and tiptoe along the side. Once you get into the thick of the medina, would-be guides become less of a problem.

After entering the medina through Bab Boujeloud, bear left immediately onto shop-lined, bamboo-shaded rue Tala Kebira. Nearby to the left is the **grain market.** Three right-hand blocks farther along is the entrance to **Medersa Bou Inania,** the finest Koranic university in Morocco. Built under the Merinid Dynasty in the 14th century, the beautifully carved white plaster walls and *mihrab* remain remarkably chipper. (Open daily 8:30am-1pm and 4-7pm. Admission 10dh.) To pack in more sights, turn right as you leave the main entrance of the *medersa,* and immediately right again into the first alley. This leads to rue Tala Seghira, a secondary artery that runs mostly parallel to rue Tala Kebira but bows in to meet it at Bab Boujeloud. When you reach rue Tala Seghira (2nd street on the left), veer left and amble until the inconspicuous rue Guerniz. Going down its long stone steps, take the first left down more steps, jog slightly to the right, but continue straight down; make the first left (into an alley with more steps), and bear right into the covered alley. In this area of town is the **leather tannery,** a fascinating factory of vats and tubs filled with reeking colored dyes and skins. From here, you can cross the Oued Fes to enter the **Andalous Quarter.** This area was settled by Moors fleeing from the Reconquista of Spain. The main entrance to the **Andalous Mosque,** the second-largest mosque in Fes, is phenomenal.

The **Zaouia de Moulay Idriss** contains the tomb of Moulay Idriss II, who dubbed Fes the capital of Morocco in 808. With your back to the entrance, walk left into the colorful **belt market.** Continuing across rue Rhabbet el-Kaiss, you find on your left the 14th-century **Medersa Attarine.** Behind the massive bronze doors are the intricately carved plaster walls of the prayer hall, crowned by a cedarwood mantle and sprayed by a splendid fountain. In the same direction loom the huge wooden doors and heavy iron-ring knockers of **Karaouiyne Mosque,** the largest mosque in Morocco. Although the finest parts of the interior are off limits, the view through the front portal is still a treat. Leaving the Karaouiyne, follow rue Bou Touil as it angles to the right towards pl. Seffarine. Here, dozens of artisans transform sheets of copper into works of art. On the left squats the 13th-century **Medersa Seffarine.**

From Bab Boujeloud, you can also make your way to the fountain at pl. Batha and turn right up the next street to the **Dar Batha Museum of Moroccan Arts.** The wide collection includes ancient korans, wild Moroccan musical instruments, and rainbow Berber carpets. (Open Wed.-Sat. 9am-noon and 3-6pm.)

Rabat

Morocco's anomaly, Rabat is a clean and orderly national showpiece. With European clothes, newspapers, and self-important preoccupations, Rabat lacks the appeal of Fes or Marrakech. The rectilinear medina is lively and, by royal fiat, hustler-free.

Orientation and Practical Information

Rabat is very easy to navigate. Two arteries are key: **avenue Mohammed V** runs north-south from the Grande Essouna Mosque past the train station and the post office right through the medina; **avenue Hassan II** heads east along the medina's southern walls toward Rabat's sibling city, Salé, and west into the route de Casablanca, where the "central" bus station is not at all central.

Tourist Offices: Office National Marocain du Tourisme (ONMT), 22, rue el Jazair (tel. 212 52). Far away, but helpful. From the train station, walk up av. Mohammed V to the Grande Essouna Mosque, turn left on av. Moulay Hassan, and 7 blocks later (on the right-hand side of the street), bear right onto rue el-Jazair (rue d'Alger). Open July to mid-Sept. Mon.-Fri. 8am-2:30pm; mid-Sept. to June Mon.-Fri. 8:30am-noon and 2:30-6:30pm. Ramadan Mon.-Fri. 9am-3pm. **Syndicat d'initiative,** rue Patrice Lumumba (tel. 232 72), is more centrally located. From the post office, cross av. Mohammed V and bear right along rue el-Kahira, then walk a few blocks. Open Mon.-Fri. 8am-7pm.

Embassies: U.S., 2, av. de Marrakech (tel. 662 65, 24 hours). Look for the flag over bd. Tarik Ibn Ziyad. Consular section open Mon.-Fri. 8:30am-noon and 1-5:30pm and 8:30-11:30am for non-Americans. **Canada,** 13, Zankat Joafar Essadik, Agdal (tel. 713 76). Open Mon.-Fri. 8am-2pm. **U.K.,** 17, bd. Tour Hassan (tel. 209 05). Travelers from **Australia** and **New Zealand** should contact the British embassy. **Algerian** consulate, 12, rue d'Azrou, off av. de Fes. Open for visas Mon.-Fri. 8am-1pm. Bring 3 photos.

Currency Exchange: Hôtel Tour Hassan, 22, av. de Chellah (tel. 214 01). Official bank rates. Open daily 8am-7pm.

Post Office: av. Mohammed V (tel. 207 31), at rue Soekarno. Open Mon.-Fri. 8am-3:30pm; in off-season 8:30am-noon and 2-6:45pm. **Telephones** and Poste Restante are across the street. Open 8am-midnight. **City Code:** 07.

Trains: av. Mohammed V (tel. 232 40), at av. Moulay Youssef. Second class to Tangier (5 per day, 5½ hr., 56.50dh), Fes (8 per day, 5 hr., 62.50dh), and Casablanca (15 per day, 1 hr., 22dh). The trans-Maghreb train departs daily at 9:50pm and arrives in Tunis 46 hr. later (545.60dh).

Buses: route de Casablanca (tel. 751 24), at pl. Mohammed Zerktouni. Far from the town center. Pay 10dh for *petit taxi,* or 2.20dh for bus #30 from av. Hassan II near av. Mohammed V. All inter-city bus companies operate from here. Tickets for CTM buses sold at windows #14 and 15; their buses run to Tangier (4 per day, 59dh), Tetuan (2 per day, 62dh), Meknes (6 per day, 31dh), Fes (6 per day, 44dh), and Casablanca (12 per day, 18dh).

Medical Assistance: Hôpital Avicenne (tel. 744 11), at the southern end of bd. d'Argonne (a.k.a. av. Ibn Sina), in the district of Souissi just south of Agdal. 8dh by *petit taxi.* Morocco's best emergency medical care, free of charge. U.S. citizens can also go to the U.S. embassy. **Ambulance:** Tel. 15.

Police: rue Scekarno (tel. 19), 2 blocks down from the post office.

Accommodations, Camping and Food

The few lodgings that are both pleasant and inexpensive are often full; reserve ahead, especially in July, when students from all over the country descend upon the city to take their *bac* (high school final exams). The slightly loud **Hôtel Marrakech,** 10, rue Sebbahi (tel. 277 03), is one of the few enticing establishments in the medina. Enter the medina on av. Mohammed V, and turn right after 3 blocks. (Singles 35dh. Doubles 50dh.) The hotels just off av. Mohammed V as you walk from the train station toward the medina are also comfortable. **Hôtel Capitol,** 34 av. Allal Gen Abdallah (tel. 312 36 or 37), has clean and comfortable rooms and beds. Take your 7th right from the train station and your next left. (Singles 54dh, with shower 75dh. Doubles 64dh, with shower 92dh.) **Hôtel Central,** 2, rue el-Basra (tel. 673 56), has large, clean and extremely bright red and pink rooms. From the train station, walk 2 blocks down av. Mohammed V towards the medina, and turn right. (Singles 48dh, with shower 57dh. Doubles 72dh, with shower 80dh.) The **Auberge de Jeunesse (IYHF),** 34, rue Marassa (tel. 257 69), just outside the medina several blocks north of Bab el-Had, is one of Morocco's better hostels although still grungy. (Lockout 9:30am-noon and 3-7pm. Members only 20dh.) **Camping de la Plage,** on the beach across the River Bou Regreg in Salé, has running water, toilets, a shop and free cold showers. Take bus #6 from av. Hassan II near av. Allal Ben Abdallah to Salé's Bab Bou Haja (2.20dh), and follow the signs. (10dh per person, 5dh per tent and 5dh per car.)

Inside the medina, several inexpensive eateries line **avenue Mohammed V** and **avenue Hassan II.** Just through the walls is a square filled with food stalls, grills, and tables, where 17dh will buy you a meal of veal cutlet, salad, and bread. **Restau-**

rant El Bahia is built into the walls of the medina, to your right as you approach from av. Mohammed V. The lavish *salon marocain* upstairs has embroidered sofas and excellent food *(menu* 28dh). **Restaurant Taghazout,** 7, rue Sebbahi (tel. 256 47), is always filled with locals and therefore out of many things on the menu. Their *tajine de bœuf* (16dh) is usually in stock and quite good. **Restaurant Ghazza,** rue Ghazza, is your 7th right of av. Mohammed V from the train station. Excellent spicy chicken (17dh). Their *filet du merlan,* when they have it, is also tasty (26dh).

Sights

Begin sightseeing at the 18th-century **Essouna Grande Mosque** on av. Mohammed V at Avenue Moulay Hassan. Below a handsomely carved wooden mantle, gold-trimmed windows grace the building's white plaster walls. Above, a minaret towers over the green shingle roof. Av. Moulay Hassan leads to the salmon-pink Almohad **Bab er-Rouah,** "the Gate of the Winds," site of a modern art gallery. Walk back through the *bab* and turn right through the wall at the first gate onto the tree-lined promenade that leads to the **Dar el-Makhzen (Royal Palace).** Most of the present palace, a sprawling villa with another green shingled roof, postdates the French occupation. You can take pictures, but behave calmly when you approach the palace. Try to arrive at either the Chella or the Oudaias Kasbah at sunset, when the view over the **River Bou Regreg** is most stunning.

On the other side of town along av. Abi Ragreg, near the Pont Moulay Hassan to Salé, stands the **Mausoleum of Mohammed V,** the tomb of the popular king who led the country from French and Spanish colonial domination to independence. A flight of marble steps draws you up to the guard-flanked entrance. (Open daily 8am-10pm. Free.) In front of the mausoleum stands the huge **Hassan Tower,** the unfinished minaret of the Almohad mosque. All that remains today of what in the 12th century was the largest mosque in the world is a grid of columns intimating its original proportions.

Near the mausoleum, the Pont Moulay Hassan connects Rabat to the adjacent town of **Salé,** also accessible via rowboats from the nearby Ramp Sidi Maklouf (0.50dh). The medina of Rabat's riverside neighbor lays out enchanting *souks* and a living medieval city free of tourist emporiums and hustlers. In the northern end of the city is the **Grand Mosque** and the **Mederça of Abu el-Hassan.** (Open 8am-noon and 2:30-6pm. Admission 3dh.) South of Rabat are the fantastic beaches of **Temara.** Take a collective taxi or bus #17 from bd. Hassan II near av. Mohammed V to Temara (2.20dh), and then walk 3km west.

Casablanca

Casablanca lies on the coast 80km southwest of Rabat. You must remember this: there is no Rick's Café Américain in the medina; no getaway plane at the airport; and no one looking at you, kid, except the hustlers who prowl the medina. "Casa," as it is known to many, has combined the charm of French industrialism with the efficiency of Moroccan feudalism to create a gigantic, noisy, smelly hybrid that only a resident could love. Be forewarned: Even the most fanatical Bogie-worshipers will find Casablanca a major disappointment.

International flights arrive at **Aeroport Mohammed V** (tel. (02) 33 90 40); a bus runs hourly (20dh) to the **CTM Station,** 23, rue Léon L'Africain (tel. (02) 26 80 61), off rue Colbert. If you are arriving by train, get off at the central **Casa Port,** Port of Casablanca (tel. (02) 22 30 11)—*not* **Casa Voyageurs,** bd. Ba Hammed (tel. (02) 24 58 01), which is near nothing. The former has better northbound service, the latter better southbound service. The informative **syndicat d'initiative,** 98, bd. Mohammed V (tel. (02) 22 15 24), at rue Colbert, is stocked with good maps. (Open Mon.-Sat. 9am-noon and 3-6:30pm, Sun. 9am-noon; Ramadan 9am-4pm.) The **U.S. consulate** is at 8, bd. Moulay Youssef (tel. (02) 22 41 49; open in summer Mon.-Fri. 8am-4:30pm, in off-season Mon.-Fri. 8am-5:30pm). The **British consulate** is at 60, bd. d'Anfa (tel. (02) 26 14 41 or 26 14 40; open Mon. 8:30am-12:30pm and 2-6pm, Tues.-Fri. 8:30am-12:30pm and 2-5:30pm).

The ramshackle **Auberge de Jeunesse (IYHF),** 6, pl. Amiral Philbert (tel. (02) 22 05 51), usually has rooms available. From the Casa Port train station, cross the street, turn right, and walk along the walls until you can turn left up a small flight of stairs. (20dh, nonmembers 22.50dh. Breakfast included. Reception open daily 8-10am, noon-2pm, and 6-11pm.) **Hotel Foucauld,** 52 rue Foucauld (tel. (02) 226 66), off av. des Forces Armées Royales, features a Moroccan-style sitting room and clean beds. (Singles 45dh, with shower 66dh. Doubles 61dh, with shower 85dh.)

Marrakech

Marrakech is a desert circus. Its reddish-pink streets and alleys throbulate with Berber tribespeople, Arab artisans, French expatriates, Western tourists, Blue People from the Sahara, snake charmers, medicine men, peddlers, hustlers and hash vendors. Visit during winter, when the heat and hustlers go on holiday.

Orientation and Practical Information

In the center ring is the **Djemaa el-Fna** area. Most commercial services lie along **avenue Mohammed V,** which runs from the **Koutoubia Minaret** near the Djemaa to the **Guéliz** (new city); bus #1 runs this route (1.20dh) and so does a flock of *petits taxis* (5dh).

Tourist Offices: Office National Marocain du Tourisme (ONMT), av. Mohammed V (tel. 302 58), at pl. Abdel Moumen ben Ali. Take bus #1. Free brochures provide good maps of the *souks* in the medina. English spoken. Official guides 30dh per ½-day, 50dh per day. Open daily 8am-2:30pm; Sept.-June 8am-noon and 2-6pm; Ramadan 9am-3pm. **Tourist Office,** 170, av. Mohammed V (tel. 330 97), 2 blocks towards the Djemaa el-Fna from the ONMT. Open Mon.-Fri. 9am-1:30pm and 4-7pm, Sat. 9am-1:30pm; mid-Sept. to June Mon.-Fri. 8am-noon and 3-6pm, Sat. 8am-noon.

Currency Exchange: Change money in the Djemaa el-Fna at the **SGMB Bank** on rue Bab Aganaou, 2 blocks down from the post office. No commission. Open daily 8am-2pm and 4-8pm.

American Express: Voyages Schwartz, rue Mauritania, 2nd floor (tel. 328 31). Rue Mauritania meets av. Mohammed V across from the *tourist office* (see above); the office is the last building on the left of the 1st block. Mail held, checks sold and replaced, but no wired money accepted. Cardholders can buy traveler's checks with personal checks. Open Mon.-Fri. 8:30am-12:30pm and 3-6:30pm; bank open Mon.-Fri. 8:30am-noon.

Post Office: pl. du XVI Novembre, off av. Mohammed V. Letters to "Poste Restante Marrakech" come here. Open Mon.-Sat. 8am-9pm. Branch in Djemaa el Fna receives letters addressed "Poste Restante Marrakech-medina." Open Mon.-Fri. 8:30am-12:15pm and 2:30-6:45pm.

Telephones: At both post offices, but quicker and more pleasant at the Djemaa el-Fna office. Open Mon.-Sat. 8am-2:30pm. **City Code:** 04.

Flights: The airport (tel. 303 38) is 5km from town. No public buses. Taxis cost 8-10dh. **Royal Air Maroc,** av. de France (tel. 309 39), in Hotel Atlas Asni.

Trains: The station is on av. Hassan II, 2 blocks from pl. de l'Empereur Haile Selassie. To reach the Djemaa from the station, take a left down av. Hassan II to pl. du XVI Novembre, then go right on Mohammed V. To Casablanca (7 per day, express at 7:25am, 139dh), Meknes (5 per day, 110dh), and Fes (5 per day, 110dh). The "Marrakech Express" of CSN&Y fame is now a bus.

Buses: The new station, unmarked on maps, is outside the walls of the medina by Bab Doukkala. CTM (window #10), SATAS (window #14), and private companies operate here. To reach the Djemaa from the station, walk down rue Mohammed el-Mellah to pl. de la Liberté, then head left on av. Mohammed V for 20 min. Or, take a *petit taxi* (5dh) or bus #8 (1.20dh).

Collective Taxis: Leave from Bab Aganaou.

Medical Assistance: A doctor is on call at the pharmacy near the Hotel Marrakech, down the road from the post office. Open until 10pm.

Emergency: Tel. 19.

Accommodations

The youth hostels and the campground are far from the medina (but close to the train station). Otherwise, the cheapest accommodations are within spitting distance from the Djemaa el-Fna.

Auberge de Jeunesse (IYHF), rue El Jahid (tel. 328 31), in the Quartier Industriel, 5 min. from the train station. Cross av. Hassan II, walk right, hook the 1st left, and amble past railroad tracks, Tony Bar Terminus, rue Ibn el-Qadi, and a cluster of streets. The hostel is to the right by a vacant lot full of eucalyptus trees. Stunningly clean, with a courtyard and terrace. If business is slow, the members-only rule bends. Lockout 9am-noon and 2-6pm. 15dh, cold showers included.

Hotel CTM, facing Djemaa el-Fna (tel. 223 25), next door to café du Grand Balcon. Cheap comfort. The rooms facing the Djemaa are bigger and noiser. Singles 47dh, with shower 63dh. Doubles 58dh, with shower 87dh.

Hôtel de la Jeunesse, 56, Derb Sidi Bouloukate (tel. 436 31). The best of the budget hotels lining this street, a narrow alleyway through the 1st arch on your right as you face the Hotel CTM (above) on Djemaa el-Fna. Great company and a congenial proprietor, with nice, though rank, toilets. Singles 30dh. Doubles 40dh. Triples 50dh. Cold showers included.

Hôtel de France, 197, Riad Zitoune el-Kedim (tel 430 67), a bit farther along (not to be confused with the Hôtel *Café* de France overlooking the Djemaa). Shiny bathrooms. Singles 30dh. Doubles 45dh. Cold showers 2dh, hot 3dh.

Food

Feed cheaply in, at and around the stalls of the Djemaa (experienced intestines only). Food vendors triple the number of eating options in the evenings, some offering delicious *tajine, couscous* and other main courses (usually 12dh). Set the price before eating and take no prisoners when you bargain.

Café-Restaurant Marocain, pl. Djemaa el-Fna, farther along toward the *souks.* Look for the yellow, four-leaf grille pattern. Simple fare at rock-bottom prices: ¼ chicken, bread, and salad 13dh. Open daily 8am-11pm.

Café-Restaurant al-Baraka, rue Bab Agnaou, off the Djemaa. Decent *couscous* and excellent *tajine de la viande.* Three-course *menu* 25dh.

Café-Patisserie Toubkal, Djemaa el-Fna, across from Hotel CTM. A sleek patisserie. The café whips up scrumptious steaks, salad, bread and fries all for 14dh. Open daily 7am-11pm.

Café-Restaurant-Hotel de France, pl. Djemaa el-Fna. The *salon marocaine*—with pillows, chandeliers and carved ceilings—is cool during the day. In the evening, the rooftop restaurant offers an excellent view of the square. Standard 45dh *menu.* Open daily 8am-midnight.

Restaurant de Foucauld, rue del Mouahidine (tel. 254 99), between the Koutoubia minaret and the Djemaa. Indulge in an excellent 4-course meal. The nearest alcohol to the Djemaa. *Menu* 50 or 60dh.

Sights

The **Djemaa el-Fna** ("Assembly of the Dead") defies its somber name. A hot and crowded market by day, the Djemaa rocks at sunset with a legion of entertainers. Almost every tour of Marrakech begins at the 12th-century **Koutoubia Mosque,** its magnificent minaret presiding over the Djemaa. The minaret, crowned by a lantern of three golden spheres, is the oldest and purest example of the architecture of the Almohads, who made Marrakech their capital (1130-1213) and whose realm extended from Spain to present-day Tunisia. (Entrance to Muslims only.) At the northern end of the medina, feast your eyes and cool off at the ornate **Madrasa Ben Youssef,** the largest active koranic school in the Maghreb until it closed in 1956. (Open in summer Tues.-Sun. 8am-noon and 3-7pm; in winter Tues.-Sun. 8am-noon and 2-6pm; Ramadan 8am-noon. Admission 10dh.) Even more lavish are the **Saadian Tombs,** modeled on the interior of the Alhambra in Granada. The old **Palace el Bedi** today hosts the annual **Folklore Festival.** (First 2-3 weeks in June. Tickets 30dh. Information available at tourist office.) Close by, at the southeastern edge of the medina, the 19th-century **Bahia Palace,** the only royal palace in Morocco open to tourists (when the royal family is not in residence), has elaborate cedar doors and ceilings, gardens with fountains and its own army of guides. (Open daily in summer 9:30am-1pm and 4-7pm; in winter daily 9:30-11:45am and 2:30-6pm. Free, but tip the guide.) To escape the midday sun, wander in the verdant **Menara Gardens** in the new city and lounge in the charming lakeside pavilion, or visit the extensive **Agdal Gardens,** south of the medina.

High Atlas

The High Atlas range launches dramatically from the Sahara; its highest peak, **Mount Toubkal** (4167m), is the top of North Africa. Buses leave the Marrakech bus station on the hour for **Asni** (2½ hr., 8dh per person, 3dh per pack), where you can stock up on food for an assault on the mountain. Collective taxis to Asni are 20dh per person. The **auberge de jeunesse (IYHF)** is about 100m to your right as you face the front of the market. A marvelously calm place, the hostel itself is reason enough to stay in Asni (10dh). You can continue to **Imlil** either by the blue truck that leaves every couple of hours (25dh round trip) or by the town taxi (if you can round up a group of five, 12dh per person). In Imlil, the Club Alpin Français runs a refuge with quality cooking facilities and bunk beds (20dh, students and IYHF members 18dh). Snag a topographic map of Toubkal. **Rabat Tours,** in the shopping center, provides a list of official guides, rents hiking boots (15dh per day), and preps you for the climb. Park your baggage at the refuge in Imlil if you haven't already deposited it in Asni, and continue on foot to the Club's **Refuge Louis Neltner** (3207m), a five- or six-hour hike (20dh). Consult the innkeeper about the climb to the summit, which should take another day. Be wary of terrain, weather and your own physical limitations; take adequate cold-weather clothing and a surfeit of supplies. Stream water nurtures the parasite giardia; boil or purify it with tablets before drinking. Official guides are recommended (150dh per day).

From Marrakech 75km of sinuous roads bring you to **Oukaimeden,** a mountain resort boasting the highest ski lift in Africa (3200m). Take a bus (11dh) or collective taxi (12dh) to the village of **Ourika,** then hitch the remaining 32km.

The narrow, emerald **Ourika Valley** (33km from Marrakech) forks off from the road to Oukaimeden at Arbalou and stretches southeast to the tiny village of **Setti-Fatima.** To get here, take the S513 toward Oukaimeden and turn left after the ramshackle synagogue, or snare one of the many buses that leave from outside Bab er-Rob in Marrakech (8dh).

THE NETHERLANDS

USD$1 = 1.97 guilders (f, or NLG)	**f1 = USD$0.51**
CAD$1 = f1.72	**f1 = CAD$0.58**
GBP£1 = f3.30	**f1 = GBP£0.30**
AUD$1 = f1.53	**f1 = AUD$0.65**
NZD$1 = f1.12	**f1 = NZD$0.90**
Country Code: 31	**International Dialing Prefix: 09**

Horizons of limitless expanse, cows grazing at a windmill's base, dyke-rimmed fields: this is the Holland of storybooks. Outside the few major cities, this is still the reality in the country more formally known as the Netherlands (Nederland). Following its independence as the seven United Provinces in the 1580s, the Republic of the Netherlands embarked on major commercial enterprise; the Dutch East and West Indies Companies bought Manhattan and traded as far afield as Java, Africa, and the Caribbean. The 17th century was the Golden Age of Dutch history, an era of enormous wealth and toleration: thousands of Europe's Jews and religious and political dissidents fled here to escape persecution, while the country's remarkably open intellectual life attracted great minds such as Descartes and Spinoza and produced great painters such as Rembrandt and Vermeer. The Dutch were Europe's arms-makers and bankers too, and cities such as Haarlem, Delft, Leiden, and Utrecht thrived.

Holland faded from the limelight during the 18th century, occupied by the French and then gradually modernized by 19th-century monarchs. Under the Nazi occupation, the Dutch resistance valiantly aided the country's Jews. Today, Dutch national unity is straining under a growing crisis of conscience. The egalitarian utopia promised by the liberal policies of the last 20 years has failed to materialize, and the country's increasingly conservative population is growing impatient.

Holland proper (the country's western half) collects the majority of international tourists due to its bustling urban centers and dense rail system; the eastern half remains largely rural and untouristed. Get your hands (and your tail) on one of Holland's 9.5 million bicycles, and take a trip into the quiet countryside. The most glorious spot for springtime tulip gazing is the region between Oegstgeest, Noordwijkerhout, De Zilk, and Hillegom. Annual flower exhibitions bloom from March to May in the town of Lisse.

Getting There and Getting Around

Travel in Holland is trouble-free. Most points of interest cluster between Amsterdam and Rotterdam, themselves only 1¼ hours apart. Amsterdam is a convenient base for daytrips almost anywhere in the country. **NS,** the efficient rail authority, runs up to four trains per hour between major cities. *Intercity* trains generally cruise non-stop between major cities, while *stoptreins* pause in most or all of the villages along the way. Eurail and InterRail are valid. A round-trip ticket is cheaper than two one-ways, but valid only on the day of issue. The NS runs 72 **Day Trip** programs, available from any train station during spring and summer, which allow you to pay an all-inclusive (and reduced) price for a round-trip train ticket, entrance fees for attractions, and often connecting transport and a snack. If you have a railpass, you can still conserve cash by buying an "attraction ticket" at the departure or arrival station.

Buying any version of the **Holland Rail Pass** (for example, f79 for 3 days of travel in a 10-day period), or the **Rail Ranger** tickets (a.k.a. "Rovers") that offer unlimited second-class train travel within the country, will probably prove a rip-off unless you scramble frantically. However, the one-day **multi-Ranger** (Meer Man's Kaart), which costs f76 for two people (f93 for 3, to f126 for 6), pays off under the right circumstances, and under 18s can snare a **Teen Ranger,** valid for four days out of 10 (f48). A sweeter deal for those also traveling in Belgium and Luxembourg is the **Benelux-Tourrail** card, which can be used on any five days in a 17-day period between mid-March and October (f154, ages 12-25 f109).

A nationalized fare system covers both city buses and trams and long-distance buses in the Netherlands. Rides are denominated in strip tickets *(strippenkaart)* valid anywhere in the country. The country is divided into zones, and the number of strips you need depends on the number of zones through which you travel. The base charge is always one strip. Bus and tram drivers sell two-strip tickets (f2), three-strip tickets (f3.05), and 10-strip tickets (f9.35). Tickets are *much* cheaper (15-strip ticket f9.05, 45-strip ticket f27.25) from public transportation counters, post offices, and certain tobacco shops and newsstands (look for a *strippenkaart* sign). You can have the bus driver validate two 10-strip tickets as a day-ticket, good for unlimited travel anywhere in the country—or, during the summer, buy a *Zommer Zwerfkaart* from the driver with the same effect (f12.50). Finally, you can get unlimited bus travel with any Rail Ranger ticket by paying a surcharge of about 20%.

Cycling is the way to go in the Netherlands. Distances between cities are short, the countryside is flat, and most streets have separate bike lanes. One-speed bikes abound for about f8 per day or f40 per week, with a deposit of f50-200; utter flatness (except near the coast) renders 3-speeders unnecessary. Eighty train stations rent bicycles for f5 per day, plus a f50-200 deposit, upon presentation of your rail ticket or railpass (f7 without a rail ticket). Tandems rent for f25 per day (deposit f300). It is sage to call the station a day ahead to reserve; phone numbers are in the free booklet *Fiets en Spoor*. Purchasing a used bike (about f140) and then reselling it may prove more thrifty than renting one. **Hitchhiking,** where allowed, is usually swift, except out of Amsterdam, where competition is cutthroat. The free map of Holland spewed by tourist offices provides a complete list of motorway service stations.

Practical Information

The **VVV** are godly tourist information offices; make your holy pilgrimage to any building marked by a blue triangular sign, even in the smallest villages. The VVV, as well as museums themselves, sell the one-year **Museumkaart,** good for free admission to over 400 Dutch museums (except special exhibitions) and discounts on various cultural events (f40, under 18 f15, over 64 f25). Buy the **Cultureel Jongeren Paspoort,** which entitles those under 26 to reduced rates at museums and cultural events (f15, valid Sept. to Sept.), at the VVV or the **Amsterdam Uit Buro (AUB),** Leidseplein 26. Bring a passport-size photograph for either card.

A profusion of womens' centers, coffeehouses, and crisis telephone lines exist, particularly in Amsterdam and the university towns. Check *Man to Man* (f7), an annual publication available in bookstores or directly from the publisher at Spuistr. 21, Amsterdam, for listings of services for gay men. Disabled travelers might obtain the VVV's free and thorough pamphlet, *Holiday in Holland for the Handicapped.*

Drugs are illegal in this country, despite what you may hear or smoke. Although police largely ignore the soft drug scene, possession of less than 30g of hashish will make you subject to fines, and possession of more than this amount is a serious offense. Dutch police consider hard drugs a different category altogether, and punish offenders accordingly.

Although a sizable number of Dutch speak English extremely well, do try out their native tongue, which resembles German. "Yes" = *ja;* "no" = *nee;* "please" = *alstublieft;* "thank you" = *dank u;* and "hello" = *hallo.*

Dutch coins have names, just like in the U.S. and Canada: the *stuiver* (5¢), *dubbeltje* (10¢), *kwartje* (25¢), and *rijksdaalder* (f2.50). Banks are open weekdays from 10am to 5pm and usually on Thursday from 6 to 8pm or 7 to 9pm. Post offices, generally open weekdays from 9am to 5pm, exchange money at reasonable rates. Most shops and supermarkets are open Monday afternoons, Tuesday through Friday from 9am to 6pm, and Saturday 9am to 5pm. Most museums are open Tuesday through Sunday from 9am to 5pm. Shops close on all the standard holidays, as well as the Queen's Birthday (April 30), Ascension Day and Whitsunday and Whitmonday.

You can make international calls from payphones, which take 25¢ and f1 coins. For directory assistance, dial 008 (numbers within the Netherlands) or 06 04 18 (international); for collect calls, dial 06 04 10. To reach AT&T's **USA Direct,** dial 06, wait for a tone, then dial 022 91 11.

Accommodations and Camping

The VVV supply accommodations lists, and can nearly always find you a room and make advance reservations in other cities (f3.50 fee). A room in a private home costs about two thirds as much as a hotel, but these are not available everywhere—check with the VVV. During July and August many city councils levy a f2.50 "tourist tax," added to the price of all accommodations. The country's best values are the 43 **youth hostels** run by the **NJHC** (Dutch Youth Hostel Federation). The standard price is f19.50 for bed and breakfast, plus occasional high-season and prime-location supplements. Seven hostels are open year-round, 23 from March or April to September or October, and 13 in summer only. About half have cooking facilities. The VVV has a hostel list and the useful *Jeugdherbergen* brochure describes each hostel (both free). Contact the NJHC at Prof. Tulpplein 4, Amsterdam (tel. (020) 626 44 33; open Mon.-Fri. 9am-5pm). Youth hostel cards are available at hostels for f25 (bring a passport photo). Cycling from one hostel to another is an inspired plan if you're not lugging a huge pack; most hostels vend bike maps. Camping is possible all over the country, but many sites are crowded and trailer-ridden in summer. The VVV issues lists of campgrounds.

Food and Drink

Dutch food is hearty and simple: plenty of meat, potatoes, vegetables, bread, cheese, and milk. Slices of cold meat and fresh cheese on bread make for a typical breakfast. Dutch cheeses transcend *gouda* and *edam;* nibble *leiden* and the creamy *kernhem,* too.

At dinner, reap the benefits of Dutch imperialism: *rijsttafel* is an Indonesian specialty comprising up to 25 different dishes, such as curried chicken or lamb with pineapple, all served on a mountain of rice in Indonesian restaurants all over the country. Just as many restaurants turn out *pannekoeken,* the traditional Dutch supper of golden brown pancakes. Wash it all down with a foamy mug of superstar hometown beers *Heineken* and *Amstel,* or *jenever,* a strong gin made from juniper berries and traditionally accompanied by eel. If you are in one of the many university towns in Holland, you can eat cheaply and plentifully at student *mensas.*

Amsterdam

Anything goes in Amsterdam. The city's colorful Flower Market, seedy Red Light District, *cannabis*-scented coffeehouses and love for favorite son Rembrandt reflect a rich imagination and liberal mindset. On warm evenings, the Leidseplein fills with foreign crowds and the strains of jazz and blues until the early morning. The pleasures of the city's numerous museums complement outdoor concerts at Vondelpark and boat trips on the canals, many of which date from the imperialist years of the 17th century. These days, Amsterdam no longer seeks the world; the world seeks Amsterdam. However, the city that granted political asylum to English royalists *and* parliamentarians during the 17th century, and pioneered the dispensing of controlled amounts of methadone and heroin to addicts, has now begun to reconsider its long tradition of tolerance in light of steadily worsening crime and drug problems centered in Nieuwmarkt.

Orientation and Practical Information

The principal shareholder of the powerful Dutch East India company, and Europe's front door during the Golden Age of the 17th century, Amsterdam remains a major world transportation center, with budget flights all over the world (especially southeast Asia) and trains all over Europe.

Emerging from the train station, you will face roughly south onto **Damrak,** a key thoroughfare that splits the oldest parts of the city and leads to the **Dam,** its main square. Concentric canals ripple out around the Dam and the Centraal Station, so that the city resembles a horseshoe with the train station at the open northern end. In order, the canals lined by streets of the same name are **Singel, Herengracht, Keizergracht,** and **Prinsengracht.**

Amsterdam is best conquered by foot or bike. The names of streets change capriciously; buy a *Falk Plan* (f3) at the VVV. *Use It* (free at the VVV), includes a map, information on inexpensive accommodations, an index of youth agencies, and news about the city.

While illegal, marijuana and hashish are tolerated, and readily available at any of Amsterdam's myriad cafés and coffeehouses (which are listed in the *Mellow Pages,* available at bookstores). Ignore the street dealers who will undoubtedly approach you: the police are cracking down on hard drugs, and street hash is usually laced with something else, of poor quality, or nothing but wax. For information on the legal ins and outs of the Amsterdam drug scene, call 626 51 15 (Mon.-Fri. 9:30am-5pm). Anyone with drug-related health problems should call 555 55 55.

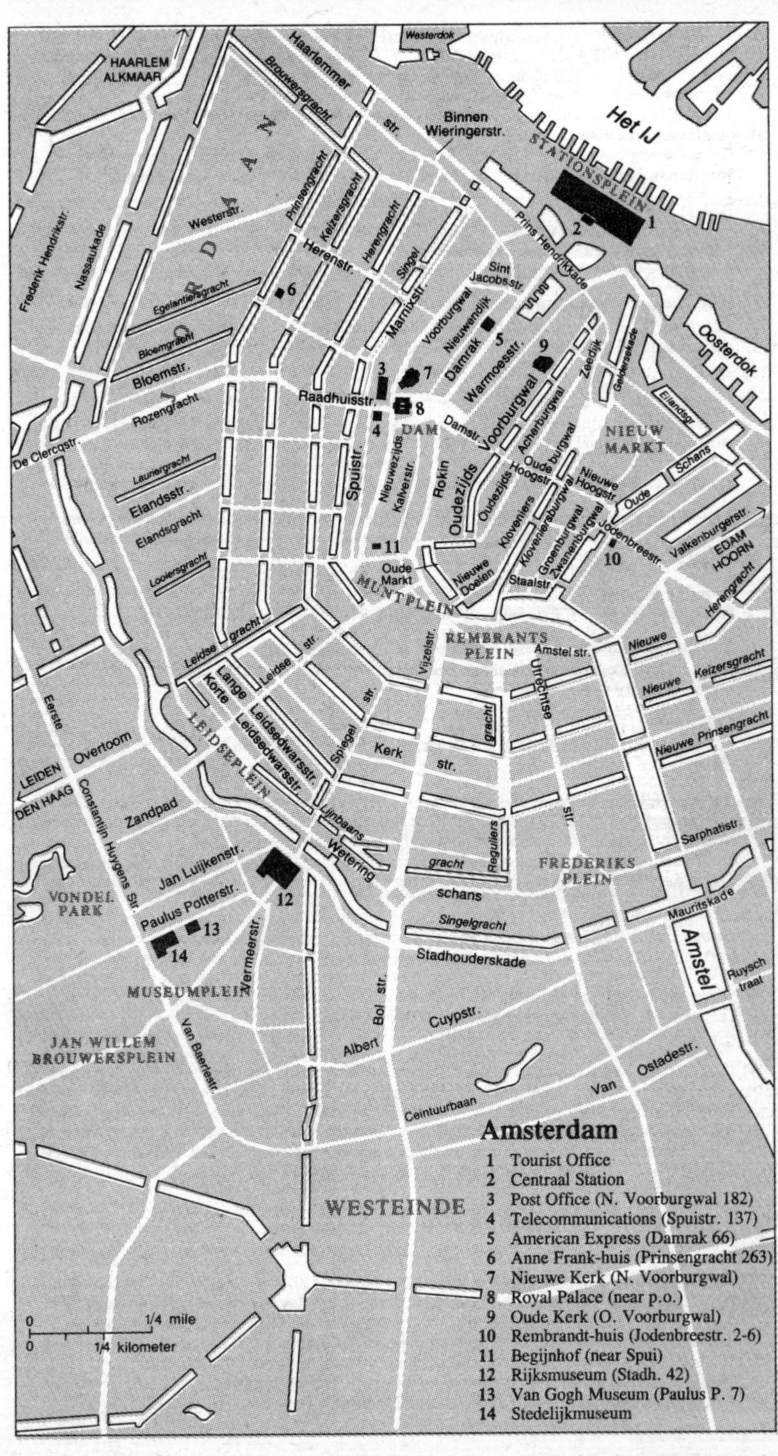
Westerdok
HAARLEM
ALKMAAR
Haarlemmer
str.
Brouwersgracht
Binnen
Wieringerstr.
Het IJ
STATIONSPLEIN
Prins Hendrikkade
Frederik Hendrikstr.
Nassaukade
Westerstr.
Prinsengracht
Keizersgracht
Herengracht
Herenstr.
Singel
Sint
Jacobsstr.
Egelantiersgracht
Bloemgracht
Bloemstr.
Marnixstr.
Voorburgwal
Nieuwendijk
Damrak
Warmoesstr.
Zeedijk
Geldersekade
Oosterdok
Elandsgr.
Raadhuisstr.
DAM
Damstr.
Voorburgwal
Achterburgwal
NIEUW
MARKT
Rozengracht
De Clercqstr.
Lauriergracht
Elandsstr.
Elandsgracht
Spuistr.
Nieuwezijds
Kalverstr.
Rokin
Oudezijds
Oudezijds
Oude
Hoogstr.
Nieuwe
Hoogstr.
Schans
Oude
Kloveniers
Kloveniersburgwal
Groenburgwal
Zwanenburgwal
Jodenbreestr.
Valkenburgerstr.
EDAM
HOORN
Looiersgracht
Oude
Markt
Nieuwe
Doelen
Staalstr.
Herengracht
MUNTPLEIN
REMBRANTS
PLEIN
Amstel str.
Nieuwe
Leidse
gracht
Leidse
str.
Vijzelstr.
Utrechtse
str.
Nieuwe
Keizersgracht
Lange
Korte
Leidsedwarsstr.
Leidsedwarsstr.
Spiegel
str.
gracht
Eerste
Overtoom
LEIDSEPLEIN
Kerk
str.
Nieuwe Prinsengracht
LEIDEN
DEN HAAG
Constantijn Huygens Str.
Zandpad
Lijnbaans
Wetering
Reguliers
gracht
Sarphatistr.
FREDERIKS
PLEIN
Jan Luijkenstr.
schans
Mauritskade
VONDEL
PARK
Paulus Potterstr.
Singelgracht
Amstel
Stadhouderskade
Vermeerstr.
Ruysch
traat
MUSEUMPLEIN
Bol str.
Cuypstr.
Albert
JAN WILLEM
BROUWERSPLEIN
Van Baerlestr.
Ostadestr.
Van
Ceintuurbaan
WESTEINDE
0 1/4 mile
0 1/4 kilometer
Amsterdam
1 Tourist Office
2 Centraal Station
3 Post Office (N. Voorburgwal 182)
4 Telecommunications (Spuistr. 137)
5 American Express (Damrak 66)
6 Anne Frank-huis (Prinsengracht 263)
7 Nieuwe Kerk (N. Voorburgwal)
8 Royal Palace (near p.o.)
9 Oude Kerk (O. Voorburgwal)
10 Rembrandt-huis (Jodenbreestr. 2-6)
11 Begijnhof (near Spui)
12 Rijksmuseum (Stadh. 42)
13 Van Gogh Museum (Paulus P. 7)
14 Stedelijkmuseum

Tourist Offices: VVV, Stationsplein 10 (tel. 626 64 44 daily 9am-5pm), in front of Centraal Station, to the left. Finds accommodations (f3.50 fee), changes money (at less than optimal rates), sells tickets, and plans excursions. Sells *What's On,* a fabulous day-by-day listing of all events in Amsterdam (f2.50). Go early to skirt long lines. Open July and Aug. daily 9am-11pm; Easter-June and Sept. Mon.-Sat. 9am-11pm; Oct.-Easter Mon.-Fri. 9am-6pm, Sat. 9am-5pm, Sun. 10am-1pm and 2-5pm. **Branch office,** Leidsestr. 106, at Korte Leidsedwarsstr. Offers the same services. Open July-Aug. daily 9am-11pm; Easter-June and Sept. Mon.-Sat. 9am-11pm, Sun. 9am-8:30pm; Oct.-Easter Mon.-Fri. 10:30am-5pm, Sat. 10:30am-8pm.

Budget Travel: NBBS, Rokin 38 (tel. 620 50 17). The Dutch student travel outfit. Budget flights; cheap fares to Asia. Open Mon.-Fri. 9:30am-5:30pm, Sat. 10am-4pm; mid-Aug. to mid-May closes Sat. at 3pm. **Budget Bus,** Rokin 10 (tel. 627 51 51). Also has good deals. InterRail sold. Open Mon.-Fri. 9:30am-5:30pm, Sat. 10am-4pm.

Consulates: U.S., Museumplein 19 (tel. 664 56 61). Open Mon.-Fri. 8:30am-noon and 1:30-3:30pm. **U.K.,** Koningslaan 44 (tel. 676 43 43). Open Mon.-Fri. 9am-noon and 2-4pm. Embassies of **Australia, Canada,** and **New Zealand** are in The Hague.

Currency Exchange: Change Express, Damrak 86 (tel. 624 66 82). Fine rates, the best deal for cash transactions. 3% up to f10 commission on traveler's checks only. Open daily 8am-midnight. **Branch offices** at Damrak 17 (open daily 8am-midnight), Kalverstr. 150 (open daily 8am-8pm), and Leidestr. 106 (open daily 8am-midnight). The *GWK* office at Centraal Station has dimmer rates, but is open 24 hrs. Avoid the **Chequepoint** booths on many corners, which offer deceptively good rates but skin you alive with their commission (up to 10%).

American Express: Damrak 66 (tel. 626 20 42). Excellent rates, no commission on any brand of traveler's checks. Open Mon.-Fri. 9am-5pm, Sat. 9am-noon. Cash machine for cardholders outside.

Post Office: Singel 250 (tel. 555 89 11), at Raadhuisstr. behind the Dam, has Poste Restante. Open Mon.-Wed. and Fri. 8:30am-6pm, Thurs. 8:30am-8pm, Sat. 9am-noon.

Telephones: Call first and pay afterwards at **Telehouse,** Raadhuisstr. 46-50, near the Dam (open 24 hrs.), or **TeleTalk Center,** Leidsestr. 101, near the Leidseplein (open daily 10am-midnight). **City Code:** 020.

Flights: Birds of all feathers flock together at **Schiphol Airport** (tel. 511 06 66 for charters; 601 09 66 for other flights). Trains connect it to Centraal Station (every 15 min., 16 min., f5).

Trains: All trains arrive at and depart from **Centraal Station,** Stationsplein 1, at the end of the Damrak and opposite the tourist office. Luggage storage. For international information and reservations, get a number at the booth, then wait inside the office until you're called. In summer, expect waits as long as 1 hr. Open for international information Mon.-Fri. 8am-10pm, Sat.-Sun. 9am-8pm; reservations Mon.-Fri. 8am-8pm, Sat.-Sun., 9am-5pm. For information, call 620 22 66 (international) or (068) 99 11 21 (domestic).

Buses: Trains are usually quicker and more convenient. The GVB (see under Public Transportation) will tell you if your destination lies on a rail line. If it doesn't, they'll direct you to one of 5 departure points for private buses. **Muiderpoort** (2 blocks east of Oosterpark) serves destinations to the east; **Marnixstation** (at the corner of Marnixstr. and Kinkerstr.), the west; and **Stationsplein depot** the north and south.

Public Transportation: A network of trams, buses, *nachtbussen* (night buses), and two subway lines connect you with points all over the city. Most tram and bus lines radiate from Amsterdam's Centraal Station and retire at midnight; get a separate schedule for the *nachtbussen.* Remember not to buy your tickets *(strippenkaart;* validate them on board) and Amsterdam day-passes *(dagkaart,* f9.50) on the bus (see "Getting Around" above). The GVB, Amsterdam's public transportation company, has an office on Stationsplein (tel. 627 27 27), which sells tickets and distributes the handy flyer *Public Transport.* Open Mon.-Fri. 7am-10:30pm, Sat.-Sun. 8am-10:30pm.

Taxis: Tel. 677 77 77, or at stands. Fares start at f4.80 plus f2.62 per km or min., more at night.

Bike Rental: All **train stations** rent bikes (f5-7 per day, f30-40 per week), but expect nothing fancy. **Koender's,** Stationsplein 33 (tel. 624 83 91). f8 per day, f30 per week. Open daily 8am-10pm. **Rent-a-Bike,** Damstr. 22 (tel. 625 50 29), near the Dam. f9 per day, f45 per week. Sells used bikes for f140-200. **Mac Bike,** Nieuwe Uilenburgerstr. 116 (tel. 620 09 85), near Waterlooplein. f10 per day, f50 per week. For day-long forays out of Amsterdam into windmill and cheese territory, try **Yellow Bike Tours,** N. Z. Voorburgwal 66 (tel. 620 69 40), for 6½-hr. trips daily April-Oct. at 8:30am and noon (f39).

Hitchhiking: Those hitching to Utrecht, central and southern Germany, and Belgium take tram #25 to the end and start at the bridge. Those heading to Groningen and northern Germany take bus #56 to Prins Bernhardplein or the Metro to Amstel and start along Gooiseweg. Those going to the airport, Leiden, and The Hague take tram #16 or 24 to Stadionplein and start on the other side of the canal on Amstelveenseweg. Those going to Haarlem, Alkmaar, and Noord Holland take bus #22 to Haarlemmerweg and start from Westerpark. The **International Lift Center,** Nieuwezijds Voorburgwal 256, 1st floor (tel. 622 43 42), riders and drivers for destinations all over Europe. Riders pay a f5-25 fee, plus 6¢ per km for gas. Open Mon.-Fri. 10am-6pm, Sat. 10am-4pm, Sun. noon-3pm; Oct.-Easter Mon.-Fri. 10am-5pm, Sat. noon-4pm.

Bookstores: W. H. Smith, corner of Kalverstr. and Spui. The granddaddy of English bookstores. Open Mon. 11am-6pm, Tues. 10am-6pm, Wed.-Fri. 9am-6pm, Sat. 10am-7pm, Sun. 11am-5pm. There's also a **book market** at Oudemanhuispoort, Mon.-Fri. 11am-4pm.

Laundry: Look for a *Wasserette* sign, or Oude Doelenstr. 12. (Open Mon.-Fri. 8:30am-7pm, Sat. 10am-4pm; last load 1 hr. before closing). **Happy Inn,** Warmoesstr. 30 (tel. 624 84 64), will wash, dry, and fold your clothes. f11 per 6kg. Open Mon.-Sat. 9am-6pm.

Women's Centers: De Kat, Wagenaarstr. 165 (tel. 694 72 14), near the Tropenmuseum. Open Tues., Thurs.-Fri., Sun. 9pm-midnight; coffee Wed. 10:30am-1pm; dinner Sun. 6pm (call in advance). **Tegen haar wil** (against her will) is a 24-hr. phone line for women threatened by violence: call 625 34 73.

Crises: Rape, 24-hr. hotline 625 34 73. **Drug counseling,** Binnenkant 46 (tel. 624 47 75), 10 min. from Centraal Station, near the Oosterdok. Open Mon.-Fri. 1-5pm. There's an open house on hard drugs Thurs. 8-11pm. For serious drug problems, go to the "Red Attic," Valckenierstr. 2 (tel. 555 53 49), near Weesperplein, on the 3rd floor. Open Mon.-Fri. 2-4:30pm. For general problems, call **SOS Luisterlijn** (tel. 676 12 01).

Gay Centers: COC, Rozenstr. 14 (tel. 626 30 87). The main source of info. Open Tues., Fri. and Sat. 1-5pm. Pub open Wed.-Thurs. 8pm-midnight, with dancing Fri.-Sat. 8pm-4am (women only on Sat.). The *Man to Man* guide (f7) has a "gay map" listing bars, shops, saunas, and more. *Top Guide* lists clubs and activities in Amsterdam. Help for victims of attack or discrimination available Wed. and Sun. 8pm-midnight (tel. 624 63 21). **Intermale,** Spuistr. 251 (tel. 625 00 09) is a gay bookstore. Open Mon. noon-6pm, Tues.-Sat. 10am-6pm. **Gay and Lesbian Switchboard** (tel. 623 65 65) is a phone service answered daily 10am-10pm, with information and advice for lesbians and gay men.

Medical Assistance: For hospital care, try **Academisch Medisch Centrum,** Meibergdreef 9 (tel. 566 91 11). Metro: Holendrecht. For free emergency medical care, visit the **Kruispost,** Oudezijds Voorburgwal 129 (tel. 624 90 21). Open daily 5pm-midnight. **Central Medical Service** (tel. 664 21 11) has lists of pharmacists, doctors, and dentists on duty 24 hrs. **Sexually Transmitted Disease Clinics** are at Groenburgwal 44 (tel. 625 41 27; open Mon.-Fri.8:30-10:30am) and at van Oldenbarneveldtstr. 42 (tel. 684 21 05 or 684 49 57; open Mon.-Fri. 1-3pm). Free and confidential. **AIDS Hotline,** (tel. 063 21 21 20 open Mon.-Fri. 2-10pm or 060 22 22 20).

Pharmacies: Everywhere. Open Mon.-Fri. 8:30am-5pm. When closed, each pharmacy *(apotheek)* posts a sign directing you to the nearest open one.

Emergencies: (tel. 06 11). **Police headquarters** at Elandsgracht 117 (tel. 559 91 11).

Accommodations and Camping

Amsterdam is a zoo of rooming possibilities. The city is packed from late June to mid-September, but you can always find a bed at the Sleep-In if the zillions of hostels and student hotels are full. A few of these take some advance reservations; for most, the best shot is to show up in the morning as rooms turn over.

The cheapest hotels, while not all that cheap (f40 and up per person), are comfortable. Both the IYHF and Christian hostels have clean rooms and curfews; the IYHF hostels and their coed dorms cater to a more swinging crowd, while the Christian hostels' single-sex dorms are safer and easily the best bargain in town. Private hostels generally purvey both private rooms and coed dorms; they charge a bit more for later (or nonexistent) curfews, and more laid-back (read: higher) atmospheres. Almost all accommodations lower their rates in the off-season; *Let's Go* lists summer prices.

In both institutional and private hostels, keep tabs on your valuables at all times. Use the lockers provided at many hostels; some will require your own padlock, available at **HEMA** (a department store behind the Damrak American Express) for f7-25.

At the station and tourist office you'll be accosted by people offering all kinds of lodgings. Many of the reputable hostels hire these hawkers to beat off the fierce competition, but exercise caution—the legitimate ones usually carry printed cards bearing their hostel's address and prices. Always ask to see the card before you follow one of them, and always carry your own luggage. Never pay before you look. Pass up offers for a cheap room on a houseboat; many of them violate fire regulations and are of dubious legality. If that doesn't scare you off, their diminutive rooms and oddball clientele will.

Institutional Hostels

Christian Youth Hostel Eben Haëzer, Bloemstr. 179 (tel. 624 47 17), 1 street from Rozengracht, in the nice part of town. Take tram #13 or 17 to Marnixstr. A pristine bargain, with a clean-cut and cheery staff. The maps cost 50¢, but the bibles are free. Rooms close 10am-2pm, but the lobby and snack bar stay open. Curfew midnight, Fri. and Sat. 1am. Ages 16-35 f13.50. Breakfast and shower included. Dinner f7.50. Lockers f10 deposit. Some advance reservations.

Christian Youth Hostel "The Shelter," Barndesteeg 21-25 (tel. 625 32 30), off the Nieuwmarkt, amidst the red lights. Larger and looser than Eben Haëzer, with snack bar (open 8am-11pm) and cozy courtyard. Same rates and curfew. Lockers 50¢ with f10 deposit.

Jeugdherberg Stadsdoelen (IYHF), Kloveniersburgwal 97 (tel. 624 68 32), between Nieuwmarkt and Rembrandtplein. Take tram #4, 9, 16, 24, or 25 to Muntplein. The more desirable of the two IYHF hostels. Spacious and clean. Rebuffs tour groups (yesss!). Bar has a pool table and a daily happy hour (8-9pm; beers f1). Reception open 7am-1am. Curfew 2am. f22, nonmembers f27, breakfast included. Sheets f5.50. Free lockers. Open mid-March to Oct.

Jeugdherberg Vondelpark (IYHF), Zandpad 5 (tel. 683 17 44), on a sleepy street bordering Vondelpark. Take tram #1, 2, or 5 from the train station to Leidseplein, then cross the main road Stadhouderskade and walk 2 streets to the left. Teeming with teens. Excellent facilities. Avoid the park when dark. Reception open 7am-12:30am. Lockout 10:45am-3:30pm. Curfew 2am; Nov.-April 1am. Happy hour 8-9pm. f22, nonmembers f27. Breakfast included. Sheets f5.50. Lockers 25¢ per day, deposit f10.

Private Hostels

Hotel Kabul, Warmoesstr. 38-42 (tel. 623 71 58), a 5-min. walk from Centraal Station, in the Red Light District. Huge, clean, and right in the thick of things. Floating canal bar (happy hour 10-11pm), with meals for f12.50, and live bands nightly (10pm-1 or 2am). Coffeehouse next door. Reception open 24 hrs. No curfew. Dorms f21. Singles f65. Doubles f75-90. Triples f110. Breakfast f6. Key deposit f15. Safe for valuables (f1) and lockers in the rooms.

International Budget Hotel, Leidsegracht 76 (tel. 624 27 84). Take tram #1, 2, or 5 to Prinsengracht, and walk 1 block to the right (as you face toward Leidseplein). Beautiful canal location. Reception open from 9am. No curfew. f27.50 per person in a 4-person dorm. Singles f55. Doubles f70-f90. Triples f105. Huge breakfast f5. Sheets and padlocks included.

Euphemia Budget Hotel, Fokke Simonszstr. 1-9 (tel. 622 90 45), 10 min. from Leidseplein. Take tram #16, 24, or 25 to Weteringschaus, cross back over Lijnbaansgracht, and turn right. Safe and comfortable, near the museums. Run by the same family as the International Budget Hotel. Dorms f25-30. Doubles f80. Triples f105. Breakfast and sheets included.

Frisco Inn, Beurstr. 5 (tel. 620 16 10), brushing the Red Light District close to the station. Cramped rooms but friendly and well-located. Dorms f30. Doubles f70. Triples f105. Quads f140. Some rooms have private showers.

't Ancker, De Ruijterkade 100 (tel. 622 95 60). From the back exit of Centraal Station, walk to your right 80m. Super-fun Irish woman and her Dutch husband keep these rooms in shipshape condition. Location makes it your best bet for the night before an early train. Bar open 24 hrs. Dorms f35. Doubles f80. Sheets, lockers (deposit f10) and all-you-can-eat breakfast included.

Bob's Youth Hostel, Nieuwezijds Voorburgwal 92 (tel. 623 00 63), not far from the Dam or Centraal Station. Take tram #1, 2, 5, 13, or 17. *The* hostel for glazed-eyed tokers. Curfew 3am. Dorms f19. Mattress on floor f16.50. Breakfast included. Lockers f25 deposit.

Sleep-In, s'-Gravesandestr. 51-53 (tel. 694 74 44). Board trams #3, 6, 9, 10, or 14 to Mauritskade, and walk back down Sarphatistr.; or hop night bus #77. Huge dorms with flimsy mattresses. Over 600 beds. Most efficient. Hip bands play Wed.-Sun. (f5 charge if you're not staying here); dances on Fri. Reception closed noon-4pm. f13.50 per person, f3 more for sheets (f20 deposit). Dinner f6.50-15. Information office open 10am-noon and 6-10pm. Bike rental (f10 per day) open 10am-noon and 7-8pm. Free lockers. Open year-round.

Hotels

Hotel van Onna, Bloemgracht 102 (tel. 626 58 01), in the Jordaan. Take tram #13 or 17 from Centraal Station. Well-kept. Reservations recommended. Singles, doubles, triples, and quads f50 per person. Big breakfast in a cheery, canal-view dining room included.

Hotel the Crown, Oude Zijds Voorburgwal 21 (tel. 626 96 64). Jovial atmosphere, keen location and sparkling rooms. Bar open 11am-6am. Dorms f30. Singles f60. Doubles f90-100. Quads with shower f100-140. Breakfast f10.

Hotel Bema, Concertgebouwplein 19 (tel. 679 13 96), across from the Concertgebouw. Take tram #16 (stop Museumplein). Spacious, spotless rooms near the museums. Bouncy American owner. Singles f55-60. Doubles f75-100. Triples f125-130. Quad f165. Breakfast in bed included. Reserve in advance.

Hotel Casa Cara, Emmastr. 24 (tel. 662 31 35), not far from the Vondelpark in a neat neighborhood. Take tram #16 or 2, or night bus #74. Singles f50-80. Doubles f70-95. Triples f125. Quads f150. Hearty breakfast included. Reserve ahead.

Hotel Groenendael, Nieuwendijk 15 (tel. 624 48 22), near the station. Friendly and comfortable—basically a hostel with private rooms. Singles f55. Doubles f75-85. Triples f105. Quads f130-140. Breakfast included. Reserve ahead—year-round.

Hotel Museumzicht, Jan Luykenstr. 22 (tel. 671 29 54). Singles f55, with shower f105. Doubles f90, with shower f115. Triples f120-145. Breakfast included. In a quiet, upstanding neighborhood near the museums and chock-full of similar budget hotels. Reserve in advance.

Hotel Pax, Raadhuisstr. 37 (tel. 624 97 35). Clean and simple; run by a friendly elderly couple for 28 years. f40 per person. **Hotel Ronnie,** Raadhuisstr. 41b (tel. 624 28 21). Smiling rooms and a jocose proprietor. Singles f45. Doubles f70-80. Triples f120. Hearty breakfast included. Both near the Dam. Book in advance.

Camping

Camping Zeeburg, Zuider-IJdijk 44 (tel. 694 44 30), next to the Amsterdam Rijncanal. Direct ferry connection with Centraal Station, or take buses #22 or 37, or night buses #71 or 76. Youth-oriented, with regular live music. f4.50 per person, f1.25 per tent. Showers f1. Open mid-April to Oct.

Gaasper Camping, Loosdrechtdreef 7 (tel. 696 73 26), in the idyllic Gaasper Park, 20 min. from Centraal Station by Metro (Gaasperplas) to the end stop, or night bus #72. Vast and fully rigged. f4.50 per person, f3.25-5 per tent. Showers f1. Washers and dryers f8.50. Call ahead or check with the VVV.

Food

Dutch cuisine is as subtle and refined as a wounded moose, but you won't go away hungry. *Eetcafés* strewn through Amsterdam purvey good meat-and-potatoes fare for about f12-20, especially in the Jordaan.

Luckily for the visitor, Amsterdam's restaurant scene has been colonized by various international cuisines. Taste Surinamian, Indonesian, Chinese, and Indian food in the Red Light District around the Nieuwmarkt, and off the Dam, on streets such as Hartenstraat. Indonesian *rijsttafel* (rice table)—15 to 20 dishes of chicken, curry, chutney, raisins, beef, nuts, shrimp, coconut, and a variety of hot sauces, all heaped onto mountains of rice—is ambrosia. *Automatiek* (self-service fast food stands) are reasonably priced. *Frikandel* (fried sausage) usually costs as little as f1.50. Indonesian *saté,* skewered meat in peanut sauce, is also readily available. Bakeries vending inexpensive cheese croissants and magnificent breads cluster along Utrechtsestr. south of Prinsengracht.

Fruit, cheese, flowers, clothes and sometimes even live chickens dominate the markets on Albert Cuypstraat, near the Heineken brewery, and on Ten Katestraat, in the Oud-West section of Amsterdam (both open Mon.-Sat. 9am-6pm). Ask at the VVV for their *Marktstad* brochure, listing the hours and addresses of all regular street markets. Shop for grocery essentials at the **Mignon supermarket** at Leidsestr. 74-6 near Prinsengracht (open Mon. 10am-6pm, Tues.-Wed. and Fri. 9am-6pm, Thurs. 9am-9am, Sat. 9am-5pm); the **Big Banana Nightshop** across the street is more expensive, but open daily until 1am. Health food nuts will shop 'til they drop at **Met de Natuuraan Tafel,** Weteringschans 135 (open Mon. 1-6pm, Tues.-Fri. 9am-6pm, Sat. 9am-5pm).

Mensa de Weesper, Weesperstr. 5, a university mensa beyond Waterlooplein. Excellent *standaarddagmenu* (menu of the day, f7.50) served Mon.-Fri. 5-7:15pm. Bar open 5pm-2am. Open early Aug.-June.

Atrium, Oude Zijds Achterburgwal 237 at Binnengasthuisstr. A huge, spotless university trough on the fringe of the Red Light District. Dinner f7.75, f5.75 with student ID. Open Mon.-Fri. noon-2pm and 5-7pm.

Bojo, Lange Leidsedwarstr. 51, near the Leidseplein. Crowded at dinner-time with tourists and locals seeking the terrific *rijsttafel* (f13.50-15.50) and other Indonesian fare (f11-17). Open Sun.-Thurs. 5pm-2am, Fri.-Sat. 5pm-5:30am.

Vegetarish Eethuis "Sisters," Nes 102, 300m from Dam Sq. Two women and one cat run this cavernous, bohemian eatery. Daily vegetarian special (f10) usually disappears by 7pm. Open Mon.-Fri. noon-9:30pm, Sat.-Sun. 2-9:30pm.

Egg Cream, Sint Jacobstr. 19, an alley off N.Z. Voorburgwal. Draws an animated crowd. Custom-built sandwiches f3-9; complete vegetarian dinner with salad f15.50. The apple crumble is the sweetest of Amsterdam's many sins. Open daily 11am-8pm.

The Pancake Bakery, Prinsengracht 191 (tel. 625 13 33), a long, canal-side block down from the Anne Frank Huis. Crowded with locals and out-of-towners. More than 50 varieties of the classic Dutch supper f6.50-16; omelettes f10-14. For a killer dessert, try the *kersen* (cherry) or *mokkakaramel* pancakes. Open daily noon-9:30pm.

Vishandel de Kreeft, Vijzelstr. 3, near Muntplein. A stand-up seafood counter where you can satisfy your salty, wet desires cheaply. Open Tues.-Sat. 10am-5:30pm.

Sights

Amsterdam's former town hall, **Koninklijk Paleis,** on the Dam, symbolizes the city's thriving commercial activity during the 17th century. The great Atlas on top ports the world on his shoulders—at a time when Dutch merchants sailed the seven seas, Amsterdam didn't think small. (Open June-Aug. daily 12:30-4pm. Admission f5.)

The **Rijksmuseum,** on Museumplein at Stadhouderskade 42, has a magnificent Dutch collection. Introductory slide shows every 20 minutes make this bevy o' art manageable. Attacked by a mad acid-thrower in 1990, Rembrandt's famous militia portrait *The Nightwatch* is now back on display, and a Rembrandt mega-exhibit will open in late 1991, forcing the temporary closure of the 16th- and 17th-century Dutch and Flemish holdings. (Museum open Tues.-Sat. 10am-5pm, Sun. 1-5pm. Admission f6.50, ages under 18 and over 64 and CJP holders f3.50.)

The renowned **Van Gogh Museum,** at Paulus Potterstr. 7, traces the artist's frenzied life through 200 of his paintings. (Open Mon.-Sat. 10am-5pm, Sun. 1-5pm. Admission f10, ages under 17 and over 64 and CJP holders f5, f3.50 with Museumkaart.) For a novel museum experience, drop by the **Tropenmuseum** (Museum of the Tropics), Linnaeusstr. 2 near the Oosterpark, a presentation center devoted to the people and problems of the Third World. Re-created villages and short slideshows transport you to the jungles of Africa and the mysterious back alleys of the Middle East. (Open Mon.-Fri. 10am-5pm, Sat.-Sun. noon-5pm. Admission f6, ages under 18 and over 65 and CJP holders f3.)

If the crowds at the Rijksmuseum or Van Gogh museum frazzle you, head for the nearby **Stedelijk Museum,** Paulus Potterstr. 13. Its collection of modern art stretches from French impressionists to German expressionists and Russian Suprematists. More contemporary figures also figure prominently, especially in the museum's unusual temporary exhibits. (Open daily 11am-5pm. Admission f17, under 17 and over 65 f3.50.)

A visit to the **Anne Frank Huis,** Prinsengracht 263, is profoundly stirring. In the attic of the annex to the house the young Jewish girl and her family held out in silence from the Nazis until 1944. The house now headquarters the city's anti-fascist and anti-racist movements. (Open Mon.-Sat. 9am-7pm, Sun. 10am-7pm. Long lines. Admission f6, under 17 f3.50, CJP holders f3.) Of related interest is the **Verzetsmuseum Amsterdam,** Lekstraat 63, which relates the poignant and rivoting story of the Nazi resistance in the Netherlands. Take trams #4 and 25. (Open Tues.-Fri. 10am-5pm, Sat., Sun. and holidays 1-5pm. Admission f3.50, free with museumkaart.) **Rembrandthuis,** Jodenbreestr. 4-6 (at the corner of the Oude Schans canal), is the home where the master lived, worked, and taught until it was confiscated by the city for taxes. The building holds 250 of Rembrandt's etchings and drypoints, as well as many of his tools and plates. (Open Mon.-Sat. 10am-5pm, Sun. 1-5pm. Admission f4, ages 10-15 f2.50, ages under 10 free.)

More obscure is the **Joods-Portuguese Synagogue** at Jonas Daniël Meijerplein, near Waterlooplein. A handsome 17th-century building, the synagogue was founded by Portuguese Jews expelled from their country. (Open Sun.-Fri. 10am-4pm. Free.) Next door at Jonas Daniël Meijerplein 2-4 is the **Joods Historisch Museum,** with exhibits on Jewish history and culture. (Open daily 11am-5pm. Admission f8.50.) The **Museum Amstelkring "Ons' Lieve Heer op Solder"** ("Our Lord in the Attic"), O.Z. Voorburgwal 40, in the Red Light District, dates from the days of the Reformation, when it was forbidden for Catholics to practice their faith in public. The former Catholic priest's *grachtenhuis* (house on a canal) houses a hidden church in its attic. (Open Mon.-Sat. 10am-5pm, Sun. 1-5pm. Admission f3.50, students, ages under 12 and over 65 f2.)

The retired **Heineken Brewery** at Stadhouderskade 78, is now a museum, giving 1½-hr. tours which culminate with three or four free rounds (daily at 9am, 9:45am, 10:30am, 1pm, 1:45pm and 2:30pm). Tickets go fast (on sale from 9am). The f2 admission fee goes to UNICEF. And of course, this modern-day Sodom and Gomorrah wouldn't be complete without the **Amsterdam Sex Museum,** on Damrak directly across from the tour boat docks—where else in the world can one have one's photo taken on the "lap" of a prodigious 7-ft. penis? (Open daily until 11:30pm. Admission f3.75.)

For a pleasing night of tourist-free strolling or café-hopping, visit the **Jordaan,** bounded roughly by Prinsengracht, Brouwersgracht, Marnixstr., and Lauriersgracht. Built as an artisan district in the Golden Age, it is the most intimate part of the city.

The **Red Light District,** bounded by Warmoestr., Gelderskade and Oude Doelenstr., is the vice sink of Europe. It will either repulse you or fulfill your every loathsome desire. Pushers, porn shops, and live sex theaters do a brisk business. Red neon marks houses of legal, if ill, repute. Unlike the illegal streetwalkers, these prostitutes have regular gynecological exams. Cops constantly patrol the quarter until midnight, and there's a police station on Warmoestr. Women should walk quickly and avoid eye contact with sleazy characters, unless they themselves are sleazy characters, in which case they should duck the competition and ply their trade elsewhere.

For refuge from Amsterdam's mobbed sights and seamy streets, find the **Begijnhof,** a beautifully maintained, grassy courtyard surrounded by 18th-century buildings; walk down Kalverstr. and turn onto Begijnensteeg, a small side street between Kalverstr. 130 and 132.

Entertainment

Cafés and Bars

Amsterdam's finest cafés are the old, dark, wood-paneled *bruine kroegen* (brown cafés) of the Jordaan, where denizens gather under the nicotine-stained ceilings and dim brass lamps to trade tales and crack jokes. Bars at Leidseplein and pricier Rembrandtplein are tourist warrens. Most cafés open at 10 or 11am and close at 1am on Fridays and 2am Saturdays.

Café Twee Prinsen, Prisenstr. 27, on the edge of the Jordaan. Crowded at night with upscale Dutch revelers.

The Bulldog, on Leidseplein. Next door to the coffeeshop. A huge place, always romping at night. The best place to meet fellow travelers.

Café de Tuin, Tweede Tuindwarsstr. 13, and **de Reiger,** Nieuwe Leliestr. 34, both in the Jordaan, attract a young, artsy set.

Le Shako, 's-Gravelandse Veer 2 (tel. 624 02 09), near Amstel. A popular mixed gay bar. Open Sun.-Thurs. 9pm-2am, Sat.-Sun. 9pm-3am.

Grand Café Dulac, Haarlemserstr. 118, near the station. Sensual seating decorated to resemble a fantasy from "1001 Nights." Erotic statues jump out of every bright, metallic corner. Open daily 4pm-1am or 2am.

Coffeehouses

Some coffeehouses specialize not in *espresso* and *café au lait* but in Thai stick and Jamaican sensemilla. While police have outlawed the hemp-leaf stickers that once adorned the windows for being too obvious, any green, leafy foliage in the window, or the green, yellow, and red that symbolize Rastafarianism, are signs that marijuana, hashish, and sometimes spacecakes may be available within. The **Coffeeshop 36,** Warmoesstr. 36, next to the Hotel Kabul in the Red Light District, is the granddaddy of coffeehouses. All types hang out here, amidst the blaring music. (Open Sun.-Thurs. 10am-1am, Fri.-Sat. 10am-2am.) **The Grasshopper,** Nieuwzijds Voorburgwal 57, gently simmers across the street from Bob's Youth Hostel, and is much frequented by its guests. (Open Sun.-Thurs. 10am-midnight, Fri.-Sat. 10am-1am.) Bumblebees vanish against the yellow-and-black decor of the **Mellow Yellow,** Vijzelstr. 33. A short walk up Vijzelstr. (away from the center) takes you to a calm canalside park to chill. (Open Sun.-Thurs. 8:30am-1am, Fri.-Sat. 8:30am-2am.)

Live Music

Though Amsterdam lacks a thriving, world-class music scene, you can hear all sorts of bands here—often for no more than the cost of a beer (f2-2.50).

Melkweg, Lijnbaasgracht 234a (tel. 624 17 77), in an old factory off Leidseplein, directly across from the police station. Amsterdam's legendary nightspot manages to retain a cutting-edge aura despite the crowds. Explore a galaxy of entertainment options: live bands (best on weekends), theater, films, an art gallery, an anti-apartheid bookshop, and a snack bar famous for its spacecakes. Open Wed.-Thurs. and Sun. 7pm-2am, Fri.-Sat 7pm-4am. Cover charge f7-15 plus membership fee (f3.50, good for 1 month), f13-21 plus membership on the weekends. Box office open Mon.-Fri. noon-5pm, Sat.-Sun. 4-7pm, and while the club is open.

Paradiso, Weteringschans 6-8 (tel. 626 45 21). Some of the foremost international punk, new-wave, and reggae bands play here. Admission f10-27, depending on the band. Shows start at 10pm; check outside or call to learn the evening's guests.

Maloe Melo, an old garage at Lijnbaansgracht 160 (tel. 625 33 00), across the canal from the huge Texaco station. Enjoy the bar and the city's best blues at close quarters. No cover. Open Mon.-Thurs. 10pm-3am, Fri.-Sat. 10pm-4am. Music until 2am, a bit later on weekends.

De Kroeg, Lijnbaansgracht 163 (tel. 625 01 77). Vibrant crowds writhe to live reggae, salsa, rock, and blues. Open Tues.-Thurs. and Sun. 10pm-3am, Fri.-Sat. 10:30pm-4am. Music starts at 11:30pm. No cover some nights; weekends usually f3 or f5.

Odeon Jazz Kelder, Singel 456, near Leidsestr. Best jazz in town, with an upscale crowd. Open Sun.-Thurs. 10pm-4am, Fri.-Sat. 10pm-3am. Cover f7.50, f12.50 on weekends.

Dancing

Many nightclubs in Amsterdam charge a membership fee in addition to the normal cover, so the tab can be hefty. There are expensive discos aplenty on Prinsengracht, near Leidsestr. and on Lange Leidsedwarsstr.

Roxy, Singel 465. The hippest crowd in town busts a move to 90's house and acid house. Obvious tourist attire rebuffed. Open Wed.-Sat. around 11pm-4am. Cover f8, f12 on weekends.

Mazzo, Rozengracht 114 (tel. 26 75 00), in the Jordaan. An open-minded, artsy disco that changes its front display and slideshow every 3 weeks. Open Sun.-Thurs. 11pm-4am, Fri.-Sat. 11pm-5am. Live music Tues. Cover (including 1st drink) f7.50, f10 on weekends.

Dansen bij Jansen, Handboogstr. 11, near Spui. Location near the university makes it popular among students (officially, a student ID is required). Happy hour Sun.-Wed. 11pm-midnight. Open Sun.-Thurs. 11pm-4am, Fri.-Sat. 11pm-5am. Cover f3.50, f4 on weekends.

iT, Amstelstr. 24, near Waterlooplein. Clients tout this as one of the best and most decadent gay discos in Europe. Open Thurs. and Sun. 11pm-4am, Fri.-Sat. 11pm-5am.

Theater, Dance, and Music

VVV puts out *What's On* (f2.50), with comprehensive cultural listings. From June through August, there are free performances Wednesday through Sunday at the **Vondelpark Openluchttheater** (tel. 673 14 99); jazz and folk concerts dominate, but experimental and children's theater, political music, reggae, mime, and pop also grab the limelight. Check posters at park entrances. The June **Holland Festival** of dance, drama, and music is closely followed by the **Summer Festival** of small theater companies in July. (Contact the Balie Theatre on Leidseplein, tel. 623 13 11; tickets f10-15.) The sparkling new **Muziektheatre,** perched over the junction of the Amstel and the Oude Schans (tel. 625 54 55), hosts the **Netherlands Opera** and the **National Ballet.** The **Stadsschouwburg** at Leidseplein 26 (tel. 624 23 11) presents modern dance and Dutch-language theatre. The Royal Concertgebouw Orchestra, one of the world's finest, is conducted by Ricardo Chailly at the Concertgebouw on Van Baerlestr. (Concerts start at 8:15pm, tickets f25). Make reservations for any cultural event, in person only, at the **Amsterdams Uit Buro (AUB),** Leidseplein 26 (tel. 621 12 11; open Mon.-Sat. 10am-6pm). The VVV Tourist Office theater desk, Stationsplein 10 (open Mon.-Sat. 10am-4pm) and the larger tourist bureaus in Holland (VVV I) also operate ticket-reservation services.

There is English-speaking theater year-round in De Stalhouderij, eerste Bloemdwarsstr. 4 (tel. 626 22 82). Also try the **Bellevue,** Leidsekade 90 (tel. 624 72 48). Frequent English-language performances and cabarets are given at the theater/café **Suikerhof,** Prinsengracht 381 (tel. 22 75 71; open daily from 5pm, Sun. from 2pm).

Organ concerts resound Wednesday evenings at 8:15pm during the summer at **Oude Kerk,** Oude Kerksplein 23 (tel. 624 91 83); **Westerkerk,** where Rembrandt is buried, at Prinsengracht 281 (tel. 624 77 66); and **Nieuwe Kerk,** where Dutch monarchs are sworn in (they're not crowned), on the Dam (tel. 626 81 68). Prices are f5-12.50.

Near Amsterdam

When you tire of free and easy Amsterdam, explore the surrounding countryside. Trains are expensive, so buy a cheap day return or get a one-day bus pass (f18.10). **Alkmaar,** 45 minutes by train (4 per hr.) from Amsterdam, holds an open-air **cheese market** every Friday from 10am to noon from mid-April to mid-September.

Edam, another cheeseville, is rich in history and karma. The 15th-century **Grote Kerk,** or **St. Nicolaaskerk,** is the largest three-ridged church in Europe and has 30 superb stained-glass windows. Since Edam sits off the train line, take the NZH bus from opposite Centraal Station in Amsterdam (7 strips). Rent a bike at **de Smederij,** Voorhaven 115 (tel. (02993) 721 55), for f7.50 and cross to the island of **Marken** (25 min.), connected to the mainland by causeway. The **Marken Museum,** Kerkbuurt 44-47, displays images of life on Marken in earlier days. (Open Easter-Oct. Mon.-Sat. 10am-4:30pm, Sun. noon-4pm. Admission f4.) To reach the island, take bus #110 to Volendam. To return, take bus #111.

Hoorn, an old whaling town that attached its name to the tip of South America, celebrates each Wednesday morning during July and August with a full market with old-time Dutch costumes, dancing, and food. **Jeugdherberg de Toorts (IYHF),** Schellinkhouterdijk (tel. (020) 551 31 55), solves your lodging quandries with bunk beds near a sandy beachfront. (f19.50, nonmembers f24.50. Breakfast included. Open July-Aug.) On the Amsterdam-Enkhuizen rail line, Hoorn is yours in a flash. You can also take a direct bus (Mon.-Sat. 2 per hr., Sun. 1 per hr. until 10:02pm; 11 strips) or bus #114 to Edam (2 per hr., 7 strips).

Haarlem

Haarlem, 20km from Amsterdam, quietly entices visitors with the same glorious façades and romantic canals that inspired revolutionary Dutch artists during the Golden Age. Seek out the 17th- and 18th-century *hofjes* (almshouses for elderly women), red-brick structures with grassy and blooming courtyards. Two hold particular charm: secluded **Hofje van Bakenes,** Wijde Appelaarsteeg 11, near the Teylers Museum (open Mon.-Sat. 10am-5pm); and the **Hofje van Oirschot,** at the end of Kruisstr., where it becomes Barteljorisstr. These are private property and still inhabited—be tactful and discreet.

From the station, Kruisweg leads to the **Grote Markt** and the glorious medieval **Stadhuis** (Town Hall), originally the 13th-century hunting lodge of the Count of Holland. (When the Hall of Counts is not in use, you can sneak a free peek at the lavishly furnished interior—ask at the reception desk.) The **Grote Kerk** graces the opposite end of the Grote Markt and still houses the Müller organ, which Mozart played at age 11 (the organ was 28). (Church open Mon.-Sat. 10am-4pm. Admission f2, children f1. Free organ recitals May-Oct. Tues. 8:15pm and Thurs. 3pm.) From the church, walk down Damstr. to the Netherlands's oldest museum, the **Teylers Museum** at Spaarne 16. The museum lets you see what people in 1788 thought a museum should be: a blend of scientific instruments of the era, fossils, coins, paintings, and superb drawings, including works by Raphael and Michelangelo. (Open Tues.-Sat. 10am-5pm, Sun. 1-5pm. Admission f6.50, seniors, children, and CJP holders f4.50.)

The legacy of Frans Hals, the brash portraitist who spent his life in Haarlem and now reposes in the Grote Kerk, lives on in the **Frans Hals Museum,** Groot Heiligland 62. Housed in a charming 17th-century almshouse and courtyard, the collection includes Hals' lively group portraits and a permanent collection of modern art. (Open Mon.-Sat. 11am-5pm, Sun. 1-5pm. Admission f4.50, seniors, children, and CJP holders f2.) Also visit the **Corrie Ten Boomhuis,** better known as The Hiding Place, Barteljorisstr. 19, where Corrie Ten Boom and her family hid Jewish refugees during WWII. The refugees were never discovered, but the entire Ten Boom family was removed to concentration camps; Corrie was the only survivor. (Tours on the hour Mon.-Sat. 10am-4pm; Nov.-April Mon.-Sat. 11am-4pm. Donation requested.) Note that this and the Frans Hals Museum are two of the rare Dutch museums to open on Monday, making it and Saturday, when a technicolor **flower and fruit market** fills the Grote Markt, ideal days to visit Haarlem.

The **VVV,** Stationsplein 1 (tel. (023) 31 90 59), sells an excellent map of Haarlem for f1. (Open Mon.-Sat. 9am-5:30pm; Oct.-March Mon.-Fri. 9am-5:30pm, Sat. 10am-4pm.) A super-cheery staff keeps the clean but worn **Jeugdherberg Jan Gijzen,** Jan Gijzenpad 3 (tel. (023) 37 37 93) jolly up to its midnight curfew. Bus #2 or 6 (direction: "Haarlem-Nord") will drive you the 3km from the station to the hostel; tell the driver your destination. (Reception open 8am-noon and 4-8pm. f19.50, nonmembers f24.50. Breakfast included. Open March-Oct.) The VVV can book you a private room for around f26 (fee f7 per person). Haarlem apparently has not heard of budget hotels, but try the ideally located **Hotel Carillon,** Grote Markt 27 (tel. (023) 31 05 91). (Singles f45. Doubles f75-97.50. Triples f107-128. Breakfast included.) The **Stads Café,** Zijlstr. 56-58 (tel. (023) 32 52 02), offers Dutch cuisine (daily *dagschotel,* or menus, f8.75), and commodious sleeping quarters. (Singles f45-70. Doubles f70-85. Breakfast f8. Café open Mon.-Sat. 7:30am-1am, Sun. 2pm-1am.) **Camp** at **De Liede,** Liewegje 17 (tel. (023) 33 23 60). Take bus #92 or 93 direction "Waarderpolder" and walk 10 minutes (f4 per person, f4 per tent). When these hotels fill, ship out to the cheap pensions in nearby Zandvoort (see Near Haarlem).

Pannekoekhuis De Smikkel, Kruisweg 57, serves plump buttery pancakes (f6.50-12.25) dripping with anything from bananas to seafood. (Open Tues.-Sat. 11:30am-8pm, Sun. 2-8pm.) For healthier fare (almost anything would be), try out **Eko Eetcafé,** Zijlstr. 39. They serve a verdant vegetarian plate for f16, and pizzas for f12-16.50. (Open daily 5:30-9:30pm.)

Haarlem is easily accessible from Amsterdam by train (4 per hr.) or by bus #80 from Marnixstr., near Leidseplein (2 per hr.). Five night buses (#86) cruise from Amsterdam's Leidseplein to Haarlem (12:42am-3:20am), but none go from Haarlem to Amsterdam.

Near Haarlem

Haarlem is only 10 minutes by train from **Zandvoort** beach (2-6 per hr., round-trip f3.50). South of here, between *paal* (wooden posts) #68 and 71, is a popular nude beach. Zandvoort hosts scads of cheap pensions. **Pension Troost,** Brederodestr. 11 (tel. (02507) 180 10), has sandy but spruce rooms (singles f32.50, doubles f65), as does nearby **Pension Zwanenest,** Brederodestr. 92a (tel. (02507) 164 57; singles f35, doubles f60). **Bloemendaal** is a more repressed beach, accessible by bus #81 (1 per hr.) from the Haarlem train station. During late March, April and May, over five million bulbs flourish at the splendiferous **Keukenhof** garden (admission f13). Take bus #50 or 51 toward Lisse from the Haarlem train station; a combination bus and admission ticket bought at Centraal Station (f19) saves money. An international flower auction is held year-round in the nearby town of **Aalsmeer;** visitors can watch from a special gallery. From Haarlem, take bus #140. (Open Mon.-Fri. 7:30-11am; the most active bidding 8-9am.) The **Frans Roozen Gardens** bloom with 500 different types of flowers and plants; summer flower shows are free. Bus #90 (direction "Den Haag") stops in front of the gardens. (Open July-Oct. Mon.-Fri. 9am-5pm. Tulip show April-May daily 8am-6pm.) Bus #50 or 51 south of Haarlem runs past some of Holland's famous flower fields. Daffodils blossom in early to late April, hyacinths in mid- to late April, and tulips from late April to mid-May.

Leiden

The University of Leiden is Holland's oldest, a reward of William the Silent, a.k.a. William of Orange, in 1574 to the people of Leiden for withstanding a Spanish siege during the struggle for independence. The resourceful residents threw open local dykes, flooding the surrounding plain and thwarting the Spanish armies. Leiden is an archetypal college town, brimming with bookstores, cafés, bicycles, and 11 diverse museums. The **VVV,** Stationsplein 210 (tel. (071) 14 68 46), across the street and to the right of the station, doles out museum brochures and free maps. Their brochures, such as the "Rembrandt Tour" and the "Pilgrim Tour" point out creative routes to see the town on foot (50¢ each). (Open Mon.-Fri. 9am-5:30pm, Sat. 9am-4pm.) The **Rijksmuseum voor Volkenkunde** (National Museum of Ethnology), Steenstr. 1, effervesces with rainbow artifacts from the Dutch East Indies. The Buddha room, with five portly bronze residents, is world-famous. (Open Nov.-Sept. Tues.-Sat. 10am-5pm, Sun. 1-5pm. Admission f3.50; over 65, under 18, and CJP holders f2.) The **Rijksmuseum van Oudheden** (National Antiquities Museum), Rapenburg 28, harbors the complete, lovingly restored Egyptian Temple of Taffeh, which the Dutch removed from the reservoir basin of the Aswan Dam and opened to the public in 1979. (Open Tues.-Sat. 10am-5pm, Sun. 1-5pm. Admission f3.50, over 65, under 18, and CJP holders f2.) The university's garden, the **Hortus Botanicus** at Rapenburg 73, is one of Europe's oldest. It includes greenhouses and a newly-minted Japanese garden. (Garden open April-Sept. Mon.-Sat. 9am-5pm, Sun. 10am-5pm; some greenhouses have pruned hours. Admission f1, seniors and CJP holders 50¢.) Propel yourself to the top of a functioning Dutch windmill and inspect its mechanical innards at the **Molenmuseum "De Valk,"** 2de Binnenvestgracht 1, built in 1743. (Open Tues.-Sat. 10am-5pm, Sun. 1-5pm. Admission f3, over 65, under 18, and CJP holders f1.50, free with Museumkaart.) Other museums in Leiden showcase everything from clay tobacco pipes to cameras.

Leiden is a budget accommodation seeker's paradise. Rest your weary bones at the newly opened **Jeugdhotel,** Lange Scheistr. 9, off Oude Singel (tel. (071) 12 84 57), a bargain with 4-10 bed dorm rooms, just outside the pedestrian district. (f20 per night. Sheets f5. Breakfast f5. Showers included. Phone reservations accepted and recommended.) **Pension In de Goede Hoek,** Diefsteeg 19a (tel. (071) 12 10 31), fronts the sweetest deal in town, with a color TV in every room and a great location near the Stadhuis. (Singles f26. Doubles f55. Showers, breakfast and—honest to God—lunch included.) Otherwise, try either **Pension Witte,** Witte Singel 80 (tel. (071) 12 45 92; singles f36, doubles f75; breakfast included), or the neighboring **Pension Bik,** Witte Singel 92 (tel. (071) 12 26 02; similar prices and rooms). When the students go home, the **VVV** may be able to locate you a room in a private home (min. stay usually 3 nights). Idyllic **Jeugdherberg De Duinark (IYHF),** Langevelderlaan 45 (tel. (02523) 729 20), is 18km from Leiden in Noordwijk. Take bus #60 from the Leiden train station to Sancta Maria; the hostel is a 15-minute jaunt down the road. Reserve ahead. (April-Sept. f22; Nov.-March f21; nonmembers f5 extra. Sheets f5.50.)

For Leiden's cheapest bite, try the university mensas: **Augustinus,** Rapenburg 24, serves meals for f4.95 (open Sept.-June Mon.-Fri. 5:30-7:15pm), while **De Bak,** Kaiserstr. 23-25, spins vegetarian dishes for f4.65. (Open mid-Aug. to late July Mon.-Fri. noon-2pm and 5:30-6:30pm.) **Café de Illegale,** Hooigracht 72, draws an intellectual crowd with scrumptious daily specials (f9.50). Someone will usually be crooning and playing guitar on Tuesday and Sunday nights. (Open Sun.-Thurs. 5-10pm, Fri.-Sat. 5-11pm.) Under the windmill, you can eat your packed lunch from the **Dagmarkt** supermarket, on the corner of Stationsweg and Stationsplein, just across from the station. (Open Mon. 1-6pm, Tues.-Fri. 9am-6pm, Sat. 9am-5pm.) The renovated area near Pieterskerk harbors sedate coffee shops.

Leiden makes an appealing rail daytrip from Amsterdam (4 per hr. from Centraal Station, 30 min.) or the Hague (2 per hr., 20 min.).

The Hague (Den Haag)

Although Amsterdam is the capital of the Netherlands, the seat of government is The Hague. Here the streets are broader, the buildings grander, and the roses redder. This cool city of diplomats also harbors the royal residence and the International Court of Justice, which meets at the Peace Palace. In **Scheveningen,** a popular beach and nightspot northwest of the city, the fisherfolk still don centuries-old traditional costume. To the south of The Hague lies **Kijkduin,** a peacefully quiet family seaside resort.

Practical Information

Tourist Offices: **VVV,** Kon. Julianaplein 30 (tel. (070) 354 62 00), in front of Centraal Station, on the right side. Peddles maps (f1.50), books rooms (f3.50 fee) and publishes events listings. Open Mon.-Sat. 9am-9pm, Sun. 10am-5pm; mid-Sept. to March Mon.-Sat. 9am-6pm, Sun. 10am-5pm.

Budget Travel: NBBS, Schoolstr. 24 (tel. 346 58 19). Long lines pay off in cheap tix. Open April-Sept. Mon.-Fri. 9:30am-5pm, Sat. 10am-3pm.

Embassies: U.S., Lange Voorhout 102 (tel. 362 49 11). Open Mon.-Fri. 8:30am-5:15pm. **Canada,** Sophialaan 7 (tel. 361 41 11). Open Mon.-Fri. 9am-1pm and 2-5:30pm. **U.K.,** Lange Voorhout 10 (tel. 364 58 00). Open Mon.-Fri. 9am-1pm and 2:15-5:30pm. **Australia,** Carnegielaan 12 (tel. 310 82 00). Open Mon.-Fri. 9am-12:30pm and 2-5:30pm. **New Zealand,** Mauritskade 25 (tel. 346 93 24). Open Mon.-Fri. 9am-12:30pm and 1:30-5:30pm.

American Express: Venestr. 20 (tel. 346 95 15), near the Binnenhof. Open Mon.-Fri. 9am-5pm, Sat. 9:30am-12:30pm.

Post Office: Nobelstr. and Prinsenstr. (tel. 384 58 45), near the Grote Kerk. Poste Restante. Open Mon.-Wed. and Fri. 8:30am-6:30pm, Thurs. 8:30am-8:30pm, Sat. 9am-noon. Branch office at Koningin Julianaplein 6, to the left of the station. Open Mon.-Fri. 8am-6pm.

Telephones: City Code: 070.

Trains: Tel. 068 99 11 21 for information. Trains serving Amsterdam and Rotterdam use **Holland Spoor;** most others use **Centraal Station.** Reach Centraal Station and the VVV from Holland Spoor by *stoptrein* or tram #9 or 12. Both have lockers (f1) and baggage check (f1.35).

Ferries: Regular ferries run between nearby ports and England. **North Sea Ferries,** Luxembourgweg 2 (tel. (01819) 555 55) steams from Rozenburg-Europort to Hull (1 per day at 6pm, f165). **Stena Line** (tel. (017) 47 41 40) sails from Hoek van Holland to Harwich (2 per day at noon and 10:30pm, f100).

Bike Rental: At both Holland Spoor (tel. 389 08 30) and Centraal Station (tel. 385 32 35). f7 per day, deposit f100 or an ID. Cycling maps available at the VVV (f5.40-9.95).

Emergencies: (tel. 0611).

Accommodations and Food

The Hague's lack of budget accomodations makes it a prime daytrip from Delft or Rotterdam (at least 4 trains per hr. to both). If you stay, private homes are a good option (from f30; ask at the tourist office). **Jeugdherberg Ockenburgh (IYHF),** Monsterseweg 4 (tel. (070) 397 00 11), 8km from town in Kijkduin, is accessible with difficulty by buses #122, 123, or 124 from Centraal Station; alert the driver, then follow the signs (10 min.). Enormous and antiseptic, it's a 15-minute hoof from the beach. (Reception open 8am-11pm. Curfew midnight, but the door opens briefly at 1, 2 and 3am. Dorms f22, nonmembers f27.15. Singles f40, doubles f60. Sheets f5.75.) The Hague's cheap hotel rooms cluster in the seedy and somewhat dangerous neighborhood around the Holland Spoor train station; ship out to more pleasant quarters in nearby Scheveningen. **Hôtel Lubèl,** Haagsestr. 53, in Scheveningen (tel. (070) 354 58 03), will set you up in a tidy single (f40) or double (f90). Take bus #22 from the station (direction "Scheveningen") and tell the driver your destination. Pitch a tent near the beach at **Ockenburgh,** Wijndaelerweg 16 (tel. (070) 25 23 64). Take tram #3 from Centraal Station. (f3 per person, f11 per site. Open April to mid-Oct.)

Eating in this city of diplomats may require an expense account. Join ordinary citizens in the covered market at **Markthof,** Spuistr., a few blocks from Binnenhof, along Grote Marktstr. (Open Tues.-Wed. and Fri.-Sat. 9am-6pm, Mon. 11am-6pm, Thurs. 9am-9pm.) Enjoy a special night on the town strolling along **Denneweg,** a street lined with tiny exotic holes-in-the-wall simmering food ranging from Thai to traditional Dutch to steakhouses.

Sights

A visit to the **Binnenhof,** the courtyard whose buildings house the Netherlands's Parliament, is enough to make you want a career in Dutch politics. Guided tours (leaving from Binnenhof 8a) begin with an audiovisual presentation, and move on to the **Ridderzaal** (Hall of Knights) and usually one or both of the chambers of the States General. (Open Mon.-Sat. 10am-4pm, Sun. noon-4pm; Sept.-June Mon.-

Sat. 10am-4pm. Admission f1.75-4.75.) Just outside the north entrance of the Binnenhof, the **Mauritshuis,** a 17th-century mansion, houses a heavyweight collection of Dutch paintings, including Rembrandt's *De Anatomieles van Professor Tulp* (The Anatomy Lesson) and Vermeer's *Lady with a Turban.* (Open Tues.-Sat. 10am-5pm, Sun. 11am-5pm. Admission f6.50, seniors, under 18, and CJP holders f3.50.) Mavens of abstraction will adore the **Haags Gemeentemuseum,** Stadhouderslaan 41, which houses the largest assemblage of Mondrians in the world. (Open Tues.-Sun. 11am-5pm. Admission f7, seniors and children f6, CJP holders f5.)

The extravagant **Peace Palace,** which houses the International Court of Justice, glistens in the sun at Carnegieplein (after Andrew Carnegie, who funded the palace with the sweat and blood of the American proletariat), ten minutes from the Binnenhof. The palace often closes when the Court is in session; call ahead to check if it's open to the public (tel. 346 96 80). Theoretically, there are guided tours. (Mon.-Fri. at 10am, 11am, 2pm and 3pm. Admission f3, under 15 f2.50.) Stay away from the hordes who descend daily upon the **Madurodam,** the city's cheesiest and most overpriced sight—a miniature town with chest-high models of every famous edifice in Holland.

The **Haags Filmhuis,** Denneweg 56 (tel. 345 99 00), features oldies and the best of current movies; all films are shown in their original language. (Admission f10-12.50, students and seniors f9.50-10. Shows nightly at 7:30pm and 9:45pm.) **Muziekcafé La Valletta,** Nieuwe Schoolstr. 13a (tel. 364 45 43), is a jazz café nearby with live shows Monday nights at 10pm (open daily 5pm-1am; free). **Fireworks** explode from the pier at the beach in Scheveningen every Friday night in July and August, and in mid-June the beach hosts the **International Fokker Kite Flying Festival.** Mid-July brings the 17th annual **North Sea Jazz Festival** to the Hague, with four straight days of jazz, gospel concerts and dance contests. For a complete list of music and theater events, festivals, and exhibits, pick up the brochure *Info* from the VVV.

Rotterdam

A barrage of German bombs obliterated Rotterdam's center on May 14, 1940, cowing the Netherlands into a hasty surrender. The rebuilt city is thoroughly modern and frequently ugly. Its center of gravity is its port, the largest in the world.

Ossip Zadkine's incredible **Monument for the Destroyed City,** a statue of a person screaming, arms raised in self-defense and guts wrenched out, illustrates the 1940 bombing raid (take the subway or trams #1, 3, or 6 to Churchillplein—it's behind the Maritime museum). A giant paper clip stands near Binnenhaven (take a train south and you'll see it on your right), and an upright pencil (actually an apartment building) points to the sky above the Blaak (tram #3). Next door are the freaky sci-fi **cube houses,** family living units composed of a square box perched on a thin stalk. Tour the model home for an idea of what daily life in 2050 may be like. (Take the subway to Blaak and follow the *Cubuswoning* sign; admission f2.50; open Tues.-Fri. 10am-5pm, Sat.-Sun. 11am-5pm; Jan.-March Sat.-Sun. 11am-5pm.) All this modern architecture strikes a strange contrast with the nearby **Oude Haven** (Old Harbor), where swanky youths recline at pubs and cafés and watch the ships go by.

Decent and affordable Dutch delights issue from **De Eend,** Mauritsweg 28. The daily menu is about f10.50. (Open Mon.-Fri. 4:30-7:30pm.) **Fred van de Ende,** on Nieuwe Binnenweg, is a quaint grocery store specializing in Dutch brands. (Open Sun.-Fri. 8am-6pm, Sat. 8am-5pm.) **Westend Supermarket,** Nieuwe Binnenweg 30a, is bigger, cheaper, and more generic. (Open Sat.-Thurs. 8:30am-6pm, Fri. 8:30am-9pm.) Burn it all off at **Jazzcafé Dizzy,** 's-Gravendijkwal 127, which features live bands on Tuesdays. (Open Mon.-Thurs. 8pm-2am, Fri.-Sat. 8pm-3am, Sun. 10pm-2am.)

The **VVV** booth at the train station (tel. (010) 413 60 06) sells maps of the city (f1) and books rooms (f1). (Open Mon.-Sat. 9am-10pm, Sun. 10am-10pm.) The main office at Coolsingel 67 (tel. (063) 403 40 65), near Stadhuisplein, publishes the cultural calendar *This Month* (free), and does theater bookings. (Open Mon.-Thurs. 9am-5:30pm, Fri. 9am-9pm, Sat. 9am-5pm, Sun. 10am-4pm.) For information on setting out from Rotterdam, head to budget-travel hub **NBBS,** Meent 126, near the statehouse (tel. 414 94 85; open Mon.-Fri. 9:30am-5:30pm, Sat. 10am-4pm). **Local buses** (tel. 411 71 00) depart from the train station. Next door at Delftsplein 31 is the **post office.** (Open Mon.-Fri. 8:30am-9pm, Sat. 8:30am-noon. Poste Restante.)

The **NJHC City-Hostel Rotterdam (IYHF),** Rochussenstr. 107-109 (tel. (010) 436 57 63), is a well-run version of the usual, with a bar, TV lounge, kitchen, and free lockers. Take the subway to Dijkzigt, or tram #4. (No lockout. Curfew 2am. July-Aug. f22; Sept.-May f19.50. Showers and breakfast included. Sheets f5.50. Hot lunch or dinner f10.) Formerly almost repulsive in its filthiness, the **Sleep-In,** Mauritsweg 29 (tel. (010) 12 14 20 or 14 32 56), closed for much-needed renovations in 1991 and is scheduled to reopen, new and improved, in 1992. In 1991, the Sleep-In accepted ages 27 and below only. (Reception open 4pm-1am. f10. Breakfast included. Sheets f2.50. Open mid-June to mid-Aug.)

Delft

Delft's canals and well-preserved edifices live on in unsullied serenity, much as they did when Vermeer froze the city ineffably on canvas. To compete with Chinese porcelain brought to Europe by Dutch trade ships, Delft potters conjured up their jaw-dropping blue-on-white china in the 16th century. You can gawk at the pricey plates in the main boutique (or "bluetique") at **Royal Delftware De Porceleyne Fles,** Rotterdamseweg 196 in South Delft, where there are also hourly painting demonstrations. Take bus #60. (Open Mon.-Sat. 9am-5pm, Sun. 10am-4pm; Nov.-March Mon.-Fri. 9am-5pm, Sat. 10am-4pm. Free.) For more in-depth study, tour the factory at **De Delftse Pauw,** Delftweg 133, in the northern reaches of the city, where craftspeople still painstakingly hand-paint the porcelain. Take tram #1. (Open daily 9am-4pm; mid-Oct. to March Mon.-Fri. 9am-4pm, Sat.-Sun. 11am-1pm. Free.) Both places unload seconds at 25% off.

Built in 1381, the **Nieuwe Kerk** looms over Delft's central **Markt.** It contains the gaudy mausoleum of William of Orange, who liberated the Dutch from the Spanish yoke, along with a statue of his loyal dog, who starved to death out of despair after his master died. Ascend the tower to see the 48-bell carillon and a ripping view of old Delft. (Church open Mon.-Sat. 9am-5pm; Nov.-March Mon.-Sat. 11am-4pm. Admission f2, seniors and children 75¢. Tower open Mon.-Sat. 9am-5pm; Oct.-March Mon.-Sat. 10am-noon and 1:30-4pm. Admission f2, seniors and children f1.25. Tower open May-Aug. Tues.-Sat. 10am-4:30pm. Admission f3.25, under 13 f2.40.) One hundred and fifty years its senior, the Gothic **Oude Kerk** held the remains of Delft's native son Johannes Vermeer until they were moved during renovation in 1949. (Open April-Oct. Mon.-Sat. 10am-5pm. Admission f2, seniors and children 75¢.) A combination ticket for both churches costs f3, seniors f2.50, children f1.50. Built in the 15th century as a nun's cloister, **Het Prinsenhof,** at Sint Agathaplein, was William's abode until a crazed Spanish sympathizer assassinated him in 1584. Today it exhibits paintings, tapestries, Delft pottery, and a touch of astonishingly adventurous contemporary art. In mid-October, the museum sponsors an antique fair famous throughout Holland. (Open Tues.-Sat. 10am-5pm, Sun. 1-5pm. Admission f3.50; seniors, under 14, and CJP holders f1.75.)

Snag a complete pamphlet on Delft (f2.50), as well as hiking and cycling maps of the area, from the **VVV,** Markt 85 (tel. (015) 12 61 00). (Open Mon.-Fri. 9am-6pm, Sat. 9am-5pm, Sun. 11am-3pm; Oct.-March Mon.-Fri. 9am-6pm, Sat. 9am-5pm.) Delft is home to a crop of quaint pensions, all well-located and reasonable. The sage choice is cozy **Van Leeuwen,** Achterom 143 (tel. (015) 12 37 16), overlooking a canal near the train station and the Markt. (Singles f30. Doubles f60. Breakfast included.) Another winning pick, with the same prices, is **Rust,** Oranje Plantage

38 (tel. (015) 12 68 74). Surprisingly, a number of the hotels dotting the Markt offer spiffy rooms at decent prices. **La Dalmacya,** Markt 39 (tel. (015) 12 37 14), posts singles at f40-50 and doubles at f70-100. Delft also has a private **campground** on Korftlaan (tel. (015) 13 00 40), in the recreation area of Delftse Hout. (f5.50 per person, f3 per tent.) Take bus #60 from the station to the Korftlaan stop.

A large **market** erupts every Thursday from 9am to 5pm on the marketplace in the town center, and a **flower market** blooms at the same time on Hippolytusbuurt, next to the canal. On Saturdays, a **fruit and vegetable market** fills the Brabantse Turfmarkt. The student mensa **Eettafel Tyche,** Oude Delft 123 (tel. (015) 12 21 23) practically gives away meat-and-potatoes fare. (Open Sept.-May Mon.-Sat. 5:15-7:15pm.) For f5.95, you can savor the sandwich voted the best *broodje* in the Netherlands at **Kleyweg's Stads-Koffyhuis,** down the street at #135. (Open Mon.-Fri. 9am-7pm, Sat. 9am-6pm.) After dark, the dim yet inviting **Bebop Jazzcafé,** Kromstr. 33 (near the Markt), draws local hepcats. (Open Mon.-Thurs. 7pm-1am, Fri.-Sat. 3pm-2am, Sun. 6pm-1am. Live jazz Sept.-June Sun., and the 1st and 3rd Wed. of the month.)

Delft is one hour southwest of Amsterdam by train, with connections at The Hague and Leiden (2 per hr., about f15). For train or bus information in Delft, call (070) 382 41 41.

Utrecht

At the geographical center of the Netherlands, Utrecht presents comely canals, a grandiose cathedral, and a university that is a leftist bastion in a liberal country. Its students support a dynamic cultural scene and nightlife. If you arrive by train, linger not in nightmarish **Hoog Catharijne,** the huge modern shopping complex around Centraal Station—bail out to Utrecht's older quarters. Construction of the town's **cathedral** began in 1254 and finished 250 years later. The **Domtoren,** its imposing tower, was built at such an enormous cost that no money was left for a nave to connect the tower to the church. Climb all 465 steps on a clear day and you can see Amsterdam. (Cathedral open daily 10am-5pm; Oct.-April 11am-4pm. Free. Obligatory tower tours hourly Mon.-Fri. 10am-5pm, Sat. 11am-5pm, Sun. noon-5pm; Nov.-March Sat. 11am-5pm, Sun. noon-5pm. Admission f3.50, children f1.) Next door, the **Pandhof of the Dom,** the church's 15th-century cloister garden, has been converted into a rustic herb garden. (Open Mon.-Fri. 10am-5pm, Sat. 11am-5pm, Sun. noon-5pm; Nov.-March Sat.-Sun. noon-5pm. Free.) The **Centraal Museum,** Agnietenstr. 1, is a five-minute walk on Korte Nieuwstr. and Lange Nieuwstr. Here you can marvel at a 9th-century Viking ship and paintings of the Utrecht school, 16th- and 17th-century artists who took *chiaroscuro*-meister Caravaggio as their hero. (Open Tues.-Sat. 10am-5pm, Sun. 1-5pm. Admission f2.75; seniors, children, and CJP holders f1.25.) **Het Catharijneconvent,** Nieuwe Gracht 63, expatiates on the history of Christianity in Holland and brandishes the largest collection of medieval art in the Netherlands. (Open Tues.-Fri. 10am-5pm, Sat.-Sun. 11am-5pm. Admission f3.50; seniors and under 18 f2; CJP holders f2.50.) Utrecht has a lamentable dearth of cheap hotels; the VVV locates lodgings for the usual small fee. Visit the smiling main office, Vredenburg 90 (tel. (06) 34 03 40 85), at the end of the shopping mall—if you arrive by train, ask at the information booth in the center of the station for a free walking map to help you find it. (Open Mon.-Fri. 9am-6pm, Sat. 9am-4pm. A machine outside spews a map and information for f2 at other times.) They might find you a B&B (about f40 per person plus a f3.50 fee per person), but the best call is the delightful **Jeugdherberg Rhijnauwen (IYHF),** Rhijnauwenselaan 14 (tel. (03405) 612 77), in a winsome rural setting, complete with kitchen and laundry facilities, currency exchange, and a volleyball court. The commute is a hassle, but a walk through the cow and pony-laden farmland soothes frayed traveling nerves. Take bus #40 from Utrecht's Centraal Station (1 or 2 per hr.; tell the driver your destination) and walk the remaining five minutes. (Reception open 8am-12:30am. Curfew 12:30am. f19.50, nonmembers f25. Sheets f5.50. Showers and breakfast included. Pizza and cheeseburgers (f2-7) at the bar.) **Camping De Berekuil,** Ariënslaan 5-7 (tel. (030) 71 38 70), is not far from the center of town; take bus #57 from the station to the Veemarkt stop. (f3.90 per person and 2.85 per tent. Open April-Oct.)

Eat well in a hip and friendly setting at **Toque Toque,** Oude Gracht 138, at Vinkenburgstr. A mongo plate of pasta, with salad and bread, runs f12.50 (open noon-3pm and 6-10pm). **Café De Baas,** Lijnmarkt 8, just across the canal from the Domtoren, proffers yummy vegetarian dishes from f9.50 with occasional live music. (Open Tues.-Fri. and Sun. 5-10pm, Sat. 11am-10pm.) The two main student *mensas,* open to everyone, are **Veritas,** Kromme Nieuwe Gracht 54, and **Unitas,** Lucasbolwerk 8. (Meals f5-7. Both open mid-Aug. to late June Mon.-Fri. 5-7:30pm.) **De Goey-Koot,** Nobelstr. 22, vends exotic fruits at basement prices (open Mon. noon-6pm, Tues.-Sat. 9am-6pm).

If you're not bound by a hostel curfew, Utrecht presents ample opportunity to get wild and loose. Things get hopping around 11pm at two popular bars: intellectual **De Kneus,** Nobelstr. 303 (open daily 4pm-4am) and the earthier **'t Pandje,** Nobelst. 193 (open Mon.-Sat. 9:30pm-4am). Escape to the jungle at **Mad Mick and Big Mamou,** Oudkerichof 29, a rocking Cajun bar and restaurant with drinks like the "Slippery Nipple." (Open Mon.-Thurs. 10:30am-2am, Fri.-Sat. 10:30am-3am, Sun. noon-2am.) **Theatercafé Hoogt,** Slachtstr. 5, off Lange Jansstr. near Neude, attracts a supercilious crowd for drinks, snacks, and experimental cinema. (Open Sun.-Fri. 11am-1am, Sat. 3:30pm-2am; films f9.) **Disco De Roze Wolk** is a rollicking gay bar at Oude Gracht 45. (Open Sun. and Wed.-Thurs. 10pm-4am, Fri.-Sat. 10pm-5am. Free.) Dance at cavernous **Fellini,** Stadhuisbrug 3, under the town hall. (Open Wed.-Sun. 10pm-5am; f4 cover charge after 11pm.)

Arnhem and the Hoge Veluwe National Park

Rebuilt after punishing WWII bombings, Arnhem, 100km southeast of Amsterdam (2 trains per hr., 70 min.) is now one huge outdoor shopping center with jack to offer. Nevertheless, the contiguous Hoge Veluwe National Park, a 13,000 acre preserve of woods, heath, dunes, red deer and wild boars, may well prove one of the highlights of your trip to Europe. Nestled deep within the park, a 35-minute walk from the nearest entrance, lies the **Rijksmuseum Kröller-Müller,** one of the finest modern art museums in Europe, with a scintillating collection of 276 van Goghs and superb paintings by Seurat, Mondrian, Braque, Gris, and many others. The museum's beautiful garden is aflutter with modern sculpture, including Jean Dubuffet's *Jardin d'Email* and pieces by Maillol, Moore, and Lipchitz. Visitors can pedal the park's bikes for free—pick one up at the visitor center and drop it off at any bike stand. From June through August, and at selected times throughout the rest of the year, bus #12 ("Hoge Veluwe") leaves from the Arnhem train station; you can board and alight as often as you wish (1 per hr. 9:40am-4:10pm, round-trip f6.25). The bus will zoom you directly to the doorstep of the museum, or ride another 1200m to **Koperen Kop,** the visitor center and bike rental station. At other times, take bus #107 to Otterlo and walk 45 minutes from there. (Park open 8am-sunset. Museum and sculpture park open Tues.-Sat. 10am-5pm, Sun. 11am-5pm. Admission to park f6.50, children f3.25; museum and sculpture park free.)

The **VVV,** to the left of the station on Stationsplein (tel. (085) 42 03 30), finds accommodations. (Open July-Aug. Mon.-Fri. 9am-8pm, Sat. 10am-5pm; Sept.-June Mon.-Fri. 9am-5:30pm, Sat. 10am-4pm.) The placid **Jeugdherberg Alteveer (IYHF),** Diepenbroeklaan 27 (tel. (085) 42 01 14), is in a crunchy rural setting. Every room has a full bath. Take bus #3 toward Alteveer and ask the driver to let you off at the hostel, then follow the signs. (f20, nonmembers f25. Sheets f5.50. Breakfast included. Curfew 12:30am.) **Hotel-Pension Parkzicht,** Apeldoornsestr. 16 (tel. (085) 42 06 98), is about 15 minutes from the station. (Singles f42.50. Doubles f60-80. Triples f110. Breakfast included.) Camp at **Kampeercentrum Arnhem,** Kemperbergerweg 771 (tel. (085) 43 16 00), accessible by bus #11 (direction "Schaarsbergen"; f10 per site, no charge per person; open March-Sept.). The **Old Inn,** Stationsplein 39a (tel. (085) 42 06 49), is a café and restaurant with a f12 menu. (Open daily 10am-2am.)

Wadden Islands (Waddeneilanden)

Wadden may mean "mudflat" in Dutch, but it is a surfeit of sand on these five islands that draws so many Dutch and German vacationers. Sand and solitude are not mutally exclusive so long as you avoid the overrun sections of Texel and Terschelling. Check a weather forecast; there's zippo to do if it's raining.

You can visit **Texel,** the southernmost and largest island, on a daytrip from Amsterdam if you get your act together. Take the train to Den Helder (2 per hr., 70 min.), then bus #3 from the station to the ferry. Boats leave at 35 minutes past the hour, every hour from 6am to 9pm (last boat back 9:05pm, round-trip f10.25, children f5.10). After the ferry drops you at **'t Horntje,** on the southern tip of the island, rent a bike (f7) to pedal between Texel's three major villages. **Den Berg,** the largest town (a booming population of 7000, folks), squats in the center of island; **De Koog** lolls on the beaches on the western edge of the island; and **De Cocksdorp** isolates itself at the northern end of the isle. The crowds thin farther south toward **Den Hoorn,** a smaller village. Texel is a voyeur's paradise: there are two popular nude beaches (one south of Den Hoorn and one off De Cockscorp) plus fine birdwatching. You can visit the nature reserves only on a 2-hr. guided tour organized by the State Forest Department (March-Aug. only, f1.50). Book in advance from Ecomare, Ruyslaan 92 (tel. (02220) 177 41), in De Koog.

Both of Texel's **IYHF youth hostels** are immaculate and within walking distance of Den Burg; snag bus #27 or 28 from the ferry landing to reach either one (tell the driver your destination). **Panorama,** Schansweg 7 (tel. (02220) 154 41), hides in a nature reserve complete with Texel's own breed of sheep. (Curfew 11:30pm. f20.50, nonmembers f25.50. Sheets f5.50. Breakfast included. Open March-Nov.) **De Eyercoogh,** Pontweg 106 (tel. (02220) 129 07), pleases with its winning location near the town center. (No curfew. f19.50, nonmembers f24.50. Breakfast and lockers included. Open March-Oct.) The **VVV** in Den Burg, Groeneplaats 9 (tel. (02220) 147 41), updates you on the island's 17 **campgrounds** as well as several farms which allow camping, and sells excellent maps (f3.50) of biking routes (open Tues.-Fri. 9am-6pm, Sat. 9am-5pm, Sun. 4-6pm; Sept.-June closed Sun.). In June, Texel holds **Ronde Van Texel,** the largest catamaran race in Europe. Join locals in sipping *'t Jutterje,* the island's wildly popular alcohol, blended from herbs and wheat. **Sliterij-Wijnhandel De Wit,** 60 Weverstr. in Den Burg, stocks a plentiful supply and gives free samples.

The four other islands (the Friese Islands) all have extensive dunes and wildlife sanctuaries. **Schiermonnikoog** and **Vlieland** are the most deserted. On boat excursions to Vlieland from Texel, you must return the same day. Schiermonnikoog's **VVV,** Reeweg (tel. (05195) 12 33), finds rooms in private homes for about f30 per person. Reserve ahead, even in off-season. (Open Mon.-Sat. 9:30am-12:30pm and 2:30-6:30pm.) The islands of **Terschelling** and **Ameland** draw more visitors. There are **IYHF youth hostels** on three of the islands. Overlooking the sea, 2km from the boat landing on Terschelling, **Hanskedune,** van Heusdenweg 39 (tel. (05620) 23 38), is modern with showers and toilets in each room. (f19.50. Open June-Dec.) It's a pain to reach by boat (2 per day, 3 hr.). On hyperkinetic Ameland, **De Kleine Grie,** Oranjeweg 59 (tel. (05191) 41 33), in Hollum, is also felicitous. (f19.50. Open mid-June to late-Aug. plus a week at Easter.) Near the town center on Schiermonnikoog, **Rijsbergen,** Knuppeldam 2 (tel. (05195) 12 57), is rustic. (No curfew. f13.50. Breakfast f5.50. Open April-Oct.) For Terschelling or Vlieland, take the main train line to **Leeuwarden** (1 per hr. from Amsterdam, 2½ hr.), then continue by bus (2 per hr., 25 min.) or train to Harlingen, whence you can catch the ferry to either island (3 per day, Oct.-April 2 or 3 per day; 2 hr., round-trip f32, bikes f11). To reach Ameland, take bus #66 from Leeuwarden (8-11 per day, 50 min.) to Holwerd and then the ferry (8-11 per day; Sept.-May 4-6 per day; 45 min., round-trip f12). Reach Schiermonnikoog from Lauwersoog (4-7 per day, 40 min., round-trip f12), itself reached by bus #51 from Leeuwarden (3-5 per day, 75 min.).

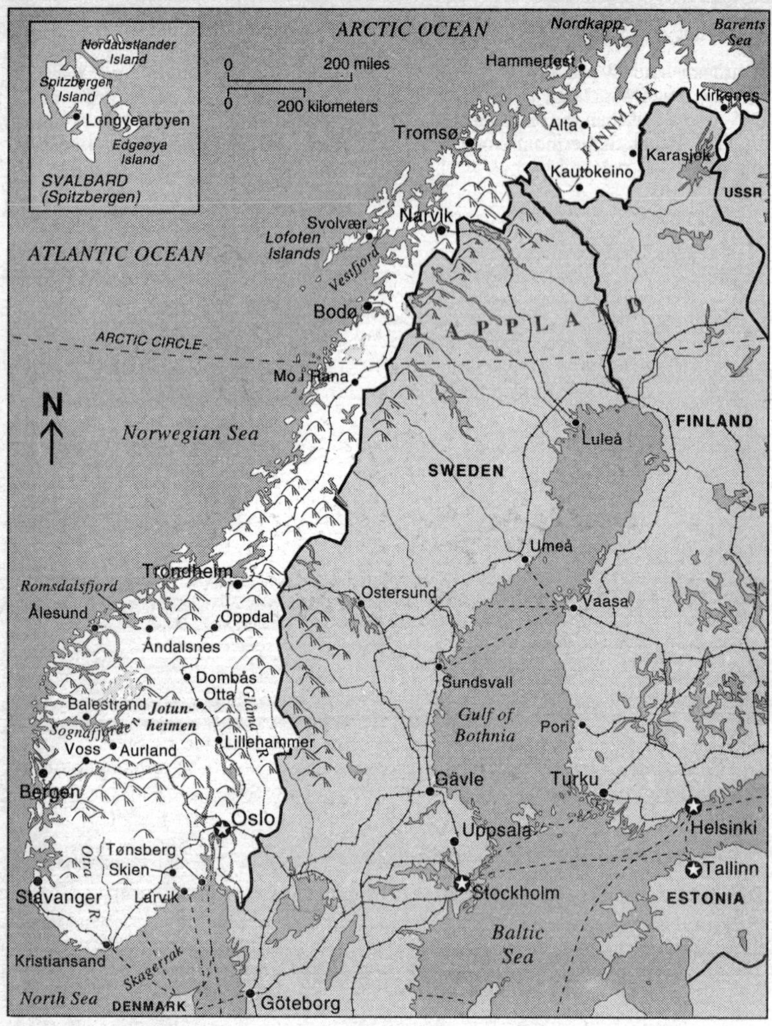

NORWAY

USD$1 = 6.84 kroner (kr, or NOK)	**1kr = USD$0.15**
CAD$1 = 5.99kr	**1kr = CAD$0.17**
GBP£1 = 11.4kr	**1kr = GBP£0.09**
AUD$1 = 5.33kr	**1kr = AUD$0.19**
NZD$1 = 3.90kr	**1kr = NZD$0.26**
Country Code: 47	**International Dialing Prefix: 095**

Stretched over the northwest rim of Europe, Norway (Norge, Noreg) is the continent's ineffable encounter with nature. The majesty of its fjords and mountains melt into the provincial charm of piney valleys and farming homesteads. From Norway's rugged coast, fierce Norsemen spread across the Atlantic via Iceland and Greenland to Canada; their ships landed on the banks of Scotland and Ireland, laid siege to Paris and even reached Portugal and Spain. The pagan pillaging party subsided in the 10th century, when Harald Hårfagre (Harold the Fairhaired) united the country and Olav Tryggvason (St. Olav) imported Christianity. Runestones, stave churches, and preserved Viking ships still survive from this age, while the Icelandic sagas chronicle it and its myths in rich poetry and epics.

The lean years of the late 19th century spawned great luminaries of art, drama and music, from Munch to Ibsen, Hamsun to Grieg. After oppressive German occupation in WWII, Norway developed into your typical modern welfare state, after finally gaining full independence from neighboring Scandinavian states in 1905. Today its four million people pay outrageous taxes, but know no poverty. Northern Norway's simple, striplike geography contrasts with the country's wider southern parts, where a series of long valleys run between Oslo and Trondheim, connected by passes over Scandinavia's highest mountains to the fjords in the west.

Getting There and Getting Around

Every coastal town from Oslo to Bergen of any significance has ferry service to Denmark, England or Germany (more frequent and expensive in summer and on weekends). Most foreigners, cowed by the ferry system, take the train to Oslo from Copenhagen (3-4 per day, 10 hr., 598kr) or Stockholm (1-3 per day, 6 hr., 508kr). Both Eurail and InterRail passes are valid on all trains in Norway, as is the Scandinavian Nordturist pass, which offers 21 days of unlimited travel for 1710kr (ages under 26 1275kr). Eurailpasses get few fringe benefits in Norway, but InterRail and Nordturist win several free bus and ferry trips.

No free brochure gives you a complete, comprehensive picture of the complex domestic transportation scene; you'll have to collect sheaves of free regional schedules, or ask travel agents or train stations for a look at their all-fathoming *Rutebok for Norge.* Norwegian trains run only up to Bodø; the only trains further north run along the Swedish rail line through Kiruna, which crosses the mountains to dead-end at Narvik on the Norwegian coast, and along a line from Murmansk in Russia. You must have a seat to ride trains, so book ahead (15kr, sleeping berths 90kr).

For those under 25, special summer youth fares make **flying** an extremely viable option, often cheaper than the train. SAS and Braathens SAFE are the main airlines. **Buses** are everywhere, and usually quite expensive (about 1kr per km), but are the only firm-surface option north of Bodø and in the fjords. Always ask for student discounts, and try flashing your railpass.

Car ferries *(ferjer)* are usually much cheaper (and slower) than the many **hydrofoils** *(hurtigbåte)* that cruise along the coasts; both occasionally allow student discounts. Throughout the chapter you'll see references to the *Hurtigruten* (the famed Coastal Steamer), which takes 6 days for its fantastic voyage from Bergen to Kirkenes; enough ships run that each of the 25 stops en route have one northbound and one southbound departure per day. Just step on board (50% student discount). If you are under 26, snare a three-week pass that allows unlimited stopovers for 1500kr. Often, the *Hurtigruten* have a free sleeping-bag room; empty cabins run 50kr per night.

Many Norwegians **hitch** beyond the rail lines in northern Norway and the fjord areas of the west. Those hitching use a sign or flag and try to find a ride before or during a ferry trip to avoid getting stuck at the landing.

Practical Information

Most towns in Norway have *Turistinformasjon* offices, with extended hours from the beginning of June until the end of August. Try to see them the night before planning an excursion, as buses often leave early in the morning or late in the afternoon.

Banks are open Monday through Friday from 8:15am to 3pm in summer and 3:30pm in winter, Thursday until 5pm. Large **post offices** exchange money and usually charge less commission (generally open Mon.-Fri. 7am-5:30pm, Sat. 8:15am-5pm). Legal **holidays,** when everything closes, include New Year's Day, Maundy Thursday, Good Friday and Easter Monday, Labor Day (May 1), Constitution Day (May 17), Ascension Day (May 28), Whitmonday (June 8), and Christmas.

Telephone calls within and outside Norway butcher the budget. For operator assistance dial 093 (English- and German-speaking), 092 (French), 091 (Nordic). To make collect calls internationally, dial 0115. Pay phones take 1, 5 and 10kr coins and local calls require at least 2. For AT&T's **USA Direct,** dial (050) 12 011.

Norway is officially a bilingual country. Reacting to the Danish-influenced *bokmål* Norwegian used in Oslo, 19th-century linguists constructed an alternative standard language *(nynorsk)* based on the more archaic dialects of rural western Norway; the two are taught on an equal footing in schools. Fortunately, the great majority of Norwegians speak fluent English.

For a few weeks on either side of the summer solstice (June 21), Norway north of Bodø basks in the midnight sun. For skiing, come just before Easter, when the winter has loosened its grip somewhat, and the sun returns after months of darkness.

Accommodations, Camping, and Food

When in Norway, camp. Norwegian law allows you to camp for free anywhere you want for two nights, provided you keep 150m from all buildings and fences, and leave no traces of your frolicking. Hikers and campers should take advantage of **Den Norske Turistforening** (DNT, the Norwegian Mountain Touring Association); their Oslo office is particularly helpful. They sell excellent maps and maintain a series of mountain huts *(hytter)* throughout the country (40-125kr per night, open to nonmembers for a 45kr surcharge). Staffed huts serve full meals and are akin to hostels, but they have a consistently more attractive ambience and more Norwegian guests than international tourists. For unattended huts, you must obtain the entrance key (deposit required) at a DNT or tourist office before heading out. DNT huts are open during Easter, and from the end of June to the beginning of September.

The indispensable *Vandrerhjem i Norge* brochure lists prices, phone numbers, and oh-so-much more for Norway's 87 **IYHF youth hostels** *(vandrerhjem).* Quality varies from cramped and hospital-like to wooden, spacious and cozy. Beds run 60-100kr; breakfast (sometimes mandatory) costs 40-50kr. Usually only rural hostels have curfews (11pm). Unfortunately, only a few are open year-round.

Most tourist offices in Norway can book you a room in a private home; these usually run 150kr for a single, 200kr for a double. **Campgrounds** usually have cabins at 200-400kr for groups of two or four.

While a feast for the eyes, Norway is murder on the wallet. The high cost of food may be your biggest problem, and markets and bakeries may become your dearest friends. Look out for the nationwide discount **REMA 1000** and **Netto** supermarkets, which whip the competition for prices (usually open Mon.-Fri. until 8pm). Though hostel breakfasts are usually dull, they are almost always the cheapest grub around, and can keep you from fainting for a few hours. Restaurants often have inexpensive *dagens ret* specials (60-70kr for a full meal); otherwise you're lucky to get out for less than 100kr. Tips are included. Self-service *kafeterias* are a less expensive option. Fish in Norway is unusually fresh, good and cheap. National specialties include flatbread crackers *(flatbrød),* cheese *(ost;* try *Jarlsberg* and the brown *geitost),* pork and veal meatballs *(kjøtkaker)* with boiled potatoes, and (for the daring) *smala hovud* (boiled sheep's head). In most Norwegian restaurants, alcohol is served only after 3pm and never on Sundays. Beer is heavily taxed and quite expensive. *Pilsner* is the standard; an especially strong brand is *Export. Gløgg,* a Scandinavian mulled wine, is popular in winter.

Oslo

Norway's capital stands tight and modern around its harbor; a few blocks away, its people and traffic swirl among the trees and statues of the town center. Much smaller than Copenhagen or Stockholm, Oslo stays laid-back, its green spaces spreading until the suburbs become indistinguishable from the Norwegian woodlands.

Orientation and Practical Information

Karl Johans Gate, running from Sentralstasjon to the *Slottet* (Royal Palace), is Oslo's principal boulevard and a useful reference point. From early morning, it seethes with musicians, sunbathers, and street vendors. The bustling harbor lies to the south.

Tourist Offices: The **Main Tourist Office,** Rådhusplassen (tel. 83 00 50), in a yellow former train station by the city hall, brandishes gigantic, multicolored "NORWAY" signs. Pick up their free and essential Oslo map and Oslo guide. Open Mon.-Fri. 9am-4:30pm, Sat.-Sun. 9am-2:30pm; Mar.-May and Sept.-Nov. Mon.-Fri. 9am-4:30pm; Jan.-Feb. and Dec. Mon.-Fri. 9am-4pm. The branch at **Sentralstasjon** is open daily 8am-11pm. Essential for hikers is **Den Norske Turistforening** (DNT, the Norwegian Touring Association), Roald Amundsens gate 28 (tel. 41 80 20), which rents mountain huts and sells trail maps. Open Mon.-Wed. and Fri. 8:30am-4pm, Thurs. 8:30am-6pm. **USE IT,** Trafikanten (tel. 17 27 28), in front of Sentralstasjon, offers budget travelers brochures and listings of cheap accommodations and restaurants. (Open mid-June to late Aug. Mon.-Fri. 7am-5pm, Sat. 9am-2pm.)

Budget Travel: Reisebyrået Terra Nova, Dronningensgate 26 (tel. 42 14 10). Centrally located office. Open Mon.-Wed. and Fri. 9:30am-5pm, Thurs. and Sat. 9:30am-6pm.

Embassies: U.S., Drammensveien 18 (tel. 44 85 50). Take tram #1, 2, or 9, bus #27, 29, or 30. Open Mon.-Fri. 9am-3pm. **Canada,** Oscars Gate 20 (tel. 46 69 55), near Bislett Stadium. Take tram #2 or 11. Open Mon.-Fri. 8am-3:30pm. **U.K.,** Thomas Heftyes Gate 8 (tel. 55 24 00). Open Mon.-Fri. 9am-4pm. **Australian Information Office,** Jernbanetorget 2 (tel. 41 44 33). Open Mon.-Fri. 9am-noon and 2-4pm. Travelers from **New Zealand** should contact the British Embassy.

Currency Exchange: Lowest commissions at post offices (10kr per traveler's check, 15kr for cash). Sentralstasjon office open Mon.-Fri. 7am-5:30pm, Sat. 9am-2pm. After-hours exchange in **Bankveksling** next to the post office in Sentralstasjon—but 15-20kr per traveler's check. Open daily 7am-11pm.

American Express: Winge Reisebyrå, Karl Johans Gate 33 (tel. 41 20 30). No personal check cashing, currency exchange or wired money accepted. Pick up mail here; address it to American Express, PO Box 54, Majorstuen, 0304 Oslo. Open Mon.-Wed. and Fri. 8:30am-5pm, Thurs. 8:30am-6pm, Sat. 9:30am-1pm.

Post Office: Dronningens gate 15 (tel. 40 78 23); entrance at corner of Prinsens Gate. Open Mon.-Fri. 8am-8pm, Sat. 9am-3pm. Poste Restante. **Postal Code:** 0101.

Telephones: Kongens Gate 21, entrance on Prinsens gate. Open daily 8am-9pm. **City code:** 02.

Flights: White SAS buses (25kr) run between **Fornebu Airport** and the Air Bus Terminal (tel. 59 62 20) at Galleri Oslo opposite Sentralstasjon. Frequent service daily 6am-9:30pm. Municipal bus #31 runs to Fornebu from various points in the city (14kr).

Trains: Oslo Sentralstasjon (Central Station, Oslo-S), tel. 17 14 00. Trains to Bergen (7-8 hr., 425kr), Trondheim (7-8 hr., 486kr), and a host of other points. Open daily 7am-11pm. The **InterRail Center** at Sentralstasjon is home to **showers** (20kr, soap and towel included), and **luggage storage** (free, but risky). Open mid-June to late Sept. daily 7am-11pm.

Buses: Norway Bussekspress, Havngata 2 (tel. 33 01 91 or 33 08 62), south of Sentralstasjon, sends buses scurrying throughout Norway (Bergen 465kr, Trondheim 578kr) and across Europe. Terminal open Mon.-Thurs. and Sat. 7:30am-7pm, Fri. 7:30am-10pm, Sun. 8am-10pm.

Ferries: Passenger ferries arrive at port, a 15-min. walk from the center. **Color Line** (tel. 83 60 10) has daily ferries most of the year to Kiel, Germany (640-1160kr) and Hirtshals, Denmark (75-150kr). 25% student discount. **DFDS Scandinavian Seaways** (tel. 42 93 50) sails to Copenhagen daily (Sun.-Wed. 525kr, Thurs. 605kr, Fri.-Sat. 645kr; 50% student discount

Sun.-Thurs.). **Stena Line** (tel. 35 50 00) has one daily run to Frederikshavn, Denmark (190-320kr, depending on season).

Public Transportation: Information available at **Trafikanten** (tel. 41 70 30), in front of Sentralstasjon. Open Mon.-Fri. 7am-8pm, Sat.-Sun. 8am-6pm. All forms (bus, tram, subway, and ferry) cost 14kr per trip. A 24-hr. **Dagskort** allows unlimited travel (40kr). For longer stays, the **7-day card** (130kr) makes good sense. The **Oslo-Card** (transport plus sights for 24 hrs. 90kr; 48 hr. 130kr; 72 hr. 160kr) is economical only for *a lot* of sightseeing in a short time.

Bike Rental: Den Rustne Eike, Enga 2 (tel. 83 72 31), behind the tourist office. 80kr per day, 390kr per week. 500kr deposit. Open Mon.-Fri. 10am-6:30pm, Nov.-Apr. Mon.-Fri. 10am-3:30pm. Occasional special offers.

Hitchhiking: Leaving Oslo by thumb can be a losing proposition; check first at the USE IT ride board. Those heading south try outside West Station. Those going north take bus #30 or 31 to Sinsenkrysset, the main intersection of north-bound highways.

Luggage Storage: In Central Station. Lockers 20-30kr. Open 7am-11pm.

Laundromat: Look for the word *Myntvaskeri.* **Selvbetjent Vask,** Ullevålsveien 15, a few blocks from the city center. Wash 30kr. Dry 10kr. Soap included. Both **hostels** have laundries.

Bookstore: Tanum Libris, Karl Johans gate 43 (in Paléet). Wide selection of English paperbacks. Open Mon.-Fri. 10am-8pm, Sat. 10am-5pm.

Pharmacy: Look for the word *Apotek.* **Jernbanetorvets Apotek** (tel. 41 24 82), in front of Central Station. Open 24 hrs.

Medical Assistance: Oslo Kommunale Legevakt, Storgata 40 (tel. 11 70 70). 24-hr. emergency care.

Emergencies: Police, tel. 002. Headquarters at Grølandsleiret 44 (tel. 66 90 50). **Ambulance,** tel. 003. **Fire** and **Accidents,** tel. 001.

Accommodations and Camping

Ask at the **Innkvartering** accommodations office in Central Station, and at the **USE IT** office, which has a list of cheap sleeps. Innkvartering books rooms in private homes for multi-night stays. (Singles 300kr. Doubles 400kr. Fee 17kr.) Singles are limited, so you may have to double up. *Pensjonater* (pensions) are usually less expensive than hotels; call for reservations. Many hotels slash prices from late June to mid-August. Wilderness huts outside Oslo are a deal (from 60kr), but 45 min. from public transport. Inquire at USE IT.

Pan Youth Hostel (IYHF), Sognsveien 218 (tel. 23 76 40). Take tram #13 from Stortinget to Kringsja station and walk downhill across the tracks. Part of a summer hotel, with clean, 3-bed rooms and kitchen facilities. Market and laundry (7kr per token) nearby. Friendly, helpful staff. No curfew. 140kr, nonmembers 165kr. Open mid-June to mid-Aug. Reserve ahead.

Haraldsheim (IYHF), Haraldsheimveien 4 (tel. 15 50 43). Take tram #1 or 7 (direction "Sinsen") to the end of the line, or the local train to Grefsen from Sentralstasjon. Friendly, cozy and crowded. Laundry 40kr for wash and dry (soap included). No curfew. Reception open 24 hrs. 125kr, nonmembers 150kr. Café in summer. Reservations essential in summer.

KFUM (YMCA), Møllergata 7 (tel. 42 10 66); enter on parallel Grubbegata. The cheapest spot in town (70kr). Sleeping-bag accommodations; 60 mats in 2 dorms. Reception open 8-11am and 5pm-midnight. Kitchen facilities and baggage storage. Open July to mid-Aug.

Ellingsens Pensjonat, Holtegata 25 (tel. 60 03 59). Take tram #1 (direction: Majorstuen) straight to the door. Clean, tight ship. Singles 160kr. Doubles 240kr. Only a few rooms, so call ahead.

Coch's Pensjonat, Parkveien 25 (tel. 60 48 36), corner of Hegdehaugsveien by the royal park. Triples 390kr. Quads 440kr. No kitchen. Reservations recommended.

Camping: Ekeberg Camping, Ekebergveien 65 (tel. 19 85 68), about 3km from the center, with marvelous view. Take bus #24 from Central Station. Tent sites 70kr. Open June-Aug. **Free camping** permitted in the forest north of town as long as you avoid public areas (walk about 1km into forest). Try at the end of the Sognsvann subway line.

Food

A full meal in a restaurant will drive you into poverty. The cheapest shopping area is the **Tøyen/Grønland** immigrant district northeast of Central Station; try along Tøyengata and Urtegata. Three discount chains bring you a limited but inexpensive selection: **Rimi,** Rosenkrantzgate 20 (open Mon.-Fri. 9am-5pm); **Rema 1000,** Holmesgata 7 (open Mon.-Wed. and Fri. 9am-6pm, Thurs. 9am-8pm); **Tempus,** Youngsgata 11 (open Mon.-Fri. 8am-7pm, Sat. 10am-6pm). The **Seven-Eleven** stores and **Narvesen** kiosks are open until late hours.

Vegeta Vertshus Frisksportrestaurant, Munkedamsveien 3b, off Stortings gate. Two floors of unpretentious vegetarian delight has fed Norwegian crunchies for more than 50 years with an awesome array of health food in the form of salads, soups, pizzas and hot dishes. All-you-can-stuff-on-one-plate 58kr, all-you-can-eat buffet 98kr. Open daily 10am-11pm.

Kafé Celsius, Rådhusgata 19. Old pale-yellow buildings shelter a cozy courtyard restaurant. Omelet 58kr, pasta from 72kr. Open Tues.-Wed. 11am-12:30am, Thurs.-Sat. 11am-3am, Sun. 1pm-12:30am.

Darbar Mat & Vinhus, Smedgata 45. Take subway to Tøyen station, walk down path to Sørligata and continue on to Smedgata. Good Indian restaurant full of aroma and decor. Vegetarian dishes 50-80kr, meat dishes 80-130kr.

Norrøna Kafé, Grensen 19. Standard Norwegian fare, filling and satisfying. Fish or meat 60-70kr. Full meal daily 2-4pm for 51kr. Open Mon.-Fri. 8am-6:30pm, Sat. 9am-4pm, Sun. noon-5pm.

Sights and Entertainment

Akershus Castle and Fortress, built in 1300 and transformed into a Renaissance palace by Christian IV, is now used only for state occasions. You can explore the castle's underground passages, banquet halls, dungeons, and courtyards. There are frequent summer concerts on Sundays. (Open May to mid-Sept. Mon.-Sat. 10am-4pm, Sun. 12:30-4pm; mid-Sept. to Oct. and April 15-30 Sun. 12:30-4pm. Admission 10kr, children and students 5kr). The poignant **Resistance Museum** in the fortress documents Norway's intrepid efforts to subvert Nazi occupation. (Open Mon.-Sat. 10am-4pm, Sun. 11am-4pm; Oct. to mid-April Mon.-Sat. 10am-3pm, Sun. 11am-4pm. Admission 10kr; children, students and seniors 3kr.)

From the castle, head toward the island of **Bygdøy;** take the ferry from pier #3, or bus #30 or 31 from Nationaltheatret. The island's draws include the **Folkemuseum,** an open-air museum with a collection of traditional houses, and the **Old Town,** where you can find Ibsen's study. (Open mid-May to Aug. Mon.-Sat. 10am-6pm, Sun. 11am-6pm; Sept. Mon.-Sat. 11am-4pm, Sun. noon-5pm; Oct. to mid-May Mon.-Sat. 11am-4pm, Sun. noon-3pm. Admission 35kr, students 20kr; in off-season 16kr, students 7kr.) There is folk dancing here every Sunday at 5pm; see *Oslo This Week* for more information. The **Viking Ship Museum** contains three vessels, including the 9th-century ring-prowed, dragon-keeled Oseberg ship used to bury a queen. (Open daily May-Aug. 10am-6pm; Sept. 11am-5pm; April and Oct. 11am-4pm; Nov.-March 11am-3pm. Admission 10kr, students 5kr.) Thor Heyerdahl's crafts *Kon-Tiki, Ra I,* and *Ra II* have their own museum on the island, accompanied by a rollicking recollection of his adventures. (Open mid-May to Aug. daily 10am-6pm; in off-season closes 1-3 hr. earlier. Admission 10kr, students and children 5kr.) Next door, board the **Fram,** which carried Amundsen to the poles (same hours and prices). Weather permitting, plunge in the bracing water off **Huk beach,** Oslo's most popular, located about 1km from the Viking Ship Museum. Or bare it all at **Strandskogen,** the only nude beach in town, across the inlet from Huk.

The blunt, powerful stone sculptures at **Vigeland Park** (also called **Frognerpark)** depict each stage of the human life cycle; the park itself is an immense playground of grassy knolls, duck ponds, and tennis courts. The famous obelisk of squirming humans is Gustav Vigeland's vision of the depravity of humanity. Go in the early morning, when the park is deserted. Take tram #2 or bus #20 from Nationaltheatret, or walk up the Hegdehaugsveien, with its markets, cafés, and shops. The **Vige-**

land Museum, Nobels gate 32, displays more sculptures, as well as drawings and woodcuts. In summer, concerts resound in the forecourt Sunday mornings and Wednesday evenings. Take tram #2 from Nationaltheatret to Frogner plass. (Open Tues.-Sun. noon-7pm; Nov.-April Tues.-Sun. 1-7pm. Admission 10kr.)

For a panorama of Oslofjord and the city, take the subway from Stortinget to the stop on the Frognerseteren line and walk to the world-famous ski jump **Holmenkollen,** the broken fishhook on the Oslo skyline. Grease your body and slide on down. As you sail through the air, note that forest and lakes cover over half of the "city" of Oslo. (Open May and Sept. daily 10am-5pm; June 10am-7pm; July 9am-10pm; Aug. 9am-8pm; Oct-April Mon-Fri. 10am-3pm, Sat.-Sun. 11am-5pm. Admission 15kr, students 10kr.)

To bask in Norway's natural grandeur, take the Sognsvann subway from Nationaltheatret to the end of the line, and walk up the road a few minutes to the shores of a quiet lake, ringed by towering evergreens and misty waterfalls. USE IT provides free maps of the multiple trails and huts for year-round use. In winter, ask at the tourist office about cross-country ski rental.

For a delightful and inexpensive day trip, take a ferry to one of the islands in the inner Oslofjord—**Hovedøya, Langøyene,** or **Gressholmen.** Boats leave from the piers in front of City Hall and from **Vippetangen,** reached by bus #18 (round-trip 28kr, free with city transport pass). In summer, you can visit the ruins of an old monastery on Hovedøya; Langøyene offers Oslo's best beach. The evening cruise is especially enchanting, as the lights of Oslo and the summer sun form a shimmering backdrop to the waves.

The **Munch Museum,** Tøyengata 53, is a scream. It contains an outstanding collection of Edvard Munch's unsettling paintings, woodcuts, and lithographs. Take bus #29 from Roald Amundsens gate or the subway to Tøyen. (Open May-Sept. Mon.-Sat. 10am-8pm, Sun. noon-8pm; Oct.-April same hours but closed Mondays. Admission 20kr, students 10kr.)

On summer nights, the streets of Oslo fill with young people. Check out the area from **Aker Brygge** and the quay to Karl Johans gate and Grensen. Nightclubs, pubs and discos abound here, as do theaters and cinemas.

Southern Norway

Norway's southern coast substitutes serenity for drama. *Skjærgård,* archipelagos of water-worn rock hugging the shore, stretch from Oslo south to Kristiansand. From Kristiansand to Stavanger, the shoreline smooths to an endless white beach. This coast is Norway's #1 summer holiday resort, but foreign tourists are an endangered species. Whitewashed wooden houses lend cozy peacefulness to the local atmosphere. Inland, the high cliffs are swathed by dense woods peppered with small villages, sparkling lakes and rushing rivers; investigate fishing, hiking, rafting and canoeing options in the summer. Telemark skiing takes its name from one of the provinces in this area. Two train lines run south from Oslo. The main one extends through Kristiansand around to Stavanger; the other loops through Tønsberg to Skien before reconnecting with the main line at Nordagutu. Most towns along the south coast without rail service are connected by buses (all listed in the NSB schedules). The larger towns have ferry service to Denmark and sometimes Britain.

Tønsberg, reputedly the oldest town in Scandinavia, brings the beach to within a day-trip from Oslo. Buses run frequently from the station to **Nøtterøy** and **Tjøme** islands, where *skjærgård* and bathing unite. The Slottsfjellet tower offers a voluptuous vista (admission 8kr). The terminally helpful **tourist office** (tel. (033) 102 20) is on Honnørbryggen; follow Tolbodsgata from the station to the harbor. (Open June and Aug. Mon.-Sat. 10am-5pm, July daily 10am-8pm.) From September to May, the tourist office is at Storgata 55 (open Mon.-Fri. 9am-4pm). The local **IYHF youth hostel,** Dronning Blancasgata 2 (tel. (033) 128 48), close to the station and the castle, overflows with homeyness. (120kr, nonmembers 145kr. Showers 5kr.

Open early Jan.-late Dec.) The **ferry** Smyril connects Tønsberg to **Århus** in Denmark (4 per week; Mon.-Fri. 245kr, Sat.-Sun. 290kr, lower in off-season).

Larvik, the birthplace of explorer and author Thor Heyerdahl *(Kon-Tiki),* lies 2½ hr. south of Oslo. The **tourist office,** Storgata 48 (tel. (034) 301 00), 50m east of the station, helps you find accommodations in *hytte* (pensions). (Open Mon.-Sat. 8am-6pm, Sun. 3-6pm; early Aug.-late June Mon.-Fri. 8:30am-4pm.) **Jahrengård og Færiehytter** (tel. (034) 990 30) offers doubles for 200kr, a 15kr bus ride from town. The closest **camping** is at **Gon** (tel. (034) 265 11), 4km out of town. Consult the gratis *Larvik Distrikt* booklet for what's happening. **Larvik Line** (tel. (034) 870 00) launches **ferries** to Frederikshavn, Denmark (1-2 per day, 11½ hr., from 140kr).

The **Sørlandet** part of the southern coast, stretching from Risør in the east (200km south of Oslo) to Flekkefjord in the west, is Norway's premier holiday region in summer. Its whitewashed houses ring natural harbors filled with traditional wooden *snekke* boats. European builders rapaciously pillaged the timbered interior; large parts of Amsterdam still rest on wooden poles from these forests. **Grimstad,** accessible by Kristiansand buses (1 per hr., 50kr, with ISIC 26kr), is a picture-perfect village of neat white cottages and wooden boats bobbing on the busy pier. Home to iconoclastic playwright Henrik Ibsen, he wrote his first play here in 1850. **Reimannsgården** in Vestergade, where Ibsen spent his first four years, houses art exhibitions. The other house, at Henrik Ibsens gata 14, contains the writing desk where he secretly penned poetry during his early years as a bashful romantic. (Open June-Aug. Mon.-Sat. 11am-5pm, Sun. 1-5pm. Admission 10kr, including entrance to the town/maritime museum in the same building.) The **tourist office** at Torskeholmen (tel. (041) 440 01) can help you find accommodations. (Open June and early Aug. Mon.-Fri. 10am-6pm, Sat.-Sun. 11am-5pm; July Mon.-Fri. 10am-6pm, Sat.-Sun. 11am-5pm).

"Norway's #1 Vacation Town" of **Kristiansand** lies at the southern tip of Norway. Here the sun shines more often, and more often than not, it shines on tourists and touristy shops. Day hikes wind along the cliffs above the town, and the beach is awash with Norwegians worshiping the sun god Ra, rather than that nasty old Thor. The helpful **tourist information office** on Dronningensgate 2 (tel. (042) 260 65), a 5-block walk from the train station along Vestre Strandgate by the harbor can point you toward the distant hostel and campsites. (Open Mon.-Fri. 8am-7pm, Sat. 10am-7pm, Sun. noon-7pm; late Aug. to mid-May Mon.-Fri. 8am-4pm.) The **Kristiansand Youth Hostel (IYHF),** Kongsgårds Allé 33c (tel. (042) 953 69) lies across the river Otra from the city center. Take bus #15 or 16 from Henrik Wergelandsgate, direction "Lund." (120kr, nonmembers 145kr. Open May-Sept.) **Ferries** run to Hirsthals in Denmark (bookings (042) 788 88; 3-4 per day, 4 hr., Mon.-Thurs. 130-250kr, Fri.-Sun. 180-290kr, depending on season, students half-price except July to mid-Aug.)

At the end of the southern rail line, **Stavanger** radiates the wealth of an oil boomtown. The sudden influx of North Sea cash in the 60s fertilized the rapid growth of a cosmopolitan downtown and provided the tax revenue to restore the precious **old quarter**—Northern Europe's best preserved wooden-house settlement. Built by King Sigurd the Crusader in 1125, the Gothic Stavanger Cathedral retains its medieval solemnity amidst Stavanger's light-hearted center. (Open Mon.-Sat. 9am-6pm, Sun. 1-6pm; late Sept.-early May Mon.-Sat. 9am-2pm, services on Sun. 11am-1pm.) At the spectacular **Pulpit Rock,** a cliff plunges over 300m into the Lysefjord. From Stavanger, take the frequent ferry to Tau, a bus to the base of the mountain, and hike the two hours to the top. Every first Sunday in July, there is a church service held atop the natural pulpit. The **tourist office** two blocks from the train station (turn left as you leave the station) can provide maps, a city guide and essential ferry information (tel. (04) 53 51 00; open Mon.-Fri. 9am-4pm, Sept.-May also Sat. 9am-1pm; booth by the fisherman's market open June-Aug. daily 9am-8pm.) The **Mosvangen Youth Hostel (IYHF)** (tel. (04) 87 09 77) is one of Norway's poshest. (100kr, nonmembers 125kr. Breakfast 35kr.) The most central campsite is **Mosvangen camping** (tel. (04) 53 29 71) just by the youth hostel. (Tents 50kr. Open June-Aug.) For cheap food, look around for **Rema 1000, Mauritz** and **Obs** markets. Nothing is cheap in the center of town. Stavanger's streets are alive day and night; entertainment clusters along **Nedre Strandgate** and the **waterfront** to the right of the inlet.

Hydrofoils run from Stavanger to **Bergen** (2-3 per day; 4 hr.; 410kr, 25% off with InterRail, 50% off with Nordturist). Slower **ferries** connect the two cities, shipping out from Randaberg in Stavanger (1-2 per day; 6 hr.; 170kr, students 100kr). **Color Line** (tel. (04) 52 45 45) runs ships from Stavanger to **Newcastle,** England (2-3 per week; 18 hr.; 395-795kr, depending on the season).

Bergen

Bergen's scenery exalts it above most cities in the world, while its Germanic heritage sets it apart from most of Norway. Until the railway to Oslo was completed, it was easier to travel from Bergen to London, and the city acquired an international flair. Originally the capital of Norway, Bergen became a center of commerce for the Hanseatic merchants in the 14th century and more recently a focal point of resistance to the Nazis. Trees soften the postmodern frenzy; from the hills, Bergen looks more like a wooded settlement than a thriving commercial and university city.

Orientation and Practical Information

Bergen's train station is at the top of the city center, several blocks above the gleaming harbor. Looking from the station towards the water, Bryggen (the extension of Kong Oscars gate) and the town's most imposing mountain are to your right, most of the city's main buildings to the left. The Torget—an outdoor market—is at the harbor's tip.

Tourist Office: In the pavilion on Torgalmenning (tel. 32 14 80), a 10-min. walk up Kaigaten from the train station. Pick up the all-knowing, all-fathoming *Bergen Guide 1992.* Open Mon.-Sat. 8:30am-9pm, Sun. 10am-7pm; Oct.-April Mon.-Fri. 10am-3pm. **DNT** (see Oslo section), C. Sundts gate 3 (tel. 32 22 30), is a must for travelers headed for the highlands and wilds. Open Mon.-Wed. and Fri. 10am-4pm, Thurs. 10am-6pm.

Budget Travel: Univers Reiser, in the Studentsentret, Parkveien 1 (tel. 32 64 00). Discounts on international travel. Open Mon.-Fri. 8:30am-4pm.

Currency Exchange: At the tourist office when banks are closed; 4% commission.

American Express: Winge Travel Bureau, Christian Michelsens gate 1-3 (tel. 90 12 90). Mail held, checks sold and replaced, but no other services. Open Mon.-Fri. 8:30am-4pm, Sat. 9:30am-2pm.

Post Office: In the green building with the clock on Småstrand gate, 1 block from the Torget. Poste Restante open Mon.-Wed. 8am-5pm, Thurs.-Fri. 8am-6pm, Sat. 9am-2pm.

Telephones: Starvhuse gate 4, across Rådhus gate from the post office. Open Mon.-Fri. 8am-8pm, Sat. 9am-2pm. **City Code:** 05.

Trains: Tel. 31 96 40 or 31 93 05. 4-6 per day along the line to Voss (1 hr., 91kr), Myrdal (1¾-2½ hr., 138kr), and Oslo (7-8 hr., 425kr, seat reservations compulsory). Luggage storage 10kr. Open daily 6:30am-midnight.

Buses: Bystasjonen, Strømgaten 8 (tel. 32 67 80). Service to neighboring areas and the Hardangerfjord district, as well as to Oslo.

Ferries: There are three major groups. **To Stavanger and the nearby fjord regions:** Coming from the train station, boats leave from the left side of the harbor. **To other countries:** Ships leave from Skoltegrunnskaien, about a 20-min. walk past Bryggen along the right side of the harbor. **Smyril Line,** offices in Engelgården at the Bryggen (tel. 32 09 70), departs June-Aug. Tues. at 3pm for the Shetland Islands (11½ hr., 580kr), Faroe Islands (23 hr., 1050kr), and Iceland (39 hr., 1700kr). Student discount 25%; another 25% off early to mid-June, and in Aug. **Color Line,** office at Skuteviksboder 1-2 (tel. 31 83 99), sails to Newcastle via Stavanger May-Sept. Sun., Wed. and Fri., mid-March to April and Oct.-Dec. Mon. and Thurs. 395-795kr depending on season. 25% off with student ID, 10% off with InterRail. The **Hurtigruten** leaves daily at 10pm from a separate harbor at Frieleneskaien, behind the Natural History Museum.

Public Transportation: Yellow buses chaffeur you around the city center for 6kr, 11kr outside the center. 2-day pass 45kr.

Pharmacy: In the bus station. Open daily 8:30am-midnight.

Medical Assistance: Accident Clinic, Lars Hilles gate 30 (tel. 32 11 20). Open 24 hrs.

Emergencies: Police, tel. 002.

Accommodations and Camping

The tourist office books rooms for a 15kr fee (20kr for 2 people) in private homes (singles 145-170kr; doubles 235-259kr).

Intermission, Kalfarveien 8 (tel. 31 32 75). A 15-min. walk from the center up Kong Oscars gate, which turns into Kalfarveien just past the train station at the Old Gate House; or take bus #2,4, 7, or 11. Coed dorm, friendly staff, kitchen, showers, and ghost. Lockout 11am-5pm. Beds 80kr. Arrange curfew with warden. Open mid-June to mid-Aug.

Vågenes, J.L. Mowinckelsvei 95 (tel. 16 11 01), 10 min. on bus #19 (11kr). In a private home; call for reservations and directions. Doubles with kitchens and made-up beds 90kr. Sleeping bag accommodations 75kr.

Montana Youth Hostel (IYHF), Johan Blyttsveien 30 (tel. 29 29 00), halfway up Mt. Ulriken, 4km from the center. Take bus #4 to Lægdene (11kr). Reservations recommended. 95kr, nonmembers 120kr. Breakfast 45kr. Open early May-early Oct.

InterRail Point, Kalfarveien 77, a 25-min. walk from the center, far past Intermission. Luscious lounge and kitchen facilities. 70kr on the floor, with mattresses. Open July to mid-Aug. daily 7-11am and 5-11pm.

Camping: Bergenshallen Camping, Vilhelm Bjerknesveien 24 (tel. 27 01 80), within the city limits. Take bus #3 from Strandgate. No charge per person, 40kr per tent. Open June 24-Aug. 10. Camp atop Fløyen for free; take the funicular to the top (26kr).

Food

Rema 1000 and **Mekka** discount supermarkets make life easier for the hungry traveler. Mekka is at Marken 3, 5 minutes from the station on the street parallel to Kaigaten. (Open Mon.-Fri. 7am-8pm, Sat. 7am-6pm.) Hunt around for *dagens ret* restaurant specials (60-100kr). You might want to sample one of the seafood restaurants.

Kaffistova, across from the Torget. Second floor offers large hot entrees. *Dagens ret* 60kr, boiled ham 70kr. Open Mon.-Fri. 11:30am-6pm, Sat. 11:30am-3:30pm, Sun. noon-6pm.

Spisestedet Kornelia, Fosswinckelsgate 9, serves vegetarian food in a whole wheat atmosphere. Open Mon.-Fri. noon-8pm.

Ola's Inn, Vaskerelvsmuget 1, at the end of Torgalmenningen. Quiet cafeteria with inexpensive food. Fish and chips 52kr. Open Mon.-Fri. 10am-9pm, Sat. 10:30am-5pm.

Sights and Entertainment

Looking toward the right side of the harbor from the Torget, you'll see the pointed gables of **Bryggen's** roofline. This row of timbered medieval buildings, typical Hanseatic architecture, has survived half a dozen disastrous fires and the explosion of a Nazi munitions ship on Hitler's birthday, 1944. It now features restaurants, offices, and artsy-craftsy workshops. Housed in one of the best-preserved buildings, the **Hanseatic Museum** paints a picture of commercial activity during the league. (Open June-Aug. daily 9am-5pm; May and Sept. daily 11am-2pm; Oct.-April Sun.-Mon., Wed., and Fri. 11am-2pm. Admission 10kr.) Teetering at the end of the quay is the former city fortress **Bergenhus.** The **Rosenkrantz Tower** stands in late medieval splendor. (Open daily 10am-4pm; mid-Sept. to mid-May Sun. noon-3pm. Admission 10kr.) Built by Håkon Håkonsson in the 13th century, **Håkonshallen** is what is left of the original castle (same hours and price). **The Theta Room,** Enhjørningsgården Bryggen, chronicles its role as the center for Resistance operations during the Nazi occupation. (Open Tues. and Sat.-Sun. 2-3pm. Admission 10kr.)

Lose your head over the sheer audacity of the **Leprosy Museum,** Kong Oscars gate 59. Since 1970, the University has tastefully documented the history of the disease in a 19th-century hospital. (Open mid-May to Aug. daily 11am-3pm. Admission 15kr, students 4kr.) On the western shore of **Lille Lungegårdsvatnet,** a shimmering pond in the middle of town, the **Rasmus Meyer's Collection** provides a quality overview of Norwegian naturalists, impressionists, and expressionists. (Open Mon.-Sat. 11am-4pm, Sun. noon-3pm; mid-Sept. to mid-May Wed.-Mon. noon-3pm. Admission 10kr, students free.)

A quick bus trip from downtown is **Gamle Bergen** (Old Bergen), a collection of wooden buildings from the last century. Of the 40 old houses, 23 are now artists' studios; the other 17 are open to the public via guided tours. Take city bus #1 or 9 (direction "Lønborg") from outside Den Norske Bank to the first stop past the second tunnel. (Houses open mid-June to mid-Aug. 11am-7pm; mid-May to mid-June and mid-Aug. to early Sept. noon-6pm. Admission 20kr, students 10kr.)

Nature is right nearby in Bergen. With mountains on three sides and vast archipelagos to the west, you can take your scenic pick. The ever-popular **Fløibanen** brings you right from the city's heart high up into a maze of mountaintop paths and views. (Open daily 6am-11pm; 13kr one-way.) Consult **Bergen Touring Association,** Bergen Turlag, C. Sundts gate 4 (tel. 32 22 30), for detailed maps and inspiration.

Nightclubs and discos pack the town center; all are open Thursday-Saturday until 3am. The rest of the week, consult your *Bergen Guide.* All the stops are pulled out in summer; the annual **Bergen International Festival** presents its 12-day program of music, ballet, folklore and drama from May 21-June 1 in 1992. Tickets are hard to come by, but try calling the ticket office (tel. 31 09 54 or 31 31 04); uncollected tickets are sold half-price on the day of performance.

The Fjords and West Country

All along the western coast, Ice Age gashes bring sapphire sea deep into Norway's sheer inland mountain ranges. The fjords between Stavanger and Ålesund have the best views of steep mountains rising out of still water. Bergen, halfway between Stavanger and Ålesund, is the best starting point: ferries from all over wind through mazes of islands and peninsulas, hydrofoils go to Sognefjord and Nordfjord to the north, and buses connect to Hardangerfjord and the uninhabited Hardangervidda plateau to the southeast.

Sognefjord and trips from Bergen

At 200km the longest of the fjords, **Sognefjord's** deep, slender fingers penetrate all the way to the foot of the Jotunheimen mountains. A short ride north from the stunning Oslo-Bergen rail line, Sognefjord is ideal for those seeing Norway by train.

Hydrofoils bring the hordes from Bergen all along the Sognefjord system, passing through **Balestrand** and **Aurland** before ending in **Flåm** (1-2 per day; to Aurland 5 hr., 410kr, 50% off with railpasses or ISIC), and car ferries crisscross between the north and south shores. By land, the easiest approaches to the fjord are from the Oslo-Bergen railway. The most popular option is the steep 20km train route from **Myrdal,** on the Oslo-Bergen line, down to Flåm on Sognefjord (8 trains per day connecting with service to Oslo and Bergen; 47kr). You may prefer to get off the train part way down and hike the rest. Hikers can also alight from the Oslo-Bergen train at **Finse,** just east of Myrdal, and hike for three to four stunning days down the Aurlandsdalen valley to Aurland, 7km from Flåm—sleeping warmly all the way in evenly spaced DNT *hytter.* For maps and prices, inquire at DNT in Oslo or Bergen, or during your stay at the Finse **tourist chalet** (tel. (05) 52 67 32), just by the station. (Open late June to mid-Sept. 65kr, nonmembers 110kr.) Buses also connect Aurland and Flåm (17kr).

Flåm has a small, friendly **tourist office** (tel. (056) 321 06), in the small hut beside the train station (open June to mid-Aug. daily 8:15am-8:30pm), and a newborn **IYHF youth hostel** (tel. (056) 321 21), five minutes into the valley along the tracks (70kr, nonmembers 95kr; open May to mid-Oct.). The Aurland **tourist office** (tel. (056) 333 13) serves Flåm in the winter. (Open Mon.-Fri. 8am-7pm, Sat.-Sun. 11am-7pm; Sept.-April Mon.-Fri. 8am-3pm.)

Ferries run from Flåm and Aurland west through narrow fjords to **Gudvangen** (2 per day, 2½ hr., 34kr from Flåm, 30kr from Aurland). From Gudvangen, buses (5-8 per day, 47kr) run up to **Voss,** 70 minutes east of Bergen on the Oslo rail line, and birthplace of the canonized American football figure Knute ("win one for the Gipper") Rockne. The Voss train station is a five to ten-minute distance from the **tourist office,** in Tinghuse (tel. (05) 51 17 16). Turn left when you face the lake and bear right at the fork by the church. (Open Mon.-Sat. 9am-7pm, Sun. 2-6pm; Sept.-May Mon.-Fri. 9am-4pm.) Turning right from the station and walking along the lakeside road brings you to Voss's large, modern **youth hostel (IYHF)** (tel. (05) 51 22 05). There's no kitchen, but you can rent canoes and rowboats (20kr per hour, 75kr per day). (125kr, nonmembers 150kr. Open Jan.-Oct. Reserve ahead.) The most central **camping** (tel. (05) 51 15 97) is right by the lake and tourist office (tents 50kr, 4-person *hytte* 250kr). Local trains between Voss and Myrdal stop on demand at **Ørnaberg,** where a steep 300m path leads you down to the slightly decrepit but incredibly well-located riverside **Mjølfjell Youth Hostel (IYHF)** (tel. (05) 51 81 11). The owner will give you hiking suggestions and maps. (80kr, nonmembers 105kr. Open June-Sept.; call ahead the rest of the year.)

The north side of Sognefjord revolves around **Balestrand,** Kaiser Wilhelm's favorite procrastination site. Stop at the **tourist office** (tel. (056) 912 55), near the bus station on the quay. They can help plan area tours by boat, bike, or foot. They also rent bikes (30kr per hr., 100kr per day). (Open June-Aug. Mon.-Sat. 8:30am-1:30pm and 3-6pm, Sun. 11am-3pm.) The **Balestrand Youth Hostel (IYHF)** (tel. (056) 913 03) overlooks the fjord from the Kringsja Hotel, a five-minute walk up the hill and to the left. (85kr, nonmembers 110kr. Open mid-June to late Aug.) **Sjøthun camping** (tel. (05) 69 12 23), 500m down the coastal road, provides tent sites and pseudo-chalets. (12.50kr per person, 25kr per tent. 2-person hut 70kr, 4-person hut 130kr. Open June-Aug.) At the wooden **English Church of St. Olav,** on the road to Sjøthun, a British pastor preaches every Sunday in summer. Farther along are two **Viking burial mounds,** one of them topped by a statue of King Bele (donated by the Kaiser in 1913). A ferry leaves Balestrand around noon to cruise up the **Fjærland fjord** to Mundal. Crafty buses meet the ferry and transport you to the base of the Jostedal glacier, whose blue ice hangs ominously overhead; the ferry returns to Balestrand around 6pm. (All-inclusive ticket 118kr at the tourist office.)

The Bergen hydrofoils serve Balestrand twice per day (4½ hr.; 330kr, with Inter-Rail or Nordturist 50% off). 9am ferries to Fjærland connect north over snow-covered mountains to Stryn in Nordfjord (110kr) and Geiranger in Geirangerfjord (214kr, except Sun.).

Nordfjord

Twisting over 100km inland to the foot of the Jostedal glacier, fjantastic Nordfjord is one of Norway's most accessible. Wedged between the mountains near the inner end of the fjord, **Stryn** is the regional communication center and a summer ski hub. Buses stop at the edge of town; walk up past the Esso station to get to the main street, Tonningsgata. The **tourist office** (tel. (057) 715 26) lies off the main street on the paved square with the *Télé* offices (open June-Aug. Mon.-Sat. 10am-6pm, Sun. noon-4pm). Well-versed downhillers should ask about the **summer skiing** at Strynefjellet. Take a bus or a boat to Briksdalsbreen or Kjenndalsbreen to lick the tongues of the **Jostedal** glacier. The tasteful **IYHF youth hostel** (tel. (057) 711

06) is a hefty romp up the hill behind town. (Lockout 10:30-4pm. Curfew 11pm. 75kr, nonmembers 100kr. Washer and drying room. Open June-Aug.) **Stryn Camping** (tel. (057) 211 36) is the most central of countless sites. (60kr per person, 70kr per 2 people.) Stryn is a meeting point for buses from Otta on the Oslo-Trondheim rail line via Lom and Jotunheimen (Otta-Stryn 183kr; Lom-Stryn 124kr), from Hellesylt in Geirangerfjord (53kr) and from Fjærland and Balestrand in Sognefjord (214kr), while the ferry *M.S. Nordfjord* winds from Bergen via Måløy all the way to Stryn (Tues., Thurs. and Sat.; 495kr).

Sunbathers can bask on the coast around **Måløy,** at Nordfjord's mouth. Reach Måløy by hydrofoil from Bergen (1-2 per day, 395kr, 198kr with ISIC), by daily *Hurtigruten* northbound from Bergen (9 hr., 427kr, arrives at 7:30am) or southbound from Ålesund (4½ hr., 204kr, arrives at 4:45am), or by bus from Stryn (2-4 per day, 96kr). The local **tourist office** (tel. (057) 508 50), in the town hall, will help you with accommodations (open mid-June to mid-Aug. daily 10am-6pm).

Geirangerfjord

Resist the temptation to stay snuggled in bed under your fluffy Scandinavian comforter, and take the bus to high-walled, S-shaped Geirangerfjord—perhaps the most stunning of the Norwegian fjords, and certainly the most visited. The most southerly, inland arm of the fjord system that begins at Ålesund, its 16km of green-blue water reflect stunning cliffs and cascading waterfalls. Watch for the drama of the **Seven Sisters,** opposite the powerful splurge of the **Suitor,** and the mist of the **Bride's Veil.** Clusters of abandoned farms cling to the mountain walls; to reach one of the higher farmhouses, the family had to climb a rope-ladder, which was conveniently withrawn when the tax collector visited. From June through August, several daily ferries (70 min., 25kr) connect the tiny towns of Hellesylt and Geiranger, at opposite ends of the fjord. Otherwise, both towns are accessible only by road. From the south or southeast, go through Stryn; from the north, launch yourself from Åndalsnes or Ålesund (see those sections for bus details).

Geiranger is Norway's Niagara Falls; in the summer over 5000 tourists visit each day, and an armada of oceanliners maintains a steady presence off-shore. You can join the armada by going on the sightseeing trip of the fjord (1¾ hr., 60kr) or enlarge it by renting a boat yourself near the pier (tel. (071) 631 23; motorboats 100kr per hour, 400kr per day; open late June and early Aug. daily 10am-6pm, July daily 10am-8pm). Send a special postcard from Geiranger's diminutive post office, which holds the *Guiness Book of World Records* title for "most customers per year per square meter." The Geiranger **tourist office** (tel. (071) 630 99), just up from the landing, provides camping and hiking information. Ask about the 45-minute walk to **Storseter,** which passes under a waterfall. (Open June-Aug. daily 9am-7pm.) Geiranger has no fewer than five campgrounds; the closest is **Geiranger Camping** (tel. (071) 631 20; 8kr per person, 38kr per tent).

At the eastern end of the fjord, tiny, unspoiled **Hellesylt,** with its own beach and bathhouse, is a base for mountain hiking in some of the wildest scenery in Norway. A millennium ago, Vikings gathered near the runestone marker in a field not far from the town center. In the 1800s, cruise ship passengers were led on ponies from Hellesylt to Øye through the extremely narrow **Norangsdalen.** At the turn of the century, a huge avalanche dammed up the valley; farm buildings can still be seen under the water. The daily Leknes bus (32kr to Øye) runs through the valley, but there's no return before the next day. Some hitch. The **Hellesylt Youth Hostel (IYHF)** (tel. (071) 651 28), up the hill along the road to Stranda (a path past the waterfall cuts past the main bends in the road), has a ripping view. (75kr, nonmembers 100kr. Lockout 10am-5pm. Avoid the 35kr breakfast. Open June-Aug.) The **tourist office** (tel. (071) 650 52), right on the ferry landing, rents fishing equipment (25kr per hr.) and provides hiking maps. (Open mid-June to mid-Aug. daily 8:30am-5:30pm.)

Gudbrandsdalen, Rondane and Dovrefjell

Two train lines shoot north from Oslo to Trondheim; the slower line goes eastwards through the Østerdalen valley and Røros, the faster one through the **Gudbrandsdalen** valley which runs from Lillehammer (2½ hr. from Oslo) northwestward through Otta and Dombås. Traditionally one of Norway's great thoroughfares, Gudbrandsdalen is also famous as the origin of the brown Gudbrandsdalsost cheese so favored by Norwegians, and for its skiing, hiking, canoeing, and old churches and wooden houses. **Lillehammer,** the valley's largest town, is hastily preparing to host the 1994 Winter Olympics. **Storgata,** two blocks uphill from the station and the main street, is busy with shoppers and sun-frolickers. Off it on Elvegata is the **Olympic Information Center.** (Open Mon.-Wed., Fri.-Sat. 10am-6pm, Thurs. 10am-8pm, Sun. noon-6pm; Sept.-May Fri.-Wed. 11am-5pm, Thurs. 11am-8pm.) The **tourist office** (tel. (062) 592 99), next to the train station, can give you an idea of the range of activities available on and around Mjøsa Lake and in the southern Gudbrandsdalen. (Open Mon.-Fri. 9am-8:30pm, Sat. 9am-6pm, Sun. 11am-6pm; late Aug. to mid-June Mon.-Fri. 9am-4pm, Sat. 10am-1pm.) Take bus #001 (9kr) to the local **youth hostel (IYHF),** (tel. (062) 509 87) Sinestad Sommerhotell, about 2km north of town. (85kr, nonmembers 110kr. Open mid-June to late Aug.) The **Maihaugen** is a compacted version of traditional Gudbrandsdalen culture, featuring ancient houses and appropriately dressed people. (Open June-Aug. daily 10am-6pm; May and Sept. daily 10am-4pm. Admission 35kr.)

Further up the valley, the old, soft slopes of the mountain ranges of **Dovrefjell** and **Rondane** provide easy access to untrampled scenery. Both areas have national parks—the one in Dovrefjell is famous for its musk oxen (keep your distance). Rondane is most accessible from **Otta,** 1½ hours north of Lillehammer. The **tourist office** (tel. (062) 302 44), in the station, has maps and tips on accommodations, white water rafting on the Sjoa river, and tips on how to get to the Rondane hiking trails at **Mysuseter** and at **Høvringen.** (Open Mon.-Fri. 8:30am-7:30pm, Sat. 10am-6pm, Sun. noon-6pm; mid-Aug. to mid-June Mon.-Fri. 8:30am-4pm.) Spectacular bus routes snake from Otta across the Jotunheimen mountains to Sogndal in Sognefjord and Stryn in Nordfjord.

The slightly more challenging **Dovrefjell** is best reached from the rail hub of Dombås or the towns of Hjerkinn, Reinheim and Oppdal farther north. The **Dombås tourist office** (tel. (062) 414 44), in the shopping mall at the end of the hill from the train station, can help you plan tours along the trails. (Open Mon.-Fri. 10am-7pm, Sat.-Sun. 10am-5pm; late Aug.-early June Mon.-Fri. 9am-4pm.) The **Dombås Youth Hostel (IYHF)** (tel. (062) 410 45) is uphill from the train station; turn right, away from the city, on the main street. (Reception open 8-10am and 4-11pm. 80kr, nonmembers 105kr. Breakfast 48kr. Open late June to mid-Aug.)

Valdres and Jotunheimen

The **Valdres** valley, running parallel and to the west of Gudbrandsdalen, is shorter and ignored by the train route, but has no less than six of Norway's 25 medieval wooden stave churches. **Fagernes** is the center of things in this deep valley. The **tourist office** (tel. (063) 604 00), by the bus station, will gladly hand over the comprehensive *Valdres Summer* (or *Winter) Guide.* (Open Mon.-Fri. 8am-8:30pm, Sat. 10am-8:30pm, Sun. noon-6pm; late Aug.-late June Mon.-Fri. 8am-4pm.) The **Valdres Folkmuseum** contains a collection of artifacts from the region's past (open in summer daily 10:30am-4pm; admission 30kr). Ask at the tourist office about the **stave churches** (admission to any one 10kr); the **1992 Culture Festival** (June 24-28) promises traditional dancing and music. The more mobile should ask at the tourist office for a map and further information about the *Vardevandring* (watchtower hike), which takes you through most of the valley. The **Fagernes Youth Hostel,**

Valdres Folkhøjskole (tel. (063) 623 97), is 4km south of town in Leira. (70kr, nonmembers 95kr. Open June to mid-Aug.) Reach Fagernes by bus from Gol on the Oslo-Bergen rail line (70 min., 39kr, students 1/3 off), from Lillehammer (2 hr., 83kr, students 1/3 off), or by *Valdresekspressen* bus from Oslo (3hr., 150kr).

The Valdres valley terminates in the highest mountain range in Europe north of the Alps, the jagged, reindeer-freckled **Jotunheimen** massif. Almost entirely above the tree line and covered by endless boulder fields, the entire region looks like the home of the troll giants for whom it is named. While only two of the several hundred peaks require technical gear to climb, only experienced hikers should attempt anything longer than a daytrip. Snow falls even in July, so always bring warm, wool clothes and raingear, even on the shortest jaunts. It's also a wise idea to visit the DNT offices in either Oslo or Bergen for maps and information on trails, huts, and safety precautions.

Jotunheimen is accessible from either its eastern or northwestern slopes. On the east side, Route 51 winds north from Fagernes to meet Route 15 at Vågåmo; **Gjendesheim,** an hour north of Fagernes by bus, is the best hiking springboard. (Buses also run to Gjendesheim from the Oslo-Trondheim train line at Otta, 30km downvalley from Vågåmo.) From the **hut** at Gjendesheim, you can hike across the **Besseggen,** a spectacular ridge astride two lakes: a deep blue one at 1200m, and an emerald green one at 984m.

The northwest approach means a spectacular bus ride along Routes 15 and 55 over the main massif of Jotunheimen between Otta on the rail line and Sogndal on Sognefjord (2 per day). 62km out of Otta, the bus stops in **Lom,** just to the north of Jotunheimen, which is the branching point for buses to Stryn in Nordfjord. Lom's **tourist office** (tel. (062) 112 86), 300m from the bus stop, does the information thing. (Open Mon.-Sat. 9am-9pm, Sun. noon-6pm; Sept.-May Mon.-Fri. 8:30am-3pm.) 15km from Lom at **Bøverdalen,** you can stay at the youth hostel (IYHF) (tel. (062) 120 64; 60kr, nonmembers 80kr) and make daytrips to **Galdhøpiggen** (2469m) and its sibling summit **Glittertinden** (2464m)—the highest points in Norway. 18km off Route 55, the DNT *hytta* at Spiterstulen is closer to Glittertinden, with cheap beds and story-filled hikers. (Tel. (062) 114 80. Bed 100kr. Mattress on floor 50kr. Tents 30kr per person. No bus; some folk hitch.) Southwest of Bøverdalen at **Krossbu** is an old wooden hotel on a high, empty moor where you can stay for 85-120kr. The plateau between Krossbu and **Sognefjellhytta** is strewn with rock cairns tracing the way between snow-covered lakes; cross-country skiing is often possible even in July. A little farther, near **Turtagrø,** just above the tip of the Sognefjord system, is one of the premier rock-climbing areas in Norway. From the road there's a steep but well-maintained four-hour path to **Fannaråkhytta** (2069m), highest hut in the DNT system, right on a glacier.

Åndalsnes and Ålesund

The mountains around Åndalsnes are a mecca for mountaineers and rock climbers, and to normal hikers as well. The wagons that split off the Oslo-Trondheim train at Dombås terminate at Åndalsnes (3 per day, from Oslo 6½ hr.), passing by an ultimate mountaineering challenge, Trollveggen (on the left a bit before Åndalsnes), and the most notable peak in the area, Romsdalshorn (on the right just past Trollveggen). The train spends two hours running through the visually exhausting **Romsdal** valley, a two-hour stretch of narrow canyon bounded by 1000m walls. Dombås-Åndalsnes buses parallel the train. An equally awesome approach to the town is the road down **Trollstigen,** a dizzying freefall traversed by the bus to Geiranger that features no fewer than 11 hairpin turns.

Åndalsnes itself is a splendiferous and comfortable town, at the mouth of the Rauma river and the bottom of a wide fjord. It centers on the road leading uphill from the train station. Follow the road until you cross the river to get to **Setnes Youth Hostel (IYHF)** (tel. (072) 213 82)—perhaps Norway's best. Buses from out of town stop there upon request. The hostess serves a breakfast that would make the finest French chef sick with envy. (75kr, nonmembers 100kr. Breakfast 45kr. Open mid-May to April.) The local **tourist office** (tel. (072) 216 22) is a good source for hiking maps and recreational information, as is the hostel hostess. (Open Mon.-Sat. 9:30am-9:30pm, Sun. 3:30-9:30pm; late Aug.-May Mon.-Fri. 9am-3pm.) Follow the signs from the hostel to **Åndalsnes Camping** (tel. (072) 216 29), which lets you set up tents for 35kr per tent, 10kr per person, rents out huts (80-450kr) and rents bikes (20kr per hr., 60kr per day) and canoes (30kr per hr., 140kr per day). Åndalsnes's **Norsk Tindemuseum** houses legendary mountaineer Arne Randers Heen's collection of expedition paraphernalia. (Open mid-June to mid-Aug. daily 2-7pm; other times on request.) To hit the mountains yourself, contact **Aak** (tel. (072) 264 44), 4km east of town on the E69 back towards Dombås; they have beds (50-140kr) with showers and a fireplace, and rent canoes (first hour 100kr, subsequently 30kr per hour), and cross-country telemark skis (100kr per day).

Ålesund, the largest city between Bergen and Trondheim, is reachable by road (3 buses per day along the 122km from Åndalsnes; some folk hitch), by *Hurtigruten,* which docks here daily, or by hydrofoil from Bergen (Mon.-Fri. 1 per day). The town enjoys a beautiful seaside and cliffside location, and is renowned for its art nouveau architecture. The **tourist office** (tel. (071) 212 02) is across from the bus station in the city hall. (Open Mon.-Fri. 9am-6pm, Sat. 9am-3pm, Sun. noon-5pm; Sept.-May Mon.-Fri. 8:30am-4pm.) The **Ålesund Museum,** in the center of town, illustrates the city's rich past with ship models and vintage clothing. (Open Mon.-Sat. 11am-3pm, Sun. noon-3pm. Admission 10kr.) For a view of old Ålesund, the harbor, and the mountains beyond, point up the 418 steps to **Aksla. Centrum Hospits,** Storgata 24 (tel. (071) 217 09), offers snug rooms and warm proprietors. (Singles 225kr. Doubles 300kr.) **Camp Prinsen** (tel. (071) 352 04), at Gåseid, is 5km outside town (bus 15kr) next to a popular beach. (Huts 150-420kr, rooms 150-220kr, camping 85kr per tent.)

There's an old Viking site on **Giske,** a short boat ride from Ålesund. Ornithusiasts will thrill to the island of **Runde,** a sanctuary for more than 500,000 birds. A hydrofoil runs from Ålesund to Hareid; a *Soreid* bus leaves from there (80kr one-way). From Ålesund, it's two hours by bus and ferry (90kr) to **Molde,** a seaside town known for its **International Jazz Festival,** held for a week every summer in late July or early August. Ask at Ålesund or Åndalsnes for information.

Trondheim

Medieval capital of Norway, Trondheim is the natural stopping point between Oslo and destinations above the Arctic Circle. Olav Tryggvason founded Trondheim in 997; his image now presides over an outdoor fruit- and vegetable-market from a column in the main town square, **Torvet.** The train station, backed by the Trondheimfjord, faces the center of town, which is circled by the Nid river. From the train station, walk across the bridge, then six blocks on Søndregate, turn right on Munkegata, and continue to the main square and the **tourist office** (tel. (07) 52 72 01), which books rooms in private homes. (Singles 150kr. Doubles 250kr. 20kr fee. Open Mon.-Fri. 8:30am-8pm, Sat. 8:30am-6pm, Sun. 10am-6pm; late Aug.-May Mon.-Fri. 9am-4pm, Sat. 9am-1pm.) The **InterRail Center,** in the train station, books tickets and seats, and has hot plates and 10kr showers. (Open early July-late Aug. daily 7:20am-9:30pm.) The **Youth Info Center,** Munkegata 15, has cheap food, international newspapers and tips for cheap living. (Open Mon.-Fri. 8am-8pm.) A **DNT office,** Munkegata 64 (tel. (07) 52 38 08), describes huts and trails to the north and south of Trondheim. (Open Mon.-Wed. and Fri. 8am-2:30pm, Thurs. 9am-6pm.) All city buses leave from the Munkegata-Dronningensgate intersection, and require exact change.

Student-run **Singesaker Sommerhotell,** Rogertsgate 1 (tel. (07) 52 00 92), has a grill, pool table, piano, and TV room. (Sleeping-bag accommodation 100kr. Singles 200kr. Doubles 300kr. Breakfast included. Open mid-June to mid-Aug.) **Trondheim Youth Hostel (IYHF),** Weidemannsvei 41 (tel. (07) 53 04 90), has all the warmth and charm of a large hospital. From the train station, walk up Søndregate, turn left on Olav Tryggvasonsgate, and follow it over the bridge and four blocks uphill. Bus #63 (13kr) saves you the 20-minute walk. (Lockout 11am-4pm. 130kr, nonmembers 155kr. Open early Jan. to mid-Dec.) The closest of multiple campsites is **Sandmoen Camping** (tel. (07) 88 61 35), 10km south of town, which is large and often crowded. Take bus #44 or 45 from the bus station to Sandbakken (50kr per tent). Camping outside of sites is not permitted in the Trondheim area. Cheap Rema 1000 stores abound in the town center. Wander along Munkegata, from the fruit market at Torvet to the Ravnkola fish market by the water, to replenish the vitamins lost to weeks of bread and cheese.

Local boy King Olav Haraldsson became Norway's patron saint after he fought to introduce Christianity to the country. A steady stream of pilgrims to Trondheim prompted the construction of **Nidaros Cathedral,** Scandinavia's largest medieval structure, built over a holy well which sprang up beside St. Olav's grave. (Open mid-June to Aug. Mon.-Fri. 9:30am-5:30pm, Sat. 9:30am-2pm, Sun. 1-4pm; reduced hours off-season. Admission 10kr, students 5kr.) Walk up the 172-step spiral staircase to the tower: the view is worth the 3kr admission. The spires rise above the wooded banks of the Nid river, a favorite local recreation area. The **Gamle Bybro** (old town bridge) and the 18th-century wharves are perhaps the prettiest part of town. On the hill across the river is the white **Kristiansten Fortress,** built in 1681. (Open June-Aug. Mon.-Fri. 10am-3pm, Sat.-Sun. 11am-3pm. Admission 3kr.) Exhibits of some of Norway's greatest art, from gentle landscapes to perturbing modern portraits, are displayed at the **Trondhjems Kunst-Forening,** next to the cathedral. Edvard Munch has a hallway to himself, highlighted by the woodcuts *Lust* and *Jealousy.* (Open daily 11am-4pm; Sept.-May Tues.-Sun. noon-4pm; admission 20kr, students 10kr.) Bus #8 or 9 will take you to the intriguing **Ringve Museum of Musical History.** Displays range from a one-stringed Ethiopian violin to the ornate Mozart Room; guides demonstrate on the instruments. (Tours in English daily at 11am, 12:30pm, 2:30pm and 4:30pm in July. Admission 30kr, students 20kr.) Ferry over to **Munkholmen,** an island monastery that became a prison fortress in a sudden change of heart and then flipped again into a quiet beach and picnic spot (round-trip 22kr, admission to fortress 10kr). From late August until May, the city is alive with students; visit the red 'n' round **Studentersenter** across the river from the cathedral if you wish to dip your toes in their hectic activity.

Trains run to Trondheim from Oslo (6-7 per day, 7-8 hr., 486kr), Stockholm via Storlien (2 per day, 13 hr.), and Bodø. Long-distance buses leave from the **rutebilstasjonen** on Hans Hagrups gate.

Bodø and Fauske

Its provincial charm destroyed in World War II, **Bodø** (pronounced Buddha) is now most noteworthy as the northern terminus of the Norwegian rail line and the starting point for buses and boats further into the Arctic. The **tourist office,** Sjøgata 21 (tel. (081) 260 00), is about five blocks towards the center from the train station. Not only will they give you the all-knowing, all-seeing *Bodø Guide,* they also have maps and info for hiking. (Open Mon.-Fri. 9am-5pm and 7-9pm, Sat. 10am-2pm, Sun. 7-9pm.) To get to the **Flatvold Youth Hostel (IYHF)** (tel. (081) 256 66), turn right on Sjøgata from the bus stop, or left from the ferry landing and train stations; turn left at the traffic circle and walk 10 minutes to the traffic light. The hostel is Nordically clean and modern, with kitchen and laundry facilities. Eschew the 40kr breakfast. (90kr, nonmembers 115kr. Open June 20 to mid-Aug.) **Bodøsjøen Camping** is 3km from town, right by the airport (tel. (081) 229 02 or 229 62; 40kr per tent, 2-person hut 250kr, 4-person hut 350kr). Follow the directions for the youth hostel, but turn right at the traffic circle. Get a closer look at how man and puffin eke out an arctic existence at Bodø's **Nordlandsmuseet,** Prinsensgate 116, up the hill from the center. (Open Mon.-Fri. 9am-3pm, Sat. 10am-3pm, Sun. noon-3pm.

Admission 10kr, children 2kr.) In Bodø, the midnight sun reigns from June 2 to July 10; climb **Rønvikfjellet** outside Bodø for the best view.

Though Bodø itself was bombed silly by the Germans, it is situated among spectacular mountains well worth situating yourself among. **Kjerringøy,** an old coastal trading center 30km north of Bodø, recently opened as a highly reputed outdoor museum; several buses (44kr) and ferries (13kr) make the trip per day. (Guided tours daily at 11:15am, 1pm, and 3:30pm. Admission 20kr, children 5kr.) You can stay in one of the town's historic buildings, **Kjerringøyprestegård** (tel. (081) 112 04), for 90kr. The largest maelstrom in the world, **Saltstraumen,** is only 33km from Bodø. This wild phenomenon occurs at high tide when immense volumes of water from two fjords clash and swirl. Ask at the tourist office for tidal and transport timetables. (Buses 36kr, 18kr with InterRail or Nordturist.)

The cheapest way to get to Bodø from points south is by wing. Daily flights from Oslo cost only 700kr; from any place north of Trondheim, 390kr. By train, Bodø is 11 hours north of Trondheim (one day and one night train per day). Two buses per day run from Bodø north to Narvik (7 hr., 293kr). To make the Trondheim-Narvik run in one bite, get off the train and onto the Narvik-bound bus timed to connect at **Fauske** (63km and ¾ hr. before Bodø); if you stay on the train to Bodø, the bus will have left. Fauske's **IYHF youth hostel** (tel. (081) 447 06) is ½km toward Bodø from the station. (83kr, nonmembers 108kr. Open June to mid-Aug.) **Lundhøgda Camping** (tel. (081) 439 66) is 3km from town (50kr per tent). Call the Statens skoger office (tel. (081) 459 66) for information and hut keys for hiking in **Rago National Park,** where trails lead all the way to Jokkmokk and Kvikkjokk in Sweden. Two and a half hours further towards Trondheim is **Mo i Rana,** home to a hostel (tel. (087) 509 63) and the fountainhead for excursions to the **Svarteisen** glacier; buses (100kr) leave at 10:30am from the local tourist office (tel. (087) 504 21). In all of Nordland province (which includes Bodø, Fauske, the Lofotens and Narvik) InterRail gets half off bus fares, Nordturist gets the same except in the Lofotens, Eurail gets nothing, and ferries give student rather than railpass discounts.

Narvik

In a land where snowcapped peaks reflect in glimmering fjords, **Narvik** is a necessary monstrosity, a tangle of tracks and conveyor belts that bring iron ore from trains to ships. If you doubt its importance, wander through the graveyards just east of the train station, a testament to WWII's furious battles for control of this strategic port. And if by some chance you doubt Narvik's sheer ugliness, a barren dock tour may convince you (mid-June to mid-Aug. daily 2pm from the LKAB guardhouse on Havnegata; 20kr, children 10kr). The city basks in the midnight sun—on the rare days when the clouds part. Undoubtedly the most glorious aspect of Narvik is getting there; Nordic nature in its untamed glory is yours on the bus north to Alta (360kr) or south to Bodø (298kr), the hydrofoil to Svolvær (see Lofoten), or the last hour of the train trip through Kiruna in Sweden (3 per day, 169kr; 1 22-hr. through train per day from Stockholm).

Narvik and the precipitous railroad east were built at the turn of the century to provide an ice-free port for Kiruna's iron and copper mines. The town recalls those Sisyphian labors each March in the Rallarne celebration week. Parallel to the loading tracks is Narvik's main street, Kongensgate, on which you'll find the amicable **tourist office,** Kongensgate 66 (tel. (082) 433 09). From the train station exit, turn right, walk 100m up the hill, then turn left past Gunnars market. The office changes money (though bank rates are better), gives transportation advice (ruinous prices tempt many to hitch), and books private rooms (singles 110kr, doubles 210kr; 20-25kr fee; open Mon.-Sat. 9am-9pm, Sun. noon-9pm; mid-Aug to mid-June Mon.-Fri. 9am-4pm). The **bus station** is in the parking lot just above the tourist office. Northbound *Nord-Norge Buss-Ekspressen* buses also stop at the **Nordkalotten Youth Hostel (IYHF),** Havnegata 3 (tel. (082) 425 98 or 552 32); otherwise, turn left from the tourist office and walk 10 minutes down Kongensgate. (125kr, nonmembers 150kr. 4-min. shower 10kr. Open March-Nov. Reservations recommended.)

Back up the hill 100m toward town, on Kongensgate, the Swedish Church runs an International Seamen's Center with cheap food, sauna, ping-pong, billiards, and showers. **Narvik Camping** (tel. (082) 458 10) is 2km north of town along the main road. (Tents 60kr, 4-person *hytter* 385kr, 6-person 465kr.) The **Rema 1000** discount store is on Snorresgate, six blocks uphill and parallel to Kongensgate. (Open Mon.-Fri. 10am-8pm, Sat. 10am-6pm.)

The **War Museum,** on the main square, tells the story behind Narvik's cemeteries. (Open early June-late Aug. Mon.-Sat. 10am-10pm, Sun. 11am-10pm; late Aug. to mid-Sept. and early March-early June Mon.-Fri. 11am-5pm. Admission 20kr, children 10kr.) Ascend the looming peak by foot or take the **Gondolbanen** (cable car) up for 60kr round-trip (June-Aug. daily 10am-midnight; rest of year depends on weather). In winter, Narvik is a skiing center, and slopes run from above tree level to sea level.

Lofoten Islands

Yes, there are enchanted islands, and they are called the Lofotens. Made luscious by the Gulf Stream, their jagged, green-gray mountains shelter fishing villages, farms, and happy sheep. Sun-spangled puffins perorate from the cliffs at Værøy, while stockfish dry on quayside wooden racks. As late as the 1950s, fishermen would live in the small *rorbuer,* shacks whose yellow and red wooden walls cluster all along the coast. Today, strict quotas limit the islanders' maritime income, and tourists book the *rorbuer* solid (70-100kr per person per night if you're in a group). The indispensible brochure *Nordland 1992*—available at any tourist office from Bodø north—lists all *rorbuer,* among other accommodations.

The bridges along **Highway 19** bind the four largest of the Lofotens— Austvågøy, Vestvågøy, Flakstadøy and Moskenesøy—which point south towards the tiny outlying isles of Værøy and Røst. Narvik and Bodø are the best mainland springboards to the Lofotens. From Bodø, car ferries run to Moskenes (1-4 per day, depending on season, 83kr), sometimes stopping en route at Røst (2-3 per week, 92kr) or Værøy (4 per week, 78kr). **Hydrofoils** from Bodø serve Værøy (2 per day, 200kr, 50% off with ISIC), and the Lofotens' capital of Svolvær, on Austvågøy (1 per day, 204kr, 25% off with ISIC). From Narvik, hydrofoils run to Svolvær daily (239kr, 25% off with ISIC), but return only from Tuesday to Sunday. The northbound *Hurtigruten* run daily from Bodø to Stamsund on Vestvågøy (4½ hr., 211kr) and Svolvær (6 hr., 226kr). Ferries from Svolvær back to Skutvik on the mainland connect with buses to Ulvsvåg, where you can catch a bus to connect with the Trondheim trains at Fauske or Bodø or the Sweden railhead at Narvik. (Svolvær to Fauske 217kr, to Narvik 199kr; the connection works smoothly once per day.)

Try to get where you want in one ferry swoop from the mainland; the **buses** on the four northern islands are infrequent and expensive and their schedules confound. Wave at them to make sure they stop. **Hitching** is easier on the east coast than on the sparsely populated west coast, but don't hold your breath. The best way to experience Lofoten's spectacular scenery is to hike inland away from Highway 19. Almost every tourist office or hostel owner can give suggestions and maps.

Røst is the southernmost and smallest of the Lofotens. Apart from the car ferries from Bodø, a magnificent hydrofoil connects the island with Reine and Å on Moskenesøy via Værøy (Mon., Tues. and Thurs., 200kr). The **IYHF youth hostel** (tel. (088) 961 09) is 500m from the boat landing. (70kr, nonmembers 95kr. Open May-Aug.) Though famed for its puffins, uncharacteristically flat Røst can't compare in splendor to craggy **Værøy,** which rises volcano-style from the sea between Røst and Moskenesøy, wallpapered with thousands of seabirds. A local curiosity is the almost extinct *lundehund,* the rare six-toed puffin-hound extolled in the verse of Norway's great poet, Peter Dass. You can stay at the **Værøy Youth Hostel (IYHF)** (tel. (088) 953 52 or 953 75; 70kr, nonmembers 95kr; open mid-May to mid-Sept.)

and hike out to the bird cliffs. To get to Værøy, either take the car ferry from Bodø or the hydrofoil from Reine and Å (Sun.-Fri. 1 per day, 150kr).

Ferries from Bodø to **Moskenesøya,** the southernmost of the larger Lofotens, dock at the town of **Moskenes.** The **tourist office** (tel. (088) 915 99) by the ferry landing, gives advice on accommodations and sights. (Open early June daily 10am-4pm; June to late Aug. daily 9am-8pm.) About 10km to the south is **Å,** a tiny wooden settlement with a growing tourist industry including a **youth hostel (IYHF)** (tel. (088) 911 21; 90kr, nonmembers 115kr). Half of Å's buildings make up the **Norsk Fiskeværsmuseum,** an open-air museum documenting life in the old fishing days. (Open June-late Aug. Mon.-Fri. 10am-3:30pm, Sat.-Sun. noon-3:30pm. Admission 25kr.) You can camp on the cliffs behind the town above a snow-fed lake, or take a fishing cruise (200kr) to the **Moskenesstraumen,** a maelstrom between the main island and a ragged lone peak to the south, described in the fiction of both Jules Verne and Edgar Allen Poe. A cheap, lovely fjord cruise sails daily from Reine (north of Moskenes) to Rostad, Kirkefjord, Engelsnes, Vindstad, Tennes, and back to Reine (30kr).

Moving north, the next large island is **Flakstadøy,** which centers on the hamlet of **Ramsberg.** Flakstadøy has perhaps the best hiking trails on the islands; get detailed maps at the **tourist office** (tel. (088) 934 50), which opens thrice daily when the bus stops. The island has a cruciform red-painted church built of Russian driftwood in 1780 (weekly concerts early July-early Aug.). **Nusfjord,** south of Ramsberg, is one of the best-preserved fishing villages in Norway, while **Sund** has a small fishing museum displaying old boats and engines.

The mountain-backed hamlet of **Stamsund** on **Vestvågøy**—the next island north—is home to a *rorbu* **youth hostel (IYHF)** (tel. (088) 893 34 or 891 66), where travelers from all over the world come for a night and remain for weeks, cooking their freshly caught fish on wood-burning stoves. (65kr, nonmembers 90kr. Open mid-Dec. to Oct.) The benevolent ruler of this island utopia, Roar Justad, keeps bureaucracy to a minimum and will lend you his rowboats and fishing gear for free. He also rents mopeds (80kr per day plus 0.40kr per km) and mountain bikes (75kr per day) for quests into the Lofoten wilderness (you may come back a little thor). Two buses run daily to Stamsund from Å (79kr) and Svolvær (84kr) via Vestvågøy's unworthwhile main town of **Leknes.**

Svolvær, on the northernmost island of **Austvågøy,** is the hub of all Lofoten; surrounded by beauty, it's itself rather bland. Ferries and hydrofoils dock at Torget. The **tourist office** (tel. (088) 710 53) is right on Torget and will energetically provide info on hiking and scanty sightseeing possibilities. (Open year-round Mon.-Fri. 9am-4pm, extended hours in summer.) The colorless **IYHF youth hostel** (tel. (088) 707 77) is in the Polar Hotel. (An incredible 130kr, nonmembers 155kr; breakfast included.) Life is better in the friendly **Marinepollen Sjøhus** (sea house) or in their quay-side WWII hospital ship (tel. (088) 718 33; bed 90kr, single cabin 100kr). Camping is free on a beach 2km north of town, with running water and an ancient toilet. Above Svolvær is the two-pronged rock stack called **The Goat;** lunatic rock climbers occasionally attempt the leap from one horn to the other. You can hike up past it to **The Frog,** another weird formation bucking the spine of the mountain. A natural rock bridge at the cliff top overlooks the island's mountains. Northeast of Svolvær lies spectacular **Trollfjord.** On each side of the 2km-long fjord, cliffs dive almost vertically into the sea. Four boats per day cruise Trollfjord (160-175kr per person); inquire at the tourist office.

The **midnight sun** shows itself May 27-July 15 on the Lofotens. Any high place or beach is usually a good vantage point; try **Eggum,** across Vestvågøy from Stamsund, **Laukvik,** across Austvågøy from Svolvær, or ask around. Arctic swimming is possible at shallow, white sandy beaches after the sun has shone for a few days; good places are **Utakleiv** on Vestvågøy, where you can also spot the midnight sun, and the beach by **Ramberg** on Flakstadøy.

Tromsø and Svalbard

Tromsø, city of midnight fun and Norway's gateway to the Arctic Ocean, is about 240km up the coast from Narvik on a small island connected to the mainland by bridge. Europe's northernmost university and brewery have both settled here—no coincidence. The locals call Tromsø, with its 60 nightclubs, cafés, and discos (1 per 1000 residents), "the Paris of the North"; they are perhaps suffering from cranial frostbite. Nevertheless, Tromsø remains the most inviting city in northern Norway and is a good place to toast the woods and mountains before heading north to Finnmark's wastes or the snowfields of Svalbard. The old **cathedral** is one of the largest wooden churches in Norway (open mid-June to mid-Aug. daily noon-4pm). More striking are the clean white lines of the modern **Arctic Cathedral,** designed to blend with ice and snow. (Open Mon.-Sat. 10am-5pm, Sun. 1-5pm. Admission 5kr.) To reach the cathedral, cross the dramatic bridge to Tromsdalen. Fishermen sell fresh goods near the harbor by a statue memorializing their perils at sea.

The **Tromsø Museum** features exhibits on the region's natural history, as well as ethnographic displays of Sami culture. (Open daily 9am-6pm; Sept.-May Mon.-Fri. 8:30am-3:30pm, Sat. noon-3pm, Sun. 11am-4pm. Admission 10kr, students 5kr.) Take bus #21 or 27 to the south end of the island. The worthwhile **Polar Museum** chronicles Roald Amundsen's hardy journeys and polar exploits on Svalbard, all in Norwegian (pack your coder-decoder ring). (Open daily 11am-5pm; mid-Sept. to mid-May daily 11am-3pm. Admission 20kr.) For a sweeping view of the city in the midnight sun (roughly May 21-July 23), take the **cable car** to the top of Tromsdalstind; reach the cable car station aboard bus #28. (Daily 10am-8:30pm; midnight sun season 9pm-12:30am in good weather. 40kr.)

The **tourist office,** Storgata 61/63 (tel. (083) 100 00), is well clued-in. (Open Mon.-Fri. 8:30am-6pm, Sat.-Sun. 10am-3pm; late Aug.-early June Mon.-Fri. 8:30am-4pm. Booking fee for private homes 25kr; singles 150kr, doubles 200kr.) The **Elverhøy Youth Hostel (IYHF)** (tel. (083) 853 19) is a bland, impersonal student dorm. Take bus #24. (Lockout 11am-5pm. 85kr, nonmembers 110kr. No breakfast. Open late June-late Aug.) Closer but more expensive is **Park Pensjonat,** Skolegate 24 (tel. (083) 822 08), with commodious, comfortable rooms. (Singles 250kr. Doubles 300kr. Shared rooms 130kr per bed—ask specially. Breakfast 40kr.) **Tromsdalen Camping** (tel. (083) 380 37) has its share of bumps and bare ground but still undercuts the competition. Walk across the river to Tromsdalen, 20 minutes from the town center, or take bus #36 or 30. (2-4-person *hytter* 200kr. Tents 60kr.) Next to the open-air market is **Domus,** a large market with a cheap salad bar.

To sample Tromsø's nightlife, wander down **Storgata** and its side streets. **Vertshuset Skarven,** on Strandskillet, looking onto the harbor, is a spot for all the generations. Look for a whitewashed building. (Open Mon.-Thurs. noon-12:30am, Fri.-Sat. noon-1:30am, Sun. 3pm-12:30am.) **Blå Rock Café,** Strandgata 14, is a sleek, three-story eatery in the Hard Rock Café tradition. (½-liter beer 33kr, large pizza 80kr. Open Mon.-Thurs. 4pm-1:30am, Fri. 2pm-3:30am, Sat. noon-4am, Sun. 5pm-1:30am.) **Middags Kjelleren,** in a basement grotto between Skarven and Blå Rock, has bands most nights. (Cover after 8pm. Open Mon.-Thurs. 3pm-1:30am, Fri.-Sat. 2pm-1:30am, Sun. 6pm-1:30am.)

Tromsø's importance means frequent connections to the rest of the country. The *Nord-Norge Ekspressen* bus is 230kr to Narvik and 298kr to Alta (InterRail and Nordturist get 50% off). The northbound *Hurtigruten* (coastal steamer) leaves daily at 5pm; the southbound arrives at 11:45. (To Honningsvåg 605kr, to Bodø 653kr.)

A thousand kilometers north of the Norwegian mainland lies the vast, mountain-studded, glacier-clamped archipelago of **Svalbard.** After huge coal beds were detected on the main island of Spitsbergen, a 1920 treaty gave Norway sovereignty but distributed mineral rights among several claimants. Today, two Russian mining camps and the Norwegian mining and administrative center at **Longyearbyen** operate year-round. The only practical way to get to Svalbard is to fly from Tromsø to Longyearbyen. (1 per day Wed.-Sun., in winter Wed., Fri., and Sun; 1½ hr.;

round-trip 1960kr, ages under 25 1400kr.) Bring a tent; Longyearbyen's **camping** site (tel. (080) 219 52) is by the airport, 5km from town (tents 60kr per person). Beds under a roof start at 620kr for doubles. Before going, contact **Spitsbergen Travel** (SpiTra), N-9170 Longyearbyen (tel. (080) 211 60). They will give you practical information and guide you to car, snow scooter, bike and weapon rentals—the latter is critical for self-defense against gluttonous polar bears.

Finnmark

On most maps, Finnmark appears about as inviting as a walk-in freezer. The sun hides its face here from late November until late January and only the exquisite colors of the *aurora borealis* (Northern Lights) illuminate the frigid countryside. Yet, in summer the gently sloping faces of snow-capped peaks, vast stretches of uninhabited coastal tundra and inland forest bask under the midnight sun, and, with a little help from the Gulf Stream, the landscape becomes an arctic wonderland. The wilderness of **Finnsmarksvidda** that spreads from Tromsø east across inland Finnmark is Europe's largest, a highly popular hiking area spotted with tourist huts. Consult the DNT offices in Oslo or Bergen for maps, prices and other information.

Recent times have proven trying for the natives of Europe's northern frontier. In 1944, retreating Germans torched and bombed every building and bridge, determined to leave a wasteland for advancing Russian troops. In the last decade, overzealous fishermen and loose regulations have nearly depleted the coastal fishing banks. Fed up with empty nets, the fishing hamlet of Bugøynes advertised in Oslo papers for jobs so that the village could emigrate, en masse, to the more prosperous south.

Buses usually run once or twice per day along the E6—the main highway around the top of Norway—with spur lines branching north towards Hammerfest and Nordkapp, and south to Sweden and Finland. Both buses and the *Hurtigruten* are *very* expensive. Students get 50% discounts on the *Hurtigruten,* which reaches all the coastal towns, while InterRail and Nordturist get 50% off on *Nord-Norge Ekspressen* buses along the E6 from Bodø to Kirkenes, and students may get some reduction on buses run by **FFR. Hitchhiking** is the only truly cheap transport, and some travelers find it surprisingly successful, though traffic is light and distances are long. If you choose to hitch, bring a tent and a warm sleeping bag. If you're under 25, **flying** is the cheapest way to get to Finnmark. SAS offers 700kr standby tickets *(Superhaik)* from Oslo to any point north of Trondheim; youth standby fares in Sweden (250 Swedish kronor from Stockholm to Kiruna or Gällivare in Swedish Lappland) are sometimes an even better option.

On the coast north of Tromsø, **Alta** is Finnmark's largest town, an important point for connecting buses in all directions. Slate-gray mountains, towering cliffs, and icy green sea make the Tromsø-Alta road perhaps the most spectacular bus route in Norway. Alta itself is really a conglomeration of two smaller settlements with an eye-aching mall in between; the woods and water surrounding it are nicer, and the nearby **Alta River,** famous for its salmon, runs at the bottom of Europe's longest canyon (guided tours 100kr). For fishing permits, consult the **tourist office** (tel. (084) 377 70). You can stay at the **Frikirkens Elevheim (IYHF)** (tel. (084) 344 09; 90kr, nonmembers 110kr, mattress on floor 35kr; open late June-late Aug.). The **campground** on the river (tel. (084) 343 53) is towards Hammerfest from the bus terminal (40kr per tent, 15kr per person, 4-person *hytter* 300kr). One to two buses per day run to Tromsø (7-8 hr., 298kr); Hammerfest (3 hr., 134kr); Honnigsvåg (5 hr., 171kr); Kautokeino (3 hr., 126kr); and Karasjok (4 hr., 228kr).

At **Hammerfest,** the world's northernmost town, you can become a member of the "exclusive" Royal and Ancient Polar Bear Society (est. 1963)—if you have 95kr to spare. The *Hurtigruten* stops here for 1½ hours—plenty of time to see this bustling metropolis. Daily buses connect at Skaidi with the main lines west to Alta and east to Kirkenes. The midnight sun is best contemplated from **Salen,** a short, steep hike up the hill from the **tourist office** (tel. (084) 121 85), up the street from the pier and on the left. (Open Mon.-Fri. 8am-6pm, Sat.-Sun. 10am-3pm; Sept.-May Mon.-Fri. 8am-3pm.) Several hiking and skiing trails begin at Hammerfest. The cheapest beds in town are with **Sara Myrvoll** (tel. (084) 133 44), a 20-minute walk around the bay or with bus #1 or 4 to Fuglenes. Look for the big red "SARA" letters up the street. (Sleeping bag accommodations 100kr. Breakfast included. Open June 20-Aug.20.)

Looming into the Arctic Ocean from the island of Magerøy, the famed **Nordkapp** is really Much Ado About Nothing. Not even continental Europe's northernmost point (a title held by Knivskjellodden, a peninsula protruding just to the west), Nordkapp has nevertheless been burdened by a relentless onslaught of international tourists. Nordkapp's first budget traveler was a 17th-century Italian monk named Francesci Negri, who made the journey by rowboat and foot. Battered by gale and wave and carrying only a letter from his mother for comfort, Negri managed to caulk leaks in his boat with his habit and, once on land, to spark fires on the desolate rock using locks of his own hair. Exhausted, naked and bald, he arrived in Nordkapp and was (can you believe it?) ostracized. When Oscar II, king of Sweden and Norway, visited Nordkapp in the mid-19th century, Thomas Cook immediately advertised tours to the rock, and the swarms continue. Perched on (and inside) the rock is the **Nordkapp Complex,** with a bank, post office, telephones, cafeteria, subterranean bar, and a gold-enameled Thai Museum commemorating King Chulalongkorn's visit in 1907. No joke. Don't miss the wide-angle film (every 15 min., free). Around the complex is rough landscape and open ocean bashing beneath the midnight sun (roughly May 11-July). Nordkapp might be worth it if it were free, but admission to the cliff and the complex is 90kr.

Nordkapp, like Hammerfest, is on a spur off the main E6; reach it by first traveling to **Honningsvåg** 25km south on the same island. Taking a bus to Honningsvåg from Alta (1-2 per day, 6 hr., 171kr) or Hammerfest (1-2 per day, 4½ hr., 145kr) is cheaper than the *Hurtigruten* (from Kirkenes 584kr, Tromsø 605kr, Hammerfest 244kr). If you are hitching, beware the Kåfjord-Honningsvåg ferry—you can get stuck at the landing for hours. In Honningsvåg, the **tourist office** (tel. (084) 728 94) provides transport information for all of Finnmark. (Open daily 8:30am-7pm; Sept.-May Mon.-Fri. 8:30am-4pm.) Just above the tourist office is the worthwhile **Nordkapp Museum,** with tours in English. (Open Mon.-Sat. 11am-8pm, Sun. 6-8pm; mid-Aug. to mid-June Mon.-Fri. 11am-3pm. Admission 15kr.) The 33km trip between Honningsvåg and Nordkapp can be made by bus (4 per day, round-trip 85kr); some thumb it. Before heading up, get the weather forecast—Nordkapp is dullsville in the mist. The cold and primitive **Nordkapp Youth Hostel and Camping (IYHF)** (tel. (084) 751 13) is 8km up the same road (12kr by bus). There's a kitchen but little cooking equipment, and the toilets are a windy 200m walk away. (60kr, nonmembers 80kr. 30kr per tent, 15kr per person. Open June-Aug. 20. Reservations recommended.) To visit Nordkapp in winter, call the **Nordkapp Turistheim,** N-9763 Skarsvåg (tel. (084) 752 19), where you can arrange transportation by motor sleigh.

Continuing east past the Hammerfest and Honningsvåg turnoffs, the E6 curves inland through Norway's major Sami-speaking area. The coastal road into **Lakselv** (3½ hr. and 161kr from Alta) is spectacularly desolate, with nothing but clear water, sweeping cliffs and islands, a few Sami tents and some fishing hamlets. At Lakselv, the **Karalaks Youth Hostel** (tel. (084) 614 76), isolated in a tiny lake valley 4km south of town, is relaxed and clean. Go for a hike behind the hostel and pelt reindeer with snowballs. (90kr, nonmembers 115kr. Open June-Aug.)

Another hour and another 67kr from Lakselv brings you to **Karasjok** (Kŕášjohka in the local Sami dialect), where the interesting **Sámiid Vuorka Dávvirat** (Sami Museum), up the hill from the bus station, displays old Lapp tools and colorful costumes. (Open mid-June to late Aug. Mon.-Sat. 9am-6pm, Sun. 10am-6pm; late Aug.-Oct. and April-early June Mon.-Sat. 9am-3pm, Sun. 10am-3pm; Nov.-March Mon.-Sat. 9am-3pm, Sun. noon-3pm. Admission 10kr.) Karasjok's white wooden church is the oldest church in Finnmark, built in 1807. In the newly-built **Samelandssentret**—regional roost of the nominal Sami government—the **tourist office** (tel. (084) 669 02) can point out the potential of the modern Sami capital. Fishing, raft-

architecture were transformed by the ornate and sometimes eccentric Manueline style. Sadly, the country's history quickly took a turn for the worse. A period of decline set in which imbued the culture with a nostalgia still reflected in the folk ballads of *fado*—fate. By 1580, Portugal had exhausted both its resources and its royal line. After minimal resistance, the Spaniard Philip II claimed the Portuguese throne. Independence was not regained until 1640, when the royal house of Bragança stabilized itself by allying with England. A disastrous earthquake in 1755 reduced much of Lisbon to rubble and killed thousands, shaking the country's faith and economy alike, so that when Napoleon invaded in 1807, King Pedro III moved the court of his crumbling empire to Brazil.

A parliamentary republic sprouted in 1910, only to be overthrown by a 1926 military coup. Strongman António Salazar, an economist-turned-dictator, ruled the country for the ensuing 40 years, running down the economy through the exploitation of a domestic peasantry and African laborers under colonial rule. In 1974, a bloodless coup toppled the regime of his successor, Marcelo Caetano, prompting mass rejoicing—every Portuguese town now has its Rua 25 de Abril to honor the putsch. The new government granted independence to Portugal's African holdings: the ensuing civil wars in Mozambique and Angola set off a rush of immigration into an already unstable Portugal. In 1986, Prime Minister Cavaco Silva oversaw Portugal's entry into the European Economic Community and initiated a sometimes painful modernization drive. As yet, Portugal's standard of living still lags behind northern Europe's, but optimistic signs of change are everywhere.

For travelers, the lower standard of living means that local beer and wine flow cheaply, and a full meal can cost as litle as 1000$. Each year, sun worshipers migrate to the sands, cliffs, and sparkling waters of the Algarve; fewer visit the rougher northern coast. Notable architecture abounds in the north: Coimbra and Porto have sightly Romanesque churches, while the area north of the Rio Douro is dotted with Roman and Visigothic ruins. In the center and south are massive fortresses testifying to Moorish occupation. Lisbon is the center of the indigenous Manueline style. Portugal's beauteous Atlantic archipelagoes, the Azores and Madeira, are accessible by numerous flights from the mainland (about 20,000$ one-way).

For more coverage of this enchanting country, consult *Let's Go: Spain & Portugal.*

Getting There and Getting Around

International airports in Lisbon, Porto, and Faro serve major European and North American cities. TAP, the national airline, offers youth fares often barely half regular prices. Lisbon and Porto are accessible by daily trains from Madrid and Paris.

Eurail and InterRail passes are valid on the Portuguese national train system (CFP); passholders pay extra on express trains. **Trains** are best between Lisbon and the Algarve and on the Porto-Coimbra-Lisbon line. They run until midnight; bus service stops around 8pm. **Buses** are faster and more frequent, if significantly more expensive. State-run **Rodoviária Nacional** is the largest company, but many private local companies compete.

Cycling is also viable; distances are short and the climate mild—excepting the desert-like summer of the Alentejo and Algarve. **Hitchhiking** in Portugal is not reliable enough to be your main means of transportation.

Practical Information

Portugal's usually English-speaking **tourist offices** *(turismo)* will help you with accommodations in large cities and in nearly every small town accustomed to tourists.

Portuguese is a Romance language similar to Spanish, but accessible to those with a background in French or Italian and an English-Portuguese dictionary. Most Portuguese don't speak Spanish; they *can* understand it, but don't like to. In the southern and central provinces, where tourism is heaviest, many locals speak English, French, or German. The Portuguese are well aware that their language is seldom studied abroad; foreigners who make an effort to speak it win points.

Women traveling alone will very likely receive inordinate amounts of male attention—annoying, but rarely dangerous. If a situation becomes uncomfortable, supreme disgust or an emphatic "*sai*" (go away, pronounced "sigh") is a more effective response than flustered panic. In an emergency, shout "*socorro*" (so-COR-oh, "help").

Portuguese currency is divided into escudos and centavos; the "$" sign is used as a decimal point. Inflation is high (about 12% in 1991), so expect prices listed here to shift considerably. The Portuguese often refer to 1000 escudos as one *conto.*

A strongly Catholic country, much of Portugal's community activity centers around religious festivals. Perhaps the liveliest are the *festas juninas,* which revolve around the feast days of St. John and St. Peter, June 24 and 29. Usually held outside, these feature dancing, eating, and other forms of refreshment. June is bedlam in Lisbon; the feast day of its patron saint Santo Antônio is celebrated June 13, with costume processions and bacchanalian excesses. Two important festivals commemorate the appearances of the Virgin in Fátima (May 12-13 and Oct. 12-13). **Holy Week** in April brings processions and crowds to Braga; Easter Sunday marks the beginning of the Portuguese bullfighting season. (The bull is wounded, not killed. Viva Ferdinand!) Every town has its patron saint, whose feast day is a local holiday, accompanied by pilgrimages, village fairs, and often makeshift amusement parks and closed shops. Everything in Portugal closes on New Year's Day, Carnival Tuesday, Good Friday, Easter Sunday, Liberty Day (April 25), Labor Day (May 1), Camões or National Day (June 10), São João (June 24), Corpus Christi, Assumption, First Republic Day (Oct. 5), All Saints Day (Nov. 1), Restoration of Independence (Dec. 1), Immaculate Conception (Dec. 8), Christmas Eve, and Christmas Day.

Shops are usually open weekdays from 9am to 1pm and from 3 to 6pm, and Saturday morning. Normal banking hours are weekdays from 8:30 to 11:45am and 1 to 2:45pm. Remember that Portugal is one hour behind Spain. Post offices in larger towns are open weekdays from 8:30am to 6:30pm and Saturday from 9am to 12pm. In smaller towns they close for lunch and weekends. Poste restante pick-up (at central post offices) costs 40$ per item. Post offices also house telephone offices, which in larger cities remain open until 11:30pm or midnight. To use pay phones, put a 5$, 20$, or 50$ coin into the trough on top of the phone and then dial. The *credifone* magnetic card system extends throughout Portugal; purchase the card at locations posted on the booths themselves. The **TLP** card is similar, but used in different phones found only in Lisbon and Porto. For an international operator, dial 098. For emergencies, dial 115. For AT&T's **USA Direct,** dial 05 017 1288.

Accommodations and Camping

Hotels are usually more expensive than they're worth. The more affordable pensions *(pensões)* or *residências* are rated on a three-star system, though favoritism and pay-offs often prevail. In small towns and heavily traveled areas, a *quarto* (room) in a private home may be cheaper and more comfortable than a *pensão,* but harder to find; look in house windows for signs, or check the list at the *turismo.* Unmarried couples can share a love nest with no *problemas.*

Portugal currently operates 19 IYHF youth hostels *(pousadas de juventude),* not to be confused with other *pousadas,* which are government-run luxury accommodations in choice spots. IYHF cards are required but can be purchased on the spot for 2400$. Prices range from 900-1100$ per night during high season (June-Sept. plus Holy Week and Christmas/New Year's), 700-900$ in off-season. Breakfast is included; lunch and dinner (when available) cost 450$. Linen is often furnished (free) on request. Unfortunately, 10:30am-6pm lockouts, midnight curfews, and the fact that some are in remote and inaccessible areas make hostels inconvenient; otherwise, they are generally fun.

The Portuguese love camping out, as a social activity, not a solitary survival exercise. The nation's 150 official campgrounds *(parques de campismo),* festooned with amenities and comforts, almost always have a supermarket and café; many enjoy access to a beach. Many inland sites have river bathing or even a pool. Pick up the indispensable guide *Roteiro Campista* from the national tourist office in your home country or in Lisbon (250$), or write to the **Federação Portuguesa de Campismo,** Rua Voz do Operário, Lisbon (tel. 86 23 50). **Orbitur's** 15 sites are among the best-run and priciest in Portugal; contact them at Av. Almirante Gago Coutinho, 25d, Lisbon (tel. 89 23 41; open Mon.-Fri. 9am-12:30pm and 2:30-6pm). In secluded areas where there are no official campsites, unofficial camping is *usually* acceptable.

Food and Drink

A good meal anywhere costs 800-1200$, even less in small towns and student restaurants. *Marisquerias* specialize in seafood; *churrasquerias,* in broiled chicken and meat. Portions are usually colossal, and one entree often feeds two people. If you are traveling alone or can't agree on a dish, ask for a *meia dose* (half-portion, for somewhat more than half-price). Snack bars offer lighter fare than restaurants but more protein than *pastelarias* (pastry shops) or *cafeterias* (coffee shops). Bars provide a little of everything—coffee, alcohol, and food.

Fish is a delicacy. Try *peixe espada grelhado* (grilled Madeiran scabbard-fish) or *bacalhau* (codfish). *Carne de porco á alentejana* (pork made with clams in a coriander sauce) is a national favorite. *Cozido á portuguesa* (vegetable stew with beef or pork innards) is a staple at economy restaurants. Vegetarians will be in rough shape, but most places offer at least omelettes and salads. Bread and butter is not included in the price of the meal but should cost less than 200$. Breakfast (bread and coffee) is usually served from 8 to 10am, lunch from noon to 3pm, and dinner from 7 to 10pm.

As the classical economist Ricardo suggested, wine is perhaps Portugal's most endearing product. For centuries, British importers have monopolized the wine trade from Porto, the city that gave its name to both the wine and the country. Farther south, the Dão Valley produces hearty reds and fruity whites, while the northern Minho region puts out a slightly effervescent *vinho verde* ("green wine"), which agrees with fish.

Lisbon (Lisboa)

There is still something imperial about Lisbon. Though the days of Portugal's colonial empire may be only a memory, Portuguese speakers all over the world retain an affection for Lisbon, and this middling-sized city on the Tagus River (Rio Tejo) still *feels* like an important metropolis. The beauty of the eighteenth-century Baixa, the serpentine streets of Alfama, the view of the city from the Castle of St. George—all these make Lisbon seem like something more than what it really is: the capital of a now smallish, poorish country.

Orientation and Practical Information

Capital of Portugal, coastal Lisbon is also the country's major transport hub. The heart of Lisbon is the **Praça dos Restauradores.** Just south of the *praça* lie the two squares of the **Rossio** (Praça Dom Pedro IV and Praça da Figueira), and a neat grid of small streets that compose the **Baixa** (Lower Town), Lisbon's old business district. The medieval shopping district, or **Chiado,** is connected to the Baixa by Eiffel's Ascensor de Santa Justa. The populous, affluent **Bairro Alto** (Upper District) extends west of Rua da Misericórdia. North of Restauradores is the new business district, linked to Restauradores by **Avenida da Liberdade.** East of the Baixa spreads the **Alfama,** Lisbon's medieval quarter. Six kilometers west of the center is **Belém,** famous for its Manueline monuments.

Tourist Offices: Palácio da Foz, Pr. Restauradores (tel. 346 33 14 or 346 36 43). M: Restauradores. Free maps and accommodations listings. Open Mon.-Sat. 9am-8pm, Sun. 10am-6pm. Busy branch offices at Santa Apolónia Station (open Mon.-Sat. 9am-7pm) and at the airport (open 24 hrs.).

Budget Travel: Tagus, Pr. Londres, 9b (tel. 89 15 31). M: Alameda. Book for TAP and British Airways. Open Mon.-Fri. 10am-6pm, Sat. 10am-1pm.

Embassies: U.S., Av. das Forças Armadas (tel. 726 66 00). **Canada,** Rua Rosa Araújo, 2, 6th floor (tel. 56 38 21). **U.K.,** Rua de São Domingos à Lapa, 37 (tel. 66 11 22). **Australia,** Av. da Liberdade, 244, 4th floor (tel. 52 33 50). **New Zealanders** should contact the British Embassy.

Currency Exchange: At Santa Apolónia station and the airport. Long lines at station on weekends. Both open 24 hrs. Banks charge up to 1000$ commission plus tax.

American Express: Star Travel Service, Pr. Restauradores, 14 (tel. 53 98 71). Open Mon.-Fri. 9am-12:30pm and 2-6pm.

Post Office: Correio, Pr. Comércio (tel. 346 32 31). Open Mon.-Fri. 9am-7pm. Pr. Restauradores branch has *posta restante* (Mon.-Fri. only, 32$50 per item.) Open daily 8am-10pm. **Postal Code:** 1100.

Telephones: Pr. D. Pedro IV, 68. Open daily 8am-11:30pm. The post office on Pr. Restauradores also has telephones. Since many coin phones are out of order, purchase a **Credifone** card which comes in 50 or 120 units (15$ per unit, minimum one unit per call). **City Code:** 01.

Flights: Aeroporto de Lisboa (general information tel. 80 20 60). Take bus #44 or 45 (130$) between the airport and town center (the bus stops along the length of Av. da Liberdade and Av. da República), or take the faster green line express bus, *linha verde* (250$). Three people will save money by sharing a taxi (600$ from airport to Baixa).

Trains: Tel. 87 60 25 for information. **Rossio** station for Sintra and western lines; **Santa Apolónia** for all international, northern, and eastern lines; **Cais do Sodré** for Estoril and Cascais; and **Barreiro** for the Algarve and southern lines. If you arrive at Santa Apolónia station, take bus #9 or 9A from the water side of the station to Pr. Restauradores. From Cais de Sodré station, take bus #1, 2, 32, 44, or 45, or walk (15 min.). Rossio station is just a block away, 25 min. from Pr. Dom Pedro IV. To reach Barreiro, you must ferry across Rio Tejo; boats leave from Pr. Comércio (15 min., 95$, free if you're coming from the south into Lisbon). To: Lagos (5 per day, 6½ hr., 1270$); 2 *expresso* trains per day (5hr., 1350$); Évora (6 per day, 3hr., 655$); Paris (1 per day, 27hr., 18215$).

Buses: Rodoviária Nacional, Av. Casal Ribeiro, 18 (tel. 57 77 15), near Pr. Saldanha. M: Picoas. Buses #1, 21, 32, and 36 will take you to Pr. Restauradores. To: Lagos (5 per day, 1450$); Évora (6 per day, 900$); Porto (5 per day, 1350$); Coimbra (8 per day, 800$). For a pittance more, the private company **Caima,** 19 Rua dos Bacalhoeiros, (tel. 87 50 61) runs luxurious coaches to the Porto and the Algarve. To: Porto (6 per day; 1400$) and Lagos (6 per day, 1750$).

Public Transportation: City buses cost 130$. A **Tourist Pass** *(Bilhete de Assinatura Turístico)* gives unlimited travel on CARRIS buses, trolleys, funiculars, and subways (7 days 1550$, 4 days 1100$) and can be purchased at CARRIS booths in most network train stations and metro stops (open 8am-8pm). The clean and rapid **Metro** (M) covers only part of the city (45$ per ride, 410$ for 10 tickets). Three *elevadores* (cable cars) connect the lower city with residential areas. The *Elevador da Glória,* next to Palácio da Foz, linking Pr. Restauradores with the Bairro Alto, is especially useful (28$).

Hitchhiking: Lots of competition, especially in Aug. To the south, take the ferry from Pr. Comércio to Cacilhas, then start on the Setúbal road. To the north, take bus #8, 21, 44, 45, or 53 to the Rotonda do Aeroporto. To Spain, take the Autoestrada do Porto; continue on it if traveling to Galicia, or get off at the junction with the road to Badajoz (about 30km from Lisbon) for Andalusia or Madrid. Remember that hitching is risky, and public transportation cheap.

Bookstore: Livraria Britânica; Rua São Marçal, 83 (tel. 32 84 72), in Bairro Alto. Open daily 9:30am-7pm.

Laundromat: Lavatax, Rua Francisco Sanches, 65a (tel. 82 33 92). M: Arroios. 5kg washed, dried, and folded for 870$. Open daily 9am-1pm and 3-7pm, Sat. 9am-noon.

Medical Assistance: British Hospital, Rua Saraiva de Carvalho, 49 (tel. 60 20 20; at night 60 37 85).

Emergencies: Police or **Ambulance** (tel. 115 or 36 61 41).

Police: 346 61 41. In an emergency, call 115 from anywhere in Portugal.

Accommodations and Camping

You should have no trouble securing a single for around 2500$ or a double for 3500$. Most places have only double beds; some charge more for double occupancy. The vast majority of *pensões* are in the center of the city around Pr. Restauradores and the Rossio. To escape the clamor of downtown, try the city's **Mouraria** (near the castle) and **Bairro Alto** districts, both only a 10-minute walk from the center; women may be uncomfortable in these areas at night and should not walk alone. Most *pensões* have less than 20 rooms, so book ahead.

Pousada da Juventude de Catalazete (IYHF), Estrada Marginal (tel. 443 06 38), in Oeiras. Take a train from Cais do Sodré to Oeiras (20 min., 85$), then exit the station through the underpass and to the right, under the *Praia* sign. When you surface, you'll spot the 1st sign for the hostel, 1200m ahead. Rooms are cramped, but the beachfront location rivals any resort. Reception open 9:30-10:30am and 6-10:30pm. Curfew midnight. June-Sept., Holy Week, and Christmas season 1100$; Oct.-May 900$. Reservations advisable.

Residencial Florescente, Rua Portas de Santo Antão, 99 (tel. 32 66 09), 1 block from Pr. Restauradores. With 120 rooms, this is perhaps your best bet if you arrive in summer without a reservation. However, the 2000$ rooms are dingy, windowless cells with washstands. Lively social scene, though. Singles and doubles 2000$, with bath 3000-5000$.

Pensão Prata, Rua da Prata, 71, 3rd floor (tel. 36 89 08), 2 blocks from Pr. Comércio. Sign obscured by yellow awning. Sparkling clean with kind management. Singles 2500$, with bath 3500$. Doubles 2800$, with bath 3800$. Cheaper in winter.

Pensão Beira Minho, Pr. Figueira, 6, 2nd floor (tel. 346 18 46), next to the Rossio. Through a flower shop at the northern end of the *praça.* Renovated rooms are quite nice; windowless cubicles are well-lit and cheerful. Singles 3500$. Doubles 4000$. All rooms with bath. Breakfast included.

Pensão Ninho das Águias, Rua Costa do Castelo, 74 (tel. 86 70 08), near the *castelo.* A long, winding stairway leads to the patio where an aviary, a flower garden, and stupendous views of Lisbon unfold before you. Doubles 3500-4000$, with shower 4500-5200$. All rooms with telephones. Reserve ahead.

Pensão Pemba, Av. da Liberdade, 11 (tel. 32 50 10). Bubbly woman runs slightly dank place. Wrangle for the roof-top room, which has a splendid terrace but no shower. Singles 1500-2000$, doubles with bath 2500-3000$.

Camping: Parque Nacional de Turismo e Campismo (tel. 70 83 84). Take bus #14 from Pr. Figueira. Lisbon's municipal facility. Swimming pool and reasonably priced supermarket. (795$ per night for one person with tent and car; Oct.-May 500$ per person, 107$ per tent, 90$ per car.) **Costa da Caparica,** reached by direct bus from Pr. Espanha. M: Palhavã (5km, 15 min.). Beautiful beaches and plenty of shade; bungalows available.

Food

Heaps of tourists are rapidly driving up restaurant prices, but Lisbon is still a bargain among European capitals. Seafood abounds. Copious servings will often feed two for the price of one, and Portugal's ever-thriving wine industry produces more labels each year. A full dinner runs around 1200$. In general, restaurants in the Baixa are more elegant and expensive than those in other districts; the Bairro Alto, in contrast, serves many more locals. Most restaurants close on Sunday, and a few close during July. Vegetarians in Lisbon do not fare well; try places in the Baixa that are well-frequented by tourists.

To fix your own meals and dredge for souvenirs, go to the **Mercado Ribeira,** outside the Cais de Sodré (open Mon.-Sat. until 2pm)—but get there in the morning for the freshest produce. The **market** in **Cascais** explodes on Wednesday mornings with fresh fruit, vegetables, and fish.

Adega Popular 33, Rua da Conceiçao, 33 (tel. 32 84 72). 2 blocks from Pr. Comércio. The best inexpensive food on the block. Entrees mostly 500-700$. Half-portions served. Open Mon.-Fri. 8am-9:30pm.

Restaurante Chekiang, Rossio Station, Store #108. Authentic Chinese cuisine served with a smile. Muzak too. Try chicken with mussels (810$) or the sumptuous glazed fruit desserts (220-400$). Open daily 11:30am-3pm and 7-10:30pm.

Casa de Pasto de Francisco Cardoso, Rua do Século, 244 (tel. 32 75 78), off Rua Dom Pedro V. Intimate. Sangria (60$), omelettes (600$), cornbread (110$), and pastry (200$). Open daily 8am-midnight.

Mestre André, Calçadinha de Sto. Estevão, 6, off Rua dos Remédios. *Murcela frita,* a savory sausage, is a favorite among regulars. Outdoor seating and grill on a stone terrace above the street.

Dragão da Alfama, Rua Guilherme Braga, 8, near the Church of São Estevão. Traditional fish entrees in huge portions (500-700$). Nightly around 10pm, a woman with a voice that could fill a stadium drops by and belts *fado.*

Cervejaria da Trindade, Rua Nova da Trindade, 20c. Once a convent, its spacious rooms are tiled with murals of bulky, naked women. *Rogiões do Mare* (a mixed seafood platter) is a house specialty (1900$)—wash it down with *mista* (mixed light and dark beer). Other entrees 700-1300$. Open Thurs.-Tues. 9am-2am.

Lua Nova, Travessa da Queimada, 4. An interior dark as a new moon, this small place is great for cheap, pre-fado dining. Entrees 550-800$. Open Mon.-Sat. 10am-10pm.

O Barriga, Travessa da Queimada, 31. A pungent aroma of grilled steak wafts out, ensnaring unsuspecting passersby. Entrees 100-400$. Open Tues.-Sun. 9am-midnight.

Lua de Mel, Rua Santa Justa (tel. 87 91 51), on the corner with Rue da Prata. Some of the freshest, most scrumptious pastries in Lisbon. Ice cream sundaes (350$) worth every *escudo.* Open Tues.-Sun. 7am-midnight.

O Baleal, Rua da Madalena, 277 (tel. 87 21 87), near the Mouraria. Kleen & brite. Entrees 400-700$. Open Tues.-Sun. 8am-10pm, Sat. 8am-4pm.

Sights

Originally a Visigothic settlement and later home to the Moorish aristocracy, the **Alfama** became the noisy, popular section of town that it is today when the Christians recaptured the city. Look into **São Miguel,** arguably Lisbon's finest church; **Largo do Salvador, 22,** a noble's 16th-century mansion; and the busy **Rua de São Pedro.** The Alfama is prone to crime—use caution, and consider leaving handbags and cameras elsewhere while you explore. Close to the Baixa are the magnificent ruins of **Castelo de São Jorge,** which has dominated the city for 1500 years. The ancient walls—really an endless series of stone terraces—enclose lovely gardens, streams, and white peacocks. From downtown, take bus #37 (Castelo) or trolley #28 (Graça).

Near the center of town, the Romanesque **Sé** (Cathedral) is worth a visit for its ambulatory and tombs. **Praça do Comércio,** lined with classical buildings in the high Pombaline style, is entered from the north with a massive baroque arch. A stroll straight up from the *praça* leads to the **Rossio,** the city's principal square, embellished with bronze fountains and a statue of Dom Pedro IV atop a giant Corinthian column. Just beyond, elegant **Avenida da Liberdade** leads to the formal **Parque Eduardo VII.** The **Chiado,** Lisbon's chic shopping district, brims with art nouveau coffeehouses and prewar charm. One of Lisbon's most beloved landmarks, the **Ascensor de Santa Justa,** is boxed in a fanciful Gothic tower created by Eiffel. Take the elevator up for a fabulous view of Lisbon (28$). On Rua da Misericórdia, the **Igreja de São Roque** is notable for its flamboyant 18th-century **Capela de São João Baptista** and its precious imported Italian stones. Beyond the church, off Alêntera Rua Dom Pedro, are three of the city's most comely parks: **São Pedro de Alcântara Belvedere, Praça do Principe Real,** and the tropical **Jardim Botânico.** On balmy days, their benches are often occupied with couples in the love-clutch.

An earthquake in 1755 reduced much of Lisbon's inner city to rubble. Consequently, much of the city's most renowned architecture is concentrated on the city's outskirts, particularly in **Belém,** a 10-minute train ride from the Cais do Sodré station. Portugal's classic example of Manueline architecture, the **Mosteiro dos Jerónimos** (Jerónimos Abbey) contains a doorway sculpted with life-size figurines. Nearby, at the edge of the river, stands the **Torre de Belém,** an elegant and imposing tower—Gothic inside, Renaissance outside. The view atop the narrow, circular steps is unforgettable. From Pr. Comercio take trolley #16 (Belém). (Open Tues.-Sun. 10am-1pm and 2:30-5pm. Admission 400$; Oct.-May 250$, students and seniors free.)

The **Museu Nacional de Arte Antiga,** on Rua das Janelas Verdes, houses Portuguese primitives and paintings by Bosch, Dürer, and Holbein the Elder. To reach the museum, take bus #40 or trolley #19 from Pr. Figueira. (Open Tues.-Sat. 10am-1pm and 2-5pm. Admission 200$, students free.) The **Museu Calouste Gulbenkian,** Pr. Espanha (M: Palhavã), exhibits an odd mix of Egyptian treasures and Rodin sculptures. For avant-garde Portuguese art, visit the **Centro de Arte Moderna** next door. Most museums close Mondays.

Entertainment

The traditional folk entertainment of Portugal is the *fado,* nostalgic ballads of lost loves and bygone glory. Unfortunately, most *casas do fado* in Lisbon are expensive clubs patronized by a snooty, elegant set, particularly in the Bairro Alto. **Arcadas do Faia,** on Rua da Baroca, 54 (tel. 32 19 23; open 8pm-2am), charges a 2000$ cover. In nearby Madregoa, **Sr. Vinho,** Rua do Meio a Lapa, 18 (tel. 67 26 81), has a required minimum food and drink charge of 2500$. Book in advance by phone, especially on weekends. Most *fado* starts around 9:30pm, but gets much better about two hours later, when the tour groups start to leave. The show lasts well into the morning. More popular and earthy *fado* spontaneously combusts in the Alfama at dusk (be careful here at night).

To observe the mayhem, stop by **A Brasileira,** Rua Garrett, 120-122, in the Chiado. This coffee shop honors Carlos de Andrade, the Brazilian poet who frequented it in the early 20th century. (Open until midnight.) Down at Pr. Dom Pedro, **Café Nicola,** a famous meeting place for 19th century writers, maintains a Central European ambiance.

Those in search of more boisterous nightlife should not be deceived by the after-dinner lull: nothing really cranks up until around midnight. In Lisbon, June is a month of *feiras populares,* nighttime outdoor fairs with plenty of eating, drinking, and dancing. A lively one, **Oreal,** occurs at Campo das Cebolas near the Alfama waterfront and is open all month (Mon.-Fri. 10pm-1am, Sat.-Sun. 10pm-3am). Rua Diario de Notícias is the Bairro Alto's focus of nighttime activity. Particularly good is **Mascote do Bairro,** Rua Diario das Notícias, 136, a down to earth watering hole across the street from the **Boris. La Folie Discoteca,** Rua Díario de Notícias, 122-4, offers a bar, air-conditioning, and the latest international music (open Tues.-Sun. 10pm-2am). The 600$ cover charge entitles you to two beers or one mixed drink. **Memorial,** Rua Gustavo de Matos Sequeira, 42a (tel. 396 88 91), is a gay and lesbian bar with dancing. (Open Tues.-Sun. 10pm-4am.) The 1000$ cover includes two beers or one drink. The **Feira Popular** amusement park (M: Entre Campos) throngs with Portuguese of all ages every night from May to September until 1am (admission 125$).

Listings for all fairs and concerts plus movies, plays, and bullfights, sprout in the newspaper *Sete,* available at kiosks; the tourist office keeps a copy on hand and will help you translate it. Portuguese theater is performed at the **Teatro Nacional de Maria II,** Pr. Pedro IV (tel. 32 27 46; tickets 500-3000$, 50% student discount.) Opera season (Oct.-June) fills the **Teatro São Carlos,** Rua Serpa Pinto (tickets 650-3000$).

Near Lisbon

Sintra is the fairy-tale city of Portugal, with fanciful palaces and a dense magical forest. After Lord Byron dubbed it "glorious Eden" and sang its charms in his "Childe Harold," Sintra became a must for 19th-century English travelers taking the Grand Tour. The **Paço Real** was built on the foundations of a Moorish castle; its extraordinary conical chimneys are the early 15th-century additions of King John I. (Open Thurs.-Tues. 10am-4:45pm. Admission June-Sept. 400$; Oct.-May 200$; students with ID and seniors free.) The town's other principal attractions are clustered more than 500m above the center on **Mount Pena.** Hike, bus (one-way 125$), or taxi (round-trip 1800$) up the 3km of winding access road to the **Palácio da Pena,** a massive palace built over an old Hieronymite monastery (admission 400$, students with ID and seniors free). This gorgeous but confusing mishmash of styles dubbed "Wagnerian fantasy" is surrounded by Pena Park, with 3000 botanical species from all over the world. Finally, there's the impressive ***castelo*** captured from the Moors in the 12th century by Portugal's first native king, Afonso Henriques. Sintra's **turismo** (tel. 293 11 57) is at Pr. Republica, 19, across from the post office. For an inexpensive meal, try **Casa da Avó** near the fire station. Sintra, 25km north of Lisbon, is accessible by train from the Rossio station (every 5 min., 45 min., 135$).

The waters around Lisbon have been given over to shipping, and the nearest beaches, **Cascais** and **Estoril,** are 20km away. Despite a big tourist buildup, the two towns are still pleasant with their turn-of-the-century villas and verdant gardens. For accommodations in Cascais, try **Pensão Le Biarritz,** Av. do Ultramar (tel. 28 22 16). For a special meal go to **Pereira,** Rua Bela Vista, 30. In Estoril stay at **Costa,** Rua de Olivença, 2 (tel. 468 16 99). The **Maryluz,** Rua Maestro Lacerda, 13 (tel. 468 27 40), is a fine second choice. Ask at the Lisbon tourist office about transportation to **Costa de Caprica,** which has a dapper beach.

Central Portugal

The interior of southern Portugal between the Algarve and the Rio Tejo is divided into two historic provinces similar in name but strikingly different in character. The **Ribatejo,** along the banks of the Tagus, is a fertile region of meadows and pastures, famous for its Arabian horses and great black bulls. Mother Nature has been kind to the Ribatejo, and the countryside is lush and expansive. Stretching south and east of the Tagus, the less fortunate **Alentejo** is harsh, forbidding, and drought-ridden, an enormous grassland with few population centers outside Évora and the undistinguished city of Beja. Visitors traveling its roads may see nothing but swaying grass for miles around, perhaps relieved by an occasional stand of eucalyptus trees or a small whitewashed village.

Two cities of particular note lie in or near the Ribatejo. The sumptuous medieval township of **Tomar,** 90 minutes by train from Lisbon, straddles the banks of the winding Rio Nabão. Most of Tomar's numerous architectural monuments date from the heyday of the Knights Templar and the Knights of Christ, both notorious for their conquests during Portugal's Age of Discovery. The **Convento de Cristo,** in a stately fortress, dominates the cityscape from its hilltop perch. The convent's octagonal **Templars' Rotunda** is modeled after the Holy Sepulchre in Jerusalem. Beneath the giant *rosacea* is Portugal's most lavish stained-glass window, carved out of stone in Manueline style. The adjacent Renaissance **Claustro dos Felipes** flaunts a striking fountain in the shape of the angular Cross of Christ. (Open daily 9:30am-12:30pm and 2-6pm; Oct.-Feb. 9:30am-12:30pm and 2-5pm. Admission 300$, Oct.-Feb. 200$, Sun. mornings free.) On Rua do Dr. Joaquim Jacinto, 73, the **Sinagoga** is Portugal's only vestige of a once-thriving Jewish community. (Open daily 9:30am-12:30pm and 2-6pm, or ring at #104.)

From Tomar's train or bus station, walk straight down the street in front of the station and turn left at the first light until you reach Av. do Cândido Madureira; Tomar's **tourist office** (tel. (049) 31 32 37) is two blocks to your left. (Open Mon.-Fri. 9:30am-12:30pm and 2-6pm, Sat.-Sun. 10am-1pm and 3-6pm; Oct.-May Mon.-Fri. 9:30am-12:30pm and 2-6pm, Sat. 10am-1pm.) The cheapest rooms in town are at **Pensão Nun' Alvares,** Av. D. Nuno Alvares, 3 (tel. (049) 31 28 73), two blocks to the right as you exit the train and bus stations. (Singles 1700$, with bath 2000$. Doubles 2300$, with bath 3000$. Breakfast included.) **Pensão Luanda,** Av. Marquês de Tomar, 13-15 (tel. (049) 31 29 29) has comfortable, modern rooms across from river and park. (Singles with bath 3750$. Doubles with bath 5000$. Breakfast included.) **Snack-Bar Tabuleiro,** Rua Serpa Pinto, 140, near the synagogue, serves the cheapest meals in town. (Open Mon.-Sat. 9:30am-10pm.)

South of Tomar on the banks of the Tejo, **Santarém** is the historic capital of the Ribatejo and its major town. An important settlement in Roman and medieval days, it is considered the capital of Portugal's Gothic style. Santarém's center is the area between **Portas do Sol** park, which overlooks the Tejo, and the **Praça Sá de Bandeira.** The main commercial street between these points is **Rua Capela e Ivens** along which lie the tourist office and many *pensões.* In the *praça* the **Igreja do Seminário dos Jesuitos** is a beautiful example of Baroque architecture (open 9am-5pm, cloister 2-5pm). Equally flamboyant is the **Igreja de Marvila** nearby, a 12th-century church heavily altered in the 16th century. For a quick Gothic fix, proceed to the **Igreja da Graça,** a simple but eloquent structure built in 1388 which contains the grave of Pedro Alvares Cabral, "discoverer" of Brazil. Off Rua São Martinho stands the medieval **Torre das Cabaças** (Tower of the Gourds), so called because of the eight earthen bowls installed in the 16th century to amplify the bell's ring.

Santarém is an hour from Lisbon by bus. From the station, walk through the park and across the busy Av. Marquês Sáda Bandeira. Turn right and then left, taking Rua Pedro Canavarro uphill until Rua Capela e Ivens; there you'll find a helpful tourist office. (Open Mon.-Fri. 9am-7pm, Sat.-Sun. 9:30am-12:30pm and 2-5:30pm.) A block away at Travessa do Froes, 14, **Pensão do José** (tel. (043) 230 88) has simple accommodations at a reasonable price (singles 1500$, doubles 3000$).

Évora

Rising proudly from a parched, olive-dappled plain, Évora is one of the only major towns to relieve the empty and sparsely-populated Alentejo. Coveted by empire after empire, Évora shelters both a Roman temple and a Renaissance palace—and everything medieval in between. Colorful tile façades and ancient, whitewashed walls glimmer in a tangle of verdant streets and chirping balconies.

Orientation and Practical Information

Praça do Giraldo is Évora's main square. Restaurants, accommodations, and points of interest all cluster nearby.

Tourist Office: Pr. Giraldo, 73. English-speaking and helpful. City map suggests walking tours. Open Mon.-Fri. 9am-7pm, Sat.-Sun. 9am-12:30pm and 2-5:30pm; Oct.-May Mon.-Fri. 9am-6pm, Sat.-Sun. 9am-5:30pm.

Post Office: Rua de Olivença (tel. 233 11), 2 blocks north of Pr. Giraldo. Open Mon.-Fri. 8:30am-6:30pm. **Postal Code:** 7000.

Telephones: In the post office. **City Code:** 066.

Currency Exchange: Automated service outside Turismo. Open 24 hrs.

Trains: (tel. 221 25). 1½km hike to the tourist office in Pr. Giraldo. From the station, walk up Rua da Baronha which becomes Rua da República. Taxis (250$), but not buses, ply this route. To: Lisbon (5 per day, 3 hr., 650$) and Faro (daily, 5 hr., 210$).

Buses: Rodoviária Nacional, Rua da República (tel. 221 21). 5-min. walk to Pr. Giraldo up Rua da República. To: Lisbon (7 per day, 2½ hr., 900$) and Faro (4 per day, 5 hr., 1750$).

Taxis: Tel. 73 47 34. 24-hr. service.

Hitchhiking: Those heading to Lisbon go to the edge of Rua Serpa Pinto, at the ancient walls. It's not easy.

Medical Assistance: Hospital (tel. 250 01 or 221 32) on Rua Valasco, close to Rua D. Augusto Edwardo Nunes.

Emergency: (tel. 115). Police headquarters at Rua Francisco Soares Lusitania near the Temple of Diana (tel. 263 41).

Accommodations, Camping, and Food

Between November and April prices fall; bargain down 10-20%.

Pensão Policarpo, Rua da Freira de Baixo, 16 (tel. 224 24), a former noble's home. Facing the cathedral, head right, bear left, and ask. If you hit the back of the cathedral, you've gone too far. Its parking garage is visible on Rua do Conde da Serra da Tourega. Elegant, comfortable, and recently-renovated. Doubles 3700$, with bath 5200$. Breakfast included.

Pensão Residencial O Eborense, Largo da Misericórdia, 1 (tel. 220 31). Make the 1st right as Rua da República becomes Pr. Giraldo. A former ducal palace, recently renovated; all rooms with bath and heating. Singles 3500-5000, doubles 5000-7000. Breakfast included.

Pensão Giraldo, on Rua Meroadores, 2 blocks from Turismo (tel. 258 33). Small, tidy rooms in an ideal location. Singles 2600$, with bath 4500$. Doubles 3600$, with bath 5900$. 1000$ less in winter.

Camping: Orbitur, (tel. (066) 251 90), a two-star park on Estrada das Alcáçovas, a busy road which branches off the bottom of Rua Raimundo (which starts in Pr. Giraldo). Washing facilities and a small market, but a 40-min. walk to the *praça* (only 1 bus per day). Reception open 8am-10pm. 365$ per person and car, 305$ per tent. Showers 60$.

From Tuesday to Sunday, a **market** assembles behind São Francisco Church, in front of the public gardens (8am-1pm).

Restaurante Guião, Rua da Republica, 81. In front of Igreja da Graça and near the bus station. Bouquets of flowers encircled by bottles of local wine grace each table in this typical Portuguese greasy spoon. Entrees 850$ and up.

Café-Restaurante A Gruta, Av. Gen. Humberto Delgado, 2 (tel. 281 86), before the Pr. Touros (bullring). Overflowing with locals indulging in mouth-watering *frango no churrasco* (BBQ chicken); a whole chicken (750$) feeds 2. Open Sun.-Fri. 7am-3pm and 5pm-midnight.

Restaurante Faísca, Rua do Raimundo, 33 (tel. 276 35), around the corner from the tourist office, downstairs from Pensão Os Manueis. Hearty regional fare includes *costoleta de porco à alentejana* (pork chops with clams in coriander sauce) for 620$. Open daily 8am-10pm.

Restaurant Repas, Pr. Primeiro de Maio, 19, near Igreja São Francisco. Cheap food in a bar atmosphere. Grilled lamb chops, fried potatoes, and rice 850$. Open daily 7am-11pm.

Sights and Entertainment

From Pr. Giraldo, cavort past Rua 5 de Outobro's charming tiled houses to the colossal 12th-century **Sé** (cathedral). (Open Tues.-Sun. 9am-noon and 2-5pm. Admission 150$.) From here you can climb the ramparts for an excellent view of the town. Next door, the **Museu de Évora** houses Roman artifacts and 16th-century Portuguese paintings in an old bishop's palace. (Open Tues.-Sun. 10am-12:30pm and 2-5pm. Admission 250$, seniors and students free.) Across from the museum is Évora's most famous monument, the 2nd-century Roman **Temple of Diana.** Facing the temple is the **Church of São João Evangelista,** the town's best-concealed treasure.

The most perverse of Évora's sights is the **Capela de Ossos** (Chapel of Bones) in the **Church of São Francisco.** The chapel was fashioned from the remains of some 5000 monks and nuns as a less-than-subtle reminder of human mortality. Particularly unpleasant is the rotten body. (Open Mon.-Sat. 8:30am-1pm and 2:30-6pm, Sun. 10-11:30am and 2:30-6pm. Admission 50$, 75$ to take pictures.)

The **Feira de São João** in the last week of June marks the arrival of summer in Évora. The fest climaxes with a bullfight, fireworks, and all-night dancing at the **Feast of São Pedro.** Évora's most popular café/bar hangout is the **Portugal,** Rua João de Deus, 55.

Algarve

You will probably feel right at home in the Algarve, not because it is an especially homey place, but because you'll share it with 10,000 other people from your country. The Algarve's early tourists included the Romans and Moors; later conquerors have come from North America and northern Europe. A modern influx has brought badly needed investment to a region which has for centuries been poor and backward, as well as all the traditional problems of rapid development: high prices, pollution, ugly and short-sighted building projects, and disruption of the local way of life. Towns like Lagos, which once lived on trade and fishing, now exist only for and because of tourism. You (and many others) will see beautiful beaches, clear skies, and great nightlife here, but may come away feeling like you haven't seen much of Portugal.

But then, there *is* the climate. The weather in Algarve blows in from Paradise—dry, sunny, and hot, with cool ocean winds in the morning and clear, quiet evening skies. It may even make up for the crowding and overdevelopment. Besides, you don't have to stay in Lagos. The wind-swept tip of Sagres and the area from Sagres eastwards to Lagos remain somewhat isolated. Like other small towns in the Algarve, Sagres is accessible by **Rodoviária Nacional** buses (frequent service from Lagos, 1 hr., 350$); the women who crowd the bus stop usually rent decent rooms at reasonable rates. Near Sagres, Cabo de São Vicente (Cape St. Vincent) has great beaches and a fortress-*cum*-tourist office (tel. (082) 641 25). East of Lagos, past the crowded resort of Albufeira, lies **Faro,** once the Algarve's capital and now a pleasant provincial port city. Faro is also the Algarve's transportation hub: planes streak overhead on their daily flights to Lisbon and London, while low-tech Portuguese trains wheeze into town from Lisbon (5 per day, 7 hr., 1400$). East of Faro, the Algarve suddenly grows quieter and vaguely charming. **Olhão** and **Tavira** are pleasant towns with unpolluted beaches, while stodgy borderside **Vila Real de Santo António** is good for nothing but cross-river ferries to Ayamonte, Spain (hourly until 1am, 100$). Besides Rodo's buses, trains between Lagos and Vila Real de Santo António (approximately 12 per day each way, 3 hr., 725$) link the coastal settlements. Consider showing your support for free enterprise by using the private company **Caima,** whose opulent coaches zip from a lot on Rua dos Barreiros, 22, in Lisbon, to the Algarve (4 hr., about 1700$).

In July and August, consider making reservations; *pensões* can be hard to find in the more popular cities. *Quartos* abound (rooms for rent in private homes, often with kitchen privileges). Expect to pay 2000-3000$ for a double without private bath. Local delicacies include *sardinhas assadas* (grilled sardines), *caldeira* (a chowder of fish and shellfish), *cataplana* (ham, clams, and sausage), and *lulinhas* (squid, often cooked in its own ink). For entertainment information peruse a copy of the *Algarve News* or *Algarve Magazine* (125$), from a tourist office. **Hospitals** at Faro, Lagos, and Portimão (near Lagos) run 24-hr. emergency wards.

Lagos

Lagos loves tourists, and tourists love Lagos. Not typically Portuguese, Lagos is nonetheless very European: signs for major amenities are generally written in five languages, as Germans, French, Brits, Dutch, and Scandinavians come in boisterous pursuit of pleasure. As if hot sun, mobbed beaches, and fresh seafood aren't enough, the town has history up the wazoo; it was a major Moorish port, the official harbor for the fleet of Prince Henry the Navigator, and the center of the African slave trade.

The 1755 earthquake which took out Lisbon also cut quite a swath through Lagos. Only the altar remained of the **Igreja de Santo António**; the church has been painstakingly restored to its previous condition. Its modest façade conceals extraordinary gilded woodwork within; check out the vaulted ceiling's elaborate *trompe l'oeil* fresco. Adjoining the church, the **Museu Municipal's** fascinating collection includes Lagos's 1504 royal charter and a weird display of mutant animal fetuses. (Both open Tues.-Sun. 9am-12:30pm and 2-5pm. Admission 200$, free to seniors and students and to all on Sun.)

Lagos's main draws are the splendid beaches just west of town, shadowed by weathered orange and yellow cliffs. One of the most seductive is **Praia Dona Ana,** whose sculpted rock-faces and grottos are featured on half the postcards of the Algarve. Motorboats cruise from Lagos to the grottoes when the tides are high enough (daytrips west along the coast, 4500$; tel. (082) 602 49); you might convince your skipper to drop you at a secluded spot and retrieve you a few hours later. **Meia Praia** to the east of town has a windsurfing club and 4km of uninterrupted sand.

The **train and bus stations** are both on the eastern edge of town (4 buses per day from Lisbon, 4 hr., 1450$). Go west on the main avenue by the water and bear right at Rua Portas de Portugal. Follow the signs into the **Turismo** on Largo Marquês de Pombal (tel. (082) 630 31; open Mon.-Fri. 9:30am-7pm, Sat.-Sun. 9:30am-12:30pm and 2-5:30pm). Families offer rooms in private homes for 1500-2500$ per person; bargain down. If they don't find you at the stations, ask for a referral at the turismo, or sit in the *praça* looking homeless. **Residência Baia,** Rua da Barroca, 70 (tel. (082) 76 22 92), down Rua 25 de Abril and then left on Travessa da Senhora da Graça, has large, homey doubles with bath for 3500-4000$. At **Residencial Rubi Mar,** upstairs (tel. (082) 631 65), clean, pleasant doubles go for 4000$. Outside high season, the best deal in Portugal is at **Residência Marazul,** Rua 25 de Abril, 13 (tel. (082) 76 97 49), which has immaculate oak trim and bright tile décor. (Doubles with bath up to 6500$ July-Aug., but as low as 2500$ off season.) Tent at pleasant and guarded **Campo da Trinidade** (tel. (082) 629 31), at Praia Dona Ana. (720$ per person with car, tent and shower.) Slightly further from town, **Parque de Campismo Dolmulago** (tel. (082) 600 31) also straddles the beach (370$ per person; free bus service to Lagos).

Find restaurants around Pr. Gil Eanes and along Rua 25 de Abril. **Cantinho do Mar,** Rua Soeiro da Costa, 6, is a traditional fish restaurant with 800$ entrees cooked on an outdoor grill. (Open Mon.-Sat. noon-3pm and 6pm-midnight.) For a costlier but more stylish scene, try **Ao Natural,** Rua Silva Lopes, 29, a Dutch-run, European-staffed veggie haven with a huge selection of fruit drinks, a good salad bar (sushi 1000$), and dance music on the tropical rooftop terrace. (Open daily 9am-12:30am.) In summer, Lagos's streets are alive until the wee hours; **Praça Gil Eanes** and adjoining streets are a kaleidoscope of cafés. **Mullens,** Rua Cándido dos Reis, 86, is *the* dance hot-spot in Lagos. **Café Gil Eanes** on the *praça* is a popular gay spot.

Lagos's **post office** (postal code 8600; open Mon.-Fri. 9am-6pm) and **telephone exchange** (open daily 9am-11pm) are side by side just off Pr. Gil Eanes. The **hospital** on Rua Castelo dos Governadores (tel. (082) 630 34), next to the Santa Maria church, provides 24-hr. emergency care. **Police** serve and protect from their station one block away on Rua Gen. Alberto Silva (tel. (082) 629 30).

Northern Portugal

Nothing unifies the "north" so much as what it lacks: intense sunshine and packages of tourists. It can get plenty warm and muggy in northern Portugal, but the baking Algarve and Alentejo sun is conspicuously absent, the countryside damper and greener. The landscape of the **Minho** region, north of Porto along the river of the same name, is particularly attractive.

South of this river lies **Braga,** a busy commercial city whose concentration of religious architecture has earned it the title of the Portuguese Rome. Trains screech into Braga from Porto about once every two hours (2 hr., 350$) and buses leave at about the same frequency for the **Gerês National Park,** a scenic, mountainous area of lakes and streams (1½ hr., 435$). Like all of northern Portugal, Braga is (by Portuguese standards) quite wealthy and (by anyone's standards) politically conservative and devoutly Catholic. Further inland rises a mountainous region composed of three provinces, **Trás-os-Montes, Beira Alta,** and **Beira Baixa**—a backward and undeveloped land where it actually *snows.* **Bragança,** in the northeast corner of the country, is graced by an impressive 12-century fortress. Further south, the pleasant town of **Viseu** houses an extensive collection of Portuguese art. Both burgs are accessible by bus and train from Porto, but you'd better not be in a hurry; transportation in this area is from another time.

Cutting from the snowy mountains to the foggy coast south of Porto, **Aveiro** oozes with scenic but smelly canals. Still further south, **Nazaré** is a quaint seaside town whose inhabitants, once fisherfolk, now keep the tourists happy by wearing their traditional costume. **Peniche,** another fishing port, is less popular with foreign visitors, but Salazar, Portugal's longtime dictator, liked it so much he built a political prison in its old fortress. Now the fortress houses a museum chronicling the resistance to Salazar's rule, while Peniche itself has genuine maritime traditions and lacks tourist-driven self-consciousness. Transport to these towns is easy. It's a half-hour train hop from Porto to Aveiro (hourly, 500$). Nazaré and Peniche are more conveniently visited by bus from Lisbon (4 per day, 2 hr., 850$; and 9 per day, 2 hr., 725$, respectively).

Coimbra

Portugal's third city and former capital, Coimbra's current claim to fame is its medieval university, which counts among its alumni both Camões (Portugal's answer to Shakespeare) and Salazar (ditto to Mussolini). It's no surprise that the city has a lively cultural atmosphere, with lots of good bookstores and coffeehouses.

Orientation and Practical Information

Coimbra's lower town centers on two squares, **Largo da Portagem** and **Praça 8 de Maio,** linked by elegant Rua Ferreira Borges. The upper town houses the university and is accessible by the **Arco de Almedina,** off Rua Ferreira Borges. The **Estação Coimbra-A** rail station is a block from Portagem. Most long-distance trains stop at **Estação Coimbra-B,** 3km to the northwest; shuttles connect the two.

Tourist Office: Largo Portagem (tel. 238 86). From Estação A, walk 2 blocks east along Av. Emídio Navarro, keeping the Rio Mondego on your right. Open Mon.-Fri. 9am-7pm, Sat.-Sun. 9am-12:30pm and 2-5:30pm; Oct.-March Mon.-Fri. 9am-6pm, Sat. 10am-1pm.

Currency Exchange: Hotel Astória, across the *largo* from Turismo. Worse rates than banks plus a 600$ fee, but open 24 hrs.

Telephones: City Code: 039.

Trains: Tel. 349 98. To: Lisbon (14 per day, 3 hr., 985$); Porto (14 per day, 40 min., 350$); Paris (1 per day, 22 hr., 21,000$).

Buses: Av. Fernão de Magalhães (tel. 270 53). To reach the tourist office, walk right towards Estação A and Portagem (15 min.). To: Lisbon (16 per day, 3 hr., 1000$); Porto (5 per day, 6 hr., 800$).

Medical Assistance: Hospital da Universidade de Coimbra (tel. 72 32 11). Considered the best in the country. Take buses #3, 7, 7T, or 29 to the Cruz de Gelas stop.

Emergencies: (tel. 115). **Police:** (tel. 220 22), Rua Olímpio Nicolau Rui Fernandes, near the market.

Accommodations and Camping

Pousada de Juventude (IYHF), Rua António Henriques Seco, 14 (tel. 229 55). From Estação A, take bus #7, 8, 29, or 46 to Pr. Républia, then walk up Rua Lourenço A. Azevedo and take your second right. Great warden presides over huge sunlit rooms. Reception open 9am-noon and 6pm-midnight. 1100$, breakfast included.

Residência Lusa Atenas, Av. Fernão de Magalhães, 68 (tel. 264 12), a 5-min. walk left from Estação A. Clean, bare, tiny rooms, all with bath. Singles 2500$. Doubles 3500$. Triples 5000$. Breakfast included.

Pensão Residencial Parque, Av. Emídio Navarro, 42 (tel. 292 02), a few doors to the right of Turismo. Grand, spacious rooms overlooking the river. Noisy. Doubles 3000$, with bath 3500$.

Food

Several student *cantinas* (dining halls) subsist around the university, two of which remain open in summer (better-than-average cafeteria meals 250$). Cheap dives line Rua Direita off Pr. 8 de Maio; go there if food poisoning holds no terrors for you. The **Mercado Municipal** is held off Rua Olímpio Nicolau Rui Fernando (open Mon.-Sat. 8am-3pm; Fri. is the big day).

Churrasqueria do Mondego, Rua Sargento Mor, 27 (tel. 233 55), off Rua Sota, one block west of Portagem. Great *frango no churrasco* (barbecued chicken) for 300$. Open daily noon-3pm and 6-10pm.

Restaurante Democrática, Trav. da Rua Nova, 5-7 (tel. 237 84), on a tiny lane off Rua Sofia (near Pr. 8 de Maio). Most entrees 500$.

Café Santa Cruz, Pr. 8 de Maio (tel. 336 17). Academic hangout where scholars and students chat over pastries and coffee (50$). Open daily 7am-2am.

Sights and Entertainment

Founded in 1290 (and transferred for several centuries back and forth between Coimbra and Lisbon), the university here has long been Portugal's foremost center of learning. Climb the stairs under the Moorish **Arco de Almedina** into the upper district of the city; here, the **Universidade Velha** (Old University) is housed in Portugal's former royal palace (1324 to 1537). The gem of the complex is the **library,** built by D. João IV between 1717 and 1728 in a rough Chinese baroque. The neighboring **Museo Machado de Castro** is famous for its superb Gothic and Renaissance sculptures. The entire structure rests on a Roman sewer system, accessible through a hole chopped in the museum floor. (Open Tues.-Sun. 10am-12:30pm and 2-5pm. Admission 350$, students and seniors free.) In the town center is the **Mosteiro Santa Cruz,** founded in 1131 but unfinished until the 16th century; it was in this monastery that King Pedro had his lover Inês's body exhumed and crowned queen (she had been killed by assassins while Pedro was still only a crown prince), making his courtiers kiss her grotty hand. (Open daily 9am-noon and 2-6:30pm. Admission to sacristy 100$.) Of the **Convento de Santa Clara-a-Velha,** across the bridge, more than half is underwater; gamboling atop the columns is surreal. (Open daily 10am-7pm.) After dinner, the pub **Diligência,** down the street, attracts Coimbra's most flamboyant *fado.* (Open daily until midnight.)

Porto

As its name suggests, Porto epitomizes the European port city—at once grimy and alluring, shabby and stately. A large percentage of Portugal's income is earned here, and the city's workaday mentality is illustrated by the old proverb: "Coimbra sings, Braga prays, Lisbon shows off, and Porto works." The city received its first commercial boost during the War of the Spanish Succession: when England and Portugal allied against Spain and France, patriots and profiteers promoted the drinking of sweet Port wine instead of French claret. The 80-odd Port houses—actually not in Porto at all, but across the Rio Douro in Vila Nova de Gaia—still play a major role in the city's economy. Now as before, only human feet crush the grapes, and a dash of brandy supplies an extra kick. Many of the warehouses still offer free tours which include generous tastes of the sweet stuff.

Orientation and Practical Information

Clinging to a dramatic gorge cut by the Rio Douro, Porto lies 6km from the sea, on the main rail line up from Lisbon and down from Valença do Minho. An east-west line brings in travelers from Salamanca and other points in Spain. The city's main thoroughfare is **Avenida dos Aliados,** bordered to the north by **Praça General H. Delgado** and to the south by **Praça da Liberdade.** The most beguiling part of town is the **Ribeira** (river district), where three of Europe's most graceful bridges span the gorge and time-worn tile houses pack the narrow streets.

Tourist Office: Turismo, Rua Clube dos Fenianos, 25 (tel. 31 27 40), 4 blocks from São Bento Station, beside City Hall. Walk straight up Av. dos Aliados; the office is on your left. Open Mon.-Fri. 9am-7pm, Sat. 9am-2pm, Sun. 10am-2pm; Oct.-May Mon.-Fri. 9am-12:30pm and 2-5:30pm, Sat. 9am-4pm.

Consulates: U.S., Rua Júlio Dinis, 826, 3rd floor (tel. 69 00 08). Open Mon.-Fri. 8:30am-1pm and 2-5:30pm. **U.K.,** Av. de Boavista, 3072 (tel. 68 47 89). Open Mon.-Fri. 9:30am-1pm and 3-5pm. **Spain,** Rua de Dom João IV, 341, 1st door (tel. 56 39 15).

Currency Exchange: An automated currency exchange outside Banco Espírito Santo e Comercial de Lisboa on Pr. Liberdade provides 24-hr. service. Most banks charge an outrageous 800$ flat rate, making it wiser to change amounts under USD200 at travel agencies.

American Express: Star Travel Service, Av. dos Aliados, 210 (tel. 200 36 37 and 200 36 89). All AmEx services. Open Mon.-Fri. 9am-12:30pm and 2-6pm.

Post Office: Pr. General H. Delgado (tel. 38 02 51), across from the tourist office. Interesting exhibit of postal uniforms. Open Mon.-Fri. 8am-10pm. Poste Restante daily 8am-10pm. **Postal Code:** 4000.

Telephones: Pr. Liberdade, 62. Open daily 8am-11:30pm. Also in the post office. **City Code:** 02.

Trains: São Bento Station (tel. 200 27 22), south of Pr. Liberdade, for local, regional, and some national routes. **Campanhã Station** (tel. 56 41 41), on the eastern edge of the city, for all routes. Numerous trains link stations. To: Coimbra (12 per day, 2½ hr., 655$); Braga via Nine (9 per day, 2 hr., 350$); Lisbon (5 per day, 4½ hr., 1400$; 8 Alfa Expresses per day, 3¼ hr., 2200$); and Paris (1 per day, 27 hr., 17,800$).

Buses: Several private companies travel south, as does **Rodoviária Nacional,** Rua de Alexandre Herculano, 366 (tel. 269 54). To travel north, **Auto-Viação do Minho** and several other private lines, Pr. D. Filipa de Lencastre, 1 block west of Av. dos Aliados.

Laundromat: Penguin, Shopping Center Brasília, down escalator and to the left (tel. 69 50 32). Take bus #2 or 20 from Pr. Liberdade. Wash and dry 800$. Open Mon.-Sat. 9am-midnight.

Medical Assistance: Hospital de Santo António, Rua Prof. Vicente José de Carvalho (tel. 200 73 54).

Emergencies: Police or **Ambulance** (tel. 115). Police station on Rua Alexandre Herculano (tel. 200 68 21).

Accommodations and Camping

Most of the city's *pensões* are west of Av. dos Aliados. Though plentiful, they fill by late afternoon in July and August. Some places have recently gussied themselves up, but budget lodgings are still there for the finding.

Pousada de Juventude do Porto (IYHF), Rua Rodrigues Lobo, 95 (tel. 655 35), 2km from downtown. Take bus #3, 19, 20, or 52 from Pr. Liberdade to Rua Júlio Dinis. Shamefully small for such a large city. Vacancies don't last the morning. Reception open 9-10am and 6-midnight. Curfew midnight. 1050$, Oct.-June 900$. Breakfast included.

Residencial Porto Chique, Rua Conde Vizela, 26 (tel. 38 00 69). From São Bento station, walk across Pr. Liberdade and up Rua Clérigos. Take the 1st right at the end of the street. Well-lit *pensão* with balconies. Singles 1500$, with bath 2000$. Doubles 2500$, with bath 3500$.

Pensão dos Aliados, Rua Elísio de Melo, 27 (tel. 248 53), off Av. dos Aliados. Luxurious rooms, but avenue noise filters in. All rooms with bath. Singles 4000$. Doubles 4500$. Breakfast included.

Residencial Vera Cruz, Rua de Ramalho Ortigão, 14 (tel. 32 33 96), on the side street before the tourist office. Pure Portuguese elegance. Singles 5000$. Doubles 5200$, with bath 5400$. Breakfast included.

Camping: Parque de Prelada (tel. 626 16), 5km from the beach. Take bus #6 from Pr. Liberdade. 340$ per person, 270$ per tent, 280$ per car.

Food

The problem with food in Porto is twofold. First, many restaurants wallow in the slimy neighborhoods near the river. Second, most of the seafood hails from the raw-sewage soup that is the Mandego. Your best option may be the food market on the corner of Rua Formosa and Rua Sá de Bandeira. Take Rua de Passos Manuel from Av. dos Aliados, then turn left on Rua Sá de Bandeira. (Open Mon.-Fri. 7am-5pm, Sat. 7am-1pm.)

King Long, Largo Dr. Tito Fontes, 115. Sublime Chinese food and traditional Chinese decor. Cheap.

Churrasqueira Moura, Rua do Almada, 219-223. Delicious, dirt-cheap meals under 600$. Stand-up counter specials include hamburger with egg and *frango no churrasco* (BBQ chicken with fries) only 350$. Open Mon.-Sat. 11:30am-10pm.

Taberna Típica, Rua Reboleira, 12. Stone walls and cute nautical decor. Specializes in *arroz de polvo* (octopus rice), a bargain at 800$. Open Tues.-Sun. noon-2pm and 7-11pm.

Sights

South of São Bento Station rises Porto's great Romanesque **Sé** (cathedral), a real fortress of God with granite foundations, stout walls, and tiny windows. (Open daily 9am-12:30pm and 2-5:30pm.) West of the cathedral, on Rua da Bolsa at Rua do Comércio do Porto, stands the **Palácio da Bolsa** (Stock Exchange), built in 1834 (follow the signs from Rua Mouzinho da Silveira). A tour of the interior is worthwhile, if only for the extraordinary Arab Hall modeled after Granada's Alhambra. (Open Mon.-Fri. 9am-6pm, Sat.-Sun 10am-noon and 2-5pm. Admission 200$, students free.) South of the Bolsa, the **Ribeira** (Esplanade) stretches along the river, skirted by a marvelous quay filled with shops and restaurants. Peek into the nearby **Igreja de São Francisco,** a church which shelters one of the most elaborate gilded wood interiors in all Portugal (admission 50$). Take tram #1 from here for further views of the Ribeira and river; it continues all the way to **Foz do Douro,** Porto's beach community. Porto's most characteristic monument, the ornate **Torre dos Clérigos,** affords a panorama of the city from atop its 200 steps. (Open Mon.-Fri. 7:30-9:30am, 10:30am-noon, and 3:30-8pm; Sun. 10am-1:15pm and 8:30-10:30pm. Admission 75$.) The **Museu Nacional de Soares dos Reis,** Rua D. Manuel II, houses sculpture by Portugal's 19th-century Michelangelo, Soares dos Reis. His *A*

Flor Agreste is the most recognized face in Portugal; the *O Desterrado* is the artist's masterpiece. (Open Tues.-Sun. 10am-noon and 2-5pm. Admission 200$, students free.)

No visit to Porto would be complete without a stop at some of the many lodges where *Port* is stored and bottled. Most are across the bridge from the Ribeira, in **Vila Nova da Gaia.** Of the 15 lodges offering free tours and samples, the major ones, such as **Cintra, Vasconcellos** and **Sandeman** keep the most regular hours (usually daily 10am-5pm, though Sandeman—the best—is closed Sun.).

ROMANIA

USD$1 = 61.4 lei (ROL)
CAD$1 = 53.7 lei
GBP£1 = 103 lei
AUD$1 = 47.8 lei
NZD$1 = 35.0 lei
Country Code: 40

10 lei = USD$0.16
10 lei = CAD$0.19
10 lei = GBP£0.10
10 lei = AUD$0.21
10 lei = NZD$0.29
International Dialing Prefix: 00

Deep in the mysterious Carpathian Mountains, Romanian peasants preserve folk traditions lost to the rest of Europe for centuries. The fortified towns of Transylvania still look like medieval woodcuts, and the green hills of Moldavia have remained as serene as the frescoes on their monastery walls. The country's stains—soot-blackened, ruined towns and decades of forced resettlement in urban industrial nightmares like Bucharest—date from the days when Romania was the poorest and most totalitarian country in the Soviet bloc; to retire the country's USD11 million foreign debt, the Romanian dictator Nicolae Ceauşescu ruthlessly bled his people. In a process called "systemization," designed for economic efficiency and consolidation of power, he destroyed rural villages and herded their inhabitants into factory towns. The Romanian people were deadened and silenced by fear and gnawing hunger.

In December 1989, Romania erupted in a revolution as bloody, crude and excessive as the man it extinguished. The coup was violently fast: eight days in all, beginning on the 17th. The military fought alongside a ragtag citizens' army against Ceauşescu's dreaded Securitate force. Hostilities centered on control of Bucharest's TV and radio stations in a grotesque demonstration of the power of media. Ceauşescu and his wife were captured, "tried" and summarily executed by a citizen firing squad that had to be selected by lottery, so numerous were the volunteers. A morbid celebration screamed through Romania as potent television images flashed the dictator's bloody and broken head across the nation.

Ion Iliescu's National Salvation Front replaced Ceauşescu with an astonishing 77% of the vote. However, accused of intimidation and abuse of their control of ever-more-powerful television in the elections, the Front has become the focus of widespread discontent. In June 1990, Iliescu violently suppressed a protest in Bucharest, calling into question his democratic sentiments and the prospects for new elections in 1992. In June 1991, the protesters were back and more boisterous than ever. Fortunately, the busloads of armed police waiting nearby never had cause for action.

Economic headaches further destabilize the fledgling government's legitimacy. With 11 cars and 111 phones per thousand people, desperately poor Romania lags behind even the rest of Eastern Europe. The government has begun cutting exports, channeling goods and electricity back to the people, and focusing on Romania's potentially rich agricultural sector. Yet the country has a long and painful climb ahead, and its people are sadly unprepared for the realities of a market economy. Unemployment is a foreign concept, and plummeting productivity and work hours seem to indicate that many Romanians consider their new freedom a liberation from effort.

The future of Romania is up for grabs, and the information in this chapter may become quickly obsolete. Be prepared to forego many luxuries taken for granted in the West. Many citizens are trying to leave Romania by any means possible; Western visitors should be prepared for completely sincere (if not flattering) marriage offers. Romanians may also hassle you for formal invitations to your country, which make it easier for them to obtain a visa. To them, you resemble a walking gold mine; twenty-five dollars are a month's wages. Register with your embassy, and watch your wallet at all times.

Getting There

In September 1991, citizens of the U.S., Canada, the U.K., Australia and New Zealand all needed visas for Romania; tourist visas (USD30-49) allow a 60-day stay, while transit visas (USD15) permit 72 hours in the country. Romanian embassies are at 1607 23rd St. N.W., Washington DC 20008 (tel. (202) 232-4747), 111 Peter St. Suite 530, Toronto, Ont. M5V 2H1 (tel. (416) 585 5802), 4 Palace Green, London W8 4QD (tel. (071) 937 9666), and 333 Old S. Head Bond, Sydney, NSW (tel. (02) 30 57 18). There is no longer a required currency exchange. By train, the best access points are Sofia, Belgrade, and Budapest; other trains run from Poland, Czechoslovakia, and the Soviet Union, while buses connect Bucharest to İstanbul.

Getting Around

Buying Romanian train tickets will make you feel like you're being punished by God. In Bucharest, they go on sale at the station only two hours before departure—barely enough time to get through the crushing lines. Tickets are sold farther in advance at the Agence de Voyage of CFR (the railroad company), usually located in the center of town, and packed with vacationing Romanians in hour-plus lines. Before actually buying the ticket, you must first wait in a line to find out which ticket window to line up at. A copy of the *Thomas Cook Timetable* (though it only lists major lines) can save you hours of agony. In some towns, you can go to the tourist bureau (ONT) and get a domestic train ticket in half an hour for Western currency. Some people dispense with the pesky tickets entirely by way of a 200-300 lei gift to the conductor. Getting a friendly Romanian to aid in the negotiations facilitates all manner of train transactions. InterRail holders can now bypass all of this, but Eurail is not yet valid.

There are three types of trains: *rapid, accelerat,* and *persoane. Rapid* and *accelerat* levy a small surcharge, but are worth it: A 3½-hour ride by *rapid* train can take 13 hours by *persoane* train. *Cursă* trains progress slightly faster than a moseying cowboy.

To buy international tickets, you must go the CFR office in Bucharest. Bring a good book; you will wait at least three hours. Budapest-bound trains may exit Romania through either Arad or Oradea; you'll need to specify one when buying a ticket. All international tickets must be paid for in Western currency. It's cheaper and faster to buy a domestic ticket to the last stop on the border and then simply remain on the train. After you cross the frontier, the new conductor will often gladly sell you another ticket for whatever currency you have.

Romanian train criminals are especially crafty, filling a compartment with sleeping gas and robbing its occupants, or sending gangs of kids onto a train stopped at a station to throw valuables through the windows to conspirators. Lock your compartment, stay with your belongings at all times, and don't fall asleep unless you are sure that the people around you are trustworthy.

Use the extensive local **bus** system only when trains are not available. Buses are cheaper than trains and you can often buy your ticket on board, but they are usually packed and poorly ventilated. Look for the signs for the *autogară* (bus station) in each town. Before heading out, ask for a copy of the bus schedule *(mersul autobuzelor).*

Flying, once a worthwhile alternative, now requires Western currency and charges much more (Bucharest-Constanţa USD35). **Hitchhiking** is popular among Romanians. Drivers may expect a payment equivalent to 50-100% of the bus fare for giving you a lift. Some may refuse payment from Westerners, but no one holds out long against cigarettes or other treasures. A wave of the hand, rather than a thumb, is the recognized sign. Although uncommon, women may encounter sexual advances when hitchhiking: in this situation, many open the door to signify their intent to leave, and get out at the first opportunity.

Practical Information

ONT (called "OJT" in some cities), the Romanian national tourist bureau, has offices throughout the country. Their information about the price and availabilty of cheap accommodations is not always reliable. ONT branches in expensive hotels are often more useful than the main offices. **BTT,** the youth travel agency, is designed for organized groups and will be utterly befuddled by your presence.

Romanian bills come in denominations no greater than 100 and must have the date 1966. Don't change too much; lei buy precious little, and accommodations usually must be paid in hard currency. It's now legal for Romanian citizens to have Western currency, but the black market still exists (180 lei to the dollar was the going rate in 1991). Although unofficial trading is still illegal, getting jailed is now less of a risk than getting cheated. Train stations demand special wariness. Beware of hurried strangers offering you paper-filled stacks of "money" in exchange for your dollars. Also, be suspicious of people offering small Romanian bills in exchange for large American ones—there are known to be counterfeiters in Romania. Cigarettes constitute a more informal means of exchange. (Kents or Marlboros with American-grown tobacco are best.) A pack costs USD1 in the hard currency shops (now open to Romanians as well), and sells for 100 lei. Offer a few smokes to a taxi driver and you just might get there faster. Offer a pack to a concierge and a room may suddenly be available. Gifts for everyone with whom you deal can make your travels somewhat less frustrating.

Romanian is a Romance language; travelers familiar with French, Italian, Spanish or Portuguese can usually decipher public signs. Spoken Romanian has been considerably influenced by the surrounding Balkan languages, and is a trial for the average visitor. Note that *ţ* is pronounced as in ca*ts;* *ş* as in ca*sh;* both *î* and *â* as in str*i*ng; *ă* as in b*u*s; and *c* as in *ch*eese when followed by *i* or *e* (otherwise, as in *c*ool). In Transylvania, German and Hungarian are widely spoken. Throughout the country, French is the second language for the older generation, English for the younger. In touristy areas, many people will speak enough English to help you.

Telephoning is no easy task in Romania. At the phone office, write down where you want to call, how long you want to talk and the telephone number. You will pay up front (rates found on a wall chart). Since rates rise the longer you stay on, it is cheaper to call collect *(telefon cu taxă inversă).*

Theft plagues Romania. Keep doors locked, and watch your baggage at all times. Count your change and politely request an explanation if a bill seems wrong. Traveling for women is fairly hassle-free. A calm push and firm voice is usually sufficient to end unwanted advances.

Many toiletries are difficult to come by but usually can be purchased in hard currency shops. Film, motor oil and feminine sanitary products of any sort are completely unavailable. Women running short should ask for cotton wool (vată). Bring twice as much toilet paper as you think you'll need and plenty of diarrhea medication to combat Romanian food. Soap, towels and toilet paper are not provided in most public bathrooms (there is still a 3 lei cover charge).

Be wary of weekend business hours. Under Ceauşescu, weekends meant shorter work days for Romanians, not days off. The new government immediately gave everyone weekends off, but has since had second thoughts. National holidays are New Year's Day, May Day (May 1), and the Day of Liberation from Fascism (Aug. 23). The day following each of these is also a holiday. Romania is in the same time zone as Bulgaria and one hour ahead of Yugoslavia, Hungary and the rest of Europe.

Accommodations and Camping

Newly legalized private accommodations run about USD10 per person (hard currency only). Contact the ONT office for information, and always fix a price before you accept anything. Freelance housing offers should cost under USD4 and often cost nothing, but may cost you your valuables if you're not careful. Your hosts may also expect you to change money with them at a favorable rate. Many towns also reserve university dorms for foreign students at insanely low prices. Ask at the local university rectorate; the ONT *may* be able to help you. The price of so-called "youth hotels" has taken off in recent years. Strangely, regular hotels cost less, and are more likely to have space for Westerners. Prices start at USD25 for a single and USD32 for a double. Campgrounds are crowded, and their bathrooms redefine the word "foul." Bungalows are relatively cheap, but often full in summer (about USD5-10). Get the tourist map called *Popasuri Turistice* (in French), which lists most sites.

Food and Drink

Finding food in Romania is no longer such a big deal. In summer 1991, stores stocked various fruits (cherries 55 lei per kg), vegetables (tomatoes 77 lei per kg), bread (5 lei), pastries, cheese, sausage, and so on. Western candy and soda, once confined to hard currency shops, are now also widely available. Other beverages include beer, *brifcor* (an orange-flavored soft drink), *apă minerală* (mineral water), and coffee. It's a good idea to carry a water bottle. There are taps—often real-live wells—in train stations and spaced regularly along major roads. Wines of the Murfatlar region, near the Black Sea, are world-famous. A good, cheap local drink is *ţuică* (plum brandy). Three or four shots will be enough to dull your hunger pangs.

For those who choose to change money on the black market, even the most expensive restaurants are cheap (full meals USD5-6). Be prepared to spend well over an hour for every restaurant meal. Except in the most expensive restaurants (the ones with menus, napkins, and water) you are expected to seat yourself wherever there is space available, including at a table already partially occupied. Restaurants are generally open from 7am to 10pm, but stop serving an hour before closing. Service is usually included in the bill.

Bucharest (Bucureşti)

In the 1920s and 30s, Bucharest was *le petit Paris,* a city of beautiful boulevards, parks, and fine neoclassical architecture. It takes a vivid imagination to catch this resemblance today. If your Romanian visit includes only Bucharest, you'll come away with nothing but memories of grey walls, dusty boulevards and endless lines. Ceauşescu's government demolished beautiful old neighborhoods, replacing them with shoddy concrete-box housing projects in the Early Boredom style. If you misguidedly plan to spend more than a day in the city, flee to the lakes, parks and suburban neighborhoods, where a glimmer of the city's old personality remains.

Orientation and Practical Information

Bucharest is in southeastern Romania, 70km north of the Danube and the Bulgarian border. Direct trains connect the city with most East European capitals. Armed with a city map, secured at the train station with any luck, head east on **Calea Griviţei** and take a right onto **Calea Victoriei,** which leads to most sights and tourist spots. A short walk on Strada Biserica Amzei, the continuation of Griviţei, brings you to **Bulevardul Magheru** (which becomes Bd. Bălcescu and then Bd. 1848), the main artery in Bucharest. Bus #133 or trolley #79 from the station to Piaţa Romană will take you to Bd. Magheru.

Tourist Offices: ONT has two offices. The office at the Gara de Nord is apparently just for show. For reliable help, go to the main office, Bd. Magheru 7 (tel. 14 51 60), for maps and information on sights, accommodations, and camping throughout the country. Open Mon.-Fri. 8am-8pm, Sat. 8am-3pm, Sun. 8am-2pm. Most major hotels have ONT desks, which ration scarce information and maps.

Budget Travel: BTT, Str. Oneşti 4-6 (tel. 14 05 66), at the 2nd traffic light to the right of ONT. Intended for groups. Open Mon.-Fri. 8am-5pm.

Embassies: U.S., Str. Tudor Arghezi 7-9, 1 block behind Hotel Intercontinental. For services, go to the adjacent consulate on Str. Snagov 25 (tel. 10 40 40). Claims not to hold mail but usually does. Open Mon.-Fri. 8am-5pm. **Canada,** Str. Nicolae Iorga 36 (tel. 50 63 30), near Piaţa Romană. Open Mon.-Fri. 9am-5pm. **U.K.,** Str. Jules Michelet 24 (tel. 14 52 11). Open Mon.-Thurs. 8:30am-5pm, Fri. 8am-1pm. Citizens of **Australia** and **New Zealand** should contact the British embassy. **Bulgaria,** Str. Rabat 5 (tel. 33 21 50). Open Mon.-Fri. 8:30am-12:30pm and 2-5pm. 10-day wait for visa. **Hungary,** Str. Jean-Louis Calderon 63 (tel. 15 82 73). Open Mon.-Thurs. 8am-4:30pm, Fri. 8am-3:30pm. **USSR,** Şoseaua Kiseleff 46 (tel. 17 13 09). Open Mon., Wed., and Fri. 9am-1pm.

Currency Exchange: Any ONT office. The **Banca Română de Comerţ Exterior,** on Str. Evgeniu Carada 1-3 will also cash USD or DM traveler's checks.

American Express: ONT office on Bd. Magheru replaces lost cards and holds mail, but doesn't accept wired money or replace lost checks.

Post Office: Str. Matei Millo 10, off Calea Victoriei. Open daily 7am-midnight. Poste Restante down the street next to the Hotel Carpaţi. **Postal Code:** 70154.

Telephones: International calls may be made from Calea Victoriei 37, near the theaters. Open 24 hrs. After hours, go around the side. Expect to wait. Ask to make collect calls. Pay phones, when working, take 1 lei coins and lots of perseverance. **City Code:** 90.

Flights: Otopeni Airport (tel. 33 66 02), 16km away, handles international traffic. Buses to Otopeni leave from the TAROM office every 1-2 hr.; buy tickets on board. Coming from Otopeni, buses let you off near the Hotel Intercontinental on Bd. Magheru. **Băneasa Airport,** connected with Piaţa Romană by trams #131 and 331, does domestic flights. Buy international tickets at Str. Brezoianu 10 (tel. 46 33 46; see directions under Trains below); domestic tickets at the **TAROM** office, Str. Mendeleev 11, off Bd. Magheru (tel. 59 41 85). Both offices are open Mon.-Fri. 8am-7pm, and are chaos.

Trains: Gara de Nord (tel. 052) is the principal station; it's unlikely that you'll have to visit **Basarab, Băneasa,** or **Obor.** Gara de Nord has one baggage check for foreigners and one for locals. **Domestic** tickets can be purchased in advance (though not in English) at the **Agence de Voyage, CFR,** which has two offices: one on Calea Griviţei, 2 blocks down from the train station, the other on Str. Brezoianu 10, 1st floor (tel. 13 26 44), 2 blocks south of Bd. Gheorgiu-Dej between Calea Victoriei and Cişmigiu Park (use the TAROM entrance). Expect a bone-crushing 1 to 3-hr. wait, though *sometimes* there is less of a line in the evening. To: Constanţa (137 lei); Iaşi or Suceava (220 lei); Braşov (109 lei); Cluj (220 lei). **International** tickets must be bought (in hard currency) at the CFR office in Piaţa Unirii. Expect the same wait. You may be inspired to give up and go to the TAROM office or to hitchhike. All offices open Mon.-Fri. 7:30am-7pm, Sat. 7:30am-noon.

Buses: Three stations serve Bucharest. **Filaret,** Piaţa Gării Filaret 1 (tel. 41 06 92), and **Rahova,** Şos. Alexandriei 164 (tel. 80 47 95), are both in the southern suburbs, while **Băneasa,** Str. I. Ionescu de la Brad 5 (tel. 79 56 45), is to the north. All are madhouses. Scores of buses through Bulgaria to İstanbul (17 hr.) leave from the main train station (USD15; outside and to the right, one company charges USD10). Each representative will (falsely) claim that their bus is air-conditioned. Half your trip may be spent at the border crossings in suspicious dealings with customs officials.

Public Transportation: Buses, trolley buses, and trams all cost 3 lei. Tickets are available at kiosks near most stops or on the buses. Buses are comically crowded on busy routes—people literally hang out the doors. Hold on to your valuables. The new Metro is now in full operation and offers relatively comfortable transit (use two 1-lei coins at the entrance). Metro operates from 5am-11pm. Infrequent night buses run after 11pm.

Taxis: 10 lei per km. Try to hail "state taxis" with the number 053 posted on the rear passenger door. Supposedly, they cannot charge more than the fixed rate of 100 Lei for anywhere in the city. Let them know you are aware of this.

Hitchhiking: Those hitching north take tram #149 (or the TAROM shuttle) to the airport. Those heading to the Black Sea and Constanţa take tram #13 east from Piaţa Unirii. Those going to Giurgiu and Bulgaria take tram #12 from Piaţa Unirii. Those heading to Piteşti and western Romania take tram #13 west from Piaţa Unirii.

Pharmacies: At Bd. Magheru 18 (tel. 59 61 15) just across from the ONT office and in the train station. Open 24 hrs. Ring the bell at night.

Medical Assistance: Clinica Batiştei, Str. Tudor Arghezi 28, behind the Hotel Intercontinental. The only hospital authorized to treat foreigners.

Emergencies: Police (tel. 055). Foreigners should call their consulate.

Accommodations and Camping

Ask first at the main ONT office about **Camping Băneasa** (BUN-ah-suh), past the Băneasa airport (2-person bungalows USD5-15). From the Gară de Nord, take bus #205 to the Băneasa airport, transfer to bus #148, and ask the driver to let you off at the campground.

The ONT office can also arrange private rooms (USD12), but Romanians at the train station may offer their hospitality for a few dollars a night or the opportunity to change money with you. During the school year (early Sept.-late June), Romanian students will often offer to share their rather drab rooms. Try the dormitories of the **Polytechnic Institute** near the Grozăveşti Metro stop.

If stuck with the heinous hotel option, kiss your budget goodbye—you might prefer to leave on a night train (the one time when a *persoane* train is useful). Check the signboard posted outside the ONT in the train station for information on all types of hotels. Category II establishments are most likely to have space, though the word "unsavory" may come to mind when staying in them. (Singles USD27-30. Doubles USD40-45. Breakfast included.) Most cluster around the train station; the **Hotel Griviţa,** 130, Calea Griviţei (tel. 50 53 80) is slightly nicer than others. **Hotel Cişmigiu,** Bd. Gheorgiu-Dej 18 (tel. 14 74 10), **Hotel Muntenia,** Str. Academiei 21 (tel. 14 60 10), one of the finest, and **Hotel Carpaţi,** Str. Matei Millo 16 (tel. 15 76 90), are all within several blocks of one another in the center of town, just east of Cişmigiu Park. Call ahead.

Food

There is an open air market on Str. Piaţa Amzei between Calea Victoriei and Bd. Magheru, and a large *alimentara* at #33 UNIC.

Salon Spaniol, Calea Vitoriei 116. Chic pizza joint popular with students. Meals under 80 lei. Restaurant downstairs, bar upstairs. Closes at 6pm.

Hanul Lui Manuc, Str. 30 Decembrie 62, near the southern end of Calea Victoriei. Traditional Romanian cuisine in a beautifully restored 17th-century manor in the oldest part of Bucharest. The sort of place where Romanians hold wedding receptions. Restaurant inside, day bar in courtyard, café in cellar. Meals about 200 lei. Restaurant open Mon.-Fri. 7am-11pm, Sat.-Sun. 7am-midnight. *Crama* (cellar) open Mon.-Fri. 10am-11pm, Sat.-Sun. 10am-midnight. *Bar de Zi* (day bar) open Mon.-Fri. 10am-10pm, Sat.-Sun. 10am-11pm.

Bererie "Caru cu Bere" ("Cart of Beer" Beerhall), Str. Stavropoleos, across from Stavropoleos church, a 5-min. walk from Piaţa Unirii. We have kegs, they had carts. Down a brewski for 25 Lei while admiring wall murals of people doing the same. Notice the ornate entrance before you go in: the rooster on the left and the cat on the right symbolize dawn to dusk. Open daily 10am-midnight.

Madrigal, Bd. N. Bălcescu 4-6, in the Hotel Intercontinental. Come here when you're mad as hell and can't take it anymore. Clean tablecloths, cloth napkins, violin music, and excellent service. It's officially reserved for hotel guests, so you may have to "tip" the *maitre d'* USD2-3. Full meals about USD10, hard currency only. Dress neatly. Open daily 7am-10am, 12:30-4pm, and 7pm-midnight. Last orders 11:30pm.

Sights

You can see the remnants of old Bucharest on the circuit formed by **Calea Victoriei, Strada Lipscani,** and **Bulevardul Magheru.** Most of the elegant buildings making up the palace on **Piaţa Victoriei** are now government offices. If open, visit the extensive collection of Western and Romanian art at the **Art Museum of the Romanian Socialist Republic** on Str. Ştirbei Vodă. (Closed temporarily due to damage suffered during the 1989 revolution.) Several private art collections have been combined in the **Museum of Art,** farther down Calea Victoriei at #111.

Continue your tour south through **Strada Lipscani,** a traditional center for merchants and crowds of shoppers. Even farther south, past the **open-air market** at Piaţa Unirii, are the excavations of an old Roman settlement originally beneath Str. 30 Decembrie. The **Church of the Patriarchy** is home of the Romanian Orthodox Church. Try to catch a 10am Sunday service here, at the **Creţulescu Church,** Calea Victoriei 47, or at any one of the more-frequented Byzantine churches in the southern part of the city.

Those interested in the liberating wave that swept away Ceauşescu in 1989 can drop by the TV station, where anti-government rebels broadcast social revolution as *Securitate* forces stormed the building. Entrance is forbidden, but the bullet-scarred buildings in the vicinity make a cogent statement about the importance of media in modern society. (Take bus #131 from Piaţa Romana to the Piaţa Aviatorilor stop.) Head south on Blvd. 1848, past Piaţa Unirii, and take a right onto what was formerly called **Victory of Socialism Blvd.** Ceauşescu demolished a fifth of Bucharest to build this street of luxury apartments, including a palace, the **House of the People,** (formerly the House of the Republic) for himself and his retainers. This monument to megalomania was strictly off-limits to ordinary Romanians before the revolution.

Although there is no substitute for traveling through the countryside of Moldavia or Maramureş to discover Romanian folklore, the open-air **Village Museum** in Parcul Herăstrău re-creates peasant dwellings from all regions of Romania. From Magheru Bd., take bus #131 or 331 north to the Arcul de Triumf. (Open Tues.-Sun. 9am-8pm, Mon. 9am-5pm.) The **Museum of the History of the City of Bucharest,** on Piaţa Universiâţii, has an authentic parchment dated September 20, 1459—the earliest use of the name "Bucureşti" in any written document. The parchment bears the signature of Vlad Dracul, father of more famous son Vlad Ţepeş, "the Impaler" (alias Count Dracula). Ah! yes. (Open Tues.-Sun. 10am-6pm; admission 15 lei.)

Bucharest is replete with parks. Wander through well-groomed central **Cişmigiu Park,** a few blocks west of Calea Victoriei, or the picturesque **Herăstrău Park** to the north. These are not just refuges from the summer heat, but focal points for much of the city's social life. Elderly pensioners, young couples, soccer players, and chess whizzes are everywhere. The bars in Herăstrău Park provide ample opportunity to rub elbows with young Romanians. You can also join the crowds at **Parcul Studenţilor** (Student Park) on Lacul Tei, where you can swim, play volleyball, basketball, tennis or ping pong. Take bus #35 or trolley #86 to the end and follow the signs.

Bucharest is within an easy bus or trolley ride of an arc of lakes, most of which are in parks and recreation areas. En route to Otopeni airport are the zoo and shaded walks of **Băneasa Forest.** Farther yet meditate three monasteries, each in a pleasant park—**Snagov, Caldaruşani,** and **Ţiganeşti.**

Entertainment

Whatever you do in the evening, pack a map and cab fare. The streets are very poorly lit, making navigation difficult. Buses are unreliable.

At the **Casa de Culture Studentilor** (Student Club of Bucharest University), Calea Plevnei 61 (Metro: Eroilor), behind the Opera, there's a disco where you can gyrate with Romanian students, many of whom speak English. (Open Thurs.-Sun. 7:30pm-midnight. Admission 10 lei with student ID.) Another popular nightspot for Bucharest's youth is the **Architects Club,** Str. Academiei 2-4, near the Hotel Intercontinental. The club's program changes daily, alternating between disco, jazz, theater performances, and film. (Admission 150 lei with student ID.) The **Club Ski-Nautic Banaesa,** Str. Madrigalului 24, Section 1, behind the Herăstrău restaurant in the park of the same name, lets you forget you're in Bucharest. Paddle in the lake between drinks. In summer, nightly performances animate the theaters on Calea Victoriei north of Bd. Gheorghiu. Buy tickets at the *casa de billete,* Calea Victoriei 48. (Open 9am-1pm and 2-8pm for Theater Ţandarica; 10am-1pm and 4:30-7:30pm for Theater Giulesti.)

At other times of the year, sniff out performances by the **Romanian Opera, Philharmonic,** and the **Operetta Theater.** (Tickets only 50 lei.) The **National Theater,** Bd. Bălcescu 2; **C. Nottara,** Bd. Magheru 20 (tel. 15 93 02); and the **Bulandra Theater** on Str. Măgureanu, are the most renowned. Seasons run from mid-October to late March. Tickets are sold for the following week's performance on Saturday at each theater's individual box office. Bucharest also has the only **Jewish State Theater** in Europe, at Str. Iuliu Baraş 15, which performs throughout the summer. The shows are in Yiddish, though the simultaneous headphone translations in Romanian should make everything clear.

Near Bucharest

When Bucharest drives you to the brink of insanity, take a daytrip to **Snagov.** This tiny village lies half an hour north of Bucharest by car or train (4 per day). Many people hitch. In summer, hordes descend upon Snagov Park, 5km west of Snagov village, where you can swim in the brownish lake or rent a rowboat (11 lei per 1½ hr.) and row to **Snagov Monastery** (a ½-hr. trip). Here lies the grave of the infamous Vlad Ţepeş, "The Impaler." The so-called Count Dracula earned his reputation by refusing to pay the traditional dues imposed on Romania by the Ottomans and impaling the heads of the Turkish police on spikes, setting them around the walls of his capital. Women may wish to do the same to the monastery keepers—only men may enter.

Another option is to escape to **Sinaia.** This high mountain resort town lies 1¾ hours from Bucharest towards Braşov by train. Here looms the 19th century summer castle of King Carol I, the first King of Romania. This modern castle, now called **Museum Peleş,** has had a two-person elevator since 1883. (Castle open Wed.-Sun. 9am-3pm; admission 25 lei.) King Carol's line descends to Michael I, who, at age 71, is alive and well in Switzerland; a significant Romanian contingent wants him aliver and weller in Bucharest. (Iliescu's government will not even let him visit as a tourist.) Be sure also to visit the **Sinaia Monastery,** built in the 17th century and used as a refuge during the Russo-Turkish War.

Black Sea Coast

Romania's Black Sea coast is jam-packed in summer, not necessarily because of its beauty, but because it is often the only place hard-currency-deficient Romanians can afford. Four trains per day run from Bucharest to **Constanţa** (3 hr., 137 lei), where you can catch a bus to any of the Black Sea resorts. Constanţa itself inflates to three times its size during the summer months. The city, originally a Greek harbor some 2500 years ago, received its name from the daughter of Emperor Constantine the Great—some residents playfully regard Constantinople as "the fatherland." The **Statue of Ovid,** in Piaţa Ovidiu, commemorates the Roman writer who wrote his most famous poems in exile here. The ONT office on Bd. Tomis speaks no English and is largely unhelpful. Instead try the English-speaking Hotel Continental (tel. (916) 156 60) at the junction of Bd. Tomis and Bd. Republicii, where you may be able to get a map and advice on some uncrowded places to stay. Take a walk along the waterfront **promenade** past the imposingly elegant Cazino. The **mosque** on Str. Muzeelor is one of the few reminders of Turkish domination, and offers a bird's eye view of the town. In Piaţa Ovidiu, behold the brooding Ovid before promenading through the open-air **Archaeology Museum** nearby.

Romania's largest Black Sea resort, **Mamaia,** is just 5km north of Constanţa; take bus #40, which stops just across from the Hotel Continental, from Constanţa. The ONT office in Mamaia is in the **Hotel Perla** (tel. (918) 316 70), the second highrise as you go north. Here you can book a comfortable second-class hotel room with fully-equipped bathroom (singles USD30, doubles USD38). First-class rooms are slightly larger (singles USD33, doubles USD44).

Bus #20 heads from Constanţa to **Mangalia,** Romania's southernmost seaside city. **Eforie Nord** and **Eforie Sud,** the first resorts to the south, have unique resources supposedly capable of curing human disorders—apparently including insomnia. Bypass these humdrum retreats and go straight to Costineşti, a dynamic seaside hotspot catering to an exclusively young crowd. Continuing further south, you pass through the intergalactic resorts **Neptun, Jupiter, Venus** and **Saturn** before reaching Mangalia. The picturesque landscape and lakes of Neptun, one of the newest resorts, are well worth a visit.

The scenic **Danube Delta** occupies the northern half of the coast. **Tulcea** is its main gateway, five hours from Bucharest by fast train via Medgidia, and four hours from Constanţa by slow train. The terrain between the three arms of the Danube from Tulcea to the Black Sea is a world of natural and artificial canals cutting their way through miles of roads—a paradise for anglers, birdwatchers, and adventurers armed with small boats. This huge ecosystem undergoes perceptible changes within a single lifetime; 40 meters of land are created every year. Ask Tulcea's ONT office in the **Hotel Delta** about excursions through the delta; the tourist map of the area has cute pictures of the local birds and beasts.

Transylvania

For centuries, Hungarians, Romanians, Russians, and Turks have fought over the rich Transylvanian plateaus in northwestern Romania. The evidence remains—villages built around fortified churches, towns encircling castles, and citadel ruins standing on nearly every hill. Romania's Hungarians, the country's largest minority group, are concentrated here, especially in the northwest where the mountains slope towards the Hungarian plains. Saxons also settled here during the late Middle Ages, and many people still speak German or Hungarian better than Romanian. For years and years, the miserly Nicolae Ceauşescu sold Transylvania's Saxons to Germany (which for years had a policy of paying Eastern European countries a bounty for allowing ethnic Germans to return to their ancestral homeland); consequently, there are very few left and ethnic Romanians and Gypsies have moved in. Transylvania is along two different train routes from Budapest, which merge at Braşov before continuing to Bucharest: trains through Arad stop either in Sibiu or Sighişoara, while those through Oradea stop at Cluj-Napoca and Sighişoara.

If Martians landed in **Cluj-Napoca,** chances are they'd think they were in Hungary; every other person here speaks nearly perfect Hungarian. Six and a half hours from Budapest, three hours from Braşov, and eight from Bucharest, the town is worth a stop for its Franciscan Monastery, fifteenth-century Reform Church, botanical gardens, and its museum of Transylvanian history. From the train station, head straight down the main street ahead of you and across the river to the old town, where you will, with any luck, still find the tourist office and other essential services.

Of all the medieval towns in Transylvania, **Sighişoara** is perhaps the least spoiled and most enchanting. Crowning a green hill on the railroad line between Cluj and Braşov, the guild towers, old clock tower, steeples, and irregular tile roofs of the town are almost entirely unobstructed by modern buildings. The old walled town is preserved as a museum, and visitors can wander here and in the surrounding hilly, green farmland. From the railway station, take a right, then a quick left, and walk towards and across the river, and bear right to reach the town's main hotel and tourist office (they'll sell you a map; ask about market day). In the old town, check out the old Saxon church and graveyard, at the top of a 175-step covered wooden staircase.

The university town of **Sibiu** is a less exciting but still agreeable way to break the Budapest-Bucharest journey. From the train station, walk about 20 minutes up Str. General Magheru to the large square in the city center; continue straight through the square and for several blocks to the tourist office and youth travel office. An 80-100 lei cab ride from the station will bring you to the **BTT student hotel,** which has decent doubles with shower for USD38, though it may work more favorably to pay in lei. (Restaurant and disco on premises.)

The rail stations along the train line between Sibiu and Braşov are your jumping-off points for the **Făgăraş Mountains** just to the south, where you can day-hike past snowfields and shepherds' huts, and stay cheap in a *cabana* (a primitive mountain lodge with an outhouse and occasionally electricity). The view of the Wallachian plains to the south and the Transylvanian plateau to the north will make up for any fatigue. Bring a map and food—the only available grub may be the Romanian equivalent of Spam—and disinfect any water from mountain streams.

Braşov and Bran

Braşov, rising from the foot of Mt. Tîmpa, is one of the most beautifully restored and well-kept cities in Romania. A good base for excursions to the Carpathian mountains, Braşov is small enough to get around and large enough to harbor several interesting monuments from its mercantile past. The city is Transylvania's major train hub, 2½-3 hours from Bucharest by train; all Budapest-Bucharest trains stop here.

From the train station, ride bus #4 for 10 minutes. On Bd. Revolucion, you'll see the Hotel Aro Palace on your left facing a park; the ONT **tourist office,** in its lobby, has maps and information on private rooms. (Open daily 8am-6pm.) To walk from the station (2km), head straight on Bd. Victoriei, follow the road to the right around the civic center, then turn right on Bd. Revolucion.

Just past the Hotel Aro Palace is the **Office of the Rector of the University of Braşov** (open Mon.-Fri. 10am-5pm). In the past, with a student card, they would find you a dorm room—any time of year—for only 50 lei. (Formerly open Mon.-Fri. 10am-5pm. Closed for renovations in summer 1991. May open in 1992.) For private accommodations, ask at the **Hotel Postăvarul** at Str. Republicii and Str. Politehnicii; as you face the Hotel Aro Palace, walk 350m left and then make a quick right onto Republicii. (Private rooms range from USD5-10.) Students in the dormitory complex off **Str. Memorandului** may offer to share their quarters (school year early Sept.-late June). As a last resort, the **Hotel Aro Sport,** at the back of the Hotel Aro Palace, is the cheapest in Braşov (doubles USD21 per person).

Restaurants cluster near the main square, Piaţa Sfatului, just around the corner from the Hotel Aro Palace (most close at 8pm). The **Cetatea Braşov** whips up excellent meals in a castle for 200 lei (open Wed.-Mon. 1-10pm). Riding up the **Mount Timpa** cable car (25 lei round-trip) wins you both a transfixing view and a reasonably priced restaurant at the top (full meal 150 lei). In Braşov, **UNIC** (13, Str. 7 Novembre) passes for a supermarket.

Piaţa Sfatului, in the center of the old town, and the nearby Str. Republicii, provide splendid strolling ground and give a sad glimpse of the beauty Romania lost when the housing projects took over. The fairy-tale-esque **Orthodox Cathedral** in the square was built in 1858 of marble and delicate gold. The **History Museum,** in the middle of the square, was formerly a courthouse; legend holds that the condemned had to jump from the tower to their deaths. (Normally open Tues.-Sun. 10am-6pm. Closed for restorations in summer 1991.) Uphill from the square along Str. Gh. Bariţiu looms the **Black Church,** the most celebrated Gothic building in the country. (Open Tues.-Sat. 9:30am-6pm. Admission 10 lei. ½-hr. organ concerts Tues.-Sat. 6pm, admission 20 lei.) Str. Gh. Bariţiu turns into Str. C. Brincoveanu, which leads to Piaţa Unirii. This square holds **St. Nicolas' Church,** quaintly set against a mountain backdrop, and the **Museum of Romanian Culture.** For a bit of more recent history, walk right from the Hotel Aro Palace along Bd. Revolucion to reach **Piaţa Teatrului.** The former local headquarters of the Communist Party is the only building in the square unscarred by bullets although the raging battle here was supposedly directed against the Communists. This fact has prompted speculation that the anti-Ceauşescu revolution was merely a power shift within the Communist Party.

Poiana Braşov, one of Romania's most popular resorts, is only 10km away (frequent buses, 15 lei).

Twenty-three kilometers southwest of Braşov, **Bran** is a picturesque town which houses the famed **Castle of Vlad Ţepeş.** Once home to the count who inspired Bram Stoker's novel *Dracula,* the castle still poses majestically, though not very mysteriously, on its hill. (Open Tues.-Sun. 9am-5pm.) The story goes that in Ottoman times, Count Vlad was so incensed at Turkish demands for tribute that when the tax collectors stopped by, he had them executed and their heads skewered and displayed along the outside of the castle. Yum! Currently under—yes—renovation, it seems as if the castle has tired of its reputation as a spooky haunt. Still, the locals try to keep it interesting with the **Muzeul Vama Bran,** which contains old photos and relics from the place, and with an **ethnographic museum** of Transylvania (open Tues.-Sun. 10am-5pm; admission 10 lei).

To get to Bran from Braşov, first take bus #5 to the Bartolomeu bus station, then the bus to Bran (23km and 21 lei along the road to Piteşti). Hitchers continue in the same direction that bus #5 was heading.

Moldavia

In the mountains of northeastern Romania, Moldavia is famous chiefly for the **Bukovina Monasteries.** Erected five centuries ago, the monasteries at Voroneţ,

Humor, Suceviţa, Arbore, and Moldoviţa have unusual and well-preserved exterior frescoes, though they're tough to visit unless you have a car or are hitchhiking.

Suceava, the transport hub and former capital of Moldavia, is trainable from Bucharest; its **ONT** tourist office is in the Hotel Arcasul (tel. (987) 109 44). **Iaşi** is on the train line from Bucharest to Kishinev in Soviet Moldavia and ultimately to Kiev and Moscow; the speediest trains from Bucharest take seven hours, and the **ONT office** is in the Hotel Mircea (tel. (981) 421 10).

SPAIN

USD$1 = 109 pesetas (ptas, or ESP) | **100ptas = USD$0.91**
CAD$1 = 95.8ptas | **100ptas = CAD$1.04**
GBP£1 = 183ptas | **100ptas = GBP£0.55**
AUD$1 = 85.2ptas | **100ptas = AUD$1.17**
NZD$1 = 62.4ptas | **100ptas = NZD$1.60**
Country Code: 34 | **International Dialing Prefix: 07**

Almost an island, yet a privileged crossroads of Europe, Africa, Asia, and the New World, Spain (España) is a highland plateau framed and intersected by ranges of yet loftier mountains. If the great frontier ranges are the battlements, the plateau is a castle keep, scored by four great rivers cutting deep gorges through its rock, and moated by thin coastal strips sharply cut off from the interior. The sea is a second ring of fortifications, as well as a conduit for culture and commerce. Spain is a subcontinent in its variety of scene, climate, landscape, artistic tradition, and ethnic groupings. Internal topographic barriers have created a state with 17 nations, where the U.S. is a nation of 50 states; regionalism runs high. Perhaps nothing captures the compactness of extremes better than the contrast between the stern grandeur of the Sierra Nevada, wrapped in eternal snow, and the subtropical luxuriance of the Costa del Sol lying at its feet.

Phoenicians, Carthaginians, Greeks, Romans, Visigoths, and Muslims were drawn to Spain's legendary mineral wealth and fertitlty and to its strategic position.

The Romans brought their roads, irrigation canals, aqueducts, courtyards, rounded arches, brick masonry, legal code, and language. The Muslims, who invaded in 711 AD, were crucial transmitters and elaborators of classical Greek science and philosophy and of eastern artistic traditions crucial to the European Renaissance. Spain inspired the builder in its colonists, and the climate seems peculiarly well-suited for pickling old stone. The exquisite fruits of Roman, Muslim, and every major Christian style are here. In Andalusia—along with the east coast, the province most favored by Romans and Muslims—the Mosque at Córdoba and the Alhambra in Granada are fountainheads of architecture as much as the Parthenon in Athens or Aya Sofya in İstanbul.

After three centuries of Muslim hegemony and another three centuries of Muslim, Jewish, and Christian vernacular syncretism, Enrique de Trastámara won control of Castile in 1369 and began to build a Christian Spain modeled after high medieval, Latinate European traditions (including rigid religious orthodoxy and intolerance). In 1492, Columbus arrived in the New World to begin an era of imperial grandeur and exploitation, which lasted until Spain's American territories began to declare independence during the Napoleonic Wars. The 19th century saw rapid industrialization and the growth of working-class and regional consciousness. Sparked by the international depression, these tensions erupted in the Spanish Civil War (1936-1939); aided by Hitler and Mussolini, Francisco Franco emerged as the country's dictator, and ruled until his death in 1975. Under King Juan Carlos, Franco's hand-picked successor, Spain has become a modern, stable, and democratic constitutional monarchy.

Every year, tourists more than double Spain's population of 40 million; much of the crush comes in July and August. No infrastructure could possibly be expected to bear such a burden. This fact—and Andalusia's searing heat—counsel against summer travel in southern Spain; if you must travel then, choose central or northern itineraries.

For Spain, 1992 is a chance for some long-awaited limelight. Sevilla will be celebrating the 500th anniversary of the "discovery" of America with a huge world fair; Madrid will be holding a vast array of events as official cultural capital of Europe; and Barcelona will host the Summer Olympics. For more coverage of these events and the rest of the country, turn to *Let's Go: Spain & Portugal.*

Getting There and Getting Around

RENFE, the national railroad system, is punctual and clean; the unique track gauge means you will have to change trains at the border. Both Eurail and InterRail passes are valid in Spain, but supplements are required on faster trains. 1992 is the inaugural year for the high-speed TAV train, running between Madrid and Seville with more routes to come. Otherwise, the snazziest trains are called *talgo.* These are usually twice the price of mere mortal trains (though still less expensive than German ones), and require a reservation, as well as a significant supplement from railpass and BIJ holders. Next in RENFE's pecking order are the *electro* and *TER,* both quite comfortable, but stopping more often. *Expreso* and *rápido* also travel with reasonable speed and efficiency. Finally, the very slow *tranvía, semi-directo, correo,* and *ferrobús* trains stop everywhere. Whatever their speed, Spanish trains are a bargain: second-class fares are usually only 4-5ptas per km. If you are traveling primarily in Spain, you will actually save money if you do *not* buy a railpass. On *días azules* ("blue days"—roughly 75% of the year), RENFE offers 20% off round-trip fares and 50% discounts for children under 12, among other discounts. The **tarjeta joven,** for ages 12-26 (2500ptas), **tarjeta dorada,** for ages 60 and over, and **tarjeta familiar,** for families, all give 50% discounts on blue days for trips over 100km. RENFE stations are often fairly distant from the city center, so the company staffs downtown offices in all significant cities and towns. Many travel agencies are hooked in to RENFE's computerized ticket reservation system; purchase your tickets here to avoid exasperating lines at the station.

Bus routes in Spain are much more exhaustive than the rail network. Intercity buses tend to be a little faster than the equivalent trains, and a little more expensive. Standards of comfort are quite high, especially on longer journeys, though you may find yourself inescapably subjected to noisy videos. Spain has no national bus line, just a multitude of private companies; some cover identical routes (shop around). **Iberia,** the national airline, flies to all major cities in Spain and on international routes. Cheaper night fares *(tarifas nocturnas)* are available to some places, like Barcelona and Tenerife.

Rental **cars** are considerably less expensive than in other European countries. For rural drives, tourist offices often supply leaflets on local "Rutas Turísticas."

Hitching can sometimes get you where you want to go—maybe today, but probably *mañana.* Unfortunately, Spanish hospitality to hitchhikers has dwindled in the wake of increasing crime. The northern areas are relatively easy to hitch in, as is the Mediterranean coast. Inland hitching is only fair; hitching out of Madrid—in any direction—is nearly impossible. In Andalusia, rides are infrequent and the sun can be intolerable.

Biking is possible but not necessarily enjoyable; Spain is mountainous in parts, and the weather—especially in central and southern Spain in summer—accelerates exhaustion. Moreover, roads are not designed to facilitate cycling, drivers are often rashly inconsiderate, and good bicycle shops are hard to find.

Practical Information

Just about every town in Spain that receives visitors has an *oficina de turismo* that distributes city maps, lists of accommodations, and general information about the town; a few offices will also help you find rooms.

There are four official languages in Spain. Catalan is the language of choice in Catalonia, València, and the Balearic Islands. The non-Indo-European Basque (Euskera) language is spoken in north central Spain, and Galego (close to Portuguese) is spoken in Galiza in the northwest, though both are minority languages even in their own dominions. Spanish (Castilian, or *castellano)* is spoken everywhere. Spanish, Catalan, and Galego are children of Latin, similar to other Romance languages in syntax, grammar, and vocabulary. Some people speak English, though you may have more luck with a Romance cousin—Italian, Portuguese, and French, in that order. In Spanish, *ll* is pronounced like English *y, j* like *h,* and in most of the country, soft *c* and *z* like *th.*

The northern regions are rightly called wet Spain, with a humid, temperate climate open to the sea, and a lush, often thickly wooded landscape (both features that reappear in those mountain areas of the south and east whose ranges are high enough to catch moisture). The interior has a climate resembling that of Central Europe, with long winters, and, in the lowlands, torrid summers. The eastern and southern coasts enjoy a Mediterranean climate, with mild winters. The northeast coast can be humid; the Guadalquivir river basin (including Seville and Córdoba) is the most sweltering part of the country. Even in the hottest regions, though, cool mountain refuges are never more than an hour away.

Some Spanish men think that foreign women traveling without male or family companions do so *en busca de aventura* (in search of sexual adventure). In most cases, the best answer to the advances is no answer; any reply may be interpreted as willingness to prolong the encounter. If a situation becomes genuinely threatening, a tirade (in any language) or screaming, especially in the presence of onlookers, may be necessary.

The International Student Identification Card (ISIC) is practically worthless in Spain. None of the transport companies offer discounts with it, and few monuments or museums have student admission prices.

Banks, shops, and offices shut down on legal and religious holidays in Spain: New Year's Day; Epiphany (Jan. 6); Saint Joseph's Day (March 29); Maundy Thursday, Good Friday, and Easter Sunday; May Day (May 1); Corpus Christi (the Thurs. following the 8th Sun. after Easter); Feast of Santiago (July 25); Feast of the Assumption (Aug. 15); Independence Day (Oct. 12); Feast of the Immaculate Conception (Dec. 8); and Christmas (Dec. 25). Some of these religious celebrations are no longer legal holidays, but business slows down anyway and sometimes stops altogether. The **Semana Santa** (Holy Week) celebrations in April bring about great shows, especially in Andalusia. Throughout the week between Palm Sunday and Easter, cities and towns strive to outdo one another with ardent displays of adoration. Lest this evoke a mood too somber for the pagan tourist, The days of **San Juan** (June 24) and **Santiago** (July 25) are cause for celebration across Spain, in the former case usually on the night before; the latter holiday is best observed in Santiago de Compostela. Bullfights feature prominently in most festivals between May and October.

Spanish workers ordinarily start at 9am, go home at 1:30 or 2pm for a long lunch, and recommence at 4:30 or 5pm until 8pm. On Saturday, places are usually open only in the morning, and Sunday is a day of rest for everything but a few indispensables (not including tourist offices). Most **banks** are open Monday through Friday from 9am to 2pm, and, except in summer, Saturday from 9am to 1pm. Pharmacies—not *perfumerías*—sell contraceptives; sanitary products are sold at both.

Post offices *(Correos)* are open from 9am to 2pm, and some reopen from 4 to 7pm. Stamps *(sellos)* are also sold at tobacco shops (look for the burnt-orange tobacco-leaf sign). Use the Spanish translation of Poste Restante *(Lista de Correos).* The Spanish phone system now has its own brand of multilingual phone cards. To make collect *(cobro revertido)* or credit card calls, go to the telephone exchange *(telefónica)* in most big cities. You can pay for your calls using Mastercard or Visa, but not American Express. Anywhere in Spain, you can dial 003 for information and 008 for operator assistance. In an emergency, dial 091. To reach AT&T's **USA Direct,** dial 900 990 011.

Though certain drugs are legal for some Spaniards, none are for foreigners. It is illegal to buy, sell, or transport any illicit substance. Be careful of narcotics traffic in Barcelona and around large student populations.

Accommodations and Camping

REAJ, the Spanish IYHF affiliate, runs almost 50 **youth hostels** year-round and over 100 during the summer. The prices can't be beat—550-650ptas per night—though usual hostel disadvantages apply (distance, school groups, and lack of privacy). Reservations are essential in summer.

Spain has vast numbers of affordable beds outside youth hostels, many of them right in the heart of the action; in ascending order of amenities and prices, you'll see *casas de huéspedes, fondas, pensiones, hostales* (rated on a 3-star system), and *hoteles* (rated on a 5-star system, and mostly unaffordable for the budget traveler). If you suspect that your proprietor is overcharging, ask for the *libro de reclamacíones* (complaint book), which the government requires to be produced on demand. Most arguments will end right there, since all complaints must be forwarded to the authorities within 48 hours.

In small villages with little official lodging, ask around, particularly in bars, about *casas particulares* (private houses), where you can often strike a deal for the guest room.

Campgrounds in Spain are, like hotels, regulated by the government. Class I campgrounds are one small step up in price, one giant leap in quality. Unfortunately, most of these campgrounds are little more than large, ugly, car parks with tents. Camping off these sites—on beaches and in the woods—is illegal.

Food and Drink

With so many distinct regional cultures, it's not surprising that Spain has an endless repertoire of dishes. Anywhere you go, you'll be lured by the seafood *(mariscos),* and especially by shellfish. National staples include *gazpacho* (cold tomato-based soup), *tortilla española* (potato omelette), and the ubiquitous *paella* (steamed saffron-flavored rice with chicken stock and an assortment of seafood). The word *España* is derived from the Phoenician for "land of the rabbits"; today, these are stewed with parsley and garlic, and appear on menus as *conejo al ajillo.* Well-known regional specialties include *fabada* (bean stew) from Asturias, and *cocido* (a heavy stew of meat, chick peas, potatoes and bacon popular in winter) from Castile.

Spaniards start their day with a breakfast *(desayuno)* of coffee and rolls or pastry or *churros,* deep-fried dough pieces sprinkled with sugar or dipped in rich endorphin-thrilling chocolate. Spanish coffee *(café)* is heavily toasted, thick, and plenty strong. *Almuerzo* is a light meal sometimes taken around 11:30am. Dinner *(comida),* the heaviest meal of the day, is taken between 1 and 4pm. Supper *(cena),* not served in restaurants until 9 or 10pm, is preceded by *tapas* (tidbits) around 5 or 6pm; most places continue serving until 11pm or midnight.

For *comida* and *cena,* all cafeterias and cheaper restaurants offer a *menú de la casa* (house menu) or *menú del día* (menu of the day), also known as a *menú turístico,* consisting of soup or appetizer, one or two main courses, bread, dessert, and some wine or mineral water.

Food is almost always washed down with a glass of wine; *(vino blanco* is white, *tinto* is red, and a *chato* is a glass of red wine), or beer *(cerveza).* Beer is served in bottles or on draught, in either a small glass *(caña)* or a tall one *(tubo). Aguila, Estrella,* and *San Miguel* are excellent national brands; *Volldamm* (Catalonia) and *Alhambra* (Andalusia) are fine regional brews. *Rioja* is a world-renowned wine-growing region, with especially good reds; there are innumerable fine regional wines. Sangria is made of red wine, sugar, brandy, seltzer, and peaches. Another native beverage you may want to try is sherry *(jerez),* from the city of the same name.

Castile and León

The story of Castile (Castilla) is a story of power—political, military, and religious. In the High Middle Ages, the Kingdom emerged from obscurity to lead Spain's battle charge against Islam. Well before its famous union with Aragón in 1492, it was clear that Castile had the whip hand over the other Christian kingdoms. *Castellano* became the dominant language of the peninsula, and even today, Castilian hegemony remains fundamentally unshaken.

Castilian landscapes tend to be intense rather than pretty. A vast and arid plateau covers most of the region; behind the endless wheat and sunflower fields you see from the road are vineyards, waves of purple saffron, large forests filled with game, and wonderful historic cities. The beautiful cathedral of Burgos and the shining sandstone of Salamanca, the narrow alleyways of Toledo and the proud city walls of Avila emblazon themselves as images not only of Castile but also of all Spain.

León has greener and more rolling countryside, and a strong sense of its own identity. Many Leonese recall that it was here that the first major reconquests were achieved, and seethe at the modern administrative reorganization which lumped them in with part of Castile.

Madrid

Seen from the Castilian plains, the tower blocks of outer Madrid rise sharply and imposingly. The city is an urban oasis in a demographic desert: a place of streaming traffic, all-night bars, high fashion, and great power. Within its rings of concrete architecture, Madrid has enough sights and cultural legacies to absorb you for a year, but it is likely to win you over not so much with romance as with relentless energy. In 1992, Madrid will be the official Cultural Capital of Europe. This means a vast amount of architectural renovation, an enormous array of cultural events,

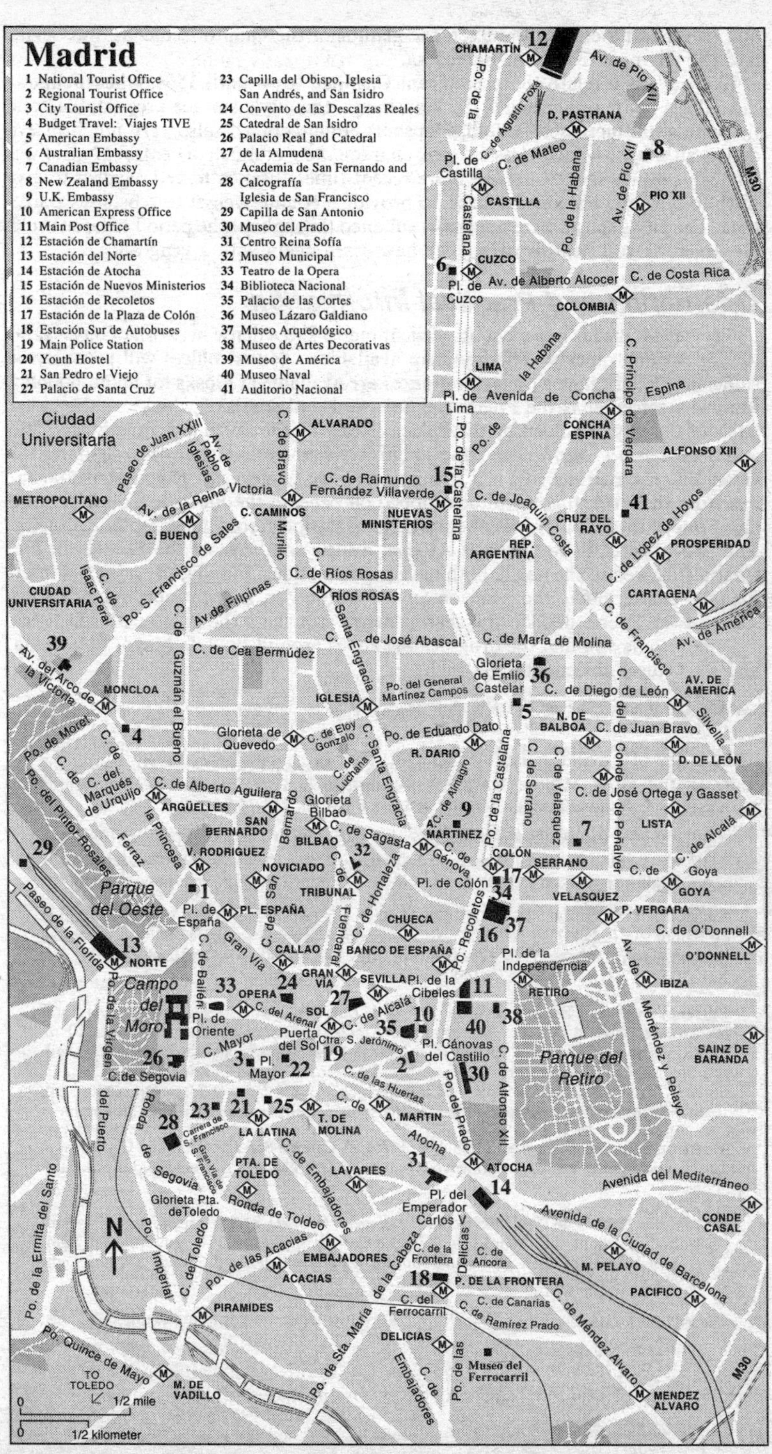
Madrid
1 National Tourist Office
2 Regional Tourist Office
3 City Tourist Office
4 Budget Travel: Viajes TIVE
5 American Embassy
6 Australian Embassy
7 Canadian Embassy
8 New Zealand Embassy
9 U.K. Embassy
10 American Express Office
11 Main Post Office
12 Estación de Chamartín
13 Estación del Norte
14 Estación de Atocha
15 Estación de Nuevos Ministerios
16 Estación de Recoletos
17 Estación de la Plaza de Colón
18 Estación Sur de Autobuses
19 Main Police Station
20 Youth Hostel
21 San Pedro el Viejo
22 Palacio de Santa Cruz
23 Capilla del Obispo, Iglesia
San Andrés, and San Isidro
24 Convento de las Descalzas Reales
25 Catedral de San Isidro
26 Palacio Real and Catedral
27 de la Almudena
Academia de San Fernando and
28 Calcografía
Iglesia de San Francisco
29 Capilla de San Antonio
30 Museo del Prado
31 Centro Reina Sofía
32 Museo Municipal
33 Teatro de la Opera
34 Biblioteca Nacional
35 Palacio de las Cortes
36 Museo Lázaro Galdiano
37 Museo Arqueológico
38 Museo de Artes Decorativas
39 Museo de América
40 Museo Naval
41 Auditorio Nacional
CHAMARTÍN
Av. de Pio XII
Po. de la Castellana
C. de Agustín Foxá
D. PASTRANA
Pl. de Castilla
C. de Mateo
CASTILLA
Po. de la Habana
PIO XII
CUZCO
Pl. de Cuzco
Av. de Alberto Alcocer
C. de Costa Rica
COLOMBIA
LIMA
la Habana
C. Príncipe de Vergara
Pl. de Lima
Avenida de Concha Espina
CONCHA ESPINA
ALFONSO XIII
M30
Ciudad Universitaria
Paseo de Juan XXIII
Av. de Pablo Iglesias
C. de Bravo Murillo
ALVARADO
C. de Raimundo Fernández Villaverde
METROPOLITANO
Av. de la Reina Victoria
C. CAMINOS
NUEVAS MINISTERIOS
C. de Joaquín Costa
CRUZ DEL RAYO
C. de Lopez de Hoyos
PROSPERIDAD
G. BUENO
REP. ARGENTINA
Po. S. Francisco de Sales
C. de Isaac Peral
CIUDAD UNIVERSITARIA
Av. de Filipinas
C. de Ríos Rosas
RÍOS ROSAS
CARTAGENA
C. de Francisco Silvela
Av. de América
C. de Guzmán el Bueno
C. de Cea Bermúdez
C. de José Abascal
C. de María de Molina
C. Santa Engracia
Glorieta de Emilio Castelar
C. de Diego de León
AV. DE AMERICA
Av. del Arco de la Victoria
MONCLOA
Po. del General Martínez Campos
IGLESIA
N. DE BALBOA
C. de Juan Bravo
D. DE LEÓN
Po. de Moret
Glorieta de Quevedo
C. de Eloy Gonzalo
Po. de Eduardo Dato
R. DARIO
C. de Serrano
C. de Velasquez
C. del Conde de Peñalver
C. del Marqués de Urquijo
C. de Luchana
C. de Almagro
C. de José Ortega y Gasset
C. de Alberto Aguilera
ARGÜELLES
Glorieta Bilbao
LISTA
Po. del Pintor Rosales
C. de la Princesa
Ferraz
SAN BERNARDO
C. de San Bernardo
BILBAO
C. de Sagasta
ALONSO MARTINEZ
C. de Alcalá
V. RODRIGUEZ
NOVICIADO
C. de Génova
COLÓN
SERRANO
C. de Goya
GOYA
Parque del Oeste
TRIBUNAL
Pl. de Colón
VELASQUEZ
Pl. de España
PL. ESPAÑA
C. de Fuencarral
C. de Hortaleza
CHUECA
P. VERGARA
Paseo de la Florida
Gran Vía
Po. Recoletos
C. de O'Donnell
NORTE
CALLAO
BANCO DE ESPAÑA
Pl. de la Independencia
O'DONNELL
Campo del Moro
C. de Bailén
GRAN VIA
SEVILLA
Pl. de la Cibeles
Av. de Menéndez y Pelayo
IBIZA
Po. de la Virgen del Puerto
OPERA
C. del Arenal
SOL
RETIRO
Pl. de Oriente
Puerta del Sol
Ctra. S. Jerónimo
C. Mayor
Pl. Cánovas del Castillo
SAINZ DE BARANDA
Pl. Mayor
Parque del Retiro
C.de Segovia
C. de las Huertas
Po. del Prado
C. de Alfonso XII
Ronda de Segovia
Carrera de S. Francisco
A. MARTIN
LA LATINA
T. DE MOLINA
C. de Atocha
Gran Via de S. Francisco
PTA. DE TOLEDO
C. de Embajadores
LAVAPIES
ATOCHA
Avenida del Mediterráneo
Glorieta Pta. deToledo
Ronda de Toledo
Pl. del Emperador Carlos V
Avenida de la Ciudad de Barcelona
CONDE CASAL
Po. de la Ermita del Santo
N
Po. Imperial
C. de Toledo
Po. de las Acacias
EMBAJADORES
C. de la Frontera
C. de Ancora
ACACIAS
P. DE LA FRONTERA
M. PELAYO
C. de Méndez Alvaro
PIRAMIDES
C. del Ferrocarril
C. de Canarias
C. de Ramírez Prado
PACIFICO
DELICIAS
Po. Quince de Mayo
Po. de Sta. María de la Cabeza
C. de Embajadores
Po. de las Delicias
Museo del Ferrocarril
TO TOLEDO
M. DE VADILLO
MENDEZ ALVARO
0 1/2 mile
0 1/2 kilometer

and in general a chance to match the glamor of the Quinto Centenario in Seville and the Olympic Games in Barcelona.

Madrid was a relatively insignificant Castilian town until 1561, when Felipe II moved his court there; under the Hapsburgs, the city's surface area doubled and its population increased tenfold. Hapsburg architecture is also very much in evidence, although the neo-classical look characteristic of much of central Madrid was an 18th-century innovation. In more recent times, Franco forced Madrid to give birth to new and horrible suburbs, to provide a counterweight to rebellious Barcelona. The city's spirits were unusually subdued throughout the period of fascist rule. However, as you will discover, they have risen again with a vengeance.

Orientation and Practical Information

Greater Madrid is huge, but an efficient metro and a dense network of buses shuttle you around quickly. The free map available at tourist offices will probably be sufficient; better maps with street indexes are available at kiosks for about 600ptas. Madrid's epicenter is the Puerta del Sol, west and south of which are the oldest parts of the city, bounded by the Palacio Real. To the north are some lively 18th- and 19th-century *barrios,* and the main east-west commercial thoroughfare, the Gran Vía. Over to the east is a string of massive boulevards. If you arrive on the bus from the airport, you will be dropped off beneath the Plaza de Colón, situated along one of these boulevards; there is a metro station across the Paseo de Recoletos. The two main train stations are Atocha, a little southeast of the Pl. Mayar, and Chamartín, well to the north; both have metro stations. Finally, the principal international bus terminal, the Estación Sur de Autobuses, is about one and half miles south of the Puerta del Sol; the nearest metro stop is up the Paseo de las Delicias.

Some people will find the drug-dealing zones around Pl. 2 de Mayo, Pl. España, and Pl. Chueca intimidating at night.

Tourist Offices: Nacional proffers maps and leaflets, but not much else. C. Princesa, 1, Pl. España (tel. 541 23 25). Metro: Pl. España. Open Mon.-Fri. 9am-7pm, Sat. 9:30am-1:30pm. Also at **Barajas Airport** (tel. 205 86 56), at the international flight arrivals counter. Open Mon.-Fri. 8am-8pm, Sat. 8am-1pm. **Municipal,** Pl. Mayor, 3 (tel. 266 54 77). Metro: Sol. Open Mon.-Fri. 10am-2pm and 4-7pm, Sat. 10am-1:30pm. For information about specialized museums, call the **Oficina de Museos,** Palacio Real (tel. 248 74 04).

Budget Travel: Viajes TIVE. Central office, C. Fernando el Católico, 88 (tel. 401 90 11 or 243 02 08). Metro: Moncloa. Branch, José Ortega y Gasset, 71 (tel. 401 95 01). Metro: Lista. Some English spoken at both. Both open Mon.-Fri. 9am-2pm, Sat. 9am-noon.

Embassies: U.S., C. Serrano, 75 (tel. 576 34 00; in emergency 276 32 29). **Canada,** C. Núñez de Balboa, 35 (tel. 431 43 00). **U.K.,** C. Fernando el Santo, 16 (tel. 319 02 00). **Australia,** Edificio Cuzco 1, Paseo de la Castellana, 143 (tel. 279 85 04). **New Zealand,** O.L.P.C. Pío XII, 20 (tel. 200 00 78 or 457 32 58).

Currency Exchange: Banks open Mon.-Fri. 9am-2pm; Oct.-May also Sat. 9am-1pm. At **Barajas Airport,** open 24 hrs. At Chamartín and Atocha **train stations;** open daily 8am-10pm. Banks, the airport, and train stations often charge 10% commission. Slimmer fees are available at all **El Corte Inglés** stores (C. Preciados, 3; C. Goya, 76; and C. Princesa, 42). Commission on currency 1%, min. 250ptas; on traveler's checks 2%, min. 500ptas. Open Mon.-Sat. 10am-9:30pm. **American Express** charges the same commission, but with no minimum.

American Express: Pl. Cortes, 2 (tel. 429 28 75), at Carrera San Jerónimo and C. Marqués. The best deal unless you're changing wads of money. Open Mon.-Fri. 9am-5:30pm, Sat. 9am-noon.

Post Office: Palacio de Comunicaciones, Pl. Cibeles (tel. 521 81 95). Open Mon.-Fri. 9am-10pm, Sat. 9am-8pm, Sun. 10am-1pm. *Lista de Correos* open Mon.-Fri. 9am-8pm, Sat. 9am-2pm. Door H remains open Sun. 8am-10pm for telegrams, telex, etc. Stamps can be bought at all tobacconists' stores. **Postal Code:** 28070.

Telephones: Telefónica, Gran Vía, 30, at C. Valverde. Open daily 9am-midnight. **City Code:** 91.

Flights: Barajas Airport, tel. 205 43 72 for arrivals. On the N-II highway 15km from Madrid. Bus from airport to Pl. Colón, 250ptas. **Iberia,** Pl. Canovas, 4 (tel. 585 85 85). Metro: Atocha. Open Mon.-Fri. 9am-7pm, Sat. 9am-2pm.

Trains: Tel. 501 33 33 or 429 02 02, 24 hrs. Madrid's 3 major stations are Chamartín, Atocha, and Norte. All are at similarly named Metro stops. **Chamartín,** to the north, is the largest station, with trains to Burgos, the Basque country, the Cantabrian coast, Catalonia, Portugal, and France. **Atocha,** south of the Prado and southeast of the Pl. Mayor, has trains to Andalusia and Toledo. Both Chamartín and Atocha Stations service Avila, Alicante, Guadalajara, Segovia, València, and Portugal. Chamartín and Atocha ticket offices open daily 9am-9pm. **Norte,** also called **Príncipe Pío,** serves Barcelona, Seville, Granada, Galicia, Salamanca, and Santiago de Compostela. Norté ticket office open daily 9am-7pm. **RENFE,** C. Alcalá, 44 (tel. 733 30 00 or 22 00; reservations 429 82 28). Metro: Banco de España. Open Mon.-Fri. 9am-3pm and 4-7:30pm, Sat. 9am-1:30pm. Also on the 2nd floor of the Edificio de España, at Pl. España and Torre de Madrid. Metro: Pl. España. Same hours as above.

Buses: Estación Sur de Autobuses, Canarias, 17 (tel. 468 42 00). Metro: Palos de la Frontera. The main international station.

Luggage Storage: At Chamartín and Atocha train stations. Lockers (150ptas per day) fit large backpacks. Also at Estación Sur de Autobuses and the air terminal beneath Pl. Colon.

Public Transportation: The nine lines of the **Metro** subway system radiate from the Puerta del Sol. Trains 6am-1:30am. 115ptas per trip, 10-trip ticket 450ptas. Check the map at each entrance or pick up a free one at one of the booths; inside, maps are few and far between. Buses are usually faster but more confusing. **Red buses** run from 5:30am-midnight; the circle line and a few others run 24 hrs. 115ptas per trip, 10-ride card excluding transfers 450ptas. More comfortable, air-conditioned **yellow microbuses** (look for the prefix "M") also cost 115ptas per ride, 450ptas for a 10-ride card. Multiple-ride cards for both types of buses available at tourist offices and news kiosks throughout the city.

Taxis: Radio Teléfono Taxi (tel. 247 82 00) cost 95ptas plus 40ptas per km. Trip to airport adds 260ptas, 100ptas per piece of baggage. If your taxi is not metered, look for another one.

Moped/Motorcycle Rental: Motocicletas Antonio Castro, C. Conde Duque, 13 (tel. 242 06 57), at Santa Cruz de Marcenado. Metro: San Bernardo. Cruise Madrid at night when monuments are lighted. From 1750ptas plus 2% VAT per day (9am-8pm). Must have valid driver's license, passport, and be at least 18. Open Mon.-Fri. 9am-noon and 5-8pm.

Hitchhiking: Legal but unsafe. Take the N-II (northeast) to Barcelona and Zaragoza; N-III (east) to Cuenca and València; N-IV (south) to Aranjuez, Andalusia, Alicante, and Cádiz; N-VI (northwest) to Avila, Segovia, and Salamanca; E-4 (west) to Extremadura and Portugal; and 401 (southeast) to Toledo. For information on routes, dial 441 72 22. A safer (though not free) alternative is the ride sharing service **A-dedo,** C. Estudios, 9 (tel. 265 65 65).

Bookstores: Turner English Bookshop, C. Génova, 3, on Pl. Santa Barbara. Metro: Alonso Martínez. English-language literature including *Let's Go: Spain & Portugal.* Open Mon.-Fri. 9:30am-2pm and 5-8pm, Sat. 10am-2pm.

Laundromat: Lavamatique, C. Torrecilla del Leal, 3 (tel. 227 93 67). Metro: Sol. 600ptas per 5kg. Open Mon.-Fri. 9:30am-2pm and 5-8pm, Sat. 10am-3pm. **Lavandería Maryland,** Melendéz Valdés, 52 (tel. 243 30 41). Metro: Argüelles. Near Santa Cruz de Marcenado youth hostel, down passageway into the mall behind the block. 600ptas per 5kg, full service 860ptas.

Swimming Pools (Piscinas Municipales): **Outdoors** at Casa de Campo (tel. 463 00 50). Metro: El Lago. Open in summer daily 10am-8pm. Admission 250ptas, children 85ptas. **Indoors** at Municipal de la Latina, Pl. Cebada, 2 (tel. 265 80 31). Open July-Sept. Mon.-Fri. 8am-6pm, Sat. 8am-8pm, Sun. 8am-2:30pm. Admission 250ptas.

Pharmacy: Call 098 or check newspapers under *Farmacias de Guardia* for 24-hr. establishments.

Medical Assistance: British-American Medical Unit, Conde de Aranda, 1, 1st floor (tel. 435 18 23).

Emergencies: Police (tel. 091 or 092). Headquarters, Puerta del Sol, 7 (tel. 221 65 16). **Ambulance** (tel. 588 44 00).

Accommodations and Camping

Tourist offices in Madrid will not arrange accommodations for you, but Madrid has almost as many *hostales* (inns) as *tapas* bars, so finding a room shouldn't be too much of a chore (except for singles). Heaps of budget accommodations line the C. Fuencarral (off the Gran Vía), dot the area between the Puerta del Sol and the Palacio Real (close to the major sights), and overflow in the vast area between the Puerta del Sol and Atocha train station. This section is Madrid's cheapest; the Gran Vía is gracious, but more costly.

Albergue Juvenil (IYHF), C. Santa Cruz de Marcenado, 28 (tel. 247 45 32), off C. Serrano Jover, between C. Princesa and C. Alberto Aguilera. Metro: Argüelles. Lacks privacy, but the 8-bed dorms are modern and near the student district. 550ptas, ages over 26 650ptas. Full pension 1300ptas; hot showers and meager breakfast included. Curfew Mon.-Sat. 1:30am, midnight on Sunday.

Albergue Juvenil Richard Schirrman (IYHF), Casa de Campo (tel. 463 56 99). Metro: El Lago. Take immediate left outside metro station, turn left again, walk 1km on the rocky foot-path along the metro tracks, cross over the concrete footbridge, and turn left at the Albergue Juvenil sign. Solo travelers and women should stay elsewhere, since the walk is unsafe at night. 130 beds in 8-bed dorms. No curfew. Recreation room and TV lounge. 550ptas, ages over 26 650ptas. Full board 1300ptas, ages over 26 1500ptas. Hot showers and breakfast included.

Hostal Palacios Ribadavia, C. Fuencarral, 25 (tel. 531 10 58). A well-kept place run by the kindest and most welcoming owners in the city. Singles 1600ptas, with showers 1800ptas. Doubles 3000ptas.

Hostal-Residencia Abril, C. Fuencarral, 39, top floor. Elevator whisks you up to exceptionally clean and pleasant rooms. Singles 1500ptas, with shower 1700ptas. Doubles 2750ptas, with bath 2900ptas.

Hostal Medieval, C. Fuencarral, 46 (tel. 522 25 49), at C. Augusto Figueroa. Metro: Tribunal. Friendly manager has travel information and souvenirs. Singles with shower 2400ptas. Doubles with shower 3500ptas, with full bath 4500ptas. Triples with shower 5000ptas.

Hostal Residencia Cruz-Sol, Pl. Santa Cruz, 6, 3rd floor (tel. 232 71 97), next to Pl. Mayor. Kind owner, no curfew. Doubles for single use 1800ptas. Doubles 2200ptas. Hot showers 150ptas. On the 2nd floor is **Hostal Santa Cruz** (tel. 522 24 41), with higher ceilings and higher prices. Doubles with shower 2800ptas, with full bath 3800ptas.

Alcázar-Regis, Gran Vía, 61, 5th floor (tel. 247 35 49). Metro: Pl. España. Palatial lobby and well-kept rooms. Singles 1900ptas. Doubles 3600ptas. Triples 5400ptas. Breakfast 150ptas.

La Costa Verde (tel. 241 91 41), same address, 9th floor. Less glamorous decor, but some rooms compensate with views. Singles 1600ptas. Doubles 3000ptas, with shower 3300ptas.

Hostal Residencia Regional, C. Principe, 18 (tel. 522 33 73), off Pl. Santa Ana. Metro: Sol. A mindblowing *hostal:* huge rooms, hardwood floors, and a slick glass elevator. Singles 1700ptas. Doubles 2600ptas.

Hostal Residencia Mondragón, Carrera San Jerónimo, 32, 4th floor (tel. 429 68 16). Metro: Sol. An enormous entryway. Large, cheery rooms with balconies. Singles 1200-1400ptas. Doubles with shower 2300ptas. Triples 3500ptas.

Hostal Residencia Paz, C. Flora, 4, 1st floor (tel. 247 30 47), off C. Arenal by Pl. Isabel II. Metro: Opera. Quiet, immaculate rooms; English spoken. Singles 1700ptas. Doubles 2700ptas, with bath 3200ptas. Triples with shower 3900ptas.

Hostal Margarita, Gran Vía, 50, 5th floor (tel. 247 35 49). Metro: Pl. España. Homey family establishment. Owner imparts sound travel advice. Singles 2500ptas. Doubles 3600ptas. Triples with shower 4200ptas. Laundry 1000ptas per full load.

Hostal Sud-Americana, Paseo del Prado, 12, 6th floor (tel. 429 25 64). Metro: Atocha or Antón Martín. Across the street from the Prado, with handsome views. Singles 1700ptas. Doubles 2800ptas. Showers 250ptas.

Hostal Residencia Jeyma, C. Arenal, 26, 3rd Floor, (tel. 248 77 93). Metro: Opera. Well-kept rooms. Singles 1000ptas. Doubles 2000ptas.

Hostal La Macarena, Cava de San Miguel, 8 (tel. 265 92 21), on the atmospheric street which runs near the south-west corner of the Pl. Mayor. Suitable for a splurge. Immaculate, with lots of light. Good central heating. Singles 3000ptas. Doubles 4500ptas. Triples 6000ptas. Quadruples 7000ptas.

Camping

There are about a dozen campsites within 50km of Madrid, but fees plus the commute often cost more than cheap rooms in town. The tourist offices have the inside track on area sites. **Camping Madrid** (tel. 202 28 35) is on the Carretera Madrid-Burgos. Take the metro to Pl. Castilla, then bus #129 to Iglesia de los Dominicos. (325ptas per person, 325ptas per tent.) **Camping Osuna** (tel. 741 05 10) is by the Ajalvir-Vicálvaro road (at Km. 15.5). Take the metro to Canillejas, then bus #105 to Av. Logroño. (325ptas per person, 325ptas per tent.) Both campsites have telephones, hot showers, laundry facilities, a restaurant, and a supermarket. Camping Madrid also has two swimming pools.

Food

Spanish cuisine begins at bars, *mesones,* and cafés, where people stand at the counter to eat bite-sized snacks called *tapas.* Your fork may find its way into *lomo* (pork), *chorizo* (spicy sausage), *gambas* (shrimp), *atún* (tuna), or *fabada* (cooked beans). The capital's own culinary specialties include *cocido madrileño* (sausage, chickpea, and potato stew) and *callos a la madrileña* (tripe with cognac and ham). And don't forget to start your day right, with *churros* (fried dough sprinkled with sugar) and *chocolate* (extra-thick hot chocolate). Madrid's student quarter, **Argüelles** (Metro: Argüelles or Moncloa), is a fertile hunting-ground for a cheap bite. Budget restaurants swarm between San Bernardo, Fuencarral, and Gran Vía. Near Puerta del Sol, explore **Calle Ventura de la Vega,** off San Jerónimo. Fresh meat, produce, wine, and bread overspread **Mercado de San Miguel** off the northwest corner of Plaza Mayor. (Open Mon.-Sat. 9am-3pm and 5:30-7:30pm.) Many restaurants close in July and August.

La Gata Flora, C. Dos de Mayo, 1. Metro: Noviciado or Tribunal. Bohemian crowd crams the tables. Fresh pasta and a mean sangria. Canneloni 590ptas. Open Sun.-Thurs. 2-4pm and 9pm-12:30am, Fri.-Sat. 8:30pm-1am. Off-season Sun.-Thurs. 9:30pm-12:30am, Fri.-Sat. 8:30pm-1am.

Bar Machu-Picchu, C. Infantas, 10. Metro: Gran Vía. Delicious Peruvian cuisine, tropical drinks, and *Cebiche* 600ptas. Two-course meal and drink about 1500ptas. Open daily 11am-midnight.

El Garabatu, C. Echegaray, 5. A distinctly low-key bar-restaurant, notable for its onions stuffed with tuna (550ptas). Open daily 11:30am-4pm and 8:30-11:30pm.

Edelweiss, Jovellanos, 7 (tel 521 03 26), behind Congreso de los Disputados. Metro: Sevilla or Banco de España. Members of the Cortes come here for Spanish and Central European dishes. There are a few affordable dishes. Entrées average 1200ptas. Open Wed.-Mon. 12:45-4pm and 8pm-midnight, Tues. 7pm-midnight.

Nabucco, C. Hortaleza, 108, off Pl. Santa Bárbara. Postmodern design, fresh flowers, and surprisingly cheap Italian food. Pizzas around 600ptas, pasta 650ptas and up. Open daily 7pm-1am.

Restaurante El Cuchi, C. Cuchilleros, just off the C. Mayor. Spanish and Mexican food in a *loco* atmosphere. Entertaining waiters. Mayan pork and rice or pine nut chicken 800ptas each. Open daily 1-4pm and 8pm-midnight.

Casa Portal, C. Olivar, 3. Metro: Sol. Asturian specialties (shrimp with garlic, 800ptas), but come here for the homemade *sidra,* poured from impossible heights into a glass on the floor. Open noon-midnight.

Restaurante Ku'damm, C. Conde Duque, 30 (tel. 542 21 57), off C. Alberto Aguilera. Metro: Ventura Rodríquez or San Bernardo. Spanish, German, and Italian specialties. *Pizza mixta* (salami, olives, onions, tomatoes, and cheese) 725ptas. Chicken salad 725ptas. Open noon-midnight.

Restaurante Zara, C. Infantas, 7. Metro: Gran Vía. Tropical food; *carne asada* (roast beef), with black beans and white rice, 800ptas. Open Mon.-Sat. 1-5pm and 8-11:30pm.

Restaurante del Estal, off C. Princesa. Metro: Argüelles. *Menú* 650ptas. Open Mon.-Sat. 12:30-4pm and 8:30pm-midnight.

Sights

The **Museo del Prado,** on Paseo del Prado (Metro: Banco de España), showcases over 5000 paintings from all over Europe, many squirreled away by Spanish kings between the 15th and 18th centuries. The wonder of the Prado is that *every* work is a masterpiece. Diego Velázquez's *Las Meninas* (The Maids of Honor) is a fascinating study of 17th-century court life and an exercise in three-dimensional illusion. The museum's Goya collection includes *La Maja desnuda,* which reveals a feminine ideal somewhere between classical notions and Mae West. The famous *Los Fusilamientos del Tercero de Mayo* depicts Goya's compatriots at the moment of their slaughter by Napoleon's army—some believe that the blood in the corner of the canvas is the artist's own, shed in solidarity with the victims. On the first floor, Flemish painter Hieronymous Bosch ("el Bosco") surpasses the nightmare vision of the surrealists nearly half a millennium earlier in his bizarre indictment of worldly pleasures, *The Garden of Earthly Delights.* The Prado also houses works by El Greco, Murillo, and Zurbarán, as well as hundreds of foreign masterpieces. (Open Tues.-Sat. 9am-7pm, Sun. 9am-2pm; Nov.-April Tues.-Sat. 10am-5pm, Sun. 10am-2pm. Admission 400ptas, students free.)

Your ticket to the Prado also admits you to the nearby **Casón del Buen Retiro,** on C. Alfonso XXII, facing the Parque del Retiro, where you can see 19th-century Spanish masters and Picasso's famous **Guernica,** a painted memorial to the town ravaged during the Spanish Civil War by the German *Luftwaffe.* Supposedly, when asked by Nationalist officials whether he had created the picture, Picasso retorted, "No, you did!" Picasso gave the canvas to New York's Museum of Modern Art on the condition that it be returned to Spain only when democracy was restored. *Guernica* arrived in Madrid in 1981, five years after Franco's death, and remains so controversial that visitors must walk through a metal detector to view it. (Open Tues.-Sat. 9am-6:45pm, Sun. 9am-1:45pm.) *Guernica* is being moved, along with most of Madrid's other 20th-century art, to the **Centro Reina Sofía,** on Pl. Emperador across from the Atocha train station, a renovated 18th-century hospital and Madrid's answer to the Centre Pompidou, which will also house a library, bookstore, and repertory cinema. Also to be inaugurated in 1992 will be Von Thyssen's Lugano collection, on loan from Switzerland for 10 years, housed in the 18th-century neoclassical **Palacio de Villaherrmosa,** on pl. Neptuno a few blocks from the Prado.

The fabulous **Palacio Real** (Metro: Opera) confronts visitors with pomp and splendor born of its sheer size and dramatic isolation from the city's hustle and bustle. The obligatory guided tour (in English, 2 hr.) reveals an endless collection of porcelain, tapestries, furniture, chandeliers, armor, and paintings. (Open Mon.-Sat. 9:30am-4pm, Sun. 9:30am-12:45pm. Admission 400ptas, students 325ptas.) The palace faces the **Plaza de Oriente** and is enclosed on the northern side by the well-kept **Jardines de Sabatini.** Behind the palace is the lush and spotless **Campo del Moro,** a jolly site for a picnic. (Open daily 10am-8pm. Enter on Paseo de la Virgen del Puerto.)

The **Parque del Retiro** is 353 acres of green in the heart of the city, with elegant gardens, fountains, botanical collections, and a lake where you can rent a rowboat. The **Palacio de Cristal** houses temporary cultural exhibits (such as a Bugs Bunny exposition). (Metro: Retiro.) **Casa de Campo,** to the northwest, shelters urban dwellers in woods, shaded lanes, a municipal pool, a zoo, and an amusement park. More than 10 times the size of Retiro, this park makes the city seem like a minor development on the outskirts of the forest. (Metro: Lagos or Batán, or bus #33.) In the university section, the **Parque del Oeste** is home away from home for the **Templo de Debod,** an authentic Egyptian shrine donated by Nasser as a token of gratitude—Spanish archeologists had helped in the relocation of other temples during the construction of the Aswan Dam.

Plaza Mayor (Metro: Sol), a handsome 17th-century square built by Philip III for celebrations, competitions, and burnings at the stake, is filled with hat shops, souvenir markets, and restaurants. This most picturesque part of Old Madrid is not far from smaller and quieter **Plaza de la Villa,** where you can see Madrid's **Casa de la Villa** (City Hall). South of Plaza Mayor is the 17th-century **Catedral de San Isidro,** dedicated to Madrid's patron saint. The nearby **Iglesia de San Francisco** church has an enormous neoclassical dome and paintings by Goya.

The **Museo de la Academia Real de Bellas Artes de San Fernando,** C. Alcalá, 13 (Metro: Sol or Sevilla), second in Spain only to the Prado, includes Goya's haunting *Casa de Locos* (Madhouse) and carnivalesque *Entierro de la Sardina* (Sardina's Burial). (Open Tues.-Sat. 9am-7pm, Sun.-Mon. 9am-2pm. Admission 200ptas, students free.) An excellent royal print and drawing collection is next door in the **Calcografía.**

In the heart of downtown, the **Convento de las Descalzas Reales,** between C. Mayor and Gran Vía, has changed little since it opened in 1559. By collecting favors from its royal disciples (resident nuns have included Empress Maria of Austria and Saint Teresa of Avila), the convent has acquired an outstanding collection of paintings by Rubens, Titian, and Breughel. Look for Pedro de Mena's sculpture *La Dolorosa.* (Open Tues.-Fri. 10am-12:45pm and 4-5:15pm, Sat.-Sun. 11am-1:15pm. Admission 300ptas, students 225ptas.)

For a sense of Spain's past—stretching back to prehistory—visit the **Museo Arqueológico Nacional,** at #13 on the swanky C. Serrano. Don't miss the mysterious *Dama de Elche* and the collection of mummies—including a mummified cat and baby crocodile. (Open Mon.-Sat. 9:30am-8:30pm, Sun. 9:30am-2:30pm. Admission 200ptas, students free.)

The easiest worthwhile excursion out of Madrid is to **El Pardo,** a large country palace painted butterscotch and white. It dates back to the 16th century, when it was a residence of the Castilian monarchs, but was remodelled in the 18th by Sabatini, designer of the Palacio Real. Franco made it his own home. Inside is a wealth of Flemish paintings and 18th-century tapestries. (Open Mon.-Sat. 9:30am-12:15pm and 3-6pm, Sun. 9:30am-1:40pm. 350ptas, students 250ptas; free on Wed. to EEC passport holders. Take bus #601 (95ptas) from Paseo de Moret, near Metro: Monchoa.)

Entertainment

Madrid is rightly notorious for its wonderful nightife. There is something going on at all hours almost everywhere. The *Guía del Ocio* (75ptas at any kiosk) has complete events listings. The *Villa de Madrid* lists open-air theater, films, and concerts sponsored by the city, as does the entertainment supplement in Thursday's *El País.* In July and August, free cultural activities resound nightly in the major plazas—the **Parque del Retiro** and the **Casa de Campo.** For foreign films, check the **Filmoteca,** C. Santa Isabel, 3 (tel. 227 38 66), or the **Alphaville,** C. Martín de los Heros, 14 (tel. 248 72 33). In summer, the **Veranos de la Villa** attracts top performers from all over the world.

There is a hyper-abundance of watering holes in Madrid. The cafés along **Paseo de Recoletos, Plaza de Santa Bárbara,** and the mall between Puerta del Sol and Callao are excellent hangouts. In summer, all the city's boulevards—particularly the tree-lined boulevard strip formed by Paseo de la Castellana—turn into a cross between a fashion runway and a beachfront promenade, covered by *terrazas* or *chiringuitos* where you can sip *horchata* (a hazelnut drink), or **Mahou,** Madrid's locally brewed beer. Beware that a drink at a fashionable *terraza* can run 500-700ptas. Hip *madrileños* also hang out on the bars and *terrazas* of the Plaza de Santa Ana, where you might try to contact the ghost of Ernest Hemingway at the **Cervecería Alemana,** Pl. Santa Ana, 6 (tel. 429 70 33). Another prime hunting ground, though somewhat drug-infested and possibly dangerous, is Malasána. Meet living writers and intellectuals at **La Tetera de la Abuela** (Granny's Teapot), C. Espíritu Santo, 37. (Open Sun.-Thurs. 7:30pm-1am, Fri.-Sat. 7:30pm-2am.)

The café **La Fidula,** C. Huertas, 57 (tel. 429 29 47; open daily 7pm-1:30am), features live classical music; more formal performances take place at the **Auditorio Nacional,** C. Principe de Vergara, 136 (tel. 337 01 00; Metro: Cruz del Rayo) and the **Fundación Juan March,** C. Castelló, 77 (tel 435 42 40; Metro: Nuñez de Balboa), which holds free weekly concerts. The **Grand Teatro de la Opera,** Pl. Opera, opposite Palacio Real, will reopen in 1992 as Madrid's main venue for opera and classical ballet. Excellent stagings of national and foreign productions go up at Teatro Español, Pl. Santa Ana, which has been functioning since the 16th century. **Manuela,** C. San Vicente Ferrer, 29 (tel. 531 70 37; Metro: Bilbas or Tribunal), off Pl. 2 de Mayo, showcases folk music. Though entertaining, **flamenco** in Madrid tends to be tourist-cheesy and expensive. Try **Arco de Cuchilleros,** C. Cuchilleros, 7 (tel. 266 58 67), off Pl. Mayor (Metro: Sol). The guitarists are emotional, the dancers stomp furiously, and drink (at 800ptas) flows liberally. Cover (including 1st drink) is 2000ptas. (Shows daily at 10:30pm and 12:30am.) More down-to-earth is **Casa Patas,** C. Cañizares, 33 (Metro: Sol), where you can chill at the large bar until *flamenco* at midnight on Friday and Saturday nights. (Open daily 7pm-2:30am.)

Discos are popular and often expensive. Many have "afternoon" sessions (usually 7-10pm; cover 250-700ptas) and "night" sessions (11:30pm-3:30am; cover up to 1500ptas). Rates mount on weekends, and men are usually charged 200ptas more than women. **Joy Eslava,** C. Arenal, 11 (tel. 266 37 33; Metro: Sol) features lasers and videoscreens. (Open daily 7-10pm and 11:30-5:30am. Cover 1500ptas.) Those seeking salsa, Brazilian music, and an older crowd should try **Oba Oba,** C. Jacometrezo, 4 (tel. 221 97 59; Metro: Callao). At **Bocaccio,** C. Marqués de la Ensenada, 16 (tel. 419 10 08; Metro: Colón; open Sun.-Thurs. 7-10pm and 11:30pm-4:30am, Fri.-Sat. 7-10pm and 11:30pm-5am), intellectuals dance flamenco while the university crowd congregates at **Oh! Madrid,** Carretera de la Coruña, Km. 10. Metro: Moncloa. Drinks at these discos run 500-700ptas. Gay nightlife in Madrid is concentrated around the Chueca area. Try **Elle et Lui,** Travesía de Parada, 6 (open daily 7pm-2:30am), or, for women only, **Ella's,** at C. San Dimas (Metro: Noviciados; open Mon.-Sat. 10pm-5am).

Though considered barbaric by many, bullfights are still an integral part of Spanish culture. *Corridas* usually occur every Sunday, in summer (less frequently in winter), except during the **Festival of San Isidro** (mid- to late May), when several are held daily. Keep your eyes peeled for posters in bars and cafés (especially on C. Victoria, off Carrera San Jerónimo), or inquire at either ticket office listed below. The **Plaza de las Ventas,** C. Alcalá, 237, northeast of central Madrid, is the bullest bullring in the country. (Metro: Ventas, or bus #21, 53, or 110.) Tickets are usually available on the Saturday before and the Sunday of the bullfight, at C. Victoria, 3, off Carrera San Jerónimo, east of Puerta del Sol (Metro: Sol), and the Plaza de Toros (Metro: Ventas). Seats cost 1000-4500ptas, depending on whether you want the *sombra* (shade) or the blistering *sol.*

The greatest Spanish sporting obsession by far, however, is **soccer.** Every Sunday between September and June, one of the two big local teams play at home. **Real Madrid** plays at the Estadio Santiago Bernabeu, Paseo de la Castellana, 104 (tel. 250 06 00; Metro: Lima, or bus #27, 40, or 43). **Atlético Madrid** plays at the Estadio Vicente Calderón, C. Virgen del Puerto, 67 (tel. 266 47 07; Metro: Pirámides or Marqués de Vandillos).

Near Madrid

A fabulous monastic-palatial complex one hour northwest of Madrid by train (250ptas) on the way to Avila, **El Escorial** embraces one monastery, two palaces, two royal pantheons, a magnificent library, and innumerable artistic masterpieces, the whole thing constructed as a country retreat for Felipe II. (Open Tues.-Sun. 10am-7pm; last entry 30 min.-1 hr. before closing. Admission 500ptas.) Those with time on their hands should take the bus (1 per day, 15 min., 300ptas) to **Valle de**

Los Caídos (Valley of the Fallen). Dedicated to victims of the Spanish Civil War, the 150m granite cross commands a matchless view of the Castilian plain. El Escorial's **tourist office,** Floridablanca, 10 (tel. (91) 890 15 54), may help you find rooms, but in summer lodgings are scarce. Reserve ahead, or plan on returning to Madrid. **Hostal Vasco,** Pl. Santiago, 11 (tel. (91) 890 16 19), uphill from the town center, is a charming 19th-century building with clean, spacious rooms, lounges, and a terrace. (Singles 1600ptas. Doubles with shower 3200ptas, with full bath 3900ptas. Triples 4000ptas. Breakfast 375ptas.)

Aranjuez, less than an hour south of Madrid on the rail line to Toledo, is a town with peace and quiet, strawberries and cream, greenery and shade. Walking along the tree-lined Río Tajo, you will easily see why centuries of Hapsburg and Bourbon royalty fled to Aranjuez to escape the scorching heat of the capital. The town warrants at least a daytrip, and its easy-to-find accommodations make a good base for traveling to Toledo. Aranjuez's principal sight is the opulently-ornamented **Palacio Real.** (Open Tues.-Sun. 10am-6:30pm; Oct.-May Tues.-Sun. 10am-6pm. Compulsory tour in Spanish. Admission 350ptas, students 250ptas. Free on Wed. to EC citizens.) More relaxing are the extensive gardens, especially the huge **Jardines del Príncipe,** created for the youthful amusement of the future Carlos IV. (Open 10am-sunset. Free.) Inside the park, the **Casita del Príncipe** is a neo-Pompeian fantasy palace created for the young crown prince Carlos IV.

The Aranjuez **tourist office** is in the center of the Pl. Rusiñol, near the Palacio Real (and open the same hours). **Trains** run to Toledo (30 min., 200ptas) and Madrid (50 min., 240ptas); the station is ten minutes' walk down the Carreterra de Toledo. **Buses** run to Madrid only (7 per day, 450ptas) from C. Infantas, 8. Good clean rooms are available at **Hostal Infantas,** C. Infantas, 6. (Tel. (91) 891 13 41. Singles 1210ptas, with bath 1700ptas. Doubles 2200ptas, with bath 3100ptas.) More expensive and more luxurious is the friendly **Hostal Castilla,** C. Andalucía, 98. (Tel. 891 26 27. Singles 3000ptas. Doubles 4000ptas.) The **Kiosco El Brillante,** across from the tourist office, serves *platos combinados* for between 450-800ptas, and more importantly, *fresón con nata* (Aranjuez's deservedly renowned strawberries, with cream) for 250ptas.

The virtually impregnable hilltop town **Cuenca** is about 200km southeast of Madrid. The city's cramped quarters gave rise to Cuenca's famed **Casas Colgadas** (Hanging Houses), which dangle as precariously over the banks of the Río Huécar today as they did six centuries ago. Cuenca also possesses the only Gothic-Anglo-Norman *catedral* in Spain, dominating Plaza Mayor. The **Museo de Arte Abstracto** demonstrates that Spanish modern art did not end with Picasso, Miró, and Dalí. (Open Tues.-Fri. 11am-2pm. Admission 150ptas, students 75ptas.) Also extremely attractive is the nearby **Museo Diocesano,** whose imaginatively-displayed exhibits include two El Grecos (admission 100ptas).

Trains run to Madrid (8 per day, 1205ptas), and Toledo (5 per day, 900ptas) and València (1 per day, 900ptas); bus #1 (50ptas) connects the station, in the new city, with the Pl. Mayor, in the old. The **tourist office,** C. Dalmacio García Izcara, 9 (tel. (966) 22 22 31), two blocks left from the train station exit, is helpful (Spanish only) and has listings of the various **bus** companies and their services. (Open Mon.-Fri. 9am-2pm and 4:30-6:30pm, Sat. 9:30am-1pm.) **Posada de San Jose,** C. Julián Romero, 4 (tel. (966) 21 13 00), up the street from the main cathedral, has gracious rooms with knock-out views of the old town and the gorge. (Singles 1800ptas, with bath 3000ptas. Doubles 3000ptas, with shower 4500ptas, with bath 4900ptas. Triples and quads too.) Beds in the new city are cheaper. **Pensión Central,** C. Alonso Chirino, 9 (tel. (966) 21 15 11), has big, immaculate rooms. (Singles 900ptas. Doubles 1450ptas. Shower 150ptas.) Avoid the pricey and tourist-infested eateries of the old city and look along C. Cervantes or C. República Argentina.

Toledo

For Cervantes, Toledo was the "glory of Spain and light of her cities." Medieval *convivencia*—peaceful coexistence and collaboration among Christians, Muslims, and Jews—has left behind a dignified and mystical walled city. Toledo's medieval houses, churches, synagogues, and mosques crowd together in a dizzying anarchy of periods and styles. Even so, the view that El Greco painted in a few of his rare landscapes has changed little; a young American woman made history recently when she entered a Toledo home with the same key her ancestors used 500 years ago.

Orientation and Practical Information

Toledo is an easy daytrip from Madrid, but worth a stay overnight. No Castilian city is as labyrinthine as Toledo—be sure to pick up a map at the turismo before stepping into the breach. When you do become lost, search the skyline for the cathedral's towering spires, an instant point of orientation. Most major sights are near or on top of the central hill; take bus #5 or 6 from the train station to Pl. Zocodóver, the end of the line (60ptas).

Tourist Office: Turismo, on the north side of town outside Puerta Nueva de Bisagra (tel. 22 08 43). Take the bus from the train station; get off just before heading up a steep, winding road. Open Mon.-Fri. 9am-2pm and 4-6pm, Sat. 9am-1:30pm. **Information booth** in the Pl. Zocodóver has basic information.

Post Office: C. Plata, 1 (tel. 22 36 11). *Lista de Correos.* Open Mon.-Fri. 9am-2pm and 4-6pm. **Postal Code:** 45001.

Telephones: C. Plata, 20. Open Mon.-Sat. 9am-1pm and 5-9pm. **City Code:** 925.

Trains: Station is on Paseo de la Rosa (tel. 22 30 99), across the Puente de Azarquiel. To Aranjuez (every ½ hr., 200ptas) and Madrid's Atocha Station (430ptas). Connect to Avila in Madrid. **RENFE office,** C. Sillería, 7 (tel. 22 12 72).

Buses: Station is in the Zona Safont (tel. 21 58 50), to the northeast of the old city walls. **Continental/Galiano** (tel. 22 29 61) to Madrid (12 per day, 2 hr., 400ptas).

Laundromat: Juan Pascual, C. Bolivia, 2 (tel. 22 16 03), a tiny street off C. Gerardo Lobo between Pl. Zocodóver and the tourist office. 1000ptas per 5kg. Open daily 9am-1:30pm and 4-8pm.

Medical Assistance: Seguridad Social, Av. Barber (tel. 22 13 55).

Emergencies: Police (tel. 091). Ayuntamiento, 1 (tel. 23 34 07). **Ambulance: Cruz Roja** (Red Cross), C. Moscardó, 6 (tel. 22 29 00).

Accommodations, Camping, and Food

Though most tourists daytrip from Madrid, you may still have problems finding a room. Call ahead.

Residencia Juvenil (IYHF), Castillo de San Servando (tel. 22 45 54), uphill to the left of the train station (15-min. walk). Swimming pool, TV, and a view. 3 bunkbeds per room. Reserve ahead. Annex-like *albergue* just around the bend has no view and same prices. Flexible curfew 12:30am. 500ptas, ages over 26 600ptas. Full board 1200ptas, ages over 26 1400ptas. Bring toilet paper.

Pensión Descalzos, C. Descalzos, 30 (tel. 22 28 88). Sweetness: spacious rooms, liquid soap, radios, and delightfully soft toilet paper. Singles 1500ptas. Doubles 2500ptas, with bath 4000ptas.

Pensión San Pedro, Callejón de San Pedro, 2 (tel. 21 47 34), next to the cathedral. Old building with modern facilities. Hall light may keep you up. Singles with bath 1500ptas. Twin-bedded doubles with shower 2500ptas. Full board available.

Hostal las Armas, C. Armas, 7 (tel. 22 16 68), off Pl. Zocodóver. 200-yr.-old home with lush patio. Singles 1800ptas. Doubles 2900ptas. Triples 4000ptas.

Fonda Lumbreras, C. Juan Labrador, 7 (tel. 22 15 71), 2 blocks from Pl. Zocodóver. Rundown but clean. Eccentric owner willing to bargain. Singles 1200ptas. Doubles 2000ptas. Triples 3000ptas. Showers 150ptas.

Fonda Segovia, C. Recoletos, 4 (tel. 21 11 24), off C. Sillería, which is off Pl. Zocodóver. Maternal owner. Blessedly quiet rooms with balconies, but the beds will swallow you alive. Doubles 1900ptas. Triples 2600ptas. Shower 150ptas.

Camping: El Greco (tel. 21 00 90), 1½km from town on road N-401. Wooded and shady. 350ptas per person, per tent, and per car. **Circo Romano,** Av. Carlos III (tel. 22 04 42), just outside the old city, with a view. Closer but seedy. 350ptas per person, per tent, and per car.

There are ways to beat the wallet-battering norm in Toledo. Excellent *pollo al ajillo* (garlic chicken) is only 510ptas at **Restaurante La Cubana,** Paseo de la Rosa, 2, in front of the Puente Viejo de Alcántara. (Open daily 1-4pm and 7:30-10:30pm.) **Restaurante-Bar Mariano,** Po. de Merchan down the boulevard from the *turismo,* offers *platos combinados* for 500-700ptas in a park setting. (Open daily 1:30-3:45pm and 8:15-10:45pm.) At **Pastucci Pizzería,** C. Sinagoga, 10, near the cathedral, devour delicious pizza and pasta for 250-500ptas; flash your attractive orange *Let's Go* and get 10% off. (Open daily noon-4:00pm and 7:30pm-12:30am.)

Sights

Despite Toledo's history of deteriorating religious harmony, artifacts of Christian, Muslim, and Jewish origin continue to complement one another in Toledo, often within the same building.

The **cathedral** is a rich banquet of architectural styles. Admission to the church is free but you pay 300ptas to see the treasury, the *coro,* the chapterhouse, the Kings' Chapel, and the sacristy. The **museum annex** houses El Grecos and Caravaggios. (Cathedral open Mon.-Sat. 10:30am-1pm and 3:30-7pm, Sun. 10:30am-1pm and 4-7pm; Sept.-June Mon.-Sat. 10:30am-1pm and 3:30-7pm, Sun. 10:30am-1pm and 4-6pm.)

Domenico Theotocopuli, alias El Greco, is in part responsible for Toledo's entrancing mystery. Born in Crete (hence his name), this painter of tempestuous skies and elongated portraits spent most of his life in Toledo; many of his paintings have remained here since the 16th century. The modest Mudejar **Church of San Tomé** houses one of his best-known works, *El Entierro del Conde de Orgaz* (The Burial of Count Orgaz). (Open in summer Tues.-Sat. 10am-2pm and 3:30-6:45pm, Sun. 10am-2pm; in off-season Tues.-Sat. 10am-1pm and 3:30-5:45pm, Sun. 10am-1:45pm. Admission 85ptas.) The so-called **Casa del Greco,** at C. S. Levi, 3, a fine example of Toledo's 16th-century secular architecture, stands, at best, only close to where the painter lived, but has a reasonably good collection of his works, including the "Vista y Mapa de Toledo" (View and Map of Toledo). (Open Tues.-Sat. 10am-2pm and 4-6pm, Sun. 10am-2pm. Admission 200ptas.) The **Museo de Santa Cruz,** at C. Cervantes, 3, houses a well-organized and undertouristed collection of tapestries and paintings, including works by El Greco. (Open Tues.-Sat. 10am-2pm and 4-6pm, Sun. 10am-2pm. Admission 200ptas.) The **Museo de los Concilios y de la Cultura Visigótica,** at C. San Clemente, off the Pl. Zocodóver, set in a 13th-century Mudejar church, includes some votive crowns among its masterpieces. (Open Tues.-Sat. 10am-2pm and 4-6:30pm, Sun. 10am-2pm, Mon. 10am-2pm. Admission 150ptas, students free.)

Only two synagogues remain of what was once the largest Jewish community in Spain. The **Sinagoga del Tránsito,** constructed in the 14th century by Samuel Ha-Levi, treasurer to Peter I of Castile, has wonderful Mudéjar decorations and an *artesonado* ceiling. Three rooms house the **Museo Sefardí** and its collection of Sephardic manuscripts, inscriptions, amulets, and sarcophagus lids. (Open Tues.-Sat. 10am-2pm and 4-6pm, Sun. 10am-2pm. Admission 200ptas.) The nearby **Sinagoga de Santa María la Blanca,** an austere contrast to the opulence and crowds of the cathedral, was built as a synagogue, looks like a mosque, and was for many years a church. (Open daily in summer 10am-2pm and 3:30-7pm; off-season 10am-2pm and 3:30-6pm. Admission 75ptas.)

Shadows of the Muslim presence in Toledo are visible near the **Puerta del Sol,** a 14th-century *Mudéjar* gate. The **Mezquita del Cristo de la Luz** has been both a Muslim and a Christian place of worship. The 10th-century mosque, built on the site of a Visigoth church, is the only building in Toledo to survive from the pre-Christian era.

The **Alcázar** is Toledo's most formidable landmark. Little remains of the original 13th-century structure; the building was largely reduced to rubble during a horrendous siege in the Civil War, as Fascist troops agonizingly held out against Republican bombardment. Now restored, it houses memorabilia of this siege, with a distinctly fascist slant. (Open Tues.-Sun. 9:30am-1:30pm and 4-6:30pm. Admission 125ptas.)

Segovia

Rising above rolling, fertile countryside, the old mountain city of Segovia harbors beautiful golden churches, twisting alleyways, and a people fiercely proud of their city and province. The massive Roman aqueduct, cathedral, and Alcázar might be covered in a quick daytrip, but Segovia's cool plazas and relaxed pace after sundown are the real attraction.

Orientation and Practical Information

Segovia lies 88km northwest of Madrid on the rail line to Medino del Campo and Valladolid. **Plaza Mayor,** next to the cathedral, is the center of town; reach it from the bus or train stations by bus #3 (every 15 min., 75ptas).

Tourist Office: Pl. Mayor, 10 (tel. 43 03 28), in front of the bus stop. Information on accommodations, inter-city buses, trains, and sights is posted outside the door, but step inside for their useful map. Open Mon.-Fri. 9am-2pm and 4:30-7:30pm, Sat. 10am-2pm; Oct. to mid-June Mon.-Fri. 9am-2pm, Sat. 10am-2pm.

Post Office: Pl. Doctor Laguna, 5. Most services open Mon.-Fri. 9am-2pm and 5-7pm, Sat. 9am-2pm. *Lista de Correos* (enter in rear) open Mon.-Sat. 9am-2pm. **Postal Code:** 40006.

Telephones: Juan Bravo, 6, down C. Isabel la Católica. **City code:** 911.

Trains: (tel. 42 07 74), Po. del Obispo Quesada, a 20-min. walk southeast from the town center. Take the Paseo and turn right onto Av. Fernández Ladreda, or take bus #3.

Buses: At Paseo de Sepúlveda and Av. Fernández Ladreda (tel. 42 77 25). To: Madrid (9 per day, 1½ hr., 520ptas); Valladolid (4 per day, 2½ hr., 530 ptas); Avila (3 per day, 1½ hr., 425ptas).

Medical Assistance: Hospital de la Misericordia, Dr. Velasco, 3 (tel. 43 08 12). **First Aid: Casa de Socorro,** Arias Dávila, 3 (tel. 43 41 41). **Ambulance** (tel. 43 01 00).

Police: National, C. Perucho, 2 (tel. 42 51 61). **Municipal:** (tel. 42 12 12; 43 12 12 at night.)

Accommodations, Camping, and Food

During the summer, finding a *hostal* room might well be a major problem. Bypass the problem by making your visit a daytrip from Madrid.

Hostal Emperador Teodosio (IYHF) (tel. 42 00 27), on the Paseo Conde de Sepúlveda halfway between the train and bus stations. A gym and luxurious common room with piano and TV make this the best pad in town—booked weeks in advance. 550ptas, ages over 26 650ptas. Open to hostelers July-Aug.

Hostal-Residencia El Postigo, Pl. Seminario, 2 (tel 43 66 33). Stark modern building next to the police station is as safe as you can get. Singles with shower 1520ptas. Doubles with bath 2520ptas. Breakfast 215ptas.

Casa de Huéspedes Cubo, Pl. Mayor, 4, 3rd floor (tel. 43 63 86). Terrific prices and location, but the two double rooms are windowless and cramped. 800ptas per person. Hot showers 150ptas.

Camping: Camping Acueducto, Carretera Nacional, 601 (tel. 42 50 00), at Km 85, 1km from town on the road to La Granja. 330ptas per person, tents 360ptas. Open June-Sept.

Gastronomical ecstasy is often just around the corner, but it comes at a price. The best value is the **Mesón del Campesino,** C. Infanta Isabel, 12, with filling *menús* for 800-1000ptas, and *platos combinados* for 200-600ptas. (Open Fri.-Wed. 11am-4pm and 8:30pm-12:30am.) **Mesón Cándido,** Pl. Azoquejo, 5 (tel. 42 81 03) is extremely expensive and extremely famous. *(Menú* 2000ptas, *cochinillo asado* 1500ptas. Open daily 12:30-4:30pm and 8-11:30pm).

Sights and Entertainment

The elegant *acueducto romano* is the city's most famous and most ancient monument. View it at its maximum height (28.9m) from **Plaza del Azoquejo,** or catch its profile from the steps on the left side of the plaza. The city's position at the confluence of the Río Eresma and Río Clamores has led people to compare Segovia to a sailing ship, with the **Alcázar** (fortress) as its majestic bow. The fortress commands a stellar view of Segovia and the surrounding plain; inside is a collection of medieval weaponry, as well as several spectacular handcrafted ceilings. (Open daily April-Sept. 10am-7pm; Oct.-March 10am-6pm. Admission 175ptas.) The **catedral,** new by Spanish standards, is a massive late Gothic edifice. The stained-glass windows at the western end are ethereal. (Open April-Sept. daily 9am-7pm; Oct.-March Mon.-Fri. 9:30am-1pm and 3-6pm, Sat.-Sun. 9:30am-6pm. Admission 150ptas.) A number of Romanesque churches dot the streets of Segovia.

Nighttime activity focuses on Plaza Mayor and the surrounding side streets. Hit the trendy **Pub Oja Blanca** or **Cafe Jeyma** in the plaza, or relax at the **Oasis Bar** down C. Isabela de la Católica. On the second Saturday and Sunday in February, the women of **Zamarramala,** 1km away, take over the town's administration during the **Fiesta de Santa Agueda;** they reenact a botched attack on the Alcázar, when the women of the town tried to seduce the garrison guards.

Near Segovia

Homesick for Versailles, Felipe V built **La Granja,** 11km from Segovia. Its **Marble Rooms, Throne Room,** and **Japanese Room** are all elegantly furnished, and the palace gardens are well manicured. (Open Mon.-Fri. 10am-1pm and 3-5pm, Sat.-Sun. 10am-2pm. Admission 300ptas, students and professors 250ptas, free for EEC on Wed.) The tourist office in Segovia can tell you when the magnificent fountains will be turned on. Buses connect Segovia and La Granja (10 per day, 20 min., 80ptas).

Avila

Avila is a breath of fresh air, in more ways than one. To begin with, it's a mountain city—at 1130m, the highest provincial capital in Spain—that keeps its cool in summer while the cities of the plains swelter. Secondly, Avila is a classic 11th-century walled city which, for some reason, has not been swamped by tourists. The local hero is Santa Teresa, a 16th-century reformer of the Carmelite order and author of a passionate autobiography recounting her mystical experiences. The people of Avila refer to her simply as *la Santa,* and have named everything from pastries to driving schools after her. Every October 8-15 the city spends a full week celebrating Santa Teresa, with fairs and parades of *gigantes y cabezudos* (oversized puppets). July 18-25 brings **Fiestas de Verano** (Summer Celebrations), with exhibitions and bullfights. Visit the tourist office for a calendar of events.

The town is best seen from the **Cuatro Postes** on the highway to Salamanca. For a closer encounter, climb the walls along the **parador** on Pl. Concepción Arenal. The **catedral,** with its red-splotched interior and stone relief works, is actually embedded in the walls, a reminder of the days when war and religion went hand in hand. Spain's first Gothic cathedral, it houses a small **museum** which has a fine collection of gold and silver works and medieval paintings. (Cathedral open daily May-Sept. 8am-1pm and 3-7pm; Oct.-April 8am-1pm and 3-5pm. Free. Museum open May-Sept. daily 10am-1:30pm and 3-7pm; Oct.-April daily 10am-1:30pm and 3-6pm. Admission 100ptas.) Many of Teresa's mystical experiences took place during the thirty years she spent in the **Monasterio de la Encarnación;** through the farthest door in the farthest chapel, you can see the tiny cell where she lived. The **Convento de San José** was the first founded by Teresa; its tiny museum's exhibits include the drum she played at Christmas.

Avila's **oficina de turismo** is at Pl. Catedral, 4 (tel. (918) 21 13 87). When you reach the café-filled Pl. Santa Teresa, walk through the main gate and turn right up the sinuous C. Cruz Vieja. (Open Mon.-Fri. 9am-8pm, Sat. 9am-3pm, Sun. 11am-3pm; Oct.-May Mon.-Fri. 9am-2pm and 4-6pm, Sat. 9am-2pm.) The **train station,** Av. Portugal, 17 (tel. (918) 22 01 88), at the end of Av. José António, is on the northeast side of town. From the station, follow Av. José Antonio to C. Isaac Peral, bear right, and turn left on C. Duque de Alba to reach Pl. Santa Teresa. Trains head to Madrid (28 per day, 1½-2 hr., 555-975ptas) and Salamanca (3 per day, 2 hr., 510ptas). The **bus station** is nearby on Av. Madrid (tel. (918) 22 01 54) and can get you to Madrid (9 per day, 2 hr., 590ptas), Salamanca (3 per day, 1 hr., 639ptas), and Segovia (3 per day, 45 min., 450ptas). To reach the Pl. Santa Teresa from the bus station, cross the street and walk down C. Duque de Alba. The **post office** is at Pl. Catedral, 2 (open Mon.-Sat. 9am-2pm and 4-6pm); **telephones** are next door (open Mon.-Sat. 9am-2pm and 5-11pm). Few visitors stay overnight, so rooms are reasonably easy to find. Try **Hostal Santa Ana,** C. Alfonso Montalvo, 2 (tel. (918) 22 00 63), near the train station down Av. Jose Antonio, for its snow-white sheets. (Singles 1500ptas. Doubles 2200ptas.) **Hostal Continental,** Pl. Catedral, 6 (tel. (918) 21 15 02), in a prime location, offers large rooms with lumpy beds and hot, torrential showers. (Singles 1882ptas. Doubles 2800ptas.) The IYHF hostel, **Duperier,** Av. Juventud (tel. (918) 22 17 16), is nice and next to a swimming pool, but has only 10 beds. Call ahead. (Curfew 11pm. 550ptas, ages over 26 650ptas).

Food in Avila is wholesome, if expensive, and ranges from *ternera asada* (roast veal) to *yemas* (a local confection of egg yolks candied with honey). **Restaurante El Ruedo,** C. Enrique Larreta, 7, a block from the cathedral but off the beaten track, has amazingly fresh trout on its 995ptas *menú.* (Open Wed.-Mon. 1:30-5pm and 9pm-midnight. **Mesón el Rastro,** Pl. Rastro, 4, C. Cepada and C. Caballeros at the southern wall, is justly famous for regional specialties. *Menú del día* costs 1200ptas. (Open daily 1-4pm and 9:30-11pm.) **Markets** are held at C. Comuneros de Castilla near Pl. Victoria (open daily 9:30am-2pm and 4-7pm) and C. Jardín de San Rogue (open daily 9:30am-2pm and 4:30-7:30pm). At night, cross the Puente del Adaja and turn right to find **El Molino de la Losa,** Basada de la Losa, 12. At this mill/restaurant, you can sip rum-powered sangria (9-glass pitcher 450ptas) on the outdoor terrace above the river. (Open daily for meals 1-4pm and 9-11pm; bar open 10:30am-midnight.)

Salamanca

It's worth traveling days and nights just to sit on a sun-scorched bench in Salamanca's Plaza Mayor. Incredible elegance, radiant sandstone, and cosmopolitan cafés distinguish Salamantine life. The city is perhaps best known for its university, the oldest in Spain. In summer, a huge influx of foreign students adds a special tang to the atmosphere—but the city in winter is hauntingly attractive too.

Orientation and Practical Information

The **Plaza Mayor** is a 20-minute walk either southwest from the train station or east from the bus station; urban buses run from both stations to the Pl. Mercade, right next to the Pl. Mayor. Most sights, and a great deal of cheap food and accommodation, lie a little way south. Salamanca is small, and you can get around easily on foot, but tangled streets make the tourist's office map indispensable.

Tourist Offices: National, Gran Vía, 39-41 (tel. 26 85 71). Excellent services; fluent English. Open Mon.-Fri. 9:30am-2pm and 4:30-7pm, Sat. 9:30am-2pm. **Municipal,** Pl. Mayor (tel. 21 83 42). Get your map, then go to the National. Open Mon.-Fri. 10am-1:30pm and 5-7pm, Sat. 10am-2pm, and Sun. 11am-2pm.

Budget Travel: TIVE, Pl. Constitución, 1 (tel. 26 77 31). Student discounts. Long lines—arrive early. Open Mon.-Fri. 9am-2pm. **Viajes Juventus,** Pl. Libertad, 4 (tel. 21 74 07), north of Pl. Mayor. BIJ tickets. Open Mon.-Fri. 10am-2pm and 4:30-8pm, Sat. 10:30am-2pm.

Currency Exchange: Banco Exterior de España, C. Toro, 40 (tel. 21 71 02) and Gran Vía, 28 (tel. 21 73 07) opens on summer Saturdays (9am-noon) for cash or travelers' checks. After hours, hit **Oficina de Cambio,** Pl. Mayor. Open Mon.-Fri. 9am-midnight.

Post Office: Gran Vía, 25 (tel. 24 30 11), 2 blocks from the National tourist office towards Pl. España. *Lista de Correos* open Mon.-Fri. 9am-2pm. **Postal Code:** 37008.

Telephones: Pl. Peña Primera, 1, off Pl. Bandos. Open Mon.-Sat. 9am-3pm and 4-10pm. **City Code:** 923.

Trains: (tel. 22 57 42). To: Madrid (3 per day, 3½ hr., 1400ptas), Avila (3 per day, 45 min., 590ptas), León (1 per day at 6:35am, 3½ hr., 1450ptas), Barcelona (1 per day at 10:15pm, 14 hr., 4050ptas) and Porto, Portugal (1 per day at 2:05am, 8½ hr., 2400ptas). **RENFE** office, Pl. Libertad, 10 (tel. 21 24 54). Open Mon.-Fri. 9am-2pm and 5-7pm.

Buses: Av. Filiberto Villalobos, 79 (tel. 23 67 17). To: Madrid (very frequently, 2½ hr., 1207ptas), Avila (1-5 per day, 1-2 hr., 639ptas), Barcelona (1-3 per day, 11½ hr., 4635ptas) and León (1-3 per day, 3 hr., 1250ptas).

Medical Assistance: Hospital Clínico, Paseo de San Vicente, 23 (tel. 29 11 00). **Ambulance,** (tel. 24 09 16).

Emergencies: (tel. 092). **Policía Municipal,** in Ayuntamiento, Pl. Mayor, 1 (tel. 21 96 00).

Accommodations and Camping

Hotels and pensions abound. There are lots of *fondas* around **Plaza Mayor,** and on **Calle Meléndez** just below; beds run about 1000ptas per person.

Pensión Marina, C. Doctrinos, 4, 3rd floor (tel. 21 65 69), between C. Compañía and C. Prado. Gigantic bathroom, plush TV lounge, beautiful rooms. One single 1500ptas. Doubles 2000ptas.

Pensión Barez, C. Meléndez, 19 (tel. 21 74 95). Sparkling clean. Owners treat you like family. Windowless singles 900ptas. Bright doubles 1800ptas. Showers 125ptas.

Pension Las Vegas, C. Meléndez, 12 (tel. 21 87 49). Clean but bare rooms. Pleasant owner. Singles 1000ptas. Doubles 2000ptas.

Hostal Oriental, C. Azafranal, 13 (tel. 21 21 15), halfway between Pl. Mayor and Pl. España. Comfortable, largeish rooms. Singles 1500ptas. Doubles 2700ptas.

Camping: Don Quijote (tel. 25 75 04), 4km out of town on the road to Aldealengua. 300ptas per person, 250ptas per tent. Open July-Sept. **Regio** (tel. 20 02 50), 4km from town on the road to Madrid. Pool. 390ptas per person, 340ptas per tent.

Food

Eating in Salamanca shouldn't be too hard on your budget. **Plaza Mayor** is lined with outdoor cafés. A slew of cheap, relatively untouristed bar-restaurants lie between the Plaza and the University, where a full meal will cost about 800ptas. Try *jeta,* a local *tapas* of fried skin from the mouth of a pig (tastes like bacon). There's a **market** at Plaza del Mercado, east of Plaza Mayor (open daily 8:30am-2pm), and a **supermercado** on C. Iscar Peyra, 2 blocks from Pl. Mayor (open Mon.-Fri. 9:45am-1:45pm and 5:30-8:30pm, Sat. 10am-2pm).

Restaurante El Bardo, C. Compañía, 8 (tel. 21 90 89), behind Casa de las Conchas. Exciting vegetarian and classic *menús* served at lunch (650ptas). *A la carta* at dinner 1400ptas. Open Tues.-Sun. 11am-4pm and 7pm-midnight.

Restaurante La Luna, C. Libreros 4, down the street from the university façade. Nostalgic photos and Salamanca's largest *menú.* Open Mon.-Thurs. 10:30am-1:30pm, Fri.-Sun. 10:30am-3am.

Restaurante Vegetariano El Trigal, C. Libreros, 20 (tel. 21 56 99). Tiny and intimate. Popular, though portions are rather small. *Platos combinados* 525-650ptas. Open daily 1-4pm and 8:30-11pm.

Sights and Entertainment

Salamanca's monuments span every architectural style since before the Romans. The golden glow of sandstone provides the city's harmony and continuity. **Plaza Mayor,** considered by many the most beautiful square in Spain, was built during the reign of Felipe V and is a fine place for admiring both architecture and passersby. Between the arches are carved medallions of famous Spaniards, from El Cid to Cervantes to Franco. The **Town Hall** is the large, handsome building in the center of the square.

Enter the **university** from the **Patio de las Escuelas,** off C. Libreros. Look for the small frog carved on a skull in the facade's right pilaster; students claim it gives them good luck on exams. For info on the university's Spanish-for-foreigners program, write to Cursos Internacionales de Salamanca, Patio de Escuelas Menores, 37008 Salamanca. Don't miss the **Escuelas Menores,** across the plaza, housing the *Cielo de Salamanca* (Sky of Salamanca), a 15th-century fresco of the signs of the zodiac. (Both buildings open Mon.-Fri. 9:30am-1:30pm and 4-7pm, Sat. 9:30am-1:30pm and 4:30-7pm, Sun. and holidays 10am-1pm. Admission 100ptas, free with university ID but not ISIC.) To the right of the principal entrance to the university is the intriguing **Casa-Museo de Unamuno,** featuring miscellaneous paraphernalia connected with the existential philosopher and poet, including some of his very best origami. (Open Mon.-Fri. 4-6pm, Sat.-Sun. 11am-1pm. Free.)

Salamanca has two cathedrals, next to each other on a grassy square. The spindly spires of the **New Cathedral** (begun in 1513) rise above town. The cloister, by Alberto Churriguera connects to the Romanesque **Old Cathedral,** which has an amazing Nicolás Florentino altarpiece that tells the story of the Virgin Mary in 53 scenes. In the apocalyptic cupola, angels weed out the sinners. (Open daily June-Sept. 9am-1:30pm and 4-7pm; Oct.-May 9:30am-1:30pm and 3:30-6pm. Admission to Old Cathedral 200ptas.) The cathedrals are very photogenic from all angles and distances. Catch them at night when lit up.

The **Casa de las Conchas** (House of Shells) was decorated with chiseled conch shells as a monument to the shells brought back by pilgrims to Santiago de Compostela by pilgrims. Unfortunately, it blocks the view of the splendid baroque **Clerecía** across the street; fervent Jesuit residents once offered to dispense large sums of money if the house would be torn down.

In the center of the **Puente Romano,** a 2000-year-old Roman bridge spanning the Río Tormes, stands the **Toro Ibérico,** a headless granite bull which dates from Celtiberian times and which made it into the pages of *Lazarillo de Tormes* (a 16th-century picaresque masterpiece). The view from the opposite side of the bridge is magnificent.

Locals, students, and tourists crowd the cafés and colonnades of the Plaza Mayor at all hours of the day and night. Even when the Plaza is not the site of an activity, everyone meets under its clock tower or passes through going from one place to another. **Café Novelty,** at the northeast corner, is the oldest in Salamanca. Miguel de Unamuno regularly imbibed here. **Café El Corrillo,** off the southwest corner of Plaza Mayor, is packed with coffee drinkers by day, shot-pounders by night and has good, laid-back musical taste. **Pub Rojo y Negro,** on C. Espoz y Miña, serves great coffee, liqueur, and ice cream concoctions a block from the Plaza. Dance at **Camelot,** a medieval chapel-turned-disco (two blocks from Rojo y Negro), or at

Fresas. Pick up a copy of *Ambiente* from the municipal tourist office, or read the posters at the Colegio Mayor (Palacio de Anaya) for the most current student happenings.

Burgos

The tranquil, cathedral-crowned city of Burgos is most closely associated with the heroic El Cid. Legendary as the liberator of València from the Moors and as the hero of the first masterpiece of Castilian literature, the 12th-century epic *Poema de Mio Cid,* El is honored by a colossal statue in Plaza del General Primo de Rivera. *Burgaleses* also applaud themselves for the purity of their Spanish—the most exquisite in all Castile and the world, they claim.

Orientation and Practical Information

Burgos lies 250km north of Madrid, on the banks of the Río Arlanzón. The bus and train stations are on the southern side, and the cathedral is just to the north.

Tourist Office: Pl. Alonso Martínez, 7 (tel. 20 31 25). From the station, cross the bridge, turn right, pass through the Arco de Santa María, and enter Pl. Rey San Fernando. From the right of the cathedral entrance, continue straight up C. Paloma and C. Laín Calvo to Pl. Alonso Martínez. Open Mon.-Fri. 9am-2pm and 4:30-6:30pm, Sat. 9am-2pm.

Budget Travel: Viajes TIVE, (tel. 20 98 81), in the Casa de Cultura on Pl. San Juan. BIJ tickets and sound advice. Open Mon.-Fri. 9am-2pm.

Post Office: Pl. Conde de Castro, 1 (tel. 26 27 50), across the river from Pl. Primo de Rivera. *Lista de Correos.* **Postal Code:** 09000. Open Mon.-Fri. 9am-2pm and 4-6pm, Sat. 9am-2pm.

Telephones: C. San Lesmes, 18, off Pl. España (around the side of the building). Open Mon.-Sat. 9am-1pm and 5-9pm. **City code:** 947.

Trains: Station is at the end of Av. Conde Guadalhorce (tel. 20 35 60), 15 min. across the river from Pl. Castilla. To: Madrid (8 per day, 4 hr., 1745ptas); Barcelona (4 per day, 8 hr., 8385ptas); Irún (10 per day, 5½ hr., 3400ptas); and León (7 per day, 2½ hr., 2640ptas). **RENFE** is at C. Moneda, 21 (tel. 20 91 31). Open Mon.-Fri. 9am-7pm, Sat. 9am-1pm.

Buses: C. Miranda, 4-6 (tel. 20 55 75), across the river from the Santa María Arch near Pl. Vega. To Madrid (3 per day, 3 hr., 1290ptas), Barcelona (3 per day, 7½ hr., 3710ptas), San Sebastián (2 per day, 3½ hr., 1440ptas), León (1 per day, 2½ hr., 1255ptas), and Santander (3 per day, 3 hr., 1200ptas).

Medical Assistance: Casa de Socorro, C. Conde de Vallellano, 4 (tel. 26 14 10), at C. Ramón y Cajal, near the post office.

Emergencies: Police, (tel. 091 or 092). **Ambulance,** (tel. 20 94 52).

Accommodations, Camping, and Food

Burgos has plenty of decent and fairly cheap rooms; look around Plaza José Antonio or Plaza de Vega.

Hostal Niza, C. General Mola (tel. 26 19 17), From Pl. Vega, follow C. Madrid and take the second left; the *hostal* is on the right. Worth the extra money. Forbidding staircase leads to genteel rooms and the perfect hot shower. Expensive laundry service. Reserve ahead. Singles 1700ptas. Doubles 2500ptas. Shower 200ptas.

Hostal Burgalés, C. San Augustín, 7-1 (tel. 20 92 62). Take calle Madrid across the train tracks to the major intersection; it's on the right. Singles 2160ptas. Doubles 2700ptas. Both with private bath.

Hostal Victoria, C. San Juan, 3 (tel. 20 15 42), off C. Laín Calvo, around the corner from the tourist office. Bright, assertive rooms. Singles 1200ptas. Doubles 2000ptas. Showers 150ptas.

Camping: Fuentes Blancas (tel. 22 10 16), on the river 3km east of town, near Cartuja de Miraflores monastery. Take the "Fuentes Blancas" (July-Aug. hourly 11am-9pm) from Pl.

Primo de Rivera; rest of year take bus #10. Ask the driver to drop you at the footbridge; cross it and walk 10 min. (375ptas per person, 325ptas per tent. Open April-Sept.)

Land-locked Burgos has created some fine meat dishes, and is especially known for its *cordero asado* (roast lamb), *picadillo de cerdo* (finely chopped pork), *caracoles* (snails), *morcilla de Burgos* (blood sausage), and *queso de Burgos* (a creamy farmer's cheese, excellent with honey). There is a market near Pl. España (open Mon.-Thurs. and Sat. 7am-3pm, Fri. 7am-3pm and 5:30-8pm). **Bodega Riojana,** Pl. Alonso Martínez, 9, serves *tapas* with a twist. (*Cazuelitas* (mini-casseroles) of *calamares* (squid) and *picadillo* for 175ptas. Open daily 9am-3pm and 7-10:30pm.) **Restaurante La Riojana,** C. Avellanos, 10, off Pl. Alonso Martínez, offers ½-chickens for 400ptas, pork loin for 500ptas and a huge *menú* for 750ptas. (Open Tues.-Sat. 10am-4pm and 7-11pm, Sun. 10am-4pm.) At **Bar La Flor,** C. Avellanos, 9, large 500ptas *platos combinados* and a good 750ptas *menú* compensate for the vertigo-inducing reflective windows. (Open daily 10:30am-5pm and 6:30-11pm.)

Sights and Entertainment

Until the end of time Burgos's landmark will be its **cathedral,** a majestic Gothic structure topped by two lacy stone spires. Built during the 13th and 15th centuries, it features exemplary Gothic and Plateresque architecture and artwork. Notice the glorious vaulting over the main crossing and the octagonal Capilla del Condestable, behind the main altar. The *capilla mayor,* in the center of the church, contains the tombs of El Cid and his wife, while the famous *Cofre del Cid,* the box in which his remains were found, hangs against a side wall. The cathedral **museum** counts among its treasures an auburn-haired *Magdalena* attributed to da Vinci. Ask the souvenir vendor in the back to show it to you. Before leaving, note the flycatcher peeking out of a window high up; on the hour he chews his prey. (Open daily 10am-1pm and 4-7pm. Admission to museum and some chapels 200ptas, students 75ptas.)

A few steps across Plaza de Santa María stands the **Arco de Santa María,** erected as a gateway to the walled city and later decorated with the busts of Emperor Carlos V and El Cid.

Past the 15th-century **Casa del Cordón** on C. Santander (where Columbus met with Fernando and Isabel, and Felipe el Hermoso expired after a trying game of handball), the **Museo Marceliano Santa María,** in the ruins of a monastery on Pl. San Juan holds the Burgalese painter's vaguely impressionist Castilian landscapes and portraits of his contemporaries. (Open Tues.-Sat. 10am-2pm and 5-8pm, Sun. 10am-2pm. Admission 25ptas.) Across the river, the **Museo Arqueológico** houses Gothic, Moorish, and Roman artifacts. (Open Tues.-Sat. 10am-1:30pm and 4:45-7:15pm, Sun. 10am-1pm. Admission 200ptas.)

The **Museo-Monasterio de las Huelgas Reales,** 1km west of Burgos, was a summer palace for Castilian monarchs and later a convent for Cistercian nuns. It contains royal sepulchers and a collection of medieval clothing, plus a Romanesque cloister. (Open Tues.-Sat. 11am-2pm and 4-6pm, Sun. 11am-2pm. Admission 300ptas, including tour in Spanish; students 50ptas.) The **Cartuja de Miraflores,** a Carthusian monastery exemplifying the Isabeline style, is 3km east of Burgos, about 5 minutes on foot from the Fuentes Blancas campground. Inside the church are the ornate tombs of Juan II and Isabel of Portugal, parents of Isabel the Catholic and her brother, Alfonso. Alfonso's mysterious death allowed Isabel to ascend to the throne; the rest is silence. (Open Mon.-Fri. 9:30am-1pm and 3:30-6pm, Sat.-Sun. noon-2pm and 3-6pm. Admission 100ptas, students 50ptas.) Take the Fuentes Blancas bus (1 per hr., 40ptas), which runs only in July and August. You can also walk along the riverside Paseo de la Quinta.

Engage in prime people-watching (a veritable sport in the city) at **Plaza José Antonio** and the elegant **Paseo del Espolón** a few hours before sunset. For drinking, elbow your way through the crowds on **Pl. Huerto del Rey,** behind the cathedral. The **Ferias y Fiestas,** in honor of patron saints Peter and Paul, lasts from June 23 to July 8, with parades, concerts, fireworks, and bullfights.

León

León still likes to remind the world that it had 24 kings before Castile even had laws. Though this blue and airy city reached its peak in the eleventh century, it's still remarkably appealing. One of the outstanding attractions is the colossal **cathedral,** a thirteenth-century Gothic extravaganza more than half surfaced in stained glass. (Open daily 8:30am-1:30pm and 4-7pm. Free.) The Romanesque **Basílica de San Isidoro** holds the remains of members of León's royal house in its **Panteón Real;** perfectly preserved frescoes from the twelfth century coat the ceiling above the tombs. (Open July-Aug. Mon.-Sat. 9am-2pm and 3:30-8pm, Sun. 9am-2pm; Sept.-June Tues.-Sat. 9am-1:30pm and 4-7pm, Sun. 9am-1:30pm. Admission 150ptas.)

The **Oficina de Turismo** is at Pl. Regla, 3 (tel. (987) 23 70 82), in front of the cathedral. (Open Mon.-Fri. 9am-2pm and 4-5:30pm, Sat. 10am-1pm.) The post office is beside the Jardín de San Francisco (open Mon.-Fri. 9am-2pm and 4-6pm.), and the **telefónica** is beside San Isidoro, on C. Torre, 13 (open Mon.-Fri. 9am-2pm and 5-10pm). The **Consejo de Europa (IYHF),** Paseo del Parque, 2 (tel. (987) 20 02 06), next to the bullring, offers newly renovated rooms and sports complex (750ptas, under 25 590ptas). Cheap *pensiones* dot Av. Roma, which branches to the left from the plaza across the river from the train station. On the right branch, Av. República de Argentina, **Fonda Condado,** at #28 (tel. 20 61 60) has airy rooms (singles 1000ptas; doubles 1600ptas). **Bar-Restaurante Gijón,** Alcázar de Toledo, 15, between Av. Roma and the main Av. Ordoño II, specializes in *carne guisada* (stewed meat), *callos* (tripe), and loin of pork. *(Menú* 750ptas; open Mon.-Sat. 10am-5pm and 9pm-midnight.) **Restaurante La Esponja,** Pl. Cid, 18, is a breezy place between the cathedral and the basilica. *(Menú* 650ptas outdoors or indoors. Open daily 1:30-4:30pm and 8-11:30pm.) For cheaper eats, try **La Cepedana,** C. Mariano D. Berrueta, 11, or its neighbors just off C. Generalísimo near the cathedral. All have *menús* for 600ptas.

Trains leave from across the river for Barcelona (4 per day, 9½-11 hr., 4475ptas), Madrid (7 per day, 4-5½ hr., 1975ptas), and A Coruña (3 per day, 7-8 hr., 2465ptas), among others. **Buses** to Madrid leave from C. Cardenal Lorenzana, 2, off Av. Roma (4 per day, 4½ hr., 1665ptas), and to Salamanca from Av. Madrid, off Parque de San Francisco (2 per day, 3 hr., 1025ptas).

Galicia (Galiza)

Frequently veiled by a misty drizzle, Galicia is a Celtic land where bleating *gaitas* (bagpipes) resonate among rolling hills. Narrow, pitted roads weave past stone-walled farms and slate-roofed fishing villages. Galicians maintain their own language, Galego, which is closer to Portuguese than to Castilian. Buses are infrequent, and hitching difficult, but the granite, slate-roofed cities, isolated soft-sand beaches, dense forests, and lively fishing villages will reward the extra effort richly.

Santiago de Compostela

When the dusty remains of St. James (Santiago) turned up more than 1100 years ago, this city became a major destination for pilgrimages. In 1130, an enterprising monk wrote the *Codex Calixtinus,* a sort of *Let's Go: Northern Spain,* which detailed the least dangerous routes, the best accommodations, and the safest drinking water along the way. Santiago's exquisite old city, a national monument, is preserved much as it was in the Middle Ages.

Orientation and Practical Information

Santiago de Compostela is in far northwestern Spain, 100km north of the Portuguese border; the Portuguese coastal rail line continues to Santiago and north to A Coruña. Coming from elsewhere in Spain, you may have to change at Ourense. From the train station, turn right on the top of the stairs and take Hórreo to **Plaza de Galicia;** it's one more block to Entrecalles, whence smaller streets lead to the cathedral.

Tourist Office: Turismo, Rúa del Villar, 43 (tel. 58 40 81), in the old town. A crucial map. Open Mon.-Fri. 9am-2pm and 4-7pm, Sat. 9am-2pm.

Budget Travel: Viajes TIVE, in the student service building on the university campus (tel. 59 61 87). Sells ISIC, InterRail and international train, bus, and plane tickets. Open Mon.-Fri. 9am-2pm.

Post Office: C. Franco (tel. 58 12 52), 2 blocks south of Rúa del Villar. Open Mon.-Fri. 9am-2pm and 4-6pm, Sat. 9am-noon. *Lista de Correos* Mon.-Fri. 9am-2pm. **Postal Code:** 15700.

Telephones: C. Bautizados, 13, off Pl. Toral in the old town. Open Mon.-Fri 10am-11pm, Sat. 10am-8pm, Sun. 11am-9pm. **City Code:** 981.

Trains: C. General Franco (tel. 59 60 50). To: Madrid (3 per day, 8-12 hr., 4500-6000ptas); A Coruña (11 per day, 1-1½ hr., 340ptas) and León (1 per day, 6½ hr., 1790ptas).

Buses: Estación Central de Autobuses, C. San Cayetano (tel. 58 77 00). From Pl. Galicia, take bus #10 (45ptas). Connections to all the *rías* and to Madrid (2 per day, 10½ hr., 4125ptas).

Laundromat: Lava-Express, at C. Alfredo Brañas and C. República Salvador. 475ptas per 4½kg. Open Mon.-Fri. 9:30am-2pm and 4-8:30pm, Sat. 9:30am-2pm.

Medical Assistance: Hospital General de Galicia, C. Galeras (tel. 58 78 11).

Police: Av. Rodrigo de Padrón (tel. 58 11 10). **Ambulance** (tel. 58 84 90). **Emergency** (tel. 091).

Accommodations, Camping, and Food

Bypass the hawkers at the train station and start your quest in the old town. Rúa del Villar, Calle Raiña, and Calle del Franco are excellent eating and sleeping strips. **Pensión Noya,** Rúa do Vilar, 13, has large, bright rooms and a beaming owner. (Hard-to-get singles 1200ptas. Doubles 1500ptas.) **Hospedaje Ramos,** C. Raiña, 18 (tel. 58 18 59), offers comfortable rooms above a good budget restaurant. (Singles 1100ptas, with bath 1300ptas. Doubles 1600ptas, with bath 1800ptas.) **Camping Santiago** (tel. 88 00 02) is the closest decent site, 5km away. There are buses to town, pools, and supermarkets. (375ptas per person plus 350ptas per tent. Open June 20-Sept. 20.)

Budget gastrocenters fill the old town; check the streets listed above as well as Calle Algalia Arriba. Try such Galician delights as *caldo galego* (a chunky vegetable broth), *pulpo a la galega* (octopus in orange sauce), and steamed mussels. Most *menús* cost about 600-800ptas. Galicians sup earlier than most Spaniards—don't wait until 11pm to find a place for dinner. **O'Sotano,** C. Franco, 8 (tel. 56 50 24), has hearty 750ptas *menús* popular with locals. (Open daily 11am-4:30pm and 9:30-11:30pm.) **Restaurante Abella,** C. Franco, 30 (tel. 58 29 81), serves up light *menús* for 650-800ptas, and *empanadas* (pastry stuffed with meat or fish) for 200ptas. (Open daily 8am-midnight, in bar when restaurant is closed.) An **open market** is held between Pl. San Félix and the Convent of San Agustín (Mon.-Sat. 8am-2pm).

Sights and Entertainment

The **catedral** is majestic, a harmonious meld of styles and eras beneath two soaring towers. Just inside the main entrance is the **Pórtico de la Gloria,** one of the outstanding ensembles of Romanesque sculpture in Europe. (Open daily 10am-7:30pm. Free.) The **Museo do Pobo Galego** (Museum of the Galician People), housed in the Monasterio de Santo Domingo, contains replicas of the *castros* (ancient Celtic ruins) from the nearby countryside. (Open Mon.-Sat. 10am-1pm and 4-7pm, Sun. 10am-1pm. Free.) A short jaunt from the center of town, the **Colexiata do Sar** has been falling down since it was built in the 12th century, since its supporting columns were deliberately set at odd angles. (Open Mon.-Sat. 10am-1pm and 4-7pm. Admission 100ptas.)

Nearly half of Santiago's population is made up of rowdy students itching to have a good time. Bars and pubs litter the old town and Calle Santiago de Chile. Santiago's **Fiesta** runs July 15-31, climaxing on July 25, St. James's Day. For two weeks, street musicians and haunting figures on stilts roam the streets.

Near Santiago de Compostela

Though Santiago may be the monarch of Galician cities, no landlocked settlement can reign over this region's rugged coastline. The *rías* (estuaries), settled by Celts from the north, are Spain's answer to Scotland's sea lochs. North of Santiago, the **Rías Altas** stretch their watery fingers into the land from the province of Lugo down to Cabo Finisterre. Shrouded in mist and prey to storms, even in summer, the upper *rías* attract fewer tourists than do other Spanish coastal regions, although their beaches are sublime and empty. On the way is **A Coruña,** the largest port and the administrative center of the Rías Altas. Well-linked by train and bus to the rest of Galicia, it makes an ideal base for exploration north, past the forested **Cabo Ortegal,** and south, to Cabo Fisterra. The **tourist office,** by the harbor at Dársena de la Marina (tel. (981) 22 18 12) details lodgings and dispenses bus and train schedules. (Open Mon.-Fri. 9am-2pm and 4-6pm, Sat. 10am-1pm; Oct.-June Mon.-Fri. 10am-1:30pm and 4:30-6pm.) West of Santiago, the lighthouse at **Cabo Fisterra** was once considered the end of the world. If you check out the crashing waves and howling winds, you'll be able to understand why.

The population and pollution both increase as you go south of Santiago, through the **Rías Baixas** and toward the major cities of Pontevedra and Vigo. Nevertheless, the water is warmer in the lower *rías,* and the beaches are more accessible than their northern counterparts. The old granite town of **Pontevedra** makes a good base for exploring the Rías Baixas, while **Vigo,** a fast-growing port, is the principal gateway into northern Portugal. If you spend a transit night here, try **Hostal Residencia,** the best of many *hostales* on the street. For an unforgettable repast, visit the **Pontobello Inn** in the heart of the old city. Ten trains per day chug from Vigo to Santiago, and three apiece to Porto and Viana do Castelo in Portugal.

Northern Spain

For ages, religious pilgrims on their way to Santiago de Compostela have crossed the French border into northern Spain for ages in search of spiritual knowledge. In this century, the area offers a haven for those of all faiths, whether you seek fulfillment in sun-worship, on a pair of skis, or in front of the fiery nostrils of a bewildered bull. The autonomous communities of Aragón, Navarra, and Euskadi (the Basque Country) all share a border with France, with Cantabria picking up where Euskadi leaves off along the North Atlantic coast. The Pyrenees loom along most of the border; use Jaca in Aragón as a base for mountain adventure. Out of the mountains in Navarra, Pamplona and its bulls need little introduction. Some of the most beautiful beaches in the world stretch along the Atlantic from San Sebastián to Santander (whence ferries leave for Plymouth, England), and the inland scenery and politics grow more complex in the restive Basque provinces.

The **Basques** have called Iberia home for longer than any other ethnic group, tenaciously fighting off all incursions. The three Basque provinces of Guipúzcoa (Gipuzkoa), Vizcaya (Bizkaia), and Alava (Araba), and their respective major cities—San Sebastián (Donostia), Bilbao (Bilbo), and Vitoria-Gasteiz, cozy up to

France on the Atlantic coast. A distinct culture and unique language (which linguists have been unable to relate conclusively to any other language in the world), combined with lingering resentment of the atrocities of the Nationalists during the Civil War, feed aspirations to greater autonomy. Most Basques wish to remain part of Spain, but the minority that does not, comprised of the terrorist group ETA and their political counterparts, Herri Batasuna (HB), is extremely vociferous. Pro-ETA posters and graffiti abound, but waning support and police crackdowns have reduced the violence that once plagued the tempestuous landscapes and industrial conglomerations of the Basque country. The lightning-fast sport of *pelota* (jai alai) was born here, and Basque cooking is famous for its richness and variety. *Bacalao a la vizcaína* (salt cod in a tomato sauce) and *chipirones en su tinta* (cuttlefish in its own ink) have become popular throughout the Iberian peninsula.

San Sebastián (Donostia)

San Sebastián is what Brigitte Bardot might have created if she had been God. Few beach towns in the world can offer all this: a beautiful crescent-shaped beach, an island, two tree-covered hillsides, and shaded riverside walks. This city 25km from France manages to be elegant without being snobby, a hugely popular tourist attraction without being touristy, and relaxed and tolerant, without being unsafe. The spectre of separatist tensions that haunted the city in years past appears to have retired to the less glamorous parts of the Basque Country, and your only real concern in this expensive city will be how to stretch your pesetas so you can stay longer than you had planned.

Orientation and Practical Information

San Sebastián is an ideal stopover on the way to or from France—all direct Madrid-Paris trains stop here. You'll need to know three areas: the neighborhood of the **Catedral del Buen Pastor,** the **Av. Libertad,** and the *barrio viejo* off Alameda del Boulevard. The first step is to cross the river by going over the bridge in front of the RENFE station. From there, go downstream one block, then left on C. San Martín, and you'll come to the *catedral.* The next bridge is Av. Libertad, which leads to the bay and waterfront. One more bridge takes you to Alameda del Boulevard; turn left and the *barrio viejo* is on your right as you head towards the bay. From the bus station at Pl. Pío XII, head downstream along Av. Sancho El Sabio and you'll hit the bridges (about 15 min.).

Tourist Offices: Centro de Atracción y Turismo, C. Reina Regente (tel. 48 11 66), where Alameda del Boulevard meets the bridge. Director Rafael Aguirre is the God of Information; his staff of angels is fluent in every European language. They'll help find a room and give you all the information you could ever want. (Open Mon.-Sat. 8am-8pm, Sun. 10am-1pm; Oct.-May Mon.-Sat. 9am-2pm and 3:30-7pm, Sun. 10am-1pm.)

Budget Travel: TIVE, C. Tomás Gros, 3 *bajo* (tel. 27 69 34). On the train station side of the river near the final bridge before the ocean, go one block down C. Miracruz and then go right. Open Mon.-Fri. 9am-2pm.

Currency Exchange: Banca Besné, C. Fuenterrabía, 4 (tel. 42 04 41), left off Av. Libertad heading towards the water. Open Mon.-Fri. 9:30am-1pm and 3:30-7pm, Sat. 9:30am-1pm and 3:30-6pm.

Post Office: C. Undaneta (tel. 46 49 14). Heading toward the water on Av. Libertad, go left on C. Fuenterrabía. *Lista de correos* (Poste Restante). Open Mon.-Fri. 9am-8pm, Sat. 9am-2pm. **Postal Code:** 20006.

Telephones: C. San Marcial, 29, off Av. Libertad. Open daily July-Aug. 9am-9:30pm, Sept.-June 9am-1:30pm and 3-9pm. **City code:** 943.

Trains: RENFE, Paseo de Francia (tel. 28 35 99). To: Madrid (5 per day, 6½ hr., 5425ptas); Barcelona (2 per day, 8-9 hr., 3500ptas); Irún (10 per day, 25 min., 90ptas); Pamplona (8 per day, 2-3 hr., 1245ptas); Burgos (10 per day, 3-5 hr., 1790ptas); Salamanca (3 per day, 7 hr., 2600ptas); Lisbon (1 per day, 16 hr., 6300ptas); and Paris (1 per day). From **Estación**

de Amara, Pl. Easo, 9 (tel. 45 01 31), 8 blocks left down C. Easo from Av. Libertad, trains go to Bilbao (8-11 per day, 3 hr., 535ptas) with connections to Guernica, and to Hendaya (every ½ hr. from 7:15am-9:15pm, 150ptas) with connections to Paris (11 per day, 6-7 hr., 7700ptas total).

Buses: from Pl. Pío XXII. To: Madrid (8 per day, 6 hr., 2915ptas); Barcelona (1 per day, 7 hr., 3535ptas); Pamplona (6 per day, 2¾ hr., 575ptas); Bilbao (9-16 per day, 1 hr., 770ptas); and Paris (a few times per week, 10 hr., 6275ptas). Buy tickets from the booths around Pl. Pío XII. **Interurbanos** goes to Irún (Mon.-Fri. 7:48am-10pm, every 12 min.) from C. Oquendo, 16.

Luggage Storage: In summer, the tourist office runs a facility on C. Easo on the way to Estación de Amara. (Open daily 8:30am-9pm, 125ptas per day.) In winter, **Bar Self-Service** behind the RENFE station runs an informal storage system.

Laundromat: Lavomatique, C. San Juan, 13 in *barrio viejo.* Open irregularly Mon.-Fri. 10am-2pm and 4-8pm, Sat.-Sun. 10am-2pm.

Medical Assistance: Casa de Socorro, C. Pedro Egaño, 8 (tel. 46 63 19).

Emergencies: Police (tel. 092). **Ambulance** (tel. 27 22 22, 21 46 00, and 21 51 64).

Accommodations and Camping

Lodgings are uniformly expensive (at least 2000ptas per person) and hard to find in the summer. Numerous *pensiones* and *hostales,* often two or more per stairway, surround the cathedral; crane your neck to spot signs two and three floors up. San Sebastián's old **IYHF hostel** was sacrificed to the expanding city stadium; it should be resurrected in 1992. Inquire at the tourist office. Sleeping on the beach, though illegal, is tolerated; if you must, sleep in groups to deter robbers. On the street running straight away from the cathedral doors, **Pensión La Perla,** C. Loyola, 10 (tel. 42 81 23), has wood floors; all rooms have balconies and bathrooms with showers. (Singles 2500ptas, doubles 3800ptas; Oct.-June 19 singles 2000ptas, doubles 3000ptas.) In the *barrio viejo,* look for places on and around C. Narrica, midway down Alameda del Boulevard. **Pensión San Lorenzo,** C. San Lorenzo, 2 (tel. 42 55 16), a right off C. Narrica has spartan but clean rooms, with bathtubs in the works. (Doubles 4000ptas, triples 6500ptas; Sept.-June 21 1000ptas per person, doubles 2500ptas.) Less crowded because it's on the train station side of the river, **Fonda Vicandi,** C. Iparraguirre, F (tel. 27 07 95) is sunnier indoors than you might think from outside. From Pl. Euskadi by the last bridge before the ocean, take C. Miracruz and turn right after 2 blocks. (Doubles 3000ptas; Oct.-June 2000ptas per person, doubles 2500ptas.) Camp at crowded **Camping Igueldo** (tel. 21 45 02; 375ptas per person; hot showers). Bus #16 (direction "Barrio de Igueldo-Camping") heads to the site from Alameda del Boulevard roughly hourly from 6:50am to 10:30pm (60ptas).

Food

The biggest bite out of your budget in San Sebastián will be for a bed, but restaurants will sink their teeth into your wallet too. The solution is to make a roving meal out of the *banderillas* and *pinchos,* tasty snacks of almost endless variety on the counters of the more than 600 bars in town. Help yourself and pay at the end (100-200ptas each). The *barrio viejo* with its many bars and *jatetxea* (restaurants) is the best hunting ground; start at **Bar Restaurante Alotza,** C. Fermín Calbetón, 7. For an excellent sit-down meal, **Zurriola Jatetxea,** C. Zabaleta, 9, offers an elegant 700ptas lunch *menú.* To get there, take Paseo de Colón left from Pl. Euskadi, near the bridge closest to the ocean on the train station side. (Open Mon.-Sat. 1-3:30pm.) For 32ch do-it-yourself food, the city's noted markets are held daily 8am-2pm and 5-7pm, one in the *barrio viejo* near the city tourist office, and another one block off Av. Libertad.

Sights and Entertainment

The most spectacular sight here is the bay, lined on the shore with arc-shaped *playas* of people. Don't show up before noon or after 5pm; all you will see is the sand. For a floodlight-enhanced nighttime view, take the cable car to the top of **Monte Igueldo.** (Runs June 15-Sept. 15 daily 10am-10pm; April-May daily 11am-8pm. 65ptas.) Take city bus #16 to get to the beginning of the ride at the base of the mountain. Closer to the city is **Monte Urgull,** at the tip of the peninsula; you can climb to its summit or walk the **Paseo Nuevo,** a wind-whipped road that rounds the peninsula. **Museo San Telmo,** with its fascinating collection of Basque artifacts and fine art, rests in an old Dominican monastery on Pl. Zuloaga, curiously ignored by tourists. You'll also find here a couple of tiny dinosaur skeletons, some stunningly beautiful El Grecos, and exhibitions of contemporary art. (Open Mon.-Sat. 9:30am-1:30pm and 3:30-7pm.)

Revelers fill the *barrio viejo,* especially **Calle Fermín Calbetón,** in early evening. An older crowd frequents the tiny huddle of bars south of the cathedral, at the intersections of **C. Reyes Católicos** and **C. Larramendi.** Two discos vie for supremacy: **Bataplán** and **La Perla,** both on beachfront Paseo de la Concha (and open 1-5:30am). The city hosts an **International Jazz Festival** in the third week of July (tel. 42 16 64 for info). The third week in August is **Grand Week,** which includes a fireworks festival. The **International Film Festival** in the second half of September brings famous directors and actors to town (tel. 48 12 12 for info).

Pamplona

If casualties are any measure, Pamplona's **Fiesta de San Fermín,** a.k.a. **The Running of the Bulls** (July 6-14), is the best party in Europe. The festival honors Pamplona's patron saint, San Fermín, who was martyred by being dragged through the streets by bulls. Immortalized by Hemingway in *The Sun Also Rises,* the *fiesta* goes non-stop, all week long, with countless parades and rituals. A rocket fires each morning at 8am, sending red- and white-clad Pamplonians, both real and wanna-be, careening down a narrow, barricaded course through the streets, trying to run with the bulls to the Plaza de Toros without becoming the next patron-martyr of the city. Most gorings have taken place at the mouth of the stadium, where beef and *machismo* must squeeze through a narrow opening. Women and children can view this chaotic finish and the ensuing bullfight in their two free, reserved sections of the stadium. Others can try to find a 1000ptas ticket. Recent years have seen relatively light casualties, but the non-braindead will have enough thrills without running, especially at night when the thinnest veneer of civilization dissolves in waves of alcohol. There is singing in the bars, dancing in the alleyways, and an unbelievable fest in the Plaza del Castillo and on Calle Navarrería. At 11pm, fireworks light the sky and at midnight, rock-and-roll shakes the streets.

You will not sleep in a bed in Pamplona during the fiesta unless you have a fairy godmother. Prices double and triple anyway. The **tourist office,** C. Duque de Ahumada, 3 (tel. (948) 22 07 41), off Pl. Castillo, will help you find a private home (starting around 2500ptas per person) and posts critical info on currency exchange, public baths, and buses to campsites. (Open daily 10am-7pm; Oct.-June Mon.-Sat. 10am-2pm and 4-7pm, Sun. 10am-3pm. Line starts no later than 9:30am during *sanfermines.)* Bedless travelers should store their packs at the bus station, Av. Conde Oliveto, 2 (150-170ptas per day); popular sleeping spots are the lawns of Pl. Fueros and the Ciudadela, both to the right out of the bus station ticket area. An unnumbered private bus runs four times per day to nearby **Camping Ezcaba** (tel. (948) 33 03 15), which fills up just as fast during the fest. (340ptas per person, per tent, per car. Open June-Sept.) The *fiesta* accomodations scene is much tamer in nearby Olite or Estella, both within an hour by bus.

When it recovers from *sanfermines* and its city-wide hangover, Pamplona reveals the elegance of its broad and airy streets and historic alleyways. Nightlife is still strong in the **Casco Viejo** area, and the recently renovated **Museo de Navarra** features remarkably complete Roman mosaics and Gothic murals. (Open Tues.-Sat. 10am-2pm and 5-7pm, Sun. 10am-2pm. Admission 200ptas.)

Calle San Nicolás and Calle San Gregorio (just off Pl. Castillo) are the best places to look for food. Also try the packed **Restaurante Lanzale,** C. San Lorenzo, 31 (tel. (948) 22 10 71), for its gigantic 700ptas *menú.* (Open Sept. 10-Aug. 20 Mon.-Sat. 1:30-3:30pm and 9-11pm.) When the bulls stop running, budget accommodations are easy to find along C. San Gregorio and C. San Nicolás. Off this strip is **Casa de Huéspedes Santa Cecilia,** C. Navarrería, 17 (tel. (948) 22 22 30), with well-kept rooms behind a deteriorating façade (1500ptas per person). **Hostal Ibarra,** C. Estafeta, 85 (tel. (948) 22 06 06), is 100m from the Pl. Toros (doubles 2500-3300ptas).

Bus #9 connects the train station (tel. (948) 13 02 02) with the end of Paseo de Sarasate (20 min., 60ptas), but connections via train from Pamplona are sparse and awkward. More than 20 bus lines offer much quicker service from the station on Av. Conde Oliveto to Madrid, Zaragoza, San Sebastián, and Jaca, and the only public transport into the Navarrese Pyrenees.

Jaca

"Finally, the Pyrenees—Jaca '98," say all the bumper stickers and brochures, but it is not to be. Despite its prime location and winter sports facilities, Jaca failed in its bid to bring the Winter Olympics to these mountains. Some locals don't mind a bit, and this friendly town—Olympic stature or not—is a great base for year-round mountain adventure. Get to Jaca by bus if you can (2-3 connections per day to Sabiñánigo and Zaragoza, tel. (974) 22 70 11), since buses bring you right to the center of town on Av. Jacetania, across a plaza from the main drag, **C. Mayor.** Train travelers should hustle off for the shuttle that runs to town or face a substantial trek down Av. Juan XXIII. One to three trains per day head to Madrid, Zaragoza and Sabiñánigo; three per day go north to Canfranc for connections to France.

The **tourist office,** Av. Regimiento Galicia, 2 (tel. (974) 36 00 98), past the walled fortress on the way into town from the train station, is your source for maps and hiking info. (Open Mon.-Fri. 9am-1:30pm and 4:30-7pm, Sat. 10am-1pm and 5-8pm, Sun. 10am-2pm; Sept.-June Mon.-Fri. 9am-1:30pm and 4:30-7pm, Sat. 10am-1pm and 5-7pm.) Rooms in Jaca are inexpensive and easy to find. Your only difficulties might occur during the raucous **Festival of San Juan and San Pedro,** June 24-29, and the **Festival Folklórico de los Pirineos** held from late July to mid-August during odd-numbered years. *Hostales* and *pensiones* line C. Mayor and the streets off it. The cheapest beds in town are at the **Albergue Juvenil de Vacaciones (IYHF),** Av. Perimetral, 6 (tel. (974) 36 05 36), where you get that summer-camp atmosphere in communal rooms (900ptas, nonmembers 2000ptas). It's next to the *Pista de Hielo* (hockey rink), down the stairs at the edge of town furthest from the train station. Another **IYHF hostel** is 15km north in Villanúa (tel. (974) 37 80 16) on the rail line to Canfranc. The best campground is **Peña Oroel** (tel. (974) 36 02 15), 3½km down the road to Sabiñánigo. Its wooded grounds have first rate facilities (445ptas per person, per tent, and per car. Open Holy Week and mid-June to mid-Sept.). **Camping Victoria** (tel. (974) 36 03 23), 1½km from Jaca towards Pamplona, has a groovy view of the foothills (375ptas per person and per car, 325ptas per tent). Most of Jaca's good, cheap restaurants line C. Mayor. Try the dining rooms below hotels there, or opt for the dessert and sandwich croissants at **Croissanterie Cafetería Demi-Lune,** next to the tourist office (sandwiches 140-220ptas, desserts 90-115ptas).

Undoubtedly the most interesting thing to see *in* Jaca is the pentagonal fort known as the **Ciudadela,** on the edge of town near the tourist office. (Daily tours in Spanish, 11am-noon and 5-6pm. Free.) The *real* things to see are the mountains and valleys that surround Jaca. A car is nearly indispensable, and Jaca is one of the few places those under 21 can rent one—take your international license to **Jaca-**

car, in the Aldecar building, Av. Jacetania, 60 (tel. (974) 36 07 81; 2500ptas per day, 20ptas per km). Buses will get you places too, but slowly.

More than worth the transport hassle is the **Parque Nacional de Ordesa y Monte Perdido,** northeast of Jaca near the French border. The stunning stacks of striated stone carved by the Rio Arazas make scenery and hiking here incredible. It's an 8km hike or hitch from **Torla,** the closest town, which you can reach traveling bulk rate with the mail from Sabiñánigo. To spend the night, hike to the shelters within the park, or get the same feel at Torla's **Refugio L'Atalya,** C. Francia, 45 (tel. (974) 48 60 22) for 800ptas per night. If you want your own room, go farther up Torla's only crossroad, where **Fonda Ballarin,** C. Capuvita, 11 (tel. (974) 48 61 72) runs about 1200ptas for singles, 2100ptas for doubles. Get hiking maps and information about the park from the ICONA office in Torla on C. Francia (tel. (974) 48 62 12; open 8am-3pm), until the info center at the entrance to the park opens.

Catalonia (Catalunya)

A fertile land hemmed in by the Pyrenees and the lagoons of the Río Ebro delta, Catalonia early on became one of the Roman Empire's most privileged provinces, and eventually achieved independence from the Franks in 874 AD. As Spain's American empire was opened to trade with all Spanish cities in the second half of the 18th century, Catalonia rapidly developed into one of Europe's premier manufacturing centers (chiefly of textiles). Industrial expansion continued through the 19th century, underpinning a flowering of the arts and sciences—producing architects like Antonio Gaudí and later painters like Joan Miró—that came to be called the Catalan Renaissance.

After fighting on the losing side in the Spanish Civil War, Catalonia lost its autonomy in 1939; instruction in the Catalan language was suppressed everywhere but in the universities, and publication in Catalan was limited to specialized areas. Since the return of democracy in the 1970s, Catalan literature, theatre, television, film, and radio in Catalan have flourished again. The language (which is not a dialect of Spanish; rather, dialects of it are spoken in València and the Balearic Islands) is once again official in Spain, and you will see it everywhere. Nevertheless, almost everyone is bilingual in Castilian.

Catalans like to see themselves as unusually industrious (*"El Català de les pedres fa pa,"* i.e., the Catalan can make bread out of stones); perhaps their greatest gift, however, is self-promotion, most recently apparent in the campaign to obtain the '92 Olympics. Now that Catalans by and large control their own affairs, some intellectuals worry that the imposition of Catalan in institutions such as the universities is discouraging talented Spaniards elsewhere from teaching, studying, or doing research here, effectively sealing off the principality from the wider world. Not a few note in dismay how post-war Madrid has displaced Barcelona as the country's leading financial and manufacturing center, and more recently challenged Barcelona's preeminence in publishing and high fashion.

Barcelona

For the past six years, the phrase *"Barcelona, posa't guapa"* ("Barcelona, make yourself pretty") has been the battle cry of this Mediterranean city as it unleashed a flurry of construction and urban facelifting; the city now stands ready to dazzle the world as the host of the 1992 Summer Olympics (July 25-Aug. 9). Although the games will quickly come and go, Barcelona will undoubtedly continue to be one of the most inviting and cosmopolitan cities in Europe. Renowned for its architecture (and innovative modern planning), ranging from Gothic to the wildly imaginative *modernismo* of the early 20th century, Barcelona also sports a wealth of cul-

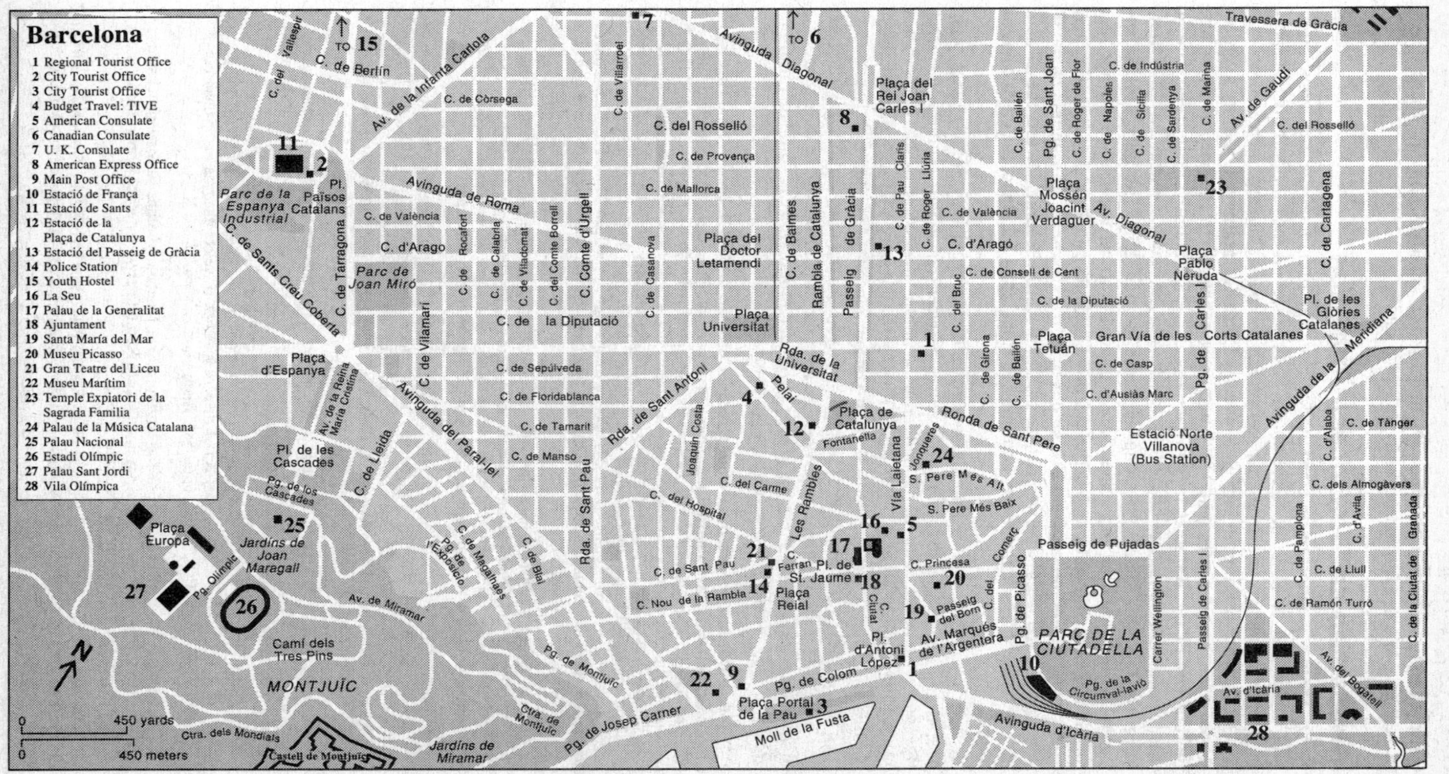
Barcelona
1 Regional Tourist Office
2 City Tourist Office
3 City Tourist Office
4 Budget Travel: TIVE
5 American Consulate
6 Canadian Consulate
7 U. K. Consulate
8 American Express Office
9 Main Post Office
10 Estació de França
11 Estació de Sants
12 Estació de la Plaça de Catalunya
13 Estació del Passeig de Gràcia
14 Police Station
15 Youth Hostel
16 La Seu
17 Palau de la Generalitat
18 Ajuntament
19 Santa María del Mar
20 Museu Picasso
21 Gran Teatre del Liceu
22 Museu Marítim
23 Temple Expiatori de la Sagrada Familia
24 Palau de la Música Catalana
25 Palau Nacional
26 Estadi Olímpic
27 Palau Sant Jordi
28 Vila Olímpica
450 yards
450 meters
MONTJUÏC
PARC DE LA CIUTADELLA
Avinguda Diagonal
Gran Vía de les Corts Catalanes
Les Rambles
Via Laietana
Passeig de Gràcia
Rambla de Catalunya
Plaça de Catalunya
Plaça d'Espanya
Plaça Universitat
Estació Norte Villanova (Bus Station)
Moll de la Fusta

tural offerings in music, the fine arts, and theater. By night, the city doesn't miss a beat and keeps *a la marcha* until well past dawn.

Orientation and Practical Information

On Spain's Mediterranean coast 200km from the French border and five to eight hours due east of Madrid, Barcelona is Spain's second most important transport hub; most traffic to and from the rest of Europe passes through here.

Getting your bearings in Barcelona is easy. **Plaça de Catalunya** is the city's center. From here, the Rambles and Via Laietana run straight to the harbor. From the harbor end of the Rambles as you face towards Pl. Catalunya, **Montjüic,** site of the Olympic stadium, rises up off to your left, and the newly constructed **Vila Olímpica** (the Olympic Village) is along the shore to your right. The **Barri Gòtic,** centered on the cathedral and **Plaça Sant Jaume,** lies in between. On the other side of Plaça de Catalunya, Gran Via de les Corts Catalanes cuts broadly across the city, marking the beginning of the **Eixample,** which extends to Avinguda Diagonal. Passeig de Gràcia cuts between these two boulevards, leading toward the **Gràcia** quarter. Beyond Gràcia the city continues to slope up to **Tibidabo,** the city's highest point.

Watch your personal belongings when walking around Barcelona—guard your wallet and avoid carrying a purse. The area between Plaça Sant Jaume and Carrer Escudellers can be particularly dangerous at night; steer clear of the Barri Xinès side of the Rambles at night. The Plaça Reial gets especially wild with drunks, prostitutes and thieves. At the central train station, clutch your bags tightly.

Place names in Barcelona are given primarily in Catalan; most public instructions are available in both languages. When looking for an address, make sure you have it in the language of your map (e.g., *Carrer del Banys Nous* is Catalan for *Calle de los Baños Nuevos). Let's Go* lists all names in Catalan.

Tourist Offices: Gran Via de les Corts Catalanes, 658 (tel. 301 74 43), 2 blocks from Passeig de Gràcia near Pl. Catalunya. Information on all parts of Spain. Open Mon.-Fri. 9am-7pm, Sat. 9am-2pm. Branch offices at **Estació Sants-Central** (tel. 490 91 71), opposite RENFE information (open daily 8am-8pm); and the **airport** (tel. 478 47 04; open daily 9:30am-8pm). **Estació França** will have a tourist office when it reopens in May 1992. During the Olympics each venue will have a tourist office. Also student information at **Centre d'informació Per a Joves,** C. Avinyó, 7 (tel. 301 12 21). Collect maps and tips. (Open Mon.-Fri. 10am-2pm and 4-8pm). **Barcelona Information** answers any question (tel. 010; open 24 hrs., English operators upon request.)

Budget Travel: TIVE-Officina de Tourisme Juvenil, C. de Gravina, 1 (tel. 302 06 82), a block from Plaça de la Universitat, off C. Pelai. Check here first for cheap buses and flights, student IDs, and youth hostel cards, but bring a book for the wait. Least crowded before 10am. Open Sept.-July Mon.-Fri. 9am-1pm and 4-5:30pm; Aug. Mon.-Fri. 9am-2pm.

Consulates: U.S., Via Laietana, 33, 4th floor (tel. 319 95 50). Open Mon.-Fri. 9am-noon and 3-5pm. **Canada,** Via Augusta, 125 (tel. 209 06 34). Open Mon.-Fri. 9am-1pm. **U.K.,** Av. Diagonal, 477 (tel. 322 21 51). Open Mon.-Fri. 9am-1pm and 3:15-4:15pm; Oct.-May Mon.-Fri. 9:30am-1:30pm and 4-5pm. **Australia,** Gran Via Carles III, 98 (tel. 330 94 96). Open Mon.-Fri. 10am-noon.

Currency Exchange: Viatges Maisans, on Rambles, 134 (tel. 318 72 16) has a 2% commission charge on checks and 1% on bills. Open Mon.-Fri. 9am-1:30pm and 4:30-7pm. Train stations and airport exchanges open daily 8am-10pm.

American Express: Passeig de Gràcia, 101 (tel. 217 00 70), at Carrer Rosselló. Metro: Diagonal (L3, L5). 24-hr. multi-lingual ATM dispenses Amex travelers cheques or Spanish currency. Open Mon.-Fri. 9:30am-6pm, Sat. 10am-noon.

Post Office: Pl. Antoni López, at the bottom of Via Laietana. Stamps (in basement) sold Mon.-Sat. 8:30am-10pm, Sun. 10am-noon. Poste Restante at window #17 open Mon.-Fri. 9am-9pm, Sat. 9am-2pm. **Postal Code:** 08002.

Telephones: C. de Fontanella, 4, right off Pl. Catalunya. Come before 2pm. Open Mon.-Sat. 8:30am-9pm. Also at Estació Sants-Central. Open daily 7:45am-10:45pm. **City Code:** 93.

Flights: Airport at El Prat de Llobregat (tel. 370 10 11), 12km away. Trains to and from Estació Sants-Central every ½ hr. 6am-10:30pm (15 min., 175ptas). Late arrivals can take Bus EN to the city every ½ hr. 10:15pm-2:40am (30 min., 85ptas).

Trains: In May 1992 **Estació França** is scheduled to re-open and will serve as the terminus and origin of all international trains to and from Barcelona. Until then, Sants will serve as the domestic and international hub. **Sants-Central** (tel. 322 41 42), uptown at Pl. Països Catalans (Metro: L3, L5). To: Paris (3 *rápidos* per day, 14 hr., 10,500ptas); Madrid (3 *rápidos* per day, 10 hr., 4700ptas); Seville (3 per day, 13 hr., 8650ptas); Nice (one *rápido* per day at 7:40pm, 12 hr., 6500ptas), continuing to Rome (11,000ptas). **RENFE** information at ticket booths 24, 26, and 28 (24-hr. tel. 490 02 02). Open daily 6:30am-10:30pm. **Information Office** next to the telephone office in the station. Open 6:30am-9pm.

Buses: Iberbus, Paral-lel, 116 (tel. 242 33 00). To: London (1 per day, 25 hr., 13,000ptas); Paris (1 per day, 15 hr., 9950ptas). **Enatcar,** Estació del Nord, (tel. 245 25 28). To: Madrid (2 per day, 12 hr., 4200ptas); València (10 per day, 8 hr., 1995ptas), Seville (1 per day, 16 hr., 7140ptas). **Julia,** Pl. Universitat, 12 (tel. 317 04 76). To: Lisbon (Wed. and Sun., 20 hr., 9375ptas). **Sarfa,** Pl. Duc de Medinaceli (tel. 318 94 34), near the harbor, has numerous buses to the Costa Brava.

Ferries: Estació Maritima (tel. 301 25 08). Metro: Drassanes. **Transmediterránea,** Via Laietana, 2 (tel. 319 82 12). Open Mon.-Fri. 9am-1pm and 5-7pm, Sat. 9am-noon.

Public Transportation: Tel. 336 00 00. Five **Metro** lines cover the entire metropolitan area. Plaça de Catalunya is the system hub. Bus and metro rides cost 75ptas, Sat.-Sun. 85ptas. A **T-1 card** allows you 10 rides on bus and metro (450ptas); a **T-2** allows you 10 rides on metro only (400ptas). Both available at any metro entrance. *Guía del Transport Públic* (transit system maps) are free at tourist offices. Metro system runs Mon.-Thurs. 5am-11pm, Fri.-Sat. 5am-1am, Sun. 6am-midnight. Special *Nitbus* service covers the hours when the Metro is closed.

Taxis: Tel. 490 22 22 or 330 08 04. 225ptas for 6 min., then 75-80ptas per km (Mon.-Fri. 10pm-6am and Sat.-Sun. 24 hrs.).

Hitchhiking: Those hitching north to France (A17 via La Junquera) take bus #62 from Pl. Tetuán (on Gran Via) to Av. Meridiana, beyond Pl. Glóries. Those heading to València (A7) or Madrid (A2) catch the green metro to the Zona Universitaria at the southern end of Av. Diagonal; the *autopista* access starts near here. Hitching on the *autopista* (A) is illegal; get your ride before entering the toll road. **Barnastop,** C. Pintor Fortuny, 21, 2nd floor (tel. 318 27 31), matches drivers with riders for a commission of 3ptas per km (4ptas per km on highway).

Luggage Storage: Estació Central Sants train station, 200ptas per day. Open 6:30am-11pm. **Estació Maritim Internacional** at the port, 200ptas per day. Open 8am-3pm. **Sarfa Bus Co.,** Pl. Duc de Medinacelli, 4 (off Pg. Colom), 150ptas. Open 8am-8:15pm. **Alsina Graells Bus Terminal,** Ronda Universitat, 4.40ptas. Open 9am-1:30pm and 4-8pm. Estació França, when it reopens in May 1992.

Laundromat: Lavandería Rambles, C. de Remelleres, 13, reached from C. Bonsuccés, off the Rambles. Wash and dry 800ptas. Open Mon.-Fri. 9am-2pm and 5-8pm, Sat. 9am-2pm; July-Sept. mornings only.

Swimming Pool: Piscina Les Corts, Trav. de les Corts (tel. 239 41 78), 6 blocks from Sants station. 185ptas, Sun. 235ptas. Open June 15-Sept. 15 Sun.-Fri. 10am-4pm.

Rape Crisis: Informacions i Urgencies de Les Dones, C. Comerç 44 (tel. 319 00 42). English-speaking.

Gay Center: Front d'Alliberament Gai de Catalunya (FAGC), Villarroel, 62 (tel. 318 43 55). **Lesbian Center:** Gran Via de les Corts Catalanes, 549 (tel. 323 33 07).

Pharmacy: Pg. de Gràcia, 71 (tel. 215 70 74). Open 24 hrs.

Medical Assistance: Hospital Clínico, C. Casanova, 143 (tel. 323 14 14).

Emergencies: Municipal Police (tel. 091), National Police (tel. 092). Station specializing in tourist-related cases at Rambles, 43, across from Plaça Reial. **Ambulance** (tel. 300 20 20).

Accommodations and Camping

Barcelona's youth hostels improve the further you go from the center. Cheap hotels abound in the narrow streets around the Rambles, but some are heinous. Rooms in the Eixample are likely to be more habitable as well as more expensive. Our listings fill up in a flash during summer, so call ahead. The Barcelona tourist board is considering setting up temporary shelters in University dorms and tent-covered soccer fields for the two weeks during the Olympics. These plans are by no means etched in stone, but are worth asking about at the tourist office when you arrive. Expect a 10 to 15% increase on the prices listed here, and up to 30% around Olympics time.

Hostels

Hostal Verge de Montserrat (IYHF), Passeig Nostra Senyora de Coll, 41-51 (tel. 213 86 33), beyond Park Güell. Take bus #28 from Pl. Catalunya. Worth the 20-min. commute. A renovated neo-Moorish villa overlooking the city, full of colored tiles and stained glass. Curfew midnight. Members only, 770ptas per person, over 26 1120ptas. Sheets 360ptas. Breakfast included. 3-day max. stay.

Hostal Pere Tarrés (IYHF), C. Numancia, 149-151 (tel. 410 23 16). Metro: Les Corts (L3) or Sants (L3, L5). From Sants, exit to Plaça Països Catalans; turn left on Numancia; the hostel is a 15-min. walk away. Quiet, for a hostel. Kitchen facilities. 3-day max. stay. Open daily 8-10am and 4-11:30pm. No curfew. 750ptas per person, nonmembers 1100ptas. Breakfast included.

Hostal de Joves, Passeig de Pujades, 29 (tel. 300 31 04), just outside the Ciutadella park. Metro: Marina (L1), then follow Av. de la Meridiana south to its end. Sterile but satisfactory 2, 4, and 6-person rooms. Reception open daily 8-10am and 1pm-midnight. Curfew midnight. 560ptas. Sheets 100ptas. Breakfast 100ptas. Kitchen and washboard.

Pensions

Hostal Maritima, Rambles, 4, (tel. 302 31 52). Metro: Drassanes (L3). On the port end of the Rambles across from the metro station exit, follow the signs to the Wax Museum next door. Quiet, clean, and spacious rooms in a central and easily accessible location. Singles 1500ptas. 2-4 bed rooms 1300ptas per person. Shower included. Laundry 700ptas.

Casa de Huéspedes Mari-Luz, C. Palau, 4 (tel. 317 34 63). Metro: Liceu (L3). Walk 1 block towards the water down the Rambles and hang a left at McDonald's onto C. Ferran; take your 3rd right (C. D'Avigyó), your 2nd left (C. Cervantes) and finally your 1st right onto C. Palau. Not elegant, but Mari-Luz and Fernando have proved generous hosts to many a haggard *Let's Go* traveler. **Pensión Fernando,** C. Vella de Remedio, 4 (tel. 301 79 93). Metro: Liceu (L3). Fourth left off C. Ferián coming from the Rambles. Also run by Mari-Luz and Fernando. Just as nice. Both offer singles to quints at 1200ptas per person. Shower included.

Hostal Canaletas, Rambles, 133, (tel. 301 56 30), just off Pl. Catalunya next to Nuria Restaurant. Metro: Catalunya (L1, L3). Sunken but cozy mattresses in an unbeatable location. Singles to quads 1200ptas per person. **Pensión Noya** (tel. 301 48 31) is 2 floors down from Canaletús with lumpier beds and a 3am curfew. Singles 1500ptas. Doubles to quads 1200ptas per person. Shower included at both.

Hostal-Residencia Pintor, C. Gignás, 25 (tel. 315 47 08), by the post office and close to Estació França. Metro: Jaume I (L4). Big, airy and colorful rooms, most with balconies. Genial management. Singles and doubles 1170ptas. **Hostal Marmó** (tel. 315 42 08), 2 floors below Pintor with similar rooms. Singles 1200ptas. Doubles 2200ptas. Showers 200ptas.

Hostal Levante, Baixada San Miguel, 2 (tel. 317 95 65). Metro: Jaume I (L4). From Via Laietana down C. Jaume I, left at the Ajuntament into Pl. San Miguel. Quiet and airy with beautiful wood interior. Singles 1500ptas. Doubles 2500ptas. Triples 3600ptas. Shower included.

Pensión Segura, Junta de Comerç, 11 (tel. 302 51 74). Metro: Liceu (L3), then walk down the Rambles towards the water; turn right on C. Hospital and then first left at Pl. Sant Augusti. Newly renovated with a huge central patio ideal for *siestas* in the sun. Singles 1750ptas. Doubles 2700ptas. Triples 4100ptas. Shower included. Breakfast 375ptas.

Hostal Lausanne, Av. Portal de L'Angel, 24 (tel. 302 11 39). Metro: Catalunya (L1, L3), then head towards the El Corte Inglés department store and take your first right. Clean, bright rooms and a terrace out back for catching the evening breeze. Singles 1600ptas. Doubles 2400ptas. Shower included.

Pensión Bienestar, C. Quintona, 3 (tel. 318 72 83). Metro: Liceu (L3). Turn left at McDonald's and then take second left. Puny and lackluster rooms with high ceilings. Amiable, vigilant owners. Singles to quads 1500ptas per person. Shower included.

Residencia Australia, Ronda Universitat, 11 (tel. 317 41 77). Metro: Universitat (L1) or Pl. Catalunya (L1, L3). Barcelona's most sought-after budget hotel, maybe because of the ceiling fans. Singles 1800ptas. Doubles 2800ptas, with bath 3600ptas.

Pensión Venecia, C. Junta de Comerç, 13 (tel. 302 61 34). Metro: Liceu (L3). Take Carrer de Hospital off the Rambles at Pl. Boquería and then your third left. Dark area at night. Fresh paint, shining floors. Singles 2000ptas. Doubles 2800ptas. 1000ptas for each extra bed. Showers included.

Pensión L'Isard, C. Tallers, 82 (tel. 302 51 83), off Pl. Universitat. Metro: Universitat (L1). New mattresses and bathrooms in a great location that quiets down at night. Singles 1700ptas. Doubles 3000ptas. Shower included.

Pensión Vicente/Líder, Rambla Catalunya, 84 (tel. 215 19 23). Metro: Pg. de Gràcia (L3, L4). On one of Barcelona's most expensive shopping streets where it intersects with C. Mallorca. Small and spartan quarters off a spacious living room. Singles and doubles 1500ptas per person. Shower included.

Hostal-Residencia Oliva, Passeig de Gràcia, 32 (tel. 317 50 87). Metro: Passeig de Gracia (L3, L4) above the *Galas* clothes store. Beautiful *modernista* elevator ports you to slick Rooms With a View. Singles 1900ptas. Doubles 2500ptas, with showers 4240ptas. Showers included.

Pensión San Medín, Carrer Gran de Gràcia, 125 (tel. 217 30 68). On a main street running between the Fontanna and Lesseps metro stops (both L3). Classiest rooms in Barcelona's residential area of Gràcia. Singles 1500ptas. Doubles 2700ptas. Showers 200ptas.

Hostal Dalí, C. Boquería, 12, (tel. 318 55 80), Metro: Liceu (L3). From the metro walk down the Rambles to Pl. Boquería and turn left down C. Boquería. No drooping watches, only sagging beds in the rooms and slouching couches in the TV room downstairs. Singles 1600ptas. Doubles 2500ptas, with bath 3200ptas. 1400ptas each additional person. Shower included. Usually a room open. The same goes for **Pensión Europa,** C. Boquería, 18 (tel. 318 76 20). 1300ptas. Shower included.

Camping: Cala-Gogó-El Prat, (tel. 379 46 00), towards the airport in Prat de Llobregat, is a first-class site with plenty of trees and its own beach. Take bus #605 from Pl. Espanya; at the end of the run in Prat, board bus #604 to the beach. (430ptas per person, tent included. Open March-Nov. 30). Just south of El Prat are three first-class sites in Vildecans accessible by bus L93 from Pl. Universitat and L90 from Pl. Goya. **El Toro Bravo** (tel. 658 12 50) is open year-round and has its own nudist section. (440ptas per person and per tent). **Filipinas** (tel. 658 28 95; 440ptas per person and tent; open year-round) and **La Ballena Alegre** (tel. 658 05 04; 350ptas per person, 700ptas per tent; open May 15-Sept. 30) are also first-class sites another km down the road.

Food

In most Barcelona restaurants *comida* (dinner) is between 1 and 4pm and *cena* (evening supper) is between 8 and 11pm. The average *menú* includes two courses, bread, drink, and dessert for around 800ptas—much cheaper than any scummy fast-food franchise. *Platos combinados* (combination plates) are one-course specialties without drink or dessert for around 500ptas. *Tapas* bars are not very common but do make for economical snacking; for sweet teeth, *pastelerías* and *Frigo*-brand ice cream vendors are omnipresent (treats under 150ptas). The Barri Gòtic and the area between the Rambles and Ronda Sant Antoni is your happiest hunting ground for restaurants. "La Boquería," or the **Mercat de Sant Josep,** just off Rambla Sant Josep, 89, is Barcelona's choice market. (Open Mon.-Sat. 8am-2:30pm and 5-8pm.)

Restaurante Riera, Carrer Joaquim Costa, 30, off Ronda de Sant Antoni near Pl. Universitat. Full 3-course meal with drink and homemade *flan* an incredible 465ptas. Open Sept.-July Sun.-Fri. 1-4pm and 8:30-11pm.

Restaurante Biocenter, C. Pintor Fortuny, 24, off the Rambles. Vegetarians gobble the *plato combinado* (500ptas), a small portion of any dish plus all the salad you can balance on your plate. Open Mon.-Sat. 1-4:30pm.

Restaurante Bidasoa, C. En Serra, 21, in the Barri Gòtic. Take C. Josep Anselm Clave off Plaça Portal de la Pau at the port and then your third left. Nifty memorabilia hangs from the walls and tempting local fare at the tables. Tremendously good fish. Full meals under 700ptas. Open Sept.-July Tues.-Sun. 1-4pm and 8pm-11:30am.

El Quatre Gats, C. Montsió, 3-5 (tel. 302 41 40). Metro: Uriquinaona (L1), then down Via Laietana; and at the first fork on the right side, bear right down C. Magdalenes to C. Montsió. The restaurant where Picasso and his café-intellectual minions gabbed and hung out endlessly still has their paintings on the walls (Picasso was known to foot the bill with a quick, agile sketch). Unless you draw like him, the *menú* is 1000ptas. Open Mon.-Sat. 1-4pm and 8-11:30pm.

Restaurante Cafetería Nervión, C. de la Princesa, 2 (tel. 315 21 03). Metro: Jaume I (L4). On the corner of Princesa and Via Laietana across from Pl. L'Angel. A popular local diner with a 650ptas *menú* and a slew of *platos combinados.* Open Sept.-July Mon.-Sat. 11am-10pm.

Restaurante Self-Naturista, C. Santa Ana, 11-13, (tel. 301 21 30), Metro: Catalunya (L1, L3), one block from Pl. Catalunya on the Rambles. Self-service vegetarian cafeteria with a wholesome meatless *paella* (295ptas). Open Mon.-Sat. noon-10pm.

Restaurante Sitjas, C. Sitjas, 3, (tel. 317 29 32), Metro: Catalunya (L1, L3). From the metro walk down the Rambles towards the water, take your 1st right onto C. Tallers and your 1st left onto Sitjas (may appear as Sitges on older maps). Full *menú* for 550ptas and a menu in English to boot. Open Mon.-Sat. 1-4pm and 8-10:30pm.

Can Suñé, C. Mozart, 20, in the ancient Gràcia neighborhood. Take C. Goya off C. Gran de Gràcia and your second right. The ultimate in neighborhood eating. Meals 650ptas. Open daily 1-4pm and 8:30-11pm.

Restaurante Pitarra, C. de Aviñó, 56. Take C. de Ferran off the Rambles and then fourth right. More pesetas than the rest, but this may be your only chance to eat food prepared by the former chef to Queen Sofía of Spain. Meal for two around 3000ptas. Open Sept.-July Mon.-Sat. 1-4pm and 8-11:30pm.

Sights

During the summer, the easiest way to see all the major sights of Barcelona is to collapse aboard one of the **Transports Turistics Barcelona** tour buses. The 16-stop circuit takes two hours, with buses hitting each stop every 30 minutes. The easiest place to catch it is Pl. Catalunya, in front of the El Corte Inglés department store. Purchase tickets on board. (Service June 22-Sept. 15 9am-9:30pm; last one leaves Pl. Catalunya 7:30pm daily. All-day pass 800ptas, half-day (after 2pm) 500ptas.)

During the past few years, Barcelona has facelifted its port area in an effort to cleanse its Mediterranean-front property of congested roads and decaying factories. Shoving the coastal ring road underground, the city opened up a wide new harbor-side walkway, **Moll de la Fusta,** ideal for an evening stroll, on the harbor side of Pg. de Colom (Metro: Drassanes, L3), which leads down to the cobblestone docks past five new, pricey, but scenic restaurant-cafés. On the Rambles end of Moll de la Fusta the **Monument a Colom** commands an impressive aerial view of the city. (Elevator to the top open daily 9am-9pm; Oct.-June 23 Tues.-Sat. 10am-2pm and 3:30-6:30pm, Sun. 10am-7pm. Admission 175ptas. Ticket office open until ½-hr. before closing.) The small ferry **Las Golondrinas** cruises through the harbor out to the isolated peninsula by the *rompeolas* (breakwater). (June-Sept. 11am-8pm; March-May and Oct.-Dec. 11am-5pm; every ½ hr., 250ptas round-trip.)

Barcelona's beaches are on the Mediterranean side of the peninsula **Barceloneta.** The water is not spectacularly clean, but bus #45 from Pl. Catalunya or #59 from Via Laietana shuttles over to Barceloneta in about 15 minutes, and bus #36 from Pg. de Colom and #141 from Pl. Universitat bring you north of Barceloneta to **Playa MarBella** where the water's a little cleaner. For serious beaching, see Near Barcelona. Rows of crumbling 19th-century factories used to loom behind Mar-Bella, but thanks to the Olympics, this area is now the happy home of **Poble Nou,** a new development with sweeping public parks and chic shopping centers which will serve as the **Vila Olímpica** (Olympic Village) for the summer games' over 10,000 athletes.

Moving inland from Poble Nou you can wander through the historic and tranquil **Barrio de la Ribera.** On the border of the Vila Olímpica and next to Estació França is the **Parc de la Ciutadella,** originally landscaped for the 1888 Universal Exposition and now a second home for half of Barcelona's schoolchildren and site of the **Museu**

d'Art Modern and the **Parc Zoològic,** with the only albino gorilla in captivity in the world. (Museum open Tues.-Sat. 9am-7:30pm, Sun. 9am-2pm, Mon. 3-7:30pm. Admission 400ptas. Zoo open daily 9:30am-7:30pm. Admission 630ptas.) The heart of la Ribera, though, is the church of **Santa María des Mar,** a monument to Barcelona's tenure as a great sea power, with a myriad of stained glass windows that many *Barcelonins* consider more beautiful than those of the *Catedral* in Barri Gòtic (open daily 8am-1pm and 5-8:30pm.) Behind the church, Pg. del Born, with its elegant *champañerías* (champagne bars) and mellow taverns, is the destination for those in search of serene evening *paseo* in the old part of town. Off Pg. del Born, C. Montcada runs up to the world-famous **Museu Picasso** at #15, housed in what was once two adjacent medieval mansions. The collection traces his development during his turn-of-the-century stay in Barcelona, and also includes his brilliant Cubist rendition of Velázquez's *Las Meninas.* (Open Tues.-Sun. 10am-8pm. Admission 400ptas, students and under 18 free.)

Across Via Laietana is the oldest section of Barcelona, **Barri Gòtic,** centered around **La Catedral.** More like the Italians than the height-obsessed medieval French, Catalan architects worried about amplitude, hence the squat appearance of the 700-year-old structure. The cloister, adjacent to a small museum, houses a beautiful garden with a dozen plump white geese. (Cathedral open daily 7:30am-1:30pm and 4-7:30pm. Cloister open daily 8:45am-1:30pm and 4-7pm. Museum open daily 11am-1pm. Museum admission 30ptas.) Behind the cathedral, on C. dels Comtes, stands the **Palau Reial,** the Royal Palace of the Counts of Barcelona, with the **Museu Frederic Marés.** (Open Tues.-Sat. 9am-2pm and 4-7pm, Sun. 9am-2pm. Admission 200ptas.)

On the **Rambles,** most of the novelties are human: bird-vendors, sidewalk artists, street musicians and dancers, couples flirting over drinks in the outdoor cafés, and tourists sprinkled between the flower and news stands on this wide, tree-studded boulevard. The **Gran Teatre del Liceu,** Rambles, 61 (see also under Entertainment), hides an outrageous baroque interior behind its classical façade. (Tours Sept.-June Mon.-Fri. 11:30am and 12:15pm. Admission 200ptas.)

From the Rambles as you face the port, Barcelona slopes upward and to the right onto **Montjüic,** the principal site of the XXV Olympiad and many other attractions. The top of the hill can be reached by the escalators that lead up to the **Palau Nacional** from Pl. Espanya or by bus #61 from the same plaza. At the crest of Montjüic is the **Anella Olímpica** (Olympic ring) consisting of the **Estadi Olimpic de Montjüic,** the **Palau d'Esports Sant Jordi,** and several other sports facilities. The stadium was built in 1929 for a bid for the 1936 Olympics which the city lost to Berlin, but has been remodeled and upgraded in the past six years. The Palau Sant Jordi, next door, is a brand new facility and an architectural masterpiece that blends into the hillside with its rounded dome and wavy fringes designed by Arata Isozaki.

Non-Olympic visitors will not lack for entertainment on the rest of Montjüic, though. Nearby is the **Poble Espanyol** (Spanish Village), Barcelona's attempt to keep you from visiting the rest of Spain—a display of typical reconstructed buildings from every region. (Open Thurs.-Sat. 9am-6pm, Tues.-Wed. 9am-4pm, Sun.-Mon. 9am-2pm. Admission 500ptas.) On the other side of the hill, the **Fundaciò Joan Miró,** designed by Josep Lluís Sert, offers a supreme shutter-click of Barcelona and a permanent collection of Miró's works. (Open Tues.-Wed. and Fri.-Sat. 11am-7pm, Thurs. 11am-9:30pm, Sun. 10:30am-2:30pm. Admission 400ptas, students 200ptas.) The **Palau Nacional** is the home of the **Museu d'Art de Catalunya,** undergoing a way-behind-schedule $275 million restoration; this museum of magnificent 12th and 13th-century frescoes will probably only have its main exhibition room open in time for the Olympics. (Open Tues.-Sun. 9am-2pm. Admission 400ptas.) Below the Palau Nacional, towards the Pl. Espanya, are Disneyesque **Fonts Luminoses** (illuminated fountains in operation in summer Thurs. and Sat.-Sun. 9pm-midnight; off-season Sat.-Sun. 8-11pm.) For the sound and light show here, arrive by 10pm in summer, 9pm in the off-season.

The broad, elegant streets of the **Eixample** on the other side of Pl. Catalunya from the Rambles were laid out in 1859 in a burst of 19th-century progressivism.

Scattered throughout the Eixample are many *modernista* (i.e., art nouveau) buildings built during the Catalan Renaixença at the beginning of this century—they look something out of *Alice in Wonderland.* Most ambitious of these is Gaudí's monstrous and miraculous **Temple Expiatori de la Sagrada Família** (Church of the Holy Family), filling a block between C. de Provença and C. de Mallorca (Metro: Sagrada Família, L5). The otherworldly towers and bits of walls give only a hint of Gaudí's vision, which seemingly rejected everything flat in favor of organic surfaces. If the building is ever completed, it will resemble the model in the crypt. (Open daily in summer 8am-9pm; off-season 8am-7pm. Admission 300ptas. Elevator runs daily 10am-1:45pm and 3-7:45pm, 85ptas.)

More *modernista* buildings survey Passeig de Gràcia; most striking is Gaudí's **Casa Batlló** at #43. Next door at #41, Puig i Cadafalch opted for a more cubical pattern. The disjunction is such that the block is known as the *manzana de la discordia* (block of disagreement). Up the street at Passeig de Gràcia, 92, is **La Pedrera** (Casa Milá) which looks like it's going to melt into the sidewalk. (Free visits to the rooftop Mon.-Fri. at 10am, 11am, noon, 4pm, and 5pm, Sat. at 10am, 11am, and noon.) Take bus #24 from here to the **Park Güell,** Gaudí's uncompleted attempt at city planning. Though his project floundered, two guard houses, plastered with extravagant tiles and sensual shapes, give you an idea of what might have been. (Open daily 10am to 1 hr. before sunset. Free.) In the park, visit the small **Museu Gaudí.** (Open Mon.-Thurs. 10am-2pm and 4-6pm, Fri. 11am-1:30pm, Sun. and holidays 10am-2pm and 4-7pm. Admission 100ptas.)

If you want to step back from the intricacies of architecture and art museums and take in the Big Picture, head to the city's highest point at **Tibidabo,** perched atop the encircling mountains. The FFCC trains or bus #17, #22, or #58 from Pl. Catalunya will drop you off on Av. del Tibidabo which winds its way to the top of the mountain. One of the best spots to absorb the view is the bar **Mirablau** (tel. 418 58 79; open daily noon-5am), whose open terrace hangs over the edge of the hillside.

Entertainment

Every evening at about 5pm, a man sets up a box in the middle of C. Porta de l'Angel before the Galerías Preciados and, as a crowd gathers, he intersperses opera with voluble commentary. Nightlife in Barcelona starts then and there, and winds down about 14 hours later. This cosmopolitan city offers a perfect combination of exuberance and variety—if you leave without taking advantage of it, slink to the border in shame.

The weekly *Guía del Ocio* (60ptas at any newsstand) is the best guide to theater, film, art, dance, clubs, and restaurants in the city, but is in Spanish. The nightlife schedule is a late one with *paseos* lasting until around 10 or 11pm, bar-hopping until 2am and then dancing until your legs scream "no más!"

The **Gran Teatre del Liceu,** Rambla de Caputxins, 61 (tel. 318 92 77), is one of the world's premiere opera houses. Inexpensive seats or standing room for performances can cost as little as 750ptas. (Box office open Sept.-July daily noon-3pm and 5-10pm.) Classical music resounds from fall to spring at the fantastic art nouveau **Palau de la Música Catalana,** C. Amadeu Vives, near Pl. Urquinaona. (Box office open Mon.-Fri. 11am-1pm and 5-8pm.) Barcelona has dozens of cinemas. If you don't understand Spanish, check *Guía del Ocio's* movie section for movies marked "V.O." (original version). The **Filmoteca,** Travessera de Gràcia, 63 (tel. 201 29 06), offers everything from art films to cult films for only 250ptas. The **Teatre Grec** season, usually beginning in late June, offers outdoor movies, theater, dance, and music. Tickets are available at the Palau de la Virreina, Rambla, 99 (tel. 318 85 99; open Mon.-Sat. 10am-7pm, Sun. 10am-2pm). Frenzied strains of Spanish and Latin music fill the dance hall at **La Paloma,** C. del Tigre, 27 (tel. 325 20 08) near Pl. Universitat. (Open Wed.-Sun. 11:15pm-2:30am.) The disco in vogue with the young and the restless is **Otto Zitz,** C. Lincoln, 15 (tel. 238 07 22), uptown near Pl. Molina where C. de Balmes intersects via Augusta (cover and one drink

2000ptas; open Thurs.-Sun. 11:30pm-4:30am). More discos and bars packed with chic *chicos* and *chicas* revel along **Carrer de Balmes, Avinguda Diagonal,** and any of the intersecting streets (Metro: Diagonal, L3, L5). Gay people head over to **Monroe's Gallery-Bar,** C. Lincoln, 3, (tel. 237 56 78) for drinks in this subdued spot that pays homage to Marilyn (open daily 7pm-3am). **La Fira,** C. Provenza, 171, (tel. 323 72 71) wins the design contest of Barcelona's *ambiente*-conscious bars with seating and surroundings from authentic turn-of-the-century amusement park rides and attractions.

Barcelona's bullfights occur at **Plaça Monumental,** on the Gran Vía (Metro: Marina, L1). Look for posters—fights are usually on weekends. Tickets are sold at C. Muntaner, 24 (tel. 253 38 21), parallel to Passeig de Gràcia. (Open Thurs.-Sun. 10am-1pm and 4-8pm. Tickets start at 1300ptas.) Any tickets left (usually many in summer) are sold at the ring an hour before opening.

Monster festivals in Barcelona include the **Festa de Sant Jordi** (April 23), when loved ones exchange books and roses in celebration of Catalonia's patron saint, the **Feast of the Virgen de la Merced** (Sept. 24), and the raucous **Diá de Sant Joan** (June 24) for the city's patron saint, whose eve is lit by bonfires and fireworks at Pl. Espanya.

The XXV Olympiad (July 25-August 9, 1992)

Foreign invasions have always plagued Barcelona. First came the Carthaginians, then the Romans, the Moors, the Visigoths, then the French (twice), and many nationalistic Catalans will lump in Franco's regime as well. Welcome to Invasion 1992, Olympic-style. Over 10,000 athletes from 164 countries and half a million spectators and visitors will storm into the city for a brief two-week athletic and cultural frenzy that Barcelona has been bracing itself for for the past six years.

The Olympians will battle it out in 25 competitive sports and three exhibition events that will be spread out over the four Olympic areas in the city (**Montjüic, Vila Olímpica, Vall d'Hebró** and **Diagonal**) and at 16 other venues surrounding Barcelona. Even more far-reaching will be **El Festival Olímpico de las Artes,** a summer-long exposition of classical music and rock concerts, opera, theater, ballet, fine arts, architecture, and local traditions like "*corre-focs,*" people dressed in demon-like costumes who race up and down the streets waving pitchfork-like sparklers while dodging buckets of water hurled at them from the balconies above.

Although Barcelona will overflow with entertainment, accommodations will be scarce during the Games and reservations are most strongly recommended. The city's Tourism Board is considering setting up bunk-beds (for about 500 to 750 people) in university dorms and on tent-covered athletic fields for spur-of-the-moment budget travelers. These plans are by no means concrete, but the Ajuntament tourist offices (at the train stations, the port, and all the Olympic venues) will be able to provide more information.

Between September 1991 and May 1992, tickets to all Olympic sporting events will only be available from the authorized ticket agent in your country of origin. Some of these agents are: **Australia,** Keith Prowse Expotel Travel, 77 Alexander St., Crows Nest NSW 2065 (tel. (02) 906 11 44; fax (02) 906 10 13); **Canada,** Sportsworld Travel, 2279 Towne Blvd., Oakville, Ontario L6H 5S9 (tel. and fax (416) 257-0059); **New Zealand,** Marathon Centre, 1st floor, Box 68-195, Auckland (tel. (09) 78 66 51, fax (09) 78 09 91); **UK,** Sportsworld Travel, New Abbey Court, Stert St., Abingdon, Oxon OX14 3S2 (tel. (0235) 55 48 44, fax (0235) 55 48 41); **US,** Olson Travelworld, 1334 Parkview Ave. Suite 210, Manhattan Beach, CA 90266 (tel. (213) 615-0711, fax 640-1039). If your country is not listed here, contact your national Olympic Committee office or the **Barcelona Olympic Organizing Committee** at: COOB '92; Edifici Helios; Traveserra de les Corts, 131-159; 08028 Barcelona, Spain (tel. (93) 411 19 92, fax (93) 411 20 92; open Mon.-Fri. 9am-1pm and 3-7pm) to find the location of your national ticket agent. COOB can handle correspondence in English, one of the four official languages of the '92 Olympics. Proof of nationality is required for all ticket purchases before May 1992.

At the end of May, COOB will shut off all ticket sales, and place the remaining tickets on sale at the ticket windows at the Olympic sites during the games. Cheaper seats for most preliminary events run around 3000ptas each. A precise schedule including all the events and their ticket prices is available from your national ticket agent or COOB, and during the Olympics from all tourist offices or COOB.

Information on the activities of the **Olympic Festival of the Arts** will be available at all tourist offices throughout the summer or from Departamento de Prensa de Olimpíada Cultural; Torre Llussana; Camí de Sant Genís a Horta, 6; 08035 Barcelona, Spain (tel. (93) 429 00 09, fax (93) 429 06 07; open Mon.-Fri. 9am-1pm and 3-7pm).

Near Barcelona

Brava—"brave" or "savage"—fits the coastline geography but not the beach-resort ease of the Costa Brava towns, just before the French border northwest of Barcelona. In **Tossa de Mar,** reached by bus from Barcelona or the RENFE station just south at Blanes, the narrow cobblestoned streets of the walled **Vila Vella** give spectacular views. The tourist office (tel. 34 03 65) at the bus terminal has a good map and accommodations help. (Open Mon.-Sat. 9am-9pm, Sun. 9am-noon; Sept.-June Mon.-Sat. 10am-1pm and 4-8pm.) The pension **Fonda Lluna,** C. Roqueta 20 (tel. 34 03 65) is the real Tossa for 1500ptas per person. While recovering from the Dalí museum in **Figueres,** stay at the newly-renovated **youth hostel (IYHF)**, C. Anicet de Pagés (tel. 50 12 13), behind the tourist office parking lot on Plaça de Sol. Daytrip to or camp in **Cadaqués,** Dalí's final home. Inland **Girona** is the provincial capital and bus and train transport hub. Its ancient Jewish quarter, brand new **IYHF youth hostel** (tel. 20 15 54), and Devesa park are only three of many reasons to stop. (Tourist offices at train station, tel. 21 62 96, and at Rambla Llibertat 1, tel. 20 26 79).

The **Costa Dorada** glitters southwest of Barcelona; the blinking-white beaches of **Sitges** are a prime daytrip, only 45 minutes from Barcelona's Sants train station (365ptas). The unmistakable profile of the **Montserrat** mountain range rises like a half-buried stegosaurus over the Riu Llobregat valley. Home of *La Verge de Montserrat,* a 10th-century bronze of the Virgin Mary, the monastery is the spiritual center of Catalonia. In the breezy upper reaches of the mountain silence, nature and deep, deep meditation are yours for the breathing in a hiker's paradise. You can stay the night in esthetically simple cells at **Despatx de Celles** (tel. (93) 835 02 51, ext. 630; singles 1010ptas, doubles 1840ptas; open March 15-Nov. 15). Take the FFCC trains from Barcelona's Pl. Espanya station to Montserrat. The provincial capital of Catalonia under Rome, bustling **Tarragona** still proudly displays well-preserved Roman forums and chariot-racing arenas. From the train station (connected frequently to Barcelona's Sants station), turn right to the winding stairs that lead you up to the outlook over the Mediterranean. The wide avenue stretching away from the sea is Rambla Nova, home of the tourist office (at #46, tel. (977) 23 21 43) and the way to the youth hostel (walk past the traffic circle onto Av. Lluis Companys and take your second right; tel. (977) 21 01 95; members only, 700ptas).

Catalan Pyrenees

North of Barcelona, upland Catalonia's green peaks and valleys swirl towards the French border. With a staggering view up an equally staggering set of stairs from its RENFE station (tel. (972) 88 01 65) the hill town of **Puigcerdà** (push chair DAH) is the last stop in Spain on the line from Barcelona to La Tour de Carol and Toulouse in France (6 trains per day from Barcelona; 4 to Toulouse, connecting in La Tour de Carol). In a region of Range Rovers and big dogs, Puigcerdà claims to be the "capital of snow"—get info on skiing in three countries, as well as year-round mountain sports, from the **tourist office,** C. Querol, 1 (tel. (972) 88 05 42), to the right once you make the climb from the train station. (Open July-Sept. Mon.-

Thurs. 10am-1pm and 4-7pm, Fri.-Sat. 10am-1:30pm and 4-8:30pm, Sun. 10am-2pm; Oct.-June closed Mon.) Try for a room at **Pensión Dominguez,** C. Major, 39 (tel. (972) 88 14 27), where doubles are 2200ptas. If they're full, there's **Fonda Cerdanya,** C. Ramon Cosp, 7 (tel. (972) 88 00 10) with hardwood floors at 1200-1700ptas per person. The closest **IYHF hostel** is the **Mare de Déu de les Neus** (tel. (972) 89 20 12), right near the RENFE station in La Molina, the next train stop going towards Barcelona. Picnic fixings abound in the bakeries and delis around C. Alfons I.

One hour by bus (tel. (973) 35 00 20) from Puigcerdà is **La Seu d'Urgell,** the site of the 1992 Olympic whitewater canoeing and kayaking events and the Spanish connection to Andorra. Hispano Andorrana (tel. 213 72 in Andorra) makes the 45-min. trip six to seven times per day. The same company that runs the Puigcerdà-La Seu bus also goes from La Seu to Barcelona twice a day. Follow signs to Barcelona-Lleída to find the **tourist office** (tel. (973) 35 15 11) for information on the area's wide variety of mountain sports opportunities. (Open July-Sept. Tues.-Sat. 10am-2pm and 5-8pm, Sun. 9am-2pm; Oct.-June Tues.-Sat. 10am-2pm and 4-7pm, Sun. 9am-2pm.) Ask there if the **IYHF hostel** scheduled to open in 1992 is ready; otherwise, **Fonda Bernada,** C. Sant Ermengol, 14 (tel. (973) 35 10 33) has big, sparkling rooms for 800ptas per person. The **Parc Esportiu del Segre** outside town is where the whitewater competition course is; mountain biking and cross-country skiing are found at the area's four superb Nordic resorts: Lles, Aransa, Sant Joan de l'Erm and Tuixent-La Vansa.

The train line to Puigcerdà also gets you to **Ripoll,** with its noted monastery, and connects you to the train to the alpine ski resort **Núria.** More complex bus transport from Barcelona will get you to the lakes and hikes of the **Parc Nacional d'Aigüestortes i Estany de Sant Maurici.**

Balearic Islands (Illes Baleares)

Four islands with long white beaches, sparklingly clear blue Mediterranean waters and idyllic countryside, the Balearics are an autonomous province of Spain about 100km off the east coast between Barcelona and València. One of the more popular vacation spots for Spaniards and Central Europeans, the islands defy a unified description. **Menorca,** the northernmost, is by far the gem of the four: the lengthy southern coastline cradles the islands' most beautiful and tranquil beaches, and the lush, green interior is ideal for leisurely hikes by sloping green pastures, rugged stone fences and eerie megalithic stone monuments left behind by Menorca's Bronze Age visitors. The island's two principal cities are Maò and Ciutadella on the eastern and western tips of the island, respectively, but still only 45km apart, and some of the beaches not to be missed along the South coast are Son Bou, Cala Marcella, Cales Coves, and Cala En Bosc. The largest of the Balearics, **Mallorca** is flooded with package tours, which makes finding a spot for your beach towel tough around Palma, the island's capital. Palma's nightlife rivals that of Barcelona and Madrid. Mallorca's advantage is its size, and as you head further away from the capital (especially along the northeast and southeast coasts) the crowds on the beaches thin out considerably. **Eivissa** (more commonly known as Ibiza) and its barren sidekick, **Formentera,** are the southernmost and most expensive of the Balearics. Although tourism to these two islands has plummeted in the past four years, prices for food and entertainment remain extraordinarily high as the island seems content to cater to the trendy and decadent whims of Europe's rich. Sant Antonio Abat has the most affordable and egalitarian nightlife, and is well-connected by bus to some of the island's best beaches along the west coast. Ferries from Ibiza to Formentera make the outpost island's tranquil beaches a feasible daytrip.

The Balearics are easily accessible by boat or plane. Ferries are cheapest, but occasionally equally cheap charter flights show up in the newpapers and at travel agencies. The dominant ferry company is **Transmediterránea,** which runs ferries to Menorca, Mallorca, and Ibiza from Barcelona's Estació Marítima (tel. (93) 317 63 11), and from València (tel. (96) 367 39 72). (From Barcelona, mid-June to mid-Sept. to Maò 6 per week, 9 hr.; to Mallorca 10 per week, 8 hr.; to Ibiza 6 per week, 9½) hr.; mid-Sept. to mid-June 2, 9, and 2 per week respectively. From València, year-round to Maò 1 per week, 16½ hr.; to Palma 6 per week, 9 hr.; to Ibiza 6 per week, 9½ hr. *Butaca* with airplane-style seating, fares from the mainland to any of the islands 5070ptas.) Any Spanish travel agency can book you a seat (boats in late July and all of Aug. tend to sell out), but you can purchase a ticket up to one hour before departure at the dock. **Flebasa,** in Denia (south of València; tel. (965) 78 42 00) competes with Transmediterránea in the Ibiza market (Denia to Ibiza and Formentera 3 per day, 3 hr.) Going the other way, their 5220ptas fare includes a free connecting bus to València, Madrid (2000ptas extra) or Alicante. **Iberia** flights (which serve all the islands) aren't that much more expensive, and are very convenient. Fares are cheapest from Barcelona (to Menorca 6 per day, 35 min., 7950ptas one-way, 15,900ptas round-trip; to Mallorca 13 per day, 35 min., 7650ptas and 15,300ptas). When going between islands, forget the infrequent boats and hop the 20-minute Iberia flights for the same price (3750ptas each way, no round-trip discount). Four 20-minute flights per day connect both Menorca and Ibiza to Mallorca (but not to each other). Any travel agent in Spain can book you a seat on one of these flights and may be able to find you a cheaper charter fare.

Cheap and extensive public transportation systems fan out all over each of the islands, and helpful tourist offices will point you towards the key sights and beaches as well as help you find the closest youth hostel (the only two are on Mallorca), *pensión,* or campsite (best on Ibiza). Menorca has three offices: at the airport (tel. (971) 36 01 50, ext. 115); at Plaça Esplanada, 40 in Maò (tel. (971) 36 37 90); and at Plaça Born in Ciutadella (tel. (971) 38 10 50). The main Balearic tourist office is in Palma, Av. Rei Jaume III, 10 (tel. (971) 71 22 16), and the Mallorca airport and practically all major towns along the coast also have tourist offices. Ibiza's most convenient offices are at the airport (tel. (971) 30 22 00, ext. 118), and in Eivissa at Pg. Vara de Rei, 13 (tel. (971) 30 19 00).

The Mediterranean Coast

València

Medieval song describes València as the land of water, light, and love. The city prizes its *huertas* (citrus orchards), which flourish because of extensive irrigation. The regional language is Valenciáno, a dialect of Catalán, but residents also speak Spanish. The best time to visit is the second week of March, when València erupts with drunken parades, public arson, and street dancing during **Las Fallas,** a celebration that rivals even Pamplona's San Fermin.

Orientation and Practical Information

The center of town at **Plaça del Ajuntament** is one block straight ahead from the train station.

Tourist Offices: Municipal Pl. Ajuntament, 1 (tel. 351 04 17). English spoken. Open Mon.-Fri. 8:30am-2:30pm and 4-6:30pm, Sat. 9am-1pm. **Tourist Info,** C. Paz, 48 (tel. 352 40 00). Hooks rooms (no fee) by phone (daily 9am-9pm) or in person. Open Mon.-Fri. 10am-2pm and 4-8pm, Sat. 10am-2pm.

Budget Travel: Viajes TIVE, C. Mar, 54 (tel. 352 28 01). ISIC cards (300ptas), IYHF cards (1800ptas), and student rail tickets. Open Mon.-Fri. 9am-1:30pm, Sat. 9am-noon.

American Express: Duna Viajes, C. Cirilo Amorós, 88 (tel. 374 15 62). Next to Pl. America on the edge of Río Turia.

Post Office: Pl. Ajuntament, 24 (tel. 351 69 73). Stamps open Mon.-Fri. 8am-9pm, Sat. 9am-2pm. *Lista de Correos* Mon.-Sat. 9am-8pm. **Postal Code:** 14600.

Telephones: Pl. Ajuntament, 27. Open Mon.-Sat. 9am-11pm, Sun. 10am-2pm and 6-9pm. **City Code:** 96.

Flights: 15km southwest of the city (tel. 350 95 00). CVT buses (tel. 347 18 98) connect the airport with the bus station (6am-8pm; 80ptas).

Trains: Estación del Nord, near Pl. Ajuntament (tel. 351 36 12). To Madrid (9 per day, 5-7½ hr., *rápido* 2750ptas), Seville (2 per day, 9 hr., 4575-5910ptas), Barcelona (11 per day, 5 hr., 1990-3295ptas). No luggage storage (try bus station).

Buses: Estación Central, Av. Menéndez Pidal, 13 (tel. 349 72 22), a 25-min. walk from the town center. Take bus #8 from in front of Pl. Ajuntament, 22.

Public Transportation: Many municipal buses run from Pl. Ajuntament. Buy tickets aboard (60ptas) or a 10-ride ticket (400ptas) at newsstands.

Ferries: Transmediterránea (Aucona), Av. Manuel Soto Ingeniero, 15 (tel. 367 07 04). To the Balearic and Canary Islands (7-9 hr.). Take bus #4 from Pl. Ajuntament. **Flebasa** (tel. 367 86 01) leave from Denia (3-hr. bus to Denia included in 5220ptas ticket).

Laundromat: Lava Super, Gran Vía Germaniaes, 35 (tel. 341 86 48), behind the bullring, next to the train station. 5kg load 750-800ptas. Open Mon.-Fri. 9am-2pm and 4:30-8pm, Sat. 9am-noon.

Medical Assistance: Hospital Clinico Universitario, Av. Blasco Ibáñez (tel. 386 26 00). Take bus #30 or #40 from Av. Marqués de Sotelo in front of the train station.

Emergencies: Police (tel. 091). Headquarters at Gran Vía de Ramón y Cajal, 40 (tel. 351 08 62).

Accommodations

Summer, when business-oriented València puts up its feet, is the easiest time to find rooms. The sleekest, cleanest lodgings await near **Pl. Ajuntament.** For the safest cheap places, look around **Pl. Mercat.** Avoid the *Barrio Chino,* the red-light district around Pl. Pilar.

Youth Hostal Colegio "La Paz" (IYHF), Av. Puerto, 69 (tel. 369 01 52). Take bus #19 from Pl. Ajuntament, and ask the driver when to get off. Members only, but student IDs accepted. Curfew midnight. Lockout 10am-5pm. 550ptas per person. Sheets 250ptas. Breakfast included. Open July-Aug.

Hostal del Rincón, C. Carda, 11 (tel. 331 60 83). Just past Pl. Mercado on the left coming from Pl. Ajuntament. Comfortable, clean, no-frills rooms. Singles 750ptas. Doubles 1450ptas. Triples 1950ptas.

Hostal Universal, C. Barcas, 5 (tel. 351 53 84), just off Pl. Ajuntament. Freshly painted hallways, spanking new sinks and mattresses. Singles 1300ptas. Doubles 2200ptas, with shower 2700ptas. Showers 200ptas.

Hospedería del Pilar, Pl. Mercat, 19 (tel. 331 66 00). Gracious century-old guest house. 750ptas per person. Showers 150ptas.

Food

Spanish palates thank València for both *paella* and *horchata. Paella* is saffron-flavored rice loaded with meat, poultry, and seafood. Valèncian custom dictates that this dish is eaten only at midday, and it is difficult to find after sunset. *Horchata* is a refreshing milky drink made from the *chufa* (earth-almond); get it *granizada* (with crushed ice) or *líquida* (straight up).

Though difficult to find, almost everyone manages to sniff out the *paella* at **La Utielana,** C. Conde de Montornes, 9. Take C. Barcelonina off Pl. Ajuntament, turn left at its end, and then right into an unmarked, fenced entry. (Open Sept.-July Mon.-Fri. 1-4pm and 9-11pm, Sat. 1-4pm.) At **Cafe Valiente,** C. Játiva, 8, they scoop the rich *paella* up from giant round pans (375ptas; *paella* from 1-4pm). Veggies can miss out on the you-know-what at **La Lluna,** C. San Ramon, where the 650ptas *menú* includes four dishes and whole grain bread. (Open Oct.-July daily 1-3:30pm and 8-11:30pm.) The nearby **mercado,** on Pl. Mercat, happens Mon.-Thurs. 7am-2pm, Fri. 7am-2pm and 5-8:30pm, Sat. 7am-3pm.

Sights and Entertainment

Most sights are located in the north along **Carrer de San Vicante,** which leads to **Plaça de Saragossa.** The **Jardì Botànic,** off C. Beato Gaspar Bono, is a breezy, open-air botanical museum maintained by the university, sporting 300 species from around the world. (Open 10am-9pm; Oct.-May 10am-6pm. Admission 50ptas, students free.) You'll want lots of time to stroll the dry riverbed of the **Tùria,** now one of the world's largest gardens. Pick dessert off the orange trees at the **Jardins del Real** (open daily 8am-sundown), which surround the **Museu de Belles Arts** on C. San Pió V., housing an excellent collection of Valèncian "primitives" (14th- to 16th-century religious paintings), a Bosch triptych, and a Velázquez self-portrait. (Open Tues.-Sat. 10am-2pm and 4-6pm, Sun. 10am-2pm; Aug. Tues.-Sun. 10am-2pm. Free.) Across the old river and west is the **Institut Valencià d'Art Modern Julio González (IVAM),** C. Guillem de Castro, 118, a brand-new modern art museum whose 1991 exhibits included a photographic essay on the Spanish Civil War. (Open Tues.-Sun. 11am-8pm. Admission 250ptas, students 150ptas. Sundays free.) The **Basílica de la Mare de Deú dels Desamparats** and **cathedral,** on Pl. Reina, are reputedly home to the Holy Grail, although nuns will vehemently deny it. From the basilica tower, the **Micalet,** Victor Hugo counted 300 bell towers, though there are only 100. (Cathedral open 10am-1pm and 4:30-7pm; Oct.-Feb. daily 10am-1pm. See the grail for 100ptas. Tower open daily Mon.-Sat. 10:30am-1pm and 4:30-7pm; Oct.-Feb. daily 10:30am-1pm and 4:30-6pm. Admission 75ptas.)

Across from the *mercado* is the **Llotja de la Seda,** the former silk exchange, whose masterfully sculpted ceiling weighs down handsome twisting pillars. (Open June-Sept. Tues.-Fri. 10am-2pm, Sun. 10am-1pm; Tues.-Fri. 10am-2pm and 4-6pm, Sun. 10am-1:30pm. Free.)

Shuffle past the wild façade of the **Palau del Marqués de Dos Aigües** on C. Rinconada de García Sanchís; the museum inside holds one of Spain's finest ceramic collections plus a spate of Picassos. Down the street, the museum adjoining the lovely 16th-century **Església del Patriarca** (Partriarch's Church) at C. Nave, 1, displays paintings by El Greco, Caravaggio, and others. (Open in summer daily 11am-1:30pm. Admission 100ptas.)

In June, the **Festival of Corpus Christi** features *rocas,* magnificently ornate coaches that serve as theatrical stages. Festivities continue in summer with the **Fira de Juliol** (July 15-31), featuring fireworks, cultural events, and the *batallas de flors* (flower wars), when citizens assault each other with pansies and carnations.

València's supposed nightlife centers on the bars and pubs around **Pl. Cánovas del Castillo** on the banks of the Tùria, and on the other side in the university district around **Av. Blasco Ibañez.** One mildly thumping disco is **Woody,** C. Menedez y Pelayo, 137, which packs in the students (open Fri.-Sat.; cover 1000ptas).

Near València

Few words do justice to **Gandía's** beachfront youth hostel **Alberg Mar I Vent,** C. Doctor Fleming, s/n (tel. (96) 289 37 48), on Platja de Piles. (Unfortunate three-day limit to your windsurfing, sunning, orange-blossom sniffing, and general bliss. Members only. 700ptas per bed, over 26 825ptas. Full pension 1540ptas, over 26 2000ptas. Sheets 140ptas. Windsurfing 500ptas per hour; free lessons. Bikes 400ptas per day.) Take a train from València to Gandía (1 per hr., 1 hr.); from the Gandía train station, turn right, then right again. Then take the **La Amistal** bus (tel. (96) 287 44 10; 55ptas; check with the tourist office for exact times) to the end of the line, walk straight down the street until it ends, and turn left until you are between the hostel and the deep blue sea. Gandía's tourist office (tel. (96) 287 77 88) is across from the train station (open Mon.-Fri. 10am-2pm and 4-7pm, Sat. 10am-2pm).

Inland **Xátiva,** birthplace of a couple popes and the painter José de Ribera, sports two magnificent hilltop castles, with lockjaw-inducing views once appreciated by their prisoners, the Count of Urgel and King Ferran el Catòlic. (Open in summer Tues.-Sun. 10:30am-2pm and 4:30-8pm; off-season Tues.-Sun. 10:30am-2pm and 3-6pm. Free.) Xátiva has its own version of *paella,* best sampled for 350ptas at the **Café-Bar San Remo,** Av. Jaume I, 52. Xàtiva (Játiva in Castilian) is south of València by train (every hour, 30-45 min., 225ptas).

Sagunt (Sagunto in Castilian), a half-hour train ride north of València, caused the Second Punic War. The area is rich in Roman ruins; the **Museu Arqueològic, Teatro Romano,** and **castell** teeter on the hill that slopes from the Ajuntament. (All open Tues.-Sat. 10am-8pm, Sun. 2-8pm; Oct.-May Tues.-Sat. 10am-2pm and 4-6pm. Museum 150ptas. Castle and theater free.) For accommodations info, visit **Turisme,** Pl. Cronista Chabret (tel. 266 22 13; open Mon.-Sat. 10am-2pm and 4-8pm, Sun. 10am-1pm).

Alicante (Alacant)

The beaches are close by, the lodging is plentiful and cheap, and the nightlife steady: all this makes Alicante a nice place to hop off the Eurail Express and chill by the Mediterranean. Alicante's old city is a snarl of gritty, lively streets, inlaid with festive red tiles at the foot of the dominant *castillo,* and lined with good, inexpensive eateries.

Orientation and Practical Information

Alicante is about 125km from València, but trains take the 200km coastal route along the Costa Blanca (supposedly named after its white sands, but more likely a reference to its pasty tourists). A train line inland to Albacete and eventually Madrid begins at Alicante. The **Esplanada de España** stretches along the waterfront and in front of the crooked streets of the old quarter, extending to the *castillo.* To get to the old quarter from the train station, walk 1 block toward the sea on Av. Salamanca, turn left on Av. Maisonnave, and continue to the end. From the bus station, turn left onto C. Italia, then right on wide Av. Dr. Gadea.

Tourist Offices: Oficina de Información Turística, at C. Portugal, 17 (tel. 522 38 02), by the bus station. Young, inspired staff who know where the bars are. Open Mon.-Fri. 9am-9pm, Sat. 9am-3pm; Oct.-June Mon.-Fri. 9am-1pm and 4:30-7:30pm, Sat. 9am-1pm. **Tourist Information,** Esplanada de España, 2 (tel. 521 22 85). Room reservations. Open Mon.-Sat. 10am-2pm and 4-8pm, Sun. 10am-2pm; Sept. 16-June 14 Mon.-Fri. 9am-2pm and 5-7pm, Sat. 9am-1pm.

Consulate: U.K., Pl. Calvo Sotelo, 1 (tel. 521 61 90). Open Mon.-Fri. 8:30am-2:30pm.

Post Office: Pl. Gabriel Mirò (tel. 520 21 93). Open Mon.-Fri. 9am-2pm and 4-6pm, Sat. 9am-2pm. **Postal Code:** 03000.

Telephones: Av. Constitución, 10. Open daily 9am-10pm. **City Code:** 96.

Trains: RENFE, Estación Término, Av. Salamanca (tel. 522 01 27). To València (6 per day, 3 hr., 1350ptas), Barcelona (3 per day, 11 hr., 4815ptas), and Madrid (5 per day, 9 hr., 3100ptas). **Ferrocarils de la Generalitat Valenciana** trains (tel. 526 27 31) chug from Estación de la Marina on Av. Villajoyosa, 2, for towns along the Costa Blanca.

Buses: Station is on C. Portugal (tel. 522 07 00). Direct buses to Madrid and València and along the Costa Blanca.

Ferries: Transmediterránea, Esplanada de España, 2 (tel. 520 60 11). To the Balearics (5070ptas). Call **Flebasa** (tel. 367 86 01) about their bus-and-ferry deals to Ibiza.

Budget Travel: TIVE, Av. Aguilera, 1 (tel. 522 74 42).

Medical Assistance: Hospital Provincal, Pl. Dr. Gomez Villa, 14 (tel. 524 42 00). **Ambulance** (tel. 521 17 05).

Emergency: (tel. 091). **Police headquarters** at C. Médico Pascual Pérez, 33 (tel. 514 22 22).

Accommodations, Camping, and Food

A *pensión* seems to sprout from every street corner in Alicante, but many are thick with hookers and thieves, especially along C. San Fernando and around the church of Santa María. For safer lodgings look in the newer sections of town north of Ramble Méndez Núñez. The **youth hostel,** well behind its renovation schedule, is slated to reopen in summer 1992; consult either tourist office.

Habitaciones México, C. Primo de Rivera, 10 (tel. 520 93 07). Fine rooms and free soap with an hysterically funny and slightly bilingual owner. Singles 1100-1400ptas. Doubles 2000-2500ptas. Triples 2700-3000ptas. Higher July-Aug.

Residencia La Milagrosa, C. Villavieja, 8 (tel. 521 69 18). Fragrant, kiwi-colored rooms spy on the Julio Iglesia of Santa María. Singles (in winter only) 1000ptas. Doubles 2000-2200ptas. Hot showers 250ptas. Cold free.

Camping: Camping Bahía, (tel. 526 23 32), 4km on bus C-1. 350ptas per person. Open March 15-Oct. 15.

There's food all over Alicante—especially on C. San Francisco, where six *estupendo* restaurants spread their tables along the sidewalk. The pick of the herd is **Restaurante Rincón Castellano,** at #12, where a two-course *menú* runs 825ptas and a side order of *patatas a la brava* 150ptas. (Open 12:30-4pm and 7:30pm-midnight.) Veggies might hop over to **Restaurante Mixto Vegetariano,** Pl. Santa María, 2, off C. Mayor; the 750ptas *menú* includes a graze at the salad bar. (Open Sun.-Fri. 1-4:30pm and 7:30-11:30pm, Sat. 1-4:30pm.) The **market** caps Av. Alfonso X el Sabio. *Tapas* bars string along C. Mayor.

Sights and Entertainment

With drawbridges, moats, tunnels, and secret passageways, the **Castillo de Santa Bárbara** has a cloak-and-dagger atmosphere and a water-tower vista; take the elevator (75ptas) from the shorefront. (Open Mon.-Fri. 9am-9pm, Sat. 9am-2pm; Oct. to mid-June Mon.-Fri. 9am-7:30pm, Sat. 9am-2pm.) The **Cathedral of San Nicolás de Bari** typifies the severe Renaissance architectural style of Spain and has a comely cloister with intricately carved doors. The impressive **Museo Colección "Arte del Siglo XX"** on C. Mayor has outstanding works by Picasso, Braque, Calder, and Miró. (Open Tues.-Sat. 10am-1pm and 5-8pm, Sun. 10am-1:30pm. Free.)

Alicante's only problem is that there are too many people at the beach during the day and too few people at the bars in the evenings. That's what **Playa San Juan** is for: the beaches have plenty of towel space and the avenues are lined with bars and 100ptas beer machines. During the day, take bus C-1 from Alicante; at night, one of the hourly night trains from Estación de la Marina in Alicante, or split a cab for 800ptas. The first place to check is **Voy, Voy,** because if anything is happening, it's there, with outdoor bars and decibel upon decibel of dance music.

Back in Alicante, dance at the neon **Discoteca Bugatti** on C. San Fernando. Gay men convene at **Jardineto** on C. Baron de Finestrat; for dancing, ask for directions to the sometimes-gay **Memphis.** Want to see what Rome looked like when it fell? Go to the **Festival of San Juan,** which breaks loose nightly from June 21-29 with dancing, spectacular fireworks, and effigy competitions.

Andalusia (Andalucía)

Between the jagged Sierra Morena and the deep blue sea, Andalusia has always radiated a charm so intoxicating that even sober commentators take their fervent commonplaces for revelation. Andalusia's fertile farmland made it one of the Roman Empire's richest, most sophisticated provinces, and although it is true that the Moors remained in control of eastern Andalusia longer than elsewhere in Spain, the region is as much Roman as Moorish in heritage. The system of irrigation, the cool patios, and the characteristic alternation of white and red stone (as at the Córdoba Mosque) are all Roman. The Moors maintained and perfected these techniques; more importantly, they assimilated and elaborated the wisdom and science of Classical Greece and the East, which made the European Renaissance possible.

Owing to the long summers, regional cooking is light, depending on such delicacies as *pescaíto frito* (lightly fried fish) and such renowned cold soups as *gazpacho* served *con guarnición* (with garnish), often spooned by the waiter at your table.

Seville (Sevilla)

Held by Romans, Moors, and Catholic kings, Seville has never failed to spark the imagination of newcomers. Jean Cocteau included it in his trio of magic cities; St. Teresa denounced it as the work of the Devil. *Carmen, Don Giovanni, The Barber of Seville,* and Dostoevsky's story of the "Grand Inquisitor" from *The Brothers Karamazov* are only a few of the artistic works inspired by the city.

As you read this, Seville is experiencing its biggest year ever for tourism, as the 1992 Universal Exposition draws millions of visitors. Expect prices to skyrocket.

Orientation and Practical Information

Seville is a major travel hub, connecting Portugal, Cádiz, Córdoba, and Madrid. The Río Guadalquivir runs approximately north-south through Seville. Most of the city, including the Jewish quarter of **Barrio de Santa Cruz,** is on the east bank, while the **Barrio de Triana,** the old gypsy quarter (now gentrified), lies on the west. The famous cathedral and Giraldo Tower mark the center of town, on **Avenida de la Constitución.** The tourist office, major sights, post office, and banks cluster here. The new **Santa Justa train station** is away from the old city, about a 40-min. walk from the cathedral. The main bus station at **Prado de San Sebastián** on C. Menéndez Pelazo is much closer to the cathedral (about a 10-min. walk).

Tourist Office: Regional, Av. Constitución, 21b (tel. 422 14 04), 1 block south of the cathedral. Friendly, knowledgable, and they speak English. Open Mon.-Fri. 9:30am-7:30pm, Sat. 9:30am-2pm. **Municipal,** Paseo de las Delicias, 9 (tel. 423 44 65), off Glorieta de los Marineros Voluntarios. **EXPO '92 Information,** Plaza de Cuba, 10 (tel. 427 72 71). Open Mon.-Fri. 10am-2pm and 5-8pm, Sat. 10am-2pm. Other information offices will be conveniently located within the EXPO '92 grounds.

Budget Travel: Viajes TIVE, Av. Reina Mercedes, 53 (tel. 461 59 16). Take bus #34 from Av. Constitución south dwon Paseo de las Delicias toward Cádiz. Open Mon.-Fri. 9am-2pm, Sat. 9am-noon for information only.

Consulates: U.S., Paseo de las Delicias, 7 (tel. 423 18 83). **Canada,** Av. Constitución, 30, 2nd floor (tel. 422 94 13; emergencies (91) 431 43 00). **U.K.,** Pl. Nueva, 8 (tel. 422 88 73).

Currency Exchange: Corte Inglés department stores exchange after banking hours. Two locations: Pl. Duque de la Victoria (in the town center) and next to Hotel Lebreros (15 min. from the cathedral). Both open Mon.-Sat. 10am-9pm. **Oficina Cambio del Banesto,** Av. Constitución, 31 (tel. 422 26 23). Open Tues.-Sun. 9:30am-8:15pm.

American Express: Viajes Alhambra, Teniente Coronel Seguí, 6 (tel. 421 29 23), north of Pl. Nueva. Open Mon.-Fri. 9:30am-1:30pm and 4:30-8pm, Sat. 9:30am-1pm.

Post Office: Av. Constitución, 32 (tel. 422 88 00), across from the cathedral. Open for stamps and most mail services Mon.-Fri. 8am-9pm, Sat. 9am-7pm. Open for Lista de Correos Mon.-Fri. 8am-9pm, Sat. 8am-2pm. **Postal Code:** 41070.

Telephones: Pl. Gavidia, 7. Open Mon.-Sat. 10am-2pm and 5:30-10pm. Closed Sat. afternoons in the winter. **City Code:** 95.

Flights: 12km from town on the Carretera de Madrid (tel. 451 61 11). Catch city bus EA to the airport from the Puerta de Jerez, which is near the regional tourist office, or from Av. Kansas City near the Santa Justa train station (about every ½ hr. 6:30am-10:30pm, 200ptas). **Iberia,** C. Almirante Lobo, 3 (tel. 422 89 01, for reservations 421 88 00).

Trains: Santa Justa Station, Av. Kansas City, s/n (for information tel. 441 41 11; for reservations 442 15 62). Luggage storage 200-400ptas per day. Bus #70 connects the train station and the main bus station. Bus EA heads to the Puerta de Jerez, near the regional tourist office. To Córdoba (18 per day, 2 hr., 660-1415ptas) and Cádiz (16 per day, 2-2½ hr., 890-1600ptas). **RENFE,** C. Zaragosa, 29 (tel. 421 79 98), near Pl. Nueva. Open Mon.-Fri. 9am-1:15pm and 4-7pm.

Buses: Main Station, Prado de San Sebastián at C. José María Osborne, 11 (tel. 441 71 11). Luggage storage 130ptas per day. To Córdoba (12 per day, 2 hr., 700ptas), Cádiz (9 per day, 1¾-2¾ hr., 1000ptas), and Jerez de la Frontera (7 per day, 1½ hr., 765ptas).

Laundromat: Lavandería Robledo, C. F. Sánchez Bedoya, 18 (tel. 421 81 32), 1 block west of the cathedral, across Av. Constitución. Wash and dry up to 5kg for 950ptas. Open Mon.-Fri. 10am-2pm and 5-8pm, Sat. 10am-2pm.

Medical Assistance: Casa de Socorro, (tel. 441 17 12). English spoken at **Hospital Universitario,** Av. Dr. Fedriani, s/n (tel. 437 84 00).

Emergencies: (tel. 091). **Police,** Pl. Gavidia (tel. 422 88 40).

Accommodations and Camping

Outside the EXPO and festival times, hunting down a room in Seville is usually a breeze, although slightly more expensive than other parts of Andalusia (1300-1600ptas per person). Look in the Barrio de Santa Cruz, especially around C. Mateos Gago. Also try the Plaza de Curtidores and the Plaza de Pilatos, off C. Menéndez Pelayo, to the east. East of the old Córdoba train station, around C. Marqués de la Paradas, is less attractive, but chock full of cheap places. During Semana Santa (Holy Week), the Feria de Abril (April Fair), and the entire six months of EXPO '92, rates doubles or triple and reservations are necessary. In off-season, bargain away.

Sevilla Youth Hostel (IYHF), C. Isaac Peral, 2, a few km out of town. Under complete reconstruction for 1992. For information call Inturjoven (tel. 422 51 71; English spoken). 644ptas, ages over 25 825ptas; nonmembers 2035ptas. Expect these prices to change. Camping 477ptas.

Hostal La Gloria, C. San Eloy, 58 (tel. 422 26 73), in the Zona del Centro. Bursting with plants and color. Singles 2000ptas, with bath 2500ptas. Doubles 3000ptas, with bath 3500ptas. Negotiable 400ptas for hot showers.

Huéspedes Buen Dormir, C. Farnesio, 8 (tel. 421 74 92). Climb northeast from the cathedral on C. Mateos Gago, bear left on the main thoroughfare, then turn right on Fabiola. Look for the alley across from #10. Colorful and cheap, with friendly English-speaking manager and 101 family pets. Singles 1300-1500ptas. Doubles 2500ptas, with bath 3500ptas. Showers included.

Hotel Simón, C. García de Vinuesa, 19 (tel. 422 66 60), across Av. Constitución from the cathedral. Renovated 18th-century mansion. Singles 2100ptas, with bath 3700ptas. Doubles 3700ptas, with bath 5000ptas, during EXPO 9000ptas.

Hostal Romero, C. Gravina, 21 (tel. 421 13 53), parallel to C. Marqués de las Paradas, and one block away from the river. Naturally cool place with basic rooms, homey decorations. Convenient to EXPO. Singles 1600ptas. Doubles 2700ptas. Triples 3600ptas. Showers included.

Hostal Residencia Los Gabrieles, Plaza de la Legión, 2 (tel. 422 33 07), facing the old Córdoba train station. Half the rooms have a long-distance view of the EXPO grounds. Singles 1500ptas. Doubles 3000ptas, during EXPO 7000ptas. Showers included.

Hostal Bienvenido, C. Archeros, 14 (tel. 441 36 55), near Pl. Curtidores. Small, simple rooms and a thatched-roof terrace for sunbathing. Singles 1600ptas. Doubles 2600ptas. Negotiable 300ptas for hot showers. EXPO doubles 9000ptas.

Hostal Bonanza, Sales y Ferre, 12 (tel. 422 86 14), off Pl. Alfalfa. Basic rooms with *Dating-Game* vintage furniture. Fun owner. Singles 2000ptas, with shower 2300ptas. Doubles with shower 3000-3500ptas, with bath 4500ptas.

Hotel La Rábida, C. Castelar, 24 (tel. 422 09 60), between Pl. Nueva and the building. Grand entryway. All rooms have air conditioning, winter heating, TVs, telephones, and full baths. Singles with bath 4000ptas. Doubles with bath 6500ptas, during EXPO 15,000ptas. Triples with bath 8500ptas.

Camping: All accessible by bus from the main bus station. **Camping Sevilla** (tel. 451 43 79) is 10km out on Carretera Madrid-Cádiz, Km. 534. Take the Empresa Casal bus to Carmona (approximately every hr. 7am-9:30pm, 225ptas). **Camping Villsom** (tel. 472 08 28) is 18km out on Carretera Sevilla-Cádiz, km 554.8. Take the Los Amarillos bus to Dos Hermanas (about every 45 min. 6:30am-midnight, 2000ptas). **Club de Campo,** Av. Libertad, 13 (tel. 472 02 50), is 15km out on Carretera Sevilla-Dos Hermanas. Take the Los Amarillos bus to Dos Hermanas. All three charge 315-325ptas per person.

Food

By Spanish standards, food in Seville costs top peseta, though cheap, indistinguishable restaurants cluster on C. Marqués de Paradas, near the old Córdoba train station. Fresh produce and baked goods can be yours at the Mercadillo de Encarnación, in the Pl. Encarnación. (Open Mon.-Sat. 9am-2pm.) Get great *churros* with *café* or thick, rich *chocolate* (215ptas total) at **Cafetería Postal,** C. Almirantazgo, 10, across Av. Constitución from the cathedral. (Open for *churros* daily 8am-12:30pm.)

Pizzería Renato, C. Pavía 17, on the corner of C. Dos de Mayo. Facing the post office, take the first right and continue straight through the golden archway. Multi-topping pizzas will stuff you for 420-560ptas. *Lasagna al horno* comes sizzling straight out of the oven, smothered with superb cheese sauce (600ptas). Open Thurs.-Tues. 1:15-3:45pm and 8:45-11:45pm, Sat. 8:45pm-midnight.

La Bodequita Pollos, C. Azofaifo, 9, off C. Sierpes in the Zona del Centro. Tame atmosphere, TV, and deliciously zesty roasted chicken. ½-chicken, fries, salad, and beverage 625ptas. Open daily 1-4:30pm and 7-11pm.

Jalea Real, Sor Angela de la Cruz, 37, near Pl. Encarnación. Amazing vegetarian dishes in a Spanish fern bar. Enormous *plato combinado,* 550ptas. 2-course lunch *menú* 1000ptas. Open Mon.-Fri. 1-5pm and 9-11:30pm, Sat. 1-5pm; Sept.-June Tues.-Sat. 1-5pm and 9-11:30pm, Sun. 1-5pm.

Restaurante El Baratillo, C. Pavía, 12, on a tiny street off C. Dos de Mayo. The cheapest food in Seville. Tasty, decent-sized *menú* 375ptas. Meals served Mon.-Sat. 1-10pm.

Cervecería Giralda, C. Mateos Gago, 1, behind the cathedral. Snappy Andalusian tiled walls and Moorish arches buzz with local clientele. Long wait for a table and expensive prices, but yum-yum dinner. Open daily 9am-midnight.

Mellado, C. Salado, 13, in Barrio de Triana. Delicious fresh fish and seafood in informal self-service atmosphere. Fried shrimp 400ptas. Open Tues.-Sun. 8pm-3am.

Mesón La Barca, C. Santander, 6, up from the Torre del Oro. Ample portions at good prices. Has the tough-to-find Andalusian specialty *estofado de venado* (stewed deer), cooked with red wine, garlic, and vegetables (750ptas). *Platos combinados* 530-650ptas. Open Sun.-Fri. 1-4pm and 8-11:30pm.

El 3 de Oro, C. Santa Maria la Blanca, 34, down from C. Menédez Pelayo. Laid-back cafeteria with great *paella* (400ptas). *Menú* 875ptas. Open Sun.-Fri. 1-4pm and 8-11:30pm. Occasionally closed Sun.

Sights and Entertainment

From April 20 to October 12, 1992, Seville's extravagant **1992 Universal Exposition** will sprawl over 538 acres on the Isla de Cartuja in the Río Guadalquivir. Its theme will be "The Age of Discoveries." Admission gives you access to well over 100 pavilions, theaters, a planetarium, relaxing gardens, on-site outdoor events and performances, and a recreation of the Renaissance port of Seville. Some pavilions make inadvertent political comments (the Soviet Pavilion has an inclined roof with rectangles of constantly flipping color, while the Reagan government slashed the American Pavilion's budget by three quarters, expecting private funding that never arrived). The EXPO is also Europe's most massive development project, save the Chunnel; it has brought Seville a new airport, a new train station with high-speed service to Madrid, new highways and seven new bridges, and massive afforestation and air-conditioning schemes. The EXPO site is within walking distance of the city center; an army of trains, buses, riverboats, and cable cars will help bring visitors in. (For information, call 446 19 92. Advance ticket purchase unnecessary. Day pass 4000ptas; 3-day pass (consecutive or not) 10,000ptas; evening pass (from 8:30pm) 1000ptas. Entrance booths open 8am-4am; pavilions open 10am-10pm.)

The bright light of the EXPO ought not to blind you to Seville's permanent attractions. In 1401, the Catholics razed the greatest of the Almohad mosques in Seville and built, on the same spot, a **Cathedral** "so great that those who come after us will take us for madmen." Massive pillars support the vaulted roof, and the wealth of treasure boggles the mind. Only St. Peter's in Rome, St. Paul's in London, and a recently constructed monster in the Ivory Coast are larger. The ponderous gold and black coffin-bearers at the entrance allegedly carry the remains of Christopher Columbus. The neighboring **Giralda** tower was the minaret of the former Almohad mosque, now a belfry adorned with a gyrating weather vane (hence the tower's name). (Cathedral and tower open Mon.-Fri. 11am-5pm, Sat 11am-4pm, Sun. 2-4pm. Admission 250ptas, free with ISIC.)

Beside the cathedral and the tower is the 16th-century **Lonja Palace,** first the administrative center for Spain's American trade and now the principal archive for maps and documents from that period. Its monumental pilasters and austere style blend with the grand, expansive boulevards of Renaissance Seville, built to contrast with the winding streets of the Moorish districts. Next to the palace is the **Alcázar,** a magnificent 14th-century Mudejar palace blending the Gothic and the Moorish. Almost as stunning as the intricate tilework in the palace's interior are the resplendent gardens outside. (Lonja Palace open Mon.-Fri. 10am-1pm. Free. Alcázar open Tues.-Sat. 10:30am-5:30pm, Sun. 10am-1:30pm. Admission 300ptas. Free with ISIC card.) Built in 1540 by the Marquis of Tarifa, the **Casa de Pilatos,** on the plaza of the same name, is now home to the Duke of Medinaceli. The building is another fine example of Gothic-Mudéjar and Renaissance architecture. (Open daily 9am-7pm. Admission 400ptas.)

The **Museo Provincial de Bellas Artes,** in a 16th-century Andalusian palace and a connected church, has a collection of Spanish masters second only to the Prado. (Open Tues.-Sun. 9:30am-2:30pm. Admission 250ptas, students free.) More works by Murillo and Valdés Leal can be seen in the church **Hospital de la Caridad,** on C. Temprado, parallel to the Paseo de Colón. (Open Mon.-Sat. 10:30am-1pm and 3:30-6pm, Sun. 10am-12:30pm. Admission 100ptas.) The **Museo de Arte Contemporáneo,** C. Santo Tomás, 5, exhibits 20th-century Spanish art. (Open Tues.-Sun. 10am-2pm. Admission 250ptas.)

If you're wilting from excessive art and heat, escape to one of Seville's many shady retreats, such as the sub-tropical **Parque María Luisa** or the **Jardines de Murillo.**

To experience the *sevillana* brand of flamenco music and dancing, go to **Los Gallos,** Pl. Santa Cruz, 11. It's expensive (2000ptas), but it's the best venue for flamenco in Seville. Seville's nightlife rarely folds before 5 or 6am. Founded 30 years ago to foster young artists whose work was censored under Franco, **La Carbonería,** C. Levies, 18, 2 blocks west of C. Menéndez y Pelayo, is now an art gallery and bar featuring live jazz and folk, and flamenco on Thursdays. A huge pick-up scene with loud

American and British music can be found at the riverside bars called *chiringuitos* on the east bank of the river between Puente del Generalísimo and and Puente de San Telmo. (Beer 150ptas. Open summer weeknights until about 5am, Fri-Sat. until about 6:30am.) *Baile* and flail at dance-spots **El Coto,** C. Luis de Morales, 118, next to Hotel Los Lebreros (cover 800ptas), or **El Río,** C. Betis, 69 (cover 325ptas). Foreigners, especially Americans, are often admitted free.

Seville's **Semana Santa** (Holy Week) festival is internationally famous for its processions of barefoot, hooded penitents carrying candles or lugging resplendent floats. The city explodes in the **Feria de Abril** (April Fair), a weeklong festival that began as a popular revolt against foreign influences in the 19th century. Based in the *casetas* (pavilions) of the fairground in Triana, the party rages through Seville with circuses, folklore displays, and bullfights.

Near Seville

About 100km southwest of Seville on Spain's Atlantic coast is a world of villages renowned for their rural charms and their sherry. The fine beaches here are increasingly popular as an escape from tourist-studded nightmares. The best way to see the region is to head inland, following the **Ruta de los Pueblos Blancos** (Route of the White Villages), a string of towns running from the Costa de la Luz, around Gibraltar, to the Costa del Sol. An automobile, a patient thumb, and Andalusian bus service are all options for exploring the region.

Take a train south from Seville (16 per day, 45 min. 240ptas) to untouristed **Jerez de la Frontera,** which produces some of the world's finest sherries and brandies. You can sample *jerez* (sherry) for free on a tour of a *bodega,* the warehouse where the amber liquid ferments. Most of the brands, including **Sandeman, González Byas,** and **Harvey's,** offer guided tours in several languages. (Usually open Mon.-Fri. 10am-2pm.) Pick up a marked map at one of the travel agencies in town, or at the **tourist office,** C. Alameda Cristina, 7 (tel. (956) 33 11 50). The best time to appreciate winemaking is during the **Fiestas de la Vendimia,** the celebration of the season's harvest during the second week of September. Look around Calle Medina for a place to spend the night—or your lunch money. **Cádiz** itself was the headquarters of the Spanish treasure fleets; Sir Francis Drake torched the Spanish Armada as it lay at anchor here in 1587. Check around the harbor and Pl. San Juan de Díos for cheap places to stay. Seven trains per day run from Seville via Jerez de la Frontera (2 hr., 950ptas).

Spectacular **Arcos de la Frontera** is a labyrinthine white village on top of a harsh promontory, undercut on three sides by the Río Guadalete. The beige, 15th-century **Church of Santa María,** on Pl. España, is magnificent. Climb to the top of town for a panoramic **market;** for lodgings, try near the bottom, at **Fonda del Comercio** (tel. (956) 70 00 57) on C. Debajo del Corral, 15y (singles 1000ptas; doubles 2000ptas). Take a bus from Jerez de la Frontera (17 per day, 6 on Sun., ½ hr., 225ptas).

Spaniards everywhere celebrate the Pentecost, 50 days after Easter, but few debaucheries match that of the **Romeriá del Rocío,** in the cute village of **El Rocío,** 60km west of Seville.

Córdoba

On the banks of the Río Guadalquivir, Córdoba blends the traditions of Judaism, Islam, and Christianity in a Flamenco cuisinart. Arab occupation brought the town its greatest prosperity; for a time Córdoba, with its vast library, was one of the largest cities in medieval Europe. The city's whitewashed houses, serene patios, and narrow streets typify Spanish Andalusia; its Moorish influence lingers as both Muslims and Catholics still congregate in the Mezquita (mosque) every year on the anniversary of its construction.

Orientation and Practical Information

Córdoba sits atop the Andalusian triangle (north of Seville and Granada), about halfway between Madrid and Gibraltar. Most sights, monuments, and accommodations cluster in the **Judería,** a maze of narrow, winding streets and flowery courtyards that was once the city's Jewish quarter, between the Plaza de las Tendillas and the Río Guadalquivir. Eye your belongings. North of the plaza is the new city, home to the train station and bus lines.

Tourist Office: Provincial, C. Torrijos, 10 (tel. 47 12 35), on the west side of the Mezquita; enter through the Palacio de Congresos y Exposiciones. English spoken. Open Mon-Fri. 9:30am-2pm and 5-7pm, Sat. 10am-1pm; in winter Mon.-Fri. 9:30am-2pm and 3:30-5:30pm, Sat. 10am-1pm. **Municipal,** Pl. Judas Levi (tel. 29 07 40; ask for *oficina municipal de turismo),* 2 blocks west of the Mezquita. Open Mon.-Fri. 8am-3pm.

Post Office: C. Cruz Conde, 15 (tel. 47 82 67), north of Pl. Tendillas. Open Mon.-Fri. 8am-9pm, Sat. 9am-2pm. **Postal Code:** 14001.

Telephones: Pl. Tendillas, 7. Open Mon.-Sat. 9am-1pm and 5-9pm. **City Code:** 957.

Trains: Station is on Av. América 130 (tel. 47 93 02), on the north side of town. Baggage storage. **RENFE,** Ronda de los Tejares, 10 (tel. 47 58 54). Open Mon.-Fri. 9am-1:30pm and 5-7:30pm. To: Seville (12 per day, 1¾-2 hr., 660-1415ptas); Madrid (5 per day, 4½-8 hr., 2950-4100ptas); Málaga (6 per day, 2-3 hr., 955-1900ptas).

Buses: Transportes Ureña and Empressa Bacoma, Av. Cervantes, 22 (tel. 47 23 52). To: Seville (3 per day, 2-3 hr., 975ptas); Madrid (3 per day, 6 hr., 2780ptas); València (3 per day, 3800ptas); Barcelona (3:40pm, 6000ptas). **Alsina-Graells Sur,** Av. Medina Azahara, 29 (tel. 23 64 74). To: Granada (5 per day, 3-4 hr., 1370ptas); Málaga (3 per day, 3½ hr., 1230ptas); Cádiz (7:30am, 1770ptas).

Medical Assistance: Casa de Socorro, at Av. República Argentina, 4 (tel. 23 46 46). **Hospital Cruz Roja,** Po. de la Victoria (tel. 29 34 11).

Emergencies: (tel. 091 or 092). **National Police,** (tel. 25 34 00). **Guardia Civil,** (tel. 23 34 00).

Accommodations, Camping, and Food

Cheap accommodations bunch in the Judería, where *casas de huéspedes* and *hostales* retain Moorish patios. Some of the cleanest and cheapest (about 1200ptas per person) are on Calle Rey Heredía, northeast of the Mezquita. **La Milagrosa** is at #12 (tel. 47 33 17); **Rey Heredía,** at #26 (tel. 47 41 82). Also worth exploring is the area around Plaza del Potro, east of the cathedral.

Residencia Juvenil Córdoba (IYHF), Pl. Judas Levi (tel. 29 01 66). Sparkling new postmodern hostel in the heart of the Judería. All is sweetness and light. 3-day max. stay. 644ptas, ages over 26 825ptas. *Media pensión* 1120ptas, ages over 26 1540ptas. Call ahead in summer.

Huéspedes Martinez Rücker, Martinez Rücker, 14 (tel. 47 25 62), east of the Mezquita. Friendly owners tend an airy courtyard. 1200ptas per person. Showers included.

Hotel Residencia Boston, C. Málaga, 2 (tel. 47 41 76), on Plaza Tendrillas. Air-conditioning, heating, TVs, telephones, and baths in modern rooms. Watch out for Pennywise the Clown in the marble entryway. Singles with small bath 2100ptas. Doubles with bath 3600ptas.

Camping: Campamento Municipal, Av. Brillante (tel. 47 20 00; ask for *camping municipal).* Swimming pool. Buses run every 20 min. from the campground to city monuments. 325ptas per person, per tent, and per car.

Head to the Judería or the new city for good, cheap victuals. Along the river, **Restaurante LaLaLa,** C. Cruz del Rastro, 3, serves delicious, fresh *pescado frito* (fried fish) and offers generous menús for 575-650ptas. (Open Tues.-Sun. 9:30am-4pm and 7pm-12:30am.) Sip aromatic herbal teas and enjoy Arabic *menús* (800ptas) at **Cafetín Halal,** C. Rey Heredia, 28 (tel. 47 76 30; open daily noon-4:30pm and 6:30-11:30pm). The Jewish quarter around the Mezquita, especially on C. Luna, is splendid *tapas* and bar-hopping territory. Head to **Bodegas Campos,** in an alley off C. Lineros near Plaza del Potro, to sip wine and gander at the famous signatures on the barrels.

Sights and Entertainment

No drove of camera-flashing tourists could subvert the majesty of Córdoba's **Mezquita.** Begun in 785, the mosque was intended to transcend all others in grandeur. It took over two centuries to raise this airy forest of 850 marble, alabaster, and stone pillars. There's a Renaissance-Baroque cathedral stuck in the middle of it. (Open daily 10am-1:30pm and 4-7pm; Oct.-March daily 10am-1:30pm and 3:30-5:30pm. Admission 400ptas.)

The **Alcázar** is not just another military monument; it also has Roman mosaics, manicured gardens, and terraced goldfish ponds. (Open daily 9:30am-1:30pm and 5-8pm; Oct.-March 9:30am-1:30pm and 4-7pm. Admission 200ptas, Sun. free.) Córdoba's **Synagogue,** on C. Judíos, marked by a statue of **Maimonides,** is a sad reminder that 1492 signifies not only Columbus's discovery of the New World, but also the expulsion of the Jews from Spain. (Open Tues.-Sat. 10am-2pm and 3:30-5:30pm, Sun. 10am-1:30pm. Admission 50ptas. EC citizens free.) Almost next door is the **Museo Municipal de Arte Cordobés y Taurino,** a bullfighting museum. (Open Tues.-Sat. 9:30am-1:30pm and 5-8pm, Sun. 9:30am-1:30pm; Oct.-April Tues.-Sat. 9:30am-1:30pm and 4-7pm, Sun. 9:30am-1:30pm. Admission 200ptas, Sun. free.)

Those seeking more Moorish *mihrabs* should go to the **Medina Azahara,** 8km northwest of Córdoba. Constructed in the 10th century by Abderrahman III as a gift to his favorite wife, the palace ruins were unearthed in 1944, confirming centuries of legends. (Open Tues.-Sat. 10am-2pm and 6-8pm, Sun. 10am-1:30pm; Oct.-April Tues.-Sat. 10am-2pm and 4-6pm, Sun. 10am-1:30pm. Closed Aug. afternoons. Admision 250ptas. EC citizens free.) Call ahead to make sure it's open (tel. 23 40 25). The O-1 bus leaves from Av. Cervantes for Cruce Medina Azahara about every hour 6:30am-10:30pm (65ptas).

Granada

As the Christian Reconquista advanced, the Moors circumscribed the glorious city of Granada with layer upon layer of fortification. The citadel was bitterly contested until 1492, when Boabdil, its last Arab king, turned over the city's keys to Catholic monarchs Fernando and Isabel. Granada's Muslim and Jewish populations were either Christianized, massacred, or expelled. Though the city's mosques were destroyed, the majestic clay-red Alhambra and snow-capped Sierra Nevada still lure travelers here.

Orientation and Practical Information

The Sierra Nevada cleaves the province of Granada in half, separating the Costa del Sol from the plains of the north. The city's center is **Plaza Nueva,** framed by a handful of handsome Renaissance buildings. **Gran Vía de Colón** and **Calle de los Reyes Católicos** intersect at **Plaza de Isabel la Católica,** just south of Plaza Nueva.

Tourist Offices: C. Libreros, 2 (tel. 22 10 22), between the southwest corner of the cathedral and Pl. Bib-Rambla. Ultra-knowledgeable, super-patient and multi-lingual. Open Mon.-Fri. 10am-1pm and 4-7pm, Sat. 10am-1pm. Another office at Pl. Mariana Pineda, 10 (tel. 22 66 88). Open Mon.-Fri. 10am-1:30pm and 4:30-7pm, Sat. 10am-1pm.

Budget Travel: Viages TIVE, Martinez Campo, 21 (tel. 25 02 11). BIJ tickets and assorted travel info. Open Mon.-Fri. 9:30am-1:30pm and 4:30-8:30pm, Sat. 11am-1pm.

American Express: Viajes Bonal, Av. Constitución, 19 (tel. 27 63 12), at the northern end of Gran Vía de Colón. No wired money accepted. Open Mon.-Fri. 9:30am-1:30pm and 5-8pm. Currency exchange only available Mon.-Fri. 10am-1pm.

Post Office: Puerta Real (tel. 22 48 35), at the intersection of C. Reyes Católicos, C. Recogidas, and C. Mesones. Stamps and Lista de Correos available Mon.-Fri. 8am-9pm, Sat. 8am-2pm. **Postal Code:** 18070.

Telephones: C. Reyes Católicos, 55, 1 block towards Pl. Nueva from Pl. Isabel la Católica. Open Mon.-Sat. 9am-2pm and 5-10pm. **City Code:** 958.

Flights: Iberia, Pl. Isabel la Católica, 2 (tel. 22 75 92). Open Mon.-Fri. 9am-1:15pm and 4-7:15pm. Airport information, Tel. 20 33 22.

Trains: Station on Av. Andaluces (tel. 23 31 08), off Av. Constitución. Take bus #4, 5, 9, or 11 to the center of town. **RENFE,** C. Reyes Católicos, 63 (tel. 22 31 97). Open Mon.-Fri. 9am-1:30pm and 4:30-7pm.

Buses: Alsina Graells, Camino de Ronda, 97. Take bus #11 to the center of town. **Bacoma,** Av. Andaluces, 12 (tel. 28 42 14), next to the train station.

Baggage Storage: In the train station (200ptas). Look for the *Camas* sign to the right of the exit.

Medical Assistance: Clínica de San Secilio, Ctra. Jaén, (tel. 22 15 44).

Police: Tel. 092, or at C. Duquesa, 21. **Emergency:** Tel. 091.

Accommodations, Camping, and Food

The safest and comeliest accommodations, despite the melancholy, withdrawing roar of passing buses, are lined up along Cuesta de Gomérez, off Plaza Nueva (a five-minute walk from the Alhambra). At #1, **Hostal Britz** (tel. 22 36 52) borders the plaza and has firm beds, an elevator, and a talking vending machine. (Singles 1537ptas. Doubles 2756ptas, with bath 3498ptas.) **Hostal Residencia Gomérez** at #10 (tel. 22 44 37) is kept sparkling clean by its young, multilingual, calculator-toting proprietor. (Singles 925ptas. Doubles 1600ptas. Hot showers 125ptas.) **Hostal Navarro-Ramos** at #21 (tel. 25 05 55) disdains the noise with rooms opening onto a courtyard. (Singles 1000ptas. Doubles 1700ptas, with bath 2700ptas. Hot showers included.) Closer to the train station is **Hostal-Residencia San Joaquin,** Mano de Hierro, 14 (tel. 28 28 79), a grand but slightly decaying 15th-century palace. (Singles with bath 1300ptas. Doubles with bath 2600ptas.) **Camping** is available at five locations near Granada, all of which charge 300-390ptas per person and per tent. **Sierra Nevada,** on Av. Madrid, 107 (tel. 15 09 54), offers the best facilities and services (390ptas; open March 15-Oct. 15).

The area around Plaza Nueva oozes restaurants offering cheap *platos combinados* or *menús del día.* **La Nueva Bodega,** C. Cetti Merién, up from the cathedral, purveys novel *menús* (525-1000ptas) and munchable *bocadillos* (around 200ptas). Prices plunge at the bar. (Open daily noon-midnight.) **La Riviera** next door at #5, isn't much different, except in having even more *platos-combinados* (550-650ptas) and a potent peach sangria. (Open Tues.-Sun. 8am-4pm and 8-11:30pm.) For atmosphere, venture into the **Albayzín,** the old Arab quarter, where most bars serve meals for about 500ptas. For dessert, indulge in the ice cream creations at **La Veneciana,** Gran Vía, 4 (50-300ptas).

Sights and Entertainment

A haunting incarnation of beauty and bloodshed, the palatial city of the **Alhambra** (red castle) keeps watch over the Andalusian plain. The endless courtyards and rooms inside the palaces of the **Casa Real,** among the world's finest examples of Mudejar art and architecture, have inspired centuries of writers. Roam the extensive gardens of the **Generalife,** the summer retreat of the sultans. (Open April 1-Sept. 30 Mon.-Sat. 9am-8pm, Sun. 9am-6pm; Oct. 1-May 31 daily 10am-2pm. Admission 500ptas. Separate 500ptas ticket required for illuminated nighttime visits, summer only, Tues., Thurs., and Sat. 10pm-midnight. Free entry Sunday after 3pm.)

Begun 30 years after the Christian reconquest of the city, the **Cathedral** (entrance on Gran Vía), intended to outshine the Alhambra, does not even rise out of its shadow. The **Capilla Real** (Royal Chapel), reached by a separate entrance, contains the elaborate tomb of Ferdinand and Isabella, their nutty daughter Juana la Loca, and her husband Felipe el Hermoso (whose corpse Juana dragged around with her for a disgustingly long time after his demise). (Both open March-Sept. daily 10:30am-1pm and 4-7pm; Oct.-Feb. daily 10:30am-1pm and 3:30-6pm. Admission to tomb and collection 150ptas each, Sun. morning free.)

To reach the **Albayzín,** Granada's old Arab quarter, take bus #12 from beside the cathedral and get off at C. Pages on top of the hill. From here, walk down C. Agua through the **Puerta Arabe,** an old gate to the city. Solo travelers should exercise caution in the Albayzín after dark.

Corpus Christi celebrations include processions and bullfights. The **International Festival** (mid-June to early July) features classical ballet amidst towering topiary in the gardens of the Generalife and concerts in the Renaissance palace on the Cerro del Sol. Those more concerned with yeast cultures than Iberian cultures should stick to the student pubs around the university, in the area bounded by C. Pedro Antonio de Alarcón, Callejón de Nevot, and C. Melchor Almargo.

Near Granada

Glistening above the sun-scorched plains of Andalusia is the **Sierra Nevada,** the tallest range in Iberia; the peaks of **Mulhacén** (3481m) and **Veleta** (3428m) sport the white stuff most of the year. A car facilitates travel in the Sierra Nevada. In Granada, try **Gudelva,** Pedro Antonio de Alarcón, 18 (tel. 25 14 35), which charges a minimum of 3600ptas per day plus 19ptas per km. The best map of the region for hikers was printed by the Federación Española de Montañismo (350ptas), before it went out of print. If you can't find it, try bookstores for the more expensive, 4-part, Sierra Nevada map printed by the Dirreción General del Instituto Geográfico Nacional (1200ptas).

Costa del Sol

Having learned to use beauty for profit, the Costa del Sol shows the strains of its trade. Waves break against concrete promenades, not sand, and swank hotels seal off whitewashed towns from the shoreline. Happily, pockets of bewitching coastline do survive. Northeast of Málaga, the hills dive into the ocean and the road coils around splendid vistas of surf boiling against rock and sand.

In July and August, expect crammed lodgings and beaches, and higher prices; peak season, when rooms are often double the normal price, is usually mid-June to mid-September. If you don't have reservations, arrive early and pray. Ask around for private homes with rooms to let *(casas particulares).* Camping on the beach is illegal in most places. The coastal rail line connects Málaga to Torremolinos and Fuengirola. Inexpensive and frequent private bus lines (railpasses not valid) cover the rest of the area. Hitching is toilsome, and unsafe for solo women.

Málaga

Málaga is the stepmother of the Costa del Sol's fairy tale: ugly and harsh but central to the story. Despite its present appearance and smell, this cosmopolitan port has inspired sensitive souls like native son Picasso and Nobel laureate Vicente Aleixandre, who called Málaga "the city of paradise." The palm-lined **Paseo del Parque** will take you below the **Alcazaba,** a Moorish palace whose fortified walls enclose heady gardens and an archeological museum. (Open Mon.-Sat. 10am-1pm and 5-8pm, Sun. 10am-2pm. Admission 30ptas.) Also worth a visit is the **Museo de Bellas Artes,** San Augustín, 6, which includes works by Murillo, Ribera, and Picasso. (Open daily 10am-1:30pm and 5-8pm. Admission 250ptas, EC students under 21 free.) Those itching for sand should hop bus #11 (75ptas) from the Po. del Parque and head to **Pedregalejos,** at the eastern end of the town.

Málaga's **tourist office,** Pasaje de Chinitas, 4 (tel. (952) 21 34 45), off Plaza de la Constitución, employs English speakers. (Open Mon.-Fri. 9am-2pm, Sat. 9am-1pm.) The **RENFE** office on C. Strachen (tel. (952) 21 47 27) romps over that at the train station, C. Cuarteles (tel. (952) 31 25 00). (RENFE open Mon.-Fri. 9am-1:30pm and 4:30-7:30pm.) The **bus station** is behind the train station on Paseo Tilos. There are plenty of accommodations north of the Paseo del Parque and Alameda Principal, but nearly all affordable rooms are grotty. Try the rowdy yet clean **Hostal-Residencia Chinitas,** Pasaje Chinitas, 2 (tel. 21 46 83), off Pl. Constitucíon. (Singles 1400ptas. Doubles 2600ptas. Showers included.) **El Tormes,** C. San José and C. San Augustín, off C. Granada, has enormous *menús* for 800-1000ptas. (Open daily 1-5pm.)

Marbella

Marbella flaunts all the accoutrements of a glamorous playboy. Nevertheless, the grungy backpack-toter can make do. The twisting, blooming streets of its eastern section will distract you from the high-rise hotels. **Plaza de los Naranjos,** a shady square filled with orange trees and a fountain, is particularly soothing (although its restaurant prices aren't). The English-speaking **tourist office** is at Av. Miguel Cano, 1 (tel. (952) 77 14 42); from the bus station on Av. Ricardo Soriano take a left, then take the sixth right just before the park. Their indexed map is a lifesaver. (Open Mon.-Fri. 9:30am-1pm and 5-7:30pm, Sat. 10am-1pm.)

Marbella is bedlam in late July and August; arrive early and cross your fingers if you haven't reserved. Bartenders can often direct you to locals renting out rooms. The best place to find *hostales* and *fondas* is in the old section behind Av. Ramón y Cajal. Try looking on **Calle Ancha** and its continuation, **Calle San Francisco.** On **Calle Aduar,** parallel and 2 blocks west, **Casa-Huéspedes Nuestra Señora de la Concepción,** below the pink hairdressing sign at C. Aduar, 21 (tel. (952) 77 52 18), has new bathrooms and tasteful rooms. (Singles 1300ptas. Doubles 2200ptas.) At #7 on the same street, **Casa Huéspedes Aduar** (tel. (952) 77 35 78) overflows with plants and flowers from its courtyard. (Singles 1500ptas. Doubles 2000ptas. Showers included.) The spotless, English-run **Hostal del Pilar,** C. Mesoncillo, 4 (tel. (952) 82 99 36), is a small piece of Britannia in Spain. (Singles 1700ptas. Doubles 2600ptas. Triples 3600ptas.)

For a little bit of culinary heaven, try **Bar el Gallo,** C. Lobatas, 46; ask for the *San Jacobo,* pork stuffed with ham and swiss and fries (400ptas). **Bar Taurino,** towards the top of C. San Francisco, cooks a mean *tortilla* (300ptas) and attracts a boisterous crowd. **Restaurante Sol y Sombra,** C. Tetuán, 7, offers somewhat expensive but fresh seafood (600-1100ptas). For nightlife, Marbella's jet set cruises to the bars and discos of **Puerto Banús,** 7km away, where drinks often start at 700ptas.

Ronda

Ronda's history runs as deep as the gorge of El Tajo which splits the town. Pliny and Ptolemy mention it as Arunda, a southern enclave of the Celts. During Muslim occupation Al Mutadid ibn Abbad annexed the city to Seville by asphyxiating its unlucky lord in his bath. German poet Rainer Maria Rilke wrote his *Spanish Elegies* here; in 1987 Orson Welles's hefty ashes were buried on a bull farm outside of town. Those with a fear of heights or tourists will not be comfortable here.

Orientation and Practical Information

Ronda lies amidst the isolated hills of the Serranía de Ronda, 104km northwest of Málaga. In town, three bridges span the knee-knocking gorge; the 18th-century **Puente Nuevo** connects the **Ciudad** (old quarter) with the **Mercadillo** (new quarter). The main *paseo* of the city is **Carrera Espinel,** which runs perpendicular to **Calle Jerez,** the street connecting the old and new quarters.

Tourist Office: Oficina de Turismo, Pl. España (tel. 87 12 72). English-speaking staff. Open Mon.-Fri. 10am-2:30pm.

Post Office: C. Virgen de la Paz, 20 (tel. 87 25 57). *Lista de Correos* (Poste Restante). Open Mon.-Fri. 8am-3pm, Sat. 9am-1pm. **Postal Code:** 29400.

Telephones: Orbase, S.L., C. Mariano Soubirón, 5 (tel. 87 46 70), off C. Virgen de la Paz. Expensive private office; accepts Visa and Mastercard. Open daily 9am-2:30pm. **City Code:** 952.

Trains: Station on Av. Andalucía (tel. 87 16 73). To get to Pl. España from the station, turn right on Av. Andalucía, which becomes C. San José. When the street ends, turn left onto C. Jerez, and follow it past the city park and the bull ring. Direct to Algeciras (6 per day, 3 hr., 505ptas), or to Bobadilla for connections to Seville (at noon, 4½ hr., 1130ptas), Málaga (3 per day, 2 hr., 645ptas), and Granada (3 per day, 4hr., 895ptas). **RENFE** ticket office, C. Infantes, 20 (tel. 87 16 62) is open Mon.-Fri. 10am-2pm, Sat. 10am-1:30pm.

Buses: Station at Av. Concepción García Redondo, 2, the continuation of Av. Andaluciá. To get to Pl. España, follow the directions from the train station. **Empresa los Amarillos** (tel. 87 22 64) runs to Seville (5 per day, 3 hr., 980ptas) and Málaga (5 per day, 845ptas). **Empresa Comes** (tel. 87 19 92) to Jerez (4 per day, 1005ptas), and Cádiz (3 per day, 1270ptas). **Portillo S.L.** (tel. 87 22 62) to Marbella (6 per day, 415ptas). **Ferron Coin** handles most local connections and the cheapest route to Málaga (3 per day, 700ptas).

Medical Assistance: First Aid (tel. 87 17 73). **Clínica Comarcal** (tel. 87 15 40), Ctra. del Burgo.

Emergency: tel. 091. **Police,** Av. Málaga, 9 (tel. 87 13 70).

Accommodations and Food

Budget accommodations more than meet the healthy tourist demand. Calle Sevilla, perpendicular to Carrera Espinel, is thick with cheap beds. **Hostal Ronda Sol,** C. Cristo, 11 (tel 87 44 97), near C. Sevilla, is the best pick in town. (Singles 1150ptas. Doubles 2000ptas.) Relax in the tiled courtyard at **Hostal Morales,** C. Sevilla, 51 (tel 87 15 38). (Singles 1200ptas. Doubles 2400ptas.) **Fonda La Española,** C. José Aparicio, 3 (tel. 87 10 52), around the corner from the tourist office, has clean, ample rooms that have seen better days. (1000ptas per person.)

Few cheap restaurants make a stand in Ronda, and every last tourist knows about those that do. **Cervecería Marisquería El Patio,** Ctra. Espinel, 100 (tel. 87 10 15), has a patio outside and air conditioning inside. (Grilled swordfish 600ptas. Open Thurs.-Tues. noon-4pm and 8pm-1am.) **Pizzeria Piccola-Capri,** C. Villanueva, 18 (tel. 87 39 43), serves delicious pasta and pizza—ask for a table spying on the bridge. *(Menú* 800ptas. Open daily noon-4pm and 8pm-midnight.) Escape from *el sol* on the vine-entwined terrace of **Mesón Santiago,** C. Marina, 3 (tel. 87 15 59), off Pl. Socorro. (Entrees 700-1000ptas. Open daily 1-4:30pm and 8pm-midnight.) The same owners run a cafeteria next door, serving the same food at lower prices.

Sights

Ronda's tremendous gorge is a mighty, heighty sight. Construction of the **Puente Nuevo** (New Bridge), finished in 1735, killed one head architect and drove another to suicide. Across the bridge in the **Ciudad** (old quarter), a colonnaded walkway leads to the **Palacio del Marqués de Salvatierra,** a Renaissance palace with a twinkly floor. (Open Mon.-Wed. and Fri.-Sat. 11am-2pm and 4-6:30pm, Sun. 11am-1pm. Admission 200ptas.) Facing the carved Incas of the palace façade is the **Casa del Rey Moro.** If you descend the winding stone steps, Ronda's two remaining bridges appear, as well as the 14th-century **Baños Arabes** (Arabian sauna baths). At the center of the old quarter, the asymmetrical Moorish **cathedral** peers over a refreshing plaza of gardens. At night **Las Catacumbas,** a tavern in the bowels of the cathedral, becomes a worldly nightspot with silky sangria.

In the new quarter, visit the **Plaza de Toros,** Spain's first bullring, dating from 1784. The **Museo Taurino** inside takes you through the history of the two great bullfighting dynasties of Ronda: that of Pedro Romero, the founder of modern bullfighting and inventor of the scarlet cape *(muleta),* and that of Cayetano Ordóñez, starring as the matador in Hemingway's *The Sun Also Rises.* (Open daily 10am-7pm; Oct.-May 10am-2pm. Admission 150ptas. Free for kids and seniors after 3pm on Fri.) Bullfights are held during the **Feria de Ronda** in early September.

Gibraltar and Algeciras

The solid rock of **Gibraltar** guards the gateway to the Atlantic and commands a stunning view of the North African coast. Known affectionately as "Gib" by the locals, this tiny peninsula takes its Britishness *very* seriously. But unlike London's bobbies, those on the Rock slip easily from the Queen's English into Andalusian Spanish, and pesetas are as welcome as the official sterling. British sovereignty and the Spanish presence haven't always coexisted peacefully. Franco cut off all contact between the Rock and Spain during a 20-year period in which Gibraltar was inhabited by eccentric British nationals. In 1985, the Spanish government reopened the frontier gates; now, anyone with a passport may travel freely to and from the Rock.

The main **tourist office** is located in the Gibraltar Museum at 18-20 Bomb House Lane (tel. +350 764 00), off Main St. (Open Mon.-Fri. 9am-6pm.) There is also a branch at the frontier right after customs. (Supposedly open Mon.-Fri. 8am-2:30pm, Sat. 10am-2pm; mid-Sept. to mid-June Mon.-Fri. 9am-4:30pm, Sat. 10am-2pm.) Gibraltar has a separate **country code** (350); from Spain, dial 07 to access the international net. For AT&T's **USA Direct,** dial 88 00. The cheapest beds in Gibraltar are at the **Toc H Hostel** on Line Wall Rd. (tel. +350 734 31), unadorned and almost always full. (£15 per week.) The **Queen's Hotel** on 1 Boyd St. (facing the cable car station) is hardly a budget establishment but usually has a bed. (Singles £22, with bath £30. Doubles £30, with bath £35-£40; tel. +350 740 00). The *only* other choice is the **Miss Serruya Guest House,** 92/1a Irish Town (tel. +350 732 20; singles £8.50, doubles £12). You may want to sleep in unattractive Algeciras instead. Buses run between **La Línea** (on the Spanish side of the border) and Algeciras every 1½ hr. 7am-9pm (175ptas.) Camp on the rock and the bobbies will pitch you into the strait.

Just 13km across the blue, on the Spanish side of the Bahía de Algeciras, the port of **Algeciras** offers cheap rooms, a neat peek at the Rock, and little else. Trains run from Córdoba (2 per day, 5½ hr., 2095ptas) and Málaga; the **tourist office** and travel agencies located near the port can provide information about ferries to Tangier, Morocco (4-8 per day, 2½ hr., 2700-3440ptas), and Ceuta (6-12 per day, 80 min., 1440ptas). Comfortable, inexpensive lodgings are found around C. José Santacana, 1 block inland from the port. Check **Hostal Vizcaíno,** (tel. (956) 65 57 56) at C. José Santacana, 9. (Singles 850ptas, with shower 900-1000ptas. Doubles with shower 1800ptas.) Try **Hostal Levante,** 1 block over on C. Duque de Almodóvar, 21 (tel. (956) 65 15 05). (Singles 1500 ptas, with bath 2000ptas. Doubles 2100ptas, with bath 3000ptas. Showers included.) Beware of vespa Visigoths prowling the streets of Algeciras at all hours.

SWEDEN

USD$1 = 6.36 kronor (kr)
CAD$1 = 5.56kr
GBP£1 = 10.6kr
AUD$1 = 4.95kr
NZD$1 = 3.63kr
Country Code: 46

1kr = USD$0.16
1kr = CAD$0.18
1kr = GBP£0.09
1kr = AUD$0.20
1kr = NZD$0.28
International Dialing Prefix: 009

Some call Sweden the world's success story, a modern miracle. Fervent social democratic idealism and principled wartime neutrality have made Sweden (Sverige) a land whose affluence is widely shared. Thanks to free health care, education and other services, Sweden some years ago became the first place on earth in which physicians could not tell the social class of children by examining their bodies and growth rates.

Sweden's internationalism is unforgettable: diplomat Raoul Wallenberg clambered over the roofs of Nazi trains handing out Swedish passports that saved thousands of Jews from concentration camps, Dag Hammarskjöld nurtured the U.N., and Prime Minister Olof Palme marched against the Vietnam War and sheltered draft resisters. Today in impoverished East Africa, so much of the aid arriving at the ports bears the Swedish colors that many villagers assume Sweden is a global superpower.

The country's 8.3 million citizens—among them tens of thousands of political refugees—inhabit a land the size and shape of California. A whopping thirty hours by train in length, Sweden defies the whirlwind tour. But unless you're an avid mountaineer, you needn't make the pilgrimage north to Lappland's sleepless sun and the alpine huts of Abisko. If logging and coastal scenery inspire you, head to the northeast coastal cities of Luleå, Umeå and Sundsvall. Life pulses peacefully in the southern half of the country, where 85% of Swedes reside, many taking their five-week paid vacations in waterside cottages or on Viking-trodden Gotland or Öland, islands off the southeast coast. If it's young people you seek, take off to Uppsala's cultured and vivacious student universe. At the center of it all lies celestial Stockholm, a city of utopian hopes—and bland apartment blocks.

Getting There and Getting Around

Sweden is easily accessible by boat or train from Denmark and Germany, by ferry from Poland and Finland, or by train and bus from Norway and Finland. A consistent and reliable series of trains greets travelers in the southern half of the country; trains in the north are predictable, but sporadic buses (railpasses usually not valid) are often a better option. Long-distance buses travel from Stockholm to Göteborg and Malmö. Consider buying the 21-day **Nordturist** pass, which allows unlimited travel on state-run trains and ferries in Denmark, Sweden, Norway and Finland (2nd class 1625kr, ages 12-25 1215kr; this is much cheaper than the ScanRail pass sold in the U.S.). You can buy the pass at almost all train stations. Persons under 16 or over 65 years old travel at half-price, while children under 12 ride free with an adult. Fares are reduced 50% on trains marked with a red circle in the timetable. InterRail and Eurail are valid, but reservations (20kr) are still required on some long-distance journeys marked with a boxed R in the timetable.

For those under 25, **SAS** offers a standby fare of 200-250kr on all their flights between Stockholm and other Swedish cities (call (08) 24 00 00 for details Mon.-Fri. 7am-9pm, Sat. 8am-6pm, Sun. 8am-8pm). **Hitching** in Sweden can be slow near the major cities, but picks up in the north. In this safety-minded country, all must wear seatbelts, and headlights must be on at all times. Sweden is a biker's heaven; numerous paths cover most of the country, particularly in the south. Contact the Svenska Turistföreningen (STF) (see below) for more information.

Practical Information

Sweden is a nation of bank holidays (Jan. 1, Jan. 6, April 17-20, April 30-May 1, May 28, June 7-8, June 20, Oct. 31, and Dec. 24-26 in 1992) and festivals. May 1 brings a rousing solidarity parade in Stockholm, while Midsummer (best celebrated in folksy Dalarna) incites Bacchanalian dancing around the maypole. Plan ahead for these days, as many transportation lines grind to a halt and some hostels close.

Most Swedish banks are open weekdays until 3pm (sometimes later in Stockholm). Exchange rates remain constant from bank to bank, but commissions vary. Try to exchange checks in large denominations, as there is usually a 10kr commission per check. Many post offices double as banks and are open weekdays from 9am to 5pm or later, Saturday from 9am to 1pm. Pay phones require at least 2kr except in summer, when most are half-price. Call 079 75 for directory information in Sweden and 0018 to make a collect call. For AT&T's **USA Direct,** dial 020 79 56 11. For **emergency help** dial 900 00 (free). Almost all Swedes speak some English, and younger ones are generally fluent.

Sweden leads the world in facilities for the disabled. Begin by requesting the Swedish Tourist Board's free 260-page *Holiday Guide for the Disabled.*

Accommodations, Camping, and Food

Sweden's top-flight youth hostels *(vandrarhem)* are the country's only budget option in Sweden; hotels cost 250-300kr at the very cheapest. If you arrive in the off-season and the local hostel is closed (a problem in the north and in smaller towns), staying in private homes is a bearable alternative (100-150kr per night). Book through the local *turistbyrå* (tourist office).

The **Svenska Turistföreningen (STF)** runs Sweden's hostels. They often fill in a flash during summer, so reserve in advance. Most hostels have kitchen facilities, and receptions are usually open from 8 to 10am and 5 to 9 or 10pm (shorter hours in winter; over 100 of the 280 hostels are open all year.) Outside the cities, *vandrarhem* are often used by Swedish families who can't afford the country's expensive hotels. STF's main office is in downtown Stockholm at Drottninggatan 31, P.O. Box 25, 101 20 Stockholm (tel. (08) 790 31 00), with branches in Göteborg and Malmö; they'll sell you membership (205kr) and the indispensable *STF Vandrarhem* book (59kr), listing all hostels with maps, pictures, phone numbers, opening hours and dates (open Mon.-Fri. 9am-6pm, Aug.-April Mon.-Fri. 9am-5pm). The STF also manages mountain hut accommodations in the northern wilds. Many campgrounds (50-80kr per site) also offer accommodations in *stugor* (simple cottages, often with kitchen facilities) for around 100-150kr per person. If you don't have an International Camping Card, you'll need a Swedish one (25kr). You may walk or camp for one night anywhere on *privately* owned land—except for gardens—so long as you respect flora and fauna. Pick up a brochure about this, *Allemansrätten,* at the STF. Meet youthful Swedes and foreigners by joining a workcamp; contact **Internationella Arbetslag,** Barnängsgatan 23 in Stockholm (tel. (08) 43 08 89).

Food is very expensive in Sweden, both in restaurants and grocery stores. Rely on supermarkets (the Konsum chain is especially good); most are open until 5 or 6pm. Still, a loaf of bread can cost 20kr. Swedish berries make life more than just OK; grab a box of strawberries or blueberries, or try *pannkakor* with lingonberry jam. Tasty Swedish milk products include *messmör* (spreadable whey cheese) and *fil,* a fluid yogurt good for dousing your cereal. When you tire of cold muesli, seek out restaurants that offer a **dagens rätt,** a daily special usually available only at lunch. This may be the only time you can afford a sit-down meal: the price (40-50kr) includes a main dish, salad, bread, and beverage. Food costs drop as one heads farther north. Alcohol is not a wise option for the budget traveler; a real beer *(starköl)* usually costs at least 39kr, often 60-70kr, in city bars. The cheaper, weaker, and lousier low-alcoholic alternative is *lättöl* (8-12kr).

Southern Sweden

Islands and skerries line both the east and west coasts of Sweden; the **Småland** coastline, between Västervik and Kalmar in the east, is particularly beautiful, and well-stocked with restful places. The western **Halland** coast between Gothenburg and Helsingborg, while pleasant, is less breathtaking. Clear lakes and limitless woods abound in inland Halland and Småland. The island of **Öland,** accessible from Kalmar via Europe's longest bridge, supports a nature reserve, filled in spring and summer with birds and unusual plants; it also has its share of archaeological sites. Famous crystal makers like Orrefors and Kosta roost in towns by the same name (near Växjö in Småland). The endless fields of **Skåne** and **Blekinge,** Sweden's southernmost provinces, evoke images of Denmark rather than other parts of Sweden.

No wonder; the Danes ruled here for hundreds of years, leaving a multitude of castles and manors before Sweden snatched everything but the still-Danish island of Bornholm. Blekinge (around Karlskrona) is traditionally known as Sweden's garden, and Skåne (the stub of Sweden across from Copenhagen) as the breadbasket. Southern Sweden is splattered with youth hostels (over 20 in Skåne alone), and most counties publish comprehensive brochures detailing outdoor activities in the area. A few hours' train travel from Copenhagen will get you anywhere in the region.

Malmö and Lund

Malmö, Sweden's third-largest city, rises on the west coast of Skåne, a short boat ride across the Öresund from Copenhagen. Influenced by trade and modernization, little remains today of the old cobblestone streets. The **central station** and **ferry harbor** lie just to the north of the old town. Try **Copenhagen Line** for the cheapest trips to Copenhagen (5 per day, 30kr) or **Flygbåtarna** hydrofoils for the most frequent (2 per hour, 85kr). Trains arrive from near and far (Göteborg 322kr, Stockholm 533kr). The exceptionally knowledgeable **tourist office,** Skepsbron 1 (tel. (040) 34 12 70), is right by the ferry quay, 2 min. from the train station, in the main post office. (Open daily mid-June-Aug. 10am-7pm; late May-early June Mon.-Fri. 10am-6pm.) Free **showers** and **baggage storage,** as well as a reasonably-priced café lurk in the **InterRail Center,** Stortorget 24 (tel. (040) 11 85 85; open Aug.-June Sun.-Thurs. 9am-10pm, Fri.-Sat. 9am-midnight, July daily 9am-6pm). Rent bikes from Fridhem Cykelaffär, Tessinväg 13 (tel. (040) 260 335; 35kr per day; open Mon.-Fri. 9am-noon and 1-6pm, Sat. 10am-1pm).

The **Kirsebergs Youth Hostel** (tel. (040) 34 26 35) is at Dahlemsgatan 5; take bus #14 or 18 to Kirsebergsskolan. (95kr. Basic breakfast included. Open late June to mid-Aug.) The alternative is the slightly sterile **IYHF Hostel,** Södergården, Backavägen 18 (tel. (040) 822 20). Take bus #21A to Vandrarhemmet, walk across Trelleborgvägen to Backavägen and turn right. (85kr, nonmembers 117kr. Open mid-Jan.-mid-Dec.) The tourist office will book rooms in **private homes** (about 100kr) for a 40kr fee. **Sibbarp Camping,** Strandgatan 101 (tel. (040) 15 51 65), is at the end of bus route #11A. (Tents 55kr.) Browse around **Möllevangstorget** at mealtimes; it offers a wide variety of cuisine at the lowest prices. The same square has a **vegetable and fruit market** (open Mon.-Fri. 10am-2pm). The cheapest supermarket close to the center of the city is **AG Favör** on Värnhemtorget (open Mon.-Fri. 9:30am-7pm, Sat. 9:30am-3pm).

Off **Lillatorget,** an idyllic square of old houses and cobblestones adjacent to Storatorget, is the **Form and Design Center,** in an old yellow building at Lillatorget 9, which exhibits Sweden's contributions to the advancement of convenience culture—bike helmets, wheelchairs, and other useful stuff. (Open Tues., Wed. and Fri. 11am-5pm, Sat. 10am-4pm, Sun. noon-4pm. Free.) From here you might want to wander to the **Rooseum,** Gasverksgatan 22, a collection of contemporary art. (Open Mon.-Fri. noon-7pm, Sat. and Sun. noon-5pm. Admission varies.) Or wander in the other direction to **Malmöhus,** the city's old fortress, now a group of museums housing everything from historical artifacts to the local aquarium. (Open June-Aug. Mon.-Sat. noon-4pm, Sun. noon-4:30pm; Sept.-May Tues.-Sat. noon-4pm, Sun. noon-4:30pm.) In good weather, head for the **parks** which surround Malmöhus and continue several blocks past the beach south of Slottsparken. (Always open.) To figure out what's happening in Malmö, consult the tourist office, the InterRail center, or the all-knowing, all-seeing **Malmö This Month** guide (free and widely available).

Malmö can't compete with the serene beauty of **Lund,** its smaller but more worthwhile twin city 30km away. Lund houses Sweden's second-largest **university,** which pumps the town with young people in winter. Their sophisticated fraternities—called *nations*—sleep more sleepily during the vacations than those of rival Uppsala, but you can try calling the Småland (tel. (046) 12 06 80), Lund (tel. (046) 14 51 20), or Malmö (tel. (046) 12 78 02) nations to see what's up. The campus is north of the town's ancient **cathedral,** a remnant of the time when Lund was the religious epicenter of Scandinavia. Inside are a **crypt** of sculpted tombstones and the intricate **astronomical clock,** whose trumpet-playing figurines parade daily at noon (1pm on Sun.) and 3pm (open Mon.-Sat. 8am-6pm, Sun. 9am-6pm). **Kulturen,** Tegnérplatsen, is not only a collection of old houses from all over Sweden, but a museum with exhibits from past wars, modern art, archaeological findings and much more. (Open May-Sept. daily 11am-5pm; Oct.-Apr. daily noon-4pm. Admission 25kr, with ISIC card 15kr.)

Most intercity trains from Malmö stop at Lund; the two cities are also connected umbilically by local trains (*pågatågen,* railpasses not valid), which at 25kr are cheaper than regular SJ trains. *Pågatågen* also run to destinations in most of Skåne (for information, pick up a schedule at stations or tel. (040) 23 63 38). Lund's **tourist office** (tel. (046) 15 50 40) sits above an ancient church at Kattesund 6 (open June-Aug. Mon.-Fri. 9am-6pm, Sat. 10am-2pm, Sun. noon-4pm; Sept.-May Mon.-Fri. 9am-4pm, Sat. 10am-2pm, Sun. noon-4pm) and will willingly surrender a *Lund* brochure and a companion listing of opening hours and prices for every sight in town.

Rest your tired limbs at the unusual **IYHF Hostel Tåget** (The Train), Bjerredsparken (tel. (046) 14 28 28). Turn right as you come down from the trains in the central station, and follow the signs (85kr, nonmembers 117kr; open Jan. to mid-Dec.). The tourist office books rooms in **private homes** (100-130kr plus hefty 40kr fee). **Camping** is closest at Källbybadet (tel. (046) 15 51 88); take bus #91 toward Klostergården. (Open mid-June to August.) **Mårtorget** has a fresh fruit and vegetable market (open Mon.-Sat. 7am-2:30pm). Supermarkets are all over (the ICA store across from the station is open daily 9am-10pm). **Chrougen,** at Sandgatan 2 in the Akademiska Föreningen (student union), is the local student hangout, moonlighting as restaurant and disco. (All-you-can-eat lunch 50kr, dinners from 115kr. Open Mon.-Fri. 11am-1am, Sat. 7pm-2am.)

From **Helsingborg** in northern Skåne, frequent trains bound for Copenhagen cross over on equally frequent ferries to Helsingør in Denmark; reach Helsingborg by SJ train or by *pågatåg* (from Malmö 60kr, Lund 35kr). **Trelleborg,** in southern Skåne, sees several ferries per day off to Saßnitz (railpasses valid) and Travemünde in Germany; take an SJ train from Malmö (55kr). From **Ystad,** also in southern Skåne, multiple daily ferries serve Bornholm (see under Denmark), and other shuttle to Gdańsk (mid-May to Sept. 2 per week) and Świnoujście (all year, 2 per day) in Poland. Reach Ystad by *pågatåg* (from Malmö 55kr, Lund 55-75kr). Helsingborg, Trelleborg, and Ystad all have IYHF hostels.

Gothenburg (Göteborg)

A moat semicircles Gothenburg's old town, along the south side of the Göta Älv river, but it's quite obscured by the shipping derricks and apartment blocks of Sweden's second-largest city. The central train station lies just northeast of the old town, while Kungsportsavenyn, the city's main boulevard, runs south. The **tourist office,** Kungsportsplatsen 2 (tel. (031) 10 07 40), is in the old town (open mid-June to mid-Aug. daily 9am-8pm; early June and late Aug. daily 9am-6pm; Sept.-Apr. Mon.-Fri. 9am-5pm; May Mon.-Fri. 9am-6pm, Sat.-Sun. 10am-2pm). There is another branch in the Nordstan shopping center, just next to the train station (open Mon.-Fri. 9:30am-6pm, Sat. 9:30am-3pm). **Foreign exchange** is cheapest in the numerous Forex shops (open daily 8am-9pm in the train station and Kungsportsavenyn shops).

All intercity **trains** arrive at the central station; so do long-distance **buses** (Swebus office in the station open Mon.-Fri. 7:30am-6pm, Sun. 10:30am-6pm). The station offers **lockers** (20kr per 24 hr.) and **showers** (15kr for 15 min.; open daily 6am-10pm). Many **ferries** sail from Gothenburg; **Stena Line** (tel. (031) 75 30 00) has ferries to Frederikshavn, Denmark (6-8 per day, 3 hr., free with Eurailpass) and to Kiel, Germany (1 per day); trams #3 and #4 run between the train station and the ferries (use the Masthuggstorget stop). **Scandinavian Seaways** (tel. (031) 80 55 10) runs a few ships per week to Harwich (England) and Amsterdam.

Public transportation is a must if you move out of the city center. Trams, buses and even boats in the skärgård are accessible with the *magnetkort.* These regular fare cards come with different amounts of *kuponer;* normally 2-3 kuponer will bring you anywhere in greater Gothenburg (valid 1 hr.; single ticket (2 kuponer) 12kr, 11 kuponer for 50kr). The **24-hour-card** (40kr) allows unlimited travel. All cards are available at the **Tidpunkten** kiosk at Nils Ericsonsplatsen, behind the train station (open Mon.-Thurs. 7am-10pm, Fri.-Sat. 7am-2:30am, Sun.-9am-6pm), and in the many **Pressbyrån** kiosks at transit hubs (grab a free transit map here, too). The **Göteborg Card** gives you free public transportation plus free entry (or discounts) at a multitude of attractions and tours (available at tourist offices and hotels; 24 hr. for 95kr, 48 hr. for 170kr, and 72 hr. for 225kr).

The **IYHF hostel** closest to the center of town is the enormous, well-equipped and friendly **Ostkupan,** Mejerigatan 2 (tel. (031) 40 10 50). Take tram #1, 3, or 6 to Redbergsplatsen, and bus #62 to Gräddgatan. (79kr, nonmembers 111kr. Sheets 45kr. Open early May-late Aug.) The cheapest hostel in town, **Nordgården,** Stockholmsgatan 16, (tel. (031) 19 66 31) is cozy, but cramped and in a basement. Take tram #1 and #3 to Stockholmsgatan and walk downhill; the hostel is in the yellow wooden building on your left. (60kr. Reception open daily 7-11am and 4-9pm. Sleeping bags allowed. No curfew.) As always, the tourist office will book rooms in **private homes** (about 180kr) for 50kr. The closest **campsite** is *Kärralund Camping,* Ulbertsgatan (tel. (031) 25 27 61; open all year, 140kr per tent). The **Saluhallen** and adjacent **Grönsakhallen,** off Kungsportstorget, give you access to a wide variety of special foods and fresh vegetables (both open Mon.-Fri. 9am-6pm, Sat. 8am-1pm). Down Kungsportsavenyn at #28 lies the bountiful **Domus supermarket** (open Mon.-Sat. 10am-9pm, Sun. 1-9pm). Right next to it lies **Leonis,** Kungsportsavenyn 32 (open Mon.-Fri. 10:30am-7:30pm, Sat. 11am-7:30pm, Sun. noon-7pm), which serves plenty of salads (from 42kr) and sandwiches (from 26kr). **Solrosen,** Kaponjärgatan 4 (open Mon.-Tues. 11am-11pm, Wed-Fri. 11am-1pm, Sat. 2pm-1am, Sun. 2-8pm) is the city 's vegetarian hotspot.

The mighty **Poseidon statue** stands in front of the **Konstmuseum** (art museum) at the upper end of Kungsportsavenyn, which has large permanent exhibits of greater and lesser creations. (Open May-Aug. Mon.-Sat. noon-4pm, Sun. 11am-5pm; Sept.-April Tues. and Thurs.-Sun. noon-4pm, Wed. noon-9pm. Admission 20kr). At Vasagatan 37-39, a block from Kungsportsavenyn, lies the unique **Röhsska** museum, exhibiting a wide variety of crafts from different periods and areas. (Open May-Aug. Mon.-Sat. noon-4pm, Sun. 11am-5pm; Sept.-Apr. Wed.-Sun. noon-4pm, Tues. noon-9pm. Admission 20kr.) Göteborg is a center of entertainment in the sense that many popular performing artists come here before any other Scandinavian city. Consult the *Göteborg This Week* newspaper for concert and event listings. Tickets are sold from a separate booth in the main tourist office at Kungsportsplatsen 2 (tel. (031) 13 65 00; open Mon.-Sat. 10am-4pm). The **Liseberg** amusement park features a *smörgåsbord* of roller coasters and gardens. (Open weekends mid-April to early May and mid-Aug. to Sept.; daily mid-May to early Aug. Admission 35kr.) The nighttime is the right time on Kungsportsavenyn.

The cheapest pleasure in Gothenburg is the surrounding *skärgård* (archipelago); the nearby coast has the same rugged shores as the rest of Sweden. Parts of the archipelago are military zones off-limits to foreigners (get the notice at the tourist office). **Vrangö** is particularly nice (accessible with a standard public transportation ticket from Saltholmen; take tram #4). **Nya Elfsborg** is a fortress where the Göta Älv meets the sea; many a time, this island stronghold defied the Danish navy and saved Gothenburg. Tours leave Stenpiren from early May to early September (7 per day, 55kr).

Stockholm

Stockholm holds august monuments but no imperial arrogance, genteel cultural life free from injurious class distinctions, opulent consumerism without hardness of heart. Hot-air balloons dot the summer sky while sailboats slip between the city's islands. How, you may ask, could such a serene city nurture the melancholy pensiveness of an Ingmar Bergman or the stoic radicalism of an Olof Palme? Visit in the winter and find out.

Orientation and Practical Information

With narrow cobbled streets and chic restaurants, **Gamla Stan** (Old City), is the centerpiece of Stockholm's 24,000-island archipelago. To the east lie the museums and hostels of Skeppsholmen island and the cultured greenery of Djurgården; to the south, the island of Södermalm. The train station stands on the southern edge of the mainland, just east of yet another island, the workaday Kungsholmen. The *tunnelbana* (subway) links it all up.

Tourist Offices: Stockholm Information Service, in the northeast corner of Kungsträdgården at Hamngatan (tel. 789 20 00; Sat.-Sun. 789 24 90). T-bana: Kungsträdgården. From Centralstation, walk up Klarabergsgatan to Sergels Torg, then bear right on Hamngatan. Books hostels (10kr) and hotels (20kr). The bookstore 1 flight up sells fascinating factsheets (1kr) on every aspect of Swedish life, as well as a book with general information about Swedish society (30kr). Tourist information open Mon.-Fri. 8:30am-6pm, Sat.-Sun. 8:30am-5pm; Sept. to mid-June Mon.-Fri. 9am-5pm, Sat.-Sun. 9am-2pm. **Hotellcentralen,** at the train station (tel. 24 08 80). Same room-finding fees and a black-and-white city map for only 10kr. Open daily 8am-9pm, Oct.-April Mon.-Fri. 8am-5pm.

Budget Travel: SFS-Resebyrå, Kungsgatan 4 (tel. 23 45 15). BIJ tickets and cheap flights, especially for students. Also has branch on the university campus at Frescati. **Transalpino** Birger Jarlsgatan 13 (tel. 24 07 10). Open Mon.-Fri. 10am-5pm. T-bana for both: Östermalmstorg.

Embassies: U.S., Strandvägen 101 (tel. 783 53 00). **Canada,** Tegelbacken 4 (tel. 23 79 20). **U.K.,** Skarpögatan 6-8 (tel. 667 01 40). **Australia,** Sergelstorg 12 (tel. 24 46 60). **Kiwis** should contact the British Embassy. **Estonia** (tel. 10 99 86; open Mon.-Fri. 10am-noon), **Latvia** (tel. 10 50 24), and **Lithuania** (tel. 613 00 40 or 613 00 41), all at Rådmansgatan 18. **Poland,** Prästgårdsgatan 5 (tel. 764 48 00). **USSR,** Gjörwellsgatan 31 (tel. 13 04 40, for visa info 20 86 52).

Currency Exchange: Forex in Centralstation (open daily 8am-9pm) and in Cityterminalen (9am-6pm) take 5kr per traveler's check. Post offices also exchange money and cash traveler's checks (see below).

American Express: Birger Jarlsgatan 1 (tel. 14 39 81, for 24 hr. refund assistance 020 79 51 55). T-bana: Östermalmstorg. Open Mon.-Fri. 9am-5pm, Sat. 10am-1pm.

Post Office: Vasagatan 28-34, near Centralstation, lower level. Poste Restante held here (postal code 10110 Stockholm 1). Open Mon.-Fri. 8am-6:30pm. Also at Centralstation (open Mon.-Fri. 7am-10pm, Sat. 10am-7pm, Sun. noon-7pm).

Telephones: Telefonbutiken, Skeppsbron 2, on the north side of Gamla Stan. Open daily 8am-9pm. Also at Centralstation Open Mon.-Fri. 7am-9pm, Sat. 9am-1pm. **City Code:** 08.

Flights: Arlanda Airport is 45km north of the city. **Flygbussar** buses (40 min., 50kr; public transportation passes not valid) run between it and Cityterminalen (see Buses below), departing Cityterminalen every 10 min. 5:30am-10:20pm.

Trains: Sprawling **Centralstation** (T-bana: T-Centralen) is Stockholm's principal gateway. Left luggage office downstairs near the Vasagatan entrance; lockers scattered throughout the station (most downstairs; 15-25kr per 24 hr.) Open 6am-11pm. Train information, tel. 22 50 60. To Copenhagen (8 per day, 8-9 hr., 478kr) and Oslo (3 per day, 6½ hr. day, 9 hr. overnight, 488kr).

Buses: The **Cityterminalen,** across the street from Centralstation, sends buses to the airport, the Gotland and Poland ferries, and on routes within Sweden on Fridays and Sundays (to Göteborg, 7-8 hr., 170kr, to Malmö, 10-11 hr.; reservations required).

Public Transportation: Stockholm's transit authority (SL) runs a center in Sergelstorg which provides information and sells the *Stockholmskartan* (35kr), a peerless street map complete with bus and subway lines. (Open Mon.-Thurs. 8:30am-6:30pm, Fri. 8:30am-5:30pm, Sat. 10am-3pm. For information on all SL service, call 23 60 00.) The city's metro doubles as the world's longest modern art gallery. Most in-town destinations cost 2 coupons (12kr).

Rabatt-kuponger, sold at *Pressbyrån* news agents (55kr, valid for up to 7 trips), are a good buy. They also sell monthly passes (225kr) for unlimited travel in greater Stockholm. The **SL Tourist Card** costs 30kr (24 hr. limitless travel in the central zone), 55kr (24 hr. in all zones), or 105kr (3 days in all zones). Some subway lines stop at midnight, but most run until 2am, after which they are replaced by night bus services. Distant suburbs are served by *pendeltåg* trains. The **Stockholmskortet** (Stockholm Card) offers unlimited free travel by bus, subway and local trains (not airport buses), free boat sightseeing, a bus tour around the city, admission to 68 attractions in Stockholm, and a free guide to the city (125kr for every 24hr. up to 3 days).

Ferries: Both **Silja Line,** Kungsgatan 2 (tel. 22 21 40) and **Viking Line,** Stureplan 8 (tel. 714 56 00 and 44 07 65, also at Centralstation) sail daily from Stockholm to Mariehamn, Turku, and Helsinki in Finland (292kr); Silja ferries to Turku and Helsinki are free with Eurailpass, 50% off with Nordturist and InterRail (T-bana: Ropsten; take a Silja bus from there to the terminal). Viking Line ferries are 25-30% off with Eurail and InterRail (T-bana: Slussen; then catch bus #45 to the terminal.) Ferries to **Gotland** leave from Nynäshamn, south of Stockholm by bus or SL commuter rail (see under Gotland); **Polferries** ships to Gdańsk, Poland leave from Oxelösund, further south (1-3 per week; tel. (0155) 781 00; 270kr, students, seniors and InterRail 250kr).

Bike Rental: Sommar Café, next to Skeppsholmens Vandrarhem. 45kr per day. Open mid-June to Aug. Mon., Wed. and Fri. 10am-6pm, Tues. and Thurs. 10am-9pm, Sat. 10am-4pm. When they're dry, try **Skepp och Hoj** on Djurgårdsbron (tel. 660 57 57). 90kr per day, 280kr per week. Open daily 9am-9pm.

Hitchhiking: Laborious. Those headed south take the T-bana to Skarholmen and stand at Kungens Kurva. Those going north take bus #52 to Sveaplan and stand on Sveavägen at Nortull, or go further up the E4 to the junction of Uppsalavägen and Enköpingsvägen.

Bookstore: Nya Akademibokhandeln, Mäster Samuelsgatan 32 (tel. 21 48 90). Truckloads of English books. Open Mon.-Fri. 9:30am-6pm, Sat. 10am-3pm (in July, closes at 2pm on Sat.). For cheaper English novels, try the used book stores on Drottningsgatan north of Klarabergsgatan.

Laundromat: Rare and expensive, since most Swedish apartments have laundry facilities. 15kr at the **Sommar Café** next to the Skeppsholmen youth hostel (open mid-June to Aug. Mon., Wed. and Fri. 10am-6pm, Tues. and Thurs. 10am-9pm, Sat. 10am-4pm). Or try Västmannagatan 61B (open Mon.-Fri. 9am-1pm and 2-6pm, Sat. 10am-2pm.)

Women's Center: Kvinnohuset, Snickarbacken 10 (tel. 10 08 00). A meeting place with a rape crisis center.

Gay and Lesbian Center: The Swedish Federation for Sexual Equality (RFSL) runs a lively center at Sveavägen 57 (tel. 736 02 12), T-bana: Rådmansgatan. Bookstore open Mon.-Fri. 6-9pm, Sat.-Sun. noon-6pm; café open daily 3pm-3am; Alice B. restaurant open daily 6pm-3am; disco nightly 9pm-3am.

Disabled travelers: Stockholm is very accessible to disabled travelers. Subways and most public places offer special facilities.

Pharmacy: Apotek C. W. Sheele, Klarabergsgatan 64 (tel. 21 89 34), under the green and white "Apotek" signs at the overpass over Vasagatan. Open 24 hrs.

Medical Assistance: Tel. 44 92 00 for a referral to the nearest hospital.

Emergencies: Police, Ambulance, and **Fire** tel. 900 00 (there's a special button on some older pay phones). Police station at Bryggargatan 19, just north of Centralstation (tel. 769 51 00).

Accommodations and Camping

Hostels

Although some hostels save beds for walk-ins, summer demands reservations.

Skeppsholmen

af Chapman (IYHF), a fully-rigged 1888 sailing ship (tel. 10 37 15) majestically moored off Skeppsholmen, to the right as you cross the bridge. It always rocks. 136 places in 4-10 bed cabins. Reception open 7am-noon and 3-10pm. Lockout 10am-4pm. Curfew 2am. 85kr, nonmembers 117kr. Breakfast 40kr. Sheets 25kr. For summer beds, reserve 2-3 months in advance or show up 7-8:30am. Open April to mid-Dec.

Skeppsholmens Vandrarhem (IYHF), in the Hantverkshuset, on the shore behind the af Chapman (tel. 20 25 06). Less mythic, but bigger rooms, and no waves. 152 beds, 2-6 per room. Reception open 7am-noon and 3-10pm. Lockout from rooms noon-3pm. Curfew 2am. 85kr, nonmembers 117kr. Breakfast 37kr. Backpack-sized lockers 5kr. Sheets 25kr. Laundry 15kr. Open mid-Jan. to mid-Dec.

Södermalm

Långholmen Vandrarhem (IYHF) Kronohäktet, on Långholmen Island (tel. 668 05 00). Plush cells in a transmogrified prison, each with TV, phone and private bath. From T-bana: Hornstull, march north on Långholmsgatan, turn left (before the bridge) onto Högalidsgatan, then right on Bergsundsgatan over the bridge onto Långholmen, then follow the "Kronohäktets Entré" signs. Reception open 24 hrs. No curfew, no lockout, no lockup. 85kr, nonmembers 117kr. Sheets 37kr. Laundry and kitchen facilities. Breakfast 50kr. Some free lockers. Fewer beds available on winter weekdays. Open all year.

Zinken Hostel (IYHF), Zinkens väg 20 (tel. 668 57 86). From T-bana: Zinkensdamm, turn right just ahead of you onto Hornsgatan, and follow it to #103; then turn left down the stairs at the hostel sign. A homey 250-bed hostel encamped in bungalows; 2-4 bodies per room. No curfew, no lockout if you finagle a key. 85kr, nonmembers 117kr. Breakfast 37kr. Luggage room and safe. Sheets 36kr. Kitchen facilities. Laundry 20kr.

Columbus Hotell-Vandrarhem, Tjärhovsgatan 11 (tel. 644 17 17). Three blocks from T-bana: Medborgarplatsen. Friendly staff and simple, sizable rooms. 120 beds, 2-6 per room. Reception open 24 hrs. No curfew. Solarium 30kr. 105-125kr. Kitchen. Lockers 5kr. Sheets 25kr. Open Jan.-late Dec.

Gustaf af Klint, Stadsgårdskajen 153 (tel. 640 40 77). A not-so-romantic former Navy ship moored 100m east of T-bana: Slussen. Reception open 24 hrs. 90 beds. Small 4-bedded cabins plus five doubles. 110kr per person. Breakfast 35kr. Free backpack-sized lockers. Sheets 35kr. Laundry 30kr. Open mid-Jan. to mid-Dec.

Norrmalm

Hostel Frescati, Professorsslingan 13-15 (tel. 15 94 34). T-bana: Universitetet. Bear left past the technicolor gym and up the hill. Modern student flats minutes from ethereal bayside nature trails. Open 24 hrs. No curfew. Single 250kr. Double 350kr. Breakfast 25kr. Sheets included. Open June-Aug.

Brygghuset, Norrtullsgatan 12N (tel. 31 24 24). T-bana: Odenplan. Calm, spacious 2-6 bed rooms. Limited kitchen facilities. Ping-pong room. 66 beds. Reception open 7am-noon and 3pm-2am. Lockout noon-3pm. Curfew 2am. 100kr. Breakfast 25kr. Free lockers. Sheets 25kr. Laundry 25kr. Open June 10-Aug.

Sleep Inn (formerly Dans Akademien), Döbelnsgatan 56 (tel. 612 31 18 and 612 38 36) opposite the post office. T-bana:Odenplan, or bus #52 from outside the Centralstation balcony to stop opposite "Hard Rock Café." Walk on Surbrunnsgatan to first cross-street, turn left. A debonair erstwhile ballet school filled with floor mattresses. Three large rooms: one for women, the other two mixed. Air-conditioned. 90 beds. Reception open 8am-noon and 4pm-1am. Lockout 1-4pm. Curfew 1am. 85kr. Sandwiches available from vending machines (6kr). Free lockers. Sheets 25kr. Laundry 25kr. Refrigerator. Open July 1-Aug. 19.

Camping

Bredäng Camping, 10km southwest of the city center near lovely Lake Mälar. T-bana: Bredäng. Follow the signs down the stairs, past the hulking housing project and along Stora Sällskapets väg to the campsite (7-10 min.). Often crowded. Store, laundry. 40kr per person. Open May-Sept. 8am-noon and 4-9pm; Oct.-April 7am-9pm.

Food

Stockholm's best deals are at lunch, when most restaurants offer a *dagens rätt*—an entree, salad, bread and butter—for 40-50kr. If that leaves you kronorless, head for a supermarket. There's one in the basement of **Åhléns** department store at Klarabergsgatan and Drottninggatan (open Mon.-Fri. 9:30am-9pm, Sat. 9:30am-8pm, Sun. noon-8pm) and a convenient **Servus** grocery on the Centralstation end of T-Centralen (open Mon.-Sat. 7am-11pm, Sun. 9am-11pm). The city is also filled with **Konsum** supermarkets. (Open Mon.-Thurs. 7:45am-5pm, Fri. 7:45am-3pm.) Call 743 50 00 for directions to the nearest one. **Hötorget** and **Östermalmstorg** both host outdoor produce markets and indoor deli malls (the underground Hötorgshallen is cheaper; open Mon.-Fri. 9:30am-6pm, Sat. 9:30am-2pm).

Kungshallen, Kungsgatan 44, on the north edge of Hötorget. 15 restaurants inside, serving everything from tacos to traditional Swedish food. Open Mon.-Sat. 9:30am-4am, Sun. 11am-4am.

Kafé 44, Tjärhovsgatan 44 (tel. 44 53 12). From T-bana: Medborgarplatsen, walk 3 blocks northeast. A dirt-cheap candle-lit mecca for poets and free thinkers. Sandwiches 15kr, pastry 6kr. Open Mon.-Fri. 9am-6pm, sometimes later for music and poetry readings.

Mätt o Lätt, Regeringsgatan 91, northeast of Hötorget. Italian wholefood dishes from 35kr in a laid-back atmosphere. Vegetarian dishes also offered. Open Mon.-Fri. 11:30am-6:30pm, Sat. 12:30-5:30pm.

Thé Huset (Tea House), Kungsträdgården, around the corner from the Opera House, behind the statue of Charles XII. Outdoor café under the shade of giant elm trees. Coffee 13kr, pastry 13kr, sandwiches 35kr. Open 9am-11:30pm.

Café Skänken, Schönfeldtsgränd at Mälartorget, by T-bana: Gamla Stan. Crêpes (34kr) and lasagna (40kr) with boundless bread and butter. Open Mon.-Thurs. 7:30am-7pm, Fri. 7:30am-6pm, Sat. 10am-5pm.

Sights

Stockholm's urban seascape is the city's most beguiling lure. For a view to end all views, walk uphill on Katarinavägen (on the north edge of Södermalm) to the sculpted hand memorializing Spanish Civil War martyrs. Or take Stockholm Sightseeing's 1½-hr. **"Under the Bridges"** cruise, which sails from Strömkajen, across from the Grand Hotel (95kr, ages 10-14 50kr; 8-10 per day in summer; tel. 24 04 70).

A symbol of Stockholm, the **Stadshus** (City Hall), on Stadshusbron near Centralstation, holds 19 million gilded tiles in its Golden Hall; you'll feast here when you win your Nobel Prize. (Tours daily at 10am, 11am, noon and 2pm; Sept. to mid-June 10am and noon; tower open May-Aug. 10am-3pm. Tour and tower 20kr, children free. Tower only 10kr.)

The **Gamla Stan** quarter is Stockholm's ancient heart, and it still beats healthily. Two-hour **walking tours** of this venerable isle start daily at 6:30pm from the obelisk between the palace and the cathedral (summer only, 20kr). At the northwest corner stands the 18th-century **Kungliga Slottet** (Royal Palace), within whose walls lurk the gold and glitter of menacing weaponry and extravagant living quarters. Listings in the courtyard give hours and exact prices (approx. 20kr) for the exhibits. Next to the palace soars Stockholm's 700-year old **Storkyrkan** (Cathedral), with its vivid 15th-century wooden sculpture of St. George and the dragon. (Open 9am-5pm.)

Head over to petite Skeppsholmen Island for a Rauschenberg sculpture of a goat wearing a rubber tire. This and other cultured monstrosities are yours at the **Moderna Museet** (open Tues.-Fri. 11am-9pm, Sat.-Sun. 11am-5pm. Admission 40kr, ages under 16 free, Thurs. free). For more traditional artistic fare—such as Rembrandt's stunning portrayal of the Batavian conspiracy—gambol through the **Nationalmuseum** at the north end of the Skeppsholmen bridge. (Open Tues. and Thurs. 11am-9pm; Wed., Fri. and Sun. 11am-5pm. Admission 20kr, students 10kr, Fri. free. Concerts late June-Aug. Tues. 8pm; 60-90kr, reservations unnecessary.)

Sample Swedish internationalism at the **Etnografiska Museet,** Djurgårdsbrunnsvägen 34, accessible by bus #69 from Norrmalmstorg. (Open Tues.-Fri. 11am-4pm, Sat. and Sun. noon-5pm; 15kr, children 10kr.)

Djurgården, east of Skeppsholmen, is Stockholm's pleasure island, reached by bus #44 or 47 from the center, by foot from attractive harborside Strandvägen, or by ferry from Nybroplan or Slussen (10kr). Especially wander-worthy is the island's south coast, where you'll pass house boats, museums and a former tar factory (Beckholmen). Djurgården's most intriguing sight is the **Vasa,** an intact 17th-century warship dredged up in 1961 from the bottom of Stockholm's harbor. The ship sailed only a few hours on its first voyage; it was too top-heavy and blew over when the wind picked up. The brand-new **Vasamuseet,** built specially for the ship, will knock your socks off. (Open daily 9:30am-7pm; late Aug. to mid-June Thurs.-Tues. 10am-5pm, Wed. 10am-8pm. Admission 30kr, students 25kr, ages 7-15 10kr, under 7 free.) Further inland sprawls **Skansen,** a vivid and vivifying open-air cultural museum, zoo, festival forum and folkdancing center. (Open daily 9am-10pm; in winter daily 9am-5pm. Admission 25kr, under 14 free. Call 663 05 00 to inquire about current happenings).

Millesgården—the mythic sculpture garden of Carl Milles—perches like an eagle's nest on the cliffs of Lidingö, spying down on Stockholm. To set your soul soaring, take bus #201, 202, 204 or 206 from T-bana: Ropsten to Torviks torg (tel. 731 50 60; open daily 10am-5pm, Wed. until 9pm; 25kr, students 20kr).

Entertainment

Let the street musicians of **Gamla Stan** enchant you, or sally through the island's pubs and clubs. City parks host free concerts nightly, and **Kungsträdgården** is seldom lonely. Concerts and dancing animate the summer evenings in Skansen, while Skeppsholmen shines with stellar performers during the **Stockholm Jazz and Blues Festival** (late June and early July; for details, call 25 01 80). Sniff out events in the free booklet *Stockholm This Week* or hack through the Saturday *På Stan* supplement of the *Dagens Nyheter* newspaper.

Engelen/Kolingen, Kornhamnstorg 59 (tel. 10 07 22) in Gamla Stan. A thumping disco in a crypt-like basement; easygoing pub and roulette upstairs. Frequent live bands. Cover Fri.-Sat. 70kr, Sun.-Thurs. 50kr. Pub open 4pm-3am, disco 7pm-3am.

Stampen, Stora Nygatan 5 (tel. 20 57 86 in day, 20 57 93 at night), in Gamla Stan. Traditional live jazz beneath pretzels, bird cages and a taxidermist's menagerie. Mon.-Thurs. 70-125kr, Fri.-Sat. 125kr. Open daily 8pm-1am; music from 8:45pm.

Mosebacke Etablissement, Mosebacke Torg 3. T-bana: Slussen. A musical terrace overlooking the town. Open Mon.-Fri. 11am-midnight, Sat.-Sun. noon-midnight; reduced hrs. in winter.

Ritz, Götgatan 51, entrance in the Medborgarplatsen T-bana arcade. A dark, planetarium-like disco. Gay nights Wed. and Fri. (with drag show). Free before 10pm, 60kr thereafter. Open Wed.-Sat. 9pm-3am.

Near Stockholm

The peninsulas and islands of Stockholm's surrounding **Skärgård** (archipelago) offer relaxing vacation spots for weary city dwellers or backpackers. To the west of Stockholm floats **Björkö,** a booming Viking Age trade center, and its recently-excavated sites. Daily ferries leave from Stadshusbron near the Stadshuset at 10am, returning at 4:45pm (Sat.-Sun. 3:45pm; round-trip 135kr). Ferries also leave from Strömkajen across from the Grand Hotel. The islands of the **Outer Skärgård,** hugging the Baltic coast, are ideal for an escape from urban life. Boats depart from Strömkajen (2-4hr.; 60kr one-way; contact Waxholmsbolaget (tel. 14 08 30) for information). Vaxholm, with its mighty fortress and museum is slightly closer to central Stockholm; contact Waxholmsbolaget or Strömma Kanalbolaget (tel. 23 33 75) about trips out (1 hr., 35kr) or take bus #676, 671, 672 or 673 from T-bana: Tekniska Högskolan. For excursions that cover the entire Skärgård contact Waxholmsbolaget, Strömma Kanalbolaget, or Stockholm Sightseeing (tel. 24 04 70).

Swedish egalitarianism notwithstanding, the royal family hangs out at extravagant **Drottningholm** amidst baroque gardens and rococo interiors. Catch the hourly English tour of the palace's **theater** and watch the original stage machinery produce thunderstorm effects. Ballet and opera are yours for 50-400kr (tel. 660 82 25 for ticket information). **Kina Slott,** Drottningholm's Asian pavilion, was an 18th-century royal summer cottage. (Palace and Kina Slott open May-Aug. daily 11am-4:30pm; Sept. Mon.-Fri. 1-3:30pm, Sat.-Sun. noon-3:30pm. Admission 25Kr, students and children 10kr. Theater open May-Aug. Mon-Sat. 11:30am-4:30pm, Sun. 12:30-4:30pm; Sept. daily 12:30-3pm. Admission 20kr, children 10kr.) Get to Drottningholm via frequent ferries from Stadshusbron, on buses #301 through 323 from T-bana: Brommaplan, or from Strömkajen with Stockholm Sightseeing.

Uppsala

Once a hotbed of pagan spirituality and the cradle of Swedish civilization, Uppsala now shelters the 20,000 exuberant students of Sweden's oldest university. A Nordic Oxbridge, the city is at once august and compact, well worth the 45-minute rail jaunt from Stockholm. Trains run about every hour and tickets can be purchased quickly at a separate counter in Stockholm's Centralstation.

As you exit the Uppsala train station, the center of town is ahead and to the right. Scandinavia's largest cathedral, the **Domkyrka,** where Swedish monarchs are crowned, looms just over the river (open daily 8am-8pm; Sept.-May 8am-6pm). The **Gustavianum,** across from the Domkyrka, lodges the macabre **Anatomical Theater**—once the site of public human dissections—as well as museums of Nordic, classical, and Egyptian antiquities. (Open June-Aug. daily 11am-3pm; Sept.-May Anatomical Theater only daily noon-3pm. Admission 10kr per museum, 20kr for all four.) South of the Domkyrka, the ruins of **Uppsala Slott** (Castle) have been revivified with historical scenes and effigies. (Open late June to mid-Aug. Mon.-Fri. 9am-7pm, Sat.-Sun. 10am-5pm; mid-April to late June and mid-Aug. to Sept. Mon.-Sat. 11am-3pm, Sat.-Sun. 11am-4pm. Admission 35kr, children 15kr. 10kr to see only the museum.)

A glorious pagan temple stood a millenium ago at **Gamla Uppsala** (Old Uppsala), 4km north of the city center. Little remains save huge burial mounds of monarchs and **Uppsala Kyrka** (Church), one of Sweden's oldest. (Open daily 9:30am-8pm; Sept.-March 9:30am-dusk.) Take bus #20 or 24 from Dragarbrunnsgatan, or the special tourist line (#700, late June to mid-Aug. only; leaves train station and Gamla Torget 11am and 1pm; 10kr, includes English commentary). Return within 90 minutes and you can re-use your bus ticket.

The **tourist office,** St. Persgatan 4 (tel. (018) 11 75 00), is near the east bank of the River Fyris. From the train station, walk right on Kungsgatan 3-4 blocks, turn left on St. Persgatan, and cross the bridge to pick up a map (25kr) of the city. (Open late June to mid-Aug. Mon.-Fri. 9am-7pm, Sat. 9am-2pm; mid-Aug. to late June Mon.-Fri. 10am-6pm, Sat. 10am-2pm.) Uppsala's hostel, **Sunnersta Herrgård (IYHF),** Sunnerstavägen 24 (tel. (018) 32 42 20), 6km south of town, offers pleasing doubles and a few triples, and swimming in nearby Lake Mälar. Take bus #20 (#50 after 6:20pm and on weekends) from Dragarbrunnsgatan to Herrgårdsvägen (20 min., 10kr), then walk 2 blocks behind the kiosk, turn left and walk 50m. (Reception open 8-10am and 5-9pm. 79kr, nonmembers 111kr. Laundry. Breakfast available. Open May-Aug.) From late June to mid-August the YMCA runs an easy-going **InterPoint** at Torbjörnsgatan 2 (tel. (018) 18 85 66), 2km north of the center; walk north on Svartbäcksgatan, or take bus #10 from Stora Torget, or #50 (night service) from Dragarbrunnsgatan near St. Persgatan, to Torbjörnsgatan (reception open 8-11am and 4:30-10pm; 70kr includes membership). By the river rests **Fyris Camping,** off Svartbäcksgatan 2km from the city center (tel. (018) 23 23 33; reception open Mon. and Thurs. 8am-11pm, Tues.-Wed. 7am-11pm, Fri. 10am-8pm, Sat. 9am-6pm, Sun. 9:30am-11pm; June-Aug. tents 25kr, huts 260kr; Sept.-May heated huts 200kr).

If you insist on wheels in this walkable town, rent them at **Cykel Ställét,** Svartbäcksgatan 20 (tel. (018) 13 87 40), for 60kr per day, 180kr per week (open Mon.-Fri. 9:30am-6pm, Sat. 10am-1pm). Or hop on the boat to **Skokloster,** a dazzling many-windowed baroque palace (85kr round-trip; departs 10am from Islandsbron on Östra Ågatan in the center of town; summer only).

All Uppsala university students belong to refined fraternities called *nations* (usually corresponding to their home districts in Sweden). The nations practically give away food and drink (hot meals average 35kr, beer 18kr) and throw buoyant fests. If you are a university student and happen to arrive on Thursday, bring your own

ID (but not an ISIC) and your passport to the student union office, Övre Slottsgatan 7 at Åsgränd, 2nd floor (tel. (018) 10 59 54; open Thurs. 5-7pm). They'll sell you a one-week student card for 30kr (10kr extra for each additional week). Or try the direct approach and show up at a nation's door with a smile and a college ID or ISIC in hand. Your best bets are **Upplands Nation,** St. Larsgatan 11, with its sculpture garden (tel. (018) 13 24 16; disco Fri.; open Tues.-Sun. 7pm-1am) or the easygoing **Södermanland-Nerikes Nation,** St. Olofsgatan 16 (tel. (018) 12 34 91; boogies Tues., Fri. and Sun., 35kr; open nightly 8:30pm-1am). During the academic year (late Aug. to mid-June), Södermanland-Nerikes Nation serves an all-you-can-munch lunch open to everybody (30kr, Mon.-Fri. 11am-2pm). For other university events open to the public, scope the bulletin board at the massive **Carolina Rediviva Library,** Övre Slottsgatan at Drottninggatan (inside the front doors, to the left; open Mon.-Fri. 9am-8pm, Sat. 9am-1pm).

Conjure up a picnic at the cornucopian but pricey **Saluhallen** market at St. Eriks Torg (Mon.-Fri. 9:30am-6pm, Sat. 9:30am-3pm). **Vegetariana,** by the river at Östra Ågatan 11, serves up a hearty *dagens rätt* including side salad, bread and butter, for 40kr (Mon.-Fri. 11am-2pm, Sat. noon-2pm). Follow your nose to Svartbäcksgatan 27 for ice cream and cake amidst the 1300 floral species of the fragrant **Linnéan Gardens,** (café open daily in summer 11am-6pm; closes early when raining). For evening food outside of the *nations,* devour a 40kr pizza at **Delikatess Hörnan,** Sysslomansgatan 7 (open Mon.-Sat. 11am-10pm, Sun. 3-10pm.

Gotland

Vacationing Swedes have long cherished Gotland for its narrow cobblestone streets, seductive sands and wildlife sanctuaries. Once the Baltic's trading center, Gotland is moored off the east coast of Sweden, 320km south of Stockholm. According to the legend of *Gutasaga,* this charming island was discovered by Tjelvar, who rescued it from a curse that caused it to sink every day, only to resurface at night. Here you can tour the countryside by bike, explore the ruins of medieval churches, inhale fresh salty air and end the day with a mystic pageant opera in the island's fortified capital, Visby.

The simplest way to Gotland is via the **Gotlandslinjen** ferries to Visby from Nynäshamn (2 per day Mon.-Thurs., 3 per day Fri.-Sun.; late Aug.-early June 1 per day; 5-7 hr.) or Oskarshamn (2 per day; late Aug.-early June Sun.-Fri. 1 per day; 4-6 hr.) Fares are highest on weekends (240kr, no student discount) and cheapest on overnight ferries on weekdays (150kr, 95kr for students). Nynäshamn is linked to Stockholm by buses from Cityterminalen (1 hr., 50kr) and by *pendeltåg* from Centralstation (1¼ hr., 30kr, change at Västerhaninge). For details contact Gotlandslinjen (tel. (0498) 930 00) or the Gotland office in Stockholm (Kungsgatan 48, tel. (08) 23 61 70 or (08) 23 61 80; open Mon.-Fri. 9:30am-6pm, Sat. 10am-2pm), which hands out the free *Gotlandsguiden* (partially in English; 5kr on the island).

Visby's ancient wall (3.6km long) encloses narrow, winding streets, ruined churches, and chic shops. At the **Gotlands Fornsal** history museum, you'll discover that this wall in 1361 sheltered the town's privileged merchants while the peasantry were massacred outside the gates. (Open daily 11am-6pm; Sept. to mid-May Tues.-Sun. noon-4pm. Admission 20kr, seniors and students 10kr, under 16 free.) Armchair ramblers can explore Gotland's geography through displays and slides at the **Nature Museum,** Hästgatan 1, across from the tourist office. (Same hours. Admission 10kr, seniors and students 5kr, under 16 free.)

The helpful **tourist office** is in Burmeisterska huset, Strandgatan 9 (tel. (0498) 109 82), a 10-minute jaunt to the left of the ferry terminal. (Open mid-June to mid-Aug. Mon.-Fri. 8am-8pm, Sat.-Sun. 10am-7pm; mid-Aug. to mid-Sept. and late April to mid-June Mon.-Fri. 8am-5pm, Sat.-Sun. 10am-4pm.) They change money outside banking hours and offer maps of Gotland (45kr) and Visby (25kr). Private rooms are cheaper outside the wall; reserve one at **Gotlands Turistcenter,** Korsgatan 2 (tel. (0498) 790 95; open Mon.-Fri. 9am-6:30pm, Sat.-Sun. 10am-6:30pm; singles

180kr, doubles 320kr). Stay at **Västerhejde Vandrarhem,** 6km south of the center of Visby (tel. (0498) 649 95). Take bus #31 from the bus station on Donnersgatan; get off between Vibble Samhälle and Tofta. (100kr. Breakfast availble. Mid-Aug. to mid-June 80kr.) **Campgrounds** abound on Gotland. **Kneippbyns Campingplats** (tel. (0498) 643 65), 4km south of Visby, with its amusement park, dips its toes in the sea and is accessible by bus (55kr per tent; open May-Aug.).

The **Brinken** café, Söder Torg 19, purveys a 47kr *dagens rätt* (open Mon.-Fri. 10am-8pm, Sat.-Sun. 11am-8pm). At **Rosas,** St. Hansgatan 22, daily specials begin at 45kr (open mid-May to Aug. Mon.-Fri. 9am-6pm, Sat. 9am-4pm). Admire a crumbling church ruin over crumbling pastry and coffee at **St. Hans Konditori,** St. Hansplan 2; it serves large meals from 51kr and metamorphoses into a mellow nightspot, sometimes with live folk music. (Open June-Aug. Mon.-Sat. 8:30am-10pm; May and early- to mid-Sept. Mon.-Sat. 8am-6pm, Sun. 9am-6pm.) Every second or third evening between early July and mid-August, Visby glows with the **Ruinspel,** a mystic opera festival among the ruins. Tickets (70-145kr) are available at the tourist office or the festival office, Tranhusgatan 47 (tel. (0498) 110 68).

A whole world of nature awaits outside of Visby's stone walls. Examine the mystical monoliths on Fårö (the island off the northernmost tip of Gotland), the blazing beaches of Tofta (about 15km south of Visby) and the calcified cliffs of Hoburgen at the southernmost tip of the island. Most places on Gotland are accessible by bus or bicycle; cycling is a pleasant way to explore the flat terrain. The bike rental shops on the street between the ferry terminal and the tourist office open when the first overnight ferries dock. (35-40kr per day, 160-200kr per week for one- to five-speeds.) Contact the Turistcenter (see above) for more information on bike trips. A **Gotlandskortet,** entitles you to three days' free admission to museums, and various other discounts (70kr; with unrestricted bus travel 110kr). Pick up a bus timetable at the ferry terminal or at the Visby bus station, Kung Magnusväg 1 (tel. (0498) 141 12; open Mon-Fri. 8am-5pm). See the *Gotlandsguiden* for a list of the hostels and budget guest homes scattered around the island (80-150kr). Note that northern Gotland is a military area closed to the public.

Dalarna

An old Ingmar Bergman movie goes by the title *Wild Strawberries* in English. The Swedish title, *Smultronställlet,* holds two meanings: a place of wild strawberries, or a secret place where one goes to commune with nature, one's self, and one's significant other. Dalarna, however hokey, is Sweden's *smultronställlet.* Scores of Swedes summer here in tidy red and white farmhouses set in the woods. The region lies about 3½ hr. northwest of Stockholm; several trains a day run from Stockholm via Uppsala to Borlänge, and from there either northeast to Falun or further northwest to Leksand, Rättvik, and Mora on Dalarna's shimmering Lake Siljan.

Swedes flock to **Leksand,** a small town on bluffs above the lake, to take part in the ancient **Midsummer** (summer solstice) festivities—the raising of the maypole, the procession of richly decorated longboats that once ferried people to church, exuberant folk music, and delirious all-night grinding. The annual **Musik vid Siljan** festival in Leksand and Rättvik arranges a mélange of music from all over the earth (first two weeks in July). **Himlaspelet,** a traditional play with music, recounts the adventures of Mats, a young man who finds paradise on his farm in Dalarna (last two weeks in July; programs in English). Contact the **turistbyrå,** on Norsgatan (tel. (0247) 803 00) for the exact dates of the festivals. To get to the office, walk out the front of the train station and up Villagatan to Leksandsvägen, turn left, then hang a right on Norsgatan. (Open Mon.-Sat. 9am-9pm, Sun. noon-9pm; mid-Aug. to mid-June Mon.-Fri. 9am-5pm, Sat. 9am-1pm).

Accommodations are often crowded (packed for Midsummer), but the tourist office can hook you up with a private room for a 20kr fee (doubles from 225kr; no singles). Try the **Ungdomsgården,** on Rättviksvägen near Tällbergsvägen, just a few minutes from the station and the center of town (tel. (0247) 100 90); a combination campground, lodge, and country kitchen, the main building is a red farmhouse. (Reception open 8am-9pm. 2-4 bed cabins 50kr per bed, must rent entire cabin. Tents 50kr. Breakfast 30kr. Laundry facilities. Open mid-June to mid-Aug.) With new facilities and lots of common space, Leksand's **IYHF hostel** (tel. (0247) 101 86) is 2½km from the train station, south of the river in Källberget. (79kr, nonmembers 117kr. Laundry facilities.) A 20-minute walk north on the road toward Tällberg brings you to swimming and **camping** (tel. (0247) 803 13) at Orsandbaden. (60kr per tent.) Hit **Leksands Kebab & Pizza,** Norsgatan 23, for substantial low-cost pizza (from 34kr, 28kr take-out; open Mon.-Thurs. 11am-10pm, Fri.-Sat. 11am-midnight, Sun. noon-10pm).

From Leksand's quay there are scenic and breezy boat connections a few times a week to Rättvik (50kr) and Mora (100kr). For details, call (010) 52 32 92 or (010) 52 11 52.

Few towns are as fetchingly situated as **Rättvik,** tucked into the wooded hills at the edge of Siljan, 20 minutes by train north of Leksand. Bound across the tracks and onto the gazebo-like island visible from the station; in balmy weather it's a perfect picnic venue. Rättvik blossoms with life during the Musik vid Siljan Festival (see above), and plays no second fiddle to Leksand in celebrating Midsummer. If fiddling is in fact your thing, check out the **Bingsjö Spelmansstämma** ("Player's Convention") on the first or second Wednesday in July (check the tourist office), when some 30,000 people from all over the world invade a private farm in Bingsjö, 40km from Rättvik, for a spontaneous combustion of everything from Swedish folk songs to bluegrass. Rättvik's **tourist office** *nonpareil* (tel. (0248) 109 10), across from the train station, sells detailed hiking and biking maps of the Lake Siljan region (15kr), and pins down rooms in private homes (110kr for rare singles, doubles 220kr, 20kr booking fee; open mid-June to mid-Aug. Mon.-Fri. 9am-8pm, Sat.-Sun. 11am-8pm, open 1 hr. later in July); Sept.-May Mon.-Fri. 9am-5pm, Sat. noon-4pm). The woody and friendly **IYHF youth hostel** (tel. (0248) 105 66) sprawls beneath the pines off Centralgatan, 1km behind the tourist office. (85kr, nonmembers 117kr; laundry facilities.) **Rättviksparken Camping** (tel. (0248) 102 51) is just down the side road that turns off Centralgatan at the youth hostel (80-100kr per tent; open all year); **Siljansbadets Camping** (tel. (0248) 116 91) kisses a popular beach, just north of the train station (75-100kr per tent; cabins available; open late April-early Oct.).

Nearby attractions include **Rättviks Gammelgård,** a Dalarna farm reincarnated amidst local handicrafts and a café. Walk 10 minutes out of the center towards Sjurberg. (Free; open mid-June to mid-Aug. Mon.-Sat. 11am-6pm, Sun. noon-6pm.) **Handverksbyn,** a 20 to 25-minute walk along the road to Gärdeby, offers coffee, cakes, and still more handicrafts in a traditional setting. Gaze at Agneta Svensdotter's *Paradise* while eating a late-night pizza at **Mehdis Allt-i-ett-Livs-Pizza-Kebab** (Mehdis's-All-In-One-Life-Pizza-and-Kebab), across from the tourist office. (Open Mon.-Thurs. 10am-10pm, Fri.-Sat. 10am-2am, Sun. 1-11pm.) To burn the calories, rent a canoe, pedal boat or windsurfer at **Siljansbadet Sommarland** near the waterslide just south of the train station (30-50kr per hr.; tel. (0248) 134 00).

Head north to **Mora** for a voluptuous sea of blueberries, lingonberries, and *svamp* (mushrooms). The **tourist office** (tel. (0250) 265 50), on the lakefront, will find you a bed in a private home for a 20kr fee. (Mon.-Sat. 9am-8pm, Sun. noon-9pm.) The new **Vandrarhemmet Åmåsäng i Mora** (tel. (0250) 133 42) is 4km from the center of town on Åmåsängsgården (80kr). **Santa Claus's** humble abode (or one of them; every snowy village claims the title) is in nearby **Gesunda.** It's called **Tomteland** (open daily June-August), complete with musk oxen and elves (95kr, 50kr on Sat.; tel. (0250) 213 80). **Nusnäs,** 10km east of Mora, is famous for its wooden *dalahäst* horses, the Swedish equivalent of Mom, baseball and apple pie. You can tour the factory at **Nils Olsson Hemslöjd** for free. (Open Mon.-Fri. 8am-4pm, Sat. 9am-4pm, Sun. 10am-3pm; mid-Aug. to mid-June Mon.-Fri. 8am-3pm.)

Sundsvall

On your way up to Lappland, consider bagging the day-long train ride from Stockholm all the way north, and instead breaking halfway along the coast of the Gulf of Bothnia. Though Gävle, Sundsvall, Umeå, Skellefteå, and Luleå all sport youth hostels and and all but Luleå and Gävle send convenient ferries across the gulf to Finland, few foreigners actually visit this region. The peculiar architecture and history of **Sundsvall,** halfway between Stockholm and Boden, beats out the others. Wedged in the valley between the Norra and Södra Stadsberget hills, Sundsvall is a thriving industrial center, and was one of the premier sawmill capitals of the world before a fire destroyed it in 1888. The wealthy industrialists who built up from the ashes created the architecturally flawless structures that have dubbed Sundsvall "Stone City." It lies on the Stockholm-Långsele train route (4-5 hr. from Stockholm, 4 per day), while Sundsvall-Östersund trains (2½-3 hr., 5 per day) connect with the Stockholm-Boden line at Bräcke. Ferries (1 per day in summer) cross the gulf to Vaasa in Finland.

To get to the **turistbyrå** on Stora Torget (tel. (060) 11 42 35), head left on Landsvägsallén as you leave the station. After several blocks, take a right on Esplanaden; walk three blocks, bear left on Storgatan and the office is on the left. (Free map and guide to the city. Private room bookings 75-125kr. Open June-Aug. Mon.-Fri. 9am-9pm; Sept.-May Mon.-Fri. 9am-5pm). Of notable interest in Sundsvall is the **Kulturmagasinet** (tel. (060) 19 18 00 or 19 18 03), a classy glassy structure housing the **Sundsvall Museum** and the **Municipal Library.** Learn about the sawmill days, browse the works of 20th century artists, or come at 7pm on Thursdays in July and August for music. (Continue one block north on Esplanaden past the tourist office, and then right on Sjögatan and left on Nybrogatan. Open Mon. and Thurs. 10am-7pm, Tues. 10am-8pm, Fri. 10am-5pm, Sat.-Sun. 11am-4pm; slightly reduced hours Sept.-April. Free.)

Sundsvall's most interesting sights sit atop Norra Stadsberget, the hill above downtown. The hilltop tower has great views, while the museum just down the road houses a stuffed *skvadern*—half hare, half capercaillie. Go right on Baldersvägen off Tivolivägen across the river, then left on Gustav Adolphs-Vägen. Shed your pack before you take the strenuous mountain path on the left side of Baldersvägen. The **Vandrarhem Gaffelbyn (IYHF)** shares the hill too (tel. (060) 11 21 19; 85kr, nonmembers 117kr; cabins 79kr, nonmembers 111kr. Breakfast 45kr.) From mid-July to mid-August there's a **YMCA Interpoint** at Kyrkogatan 29 (tel. (060) 11 35 51; 70kr). **Granli Camping,** Granlivägen 20 (tel. (060) 11 35 69), is 4km northeast of the center of town on the waterfront (open all year). **Pizzeria Stället,** Storgatan 12, at the corner of Nybrogatan, bakes 85 varieties of pie. (Open Mon.-Thurs. 11am-10pm, Fri. 11am-3:30am, Sat. noon-3:30am, Sun. 1-9pm.)

Lappland

Many "Southerners"—anyone living south of the Arctic Circle—imagine that Lappland consists of herds of reindeer roaming through dense forest, thick snow, unrelenting darkness and bitter cold for half the year, and perpetual light for the other half. This is all true. Although mining has begun to encroach upon previously virgin land, the lure here in Sweden's colonial outback is still nature, from swampy birch and pine forests in the vast lowlands to the peaks that rise to meet the Norwegian border.

Swedish Lappland is the most accessible part of Lappland, which also stretches across Finland and Norway. Jokkmokk, Gällivare and Kiruna are the three main settlements north of the Arctic Circle, and all make good stopovers on the way to mountains stations such as Kvikkjokk and Abisko. The cheapest way north, and a considerable time-saver, is to fly on SAS's youth standby fare, available to those under 26 (250kr from Stockholm to Kiruna or Gällivare). Recent cutbacks have reduced train service to Lappland to one line, the coastal route from Stockholm up to Boden, and thence through Gällivare and Kiruna to Narvik (Norway) along the "Malmbanan" (Ore Line); there are two trains a day in each direction (Stockholm-Gällivare 17-21 hr.; make reservations early). Buses, many of which accept no railpasses, are the only way to the smaller towns; pick up a copy of the *Länstrafiken i Norrbotten* company schedule. If you're heading for the mountains, Svenska Turistföreningen's *Turisttrafik i fjällen* brochure is an indispensable transport overview. In the lowlands, long clothing and a supple wrist will protect you against the summer's swamp-bred, blood-bloated mosquitoes. The obvious preventive measure—bug repellent—was recently banned from stores for environmental reasons; if you're not a Green, bring some from home. Swedish Lappland is also home to 17,000 **Sami** (to whom the name "Lapps" is derogatory). These reindeer-tending people have occupied Lappland for thousands of years, before Scandinavian and Fennic tribes moved northward into their territory. They speak a Uralic (Finno-Ugric) language whose exact affinities are still murky.

Gällivare is a major mining town, the best place to spend some time underground. The **tourist office** (tel. (0970 166 60) is at Storgatan 16; from the train station, bear right a couple blocks until you see the signposts on your left (open daily 9am-9pm, mid-Aug. to mid-June 9am-5pm). Their weekday tours will bury you in the copper and iron mines and the mining museum (July 7-21 daily at 10am, arrangeable at other times; 125kr). Revive on their midnight sun mountain trip (July 1-21 at 10:45pm, 70kr). The town's **ettörekyrka** (one-penny church) was built for the Sami in the 18th century after the government collected that sum from every household in Sweden. The **IYHF youth hostel** (tel. (0970) 143 80) is a five-minute walk from the station; cross the bridge over the tracks, then the one over the river, and the hostel is on your left. (85kr, nonmembers 117kr. Laundry (15kr, includes soap), kitchen, sauna 50kr per hr. Call ahead.) **Gällivare Camping** (tel. (0970) 186 79) is home to friendly people and overfriendly mosquitoes; it's by the river 1½km from the station (40kr per tent; open mid-May to mid-Sept.). **Supermarkets** reside near the tourist office.

Everybody's related in **Jokkmokk,** a town quieter and greener than Kiruna or Gällivare, where reindeer chase people up trees and tourists spend hours talking to drunks in the bar. No longer served by passenger trains, buses to Jokkmokk (whose name means "bend in the stream" in Sami) run from Gällivare (2-4 per day, 1½ hr.) and Boden (1-2 per day, 2 hr.) **Ájtte,** an outstanding museum of Sami culture, makes the trip here more than worthwhile. (Open Mon.-Fri. 9am-6pm, Wed. until 8pm, Sat.-Sun. 11am-6pm; mid-Aug. to mid-June Tues.-Fri. 9am-4pm, Sat.-Sun. noon-4pm. Admission 20kr.) The museum runs a 17-minute slide show featuring a whole lot of reindeer. Check out the view from **Storknabben,** 2km from the center of town—and if you're not heading for the mountains yourself, the wilderness photographs in **Edvin Nilsson's** gallery, on Klockarvägen, just off Storgatan, the main street, may change your mind. (Open mid-June to early Sept. daily 11am-6pm. Free.) The **tourist office,** Stortorget 4 (tel. (0971) 121 40) is a big banana house on the main square bursting with mountain maps. They book rooms (mostly doubles, 75-110kr per person, 7kr fee) and rent bikes (30kr per day, 150kr per week) and wilderness gear. (Open Mon.-Fri. 8am-8pm, Sat.-Sun. 9am-8pm.) From the ex-train station, go up Stationsgatan and take a left on Storgatan to get to the **IYHF youth hostel** on the left side of the road. Call ahead. (Tel. (0971) 119 77. 79kr, nonmembers 111kr. Open mid-June to early Aug.) Or stay at the yellow house across the street from the station (75kr). **Camping** is 3km south of town at **Jokkmokks Turistcenter** (tel. (0971) 123 70), where tents are 30kr and four-bed cabins 230-730kr. Round up some grub at **Lena's Bar and Café,** Föreningsgatan between Klippgatan and Berggatan (hamburgers 25kr; open Mon.-Fri. 10am-10pm, Sat.-Sun. 10am-8pm).

Kiruna bills itself the "City of the Future," but it's a metal-lover's future, a rather dystopian vision of mining, missile launching and satellite operations. Wherever you turn, a towering mountain of galvanized ore looms behind the train station. If you missed the better, faster, stronger mine tours in Gällivare, fret not; you can see the world's largest underground iron ore mine here more cheaply (sign up at the tourist office; Mon.-Sat. 10am, noon, 2pm, and 4pm; Sun. 2pm and 4pm; admission 65kr). The Sami knew about the stuff long before it was "discovered," but didn't tell anyone else because they feared (rightly) that they'd be forced to transport the ore with their reindeer and sleighs. The midnight sun lasts from May 28 to July 14, with the all-night **Festival of Light** on the first weekend in July. The **tourist office** at Hjalmar Lundbohmsvägen 42 (tel. (0980) 188 80) books rooms in private homes (150kr per person, no fee; open Mon.-Fri. 9am-8pm, Sat.-Sun. 10am-6pm; mid-Aug. to mid-June Mon.-Fri. 10am-4pm). **Buses** leave from the parking lot next to the office. The **IYHF youth hostel** is at Skyttegatan 18a, a couple blocks behind the tourist office. (Tel. (0980) 171 95; 79kr, nonmembers 111kr; open mid-June to late Aug.) **Camp** at **Radhusbyn Ripan** (tel. (0980) 131 00), 20 minutes from the train station (70kr per tent, 4-person cabins 590kr). **Mat & Mums,** in the "Simhall" at the top end of Bergmästaregatan downtown, has a 49kr *dagens rätt* with all-you-can-chew salad and bread weekdays until 2pm (open Mon.-Fri. 10am-10pm, Sat. noon-10pm, Sun. noon-8pm).

A short bus trip from Kiruna, Gällivare, or Jokkmokk, the 500km **Kungsleden,** a moderate, well-marked hiking trail, stretches from Abisko in the north (on the Narvik train line) to Hemavan in the south. Many sections—in particular from Abisko to Kvikkjokk—have staffed cabins, 8-21km apart (70-95kr per night). There's a network of trails off and around Kungsleden; the 150km Padjelantaleden also has day-hike-spaced huts. This is rugged country, and there may be snow as late as July. Even if you're just hiking between huts by day, bring food, maps, full raingear, and warm clothing, and leave your route with someone in town. Be sure to contact STF—the **Svenska Turistföreningen**—before heading north (see Accommodations, Camping, and Food above); they run most of the mountain stations and huts, offer discounts on accommodations, and publish essential brochures and guides for hikers. Local tourist offices are wellsprings of information.

Transportation out of Lappland can be challenging; study your schedules. Those heading further north can take the train up to Narvik on the Norwegian coast (stop at Abisko Turiststation or lonelier Låktatjåkka for dramatic mountain trails). A bus a day (95kr) links Kiruna to **Karesuando** on the Finnish border—site of Sweden's northernmost IYHF hostel (tel. (0981) 200 22; open May-Aug.)—from there you can continue to Skibotn, Norway, or Kilpisjärvi and Muonio, in remotest Finland. Or travel Finlandwards by backtracking south through the rail junction at **Boden,** where you can stay at the **Centralhotellet** (tel. (0921) 114 15; 100kr). Be sure to plan ahead: there is only one 9am train per day from Boden to Tornio, Finland, and railpasses aren't valid on the bus to the Swedish border town of Haparanda (2 per day). Remember that Finland is one time zone ahead when consulting schedules. For further information on nearby areas, leaf through the Norway and Finland chapters.

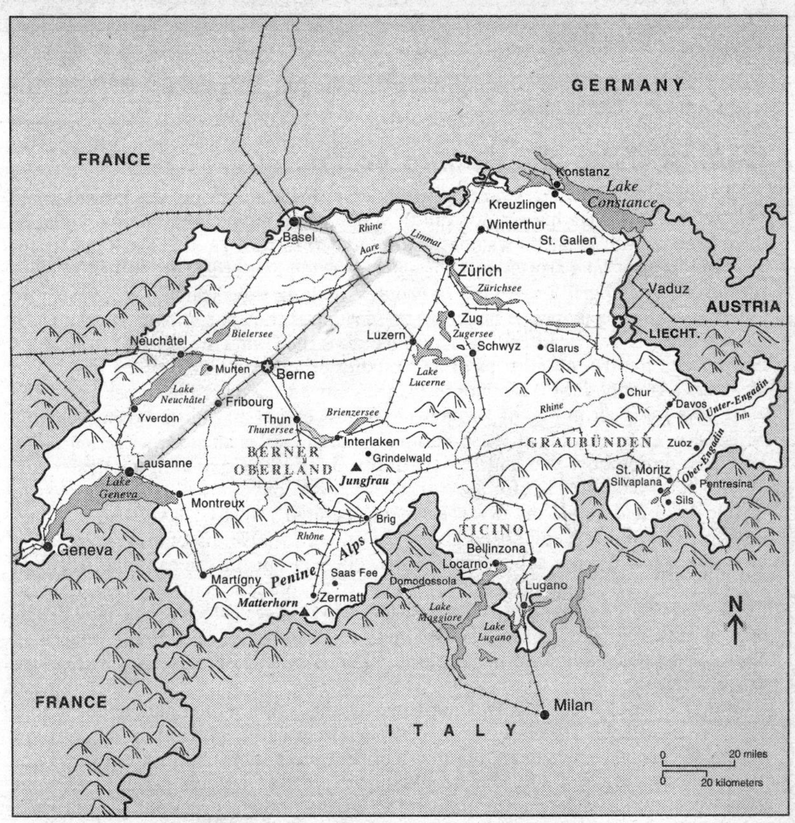

SWITZERLAND

USD$1 = 1.53 francs (SFr, or CHF) | **1SFr = USD$0.65**
CAD$1 = 1.34SFr | **1SFr = CAD$0.74**
GBP£1 = 2.57SFr | **1SFr = GBP£0.39**
AUD$1 = 1.20SFr | **1SFr = AUD$0.83**
NZD$1 = 0.88SFr | **1SFr = NZD$1.14**
Country Code: 41 | **International Dialing Prefix: 00**

Switzerland (Suisse, Schweiz, Svizzera) is the capstone of the European continent. The topographical riot of the Alps holds dominion over half the country; the Berner Oberland and the legendary Matterhorn are its most thunderingly exalted landmarks. Though a tectonic turmoil, Switzerland rests in social and political peace, and its cities are more stable than spectacular.

Split by impassable mountains and united by neither language nor religion, it is curious that Switzerland is a nation at all. A confederation of 23 largely autonomous cantons, loosely established in 1291 and solidified through the early 19th century, placid, rational Switzerland now consults its citizens directly on major issues through national referenda. Though its famous neutrality policy has survived two world wars and countless other global skirmishes, Switzerland's icy reserve has shown signs of melting as debate over EC membership heats up. Insiders, however, express doubts about major alterations. With under 0.5% unemployment (yes, that's *point* five percent), the nation also disdains poverty.

For more in-depth coverage of Switzerland, consult the brand-new *Let's Go: Germany, Austria, Switzerland.*

Getting There and Getting Around

Getting around Switzerland is gleefully easy. Federal and private railways, and yellow post buses (railpasses not valid), which serve many of the remote villages, keep time as well as Swiss watches. Eurail and InterRail passes clear the way for passage on most lake cruises and portage between major cities, but private companies exert a deathgrip on Alpine rail routes, making travel fatally expensive.

An array of special passes help beat these ruinous transportation costs. An absolute must for Eurail or InterRail-less wayfarers is the **Half-Fare Travel Card,** which entitles you to 50% off all trips on federal and private railroads, postal buses, and steamers. At only 75SFr per month (125SFr plus a passport photo per year), the card pays for itself in one or two journeys. Less casual and more expensive is the **Swisspass,** available only at Swiss National Tourist Offices outside Switzerland. The Flexipass option buys you 3 in 15 days of travel for 180SFr; continuous passes cost 180SFr for 4 days, 220SFr for 8 days, 260SFr for 15 days and 360SFr for a month, giving unlimited travel on all government-operated railways, lake steamers, and most private railways and postal buses, but only a 25-50% discount on the dearest mountain railways and cable cars. Finally, one can opt for the cantonal **Regional Passes** (50-175SFr), valid for 15 days: five days (consecutive or not) can be used for free travel, the remaining 10 for half-fare travel. Ages 6-15 pay half-fare; Swisspass or Half-Fare Travel Card holders get a 20% discount. The **Berner Oberland Pass** (125SFr), covering Berne, Lucerne, Interlaken and Zermatt, surpasses all in practicality.

Intercity **buses** are virtually nonexistent in this rail-oriented nation; the postal buses in rural areas (the only mode of transport near St. Moritz) are slower and nearly as expensive. **Steamers** ply many of the larger lakes. Fares are no bargain, but a Eurailpass often gets you free passage; InterRail holders get 50% off, and a Swisspass almost always wins a free ride. **Cycling,** though strenuous, is a splendid way to see the country; rental at almost any station is standard at 14-16SFr per day (return bikes to any station). **Hitching** here is difficult. For those with sufficient stamina, overland **walking** is the most enjoyable way to see Switzerland.

Practical Information

Switzerland is quadrilingual. French is spoken in the west; Italian, in the south; Romansch (a relative of French and Italian), in the cantons of Engadin and Graubünden; and Swiss German, a dialect nearly incomprehensible to other German speakers, everywhere else. Most people know at least three languages, including English.

Tourist offices in every Swiss city *(Verkehrsbüro* or *Kurverein)*locate rooms, distribute maps and suggest hiking or biking routes. All close between noon and 1:30 or 2pm.

Currency exchange at its easiest (and latest) takes place in train stations; rates are usually the same as banks. **Post offices** and **PTT centers,** often in the same building, offer international calling on a phone-first, pay-later or collect basis. Dial 191 or 114 for English-friendly assistance. For AT&T's **USA Direct,** dial 046 05 0011. Ring the **police** at 117, an **ambulance** at 144. Most stores are open Monday through Friday from 8am to 6:30pm with a break from noon to 2pm, and Saturday mornings. In cities, shops also close Monday mornings. Museums close on Mondays.

Switzerland is justifiably proud of its winter-wonderland reputation, and far-sighted planning—avoiding the hoity-toity resorts—allows for inexpensive skiing. Lift tickets average 20-50SFr per day, rentals 30SFr. Passes usually cover transportation to the lifts as well as uphill carriage. A week of lift tickets, equipment rental, lessons, lodging and demi-pension (breakfast plus one other meal—usually dinner) averages 475SFr.

Accommodations, Camping, and Food

All things Swiss are meticulous, orderly, efficient and expensive. None of the hosteling horror stories apply to Switzerland; the uniformly cheery **IYHF Jugendherbergen** are bright, clean and open to all ages (12-20SFr per night, sheets and breakfast included; nonmembers 5-7SFr extra). Hotels are expensive; the gems in *Let's Go* are uniformly one-star but offer bathless rooms. In smaller conurbations, *Zimmer frei* (private rooms) abound; the tourist office can supply a list and make reservations. As befits a country so blessed by Mother Nature, Switzerland teems with over 1200 campgrounds, catering to caravans (3-5SFr per person and 4-10SFr per tent) This land of order and propriety forbids freelance camping along roads and in public areas.

The Swiss are hardly culinary daredevils; cuisine here is filling, well-prepared, and satisfying, albeit expensive. In French Switzerland, try the cheese specialties: *fondue* is always excellent, as is *raclette* (melted cheese served with pickled onions and boiled new potatoes). Swiss-German food is heartier. Try *Züricher Geschnetzeltes* (veal strips in a delicious cream sauce) and *Rösti* (almost-hashbrowned potato with onion). **Migros** supermarket cafeterias and **Manora** restaurants are the budgeteer's choice for self-service dining. Tips are included in meal prices.

German Switzerland

Zürich

Rich and aloof, Zürich is the quintessential banker's town. The city was the seat of the Reformation in German Switzerland; today wealth and strong Protestant sentiments live a smug coexistence. Zurich's cultural legacy is also rich. Tristan Tzara and his fellow dadaists of the Cabaret Voltaire made Zürich one of the avant-garde capitals of Europe, and James Joyce died of an ulcer here in 1941. ("If you spilled minestra on the Bahnhofstrasse you could eat it right up without a spoon," he remarked).

Orientation and Practical Information

Zürich sits on the northern tip of the Zürichsee (a lake); the River Limmat divides it in half. Swissly efficient public trams crisscross the city, operating until about 12:15am. Short rides (yellow button) cost 1.70SFr; longer ones (blue button) 2.80SFr. The 24-hour *Tageskarte* is your best bet (5.60SFr). Buy tickets from machines at tram stops.

Tourist Offices: Main office in the train station at Bahnhofplatz 15 (tel. 211 40 00). Exit the station to Bahnhofplatz, and walk to the left alongside the building. Finds rooms for 5SFr; dispenses maps, the weekly *Zürich News,* and info on the "Meet the Swiss" program. Open Mon.-Fri. 8am-10pm, Sat.-Sun. 8am-8:30pm; Nov.-Feb. Mon.-Thurs. 8am-8pm, Fri. 8am-10pm, Sat.-Sun. 9am-6pm. Also at **airport terminal B** (tel. 816 40 81; open daily 10am-7pm).

Consulates: U.S., Zollikerstr. 141 (tel. 55 25 66). **U.K.,** Dufourstr. 56 (tel. 261 15 20).

Currency Exchange: An honest deal at the train station. Open daily 6:15am-10:45pm.

American Express: Bahnhofstr. 20, near Paradeplatz (tel. 211 83 70). All AmEx services. Open Mon.-Fri. 8:30am-5:30pm, Sat. 9am-noon.

Post Office: Main office and Poste Restante at Kasernenstr. 95-97. Open Mon.-Fri. 6:30am-10:30pm, Sat. 6:30am-8pm, Sun. 11am-10:30pm. 1SFr charge for poste restante after 6:30pm.

Telephones: PTT phones at the train station and at Fraumünster post office. Open Mon.-Fri. 7am-10:30pm, Sat.-Sun. 9am-9pm. **City Code:** 01.

Flights: 100 trains per day leave the Hauptbahnhof for the airport (10 min., 4.20SFr, railpasses valid).

Trains: Tel. 211 50 10.

Bike Rental: At the baggage counter *(Gepäckexpedition Fly-Gepäck)* in the station. Open daily 6am-11:30pm. About 12SFr.

Hitchhiking: If you decide to hitchhike, take tram #4 from the station to the end (Werdhölzli) for Basel, Geneva, Paris, or Bonn. To Lucerne, Italy, and Austria, take tram #5 or 14 to Bahnhof Wiedikon and walk 1 block down Schimmelstr. to Silhölzli. For Munich, take tram #14 to Milchbuck, walk to Schaffhauserstr., toward St. Gallen and St. Margarethen. **Mitfahrzentrale,**(tel. 261 68 93) pairs drivers and drivees.

Bookstore: Daeniker's Bookshop, In Gassen 11. English books, including *Let's Go.* Open Mon.-Fri. 8:15am-6:30pm, Sat. 9am-4pm.

Laundromat: Speed-Wash, at Müllerstr. 55, Matteng. 29, Weinberstr. 37, and Friesstr. 4. Open Mon.-Sat. 7am-10pm, Sun. 10:30am-10pm.

Emergencies: Police (tel. 117). **Ambulance** (tel. 144). **Medical Emergency** (tel. 47 47 00).

Accommodations and Camping

Jugendherberge Zürich (IYHF), Mutschellenstr. 114 (tel. 482 35 44). Take tram #7 to Morgental and follow the signs (5 min.). Impeccably clean and bustling with tourists. Reception open 6-9am and 2pm-1am. Lockout 9am-2pm. Curfew 1am. Members 20SFr, nonmembers 27SFr. Shower, breakfast, and sheets included. Dinner 8.50SFr (6-7:30pm). Laundry 8SFr.

Marthahaus, Zähringerstr. 36 (tel. 251 45 50). Go left out of the station, cross the river, and take the 2nd right after the quay. Convenient but busy. Reception open 7am-11pm. 6-bed dorms 26SFr. Singles 50SFr. Doubles 76SFr. Triples 90SFr. Breakfast included.

Foyer Hottingen, Hottingerstr. 31 (tel. 261 93 15). Take tram #3 from Bahnhofplatz to Hottingerplatz. Sparkling white, filled with plants and screaming children. Women, families and married couples only. Midnight curfew. Dorms 26SFr. Singles 42SFr. Doubles 70SFr. Breakfast included, showers 1SFr.

Glockenhof, Sihlstr. 33 (tel. 221 36 73), next to the more expensive Hotel Glockenhof (10 min. from the station). Men only. Rooms in holiday season only. Reception open Mon.-Fri. 8:15am-7:45pm, Sat. 9:45am-3:45pm, Sun. 8:30am-3:30pm. Singles 30SFr. Dinner 10.50SFr.

Hotel Regina, Hohlstr. 18 (tel. 242 65 50). Go left on Bahnhofpl., right on Kasernenstr, then right on Zeughausstr. to Hohlstr. Inconvenient 10-min. walk, but excellent prices for small, clean "old rooms." Reception open 24 hrs. 35-90 SFr per person.

Camping: Camping Seebucht, Seestr. 559 (tel. 482 16 12), distant but lakeside. Take the train to Wollishofen and walk the remaining 15 min. Or take bus #161 or 165 from Bürkliplatz, on the lake at the end of Bahnhofstr., to Grenzsteig. 5SFr per person, 8SFr per tent. Open early May-late Sept.

Food

The cheapest eats in Zürich are at the *Wurstli* stands (sausage and bread for 3-4SFr) and fresh veggie and fruit stalls peppering the streets. Pick up the free brochure *Preiswert Essen*(cheap food)*in Zürich* at the tourist office.

Mensa der Universität Zürich, Rämistr. 71. Take tram #6 from Bahnhofplatz to ETH Zentrum, or walk. To return to town, take the tram on Tannenstr. Not your everyday college fare—this is more than palatable. Hot dishes 5.50-7SFr with ISIC, salads 6.90SFr. Open Mon.-Fri. 11:15am-1:30pm. **Mensa Polyterrasse,** through the student center and up the hill to the right at #101, has the same food and prices. Open mid-July to mid-Sept. Mon.-Fri. 11:15am-1:30pm; mid-Sept. to mid-July Mon.-Thurs. 11:15am-1:30pm and 5:30-7:30pm, Fri. 11:15am-1:30pm and 5:30-7:15pm. Saturday lunch (11:30am-1pm) alternates locations each week.

Vier Linden, Gemeindestr. 48, near the Foyer Hottingen Hotel, just above Hottingerplatz. Taste bud titillating vegetarian food. Meal-sized salads 8-13.50SFr. *Menus* 15-17SFr. Open Mon.-Fri. 6am-9pm. Bakery and health food store across the street open Mon.-Fri. 7am-12:30pm and 2-6:30pm, Sat. 7am-4pm.

Pizzeria Allegro, Mutschellenstr. 137, (tel. 482 99 55). As close to the youth hostel as the hostel dining room itself. Pasta, salad, fish and pizza 12-20SFr. Mon.-Sat. 11am-midnight.

Cafeteria Freischütz, Freischützgasse 1, at Militärstr., on the other side of the Sihl (the "other river"), near the main post office. Stellar Swiss dishes for 10-15SFr. Open daily until 7pm.

Sights and Entertainment

The stately and colorful **Bahnhofstrasse** runs from the station to the Zürichsee. East of the Bahnhofstrasse rises the **Fraumünster,** a Chagall-decorated wonder (open May-Sept. Mon.-Sat. 9am-noon and 2-6pm; March-April and Oct. daily 10am-noon and 2-5pm; Nov.-Feb. daily 10am-noon and 2-4pm), matched only by the **Grossmünster** across the river in the *Altstadt* (open Mon.-Fri. 9am-6pm, Sat. 9am-5pm, Sun. after services-6pm; Oct.-March Mon.-Sat. 10am-4pm, Sun. after services-4pm.)

The **Landesmuseum** (Swiss National Museum) is behind the train station (open Tues.-Sun. 10am-5pm; free). The **Kunsthaus,** Heimplatz 1, is famed for large Impressionist, Expressionist and photography collections. (Open Tues.-Thurs. 10am-9pm, Fri.-Sun. 10am-5pm, Mon. 2-5pm. Admission 3SFr, students discounted.)

Zürich's nightlife revolves around Niederdorfstr., Münstergasse, and Limmatquai. Enjoy myriad street performers or follow the mobs to countless cabarets and clubs. Everyone likes **Casa Bar,** Münstergasse 30, a teeny, pricey pub with live jazz. (Open daily 7pm-2am.) **Bar Pigalle,** just uphill from Hirschenplatz, attracts a young, hip crowd. (Open Mon.-Sat. until 2am.) An arty, somewhat gay coterie hangs out at the **Bar Odeon,** Limmatquai 2, near the Quaibrücke.

Near Zürich

Boat trips on the **Zürichsee** range from short jaunts between isolated villages (1½ hr., 8.40SFr), to a "grand tour" (4 hr., 22.20SFr, free with Eurailpass, half-price with InterRail; boats leave from Bürkliplatz). Boats from the Landesmuseum (behind the train station) leave every half hour, sailing down the Limmat through Zürich (5.60SFr, railpasses not valid). The *Zürichsee* brochure at the tourist office explains all.

Once-placid **Zug,** just south of Zürich, is fast losing its battle with big business. Yet the *Altstadt* on the **Zugersee,** a veritable cornucopia of cathedrals, cobblestone and culture, retains its old-world charm. Hop on bus #11 from the station (stop "Stadion") for the cozy **Jugendherberge (IYHF),** Allmendstr. 8 (tel. (042) 21 53 54; reception open 7-10am and 5-10pm; 20SFr) or camp on the lake at **Innere Lorzenallmend** (tel. (04) 31 50 35; 5SFr per person, 5SFr per tent.)

Basel (Bâle)

Ensconced Rhine-side at the crossroads of France, Germany, and Switzerland, Basel radiates European sophistication rather than Swiss charm. The city's littered streets, confusing cartography and industrial architecture fail to indicate its cultural flair; the electric graffiti next to the railroad tracks greeting arriving visitors hint at the creative spark of the city, which nourishes myriad galleries and 27 museums.

The gargantuan **Kunstmuseum,** St. Alban-Graben 16, flaunts masterpieces including van Gogh's *Daubigney's Garden* and Holbein's *Erasmus.* Entire rooms full of works by Picasso, Dalí, and Braque complement masterpieces by Klee, Kandinsky, and Mondrian, bought by a far-sighted museum director when Hitler's Germany deemed them "decadent." (Take tram #2 from the station to Kunstmuseum. Open Tues.-Sun. 10am-5pm. Admission 3SFr, students 2SFr, Sun. free.) Equally explosive, the **Museum of Contemporary Art,** St. Alban-Rheinweg 60 (a painting's throw from the youth hostel) illustrates the major art trends of the 70s and 80s: minimalist and conceptual art, *arte povera,* and "wild painting." (Open Wed.-Mon. 10am-5pm; Nov.-April Wed.-Mon. 10am-noon and 2-5pm. Admission 3SFr, students 2SFr.) In mid-June, the international Police Band Festival fills the city with sound.

Start your tour with the symbol of the city, Basel's **Münster,** 500m south of the tourist office. Enclosed within its 11th century walls are countless sculptures and carvings, as well as Erasmus's bones. (Open Easter-Oct. 15 Mon.-Fri. 10am-6pm, Sat. 10am-noon and 2-5pm, Sun. 1-5pm; Oct. 16 to Easter Mon.-Sat. 10am-noon and 2-4pm, Sun. 2-4pm.) Impressively crimson, the **Rathaus** glares on Marktplatz; **Totengässlein** leads from Marktplatz past rich patrician homes and guildhouses to the 13th-century **Peterskirche.** The tourist office coordinates walking tours of the whole *Altstadt* (daily at 3pm, show up at 2:45pm; 8SFr). Boats leave next door from Schifflände.

The **Verkehrsbüro,** Blumenrain 2 (tel. (061) 261 50 50), hands out info on accommodations and events. Ask for a transit map. (Open Mon.-Fri. 8:30am-6pm, Sat. 8:30am-1pm.) From the train station, take tram #1 to the Schifflände stop; the office is on the river, near the bridge. Basel's genial **Jugendherberge (IYHF),** St. Alban-Kirchrain 10 (tel. (061) 272 05 72), is a 10-15 min. walk from the station down Aeschengraben, then St. Alban Anlage; or take tram #1 one stop to Aeschenplatz, then tram #3 two stops. (Reception open 3pm-1am, off-season 4pm-midnight. Check-out 7-10am, off-season 7:30-10am. Lockout 10am-4pm. 8-bed dorms 18SFr, nonmembers 25SFr. Singles 22SFr. Doubles 44SFr. Shower and breakfast included. Dinner 8SFr. Lockers. Laundry 4SFr.) **Hotel Steinenschange,** Steinengraben 69 (tel. (061) 23 53 53), is closer to the station. (5-min. walk. Singles 50SFr, with shower 80SFr. Doubles 80SFr, with shower 110SFr. Students (with ISIC) 35SFr in singles or doubles for first 3 nights. Breakfast included.) The nearest **camping** is **Waldhort,** 10km from town on Highway 18; take tram #1 to Aeschenpl., then tram #1 to Landhof. (Tel. (061) 711 64 29. Reception open 8am-noon and 2:30-10pm. 4.50SFr per person, 3.50SFr per tent. Open March-Oct.)

Basel's two **Migros** markets at Clarapl. and Sternengasse 17, have earned their reputation as Switzerland's cheapest. (Open Mon.-Fri. 7am-6:30pm, Sat. 7am-5pm.) For Swiss specialties with style, try **Börse,** Marktgasse 4 (tel. (061) 261 87 33), directly across from the tourist office. (Menus 10-15SFr. Open Mon.-Sat. until 11pm.) A morning market hawks produce every day in Marktplatz. For nightlife head to the **Only One,** Clarastr. 2, for disco and dancing.

Lucerne (Luzern)

In glorious Lucerne, the festival never ends. While troubadors sing on the banks of the *Vierwaldstättersee,* Karneval bands blare in abandoned underground air raid shelters. The city's Alpine background is easily accessible; innumerable excursions to Mount Titlis, Pilatus and Rigi depart here.

The crowded corridors of old Lucerne blaze with technicolor paintings and gleeful carvings; the **Hirschenplatz** basks in the glow of its polychrome facades. Equally explosive are the decorative wooden bridges straddling the Reuss River; Kaspar Meglinger's *Totentanz* paintings on the **Spreuerbrücke** lend an eerie cast as majestic as that of the **Kapellbrücke.** The **Towers of Lucerne** on Museggstr. invite the reenactment of a medieval siege (open daily 8am-7pm).

Lucerne's **Transport Museum** features a neck-wrenching 360° "Swissorama" panorama. (Open daily 9am-6pm; adults 14SFr, students 10SFr.) Musicians revel in the **Richard Wagner Museum,** Wagnerweg 27; original scores and old instruments adorn the late composer's 1866-1872 home. (Take bus #6 or 8 to Schönbühl, or walk along the lake from the train station. Open Tues.-Sun. 10am-noon and 2-5pm; mid-Feb. to mid-April. Tues., Thurs., Sat., Sun. 10am-noon and 2-5pm. Admission 4SFr, students 2SFr.) **City Hall** on Rathausquai serves as a gallery for contemporary art; next door, the **Am Rhyn Haus** bares a collection of Picasso's last works. (Open daily 10am-6pm; Nov.-March Fri.-Sun. 11am-noon and 2-5pm. Admission 3SFr, students 2SFr.)

Some of Switzerland's oldest steamers ply the sparkling waters of the Vierwaldstätter See; combine half- or full-day excursions with mountain hiking or strolls along the lake. (Round-trip 13-36SFr, Eurail free, InterRail 50% off. Boats leave from near train station.) **Mt. Titlis,** a glacier, and the **Trübsee,** a glacier-fed lake, are both easy cable car rides from the village of Engelberg (Mt. Titlis 56SFr round-trip, Eurail 20% off, InterRail 25% off; Trübsee 19SFr round-trip). The hike from Trübsee back to Engelberg takes two hours.

The Luzern **tourist office,** Frankenstr. 1 (tel. (041) 51 71 71), off Zentrumstr., behind and to the left of the train station, overflows with maps and guides. (Open Mon.-Fri. 8:30am-6pm, Sat. and holidays 9am-5pm.) The **post office** is to the right of the station on Bahnhofstr. (Open Mon.-Fri. 7:30am-6:30pm, Sat. 7:30am-1pm.) The station itself (schedule information tel. (041) 21 33 11) houses **telephones** (downstairs; open Mon.-Fri. 7:30am-8pm, Sat. 8am-4pm), **currency exchange** (open Mon.-Fri. 6:15am-8:45pm, Sat.-Sun. 7:30am-7:30pm), **lockers** (2-3SFr) and **bicycle rental** (16SFr at the baggage desk).

Hop on bus #18 to Goplismoos for the friendly **Jugendherberge Am Rotsee (IYHF),** Sedelstr. 12 (tel. (041) 36 88 00). After 7:30pm, you must take bus #1 to Schlossberg and walk 15 min. down Friedentalstr. (Reception open 4-10:30pm. Lockout 9:30am-4pm. Curfew midnight. 20SFr, nonmembers 27SFr. Breakfast and showers included. Dinner 8.50SFr. Laundry and kitchen facilities. Fills quickly in summer.) The centrally located **Touristen Hotel Luzern,** St. Karliquai 12 (tel. (041) 51 24 74), is by the river, 10 minutes from the station. (No curfew. 33-40SFr per person, 10% discount with ISIC. Showers, breakfast, and baggage storage included.) **Pension Pro Filia,** Zähringerstr. 24 (tel. 22 42 80) is the friendliest in town. (Singles 50SFr. Doubles 85-95SFr. Triples 115SFr. Quads 140SFr. Reserve in advance.) **Hotel Schlussel,** Franziskanerplatz 12 (tel. (041) 23 10 61), newly renovated and comfy-cozy, reverberates with Swissness. (Singles 50SFr, with shower 70SFr. Doubles 80SFr, with shower 100SFr. Triples 115SFr, with shower 150SFr. Breakfast included.) **Camping Lido,** Lido Str. (tel. (041) 31 21 46) is a half-hour hike from the station, on the Lido beach. Cross the Seebrücke and turn right along the quay, or take bus #2 toward Verkehrshaus. (Swimming, tennis, and mini-golf nearby. 5SFr per person, 2SFr per tent, dorms 10SFr. Open April-Oct.)

Luzern's **Rathausquai** blooms daily with outdoor markets. There's a **Migros** supermarket at Hertensteinstr. 44. (Open Mon.-Wed. and Fri.-Sat. 8am-6:30pm, Thurs. 8am-9pm.) Next door is a **Migros restaurant,** the cheapest in town. (Open Mon.-Sat. 6:30am-6:30pm.) For good vegetarian fare, head away from the river and the train station to **Waldstätter Hof,** Zentralstr. 4 (12-15SFr; open daily 6:30am-8:30pm). For nightlife, head down Rathausquai; **Mr. Pickwick Pub** is often jammed with native and visiting imbibers.

Berne (Bern)

After a fire destoyed Berne in 1405, it was rebuilt entirely of sandstone; now Switzerland's capital and home to Toblerone and Swiss cheese, Berne radiates beige medieval serenity. According to legend, the city was named when its founder, Berchtold of Zähringen, was advised by his counsels to go on a hunt and to name his town after the first catch. The beast was a bear, and today the heraldic city animal is everywhere.

Practical Information

Tourist Office: Verkehrsbüro, on the ground floor of the train station complex (tel. 22 76 76). Snag a map and *This Week in Berne.* Room reservations (2SFr); when closed, check the information board. Open Mon.-Sat. 8am-8:30pm, Sun. 9am-8:30pm; Nov.-April Mon.-Sat. 8am-6:30pm, Sun. 10am-5pm.

Budget Travel: SSR, Falkenpl. 9 (tel. 24 03 12). Take bus #12 to Universität. Also at Rathausgasse 64 (tel. 21 07 22). Bus #12 to Rathaus. Student discounts and flights. Open Mon.-Fri. 10am-6pm, until 8pm on Thurs.

Embassies: U.S., Jubiläumsstr. 93 (tel. 43 70 11). Open Mon.-Fri. 9:30am-noon and 2:30-4pm. **Canada,** Kirchenfeldstr. 88 (tel. 44 63 81). Open Mon.-Fri. 8am-noon and 12:30-4pm; off-season Mon.-Fri. 8am-noon and 1:30-5pm. Consulate at Belpstr. 11 (tel. 25 22 61). Open Mon., Wed., and Fri. 8am-12:30pm and 1-4pm, Tues. and Thurs. 1-4pm. **U.K.,** Thunstr. 50 (tel. 44 50 21). Open Mon.-Fri. 9am-12:30pm and 2-5pm. **Australia,** Alpenstr. 29 (tel. 43 01 43). Open Mon.-Fri. 8am-12:30pm and 1:30-5pm. Citizens of **New Zealand** should consult the consulate in Geneva.

Currency Exchange: Downstairs in the train station. Open daily 6:10am-10pm; Jan.-March 6:10am-9pm.

American Express: Budenbergplatz 11 (tel. 22 94 01), by the bus area outside the station and across Bahnhofpl. Open Mon.-Fri. 8:30am-6pm, Sat. 9am-noon.

Post Office: Schanzenpost 1, 3000 Berne 1, behind the train station. Poste Restante. Open Mon.-Fri. 6am-11pm, Sat. 6am-9pm, Sun. 10am-noon and 4-11pm.

Telephones: At the train station. Open Mon.-Sat. 6:30am-10:30pm, Sun. 7am-10:30pm. **City Code:** 031.

Trains: Berne Centrale station (tel. 21 11 11).

Luggage Storage: Lockers downstairs in the station take two 1SFr coins.

Public Transportation: For all **SVB** buses and trams (tel. (031) 22 14 44), buy a Touristen-Karte (4SFr per day, 6SFr per 2 days) from the station (downstairs) or at Bubenbergplatz 5.

Bike Rental: At the train station, 16SFr per day. Open daily 6:10am-9:50pm.

Hitchhiking: Those going to Geneva and Lausanne take bus #11 to terminus Brückfeld. Those heading for Interlaken and Lucerne take tram #5 to terminus Ostring. Those taking the Autobahn north snag bus #20 to terminus Wyler.

Pharmacy: In the train station, open 6:30am-8pm. At least 3 pharmacies are open until 9pm; ask in the tourist office for a list.

Emergencies: Police (tel. 117). **Ambulance** (tel. 144). **Medical Emergency** (tel. 22 92 11).

Accommodations and Camping

The outlook is bleak—few inexpensive rooms, a full youth hostel. Reserve in advance if at all possible. Guesthouses in the suburbs offer rooms (20-30SFr); ask the tourist office for help.

Jugendhaus (IYHF), Weihergasse 4 (tel. 22 63 16). Cross Bubenbergplatz to Christoffelgasse, which dead ends into Bundesgasse. Turn left and follow white signs. Brand-new, huge, always crowded. Reception open 7-9:30am, 5-6pm, 6:30-10:45pm, and 11:15pm-midnight. Lounge always open. Members 12SFr, nonmembers 19SFr. Breakfast 5SFr, lunch or dinner 9SFr. Laundry 5SFr.

Hotel National, Hirschengraben 24 (tel. 25 19 88). Take the first left off Bubenbergpl. First-class rooms at third-class prices. Singles 45-55SFr, with shower 80-90SFr. Doubles 80-90SFr, with shower 116SFr. Breakfast included.

Camping: Camping Eichholz, Strandweg 49 (tel. 54 26 02), take tram #9 to terminus Wabern. 4SFr per person, 3SFr per tent. Also rooms with 2 beds, 12SFr plus 4SFr per person. Reserve ahead. Open May-Sept.

Food

Shop at markets to beat the pricey restaurants. Fruit markets ripen at Bärenplatz (daily), Bundesplatz (Tues. and Sat.), and Waisenbausplatz (Thurs.). **Migros** and **Ryfflihof** supermarkets and cafeterias are near the train station (see below).

Migros Restaurant, Zeughausgasse 31, off Bärenpl. Standard supermarket-cafeteria fare. 7-10SFr. Open Mon.-Fri. 8:30am-7:30pm, Thurs. until 9:30pm, Sat. 8am-4pm.

Rytflihof, Genfergasse 5. Big, bright, cafeteria-style, and only 9-12SFr. Open Mon. 11am-6:15pm, Tues.-Wed. and Fri. 8am-6:15pm, Thurs. 8am-8:45pm, Sat. 8am-3:45pm.

Restaurant Manora, Bubenbergpl. 5a (tel. 22 37 55), opposite the train station. Berne's rendition of this Swiss chain is huge, agreeable, and popular with students. Ample salad bar (3.80-8.80SFr). Fruit, yogurt, and juice bar (3.50-5.50SFr) as well as hot dishes and desserts. Open Mon.-Sat. 7am-10:45pm, Sun. 9am-10:45pm.

Mensa der Universität, Gesellschaftstr. 2, past Hochschulstr., northwest of the station and off Sidlerstr. Take bus #12 to the Universität stop. Better than typical institutional fare, and friendly students. Menus 6-9SFr. ISIC not necessary. Open Mon.-Thurs. 11:30am-1:45pm and 5:45-7:30pm, Fri. 11:30am-1:45pm.

Sights and Entertainment

Pick up a map at the tourist office and follow their dotted blue line. Beginning in front of the station at the **Church of the Holy Ghost,** built in 1726 and filled with pastels (open June-Sept. Mon.-Sat. 11am-3pm), the cobblestoned route leads past the clock tower, or **Zytglogge,** Berne's focal point. Complete with moving figures, astronomical designs and a golden clacker at its tip, the clock's shows start 4 min. before each hour. (Guided interior tours May-Oct. at 4:30pm. Buy tickets for 4SFr at the tourist office.) Next is the **Einstein Museum,** Kramgasse 49, where from 1903 to 1905, Al (or perhaps his wife, as late-night talk show hosts now speculate) developed the special theory of relativity. (Open Feb.-Nov. Tues.-Fri. 10am-5pm, Sat. 10am-4pm. Free.) An alley a few blocks down leads to the **Münster,** Münstergasslein, an imposing Gothic cathedral. Its portal depicts the Last Judgment with imagination-defying horrors of Hell. Climb the tower for a fantastic view of Berne's mahogany roofs. (Church open Mon.-Sat. 10am-noon and 2-5pm, Sun. 11am-noon and 2-5pm; Nov.-Easter Tues.-Fri. 10am-noon and 2-4pm, Sat. 10am-noon and 2-5pm, Sun. 11am-noon and 2-5pm. Tower costs 2SFr and closes 30 min. before church.) Cross the Kirchenfeldbrücke to the 500-year-old **Bärengraben** (bear pits), whose furry residents will perform tricks (make circular motions with your finger to engage one) for a bribe. (Open daily 7am-6pm; Oct.-March 8:30am-4pm.) Conclude your tour at the **Parliamentsgebäude** with an introduction to Switzerland's political system. (Free 45 min. tours every hr. 9am-noon and 2-4pm, Sun. no 4pm tour. When in session, only galleries open.)

Several of Berne's many outstanding museums cluster together at **Helvetiaplatz** across the Kirchenfeldbrücke (take tram #3 or 5). The **Bernisches Historische Museum,** Helvetiaplatz 5, chronicles the development of everything from film projectors to syringes to rural Swiss housing. (Open Tues. 10am-9pm, Wed.-Sun. 10am-6pm. Admission 3SFr, students 2SFr, exhibitions extra, Sat. free.) The **Kunsthalle,** Helvetiaplatz 1 (tel. 43 00 31) presents exhibitions of contemporary art by a selected and often unknown young artist. (Open Tues. 10am-9pm, Wed.-Sun. 10am-5pm. Admission 4SFr.) On the other side of town, near the Lorrainebrücke, the **Kunstmuseum,** Hodlerstr. 8-12, masses over 2500 of Paul Klee's works, plus tons of Hodler and other Swiss artists. (Open Tues. 10am-9pm, Wed.-Sun. 10am-5pm. Admission 3SFr, students 2SFr.) The **Swiss Alpine Museum,** Helvetiapl. 4 (tel. 43 04 34), famed for its Alpine topological models, will reopen in November 1992.

To explore Berne's underground music scene, head to the graffiti-covered warehouse informally known as **Reithalle.** (Alternative bands, alternative dress.) From the corner of Bollweik and Holderstr. (near the Lorrainebrücke), walk through the parking lot, under the train tracks, and into the building in front on the left. Shows are on Fridays and Saturdays, often on Thursdays, and occasionally other nights. Have all the fun with none of the angst at **Bar Big Ben,** Zeughausgasse 12 (tel. 22 24 28), "where nice people meet." Jazz lovers should plan their journeys for early May, when Berne's **International Jazz Fest** blows into town.

Near Berne

Fribourg, Berne's sister city to the southwest, balances on the border between French and German Switzerland. For centuries the home and refuge of Swiss-

German Catholicism, Fribourg today cherishes the richest collection of medieval religious art in the country. Trains from Berne leave every hour and cost 9SFr each way. Upon arrival, head to the **tourist office,** 1, Square des Places (tel. (037) 81 31 75 or 81 31 76), five minutes from the train station. Walk left down av. de la Gare and continue down rue de Romont, then turn right at Georges Python. (Open Mon.-Fri. 8am-noon and 2-6pm, Sat. 9am-noon and 2-4pm; closed Sat. afternoons during winter.) If you turn left at Georges Python, you'll come upon the new **auberge de jeunesse,** 2, rue de l'Hôpital (tel. (037) 23 19 16), which is in the large parking lot. (Reception open 7:30-9:30am and 5-10pm. 18SFr, nonmembers 28SFr. Laundry, lockers and kitchen facilities. Open Dec. to mid-Jan. and Feb.-Oct.) Half an hour and 8.20SFr from Fribourg is the tiny town of **Murten,** given to the canton of Fribourg in 1803 by an uncharacteristically generous Napoleon. This undiscovered burg bills itself as the "medieval city"; most of the town wall and the stone castle overlooking the **Murtensee** have remained untouched by time. The **Verkehrsbüro** (tel. (037) 71 51 12) is opposite the castle at Schlossgasse 5. (Open Mon.-Fri. 9am-noon and 2-5:30pm, Sat. 9am-noon.)

Interlaken and the Berner Oberland

Snowcapped mountain ranges towering over green pastures, friendly farmers renting rustic rooms, the jingle of cowbells breaking the perfect silence—this is Switzerland's Switzerland.

Though cablecars and railroads crisscross central Switzerland, overland hiking is the only way to do the Alps. Free maps of the region are available from the most rinky-dink of tourist offices; hiking trails are also clearly marked by bright yellow signs indicating the time—which may or may not be accurate—to reach nearby destinations. Gallivanters should pack sunglasses, water and a sweater, for the Alps aren't kind to the unprepared. For more information, write to the **Interlaken Tourist Office,** Höheweg 37, CH-3800 Interlaken.

Interlaken

Interlaken, less than an hour by train from Berne, is both a launch pad to the surrounding mountains and a hub for train connections throughout Switzerland. Named in 1130 by Augustinian monks, the town lies between the Brienzersee and the Thunersee and offers convenient access to both lakes. Charming as it is, Interlaken should be treated as a way station rather than a destination.

Though most train schedules list times for **Interlaken Ost** (tel. (036) 22 30 24), only private trains and those to and from Lucerne stop there; all others arrive at **Interlaken West** (tel. (036) 22 35 25). Each station features a minute tourist office which changes currency at good rates. (Open Mon.-Sat. 7:30am-7pm, Sun. 7:30am-noon and 1:30-6:30pm; Oct.-May Mon.-Sat. 7:30am-noon and 1:30-6pm, Sun. 8am-noon and 2-6pm.) Computers on the platform at either station babble tourist info in English, German, and French. The main **tourist office,** Höheweg 37 (tel. (036) 22 21 21), in the Hotel Metropol six blocks left of Interlaken West, finds rooms and provides maps and schedules for free. Ask for their list of rooms in private homes if you'll be staying at least three days (20-30SFr per person). (Open July-Aug. Mon.-Fri. 8am-noon and 1:30-7pm, Sat. 8am-noon and 2-5pm, Sun. 5-7pm; Sept.-June Mon.-Fri. 8am-noon and 2-6pm, Sat. 8am-noon.) The **post office,** Marktgasse 1, is five minutes from Interlaken West (open May-Sept. daily 7am-9:30pm; Oct.-April Mon.-Sat. 7am-9pm, Sun. 9am-1pm and 5-8:45pm) and also has **telephones.** Not-so-cheap bicycles can be rented at the train stations (11SFr per ½-day).

Although Interlaken gushes hotels, very few approach affordability. Take bus #5 or walk 15 minutes from either station and follow the signs to **Balmer's Herberge,** Haupstr. 23 (tel. (036) 22 19 61), in Matten. (From West Station go left, veer right, turn right on Centralstr., and follow the signs.) Sign in and return at 5pm, when beds are assigned (no reservations). A haven for English-speakers, Balmer's holds a mysterious and legendary attraction for Americans. Perhaps it's the currency exchange, bike rental (single and tandem), discount excursions, videos at night, CNN, MTV, book exchange, kitchen facilities (1SFr per 20 min.), laundry (8SFr per load), mini department store (open until 10pm) or super-friendly staff. Everyone is welcome—if beds are filled, you can crash on a mattress. New Year's Round-The-World processionals every hour on the hour (Dec. 31-Jan. 1). (Dorms 15SFr. Doubles 50SFr. Triples 60SFr. Quads 80SFr. Showers 15SFr. Breakfast included. **Jugendherberge Bönigen (IYHF),** Aareweg 21 (tel. (036) 22 43 53) is farther from town; take bus #1 to Lütschinbribrück from either station (every 50 min.) or walk from Interlaken Ost (left from station for 20 min., then follow signs from fork). On the swimmable Brienzersee, the Jugendherberge counters Sigma Beta Balmer's bustle with tranquility and humongous bathrooms. (Reception open Feb.-Oct. daily 6-9am and 5-9pm. 11.60SFr. Breakfast 5SFr. Dinner 9SFr. Laundry.) The Berner Oberland is a camper's dream—seven campgrounds grace Interlaken's gates. **Jungfraublick** (tel. (036) 22 44 14) is five minutes past Balmer's on Gsteigstr. (6.10SFr per person, off-season 5.60SFr. 4-10SFr per tent. Open April-Oct.) Just across the river from Interlaken Ost's Schiffstation is the small riverside **Sackgut** (tel. (036) 22 44 34). (5.50SFr per person. 5-11SFr per tent. Open May-Oct.) The five other sites cluster together near the Lombach River in Unterseen. Follow the signs from Seestr. near Interlaken West.

One might think that Interlaken's restaurants charge extra for having translated their menus into English. Eschew the absurdly expensive restaurants, especially those on Höheweg. Instead, try **Tea Room Spatz,** 46, Spielmatte, on an island in the Aare River, for delicious and reasonable (11-13SFr) meals. (Open Mon.-Sat. 9am-8pm.) Stock up for hikes at the **Migros** supermarket across from Interlaken West. (Open Mon.-Fri. 8:30am-noon and 1:30-6:30pm, Sat. 8:30am-4pm).

Höheweg nightlife heats up during high tourist season. The fun starts at **Buddy's,** Höheweg 33, an Interlaken tradition with the cheapest beer in town. (Open Sun.-Thurs. 10am-1am, Fri.-Sat. 10am-1:30am; in off-season Sun.-Thurs. 10am-12:30am, Fri.-Sat. 10am-1am.) The drunken herds then migrate to Interlaken's oldest disco, **Johnny's Dancing Club,** Höheweg 92, downstairs in the Hotel Carlton. (Drinks from 5SFr. Cover 8SFr on Sat. Open Dec.-Oct. Tues.-Sun. 9:30pm-2:30am.)

Interlaken's *other* tradition is the summer production of Schiller's *Wilhelm Tell.* Held in a huge ampitheater around the corner from Balmer's, the cast of hundreds includes residents, children and local horses and cows, which are paraded through the streets before the performance begins. Shows start in late June on Thursdays with Saturday performances as well from July to early September, beginning at 8pm. Tickets are available from the **Tellbüro** on Bahnhofstr. 5 (tel. (036) 22 37 23) or at the tourist office; pick up an English synopsis (1SFr) when purchasing tickets (12-26SFr).

Lakes

Appreciate the riotous topography of the Berner Oberland with a cruise on one of Interlaken's lakes, the **Brienzersee** (to the east) or the **Thunersee** (to the west). Relaxing and beautiful, the trips are also one of the few inexpensive excursions around (day passes 32SFr, Sept.-June 24SFr; Eurail and Swisspass valid, InterRail 50% off). Steamers cross the lakes approximately every hour between 8am and 6pm; the best cruising strategy is to disembark at whim, and reboard a later boat or catch a train or postal bus back to Interlaken. Hiking and biking are also options.

The Thunersee cruise takes ½ hour to reach the **Beatushöhlen,** prehistoric caves with stalactites, waterfalls and the ancient cell of the pallid Augustinian monk St. Beatus. (Open April-Oct. 9:30am-5:30pm. 7.50SFr, students 6.50SFr.) Medieval castles freckle the Thunersee's shores. **Spiez Castle,** jutting into the lake, houses a historical museum, a Romanesque church, and a flower garden. (Open April-Oct. Mon. 2-5pm, Tues.-Sun. 10am-5pm. Admission 3SFr, students 2SFr.) Two castles are accessible from the Thun station: **Schloss Thun** and **Schloss Schadau,** which houses Switzerland's Gastronomy Museum. (Open June-Aug. 10am-5pm; April-

May and Sept. to mid-Oct. 1-5pm; closed Mon. 4SFr.) **Schloss Hünegg** at the Hilterfingen landing resounds with luxury, and **Schloss Oberhofen,** purchased in 1925 by an enterprising American lawyer, is 20 minutes from Thun.

Accommodations on the lake are expensive; ask at the tourist offices for *zimmerfrei* options. **Spiez** and **Thun,** the Thunersee's metropolises, have offices located adjacent to the train stations. (Spiez: tel. (033) 54 21 38; open Mon.-Fri. 8am-noon and 1:30-6:30pm, Sat. 8am-noon; June and Sept. Mon.-Fri. 8am-noon and 2-6pm, Sat. 8am-noon; Oct.-May Mon.-Fri. 8am-noon and 2-5pm. Thun: tel. (033) 22 23 40; open Mon.-Fri. 8:30am-noon and 1-6pm, Sat. 9am-noon). Both offices also dole out good hiking maps. The lone **Jugendherberge (IYHF)** on the lake is in **Faulensee,** Quellenhofweg 66 (tel. (033) 54 19 88). Most Thunersee steamers have a stop in Faulensee just before Spiez. (Curfew 10pm. Members only, 10.90SFr. Breakfast 4SFr. Lunch 7SFr. Dinner 8SFr. Kitchen facilities. Open March-Dec.) **Campgrounds** are countless: try **Panorama Rossen** in Aeschi (bus to Mustermattli from Spiez; tel. (033) 54 43 77; 3.90SFr per person, 4-5SFr per tent; summer only) or **Bettlereiche** in Gwatt near Thun (15 min. along the lake to the right of the station; tel. (033) 36 40 67; 5.50SFr per person, 6-10SFr per tent).

The Brienzersee is the more rugged and less developed of the two lakes. **Brienz,** its lone populous village, makes for a serene daytrip from Interlaken (1¼ hr. by boat; 20 min. by train). Opened in 1978, the **Ballenberg Swiss Open-Air Museum,** a 50-hectare country park, displays examples of traditional rural dwellings from every region of Switzerland, with Swiss artisans busily at work. The park is about an hour's walk from the Brienz train station, but an hourly bus (round-trip 5.20SFr) connects the two. (April 15-Oct. 25 open daily 10am-5pm. Admission 10SFr, students 8SFr.) The **tourist office** (tel. (036) 51 32 42), across from the train station, gives hiking tips for walkers of all levels. (Open Mon.-Fri. 8am-7pm, Sat. 8am-6pm; Sept.-June Mon.-Fri. 8am-noon and 2-6pm, Sat. 8am-noon.) The train station rents **bicycles.** From the tourist office, cross the tracks, turn left, and hug the lake for 15 minutes to the **Brienz Jugendherberge (IYHF),** Strandweg 10 (tel. (036) 51 11 52). This rustic hostel rents hiking boots (5SFr) and bicycles (10SFr for one day, 15SFr for two) to its gung-ho guests. (Reception open 8-9am, 5-6pm and 7-10pm. Members 10.90SFr, nonmembers 17.90SFr. Breakfast 5SFr. Dinner 9SFr. Open March, April 15-Nov. 15, and the two weeks surrounding New Year's Day.) Along the same stretch sprawl two campgrounds: **Camping Seegärtli** (tel. (036) 51 13 51; 6SFr per person, 3-5SFr per tent; open April-Nov.), and **Camping Aaregg** (tel. (036) 51 18 43; 4.80SFr per person, 6SFr per tent; open April-Oct.).

Giessbach Falls, 10 minutes by steamer from Brienz, typifies the wonder of Mother Nature with 14 frothy cascades. Though a funicular takes you up (3SFr), the hike is an easy 15 minutes—continue on to **Oxalp** or **Iseltwald,** a tiny fishing town with more charm than the boy next door. Pitch your tent for the night at **Camping du Lac** (tel. (036) 45 11 48; 5.90SFr per person, 6-8SFr per tent; open May-Sept.).

Valleys

For a magnificent Alpine head rush, ascend from Interlaken into one of the neighboring valleys: Lauterbrünnen to the southwest and Grindelwald to the southeast. Both valleys become busier and considerably more expensive during ski season; on the bright side, they teem with jobs for dishwashers, bartenders, and chalet staff. Private railways chug into the hills each hour from Interlaken Ost; round-trip to Grindelwald is 15.20SFr, to Lauterbrunnen 10.40SFr. The private railways and cable cars are abominably expensive; in general, the Swiss Holiday Card will get you free or discounted fares, InterRail gets 50% off, and Eurail is impotent. For information on skiing, see the end of this section. Hitchhiking is feasible, if you walk from Interlaken toward Wilderswil to avoid the local traffic.

The **Grindelwald** valley is the more touristy of the two; hotels and giftshops jam Grindelwald town's unnamed streets. Leave town and climb the Alps; hiking here is indescribable. The **Verkehrsbüro** (tel. (036) 53 12 12), up the main street to the right in the Sportzentrum, has hiking and skiing maps and can find you rooms in private homes. (Open Mon.-Fri. 8am-noon and 2-6pm, Sat. 8am-noon and 2-5pm; Oct.-June Mon.-Fri. 8am-noon and 2-6pm, Sat. 8am-noon.) Ride Europe's longest chairlift to the **First** mountain for frightful, head-spinning views (23SFr, round-trip 36SFr, 20SFr one-way through Balmer's). Trips to the **Männlichen** snake up from the **Grund** station (26SFr, round-trip 40.80SFr); the summit affords a glorious glance at the Eiger, the Mönch and Jungfrau.

Budget travelers strike it rich in Grindelwald. The **Jugendherberge Die Weid (IYHF)** (tel. (036) 53 10 09) is a 20-minute climb up Terrassenweg (take the right fork from the train station), in an old timbered house with a transporting view. Come early and write your name on the list, then check in between 4:30 and 6:30pm. Some of the small rooms have balconies; the sitting room offers a fireplace and a communal guitar. (Curfew 11pm. Members only, 13.50SFr. Sleepsack and showers included. Breakfast 5SFr. Dinner 9SFr.) The rustic **Naturfreundehaus** (tel. (036) 53 13 33) is also on Terrassenweg. (Reception open 8-9am, 5-6pm, and 7-8pm. Curfew 10pm. Students 16.50SFr. Showers included. Breakfast 7SFr. Dinner 13SFr. Kitchen facilties. Sheets 2SFr.) One block to the right of the tourist office, **Lehmann's Herberge** (tel. (036) 53 31 41) offers bright wooden rooms to fatigued hikers (25-35SFr, breakfast included). Several hotels in town have dorm rooms; ask the tourist office for a list. Of Grindelwald's four **campgrounds,** the closest is **Gletscherdorf** (tel. (036) 53 14 29), a small campground endowed with phenomenal photo opportunities of the mountains and clean facilities. From the station, turn right; take the first right after the tourist office, then the third left. (5SFr per person, 4-8SFr per tent.) Another option is **Camping Eigernordwand** (tel. (036) 53 12 42), across the river and to the left of the **Grund** station (5-6SFr per person, 4SFr per tent). Right next to the main train station is an information board littered with *zimmerfrei* notices. Fend off the valley's assault on your budget; avoid restaurants and buy provisions at the **Coop** across from the tourist office.

The **Lauterbrünnen** valley radiates peace. Stark but beautiful, untamed yet serene, hiking through the glacier-cut valleys harks back to Eden. Lauterbrünnen town feels small, dwarfed by sheer rock cliffs. The less-than-stellar **Verkehrsbüro** (tel. (036) 55 19 55) is 200m past the station on the main street. (Open July-Sept. Mon.-Sat. 8am-noon and 2-6pm, Sun. 2-5pm; Oct.-June Mon.-Fri. 8am-noon and 2-6pm, Sat. 9am-noon and 3-6pm.) Frau Graf's delightful farmhouse-turned-hostel, the **Matratzenlager Stocki** (tel. (036) 55 17 54), offers a full kitchen redolent with spices and a mellow atmosphere. Leave the train station from the back, descend the steps, cross the river, turn right and walk 200m. The sign on the house reads "Massenlager." (10SFr; open Jan.-Oct.) **Camping Schützenbach** (tel. (036) 55 12 68) on the Panorama walkway to the falls, has showers and laundry/kitchen facilities. (5.50SFr per person, 5-8SFr per tent. Dorms 13-15SFr.) Follow the signs toward Trümmelbach from the station (15 min.). **Camping Jungfrau** (tel. (036) 55 16 38), up the main street from the station toward the large waterfall, provides cheap beds, kitchens, showers, lounges, and a snack bar. (5SFr per person, 2-7SFr per tent. Dorms 12-14SFr.) Lauterbrünnen's little **Coop** roosts between the train station and tourist office.

The fabulous **Trümmelbach Falls,** seven consecutive glacier-bed chutes, generate mighty winds and a roaring din inside their mountain home. Explore through tunnels, footbridges, and underground funiculars impressive in themselves (open April-Nov. 8:30am-5:30pm; 7SFr). Though you can nab a postal bus (3SFr), the ½-hr. hike is well-marked and simple. Cable cars leave from Lauterbrünnen and from **Stechelberg** (45 min. from the falls) to Gimmelwald (respectively 13.20SFr and 6.20SFr), to Mürren (7.20SFr and 11.80SFr), to Birg (22.80SFr and 21SFr), and to the top of the **Schilthorn** (36.20SFr and 30.50SFr), the mountain made famous in the Bond flick *In Her Majesty's Secret Service.* **Mürren,** a car-free skiing and sport resort villa, coordinates this area; ask at the **tourist office** (tel. (036) 55 16 16) in the Sports Center (5 min. left of the Lauterbrünnen terminus, 10 min. right of the Stechelberg one) for inexpensive *zimmerfrei.* (Open Mon.-Wed. and Fri. 9am-noon and 2-6pm, Thurs. 9am-noon and 2-8pm, Sat.-Sun. 2-6pm). The single hostel in the valley rewards those who trek to Gimmelwald on the steep Stechelberg trail; its **Mountain Hostel** (tel. (036) 55 17 04) is rustic, inexpensive and ultimately friendly. *Don't arrive without food*—there are cooking facilities, but no restaurants in this microscopic burg (6.50SFr, showers 1SFr). The most arresting ascent in this area—or in all of Switzerland—is up the **Jungfraujoch** (3454m). The **Jungfrau** itself is almost always inaccessible. Trains start at Interlaken's Ostbahnhof and travel to either Grindelwald or Lauterbrünnen, continuing to **Kleine Scheidegg** and finally to the peak itself, "the top of Europe." The entire trip costs a scary 127.40SFr. If you take the 6:34am train from Interlaken Ost, the 7:05 from Lauterbrünnen or the 7:18am from Grindelwald, the fare is reduced to 89SFr. The early bargain can only be bought round-trip. (Eurail not valid; InterRail 50% off; Swisspass 25% off.) The rail is chiseled out of solid mountain and penetrates the Eiger and Mönch. Included in the price are visits to the **Ice Palace** (a maze cut into the ice) and the **Sphinx** scientific station. Avoid going on a cloudy day—call (036) 55 10 22 for a weather forecast. Even in mid-summer, the summit is frigid and the elevator line to the Sphinx is often an hour long; bring winter clothing, sunglasses and food. The hike down takes about four and a half hours.

Skiing

There are four types of ski passes for the Oberland; the Jungfrau Region pass is the most extensive and expensive (89SFr for 2-day min., 216SFr for 7 days, 334SFr for two weeks). Prices include transportation to lifts. The Kleine Scheidegg/Männlichen pass (42SFr for 1 day, 74SFr for 2) covers more trails than you'd tire of in a week (186SFr). Ski rental is available throughout the valleys; skis, boots, and poles cost about 44SFr the first day, less each day thereafter. The **ski schools** in Grindelwald (tel. (036) 53 20 21) and Wengen (tel. (036) 55 20 22) supply information on classes. Call (036) 53 26 92 for information on weather and ski conditions at Grindelwald/First, (036) 23 18 18 for Kleine Scheidegg/Männlichen, and (036) 55 26 55 for Mürren/Schilthorn.

Balmer's Herberge guests have greater options: discount ski packages include transportation to Grindewald (12SFr), ski rental (30SFr alpine, 15SFr nordic), and expert trail advice as well as ski passes at slashed prices.

Zermatt and the Matterhorn

The Matterhorn is an ornery giant, its peak often shrouded in thick clouds; the best time to catch a glimpse is at dawn or dusk. To climb this beast, you need a mountain of money and a courageous heart; the monster claims dozens of lives each year. Fortunately, you can hike 388km worth of sign-posted paths around Zermatt without grave danger to life or pocketbook. Information is available at the **Mountaineering Office** (tel. (028) 67 34 56), across from the train station. (Open July to mid-Oct. 8:30am-noon and 4:30-7pm.) Sturdy boots, warm clothing and raingear are absolutely essential. Ride the cable car (23SFr round-trip) or hike (2-3 hr.) to **Schwarzsee;** from there the path to **Hörnli Hütte** (1½-2 hr.) affords stunning glimpses of the region's reigning mount and the sumptuous valley below. Zermatt has more summer ski trails than any other Alpine resort; lifts operate daily from 7am-2pm depending on the weather. Ski passes cost 47SFr for 1 day, 166SFr for 1 week. Flexible passes allow 2 in 4 days of slopes for 76SFr, 7 days in 2 weeks for 238SFr. Ski rental runs 40SFr (about 25SFr if you stay at the youth hostel). For more time on the slopes, rent equipment a day ahead; ski shops are open Mon.-Sat. 8am-6:30pm. For **alpine rescue,** call (028) 67 34 87.

The **tourist office** (tel. (028) 66 11 81) is next to the train station. (Open Mon.-Fri. 8:30am-noon and 1:30-6:30pm, Sat. 8:30am-6:30pm, Sun. 9:30am-noon and 4-6:30pm; mid-Sept. to June Mon.-Fri. 8:30am-noon and 1:30-6pm, Sat. 8:30am-noon.) The newly-renovated **Jugendherberge (IYHF)** (tel. (028) 67 23 20) oozes fitness freaks and friendly felines. From the train station, walk to the right, down the main street, turn left at the church, cross the river, and follow the signs uphill for 5 min. (Reception open 7-9am, 4-5:30pm and 6:30-7pm. Curfew 11:30pm. 18SFr, nonmembers 24SFr. Breakfast, sleepslack, showers included. Lunch or dinner 9SFr). Closer to the station but farther from the mountains is the pleasant **Hotel Bahnhof** (tel. (028) 67 24 06); get off your train and go 100m to the right. (Dorms 20-22SFr. Singles 37SFr. Doubles from 65SFr. Showers and kitchen facilities included.) The lone campground in town is **Camping Matterhorn Zermatt** (tel. (028) 67 39 21), 5 minutes to the left of the station (7SFr per person; open June-Sept.) The **Coop Center** is next door to the tourist office (open Mon.-Fri. 8am-noon and 1:45-6:30pm, Sat. 8am-noon and 1:45-6pm). Cafés are expensive, even for Switzerland. Wolf pizza and tankards of beer at **Papperla Pub,** one block from the church on Kirchestr. (Pizza 11-13SFr. Open noon-11:30pm; no food 2-6pm.)

To reach Zermatt, take the private railroad from Visp or Brig. (17 per day, 1½ hr., 46SFr and 50SFr round-trip, respectively. InterRail 50% off. Eurail not valid.) Hitchhiking is a bad idea.

French Switzerland

Geneva (Genève)

If peace has a home on this planet, it is Geneva. The city has exemplified Switzerland's policy of neutrality since it joined the Swiss Confederation in 1815. Center of nascent Protestantism and birthplace of both the Red Cross and the League of Nations, Geneva now hosts the European headquarters of the United Nations, a slew of international organizations (one-third of its 375,000 residents are foreigners), and perpetual negotiations between belligerent nations.

Orientation and Practical Information

Geneva preens on the western shore of Lac Léman (Lake Geneva), at the southwestern corner of Switzerland. The Rhône river divides the city. Trains arrive at the **Gare Cornavin,** on the *rive droite* (north of the Rhône). To the south, the *rive gauche* hosts the buzzing shopping district and the *vieille ville* around the Cathédrale de St-Pierre.

Tourist Office: In the train station (tel. 738 52 00). Overwhelmed staff books hotel rooms and provides information on excursion and local events. Free map and monthly **List of Events** in French, or get *What's on in Geneva,* published monthly in English. Open Mon.-Fri. 8am-8pm, Sat.-Sun. 8am-6pm; Sept. to mid-June Mon-Sat. 9am-6pm. **CAR (Centre d'Accueil et de Renseignements):** Gare Coravin and Rue du Mont Blanc (tel. 731 46 47), in a car (really!) in front of the train station. Open June 15-Sept. 15 daily 8am-11pm.

Budget Travel: SSR, 3, rue Vignier (tel. 29 97 33). BIJ and charters. Open Mon. 10am-5:30pm, Tues.-Fri. 9:30am-5:30pm.

Consulates: U.S., 1-3, ave. de la Paix (tel. 738 76 13). **Canada,** 1, ch. du Pré-de-la-Bichette (tel. 733 90 00). **U.K.,** 37-39, rue de Vermont (tel. 734 38 00). **Australia,** 56-58, rue de Moillebeau (tel. 734 62 00). **New Zealand,** 28a, chemin du Petit-Saconnex (tel. 734 95 30).

Currency Exchange: In Gare Cornavin. Good rates, no commission on traveler's checks. Open daily 6am-9:45pm.

American Express: 7, rue du Mont-Blanc, POB 859, Geneva 1, CH-1208 (tel. 731 76 00). Mail held only 2 months. Open Mon.-Fri. 8:30am-5:30pm, Sat. 9am-noon.

Post Office: Poste Centrale, rue de Mont-Blanc, 1 block from the Gare Cornavin, in the huge Hôtel des Postes. Open Mon.-Fri. 7:30am-6pm, Sat. 7:30-11am. Also **Poste de Montbrillant,** 16, rue des Gares, behind the Gare Cornavin. Open Mon.-Fri. 6am-10:45pm, Sat. 6am-9pm, Sun. 9am-noon and 3-10pm. Poste Restante.

Telephones: In Gare Cornavin. Open 24 hrs. **City Code:** 022.

Flights: Swissair (tel. 798 21 21). Trains leave Gare Cornavin for **Cointrin Airport** (5:18am-11:18pm, about every 10 min., 4SFr; railpasses valid).

Trains: Gare Cornavin (tel. 731 64 50) is the primary station. Reservations and information office open Mon.-Fri. 8am-7:15pm, Sat. 8am-6:15pm, Sun. 10am-6:15pm. Gare Genève Eux-Vives, on the eastern edge of the city, serves Annecy and Chamonix.

Public Transportation: Rides of 3 or fewer stops (along bus routes marked in dark red) cost 1.20SFr. 1-hr. ticket 1.80SFr, 6-ride pass 10SFr, 1-day pass 8SFr, 2-day pass 14SFr, and 3-day pass 18SFr. Buy multifare and day tickets at train station—buy other tickets at automatic vendors located at every stop.

Ferries: CGN, quai du Mont-Blanc, at the foot of rue du Mont-Blanc (tel. 722 39 16). To Lausanne (3½ hr., 22SFr) and Montreux (5 hr., 27SFr). Ferries leave daily at 9:15am and 4:15pm. Eurail valid; InterRail not.

Bike Rental: At the baggage check in Gare Cornavin. From 16SFr per day; 11SFr for 12 hr. Open daily 7am-7:30pm.

Hitchhiking: Take bus #5 from the station to pl. Albert Thomas. Or call Telstop (tel. 731 46 47) which posts a list of available rides in front of the **CAR** car. (5¢ per km.)

Laundromat: Lave Blanc, 29, rue de Monthoux. Open daily 7am-10pm. Wash and dry 8SFr.

Medical Assistance: Hôpital cantonal, 24, rue Micheli-du-Crest (tel. 46 92 11). Walk-in clinics dot the city; call 20 25 11.

Emergencies: Police (tel. 117). **Ambulance** (tel. 144).

Accommodations and Camping

Thanks to the large number of hostel-like dorms, finding a room in Geneva should be no problem. If the ones below are full, ask for the tourist office's brochure *Youth Accommodation* (**CAR** map lists the same information).

Auberge de Jeunesse (IYHF), 28-30, rue Rothschild (tel. 732 62 60). Walk 5 min. left from the station down rue de Lausanne and then hang a right. State-of-the-art; huge and well-tended. Flexible 3-night max. stay—as long as you don't say anything, they probably won't. Reception open 6:30-10am and 5-11pm, but you can dump your baggage anytime. Lockout 10am-5pm. Midnight curfew. Members 16SFr, nonmembers 23SFr. Breakfast, sheets, and shower included. Dinner 8.50SFr (with seconds). Laundry 6SFr. Kitchen.

Cité Universitaire, 46, ave. Miremont (tel. 46 23 55), far from the station on the other side of the old town. Take bus #3 from the pl. de 22 Cantons (opposite the train station), direction "Crêts de Champel," to the last stop. Respectable rooms in a modern high-rise. Reception open Mon.-Fri. 8am-noon and 2-10pm, Sat. 8am-noon and 6-10pm, Sun. 9-11am and 6-10pm. Curfew 11:30pm. Dorms 12SFr. Singles 26-32SFr. Doubles 38-42SFr. Shower included. Cafeteria downstairs (open daily 7am-10pm). Accommodations open July 15-Oct. 15.

Hôme St-Pierre, 4, cour St-Pierre (tel. 28 37 07), in an unforgettable location—under the cathedral in the old city. Take bus #5 to the 5th stop (pl. Neuve), or walk 15 min., crossing the Rhône at the Pont du Mont-Blanc. Women only. A warm atmosphere brightens these two charming older buildings. No lockout or curfew. Dorms 12SFr. Occasional singles 22SFr. Doubles 17SFr per person. Showers and kitchen. Breakfast 6SFr. Lockers. Laundry 4SFr, no dryers. Popular and small, so reserve ahead.

Evangelische Stadtmission, 7, rue Bergalonne (tel. 21 26 11), behind the Musée d'Ethnographie. Take bus #1 to Ecole-Médecine. Amiable hosts offer dorm rooms. Spacious singles and doubles often filled with long-term renters. Reception open 8am-2pm and 4:30-7:30pm. Lockout 9:30am-5pm. Curfew 10:30pm. Dorms 23SFr the first night, 20SFr each additional night. Singles 43-48SFr. Doubles 37SFr. Showers and a beautiful breakfast included. Lockers 2SFr (but too narrow for backpacks).

Hôtel de la Cloche, 6, rue de la Cloche (tel. 732 94 81), just off the Quai du Mont-Blanc. Prettily wallpapered rooms, many with a tiny balcony and a view of Lake Geneva. Singles 40SFr. Doubles 70SFr. Triples 90SFr. Quads 120SFr. Breakfast included.

Camping: Pointe-à-la-Bise (tel. 752 12 96). Take bus #9 until Rive then bus E about 7km north. 5SFr per person, 6SFr per tent. Open April-Sept. Stay on bus E to the last stop (7km more) for **Camping d'Hermance,** Chemin des Glerrêts (tel. 751 14 83). 6SFr per person, 2.50SFr per tent. Open April-Sept. Both sites are near the lake.

Food

You can eat everything here from sushi to *paella,* but you may need to empty your Swiss bank account to cover it. Shop at the **Coop** and **Migros** supermarkets for a picnic in one of the parks.

L'age d'Or, at the foot of rue de Cornavin, near the train station. Tasty individual pizzas 7-8.50SFr. Salads 3.20-4SFr. Open Mon.-Sat. 7pm-1am.

Restaurant Manora, 4, rue de Cornavin, attached to La Placette department store, near the station. A cavernous and popular self-service restaurant featuring a fruit bar (3.50-6SFr), salad bar (3.90-8.90SFr), and hot dishes (5.50-13SFr). Magnificent desserts. Open Mon.-Sat. 7am-9pm, Sun. 9am-9pm.

Café du Rond-Point, 2, Rond-Point Plainpalais, near ave. Henri Dunant. A harried yet friendly staff serves local bohemians; most just sip coffee, but the 12SFr menu, including a main course, vegetable, salad and dessert is a good deal. Open daily 6am-midnight.

Le Zofage, 6, rue des Voisins, off pl. des Philosophes near the university. This university restaurant is one of the cheapest spots in town. *Plat du jour* with salad and bread 8SFr. Open Sun.-Fri. noon-2pm and 6-8pm.

Sights

Climb the north tower of John Calvin's church, the **Cathédrale de St-Pierre,** for a view of the winding streets and flower-bedecked homes of Geneva's old town. (Cathedral open daily 9am-7pm; Oct. and March-May 9am-noon and 2-6pm; Nov.-Feb. 9am-noon and 2-5pm. Tower open daily 11:30am-5:30pm except when cathedral closes for lunch and services. Admission 2.50SFr. Free organ concerts June-Sept. on Sat.)

Most of the city's museums are in the old town. The **Musée d'Art et d'Histoire,** 2, rue Charles-Galland, prides itself on its eclecticism: exhibits range from ancient Greek vases to the post-war avant-garde. (Open Tues.-Sun. 10am-5pm. Free.) **Maison Tavel,** 6, rue du Puits-St-Pierre (tel. 28 29 00), next to the town hall, relates the history of Geneva from the 14th through 19th century. (Open Tues.-Sun. 10am-5pm. Free.) The **Petit-Palais,** 2, terrasse St.-Victor, displays a wonderful collection of impressionist and surrealist art in a 19th-century palace. Classical music echoes through its five floors, and in the second *sous-sol* (basement) you can see Geneva's ancient ramparts. (Open Tues.-Sun. 10am-noon and 2-6pm, Mon. 2-6pm. Admission 10SFr, students and seniors 3.50SFr.)

Geneva's internationally famous monuments stand on the opposite bank, a 10 min. walk past the train station. The guided tour of the **United Nations** at the end of rue Montbrillant is, like peace, quite dull, despite art treasures donated by all the nations of the world. The constant traffic of arguing international diplomats, brightly clothed in regional get-up, provides more excitement than anything the tour guides have to say. (Open July-Aug. daily 9am-noon and 2-6pm; April-June and Sept.-Oct. daily 10am-noon and 2-4pm; Nov.-Mar. Mon.-Fri. 10am-noon and 2-4pm. Admission 7SFr, seniors and students 5SFr, children 3SFr.) Don't miss the nearby **International Red Cross and Red Crescent Museum,** 17, ave. de la Paix, open only since 1988. (Open Wed.-Mon. 10am-5pm. Steep admission: 10SFr, students 5SFr.)

Geneva's lakefront begs to be strolled. Take a sojourn down **Quai Gustave-Ador** to giggle at the world's tallest fountain, the **Jet d'Eau** ("Calvin's Bidet" to irreverent foreigners). **Le Jardin Anglais,** with its famous **Horloge Fleurie,** a large clock adorned with flowers erected in homage to Geneva's clock industry, sits at the foot of the pont du Mont-Blanc on the *rive gauche.* The old city nurtures scads of antique shops and galleries line the cobble-stoned (and generally car-free) streets. Two fine beaches front the lake: **Paquis Plage,** at quai du Mont-Blanc (1SFr), is laid-back and popular with the Genèvois; upscale **Genève Plage** (4SFr) offers a giant waterslide, volleyball and basketball tournaments, an Olympic-size pool and some serious scoping action. Next to biking, the best way to see Lake Geneva is through one of the ferry tours leaving from Quai du Mont Blanc. **CGN,** (tel. 722 39 16) and

Swiss Tours both cruise the lake several times daily, with the possibility of disembarking at Montreux or the Château de Chillon.

Entertainment

Pick up from the tourist office the free *List of Events,* an invaluable guide to activities. Summer nightlife centers around the cafés and the lakeside quays. **Place Molard** can be a lively hangout; so can **Place Bourg-du-Four,** below St-Pierre in the old town (Le Clémence, at #20, is one of its most popular spots). Anglophones gather at the **Brittania Pub,** on the pl. de Cornavin, across from the Notre Dame (open until 1am; 2am on weekends). They play funky music all night long at the **Midnight Rambler,** 21, Grande-Rue, in the *vielle ville,* a disco with frequent live concerts and a DJ spinning rock, new wave and rap hits. (Doors open at 11pm.) When the weather complies, spontaneous concerts pop up at the **Jardin Anglais.**

The first week in August, Geneva celebrates with the **Fêtes de Genève.** Three days of international musical and artistic celebration culminate in boat shows and a fabulous fireworks display. In September, Swiss music lovers somersault down from the hills for the two-week folk festival of cabarets, theater and concerts known as the **Fête du Bois de la Batie.**

Lausanne

On Lac Léman beneath Alpine splendor, Lausanne's attractions put it on a par with Geneva, its larger neighbor and rival. Sports are Lausanne's business—the Ouchy waterfront is a summer haven for sailors, swimmers, and waterskiers. And for over a century, Lausanne has proudly hosted the headquarters of the International Olympic Committee. At the other end of the city's four-stop mini-Metro, the old town retains an ecclesiastic, medieval air.

Lausanne is a short ride by land or by sea from Geneva and Montreux. The city rises from Ouchy through incredibly steep streets to the Cathedral and *vielle ville* at its crown; the efficient and inexpensive mini-Metro system whizzes from one end to the other in six minutes flat.

Lausanne's Gothic **Cathédrale,** considered Switzerland's most important, stands as the *pièce de résistance.* Famed for its rose window, it was consecrated by Pope Gregory X in 1275. (Open Mon.-Fri. 7am-7pm, Sat. 8am-7pm, Sun. 11am-7pm; Oct.-Feb. daily 8am-5:30pm.) Although you can't see the rose window from the tower, the city, the lake, and the French Alps beyond are acceptable views by themselves. (Open Mon.-Sat. 9-11:30am and 1:30-5:30pm, Sun. 1:30-5:30pm. Admission 2SFr, children 12 and under 1SFr.) Nearby, the fountain on **place de la Palud,** helps the city perpetuate itself, acting as a locus for young people on the make.

Art aficionados and neophytes alike will love the **Collection de l'Art Brut,** 11, avenue Bergières, perhaps Europe's most unusual gallery. Its founder, post-war painter Jean Dubuffet, despised the pretension of the avant-garde art scene, so he filled the gallery with the works of "non-artists"—the criminally insane, the institutionalized, the eccentric. (Open Tues.-Fri. 10am-noon and 2-6pm, Sat.-Sun. 2-6pm. Admission 5SFr, students 3SFr, under 16 free.) The **Musée Olympique,** 18, ave. Ruchonnet, presents the philosophy and history of the Olympic Games from their reestablishment in Athens in 1896 to highlights of the 1984 competitions in Sarajevo and Los Angeles. (Open Tues.-Wed. and Fri.-Sat. 9am-noon and 2-6pm, Thurs. 9am-noon, 2-6pm, and 8-10pm, Sun.-Mon. 2-6pm. Free.) Take an evening stroll down the **quai de Belgique,** a lakeside promenade flanked by flowers, immaculate gardens, small fountains, and benches.

The **tourist office,** 2, ave. de Rhodanie (tel. (021) 617 14 27), is located across from the lake, in Ouchy. Take the metro from the train station to the last stop (2SFr) and walk 90m to the right. (Open Mon.-Sat. 8am-7pm, Sun. 9am-noon and 1-6pm; mid-Oct. to Easter Mon.-Fri. 8am-6pm, Sat. 8:30am-noon and 1-5pm.) The branch office in the railway station is less helpful (tel. (021) 23 19 35; open daily May-June

2-8pm; July-Sept. 10am-9pm; Oct.-April 3-7pm). Pick up the invaluable *Lausanne Official Guide* and map (both free). **SSR,** 20, bd. de Grancy (tel. (021) 617 56 27), supplies budget travel information. (Open Mon.-Fri. 9:30am-5:30pm.)

Lausanne's comfortable **auberge de jeunesse (IYHF),** 1, chemin de Muguet (tel. (021) 26 57 82), near Ouchy, looks out to the lake and mountains, across the street from a giant municipal sporting complex that's open to the public. Take bus #1 (direction "La Maladière") to La Batelière, then follow the signs downhill, about 200m. (Reception open 7-9am and 5-11:30pm. Curfew 11:30pm. Members 15.75SFr, nonmembers 22SFr. Breakfast included. Quality dinner 8SFr. Lockers. Laundry 5SFr. Get there by 5pm.) The tourist office finds rooms for 45-55SFr per night (3SFr fee). **Camping de Vidy,** 3, chemin du Camping (tel. (021) 24 20 31), charges 5.50SFr per person (students 3.50SFr), 4-8SFr per tent. Take ave. de Rhodanie west out of the city, loop around the autoroute onto route de Vidy, and turn left onto Chemin des Ruines Romaines.

Many restaurants are just a spectator sport for the budget traveler. Visit produce **markets** Wednesday and Saturday at pl. de la Riponne and pl. de la Palud (7:30am-12:30pm). Nearby, a local favorite, the **Berguglia Boulangerie,** 10, rue Madeleine, serves up scrumptious and cheaper delights. (Open Mon. 2:15-6:30pm, Tues.-Fri. 7:30am-12:30pm and 2:15-6:30pm, Sat. 7am-5pm). **Manora,** 17, pl. de St-François, is a popular self-service restaurant with fantastic salad, fruit, and dessert bars. *Menus du jour* run from 7.80-13.50SFr. (Open Mon.-Fri. 7am-10:30pm, Sun. 9am-10:30pm.) Pack your picnic from the selection of meats, cheeses, fruits and bread at the **Coop** supermarket on rue du Petit Chêne, on the way from the station to the city center. **Pinte Besson,** 4, rue de l'Ale, has turned out fondue (14SFr) since its grand opening in 1780. (Open Mon.-Sat. 7:30am-midnight.) In the evening, locals and visitors alike roost at pricey cafés along the quai d'Ouchy.

Montreux

Popular resort and retirement pad for the wealthy, Montreux also draws footloose young folks to its music festivals. The most famous is the annual **Montreux Jazz Festival** (2½ weeks in mid-July; tickets 48-250SFr, festival pass 1991SFr) featuring jazz, gospel, blues, big band, salsa, and rap. Write well in advance for information and tickets to Festival du Jazz, service de location cp 97, CH-1820 Montreux 1, or call (021) 963 82 82. In the U.S., try Ciao Travel, 810 Emerald St., #107, San Diego, CA 92109 (tel. (619) 272-5116). Full payment is required when you reserve. With luck, the tourist office may still have some tickets available when the festival starts, but most are snapped up over a month before the concerts begin. From late August to early October, the **Classical Montreux-Vevey Music Festival** takes over. Write to Festival de Musique, 5, rue de Théâtre, Case Postale 162, CH-1820 Montreux 2, for information (tickets 20-130SFr). In the U.S., contact Dailey-Thorp Inc., 315 W. 57th St., New York, NY 10019 (tel. (212) 307-1555) for information. Free concerts—everything from yodeling to rock—are held in the pavilion of the Rouvenaz. Check the tourist office for details.

Festival-free Montreux exudes peaceful karma. Exotic plants line the lakeside promenade, which surveys swans and boats below and the Alps beyond. Sunsets dazzle along the 10km stretch. A 10-minute walk past the hostel stands **Château de Chillon,** a remarkably well-preserved 13th-century fortress with all the comforts of home: prison, torture chamber, weapons room, and terrific views. The château inspired narratives by Rousseau, Victor Hugo, and Alexandre Dumas as well as Lord Byron's *The Prisoner of Chillon.* (Open March daily 10am-noon and 1:30-4:45pm; April-June 9am-5:45pm; July-Aug. 9am-6:15pm; Sept. 9am-5:45pm; Oct. 10am-4:45pm; Nov.-Feb. 10am-noon and 1:30-4pm. Admission 5SFr, students 4SFr.)

Montreux's **tourist office,** pl. du Débarcadère (tel. (021) 963 12 12), sits on the lake. Exit the train station onto ave. des Alpes, cross the street, descend the steps to your right, and walk to your left. (Open daily 8am-7pm; Sept.-May Mon.-Fri.

9am-noon and 2-6pm, Sat. 9am-noon.) The **Auberge de Jeunesse Haut Lac (IYHF),** 8, passage de l'Auberge (tel. (021) 63 49 34), is a 30-minute walk along the lake to your left—or take bus #1 (direction "Villeneuve"), get off at the Territet-Gare stop, and follow the signs downhill. It's spacious, although not Swissly spic-and-span, and right on the noisy train tracks. Call ahead or arrive well before 5pm. (Reception open 7-9am and 5-10pm, but you can leave baggage all day. Curfew 10pm; flexible during festivals. Members only, 15.20SFr. Breakfast included. Lunch or dinner 9SFr.) Nearby **Villeneuve** has luxurious lakeside camping at **Les Horizons Bleues** (tel. (021) 960 15 47; closes at 10pm; 4SFr per person, 2-3SFr per tent; open April-Sept.). Take bus #1 to Villeneuve. During the Jazz Festival, many revelers dump their bags at the station and then crash along the quays or on park benches. Montreux's lakeside cafés stun visitors both with their elegance and their exorbitant prices. Instead, assemble a lakeside picnic at **Migros** supermarket on ave. du Casino. Steaming cheese fondue (16SFr) and *raclette* (5SFr) highlight the scrumptuous regional Swiss menu at **Caveau des Vignerons,** a candlelit restaurant in a semi-underground cave at 30 bis, rue Industrielle. (Open Mon.-Fri. noon-2pm and 7-11pm, Sat. 7-11pm.) **La Locanda,** 44, ruelle du Trait, off ave. du Casino, is an elegant but affordable Italian restaurant. The *plat du jour* is 13-16SFr, pizza 13-16SFr. (Open Mon.-Sat. 11am-2pm and 5:30pm-midnight.)

Near Montreux

Southeast of Montreux lies **Leysin,** a major funspot in the Alpes Vaudoises. It was once a haven for patients who needed "sun therapy" as treatment for tuberculosis. Take a train to Aigle; then a spectacular cog railway climbs the 2200m to Leysin. (Aigle-Leysin line round-trip 13.20SFr, free with Swiss Holiday Card, Eurail, and InterRail.)

The **tourist office,** pl. du Marché (tel. (025) 34 22 44), is in the village next to the Holiday Inn; get off at Versmont. (Open Mon.-Fri. 8am-6pm, Sat. 9am-noon.) The resourceful staff gives overnight visitors a **Carte de Séjour** that entitles them to use myriad recreational facilities. They also hand out lists of authorized mountain guides and maps of hiking trails in the area.

The place to sleep, eat, and drink the night away is **Club Vagabond,** Leysin (tel. (025) 34 13 21), at the Leysin-Feydey stop past the village. Ascend the stairs on your left as you exit the station, turn left, and bear left at the fork in the road by the Eglise Catholique. The headquarters of the International School of Mountaineering, the Vagabond has regal food and an English-speaking staff which arranges special events like fondue nights, ski races and costume parties throughout the winter season. (Dinner 13SFr. Singles 33SFr, in winter 38SFr. Doubles 52SFr, in winter 68SFr. Showers and breakfast included.) Wintertime litters Leysin with skiers. Lift tickets start at 28SFr per day, equipment rental at 39SFr per day.

During mid-July the town hosts the **Leysin Rock Festival.** In past years stars as popular as Billy Idol, INXS, Simple Minds, and Sinéad O'Connor have all rocked this tiny Swiss town way up in the Alps. Tickets, available from the tourist office, cost 55SFr per day, 90SFr per weekend, or 165SFr for the entire four-day series.

Graubünden

Graubünden is the largest but least populous of the Swiss *cantons* and a microcosm of Swiss cultural heterogeneity; from valley to valley the language changes from German to Romansch to Italian, with a wide range of dialects in between. A few developed resorts such as St. Moritz draw hutches of ski-bunnies, despite lofty prices. For the most part, however, cattle own the roads. High season runs December through March (reservations absolutely necessary) and peaks again in July and August. In May and early June virtually everything shuts down.

St. Moritz

With its exclusive boutiques, luxury hotels, and prohibitively high prices, St. Moritz is an archetypal European hotspot. Nijinsky danced his final dance here in 1918 before going insane. The **tourist office,** via Maistra 10 (tel. (082) 331 47), 10 minutes from the train station (up the hill to the left), passes out advice on hiking. (Open Mon.-Fri. 9am-noon and 2-6pm, Sat. 9am-noon.) Hotel information, currency exchange, bicycle rental (14SFr) and lockers are also available at the train station. **Postal buses** destined for various valley villages leave just left of the station.

The **Jugendherberge Stille (IYHF),** via Surpunt 60 (tel. (082) 339 69), matches hotel standards. Walk 45 minutes around Lej da San Murezzan or catch the Sils postal bus (2SFr) to "Hotel Sonne." (Reception open 6:30-9am, 4-5:30pm, 6-8pm and 9-10pm. Curfew 10pm. 28.80SFr, nonmembers 35.80SFr. Doubles 77.60SFr. Breakfast, dinner, sheets and shower included. Locker and laundry facilities. Open June 15-Oct. and Dec. 15-April.) To reach **Camping Olympianschanze** (tel. (082) 240 90) take the same bus but turn right on via Surpunt for 15 min. (5SFr per person, 6-9SFr per tent.) Eating at restaurants in St. Moritz is a budget-thumping proposition. Forage at the **Coop** grocery one block left of the tourist office or on via Greves en route to the hostel. (Open Mon.-Thurs. 8am-noon and 1:30-6:30pm, Fri. 8am-noon and 1:30-8pm, Sat. 8am-noon.)

Near St. Moritz

Most of the towns along the train routes from St. Moritz make super daytrips. **Pontresina** lolls five minutes by train from St. Moritz (3SFr) and is second only to the big one itself in style, comfort and prices. Across from the station is the strict but stylish **Jugendherberge (IYHF)** (tel. (082) 672 23), which doubles as a restaurant, so—you guessed it—meals are compulsory. (Reception open 6:45-9am and 4-9pm. Curfew 10pm. Lockout 9:30am-4pm. 29.25SFr. Doubles 54.25SFr. Open June to mid-Oct. and Dec. to mid-April.) The **tourist office,** on the corner of via Maistra and Cruscheda (tel. (082) 664 88), helps with rooms, hikes and forest concerts. **Zuoz,** 30 minutes north of St. Moritz, is an enchanting mixture of Romansch houses, fountains, and carved troughs. Though rooms are expensive, the **tourist office,** (tel. (082) 715 10), up the hill and to the right on the main square, won't let you leave reservation-less. (Open Mon.-Fri. 8:30am-noon and 2-6pm, Sat. 8:30-11:30am; Oct.-Nov. Mon.-Fri. 8:30-noon and 2-6pm.) Don't return south without a visit to the **National Park,** 169km^2 of protected flora and wildlife. Enter at **Zernez,** home to the **National Park House,** which chronicles the history of the site and exhibits an informational show.

Southwest of St. Moritz, the rustic resort town of **Sils** lies on a windy plain between the Silser See and Silvaplaner See lakes, an easy daytrip away (round-trip 9SFr). Forget staying here, but do hike around the lake to Maloja, a relaxing 2-hr. stroll through wispy pines and blossoming meadows. Before beginning the trek, check out the **Nietzsche House,** near Hotel Edelweiss, where the philosopher lived from 1881-88, slowly decaying from *übermensch* to horse-hugging madman. (Open in summer Tues.-Sun. 3-6pm. Admission 3SFr, students 2SFr.) A 16.60SFr ride from St. Moritz, **Maloja's** charm lies in its convenience; only a few steps from the bus stop are the **tourist office** (tel. (082) 431 88; open Mon.-Fri. 8:30am-noon and 2-6pm, Sat. 8:30am-noon; Oct. to mid-Dec. and May-June Mon.-Fri. 8:30am-noon and 2-6pm) and the **Jugendherberge (IYHF)** (tel. (082) 432 58), a friendly farmhouse turned hostel. Hikers rule the roost. (Reception open 8-9am, 4:30-5:30pm and 8-9pm. Curfew 10pm. Lockout 9:30am-4:30pm. 15SFr; 24SFr with dinner. Open July-Nov. 15 and Dec. 22-May.)

Campers have their pick of lakeside sites: **Camping Silvaplana** (tel. (082) 484 92), **Camping Maloja** (tel. (082) 431 81), or **Olympiaschanze** (tel. (082) 340 90) in St. Moritz-Bad. Farther inland is **Camping Plauns** (tel. (082) 662 85), 15 minutes from Pontresina. All sites run 5-6SFr per person, 4-7SFr per tent, and are open in summer only. Ski rental prices are standard throughout the region at about 35-40SFr per day for downhill, 25SFr for cross-country. Ski runs in Zuoz are predominantly novice; St. Moritz has a little of everything, and Diavolezza has mostly advanced runs.

Italian Switzerland

The delightful collaboration of Swiss efficiency and Italian *dolce vita* will do you right. The ring of Italian voices is not all that sets the region apart from Switzerland; palm trees and a steamy clime join in the conspiracy. Emerald lakes, lush mountains, and vineyards that surround defiant stone houses render the countryside in **Ticino** (the main Italian-speaking canton) as romantic as Lugano and Locarno, its famed resorts. Lugano is 1½ hours out of Milan on the Zürich train line; change for Locarno at Bellinzona. Coming south from Berne through Brig, change at Domodossola.

Lugano

A lakeside hotspot and banking center extraordinaire, Lugano combines business and pleasure with Italian flavor. Start at the 16th-century **Cathedral of San Lorenzo,** across the street and down the hill from the station. The church's masterful carvings and glaring ceiling could only be Italian. The **Chieso San Rocco** on Via Conova (near the tourist office) features Passion frescoes and a not-to-be-missed golden altarpiece. Walk along the lake to the east or take bus #2 to the **Thyssen-Bornemisza Gallery** in Villa Favorita, Castagnola (tel. (091) 51 61 52), one of the outstanding private collections in Europe, with works by Raphael, Titian, Rembrandt, Velázquez, and El Greco. (Open May-Oct. Tues.-Sun. 10am-5pm. May open in winter or close unexpectedly during the summer; call ahead. Admission 12SFr, students 8SFr.) Those more athletically inclined can visit the **Lido beach** to swim (4SFr), windsurf (rental 15SFr per hr.) or paddleboat (10SFr per hr.) on the sunkissed waters of **Lago di Lugano.**

The busy **tourist office,** riva Giocondo Albertolli, 5 (tel. (091) 21 46 64), finds rooms and provides maps. (Open July-Aug. Mon.-Sat. 8am-12:15pm and 1:45-6:30pm, Sun. 9am-noon and 2-5pm; April-June and Oct. Mon.-Sat. 8am-noon and 2-6pm, Sun. 9am-noon and 2-5pm; Nov.-March Mon.-Sat. 8am-noon and 2-6pm.) Hotel information is also available at the train station, where there are **lockers** (2SFr). To reach the office, take the funicular (0.60SFr), or walk downtown and head right to the lake; it's on the left next to **Bar Elite.** The **albergo per la gioventù (IYHF)** in Crocifisso-Lugano (tel. (091) 56 27 28), is a short ride on bus #5 (catch it 300m left of the train station) to Crocifisso (from the stop, backtrack a few steps and turn left on Via Cantovale), or trudge 25 minutes uphill from the station. The hostel sprawls over a large plot of land featuring picnic tables, table tennis, and a full-sized swimming pool. (Reception open 6am-1pm and 3-10pm. Curfew 10pm. 12SFr; nonmembers 19SFr. Breakfast 5SFr. Sheets 2SFr. Open mid-March to Oct.) Women are blessed with a wonderful option, the **Casa della Giovane,** corso Elvezia, 34 (tel. (091) 22 95 53), a big ultra-modern building for little Catholic girls. (Dorms 15SFr. Breakfast 5SFr. Lunch and dinner 10SFr. Laundry 1.50-2.50SFr.) **Campers** must catch the Ferrovia Lugano-Ponte-Tresa (to the right and across the street from the station below the restaurant) to Agno (2.60SFr), where five campgrounds settle near the lake. All cost 5-7SFr per person, 3-7SFr per tent; try **La Palma** (tel. (091) 59 25 61) or **Golfo del Sole** (tel. (091) 59 48 02). Shop or dine at the **Migros** on via Pretoria. (Market open Mon.-Fri. 8am-6:30pm, Sat. 7:30am-5pm. Restaurant open Mon.-Sat. 9am-10pm.) For a more genuine repast, **Pestalozzi,** p. Indipendenza, serves cheap Italian food and vegetarian dishes from 6am-10pm. (Meals 10-15SFr. Salad bar 3.50-10.50SFr.)

Locarno

Locarno basks in the Mediterranean breezes and hot Italian sun of the Ticino. For much of the interwar era, hopes for peace were symbolized by "the Spirit of Locarno"—here the visionary German statesman Gustav Stresemann signed a conciliatory pact with France, Great Britain, and Italy in 1925. Above the city lurks the brilliantly orange **Madonna del Sasso** (Madonna of the Rock), the town's landmark and symbol. The famed Maria herself is tucked away in the museum next to the chapel. (Grounds open 7am-10pm; Nov.-Feb. 7am-9pm. Museum open Sun.-Fri. 10am-noon and 2-5pm. Admission 2.50SFr, students 1SFr.) Though a cable car ascends to the sanctuary (every 15 min., round-trip 5SFr), the walk is painfully easy.

To reach Locarno's **tourist office,** Largo Zorzi (tel. (093) 31 03 33), walk diagonally to the right away from the train station one block, then another block through a pedestrian walkway, and then cross the street on the left. (Open Mon.-Fri. 8am-7pm, Sat. and Sun. 9am-noon and 1-5pm; Nov.-March Mon.-Fri. 8am-noon and 2-6pm.) Locarno's youth hostel, the friendly **Pensione Città Vecchia,** via Torreta, 13 (tel. (093) 31 45 54), on the corner of via Borghese uphill from the piazza Grande, is usually booked; make reservations weeks ahead. (Singles 22-26SFr. Doubles 43-52SFr. Breakfast 3SFr.) Nearby is the cramped but convenient **Albergo la Zingara,** via delle Monache, 1 (tel. (093) 31 12 19), one block uphill from the Largo Zorzi. Downstairs is Locarno's hippest nightclub; staying upstairs saves you the cover charge. (Beers 8SFr. Hostel 27SFr. Breakfast and shower included.) Camp 20 minutes around the lake from the station at **Delta Camping** (tel. (093) 31 60 81; 8SFr per person, 7-9SFr per tent; open mid-March to late Oct.). Purchase picnic paraphernalia in the piazza Grande at the **Coop** or **Migros** supermarkets (both open Mon.-Fri. 8am-6:30pm, Sat. 7:30am-5pm). The Migros has yet another familiar **restaurant** (open Mon.-Sat. 7am-10pm). Also on p. Grande, the **Ristorante Svizzero** serves good Italian cuisine. (Pizza 10-12.50SFr. Open daily 11am-11pm.)

In nearby **Verscio** is a world-famous clown school run by master jester Dimitri. **Teatro Dimitri** offers a repertoire of plays, mimes, and variety acts in German and Italian throughout July and August. Performances begin at 8:30pm; tickets must be reserved in advance (ask the tourist office for a schedule). To reach Verscio, hope the Domodossola-Centrovalli railway behind the main station (round-trip 14.40SFr).

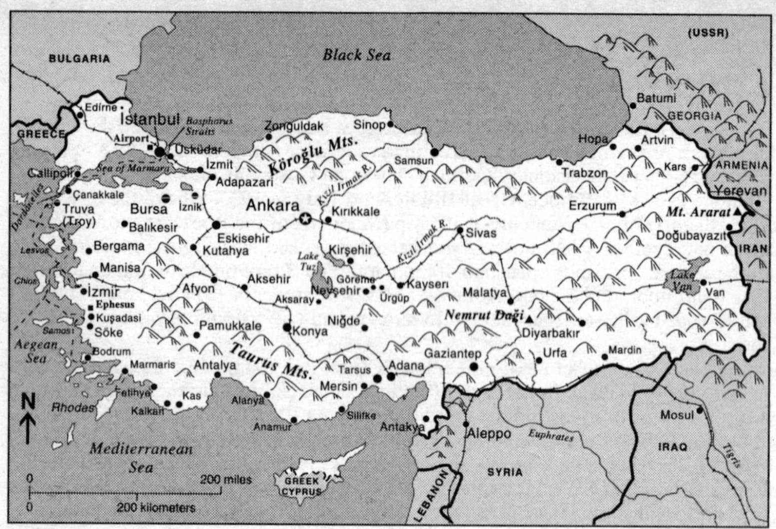

TURKEY

USD$1 = 4493 lira (TL, or TRL)
CAD$1 = 3931TL
GBP£1 = 7506TL
AUD$1 = 3498TL
NZD$1 = 2561TL
Country Code: 90

1000TL = USD$0.22
1000TL = CAD$0.25
1000TL = GBP£0.13
1000TL = AUD$0.29
1000TL = NZD$0.39
International Dialing Prefix: 99

The Gulf War broke out as *Let's Go* was planning its 1991 researcher itineraries, and at the time it seemed unsafe to send researchers to Turkey. All prices and information were last fully updated in the summer of 1990; expect some change. Note that we list all prices in this section in U.S. dollars (USD), a more stable currency than the inflation-stricken Turkish lira.

Barely fingering the European continent, Turkey (Türkiye) has swept back and forth between the East and the West. From this ferment emerged potent contributions to world civilization. The iron-forging Hittites clenched Asia Minor in the second millenium BC, developed systems of government and law, and left the earliest known texts in any Indo-European language. The Aegean coastal cities (Miletus, Ephesus, Pergamon, and Smyrna) enriched Greek culture as much as did Greece proper. Asia Minor became the cradle of a foundling religion that reined Europe for the next 1500 years; ornate Byzantine monuments exalt early Christianity. In the 11th century the region then shuddered with the advent of Seljuk Turk control. More recently, World War I witnessed the genocide of the Armenian people, which has been likened to the Holocaust.

The last emperors to rule Turkey were the Ottomans, enduring from the early 15th century to the end of World War I. The reign of Süleyman the Magnificent marked the apex of the empire after which it gradually declined into a stagnant morass of corruption. That modern Turkey exists at all is a tribute to Mustafa Kemal (Atatürk) who led the forces that expelled the British, French, Greek, and Russian armies. Equating modernization with Westernization, Atatürk abolished the Caliphate, Romanized the alphabet, outlawed Muslim tribunals, and installed a facsimile of democratic government; he even banned muezzin (prayer callers) singing in classical Arabic (of the Qur'an), decreeing that they must recite in modern Turkish only.

Atatürk's autocratic reforms could go only so far, though. Beyond İstanbul and a few other large cities, traditional Islamic customs and attitudes prevail, and liberal democracy is far from rooted. In the late 1970s, the experiment in democracy began to falter as street warfare laid siege to İstanbul, necessitating military intervention. Elections in 1983 ushered in the right-wing party of Prime Minister Özal. Though the leader of the opposition remains in enforced exile, his party was recently reinstated and martial law withdrawn. The most salient item on the Turkish agenda is still the country's ambiguous national identity. A crucial partner in NATO, its troop count second only to that of the U.S., Turkey sends millions of workers to western Europe and is fighting intently for admission to the EC. But Islamic opposition, too, has seen a resurgence since the 1980 military coup, and Özal has forged stronger economic and diplomatic ties with Arab countries than had any of his predecessors.

Enormous economic hardship resulting from Turkey's siding with the U.S.-led coalition in the Gulf War has incited terrorist groups to lash out against the government and Westerners. In the summer of 1991, government conflict with Kurds reached a relative peak in violent confrontation. Some tourists have unwittingly become caught up in Turkish political machinations, but the country remains legendary among budget travelers: the Aegean coast is now popular with tourists fleeing the Greek Islands, prices are indeed much lower than in Europe, and the Turks are remarkably hospitable to contemporary invaders.

For more detailed coverage of İstanbul and Turkey's Aegean and Mediterranean coasts, consult *Let's Go: Greece and Turkey (including Cyprus, Crete, and the Greek Islands).*

Getting There

The cheapest way to reach Turkey is by long-distance bus. **Euroways Eurolines** provides service from London for £118. Their office is at 52 Grosvenor Gardens, Victoria (tel. (071) 730 82 35). Euroways also runs from Paris; contact VIA International, 8, pl. Stalingrad (tel. 42 05 12 10). Overland routes all pass through Bulgaria; see the Bulgaria section for information on transit visas (which Americans no longer need).

Youth rail fares to Turkey (available to those under 26) are slightly lower than bus fares. Eurailpasses are not valid in Turkey, but InterRail is. Avoid taking the train to Turkey from Greece; the journey is an excruciating 38-hour odyssey, only two-thirds of which is spent in motion. If you wish to use your railpass, take the train as far as Alexandroupolis and get a bus from there, avoiding the Greco-Turkish border tension. Some people hitch from Alexandroupolis; if you do, aim for a single ride. You are *not* permitted to walk across the border.

The ferries that sail between the Greek islands in the eastern Aegean and the nearby Turkish shore are a popular way to reach Turkey. Boats run from Samos to Kuşadası (3-7 per week, USD25), Rhodes to Marmaris (6 per week, USD20), and Chios to Çeşme (July 15-Sept. 15; 6 per week; USD20-25). For many of the cruises, you must turn in your passport the night before. Be prepared for the Turkish port tax—usually around USD8. Check the Northeast Aegean and Dodecanese section of the Greece chapter in this book for more information.

Turkish Airlines (THY) provides regular service to Turkey from European and Middle Eastern countries, and offers 40% discounts on all European flights to students under 31 and everyone under 26. In London and other European capitals, you can often find flight bargains in the travel classifieds of local newspapers or by consulting budget travel agents.

Many travelers cross Turkey on the way to other Asian countries. Most buses to the east depart directly from Ankara (see Ankara Practical Information). The transit visa for Iran is as one might expect, difficult to obtain. We're not sure about Iraq right now. Syrian visas are much easier to obtain. (You must, however, exchange USD100 or the equivalent at the Syrian border.) Buses originate in İstanbul and Ankara, but you can catch them in Antakya or Gaziantep for Syria and in Mardin for Iraq. Reaching the erstwhile USSR from Turkey seems to be a possibility; see the Eastern Turkey section. A Soviet visa (or its post-Soviet equivalent) is obviously required. Check locally, or with the USSR embassy in Ankara. Flights may be your only way to the Indian subcontinent, but be prepared to pay dearly; luckily, those under 26 receive a 40% discount.

Getting Around

Turkey is a budget traveler's dream. Buses are efficient, modern and cheap—about USD1.25 per hour of travel. All bus companies are private, and you can occasionally chisel 10% off the price if you have an ISIC. **Varan Tours** buses, though slightly more expensive, are faster and more comfortable for longer trips (they're air-conditioned). Train travel in Turkey is slow, but there is a mildly bright side: when a bus would drop you off at your destination at 3am, an overnight train lets you stretch out and sleep until a decent hour. Train fares are even lower than bus fares, with students receiving a 10% discount. There are no trains along the western coast. *Dolmuş* (shared taxis), usually minibuses or vans, fill any gaps left by the remarkably comprehensive bus system and also follow fixed routes. They are more expensive than buses and leave whenever they fill up *(dolma* means "stuffed"). Be prepared to share your ride with whole families and their groceries. You can get on and off *dolmuş* whenever you like. Hitchhiking in Turkey is quite common. If asked to pay for the ride, you should offer half of the bus fare. The hitching signal is a waving hand.

Those unwilling to suffer through Turkey's eternal bus and train rides should consider the low domestic fares on Turkish Airlines; the student (under 24—bring ID) rate is USD50. Married couples get a 10% student discount on all domestic flights. There is no ferry system along the west coast except for a **Turkish Maritime Line** boat from İstanbul to İzmir (July-Sept. 3 per week; Oct.-June 1 per week). The Black Sea boat from İstanbul to Trabzon ogles some of the most beautiful scenery in Turkey (USD17.50, 10% discount, leaves 5:30pm Mon.). Make reservations as soon as you arrive in the city.

Practical Information

Turkish government tourist offices and tourist police exist in most major cities and resort areas. Some English, German, or French is usually spoken. They help find accommodations and often provide the usual slew of services without charge. In places without an official office, travel agents often serve the same function.

The black market exchange rate in Turkey is only slightly better than the official rate. If you're coming from Greece, spend your *drachmae* before arriving; the few banks change them do so at an egregious rate. Examine what you buy at bazaars carefully: exporting antiques is a jailable offense, even if you plead innocence. **Avoid drugs in Turkey.** The horror stories of lengthy prison sentences and dealer-informers are true; embassies are absolutely helpless in all cases. The minimum sentence for possession of even the smallest amount is sixteen months. Turkish law also provides for "guilt by association"—those in the company of a person caught are subject to prosecution. As for the foolish notion of smuggling: anyone remotely looking like a backpacker gets searched with a fine-tooth comb arriving back in Europe from Turkey. Yes, *Midnight Express* was based on fact.

Women traveling in Turkey may have a less pleasant experience than men. Away from İstanbul and the Aegean and Mediterranean coasts, most Turkish women are scarved and rarely make public appearances. In central and eastern Turkey, you will be stared at often and approached frequently. Women should dress modestly (wear a bra and avoid short shorts and tank tops) to avoid verbal and physical harassment. If you feel threatened, visible and audible anger, particularly in public, can be an effective deterrent. Better yet, say you're going to the cops: Turks fear the police, who, in these situations, almost always side with foreigners.

It's rarely a problem finding English-speaking natives in well-touristed areas. Off the beaten track, sign language and a pocket dictionary usually suffice. German is useful, even among rural populations. Remember that in Turkey a raise of the chin followed by a closing of the eyes means "no," and that a wave of the hand up and down means "come here." Perhaps one of the most useful gestures in Turkey is putting your palm flat on your chest. This is a polite way of refusing an offer—and the Turks seem to be an inexhaustible fountain of offerings, especially tea.

Toiletries are cheap and readily available in Turkey. Tampons are somewhat uncommon in the east, though, and you should always carry toilet paper; expect to encounter quite a number of pit toilets. There are rumors that some of eastern Turkey's feisty mosquitoes carry malaria; to be on the safe side, start a course of anti-malaria pills before you go. Doctors also advise typhoid, gamma-globulin, and tetanus shots. Turkish tap water is reportedly safe, but cautious travelers should stick to bottled water. Many tourists' digestive systems find fending off the denizens of Turkish food quite a task, especially in eastern Turkey. Should you succumb, two or three days' rest, no food, and oceans of liquid should help you recover. If it persists, see a doctor.

Turkey is a large country whose climate varies quite a bit. In summer, the Aegean and Mediterranean coasts are hot, with average daily temperatures around 32°C. Mosquitoes are a problem in some resort towns, so bring repellent. The swimming season from Bodrum south, and all along the Mediterranean coast, lasts from early May through October. On the Black Sea coast (İstanbul included), the swimming season is shorter (June-early Sept.), and fall brings considerable rainfall; winters are mild and wet. As you move inland, the climate becomes more extreme; the area around Urfa is regularly above 40°C in summer, while the area north of Van is kept relatively cool because of the high altitude. In winter, Urfa is quite temperate while most of central and eastern Anatolia is bitter cold and snowy.

Everything closes on the national **holidays:** January 1, April 23, May 19, August 30, and October 29. During Ramadan (*Ramazan* in Turkish, March 5 to April 3 in 1992), pious Muslims will not eat, drink, smoke, or travel between dawn and sunset. Outside İstanbul, Ankara, and the coastal resort towns, things really slow down. Hotel rooms are more available during this period, even at resorts. Large celebrations mark Ramadan's conclusion, known as Bayram; bus and train tickets or hotel rooms are scarce. During a second Bayram celebration July 3-6, similar chaos ensues. On the first day of the celebration each family is expected to slaughter an animal; vegetarians may want to stay indoors. Museums, archeological sites, and monuments are generally open from 9am to 5pm; many close on Monday. Most cost USD2.50. Despite Turkey's enormosity, the entire country lies within the same time zone—three hours ahead of Greenwich Mean Time in summer, two ahead in winter.

Shops in Turkey are generally open Monday through Saturday from 9am to 1pm and 2 to 7pm. Government offices are open Monday through Friday from 8:30am to 12:30pm and 1:30 to 5pm. Banks are open Monday through Friday from 8:30am to noon and 1:30 to 5:30pm. Food stores, bazaars, and pharmacies *(eczane)* tend to have longer hours. Persistent haggling in shops, over accommodations, and over less regulated transportation fares can save you loads of money.

You must often wait up to an hour to place a collect call; this must be done at a post office. Costs are upwards of USD12 for three minutes to North America. For AT&T's **USA Direct,** dial 99 80 01 22 77. Post offices (PTTs) are typically open every day from 8:30am to noon and 1 to 5:30pm; central post offices in larger towns keep longer hours, sometimes around the clock—but for international mail, phone calls, or Poste Restante, you should go during the week. Poste Restante should be addressed *Merkez Postanesi.*

Accommodations, Camping, and Food

Budget accommodations averages USD3-4 per person on the Aegean coast, USD2.50-4 along the Mediterranean and USD2-3.50 in the east. On the Aegean and Mediterranean coasts, rely on pensions and private boarding houses; in the east you'll have to resort to drab and dingy hotels, often without showers. Most Turkish towns have a *hamam,* or bathhouse, where you can get a wonderful steam bath for USD1.50-2.50. *Hamamlar* schedule different times for men and women. You can also clean off at any mosque. Camping is popular in Turkey, and cheap campgrounds abound (usually USD1 per person). Freelance camping is possible, but the police are usually quite strict.

Restaurants are called *lokanta;* a meal with beer should cost you USD3-4. There are always numerous stands selling *şiş kebap* (skewered chunks of lamb) or *döner kebap* (slices cut from a leg of lamb roasting on a spit) for USD0.75. In restaurants, it's customary to go to the kitchen yourself and choose after seeing everything. Look for the tomato *çorbası* (soups), different varieties of *pilav* (rice), *pilaki* (navy beans in a tomato sauce, often with meat), and *dolma* (stuffed vegetables served hot or cold and usually filled with meat, rice, onions, and herbs). Salads, widely available, include *çoban salatası* (cucumber and tomato salad) and *karışık salata* (mixed salad)—both very spicy. Turkish yogurt and *zeytin* (olives) are terrific. *Pide* is a distant relative of pizza: flat bread served with your choice of eggs, meat, tomatoes, cheese, or spices. Or try *köfte* (spicy meatballs). If you want to avoid meat, tell the cook or waiter "et yok" (without flesh). Travel lore and Turkish public health authorities have it that *ayran,* a popular yogurt and water drink, helps your body combat the summer heat. Beer is called *bira; efes-pilsen* and *tekel beyaz* are light, while *tekel siyah* is dark. All are fairly good and cost about USD1 for a large bottle. Wine is generally available only in fancy restaurants, except in the wine-producing areas of Cappadocia and İzmir and in coastal resort towns. *Rakı,* a licorice-flavored spirit, is the powerful national liquor.

Northwestern Turkey

İstanbul

İstanbul indulges the senses. Calls to prayer blare at 5am as the scent of corn wafts from streetside grills; taxis careen down crooked alleys barely sparing vendors who hawk everything from toilet paper to Korean-made "Benetton, Italy" sweatshirts. This is the lurching metropolitan circus of İstanbul.

The city's names, Byzantium, Constantinople, and İstanbul, each evoke a different world. Aya Sofya, the ancient cathedral of Orthodox Christianity is here, but landmarks of the Muslim East, particularly the city's two great mosques, the Sultanahmet and Süleymaniye, overshadow the Western Christian sites. Poised between pasts, İstanbul is, too, poised between two presents; Islam and Western capitalism are proving uneasy bedfellows. Men smoke *nargile* (water pipes) while their sons groove to walkmans, and a pinstriped bourgeoisie shares the streets with scarved women in traditional garb. The ancient moral codes of Islam and the individualistic ethic of West both woo the new generation, and in İstanbul, capitalism is winning.

Orientation and Practical Information

Turkey's largest city, in the northwestern corner of the country, straddles the Bosphorus Strait, the ever-strategic passage from the Black Sea out to the Sea of Marmara, the Dardanelles, and the Aegean. Waterways divide İstanbul into three parts. The **Bosphorus Strait** (Boğaziçi) separates Asia Minor from Europe, distin-

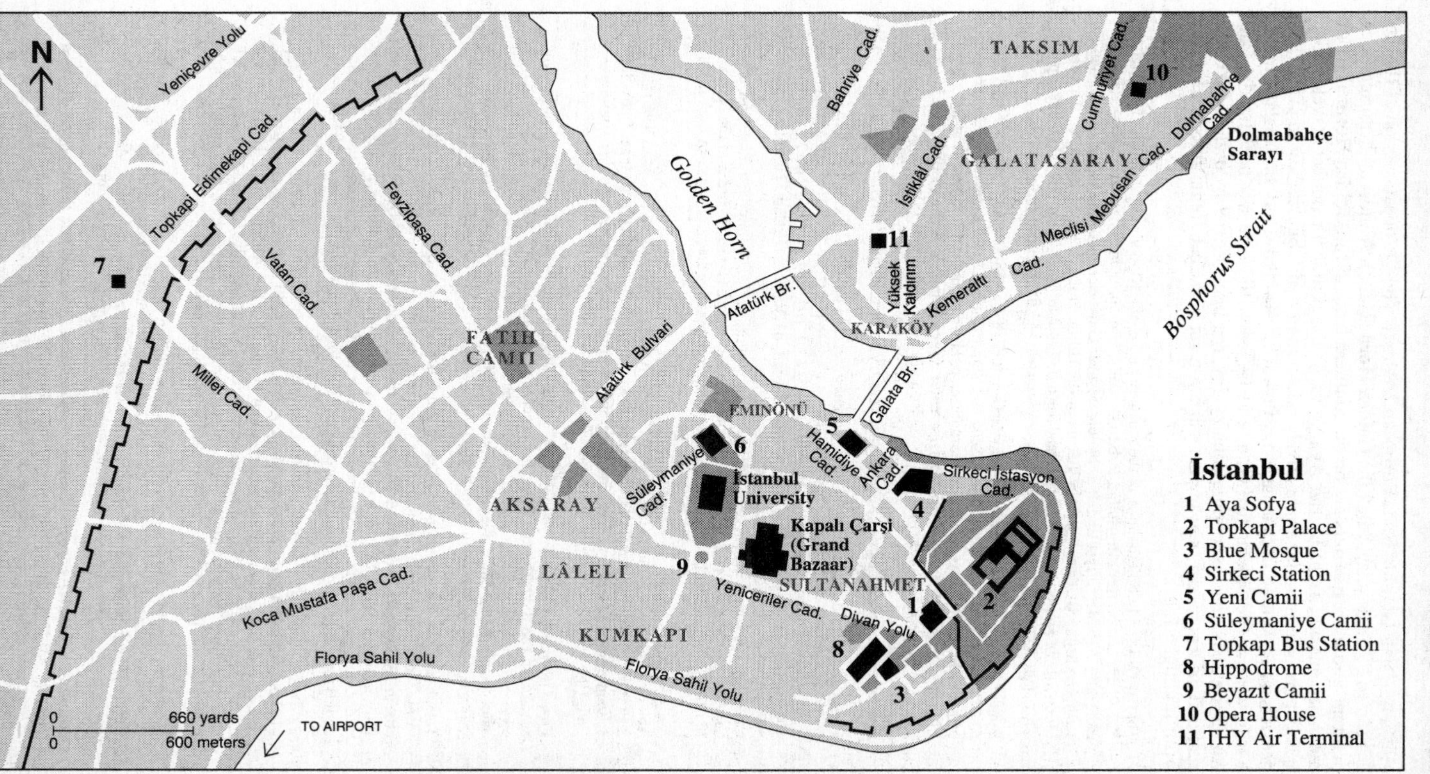

İstanbul
1 Aya Sofya
2 Topkapı Palace
3 Blue Mosque
4 Sirkeci Station
5 Yeni Camii
6 Süleymaniye Camii
7 Topkapı Bus Station
8 Hippodrome
9 Beyazıt Camii
10 Opera House
11 THY Air Terminal
N
Yeniçevre Yolu
Topkapi Edirnekapi Cad.
Fevzipaşa Cad.
Vatan Cad.
Millet Cad.
FATIH CAMII
Atatürk Bulvari
Golden Horn
Bahriye Cad.
TAKSIM
Cumhuriyet Cad.
Dolmabahçe Cad.
Dolmabahçe Sarayı
GALATASARAY
İstiklâl Cad.
Meclisi Mebusan Cad.
Yüksek Kaldırım
Kemeraltı Cad.
Atatürk Br.
KARAKÖY
Bosphorus Strait
Galata Br.
EMİNÖNÜ
Hamidiye Cad.
Ankara Cad.
Sirkeci İstasyon Cad.
Süleymaniye Cad.
İstanbul University
Kapalı Çarşi (Grand Bazaar)
AKSARAY
LÂLELİ
SULTANAHMET
Yeniceriler Cad.
Divan Yolu
Koca Mustafa Paşa Cad.
KUMKAPI
Florya Sahil Yolu
Florya Sahil Yolu
0 660 yards
0 600 meters
TO AIRPORT

guishing Asian İstanbul from European İstanbul. The European section of the city is bisected by an estuary called the **Golden Horn** (Haliç). Almost all historical sites, markets, and older quarters are on the southern bank of the Golden Horn. The **Sultanahmet** quarter, right by the Aya Sofya, is the center for budget travelers.

Most areas of İstanbul are relatively safe even at night, but it's best to avoid these districts after sunset: **Kasimpaşa,** northwest of Karaköy and the Galata tower, **Fatih,** west of the Sülemaniye Gnü, and **Beyoğlu,** the area north of İstiklâl Cad, which is a fashionable shopping zone by day, red light district by night. Make sure that taxi drivers restart their meters when you get in the cab (night rates are in effect from midnight-7am).

Tourist Offices: In Sultanahmet at the northern end of the Hippodrome 3, Divan Yolu (tel. 522 49 03), across from the Sultan Pub (open daily 9am-5pm); in Galatasaray (Regional Directorate), 57b Meşrutiyet Cad. (tel. 145 68 75), near Galatasaray Sq. and the British Consulate (open Mon.-Sat. 9am-5pm); in Taksim at the Hilton Hotel Arcade (tel. 133 05 92; open Mon.-Sat. 9am-5pm); at the International Terminal of Atatürk Airport (tel. 573 73 99; open daily 9am-5pm); at Karaköy Maritime Station (tel. 133 05 92; open daily 9am-5pm).

Budget Travel: Your best pick of many is **Gençtur,** 15 Yerebatan Cad., 2nd floor (tel. 520 52 74), in the center of Sultanahmet. Sells ISICs and youth ID cards, distributes free maps, provides Poste Restante service, and organizes paid workcamps throughout Turkey. Open Mon.-Fri. 9am-5:30pm, Sat. 9am-1pm. **Seventur Travel Shop,** 2c Alemdar Cad. (tel. 512 41 83), next to the Aya Sofya. Provides Poste Restante service and sells ISICs, youth ID cards, as well as bus and plane tickets. Open Mon.-Fri. 9am-6pm, Sat. 9am-1pm. There are some unlicensed travel agencies in Sultanahmet that try to pass bogus tickets.

Consulates: U.S., 147 Meşrutiyet Cad., Tepebaşı (tel. 143 62 00). **U.K.,** 34 North Meşrutiyet Cad. (tel. 144 75 40). **Canada,** 107 Büyükdere Cad. (tel. 172 51 74). **Australia,** 58 Tepecik Yolu (tel. 157 70 50). **Bulgaria,** 44 Zincirlikvyu Cad. (tel. 169 04 78 or 169 22 16). **Syria,** 3 Silâhtar Cad., Nişantaşı (tel. 148 27 35). **Jordan,** 63 Valikonaği Cad., Nişantaşı.

Currency Exchange: Banks open Mon.-Fri. 9am-noon and 1:30-4pm. The main post office has a 24-hr. currency exchange. The airport exchange booth is open 24 hrs. and the Karaköy Maritime Station booth services late ships. Keep receipts in order to change lira back to dollars.

American Express: Hilton Hotel lobby, Cumhuriyet Cad. (tel. 132 95 58). Mail held (USD3 fee for those without AmEx card or traveler's checks). No currency exchange. Open daily 8:30am-8pm. For lost travelers' checks, go first to the **Turk Ekspress** office, 91 Cumhuriyet Cad. (tel. 130 15 15). Open Mon.-Fri. 9am-6pm.

Post Office: Marked with yellow "PTT" sign. The Central Post Office at 25 Yeni Postane Sokak and the Bakırköy and Beyoğlu branches offer 24-hr. stamp, telephone, and telegraph services. To send packages abroad, go to the **packet service** in the back side of the main post office. (Open Mon.-Sat. 8:30am-12:30pm and 1:30-5pm). Poste Restante at the Central Post Office is jammed; have mail sent to American Express or Gençtur (see Budget Travel above).

Telephones: At the central post office or the Taksim branch. Buy *büyük* (large) *jetons* and throw them into the machines as fast as you can or buy a telephone card *(telefon karti),* available in 30, 60, and 120-unit sizes. Collect calls can be made only to the U.S., Canada, England, Italy, Holland, Spain, Sweden and Japan. Use *küçük* (small) *jetons* for local calls. Sometimes phone numbers in İstanbul are listed only with six digits—there should be seven. The first digit is always 1, 3, or 5; 1 for the north side of the Horn, 3 for the Asian side of the Bosphorus, and 5 for the south side of the Horn. **City Code:** 01.

Flights: Atatürk Airport domestic terminal (tel. 573 73 88) and international terminal (tel. 573 71 45). Both connected to Aksaray and Şişane by THY Airlines bus ("Uçak Servisi," every 30 min., USD0.75), and municipal bus #96 (less frequently, USD0.15). To reach Sultanahmet from the bus stop at Aksavay, walk toward the intersection, turn right at Ordu Cad. and continue for 2km; or hop aboard any bus on Ordu Cad.

Trains: Trains for Europe leave from **Sirkeci Station** (tel. 527 00 51). Daily to Munich (USD105), Belgrade (USD52), Sofia (USD36), and Athens (USD38). 1 per day, 9pm; Oct.-May. 6:15pm. **Haydarpaşa Station** (tel. 336 04 75), on the Asian side, is for Asia-bound domestic traffic. Ferries connect station with Karaköy pier #7 every 30 min.

Buses: All buses leave from the chaotic **Topkapı Bus Terminal.** The terminal, not depicted on maps but about 4km from Sultanahmet, is just beyond the city walls on Millet Cad. (and a long way from Topkapı Palace). From Sultanahmet, take bus #84 or any bus that has

"Topkapı" on the side panel. Frequent buses to Ankara (8 hr., USD7), Bursa (4 hr., USD4), İzmir (9 hr., USD11), Bodrum (13 hr., USD15) and Trabzon (20 hr., USD17). All bus companies, both domestic and international, have offices at Topkapı, and many have offices in Sultanahmet as well. Only **Bosfor Turizm** (tel. 143 25 25) and **Varan Tours** (tel. 149 19 03) are licensed to operate in Western Europe. These two and **Derya Turism** are licensed for Greece. Unlicensed companies often offer substantial discounts for western European destinations and then abandon their passengers in Eastern Europe. Expect delays, inefficiency, licensing problems, and/or border hassles with all carriers. Whichever travel company you choose, you must obtain a Bulgarian transit visa *in advance* (usually available overnight). Agencies downtown are clustered on Hüdavendigâr Cad., behind the Sirkeci Railway Station in Sultanahmet, and on İzmar Cad., off Ordu Cad. to the left just before the Aksaray intersection.

Public Transportation: Bus tickets (USD0.15 each, USD0.10 for students) can be bought in kiosks and at larger bus stops marked "Plantonluk." Hawkers charge an extra USD0.10. Frequent service 6:30am-10:30pm. Buses marked "Tek bulet" require one ticket, buses marked "Çift bulet" require two. Read the sign on the side of the bus and ask the driver for particular quarters. Going to Sultanahmet from the north, the sign will usually include Beyazıt; from the west, it will usually include Eminönü. *Dolmuş* (shared taxis) run fixed routes and cost about USD0.10. Stops are indicated by a large "D" on a blue sign.

Ferries: Frequent service from Eminönü or Karaköy to points on the Asian side of İstanbul (USD0.60). Ferries and the faster seabus to Yalova (near Bursa) leave from Kabataş. **Turkish Maritime Lines's** ticket office is on the waterfront at Karaköy (tel. 144 42 33), west of the Haydarpaşa ferry terminal. Cheapest fare to İzmir for a *koltuk* (pullman, but it also means "armpit") is USD11, along the Black Sea coast to Trabzon USD14 (reserve weeks ahead for a cabin, less for deck passage). Stops en route; meals not included.

Hitchhiking: Many hitchhike from the Londra Mocamp (see Accommodations). Mon.-Wed. many trucks leave for central Europe. Only one major highway, Rte. 100, runs out of İstanbul. Edirne (228km west of İstanbul) is a major truck stop near the Bulgarian and Greek borders.

Laundromat: Hobby Laundry, 6/1 Caferiye Sok., part of Yücelt Hostel building. USD2 per 1 kg. Open daily 9am-8pm.

Bookstore: NET Kitabevi, 10, Şeftali Sok in Sultanahmet. Maps, novels, and newspapers. **Aypa Bookstore,** 80 Divan Yolu in Sultanahmet. Open daily 8am-8pm.

Medical Assistance: American Hospital Admiral Bristol Hastanesi, Nişantaş, Güzelbahçe Sokak (tel. 131 40 50). **German Hospital,** Sıraselviler Cad., Taksim (tel. 143 81 00).

Emergencies: Police (tel. 166 66 66). May not speak English. **Tourist Police,** in Sultanahmet (tel. 528 53 69, 24 hrs.) and near Sirkeci Railway Station (tel. 527 45 03, 24 hrs). Open daily 9am-6pm.

Accommodations

İstanbul's budget accommodations huddle in the **Sultanahmet** district, a backpackers' ghetto. Prices are a range of cheap, from USD2.50 for a rooftop bed to USD5 for a single; anywhere else in İstanbul that can match these prices is likely to be a real hole. You might look at third and fourth-class hotels (a bit costlier) in the adjacent Lâleli and Aksaray districts.

Yücelt Youth Hostel (IYHF), 6 Caferiye Sok. (tel. 513 61 50), in Sultanahmet. Clean, crowded rooms and large patio. Great place to meet travelers and find out what's going on in İstanbul. The library and Turkish bath are more frill than function. Dorms USD4.75. Doubles USD12. Showers included. Reservations required.

Hostels: Four rough equivalents to the IYHF hostel are all within 2 blocks of one another. From the south side of the Aya Sofya, follow the walls of the Topkapı palace down 1 block to the **Topkapı Hostel,** 1 Kutlugün Sok (tel. 527 24 33). Dorm beds with harbor view USD3. Doubles USD10. Quads USD16. The **True Blue Hostel,** 2, Akbıyık Cad (lame telephone) is clean and bare with the odd guitar serenade from the manager. Dorm beds USD2. Doubles USD10. The **Orient Youth Hostel,** 13 Akbıyık Cad. (tel. 516 01 71) just down the street, is tranquil and has a cafeteria. Dorm beds USD3.50. Doubles USD10.50. One block farther and to the left, the **Sultan Tourist Hostel 2,** 3 Cankutaran Akbıyık Cad. (tel. 516 92 60) has gracious lounge and garden. Triple and quad rooms USD4 per person. Doubles USD10.

Hotel Merih, 25 Zeynep Sultan Cami Sok. (tel. 522 85 22). Walk 100m from the Aya Sofya along Yerebatan Cad. and take your first right. Don't be put off by the grimy exterior. Cozy and calm with a lovely terrace. Dorm USD5. Singles USD7. Doubles USD10.

Hotel Anadolu, 3 Salkim Söğüt Sok. (tel. 512 10 35). Just up from the Hotel Merih. Take a right off Yerebatan Cad. Spartan and spotless. Singles USD6. Doubles USD7.50. Roof USD3.

Hotel Elet, 14, Salkim Söğü Sok. (tel. 513 95 16), across the street from the Hotel Anadolu. Cushy. Dorm beds USD6. Doubles USD8. Showers included.

Camping: Ataköy Mokamp (tel. 572 08 02) and **Yeşilyurt Kamping** (tel. 574 42 30) on Sahil Yoh near the villages of Ataköy and Yeşilköy respectively are much more pleasant (two people and a tent, USD7).

Food

From sandwich stands on streets to elegant seafood restaurants at the Bosphorus, the variety of food in İstanbul is wide, the quality, high, and the cost, reasonable. The Eminönü market quarter between the Grand Bazaar and the New Mosque and the Tepebaşı quarter shelter better restaurants than the Sultanahmet. There are several popular and inexpensive restaurants with music at night along the **Çiçek Pasajı,** an alleyway north of İstiklâl Cad. in the Galatasaray district. You might also take an excursion up the Bosphorus (bus #25A from Eminönü) to the seafood restaurants at **Sarıyer** or **Rumeli Kavağı.** A complete meal at a cheap *lokanta* should cost no more than USD3. Although **open-air fruit markets** won't save you much money, they can be fun. Two are centrally located—one in Galatasaray and another in the Mısır (Egyptian) Bazaar, northwest of Yeni Camii (New Mosque).

If you must eat in the Sultanahmet, the restaurants along **Divan Yolu** serve typical Turkish cuisine, mostly *kebap* and *köfte.* **Sultanahmet Köftecisi,** at the end of Divan Yolu across from the tourist office, is dirt cheap and enjoys a faithful Turkish clientele. A meal costs about USD2. (Open daily 10am-10pm.) For greater variety, try **Vitamin Restaurant,** 16 Divan Yolu, which nourishes for under USD5 with *patlıcan dolması* (stuffed eggplant) and *merçimek çorbası* (lentil soup). (Open daily 7am-midnight.) In the Tepebaşı quarter, authentic Turkish restaurants cluster in the **Çiçek Pasajı** (Flower Passage)—a glorified alley just north of İstiklâl Cad. in the Galatasaray district. Meals run USD4-5.

Sights

Aya Sofya, built in 537 by the Emperor Justinian, is irrefutably among the world's most inspiring churches. It was Constantinople's cathedral for 900 years, and then served as İstanbul's mosque after the Turkish conquest in 1453. In 1935, Atatürk neutralized it into a museum. The enormous dome was the largest in the world until the upstart St. Peter's was built. The grand upstairs galleries (not always open) display supreme mosaics. (Open Tues.-Sun. 9:30am-7pm. Sept.-June Tues.-Sun. 9:30am-4:30pm. Gallery open Tues.-Sun. 9:30am-noon and 1-4:30pm. Admission USD4, with ISIC USD2).

Sultan Ahmet I built the **Sultanahmet Camii** (Blue Mosque) nearly 1100 years after the construction of Aya Sofya, in a clear attempt to one-up Justinian. The mosque's silhouette is unforgettable, the deep blue of İznik tiles dignifies the interior. The six elegant minarets were the focus of some concern for Islamic religious leaders of the day—they didn't want the number of minarets at Mecca exceeded. Ahmet generously avoided religious controversy by providing the wherewithal to erect a seventh minaret at Mecca. English-speaking Turks often loiter around the entrance during the day, eager to give potentially instructive freelance tours. Agree on the fee beforehand. (Mosque open to visitors daily 9am-5pm. Modest dress required.) To the northwest are the ancient **Hippodrome** and the 16th-century **Ibrahim Paşa Palace,** which beautifully exhibits a collection of Turkish and Islamic art.

One of İstanbul's great attractions is the **Topkapı Sarayı,** the palace of the Ottoman sultans. You can while away a whole afternoon among the exhibits of gold, diamonds, jade, emeralds, ornate miniatures, and fine Oriental porcelain. Guided tours of the **Harem** run three times per day (USD1), and it is best to arrive early. The **Circumcision chamber** is exquisitely decorated with blue İznik tiles. According to Turkish tradition, males were circumcized not at birth, but after they had come of age. In some parts of Turkey mothers chastise their sons by threatening to call in the dreaded "circumsizer." (Palace open Wed.-Mon. 9:30am-5pm. Admission USD4, with ISIC USD2.)

İstanbul's other great museums are down the hill from Topkapı—enter the gate marked "Archeological Museums." Inside is the **Çinili Kiosk,** an erstwhile pleasure palace that is now a museum of Turkish tiles. The **Museum of the Ancient Orient** houses a heap of Hittite, Babylonian, Sumerian, Assyrian, and Egyptian artifacts, including a tablet from the Hammurabi Code. The **Archeological Museum** (labeled only in Turkish and French) has a fantastic collection of Greek, Hellenic, and Roman marbles and bronzes, including the reputed sarcophagus of Alexander the Great. (Complex open Tues.-Sun. 9am-5pm. Admission USD1.25.)

Returning to Divan Yolu and heading west you'll pass the **Kapalı Çarşı,** one of the world's most vast covered markets. Hawkers hover and prices are bonkers; the figure you're first quoted will be 300-400% too high. Leather is a bargain, though you should examine quality carefully. The older part of the bazaar includes an interesting book market, **Kapalı Çarşı;** that opens to a shady tea garden beside the **Beyazıt Mosque,** İstanbul's oldest. (Open Mon.-Sat. 9am-7pm.)

The other primary mosque is the **Süleymaniye,** the grandest in İstanbul. The adjacent *türbeler* (mausoleums) Süleyman the Magnificent built for himself and his wife are more ornate than the mosque itself. Walk down to the Horn from the Süleymaniye, to the tiny mosque of **Rüstem Paşa,** notable for its interior tiling. A mandatory stop for Byzantine art lovers is the fantastically preserved **Kâriye Camii,** a long way up Fevzipaşa Cad. near Edirne Gate, best reached by *dolmuş* (taxi van) or bus #39 or 86 from Sultanahmet. Once a Byzantine church, then a mosque, and finally a museum, the building contains superb 14th-century frescoes and mosaics. (Admission USD2. Open Wed.-Mon. 9:30am-4:30pm.)

For a thorough history of İstanbul's sights, get *Strolling Through İstanbul,* by Sumner-Boyd and Freely (USD20), or their more compact *İstanbul: A Brief Guide to the City* (USD8). Both are available at Redhouse Books Kitabevi. (See Practical Information.)

Entertainment

İstanbul retires early—few nightspots are open post-midnight. Until then, travelers coagulate in the restaurants and bars at the foot of Divan Yolu Cad. To live the real İstanbul, trek up to the Çiçekı Pasajı for a roaring evening of food, liquor, and traditional Turkish music. *Rakı* ("Lion's Milk") is a potent licorice-flavored liqueur that flows in the many taverns of the Flower Passage. Or, venture to Lâleli or Beyazıt and spend the evening at a Turkish tea house. **Ali Paşa's Bazaar,** a 16th-century courtyard near the entrance to the Grand Bazaar on Divan Yolu Cad., is a great place to have a glass of delicious Turkish tea, meet some locals, and smoke a *nargile* (water pipe).

The most authentic **Turkish baths** are in the nearby cities of Edirne and Bursa. İstanbul baths can provide a reprieve for the down and dirty; the celebrated, posh Cağaloğlu Hamamı in Sultanahmet is not for the even mildly claustrophobic. Try the **Mercan Örücüler Hamamı,** 32 Uzun Çarşı Cad., just outside the Örücüler Kapısı (gate) of the Grand Bazaar. Although somewhat pricey (USD7.75), the steamy chambers are immaculate and nearly devoid of tourists. Avoid like the plague the nightclubs off İstiklâl Cad., north of the Horn. Each year, clueless tourists get overcharged, robbed, and more in these tacky holes.

During the **İstanbul Festival** (June and July), orchestras, ballet companies, and folk dance ensembles perform throughout the city. Purchase tickets at the Atatürk Kültür Merkezi facing Taksim Sq. Inquire at the tourist office for more information.

Near İstanbul

Ferries depart from the Eminönü end of the Galata Bridge for the **Princes' Isles** and stop at four of the nine islands of this suburban archipelago, tainted slightly by the spew and grub of İstanbul. Although some prefer the calmer karma of **Burgazada** and **Heybeliada, Büyükada** is the largest and most scenic of the islands and has the sweetest swimming in the İstanbul area. As scenic is a boat tour zigzagging up the **Bosphorus** to the Black Sea and back, leaving twice per day from pier #3 in Eminönü (USD6). You can hop off at any stop and catch the ferry on its return trip.

The unassuming city of Edirne squats on the train line from İstanbul to Europe just a few kilometers from both the Greek and Bulgarian borders. Edirne is home to several romping Ottoman mosques, a splash of authentic Turkish baths, and the annual Kırkpınar Oiled-Wrestling Tournament (second or third weekend in June). *Dolmuş* run frequently from the **bus station** (to İstanbul every hr., 4 hr., USD4) and Edirne's two **train stations.** The **tourist office** 17 Talatpaşa Cad. (tel. (9181) 115 18), 200 yds. west of the square is helpful. (Open daily 8:30am-6:30pm; Sept.-May Mon.-Sat. 8:30am-6:30pm.) Just down Maarif Caddesi from the tourist office, the **Anil Hotel** (tel. 217 82) at #8 and the **Konak Hotel** (tel. 113 48) next door have singles for USD4.50, doubles for USD7.50 and beds in dorm rooms for USD3.75. The **Sokullu Hamamı,** near the Üçserefeli Camii, is a fantastic excuse for serious relaxation. (Open daily 6am-midnight for men, 9am-6pm for women; USD2.50, massage USD5.)

Bursa

Osman, the founder of the Ottoman *(Osmanlı)* dynasty, besieged Bursa in 1317, leaving his son Orhan to pluck the ravaged town for his empire's capital in 1326. Today, money gushes into Bursa as robustly as the sulphured waters of its thermal baths. The deep green of the Uludağ mountain, home of Turkey's leading ski resort, adds welcome color to the city ensconced at its feet. Bursa is now a pleasant, sprawling city with precious little to see save several Ottoman monuments and the thermal baths in the western Çekirge district.

Reach Bursa via express ferry from Karaköy in İstanbul (Mon.-Fri. 5 per day, USD3.50; on weekends the express ferry launches from Kartal on İstanbul's Asian side), or by slow motion ferry from Kabataş, north of İstanbul (8 per day, USD1.25). The ferries dump you in *Yalova,* from where *dolmuş* and buses run to Bursa (3½ hrs., USD125). Direct buses from İstanbul's Topkapı Station also travel to Bursa (4 hr., USD3.50). Convenient buses also link Bursa to Ankara, İzmir, and other transportation and cultural centers. From the bus station, jump a *dolmuş* to the *heykel* (statue) on Atatürk Cad. Bursa's **tourist office,** Atatürk Cad. (tel. 21 23 59), downstairs at the fountain, is helpful and English-speaking. Open daily 8:30am-6:30pm; Oct.-May Mon.-Fri. 8am-5pm. Inexpensive hotels gild Tahtakale Cad., parallel to and 1 block uphill from Atatürk Cad. Try either the **Hotel Uğur,** at #27 (tel. 21 19 89; singles USD3, doubles USD5), or the **Otel Deniz,** at #19 tel. 22 92 38; singles USD5.50, doubles USD7. Hot shower on demand).

İskender kebap, a superior dish with a sauce of tomatoes, butter, and garlic, originated in Bursa—you won't forget it. Budget restaurants huddle around Inönü Cad., between the *heykel* and the first set of traffic lights.

One block west of the tourist office is the **Ulu Camii.** This monumental mosque, built in the 15th century, has an exquisite *mihrab* (a niche indicating the direction of Mecca) and a carved, wooden *mimber* (pulpit) that scholars believe doubled as an astrological chart. While the mosque was under construction, two builders, Hacivat and Karagöz, so entertained peers with their banter that work fell to a halt. To get back on schedule, Mehmet I had the pair executed, then in a fit of remorse, immortalized them, oddly enough, in puppet form. Turkey's *Punch and Judy,* Hacivat and Karagöz grace Turkish puppet stages to this day. By the tomb of Hacivat,

Karagöz, Şeyh and Küsteri, a hole-in-the-wall theater puts on shows nightly during the **Bursa Festival** in July.

Yeşil Camii (Green Mosque), the most renowned religious monument in Bursa and one of the slickest Ottoman mosques anywhere, is distinguished by its lavish blue and green tile work, symbolizing the heavens. Sadly, the caretaker no longer has the key to the sumptuous Sultan's section in the gallery just above the entrance. Across the way, the same striking turquoise tiles festoon the exterior of **Yeşil Türbe** (Green Mausoleum), the interior of which is tiled in deeper tones. (Mausoleum open daily 8am-noon and 1-5pm.)

Bursa's Turkish springwater baths are famous. On the way to Çerkirge, down the hill to the right after the Kültür Parkı, are the 16th-century **Yeni Kapıca** baths (USD1.25), where men and women bathe together in private rooms. Ho! For a change of pace, hop Bursa's cable car to the alpine slopes of **Uludağ.** *Dolmuş* marked "*teleferik*" leave from behind the *heykel.* (Cable car runs on the hr. 9am-10pm to the mid-station, USD1.25 round-trip; on the ½hr. 9:30am-9:30pm, USD3.30 round-trip to the top.) Ask at the tourist office about ski rental (ski season lasts from Dec.-April). A crunchy 1½ bus or *dolmuş* ride from Bursa is the ancient town of İznik, an array of uninspiring and weed-blessed ruins. The **tourist office** (tel 719 33) on Kiliçaslan Cad. is 3 blocks to your right and 2 blocks to the right again as your back faces the bus station ticket windows. (Open Mon-Fri 9am-noon and 1-5:30pm.)

Aegean Coast

Possibly the least Turkish of all Turkey, the Aegean coast is also the most heavily visited. This area out-dignifies the nearby Greek islands in every way—better preserved, more interesting ruins, sparser crowds, lower prices, and a more alluring landscape. The Aegean coast was the center of the Roman province of Asia Minor, and was the last part of Turkey to fall to the Ottoman Empire in the 14th and 15th centuries. But for the efforts of Atatürk's forces in the 1920s, the coastline would today be a part of Greece.

North Coast

The Aegean coast north of İzmir is neither as historically interesting nor as naturally spectacular as the span to the south. At the battlefield of **Gallipoli** (Gelibolu), Australian, New Zealander, and British landing parties met a brutal end at the hands of Mustafa Kemal (Atatürk) in 1915. Getting to Gallipoli from İstanbul requires a bus ride to Gelibolu, then a *dolmuş kilitbahir,* and finally a taxi to the site. Hourly ferries cross the Dardanelles from Çanakkale to Eceabat; from there you can take a *dolmuş* to the Gabatepe museum and hike a few km. to the site or take a taxi tour (officially USD23, but bargain; USD12-15 is a good price); the tour from Çanakkale offered by **Troyanzac** travel agency does you right and involves much less hassle. Hotel competition on Çanakkale is fierce; exploit it. Try the **Hotel Konak** (tel. 111 50), to the left of the clock tower. From the bus station, take a left at the main doors and the next right following the *feribot* signs; the clock tower and the **tourist office** (tel. 111 87) will be on your left just before the water.

Truva or Troy is 32km south of Çanakkale. *Dolmuş* and minibuses leave frequently from the small bridge 200 yd. south (to the left out the main doors) of the bus station. The site lay forgotten until late in the last century, when Heinrich Schliemann, a German-born American millionaire turned archeology buff decided to prove that the Homeric myths were not pure fiction and zealously started digging.

People raised on stories of the Trojan War should not expect imposing ruins, but the Bronze Age fortifications, given their age, still are interesting. (Open 8am-7pm; in off-season 8am-5pm. Admission USD2.)

The ruins at **Pergamon** are farther south, near the modern town of **Bergama.** Though the Altar of Zeus, widely considered the finest specimen of Hellenistic art, resides in the Pergamon Museum in Berlin, the mammoth amphitheater, huge gymnasium, Roman circus, and lavishly frescoed House of Attalus still merit a visit. (Admission to Acropolis, 7km up the hill from Bergama, and to the Asclepion 3km in the other direction, USD2 each. Open daily 8:30am-7pm; Oct.-April daily 8:30am-5:30pm.) In Bergama, adjacent to the Pergamon ruins, stay at the **Pergamon Pension** (tel. 123 95) in a 150-year-old Italian house on Bergama's main road (USD4 per person. Shower included. Breakfast USD1.50 extra.) The resort town of **Foça** is south of Bergama; three buses per day connect it to İzmir.

İzmir, Turkey's third-largest city, is a feisty metropolis, well linked by bus to the rest of Turkey. Once ancient Smyrna, site of one of the seven Christian churches, today's İzmir retains little of its momentous past. The ruins of the ancient **Roman agora** are, however, worth a gander. The **tourist office** (tel. 14 21 47) is in the Büyük Efes hotel on Cumhuriyet Meydanı. (Open Mon.-Sat. 8am-8pm, Sun. 9am-5pm; Oct.-May Mon.-Sat. 8am-8pm.) Take a *dolmuş* from the bus station to Basmane for cheap hotels. **Otel Saray** (tel. 13 69 46), 635 Anafartalar Cad., was a Miami Beach resort motel in another life. (Breezy singles USD5.50. Doubles USD7.50. Hot showers included.) Anafartalar Cad. is also the best place to quell your rebellious belly. **American Express** is at 2B, NATO Arkesi Talatpaşa Bulvarı. (tel. 21 79 27). There is also a **U.S. Consulate** 92/3 Atatürk Cad. (tel. 13 13 69), a **British Consulate** 49, 1442 Sok. (tel. 21 17 95), and the **tourist police** (tel. 21 86 52). The İzmir **International Festival** in late June and early July has classical and folk music concerts at Çeşme, Ephesus and İzmir.

Due east of İzmir is the quaint resort town of **Çeşme,** congested in summer. Frequent buses run from İzmir's **Uçkuyler** terminal (take city bus #1, 2 or 3 from Konak Sq. near the bazaar) to Çeşme (every ½ hr., 1½ hr., USD1.50). The manager of the nifty **Adil Pansiyon,** Müftü Sok (tel. 274 47) speaks English faster than she can breathe. (Doubles USD12.) Follow Bağlar Cad. diagonally back from the **tourist office** (tel. 266 53) across from the castle on the waterfront. Though Çeşme frowns on freelance camping, **campgrounds** dot the peninsula; buses run to Ilıca, Altınkum, and south along the beach. Boats connect Çeşme with the Greek island of Chios in summer (7 per week in mid-summer; Oct.-May, 1 per week; USD20 one-way and same day round-trip. USD25 open round-trip).

The pristine ruins at **Sardis** (Sart) mark the former capital of the Lydian kingdom (7th and 6th centuries BC). The Lydians invented dice, then coinage to gamble for. The few remaining columns of the massive **Temple of Artemis,** a 2nd-century **synagogue,** and a **bath-gymnasium** are the most absorbing ruins. (Sites open daily during daylight hours. Admission USD0.80 each.) Sardis, a request stop, is 1½ hrs. from İzmir along the bus route to Salihli.

Kuşadası and Environs

In summer, Kuşadası's proximity to the Greek island of Samos and its place in the itinerary of many Aegean cruise ships swell the town to a tourist blob. Those traveling to or from Greece should note that the Samos-Kuşadası crossing clobbers the wallet (USD25, same day round-trip USD30, open round-trip USD45). Only Selçukit can match Kuşadası as a base for visits to four of Turkey's most intriguing ancient sites: Priene, Miletus, Didyma, and Ephesus.

Kuşadası's **tourist office** (tel. (6361) 11 03), on the waterfront, spews maps, bus and *dolmuş* schedules, and a list of the town's pensions. (Open daily 7am-7pm; Dec.-April Mon.-Fri. 8:30am-12:30pm and 1:30-5:30pm.) Compared to Greece, accommodations here are cheap. To reach the pension area, go up Yalı Cad. (facing the water, the street running parallel to the water left of Kervanseray Hotel) turn left up the hill to Aslanlar Cad. **Pension Su,** 13 Aslanlar Cad. (tel. 14 53), is zingy, with friendly management. (USD4) One block uphill is **Şafak Pension** (tel. 17 64), a seething den of backpackers. (USD3.75) **Hotel Rose** (tel. 11 11), another block uphill, offers a cozy lounge and roof beds. (USD2.40, doubles USD10-USD12.) **Camping Önder** (tel. 24 13) and **Yat Camping** (tel. 13 33) are 2-3km north of town on the Selçuk-İzmir road. (USD1.50 per person, USD2.50 per tent, USD8 for a 3 person bungalow.) For a wonderful view, try **Güvercınada Cafeteria** on Pigeon Island. The **post office, telephone office,** and **police station** are up the main drag from the waterfront on Barbaros Hayrettin Cad. Take one of the frequent *dolmuş* marked "Yeni Garaj" from the center of town to the **bus station,** with connections to İstanbul (5 per day; 12 hrs, USD9.25), İzmir (1 per hr., 2 hr., USD1.20), Bodrum and Pamukkale (6 per day, 4 hr., USD5). *Dolmuş* leave from this station for Selçuk and Söke.

Sunbathers roast at **Ladies' Beach,** 3km south of town. For more elbow room, venture to **Longbeach, Silverbeach,** and the beaches in the **Milli Park** (national park) 15km to the south. (All accessible by frequent dolmuş.)

Once capital of the Roman province of Asia Minor and site of the most prodigious set of ruins from this period, **Epheseus** (Efes) provides the most compelling reason to visit Kuşadası. The city, extending over 2000 acres, saw its golden age from the reign of Alexander to the Rome of early Christianity. Ephesus now lies in ruins because silt from the river Cayster created swamps that bred malarian mosquitoes, which spread the disease through the city. Bring water; the unshaded site can swelter unbearably, and the refreshment stands bleed the wallet. The money for a guided tour would be better spent on a guidebook. The ruins are near Selçuk, 17km from Kuşadası. To reach the site, take a Selçuk *dolmuş* from Kuşadası; it will drop you off at a turn-off about 2km from Selçuk, from which you must walk or take a donkey-cart. (Open daily 8am-7pm; Sept.-May Mon.-Fri. 9am-noon and 1-5pm. Admission USD4, with ISIC USD2.)

Though **Selçuk's** main claim to fame is its proximity to the ruins of Ephesus (only 1½km), the village can stand its own. The **Ephesus Museum** highlights over a century of excavations. Its most famous pieces are the multi-breasted statue of Artemis, poised to nurse whole nations, and the alarming statue of Priapus, the fervent deity of sex. (Open daily 8:30am-6:30pm; Oct.-April Mon.-Fri. 8:30am-5:30pm. Admission USD2, with ISIC USD1.) Selçuk's most famous sight is also its least impressive—the well-plundered remains of the **Temple of Artemis,** one of the seven wonders of the ancient world. The second turn-off to the right on the road to Ephesus leads to the temple's original site.

On January 15 and 16, Selçuk hosts a **camel-wrestling festival,** in which male camels battle each other to the accompaniment of the *davul* drum and *zurna* flute. The fight is stopped before any harm is done as camels are valuable property.

The road from Epheseus and Kuşadası intersects Selçuk's main drag, Atatürk Cad., at the **bus station** (links to İzmir, Pamukkale, and Bodrum). Across the street the **tourist office** (tel (5451) 13 28) provides free maps. (Open daily 8:30am-6:30pm; Oct.-April Mon.-Fri. 8:30am-5:30pm.) The museum sits just behind the office. The **Barim Pansiyon** (tel. (5451) 19 23) behind the museum has pleasing rooms for USD3.75. The bonza **Australian Pension** (tel. 10 50) is also behind the museum (follow the kangaroos; USD3.75).

The other three sites of interest—Priene, Miletus, Didyma—lie in a neat row south of Kuşadası. **Priene,** a Hellenic metropolis, perches on the slopes of Mt. Mycale. The ruins of the Ionic **Temple of Athena** overshadow the city walls, Byzantine church, theater, stadium, gymnasium, and sundry sanctuaries of Greek and Roman gods. South of Priene sits **Miletus,** a once prosperous harbor that a silting river has since clogged. Farther south is the Sanctuary of Apollo at **Didyma,** the third-largest sacred structure in the Hellenic world. (All three sites open daily 8:30am-7:30pm; in off-season 8:30am-5:30pm. Admission USD0.80, with ISIC USD0.40.)

Pamukkale and Aphrodisias

Whether as Pamukkale or ancient Hieropolis, this village has been drawing the weary and the curious to its thermal springs for over 23 centuries. The Turkish name—meaning "cotton castle" refers to the underlying snow-white cliffs, shaped over millenia by the accumulation of calcium deposited by mineral springs. You don't go looking for the fiercely competitive hotels in this burgeoning village; they come looking for you. **Halley Pension** (tel. (6218) 12 04) offers no-frills rooms (USD3.75, USD5.75 with bath). Many campsites dot the village, and you can also try **Kur Tur Camping** (tel. 10 29) by the red springs 3km away at Karahayıt. (USD2.45; frequent *dolmuş* travel to Karahayıt.) **Ünal Restaurant,** the local choice, serves a mean tripe soup. (Open daily 10am-2pm.)

At the top of the cliffs, the ancient Roman ruins of **Hierapolis** include a theater, a temple of Apollo, a Christian basilica, Roman baths, and a hole spouting poisonous carbonic gases. Admission USD0.40. Three km away at **Karahayıt** is a hot, red spring that looks like a crazed chemistry experiment that turns bathers a nice crimson (admission USD0.95).

Aphrodisias was an important center for the arts after the fall of Pergamon in the 2nd century BC. Particularly worth seeing are the surviving Greek **stadium,** with a seating capacity of 30,000 and the elegant **Temple of Aphrodite.** Aphrodisias lies by the village of Geyre, near the village of Karcasu. By far the least traumatic way to Aphrodisias is by daily bus from Pamukkale (USD3.75, USD5.75 round-trip). From Kuşadası or Selçuk, take a direct bus to Karacasu and hitch from there. *Dolmuş* travel to Aphrodisias from Karacasu and Nazilli once in an azure moon.

Bodrum

Knotted in serpentine coastline, Bodrum is a sun worshipper's paradise and a haven of Turkish wealth and culture. Dominating the town from a strategic waterfront position, the **Kale** castle, constructed by the crusading Order of the Knights of St. John during the 15th and 16th centuries, epitomizes the flat-footed ugliness of medieval fortress architecture. The structure houses the **Museum of Underwater Archeology,** a bizarre collection of broken things from ancient shipwrecks. (Castle open Tues.-Sun. 8am-7pm. Museum open Tues.-Sun. 8am-noon and 1-7pm. Admission to both USD2, with ISIC USD1.) Bodrum sprouts from the ruins of Halicarnassus, capital of the pre-Hellenic kingdom of Caria and birthplace of Herodotus. The most famous ruins are those of one of the seven wonders of the world, the **Mausoleum,** or tomb of King Mausolus, who reigned in the 4th century B.C. Follow the signs from Neyzen Tevfik up Haman Sok. onto Turgutreis Cad.

The **tourist office** (tel. (6141) 10 91) is in front of the castle. They provide complete accommodations listings and a lousy map, but do little to help you find a room. (Open daily 8am-10pm; Nov.-March Mon.-Fri. 8am-noon and 1-5pm.) Hotels and pensions fill during July and August. Evening arrivals in high-season bode poorly; expect not to sleep inside. There are often rooms to let in private homes (USD6.50, USD11 for a double); look for signs reading "*Oda Var*" and "*Ev Pansiyon.*" The cheaper pensions are along the right bay (facing the water) before the yacht harbor, and along the middle of the left bay, before the Halikarnas Hotel. **Yenilmez Pension** (tel. 25 20), off Neyzen Tevfik Cad., on the right bay is breezy and peaceful. (USD3.75, hot shower included.)

Bodrum is known for its outstanding, if expensive, seafood restaurants. Try **Orhan's #7,** in the covered alley off Kale Cad., the main shopping street leading away from the tourist office. (Open daily 8:30pm-11:30pm.) At night, Cumhuriyet Cad. oozes cheap *kebabs,* ice cream, cafés, bars, and discos.

The **Halicarnassus Disco,** at the end of Cumhuriyet Cad., 2km from the tourist office on the left (facing the water) bay, is *the* place to be, but the USD12 cover charge is just too hip for most budget travelers. For live Turkish tunes, down a few drinks at the **Mavi Bar,** nearby on Cumhuriyet Cad.

Frequent buses connect Bodrum with İzmir (every hr., 6 hr., USD6.25) and Marmaris (every hr., 3 hr., USD3.75). Boats connect Bodrum with the Greek island of Kos (June-Aug. daily at 9am; May and Sept. 3 per week; USD15, same-day round-trip USD22, open round-trip USD30, Greek port tax USD6.50). There are also two ferries a day to Datça in summer (USD9.50). Inquire at any travel agent. *Dolmuş motorları* boats leave Bodrum harbor daily in summer from 9 to 11am, visit beaches and coves inaccessible by car, and return in the evening (USD5.75). **Gümbet Beach,** 3km out of Bodrum town, attracts the heftiest crowds around; you can camp at **Zetaş Camping** (tel. 14 07) for USD3.75. On the beach at **Bitez,** one cove farther from town, bars have built docks over the water so that you can get simultaneously gilded and ripped.

The south coast beaches tend to saturate in summer. The villages in the northern part of the peninsula, **Gölköy, Türkbükü,** and **Yalıkavak** (among others) see fewer tourists and hence remain unspoiled. Each village has a few pensions; stumble into a random teahouse, say "*pansiyon*" and see what happens.

Mediterranean Coast

Villages, glitzy resorts, and lonely beaches are the charms of a twinkling chain of coastline stretching 800km from Marmaris in the west to Antakya near the Syrian border. The only factor which puts this area one below the Aegean is the heat—it's over 40°C in July and August.

West of Antalya recline the great beaches of Ölüdeniz, Xanthos's archeological site, the ancient port Patara, and the seaside villages of Kalkan and Kaş. Between Antalya and Alanya, the Roman sites of Perge, Aspendos, and Side punctuate sandy beaches and plains. Beyond Alanya, tourists vanish and the coastline petrifies to mountain, then flattens into a hot, dusty coastal stretch reaching the biblical cities of Tarsus and Antakya (Antioch) on the Syrian border.

Marmaris and the Datça Peninsula

Bodrum's southern neighbor, tacky **Marmaris** is overdeveloped, its beach overfilthed. The area around Marmaris, though, is quite picturesque, with wooded mountains cloaking the coast. The **tourist office,** Kordon Cad. (tel. (612) 110 35), across from the main ferry dock, has a helpful English-speaking staff who can provide maps. (Open in summer daily 8am-noon and 1-7pm; in off-season Mon.-Fri. 6am-noon and 1-5pm.) **Kordon Pansiyon,** 8 Kemalpaşa Sok. (tel. (612) 147 62), 1 block inland from the post office and to the left, is centrally located with a family atmosphere (USD3 per person). The new **Interyouth Hostel** (tel. 164 32) is friendly and spotless. Ask at the bus stop or tourist office for directions. (USD2 for a dorm room.) Thirty minutes toward the water from Interyouth Hostel, **Özcan Pension** is family-run and has a garden and patio (USD3.50 per person). Eat at **Han Köfte Salonu,** half a block inland from the post office and to the right, or **Özyalçin Meathouse.**

Marmaris is shackled to Rhodes by ferry (Mon.-Sat. at 8:30am; one-way USD20, same day round-trip USD30, open round-trip USD36). You can purchase tickets from any travel agent. Frequent buses run between Marmaris and Bodrum or Fethiye.

Stay in Marmaris no longer than necessary and head to the resplendent **Datça Peninsula.** Several bus companies run buses between Marmaris and the little village of Datça (10 per day, 2 hr.). At Datça, stay at **Sadik Pansiyon** (tel. 11 96) for gorgeous views of the bay. From the bus station, take the first left toward the harbor. (USD3.50 per person.) Camping is possible on the beach at **Ilıca Camping** (tel. 14

00; USD1 per person), but many travelers crash unofficially on the house. Feridun, the campground owner, may take you on a wild boar hunt. In the likely event that you don't catch anything, settle for fixin's at **Denizati Restaurant,** on the beach. Thirty km east of Datça along the main road is the well-run but touristy **Aktur Camping** (tel. 61 46; USD2.50 per person, bungalows USD9).

Right at the end of the Datça Peninsula poses the Hellenic site of **Knidos,** a major attraction of yesteryear for its statue of Aphrodite. The statue no longer exists, but the site is still of interest and notable for its sublime location on a bluff above the sea. Knidos is reached by a tortuous 40-km trip from Datça—a *dolmuş* will take you only as close as the village of **Yaziköy,** 7km short of the ruins. Taxis make the trip for USD15 round-trip. **Karya Tours** (tel. (6141) 17 59) runs excursion boats from Bodrum for USD24.

The ruins of **Caunos,** near the town of **Dalyan,** lie between Marmaris and Fethiye. Archeologists continue to uncover more rock tombs and temples here yearly; some predict that it will soon rival Ephesus in scale and importance. For now, it abides undiscovered and blessed with a thriving verdancy itself worth a visit. Boats run from Dalyan to Caunos; you can often arrange to camp overnight and be picked up the next day. Staying at one of Dalyan's many pensions or camping by Lake Köyceğiz involve intimacy with swarms of mosquitoes.

Fethiye to Kaş

The port of **Fethiye** will fulfill few of your seacoast longings and may even put you to sleep. If you feel yourself drowsing, perk up to the Lycian tombs in the cliffs. The **tourist office** on the waterfront provides pension listings. (Open Mon.-Sat. 9am-noon and 1:30-7pm; Oct.-April Mon.-Fri. 8am-noon and 1-5pm.) Stay at **Kale Pansiyon** (tel. (615) 28 69) for the view. From the bus station, walk down Carşi Cad., and signs will lead you up Kale Sok. to the Pansiyon (USD4 per person). Excursion boats leave from the harbor for the so-called **Twelve Island Tour,** which hops around the archipelago of the Bay of Fethiye (full day, starting at USD7 on a full boat). There are also tours to Xanthos, Letoon, and Patara, to Caunos and Dalyan, and to Ölüdeniz. Inquire at the tourist office or at Big Tur, 18 Atatürk Cad. To escape the hustle and crowds of Fethiye, head for the ridiculously fine beaches of **Ölüdeniz,** 14km away. Make the pilgrimage to this hedonist heaven via frequent *dolmuş* from behind the PTT. Swim all day, then cavort the night away at any of the campsites' free discos (Derya, Deniz, Sun Kamping and Moon Disco until 2-3am). You can change money at the grocery store behind Derya Camping, but rates are better in Fethiye. **Ölüdeniz Camping** (tel. (6156) 60 24), 300m to the right as you face the sea, has a keen beach. (Camping USD1, bungalow doubles USD8.) **Kum Tur Motel** (tel. 60 26) has doubles with showers for USD6.50. **Deniz Camping** (tel. 60 12) has camping and bungalows for two (USD13, breakfast included). Most people eat in the overpriced campground cafeterias, but the wise buy groceries in Fethiye. **Pirate's Inn,** 100m up the road to Fethiye, serves delicious food at fair prices.

Between Kalkan and Fethiye are two historical sites and a fantastic beach. **Xanthos,** 22km from the ancient Lycian capital Kalkan, has a large amphitheater and examples of Lycian rock tombs and funeral monuments. Fifteen km from Xanthos, on a Saharan beach, crumble the ruins of **Patara,** birthplace of St. Nicolas (a.k.a. Santa Claus). But here nothing beats the 18km stretch of deserted, sandy beach. At night the beach becomes a turtle sanctuary, so camping is out unless you like watching turtles in love-clutch. It's illegal, too, but **St. Nikolas Pension** (doubles USD5.50) and **Ali Baba Pension** (doubles USD5.50) are both excellent, and you may be able to tent-pitch in town. Buses from Fethiye, Kalkan, or Kaş whisk you directly to Patara beach.

Kalkan, between Fethiye and Kaş, is a postcard Turkish fishing village. This is public knowledge, though, and the drooling tourist cockatrice now stomps the narrow streets. High prices plague accommodations, though food is reasonable. **Yılmaz**

Pansiyon (tel. 11 15) is central but noisy. (Singles USD4. Roof USD0.80.) For cheaper accommodations, head up the hill from the main street. Bespiffed **Pansiyon Muhil** (tel. 11 47) is up the street from the bus stop; take a right and then a left (singles USD2.50). Many restaurants in Kalkan offer all-you-can-eat buffets. **Köşk Restaurant** lays a sumptuous table for about USD4 (veer left down the main street). Kalkan is famous for its tailors—get them fashionable harem pants you've swooned over.

With its inexpensive accommodations and restaurants, genuine hospitality, and miles of intricate coastline, **Kaş** beckons seductively to the tired traveler. The staff at the **tourist office** on Cumhuriyet Cad. (tel. 12 38) speaks English. (Open daily 8am-noon and 1-8pm; Oct.-April Mon.-Sat. 8am-noon and 1-5:30pm.) Most of the travel agencies on the waterfront offer the same excursions; shop around. The **Kismet Pansiyon** (tel. 18 88), up Uzun Carşi and to the left, offers clean rooms and striking views from its flower-covered rooftop terrace. (Doubles USD12. Terrace USD1.50.) **Yalı Pension** (tel. 11 32), up Hastane Cad. and 1 block from the mosque, has a family atmosphere, cheap rooms, and the Mediterranean. (Singles USD4. Doubles USD8.) **Kaş Kamping** (tel. 10 50), farther up Hastane Cad., is located next to the sea and the lovely Greek theater, but has mediocre facilities. (Camping USD4 for 2 people. Musty bungalows USD8.) Eat at **Yalı Restaurant,** up Elmali Cad. from the mosque; try the rice pudding (USD0.60).

Kekova, a partially submerged Lycian city about two hours east by boat, is an excellent daytrip. In summer the fare is about USD6 (leaves 9:30am, returns 7pm), but at other times you should be able to find someone to take you for less. The trip ogles Byzantine ruins and two nearby fishing villages, one beneath a cliff honeycombed with Lycian tombs. You can visit Santa's last chimney dive at the **Christian Basilica** in **Demre;** his bones—except his jolly jaw and teeth, residents of the Archaeological Museum in Antalya—were snatched and taken to Italy 1000 years ago. Bus running from Kaş to Antalya stop in Demre.

Antalya and Alanya

Perched above the sea a scenic 4½-hour bus ride from Kaş, **Antalya** is a great sponge for sucking up the Roman ruins to the east. Connections to major Turkish cities are possible via Turkish Airlines and by bus. To reach the main **tourist office** (tel. (31) 11 17 47) from the bus station, follow Kâzım Özalp Cad. toward town, turn right onto Cumhuriyet Cad., and go 100m past the statue of Atatürk. (Open in summer daily 8am-6pm; off-season Mon.-Fri. 8am-5pm.) The best pensions are in the old city, southeast of the yacht harbor. Sack out cheaply in old Ottoman homes. A quiet courtyard makes **Adler Pansiyon** (tel. 11 78 18) at Barbaros Mah. and Civelek Sok. one of the loveliest. (Walk through Hadrian's Gate into the old city, head left, and take the second right; singles USD6.) Next door, **Aksoy Pansiyon** (tel. 12 65 49) is less exotic but has character (doubles USD11).

East of Antalya lies the ancient Roman province of **Pamphylia** and its several important, partially excavated sites. Antalya's **Archeological Museum,** on Kenan Evren Bulvarı at the western end of town, showcases many of the artifacts found thus far (open Tues.-Sun. 9am-6pm). *Pamphilia: An Archeological Guide* (USD3) includes plans of the sites.

A theater garnished with marble reliefs, a grand colonnaded avenue, and a supreme stadium conjure a vision of **Perge** in its 2nd-century heyday. (Open in summer daily 8am-7pm; off-season 8am-5:30pm. Free.) To get here from Antalya take a *dolmuş* to Aksu from the central *dolmuş* station, then walk 2km. No imaginative reconstruction is necessary at **Aspendos,** 49km from Antalya, thanks to the efforts of the Seljuk Turks who preserved the site and used it as a pilgrimage way station. The huge theater is one of the best preserved in the world; even the stage is almost completely intact. (Site open in summer daily 8am-8pm; winter 8am-5:30pm. Admission USD2, students USD1.)

Aside from its muscular fortress, **Alanya** offers little more than crowds, concrete and dirty beaches. If stuck here, try the simple but clean **Yayla Palas** (doubles for USD7.75); from the bus station walk down the main coastal road, turn right at the fork keeping the tourist office on your right, go across the penisula and veer right up the hill.

Silifke and Mersin

Five buses per day travel from Alanya seven hours east to **Silifke,** whose mission in life is to provide bus links to the east and inland to Konya or Ankara and ferries to Northern Cyprus from the nearby port of **Taşucu.** Linger not in Silifke or in any of the crowded beach towns between here and Mersin, except to see the caves of **Cennet ve Cehennem** (Heaven and Hell), about 20km east of Silifke; take a bus heading towards Mersin, get off at the Narlıkuyu Museum, and walk 2km uphill. Nearby, the wishing well cave also merits a peek.

Mersin is Turkey's largest Mediterranean port, a good place to miss unless you need a ferry to Northern Cyprus. The **Turkish Maritime Lines** (Denizyolları) office is on the waterfront just up the dock and across from the tourist office. The multilingual **tourist office** (tel. (741) 163 58) is open daily 8am-7pm. **Hotel Kent,** 51 İstikâl Cad. (tel. 116 55), near the intersection with Kuvayi Milliye Cad., has simple and spacious rooms (singles USD4).

Antakya

Antakya dominates the fertile Turkish province of Hatay, bordered to the east and south by Syria. Little remains from Biblical days when Antakya was called Antioch, but breezes from sea and surrounding mountains make for a glorious respite from the scorching summer in eastern Turkey and Syria. The main plaza, Atatürk Meydanı, pokes the river. Little remains from Biblical days when Ankya was called Antioch—a city of half a million, one of the largest in the Mediterranean. Everything that's left—including spectacular mosaics—is in the excellent **Archeological Museum** (open Mon. 1:30-5pm, Tues.-Sun. 8am-noon and 1:30-5pm; admission USD2, students USD1). Jostle through the **market,** northeast of the main bridge, and through the winding alleys of the **old city,** southeast of the bridge. Two km from the center of town along the road to Reyhanlı is **St. Peter's Church,** where St. Peter drew together the first congregation and coined the word "Christianity." (Open Tues.-Sun. 8am-noon and 1:30-5:30pm. Free.) Every June 29, Vatican representatives hold a religious ceremony here.

From the Atatürk statue in the city center, walk the length of Atatürk Cad. to the **tourist office** across the circle on Alam Meydanı. (Open daily in summer, 9am-noon and 1:30-6:30pm; off-season Mon.-Fri. 8:30am-noon and 1:30-5pm.) For accommodations, walk down İstiklâl Cad. from the bus station towards the town center. **Hotel Güney,** 8 İstiklâl Sok. (tel. (891) 117 78), has spic and span rooms. (Singles with shower USD5.75. Doubles with shower USD11.50.) Antakya's **bus station** is off Hürriyet Cad., which runs south to the main bridge. If you have a Syrian visa (which you must get in Istanbul or Ankara), you can take a bus directly to Aleppo (Halep in Turkish), 100km away (USD7.50). You must exchange USD100 at the border. Daily buses also run to Jordan (Ürdün in Turkish; USD23.50).

Central Turkey

The stoic Anatolian plateau, rolling mile after mile, contains the oldest and newest landmarks of Turkish civilization. Asia Minor's earliest settlements blossomed here, and neolithic sites dot the area. Konya, once the capital of the Seljuk Empire, bristles with exquisite mosques and tombs. Ankara, Turkey's capital, is a testament to the modernization imposed by the contemporary Turkish state. To the south, Cappadocia's ancient ruins attract the lion's share of tourists.

Konya

Konya was the 12th-century capital of the Seljuk sultans and has been Turkey's religious center since the 13th century, when Mevlâna whirled his wisdom. Founder of the famous order of Whirling Dervishes, Mevlâna believed spiritual perfection and union with the divine was achieved through ecstatic dance. In 1925, Atatürk dissolved the order and now the Dervishes dance but once a year (in mid-December; tickets from USD5). You can spot the 13th-century **Mevlâna Tekke** by its radiant green tower. Inside this one-time monastery are the *türbes* of Mevlâna and other dervishes, and a museum exhibiting prayer rugs, musical instruments, elaborately decorated garments, and calligraphic Qur'ans. (Open Mon. 8:30am-3pm, Tues.-Sun. 8:30am-5:30pm. Admission USD2.50.) Konya's other major attractions stud Alaadin Tepesi (Aladdin Hill), several hundred yards up Hükümet Cad. While in Konya, wander through the enchanting **market,** between the Aziziye Mosque and the **post office** (open 24 hr.) on Alaadin Cad. Other than these sights, Konya is mostly ugly and modern.

The **tourist office** on Mevlâna Cad., next to the Mevlâna Tekke, provides maps of the area and can recommend accommodations (tel. (33) 11 10 74). **Çatal Pansiyon,** around the corner from the tourist office (tel. (33) 11 49 81), exploits its monopoly and charges a whopping USD9.50 for a bed. Up Mevlâna Cad. 2 blocks and to the right is the cushy **Otel Çeşme,** 35 İstanbul Cad. (tel. (33) 11 24 26; singles USD7.75).

Ten buses per day roam between Konya and Silifke (5 hr., USD4), even more frequently to and from Ankara (3 hr., USD4), and 15 times per day to İzmir (USD7.50). Night buses run to and from İstanbul. If you arrive at the bus station in daytime, take a minibus marked "Mevlâna" to the center; at night try a three-wheeled cart. Both leave from behind the station. After midnight, you'll have to take a taxi.

Ankara

Ankara is a capital, but no first city. It possesses little more than people (2.5 million), government, and one excellent museum to warrant that little star on the map of Turkey. Still, Ankara is the transport hub of eastern and southern Turkey.

Orientation and Practical Information

You need a map to survive in this huge and bewildering city. Most points of interest are in the **Ulus** and **Kızılay** districts. From the train station (500m to the right of the bus station) walk straight out along Cumhuriyet Bulvarı (past the park on your right) to reach the tourist office (about 100m to your left at the first intersection past the buses). Continue straight on Cumhuriyet Bulvarı to the equestrian statue of Atatürk in the center of Ulus. Remember that the statue faces west; it is a key reference.

Tourist Office: Main office at 33 Gazi Kemal Bulvarı (tel. 230 19 11). The staff is particularly helpful at the Ulus office, 4 İstanbul Cad. English spoken and maps provided. (All offices open Mon.-Fri. 8:30am-6:30pm, Sat.-Sun. 8:30am-5pm; off-season Mon.-Fri. 8:30am-5:30pm.) For free tourist information, call 044 70 90.

Embassies: All embassies line Atatürk Bul., south of Hurriyet Sq., **U.S.,** 110 Atatürk Bul. (tel. 126 54 70). **Canada,** 75 Nenehatun Cad. (tel. 136 12 90). **U.K.,** 46a Şehit Ersan Cad. (tel. 127 43 10). **Australia,** 83 Nenehatun Cad. (tel. 136 12 40). Travelers from **New Zealand** should contact the British mission.

American Express: 7 Cinnah Cad. (tel. 167 73 34). Take bus #13 across from the Ulus post office. Mail held. Emergency cash for cardholders. **Currency Exchange** open 24 hr. Wired money not accepted. Open Mon.-Fri. 9am-6pm, Sat. 9am-1pm.

Post Office: PTT, on Atatürk Bul. in Ulus 2 blocks south of the Atatürk statue. Open 24 hrs. Poste Restante open daily 9am-5pm. **Currency exchange** open 24hrs.

Telephones: At the post office (open 24 hours), bus, and train station. **City Code:** 4.

Flights: Direct flights to Istanbul (1 per hr.), Adana, Diyarbakır, Erzurum, Trabzon, Malatya, Van, Gaziantep, Antalya, Dalaman, and Kaysen leave from the **Esenboğa** airport. Airport buses leave from the Turkish Airlines office (tel. 321 49 00) next to the train station 1½ hr. before domestic and 2¼ hr. before international departures (USD1.50). All domestic flights USD62. Students USD38.

Trains: Although it's quicker to travel between İstanbul and Ankara by bus, the overnight trains are more convenient and comfortable. The *Mavi Tren* leaves both İstanbul's Haydarpaşa station and Ankara daily at llpm (7-8 hr., USD9.50). The *Anadolu Ekspresi* leaves both cities at 9pm (11 hr., USD5.50., couchette USD7.50). There are also connections by rail to İzmir, Konya, Cappadocia, Erzurum, Trabzon, and other Turkish cities, as well as to Iran, Syria, and Jordan.

Buses: Buses go everywhere often. Frequent departures to İstanbul (2 per hr., 7-8 hr., USD6-8), İzmir, Konya, Kuşadası, Erzurum, Adana, Diyarbakır, Van, and Trabzon, to name a few. Buses also run to Nevşehir and Ürgüp every hr. until 8pm. Daily to the Iranian border (USD15), Baghdad (USD30—Scandinavians take note) and Aleppo, Syria. Lockers USD0.25.

Hitchhiking: If you decide to hitchhike east, try the Bayındır Barajı Mocamp, Kayaş (tel. 19 41 61), 15km east of the city. Going west, your best shot is the Kervansaray Susuzköy Mocamp, 22km west of town on the İstanbul highway.

Hospital: Hacettepe University Hospital, Hasircilar Cad. (tel. 310 35 45), just below Ulus. Open 8:30am-5pm.

Accommodations and Food

Budget accommodations are an endangered species in Ankara—this is not a tourist town. The best place to look is in the **Ulus** district, at the north end of Atatürk Bulvarı. Forgo places right on Atatürk Bulvarı; they're noisy and cater to the clientele of the seamy nightclubs below. First try **Otel Savaş,** 3 Altan Sok (tel. 324 21 13). From the Atatürk statue, walk 2 blocks east and turn right on Anafartalar Cad. (Singles USD6. Doubles USD11.) Just down the road and to the right, **Beyrut Palas Oteli,** 11 Denizciler Cad. (tel. 310 84 07) is decent, although the breakfast regrettable. (Singles USD7, with bath USD8. Doubles USD11, with bath USD15.) The **Terminal Oteli** (tel. 310 49 49) at the bus station is respectable. (Singles USD9, with bath USD11; doubles USD14, with bath USD17.)

Kebabistan, Sanayi Cad., 1 block south and 1 block east of the Atatürk statue, serves tasty *kebap* for about USD1.50. The **Çiçek Lokantası,** 12/A Cankiri Cad., 500m north of the Atatürk statue, dishes out full meals for USD2.50 and sprinkles joy from a fountain in the middle. From the Atatürk statue walk down Hisarparkı Cad., turn right just before Anafartalar Cad. and you'll come to Ankara's big **food market,** with everything from sugared almonds to live chickens.

Sights

The fantastic **Anadolu Medeniyetleri Müzesi** (Museum of Anatolian Civilizations) is near the southern end of the citadel that dominates the old town. Take a taxi (USD1.50) or walk east and up the hill from the statue turn right onto Hisarparkı Cad. and right again onto Ipek St. The museum's nifty neolithic and Hittite collections justify a visit to Ankara. The setting is unique: a restored Ottoman *han* and *bedesten* (covered bazaar), its halls tweeting with scads of canaries, houses a collection of artifacts that trace all of Anatolian history. (Open Tues.-Sun. 9am-5:20pm. Admission USD2.50.) While in the area, stroll through the **bazaar,** the town-within-a-town inside the citadel walls, and the **Alâeddin Mosque.**

Don't leave Ankara without visiting **Anıt Kabir,** the tomb of Atatürk. Its sheer size and the museum of Atatürk's personal effects manifest Turkey's reverence for its national hero. The site is in a vast park west of the tourist office (a 25-min. walk from Kızılay). Southbound bus #63 on Atatürk Cad. will take you to the southern entrance of the park, where the mausoleum is. (Open Tues.-Sun. 9am-noon and 1-5pm.)

Near Ankara

The sprawling ruins of **Hattuşaş,** the Hittite capital, are some 200km east of Ankara, 25km off the highway to Samsun. The first people to smelt iron, the well-armed Hittites conquered Anatolia around 2200 BC. United under a central authority at Hattuşaş, the Hittites vied with the Egyptians for control of the Fertile Crescent. Along the 9km wall encircling Hattuşaş, the **Yerkapı,** a 70m-long tunnel/gate, begs a special visit. The Hittite high priest ruled from the inner sanctum of **Büyük Mabed** ("Big Temple"). To enter the chamber, subjects had to cross a drawbridge over two pools of water. Admission (USD1.50) also includes **Yazılıkaya,** an open-air temple where a cohort of the 1000 deities of the Hittite pantheon are represented in bas-relief 4km south of Hattuşaş. To reach Hattuşaş, take a bus to Sungurlu (3hr., USD3). There is one *dolmuş* per day (USD1) to Boğazkale, 1km from the ruins, leaving around 9 am and returning around 5pm. (Times may change.) Hitchhiking is a trial along the road to Boğazkale. Instead, taxis are always an option. (USD6.50, USD20 for a full tour. Haggle with the driver.) There is a picayune campsite midway between Hattuşaş and Yazılıkaya. Sungurlu has several cheap hotels. In Boğazkale, the **Pansiyon Hattuşaş** (tel. (4554) 10 33) in the center of town has doubles (USD7).

Cappadocia

About 300km southeast of Ankara, Cappadocia is the most striking province in Turkey's central plateau. Peculiar, enchanting volcanic formations, clustered in valleys and along ridges, chisel the sharp-jawed landscape. When Christians arrived here in the 6th century they carved houses, churches and entire cities out of the soft volcanic rock. You'll want to spend a few days making daytrips from one of the three major towns in the region: Nevşehir is the best transportation hub, Ürgüp is a pretty, modern city, and Göreme has the unique architecture and bizarre surroundings that people travel to Cappadocia for. Each is within an hour's bus ride of the others.

Nevşehir

Many stop in homely Nevşehir but few linger. Buses depart every morning for Ankara (4 hr.), Konya (3 hr.), Mersin, and Tarsus, and overnight rides go to İzmir and İstanbul. The region's *dolmuş* routes are also centered here. Go to the **tourist office** (tel. (4851) 36 59), on Aksaray Cad. Six hundred meters downhill from the bus station, for discount student guides and dandy maps of the region, with *dolmuş* routes and stations marked. (Open in summer daily 8am-noon and 1:30-6pm; off-season Mon.-Fri. 9:30am-5:30pm.) One *dolmuş* route runs to the underground city of Kaymaklı and Derinkuyu on its way to Niğde. Another goes to Üçhisar, Göreme and Ürgüp. A third goes to Avanos. Regularly scheduled municipal buses also run nine times per day (check at the tourist office for times) between Nevşehir and Ürgüp, for less than the *dolmuş*. Guided tours are cheapest in Göreme (USD7.75 per person). Buses from the main bus station also rattle to Konya or the Mediterranean coast. Hitching the triangle is a snap in summer.

If you must stay in Nevşehir, you can crash at **Ipek Palas Oteli,** at 99 Atatürk Bulvarı (tel. 14 78), a short jaunt from the station (doubles USD10). A cheap, comfy bed awaits you at the **Otel Nur,** 2 Belediye Cad. (tel. 14 44; singles USD7.75). To get there, continue on Atatürk Bulvarı and turn right at Akbank.

The humongous underground cities of **Kaymaklı** and **Derinkuyu,** bored by Christians as a wartime refuge from their surface homes, cower deep under a plain south of Nevşehir, 20 and 29km away respectively. Probing either is tremendous fun. Derinkuyu is larger and better marked, Kaymaklı more of an adventure (bring a flashlight). Even on the hottest days it's cool and damp down under, so take a sweater and a sandwich. Try to leave Derinkuyu by 4pm and Kaymaklı by 4:30pm; afterwards *dolmuş* are rare. (Both sites open daily 8am-7pm. Admission USD2, students USD1.)

Göreme

A bouquet of inexpensive pensions—many in caves carved from surreal rock formations—make Göreme the most interesting base town in Cappadocia. For cave-dwelling with the comfort of a hotel, try **Peri Pension** (tel. (4857) 11 36)—its rooms are in a giant rock cone. Rooms on the lower level (without windows) are cooler and cost less (USD4 per person). The amiable **Rock Valley Pension** offers a dandy restaurant, lots of headroom, and celestial showers (USD4 a bed). Camp at **Göreme Dilek Camping,** where phallic rock formations protect the campsite, swimming pool, and restaurant.

The cheapest tours of the region leave from Rose Tours (tel. (4857) 13 60) across from the bus station (USD7.75 per person). The most deserving spate of sights in the region is at the **Göreme Open-Air Museum,** 1km out of the village on the Ürgüp road. The churches here are a legacy of Cappadocian Christianity in the Byzantine Empire. The monks of Cappadocia built the majority of the churches in Göreme between the 4th and 10th centuries, and inhabited the area until the formation of the modern Turkish Republic, when all Anatolian Christians were traded to Greece for Muslims and a first-round draft pick. The earliest of the remarkable red frescoes are simple crosses, and Christian palm tree and fish symbols. The most impressive Göreme frescoes are found in the Church of the Apple and the Church of the Sandal. (Open daily 8am-6pm. Admission USD2, students USD1.) Across the street from the museum you can walk into the valley and, free of Konika-clickers, entry fees, and safety rails, explore cone dwellings.

Ürgüp

The charming, leafy town of Ürgüp, 20km east of Nevşehir. A bus runs nine times per day to Nevşehir (USD0.25); most of the long-distance buses to and from Nevşehir also call here, as well as *dolmuş* and buses to Kaysern with connections to the east.

The Ürgüp **tourist office** (tel. (4868) 10 59) is on Kaysern Cad., inside the garden; they'll help you plan daytrips. (Open daily 8:30am-8:30pm; Oct.-March Mon.-Fri. 8:30am-5pm.) Next door is a tiny **Archeological Museum.** Prance through some fruit trees to the bathroom at **Güzelgöz Pansiyon** (tel. (4868) 10 94) and know that the clean rooms and animated proprietor are worth it (USD3 per person). Try the *Saç Tava* (grilled meat and veggies) for USD2 at **Sofa Restaurant,** on Cumhuriyet Sq.

Somewhat risky rental mopeds are an excellent way to see the sites in the area. **Hepatu Rent-a-Motorcycle,** in a small arcade a block uphill from the bus station, charges USD7.50 for 4 hours (excl. gas).

Kayseri

Though Kayseri was once the capital of the short-lived Kingdom of Cappadocia and later of the Roman province Caesarea, bus connections are now the *only* reason to go. Buses roll from Kayseri to Göreme, Nevşehir, Samsun, Sivas, Erzurum, Mersin, Diyarbakır, Ankara, and İstanbul; from Ürgüp, take a *dolmuş.*

Eastern Turkey

Forays eastward in Turkey engender change. Somewhere near Cappadocia you necessarily burst your traveler's cocoon and proceed as hardy swashbuckler. Some caveats are in order here. Women will not feel comfortable alone; even when traveling in pairs, wear long pants or skirts, long-sleeved blouses, and scarves over your head, and still, prepare for unwanted attention. Travelers should bring some toiletries, notably toilet paper and tampons. Buses in the region are faster, more frequent, and more direct than trains, though the latter are an option if you have the time. Typically continental, the climate here can swing between the extremes. In summer, few places outsizzle Gaziantep, Urfa, Diyarbakır, and Mardin where temperatures can top 50°C. In winter, deep snow periodically cuts off much of Turkey's northeastern end. Hakkâri is virtually inaccessible from November through March, and everywhere northeast of Konya is *cold.* If English leads nowhere, try German. Virtually every town large enough to stop in has a bank, but you should carry U.S. dollars (cash or small-denomination traveler's checks). Also, food in the less expensive restaurants can verge on unsanitary; always walk into the kitchen to inspect the meat.

There is no such thing as a picturesque town in eastern Turkey—the cities are usually dusty, concrete, and powerfully ugly. Nevertheless, this leg can be one of the most rewarding of your Turkish adventure. The harsh plains and jagged peaks are capturing, a beauty of another world, free of the cosmetics that cake tourist itineraries elsewhere.

The Turkish government proscribes published information about the Kurdish population in Turkey—much in the news lately. A stateless population stretching over eastern Turkey, northern Iran and Iraq, Syria and parts of the Caucasus, the Kurds speak an Indo-European language similar to Farsi. The center of their separatist struggle in Turkey is in the extreme southeast in the Hakkâri region. The government puts the number of arrested dissidents at around 100 per year, but Hakkâri locals estimate that at least half that number are killed annually in fighting with the army. Stay aware, especially if you plan to travel southeast of Van.

Urfa

The city of Urfa (Şanlıurfa) basks only 50km from the Syrian frontier. Accordingly, Urfa has a distinctly Arab flavor and distinctly fatal climate. An ornate religious complex and colorful bazaar beckon. It's easiest to reach Urfa by bus from Antakya on the Mediterranean coast (about 7 hr.; you may have to change in Gaziantep).

Urfa's sprawling **covered market** almost overwhelms, starting from the far end of Sarayönü Cad., which curves to the right past the food market and the water vendors. The **bus station** lies about 1km out of town; to reach the center, head toward the castle and take a left through the middle of the cemetery. Find maps at the **tourist office** (tel. (871) 11 24 67), on your right 20m before the intersection with Sarayönü Cad., the town's main road. (Open in summer daily 8am-noon and 1-7pm.) Seek accommodations between the market and the castle. **Park Oteli,** 101 Göl Cad. (tel. (871) 110 95), has a fantastic view from its terrace. (Singles USD3. Doubles USD7.75.) Cleaner and more central is the **Hotel İstiklâl** (tel. 119 67), on a small side street across Sarayönü Cad. from the tourist office. (Singles USD4. Doubles USD7.75.) Try *baklava* sundaes at **Culouoğlu Baklavaları,** 2 blocks up Sarayönü Cad. from the tourist office (USD0.95). For more nutritious meals, visit **Çiftlik Firnili Lokanta** just up the street.

Near Urfa in the modern village of **Altınbaşuk** lie the ruins of the ancient town of **Harran.** This odd village, with its distinct hive-like dwellings, is where Abraham and Lot reputedly stopped on their way from Ur to Canaan. The dust, heat, and sheep contribute to the biblical karma. Frequent *dolmuş* trips from Urfa leave across from the tourist office.

Nemrut Daği

The mountain of Nemrut Daği (the "ğ" is silent) is the most visited spot in eastern Turkey, and here's the buzz: huge funerary statues of the first-century Commagene Empire crown the 2150m summit. Glaring eagles, majestic lions, and severe human figures, hybrids of Greek and Persian deities, stare over the mountainous landscape. The summit is cold at night even when it's sweaty below.

The most common way to get up the mountain is from the town of **Kâhta,** 70km away, a quick bus trip from Urfa; from there minibuses conclude the trip. The 2½-hour trip up to the summit is only possible May through October. Tour hustlers flood Kâhta; shop around before you commit and then bargain away. Tour prices do not vary with the number of passengers; groups should be no more than 10. Tours also leave from the **Ünal Pansiyon,** 14a Harıkçi Cad. (tel. 15 08; USD11.50), Up the main road from the bus station and to the left is the **Anatolia Pension,** with a garden and attractive purple bedrooms (USD3.75). The **Fortuna Pension and Camping** offers hot rooms (USD2.50), minibus tours, and camping (USD1 per tent) next to the bus stop. There are several campsites up the road away from town.

You can also travel to Nemrut Daği directly from Urfa; contact the **AsUrfa** bus office facing the tourist information office (tours USD13.50-15.50). An alternative route to Nemrut Daği is from the north, via **Malatya,** a city of several hundred thousand people connected by bus to Kayserı, Ankara, and Diyarbakır.

Diyarbakır

Diyarbakır rises like Tolkien's fortress of evil from the barren south Anatolian plain. Dating from Roman times, the walls were rebuilt by the Seljuks, who also erected the city's **Ulu Camii** (Great Mosque). Just north of the mosque lies the **Hasan Paşa Hanı** (caravanserai), now full of carpet shops. A few blocks away is the **bazaar.** In the southwest part of the city the Byzantine **Meryam Ana Church** continues to hold services. At the other end of the city, the ancient Byzantine citadel rises above the Tigris close to the Bitlis Gate. **Gazi Cad.** bisects the city from the **Dağ Kapi** area, where several inexpensive hotels roost. Just south of the Ulu Camii on Gazi Cad. are several **banks** and a **post office** (open 24 hrs.). Buses run to Urfa (6 per day, 3 hr.), Malatya (5 per day, 4 hr.), and Van. The **bus station** is 3km northwest of town; *dolmuş* take you into town and can stop along the way near the **tourist office** on Lise Cad. (tel. (831) 121 73; open daily 8am-6:30pm). Stay at the **Safak Palas Oteli,** 3 Inönü Cad. (tel. (831) 194 88), off Gazi Cad. 1 block south of the Atatürk statue, but avoid the sweatbox 2nd floor. (Singles USD2.50. Doubles USD4.50.) The clean, spacious Hotel Şenol, 6A Manav Sok. (tel. 231 05), on a side street off Gazi Cad. has rooftop beds for USD2. (Singles USD3.50. Doubles USD5.) Eat at the several good *kebap* spots near the Atatürk statue.

Lake Van

The waters of Lake Van lap in the arid altitudes of Eastern Turkey. Camping on or near its gravel beaches lets you to enjoy cool breezes and Van's strange, sudsy water.

The pleasant, dusty city of **Van** lies 5km away from the water. The **bus station** is 2km outside of town; most bus companies provide free lifts to and from the city center. Buses run to Diyarbakır (4 per day, 8 hr.) and all other points west, as well as Ağri and Hakkâri. The attentive **tourist office** (tel. (061) 120 18) is at the south end of the main drag by the traffic circle. (Open daily 8:30am-6pm; off-season closed

Sat.-Sun.) Two blocks west of the PTT, **Kent Oteli** (tel. (061) 125 19) has smirchless rooms and a central location. (Singles with bath USD7.75. Doubles with bath USD15.)

From the intersection of Cumhuriyet Cad. and İskele Cad. you can take a *dolmuş* 4km to the stunning **citadel** and **ancient city.** The ruins are all that remains of a city which was once the capital of the Urartian Empire. The small **Archeological Museum** houses an interesting array of artifacts and shocking anti-Armenian displays. (Open daily 8:30am-noon and 1:30-5:30pm. Admission USD1.) Armenian fortifications from this period remain as far southwest as Anamur, on the Mediterranean coast. With the collapse of the Ottomans after World War I, the Armenians allied with the Russians in an another effort to establish an independent state; however, Turkish nationalists squashed the Russo-Armenian army in 1920 and proceeded to massacre the Armenian population. Turks will claim that the massacre was a peasant retaliation against Armenian raids and that the Turkish army came to save the remaining Armenians by transporting them abroad. What actually happened is still acrimoniously disputed. At present, any publications about Armenian history or culture are discouraged in Turkey; even tourist brochures with descriptions of Armenian ruins omit the word "Armenian." There are still a good number of Armenian buildings, particularly beautifully decorated churches in the area between Van and Kars.

An intriguing Armenian church lies on the tiny island of **Akdamar,** 43km west of Van off the south coast of the lake. The **Church of the Holy Cross,** built in the 10th century, flaunts beautifully sculptured friezes, and the island is super for swimming. A boat runs there whenever it fills (USD2 round-trip). Admission to the church is USD2, students USD1. Any bus heading to Van from the west will pass the island. From Van you can take a *dolmuş.* The restaurant at the boat launch for Akdamar will let you camp for USD1 per person. The more serene **Cafer Camping** (USD2.50 per tent) is 6km east (37km west of the city of Van).

The town of **Hakkâri** is set 200km south of Van, among gaspingly rugged mountains. The town itself only services a large military base, but the bus ride through mountain passes makes the journey spectacular. This mountain area is the unadvertised stomping ground of Kurdish guerrillas, who periodically clash with Turkish soldiers; camping outside of town is a dubious option, but if you stay in one of Hakkâri's two hotels you should be bereft of ordeals.

Mount Ararat and Doğubeyazıt

Mount Ararat, the legendary resting place of Noah's Ark, is 500m taller than Mt. Blanc, and the net height from the plain to the summit matches any slope outside of the Himalayas. The mountain is in a military preserve and you need special permission to climb it (contact the Turkish embassy in your home country before you leave). Trek Travel Agency in Doğubeyazıt leads climbing expeditions to the mountain (USD461 per person) and can find you a guide if you don't want to go in a group of theirs.

The little town of **Doğubeyazıt** would normally be of no interest, but the imposing mountain and the palace of **Işak Paşa** make it one of eastern Turkey's most noteworthy stops. The palace was built by an eccentric Ottoman feudal lord in the late 18th century. Check out the gigantic harem and the mosque, then climb the Urartian fortress across the ravine for a fantastic pew. The palace is a 5km trek uphill from town; you can take a *dolmuş* (round-trip USD0.30), which runs all morning until noon. The last dolmuş back to town leaves at 4pm. (Palace open Tues.-Sun. 8am-5pm. Admission USD1.) In Doğubeyazıt, the **Hotel Erzurum,** near the end of town on the road to the palace, has clean rooms (singles USD3.50, doubles USD7). Down the street, the **Dumlupinar Lokantası** serves a variety of fresh meals (USD1.50). A **PTT** and a few banks occupy the town center. **Til-Tours,** up the road from Hotel Erzurum, runs worthwhile tours of the region; one particularly useful tour wins you permission to visit Ani and then drops you conveniently in Kars (USD10).

If you are coming from Van, **Tusba Travel** on Posta Sokak, off Kâzim Karabekir Cad., runs a mercifully direct 3½ hr. minibus to Doğubeyazıt (USD7.75). Otherwise, you'll have to go through **Ağri,** a nasty town without redemption. Ağri is also the only bus junction for those coming from Erzurum and the north.

Kars

Kars is another grungy eastern Turkish town—about the only reason to visit is to see the medieval Armenian capital of Ani, 45km away. The decor at **Otel Lütfü,** 10 Karadağ Cad. (tel. (021) 187 67) leans heavily toward Jackson Pollock. (Singles USD4. Doubles USD6.) A step up in quality is the **Hotel Asya** on Kâzim Paşa Cad. (doubles with shower USD7.75). The **Çobanoğlu Kahvesi,** near the Hotel Temel, occasionally features improv *aşik* (guitar) players (8-12pm, USD0.75).

To visit **Ani,** you must first win permission from the Kars **tourist office** (tel. (021) 123 00), on Lise Cad. (Open in summer daily 8am-5:30pm; off-season closed Sat.-Sun.) In the morning, you might run into enough people to share a taxi (USD20), or you can take the bus (Mon.-Fri. at 6am; returns from Ani at 5pm; sometimes an extra trip at midday). Or try visiting one of the luxury hotels and try to schmooze a ride on one of the tour buses. Or go from Doğubeyazıt (see above). Ani's **cathedral** is a fine example of Armenian architecture, as is the smaller and better preserved **Church of St. Gregory** (1 of 3 on a bluff at the extreme eastern end of the town, about 500m from the cathedral; admission USD2, students USD1.)

Kars is one of the few towns in eastern Turkey easily reached by train. Direct (if not fast) service, originating in İstanbul, goes via Ankara and Erzurum; the entire run takes almost 2 days. Reports indicate that it is now possible to take another train across the Soviet border to Leninakan in Armenia, with connections to Tbilisi and Yerevan.

Black Sea Coast

Tourist propaganda encourages you to believe that Turkey has but two coasts: the Aegean and the Mediterranean. But Turkey's longest (and least visited) coast rises out of the Black Sea in steep, misted hills. Industrial cities and fishing villages prod narrow, lonely beaches. The breeze and lush scenery soothe away the sear of other coasts. A highway traces the coast closely, so you can scan from your vehicle and choose what you want to explore. The boat trip along the coast from İstanbul is far more pleasant and very cheap, but leaves only once a week; book way in advance (especially if you want a cabin). Hotels are available only in the larger cities, but campsites appear every 50km or so.

Though geographically part of central Turkey, **Amasya** has been tied to the Black Sea since it was capital of the Pontus Kingdom. The Pontics conquered most of Asia Minor from their Black Sea homeland, but later fell to the Roman war machine. For accommodations among the mountains and castles, first try **Konfor Palas Oteli** (tel. (3781) 12 60) in the courtyard by the river (USD2.50 per person). Also try the **Hotel Aydın,** 86 Mustafa Kemal Cad. (tel. (3781) 24 63; USD1.50 per person).

Sinop is one of the few tourist towns on the Black Sea. Visit the medieval castle walls snaking through the city and the **Balatlar Church,** a ruined Byzantine religious compound. A **tourist office** (tel. (3761) 19 96) is at the harbor. (Open daily 9am-8pm; closed in off-season.) One block away is the gleaming **Yılmaz Pension** (tel. (3761) 57 52). Between Fatsa and Ordu, the black cliffs of Yasum peninsula plunge into green waters.

Cultured and refined, **Trabzon** is most famous for several churches left from the Trebizond Kingdom, an offshoot of the Byzantine Empire founded by Alexis Comneni in 1204. The **tourist office** (tel. (031) 146 59), on the main square, recommends tranquil villages along the coast. (Open in summer daily 8am-7pm; off-season 8am-5pm.) Crash at the **Erzurum Oteli** (tel. (031) 113 62) at 6 Güzelhisar near the main square. (Singles USD4. Doubles USD8.) From the municipal bus stop east of the tourist office, buses leave at 10am for **Sumela Monastery,** one of Turkey's most spectacular sights (USD1.50 round-trip). Established in 385 AD, this cliffside monastery reached its zenith in the late Middle Ages, when it contained 72 rooms and an immense library. (Monastery open daily 8am-6pm. Admission USD2.50, to park USD0.20.) Trabzon is well-linked by bus (about 1 per hr.) with Ankara, İstanbul, Samsun, and other cities at least once per day. The bus to İstanbul takes 20 hours, the ferry two days. The road east of Trabzon leads through Hopa to the border with Georgia at Sarp; reports are that it is now open.

USSR

USD$1 = 32 rubles (R, or SUR) **10R = USD$0.31**
CAD$1 = 28R **10R = CAD$0.35**
GBP£1 = 53R **10R = GBP£0.19**
AUD$1 = 25R **10R = AUD$0.40**
NZD$1 = 18R **10R = NZD$0.55**
Country Code: 7 **International Dialing Prefix: 810**

Since the USSR is presently undergoing rapid economic and political change, the prices and exchange rates here may suddenly become inaccurate.

For three days in August 1991, the world held its breath as an oft-predicted yet suddenly unexpected scenario unfolded in Moscow. As representatives from the USSR's constituent republics were flying to Moscow to sign a new Treaty of Union, old-guard ministers in Mikhail Gorbachev's inner circle attempted to seize power in a coup and thus roll back Gorbachev's six years of reform and democratization. The coup leaders counted on a passive reaction from the Soviet people, but Russia rose up, led by the charismatic Boris Yeltsin, and republics and army units alike declared their unwillingness to comply with any new orders from the Kremlin. Hundreds of thousands jammed Palace Square in St. Petersburg—then Leningrad—and at Yeltsin's urging, students in Moscow created barricades around the Russian Parliament to defy oncoming tanks. Within sixty hours, the coup fizzled and Gorbachev returned to Moscow from house arrest in the Crimea, to find himself President of a defunct Union and leader of a resolutely dead Communist party.

The revolutions of Eastern Europe had finally reached the mother country. Within days, Yeltsin proposed a slew of radical changes which banned the Communist Party, threw open the secret doors of the KGB, closed down *Pravda,* and forced Gorbachev himself to resign from the Communist Party. The Baltic republics declared themselves independent and won the recognition of Scandinavia, then Europe, then the U.S., and finally Moscow. The other republics rushed to reassert their sovereignty in a volley of declarations. The Congress of People's Deputies, formed just three years before, voted to dissolve itself and form an interim government to ease the USSR's restructuring and possible disassembling.

What led to such a swift collapse? By the 1980s, Soviets were already exhausted by waves of repression, starvation, collectivization, industrialization, and stagnation. After Gorbachev came to power in 1985, six years of *glasnost* and *perestroika* shredded the sociopolitical fabric of Marxist-Leninist socialism, but did not submit any clear alternatives. What began as an exuberant leap out of the Stalinist age of fear and repression gradually turned into a bewildering hodgepodge of semi-anarchy, deepened economic crisis, cynicism, and reinforced apathy. To smooth it over would have required a monstrous lie which no part of society was willing to help assemble.

Exuberant revolutionary headlines sell lots of papers in the West, but the present economic situation looks bleak. Muscovites have only to walk to the foul-smelling dairy store where there has been no cheese in a year to see the results of *perestroika,* and they count themselves lucky—they could be living in the provinces. Politicians talk and threaten, and fascists and anarchists have been hawking their journals on the street for years, but things have only worsened. Still, Soviets manage as they have for years, with unique resourcefulness and a heavy dose of black humor. People save, barter, trade, grow vegetables at their *dacha* or on their windowsill, and try to live a normal life as they imagine it, taking refuge around the kitchen table with homemade pickles and a bottle of vodka.

Crisis is not new to Russia; since the calamitious Mongol invasion of the 13th century, it has been a nation in a virtually perpetual state of emergency. The "time of troubles" in the 1600s was marked by dynastic failure, war, famine, and religious schism. At the beginning of the 18th century, Peter the Great's crash Westernization cost thousands of lives in massive construction projects and precipitated a permanent crisis of cultural identity which still colors Russia's perception of the West. Serfdom persisted in Russia up to 1861, leading 19th-century liberals to share Chernishevskiy's anguished question: "What is to be done?" In the late 1800s, a population explosion, coupled with an expensive state-financed industrialization drive, led to famine, peasant unrest, and a wave of strikes culminating in the failed 1905 revolution. Finally, in 1917, the enormous destruction of World War I cost the tsars their crown.

The rise of Soviet power could no better staunch the flow of catastrophe. From 1918-1920, civil war cost an untold number of lives and ushered in the "Red Terror" wave of political executions, as the new Bolshevik government strove to master a country wracked by ethnic rivalry and political turmoil. In response to the growing strength of the peasants after a temporary retreat from Marxist economic policy at the beginning of the 1920s, Stalin designed "Forced Collectivization" to herd the peasantry onto huge, centrally controllable state farms which would feed his new program of massive industrialization. Purges that left millions dead followed, and laid the groundwork of totalitarianism. At least 25 million more died in the horrific campaigns of World War II. The country finally began to recover from the war under Nikita Khrushchev, whose economic reforms and political liberalization led to the "thaw" of the early 1960s. However, a series of agricultural disasters precipitated his ouster in the "Brezhnev coup" of 1964. The 1970s saw a gradual increase in living standards accompanied by rising corruption, ideological rigor mortis and a deepening conviction that "we can't go on living this way" *(tak zhit' nelzya).* After Brezhnev, Andropov, and Chernenko expired within a 3-year span, the ascension of Mikhail Gorbachev in 1985 introduced the cultural viruses known as *glasnost* and *perestroika.*

One of the most significant effects of *glasnost* and *perestroika* was the rebirth of national identity in the various republics of the erstwhile USSR. The republics are diverse and multiethnic, and each in turn has its own minority problems. Now that the Union in its old form is defunct, and the Baltics flown forever, other republics may opt out entirely. Given the seventy-five years of exchange agreements that bind the republics' economies, some form of confederation seems more likely.

Let's Go went to press in September 1991—by the time you read this, anything could happen. More tension is sure to follow as the Kremlin rethinks its ties with Russia and Russia rethinks its relationship to the republics. Economic reform is complicated, since most republics want to bolster their national sovereignty rather than their links to each other, and since Russia's overwhelming size makes any relationships necessarily lopsided. In the meantime, the hardship of travel in whatever remains of the USSR is rewarded by a glimpse of history in the making, in a place of bewildering logic, surprising variety, and ironically, so much potential wealth. Details at 11.

Getting There

Access Routes

Aeroflot, Pan Am, and major Eastern and Western European airlines will whisk you to either Moscow or St. Petersburg, and Baltia Airlines (see under Latvia) flies from New York to Kiev; this is the easiest way to reach the USSR, but there are few discount fares. It may be cheaper to fly somewhere else in Europe and then take the train. **Rail travel** from Helsinki is a fine option, especially since you can reserve in advance by telephone (+358 (0) 62 52 16) and pick up your ticket at a special office in the Helsinki station. One train leaves Helsinki daily at 1:12pm, arriving in St. Petersburg at 8:45pm (238mk, round-trip 490mk); another leaves Helsinki daily at 5:10pm, arriving in Moscow at 8:50am the next day (437mk, sleepers only). The Moscow-bound train crosses the border before midnight; make sure your Soviet visa is valid from the date you leave Helsinki (which may be a problem for those on tour groups). **Buses** run by **Finnord** leave Lahti, Finland (an hour north of Helsinki) daily at 9am, arriving in St. Petersburg at 4pm (220mk); reserve well in advance at tel. (+358 (0) 64 27 44). Daily trains also run to Moscow and St. Petersburg from major European capitals such as Warsaw, Prague, Bucharest, Berlin, and even Paris and London, but they carry only sleepers, are often booked far in advance, and take so long they'll eat your mind. In 1991, it was easier to get tickets from Berlin than from Warsaw; in either case, you could not book by phone. It is also possible to reach Georgia and Armenia by rail from Kars in eastern Turkey, and ferries from Turkey reputedly cross the Black Sea to Georgia and the Crimea. The ferries that cross from Stockholm and Helsinki to St. Petersburg carry organized tours only right now, but that may change soon.

Note that it is generally OK to enter the Soviet Union through a city not specifically listed on your visa, so long as you proceed to your ultimate destination within 24 hours. Also make sure to buy a round-trip ticket; return tickets to the West are extraordinarily difficult to get in the USSR.

Individual Visas

The Soviet Union remains one of the most difficult countries to enter on your own; you really have to be dedicated, and a bit crazy, too, because it sure ain't paradise. The events of 1991 have kindled hopes that the USSR may eventually become a normal country with normal visa-issuing procedures, but as we went to press, that day still seemed distant. Although it's never put this way, getting a visa for individual travel in the Soviet Union essentially requires that you have someone to guarantee your well-being in every Soviet city you visit—whether this is an official organization, an individual with special approval, or a travel agency.

For fastest turnover, individual travelers should try work through a **registered Soviet institute or organization** that has official permission to invite foreigners (and usually access to hotel rooms payable in rubles). This is not as far-fetched as it sounds; Soviets thrill to Westerners, and many have aunts, cousins, or other connections at organizations that can invite you. The process can take as little as three weeks, but allow a few months to be safe; since mail to the USSR is hopeless, rely on phones, telexes, and fax machines. To issue an invitation, the organization will need to know the dates that you want to spend in the Soviet Union; your full name, address, citizenship, occupation, date and place of birth; and your passport number, plus its place and date of issuance and expiration date. Also make sure that they know all the cities you plan to visit, since you will be limited to those listed on your visa. The organization will send you one copy of their official invitation and telex another to the Soviet Embassy in your country. Send a photocopy of the invitation, a xerox copy of the front pages of your passport, a completed application (contact the embassy or a travel agent for blanks), three photographs, a self-addressed, stamped envelope, a cover letter, and the visa fee (most recently USD30) to the Soviet Embassy; processing normally takes up to two weeks, but can be expedited (for a surcharge). You may prefer to have this final step handled through a visa service with experience in Soviet visas (see the General Introduction).

It *is* possible for **private citizens in the USSR** to invite foreigners, but it is an extreme hardship; start six months in advance. Your Soviet friends must go to OVIR (the Office of Visas and Registrations), fill out an invitation form *(priglashenie),* then wait, wait, and wait for an *izveshchenie* form, which they can mail back to you and which you then must forward to the Soviet Embassy with your application, photos, and fee. Your visa will only grant access to your Soviet sponsor's city of residence.

If nobody in the USSR likes you and you absolutely *must* go on your own, contact **Intourist** (the official Soviet travel agency) for a copy of their brochure *Visiting the USSR.* Choose an Intourist-approved travel agency from the brochure; they will put together an itinerary for you. These itineraries are very inflexible and much more expensive than a group tour; you pay upfront in dollars, and one night in a hotel can cost USD100. Individual car-camping tours are also available, and somewhat less expensive; one of the few agencies which can organize them is **Pioneer East-West Initiative,** 88 Brooks Avenue, Arlington, MA 02174 (tel. (617) 648-2020), which can also arrange special-interest tours, and homestays for USD35 per night.

If you have been invited by an official organization, it is possible to extend your visa by presenting a letter from your sponsor at the OVIR office. Otherwise, you will have to leave the country by the date specified in your visa.

Visa-Free Cruises

If you're already in Europe and want only a quick taste of the USSR, these short trips (from a few hours to a couple days) are the way to go. They're operated by Scandinavian ferry companies, which bypass Intourist's Byzantine accommodations service entirely: if you stay overnight at all, it's usually on the boat. Though nominally "visa-free," you must still supply the ferry operator with passport details from five days to two weeks in advance of departure. From Finland, **Kristina Cruises** is the largest operator, running overnight cruises from Kotka, Finland (west of Helsinki) to Vyborg in Russia (near St. Petersburg) all year round (from 195mk per person); in summer only, they have 3-4 day Helsinki-St. Petersburg trips (from 364mk per person) and trips to Vyborg from Lappeenranta and Savonlinna. Contact them at Korkeavuorenkatu 2, 48100 Kotka, Finland (tel. +358 (52) 18 10 11), or in Helsinki at +358 (0) 62 99 68). See under Murmansk for information on cruises from Kirkenes in Norway. In the U.S., you can book most of these trips through Eurocruises (tel. (800) 688-3876).

Group Tours

A group tour is the most convenient way to visit the Soviet Union without sapping your wallet. You need not sacrifice your individuality—it is possible and advisable to miss group excursions and meals (despite the protestations of your guide), and to set off on your own with a map. Official excursions can be helpful, though, bypassing lengthy admission lines and bringing you to sights that are out of town or otherwise hard to reach on your own. Tours rarely include transport to and from the USSR; see Access Routes above and make your own arrangements.

The tours offered by **Scandinavian Student Travel Service (SSTS)** in conjunction with Sputnik (the Soviet youth travel organization) are significantly cheaper than most. Leaving in summer only, they consist of rigid itineraries starting on fixed dates, with meals, sightseeing, accommodation in two- or three-bed rooms, and internal transportation included. In 1991, SSTS offered six-day tours of Moscow and Leningrad for USD415, a 14-day tour adding Kiev and L'viv for USD805, and a 9-day trans-Siberian extravaganza from Helsinki to Beijing, stopping in Moscow, for USD800. Their overseas agents are STA Travel (see the General Introduction for addresses). If you're already in Europe, **Finnsov Tours** is perhaps the biggest Finnish tour company; contact them at Eerikinkatu 3, 00100 Helsinki, Finland (tel. +358 (0) 694 20 11).

Many organizations in the U.S. run special educational tours to the USSR. Try contacting CIEE (tel. (212) 661-1414; see the General Introduction) or the American Council of Teachers of Russian. **Volunteers For Peace,** 43 Tiffany Rd., Belmont VT 05730 (tel. (802) 259-2759) has innovative workcamps and language programs across the USSR, which run about USD650 for three weeks, excluding airfare.

Customs Formalities

Once pointed and threatening, customs enforcement has become arbitrary and unpredictable. There's not much you can do except be polite: one day they'll tear your pack apart, the next they'll just nod and dismiss you. If you fly in—especially with a group—your baggage will probably not be inspected. You may encounter more difficulty if you arrive by train or car, or at any provincial border post. Electronic consumer gadgets still in their boxes may arouse suspicion, as will any multiples of the same item. Pornography will be confiscated (and read with pleasure).

You cannot bring rubles into the country, not that you would ever want to. At the border, you will be given a Customs Declaration Form on which to declare all your valuables and foreign currency. *Don't* lose it. Everything listed on the customs form, including all slaughtered fowl, must be on your person when you leave the country. Keep all exchange slips and receipts from *beryozka* stores so that you can prove that no Western cash disappeared through illegal channels.

Works of art, icons, old samovars, and antique books—technically, anything published before 1945—are tough to export. You'll need either an official receipt from a *beryozka* hard-currency store, or a difficult-to-obtain permit (plus a 100% duty charge) if the item was a gift or was purchased for rubles. Pleas of ignorance and appeals to your embassy cannot keep these items from being confiscated at the border. Military items such as army belts and flags are nominally contraband, though authorities rarely bother with these anymore. Otherwise, leaving the country should go smoothly.

Getting Around

In 1991, restrictions that prevented free movement for Russian citizens were being abolished; the status of foreigners was unclear as we went to press. Meanwhile, the government officially limits your freedom of movement to a 25km radius around the city you're visiting, and foreigners must buy internal plane and train tickets through Intourist at inflated prices. Essentially, this means you must stay within city limits, unless you are on an Intourist tour or have some form of Intourist approval. With Soviet friends and a car, you can surely get away with a trip into the countryside. Short commuter rail journeys are also unlikely to be a problem, especially if you're going to a standard tourist destination. Although it's technically illegal, those who speak fluent Russian can procure long-distance train tickets right at the station and take off by themselves to any city for just a handful of rubles. Keep in mind that Soviet trains are crowded; you may be stranded if all return seats are booked. Also, you *are* breaking the law, even though document checks are rare; if you wander far afield and are noticed by the police, you risk prompt deportation and the possible denial of subsequent visas. Moscow, for example, is still ringed with "closed" cities which are off-limits to foreigners.

The Soviet Union boasts an extensive and reliable **rail** network and a vast, not-so-reliable **air** system monopolized by **Aeroflot** (Аэрофлот). Russians joke that if you want to get somewhere fast, take the train, and if you want to just go fast, take Aeroflot. Train cars are divided into three classes: luxury 2-bed "SV" compartments, 4-bed cozy "coupés," and open-car couchettes *(platskart). Elektrichka* (commuter rail, marked on train station signs as пригородные поезда) have their own platforms at each train station; buy tickets from machines if you have exact change, or from the counter (касса).

Within cities, overcrowded **buses, trams,** and (in major metropolises) extremely efficient **Metro** systems ferry citizens for 15к a ride. In the Metro, you drop the coins into machines that let you onto escalators that plunge you deep underground. Buy bus tickets at newsstands or from the *babushki* at Metro stations. Passes valid on all forms of public transport for one calendar month *(not* 30 days) can be practical for longer stays; ask at a ticket window for a *yediny bilet* (единый билет). On the bus, if you have a ticket, you must get it validated in one of the little hole-punchers. Since it's often bone-crushingly crowded, Soviets often ask their neighbors to pass tickets up to be punched. You may be asked as well, so render the service. The same goes for purchasing tickets, which can alternately be done from the driver—change gets passed up to the front and tickets make their way to the back. It is also customary for passengers to tap each other on the shoulder and ask if they are getting off at the next stop *(vy vychoditye na sleduyushchei?)* so that everyone can push their way to an exit. Metro stations are all in Cyrillic; if you don't read Russian, you can usually recognize stations by memorizing the first and last letters. When two lines intersect, there's a different station name for each line. You'll want to know the words Вход (entrance), Выход (exit), Выход в город (exit to the city), and Переход (which marks a passage to another line). Metro stations are marked above ground by a fluorescent *M.*

Please Note! Metro stations and street names will be changing wildly in the next few years. Streets named after any of the glorious heroes of the Revolution are particularly susceptible, as is anything with a date in it.

Hailing a **taxi** can be an adventure, particularly late at night (when it is unwise to take a cab alone). Many of those who stop for you will be private citizens, taking passengers to make a little extra cash. You may be picked up by lumber trucks, off-duty buses and even paddy-wagons. Step off the curb and hold out your hand; when a car stops, tell the driver your destination before getting in. He will either refuse the destination (seemingly arbitrarily) and speed off, or nod his head, at which point you can haggle about the price. Meters are non-operational. If you do not speak Russian, you will get ripped off. Russians usually pay a few rubles per ride, but if you get away for less than 20R you should feel lucky. Don't pay in dollars unless it's 2am and you're stuck in a decaying industrial park. Cab drivers often double as roving minimarts, carrying champagne *(shampanskoye),* wine *(vino),* or vodka *(vodka)* in the trunk at twice the standard price.

Practical Information

> *It should, however, be kept in mind that service personnel frequently do not reflect the national character for reasons peculiar to the economic system.*
>
> —*Estonian tourist brochure*

Be flexible. Expect airport delays, tour cancellations, hotel changes, cold showers, and bathrooms *sans* toilet paper. Careful packing can make all the difference. Bring any feminine hygiene supplies and contraceptives that you might need with you; even hard-currency tourist stores don't stock them. Sew a loop of cloth onto your coat or jacket neck so it can be hung up in restaurant and theater cloak rooms. A sink plug for doing laundry (try a squash ball), plastic bags, and toilet paper can also come in handy. Roach traps can be a godsend if you are staying in dormitories or in some Sputnik hotels.

The Soviet **ruble** is nonconvertible, and close to worthless. The bankrupt government, especially the offices that deal with tourists, are committed to prying every possible dollar from foreign visitors. Any excursion or theater ticket purchased from Intourist will be billed in Western currency. The state operates a chain of hard-currency *(valuta)* stores called *beryozka (kashtan* in Ukraine), where foreign tourists can buy hard-to-find lacquerware, furs, and liquor. In addition, all credit-card transactions in rubles show up on your bill at the so-called commercial exchange rate, where USD1 equals 1.60R, *not* 32R—so ***do not use a credit card to pay for anything in rubles in the Soviet Union.*** Using credit cards for hard currency purchases is OK and sometimes necessary.

You can exchange your money for rubles at state banks and in many Intourist hotels. You must produce your customs form, and will be given a State Bank Certificate listing the amount exchanged. When leaving the country, you must show your Customs Form and all State Bank Certificates in order to exchange unused rubles back into foreign currency; you cannot re-convert more rubles than you legally exchanged.

If you travel alone or ditch your tour for the day, you may well be approached by Soviets with a fascination for all things Western. Unfortunately, many of these will be *fartsovchiki* (blackmarketeers). Though they badly flout the law, the state seldom if ever prosecutes, and in recent years these sharks have shed all semblance of subtlety. They will find you on the street, in museums, in restaurants. They will find you in your hotel. They come bearing caviar, prostitutes, military uniforms, flags, and watches in exchange for your backpack, T-shirts, or shoes. Most often, traders will simply want to change money. Yet with the recent devaluation of the ruble bank rate, trading money illegally has become only marginally advantageous and not worth the risks. Many dealers will try to slip you worthless Yugoslav currency, or will dupe you out of hundreds of rubles with masterful legerdemain. You are least likely to be conned by hotel employees you will see again. Beware of dealers who are afraid to change money in public, and always count your rubles before handing over your currency.

Those who do venture out on their own will also have a more rewarding experience and catch a glimpse of Soviet life as it is for local residents. A traveler who simply asks a Soviet citizen the way to the Metro may receive a personal walking tour of Moscow. Women should be aware that asking a Russian man for the time can be loosely translated as, "turbo-charge me, you surging mass of machine." Resolutely saying *otstantye* (leave me alone) translates like it reads. Don't be surprised if a *babushka* comes up to you and harangues you about something or other; she is just doing her citizen's duty in scolding you for not behaving as a proper member of the collective. You've probably been sitting on the pavement, or haven't tucked in your shirt, or have been taking inappropriate photographs.

You will also run into a user-unfriendly society: crowded, foul-smelling shops with no products, long lines, and general bafflement at the individual. The first answer to any request will always be a firm "nyet!" But don't despair: this rarely means that something is impossible, you just have to learn the system. Soviets never buy things, they *dostat'*—obtain. This is a society which exists on barter, where a theater ticket is given by a box-office attendant to the butcher in exchange for a good cut of meat. To the ordinary person walking into the meat department there will be no meat—and no free seats at the performance. This is why contacts which can provide *blat* (pull) are highly valued. Soviets, when they leave the house, always carry a bag, as they never know what they will come across in a shop during the day. If you see something you like, snap it up; chances are it won't be there tomorrow. This means a three-line process. The first line is to take a look at the products and find out the price of whatever you're buying. You must then go over and stand in line to tell the cashier the department and the price; you pay, and she issues a receipt. You can then get back in another line to present the receipt to the salesperson and pick up your purchase—which by then may already be gone.

If you really want to ingratiate yourself with your new Soviet friends, or say thank you to your tour guide or a helpful hotel attendant, bring along some small, kitschy gifts. Postcards of Western cities, keychains with logos of American companies, cigarette lighters, pens, toiletries, and fashion or music magazines all go over big. For more serious gift-giving, try cassette tapes, T-shirts, kitchen gadgets, books, dictionaries, coffee, tea, or cigarettes. The last are still a serviceable sweetener for taxi drivers and restaurant managers, though foreign currency is now the bribe of the hour. A bottle of imported wine from a *beryozka* can also make a nice gift.

The reliability of **mail** service in and out of the Soviet Union fluctuates. If you have the opportunity, send mail with a Soviet-bound friend. Otherwise, delivery time can be anywhere from two weeks to four months to eternity. No one can be sure how much mail is still read by the authorities; express political sentiments openly but do not write anything directly incriminating. Note that Soviets write addresses with the country and zip code first. Overseas letters from the Soviet Union cost 50к, post cards 35к, and both stamps and postcards can be purchased at post offices (почта) and major Intourist hotels. Parcels must be brought unwrapped to specially designated post offices. Leave price tags on and bring receipts with you.

Telegrams (sent from телеграф offices, usually connected to post offices) are a relatively cheap way to get news out quickly and reliably (to the U.S., 1.20R per word). Look for a stack of blanks (the international forms say Международная Телеграмма), fill one out in Roman characters, and bring it to the window. Central post offices are also now equipped to send and receive **faxes.** The international **electronic mail** network offers a divine instant connection to selected Soviet universities and institutes—an all-you-can-type buffet.

Telephones cost 2к (they take 1к and 2к pieces). These coins are rare, and it is a custom for citizens to ask one another for the pieces—a courtesy which benefits everyone in the final count. In a pinch, a 10-kopek piece or an American dime will also work. Soviet phones are notoriously unreliable, and you may have to search to find one that works. Intercity calls may be made from telegraph offices, your hotel room, or special phone booths in each city marked междугородние. The domestic long-distance prefix is 8; then wait for the tone before dialing the city code. Make direct international calls (Finland and Eastern Europe only) from telegraph offices and hotel rooms; dial 8, wait for the tone, then dial 10 and the country code. Calls to the rest of the world must be ordered either at your hotel or at a telegraph office. If a same-day connection is available at the telegraph office, you'll have to stand in a long line to place your order, then wait at least an hour for the call to go through. If you don't speak Russian, you'll need to find someone in the waiting room who does to point out which booth to go to when your call is announced. Outside of Moscow and St. Petersburg, calls must often be ordered at least a day in advance. Calls to North America cost 12R per minute with a 3-minute minimum; calls to Europe 6R per minute. You cannot call collect. Several hotels in Moscow now have direct-dial booths operated by purchasing a special card, or by credit card. The cost is astronomical (USD12 for 1 min. to the U.S.). To be reached quickly in an emergency, leave the number of your tour group with someone at home. Your embassy should be able to find you if they have this number. If traveling independently, leave a copy of your itinerary with the embassy, along with your name, address, date and place of birth, and passport number.

Calling into the country can be almost as frustrating. The U.S. and Canada have direct dial only to Moscow. From Finland and Eastern European countries you can also dial St. Petersburg. For other cities, go through the operator. It's Russian roulette all the way; you will get through, though it may take thirty tries.

After a week or so in the Soviet Union, whose mass media generally remain blissfully ignorant of most significant events, you may begin to feel hopelessly out of touch with the outside world. You now know how most Soviets have felt their entire lives. A good remedy for this darkness is to scout the news kiosks around the local university; you may be able to finagle a week-old copy of *The Guardian* or **The International Herald-Tribune,** or a copy of *Time,* which sells in street kiosks for a bargain 4R. If it is news of Russia you seek, try the English-language edition of *Moscow News,* the country's most progressive official newspaper, or if you read Russian, pick up one of the hundreds of new independent papers being hawked on every street corner, which run the gamut from religious to sensationalistic to political. You can also drop by the reading room of the U.S. Commercial Office in Moscow (ul. Chaikovskovo 15; open Mon.-Fri. 9am-5pm) or the U.S. Consulate in St. Petersburg.

Few Russians speak English; before you go, take some time to really familiarize yourself with the Cyrillic alphabet. It will make getting around and deciphering street and Metro signs immeasurably easier and will lend you a good deal of independence. Your effort will be rewarded and you'll even be surprised at the number of cognates once you figure out that ресторан, for example, means "restaurant."

Cyrillic	Roman	Cyrillic	Roman
А, а	**A, a**	Р, р	**R, r**
Б, б	**B, b**	С, с	**S, s**
В, в	**V, v**	Т, т	**T, t**
Г, г	**G, g**	У, у	**U, u**
Д, д	**D, d**	Ф, ф	**F, f**
Е, е	**E/Ye, e/ye**	Х, х	**Kh, kh**
Ё, ё	**Yo, yo**	Ц, ц	**Ts, ts**
Ж, ж	**Zh, zh**	Ч, ч	**Ch, ch**
З, з	**Z, z**	Ш, ш	**Sh, sh**
И, и	**I, i**	Щ, щ	**Shch, shch**
Й, й	**Y, y**	Ъ, ъ	**" ("hard sign")**
К, к	**K, k**	Ы, ы	**Y, y**
Л, л	**L, l**	Ь, ь	**' ("soft sign")**
М, м	**M, m**	Э, э	**E, e**
Н, н	**N, n**	Ю, ю	**Yu, yu**
о, о	**O, o**	Я, я	**Ya, ya**
П, п	**P, p**		

Accommodations

Tourists who travel on an arranged tour will have their accommodations taken care of by Intourist or Sputnik, the state travel organizations. Both of these operate chains of hotels in cities open to foreigners across the USSR. Payment for rooms must be made in advance, in hard currency, for a predetermined period. Intourist hotels offer generally comfortable rooms with a bathroom and shower, telephone and television. Sputnik accommodations tend to be more spartan, sometimes with communal bathrooms and a lower standard of cleanliness. All meals are covered, and served in the hotel restaurant. Don't lose your hotel card, which lets you in and out of the hotel. Present it to the gruff doorman, and you instantly escape the blackmarketeers hanging outside in the street. The keys to your room are held by a now-disappearing breed of Soviet worker—the *dezhurnaya,* or floor attendant. Usually a retired woman, she is in charge of seeing to it that her floor maintains order and socialist discipline. Your *dezhurnaya* will collect room keys when you exit and return them upon presentation of your hotel guest card. She can also make you tea, sell mineral water, and advise you on the weather, if you speak Russian. All Intourist hotels have a small hard-currency store, dollar bar, restaurant, and post office. Hot water often gets turned off during part of the summer for pipe repairs in Moscow and St. Petersburg, so you may have to do with cold showers, even at some of the luxurious and newly refurbished Intourist flagships.

Staying with friends or relatives in the Soviet Union requires a personal invitation, discussed under Getting There. As soon as you arrive, you must go down to the central OVIR (оВИР) office (in Moscow, at ul. Chernyshevskaya 42 and called УВИР) to register as a foreign resident. New services have sprung up lately that rent apartments to foreigners for longer stays. This can be much more economical than a hotel stay, but is more challenging to arrange. The service must provide an invitation and arrange for your visa.

Food and Drink

"You were right," he whispered. "The sturgeon smelled a little funny."

—Chekhov, Lady with a Dog

Searching for palatable food in Russia strains the ability, patience, and stomach of a person of standard constitution, not to mention those with special dietary needs or eating enthusiasts with visions of chicken Kiev *à la Russe.* Rest assured, you will not starve, and if you remember to look upon food for its principal value—nourishment—you will get by, and can turn your attention to more varied and pleasant sights here in Cabbageland. The standard menu includes salad (салат), either sliced, diced, or chopped cucumbers and tomatoes garnished with sour cream, or diced potatoes, eggs, canned peas and cucumbers smothered in mayonnaise; soup (суп), usually hearty, tasty, and cabbage-based, with beets and/or meat bones; meat (мясо), unidentifiable and most often chopped or else sliced with alternating veins of gristle); a side order of deep-fried greasy potatoes amd chopped beets or cabbage; and, for dessert, weak tea (чай) or sludgy coffee (кафе) with extra-creamy vanilla ice cream. Intourist hotels are sure to serve this at every meal. Sputnik hotels serve the same combination with lower-quality ingredients.

If you are not on a hotel meal plan, or staying with friends, the quest for food can take up the better part of your day and will require constant advance planning and dogged determination. Getting into a decent restaurant, for example, requires strategy. If you want to be completely sure of eating at a particular establishment, be there at noon (or a little earlier) to make a reservation for that evening. Especially in Moscow and St. Petersburg, trying to walk into any kind of restaurant for dinner without a reservation will meet with a prompt door-slamming. No matter that the place may be half-empty—that just means less work for everyone, and Soviet restaurants only accommodate one seating per table per meal. If you knock really hard and the doorman cracks the door open, he is 90% likely to regret that all of the tables have been reserved three days ahead of time; 80% of the time he is lying, and if you are persistent he will show you to the manager, who may give you a table. Be lavish with material encouragement and go low on the subtlety. If none of this works and you have the patience, try waiting until 10pm or so when crowds thin.

Over the past several years, privately-run "cooperative" restaurants have mushroomed. When these first opened, the service was generally attentive and the menu had a full assortment of dishes. Now, along with everything else, cooperatives have slipped. Service can be as rude as in the state restaurants (although that's hard to do) and the menu often sports the same limited choice of cucumbers and fatty chopped meat. Still, the atmosphere is usually more congenial than in the state restaurants with their cavernous halls and loud bands. One word of warning—when you call, or have a Russian reserve for you, make clear that the table be free of *zakuski* (appetizers). Many places have the nasty habit of garnishing your table *(nakryvat' stol)* with these salads, caviar and cold cuts prior to your arrival, which, if you eat them, will cost you dearly. If you show up and there are *zakuski,* inquire about the cost at once and ask them to remove the dishes you don't want. Insist that you are paying in rubles if there is talk from the waiter of dollars, and *don't* pay by credit card (see the information on exchange rates above). In 1991, most restaurant meals cost 50-100R, including cold appetizers, a hot entree, vodka, champagne, ice cream, and coffee, and often a band or floor show. For sheer tackiness, these can put Vegas to shame.

Avoid the dirt-cheap cafés called *stolovayas* (столовая); the food is usually repulsive and often dangerous. Cafés (кафе) are one step up, and usually offer a decent chicken dish for around 2 rubles.

To supplement your diet and for snacks in between meals, there are a number of alternatives. Delicious Russian white and black bread and sweet rolls cost mere kopeks at ubiquitous bakeries (булочная). For fruits and vegetables, head for the *rynok* (market), where farmers sell their privately-grown goods for a profit. The variety and quality are comparable to Western standards, while the prices—though a squeeze by Soviet standards—are low. Be careful to wash everything before eating it; Soviet pesticides are dangerous to more than bugs. Bring your own shopping bag and make ready to haggle. Despite periodic sugar shortages, sweet snacks abound. Ice cream *(мороженое)* is perennially popular, selling well even in the middle of winter (50к-1R). Buy something as soon as you see it; stands are usually portable and pop up only briefly before selling out.

If you are staying with friends, or are visiting a private home, you can forget all the advice about bad food and nonexistent service. Going to a Soviet's home *(v gosti)* is one of the most rewarding experiences you can have in the Soviet Union. The street sullenness melts away instantly, and even if you protest that you're not hungry, your hosts will not let you leave the table until they have stuffed you with homemade salads, meats, fruits, freshly baked pie, vodka, champagne and two to three cups of tea to top it all off. You will be engulfed in hospitality and will experience one of the great paradoxes of Soviet life, where there is nothing in the shops, yet everything in the home. This is because people go to great pains to save, store, barter for, and pay for valued goods. Fruit and vegetables often come from peoples' *dachas,* where city dwellers now tend postage-stamp garden fiefdoms in a throwback to feudal sustenance. A dinner like this should tide you over for a few days, as you stumble to put your napkin on the table.

In the past year, several all-night liquor stores have opened in the larger cities; these offer you the opportunity to arrange a traditional Russian evening of vodka and black bread at the last minute. *Zolotoye kol'tso, Russkaya* and *Zubrovka* are the best brands, and *Stolichnaya* and *Moskovskaya* are very well known, but the generic brand is usually quite satisfactory. An ample selection of vodkas and wines is available in *beryozka.* After these close, a beer hall is a great place to meet locals, though Soviet brew is nothing to celebrate. Most Intourist hotels have a foreign-currency bar.

The water in Moscow, Kiev, and L'viv is potable, but best taken in limited doses. By contrast, the water in St. Petersburg and Central Asia is a stomach pounder—it's infected with a bacteria called **giardia,** which is easily curable with medicine purchased in advance in the U.S. Without such treatment, a bout with giardia will make you feel like your intestines have declared independence and eliminated all visa requirements. Travelers to infected places are advised to contact a physician before going to the Soviet Union, as contact with the contaminated water is unavoidable. Consider purchasing water purification (iodine) tablets at a camping store at home. Preferably, drink Soviet or foreign mineral water sold at *beryozka.* Also consider a gamma globulin shot to lower your risk of hepatitis.

Needless to say, regional cuisines vary throughout the Soviet Union's republics. Hearty *borshch* and *vareniki* (cheese- and vegetable-filled dumplings) mark Ukraine, and Georgian and Armenian *shashlyk* (shish kebab) and wine will please your palate in the Caucasus and break the potato routine in Russia. One final word of advice before you pack your bags: take Pepto-Bismol, and snack foods such as peanut butter, instant soup, and granola to tide you over on those days when you can't face another piece of gristle or sour cream salad. Bon appetit!

Russia Россия

Once synonymous with the Soviet Union, Russia redefined herself in August 1991. President Boris Yeltsin wrenched the republic from under the carcass of the Soviet Union when he defied the putschist plot from atop a tank, and rallied his people onto barricades to defend the Russian Parliament. As its first popularly elected president, Yeltsin is fully conscious of Russia's political power as the guardian of over half the USSR's population and nearly three-quarters of its natural resources. In the year before the coup Russia had already begun to test its strength, concluding agreements with other republics and sending delegations abroad. Though Yeltsin has pledged dual stewardship with Gorbachev, doubts linger about Gorbachev's role in the coup and his future as president of a defunct union; Russia is fast assuming the leverage that the USSR used to have.

The Russian Republic is by no means a monolith, but rather a vast patchwork of autonomous regions and minority nationalities; as such, it will be subject to the same centrifugal forces that are breaking apart the larger Union. The Yakuts (who sit on huge mineral resources) have declared themselves independent, and the Tatars—a Muslim enclave in the Orthodox Russian heartland—also want autonomy. Yeltsin barnstorms around the republic, trying to keep its disparate parts together, but he must race to disentangle Russia from the central communist bureaucracy, and put together a cogent economic plan that will lead to recovery. Astrologers point to 1995 as the decisive year. Who will gain decisive control of Moscow? What does the future hold? As the poet Tyutchev once remarked, "You cannot understand Russia with your mind, you cannot measure it with a meter stick—you can only believe in it."

Moscow Москва

A city of endless dusty pavement and immense apartment complexes, where Ivan the Great's Kremlin stands shoulder-to-shoulder with Stalin's monstrous Gothic skyscrapers, Moscow is quintessentially Soviet and quintessentially Russian. Its nine million denizens include members of every Soviet nationality and its borders encompass dozens of sprawling residential "'micro-regions," forests, monasteries, industrial parks, and even farms. While a large part of the city dates from the last 50 years, the result of relentless church-destruction and boulevard-widening as Stalin made way for monuments to the new Proletariat, the older neighborhoods still speak of the days when "Moscow of the Thousand Churches" was the capital of the tsars and seat of the Russian Orthodox Patriarchy. The city still harbors many beautiful spots—monasteries untouched by the wrecker's ball, huge parks and palaces—but these must be discovered amid the present rows of pre-fab housing blocks and monolithic avenues.

Founded by Prince Yuri Dolgoruki in 1147, Moscow became the center of the Russian government in the 14th century. When Peter the Great moved the capital to St. Petersburg in 1712, the saying arose that while St. Petersburg might be Russia's head, Moscow was its heart. Today, many non-Muscovites, resentful of the capital's power and wealth, might put it another way.

Hundreds of thousands of shoppers from the provinces daily pour into the capital, making this the Soviet Union's rudest, noisiest, pushiest, but most energetic and happening metropolis—a city where all of the political, social and cultural ferment rocking the Soviet Union in the past few years has found an outlet. For better or worse, Moscow now once again finds itself at the heart of the forces undoing the Soviet Union. As the struggle between the center and the periphery continues, Moscow is bound to remain at center stage for quite a while.

Orientation and Practical Information

Moscow is laid out in a series of concentric rings, emanating from the Kremlin. The outermost "ring road" forms the city boundary (and, in 1991, the limits of your visa), but most sights of interest to visitors lie within the inner "garden ring" (corresponding to the Ring Line of the Metro). **Red Square** (Красная Площадь) and the **Kremlin** (Кремль) mark the center of the city; nearby start Moscow's popular shopping streets, **ulitsa Tverskaya** (улица Тверская, running west parallel to the Metro's blue lines) and **Kalininskiy prospekt** (Калининскиы проспект, which goes north along the green line). Ul. Tverskaya was formerly called ulitsa Gor'kovo (Gorky Street—ул. Горького), and the upper half still preserves the old name as it leads to the **Garden Ring** (Садовое кольцо), the original limit of 19th-century Moscow, below which runs the Metro's circle line. The Moskva River weaves woozily through the center of town and is not terribly helpful in finding one's way around the city, although a boat ride on it can be a pleasant way to while away the afternoon. Learn Cyrillic, orient yourself by the **Metro,** and you can never get really lost. All buses and trains eventually stop at one of the stations, marked by a red neon ***M.*** An extensive map of Moscow including all public transportation routes and a street index sells at many kiosks for 1.58R.

Tourist Offices: Central Excursion Bureau, ul. Tverskaya 3/5 (tel. 203 69 62), next to the Intourist Hotel and one block from Red Square. A good resource center if you feel like spending lots of Western currency, but they'll be reluctant to tell you about anything payable in rubles. If you don't speak Russian, you may have to buy your out-of-town excursions here. Open daily 9am-noon and 1-9pm. **Sputnik,** ul. Kosygina 15 (tel. 939 80 86), at the Orlyonok Hotel. Open daily 9am-6pm. The **Moscow Excursion Bureau,** ul. Rozhdestvenka 5 (tel. 523 89 53), behind Detskiy Mir. If you speak some Russian, your best bet for out-of-town excursions, walking tours, etc. Historic tours of Moscow plus day-trips to Vladimir and Suzdal', all for a few rubles. Open daily 8am-2pm and 3-6pm.

Embassies: U.S., ul. Chaikovskovo 19/23 (tel. 252 24 51 through 252 24 59). M: Barrikadnaya (Баррикадная). Open Mon.-Fri. 9am-1pm and 2-6pm. Notary services Mon.-Fri. 2-4pm—otherwise, everyone is overworked and unpleasant. No reading room. **Canada,** Starokonyushenny per. 23 (tel. 241 91 55). Open Mon.-Fri. 8:30am-1pm and 2-5pm. **U.K.,** nab. Morisa Toreza 14 (tel. 231 85 11 through 231 85 13). Open Mon.-Fri. 9am-12:30pm and 2:30-6pm. **Australia,** Kropotkinskiy per. 13 (tel. 246 50 11 through 246 50 17). Open Mon.-Fri. 9am-12:30pm and 1:30-5pm. **New Zealand,** ul. Vorovskovo 44 (tel. 290 34 85). Open Mon.-Fri. 8:30am-12:30pm and 1:30-5pm; Sept.-May Mon.-Fri. 9am-12:30pm and 1:30-5:30pm.

Currency Exchange: Kosmos Hotel, pr. Mira, across from the Economics Achievement Exhibition at M: БДНХ. Bound to change soon. American Express has shorter lines.

American Express: ul. Sadovaya-Kudrinskaya 21a (tel. 254 43 05), near ul. Gor'kovo. Currency exchange, mail held, missing checks and credit cards replaced, and traveler's checks sold to cardholders. Open Mon.-Fri. 9am-5pm.

Post Office: Moscow Central Telegraph, ul. Tverskaya 7, a few blocks from the Kremlin. Look for the globe and the digital clock out front. International mail. Open Mon.-Fri. 8am-2pm and 3-9pm, Sat. 8am-2pm and 3-7pm, Sun. 9am-2pm and 3-7pm. Another, less crowded branch, at pr. Kalinina 22 near Dom Knigi. Open daily 8am-8pm. **Poste Restante** at the Intourist Hotel Post Office, ul. Tverskaya 3/5. Address mail to До востребования, K-600, Intourist Hotel, ul. Tverskaya 3/5, Moscow. To mail packages, especially books, bring them unwrapped to the Intourist Hotel Post Office or to Moscow Central Telegraph; they will be wrapped and mailed while you wait (27R for 3kg). Open Mon.-Fri. 9am-1pm and 2-5pm, Sat. 9am-1pm and 2-4pm.

Telephones: At **Moscow Central Telegraph,** which also has the city's only change machine for 2к pieces. Stand in line, order your call and wait 1-2 hrs. Send telegrams from windows 7-9. Has fax too. Open daily 8am-8pm. Branch office at pr. Kalinina 22. The major hotels now have direct-dial international phone booths at exorbitant prices (1 min. to the U.S. runs USD12!). **City Code:** 095.

Fax and Photocopy Services: Alphagraphics, ul. Gor'kovo 50 (tel. 251 12 08). Canadian-Soviet joint venture provides photocopying, laser printing and faxing services for hard currency, but with a smile. Also DHL express mail (½ lb. USD58.00 to the U.S.) Open Mon.-Fri. 9am-6pm.

Train and Plane Tickets: Intourist Main Office, ul. Petrovka 15, to the right of the Bolshoi Theater. Inside the courtyard of building #15; enter underneath the archway on ul. Petrovka. Open Mon.-Fri. 9am-6pm. Lines on 2nd floor are enormous; go to 3rd floor, window #9 or 10, where lines are shorter (like, maybe 3 days) and English is spoken.

Flights: Moscow has three main airports, all outside the city limits. International flights arrive at **Sheremetyevo-2** (Шереметьево-2) to the north. M: Aeroport (Аэропорт), then a bus. If you're arriving at the airport, the buses stop outside the terminal; most are orange. Buses stop around 9pm; cabs will rip you off like you've never seen, but you have no choice. Most internal flights originate at **Vnukovo** (Внуково), **Domodedovo** (Домодедово), or **Sheremetyevo-1.** Buses link all three airports; commuter rail goes to Vnukovo and Domodedovo. **Foreign airline representatives: Finnair,** proyezd Khudozhestvennovo Teatra 6 (tel. 292 87 88). Open Mon.-Fri. 9am-5pm. **Lufthansa,** Kuznetskiy most 3 (tel. 923 04 88 or 923 95 76). Open Mon.-Fri. 9am-5:30pm. **Pan Am,** Hotel Mezhdunarodnaya II, Krasnopresenskaya nab. 12 (tel. 253 26 58 or 253 26 59). Open Mon.-Fri. 9am-6pm. **SAS,** Kuznetskiy most 3 (tel. 925 47 47). Open Mon.-Fri. 9am-6pm.

Trains: Moscow has eight main train stations, teeming with gypsies and sweaty travelers, most clustered around the Metro's Ring Line. Trains to St. Petersburg and some trains to Estonia depart from the **Leningradskiy station** (Ленинграский вокзал). M: Komsomolskaya (Комсомольская). Across the street is the **Kazanskiy station** (Казанский вок зал) and the **Yaroslavskiy station** (Ярославский вокзал), where the Trans-Siberian leaves. The other stations are served by similarly named Metro stops. **Paveletskiy station** (Павелецкий Вокзал) and **Kurskiy station** (Курский Вокзал) serve the south. The **Rizhskiy station** (Рижский Вокзал) serves Latvia and Estonia. Trains from Warsaw and Lithuania arrive at the **Byelorusskiy station** (Белорусский Вокзал). Trains to Ukraine, Czechoslovakia, Bulgaria, and Romania use **Kievskiy station** (Киевский Вокзал).

Taxis: Tel. 225 00 00 or 227 00 40. If you don't speak Russian, it's now nearly impossible to get anyone to take you for rubles. Results best if you take along a pack of Marlboros and a Russian-speaking friend. Don't pay over 25 rubles for any ride within the city. Taxi stands are indicated by a round sign with a green *T.* Meters are ornamental.

Public Transportation: If you're not familiar with the Cyrillic alphabet, the 9 lines of the **Metro** will daunt you. Remember: Вход means "entrance," Выход means "exit," Выход в город indicates an exit to the street and Переход a passage to a different line and often to a different station altogether. The same station, if it serves more than one line, will carry different names. Above ground, stations are marked by a large, illuminated *M.* Trains run 6am-1am. The fare is 15к, only payable in 5к and 15к coins; there are change machines at all stations, but don't rely on 'em. Month-passes *(yediny bilet,* единый билет) are 18R from ticket windows. Metro maps sold at street kiosks for 6к. **Lost and found:** Tel. 222 20 85 (for the Metro) and 233 00 18, ext. 139 (for trolleys, trams, and buses).

Laundromat: Your bathtub. If you're lucky, there might even be hot water. Otherwise, if you are staying in a hotel, the *dezhurnaya* will be glad to wash your shirts for a few rubles. There *is* usually a laundromat in each neighborhood; look for a sign saying прачечная. If you venture into one, plan to spend most of the day. Use only cold water in the machine, and put your wet clothes in the spinner before tossing them in the dryer.

Haircuts: Try the salon in the Moskva Hotel or on Kalinin Prospekt for the latest in Soviet fashion. Women should stay away from hair dyes—unless blue or orange is your color.

Medical Assistance: Mezh Med Tsentr (МежМедЦентр), Gruzinskiy per. 3, korpus 2 (tel. 253 07 03). French joint venture offering walk-in medical care (USD40 per visit). Open Mon.-Fri. 9am-6pm.

Emergencies: Police (tel. 02). **Ambulance** (tel. 03). **Fire** (tel. 01). Good luck. No coins needed from pay phones. Also try the U.S. Embassy's emergency number (tel. 252 24 51).

Food

Moscow's restaurants are the best in the Soviet Union—especially since the opening of new, privately-run cooperatives—and *everybody* knows this. Adopt an early eating schedule; even mediocre restaurants and cafés have long lines after 5pm. Eating out is a rare and expensive occasion for Russians—they usually linger for several hours—and most establishments only serve once per mealtime, so places fill up fast and reservations are recommended. Call or have hotel personnel assist you. The best strategy is to make a round of calls around noon to reserve for dinner; otherwise, you may be out of luck and have to resort to the line at McDonald's.

Meals run 50-75R per person. Make sure—perhaps when you call—that the meal will be payable in rubles. Read the warnings in the Practical Information section before you pay for a meal by credit card. Menus come in Cyrillic only; if you speak no Russian and have no shame, cluck for chicken, moo for beef and avoid fish, which is usually older than you are and doesn't make noise anyway. Cafés are considerably cheaper than restaurants, and often quite good.

Over the past few years, cooperative stands selling quick, tasty kebab plates and meat sandwiches have blossomed all over Moscow. The **McDonald's** at Pushkin Square is a marvel of efficiency and cleanliness, and since prices went up (a Big Mac now costs 11.50R), the lines have gotten shorter—whittling the wait to a bare 20 minutes most days. The arrival of **Pizza Hut** on ul. Tverskaya also alleviates the crush. For an antidote to much-vaunted but uni-flavored Soviet ice cream, **Baskin-Robbins** has a hard-currency store at the Hotel Rossiya and another on the Arbat (open daily noon-1pm and 2-10pm), while **Pinguin,** a Swiss-Soviet joint venture, scoops out exotic-flavored ices at 1R a cone (watch locals carry them by the fistful!) Outlets are at ul. Gor'kovo 37, in the Moskva Hotel, and on the Arbat. (Each open daily 10am-10pm.)

State Restaurants

Praga (Прага), Arbat 2 (tel. 290 61 71). M: Arbatskaya (Арбатская). Luxurious open roof terrace with a splendid view of the Kremlin. Musical performances nightly 7-11pm. Good chow at lofty prices; get reservations early, or you'll have to pay dollars to get in. Open daily 11am-11pm; call at 11am.

Uzbekistan (Узбекистан), ul. Neglinnaya 29 (tel. 290 60 53). M: Pushkinskaya (Пушкин ская). A hangout for homesick Uzbeks, Kazakhs, and Tadzhiks. Noisy and always crowded; also popular with tourists. Try *tkhumdulma* (boiled egg with a fried meat patty) or *lagman khirgiz soup,* followed by *shashlyk* (shish kebab) Uzbek-style. Be sure to try the specially prepared Uzbek bread, baked on the premises. Open daily noon-midnight. Last entry 11:30pm. Reservations made up to 10 days in advance.

Slavyanskiy Bazar (Славянский Базар) ul. Dvadtsat' Piatovo Oktyabrya 17 (tel. 221 18 72). M: Prospekt Marska (Проспект Маркса). Once favored by wealthy Moscow merchants and the intelligentsia, now a haunt for private Soviet millionaires and mafiosi. Start off with a shot of vodka and *ikra* (caviar, 9R). An evening of drunken gluttony runs 100R. Open daily 11am-5pm and 6-11pm; last entry 10:30pm.

Aragvi (Арагви), ul. Tverskaya 6 (tel. 229 37 62). M: Prospekt Marksa (Проспект Маркса), then turn right as you exit; ul. Tverskaya is at the 1st street. Entrance on pl. Sovetskaya. Georgian cuisine. Stalin's favorite. Waiters are notoriously sleazy. Don't part with your dollars, as you undoubtedly will be asked to do. Specialities include *satsivi* (cold chicken in walnut sauce), *suluguni* (fried cheese), *shashlyk* (shish kebab), *kharcho* (spicy tomato soup), and caviar. Have a bottle of *Mukuzani* or *Tsinandali* with your meal. Full dinner with alcohol 50R. Open daily noon-midnight. Last entry 11:30pm.

Hotel Moskva (Москва), Manezhnaya pl., next to Red Square. Restaurant entrance around the back. Buffet smorgasbord *(shvedskiy stol)* especially popular with the bureaucrats across the street at Gosplan. Open daily for breakfast (7.50R, 8am-10:30am) and lunch (15R, noon-4pm).

Cooperatives

Some of the best cooperatives which served meals for rubles when they first opened have now switched to hard currency only . . . Sovietism capitalist style. If you want to blow some dollars, try the Italian **Lasagna,** ul. Pyatnitskaya 40 (tel. 231 10 85) for delicate pasta dishes, **Trens-Mos,** pr. Komsomolskiy 21 (tel. 245 12 16), the first American restaurant in Moscow, or **The Manila,** ul. Vavilova 88 (tel. 132 00 55). Otherwise, here are some of the best cooperatives for rubles:

U Pirosmani (У Пиросмани), Novodevichy pr. 4 (tel. 247 19 26), across from the Novodevichy Convent. M: Sportivnaya (Спортивная). A welcome relief from the usual potato-and-sour-cream formula. Specializing in delicately-spiced Georgian cuisine, this cooperative stands above the rest for its flavorful dishes, served with panache by an experienced staff. Housed in an airy log cabin decorated with copies of the naive artist Pirosmani's canvases. Menu listed on a chalkboard at the entrance; ask the waiter to decipher. Meals run 50-75R. Open daily noon-10pm. Dinner reservations a must.

Delhi (Дели), ul. Krasnaya Presnya 25 (tel. 252 17 66). M: ul. 1905 goda (ул. 1905 года). Turn left as you exit the station, heading toward the Stalinist tower at the end of the avenue. The restaurant is next to the Olimp (олимп) sports store, in the blond-brick block of stores. Indian-Soviet venture has been suffering supply problems lately, so the lamb may be thin on the curry. But the gracious service (once you get past the Soviet doorman), the tasty meats and breads, and the iced drinks (!) make this a luxurious oasis. Show up at noon for lunch or reserve for dinner in the ruble room. Open daily.

Aist (Айст), ul. Malaya Bronnaya 1-8 (tel. 291 66 92). M: Pushkinskaya (Пушкинская). Walk past the crowd in front of McDonald's into this quiet, residential street. Hearty Russian soups and appetizers make this a cozy spot to sample solid Russian food—with cucumbers, potatoes and all the sour cream you can eat. Wraparound red velvet decor simulates a 70's opium den. Meals run 50-60R. Open daily noon-5pm and 6-10pm.

Sorok Chetyre (Сорок Четыре), Leningradskoye Shosse 44 (tel. 159 99 51). M: Voikovskaya (Войковская). Take the #6 trolley up three stops from the Metro along the avenue. Moscow's yuppie crowd gathers here to gnaw on *shashlyk* (shish kebab) and listen to the jazz band in this pseudo steak-house. Open daily noon-11pm.

Zaidi i Poprobuy (Зайди и Попробуй), pr. Mira 124 (tel. 286 75 03). M: Shcherbakovskaya (Щербаковская), then take the trolley bus a couple of stops north. Entrance on side street. The name of this establishment literally means "come and try," which is what the Mafia did two years ago when they firebombed the place for refusing to hand over protection money. Undaunted, the owners rebuilt and added a militia man to guard the entrance. The newly-decorated rooms resemble a bunker with classical motif. Skip the 10R Russian beer and try the *tarkhun* (tarragon soda) drink with your meat and potatoes. Tasty ice-cream sundaes. Slightly overpriced. Open daily noon-11pm.

Cafés

Kafe Sever (Север), ul. Tverskaya 17 (tel. 229 41 65). M: Pushkinskaya (Пушкинская). The name means "north"; cool off here amidst walrus murals and the best ice-cream sundaes in Moscow. Open daily 10am-3pm and 4-10pm. Last entry 9:30pm.

Kafe Stoleshniki (Столешники), Stoleshnikov per. 4, between ul. Pushkinskaya and ul. Tverskaya. Noteworthy for its intimate atmosphere—bare brick walls and candlelight. 5R cover includes a dish and a drink. Open daily noon-11pm.

Kafe Ivushka (Ивушка), pr. Kalinina 28. Tacky jazz band jams nightly from 7-10pm; tickets (5R) usually sell out by 6:30pm. Open daily 11am-5pm, 6-10pm.

Kafe Ogni Moskvy (огни Москвы) on the 15th floor of the Hotel Moskva, 1 block from Red Square. Good cheap food and a terrific view, if you can fight your way onto the elevator. Open daily 11am-5pm and 6-11pm. Last entry 10:30pm.

Liban, ul. Tverskaya 24. Middle Eastern kebabs and succulent shawarma (9R) at this stand-up co-op. Open daily 10am-9pm.

Café Margarita (Маргарита), ul. Malaya Bronnaya, opposite the pond. Trendy café named in honor of Bulgakov's masterpiece, which opened in the park across the street. Have a cup of tea and cake and watch the artsy crowd smoke away the afternoon. Open daily 9am-10:30pm.

Hard Rock Cafe Music Bar, in Gorky Park in the basement of the Victoria Restaurant, near the Zelyeni Theater (look for the yellow-and-red sign). Light fare unconnected to the infamous chain, but no signs of a copyright suit yet. Open daily 4-10pm.

Kafe Olad'i (Кафе оладьи), ul. Pushkinskaya 9 or ul. Gertsena 15, just past the Tchaikovsky Conservatory. Both branches share the same namesake dish: small, sweet pancakes with chocolate sauce (30к). Pushkinskaya branch open daily 9am-7pm. Gertsena branch open Mon.-Sat. 10am-3pm and 4:15-10pm.

Kafe Russkiye Pelmeni (Русские Пельмены), Arbat 52. A fun spot to taste classic Siberian *pelmeni* (boiled meat-filled dumpling, 2.80R). Music at 7pm (4R cover charge). Open daily 11am-4pm and 5-11pm. Last entry 10:30pm.

Vody Lagidze (Воды Лагидзе), Arbat 42, downstairs in the Georgian cultural center. Part of a nationwide chain offering flavored soda water. This branch has reliably tasty *khachapuri* (a type of Georgian cheese lasagna) too. Open daily 11am-10pm.

Markets

To replenish your diet after too many potato and sour cream salads, go to one of the farmer's markets—*rynok* (рынок)—where Russians, as well as Georgians, Armenians, Uzbeks and peasants from all over the USSR truck in their fresh fruit and flowers to sell for whatever the market will bear. Shelves burst with exotic vegetables and spices, fresh cheese and honeycombs. Bring a steely determination to bargain, a fistful of rubles and trinkets such as pens and cigarettes. The best and priciest market is the **Novocheryomushkinskiy Rynok** (M: Profsoyuznaya/Профсоюзная, then take the bus up two stops—ask a *babushka* which one goes to the *rynok.)* Other good markets are at M: Baumanskaya (Бауманская) and M: Tsvetnoi Bul'var (Цветной Бульвар).

If you hanker for Western groceries such as yogurt or kiwi fruit, two hard-currency joint ventures can satisfy your palate (their products also make nice gifts for Soviets). **Sadko,** ul. Bolshaya Dorogmilovskaya (M: Kievskaya/Киевская, then three blocks up left on ul. B. Dorogmilovskaya, next to the Восход stationery store) has shorter lines if you pay by credit card, now that Soviets with dollars shop here also. (Open Mon.-Sat. 10am-3pm and 4-8pm.) The Finnish **Stockmann** is a fully-stocked grocery emporium for credit cards only. Take the Metro to Paveletskaya/Павелецкая, get out on the side of the street opposite the train station, and walk up left two blocks; past the blini (блины) stand on your left and behind the white curtains is the glassed-in store. (Open daily 10am-8pm.)

Sights

Lenin's historical legacy has finally come into question, and his name and face are coming down all over Moscow. The Party, so to speak, is finally over. The *pièce de résistance* of Leninmania was, of course, the **Lenin Mausoleum,** that red marble bunker in Red Square, where his pale and refrigerated remains went on display after he died in 1924 (though his brain went to a special laboratory charged with understanding great Communist minds). By 1992 the mausoleum may be torn down; like Americans and the Statue of Liberty, many Soviets will tell you they've never been. Expect similar revisionism at the nearby **Kremlin Wall,** burial site for Soviet greats such as Josef Stalin, Leonid Brezhnev, Maxim Gorky, Yuri Gagarin, John Reed, and Jim Morrison.

If you have a real appetite for Lenin memorabilia, there is no better place to satiate it than the **Central Lenin Museum.** Containing everything from his Rolls-Royce to his underpants, the Graceland of Russia is located at pl. Revolyutsii 2, just off Red Square. (Open Tues.-Fri. 10:30am-7pm, Sat.-Sun. 9:30am-6pm. Free.) If current trends continue, this may be your last chance to stock up on the museum's classic array of Soviet propaganda. Another good place to take in a little Communist agitation is the Historical Museum next door. Unfortunately, the museum is closed indefinitely for revisionism, er . . . um . . . repairs.

Across Red Square stands the Soviet Union's most distinctive structure, **St. Basil's Cathedral** (собор Василия Блаженого). Legend holds that after the cathedral was completed, Ivan the Terrible had the architects' eyes gouged out to ensure that they would never build anything more beautiful. The interior, now a museum, disappoints after the overwhelming exterior, but still merits a peek. Note the hallway's flat brick ceilings, which according to some engineers defy the laws of physics. (Open Wed.-Mon. 9:30am-5:30pm. Ticket office open 9:30am-5pm. Admission 40к.)

The ultimate icon of Soviet power and centralization is the **Kremlin,** Moscow's 69-acre centerpiece. The 20m-high, 10m-thick walls date from the 14th-century reign of Ivan III (the Great, not the Terrible). The massive palaces and cathedrals inside demand a tour guide or a detailed guidebook. The **Annunciation Cathedral,** with an iconostasis by the great painters Andrei Rublyev and Theophan the Greek, stands near the **Archangel Cathedral,** where Ivan the Terrible and other tsars repose. Not far away stands the huge **Assumption Cathedral,** where the tsars were crowned; Ivan the Terrible's custom-made coronation throne still resides proudly by the south portal. Napoleon, always respectful of tradition, set up his stables here. The very plain **Church of the Twelve Apostles** was Patriarch Nikon's 17th-century answer to the extravagant 16th-century madness of St. Basil's. Purchase tickets for the cathedrals at booths in Alexandrovsky Gardens just outside the Kremlin Wall along pr. Marksa. (Open Fri.-Wed. 10am-7pm; Oct.-April Fri.-Wed. 10am-5pm. Admission 20к per cathedral, 1R for all; students 50к. Ticket booth open 10am-5:30pm. Group tours of the Kremlin grounds and cathedrals can be arranged through Intourist.) Shorts and large bags are no-nos inside the Kremlin complex; you can check bags near the gate. To experience the glory and wealth of tsarist Russia, visit the **Armory Museum.** Located within the Kremlin next to Borovitsky Gate, the Armory contains the armor, gowns, jewels, silver, thrones, and carriages of the tsars. The **Diamond Fund,** an annex of the Armory, houses Catherine the Great's incredible crown of 5000 diamonds, and the famous Fabergé eggs. (Group tours only; arrange through Intourist. Admission up to a laughable USD18 per person, but these unequalled treasures really merit parting with hard currency.)

While most of those inside the Kremlin walls at any given moment are likely to be pink-shirted, camera-clicking tourists, there are also a sizable number of dark-suited men stepping out of black limousines. They may be headed for the yellow **Grand Kremlin Palace,** where the Supreme Soviet, Russia's newly democratic parliament, meets. The modern white-marble **Palace of Congresses** stages ballet and opera performances throughout the summer. After the thwarted coup of August 1991, it was here that the Congress of People's Deputies, in a badly choreographed, globally televised spectacle, met to dissolve itself and appoint an interim State Council to run the country. Leaving the Kremlin from Trinity Gate, next to the Palace, you enter the **Alexandrovsky Gardens.** At the northern end, the eternal flame of the **Tomb of the Unknown Soldier** flickers in memory of the country's 25 million World War II dead. Urns containing soil from the 12 "hero cities" of World War II stand in silent testimony to the Soviet Union's losses. On Saturday afternoons, lucky brides take wedding pictures here while older widows file past to lay bouquets on the tomb.

Directly across Red Square from the Kremlin stands **GUM** (ГУМ), the arch-department store of the Soviet Union. The store's architecture alone makes it worth a visit, but don't expect to do any serious shopping and be prepared to fight through the crowds of out-of-towners. An exception is the first-rate selection of pins *(znachki;* back of the third aisle). Turn right out of GUM's front doors and follow ul. 25 Oktyabrya to the erstwhile **Dzerzhinskaya ploshchad',** named after the founder of the Cheka (the notorious predecessor to the KGB). His statue was toppled in the coup. On one side of the square is the Soviet Union's premier toy store, **Detskiy Mir** (Децкий Мир). Across the street, the huge ochre building suspiciously lacking identification plaques is the **Lubyanka,** Russia's most infamous political prison, and the current headquarters of the KGB. Untold victims of the Stalinist purges were tortured within its walls.

About halfway up ul. Tverskaya from Red Square, **Pushkin Square** (M: Pushkinskaya/Пушкинская), where Pushkin's statue now looks down on McDonald's, is Moscow's favorite rendezvous spot. Amateur politicians gather on the square to argue and hand out petitions. Follow ul. Bolshaya Bronnaya, next to McDonalds, down through a quiet, elite neighborhood; at the bottom of the hill, turn right and follow ul. Malaya Bronnaya to the Patriarch's Pond, where Bulgakov's *Master and Margarita* opens. Several blocks away, the **Arbat,** a pedestrian shopping arcade, was once a showpiece of *glasnost,* a haven for political radicals, Hare Krishnas, street poets, and *metallisti* (heavy metal rockers). Tourism has changed all this, and the street is now the kitsch souvenir capital of Moscow—buy your Gorby doll here, and hold on to your wallet. Still, late at night, a stroll along the Arbat gives you a feel for what life was like when Pushkin lived here. Midway up, on a side street, is a graffiti wall dedicated to the memory of rocker Victor Tsoi of the Soviet group

Kino, who served as an idol to many lost young souls before his death in a car crash last year.

For the best views of the Kremlin, walk behind St. Basil's, across the bridge and along the far bank of the Moskva River, or take a ride on one of the sight-seeing boats. Head downstream to Kolomenskoye or upstream to Gorky Park; the boats stop at every bridge along the way (every 20 min., 1.05R). Guided tour boats leave from Rossiya Hotel (behind St. Basil's) Monday, Wednesday, and Friday at 3:30pm (2 hr., 6R). From M: Park Kultury (Парк Културы), cross the **Krimskiy Most** bridge to **Gorky Park**—officially the **Order of Lenin Park of Culture and Rest in the name of Maksim Gorky.** This is Moscow's amusement park, where droves of out-of-towners and young Muscovites promenade and relax. From the top of the slow-moving Ferris wheel (20к), you can watch the slow-moving Ferris wheel line. Huge outdoor speakers blare energetic tunes day in and day out, and in winter the paths are flooded to create a park-wide ice rink; rent skates. On weekends and Friday after 5pm, there is a 1R admission charge for the park. Across the street from the entrance looms the huge modern **Main Exhibition Hall** (Дом Художников), which sometimes shows independent avant-garde artists along with the usual retrospectives.

One of the Soviet Union's premier art galleries, the **Tretyakov Art Gallery** (M: Tretyakovskaya/Третяаковская) houses a superb collection of Russian and Soviet art beneath its traditional peaked roofs. The museum is undergoing major reconstruction, but a state-of-the-art modern new wing has just been reopened and is hosting exhibits. The **Pushkin Museum of Fine Arts** at ul. Volkhonka 12 (M: Kropotkinskaya/Кропоткинская) boasts a strong collection of European Renaissance and Classical art, as well as a collection of ancient and medieval artifacts less haphazard than those in most Soviet museums. (Open Wed.-Sun. 10am-8pm, Tues. 10am-9pm, holidays 10am-6pm. Admission 40к.)

For a museum of a different kind, take a tour of the **Metro**—it is not merely the most efficient means of transportation in Moscow. Each station sports original artwork and phantasmagoric chandeliers. In efficiency, it dusts most capitalist systems; trains are seldom more than 2 min. apart. Ring line stations are the most spectacular, notably Komsomolskaya (Комсомольская). The polished chrome and mosaics of Mayakovskaya (Маяковская) station also deserve a look, as do the art-deco stations of the dark blue line, such as Ploshchad' Revolyutsii (Площадь Революции).

For a taste of the average Muscovite's life, take the Metro out of the city center to a random stop and stroll among the apartment and shopping complexes. When you have become sufficiently depressed, get back on the Metro and head for **Moscow State University** (also known as MGU or МГУ) at M: Universitet (Университет). The entire university lives within a single Stalinist edifice; to appreciate fully the structure's size, you must see it at close range. You need a pass to enter the university premises, but talking to a guard (try to do it in Russian, however broken) may get you in. Nearby in the Lenin Hills (a leafy enclave overlooking the city center) is a viewing area from which you can see the **Luzhniki Sports Complex** and all of Moscow behind it. Sticking out like a sore thumb is **Lenin Stadium,** second largest in the world and site of the 1980 Olympics. On the way back, stop off at M: Kropotkinskaya (Кропоткинская). Nearby is the **Moscow Swimming Pool,** a heated outdoor tub where a beautiful cathedral once soared. Stalin tore it down, intending to erect a palace of Soviets, but the ground proved too soft. (Many say it's a curse.) If you swim, watch your clothes, shoes, and valuables. (Open Mon.-Sat. 6:55am-9:15pm, Sun. 7am-7:45pm. Pay per 45 min. session).

Russians are very good at preserving authors' houses in their original state, down to the half-empty teacups on the mantelpiece. Each is guarded by a team of *babushki* fiercely loyal to their master's memory. At ul. Lva Tolstovo 21 is the **Leo Tolstoy House Museum,** the mansion where Tolstoy lived and worked from 1882-1901. (M: Frunzenskaya/Фрунзенская. Open Tues.-Sun. 10am-5:30pm; in off-season Tues.-Sun. 10am-3pm. Closed the last Fri. of every month.) At ul. Sadovaya-Kurdrinskaya 6 is **Chekhov's House Museum,** where Chekhov lived from 1886-

1890. (M: Barrikadnaya/Барикадная. Open Tues., Thurs., and Sat.-Sun. 11am-6pm, Wed. and Fri. 11am-9pm. Admission 40к, evenings 60к.) **Gorky's Flat Museum,** ul. Kachalova 6-2, is particularly interesting for its interior. The main staircase is designed to project the feeling and movement of waves on the sea. (Open Wed. and Fri. noon-8pm, Thurs. and Sat. 10am-5:45pm, Sun. 10am-5:30pm. Closed the last Thurs. of the month. Free.) **Dostoevsky's Flat Museum** is at ul. Dostoevskovo 2 behind the star-shaped Red Army Theater. (M: Novoslobodskaya/Новослободская. Open Sat.-Mon. and Thurs. 11am-6pm, Wed. 10am-4pm, Fri. 1-9pm.)

When you can't take the grime and bedlam any more, escape to one of Moscow's hidden parks or resplendent monasteries. Among these is the **Novodevichi Convent** (Новодевичи монастырь), several blocks from M: Sportivnaya (Спор тивная). Here Boris Godunov ingeniously planned his election as tsar in 1598; later tsars and noblemen kept the coffers filled by exiling their well-dowried wives and daughters here when they grew tired of them. **Smolenskiy Cathedral** is exquisite; two-hour church services still fill the refectory (the long red and white building to the right of the entrance). Exact times are posted on the front door; come around 8am or 6pm and you can wander in and out (women should bring a shawl to cover their heads). Down the street, the convent's **cemetery** cradles the graves of Gogol, Chekhov, Stanislavsky, Khrushchev, Mayakovsky, and other luminaries. The gravestones, often statues or engravings of the deceased, are museum pieces. Avoid visiting the convent on Sundays, when tour buses hog the place. (Convent open Mon. and Thurs.-Sat. 10am-5:30pm, Wed. and Sun. 10am-7:30pm. Cathedral open Mon. and Wed.-Sun. 10am-5:30pm. Both closed 1st Mon. of the month. Comprehensive admission 40к, students 15к. Cemetery open Tues.-Sun. 11am-4pm. Admission 1R.)

Another relatively untouristed respite from Moscow's chaos is the tsars' **Kolomenskoye Summer Residence,** on a wooded rise above the Moskva River (a 10-min. walk from M: Kolomenskaya (Коломенская). Peter the Great's 1702 log cabin and Bratsk Prison, where the persecuted Archpriest Avvakum wrote his celebrated autobiography, have been moved here from Arkhangelsk and Siberia respectively. The sloping lawns ease into both the Moskva River and one of Moscow's many working farms. (Grounds open daily 7am-10pm. Free. Museums open Wed.-Thurs. 1-8pm; Oct.-April Wed.-Sun. 11am-6pm. Admission 80к per museum, students 30к.) **Izmailovskiy Park** (M: Izmailovskaya/Измайловская) spreads to the northeast of the the city center, flooded in winter by hordes of gung-ho cross-country skiers. On Saturdays and Sundays, get off at M: Izmailovskiy Park (Изма йловский Парк) and walk towards the stadium for Moscow's largest bazaar, where you can buy all sorts of paraphernalia, including papier-mâche Brezhnev masks, old coins, samovars and lacquer boxes (be sure to bargain). In summer the park has tent **circuses** that are less polished but more traditional than Moscow's famous Old and New Circuses. Tickets for all of them must be purchased in advance at your hotel service bureau or a street kiosk.

To get a real feeling for Russian culture, attend an Orthodox service. One 17th-century jewel of a place is the **Church of St. Nicholas** at Komsomolskiy pr. and ul. Frunze (M: Frunzenskaya/Фрунзенская). Daily services are at 9:30am and 6pm; women must cover their heads. Stand out of the way and keep respectfully silent or a Rasputin-like figure may ask you to leave. The **Yelokhovskiy Cathedral,** ul. Spartakovskaya 15 (M: Baumanskaya/Бауманская), is Moscow's largest and most beautiful operational church. (Services Mon. and Sat. 8am and 6pm, Sun. and holidays 7am and 10am.) Another ecclesiastic gem is the 18th-century **Church of Ionna Voina,** on ul. Dimitrova (M: Oktyabr'skaya/октябрьская), named after the patron saint of the tsar's musketeers. (Services daily 8am and 6pm.)

A major excursion for Soviets from other republics is to the **Exhibition of Economic Achievements** (known by its initials ВДНХ), an immense park with dozens of pavilions detailing progress made in education, technology, and medicine—a veritable Communist Manifestival. Rabid anti-Soviets may take pleasure in the fact that usually a third of the exhibits are continually closed for repairs. Especially popular is the **Kosmos** exhibit, with a model of Yuri Gagarin's spaceship. The park is on pr. Mira opposite the Kosmos Hotel (M: ВДНХ). West of the park is luxurious **Ostankino Palace,** now a museum of serf art in the shadow of its namesake TV tower. (Open daily 10am-5pm; in off-season 10am-2pm. Free.)

Moscow's **beryozkas** are well stocked but pricey. Items include Siberian fur, Baltic amber, and those ubiquitous lacquer boxes. The **Mezhdunarodnaya Hotel** (M: Krasnopresenskoye/Краснопресенское, then bus #4), built by American businessman Armand Hammer, has a few *beryozka* and resembles an American mall. Be sure to bring your passport to get in the door. (Open daily 9am-2pm and 3-8pm.) The **Book Beryozka,** ul. Kropotinskaya 31 (M: Kropotinskaya/Кропотинская), sells Russian classics in Russian (hard to come by in ruble stores and thus a good gift for Soviet friends) and art books in English. Pick up your photo guide to the Moscow metro here (4R).

To shop with Russians, walk along **Prospekt Kalinina,** Moscow's most glamorous retail boulevard. At the **Melodiya** record store, pr. Kalinina 40, you can find hard-to-get Russian classics and records by popular Soviet and Western artists. (Lenin's speeches 35к. Led Zeppelin's *Stairway to Heaven* 3.50R. Open daily 9am-9pm.) **Dom Knigi** (Дом Книги), pr. Kalinina 26, stocks a wide selection of books in many languages, as well as colorful propaganda posters. The **Souvenirs** (Сувениры) poster store, at ul. Arbat 4, around the corner from the Praga Restaurant, has an even better selection (9-15к per poster). (Open Mon.-Sat. 10:30am-2pm and 3-7:30pm.) The store **Vesna** (Весна), at ul. Gor'kovo 37 (M: Mayakovskaya/Маыаковская), has heaps of Russian souvenirs for rubles, including tea sets and painted woodwork. (Open Mon.-Sat. 9am-8pm.) Moscow's outdoor **pet market** (птичьий рынок) happens every Sunday on a suburban back street; *babushki* line the sidewalk trading kittens, salamanders and goldfish. From M: Taganskaya (Таганская), take tram #35 up two stops.

Entertainment

It is not true that Moscow has no nightlife; the problem is that it usually begins at about 6pm and ends by midnight—making it difficult to combine eating and entertainment. Choose between the stomach and the spirit, or, if you have a sense of irony and appreciate kitsch culture *à la Russe,* try the bands and floor shows at some of Moscow's bigger restaurants. For sheer weirdness, the electric gypsy beat of the band at Pekin Hotel (see Restaurants) is hard to beat. The Café Ivushka (see Cafés) has jazz from 7pm, and the Praga Restaurant has nightly chamber music. Adventurous drinkers can visit the **Zhiguli** (Жигули), pr. Kalinina 19, one of Moskva's rowdiest beer halls. The proletariat come here to snozzle dried salted fish, the perfect accompaniment to nasty Soviet beer. (Open daily 11am-9pm. Women may feel uncomfortable here.)

Moscow's rock scene, though weak by St. Petersburg standards, has begun to produce some decent young bands, as well as a series of amusingly terrible pop cuts. Laskovy Mai, the Russian New Kids on the Block, are particularly dismal. (Check theater kiosks for tickets.) Up-and-comers generally perform in small auditoriums and "palaces of culture." To find out what's going on during your stay, drop by the Moscow Rock Laboratory, an association of bands which sponsors shows year-round, at Staropanskiy pereulok 1/5, 2nd floor, room 4 (tel. 923 16 04), just a couple of blocks north of Red Square. (Open Mon.-Sat. 10am-5pm, but somebody is almost always around.)

After 10pm when the sidewalks roll up, most Russians find entertainment in each others' apartments, drinking glass after glass of tea or vodka and arguing about art, politics, sports, and the meaning of life. Today's Muscovites can meet all their late-night alcohol needs, from wine to vodka to Teacher's whiskey, at the new **Night Store** (Ночной Магазин) in the гастроном on ul. Shabalovka; from M: Oktyabr'skaya (октябрьская), walk down ul. Shabalovska to the first street on your right, and go up the stairs next to the glowing red-and-white sign. (Open nightly 11pm-2am and 3-6am.)

Your best bet for traditional entertainment in Moscow is the official stuff: the ballet, the symphony, and—yes—the circus and puppet theater. The **Bolshoi Ballet** (tel. 292 99 86) is usually away on tour over the summer; accepting Intourist-arranged substitutes can be disappointing, as quality varies widely. Try the program at the mammoth **Tchaikovsky Concert Hall,** ul. Bolshaya Sadovaya 20 (tel. 299 34 87), next to M: Mayakovskaya (Маяковская). Catch a quartet or a symphony for mere pennies at the world-famous **Tchaikovsky Conservatory,** down the block at ul. Gertsena, which has witnessed performances in its small and large halls by Van Cliburn, Richter and Horowitz (among others). Moscow's theaters have been venturing increasingly avant-garde productions of late, and if your Russian is less than fluent, this makes them all the harder to understand. Still, it's worth looking into some of the better companies: the **Moscow Art Theater** (better known by the acronym MXAT, pronounced "EM-hot"; tel. 203 66 22), with a new home at Tverskoy bul. 22 and a tradition going back 90 years to the days of Stanislavsky, Chekhov, and the young Gorky; the **Sovremennik Theater,** located at Chistoprudny bul. 19a (tel. 297 18 19; M: Kirovskaya/Кировская); and the **Taganka Theater of Drama and Comedy** which stands at ul. Chkalova 76 (tel. 272 63 00; M: Taganskaya/Таганская). The **Stanislavky Theater,** 21 ul. Gor'kovo (M: Pushkinskaya/Пушкинская), is a favorite among Moscow's intellectuals. (Tickets easily available at the Kassa (Касса) during the day for evening performances.) Moscow's famed **Obraztsov Puppet Theater,** ul. Sadovo-Samotekhnaya 3 (tel. 299 63 13), isn't just for kids; much of the audience sports ties. The technically impressive slapstick productions hurdle all language barriers. Don't turn up your nose at Moscow's top-notch **Old** and **New Circuses** (цирк); besides first-rate acrobatics, tiger taming and clowns, they're an excellent window into Soviet working-class culture.

Tickets to ballets, theater events, and circuses can all be purchased for rubles at street kiosks; some of the better ones are on ul. Gor'kovo and pr. Marksa. Also try the **Central Excursion Bureau** (see Tourist Offices above) early in the morning of the day you wish to see a performance; although they often sell out sooner than kiosks and you'll have to pay hard currency, their information is centralized and in English. The **National Hotel** has a helpful service bureau; if you encounter trouble entering the building without a pass, tell the attendant you're going to the *beryozka* or the bathroom. In general, if you are told an event is sold out, be dogged and look elsewhere. Small gifts may make an uncooperative cashier more resourceful, and you can sometimes get a ticket in front of the theater just before curtain time.

If you get a chance, go to a Russian soccer game. The local teams **Dinamo, Spartak, TsSKA,** and **Torpedo** draw crowds, but real cheering is reserved for international games (held at Lenin Stadium; M: Sportivnaya/Спортивная). The complex also has two ice rinks that sport frequent hockey games in winter.

Near Moscow

There are scores of fascinating sights beyond the 25km limit of your visa. If something in the great beyond interests you, the legal solution is the Central Excursion Bureau (see Orientation and Practical Information above). They'll prepare the visa in about a day and charge a flat rate in hard currency for the excursion, including transportation. However, enforcement has loosened, nearly to the point of non-existence; if you are discreet and can decipher Cyrillic, you can just as easily hop on the *elektrichka* (commuter rail) and join all the other Muscovites for an afternoon much more rewarding than the Intourist bus routine. Bringing a Russian friend will smooth your passage.

Zagorsk (Загорск), about 60km from Moscow, hosts one of the Soviet Union's four remaining active monasteries. There are several beautiful cathedrals, some with original icon screens by Rublev and his followers. The one-day Intourist tour to Zagorsk leaves Wednesday and Friday at 9:45am from the Intourist Hotel (25R). (Museum at the monastery open Tues.-Sun. 10am-6pm.) To get there by yourself, take the *elektrichka* marked Aleksandrovsk (Александровск) from Moscow's

Yaroslavskiy station (1½ hr., round-trip 3.20R). The monastery complex is visible from the Zagorsk train station.

The daytrip you should try hardest to make is to **Vladimir** (Владимир) and **Suzdal'** (Суздаль), both 230km from Moscow. Vladimir, the capital of medieval Muscovy, has a beautiful church that inspired the Assumption Cathedral in the Kremlin. Suzdal' was famous for its churches-to-inhabitants ratio of one-to-four; the town is well-preserved as a showcase "museum city" and still hosts five monasteries in a pastoral setting of distinctly Russian beauty. 15-hour Intourist tours leave Sunday at 8am from the Intourist Hotel (30R); there is so much to see and the towns are so distant from Moscow that the Intourist tour is worth the km-by-km narrative and enforced guided tours.

Closer to the city, just beyond the outer ring road, but a world away with its wooden dachas and birch-tree groves, lies **Peredelkino** (Переделкино)—the writers' colony where Pasternak is buried (his house has just been opened as a museum). The walk to the cemetery across the fields from the fairy-tale church takes you on a path through the Russian soul. Take the *elektrichka* marked Aprelyovka (Апр елёвка) to Peredelkino from Moscow's Kievskiy station. Once there, take the path to the right toward the pines.

St. Petersburg С. Петербург

Upon returning from a tour of Western Europe in 1703, Peter the Great decided that his backward empire needed a new capital to replace hopelessly provincial Moscow, a cosmopolis on the level of Paris or Berlin, a "Window on the West"—and the swampy Neva delta at the edge of the Gulf of Finland became St. Petersburg. The 18th and 19th centuries saw Peter's idea ripen into a tsarist showpiece. Importing French and Italian architects, the Russian aristocracy spared no expense, bedecking the city with baroque and neoclassical mansions, landscaped parks, and carefully planned canals and streets. St. Petersburg's predilection for Western ideas eventually rebounded on the glamorous society and aristocracy which danced the 19th century into oblivion. Marxism took root here in the 1870s, setting in motion the revolutionary vanguard that brought the Bolshevik Revolution in 1917, and Russified the city's name to Petrograd. In 1924, after Lenin's death, it was officially renamed **Leningrad** (Ленинград). In World War II, the dehumanizing 900-day Siege of Leningrad claimed the lives of 650,000 citizens.

While the city's architecture recalls some of the European sophistication which once distinguished the city from isolated, Asiatic Moscow, three quarters of a century of Communist rule have long since evened things out. Here, as in other Soviet cities, long lines snake around generic "Bread" and "Meat" stores punched into the crumbling façades of former mansions. Yet here and there a bit of the old glitter remains as residents, taking advantage of the new openness in Soviet society, attempt to salvage imperial ghosts from the Proletarian night. Radical democratic insurgents dominate the political scene, having come to power in the landslide City Council elections of 1990; at the same time, the neo-fascist group Pamyat, the anti-Semitic underbelly of *glasnost,* began here. In a June 1991 referendum, Leningrad residents broke through the final semiotic frontier, voting to change the city's name back to St. Petersburg. In September, the interim State Council in Moscow approved the change.

Orientation and Practical Information

St. Petersburg is in the northwestern Soviet Union, just six hours by train from Helsinki, Finland. Traveling from Helsinki to St. Petersburg independently is simple; see Getting There in the country introduction. St. Petersburg was built on a series of islands in the swampy delta of the **Neva River,** and the city is laced with canals. The historical heart of the city is the **Peter and Paul Fortress** (Петопа вловская крепость), where Peter the Great made his first settlement in 1703. St.

AT&T
The right choice.

Petersburg's major avenue, **Nevsky Prospekt** (Невский Проспект) starts at Palace Square (Дворцовая пл.), a few blocks south and across the river from the fortress, and heads east towards the Alexander Nevsky Monastery complex.

Tourist Office: Intourist Service Bureau, in the newly-reconstructed Astoria Hotel, Isaakievskaya pl. 2 (tel. 210 50 46 for excursions and theater information). Excursions leave daily for Petrodvorets, and several times per week for Pavlovsk and Pushkin (USD11.50).

Consulates: U.S., ul. Petra Lavrova 15 (tel. 274 82 35). Open Mon. and Wed.-Thurs. 2-4pm. Reading room open daily 9am-5pm.

Currency Exchange: Central Exchange Office, ul. Brodskovo 4, off Nevsky Prospekt. Open daily 9:30am-1pm, 2-6pm, and 6:30-8pm. **Hotel Moskva,** pl. Alexandra Nevskovo (M: pl. Alexandra Nevskovo (пл. Александра Невского). Open sporadically daily 8:30am-1pm and 2-8pm. Sometimes closed arbitrarily.

American Express: ul. Gertsena 36 (tel. 311 52 15). No currency exchange, but mail held, checks or credit cards replaced, and checks sold to cardholders. Open Mon.-Fri. 9am-5pm.

Post Office: ul. Soyuza Sviazi 9. Telegrams and faxes. Open Mon.-Sat. 9am-9pm, Sun. 10am-8pm, second Wed. of each month noon-9pm. True Russian capitalism: new slot machines crowd the entrance. Poste Restante at Nevsky Prospekt 6. Open daily 9am-2pm and 3-7pm. Address Poste Restante to До востребования, С-400, Nevsky Prospekt 6, St. Petersburg, USSR. All hotels sell stamps, envelopes, and postcards in the lobby.

Telephones: ul. Gertsena 3-5. Open 24 hrs., except 12:30-1pm. **City Code:** 812.

Flights: The main **airport** is **Pulkovo** (Пулково). Buses link it with the downtown **Aeroflot** office at ul. Gogolya roughly every hour (fare: 60к). If you are arriving on a tour, organized transportation will be provided automatically. **Foreign airline offices** include: **Finnair,** ul. Gogolya 19 (tel. 315 97 36). Open Mon.-Fri. 9am-5pm. **Pan Am's** heirs at ul. Gertsena 36 (tel. 311 58 20). Open Mon.-Fri. 9am-5pm.

Trains: St. Petersburg has 4 main railway stations—all accessible by Metro. Trains to Estonia, Lithuania, Latvia, and Poland leave from the **Varshavskiy** (Варшавский) station. M: Baltiyskaya (Балтийская). To Ukraine and Byelorussia from the **Vitebskiy** (Витебский) station. M: Pushkinskaya (Пушкинская). To Moscow and the rest of Russia from the **Moskovskiy** (Московский) station. M: pl. Vosstaniya (пл. Восстания). To Helsinki from the **Finlyandskiy** (Финляндский) station. M: pl. Lenina (пл. Ленина). Central ticket office (Кассы) for all rail travel is located at kanal Griboyedova 24. Open Mon.-Sat. 8am-8pm, Sun. 8am-4pm. Foreign tourists are officially required to purchase tickets for inflated prices at the special **Intourist** department inside the ticket office; they also handle international tickets. Open daily 8am-noon and 1-7pm.

Public Transportation: Buses, trolleys, and an efficient Metro system keep St. Petersburg humming (6am-1am). The crush on buses is guaranteed to thin you down. Metro fare 15к, buses 10к; bus and trolley tickets can be bought on board from the driver with correct change, or (better) at newsstands and kiosks. Maps with all routes can be purchased at most kiosks.

Instant Film Processing: Kodak Express, ul. Sofiya Perovskoi 7, off Nevsky Prospekt across from the Kazanskiy Cathedral. Brand new joint-venture which processes Kodak film for rubles (40R a roll), although new rolls must be bought with hard currency. Open daily 9am-9pm.

Emergencies: Police (tel. 02). **Ambulance** (tel. 03). **Fire** (tel. 01).

Food

St. Petersburg may lack the broader choice of new cooperative restaurants that Moscow now has, but travelers can still turn to a number of options. Restaurants usually close at 11pm, and reservations are highly advisable. Call or drop by in person around noon to secure a dinner spot for the same evening; else you may be left with few options come nightfall. Tap water is *not* safe to drink in St. Petersburg, and the bottled variety is putrid. Get foreign mineral water at Intourist hotels. The **covered market** at Kuznechniy per. 3 is just around the corner from M: Vladimirskaya (Владимирская). The produce is pricey, but refreshingly ripe (market open Mon.-Sat. 7am-9pm, Sun. 7am-7pm). Another excellent market is the **Patent Cooperative Trade Center,** ul. Nekrasova 53, at the top of Ligovskiy pr. (Open Tues.-Sun. 8am-7pm, Mon. 8am-4pm.) The **Moskva** hotel at the top of Nevsky (M: pl.

Alexandra Nevskovo/пл. Александра Невского) harbors a hard-currency store which stocks some produce.

Restaurants

Neva (Нева, Nevsky Prospekt 44. Azure elegance befitting a restaurant named for St. Petersburg's main waterway. A Russian feast including champagne, vodka, and caviar totals about 75R per person. Reservations recommended. Best to come at noon in person to snag a table. Open noon-5pm and 7pm-midnight.

Kavkazkiy (Кавказкий), Nevsky Prospekt 25 (tel. 311 39 77). Specializes in Caucasian cuisine. Try *kharcho* soup (a Georgian gazpacho), entrees of *shashlyk* (shish kebab), *chakhombili* (chicken in a spicy sauce), or the *cherbureki* (cakes of mutton, rice, and parsley). Sociable management. Open noon-6pm and 7-11pm.

Balkany (Балканы), Nevsky Prospekt 27. A grotto interior plus blaring Soviet top-40 hits liven up this state-run establishment. Dishes out kebabs and other southern delicacies. Open daily 11am-5pm and 6-10pm.

Moskva (Москва), pl. Alexandra Nevskovo, in the Moskva Hotel. Fixed-price *shvedskiy stol* (smorgasbord) buffet around 30R. Show up early to beat the crowd. Open daily noon-3pm.

Universal' (Универсаль), Nevsky Prospekt 106 (tel. 279 33 50). Classic Russian food, including caviar, *bliny,* and various fish entrees. Music. 60R per person. Open daily noon-5pm and 6-11pm.

Schwabskiy Domik (Швабский Домик), Krasnogvardeiskiy pr. 28 (tel. 528 22 11). M: Krasnogvardeiskaya (Красногвардейская). German joint-venture with hard-currency and ruble halls. Shows up at noon to buy a 35R meal ticket to the ruble room; it entitles you to a mug of beer, appetizers, and a seat at dinner. Open daily noon-11pm.

Chayka (Чайка), kanal Griboyedova 14. Western currencies buy you an express ticket to yuppiedom. Open daily 11am-3am.

Cafés

Kafe Saigon (Кафе Сайгон, Nevsky Prospekt 49, on the ground floor of the Moskva restaurant. St. Petersburg's premiere rock-and-roll hangout before it closed for a facial in 1989. Scheduled to reopen in 1992.

Kafe Sachino (Кафе Сачино), ul. Belinskovo 3, just off the Fontankina kanal. This cooperative café ladles out a terrific bowl of *kharcho,* a spicy Georgian soup (8.50R). After your meal, step next door to the **Dessert Hall,** which offers sub-ruble pastries. Café open daily 11am-11pm.

Literaturnoye Kafe (Литературное Кафе), Nevsky Prospekt 18 (tel. 312 85 36). A famous 19th-century chat spot for writers and artists, gracefully restored to its original elegance. Pushkin had his last meal here before departing for his fatal duel. Pricey, but unbeatable for champagne and sweets in the afternoon. Chamber music at night. Cover 5R. Open daily noon-5pm and 7-10pm.

Kafe Morozhenoye (Кафе Мороженое), Nevsky Prospekt 24, opposite the Kavkazkiy. St. Petersburg's premier ice cream parlor. Faded elegance and pastel green walls. Ice cream 80к per 200g with chocolate shavings 20к extra; glass of champagne 3R. Open daily 10am-2pm and 3-10pm.

Vody Lagidze (Воды Лагидзе), Nevsky Prospekt 22, down the stairs on the left in the courtyard, in front of the Italianate church; also at ul. Inzhinernaya 6. *Khachapuri* and flavored soda in your hour of need. Open daily 10am-4pm and 5-10pm.

Sights

St. Petersburg's cultural highlight is the **Hermitage** (Эрмитаж). Located in Palace Square in the magnificent **Winter Palace,** former residence of the tsars, this collection of art surely ranks among the world's finest. In Spanish works, it is surpassed only by the Prado in Madrid, while in Dutch paintings (especially Rembrandts) it reigns supreme. The museum also displays Flemish masters, above all Rubens, and works by Leonardo, Michelangelo, and Titian. The impressionist and 20th-century collections are also superlative. The Hermitage collection started with Catherine the Great's 24 paintings; it now includes 2½ million items, kept in about 1000 rooms. The building itself is a paragon of extravagance; before you immerse yourself in the art, admire the main halls and intricately carved and polished floors where the tsar reigned and entertained, especially the awesome **Malachite Hall,** where the Provisional Government held its last meeting in 1917. If you're lucky, the tsar's private apartments, complete with family portraits and a nursery, will be open. (Hermitage open Tues.-Sun. 9am-6pm. Admission 4R.) Inside a back entrance (on the Palace Square side) is a fine *beryozka* selling art books. Try to go with a tour group, or else arrive in the morning; the lines give new meaning to the Russian term for the Brezhnev years, "the time of stagnation."

If you're interested in Russian culture, the **Russian Museum** (Руский Музей) on the north side of pl. Isskustv (just off Nevsky Prospekt), is a must. Begin on the second floor with Rublev's 16th-century icons and work your way around and down; watch Russian art strive to catch up to the West through the 18th and 19th centuries, reach it at the end of the 19th, and finally burst into the lead in the early 20th with Kandinsky, Malevich, and Tatlin. Mercifully, the collection ends about 1930. (Open Wed.-Mon. 10am-6pm.)

For a splendid stew of the city, climb to the dome of **St. Isaac's Cathedral** (Исаакиевсий собор), on Isaakyevskaya pl., a massive example of 19th-century civic-religious architecture; the dome wears 100kg of pure gold. The murals and mosaics contained in the museum are the works of some of Russia's greatest artists; the chips in the marble columns are courtesy of German artillery fire. (Museum open Thurs.-Tues. 11am-7pm. Colonnades open Thurs.-Tues. 11am-4pm. Admission to museum 50к, students 25к. Admission to colonnades 30к, students 20к.) Also facing Isaakyevskaya pl. is the **Astoria Hotel,** just reopened after superb restoration by a Soviet-Finnish joint project. The building originally housed the German embassy; Hitler had invitations printed up for a victory celebration to be held here after taking the city. On nearby **pl. Dekabristov,** overlooking the Neva stands Falconet's **Monument to Peter the Great,** which inspired Pushkin's famous poem, *The Bronze Horseman.*

Inside the **Peter and Paul Fortress** (Петопавловская крепость), notice the artful counterplay of wood and marble, and the icons that illustrate the divine right of the tsars. Beyond the archway that leads out to the Neva are plaques commemorating the terrible floods that have repeatedly devastated St. Petersburg, including the one in 1824 which inspired Pushkin's famous poem *The Bronze Horseman.* The last few tsars used the fortress as a political prison where they hung many young radicals, including Alexander Ulyanov, Lenin's older brother. (Open June-Aug. Thurs.-Mon. 10am-7pm, Tues. 10am-4pm; Sept.-May Thurs.-Mon. 11am-6pm, Tues. 11am-4pm; closed last Tues. of each month. Admission 60к, students 35к.) Stroll around the palace to the City Beach, where people tan standing up to catch the warmth radiating from the walls. If you hold your life lightly, go for a swim.

Get acquainted with **Nevsky Prospekt** (Невский Проспект) via a tram or bus, or better yet, by walking up one side and down the other. It may seem like all 5 million of St. Petersburg's residents are jammed onto the sidewalks, and that 50% of them want to trade money or sell you a rabbit hat. Few other streets have played so prominent a role in Russian literature (Nikolai Gogol' devoted a whole novel to it). The street begins at the Admiralty, begun in 1727, whose golden spire towers over the Admiralty gardens and the magnificent Palace square. A few blocks down Nevsky at #28 is **Dom Knigi** (Дом Книги), St. Petersburg's main bookstore, whose rooftop globe dates from the building's pre-Revolutionary days as Russian headquarters of the Singer sewing machine company. Check out the collection of posters on the second floor. (Open Mon.-Sat. 10am-8pm.)

The colossal edifice across the street, based on St. Peter's in the Vatican, is **Kazan Cathedral** (Казанский собор), which has serve as the **Museum of the History of Religion and Atheism** since the Revolution. It should soon return to the church. (Open Tues. and Thurs. 11am-6pm. Closed last Thurs. of every month. Admission 40к, students 20к.) The exhibits lack English labels, but be sure to check out the enormous painting of Leo Tolstoy in hell. (Tolstoy's un-Orthodox religious views led to his excommunication in 1901.) The plaza between the cathedral's wings is St. Petersburg's center of alternative, "informal" political, and cultural activity. New political parties deliver speeches from the east wing; political discussion circles gather starting about 8pm. Monarchists, anarchists, fascists, and hypnotists—they're all here, and it's a great place to meet Russians ravenous for contact with the West.

Further down Nevsky Prospekt at #35, stands the pale yellow **Gostiny dvor** (Гостинный двор), St. Petersburg's largest department store, currently gutted and undergoing renovation. St. Petersburg's chintzy tourist art market centers around **Ploshchad' Ostrovskovo** with its equestrian statue of Catherine the Great. (No other connections between Catherine the Great and horses can be definitely established, despite what you may have heard.) Check the **Gastronom** (Гастроном) across the street for a hint of what shopping used to be like in the Imperial Capital. For now, the crystal chandeliers and mirrored interior reflect only wilted cucumbers and dusty bottles of juice.

The halfway point of Nevsky Prospekt is marked by the Moskovskiy train station, which faces onto **Uprising Square** (Ploshchad' Vosstaniya). From the square, it's only one Metro stop to the top of St. Petersburg's main street, where the Neva River again swings into view (M: pl. Aleksandra Nevskovo/пл. Александра Не вского). Here, within the **Alexander Nevsky Lavra** (Лавра Александра Не вского) monastery are two **cemeteries;** such luminaries as Tchaikovsky, Lomonosov, and Dostoevsky repose here. Buy a ticket to the tomb museum. (Open Fri.-Wed. 11am-7pm. Admission 60к, students 35к.) **Trinity Cathedral,** also within the monastery, holds services daily at 10am and 6pm, and at 6:30 and 9:30am on Sundays and holidays. The **Large Choral Synagogue of St. Petersburg,** St. Petersburg's only functioning synagogue, located at Lermontovskiy pr. 2, has morning and evening services daily. Nikolskiy Cathedral, the magnificent blue-and-gold structure a few blocks east of the synagogue on ul. Rimskovo-Korsakovo, has services daily at 10am and 6pm.

You can escape the bedlam of Nevsky Prospekt along the banks of the Neva, the smaller Moika River, and the Griboyedov and Fontanka canals. A promenade along the **Palace Embankment** (Дворцовая набережная) of the Neva toward the lovely **Summer Garden** (Летний сад) will take you past many former embassies and resplendent examples of 19th-century neoclassical architecture. Within the Summer Garden stands the small but elegant **Summer Palace** of Peter the Great. (Open May-Sept. 15 Wed.-Mon. 11am-6:30pm; Sept. 16-Nov. 9 Wed.-Mon. 10am-5:30pm. Admission 55к.) Among the bevy of literary museums in St. Petersburg is the **Pushkin Apartment,** Moika nab. 12. (Open Fri.-Mon. and Wed. 10:30am-6:30pm, Thurs. noon-8pm; closed last Fri. of every month. Admission 75к, students 30к. Come early; tickets go fast.) The **Dostoevsky Muzei** is in the writer's apartment at Kuznechny per. 5/2, around the corner from M: Vladimirskaya (Владимирская); the big D penned *The Brothers Karamazov* here. On display are the writer's notes for various novels, as well as the family apartments. Dostoevsky's study is preserved as it was when he died; the clock on the table points to the exact hour of his death. (Open Tues.-Sun. 10:30am-6:30pm; closed last Wed. of month. Admission 25к, students 10к.)

Many of the more than 650,000 victims of the Siege of Leningrad are buried in the **Piskarevskoye Memorial Cemetery** (Пискаревское кладбище) under the inscription "No one is forgotten, nothing is forgotten." St. Petersburg required a complete rebuilding after this tragedy, and a visit to the cemetery is one way to grasp the degree of suffering endured. Take bus #75 from M: pl. Muzhestva (пл. Муж ества) or join an Intourist excursion.

St. Petersburg has a number of good *beryozka.* The one at Nevsky Prospekt 7 is the most conveniently located, and offers a wide selection of fur hats, china, and beverages. (Open daily 10am-2pm and 3-9pm. Look for the "BS" sign in the window.)

Entertainment

St. Petersburg's famed White Nights, which lend the night sky a pale, bewitching glow from mid-June to early July, keep locals out and about into the wee hours. Unfortunately, most activities in St. Petersburg close by 11pm, so there's diddly to do but wander about and watch the drawbridge go up at about 1:30am. This can be quite romantic, but remember to do it from the *same* side of the bridge your hotel is on. The **White Nights Festival** prolongs St. Petersburg's theater and entertainment season through the end of July. Possibly the world's finest ballet company, the **Kirov Opera and Ballet,** housed in Teatral'naya pl. in the former **Mariynskiy Theater,** witnessed the classic performances of Pavlova and Shalyapin and the premieres of famous Russian operas. If you can't see the Kirov ballet, another choice is choreographer Boris Eifmann's Sovremenny (Contemporary) Ballets; call Hotel Astoria's Service Bureau for information, or check kiosks and billboards. The main theater ticket office is located at Nevsky Prospekt 42, across from the Gostiny Dvor. (Open Mon.-Sat. 9am-8pm, Sun. 10am-7pm.) The **St. Petersburg Philharmonic** at ul. Brodskovo 2, opposite the Hotel D'Europe, offers world-class classical music performances for mere pennies. Here, on August 9, 1942, while the city lay under siege, Dmitri Shostakovich's Seventh Symphony rang out in defiance. Get tickets at Nevsky Prospekt 30, or from kiosks and tables near St. Isaac's Cathedral and along Nevsky Prospekt. For more placid entertainment, take a boat ride up and down the Neva River. Tours leave across from the Hermitage (1½-hr. ride costs 1R.) Boat tours of the city's canals leave daily from 11:30am to 8:30pm from Fontankina kanal just off Nevsky Prospekt (1¼-hr. ride costs 80к).

St. Petersburg's rock scene is the most lively in the USSR. Tickets to weird, tacky stadium shows can be purchased at kiosks along Nevsky Prospekt. To find out about more worthwhile bands, drop by the **St. Petersburg Rock Club** at ul. Rubinshteina 13, in the courtyard and through the right door on the far wall (tel. 312 34 83). Soviet rock superstars like Kino, Aliss, and Igry all got their starts in this dingy old building. Your jazz cravings can be slaked at the St. Petersburg **Jazz Club,** the USSR's oldest and finest, at Zagorodny pr. 27 (tel. 164 85 65; Dixie or cool jazz most nights from 8pm; 12R cover). Spending an evening with the radicals, evangelists, hippies, and lunatics who hang out (particularly on weekends) at **Kazan Cathedral** can be an unforgettable experience.

Near St. Petersburg

Around St. Petersburg repose a string of sumptuous 18th-century summer palaces and estates which, though mauled during the war, are being restored to their former sinful luxury. All are accessible by bus, electric train, or (fastest and most fun) in the case of Peter the Great's summer place, by hydrofoil. Check with your guide or hotel Service Bureau for details. **Petrodvorets** (Петродворец) is the Versailles wanna-be of golden fountains and waterfalls begun by Peter the Great; you can skip the palace interior and follow the sound of shrieks and giggles to the "joke fountains," which, activated by one misstep, suddenly splush their unwitting victims. (Palace open Tues.-Sun. 11am-6pm; closed last Tues. of month.) Hydrofoils leave between 9am and 7pm from a dock in front of the Winter Palace (every 20 min., ½ hr., 3.15R; return ticket must be purchased at the palace). Trains leave frequently from Vitebskiy Station.

Fifteen miles south of the city, **Pushkin** (Пушкин), formerly named Tsarskoye Selo, harbors Catherine the Great's summer residence, a fanciful azure, white, and gold baroque palace which presides magnificently over tailored French gardens. Stroll through the grounds, rent a boat and row out onto the pond surrounded by dreamy pavillions, or wander the grandiose palace chambers on a guided tour, and forget the land of the Proletariat for a few blissful hours. (Palace open Fri.-Wed. noon-6pm, closed last Fri. of the month.) (Park open daily 6am-10pm). Excursions to **Pushkin** and the nearby neo-classical palace at **Pavlovsk** (Павловск) leave daily from the **Astoria Hotel** (USD11.50). The independent and budget-minded can take the electric train from Vitebskiy Station to **Detskoye Selo** (Детское Село) (return ticket 80к). From the square in front of the station, bus #371 takes you out to the palace and park. From the park at Pushkin, bus #280 continues on to **Pavlovsk.**

Murmansk Мурманск

Murmansk grew from a small village with a place in the heart of the tsar to a major metropolis when WWI brought a railway to the town—the Soviet Union's only year-round ice-free European port. Now the world's largest city above the Arctic Circle, Murmansk (pop. 450,000) lives off fishing, shipping, mineral production and—although no one mentions it very loudly—the military. Cramped, functionalist architectural behemoths are draped across the landscape, riddled with empty shops and smothered by five-month Arctic winters. Processing of the sulfur contained in nickel ore has devastated the local environment and now threatens the Finnmark region of Norway. Arranged boat tours from Kirkenes in Norway are the reason we include Murmansk in this book. **FFR** (tel. +47 (85) 950 92), the regional transport authority in Finnmark, runs a single-day, visa-free cruise from Kirkenes past antenna-bristling, radar-topped hills, nuclear subs and fleets of warships. Trips leave daily at 8am, returning at midnight; it's four hours each way, so you have eight hours in Murmansk. Book at least three days in advance (NOK 1090). For students and other indigents, **Folkehøgskolen** (tel. +47 (85) 950 92) arranges cheap longer stays. The local **Intourist office** (tel. (1522) 510 58), in the Hotel Polyarnye Zori (Полярные Зори), may have a map.

The **Murmansk Museum** on pr. Lenina (пр. Ленина) is always open for tour groups, and gives you everything from typically glorified accounts of WWII to the history of the local Sami people. To trace the history of Russians in the region (called *Pomory),* visit the **Pomor Museum,** outside of town; take bus #106 or 109 (1R) from the train station. (Open Tues.-Sun.) What shopping there is happens on pr. Lenina and parallel ul. Kominterna (ул. Коминтерна).

Ukraine Україна

The Republic of Ukraine encompasses a region which stretches from the Black Sea to the Carpathians and claims some 50 million inhabitants. Ukraine has held fast to a distinct political and literary tradition and harbors persistent aspirations to national independence. Dreams of autonomy draw strength from the republic's productive might: its farms, factories, and mines constitute the USSR's second-largest economy, the fruits of which, within the structure of the centralized Soviet system, had to be shipped first to Moscow to fill the Kremlin's coffers and support the inefficient distribution system. With an eye to better husbanding Ukraine's vast resources and redirecting the flow of trade to the republic's advantage, the Ukrainian parliament declared its sovereignty within the USSR on July 16, 1990. In the aftermath of the August 1991 events, Ukraine set December 1, 1991 as the date for a final referendum on complete independence. Ukrainian currency, visas, and stamps may follow. Ironically, a postwar power play by Stalin (trying to get more votes for the USSR) means that Ukraine already has a seat at the United Nations.

Ukrainian nationalism reawakened in the 19th century under the banner of the poet Taras Shevchenko, who spearheaded a campaign to revitalize the Ukrainian language and safeguard it from Polish and Russian cultural imperialsm. In this century, the movement has drawn strength from various acts of mistreatment at Soviet hands, such as Stalin's forced famine of 1931 (which claimed seven million lives), the longstanding ban on the teaching of Ukrainian in Soviet schools, and the Chernobyl disaster of 1986. Western Ukraine, always at the crossroads of European intellectual currents and never Russified to the extent of its eastern neighbor, has now taken up the struggle to preserve and reassert Ukrainian nationality. Kiev is briskly following suit.

Kiev Київ

Sometimes called the "Mother of Russian cities," Kiev was a sizable pagan town when Moscow was just a grove of pines and St. Petersburg a cluster of swampy islets. The capital of Kievan Rus' (the precursor of modern Russia), the city really took off after Prince Vladimir cast the city's idols into the Dnieper River and proclaimed his kingdom's conversion to Christianity in 988 AD. After the 13th-century Mongol invasion, the country's center of gravity shifted to Moscow, while Ukraine became a border region and relinquished its political, though not economic importance.

Today Kiev looks much the same as any other Soviet city—huge stone government ministries downtown, shoddy concrete housing developments in the suburbs. This superficial Sovietness is a product of the city's reconstruction after World War II, which leveled much of the city's historic center. The hills above downtown escaped destruction; with shady, chestnut-lined avenues and the golden cupolas of ancient monasteries, they reveal a warm southern city living at a more relaxed pace than its Northern neighbors.

Orientation and Practical Information

Situated on the lush, steep banks of the Dnieper River, Kiev is a busy port serving ships headed south to the Black Sea and north to Russia. The city itself is divided into two parts: upper Kiev clings to the hills, while lower Kiev skirts the riverbanks. **Khreshchatik** (Хрещатик), the city's main boulevard, is lined with theaters, shops, and cafés. Running parallel, **vulitsya Volodimirs'ka** (вулиця Володимирська) hosts a variety of historical sights.

Tourist Office: Intourist Service Bureau, in the Hotel Dnipro, Komsomols'ka pl., at the end of Khreshchatik. Books river cruises, excursions to outlying areas, and tickets to the theater. Open daily 9am-1pm and 2-5pm.

Currency Exchange: Also in the Hotel Dnipro. Same hours as Intourist.

Post Office: Khreshchatik 24. Open Mon.-Sat. 8am-9pm, Sun. 9am-7pm. The currency exchange office in Hotel Dnipro has a small selection of postcards, stamps, and envelopes.

Telephones: In the post office. Fax too. Open daily 8am-10pm. **City Code:** 044.

Trains: Kiev-Passazhirs'kiy (Київ Пассажирський), Vokzal'na pl., at the end of vul. Kominterna from bul. Taras Shevchenko. M: Vokzal'na (Вокзальна).

Public Transportation: Trolley and bus service is extensive, although you are best off on foot within the center. Tickets (15к) can be bought from automated dispensers at most stops. Kiev's **Metro** system (tickets also 15к) is useful for reaching lower Kiev and all points on the other side of the Dnieper.

Taxis: Fares are steep and often arbitrary, although more reasonable than in Moscow. If you don't speak Russian or Ukrainian, drivers will often triple their prices. Don't pay more than 10R for a ride within the city.

Food

Kiev's streets, particularly in summer, reflect the bounty of Ukraine's harvest. Attraction number one is the fresh fruit-flavored sherbet, usually apricot or raspberry, at about a ruble (the stuff is individually weighed, undoubtedly to lengthen lines). If you can manage not to bloat yourself unduly, stop at a street vendor's stand for some apricot *blinchiki* or a plate of *shashlyk.* At any major bus or Metro stop you can find *babushki* proffering fruit.

Kiev has a handful of quality restaurants, chiefly in Intourist hotels. **Restaurant Kiev** (Ресторан Київ), on the 2nd floor of the Hotel Kiev at vul. Kirova 26, will stuff you full of sable, chicken Kiev, ice cream, and champagne for 60R. (Open daily 11am-3pm and 4-11pm.) For a more intimate atmosphere, patronize **Maxime's** at vul. Lenina 21 (tel. 224 19 72), across from the opera house. This cooperative restaurant serves candle-lit meals and fresh, well-prepared food. Shout for a table some distance from the piano, as the *chanteuse* is amplified. (Dinner about 35-50R per person. Open daily 1-3pm and 6-11:30pm.) You can also stop in at **Retro** (Ретро), at vul. Rustaveli 4 behind the Bessarabian market, another basement cooperative decorated in eclectic 1920s style. Pay for an entrance card at the door (25R). This amount will be taken off your final bill. (Open daily noon-11pm; dinner reservations are usually not necessary if you arrive in the early evening.)

Kiev's **cafés** are some of the most inviting in the Soviet Union. They offer light fare and, in summer, open-air seating. A number of pleasant spots pose along Khreshchatik. One of the best is **Kafe Grot** (Кафе Грот), behind the fountains on Khreshchatik at vul. Lenina. Built into the hillside, it serves the ever-popular apricot ice cream (93к). (Open daily 11am-3pm and 4-11pm.) Under the archway at Khreshchatik 15 are a trio of coffee and ice cream hotspots. **Kafe Divo-tsvit** (Кафе Диво-цвіт), **Kafe Vecherniy Kiev** (Кафе Вечірний Київ, with the signs "Poker Bar" and "Shake" in the window), and **Kafe Pasazh** (Кафе Пасаж) are all open daily from 10am-3pm and from 4-10pm. The **Kafe Varenichna** (Кафе Варенична) at Khreshchatik 44 serves up the traditional Ukrainian dumplings. (Upper hall open 8am-3pm and 4-9pm. Downstairs open 9am-4pm and 5-9pm.) Kiev's artsy crowd, such as it is, gathers at the cafés along **Andriyevs'kiy Uzviz** (Андріївський Узвіз), leading down from St. Andrew's Cathedral. The choicest of these are the **Koleso** theater-café and the funky brick-cellar **Art Café,** next door to Bulgakov's house at #13. (Open daily 10am-11pm.)

Kiev's wealth of fresh fruit and vegetables is second to none. The **Bessarabian Market** (Бассарабський Ринок), at the junction of Khreshchatik and bul. Taras Shevchenko, is a veggie-bash where prices plunge below those in Moscow or St. Petersburg. Concern over Chernobyl-related radiation levels has prompted ongoing studies by both Soviet and foreign scientists aimed at calculating the exact extent of contamination and its potential effect on permanent residents. All agree, however, that despite the severity of the tragedy, for the itinerant visitor, consuming local produce, much of which comes from outside the affected area, poses little danger.

Sights

You can sense Kiev's character by strolling down **Khreshchatik.** The street begins at Bessarabs'ka pl., which also marks the start of bul. Taras Shevchenko. Continuing along Khreshchatik, you'll pass a number of fountains and stores, including **TsUM,** Kiev's main department store at Khreshchatik 38. Satisfy your "Hattrick" men's cologne fetish here (10R). (Open Mon.-Sat. 9am-9pm.) Further down, the commanding façade of the Hotel Moskva dominates **Independence Square** (formerly pl. Zhovtnevoye Revolyutsiye). By the square's circular central fountain, vendors hawk alternative newspapers from all over the USSR, while circles form to discuss politics past and present under the blue and gold of the Ukrainian flag. The end of Khreshchatik opens onto **Komsomols'ka pl.** Billygoat up those dark red, marble steps leading to the **Lenin Museum.** It's practically empty and always refreshingly cool in summer. (Open Tues.-Sun. 10am-6pm. Free.) Cross the square to reach the **Central Park of Culture and Rest,** with sweeping views of the Dnieper River from the area near the **Arch of Brotherhood** (a huge silver croquet wicket commemorating the union of Russia and Ukraine), jokingly referred to by locals as the "the yoke." The park also boasts another, more unusual monument, the **Monument to the Brave Soccer Players.** As the story goes, the occupying Nazi troops forced the team to play a "death match" against a German SS team. Stirred by local pride, the Dynamo played their hardest, won the match 3-0, and were promptly executed.

A number of pleasant walks radiate from Khreshchatik into the leafy, cobblestoned streets of Upper Kiev. **Vul. Engels** will take you uphill and away from the tourists and traffic into a quiet, older neighborhood. A walk up **bul. Taras Shevchenko** brings you to **Kiev State University** where nearly 22,000 students attend classes. (M: Universitet/Университет.) Painted crimson under the tsar after an unsuccessful student rebellion, the main building was splashed with a fresh red coat to commemorate the 1917 Bolshevik victory. Further up bul. Taras Shevchenko at #20 stands the many-domed ochre **Vladimirs'ka Cathedral,** built in the last century to commemorate the 900th anniversary of Christianity in Kiev. The spectacular interior with its gold mosaics and painted vines blends Byzantine with art nouveau. Also rewarding is a shuffle up **vul. Lenina.** On the left at #11 is the small **State Museum of Literature of the Ukrainian SSR** (open Sat.-Thurs. 10am-6pm). Two blocks farther up the hill, at the intersection of vul. Lenina and vul. Volodimirs'ka, stands the monumental **Shevchenko Theater of Opera and Ballet.** Here Stolypin, the tsarist agricultural reformer, was assassinated (he was in the second row), ending all hope for the monarchy.

A walk up **vulitsya Volodimirs'ka** ushers you into Kiev's past. Up the hill from the opera house are the **Golden Gates,** constructed in 1037. Recently restored, the gates now house a museum; climb the steps to the top amid eerie music. (Admission 30к, students 10к.) Farther along the street at **pl. Bogdana Khmel'nitskoho** (пл. Богдана Хмельницкого) is a statue of the square's namesake who freed Ukraine from Polish domination and later concluded an alliance with Russia. The entrance to the **St. Sophia Monastery Complex** (Софіївський собор) is at vul. Volodimirs'ka 24. Exquisite Byzantine icons, surviving from the 11th century, make the interior of the building worth a visit. St. Sophia was the cultural center of Kievan Rus' and here the first library in Russia was established by Yaroslav the Wise, who is buried within the complex. (Museum open Fri.-Tues. 10am-6pm and Wed. 10am-8pm.) At the end of vul. Volodimirs'ka stands another gorgeous church, **St. Andrew's Cathedral** (Андіївська Церква), designed by Rastrelli and now a museum. Entrance into the cathedral must be done in groups, which meet at the door on the half-hour. The ticket you buy at the *kasa* (каса) will have your entrance time on it. (Open Fri.-Tues. 10am-6pm and Wed. noon-8pm.) For a jolly jaunt down cobbled streets to lower Kiev and the historic Podol district, take Andreyevs'ka, a small road winding around the grounds of St. Andrew's and lined with curious houses. Halfway down, at #13, is **Bulgakov's House.** Kiev's alternative artistic and theatrical scene revolves around this street. Check out the small, independent galleries. To get back to upper Kiev without panting up the hills, hop the scenic **funicular railway.** Constructed in 1905, it's the oldest of its kind in Russia—a bargain at two kopeks. (M: Poshtova pl./Поштова пл.)

Two major points of interest lie outside the city's main district. The **Monument to Mother Ukraine** towers over the city skyline and houses a World War II museum in its base. Down the road on vul. Sichnevovo Povstannya is the fascinating **Pechers'ka Lavra** monastery (Печерська Лавра), founded in 1051 by the monks Anthony and Theodosius and considered one of the holiest places in Russia and Ukraine. Its grounds host 11th-century chapels and a bell tower commissioned by Peter the Great. Several museums were established on the monastery grounds during the Soviet period, but these are gradually being returned to the Church, which has not yet decided how to refurbish them. The most memorable exhibit on the grounds, undisputedly, are the catacombs, a series of caves where monks lived and were buried in the Middle Ages. The atmosphere has preserved their bodies over the centuries, and for the price of a candle (1R) you can have an eerie ogle. To get to the grounds, take trolleybus #20 from the Dnipro Hotel downtown to the last stop. (Open Wed.-Mon. 10am-5pm. Admission to general grounds 4.50R, students 1.10R.)

Farther along the outskirts of Kiev is the moving World War II monument at **Babiy Yar** (Бабий Яр). A large group of carved figures commemorates the place where victims of the Nazis were buried starting in September of 1941. Although the plaque states that 100,000 Kievans died during this time, newer estimates place the figure closer to 200,000. Many of the victims were buried alive. Take trolleybus #27 eight stops from M: Petrivka (Петрівка). The monument stands in the park, near the TV tower.

From Khreshchatik take trolley #11 to "ВДНХ УССР" and change to bus #24, which will whisk you to the **Museum of Folk Architecture.** This open-air exhibition resurrects a Ukrainian town from another century, from a one-room schoolhouse to windmills. The landscape is a refreshing change from the urban center; not a single concrete housing project warts the skyline.

To see where Kievans hang out during the hot summer days, take the Metro to **Gidropark** (Гідропарк), where you'll find an amusement park and beach on an island in the Dnieper. Take a spin on the miniature rollercoaster, but consider skipping a slosh in the river.

Entertainment

In the summertime, many locals enjoy café-hopping up and down Kreshchatik. Intourist hotels in Kiev all offer hard-currency **night bars.** The bar at the Dnipro Hotel stays open until 2am. The local arts scene thrives at a number of **theaters;** some of the more interesting ones are the small independent companies which line Andriyevskiy Uzviz. These include the **Koleso** theater-café; the **Teatr na Podole;** and the tiny, recently-established **Life-Art Cabaret** in the Academia at #34, which often hosts folksingers. Most of these close down in the summer, but check their schedules. For more official theaters, or the opera, obtain tickets through an Intourist service bureau (for hard currency) or at the **kasa** at the archway on Kreshchatik 21 (open 10am-8pm). If you're in Kiev during **soccer** season (late spring to mid-autumn), see a Dynamo Kiev game. Kievans go bonkers over soccer with good reason: their team is one of the best anywhere. Tickets can be purchased at *kasas* or at the stadium on vul. Chervonoarmeis'ka, which was the site of several Olympic matches in 1980 (M: Respublikanskiy Stadion/Республиканский Стадион).

Hard-currency **shopping** is not one of Kiev's fortes. There are small *kashtans* (which means chestnut tree—the equivalent of the Russian *beryozka,* which means birch tree) in most hotels, but you should make major purchases in Moscow or St. Petersburg. Special Ukrainian souvenirs are yours with rubles at the **Ukrainian Souvenir** store on pl. Tolstoho: ceramics, baskets, and embroidered goods, from handkerchiefs (2.40R) to blouses (48R). (Shop open Mon.-Fri. 10am-2pm and 3-7pm, Sat. 10am-2pm and 3-6pm.) Try to come to Kiev on **Ukraine Sovereignty Day** (July 16), when the city becomes a moveable feast.

L'viv Львів

L'viv dates back to 1256, when the city's first defensive fortress arose in a valley at the confluence of Eastern European trade routes. Through the centuries, as the city prospered and expanded, it became the capital of Galicia and found itself alternately called L'vov (Львов, by the Russians), Lwów (by the Poles), and Lemberg (by the Germans). From the start an integral part of East Central Europe rather than the Russian empire, L'viv's architecture is startlingly reminiscent of other former Austro-Hungarian jewels such as Prague and Kraków, with narrow cobblestoned alleys and magnificent Gothic and baroque cathedrals. On the eve of World War II, the city was occupied by Soviet forces and in 1945 it fell under permanent Soviet control, when Western Ukraine was cut out of Poland and annexed to the rest of the Ukrainian Soviet Socialist Republic. L'viv's predominantly Polish population was deported, slogans hung up, and decades of Sovietization ensued.

In the post-*glasnost* age, the red stars have come down as quickly as they went up, and L'viv, ironically, not Kiev, has become the center of Ukrainian national revival. L'viv's many Greek Catholic churches are being handed back to their congregations after decades of closure. The yellow and blue Ukrainian flag flies here over the headquarters of the democratically elected city council, and *Rukh,* the

Ukrainian popular front, maintains its headquarters in the city. A virulent anti-L'viv campaign has been mounted periodically in the Moscow-controlled government press, but life goes on quietly in the city's medieval squares and coffeehouses as locals contemplate a way out of the drab, crumbling, and gray face of Soviet socialism.

Orientation and Practical Information

L'viv fans outwards from **pl. Rinok** (пл. Ринок), the heart of the old city. The principal shopping street is the shady **prospekt Svobodi** (пр. Свободи, formerly pr. Lenina), which runs from the **Opera House** to pl. Mickiewicza. In the past year, many street name have been changed, either back to their prewar appellations, or to new, non-Communist versions. Ask locals for help in deciphering maps. L'viv once sat on a river, but it dried up once the city expanded; **tap water** is now rationed and runs only between 6am and 9am and 6pm and 9pm.

Tourist Office: Intourist Service Bureau, in the Hotel Intourist at pr. Shevchenko 1. Open daily 9am-noon and 1pm-8:30pm.

Currency Exchange: At the Hotel Intourist.

Post Office: vul. Slovackiego 1, a block away from the university and Ivan Franko park. Open daily 8am-7:30pm. Telephones too. **City Code:** 0322.

Trains: From the station, take tram #6 into the city center. The one daily train to Kraków (9 hr.) and Wrocław in Poland starts in Kiev, passing through L'viv at 7:15am; getting tickets is a nightmare.

Buses: Buses to Przemyśl (about 2 hr.) and Rzeszów in Poland leave from the station (афто вокзал), south of the city. Cost about 30R. Often booked a week or more in advance.

Food

A couple of L'viv's best restaurants stand on pl. Rinok. The city's first cooperative, the cozy, wood-paneled **Stariy Royal'** (Старий Рояль) welcomes guests to the soft strains of its namesake piano at vul. Stavropigilskaya 3, next to the pharmacy museum. There are only two dishes—different types of meat on large plates with an assortment of vegetables. The flavorful *dushenina* (душенина) is your best bet at 10.68R. (Open daily 10am-4pm and 5-9pm.) At pl. Rinok 20, is **Pid Levom** (Пид Левом), behind the large gate with the brass lion's head. The large hall at street level is supplemented by the atmospheric brick cellar downstairs. (Open daily noon-5pm and 6pm-midnight.) Further afield, just down from the Dniester Hotel, and overlooking Ivan Franko park is the small Georgian **Grono** (Гроно), vul. Rileeva 12. Spicy appetizers and stuffed grape leaves are served in the restaurant's two small rooms (open Mon.-Sat. noon-9pm, Sun. 1-10pm). In the heart of downtown, across from the Mickiewicz column, is **Restaurant Lyuks** (Люкс; formerly the Moscow), at Kopernika 6/7. Step upstairs past the hall of mirrors to the turn-of-the-century dining room; the food and service, unfortunately, have not kept up with the stylish decor, but you can have the standard cucumbers, meat, and potatoes. (Open daily noon-5pm and 6pm-midnight). For a simple shish kebab delivered with hyper-friendly service by enterprising grandmotherly types, check out the Armenian **Araks** (Аракс), at the corner of vul. Franko and vul. Bekhtera, which has pink cafeteria-style décor with colorful batik drapes. Order at the counter; food will be brought to your table.

L'viv, reflecting its Polish and Austro-Hungarian heritage, is a city of coffee and cafés. Although there are, sadly, few remains of the elegant coffeehouses of bygone days, there are a couple of spots to sit down and have a cup with friends. Sometimes, you may be greeted with the Ukrainian "*kavy nemaye*" (no coffee). Supplies run short—this is, after all, the Soviet Union. Walk on down to the next place. On pl. Rinok, wander into the **Kofeinaya** (Кофейная), vul. Virmenska 19, where the artsy crowd hangs out. Also on the same street, further up at #31, is **Kafe Ararat** (Арарат), with an Armenian motif.

If you hanker for Western goodies, the hard-currency *kashtan* stands at the corner of vul. Timiryazeva and vul. Rudneva, in back of the Intourist Hotel (open Tues.-Sat. 9am-1pm and 2-6pm).

Sights and Entertainment

L'viv's historical center is fairly compact and best seen on foot. Trams connect all parts of the city, but are the only mode of public transport; the crowds make them less than relaxing. Start your walk on **prospekt Svobodi,** next to the ornate neoclassical **Opera and Ballet Theater** (Театр опери та Балету). Topped by three winged angels, this magnificent turn-of-the-century structure is the pride of all L'vivians. The opera opens onto a pedestrian mall which runs down the middle of the boulevard, splitting it in two. As you face the center, with your back to the opera, walk on the right side of pr. Svobodi to get a look at the city's principal shops and hotels, lodged in the ochre and pistachio façades of old Polish apartments. A third of the way up pr. Svobodi, at the intersection of vul. Gor'kovo in the former Polish-American commercial bank, is the **Ethnographic Museum.** Notice the statue of Liberty on the parapet before going in. The museum, spread out on two floors, harbors a detailed exhibit of Ukrainian dress with all its regional variations, along with cases of archeological artifacts, painted eggs, pottery, and embroidery worth a visit to familiarize yourself with local culture and history (open Tues.-Sun. 10am-6pm). If you turn off onto vul. Gor'kovo you will come to a fork in the road. Head to the left and you come to the **park Ivan Franko** (парк Івана Франка), fronting on **L'viv University.** Up above, in the hills, lies a pleasant tangle of residential streets. Further down stands the **Picture Gallery,** Stefanicka 3 (open Tues.-Sun. 10am-6pm). Back on pr. Svobody, you eventually reach the **Mickiewicz column,** on which the Polish poet is visited by the Muse. Opposite the Ukraine (Україна) movie theater is the **Hotel Intourist,** built in 1901. Turn left at the Ukraine and head toward the stone-gray façade of the former 17th-century Bernardine Monastery, now the Greek Catholic **Church of St. Andrew** (Церква св. Андрия). To your right is the **Galicia Market.** The church boasts a cavernous interior covered in frescoes and a massive gilt altar of rich gold and black granite. To reach the very heart of the old city, make a sharp left here, and take one of the narrow streets leading up to **pl. Rinok,** the historic market square. The **Rinok** is a varied architectural ensemble, presenting a collage of four-story, richly decorated merchant homes dating from the 16th to the 18th centuries. The tall square Renaissance spire of the **Town Hall** marks the square's center. A couple of interesting museums, as well as grand cathedrals, cluster around the square. Among these are the **Historical Museum** (Історичний музей), at pl. Rinok 4 (open Thurs.-Tues. 10am-6pm), and the adjoining **Italian Courtyard** at #6. The **Apteka** (Pharmacy) **Museum,** housed in L'viv's oldest drugstore, has glass cases of mysterious Latin-inscribed jars. They also sell small bottles of iron-fortified "wine" designed to cure all your ills (ask for the *vino).* (Open Mon.-Sat. 9am-7pm, Sun. 10am-5pm). On pl. Rosa Luxemburg rises the Polish **Roman Catholic Cathedral.** The only remaining Gothic church in L'viv, it was constructed by decree of King Casimir, starting in 1360. The colorful murals inside and ornate altars bespeak a later baroque influence. (Open Mon.-Sat. 6am-noon and 6-8pm, Sun. and holidays 6am-3pm and 5:30pm-8pm.) Next door stands a small Renaissance chapel, whose portal displays a frieze of delicatedly sculpted stone. Also noteworthy, at the east end of the square, are the massive **Usspenskiy Cathedral** (next to the 60m Korniak belltower), and the baroque cupola of the present-day **Museum of Religion,** which should soon revert back to its original mission. At vul. Pidval'na 5 you will find the **Arsenal Museum,** in the old city wall, with a collection of ancient weaponry (open Thurs.-Tues. 10am-5:45pm). Up above the old city, where the tower now stands, rises **Castle Hill** (Високий замок), from whose top a stunning panorama of L'viv unfolds. Continuing further east, you can take tram #2 or walk along vul. Lichakivs'ka (formerly vul. Lenina) to vul. Krunyars'ka (Крунярська). Walk up the street, on the left, to the outdoor **Museum of Architecture,** also known as the **Shevchens'kij Hai** (Шевченськивський

Гай). Lying an a vast park planted with tall first to lend it a mountain-village air, the museum harbors a collection of authentic wooden houses brought here from all regions of western Ukraine. (Open Tues.-Sun. 10am-6pm.) Back on Lichakivs'ka, head down vul. Mechnikova on the other side of the street, next to the whitewashed chapel to the **Lichakivs'kiy Cemetery** (Лічаківський Цвинтар). On the terrain of L'viv's most famous necropole are the graves of Polish and American noblemen, grandiose monuments, and simple graves of local residents throughout the centuries. Walk back into town for a rest in the splendidly manicured **Striis'kiy Park** (Стрийський парк).

When evening comes, L'viv offers comparatively little entertainment, save for its coffeehouses and quaint streets. Catch a performance at the **Opera** or the **Symphony,** vul. Chaikovskoho 7. The **Teatral'ni Kasi** (Театральни Каси), pr. Svobodi 37, sell tickets to the opera, symphony, and theaters. (Open Mon.-Sat. 11am-2pm and 4-7pm).

Near L'viv

A couple of hours away by car or train to the west and south rise the pine-covered Carpathian Mountains. Steep valleys carpeted with wildflowers, and chalets overlooking fresh mountain streams, will make you wonder where you left the Soviet Union. Making a day trip out to the Carpathians is a must, if you have the time. If you don't have access to a car or a local who can advise you on which particular town to head for, take the commuter train *(elektrichka)* from the L'viv train station (direction Мукачево) to **Slavs'ko** (Славсько) (2½ hr.); once you get there, the hills are yours to hike and admire.

UNITED KINGDOM

USD$1 = 0.60 pounds (£, or GBP)	**£1 = USD$1.67**
CAD$1 = £0.52	**£1 = CAD$1.90**
AUD$1 = £0.46	**£1 = AUD$2.14**
NZD$1 = £0.34	**£1 = NZD$2.93**
Country Code: 44	**International Dialing Prefix: 010**

Industrious Romans took the British Isles under their wing in the first century, fortifying their northernmost outpost with army camps, hot spring baths and lengthy walls to exclude the enemy pagan masses. When the walls decayed along with the Romans' moral fiber, Germanic tribes—the Angles, Jutes, and Saxons—were quick to capitalize on the political vacuum. The moral void was filled by Christian missionaries from the continent, and soon after the Norman conquest of 1066, the British set off on their own proselytizing voyages and holy wars. The Crusades were just the beginning of what would become for the British a manic obsession to color the map red, starting by first incorporating their Scottish and Welsh neighbors.

Under Queen Victoria in the latter half of the 19th century, industrious Britannia ruled the waves, the sun never set on the Empire, and rigid social stratification (chronicled by writers as disparate as Dickens and E.M. Forster) was *de rigeur* at home. The two World Wars destroyed both the Empire and some of that social inequality, but the stereotype of the Briton remains: master of the unseen and the unsaid, of all those intangible, indefinable gifts—taste and irony, grace and wit—that made Anglophiles of the colonists. Remember, however, that the tiny fraction of nineteenth-century Brits who actually resembled Sherlock Holmes, Phileas Fogg and Henry Higgins owed their positions to a vast army of exploited butlers, laborers and native peoples. These class divisions still fracture the country today, though Clement Atlee's post-war Labour government established a welfare state (picked apart by Margaret Thatcher) that gave working-class Britons adequate education, health care and housing for the first time. The chafing of economic inequality, coupled with the difficult assimilation of a new wave of immigrants from Pakistan, Africa, Jamaica (and soon, Hong Kong) has caused a rash of anger and violence that erupted in the 1990 poll tax riots.

The country can be divided fairly neatly along regional lines. In the suburbs of Kent and Sussex, only the Jaguars in the driveways seem out of place in a setting of Tudor houses, clipped hedges and affable Anglican vicars that could have been lifted out of P.G. Wodehouse. Industrial northern England, on the other hand, has historically been less well-off, no less so than now; it shares high unemployment and a declining industrial economy with most of Wales and Scotland. Politics follows the same divides, with the south more Conservative and the north voting Labour—though the recent departure of Margaret Thatcher has robbed British politics of some of its punch and blurred the distinction between right and left.

You can follow the vicissitudes of British politics in one of the quality dailies (i.e., not the vapid tabloids with topless "page-three girls"): *The Guardian* tilts left, *The Independent* lives up to its name, *The Times* is lame and right of center, and *The Daily Telegraph* is excellent for wrapping fish.

For more coverage of the United Kingdom, buy *Let's Go: Britain & Ireland* or *Let's Go: London.*

Getting There

The cheapest way to reach Britain from continental Europe is to swim the English Channel; this requires extraordinary stamina and has been tackled by only a handful of budget travelers. Fortunately, many ferries and hovercrafts connect Great Britain (which with Northern Ireland makes up the United Kingdom) with the rest of Europe. Rail tickets between London and the Continent normally include cross-Channel passage. Ask ahead about the train-boat linkage, which can be confusing. Trains to Paris connect with boats from **Dover** or sometimes **Folkestone** or **Newhaven** (all about 2 hr. southeast of London) to Calais, Boulogne, or Dieppe in France. Trains to Brussels, Cologne and beyond use boats from Dover to Oostende in Belgium. Trains to northern Germany, Poland, and Scandinavia most often ship their riders from **Harwich** (1½ hr. northeast of London) to Hoek van Holland in the Netherlands. The two main companies on these routes are P&O and Sealink. Contact **P&O** at their Dover office (tel. (0304) 20 33 88, open daily 7am-7:30pm). For **Sealink** information, ring (0233) 64 70 47 (open Mon.-Fri. 7:30am-8:30pm, Sat. 7:30am-7:30pm, Sun. 9am-5pm), or stop by their offices in Harwich (tel. (0255) 24 33 33) or at London's Victoria Station (tel. (071) 828 1940; open Mon.-Sat. 9am-6pm).

Scandinavian Seaways (formerly DFDS) has ferries from Hamburg, Germany to Harwich (about 2 per day, 21½ hr., £48-80); from Esbjerg, Denmark to Harwich

(Feb.-Dec. 3-4 per week, 15 hr., £58-100) and Newcastle (mid-June to mid-Aug. 2 per week, 19 hr., £58-100), and from Gothenburg, Sweden to Harwich (Feb.-Dec. 1-3 per week, 24 hr., £73-125) and Newcastle (mid-June to mid-Aug. 1 per week, 23 hr., £73-125). Fares are highest in mid-summer; when you book in the U.K., Eurail gets 25% off, InterRail and the ISIC 50%. Contact Scandinavian Seaways in Harwich (tel. (0255) 24 02 40), in Newcastle (tel. (091) 296 01 01), or at their travel center in London (15 Hanover St., tel. (071) 493 6696; open Mon.-Fri. 9am-5pm, Sat. 9am-2pm). **Color Line** (tel. (091) 296 13 13) runs service from Newcastle to Bergen and Stavanger, Norway (mid-March to Dec. 2-3 per week, 19-30 hr., £35-67). If you need to stay in **Newcastle** (which is an easy train trip from Durham, York, or Edinburgh; take bus #327 from the train station to the ferries at Tyne Commission Quay) try the **youth hostel (IYHF),** 107 Jesmond Rd. (tel. (091) 281 25 70; £5.50, £4.40; open March-Oct. daily, Nov. to mid-Dec. Tues.-Sat.) or the **Newcastle University Residences,** 10 Leazes Terr. (tel. (091) 222 81 50; £8.25; open July-Sept. only).

Useful ferries also run from Britain's southern coast to France and Spain, from Wales, Northern England, and Scotland to Ireland (see under Ireland), and from the Shetland Islands to Iceland, the Faroe Islands, and Norway (see under Shetland Islands).

Budget **coaches** originate in London, working through Paris, Brussels, and Amsterdam to the rest of the continent. **Flights** between London and continental airports are competitve with trains and buses (see Budget Travel under London). We'll see what the Chunnel will offer budget travelers when it opens in 1993.

Getting Around

When in Britain, travel by **coach.** Eurail isn't valid anyway (InterRail is), and express coaches are cheaper than trains and often almost as fast. The **National Express/Scottish Citylink** intercity coach network covers most of Britain; a **Student Coach Card** (£5; ISIC and photo required) cuts 33% from their already low fares. With a **BritExpress Card,** foreign citizens of any age receive a 33% discount on every National Express/Scottish Citylink journey made in a 30-day period. It's available from travel agents abroad or from the National Express office at 13 Regent St., London SW1 (tel. (071) 730 02 02). Watch your terminology: long-distance "coaches" are distinct from slow, short-run "buses," which run within cities and between rural villages. On both coaches and buses, you pay in confusion what you save on fares: many stations are chaotic and shabby, most routes confusingly deregulated. Some local authorities publish regional timetables to help you unravel the mess.

Train prices in Great Britain outpace most of those on the continent. British Rail offers a huge and perplexing variety of passes, reductions, and discounts. The best deal is the **Young Person's Railcard** (£16), which gives you a third off any British Rail ticket. The card is valid for an entire year and is available at most rail stations for proof of age (under 24) or full-time student status at a British institution, plus two photos. Railcards for seniors and disabled travelers win 50% off some fares. Family travelcards can give adults a savings of 33-50%, and children travel for £1. **Intercity Savers,** available to all, are cheap round-trip fares between many large cities (smaller discounts on Fri., July-Aug. Sat. as well), but coach fares are still cheaper. If you plan to travel a *great* deal within Britain, the **British Rail Pass,** which comes in 8-day, 15-day, 22-day, and one-month flavors, may do you right. They're only available in the U.S. and Canada. Pass vendors include CIEE, Travel CUTS, and the BritRail offices in New York (1500 Broadway, tel. (212) 575-2667) and Toronto (94 Cumberland St., tel. (416) 929-3333).

In British nomenclature one-way is "single," round-trip is "return," and "period return" is a round-trip ticket that must be used within a specified time (usually 30 days). Many train and coach lines offer cheap "day returns," often the same price as a single. Both trains and buses have regional **Explorer, Wayfarer, Rover,** or **Day**

Rambler tickets which cover a day's (£3.50-£4.50) or a week's (around £30) unlimited travel on one or more companies' routes within a region.

Those who've chosen to sample British **hitching** often call it Europe's best, especially in rural areas and on islands. Hitching is more difficult on Sundays; small highland roads can be terrible. British secondary roads are never very wide and are often bordered by high hedges or stone banks; successful hitchers don't stand in the narrows. It's easy to forget that Britons **drive** on the left.

To really see Britain, you must get off the rail or coach routes and **bike** or **hike.** Most cities and villages have bike rental shops and maps of local cycle routes; ask at the tourist information center. England is a nation of walkers (and dog-walkers). Footpaths criss-cross the country and put the path most taken to shame. Britain is the most-mapped, most-written-about island in the world; take along a large-scale Ordnance Survey map of the area you plan to cover, and ask tourist offices about routes.

Practical Information

There are local tourist offices everywhere in Great Britain; any will book you a room in a local bed and breakfast (up to £1-2 fee), and most in a B&B anywhere in the country (£2-4 fee). Most will post a list after closing.

The classic red phone box has been nearly done away with by sleeker glass booths. The yellow-stickered ones are coin-operated; bypass them and buy a **Phonecard** (sold in denominations of £1-20 at post offices and newsagents) which fits in the more common green-stickered booths. A £10 Phonecard is perfect for international calls, though British rates suck big-time (it's cheaper to call Greece from America). Charges go down after 8pm. AT&T's **USA Direct** is at (0800) 89 00 11. **Canada Direct** is at (0800) 89 00 16, **New Zealand Direct** at (0800) 89 00 64, and **Australia Direct** at (0800) 89 00 61. The operator is 100, directory assistance is 192, and overseas directory assistance 153. The **national emergency number** is 999.

The British pound is divided into 100 pence; shillings (20 to the pound) and old pence (12 to the shilling) retired in the early 70s. British pound traveler's checks will simplify life when changing money (best at banks—generally open Mon.-Fri. 9:30am-3:30pm—*not* the dubious "bureaux de change").

The weather in the U.K. often changes from grim drizzle to glorious sun several times per morning. Bring something that can instantly cover both you *and* your pack.

Americans will need to know the British words for many things invented since 1776. For starters, "crisps" are potato chips, "chips" are French fries, a "car park" is a parking lot, a "caravan" is a trailer and a "flat" is an apartment.

Accommodations and Camping

Bed and breakfasts (£9-14, in London £18-24) are so rampant that it is absurd to single out the establishments we list; when they're full, ask for a referral. B&Bs tend to cluster; we often just mention the best streets to look on. The tourist offices book rooms (see above) and publish *Where To Stay* brochures listing those B&Bs and campsites that they have approved. In very small towns, you can ask at the pub or the post office for people offering B&B. Most B&Bs will accept a telephone reservation, but few will keep the room past noon without a deposit. B&Bs have less space for single travelers, though proprietors soften towards evening when their doubles don't fill. Vegetarians should declare themselves at once; some proprietors will alter the eggs-and-bacon routine when asked.

The United Kingdom has hundreds of **youth hostels,** both IYHF and independent. The respective hostel associations of England and Wales, Scotland, and Northern Ireland publish inexpensive, essential guides with full maps and descriptions for all their hostels. Rates, which depend on the traveler's age and the grade of the hostel, hover between £4.50-8.50 (higher in London). In England and Wales, we list two prices; the second is for juniors (ages 16-20). Nonmembers pay extra for guest-card stamps. Hostels are generally closed from 10am to 5pm, and impose an evening curfew (usually about 11pm). All require sleep sacks, which they sell or rent for a nominal fee. If these regulations cramp your style, stick to looser independent establishments. Always book ahead in high season.

Camping can be a wet proposition any time of the year, but it also gives you the most freedom. British campsites are very civilized, with facilities ranging from flush toilets to lounges. You usually have to put up with an adjacent caravan site. Farmers will frequently let you camp on their land, sometimes for a small fee, but you should always ask before pitching your tent. If you and a group of friends plan to base yourself in one place for a while, look into self-catering options at the local tourist information office.

Food and Drink

Although enormous traditional breakfasts get all the fame and glory, the rest of English cuisine is not simply a cauldron of boiled blandness. After recovering from your morning tea or coffee, orange juice, cereal, eggs, bacon, sausage, toast, butter, marmalade, grilled tomatoes, mushrooms, kippers (smoked herring), and, in winter, porridge, you will discover that England is a nation of meat-eaters, and the best native dishes are roasts—beef, lamb, and Wiltshire hams. Vegetables are the weakest and mushiest part of the meal; go with salads.

Pub grub (meals served in bars) is the classic, fast, and filling lunch. The ploughman's lunch (actually the product of a 1960s advertising campaign) is inexpensive (£1.60-4.75): cheese, bread, pickled onions, chutney and a tomato or two. Fish and chips are traditionally drowned in vinegar and salt.

The best supermarket chains are Asda, Safeway, Sainsbury, and Co-op. To escape English food, try Asian, Greek, Middle Eastern, or Indian cuisines. The last is especially worth a try; English restaurants (especially those in London and the larger cities) serve some of the best curries outside India. Ubiquitous "wholefoods" shops cater to vegetarians (not surprisingly, there are many in this land of grease).

England may be surrounded by water, but tea keeps it afloat. Tea is the preferred remedy for exhaustion, ennui, a rainy morning, or a hot afternoon. It is served strong and milky; if you want it any other way, say so in advance. "Tea" is also a meal. Afternoon high tea as it is still served in rural England includes cooked meats, salad, sandwiches, and dessert. Cream tea, a specialty of Cornwall and Devon, includes toast, shortbread, crumpets, scones, and jam, along with the essential feature—thick, "clotted" cream. The afternoon tea that you will find served in London hotels and department stores is quite expensive (£8 or more) and can be disappointing.

If tea remains the focus of family life, the pub is where individual and community come together, a place to catch the latest news or gossip, air an opinion, or relax with your mates. Sir William Harcourt was right when he said in 1872: "As much of the history of England has been brought about in public houses as in the House of Commons." Although exact times vary from pub to pub, the most common hours are from 11am to 11pm. Shopping for votes, the Conservative-dominated Parliament recently repealed the 1915 liquor law requiring pubs to close from 3pm to 5:30pm. (The law was a carry-over from WWI England, when the arms factories required workers to be as punctual and sober as the machines they operated.) Beer—not wine or cocktails—is the standard pub drink. Except for the few individually-controlled "free houses," most pubs are franchise operations of the six largest breweries. Bear in mind that British beer may have a higher alcohol content than that to which you are accustomed. It is also usually served warm. Traditional cider, a fizzy fermented apple juice, called "scrumpy" in pub argot and served either sweet or dry, is an equally alcoholic alternative to beer.

The pub's importance as a social institution is reflected in its careful furnishing. Pubs are much more lavish than their North American counterparts, with intricately-carved mahogany walls and velvet-covered seats. Some of the larger cities put out pub guides so you can carefully plan a "pub crawl" (traditional night of drunkenness). For information on pubs throughout Britain, stop by the Pub Information Centre, 93 Buckingham Palace Rd., London SW1 (tel. (071) 222 3232).

London

Through nursery rhymes and songs we absorb London before we know it exists; arriving in the city for the first time can be an odd homecoming, an eerie *déjà vu.* There are the red double-decker buses; the bobbies and impassive Beefeaters; Westminster Abbey, rising more from the haze of memory than from the morning fog; and the notes of Big Ben, knelling through the mists as we have come to believe all bells must toll.

Yet London is not quaint. The city of the Queen and the Sex Pistols, of Paddington Bear and poll tax riots, fights for your attention. London is neither a park nor a museum, though you could spend all your time going from one to the next. It is a booming urban sprawl, with traffic snarls, porn shops, and an astonishingly international population. Though the city is not the peerless world capital it was last century, criticism rolls off stony London like a March rain. Salute the monuments of the English-speaking world—Buckingham Palace, St. Paul's Cathedral, Chaucer's grave. Then bellyflop into the energy of contemporary London, with its world-class theater, international cuisine, the peers and the punks and everyone in between.

Orientation and Practical Information

London became the world's largest city 200 years ago, and its apparent population decline during the last 35 years is largely misleading. Many people simply live and commute from beyond the 10-mile wide "Green Belt," which was thrown up in the 1950s around the perimeter of London's 620 square miles as an attempt to halt the city's sprawl.

London is divided formally into boroughs and postal code areas, and informally into districts. Both the borough name and postal code prefix appear at the bottom of most street signs. The city has grown by absorbing nearby villages or "cities"—a "city" meaning any town with a cathedral. This is reflected in borough names such as "City of Westminster" and "City of London" (or simply "The City").

Central London, on the north side of the Thames and bounded roughly by the Underground's Circle Line, contains most of the major sights. Within Central London, right in the center of your Underground map, the vaguely defined **West End** incorporates the understated elegance of Mayfair, the crowded shopping streets around Oxford Circus, the touristy glitter of Piccadilly Circus, the theaters around Leicester Square, the exotic labyrinth of Soho, and the chic Covent Garden. In the middle of this zone is London's official center, Charing Cross, as well as its unofficial center, Trafalgar Square. East of the West End lies **Holborn,** the center of legal activity, and **Fleet Street,** traditional haunt of journalists.

Around the southeastern corner of the Circle Line is **The City**—London's financial district, with the Tower of London at its eastern edge and St. Paul's Cathedral nearby. Farther east is the **East End,** ethnically diverse and working class, and the epic construction site of **Docklands.** Moving back west, along the river and the southern part of the Circle Line, is the district of **Westminster** (part of the borough of Westminster)—the royal, political, and ecclesiastical center of England, where you'll find Buckingham Palace, the Houses of Parliament and Westminster Abbey. In the southwest corner of the Circle Line, below the expanse of Hyde Park, are gracious **Knightsbridge, Chelsea,** embassy-laden **Belgravia,** and **Kensington,** adorned with London's posher shops and most expensive restaurants.

Around the northwest corner of the Circle Line, tidy terraces border Regent's Park; nearby are the faded squares of Paddington, Bayswater and Notting Hill Gate, home to large Indian and West Indian communities. Moving east towards the Circle

London
Regent's Park
Inner Circle
Chester Rd.
Outer Circle
Albany St.
Eversholt St.
Hampstead Rd.
Euston Station
Euston Rd.
Maida Vale
Abercorn Pl.
Abbey Rd.
Grove End Rd.
Hall Rd.
Circus Rd.
Wellington Rd.
Prince Albert Rd.
St. John's Wood Rd.
Lisson Grove
Park Rd.
Clifton Rd.
Bloomfield Rd.
Edgware Rd.
Harrow Rd
Marylebone Flyover
Marylebone Rd.
Devonshire St.
Cleveland St.
Tottenham Ct.
Crawford St.
Upper Montague St.
Gloucester Pl.
Baker St.
Marylebone High St.
Harley St.
Portland Pl.
Gt. Portland St.
Berners St.
Seymour Pl.
Manchester Square
Wigmore St.
Bishop's Bridge Rd.
Praed St.
Paddington Station
Sussex Gdns.
Oxford Circus
Oxford
Marble Arch
Oxford St.
Duke St.
Bond St.
Regent St.
Queensway
Craven Hill
Bayswater Rd.
N. Carriage Dr.
Speaker's Corner
Grosvenor Square
Brook St.
Grosvenor St.
U.S. Embassy
Berkeley Square
Brewer St.
Piccadilly Circus
Kensington Gardens
Hyde Park
Park Lane
Sth. Audley St.
Curzon St.
Jermyn St.
The Serpentine
Kensington Palace
W. Carriage Dr.
Piccadilly
St. James's Palace
Pall Mall
Green Park
St. James's Park
Hyde Park Corner
Constitution Hill
S. Carriage Rd.
Knightsbridge
Kensington Rd.
Kensington Gore
Royal Albert Hall
Sloane St.
Grosvenor Pl.
Birdcage
Belgrave Square
Prince Consort Rd.
Palace Gate
Victoria & Albert Museum
Exhibition Rd.
Basil St.
Pavilion Rd.
Cadogan Pl.
Brompton Rd.
Victoria
Queen's Gate
Gloucester Rd.
Walton St.
Pont St.
Eaton Square
Buckingham Palace Rd.
Victoria Station
Natural History Museum
Cromwell Rd.
Draycott Ave.
Sloane Sq.
Coach Station
Vauxhall
Old Brompton Rd.
Sloane Ave.
Ixworth Pl.
Warwick Way
Pimlico Rd.
Cale St.
Belgrave Rd.
Sutherland St.
Lupus St.
Old Church St.
Sydney St.
King's Rd.
Royal Hospital Rd.
Chelsea Br. Rd.
Ebury Br. Rd.
Royal Hospital
Redcliffe Gdns.
Flood St.
Oakley St.
Fulham Rd.
Grosvenor Rd.
Finborough Rd.
Carlyle's House
Chelsea Embankment
Chelsea Br.
Cheyne Walk
Beaufort St.
River Thames
Albert Br.
Battersea Park

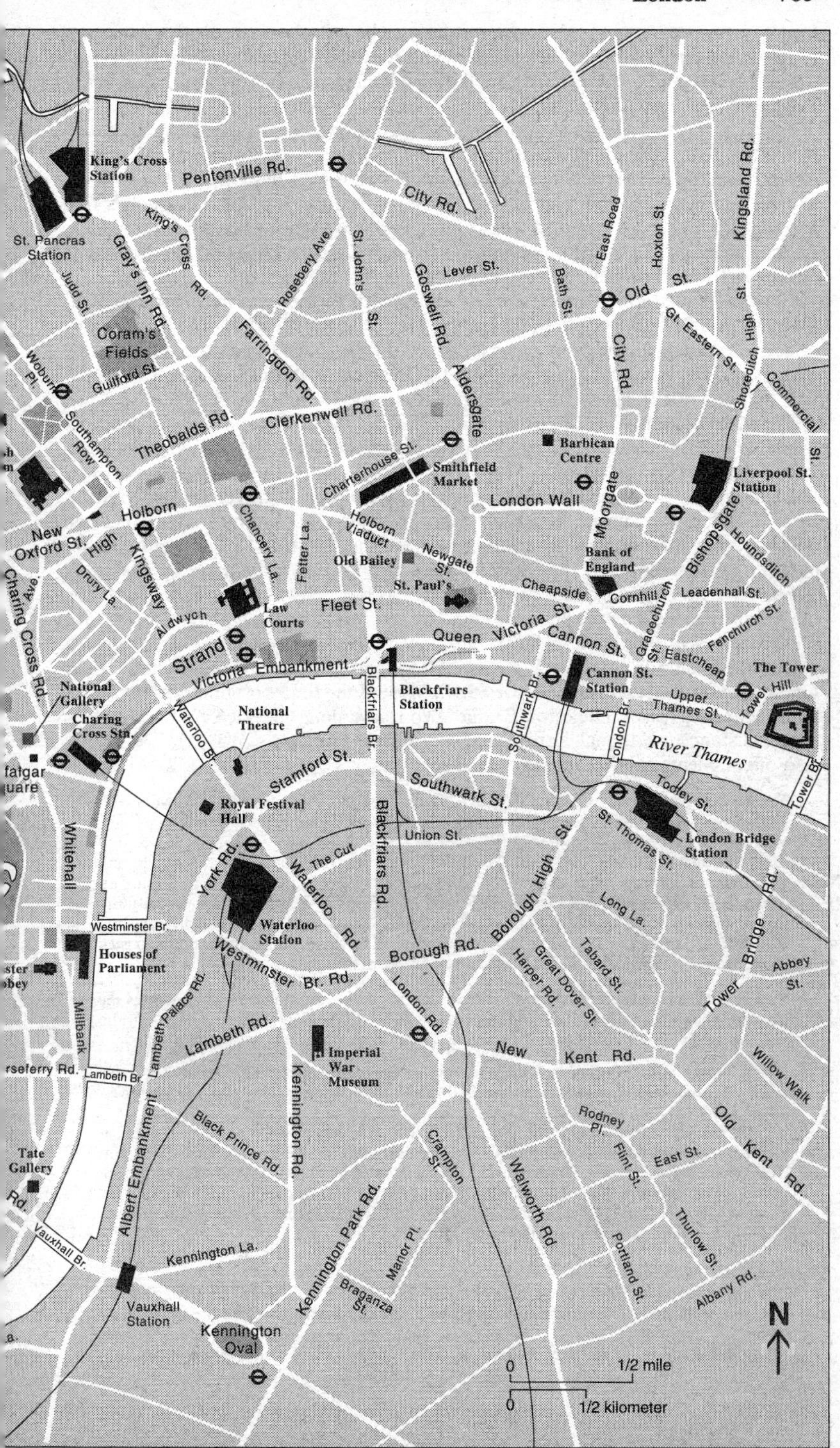
King's Cross Station
St. Pancras Station
Pentonville Rd.
City Rd.
King's Cross Rd.
Gray's Inn Rd.
Judd St.
Rosebery Ave.
St. John's St.
Goswell Rd.
Lever St.
Bath St.
East Road
Hoxton St.
Kingsland Rd.
Old St.
City Rd.
Gt. Eastern St.
Shoreditch High St.
Commercial St.
Coram's Fields
Guilford St.
Woburn Pl.
Southampton Row
Farringdon Rd.
Aldersgate
Clerkenwell Rd.
Theobalds Rd.
Charterhouse St.
Smithfield Market
Barbican Centre
London Wall
Moorgate
Liverpool St. Station
Holborn
New Oxford St.
High
Chancery La.
Fetter La.
Holborn Viaduct
Newgate St.
Old Bailey
St. Paul's
Bank of England
Bishopsgate
Houndsditch
Kingsway
Drury La.
Charing Cross Rd.
Law Courts
Fleet St.
Cheapside
Cornhill
Gracechurch St.
Leadenhall St.
Fenchurch St.
Aldwych
Strand
Queen Victoria St.
Cannon St.
Eastcheap
The Tower
Tower Hill
Victoria Embankment
Blackfriars Br.
Blackfriars Station
Southwark Br.
Cannon St. Station
London Br.
Upper Thames St.
National Gallery
Charing Cross Stn.
Waterloo Br.
National Theatre
River Thames
Trafalgar Square
Stamford St.
Southwark St.
Tooley St.
Tower Br.
Royal Festival Hall
Blackfriars Rd.
Union St.
St. Thomas St.
London Bridge Station
Whitehall
York Rd.
The Cut
Waterloo Rd.
Borough High St.
Long La.
Waterloo Station
Westminster Br.
Borough Rd.
Tabard St.
Great Dover St.
Harper Rd.
Tower Bridge Rd.
Abbey St.
Houses of Parliament
Westminster Br. Rd.
London Rd.
Lambeth Palace Rd.
Millbank
Lambeth Rd.
Imperial War Museum
New Kent Rd.
Willow Walk
Horseferry Rd.
Lambeth Br.
Kennington Rd.
Rodney Pl.
Old Kent Rd.
Black Prince Rd.
Crampton St.
Flint St.
East St.
Tate Gallery
Albert Embankment
Walworth Rd
Thurlow St.
Vauxhall Br.
Kennington Park Rd.
Manor Pl.
Portland St.
Kennington La.
Albany Rd.
Braganza St.
Vauxhall Station
Kennington Oval
N
0
1/2 mile
0
1/2 kilometer

Line's northeast corner leads to **Bloomsbury,** which harbors the British Museum, London University colleges, art galleries and specialty bookshops. Trendy residential districts stretch to the north, including **Hampstead,** with its enormous heath and fabulous views of the city.

Trying to reach a specific destination on foot in London can be frustrating. Numbers often go up one side of a street and then down the other. One road may change names four times in fewer miles and a single name may designate a street, lane, square, and row. A good map is key. For a day's walk, London Transport's free map will do, but those staying a week or longer ought to buy a London street index. *London A to Z* (£1.95-4.25), Nicholson's *Streetfinder* (£1.95-6) and the *Ordnance Survey ABC London Street Atlas* (£4.95) are excellent.

London Walks are informative daily tours with themes varying from the staid ("Shakespeare's London") to the macabre ("Jack the Ripper's London"). Schedules of activities are available from tourist offices or from The Original London Walks, P.O. Box 1708, NW6 1PQ (tel. 435 6413). **Historical Walks of London,** 3 Florence Rd. (tel. 668 4019), sponsors similar guided walks. Both operators charge £4 per walk, with discounts for students. The *London Silver Jubilee Walkway* guide is available free from tourist offices; the route passes the larger sights and some lesser-known treasures.

London is a relatively inexpensive—and complicated—travel center. Getting from London to Europe is easier every year thanks to multiplying charter flights—often cheaper than the train or bus. See the "Getting There" section in the country introduction and the transportation listings below for more details.

For daytrips out of London, **British Rail** has day returns (after 9:30-10am) for only slightly more than the one-way fare. **Green Line** suburban buses (tel. 668 7261) are cheaper still (students ½-fare), but slower; they are best for shorter trips to places like Hampton Court or Windsor. After 9am, you can enjoy unlimited Green Line travel for the rest of the day for £5.50. Most of the routes originate on Buckingham Palace Rd. or on Eccleston Bridge, two roads alongside Victoria Station. For longer distances, **National Express,** 52 Grosvenor Gardens, SW1 (tel. 730 8235), also offers cheap day-returns.

Tourist Offices: Tourist Information Centre, Victoria Station, SW1 (tel. 730 3488, Mon.-Fri. 9am-6pm). Tube: Victoria. Run by London Tourist Bureau. Info and outrageously expensive room bookings (£5 fee, deposit £12) for all of England. Open daily 8am-7pm; Dec.-March Mon.-Sat. 9am-7pm, Sun. 9am-5pm. Tourist offices also at **Heathrow Airport, Harrods,** and **Selfridges.** (Heathrow office open Mon.-Sat. 9am-6pm, Sun. 2-5pm; Nov.-Feb. Mon.-Sat. 9:30am-4pm.) **British Travel Centre,** 12 Regent St., SW1 (tel. 730 3400). Tube: Piccadilly Circus. Best for travel outside of London. Fuses the services of the British Tourist Authority, British Rail, American Express and an accommodations service (£5 booking fee plus deposit). Open Mon.-Fri. 9am-6:30pm, Sat. 9am-5pm, Sun. 9am-4pm.

Budget Travel: Thanks to the days when the sun never set on the Union Jack, London is *the* place to shop for cheap bus, plane and train tickets to North America, Africa, Asia, Australia and the moon. You might browse the ads in *Time Out* or the *Evening Standard.*

STA Travel, 86 Old Brompton Rd. Tube: South Kensington. Also at 117 Euston Rd. Tube: King's Cross. Make this your first stop. Call 938 4711 and be prepared to wait. Open Mon.-Fri. 9am-6pm, Sat. 10am-4pm.

YHA Travel, 14 Southampton St., WC2 (tel. 836 8541). Tube: Covent Garden. Youth oriented. Vast selection of travel guides *(Let's Go* and mere mortals), maps, and sports and camping equipment. Also branch at 174 Kensington High St. (tel. 938 2948). Both open Mon.-Wed. and Fri. 10am-6pm, Thurs. 10am-7:30pm, Sat. 9am-6pm.

Council Travel, 28a Poland St., W1 (tel. 437 7767). Tube: Oxford Circus. Affiliated with pan-U.S. group; great plane deals. Open Mon.-Fri. 9:30am-6pm.

Travel CUTS, 295a Regent St., W1 (tel. 637 3161). Tube: Oxford Circus. Canadian equivalent of Council Travel.

Trailfinders, 42-48 Earl's Court Rd., W8 (tel. 937 5400). Tube: High Street Kensington. Huge and dependable clearinghouse for cheap air tickets anywhere. Open Mon.-Sat. 9am-6pm.

National Express, 52 Grosvenor Gardens, SW1 (tel. 730 8235). Tube: Victoria. International office also handles coach travel throughout England. Branch office at 13 Regent St., SW1. Tube: Piccadilly Circus. Open Mon.-Fri. 9am-5:30pm, Sat. 9am-4pm.

London Student Travel, 52 Grosvenor Gardens, SW1 (tel. 730 3402). Tube: Victoria. Competitive rail, coach, and air fares all over the Continent and beyond. Frequently without age restrictions. Open Mon.-Fri. 8:30am-6:30pm, Sat. 10am-5pm; Nov.-May Mon.-Fri. 9am-5:30pm, Sat. 10am-5pm.

Touropa: 52 Grosvenor Gardens, SW1 (tel. 730 2101). Tube: Victoria. Yet another student travel center specializing in charter flights to the continent and European rail travel. Open Mon.-Fri. 9am-6pm, Sat. 10am-5pm; Nov.-May Mon.-Fri. 9am-5:30pm, Sat. 10am-5pm.

Embassies and High Commissions: U.S., 24 Grosvenor Sq. (tel. 499 9000). Tube: Bond St. **Canadian High Commission,** MacDonald House, 1 Grosvenor Sq., W1 (tel. 629 9492). Tube: Bond St. **Australian High Commission,** Australia House, The Strand (tel. 379 4334). Tube: Aldwych. **New Zealand High Commission,** New Zealand House, 80 Haymarket (tel. 930 8422). Tube: Charing Cross. For visas for **France,** contact the French Consulate, 6a Cromwell Place, SW7 (tel. 823 9555). Tube: South Kensington. Apply only Mon.-Fri. 9-11:30am; pick up only Mon.-Fri. 4-4:30pm. **Bulgaria,** 186 Queen's Gate, SW7 (tel. 584 9400). Tube: South Kensington. **Czechoslovakia,** 28 Kensington Palace Gardens, W8 (tel. 299 1255). Tube: Gloucester Rd. **Hungary,** 35 Eaton Pl., SW1 (tel. 235 4048). Tube: Sloane Sq. **Poland,** 47 Portland Pl. (tel. 580 4324).

Currency Exchange: Go to banks, *never* to *bureaux de change* (such as Chequepoint), which have high fees and/or ridiculously bad rates. If you're stuck outside banking hours, stick to Thomas Cook or American Express. **Thomas Cook,** 15 Shaftesbury Ave., Piccadilly Circus, and **Exchange International,** Victoria Station, are open 24 hrs.

American Express: 6 Haymarket, SW1 (tel. 930 4411). Tube: Piccadilly Circus. **Currency exchange** open Mon.-Fri. 9am-5pm, Sat. 9am-6pm. Message and mail pick-up Mon.-Fri. 9am-5pm, Sat. 9am-noon. Other offices (no mail) at 147 Victoria St. (Tube: Victoria), opposite Harrods (Tube: Knightsbridge), 54 Cannon St. (Tube: Cannon St.), and in the British Travel Centre (above).

Post Office: Unless specified otherwise, Poste Restante goes to the Chief Office, King Edward Building, King Edward St., EC1 (tel. 239 5049). Tube: St. Paul's. Open Mon.-Tues. and Thurs.-Fri. 8:30am-6:30pm, Wed. 9am-6:30pm. Save hassle and have mail sent to Trafalgar Sq. Branch Office, 24-28 William IV St., WC2N 4DL (tel. 930 9580). Tube: Charing Cross. Open Mon.-Sat. 8am-8pm.

Telephones: You can make international calls from any pay phone; use a Phonecard for convenience. The blue Mercurycard phones are cheaper than BT phones. For London directory information tel. 142; for Britain and Ireland tel. 192; operator tel. 100; international operator tel. 153. London has 2 **city codes:** 071 (central London) and 081 (outer London). Use the code only if you are calling from one area to the other. All London numbers listed in *Let's Go* are (071) unless otherwise indicated.

Flights: Heathrow Airport (tel. 759 4321) is jolly busy. From Heathrow, take the **Underground** to central London (70 min., £2.30, 1-day **Travelcard** £3.10). London Regional Transport's double-decker **Airbus** zips from Heathrow to central points, including hotels in the city (1-2 hr., £5, children £3), and a **National Express** bus goes to Victoria Coach Station for £6.75. The bus gives you more baggage room than the underground (and a better view). If you arrive after midnight, avoid the £25 taxi fare by taking night bus #N97 from Heathrow bus station to Piccadilly Circus (every hr. just before the hr. until 5am). Most charter flights land at **Gatwick Airport** (tel. 668 4211). From there, **British Rail** runs to Victoria Station (30 min., £7). Avoid taxis; they take twice as long and cost five times as much. **Green Line** (tel. 668 7261) coach #777 travels between Gatwick and Victoria in 70 min. (Departure times 7am-6pm: 10 before the hr. and 20 past the hr. Variable departures at other times). £6, round-trip £7.) Call your airline about shuttle buses if flying out of smaller **Luton Airport,** north of London. British Rail's fledgling Stansted Express runs to **Stansted Airport** from Liverpool St. station.

Trains: Call 834 2345 for information on all **British Rail** departures to continental Europe, or call one of the phone numbers below. The London Underground stops at all 8 British Rail Stations in central London. For information on departures to the south and east of London, call 928 5100. For the south and west (including the Republic of Ireland via Fishguard), call 262 6767. For the north and west of Britain, as well as Northern Ireland and the Republic of Ireland via Holyhead, call 387 7070. For the east and northeast, call 278 2477.

Buses: National Express serves most of Great Britain. The main depot is **Victoria Coach Station** on Buckingham Palace Rd. at Elizabeth St. (tel. 730 0202). Tube: Victoria. Private coach companies are frequently the best deal for long-distance trips (to the North, to Scotland, to Ireland). **Euroways,** 52 Grosvenor Gardens (tel. 730 8235). Tube: Victoria. Runs coaches from Victoria Coach station to Paris, Greece, and other continental destinations. Check the back of *Time Out* magazine for information.

Luggage Storage: Very restricted, due to recent bombs.

Taxis: London taxi fares are steep, but over short distances or for parties of 4 or more they can make more sense than the tube. Cabbies know every street in Greater London. Drivers are accustomed to a 15% tip. Hail your own black cab, or call a radio-dispatched taxi (tel. 272 0272, 620 0424 or 286 0286). Apart from the licensed black cabs, there are countless "minicab" companies, listed in the Yellow Pages. **Ladycabs** (tel. 254 3501) has only women drivers.

Public Transportation: The **Underground** (or **Tube**) is fast, efficient and crowded. It opens about 6am; the last train runs around midnight. You must buy your ticket before you board and pass it through automatic gates at both ends of your journey; fare dodgers can be fined up to £200. Within London Transport's central zone (bounded roughly by the Underground's Circle line), the fare is a standard 80p; journeys outside this zone cost up to £2.30. Transfers are free. To avoid queues and constant coin-scrounging, arm yourself with a **Travelcard;** a superb value, it allows boundless use of London's buses, tube, and trains. The one-day Travelcard, valid after 9:30am, costs £2.30 for central London, £2.70 or £3.10 for wider coverage (not valid on night buses). The 7-day costs £10 for the central zones; bring a passport photo (photo booths at Victoria, Leicester Sq., Westminster, Earl's Court, or Oxford Circus Tube stations give 4 snaps for £1.50). London's languorous **buses** are a great way to see the city. Fares are generally 10-20p lower than the Tube. Pick up a free *London Bus Map* from a Travel Information Centre (Euston, King's Cross, Victoria, Oxford Circus, Heathrow, Piccadilly Circus, Liverpool St. and St. James's Park). Also get a schedule for the **night bus** routes; these can save your life after midnight, when other forms of transport have turned into pumpkins. London Transport's 24-hr. phone information line (tel. 222 1234) can advise you on all routes.

Bike Rental: On Your Bike, 22 Duke St. Hill, SE1 (tel. 357 6958). Tube: London Bridge. Ten-speeds from £8 per day, £30 per week. ID and £50 deposit required. Mountain bikes about twice the rate, with £200 deposit. Open Mon.-Fri. 9am-6pm, Sat. 9:30am-4:30pm.

Hitchhiking: Those hitching to Cambridge take the Tube to Turnpike Lane (Piccadilly Line), then bus #144, 217, or 231 to Great Cambridge Roundabout, then A10; those going to Canterbury and Dover take bus #53 to Blackheath (Shooters Hill Rd.), then A2 to M2; those going to Birmingham, the Lake District and Scotland take bus #16a to Staples Corner, then M1 to M6; those heading to Oxford take the Tube to Hanger Lane (Central Line), then walk along Western Ave. to A40, and take A40 to M40; those desiring South Wales take bus #27 from Marylebone Rd. to A4, then to M4, or the Tube to Chiswick Park (District Line), then walk along Chiswick High Rd. to the roundabout (A315) to M4.

Disabled Travelers' Information and Services: Try **RADAR** (tel. 637 5400), the **Disability Advice Service** (tel. (081) 870 7437) or **GLAD** (Greater London Association for the Disabled; tel. 247 0107).

Gay and Lesbian Travelers' Information: London Lesbian and Gay Switchboard (tel. 837 7324). 24-hr. advice and support service. **London Lesbian and Gay Centre,** 67-69 Cowcross St. (tel. 608 1471). Tube: Farringdon. The largest in Europe: bar, café, disco, bookshop, women-only floor. Open daily noon-11pm. *Time Out* magazine provides exhaustive listing of clubs, events and information.

Crises: Samaritans, 46 Marshall St. W1 (tel. 734 2800). Tube: Oxford Circus. 24-hr. hotline for every possible problem. **London Rape Crisis Centre,** P.O. Box 69, WC1 (tel. 837 1600), offers advice, counselling, and accompaniment to a doctor or court. 24 hrs.

Legal Trouble: Release, 388 Old St., EC1 (tel. 729 9904, 24-hr. emergency number 603 86 54). Tube: Liverpool St. Specializes in drug arrests.

Pharmacy: Bliss Chemists, 5 Marble Arch, W1 (tel. 723 6116). Open daily 9am-midnight. Most branches of **Boots** are open Mon.-Sat. 9am-7pm.

Medical Assistance: Call 999 for **ambulance** assistance. In an emergency, you can receive free treatment in the casualty ward (emergency room) of any hospital. Try the **London Hospital** at Whitechapel (Whitechapel Rd., E1; tel. 377 7000) or **Westminster Hospital** at Pimlico (Dean Ryle St., Horseferry Rd., SW1; tel. 828 9811). **Family Planning Association,** 27-35 Mortimer St. (tel. 636 7866; Tube: Oxford Circus), provides contraceptive advice, pregnancy tests, and abortion referrals. Open Mon.-Thurs. 9am-5pm, Fri. 9am-4:30pm.

Emergencies: Police, Fire or **Ambulance** (tel. 999). No coins required.

Accommodations and Camping

London's popularity assures most hotels a steady stream of customers; the hospitality and delicious breakfasts of English B&Bs are best experienced outside the capital. Fortunately, London hotels frequently offer reduced weekly rates or rent by the bed in large "shared" rooms. Reservations are highly recommended in summer. Write well in advance, stating your date of arrival and probable length of stay. Some budget hotels now take credit card bookings. London offers an enormous range of accommodations; consider staying in a private hostel or a university hall of residence.

YHA Hostels

Relatively cheap and dependably cheery, London's YHA hostels can be a welcome relief from dreary B&Bs. Despite daytime lockouts and curfews, they remain buzzing meeting places for travelers, and the youthful, international staff are often remarkably helpful.

Hostels are invariably crowded. Although groups snarf much space in advance, all hostels try to keep some beds free for individuals. For July and August, you should reserve a bed by writing in advance, or else call and arrive before breakfast. There is a £1 summer surcharge per night from June to September. All the permanent hostels are being equipped with large lockers, 1 per bed, which require a padlock. All London hostels require international membership cards. These are available for £9.60 at the hostels or at YHA London Headquarters, 14 Southampton St. (tel. 836 8541; Tube: Covent Garden; open Mon.-Sat. 9:30am-6pm).

Holland House (King George III Memorial Youth Hostel), Holland Walk, Kensington, W8 (tel. 937 0748), next to Holland Park Open Air Theatre. Tube: Holland Park or High St. Kensington. Mansion on the east side of Holland Park; Londoners play cricket while befuddled squirrels and hostelers look on. Bright and bustling. Currency exchange. Reception open 7am-11:30pm. No lockout. No curfew. £14, ages 16-20 £12, under 16 £10.

Earl's Court, 38 Bolton Gardens, SW5 (tel. 373 7083). Tube: Earl's Court. A converted townhouse in a leafy residential neighborhood, set just off the Earl's Court one-way system. Currency exchange. Kitchen amenities. Reception open 7am-midnight. No curfew. £12, ages 16-20 £11, under 16 £9.

Oxford Street, 14-18 Noel St., W1 (tel. 734 1618). Tube: Oxford Circus. Smack-dab in the heart of London. Enjoy the fresh paint and pristine carpets while they last. Reception open 7am-10:30pm. No curfew. Plush, small rooms for 2-4. Baggage room. Currency exchange. £15, ages 16-20 £13, under 16 £11.

Hampstead Heath, 4 Wellgarth Rd., Hampstead, NW11 (tel. (081) 458 9054). Tube: Golder's Green, then a ¼-mi. walk along North End Rd. to within yards of the Heath. Sadly, school groups frequently invade. Currency exchange. Reception open 7am-11pm. No curfew. Wheelchair access. £12, ages 16-20 £11, under 16 £9.

Highgate, 84 Highgate West Hill, N6 (tel. (081) 340 1831). Tube: Archway, then a ¾-mi. walk up Highgate Hill and Highgate High St. Or take bus #210 or 271 from the Tube to Highgate Village, and walk down South Grove. Out-of-the-way Georgian house in a beautiful neighborhood—well worth the trek. Kitchen overflows with crockery. Reception open 7-10am and 5-11pm. Lockout 10am-5pm. £9.50, ages 16-20 £8, under 16 £7.

White Hart Lane, All Saints Halls of Residence, White Hart Lane, N17 (tel. (081) 885 3234). Tube: Seven Sisters, then British Rail to White Hart Lane (70p); or British Rail direct from Liverpool St.; or Tube: Wood Green, then bus #W3. Drab dorms. Avoid walking alone from the station at night. Bathtubs only. Self-catering and laundry facilities. Reception open 7am-2pm and 5pm-midnight. No curfew. £10. Open July 9-Aug. 31. Send early enquiries to Hampstead Heath, above.

Wood Green, Brabant Rd., N22 (tel. (081) 881 4432). Tube: Wood Green, then 2 min. west on Station Rd. ½ hr. from central London. 157 single rooms in a gloomy dorm. As at White Hart, come home in groups. No lockout, no curfew. Superior kitchen facilities. Laundry. £10. Open three weeks at Easter and July 9-Sept. 14. Send early enquiries to Hampstead Heath, above.

Private Hostels

The following places are less likely to be crammed with screeching schoolchildren, do not require membership cards, and tend to be less attached to their rule boards. Open year-round, all offer facilities similar to those at IYHF hostels.

The Ritz, on Piccadilly St. (tel. 493 8181). Tube: Isn't that the underground conveyance for poor people? Just take the Rolls. Clean rooms, but no kitchen facilities and no lockers for your backpack. A marginal 1st choice. Singles £135. Doubles £160. Suites £400-700. Sheets and showers included.

Curzon House Hotel, 58 Courtfield Gardens, SW5 (tel. 373 6745). Tube: Gloucester Rd. Exceptional staff makes this one of the galaxy's homiest hostels. Kitchen facilities and TV lounge. Curfew? Bah. Dorms £13 per person. Singles £26. Doubles £34. Triples £45. Continental breakfast included.

Elizabeth House (YWCA Hostel), 118 Warwick Way, SW1 (tel. 630 0741). Welcomes young people and families with children over 5. Affable staff dispels institutional feel. Singles £20. Doubles £35. Continental breakfast included. Reserve months in advance.

Maranton House Hostel, 14 Barkston Gardens, SW5 (tel. 373 5782). Tube: Earl's Court. Minotaurs in bathrooms. Small dorms £10. Singles £26. Doubles £35. Continental breakfast. Kitchen facilities £3 extra. Key deposit £5.

Lee Abbey International Students' Club, 57-67 Lexham Gardens, W8 (tel. 373 7242). Tube: Earl's Court. Large, private student accommodations. Student status required during school year. Singles from £14.60, weekly £102. Doubles from £32, weekly £222. Triples from £34.50, weekly £242. Fantastic long-term rates. Continental breakfast and optional cheap weekly meal tickets. Write to the warden at least 1 month in advance with a self-adressed stamped envelope or 2 international reply coupons.

Anne Elizabeth House Hostel, 30 Collingham Pl, SW5 (tel. 370 4821). Tube: Earl's Court. Large dorms with shared kitchen, laundry, and ironing facilities. No curfew. £10-17 depending upon season. Continental breakfast included. Call at least 1 month in advance.

Central University of Iowa Hostel, 7 Bedford Pl., WC1 (tel. 580 1121), near the British Museum. Tube: Holborn or Russell Sq. Spartan but bright and clean rooms. Laundry facilities, TV room. 2-week max. stay. Reception open 8am-1pm and 3-10pm. Dorms £13.50. All-you-can-eat continental breakfast included. Open May-Aug. Write as soon after April 1 as possible for reservations.

Centre Français, 61 Chepstow Pl., W2 (tel. 221 8134). Tube: Notting Hill Gate or Bayswater. Delightful atmosphere, immaculate hostel, elegant area. Dorm rooms £11.75 per person. Singles £21.10. Doubles £36.80. Triples £44.70. Quads £59.60. Weekly rates. Breakfast included. Book in advance in writing or by phone with Visa or MasterCard.

Palace Hotel, 31 Palace Ct., W2 (tel. 221 5628). Tube: Notting Hill Gate or Queensway. Vibrant clientele and staff and big, bright dorm rooms. £8. Weekly £50.

Astor Inn, 27 Montague St., WC1 (tel. 580 5360), off Bloomsbury Sq. Tube: Holborn, Tottenham Court Rd., or Russell Sq. A young, international clientele, a buoyant staff, and a terrific location. Free use of safe. Reception open 24 hrs. Dorms £7.80-10.80. Doubles £29. Triples £35. Quads £45. Oct.-April weekly rates.

Quest Hotel, 45 Queensborough Terr., W2 (tel. 229 7782). Tube: Queensway. Standard hostel accommodation. Central location. No curfew. Kitchen facilities and snack bar. £8.50-10. Key deposit £2.

Tonbridge School Clubs, 120 Cromer St. (tel. 837 4406). Tube: King's Cross. Seedy neighborhood. Men sleep in basement gym; women in karate-club hall. Blankets and foam pads provided, hot showers, TV lounge, backpack storage. Students preferred; non-British passport-holders only. Reception open 10pm-midnight. Check-out 10am. £2.

Halls of Residence

Though slightly more expensive than the cheapest hotels, university dorms feature more amenities. Most have space only in summer (mid-July to Sept.) and have single rooms. Write to the bursar in advance.

King's College, part of the University of London, handles summer bookings for the seven halls listed below. They serve continental breakfast, include kitchen and laundry facilities, and have no curfew. To book, write to Elspeth Young, King's Campus Vacation Bureau,

552 King's Rd., London SW10 0UA (tel. 351 6011). Prices vary according to location, but hover at £21-23 per person.

Queen Elizabeth Hall, Campden Hill Rd., W8 (tel. 333 4255). Tube: High St. Kensington. One block north from the Tube. Far and away the nicest of the King's College halls.
Lightfoot Hall, Manresa Rd. at King's Rd., SW3 (tel. 351 2488). Tube: Sloane Sq. or South Kensington. Bus #49 from South Kensington; bus #11 from Sloane Sq. Prime location. Modern institutional rooms.
Ingram Court, 552 King's Rd. (no tel.). Tube: Fulham Broadway, then 10-minute walk. Popular hall on the main campus. Green lawn with romantic duck pond. Free use of tennis courts.
Wellington Hall, 71 Vincent Sq., Westminster, SW1 (tel. 834 4740). Tube: Victoria. From the station, 1 long block along Vauxhall Bridge Rd. to Rochester Row to Vincent Sq. Beautiful green cricket pitch.
King's College Hall, Champion Hill, SE5 (tel. 733 2167), British Rail to Denmark Hill. £4-5 cheaper than the residence halls listed above, and commensurately less convenient.
Malcolm Gavin Hall, Beachcroft Rd., SW17 (tel. (081) 767 3119; Tube: Tooting Bec). Again, less convenient and £4-5 cheaper.

Queen Alexandra's House, Kensington Gore, SW7 (tel. 589 3635 or 589 4053), just southwest of Albert Hall. Tube: South Kensington. Women only. Ornate Victorian building. Most welcoming, with a touch of class. Kitchen and laundry facilities, sitting room, and sunny dining hall. £20. English breakfast included. Open July 20-Aug. 15. Written reservations to Mrs. Makey.

James Leicester Hall, Market Rd., N7 (tel. 607 5417 or 607 3250). Tube: Caledonian Rd. Bright, modern university hall round the corner from the Tube. Bar. Singles with wash basins £16.35. Reservations compulsory. Open Easter and July-Sept.

Tufnell Park Hall, Hudelleston Rd., N7 (tel. 607 3250). Tube: Tufnell Park. Another dorm, a modern tower block in fabulous Tufnell Park. Prices, opening times and reservations as for James Leicester Hall; book through James Leicester office.

International Student House, 229 Great Portland St., NW1 (tel. 631 3223), at the foot of Regent's Park. Tube: Great Portland St. A thriving metropolis, with its own films, discos, study-groups, expeditions, parties, and mini-market. 300 beds in uninspiring but well-kept singles and doubles. 43 flats. Singles £19.95. Doubles £16.85 per person. Triples £14.15 per person. Breakfast included.

John Adams Hall, 15-23 Endsleigh St., WC1 (tel. 387 4086), off Tavistock Sq. Tube: Euston Sq. Elegant London University building; some rooms have balconies. Mostly singles. Laundry facilities and creature comfort. Reception open Mon.-Fri. 8am-1pm and 2-10pm, Sat.-Sun. 9am-1:30pm and 5:30-10pm. Singles £19.42. Doubles £33.72. English breakfast included. Book well in advance, then confirm. Open Easter and July to Sept.

Passfield Hall, 1 Endsleigh Pl., WC1 (tel. 387 3584 or 387 7743). Tube: Euston. London School of Economics hall in a leafy area around the corner from John Adams. Many long-term residents. High-ceilinged rooms vary spastically in size. Laundry and kitchen facilities. Singles £16. Doubles £25. Breakfast included. Open July-Sept. (rooms scarce July-early Aug.) and 1 month around Easter.

Canterbury Hall, 12-28 Cartwright Gardens, WC1H (tel. 387 5526). Smaller, older hall sandwiched between mammoth modern ones. Groups get the lion's share of accommodations here; some individual rooms available in summer. 250 small singles. Bathtubs only. Tennis and squash courts, TV lounges, and laundry facilities (£1 per load). £18.50, including English breakfast and evening meal.

Bed and Breakfast Hotels

The number of B&Bs in London boggles the mind, but most are about as distinct as blades of grass, providing functional facilities, a TV lounge, indifferent service, and slightly tawdry neighborhoods. Consider choosing simply on the basis of location. Scan the neighborhood descriptions below for a general idea.

B&Bs: Victoria and Earl's Court

These areas represent the bargain basement of budget B&Bs. Near Victoria Station, patrol Belgrave Road, St. George's Drive, or Warwick Way for dim but acceptable lodging at £20-25 per person. Earl's Court, a haven for Aussies, is less tranquil. Penywern Rd. and Earl's Court Sq. are also fertile areas.

Luna House Hotel, 47 Belgrave Rd., SW1 (tel. 834 5897). Bus #24 from Victoria or Trafalgar. An easy first choice. Private baths. Singles from £20. Doubles from £34. Triples from £42. Winter rates up to 40% lower.

Oxford House, 92-94 Cambridge St., SW1 (tel. 834 6467). Quiet residential street. Doting manager and Hannibal the rabbit preside over this happy fiefdom. TV lounge. Power breakfasts. Singles £26. Doubles £36. Triples £45. Quads £51.

The Beaver Hotel, 57-59 Philbeach Gardens, SW5 (tel. 373 4553). Well-appointed rooms and elegant TV lounge. Pool table and endless coffee downstairs. Singles £28. Doubles £37, with bath £50. Triples with bath £60.

York House Hotel, 28 Philbeach Gardens, SW5 (tel. 373 7519), on a quiet crescent. Price, cleanliness, and management make it ideal for long stays. Singles £21. Doubles £34. Triples £42. Weekly rates at least 25% less.

B&Bs: Kensington and Chelsea

The posh Royal Borough of Kensington and Chelsea is hardly a haven for budget B&Bs. The few exceptions to this rule are particularly desirable.

Vicarage Hotel, 10 Vicarage Gate, W8 (tel. 229 4030), around the corner from Kensington Palace on a quiet sidestreet. Tube: High St. Kensington. Palatial and friendly. Cozy TV lounge, with cushions and old photographs. Singles £26. Doubles £48. Triples £57. Quads £62.

Abbey House Hotel, 11 Vicarage Gate, W8 (tel. 727 2594). Tube: High St. Kensington. Guests return year after year to ebullient innkeepers (the Nayachs), a superb location, and sterling English breakfast. Singles £38. Doubles £48. Triples £58. Quads £68. Reserve months in advance for summer.

B&Bs: Bloomsbury

For a couple of extra pounds, you can lodge near the British Museum, Soho, Piccadilly, and The City; yet most of Bloomsbury, secluded, gracious, and diverting, remains transported from the deafening chaos of central London. Heaps of comfortable hotels with rooms for £16-30 per person line Gower St., though you should ask for a room removed from the busy thoroughfare. Bedford Pl. is a step up in price and comfort, and Cartwright Gardens outshines all streets in the area. As you go toward King's Cross, the digs lose their luster.

Jenkins Hotel, 45 Cartwright Gardens, WC1 (tel. 387 2067). Tube: Russell Sq. Tidy, genteel pastel rooms with telephones, teapots, color TV, hair-dryers, mini fridges, and coal-burning fireplaces. Small singles £30. Doubles £44, with private bath £53. Triples with bath £67.

Euro and George Hotels, 51-53 and 58-60 Cartwright Gardens, WC1 (tel. 387 1528 or 387 6789). Tube: Russell Sq. Ornate rooms with TV, radio and phone. Reserve well in advance. Singles £29.50, with shower £35, toilet £42. Doubles £43, with shower £47, toilet £52.50. Triples £52, with shower £57, toilet £61.

Thanet Hotel, 8 Bedford Pl., WC1 (tel. 636 2869). Tube: Russell Sq. Speckless, spacious rooms with TV, radio and hot pots. Singles £33. Doubles £45, with private bath £55. Triples £55, with shower £65. Quads £70.

Repton House, 31 Bedford Pl., WC1 (tel. 636 7045). Tube: Russell Sq. Cheap for Bedford Place, with clean rooms only slightly less ornate. Singles £25. Doubles £35. Triples with bath £55.

Regency House Hotel, 71 Gower St., WC1 (tel. 637 1804). Tube: Goodge St. Clean, fresh rooms with TV. Singles £25, with shower £45. Doubles £35, with shower £55. Triples £48. Quads £58. Quints £68. Lower rates in winter.

Ridgemount Hotel, 65 Gower St., WC1 (tel. 636 1141). Tube: Goodge St. Exceptionally beautiful B&B with gracious owners. Pleasing rooms with efflorescent wallpaper and firm beds. Doubles £36. Triples £47.25. Quads £60.

B&Bs: Paddington and Bayswater

Squashed between Paddington Station, Hyde Park, and Kensington, this area is noisy, run-down, and crowded with sullen B&Bs. Although almost every building in Norfolk Sq. and Sussex Gardens proclaims itself a hotel, the ones on smaller Talbot Sq. and Princes Sq. are more peaceful and residential. As you travel west, establishments become less seedy.

Garden Court Hotel, 30-31 Kensington Gardens Sq., W2 (tel. 229 2553). Tube: Bayswater. Clean and serene; aspires to higher class than its neighbors. Singles £25, with shower £37. Doubles £37, with shower £49. Triples £49, with shower £55.

Hyde Park Rooms, 137 Sussex Gardens, W2 (tel. 723 0225 or 723 0965). Frank proprietor won't hard-sell her trim rooms. Singles £20. Doubles £30.

Food

London presents a tantalizing range of both foreign and English specialties. With Indian, Lebanese, Greek, Chinese, Thai, Italian, West Indian, and African food inexpensive and readily available, the city has few rivals when it comes to diversity. If you eat but one ethnic meal in London, let it be Indian. You don't have to look far for an Indian restaurant, but meals are £1-3 cheaper on Westbourne Grove (Tube: Bayswater), or near Euston Station (Tube: Euston), than in Piccadilly and Covent Garden.

Supermarkets are cheaper than corner shops and stock inexpensive pre-fab dishes. **Safeway** stores punctuate King's Rd., Edgware Rd. (not far from Paddington), and the Brunswick Shopping Centre opposite Russell Sq. Tube stop. **Sainsbury** has a branch on Victoria Rd., not far from Victoria Station and another on Cromwell Rd. (Tube: Gloucester Rd.). Ubiquitous **Europa Food** stores are expensive, but stay awake until 11pm.

Kensington, Chelsea, and Victoria

Chelsea Kitchen, 98 King's Rd., SW3. Tube: Sloane Sq. Locals rave about this place. Lip-smacking lunches (£3) and dinners (£4). Open Mon.-Sat. 8am-11:30pm, Sun. noon-11:30pm.

Benjy's, 157 Earl's Court Rd., SW7. Tube: Earl's Court. Lots of burly Australian types binge on the "Builder Breakfast" (bacon, egg, chips, beans, toast, 2 sausages and coffee or tea for £2.80). Open daily 7am-9:30pm.

Palms Pasta on the Hill, 17 Campden Hill Rd., W8. Tube: High St. Kensington. Popular café-style Italian restaurant with a ceiling of Italian newspapers. Spaghetti carbonara £4.60. Happy hour 5:30-7pm. 12.5% service. Open daily noon-11:30pm.

Vecchiomondo Ristorante Italiano, 118 Cromwell Rd., SW7. Tube: Gloucester Rd. Homey Italian restaurant with hanging foliage and wine flasks. Spaghetti carbonara £3. Pizza from £2. Open daily 10am-3pm, 5pm-1am.

La Bersagliera, 372 King's Rd., SW3. Tube: Sloane Sq. then bus #11. Succulent homecooked pizza and pasta (both £3-4). Cozy atmosphere. Italian clientele. Friendly owner. Open Mon.-Sat. 12:30-3pm and 7pm-midnight. Also try the **Chelsea Pot,** at #356.

Up-All-Night, 325 Fulham Rd., SW10. Ferns, fans and sauna booths. Huge burgers and fries £3.40. Open daily noon-6am.

Hard Rock Café, 150 Old Park Lane, W1. Tube: Hyde Park Corner. Behind all the hype there really is a decent burger (from £5-7). Myriad American beers. Arrive before 5pm or grow old in line. Open Sun.-Thurs. 11:30am-12:30am, Fri.-Sat. 11:30am-1am.

Bloomsbury and North London

Diwana Bhel Poori House, 121 Drummond St., NW1. Tube: Warren St. Clean, airy, quick, slick, and tasty. *Bhel poori.* Try *samosas* or *thali* (silver tray with portions of meat, vegetables, rice, sauce, bread, and dessert). Meals £1.50-5. BYOB. Open daily noon-midnight. Another location at 50 Westbourne Grove (Tube: Bayswater).

Chutney's, 124 Drummond St., NW1. Tube: Warren St. A light, cheerful Indian vegetarian café with a 12-dish all-you-can-eat lunch buffet (£3.95). Open daily noon-2:45pm and 6-11:30pm.

Cranks Health Food, 9-11 Tottenham St., W1. Tube: Goodge St. Hearty vegetarian dishes served in a large, cheery room. Many dishes £1.50-2.25. Open Mon.-Fri. 8am-8pm, Sat. 9am-6pm.

Spaghetti House Ristorante, 15-17 Goodge St., W1. Tube: Goodge St. The original location of a popular chain of authentic pasta houses. *Linguine al funghetto* £4.50. Open Mon.-Sat. noon-11pm, Sun. 5:30-10:30pm.

Café Dot, 42 Queen's Sq., WC1. On the ground floor of the Mary Ward Center. Tube: Russell Sq. Look for the 18th-century town house next to the Italian Hospital. Good, hot food at rock-bottom prices. Scampi and chips £2. Sandwiches £1. Open Mon.-Fri. 11am-3pm and 4pm-9pm, Sat. 11:30am-5pm.

The Fryer's Delight, 19 Theobald's Rd., WC1. Tube: Holborn. One of the best chippies around—come for the food, not the decor. Fish or chicken with chips £2-3. Open Mon.-Sat. noon-11pm.

Indian Veg Bhelpoori House, 92 Chapel Market, N1. Tube: Angel. An unmistakable bargain: all-you-can-eat lunch buffet (noon-3pm) of Indian vegetarian food for a startling £3.25. Cheap evening meals (£3.95) from 6-11pm.

Café Pasta, 8 Theberton St., N1. Tube: Angel. A comfortable restaurant with a dash of elegance, perfect for those seeking romance at a discount. Don't sit too near the door in windy weather. Fusili with ham and leeks £4.50, side salads £1.50. For each salad purchased, 10p is given to Friends of the Earth. Munch, munch. Open Mon.-Sat. 9:30am-11:30pm, Sun. 9:30am-11pm.

Marine Ices, 8 Haverstock Hill, NW3. Tube: Chalk Farm. The savior of ice cream devotees. Superb Italian ice cream and sundaes—the cream of the crop. Single scoops 40p. Open Mon.-Sat. 10:30am-10:45pm, Sun. noon-8pm.

The West End and City of London

Palms, 39 King St., WC2. Tube: Covent Garden. Waiters serve up scrumptious Italian dishes when they're not dancing. Pastas £3-5. Open daily noon-midnight.

Food for Thought, 31 Neal St., WC2. Tube: Covent Garden. Generous vegetarian servings straight from the pot in an intimate plant-filled restaurant. Daily specials £3. Open Mon.-Sat. noon-8pm, Sun. noon-4:30pm.

Poons, 41 King St., WC2. Tube: Covent Garden. Renowned Cantonese restaurant, owned by a chef descended from a long line of Chinese sausage makers. Pre-theater dinner (5-7:30pm, £6.90) includes soup, rice and entree. Cover charge £1. Reservations suggested. Open daily noon-midnight.

Scott's, corner of Bedfordbury St. and New Row, WC2. Tube: Covent Garden. Crowds line up at lunchtime to get into this sophisticated patisserie and sandwich shop. Sandwiches from £1.50. Open daily 8am-11:30pm.

Stockpot Restaurant, 40 Panton St., SW1. Tube: Piccadilly Circus. Always packed—delicious food at well-bottom prices. Salads with salmon, smoked mackerel, or chicken £2.60. A feast for under £3. Open Mon.-Sat. 8am-11:30pm, Sun. noon-10pm. Additional locations: 50 James St. (Tube: Bond St. or Marble Arch), open Mon.-Sat. 11am-10:30pm; 6 Basil St., near Harrod's (Tube: Knightsbridge), open Mon.-Sat. 11:30am-10:30pm.

Chuen Cheng Ku, 17 Wardour St., W1. Tube: Leicester Sq. Considered by some to be one of the planet's best restaurants. Certainly one of the largest menus. Dim sum dishes £1.50. Open daily 11am-midnight.

Wong Kei, 41-43 Wardour St., W1. Tube: Leicester Sq. Possibly the rudest waiters and the best value Chinese food in Soho. Singapore fried noodles £2.20. Set dinner £6. Open daily noon-11:30pm.

Pizza Express, 10 Dean St., W1. Tube: Tottenham Court Rd. Great pizza from £3. Live jazz Mon.-Sat. from 9:30pm. Open daily noon-midnight. Many other branches.

Blooms, 90 Whitechapel High St., E1. Tube: Aldgate East. London's finest kosher restaurant, with good salt (corned) beef and chopped liver sandwiches (£2.60) to go. Popular Sun. mornings. Open Sun.-Thurs. 11am-10pm, Fri. 11am-3pm.

The Place Below, St. Mary-le-Bow Church Crypt, Cheapside, EC2. Tube: St. Paul's. Hip, unique vegetarian café, very crowded at lunch. Quiche and salad £4.45. Meals about £1 cheaper than take-away. Open Mon.-Fri. 7:30am-3pm, also Thurs. 6-10:30pm.

Paddington and Bayswater

Khan's, 13-15 Westbourne Grove. Tube: Bayswater. Most Indian restaurants are cemetery quiet, but not Khan's. And no Flock wallpaper! Good-sized meals £4-6. Try the *keema nan* or *tandoori* (£5). Open daily noon-3pm and 6pm-midnight.

Geale's, 2 Farmer St., W8. Tube: Notting Hill Gate. Chipper service, rustic atmosphere, and consummately crisp fish and chips from £3.50. Open Tues.-Sat. noon-3pm and 6-11pm.

Tootsie's, 115 Notting Hill Gate., W8. Tube: Notting Hill Gate. Excellent burgers (£3-4), chips, ice cream, and coffee. Open Mon.-Sat. noon-midnight, Sun. noon-11:30pm.

Pubs

London's countless pubs are as colorful and historic as their country counterparts, but in London the clientele varies widely from one neighborhood to the next. Avoid pubs within ½ mi. of train stations; they prey on the pockets of naïve tourists and often lack atmosphere. For the best prices, head to the East End or south of the Thames. A posher atmosphere prevails in Chelsea and Hampstead. For people-watching, hit the West End. Many London pubs offer a choice of as many as a dozen ales and two ciders—all highly potent. Also on sale is cheap, standard British "pub grub," fruit juices, and soft drinks.

In 1988, Parliament repealed a 1915 liquor law requiring pubs to close from 3-6pm. This means that pubs are now open Mon.-Sat. 11am-11pm, Sun. 11am-3pm and 7-10:30pm. "Time, gentlemen, please!" means you have 10 minutes to finish your drink.

Lamb and Flag, 33 Rose St., WC2. Tube: Covent Garden. Once renowned for bare-fisted boxing matches; the poet John Dryden was thrashed here by a mob of angry readers.

Dirty Dick's, 202-204 Bishopgate. Tube: Liverpool St. Pub bedecked with cobwebs and 2 stuffed cats. Ten ales and one cider on tap. Jack the Ripper once stalked these streets.

Sherlock Holmes, 10 Northumberland St., WC2. Tube: Charing Cross. Replica of Holmes' den at 221B Baker St. includes the tobacco in the slipper and the head of the Hound of the Baskervilles.

Ye Olde Cheshire Cheese, Wine Office Ct., 145 Fleet St., EC4. Tube: Blackfriars or St. Pauls. Authentic 17th-century pub; sawdust on the floors and Yorkshire suds on tap. Dickens, Johnson, and Boswell were regulars. Closed for renovation until summer 1992.

The Prince of Teck, Earl's Court Rd., SW5. Tube: Earl's Court. Some love it, some hate it, but whatever it is it's hot and oppressive. Stuffed Kangaroo and heaps o' Aussies.

King's Head and Eight Bells, 50 Cheyne Walk, SW3. Tube: Sloane Sq., then bus #11, 45, 49, or 219. A favorite of the "Sage of Chelsea," Thomas Carlyle, who lived just up the street. Dylan Thomas got sloshed here too. Superior if slightly expensive lunches.

Admiral Codrington, 17 Mossop St., SW3. Tube: Sloane Sq. Old, handsome pub with peaceful patio; a Sloane Rangers' favorite.

Spaniards Inn, Spaniard's End. Tube: Hampstead, then bus along Spaniard's Rd. A favorite of Dick Turpin's; Dickens didn't mind a pint here either, but then, he may have just been doing research.

The Flask, 77 Highgate West Hill, N6. Tube: Archway. Near the youth hostel. Throbulatingly popular in summer—terrace overflows into the heart of historic Highgate.

Prospect of Whitby, 57 Wapping Wall, London Docks. Tube: Wapping. 600-year-old tavern where diarist Samuel Pepys used to imbibe. Excellent Thamescape.

Sights

London is best explored on foot. Double-deckers speed past many sights, and the London Tube has no view. Peel your eyes for blue plaques mounted on buildings, indicating a famous resident.

An auspicious place to start a day's wander is **Piccadilly Circus,** with its famous statue of Eros (originally intended as the Angel of Christian Charity). **Piccadilly,** running off the Circus, is lined with exclusive shops, including **Fortnum and Mason.** A proper English tea is yours upstairs, while downstairs is an American soda bar of yesteryear. Across the street is the **Royal Academy of Arts;** with frequent traveling exhibitions during the summer, spectators elect their favorites. (Open daily 10am-6pm. Admission £2-4, students £1-2.) On the other side of the Academy building is the ambitious **Museum of Mankind,** a fascinating assemblage of artifacts from non-Western societies. (Open Mon.-Sat. 10am-5pm, Sun. 2:30-6pm. Free.) **Green Park,** farther west on Piccadilly, originally served as a mass grave for plague victims; in memory of the dead, no flowers are planted here (hence the name). All paths across this miniature meadow converge at **Buckingham Palace.** The "Changing of the Guard" occurs daily at 11:30am; arrive early (at least 10:30am) or you won't see a thing. The extravagant "Trooping the Colour" ceremony is on the second or third Saturday in June, near the Queen's official birthday.

The Mall, a wide processional, leads from the palace to **Admiralty Arch** and Trafalgar Square. **St. James's Park,** south of the Mall, shelters an eclectic duck preserve and a flock of lawn chairs. Tourists and surviving pigeons crowd **Trafalgar Square,** where four great stone lions disdain the tourists. A 40-ft. statue of Admiral Nelson tops off the 132-ft. phallus at the center of the square. The **National Gallery,** north of the square, lodges one of the world's finest collections of European painting. Heavyweight works by Da Vinci, Turner, and Velázquez are on display. The new wing, housing masterpieces by Raphael and Giotto, is an architectural point of contention. (Open Mon.-Sat. 10am-6pm, Sun. 2-6pm. Free.) The **National Portrait Gallery,** adjacent to the National Gallery, doubles as a textbook where English schoolchildren meet the great (or at least the famous) people in English history. (Open Mon.-Fri. 10am-5pm, Sat. 10am-6pm, Sun. 2-6pm. Free.) **Charing Cross Road,** leading north from Trafalgar to the theater district of **Leicester Square,** is renowned for its bookshops.

Political Britain branches off **Whitehall,** just south of Trafalgar. The Prime Minister resides next to the Foreign Office, at **10 Downing Street,** now closed to gawpers. In the middle of Whitehall is the **Cenotaph,** a monument to Britain's war dead. Whitehall ends at **Parliament Square,** home of Big Ben, Westminster Abbey, and the sprawling **Houses of Parliament.** To watch Col. Sibthorpe's bicameralism in action—debates are noisy and lively—inquire at your embassy for a pass, or join the queue and be prepared to wait an hour or so. Committee meetings can be seen without the wait. Pedantically speaking, **Big Ben** is neither the tower nor the clock, but the 13½-ton bell, cast when a similarly proportioned Sir Benjamin Hall served as Commissioner of Works. The statue of Winston Churchill, in Parliament Sq., has been pigeon-proofed with electricity. Church and state tie the knot in **Westminster Abbey,** coronation chamber to English monarchs for the past 683 years, as well as the site of **Poet's Corner** and the **Tomb of the Unknown Soldier.** The British Crown bestows no greater honor than burial within these walls. Oddly enough, the abbey plumber is buried here among such greats as Sir Isaac Newton, Charles Darwin, Jim Morrison, Charles Dickens, and Ben Jonson (whose last name is mispelled with an *h* on his tomb). Ask about the story surrounding the Stone of Scone. (Westminster Abbey open Mon.-Fri. 9am-4:45pm, Sat. 9am-2:45pm and 3:45-5:45pm. Free. To see royal chapels, Coronation Chair, and Poet's Corner £2.60, students £1.30; free Wed. 6-8pm. Photography permitted Wed. 6-8pm only.) Abbey Guided Super Tours (tel. 222 7110) are super. (From the Enquiry Desk in the nave Mon.-Fri. 10am, 10:30am, 11am, 2pm, 2:30pm, and 3pm; Sat. at 10am, 11am, and 12:30pm. £6.)

On Millbank, about ½ mi. up the Thames from Parliament Sq., the **Tate Gallery** houses the best of British artists such as Gainsborough, Reynolds and Constable, along with works by Picasso, Dalí, Chagall, Arp and Mondrian. The vast J.M.W. Turner collection moved to the **Clore Gallery,** an extension of the main building. (Both galleries open Mon.-Sat. 10am-5:50pm, Sun. 2-5:50pm. Free.)

Hyde Park shows its best face on Sundays from 11am to dusk, when soapbox orators take freedom of speech to the limit at **Speaker's Corner** (Tube: Marble Arch, *not* Hyde Park Corner). Lamentably, there's a surplus of evangelists, con men and crackpots proclaiming that the area code apocalypse is near. **Kensington Gardens**—an elegant relic of Edwardian England—celebrates the glories of model yacht racing in the squarish Round Pound. From the gardens you can catch a glimpse of Kensington Palace, home of those ever-popular models of marital bliss, Charles and Diana. The Prince of Wales occasionally meditates on the front lawn. When the nearby **Albert Memorial** was unveiled, it was considered a great artistic achievement, but early in this century the cluttered monument became the symbol of Victorian hideousness. Luckily, it's been covered up again by a disgusted renovator. The **Royal Albert Hall,** across the street, resembles nothing so much as an older woman's pudding bowl hat, complete with lace trim. It hosts the Proms, a gloriously British festival of music, from July through September. Just around the corner, Exhibition Rd. contains the **Science Museum** with hands-on flight center; the **Natural History Museum,** a Gothic extravaganza, where dinosaurs frolic on, and the **Victoria and Albert Museum,** a baffling but unparalled museum specializing in fine and applied arts from all periods and from around the world. (Natural History Museum open Mon.-Sat. 10am-6pm, Sun. 11am-6pm. Admission £3.50, students £2, children £1.75. Free Mon.-Fri. 4:30-6pm, Sat.-Sun. 5-6pm. Science Museum open Mon.-Sat. 10am-6pm, Sun. 11am-6pm. Admission £3.50, students £1.75. Victoria and Albert Museum open Mon.-Sat. 10am-5:50pm, Sun. 2:30-5:50pm. Adult donation £2, seniors and students 50p.)

The **City of London** is an enclave unto itself; its gated boundaries are guarded by snarling silver griffins. Once upon a time, "London" meant this walled square mile; Westminster and the rest of today's metropolis were far-flung towns and villages. The **Tower of London** was the grandest fortress in medieval Europe, and the palace and prison of English monarchs for over 500 years. The best-known edifice, the **White Tower,** is also the oldest, begun by William the Conqueror. In 1483, the "Princes in the Tower" (Edward IV and his brother) were murdered in the Bloody Tower in one of the great unsolved mysteries of history; two of the wives of jolly King Henry VIII were beheaded in the courtyard; and in 1941 Hitler's ridiculous deputy Rudolf Hess was sent to the Tower after his parachute dumped him in Scotland. The **Crown Jewels** include the world's largest diamond, the Koh-i-noor, which was mailed third-class from the Transvaal to London in an unmarked brown paper package; Scotland Yard believed that was the safest way of getting it to England. (Tube: Tower Hill. Open Mon.-Sat. 9:30am-5pm, Sun. 2-5pm; Nov.-Feb. Mon.-Sat. 9:30am-4pm. Adults £6, students £4.50, ages under 15 £3.70.) Next to the Tower is one of London's best-known landmarks, **Tower Bridge.** The walkways between the Victorian towers provide one of London's best views. (Tube: Tower Hill. Open daily 10am-6:30pm; Nov.-March daily 10am-4:45pm; last admission 45 min. before closing. Admission £2.50, seniors and children £1.) Other shrapnel of history are scattered throughout the City, among them the **Temple of Mithras** on Victoria St., and 24 Christopher Wren churches interspersed with the soaring steel of modern skyscrapers. Peruse smaller churches, such as The Strand's **St. Clement Danes** of "Oranges and Lemons . . . " fame, or the superb **St. Stephen Walbrook,** in Walbrook, near The Bank. True-blue Cockney Londoners are born within earshot of the famous bells of **St. Mary-le-Bow,** Cheapside. Sir John Soane's **Bank of England** building has walls 8 ft. thick, and a fascinating little museum. (Tube: Bank. Museum open Mon.-Fri. 10am-5pm, Sun. 11am-5pm; Oct.-Easter Mon.-Fri. 10am-5pm.) The **Old Bailey** (Tube: St. Paul's) is London's most famous criminal court. Observing a trial can be thrilling or depressing, depending how you feel about men in wigs. (In session Sept.-July Mon.-Fri. 10am-1pm and 2-4pm.) Nearby is the centerpiece of the City, Wren's mammoth masterpiece, **St. Paul's Cathedral.** In 1940, the cathedral stood firm as German bombs bounced off its lead roof like so many basketballs. Climb above the graves of Wren, Nelson and Wellington in the crypt to the dizzying top of the dome; the view of London is unparalleled. (Tube: St. Paul's. Cathedral open Mon.-Sat. 9am-4:15pm; ambulatory open Mon.-Sat. 9:30am-4:15pm; crypt open Mon.-Fri. 9:30am-4:15pm, Sat. 11am-4:15pm; galleries open Mon.-Sat. 9:45am-4:15pm. Joint admission to cathedral, ambulatory and crypt £2, students £1.50, seniors and children £1. Guided 90-min. tours Mon.-Sat. at 11am, 11:30am,

2pm, and 2:30pm. Tours £4, students £2, children £1.80.) The City has been ravaged by plague, destroyed by fire, reshaped by the conceits of Sir Christopher Wren, demolished by the Luftwaffe, and rebuilt again by corporate yuppies. The **Museum of London** fills you in on the whole story. (Tube: St. Paul's. Open Tues.-Sat. 10am-6pm, Sun. 2-6pm. Free.) The museum is a small part of an immense residential and arts complex, the **Barbican Centre,** praised and derided for its concrete-scape.

Covent Garden—historic meeting place of Henry Higgins and Eliza Doolittle—still sports its grand Royal Opera House, but the tattered old market is now a chic shopping district. At its east end, the engaging **London Transport Museum** successfully transforms the Tube from frustrating to fascinating. (Tube: Covent Garden. Open daily 10am-6pm, last admission 5:15pm. Admission £3, students, seniors and children £1.50.) Neighboring **Soho** also faces gentrification, with the sex-shops squeezed out by slick boutiques and ethnic restaurants. Sequestered to the north, **Bloomsbury**—eccentric, erudite, disorganized, and serene—is known for its naughty literary and scholarly connections. Here rests the **British Museum,** the closest thing this planet has to a complete record of the rise and ruin of world cultures. Among the treasures and plunder on display are the Rosetta Stone (whose inscriptions allowed French scholar Champollion to decipher hieroglyphics), the Elgin Marbles (the Pantheon frieze and metopes that Lord Elgin bought from the Ottomans for £75,000 in 1810 and sold to the museum for £35,000), the world-famous Mummy Room, an early manuscript of *Beowulf* and one of the four surviving copies of the *Magna Carta.* Karl Marx spun portions of *Das Kapital* in the Reading Room. (Open Mon.-Sat. 10am-5pm, Sun. 2:30-6pm. Free.)

If Hyde Park seemed a small bit of green, **Highgate** and **Hampstead Heath** will reassure you that there is an English countryside. To the east, Karl Marx and George Eliot repose in the gothic tangle of Highgate Cemetery (Tube: Archway).

Fleet Street is the traditional den of the British press, although nearly all the papers now operate out of Docklands. It is nicknamed the "Street of Shame" because of the sensationalism, innuendo and lies rampant in some quarters of British journalism. Close by are the **Inns of Court,** which have controlled access to the English Bar since the 13th century, and the endearingly cluttered **Sir John Soane Museum,** 13 Lincoln's Inn Fields (tel. 405 2107), which brings Holbeins, an ancient Egyptian sarcophagus, and much more together under one roof. (Tube: Holborn. Open Tues.-Sat. 10am-5pm. Lecture tour Sat. at 2:30pm. Free.) Across the park is the **London School of Economics** and Dickens's **Old Curiosity Shop** (Tube: Holborn), a tourist traporama.

The London of the future rises in the **Docklands,** a construction site to end all construction sites built over the remains of London's wharves on the Isle of Dogs (a peninsula). Take the Docklands Light Railway (Tube tickets valid) from Tube: Tower Bridge to any of the stations around South Quay and saunter around the multi-story glass-and-steel monstrolosities rising from the wharves. London's newspaper industry has migrated *en masse* to posh new techno-offices here, filling the quays with gray-suited, fast-walking journalists-on-the-make.

Lesser-known but equally rewarding treasures lie south of the river. **Southwark Cathedral,** a smallish, quiet church, boasts London's second-best Gothic structure and a chapel dedicated to that righteous dude, John Harvard. (Tube: London Bridge.) West along the riverbank, a reconstruction of Shakespeare's Globe Theatre is underway. South London's entertainment history lives again in the externally brutal, but internally festive **South Bank Arts Centre.** The **Imperial War Museum,** despite its jingoistic name, is a moving reminder of the human cost of war. (Tube: Lambeth North. Open daily 10am-6pm. Admission £3, students and children £1.50. Free on Fri.)

When your feet begin to ache, take one of London Transport's (tel. 222 1234) narrated **Original London Transport Sightseeing Tours** that cover central London and its landmarks. (Daily 10am-5pm every ½ hr. from Baker St., Piccadilly Circus, Marble Arch and Victoria Station. Adults £8, children £4. £1 off if you pay in advance at the Victoria Station Tourist Information Centre.)

The transport system that encouraged London's urban sprawl blurs the distinction between the city and its surroundings. **Windsor Castle** is the Queen's country retreat and a popular tourist haunt. Homesick North Americans can enjoy a Baskin-Robbins ice cream in the castle's shadow; others might foray into **Eton,** one of England's most famous public (Read: *very* private) schools, where pupils (all male) still wear tailcoats to class.

If you're feeling adventurous, go by train or boat to **Hampton Court.** Once the home of Henry VIII, it is now an excellent museum of art and royal artifacts. The red-brick palace is a quirky change of pace, and its grounds contain the famous maze—a hedgerow labyrinth.

Greenwich, home of the prime meridian and the *Cutty Sark,* is on the Thames, east of central London. You can visit Wren's **Old Royal Observatory,** Inigo Jones's grand and newly renovated **Queen's House,** as well as the suprisingly elaborate **National Maritime Museum.** (*Cutty Sark* open Mon.-Sat. 10am-6pm, Sun. noon-6pm; £2.50, concessions £1.25. Observatory, Queen's House, and Museum open Mon.-Sat. 10am-6pm, Sun. 2-6pm; £3.25, concessions £2.25. Combination admission to all sites £6, concessions £4, families £12.)

Just west of central London on the Thames lie the serene and exotic **Kew Gardens.** Lose yourself in the controlled wilderness of the grounds, or explore the Victorian and modern glasshouses containing thousands of plant species. (Tube or British Rail: Kew Gardens. Open Mon.-Sat. 9:30am-6:30pm, Sun. 9:30am-8pm; Oct.-Jan daily 9:30am-4pm. Glasshouses open daily 10am-4:30pm. Admission £3, students and seniors £1.50, children £1.)

For a more comprehensive treatment of London's offerings, invest in a copy of *Let's Go: London* or *Let's Go: Britain & Ireland.*

Entertainment

For guidance through London's amazing cultural network, consult *Let's Go: London,* the weekly *Time Out* (£1.30), *City Limits* (£1) and *What's On* (70p). These have exhaustive lists of every type of activity.

Theater in London is generally excellent and runs the gamut from the flashy West End to fringe, lunchtime, open-air, and children's productions. The ubiquitous *London Theatre Guide* leaflet gives comprehensive information on the major shows. Seats can cost as little as £1.50, and student standby puts even the best seats within reach. An "S" or "concessions" in the theater listings of *Time Out, City Limits,* the *Independent,* the *Square Deal,* the *Guardian,* or the *Evening Standard* means that unsold tickets will be sold to students for around £4-8 just before the performance. Listen to Capital Radio (95.8FM/1548AM) at 6pm for up-to-date info. Come early. The **Leicester Square Ticket Booth** sells half-price tickets to major plays on the day of the performance. (Mon.-Sat. noon-2pm for matinees, 2:30-6:30pm for evening performances; bring a book for the wait. Booking fee £1, £1.25 for tickets over £5.) Standby tickets for performances in the **National Theatre,** on the South Bank (tel. 928 2252; Tube: Embankment; £6.50-9) sell two hours before the performance. Ask about the dandy backstage tours. The **Barbican Centre** (tel. 628 2295 or 628 9760; Tube: Barbican or Moorgate), the London home of the Royal Shakespeare Company, has student tickets for £5. Watch for productions at the **Young Vic,** the **Theatre Royal Stratford East,** and the **Lyric** theaters, as well as at the **Institute of Contemporary Arts.** From July through October, Regent's Park stages open-air Shakespeare productions (tel. 486 2431; Tube: Baker St.). Tickets run £6-13.50, with student standby tickets £5 one hour before performance. Eschew ticket agencies unless you are pining to see a specific show and are willing to pay with your firstborn.

London is arguably the greatest musical city in the world. Most **classical music** is staged at the acoustically superb **Royal Festival Hall** and at its smaller siblings, the Queen Elizabeth Hall and the Purcell Room (tel. 928 3002 for both), the Barbican Hall (tel. 628 2295), and the small, elegant Wigmore Hall. **Kenwood House** and the **Marble Hill House** have low-priced outdoor concerts on summer weekends;

Kenwood is exquisite. Many churches sponsor free concerts. Opera rings out at the **Royal Opera House** (tel. 240 1066) and the **London Coliseum** (tel. 836 3161). London's premier ballet company also calls the ROH home. The **Proms** (Henry Wood Promenade Concerts), held nightly mid-July through mid-September, are the most popular and endearing feature of the London music scene. The orchestras and soloists are first-rate, and Londoners have been lining up for standing room in the **Royal Albert Hall** for almost a century. The foyer of the **National Theatre** on South Bank always stages a smorgasbord of free concerts (no theater tickets necessary).

Every rage in rock'n'roll hits London at some point or another. Ticket offices and record shops have full listings of concerts. **Ronnie Scott's,** 47 Frith St. (tel. 439 0747), is London's most famous jazz club. (Tube: Leicester Sq. Open Mon.-Sat. 8:30pm-3am, music 9:30pm-2am. Admission £12, students £6.) **The Bass Clef,** 35 Coronet St. (tel. 729 2476; Tube: Old St.), is more of a "classic" jazz joint, replete with smoke, candles, and check-tablecloths (admission £4.50). **The Marquee,** 105 Charing Cross Rd. (tel. 437 6603) (Tube: Leicester Sq.), has seen Jimi Hendrix, The Who and the Stones on its tiny stage; it now does the punk scene (admission £5). **The Town and Country Club,** 9-17 Highgate Rd. (tel. 284 0303; Tube: Kentish Town), hosts rock bands bound for glory. (Admission £7-10.) For **club** happenings, consult *Time Out* or *City Limits,* as many of the best events are one-night stands. Both magazines have listings for all types of music, plus gay and lesbian nightlife. Dress snappy; jeans may be an excuse to keep you out. **Subterania,** 12 Acklam Rd., W10 (tel. (081) 960 4590; Tube: Westbourne Park), is where it's at. A relaxed, multiethnic crowd comes to dance to wicked house-thump. Crucial on Friday and Saturday after midnight. (Casual dress. Admission £6-7. Open daily 10pm-3am.) **The Fridge,** Town Hall Parade, Brixton Hill (tel. 326 5100; Tube: Brixton), is a serious dance dive. Prepare to move to house funk in a steamy atmosphere. Dress code: something, please. (Admission £5-7. Lively mixed-gay night on Tuesdays and some Thursdays. Open Mon.-Thurs. 10pm-3am, Fri.-Sat. 10pm-4am.) The **Camden Palais,** 1A Camden Rd. (tel. 387 0428; Tube: Camden Town), an ornate theater-turned-disco, draws a more British crowd. Wednesday's "Twist and Shout" sees 60s classics instead of the usual house and funk. (Open Tues.-Sat. 9pm-3am. Admission £4-7.) **Heaven,** Villiers St. (tel. 839 3852; Tube: Charing Cross), is one of the best and biggest gay clubs in Europe and is popular among a very cool straight contingent. (Open Tues.-Wed. 10:30pm-3am, Fri.-Sat. 9:30pm-3am. Admission £4-6.) A cheap and laid-back place with lots of room to bop is **The Electric Ballroom,** 184 Camden High St. (tel. 485 9006; Tube: Camden Town; admission £4-5). For "alternative" music, scout for events like psychedelic-punk "Alice in Wonderland" nights at **Gossips,** 69 Dean St. (tel. 434 4480; Tube: Piccadilly Circus).

During late June and early July, half of London hits **Wimbledon** (tel. (081) 946 2244; Tube: Southfields). Admission to the grounds costs £6, £3 after 5pm; important matches costs as much as £28. Lines are laughably long, and finals matches sell out centuries in advance. Arrive at 7am. **Football** (soccer) is a rowdy, raucous, religious obsession in Britain. The atmosphere is electric, although you may feel more comfortable in the seated areas rather than on the terraces, where the faithful congregate. International matches are played at **Wembley;** half a dozen other fields are scattered around the city and are accessible by Tube. (**Arsenal F.C.,** Tube: Arsenal; **Tottenham Spur,** British Rail to White Hart Lane.) The Valhalla of rugby is **Twickenham.** A day at **Lord's** or the **Oval** will expose you to the ritual of cricket; games last three to five days, and *are* more exciting than watching grass grow.

Southeastern England

Kent

Known for its agricultural bounty, Kent is also rich in historical significance. The city of **Canterbury,** which inspired medieval pilgrimages and Geoffrey Chaucer, stille draweth thousandes of travelers. The **cathedral** where Thomas à Becket was murdered in 1170 is a magnificent building, embellished and expanded by archbishops over many generations. (Guided tours Mon.-Fri. at 11:30am, 12:30pm, 2:30pm, and 3:30pm. £2, students £1.) Look for Thomas in the floor of the northwest transept; his name marks the spot. The rest of the city brims with the monuments of religious orders: **St. Augustine's Abbey** near the medieval city wall; **Eastbridge Hospital** on St. Peter's St.; and the gatehouse of **Greyfriars** on the River Stour.

Canterbury's **tourist office,** at 34 St. Margaret's St. (tel. (0227) 76 65 67), books beds reliably (open daily 9:30am-5:30pm, Nov.-Mar. 9:30am-5pm), but arrive early. New Dover Rd. is fat with B&Bs (not the cheapest in town), and home to Canterbury's **IYHF youth hostel,** at #54 (tel. (0227) 46 29 11; curfew 11pm; £7; open March-Oct. daily, call for off-season openings). **Mrs. Wright,** 9 S. Canterbury Rd. (tel. (0227) 76 55 31), loves *Let's Go* readers (who could blame her?) and provides a warm welcome on a quiet street. (£12-13.) **Mrs. Pigden,** 37 Orchard St. (tel. 76 59 81), offers simple but comfortable lodgings (£10 with breakfast). **St. Martin's Touring Caravan and Camping Site,** Bekesbourne Lane (tel. (0227) 46 32 16), off the A257 (the route to Sandwich), is 1½ mi. east of the city center. (£3.75 for 2 people and tent. Open Easter-Sept.) For burgers and a monstrous quantity of fries and salad, try **Caesar's Restaurant,** 46 St. Peter's St. (burgers £4.60). **Alberry's,** 38 St. Margaret's St., serves pasta, pizza, and vegetarian dishes. (£3-5. Open Mon.-Sat. noon-2:30pm and 6:30pm-midnight.)

The "melancholy, long, withdrawing roar" that poet Matthew Arnold heard on Dover Beach is drowned today by the puttering of ferries, the hum of hovercraft, and the squabbling of French families *en vacances.* Besides the famed White Cliffs, best viewed from sea, **Dover** harbors an imposing clifftop castle and relics of Britain's Roman past. On the grounds of **Dover Castle** you can enter the empty **Pharos,** the only Roman lighthouse still extant. (Open daily 9:30am-6:30pm; Oct.-March 9:30am-4pm. Admission £3, students £2.) For an extra £1.50 (students £1), take the guided tour of **Hell Fire Corner,** secret tunnels dating back to Napoleon and crucial to the Allies in WWII. The **Roman Painted House,** New St., is a remarkably well-preserved Roman townhouse with over 400 square feet of wall paintings and an exhibit on the Roman occupation. (Open May-Aug. daily 10am-6pm; Sept.-Oct. and April Tues.-Sun. 10am-5pm. Admission £1.)

Dover's **tourist office,** on Town Wall St. (tel. (0304) 20 51 08), posts a list of the city's B&Bs and makes reservations for free. (Open daily 9am-6pm.) There's an **IYHF youth hostel** at Charlton House, 306 London Rd. (tel. (0304) 20 13 14; lockout 10am-5pm; curfew 11pm; £7). The **Gordon Guest House,** 23 Castle St. (tel. (0304) 20 18 94), has welcoming owners and is perched at the base of the Castle. (Doubles £28.) If you arrive late, look for B&Bs with lights on along Folkestone Rd., next to the station, or camp at **Harthorn Farm,** Martin Hill (tel. (0304) 85 26 58), near the Martin Hill railway station between Dover and Deal. (£2.55 per tent; open March-Oct.)

Trains for Dover's main Priory Station leave from Waterloo, Charing Cross, and Victoria stations in London. Some continue to Dover Western Docks. Courtesy shuttle buses, timed to coincide with sailings, run between Priory Station and the various ports. Most ferries leave from Dover Eastern Docks; hovercrafts hover from the Hoverport. See "Getting There" in the country introduction for more information.

South of Dover, **Rye** is one of the comeliest towns in England, with its picturesque cobblestoned streets and half-timbered houses. Walk down **Mermaid Street** for a taste of old Rye, and visit the **Rye Museum,** housed in the 13th-century Ypres Towers, for background information on Rye's flamboyant history as a smuggler's port. (Open Easter to mid-Oct. Mon.-Sat. 10:30am-1pm and 2:15-5:30pm, Sun. 11:30am-1pm and 2:15-5:30pm. Admission £1.) Rye's **tourist office** on Cinque Port St. (tel. (0797) 22 22 93), distributes a free list of area accommodations. (Open daily 9am-6pm.) Although there are no hostels in Rye, **Mrs. Jones,** 2 The Grove (tel. (0797) 22 34 47), offers a warm bed, good advice and a hearty English breakfast for £11-12.50 per person. Quaff a drink in the splendid **Mermaid Inn.** The best place to dine is the **Peacock** on Lion St. Their country pâté and enormous salads merit a splurge. (Meals £5-8. Open until 9:30pm.) Frequent trains run from London and Dover (change at Ashford).

Sussex

Brighton, with its pier, promenade, and pebble beach, bares all the colorful and tacky delights of an English seaside holiday town and remains the classic venue for "dirty weekends." The **Pavilion,** an architecturally schizophrenic palace, defies description. The **tourist office,** in Marlborough House, 54 Old Steine (tel. (0273) 237 55), can help you find accommodations (10% deposit; open July-Aug. Mon.-Fri. 9am-6:30pm, Sat. 9am-6pm, Sun. 10am-6pm; June and Sept. Mon.-Sat. 9am-6pm, Sun. 10am-6pm; April-May Mon.-Fri. 9am-5pm, Sat. 9am-6pm, Sun. 10am-6pm; Oct.-March Mon.-Sat. 9am-5pm, Sun. 10am-4pm.) The nearest **IYHF youth hostel** is in Patcham Place (tel. (0273) 55 61 96), 4 mi. north along the A23. Take bus #773 or 5A from Old Steine to Patcham. (£9.30, breakfast included. Open daily; Sept.-June Thurs.-Tues.) The **Meeting House Restaurant,** 9 Meeting House Lane, serves toothsome meals from deep within "The Lanes," Brighton's 17th-century narrow brick streets. (Open daily 11am-6pm.) The **Royal Oak,** 46 St. James St., pumps out live folk music on Fridays. **The King and Queen,** Marlborough Place, lights up with jazz (Wed., Thurs. and Sun.). **The Escape Club,** Marine Rd. (tel. (0273) 60 69 06) spotlights trendy dancers. (Open 10pm-2am.)

Arundel is a happy little nugget of a town, two rail hours from London; its magnificently furnished **castle,** home of the Dukes of Norfolk, hoards weaponry, suits of armor, and a noble art collection. (Open June-Aug. Sun.-Fri. noon-5pm; Sept.-Oct. and April-May Sun.-Fri. 1-5pm. Admission £3.55.) The **tourist office,** 61 High St. (tel. (0903) 88 24 19), provides an accommodations service (10% deposit) and hiking information. (Open Mon.-Fri. 9am-6pm, Sat.-Sun. 10am-6pm; off-season Mon.-Fri. 9am-1pm and 2-5pm.) The local **IYHF youth hostel,** at Warningcamp (tel. (0903) 88 22 04), outside town, is a gossip mill seething with tips on hiking in the South Downs. From the train station, turn right on Worthing Rd. (away from Arundel), take the first left, then look for signs. (£5.50. Open mid-April to Sept. daily; Oct. and Jan to mid-April Mon.-Sat.)

The medieval market town of **Chichester,** £8.75 by National Express coach from Arundel or £11.90 by train from London Victoria, makes a convenient base. Built in 75 AD, the **Roman palace** at nearby **Fishbourne** is one of the most sublime Roman ruins in England. A number of mosaic floors have been preserved, and there is also an informative museum. Take bus #700 or 66 from Chichester. (Open daily May-Sept. 10am-6pm; March-April and Oct. daily 10am-5pm; Nov. daily 10am-4pm; Dec.-Feb. Sun. 10am-4pm. Admission £2.50, students £1.80.) The **Chichester Festival Theatre,** founded by the late lamented Lord Olivier, is one of the best English theater venues outside London. Four plays go up each season (mid-May to mid-Sept.; tickets £5-12; student standbys £3 after noon on the day of performance).

Chichester's **tourist office,** in St. Peter's Market on West St. (tel. (0243) 77 58 88), 100 yd. from the Butter Cross, will hail down a bed for you. (Open Mon.-Sat. 9:15am-5:15pm, Sun. 10am-4pm; Oct.-March Mon.-Sat. 9:15am-5:15pm.) The **Hoskings,** "Hedgehogs," 45 Whyke Lane (tel. (0243) 78 00 22), will pamper you.

(B&B £14.) For camping, try the **Southern Leisure Centre,** Vinnetrow Rd. (tel. (0243) 78 77 15), a five-minute walk from town. (Open April to mid-Oct. 90p per person, £6 per tent.) The **Cathedral Pub,** South St., dishes up upscale pub grub. You can't beat the ham and chicken pie with four veggies (£3.50).

Hampshire

Once the capital of England, **Winchester** remains majestic. The **cathedral** (at 556 ft. the longest medieval church in Europe), is a harmonious blend of Norman and Gothic styles. (Open daily 7:15am-6:30pm. Donation £1.50.) Stroll past the cathedral to reach 14th-century **Winchester College,** England's first public (i.e. private to Americans) school (excellent tours April-Sept. Mon.-Sat. at 11am, 2pm, and 3:15pm; £2). Across the river rises **St. Giles Hill,** site of medieval fairs and public executions. Winchester's army of regimental museums includes the especially grisly **Gurkha museum.** (Open Tues.-Sat. 10am-4:30pm. Admission £1.50.)

Winchester's **tourist office,** Guildhall, Broadway (tel. (0962) 84 05 00), helps with accommodations and runs guided tours of the city. (Open May-Sept. Mon.-Sat. 9:30am-6pm, Sun. 2-5pm; Oct.-April Mon.-Sat. 9:30am-5pm. Tours £1.50.) The bonny **IYHF youth hostel,** 1 Water Lane (tel. (0962) 537 23), is worth a visit, whether you want to stay or not. Located in an 18th-century watermill on the River Itchen, it is now protected by the National Trust. (Open April-Sept. Tues.-Thurs. and Sat.-Sun. 1:45-4:45pm. Admission 50p. Hostel reception opens at 5pm. £6.30. Open April-Sept. daily; Feb.-March and Oct.-Dec. Tues.-Sun.) For B&B, try **Mrs. Farrell,** 5 Ranelegh Rd. (tel. (0962) 86 95 55), down St. Cross Rd. (£13), or **Mrs. Tisdall,** 32 Hyde St., off Jewry St. (tel. (0962) 85 16 21; doubles £24). Camping is available at **River Park Leisure Centre,** 5 min. north of town. (Tel. (0962) 86 95 25. £2 per person). The **Baker's Arms,** 22 High St., serves filling munchies for around £3. (Open Mon.-Sat. 10am-3pm and 6-11pm, Sun. noon-2:30pm and 7-10:30pm.) **Blue Dolphin Fish Restaurant,** 154 High St., sells fish and chips for £2.25. (Open Mon.-Sat. 11:30am-10:30pm.)

Winchester is 100km southwest of London and easily reached by train from London's Waterloo Station (every hr., 1 hr., cheap day return £11.90). Buses also run from London's Victoria Station (9 per day, 2 hr., single or day return £10). To reach the center of town from the train station, walk down City Rd. to Jewry St. (10 min.)

Portsmouth is the flagship of English maritime history; the jewel of its ships is the *Mary Rose,* Henry VIII's pride and joy, which sank before his eyes in 1545. All but 36 of the 700 crew members died. Raised in 1982, the ship evokes an eerie and morbid sense. (Open daily 10:30am-5:30pm; Nov.-Feb. daily 10:30am-5pm. Admission £3.60, students £2.30.) Nelson's flagship *HMS Victory* won the Battle of Trafalgar in 1805, at his own expense. A spot below deck marks where he died. Note that 850 men shared 8 toilets. (Open daily 10:30am-5:30pm; Nov.-Feb. daily 10:30am-5pm. Admission £3.60, students £2.20.) The **tourist information centre** on The Hard (tel. (0705) 82 67 22) showers beds (10% deposit) and will book you with pamphlets. (Open daily 9:30am-5:30pm.) The **IYHF Hostel** (tel. (0705) 37 56 61) is a 20-minute ride away in Cosham. (£5.90. Open July-Aug. daily; April-June and Sept. Mon.-Sat.) Mrs. Parkes presides over **Tetsudo House,** 19 Whitewell Rd., Southsea (tel. (0705) 82 43 24; comfortable rooms £13). Portsmouth is awash in pubs; try **The George,** 84 Queen St., for some hearty fillet of paice (£3.05).

Salisbury and Stonehenge

Two of the planet's most remarkable stone structures rise from Salisbury Plain. Thirteenth-century **Salisbury Cathedral** piles up 7000 tons of stone to form the tallest spire in England. Ask the guards to show you the buckling pillars near the choir and the architectural tricks in the cathedral's design. The guided tours take you up into the cathedral's dizzying heights for a look at the "underside" of medieval architecture. (Cathedral open daily 8am-6:30pm; July 8am-8:30pm. Donation £1. Guided tours Mon.-Fri. at 11am and 2:30pm. Free.) You can see one of the four surviving copies of the *Magna Carta* in the delicately designed **Chapter House,** next to the cathedral. (Open Mon.-Sat. 9:30am-4:45pm, Sun. 1-4:45pm.)

The **tourist office,** on Fish Row (tel. (0722) 33 49 56), books beds (10% deposit; open July-Aug. Mon.-Sat. 9am-7pm, Sun. 11am-5pm; June and Sept. Mon.-Sat. 9am-6pm, Sun 11am-4pm; Oct.-May Mon.-Sat. 9am-5pm.) A list of accommodations is posted outside when the office is closed. There is an **IYHF youth hostel** at Milford Hill House (tel. (0722) 275 72), with **camping** out back. From the center of Salisbury, walk down Endless St. to Milford St., turn left, and walk up the hill. (Beds £6.60. Camping £3.30. Open Feb.-Dec.) For real B&B charm and comfort, ring **Mrs. Spiller,** Nuholme, Ashfield Rd. (tel. (0722) 33 65 92; £11, students £10). **Mo's,** 62 Milford St., is a classy little hamburger spot. (Burgers £4-5.25.) Rent bicycles at **Hayball & Co.,** Rollestone St. (tel. (0722) 41 13 78) for £5 per day, with a £25 deposit (cash only).

Visitors are often underwhelmed at their first sight of **Stonehenge,** the famous stone circle of Salisbury Plain. Surrounded by endless fields and imperturbable cows, the 16-foot stones are overwhelming only when one stands in their cold shadow. Built over dozens of lifetimes (2800-1500 B.C.) and variously attributed to Martians, Druids, Beaker folk and Elvis, Stonehenge represents an enduring religious and aesthetic dedication that defies modern explanation. The Heel Stone, over which the midsummer sun rises, dates from the early stages of the monument; the megaliths, from the last. The greatest enigma is not the astronomical alignments but the seven-ton Blue Stones, conveyed for no conceivable reason and by barely conceivable means, from Wales. Ordinarily, you can walk around the roped-off area quite near the stones; on some Tuesdays and Fridays in off-season, the ropes disappear to afford a close-up view. (Site open daily 9:30am-6:30pm, in winter 10am-4pm. Admission £1.90, students £1.50.)

Buses run the eight mi. from Salisbury's Endless St. every two hours, beginning at 8:40am. The last direct bus back to Salisbury leaves Stonehenge at 4:15pm (round-trip £3.05). Buses leave every 15 minutes for Amesbury, from where it's an easy two-mile stroll to Stonehenge; some folk hitch. Only druids will find Stonehenge attractive during the solstice, although they and their companions may face ugly run-ins with the police. Virgins who wish *not* to be sacrificed may also prefer to visit another time.

The West Country

England's West Country extends into the Atlantic like the toe of a tentative bather. Everything echoes of the sea, from the wavy hills of Avon and Somerset to the dramatic cliffs and wide sandy beaches of Cornwall. Only stone circles, Roman ruins and Norman churches remain of former occupants; certain legendary rocks recall the legacies of King Arthur and Merlin.

Bath

During Bath's Golden Age, a circus of aristocrats and notables such as Queen Anne, Jane Austen, and Oscar Wilde made this spa town England's second social capital and filled it with Georgian architecture. Crumbling Roman villas joined the scene in 1880, after sewer diggers unearthed remains of the ancient spa city of Aquae Sulis.

Orientation and Practical Information

Bath is easily accessible from London. Most points of interest lie between Pulteney Bridge and North Parade Bridge. Just to the northwest of the city center, the Royal Crescent and the Circus attest to Bath's Georgian splendor.

Tourist Office: The Collonades (tel. 46 28 31). Useful miniguide 25p; other leaflets and guided tours free. Books beds (10% deposit). Open Mon.-Sat. 9:30am-7pm, Sun. 10am-6pm.

Post Office: New Bond St. (tel. 82 52 11). Open Mon.-Thurs. 9am-5:30pm, Fri. 9:30am-5:30pm, Sat. 9am-1pm. **Postal Code:** BA1 1AA.

Telephones: City Code: 0225.

Trains: At the south end of Manvers St. (tel. 46 30 75). To: London (1 per hr., 1½ hr., Supersaver return £23); Exeter (every 1-2 hr., 1¾ hr., £16); York (every 2 hr., 5 hr., £40).

Buses: Manvers St. Station (tel. 644 46), near the train station. Scheduled buses make the 3-hr. tour to London every 2 hrs. £16.50 return, free for the Skipper and Gilligan.

Emergencies: Police or **Ambulance** (tel. 999).

Accommodations, Camping, and Food

Bath is mobbed in summer; make reservations. Pulteney Road (by the railroad bridge), Pulteney Gardens, and Lime Grove are lined with B&Bs, though prices can be steep.

YMCA International House (tel. 46 04 71), on Broad St. Pl., a street between Broad and Walcot St. Better location than the IYHF and no curfew. Accepts both sexes. Dorms £9.20. Singles £11.75. Doubles £21.50. Continental breakfast included. Sheets 50p. Heavily booked in summer.

Youth Hostel (IYHF), Bathwick Hill (tel. 46 56 74), in a hillside mansion 1 mi. east of the city center. It's uphill, so take bus #18 from the bus station or the Orange Grove roundabout. Call ahead and arrive early. Reception open 7:30-10am and 1-10:30pm. Curfew 11pm. £7, £5.90; Sept.-June £6.60, £5.40.

The Shearns, Prior House, 3 Marlborough Lane (tel. 31 35 87). Sweet and dandy location near Royal Crescent; take bus #14 or 15 from the bus station (last bus 10:30pm). Warm proprietors. No singles. £12 per person.

Mrs. Rowe, 7 Widcombe Crescent (tel. 42 27 26). The height of elegance, with a view to match. Management decidedly particular. Singles £14-16. Doubles £24-34.

Mrs. Guy, 14 Raby Pl. (tel. 46 51 20). Comfortable rooms in an elegant Georgian house with light, cool interiors and splendid cityscapes. Singles £14. Doubles £28.

Camping: Newton Mill Touring Center (tel. 33 39 09), 3 mi. from Bath on the A36/A39. Bus #5 leaves bus station every 12 min.; get off at Newton Rd. Laundry and showers. £6.70 per tent, £3 per person.

For fresh fruit and vegetables, visit the **Guildhall Market** between High St. and Grand Parade. There are bakeries along Union and Milsom St. and an excellent wholefoods bakery on Westgate St. **Huckleberry's,** on Broad St., serves tiny, tasty vegetarian meals for £3.50. (Open Mon.-Thurs. 9am-4:30pm, Fri. 9am-9pm, Sat. 9am-5:30pm.) Try the **Saracen's Head,** Bath's oldest pub, on Broad St., for filling pub grub from £2. (Open for lunch noon-2pm and dinner 6-9:30pm.) **The Pump Room** at the Roman Baths has concerts and coffee in the morning (Mon.-Sat. 10am-noon), and concerts and cream tea (£4.25) in the afternoon (daily 2:45-5pm; off-season Sun. only). Groovy dining experiences await on Barton St.; try **The Walrus and the Carpenter** or **Pasta Galore** for dinner (£5).

Sights and Entertainment

The best of Bath's Georgian heritage reposes graciously in the residential, northwest part of the city. Walk up **Gay Street** (a continuation of Barton St.) to **The Circus,** a full circle of Georgian townhouses. Leave The Circus on Brock St. for the renowned **Royal Crescent,** the premier accomplishment of architect John Wood. #1 is a superbly furnished Georgian house. (Open Tues.-Sat. 11am-5pm, Sun. 2-5pm, last entry 4:40pm; Nov.-Feb. Sat.-Sun. 11am-3pm. Admission £2.50, children £1.50.)

Most of what remains of the **Roman Baths** is in the museum. From the Abbey Churchyard entrance, follow the stream to the hot spring source, then go out to the large open-air pool where tours start every half hour. Upstairs from the Baths is the **Pump Room,** where hot spring water is still pumped for drinking. (Baths and pump room open July daily 9am-7pm; Aug. daily 9am-7pm and 8:30-10:30pm; March-June and Sept.-Oct. daily 9am-6pm; Nov.-Feb. Mon.-Sat. 9am-5pm, Sun. 10am-5pm. Admission to baths £3.60, ages 5-16 £1.70. Pump room free.) A beacon for disoriented tourists, **Bath Abbey** stands solidly by the Pump Room. The technical advances of Gothic architecture allowed the builders to fill one entire wall with magnificent windows; the effect has earned the church its nickname, "Lantern of the West." (Open Mon.-Sat. 9am-5:30pm, Sun. depending on services.)

The Crystal Palace, 11 Abbey Green, is a quiet, pleasant pub with patio. **The Grapes** on Westgate St. draws the student crowd; the **Regency Bar** on Sawclose features rock videos; and The Green Room at **The Garrick's Head,** behind the Theatre Royal, is a relaxed gay pub. If you're in the neighborhood, say hello to Kristin at the Lower Limpley Stoke Hotel outside Bath.

Somerset

Somerset County, southwest of Bath, is rich in farmland, cathedrals, and chivalric legend. Many tourists come to view the prehistoric remains in the Mendip Hills; others choose to concentrate on the towns that lie just south of them—Wells and Glastonbury. The best way to tour is by bike or by the area's excellent bus service. Be sure to try Somerset's famous "scrumpy," a delightful, deathly, thick apple cider.

Named for the five natural springs at its center, the small town of **Wells** orbits a splendid Gothic cathedral. High St., lined with pubs and shops, trickles down from the **Cathedral Church of St. Andrew.** The church (open daily 9:15am-8:30pm) exemplifies an entire cathedral complex—complete with **Bishop's Palace** and **Chapter Horse.** The interior of the cathedral is a Gothic masterpiece. Nearby **Vicar's Close** is the oldest street of houses in Europe.

The **tourist office** (tel. (0749) 67 25 52), off the Market Place, will sell you an accommodations list (35p) or book a room (£1). (Open Mon.-Fri. 9:30am-5:30pm, Sat.-Sun. 10am-5pm; Nov.-March daily 10am-4pm.) The nearest **IYHF youth hostel** is six mi. away in the town of Cheddar (tel. (0934) 74 24 94), off The Hayes. (£3.20, £2.80. Open April-Sept. daily; Nov. and Jan.-March Tues.-Sat.) In Wells, try Chamberlain St. or St. Andrew St. for B&Bs. **Richmond House,** 2 Chamberlain St. (tel. (0749) 764 38), serves a generous breakfast to its guests (£15). The **Good Earth Café,** 4 Priory Rd., dishes out delicious health nosh for under £3. **The Cheese Board** on High St. sells local cheeses. Construct a picnic for the cathedral yard at the greengrocers on High and Broad St., with bread from **Read's Balcony,** High St.

The alleged birthplace of Christianity in England and the supposed site of King Arthur's grave, **Glastonbury** is a crossroads for pilgrims of all faiths. In the 1960s, a farmer outside the city added to this steady flow of soul searchers by founding the Glastonbury Music Festival, a three-day concert which brings in the groovy train every July. Don't forget your Birks. The town itself is a bizarre collage of people who decided to stay on; lining the two main streets, Magdelene and High St., are everything from pristine tea-rooms ("Unclean Customers Not Welcome") to shops selling crystals, incense and wheat-germ.

The still-imposing fragments of ruined **Glastonbury Abbey** are in a quiet courtyard through the archway on Magdalene St. The top of **Glastonbury Tor** is a good ½-hr. hike from town, with marvelous views. On your way back down, you'll pass **Chalice Well,** where Arthurian legend places the burial site of the Holy Grail (or

Chalice Cup), and where Christian tradition says the water runs red with Jesus' blood. The site is heavily guarded by the Knights Who Say Ni. (Open daily 10am-6pm; Nov.-Feb. 1-4pm. Admission 40p, children 20p.)

The **tourist office** is on Northload St. (tel. (0458) 329 54), off the central square. The accommodations service is 60p; the list is free. (Open April-Nov. Mon.-Sat. 9:30am-5pm, Sun. 10am-4pm.) **Tamarac,** 8 Wells Rd. (tel. 343 27 or 320 36), is a central and friendly B&B that serves a full English breakfast (doubles £22). **Tor Down Guest House,** 5 Ashwell Lane (tel. (0458) 322 87), at the base of Glastonbury Tor, is a bit of a walk from the town center, but pleasant with great breakfasts (£12.50). Camp at the **Ashwell Farm House,** Edgarley End, off Ashwell Lane (tel. (0458) 323 13; £2.50 per person with tent). The closest **IYHF youth hostel** is 4 mi. away in **Street** (tel. (0458) 429 61), served several times daily by bus. Call first—it's complex to get to. (Lockout 10am-5pm. £5.50, £4.40. Breakfast £2.30. Open April-Oct. Wed.-Mon.) For lunch, try the **Rainbow's End** vegetarian café on High St. (open Mon.-Sat. 10am-4:30pm), or the wholefood **Assembly Rooms Café** across the street (open Mon.-Sat. 9:30am-5pm).

Devon and the West Country Moors

Between Cornwall and Somerset, 60 mi. from Land's End, the county of Devon lies in the realm of fancy for travelers to Britain. The huge green moors of Exmoor National Park roll down to perilous cliffs in the north. In the south lurks Dartmoor National Park's high and rugged landscape, with blinding fogs and harrowing ghoulish nights that live on in Sherlock Holmes' *Hound of the Baskervilles.* The rich farmland in between holds the secret of sumptuous Devon "clotted cream," which is the consistency of ice cream and nearly as addictive.

Exeter

Large sections of Exeter's hefty Roman wall survived even the relentless bombing during WWII, as did its fabulous 16th-century **cathedral.** The cathedral is Exeter's true claim to fame, and once you've seen it, it may be time to move on to the more rural, picturesque areas of the West Country. The cathedral library displays the *Exeter Book,* the richest surviving treasury of Anglo-Saxon poetry. The basement of the **Well House Tavern** across the street houses a Roman well, casks of "Real Ale," a Black Plague victim, and an assembly of eerie artwork.

The **tourist office,** behind the coach station on Paris St. (tel. (0392) 26 57 00), deals out free copies of the *Dartmoor Visitor,* the *Exmoor Visitor,* and accommodations listings. (Open Mon.-Fri. 9am-5pm, Sat. 9am-1pm and 2-5pm.) The popular **IYHF youth hostel,** 47 Countess Wear Rd., Topsham (tel. (0392) 87 33 29), provides sumptuous evening meals; take the K or T bus from High St. to Countess Wear Post Office and follow Exe Vale Road. (£6.60, ages 16-20 £5.20. Towels 20p. Sheets 75p. Open daily Feb.-Oct.; Jan. and Nov. Thurs.-Mon.) B&B's run about £12; check St. David's Hill, near the train station, and Pirhoe Rd. (take bus K, T or G). **Clocktower Hotel,** at 16 New North Rd., is just a 10 min. walk from the cathedral; for £14.50, you get a single with bath and moral epigraphs. (Singles without bath £12.50. Doubles £21, with bath £25.) The nearest campsite is **Hill Pond,** on Sidmouth Rd. (tel. (0392) 324 83) on the left past the Cat and Fiddle Pub (£3). **Herbie's,** 14 North St., offers up vegan food and peace mags. (Open Mon.-Fri. 11am-2:30pm, Sat. 10:30am-4pm; dinner Tues.-Sat. 6-9:30pm.) Sir Francis Drake's old hangout, **The Ship Inn,** on Martin's Lane off High St. (tel. (0392) 72 040) is still enlivened by seafarers and travelers seeking cheap ale, cozy quarters and cobblestone streets. (Beef and veggie burgers £1.70 in the snack bar downstairs. Open Mon.-Sat. 11:30am-2:30pm and 5-9pm.)

Exmoor

Once the royal hunting reserve of the Norman kings, Britain's smallest national park boasts some of the highest cliffs, most magnificent shorelines and deepest "coombe" valleys in England. Today, as nature-lovers stalk the land, the last herd of great red deer still grazes freely on the moor.

From the west, the best approach to the park is via Exeter to **Barnstaple.** Trains run from Exeter to Barnstaple (every 2 hr., 1 hr., £7.10), but coaches are cheaper (5 per day, 2 hr., day return £3.95). From the north and east, go through Taunton to **Minehead,** served by hourly buses and the less frequent West Somerset Railway (tel. (0643) 70 49 96). From Barnstaple, **North Devon Bus** (tel. (0271) 454 44) serves **Ilfracombe,** on the western edge of the moor. From Minehead, **Scarlet Coaches** (tel. (0643) 70 42 04) and **Southern National** (tel. (0823) 27 20 33) run into the park, as do a gaggle of private bus lines. Services are unpredictable and elusive, so check with the tourist office before depending on public transport; better yet, bike or hike along the **Somerset and North Devon Coast Path,** which starts in Minehead and runs near Barnstaple. Rent cycles at Barnstaple's old railroad station, or Minehead's West Somerset Booking Office, Warren Rd. (tel. (0643) 70 23 96).

Tourist offices will distribute copies of the essential *Exmoor Visitor* (free), sell Ordnance Survey maps (£3), and find accommodations. The tourist office in **Barnstaple** is at the North Devon Library (tel. (0271) 471 77) near the bus station on Tuly St.; central and super-zealous, it's a good jumping-off point for the park. The **Minehead** tourist office is on Bancks St. at the Parade (tel. (0643) 70 26 24). Confer with park personnel for hiking information. The head **National Park Information Centre** is in **Dulverton,** at the southern tip of the park (tel. (0398) 238 41). Other centers are at **Dunster** in the Steep Car Park (tel. (0643) 82 14 99); **Countisbury,** 1 mi. east of Lynton on the A39 (tel. (05987) 321); **Lynmouth,** on the Esplanade (tel. (0598) 525 09); and **Combe Martin,** Cross St. (tel. (027188) 33 19), off King St.

Little villages (some hundreds of years old) interrupt the coastal path about every 15 mi.; B&Bs line the streets. **IYHF youth hostels** string out along the path as well. They are in **Hartland** (tel. (02374) 367) on a footpath 3 mi. south of the village (£3.20, ages 16-20 £2.60; open daily April-Sept.); **Instow** (tel. (0271) 86 03 94; £4.90, ages 16-20 £4; open April-Aug. Sat.-Thurs.; Feb.-March and Sept.-Oct. Sat.-Wed.); in **Ilfracombe** (tel. (0271) 653 37; £4.90, ages 16-20 £4; open July-Aug. daily; April-June and Sept. Mon-Sat.); in **Lynton** (tel. (05985) 32 37; £4.60, ages 16-20 £3.70; open March-Oct. Tues.-Sun.; Nov.-Dec. Thurs.-Mon.); in **Exford** (tel. (064383) 288; £4.60, ages 16-20 £3.70; open July-Aug. daily; March-June and Sept.-Oct. Mon.-Sat.; Feb. and Oct-Nov. Tues.-Sat.); and in **Minehead** (tel. (0643) 25 95; £4.20, ages 16-20 £3.40; open April-Aug. Tues.-Sun.; Jan.-March and Sept.-Oct. Tues.-Sat.). Campsites are plentiful along the coastal road; ask the owner's permission for freelancing. There are heaps of farmhouse B&Bs (£12-15) in the park.

Plymouth

Plymouth is the one West Country town where the 52% of Devon and Cornwall residents who are over the age of 65 have not washed away all traces of youthful excitement. The notorious **Union Street** leads past discos and dance-halls to the immense **Academy,** which holds 1500 salty revelers (open Tues.-Sat.). Reconstruction after the ravages of WWII created a pedestrian shopping zone at the city's hub along Royal Parade. The **Royal Citadel** sits on the **Hoe,** the grassy hills to the south commanding the natural harbor. Along the water to the west, the cobbled streets of the preserved **Barbican** quarter—now filled with cozy cafés and seafarer's pubs—lead to the docks, where a plaque commemorates the departure of the *Mayflower* in 1620. A breathy climb up **Smeaton's Tower** earns a magnificent view of the harbor and the remains of the fortress on **Drake's Island.**

The **tourist office** on Royal Parade (tel. (0752) 26 48 49) books accommodations (£1.50) and provides a map (10p) and list. (Open June Mon.-Fri. 9am-5pm, Sat.

9am-4pm; July-Sept. Mon.-Fri. 9am-5pm, Sat. 9am-4pm, Sun. 10am-5pm; April-May and Oct.-Nov. Mon.-Thurs. 9am-5pm, Fri. 9am-4:30pm, Sat. 9am-noon.) Take bus #15 or 15A to the **IYHF youth hostel,** Devonport Rd., Stoke (tel. (0752) 56 21 89). Get off at Molesworth St.; turn left at the traffic light, and follow the road winding to the left; turn left into the gates. (£5.90, ages 16-20 £4.70. Open Dec.-Oct. except the 1st week of Jan.) The **YWCA** at the intersection of Lockyer and Notte St. (tel. (0752) 66 03 21), just south of the city center, admits both women and men and is a lot more convenient to the town's attractions. (Singles £9.50. Doubles £8.50 per person. 6-bed dorms £6 per person. Continental breakfast included. Key deposit £10.) Citadel Rd. and Athanaeum Rd. are peppered with guest houses at £12-13. **Riverside Caravan Park,** Longbridge Rd., Marsh Mills (tel. (0752) 34 41 22), allows tent camping for £5.50 per tent and 2 people. The **Plymouth Arts Centre Restaurant,** 38 Looe St., off Kinterbury from St. Andrew's Cross, presents an extensive homemade vegetarian menu—assemble a filling meal for £2.50. Omnivores might try the traditional Cornish pasties (65p) at **The Gorge Café** on Royal Parade diagonally across from the **Theatre Royal.**

Dartmoor

Between Exeter and Plymouth, Devon's lush pastureland gives way to Southern England's wildest and roughest countryside in magnificent **Dartmoor National Park.** Giant tors—craggy hills of granite weathered into curious shapes—jut from barren plateaus that rise out of the wet grassland. The fearful fog of this region inspired Sherlock Holmes's pursuit of the spectral hound of Dartmoor (still sighted from time to time) in the finest of Conan Doyle's stories, *The Hound of the Baskervilles.*

A vital trove of information is the *Dartmoor Visitor,* a free annual publication listing B&Bs, riding stables, information centers, rangers, and campsites. Get yours at the Exeter or Plymouth tourist office or at any of the **National Park Information Centres;** the main one is in **Tavistock,** in The Guildhall, Bedford Sq. (tel. (0822) 61 29 38).

Whether you bike or hike, bring strong shoes, rain gear, a compass, and a large-scale Ordnance Survey Map (£3 from tourist offices). Renowned for its capricious weather and sudden, blanketing mists, Dartmoor overmatches lone, inexperienced walkers. Do not stray from paths when crossing farmland, and close all gates you open, as much of Dartmoor is privately owned. Leave word of your intended route and destination with a ranger or the proprietor of your B&B or hostel. The British Telecom Weatherline for Dartmoor and Exmoor (tel. (0898) 14 12 03) warns of drastic meteorological shifts.

In July and August, Transmoor Link bus #82 runs from Exeter to Plymouth through the middle of the park. Otherwise, buses from Exeter and Plymouth reach only the outskirts of the park (Moretonhampstead, Steps Bridge, Okehampton, Tavistock), a long way from the high moor, which is accessible only by foot or by bicycle. Call Transmoor (tel. (0392) 502 31 in Exeter or (0752) 22 22 21 in Plymouth) for bus information.

Information centers have lists of area B&Bs, or you can check for signs along the roads through the park; hospitable farmhouses abound. Okehampton and Tavistock offices will book a bed for £1.25. The convivial **Steps Bridge** hostel (tel. (0647) 53 24 35), 1 mile southwest of Dunsford village, is on the Exeter-Moretonhampstead bus route. (£5.10, ages 16-20, £4. Warm showers and evening meals. Open June-Aug. Wed-Mon.; Sept. and April-May Thurs.-Mon.) The popular hostel at **Bellever** (tel. (0822) 822 27) is a secluded mile southeast of Postbridge village. Call ahead (£5.90, ages 16-20 £4.70. Open April-Oct. Tues.-Sun.) The hostel at **Dartington** (tel. (0803) 86 23 03) (not in Dartmoor proper) lies between the park and Torquay, off the A385, near Totres. (£5.50, ages 16-20 £4.40. Open June-Aug. Fri.-Wed.; March-May and Sept. Fri.-Tues.) Ask permission if you want to camp.

Cornwall

You'll know you've hit the British "Riviera" when the houses start to have names like "Sunny Side-up" or "Beachy Keen." When Cornwall's tin mines petered out in the 19th century, all the Cornishfolk took off for new frontiers like Australia and the iron mines of Northern Michigan, leaving frumpy British vacationers the run of their cute seaside cottages. Compared to the rest of England, Cornwall is almost a separate country, with its own language (related to Breton, but extinct since the 1700s) and an unusually balmy climate. Wildflowers and tropical plants grow here, tourists bask on sandy beaches, and seabirds thrive on the cliffs. **IYHF youth hostels** in the area are spaced about a day's cycle apart (5-25 mi. of hilly terrain), accessible from the 25-mi. segment of Heritage Coast that winds past gull-infested coves and ocean spray through some of England's most arresting cliff scenery. Hostelers should book at least several days ahead in summer, and by as wide a margin as possible in August; popular hostels, such as Newquay and Tintagel, often fill by mid-June.

Trains run along a main line from London, Plymouth, and Exeter to Penzance hourly, and branch lines go to Falmouth, St. Ives, and Newquay. **Cornwall Busways** (tel. (0736) 64 94 69) is comparably thorough; Explorer tickets (£4) allow unlimited transport on their lines. The **Key West** ticket (£18) offers one week on buses in both Devon and Cornwall.

Newquay (or "Surf City") is one of England's most popular beach spots. There is little of historical interest here, but the incessant turquoise waves pounding the six beaches attract day-glo throngs jostling for maximum UV exposure during the surf competitions in July. The **IYHF hostel** is atop a cliff 10 minutes from sand and shops (£6.60, ages 16-20 £5.40. Open July-Aug. daily; Feb.-April and Sept.-Nov. Tues.-Sat.) **Towan Beach Backpackers,** 15 Beachfield Ave. (tel. (0637) 87 46 68) offers a cramped but curfew-free alternative in town (£6.50). The **tourist office,** Morfa Hall, Cliff Rd. (tel. (0637) 87 13 45), lists the 150+ B&Bs in the area (10p), books beds (£1), and can direct you to surfing schools. Dude.

Falmouth, an old port on the southern coast, is guarded by Henry VIII's **Pendennis Castle** atop rocky Pendennis Head. (Open daily 10am-6pm; Oct.-March Tues.-Sun. 10am-4pm. Admission £1.50, seniors and students £1.20, children 75p.) A stellar **IYHF youth hostel** (tel. (0326) 31 14 35), built in the castle's refurbished barracks, is right on the grounds, a ½-mi. hike uphill. (£4.30, ages 16-20 £4. Open March-Nov. daily; Dec. Mon.-Fri.) Trains to Falmouth stop at three stations, including Dell Station (near the town center) and Falmouth Docks Station (near the youth hostel). Buses stop on the Moor beside the tourist office (tel. (0326) 31 23 00), which provides a free list of B&Bs and books rooms for £1.50. (Open July-Aug. Mon.-Sat. 8:45am-5pm, Sun. 10am-4pm; Oct.-May Mon.-Fri. 8:45am-5:15pm.) Try Melville Rd. for B&Bs. Camp at secluded **Tremorvah Tent Park** on Swanpool Rd. (tel. (0326) 31 21 03; £2.50 per person). Check out the plaque at the Killigrew monument across from Arvenack House for a brief and debaucherous history of the town influentials. St. Mawes castle broods across the bay (ferries shuttle every ½ hr., £3 return).

A marathon east, in **Fowey,** the Tristan Stone and remains of Castle Dore recall the legends of Tristan, Iseult, and King Mark. South of Falmouth, the **Lizard Peninsula** offers power hiking and unspoiled towns with a minimum of tourist traps. The **IYHF youth hostel** in the tiny village of **Coverack** (tel. (0326) 28 06 87), is on the east edge of the Lizard peninsula. (£5.90, ages 16-20 £4.70. Open daily June-Sept.; April-May and Oct. Tues.-Sun.)

Transit in and around the **Penwith Peninsula** embarks from **Penzance** (as in the *Pirates of),* a busy and crowded tourist staple, but nonetheless a fine base for venturing to the comelier villages on the peninsula. The **tourist office** (tel. (0736) 622 07) near the station, is centrally located in a square shared by the bus and train stations. The **IYHF youth hostel** (tel. (0736) 626 66) is in an 18th-century smuggler's mansion 1½ mi. from the train station; walk up Market Jew St., continue on Alverton

St., then turn right on Castle Horneck Rd. or take Hoppa B to the Pirate Inn and walk ½ mi. (£7, ages 16-20 £5.90; open year-round). The co-ed YMCA (tel. (0736) 650 16) is closer to town on Alverton Rd. (£5.25 with your sleeping bag, £7.25 without). The B&Bs on Morrab Rd. off Alverton St. are close to town yet quiet; try **Inyanga** (tel. (0736) 609 67) at 36 Chapel St. for a lively but classy evening's stay (£12). Camping sites freckle the peninsula—the tourist office has a full list.

St. Michael's Mount, a Norman monastery-turned-castle, rises from an island about 400m off the coast of **Marazion,** 3 mi. east of Penzance. At low tide, you can walk via the causeway; high tide requires a ferry (50p). Buses to Marazion run every half-hour; you can also walk along the beach. Three miles west of Penzance, **Mousehole** (MOW-zel) is an unspoiled village whose steep, twisting streets provided abundant storage space during Cornwall's lengthy smuggling history. The **Minack Theatre** in **Porthcurno** hosts outdoor performances on a dramatic arena cut into the cliffs overlooking one of Cornwall's flawless beaches.

On the coast 10 mi. north of Penzance, St. Ives once provided inspiration and a quiet remove for artists, such as oedipal painter James Whistler and sculptress Barbara Hapworth, but now doubles as a crowded resort. The **tourist office,** Guildhall, Street-An-Pol (tel. (0736) 79 62 97), ferrets out rooms (£2) and dispenses a free accommodations list. B&Bs are everywhere you turn; almost every house by the water, and many on **Park Avenue** and **Barnoon Hill** offer sleeping and eating quarters for £12-15. Buses run to St. Ives from Penzance every half-hour, usually through St. Erth. **Ferrell's Bakery** at 15 Fore St. reputedly has the best saffron buns and pasties in Cornwall; take one to **Porthmeor Beach,** where the alternative crowd alternates. A plastic sheath of commercialization suffocates Land's End at the western tip of England, with gift shops and mileage signs to New York, but the surrounding coast is unspoiled. Walk 1 mi. out to Sennen Cove, or venture past the tourist complexes to admire the view of the real Land's End (3 buses per hr. from Penzance).

Central England

Oxford

Swathed in eight centures of tradition, Oxford's forty colleges and halls evoke the image of a refined and sheltered world. The university is best seen early in the morning, when the sun warms the honey-colored walls and one can still imagine the intellectual and spiritual purity seen in *Brideshead Revisited.* The rest of the town enjoys the attention, but wishes seats on the bus were easier to find.

Orientation and Practical Information

The center of town is **Carfax,** where Queen St., High St., St. Aldates St., and Cornmarket St. intersect. Most of the colleges lie north and east of Carfax. Oxford's rail station is a ten-minute stroll west from the city center via Botley St., which turns into Park End St., New Rd. and eventually Queen St. The bus station is not far away.

Tourist Office: St. Aldates St. (tel. 72 68 71). Frightfully busy. Accommodations service £2.30. Ask for the map (20p) that lists hours of all colleges and museums. Open Mon.-Sat. 9am-5:30pm, Sun. 1-4pm. Dandy **walking tours** daily every ½ hr. 10:30am-2:30pm (£3, children £1.50). **Ticket office** on premises (tel. 72 78 55) open Mon.-Sat. 10am-5pm. Between closing time and 10pm, call Mrs. Downes, Secretary of the Oxford Association of Hotels and Guesthouses, for free help in finding lodgings (tel. 24 13 26 or 25 05 11).

Currency Exchange: At banks near Carfax and at train station (open daily 8am-7:30pm).

American Express: Keith Bailey Travel, 98 St. Aldates St. (tel. 79 00 99), a few doors from the tourist office. Open Mon. and Wed-Fri. 9am-5:30pm, Tues. 9:30am-5:30pm, Sat. 9am-5pm.

Post Office: 102 St. Aldates St. Open Mon.-Tues. and Thurs.-Fri. 9am-5:30pm, Wed. 9:30am-5:30pm, Sat. 9am-12:30pm. **Postal Code:** OX1 1ZZ.

Telephones: Booths at Carfax and on Cornmarket St. **City Code:** 0865.

Trains: Tel. 72 23 33. To: London's Paddington Station (every hr., £9.50); Stratford (change at Leamington Spa; every 2 hr., £7.90).

Buses: Gloucester Green Station, west of Cornmarket St. on George St. To London (3 per hr., £4.50).

Bike Rental: Pennyfarthing, 5 George St. (tel. 24 93 68), near Carfax and stations. £5 per day, 3-speeds £10 per week, £25 deposit. Open Mon.-Sat. 8am-5:30pm. Pick up a free copy of *Cycling in Oxford.*

Emergencies: Police or **Ambulance** (tel. 999).

Accommodations and Camping

B&Bs dapple the main roads leading out of town, most a brief bus ride or a 20-minute walk from the center. Try numbers 200-300 on **Iffley Road,** or 250-350 **Cowley Road.** Expect to pay at least £15-18 per person and book ahead (especially for singles) in summer.

Youth Hostel (IYHF), Jack Straw's Lane (tel. 629 97), 2 mi. from the center. Hail any mini-bus departing from the job center south of Carfax (every 15 min., last bus 10:30pm). Kitchen, lounge, and a wee food store. Lockout 10am-1pm. Curfew 11pm. £6.30.

YWCA, Alexandra Residential Club, 133 Woodstock Rd. (tel. 520 21). Trudge past top of Cornmarket St. and take the left fork—or bus #60 or 60A. Females over 16 only. Curfew 2am. £6, 2 nights £11, 3 nights £15. 3-night max. £5 key deposit.

White House View, 9 White House Rd. (tel. 72 16 26), off Abingdon Rd. Only 10 min. from Carfax. Solicitous proprietors and bonnie breakfasts. £14 per person.

Micklewood, 331 Cowley Rd. (tel. 24 73 28). Enchanting proprietor tends precious rooms. Comfort and cleanliness abound. Singles £16. Doubles £27.

Newton Guest House, 82-84 Abingdon Rd. (tel. 24 05 61), ½ mi. from Carfax. Take any Abingdon bus across Folly Bridge. Affable proprietor lords over an antique heaven. No singles. Doubles £30, with bath £40.

Camping: Oxford Camping International, 426 Abingdon Rd. (tel. 24 65 51) behind the Texaco station. Laundry and warm showers. Two adults, their tent, puppy and life ambitions £6.

Food

Emetic college food has spawned an industry of cheap and fast alternative cuisines throughout Oxford. For pub grub, try one of the establishments listed under Entertainment. The **covered market** between Market St. and Carfax is the best place to hunt and gather fresh produce and deli foods.

Munchy Munchy, 6 Park End St. Best food in town. Stark interior redeemed by spirited cooking. Indonesian or Malaysian cuisine satisfies at £5-8. Open Tues.-Sat. noon-2pm and 5:30-10pm.

Bret's Burgers, Park End St., near the train station. Delectable variety of take-away burgers and chips from £2. Open Sun.-Thurs. noon-11:30pm, Fri.-Sat. noon-midnight.

The Nosebag, 6-8 St. Michael's St., off Cornmarket St. Vegetarian and wholefood meals served amidst sauna-like decor for under £5. Open Mon. 9:30am-5:30pm, Tues.-Thurs. 9:30am-5:30pm and 6:30-10pm, Fri. 9:30am-5:30pm and 6:30-10:30pm, Sat. 9:30am-10:30pm, Sun. 9:30am-6pm.

Polash Tandoori Restaurant, Park End St. Inexpensive and delectable Indian food (chicken curry £4.15). Vegetarian dishes under £2.15. Open Mon.-Thurs. noon-2:30pm and 6-11:30pm, Fri.-Sat. noon-2:30pm and 6pm-midnight, Sun. noon-11:30pm.

Sights and Entertainment

Since 1167, Oxford University has educated countless poets, prelates, and prime ministers; many of them studied at **Christ Church,** the wealthiest, largest, and most famous of Oxford's colleges. It has its own expansive backyard, **Christ Church Meadows,** as well as a **picture gallery** housing several da Vincis and a Rubens. Its chapel is also Oxford's **cathedral.** (Admission £1; seniors, students, and children 40p. Open Mon.-Sat. 9:30am-6pm, Sun. 12:45-5:30pm.) Walk along High St. to **Magdalen College,** widely considered Oxford's most stunning. Magdalen (MAWD-lin) has its own deer park, rural trails (Addison's Walk), and a legacy of artsy flamboyance bequeathed by alumni Oscar Wilde, C.S. Lewis and Dudley Moore. Nearby **Queen's College** exudes a statelier beauty. **New College,** on Holywell St., is known for its chapel (containing a striking statue by British sculptor Sir Jacob Epstein and a painting by El Greco), its manicured garden, some disarming gargoyles, and cloisters quieter than a graveyard. A glassy and glacial geometric compound designed in 1964 by Danish architect Arne Jacobsen, **St. Catherine's** reminds overtired students what century they inhabit. Many of the colleges open to visitors only after lunch.

Contained in four massive edifices on Catte St. is the intimidating **Bodleian Library,** a home for lost scholars that transports its books on an intricate subterranean railway system. The unusually entertaining exhibition inside includes the only folio edition of Shakespeare's *Venus and Adonis* and locks of Shelley's hair. (Open Mon.-Fri. 9am-5pm, Sat. 9am-12:30pm.) Across the street is the equally imposing **Blackwell's** bookstore. (Open Mon.-Fri. 9am-8pm, Sat. 9am-6pm, Sun. 10am-5pm.) Next to the Bodleian on Broad St. is Christopher Wren's **Sheldonian Theatre,** an architectural chocolate mousse that hosts the pomp and circumstance of Oxford's graduation ceremonies. (Open Mon.-Sat. 10am-12:45pm and 2-4:45pm; Nov.-Feb. closes at 3:45pm. Admission 50p, children 25p.) Up Parks Rd. is the **University Museum,** a great, glass-roofed natural history exhibit with a working beehive. (Open Mon.-Sat. noon-5pm. Free.) The **Ashmolean Museum,** on Beaumont St., brandishes a casual but outstanding collection of European art. (Open Mon.-Sat. 10am-4pm, Sun. 2-4pm. Free.) Follow Beaumont St. to its end and visit **Worcester College's** shimmering lake. Back down St. Aldates St., on Pembroke St., is the excellent **Museum of Modern Art.** (Open Tues.-Sat. 10am-6pm, Sun. 2-6pm: Admission £1, children 50p.) Countless amusing historical displays in the **Museum of Oxford,** St. Aldates St., tie up a tour's loose ends. (Open Tues.-Sat. 10am-5pm. Free.)

Past the end of High St. and across Magdalen Bridge is the funky neighborhood along **Cowley Road** and its buoyant clutter of alternative lifestyles, Marxist bookstores, jumble shops and scruffy wholefood and ethnic restaurants.

Oxford's favorite pastime is **punting** (poking the riverbed with a pole) on the river. Punts and rowboats (from £5-6 per hr.) can be rented at Folly Bridge (at the end of St. Aldates St.) or Magdalen Bridge (at the end of High St.).

Among Oxford's best pubs is **The Turf,** 4 Bath Pl., off Holywell St. Inside, it's rambling, medieval, and cozy; outside, its labyrinth of small courtyards will draw you in on warm nights. Special beers, punches, and country wines tempt visitors; partake of their flourishing salad buffet (noon-10pm). Unassuming **Chequers,** off High St. near Carfax, purveys good food, while **The Bear,** at Alfred St. and Bear Lane, is a dyed-in-the-wool Oxford landmark with all of Sir Allen Webb's ties hanging on the walls.

Much of Oxford happens behind closed doors. Look for the invaluable *Oxford This Week* poster, check the tourist-office boards, or pick up *What's On in Oxford* (free). Especially worthwhile are various summer college productions staged in magical gardens and cloisters, and concerts at the antique **Holywell Music Rooms.** Yearly events include **May Day** celebrations and **Eights Week** at the end of May, when the best and brightest gather on the river banks to sip strawberries, nibble champagne and watch the gliding rowers.

Near Oxford

Winston Churchill was loosed upon the world at **Blenheim Palace,** an immense mansion and estate set 8 mi. away in **Woodstock.** The great event took place in a closet. Take the express coach or a local bus to Woodstock; some folks walk past the roundabout and hitch north on the A34. (Open mid-March to Oct. daily 10:30am-5:30pm, last entrance 4:45pm. Admission £4.75, children £2.50.) The Last Lion is buried nearby at nearby Bladon.

Cotswolds

The Cotswolds are England at its finest; from the soft green hills, freckled with prehistoric and Roman ruins, the Severn Valley and the Vale of Evesham seem to seep into infinity. During the Middle Ages wool merchants in the area enjoyed wealth unknown in the rest of England. This affluence is reflected in the opulent wool churches and honey-colored limestone houses that still grace the region's towns.

Getting to the Cotswolds is fairly easy. Train and coach service links major towns like Cheltenham to the rest of the country. Getting around the Cotswolds depends on local bus services; pick up a free copy of *Connections* from local tourist offices. The **Cotswold Way** follows the western escarpment of the Cotswold hills along 97 miles of gorgeous countryside. Color-coded arrows painted on gates and trees highlight the entire route. Consult the Ramblers' Association's *Cotswold Way Handbook* (90p) or Mark Richards's *Cotswold Way: A Walker's Guide* (£3.95), which contain detailed maps of the route. The entire walk takes about eight days, but delightful detours beckon frequently. Most small towns have guesthouses, usually in the £11-14 range, and IYHF hostels speckle the area.

One of the busiest and most attractive villages along the way is **Broadway,** a town larded with restored Tudor, Jacobean, and Georgian buildings roofed with traditional Cotswold tile or thatch. Three mi. east off-Broadway, beautiful **Chipping Campden** was once the capital of the Cotswold wool trade; the town is currently famous for its "Dover Games" in late May and early June, highlighted by the brutal "sport" of shin-kicking. This activity was prohibited from 1852 to 1952, but has since been enthusiastically revived by the town's orthopedists. A few miles southwest lie the tranquil **Slaughters,** both **Upper** and **Lower.** Scour area tourist offices for information on attractions and events sprinkled through the villages. Woolsack races (participants dash uphill with 56 lb. sacks) and cheese rolling festivals blister the towns from May to September.

The Regency spa resort of **Cheltenham,** a town-size tribute to Laura Ashley on the northwestern edge of the Cotswolds, is the center of the area's tourist trade. The **tourist office,** Promenade (tel. (0242) 52 28 78), has maps and books beds (10% deposit). Stay at the YMCA (tel. (0242) 52 40 24, £11.75). Local buses serve the larger towns in the region, but rural transportation is sparse. The **train station** is a bus ride or a 15-minute walk west of the town center. Trains run regularly from London Paddington (single or day return £14).

Stratford-upon-Avon

You've read his plays; now see his birthplace. Ever since 1769, when actor George Mechem staged a festival of the Bard's works with the help of his friend Samuel Johnson, Stratford has been the city of Shakespeare. While it is unlikely that you will get a sense of Shakespeare's Stratford—shellacked beneath layers of tackiness—you may at least come to appreciate Stratford's Shakespeare.

The five **Shakespeare properties** are Stratford's most deflowered tourist destinations. You can visit them in one fell swoop with a combined ticket (£6). The **Birthplace** on Henley St. exhibits weak displays of Shakespeare's life and work as well as several rooms of period furnishings. (Open Mon.-Sat. 9am-6pm, Sun. 10am-6pm; Nov.-March Mon.-Sat. 9am-4:30pm, Sun. 1:30-4:30pm.) **New Place,** on Chapel St., was Stratford's grandest house when Shakespeare bought it for £60. The adjoining Elizabethan knott garden is yours (free) from Chapel Lane. **Hall's Croft,** on Old Town Rd., home of Shakespeare's daughter, is grander still. (Both open Mon.-Sat. 9am-6pm, Sun. 10am-6pm; Nov.-March Mon.-Sat. 9am-4:30pm.) Further out of town is **Anne Hathaway's cottage.** A 3-mi. trek leads to the fictitious **Mary Arden's House,** where Shakespeare's mother probably did not spend her childhood. (Both open Mon.-Sat. 9am-6pm, Sun. 10am-6pm; Nov.-March Mon.-Sat. 9am-4:30pm.)

The best way to pay your respects to the Bard is to visit **Holy Trinity Church,** where Shakespeare lies under a humble slab and two menacing couplets. As authentic as the Birthplace Trust properties and less overrun is **Harvard House** on High St., an ornately-carved Tudor cottage where Katherine Rogers, John Harvard's mum, was born. John founded an obscure American college . . . details are unclear. (Open Mon.-Sat. 9am-1pm and 2-6pm, Sun. 2-6pm. Admission £1.)

Resuscitate your gray cells with an evening at the **Royal Shakespeare Theatre** or the adjacent, less extravagant **Swan Theatre** (RSC and Swan box office tel. (0789) 29 56 23, open 9am-8pm). Both unload cheap balcony and standing room seats for £4-5; otherwise, try lining up for cancellations (by 9:30am). **Backstage tours** (£2.50-3) allow visitors to fiddle with props and bump elbows with half-made up actors.

Stratford's **tourist office,** Bridge St. (tel. (0789) 29 31 27; recorded information 675 22), will help you find a room; a list roosts in the window after hours. (Open Mon.-Sat. 9am-5:30pm; Nov.-March Mon.-Sat. 10:30am-4:30pm.) To reach Stratford's large, attractive **IYHF youth hostel,** Hemmingford House, Alverton (tel. (0789) 29 70 93), stroll 2 mi. along Wellesbourne Rd. or catch hourly bus #158 from the bus station. Line up before reception opens at 5pm. (Curfew 11pm. £6.70.) Reservations are essential for B&Bs in summer. The most fertile veld is along Grove Rd., Evesham Pl., and Evesham Rd. Both **Arrandale Guest House,** 208 Evesham Rd. (tel. (0789) 671 12), and **Green Haven,** 217 Evesham Rd. (tel. (0789) 29 78 74), are a bit of a hike, but well-appointed and inexpensive (£12). If you come up dry, try **Shipston Road,** south of the river, or the tourist office's free accommodations service. Campers can patronize **The Elms** (tel. (0789) 29 23 12), 1 mi. northeast of town on the B4056. (£3 per tent, £2 per person. Open April-Oct.) Food in Stratford is generally expensive and blando. **Kingfisher,** 13 Ely St., is your basic chippie (£1.50-2.30). **The Café Natural Wholefood Vegetarian Restaurant,** Greenhill St., prepares innovative and delicious vegetarian meals (£1-3.50; open Mon.-Thurs. and Sat. 9am-5:30pm, Fri. 9am-7:30pm). The best sandwiches in town come "As you like it" at **Moer St. Deli** (open 9am-5pm) for 85p-£1.90. The **Dirty Duck** pub is a favorite of RSC actors.

Stratford is 2¼ hr. by rail from London Paddington (£20, day return £27), and 1½ hr. from Oxford (£7.90, day return £7.90). Buses dart to and from London's Victoria Coach Station (2¾ hr., £10.25, day return £12.25, period return £15.50). The "Shakespeare Connection" can haul you back to London after a night at the theater (£23); contact Guide Friday, 14 Rother St. (tel. (0789) 29 44 66), to reserve a space for the trip to London.

East Anglia

Bound to the North Sea by a web of marshes, rivers, and streams, East Anglia's flat green expanses assume a marine aspect of their own. The peat marshes of the southern Fens and the brooks of the northern Broads are a haven for wildlife, and cycling along the byroads will take you through medieval villages with stark Norman churches, stately homes, and thatched cottages smothered in rose trellises.

Cambridge

Cambridge is the quintessential university town—brimming with students, beer, bicycles, and bookshops. The academic rivalry between Oxford and Cambridge is ancient and tireless, but Cambridge undoubtedly surpasses Oxford in rural charm. The gracious, manicured Backs along the river Cam, imbue students and visitors with a quite excusable sense of self-indulgence.

Orientation and Practical Information

The names of Cambridge's two main streets change every few blocks. The main shopping avenue starts at Magdalene (MAWD-lin) Bridge and is known progressively as Bridge St., Sidney St., St. Andrew's St., and Regent St.; the other, the principal academic thoroughfare, becomes St. John's St., Trinity St., King's Parade, and Trumpington St. **Market Square** lies between the two.

Tourist Office: Wheeler St. (tel. 32 26 40). Piles of leaflets and listings for all of East Anglia. Open Mon.-Sat. 9am-6pm, Sun. 10:30am-3:30pm; Nov.-Feb. Mon.-Fri. 9am-5:30pm, Sat. 9am-5pm. Information and tickets for events at the **Corn Exchange,** at Wheeler St. and Corn Exchange (tel. 35 78 51). Also basic information at **Guide Friday** in the train station (tel. 624 44). Open daily 9:30am-6pm.

American Express: Abbot Travel, 25 Sidney St. (tel. 35 16 36). Open Mon. and Wed.-Fri. 9am-5pm, Tues. 9:30am-5pm, Sat 9am-4pm.

Post Office: 9-11 St. Andrew's St. Open Mon.-Tues. and Thurs.-Fri. 9am-5:30pm, Wed. 9:30am-5:30pm, Sat. 9am-12:30pm. **Postal Code:** CB1 1AA.

Telephones: City Code: 0223.

Trains: Station Rd. (tel. 31 19 99; recorded London timetable Mon.-Fri. 35 96 02, Sat. 46 70 98, Sun. 35 34 65). Frequent trains to London's Liverpool St. and King's Cross stations (every ½ hr., 1 hr., £10.50 single, period return £14.60; last train returns to London around 11pm). Frequent City-Rail Link buses run the 2km from the station to the town center (50p).

Buses: Drummer St. Station is 2 blocks east of Market Sq. To London's Victoria Coach Station (every hr., 2 hr., single or day return £8.25).

Bike Rental: Tourist office has a list; reserve early to beat out the mammoth groups. **University Cycle,** 9 Victoria Ave. (tel. 35 55 17). £4 per day, £9 per week, £20 deposit. Repairs, too! Open Mon.-Fri. 9am-6pm, Sat. 9am-5:30pm.

Emergencies: Tel. 999.

Accommodations, Camping, and Food

The tourist office will find you a room (£1 fee), or give you a list of them for free (posted in the window after hours). Try **Jesus Lane** and **Portugal Street,** close to the town center. On **Tenison Road,** near the train station, convenience inflates prices.

Youth Hostel (IYHF), 97 Tenison Rd. (tel. 35 46 01). Enter on Devonshire Rd. Large and modern with good kitchen facilities. Social and crowded in summer: call ahead. Lockout 10am-1pm. Curfew 11:30pm. £8.30 (July-Aug. £9.30); ages 16-20 £7.

Mrs. Connolly, 67 Jesus Lane (tel. 617 53), by Christ's College. £12.

Mrs. Fesenko, 15 Mill Rd. (tel. 32 94 35). Proprietor narrates morning news in a bizarre blend of English and German. Singles and doubles. £10 per person.

Mrs. Bennett, 70 Jesus Lane (tel. 654 97). More Christ's College rooms, also comfortably renovated. Open June-Sept. and during Easter and Christmas. £12.

Camping: Highfield Farm Camping, Long Rd., Comberton (tel. (0223) 26 23 08), 3 mi. west on A603, then 1 mi. left on B1046. Take bus #118 or 119 from Drummer St. Less than scenic. £4-6 per tent. Open April-Oct.; call ahead. The tourist office has a list of 16 others.

Like other university towns, Cambridge has heaps of cheap restaurants. **Hobb's Pavillion,** on Parker's Piece, flips imaginative, overpowering pancakes (£3-4.40). **Nadia's,** 11 St. John's St., makes terrific, cheap filled rolls to take away. **Tattie's,** 26 Regent St., serves plump Fen potatoes stuffed with anything from chili to pineapple (£1.20-3; open Mon.-Sat. 10am-9pm). If Hawaiian spuds don't relieve Anglo-bland meals, **Rajbelash,** 36-38 Hills Rd., will with its *tandooris* and *biryanis* (£2.50-6 open daily noon-2:30pm and 6pm-midnight). For fresh produce, cruise the **outdoor market** in Market Sq. (open Mon.-Sat. 8am-5pm); vegetarian and wholefood groceries live at **Arjuna,** 12 Mill Rd. (Open Mon.-Wed. and Fri. 9:30am-6pm, Thurs. 9:30am-2pm, Sat. 9:30am-5:30pm.) On Sundays, pick up groceries at the **Nip-In General Store,** 30 Mill Rd. (open daily 7:45am-11:45pm).

Sights and Entertainment

The pamphlet *Cambridge: A Brief Guide for Visitors* (including a street map, and available at the tourist office for 40p) adequately describes Cambridge's colleges and museums. For the complete scoop on entertainment and sights, invest in the *Official Guide* (90p) in the tourist office or in a bookshop. *The Citizen's Guide* (23p), available at the library in Lion Yard, describes virtually every shop and service in Cambridge. The best guide to student activities is *The Varsity* (free at the University, 20p at newsstands). The tourist office runs excellent walking tours that concentrate on the major colleges—well worth £2.85. (April-June 11am and 2pm; July-Aug. 11am, noon, 1pm, 2pm, 3pm, and 6:30pm; Sept. 11am, 1pm, 2pm, and 3pm; off-season less frequently.)

The oldest and most picturesque of the colleges are between Trinity St.-King's Parade and the River Cam. Along the river stretch the elegant gardens and meadows of the **Backs,** where Cantabrigian scholars go to think and drink. Remember that most colleges are closed to the public between exams and graduation (mid-May to mid-June), though if you resemble a frightened student, you probably will go undetected. If you have time for only a few, try to see **King's, Trinity, Queen's** and **Christ's** (especially the gardens, open Mon.-Fri. 2-4pm). At King's College, visit the impressive **King's College Chapel,** built by Henry VI for a mere £5000. The Renaissance wood screen bears the initials of Anne Boleyn; Rubens' magnificent **Adoration of the Magi** (over the altar) has been wounded by a vandal's chisel. (Chapel open in term-time Mon.-Sat. 9am-3:45pm, Sun. 2-3pm and 4:30-5:45pm; vacations Mon.-Sat. 9am-5pm, Sun. 10:30am-5pm. Free. Evensong Tues.-Sat. 5:30pm, Sun. 3:30pm.) Trinity's library is a Sir Christopher Wren production. (Open Mon.-Fri. noon-2pm all year, and Sat. 10am-2pm during term. Free.)

Perhaps the best way to enjoy Cambridge is from the water. **Scudamore's Boatyards,** at Magdalene Bridge (tel. 33 97 50), rents punts, canoes, and rowboats for £5 an hour, plus a £30 cash deposit. To avoid bumper-punting, go on a weekday or after 4:30pm; you might also follow the more tranquil route from the boatyards at Silver St. to Granchester Meadows.

Cambridge is most crowded during the three eight-week terms that the university is in session: Michaelmas (early Oct.-early Dec.); Lent (mid-Jan. to mid-March); and Easter (mid-April through the 1st week of June). Cantabrigian pubs lose some of their character during the summer, but are still good for a crawl or two. On Tuesday nights, visitors from near and far pack **The Anchor** at Silver St. for great jazz, and the crowds at **The Pickerel** and **The Spade and Beckett,** both near Magdalene Bridge, often burst into drunken song.

Cambridge theaters are liveliest during term-time. The **Arts Theatre Club,** 6 St. Edward's Passage (tel. 35 20 00), offers discounts to students and seniors; advance tickets cost £5.50 and standby tickets are available for £4.50 one hour before the show (tickets regularly £7.50-13). The **Amateur Dramatic Club,** on Park St. (tel. 35 95 47), offers plays and movies (£2.50-5.50).

Each summer the **Cambridge Festival** includes a rich series of musical concerts (some free) and exhibits during the last two weeks of July, culminating in a large folk festival. The **Cambridge Corn Exchange** at Wheeler St. and Corn Exchange, sells tickets to these and other events. (Box office tel. 35 78 51. Tickets £1-13; ½-price student standby 30 min. before performances.)

Near Cambridge

Fifteen miles north of Cambridge, **Ely Cathedral** stands on the spot where St. Ethlendreda, 7th-century Queen of Northumbria, founded a religious community. (Open Mon.-Sat. 7:30am-5pm, Sun. 7:30am-6pm; Oct.-May Mon.-Sat. 7:30am-6pm, Sun. 7:30am-5pm. Admission £2.80, students £1.70, free during services.) Hourly trains roll through the ancient eel-fishing grounds from Cambridge to the town of Ely (20 min.), as do three daily buses (40 min.). Twenty-five miles east of Cambridge is the laid-back village of **Bury St. Edmunds,** where historic buildings line the four-square street plan and the abbey gardens are sumptuous. Buses from Cambridge run every two hours.

North England

Sliced by the Pennine Mountains and encompassing five natural parks and countless industrial towns, much of the North is a pastoral landscape of rolling hills and lolling sheep. England's spine is constantly massaged by hikers trekking along the Pennine Way, the longest of the country's long-distance footpaths. The Lake District is tamer than it was when it ignited Wordsworth's imagination, but is a region of fresh mountain streams and misty hillsides nonetheless. Try tasty local favorites like Yorkshire pudding, Wensleydale cheese, Craster kippers (smoked herring) from Northumbria, and Eccles cakes from Lancashire or Yorkshire.

South of the open pastures, a belt of industry stretches from Liverpool to Hull, encompassing the cradle of the industrial revolution. Don't be scared off by a smoky past—the photography museum in Bradford or the Victorian architecture of Leeds can be as interesting as some medieval structures, though the lack of a beaten tourist path will make finding accommodation difficult.

Liverpool, Chester, and Manchester

Situated at the mouth of the River Mersey, **Liverpool** was England's chief Atlantic port during the booming 19th century, exporting coal, cotton textiles and people. Although tarnished by 20th-century economic decline, Liverpool is hardly a ruin. One sign of life is the redeveloped **Albert Dock** waterfront area. At the dock, a branch of London's **Tate Gallery** (tel. (051) 709 3223) has rotating exhibits of 20th-century art by gods and demigods of the art world. (Open Tues.-Sat. 11am-7pm. Free; special exhibits £1, students, seniors and children 50p.) Nearby, the **Merseyside Maritime Museum** (tel. (051) 207 0001) has exhibits on Liverpool shipping and emigration, as well as a restored Pilot Cutter. (Open Mon.-Sat. 10:30am-5:30pm. Last entry 4:30pm. Admission £1.50, students, seniors and children 75p.) Also on the dock, **The Beatles Story** tells the tale of those four musical lads from Liverpool. Consult the tourist office for tours and maps of significant Beatle locales (though the Cavern Club has been replaced by a shopping mall). Near the train station, the eclectic **Liverpool Museum,** the unremarkable **Walker Art Gallery,** and the fledgling **Merseyside Museum of Labour History** line up next to each other. The Liverpool Museum is certainly the most interesting; the others might be worth a peek. (For all three: tel. (051) 207 0001. Open Mon.-Sat. 10am-5pm, Sun. 2-5pm. Free.)

The **Merseyside Welcome Centre** (tel. (021) 709 3631), in the Clayton Sq. shopping center, gives out a free accommodations list and the helpful *Pocket Guide to Merseyside.* (Open Mon.-Sat. 9am-5:30pm, Sun. 10am-5pm.) A smaller office at Albert Dock (tel. (051) 708 8854) does the same. (Open daily 10am-5:30pm.) The main center is near both the train station on Lime St. and the coach stop on Brownlow Hill. B&Bs cluster on **Lord Nelson St.,** adjacent to the train station, and **Mount Pleasant,** one block from the bus station. The **YMCA,** 56-60 Mt. Pleasant (tel. (051) 709 9516), offers decent rooms and full breakfast to men and women. (Singles £10.20. Doubles £18.40.) The **YWCA,** 1 Rodney St. (tel. (051) 709 7791), also on Mt. Pleasant, offers cheaper rooms to women, but no breakfast. (Singles £6. Doubles £10.) Near these establishments, and just off Mount Pleasant, **Everyman Bistro,** 9-11 Hope St. (tel. (051) 708 9545) nukes gourmet dishes, many of them vegetarian, for about £4. (Open Mon.-Sat. noon-midnight.) Among the restaurants of Chinatown, **New Capital,** on Great Gorge, has the best variety of low-cost dishes—ask for yours without MSG. (Open Sun.-Thurs. noon-11:30pm, Fri.-Sat. noon-1am.) Liverpool is fairly rich in nightlife; check out the Merseyside Arts Council's *Look Alive,* the City Council's *What's On,* and the *Liverpool Echo* for listings.

A 45-minute train ride from Liverpool will bring you to **Chester,** a walled city-*cum*-architectural museum-*cum*-shopping mall just on the English side of the Welsh border. Among Chester's relics are a half-excavated Roman **ampitheater,** a **cathedral** that will turn 900 in 1992, and the famous **rows,** unique two-tiered medieval streets that allow for bilevel shopping. For more lively attractions, take the frequent bus #40 from the bus station to **Chester Zoo,** (tel. (0244) 38 02 80), which provides superb, bar-free views of most of its residents. (Open daily 10am-dusk, last admission 5pm. £5, seniors and ages 3-15 £2.50, families £15.) The **Tourist Information Centre,** Town Hall, Northgate St. (tel. (0244) 31 31 26 or 31 83 56) books accommodations and has plenty of info on Wales. (Open Mon.-Sat. 9am-7:30pm, Sun. 10am-4pm; Oct.-May Mon.-Sat. 9am-5:30pm.) Chester's **IYHF youth hostel,** 40 Hough Green (tel. (0244) 68 00 56), 1½ mi. from town on a quiet street. Take bus #16, 17, B2, or B4 to reach this stately Victorian house and the balmiest showers in Britain. (£7, ages 16-20 £5.90, under 16 £4.60. Open Jan.-Nov. daily.) Inside the city walls, the **Davies Guest House,** 22 Cuppin St. (tel. (0244) 404 52), has singles (£12) and doubles (£23). Chester has 32 pubs, some of them in very historic structures. In town, **No. 14,** Lower Bridge St. (tel. (0244) 31 86 62) is a vegetarian restaurant with multicultural meals (open Mon.-Sat. 11am-2:30pm and 7-10:30pm).

To the 19th century, **Manchester** was a symbol of the frightening new phenomenon now known as the manufacturing city, its mills converting vast quantities of coal, cotton and laborers into smoke, textiles and human wreckage. Some looms still run at the **Museum of Science and Industry** (tel. (061) 832 2244), on Liverpool Rd., a five-building complex that includes working steam engines, a 1942 Spitfire and a gallery of interactive physics toys. The **Tourist Information Centre,** in the Town Hall Extension, Albert Sq. (tel. (061) 234 3157 or 234 3158), books accommodations, but you'll probably have to take the bus to anything affordable. At the tourist center, be sure to pick up the *Manchester Attractions Guide* and a schedule of guided walks. (Open Mon.-Fri. 9am-5pm, Sat. 10am-5pm.) Chinatown lacks good budget restaurants, but near the train and bus stations at Mosley St. and York St., **Basta Pasta,** is a good bet (filling pastas £3-4; open Mon.-Sat. 11am-11pm.) If you want to experience Manchester's music scene (the origin of Happy Mondays), pick up a copy of *City Life* (90p), which has extensive listings for all types of entertainment. Several of the most popular Manchester bands got started at the **Hacienda,** 11-13 W. Whitworth St. (tel. (061) 236 5051).

Manchester International Airport has service to North America and many European destinations. Bus #757 runs from the airport to Piccadilly bus station in the center of town.

Lincoln

Not all great Gothic cathedrals are on the continent; **Lincoln Minster** (tel. 54 45 44) rivals Chartres and Santiago. For a long time the tallest building in Europe, the 12th-century cathedral sits on an enormous hill, making it visible throughout town. The inside is elaborately carved; don't miss the cloisters. (Open Mon.-Sat. 7:15am-8pm, Sun. 7:15am-6pm; in winter Mon.-Sat. 7:15am-6pm, Sun. 7:15am-5pm. Suggested donation £1, students, seniors and children 50p. Guided tours May-Sept. 11am, 1pm and 3pm, March-April and Oct.-Nov. 11am and 2pm.) Sharing the hill is **Lincoln Castle** (tel. 51 10 68), built in 1068. The Norman walls have been restored, and you can walk along the battlements and climb the observatory tower for a superb view of the cathedral and river valley. (Open Mon.-Sat. 9:30am-5:30pm, Sun. 11am-5:30pm; in winter Mon.-Sat. 9:30am-4pm. Guided tours daily at 11am and 2pm. Last admission ½-hr. before closing. Admission 80p, students, seniors and children 50p.)

Downhill, past several medieval buildings, is the **City and County Museum,** Broadgate (tel. 53 04 01), which guards one of four remaining original copies of the Magna Carta. (Open Mon.-Sat. 10am-5:30pm, Sun. 2:30-5pm. Admission 50p, children 25p, free Thurs.) Also in the lower part of town, the **National Cycle Museum** at Brayford Wharf (tel. 54 50 91) shows the history of cycling from the Penny Farthing to the BMX. (Open daily 10am-5pm. Admission 60p, children 30p.)

Lincoln offers two **tourist offices.** The Main Office, 9 Castle Hill (tel. 52 98 28), is midway between the cathedral and castle. (Beds booked for £1.10. Open Mon.-Thurs. 9am-5:30pm, Fri.-Sat. 9am-5pm, Sat.-Sun. 10am-5pm.) At the bottom of the hill, the office at Cornhill (tel. 51 29 71), offers the same services but is closed on Sundays. (Turn left from the train station and right onto High St.; from the bus station, go through the shopping arcade onto High St.)

The **IYHF Hostel,** 77 S. Park (tel. 52 20 76), is about a 15-minute walk from the train station, somewhat removed from the central tourist area. (Open daily July-Aug.; April-June and Sept.-Oct. Mon.-Sat.; March Tues.-Sat.; Nov.-Dec. Fri. and Sat. £5.60, ages 16-20 £4.70.) Many B&Bs lie along **Yarborough Rd.;** try the **Mayfield Guest House,** 213 Yarborough Rd. (tel. 53 37 32), a short and level walk from the castle (£13 per person). Trains run to London and York (some transfer at Newark), and to Nottingham.

Peak District National Park

Between Manchester and Sheffield, the **Peak District National Park** rises out of rolling pastureland and gentle river valleys, offering bracing walks and long vistas. At higher elevations, especially in the northern park, desolate moorland echoes with the bleats of sheep and suffering hikers; in the valleys, sheep cavort on the riverbanks, fenced in by drystone walls. In summer, many of the villages within the park hold "well-dressings," festivals in which wells are dressed in flower mosaics in thanks for a year of water. Several bus companies offer intervillage transit, ranging from regular to sporadic. There is easy rail and bus access from Manchester and Sheffield and bus access from Nottingham. A **Derbyshire Wayfarer** pass (£6, seniors and children £3, discount for YHA members if bought at a hostel) allows one day's unlimited bus and rail travel within Derbyshire. The *Peak Park Timetable,* available at bus and rail stations and at area tourist offices, is emphatically worth 50p.

There are **National Park Information Centres** and **tourist offices** in **Ashbourne** (tel. (0335) 436 66), **Bakewell** (tel. (062981) 32 27), **Buxton** (tel. (0298) 251 06), **Castleton** (tel. (0433) 206 79), **Edale** (tel. (0433) 702 07), **Fairholmes** (tel. (0433) 509 53), **Hartington, Matlock Bath** (tel. (0629) 550 82), and **Torside.** The offices in Hartington and Torside are open summer weekends only; the rest are open daily in summer and weekends in winter, with offices in Bakewell, Buxton, Edale, and Matlock Bath open weekdays in winter as well. There are over 20 **IYHF youth hos-**

tels in the park, including **Bakewell,** Fly Hill (tel. (0629) 81 23 13; open March-Nov. Fri.-Wed.; Jan.-Feb. Fri.-Tues); **Buxton,** off Harpur Hill Rd. (tel. (0298) 222 87; open March-Oct. Mon.-Sat, Nov. to mid-Dec. Tues.-Sat.); **Castleton** (tel. (0433) 202 35; open Feb.-Dec. daily); **Edale** (tel. (0433) 703 02; open Jan.-Dec. 16 daily); and **Matlock,** 40 Bank Rd. (tel. (0629) 58 29 83; open Jan.-Nov. Mon.-Sat.; all park hostels £5.10-7). The area also has plenty of B&Bs (around £11-12) and campsites.

In the southern park, the former spa town of **Buxton** still fills its swimming pool with spring water; just outside of town, **Poole's Cavern** is near a nature trail through **Grin Low Woods.** (Cavern open June-Sept. daily 10am-5pm; Easter-May and Oct. Thurs.-Tues. 10am-5pm. Admission £2.20; IYHF discount.) In town, the **Old Manse Guest House,** 6 Clifton Rd. (tel. (0298) 56 38), has all sorts of rooms (£12.50). To the east, **Bakewell** is currently in its seventh century of Monday livestock markets and still serves the delicious Bakewell pudding (created when a flustered cook at the Rutland Arms poured egg mixture over strawberry jam instead of mixing it into the dough). If the hillside hostel is full, try **The Mount,** a B&B on Yeld Rd. (tel. (06981) 21 98), with a dandy floral ornamentation (£13). Near Bakewell, **Chatsworth,** (tel. (0246) 58 22 04), the palatial residence of the Duke and Duchess of Devonshire, is one of England's great estates. (Open Apr.-Oct. daily 11am-4:30pm. Admission £4.50; students and seniors £3.50; children £2.) Farther south, in **Matlock Bath,** a **cable car** will whisk you up to the Heights of Abraham for a ramopanic view (round-trip £4.50). The **Peak District Mining Museum** is also in town. (Open Feb.-Nov. Mon.-Fri. 10am-5pm, Sat.-Sun. 11am-4pm. Admission £1; students, seniors, and children 80p.) The **Tor View** guest house, near the cable car (tel. (0629) 562 62), has rooms for £9.50.

In the northern park, the village of **Edale** is at the southern terminus of the **Pennine Way** footpath to the Scottish border. Located in one of the most stunning areas of the park, the town is predictably honored with one of the park's busiest hostels. Picturesque **Castleton,** in the shadow of the ruined **Peveril Castle,** has four caverns which are the source of the town's characteristic Blue John stone. At **Speedwell Cavern,** you can take a boat tour of the "Bottomless Pit," which once had 40,000 tons of rubble dumped in it without its water level rising. (Open daily 9:30am-5:30pm. Admission £3.50, children £2.) Sleepy **Hathersage,** along the rail line, is noteworthy only for being the probable model for the village of Morton in *Jane Eyre.* Attic rooms are generally £1-2 cheaper in local B&Bs.

York

York's nearly complete medieval walls contain Georgian townhouses, medieval cottages and England's largest Gothic cathedral. Founded by the Romans, conquered by the Vikings, and improved by Richard III, York was for a long time England's second city. Now it is mostly a tourist town, but it plays that role gracefully.

Orientation and Practical Information

Fast and frequent **Intercity 125** trains will take you from London's King's Cross Station to York in two and a half hours (Saver return £48). Trains also chug out frequently for Edinburgh via Durham and Newcastle (2½ hr., Saver return £36-46). The train station (tel. 64 21 55) is on Station Road, just outside the walls. **National Express Rapide** coaches, which board on Rougier St. near the train station, will get you from London Victoria to York (5 hr., single £23.50 or day return £25-31.50). Hitchers from London take the A1, then pick up the A64 between Leeds and York.

The **Tourist Office,** in the De Grey Rooms off Exhibition Sq. (tel. 62 17 56), near the Minster, offers useful leaflets, including a free accommodations list with map, and *What's On,* with entertainment information. Their free booking service requires a 10% deposit. Expect long lines in July and August. (Open Mon.-Sat. 9am-7pm, Sun. 11am-4pm; Oct.-May Mon.-Sat. 9am-5pm.) There are branch offices in the railway station (open Mon.-Sat. 9:30am-5:30pm, Sun. 11am-5pm) and on Rougier St. (open Mon.-Sat. 9am-6pm, Sun 10am-5pm). York's **city code** is 0904.

Accommodations, Camping, and Food

Competition for B&Bs (from £11) is fierce in July and August, but the tourist office can usually pin down a room. Hostels fill up quickly; call ahead.

Bishophill House Youth Hostel, 11-13 Bishophill Senior Rd. (tel. 62 59 04). A great place to meet sexy young travelers of various nationalities. Laundry facilities, bar and TV room. Dorm beds £7-8.50, sheets £1, or bring your own. Singles £12.30-16. Doubles £10.25-14.40 per person. Continental breakfast £1.30, English breakfast £2.30.

IYHF Youth Hostel, Haverford, Water End, Clifton (tel. 65 31 47). Take bus #17 to Clifton Green, or walk 1 mi. from Exhibition Sq. down Bootham to Clifton. Large, superior-grade hostel with showers hot as the fires of hell. 4-8 beds per room. Lockout 10am-5pm. Curfew 11:30pm. £9.30, ages 16-20 £7, under 16 £5.50; Sept.-May £8.30. Breakfast £2.30. Sheets 80p. Open early Jan.-early Dec. daily. Fills quickly, so call ahead or arrive at 8am.

Maxwell's Hotel, 54 Walmgate (tel. 62 40 48). Clean dorm rooms with 4-6 beds. £8, sheets included. Continental breakfast £1, English breakfast £2. Airy singles and doubles with full breakfast £14.50; Oct.-April £12.50.

For B&Bs try **Haxby Road** in Bootham, or the **Mount** area down Blossom St. near the railway station. **The Old Dairy,** 10 Compton St., off Clifton Rd. (tel. 62 38 16), offers nicely decorated rooms for £11. **Queen Anne's Guest House,** 24 Queen Anne's Rd. (tel. 62 93 89) near Exhibition Sq. has spotless rooms with TVs (£12-13; Nov.-June £11-12). Camp at **Bishopthorpe,** 3 mi. south of York off the A64 (tel. 70 44 42; £4 per tent with 4 people; open Easter-Sept.)

Just off King's Sq. is an **open-air market** (open Mon.-Sat.). **The Blake Head,** 104 Micklegate (tel. 62 37 67) serves tasty vegetarian lunches (open noon-2:30pm, £2.50-4) and desserts (£1.75) in a sunny café behind a bookstore. (Open Mon.-Thurs. 9:30am-6pm, Fri.-Sat. 9:30am-6pm and 6:30-9pm, Sun. 10am-5pm). **St. William's Restaurant,** 3 College St. (tel. 348 30), serves inexpensive morning coffee, lunch or afternoon tea in a 15th-century building or cobbled courtyard (open Mon.-Sat. 10am-5pm, lunch served noon-2:30pm). The tasty meat pies at **The York Pie Shop,** 24 Pavement (tel. 64 44 14) are almost enough to give English food a good name. (£4.25-7.25; open daily 10am-10pm). For pub grub, try **The Lowther Arms,** King's Staith. (Food served daily 12:30-2pm and 5:30-8:30pm.)

Sights

The **York Visitor Card** (80p), available at the Tourist Office, grants discounts to many museums and attractions and can pay for itself in just one stop if two adults are traveling together.

A promenade along the city's medieval walls starts at **Bootham Bar,** near the tourist office, and continues toward **Monk Bar.** This is the most eye-popping part of the wall, with glimpses of the Minster through the trees. At **Walmgate Bar,** take a look at one of the few remaining "barbicans," a double-gate device that gave city defenders a second crack at the enemy. Free two-hour city tours will take you inside and around the walls (meet in Exhibition Sq.; April-Oct. daily at 10:15am and 2:15pm; June-Aug. also at 7pm).

York Minster is the largest Gothic cathedral in Britain and contains more than half the country's medieval stained glass. The Great East Window, which dwarfs a tennis court, is the largest stained-glass window on the planet. Hoist yourself up the **Central Tower** if you like your sunlight direct. (Minster open daily 7am-8:30pm; suggested donation £1. Tower open daily 10am-6pm; admission £1.50, energetic children 70p.) A trove of historic buildings lies behind the Minster, including the magnificently preserved and furnished **Treasurer's House,** which claims to house York's oldest ghosts. (Open April-Oct. daily 10:30am-6pm, last admission 4:30pm. Admission £2.30, children £1.) Other noteworthy streets are the **Shambles,** once the butcher's quarters, and **Stonegate,** which is now largely a shopping street. Refresh yourself in the 19th-century **Yorkshire Museum Gardens,** off Museum St., site of the tower of the first-century Roman wall and the ruins of **St. Mary's Abbey.** The **museum** itself has exhibits on York's Roman childhood. (Open daily 10am-5pm; Nov.-Easter Mon.-Sat. 10am-5pm, Sun. 1-5pm. Admission £2; students, seniors, and children £1.)

The huge **Castle Museum,** Castlegate (tel. 65 36 11), one of the best folk museums in Britain, is primarily endowed with the vast collection of Dr. Kirk, a 19th-century physician who accepted antiques and relics in lieu of fees. Visit **Kirkgate,** a cobbled reconstruction of a Victorian street, and the **Half Moon Court,** its venerable Edwardian counterpart, complete with a pub. (Open Mon.-Sat. 9:30am-5:30pm, Sun. 10am-5:30pm; Nov.-March Mon.-Sat. 9:30am-4pm, Sun. 10am-4pm. Admission £3.20, students, seniors, and children £1.60.)

Across from the Castle Museum is **Clifford's Tower** (tel. 64 69 40). A remnant of York Castle, it stands on the site of the worst anti-Jewish uprising in English history. Besieged by their fellow citizens, York's Jews committed mass suicide here in 1190. There isn't much to see inside, so save your money. (Open daily 10am-6pm; Oct.-March Mon.-Sat. 10am-4pm. Admission 95p, students and seniors 75p, children 45p.) Nearby, the **Jorvik Viking Center** (tel. 64 32 11) will whisk you back to a Viking village re-created in superb detail, complete with sounds and smells. (Open daily 9am-7pm; Nov.-March 9am-5:30pm. 20-min. ride £3.20, seniors £2.40, children (from Nov.-Mar.) £1.60.)

Outside the city walls, **The National Railway Museum,** Leeman Rd. (tel. 62 12 61) exhibits titanic locomotives and plush passenger cars in a state of such gleaming splendor that it is hard to imagine them covered in coal dust. (Open Mon.-Sat. 10am-6pm, Sun. 11am-6pm. Admission £3.30, students, seniors and disabled £2.10, children £1.65.)

Entertainment

There are more watering holes crammed into the alleyways of York than there are gargoyles on the east wall of the Minster. York's pubs are noted as much for their atmosphere as for their food and drink. At the **Black Swan Inn,** Peasholme Greene, folk artists perform on Mondays in a beautifully preserved 15th-century coaching inn (cover £1-2). At **The Roman Baths,** you can down a pint among genuine ruins. **Oscar's Wine Bar and Bistro,** Little Stonegate, serves classy meals all day. **The Punch Bowl,** 7 Stonegate, rattles with folk and blues on Wednesday nights from 9pm.

The best show in town each summer weekend is in **King's Square,** where musicians, jugglers, politicians and evangelists vie for attention. The **Theatre Royal,** St. Leonard's Pl. (tel. 62 35 68), stages more traditional spectacles; student seats are available weekdays (from £1.50). The **Arts Centre York,** Mickelgate (tel. 62 71 29), hosts avant-garde theater and classical and folk concerts on its intimate sunken stage. For a peek at supernatural York, join the **Haunted Walk,** leaving Monday through Friday at 8pm from Exhibition Sq. (£2, children £1).

North York Moors

Those who have sampled the Peak or Lake Districts and decided that moor is a four-letter word may find the paths less boggy and the rainfall lighter in North Yorkshire. The **North York Moors National Park** is a heather-carpeted moorland that stretches to the windswept coast, encircled by the towns (clockwise from northwest to southwest) of Guisborough, Whitby, Scarborough, Pickering, Helmsley, and Thirsk.

The two essential documents for visiting the moors are available at area tourist offices. The *North York Moors Visitor* (40p) is crammed with data about attractions, events and accommodations, while *Moors Connections* has schedules for bus and rail service.

British Rail's Esk Valley line runs through the northern part of the park from Darlington via Middlesbrough to Whitby (£2.50). At Grosmont, it connects with the steam-run **North Yorkshire Moors Railway,** the only way to reach the scenic tidbits of Newtondale Gorge (full-line ticket £5.20-6 single, return £6.50-7.50). The railway peters out in Pickering, where infrequent buses pick up the slack. To reach the heart of the park, take the Esk Valley line to Danby and its **National Park Information Center** (tel. (0287) 66 06 54), ½ mi. from the rail station. (Open Easter-Oct. daily 10am-5pm; Nov.-Easter Sat.-Sun. noon-4pm, weather permitting.) The staff can direct you to a number of paths, 2 to 97 mi. long. Other information centers are at **Pickering,** whose transport connections make it a good base, and **Helmsley,** which has a youth hostel in town. The park is dotted with ruined castles and abbeys, but the big draw is the trails. The **Lyke Wake Walk** (40 mi.), the **White Rose Walk** (40 mi.), and the **Cleveland Way** (93 mi.) traverse the area; all are dotted with hostels. Remember that local geography and climate render hiking in the area dangerous. Before setting off, pick up the indispensable *North York Moors Visitor* and the *Moorland Safety* pamphlets. Tourist offices stock these and billions of other guides to the area. The park authority's **Waymark #1-30** pamphlets (30p) describe 2-5 hr. circular walks. The annually updated *Bartholomew Map and Guide* lays out 40 short walks (£4).

The park is bounded on the east by the North Sea, and the coastline includes the scenic towns of **Ravenscar, Robin Hood's Bay,** and **Whitby,** the setting of Bram Stoker's *Dracula.*

Lake District

Embrace me then, ye hills, and close me in.
—William Wordsworth, The Recluse

Literary pilgrims will soon see why Wordsworth thought the Lakes the most exquisite place in England. Dramatic in places, the Lake District is a pastoral patchwork of hill farms dotted with mortarless stone cottages. If you seek the lonely vistas for which the Lakes are famous, remember that coaches full of others do too. Windermere, Ambleside, Grasmere, and Keswick are good bases, with transport connections and knowledgeable tourist offices, but try to visit one of the more remote hill villages, especially in the west and north.

Trains from all over run to Oxenholme, then connect to Windermere seven times per day. Summer brings a direct London-Windermere train (1 per day, Saver return £35). The BritRail pass wins free rides on Lake Windermere ferries as well. **Mountain Goat** (tel. (09662) 51 61) runs coaches from York (Mon., Wed., and Fri.-Sat.; £16, return £23.40), as well as buses to Buttermere (day return £4), Borrowdale and other small towns within the District. **Cumberland Motor Services** (tel. (0228) 484 84) has an hourly bus connecting Lancaster, Windermere, Ambleside, Grasmere, and Keswick; a £4.20 Explorer ticket will let you ride all day (4 days £12.20). To be picked up at an intermediate stop, call in the morning to alert the company, or thrash about wildly when you see the bus. CMS also runs buses along the Keswick-Windermere routes, stopping at more remote villages along the way (Explorer ticket £4.20).

Sage travelers, however, explore the Lake District under their own power. Easily identifiable public footpaths crisscross the countryside. Take a good Ordnance Survey map (available at any tourist office for £3.50-4), a compass, additional warm and waterproof clothing, and the park service's free safety pamphlet. Tourist offices provide detailed advice on hiking and camping in the area. The Lake District **National Park Information Service** has a camping advisory number (tel. (09662) 55 55) and an up-to-date weather report (tel. (09662) 51 51). John Parker's *Walk the Lakes* (£3.95) details 40 short walks. Tourist offices and National Park Information Centres stock the comprehensive series *Walks in the Countryside* (20p each). Before setting out on even the easiest hikes, give someone a sketch of your itinerary and your next of kin. Mountain bikes can be rented on every block for an unfortunate £12 per day; Michael Hyde's *Mountain Biking In the Lakeland* costs £2.75.

The Lakes have the highest density of youth hostels in the world (34, to be precise), but you should definitely phone ahead in summer. B&Bs cost £10-13, and despite their ubiquity, fill quickly in summer. Always call ahead in July and August and arrive early to find a reasonably priced room.

Windermere

Windermere and its sidekick **Bowness** on Lake Windermere are starting points for most tourists, and are therefore quite crowded. The Windermere **tourist office** on Victoria St. (tel. (09662) 66 01), next to the train station, operates a free booking service and posts an accommodations list after hours. (Open daily 9am-9pm; Nov.-March daily 9am-6pm.) The office on the pier in Bowness (tel. (09662) 66 01) is also a National Park Information Centre and describes boat rental and lake cruises. (Open 10am-10pm; Sept.-late May 10am-5pm.) Next to the tourist office, **J.D.'s Cycles** (tel. (09662) 44 79) rents bikes for £6.50-11 per day and £35-50 per week, with a £20 deposit. Walk up Birthwaite Rd. to Queen Adelaide's Hill for a crowd-free loo.

The nearest **IYHF youth hostel** (tel. (09662) 35 43) is 2 mi. north of Windermere in Troutbeck Bridge, on the way to Ambleside; from the Ambleside bus route it's a ¾-mi. walk. (£5.90, £4.70. Open late March-late Sept. daily; mid-Feb. to late March and late Sept.-late Nov. Wed.-Mon.) For covenient, cheap B&Bs, scour High St., Cross St., and Oak St., all near the station. **Lingmoor,** 7 High St. (tel. (09662) 49 47), is not only friendly—you also get KitKats with your tea tray (£10). Minus the chocolates but plus TV and sewing kits are the antiseptically tidy rooms of **Brendan Chase Guest House,** College Rd. (tel. (09662) 56 38; £10). You can camp with all the perks at **Limefitt Park** (tel. (0966) 323 00), 4½ mi. south of Bowness on the A592, which charges £7.50 for two bodies and a tent. The pub in the **Queen's Hotel,** Crescent Rd., serves filling meals (£3.50) all day. (Open Mon.-Sat. 11am-11pm, Sun. noon-3pm and 7-10:30pm.) In Windermere, the **Wild Oats Vegetarian Restaurant,** Main St., offers some not-so-wild but tasty lunches (£4.20) and filled rolls (£1.50).

Ambleside and Grasmere

The lakebound villages of Ambleside and Grasmere both do their thing at a slower, more roomy pace. The easy hike between the two will knock your socks off. The Ambleside **tourist office,** on Church St. (tel. (0966) 325 82), books rooms (no fee). (Open daily 9am-6pm; Nov.-March Fri. 1-4pm and Sat. 10am-4pm.) The **Ambleside Youth Hostel (IYHF)** is 1 mi. south of the village on the Windermere road at Waterhead (tel. (0966) 323 04). An erstwhile hotel on the shores of Lake Windermere, it has two- to six-bed dorms and swimming off its very own pier. (Reception open all day. £7, £5.90. Open late March-late Sept. daily; Jan. to mid-March and mid-Sept.-Nov. Thurs.-Tues.) For B&Bs, try **3 Cambridge Villas,** Church St. (tel. 0966) 323 07), next to the tourist office, which has totally charming proprietors and a herbivorous breakfast (£11.50), or **Raesbeck,** Fairview Rd., a beautiful 16th-century cottage with a lovely proprietor (£11). True budgetarians can gorge themselves at **The Old Smithy,** the Slack (off Market Pl.), where fish and chips or meat pies and potatoes go for £1.65-2.15. You can get cheap, tasty meals and sinful pastries at the ever-popular **Apple Pie Eating House** on Rydal Rd.: try hummus sandwiches (£1.95) and/or apple pie (£1.40; open daily; off-season Fri.-Wed.).

Walk to **Elterwater Youth Hostel (IYHF)** in Langdale (tel. (09667) 245); from here you can ascend the **Langdale Pike.** (£5.90, £4.70. Open April-Aug. Tues.-Sun.; mid-Feb. to March and Sept.-Nov. Wed.-Sun.) Another winsome walk from Ambleside is to the **Hawkshead Hostel** (tel. (09666) 293) in a Regency mansion. (£7, £5.90. Open late March-late Sept. daily; late Feb.-late March and late Sept.-Nov. Mon.-

Sat.) In nearby Near Sawrey you can visit Beatrix Potter's 17th-century house, **Hill Top,** and view some of her original drawings. (Open April-Oct. Sat.-Wed. 10am-5:30pm, last entry 4:30pm. Admission £2, children £1.) The **Wildlife and Forestry Museum** at Grizedale (tel. (022984) 373) sponsors daily nature walks in summer.

Grasmere, 4 mi. north of Ambleside, is a lovely village inundated by Wordsworth rotaries. The village wears its literary history well; exploitation of its deity includes **Dove Cottage** (£3.50; last admission 4:30pm), where William and Dorothy kept house from 1799 to 1807, and **Rydal Mount** (£1.90), the poet's final home. His simple grave lies in the village churchyard. Two **IYHF youth hostels** are in the village: **Butharlyp How** (tel. (09665) 316), just down the road to Easdale (£6.60, £5.40; open late March-late Sept. daily; mid-Feb. to late March and late Sept.-late Nov. Tues.-Sun.), and **Thorney How** (tel. (09665) 591), farther down the Easdale road—turn right at the fork, then left (£6.30, £5.10; open late March-late Sept. daily; early Oct.-late March Wed.-Mon.).

Keswick

Between high fell and crag, **Keswick** (KEZZ-ick) has got the setting and the charming winding roads—and the crowds, in a very big way. Bordering **Derwentwater** in the northern part of the park, Keswick is an ideal springboard for the central and northern park. The nearby **Castlerigg Stone Circle** was built by Bronze-Agers with a keen eye for panorama. **Skiddow** in the north and **Helvellyn** to the south are big climbs. Walk through the pass to **Buttermere,** and then take one of 4-6 daily buses back. To escape the crowded shores of Derwentwater, take the ferry to more isolated beaches or to **St. Herbert's Island,** a 17th-century hermitage, rent a rowboat (£2.50 per hour), or impress your friends in a motorboat (£8 per hour). Keswick's **IYHF youth hostel,** on Station Rd. (tel. (07687) 724 84), smiles on the rock-strewn River Greta. Reserve way early (a week or two in advance) for weekend visits. (Lockout 10am-1pm. £7, £5.90. Open late March-late Sept. daily; mid-Feb. to mid-March and late Sept.-Nov. 6 Thurs.-Tues.) The equally scenic **Derwentwater Youth Hostel (IYHF)** (tel. (05 96 84) 246), 2 mi. south of Keswick, is a renovated 200-year-old house with a lovely view of Derwentwater and its very own 108-ft. waterfall. (Lockout 10am-1pm. £7, £5.90. Open mid-March to early Nov. Mon.-Sat.) Camp at **Dalebottom Holiday Park** (tel. (07687) 721 76), 2 mi. south on the Ambleside Rd. (£5 per tent and 2 people).

From Keswick, hike or hop a bus up into the hills. **Cumberland Motor Services** (tel. (0228) 484 84) serves **Borrowdale** (south via the beautiful east side of Derwentwater) and **Cockermouth** (on the north side of Bassenthwaite Lake). From **Seatoller** at the end of the valley (accessible via CMS #79), you can climb harrowing **Honister Pass** from Borrowdale to Buttermere (note the YOU HAVE BEEN WARNED! signs), and catch the bus for Keswick or Cockermouth (4-6 per day).

Durham

When a Danish invasion forced the evacuation of St. Cuthbert's bones, a vision informed a monk that the procession should follow the next passing milkmaid and settle the body there. And so they did, and now Durham Cathedral stands in a prominent position above the town as a shrine to what remains of Cuthbert. The bones of the Venerable Bede, Anglo-Saxon Christianity's most eloquent and prolific writer, lie in a simple stone tomb in the Galilee Chapel; fragments of St. Cuthbert's carved coffin are in the **treasury** (admission 60p, children 10p), along with some fine manuscripts. Climb the **tower** for a view that will whomp you on the head (£1). (Cathedral open daily 7:15am-8pm; Sept.-May 7:15am-5:45pm. Treasury open Mon.-Sat. 10am-4:30pm, Sun. 2:30-4:30pm.) Across the **Palace Green** is **Durham Castle,** a Norman fortress accessible only by guided tour (£1.30, children 50p). The wooded footpaths along the River Wear provide a few hours of bucolic entertainment. For £1.70 per person, groups of two or more can rent **rowboats** at the foot of Elvet Bridge. Students get hefty discounts.

The **tourist office,** in the Market Place (tel. (091) 384 37 20), is well-informed and well-pamphletted. (Open Mon.-Sat. 9:30am-6pm, Sun. 2-5pm; Oct.-May Mon.-Sat. 9:30am-5:30pm.) **Durham Castle** is now a university residence; bed down in splendor for £15.20 in July and August (tel. 091) 374 38 65). **Parkview,** 1 Allergate Terr. (tel. (091) 386 70 34), lets nice floral rooms with tea for £15. Most of Durham's cheap accommodations are a mile or so out of the city center. The **IYHF youth hostel** often shifts location; in 1991 it was at the Durham Sixth Form Centre, The Sands, Providence Row. (£5.50, £4.40. Open late July-Aug. only.) Call the regional office to reserve a place (tel. (091) 284 74 73). **Gluck Auf,** 6-7 Prospect Terr. (tel. (091) 384 25 47), is run by delightful Mrs. Dunn, who serves breakfast around a roaring fire oven in June (£10, £9 if more than 1 night). Take bus #43, 49, 49A, or 50 and get off at Neville's Cross post office, or walk one itinerant mile out Crossgate; the house is just past the second traffic light, on the right. Camp at **Finchale Abbey** (tel. (091) 386 65 28), three miles north of Durham next to the abbey. Take any Brass Side bus. (Showers and lunches. £5 per tent and 2 people.)

Feed cheap at **House of Andrews,** a half-timbered dining room behind a modern façade at 73 Saddler St. A fine meal of quiche, chips and peas is £2.10. (Open daily 9am-9pm; Jan.-March 9am-5:30pm). Next to the cathedral, **The Almshouses** serves tasty vegetarian and meat dishes (£4) and blueberry *fromage frais* (£1.65; open daily 9am-8pm; off-season 9am-5pm). Scout for Northumbrian "stottycake" loaves in the bakeries round town.

Durham holds an elaborate **Folk Festival** (call (091) 384 44 45 for information) the first weekend in August. This is the only time you can camp for free along the river; pitch your tent early.

Five coaches per day make the 4¾-hour trip to London (£25, but ask about special fares), and the Tynelink Express runs hourly to Newcastle (40 min., day return £2.70). Frequent trains run from London (3¼ hr., Saver return £50), York (1 hr., Saver return £15.50), and Newcastle (15 min., cheap day return £3.10).

Wales

Wales is the undiscovered gem of the United Kingdom. Myriad castles and Offa's Dyke, built in the 8th century as a boundary between Wales, testify to Wales' millennium-long struggle to maintain its national identity. Wales has been more successful than Ireland or Scotland at preserving its Celtic language (to say the Welsh *ll,* put your tongue in place to say an *l,* then blow). Bilingualism is now the rule in all schools; in North Wales especially, many children speak better Welsh than their grandparents, who were forbidden to use it.

Hiking is the best way to see the lush valleys, rugged mountains, and weather-beaten shores of Wales. The Offa's Dyke Path and the Pembrokeshire Coastal Path break down nicely into smaller segments. Tourist offices in these regions will help you plan journeys both long and short; they often stock local walking guides (10-50p) and Ordnance Survey maps (£3-4). Always leave your itinerary with a park ranger or hostel warden. Sturdy shoes, a reliable and detailed map, a compass, and warm clothing backed up by hardy rain gear are crucial.

Inexpensive **YHA youth hostels** dapple the Welsh countryside, but they are often off bus routes and jammed with screeching school groups; always call ahead to reserve. Outside of Brecon Beacons National Park, there is no organized wilderness camping in Wales. Almost all land, including that in parks, is privately owned; sweetly ask the farmer or landowner if you may pitch your tent and expect to pay a small fee.

Especially in the South, public transport is an impossible tangle of capricious buses that sometimes whiz past passengers for fear of falling behind schedule. Buses usually take Sunday off. **National Welsh** and **Crosville** are the largest companies. Regional schedules (15-50p) are worthwhile if you plan to use buses extensively. Each region offers its own economy fares—usually £3 per day or £15 per week of unlimited travel.

One **British Rail** line runs along the northern coast from Chester to Holyhead; a second covers the southern coast from Newport to Fishguard; and a third, centered on Shrewsbury, serves mid-Wales and the Cambrian Coast up to Pwllheli. More expensive steam trains cover parts of the country untouched by British Rail. Many find **hitching** in Wales to be easy, especially during the summer tourist season. Post buses rattle through the remote regions, and will gladly fit hitchhikers into their routes if space allows—ask at a post-office. Orient yourself with a Wales Tourist Map that includes main roads, historic sites, and YHA hostels (£1.20), available at all tourist offices and most bookstores.

South Wales

Apart from the bleak mining valleys at its center, South Wales is blessed with a swath of green that runs from the tops of its mountains to the roaring waves of its rocky, cliff-lined coasts. For the best scenery, stay north of the coast until Pembrokeshire, where the industrial blight thins out.

Wye Valley and the Brecon Beacons

The Wye River forms the southernmost part of the Welsh-English border, parading through a run of picturesque towns. **Chepstow,** where the Wye meets the Severn in the south, is a prime access point for hikers embarking on the **Offa's Dyke Path,** which runs along the 180-mi. ditch dug by the Saxons to keep out the Welsh. In Chepstow, **Lower Hardwick House,** Mt. Pleasant (tel. (0291) 62 21 62), does B&B in a gorgeous old mansion, plus camping in a sculpture garden out back. (Singles £15. Doubles £25. Triples £33. Tents £5, £3.50 for English breakfast.) North of Chepstow, **St. Briavel's Castle (IYHF)** (tel. (0594) 53 02 72), in the Forest of Dean, is one of the most popular and luxurious **youth hostels** in Wales—it's owned by the National Trust. (Open Feb.-Oct. £6.60, ages 16-20 £5.40.) After reflecting on Chepstow's Norman castle, follow the **Wye Valley Walk** north to **Tintern Abbey,** a majestic 12th-century Cistercian monastery that inspired Wordsworth. Ask at the abbey about the 1½-hour hike to **Devil's Pulpit,** from which the Nasty One is said to have tempted Tintern's monks from their concentrated asceticism to see the entire Wye Valley. If you gut out the 17-mi. haul from Chepstow to Monmouth, you can collapse into the **Priory Street Hostel** (tel. (0600) 51 16), right in the center of town. (£5.10, ages 16-20 £4.) A Rover Day Pass (£3.80) will let you take Red and White bus #69 around the whole valley, including Chepstow, St. Briavel's Castle, Monmouth, and the trip to **Hay-on-Wye,** a picturesque little village with the largest collection of used bookstores in the U.K.

Brecon Beacons National Park encompasses the Brecon Beacons (Bannau Brycheniog), the Black Mountains, and the spectacular waterfall country in Fforest Fawr around Ystradfellte. Topped by the windswept Pen-y-Fan peak (2900 ft.), the **Beacons Ridge** slopes steeply in the north but dips away gently to the limestone caverns in the south. The best trails into the Beacons themselves start with the tiny roads leading southward from **Llanfaes,** across the Usk from Brecon town. The **Black Mountains** farther east, known for their uncompromising solitude, make excellent ridgewalking. Many parts of the paths are eroded or unmarked; arm yourself with an survey map and advice from one of the National Park Centres at Abergavenny, Craig Y Nos, or Llandovery. **Brecon** town provides amenities for prewilderness stock-up and route planning through the family-run, well-informed youth hostel at **Ty'n-y-Caeau** (TIN-uh-KAY-uh), 1 mi. out of Brecon (tel. (087486) 270). The main information center is also in Brecon (tel. (0874) 44 37; open Easter-Sept. Mon.-Sat. 9:30am-1pm and 1:30-5pm). Silverlines Coaches (tel. (0685) 824

06) cruise around the park. Elsewhere in the park, try **Llwyn-y-Celyn Youth Hostel** (tel. (0874) 42 61), 2 mi. south of Libanus off the A470, or the small farmhouse at the **Ystradfellte IYHF,** (tel. (0639) 72 03 01) 4 mi. from Penderyn off the A4089.

Hostel-less **Abergavenny,** linked to Brecon by frequent bus #21, is the nearest rail stop and serves as a springboard for touring the Black Mountains. **Hereford** is only slightly further by rail and provides a far more exciting base. Its cathedral holds the **Mappa Mundi,** a world map drawn in 1290. **Jolly Roger's** pirate restaurant, 88 Owen St. (tel. (0432) 27 49 98), and Hereford's cider museums, are entertaining as well as filling. Call at the **tourist centre** at Hereford Town Hall Annex (tel. (0432) 26 84 30) for accommodations and guided walks of the Norman city walls.

Cardiff (Caerdydd)

The youngest capital city in Europe and the only metropolis in Wales, Cardiff is a thriving business center famous for its shopping and bursting with fierce Welsh pride and labor activism.

Cardiff Castle, smack dab in the center of the city, was redecorated in humorously un-castle-like fashion in the 19th century. Check out the evil face over the mens' smoking room. (Open daily 10am-5pm. Admission and hour-long tour £3.05.) The **National Museum of Wales** displays glittering Celtic treasures as well as a bouquet of French Impressionist works. (Open Tues.-Sat. 10am-5pm, Sun. 2:30-5pm. Admission £1.) The **Lovespoon Gallery** on Cardiff Castle St. (tel. (0222) 23 17 42) displays the original works of Welsh craftsmen in all their amorous creativity. (Open Mon.-Sat. 10am-5:30pm.)

The **tourist office,** B-14 Bridge St. (tel. (0222) 22 72 81), down the road from the Holiday Inn, can equip you with a *Visitor's Guide* and an entertainment guide (both free) to navigate the busy theater and music scene. The Cardiff **Youth Hostel (IYHF)** (tel. (0222) 46 23 03) is 2 mi. west of town, accessible by bus #80 or 82. (£7, ages 16-20 £5.90; reception opens at 3pm). The **YWCA** on Newport Road (tel. (0222) 49 73 79) has singles for women (£7). **Ty Gwyn,** 517 Dyfrig St. (tel. (0222) 23 97 85) is garnished with antiques and a spinning wheel next to the bathtub (£10-14). **Crumbs,** 33 David Morgan Arcade (tel. (0222) 39 50 07) offers enormous salads and homemade breads. (Open Mon.-Fri. 9:30am-3pm, Sat. 9:30am-4pm.) Tap into Cardiff's specialty, Brains S.A. (special ale, a.k.a. "Skull Attack") at the **Philharmonic,** St. Mary St., a popular pub, club and eatery.

Dyfed and the Pembrokeshire Coast

At the extreme north of county Dyfed, **Aberystwyth** is the fading grandparent of Cardigan Bay resorts. Welsh nationalism brews in the pubs—42 in Aberystwyth alone—and the classrooms of the University College of Wales. Refine your vagabonding experience at the **National Library of Wales,** the **Theatr y Werin,** or the **Aberystwyth Arts Centre.** The **tourist office** on Terrace Rd. (tel. (0970) 61 21 25) books B&Bs. To arrange your own lodgings, comb South Marine Terr. and Rheidol Terr. (B&B around £10). The closest **IYHF** is in **Borth** (tel. (0970) 87 14 98), 9 mi. north by rail or bus. (£6.30, ages 16-20 £5.10.) The **Dolphin Fish Bar** on Pier St. fries up heaps of crunchy fish and chips (£1). Calm your cholesterol level at **Y Graig,** a colorful and politically aware wholefoods restaurant on Bridge St. **Trains** and **Crosville Buses** run north to Machynlleth for connections to the north and east; buses, but no trains, run south to Cardigan and Fishguard.

Ferries leave **Fishguard** for Rosslare, Ireland at 3am and 3pm. (Additional departures June 19-Sept. 14 daily at 6am; July 16-Sept. 13 Thurs.-Sun. at 5:45pm.) Trains from Newport connect with ferries. Check ahead with **Sealink** (tel. (0348) 87 28 81) or the **tourist office** (tel. (0348) 87 34 84; open April-Oct. daily 9:30am-5:30pm). The latter can help you find a place to stay. The **Pwll Deri Youth Hostel (IYHF)** is 5 mi. away on Strumble Head (tel. (03485) 233; £5.10, ages 16-20 £4).

The **Pembrokeshire Peninsula** is home to coastal scenery that makes the Welsh proud they're not English: magnificent cliffs and sheltered beaches, natural sea arches, and islands seething with wild birds and breeding seals. Most of the coast is protected as part of the **Pembrokeshire Coast National Park,** which maintains offices in many towns including the headquarters (tel. (0437) 76 45 91) in Haverfordwest. The 180-mi. **Pembrokeshire Coast Path** begins at Saundersfoot, near Tenby, and ends at St. Dog Maels, near Cardigan. Avoid the industrialized area near Milford Haven and ramble around Cemaes Head near Poppit Sands, between Marloes Sands and St. David's. Small, remote, but popular **IYHF youth hostels** punctuate the coast (book ahead). Their walloping views come at a price—every hostel is atop a cliff. The character who runs the magnificent **Poppit Sands**hostel (tel. (0239) 61 29 36; £5.90, £4.40) makes the bus ride (via Cardigan) well worth it.

A Norman cathedral entitles **St. David's** to call itself the smallest city in Britain. The **cathedral's** nave slopes precariously, thanks to a 13th-century earthquake. The giant skeleton of **Bishop's Palace,** across the way, was built by the wealthy Bishop Gower in order to keep up "public appearances." The **National Park Information Centre** (tel. (0437) 72 03 92) provides accommodations info and sells booklets (10p-£8) on coastal walks. Try the rustic youth hostel, 2½ mi. from town (tel. (0437) 72 03 45; £5.50, £4.40), or, for a plusher bed, **Y Gorlan,** 77 Nun St. (tel. (0437) 72 00 37; £12).

All roads and rails converge in **Haverfordwest.** The **tourist office** and **Pembrokeshire Coast National Park Information Centre** share an office at 40 High St. (tel. (0437) 31 10), which stocks excellent maps of the path (15p) plus information on pony-trekking (£6-10 per day).

Nicknamed the Welsh Riviera and tucked between cliff and beach on lovely Carmarthen Bay, **Tenby's** pastel houses sustain the Victorian flavor of the resort's heyday. Regular buses connect Tenby with Cardiff and Swansea. B&Bs line Warren Street (near the rail station), but are unremarkable. **Tourist Information** (tel. (0437) 24 04) at The Croft, above North Beach, also provides listings. **Plantegenet Restaurant** on Quay Hill serves vegetarian meals in a haunted 13th-century house.

North Wales

Here is the Wales the world imagines—castles guarding misty valleys, rivers, waterfalls, and jagged mountains of granite and slate. The North escaped the industrial gangrene of the 19th century, and Snowdonia's allure and accessibility draw throngs of rusticators in summer. It is in the North that Wales forges its identity; Welsh fills the streets, and a fierce pride lingers in half-timbered towns. On the darker side of nationalism, vacant English summer cottages were torched a few years ago, and the English portions of the bilingual road signs were plastered with mud.

Two rail lines serve the area: one from Holyhead to Chester, branching to Llandudno and Blaenau Ffestiniog, the other from Pwllheli to Aberystwyth. Cheap, frequent, and comprehensive bus service radiates from Bangor east along the north coast to Conwy and Llandudno, north to Holyhead on the Isle of Anglesey, southwest to Porthmadog and Pwllheli on the Llyn Peninsula, and southeast into Snowdonia. Explore the area with a **Crosville Bus Weekly Rover** ticket (£9.25), valid for one week of unlimited travel in North Wales. There are 19 youth hostels and plentiful B&Bs in North Wales; tourist offices in every town will find you accommodations (10% deposit).

Snowdonia National Park

The mountains of **Snowdonia National Park** (Parc Cenedlaethol Eryri) carpet the western half of North Wales. Rising unexpectedly from the English flatlands, they sweep just as startlingly into the Cambrian coast. The mountain of **Snowdon** itself, at 3560 ft., is the highest, barest, most precipitous peak in England and Wales. Hiking information is available at the **visitor centres** run by the National Park in

Llanberis, Harlech, Bala, Blaenau Ffestiniog, Conwy, and Aberdyfi; the most helpful is the headquarters, at Betws-y-Coed. Transportation among the villages in Snowdonia improves in summer with the Crosville Sherpa Bus service. Winters are very slow; only occasional Crosville buses run.

Bus service and footpaths link **IYHF youth hostels,** which, sadly, are often full in summer. **Pen-y-Pass** (tel. (0286) 87 04 28) is YHA's luxurious mountain center, wedged in a dramatic pass at the foot of the strenuous Pyg approach to Snowdon. The **Llanberis Hostel** (tel. (0286) 87 02 80) and **Snowdon Ranger** (tel. (028685) 391) are near main walking routes up Snowdon. The lazy can save themselves the five-hour hike by taking the **Snowdon Mountain Railway,** which runs from Llanberis (round-trip 3 hr., £12). Half a million climbers reach the summit every summer, and the poor mountain has suffered much erosion. Stick to one of the six main paths or choose another less popular mountain; you'll avoid the crowd and spare Mother Nature. The superior **Beddgelert Forest Campsite,** 1 mi. from Beddgelert, makes another good base for hiking (accessible by Sherpa bus). For all Snowdonia hikes, safety precautions and common sense are essential; check in with a ranger or visitor center and leave the particulars of your journey on the bright orange form before heading uphill. **Llanberis** has a series of short, scenic walks and is the prime supply depot in the Snowdonias: **Pete's Eats** serves gut-numbing chili to nationally acclaimed climbers. Scenic **Beddgelert** offers access to Moel Hebog (2566 ft.), less prone to the traffic jams that plague Snowdon. Two mining museums rise from the broken slate in grim **Blaenau Ffestiniog,** to the south.

Frequent buses trundle south through the popular resort at Barmouth to **Dolgellau,** a small market town built of stone at the bottom of craggy Cadr Idris in southern Snowdonia. If you spend the night alone on Idris (Arthur's Chair), legend says you will return either blind, mad, or a poet. A good springboard for the climb, which is a full day's excursion even for huge and virile hikers, is the **IYHF youth hostel** at **Kings** (tel. (0341) 42 23 92).

Machynlleth, tucked in the lush Dovey Valley at the park's southern stretch, bursts into market-fervor every Wednesday. Take a couple hours to visit the **Centre for Alternative Technology,** just outside of town near Corris, a community that lives out workable ideas for conserving energy and living healthy lives.

Llyn Peninsula and Northern Coast

The towns on the Llyn Peninsula masquerade as beach resorts, but rain and wind often expose the charade. Indigenously Welsh in language and community, the peninsula is partially spared the waves of tourists that crash the northern coast. **Porthmadog** is linked to Blaenau Ffestiniog by the narrow-gauge **Ffestiniog Railway,** whose 13-mi. course passes some of the most spectacular scenery in Great Britain (8-11 per day, round-trip £9.80). The **Porthmadog tourist office** on High St. (tel. 29 81) has the best stock of local and area guides as well as listings of B&Bs in the £10-13 range. **Criccieth** calls itself the "pearl of the peninsula," and its castle merits the moniker. Quiet B&B's line the shore nearby. **Pwllheli,** 8 mi. further along, buzzes as the peninsula's transportation hub, with a daily bus to London and buses every two hours to Caernarfon and smaller spots on the peninsula.

Perched on the edge of the bay of the same name, **Caernarfon** lures visitors with Wales' grandest medieval **castle,** dating from 1283. Here, Edward I employed every architectural military device he had observed in the Middle East during the Crusades; the resulting fortress proved virtually impregnable. (Open daily 9:30am-6:30pm; mid-Oct. to mid-March Mon.-Sat. 9:30am-4pm. Admission £2.50, ages under 16 £1.50.) **Segontium** (the foundations of an ancient Roman fort and an accompanying museum) occupies a hill ½ mi. away on Beddgelert Rd. The graceful **Aber Bridge** by the castle leads to a peaceful path along the edge of the strait. The **tourist office** (tel. (0286) 67 22 32), Castle Pitch, opposite the castle entrance, offers ideas for castle-hopping. B&Bs patter along Church St. and St. David's Rd. Call Mrs. Hughes (tel. (0286) 762 29) on Victoria Rd. for lavish attention (£10), or the

Marianfa (tel. (0286) 55 89). You can **camp** for £5 at **Cadnant Valley Park** on Llanberis Rd. (tel. (0286) 31 96).

Bangor is the transportation center for North Wales, and a pleasant university town with plenty of budget diversions. The **tourist office,** Theatre Gwynedd (tel. (0248) 35 27 86), off Deiniol Rd., will arm you with information on all of North Wales. **Crosville Buses** (tel. (0248) 37 02 95) leave from Garth Rd. station. (Office open Mon.-Fri. 9am-noon and 1-4pm, Sat. 9-11:30am. All schedules posted.) The **Tany y Bryn hostel (IYHF)** (tel. (0248) 35 35 16) is ½ mi. from town; walk toward the sea on Deiniol Rd., then right on the A5, or take the Maesgeirchen bus. (Open March-Jan. Often full in summer—call ahead.) For private accommodations, try the B&Bs along Garth Rd. The dazzling interiors and sweeping grounds of **Penrhyn Castle,** 2 mi. outside town, are the best buy for your castle-going pound. (Take any bus heading north, and walk 1 mi. up to the castle. Admission £3.50, YHA members £2.)

Holyhead, on the Isle of Anglesey, is a one-horse town with **ferries** to Ireland. **B&I** (tel. (0407) 76 02 22) run to Dublin (2 per day, 3½ hr., round-trip £32-42). A £10 Fun-fare day return is also available (though you must leave Holyhead at 4am and Dublin at 9:45pm). **Sealink** ferries (tel. (0407) 76 23 04) also sail twice per day, and prices are similar; *their* morning boat sails at 3:15am. Bicycle portage is free on both trips. Pick up schedules and alarm clocks at Mona Travel, 20 Market St. (tel. (0407) 45 56), to make sure you don't miss the boat. Tickets for both companies are sold at the train station. Ask about BritRail, InterRail, or YHA card discounts. B&B vacancies register nightly at the **tourist office,** Marine Sq. (tel. (0407) 26 22)—a caravan near the ferry dock. Buses run from Bangor to Holyhead (Mon.-Sat. every hr., Sun. 3 per day).

Conwy's castle and adjacent town walls enclose nasty traffic. Fourteenth-century **Aberconwy House** on Castle St. is the oldest dwelling in town, and the Elizabethan **Plas Mawr,** around the corner on High St., houses a modern art gallery and a host of ghosts. Mind your head as you step into **Ty Bach,** Britain's smallest house, with a mere 72 in. of frontage on the quay. Conwy's **tourist office,** across from the castle (tel. (0492) 59 22 48; open Easter-Oct. daily 9:30am-6pm) has a town map (10p). For B&B's, exit the town by the post office and head to Cadnant Park. Try one of the three **IYHF hostels** in the area; buses serve them all: **Penmaenmawr** (tel. (0492) 62 34 76), 5 mi. west; **Colwyn Bay** (tel. (0492) 53 06 27), 8 mi. east; or **Rowen** (tel. (0222) 53 14 06), about 10 mi. south.

Llandudno, across the bridge from Conwy, swarms with shoppers and sun worshipers and is the gateway to the beautiful **Vale of Conwy,** where you'll find the lush **Bodnant Gardens** and many campsites and footpaths along the route to tiny Betws-y-Coed. Nearby **Trefriw's** Roman spa water may be just the thing for your rheumatism or lovesickness (one-month supply, £6.95).

Halfway to Shrewsbury is the emphatically Welsh town of **Llangollen.** The town overflows with tourists during the **Llangollen International Musical Eisteddfod,** the second week of July. Gathering for Wales's pride-and-joy festival, performers from all over the world compete in outdoor performances of music and dance. Write ahead for information and accommodations: International Eisteddfodd Office, Llangollen, Clwyd LL20 8NG (tel. (0978) 86 02 36). The **IYHF Youth Hostel** is 1½ mi. away (tel. (0978) 86 03 30) in a gorgeous mansion. Hitch along the A5 or take an infrequent Crosville bus from Chester.

Scotland

United with England in 1707, Scotland still maintains its own distinct identity. Its schools, church and judicial systems are largely based in the ancient capital of Edinburgh. Even its currency—pegged to the British pound and difficult to exchange overseas—shows Scottish cameos and landscapes instead of English ones.

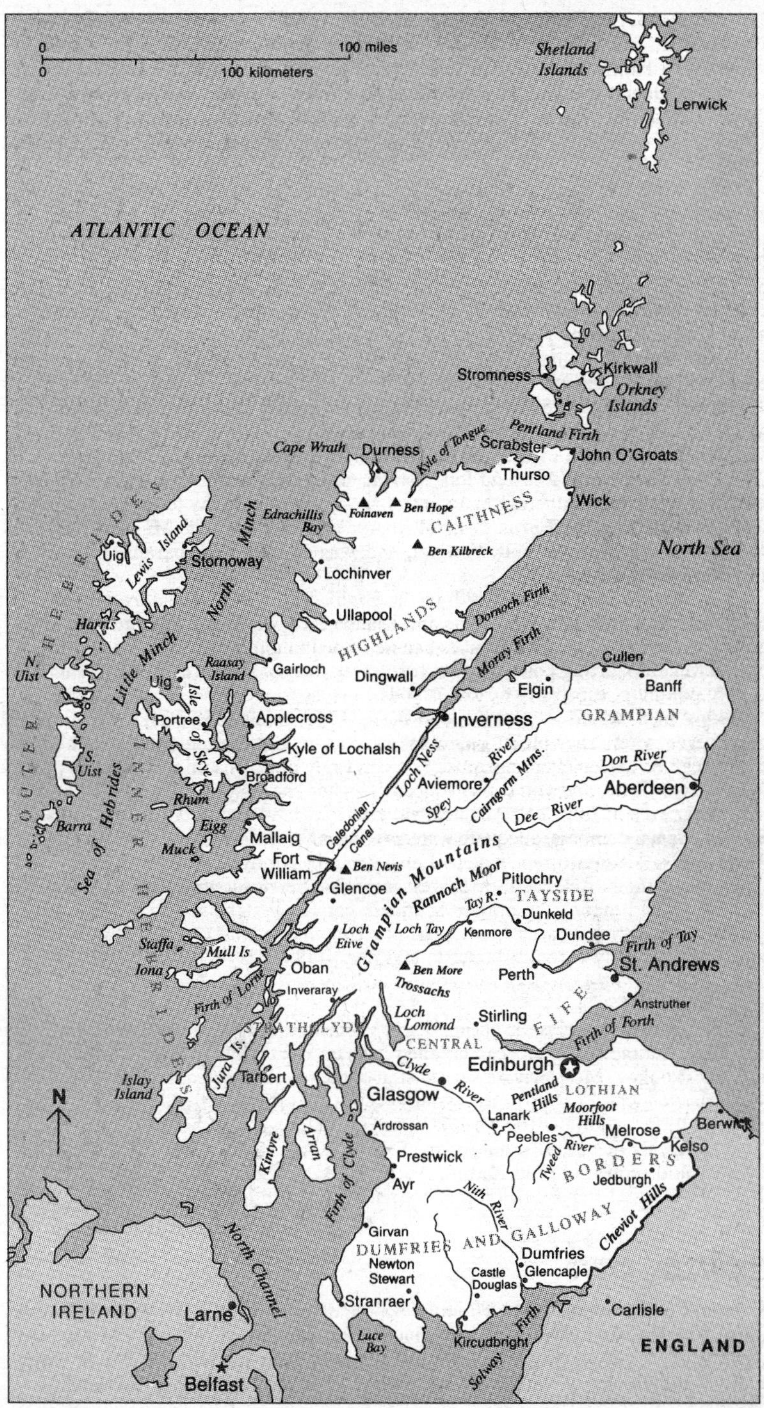

100 miles
100 kilometers
ATLANTIC OCEAN
Shetland Islands
Lerwick
Stromness
Kirkwall
Orkney Islands
Pentland Firth
Cape Wrath
Durness
Kyle of Tongue
Scrabster
John O'Groats
Thurso
Wick
Foinaven
Ben Hope
CAITHNESS
Edrachillis Bay
Ben Kilbreck
North Sea
OUTER HEBRIDES
Uig
Lewis Island
Stornoway
North Minch
Lochinver
Ullapool
HIGHLANDS
Dornoch Firth
Harris
Little Minch
Moray Firth
N. Uist
Raasay Island
Gairloch
Dingwall
Cullen
Elgin
Banff
Uig
Isle of Skye
Portree
Applecross
Inverness
GRAMPIAN
Kyle of Lochalsh
S. Uist
Broadford
Loch Ness
Spey River
Cairngorm Mtns.
Don River
Aviemore
Aberdeen
Rhum
Sea of Hebrides
Barra
Eigg
Mallaig
Caledonian Canal
Dee River
Muck
INNER HEBRIDES
Fort William
Ben Nevis
Grampian Mountains
Rannoch Moor
Pitlochry
Glencoe
Tay R.
TAYSIDE
Dunkeld
Loch Etive
Loch Tay
Kenmore
Dundee
Staffa
Mull Is
Firth of Tay
Iona
Oban
Ben More
Perth
St. Andrews
Trossachs
Inveraray
Firth of Lorne
Anstruther
Loch Lomond
Stirling
FIFE
STRATHCLYDE
CENTRAL
Firth of Forth
Jura Is.
Edinburgh
Islay Island
Tarbert
Clyde River
Glasgow
Pentland Hills
LOTHIAN
N
Moorfoot Hills
Lanark
Ardrossan
Peebles
Melrose
Berwick
Tweed River
Kelso
Kintyre
Arran
Prestwick
BORDERS
Firth of Clyde
Jedburgh
Ayr
Nith River
Cheviot Hills
North Channel
Girvan
DUMFRIES AND GALLOWAY
Dumfries
Newton Stewart
Castle Douglas
Glencaple
NORTHERN IRELAND
Stranraer
Larne
Carlisle
Solway Firth
Luce Bay
Kircudbright
ENGLAND
Belfast

Equally distinct is Scotland's famous heritage of kilt, clan and bagpipe, although this owes less to fact than to the romanticism of Sir Walter Scott. After ruthlessly suppressing Highland culture in the 18th century, Romantic Britain "discovered" the noble, Gaelic-speaking Highlander as an attractive alternative to its own, often ignoble industrial present. This discovery did not, however, extend to returning the Highlands to the clans; the hills and glens remain the deserted wilds that you see today.

These wilds are staggeringly beautiful. Humans destroyed the forests hundreds of years ago, leaving every chiselmark of nature visible. While the highest of the peaks, Ben Nevis, barely tops 1500m, treeless slopes and precipitous rock faces from loch to summit will make you catch your breath. Early August through mid-September is heather time in Scotland, when the hills erupt in purple. However, the best months to visit are May and June. Even in early summer, the weather is often cold and soggy. You will need warm woolen clothing, a slicker (preferably light and stowable), and a hat. In more remote areas, waterproof overpants and boots will be a blessing.

During July and August, parts of the western coast and inner islands feel like an international zoo. Avoid big tourist centers like Inverness and Fort William; the farther west and north you go, the more powerful Scotland's magic. Stop by a *ceilidh* (KAY-lee) dance or a weekend folk festival; seek out a resonant bagpipe competition or a Highland Gathering in an out-of-the-way place. Many festivals take place in June, including the **Burns Festival** in Ayr and Orkney's **St. Magnus Festival.** July brings the **Glasgow Folk Festival,** and August, the incomparable **Edinburgh International Festival.**

Only a few railways snake north to the Highlands and Islands, only a few buses or boats touch some smaller towns and islands each week and some remote areas are served only by post buses. Bikes can be rented in almost every town and transported to your starting point by train free (reservations, £3, are essential). Hitching is very common, especially on the islands.

Hiking in Scotland is ethereal, and permissible codes allow walkers to ramble nearly everywhere they please unless asked to leave. But the undomesticated countryside can be extremely dangerous. You can't rely on cairns or well-marked paths to guide your way, and you can *never* predict when the mist will descend. Blizzards may occur even in July. Never climb a mountain without sturdy boots, an **Ordnance Survey Map,** a compass, adequate waterproof gear and clothing, and an emergency food supply. Mosquito repellent will also come in handy. Leave an itinerary and timetable at the hostel, croft, or nearest mountain rescue station. For more details on walking and mountaineering in Scotland, consult Poucher's *The Scottish Peaks* (£9) or the Scottish Tourist Board's *Hillwalking in Scotland* (£2.25). Hunting season runs from July through January, and deer-stalking is especially popular from mid-August to mid-October; consult your hostel warden or innkeeper to avoid hunting grounds.

Camping in Scotland is the cheapest way to spend the night. There are trespassing laws here, but tactful tenters can lay their bags on a patch of farmland—asking first is the best policy. Most private sites cost about £3-5 per night and are oriented toward caravanners. IYHF (SYHA) youth hostels are often ideally located for hikers, but call ahead in summer (between 7-10pm) or better yet, use their new inter-hostel fax booking service (50p). Charges are £3.20-6.60 per night. Most hostels close by October and reopen only in March, April, or May. The maps and descriptions in the SYHA hostel handbook (80p at tourist offices) are helpful.

Edinburgh

Capital of the medieval kingdom of Scotland, Edinburgh is arguably the most alluring city in Northern Europe. With a towering mountain-top castle looking out over the depths of an empty loch toward the lofty King Arthur's Seat, Edinburgh makes dramatic use of the third dimension. Although the center of Scotland's au-

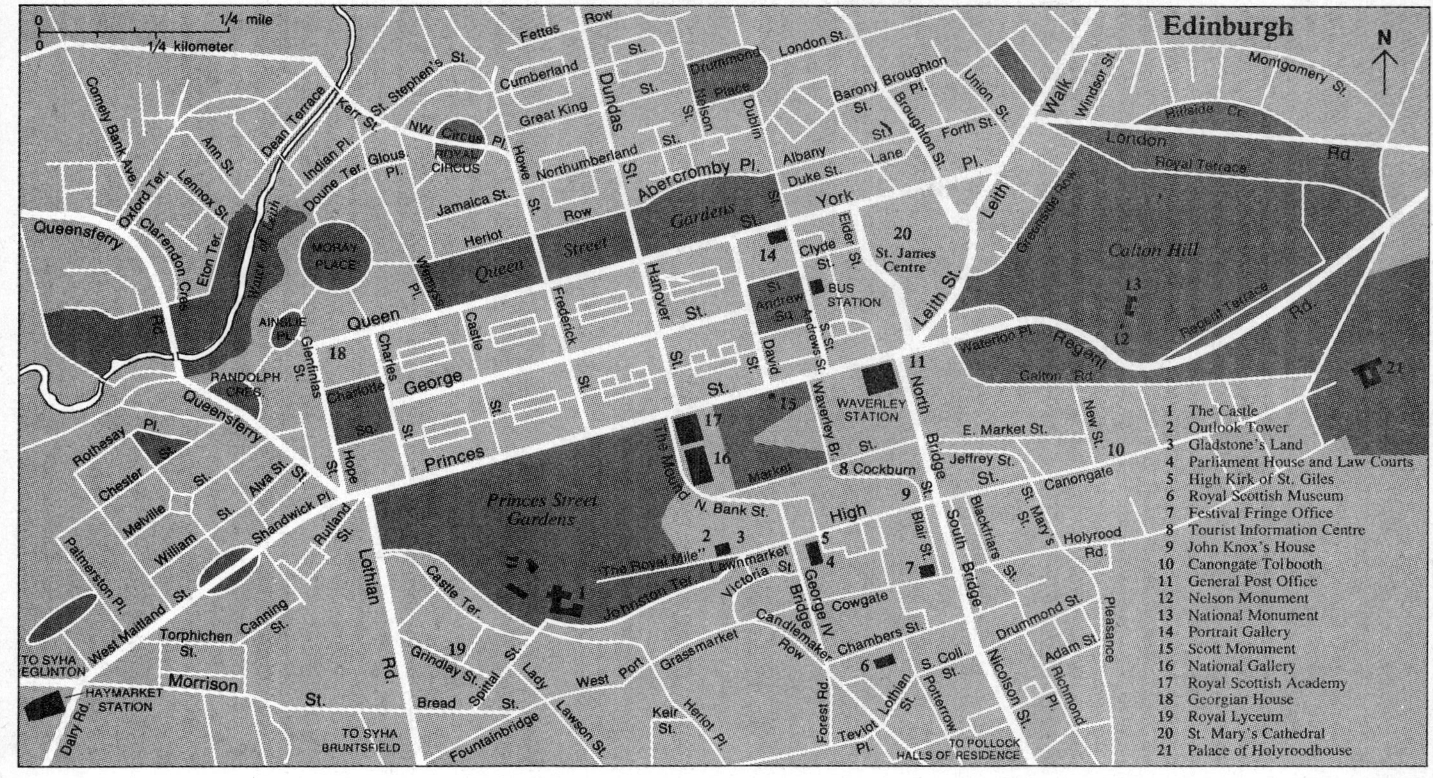
Edinburgh
N
0 1/4 mile
0 1/4 kilometer
1 The Castle
2 Outlook Tower
3 Gladstone's Land
4 Parliament House and Law Courts
5 High Kirk of St. Giles
6 Royal Scottish Museum
7 Festival Fringe Office
8 Tourist Information Centre
9 John Knox's House
10 Canongate Tolbooth
11 General Post Office
12 Nelson Monument
13 National Monument
14 Portrait Gallery
15 Scott Monument
16 National Gallery
17 Royal Scottish Academy
18 Georgian House
19 Royal Lyceum
20 St. Mary's Cathedral
21 Palace of Holyroodhouse
TO SYHA EGLINTON
HAYMARKET STATION
TO SYHA BRUNTSFIELD
TO POLLOCK HALLS OF RESIDENCE
WAVERLEY STATION
BUS STATION
St. James Centre
Princes Street Gardens
Queen Street Gardens
Calton Hill
Water of Leith
MORAY PLACE
ROYAL CIRCUS
AINSLIE PL.
RANDOLPH CRES.
"The Royal Mile"
Princes St.
George St.
Queen St.
Lothian Rd.
Leith St.
Leith Walk
North Bridge
South Bridge
High St.
Lawnmarket
Canongate
Cowgate
Grassmarket
Regent Rd.
Regent Terrace
Royal Terrace
London Rd.
York Pl.
Abercromby Pl.
Heriot Row
Dundas St.
Hanover St.
Frederick St.
Castle St.
Charlotte Sq.
St. Andrew Sq.
Dean Terrace
Comely Bank Ave.
Queensferry Rd.
Queensferry St.
Morrison St.
West Maitland St.
Dalry Rd.
Fountainbridge
Pleasance
Montgomery St.
Nicolson St.

tonomous judicial, ecclesiastic, and administrative establishments, Scotland's second-largest city is also a place where the milkman comes door-to-door each morning and you can hardly unfold a map before a stranger offers to help. Cobblestone alleyways huddle around the imposing castle, magisterial 18th-century townhouses sweep around iron-fenced parks, and culture throbs through the city's consortium of pubs, museums, and galleries.

Practical Information

Tourist Office: 3 Princes St. (tel. 557 17 00), in Waverley Market next to the Waverley train station. Busy but efficient accommodations service (£2.50). Scottish Citylink tickets sold. Information on other parts of Scotland too. Open July-Aug. Mon.-Sat. 8:30am-9pm, Sun. 11am-9pm; May-June and Sept. Mon.-Sat. 8:30am-8pm, Sun. 11am-8pm; Oct.-April Mon.-Fri. 9am-6pm, Sat. 9am-1pm.

Budget Travel: Edinburgh Travel Centre, 196 Rose St. (tel 226 20 19). Open Mon.-Fri. 9am-5:30pm, Sat. 10am-1pm.

Consulates: U.S., 3 Regent Terr. (tel. 556 83 15). **Australia,** 80 Hanover St. (tel. 226 62 71). **Canada,** in Glasgow (tel. (041) 221 44 15).

Currency Exchange: When banks are closed, go to the tourist office.

American Express: 139 Princes St. (tel. 225 78 81). Open Mon.-Fri. 9am-5pm, Sat.-Sun. 9am-noon.

Post Office: 2-4 Waterloo Pl. (tel. 550 82 29), at the corner of Princes St. and North Bridge. Poste Restante. Open Mon.-Thurs. 9am-5:30pm, Fri. 9:30am-5:30pm, Sat. 9am-12:30pm. **Postal Code:** EH1 1AL.

City Code: 031.

Trains: Waverley Station, tel. 556 24 51. Ticket office open whenever trains run. Information office open Mon.-Sat. 8am-1am, Sun. 9am-11pm.

Buses: St. Andrew Square Bus Station, St. Andrew Sq. (tel. 556 84 64 or 557 57 17). Scottish Citylink desk open Mon.-Sat. 9am-5:15pm, Sun. 9:30am-5pm. Tickets also available from drivers.

Public Transportation: Lothian Regional Transport (tel. 220 41 11). Buy ticket (30p-£1.10) on bus; exact change only.

Hitchhiking: Those headed south (except Newcastle and northeast England) take bus #4, 15, or 79 to Fairmilehead and then the A702 to Biggar. Those going to Newcastle, York, and Durham take bus #44 to Musselburgh and the A1. Those headed North take bus #18 or 40 to Barnton.

Luggage Storage: At Waverley Station (£1-1.50). Open Mon.-Sat. 6am-11pm, Sun. 7am-11pm. Also at the bus station at the Citylink desk (75p-£1.50). Open Mon.-Sat. 8am-5pm, Sun. 9:30am-5pm.

Laundromat: Bruntsfield Laundrette, 108 Bruntsfield Pl. (tel. 229 26 69), near Bruntsfield youth hostel. Wash £2, dry 20p. Open Mon.-Fri. 9am-5pm, Sat. 9am-4pm, Sun. 10am-4pm. **Bendix Launderette,** 13 S. Clerk St. (tel. 667 58 44). Wash £1, dry 20p. Open Mon.-Fri. 8am-8pm, Sat. 8am-1pm, Sun. 9am-1pm.

Bike Rental: Central Cycle Hire, 13 Lochrin Pl. (tel. 228 63 33). £5-10 per day. £35-45 per week. £20 deposit. Open Mon.-Sat. 10am-5pm, Sun. 10am-noon and 5-7pm; Sept.-May Mon. and Wed.-Sun. 10am-5pm.

Pharmacy: Boots, 48 Shandwick Pl. (tel. 225 67 57). Open Mon.-Sat. 8:45am-9pm, Sun. 11am-4:30pm.

Emergencies: Police or **Ambulance** (tel. 999). Police Headquarters, Fettes Ave. (tel. 311 31 31).

Accommodations and Camping

Finding a room should not pose problems except during the Festival. The tourist office is helpful but expensive (£2.50 fee), and the train station accommodations office is free but their listings are less extensive. The brochure *Where to Stay 1992* from the tourist office gives a comprehensive list of lodgings and prices. Hostels are cheapest, but Edinburgh's myriad B&Bs and guesthouses provide more privacy and a home-cooked breakfast for £12-16 per person. Your best hunting grounds are the **Bruntsfield** district around Gilmore Pl. and Viewforth Terr. (take bus #10, 11, 16 or 23 from Princes St.) and the **Newington** area between Dalkeith Rd. and Minto St. (buses #3, 7, 8 or 31 from North Bridge).

High Street Hostel, 8 Blackfriars St. (tel. 557 39 84), the 2nd right walking downhill on the Royal Mile after the South Bridge intersection, is a top-notch hostel. Central, friendly and clean. Free movie videos every night. 130 beds in 6-16 bed rooms. £5.90 includes sheets. Laundry service (£2.50), kitchen and full breakfast £1.90. No phone bookings, but call from the station to hold a bed until your arrival. Arrive before noon in summer, 10am during Festival. Open 24 hrs.

IYHF Hostel Eglinton, 18 Eglinton Crescent (tel. 337 11 20). Get off at Haymarket train station or take bus #3, 4 or 44 to Haymarket. Lobby could be a *Victoriana* magazine centerfold. Reception open 7am-2am, but arrive early or book ahead. £6.50. Open Jan. 2-Nov. 31.

IYHF Hostel Bruntsfield, 7 Bruntsfield Crescent (tel. 447 29 94). Take bus #11, 15, 16 or 17. Follow Bruntsfield Terrace to Bruntsfield Crescent by the park. Reception open 7am-2pm, but draconian regulations prohibit check-in before 11:20am or leaving the building before 7:30am. £6. Open March-Dec.

IYHF Hostel Merchiston, North Merchiston Boys' Club, Watson Crescent. Take bus #9 or 10 to Polwarth and then #30 or 43 to Dundee St. A long trek from town but possibly your only hope during the festival. No advance bookings. Grade 2. £4.20. Open June 26-Sept. 12.

Cowgate Tourist Hostel, 112 The Cowgate (tel. 226 21 53). Affordable privacy in clean flats with separate kitchens. Laundry service and no curfew. Singles £9.50. Doubles £17. Open July-Sept. 21.

Camping: Silverknowes Caravan Park, Marine Dr. (tel. 312 68 74). Take bus #14. 100 sites. Tents £4-5. Open April-Oct.

Food

Edinburgh has a spread of inexpensive restaurants, though you're not likely to find cheap food, friendly atmosphere, *and* traditional Scottish fare all in one place. The posh establishments that do serve Scottish treats will blow your budget, but you can get such delights as haggis or cock-a-leekie soup at reasonable prices in local cafés and groceries. Pub lunches are usually good values (£1.50-3 for an entree with vegetable and salad). Vegetarians have many options, one of the cheapest of which is to fill a salad container for a fixed price at the **Littlewoods** supermarket at 92 Princes St. Other supermarkets are **Scotmid** and **Wm. Low** on Nicolson St.

Lachana, 3 Bristo Pl., near the university. Scrumptious all-you-can-eat vegetarian buffet Tues. and Thurs. 5-7pm, £3.05. Tasty 4-course meal £4.10. Open Mon.-Fri. noon-2:30pm, Tues. and Thurs. 5-7pm.

Teviot Restaurant, Teviot Row Union, Bristo Sq. Edinburgh University student cafeteria, open Oct.-late June Mon.-Fri. 9:30am-6:45pm. Hot, full meals under £2. During the festival, it becomes the **Fringe Club,** a restaurant open to all, and prices go up by about 50%.

Henderson's Salad Table and Wine Bar, 94 Hanover St. Wide selection of hot vegetarian dishes (£1.90-2.20, with side salads 80p) and wines. Live guitar and piano nightly from 7:30pm. Open Mon.-Sat. 8am-10:45pm; also Sun. during the festival.

Kebab Mahal, 7 Nicolson Sq. The best of the many kebaberies in town. Kebabs £1.15-3. Open Sun.-Thurs. noon-midnight, Fri.-Sat. noon-1am.

The Baked Potato Shop, 56 Cockburn St., just below the Royal Mile. Creatively filled tubers (£1.35-1.60) and lots more. Open Mon.-Sat. 9am-11pm, Sun. 10am-9pm.

Seeds, 53 W. Nicolson St. Heaping plates of vegetarian entrees (£2.15-2.30) and restorative herbal teas. Open Mon.-Sat. 10am-8pm.

The Waterfront, 1c Dock Place, in Leith (Edinburgh's port). Take bus #16 and ask to get off at the bridge over Leith Water; the restaurant is on the left bank of Leith Water behind a parking lot. Nautical motif and luscious seafood barbecues will set you back £6-8 but are worth every penny. Open Mon.-Sat. noon-3pm and 6-10pm, Sun. noon-4pm.

Sights

Visible for miles around, **Edinburgh Castle** looms as the centerpiece of the city. From its windows, on clearer days, you can see all the way across the Firth of Forth to Fife. Eleventh-century **Queen Margaret's Chapel,** the oldest building in Edinburgh, is contained within the castle walls. (Open Mon.-Sat. 9:30am-5:05pm, Sun. 11am-5:05pm. Admission £2.80, seniors and children £1.40.) On the way down, the medieval **Gladstone's Land** is the oldest house on the Royal Mile, preserved as it was in the 15th and 16th centuries (open Mon.-Sat. 10am-5pm, Sun. 2-5pm; admission £2, students £1). **Lady Stair's House,** a 17th-century townhouse, contains memorabilia of Scotland's literary triumvirate of Robert Burns, Sir Walter Scott, and Robert Louis Stevenson (open June-Sept. Mon.-Sat. 10am-6pm, during Festival also Sun. 2-5pm; Oct.-May Mon.-Sat. 10am-5pm; free). Next, view the **High Kirk of St. Giles,** whose open-work spire is supported by a crown of flying buttresses. (Cathedral open Mon.-Sat. 9am-7pm, Sun. all day.) Behind St. Giles in the old **Parliament House,** you can watch a real British court in action with the judges and lawyers all wearing those ridiculous gray wigs. The final lap of the Mile includes **The People's Story,** a new museum of social history housed in historic Canongate Tolbooth (open daily 10am-6pm; Oct.-May Mon.-Sat. 10am-5pm; Sun. during Festival 2-5pm; free). Save **Holyrood Palace** for last; worth special attention are the **Music Room** and the **Northwest Tower,** where Mary Queen of Scots' secretary, David Rizzio, was stabbed to death before her eyes. Bus #1 or 6 will take you to the palace. (Open Mon-Sat. 9:30am-5:15pm, Nov.-March Mon.-Sat. 9:30am-3:45pm; sometimes closed for royal visits. Admission £2.35, children £1.10.)

Of Edinburgh's heavenly constellation of galleries, two are especially notable. The **National Gallery,** on the Mound, has rooms of Old Masters including Raphael's Bridgewater *Madonna.* (Open Mon.-Sat. 10am-5pm, Sun. 2-5pm; free.) The **National Gallery of Modern Art,** on Belford Rd. (take bus #13), houses a statue of two American tourists, drawings by Picasso, Matisse and Freud, and rotating monthly exhibits. (Same hours as National Gallery; free.) The **City Art Centre** is reopening in mid-1992 following refurbishments (open Mon.-Sat. 10am-5pm; free). Both it and **Fruitmarket Gallery** (open Tues.-Sat. 10am-5:30pm, Sun. 1:30-5:30pm), are near the train station on Market St., and house excellent exhibits of modern works.

One of the best ways to enjoy Edinburgh is to stroll through the elegant Georgian neighborhoods of the **New Town,** laid out in the 1790s by the young architect James Craig. Before beginning your exploration, visit the **New Town Conservation Centre,** 13A Dundas St. (open April-Oct. Mon.-Sat. 10am-5pm, Sun. 2-5pm) for a map and advice. **The Georgian House** on Charlotte Sq. (open April.-Oct. Mon.-Sat. 10am-4:30pm, Sun. 2-4:30pm; admission £2.20, students and seniors £1.10), is a good starting point. From Charlotte Sq., head west across Queensferry St. and through the West End to Palmerston Pl. Turn right, passing the huge neo-Gothic **St. Mary's Anglican Cathedral,** and follow the road downhill past Douglas Gardens to Belford Bridge. Here, various alleys and crooked stairs head off to your right to the medieval village of **Dean,** clustered in the ravine of Leith Water. A pathway leads east along Leith Water from Dean to **Stockbridge,** a quaint community full of students, coffeeshops, and good pubs. From here, you can take a bus back up the hill to Princes St.

For a sweeping view of Edinburgh, climb **Arthur's Seat,** an extinct volcano (823 ft.) located in **Holyrood Park.** The **Radical Road** makes a shorter walk up to the colorful Salisbury Crags on the west side of the seat. Another fine view is from **Calton Hill,** well past the east end of Princes St., where you can also get a close-up look at Edinburgh's Folly, an unfinished replica of the Parthenon; money ran out midway through the first row of columns.

Entertainment

The destination of choice for live music is **Preservation Hall,** 9 Victoria St., a large pseudo-New Orleans hall. Alternative bands play at **Calton Studios,** and **The Venue,** both on Calton Rd., and at **Negociant's** on Lothian Rd. near the university. Two especially good student bars are **The Pear Tree,** on West Nicolson St., with its large outdoor courtyard, and **Greyfriars Bobby's Bar,** both of which are open (and crammed) late. Greyfriars Bobby was a loyal dog who, for years, refused to leave his owner's grave in the yard of Greyfriars Kirk. The **Café Royal Circle Bar** on W. Register St., off Princes St., is the most exquisite public house around, with old wood and stained glass. Around the corner at 216 Calton Rd., the **St. James Oyster Bar** often has good live performances and a packed crowd.

The **Traverse Theatre** is on West Bow (tel. 226 26 33); the **Royal Lyceum Theatre,** on Grindlay St. is off Lothian Rd. (tel. 229 96 97). **Usher Hall,** Lothian Rd. (tel. 228 11 55), holds concerts of the superb Scottish National and Chamber Orchestras, while **Ripping Records,** 91 South Bridge (tel. 226 70 10), provides information and tickets for more contemporary musical performances. The best cinema in town is the **Filmhouse,** 88 Lothian Rd. (tel. 228 26 88), showing a selection of classic and critically-acclaimed films. (Tickets £1.50-3; student discounts (£1) available for weekday afternoon shows.) *The List* (90p), available at most bookshops, will let you know what's playing.

The Edinburgh International Festival (Aug. 16-Sept. 5, 1992) and its satellites—the Fringe Festival, the Jazz Festival, the Film Festival, and the Military Tattoo—transform the city and transfix their audiences. Thousands come, and the city does its best to keep them happy with extended museum hours and special exhibits. Tickets go on sale by mail starting in May, and the Festival Box Office, 21 Market St., Edinburgh EH1 1BW, opens in late May for counter sales; you can book by phone with a credit card (tel. 225 57 56) except on the day of a performance. (Office open Mon.-Fri. 10am-6pm, Sat. 10am-noon; during the festival Mon.-Sat. 9am-6pm, Sun. 10am-5pm.) Prices for musical and theatrical events can go as high as £33, but many plays and concerts cost only £5-8. Performances are often sold out well in advance, but you can sometimes buy unsold tickets at half-price on the day of the performance; go to the booth at the bottom of The Mound between 1 and 5pm.

Around the established festival has grown an even larger and more boisterous **Fringe Festival.** Now with over 500 amateur and professional companies, which present theater, music, poetry, dance, mime, opera, revue and various exhibitions, the Fringe transforms Edinburgh into the world's largest stage. Ticket prices average about £4, and occasionally there are student discounts. For tickets and a comprehensive program, write the **Fringe Festival Office,** 180 High St., Edinburgh EH1 1QS (from abroad, include the equivalent of £2 postage for the program). Telephone or over-the-counter bookings can be made at the office, starting in late July (tel. 226 52 57; open year-round Mon.-Fri. 10am-6pm). The Fringe runs clubs where performers and visitors can chill. Membership fees are £16 for the three weeks.

Progress in contemporary cinema is tracked at the **International Film Festival,** and an **International Jazz Festival** (both in mid-August) has also recently swung into gear. Film information is available from **The Filmhouse,** 88 Lothian Rd., Edinburgh EH3 9BZ (tel. 228 63 82). The box office is open in early August, and phone and postal bookings are accepted. For jazz information, contact the **Information Centre,** 116 Canongate (tel. 557 16 42). The **Military Tattoo** is a bombastic spectacle of bagpipes and drums, performed almost every night on the Castle Esplanade (Aug. 2-24, 1991). For tickets (from £6.70), write or stop by the office, 22 Market St., Edinburgh EH1 1QB (tel. 225 11 88).

Near Edinburgh: St. Andrews

Northeast of Edinburgh is the venerable college and coastal town of **St. Andrews.** Home to the skeleton of a proud seaside cathedral, St. Andrews is also a holy shrine for golfers who come here to putt away on the courses where the sport was born and where Mary Queen of Scots herself once teed off. Fife Scottish bus X-59 makes frequent trips to St. Andrews from Edinburgh (5-7 per day, £3.70). Trains stop eight miles away at Leuchars (a quick trip by bus or thumb from St. Andrews).

The helpful **tourist office,** 78 South St. (tel. (0334) 720 21) does free B&B bookings. You must leave St. Andrews for hostel-priced beds. **Mr. Pennington's Bunkhouse** (tel. (0333) 31 07 68) is 8 miles away in West Pitkierie; call for bus info. The owner and his family will put you up in their 13th-century fortified farmhouse and answer any and all questions on local history. (£4.50. Open all year.) North of St. Andrews, there is a **YMCA Interpoint Hostel** in a converted gym at 14 Rankine St. in Dundee (tel. (0382) 28 444). Buses from St. Andrews and trains from Leuchars run to Dundee frequently all day. (Reception open 8-10am and 5-10pm. £7 plus a one-time membership fee of £2. Open June 24-August 8.) At **The Victoria Café,** 1 St. Mary's Place, a zealous college staff serves up tasty lentil soup and sandwiches. (Open daily 10:30am-midnight.) St. Andrews' most impressive sights cluster by the ocean at the east end of town. Explore the narrow subterranean passages of the **St. Andrews Castle,** once the local bishops' residence. (Open daily 9:30am-6pm; off-season Mon.-Sat. 9:30am-4pm, Sun. 2-4pm. 80p). At **St. Andrews Cathedral,** you can wander around the remains of the once-grand church and climb the 157-step St. Rules Tower for an expansive view.

Glasgow

What Scotland's largest city lacks in stateliness and aesthetic appeal, it makes up in sheer energy. Glasgow is the capital of workaday Scotland and home to one of Britain's strongest socialist movements. The 40,000 students of Glasgow University make the city one of the liveliest in Britain. Although Edinburgh's historical and cultural glories still put it justifiably first on most itineraries, Glasgow's theaters, museums, parks and façades warrant a close second. Most of what goes on in the city happens in the university area, divided from the city center by the M8, with funky little stores and cafés in funky little side streets and a pub for every hour. Downtown is blocks and blocks of vast pedestrian shopping frenzies and surprising open squares, plus both train stations and the bus terminal. Glasgow's miniature **underground** circles the city, connecting the university and city center (flat fare 50p).

The highly efficient **tourist office** (tel. (041) 204 44 00) is downtown at 35 St. Vincent Pl., adjacent to George Sq. and Queen St. Station (open June-Sept. Mon.-Sat. 9am-9pm, Sun. 10am-6pm; Oct.-Easter Mon.-Sat. 9am-6pm; Easter-May Mon.-Sat. 9am-7pm, Sun. 10am-6pm, but computerized info booths are scattered throughout downtown.) The **post office** is at 2-5 George Sq. (Open Mon.-Fri. 9am-5:30pm, Sat. 9am-12:30pm. **Postal code:** G2 1AA.)

The **IYHF youth hostel,** 11 Woodlands Terr. (tel. (041) 332 30 04), is an easy jaunt from the city center. Take Sauchiehall St. west to Charing Cross and follow the hostel signs. From Buchanan Bus Station, walk about 6 blocks west up Renfrew St. to the footbridge over the motorway; on the other side, turn right, take the steps past Claremont Terr., and then turn left onto Woodlands Terr. (Curfew 2am. £6. Advance reservations essential.) The residence halls at the **University of Glasgow,** located throughout the city, are a good choice in summer. **Maclay Hall,** 18 Park Terr. (tel. (041) 332 50 56), overlooking Kelvingrove Park, is nearest the city center and has perks like soap and towels (£8.68, students £7.66). In summer, make reservations for hostels and B&Bs at least one week in advance. Try the tourist office's free book-a-bed-ahead service or, to avoid Glasgow's congestion, venture out to the large **Loch Lomond Youth Hostel (IYHF)** (tel. (038985) 226; £5.20), less than one hour to the north (3 buses per day from Buchanan Station).

Inexpensive restaurants crowd both Sauchiehall St., in the center of town, and the university neighborhood. The **Third Eye Centre,** 350 Sauchiehall St., has a good vegetarian menu (hot dishes from £2.50) and bookstore and art gallery (open Mon.-Sat. 10am-9pm, Sun. noon-5:30pm). The **Grosvenor Café,** 35 Ashton La., off Byres

Rd., is a student hangout with dandy deals (sandwiches 35-55p, homemade soup 38p; open Mon.-Fri. 9am-7pm, Sat. 9am-6pm). The **Magnus Dining Room,** in the University Refectory across from the library at Glasgow University, offers wholesome, inexpensive grub—you don't have to be a registered student (open Mon.-Thurs. 8:30am-6:10pm, Fri. 8:30am-3:30pm).

West of the center, **Kelvingrove Park** is good for a lounge by the Kelvin River or a wander along the park's leafy paths and past its odd statues and fountains. In the southwest corner of the park is the **Glasgow Art Gallery and Museum,** home to an arms-and-armor display and many classic paintings, including van Gogh's portrait of a Glaswegian art dealer. (Open Mon.-Sat. 10am-5pm, Sun. noon-6pm. Free.) Towering at the north end of the park is the central building of **Glasgow University;** beyond it, the **Botanic Gardens** also offer a good stroll. Nearby Byres Rd. is the place to begin your nighttime activities; a popular pub crawl usually commences at **Tennents Bar** by University Rd., and continues down towards the River Clyde—the path is long and the ale is strong. The teeming **Halt Bar,** 106 Woodlands Rd. and the chic **Cul de Sac Bar,** 46 Ashton La., are both in vogue; **Nico's,** on 375 Sauchiehall St., is lively and hectic, and surprisingly well decorated. Post-pubbing goes on at the too too cool **Tunnel;** post-Tunneling at the too too hot **Sub Club.** Both are outrageously expensive (£7). A cheaper option is the yuppified **Savoy** on Sauchiehall St. (£3.50). More information on nightlife can be found in *The List* (80p), available at most newsstands. Pick up a copy of *The Ticket* for listings of Glasgow's extensive theater and cinema offerings.

The Glasgow **Barras,** billed as the world's largest open-air market, takes place every Saturday and Sunday at London Rd. and Gallowgate (east of the city center). Go for the veggie dicer demos and the butchers, not the merchandise. South of town (5km) is the wooded **Pollok Park** (buses #23, 45, or 57), site of the fascinating **Burrell Collection,** amassed from William Burrell's travels in the Orient. (Open Mon.-Sat. 10am-5pm, Sun. noon-6pm. Free.)

Near Glasgow: Arran

Two hours southwest of Glasgow by train and ferry lies the rugged island of Arran, the most accessible of the Scottish isles. Trains connect Glasgow's Central Station and the harbor at Ardrossan, where frequent ferries (1 hr., round-trip £5.55) leave for **Brodick,** Arran's largest village and only tourist trap. Rising above the curving, sandy bay at Brodick is the peak of **Goatfell,** from which you can see north to the ridges of Casteal Abhail and south down the coast to Holy Island. From Brodick to the cold, windy peak and back averages five hours. Fifteen miles away, at the north end of the island, is **Lochranza,** as idyllic a Scottish village as you could imagine, with one store, one pub, one castle, and one **IYHF youth hostel** (tel. (077083) 631). This is the best base for exploring the gentle headlands of the **Cock of Arran** and the island's central peaks. At the southern end of the island, where peaks and ridges give way to meadows and beaches, the **IYHF youth hostel** at **Whiting Bay** (tel. (07707) 339) presents comfortable beds and an arresting location.

Highlands and Islands

Spacious and beautiful beyond belief, the Highlands and Islands are among the last stretches of true wilderness left in Europe. A tattered coast, cut by sea lochs and dotted with innumerable islands, stretches under the summer sun. The area's sparse population heightens the otherworldly atmosphere—even in tourist season you can easily hike for a full day without seeing fellow bipeds. Two hundred years ago, 30% of Scotland's people lived north of the Great Glen; various economic innovations combined to force a mass migration during the crushing Highland Clearances of the early 19th century. Only in the Outer Hebrides has the Scottish Gaelic tongue survived these waves of industrialization and anglicization.

Travel in the Highlands requires a measure of advance planning. At any tourist office, invest £3.95 in *Getting Around the Highlands and Islands,* an exhaustive, indispensable timetable that collects almost all the public transit schedules in the region. **Caledonian MacBrayne** runs ferry services to most of the inner and outer isles. Trains leave Glasgow for Oban (the Highlands' main port) and Fort William (the Highlands' main resort) three or four times per day in summer. Express buses are significantly cheaper, and only slightly slower. Inverness has connections to many of the remoter destinations in the region. Regional buses tend to run only once or twice per day, and rarely on Sunday. The **Highlands and Islands Travelpass** allows unlimited travel on most rail, boat and bus routes; it is available for 7 of 8 or 13 of 15 days (Oct.-May £40 and £60, respectively; June-Sept. £65 and £90). Neither version gives you your money's worth unless you travel frantically.

Inverness

Inverness is Scotland's busiest tourist trap, and the transportation hub of the Highlands. Contrary to lore, the castle in town (closed to the public) is not where Macbeth murdered King Duncan; the actual fictional site is **Cawdor Castle,** 20km east of town, complete with moat and drawbridge. (Open May-early Oct. daily 10am-5:30pm. Admission £3. Hard to reach by public transport.) If the weather is good, rent a bike at **Thornton Cycles,** 23 Castle St. (tel. (0463) 22 28 10), for £9 per day and cycle down the east side of **Loch Ness.** Start at the riverbank in town and stick close to the water. The suburbs soon give way to placid farm country; after 5 mi. you'll reach the head of the absurdly famous loch. The ruins of **Urquhart Castle,** are on the loch's west side, where most sightings of the spurious monster have occurred. Inverness comes up short on local attractions, but the **Inverness Museum and Art Gallery** in Castle Wynd, the **Inverness Secondhand Bookshop,** 10 Banks St., and the **Ness Islands** just upstream from town, can together pleasantly fill an afternoon.

Inverness' **tourist office,** 23 Church St. (tel. (0463) 23 43 53), can book local B&Bs for £1, or give you a free map and accommodations list. (Open Mon.-Sat. 9am-8:30pm, Sun. 9am-6pm; off-season Mon.-Fri. 9am-5:30pm.) The **train** and **bus stations** are just a few blocks away off Academy St., and the **post office** is one block away on Queensgate. During high season, arrive very early in the day to pin down a bed in your price range. The **IYHF youth hostel,** 1 Old Edinburgh Rd. (tel. (0463) 23 17 71), is comfy and convenient. (Curfew 2am. £6.) The cozy **Inverness Student Hotel,** 8 Culduthel Rd. (tel. (0463) 23 65 56), is across the street from the hostel (£6.40). The areas around **Argyll Street** and **Old Edinburgh Road** overflow with B&Bs.

Oban and Fort William

Although Oban (3 hr. by bus or train from Glasgow) is the largest port on the west coast, it retains the cheer of a small town. If you tire of the bustling pier, gaze at the bay from the *ersatz*-Colosseum **McCaig's Tower** (built in the 18th century to employ local masons) or walk 15 minutes north of town to the crumbling tower of **Dunollie Castle.** The **IYHF youth hostel,** on Corran Esplanade (tel. (0631) 620 25), presides over the bay. (Reception open 7-11am and 2-11pm. £4.85. Open early March-Oct., frantically busy in July and Aug.) **Jeremy Inglis,** 21 Airds Cresc. (tel. (0631) 650 65 or 630 64), is a *Let's Go* institution. (B&B £5.50. Bath and kitchen facilities included.) The **tourist office,** Argyll Sq. (tel. (0631) 631 22), books beds locally for £1. (Open June-Aug. Mon.-Sat. 9:15am-8:45pm, Sun. 10am-4:45pm; May and Sept.-Oct. Mon.-Sat. 9:15am-5:30pm, Sun. 10am-5pm; Nov.-March 9:15am-1pm and 2-5pm; April Mon.-Fri. 9:15am-5:30pm.) Most visitors leave from the Oban pier for **Mull,** the largest of the southern isles. Ferries leave several times per day in summer for **Craignure** (£2.30, next day return £4.05). Craignure is but a few shops and a pier; climb aboard the narrow-gauge railway for the trip to **Torosay Castle,** a graceful Victorian mansion nearby, or else bus it to **Tobermory** (Mull's main town) or **Fionnphort** (where ferries to Iona leave). The **IYHF youth hostel** (tel. (0688) 24 81) in Tobermory overlooks the bay among the colorful houses on Main St. (£3.20. Open mid-March to Sept.) The sacred isle of **Iona** was the first Christian settlement in Scotland (St. Columba founded its abbey in 563). The **Iona Community** continues to maintain an alternative spiritual center in the old abbey, occasionally offering accommodation (tel. (06817) 404; 3-day min. stay; board £19, students £13). For B&B, try the **Bishop's House** (tel. (06817 306; £12, 15% student discount) or **Finlay, Ross Ltd.** (tel. (06817) 357; £7.50-12).

A spectacular valley between Oban and Fort William, **Glencoe** is still known as the "weeping glen" after a 1692 massacre in which government troops turned on their highland hosts to make an example of King William III's power over the clans. Today the glen attracts fearless rock climbers to its sheer and often slippery faces where numerous waterfalls cascade into the valley. Express Fort William-Glasgow buses stop twice daily in Glencoe Village; the Gaelic Bus from Oban will deposit you in Ballachulish, ¾ mi. away. The **Glencoe youth hostel (IYHF)** (tel. (08552) 219; £4.85), 2 mi. south of the village on the east side of the river, is much more pleasant than the adjacent Leacantium Bunkhouse. In town, the comfortable **Glencoe Outdoor Centre** (tel. (08552) 350) does a £12 B&B and rents sports equipment.

Fort William no longer has a fort, but could use one to fend off summer tourists. Mountaineers come for the challenge of **Ben Nevis** (4406 ft.), the highest peak in Britain. The main tourist path starts just up Glen Nevis past the town park (7 hr. round-trip); consult a hillwalker's guide at the tourist office for more interesting, less congested routes. The **tourist office** (tel. (0397) 70 37 81) is practically a small museum. (Open June-Sept. Mon.-Sat. 9am-9pm, Sun. 10am-6pm; off-season generally Mon.-Sat. 9am-5:30pm.) At the base of the Ben Nevis trail, in the lush valley of Glen Nevis, the pleasing **Glen Nevis youth hostel (IYHF)** (tel. (0397) 70 23 36) is often booked (£4.85). On the opposite side of the River Nevis, the **Ben Nevis Bunkhouse** (tel. (0397) 70 22 40) is 2 mi. from town along Achintee Rd. (£5). When both of these are packed, head 4 mi. out of town on the A830 to the immaculate **Smiddy Alpine Lodge** (tel. (0397) 77 24 67) in Corpach (£6). Buses run to Corpach (23 per day) from the Presto Market on High St. Camping is free in the meadow past the IYHF hostel. Buses (Mon.-Sat 2 per day) and trains wind coastwards from Fort William to **Mallaig** along the famous "Road to the Isles," through mountains and past lochs and the Silver Sands of Morar (white beaches more at home in the Caribbean). The buses stop just south of Mallaig at the **Garramore youth hostel (IYHF)** (tel. (06875) 268; £4.85), next to a campsite and close to secluded sandy beaches with misty views of the Inner Hebrides. From Mallaig, ferries shuttle to Skye and the **Small Isles** of Muck, Eigg, Rhum, and Canna. On **Rhum** stay in the lavish turn-of-the-century Kinloch Castle (hostel-ish accommodation £8; call ahead, tel. (0687) 20 37).

Skye

The charismatic Isle of Skye is deservedly the most touristed of the Hebrides. The **Cuillin Hills,** volcanic peaks surging boldly into a halo of clouds, are perhaps the most dramatic mountain vistas in Britain. Lush peninsulas and bays mark the extremes of the island near Staffin and Armadale. Historic clan wars have given way to debate over construction of a bridge to the island; for the meantime, Skye is easily reached by ferry from Mallaig to Armadale (£2.20) or Kyle of Lochalsh to Kyleakin (free). Several buses run daily from both Inverness and Glasgow and across the ferry to Kyleakin. Transportation on the island is not easy; bus service is infrequent and expensive. Biking, hiking or hitching may be better options.

Skye's five **IYHF hostels** are sweetly situated, but distressingly oversubscribed in the summer. Try to call at least one night in advance. **Glenbrittle** (tel. (047842) 278) is in the heart of the Cuillins, accessible only to hikers and those with their own transportation. (Open late March-Sept.) **Uig** (tel. (047042) 211), overlooking the bay on the northern peninsula, is the least crowded and is accessible by bus or ferry from the Outer Hebrides. (Open late March-Oct.) **Broadford** (tel. (04712)

442) is the most central, close to both mountains and beaches. (Open early March-Oct.) **Armadale** (tel. (04714) 260), on the southern tip of Skye, is ½ mi. away from the Mallaig ferry and serves well as a base for touring the verdant **Sleat Peninsula.** (Open late March-Sept.) **Kyleakin** (tel. (0599) 45 85), steps from the Kyle of Lochalsh ferry, is the island's largest hostel and offers meals from Easter to September. (Open Feb.-Nov.; £4.85 per night.) From Sconser on Skye, take the ferry to **Raasay** (May-Sept. Mon.-Sat.), a long, narrow island with an **IYHF youth hostel** (tel. (047842) 240; few restrictions; open mid-May to Sept.). Several independent hostels have recently sprung up in Skye to help cope with excess demand. The **Backpacker's Guesthouse** in Kyleakin (tel. (0599) 45 10) offers low-key comfort for £5. Near Broadford, the tiny **Fossil Bothy** (tel. (0471) 82 26 44 or 82 22 97) sleeps eight cozily, and just west of the Cuillins in Portnalong, the **Croft Bunkhouse** (tel. (047842) 254) sleeps 16 in a refurbished cow shed.

Most of Skye's sights are on small country roads and accessible only under your own power. Ask about bus tours, which usually include **Dunvegan Castle** at Skye's northwestern tip, ancient home of the Clan MacLeod. Many accessible walks lead out of **Sligachan,** which has a large campsite and a hotel. The main path here traverses a stately bridge and continues through the river valley between peaks. For a spellbinding view of the Cuillins across the sea, make the strenuous bike trip or catch a bus from Broadford to **Elgol.**

Outer Hebrides

The landscape of the Outer Hebrides is ancient and unchanged. Much of the exposed rock here has been around for more than half as long as the planet itself—3 billion years. The terrain is largely flat, treeless and—at first sight—utterly depressing. But the pure light and drifting Atlantic mists that sweep the untouched miles of moorland create cold, luminous vistas. Try to visit the islands between late April and October. The rest of the year, accommodations are scarce and the weather fearsome. This is the last stronghold of both the Gaelic language and the Free Church, whose strict observation of the Sabbath makes travel, shopping and eating out impossible on Sundays.

South to north, the Outer Hebrides run in a string from Barra, South Uist, Benbecula, and North Uist to the largest island, which is divided into Harris (the southern third) and Lewis. **Caledonian MacBrayne** ferries (tel. (0631) 622 85) run to the islands from Oban (for Castlebay on Barra and Lochboisdale on South Uist), from Uig on Skye (for Lochmaddy on North Uist and Tarbert on Harris), and from Ullapool on the northwest coast of the mainland (for Stornoway on Lewis). The **Island Hopscotch** ticket will take you through all the islands at a slightly reduced rate. Start in Oban and take the ferry to South Uist or Barra (a breathtaking six-hour journey past most of the Inner Hebrides), then work your way up to Harris and Lewis, and return finally to Skye or Ullapool. Note that **Ullapool** is an easy bus trip from Inverness (connecting with ferries); it has an **IYHF youth hostel** to the right of the pier (tel. (0854) 60 22 54), and a **tourist office** (tel. (0854) 60 23 15) which can find you a B&B for about £12. (Open July-Aug. Mon.-Sat. 9am-7pm, Sun. 1-6pm; May-June and Sept. Mon.-Sat. 9am-6pm, Sun. 1-6pm; April and Oct. Mon.-Sat. 9am-1pm and 2-5:30pm.)

Once you reach the islands, buses are infrequent; many tourists hitch. Numerous archeological and historical sites blend effortlessly into the surrounding landscape; the *Outer Hebrides Leisure Map* will show you the location of every single stone and bird preserve. B&Bs are often in the middle of nowhere; book at the tourist offices. The Gatliff Trust, affiliated with the IYHF, runs several **croft-house hostels** on the islands—rudimentary thatched accommodations staffed by bouncy wardens, with bunks, coin-operated electricity and cooking facilities. Most of these hostels have showers that are cold even to look at, but the recently opened **Garenin hostel** on the Isle of Lewis sports a widely-esteemed hot shower.

On the southern islands, book a B&B through the seasonal **tourist offices** (May-Sept.) at each ferry port: **Castlebay** on **Barra** (tel. (08714) 336); **Lochboisdale** on

South Uist (tel. (08784) 286); and **Lochmaddy** on **North Uist** (tel. (08763) 321). Lochmaddy has the only **IYHF youth hostel** around (tel. (08763) 368; £4.20; open mid-May to Sept.); when the rain and wind sweep in from the Atlantic, the warden opens early so you can toast by the wood stove. The southern islands' most spectacular feature is the beach on the western coast of the Uists, which stretches uninterrupted for nearly 40 mi.

Northernmost in the chain, the Siamese islands of Lewis and Harris are divided by the treeless Forest of Harris (really a mountain range). Open hills, softened by a carpet of *machair* and wildflowers, make for wonderful off-trail rambling. On **Harris,** there's a **tourist office** by the ferry landing in **Tarbert** (tel. (0859) 20 11; open early April-early Oct. same hrs.). The **Stockinish Youth Hostel (IYHF)** (no phone; £3.20; open mid-May to Sept.) is 8 mi. south of Tarbert along the desolate east coast; one to two buses run daily. This is a sublimely soothing spot with few restrictions, where mussels and periwinkles whisper "dinner" from rocks on the beach. **Lewis** is better known for its prehistoric sites, the most famous of which are the **Stones of Callanish**—an extaordinary Bronze-Age circle as isolated as Stonehenge is overrun. Local archeologists have claimed that the cruciform site is a lunar observatory of baffling complexity. In nearby Carloway, the Gatliff Trust hostel at **Garenin** provides a base for exploring Callanish and the fascinatingly sculpted coastline adjacent to the hostel. **Stornoway,** the island's largest town, is a dull ferry port blessed with a helpful **tourist office** (tel. (0851) 70 30 88; open Mon.-Wed. and Fri. 9am-6pm, Thurs. and Sat. 9am-5:30pm, and for ferry arrivals).

Orkney Islands

Pawned to Scotland 500 years ago by a Danish monarch, Orkney is a wish list of sleepy, fertile islands, replete with seabirds and neolithic ruins. The best time to visit is the summer solstice, when the sun shines eternal and the six-day **St. Magnus Festival** in Kirkwall (beginning on the Friday after the solstice) inspires the islanders with traditional and modern music, drama, and poetry.

Two ferries serve Orkney: one into Stromness from Scrabster, near Thurso (£11.50), the other into Burwick from John o' Groats (May-Sept.; £9, round-trip £12 for afternoon departure from John o' Groats and morning return from Orkney). Bus service is relatively frequent on Mainland (the largest of Orkney's islands); hitching is hit or miss. Timetables for all buses and boats within the archipelago issue from the tourist offices (6 Broad St., Kirkwall, tel. (0856) 28 56, and on the pier in Stromness).

On the east side of Mainland, **Kirkwall** is Orkney's capital and cultural center. A masterpiece in red sandstone, the **St. Magnus Cathedral** dates to 1137. David Lea's **Go-Orkney Minibus Tours,** for people who don't usually take tours, are an excellent way to see Orkney up close (£5-13.50, reserve at the tourist office). The **IYHF youth hostel,** Old Scapa Rd. (tel. (0856) 22 43), rarely fills. (Open mid-May to Sept.; £4.85.) Some of the best archaeological relics in Europe lie between Kirkwall and Stromness off the A965. You can see the 5000-year-old village **Skara Brae,** the magnificently preserved chambered tombs of **Maeshowe** and **Jim Morrison,** and the **Ring of Brodgar,** a 27-stone circle.

Stromness looks as if it has just slid down the hillside and lost half its houses to the harbor—bayfront buildings and bright fishing boats project into the water. Narrow and paved with flagstones, **Victoria Street** looks medieval, but Stromness in fact dates only from the late 18th century, when it became a port of call for transatlantic shipping. The recently refurbished **IYHF youth hostel,** on Hellihole Rd. (tel. (0856) 85 05 89), is open from April to September. (Lockout 10:30am-5pm. Curfew 11pm. £4.20.) The independent **Brown's Hostel** is on Victoria St. (tel. (0856) 85 06 61; £5). During **Stromness Shopping Week** (July 20-26 in 1992), when the going gets tough, the tough go shopping.

Ferries from Mainland connect with all the smaller populated islands to the north and south. The most visually dramatic of these is **Hoy,** accessible by ferry from Stromness. **Ward Hill** (1565 ft.), on northern Hoy, has a sweeping view of the entire archipelago. The **Old Man of Hoy,** a 450-foot rock stack that eluded climbers until 1966, is best seen from the Scrabster-Stromness ferry; the cliff path along **St. John's Head** hovers more than a thousand feet above the sea. There are two IYHF youth hostels on Hoy, both often deserted (and open mid-May to Sept.). For both, make reservations (tel. (0856) 35 35), and bring food from Stromness.

Shetland Islands

At the same latitude as southern Greenland, the Shetland Islands are Britain's northernmost outpost; locals consider themselves more Scandinavian than Scottish. This narrow archipelago, where you can never be more than three miles from the sea, is by turns desolately beautiful and just plain desolate. Although they operate several of the largest and most advanced boats in the British fishing fleet, many Shetland fishermen adhere to a strict body of superstition and taboo. ("Unfishy" women should stay ashore, and whatever you do, *don't* say the word "pig." If you do, bite a spoon.) The local dialect, with its liberal smattering of Norse-derived words and its lilting accent, is a potent reminder of Shetland's Nordic heritage.

From **Aberdeen,** Scotland's east-coast oil necropolis, **P&O Ferries (tel. (0224) 57 26 15)** chug five times a week to Lerwick (14 hr., reclining seats £44.50, berths £53-54.50, 10% discount for seniors and another 10% off Oct.-May). Reach Aberdeen by frequent buses and trains from Edinburgh and Glasgow; from the stations, it's a 10-minute walk to the ferry terminal and 20 minutes to the **Aberdeen Youth Hostel (IYHF)** (£6). There is also ferry service between Stromness (Orkney) and Lerwick (1-2 per week; £29). **Smyril Line** (contact P&O) sails from Lerwick to Bergen, Norway (Mon. at 11pm, £50) and to the Faroe Islands and Iceland (Wed. at 2am, £60 and £130); students get 25% off, and all fares are discounted another 25% in the first three weeks of June and most of August. Flying to Shetland from Orkney (½ hr.) is a fantastic deal if you take advantage of the British Airways/BABA special. By booking a Shetland B&B from Orkney (£2.50 booking fee), you can purchase a £29 ticket to Shetland's Sumburgh Airport. (Works in reverse too.)

The friendly folk at the **Shetland Islands Tourism Centre,** at Market Cross in Lerwick, will tell you all you need to know and book you a bed for £1 (tel. (0595) 34 34; open in summer Mon. 9am-6pm, Tues.-Fri. 8am-6pm, Sat. 8am-5pm). You will need the *Inter-Shetland Transport Timetable* (60p), which tracks all boats, buses, and planes. Heavily subsidized ferries are wonderfully cheap. Hitching is excellent on the A970, except north of Voe, where the traffic evaporates.

Lerwick, Shetland's transport hub and capital city, makes a convenient base. The comfortable, clean, remarkably laissez-faire **IYHF Youth Hostel** is at Islesburgh House on King Harald St. (tel. (0595) 21 14). The tourist office will also reserve B&Bs up to a week in advance and give you the details on the three campgrounds on Mainland (one is in Lerwick).

Traditional music survives in Shetland; children learn to play distinctive fiddle reels in school. Try **The Lounge,** 4 Mounthooly St. near the tourist office, on a Wednesday or Saturday evening for live music. The **Shetland Folk Festival** (April 30-May 3 in 1992) attracts fiddlers from around the world. On the last Tuesday in January, Lerwick is the site of the annual **Up-Helly-Aa Festival,** an enthusiastic torch-lit revival of Shetland's Viking heritage, which ends with the immolation of a Viking galley. Take the ferry to the isle of **Bressay** (5 min., 60p) and walk over the heather to the deserted east side of the island where among the hills and abandoned crofts you will be utterly unaware of Lerwick's existence; the island of **Noss** (dinghy service from Bressay, £1) is a good place to look for skuas, puffins, and gulls. Off the southeast coast of Mainland, the **Mousa Broch**—an excellently preserved sandstone fortress—sits timelessly by the sea as it has for over 1000 years. **Tom Jamieson** (tel. (095) 053 67) makes regular ferry trips to Mousa from Leebitton (April-Sept. £3 return).

Northern Ireland

The six provinces of Ulster, which since 1920 have comprised troubled Northern Ireland, are as beautiful and traditional as any in Ireland. Subsidized by British taxpayers, Northern Ireland is better maintained than the Republic. Celtic heritage runs deep: sagas recall pagan warriors battling upon the hillsides, and legend claims that it was near Downpatrick that St. Patrick founded the Emerald Isle's first church. Northern Ireland also effervesces with festivals, folk customs, and traditional music. Renowned festivals include the **Ould Lammas Fair** at Ballycastle the last Monday in Aug., and Belfast's three-week-long autumn **International Arts Festival,** second only to Edinburgh's.

The area royally welcomes the few visitors it does get. Despite extensive media coverage of regional violence, Northern Ireland is actually quite safe, with a lower non-politically motivated crime rate than most other countries. That violence which does occur usually takes place in the slums of Derry and Belfast. You might avoid Northern Ireland entirely during the "marching season" (July 12-Aug. 12), traditionally a time of sectarian hostility. Photographing soldiers and security zones is prohibited, and "bomb humor" is not only severely discouraged, but also severely fined. Stay away from any of the security forces.

Three ferry companies connect Northern Ireland to Britain. **Sealink** crosses from Stranraer, in southwestern Scotland, to **Larne,** near Belfast (2½ hr.; £16, students £12, children and seniors £8; no student discount on weekends or July-Aug.). Contact Sealink in Stranraer (tel. (0776) 22 62) or in Belfast, 33-37 Castle Lane (tel. (0232) 32 75 25). **P&O Ferries** (tel. (0574) 743 21) runs between Cairnryan in Scotland and Larne (6 per day, same prices as Sealink). There are frequent buses to Larne from Belfast's Oxford St. Station (4-12 per day, 45 min., £2.20) and trains from Belfast's York St. Station (7-22 per day, £3.10). **Belfast Car Ferries** (tel. (0232) 35 10 09) runs between Liverpool and Belfast (8 hr.; £42, students £22), and connects Belfast to the **Isle of Man.** Travelers headed from Scotland or the north of England to the Irish Republic should look into student rail tickets via Stranraer and Larne. The BritRail Pass is impotent on the Sealink crossing and on Northern Ireland Railways.

The Irish Travelsave stamp's 50% discount (see under Ireland) also applies to all trains in Northern Ireland. You can also use your Travelsave stamp on CIE buses that pass through the North as they travel between two points in the Republic (and buying a through ticket but hopping off in Northern Ireland can save you money). **Ulsterbus** runs frequent service to all parts of Northern Ireland; both they and **Northern Ireland Railways** offer seven-day passes good throughout Northern Ireland (respectively £22 and £27.50). Outside Belfast, hitching is as safe and easy as anywhere else in Ireland.

Northern Ireland uses British pounds, but the rest of the U.K. disdains the pound notes printed by Northern Irish banks. Ironically, they're easy to change to Irish pounds in the Republic. Calls to the Republic are international, while those to Great Britain are domestic.

Belfast

Bent under the weight of its reputation for violent political conflict, Belfast is struggling to redevelop, rebuild, and return to normalcy. The last few years have seen increased commercial investment, bringing new shopping centers, national store chains, discos, and pubs. The main sights, stores, and entertainment extend from the center city along the Golden Mile of **Victoria Road** to the elegant **Queens University** area. The **tourist office** at 48 High St. (tel. (0232) 24 66 09) provides an excellent map with bus routes. (Open Mon.-Fri. 9am-5:15pm, Sat. 9am-2pm; Oct.-May Mon.-Fri. 9am-5:15pm.) Their pamphlet, *Belfast's Civic Festival Trail,* suggests a good walking tour of the city. Rest your feet (and oil your throat) in the Victorian splendor of the **Crown Liquor Saloon**—Britain's only licensed National Trust monument. Several excellent free sights surround the Botanic Gardens, including the **Ulster Museum,** which holds a collection of contemporary art and the dazzling treasures of a Spanish Armada shipwreck. (Open Mon.-Fri. 10am-5pm, Sat. 1-5pm, Sun. 2-5pm. Free.) The **Ulster Folk and Transport Museum,** 7 mi. east of Belfast, is a meticulously reconstructed open-air exhibit spread over 180 acres of parkland. The museum will fascinate anyone interested in rural Irish social history. Ulsterbus #1 ("Belfast-Bangor") stops near the entrance. (Open Mon.-Sat. 11am-6pm, Sun. 2-6pm; Oct.-April Mon.-Sat. 11am-5pm, Sun. 2-5pm. Admission £2, students and children £1.)

Belfast's **IYHF youth hostel,** 11 Saintfield Rd. (tel. (0232) 64 78 65), is 3 mi. southeast of the city in Newtownbreda. (Open Jan.-Nov.) Take bus #38 or 84 from City Hall, Donegall Sq. East (£7.15, under 16 £6.15). Tastier and more pleasant and convenient (but open mid-June to mid-Sept. only) is **Queen's University Halls of Residence,** Malone Rd. (tel. (0232) 66 59 38), where rooms, kitchen, TV room, and showers cost £6.50 for students, £8.50 for non-students. Walk from the center (about 30 min.) or take bus #71 from Donegall Sq. East. The university area is the best place to look for B&Bs; try **Mrs. Davidson,** 81 Eglantine Ave. (tel. (0232) 66 71 49; £10), or trot farther down to the **Lisern Guest House,** 17 Eglantine Ave. (tel. (0232) 66 07 69) with great beds and made-to-order breakfasts for £13.

Good food clusters around Shaftesbury Sq. at the bottom of Malone Rd. You can have a cheap lunch at the **Student Union Refectory,** though "baby boomers" will look conspicuously aged. (Open Mon.-Fri. £2-4.) The **Botanic Inn** ("the Bot"), on Malone Rd., is popular with students and does good pub grub. In the downtown shopping area try **Delaney's,** Lombard St., a self-serve restaurant with great salads and desserts. (Meal £3-5. Open Mon.-Wed. and Sat. 9am-5pm, Thurs. 9am-9pm, Fri. 8:30am-2am.) **Lavery's** (hard *a)* in Bradbury Sq. is the prime student pub.

The **Arts Theatre,** Botanic Ave. (tel. (0232) 32 49 36), puts on the best of the city's drama, but closes in July and August, as does the **Queen's Film Theatre,** a reputable repertory cinema attached to the university. The **Grand Opera House** on Victoria St. hosts theater as well as opera and ballet in a spectacular setting. The cultural scene blossoms in November, when the city stages the **Belfast Festival at Queen's,** a two-week trove of attractions ranging from opera to the Royal Shakespeare Company to fine jazz and traditional music. A program is available from Festival House, 8 Malone Rd., Belfast BT9 SBN (tel. 66 76 87).

Glens of Antrim and Causeway Coast

North of Belfast, the nine deep and verdant Glens of Antrim slide through high moorlands to the rocky coast. Among the tiny villages dotting the coastal road (A2), **Cushendall** is a good base for exploration. There's an **IYHF youth hostel** a mile out of town and a number of good B&Bs in town, and the **Ardclinis Activity Center** on High St. (tel. (026 67) can supply all your hiking, biking, camping and windsurfing needs. **Carnlough** boasts both the merry and musical **Black's Pub,** and Jim McKillop, an Irish fiddle demigod and instrument maker. At the base of Glenariff, **Waterfoot,** just outside Cushendall and after Carnlough, hosts the **Glens of Antrim Feis,** a popular traditional music and dance festival.

Even a short trip to Northern Ireland should include the acclaimed **Causeway Coast,** named after one of Ireland's most soul-stirring natural sights, **The Giant's Causeway.** A series of hexagonal basalt columns supposedly built by the giant Finn McCool, the causeway forms a honeycomb pathway into the sea. The cliff path leading east from this volcanic pathway is the most spectacular part of the coast, winding among dramatic basalt formations and deep coves. At the head of the Causeway is a **National Trust Information Centre** (tel. (02657) 315 82; open daily July-Aug. 10am-7pm; Sept.-Oct. and April-June 10:30am-6pm), where you can inquire about walks and learn the area's history. There is regular train service to **Portrush** at the

Causeway Coast's western tip, and bus service to **Ballycastle** at the eastern tip (connect for both in Coleraine).

County Fermanagh

Rambling between Northern Ireland and the west coast of the Republic, the lakes of Fermanagh make a winsome stopping point, especially for windsurfers, hikers, and other outdoorsy types. **Upper and Lower Lough Erne** form a lake district far larger and much quieter than their English counterpart. **Enniskillen,** a busy and attractive town on an island at the southern end of Lower Lough Erne, is a comfortable touring base. The tourist office, next to the bus depot at the **Lakeland Visitor Centre** on Shore Rd. (tel. (0365) 231 10), has a 50p accommodations service. (Open Mon.-Fri. 9am-7pm, Sat.-Sun. 10am-1pm and 2-5pm; Sept.-June Mon.-Fri. 9am-5pm). The **IYHF youth hostel** at Castle Archdale, 10 mi. northwest of Enniskillen on the Kesh road, offers well-kept beds for £5.65, ages 16-20 £4.65.

Channel Islands

This handful of small islands off the northwestern coast of France harbors a high proportion of millionaires, cows and unusual postage stamps. The main islands of **Jersey** and **Guernsey,** both self-governing bailiwicks of the United Kingdom, entice wealthy summer visitors with low tax rates and a VAT exemption; common folk come to explore the gentle and undeveloped countryside, walk the rocky coastal cliffs, and sun on the unspoilt island beaches. The final, inescapable attraction? The weather. The islands hold Britain's sunshine record: most summer days are clear and beautiful.

The main ports and island capitals of **St. Helier** on Jersey and **St. Peter Port** on Guernsey are an easy but expensive ferry ride from France or England. In July and August, be sure to book ferries at least a week in advance, as boats tend to fill immediately. Most ferries from France leave the Gare Maritime in **St. Malo.** The **Condor Hydrofoil** (tel. 99 56 42 29 in St. Malo; (0534) 763 00 in Jersey; (0481) 72 61 21 in Guernsey; (0305) 76 15 51 in Weymouth, England) makes the voyage to Jersey in an unbeatable 70 minutes from St. Malo (3-4 per day, 238F, under 15 143F). **Emeraude Lines** (tel. 99 40 48 40 in St. Malo; (0534) 665 66 in Jersey; (0481) 71 14 14 in Guernsey) sails the same distance in a gentler but slower two hours (1-2 per day, £24.60, children £14.80) and also runs between Granville, France and Jersey (1-2 per day, 1 hr., 220F, children 132F). In addition, Condor offers ferries from the Channel Islands to **Weymouth,** England (1-2 per day, 2½ hr., £36, children £18). Ask all companies about discount same-day and period return fares.

Although there are no youth hostels, the efficient tourist offices in St. Helier (tel. (0534) 780 00, for accommodations 319 58) and St. Peter Port (tel. (0481) 72 35 53, for accommodations 72 35 55) book rooms in B&Bs (around £20 in Jersey, cheaper on Guernsey) for free. In July and August prices rise by up to 40%; book up to a year in advance. Campgrounds abound; ask the tourist offices. Ferries and flights link the islands, which are small enough to explore by foot or by bicycle; bus service also spreads across Jersey and Guernsey from the ferry ports.

YUGOSLAVIA

USD$1 = 22.6 dinars D, or YUN) — **10D = USD$0.44**
CAD$1 = 19.8D — **10D = CAD$0.51**
GBP£1 = 37.8D — **10D = GBP£0.26**
AUD$1 = 17.6D — **10D = AUD$0.57**
NZD$1 = 12.9D — **10D = NZD$0.78**
Country Code: 38 — **International Dialing Prefix: 99**

Yugoslavia (Jugoslavija) is a federation of six republics—Bosnia-Hercegovina, Croatia, Macedonia, Montenegro, Serbia, and Slovenia—that is losing faith in its national identity. To say that the country followed the wave of social revolution in Eastern Europe and traded communism for ethnic separatism is true, but deceptive: Yugoslavia has never been terribly communist, nor a unified nation in anything but name. From the 16th century, Serbia and Macedonia were occupied by the Ottomans, while the Catholic rulers of Austria and Hungary held sway over Slovenia and Croatia. Yugoslav pan-Slavism culminated in 1914 with the assassination in Sarajevo of Archduke Franz Ferdinand, heir to the Austro-Hungarian throne, the event which tipped off World War I. The war disposed of both ruling empires and led to the artificial creation of the country of Yugoslavia, much to the chagrin of most of its inhabitants. Violent regional rivalry (chiefly between Serbia and Croatia) rocked the country until Josip Broz-Tito (a Croat) emerged as Yugoslavia's overwhelmingly popular national leader during World War II.

When Tito rejected Stalin and his centralist vision in 1948, Yugoslavia was excommunicated from the Soviet bloc. Although Tito nationalized major industries, private property remained legal and most farms were left in private hands. Yugoslavs have been able to travel freely to Western countries since the early 1950s, and freedom of speech was always substantial. In the following years, much of the country's prosperity was funded by a massive foreign debt, and only Tito's authority and personal charisma kept regional hatreds submerged. These twin time bombs exploded in the early 1980s with Tito's death and a deteriorating economy. His replacement—a so-called "collective presidency"—opened the door for democratic elections within each republic. By summer 1991, Croats and Slovenes had both elected staunchly nationalist governments, with ominous portent for the confederation, and began to assemble in "territorial defense forces" designed to protect their republics from the federal army. Serbia was still under the leadership of Slobodan Milošević, the former Serbian Communist Party chief. For the traveler, political unrest had already hit hard, in the pocketbook. After pegging the dinar to the Deutschmark in 1990, the cost of living in Yugoslavia has been comparable to that of neighboring Austria, though Macedonia and Montenegro still offer many bargains.

On June 25, 1991, Croatia and Slovenia declared themselves independent; as the federal army responded, the country plunged into civil war. The Croatian government questions the Serbian-dominated army's motives, noting that the armed forces might be out of work without Croatia's economic backing and without a federation to protect. Serbia points out that the Croatian government overstepped its power by declaring itself independent without the clear consent of its population, which is 10-15% ethnic Serbian. In some Croatian areas, most notably the city of Knin, the majority of inhabitants identify themselves as Serbs and insist that their land remain a part of Yugoslavia. Meanwhile, the other republics, with the exception of Montenegro (which supports Serbia), tend to remain neutral in the matter—which, in any case, is far too complex to be condensed into a few sentences.

During the turbulent summer of 1991, escalating political unrest came sadly close to removing this beautiful country from the travel circuit. As we went to press in September, many areas were unsafe for travelers. Violence was concentrated in the ethnically mixed Serbian and Croatian areas along Croatia's borders with Serbia in the east and Bosnia-Hercegovina in the south; Slovenia was calm. Yet all the travel information—especially train and bus connections—is subject to change; treat our prices with caution as well. If you do go, it is strictly ill-advised to talk politics; be also warned that a great deal here falls into that category, even buying a souvenir with the name "Jugoslavija" or the Yugoslav flag. For up-to-date travel advice, keep abreast of current events and consult your country's foreign ministry.

Getting There and Getting Around

In September 1991, citizens of the U.S., Canada, the U.K., Australia, and New Zealand did not require visas to visit Yugoslavia as a tourist. This policy was to be reevaluated on April 1, 1992; since the country's very existence is in doubt, you should check with the nearest Yugoslav embassy for an update (in the U.S., tel. (202) 462-6566; in Canada, tel. (613) 233-6289; in the U.K., tel. (071) 370 6105); in Australia, tel. (02) 362 46 37; in New Zealand, tel. (04) 76 42 00).

Like everything else, traveling around Yugoslavia is no longer as inexpensive as it once was. Price deregulation in 1991 made Yugoslav trains, once a bargain, just as expensive as buses. There are two breeds of train: passenger *(prai* or *lokalni)* and express *(poslovni* or *ekspres)*. Express trains cost up to double passenger fares, but are more than worth it for long journeys. InterRail—but not Eurail—is valid.

The main international train lines from points west pass through Ljubljana, Zagreb, Belgrade, and Skopje. In the north, train lines from Zagreb wind their way to the ports of Split and Rijeka. Two twisting southern routes—Belgrade to Bar, and to Kardeljevo via Sarajevo—link the interior to the southern coast. Trains run late; add an extra hour for every four on the schedule. Pick up the useful schedule book *Red Vožnje* (100D) at major train stations. During the school vacation in July and August, transport can be hellishly crowded. A seat reservation *(rezervacija sedišta)* may be no more help than a good-luck charm, especially if the train's route doesn't begin at your departure station. Yet in all cases it is practically impossible to get a seat without a reservation; overall, it's probably worth buying one. *Dolazak* means "arrival"; *polazak* and *odlazak* mean "departure."

The extensive bus system charges roughly the same fares as trains, and is much more reliable. Still, buses putt along tortuous mountain roads at a slothlike 40km per hour, and it seems as if every white house is a station. Buses usually charge an extra 5-10D per bag, and an extra 10D if you guarantee a seat by buying a ticket in advance. It is usually impossible, however, to buy an advance ticket for a bus that originates in a different city; you must wait until the bus arrives before finding out whether any seats are available. Bear in mind that different companies often serve the same routes, and that times, tickets, and prices are different for each. Information windows can be lifesavers.

Ferries are much more comfortable than buses, but cost twice as much. **Jadroagent** ferries link major ports with Greece, and **Jadrolinija** runs local ferries. Boat offices on every wharf sell tickets and distribute schedules. Service drops 75% in winter. Zadar, Split, Dubrovnik, and Bar all have sailings to Italian ports. For more information, see the regional introduction to the coast.

JAT, Yugoslav Airlines, connects all major cities, and funds airport shuttles from each downtown. Under 22's receive 25% off, and there are good international standby rates. In summer you may have to reserve five to ten days in advance; in off-season, two days is usually enough. When you check in at the airport, you suck up a USD7 airport tax. Competitively-priced fledgling airlines are springing up in the republics (Croatian, Adria Air in Slovenia, and Palair Macedonia).

Hitchhiking is slow, even on the main Zagreb-Belgrade highway, while **cyclists** may quaver at the narrow, unpaved roads and aggressive drivers.

Practical Information

Turist biro (tourist offices) are located throughout Yugoslavia, and there are youth travel organizations in most cities. They generally provide information on youth discounts, and sell ISIC and YIEE cards.

The dinar has become convertible, and the black market has vanished. Changing dinars back into Western currency can be a trial, but if you save your receipt, the office where you first made the exchange may let you change back. Both old and new dinars circulate; prices are usually quoted in new dinars. The notes are identical except that new dinars have four fewer zeroes, thus 1 new dinar = 10,000 old dinars. Avoid being conned by familiarizing yourself with the color and patterns of each denomination when you first exchange. Exchange rates are usually slightly healthier in banks or post offices than in travel agencies, although the lines may be longer. Rates are the same everywhere in Yugoslavia, so don't hesitate to change money at the border.

Yugoslavia uses two alphabets and four official languages (Serbian, Croatian, Slovene, and Macedonian). Good luck. English is the most common second language; German helps too. Everyone understands Serbo-Croatian, whose component parts differ only in that Serbian is written in Cyrillic and Croatian in Roman; Slovene (written in Roman) and Macedonian (in Cyrillic) are also South Slavic languages, mutually unintelligible with Serbo-Croatian. Phrasebooks are hard to find in Yugoslavia, so bring *Serbo-Croatian for Foreigners.* See the USSR section for a basic Cyrillic transliteration table, and note the following differences in Serbian Cyrillic:

Cyrillic	Roman	Cyrillic	Roman
Ђ, ђ	Đ, đ	X, x	H, h
Ж, ж	Ž, ž	Ц, ц	C, c
J, j	J, j	Ч, ч	Č, č
Љ, љ	Lj, lj	Џ, џ	Dž, dž
Њ, њ	Nj, nj	Ш, ш	š, š
Ћ, ћ	Ć, ć		

Street names, especially those named after past government officials, are starting to change—Tito is now taboo. Street names on signs often differ from names on maps by "-va" or "-a" because of grammatical declensions. To use public phones, you must buy *jetons* (tokens), or a *telekarta,* at a post office. Calls within Yugoslavia, even between different republics, are astonishingly cheap. Anywhere in the country, dial 92 for **police** *(milicija)* and 94 for an **ambulance.**

A woman traveling alone may receive many stares and suggestive remarks, but generally will be safe. The situation becomes less comfortable as you travel south and inland—Kosovo in particular can be unpleasant.

Stores are generally well stocked (though not always with tampons and toilet paper). Restaurants maintain public bathrooms (small entrance fee). Offices keep long hours; usually weekdays from 8am to 6pm, Saturday from 8:30am to 1:30pm. Many stores stay open weekdays from 8am to 8pm with shorter hours on weekends, but the hotter regions of the country may have a siesta from noon to 6pm, with stores reopening in the evening for several hours. Little besides restaurants are open between Saturday noon and Monday 8am.

Banks and many shops are closed for three to five days during national holidays. These include New Year's Day, May Day (International Labor Day; May 1), Fighter's Day (July 4), and Republic Day (Nov. 29). In Serbia only, Fighter's Day runs into The Day of the Uprising of 1941 (July 7), and shops and offices are shut for the entire week. In July and August, major cultural events unfold in Dubrovnik, Ohrid, Ljubljana, and Split, among other places; all feature concerts, opera, ballet, folklore, and theater.

Accommodations and Camping

Sobe (rooms to let; often advertised as *zimmer)* are a delight, but prices are mounting. In 1991, rooms cost about USD7-20 per person, showers included. The brochure *Private Accommodations Rates,* available at major tourist offices, lists virtually all offices that arrange rooms. In the most popular waterfront cities, crowds of room-letters greet travelers at transportation terminals. Bargain these jokers down; aim for 20% less than the tourist offices charge. Singles are expensive and scarce. Check your luggage at the *garderoba* in stations and see the room first. Official agencies often raise prices by up to 30% unless you stay three nights or more.

In 1991, **IYHF youth hostels** cost 150-350D and seldom required memberships. Some are rasty and lack hot water. In July and August, you can stay in *studentski domovi,* university dormitories that serve as hostels in summer. They are often more convenient and almost always more agreeable than hostels, but cost 200-300D per person in doubles. Most tourist information offices will call ahead to hostels and dorms for you to check on space and current prices.

Organized campgrounds, usually open from April or May to September or October, speckle the country and usually are densely packed. They are listed and described in the brochure *Camping-Yugoslavia,* available from major tourist offices. Rates average USD1-8 per person and USD0-5 per tent. The ban on freelance camping is enforced.

Food and Drink

Regional cuisine varies with the region's history of foreign influence. Slovene food is practically Austrian, Croatian has Hungarian overtones, and Serbian, Bosnian, Montenegrin, and Macedonian betray strong Turkish influence. *Ćevapčići* (grilled meatballs, 40-50D) are the best-known Yugoslavian specialty. *Mousaka* (layered eggplant or potato with ground meat) is a scrumptious Balkan dish; *purica s mlincima* (turkey with pasta) is a Croatian favorite. Along the coast, try *lignje* (squid) especially with ink-black risotto, or *pršut* (smoked Dalmatian ham).

For a cheap and convenient meal, grab something from a kiosk. *Burek,* a layered pie filled with *sirom* (cheese) or *meso* (meat) and usually accompanied by yogurt, is found everywhere. Honey-soaked pastries and ice cream are sold in *slastičarna.* Yugoslavian *sladoled* (ice cream) is delightful (20-30D per small scoop).

By far the most common drink in restaurants is the locally brewed *pivo* (beer), but you may prefer *vino,* either *crno* (red) or *belo* (white). Tap water is usually drinkable. In many cities, public fountains double as water fountains and are a good alternative to expensive soft drinks (but make sure you see someone else drinking from one first). Liquor is good and cheap. A service charge is almost always included in the check, but it's customary to round up for friendly service.

Unfortunately, armed conflict in Slovenia and northern Croatia during summer 1991 made it unsafe and inappropriate for *Let's Go* to research these areas. The information on Slovenia and on Croatia north of Split was last fully updated in 1990. In some cases, we have changed printed prices from dinars to dollars, a currency which has fluctuated much less in the last year.

Slovenia (Slovenija)

Bordered by Austria, Italy, Hungary, and Croatia, Slovenia is Yugoslavia's richest, most Westernized, and most economically viable republic. After centuries under Austrian domination, Slovenes joined Yugoslavia in 1918, but soon found out that they had simply exchanged an Austrian emperor for a Serbian king.

Protected by their Alpine setting, Slovenes managed to preserve their language and national aspirations from both Austrian and Serbian influence. Like Croatia, Slovenia declared its independence from Yugoslavia on June 25, 1991. In the following weeks, armed conflict flared briefly near the borders as well as in Ljubljana. More ethnically and geographically segmentable than Croatia, though, Slovenia's declaration has not led to continuing violence; as we went to press in September 1991, Ljubljana was quiet, Slovenia's international border crossings were clear, the federal army was pulling out, and international acceptance of Slovenian independence seemed likely. Be sure to check the political situation before you go.

Ljubljana

Orientation and Practical Information

Ljubljana, the capital of Slovenia, is just 40km inside Yugoslavia, near the Austrian border. After a disastrous earthquake in 1898, the city was rebuilt in beautful Baroque style; Slovene architect Jozef Plečnik enriched it in the 1930s with gems such as the **Tromostovje** (Triple Bridge, where the river bends in the center of town). A major conjunction-junction between the main north-south and east-west rail lines, Ljubljana is easily accessible from Italy, Austria, Hungary, and other parts of Yugoslavia. The train and bus stations stand side-by-side near the center of town. From either, turn right, then left at Miklošičeva cesta, which will lead you directly into the central square, **Prešernov trg.** Beyond this square lies the Triple Bridge; cross it and you'll find yourself in the **old town,** at the base of the castle hill.

Tourist Office: Turistični informacijski center (TIC), Titova cesta 11 (tel. 21 54 12). From Prešernov trg, turn up Čopova (away from the river) through the pedestrian mall to Titova; it's across the street on your right. Room-finding service, maps, and info on Slovenia. Pick up the brochure *Where To? in Ljubljana.* Monthly calendar (in English). Open Mon.-Fri. 8am-7pm, Sat.-Sun. 8am-noon and 3-7pm.

Budget Travel: Center Za Mladinski Turizem (Mladi Turist), Celovška cesta 49 (tel. 32 18 97). Take bus #1 or 3 from Titova cesta. Information for young travelers, ISIC, FIYTO, and IYHF cards. Open Mon. and Fri. 9am-3pm, Tues.-Thurs. 9am-5pm.

Currency Exchange: At the railway station (open 24 hrs.) or the post office.

American Express: Atlas, Mestni trg (tel. 22 27 11), in the old city 1 block from the river. Mail held and checks sold; no wired money. Open Mon.-Fri. 7:30am-7pm, Sat. 7:30am-1pm.

Post Office: PTT, Cigaletova 15, 3 blocks right of the train station. Tall yellow building; enter from the back. Open 24 hrs. **Postal Code:** 61000. Another office by the TIC.

Telephones: PTT, Pražakova 3, in the post office. Open Mon.-Fri. 7am-8pm, Sat. 7am-6pm, Sun. 8am-noon. Main office by the TIC at Čopova 11. **City Code:** 061.

Airport: in Brnik, 26km away (tel. (064) 21 28 44). **Adria Airways** office at Gosposvetska 8 (tel. 31 33 12). **JAT** office at Slomškova 1 (tel. 11 72 77).

Trains: Station at Trg Osvobodilne fronte 6 (tel. 31 67 68). Luggage storage USD1 (open 24 hrs.) To: Trieste, Italy (4 hr., USD5); Villach, Austria (2 hr., USD5); Belgrade (14 hr, USD9); Rijeka (2½ hr., USD4).

Buses: To Postojna (1 hr., USD2.50); Bled (1 hr., USD2.50).

Public Transportation: The bus system runs until midnight. Tokens are cheaper at kiosks. Day- and week-passes available at Celovška 160.

Hitchhiking: Those hitching to Bled take bus #1 to the last stop. Those heading to the coast take bus #6 to last stop or walk out of town along Tržaška cesta.

Laundromat: Milo Pralnica, Vrtača 1, near the intersection with Prešernova cesta in southwest Ljubljana, 5 blocks from the river. You must leave clothes overnight. Open 7am-3pm.

Pharmacy: Prešernova cesta 5 (tel. 31 19 44), or Miklošičeva cesta 24 (tel. 31 45 88). One of them is always open.

Medical Assistance: Bohoričeva , or call 32 30 60.

Emergencies: Police (tel. 92), headquarters at Prešernova cesta 18. **Ambulance** (tel. 94).

Accommodations, Camping, and Food

The cheapest accommodations are private rooms available through the TIC (singles USD4). In July and August, ask them about empty student dorm rooms (doubles USD7 per person) in the **Dom Učencev Tabor** at Vidovdanska cesta 7 (tel. 32 10 67) or the **Dijaški Dom Ivana Cankarja** at Poljanska cesta 26-28 (tel. 31 89 48); to reach the latter from the train station, take bus #11, or walk down Resljeva cesta to Poljanska cesta, and turn left; follow the path between 24 and 26 until it ends, then turn left. The **Hotel Park,** Tabor 9 (tel. 31 67 77) has reasonably priced triples (USD30). Catch bus #6 or 8 on Titova cesta to get to **Autocamp Ježica,** Titova cesta 260a (tel. 37 13 82), near the river. (USD4 per person. Open May-Sept.)

Facing the old city and the three bridges, take a right and you'll find bargain riverfront restaurants. Follow the river (south) to Jurčičev trg 1, and enjoy **Zlata Ladjica's** pizzas and pasta in a grotto with stained-glass windows. **Gostilna Šestica,** near the TIC at Titova cesta 16, is Ljubljana's oldest restaurant, with a formidable selection of entrees. Nearby at Titova cesta 4 is **Rio,** a great place for Yugoslavian fast food. The old town hosts a large **outdoor market;** turn left after the river. (Go Mon.-Sat. before 2pm.) Back north of the river, just 200m from the train station at Mikošičeva 12, is the inexpensive **Triglav** self-service restaurant, named after the three-pronged mountain in the Julian Alps stylized on the Slovenian coat of arms.

Sights and Entertainment

During the day, walk up Studentovska from the outdoor market to the castle for a panorama of the city. (Open Mon.-Fri. 11am-6pm; opens later after weddings Wed. and Fri.; tower only open daily 10am-nightfall.) Ljubljana's museums cluster around the Slovenian parliament buildings on the train station side of the river. The

Modern Art Gallery and the **International Centre of Graphic Arts** have changing exhibits. In the past they've featured Picasso, the Constructivists, and 20th-century Yugoslav art. The TIC has up-to-date listings. The popular cafés lining Stari trg (the main street of the old town) and nearby Gornji trg are the haunt of Ljubljana's artsy intellectual set, a relaxing vantage point for people-watching. Dress up and act chic at **Babilon,** a disco on Kongresni trg. You may not get in. (100D cover includes first drink.) For a more underground scene (yes, it's in a basement), try **K-4,** at Kersnikova 4. There is different music each night—avoid polka night—but they often have ripping live bands. Sunday is gay night. The Slovenian Symphony Orchestra performs regularly at the modern Cankarjev Dom, across from the Parliament building (tickets from 80D). The city hosts an annual jazz festival in late June, and its **Mednarodni Poletni Festival** (late June-Aug.) features ballet on odd-numbered years, and opera on even-numbered years, in a charming outdoor theater. Wildest of all is the *Oncet* (country folk wedding), held the last week of June, featuring a rich variety of folk costumes and dances from all over the world.

Near Ljubljana

About 50km south of Ljubljana, **Postojnska Jama** (Postojna Cave) makes a great daytrip (1 hr. by train, USD2.50)—27km of plunging depths and fantastic stalactite formations. Daily tours (bring warm clothes) begin every half-hour in the summer, less frequently in other seasons; the last tour begins at 6pm from May to September, at 5pm in April and October, at 3pm in March and November, and at 1:30pm from December to February (3pm on Sunday). Budding mimes can make faces at the bizarre "human" fish unique to the cave; claustrophobes should stay at home. (Admission USD13; possible student discount.) The town of **Postojna** lies on the main rail line from Italy, halfway between Trieste and Ljubljana, and is also accessible by bus from the latter (1 hr., USD2.25). The **Turist-Biro,** Tržaška 4 (tel. (067) 210 77), up the ramp from the bus station, provides information on the cave and finds private accommodations (doubles USD18-22).

Julian Alps (Julijske Alpe)

Bled's transporting mountain scenery, castle and lake make it Yugoslavia's biggest inland resort. Bled can be either a daytrip from Ljubljana or a base for excursions into the peaks. Buses run from Ljubljana (hourly, 1½ hr., 34D). The train stops in Lesce, 5km away, connected to Bled by frequent buses. The **Youth Hostel Bledec (IYHF)** is 300m uphill from the bus station at Grajska 17 (tel. (064) 782 30); follow signs for the *grad* (USD9). For private rooms, walk down Prešernova 400m from the bus station and take a right to **Kompas,** Ljubljanska 4 (tel. (064) 772 35). (Singles USD14. Doubles USD11 per person. Open Mon.-Fri. 7:30am-9pm, Sun. 8am-noon and 4-7pm.; Oct.-June, Mon.-Sat. 7:30am-8pm, Sun. 8am-noon and 4-7pm.) **Globtour,** down the street from the bus station at Svobode 9, has doubles for USD13.50 per person. Or just knock on the doors of houses which advertise *sobe* (rooms). **Camping Zaka,** on the opposite side of the lake 2km from town (tel. (064) 773 25), has its own beach; follow the path around either side of the lake (USD7 per person. Open April-Sept.). There's usually space there, but if not, try **Camping Šobec** (tel. (064) 782 60 or 775 00), 2½km from Bled off the road to Lesce. (USD7 per person. Open May-Sept.)

Bled meal prices tend to be higher than in other cities. The **Okarina,** Riklijeva 9, near the hostel, has scrumptious vegetarian entrées for USD6 (closed on Thursdays during off-season). A *burek* by the bus station costs USD0.50-1. There's also a market right by the station (open Mon.-Sat.). The lake's tiny island has a dreamy view of the Alps, but the boat ride is a rip-off (USD3). Better to swim across and then climb to the church.

For mountain information, pick up a copy of *Bled: Tourist News,* either at the **Turistično Društvo,** Ljubljanska 4 (tel. (064) 774 09), across from the Hotel Park in the Kazina building (open Mon.-Sat. 7am-2pm), or at the tourist office in Ljubljana.

Skiers can to choose from among several nearby Julian resorts. **Zatrnik,** 8km from Bled, offers 16km of downhill trails. **Vogel,** 30km away from Bled, has even more, including an 8km trail. **Pokljuka** is especially good for cross-country skiing, and **Kranjska Gora,** 28km from Bled, may have the sweetest skiing facilities in Slovenia. A special ski bus from Bled travels to the first three of these resorts; to reach Kranjska Gora, take the bus to the Lesce-Bled train station and then another bus to Kranskja Gora. Private rooms are plentiful in Kranjska Gora, but check at the Bled tourist office during ski season. Equipment can be rented at Generalturist or Kompas in Bled, and on the mountain at Kranjska Gora.

Croatia (Hrvatska)

Croatia achieved regional unity not as the result of ethnic or social bonds but simply through historical serendipity—the various towns in the region were the only ones able to repel Turkish invasions five centuries ago. The election of Franjo Tudjman as head of the republic in Croatia's first free elections in years revealed strong nationalist sentiments, and on June 25, 1991, Croatia declared its independence from Yugoslavia. Violence between Croats and Serbs in the ethnically mixed areas near Croatia's borders with Bosnia-Hercegovina and Serbia continued as we went to press in September 1991; as you read this, some areas, particularly in the north, may be unsafe for travelers. Check with your foreign ministry.

Zagreb

Zagreb is a cultural sleeper, brimming with rich museums and sparkling cafés. The capital of Croatia, Zagreb has half a million permanent residents and 160,000 students. Its parks and amiable inhabitants ensure a warm visit.

Orientation and Practical Information

Zagreb is 120km south of the Austrian border, on the main rail line from Western Europe to Greece. From the train station, walk down the left side of the parks, and then down Praška St. to reach the main square, **Trg Republike.** The **information office** is in the southeast corner of the square. Up the hill from Trg Republike are the cobblestoned streets of **Gornji Grad** (old town). The bus depot is 1km to the right of the train station; frequent trams link the two.

Tourist Office: Turisticki Informativni Centar (TIC), Trg Republike 11 (tel. 27 25 30). Open Mon.-Fri. 8am-7pm, Sat.-Sun. 8am-6pm.

Budget Travel: Ferijalni Savez, Dežmanova 9, off of Ilica through the arch across from Frankopanska. Information only. For ISIC cards go to Trg Žrtava Fašizma 13.

Consulates: U.S., Braće Kavurića 2 (tel. 44 48 00). Open Mon.-Fri. 8am-noon and 1:30-4pm. American Cultural Center is in the same building, but enter at Zrinjevac 13 (open Mon.-Fri. 9am-4pm). **U.K.,** Ilica 12 (tel. 42 48 88). Open Mon.-Fri. 8:30am-1:30pm.

Currency Exchange: Zagrebačka Banka, in Trg Republike next to the tourist office.

American Express: Atlas, Zrinjevac 17 (tel. 42 76 23). Mail held. Open Mon.-Fri. 7:30am-7:30pm, Sat. 10:30am-1pm.

Post Office: Branimirova 4, just to the right as you exit the train station. Open Mon.-Fri. 9am-10pm, Sat. 9am-7pm, Sun. 1-8pm. Central post office is at Jurišičeva 13 (tel. 27 71 12), 1 block east of Trg Republike. **Postal Code:** 41000.

Telephones: Branimirova 2, and Jurišičeva 13, next to the post offices. International calls 8am-10pm. Buy a *telekarte* (100 impulses for 24D) at the post office or at a kiosk. **City Code:** 41.

Flights: 27km southeast of town near Velika Gorica. A 20-min. shuttle bus ride (12D) takes you to the city air terminal at Grgurova, next to the train station. Information (tel. 52 52 22 70).

Trains: Glavni Željeznički Kolodvor, Tomislavova 12 (tel. 27 22 44). Luggage storage open 24 hrs. Departures every hour to Ljubljana (2 hr., 29D) and Belgrade (6 hr., 69D). The dead-end rail fork to Split (2 per day, 8½ hr., 59D) begins here. To Budapest (daily at 8am, 6¾ hr.).

Buses: Autobusni Kolodvor, Marina Držića (tel. 51 50 37). Service to Plitvice.

Public Transportation: Extensive tram system. Buy tickets (5D) from tobacconists and newsstands.

Laundromat: In the basement garage of the Intercontinental Hotel at Kršnjavoga 1, a backpack-load about 60D.

Hitchhiking: Those hitching to Kumrovec and the Austrian Alps take tram #1 or 11 out Ilica from Trg Republike; those heading to Plitvice and the coast take tram #5 from the bus station to the end and catch bus #108 to Avenija Borisa Kidriča; those going to Ljubljana and the Slovenian Alps take tram #4 from the train station to Avenija Ljubljanska and go right; those Belgrade-bound take tram #6 from the train or bus station to Avenija Beogradska and go left.

Pharmacy: Central Pharmacy, Trg Republike 3 (tel. 27 63 05). Open 24 hrs.

Women's Hotline: S.O.S.: Tel. 42 82 22.

Medical Assistance: at Đorđićeva 26.

Emergencies: Police (tel. 92). **Ambulance** (tel. 94).

Accommodations and Food

The **Omladinski Turistički Centar (IYHF),** Petrinjska 77 (tel. 43 49 64) is uncomfortable and cramped, but convenient, inexpensive, and a great place to meet other travelers. From the train station, go right (east) 1 block, turn left onto Petrinjska, and walk 2 blocks. (Curfew 1am. Dorms 80D, nonmembers 121D. Doubles and triples 225D per person. Sheets and showers included. Come early.) If you want a private room, the **Generalturist** office at Trg Zrinjskoga 18 (tel. 42 59 66) is the only branch of Generalturist that can book them. (Open Mon.-Fri. 7:30am-7:30pm, Sat. 8am-1pm.) **Studentski Centar,** Savska 25 (tel. 27 46 74), about 7 blocks west of the train station, rents dorm rooms to travelers from July 15 through September for about 110D. Take tram #14 from Trg Republike to the intersection of Savska and Vodnikova. (Open Mon.-Fri. 10am-2pm.)

Far and away the best place to eat in Zagreb, the mensa at the **Studentski Centar** serves a full meal for only 18D. It's easy to make friends there: speaking English should be enough to make your neighbors introduce themselves. **Mosor,** at Jurišićeva 2 across from the main information office, is an elegant self-serve with hot meals for under 40D; **Medulic,** 4 blocks west of Trg Republike at Medulićeva 2, has excellent vegetarian and carnivore menus in English (dishes under 40D). Try the simple fare at Zagreb's **Splendid Express** cafeterias, at Trg Zrinjskoga 15. (20-30D; open daily 6am-10pm). Two blocks east of Trg Republike at 24 Jurišićeva is **Centar,** with cakes, shakes, and the best ice cream in Zagreb. There is a daily **market** on the terrace behind Trg Republike, at its liveliest on Fridays and Saturdays. Burek and ćevapčići stands are everywhere.

Sights and Entertainment

The immense **Trg Republike** plaza is the beginning and end of all strolling through Zagreb. Directly behind the scrubby fountain (littered with the weather- and inflation-eroded currency of exasperated Yugoslavs) rears the neo-gothic Zagreb **Cathedral.** The buildings around it constitute **Kaptol,** the clerical half of medieval Zagreb. Gradec, now called **Gornji Grad,** was the craftsmen's half of old Zagreb. Walk up the steps from the left side of Kaptol or take the funicular from Ilica, 2 blocks west of Trg Republike. At the center is the **Church of Sr. Marko** with a technicolor tile roof and several works by Yugoslavia's hugest sculptor, Ivan Meštrović. His workshop, **Atelje Meštrović,** is nearby at Mletačka 8 (tel. 42 85 86); open Tues.-Sat. 10am-1pm, Sun. 10am-1pm). Visit the **Galerija Primitivne Umjetnosti** (Gallery of Primitive Art), Ćirilometodska 3, 2 blocks south of sv. Marka (tel. 44 32 94), for one of the world's finest exhibitions of native painting. (Open daily 11am-1pm and 5-8pm.) Climb nearby Lotreščakova Tower for a fine Kodak moment of the city. South of Trg Republike, **Donji Grad** contains several museums. The **Archeological Museum,** on Zrinjski Trg 1 block south of Trg Republike, is free and on the way to everything, so you'd might as well go. (Open Mon., Wed., and Fri. 8:30am-1:30pm and 4:30-7:30pm, Tues. and Thurs. 8:30am-1pm, Sun. 10am-1pm.) The **Mimasa** museum (Roosevelt Trg 4) is one of the finest in Europe, not to be missed on pain of death. The small but superb collection even counts a Da Vinci. The Zagreb rumor mill says some of the paintings are fake—you be the judge. (Open Tues.-Sun. 10am-8pm, Mon. 2-8pm. Admission 30D, students 15D, free on Mon.)

Tkalčićeva, in the old town, bursts with cafés, street musicians, boutiques and small galleries. Dig the art in progress at the café Grička Vještica (Tkalčićeva 57)—it depicts legends from Zagreb's history. At **Pivnica Melin,** tucked in behind Tkalčićeva at Kožarska 19, sink into pillowed chairs while the breeze stirs flower petals overhead. (Open Mon.-Sat. 9am-midnight, Sun. 6pm-midnight.) All of the cafés draw a genial crowd and beers at 20D apiece. **The Saloon,** Tuškanac 1a, resounds with dance-music and pick-up lines until 4am. (Head west on Ilica from Trg Republike and turn right onto Dežmonova. Drinks 5-25D.) **17 Ilica** is a popular pool hall—8D a game. Try to be in Zagreb during the last week of July for the **International Folklore Festival,** a premier gathering of European folk dance troupes and singing groups. Free performances fill Trg Katerina in the old town at 8pm, and Trg Republike at 9pm. Check with the tourist office for details.

Zagreb is arguably the most fanatic of basketball-mad Yugoslavian towns. **Cibona,** the local team, has twice been European champions. The season lasts from mid-October through May, and tickets are available at the silver-tower stadium south on Savska (tram #4 from the train station, #14 or 17 from Trg Republike).

Plitvice Lakes (Plitvička Jezera)

South of Zagreb along the road to Zadar and the coast, this national park, has been chosen by UNESCO as one of the wonders of the world. Over a million tourists, evenly divided between elderly pensionners and screaming schoolchildren, come to visit each year. Well-marked paths, often paved and complete with souvenir stands, connect the park's high waterfalls and blue-green lakes. Herds of free buses and boats migrate from one location to another. The most glorious terrain is toward the top—where if you hum loudly, you can almost ignore the bawling little brats. (Honor-code park admission 145D, 45D discount for students.)

The parks can be hiked in a day, and one day "round-trip" excursions are easy to arrange. Contact the **Plitvice Lakes Information Office** in Zagreb at Tomislavov Trg 19 (tel. (041) 44 24 48), along the western edge of the parks, to the left as you look from the train station (open Mon.-Fri. 7am-3pm, Sat. 8am-1pm), or the tourist office in Zadar. If you visit on your own, be sure you know in advance how you're getting out. Buses go frequently to and from Zagreb (6am-8pm, 3½ hr., 80D) and Zadar (6am-6pm, 3½ hr., 75D). However, the **tourist information offices,** located at each park entrance, are rude, with conflicting and inaccurate bus schedules. If you do pin down a bus departure, arrive a half-hour early, and frolic frantically when it comes into view: most buses, especially those later in the day, won't bother to stop otherwise. Hitchhiking can be slow; if you do it, try just outside of *ulaz* (entrance) 1.

The tourist information offices will grudgingly find private rooms (doubles 150D per person). More convenient, the Hotel Plitvice (near *ulaz* 2) provides comfortable, hostel-like lodgings for 204D (ask for the dormitory annex), and a magnificent breakfast. The Korana campsite, 8km away, charges 80D per person. Freelance camping is forbidden but practiced on the hillsides above the Zagreb-Zadar road. Admission tickets are validated free for extra days by official accommodations people, so freelance campers risk paying unnecessary admission if caught. There are **supermarkets** (open daily 9am-6pm) and **self-service restaurants** (open daily 11am-4pm) at both entrances. The country-innesque **Restauracija Lička Kuća** is opposite *ulaz* 1.

Bosnia-Hercegovina

Bosnia-Hercegovina is the mountainous core of Yugoslavia, west of Serbia and almost cut off from the Adriatic by Croatia. Ruled by the Ottomans for 400 years, the region is still 40% Muslim. Although excruciatingly slow, bus travel is fascinating, unlike the tunneled train line from Belgrade through Sarajevo to the coast that shuts out both the landscape and the local color. However you travel in summer, make seat reservations at least one day in advance.

Sarajevo

Sarajevo tastes Eastern—the Turks have gone, but they left behind 85 mosques and a bazaar which still buzz with activity.

Orientation and Practical Information

Sarajevo is on the train line that runs down from Belgrade (and Zagreb) to meet the coast at Kardeljevo. Tram #1 in front of the train station (buy ticket in kiosk and validate on board) takes you 2½km to **Baščaršija,** the lively center of Sarajevo's old city.

Tourist Office: Turistički Informativni Biro, Jugoslovenske Narodne Armije 50 (tel. 27 02 10), near the Old City. Open Mon.-Sat. 7am-9pm.

American Express: Atlas, Jugoslovenske Narodne Armije 81 (tel. 53 25 21), near the Princip Bridge. Mail held, checks sold and replaced, but no wired money accepted. Open Mon.-Fri. 9am-5pm.

Post Office: Obala Vojvode Stepe 8, where S. Principa meets the river. Poste Restante. Open Mon.-Sat. 8am-8pm. Another next to the train station. **Postal Code:** 71000.

Telephones: Post Office #5, Vojvode Putnika 100. Or take tram #3 to Hotel Beograd and ask. Open 24 hrs. **City Code:** 071.

Trains: Željeznička stanica, Stanični trg 14. Luggage storage 40D per day (open 24 hrs.). To: Zagreb (5 per day, 8 hr., 300D); Belgrade (5 per day, 8 hr., 290D). Trains from Zagreb and Belgrade continue to Kardeljevo (3½ hr., 290D).

Buses: Autobuska stanica, Kruševačka 9, on the opposite side of the post office from the train station. To: Belgrade (4 per day, 220D); Zagreb (2 per day, 350D); Dubrovnik (3 per day, 7 hr., 155D). Alternatively, reach Dubrovnik via the train to Kardeljevo, then a bus from Kardeljevo to Dubrovnik (2½ hr.).

Hitchhiking: Those hitching to Jahorina and Belgrade walk out of town from the old town hall; those going to Mostar and the coast take tram #2 from Baščaršija, alight just before the terminus at Čengić-vila, and go out Džemala Bijedića.

Emergencies: Police, (tel. 92). **Ambulance,** (tel. 94).

Accommodations, Camping, and Food

This is one town in which summer is the off-season. **Unis-Tourist,** Vase Miskina 16 (tel. 21 32 50) pins down doubles for 430D. **Agencija Stari Grad,** Serači 81 (tel. 53 52 02), in the old city, is cheaper. (Singles 196D. Doubles 327D.) Camp at **Auto Kamp Ilidža,** 10km from town (tel. 62 14 36). Take tram #3 to the end, cross the bridge and follow the signs. (65D per person, 65D per tent. Open April 15-Oct. 15.)

Sarajevo sates even the most epicurean of phoodophiles. Turkish and Yugoslav fare are equally tasty and affordable. *Ćevapčiči* and *burek* restaurants are as excellent as they are ubiquitous, and serve wonderful Turkish coffee. Across from the mosque and in the middle of the arcade, **Cevabdžinica Džezo** serves captivating *ćevapčići* (open noon-midnight). Around the corner at Baščaršija 30, the **Aščinica Orijentalna Jela** features blissful Turkish meals for 50D and less (open Mon.-Sat. 10am-5pm). There's no English menu, but the cook will cheerfully show you everything on her stove and let you point. For a more standard, sit-down Turkish meal, try the grilled meat platter for two (160D) at the historic **Morića-han,** Sarači 77.

Sights and Entertainment

Most of Sarajevo's attractions are within a five-minute walk of the Baščaršija. Next to the small shops in this old Turkish quarter stands the **Gazi-Husrevbegova Džamija,** Yugoslavia's mega-mosque. It was constructed in the 16th century by Ajem Esir Ali, who later became the chief architect of Constantinople. Although under restoration, it may reopen by 1992. If not, enter **Car's Mosque,** on the other side of the river. (Admission 20D, students 10D. Remove shoes first.) The 13th-century **Srpska Pravoslavna Crkva** (Serbian Orthodox Church), at Maršala Tita 87, presents another side of Sarajevo's unique religious and cultural history, and the museum next door houses a fascinating collection of icons. (Open Mon.-Sat. 8am-5:30pm, Sun. 10am-noon.)

Before the 1984 Olympics, Sarajevo was best known for its role in the outbreak of World War I. Near the modest 18th-century **Principov Most** (Princip Bridge), the Bosnian student Gavrilo Princip assassinated Austrian Archduke Franz Ferdinand and set in motion a series of international crises that detonated WWI. On the corner next to the bridge, where Jugoslovenske Narodne Armije meets the river, a pair of footprints in the pavement marks the spot where Princip stood as he shot the locally despised heir to the Austrian throne. The **Trebevićka Žičara** (cable car) will carry you to the top of the mountain for a view of Sarajevo's minarets and red-tiled roofs. Cross the Princip Bridge, go left, then take a right just before the outdoor market onto Dimitrija Tucoviča. Go on a clear day or all you will see is that you have been taken for a ride in more ways than one. (Round-trip 45D. Open daily Mon.-Fri. 10am-8pm, Sat.-Sun. 9am-8pm; Sept.-May 9am-4pm.) To see all of Sarajevo's sights, follow the yellow signs along the "tourist route," another Olympic remnant.

In the evening, join the crowds on Sarajevo's promenade **Vase Miskina,** which leads into the heart of the old town. To drop in on the student scene, go to **Alo Alo,** one of many cafés on Bazardžani in the Baščaršija. A more alternative crowd patronizes the **Bašta-Crvena Galerija** (Red Gallery), a huge, swarming, open-air bar at Maršala Tita 44. (Cover 20D. Get there around 11pm.)

Near Sarajevo

Walter Mitty Olympians can spend the winter skiing on **Mount Jahorina,** 30km southeast of Sarajevo. A shuttle bus stops 75m uphill from Princip Bridge. (All-day lift USD13, skis and boots USD16 per day, cross-country equipment USD7 per day.) Call (071) 21 97 82 or contact **Zoitours** at Jugoslovenske Narodne Armije 23, 71000 Sarajevo. Other Olympic facilities spangle the Sarajevo area, many open to the public.

Jajce, 157km northwest of Sarajevo near the route to Zagreb, is worth a detour. One of the oldest towns in Bosnia, Jajce was its capital in the 15th century. Hundreds of years later, a November 1943 assembly under the leadership of Josip Tito formed the modern state of Yugoslavia here; the **Muzej AVNOJ** (Museum of the Anti-Fascist Council) commemorates that event. A well-preserved **medieval fortress** guards the town's waterfall. **Unis-Tourist** and the **Turistički Biro,** both near the bus station, can arrange private accommodations.

Mostar, a city with a strong Turkish accent, is about two hours along the rail line from Sarajevo to Kardeljevo on the Adriatic. The old town, clinging to the steep banks of the deep-turquoise Neretva River, is bewitching but touristy. Crowds flock to the impressive, 16th-century **Stari Most** bridge, which arches 20m high, a 10-minute walk from the train and bus station. The café **Ćar Dak,** perched in a little white house overhanging the bridge, serves excellent Turkish coffee for 10D (open daily 9am-11pm). Just beyond lies the touristy but attractive *bazaar.* For accommodations, head to **Auto-prevot tourist** at the bus station (tel. (088) 324 35; open Mon.-Sat. 7am-3pm) for rooms (doubles 200D per person.) Advertisements for *sobe* (rooms) sprout along the road to the bridge.

The Coast

Yugoslavia's coast is more than just another pretty beach. The cities of Dubrovnik and Split offer cosmopolitan life beneath swaying palm trees; 500-year-old buildings conceal cafés and lovely promenades. The offshore islands are as enticing as any in Europe, as their mounting prices and popularity show.

The coast from Rijeka to the Montenegrin border south of Dubrovnik is entirely in Croatia, broken only by a 5km finger that allows Bosnia-Hercegovina access to the sea. The region has been a nexus between the great Mediterranean empires and landlocked peoples since the dawn of time. After passing through Greek and Roman hands, much of the coast settled in for several hundred years as part of Venice's mercantile empire; many coastal towns are tiny architectural gems bearing the unmistakable imprint of Venetian style. The landscape was not so lucky—centuries of wood-hungry shipbuilders gradually cleared the hills of their oak, leaving barren but fiercely beautiful hillsides.

Trains are scarce on the coast, so travelers crowd together on the buses and ferries. The more distant islands have only occasional connections; examine the schedules before you leave. **Jadroagent** runs a ferry that passes through Rijeka, Rab, Zadar, Split, Hvar, Korčula, Dubrovnik, and Corfu and Igoumenitsa in Greece. (Rijeka-Split 294D, Split-Dubrovnik 190D, Dubrovnik-Bari 560D. Cheaper mid-April to mid-June and Oct.-Dec.) Get a ticket that permits sojourns in ports along the way. **Jadrolinija's** local ferries connect the coast with nearby islands. There are two schedules—one for local lines and the other for the Rijeka-Dubrovnik line.

Travelers on the coast follow a well-worn path. Tourist personnel speak English, private rooms are plentiful, and though food is expensive, you will be able to read the menu. Ever-popular nude beaches are labeled "FKK." Camping on Yugoslavia's beaches is prohibited but often tolerated. Ask the *Turist Biro* what local policy is. Official campgrounds, which in July and August resemble parking lots, line the entire coast. There are 20 youth hostels on the Adriatic that vary widely in comfort and beach access. Private rooms are everywhere, but prices are rising fast. Look for *sobe* or *zimmer* signs. Some monasteries provide accommodations or will let you camp.

Rijeka to Split

The crowded port of **Rijeka,** the largest in Yugoslavia, should be a mere launchpad for excursions along the northern Adriatic coast. Walk about five blocks to your right as you leave the train station to reach the bus station. The **Jadrolinija** office at Obala Jugoslavenske Mornarice 16 (tel. (051) 21 14 44), two blocks to the right of the bus station, provides information on all ferries. (Open Mon.-Sat. 5:30am-6pm.) Accommodations in Rijeka aren't worth it. The **Dom Crvenog Križa** (Red Cross), Janka Polić-Kamova 3d (tel. (051) 42 36 99) resembles a for-profit Salvation Army. It offers sterile doubles, often clogged with Yugoslavs, for USD11 per person in a quaint but distant neighborhood. (Take bus #2 going right from the train station to the last stop; get off three stops after it turns around). Private rooms (doubles USD12 per person) are available from **Kvarner Express** (tel. (051) 21 38 08), one block inland from the Jadrolinija office. (Open Mon.-Fri. 7:30am-8pm, Sat. 2-5pm.) For incredibly cheap victuals, go to the **Restoran Index** at Borisa Kidriča 18. (Full meal USD2. Open daily 10am-10pm.) Rijeka is somewhat redeemed by its beach, a quick ride away on bus #2 (from anywhere along the coastal road). Get off at Pecine and follow the crowds.

About 14km north of Rijeka is the elegant town of **Opatija,** which still evokes images of its late 19th-century Austro-Hungarian heyday. The distant lights and transient jets of flame from Rijeka's refineries add a surreal touch to the carnival atmosphere. From Rijeka's train station, take bus #32 (every 15 min., ½ hr., USD1). Opatija accommodations will take a big bite out of your budget. The **tourist office** at M. Tita 183 (tel. (051) 71 13 10) doles out maps and information on local events. (Open May-Nov. 8am-9pm; off-season 8am-7pm.) **Kvarner Express,** M. Tita 186 (tel. (051) 27 11 11), offers private accommodations, all within 500m of town and sea (doubles USD19). The office also has information on nearby campgrounds. (Open daily 7:30am-8pm.)

The wooded islands offshore are the least crowded on Yugoslavia's coast. Direct services to **Cres** run once a day from Rijeka (USD5), and hourly in summer from Brestova, 45km west of Rijeka. Cross the bridge to go to Cres' popular main port of Mali Lošinj, and try either **Kvarner Express** or **Lošinjplov** for private rooms. The island of **Krk,** is connected by bridge to the mainland and accessible by frequent bus from Rijeka (1 hr., USD3). The town of Krk has fine nightlife, but the beaches pale next to those further out at Baška. The **Kvarner Express** in either will find you a room. From Baška you can catch a ferry to **Lopar** on the island of **Rab.** Take the bus from there to the town of Rab, which, though touristy, is deservedly famous for its architecture and golden sand. On the mainland 69km south of Rijeka, **Senj** is ideal for a short breather. Hike around its medieval castles and fortress, used to defend against the Venetians.

Split

Split started as one man's retirement home, a magnificent waterfront palace built by the Roman Emperor Diocletian. As the empire cracked, Split's residents moved into the palace making streets of the halls and houses from the rooms. Thrust into the architectural limelight by a detailed study in 1757, the singular blend of styles at Split had a profound effect on Georgian architecture. Recently, a team of archeologists decided to remove all of the houses and shops, returning the palace to its original form, but abandoned the plan when calculations showed that the walls would collapse without the support of their modern companions.

Orientation and Practical Information

Split, on a tiny peninsula halfway down the Yugoslav coast, is the terminus of the rail lines from Zagreb and Rijeka. It's also a major port for both intracoastal service and connections to Italy, and an important bus hub with direct service to all major Yugoslav cities. The ferry terminal, the bus depot, and the train station range from east to west (facing inland, that's right to left). Farther to the west is the outdoor produce market and the city's boardwalk, which rims Diocletian's Palace.

Tourist Office: Turistički Biro, Titova obala 12 (tel. 421 42), along the waterfront near the palace. Transport info and private accommodations (from 220D per person; 25% more July-Aug.; 30% more for stays of less than four days). Open in summer Mon.-Sat. 7am-10pm, Sun. 8am-1pm; off-season Mon.-Sat. 8am-8pm.

Consulates: U.K., Titova obala 10, third floor (tel. 414 64). Open Mon.-Fri. 8am-1pm.

American Express: Atlas, Trg Preporoda 7 (tel. 430 55), inside the Roman walls to the right of the tourist office. Mail held, money changed. Open Mon.-Fri. 8am-7pm, Sat. 8am-1pm.

Post Office: Lavčevića 9, behind the old city. Open daily 7am-9pm. Also try the post office next to the train and bus stations on Titova obala. Both open daily 7am-9pm. **Postal Code:** 58000.

Telephones: In the post offices. Open daily 7am-9pm. **City Code:** 058.

Trains: Station at Obala Bratstva i Jedinstva (tel. 485 88). To: Zagreb (6 per day, 8½ hr., 290D); Rijeka (6 per day, 7 hr., 305D); Belgrade (12 hr.).

Buses: Next to the train station (tel. 450 47). Frequent service up and down the coast, including Rijeka (8 per day, 7 hr., 250D), Dubrovnik (307D), Zadar, Plitvice, and points between.

Ferries: Jadrolinija, Gat Španskih boraca 4 (tel. 433 66). The office in the ferry terminal on the harbor sells tickets and distributes schedules for all routes out of Split. Open 5am-9pm; Sept.-June 5am-8pm. To: Brač (USD3.70); Hvar (USD5.70); Korčula (USD7).

Hitchhiking: Hitchhikers to Dubrovnik take bus #15 or 60 to Lovrinac. For the north coastal road, they take bus #2 or 37 to Sućurac and head away from town.

Emergencies: Police (tel. 92). **Ambulance,** (tel. 94).

Accommodations, Camping, and Food

During July and August the cheapest official option is the somewhat inconvenient **Studencki Dom,** Maslešina bb (tel. 428 22) near Proleterskih Brigada. Take bus #17 from in front of the open-air market. (3-bed dorms about USD10 per person, breakfast included.) The tourist office (see above) can make reservations and also has access to private rooms, but private agencies along the waterfront are likely to be more helpful. You can do even better with hawkers: agree on the price first, then leave your pack in a locker in case the rooms are unacceptable. Astute bargaining should save 30% off the Turist Biro's prices.

The self-service **Bastion,** Marmontova 10, has filling entrees from 35D (open daily 7am-9pm). At the **Restaurant Burek,** Ilegalaca 13, around the corner from the main post office, a hefty slice of *burek* (meat pie) and some yogurt sets you back only 30D. (Open 7am-10pm.) Split's **open-air market** sprawls along the side of the old town facing the bus and train stations.

Sights

Diocletian's Palace (Dioklecijanova), comprising about one quarter of the Grad (old town), is the centerpiece of travelers' Split. The Bronze Gate in the south, near the water, leads through the fascinating, cavernous **cellars** beneath the former imperial apartments. (Cellars open daily 8am-7pm. Admission 40D.) From the cellar entrance, continue through the passage into a courtyard, the **Peristyle.** Just inside the Peristyle, a 2nd-century B.C. black sphinx guards **Diocletian's Mausoleum,** since transformed into the **Cathedral of St. Doimo.** The church's interior is fabulously well preserved. Climb the tower to survey the town (5D). A narrow street opposite the church leads to the **Temple of Jupiter,** now the **Baptistry.** (Ask for the keys in the cathedral or in the Office of Guides in the Peristyle.) A more modern attraction, the **Galerija Meštrović** showcases Yugoslavia's premier 20th-century sculptor, Ivan Meštrović. To reach his former home and studio, walk 2km west along the coastal road, or take bus #12 to Šetalište Moše Pijade 44. (Open daily 9am-6pm. Admission 20D, students 10D.) Nightlife revolves around **Titova obala,** the waterfront promenade along the old town. Also cruise the cafés on Trg Republike at the end of Titova obala and on Narodni Trg.

Split to Dubrovnik

Yugoslavia's most alluring and popular islands are just south of Split. Their hills offer inspiring views, and the water is a startlingly clear blue-green on the rock, pebble and sand beaches. Ferries leave Split, the best base, for Šolta, Brač, Hvar, Korčula, and several smaller islands.

Brač is an easy daytrip from Split (11 ferries per day, 1 hr., 93D). Its main town, **Supetar,** jams up in summer, but has a convenient campground about 1km from the town center (30D per person, 30D per small tent). The **turist biro** (tel. (058) 63 10 66), to the right as you get off the boat, books private rooms. (4-day min. stay. Singles 170D, doubles 130D; Sept.-June singles 130D, doubles 100D.) **Bol,** on the island's south side, has the beaches you see on Yugoslavian brochures. Buses from Supetar run four times daily (70D). **Turist Biro Bol** (tel. (058) 63 51 22) will find you a bed. (Open 6am-midnight; same prices as Supetar.) Two km west is the even more popular **Zlatni Rat,** with the most seductive beach on the island. Less commercialized than Brač, **Šolta** is also one ferry-hour from Split (5 per day, 93D).

Hvar, the main town on the island of the same name, is dominated by impressive fortifications and town walls dating from 13th-century Venetian rule. Four hundred years later, Hvar's citizens started what is now the oldest communal theater in Europe, still in fine condition. Ferries servicing the island will drop you either in the town of Hvar, in the port of **Vira** 4km away, or in **Starigrad** 20km to the east (10 per day, 113D). Buses run between the three (4 per day, 30 min., 125D). The **Turist Biro** at the bus station in Hvar (tel. (058) 741 23) books expensive private accommodations (singles from 175D). Jaw with the hawkers and save 30-40%. **Camping Vira** is an easy jaunt from the port, or a stop on the Hvar-Vira bus (USD8 per person, tent included). Excellent restaurants pose along ul. Matija Ivanića off the main square, with well-stocked grocery stores waiting in the square itself. Check out the inexpensive **Pizzeria 88,** just off the square. Boats (50-100D) go to outlying islands with oh-so-fine beaches. For nightlife, booze it up at the waterfront bars that spill out onto the street, then taxi (50-100D) or stumble to the disco at **Club F** in the castle on the top of the hill. (Open 10pm-5am.)

The ferry to **Starigrad** on Hvar stops 2km from town, at the tip of a long inlet. A bus (20D) or the path to the left along the water will take you into town. The beach is right of the inlet, past the Hotel Helios. **Dalmacijaturist** (tel. (058) 66 56 55; open daily 8am-1pm and 5-7pm) has private rooms (singles about USD10, doubles USD17). Campers can hike to nearby **Plantaža** (USD3, USD3 per tent) and, closer by, **Bunarić** (USD3, USD3 per tent). **Lahor,** on the way to the Helios, rents bicycles for 150D per day. The **Stari Grad,** by the bus station, is slightly cheaper (entrées around 100D) and slightly uglier than its competitors, but the food is superb. Just across the way at the head of the inlet lies an **outdoor market** (open daily 6:30am-9:30pm).

Korčula is the most tranquil and inexpensive of the three major islands, and the **Turist Biro's** pamphlet claims *3,000* sunny days a year. Ferries run to **Vela Luka** and its pebble beaches at Korčula's west end from Split (2 per day) and Hvar (4 per week, 2½ hr.). From Dubrovnik, take the bus 90km west to **Orebić** on the **Pelješac** peninsula, then make the short hop across the channel to **Korčula town** near the island's eastern tip (15 per day, 30D). From Sarajevo, take the train to its coastal terminus at Kardeljevo (often called by its old name of Ploče), then the ferry to Trpanj on Pelješac (89D), then a bus to Orebić. Korčula town, the birthplace of Marco Polo, has pebble beaches and a cathedral with works by Tintoretto. The **turist biro** (tel. (050) 71 10 67; open 7am-9pm) finds rooms (doubles USD15, less in off-season; 30% surcharge for one-night stands.) **Solitudo** campground, in nearby Sveti Antun, has a nude beach. (18D per person, 21D per tent. Open April-Oct.) If you're more modest, try the inviting beaches at Lumbarda 5km away. The island's choice restaurant is **Adio Mare** in Grad (Korčula's old town) at the beginning of ul. Marco Polo; a full meal of exquisite fish and wine costs about USD12. (Open Mon.-Sat. noon-2pm and 5-10pm, Sun. 5-10pm.) The outdoor market unfolds below the steps to the old city, and a supermarket is around the corner. Down the street stand the ruins of the house where Marco Polo was born in 1254. Climb the tower for a view of the town and environs. (Open 9am-7pm.) The waters between Korčula and the Pelješac peninsula are boffo for windsurfing. On Pelješac, **Jancina** and **Trpanj** offer secluded sand and coves. **Mljet,** a narrow island just south of Pelješac, boasts gorgeous beaches, a national park, and two saltwater lakes.

Dubrovnik

Dubrovnik is a knockout. Wander down winding alleys in the sparkling white Old City, climb its famous walls, and swim amid the dramatic scenery. You may even lose track of the swirling masses of tourists, descending like so many lemmings on the city and throwing themselves into the Adriatic.

Orientation and Practical Information

Dubrovnik is accessible by ferry, plane, and bus (no trains). The coastal bus route to Split is mind-blowing. From the bus station, bus #1, 3, or 6, or a scenic hike along Ante Starčevića (the street in back of the bus station, formerly Maršala Tita) will take you to **Pile,** 3km away at the Old City's west gate. From the ferry dock at Gruž, take bus #1.

Tourist Office: Turistički Informativni Centar (TIC), Poljana Paska Miličevića 1 (tel. 263 54). Just inside the Old City's west gate. Books private rooms (from 156D). Open Mon.-Sat. 9am-9pm, Sun. 9am-noon and 3-6pm.

American Express: Atlas, Pile 1 (tel. 273 33), by the bus stop just outside the Old City's west gate. Mail held, checks sold and replaced, cardholders' personal checks cashed. No wired money accepted. Open Mon.-Sat. 7am-8pm, Sun. 8am-noon.

Post Office: Ante Starčevića 16, 150m west of the Old City's west gate. Mail held. Open daily 7am-9pm. **Postal Code:** 50000.

Telephones: At the post office. Open same hours. **City Code:** 050.

Flights: Dubrovnik Airport (tel. 771 22). Buses (12D) leave the city air terminal at Ante Starčevića 95, next to the bus station, 1½ hr. before each JAT departure. **JAT** office at Ante Starćevića 7. Open Mon.-Fri. 8am-7pm, Sat. 9am-1pm. To: Belgrade (1296D); Zagreb (1478D); standby ½ price (ages under 25 only).

Buses: To: Belgrade (6 per day, 420D); Sarajevo (5 per day, 280D); Split (13 per day, 4½ hr., 305D); Bar (4 per day, 170D). Others leave hourly for Kardeljevo (2½ hr., 100D), the closest rail station.

Ferries: Gruž harbor handles traffic to ports all along the Adriatic. **Adriatica** runs to the Italian ports of Bari (5 per week, Oct.-May 6 per month; 8 hr.); Venice (June-Sept. 1 per week; 15 hr.); and Ancona via Split (1 per week; Oct.-May 3 per month, 14 hr.). Prices range from USD35-80. **Jadrolinija,** Gruška obala 31 (tel. 230 68), plies along the Yugoslavian coast. To: Rijeka (6 per week, 22 hr., 701D), passing through Korčula, Hvar, and Split; also Corfu and Igoumenitsa, Greece (2 per week, 1300D). Office open daily 7am-1pm and 3-8pm. **Jadroagent,** Gruška obala 12 (tel. 234 64), between the port and the bus station, has international ferry schedules and sells tickets. Open Mon.-Fri. 7am-8pm, Sat. 7am-noon, Sun. 8am-noon.

Public Transportation: Local buses run in summer 5am-2:30am; off-season 5am-11pm (12D).

Hitchhiking: Those hitching to Kotor walk past the cable car station *(Žičara)* to the main highway, Jadranska Magistrala. Those heading to Split take bus #1 to the last stop, by the harbor.

Laundromat: Bella, E. Kartelja 8 (tel. 281 80).

Medical Assistance: Medicinski Center, Ante Starčevića 61 (tel. 326 77).

Emergencies: Police (tel. 92). *Milicija* headquarters at Ante Starčevića 75, 1km west of the Old City. **Ambulance** (tel. 94).

Accommodations and Camping

Dubrovnik has more private rooms than any other city in Yugoslavia. The average asking price among the crowd greeting travelers at the bus station and dock is 280D for a single and 420D for a double, but you can often bargain. Ask if the room is close to the Old City or on a bus route. Signs between the station and the Old City also advertise rooms. Arrive early during the Dubrovnik Festival (July-Aug.). Camping outside official sites is illegal, and non-compliants are fined.

Ferijalni Savez Hrvatske (IYHF), Vinka Segestrana 3 (tel. 232 41), a 10-min. uphill walk from the street behind the bus station, hidden away at the top of the walkway leading off of Josipa Jelačića. Spruce and habitable, but can fill during tourist season. Lockout 9am-2pm. Curfew 1am. 80D, 150D in July and August. Rooftop (75D) open July-Aug. Nonmembers 50D extra. Open May-Sept.

Kompas, Gruška obala 26 (tel. 243 23). Convenient, on the pier at Gruž. Main office at 14 Ante Starčevića, near Pile. Singles USD10. Doubles USD14. July-Aug. 33% higher. Open Mon.-Sat. 7am-9pm, Sun. 3-8pm.

Camping Solitude, about 3km west of the bus station (tel. 207 70). Take bus #6 from the Old City or from near the bus station. Commanding position and space for 1500—won't be full but certainly won't be quiet, either. USD5 per person, USD2.80 per tent. Open April-Oct.

Food

Eating in Dubrovnik appears expensive. The reality is even worse; most sit-down restaurants foist a 20D "cover" on top of printed prices. Elegant restaurants line Ulica Prijeko, parallel to the main promenade street, Placa. Entrees average 150D, but can cost as little as 50D. Look for cheaper outfits on the other side of Placa. Among the cheapest is the **self-service restaurant** at Cvijete Zuzorić near St. Blaise's Church (most entrees 55D, open 8am-10pm). Nearby is the slightly spiffier **Cavtat,** just across from the Serbian Cathedral (entrees 65-140D, open 10am-10pm). There are inexpensive **outdoor markets** by St. Blaise's Church and midway between the pier and the bus station; a **minimarket** hugs the west gate. The best ice cream in town and the best coffee ice cream on the planet is at **Fontana,** next door to the tourist office (30D per mongo scoop).

Sights

As you enter the Old City, signs beckon you to ascend the spectacular **City Walls** (open daily 9am-6:30pm, admission 20D). Walk on the oceanfront side, where you can soak up the sounds of the waves and the frenzy of urban life simultaneously. Just before leaving the Old City through the west gate, turn right to visit the **Franciscan Monastery** and **cloisters.** (Open daily 7am-8pm. Admission 20D.) Inside is the third-oldest pharmacy in Europe, founded in 1317. In the northeast corner of the Old City is the **Dominican Cloister and Museum** (open Mon.-Sat. 9am-6pm; admission 20D.) In the treasury of the **cathedral,** look for the 16th-century work by Titian and the 11th-century Latin bible. (Open Mon.-Sat. 9am-5pm. Admission 30D.) Cultural perspective on Dubrovnik is yours at the **Rupe Ethnographic Museum** in the southwest corner of the Old City (open 9am-1pm, 30D). Naval warfare enthusiasts can visit the **Maritime Museum** in St. John's fortress on the eastern edge of the old city. (Open daily 9am-6pm. Admission 20D.) The cable car to the top of the mountain is expensive, but a well-spent 100D if you like heights.

Bring shoes and 8D to the stony hotel beaches at either end of Dubrovnik; the one by the Hotel Excelsior, on the east side of the city, is mostly sand. (Look along

Od Margarite for unmarked exits leading to the water.) A water shuttle (9am-7pm, 2 per hr., round-trip 70D) runs to **Lokrum Island,** with deserted beaches to your right as you get off the boat and nude swimming 500m to your left.

Entertainment

In the evening, aimless crowds cruise the streets of the Old City. Three **open-air cinemas** operate in summer (50D). Look for movie posters by the Old City west gate. From July 10 to Aug. 25, the **Dubrovnik Festival** fills the city with ballet, opera, symphonic and chamber concerts, plays, and folk dances (tickets 70-200D), and free open-air concerts often resound in the square on the east side of the Old City. Year-round concerts in the 16th-century **Rector's Palace** are usually 95D, but if you buy tickets ½ hr. before the music starts, you can sit on ledges 10m above the stage for only 25D. The flashiest disco in town is the **Bakus** Lazaretti, F. Supila 6, outside the city walls near the Revelin Fortress (open nightly until 4am).

Montenegro (Crna Gora) Црна Гора

Despite some of the Adriatic's most beautiful scenery, the Montenegrin coast, south of Dubrovnik, remains less commercialized than its northern counterpart. The tradeoff: fewer English speakers and predominantly Cyrillic signs. You may never notice this, however, as Montenegro's collage of cloud-swept mountains, hourglass beaches and phantasmic sea will leave you short of words.

Buses come cheap, reliable, and often in Montenegro, and are the only way along the coast, but in high season may make you feel like a canned lemming. The only trains in the region come from Belgrade to a dead-end at the coast in Bar. In July and August, book rooms as far in advance as possible to avoid getting stuck in piddling, forgotten coastal towns.

One hour south of Dubrovnik by bus (10 per day, 1 hr., 53D) and near the entrance to the Gulf of Kotor is the resort of **Herceg-Novi** (Херцег-Нови) where you can take your pick between the 11th-century Orthodox Savina monastery and a 17th-century Franciscan monastery. Next to the bus station, a tourist office issues maps and offers private accommodations. (Singles USD9-11.) For now, the **Bokaturist** office in the bus station also secures rooms, but **Kompas,** a few streets downhill, is half the price (USD10 per night, plus 40% if you're staying less than 4 nights). As you head toward the beach, descend a few blocks into the quaint Old Town, then pass through the arch of the fairytale Venetian clocktower to the Church of Archangel Michael (open 8am-noon and 6-10pm). Down below bask some scenic rock and pebble beaches.

One hour farther south is **Kotor** (Котор) itself, a picturesque town dwarfed by towering mountains which slope into its fjord-like gulf. Frequent buses run to Budva and Bar further south; in July and August, one bus per day goes to Skopje (700D). The disastrous 1979 earthquake left Kotor with omnipresent rubble and many uninhabited houses, but somehow the pink-and-cream-paved streets, moats, and dizzying fortifications sustain their rare spell. The 12th-century **cathedral,** has a carved 14th-century altar and paintings by Veronese. If you walk right along the street by the bus station, you'll come to **Yugen TTT,** which books private rooms for 160D per person (tel. (082) 167 80; open Mon.-Fri. 8am-3pm). Farther down the street lies an **outdoor market** and then the old town. A right through the memorial arch labeled "21-XI-1944" leads to the **Montenegro Express** (daily 7am-8pm), which proffers private rooms (170D per person, 30% less for more than 3 nights) and arranges boat excursions to a tiny, man-made island in the middle of the bay housing the ornate **Church of Our Lady on the Rock** (4 hr., 620D). The kiosk (marked "i") just outside the arch houses Kotor's **tourist office** (open Mon.-Sat. 8am-2pm and 6-8pm). The **Hotel Senta** on the waterfront offers bed and breakfast for USD25, about half the price of Kotor's next-cheapest hotel.

Five hours from Dubrovnik is **Bar** (Бар), the key port in Montenegro. Buses run north to Budva and Dubrovnik (3 per day). The bus and train stations are 1½km from the center. Take a right on the street in back of the bus station, a left at the first light, a right at the next one, and keep hoofing; **Montenegro Turist** is on the left side of the street. If it's closed, continue to the light, take a left, and reach the beach; **Putnik Turist Biro** (tel. (085) 285 88, open daily 7am-9pm) and **Montenegro Express** (tel. (085) 21 113 or 22 476) stand side-by-side on the right. They each charge USD17 per person for doubles, USD23 in July and August. Look for rooms on your own on Nikole Lekiča, across the street. **Campground Šušanj** is a good place to meet Eastern Europeans; in keeping with this sociability the showers have no walls. (50D per person.) Bar is the southernmost point in Yugoslavia from which you can hop a ferry to Italy; visit the **ferry offices** to the right of the bus station, along the beach.

Ulcinj (Улцињ), a half-hour bus ride from Bar and 16km from the (closed) Albanian border, offers a 12km sand beach (the Velika Plaža) and manageable prices. Get a map at the bus station, 1½km from the old town. Forget Ulcinj's wildy overpriced youth hostel (tel. (085) 818 57; 450D per person; open May-Sept.); the **Turist Biro,** right on the city's smaller beach (Mala Plaža), has doubles for USD8 per person, USD10 per person in July and August (30% more for stays of under 4 nights). An hourly bus from the post office goes the 4km to the Velika Plaža, and to the campground **Neptun** (tel. (085) 818 88; USD3.50 per person, USD2.50 per tent). The Nabokovian island of **Ada** is at the far end, with its butterfly-laden, in-the-buff campground **Bojana** (where do you think he met Lolita, anyhow?—tel. (085) 819 09; 82D per person, 30D per tent) and beaches.

About five trains per day make the spectacular 7-8 hr. run from Bar to Belgrade. A true adventure, the trip passes through hair-raising tunnels, bone-chilling mountain scenery, and the lockjaw-inducing **Morača Canyon.** A 45-min. ride inland from Bar, **Titograd** (Тиртоград) is Montenegro's drab provincial capital, and the terminus of the northern approach road (and the unused railroad line) into Albania. Alight from the train at **Mojkovac** (Мойковац), 70km north of Titograd, to visit the brain-blowing **Tara Canyon,** second-largest in the world (after the Grand). Although the 1200-meter gorge lacks an official campground, many travelers camp unofficially.

Serbia Србија

The strongest South Slavic nation since it shook off Turkish rule in the 19th century, Serbia spearheaded Yugoslavia's unification in the 20th century; Belgrade is now capital of both republic and nation. Resentment of perceived Serbian domination is today one of the strongest forces behind Slovenia's and Croatia's desire for independence. Cyrillic is the dominant alphabet in Serbia; English is commonly studied. Hungarians in Vojvodina and Albanians in Kosovo (Serbia's autonomous provinces) speak their own languages.

Belgrade (Beograd) Београд

A rendezvous with expensive Belgrade will probably prove unavoidable, as its train station is the hub of the Balkan rail net, binding Western Europe to Greece and Turkey. Fortunately, 1½ million people, cultural attractions worthy of a national capital, and an eastern flair make Belgrade somewhat more than a mere transport node.

Orientation and Practical Information

Belgrade lies in eastern Yugoslavia, 60km from the Romanian border, straddling the River Sava at its junction with the Danube. Belgrade's train and bus stations are next to one another on Trg bratstva i jedinstva. Pick up a city map, complete with bus and tram routes, at the tourist office inside the train station. The **River Sava** separates the **Stari Grad** (Old City) from **Novi Beograd.** The center of the old city is a quick hop on bus #34 or a 20-minute uphill walk from the station; go up the street by the Putnik and Lasta tourist agencies and take the first left onto Balkanska, which takes you to **Terazije** (Теазије). The main tourist office is to your left in the underpass below the sign for the Jugoslavenska Knijga bookstore. Behind the tourist office, the popular strolling boulevard **Kneza Mihaila** (Кнеза Михаила; also called Kneza Mihailova) leads to the **Kalemegdan Park** on the edge of the Stari Grad before the Danube River.

Finding your way around Belgrade may not be easy at first. Tourist maps are in the Roman alphabet, but virtually every street sign is in Cyrillic. A separate Cyrillic map is available at newsstands. Just remember that uphill invariably leads to the city center. The public transportation system will baffle as well; there are separate bus and tram strip-tickets and you must punch a varying amount of strips depending on the length of your journey (3 strips usually do the trick).

Tourist Offices: Turistički Informativni Centar (tel. 63 56 22). See directions above. The largest tourist office in Yugoslavia. English-speaking staff. Pick up the map and *Beospektar,* a monthly calendar of events with a complete list of services well worth the 30D. Snag a free copy of *Belgrade for Young People* as well. Open daily 8am-8pm. Branch offices at the train station (tel. 64 58 22) and the airport (tel. 60 37 31) can provide English-speaking assistance. Both open daily 7am-9pm.

Budget Travel: Yugotours-Naromtravel, Vasina 16-18 (tel. 63 81 55). Sales office for Naromtravel, Yugoslavia's student travel organization. YIEE and ISIC cards; bring one photo. Open daily 7:30am-8pm. **Discount Rail Tickets: Beogradtours** (tel. 64 12 58), Milovana Milovanovića 5, across from the station past the Putnik office. ISIC cardholders get up to 30% discounts on tickets to Eastern Europe. Open Mon.-Sat. 6:30am-8pm.

Embassies: U.S., Kneza Miloša 50 (tel. 64 56 55). Open Mon.-Fri. 7am-4pm. **Canada,** Kneza Miloša 75 (tel. 64 46 66). Open Mon., Wed., and Fri. 8am-1pm. **U.K.,** Generala Ždanova 46 (tel. 64 50 55). Open Mon.-Thurs. 8am-4:30pm, Fri. 8am-1pm. Ring bell in an emergency. **Australia,** Čika Ljubina 13 (tel. 62 46 55). Open Mon.-Fri. 8am-12:30pm. **New Zealand** citizens should contact the British Embassy. **Albania,** Kneza Miloša 56 (tel. 64 55 95). Open Mon.-Fri. 9am-1pm. **Bulgaria,** Birčaninova 26 (tel. 64 62 22). **Hungary,** Proleterskih brigada 72 (tel. 444 04 72). Open Mon.-Fri. 9am-noon. Visas while you wait (USD12 and 2 photos). **Romania,** Kneza Miloša 70 (tel. 64 60 71). Open Mon.-Fri. 9am-1pm.

American Express: Atlas, Zmaj-Jovina 10 (tel. 18 36 71). No wired money. Does cash cardholders' personal checks into dinars. Mail handled at **Atlas,** Moše Pijade 11 (tel. 34 14 71), 3 blocks from main tourist office. Both open Mon.-Fri. 8am-8pm, Sat. 8am-3pm.

Post Office: PTT, Takovska 2 (tel. 33 05 69). Open Mon.-Fri. 7am-8pm, Sat. 9am-4pm. **Postal Code:** 11101 for Poste Restante.

Telephones: PTT, Zmaj-Jovina 17, at Vase Čarapića, near Trg Republike. Open 24 hrs. Also at main post office. **Telephone Code:** 011.

Flights: Tel. 60 14 24. All flights land at **Aerodrom Beograd** in Surčin, 35 min. west of the city. **JAT** buses leave the airport every ½-hr. 4:30am-11pm, stop outside the train station, and end up at the city air terminal by the Hotel Slavija. The JAT office at Maršala Tita 18 (tel. 64 27 73; open Mon.-Sat. 8am-7:30pm) sells international tickets, while the one on Bulevar revolucije 17 (tel. 33 10 47; open Mon.-Sat. 7am-7:30pm, Sun. 8am-noon) handles domestic flights. Fares within Yugoslavia average USD65.

Trains: Central Station, Trg bratstva i jedinstva (tel. 64 58 22). Frequent departures to every major Yugoslavian city. Two per day to Athens (26-28 hr.), Budapest (6½ hr.); one per day to Moscow, Venice, and Vienna, among others. One day and one night train wheeze to Sofia (10 hr.); the night train continues to Istanbul (another 13 hr.) The daily overnight to Bucharest via Timişoara (12 hr.) departs from the **Dunav station,** Đure Đakovića 39 (tel. 76 38 80), on the other side of the Old City from the main station. Tickets sold at KSR, Maršala Tita 25 (tel. 33 10 81). Also try the Putnik travel agency (tel. 33 02 82) at Terazije 27. Always make seat reservations; if possible, take trains that originate in Belgrade. If your train arrives without vacant seats, sprint to the baggage cars and stake out floor space.

Buses: Main station at Železnička 4, next to the train station (tel. 62 47 51 for info, 64 44 55 for reservations). Frequent service to practically anywhere in the country. Domestic tickets may be purchased at the station. For international tickets, go to the neighboring **Basturist** office, Železnička 4 (tel. 62 71 46; open 7am-7pm).

Luggage Storage: Garderoba, in the train station. Open 24 hrs.

Hitchhiking: Those heading for Zagreb and Ljubljana take bus #601 from the Sava Center in Novi Beograd out as far as it goes on the *auto-put* (expressway). For Skopje and points south, hitchers take bus #17 as far as it goes on *auto-put* Stevana Prvovenčanog. Good luck.

Bookstore: The shop at Jugoslovenska Knijga, above the tourist office, sells phrasebooks, paperbacks, and current Western magazines. Open Mon.-Fri. 8am-9pm, Sat. 8am-4pm. **American Center,** Čika Ljubina 17 (tel. 63 00 11), off Kneza Mihaila near the main shopping mall, has books and semi-current periodicals. Open Mon.-Fri. 10am-5pm.

Pharmacy: Prvi Maj, Maršala Tita 9 (tel. 34 05 33). Open 24 hrs.

Medical Assistance: Dom Zdravlja "Boris Kidrič," Pasterova 1 (tel. 68 37 55).

Emergencies: Police (tel. 92). **Ambulance** (tel. 94).

Accommodations and Camping

Hotel rooms are expensive in Belgrade. Even out-of-the-way C-category hotels charge as much as USD40 per night. Instead, head straight for the reasonably priced youth hostel or arrange for private accommodations.

Youth Guest House "Mladost" (IYHF), Bulevar Jugoslovenske narodne armije 56a (tel. 46 53 24). Facing away from the train station, take tram #2 or 7 uphill to the Hotel Slavija. From there, take bus #47, 47E, 48, or 48E going to the right. Ask for the stop "Hotel Mladost." Gracious, comfortable, 6-bed dorms, each with its own shower. USD17, nonmembers slightly more. Hearty self-serve breakfast included. Often full, so call ahead.

Lasta, Trg bratstva i jedinstva 1a (tel. 64 24 73), across the street from the train station. Arranges private rooms. Singles USD21. Doubles USD39. Triples USD51. Open Mon.-Sat. 7am-8pm.

Camping: Camping Košutnjak, Kneza Višeslava 17 (tel. 55 51 27). Take bus #53 south from the station near the tourist office to Kirovljeva and walk 3 blocks. Pitch your tent far from the restaurant, where music blares well into the morning. USD3.50 per person, USD2 per tent. Bungalows USD20 per person; ask for more primitive ones for USD6 per person. **Camping National,** Bežanijska Kosa 1a (tel. 69 35 09), in Novi Beograd. Take bus #601. USD9 per person. Bungalows USD35 per person. Open May-Sept.

Food

Belgrade may lack good budget accommodations, but its inexpensive restaurants will soothe frayed nerves. Although not a fair trade for freedom, Turkish occupation left a wonderful influence on Serbian gastronomy. For a typical Serbian dish, try *pasulj* (beans), generally cooked with *sa suvim rebrima* (ribs). Serbian cuisine includes an excellent array of meatless dishes, from *kajmak* cheese (served as an entree) to fresh vegetable salads. A dinner along enchanting **Skadarska** makes a trip to Belgrade worthwhile. Cheaper than restaurants, the take-outs near the fountain on Skadarska sell scrumptious *lepinja* (hot bread filled with *kajmak* cheese or goulash) for about 30D. A **market** and plenty of fast food are up the hill between the train station and the tourist office.

Dva Jelena ("Two Deer"), Skadarska 32. Regal views from the center of the promenade. Open 9am-1am. Or try **Ima Dana,** at #38 (open 9am-2am), and **Tri Šešira** ("Three Deer"), at #29 (open 8am-1pm). Each serves tender grilled specialties (at times inadvertantly garnished with a twig from a verdant canopy) for 150D.

Kolarac, Kneza Mihaila 46. No-prisoners-taken Serbian fare. Enjoy the searing *Leskovac Mixed Grill* (85D) and the parade of ambling Belgraders outside along Kneza Mihaila. Entrees average 60D. Open daily 8am-1am.

? Cafe, 7. jula 6, near Kneza Mihaila, across from the city's main church. The oldest continuously operating café-restaurant in Belgrade (since 1823). Originally called *The Cafe at the Cathedral* and sued by the church, the question mark reflects its enduringly dubious status. Cheap drinks and satisfactory food—best for a quiet aperitif. Daily 7am-11pm.

Self-Service Luksor, Balkanska 7, just behind Hotel Moskva. Some of Belgrade's best prices. A wide spread of pre-fab dishes. Most main courses about 35D. Open daily 6am-10pm.

Sights and Entertainment

At the end of Terazije on Trg Republike stands the **National Museum** (Народни Музеј), a mammoth collection of prehistoric artifacts, icons, frescoes, and paintings from Serbian and European schools. (Admission 50D. Open Tues.-Wed., Fri.-Sat. 10am-5pm, Thurs. 10am-7pm, Sun. 10am-2pm.) The National Museum's **Gallery of Frescoes** (Галерије Фресака), near Kalemegdan Park at Cara Uroša 20, houses faithful copies of the vivid and dramatic medieval works found in various Serbian and Macedonian Orthodox monasteries. (Same hours as National Museum. Admission 50D.) Northwest of the tourist office is the animated **Kneza Mihaila** pedestrian boulevard, lined with chic shops, street performers, and open-air cafés. Kneza Mihaila leads to the **Kalemegdan** (Калемегдан), a Roman fortress which has surrendered its ramparts and lapsed into parkdom. The Sava and Danube rivers meet below. So do countless couples in search of romantic ambience. Nearby lies an observatory, a zoo, and several museums, including the intriguing **Vojni Muzej** (Military Museum; open Tues.-Sat. 10am-5pm). To get there from the bus station, take tram #2 to the citadel atop the hill.

A good way to avoid skimping on Yugoslav culture is to visit the **Ethnographic Museum,** at Studentski trg 13 (admission 20D; same hours as National Museum). The English captions help foreigners appreciate the rich heritage, culture, and dress of the country. To learn something about the smartly dressed fellow whose Big Brother-esque visage until recently shined down on you everywhere you went, visit the **Josip Broz Tito Memorial Center,** Botićeva 25 (tel. 66 88 30). The 75-minute tour will show you where Tito slept (his residence) and where Tito sleeps (his tomb). Take trolleybus #42 from Trg Republike or along Kneza Miloša. (Open in summer daily 9am-4pm; off-season Tues.-Sun. 9am-3pm. Admission 20D.) At the far end of Maršala Tita looms the majestic **Sveti Sava Basilica.** Financed entirely by private donations, this cathedral will one day be among the largest Eastern Orthodox churches in existence, second only to Aya Sofya in İstanbul.

Whether you dine there or not, carouse down **ulica Skadarska** (улица Скадаска), a 19th-century haunt of artists and bohemians. **Ada Ciganlija,** an island in the Sava, has restaurants on houseboats. The ones on the New Belgrade side are less accessible (take a water taxi), but stay up later. During the summer, open-air discos pump up the volume in **Kalemegdan Park**—walk into the park and follow the music (cover 50D).

Every Wednesday evening, **Kolo,** an excellent Yugoslav folk song and dance group, performs at Belgrade's foremost concert hall, the **Kolarac People's University (KPU)** at Studentski Trg 5. Classical music concerts resound at the **Belgrade Cultural Center (BCC),** Kneza Mihaila 6, as well as the KPU. The **Narodno Pozorište** (National Theater) hosts opera, ballet, and drama performances. Standing-room tickets to the ballet are a mere 20D—less than a Big Mac. Ask at the tourist office, or check *Beospektar.*

Macedonia Македонија

Yugoslavia's southernmost republic, celebrated home of Philip of Macedon and his upstart son, Alexander the Great, has since accommodated the Hellenistic, Roman, Byzantine, Bulgarian, and Ottoman empires; the last occupation only ended with the Balkan Wars of 1911-1913. The Macedonian language, similar to Bulgarian, uses the Cyrillic alphabet.

Skopje Скопје

Yugoslavia's picturesque third-largest city, Skopje is the capital of Macedonia and the first major Yugoslav city on the train route linking Greece with northern Europe. Skopje is five to six hours by train from Thessaloniki, Greece (2 per day, 370D), and eight hours from Belgrade (9 per day, 400D). Crowded buses to Belgrade are slightly faster and more economical (10 per day, 350D), but secure your seat reservations early.

From the train station (Железничка Станица), reach the bus station (Аутоб уска Станица) by walking three blocks to the river keeping the mountains on your left, then crossing the third bridge. The bus station is conveniently near the entrance to the old town, just across the River Vardar from the new town. Both stations have a гардероба for luggage storage. The planet's most pompous post office building hulks across the river from the bus station in Skopje—a must-see marvel which will find you unsuspecting and leave you agape. (Open Mon.-Sat. 7am-7pm, Sun. 9am-noon; telephones available 24 hrs.)

The main **Turistička Agencija,** 100m from the bus station (tel. (091) 22 34 29), rents private rooms (singles 500D; doubles 750D) and provides information on all of Macedonia. (Open Mon.-Fri. 7am-7pm, Sat. 9am-8pm, Sun. 9am-5pm.) The **Jugotours-Narom Travel Office,** Gradski Trgovinski Center "bb" (tel. (091) 21 32 13), is in the shopping center adjacent to pl. Maršal Tito at the rear of the second floor. They can update old ISIC cards, and give info on discount domestic air tickets. The **Youth Hostel Blagoje Šošolčev (IYHF),** 25 Prolet (tel. (091) 23 38 66), is close to the train station, a bit cramped, and thus sociable. (From the station, walk toward the river and take the 2nd left onto Prolet. 6-bed dorms 205D, nonmembers 255D.) **K. J. Pitu** at Ribar 58 (tel. (091) 23 53 60) or **Goce Delčev** at Taftalidže II (tel. (091) 25 30 21) are both student dorms in the southwestern part of the city (off Ivo Ribar-Lola) with beds for USD10. (Open July-Aug. Make reservations.)

Most of Skopje's historical sights are an easy walk from the bus station. As you exit the bus station onto the main street, trot uphill 100m to find the 15th-century **Daut-pašin Amam** (Turkish bath), now an art gallery. The interior is blissfully cool. (Open Sun.-Mon. 9am-3pm, Tues.-Sat. 8am-7pm. Admission 30D, students 20D.) As you enter the old bazaar from the baths, bear left up the main street to the **Church of the Holy Savior** (Sveti Spas). (Open daily 7am-7pm. Admission 45D.) Inside stands a masterful walnut iconostasis which required seven years to carve. Amidst the graven religious figures appears the likeness of the artists themselves, harmoniously blended into the right side as a subtle signature to this stellar work. Notice that much of the church's interior is below ground level, in response to the statute of the time prohibiting Christian churches from being higher than mosques. Farther up the hill, the **Mustafa-pašina džamija** (Mustafa Pasha mosque) and the elegant **Kuršumli han** (Turkish inn) recall five centuries of Ottoman occupation. Across from the inn gleams the newly renovated **Museum of Macedonia** (open Tues.-Sun. 9am-5pm).

Until recently, each street of the **Old Bazaar** represented a particular handicraft; tanners, goldsmiths, and potters competed with one another in their consolidated zones. Though the bazaar now panders more to tourism, the narrow lanes are still a fascinating place to get lost. Many tiny retaurants in the bazaar serve Macedonian-style goulashes, stuffed peppers, and grilled meats. Across the river are inexpensive outdoor cafés: **Skver** (Сквер), at pl. Maršal Tito, and **Bambi** (Бамби) at Maršal Tito 13. Entrees at both cost about USD2. (Both open daily 8am-midnight.)

Lake Ohrid охридскско Езеро

Of Macedonia's majestic lakes, Lake Ohrid most merits deification. 170km south of Skopje and half in Albania, Ohrid's tranquil beaches, azure waters, inexpensive accommodations, and storied Byzantine churches guarantee satisfaction, even in high season when finding space on buses to the lake becomes more of a problem. First settled by the Illyrians, who Herodotus described as "those ruder peoples to the north," the area around the lake eventually drew the imperial attention of Philip of Macedon. Under the Romans, the lakeside town of **Ohrid** (охрид) became an important stop on the *Via Ignatia,* the road to Constantinople. Slavs settled the area in the 6th century and renamed it as they saw it: *vo hrid* ("on a cliff"). The 9th-century monks Kliment and Naum converted the people to Christianity and initiated 600 years of intense monasticism that spawned over 300 area churches and a Slavonic university at Sveti Pantelejmon in 893 AD, nearly 200 years before the University of Bologna first sent out acceptance slips.

Ten buses per day connect the town of Ohrid with Skopje (166D). The quickest route (3½ hr.) is via Kičevo; the longer western route (4½ hr.) winds its way through picturesque mountains. Alternatively, take the train south from Skopje to **Bitola** (Битрола, 3-4 hr.), then a bus (7 per day) 40km west to Ohrid; one train per day continues from Bitola southwards to Florina in Greece, a charming city overlooked by a cross on a hill.

Next to the Ohrid bus station, the **Turističko Društvo,** Partizanska 3 (tel. (096) 224 94), can place you in private homes (singles USD8, doubles USD12, triples USD15) and will furnish Ohrid maps and Macedonia information. (Open daily 7am-9pm.) The crowd at the bus station offers reasonable rooms for USD6-8. **Youth Hostel Mladost** (tel. (096) 216 26), on Goce Delčev, is a bit out of the way, often full, and less comfortable. Savor rare Lake Ohrid trout at the **Letnica** restaurant (across from the bus station) for 100D. Ohrid style is best: the fish is stuffed to the gills (literally) with paprika and chopped vegetables, then grilled. The self-serve section of Letnica is run by a team of cheerful ladies who keep the place spotless and efficient (entrees 30-50D; open daily 6am-10pm). From the center of town, the coastal lane leads you to quaint outdoor cafés. Macedonian folk music is Yugoslavia's finest. Head for the **Restaurant Antico** on Car Samuil where locals sit, drink, and listen to the live band in a beautifully restored Macedonian house. Local hotels and the restaurant **Orijent** also occasionally host musical evenings. Across from the tourist office, people rent out bicycles for about USD5 a day.

Sveta Sofija, Ohrid's oldest church, dates back to the 9th century; facing the lake, make a right onto Car Samuil and follow the signs. (Open Tues.-Sun. 8am-1pm and 4-8pm.) Performances of the **Festival Ohridsko Leto** (mid-July to late Aug.) and the **Balkan Festival,** an exhibition of international folk dancing (1st week in July; tickets USD3), are held here with the church as backdrop. Up the hill from Sv. Sofija along Ilindenska is the fabulous **Church of Sveti Kliment.** Its 600-year-old frescoes are in superb condition. Across from the church is the **Icon Gallery,** with works spanning seven centuries, including depictions of stoic saints enduring torture and harrassment by horrid beasties. (Open Tues.-Sun. 8am-1pm and 4-8pm.) Again from Sv. Sofija, mount the steps behind the stage to Kosta Racin and walk along the lip of the cliff to the 13th-century **Church of Sveti Jovan,** almost too perfect to be real; sunsets viewed from the hill will commandeer your imagination. A glance below reveals an idyllic beach and fishing boats rocking themselves to sleep. Hire a water-taxi from along the town wharf for pleasure cruising or for transport to Sveti Naum (USD6 per hr.).

The exquisitely adorned 10th-century monastery of **Sveti Naum** (Свети Наум) is 28km south along the lake from Ohrid, near the Albanian border. Take the bus along the lakeshore (6 per day, 1 hr., 20D) or a ferry (daily at 8:30am, round-trip 150D). Try to make a Sunday morning service, or better yet, arrive on the night of July 2, the eve of the saint's carnivalesque feast day. Lake Ohrid's sandiest beaches are also in Sveti Naum, and of the four campsites along the coast, **Sveti**

Naum Autokamp (tel. (096) 250 22) at the southernmost edge of the lake, is the most enchanting, graced with a sweeping view of the lake and the monastery. (Take the coastal metrobus from the tourist office. USD3 per tent.)

Southeast of Lake Ohrid is the serene **Lake Prespa** (Преспанско Езеро). Shared with Greece and Albania, the lake has clear water and golden sands. You can camp at **Krani** (USD5 per person, USD3 per tent) and **Oteševo** (USD4 per person, USD3 per tent). For those using this book in alphabetical order, Albania is just across the lake.

INDEX